U0940845

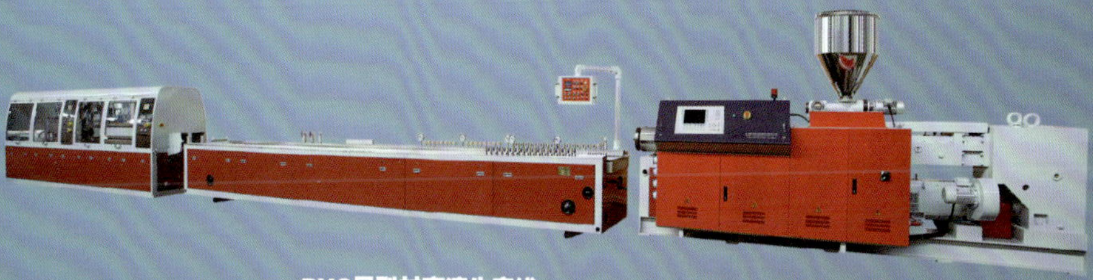

公司简介
COMPANY PROFILE

山东日科化学股份有限公司是由留日归国博士赵东日先生于2003年12月创建的集科研、生产、销售和技术服务于一体的高新技术企业，总部位于省 开发区——山东省昌乐经济开发区内，南接胶济铁路，北临济青高速。公司下设山东日科新材料有限公司、山东日科塑胶有限公司、山东日科进出口贸易有限公司三个全资子公司及控股子公司山东日科橡塑科技有限公司。公司建有山东省塑料改性工程技术研究中心和潍坊市企业技术中心，先后承担国家、省、市科技计划14项，申请国家发明专利15项（已获授权的13项），现已通过质量、环境、职业健康安全三个体系认证。

公司的主导产品有丙烯酸酯类抗冲改性剂、PVC加工助剂、PVC发泡调节剂、新型PVC抗冲改性剂ACM树脂、MBS抗冲改性剂、AMB抗冲改性剂、PMMA/ASA彩色共挤料以及ABS抗冲改性剂等系列产品，综合产能达到8万吨/年，是世界大型的丙烯酸酯类PVC改性剂制造供应商之一，也是国内塑料助剂行业大型上市企业。

公司产品国内市场占有率达到40%以上，在河北、河南、陕西、江苏、浙江、湖北、四川、广东等地均设立了客户服务中心，并出口到美国、欧盟、韩国、以色列、土耳其、印度、乌克兰、东南亚等国家和地区，出口量列国内同行业第一位。公司凭借卓越的产品质量和完善的售后服务，获得越来越多客户的认可。

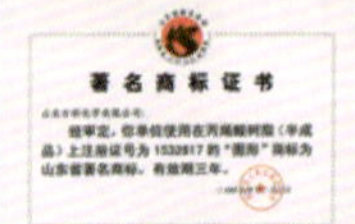

联系方式

地址：山东省昌乐县经济开发区
电话：0536-6295122　传真：0536-6295122
邮箱：office@rikechem.com　邮编：262400

YOULI
佑利

PVC-C工业及船用管道系统
PVC-C Industrial and Marine Pipe System

耐腐蚀

产品氯含量达74%（一般PVC-C产品介于63%-69%），化学稳定性上佳，因此具有超强的抗酸碱盐和抗氧化性能。在冶金和化工行业的使用环境中，表现超越金属和其他塑料管道系统。

耐火

经远东防火试验中心检测为低播焰性材料（No.FT11071）。当空气含氧量达到60%（即限氧指数，超过27%即为难燃材料；常态空气含氧量为18%）时方可到达有焰燃烧，且不易产生烟雾和有毒气体。

耐高温

受外界高温或低温环境影响较小。导热性较低，为铜管的1/400、钢管的1/200、聚乙烯管的2/3。热膨胀表现逊于钢，但优越于其他塑料材质。推荐使用于-20-93℃温度的环境中。

耐老化

机械强度和韧性超强，抗紫外线性能优越，使用寿命长于其他的塑料管道系统。

易安装

可采用胶粘、法兰、螺纹、焊接等多种方式连接，即使安装环境狭窄也可轻松完成。安装时间比热熔管道和金属管道节省1/5至1/3；成本节省1/5-1/4左右。同时避免高昂的后期维护成本。

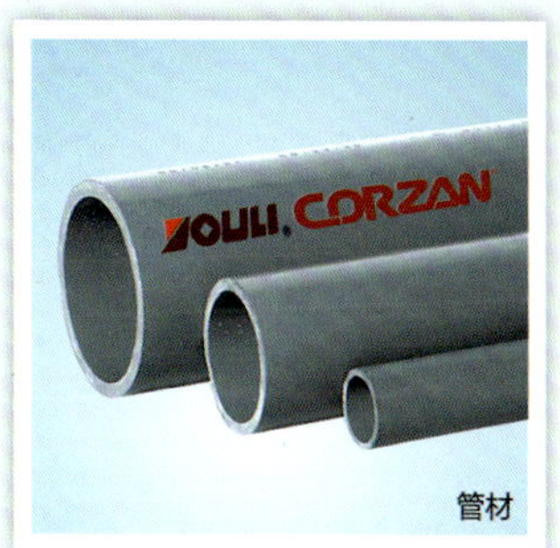

管材

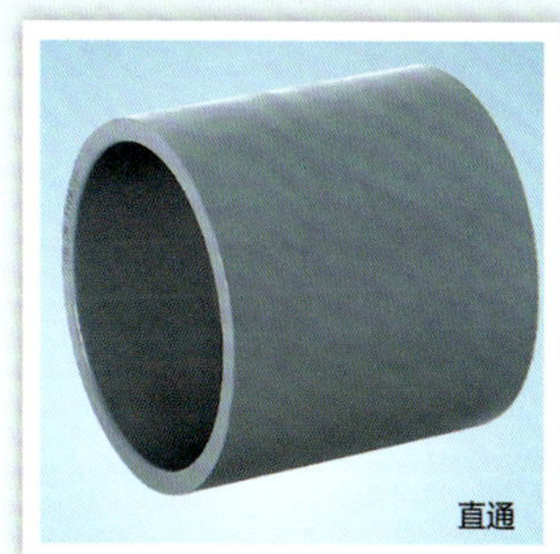
直通

异径大小头

90° 弯头

三通

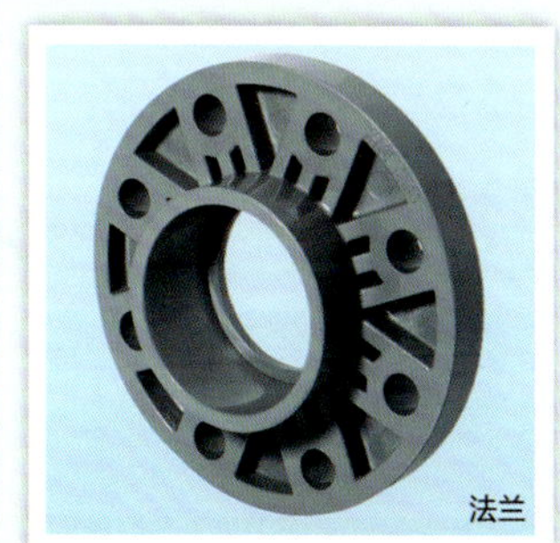
法兰

活接头

法兰式隔膜阀

电（气）动球阀

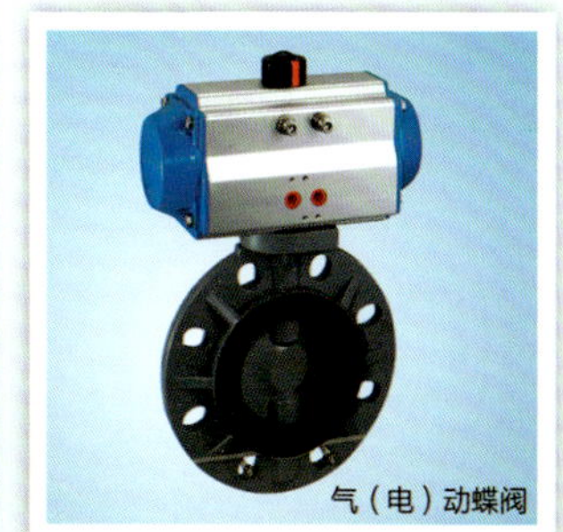
气（电）动蝶阀

常州嘉仁禾化学有限公司是中国塑料加工工业协会理事单位、中国塑协助剂专委会理事单位、台塑关系企业合格分供方、江苏省清洁化生产示范单位、省级高新企业、常州市生态园林单位。公司位于美丽富饶的江南水乡天目湖畔，被誉为现代化园林式工厂。

公司秉承德国技术，凭借公司投资创办的有中科院院士、教授、博士等数十位国内外化工专家组建的鸿博（溧阳）新材料技术研究院的技术平台，研发并生产新型材料，包括环保建材、石化产品专业用的相关助剂，适用于PVC等各种新型塑材，公司研发的具有国际先进水平的环保钙锌、钡锌和高端无酚产品，在近百家台资、大陆工厂的宽幅压延线和大型挤出、浸塑、注塑和吹塑等设备上得到成功使用，被南亚塑胶等高知名度塑胶企业确定为长期供应商。产品广泛适用于环保汽车革、发泡板、地板胶（医院、机场、学校、科研院所、舰艇等用）、人造革、透明膜、玩具膜、车身贴、PVC手套、PVC医用塑料、百叶窗、电线电缆料、油墨和涂料等。北京化工大学、东南大学、中国林化研究所和常州大学为公司产学研合作单位，是常州大学的实习基地。公司现有“常州市塑料助剂工程技术研究中心”，承担高科技新产品的开发工作，公司开发的符合欧盟市场标准的无酚产品填补了国内空白，由公司和中国林化所合作研发的无金属生态型稳定剂已被列入“十二五”规划，研发工作已全面启动。

2012年常州嘉仁禾化学有限公司承担的国家“十二五”科技攻关项目:“生物基PVC热稳定剂制备技术”是目前全球新兴的前沿战略性研究课题，我公司通过与中国林化所产学研合作研发生物基PVC热稳定剂产品已达国际国内先进水平。

公司董事长沈卫锋先生现为中国青年企业家协会会员，首届长三角年度青商人物“杰出青商“和常州市“831高层次创新创业人才”，“东南大学聘为校外辅导导师”，“常州市十大大学生创业导师”,公司现为“常州市大学生创业实践基地”。

亚通简介 ATON INTRODUCTION

福建亚通新材料科技股份有限公司创建于1994年，是一家专业从事塑料管道产品研究和制造的国家重点高新技术企业。亚通产品主要用于市政建设（道路、通信、电力、燃气、供水、排水、排污等基础设施建设）、水务投资运营（城市供水、排污、输水管网建设改造）、建筑工程、农业节水排灌系统、现代园艺等各种领域，产品种类及配套之全，位居全国同行业领先地位。

亚通经人事部批准设立博士后科研工作站，现系建设部塑料管道产业化基地，全国化学建材骨干企业，中国塑料加工工业协会副理事长单位。亚通拥有福建、北京、内蒙古、黑龙江、河南、重庆、湖北、甘肃、新疆等10多个生产基地和覆盖全国的生产、销售和服务网络。从2004年起，亚通产品陆续销往俄罗斯、马耳他、新加坡、沙特阿拉伯、圭亚那、伊朗、蒙古等国家和地区。

亚通是中国塑料管材及管件市场的知名品牌、是国家相关部门认定的“中国驰名商标”。同时亚通系列产品还荣获了“中国名牌产品”“国家重点新产品”“福建名牌产品”等多项荣誉。

公司持续以一流的产品、一流的服务，为中国现代农业、水利、电力、交通、通信、石油、化工、城市建设、环境保护和其他工业事业做出应有贡献，引导中国塑料管道行业向更高、更新水平迈进！

集团下属生产基地

亚通福建福清生产基地（总部）

亚通湖北仙桃生产基地

亚通河南开封生产基地

亚通四川彭州生产基地

亚通重庆万州生产基地

亚通甘肃张掖生产基地

亚通北京生产基地

亚通内蒙古呼和浩特生产基地

亚通福建厦门生产基地

亚通新疆昌吉生产基地

我们创造
化学新作用
让舒适生活
爱上工程塑料

华大化学
HUADA CHEM

30年前

开创聚氨酯树脂先河

现在

开创水性超纤合成革新时代

中国联塑 — 中国领先的建材家居产业集团

覆盖全国的生产基地
28家控股子公司，25个生产基地(包含已建、在建及筹建)，覆盖全国。

8大领域 打造中国领先的建材家居产业集团
8大主要产品领域：涵盖管道产品、卫浴产品、整体厨房、型材产品、门窗产品、消防器材、卫生材料、装饰板材。未来，联塑还将进军整体衣柜、防火门、保温材料、装饰辅料等泛家居领域。

服务全球 美誉典范
超过60个商务服务机构，拥有一级经销商近1000家，覆盖全国；在全球30多个国家和地区建有商务服务机构，辐射全球；先后向超过300家水务公司以及近100家电力、通信、燃气公司提供产品和服务；恒大地产、保利地产、龙湖地产等众多一线大型房地产企业都选用联塑的产品，并形成了长期稳定的合作关系。

百亿名企 蓄力向上
2011年销售额突破人民币100亿。未来，联塑将再谱新章，蓄力向上。

中国管业领导者
26年管道生产和研发经验，18个管道生产基地；建有研究院，拥有精干的研发团队，技术业内领先；专业安装公司，驻扎全国，服务各区域。

品牌管理和知识产权保护
中国联塑建立了完善的品牌战略管理及全方位的知识产权保护；拥有"联塑"、"LESSO"、"领尚"等多个品牌，600多个商标，涵盖45个产品类别，18个国家和地区；拥有授权专利近千份，涉及管道、家居等多个产品类别；"联塑"商标2005年被认定为"中国驰名商标"；2009年被推荐为“最具竞争力的商品商标”。

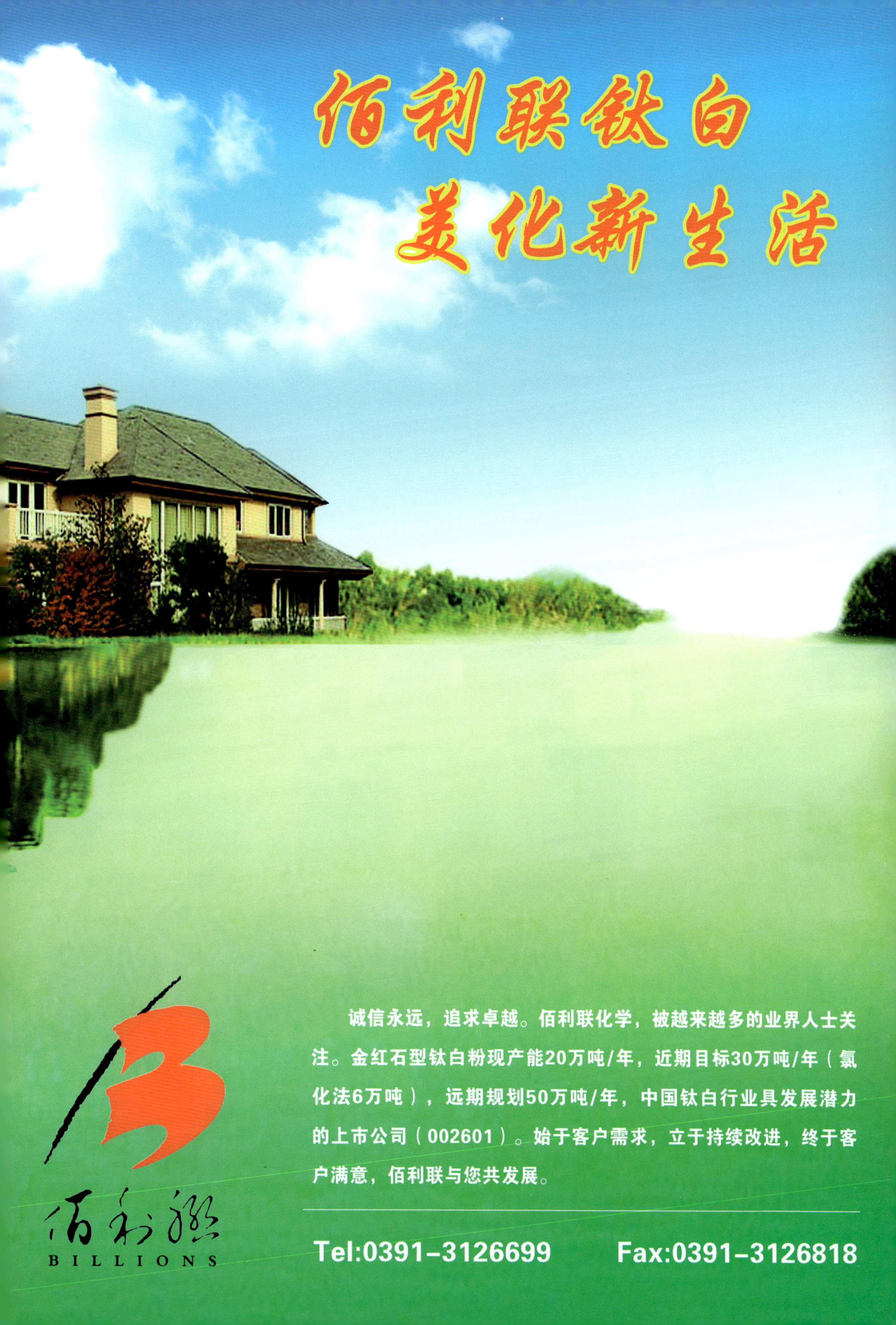
佰利联钛白
美化新生活
诚信永远，追求卓越。佰利联化学，被越来越多的业界人士关注。金红石型钛白粉现产能20万吨/年，近期目标30万吨/年（氯化法6万吨），远期规划50万吨/年，中国钛白行业具发展潜力的上市公司（002601）。始于客户需求，立于持续改进，终于客户满意，佰利联与您共发展。
佰利联
BILLIONS
Tel:0391-3126699
Fax:0391-3126818

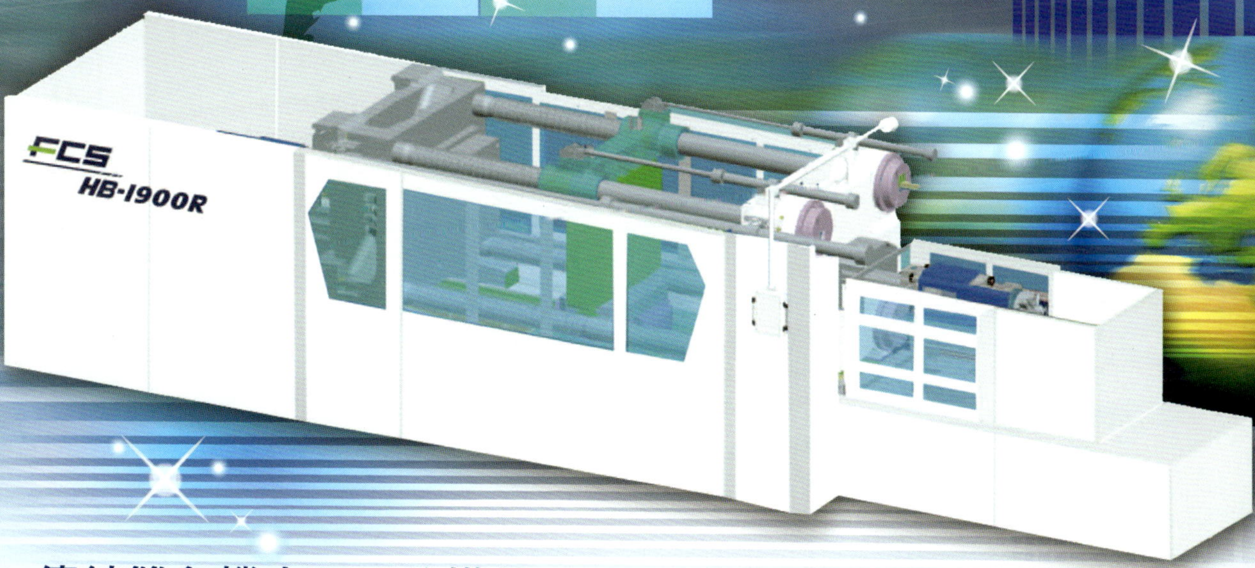

浙江明日控股集团股份有限公司

中石化、上海赛科、扬子巴斯夫、三圆石化核心客户
新疆天业浙江、安徽区域经销商
埃克森美孚化工浙江省战略合作伙伴
沙特阿美福建省战略合作伙伴

浙江明日控股集团股份有限公司为浙江省塑料行业协会会长、中国塑料加工工业协会副理事长单位，隶属于浙江省供销社，是浙江农资集团核心成员企业，成立于1998年。目前，公司总股本11600万股，总资产逾15亿元，员工500余人，主营塑料原料、化工产品贸易和塑料薄膜加工业务，汇总经营收入超100亿元，多年来年均增速达到30%水平，公司已发展成为中国塑化分销服务商行业龙头企业。

公司坚持大宗化学品为主线，与国内、国际石化企业建立了良好合作关系。目前，年经销量超120万吨，其中，聚烯烃70万吨，聚氯乙烯40万吨，ABS、PS、EVA、茂金属等5万吨，甲醇、乙二醇、橡胶等化工产品10万吨，农用薄膜、包装薄膜5万吨。

公司立足华东、面向全国，在浙江省各地市、上海、江苏、福建、安徽、江西、山东、广东、四川和宁波港、上海港、广州港、天津港等设立分销机构，在华东地区形成了畅通、高效的分销网络体系。公司还在新加坡、中国香港成立境外离岸公司，开展转口贸易、美金业务。

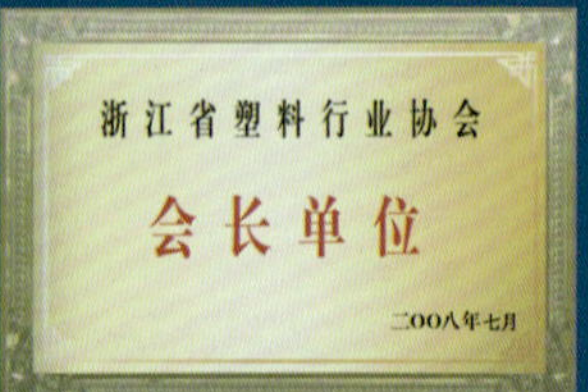

公司始终坚持"开拓、创新、诚信、共赢"的企业精神，先后被授予全国"守合同重信用"单位，2008-2012年连续被全国工商业联合会授予"中国民营企业500强企业"，2005年以来连续被浙江省工商局授予"重合同守信用AAA级单位"称号，被浙江省人行、农行评为"信用等级AAA级企业"称号。

公司正以全球化、一体化和信息化的战略眼光，努力成为提供物流支持、技术支持、信息支持的工贸结合的大宗商品分销贸易商、全国最具持续竞争力的塑化贸易商之一。

公司热诚希望与有志之士精诚合作，共创伟业！

联系方式：

地址：中国杭州市滨江区泰安路199号浙江农资大厦
电话：0571-87661222　　邮编：310052
传真：0571-87661333　　网址：www.zjmr.cn

牢固树立以客户为中心的理念，　为客户创造更多的价值

提供专业、快捷、贴心的服务，

苏州工业园区富事达塑业有限责任公司（苏州塑料一厂）

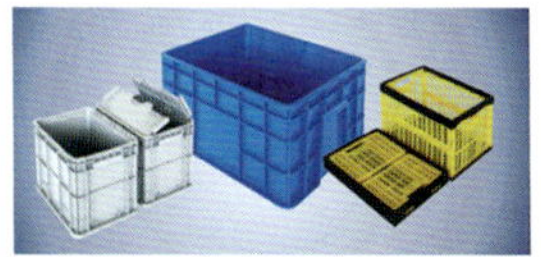
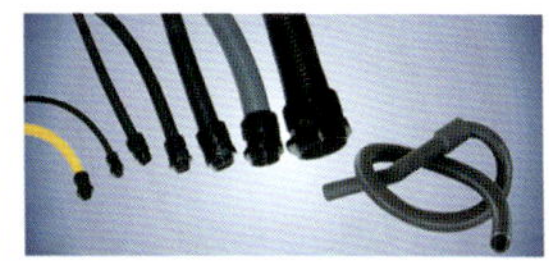

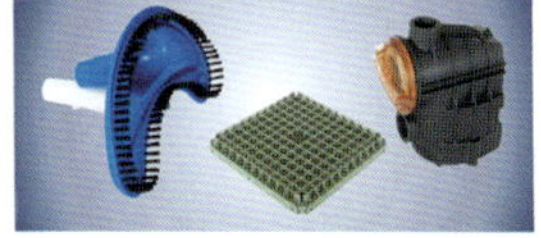

苏州工业园区富事达塑业有限责任公司（苏州塑料一厂）成立于1956年，积累了近50年的塑料加工专业技术经验。是一家专业生产工程注塑制品、波纹管、片板材和改性材料的企业。富事达公司拥有自营进出口权，是江苏省高新技术企业。公司现有员工220余人，工厂面积37000平方米，注册资金2817万元，固定资产3900万元，生产基地位于苏州工业园区。

地址：江苏省苏州市工业园区通园路198号　邮编：215001
电话：0512-67609998 65223949　E-mail:fsd@first-plastic.com
传真：0512-62889532　网址：www.first-plastic.com

贵州森瑞管业有限公司

贵州森瑞管业有限公司成立于2003年9月，位于贵州省贵阳市金阳国家高新技术开发区都匀路，是贵州省规模最大、专业从事新型塑料管材、管件研发、制造、销售和安装服务等业务的新型环保企业之一，　公司注册资本5500万元，总资产逾亿元。

公司目前装备了 40 余条国际、国内先进的管材、管件生产线和完善的检测设备，年生产量达 4 万吨以上，主要产品有聚乙烯（PE）环保健康给水用管、燃气用埋地聚乙烯（PE）管、煤矿用聚乙烯（PE）管材；市政工程排水用HDPE 双壁波纹管、PVC-U 双壁波纹管、钢带增强聚乙烯（PE）螺旋波纹管；地下通信管道用管、埋地用 PVC-C 电力电缆护套管；建筑用 PVC-U 排水管、PP-R 环保健康给水管，、难燃 PVC 电线槽、工业线槽、难燃 PVC 电工套管等。产品覆盖了国家或行业标准所列全部规格。

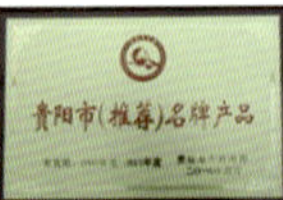

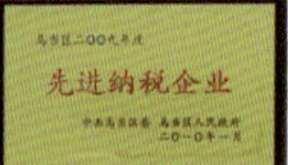

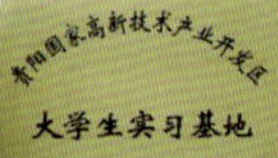

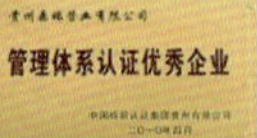

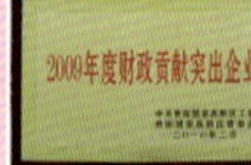

公司以“ 向社会提供环保、节能、安全、经济的塑料管道系统 ”为质量方针，先后通过ISO9001：2000 质量管理体系认证、ISO10012 计量检测体系认定、ISO14001 环境管理体系认证、OHSA18001 职业健康安全管理体系认证和压力管道元件认证。公司先后被评定为“ 国家高新技术企业 ”、“ 省企业技术中心 ”、省“ 守合同、重信用 ”单位 、“ 贵州省‘五一’劳动奖状 ”单位；国家质量监督检验检疫总局授权的“ 聚乙烯（PE）管道焊工考试委员会 ”；公司所有产品均被建设部列为“ 全国建设行业科技成果推广项目 ”、“ 贵阳市名牌产品 ”等荣誉称号。

公司坚持以“ 科技为先、质量为本 ”的经营理念，发扬“ 诚信、务实、学习、创新 ”的企业文化精神，竭诚为广大用户提供最优质的产品和服务。

联系我们：

地址：贵阳国家高新技术开发区都匀路 10 号
电话：0851-7990190/7990130
传真：0851-7990190/7990139
网址：www.gzsenrui.com

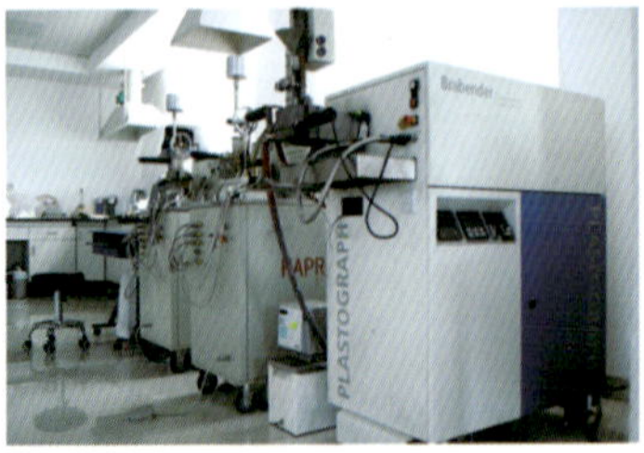

白蝶管业
WHITE BUTTERFLY PIPE

网址: www.chinappr.com

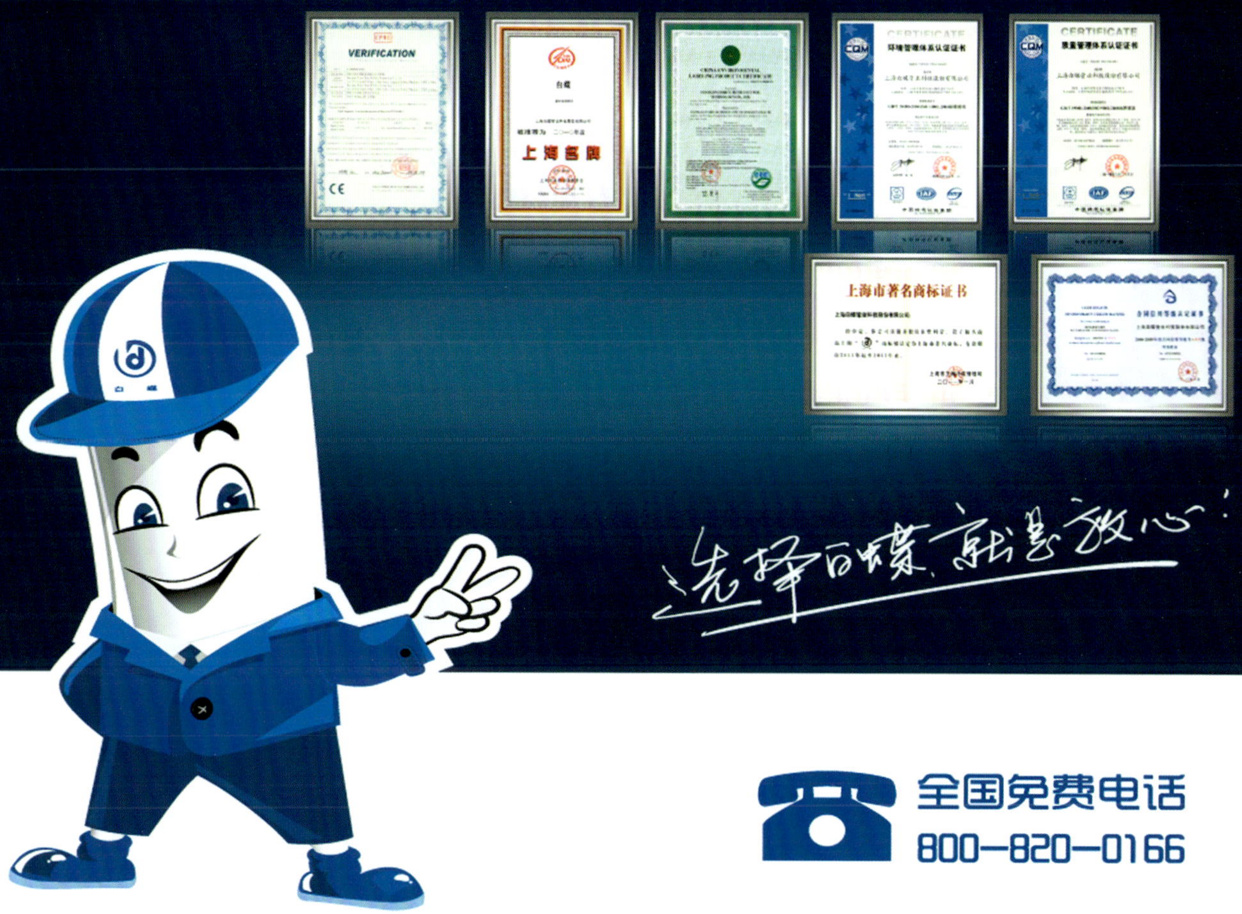

上海白蝶管业科技股份有限公司是一家从事高科技、高性能、环保型的新型管材、管件的生产和销售的股份制企业。1997年底在国内率先开发生产了“给水用三型聚丙烯（PP-R）管道”产品，广泛应用于工业及民用冷热水给水系统、纯净饮用水系统、采暖及中央空调等系统，是传统金属管道的理想替代产品。

公司建立了三大生产基地，拥有德国进口克劳斯玛菲、奥地利辛辛那提、巴顿菲尔等全自动在线检测管材挤出生产线和众多的注塑设备，并配备有多台进口管件焊制设备及检测试验设备，可生产口径自16mm～450mm多种压力等级的PP-R管、PE管、PE-RT管、PP-R稳态复合管、3S聚丙烯静音排水管、PVC-U排水管、PVC-U电工套管、β.PP-R管材和相配套的管配件，产品广泛应用于市政供水、饮用水、建筑给排水、化工、医疗、采暖等领域，进一步扩大了白蝶产品的应用领域和市场占有率。

公司作为中国塑料管道专业委员会副理事长单位，全国塑料制品标准化技术委员会（TC48/SC3）委员单位，在把产品推向市场的同时，注重了配套的应用技术和相关产品的研究开发，先后完成了“PP-R国家标准”的制订，编制了“PP-R管道设计、施工、验收规范”、“PP-R空调管施工规程”、“PP-R施工图集”等。

公司从投产塑料管道开始就把产品质量放在生产经营工作的首位，从93年开始，已连续多年通过了国家和上海地方的产品质量监督抽查，产品质量稳定、可靠，在用户中有很高的信任度，并以全国的营销网络为基础建立了售后服务体系，开设了800-820-0166的全国服务热线，以保证跟广大用户的直接联系，在用户中有很高的信任度。先后获得上海市著名商标、上海名牌产品称号。

地址: 上海市奉贤区金汇镇明星村799号　邮编: 201405　电话: (021)57586421　传真: (021)61294390　邮箱: shwb@chinappr.com

中国塑料工业年鉴

CHINA PLASTICS INDUSTRY YEARBOOK

2013

中国塑料加工工业协会主编

中国石化出版社

内 容 提 要

《中国塑料工业年鉴2013》由中国塑料加工工业协会主办、全国塑料加工工业信息中心承担组稿、编辑工作。年鉴以年度内全国塑料行业的发展和各省、市、自治区塑料加工企业的生产、经营和产品开发为主要内容,也包括合成树脂、助剂、塑料机械和模具的生产和市场情况。年鉴全面反映中国塑料工业现状,是记录中国塑料工业发展的历史文献。

图书在版编目(CIP)数据

中国塑料工业年鉴.2013/中国塑料加工工业协会主编.
—北京:中国石化出版社,2013.12
ISBN 978-7-5114-2516-4

Ⅰ.①中… Ⅱ.①中… Ⅲ.①塑料工业-中国-2013-年鉴 Ⅳ.①F426.7-54

中国版本图书馆CIP数据核字(2013)第275828号

责任编辑:韩勇
责任校对:李伟

中国石化出版社出版发行
地址:北京市东城区安定门外大街58号
邮编:100011 电话:(010)84271850
读者服务部电话:(010)84289974
http://www.sinopec-press.com
E-mail:press@sinopec.com
北京科信印刷有限公司印刷
全国各地新华书店经销
*
787×1092毫米 16开本 54.25印张 116彩页 1365千字
2014年1月第1版 2014年1月第1次印刷
定价:420.00元

《中国塑料工业年鉴》(2013)编委会名单

林荣东　泉州三盛橡塑发泡鞋材有限公司　董事长
刘丰田　山东省塑料协会　会长/研究员
谭方峰　山东省塑料工业有限公司　董事长/总经理
马之清　山东清源集团有限公司　董事长
李振平　山东蓝帆塑胶股份有限公司　董事长
刘方毅　淄博英科框业有限公司　董事长
王乐智　山东同大海岛新材料股份有限公司　总经理
赵东日　山东日科化学有限公司　董事长
丁建生　烟台万华合成革集团有限公司　总经理
符　岸　广东省塑料工业协会　会长
李建军　广州金发科技股份有限公司　研究员
黄志生　广东省皮具行业协会　会长
马镇鑫　广东金明精机股份有限公司　董事长
宋旭彬　广东海兴塑胶有限公司　总经理
林东亮　大大科技(深圳)开发有限公司　董事长
曹　阳　力劲集团深圳领威科技有限公司　集团行政总裁
左满伦　广东联塑科技实业有限公司　总裁
吴耀根　佛山佛塑科技集团股份有限公司　总工程师
林云青　康泰塑胶科技集团有限公司　总经理
李忠烈　四川省犍为罗城忠烈塑料有限责任公司　董事长
郭庆人　新疆天业股份有限公司　董事长
房　琳　中国石油化工销售有限公司　副总经理
杨卫民　北京化工大学　教授
马占峰　中国塑料加工工业协会　秘书长

委　　员：(以姓氏笔画为序)

于　健　清华大学高分子研究所　所长
王占杰　中国塑料加工工业协会 副秘书长
王长青　山东企鹅塑胶集团有限公司　董事长
王存吉　中国塑料加工工业协会　副秘书长
王德禧　中国塑协专家委员会　常务副主任兼秘书长
冯庶君　中国塑料加工工业协会　副秘书长兼会展部主任
包建成　中国塑协塑料技术协作委员会　理事长
田　岩　中国塑料加工工业协会　副秘书长兼综合业务部主任
任玥璋　中国塑协聚氯乙烯板制品专业委员会　主任
朱　瑾　中国塑协工程塑料专业委员会　主任
朱义华　中国塑协中空制品专业委员会　主任
刘　姝　中国塑料加工工业协会　副秘书长兼会员部主任
刘英俊　中国塑协改性塑料专业委员会　秘书长

李建军　中国塑协多功能母料专业委员会　主任
孔德海　新疆维吾尔自治区塑料加工工业协会　秘书长
孙冬泉　中国塑料加工工业协会　副秘书长
孙晓军　辽宁华塑实业集团有限公司　董事长
孙福荣　中国塑协人造革合成革专业委员会　主任
庄　甦　中国塑协氟塑料加工专业委员会　主任
许　琳　中国塑料加工工业协会　副秘书长兼信息部主任
吴方群　中国塑料加工工业协会　信息部副主任兼《中国塑协通讯》主编
吴家福　中国塑协密胺塑料制品专业委员会　主任
吴耀根　中国塑协双向拉伸聚丙烯薄膜专业委员会　主任
李振平　中国塑协塑料助剂专业委员会　主任
陆慧琴　中国塑协注塑制品专业委员会　理事长
陈　宇　北京市化学工业研究院　副院长
赵东日　中国塑协新材料研究开发工作委员会　负责人
赵安赤　中国塑协改性塑料专业委员会　主任
徐　斌　中国塑协聚氯乙烯板制品专业委员会　主任
徐志强　中国塑协双向拉伸聚酯薄膜专业委员会　主任
陈力辉　中国塑协塑料管道专业委员会　主任
孟庆军　中国塑料加工工业协会　副秘书长
易佩瑾　中国塑料加工工业协会　办公室副主任
林东亮　中国塑协塑料再生利用专业委员会/塑木制品专业委员会　主任
林永飞　中国塑协聚氨酯制品专业委员会　主任
林丰钦　南亚塑胶工业股份有限公司　资深副总经理
罗宏宇　中国塑协滚塑专业委员会　主任
夏　青　中国塑协降解塑料专业委员会　主任
夏嘉良　中国塑协复合膜制品专业委员会　主任
郑元和　中国塑协塑料配线器材专业委员会　主任
侯树亭　中国塑协泡沫塑料 EPS 专业委员会　主任
洪晓冬　中国塑协镀铝膜专业委员会　主任
袁建华　中国塑协异型材及门窗制品专业委员会　主任
贾润礼　中北大学塑料研究所　所长
郭庆人　中国塑协塑料节水器材专业委员会　主任
郭志宏　中国塑料加工工业协会　办公室副主任兼会员部副主任
曹志强　中国塑协农用薄膜专业委员会　主任
曹常在　中国塑协医用塑料专业委员会　主任
姜集康　中国塑协塑料编织制品专业委员会　主任
徐志强　中国塑协流延薄膜专业委员会/双向拉伸聚酯薄膜专业委员会
主任

徐　斌　中国塑协硬质PVC发泡制品专业委员会　主任

黄　锐　四川大学高分子材料系　教授

韩国林　扬州市酒店日用品协会　会长

鲍新才　宁波市塑料行业协会　会长

翦建政　湖南省塑料行业协会　理事长

主　　编：钱桂敬

副 主 编：许　琳　史立科

作　　者（以姓氏笔画为序）

孔德海　马占峰　王占杰　王存吉　王庆圆　王　浩　王梦媚　王德钧
王德禧　车忠良　韦　华　冯庶君　付志敏　史春才　田　岩　龙　洁
关平平　刘卫东　刘丰田　刘均科　刘　毅　刘英俊　刘　敏　刘汉龙
刘景芬　孙　莉　孙冬泉　许　琳　许　榕　吕　方　宋云鹤　张文雷
张明艳　张涌涛　庄　甦　李显贵　杨惠娣　杨有财　苏一凡　汪建平
邹　奇　邹文云　陈　生　陈　顶　陈俊尧　郑　静　罗崇远　周永泰
周鸿勋　倪国庆　武宏斌　孟庆君　吴耀根　郑天禄　侯芳放　姜振生
钟　雁　徐贵一　柴国樑　涂红梅　翁云宣　高坤光　郭　齐　郭金明
钱桂敬　顾大全　赵　军　赵安赤　曹广元　曹常在　符　岸　黄　勇
童人本　韩简吉　曾祥平　翟光景　唐赛珍　程田青　葛存良　昝立伟
赖汉文　黎永正

中国塑料加工工业协会

中国塑协塑料助剂专委会秘书处

中国塑料机械工业协会

出 版 说 明

2012年，是“十八大”的开局之年，是“十二五”计划关键之年，也是塑料行业承上启下实现跨越发展的关键时期，是转变发展方式、优化产业结构、全面提升产业素质和整体水平，实施产业链、产品高端化战略的重要阶段。2012年，是不平凡的一年，塑料加工业全行业认真克服全球金融危机带来的影响，紧紧围绕调结构和转方式这一主题和主线，努力拼搏，实现了稳定健康的发展好形势。

面对全球经济形势和中国塑料行业现状，中国塑料加工工业协会在2012年组织编制完成《塑料加工业“十二五”发展规划指导意见》，明确了塑料加工业在国民经济中的定位、初步理清了行业在“十二五”期间总体发展思路。在此基础上，继续组织编制了《塑料加工行业技术进步“十二五”发展指导意见》，并于2013年5月19日在中国塑料加工工业协会的理事扩大会上通过。《塑料加工行业技术进步“十二五”发展指导意见》全面总结了塑料加工业“十二五”以来技术进步取得的巨大成绩和存在的不足，全面分析了塑料加工业面临的难得的历史发展机遇和严峻的挑战，深入分析了当代塑料加工业发展趋势和最新前沿技术，在此基础上提出了“十二五”塑料加工业科技发展的总体思路。

《中国塑料工业年鉴》自创刊至今已出版了11卷。2013版为《中国塑料工业年鉴》第12卷，与前11卷在时间和内容上保持连续性。设有“综述”、“专论”、“大事记”、“全国塑料工业生产经营情况统计”、“政策法规”、“各地区塑料工业情况”、“主要制品行业情况”、“专利技术”、“重点企业”等栏目。《中国塑料工业年鉴》具有工具性特点：集手册、年表、图录、书目、索引、文摘、表谱、统计资料、指南于一身；具有资料性特点：全面、系统、准确地记述了上年度塑料行业发展状况；具有可读性特点：资料祥实、功能齐全、反应及时、连续出版，同时又肩负着“资政”、“存史”和“宣传推广”的社会责任。《中国塑料工业年鉴》全面客观地记录了上年度中国塑料工业站在新起点、抓住新机遇、展现新精神、谋求新发展的重大事件和“十二五”规划开局之年取得的丰硕成果。

《中国塑料工业年鉴》(2013)由中国塑料加工工业协会主办，中国石化出版社出版发行。中国塑协各专业委员会、中国轻工业信息中心、中国塑料机械工业协会、中国模具协会、中国氯碱协会和各省、市、自治区塑料行业协会等单位领导与专家给予了大力支持。

《中国塑料工业年鉴》编委会向所有关心、支持和参与撰稿、组织、筹划及宣传工作的领导、专家、作者和朋友们一并表示衷心的感谢。诚请广大读者对2013版《中国塑料工业年鉴》编写、出版中的不足之处给予批评、指正。

《中国塑料工业年鉴》编辑委员会

2013年9月

目　录

专　论

大 事 记

政策法规

全国塑料工业生产、经营情况统计

综　述

各地区塑料工业

主要制品行业情况

专利技术

塑料标准化

重点企业介绍

CONTENTS

Monograph

Major Events

Policies and Regulations

Statistics of China's Plastic Industrial Production and Business Operation

Review

Development of Regional Plastics Industry in China

Development Situation of Main Plastics Products

Patents

Progress of Standardization in Plastics Industry

专　　论

中国塑料工业2012年度发展报告

中国塑料加工工业协会

2012年，国内国外经济形势复杂多变，对塑料行业的发展也产生了较大的影响。行业发展需要调整结构，企业发展需要把握市场，两者都必须技术创新。中国塑料加工行业在经历了“十一五”、“十二五”以及2011年的高速增长之后，2012年遭受了严峻的考验。

一方面欧美经济复苏乏力致使塑料制品出口放缓，加上人民币升值、原材料和劳动力等成本上升以及国际贸易摩擦频出，特别是发达国家纷纷出台与塑料有关的安全法律、法规及标准等技术壁垒，导致塑料制品出口受阻，全球经济环境限制了产品的出口需求，从而放缓了行业的发展步伐。

另一方面，由于部分塑料制品产能阶段性和结构性过剩，低价竞争呈白热化趋势，而生产成本却在不断上升，国内市场内需不振等形势极大地限制了塑料制品行业的深层次发展，从而使整个产业进入常态化中速增长的阶段。

在国家一系列宏观经济政策扶持下，中国塑料加工行业努力克服了国际金融危机带来的严重冲击，下半年行业生产止跌企稳，实现了较平稳的增长，产销率维持较高水平，进出口贸易显露回暖迹象，企业效益水平有较大提升。

据国家统计局统计数据显示，2012年1～12月塑料制品规模以上企业13246个，累计完成工业总产值16757.29亿元，同比增长15.04%。与2011年相比，增长幅度回落了12.5个百分点，增长明显放缓。2012年1～12月实现销售产值16450.19亿元，产销率达到98.17%，比2011年1～12月98.04%的产销率高出0.13个百分点，产销率保持较高水平。塑料制品产量5781.86万吨，同比增长8.99%，比2011年1～12月22.35%的增长回落了13.36个百分点。

2012年1～12月塑料制品规模以上企业完成主营业务收入16310.13亿元，同比增长11.79%，比2011年1～12月主营业务收入27.52%的增长回落了15.73个百分点。实现利税1431.35亿元，同比增长17.12%。其中：利润总额为963.27亿元，同比增长15.94%。利税总额和利润总额增长分别比2011年1～12月回落了14.48和16.56个百分点。行业资产总计10412.05亿元，同比增长13.03%。从业人数233.18万人，同比下降1.55%。

据海关总署统计数据汇总显示，2012年，中国累计出口塑料制品13821.6kt，出口金额达491.85亿美元。同比分别增长5.79%和24.55%。

一、塑料制品行业产量及产、销总值增长态势平稳，呈回暖的态势

中国塑料制品产量整体保持上升趋势，但增幅比上年同期有较大的下滑。2012年1～12月，中国累计生产塑料制品57818.6kt，同比增长8.99%，比上年同期22.35%的增长回落了13.36个百分点。其中，塑料薄膜9702.5kt，同比增长9.33%，比上年同期回落1.84个百分点，其中农用薄膜1627.4kt，同比增长7.74%，比上年同期回落6.75个百分点；泡沫塑料1720.6kt，同比增长23.13%，比上年同期回落2.25个百分点；人造革、合成革3142.7kt，同比增长15.55%，比上年同期增加了5.98个百分点；日用塑料4618.4kt，同比增长14.43%，比上年同期增加了9.17个百分点；其他塑料38634.4kt，同比增长7.26%，比上年同期回落21.33个百分点。除日用塑料，人造革、合成革，泡沫塑料与上年同比增长高于10%；其他制品品种同比增长均低于10%；其中农用塑料薄膜和其他塑料制品增速最低，分别比上年同期回落了6.75和21.33个百分点。具体见表1和图1。

表1　2012年塑料制品累计产量及与上年同期比较表

塑料制品类别	1~12月累计产量/kt	累计比同期/%	增幅比同期/%
塑料制品	57818.6	8.99	-13.36
其中：塑料薄膜	9702.5	9.33	-1.84
其中：农用薄膜	1627.4	7.74	-6.75
泡沫塑料	1720.6	23.13	-2.25
人造革、合成革	3142.7	15.55	5.98
日用塑料	4618.4	14.43	9.17
其他塑料	38634.4	7.26	-21.33

来源：国家统计局

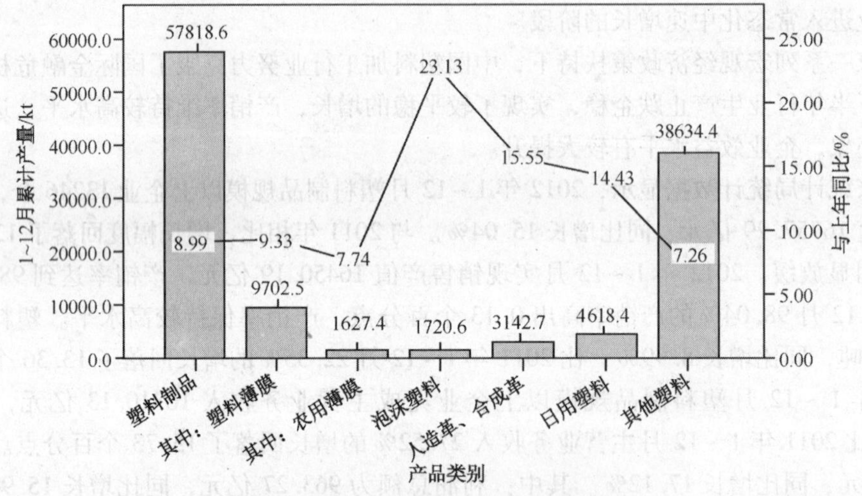

图1　2012年塑料制品累计产量同比增长示意图

从表1和图1中可以看出泡沫塑料是增速最高的制品类别，同比增长高达23.13%，但增幅比上年同期回落2.25个百分点。另外，人造革、合成革和日用塑料是两个增幅比去年同期增加的塑料制品类别，其产量累计比同期分别增加了15.55%和14.43%，增幅分别比上年同期增加了5.98和9.17个百分点。

塑料制品1~12月工业总产值为16757.29亿元，同比增长15.04%，工业销售产值16450.19亿元，同比增长14.95%。其中塑料薄膜工业总产值2222.93亿元，同比增长14.23%，工业销售产值2181.34亿元，同比增长13.99%；塑料板、管、型材工业总产值4133.52亿元，同比增长18.64%，工业销售产值4048.50亿元，同比增长18.46%；塑料丝、绳及编织品2188.23亿元，同比增长19.13%，工业销售产值2157.65亿元，同比增长19.39%；泡沫塑料732.75亿元，同比增长15.56%，工业销售产值717.05亿元，同比增长14.38%；塑料人造革合成革1085.77亿元，同比增长17.23%，工业销售产值1058.94亿元，同比增长16.98%；塑料包装箱及容器1497.17亿元，同比增长16.78%，工业销售产值

1472.72 亿元，同比增长 17.21%；日用塑料 1410.52 亿元，同比增长 13.26%，工业销售产值 1384.14 亿元，同比增长 13.49%；塑料零件 1234.80 亿元，同比增长 3.55%，工业销售产值 1215.60 亿元，同比增长 3.15%；其他塑料制品 2251.59 亿元，同比增长 11.52%，工业销售产值 2214.25 亿元，同比增长 11.54%。具体见表 2。

表 2　2012 年塑料制品累计工业总产值、工业销售产值、出口交货值及与上年同期比较表

塑料制品类别	累计工业总产值/亿元	累计比同期/%	累计工业销售产值/亿元	累计比同期/%	累计出口交货值/亿元	累计比同期/%
塑料制品	16757.29	15.04	16450.19	14.95	2140.92	2.71
塑料薄膜制造	2222.93	14.23	2181.34	13.99	258.10	3.28
塑料板、管、型材制造	4133.52	18.64	4048.50	18.46	191.91	0.16
塑料丝、绳及编织品制造	2188.23	19.13	2157.65	19.39	93.51	5.36
泡沫塑料制造	732.75	15.56	717.05	14.38	47.29	5.72
塑料人造革、合成革制造	1085.77	17.23	1058.94	16.98	87.01	-2.93
塑料包装箱及容器制造	1497.17	16.78	1472.72	17.21	122.48	18.70
日用塑料制品制造	1410.52	13.26	1384.14	13.49	459.79	5.40
塑料零件制造	1234.80	3.55	1215.60	3.15	348.07	-2.33
其他塑料制品制造	2251.59	11.52	2214.25	11.54	532.75	1.66

来源：国家统计局。

2012 年 1 ~ 12 月份累计产销率维持较高水平，达到 98.17%，比 2011 年 1 ~ 12 月 98.04% 的产销率提高了 0.13 个百分点。

从表中可以看出，2012 年 1 ~ 12 月塑料制品工业总产值、工业销售产值整体上依然保持两位数增长，只有塑料零件工业总产值同比增长 3.55%，其工业销售产值同比增长只有 3.15%。显示出塑料制品行业产、销总值增长态势平稳，虽然增速比上年同期仍有下滑，但下滑幅度已趋于放缓。2012 年 1 ~ 12 月的塑料制品出口交货值比上年同期增加了 2.71%，其中塑料包装箱及容器制造出口交货值同比增长 18.70%；只有塑料人造革、合成革和塑料零件出口交货值与上年同比是下降的，分别下降了 2.93% 和 2.33%

二、塑料制品行业主营收入仍保持两位数增长，效益水平有所提高

随着塑料制品行业止跌回升的运行态势，行业的效益水平也有所提高。

国家统计局数据显示，塑料制品行业 1 ~ 12 月主营收入为 16310.13 亿元，比上年同比增长 11.79%。其中塑料薄膜 2179.51 亿元，同比增长 10.93%；塑料板、管、型材 3960.93 亿元，同比增长 14.59%；塑料丝、绳及编织品 2172.79 亿元，同比增长 18.42%；泡沫塑料 707.48 亿元，同比增长 10.06%；塑料人造革合成革 1040.00 亿元，同比增长 11.78%；塑料包装箱及容器 1461.45 亿元，同比增长 13.11%；日用塑料 1377.94 亿元，同比增长 11.03%；塑料零件 1210.70 亿元，同比增长 1.53%；其他塑料制品 2199.34 亿元，同比增长 8.10%。由于我国政府努力实施积极的财政政策和税制改革，使整个塑料制品行业的经济效益有了较好的提升，主营收入仍保持两位数增长，企业的利润也有所提高。具体见表3、表4。

表3　2012年塑料制品主营收入及增长情况

产品名称	规模以上企业数量	主营收入/亿元	同比增长/%
塑料制品	13245	16310.13	11.79
其中：塑料薄膜	1431	2179.51	10.93
塑料板、管、型材	2504	3960.93	14.59
塑料丝、绳及编织品	1835	2172.79	18.42
泡沫塑料	747	707.48	10.06
塑料人造革、合成革	549	1040.00	11.78
塑料包装箱及容器	1405	1461.45	13.11
日用塑料制品	1335	1377.94	11.03
塑料零件	1249	1210.70	1.53
其他塑料制品	2190	2199.34	8.10

来源：国家统计局。

数据显示，2012年1～12月份塑料制品行业实现利税总额1431.35亿元，同比增长17.12%，其中利润总额为963.27亿元，同比增长15.94%。虽然经济效益指标比2011年1～12月累计指标相比有较大幅度的回落，利税总额和利润总额分别回落了14.48和16.56个百分点；但相比1－9月份又有所增加，分别增加了3.46和3.18个百分点。显示了企业效益水平有逐渐提升的趋势。所属子行业的经济效益指标为：塑料薄膜利税总额172.32亿元，同比增长10.23%，其利润总额为120.02亿元，同比增加了6.31%；塑料板、管、型材利税总额388.73亿元，同比增长21.29%，其利润总额为264.45亿元，同比增长19.20%；塑料丝、绳及编织品利税总额203.61亿元，同比增长23.98%，其利润总额为136.71亿元，同比增长27.31%；泡沫塑料利税总额67.20亿元，同比增长17.36%，其利润总额为47.14亿元，同比增长18.67%；塑料人造革、合成革利税总额95.03亿元，同比增长29.65%，其利润总额为66.56亿元，同比增长32.42%；塑料包装箱及容器利税总额141.92亿元，同比增长12.89%，其利润总额为94.67亿元，同比增长11.68%；日用塑料利税总额118.44亿元，同比增长21.66%，其利润总额为80.23亿元，同比增长22.75%；塑料零件利税总额82.54亿元，同比增加5.22%，其利润总额为49.98亿元，同比增长1.57%；其他塑料制品利税总额161.56亿元，同比增长8.46%，其利润总额为103.50亿元，同比增长4.16%。

从上述数据可以看出，塑料零件企业的效益最差，利税总额比去年同期增加了5.22%，利润总额仅比去年同期增加了1.57%，相比较今年1～9月利税总额和利润总额增速则分别回落了3.05和7.07个百分点。从中可以看出塑料零件企业的经济效益增速还在继续下降。

但从整体上看，行业的经济效益水平仍保持两位数增长。国家对企业实施的一系列扶持政策，特别是结构性减税、降低企业成本负担等政策开始显效，塑料制品行业经济效益水平有逐渐提升的趋势。具体见表4和图2。

表 4　2012 年利税利润及增长情况

行业名称	利税总额/亿元	同比增长/%	利润总额/亿元	同比增长/%
塑料制品业	1431. 35	17. 12	963. 27	15. 94
其中：塑料薄膜	172. 32	10. 23	120. 02	6. 31
塑料板、管、型材	388. 73	21. 29	264. 45	19. 20
塑料丝、绳及编织品	203. 61	23. 98	136. 71	27. 31
泡沫塑料	67. 20	17. 36	47. 14	18. 67
塑料人造革、合成革	95. 03	29. 65	66. 56	32. 42
塑料包装箱及容器	141. 92	12. 89	94. 67	11. 68
日用塑料	118. 44	21. 66	80. 23	22. 75
塑料零件	82. 54	5. 22	49. 98	1. 57
其他塑料制品	161. 56	8. 46	103. 50	4. 16

来源：国家统计局。

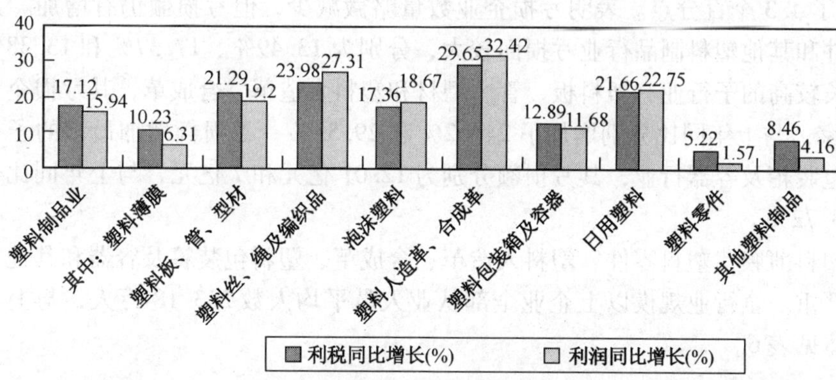

图 2　2012 年塑料制品利税总额与利润总额同比增长示意图

三、位居前八名地区的塑料制品产量占全国比例 65. 77%

分地区看，浙江、广东、山东、江苏、辽宁、福建、湖北、河南等 8 省份位居全国累计产量前八名，累计产量占比达 65. 77%，显示产业分布仍旧不平衡。具体见表 5、图 3。

表 5　2012 年塑料制品产量位居前八名地区

地　　区	本月止累计/t	占全国比例/%
全国	57818647	100. 00
浙江	9485401	16. 41
广东	9193123	15. 90
山东	4531200	7. 84
江苏	3492566	6. 04
辽宁	3238998	5. 60
福建	2745337	4. 75
湖北	2720014	4. 70
河南	2618627	4. 53
八地区总计	38025266	65. 77

来源：国家统计局。

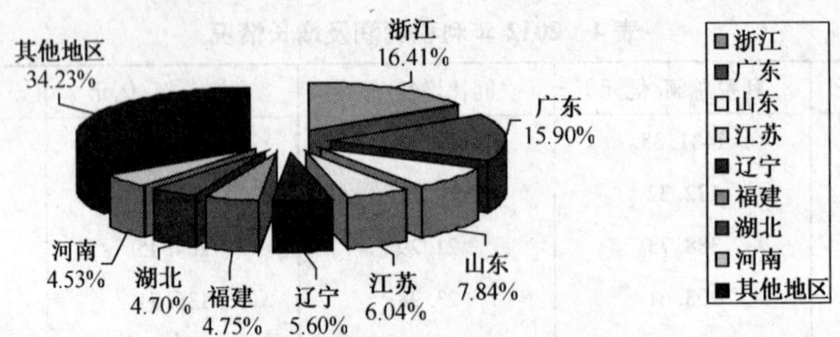

图3　2012 年塑料制品产量前八名地区占比情况示意图

四、企业亏损面和亏损企业亏损额均比今年 1～9 月份有所减少，从业人数略有减少

据对国家统计局相关资料统计，2012 年 1～12 月，主要经济指标汇总的塑料制品行业规模以上企业共 13245 个，其中亏损企业 1490 个，比去年同期亏损企业数增加了 16.59%，企业亏损面为 11.25%，比今年 1～9 月份的 13.69% 回落了 2.44 个百分点。亏损企业累计亏损额 67.25 亿元，比去年同期累计亏损额增加了 37.54%，比今年 1～9 月份亏损额同比增加的 33.24% 增加了 4.3 个百分点。表明亏损企业数量略微减少，但亏损额仍有增加。其中塑料薄膜，塑料零件和其他塑料制品行业亏损面较大，分别为 13.49%、17.37% 和 13.38%。亏损企业数同比增长较高的子行业有塑料板、管、型材和塑料人造革、合成革，其亏损企业数分别为 243 家和 57 家，与上年同比分别增加了 24.62% 和 29.55%。亏损额增加最多的子行业有塑料薄膜和塑料包装箱及容器行业，其亏损额分别为 12.01 亿元和 7 亿元，与上年同比分别增加了 78.80% 和 83.72%。

反映出塑料薄膜、塑料零件、塑料人造革、合成革、塑料包装箱及容器和其他塑料制品行业亏损较为严重。全行业规模以上企业全部从业人员平均人数 233.18 万人，与上年同比减少 1.55%。具体见表 6。

表 6　2012 年企业亏损情况及从业人员数量

行业名称	规模以上企业数量	亏损企业数量	比去年同期亏损企业数增减/%	亏损企业累计亏损额/亿元	比去年同期累计亏损额同比增减/%	全部从业人员平均人数	与上年同比增减/%
塑料制品业	13245	1490	16.59	67.25	37.54	2331784	-1.55
其中：塑料薄膜	1431	193	20.63	12.01	78.80	207169	-5.55
塑料板、管、型材	2504	243	24.62	11.54	19.95	394219	4.37
塑料丝、绳及编织品	1835	107	0.00	1.77	-3.90	323786	4.36
泡沫塑料	747	67	4.69	1.31	-8.83	89558	-4.07
塑料人造革、合成革	549	57	29.55	1.75	36.13	134940	0.68
塑料包装箱及容器	1405	162	20.00	7.00	83.72	204129	2.57
日用塑料	1335	151	9.42	4.13	8.43	277569	-1.73
塑料零件	1249	217	12.44	14.32	31.10	294375	-8.89
其他塑料制品	2190	293	21.07	13.42	42.05	406039	-5.42

来源：国家统计局。

五、2012 年塑料制品出口显露回暖迹象

据中国海关总署最新数据，2012 年中国累计出口塑料制品 13821.6kt，同比增长 5.79%；

出口额491.85亿美元，同比增长24.55%。高出我国2012年外贸出口额增速(7.9%)16.65个百分点，出口增长回暖。塑料制品的出口单价平均为3.56美元/kg，塑料制品的进口单价平均为10.27美元/kg。其进口单价是出口单价的2.88倍，说明我国出口的塑料制品仍然是以中低端产品为主，出口产品结构急需调整，但比上年同期进口单价是出口单价的3.30倍，减少了0.42倍，出口产品结构调整的些微变化逐渐显现。

由于国家实施了提高塑料制品出口退税率、取消部分产品加工贸易限制等政策，对出口企业抵御经济危机，加大塑料制品的出口起到了提振作用，塑料制品出口逐渐回暖。

六、中国塑料工业发展目标

中国塑料工业现阶段存在的急需加以认真研究和解决的问题。一是在快速发展中，产能过剩问题越来越突出，在大多数行业中普遍存在。比如双向拉伸BOPP、BOPET、塑编行业、管道行业、异型材门窗行业等。因为产能过剩造成无序竞争、恶性竞争的现象频频发生，给塑料行业带来了很大的负面影响。二是中低端产品比重过大，技术含量与国外先进水平有较大差距，市场上急需的产品还要大量的进口，产品结构、企业组织结构、区域布局不合理问题突出。三是行业急需的各种专用料还需大量进口，一些高档产品的原料如专用管道、高档薄膜的原料基本上依靠进口，严重制约了行业发展。

中国塑料工业总体发展思路，是依靠科技进步、科技创新，大力推动技术进步，推动产业升级，逐步构建现代产业体系；注重产业结构调整，加快转变发展方式，优化产品结构、区域布局和企业组织结构，突出绿色环保，着力实现循环和可持续发展；突出品牌战略，大力提高产品的档次和质量，提高整个塑料加工业的产业素质。

中国塑料工业主要发展目标，制品产量年均增长12%左右，总产值增长15%左右，考虑到塑料加工业正在进入优化结构和产业升级的关键发展阶段，该目标体现了塑料加工业将由高速增长进入平稳较快增长的趋势和特点，也是为加快技术调整、技术改造创造更好的外部环境，有利于进一步推动科技进步，技术创新，加快转变发展方式和提高发展质量。

塑料加工业在国民经济中的地位，是以塑料制品加工为核心，涵盖原料、机械、模具、助剂为一体的新兴制造业。是为工业、农业、建筑、交通运输、航天航空等国民经济各行各业提供重要产品、配件和各种新兴材料的国民经济基础性产业，也是为广大消费者提供安全可靠消费品的民生产业，是人类必须的生产资料和生活资料，是国民经济新的支柱产业之一。这里重点说明三个问题：

一是关于新兴制造业。合成树脂、合成橡胶、合成纤维三大合成高分子材料是构成现代社会的基础材料之一，是支持现代高科技发展的新型材料。塑料加工业已经由传统的初级消费品正快速向高层次消费品过度，向档次高、技术含量高的方向发展。目前塑料加工业已经成功进入工业、农业等各行各业，在高科技领域得到了广泛的应用。在未来新材料技术革命中，塑料加工业将发挥更加重要的作用。未来新材料攻关的项目中，塑料材料与制品所占的数量最大，涉及的领域最宽，因此塑料加工业已从传统制造业成长为科技含量高的新兴制造业。

二是关于塑料加工业是快速成长的国民支柱产业之一。2010年塑料加工业的总产值已经占到GDP的3.55%，距离国际上通用的5%的标准还有一定差距，一般意义上如果有一个行业产值占到国民经济的5%，那么这个产业就是国家支柱产业。显然现在塑料加工业还不能视为国民支柱产业，但国内巨大的需求和发展空间，塑料工业将继续保持快速增长。作为21世纪新材料的塑料，随着科技进步速度的加快和工业化进程的深入，其应用范围越来越广。虽然国际金融危机还没有走出危机的阴影，但是这场危机并不能从根本上改变世界经济长期发展的趋势。中国塑料加工业的比较优势将进一步得到加强，将有利于进一步扩展国际市场。塑料加工业作为朝阳产业快速发展的特点将进一步提升其在国民经济中的地位。塑料加工业应受到高度重视，应该加大培育力度，使之尽快成为国民经济的支柱产业。

三是再次明确了塑料是由合成或天然高分子化合物为原料，以增塑剂、填充剂、润滑剂、注塑剂等添加剂为辅助成分，在一定温度和压力下制成的塑性材料和少量固性材料这一论述。目的是将原料和制品加以区分，进而将合成树脂和石化产业在国民经济中的地位与塑料加工业在国民经济中的地位加以适当区分，这样塑料加工业在国民经济中的定位更加符合实际。这样做的目的是号召全行业进一步树立信心，更加重视塑料加工业在国民经济中的地位，更加坚定不移的走新型制造业的发展路子，加快成为国民经济新的支柱产业。

中国塑料工业“十二五”期间的重要任务：

(一)必须加快转变发展方式，加快结构优化调整。当前我们塑料加工业正在进入以上质量，上档次，上水平为标准的创新驱动发展的新阶段。这个阶段要求我们必须从过去依靠数量的增加和投资扩能发展的路子，坚决调整到依靠创新、依靠技术进步和优化结构的发展路子上来。十年来的高速增长是不可能一直持续下去的，20%左右的增长速度主要基于国家国民经济的高速发展和国内制品发展滞后而出现的填空式的增长。塑料加工业由持续十年的高速增长进入平稳较快增长是一个必然的趋势，这也标志着塑料加工业正由快速成长期逐步进入产业成熟期。当前要严格防止低水平产能进一步扩大。要研究市场需求，要做到理性投资，防止盲目追求大和攀比性投资。要处理好内涵和外延的关系、大和强的关系，要把工作着力点放到细分市场和实施差异化战略上来，放到依靠创新、技术进步、优化结构调整和开发新产品上来。

(二)《“十二五”规划》强调大力推进科技进步，加快创新体系建设，全面提升产业素质。塑料是未来技术革命重要的领域，要抓住国家支持新型战略产业发展的机遇，依靠科技进步，加快新技术、新工艺、新产品的开发。规划提出要集中力量对塑料加工业的共性关键技术进行攻关，力争取得阶段性的突破。如超临界发泡技术的应用、大口径交流聚乙烯管材、超高分子量聚乙烯管材加工，水性聚氨酯合成革、改性 PVC 管材、含氢氯氟烃发泡剂替代以及新的节能技术。规划对塑料加工业主要产品发展的重点和方向均作了说明，同时规划提出要紧紧围绕功能化这一核心开发新型塑料材料，功能化是塑料行业下一步发展的方向和希望。所以要高度关注并大力开发功能化技术研究和纳米材料技术研究。当前要重点关注高阻隔多层共挤纳米微层复合材料；纤维功能增强复合材料、聚合物合金等现代制造业高性能工程塑料；要关注熔体静电纺丝纳米过滤材料，纳米抗菌、阻燃、降解等功能性材料；要关注太阳能光伏发电配套材料，锂离子镍氢离子电池隔膜、光学膜以及农用多功能膜材料。规划特别强调了要加大对各种膜材料的攻关力度，要在膜材料超薄化、复合化方面进行攻关，解决功能膜发展瓶颈。“十二五”主要任务就是要通过技术进步和科技创新不断提高产业素质，提高产业核心竞争能力，为全面建设塑料加工业现代产业体系打好基础。在“十二五”规划发布之后，我们正在组织力量制定未来五年塑料加工业技术进步指南，紧紧围绕塑料加工业面临的共性、关键技术，组织攻关，实现重点突破，改变塑料加工业的面貌。围绕新材料、新工艺来开发新的产品，围绕节能减排技术，推动行业低碳绿色发展。同时要关注当代塑料加工业前沿科学技术，引导我们紧紧围绕着当前最新科技动态和前沿技术的进展把握行业发展方向。制定技术进步指南，目的就是要动员全行业和社会的科技资源共同攻关，来推动塑料加工业科技驱动发展的进程，同时我们准备在条件成熟的时候，召开塑料加工业科技大会，通过技术进步指导意见，表彰技术进步和优秀先进科技工作者。

（三）要加快结构调整和优化区域布局。当前塑料加工业区域布局不合理情况比较严重，东部产量占到74%，中部占到15%，西部仅仅10%，造成这种情况的原因有很多。中西部地区最近有很大的发展，但是区域不平衡的情况仍旧非常突出，所以“十二五”提出要在充分发挥优势的基础上实施差异化的发展。沿海地区要加强品牌建设，加快产业高端化进程，形成新的竞争优势；中部地区要抓住机遇发挥承东启西的地缘优势，要积极主动来承接沿海的产业转移；西部地区根据依托资源秉赋的特点，发挥后发优势。比如新疆，在节水灌溉农用塑料上有大的发展，能够形成布局合理各具特色的产业布局，促进塑料加工业健康发展。

特别强调一个重要任务，就是大力推进塑料制品安全工程建设。塑料制品无论是从管材、异型材及门窗到日用品各方面，都有使用安全和卫生安全的问题，这关系到广大消费者、使用者的生命财产安全，必须以高度责任感，努力提高产品质量，切实保证产品的卫生和安全。随着技术进步和生活水平的提高，对塑料产品的安全和卫生要求也越来越高，标准越来越严格，特别是与食品饮料有关的包装材料和制品成为食品安全重点监督和检测的对象。比如说PVC给水管是严格禁止使用含铅热稳定剂，必须使用符合标准的各种助剂和食品级的PVC，这个要求非常严格，在国际上，欧盟实施与食品接触塑料与塑料制品的最新法规，在去年的五月一日已经开始生效，与原法规相比，要求更加细化，检测项目变化也最大，新法规扩大了监管对象。在绿色环保方面，欧盟等地区已经对聚氯乙烯制品制定全面禁用含铅热稳定剂的路线图和时间表。塑料门窗的聚氯乙烯材料含铅的热稳定剂也不能使用。此外，各种制品的使用安全如异型材塑钢门窗、玩具、建筑保温材料、阻燃和含氢氟里昂替代等也必须引起高度关注，所以加强安全工程的建设对我们来讲任务非常艰巨，全行业要以高度社会责任感、诚信和自律，共同抵制和打击使用有毒有害物质的行为。安全工程是塑料加工业的头等大事。

七、结束语

虽然2012年塑料制品行业经济运行中的积极因素逐渐增多，企稳向好的势头日趋明显。但由于外部经济环境的不确定、不稳定因素仍然较多，我国塑料制品外贸出口下滑的局面尚未完全扭转，行业自身发展中存在的诸多问题还未得到根本性解决，如自主创新能力弱、总体装备水平偏低、产品结构不合理、科技投入不足、产品集约化程度低、行业区域发展不平衡、市场无序竞争等，产业结构调整和节能减排工作还任重道远。

China Plastics Industry Development Peport in 2012

China Plastics Processing Industry Association

In 2012, the economic situation was complicated at home and abroad, and the development of plastics industry was influenced greatly. The development of industries needed structural adjustment, development of enterprises needed to grasp market, both must depend on technique innovation. China plastics industry has experienced high growth during the 11th and 12th Five-year Plan, but was seriously challenged in 2012.

On the one hand, sluggish economic recovery in Europe and America leaded to export slowdown of plastic products, with appreciation of the RMB, rising costs of raw materials and labor, frequent international trade friction, especially developed countries have issued safety laws, regulations and technology barrier such as standards related to plastic, caused hobbling exports of plastic products. Global economic environment restricted export demand of products, slowing down the pace of development.

On the other hand, because of periodic and structural excess capacity of some plastic products, low-price competition showed superheating tendency, while the cost of production increases continually, tepid domestic demand restricted deep development of plastics industry greatly, causing all of the industry to enter normal medium-increasing stage.

With support of series of macroeconomic policies, China plastic processing industry took efforts to overcome serious impacts which were brought by international financial crisis, in the second half of 2012 achieved stabilisation, realized steady growth, the rate of production and marketing maintained higher levels, import and export trade appeared signs of recovery, benefit level of enterprises improved greatly.

According to the national statistics bureau, between Jan. and Dec. 2012, accumulated industrial output made by 13246 companies whose sales value of plastics products was more than 20 million yuan reached 1675. 73 billion yuan and increased by 15. 04 percent. Compared with the number of 2011, the growth rate has fallen about 40 percent, slowing down obviously. During the same period, sales value reached 1645. 02 billion yuan, the rate of production and marketing reached 98. 17 percent, 0. 13 percent higher than 98. 04 percent of 2011, remaining at a high level. The total output of plastics products was 57818. 6 kt, a yearly growth rate of 8. 99 percent, 13. 36 percent lower than 22. 35 percent of 2011.

Between Jan. and Dec. 2012, companies whose sales value of plastics products was more than 20 million yuan completed the main business income with 1631. 01billion yuan, up 11. 79 percent, down 15. 73 percent than the growth rate of 27. 52 percent of 2011. The profit and taxes reached 143. 14 billion, up 17. 12 percent. The total profit accounted for 96. 33 billion yuan, up 15. 94 percent. The growth of profit and taxes has gone down 14. 48 percent with the total profit down 16. 56 compared to the number of 2011. Assets of plastics processing industry totaled 1041. 21 billion, up 13. 03 percent. The number of employees reached 2331. 8 thousand, down 1. 55 percent.

According to the statistical dataprovided by Customs Bureau customs, the total exports of plastics products reached 13821. 6 kt in China, and the amount of exports reached 49. 19 billion dollar, up 5. 79 percent and 24. 55 percent respectively.

1 Output of plastics products industry and gross value of production and marketing increased steadily and appeared as warmer trend

The output of plastics products of China generally upward trended, but the growth decreased largely compared to that of last year. Between Jan. and Dec. 2012, the total output of plastics products of China was 57818. 6 kt, up 8. 99 percent, 13. 36 percent lower than 22. 35 percent of 2011. Shares of different plastics products are shown in Tab. 1. The total output of plastics films reached 9702. 5 kt, up 9. 33 percent, the growth rate went down 1. 84 percent than that of last year, of which agricultural films accounted for 1627. 4 kt, up 7. 74 percent, the growth rate went down 6. 75 percent; that of plastics foams 1720. 6 kt, up 23. 13 percent, the growth rate down 2. 25 percent; that of man-made and synthetic leather 3142. 7 kt, up 15. 55 percent, the growth rate up 5. 98 percent; that of daily articles 4618. 4 kt, up 14. 43 percent, the growth rate up 9. 17 percent; that of others 38634. 4 kt, up 7. 26 percent, the growth rate down 21. 33 percent. The output of other types increased below 10 percent except for daily articles, man-made and synthetic leather, plastics foams; the growth rate of agricultural films and others was lowest, 6. 75 and 21. 33 percent lower than that of last year respectively. For detailed data, see Tab. 1 and Fig. 1 below.

Tab. 1 Cumulative output of plastics products of 2012 and comparison with that of 2011

Product Categories	Cumulative output between Jan. and Dec. /kt	Growth Rate/%	Amplification/%
Plastics Products	57818. 6	8. 99	-13. 36
Plastics Films	9702. 5	9. 33	-1. 84
Agricultural Films	1627. 4	7. 74	-6. 75
Plastics Foams	1720. 6	23. 13	-2. 25
Man-made and Synthetic Leather	3142. 7	15. 55	5. 98
Daily Articles	4618. 4	14. 43	9. 17
Others	38634. 4	7. 26	-21. 33

Source: National Statistics

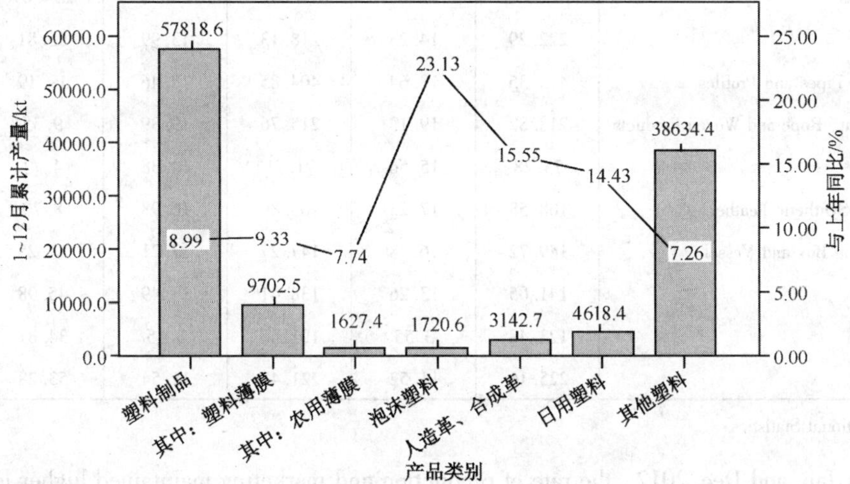

Fig. 1 Increasing sketch map of cumulative output of plastics products of 2012

Tab. 1 and Fig. 1 showed that plastics foams had the highest growth rate with 23. 13 percent year on year among all types of plastics products, while was 2. 25 percent lower than the number of last year. In addition, the growth rate of man-made and synthetic leather and daily articles was the only two increasing number, and the cumulative output increased by 15. 55 and 14. 43 percent respectively, the growth rate up 5. 98 and 9. 17 percent than that of last year.

Between Jan. and Dec. 2012, total industrial output of plastics products reached 1675. 73 billion yuan, up 15. 04 percent year on year, and sales value reached 1645. 02 billion yuan, up 14. 95 percent. Total industrial output of plastics films was 222. 29 billion yuan, up 14. 23 percent, sales value was 218. 13 billion yuan, up 13. 99 percent; industrial output of plastics plates, pipes and profiles reached 413. 35 billion yuan, up 18. 64 percent, sales value was 404. 85 billion yuan, up 18. 46 percent; industrial output of plastics filament, rope and woven products was 218. 82 billion yuan, up 19. 13 percent, sales value was 215. 77 billion yuan, up 19. 39 percent; output value of plastics foams was 73. 28 billion yuan, up 15. 56 percent, sales value was 71. 71 billion yuan, up 14. 38 percent; output value of man-made and synthetic leather was 108. 58 billion yuan, up 17. 23 percent, sales value was 105. 89 billion yuan, up 16. 98 percent; output value of plastic packaging box and vessel was 149. 72 billion yuan, up 16. 78 percent, sales value was 147. 27 billion yuan, up 17. 21 percent; output value of daily articles was 141. 05 billion yuan, up 13. 26 percent, sales value was 138. 41 billion yuan, up 13. 49 percent; output value of plastics parts was 123. 48 billion yuan, up 3. 55 percent, sales value was 121. 56 billion yuan, up 3. 15 percent; output value of other plastics products was 225. 16 billion yuan, up 11. 52 percent, sales value was 221. 43 billion yuan, up 11. 54 percent. For detailed data, see Tab. 2 below.

Tab. 2 The comparison sheet of cumulative industrial output, sales value, value of exports of plastics products in 2012 with last year

Product Categories	Industrial output / billion yuan	Growth rate /%	Sales value/ billion yuan	Growth rate /%	Value of exports / billion yuan	Growth rate /%
Plastics Products	1675. 73	15. 04	1645. 02	14. 95	214. 09	2. 71
Plastics Films	222. 29	14. 23	218. 13	13. 99	25. 81	3. 28
Plastics Plates, Pipes and Profiles	413. 35	18. 64	404. 85	18. 46	19. 19	0. 16
Plastics Filament, Rope and Woven Products	218. 82	19. 13	215. 76	19. 39	9. 35	5. 36
Plastics Foams	73. 28	15. 56	71. 71	14. 38	4. 73	5. 72
Man-made and Synthetic Leather	108. 58	17. 23	105. 89	16. 98	8. 70	-2. 93
Plastic Packaging Box and Vessel	149. 72	16. 78	147. 27	17. 21	12. 25	18. 70
Daily Articles	141. 05	13. 26	138. 41	13. 49	45. 98	5. 40
Plastics Parts	123. 48	3. 55	121. 56	3. 15	34. 81	-2. 33
Others	225. 16	11. 52	221. 43	11. 54	53. 28	1. 66

Source: National Statistics.

Between Jan. and Dec. 2012, the rate of production and marketing maintained higher levels, up to 98. 17 percent, 0. 13 percent higher than 98. 04 percent of 2011. Tab. 2 showed that cumulative industrial output, sales value of plastics products industry maintained a double-digit growth, only plastics parts industry increased by 3. 55 percent with sales value up 3. 15 percent. Statistics indicated that total value of production and marketing of plastics products industry kept a steady rising trend, although the growth rate was lower, the declining speed slowed down. Between Jan. and Dec. 2012, value of exports increased by 2. 71 percent, in which that of plastic packaging box and vessel up 18. 70 percent; only that of man-made and synthetic leather and plastics parts down 2. 93 and 2. 33 percent respectively.

2. Main income of plastics products still kept double-digit growth, benefit level increased

As theplastics products industry rebounded, benefit level also rised.

Data from National Statistics showed that main income was 1631. 01 billion yuan between Jan. and Dec. 2012, up 11. 79 percent. The main income of plastics films reached 217. 95 billion yuan, up 10. 93 percent; that of plastics plates, pipes and profiles 396. 09 billion yuan, up 14. 59 percent; that of plastics filament, rope and woven products 217. 28 billion yuan, up 18. 42 percent; that of plastics foams 70. 75 billion yuan, up 10. 06 percent; that of man-made and synthetic leather 104. 00 billion yuan, up 11. 78 percent; that of plastic packaging box and vessel 146. 15 billion yuan, up 13. 11 percent; that of daily articles 137. 79 billion yuan, up 11. 03 percent; that of plastics parts 121. 07 billion yuan, up 1. 53 percent; that of other plastics products 219. 93 billion yuan, up 8. 10 percent. As Chinese government implemented positive fiscal policy and tax reform industriously, making the economic efficiency of whole plastics products industry rise obviously. The main income kept double-digit growth, and the benefit of companies improved. For detailed data, see Tab. 3 and Tab. 4 below.

Tab. 3 Main income of plastics products and growth in 2012

Product Categories	Number of companies	Main income/billion yuan	Growth rate/%
Plastics Products	13245	1631. 01	11. 79
Plastics Films	1431	217. 95	10. 93
Plastics Plates, Pipes and Profiles	2504	396. 09	14. 59
Plastics Filament, Rope and Woven Products	1835	217. 28	18. 42
Plastics Foams	747	70. 75	10. 06
Man-made and Synthetic Leather	549	104. 00	11. 78
Plastic Packaging Box and Vessel	1405	146. 15	13. 11
Daily Articles	1335	137. 79	11. 03
Plastics Parts	1249	121. 07	1. 53
Others	2190	219. 93	8. 10

Source: National Statistics.

The data showed that profit and taxes of plastics products was 143. 14 billion yuan between Jan. and Dec. 2012, up 17. 12 percent, in which the total profit was 96. 33 billion yuan, up 15. 94 percent. Although economic benefit index fell greatly compared with that of the whole of 2011, taxes and profits decreased by 14. 48 and 16. 56 percent respectively; 3. 46 and 3. 18 percent higher than that of Jan. to Sep. of 2011 respectively. All the data indicated that enterprise's benefit level had the gradually increasing tendency.

The following showed economic benefit index of sub-sector. The profit and taxes of plastics films was 17. 23 billion yuan, up 10. 23 percent, the total profit was 12. 00 billion yuan, up 6. 31 percent; profit and taxes of plastics plates, pipes and profiles was 38. 87 billion yuan, up 21. 29 percent, total profit was 26. 45 billion yuan, up 19. 20 percent; plastics filament, profit and taxes of plastics filament rope and woven products was 20. 36 billion yuan, up 23. 98 percent, total profit was 13. 67 billion yuan, up 27. 31 percent; profit and taxes of plastics foams was 6. 72 billion yuan, up 17. 36 percent, total profit was 4. 71 billion yuan, up 18. 67 percent; profit and taxes of man-made and synthetic leather was 9. 50 billion yuan, up 29. 65 percent, total profit was 6. 66 billion yuan, up 32. 42 percent; profit and taxes of plastic packaging box and vessel was 14. 19 billion yuan, up 12. 89 percent, total profit was 9. 47 billion yuan, up 11. 68 percent; profit and taxes of daily articles was 11. 84 billion yuan, up 21. 66 percent, total profit was 8. 02 billion yuan, up 22. 75 percent; profit and taxes of plastics parts was 8. 25 billion yuan, up 5. 22 percent, total profit was 5. 00 billion yuan, up 1. 57 percent; profit and taxes of other plastics products was 16. 16 billion yuan, up 8. 46 percent , total profit was 10. 35 billion yuan, up 4. 16 percent. .

We can see from above datathat, companies which produced plastics parts had the lowest profits, profit and taxes increased by 5. 22 percent year on year, total profit only increased by 1. 57 percent, the growth rate of taxes and profits decreased by 3. 05 and 7. 07 percent respectively compared with that of Jan. to Sep. this year respectively. So the data showed benefits of companies producing plastics parts decreased continuously.

Overall, economic efficiency level still kept double-digit growth. Series of supported policies implemented by government for enterprises, especially policies such as structural tax reduction, reducing cost burden and so on began to show results. Economic efficiency level of plastics products industry had rising tendency gradually. For detailed date, see Tab. 4 and Fig 2. below.

Tab. 4 Taxes and profits and growth in 2012

Name of industry	Profits and taxes / billion yuan	Growth rate/%	Profits/ billion yuan	Growth rate/%
Plastics products industry	143. 14	17. 12	96. 33	15. 94
Plastics Films	17. 23	10. 23	12. 00	6. 31
Plastics Plates, Pipes and Profiles	38. 87	21. 29	26. 45	19. 20
Plastics Filament, Rope and Woven Products	20. 36	23. 98	13. 67	27. 31
Plastics Foams	6. 72	17. 36	4. 71	18. 67
Man-made and Synthetic Leather	9. 50	29. 65	6. 66	32. 42
Plastic Packaging Box and Vessel	14. 19	12. 89	9. 47	11. 68
Daily Articles	11. 84	21. 66	8. 02	22. 75
Plastics Parts	8. 25	5. 22	50. 00	1. 57
Others	16. 16	8. 46	10. 35	4. 16

Source: National Statistics.

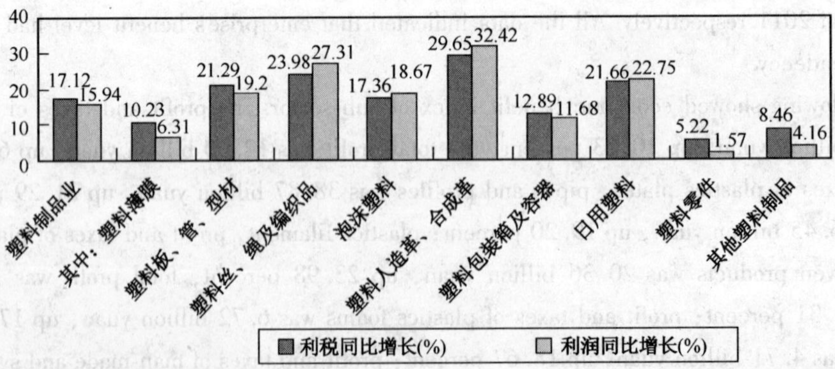

Fig. 2 The growth sketch map of profits and taxes of plastics products in 2012

3. The output of plastics products in top eight areas accounted for 65. 77 percent

From the regions, the accumulated output of provinces such as Zhejiang, Guangdong, Shandong, Jiangsu, Liaoning, Fujian, Hubei, Henan accounted for 65. 77 percent, showing the unbalanced industrial distribution.

Tab. 5 The top eight regionswith the most output of plastics products in 2012

Region	Accumulation/ton	Scale of total output/%
China	57818647	100. 00
Zhejiang	9485401	16. 41
Guangdong	9193123	15. 90
Shandong	4531200	7. 84
Jiangsu	3492566	6. 04
Liaoning	3238998	5. 60
Fujian	2745337	4. 75
Hubei	2720014	4. 70
Henan	2618627	4. 53
Total	38025266	65. 77

Source: National Statistics.

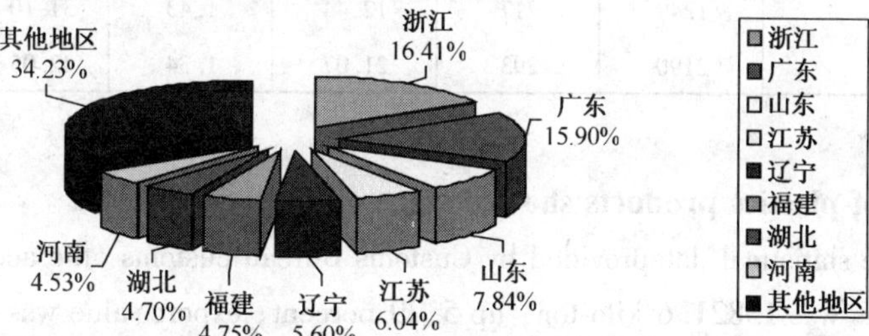

Fig. 3 The scale map of top eight regions with the most output of plastics products in 2012

4. The deficit value and deficit scale ofplastics enterprises declined compared with that of Jan. to Sep. this year, so did the number of workers

Data from National Statistics showed that, between Jan. and Dec. 2012, the number of above-scale enterprises of plastics products industry was 13245 according to main economic indexes, in which deficit enterprises 1490, up 16. 59 percent year on year, the deficit scale was 11. 25 percent, 2. 44 percent lower than 13. 69 percent of Jan. to Sep. Total deficit value was 6. 73 billion yuan, 37. 54 percent higher than that of last year, 4. 3 percent higher than 33. 24 percent of Jan. to Sep. It indicated that the number of deficit enterprises declined, but the value increased. Deficit scale of plastics films, parts and other plastic products became greater, with 13. 49, 17. 37 and 13. 38 percent respectively. The sub-industry with higher number of deficit enterprises were plastics plates, pipes and profiles and man-made and synthetic leather, the number was 243 and 57 respectively, up 24. 62 and 29. 55 percent. The sub-industry with highest deficit value were plastics films and plastic packaging box and vessel, with that of 1. 20 and 0. 7 billion yuan, up 78. 80 and 83. 72 percent.

The date reflected that plastics films, parts, man-made and synthetic leather, packaging box and vessel and other plastics products industry had great deficits. The average number of workers in above-scale enterprises of the whole industry was 2331. 8 thousand, down 1. 55 percent. Following table showed detailed data.

Tab. 6 The losses of companies and number of workers

Name of industry	Number of above-scale enterprises	Number of companies under deficit	Growth rate of number of companies under deficit/%	Deficit value/ billion yuan	Growth rate of deficit value/%	Average number of workers	Growth rate /%
Plastics products industry	13245	1490	16. 59	6. 73	37. 54	2331784	-1. 55
Plastics Films	1431	193	20. 63	1. 20	78. 80	207169	-5. 55
Plastics Plates, Pipes and Profiles	2504	243	24. 62	1. 15	19. 95	394219	4. 37
Plastics Filament, Rope and Woven Products	1835	107	0. 00	0. 18	-3. 90	323786	4. 36
Plastics Foams	747	67	4. 69	0. 13	-8. 83	89558	-4. 07
Man-made and Synthetic Leather	549	57	29. 55	0. 18	36. 13	134940	0. 68
Plastic Packaging Box and Vessel	1405	162	20. 00	0. 70	83. 72	204129	2. 57
Daily Articles	1335	151	9. 42	0. 41	8. 43	277569	-1. 73
Plastics Parts	1249	217	12. 44	1. 43	31. 10	294375	-8. 89
Others	2190	293	21. 07	1. 34	42. 05	406039	-5. 42

Source: National Statis.

5. The export of plastics products showed signs of recovery in 2012

According to the statistical dataprovided by Customs Bureau customs, the accumulated export output of plastic products was 13821. 6 kilo-ton, up 5. 79 percent; export value was 49. 19 billion dollar, up 24. 55 percent, 16. 65 percent higher than growth rate of foreign trade (7. 9 percent), the growth of export began to recover. Average import unit price was 3. 56 dollar/kg, and the average output unit price was 10. 27 dollar/kg which was 2. 88 times that of import. It indicated that export plastics products were mainly low and medium products, the export structure need to change immediately. Import unit price of last year was 3. 3 times export unit price, 0. 42 times lower, which showed micro-variation of adjustment of structure.

Because government implemented policies of promoting tax rebates of plastics products, lifting the processing trade restrictions of some products, which played a positive role in increasing exports. The exports of plastics products gradually recovered.

6. Development objectives of China's plastics industry

There are still many unsolved problems which need urgent researches in China's plastics industry. The first one, the problem of excess production capacity became apparent and existed in most industries such as BOPP, BOPET, packaging industry, profile doors and windows and so on. Because excess production capacity often led to unordered and unhealthy competition, and brought large undesirable effects to plastics industry. The second one, middle and low level products account for large part, technology content still has very great disparity compared with that of foreign, many much-needed products need to import, problems such as product structure, enterprise organizational structure, unreasonable regional distribution are prominent. The third one, imperative speciality resin needs to import, resin of some upscale products such as special pipes, upscale films mostly depends on imports which seriously restricts the development of plastics industry.

The overall idea for development of China's plastics industry is depending on technical progress and innovation, promoting a major push of technical progress, driving industrial upgrading, gradually building modern industrial system; paying attention to industrial restructuring, accelerating the transformation of development mode, optimizing product structure, regional distribution and enterprises organizational structure, extruding green, making efforts to recycle and sustainable development; extruding brand strategy, improving quality of products to enhance the quality of the whole industry.

The main aim of China's plastics industry is that production incr eases by about 12 percent on average, total output increases by about 15 percent. Considering plastics industry is entering critical stage of structure optimizing and industry up grading, the aim shows tendency and character that plastics processing industry will enter steady growth stage from rapid growth stage, also creates good outer environment for accelerating technical adjustment and transformation, is beneficial to promote technical progress and innovation, accelerates the transformation of development mode and improve development quality.

Plastics processing industry is a new manufacture which keeps the plastic products processing as the core, covering rude material, machine, mold and additive. It is the fundamental industry of national economy which can provide import products, parts and different kinds of new materials for industry, agriculture, construction, transportation, aerospace industry, etc. It is also a livelihood industry providing safe and reliable consumer goods for consumers, is one of new mainstay industries.

First is the emerging manufacturing. Three synthetic polymers like synthetic resin, synthetic rubber and synthetic fibre are the foundational materials which constitutes the modern society and support the development of modern high technology. Plastics processing industry is transiting quickly from traditional primary consumer goods to high-grade consumer goods, is developing towards highly technical direction. Now plastics processing industry has successfully entered industry, agriculture and some other industry, is applied widely in high-tech area. In the coming new materials technology revolution, plastics processing industry will play more important role. Plastics materials will account for the biggest scale and widest field in new material items. So plastics processing industry has become a new highly technical manufacturing from traditional manufacturing.

Second is about that plastics processing industry is one offast-growing mainstay industries. The total output value accounted for 3.55 percent of GDP in 2010, a little lower than international 5 percent. In general terms, if output value of an industry can account for 5 percent of GDP, it can be called mainstay industry. So plastics processing industry can't be called mainstay industry obviously, but for the large domestic demand and developing space, the plastics industry will continue to increase. As new material of the 21th century, the applied field will be wider and wider with high-speed technical progress and deeper industrialization. Although international financial crisis hasn't gone away, the crisis cann't primarily change the long-term developing tendency of world economy. Advantage of China's plastics processing industry will be reinforced, which is good for expanding international market. The position of plastics processing industry will be improved as sunrise industry with fast-developing character. We should pay more attention to plastics processing industry, enhance cultivating strength, making it become mainstay industry earlier.

Third defines the discuss that plastic is consisted of plasticized material and less solid material with synthetic or natural macromolecule compound as raw materials and additives such as plasticizer, filler, lubricant, injection agent and so on as auxiliary element. The aim is to distinguish raw material and product, further to distinguish position in national economy of synthetic resin, petrochemical industry and plastics processing industry. So the position of plastics processing industry will be more practical. The purpose is to call on all the industry to build confidence, value the position of plastics processing industry, follow the development path of emerging manufacturing firmly, accelerating speed of being mainstay industry.

The primary mission of China's plastics industry during the 12th Five-year:

1. Accelerating the transformation of development pattern, accelerating the structural optimization

In current, plastics processing industry is entering a new stage ofhigh-quality, high-grade and high-level development driven by innovation. The stage requires us to change development mode from depending on adding number of enterprises and expanding investment to innovation, technological progress and optimize structure. Ten years rapid development can't continuous, and growth of 20 percent was mainly based on domestic rapid economic development and gap-filling growth which was caused by lagging development of domestic products. It's an inevitable trend that plastics processing industry enters a steady and fast stage from a high-speed development, which marks plastics processing industry is entering maturity stage from growth stage gradually. Preventing low-level productivity enlarging is a strict task what we need do. Researching market demand, we need invest rationally to avoid pursuing big and comparing investment. Handling well the relationships between intension and extension, big and strong, and work focus should be put into subdividing market and implementing the strategy of differentiation, relying on scientific and technological progress and innovation, developing new products and optimizing the structure adjustment.

2. *The Twelfth Five-year Plan* emphasized promoting vigorously the progress of science and technology, raising the overall industrial quality. Plastic was the important field of future technological revolution, we should seize the opportunity that government supports development of strategic new industries, depend on scientific and technological progress, accelerate development of new technology, new process and new products. The plan presented that common and pivotal technology should be focused on, and we should strive for phased breakthrough. Such as application of supercritical foaming technique, large caliber crosslinking PE pipes, processing of UHMWPE pipes, waterborne polyurethane synthetic leather, modified PVC pipes, foaming agent without HCFCs and new energy-conserving techniques.

The plan made explanations on development priority and direction of main product of plastics processing industry, and presented that new plastic materials should be developed around functionality tightly. Functionality is the developing direction and hope of plastics industry. So we should pay more attention to develop functional technique and research nano-materials and technology. Now high performance engineering plastics such as high barrier multilayer co-extrusion nano-microlayer composites, functional fiber-reinforced composites, polymer alloy and so on should be given greater emphasis; functional materials such as melt electrospinning filter materials, nano-antibacterial, flame-retardant and degradative materials and so on should be focused on; Multifunctional film materials like photovoltaic generation related material, battery diaphragm of NiMH batteries and lithium-ion batteries, nimh batteries, lithium-ion batteries, optical film and so on should be paid much attention.

The plan especiallyemphasized on strengthening research efforts, researching ultrathin film materials and combination, solving development bottleneck of functional films. The task during 12th Five Year is to improve industrial quality by progress of scientific and the innovation of technology, to enhance competitiveness, to lay the foundation for overall construction of plastics processing industry modern system. After *The Twelfth Five-year Plan* was published, we are organizing forces to draft guide of technology progress for next five-year of plastics processing industry, we should make breakthroughs in common and pivotal technology which plastics industry is facing to change its appearance. Developing new products surrounding new materials and new process, driving low-carbon green growth surrounding energy-saving emission reduction technology. Meanwhile focusing on advanced technology will guide enterprises to grasp direction according to scientific and technological trends. The purpose of making guide of technology progress is to mobilize the whole industry and technical resources together to promote development process driven by guide of technology progress. When conditions are ripe, we plan to organize plastics processing industry conference on science and technology to commend advanced S&T workers according to guidelines for technological progress.

3. Speeding up restructuring process and optimizing the regional distribution. The regional distribution is seriously unreasonable, the output of east region accounts for 74 percent, that of central region 15 percent, and west region only 10 percent. There are many causes of this situation. The central and western regions develop fast, but situation of regional imbalance is still outstanding, so the plan proposed to implement differentiation development based on fully utilizing the merits. Coastal regions should reinforce construction of brand, accelerate industry high-end process, to form new competing advantage; central region should seize chance to play geographical advantages of linking East and West, undertake coastal industry transfer actively; West region should play advantages of backwardness relying on rich resources. For example, agricultural plastics used for water-saving irrigation developed quickly in Xinjiang, forming a reasonable and distinctive layout, promoting healthy development of plastics processing industry.

Particular emphasis is that safety engineering construction of plastics products should be promoted vigorously. Whether plastics pipes, profiles, doors and windows, or daily articles, all have the problem of using security and health security, which relates to the security of consumers and users´lives and properties. We should improve the quality industriously to assurance health and safety with high sense of responsibility. As the improvement of living standards and technique progress, the health and safety requirement of plastics products and standard are stricter and stricter, especially food-contacted packing polymer and plastics product become object of supervision and detection on food security. For example, PVC water supplying pipes mustn't contain lead thermal stabilizers, using standards-compliant additive and food-grade PVC, the requirement is quite strict. New laws about food-contacted and plastics products implemented by EU came into effect on May st last year internationally. Compared with old laws, requirement of new laws was much refined, and had biggest change of testing programs and enlarged regulatory objects. In environmental protection fields, EU countries and regions have made route map and timetable of banning thermal stabilizers containing lead for PVC products roundly. Also PVC used for plastics doors and windows mustn't contain lead thermal stabilizers. In addition, using security of all kinds of products such as plastics-steel doors and windows, toys, building insulation materials, a-fire-retardant materials and HCFCs substitution and so on must be paid more attention. So enhancing safety engineering construction was a big challenge for us, the industry should confirmedly outlaw and boycott actions of using poisonous and harmful substance with a high sense of responsibility, integrity and self-discipline. Safety engineering is the most important issue in plastics processing industry.

7. Conclusion

Although positive factors in plastics products industry increased in 2012, the improved tendency was gradually obviously. While because many uncertain and unsteady factors of external economic environment still existed, situation of declining foreign trade export of plastics products didn't reverse, there were still unsolved problems in self-development, such as low capability of independent innovation, low equipment level, unreasonable product structure, insufficient investment in science and technology, low degree of intensive, unbalanced regional development, chaotic competition in the market and so on. We will go a long way on adjustment of industrial structure and the energy saving and pollution reduction work.

塑料加工业技术进步指导意见(2013~2015年)

中国塑料加工工业协会

塑料加工业是以制品加工为核心，涵盖塑料原料及助剂、塑料机械及模具为一体，以创新技术为支撑的新兴制造业。塑料加工业是为工业、农业、建筑业、交通运输业、航空航天以及高科技领域提供重要产品和配件、特种材料的基础性产业，同时也是为广大消费者提供优质、安全、可靠消费品的民生产业，是国民经济新的支柱产业之一。

“十一五”期间中国塑料加工业实现了历史性跨越，跻身世界塑料工业大国行列。“十二五”期间中国塑料加工业进入了创新驱动发展的历史新阶段，将继续深入贯彻落实科学发展观，以加快经济增长方式转变为主线，加快结构调整转型升级，全面推进绿色、低碳、循环发展，建设资源节约型、环境友好型行业；全面推进自主创新，大力实施品牌战略、专利战略、标准战略，全面提升塑料加工业整体素质，加快推进由世界塑料大国向塑料加工先进大国迈进的步伐。

根据《国家中长期科学和技术发展规划纲要(2006~2020年)》、《国家“十二五”科学和技术发展规划》精神和《轻工业“十二五”发展规划》、《轻工业技术进步“十二五”发展指导意见》的要求，提出《塑料加工业技术进步指导意见》。

一、“十一五”塑料加工业技术进步取得的成绩及存在的问题

(一)“十一五”塑料加工业技术进步取得的成绩

1. 技术进步加快，初步形成以企业为主体的创新体系

——行业科技投入不断增加，以2009年为例，仅大中型工业企业新产品研发投入经费37.4亿元，新产品产值实现457.7亿元。

——申请受理与授权的发明和实用新型专利数分别达22976项和12968项。

——国家标准、行业标准的制修订取得积极进展，累计达300多项。

——至“十一五”末，全行业已通过认定的国家级技术研发中心23个，国家创新型企业9个。

——产学研结合进一步加强，由高校与企业联合开发的新产品数量稳步增长。

——开设高分子材料及加工专业的高校数量显著增多，科技成果数大幅增长，科技成果转化效果显著。

2. 节能减排、绿色环保技术推广应用效果显著

——经过近二十年的努力，塑料行业在“十一五”末完全淘汰了全氯氟烃(CFCs)发泡剂，共计约28312t，相当于减少二氧化碳排放145.02Mt，为减少消耗臭氧层物质和温室气体排放、彰显我国负责任大国形象做出贡献。

——废塑料分类与改性等高值化利用技术得到逐步提升，有力促进废塑料再生高效利用。发泡聚苯乙烯相框、聚烯烃缠绕膜、排水井盖、隔音保温墙板以及塑木步道、座椅及装饰材料等废旧塑料再生制品得到广泛应用。2006～2010年，全国回收废塑料约46Mt，进口废塑料约35Mt，两者合计超过合成树脂的年消费量。

——无溶剂与水性聚氨酯合成革、粘合剂技术在合成革、复合膜加工的产业化进程明显加快，VOC等排放大幅下降。

——绿色、高效、无污染新型助剂开发及应用取得新进展。替代重金属铅盐的绿色环保稳定剂的应用，加速了PVC制品淘汰铅盐热稳定剂的步伐；新型、环保型阻燃剂的研发应用加快了阻燃塑料绿色环保应用的进程。

——节能技术取得新进展。电磁变频加热技术、伺服驱动节能技术、锥形同向双螺杆挤出机、拉伸形变塑化技术、塑料动态成型技术、微积分成型技术等新技术节能效果显著，产品质量提高。

3. 改性、复合、聚合物合金等塑料新材料的应用拓展了塑料制品应用领域

——改性塑料在汽车、电子电器、信息、医用、轨道交通等高端应用领域份额扩大；增强增韧、阻燃、抗静电等专用功能性塑料、聚合物合金及复合材料在替代进口专用料的高科技领域用量增大。

——改性聚丙烯及其复合材料成为品种多、应用广的功能性材料；高性能共聚聚丙烯合金、聚丙烯釜内合金技术研发及产业化达到世界同类产品先进水平；耐辐射聚丙烯改性专用料、聚丙烯热罐装瓶用专用料等填补国内空白。

——碳纤维增强塑料研发与应用技术取得突破性进展，逐步缩小与发达国家差距；聚醚醚酮(PEEK)的合成打破国外技术垄断；耐高温尼龙与长碳链尼龙研发与应用技术进入世界先进水平行列。

4. 新产品、新工艺提升了行业技术水平，多项达国际先进水平

——超高分子量聚乙烯近熔点加工成型装备及系列产品技术达国际先进水平。

——先进农用塑料器材及设施、温室专用生物降解地膜、功能与寿命同步“光生态”新型棚膜等新产品得到推广应用，“膜下滴灌”节水技术成本低效率高，节水效果显著。

——高仿真定岛型复合纺丝超细纤维合成革研制成功，高密度聚氨酯合成革、生态功能型合成革、高耐寒抗水解聚氨酯合成革、动物胶原纤维高仿真聚氨酯合成革、水性聚氨酯合成革和无溶剂型聚氨酯合成革等生产取得重大技术进步。

——塑料管材行业相关专利技术超过1000项，采用新材料和复合结构设计的新型塑料管

材大量应用，超高分子量聚乙烯(UHMWPE)管材、大口径排水用钢塑复合缠绕管材、塑料与金属复合管材等产品技术已达世界先进水平。

——多项系列医用塑料产品技术国际领先，新型医疗用插管、导管关键技术及规模化生产在心脏外科体外循环和呼吸麻醉用插管、导管产品领域内取得多项科研成果并产业化。

——新型、环保型阻燃剂开发应用，环保助剂水滑石－稀土－钙/锌无毒复合热稳定剂研发成功，高阻隔药品软包装材料实现国产化，无溶剂黏合剂在复合软包装生产上实现产业化。

——降解塑料及产品开发应用与世界水平基本同步。

5. 先进制造技术取得新进展，不断缩小与发达国家差距

“十一五”期间，塑料加工高效节能、精密挤出注射成型等设备大量应用，在提高加工效率、降低成本、提升产品质量等方面发挥重要作用，提升了我国塑料加工业的整体技术水平。

——挤出成型技术不断推陈出新，大型造粒机组的成功研制打破了国外垄断；锥形同向双螺杆技术高效节能，主要性能参数达国际先进水平；多层共挤、流延、双向拉伸技术及设备取得突破性进展并替代进口。

——挤出造粒及辅助设备技术进步突出，出口增长快，国际市场占有率不断提升，优势明显；在线检测、自动计量喂料、自动化程控、CAE 辅助成型等先进辅助技术的应用促进塑料挤出技术向高端化发展，如具有超强冷却系统设计和真空定径的大口径塑料管材挤出技术。

——注塑成型技术进步显著，由单一驱动向电液混合驱动和全电动方式转变。精密注射成型技术实现了全电动、伺服节能和二板式三大系列精密塑料注射成型装备的产业化，达国际先进水平。

——三维挤吹、“一步法”注拉吹、大型挤吹、多层共注射、注吹等多种工艺的更新换代丰富了中空制品的加工手段；单层小型挤吹中空塑料成型机的技术进步重点是高效率、高生产率、多工位及多功能。

(二)“十一五”塑料加工技术进步存在问题

1. 技术创新能力薄弱

——行业缺乏技术创新总体规划引导。整体创新体系不健全造成企业和研究机构研发与创新目标缺乏前瞻性、系统性研究，对基础共性、关键瓶颈性课题的研发投入不足。科研成果转化机制不畅，科研院所、大专院校的研究成果产业转化率偏低。

——专业技术人才不足，特别在众多中小企业中技术力量薄弱问题更加突出。长期以来，塑料行业专业技术人才、基础课题研究跟不上产业快速发展的需求，一些重大课题特别是基础性关键共性课题缺乏技术带头人；产品开发能力弱，具有自主知识产权的高技术含量、高附加值产品少，中低档产品比例过大，高端装备仍需依靠进口。

2. 产品标准制、修订和检测手段跟不上行业的发展

——面对塑料加工业快速发展，新材料应用、新产品开发周期缩短和产品更新换代速度加快的现状，相应的国家标准和行业标准的制定和更新滞后矛盾突出。部分产品标准存在行业间交叉、多口管理，致使标准的制订、审定工作混乱、企业无所适从；特别是部分食品接触塑料制品企业因无标准无法及时进行 QS 认证。

——生产企业的检测设备不足，检测技术能力不强，实验室建设滞后，不能满足迅速发展的塑料加工业的需求。不少企业没有产品在线、自动检测装置和关键项目的性能检测能力，造成质量问题发现滞后，企业损失大，市场竞争力低。

3. 塑料制品安全生产工程建设亟待加强

——塑料加工业在生态化、环保绿色生产等方面的研究不足。部分包装企业对包装产品的安全性重视不够，大量采用苯溶性油墨印刷、溶剂型粘合剂复合，许多小企业对复合膜产品残留溶剂缺乏控制能力，QS 认证质量不高，对适用于不同规模、类型塑料软包装印刷复合薄膜企业的环保技术或产品缺乏有针对性的开发研究；部分小规模企业对节能减排重视力度不够，对环境保护、绿色发展缺乏认识和改进措施；国内废旧塑料的回收和利用率仅为 26%，远落后于发达国家的 30% ~70%。

4. 原材料、助剂及加工设备技术水平制约塑料加工业发展

——目前国内塑料加工业生产亟需的多种功能性树脂、特殊牌号树脂专用料人部分依赖进口。

——包括农膜用氟树脂消雾剂、抗农药型防老化剂、外涂覆消雾液，可用于食品包装材料的高分子量邻苯二甲酸酯类增塑剂、加工脱模剂、分散剂及无卤阻燃剂等高档助剂也大多进口。

——我国塑料机械产量世界第一，但以中、低端设备为主。在小型及宽幅高速双向拉伸薄膜生产设备、节能大容量挤出注塑成型机、取向聚氯乙烯(PVC - O)管等高性能塑料管道生产装备、智能型高速节能 PET 吹瓶机、大型旋模滚塑成型装备、聚酯(PET)瓶片回收及再利用设备、大型超临界 CO_2聚合物发泡挤出装备、聚合物动态反应加工技术及设备、大型多层共挤出中空塑料成型机、微纳层叠共挤出成型装备、微型/全电动注塑成型机、塑料制品在线检测设备等方面尚未有较大突破。

二、“十二五”期间行业面临形势及发展趋势

(一)难得的发展机遇与严峻挑战

1. 面临的挑战

——受国际金融危机的影响，世界经济低速增长态势仍将持续，总体需求仍然疲软，加之国外贸易保护主义抬头，对外需占相当比例而扩大内需困难的国内塑料加工业冲击很大。

——国内劳动力廉价时代的结束，使塑料加工企业面临人工成本升高、人才短缺、传统优势弱化的问题。

——多数塑料加工企业规模小、产品以中低档为主，处于产业链的低端，受原料、用户对价格的双重挤压，势微利薄，加之企业自身组织结构不合理、管理能力落后，难以适应行业及外部形势的的发展变化。

上述问题都给我国塑料加工业的未来发展和参与国际竞争带来困难与挑战。

2. 发展机遇

——塑料作为新材料技术革命的重要领域，是新型战略产业的重要支撑和组成部分

塑料在现代工业、农业、电子信息业、交通运输业以及航空航天等尖端技术领域都不可缺少。“十二五”期间，国家将新材料与节能环保、新一代信息技术、高端装备制造业、节能与新能源汽车、生物医药和新能源装备等领域一同列为战略性新兴产业，塑料加工业面临难得的发展机遇。

——作为新兴产业的塑料加工业正处于迅速发展的成长期，市场需求强劲

随着中国经济的持续、稳定、快速发展，社会对塑料制品的需求也将继续稳步增长。“十二五”期间，国家工业化、信息化、城镇化、市场化、国际化的发展战略，带动大规模基础建设、住宅建设，启动“经济适用房”、“暖房子”工程，“西气东输”、“南水北调”工程，公路、铁路网建设及城镇污水处理、节水灌溉等大型工程建设；城镇化进程的加快、居民生活水平提

高和消费结构的升级，现代农业、医疗卫生体系的快速发展，将进一步拓展塑料制品的市场空间。

——塑料加工业现代产业体系初步形成为塑料加工业快速发展奠定了坚实的基础

塑料加工行业整体技术水平的提高，技术进步、产品升级换代和结构调整步伐的加快，国家认定企业技术中心、重点实验室的增多，产学研技术创新体系的初步形成、自主创新能力的增强，给行业的快速发展提供了基本条件。

——第三次工业革命浪潮为塑料加工业发来难得的发展机遇，搭建新的创新平台

以新能源、互联网、新材料和信息技术为重要内容的第三次工业革命正迅速发展，催生并加快数字制造、智能制造和绿色制造的发展，同时当今世界正进入大数据时代，新型互联网在获取海量数据的同时，与全球计算机网络相互融合推动了云计算的发展，将大大改变信息、知识技术获取方法。这为塑料加工业发挥后发优势，努力赶超世界先进水平带来了难得的发展机遇，为塑料加工业创新驱动发展，实现上水平、上台阶、产业升级目标搭建了新的创新平台，促进与世界前沿技术紧密融合。

(二)行业发展趋势

1.“功能化、轻量化、微成型”是世界塑料加工业发展趋势

(1)功能化既是产品属性的要求，更是产品结构调整的重要方向

塑料作为21世纪新材料，是未来新材料革命中的重要领域，是节能环保、新能源、高端装备制造业、新能源汽车等领域不可缺少的配套材料。如各种高阻隔膜、电绝缘膜、电池隔离膜，各种光学膜、光伏太阳能电池封装膜等功能性薄膜，超滤、微滤等过滤膜，各种高强、高韧、耐高温、耐磨、耐腐蚀、导电、绝缘、导热、纳米合金等特种工程塑料等。随着技术进步的加快，将会赋予塑料材料和制品更多新的特殊功能，以满足国民经济发展的需要。塑料制品功能化、智能化作用将会得到更广泛发挥，其制品将会得到更广泛的应用，这是塑料加工业未来发展的重要方向。

(2)轻量化技术将为塑料加工业发展带来重大变革

各种高强度、高阻隔性树脂如茂金属线性低密度聚乙烯(m－LLDPE)、超高分子量聚乙烯(UHMWPE)、改性聚对苯二甲酸乙二醇酯(PET)、乙烯/乙烯醇共聚物(EVOH)、聚偏二氯乙烯(PVDC)等及微纳层叠共挤出、多层复合、合金等生产工艺的出现使得塑料薄膜及容器、片材向轻量化、薄壁化发展成为可能。

通过物理、化学发泡方法，特别是超临界CO_2发泡技术为代表的微发泡技术，可用挤出、注塑、吹塑及旋转模塑等多种方式生产以PVC、PS、PC、PMMA、PET和PSF等材料为基材的各种板材、片材及异型材制品，不仅显著减轻制品重量，而且将改善和提高其性能，给塑料制品的加工和应用带来革命性的变化。

低碳经济时代的到来，飞机、汽车和轨道交通的轻量化越来越成为人们关注的热点，传统材料及工艺已不能满足要求，新的环境友好、轻质高强材料加工技术成为实现轻量化及节能减排的有效途径。

(3)微成型代表着塑料加工业从设备到成型工艺最先进的技术集成

当今塑料机械的发展方向是“高速化、精密化、低耗化、自动化、智能化、网络化”，微成型作为聚合物微纳尺度制造科学的前沿技术，应用前景广阔。以毫克或微米甚至纳米为单位的微注塑成型技术，可满足光电通讯、影像传输、医疗器械、信息存储、电子产品、生物医药、精密机械等材料更昂贵、零件更细微、更节省空间的高端精微结构零件的应用需求。研究

适合微型注塑模具和微型注塑机的成型理论和制造方法、适合微型塑件生产的塑料原料，开发相应的检测元件、装置和技术，成为目前研究的热点；塑料三维打印技术可用于快速成型高精度、形状复杂、局部结构细微的塑料产品，例如航空航天特种部件、复杂汽车零部件、精密人造器官等，具有无须组装、零时间交付、便携制造、废弃材料少等优点，目前已成为最受关注的新兴技术之一。

可见，“功能化、轻量化、微成型”不仅是世界塑料加工业总的发展方向和趋势，更是世界塑料加工业先进成型技术的体现，引领行业未来科技攻关、技术创新的方向，对塑料加工业具有重要意义。

2. 低碳发展、循环发展、清洁生产是绿色塑料加工业的发展方向

发达国家对塑料加工可能产生污染的因素基本上都有明确限制规定或禁令。欧洲禁用铅/镉类重金属热稳定剂已进入倒计时，2010 年禁用了 75% 的铅盐热稳定剂，2015 年将 100% 禁止使用；《关于消耗臭氧层物质的蒙特利尔议定书》要求各签约国加速淘汰含氢氯氟烃（HCFCs）的生产和消费，涉及聚氨酯和挤出聚苯乙烯泡沫塑料制品，我国是该议定书的签约国。此外，我国还制定了回收、处理塑料及进口废塑料环境保护管理规定、《工业节能“十二五”规划》和《工业清洁生产“十二五”规划》等政策、规定。

本世纪头 20 年，我国处于工业化和城镇化加速发展阶段，面临的资源和环境形势十分严峻。这些都促使我们塑料加工业按照“减量化、再利用、资源化”的原则，在行业内进一步推进节能减排以及清洁生产技术应用，推广绿色环保、安全、无害的溶剂、助剂，进一步提高塑料材料及制品的性价比，推进循环发展，让石油及衍生的石化产品发挥最大的作用，实现以尽可能少的资源消耗和尽可能小的环境代价为目标的经济、环境和社会效益相统一。

3. 安全、卫生是未来塑料制品的生命线

随着人类对自身健康、安全关注程度的提高，社会对食品接触塑料制品的安全性要求越来越高，对其所使用的材料、助剂、加工方法要求越来越严格，相关的法律法规逐渐完善，相应的措施也愈发严厉。

美国、欧盟等国家针对食品包装材料及其添加剂的相关要求越来越严格。我国针对近年来不断发生的食品安全违法事件，将食品接触材料的生产、使用作为重点，加大了对《食品安全法》的执行和违规查处力度。国家从 2009 年开始进行食品包装材料的清理整顿工作，于 2011 年和 2012 年分别发布了《关于公布聚己二酰丁二胺等 107 种可用于食品包装材料的树脂名单的公告》（卫生部公告 2011 年第 23 号）和《关于公布硼酸等 301 种食品包装材料用添加剂名单的公告》（卫生部公告 2012 年第 5 号），对现行国家、行业标准之外的食品包装材料、添加剂新物质的使用予以规定；于 2011 年新成立了国家食品安全风险评估中心，并于 2012 年启动了对 GB 9685—2008《食品容器、包装材料用添加剂使用卫生标准》的修订工作，使国家食品接触材料的安全性管理更加规范和严格。

高度重视塑料制品的卫生和安全工作，全面、系统加强塑料制品的安全工程建设，是塑料加工业面临的头等大事。未来我们要进一步依靠技术进步，大力开发安全可靠的食品包装新材料，加快建立食品包装材料卫生安全溯源机制和方法，要加快食品包装材料标准化体系建设，将来建立食品包装材料安全评价制度和方法，以对人民生命财产高度负责和高度社会责任感，认真做好塑料制品的卫生、安全工作。

三、“十二五”行业科技发展总体思路

（一）总体思路和基本原则

1. 总体思路

深入贯彻落实科学发展观和党的十八大、全国科技创新大会精神，坚持“自主创新，重点跨越，支撑发展，引领未来”的指导方针，深入实施《国家中长期科学和技术发展规划纲要(2006~2020年)》、《国家“十二五”科学和技术发展规划》和《轻工业“十二五”发展规划》及《轻工业技术进步“十二五”发展指导意见》，紧紧围绕科学发展和结构调整这一主题和主线，加快转变发展方式，促进产业转型升级。加快建设和完善以企业为主体、以自主创新为主线的塑料加工业技术创新体系，充分发挥科技创新、技术进步对加快塑料加工业转型升级的重要支撑作用；主攻关键、共性核心技术，努力缩小差距，全面提高产业素质；大力推进塑料制品安全工程建设，全面提高产品质量和品牌影响力；强化产业优势、大力推进节能减排、绿色生产和资源高效利用，提高可持续发展能力，不断增强行业竞争能力，实现又快又好发展，推动我国塑料加工业由大向强的战略升级。

2. 基本原则

坚持以科学发展观为指导，以国家产业政策和战略发展重点为导向，以科技创新和技术进步为支撑，以政策法规为保障，实现塑料加工业上水平、上台阶，全面提升产业素质。坚持调整与发展相结合，重在促进产业结构调整和升级；坚持近期目标与长远发展战略相结合，重在促进行业持续健康发展；坚持自主创新与引进消化吸收先进技术相结合，重在推动行业的技术进步；坚持创新驱动发展和技术进步相结合，重在为全面建设塑料加工业现代化产业体系打好基础。

(二)发展目标

1. 完善科技创新体系

积极推进实施品牌、专利、标准战略，建立企业、科研机构、行业组织的联合创新机制，加快形成以企业为主体，产学研紧密结合的塑料加工业技术创新体系和服务平台，推进科研成果实现产业化转换，不断提升产业核心竞争力。

提高行业自主创新能力。重点行业研究与实验投入占收入的比重超过1%；新产品产值率和科技进步贡献率分别提高到10%和40%；国家认定企业技术中心增加到20个以上，国家重点实验室、国家工程技术研究中心实现零的突破，进一步健全企业为主体的技术创新体系，行业自主创新能力明显增强。

提高关键技术装备自主化率。重点行业关键技术和装备自主化率力争由40%提高到60%。鼓励、培育、支持行业公共科技资源共享机制和服务体系的建立，建成3个以上具有创新、咨询、检测服务等功能的科技公共服务平台。

2. 推进清洁生产和节能减排

在行业内进一步推进节能减排及清洁生产技术应用，推进新能源利用，采用环保型新材料、新工艺及新技术降低能耗。实现经济和环境、社会效益相统一。

——规模以上企业综合能耗符合国家减排指标。

——在聚氨酯、挤出聚苯乙烯(XPS)等泡沫塑料生产中积极淘汰氢氯氟烃发泡剂，配合国家实现向国际社会承诺的2015年淘汰10%用量，2030年全面停止HCFC在新产品中的使用。

——人造革合成革行业积极采用生产中排放溶剂回收技术，实现提高回收效率达95%、普及率达10%，年减少有机溶剂使用量7万吨，其中减少DMF有机气体排放量2万吨/年；大力推广水性聚氨酯、无溶剂聚氨酯用于合成革生产，水性聚氨酯应用覆盖面达到30%，生态型高端产品占生产量的20%，实现清洁生产。

——复合膜行业在大中型软包装彩印企业中推广塑料印刷、复合加工过程中废气治理和溶剂回收利用技术、推广无溶剂复合、水溶性油墨印刷生产工艺，实现年推广应用20%，减少有机溶剂使用约80%，行业年减少排放约10%。

3. 加快重点产业产品结构的转型升级

积极引进、推广国内外先进技术、工艺和设备，通过淘汰落后，优化、调整产品结构，实现产业技术和产品的安全升级；主要产品的产量满足市场需求，产品的品种与规格齐全，中、高档产品比例及产品的质量与配套水平有显著提高，部分产品达到国际先进水平。

四、“十二五”期间主要任务和产品重点发展方向

主要任务

把握当今世界塑料加工业发展方向，顺应潮流，紧紧跟踪当代最新科技动态和前沿技术进展，加快转变发展方式、优化结构调整、加快高端化进程，努力缩小与发达国家的差距，充分发挥科技创新和技术进步保证支撑作用，推动创新驱动发展，全面提升塑料加工行业整体水平，为实现塑料加工业强国目标打好基础，是“十二五”期间的紧迫任务。

(一)加快现代产业体系建设，全面提升塑料加工业整体水平

1. 把握行业发展方向，开展前沿技术研究，努力缩小与先进国家的差距

根据塑料加工行业“功能化、轻量化、微成型”的发展趋势，紧紧跟踪当代科技最新发展动态和前沿科技，组织开展具有前瞻性、先导性的前沿技术研究，主要包括：

——石墨烯低成本、环保工业化制备及聚合物/石墨烯功能高分子复合材料的制备技术，低成本石墨烯/碳纳米管等多元纳米复合化及应用技术，碳纤维基聚合物复合材料研发技术，液晶高分子原位复合增强改性技术，无阻燃剂保温、隔热、耐温、阻燃PI泡沫材料产业化技术，熔融静电纺丝制备技术，塑木用纳米纤维素产业化技术，耐腐蚀、耐磨、耐候特种涂层技术，耐高温气凝胶材料产业化开发技术等。

——绿色、环保、高效聚氨酯发泡剂技术，基于天然蛋白纤维粉体的环保高性能阻燃体系技术，高效过滤微纳米纤维膜集成化技术，氟塑料膜(PVDF、膨体PTFE)海水淡化、污水处理、除尘等用微滤、超滤膜，高档电池隔膜，航空离型用膜产业化技术，新型材质耐候、易回收地膜的研发技术，可熔接(FPVC)、取向(PVC-O)聚氯乙烯管生产技术，缠绕熔接增强PE压力管、自增强PE管生产技术，高压增强热塑性塑料管(RTP)生产技术，层叠双拉超强力膜、光学膜及层叠复合管材生产技术，天然高分子纳米晶及其增强聚乙烯醇阻隔膜产业化技术等。

——高分子材料模内层叠技术及设备开发，新型亚低温治疗血管内体温精确调控关键技术的研究与设备开发，宽幅超高分子量聚乙烯板材连续挤出技术，热塑性树脂、热致液晶聚合物、刚性高分子材料增韧热固性树脂技术。

2. 加大共性关键技术攻关力度，力争有所突破，逐步解决制约行业整体水平提升发展的瓶颈，推进科技创新与产业化

通过塑料加工业及上下游产业链的联合攻关，力争在塑料加工业关键技术和共性技术上有所突破，逐步解决制约行业整体水平提升的高端原料、助剂、装备严重依赖进口、产品安全保障能力水平不高等瓶颈问题，提升行业的整体技术水平和自主创新能力。

——石墨烯、碳纳米管导电、导热复合材料生产技术，无卤阻燃、抑烟PU泡沫、XPS、EPS材料生产技术，汽车轻量化、电子行业等领域应用的通用塑料、工程塑料和PEEK、PPS、PI、长链PA等特种工程塑料的改性、合金及制品生产技术，用于管材、异型材、板片材等制品的PVC高端改性料技术，啤酒、化妆品、医疗、食品包装及农药、汽车油箱油管用高阻隔、

抗菌等产品技术，高性能含氟聚合物新材料(太阳能背板膜、门窗户外耐候贴膜等)生产技术，功能化(阻燃、防霉等)塑木复合材料的制备技术，可降解塑料聚乳酸改性(增强、共混、共聚、复合改性)技术，纤维素纳米纤维增强纳米复合材料制备技术，土工工程用 EPS 泡沫的研发技术，高填充改性环保装潢材料、过滤材料产业化技术等。

——聚丙烯增韧增刚型 β 晶成核剂技术，硅烷改性聚醚类粘合剂研发及应用技术，薄膜高速印刷、复合用水性凹版油墨制备及应用技术，光学、电子、包装等领域高性能(透明、散热、耐电晕等)PET、PC、PI、PMMA 等薄膜生产技术，废旧 PET/PE 或 PP 共混合金及产品(编织袋、包装膜等)生产技术，高透明功能与寿命同步棚膜及高性能节水器材产业化技术，dn400 以上交联聚乙烯、dn800 以上超高分子量聚乙烯管材生产技术，分子量≥300 万超高分子量聚乙烯板材、管材近熔点挤出成型关键技术，无机纳米材料改性硬聚氯乙烯管材生产技术，长效光生态、光转换农膜生产技术，PMMA/ASA 彩色专用料在高性能推拉门窗上的应用技术，氟碳喷涂彩色珠光、氟碳耐候贴膜 PVC 异型材生产技术，塑筋材料及制品结构研究及成型加工技术等。

——可控发泡倍率的超临界 CO_2 微发泡制备 PP、PS、PI 等泡沫材料技术，异型滚塑制品及巨型滚塑制品的设计及成型技术，生物基塑料加工及装备关键技术，双螺杆反应挤出技术，塑料三维打印成型技术，PTFE 板及氟塑料制品焊接技术，超高分子量聚乙烯复合材料粘合技术等。

——生产中精确计量、连续稳定混配及车间粉尘控制系统技术，PVC 助剂无铅化替代在管材、异型材等制品的应用技术，食品、药品包装材料卫生安全性的溯源技术，低成本、可控完全生物降解地膜制备及农田应用技术，废旧地膜、一次性发泡餐盒回收管理体系的建立、完善及高值化利用技术。

3. 加快重点塑料加工装备制造的研发，提高装备自主化水平

在做好引进、消化、吸收、再创新工作的同时，以关键技术、设备和重点项目为突破口，发挥优势，集中力量开发行业高端装备，提高自主化水平，提高国产塑料机械在国际上的竞争力。

——对于处于国际领先水平的塑料动态成型加工技术与装备、高转速/高扭矩双螺杆挤出机、“木塑一步法”板材专用挤出设备、节能大容量塑筋挤出注射成型机、大型超临界 CO_2 聚合物发泡挤出装备等，要继续保持优势并不断创新。

——大面积推广应用大型聚丙烯/聚乙烯混炼挤压造粒机组、精密塑料注射成型设备、全液压四缸直锁二板式注塑机、精密挤出技术及装备、内循环两板式注塑机、锥形同向双螺杆挤出机、水性生态合成革生产装备等处于国际先进水平的设备。

——争取在熔体静电纺丝微纳米制品(微米毡、无纺布等)制造装备，大型多层共挤中空塑料成型机，巨型高分子制品旋模滚塑成型装备，微纳层叠共挤出成型装备，微型/全电动注射成型机，智能型高速节能 PET 瓶吹瓶机，PET 瓶片回收及再利用设备，小型及宽幅高速双向拉伸薄膜生产设备，PVC－O 管、大口径交联聚乙烯(PE－X)管、接枝改性聚氯乙烯(PVC－M)管等管材装备，合成革及复合膜生产溶剂排放回收装置，塑料微尺度制造装备，电加热滚塑装备，塑料制品在线检测设备等方面有更大的突破。

行业骨干企业“十二五”期间技术装备水平争取达到国际先进，行业整体先进生产线的比例进一步提高，改变国内塑料加工设备受制于人的局面，满足高效节能、节材、环保以及降低生产成本等各项要求。

4. 加快新产品新技术的开发、推广，加快产品升级换代

积极开展新产品开发，大力推广高技术含量、高附加值产品的普及，调整产品结构，推动新材料、新工艺的应用和新技术、新设备的引进，淘汰落后的技术工艺、设备。

——积极推进废塑料改性及综合利用技术、高气密性节能塑料推拉窗技术、建筑保温高效阻燃材料及产品技术、生物分解材料及其产品的应用技术、水性聚氨酯合成革及无溶剂合成革生产技术、塑木材料及产品的先进制造技术、塑料节水器材先进生产技术、微纳层叠共挤出技术、绿色建材及特种管材生产技术、塑料高效节能加工成型技术、纳米宽幅多层光生态功能膜、长效流滴消雾复合膜生产技术、新型滚塑游艇技术开发及产业化等，大力推进节能技术的普及及产业化。

——大力开展塑料的超临界CO_2微发泡制备技术，重质超强PET编织制品的产业化技术，定岛型束状超细纤维聚氨酯合成革技术，高清晰、高光度、防紫外等功能性薄膜、片材生产技术，高效无铅稳定剂生产技术，大口径交联聚乙烯及UHMWPE管材制备技术，新型环保阻燃塑料制品生产技术，多层复合滚塑产品开发及产业化技术，PVC高端改性料系列制品研发技术，低成本特种聚酰亚胺(PI)工程塑料及高性能PI薄膜制备技术，功能性肉制品塑料包装膜制备技术等，大力开发先进材料制备技术。

——通过进行生产线大型混配、精确计量及车间粉尘控制系统的技术改造，改变目前行业普遍存在特别是塑料改性、管道、异型材、再生及塑木等产品生产中出现的原料拌料不均，助剂、精细配料计量不准造成的产品质量不稳定、生产现场粉尘飞扬、污染环境等问题，逐步实现集中统一配料，以保证质量稳定。

5. 大力推行清洁生产，推进节能减排

加大重点行业推进节能、降耗、减排工作力度，利用新技术、新工艺、新材料、新设备推动节能减排。通过大力推行节能减排、清洁生产技术，降低能耗，节约生产成本，提高企业经济效益和市场竞争力。

——加强塑料产品特别是人造革合成革、复合膜制品生产全过程的低碳、绿色、生态基础理论研究。开展节能减排、生态化、绿色生产的基础理论、材料功能化、产品多功能协同发展研究，为绿色制造、发展新型低环境负荷材料和高性能复合材料提供理论指导，促进全行业的绿色转型、生态化进程。

——大力提高环保型新材料的使用率，优化原料配置。扩大环保型助剂、改性材料、多功能母料、完全生物降解塑料等新型环境友好材料的应用，保持我国塑料加工业无污染清洁生产行业地位。

——大力发展应用于环保、减排及资源充分利用技术。推动聚氨酯、XPS等泡沫塑料生产淘汰氢氯氟烃发泡剂，印刷、复合膜生产不使用丁酮、苯类有毒有害溶剂，减少对环境及人身安全的危害；加大降解塑料的研发与产业化；继续抓好人造革、复合膜行业积极推行生产中排放溶剂的回收技术；大力推广水性聚氨酯、无溶剂聚氨酯用于合成革生产和无溶剂干法复合、水溶性油墨印刷生产工艺，减少有机溶剂使用、排放；继续推进长效流滴消雾棚膜、适应建筑节能发展需求的高气密性节能塑料推拉窗及高效保温隔热塑料材料、功能性环保石塑纸、高档塑木复合材料等资源充分利用技术的产业化及推广应用。

——加快淘汰高耗能的落后生产装备，大力推广新型高效电磁变频加热技术、伺服驱动节能技术、高效节能型锥形同向双螺杆挤出技术、基于拉伸流变的塑料高效节能加工成型技术、PET瓶片免干燥节能挤出加工等低耗节能新技术；加强对塑料生产装备的更新、改造，引进消化吸收世界先进塑料加工技术并再创新，满足高效节能、节材、环保以及降低生产成本等各项要求，进一步提高先进产能生产线比例。

——加强废塑料回收体系建设，协助、配合各级政府部门做好废旧地膜、一次性发泡餐盒的回收体系建设和产品高值化再利用工作，加强废旧塑料回收自动化有水清洗和无水清洗技术推广及塑料回收利用生产工艺、设备的研发，提高生产效率，加强环保配套技术及设备的开发应用。

——加快废塑料回收利用技术研发，提高制品的性价比。推广用废聚苯乙烯泡沫塑料生产画框、相框等线材，利用回收 PET 瓶片生产塑编袋及 PET 合金，利用废塑料和废木屑等制备高性能塑木产品等，实现废塑料资源循环、增值利用。

6. 加快企业信息化改造，提高企业“两化”融合水平

建设信息化平台。加快行业经济数据库、科技项目、成果数据库、专利数据库系统建设；搞好协会网站建设，举办行业展览会，加快网络化建设，形成较为完善的科技信息资源共享平台。

加快行业信息化、数字化系统升级改造进程。积极支持鼓励企业采用先进的数字信息化系统，充分利用信息技术，推行数字化管理，实施 ERP 等先进管理信息系统，提高经济运行效率。开发和运用新型网络化平台扩大交易途径，开展多种贸易平台建设，实现增值服务。

7. 大力推进塑料制品安全管理体系建设

高度重视塑料制品特别是与食品、饮料接触的塑料薄膜、容器、管道的卫生和安全问题，在全行业组织、倡导加工企业重诺、诚信、守法，以高度社会责任感严格执行相关卫生和安全使用标准，努力提高产品质量，切实保证产品的卫生与安全。加强企业生产过程监督，加强诚信建设，确保产品安全、可靠。

——生产与食品、水、饮料接触的包装膜、容器、瓶、管道等塑料制品的企业，自觉使用符合国家卫生、安全标准的原材料和环保型助剂、填料，不使用铅盐类重金属稳定剂、低分子量邻苯二甲酸酯类增塑剂；塑料复合膜产品努力解决好溶剂残留的控制、原材料及油墨胶黏剂中小分子物的迁移量控制、异物控制和生产过程中的卫生控制。

——在企业自律的基础上，大力发展符合卫生安全的水溶性油墨、水溶性或醇溶性粘合剂，大力开发共挤技术新产品，开发共挤薄膜应用市场，促进更多的塑料包装企业走绿色包装之路。

——研究、建立食品、药品包装材料卫生安全的溯源技术管理体系，通过对塑料包装产业链尤其是食品塑料包装制品各环节禁限化学物质的指纹鉴别、含量检测，为企业的产品是否符合卫生安全标准提供检测和技术依据证明，协助企业建立完善的卫生安全管理体系，诚信守法，生产公众放心产品。

——积极宣传、倡导行业推进在 PVC 相关制品中采用环保型热稳定剂替代铅盐稳定剂，进而适时启动在全行业实施禁铅进程。

——逐步建立各类产品的风险评估、安全预警机制，有对突发塑料制品相关食品安全、专利、反倾销等类事件的应急预案，维护行业形象及产业安全。

8. 大力推进行业的标准化工作

发挥协会面向行业、企业和政府的沟通、协调作用，整合各方面资源，推动塑料加工行业标准体系完善、标准制定的工作，起到规范行业生产、限制恶性竞争，保护行业健康发展、提升行业国际竞争力，打破制约行业发展贸易壁垒的作用。

——积极推动塑料加工业国家标准、行业标准以及企业标准体系的健全与完善。协助全国

塑料制品标准化技术委员会加强已有标准体系的子行业标准体系建设与完善，尽快建立部分子行业和新兴产业的标准体系。

——积极推动塑料加工业各类标准的及时制定、修订和完善。推动塑料制品基础标准、检测方法标准的建立健全；组织研究、制定关系行业进步、生存及出口贸易等所需的安全、卫生、管理、能耗、单耗等相关标准、技术规范；加快产品标准更新速度的同时保证产品标准的质量和水平。

(二)加快行业创新资源和要素的聚集，全面推动以企业为主体的创新体系建设

(1)加快推动行业中企业研发中心的建立，在行业龙头企业创造条件率先实现国家级、普及省市级企业研发中心的认定，带动行业创新体系建设。

(2)加快推动行业人才、技术、资金等创新要素、资源的聚集，大力支持、推动行业工程技术研发中心和国家认可实验室的建立。

(3)鼓励、推进行业企业与科研院所的产、学、研、用的紧密结合，在面向市场面向行业中、在重大科研项目研发中协同作战，在行业创新体系建设中发挥带头和引领作用。

(4)充分发挥专家委员会、行业专家的把关、咨询、引领作用，发挥协会的协同组织作用，大力实施协同创新战略，加强大专院校、科研院所、企业间的联合攻关。

(三)加快人才培养，为塑料加工业持续发展、实现强国目标打好基础

人才既是重塑塑料加工行业竞争优势的关键，更是未来发展和实现塑料加工强国目标的第一要素。牢固树立人才是第一资源的思想，把培养发现人才放在重要位置，充分调动科技人员创新积极性，在科研实践中、在重大科研项目中凝聚拔尖人才。

(1)实施行业科技人才发展战略。建立企业、大学联合机制，建立、完善塑料加工行业专业人才培养基地。促进大学、企业和行业协会合作开展职业教育工程，培养高层次技术人才和高级技能型人才。在适当时机召开行业科技大会，表彰一批为行业发展做出贡献的科技人才。

(2)鼓励塑料加工企业培养和引进高级技术和管理人才，鼓励企业对产品质量及企业管理方面的改革与创新，支持企业通过内、外招聘的方式加强职工队伍素质建设，并以技术交流的方式，提高行业内科技人员的业务素质。形成尊重劳动、尊重知识、尊重人才、尊重创造的环境和氛围，逐步建立一支规模宏大、结构合理、素质优良的创新人才队伍。

(3)建设塑料行业创新人才团队。围绕产业升级，以培育自主创新能力和竞争能力为重点，形成一批具有国际先进水平的创新人才团队。依托重大科技专项、重点项目、产学研联盟等建成一批高科技人才培养基地。

重点产品发展方向

(详见附件一)

五、政策建议

(一)支持科技示范、技术创新公共服务平台的建立和发展

强化重点企业的科技引领作用，推进企业创新发展，特别是对有自主知识产权产品、有创新开发能力和新型适用专利产品的企业给予重点扶持。支持、培育行业技术创新公共服务平台的建立，鼓励企业建立国家级企业技术中心、重点实验室及工程技术研发中心、检测中心，推动自主创新；发挥大型企业在自主创新，推进行业技术进步中的带头和引领作用，鼓励、帮助行业龙头和重点企业通过资本运作组建企业集团或“产业技术创新联盟”；加强科技型示范企业、示范区域的建设并给予政策支持，促进高校院所的科研成果更快地转化为先进生产力。

(二)支持节能减排先进技术的示范与推广应用

国家应对塑料加工行业低碳技术研发及推广、应用环保新材料、新技术，对塑料生产装备的更新、改造，研发、引进消化吸收世界先进塑料加工技术等予以资金、政策支持。建议对于因使用节能、环保、低碳技术产生的产品成本上升部分，经政府和行业协会组织认定后给予部分减免税或一定补贴。

(三)引导、支持塑料废弃物再生利用有效机制的建立、运行

认真贯彻"减量化，再利用，资源化"政策，加强塑料再生利用正面宣传，引导社会、媒体正确看待废塑料；从源头抓起，促进再生资源发展与环境保护并重，认真贯彻"减量化，再利用，资源化"政策原则。建议增加塑木材料及制品、再生塑料制品的海关编码以鼓励其出口，对塑料废弃物循环再利用生产企业以减免税收或项目投资补助、塑料再生资源产品列入政府采购目录等扶植和优惠政策，引导全社会重视勤俭节约、倡导绿色低碳，创造有利环境形成适合于我国特色的塑料废弃物回收再生利用的有效运行机制，推动再生资源循环、绿色低碳发展。

(四)发挥行业协会的桥梁纽带作用，把握行业科技发展方向，为行业提供优质服务

协会在建立行业经济效益、科技项目、科技成果、专利等数据库、完善科技信息资源数据的基础上，加强对包括行业的科技发展目标、方向，资源节约、节能减排，产业布局、行业准入、风险评估、安全预警等行业重大问题的研究，把握行业科技发展方向，引领行业健康发展。积极参与国家产业政策、法规的制定，反映企业诉求，推动国家和相关部委的各项支持塑料加工行业技术进步的规划、政策、项目的制定和在塑料加工企业的落实；及时向企业传递国家、政府的相关政策、信息，抓住机遇，利用各方面的投入，有效组织以企业为主体，产学研用的行业内外科技力量开展攻关。坚持正确舆论导向，维护行业利益，为行业技术进步和健康发展提供优质服务。

(五)发挥行业协会的职能，协助政府推进行业进步

建议政府有关部门充分发挥协会在参与涉及行业产业布局、产业政策、科技政策、税收、进出口关税、退税等政策的研究与制修订方面的作用；在各类技术研发、技术改造项目的立项过程中、各项政策的实施中充分征询行业协会意见；授权并支持协会协助政府进行行业认证、行业准入及后续管理；建议政府建立同时加强与行业的沟通交流机制，做好前瞻性、安全性重大问题的研究，为行业科技创新发展不断提供激励政策，推进塑料加工业持续健康发展。

附件一　重点产品发展方向

附件二　《塑料加工业技术进步指导意见》技术目录

附件一　重点产品发展方向

"十二五"期间，从塑料助剂及制品、塑料加工设备、模具三方面概括，塑料加工行业主要包括以下重点发展方向：

1. 塑料助剂及制品

——无重金属(铅、镉等)钙锌复合热稳定剂，稀土类热稳定剂。

——无卤、低烟、低毒、高效阻燃剂，有机硅阻燃剂，纳米阻燃剂。

——真空镀铝膜新品种，硅或铝氧化物蒸镀薄膜、纳米无机材料复合膜。

——电容膜、锂电池隔膜等特种 BOPP 膜，多层共挤或无胶复合 BOPP 包装膜。

——太阳能背板膜的 PVDF 含氟基膜，气体过滤用膨体 PTFE 膜，PVDF、PTFE 高档锂离子电池隔膜，航空离型用氟塑料离型膜。

——建筑外墙用高性能 ETFE 膜，汽车、飞机表面保护用 TPU 薄膜，汽车用 PVB 玻璃夹层膜，EVA 太阳能背板封装膜，高速 PE 缠绕膜等高端流延薄膜。

——BOPET 扭结膜等环保型软包装薄膜，保温、隔热、防爆、遮避私密及安全防护等功能建筑 PET 贴膜，太阳能 TPT 背材用聚酯薄膜，耐候性聚酯薄膜，高介电强度聚酯电容膜、耐热抗老化聚酯绝缘膜、回收利用的 BOPET 热收缩膜、BOPET 膜。

——心血管支架植入手术用可扩张气囊，不含 DEHP 的 PVC 软管、肾透析用特种中空塑料透析用纤维，人造血管、关节、心脏瓣膜等医用塑料制品。

——超宽超厚消音耐磨型聚氯乙烯人造革地板，新型超细纤维合成革，高档装修用环保型具有透气功能的聚氨酯壁纸，清洁生产工艺的水性与无溶剂型聚氨酯合成革，抗菌防霉、防紫外线、阻燃、透气透湿、自洁防污、耐刮、耐候性等功能性和生态型合成革，超细纤维合成革及基材以及环保型助剂。

——高模量聚丙烯(PP)双壁波纹管、复合缠绕增强等大口径排水排污管材，PVC - M 管材，PVC - O 管材，非开挖施工技术和旧管道修复用塑料管材，用于石油输送及特种介质输送用高压增强热塑性塑料管材(RTP)，矿山用阻燃和抗静电的双抗塑料管材，分子量 >200 万的超高分子量聚乙烯(UHMW - PE)管材等。

——PVC 微发泡外墙装饰板、栅栏、室内门、室内柜体板(包括壁柜、厨柜、衣柜、书柜等)、PVC 结皮发泡建筑模板，包装用 EPS、PP 珠粒发泡产品，建筑保温用高阻燃塑料发泡材料和制品等。

——发泡、高频、交联等高性能氟塑料电线，高性能聚四氟乙烯纤维及其配套产品，各类氟塑料膜材及其组件，改性聚四氟乙烯制品，半导体用氟塑料制品。

——多层阻隔 PET 啤酒瓶，高气密性、节能、隔声推拉窗制品，石塑复合纸，纤维增强塑筋产品，用 PET 瓶片制备扁丝及编法制品，PET 与 PE 或 PP 共混合金吹塑薄膜，新型材质耐候、易回收地膜，废旧发泡聚苯乙烯制备的相框及框材产品。

2. 塑料加工设备

——注塑成型设备

微型/全电动注塑成型机，大型高效的混炼注塑一体化的塑木制品注射成型装备，带有空气辅助、水辅助装置的新型注塑机，全电动、全液压精密类注塑机，节能大容量挤出注塑成型机。

——挤出成型设备

双螺杆挤出五层、七层多层共挤薄膜生产线，高精度可熔融氟塑料挤出机及专用流延设备，发泡、高频、交联等高性能氟塑料线缆专用设备，大直径糊状挤出 PTFE 管材设备，聚合物动态反应加工技术及设备，微纳层叠共挤出成型装备，超临界 CO_2 微孔泡沫塑料挤出成型装备，小型及宽幅高速双向拉伸薄膜生产设备，PVC - O 取向增强管材生产设备、高压增强热塑性塑料管(RTP)加工设备。

——中空成型设备

大型多层共挤出中空塑料成型机，智能型高速节能 PET 瓶吹瓶机，大型挤吹塑料成型机，“一步法”注拉吹中空塑料成型机，多层共注射瓶胚设备，三维挤吹中空塑料成型机。

——滚塑成型设备

大型、多工位、自动化旋模滚塑成型装备，高效节能型烘箱式滚塑成型装备，高效多层滚塑成型设备。

——其他成型设备

大型无尘原料混配、精密计量生产系统，BOPET在线涂布设备，编织袋生产用宽幅、高速拉丝机，高速自动切袋机，高速切缝机，PET瓶片回收及再利用设备，塑料薄膜、管材等制品的在线自动检测设备，可熔性氟塑料加工设备，熔融立体三维打印成型设备。

3. 塑料加工模具

——大型化、精密化模具，多功能复合模具，热流道模具，气体辅助注射模具，高压注射成型用模具，微型、复杂模具。

附件二 《塑料加工业技术进步指导意见》技术目录

专栏1　前沿技术研究

分类		技术名称
材料	1	石墨烯低成本、环保工业化制备及聚合物/石墨烯功能高分子复合材料的制备技术
	2	低成本石墨烯/碳纳米管等多元纳米复合化及应用技术
	3	碳纤维基聚合物复合材料研发技术
	4	液晶高分子原位复合增强改性技术
	5	无阻燃剂保温、隔热、耐温、阻燃PI泡沫材料产业化技术
	6	熔融静电纺丝制备技术
	7	塑木用纳米纤维素产业化技术
	8	耐腐蚀、耐磨、耐候特种涂层研发技术
	9	耐高温气凝胶材料产业化开发技术
助剂	10	绿色、环保、高效聚氨酯发泡剂研发技术
	11	基于天然蛋白纤维粉体的环保高性能阻燃体系技术
制品	12	高效过滤微纳米纤维膜集成化技术
	13	氟塑料膜(PVDF、膨体PTFE)海水淡化、污水处理、除尘等用微滤、超滤膜，高档电池隔膜，航空离型用膜产业化技术
	14	新型材质耐候、易回收地膜的研发技术
	15	可熔接(FPVC)、取向(PVC-O)聚氯乙烯管生产技术
	16	缠绕熔接增强PE压力管、自增强PE管生产技术
	17	高压增强热塑性塑料管(RTP)生产技术
	18	层叠双拉超强力膜、光学膜及层叠复合管材生产技术
	19	天然高分子纳米晶及其增强聚乙烯醇阻隔膜产业化技术
加工	20	高分子材料模内层叠技术及设备开发
	21	新型亚低温治疗血管内体温精确调控关键技术的研究与设备开发
	22	宽幅超高分子量聚乙烯板材连续挤出技术
	23	热塑性树脂、热致液晶聚合物、刚性高分子材料增韧热固性树脂技术

专栏2 共性关键技术

分类		技术名称
材料	1	石墨烯、碳纳米管导电、导热复合材料生产技术
	2	无卤阻燃、抑烟PU泡沫、XPS、EPS材料生产技术
	3	汽车轻量化、电子行业等领域应用的通用塑料、工程塑料和PEEK、PPS、PI、长链PA等特种工程塑料的改性、合金及制品生产技术
	4	用于管材、异型材、板片材等制品的PVC高端改性料技术
	5	啤酒、化妆品、医疗、食品包装及农药、汽车油箱油管用高阻隔、抗菌等产品技术
	6	高性能含氟聚合物新材料(太阳能背板膜、门窗户外耐候贴膜等)生产技术
	7	功能化(阻燃、防霉等)塑木复合材料的制备技术
	8	可降解塑料聚乳酸改性(增强、共混、共聚、复合改性)技术
	9	纤维素纳米纤维增强纳米复合材料制备技术
	10	土工工程用EPS泡沫、高强度交联PVC泡沫等材料生产技术
	11	高填充改性环保装潢材料、过滤材料产业化技术
助剂	12	聚丙烯增韧增刚型β晶成核剂技术
	13	硅烷改性聚醚类粘合剂研发及应用技术
	14	薄膜高速印刷、复合用水性凹版油墨制备及应用技术
制品	15	光学、电子、包装等领域高性能(透明、散热、耐电晕等)PET、PC、PI、PMMA等薄膜生产技术
	16	新型耐老化、易回收地膜生产技术
	17	废旧PET/PE或PP共混合金及产品(编织袋、包装膜等)生产技术
	18	高透明功能与寿命同步棚膜及高性能节水器材产业化技术
	19	dn400以上交联聚乙烯、dn800以上超高分子量聚乙烯管材生产技术
	20	分子量≥300万超高分子量聚乙烯板材、管材近熔点挤出成型关键技术
	21	无机纳米材料改性硬聚氯乙烯管材生产技术
	22	长效光生态、光转换农膜生产技术
	23	PMMA/ASA彩色专用料在高性能推拉门窗上的应用技术
	24	氟碳喷涂彩色珠光、氟碳耐候贴膜异型材生产技术
	25	塑筋材料及制品结构研究及成型加工技术
加工	26	可控发泡倍率的超临界CO_2微发泡制备PP、PS、PI等泡沫材料技术
	27	异型滚塑制品及巨型滚塑制品的设计及成型技术
	28	生物基塑料加工及装备关键技术
	29	双螺杆反应挤出技术
	30	塑料三维打印成型技术
	31	PTFE板及氟塑料制品焊接技术
	32	超高分子量聚乙烯复合材料粘合技术
管理	33	生产中精确计量、连续稳定混配及车间粉尘控制系统技术应用
	34	PVC管材、异型材等制品用稳定剂无铅化替代技术应用及推广
	35	食品、药品包装材料卫生安全性的溯源技术
	36	低成本、可控完全生物降解地膜制备及农田应用技术
	37	废旧地膜、一次性发泡餐盒回收管理体系的建立、完善及高值化利用技术

专栏3 重点推广技术

分类		技术名称
材料	1	改性无机粉体材料在无交联聚烯烃发泡体系中应用技术
	2	食品、饮料用塑料制品高效纳米抗菌功能母料的生产技术
助剂	3	新型高效轻稀土功能助剂生产及应用技术
制品	4	TPU薄膜、PVB玻璃夹层膜、EVA太阳能背板封装膜等高端流延薄膜生产技术
	5	智能建筑、汽车用节能玻璃贴膜，太阳能TPT背材用聚酯薄膜，高介电强度聚酯电容膜，耐热抗老化聚酯绝缘膜生产技术
	6	食品、肉类等包装用环保共挤出超薄高阻隔薄膜的生产技术
	7	PVC微发泡外墙装饰、栅栏、室内门及结皮发泡建筑模板等塑木产品生产技术
	8	高耐候ASA/PVC共挤彩色门窗型材生产技术
	9	动态密封功能的TPE后共挤异型材生产技术
	10	用于80平开系列门窗的UPVC型材生产技术
	11	PE-RT耐热管道系统的工业化生产技术
	12	钢管道内衬防腐用薄壁管材生产技术
	13	1000mm大口径PVC-U双壁波纹管工业化生产技术
	14	埋地排水用钢带增强聚乙烯(PE)螺旋波纹管制造技术
	15	垃圾填埋场导渗用高密度聚乙烯管材的生产技术
	16	PVC-C环保冷热饮水管材管件制造技术
	17	大口径钢塑复合管材及管件的制造技术
	18	雨水利用的塑料管材制品生产和应用技术
	19	高压增强热塑性塑料管、抗磨塑料管生产技术
	20	纳米宽幅多层光生态功能膜研制技术
	21	涂覆型长效流滴消雾农用功能棚膜及聚合物基纳米复合涂液
	22	高性能聚碳酸酯薄膜/片材加工技术
	23	合成革用水性聚氨酯树脂及水性生态合成革制造技术
	24	定岛型束状聚氨酯超细纤维合成革生产技术
加工	25	医用导管、插管抗凝涂覆技术与应用
	26	新型滚塑游艇成型技术
	27	高效节能智能化塑料挤出草坪单丝技术

专栏4 重点节能及清洁生产技术

分类		重点节能技术名称
节能	1	基于电磁加热、拉伸流变、锥形同向双螺杆、伺服驱动、正位移输送等技术的塑料高效节能塑料加工成型技术
	2	新型建筑节能复合保温材料及节能体系(EPS/石墨复合材料、EPS模块建筑节能体系)
	3	PET瓶片免干燥节能挤出加工技术
	4	宽幅复合夹网膜制备技术
	5	电加热滚塑设备及技术
	6	农用功能性覆盖材料的功效延长技术及应用
	7	高气密性节能塑料推拉窗生产技术

续表

分类		清洁生产技术名称
清洁	1	生产车间密闭无尘粉体表面处理系统技术
	2	无重金属(铅、镉等)化环保型热稳定剂应用技术
	3	塑料薄膜高速印刷、复合用水性凹版油墨制备及应用技术
	4	水性聚氨酯与无溶剂聚氨酯应用合成革产业化技术
	5	全自动有水清洗和无水清洗技术
	6	利用废旧聚四氟乙烯材料加工聚四氟乙烯微粉技术
	7	高填充改性环保装潢材料、过滤材料产业化技术

专栏5　重点装备研发技术

分类		技 术 名 称
装备	1	熔体静电纺丝微纳米制品(微米毡、无纺布等)制造装备研发技术
	2	节能大容量塑筋挤出注塑成型机研发技术
	3	生产中精确计量、连续稳定混配及车间粉尘控制系统研发技术
	4	PVC－O管、大口径PE－X管、接枝PVC－M管等管材装备研发技术
	5	水性聚氨酯湿法生产线及自动供料系统研发技术
	6	水性生态合成革生产装备研发技术
	7	合成革、复合膜生产溶剂排放回收装置研发技术
	8	塑料微尺度制造装备及技术
	9	智能型高速节能PET吹瓶机研发技术
	10	宽幅、高速柔性双向拉伸薄膜生产线及备品备件的国产化
	11	巨型高分子制品旋模滚塑成型装备研发技术
	12	电加热滚塑装备及研发技术
	13	差速锥形螺杆塑炼技术及装备
	14	塑料动态成型加工技术与装备
	15	内循环两板式注塑机研发技术
	16	PET瓶片回收及再利用装备研发技术
	17	气体辅助挤出成型装备研发技术
	18	全电动精密塑料注射成型装备研发技术
	19	多层共挤超大型中空成型机研发技术
	20	大型超临界CO_2聚合物发泡挤出装备研发技术
	21	农膜超薄涂层用微量液体擦涂装置研发技术

关于《塑料加工业技术进步指导意见(2013～2015年)》的编制说明

中国塑料加工工业协会理事长　钱桂敬

《塑料加工业技术进步指导意见(2013～2015年)》(以下简称《意见》)的讨论稿正式提交六届三次理事扩大会审议了，现将相关情况及问题作一简要说明。

一、《意见》编制过程

2012年8月7日，中国轻工业联合会召开了全国轻工业科技大会，会议总结了“十一五”期间轻工科技工作的成就，分析了轻工科技工作面临的新形势、新问题，明确了“十二五”时期轻工科技工作思路和遵循的原则，同时发布了《轻工业技术进步“十二五”发展指导意见》及《“十二五”轻工行业重点共性关键技术研发项目指南》等指导性文件。这对于我们塑料行业的科技工作，起到了很好的促进和推动作用。

2012年中国塑料加工工业协会正式发布了《塑料加工业“十二五”发展规划指导意见》，“规划”明确了塑料加工业在国民经济中的地位、理清了行业“十二五”总体发展思路。思路突出依靠科技创新、推进技术进步、推动产业升级，着力构建现代产业体系，为推动塑料加工企业走科技创新、节能减排、品牌效益之路，不断缩小与发达国家的差距，为实现塑料加工业强国目标打好基础。2012年8月的中国塑协理事长办公会上决定组织编制《塑料加工行业技术进步“十二五”发展指导意见》，并成立了协会理事长牵头、秘书长带队、综合业务部负责、各专委会秘书长参加的起草小组，由此启动了《意见》的编制工作。

2012年8月20日协会发出中国塑协[2012]第80、81号文件，面向全行业广泛征集《塑料加工行业技术进步“十二五”发展指导意见》相关意见、内容。协会相关会员单位、行业专家和各专业委员会积极响应，就塑料加工行业的相关前沿技术、重点推广技术、共性关键技术及清洁生产、节能减排及管理等方面提出了许多好的意见建议。特别是人造革合成革、农膜、复合膜、聚酯薄膜、氟塑料、塑料管道、异型材7个专委会，还提交了完整的《行业技术进步“十二五”发展建议》的书面报告，为编制《意见》提供了重要的技术支持。

《意见》(初稿)完成后，在2013年1月25日的协会全体分支机构秘书长会上征求了意见，经各专委会补充内容，形成了《意见》(征求意见稿)。于3月15日在北京召开的有48人出席的中国塑协理事长工作会议上对《意见》(征求意见稿)进行了认真讨论，经修改后形成了《意见》(讨论稿)。希望各位理事和代表认真提出修改意见，以便进一步完善形成正式《意见》。

二、“十二五”行业科技发展总体思路

《意见》全面总结了塑料加工业“十二五”以来技术进步取得的巨大成绩和存在的不足，全面分析了塑料加工业面临的难得的历史发展机遇和严峻的挑战，深入分析了当代塑料加工业发展趋势和最新前沿技术，在此基础上提出了“十二五”塑料加工业科技发展的总体思路。

总体思路突出坚持“自主创新，重点跨越，支撑发展，引领未来”的指导方针；突出紧紧围绕科学发展和结构调整这一主题和主线，加快转变发展方式，促进产业转型升级；突出加快建设和完善以企业为主体、以自主创新为主线的塑料加工业技术创新体系，充分发挥科技创新、技术进步对加快塑料工业转型升级的重要支撑作用；突出主攻关键、共性核心技术，努力缩小差距，全面提高产业素质；突出大力推进塑料制品安全工程建设，全面提高产品质量和品牌影响力；强化产业优势、大力推进节能减排、绿色生产和资源高效利用，提高可持续发展能力，不断增强行业竞争能力，实现又好又快发展，推动我国塑料加工业由大向强的战略升级。

《意见》提出了“十二五”塑料加工业科技发展必须遵循的基本原则：

坚持以科学发展观为指导，以国家产业政策和战略发展重点为导向，以科技创新和技术进步为支持，以政策法规为保障，实现塑料加工业上水平、上台阶，全面提升产业素质。坚持调整与发展相结合，重在促进产业结构调整和升级；坚持近期目标与长远发展战略相结合，重在促进行业持续健康发展；坚持自主创新与引进消化吸收先进技术相结合，重在推动行业的技术进步；坚持创新驱动发展和技术进步相结合，重在为全面建设塑料加工业现代化产业体系打好基础。

《意见》在发展目标上，突出了完善科技创新体系；推进清洁生产和节能减排，加快重点产业产品结构的转型升级等方面的数值指标。

三、“十二五”塑料加工业重点技术研究、发展方向和重点研发内容

《意见》对重点技术研究和发展方向的确定主要考虑：一是紧紧跟踪当代科学发展趋势及前沿技术，以努力缩小与发达国家差距为目标，按照功能化、轻量化、微成型的要求，把握整个塑料行业的发展方向；二是紧紧围绕塑料加工业的关键、共性技术力争实现重点突破，并形成产业化，以改变塑料加工业面貌；三是紧紧围绕提升产业素质，大力推广新材料、新工艺、新技术、新装备；四是紧紧围绕绿色发展、循环发展、清洁生产，使我国塑料加工业节能减排迈上新台阶。

《意见》提出了“十二五”塑料加工业技术进步重点研究内容，主要有前沿技术、共性关键技术、重点推广技术、重点节能及清洁生产技术、重点装备研发技术等五个方面，同时提出重点产品发展方向，均在附件一、附件二中详细列出。

《意见》中技术方向及重点研发内容，是方向性、导向性的，也是阶段性的。随着科技进步和新技术突破，需要不断完善、补充和调整。因此塑料加工全行业要密切跟踪当代最新科技动态和前沿技术研究进程，站在科技发展制高点来把握塑料加工业发展方向，同时要面向市场，把握行业发展规律，不断做强做优、增强核心竞争力和发展后劲。

四、主要任务

《意见》提出塑料加工业未来要紧紧围绕把握当代塑料加工业发展，跟踪当代最新科技动态和前沿技术进展，加快转变发展方式、优化结构调整和加快产品和产业链高端化进程，努力缩小与发达国家的差距，充分发挥科技创新和技术进步保证支撑作用，推动创新驱动发展，全面推动塑料加工业迈上新台阶，提升行业整体水平，为实现塑料加工业强国目标打好基础。为此提出加快现代化产业体系建设，全面提升塑料加工业整体水平；加快创新资源和要素的聚集，全面推动以企业为主体的创新体系建设和加快人才培养三方面主要任务。

这里我重点说明三个问题：

（一）充分发挥科技创新和技术进步的保证和支撑作用，是塑料加工业进入创新驱动发展的历史阶段的迫切要求。

塑料加工业是以塑料制品为核心，涵盖原料、机械、模具、助剂、科研为一体的新兴制造业，既是国民经济基础性产业，也是重要的民生产业，在国民经济中具有极其重要的作用，特别在我国进入重化工业化中后期阶段，随着技术水平的提高，塑料作为二十一世纪新材料作用更加突出，塑料加工业作为新兴制造业的地位得到进一步提高，塑料加工业作为快速成长的新的支柱产业作用更加明显。目前我国已成为最大的塑料制品生产和消费大国。塑料加工业在告

别市场短缺后，已完成了数量主导型的发展阶段，正进入上水平、上质量和产品高端化的发展阶段。实现新的转型必须紧紧依靠技术进步和科技创新，必须全面提高自主创新能力。经过全行业努力，提交本届理事会审议的《塑料加工业技术进步指导意见》(讨论稿)其目的就是进一步明确塑料加工业科技发展方向和研发重点，进一步明确塑料加工业面临的关键共性攻关目标，力争实现重点突破。同时创造条件，为编制塑料加工业发展技术路线图打好基础。这是事关未来塑料加工业发展的重大问题，需要集中全行业智慧，需要整合全行业的科研力量和创新资源，通过扎实工作和艰苦努力，实现重点跨越、支撑发展和引领未来的战略目标的实现。全面推动塑料加工业的产业升级，加快推动塑料加工业强国目标的实现。

(二)紧紧围绕当代最新科技发展趋势和前沿技术进展，把握行业技术发展方向，努力缩小差距

在以互联网、计算机、空间技术、新材料和生物工程等为主要内容的第三次科技革命的推动下，作为21世纪的新材料的塑料及其制品得到快速发展。当前又迎来了以新能源、新型互联网、信息技术、数字制造、智能制造、大数据等为代表的第三次工业革命，这为塑料加工业发展带来了难得的发展机遇和空前挑战，使我们有机会瞄准塑料加工业最新技术，发挥后发优势，加快塑料加工业迈上新台阶。

当前塑料加工业发展趋势可以用“轻量化、功能化和微成型”来概括。

关于功能化，塑料是未来新材料生产中具有重要作用的关键领域之一。具体特点是，可以通过改性、复合等技术手段实现各种特种功能，以满足技术需要。在功能膜、智能膜方面，如各种高阻隔、电气绝缘用膜和各种微滤、超滤等工业用特种膜及材料；新能源生产中各种电池隔膜，光伏发电中用胶膜、背板膜；各种光学膜，如扩散膜、棱镜膜、复合膜、微透膜等。在工程塑料方面，如各种高强、高韧、耐磨、耐腐、耐高温、导电、导热、绝缘、纳米合金等特种工程塑料。

关于轻量化，是指通过结构减重和通过 CO_2超临界发泡等技术，达到减轻制品重量和提高物理、化学性能的目的。如各种保温材料、各种注塑、挤出板材发泡等。当前微孔塑料的出现更是给轻量化带来革命性变化。

关于微成型，是指毫克，微、纳米级尺度微结构成型技术。微成型代表塑料加工业从设备到成型工艺最先进的技术集成，如3D打印成型技术等，还包括精密注射等。在微成型加工技术中，塑料材料更具有优势。

“功能化、轻量化、微成型”，不仅是世界塑料加工业的发展趋势，更是塑料加工业当代世界先进技术的集中体现，既引领未来科技攻关、技术创新方向，也是塑料加工业产品结构调整的指南。

(三)加快创新资源和要素的聚集，加快以企业为主体的创新体系建设

全国科技创新大会提出：“十二五”期间，国家重点建设的工程技术研究中心和实验室，要优先在具备条件的行业骨干企业布局。使其成为企业创新能力的源泉，成为企业竞争力的核心。塑料加工业要抓住这一机遇，加快资金、技术、人才等创新要素和创新资源的聚集，加快以企业为主体的创新体系的建设。要创造条件加快企业研发中心的建立。协会将创造条件，充分发挥各大专院校、科研院所，各企业和企业家积极性、创造性，更好发挥“政、产、学、研、用”在技术创新中的作用。组织好行业联合攻关，协同攻关。通过关键、共性技术及前沿技术的攻关，聚集一流科技人才，培养一批企业创新人才，使之成为塑料加工业创新体系建设的骨干和基础。当前全球正进入大数据时代，新型互联网在获取海量信息的同时，与全球计算机网络相融合，推动了云计算的发展，这为技术创新提供了更加快捷的信息获取渠道，使我们有条件充分利用这一平台为创新服务，有条件更好推动与信息化的深度融合，有条件更好发挥后发

优势，加快缩小差距，使塑料加工业迈上新台阶。

"十二五"是塑料加工业进入承上启下、创新驱动发展的战略转型期。这种转型是塑料加工业由短缺、追赶型发展模式，向实现产销平衡、个别制品出现低端产能过剩情况下的上水平、上质量的转变。因此转型的主要任务是加快转变发展方式、优化结构调整、全面提高产业素质，加快塑料加工业现代产业体系的建设。目前，在国际金融危机影响和冲击下，国际经济增长乏力，需求下降。受此影响，我国经济下行压力加大，出口大幅下降。与此同时，生产要素成本持续上升，环境、资源、能源约束日趋增强，产能过剩矛盾越发凸现，企业生产经营困难增多，效益下降。面对严峻的经济环境，我们应冷静看到，短缺追赶型经济发展模式下的高速增长已转向中速增长。在经济增长战略转型阶段，我们必须清醒的认识到高投入、高消耗、低成本发展模式已不可持续，要加快从依靠扩大投资和规模扩张转到依靠技术进步、创新和要素升级上来，下决心全面提高全要素生产率和集约利用水平，提高发展质量和效益。

今年是"十八大"开局之年，是"十二五"规划实施关键之年，也是塑料加工业加快转型升级的关键时刻，塑料加工全行业一定要坚定信心，克服当前生产经营中遇到的困难，做好工作，力争2013年取得好成绩，为塑料加工业平稳健康发展作出贡献。

2012年中国聚氯乙烯行业经济运行分析

张文雷

一、2012年国内聚氯乙烯市场运行状况分析

2012年国内聚氯乙烯累计产量为13178kt，同比仅增长1.7%，是自2008年出现负增长以来的最低增速年份。2012年，由于受到低迷的市场需求以及长期低位的市场价格负面影响，国内聚氯乙烯产量增长并不明显，装置闲置的情况较为普遍。分析来看，市场表现不佳、企业开工率偏低是造成产能增长但产量增幅并不明显的主要原因(表1，图1)。

表1 2012年中国聚氯乙烯产量统计表 kt

	1~2月	3月	4月	5月	6月	7月	8月	9月	10月	11月	12月	合计	同比
产量	2163	1116	1090	1114	1151	1082	1087	1160	1086	1089	1126	13178	1.7%

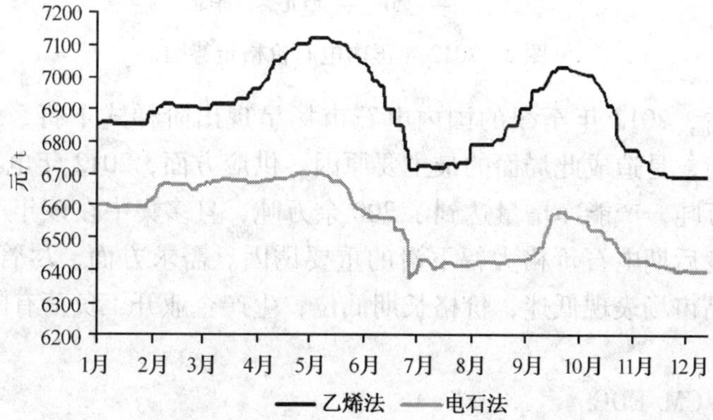

图1 2012年1~12月中国聚氯乙烯市场价格走势图

2012 年国内聚氯乙烯市场价格走向大体分为四个阶段：自年初开始，市场整体呈现震荡状态。自 5 月中旬前后受到市场供应量略有增加但需求持续低迷的负面影响，国内 PVC 价格急速转入下行通道，至 7 月初止跌企稳，并开始震荡上行。至 10 月末，随着下游行业逐渐开始进入消费淡季，需求进一步减弱，市场价格再次下滑。全年来看，国内市场供应量及下游行业需求的对比变化，成为影响市场价格波动的决定性因素。

2012 年，加工企业开工不足，下游需求行业“旺季不旺，淡季更淡”的表现，在国内市场社会库存压力不减的背景下，对聚氯乙烯市场造成了较大负面影响。目前，整个 PVC 产业链条均面临着严峻的困境：上游的电石行业面临亏损，小工厂停产避险较多，而 PVC 企业同样处于长期成本和售价倒挂，下游塑料制品行业则是在型材和管材方面的开工不饱满，出口订单匮乏。市场预期，如无重大的刺激性利好政策，PVC 产品的亏损仍将持续。

二、2012 年中国聚氯乙烯上下游产业运行情况

1. 电石

2012 年，国内电石累计产量 18692kt，同比增加 7.6%。尽管国内电石行业产能持续增长，但多数新建项目均集中在 2012 年三、四季度试车投产，产能释放率有限。加之下游 PVC 市场的低迷影响，使得大量小型电石企业被迫退出市场竞争，电石行业整体开工率难攀高位。受此影响，国内电石产量虽有增长，但增速有所减缓(表 2，图 2)。

表 2　2012 年中国电石产量统计表　　kt

	1~2 月	3 月	4 月	5 月	6 月	7 月	8 月	9 月	10 月	11 月	12 月	合计	同比
产量	3056	1677	1649	1655	1732	1523	1516.7	1635	1599	1569	1425	18692	76%

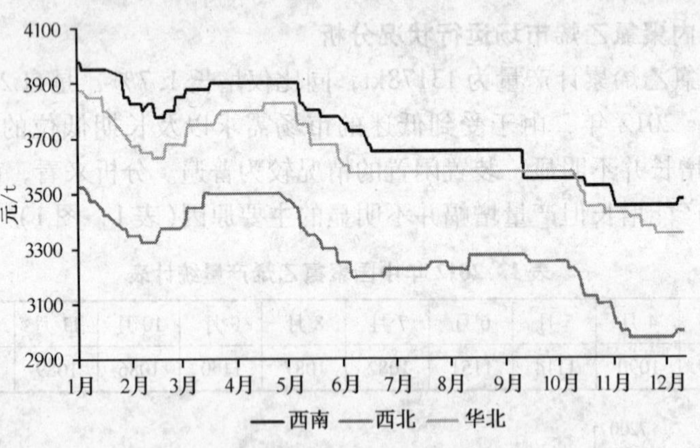

图 2　2012 年国内电石价格走势图

从市场表现来看，2012 年至今的国内电石市场呈现出阶梯式下行，价格水平一落走低。供需关系的整体失衡，是造成此局面的最主要原因。供应方面，2012 年电石产能全年新建 300 多万吨，淘汰 127 万吨，产能净增量达到了 200 余万吨，且多集中在该年三、四季度投产。供应量富余成为三季度后期电石价格大幅下滑的重要诱因。需求方面，尽管下游 PVC 产能持续增长，但受制于产品市场表现低迷，价格长期低位，生产企业开工负荷有限，更难以形成对电石市场的有效支撑。

2. 原油/乙烯/VCM/EDC

2012 年以来，随着原油、石脑油价格走低，亚洲乙烯价格具有一定优势，中国进口乙烯数量明显增加。截至 12 月份，中国乙烯进口量达到 1422kt，超过了上年全年的进口总量。

2012年中国进口EDC产品数量显著增长。尽管EDC下游溶剂行业表现平淡，但EDC价格偏低刺激PVC生产企业及部分贸易商囤货，全年数据显示的进口量已经达到557kt，超过了2011年全年进口量158kt。

2012年国际VCM市场供应整体偏紧，除7月份外，价格坚挺在高位的时间较长。中国下游PVC需求平淡，对原料采购的抵触强，故VCM进口成交在量少价高的背景下，单月度及全年进口总量均在低位。201年全年进口VCM573kt。

三、2012年主要相关下游产业运行情况

塑料型材及门窗预计“十二五”期间的建设总投资30万亿左右。从国家投资来看我国塑料建材应用有望提高一倍以上。塑料品种按平均增幅计算，塑料异型材及塑料门窗将有一倍的消费增幅。从目前5000kt/a的市场需求来看，保守估计每年将增加300~500kt(表3)。

表3　2012年中国氯碱产品主要相关下游产品产量统计表　kt

产品名称		1~2月	3月	4月	5月	6月	7月	8月	9月	10月	11月	12月	合计	同比
聚氯乙烯	塑料制品	9365	5370	5003	4865	5268	5061	4911	5068	5087	5521	5579	57818	9%

注：数据来源于国家统计局当期公布。

塑料管道行业目前加工能力超过30Mt，产业集中度高，规模企业数量多，生产能力10kt以上的企业超过了100家，有20家企业的生产能力已达到和超过100kt。

“十二五”期间塑料管材若按年均12%的平均增速增长，到2015年末塑料管材产量将达到11900kt左右。“十二五”期间，积极鼓励和支持行业内的大企业进行资源整合和对中小企业进行并购，提高产业集中度，做强做大行业内的龙头企业，促进提升大企业的核心竞争力。

四、2012年聚氯乙烯进出口状况分析

2012年，受国内下游制品行业表现欠佳的影响，其聚氯乙烯纯粉需求量有所减少。尽管年中随着国际原油价格的持续下滑，聚氯乙烯纯粉进口量有所恢复，但同比仍呈现萎缩态势(表4)。

表4　2012年聚氯乙烯纯粉进口情况月度分析表　kt

	1月	2月	3月	4月	5月	6月	7月	8月	9月	10月	11月	12月	累计	同比
进口	76.5	90.7	93.2	71.0	77.4	64.2	81.4	98.7	76.8	79.3	69.0	62.2	940.4	-10.51%

2012年，国内聚氯乙烯纯粉出口总量同比略有小幅增加。根据分析，国际市场需求面的疲软，加上并无明显优势的产品价格，对国内聚氯乙烯纯粉出口量形成了一定程度的制约(表5)。

表5　2012年聚氯乙烯纯粉出口情况月度分析表　kt

	1月	2月	3月	4月	5月	6月	7月	8月	9月	10月	11月	12月	累计	同比
出口	9.1	17.6	39.4	40.4	37.0	19.5	15.8	36.4	62.2	45.7	33.4	29.3	385.6	4.90%

五、2012年中国聚氯乙烯行业运行特点分析

1. 产能规模净增长有所减缓

根据中国氯碱网最新产能调查数据，截止到2012年12月底中国聚氯乙烯现有产能达到了23410kt(其中包括糊树脂770kt)。从统计中发现，2012年国内聚氯乙烯包括糊树脂在内的新增加产能为2960kt，在此期间，宣布正式退出的规模为1180kt，即在2011年底形成的21630kt的总产能基础上实现的净增长为1780kt。从2008年开始，国内聚氯乙烯行业的发展就不再是一味的只增不减，而是出现了“有退有进”动态增减变化。同时，较上年实现8.2%的增长速度也说明了2012年中国聚氯乙烯工业虽然也在经历后经济危机时代带来的调整阵痛，但恢复性发展仍较明显。

2. 行业企业经营状况堪忧

从氯碱行业相关上市公司公开披露的数据中可以看出，2012年以氯碱产品为主营业务的上市公司毛利率水平相比2011年继续减少。从一个侧面可以反映出氯碱行业整体经营状况的恶化。从单个企业毛利率的对比来看，盈利情况较好的上市公司主要集中在中西部地区，在氯碱产品下游需求不旺的背景下，原料、运营成本的控制成为减少亏损的重要因素。

3. 政策调控力度不减

政府部门相关的产业政策继续保持了国家在产业结构调整、节能减排等方面的延续性。与之相应，包括产能调控、电力、金融、信贷等方面的配套措施的落实和完善也在逐步推进。同时，面对目前我国出口压力持续增加，在产业安全以及对外贸易的扶持方面也增加了力度(表6)。

表6　2012年氯碱行业主要相关政策一览表

政策类别	政策名称	发布单位	发布时间	实施时间
产业调整	《关于下达2012年19个工业行业淘汰落后产能目标任务的通知》(工信部产业[2012]159号)	工信部	4月26日	
	《产业转移指导目录(2012年本)》	工信部	7月26日	
清洁生产	《工业清洁生产推行“十二五”规划》	工信部、科技部、财政部	3月5日	
	《关于荧光灯等6个行业清洁生产技术推行方案的通知》(工信部节[2012]586号)	工信部	12月25日	
安全生产	《关于进一步加强安全生产工作的通知》(安委办明电[2012]6号)	国务院安委会	2月29日	
	《关于下达2012年安全生产行业标准制修订项目计划的通知》(安监总政法[2012]42号)	安监局	4月6日	
产业安全	《关于环氧氯丙烷反倾销措施期终复审裁决的公告》(商务部公告2012年第32号)	商务部	6月27日	6月28日
	《关于终止二氯甲烷反倾销措施的公告》(2012年第48号)	商务部	8月14日	8月15日
	《关于启动进口悬浮法聚氯乙烯(PVC)日落复审的通知》(No. 21/29/2011 - DGAD)	印度商工部	10月5日	10月5日
	《关于对原产于欧盟的进口甲苯二异氰酸酯反倾销调查初裁的公告》(商务部公告2012年第79号)	商务部	11月13日	11月13日
对外贸易	《关于暂停对进出口危险品、有毒有害货物加倍收取出入境检验检疫费的通知》(发改价格[2012]1894号)	国家发改委、财政部	7月2日	8月1日
	《关于取消和免收进出口环节有关行政事业性收费的通知》(财综[2012]71号)	财政部、国家发改委	9月18日	10月1日

六、2013年国内PVC市场预测

扩能步伐未止　强弱分界明显

2013年国内计划新增PVC能力为3420kt，而内蒙古、陕西、青海、新疆四地的新增产能总和就达到了15450kt，占预期全年新增能力总和的45%。西北地区的发展模式依旧是烧碱－电石法PVC循环产业链，而沿海地区的发展模式则开始借助于进口乙烯及甲醇制烯烃等符合当地特点的最优化道路。由此可见，发展普通型号的PVC已经开始出现明显的地域强弱分化。并且西北快速扩能带来的另一问题是，当众多企业逐鹿西北，每家企业都变地域优势为自身优势时，"优势"或许就不再是纯粹的优势，同时也势必会加剧以后的价格竞争。

淘汰不经济产能成常态　未来之路仍艰巨

截至2012年底，经企业确认宣布停产搬迁、淘汰老装置、退出或作废弃处理的PVC产能总和为1180kt，和上年比明显增多。调查过程中，四川、山东、新疆地区的PVC产能减少较多，主要原因为：一是、有老厂装置停产搬迁，但设备需经过一段时间的再次安装后方可运行；二是、企业扩张建立了新园区，原老厂区的落后设备全部淘汰。

行业开工率低下　闲置能力会长期存在

经统计，2012年内长期停车或生产极不稳定的PVC企业约17家，共涉及产能总和为1680kt/a。按照业内分析，虽然有企业未表态长期闲置的产能将作为废弃处理，但整体判断如产能基数在50kt/a或以下者，未来开车的可能性也较小。而因多方制约造成装置长期停车现象的，有可能会在企业产品转型后(如：依靠大乙烯项目由电石法转为乙烯法等)才会重新选择开车。

美国页岩气革命兴起　中国PVC将遇强大挑战

自2008年以来，美国PVC产业的开工率增长主要是依赖于PVC向外出口的增加，而美国PVC之所以能够顺利向外转移的最主要原因则是廉价的成本优势。当前，借助天然气制乙烯生产PVC的强大优势，美国PVC逐步布局全球。未来，美国页岩气的开发成为世界热点，以此判断，如果美国页岩气开发高潮形成并且形成成熟的下游石化产业链，则可以进一步巩固其在国际氯碱的地位。由天然气到乙烯的成本远远低于原油制乙烯的成本，这样对美国PVC在全球的布局更加有利。

价格长期低迷　未来企业需直面压力逆势求盈利

整个2012年，国内PVC成本和售价倒挂的情况长期存在。以西北地区为例，该地区由于具备丰富的能源和资源，被称为国内PVC低成本的代表。但即使是低成本区在2012年也难以逃脱亏损的困境。2013年PVC行业仍需继续面对错综复杂的影响因素。

行业相关政策等引导和促进未来PVC产业健康、持续发展

近几年，我国氯碱行业发展已由快速的规模扩张步入了调整时期。"十二五"是中国氯碱行业发展的关键转型期，需要全方位提升行业发展水平，推动我国多种氯碱及相关产品由粗放型向精细型转变。在此过程中，国家和行业协会出台的多项关于PVC等领域的政策将对未来行业发展起到至关重要的作用。

(作者为中国氯碱工业协会副理事长兼秘书长)

生物基塑料发展前景展望

唐赛珍

进入21世纪以来，全球面临更加严峻的资源和环境压力。为应对石油资源日趋贫乏，油价不断飞涨以及环境污染、气候变暖日益恶化的问题，引发了对来源于可再生资源，既可缓解资源矛盾，又可减轻环境污染的生物基塑料(Biobased Plastics BBP)的极大关注。

1. 生物基塑料的概念、定义和分类

1.1 概念、定义

至今全球尚无统一标准化的BBP的定义和分类。

20世纪90年代末，国际材料界首先提出了生态材料(Eco materials)的概念，即任何一种材料只要经过改造，达到节约资源并与环境协调发展，就可以视为生态材料。同时也包括在生命周期各阶段由可减轻环境负荷的设计，技术和工艺过程制得的材料。

2003年11月，在日本召开的第一届生物基聚合物国际会议上，对生物基聚合物定义为：由可再生资源(如淀粉，纤维素，蛋白质等)、二氧化碳以及生物聚合物(如多糖，聚酯，聚戊二烯类，多酚以及它们的衍生物，混合物，复合物等)为原料制得的聚合物。

日本生物塑料协会(JBPA)将生物分解塑料(BDP)和BBP统称为生物塑料(Bioplastics BP)。

生物塑料：一种在拥有普通塑料使用性能的同时，不会或可减轻给环境和空气带来CO_2负担的材料("碳中性"概念参见图1)。

BBP：其原料主要源于可再生资源，通过生物化学或物理等方法制得的一类塑料，但其中一部分具有生物分解性，另一部分不具有生物分解性。

BDP：生物基或生物质塑料产品是指那些材料中的化石碳已通过植物的吸收利用实现全部或部分被替代的塑料产品，亦即在一个很短(但平衡)的可持续生态循环过程中可减少碳足迹或碳足迹达到零的材料。在一定环境条件(如堆肥化、厌氧槽、土壤和水份情况等)下，由细菌、真菌和藻类的作用而引起完全生物分解的一类塑料，但其原料既有来自可再生资源的，也有来自石油资源的(图2)。

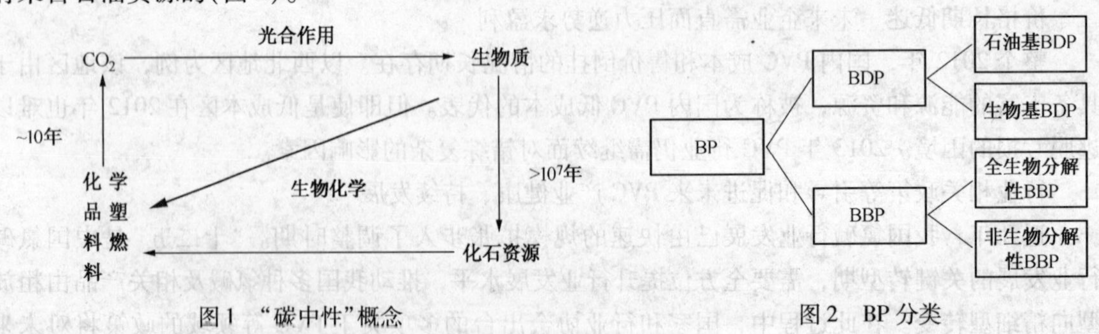

图1 "碳中性"概念

图2 BP分类

1.2 分类

目前已产业化生产的BBP主要包括以下几大类：

1.2.1 以淀粉，纤维素等天然高分子为原料，经改性后单独或以不同比例与其他生物分解塑料或石油基塑料共混(或合金化)填充等制得具有塑料特性又可完全生物分解的BBP(如热塑性淀粉、改性纤维、淀粉/BDP共混的淀粉基塑料等)或非生物分解的BBP(如淀粉/石油基塑料共混的淀粉基塑料、木塑复合材料等)。

1.2.2 以淀粉，纤维素，糖蜜等可再生资源为原料，通过微生物发酵直接制成具有塑料特性的 BDP，如聚羟基脂肪酸酯(PHA)；或先发酵制得单体，再经化学途径制得具有塑料特性的 BDP，如聚乳酸(PLA)等；

1.2.3 以淀粉，秸杆，植物油等农副产品为原料，通过生物化学或化学途径制得醇、酸等化工原料，再经化学合成制得具有与石油基塑料性能相同，或其某些性能得到改善的 BBP，如以甘蔗、淀粉等生物质为原料制得的生物聚乙烯(BPE)、生物聚酯如生物聚对苯二甲酸乙二醇酯(BPET)、生物聚对苯二甲酸丙二醇酯(BPTT)、生物聚丁二酸丁二醇酯(BPBS)等；以及以蓖麻油、大豆油为原料制得的聚酰胺 1010、聚酰胺 610、聚酰胺 11 等，但此类塑料(除 BPTT、BPET 外)不具备生物分解性能(表 1)。

表 1 有代表性的生物基塑料

名 称	生物基含量	特 点
PHA	100%	具完全生物分解性，可减少碳足迹亦或碳足迹为零。
PLA	100%	
PBS	部分	
BPTT	部分	
淀粉基塑料(淀粉/BDP)	100%	
淀粉基塑料(淀粉/石油基)	部分	具有去塑料特性，非生物分解性，但可减少碳足迹。
PLA/PP	部分	
BPE	100%	
BPP	100%	
BPET	部分	
聚酰胺 610	部分	
聚酰胺 1010	100%	
聚酰胺 11	100%	
醋酸纤维素酯	部分	
木塑复合塑料	部分	

1.3 BBP 的检测方法、标准和认证

BBP 中生物基含量的识别方法是以生物碳放射性 C-14 标记，测量产品中各组分的碳原子生物碳(C-14 衰变期短)或化石碳(C-14 衰变期长)及其含量以及其在总有机碳中的百分比。例如 50% 淀粉与 50% PE 的淀粉基塑料，其生物基的含量为 $(50\% \times 38.9\%) \div (50\% \times 85.7\% + 50\% \times 38.9\%) = 31.2\%$（式中 $C_{(淀粉)}\% = 38.9\%$、$C_{(PE)}\% = 85.7\%$）。

德国 BBP 生物基的含量分为三个等级：20% ~ 50%、50% ~ 85%、>85%；而日本共分为四个等级，25% ~ 50% 所占比例最大，约占 BBP(已登记注册的约二百个产品)总量中的 63%，其次为 >90%，50% ~ 75% 和 75% ~ 90%(参考图 3)。

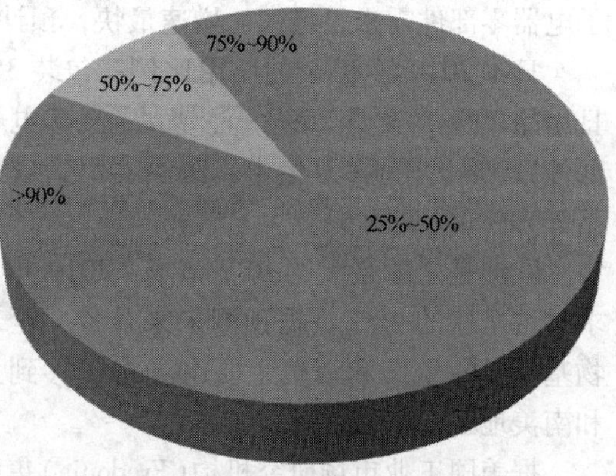

图 3 日本已登记注册的 BBP 中生物基含量组成

目前对 BBP 的认证是建立在美国测试标准 ASTM 6886 和德国的 DIN - cerleo 认证程序要求的基础上的。标识证书采用 DIN - gepruft。

我国生物基材料中生物基含量测定——液闪计数器法标准正在报批中。

2. BBP 发展概况及预测

BBP 目前全球均处于由初级发展向商业化规模发展的转型阶段。

据欧洲塑料新闻报导，2010 年全球 BBP 产能 530kt，产量约 400kt，需求量 300kt。2012 年产能有望突破 1000kt。又据欧洲生物塑料协会预测，2013 年全球 BBP 产能将达到 1460kt，其中可生物分解可堆肥的 BBP 的产能将从 2009 年的 408kt 增至 2013 年的 748kt，而不可生物分解的 BBP 则从 25kt 增至 715kt，该数据主要基于生物 PE 和生物 PP 即将投入大规模生产预测。全球 BBP 产能概况及预测如图 4 所示。

又根据有关部门市场预测，全球 2013 年 BBP 品种的市场份额：生物 PE 28%，淀粉基塑料 22%，PLA 15%，生物聚酯 8%，PHA 6%，其他(包括纤维素基塑料，木塑复合塑料等) 21%，其中增速最快的是生物 PE 和木塑复合塑料(参见图 5)。

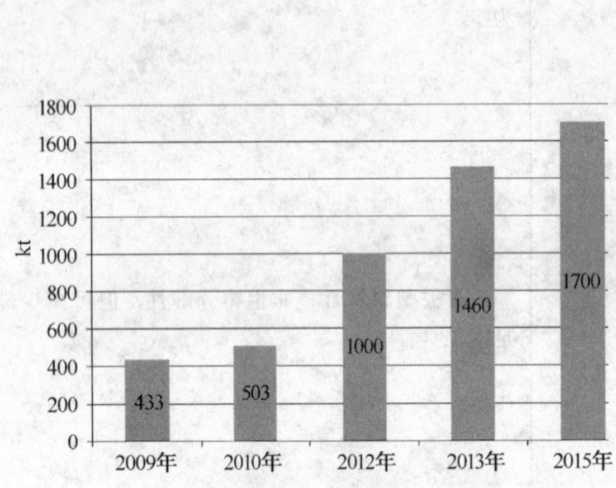

图 4 全球 BBP 产能概况及预测

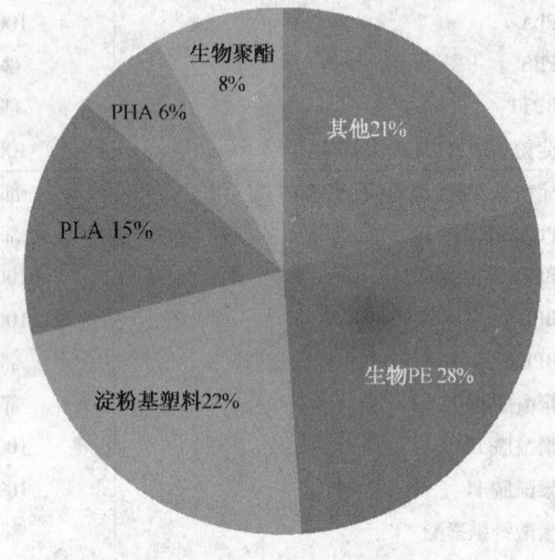

图 5 2013 年全球 BBP 品种市场份额

BBP 的市场正在迅速扩大，当前主要是一次性包装如垃圾袋、堆肥袋、包装薄膜(袋)，餐饮具、松散填充包装材料等，其次依次是日用品、文具、汽车和电子电器零部件、医用材料、农用制品等。今后可生物分解的堆肥袋，垃圾袋及不可生物分解的耐用消费品如汽车，电子电器零部件需求量最大，增速最快，预计年增长率高达 20% 以上。

日本 2010 年 BBP 的应用比例：包装 35%，日用品 29%，文具 15%，注塑品(汽车电子零部件)12%，其他(卫生巾，医用器材，农用制品等)9%(参见图 6)。

欧洲是全球最大的 BBP 市场，2010 年其需求量占全球的 48%。据预测未来几年，全球生物基塑料的生产和消费主要市场将转移到亚太和南美地区。

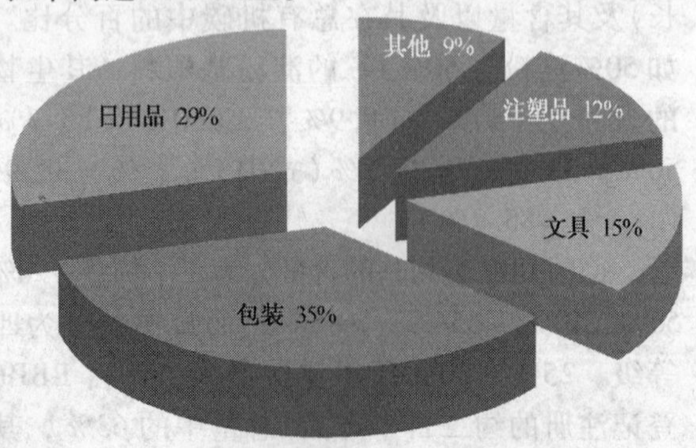

图 6 日本 BBP 应用比例

据美国工业市场研究机构(Fredonia)集团最新研究显示，美国不可生物分解的 BBP 2010 年的需求量仅 300kt，到 2020 年其需求量将超过 1300kt，在 BBP 总需求量中将占 47% 以上。

据中国塑协降解塑料专委会资料，2011 年中国 BBP 总产能约 450kt，其中 BDP 约 40 ~ 50kt。表 2 为国内外主要 BBP 生产公司的产品及产能。

表 2　国内外主要 BBP 生产公司概况

国　家	公　司	类　别	产能/(kt/a)
美国	Nature Worke Cereplast	PLA 淀粉基塑料	140
德国	BASF	PBS PBS/PLA	10
	Biotec	淀粉基塑料	—
意大利	Novamont	淀粉/PVA(EVOH) 淀粉/PCL 淀粉/纤维素	75
日本	昭和电工株式会社	PBS(生物基占 60%)	
	三井株式会社	PLA	2
	玉米淀粉株式会社	淀粉基塑料	—
荷兰	SoLANyl	PLA	40
巴西	Brasken	生物 PE	200
中国	海正生物材料股份有限公司	PLA	5
	宁波天安生物材料有限公司	PHBV	2
	天津国音生物科技有限公司	3 - PHB/49HB	10
	武汉华丽环保科技有限公司	淀粉基塑料	40
	比澳格(南京)环保材料有限公司	淀粉基塑料	10
	苏州汉丰新材料有限公司	淀粉基塑料	8

3. BBP 产业发展中存在的主要问题

BBP 作为 20 世纪末开始研发，近年来逐步兴起的一门新兴产业，发展中不可避免地存在一些问题，应当理性的看待。

3.1　BP、BDP 和 BBP 概念(定义)混淆，易产生市场误导

BP、BDP 和 BBP 之间既有密切联系，但又不能混为一谈，BP≠BDP≠BBP(详见图 7)

但当前往往有人有意无意的加以混淆，从而在投资者、消费者、终端用户以及其它利益相关者之间导致疑惑，也会对投资和市场造成误导。

3.2　当前可再生原料主要来自粮食淀粉

众所周知，粮食危机比石油危机危害更大。当前可再生资源主要以粮食淀粉为原料，这对全球口粮的供给将会造成极大冲击，危害性也极大。因此加强从广度、深度对非粮食淀粉，如稻草、秸秆、木本植物等纤维素，以及非食用油(如蓖麻油等)植物油等生物质资源的研发和规模化生产是确保 BBP 可持续发展的重要途径。

3.3　投资、成本较高，部分 BBP 对环境影响较大

根据国外《BBP 生命周期对环境影响的全面分析》结果显示，一些可再生资源的化学品在提纯、精炼过程中能耗较高、工序繁琐，造成投资和成本较高。另一些农作物在栽培过程中由

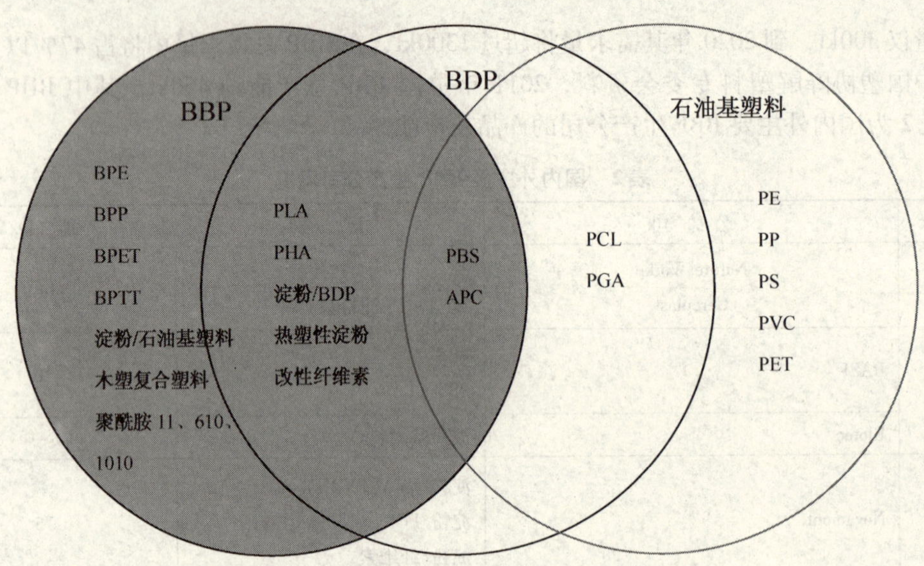

图7 BBP、BDP与石油基塑料关联示意图

于采用大量农药、化肥等，导致产品对环境影响更大。因此在选择项目投资时，必须进行生命周期对环境影响的全面分析评价。

3.4 性能与石油基塑料比较尚有一定差距

当前生物基塑料的力学性能、耐热性能、水解稳定性能、阻隔性能等与普通塑料比较尚存在一定差距必须通过必要的改性手段来实现其相应的功能和用途。

3.5 规模化生产、市场供应链有待加强

当前BBP的生产工艺虽已成功开发，但目前大部分面临装置放大、原料供应和物流支持等问题，有一些已实现规模化生产的化学品公司，则面临商业化规模及供应链建设等问题。

3.6 堆肥化设施尚待加速开发与普及

BDP的生物分解必须在一定的环境条件(如温度、湿度和菌种等等)及经历一定周期才能实现，在垃圾填埋场或土壤中也需较长时间才能完全分解。因此BDP的推广应用必须有完善的商业化规模的堆肥化体系相配合，才能真正解决庭院垃圾及城市固体废弃物中有机质垃圾的无害化及再资源化问题。但目前堆肥化作为垃圾处理方式之一，才刚刚起步，尚待加速开发和普及。

3.7 市场定位、应用开发、实用化进程有待加强

近年来，国内外一些风险投资公司和石化、生化公司仅从BBP在资源替代、节能减排方面看好其市场前景，而对产品从技术成熟程度、产品性能、成本、特别是产品定位和市场需求以及其生命周期对环境影响等缺乏全面分析或作得不够，从而引发了新一轮投资热，重复建设，盲目上线，不利于行业健康、顺利的发展。

4 BBP发展前景展望

4.1 资源、环境问题日趋加重，进一步加速BBP的快速发展

4.1.1 可再生资源作为石油资源的补充替代已成为全球关注热点

石油是一类资源有限而又正在减少、面临枯竭的不可再生资源。有资料显示，世界可开采和已探明的化石资源的储量，如按目前的消费水平计算，石油到50年后、煤炭到100年后将趋于枯竭。虽然今后还有可能探索挖掘出新的矿源，但随着人口的增长以及人民生活水平的提

高，需求量也会进一步增长。由此可推断上述预测的开采年限也势必受到一定程度的影响。因此寻找、开发新的资源，特别是可再生资源作为石油的替代补充已成为全球关注的热点。

4.1.2　BBP节能减排效果显著

随着全球经济的发展，温室效应、地球变暖的问题也日趋严峻。据美国能源情报署2006年初预测，到2025年，世界CO_2排放量将达3.88×10^7kt。中国目前排放的CO_2已达3.8×10^6 kt，到2030年可能会增至7.1×10^6kt。

在2009年《京都议定书》第5次缔约方会议上减排任务十分严峻。欧盟承诺到2020年，CO_2的排放水平将在1990年的基础上减少30%，日本减排25%，美国17%，中国比2005年减少40～50%。

实践证明，BBP具有很好的减排效果：

·BBP与普通塑料比较，可大大减少CO_2的排放详见表3。

表3　BDP与普通塑料排放CO_2的比较

类　别	有机碳含量/%	CO_2排放/%
聚丁二酸丁二醇酯(PBS)	56.8	61.1
聚乳酸(PLA)	50.0	54.7
聚碳酸亚丙酯(PPC)	47.1	51.5
聚羟基脂肪酸酯(PHA)	55.8	61.1
聚己内酯(PCL)	63.2	69.1
聚乙烯(PE)	85.7	93.8
聚丙烯(PP)	85.7	93.8
聚苯乙烯(PS)	91.4	100

·据有关研究报告显示，在生产同质、同品种产品的条件下，BBP比石油基塑料可减排CO_2 20%～30%。

·据欧洲调查显示，每吨淀粉基塑料相对于同质量的石油基PE，可节能12～40GL，可减排CO_2 0.8～3.2t。

·据美国Cereplast资料，50%的淀粉与PP共混制得的BBP，与普通PP比较，每吨可减排CO_2 42%。

据此，世界各国正加大人力、财力投入，并纷纷制定相关法律法规促进生物基塑料的发展与应用。

4.2　生物化学工艺技术的发展与创新，促进了BBP工艺改进、性能提高、成本降低

4.2.1　淀粉化学改性方式、方法有了重大突破，绿色化学改性过程减少了改性步骤及反应时间。

4.2.2　在满足应用性能前提下，大幅度提高BBP中淀粉或纤维素含量，从而可大大降低原料成本。

4.2.3　直接或间接采用非粮食淀粉，如甘蔗渣、木质纤维素等生物质为原料制得BBP，或转换成发酵用糖制PLA的工艺技术日趋成熟。

4.2.4　通过增塑、共混(合金化)、嵌段共聚、涂层、多层复合等技术创新，BBP的力学性能、耐热性能、阻隔性能以及水解稳定性能等得到了较大改善和提高。

4.3　垃圾处理方式的改变，堆肥化的快速发展与普及，加速了BDP的发展

4.3.1 近年来，许多国家在垃圾的无害化、资源化方面加强了立法，并从垃圾分类回收、清运、处理等环节逐步形成了完善而有效的管理体系。

4.3.2 1999 年欧盟发布命令要求成员国在 2016 年前将垃圾填埋量减少到 1999 年的 35%。在法规中明文规定禁止厨房剩余及庭院垃圾等进入填埋场及焚烧炉。

4.3.3 研究表明，有机质垃圾经堆肥化处理与填埋处理比较，不仅可减少填埋场占用大量土地资源，而且每吨垃圾还可以减少 250kg 的 CO_2排放。

4.3.4 BDP 垃圾袋、堆肥袋是堆肥化实施不可缺少的材料。堆肥化作为物质转换、循环利用的一种形式，并与可堆肥化的 BDP 发展相结合，已成为欧美等发达国家大规模处理有机质垃圾资源回收利用的可行方式。

4.4 产品不断增加，应用领域不断扩大

BBP 是绿色包装的典型资材，目前主要用于包装，特别是垃圾袋、包装袋、餐饮具以及松散填充料等一次性包装，今后将加速农业器材、医用器材以及从资源替代、缓解资源矛盾的视角，将更加重视不要生物分解性的耐用性商品，如交通运输、电子电器零部件等领域的发展。

综上所述，当前 BBP 作为石油基的替代品正朝着以绿色资源化利用为特征的高效、高附加值、定向转化、产业化、功能化、标准化、综合利用及环境友好等方向发展。

据世界经济组织(OECO)报告预测，到 2030 年世界生物产业经济将初具规模，届时将引发世界经济格局内重大调整和国家综合实力的重大变化，并将对人类社会带来深远影响。作为生物产业主力军之一的 BBP 被认为是可作为石油资源的补充替代、减少对石油资源的依赖，同时有利于减少 CO_2的排放、抑制温室效应，减轻环境污染及可确保可持续发展的新型绿色材料，具有光辉的发展前景。

(作者为：原中国产学研合作促进会循环经济分会副会长、中国塑协降解塑料专业委员会副理事会、联合国工业发展组织中国投资与技术促进处绿色产业专家委员会委员，现退休)

塑料技术在医疗器械中的应用现状及前景

曹常在 武宏斌 张明艳 孙 莉 黎永正 陈俊尧

医疗器械，是指单独或者组合使用于人体的仪器、设备、器具、材料或者其他物品，包括所需要的软件；其用于人体体表及体内的作用不是用药理学、免疫学或者代谢的手段获得，但是可能有这些手段参与并起一定的辅助作用；其使用旨在达到下列预期目的：(1)对疾病的预防、诊断、治疗、监护、缓解；(2)对损伤或者残疾的诊断、治疗、监护、缓解、补偿；(3)对解剖或者生理过程的研究、替代、调节；(4)妊娠控制。

医疗器械行业涉及到医药、机械、电子、塑料等多个行业，其中塑料医疗器械发展迅速，自 20 世纪 30 年代人们首次使用合成高分子材料—赛璐璐膜作为透析膜制成的人工肾应用于临床获得成功以来，高分子材料正在逐步代替传统无机材料如金属(或合金)、玻璃、陶瓷、磷灰石等用于制备医疗器械。这是因为：(1)塑料等高分子材料具有良好的物理机械性能和化学稳定性，比较适合医疗领域使用；(2)高分子材料来源丰富、价格低廉，适合制成一次性医疗用品，避免了传统材料制品因价格高昂而不得不多次使用导致的消毒和二次感染的问题；

(3)塑料具有或较容易改性得到良好的组织相容性、血液相容性制品；(4)塑料加工方便，制作成本低，适合多种成型方式，便于加工成复杂的形状和开发新型医疗产品。据英国材料协会(伦敦)统计，1995 年全球医疗器械市场(含诊断和治疗器械)已达 1000 亿美元；其中医疗材料市场已达 120 亿美元，并且以 7% ~12% 的年均增长率持续增长。

一、医疗器械塑料制备要求

作为医疗器械产品，首要要求是产品的安全性及有效性，而且有效性也必须是在产品安全性保证的基础上的有效。医用高分子材料同样必须遵循这样的原则。医用塑料产品的安全性，主要是针对产品对医护人员、患者以及产品的用后处理方面是否安全。”因此，为了满足塑料医疗器械的安全性要求，应该从产品的设计、原材料的选用(原材料的物理性能、机械强度、化学性能和生物性能等)、塑料医疗器械产品的生产工艺及加工生产过程、生产环境、产品质量技术指标是否符合要求等多方面去考量。

同普通塑料相比，医用塑料要求较高：(1)由于大部分单体及其齐聚物有毒，因此医用塑料对上述物质的残留有严格的限制；(2)塑料在聚合过程中不可避免要接触到反应釜、金属催化剂等. 常含有微量金属离子，根据医用塑料的国标要求，对锌、铅、镉、铜、钡、锡等金属离子残留情况都有明确规定；(3)用于医用塑料的树脂要求纯度较高、分子量分布较窄；(4)塑料在加工或改性过程中需要添加各种助剂，如在医用 PVC 制品中的增塑剂用量常高达 30% ~60%，因此要求尽量采用无毒助剂，长期使用时要防止或减少助剂的析出，以免影响制品性能和治疗效果；(5)根据医用塑料的使用要求，常需要使制品具用表面亲水性、抗凝血、耐辐射灭菌等特殊功能。

二、塑料医疗耗材市场现状

1. 广普类医疗耗材

包括：输液器，注射器，输血器，采血针，医用敷料，手术巾手套等。(如图 1 所示)国内主要生产企业：威高集团，新华医疗器械、成都市新津事丰，江西洪达等。

广普类医疗耗材主要以规模大，市场需要量大，使用广泛，附加值低为特点。例如国内目前生产一次性输液器企业数量超过 200 家，行业品牌数量有 300 多个。每厂每天平均生产 14 万支左右，全年约 140 亿支，除满足国内的需求外，出口约占 30%。我国一次性注射器 300 多家，其中形成自毁式注射器生产规模的约有十几家，不但能满足国内市场之需，还能大量出口。对业内主要生产企业来说，技术上已较为成熟。2006 年注射器出口 1. 21 亿美元，同比增长 47. 33%，出口区域特征明显，山东、江苏、浙江、上海四个省市所占比重达 73. 57%。

随着医疗技术水平的不断上升，产品的安全性、可靠性不断提升，人员工资薪金的不断提升，广谱类耗材现在逐步实现规模化，自动化，并不断增加技术水平，精密输液器，预填充注射器，安全采血针等新产品不仅保证了产品的安全，更增加了产品的附加值(图 1)。

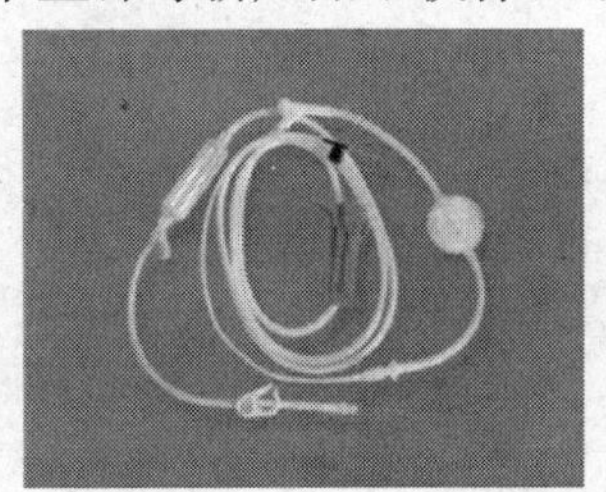
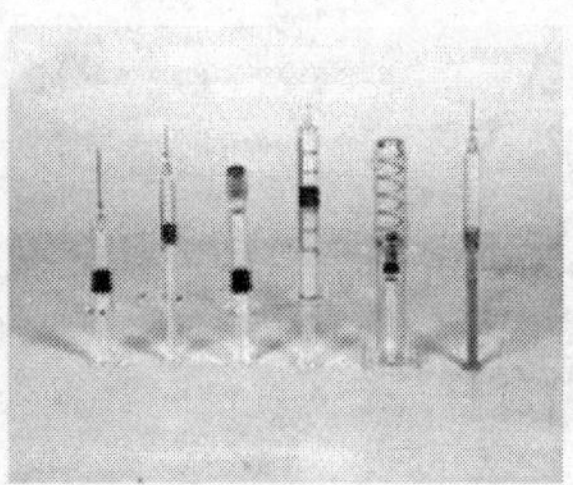
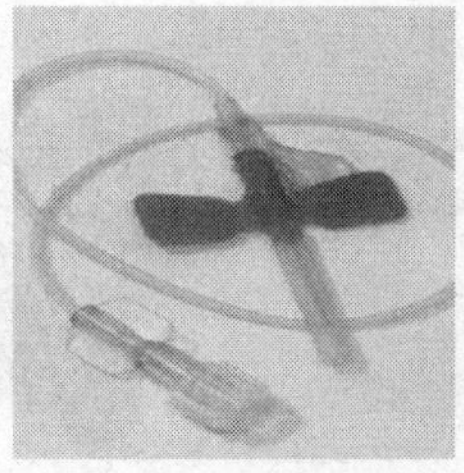

图 1　精密输液器、预填充注射器、安全采血针

2. 呼吸麻醉类

呼吸麻醉产品有：(1)气管插管(如图2所示)；(2)喉罩(如图3所示)；(3)密闭式吸痰管(如图4所示)；(4)压力延长管(如图5所示)；(5)呼吸麻醉回路(如图6所示)；(6)呼吸面罩(如图7所示)；(7)急救呼吸球(如图8所示)；(8)雾化加药器(如图9所示)；(9)气管切开插管(如图10所示)；(10)异型气管插管(如图11所示)；(11)麻醉穿刺包(如图12所示)；(12)气管插管包(如图13所示)；(13)普通吸痰管(如图14所示)；(14)双腔喉罩(如图15所示)

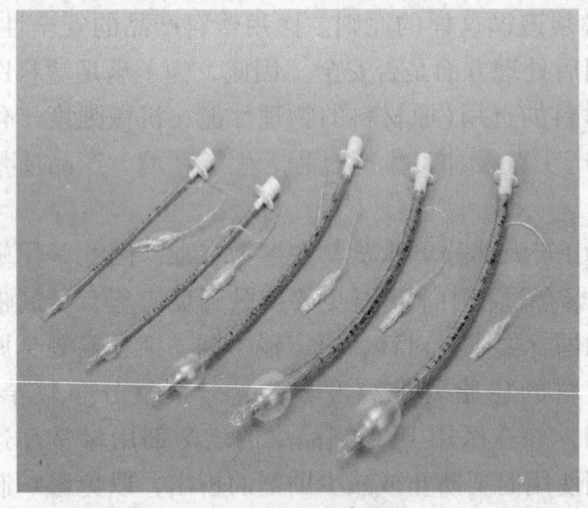

图2　气管插管图

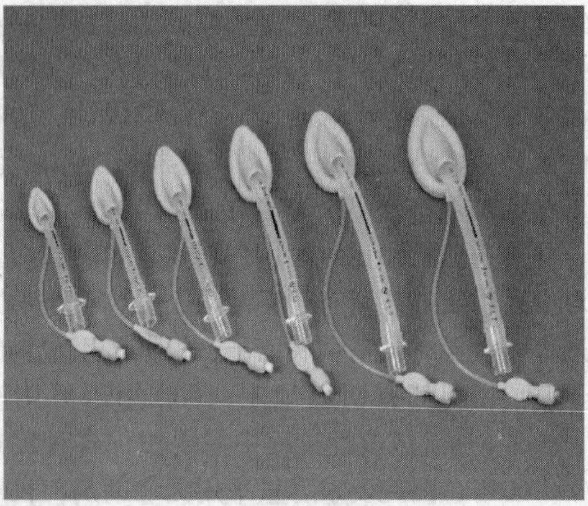

图3　喉罩图

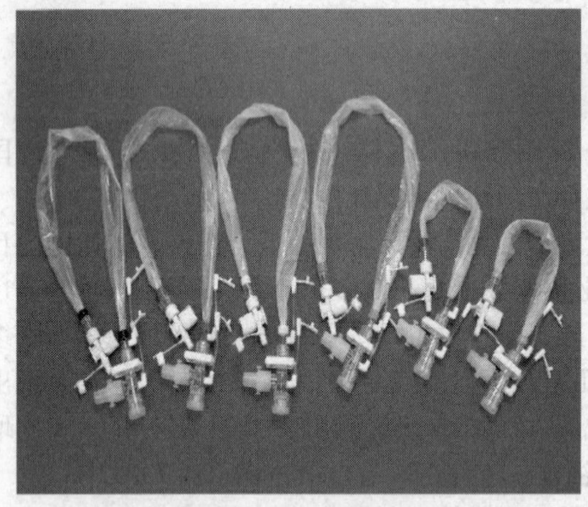

图4　密闭式吸痰管图

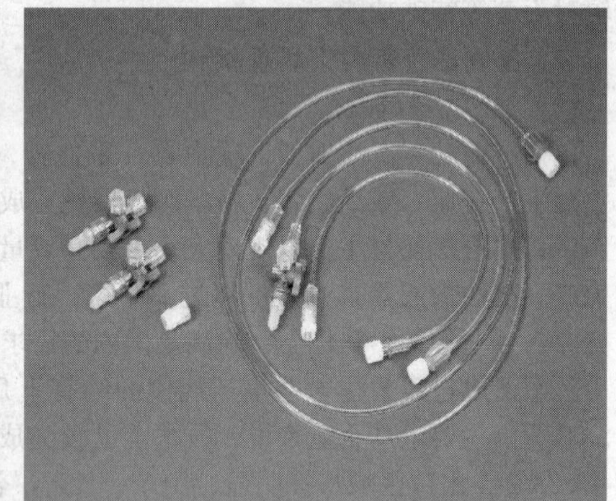

图5　压力延长管图

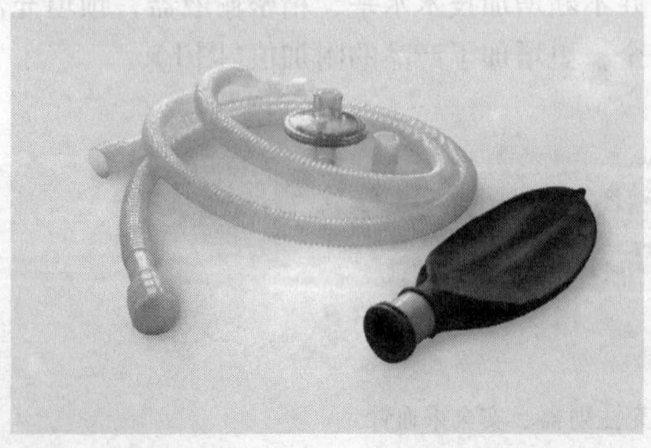

图6　呼吸麻醉回路图

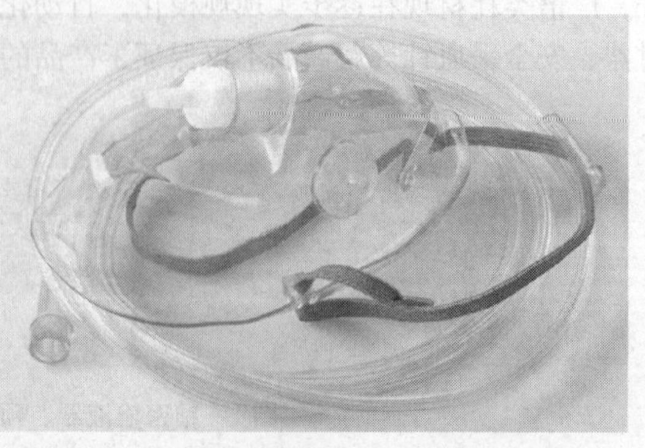

图7　呼吸喉罩图

图 8　急救呼吸球图

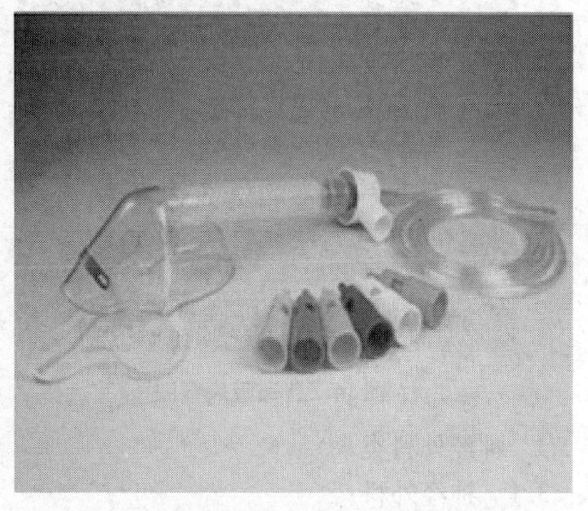

图 9　雾化加药器图

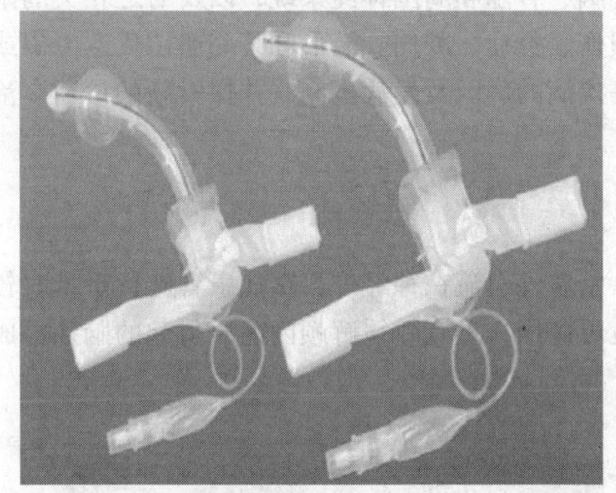

图 10　气管切开插管图

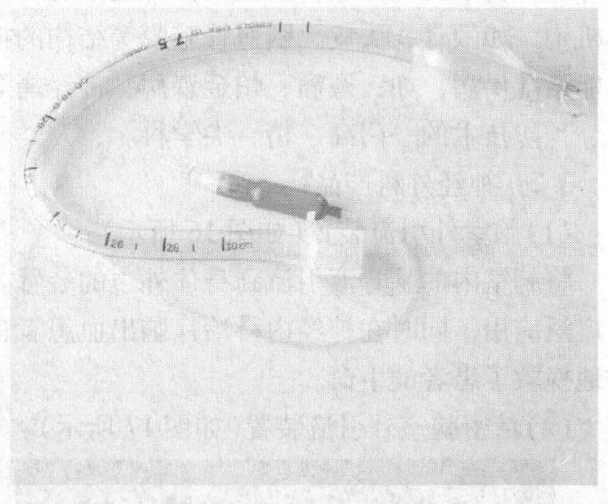

图 11　异型气管插管图

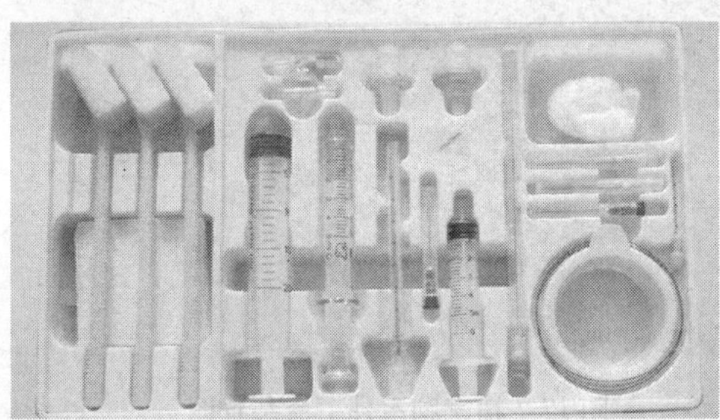

图 12　麻醉穿刺包图

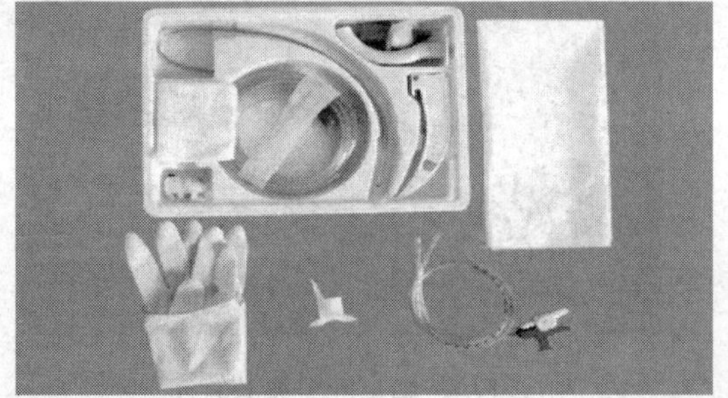

图 13　气管插管包图

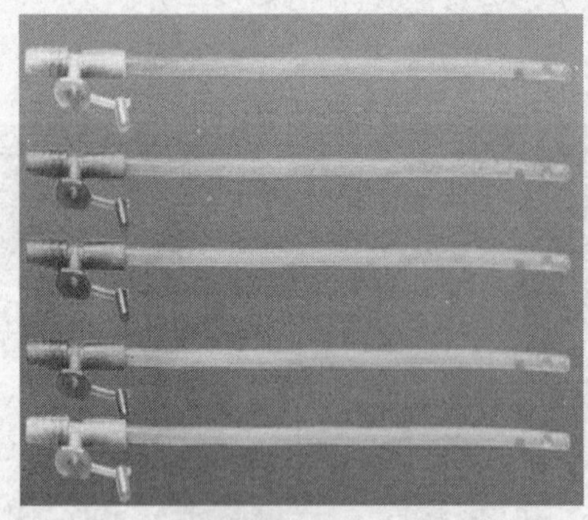
图 14　普通吸痰管图

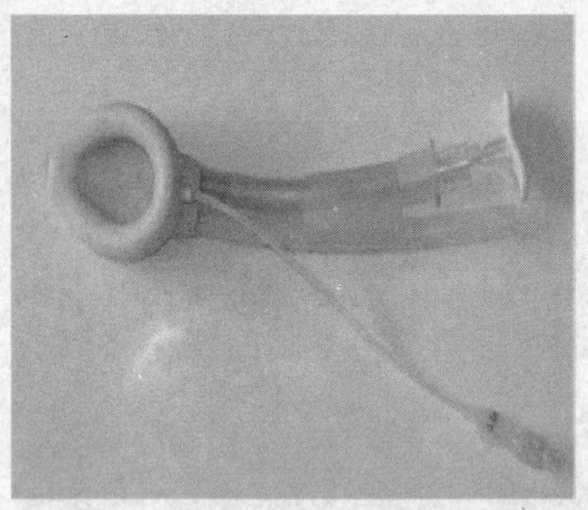
图 15　双腔喉罩图

3　神经外科类

3.1　神经外科：

神经外科是外科学中的一个分支，是在外科学以手术为主要治疗手段的基础上，应用独特的神经外科学研究方法，研究人体神经系统，如脑、脊髓和周围神经系统，以及与之相关的附属机构，如颅骨、头皮、脑血管脑膜等结构的损伤、炎症、肿瘤、畸形和某些遗传代谢障碍或功能紊乱疾病，如：癫痫、帕金森病、神经痛等疾病的病因及发病机制，并探索新的诊断、治疗、预防技术的一门高、精、尖学科。

3.2　神经外科产品：

(1)脑室外引流装置(如图 16 所示)：

将脑室内的脑脊液引流到身体外边的装置。脑室外引流在神经外科重症患者施行手术时较为广泛应用，同时在神经内科治疗脑出血患者也可应用，可有效缓解颅内高压引起的脑疝，成功地挽救了患者的生命。

(2)精密脑室外引流装置(如图 17 所示)：

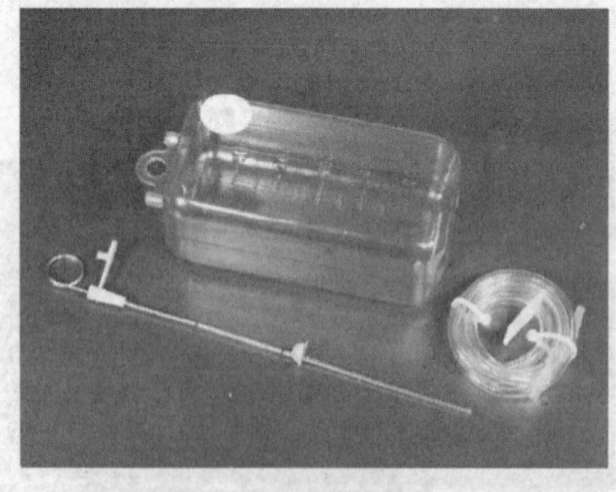
图 16　脑室外引流装置图

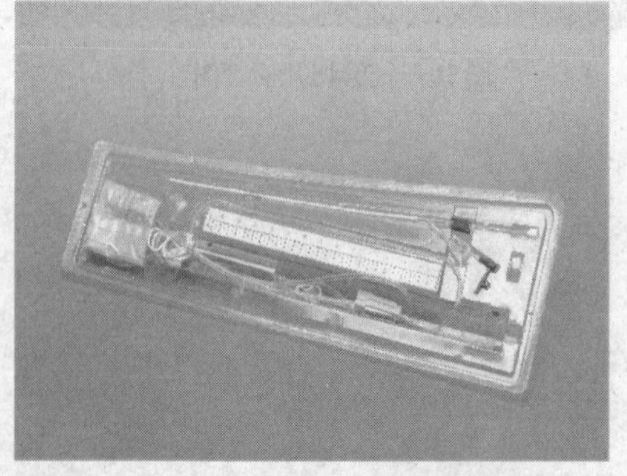
图 17　精密脑室外引流装置图

在脑室外引流装置的基础上增加了颅内压测量功能，通过重力测量患者颅内压。

(3)腰大池引流装置(如图 18 所示)：

利用颅内和腰椎内脑脊液相同的原理，从腰部实现持续引流，减轻了患者转颅的危险和痛苦。

(4)颅骨修补片(如图 19 所示)

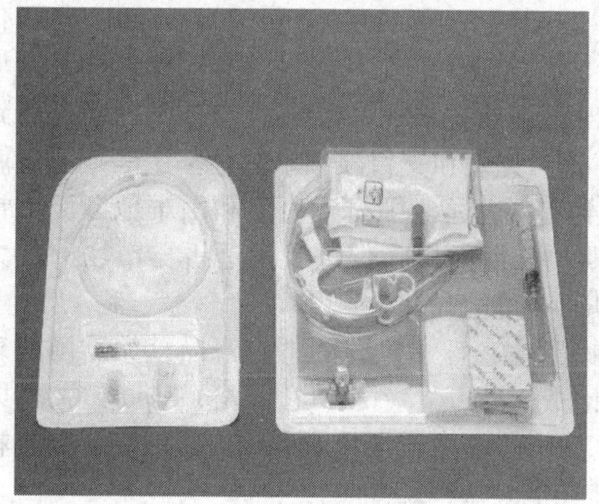

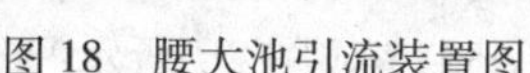

图 18　腰大池引流装置图

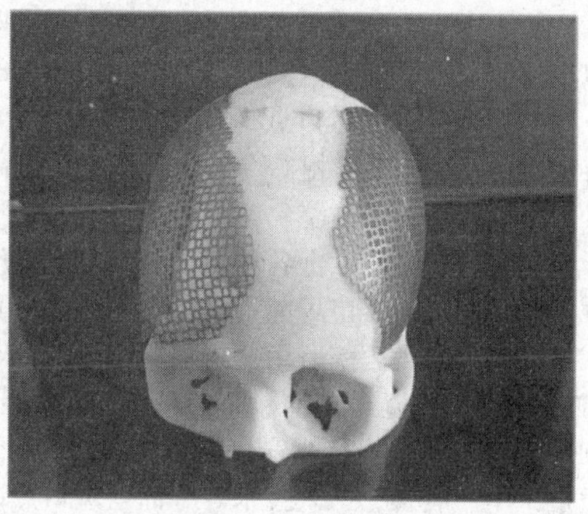

图 19　颅骨修补片

4　透析产品

4.1　血液透析

4.1.1　肾病与透析

进入 21 世纪以来，肾病已经成为人类健康的主要危害之一，而血液透析是目前及未来几十年治疗终末期肾病（尿毒症）的主要手段。造成终末期肾病的病因主要是原发性肾小球肾炎，高血压和糖尿病。目前世界上患肾病的人口已超过 5 亿，有 160 万人靠透析生存，并以平均每年 8% 的幅度增长，2010 年达到 200 万人。

4.1.2　我国肾病和治疗现状

我国慢性肾病患者总数已达到 1.21 亿。其中 1% 可能会发展为终末期肾病。40 岁以上人群慢性肾脏病的患病率高达 8% ~10%，黑龙江省慢性肾脏病患病率达 20% 以上。我国每年肾脏病发病率上升趋势很明显，例如终末期肾病患病率正在以每年 10% 速度增长。但是实际情况是我国们大量的尿毒症患者尚无经济能力实施定期的血液透析治疗，尤其在广大的农村地区。

根据联合国医疗机构统计资料指出“肾衰竭发病率占人群的万分之五”。按此计算我国 13 亿人口中有肾衰竭患者 65 万人，平均每周至少需透析 2 次，则需透析器 6760 万只。但是目前我国肾衰竭患者仅有 10% 左右能得到透析治疗，而在 20 世纪 80 年代末，美、日等发达国家 95% 以上患者已经使用透析治疗。我国肾病现状呈现“高患病率，低知晓率，低救治率”的状态。

4.1.3　我国透析市场现状和前景

血液透析治疗法的器材主要由透析机、透析器、血液回路等组成，其中透析器是血液透析设备的主要医疗耗材。2007 年全世界透析器年销售量约为 1.8 亿只。在日本、美国和欧洲等发达国家每年消耗大量的透析器，仅日本每年消耗大约 3000 万支透析器，而且还在以每年 5% ~7% 的速度增长。

中国 2008 年血液透析市场相关数据：

· 定期接受透析治疗的病人数量：65000

· 不定期接受透析治疗的病人数量：130000

· 透析器销售量：8000000

· 肾病患者增长率：每年 10%

· 市场增长率：每年 15%

我国目前年消耗透析器在 1000 万只以上。随着我国经济不断发展，人民生活水平不断提高，特别是医疗普及和医疗保险体制的进一步改革完善，进行血液透析治疗的患者人数将急剧上升。2009 年 1 月，国务院通过《关于深化医药卫生体制改革的意见》和《2009 ~ 2011 年深化医药卫生体制改革实施方案》，3 年内拟投入 8500 亿，使城镇职工和居民基本医疗保险及新型农村合作医疗参保率提高到 90% 以上。2010 年，对城镇居民医保和新农合的补助标准提高到每人每年 120 元，并适当提高个人缴费标准，提高报销比例和支付限额。健全基层医疗卫生服务体系。重点加强县级医院(含中医院)、乡镇卫生院、边远地区村卫生室和困难地区城市社区卫生服务中心建设。以上各项政府措施将在短期和长期内极大促进我国透析器市场的壮大发展。所以我国透析器市场前景是相当广阔并极具商业价值和社会意义。

目前国内各大医院所用透析器 95% 基本依赖欧美、日本等国的进口产品，如德国费森尤斯(Fresenius)，瑞典金宝(Gambro)，日本旭化成(Asahi)，日本尼普洛(Nipro)德国贝朗(B. Brau)等；国内自行生产仅占总量的约 5%，如山西华鼎，常州朗生和山东威高，而且在产品质量，生产装备，工艺技术等方面与进口产品有很大差距。

4.1.4　血液透析耗材产品包括：透析器，透析管路，瘘针(如图 20 所示)

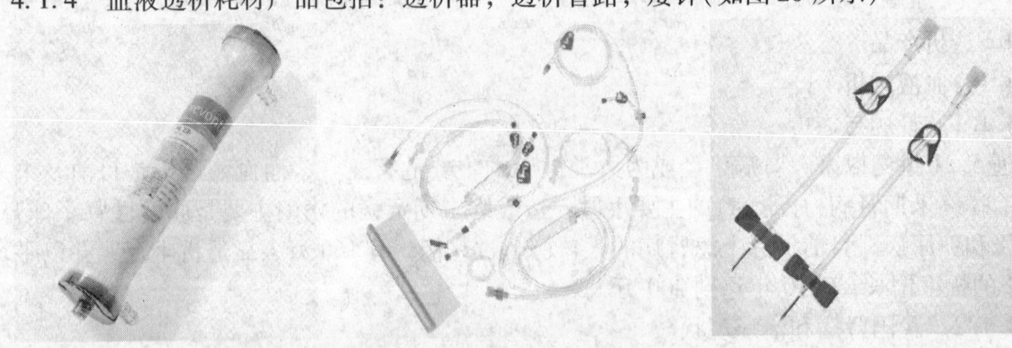

图 20　透析器、透析管路、瘘针

4.2　腹膜透析

腹膜透析是利用腹膜作为半透膜，向腹腔内注入透析液，借助腹膜两侧的毛细血管内血浆及腹腔内的透析液中的溶质浓度梯度和渗透梯度，通过弥散原理来清除溶质；通过渗透超滤原理清除水分。透出液中的代谢废物和潴留过多水分随废旧透析液排除体外，同时由腹透液中补充必要的物质。不断更换新鲜腹透液反复透析，则可达到清除毒素、脱水、纠正酸中毒和电解质紊乱的治疗目的。

1. 内置管(如图 21 所示)；2. 外置管(如图 22 所示)；3. 钛金属接头(如图 23 所示)；4. 药液袋(如图 24 所示)

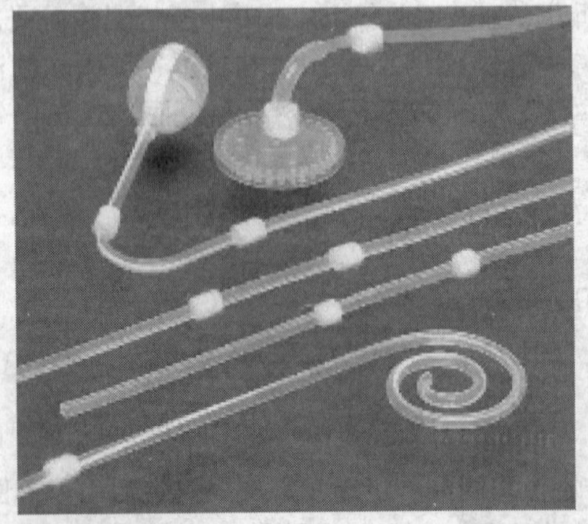

图 21　颅骨修补片图

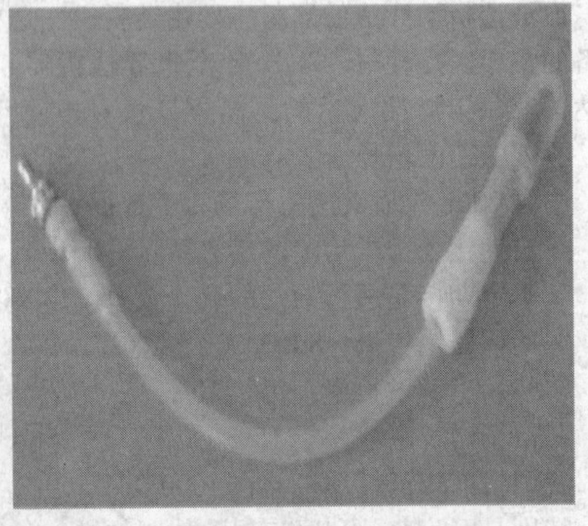

图 22　外置管图

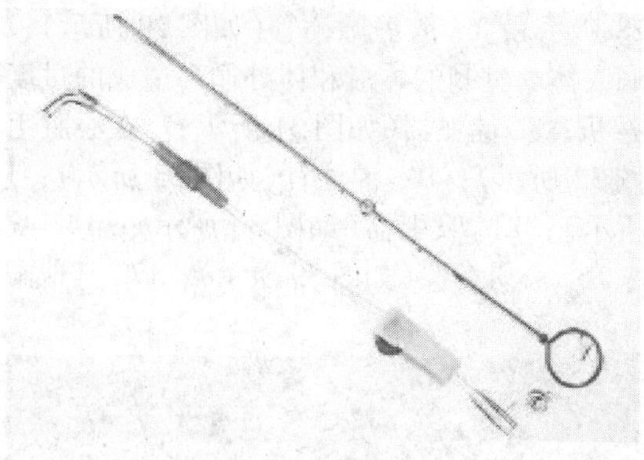

图23　外置管

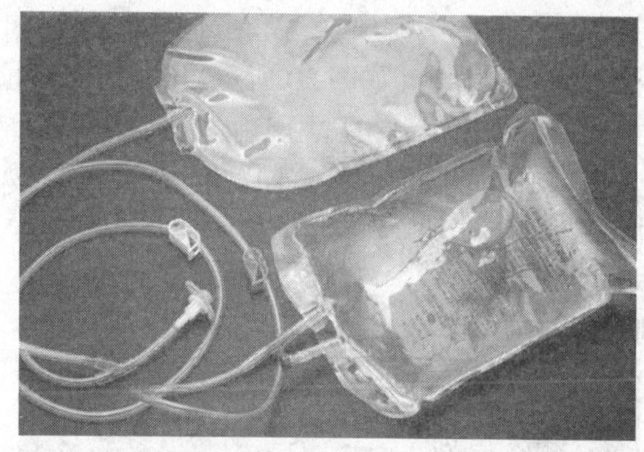

图24　药液袋

5　心血管产品

5.1　心脏外科体外循环

5.1.1　心脏外科体外循环市场

2011年我国心脏外科手术18.8万例，其中体外循环手术15万例。较2010年心脏手术17万例，体外循环手术13.8万例增长了10%，并以每年10%~15%的增幅持续增长。2011年天津心脏手术共3623例，其中体外循环2187例。

5.1.2　体外循环

体外循环是指应用人工管道将人体大血管与人工心肺机连接，从静脉系统引出静脉血，并在体外氧合，再经血泵(心肺机)将氧合血输回动脉系统的全过程，又称心肺转流，如此血液可以不经过心脏和肺而进行周身循环。心脏内因无血液流动，为外科医师提供了切开心脏进行直视手术的条件，这种方法可使心内操作时间大为延长。使一些复杂的心脏畸形的手术成为可能，主要应用于心脏、大血管手术。近年来应用领域不断扩大，如ECMO急诊急救，心肺复苏，肿瘤治疗，神经外科，一氧化碳中毒，有机磷中毒等领域。目前，全国已有600多家医院开展心血管外科手术，从事体外循环的专业人员2000多人。

5.1.3　心脏体外循环产品

1. 氧合器(人工肺)通过半透膜的作用和不同的渗透亚，使血液在膜表面进行气体交换，使静脉血(含氧量低的血液)变为动脉血(含氧量高的血液)。(如图25所示)；2. 动脉微栓过滤器(如图26所示)；3. 过滤即将进入人体的动脉血液，主要是气体或固体栓子体；4. 外循

图25　氧合器图

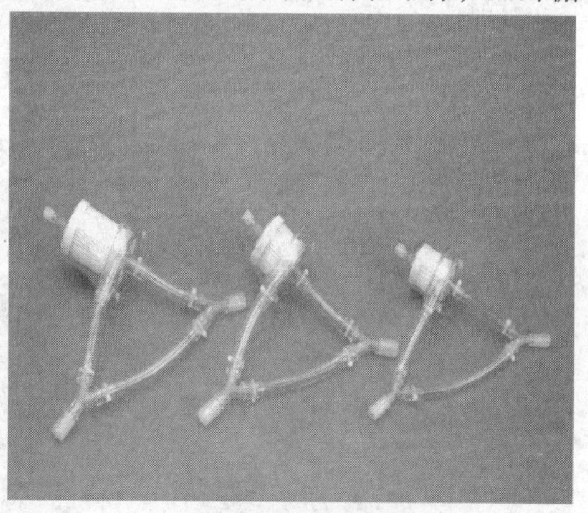

图26　动脉微栓过滤器图

环血管路(如图 27 所示)；5. 主动脉插管(如图 28 所示)；6. 腔静脉插管(如图 29 所示)；7. 血液浓缩器(超滤)(如图 30 所示)用于治疗排出病人体内过剩的体液和体外循环造成的过度稀释血液的浓缩治疗，也可用于血液的过滤和血液透析；8. 储血器(如图 31 所示)　在心脏手术中，病人血液的临时储存空间；9. 灌注装置(如图 32 所示)；10. 灌注针(如图 33 所示)；11. 阻隔器(如图 34 所示)；12. 泵前滤器(如图 35 所示)；13. 吸引器(如图 36 所示)；14. 吹管(如图 37 所示)；15. 心脏固定器(如图 38 所示)；16. 心脏瓣膜(如图 39 所示)；17. 其他配件(如图 40 所示)

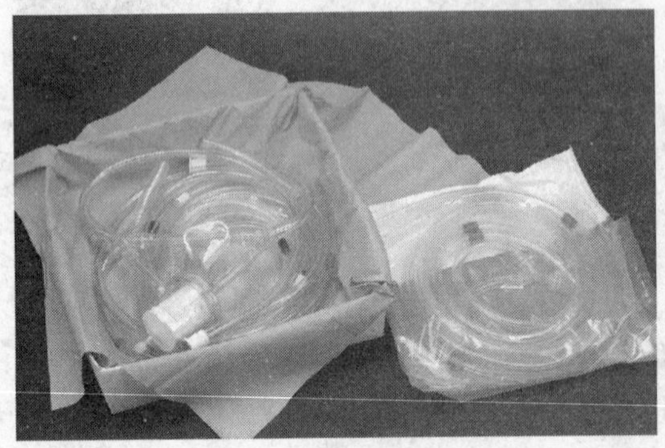

图 27　体外循环血管路图

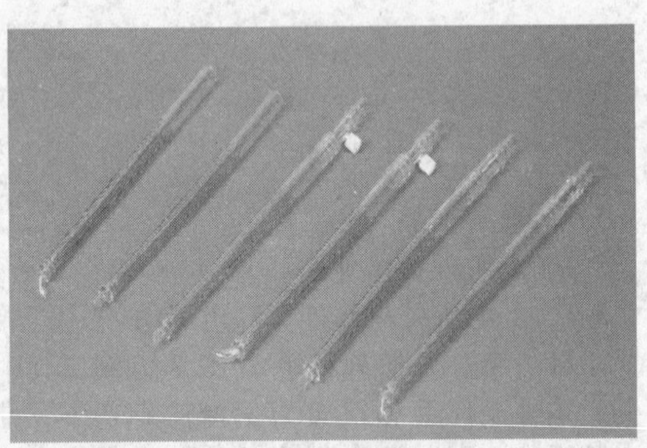

图 28　主动脉插管图

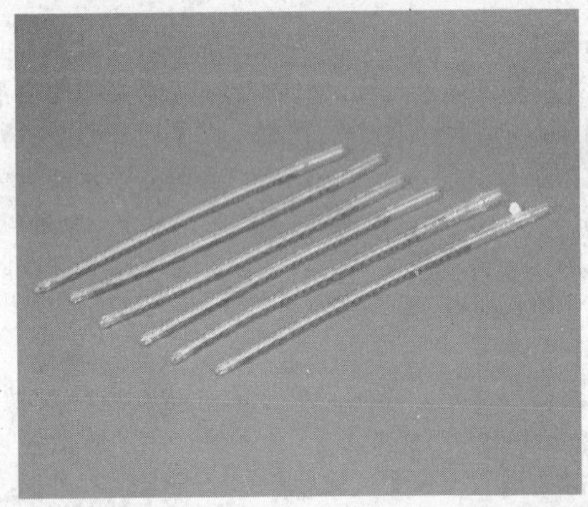

图 29　静脉插管图、双极腔静脉插管图

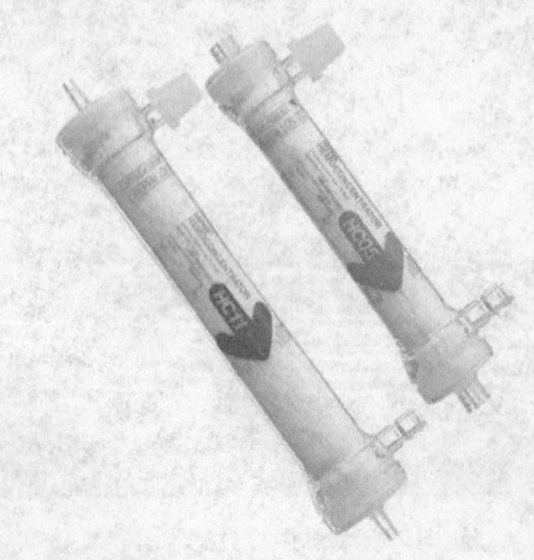

图 30　血液浓缩器(超滤)图

图 31　储血器图

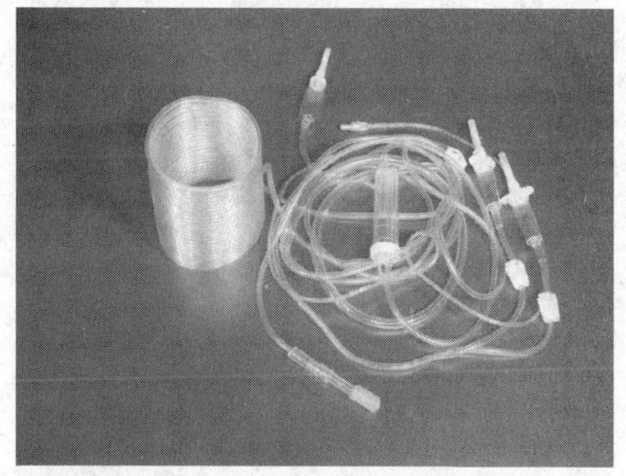

图 32　灌注装置图

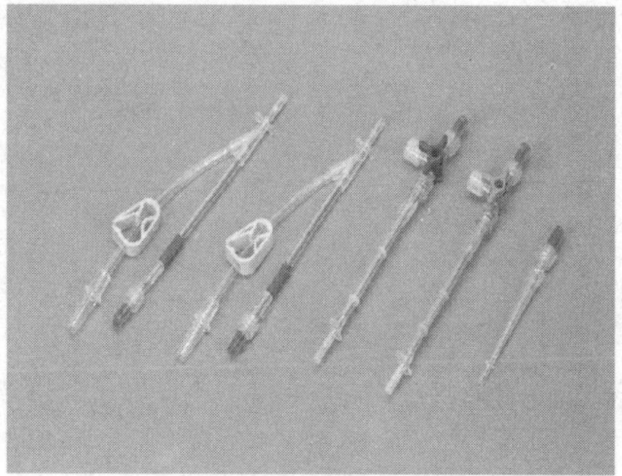

图 33　灌注针图

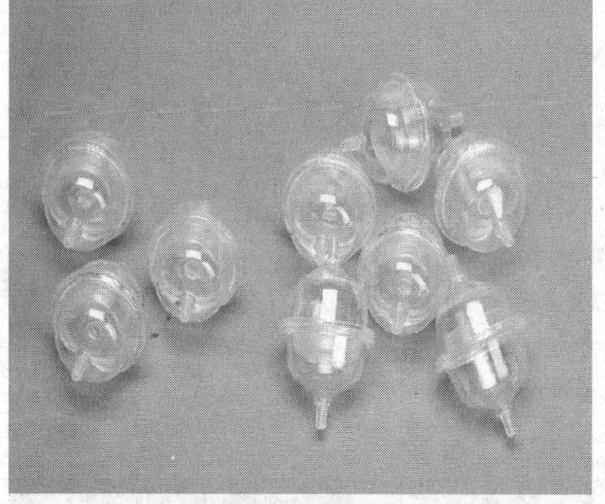

图 34　阻隔器图

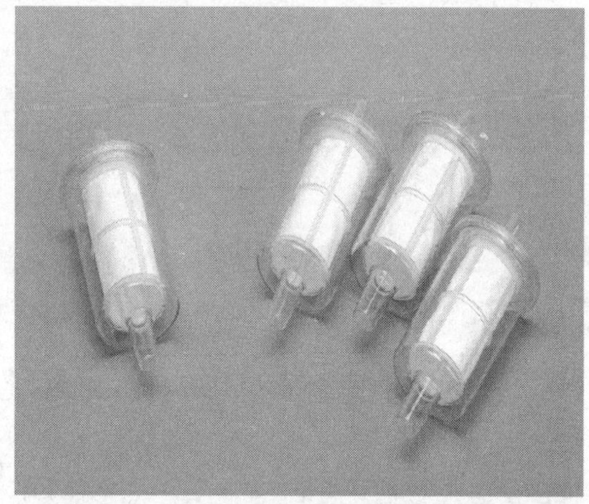

图 35　泵前滤器图

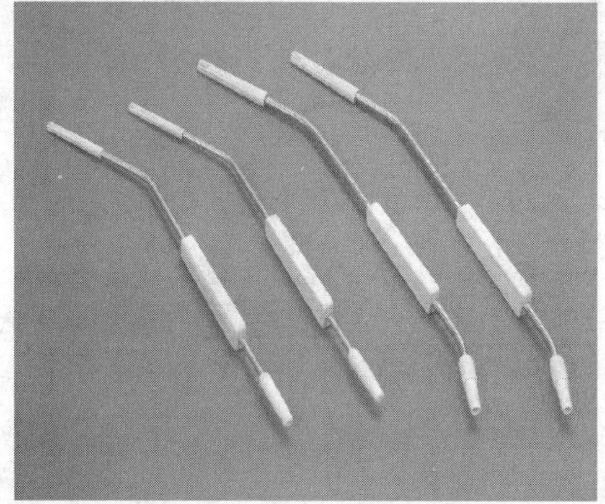

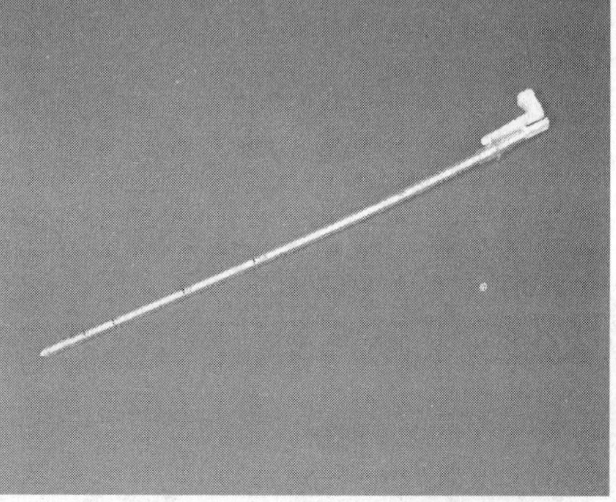

图 36　吸引管图

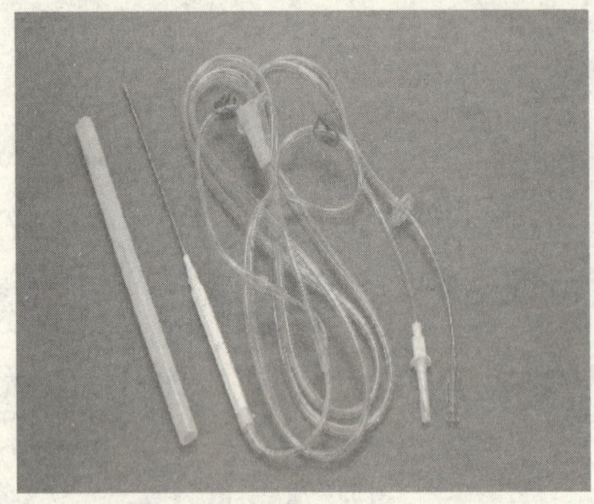

图 37　吹管图

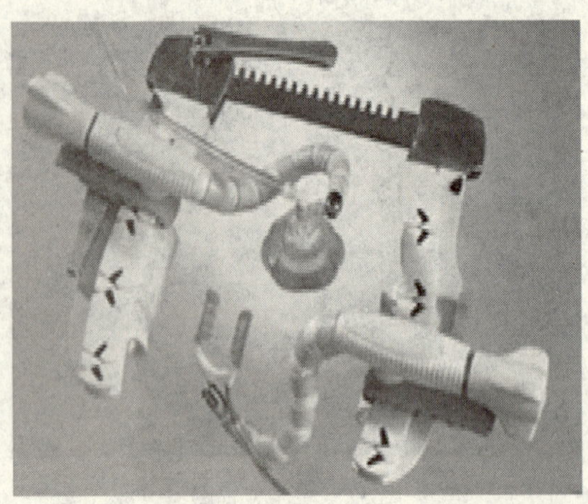

图 38　心脏固定器图

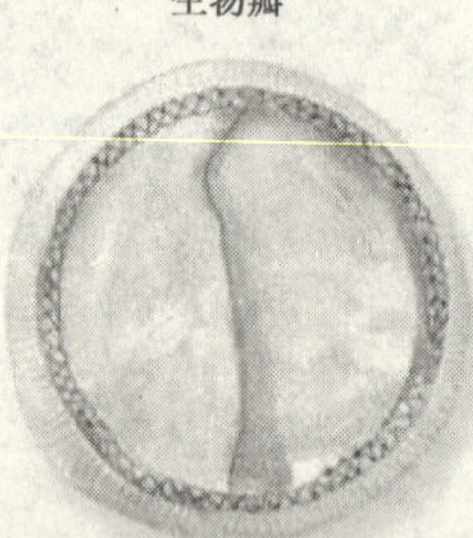

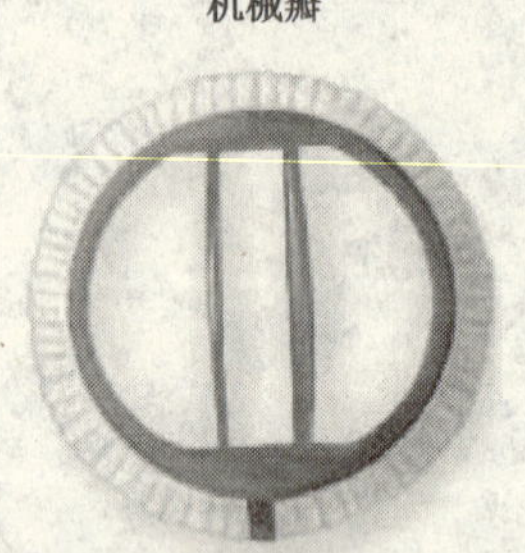

图 39　心脏瓣膜图

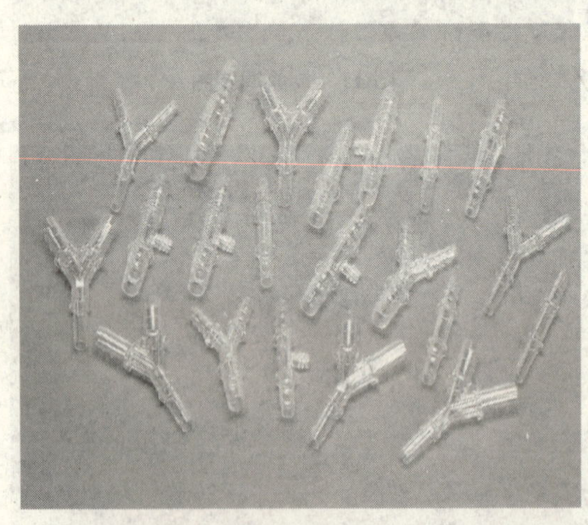

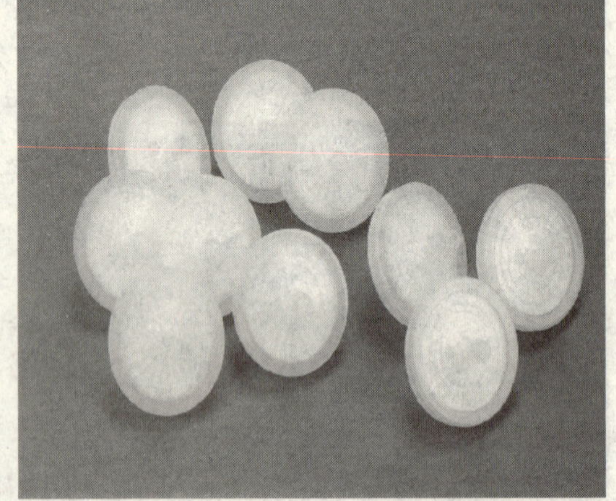

图 40　医用接头图气体过滤器图

5.2　心脏内科产品

心内科，即心血管内科，是各级医院大内科为了诊疗心血管血管疾病而设置的一个临床科室，治疗的疾病包括心绞痛、高血压、猝死、心律失常、心力衰竭、早搏、心律不齐、心肌梗死、心肌病、心肌炎、心肌梗塞等心血管疾病。

1. 心脏支架(普通型/载药性/可降解型)(如图 41 所示)；2. 心脏封堵器(如图 42 所示)；3. 造影导管(如图 43 所示)；4. 压力注射器(如图 44 所示)。

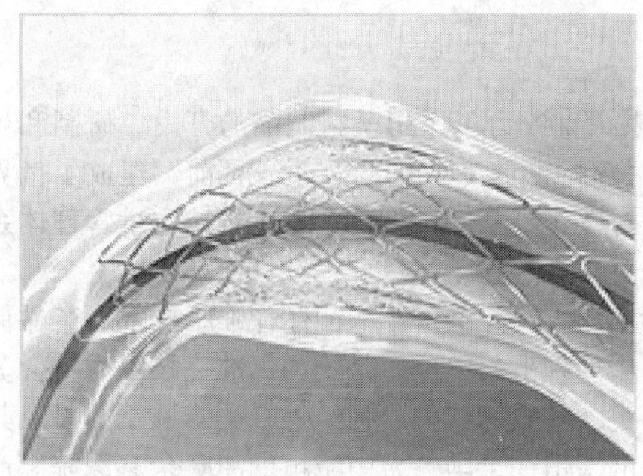

图 41　心脏支架图

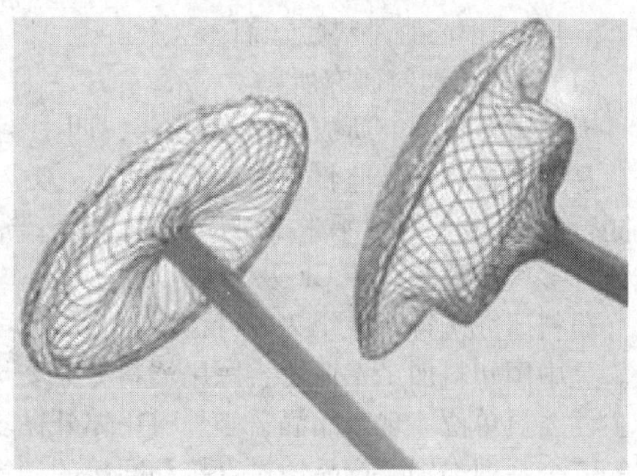

图 42　心脏封堵器图

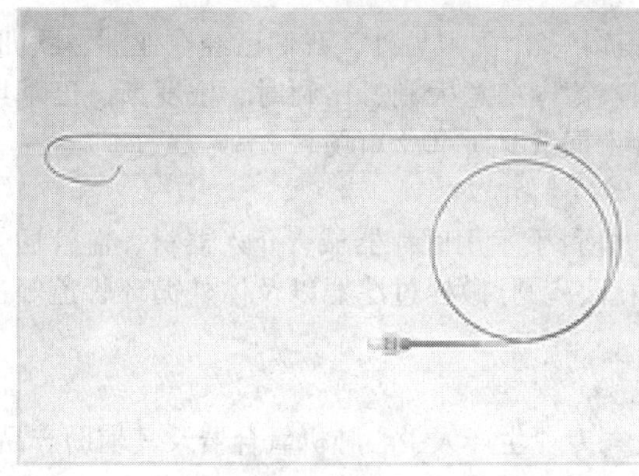

图 43　造影导管图

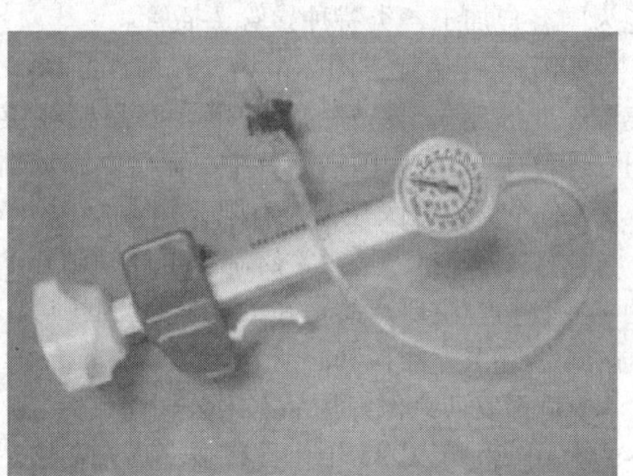

图 44　压力注射器图

5.3　国际心脏外科产品主要生产商

(1)意大利 Sorin 公司

成立于 1978 年，是意大利最大和最充满活力的生物医学公司之一。索林集团意大利有限公司的核心竞争力表现在两个重要的市场区域：它们是心肺(心脏外科)和血液管理(自体输血和机器采血)市场。心肺产品应用在成人、儿童、新生儿开心手术的体外循环中。索林在超过 80 个国家有 4800 多名雇员。

(2)泰尔茂株式会社

成立于 1921 年，总部位于日本东京都涩谷区，是医疗器械及医药制品的大型企业。产品包括一次性医用器械，输血用具系列，医药品和营养药系列，血管造影与治疗导管，医用电子产品系列，人工心肺产品系列，输液泵，注射泵，输血泵，麻醉泵，靶控泵系列，检验产品系列，家庭医疗保健产品系列等。

(3)美国美敦力

成立于 1949 年，总部位于美国明尼苏达州明尼阿波利斯市，致力于为慢性疾病患者提供终身的治疗方案。在慢性疾病医疗科技领域，美敦力中国通过提供安全可靠和有效可及的解决方案而成为值得信赖的领导者，从而保证公司和员工持续健康的共同发展。其主要产品覆盖心律失常、心衰、血管疾病、心脏瓣膜置换、体外心脏支持、微创心脏手术、恶性及非恶性疼痛、运动失调、糖尿病、胃肠疾病、泌尿系统疾病、脊椎疾病、神经系统疾病及五官科手术治疗等领域。

5.4　国内心脏外科生产商

(1)天津市塑料研究所

天津市塑料研究所成立于1965年，四十年来一直致力于医用塑料制品的开发、研制和生产。是国家食品药品监督管理局批准的“三类”医疗器械的专业生产企业。目前，建成了世界上同行业最大的5000平米10万级净化车间，通过了ISO13485:2003，医疗器械质量管理体系认证，多种产品获得了CE及FDA认证。

塑料研究所自上世纪70年代开始，从事医用塑料的研发、生产，有着雄厚技术和产品储备。是中国塑料加工工业协会医用塑料专业委员会的理事长单位，是全国标准化技术委员会分会主任委员单位。现产品涵盖心外科用体外循环类、呼吸麻醉类、神经外科类、透析类以及其它等五个系列类别。产品通过直接和间接的销售网络销往全国各大中城市的400余家医院。产品质量和技术居国内领先水平，其中自行研制的一管多腔、变径、复合挤出等专内外有技术，能为国客户加工各类特种导管、插管。

2007年开始走进国际市场，目前产品出口到三十多个国家另外，我们已经在亚洲、欧洲、美国、非洲建立了良好的客户群，产品销往英国、德国、意大利、比利时、俄罗斯、巴基斯坦、印度等30余个国家。其中，血管路，滤器等占据俄罗斯40%市场。

(2)东莞科威医疗器械有限公司

立于1993年，是一家研制、生产、销售心胸外科手术用医疗器械、介入器材、血管插管的专业公司。主要产品是在氧合器(人工肺)，插管、动脉微栓过滤器以及体外循环管道等三类体外循环医疗器械和心肌介入封堵器。

(3)西安西京医疗用品有限公司

公司成立于1995年，具有独立法人资格。公司专业生产人工心肺机氧合器及其辅助产品，近年来向有源医疗器械产品扩展。

(4)宁波费拉尔

是专业研发、生产、销售一次性使用心胸外科系列产品的企业。主要产品：一次性使用贮血滤血器、一次性使用血液微栓过滤器、一次性使用心肺转流血路(体外循环配套管路及各种规格插管)，一次性使用心脏冷停搏液灌注器等产品。净化车间700余平方米。

(5)北京米道斯医疗器械有限公司

公司成立于2012年4月，是专业从事心脏外科产品及麻醉科用品的开发、生产和销售的中美合资企业。净化车间400平米。主要产品有心脏固定器、膜式氧合器、心脏插管、体外循环管路、动脉微栓过滤器、血液停跳灌注装置等。

(6)上海祥盛医疗器械厂

该厂成立于1993年5月，是生产一次性高分子材料导管的专业厂家。目前已形成一次性心胸外科类及护理类导管二大系列共十二个产品，主要产品有：一次性使用腔静脉插管、左心房减压管、主动脉插管、人工心肺机管路、引流管、延长管、胃管、吸痰管、鼻氧管等。

(7)常州市康心医疗器械有限公司

主要产品：动静脉插管，心脏固定器，灌注针，开创保护器等。

(8)威高集团

建于1988年，以一次性医疗器械和药品为主导，发展了航天军工、房地产、证券投资等五大产业，占地面积200多万平方米，有总资产200多亿元，员工14000多人，下辖30个子公司，控股子公司山东威高集团医用高分子制品股份有限公司于2004年2月在香港创业板上市，2010年7月转主板上市。集团拥有400多种、30000多个规格医疗器械和药品，主要有输注耗材、手术缝合线、医用导管、心脏支架及心内耗材、留置针及各种异型针、血液净化设备及耗材、骨科材料、医疗设备、治疗型注射液及其它药品、生物诊断试剂、人造血浆、生物种植体、PVC 及非 PVC 原料等系列，成为中国最大的一次性使用医疗器械制造商。

三、塑料医疗器械行业的发展前景

随着经济的发展、人口的增长、社会老龄化程度的提高，以及人们保健意识的不断增强，全球医疗器械市场持续快速扩大，在经济上升时候，医疗器械行业的增长速度要快于国民经济的增长速度；在全球经济衰退时期，医疗器械产品行情仍然看好，可见医疗器械行业具有典型的正值型正周期特征，这个特征决定了国际医疗器械行业具有很大的发展潜力。其中塑料以其优良的性质、可靠的性能、方便的成型工艺在医疗领域获得了越来越广泛的应用。还正在逐渐替代各种材料继续扩大在医疗器械中的应用领域。从药品、药剂的包装，到一次性医疗器械和非一次性医疗器械的应用，都有塑料的参与，据预测今后 10 年医用塑料领域将是塑料工业最具发展潜力的领域之一。

鉴于塑料优良性质，可靠性能，方便成型，价格低廉，理应大量取代传统产品，在医疗领域有更广泛的应用。据统计全球医疗器械市场已达 1000 亿美元，医疗材料市场达 120 亿美元，并且以 7% ~12% 的平均增长率持续增长，但是国内医用塑料还是个新兴产业。我国医用塑料产值仅仅只有发达国家的 7%，我国医疗器械产值近 500 亿元，而医用塑料约 60 亿元左右，据专家推测，今后的 10 ~15 年，我国医疗器械产业将进入高速发展阶段。从 2011 年新医改提出大力发展县医院政策，受益于县医院建设对医疗设备、仪器、材料的需求增长，医疗器械业绩将更上一层楼。国家持续加大对基层医疗机构的支持力度，基层医疗机构对医疗器械的需求将持续释放。因此医疗器械市场将会增长 40%，目前全国注册医疗器械企业有 7000 多家，而生产医用塑料的企业大约只有 1000 家。由于产品精细度等因素，大部分产品只用在中小城市和广大农村地区，京津沪等大城市的市场主要应用还是进口产品，而塑料制品大多是易耗品，因此市场空间十分巨大，这将给生产医用塑料企业带来无限商机。

（作者为天津市塑料研究所有限公司）

汽车塑料制品及其加工技术的发展现状和趋势

杨有财　曹广元　车忠良　王德禧

近年来，无论国内还是国外，汽车都是发展最快的工业行业之一，行业整体呈现井喷式增长。汽车的普及、保有量的快速增长带来一些新的环境污染问题，如雾霾天气大范围出现，以及能源危机的威胁，对汽车制造业提出了要求：一是节能环保，二是提高功能，三是简化制造工序与工艺，汽车塑料化已成为国际汽车界研究开发的热门课题之一。汽车塑料化是实现汽车轻量化、环保化、节能化的必然发展趋势，汽车塑料化减轻汽车自重，提高燃油燃烧效率，汽车的自重每减少 10%，燃油的消耗可降低 6% ~8%。

塑料新材料成为 21 世纪汽车工业最佳的材料选择，塑料在汽车上的用量已经成为一个国家汽车工业技术水平的重要标志。与汽车工业发达国家相比，我国还存在很大的差距，面临巨大的挑战，德国、美国、日本等国的汽车塑料用量已达到 10% ~15%，有的甚至达到了 20% 以上，而我国塑料件仅约占汽车自重的 7% ~10%。

塑料在汽车中的应用遍及所有总成和零部件，习惯将它们分为内(装)饰件、外(装)饰件、汽车车身、功能和结构件共4种类型。塑料在汽车领域的应用日渐广泛，从部分替代金属向大部或全部替代发展，除发动机等少数部件，全塑汽车时代已经越来越近。汽车塑料制品的发展不仅有赖于新材料的开发，而且新的加工方式也至关重要，因此，本文分析研究目前国内外的汽车塑料制品及其加工新技术，期望在汽车领域，推动汽车塑料制品及其加工技术的创新和创造，汽车技术的研究重点持续向汽车塑料化发展。

1 发展现状

1.1 汽车内饰件

一辆汽车最容易出彩的是内饰件，因为汽车的外观是给别人看的，而人们真正享受的是汽车的内饰，内饰强调触觉、手感、舒适性和可视性等。汽车内饰件包括：车门内饰板、仪表板、顶棚、座椅、方向盘、门内手柄、装饰条等。内饰件用量可高达整车塑料总用量的50%左右，PC/ABS合金是最适合用于汽车内饰件的材料。

(1)国外现状

如表1所示，欧洲汽车的仪表板一般以ABS/PC及长玻纤增强PP为主要材料；美国汽车的仪表板多玻纤增强SMA，这类材料价格低，耐热、耐冲击，具有良好的综合性能；日本汽车的仪表板曾采用过ABS和增强PP材料，目前则以玻璃纤维增强的SAN为主，有时也采用耐热性更好的改性PPE[2-4]。仪表板目前多采用气辅注塑成型技术生产。

表1 国外主要汽车生产国家内饰件所用塑料种类

国 别	欧 洲	美 国	日 本
仪表板	ABS/PC，长玻纤增强聚丙烯(LGF-PP)	苯乙烯/顺丁烯二酸酐共聚物(SMA)	玻璃纤维增强的SAN，改性PPE
车门内饰板	亚麻/剑麻毡增强的环氧树脂，天然纤维预浸料	ABS或PP注塑成形	全PP车门内饰板

在美国，车门内装饰板用ABS及其合金或聚丙烯(PP)注塑成形的居多，日本最近开发成功低压注射-压缩成型、连续生产全PP车门内饰板的技术，门板包括PP内衬板、PP泡沫衬热层和PP/EPDM皮层结构，全PP车门内饰板便于回收利用[6]。在美国市场上，内饰件也都采用PP逐渐替代ABS树脂。

北欧化工一款LGF-PP产品与BMW公司自动化整体发泡注塑技术相兼容，生产全PP汽车仪表板(图1)，与全PP车门内饰板的技术类似，以长玻纤增强PP为仪表板骨架，微孔发泡PP作为填充注塑成型。

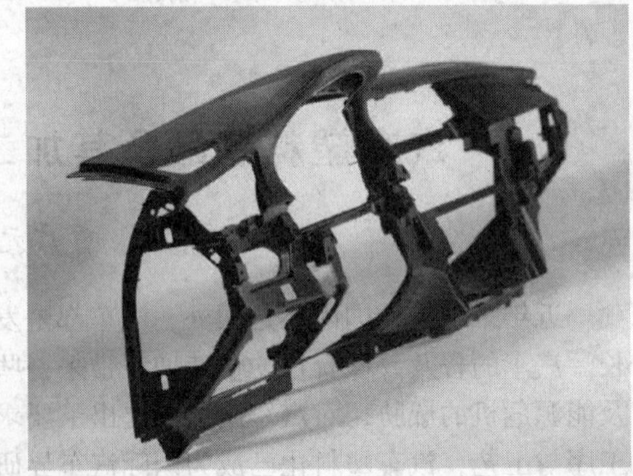

图1 BMW采用北欧化工的LGF-PP生产的仪表板

以戴姆勒-克莱斯勒公司为代表，欧洲汽车厂商已经成功地将天然纤维复合材料应用在汽车内饰件，如亚麻/剑麻毡增强的环氧树脂，使得内饰件重量减轻了20%左右，而且机械性能也得到了改善。天然纤维增强热塑性复合材料是当前国外汽车塑料的一个重要研究领域，纳入研究的天然纤维来源有纤维素、木材、亚麻、黄麻、剑麻、大麻、龙舌兰叶纤维、椰子壳纤维，以及稻草与其他农作物废料等，目前在汽车工业的应用还局限在汽车内饰件上。

(2)国内现状

我国使用的仪表板可分为硬和软仪表板两种。硬仪表板常被用在轻、小型货车、大货车和客车上，一般采用PP、PC、ABS、ABS/PC等一次性注射成型，表面需经涂装后才能使用，且最好选用亚光漆涂装[9]。另外，由于高档仪表板追求质感，所以在仪表板表面做一部分桃木饰纹将是一种发展方向[3]。

软质仪表板由表皮、骨架材料、缓冲材料等构成，ABS、玻纤增强SMA等注塑成型作为骨架，然后浇注中硬PU发泡层，表皮通常用PVC/ABS片材吸塑成型。但是，由三种以上材料构成的仪表板，材料的再生利用极为困难[3,4]，为了便于回收利用，全PP仪表板正在代替[6]。

座椅及靠背是由软质PU发泡制成，目前尚无其他更好发泡材料可以替代。

1.2 汽车外饰件

汽车外饰件包括：前后保险杠、散热器格栅、挡泥板、底部护板、后导流板、车身装饰条等。外饰件的应用特点是以塑代钢，减轻汽车自身质量，除了要具有内饰件的功能外，还要求具有高强度、高韧性、耐环境条件性能及抗冲击性能等。弹性体增韧PBT/PC合金和PET/PC合金是制造汽车外饰件的理想材料。

(1)国外现状

高耐热型PBT/PC合金和PET/PC合金的注射成型外饰件可以不用涂漆。如GE公司的PBT/PC合金，商品名为Xenoy1731在高级轿车中应用最为广泛。巴斯夫公司生产的PBT/PC合金Ultra-blend，已经大量用于制造保险杠。

散热器格栅是为了冷却发动机而设置的开口部件，位于车体最前面，往往把汽车的铭牌镶嵌其间，是表现一辆汽车风格的重要部件。有用耐候性较好的ASA(丙烯腈、苯乙烯、丙烯酸橡胶组成的三元聚合物，属于抗冲击改性树脂)材料[10]，在注塑成型后，表面可不经涂装。表面不涂装的散热器格栅，其成本将降低50%。锦湖日丽[11]开发了高抗冲的HSC7045和高耐热的HSC7079两种PC/ASA合金材料特别适合于汽车仪表板、柱式罩、散热器格栅等需要高耐候、高耐热的场合。

最近，玻纤增强材料开始大量用于汽车外饰件以塑带钢，汽车底板多采用GMT、SMC生产，戴姆勒-克莱斯勒公司采用巴斯夫的长玻纤增强尼龙生产Smart概念车轮辋(图2)，LG化学和三菱工程塑料也推出长玻纤增强材料生产的外饰件。

图2 长玻纤增强尼龙轮辋

车身侧裙板、门槛、防擦条大多采用PP+30%矿物粉。

(2)国内现状

国内保险杠主要是改性PP材料生产，扬子石化研发出直接釜内合成聚丙烯保险杠专用料[12]，产品具有成本低、能耗小、质量稳定，成功替代进口产品。

散热格栅多用ABS、ABS/PC合金注塑成型制成的，由于ABS耐候性较差，使用时需加入耐候性助剂，色泽为黑色。

挡泥板和导流板采用增韧改性 PP 和 ABS，或 FRP(纤维增强树脂)生产。

1.3　汽车车身

目前世界各国都在进行着车身塑料化(塑壳汽车)的开发研究。对塑壳汽车而言，其关键是汽车的稳定性以及车架的强度。车身材料通常是 FRP，与其他高分子材料相比具有强度高、刚度大、耐高温、成本低等优点，一直是汽车覆盖件最理想的非金属材料。玻璃纤维或碳纤维增强 PP、PET、PC/PBT、PC/ABS 等合金具有很高的力学强度和良好的综合性能可用于制造汽车车身。

(1)国外现状

德国尼奥普兰公司已研制出了全塑壳大型轿车，该车型质量只有普通轿车的43%，可节省燃料20% ~30%。它的一辆试验车横穿撒哈拉沙漠，能耐70℃的高温，且与41km/h 时速的载货汽车相撞时，驾驶员和乘客均无损伤。

英国 ELAN 运动车采用真空辅助树脂注射(VARI)成型工艺制造汽车车身及结构件，FRP 用量为150kg/辆。此外法国雷诺公司的 ESPACE MARK Ⅱ型面包车及意大利菲亚特公司的微型车等车型在大量将 FRP 用作汽车车身方面也取得了成功[8]。

目前 BMW 公司在 M3 系列车型上的顶盖和车身结构部件采用碳纤增强复合材料。日产汽车公司和丰田汽车公司都已采用碳纤增强复合材料用于轿车外饰和内饰件，并已与东丽共同开发碳纤复合材料用于车身覆盖件(图3)。

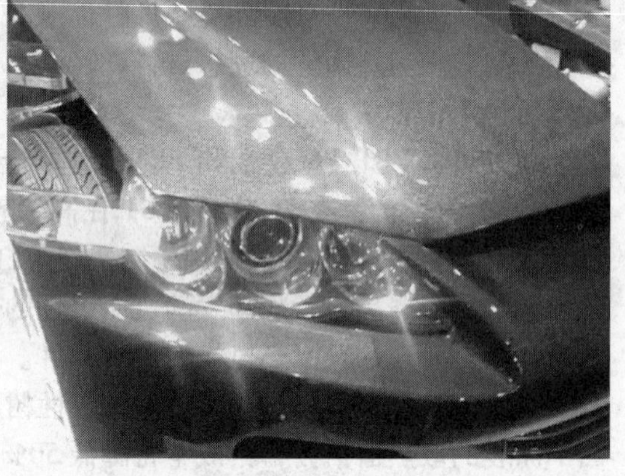

图3　东丽碳纤增强车身覆盖件

美国 GM 公司的“Ultralite”高级全塑跑车，车身材料成本为1.3万美元，骨架结构件采用碳纤增强塑料，外覆盖件采用玻纤增强塑料，全塑车身均用于高档的运动车。

(2)国内现状

北京、山东、浙江、重庆等地的汽车生产厂家，均生产过全环氧玻璃钢车身。但基本上是手工糊制，档次有待提高。东风客车公司采用手糊成型工艺生产的一款高速客车的全玻璃钢车身，每辆消耗玻璃钢约250kg；北京汽车玻璃钢有限公司采用手糊成型工艺生产驾驶室，全车身重量仅600多公斤。

1.4　功能和结构件

功能和结构件必须满足特殊的使用功能，对其材料具有特殊的要求。包括：前端模块结构件、发动机组件、传动组件、燃油箱和燃油管组件、照明系统等。国外已将工程塑料及其合金广泛作为汽车上各种功能零部件的材料。其中尼龙主要用于汽车发动机及发动机周边部件。改性聚甲醛(POM)一般用于制造轴套、齿轮、滑块等耐磨零件。改性聚苯醚(PPO)在汽车上主要用作对耐热性、阻燃性、电性能、冲击性能、尺寸稳定性、机械强度要求较高的零部件。汽车照明系统部件主要有车窗玻璃、挡风玻璃、车灯等，基本上都已经塑料化，主要采用的材料是 PC 或 PMMA 等。燃油箱具有单层或多层复合结构，耐寒、耐热、耐蠕变、耐应力开裂、耐大气老化、耐溶剂、耐化学药品腐蚀等以适应抗冲击、抗渗漏、阻燃、防爆等方面的较高要求。

(1)国外现状

欧洲采用玻纤毡增强塑料(GMT)制作汽车前端模块(图4)的用量约占汽车总用量的28%，

用 GMT 制作前端部件的优点是可将包括车头灯、风机和散热器座、发动机罩搭扣以及保险杠固定点等功能集于一体，从而取代多个金属部件，与同等强度的钢部件相比，质量可减轻 20%，生产费用可下降 10%。

德国拜耳等推出 30%～35% 玻璃纤维增强的尼龙 6 或尼龙 66，可激光焊接生产进气歧管（图 5），与铝合金比较，塑料进气歧管可以减轻 40% 左右的重量，生产成本降低 20%～30%，注塑成型后，通过激光焊接组装。

美国采用一种耐热型塑料通过玻纤及碳纤维增强，制造了大部分发动机零件，这种塑料发动机比金属发动机重量约减轻 50%，试验中省油率达到 12%～15%，而且噪声比金属发动机低 30%。

图 4　泰科纳长纤维增强塑料制作的前端模块

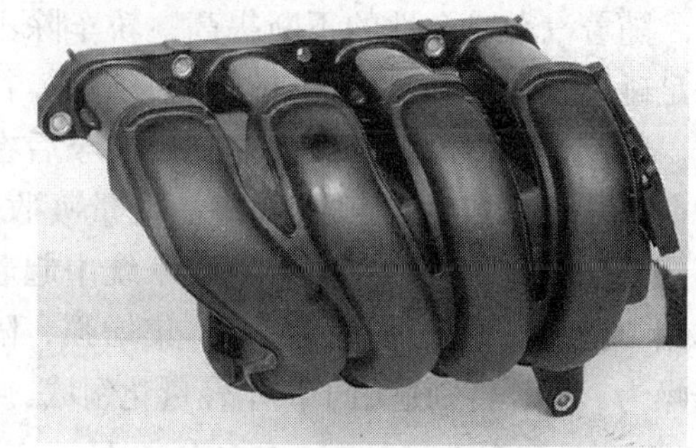

图 5　尼龙进气歧管

日本开始研究采用碳纤复合材料代替目前正在使用的铝合金，来制造汽车涡轮增压器压气机叶轮，具有强度高、耐久性和可靠性高的优点，并使叶轮质量减轻了 48%，降低了转子惯量，提高了转子加速性能，缩短了涡轮增压器的响应滞后[8]。

拜耳、三菱、帝人等开发成功用于轿车车窗的 PC 及其表面高硬度防摩擦涂层。提高了 PC 玻璃耐擦伤性和耐候性，比玻璃镜片更亮，更抗破碎，更具光学加工的准确性。1kg 的 PC 塑料可替代 2.2kg 的玻璃。

欧盟和美国油箱防渗透标准严格，通常使用具有近似零渗透的多层燃油箱，通常采用超高分子量 HDPE 基材，阻隔层 EVOH，并辅以粘接剂吹塑而成，能使防油渗透性提高到 0.8g/24h。

（2）国内现状

增强尼龙材料、长玻璃纤维增强材料国内均有比较好的基础，其性能基本接近国外同类产品的先进水平，是完全可以替代的。四川大学[13]制备的 LGF－PP 拉伸强度达到 100MP 左右，冲击强度达到 10kJ/m^2左右。金发科技等生产的长玻纤增强材料同 SABIC 公司 LGF－PP 的性能差别也不大。

上海耀华大中新材料有限公司从德国迪芬巴赫引进国内第一条的整套长纤维增强热塑性塑料直接在线模压成型（LFT－D－CM）生产线，并成功为上海通用等配套。

但是，我国主要汽车公司均为合资公司，受国外公司的影响，面临着许多技术壁垒，例如大众汽车公司新车型开发时许多材料均为指定，这让我们失去了第一次介入的机会，给今后国产化带来了很大的难度。

2　发展趋势

2.1　汽车塑料制品

世界汽车塑料制品发展的主要方向是轻量化、环保化、个性化。随着“汽车塑料化”进程的不断加速，人们对于汽车节能、减排、降耗、环保、实用、美观的要求不断提高。

(1) 实现高性能和高功能化的同时，更注重环保性和可回收性

欧盟公布一系列针对汽车环保和可回收的法规要求，如国际报废车辆指令(ELV)、RoSH指令和REACH法规，其他国家也相继颁布类似法规。今后汽车公司的材料标准有望更加完善，从过去过分追求材料高强度、高韧性，逐渐转变为考察材料的综合性能。

(2)为保障和提高车内乘员人员和路上行人安全，发展吸能泡沫及蜂窝材料技术，并要求降低噪声、振动、冲击

随着汽车安全性的不断提高，轿车除不仅要满足碰撞时车内乘员安全外，还必须保障行人安全。因此，欧盟最新安全法规规定，今后在轿车的前保险杠系统中必须装载碰撞能量吸收系统，而塑料功能泡沫材料在能量吸收系统中起着关键作用。微孔发泡聚丙烯(图6)，集增强、隔热和降噪为一体，特别适用于汽车轻量化领域。

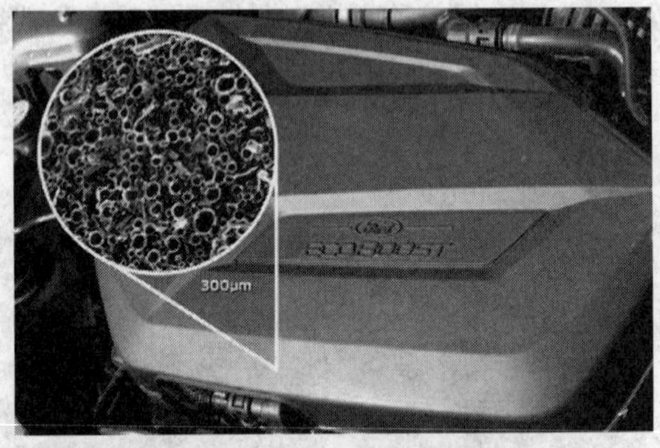

图6　微孔发泡聚丙烯用于发动机罩

(3)碳纤复合材料车身及部件技术

碳纤复合材料是目前车身轻量化效果最佳的材料，采用碳纤增强复合材料的车身重量仅172公斤，而采用钢制车身的重量为367.9kg，轻量化效果达53%以上。从实现轻量化效果方面来看，在车身部件中使用碳纤增强材料，至少可以达到降低20% ~30%或更高的减重目标。碳纤增强材料在未来环保车型的开发中，具有较强的竞争力。

(4)高阻渗性油箱技术

欧盟ECE规定的燃油渗透值≤20g/24h；美国加利福尼亚州又提出整个燃油系统的燃油损失不超过2g/24h的CARB法规，各国环保与安全要求的不断提高，对塑料燃油箱阻渗性能的要求越来越高，一些汽车制造商已经提出“零渗透”ZEV的目标，高阻渗性已成为当今汽车塑料燃油箱的发展趋势。

2.2　加工技术

汽车塑料由单一组成材料快速向复合材料方向发展，从而加快了实现汽车全塑化的步伐，促进了汽车塑料件成型加工新技术的开发。提高汽车塑化件的性能和功能是扩大塑化件应用于汽车的关键，成型加工技术的创新是提高塑化件性能和功能的重要手段。

(1)3D挤吹成型异型中空管[14]

3D挤吹异型管成型设备是适应成型形态复杂的异型中空管新发展的设备，是一种少废料或无飞边的挤出中空成型。汽车工业对形态复杂输送管件的需求增加，推动了3D挤吹异型中空管设备发展。德国SIG、瑞士ST公司主要提供3D挤吹成型异型中空管的生产设备。

3D异形燃油管向高阻隔性的多层共挤方向发展。意大利Fiat汽车公司用PA纳米复合材料作为燃油管阻隔材料替代原来的PVDF阻隔材料，多层燃油管包括PA12外层、PA6/PA12共聚物粘结层、含2%纳米粘土的PA6/PA66共聚物阻隔层、PA66内层，对汽油的阻隔性高三

倍，燃油管全都由 PA 材料组成，以便于回收。

(2)可熔型芯注射中空成型特种管材[16]

可熔型芯注射中空塑料成型，利用低熔点的金属作为注射模具的型芯来生产内外表面形状复杂并且要求光洁以及内部尺寸要求精确的中空塑料制品。

德国富吕登伯格公司汽车发动机罩下(即发动机室内)BMC 材料的进气歧管就是采用可熔型芯注射中空成型技术生产，其内表面十分光滑，有助于空气进入，使得发动机效率比用金属歧管高 15%，歧管重量减轻 1kg。

(3)低应力注射成型高性能制件

普通注塑件在高压下成型，内应力高，内应力在制件使用过程中释放，使制件变形，破坏原有的装配精度，缩短使用寿命。降低注塑件的内应力达到提高汽车安全系数。低内应力注射成型汽车塑化件，一直是当今人们热点研究的课题之一。可分为低内应力振动型注射成型、低内应力注射压缩成型、低内应力超高压注射成型 3 种，其中注射压缩成型特别适应壁厚 2mm 至 5mm 的大面积薄壁件的加工。

(4)高阻渗性油箱成型

美国 90% 以上的汽车油箱采用多层共挤出中空塑料成型件，多层油箱是 HDPE(白色)/(EVOH)/LLDPE/(EVOH)/回收料/HDPE(黑色)6 层共挤出中空成型，我国秦川塑料机械厂自主研发六层共挤中空成型机，最大可成型 200 升六层塑料汽车燃油箱(标准型)。

德国机械制造企业 Ctdnnon 公司成功开发出双片热成型法加工汽车塑料油箱，与吹塑(中空成型)法汽车塑料油箱相比，双片成型油箱由上下两片组成，在连接前可以在片材内侧附装其他部件，因而能生产吹塑法难以成型的复杂结构油箱。

LG 化学开发牌号 Hyperier 纳米复合材料成型纳米阻隔油箱，阻渗透性满足 CARB & EPA 的标准要求，其多达上千层的结构(图 7)具有优异的阻隔性能，适用于各种燃油容器，与含 EVOH 的 6 层共挤技术对比，设备投资较低。

图 7 Hyperier 纳米复合材料油箱截面结构

(5)汽车塑料玻璃成型

开发汽车塑料玻璃，首先要了解塑料原料通过何种技术处理能达到汽车塑料玻璃的性能要求。这包括，塑料车窗的表面硬化涂层处理技术、塑料车窗的模内薄膜层压技术、塑料车窗的共注射成型(共注射成型以 PC 为芯层、PMMA 为外层的三层结构的车窗，分三次注射成型)、塑料车窗的模内贴膜成型、如何生产汽车塑料车窗的低成本模具。

(6)结构件的在线配混玻纤复合材料的挤注一体成型

在汽车行业中，长玻纤增强树脂应用越来越广泛，例如仪表板和保险杠的支撑骨架、发动机和动力系统部件等。如何在注射成型加工中，充分发挥填充长玻纤增强的性能达到降低重量又提高制品的强度和刚度，成为新的注射成型的研发课题。在线配混复合材料的挤注复合塑化注射系统就是把常规的配混挤出造粒及制品的注射成形在两台设备上进行合为在同一设备上进行，可以解决这一问题。

最具代表性的是 Kraussmaffei 公司的挤注一体成型工艺设备(图 8)，采用侧喂料口加入连续长玻纤，双螺杆挤出机剪断纤维并混炼均匀后，熔体计量直接进入下端的柱塞机注射成型。我国东华机械有限公司与华南理工大学聚合物新型成型装备国家工程研究中心合作也生产了类似的设备。

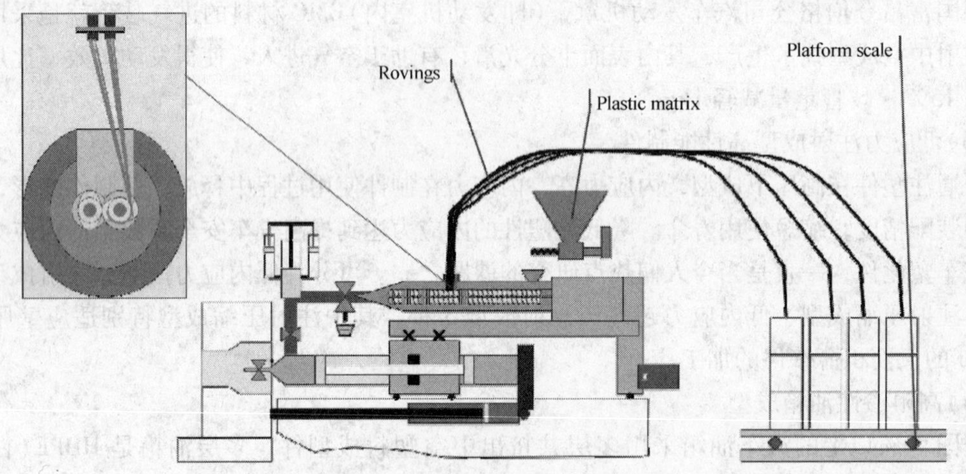

图 8　Kraussmaffei 公司在线配混玻纤复合材料的挤注一体成型工艺图

(7)特种功能件的微发泡注射成型

微发泡不同于反应发泡，主要采用物理介质，如超临界 CO_2，成核气泡为微泡沫。微发泡部件较轻、残余压力较少，尺寸精度和尺寸稳定性卓越，材料消耗较少、成型周期也较短。当采用纤维增强部件时，弯曲性较小。极宽温度范围内表现出极高的尺寸精度和尺寸稳定性。

日本马自达汽车公司开发超临界流体(SCF)发泡技术与核心反向扩展成型工艺相结合，可生产多层部件，并能更好地控制泡沫结构，改进塑料的热绝缘和声学性能。该技术可以使汽车轻量化，减少对树脂的消费量，其节约增产率高达 30%。

(8)无油漆模内薄膜装饰成型

无油漆模内薄膜装饰正在进入外观和结构零件领域，目前的趋势是将薄膜用于越来越大型的零件上。薄膜比油漆具有更好的耐候性和耐化学品性能，而且不会碎裂。

库尔兹公司(KURZ)[20]薄膜装饰材料，用于汽车复杂局部形状的装饰，还可以制作导电薄膜作为光学感应控制器，用于汽车仪表控制。

Woodbridge 集团开发出一种利用模内装饰膜生产表面具有高光泽度外装件的新工艺，该技术是在开模注入工艺的基础上发展起来的，因而具有压力机吨位小、工装成本低、工件完整性好、生产自动化程度高等优点[21]。

3　“3D 打印成型技术”加速变革汽车塑料制品及其加工技术

3D 打印使用加热喷嘴、激光束或电子束，将粉末状金属或塑料等可粘合材料融化成需要的形状，然后层层叠加来构造物件。

刚刚过去不久的 2012 年被称作 3D 打印年，这项有着 30 年历史的技术终于变得易用和大众化。但对于多数国人而言，3D 打印是一项带着“神迹”光环涌入的新事物。

3D 打印机普及程度最高的当属汽车、飞机、机械等研发领域，通常需要 2 ~ 3 周的试制品开发可以缩短到1~3天是其优势所在。Stratasys公司采用3D打印技术，为韩国现代汽车直接从3D设计图纸打印出汽车仪表板样件(图9)，3D打印已经应用到了发动机和内饰相关等各类部件的开发。

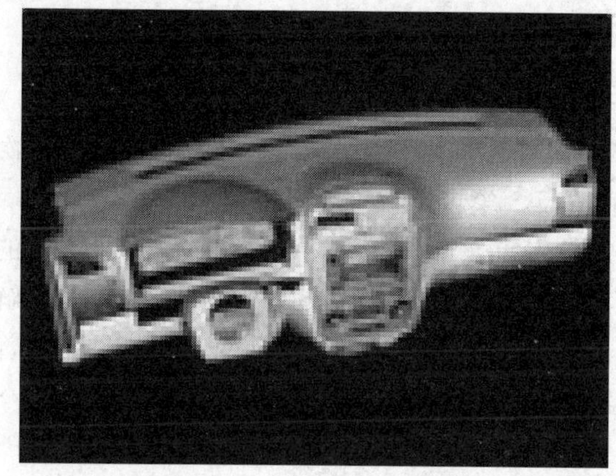

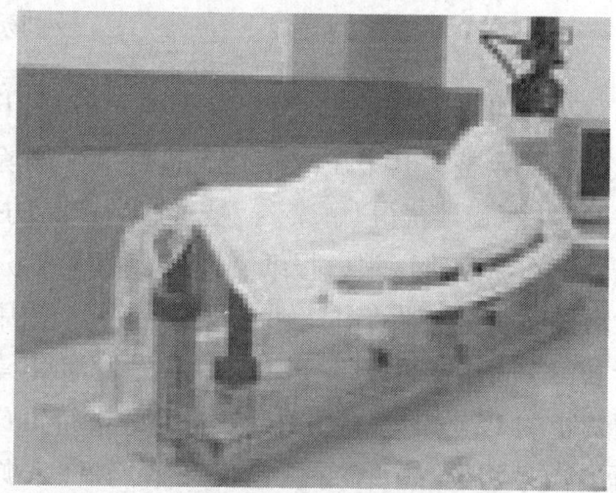

图9　汽车仪表板3D设计图及打印样品

2013年2月，世界首款3D打印汽车Urbee 2(图10)面世，它是一款混合动力汽车，绝大多数零部件来自3D打印。Urbee2依靠3D打印技术"打印"外壳和零部件，研究人员的主要工作包括组装和调试。3D打印机能"打印"出一体式的汽车车身，再将其他部件填充进去。

图10　世界首款3D打印汽车

目前3D打印技术在美国已经产业化，2011年3D打印市场规模17.1亿美元。由于3D技术可以大幅降低新产品推出的成本，减少工业模具开发的时间，因此对制造业类企业有强大的吸引力，美国有可能凭借这一技术重新吸引全球的企业家到美国投资，从而重夺制造大国的地位。

3D打印的革命意义不在于替代规模制造，而在于成就个性化的生产模式。和标准化的流水线制造相比，3D打印在一段时间内还不具备规模生产的经济性。但当这一技术将专业技术封闭的制造大门向普通个体打开时，你无法想象，它能激发出多少个性化的创意设计。而在网络交易平台和"云制造"的辅助下，这些创意转化为可以盈利的产品，或将以几何级数的速度增长。

4　结论

汽车塑料化是现代汽车科技的发展方向，可以减轻汽车重量，降低能耗，节能减排。目前汽车内饰件已经基本实现塑料化，正由内饰件向外饰件、车身、功能和结构件扩展。今后重点发展方向是开发功能和结构件，以及外饰件和车身用高性能树脂和纤维增强复合材料，并对材料可回收性和环保性高度关注，同时新成型技术不断发展出现。3D打印技术可以大幅降低新产品推出的成本，减少工业模具开发的时间，因此对汽车制造相关企业有强大的吸引力。

（作者为：中国塑料加工工业协会专家委员会、青岛中科吴泰新材料科技有限公司）

说说“禁用”和“解禁”发泡餐盒那些事

杨惠娣

2013年2月26日，国家发改委发布第21号令，对《产业结构调整指导目录(2011年本)》进行局部调整，其中在淘汰类产品目录中删除了一次性发泡塑料餐具。14年后的现在，一次性PS发泡餐具获得“解禁”，是对这一产品的公正平反，笔者举双手表示赞成！

一石激起千层浪，报纸、网络、博客，纷纷对此发表文章、言论、评论，传达出了丰富的社情民意。笔者收集了一些，列出如下：《中国化工报》2013/3/1的“PS发泡餐具14年后获解禁”；《新京报》2013/3/14的“一次性发泡餐具5月1日起解禁”；中国厨具网2013/3/1的“曾遭禁止的PS发泡塑料餐具14年后重获新生(来源：《中国化工报》)；广州化工城，2013/3/8的“‘白色污染’蜕变‘绿色包装’的启示”(来源：《中国化工报》)；甘肃化工门户的“一次性PS发泡餐具‘冷宫’14年，一朝解禁应深思”；新浪新闻中心2013/3/13的“解禁发泡餐具，主管部门要有准确说法”(来源：金羊网－羊城晚报，我有话说)；西安晚报2013/3/13的“解禁一次性发泡餐具不能不明不白”(网易新闻转载)；和讯评论2013/3/14的“魏英杰：解禁发泡餐具能否向公众说清楚”(来源：京华时报)；北京青年报2013/03/14的“发泡餐盒厂家欲跟风抢滩——‘发泡餐盒解禁令’引发市场‘暗流’涌动”(来源：YNET. com北青网)；北青网2013/3/13的“解禁一次性发泡餐具应有三个前提”；食品中国2013/3/14的“一次性发泡塑料餐具解禁，存在的问题及建议”；ChinaDaily国际频道2013/3/14的“一次性发泡塑料餐具解禁引争议，专家：回收体系极需建立”……

上面列出的一些标题说明公众对于“解禁”这件事有话说。公众的关注，是件好事情：众人的事众人议，一起来解决。因笔者经历了“禁白”和“解禁”的过程，所以，也来说说那些事。

“白色污染”是14年前“禁用”的唯一理由

1999年初，原国家经贸委颁布了《淘汰落后生产能力、工艺和产品的目录》(第一批)，将一次性PS发泡餐具作为落后产品列入目录，要求禁产、禁用，限期淘汰。人们将这一法规称为“6号令“，或更直白地称为“禁白令”。此后，在国家发改委发布的《产业结构调整指导目录》2005年版和2011年版中，一次性PS发泡餐具又两度被列入淘汰类产品。

从人们对其直白的“禁白令”的称呼，其实就透出了信息：一次性PS发泡餐具所以被禁的原因就是因它造成的“白色污染”。

6号令发布时，笔者担任一项社会工作是中国工程塑料学会降解塑料研究会秘书长，理事长是唐赛珍。当时，一次性PS发泡餐具作为一种新颖包装制品引进中国的时间还不太长，所以，笔者对于6号令将一次性PS发泡餐具列为“落后产品”而淘汰是十分地不理解、不认同的，为此，笔者与唐赛珍理事长一起走访了当时的国家经贸委，接待我们的某处长，不理会我们的解释，只是不容置疑地答复：列入目录的理由就是因为它引发的环境污染。

一次性PS发泡餐具引发环境视觉污染，铁路沿线的“小白龙”，现年40岁上下的中国坐过火车的人可能都知道。“发泡餐具最早于1986年开始在中国铁路上使用，由于废弃的塑料垃圾给铁路沿线生态以及景观造成了严重破坏，于是，铁道部于1991年开始研究治理铁路沿线“白色污染”的对策，并于1995年5月起全面禁止在铁路站车使用发泡餐具，代之以可降解餐具。”（西安晚报2013/3/13）这样，一次性PS发泡餐具首先在铁路部门被禁用了。但直接招致其灭顶之灾的是长江上漂浮的废发泡餐盒给葛洲坝的发机电组造成的故障。1998年，长江发生特大洪水，整整77天，抗洪大军上阵护堤，大量使用一次性PS发泡餐具，餐后，这些餐盒都扔到了长江，结果，沿着长江就漂到了葛洲坝……

所以，发泡餐盒被列入目录，被“禁用”是事出有因的，但是，禁用的理由是“白色污染”，背后也不排除行政命令的影子，而与落后产能无干。

当然，发泡塑料餐具造成白色污染的根源，是人，不是物。所以，6号令的唯一理由实在是站不住脚的。

禁而不止的原因何在

从上述“禁用”的理由看，6号令出台禁用发泡餐盒就存在先天不足，为以后禁而不止埋下了伏笔。但仅仅因为“禁用”理由的文不对题，还不是禁而不止存在的原因，还有一个更重要的原因在于，政府自己制订的政策发生了冲突！

当时，聚苯乙烯发泡餐盒这种工艺和产品完全是塑料行业从大陆以外引进的一种新工艺和新产品，引进主要从日本和我国台湾等国家和地区，引进方式有相当是采取合资形式，均有一定合法生产的合资期限。所以，“禁用”与合资合同存在冲突。由于这一原因，有些地区为兼顾两项政策冲突的实际情况，制订了地方的有条件继续生产的规定。

鉴于一些发泡餐盒生产企业均处于合资企业合法的合资期，或许，这就成为发泡餐盒“禁而不止”的一个重要而真实的原因。

明明白白解禁

网上不少意见对“解禁”不理解，说“被禁，容易理解；解禁，颇让人费解”、“一项明令淘汰多年的产品，为何得以重新入市？这真让人百思不得其解。”还有文章说：“政策举措的前后偏差过大，简直是‘冰火两重天’，这不能不让公众对这一解禁举措的科学性担忧。”还有人戏称：“禁白令是白禁了。”

对于“解禁”确实有必要让公众“明明白白”。

首先要解除大家疑虑的是PS发泡餐具的安全、卫生性。其实，这个问题本来是无需多说的明白事，但是，由于一些人的恶意中伤、混淆是非，个别媒体的无知传播，加之目前社会上存在的对政府诚信的怀疑，对公众的存疑不足为怪。请看北京青年报的一幅图：

图上，一名戴着防毒面具的男士和一名戴着大口罩的女士说："听说发泡餐盒又允许生产了。"形象地反映出了公众对PS发泡餐具安全和卫生性能的担忧。

当然，公众对PS发泡餐具的安全、卫生性能的关注是合乎情理的。在这里笔者可说的是，用于PS发泡餐具的材料，包括树脂PS和发泡剂，只要是按照国家标准生产的，均是无毒、无害，可与食品接触，且不会对环境产生危害的。关于这一问题有许多文章已经做了充分介绍，这里不再赘述。

再来看一下一次性PS发泡餐具的使用性能。

PS发泡餐具相比某些纸质餐具，不仅防水、隔油性好，而且与PP餐盒比，保温性和刚性好。PP餐盒刚性不足这一点，也是10多年前，火车上采用"可降解PP餐盒"替代PS发泡餐具，而最终被淘汰的原因之一。因为，送餐时，餐盒一个个摞在一起，有时要摞10多个，没有一定的刚性是不行的。发泡的PS餐具保温性好，而PP因为材料特性，在目前技术条件下不能制成发泡PP餐盒，所以，也就不可能具备PS发泡餐盒的保温性。PS发泡餐具也具有一定的耐热性，对于外卖和打包，PS餐盒的耐热性完全能满足要求，但是，比起PP餐盒，它不能进行微波加热，这大概是其唯一比不上PP餐盒的一个性能。

综上所述，PS发泡餐具的性能非常适合中餐包装。中餐的特点一是热，二是有汤水，三是有油，而对于这些合理使用条件下的要求，PS发泡餐具完全能很好满足。

再有，PS发泡餐具的环保性。PS发泡餐具生产过程清洁、能耗低、排放小，所以，符合节能减排的大方向，特别还体现在原料消费上，生产PP透明餐盒一个需要20多克原料，而发泡餐具只需4~5克，所以，PS发泡餐具符合节能减排、节约资源这一当前的方向，且价格便宜。从全生命周期看，PS发泡餐具可称得上是一种绿色环保材料产品。

废一次性聚苯乙烯发泡餐盒也是可以回收再生的。上海3分钱工程承担一次性PS发泡餐盒回收再生的中国昆山保绿塑料资源再生处理有限公司的例子可以说明，该公司采用熔融再生的方法，利用一次性废聚苯乙烯发泡餐盒为原料，制造再生废聚苯乙烯粒料，综合开发了各种应用。另一个例子是北京保绿环保塑料处理有限公司，是国内第一家发泡塑料餐具再利用工厂，产品是黏合剂。公司自1997年9月开始营运，到2001年北京市发泡餐盒的回收率就达到64%，超过既定的60%目标。北京市区"白色污染"问题明显减轻。

遗憾的是这两个企业据说均已经停止运转，原因是政策上的。但是，例子足以说明一次性PS发泡餐盒可以回收再生，关键是政策、管理。

最后说说PS发泡餐具的正确使用。

任何一个产品均有它的使用条件，而产品性能也是满足使用条件下的使用性能。换言之产品使用性能要满足使用条件，能满足使用条件就是合格产品，制订标准也是依据这个原则。而最近中央电视台有个关于不同餐盒优劣比较的节目，貌似进行科学介绍，实际有偷换概念之嫌，因为，试验都脱离了使用条件，有些采用了极端条件。不过，这些试验倒也提醒了产品不应在哪些极端条件下使用。

PS发泡餐具不能放到微波炉中使用，也不要用于蒸煮。PS发泡餐具因是发泡的，蒸煮会导致泡孔塌陷。其实，所有塑料容器等都不能像瓷碗一样放到蒸锅里去蒸。总之，尽管发泡餐具最适合中餐包装，但是，也需要正确使用。

另外，发泡餐具在日本、欧美等很多国家都在生产使用。

经过长达14年的禁用，期间不同观点长期博弈，已然充分曝露在阳光下，公众自会作出正确判断，PS发泡餐具可以明明白白“解禁”，“禁白”不“白禁”。

解禁的得益者

一次性PS发泡餐盒的解禁是否有得益者？回答应该是肯定的，确实有“得益者”。首先，节能减排、节约资源，对国家有好处；对生产餐盒企业，如果原来就生产一次性PS发泡餐盒，“解禁”是解除了“紧箍咒”，而对于生产一次性PP餐盒的企业也不必担心“影响”，它有可直接进微波炉的优势；方便面的纸质包装在南方地区，如遇到连日阴雨易返潮霉变，所以，如能使用PS发泡包装，可以解决这一问题，所以，解禁对于方便面生产企业无疑是一个福音。当然，普通消费者有一种性价比高的餐盒使用，也可算作得益者。

综上所述，解禁一次性PS发泡餐盒从得益者看是多赢的结果，值得欢迎。

清清白白回归

报纸网络上，对于解禁存在不少疑虑，或者质疑。

“一次性发泡餐具被称作“白色污染”，14年来一直禁产禁用且多次查处，但今年2月国家发改委的一纸“21号令”，却将它突然解禁。”；“‘21号令’未对删除发泡餐具的原因给出解释”，“公众疑虑重重”；“在长达14年的‘禁止’时间内，在并没有一个可以预知和令公众打消安全担忧的情况下，从‘禁止’到一夜间的‘解禁’，这样的决策本身也充满了诸多令人质疑的因素。”(西安晚报2013/3/13)

事实上，由于禁用理由说服力不强，从6号令公布至今，一些企业、专家、协会向决策部门反映，要求将一次性PS发泡餐具从《目录》中删除的意见的努力从来没有停止过。而发改委也早就在着手解禁事宜，“其实早在2011年5月，国家发改委官网针对一次性发泡餐具就曾提出，最初出台禁止一次性发泡餐具使用的环境已发生较大变化。因此在保护环境和加强回收再利用的原则下，制定一次性发泡塑料餐具的准入条件，建立和制定回收再利用的机制及相关标准等。上述工作完成后，择机将其从淘汰类目录中删除。这实际上就为此次解禁铺了路。”

另外，一些媒体也说：“资料显示，在过去十几年里，中国环境科学学会绿色包装分会和中塑协为了给一次性发泡餐具“正名”，做了大量市场调查，并多次向有关部门汇报情况”。(西安晚报2013/3/13)

综上所述，说明解禁的工作一直未间断，过程中各方还做了大量市场调查，同时国家发改委官网也有相应的网络信息披露，不是一夜之间出现的决策转变。“解禁”是清白的。

走好“解禁”后的路

“一次性PS发泡餐具终于摘掉白色污染的帽子，重新回归市场，这让业内企业欢欣鼓舞……在敞开的市场大门里，当需要我们揿下‘下一步’的按钮时，挑战依然严峻，要完成的新功课并不轻松。”“发泡餐具目前缺乏产品标准、质量安全市场准入条件以及成熟完备的回收机制”。

解禁确实面临一系列问题。首当其冲的是产品标准，其实，标准是有的。目前，2009年4月17日发布、2009年12月1日实施的GB 18006.1—2009《塑料一次性餐饮具通用技术要求》可以适用。GB 18006.1—2009《塑料一次性餐饮具通用技术要求》是代替GB 18006.1—1999《一次性可降解餐饮具通用技术条件》的新标准，标准规定了塑料一次性餐饮具定义和术语、分类、技术要求、检验方法、检验规则及产品标志、包装、运输、贮存要求。但该标准覆盖面较宽，包括了除纸之外所有种类餐盒，可考虑在现有标准基础上制订PS发泡餐盒的专用标准。据说，国家质检总局食品生产监管司也有考虑(新京报2013/3/14)。

再有，在标准基础上组织生产时，企业要严把产品质量关，保证产品的卫生安全性，坚决打击采用废旧塑料作原料生产餐盒，坚决打击荧光增白剂等添加剂的使用，行业要自律，协会要管好。

另外，一些人担心，解禁后又会造成白色污染，这种担心是多余的。因为，当前的整个环境已经与14年前发生了极大的变化。以铁路两旁小白龙的消失原因，可以知道：最后解决铁路沿线污染的是袋装垃圾和全封闭车厢等措施。所以，正如造成白色污染的是人，是管理；解决并保证不形成白色污染的同样是人，是管理。正因为如此，相关的管理部门应尽快建立和完善一次性PS发泡餐具的回收和再利用的体系，形成一条包括树脂供应、餐盒生产、消费、回收、再生利用的完整的产业链。上海3分钱的经验仍旧可以借鉴。塑料回收再生技术已经很成熟，比起技术问题，更关键的是按照“谁污染谁负责”原则建立起整个体系，才能保证可持续发展。这里应该指出的是，这里的“谁”包括树脂生产企业、餐盒生产企业、餐盒销售企业以及消费者等。

最后，进行宣传，教育消费者彻底摒弃随手丢弃垃圾的恶习，为保护身边环境贡献一份力量。

因为，毕竟禁用了14年，为更好回归，建议成立一次性PS发泡餐盒专委会，痛定思痛，为保证行业健康发展，一定要在可持续发展的框架下统筹整个行业的重建工作。

小餐盒，大民生；禁用有因，解禁必然，“禁白”不“白禁”，认识得提高；保证质量，做好回收，建立系统，持续发展！

(作者为中国塑料加工工业协会塑料技术协作委员会秘书长)

大　事　记

2012年塑料行业大事记

【1月】

2012年中央一号文件公布把农业科技摆上更加突出位置

中共中央、国务院印发了《关于加快推进农业科技创新持续增强农产品供给保障能力的若干意见》。全文共分六个部分23条，包括：加大投入强度和工作力度，持续推动农业稳定发展；依靠科技创新驱动，引领支撑现代农业建设；提升农业技术推广能力，大力发展农业社会化服务；加强教育科技培训，全面造就新型农业农村人才队伍；改善设施装备条件，不断夯实农业发展物质基础；提高市场流通效率，切实保障农产品稳定均衡供给。持续加大财政用于“三农”的支出，持续加人国家固定资产投资对农业农村的投入，持续加大农业科技投入，确保增量和比例均有提高。发挥政府在农业科技投入中的主导作用，保证财政农业科技投入增幅明显高于财政经常性收入增幅，逐步提高农业研发投入占农业增加值的比重，建立投入稳定增长的长效机制。大力推进现代农业产业技术体系建设，完善以产业需求为导向、以农产品为单元、以产业链为主线、以综合试验站为基点的新型农业科技资源组合模式，及时发现和解决生产中的技术难题，充分发挥技术创新、试验示范、辐射带动的积极作用。

2012年起中国对东盟五国聚氯乙烯实施零关税

2012年是中国—东盟自贸区成立的第三年，从2012年1月1日起，我国开始对来自泰国、马来西亚、缅甸，文莱和新加坡五国的聚氯乙烯进口关税由原有的5%降为0%。此次关税调整将不会对我国聚氯乙烯市场造成明显影响。

一方面，这五个国家历年来出口到中国的聚氯乙烯数量十分有限。2011年泰国出口到中国的聚氯乙烯纯粉总量为34kt，马来西亚为5.7kt，新加坡、缅甸、文莱共计0.03kt。相比2011年我国聚氯乙烯纯粉进口量1051kt可以说数量很少。另一方面，与国内大部分企业采用电石法制聚氯乙烯的技术工艺不同，东南亚各国普遍采用乙烯法工艺。由于近期国际原油期货价格一直处于高位动荡期，这也使得乙烯法聚氯乙烯生产企业承受着较大的成本压力。另外，目前伊朗与西方国家的紧张局势也在一定程度上起到了支撑原油价格的作用。随着我国与东盟合作的进一步深入，中国－东盟自贸区也将为双边氯碱产品贸易带来更多的机遇与挑战。

生物可降解塑料地膜“试水”云南

2012年1月18日，云南省曲靖市政府、云南(曲靖)国际农业食品科技园与世界种业巨头法国利马格兰集团在昆明签署战略合作协议，双方将就生物技术开展战略合作。目前，利马格兰生产的生物可降解塑料地膜已在云南省进行规模实验推广，此举将有效解决传统农用地膜的白色污染问题。

通过两年多时间稳步推广、逐渐扩大的实验，利马格兰研发符合云南地理、气候和土壤条件，适合玉米、烤烟、蔬菜等农作物生长特性的生物可降解塑料地膜。目前，云南省通过政府主导，免费提供给全省16个州市的农民使用，示范地膜覆盖面积达到4万多亩。

利马格兰自主研发的可广泛用于地膜等农业生产中的生物可降解塑料，原料来自全谷物以及利马格兰特有的玉米品种，是植物遗传工程与塑料加工工艺的结合，地膜在田里铺上3个月后，通过土壤微生物分解，转化成肥沃的腐殖土，实现了废物的再利用，而且不产生对环境有明显毒害作用的残留，以到达保护土壤不受污染的效果。该产品已通过欧盟OK Compost和德国Kompostierbar认证，符合EN13432标准要求。在中国，利马格兰已经与云南曲靖国际农业食品科技园合作了3年，未来计划在曲靖市建立一个专门生产生物可降解塑料的工厂。

【2月】

钛白粉行业国家地方联合实验室成立

2012年2月22日，以四川龙蟒集团钛业公司为依托组建的钛白粉清洁生产国家地方联合实验室获国家发改委授牌。

该实验室将通过建立钛白粉的清洁生产技术与应用技术开发平台，突破制约钛白粉行业发展的技术瓶颈，不断开发应用领域广、具有市场竞争力的通用型产品和高附加值的专用型产品，提高硫资源循环利用率，降低钛白粉废副处理成本，缩短产品研发到生产转化的时间，进一步提高钛白粉的生产效率。

龙蟒钛业公司曾先后参与了国家发改委“十二五”钒钛资源综合利用产业基地规划的编制，《二氧化碳颜料国家标准》、《饲料级硫酸亚铁化工行业标准》的起草，完成了国家重大产业技术开发专项项目1项、国家火炬计划项目1项、国家工业节能奖励资金项目1项、四川省重大产业技术开发项目2项，成功开发钛白粉清洁生产核心技术15项。

塑料管道产品行业指导价格公布

2012年2月23日，中国塑协塑料管道专业委员会公布塑料管道产品行业指导价格公布，2012年第

1 号：

一、给水用硬聚氯乙烯(PVC－U)管材(非铅盐稳定剂)

1. 产品标准：GB/T 10002.1—2006 给水用硬聚氯乙烯(PVC－U)管材。

2. 行业指导价格(出厂价)：11100 元/t(PVC 树脂参考价按 6700 元/t 计)。

二、排水用 PVC－U 管材

1. 产品标准：GB/T 5836.1—2006 建筑排水用硬聚氯乙烯管材。

GB/T 20221—2006 无压埋地排污、排水用硬聚氯乙烯(PVC－U)管材。

2. 行业指导价格(出厂价)：10100 元/t(PVC 树脂参考价按 6700 元/t 计)。

三、埋地排水用 PVC－U 双壁波纹管材

1. 产品标准：GB/T 18477.1—2007 埋地排水用硬聚氯乙烯(PVC－U)结构壁管道系统 第 1 部分：双壁波纹管材。

2. 行业指导价格(出厂价)：10800 元/t(PVC 树脂参考价按 6700 元/t 计)。

四、燃气用埋地聚乙烯(PE)管材

1. 产品标准：GB 15558.1—2003 燃气用埋地聚乙烯(PE)管道系统 第一部分 管材。

2. 行业指导价格(出厂价)：18000 元/t(PE 原材料参考价按 13300 元/t 计)。

五、给水用 PE 管材

1. 产品标准：GB/T 13663—2000 给水用聚乙烯(PE)管材。

2. 行业指导价格(出厂价)：17300 元/t(PE 原材料参考价按 12600 元/t 计)。

六、埋地排水用 PE 双壁波纹管材

1. 产品标准：GB/T 19472.1—2004 埋地用聚乙烯(PE)结构壁管道系统 第一部分 聚乙烯双壁波纹管材。

2. 行业指导价格(出厂价)：16300 元/t(PE 原材料参考价按 11600 元/t 计)。

七、PE 缠绕结构壁管材：

1. 产品标准：GB/T 19472.2—2004 埋地用聚乙烯(PE)结构壁管道系统 第二部分 聚乙烯缠绕结构壁管材及相关标准。

2. 行业指导价格(包括现场施工安装指导费用的出厂价)：17300 元/t(PE 原材料参考价按 11600 元/t 计)。

【3 月】

2012 年技术工作会议召开

2012 年 3 月 2 日，中国塑协塑料管道专业委员“2012 年技术工作会议”在北京召开。中国塑协常务副理事长曹俭、专家委员会秘书长王德禧、住建部科技发展促进中心高立新处长等相关单位领导、专家以及塑料管道企业代表 20 多人参加了会议。

会议讨论了《塑料管道行业“十二五”期间(2011～2015)发展建议(征求意见稿)》，听取了秘书处制定《“燃气用 PE 管道质量保障联盟”实施方案(讨论稿)》以及专委会 2012 年工作计划中有关技术交流方面的工作安排等方面汇报。“十二五”期间行业应以 PVC－U 管道和 PE 管道为发展重点，关注聚氯乙烯产能大、价格优势等特点，并大力发展改性、复合以及其他新型塑料管道，尽快完善应用的配套技术和质量保证体系。同时还应进一步加大产品创新力度，适应市场需求，重点开发、生产新材料类塑料管道、改性与复合类塑料管道、环境友好型塑料管道、新型塑料管道系统。《塑料管道行业“十二五”期间(2011～2015)发展建议》中要完善发展措施建议。

参会的一些代表对塑料管道产品标准化工作表示关注，提出要尽快完善标准体系，还应逐步建立行业的质量认证及质量承诺制度。筹备建立“燃气用 PE 管道质量保障联盟”的发展思路得到参会代表的支持，行业应用类似的方式提高行业整体水平。

首届水性生态合成革制造工程技术培训班举办

2012 年 3 月 7 日，由丽水市经济开发区管委会，中国合成革用水性树脂及水性生态合成革研发中心联合举办的“首届水性生态合成革制造工程技术培训班”在丽水开班。丽水市经济开发区管委会侯副主任作了重要讲话，丽水市多家合成革企业的技术总工，生产主管及研发中心全体人员计 100 多人参加培训。

本次培训班采取了理论学习和组织现场参观相结合的培训教学方法。由中国合成革用水性树脂及水性生态合成革研发中心常务副主任谢镇铭先生作了水性生态合成革制造基本知识的讲解，着重介绍了生态合成革的概念，水性生态合成革制造基本原材料、设备的选用以及水性贝斯的发展。随后，由“中心”所属水性生态合成革研发办主任王峰讲解了水性生态合成革工艺技术和水性生态合成革制造中常见的问题，最后由水性生态合成革研发中心孙涛介绍了水性生态合成革实验室的建设要求及进行了水性电脑配色仪介绍。还组织观看了多款用丽水市优耐克水性树脂科技有限公司的水性树脂制作的生态合成革样品。全体学员还去优耐克武义生态合成革专用生产线进行了生产现场的参观。

丽水经济开发区管委会，中国合成革水性树脂及水性生态合成革研发中心办班负责人还分别给参加本次培训班的全体学员颁发了培训结业证书。

2012锂电池、隔膜产业链市场与技术发展研讨会召开

2012年3月15日，由中国塑协双向拉伸聚丙烯薄膜专委会和中国化学与物理电源行业协会联合举办的“2012锂电池、隔膜产业链市场与技术发展研讨会”在北京召开。来自锂离子电池隔膜产业链的250多名企业负责人出席会议。

中国化学与物理电源行业协会秘书长刘彦龙，天津力神电池股份有限公司副总工程师苏金然，日本富士机械工业株式会社常务取缔役富永保昌等专家分别作了“国内外锂电池产业发展分析”、“锂离子电池不同应用对隔膜的要求”、“隔膜涂布用高精度涂布设备介绍”、“关于锂电隔膜材料发展需求与思考”、“锂离子电池隔膜在线厚度检测及控制技术”、“电池隔离薄膜专用挤出模头系统”、“制辊技术与电池隔膜工艺的优化”、“隔膜表面缺陷检查设备介绍”、“领航科技锂电池隔膜项日进展情况介绍”、“动力与储能锂电池负极材料”、“锂离子电池隔膜的制备技术进展”、“车用锂离子电池的应用与安全性”、“伊斯拉公司瑕疵检测系统在锂电隔膜行业的应用”、“锂电池正极材料发展现状及新型材料研究进展”、“扫描电镜在锂离子电池行业的应用”的精彩发言，受到与会代表的一致好评。

锦州钛业“氯化法钛白粉CR－501＋“项目获省级科技进步三等奖

2012年3月22日，锦州钛业“氯化法钛白粉CR－501＋”项目近日获得省级科技进步三等奖。该项目针对产品无机表面处理理论进行研究，选择和确定分散剂的种类、加入量等工艺条件，通过试验产品质量指标、应用性能指标的分析和检测，进一步优化包膜生产工艺。并通过生产线进行扩大试验，完善了关键生产工艺控制条件。产品的实物质量和分散性、遮盖力等应用性能都获得了显著提升，满足了客户对高档钛白产品的需求。

中国塑协塑料管道专业委员会第八届六次理事会召开

2012年3月23日，中国塑协塑料管道专业委员会第八届六次理事会议在南京召开。

中国塑协常务副理事长曹俭、中国塑协塑料管道专业委员会理事长陈力辉及专委会50家理事单位的59名代表参加会议。

中国塑协常务副理事长曹俭在会上对塑料加工行业现状作了客观的分析，并对行业发展提出希望。

中国塑协塑料管道专委会理事长陈力辉对2011年的行业工作作了总结汇报。

中国塑协塑料管道专委会秘书长王占杰做了专委会2012年工作计划汇报，并经理事会审议通过。还对专委会2012拟安排的一些活动进行了专题汇报。

通过审议，理事会表决通过，同意惠升管业有限公司、四川泰鑫实业发展有限责任公司成为中国塑协塑料管道专委会新的理事单位，同意北京拓普天品科技有限公司等54家成为中国塑协塑料管道专委会新的正式会员单位。

理事会议就《中国塑料管道行业“十二五”期间（2011～2015）发展建议》再次征求了会议代表的意见，通过讨论、交流，会议原则通过了该建议，在经过征求意见完善后，2012年年会予以发布。

理事会议讨论通过了中国塑协塑料管道专委会2012年年会策划方案。

理事会议还重点讨论了塑料管道行业产品质量参差不齐的问题，一些会议代表提出应加强企业自律，建立行业诚信体系，并通过相应途径加大产品质量监管，以减少低价竞标、恶性竞争等不良现象。

多数会议代表关注标准化进展情况，提出希望专委会加强塑料管道标准化工作，同时组织企业更多的参与塑料管道的国家、行业标准和规程的制定工作。

会议展开了《燃气用PE塑料管道质量保障联盟实施方案》的讨论。部分参会代表发言认为成立联盟等方式将会推动塑料管道行业，尤其是燃气用PE管道的健康发展，建议具体的实施方案应进一步细化。

会议组织代表参观了南京协和化学有限公司。

【4月】

中国塑协组团赴美参加2012年NPE展会及交流活动

2012年4月初，中国塑协组团赴美交流考察。团长由中国塑协常务副理事长曹俭担任，副团长由中国贸易促进委员会轻工行业分会副会长王本和担任。

代表团一行参观了2012年美国国际塑料及模具技术展览会(NPE 2012)，与美国塑料工业协会(SPI)进行了交流，共同签署了合作备忘录。考察期间，代表团还与美国塑料工程师协会(SPE)进行了交流。

NPE 2012于4月1～7日在美国佛罗里达州奥兰多市举办。代表团重点参观了国内企业的展览。通过参观、交流，使大家了解了更多的国际塑料行业现状与相关技术进展等信息。

4月2日，中国塑协与美国塑料工业协会(SPI)进行交流。国际贸易部主任MICHAEL TAYLOR代表SPI对中国塑协交流考察团前来美国参加NPE2012表示十分感谢。SPI还希望两协会在技术交流、信息交换、节能环保等方面积极有更好的合作。

中国塑协常务副理事长曹俭希望通过参加 NPE 2012 等活动，中美两国塑料行业能够进一步加强交流与合作。考察团成员还就原材料、塑料制品等方面技术、信息与美方展开了交流。

4 月 2 日下午，曹俭常务副理事长和美国塑料工业协会总裁兼首席执行官 WILLIAM R. CARTEAUX 先生分别代表中美双方共同签署了《中国塑协与美国塑料工业协会合作备忘录》。根据协议，中美两塑料行业协会将进一步促进和加强双方在技术以及贸易等领域的广泛合作。

代表团还与美国塑料工程师协会(SPE)进行了交流。SPE 首席执行官 WILLEM DE VOS 先生介绍了 SPE 的情况，曹俭常务副理事长表示，双方可以在技术交流等方面展开进一步的合作。

通过对 NPE 2012 的参观、考察、交流，代表团加深了国际塑料行业的先进生产技术、新产品的开发和应用等方面的了解，从中也看到了中国塑料加工行业与世界先进水平的差距，深刻认识到国内塑料加工企业必须提高科技水平。对于中国企业参加国外的塑料专业展览，目前主要还是以单打独斗的小团体展位为主，规模偏小、位置偏僻，展台布置、标示等方面还有待提高，还应加强工作，展示出中国塑料工业的蓬勃发展，积极进取的团体形象。还要积极发挥行业协会的作用，共同促进塑料行业的持续、稳定、健康发展。

2012 年全国电缆料配方设计及生产工艺学习研讨班举办

2012 年 4 月 11 ~ 13 日，2012 全国电缆料配方设计及生产工艺学习研讨班在杭州举办。

获国务院津贴高级工程师、上海胜华电缆集团高级技术顾问旷天申、青岛科技大学高分子科学与工程学院博士后高光涛、北京化工大学材料科学与工程学院教授苑会林、中国石化齐鲁分公司研究院高工李静、常熟市中联光电新材料有限责任公司高工张尔梅、国家质检总局 REACH 工作组组长、国务院特殊津贴获得者李聪研究员等专家授课。主要研讨内容有：(1)中国阻燃电缆技术发展概况及国外电缆料的技术进展；(2)用于电线、电缆生产的 PVC、PE、PP 等材料的性能；(3)用于电线、电缆料生产的稳定剂、润滑剂、增塑剂、抗氧剂、发泡剂和交联剂的作用原理及应用；(4)电线、电缆料的阻燃和无卤阻燃；(5)电线、电缆的着色技术；(6)电缆料的填充改性；(7)环保型助剂(钙锌、稀土稳定剂等)在电缆料中的应用；(8)电力电缆材料新技术；(9)电缆材料性能测试方法及标准；(10)橡胶电线电缆绝缘胶料、护套胶料的配方设计原理及方法；(11)橡胶电缆的生产工艺流程及参数；(12)电缆行业国际环保法规最新动态及有毒有害物质测试；(13)主要典型产品配方设计；(14)温水硅烷交联的聚乙烯电缆料(二步法)(低、中压交联电缆、控制电缆、汽车电线)；(15)硅烷自然交联的聚乙烯电缆料(一步法)(低、中压交联电缆、控制电缆、汽车电线)；(16)90℃、105℃、125℃、150℃化学交联阻燃聚烯烃电缆料(仪器、仪表、设备绝缘电线电缆)；(17)各种 PVC 辐照交联用线缆的绝缘，护层料(用于辐照交联要求耐高温场所的 PVC 线缆等)。考核合格者，由中国塑协颁发证书。

塑料混炼先进技术和设备应用研讨会召开

2012 年 4 月 15 日，中国塑料工业协会塑料技术协作委员会在上海召开了“塑料混炼先进技术和设备应用研讨会”。该领域各方专业人士 40 人参加了会议。

会议组织的主题发言有：浙江舟山通发塑料机械有限公司吴汉民董事长的“锥双同向双螺杆挤出机的开发和应用技术”、科倍隆(南京)机械有限公司位永喜代表沈君技术总监的“同向混炼双螺杆挤出机的技术进展”、上海心尔新材料有限公司王梓刚董事长的“配混料生产厂应如何选用不同的混炼设备”、南京科亚化工成套装备有限公司潘志荣工程总监的“国内同向双螺杆技术新进展”、南京科亚化工成套装备有限公司潘志荣工程总监代王秀娟的“往复式混炼机市场和技术进展”、石家庄德倍隆公司郭彦力总工代表崔鹏总经理的“三螺杆混炼设备应用特点与优势”、华东理工大学化工机械研究所谢林生教授的“双转子连续混炼造粒系统的开发及应用”、鲁谷科技(北京)有限公司张红中总经理的“变频感应加热在混炼造粒机上的应用进展”，以及北京理工大学化工与环境学院陈晋南教授的“计算机模拟技术在塑料螺杆混炼中的应用”等共 9 项内容。会议邀请了塑料混炼设备和应用方面的资深专家北京化工大学耿孝正教授、塑料技术协作委员会专家丁常楷高工等进行点评，主题发言者和参会人士进行了互动研讨，交流充分而深入，得到全体与会代表的热烈欢迎。

通过短短一天的会议：使代表对各种类型混炼设备有了进一步的认识，特别对于近年开发成功的具有我国自主知识产权并产业化的锥形同向双螺杆挤出机从不知到知之，了解了其特点，对于三螺杆挤出机、连续混炼机等混炼设备也有进一步新的认识。变频电磁感应加热器是近年发展起来的节能设备，但不少代表对其应用心存疑虑，通过介绍和互动讨论，澄清了一些模糊概念，提高了认识。北京理工大学化工与环境学院陈晋南教授的“计算机模拟技术在塑料螺杆混炼中的应用”的介绍，深入浅出、联系实际，使企业了解到其并不是高深莫测的理论，而是一项具有解决实际问题功能的应用技术，一些企业当场表示了要开展合作的意向。

2012 功能性薄膜行业市场与技术发展研讨会召开

2012 年 4 月 16 日，由中国塑协主办，中国塑协双向拉伸聚丙烯薄膜专委会、中国塑协流延薄膜专委会共同承办的“2012 功能性薄膜行业市场与技术发展研讨会”在上海召开，来自全国薄膜产业链的 320 多名企业负责人出席会议。

中国塑协双向拉伸聚丙烯薄膜专委会理事长吴耀根和双向拉伸聚酯薄膜专委会理事长徐志强致欢迎辞。中国轻工业联合会副会长、中国塑协理事长钱桂敬致开幕辞。

广东德冠薄膜新材料股份有限公司副总裁朱健民，上海永超真空镀铝有限公司总经理江谷，德国布鲁克纳机械股份有限公司高级区域销售经理普立乐，德国莱芬豪舍挤出技术公司亚洲区销售经理 Philip Neumann，德国莱芬豪舍－凯孚尔挤出技术公司 Bernd Schroeter 分别作了“独特的经营战略与企业文化，引领德冠成为功能性薄膜新材料领跑者”、“功能型镀铝膜市场与加工技术介绍”、“ 为成长中的功能性薄膜市场所提供的先进方案”、“ 多层共挤流延薄膜生产线的新进展”和“阻隔吹塑薄膜技术的最新进展”的发言。中国塑协降解塑料专业委员会秘书长翁云宣、南通新诚电容膜有限公司副总经理佘建忠、广州思肯德电子测量设备有限公司总经理王广彪、北京化工大学教授苑会林、福斯特光伏材料公司技术总监周光大、天津大学化工学院教授李保安、四川东材科技集团股份有限公司技术开发部部长罗春明、上海瀚艺集团营销总监助理张肖菲、远东宏信有限公司包装业务部中区总监戴璟、美国微觉视检测技术公司销售经理朱模军、分别作了“降解塑料现状及趋势”、“ 包装膜生产线改造电容薄膜生产线的实践”、“ 薄膜厚度在线监测及控制技术”、“功能塑料薄膜在清洁能源电池中的应用”、“ 光伏组件用 EVA 封装薄膜介绍”、“ 中国先进膜技术的发展概况”、“ 晶硅太阳能电池背板材料研究”、“ 瀚艺节能冷水系统解决方案”、“ 功能性薄膜行业投融资解决方案”和“ 视觉检测技术在功能性薄膜行业的应用”的精彩报告。

中国塑协六届二次理事会会议召开

2012 年 4 月 17 日，中国塑协六届二次理事会在上海召开。出席会议的有中国轻工业联合会副会长、中国塑协理事长钱桂敬，常务副理事长曹俭，名誉理事长廖正品以及其他六届理事会的副理事长、常务理事、理事、特聘理事及其有关理事单位的代表等。参加会议的共有 181 名代表。会议由副理事长刘景芬同志主持。

一、审议通过了《中国塑协六届二次理事会工作报告》。

会议首先听取了曹俭常务副理事长作《中国塑协六届二次理事会工作报告》。报告从制定和完善塑料加工业“十二五”发展规划指导意见，积极争取有利于行业发展的政策、布置协会评估工作，力争 2013 年达到 5A 级目标、加强行业调研，做好经济运行分析工作、积极开展行业活动，加强技术交流合作等四个方面对 2011 年工作进行了回顾，对五届理事会换届后着重做的几件大事进行了总结。协会自六届一次理事会后重点抓了：《塑料加工业“十二五”发展规划指导意见》制定，并召开了多次会议进行了修改和完善；建立健全协会规章、调整协会组织架构、召开分支机构秘书长工作会议，强化协会规范运作、提升服务能力和水平；筹备组织协会参加民政部 2013 年评估工作，力争达到 5A 级目标；做好行业产业调研工作，研究产业发展趋势加强行业信息平台建设，提升说清行业能力，做好经济运行分析工作；积极开展行业活动，加强技术交流；开展国际交流合作，密切国际同行联系，提升协会影响和凝聚力。会议明确了中国塑协 2012 年工作要点：1、认真学习贯彻中共中央十七届六中全会精神和中央经济工作会议精神，突出把握好稳中求进的工作总基调。2、按照塑料加工业“十二五”发展规划指导意见，行序渐进地做好各项工作。3、加强国际技术交流合作，积极组织塑料行业企业之间技术交流，扩大中国塑协在国际塑料行业影响力。4、加强举办展览会、博览会的工作。5、加强协会内部管理，增强服务能力，坚定信心做好行业协会评估准备工作，为争创 5A 及行业协会评估做好各项准备工作。6、加强协会秘书处日常工作，各职能部门和各专业委员会要有计划地安排各项工作，7、抓好标委会换届工作。8、抓好职工教育和培训工作。9、组织抓好行业企业信用等级评价工作。

二、审议通过了《塑料加工业“十二五”发展规划指导意见（征求意见稿）》及其编制说明。

会议听取了钱桂敬理事长对编制《塑料加工业“十二五”发展规划指导意见（征求意见稿）》进行了详细的介绍和说明。他介绍《规划》的编制首先总体思路是突出依靠科技创新，大力推进技术进步，推动产业升级，着力构建现代产业体系；突出结构调整，加快转变发展方式，优化产品结构、区域布局和企业组织结构；突出绿色、环保，着力实现循环和可持续发展；突出品牌战略，着力提高产业素质；突出平稳较快增长，为结构调整技术改造创造条件，着力推进由单纯依靠扩能发展向注重技术进步、结构优化、提高发展质量方向转变。其次规划明确了塑料加工业在国民经济中的定位是以塑料制品加工为核心涵盖原料、机械、模具、助剂为一体的新兴制造业，是为工业、农业、建筑、交通、运输、航空航天等国民经济各行各业提供重要配件和特种材料的国民经济基础性产业，也是为广大消费者提供安全可靠消费品的民生产业。是人类必须的生产资料和生活资料，是国民经济新的支柱产业之一。第三《规划》提出塑料加工业未来五年主要任务是加大高科技产品创新开发力度奠定产业技术升级基础；大力推行清洁生产，提高节能减排水平；着重培育新兴产业，提高产业高端化水平；优化产业布局，提高产业集群建设水平；推进创先体系建设，提高企业综合实力；提高出口产品附加值，优化贸易结构，大力推进塑料制品安全工程建设。

三、审议通过了《中国塑协 2011 年度财务报告》。

马占峰秘书长向会议提交了《中国塑协 2011 年度财务报告》，提请大会审议通过。

四、审议通过了中国塑协人事变动的四个议案。

1. 关于新增北京宝玛特科技发展有限公司等 87 家会员单位的议案；

2. 关于增补山东陆宇塑胶工业有限公司等 10 家理事单位的议案；

3. 关于增补上海紫东薄膜材料股份有限公司徐志强等 7 位同志为特邀副理事长的议案；

4. 关于聘任田岩、刘姝、许琳为副秘书长(专职)的议案。

中国塑协六届二次理事会对于三个工作报告和四项议案进行了审议并以鼓掌方式全部通过。

五、会议最后还对广东金发科技股份有限公司等 14 家企业获得 2010～2011 年度全国塑料行业卓越绩效先进企业进行了表彰和颁发证书；会议宣布了顾地科技股份有限公司等 19 家企业荣获中国塑料行业(第四批)3A 级企业信用并颁发了牌匾。

中国塑协六届二次理事会期间举行了《塑料加工业应用与发展论坛》。论坛会上来自国家统计局、卫生部、农业部、科技部等六位专家就当前经济形势及政策取向分析、食品包装材料的安全及标准、塑料在农业上的应用、塑料复合材料在航空领域的应用、全球化竞争下中小企业的转型与提升、“十二五”塑料行业投资机会分析等专题作了精彩的报告和演讲。

中国塑协六届二次理事会于 4 月 18 日组织参会单位参加了“第二十六届中国国际橡塑工业展览会”开幕式并组织行业会员单位参观了展览会。

第二十六届中国国际塑料橡胶工业展览会举办

4 月 18 日，亚洲第一、全球第二大的第二十六届中国国际塑料橡胶工业展览会在上海新国际博览中心开幕。中国轻工业联合会会长步正发、副会长钱桂敬、名誉会长陈士能、中国塑协常务副会长曹俭出席开幕式。

本届展会面积首次突破 200000 平方米，达 210000 平方米，本届展会有来自全球 35 个国家超过 2700 家公司参展，展示超过 2500 台机械及最新橡塑化工及原材料。此外，展会获得 13 个展团的支持，包括来自奥地利、加拿大、法国、德国、意大利、日本、中国、中国台湾省、土耳其、英国、美国，以及今年新增的泰国和韩国展团，反映全球对中国市场抱乐观态度及“CHINAPLAS 国际橡塑展”的国际化地位。

展会的主题为：橡塑科技成就未来，希望可让中外业界人士一起认识橡塑作为新型材料的广泛应用领域，唤起各界关注橡塑科技对节能环保的贡献及其对于改善未来担起的重要任务，也希望橡塑业的创新技术能推动其他行业的持续发展。

由于生物塑料市场的发展引起全球高度关注，于 4 月 18 及 19 日举行“第四届中国国际生物塑料应用研讨会”，深入探讨生物塑料最新的研发、生产、应用等成果。另外，中国车用塑料 2012 峰会已率先在 4 月 17 日成功举行，峰会主题为轻量化和电动汽车的材料和设计趋势。此外，展会同期举行超过 70 场技术交流会，主题多样化，包括塑料橡胶如何应用于汽车及汽配、轮胎、电子、光电、家电、电缆、包装、医疗及个人护理、生活用品，以至铁路、航空等领域，为各行业观众提供有效交流渠道，并为其作好企业升级转型的准备。

本届展会的海外观众来自 140 多个国家及地区，占整体观众约 20%，并迎来 100 多个中外参观团，阵容鼎盛。为期 4 天的展会吸引逾 100000 名中外专业买家到场，观摩及采购最新化工原材料及各式的橡塑机械。

第二届中国(上海)国际人造革合成革工业展览会举办

4 月 19 日，由中国塑协主办、中国塑协人造革合成革专业委员会、北京金丰益泰展览公司承办的“第二届中国(上海)国际人造革合成革工业展览会”在上海世博会主题馆大厅开幕。

开幕式由中国塑协常务副理事长曹俭主持，中国塑协副秘书长、中国塑协人造革合成革专业委员会常务副理事长兼秘书长冯庶君致开幕词，中国皮革协会会长苏超英、中国家具协会副会长兼秘书长张冰冰在开幕式上发表贺词。开幕式现场同时举行了2011年获得产业基地荣誉称号地区的颁牌仪式，福鼎市人民政府被授予中国合成革产业示范基地、中国合成革名城。

中国轻工业联合会副会长、中国塑协理事长钱桂敬宣布"第二届中国(上海)国际人造革合成革工业展览会"隆重开幕！

世界最大的合成革专业展会现场精品荟萃，充分展示了当今全球合成革新型聚合材料现代化工业发展水平。近200家来自世界各地的合成革企业参展，展位总数逾418个，展出面积12000平方米，丽水、福鼎、临海、义乌、高明、周庄等地500多人跟团参展。业内知名企业如：安利、万华、五洲、优耐克、温革、强丰、南亚塑胶、禾欣、大帝、协孚、上海华峰、万华、美特康、冠胜、国信、力发等悉数盛装亮相，台塑、意大利克莱斯皮、德国ATN等国外企业参展，形成了国内外品牌盛会、精彩纷呈的局面。

展会同期成功举办了2012人造革合成革行业特色区域发展论坛暨市区县长经验交流会、军民融合及政府绿色采购论坛、第二届中国生态合成革论坛暨产业链生态安全研讨会及中国塑协人造革合成革专委会2011年会、合成革标签与术语－中欧座谈会等会议活动。

农用地膜回收利用座谈会召开

2012年4月25日，工业和信息化部会同财政部、农业部、商务部，在北京召开了研究地膜回收利用制度及传统塑料地膜、可降解环保地膜开发应用相关扶持政策座谈会，中国塑协降解塑料专业委员会翁云宣秘书长、中国塑协农用薄膜专业委员会刘敏常务副秘书长应邀出席了会议。

工业和信息化部节能与利用司雷文副调研员介绍了基本情况，2012年3月22日温家宝总理在审计署《重要信息要目》上批示要做好农用地膜回收利用工作。刘敏常务副秘书长介绍农膜行业的现状、地膜回收利用中存在的问题及建议，使与会领导对地膜回收利用情况有了进一步了解。翁云宣秘书长介绍了地膜降解在研发、试验方面的经验和成果。

农业部科教司李波处长从地膜的起源、应用及目前部分省份回收工作的进展方面做了详细说明，并介绍了与发改委、财政部就地膜回收问题成立农业清洁生产项目，将拿出1个亿作为财政补贴。

商务部流通业发展司李嘉建调研员、工业和信息化部节能与综合利用司资源综合利用处黄建忠处长、李洪良调研员认真听取了各方介绍，黄建忠处长做了总结发言：一是大家要高度重视总理的批示精神；二是认识农膜行业目前存在问题的严重性和解决的复杂性；三是从长远考虑应加强研发推广地膜降解技术；从目前地膜回收存在的问题考虑，应从源头治理，规范现有地膜生产企业强执执行国家标准，同时修订国家标准，使其更具适用性。根据本次会议内容尽快形成书面文件上报回复总理批示。四是与发改委、财政部、农业部、商务部多部委共同协商，商讨政府给予财务税收等方面的优惠补贴；制定相关产业政策、加强地方政府监管力度，建立长效工作机制；适当的时候选择先行地区召开现场经验交流与观摩会，推动残留地膜回收工作的进展。

【5月】

福鼎获评中国合成革产业示范基地称号

2012年5月，中国塑协授予福鼎"中国合成革产业示范基地"称号。

福鼎合成革产业发展于2005年，至去年共引进合成革及配套企业47家，产值144亿元，超亿元企业36家，产品在国内占有率达25%以上，出口贸易值占总销售额的20%。目前，福鼎已形成革基布－聚胺树脂－合成革－制革品等"一条龙"的合成革产业链。预计，今年该市合成革总产值将突破200亿元大关。

中国塑协降解塑料专委会副会长会议暨"降解材料行业规划及标准研讨会"召开

2012年5月3~4日，中国塑协降解塑料专委会副会长会议暨"降解材料行业规划及标准研讨会"在北京召开。来自全国各地的近70名降解材料的专家、生产商、用户齐聚一堂，共商降解材料行业及其标准规划。

北京工商大学副校长谢志华教授、工业和信息化部消费品司谢立安处长、工业和信息化部节能与综合利用司李洪良处长、中国塑协曹俭常务副会长、中国塑协降解塑料专业委员会夏青理事长先后致辞。

会议期间，与会代表着重讨论了降解地膜的现状、应用经验、技术可行性和示范可能性，并就降解材料行业规划及其标准各抒己见、踊跃发言。

新疆祥运工贸年产600ktPVC项目奠基开工

5月18日，新疆祥运工贸有限公司年产600kt的PVC生产建设项目在库车奠基开工。这是瞄准西部经济持续增长的一项重要战略部署，也是库车县强县富民，发展化工产业，推动化工园区建设的重点引资项目。

该项目占地2500亩，总投资86.7亿元，计划配套4×15万千瓦自备电厂、烧碱、水泥厂等项目，明年建成投产。投产后，预计年均销售收入53.7亿元，建成达产后，为地方增加工业产值近百亿元，贡献利税19亿元，解决当地2500个就业岗位。

该项目走的是一条“绿色建材”节约矿产资源、能源综合利用，可持续发展的道路。配套的电石渣、电厂煤灰等废料制水泥熟料项目，将各装置产生的固体废弃物变废为宝，得到水泥产品。通过循环经济产业链，实现“一次钙资源，在电石、水泥项目中两次使用”，解决了项目废渣出路，使利用电石渣制水泥属国家“双高一优”项目。该项目具有投入产出规模大、技术含量高、创利税能力强等特点。项目建成投产后，公司在满足西部及国内市场需求的同时，亦将寻求出口能力，以在国际上取得较强的竞争优势。

中国塑协塑料管道专业委员会2012年年会召开

2012年5月24~26日，“中国塑协塑料管道专业委员会2012年年会”在重庆召开。年会主题为：“巩固‘十一五’成就规划‘十二五’发展”。来自国内外相关单位领导、专家、会员单位、塑料管道生产企业、上下游企业、行业协会、检测机构、认证单位、相关媒体等单位代表540人参加会议。

中国轻工业联合会副会长、中国塑协理事长钱桂敬在报告中详细介绍了塑料加工行业“十二五”发展规划指导意见。中国塑协常务副理事长曹俭在对塑料管道行业情况的整体介绍。重庆市经济和信息化委员会副巡视员宋嘉陵致欢迎辞。重庆市工商联副主席陈健介绍了重庆市民营经济的发展。顾地科技股份有限公司董事长林超群介绍了顾地科技的整体情况。住房和城乡建设部科技发展促进中心处长高立新介绍了“十二五”期间塑料管道的需求情况进行。水利部农村饮水安全中心高级工程师彭克奇在专题报告中围绕“十一五”农村饮水安全工程实施情况及“十二五”规划思路进行了深入的分析。中国城镇供水排水协会副秘书长兼排水专业委员会秘书长王岚作了《我国供排水管网发展面临的问题和挑战》的报告。中国城市燃气协会副秘书长马长城对我国城市燃气行业的情况作了介绍。中国建筑金属结构协会副秘书长兼给水排水设备分会会长华明九讲话。中国建筑研究设计总院机电院院长赵锂介绍了塑料排水管在建筑同层排水及特殊单立管排水系统中的应用。中国城镇供水排水协会设备材料委员会副主任白迪祺预计“十二五”期间在配置管网方面将会更多的采用塑料管材。

中国塑协塑料管道专业委员会理事长陈力辉作了《巩固“十一五”成就规划“十二五”发展》的2011年工作报告，并得到大会的通过。

中国塑协塑料管道专业委员会秘书长王占杰代表财务人员向大会作了《专委会2011年财务收支情况报告》，并得到大会的通过。王占杰公布了专委会2011年5月~2012年3月新增加的3家理事单位及27家会员单位的名单和简况。

中国建筑科学研究院认证中心认证部主任马捷作了“CABR建设工程产品认证”的情况简介，参会领导向部分获证单位授牌。

王占杰向大会汇报了塑料管道专业委员会2012年工作计划要点。介绍了《中国塑料管道行业“十二五”发展建议》的编制说明。

会议还安排了塑料管道原料、助剂、设备、新技术、检测、应用、质量管理及行业发展等方面的专题交流。

会议组织参会代表参观了重庆顾地塑胶电器有限公司的生产现场和样品展示厅。

全国塑料行业协会峰会召开

2012年5月27日，中国塑协召集全国部分省市塑料行业协会会长、秘书长在广东省东莞市召开了“全国塑料行业协会峰会”。出席会议的有中国轻工业联合会副会长、中国塑协理事长钱桂敬，中国塑协常务副理事长曹俭、名誉会长廖正品、秘书长马占峰以及中国塑协塑料管道、塑料型材及门窗制品、人造革合成革、塑料编织制品、多功能母料、专家委员会等专委会理事长、秘书长等；上海、江苏、浙江、山东、江西、安徽、新疆、西藏、广东、天津、山西、重庆、湖南、贵州、福建、甘肃、云南等17个省级塑料行业协会以及温州市、深圳市、高明区、宁波市、台州市、温岭市、厦门市、汕头市、茂名市、东莞市、顺德区、大连市、乐从镇等13个地区塑料协会的会长、秘书长等。参加会议的还有广东省塑料工业协会家居专委会、改性专委会，广东省塑协信息中心，广东省内48家塑料行业企业家等100多名代表参加了峰会。本次峰会特邀广东省民间组织管理局、省轻工业协会、大连商品交易所、广东省社会组织协会、华南理工大学、东莞虎门港管委会专家领导等。

峰会由曹俭常务副理事长主持，广东省塑料工业协会会长符岸致欢迎辞。本次座谈会是各协会以“交流合作、优势互补、共同发展”为主题的经验交流，与会省市地方协会会长、秘书长重点介绍了各自地方的行业形势和企业发展状况、介绍了各自行业组织的会员管理、会员结构以及协会自身建设的经验以及面临的问题，以及加强协会之间交流与合作和对行业企业服务建设的意见和建议等，并提议每年要召开全国塑料行业协会联谊会。大家纷纷表示将在中国塑协理事会领导下，通过科技创新、管理创新、人才培养、建立沟通机制等多方面实践推动行业经济和区域经济联动与谐发展。本次峰会是全国塑料行业协会的一次形势分析会、经验交流会、是一次团结的盛会，对于行业团结和发展必将产生积极的影响。

中国轻工业联合会副会长、中国塑协理事长钱桂敬同志作总结发言。他充分肯定了各地方协会在引导指导当地行业企业发展所取得的成绩和发挥的重要作用；对中国塑协与各省市地方协会的关系以及如何加强之间的合作、交流与配合提出了建议。总结中还对《塑料加工业"十二五"发展规划指导意见》做了详细的介绍，对协会工作者具备的各方面素质和做好服务工作提出了要求。

2012 中国塑料产业大会开幕

2012 年 5 月 30 日，由大连商品交易所、中国石化联合会和中国轻工业联合会举办的 2012 中国塑料产业大会在宁波开幕。会议重点研讨在严峻的国内外经济形势下，塑料产业面临的市场形势和未来的发展方向，同时探讨期货市场与塑料现货市场相互促进的方式。共有塑料产业链上各领域生产企业及从事塑料期货的相关人士 600 多人与会。

【6 月】

中国塑料管道行业"十二五"期间(2011 ~ 2015)发展建议

2012 年 6 月，中国塑协塑料管道专业委员会发布"中国塑料管道行业"十二五"期间(2011 ~ 2015)发展建议。主要内容如下：

一、行业发展现状

1. 生产能力强，规模企业不断增多，产业集中度提高

2. 新材料、新结构、新品种越来越多

3. 应用领域进一步拓宽

4. 生产企业仍主要聚集在经济发达地区，但已有分流迹象

5. 视技术进步，行业的整体技术水平提升

6. 骨干企业的产品质量水平和品牌意识逐步提高

7. 产品出口增加，国际化趋势逐步加强

8. 贯彻国家政策，发挥节能减排效益

二、行业目前存在的主要问题

1. 市场不规范，部分小型企业产品质量合格率低，影响行业健康发展

2. 区域发展不平衡，生产地域布局有待趋于合理

3. 原材料制约行业的发展，价格波动带来行业极大的担心

4. 市场推广工作有待加强，有限的市场竞争加剧

5. 产品研发、创新等方面还需加大投入

6. 标准化工作应进一步加强

7. 工程质量应进一步提高

三、行业发展目标建议

1. 产量目标

2. 产品结构调整目标

3. 科技进步目标

4. 技术标准制定目标

5. 产品质量目标

四、行业发展重点建议

五、主要措施建议

1. 加强宏观调控，落实相关政策

2. 加强塑料管道行业科技创新和技术进步，尽快实现产品的更新换代，提高配套水平

3. 完善标准体系，强化标准的执行力度

4. 善质量保证体系，引导市场规范化运行

5. 注重与上游行业的协调发展，实现多赢发展

6. 加强对用户的服务，促进产品的合理应用

7. 开展职业培训与交流，生产好、选好、安装好、用好塑料管道产品

8. 发挥行业协会作用，加强交流

9. 鼓励形成产业集群，防止行业过热发展

高性能纤维与复合材料在民用领域的应用暨 SAMPE 北京分会 2012 年度主题研讨会召开

2012 年 6 月 7 ~ 8 日，高性能纤维与复合材料在民用领域的应用暨 SAMPE 北京分会 2012 年度主题研讨会在中科院宁波材料技术与工程研究所召开。

高性能纤维复合材料具有轻质高强等一系列优点已被广泛应用于航空航天、航海、国防、交通运输、土木建筑、能源、化工机械、体育娱乐等领域。然而受困于成本因素，其在民用领域的广泛应用受到很大的阻碍。近些年，国产碳纤维、芳纶纤维等高性能增强材料研发与生产陆续展开，使得低成本的高性能纤维复合材料成为可能。在此形势下，如何将先进复合材料应用到更广阔的工业领域，如何推进高性能纤维与复合材料及其相关行业的可持续发展，成为面临的重要课题。

会议特邀中材科技股份有限公司副总裁薛忠民、环航复合材料股份有限公司总经理蔡科然、江苏恒神碳纤维有限公司沈真研究员、国能风力发电有限公司王专利所长、中国电力科学研究院何州文主任

工程师、全国特种纤维信息中心罗益锋主任、泰山体育产业集团总工程师龙国荣、哈尔滨工程大学佟丽莉教授、哈尔滨工业大学贾德昌教授、北京林业大学赵广杰教授、北京航空材料研究所赵文明博士和刘刚博士等做了精彩的大会报告，主题涉及复合材料在汽车、风电、核电、电缆、船舶、高铁、体育、民机、建筑等民用领域的最新应用动态和代表性的科研成果，为民用高性能纤维复合材料生产企业、终端用户、科研单位、大学院校提供一个技术交流、行业上下游商务洽谈、战略合作的平台，有力推进了高性能复合材料在工业领域得到更为广泛的工程应用和技术进步。

宁波材料所复合材料制造与装备团队范欣愉研究员和祝颖丹副研究员分别介绍了研究团队在汽车制造业用热塑性复合材料轻量化技术和纤维变角度牵引铺放技术制备变刚度复合材料的最新科研进展，包括成型技术、装备与创新思维，引起了与会者的广泛关注，并与多家单位深入交流洽谈合作。宁波材料所在热塑性复合材料成型技术与装备上的研究成果得到了与会同行的高度评价和赞誉，一致认为宁波材料所在此领域的研究工作与国际接轨，处于国内研究前沿。

大会丰富的研讨主题吸引了70余家科研院校及企业的近160位专家代表参加。

塑料检查井交流会召开

2012年6月14日，由中国塑协塑料管道专业委员会与北京市建设工程物资协会管材管件分会共同主办的“塑料检查井交流会”在全国农业展览馆新馆会议室召开。来自原料、加工设备、检测设备、塑料管道、塑料检查井生产企业，相关协会，设计院、检测机构等80多名代表参加会议。

国家化学建筑材料测试中心(材料测试部)主任魏若奇作了《塑料检查井国内外情况汇报》的主题报告。报告从国内外塑料检查井行业的基本情况，国内行业生产、应用、存在的问题，以及行业发展建议三方面介绍了有关情况。

北京市市政管理处原总工程师任明星在《赴欧洲考察塑料管道及检查井情况介绍》中，详细介绍了在德国和荷兰进行塑料管道及检查井考察工作情况。

北京市建设工程物资协会管材管件分会专家组组长王真杰，介绍了北京市地方标准《塑料排水检查井应用技术规程》的编制情况，

北京市市政工程设计研究总院副总工程师陈重在《塑料排水检查井结构设计方法简介》的报告中，分别从结构安全理念、主要结构设计规范、结构设计方法、外水压试验和轴向静荷载试验的试验压力以及回填要求方面，介绍了塑料排水检查井的结构设计。

北京市建筑设计研究总院高级工程师郑克白作了《塑料检查井在建筑小区中的应用》的报告。

承德市金建检测仪器有限公司总经理任雨峰做了《塑料检查井性能及质量检测》报告。

北京建设工程物资协会管材管件分会秘书长邹仲元在总结中指出，塑料检查井生产企业在产品开发、制定标准上应与使用者多沟通，产品质量要严格按标准生产，以便保证产品的顺利推广。

中国塑协塑料管道专业委员会秘书长王占杰在总结发言中说，针对目前塑料检查井生产企业产量供大于求的情况，建议生产企业要注重研发技术，重视产品的设计，要根据市场需求，通过发挥本身独有的优势来提高竞争力，避免产品同质化，避免恶性竞争。要共同努力，促进塑料检查井行业的健康发展。

广东仕诚“8300mm BOPP生产线技术研发及产业化”通过专家鉴定

2012年6月28日，由广东省经济和信息化委员会主持，并委托广东省轻工业协会组织，联合佛山市经济和信息化局、佛山市南海区经济促进局在广东仕诚塑料机械有限公司召开了“省级新产品新技术8300mm BOPP双向拉伸薄膜生产线技术研发及产业化”的鉴定会议。

双向拉伸薄膜简称BOPF，包括管膜法工艺和平面双向拉伸工艺。平面双向拉伸薄膜品种较多，许多结晶型聚合物和非结晶型聚合物都可拉伸成膜，目前已经产业化生产的双向拉伸薄膜包括：BOPP/BOPET/BOPA等，其中BOPP双向拉伸薄膜的需求量最大、应用范围也最广。但是目前国内高速、宽幅(速度≥450m/min，幅宽≥8300mm)双向拉伸薄膜生产设备全部依靠进口，在8300mm BOPP双向拉伸薄膜生产装备制造领域内仍属空白，远远不能满足国内双向拉伸薄膜发展的需求。

广东仕诚公司设计生产的8300mm BOPP双向拉伸薄膜生产装备，开发了高效节能双螺杆塑化挤出系统，优化了压延及横、纵拉伸系统结构，并采用了更精密的集成控制技术，研制出的国产BOPP双向拉伸薄膜生产装备，成功生产出8300mm BOPP双向拉伸薄膜，为国内首台(套)国产BOPP双向拉伸薄膜生产装备，填补了国内空白，其产品技术达到国内领先、国际同类产品先进水平。该产品幅宽达到8300mm，设计速度480m/min，薄膜厚度可精确控制在12～60μm范围内，年产能达到30000t，具备了产业化生产能力，可取得良好的经济与社会效益。

【7月】

塑料管道产品行业指导价格发布

2012 年 7 月 3 日，中国塑协塑料管道专业委员会发布塑料管道产品行业指导价格(2012 年第 2 号)：

一、给水用硬聚氯乙烯(PVC－U)管材(非铅盐稳定剂)

1. 产品标准：GB/T 10002.1—2006 给水用硬聚氯乙烯(PVC－U)管材。

2. 行业指导价格(出厂价)：11000 元/t(PVC 树脂参考价按 6600 元/t 计)。

二、排水用 PVC－U 管材

1. 产品标准：GB/T 5836.1—2006 建筑排水用硬聚氯乙烯管材。

GB/T 20221—2006 无压埋地排污、排水用硬聚氯乙烯(PVC－U)管材。

2. 行业指导价格(出厂价)：10000 元/t(PVC 树脂参考价按 6600 元/t 计)。

三、埋地排水用 PVC－U 双壁波纹管材

1. 产品标准：GB/T18477.1—2007 埋地排水用硬聚氯乙烯(PVC－U)结构壁管道系统 第 1 部分：双壁波纹管材。

2. 行业指导价格(出厂价)：10700 元/t(PVC 树脂参考价按 6600 元/t 计)。

四、燃气用埋地聚乙烯(PE)管材

1. 产品标准：GB 15558.1—2003 燃气用埋地聚乙烯(PE)管道系统 第一部分 管材。

2. 行业指导价格(出厂价)：19100 元/t(PE 原材料参考价按 14400 元/t 计)。

五、给水用 PE 管材

1. 产品标准：GB/T 13663—2000 给水用聚乙烯(PE)管材。

2. 行业指导价格(出厂价)：18200 元/t(PE 原材料参考价按 13500 元/t 计)。

六、埋地排水用 PE 双壁波纹管材

1. 产品标准：GB/T 19472.1—2004 埋地用聚乙烯(PE)结构壁管道系统 第一部分 聚乙烯双壁波纹管材。

2. 行业指导价格(出厂价)：16200 元/t(PE 原材料参考价按 11500 元/t 计)。

七、PE 缠绕结构壁管材

1. 产品标准：GB/T 19472.2—2004 埋地用聚乙烯(PE)结构壁管道系统 第二部分 聚乙烯缠绕结构壁管材及相关标准。

2. 行业指导价格(包括现场施工安装指导费用的出厂价)：17200 元/t(PE 原材料参考价按 11500 元/t 计)。

中国轻工业联合会步正发会长会见台塑集团客人

2012 年 7 月 6 日，中轻联会长步正发在北京会见了台塑集团南亚塑胶工业股份有限公司资深副总经理林丰钦一行四人，贸促会轻工行业分会副会长王本和，塑料协会常务副理事长曹俭等参加了会见。

步会长首先对林丰钦先生一行来访表示欢迎，并简要介绍了中轻联的主要职能和中国大陆塑料行业的状况。

林丰钦先生简要介绍了台塑集团南亚塑胶工业股份有限公司的基本情况：南亚塑胶工业股份有限公司成立于 1958 年，主要从事电子、化工、石化、纤维等生产工业、与台湾塑胶公司、台湾化学纤维公司等五十余家公司组成台塑关系企业，经过四十多年的努力发展，台塑关系企业已成为台湾地区最大的民营企业。目前，南亚塑胶工业股份有限公司在大陆投资开办了 21 家企业，其中 6 家是塑料加工企业。南亚塑胶和大陆有着紧密的经贸关系。

步会长指出，大陆塑料行业近几年来发展速度很快，去年大陆塑料加工行业产值占轻工行业产值的 9.8%，已成为大陆轻工业的第一大行业，出口为 1462 万吨，已成为世界上最大的塑料制品生产和消费国家。南亚塑胶较早和大陆合作，我们可以学习和借鉴南亚塑胶的一些先进的管理方法和生产技术。我们很重视海峡两岸的经贸交流与合作，这有利于促进我们共同发展，也符合两岸人民的利益。

步会长表示，随着两岸经贸交往不断深入，台资企业在大陆业务也会随之发展，遇到的新问题也会增多，中轻联愿意为台资企业提供可能的帮助。

双方就质量管理体系、产品标准等议题进行了交流。

会见结束后，曹俭副理事长等人与林丰钦先生一行进行了专题座谈。

中国塑协农膜专委会 2012 年年会暨第四届常委会换届选举会议召开

2012 年 7 月 18 日，中国塑协农用薄膜专业委员会 2012 年年会暨第四届常委会换届选举会议在白山市召开。

国家工业和信息化部消费品司轻工一处调研员谢立安、中国塑协常务副理事长曹俭、农业部农业技术推广服务中心首席科学家张真和、白山市市政府副市长陈耀辉、白山市工信局局长刘云海、白山市市政府副秘书长辛泳光、中国塑协秘书长马占峰以及中石化市场专家、中石油价格信息专家、外商驻中国代理机构和商社代表，以及全国各地的农膜企业及相关的原料、助剂、设备、科研院所等各方

面的专家、单位代表共计187位出席会议。

国家工业和信息化部消费品司轻工一处谢立安调研员介绍了代表们最关心的国家促进农业发展及农膜产业的有关政策，国家对农膜行业、地膜回收降解、节能减排等相关政策制定情况；指出应充分发挥行业协会作用，认真贯彻执行《农用薄膜行业准入条件》，对会员企业提出了希望。

四届常委会换届选举会上，全体参会代表首先听取并以鼓掌的方式审议通过了韩连贵理事长作的《中国塑协农膜专委会第三届理事会工作报告》；以鼓掌的方式审议通过了农膜专委会刘敏常务副秘书长作的《中国塑协农膜专委会第三届理事会财务报告》；审议通过了关于《中国塑协农膜专委会工作条例》修改的说明和《中国塑协农膜专委会工作条例》。审议通过了农膜专委会换届选举原则和办法；听取了四届常委会常委委员推荐名单的说明，审议并通过了四届常委会常委委员名单。

换届会还召开了中国塑协农用薄膜专业委员会四届一次常委会，选举出了四届常委会主任、副主任、秘书长。

常委会主任：白山喜丰塑料(集团)股份有限公司董事长曹志强；常委会秘书长：刘敏。常委会由47位常委单位组成，其中包括主任单位、17家副主任单位。还审议通过了关于韩连贵同志任农膜专委会名誉主任的提案。

中国塑协曹俭常务副理事长做总结讲话。他首先代表中国塑协对农用薄膜专委会2012年年会暨第四届常委会换届选举会议的成功召开表示热烈祝贺，就当前中国塑料行业的发展现状以及农膜产品质量等方面做了重要阐述，同时充分肯定了三届农膜专委会的工作和取得的成绩，并对专委会今后的工作和发展提出希望和要求。曹俭副理事长的讲话对整个行业以及专委会工作具有深刻的指导意义。

会议组织参会代表参观了白山市喜丰塑料(集团)股份有限公司。

在技术交流会上，举行了农膜原料市场分析研讨、农膜生产及相关技术等方面的论文及交流共12篇，对当前市场状况、产品研发和技术创新进行了精辟分析和阐述，开拓视野、丰富知识，加强了会员单位之间的技术交流和彼此了解与友谊。

外墙保温与节能结构技术交流推广会召开

2012年7月20～22日，由住房和城乡建设部科技发展促进中心主办的外墙保温与节能结构技术交流推广会在江苏省南京市召开

会议邀请国家有关建筑节能政策法规、标准制定主管部门以及行业内有影响的专家学者，解读国家有关建筑节能外墙保温的新政策和推广目录，分析行业发展中面临的新情况、新问题、新机遇，并由相关专家和企业介绍一批先进适用的建筑节能外墙保温新材料、新产品、新技术、新系统，以及针对满足建筑节能和绿色建筑发展新的技术要求的系统化解决方案。

会议主题为：新型墙体材料、保温隔热材料与建筑节能结构一体化和防火安全技术

会议主要交流内容：1、住房城乡建设部《关于发布墙体保温系统与墙体材料推广应用和限制、禁止使用技术的公告》(第1338号)编制背景和主要内容解读；2、外墙保温如何适应建筑节能新的标准要求和绿色建筑技术发展方向；3、建筑外墙保温与节能结构技术一体化的优化技术措施；4、节能省地型建筑科研项目《外墙外保温现状调研与政策建议研究》课题介绍；5、玻化微珠在寒冷地区建筑节能外墙保温中的应用和“城市窑洞”绿色建筑成果介绍；6、聚氨酯泡沫板在外墙外保温建筑中优化功能的系统化技术措施研究；7、节能保温与结构一体化CL体系新的发展推广前景展望；8、气凝胶超级绝热保温材料的研发实践及其在建筑节能工程中的应用前景；9、太阳能光热系统与建筑外墙保温结构一体化技术研究和应用；10、烧结保温空心砌块在建筑节能外墙保温与结构一体化中的特殊功能与发展趋势；11、发泡陶瓷板干挂无机高效保温系统在建筑节能工程中的应用；12、有机保温材料耐火试验解析；13、无机抽真空绝热保温材料在建筑节能外墙外保温中的推广应用；14、聚氨酯硬泡原料择优调整及有效提高阻燃性能技术研究；15、高密度EPS外保温现浇一体化在严寒地区的应用；16、挤出聚苯乙烯(XPS)保温板在外墙保温中的应用；17、模塑聚苯乙烯泡沫板(EPS)薄抹灰保温系统的工艺改进与功能优化研究；18、利用工业废渣生产高强度装配式新型混凝土空心砌块及其在建筑节能工程中的应用；19、无机发泡混凝土保温材料在外墙保温中的应用；20、建筑废弃物的资源化高效率利用和制造新型墙体材料技术；21、保障性安居工程示范项目建筑节能外墙保温实例介绍。

举办塑料制品性能检测培训班举办

2012年7月25～27日，由中国塑协主办的塑料制品性能检测培训班在山东淄博举办。

培训期间，特邀中国塑协、建设部科技发展促进中心、水利部农村饮水安全中心等领导参加并作重要指示。

培训班聘请国家塑料制品质量监督检验中心、国家化学建筑材料测试中心、中国石化齐鲁分公司

研究院、中国建筑科学研究院认证中心等国家权威监督检测机构的标准化及检测专家集中授课。

国家塑料制品质量监督检验中心刘山生高工教授了"塑料管材性能测试"，国家化学建筑材料测试中心魏若奇主任教授了"聚乙烯燃气管及给水管材的测试"，国家化学建筑材料测试中心黄家文 主任教授了"企业试验室检测工作的重点及意义"，中国石化齐鲁分公司研究院谢建玲副总经理教授了"塑料管道标准的变化及对原材料的要求"，中国建筑科学研究院认证中心马捷主任教授了"CABR 建设工程产品认证"等内容。

培训结束时进行考核，合格者由中国塑协颁发证书。

第七届中国塑料工业高新技术及产业化研讨会暨2012中国塑协塑料技术协作委员会年会·技术交流会中国塑协注塑制品专委会二届六次年会召开

2012年7月25~30日，第七届中国塑料工业高新技术及产业化研讨会暨2012中国塑协塑料技术协作委员会年会·技术交流会/中国塑协注塑制品专委会二届六次年会，在哈尔滨市联合召开。

中国塑协曹俭常务副理事长对大会召开表示祝贺并作了"当前中国塑料工业运行情况与对策"的报告、黑龙江省塑料公司吴勇总经理致辞并简介黑龙江塑料工业概况、中国塑协注塑制品专委会顾大全秘书长致辞并作了"中国塑协注塑制品专委会2012年年会工作报告"、中国塑协塑料技术协作委员会包建成理事长致辞并汇报了委员会一年的工作、哈尔滨哈轻塑胶有限公司总经理贾丽萍简介了公司简况并致辞、哈尔滨理工大学材料学院周浩然主任致辞并简介学院概况、北京工商大学材料与机械工程学院黄志刚院长致辞并简介学院概况。

除3篇报告外，大会共收到论文44篇，其中大会报告了32篇。另外，作为书面发言的12个报告。

会议发表论文内容包括新材料、新产品、新工艺、新技术、新设备，以及检测仪器开发和应用等，其中有不少创新点，包括：气体辅助挤出成型技术、新型同心双螺杆挤出成型机、国产伺服微发泡技术设备、国产万吨级同向双螺杆挤出机等；在检测仪器方面对Haake转矩流变仪在电性能、发泡材料性能方面的应用，以及粉体材料动摩擦系数的测试方法引起了代表的兴趣；在推进节能新技术方面，会议积极推荐变频高效加热节电系统在塑料机械上的应用以及气体辅助注射成型、微发泡注射成型、两板注射成型机等新技术。

对于当前聚氯乙烯行业中禁用铅稳定剂及其替代方案也进行了集中研讨，认为行业禁铅是必然趋势，而且，目前也已经有多种铅稳定剂替代品出现，包括钙锌复合稳定剂、复合型多功能有机锡和有机稳定剂等，但是，从经济和技术两方面还存在需要进一步解决的问题，在一些应用领域，如大规格管材挤塑和管件注塑方面还需要有所突破。

会议期间还专门安排了一单元时间进行各学科自由交流、创造深入探讨机会，推进各方技术协作。会议期间代表还参观了哈尔滨哈轻塑胶有限公司，对企业先进的管理印象深刻。

2012年PE燃气管道应用技术交流培训班举办

2012年7月26~28日，由中国城市燃气协会与中国塑协塑料管道专业委员会联合主办的"2012年PE燃气管道应用技术交流培训班"在贵阳市举办。来自燃气、管道、原料等企业的110余位代表参加了本次培训交流。

中国城市燃气协会副秘书长马长城、中国塑协塑料管道专业委员会秘书长王占杰、贵州燃气集团有限公司董事长黄友兴和枫叶控股集团有限公司总经理张文龙在讲话中分别介绍了相关情况，希望大家将学到的知识用于工作实践。

道达尔石化(中国)的技术经理赵启辉作了《PE燃气管材及管件产品标准、原材料的现状及发展》的讲座，成都城市燃气有限责任公司工程师林雅蓉介绍了《G5+合作小组在燃气聚乙烯输配系统质量控制方面所做的一些工作和经验》，国家化学建材测试中心(材料测试部)主任魏若奇讲解了《PE燃气管材及管件产品质量的鉴别、质量控制与检测方法》，枫叶控股集团有限公司技术部长闫超作了《PE燃气管材加工工艺介绍》的报告，贵州省燃气协会常务副秘书长广宏作了《PE管在贵州燃气的应用》的报告、中国城市燃气协会专家汪隆毓作了《我国PE燃气输配系统应用中需注意的一些问题》的专题报告，德国费亚泰克集团有限公司销售经理李国建作了《PE电熔管件的选用及其在燃气管网中的重要性》的讲座，亚大集团经理王志伟作了《PE燃气管道的焊接、相关标准及质量控制》的讲座。湖南颐通管业有限公司介绍了企业生产燃气用塑料管道的情况，港华辉信公司还作了塑料管道的焊接演示。培训结束后，参观了枫叶控股集团有限公司的贵州生产基地。

这次培训内容包括PE燃气管材及管件的产品标准、原料、质量鉴别及控制、检测方法、加工工艺、生产技术、市场推广、设计和应用等方面内容，为提高加工技术水平、促进更好推广应用提供了宝贵的经验。汪隆毓等专家与学员进行交流，回答大家的提问，从而进一步加深学员对本次培训内容的理解与巩固。

通过培训与交流，让更多的燃气用户深入了解PE燃气管道加工、质量控制、施工、应用等相关知识，选择好、设计好、应用好PE燃气管道，将对塑料管道行业的健康发展和燃气行业的放心使用起到很好的促进作用。

【8月】

2012全国塑编产业链技术交流与市场对接会暨沈阳康平塑编经贸展洽会会议召开

2012年8月28日，由中国塑协和沈阳市人民政府共同主办的“2012全国塑编产业链技术交流与市场对接会暨沈阳康平塑编经贸展洽会”在沈阳召开。来自国内外塑料编织制品产业链的1200多名企业代表出席会议。

开幕仪式由中国塑协常务副理事长曹俭主持。中共康平县委书记王一兵、国务院国有资产监督管理委员会研究局处长梁方、工业和信息化部消费品司副司长高延敏分别致辞。

会议进行了2011年度塑编行业二十强企业授牌仪式。由中国塑协副秘书长、中国塑协塑编专委会秘书孙冬泉宣读二十强企业名单。沈阳市人民政府市长陈海波，中国轻工业联合会副会长、中国塑协理事长钱桂敬，工业和信息化部消费品司副司长高延敏，沈阳市人民政府副市长王翔坤，辽宁省经信委副主任蔺晓刚，沈阳化工大学校长逄玉俊，国务院国有资产监督管理委员会研究局处长梁方，中国塑协副理事长曹俭，沈阳市人民政府秘书长阎秉哲，中国塑协名誉理事长廖正品，中国塑协塑编专委会会长、浙江华庆集团有限公司董事长姜集康给塑编二十强企业颁发了铜牌。

会议进行了康平县“中国塑编示范城”揭授牌仪式。由中国轻工业联合会副会长、中国塑协理事长钱桂敬和沈阳市人民政府市长陈海波共同为“中国塑编示范城”揭牌。

钱桂敬理事长在会议上发表重要讲话。陈海波市长发表讲话。

会议举行了战略合作与投资合作协议签约仪式。由康平县经济开发区领导与沈阳化工大学、广东省塑料工业协会、江苏省塑料加工工业协会、山东省塑料工业协会、浙江省塑料工业协会、常州市塑化产业商会、沧州市塑料行业协会、山东省临邑县塑料工业协会、浙江省苍南县塑料行业协会、平阳县塑料包装协会等协会负责人签署战略合作协议。康平经济开发区领导与莱阳金开塑业有限公司、温州晨光集团有限公司、山东新宇包装股份有限公司、天津华今塑业有限公司、雁峰集团有限公司、江苏中乾塑业有限公司、江苏春燕塑业有限公司、山东省德州三志塑胶有限公司、青县荣盛塑业有限公司、嵊州市德利经编网业有限公司、沈阳方科机械制造有限公司、洛阳中塑实业有限公司、沈阳恒达汇丰塑业有限公司、辽宁凌勃防腐科技工程有限公司、沈阳荣鑫塑料编织厂、沈阳国大塑业有限公司、沈阳拓源塑业有限公司、葫芦岛武祥电热技术有限公司、沈阳奕桐塑业有限公司、沈阳恒辰彩布厂等企业负责人签署了投资意向协议。共有30多个意向投资项目签约，项目总投资额超过15亿元。

会议期间，陈海波市长、钱桂敬副会长、高延敏副司长、梁方处长、辽宁省和沈阳市有关部门领导参观了展洽会的塑编机械设备和原辅料展区。

主题发言阶段，由孙冬泉秘书长主持。审议通过由中国塑协塑编专委会主任姜集康做的“2011年塑编专委会工作总结汇报”。由中国塑协塑编专委常务副理事长林增标做“关于塑编新国标制订工作的总结汇报”，新国标的制定工作历时两年，现已报国标委批复。辽宁省康平县委常委、副县长慈鸿钢作了“辽宁康平塑编产业投资环境介绍”，欢迎各企业到康平县考察、投资。江苏中乾塑业有限公司总经理王学保代表自愿参加行业自律的企业宣读“加强企业自律，促进塑编行业健康发展倡议书”。

各知名企业负责人分别作了精彩的发言，常州永明机械制造有限公司总经理何敏做“编织小我，突破自我”的主题发言，雁峰集团有限公司董事长陈志淡作“仅用1.5千瓦电机的高效节能低噪音小凸轮四梭圆织机”等主题发言，发言内容精彩纷呈，中外技术充分交流，与会代表高度赞扬。

会议安排与会代表前往沈阳康平经济开发区塑编产业集群基地参观。

29日下午两点，塑编行业“十二五”创新发展座谈会召开，由孙冬泉秘书长主持，与会代表听取了嵊州市德利经编网业有限公司副总经理丁云富对《农用塑料经编遮阳网》行标批复的说明。与会专家和企业进行了广泛的交流，专家针对企业在经营过程中出现的技术难题进行了答疑。

【9月】

2012年全国塑料异型材及门窗行业年会召开

2012年9日19~20日。2012年全国塑料异型材及门窗行业年会在河南省焦作市召开。

焦作市人民政府乔学达副市长、工信部消费品司轻工一处汪敏燕处长；中国塑协曹俭副会长；中国塑协廖正品名誉会长；中国塑协马占峰秘书长；河南佰利联化学股份有限公司许刚董事长、河南省天鹅型材有限公司拜云飞总经理。焦作市人民政府、焦作市中站区人民政府、沁阳市人民政府部分相关领导，以及来自全国各地的异型材及门窗制品行业相关的原料、助剂、设备、模具、配件、门窗、房地产等企业的代表出席了会议。参会人数比去年增加近两成。大会同期在主会场布置了小型展览，举办了技术交流会，房地产商座谈会等。会议期间参观了河南佰利联化学股份有限公司、河南省天鹅型材有限公司。

年会以绿色环保、节能、低碳为中心，以科技创新促进稳步发展为主题，举办先进技术交流会、技术讲座；进行了设备与模具，型材与门窗，五金配件与密封胶，原辅材料等产品洽谈活动。交流会期间进行了新产品、新技术、新专利介绍活动。

会议期间与部分房地产商举行了座谈会，座谈会上放映了企业产品介绍的宣传片。座谈会后到展位参观交流。

乔学达副市长对本届大会在焦作召开对促进焦作市的经济发展、和地方企业发展有着重大促进作用，对我们行业的发展现状及展望大给出了极高的评价与期盼。曹俭副会长对参会代表做出了重要指示。工信部汪敏燕处长对我国的目前工业运行经济状况以及轻工发展，国家的相关产业政策，做了简要阐述，希望我们行业在今后的国民经济转型期内，为“节能、减排、低碳、环保”作出更大贡献，对我们行业寄予重大期望。

王存吉秘书长在工作报告中分四部进行了阐述：1. 中国塑了行业“十二五”规划的核心精神；2. 行业现状；3. 重大发展态势；4. 行业存在的主要问题；5. 专委会秘书处2012年工作汇报。王存吉秘书长在工作报告中的核心内容：1. 认真分析了行业目前的经济运行情况；2. 分析了未来重大发展趋势；3. 重点分析了“第三次工业革命”与中国塑料工业；4. 认真分析了塑料异型材将成为“环境友好型”材料；5. 提请企业，现在我国的经济发展转型阶段处在初始期，行业内的骨干企业应对国际、国内的经济发展形势、政策、对经济发展转型阶段产生重大影响的因素等密切关注，透彻了解，在此基础上制定企业的发展战略、及时调整策略抓住发展机遇拓展发展空间，最大程度的规避、化解风险，伴随国家的经济发展转型实现企业的良性、快速发展。

会议同期还召开了《中国塑协异型材及门窗专业委员会六届五次理事会》。

第12届中国塑料交易会在浙江台州开幕

2012年9月22～25日，第12届中国塑料交易会在浙江台州国际会展中心开幕。本届塑交会设展位1600个，有500多家企业、3万余人参展。

相比往年，本届塑交会展览面积增加30%。展览分为机械馆、模具机床馆、原料馆、制品馆。原料、制品展区分别由去年的5000平方米增加到10000平方米。

与展会同期举办的中国（国际）塑料台州论坛，以“绿色安全，共塑未来”为主题，着重研讨浙江省工业经济运行情况、塑料行业经济运行情况、2012年塑料原料走势分析报告、贸易壁垒法律法规及应对等议题。

此前，中国塑料交易会在台州已成功举办11届，成为全面展示中国塑料产业状况的窗口。塑料原料、制品、机械、机床模具“四位一体”的塑料产业链展示格局日渐成熟。从2005至2012年，中国塑料交易会连续8年被商务部列为塑料行业重点支持的展会。

展会的塑料原料、制品、机械、模具“四位一体”的塑料产业链展示格局越加成熟；展会对塑料产业引导性越加明显，塑料产业转型升级越加迅速；展会现场世界各国专业观众和各地展商交流越加深入，台州走到了中国乃至世界塑料产业的发展前台。同期举办的中国进口废塑料国际研讨会、“中国、美国、印度”同业战略联盟论坛、第二十届亚洲塑料论坛、中国（国际）塑料台州论坛更是成为历届塑交会的“点晴之笔”。虽然2008年全球金融危机的影响，但塑交会却持续呈上升趋势，专业化、市场化、国际化、品牌化逐渐成为塑交会的发展特点。

中国塑协工程塑料专委会第三届三次理事会会议召开

2012年9月23日，中国塑协工程塑料专业委员会第三届三次理事会于在浙江台州国际会展中心召开。

中国塑协马占峰秘书长、中国塑协许琳副秘书长、中国塑协侯胜江副主任以及浙江俊尔新材料有限公司黄志杰总经理、一汽大众胡正华高级工程师、慈溪金岛塑化有限公司张曙总经理、厦门创信元橡塑有限公司刘建辉总经理，以及各个理事单位代表共计23位出席会议。

会上首先由中国塑协工程塑料专委会薛立新理事长致词，然后全票通过慈溪金岛塑化有限公司陈成良副总经理为工程塑料专委会新一任专委会秘书长，并发表就职演说。

陈成良秘书长向大会作了专委会工作报告，对专委会上半年工作进行了总结，并对下一步工作思路进行了汇报。同时请与会代表对专委会工作提出意见建议。新副理事长单位厦门创信元橡塑制品有限公司作了相关介绍。会员企业各位代表对秘书处工作提出了一下建议和意见。

最后由中国塑协马占峰秘书长讲话，对专委会的工作给予了肯定。今后，要进一步开展企业间的交流活动，为企业服务，为会员服务，做好政府与企业之间的桥梁和纽带。

2012 中国汽车用塑料及安全技术高峰论坛会议召开

2012 年 9 月 23 日至 24 日，“2012 中国汽车用塑料及安全技术高峰论坛”在台州市会展中心报告厅举行。论坛由中国塑协主办，宁波塑料行业协会及台州市国际会展中心有限公司共同协办，中国塑协工程塑料专委会承办。

工信部消费品司轻工一处处级调研员谢立安、中国塑协曹俭副理事长、台州市经济委员会副主任叶国敏、台州路桥区副区长李震杰，以及中石化市场专家、宁波海关专家老师、宁波华翔集团技术总监、浙江大学教授、上海一汽大众、上海通用汽车专家、奥托立夫中国汽车方向盘有限公司总经理、铁岭市科技局代表、巨化集团代表，以及全国各地的汽车用塑料企业及相关的原料、零部件、设备、科研院所等各方面的专家、单位代表，共计 112 位出席论坛。

中国塑协秘书长马占峰宣布会议开始，中国塑协曹俭副理事长作了重要讲话。台州市经济委员会副主任叶国敏对台州的发展及汽车领域在台州的现状作了基体的描述，对台州塑料行业提出了不足和改进的建议和意见，对台州塑料行业的发展提出了希望。

中国科学院宁波材料研究所研究员朱锦、宁波华翔集团技术总监乐俊、浙江俊尔新材料有限公司总经理黄志杰、上海一汽大众汽车有限公司高级工程师胡正华、上海通用汽车有限公司王磊、奥托立夫汽车安全系统有限公司中国汽车方向盘有限公司王立普总经理、湖南华曙高科技有限公司许小曙总裁、宁波海关统计处胡俊飞科长、中科院宁波材料所高级工程师吴飞、宁波能之光新材料科技有限公司张发饶总经理、鲁谷(北京)科技有限公司刘忠诚，分别作了“生物塑料载汽车上的应用”、“汽车零部件模具设计对材料性能的影响”、“私营汽车零部件企业的挑战与机遇”、“激光烧结技术在汽车配件中的应用”、“车用聚合物发泡材料：产业界现状和学术界技术进展”、“模具设计与注塑工艺”、“无味环保型相容剂在车用塑料中的应用”等精彩报告。

中国塑协塑料管道专业委员会组团参加在西班牙召开的第十六届国际塑料管道会议

2012 年 9 月 24 ~ 26 日，中国塑协塑料管道专业委员会组织国内相关单位参加了于在西班牙巴塞罗那举办的第十六届国际塑料管道会议。

3 天的时间，会议进行了包括 11 个 5 分钟的发言在内的 117 个论文发布。涉及到塑料管道行业的发展进程；塑料管道、新型塑料管道及管件的发展；新型结构壁管和多层复合管材；管道在燃气、供水、排水等系统中的应用；新型塑料管道设计和测试方法；传统材料的衰退、标准与规范；塑料管道工程案例分析；管道修复、环保建材、生命周期评估等方面内容。

来自 47 个国家的塑料管道原材料生产商、设备制造商、管材生产厂、管材用户、研发和测试等相关人员 465 人参加了会议。其中，欧洲参会人员 269 人，美国 72 人，亚洲 71 人，中东 26 人，澳大利亚 20 人，非洲 7 人。

除了会议的 117 个发言外，还有 22 个书面的报告展示。所有的 139 个论文中，来自欧洲 76 个，亚洲 29 个，美国 24 个，中东和澳大利亚分别 5 个。在会议室外的 33 个展览中，来自欧洲 28 个，美国 3 个，亚洲 2 个。

来自中国的参会代表共 22 人。中国共有 7 个专题报告和 2 个海报发言。国家建材测试中心(材料部)熊志敏博士作了“测试 HDPE 管材料点荷载的新方法”的报告，亚大集团王志伟经理作了“PE 管在工业领域的应用及生产质量控制程序”的报告，上海奉贤水司工程师张志浩作了“环境温度对给水用 PE 管道在应用中的影响”的报告，天津盛象公司副总经理李洪山作了“排水管道工程设计、计算及实验—天津市武清区雍阳东道”的报告，中国塑协塑料管道专委会秘书长王占杰作了“PVC - U 管道的技术进步”的报告，常州市河马公司副总经理周敏宏作了“排水用塑料检查井在中国的推广与应用”的报告，浙江中财公司副总经理陈增贵作了“高温天气下给水用 PE 管耐压验证”的报告。沧州明珠公司经理池永生作了“浅析管材挤出过程中鲨鱼皮症与口模长径比的关系”的报告，浙江双林塑料机械有限公司外贸经理李星作了“大口径缠绕增强聚乙烯管生产技术”的报告。此外博禄公司(中国)的方东宇经理作了“高模量 PP 材料在中国双壁波纹管生产中的应用”的报告。

中国另外提供的 5 个书面论文分别来自福建亚通公司陈鹊的《大口径钢塑复合排水管在中国的应用及进展》、杭州鸿雁电器有限公司盛仲夷的《新型 PP - R 熔接式管件的研究》、中国塑协塑料管道专委会王占杰的《中国塑料管道行业五年总结与下一个五年发展展望》、天津军星管业集团有限公司夏成文的《高导热系数聚乙烯管》和大庆油田有限责任公司大庆油田建设设计研究院张丽的《油田非金属管道应用技术现状及建议》。

国际塑料管道会议至今已经成功举办了16届，它是由国际塑料管道会议协会(PPCA)以及美国塑料管道协会(PPI)、欧洲PVC管道协会(PVC 4 PIPE)、PE100+协会(PE100+)、欧洲塑料管道协会(tepfa)组织的每两年一届的国际性会议。中国塑协塑料管道专业委员会组织行业参加了2008年在匈牙利的布达佩斯举办的第14届会议、2010年在加拿大温哥华举办的第15届会议，并于分别于2009年、2011年在北京成功举办了两届国际塑料管道会议的延续会议，将国际塑料管道会议上优秀的发言代表请到中国，与大家进行交流。

本次会议期间，代表团还与有关国家的行业协会、机构、企业就技术、信息、合作等方面展开了交流。

【10月】

塑料管道产品行业指导价格发布

2012年10月11日，中国塑协塑料管道专业委员会发布

塑料管道产品行业指导价格(2012年第3号)：

一、给水用硬聚氯乙烯(PVC-U)管材(非铅盐稳定剂)

1. 产品标准：GB/T 10002.1—2006 给水用硬聚氯乙烯(PVC-U)管材。

2. 行业指导价格(出厂价)：11100元/t(PVC树脂参考价按6700元/t计)。

二、排水用PVC-U管材

1. 产品标准：GB/T 5836.1—2006 建筑排水用硬聚氯乙烯管材。GB/T 20221—2006 无压埋地排污、排水用硬聚氯乙烯(PVC-U)管材。

2. 行业指导价格(出厂价)：10100元/t(PVC树脂参考价按6700元/t计)。

三、埋地排水用PVC-U双壁波纹管材

1. 产品标准：GB/T 18477.1—2007 埋地排水用硬聚氯乙烯(PVC-U)结构壁管

道系统 第1部分：双壁波纹管材。

2. 行业指导价格(出厂价)：10800元/t(PVC树脂参考价按6700元/t计)。

四、燃气用埋地聚乙烯(PE)管材

1. 产品标准：GB 15558.1—2003 燃气用埋地聚乙烯(PE)管道系统 第一部分管材。

2. 行业指导价格(出厂价)：19300元/t(PE原材料参考价按14600元/t计)。

五、给水用PE管材

1. 产品标准：GB/T 13663—2000 给水用聚乙烯(PE)管材。

2. 行业指导价格(出厂价)：18200元/t(PE原材料参考价按13500元/t计)。

六、埋地排水用PE双壁波纹管材

1. 产品标准：GB/T 19472.1—2004 埋地用聚乙烯(PE)结构壁管道系统第一部分聚乙烯双壁波纹管材。

2. 行业指导价格(出厂价)：16700元/t(PE原材料参考价按12000元/t计)。

七、PE缠绕结构壁管材

1. 产品标准：GB/T 19472.2—2004 埋地用聚乙烯(PE)结构壁管道系统第二部分聚乙烯缠绕结构壁管材及相关标准。

2. 行业指导价格(包括现场施工安装指导费用的出厂价)：17700元/t(PE原材料参考价按12000元/t计)。

2012第三届国际纸制品胶片薄膜加工印刷技术设备及材料博览会开幕

2012年10月10日，2012第三届国际纸制品胶片薄膜加工印刷技术设备及材料博览会在上海世贸商城开幕，ICE展会总监Dan Wu致开幕词。

BMB(瑞士)公司带来全球领先的涂布和层压复合设备；戴维斯标准带来为涂覆纸、复合纸及铝箔产品提供挤出和共挤的系统；保利泰带来涂布复合生产线；美国最大的气浮式干燥设备专业设计制造商——爱德旺斯向众多与会专家和买家展示其最先进、最专业的气浮式干燥技术。

随着功能性软包装材料的发展和加工技术的不断提高，软包装在许多领域正扮演着越来越重要的角色。软包装行业的进步极大地促进了食品、日化等行业的发展，这些行业的发展反过来又进一步拉动了对软包装市场的需求，使软包装行业获得了巨大的市场动力。在此基础上，软包装机械也呈现出新的发展趋势。

ICE Asia2012每两年举办一届，对纸张、薄膜、铝箔、织物和无纺布以及胶片等柔软薄片材料的处理加工和印刷的高度专业性的产业链，涵盖印刷、包装、塑料、纺织等行业中涉及柔软薄片材料的处理加工和印刷)产业国际博览会。

中国塑料包装技术与绿色包装论坛举办

10月15~18日，中国包装联合会塑料制品包装委员会在天津举办了中国塑料包装工业高新技术与绿色包装论坛暨2012中国包装联合会塑料制品包装委员会年会。

论坛针对近年来我国塑料包装行业的发展以及国内外复杂的经济形势，探讨新形势下塑料包装行业何如更好地适应经济发展的需要。论坛除涉及国

内外塑料包装行业现状及发展趋势等行业宏观层面外，还对绿色包装理念与实践、绿色智能缓释保鲜与纳米改性包装材料、薄膜行业的发展困惑与行情分析、包装行业研发资金的申请、中空包装行业发展形势、塑料包装相关国家标准与行业标准、用溯源法保障塑料包装安全、如何通过质量控制降低企业运营风险、智能包装、食品活性包装用抗菌材料技术进展、无溶剂复合设备的发展现状和趋势等进行交流。

《中国塑料工业发展史》编写工作启动

2012年10月17日，根据中国塑协〔2012〕第091号“关于提供编写《中国塑料工业发展史》相关资料的通知”精神，在成都召开了《中国塑料工业发展史》编写工作座谈会。会议前半段由杨惠娣秘书长代曹俭常务副理事长主持、后半段由曹俭常务副理事长主持，会议就《中国塑料工业发展史》的编写工作进行了热烈讨论，提出了许多建设性的意见和建议：

(1)组织编写《中国塑料工业发展史》是一件很有意义的好事；鉴于行业中的一些知情人年事已高，编写工作具有紧迫性，从某种意义上，需要积极抢救。

(2)《中国塑料工业发展史》可以按照3条线编写：一是整个行业，可从科技、新产品、生产管理、标准化、制度等方面编写，且涉及整个行业的部分，必须由协会来写；二是分地区，如北京、天津、上海、广东……包括港澳台地区；三是按照制品，如板、管、丝、膜……各类制品不要平均着力，要有重点。

(3)要写重点企业，对选那些企业的原则，认为不一定企业规模大就入选，可从产量、质量、出口量、创新性、设备先进性等多方面考虑，要有特点，对行业发展有影响。另外，历史上曾经存在过，在一段时间对行业产生过积极影响，但，现在不存在了的企业也应该写。

(4)人物如何选，有一些人对一个地区塑料工业的发展影响较大，但不一定对整个行业有较大影响，是否就写到地区篇；对有争议的人士，是否要写、是否能写，没有展开，但存不同看法，需进一步订出一些选择的原则。

(5)编写《中国塑料工业发展史》是一项很大的工程，工程量极大；所写事件等均要有出处，有证据，查实资料是必须的；如查阅档案，就很费时费力，没有专人，难于完成，建议组织专门班子，由专职人员来写。

(6)编写工作各环节均会发生费用，建议协会立项，向有关部门申请经费，申请可在编写工作开展到一定程度时进行；部分经费也可请企业赞助。

(7)关于资料征集，还可通过网络进行，广泛发动。

(8)具体编写是按照时间，还是按照事件，应该视行业具体情况、具体特点决定。

(9)建于行业规模虽大，但企业规模不大，资料保存等基础工作较差，有些内容尽量写，尽量挖，但也只能写到哪算到哪。

(10)争取再召开几次座谈会，在汇总各方意见后于今年底提出框架。

鉴于对此项工作缺乏经验，在工作过程中，要特别注意依靠行业老同志、各地方塑料协会和中国塑协专委会，随时调整工作方向，在保证质量的前提下，力争“十二五”结束时完成《中国塑料工业发展史》编写出版工作。

2012年中国塑协专家委员会二届四次会议召开

2012年10月17~20日，中国塑协专家委员会二届四次会议暨2012年塑料新材料、新技术、新成果交流会在成都召开。

会期两天，18日上午全体会议代表出席在成都市新都区木兰镇中塑·成都国际贸易中心举办的“全国发展改革试点小城镇”授牌仪式和中塑·成都国际贸易中心“西部塑料化工产业商贸总部基地”荣誉称号的授牌仪式。出席大会庆祝活动的有中国轻工业联合会党委副书记、副会长兼中国塑加工工业协会理事长钱桂敬；中国塑协常务副会长曹俭及中国塑协名誉会长廖正品；国家发改委城市和小城镇改革发展中心领导、新都区政府、木兰镇镇政府及中塑集团的各位领导及来宾300多人。中国塑协钱桂敬部长和国家发改委领导分别向中塑·成都国际贸易中心和木兰镇政府进行了授牌仪式。曹俭副会长主持了中国塑协专家委员会二届四次会议开幕仪式，并讲话。

18日下午与会的160多名专家代表听取了塑料新材料、新技术、新成果的交流报告，清华大学于建教授、北京航空航天大学詹茂盛教授和北京理工大学的陈晋南教授分别主持了三个半天的交流活动。钱桂敬部长对中国塑料产业的形势和“十二五”期间塑料产业如何发展作了重要讲话。会议《论文集》收录论文57篇，精心选择安排了24位专家进行了内容丰富、有深度、有水平的演讲，不少内容涉及了当前塑料产业共同关注的关键性、共性技术问题，如四川大学王琪教授的新型无卤阻燃高分子泡沫材料的研究，解决了XPS板材的阻燃问题。北京化工大学苑会林教授的酚醛泡沫塑料保温板材在建筑外墙外保温中的应用演讲引起了广泛的关注，苑教授介绍酚醛发泡板材满足了当今建筑外墙保温材料的所有性能的要求，是一个值得推广的保温材料。在塑机节能减排方面瞿金平院士的论文，回顾了塑料塑化输运方法从纯剪切形变加工到振动剪切形变加工再到体积拉伸形变加工的演变过程、论证了这种新型塑料加工设备能耗降低，在多相多组份复合材料、生物质复合材料等物料体系的加工方面具有独特优势，有利于实现塑料加工成型过程节能降耗。塑料微成型技术我国处于刚刚起步阶段，被认为是继 IT、生物之后，21 世纪最具发展潜力的高新技术，是未来十年高增长的新型产业，也是当前高科技发展的重要领域之一。中科院宁波材料科学与工程研究所的翟文涛研究员的超薄石墨烯高导热膜的制备、北京化工大学吴大鸣教授的聚合物微尺度成型模具设计制造技术、北京化工大学杨卫民教授的熔体静电纺丝微纳米纤维制备技术进展及德国弗劳恩霍夫学会北京技术代表张洪波先生的柔性材料的真空镀膜技术，涉及的都是微纳米材料及微纳米加工技术，是功能高分子复合材料制备的最新技术，充分体现了我国科学家勇于把高端技术和创新技术的研发有机的结合起来，这对提高我国塑料制造业的总体水平是大有好处的。

中国塑协改性塑料专业委员会 2012 年年会改性塑料新技术、新设备、新产品展示交流大会召开

10 月 19 日至 23 日，“中国塑协改性塑料专业委员会在四川成都—石棉—西昌—雅安举行，同期举办“改性塑料新技术、新设备、新产品展示交流大会”，关心、支持、从事改性塑料行业的有关企业领导及科技人员、管理人员、大专院校、科研院所专家、教授出席会议。

年会同期举办的“改性塑料新技术、新设备、新产品展示交流大会”围绕以下几个方面的问题进行宣讲和研讨：

1. 编织袋新国标《塑料编织袋通用技术要求》(GB/T－8946—2012)发布实施对填充母料行业走向的影响及应对策略

2. “石塑纸”的定位及发展态势

3. 沉淀硫酸钡在塑料薄膜中的应用及在透光、外观、手感等诸多方面的优势与特点

4. PET 瓶再生利用动态及制造编织制品的可行性

5. 节能大容量挤注成型成套设备以及废旧塑料为基料的、木丝为筋的塑筋模板成型技术

6. 可使填充塑料制品材料密度降低的发泡母料制作技术

7. 免干燥节能型 PET 瓶片增粘技术、设备及大面积熔体在线过滤器研究及应用

8. 以高铝粉煤灰为原料生产的硅酸钙微粉特点及在塑料中应用前景

9. 废弃塑料绿色环保、高值高效利用技术进展

10. “改性塑料标准手册”内容及特色

中国塑协赴越南出席亚洲塑料论坛

2012 年 10 月 21～26 日，中国塑协马占峰秘书长代表中国塑料加工工业协会应越南塑料协会邀请赴越南胡志明市出席第二十二届亚洲塑料论坛(APF)。

一、出席亚洲塑料论坛理事会

22 日出席了亚洲塑料论坛理事会议。出席会议的亚洲塑料行业成员国代表有新加坡、菲律宾、马来西亚、泰国、印尼、越南等东南亚国家与中国、印度、日本、孟加拉国、缅甸。

重要的议题主要有：

1. APF 成员国食品包装标准和法规的情况调查；

2. 会议一致通过 APF 永久秘书处设置在马来西亚，Callum Chan 先生担任秘书长，任期为 2012～2018 年；

3. Callum Chan 先生鼓励 APF 中不是“全球塑料协会解决海洋垃圾宣言”签署国的成员考虑签署这一宣言；

4. 中国塑料加工工业协会作为 APF 可持续发展委员会媒体组的牵头国，汇报了曾举办过关于密胺塑料和一次性发泡塑料餐具的新闻发布会，对于行业发展发挥了重要作用；

5. 由中国塑料加工工业协会提议，下届 APF 将于 2013 年 9 月在中国台州和第 13 届中国塑料交易会及会议一并举行。

二、出席亚洲塑料论坛

亚洲塑料论坛在 23 日举行，来自各国大约 400 余人出席了论坛，主要内容有各国塑料行业发展情况介绍与可持续发展为主题的演讲。马占峰秘书长代表中国塑协作了发言，期间与各国代表作了友好交流。

三、参观越南塑料展览会

24 日出席亚洲塑料论坛的全体代表参观了越南塑料工业展览会。该展会约一万平米左右，来自中国大陆和台湾省的参展商占到近一半的比重，与国内相关展会相比规模不大。感觉越南塑料工业起步晚，产品科技含量低，但因加工成本更低，出口更具竞争力，其原料依赖进口。我国的塑料机械和模具比其他国家产品性价比更高，在越南有广阔的市场。

中国轻工业联合会步正发会长率团访问台湾

10 月 24 日至 30 日，应台湾塑胶制品工业同业

公会的邀请，步正发会长率团赴台湾进行了访问。为欢迎代表团访台，同业公会专门组织了由蔡明忠理事长主持的座谈会，邀请包括著名企业台塑、奇美等十余家台湾塑料行业企业的负责人出席，就世界塑料行业新技术、新材料、市场状况和行业发展趋势等议题进行了交流，并共同探讨了进一步加强扩大两岸塑料行业合作的有关事宜。

座谈会上，步正发会长介绍了中国轻工业联合会的职能和开展的工作、大陆轻工业发展取得的成就和在国民经济中的重要地位，着重介绍了大陆塑料行业的发展现状。步正发会长还表示，中国轻工业联合会作为行业组织，愿意大力促进两岸塑料行业的合作交流，为台商在大陆投资提供必要的帮助。

代表团专程前往云林县和台南县，分别参观了台塑和奇美两大企业，就生产、管理、研发、市场、物流、人力资源、公益事业等有关问题进行了深入考察和交流。

通过与台湾同行的座谈和对企业的参观考察，代表团感到，随着两岸交流的日益深入，大陆经济的强劲发展和广阔市场，台商在大陆投资的不断增长，两岸的经济已经牢牢地融合在一起，密不可分，优势互补，共同发展，台湾企业有和大陆加强扩大合作交流的强烈愿望和深厚的感情基础；台塑、奇美这样的著名企业在生产和管理、科研开发、公益事业等诸方面有很多先进和独到之处，值得大陆企业学习借鉴。

王本和、曹俭、吴曼云、张蕴藏等同志陪同访问。

中国第六届国际塑木论坛举办

2012 年 11 月 2 ~5 日，由中国塑协主办、塑木制品专委会承办，第六届中国国际塑木论坛暨 2012 年中国塑协塑木制品专委会年会在宁波召开。

论坛以“资源有限、发展无限”为主题，与会演讲者围绕世界塑木发展的新动向，新技术以及塑木产品运用的新领域展开研讨，大会邀请 300 多位来自世界知名企业、科研院校、行业协会、专业研究机构的代表和高级专家，介绍行业发展情况及前景，共同交流介绍最新科研成果、生产技术以及应用技术的发展，加强企业核心竞争力，提高企业产品质量和管理能力，为企业提供一个高端的技术交流平台，和新产品推介平台。

中国轻工业联合会副会长中国塑协理事长钱桂敬出席会议并讲话。施惠芳市长等领导出席会议。

虽然我国塑木产品的生产和应用起步较晚，但几年来有了较快发展，初具规模并已初步形成了较为完整的生产体系和配套产业链，产品质量不断提高，国内市场销售量逐渐提高。但与国外塑木产业相比，还存在明显差距。正视差距实施赶超战略，努力缩小差距，全面提升塑木行业整体水平和竞争力，是塑木行业面临的重要任务。这次会议云集了塑木行业成功企业家和工程技术与管理各方精英，既是塑木产业技术交流会，也是一次新技术、新装备、新材料、新产品展示会，因此这是一次共同探讨行业发展、加强协作、促进技术进步，开创塑木行业协同、健康发展新局面的重要会议。

2012 流延薄膜、镀铝膜行业市场与技术发展研讨会召开

2012 年 11 月 4 日，由中国塑协主办的“2012 流延薄膜、镀铝膜行业市场与技术发展研讨会”在广东汕头召开。来自全国流延薄膜产业链的 400 多名企业负责人出席会议。

中国塑协常务副理事长曹俭，中国塑协流延薄膜专委会理事长、BOPET 专委会理事长徐志强，中国塑协镀铝膜专委会理事长洪晓冬，广东金明精机股份有限公司董事长马镇鑫，广东省塑料工业协会会长符岸等领导出席会议。

马镇鑫董事长致欢迎词。中国塑协常务副理事长曹俭致开幕辞。徐志强理事长、洪晓冬理事长、王全经理、曾祥平副总经理、顾春生经理、孙冬泉副秘书长、王全海经理、朱模军经理分别作了“流延薄膜产业链健康发展探讨”、“中国镀膜行业的发展趋势及展望”、“高品质多层共挤流延膜生产线”、“镀铝膜行业 2012 年发展情况分析”、“宽幅高速带来成本优势，新技术应用创造盈利空间”、“CPP 薄膜行业 2012 年分析及 2013 年发展探讨”、“流延薄膜行业综合金融服务解决方案”和“美国微觉视表面检测系统在高端薄膜行业的应用介绍”、“TPU 薄膜的性能与应用前景”、“美国 Cloeren(科罗炼)模头技术在薄膜领域中的应用”、“缠绕膜的发展现状及行业发展趋势”、“关于《夹层玻璃用聚乙烯醇缩丁醛中间膜》国家标准编制工作总结”、“Borstar® 多峰 PP 技术及高性能流延薄膜”的报告。

与会代表到金明精机股份有限公司，参观了最新研发的 3.5m 幅宽镀铝级 CPP 生产线的开机演示。

会议期间，流延薄膜专委会在 5 日晚上召开了“第一届五次理事会”和“第二次 CPP 行业骨干企业信息交流会”，会议由孙冬泉秘书长主持。会议主要交流 CPP 薄膜行业近期市场与价格情况，回顾分析了 2012 年三季度走势，探讨了 2012 年四季度 CPP 薄膜市场需求发展趋势，交流了原辅材料有关信息；探讨加强行业合作有关问题，并对流延薄膜专委会换届的有关工作进行了商讨。尤其是朱素良总经理介绍了公司如何从零做大的一些心得和体会，得到了与会企业负责人的一致肯定和称赞。与会理事讨论了关于在2013年专委会理事会换届事宜，提出应在进一步征求广大流延薄膜企业意见的基础上，在推荐好合适的牵头企业的情况下再筹备换届事宜。

国际化学品制造商协会将举办国际食品包材法规研讨会召开

11月7～8日，国际化学品制造商协会主办的“2012国际食品包装材料法规研讨会”在北京举办。来自卫生部、国家食品安全风险评估中心、国家质检总局、前美国FDA专家、美国塑料协会(SPI)、欧洲化工协会的领导和专家，和参会代表共同交流食品包装材料的法规体系和风险评估方法，推动中国的食品安全法规体系向着更科学、更健康的方式前进。

主要报告为：国家食品安全风险评估中心王竹天 研究员的“中国食品安全风险评估中心介绍及食品安全风险评估体系、卫生部卫生监督中心王永芳处长的“食品包装材料新产品申请”、国家质检总局食品生产监管司于薇处长的“市场监管及QS市场准入”、上海食品安全办公室顾振华主任的“中国食品包装材料标准框架体系及未来构想”、美国FDA食品接触材料申报(FCN)前任专家的“美国食品接触材料许可及风险评估“、欧洲化学工业协会食品接触材料专家组的“欧盟食品接触管理体系”、国家食品安全风险评估中心樊永祥博士的“GB 9685及清理工作进展，以及中国包材标准制修订计划介绍”、宁波出入境检验检疫局陈少鸿专家的“中国进出口食品接触材料的检验监管体系”

2012第七届中国塑料工业新材料新工艺新装备行业峰会召开

2012年11月9日，由中国塑协、广东省塑料工业协会、佛山市南海狮山镇人民政府主办，广东仕诚塑料机械公司承办的“2012第七届中国塑料工业新材料新工艺新装备行业峰会”，在狮山镇举行。中国塑协常务副理事长曹俭、名誉理事长廖正品、秘书长马占峰、广东省轻工行业会长杨大行、中国工程院院士翟金平；广东省塑料行业协会会长符岸及企业代表400余人出席大会，中国塑协常务副理事长曹俭致辞祝贺。

广东仕诚塑料机械有限公司是国内集研发、专业生产、营销为一体的流延薄膜设备专业生产企业。公司自2004年起从美国、英国、德国引进的多台四轴、五轴立式和卧式加工中心等大型现代化生产设备，专业生产CPP/CPE流延薄膜生产线、PVB玻璃夹层薄膜综合生产线、绿色中空阳光板生产线、EVA高粘度流延薄膜生产线和CPET流延薄膜生产线等系列产品，以其高品质、高成品率、高质量、高性价比、低耗能等优点畅销国内外，使之迅速跃升为流延薄膜设备的标志性品牌之一。2005年被国家商务部定位“重点扶持企业”。2010年被商务部及中国塑协评为三A信用等级评价企业。

狮山镇政府十分注重扶持塑料包装产业做大做强，在政策引导、规范管理、加大扶持等方面做了大量的工作，在推动了地区塑料产业发展的同时，出台了塑料包装行业发展规划，提出要坚持技术创新和企业结构创新相结合，用高新技术改造提升传统产业和发展高新技产业相结合，加速狮山镇塑料包装产品结构的调整，增强产品在国内外市场的竞争力，在加大技术创新投入的前提下，使狮山塑料包装行业在末来五年以每年18%的速度递增，形成规摸较大的塑料包装制品区域集群，成为狮山区域济发展的重要组成部份。

钱桂敬理事长在广东考察塑料企业

2012年11月16日，中国轻工业联合会副会长、中国塑协理事长钱桂敬在参加轻工业联合会在广东中山召开的“全国轻工行业特色区域和产业集群发展工作会议”后，考察了广东省相关塑料制品、及塑料机械制造企业，中国塑协曹俭常务理事长、广东省塑协符岸会长陪同考察。

上午，钱会长一行首先考察国内产量规模最大的塑料管材生产企业广东联塑科技有限公司，参观了公司产品展示厅，研发大楼的实验、检测设施，公司在顺德龙江生产基地PVC管材、管件生产车间，观看了公司宣传片。左满论总裁全面介绍了公司成功上市后发展情况，特别是今年公司在困难经营环境中的运营情况。钱会长对广东联塑公司近年来的发展表示肯定。据介绍，广东联塑去年销售已超100亿元，今年仍将有所增长。

中午，钱会长一行参观考察广东仕诚机械有限公司。张春华董事长、秦志红副总经理介绍了公司发展情况以及刚结束的“第七届中国塑料工业新材料新工艺新装备行业峰会”情况。广东仕诚公司是当地先进塑料机械装备制造代表性企业，产品全部自主研发和拥有独立自主产权，获各项专利近60项。中国塑协曾授予其“中国高端宽幅流延膜装备加工技术基地”。钱会长希望该公司能继续依靠科技创新，为振兴我国塑机制造民族工业贡献力量。

下午，钱会长受邀请来到广州博创机械股份有限公司参观考察，受到朱康健总裁的热情接待，朱康健总裁亲自驾电动车引导参观生产基地，介绍公司先进的管理模式和企业文化氛围。钱会长十分详细考察了博创公司各系列、高精度注塑机生产现场，并就塑料制品行业对塑机装备需求和高端塑料制品生产需要高精装备支撑等提出建议。博创机械公司是广州制造业转型升级、技术创新实现企业高速发展的代表性企业，也是我国塑料机械装备新崛起的领军企业。钱会长、曹俭副理事长、符岸会长还表示将与中国塑料机械工业行业和企业密切合作，为我国和广东地区塑料制造和塑料装备制造业共同发展而努力。

第五届生物基和生物分解材料技术与应用国际研讨会暨中国塑协降解塑料专业委员会2012年年会召开

2012年11月25～27日，由中国塑协降解塑料专业委员会(DPC)、全国生物基材料及降解制品标准化技术委员会、日本生物塑料研究会(JBPA)、美国生物分解塑料研究院(BPI)、韩国生物塑料协会(KBPA)主办的第五届生物基和生物分解材料技术与应用国际研讨会(ICTABP5)，暨中国塑协降解塑料专业委员会2012年年会在广东召开。

国家发改委环资司马维晨博士等领导出席会议。来自美国、日本、韩国、德国、英国和中国的360余名专家、生产商汇聚一堂，共商这一新兴产业的未来发展。参加会议的领导和嘉宾有中国塑料加工工业协会曹俭常务副理事长、国家发展和改革委员会资环司马维晨博士、中国塑料加工工业协会马占峰秘书长、北京工商大学轻工业塑料加工应用研究所所长黄志刚教授、美国生物分解塑料研究所 Steve Mojo 秘书长、韩国生物塑料协会秘书长 In－joo Chin 秘书长、德国 DIN CERTCO Miriam Sahl 女士等。大会由中国塑协降解专业委员会秘书长、北京工商大学轻工业塑料加工应用研究所检测标准中心主任翁云宣主持。

在两天的会期里，与会代表就北美地区可堆肥料的最新进展、日本生物降解和生物基塑料的发展、韩国生物降解塑料工业发展、欧洲可堆肥塑料认证及市场情况进行了交流，并对聚乳酸产品的最新进展、缩聚法合成高分子量聚乳酸及其纳米复合材料、微生物合成 PHA 材料、聚乳酸改性等学术问题展开讨论。

2012版《中国塑料工业年鉴》出版发行

由中国塑协主编的2012版《中国塑料工业年鉴》出版发行

《中国塑料工业年鉴》(2012)为《年鉴》第11卷，与前10卷在时间和内容上保持连续性。《年鉴》全面、系统、准确地记述了上年度塑料行业发展状况，设有“综述”、“专论”、“大事记”、“全国塑料工业生产经营情况统计”、“各地区塑料工业情况”、“主要制品行业情况”、“专利技术”、“重点企业”等栏目；集手册、年表、图录、书目、索引、文摘、表谱、统计资料、指南于一身；具有权威性、资料性、工具性、系统性的特点，同时又肩负着“资政”、“存史”和“宣传推广”的社会责任。为满足海外读者的需要，部分文章译成了英文，增加了英文目录。借助中国石化出版社的发行渠道，通过字里行间记载着中国塑料业的辉煌成绩。全书约800页，约1600千字，16开本精装，定价380元。

关于对“中国塑料行业(第五批)初评和(第一批)复评企业信用等级评价结果”的公告

2012年12月5日中国塑协发布“对中国塑料行业(第五批)初评和(第一批)复评企业信用等级评价结果的公告”：

中国塑料行业(第五批)初评企业信用等级评价结果

序号	企业名称	等级	编号
1	安徽万安环境工程有限公司	AAA	201209911100228
2	成都奥鑫管业有限公司	AAA	201209911100229
3	华瀚科技有限公司	AAA	201209911100230
4	江苏双星彩塑新材料股份有限公司	AAA	201209911100231
5	泉州兴源塑料有限公司	AAA	201209911100232
6	瑞金市金和塑业发展有限公司	AAA	201209911100233
7	山东东宏管业有限公司	AAA	201209911100234
8	山东陆宇塑胶工业有限公司	AAA	201209911100235
9	山东新宇包装股份有限公司	AAA	201209911100236
10	四川江瀚工业股份有限公司	AAA	201209911100237
11	台州奥博管业有限公司	AAA	201209911100238

中国塑料行业(第一批)复评企业信用等级评价结果

企业名称	等级	编号
安徽华驰塑业有限公司	AAA	394033030D00162
成都川路塑胶集团有限公司	AAA	394033030D00163
佛山高明骏腾塑胶有限公司	AAA	394033030D00164
福建融音塑业科技有限公司	AAA	394033030D00165
福建亚通新材料科技股份有限公司	AAA	394033030D00166
福建振云塑业股份有限公司	AAA	394033030D00167
甘肃大禹节水集团股份有限公司	AAA	394033030D00168

续表

企业名称	等级	编号
广东海兴塑胶有限公司	AAA	394033030D00169
鹤山市美耐德科技有限公司	AAA	394033030D00170
广东仕诚塑料机械有限公司	AAA	394033030D00171
广东炜林纳功能材料有限公司	AAA	394033030D00172
河北迪美特塑业制品股份有限公司	AAA	394033030D00173
湖南路路通塑业股份有限公司	AAA	394033030D00174
华亚东营塑胶有限公司	AAA	394033030D00175
济宁得亚利聚合体有限公司	AAA	394033030D00176
江苏联冠科技发展有限公司	AAA	394033030D00177
南雄市金叶包装材料有限公司	AAA	394033030D00178
南亚塑胶工业（郑州）有限公司	AAA	394033030D00179
汕头卜高通美实业有限公司	AAA	394033030D00180
汕头市康家宝塑料制品实业有限公司	AAA	394033030D00181
烟台万华超纤股份有限公司	AAA	394033030D00182
潍坊现代塑胶有限公司	AAA	394033030D00183
昆明普尔顿管业有限公司	AAA	394033030D00184
山东华信塑胶股份有限公司	AAA	394033030D00185
山东省塑料工业有限公司	AAA	394033030D00186
山东胜邦塑胶有限公司	AAA	394033030D00187
山东英科环保再生资源股份有限公司	AAA	394033030D00188
四川东泰新材料科技有限公司	AAA	394033030D00189
四川省海维塑胶有限公司	AAA	394033030D00190
温州市华康合成革有限公司	AAA	394033030D00191
西安高科建材科技有限公司	AAA	394033030D00192
雄县旭日纸塑包装有限公司	AAA	394033030D00193
烟台冰轮塑业有限公司	AAA	394033030D00194
义乌市大大箱包材料有限公司	AAA	394033030D00195
宏岳塑胶集团有限公司	AAA	394033030D00196

续表

企业名称	等级	编号
佛山市远华塑料实业有限公司	AAA	394033030D00197
昆山协孚人造皮有限公司	AAA	394033030D00198
福建隆上超纤有限公司	AAA	394033030D00199
山东日科化学股份有限公司	AAA	394033030D00200
黄石市鸿达塑料模具有限责任公司	AAA	394033030D00201
昆明创辉塑胶科技有限公司	AAA	394033030D00202
广东联塑科技实业有限公司	AAA	394033030D00203
天津军星管业集团有限公司	AAA	394033030D00204
山东同大海岛新材料股份有限公司	AAA	394033030D00205
温州人造革有限公司	AAA	394033030D00206
云南金恒实业有限公司	AAA	394033030D00207
广州市振兴实业有限公司	AAA	394033030D00208
江西广源化工有限责任公司	AAA	394033030D00209
康泰塑胶科技集团有限公司	AAA	394033030D00210
三斯达（福建）塑胶有限公司	AAA	394033030D00211
山东金达双鹏集团有限公司	AAA	394033030D00212
上海华峰超纤材料股份有限公司	AAA	394033030D00213
四川森普管材股份有限公司	AAA	394033030D00214
宜昌宜硕塑业有限公司	AAA	394033030D00215
义乌市鑫挺人造革有限公司	AAA	394033030D00216
云南曲靖塑料（集团）有限公司	AAA	394033030D00217
浙江经纬集团环保工程有限公司	AAA	394033030D00218
浙江龙跃科技有限公司	AAA	394033030D00219
浙江中财管道科技股份有限公司	AAA	394033030D00220
浙江中财型材有限责任公司	AAA	394033030D00221
浙江中元枫叶管业有限公司	AAA	394033030D00222
重庆顾地塑胶电器有限公司	AAA	394033030D00223
四川攀西塑胶有限责任公司	AAA	394033030D00224
广东东方管业有限公司	AAA	394033030D00225
山东天鹤塑胶股份有限公司	AAA	394033030D00226
东营大明新型建材有限责任公司	AAA	394033030D00227

第三方评价机构：北京益信健信国际信用管理有限公司。

塑料管道产品行业指导价格发布

2012 年 12 月 7 日，中国塑协塑料管道专业委员会发布塑料管道产品行业指导价格(2012 年第 4 号)：

一、给水用硬聚氯乙烯(PVC－U)管材(非铅盐稳定剂)

1. 产品标准：GB/T 10002.1—2006 给水用硬聚氯乙烯(PVC－U)管材。

2. 行业指导价格(出厂价)：11100 元/t(PVC 树脂参考价按 6700 元/t 计)。

二、排水用 PVC－U 管材

1. 产品标准：GB/T 5836.1—2006 建筑排水用硬聚氯乙烯管材。GB/T 20221—2006 无压埋地排污、排水用硬聚氯乙烯(PVC－U)管材。

2. 行业指导价格(出厂价)：10100 元/t(PVC 树脂参考价按 6700 元/t 计)。

三、埋地排水用 PVC－U 双壁波纹管材

1. 产品标准：GB/T 18477.1—2007 埋地排水用硬聚氯乙烯(PVC－U)结构壁管道系统 第一部分：双壁波纹管材。

2. 行业指导价格(出厂价)：10800 元/t(PVC 树脂参考价按 6700 元/t 计)。

四、燃气用埋地聚乙烯(PE)管材

1. 产品标准：GB 15558.1—2003 燃气用埋地聚乙烯(PE)管道系统 第一部分 管材。

2. 行业指导价格(出厂价)：19500 元/t(PE 原材料参考价按 14800 元/t 计)。

五、给水用 PE 管材

1. 产品标准：GB/T 13663—2000 给水用聚乙烯(PE)管材。

2. 行业指导价格(出厂价)：18400 元/t(PE 原材料参考价按 13700 元/t 计)。

六、埋地排水用 PE 双壁波纹管材

1. 产品标准：GB/T 19472.1—2004 埋地用聚乙烯(PE)结构壁管道系统 第一部分 聚乙烯双壁波纹管材。

2. 行业指导价格(出厂价)：16900 元/t(PE 原材料参考价按 12200 元/t 计)。

七、PE 缠绕结构壁管材

1. 产品标准：GB/T 19472.2—2004 埋地用聚乙烯(PE)结构壁管道系统 第二部分 聚乙烯缠绕结构壁管材及相关标准。

2. 行业指导价格(包括现场施工安装指导费用的出厂价)：17900 元/t(PE 原材料参考价按 12200 元/t 计)。

沈阳塑料产业协会成立大会召开

2012 年 12 月 8 日，沈阳塑料产业协会成立大会召开。中国塑料加工工业协

会常务副理事长曹俭到会祝贺。

沈阳塑料产业协会的成立是沈阳塑料工业发展的需要，也是沈阳塑料行业发展由自由竞争进入整体发展高级阶段的明显标志和重要里程碑。协会的成立，会员间通过相互学习，横向交流，可以有效提高企业的生产技术创新水平，促进科技进步，使沈阳塑料行业向环境友好型，资源节约型，科技创新型健康发展。

协会的成立为沈阳塑料行业提供了一个技术交流，企业互助的平台，为沈阳的塑料行业、企业和政府服务。

XPS 产品生产工艺及应用技术推广交流会举办

2012 年 12 月 19～21 日，XPS 产品生产工艺及应用技术推广交流会在北京举办。

会议邀请国家有关建筑节能政策法规、标准制定主管部门以及行业内有影响的专家学者，解读国家有关建筑节能外墙保温的新政策和推广目录，分析行业发展中面临的新情况、新问题、新机遇，有关专家介绍一批先进适用的建筑节能外墙保温新材料、新产品、新技术、新系统，以及针对满足建筑节能和绿色建筑发展新的技术要求的 XPS 系统化解决方案。

授课专家：住房与城乡建设部科技发展促进中心 副总工杨西伟教授级高工，中国建筑节能协会副秘书长梁 洋 ，北京化工大学材料科学与工程学院苑会林教授，北京化工大学 机电工程学院何亚东副院长，中国阻燃学会北京工商大学科技处副处长钱立军副秘书长。

会议内容：

一、《墙体保温系统与墙体材料推广应用和限制、禁止使用技术的公告》(住房城乡建设部公告第 1338 号)编制背景和主要内容解读　；

二、技术交流及推广。1. XPS 生产工艺及常见问题解决方案；2. XPS 保温材料的国家标准及质量评价；3. XPS 阻燃改性及产品阻燃检测；4. 超零界 CO2 发泡 XPS 板材生产技术介绍；5. XPS 相关的技术问题分析；6. XPS 保温板在外墙保温系统中的应用：(1)建筑节能形势与任务；(2)外墙保温系统技术现状及发展趋势；(3)外墙保温系统对保温材料防火性能要求；(4)《外墙外保温工程技术规程》JGJ 144 修订进展；(5)XPS 保温板在外墙保温系统应用的技术要求。

佛山市塑料制品国际采购中心项目奠基

12 月 21 日，佛山市塑料制品国际采购中心项目

奠基动工仪式举行，中心依托中国合成革产业基地技术创新服务中心，建设成为广东甚至我国南方地区最大的新材料物料综合性批发交易市场。

中国塑协常务副理事长曹俭、佛山市副市长宋德平、高明区委书记谭伟平、区长黄棋泰等，出席仪式并为项目奠基动土。

项目位于高明荷城沧江工业园，临近广明高速高明荷城出口。总投资15亿元，占地25万多平方米。

塑料产业是高明的传统优势产业，但由于缺乏专业市场，制约了高明塑料企业做大做强。佛山市塑料制品国际采购中心的动工建设，将打破高明没有专业性交易市场的历史，提升高明塑料行业地位，加快产业转型升级。

佛山市塑料制品国际采购中心项目总投资为15亿元，投资方广东万方投资有限公司表示，将全力确保建设资金的落实，确保首期将在两年内建成。按照规划，采购中心主要建设内容为：展销中心、微型企业孵化中心、交易服务大楼、交易行、交易大棚，以及物流中心、仓储中心、会议大厅、加工车间、酒店餐厅楼、宿舍区等。项目建成后，形成集交易、仓储、加工、配送、连锁经营、信息收发、电子结算、汇兑、生活配套、旅游会展为一体的国际性采购中心。

钱桂敬副会长出席“中国挤出模具之都”的授牌仪式

12月26日，中国轻工业联合会副会长、中国塑协理事长钱桂敬出席“中国挤出模具之都”的授牌仪式。黄石市人民政府市长杨晓波、副市长刘圣华，挤出模具企业代表出席仪式。

授牌仪式上，黄石市市长杨晓波说黄石市是我国塑料挤出模具重要生产地区之一，全市共有50多家大中型挤出模具骨干企业，产品占全国市场约60%左右的份额，远销世界25个国家和地区，具有良好的声誉。为加快挤出模具行业发展，黄石市还将规划建设中国挤出模具生产基地。该基地前期投资30亿元，预计2013年动工，基地建成后可年产各类型挤出模具10万套，产值约30亿元。基地内还将通过招商引资引进一批下游产品生产厂家，从而形成完整的挤出模具上下游产业链。

钱桂敬副会长肯定了黄石市立足本地区，充分发挥黄石市的地区优势，大力走挤出模具特色区域和产业集群发展之路，为黄石市乃至全国塑料行业的发展做出了贡献。同时介绍了我国塑料行业情况以及“十二五”我国塑料加工业发展规划，对塑料行业的科学定位进行了说明，重点阐述了塑料行业在国民经济中重要作用。钱桂敬副会长表示，黄石市在重点发展挤出模具特色产业的基础上，还要研究开发其他种类的模具，形成挤出模具系列化，打造完整的模具产业。同时注重发展塑料加工制品行业，利用黄石市钢铁冶炼优势，形成完整的上下游产业链，促进黄石地方经济的发展。

中国塑协塑料配线器材专委会一届四次会员大会暨凯迪威机械行业前沿新技术研讨会召开

2012年12月19日，中国塑协塑料配线器材专业委员会第一届四次会员代表大会在柳市镇召开，中国塑协常务副理事长曹俭出席会议并讲话。

塑料配线器材也是塑料制品中一类重要的产品。配线器材专委会成立三年多来，积极努力、开拓创新，不断加强自身建设，认真履行职责，积极拓展协会服务领域，带领全行业在制定、完成扎带产品行业标准、配合中国塑协制定海关出口加工贸易单耗标准规范行业发展，增强行业内上、下游企业间，同行业企业间的业务交流，提升专委会成员企业整体素质，宣传扎带企业形象等方面做了大量的工作，为增强行业凝聚力，促进扎带行业健康、快速发展做出了有益的贡献。据不完全统计，今年1～10月份，塑料配线器材行业克服了国际金融危机对尼龙扎带产品出口的影响，基本上实现了产销量与上年同期持平。

青岛市塑料行业协会成立

2012年12月，经过在青岛市民政局登记注册，青岛市塑料行业协会成立。协会由从事塑料制品、原料及助剂、塑料机械和模具生产及其塑料相关产品的生产、贸易、科研、咨询服务等单位及有关人士自愿参加组成的非营利行业性性社会团体。主管单位是青岛市经济与信息化委员会，业务上接受山东省塑料协会和中国塑料加工工业协会的指导。

协会现有会员单位120多家，以促进行业交流、服务企业、创建企业之家、推动行业发展为宗旨，主要业务范围：行业管理、信息交流、咨询服务、商务展览、教育培训、国际合作、市场调查、政策建议、保护行业有序竞争和促进行业发展、承办政府委托事项。

（中国塑料加工工业协会　许琳）

2012年塑料化工行业反倾销大事记

一、埃及终止对华氯乙烯聚合物地板套膜的反倾销调查

2012，埃及工贸部发布公告，决定终止对自中国进口的氯乙烯聚合物地板套膜的反倾销调查。公告称自中国进口产品存在倾销，国内产业存在实质损害，但倾销与损害间不存在因果关系。

二、印度对美国和中国台湾的苯酚作出反倾销期中复审终裁

2012年2月9日，印度商工部对原产于美国和中国台湾的苯酚作出反倾销期中复审终裁：自美国和中国台湾进口的苯酚不再对印度国内产业造成实质性损害，因此决定取消上述反倾销措施。涉案产品海关编码为2907.11、2707.99。

2011年2月，印度对原产于美国和中国台湾的苯酚进行反倾销期中复审立案调查。

（注：苯酚是重要的有机化工原料，用它可制取酚醛树脂、己内酰胺、双酚A等化工产品及中间体。）

三、美国对华光学增白剂作出反倾销终裁

2012年3月20日，美国商务部发布公告，对原产于中国和中国台湾的光学增白剂作出反倾销终裁(见下表)。

根据相关法律程序，美国国际贸易委员会将于2012年5月3日对该案作出反倾销产业损害终裁，若为肯定性裁决，美国商务部将对涉案产品发布反倾销征税令。

2011年4月20日，美国商务部对原产于中国和中国台湾的光学增白剂进行反倾销调查，涉案产品海关编码为32042080.00、29336960.50、29215940.00、29215980.90。2011年11月3日，美国商务部对该案作出反倾销初裁，裁定对中国涉案企业征收106.22%～141.08%的反倾销税。

美国对华光学增白剂作出的反倾销终裁结果

国家(地区)	生产商/出口商	倾销幅度(%)
中国	浙江宏达化学制品有限公司(Zhejiang Hongda Chemicals Co., Ltd.)	95.29
	浙江传化华洋化工有限公司(Zhejiang Transfar Whyyon Chemical Co., Ltd.)	63.98
	中国普遍	109.95
中国台湾	Teh Fong Min International Co., Ltd.	6.20
	普遍(包括 Sun Rise Chemical Ind. Co., Ltd.)	6.20

（注：光学增白剂 Optical whitener 是一类能提高白度的有机化合物，已经广泛应用在塑料等方面。）

四、韩国延长对华醋酸乙酯反倾销措施3年

2012年3月26日，韩国财政部表示，韩国将继续延长对来自中国、新加坡和日本的醋酸乙酯加征反倾销税3年，以保护本地生产商。据称，自2012年3月26日起将对来自中国、新加坡和日本的醋酸乙酯加征3.14%～14.17%的惩罚性关税，直到2015年3月26日。

2008年8月25日，韩国对来自中国、新加坡和日本的醋酸乙酯反倾销案作出肯定性终裁，征收5.81%～14.17%的关税，即2008年8月25日～2011年8月24日。醋酸乙酯是一种工业溶剂，常用于油漆，胶水和指甲油产品的生产。韩国化学品生产商拥有其国内醋酸乙酯市场约44%份额。

（注：乙酸乙酯又称醋酸乙酯，纯净的乙酸乙酯是无色透明具有刺激性气味的液体，是一种用途广泛的精细化工产品，具有优异的溶解性、快干性，用途广泛，是一种非常重要的有机化工原料和极好的工业溶剂，被广泛用于乙烯树脂、乙酸纤维树脂等的生产过程中。）

五、南非对华聚氯乙烯板、片、膜、箔及扁条进行反倾销期中复审调查

2012年3月23日，应 Austro Group Limited 的申请，南非对原产于中国的聚氯乙烯板、片、膜、箔及扁条进行反倾销期中复审立案调查。涉案产品海关编码为3920.49。

申诉方在申请书中要求，将厚度为2毫米，宽度不超过20毫米的聚氯乙烯带排除在征税范围之外。

2007年6月，南非对原产于中国的聚氯乙烯板、片、膜、箔及扁条进行反倾销立案调查；2008年4月，南非对此案作出肯定性终裁。

（注：聚氯乙烯是一种通用型合成树脂，根据添加增塑剂的不同，可分为硬质和软质聚氯乙烯两类。）

又讯：南非对华聚氯乙烯板、片、膜、箔及扁条进行反倾销日落复审调查

2012年9月21日，应 Arengo 190(Pty)Ltd. 的申请，南非对原产于中国和中国台湾的聚氯乙烯板、片、膜、箔及扁条进行反倾销日落复审立案调查。涉案产品海关编码为3920.49。

2007年6月，南非对原产于中国和中国台湾的聚氯乙烯板、片、膜、箔及扁条进行反倾销立案调查；2008年4月，南非对此案作出肯定性终裁。

六、欧盟对华双氰胺发布反倾销即将到期公告

2012年4月20日，欧盟委员会发布公告称，对原产于中国的双氰胺的反倾销措施即将于2012年11月16日到期，成员国内企业须在自本公告发布之日起，至正式到期日前3个月的时间内向欧盟委员提交反倾销日落复审申请。涉案产品海关编码为29262000。

2006年8月，欧盟对原产于中国的双氰胺进行反倾销立案调查；2007年11月，欧盟对此案作出肯定性终裁。（注：双氰胺用作环氧树脂胶黏剂潜伏型固化剂，配制单组分环氧胶黏剂等。）

（注：二氰二氨——双氰胺，缩写DICY或DCD，用作环氧树脂胶黏剂潜伏型固化剂，配制单组分环氧胶黏剂等等。）

又讯：欧盟对华双氰胺进行反倾销日落复审调查

2012年11月15日，应成员国内企业AlzChem AG的申请，欧盟对原产于中国的双氰胺进行反倾销日落复审立案调查。涉案产品海关编码为29262000。

2006年8月，欧盟对原产于中国的双氰胺进行反倾销立案调查；2007年11月，欧盟对此案作出肯定性终裁。

七、印度对华PVC胶膜进行反倾销新出口商复审调查

2012年4月12日，应海宁市天福经编织造有限公司(Haining Tianfu Wrap Knitting Co Ltd，China PR)（生产商）、Manna，Korea RP(出口商)的申请，印度对原产于中国的PVC胶膜进行反倾销新出口商复审立案调查。涉案产品海关编码为39201019、39201012、39204900、39219026、39219029、39269099、39199090、39181090、39189090、39269080。

本案的调查期为2012年4月1日~2012年9月30日。

八、墨西哥取消对华塑料卷笔刀的反倾销措施

2012年6月20日，墨西哥官方日报公布墨西哥经济部公告，决定结束对原产于中国的塑料卷笔刀的反倾销日落复审，取消原10美元/千克的反倾销税。涉案产品海关编码为8214.10.01。

九、欧盟取消对华塑料袋的反倾销措施

2012年7月13日，欧盟发布公告称，由于成员国内企业合作有限以及缺乏代表性的样本，委员会不能评估如果取消反倾销措施，成员国内企业遭受的实质性损害是否继续或再度发生，因此决定自公告发布之日起取消对原产于中国和泰国塑料袋的反倾销措施，并终止此前对华塑料袋的反倾销期中复审调查。涉案产品在欧盟合并关税编码ex39232100、ex39232910、ex39232990下。

2010年9月，欧盟对原产于中国的塑料袋进行反倾销期中复审立案调查。2011年9月，欧盟对原产于中国和泰国的塑料袋进行反倾销日落复审立案调查。

十、欧盟对中国台湾聚对苯二甲酸乙二醇酯进行反倾销新出口商复审调查

2012年7月18日，应台湾力丽企业股份有限公司(Lealea Enterprise Co.，Ltd.)的申请，欧盟委员会对原产于中国台湾的聚对苯二甲酸乙二醇酯进行反倾销新出口商复审立案调查。涉案产品海关编码为39076020。

欧盟委员会在公告中指出，将自立案公告发布之日起暂时停止对自台湾力丽企业股份有限公司进口的涉案产品征收反倾销税，并对进口自该公司的涉案产品进行登记以便裁决后，反倾销税追溯至立案之日。

（注：聚对苯二甲酸乙二醇酯简称PET，在塑料分类中，作用广泛。）

十一、印度对华4，4′-二氨基二苯乙烯-2，2′-二磺酸进行反倾销调查

2012年7月26日，应Deepak Nitrite Ltd.的申请，印度商工部对原产于中国的4，4′-二氨基二苯乙烯-2，2′-二磺酸产品进行反倾销立案调查。涉案产品海关编码为29215990、29214290、29215990。

本案的倾销调查期为2011年1月1日~2012年3月31日，损害调查期包括2008年4月~2009年3月、2009年4月~2010年3月、2010年4月~2011年3月和倾销调查期(2011年1月1日~2012年3月31日)。

十二、印度将就邻苯二甲酸二辛酯保障措施案举行公开听证会

2012年7月26日，印度保障措施局发布公告称，对邻苯二甲酸二辛酯保障措施案的公开听证会将于2012年8月7日上午11：30在保障措施局一层会议室举行，参加会议的有关利害关系方须在不迟于2012年8月2日的时间内以email形式发送到dg-safeguards@ nic. in以确认参加会议。

2012年5月，印度对邻苯二甲酸二辛酯进行保障措施立案调查。

（注：邻苯二甲酸二辛酯常被用作基于聚氯乙烯、聚氨酯、天然橡胶、苯橡胶、丁腈橡胶和氯丁橡胶的各种制品的增塑剂。）

十三、马来西亚对华聚丙烯薄膜进行反倾销调查

2012年7月27日，马来西亚贸工部决定对来自中国的双向拉伸聚丙烯薄膜进行反倾销立案调查。涉案产品海关编码为3920.20.200。

相关利害关系方应在立案公告之日起40日内提交反倾销调查答卷。有关应诉事宜，可联系中国五矿化工进出口商务法律部。电话：010-65692789。

（注：双向拉伸聚丙烯薄膜一般为多层共济薄膜，是由聚丙烯颗粒经共挤形成片材后，再经纵横两个方向的拉伸而制得的。广泛应用于包装，有“包装皇后”的美称。）

十四、巴基斯坦对华双向拉伸聚丙烯薄膜作出反倾销初裁

2012 年 8 月 14 日，巴基斯坦对原产于中国、沙特阿拉伯、阿曼、阿联酋的双向拉伸聚丙烯薄膜作出反倾销初裁(见下表)。该措施自 2012 年 8 月 14 日起正式实施，为期 4 个月。涉案产品海关编码为 3920.2010、3920.2030。

根据巴反倾销相关规定，所有利益相关方可以在初裁发布公告后 15 日内要求 NTC 披露详细信息，30 日内可要求举行听证会。在本案中，巴基斯坦将在初裁之日起 4 个月内，做出终审裁定。

2010 年 9 月，巴基斯坦对原产于中国、沙特阿拉伯、阿曼、阿联酋的双向拉伸聚丙烯薄膜进行反倾销立案调查。

巴基斯坦对原产于中国、沙特阿拉伯、阿曼、阿联酋的双向拉伸聚丙烯薄膜作出的反倾销初裁结果

国家(地区)	企业名称	临时反倾销税(%)
阿联酋	Taghleef	29.70
	普遍	57.09
阿曼	Taghleef	22.92
	普遍	22.92
中国	普遍	62.70
沙特阿拉伯	普遍	26.91

十五、阿根廷通过对华聚对苯二甲酸乙二酯反倾销调查初裁报告

2012 年 8 月 29 日，阿根廷经济和公共财政部国务秘书处照会中国驻阿根廷使馆经商参赞处，称阿方已通过对原产于韩国、中国、中国台湾、印度和泰国的特性粘度在 0.7dl/g 和 0.86dl/g 之间(包含两端)的颗粒状聚对苯二甲酸乙二酯(即 PET)进行反倾销调查的初裁报告，相关利益方可自通报之日起 10 个工作日内向阿方提交证明材料。

有关企业请与中国五矿化工进出口商会联系，电话：010-85692780；传真：010-65882821。

又讯：阿根廷完成对华聚对苯二甲酸乙二酯反倾销调查取证

2012 年 10 月 18 日，阿根廷经济与公共财政部外贸国务秘书处照会中国驻阿根廷经商参赞处，通告阿方对原产于韩国、中国、中国台湾、印度和泰国的特性粘度在 0.7dl/g 和 0.86dl/g 之间(包含两端)的颗粒状聚对苯二甲酸乙二酯(即 PET)的反倾销调查已完成取证，涉案企业可查阅有关文件。

再讯：阿根廷延长对华聚对苯二甲酸乙二酯反倾销调查期限

2012 年 11 月 15 日，阿根廷经济与公共财政部外贸国务秘书处照会中国驻阿根廷经商参赞处，通告阿方决定延长对原产于韩国、中国、中国台湾、印度和泰国的特性粘度在 0.7dl/g 和 0.86dl/g 之间的颗粒状聚对苯二甲酸乙二酯(即 PET)的反倾销调查期限。

十六、美国修改对华复合编织袋反倾销和反补贴终裁

2012 年 8 月 30 日，美国商务部发布公告，为执行世贸组织乌拉圭回合协议法案第 129 条，决定修改对华复合编织袋反倾销和反补贴终裁(见下表)。

2007 年 7 月 25 日，美国商务部对原产于中国的复合编织袋进行反补贴立案调查，涉案产品海关编码为 63053300.50 和 63053300.80。2008 年 6 月 16 日，美国商务部对该案作出终裁，裁定中国涉案企业的倾销幅度为 64.28% ~91.73%，补贴率为 29.54% ~352.82%。

美国修改对华复合编织袋反补贴终裁结果

出口商/生产商	修改前(%)	修改后(%)
淄博艾福迪塑料包有限公司(Zibo Aifudi Plastic Packaging Co. Ltd.)	29.54	83.34
青岛汉兴包装有限公司(Han Shing Chemical Co. Ltd.)	223.74	277.54
宁波永峰包装用品有限公司(Ningbo Yong Feng Packaging Co., Ltd.)	223.74	277.54
山东寿光健元春有限公司(Shandong Shouguang Jianyuanchun Co., Ltd)/山东龙兴塑胶制品有限公司(Shandong longxing Plastic Packaging Co., Ltd)	352.82	406.62
山东齐鲁塑编集团股份有限公司(Shangdong Qilu Plastic Fabric Group, Ltd.)	304.40	358.20
中国普遍	226.85	280.65

美国修改对华复合编织袋反倾销终裁结果

出口商/生产商	修改前(%)	修改后(%)
淄博艾福迪塑料包有限公司(Zibo Aifudi Plastic Packaging Co. Ltd.)	64.28	20.19
香港宝利威实业公司(Polywell Industrial Co., a. k. a. First Way (H. K.) Limited)/宝利威塑料制品厂(Polywell PlasticProduct Factory)	64.28	20.19

续表

出口商/生产商	修改前（%）	修改后（%）
淄博市临淄沃润包装制品有限公司（Zibo Linzi Worun Packaging Product Co., Ltd.）	64.28	20.19
淄博齐凯塑料制品有限公司（Shandong Qikai Plastics Product Co., Ltd.）	64.28	20.19
昌乐宝都塑料有限公司（Changle Baodu Plastics Co. Ltd.）	64.28	20.19
淄博市临淄帅强塑胶有限公司（Zibo Linzi Shuaiqiang Plastics Co., Ltd.）	64.28	20.19
淄博市临淄齐天利塑编有限公司（Zibo Linzi Qitianli Plastic Fabric Co., Ltd.）	64.28	20.19
山东友联塑编股份有限公司（Shandong Youlian Co., Ltd.）	64.28	20.19
20.19 淄博市临淄瑞通塑编有限公司（Zibo Linzi Luitong Plastic Fabric Co., Ltd.）	64.28	20.19
温州豪盛塑料有限公司（Wenzhou Hotson Plastics Co., Ltd.）	64.28	20.19
江苏豪盛塑料有限公司 I（Jiangsu Hotson Plastics Co., Ltd.）	64.28	20.19
苍南县嘉乐制袋有限公司（Cangnan Color Make The Bag）	64.28	20.19
淄博齐高塑胶有限公司（Zibo Qigao Plastic Cement Co., Ltd.）	64.28	20.19
中国普遍	91.73	47.64

又讯：美国国际贸易法院就美对华复合编织袋反倾销行政复审案作出判决

2012年12月18日，美国国际贸易法院就美国商务部对华复合编织袋反倾销行政复审案作出判决。本案诉讼双方如下：

原告：AMS ASSOCIATES，INC，经营名称为SHAPIRO PACKAGING

被告：美国政府

被告介入方：复合编织袋委员会（LAMINATED WOVEN SACKS COMMITTEE）、COATING EXCELLENCE INTERNATIONAL，LLC 以及 POLYTEX FIBERS CORPORATION

本案争议点：

该案涉及的争议点与 AMS Associates, Inc. v. United States 案（2012年7月27日作出判决）类似。原告 Shapiro 称，美国商务部第一次行政复审期间在没有根据 19 C. F. R. § 351.225 启动范围或规避审查的情况下对复合编织袋委员会订单的范围作出裁定的做法违反了其自身的相关规则。原告还认为，美国商务部责令美国海关与边境保护局暂停追溯清算以及在复审立案之前对涉案产品按估计的反倾销税征税的做法违规。被告美国政府则表示，商务部的做法是恰当的，因为调查机关有权决定是否举行正式的范围质询或调查范围以作为行政复审的一部分予以发布。被告介入方复合编织袋委员会则认为，商务部有权决定自淄博艾福迪塑料包装有限公司进口的哪些产品属于复合编织袋委员会的订单范畴。而对于追溯清算问题，商务部只是对现有的清算指令作出"澄清"。

司法权和审查标准：

原告根据 28 U. S. C. § 1581（c）恰当行使了司法权。美国国际贸易法院将支持商务部的裁决，除非"没有记录在册的实质性证据的支持，或与法律的规定不符"。"为实现对调查机关做法合理性的审查，'法院寻求对调查机关裁决的合理分析或解释，以确定一项具体的裁决是否是主观的、变化无常的或是对自由裁量权的滥用'"。

判决结果：

美国国际贸易法院认为，商务部暂停清算的做法属于越权行为。国际贸易法院将该案发回商务部重审，并责令美国海关与边境服务局撤销对2012年10月12日当事方提交文件中所罗列企业的暂停清算。本案原告所因此支付的现金保证金应当予以返还，并计算利息。

案件背景：

2007年7月19日，美国商务部对华复合编织袋启动反倾销调查，涉案产品海关编码为63053300.50、63053300.80。2008年6月16日，美国商务部作出反倾销终裁。2009年9月22日，美国商务部启动第一次行政复审；2010年9月29日，美国商务部启动第二次行政复审。2011年4月15日，美国商务部发布第二次行政复审终裁，裁定普遍税率为91.73%。

十七、印度取消对中国台湾丙酮的反倾销措施

2012年4月10日，印度商工部对原产于中国台湾的丙酮作出反倾销期中复审终裁：自中国台湾进口的涉案产品未对国内产业造成实质性损害，取消该反倾销措施不会使国内产业情况恶化，因此决定取消该反倾销措施。

2011年4月，印度对原产于中国台湾的丙酮进行反倾销期中复审立案调查。

注：丙酮是重要的有机合成原料，用于生产环氧树脂，聚碳酸酯，有机玻璃等。

十八、印度就对华尼龙扎带反倾销中期复审发布事实披露

2012 年 9 月 24 日，印度反倾销局函告中国驻印度使馆经商参赞处，该局于近日发布了对原产于或自中国进口的尼龙扎带反倾销中期复审事实披露。利益攸关方可在 9 月 26 日前通过邮件和书面形式向该局提供反馈意见。

在该披露中，印反倾销局综合考量申请方提供的原材料价格、人工成本、利率、销售费用、进口量、以及国内产业销售情况等证据材料。该局认为，即使对涉案产品征收了反倾销税，持续进口倾销仍使国内产业遭受了实际损害。建议所征收的反倾销税应能够保证为国内产业提供平等的竞争环境。

到目前为止，只有长虹塑料集团有限公司进行了应诉。

（注：尼龙扎带也称为：扎带、扎线、束线带、扎线带。尼龙扎带分为自锁式尼龙扎带、标牌尼龙扎带、活扣尼龙扎带、防拆尼龙扎带、固定头尼龙扎带、插销尼龙扎带、珠孔尼龙扎带、鱼骨尼龙扎带、耐候尼龙扎带等。）

又讯：印度对华尼龙扎带作出反倾销期中复审终裁

2012 年 10 月 3 日，印度对原产于中国和中国台湾的尼龙扎带作出反倾销期中复审终裁(见下表)。涉案产品海关编码为 39269000、39269010。

2011 年 10 月，印度对原产于中国和中国台湾的尼龙扎带进行反倾销期中复审立案调查。

印度对原产于中国和中国台湾的尼龙扎带作出的反倾销期中复审终裁结果

原产地	出口地	生产商	出口商	反倾销税（美元/千克）
中国	中国	长虹塑料集团有限公司（Changhong Plastics Group Co. Ltd.）	长虹塑料集团有限公司（Changhong Plastics Group Co. Ltd.）	2. 21
中国	任何国家(地区)	长虹塑料集团有限公司（Changhong Plastics Group Co. Ltd.）	任何企业	2. 81
		除长虹塑料集团有限公司外的任何企业	任何企业	2. 81
除中国和中国台湾外的任何国家（地区）	中国	任何企业	任何企业	2. 81
中国台湾	任何国家（地区）国家（地区）	任何企业	任何企业	2. 35
除中国和中国台湾外的任何国家（地区）	中国台湾	任何企业	任何企业	2. 35

十九、印度对华间苯二胺进行反倾销调查

2012 年 6 月 19 日，应 Aarti Industry Ltd. 的申请，印度对原产于中国的间苯二胺进行反倾销立案调查。涉案产品海关编码为 29215120。

本案的倾销调查期为 2010 年 10 月 1 日 ~2011 年 12 月 31 日，损害调查期包括 2008 年 4 月 ~2009 年 3 月、2009 年 4 月 ~2010 年 3 月、2010 年 4 月 ~2011 年 3 月和倾销调查期(2010 年 10 月 1 日 ~2011 年 12 月 31 日)。

（注：间苯二胺是一种工业染料，也是一种重要的有机合成原料，还可做环氧树脂固化剂、石油添加剂等。）

二十、印度对中国台湾的壬基酚进行反倾销日落复审调查

2012 年 8 月 9 日，应孟买 S. I Group India Limited 的申请，印度对原产于中国台湾的壬基酚进行反倾销日落复审立案调查。涉案产品海关编码为 2907. 1190、2907. 2990、3204. 1790、3810. 9090、2921. 4590、2909. 5090、3403. 1900、3402. 1300、3402. 1900。

本案的倾销调查期为 2011 年 4 月 1 日 ~2012 年 3 月 31 日，损害调查期包括 2008 年 4 月 ~2009 年 3 月、2009 年 4 月 ~2010 年 3 月、2010 年 4 月 ~2011 年 3 月和倾销调查期(2011 年 4 月 1 日 ~2012 年 3 月 31 日)。

（注：壬基酚是一种重要的精细化工原料和中间体，主要用于生产表面活性剂、也用于抗氧剂、树脂改性剂、树脂及橡胶稳定剂等领域。）

二十一、印度对华悬浮级聚氯乙烯进行反倾销日落复审调查

2012 年 10 月 5 日，应 DCW Limited（DCW）、Chemplast Sanmar Limited（Chemplast）、Reliance Industries Ltd（RIL）、DCM Shriram Consolidated Ltd.（DCM）的申请，印度对原产于中国、中国台湾、印尼、日本、韩国、马来西亚、泰国和美国的悬浮级聚氯乙烯进行反倾销日落复审立案调查。涉案产品海关编码为 3904。

本案的倾销调查期为 2011 年 4 月 1 日～2012 年 3 月 31 日，损害调查期包括 2008/09 财年、2009/10 财年、2010/11 财年和倾销调查期（2011 年 4 月 1 日～2012 年 3 月 31 日）。

二十二、印度对韩国、中国台湾和以色列的苯酚作出反倾销终裁

2012 年 9 月 28 日，印度对原产于韩国、中国台湾和以色列的苯酚作出反倾销终裁（见下表）。涉案产品海关编码为 29173500。

2011 年 4 月，印度对原产于韩国、中国台湾和以色列的苯酚进行反倾销立案调查。

印度对韩国、中国台湾和以色列的苯酚作出的反倾销终裁结果

原产国	出口国	生产商	出口商	反倾销税（美元/公吨）
韩国	韩国	爱敬油化株式会社（Aekyung Petrochemical Co.，Ltd）	Humade Corporation	0
韩国	除韩国、中国台湾和以色列外的其他国家（地区）	任何企业	任何企业	91.12
除韩国、中国台湾和以色列外的其他国家（地区）	韩国	任何企业	任何企业	91.12
中国台湾	中国台湾	南亚塑胶有限公司（Nan Ya Plastics Corporation）	南亚塑胶有限公司（Nan Ya Plastics Corporation）	63.33
中国台湾	除韩国、中国台湾和以色列外的其他国家（地区）	任何企业	任何企业	150.88
除韩国、中国台湾和以色列外的其他国家（地区）	中国台湾	任何企业	任何企业	150.88
以色列	以色列	Gadiv Petrochemicals Industries Ltd.	Gadiv Petrochemicals Industries Ltd.	17.99
以色列	除韩国、中国台湾和以色列外的其他国家（地区）	任何企业	任何企业	139.76
除韩国、中国台湾和以色列外的其他国家（地区）	以色列	任何企业	任何企业	139.76

（注：苯酚是重要的有机化工原料，用它可制取酚醛树脂、己内酰胺、双酚 A 等。）

二十三、巴西对中国和美国产聚合 MDI 作出反倾销终裁

2012 年 10 月 31 日，巴西外贸委员会发布公告，对进口自中国和美国的聚合 MDI(聚二苯甲烷二异氰酸酯)作出反倾销终裁，裁定对中国涉案企业征收 619.27 ~ 1079.68 美元/吨的反倾销税，对美国企业征收 418.73 ~ 838.08 美元/吨的反倾销税。涉案产品南共市关税号为 39093020。

(注：二苯甲烷二异氰酸酯简称 MDI，可用于合成聚氨酯胶粘剂和密封剂，二苯甲烷二异氰酸酯的初级品广泛用于聚氨酯涂料，此外，用本品制成的聚氨酯泡沫塑料，用作保暖、建材、车辆、船舶的部件等。)

二十四、阿根廷对原产中国和德国的 PVC 型材进行反倾销调查

2012 年 12 月 3 日，阿根廷经济和公共财政部发布处发布 2012 年 163 号决议，决定对原产于中国和德国的 PVC 型材发起反倾销立案调查。被调查产品的税则号为 39162000。暂定损害调查期分别为：2009 年 1 月 ~ 2009 年 12 月；2010 年 1 月 ~ 2010 年 12 月；2011 年 1 月 ~ 2011 年 12 月；2012 年 1 月 ~ 2012 年 11 月；暂定倾销调查期为 2011 年 2 月 ~ 2012 年 11 月。损害抗辩期限将在下周确定。

二十五、印度将就邻苯二甲酸酐保障措施日落复审举行听证会

2012 年 12 月 6 日，印度保障措施局发布公告，对邻苯二甲酸酐保障措施日落复审案的听证会将于 2013 年 1 月 10 日下午 15 点举行，地址：Ground Floor, Conference Hall, Bhai Vir Singh Sahitya Sadan, Bhai Vir Singh Marg, Gole Market New Delhi - 110001。

2012 年 10 月，印度对邻苯二甲酸酐进行保障措施日落复审立案调查。

(注：邻苯二甲酸酐，简称苯酐，是邻苯二甲酸分子内脱水形成的环状酸酐。苯酐为白色固体，是化工中的重要原料，尤其用于增塑剂的制造。)

二十六、美国对华聚酯薄膜作出反倾销行政复审初裁

2012 年 12 月 10 日，美国商务部发布公告，对原产于中国的聚酯薄膜作出第 3 次反倾销行政复审初裁(见下表)。

2007 年 10 月 31 日，美国商务部对原产于中国的聚酯薄膜进行反倾销立案调查，涉案产品海关编码为 39206200.90。2008 年 9 月 19 日，美国商务部对本案作出终裁，中国涉案产品的倾销幅度为 3.49% ~ 76.62%。2011 年 12 月 30 日，美国商务部对该案进行第 3 次反倾销行政复审调查。

美国对华聚酯薄膜作出的反倾销行政复审初裁结果

出 口 商	倾销幅度(%)
杜邦帝人薄膜中国有限公司(DuPont Teijin China Limited.)	2.95
绍兴翔宇绿色包装有限公司(Shaoxing Xiangyu Green Packing Co., Ltd.)	0.00
富维薄膜(山东)有限公司(Fuwei Films (Shandong) Co., Ltd.)	2.95
天津万华股份有限公司(Tianjin Wanhua Co., Ltd.)	2.95
四川东方绝缘材料股份有限公司(Sichuan Dongfang Insulating Material Co., Ltd.)	2.95

二十七、中华人民共和国商务部公告 2012 年第 7 号关于对原产于印度和中国台湾地区进口壬基酚所适用的反倾销措施进行期终复审调查的公告(二〇一二年三月二十八日)

中华人民共和国商务部于 2007 年 3 月 28 日发布年度第 11 号公告，决定对原产于印度和中国台湾地区的进口壬基酚征收反倾销税，实施期限为自 2007 年 3 月 29 日起 5 年。

商务部于 2011 年 9 月 20 日发布年度第 59 号公告，根据《中华人民共和国反倾销条例》规定，经复审确定终止征收反倾销税有可能导致倾销和损害的继续或者再度发生的，反倾销税的征收期限可以适当延长；自该公告发布之日起，中国大陆产业或者代表中国大陆产业的自然人、法人或有关组织可在反倾销措施到期日 60 天前，以书面形式向商务部提出期终复审申请。

2011 年 12 月 30 日，商务部收到江苏凌飞科技股份有限公司、常州染料化工厂有限公司代表中国大陆壬基酚产业正式递交的反倾销措施期终复审申请书。申请人主张，如果终止反倾销措施，原产于台湾地区的进口壬基酚对中国大陆的倾销行为可能继续发生；原产于印度的进口壬基酚对中国大陆的倾销行为可能再度发生；如果终止反倾销措施，原产于印度和台湾地区的进口壬基酚对中国大陆产业造成的损害可能再度发生。

依据《中华人民共和国反倾销条例》有关规定，商务部对申请人资格、被调查产品和中国大陆同类产品有关情况、反倾销措施实施期间被调查产品进口情况、倾销继续或再度发生的可能性、损害继续或再度发生的可能性及相关证据等进行了审查。申请人提出的证据表明，申请人及两家支持企业合计产量在2009年及2010年占同期中国大陆总产量的50%以上，符合《中华人民共和国反倾销条例》第11条、第13条和第17条关于产业及产业代表性的规定，申请人有资格代表中国大陆产业提出申请。调查机关认为，申请人的主张以及所提交的表面证据符合期终复审立案的要求。

根据《中华人民共和国反倾销条例》第48条规定，商务部决定自2012年3月29日起，对原产于印度和台湾地区进口壬基酚所适用的反倾销措施进行期终复审调查。现将有关事项公告如下：

一、继续实施反倾销措施

根据商务部建议，国务院关税税则委员会决定，在反倾销期终复审调查期间，对原产于印度和台湾地区的进口壬基酚继续按照商务部2007年第11号公告公布的征税范围和反倾销税税率征收反倾销税。

二、复审调查期

本次复审的倾销调查期为2011年1月1日至2011年12月31日，产业损害调查期为2007年1月1日至2011年12月31日。

三、复审调查产品范围

复审产品范围是原反倾销措施所适用的产品，与商务部2007年第11号公告中的产品范围一致，该产品归在《中华人民共和国进出口税则》税则号：29071310。

四、复审内容

本次复审调查的内容为，如果终止对原产于印度和台湾地区的进口壬基酚实施的反倾销措施，是否可能导致倾销和损害的继续或再度发生。

五、复审程序

(一)登记应诉。

就倾销调查，任何利害关系方可于本公告发布之日起20天内，向商务部进出口公平贸易局申请参加应诉，同时，被调查国家和地区的有关出口商或生产商应提供调查期内对中国大陆及其他市场出口该产品的数量及金额。

就损害调查，任何利害关系方可自本公告发布之日起20天内向商务部产业损害调查局申请参加应诉，同时，应提供产业损害调查期内的生产能力、产量、库存以及在建和扩建的计划。

(二)不登记应诉。

如果利害关系方未在本公告规定的时间内向商务部登记应诉，则商务部有权拒绝接受其提交的有关材料，并可以根据已经获得的事实和可获得的最佳信息作出裁定。

(三)利害关系方的权利。

如利害关系方对本次调查的产品范围、申请人资格、被调查国家和地区及其他相关问题有异议，可于本公告发布之日起20天内将意见书面提交商务部。

利害关系方可以到商务部反倾销公开信息查阅室查阅申请人提交的申请书等公开文本。

(四)问卷发放。

为获得调查所需信息，商务部将根据需要向相关利害关系方发放调查问卷。利害关系方答卷应当按照调查问卷规定的时间和方式提交。

(五)听证会。

利害关系方可以按照商务部《反倾销调查听证会暂行规则》和《产业损害调查听证规则》规定提出举行听证会的书面请求，商务部认为必要时也可主动举行听证会。

(六)实地核查。

商务部在必要时将派出工作人员赴境内外进行实地核查；利害关系方提交的任何材料均应包括同意接受核查的声明；核查前，商务部将提前通知有关国家和地区及企业。

(七)调查时限。

本次调查自2012年3月29日起开始，通常应在2013年3月29日前结束。

六、不合作

依据《中华人民共和国反倾销条例》第21条规定，调查机关进行调查时，利害关系方应当如实反映情况，提供有关资料。利害关系方不如实反映情况、提供有关资料的，或者没有在合理时间内提供必要信息的，或者以其他方式严重妨碍调查的，调查机关可以根据已经获得的事实和可获得的最佳信息作出裁定。

七、联系方式(略)

附件：壬基酚期终复审应诉登记表（略）

（注：壬基酚是一种重要的精细化工原料和中间体，外观在常温下为无色或淡黄色液体，略带苯酚气味，不溶于水，溶于丙酮。主要用于生产非离子表面活性剂，油溶性酚醛树脂及绝缘材料、橡胶，塑胶的防老抗氧剂TNP、抗静电ABPS、树脂改性剂、树脂及橡胶稳定剂等。）

二十八、中华人民共和国商务部公告2012年第12号 关于双酚A反倾销措施到期的公告(二〇一二年三月十九日)

2007年8月29日，中华人民共和国商务部发布2007年第68号公告，决定对原产于日本、韩国、新加坡和台湾地区的进口双酚A征收反倾销税。该反倾销措施自2007年8月30日开始实施，2012年8月29日到期。

《中华人民共和国反倾销条例》第四十八条规定，经复审确定终止征收反倾销税有可能导致倾销和损害的继续或者再度发生的，反倾销税的征收期限可以适当延长。

自本公告发布之日起，中国大陆产业或代表中国大陆产业的自然人、法人或有关组织可在该反倾销措施到期日60天前，以书面形式向商务部提出期终复审申请。申请书中应包含要求进行期终复审的明确表示和终止反倾销措施将可能导致倾销和损害的继续或再度发生的充分证据。

如中国大陆产业或代表中国大陆产业的自然人、法人或有关组织未提出复审申请，在该反倾销措施到期日前，商务部也未主动发起期终复审调查，则上述反倾销措施于2012年8月30日终止实施。

又讯：中华人民共和国商务部公告2012年第43号 关于双酚A反倾销措施期终复审立案的公告(二○一二年八月二十九日)

中华人民共和国商务部于2007年8月29日发布年度第68号公告，决定对原产于日本、韩国、新加坡和台湾地区的进口双酚A征收反倾销税，实施期限为自2007年8月30日起5年。

2007年11月22日，商务部发布年度第96号公告，决定自2007年11月23日起，由韩国(株)LG化学继承LG石油化学株式会社所适用的6.4%的反倾销税税率。

2009年12月15日，商务部发布年度第108号公告，决定自2009年12月15日起，韩国(株)LG化学的反倾销税税由6.4%调整为4.7%。

商务部于2012年3月19日发布年度第12号公告，根据《中华人民共和国反倾销条例》规定，经复审确定终止征收反倾销税有可能导致倾销和损害的继续或者再度发生的，反倾销税的征收期限可以适当延长；自该公告发布之日起，双酚A中国大陆产业可在原反倾销措施终止日60天前，向商务部提出书面复审申请。

2012年6月13日，商务部收到蓝星化工新材料股份有限公司代表中国大陆产业正式递交的反倾销措施期终复审申请书。申请人主张，如果终止反倾销措施，原产于日本、韩国、新加坡和台湾地区的进口双酚A对中国大陆的倾销行为可能继续发生，倾销行为给中国大陆产业造成的损害可能再度发生，请求商务部裁定维持对原产于日本、韩国、新加坡和中国台湾地区的进口双酚A实施的反倾销措施。

依据《中华人民共和国反倾销条例》有关规定，商务部对申请人资格、被调查产品和中国大陆同类产品有关情况、反倾销措施实施期间被调查产品进口情况、倾销继续发生的可能性、损害继续发生的可能性及相关证据等进行了审查。申请书显示，上海中石化三井化工有限公司表示支持本次复审申请。申请人提出的证据表明，申请人及支持企业合计产量在2010年及2011年占同期中国大陆总产量的50%以上，符合《中华人民共和国反倾销条例》第11条、第13条和第17条关于产业及产业代表性的规定，申请人有资格代表中国大陆产业提出申请。调查机关认为申请人的主张以及所提交的表面证据符合期终复审立案的要求。

根据《中华人民共和国反倾销条例》第四十八条，商务部决定自2012年8月30日起，对原产于日本、韩国、新加坡和台湾地区的进口双酚A所适用的反倾销措施进行期终复审调查。现将有关事项公告如下：

一、继续实施反倾销措施

根据商务部建议，国务院关税税则委员会决定，在反倾销期终复审调查期间，对原产于日本、韩国、新加坡和台湾地区的进口双酚A继续按照中华人民共和国商务部2007年第68号公告、2007年第96号公告和2009年第108号公告公布的征税范围和反倾销税税率征收反倾销税。

二、复审调查期

本次复审的倾销调查期为2011年7月1日至2012年6月30日，产业损害调查期为2007年1月1日至2012年6月30日。

三、复审调查产品范围

复审产品范围是原反倾销措施所适用的产品，与商务部2007年第68号公告中的产品范围一致，该产品归在《中华人民共和国进出口税则》(2012年版)税则号：29072300。该税则号项下的双酚A盐不在调查范围之内。

四、复审内容

本次复审调查的内容为，如果终止对原产于日本、韩国、新加坡和台湾地区的进口双酚A实施的反倾销措施，是否可能导致倾销和损害的继续或再度发生。

五、复审程序

(一)登记应诉。

就倾销调查，任何利害关系方可于本公告发布之日起20天内，向商务部进出口公平贸易局申请参加应诉，同时被调查国家和地区的有关出口商或生产商应提供调查期内对中国大陆及其他市场出口该产品的数量及金额。《倾销调查应诉登记参考格式》可在中华人民共和国商务部网站公平贸易局子网站公告栏目下载。

就损害调查，任何利害关系方可自本公告发布之日起20天内向商务部产业损害调查局申请参加应诉，同时应提供产业损害调查期内的生产能力、产量、库存以及在建和扩建的计划。

(二)不登记应诉。

如果利害关系方未在本公告规定的时间内向商务部登记应诉，则商务部有权拒绝接受其提交的有关材料，并可以根据已经获得的事实和可获得的最佳信息作出裁定。

(三)利害关系方的权利。

如利害关系方对本次调查的产品范围、申请人资格、被调查国家和地区及其他相关问题有异议，可于本公告发布之日起20天内将书面意见提交商务部。

利害关系方可以到商务部反倾销公开信息查阅室查阅申请人提交的申请书等公开文本。

(四)问卷发放。

为获得调查所需信息，商务部将根据需要向相关利害关系方发放调查问卷。利害关系方答卷应当按照调查问卷规定的时间和方式提交。

(五)听证会。

利害关系方可以按照商务部《反倾销调查听证会暂行规则》和《产业损害调查听证规则》规定提出举行听证会的书面请求，商务部认为必要时也可主动举行听证会。

(六)实地核查。

商务部在必要时将派出工作人员赴境内外进行实地核查；利害关系方提交的任何材料均应包括同意接受核查的声明；核查前，商务部将提前通知有关国家和地区及企业。

(七)调查时限。

本次调查自2012年8月30日起开始，通常应在2013年8月30日前结束。

六、不合作

依据《中华人民共和国反倾销条例》第21条规定，调查机关进行调查时，利害关系方应当如实反映情况，提供有关资料。利害关系方不如实反映情况、提供有关资料的，或者没有在合理时间内提供必要信息的，或者以其他方式严重妨碍调查的，调查机关可以根据已经获得的事实和可获得的最佳信息作出裁定。

七、联系方式（略）

再讯：中华人民共和国海关总署公告2012年第43号(二〇一二年八月二十八日)

2007年国务院关税税则委员会决定对原产于日本、韩国、新加坡和台湾地区的进口双酚A征收反倾销税，征税时间自2007年8月30日起，期限为5年。在征税期限届满之际，国务院关税税则委员会根据商务部的建议，决定在该反倾销措施期终复审期间对原产于日本、韩国、新加坡和台湾地区的进口双酚A继续征收反倾销税。现将有关事项公告如下：

自2012年8月30日起，海关对申报进口原产于日本、韩国、新加坡和台湾地区的双酚A(税则号列为29072300)，继续按照海关总署公告2007年第47号、第65号和2009年第80号的相关规定征收反倾销税。

特此公告。

还讯：商务部产业损害调查局 商调查二处函[2012]361号 关于发放《双酚A反倾销措施期终复审产业损害调查问卷(国外(地区)生产者/出口商调查问卷)》的通知(二〇一二年九月十八日)

(公司)：

2012年8月29日，中华人民共和国商务部发布2012年第43号公告，决定自2012年8月30日起对原产于日本、韩国、新加坡和中国台湾地区的进口双酚A所适用的反倾销措施进行期终复审调查。商务部产业损害调查局负责本案的产业损害调查与裁决工作。

依据《中华人民共和国反倾销条例》第五十一条和商务部《反倾销产业损害调查规定》第二十四条、第二十五条和第二十六条的规定，按照双酚A反倾销措施期终复审调查工作安排，现向你单位发放本调查问卷。请认真阅读本调查问卷，按要求如实回答问题，并于2012年10月25日前将答卷递交中华人民共和国商务部产业损害调查局。

联系地址：(略)

附：双酚A反倾销措施期终复审产业损害调查问卷(国外(地区)生产者/出口商调查问卷)(略)

(注：双酚A，也称BPA，在工业上双酚A被用来合成聚碳酸酯和环氧树脂等材料。)

二十九、中华人民共和国商务部公告2012年第13号 对原产于日本和美国的进口间苯二酚进行反倾销立案调查的公告(二〇一二年三月二十三日)

中华人民共和国商务部于2012年2月3日收到浙江鸿盛化工有限公司代表国内间苯二酚产业正式提交的反倾销调查申请，申请人请求对原产于日本和美国的进口间苯二酚进行反倾销调查。

商务部依据《中华人民共和国反倾销条例》有关规定，对申请人的资格、申请调查产品的有关情况、中国同类产品的有关情况、申请调查产品对国内产业的影响、申请调查国家的有关情况等进行了审查。同时，商务部就申请书提供的涉及倾销、损害及倾销与损害之间的因果关系等方面的证据进行了审查。申请人提供的初步证据表明，申请人浙江鸿盛化工有限公司间苯二酚产量在2010年和2011年1-9月占同期中国同类产品总产量的50%以上，符合《中华人民共和国反倾销条例》第十一条、第十三条和第十七条有关国内产业提出反倾销调查申请的规定。同时，申请书中包含了《中华人民共和国反倾销条例》第十四条、第十五条规定的反倾销调查立案所要求的内容及有关证据。

根据上述审查结果及《中华人民共和国反倾销条例》第十六条规定，商务部决定自2012年3月23日起对原产于日本和美国的进口间苯二酚进行反倾销立案调查。现将有关事项公告如下：

一、立案调查及调查期

自本公告发布之日起，商务部对原产于日本和美国的进口间苯二酚进行反倾销调查，本次调查确定的倾销调查期为2010年10月1日至2011年9月30日，产业损害调查期为2009年1月1日至2011年9月30日。

二、被调查产品及调查范围

调查范围：原产于日本和美国的进口间苯二酚

被调查产品名称：间苯二酚，又称1，3-苯二酚、雷琐辛。英文名称：M - dihydroxybenzene 或 Resorcinol。

分子式：$C_6H_6O_2$

化学结构式：(略)

物理化学特征：外观通常呈白色针状结晶体，暴露于空气当中会逐渐变红，易溶于水、乙醇、乙醚，溶于氯仿、四氯化碳，不溶于苯。

主要用途：间苯二酚是一种重要的化学合成中间体和精细化工原料，主要用于橡胶黏合剂和紫外线吸收剂的生产。

该产品归在《中华人民共和国进出口税则》：29072100。该税则号项下的间苯二酚盐不在本次调查产品范围之内。

三、登记应诉

就倾销调查，任何利害关系方可于本公告发布之日起20天内，向商务部进出口公平贸易局申请参加应诉，参加应诉的涉案出口商或生产商应同时提供2010年10月1日至2011年9月30日向中国出口本案被调查产品的数量及金额。《倾销调查应诉登记参考格式》可在中华人民共和国商务部网站进出口公平贸易局子网站下载。

就产业损害调查，利害关系方可自本公告发布之日起20天内向商务部产业损害调查局登记应诉，同时应提供产业损害调查期内的生产能力、产量、库存、在建和扩建的计划以及向中国出口该产品的数量和金额等说明材料。

四、不登记应诉

如利害关系方未在本公告规定的时间内向商务部登记应诉，则商务部有权拒绝接受其递交的有关材料，并有权根据所掌握的现有材料做出裁定。

五、利害关系方的权利

利害关系方对本次调查的产品范围、申请人资格、被调查国家及其他相关问题如有异议，可于上述登记应诉期间内将意见书面提交商务部。

利害关系方可在上述期间内到商务部贸易救济公开信息查阅室查阅本案申请人提交的申请书的非保密文本。

六、调查方式

调查机关可以采用问卷、抽样、听证会、现场核查等方式向有关利害关系方了解情况并进行调查。

七、本次调查自2012年3月23日起开始，通常应在2013年3月23日前结束调查，特殊情况下可延长至2013年9月23日。

八、商务部联系地址(略)

附件：间苯二酚反倾销调查应诉登记表(略)

又讯：中华人民共和国商务部公告2012年第83号 关于对原产于日本和美国的进口间苯二酚反倾销调查的初裁公告(二〇一二年十一月二十三日)

根据《中华人民共和国反倾销条例》(以下称《反倾销条例》)的规定，2012年3月23日，商务部(以下称调查机关)正式发布立案公告，决定对原产于日本和美国的进口间苯二酚进行反倾销调查。该被调查产品归在《中华人民共和国进出口税则》税则号：29072100，该税则号项下的间苯二酚盐不在本次调查产品范围之内。

调查机关对被调查产品是否存在倾销及倾销幅度、国内间苯二酚产业是否受到损害及损害程度、以及倾销与损害之间的因果关系进行了调查，根据调查结果和《反倾销条例》第二十四条的规定，调查机关作出初步裁定(见附件)，并就有关事项公告如下：

一、初步裁定

调查机关裁定，在本案调查期内，日本和美国的进口间苯二酚存在倾销，中国间苯二酚产业受到了实质损害，而且倾销与损害之间存在因果关系。

二、征收保证金

根据《反倾销条例》第二十八条和二十九条的规定，调查机关决定采用保证金形式实施临时反倾销措施。2012年11月23日起，进口经营者在进口原产于日本和美国的进口间苯二酚时，应依据本初裁决定所确定的各公司的倾销幅度向中华人民共和国海关提供相应的保证金。

本案征收保证金的产品归在《中华人民共和国进出口税则》：29072100，该税则号项下的间苯二酚盐不在本次调查产品范围之内。征收保证金产品具体描述如下：

调查范围：原产于日本和美国的进口间苯二酚

被调查产品名称：间苯二酚，又称 1，3 - 苯二酚、雷琐辛。英文名称：M - dihydroxybenzene 或 Resorcinol。

物理化学特征：外观通常呈白色针状结晶体，暴露于空气当中会逐渐变红，易溶于水、乙醇、乙醚，溶于氯仿、四氯化碳，不溶于苯。

主要用途：间苯二酚是一种重要的化学合成中间体和精细化工原料，主要用于橡胶黏合剂和紫外线吸收剂的生产。此外，间苯二酚还可用于生产木材黏合剂、阻燃剂和各种医药、农药的中间体等。

对各公司征收的保证金比率如下：

日本公司

1. 住友化学株式会社　40.5%
(Sumitomo Chemical Company，Limited)

2. 三井化学株式会社　40.5%
(Mitsui Chemicals，Inc.)

3. 其他日本公司　40.5%
(All Others)

美国公司

1. 茵蒂斯派克化学公司　30.1%
(INDSPEC Chemical Corporation)

2. 其他美国公司　30.1%
(All Others)

三、征收保证金的方法

自 2012 年 11 月 23 日起，进口经营者在进口原产于日本和美国的进口间苯二酚时，应依据本初裁决定所确定的各公司的倾销幅度向中华人民共和国海关提供相应的保证金。保证金以海关审定的完税价格从价计征，计算公式为：保证金金额 =（海关审定的完税价格 × 保证金征收比率）×（1 + 进口环节增值税税率）。

四、评论

各利害关系方在本公告发布之日起 20 天内，可向调查机关提出书面评论并附相关证据，调查机关将依法予以考虑。

附件：中华人民共和国商务部对原产于日本和美国的进口间苯二酚反倾销调查的初步裁定

根据《中华人民共和国反倾销条例》（以下简称《反倾销条例》）的规定，2012 年 3 月 23 日，商务部（以下称调查机关）正式发布公告，决定对原产于日本和美国的进口间苯二酚（以下称被调查产品）进行反倾销立案调查。该被调查产品归在《中华人民共和国进出口税则》税则号：29072100，该税则号项下的间苯二酚盐不在本次调查产品范围之内。

调查机关对被调查产品是否存在倾销及倾销幅度、国内产业是否受到损害及损害程度以及倾销与损害之间的因果关系进行了调查，初步调查结论如下：

一、调查程序

（一）立案及立案通知。

1. 立案。

2012 年 2 月 3 日，调查机关收到浙江鸿盛化工有限公司代表国内间苯二酚产业提交的反倾销调查申请，申请人请求对原产于日本和美国的进口间苯二酚进行反倾销调查。

经审查，调查机关认为申请人符合《反倾销条例》第十一条、第十三条和第十七条有关中国产业提出反倾销调查申请的规定。同时，申请书中包含了《反倾销条例》第十四条、第十五条规定的反倾销调查立案所要求的内容及有关证据。

根据上述审查结果及《反倾销条例》第十六条的规定，2012 年 3 月 23 日，调查机关发布立案公告，决定对原产于日本和美国的进口间苯二酚进行反倾销立案调查。调查机关确定的倾销调查期为 2010 年 10 月 1 日至 2011 年 9 月 30 日，产业损害调查期为 2009 年 1 月 1 日至 2011 年 9 月 30 日。

2. 立案通知。

在决定立案调查前，根据《反倾销条例》第十六条规定，调查机关就收到中国间苯二酚产业反倾销调查申请书一事通知了日本驻中国大使馆和美国驻中国大使馆。

2012 年 3 月 23 日，调查机关发布立案公告，并向日本驻中国大使馆和美国驻中国大使馆正式提供了立案公告和申请书的公开文本。同日，调查机关将本案立案情况通知了本案申请人及申请书中列明的日本和美国生产商、出口商。

（二）倾销及倾销幅度的初步调查。

1. 登记应诉。

根据公告要求，自公告发布之日起 20 天的登记应诉期内，被调查产品生产商日本住友化学株式会社（Sumitomo Chemical Company，Limited）、日本三井化学株式会社（Mitsui Chemicals，Inc.）和美国茵蒂斯派克化学公司（INDSPEC Chemical Corporation）向调查机关登记倾销应诉。

2. 发放问卷和收取答卷。

2012 年 4 月 12 日，调查机关向上述登记应诉公司发放了反倾销调查问卷，并要求其在 37 天内按规定提交准确、完整的答卷。

2012年4月28日，美国茵蒂斯派克化学公司向调查机关提交《无法提供间苯二酚反倾销调查答卷的函》，表示公司无法完成答卷工作，未在规定时限内提交答卷。

2012年5月18日，日本三井化学株式会社向调查机关提交《关于三井化学株式会社退出间苯二酚反倾销调查的函》，表示退出反倾销调查，未在规定时限内提交答卷。

日本住友化学株式会社未在规定时限内提交答卷。

至答卷递交截止之日，调查机关未收到3家登记应诉公司的答卷。

3. 有关利害关系方评论意见。

2012年5月18日，日本住友化学株式会社向调查机关提交《关于终止间苯二酚反倾销调查的请求》。称目前市场情况发生重大变迁，请求终止本次反倾销调查。

(三)产业损害及损害程度的初步调查。

1. 参加产业损害调查活动登记。

2012年3月23日，调查机关发出《关于参加间苯二酚反倾销案产业损害调查活动登记的通知》(商调查函[2012]82号)。在规定的时间内，调查机关共收到有效登记材料6份，其中包括国内生产者3家，分别为：湖北祥云(集团)化工股份有限公司、南通建民化工有限公司和河南新宏化工有限公司；国外生产者3家，分别为：三井化学株式会社(Mitsui Chemicals, Inc.)、住友化学株式会社(Sumitomo Chemical Company, Limited)和美国茵蒂斯派克化学公司(INDSPEC Chemical Corporation)。经审查，调查机关接受了上述利害关系方的登记。

2. 成立产业损害调查组。

2012年4月16日，调查机关成立了间苯二酚反倾销案产业损害调查组，负责本案的产业损害调查与裁决工作，并于当日发出《关于成立间苯二酚反倾销案产业损害调查组的通知》(商调查一处函[2012]114号)。

3. 发放和收回调查问卷。

根据《反倾销条例》第二十条和《反倾销产业损害调查规定》第二十四条、第二十五条的相关规定，2012年4月12日，调查机关发出《关于发放〈间苯二酚反倾销案产业损害调查问卷(国内生产者调查问卷)〉的通知》(商调查一处函[2012]102号)、《关于发放〈间苯二酚反倾销案产业损害调查问卷(国内进口商调查问卷)〉的通知》(商调查一处函[2012]103号)和《关于发放〈间苯二酚反倾销案产业损害调查问卷(国外<地区>生产者/出口商调查问卷)〉的通知》(商调查一处函[2012]104号)，向各利害关系方发放了调查问卷。调查机关同时将上述问卷送至商务部贸易救济公开信息查阅室，供利害关系方查阅。

2012年4月28日，美国茵蒂斯派克化学公司提交了《关于无法提交间苯二酚反倾销调查答卷的函》，表示决定不提交问卷答卷。

2012年5月18日，三井化学株式会社提交了《关于三井化学株式会社退出间苯二酚反倾销调查的函》，称其间苯二酚生产设备于2012年4月22日发生爆炸，已失去间苯二酚生产能力，决定不提交问卷答卷。

2012年5月2日，国内生产企业浙江鸿盛化工有限公司、湖北祥云(集团)化工股份有限公司、南通建民化工有限公司和河南新宏化工有限公司提交了《关于间苯二酚反倾销案国内相关生产企业延期提交国内生产者调查问卷答卷的请求》，申请将国内生产者问卷答卷截止期限延长至2012年5月22日。经审查，调查机关同意其延期申请。

在调查问卷规定的时间或经批准延期递交的时间内，调查机关共收回产业损害调查问卷答卷5份，包括浙江鸿盛化工有限公司、湖北祥云(集团)化工股份有限公司、南通建民化工有限公司和河南新宏化工有限公司提交的国内生产者调查问卷答卷4份；住友化学株式会社提交的国外(地区)生产者/出口商调查问卷答卷1份。调查机关未收到国内进口商调查问卷答卷。

4. 听取利害关系方意见陈述。

2012年5月2日，调查机关收到本案申请人委托代理人提交的《关于召开间苯二酚反倾销案国内产业意见陈述会的申请》。根据《反倾销条例》第二十条和《反倾销产业损害调查规定》第十七条的规定，2012年5月7日，调查机关发出《关于召开间苯二酚反倾销案国内产业意见陈述会的通知》(商调查一处函[2012]159号)。2012年5月18日，调查机关召开了间苯二酚反倾销案国内产业意见陈述会，听取了国内产业提起申请的主要理由和对产业损害调查相关问题的意见。同日，本案申请人向调查机关提交了《间苯二酚反倾销案国内产业意见陈述会汇报材料》。

2012年7月18日，日本经济产业省通商机构部及日本驻华大使馆拜会调查机关，其间就本案调查提出意见。2012年7月19日，日本驻华大使馆向调查机关提交了《宗像部长在与商务部产业损害调查局顾春芳局长会谈时的发言(关于间苯二酚反倾销调查)》。

2012年7月19日，住友化学株式会社向调查机关提交了《关于提请召开间苯二酚反倾销调查产业损害听证会的申请书》，申请就产业损害、因果关系及公共利益等问题举行听证会。2012 年 7 月 30 日，本案申请人向调查机关提交《间苯二酚反倾销案申请人对住友化学请求召开产业损害听证会申请的评论意见》，提出本案没有举行产业损害听证会的必要性，公共利益问题超出产业损害听证范围，并表示申请人将不出席会议。2012 年 8 月 2 日，住友化学株式会社提交了《住友化学株式会社关于召开间苯二酚反倾销案陈述会的请示函》，表示坚持申请在合适的时间召开产业损害调查听证会，同时考虑到申请人提出保留不参加本次产业损害调查听证会的权利，申请在 2012 年 8 月 6 日至 8 月 10 日期间召开间苯二酚反倾销案陈述会。

根据《反倾销条例》第二十条和《反倾销产业损害调查规定》第十七条的规定，调查机关于 2012 年 8 月 6 日发出《关于召开间苯二酚反倾销案住友化学株式会社陈述会的通知》（商调查一处函［2012］302 号）。2012 年 8 月 9 日，调查机关召开间苯二酚反倾销案住友化学株式会社陈述会，听取了住友化学株式会社关于本案产业损害调查相关问题的意见。2012 年 8 月 10 日，住友化学株式会社向调查机关提交了《间苯二酚产业损害陈述会书面材料》（以下称住友陈述会材料）。

5. 接收利害关系方书面评论意见。

在立案公告规定的时间内，调查机关未收到各利害关系方对立案提交的书面评论意见。

2012 年 5 月 18 日，住友化学株式会社提交了《关于终止间苯二酚反倾销调查的请求》。

2012 年 7 月 16 日，住友化学株式会社提交了《间苯二酚反倾销案无损害抗辩意见书》（以下称住友无损害抗辩）。

2012 年 9 月 20 日，本案申请人提交了《间苯二酚反倾销案申请人对住友化学株式会社相关主张和意见的评论意见》（以下称申请人评论意见）。

6. 初裁前实地核查。

根据《反倾销条例》第二十条和《反倾销产业损害调查规定》第二十七条的规定，2012 年 6 月 6 日，调查机关发出《关于间苯二酚反倾销案初裁前实地核查的通知》（商调查一处函［2012］196 号）。2012 年 6 月 18 日至 21 日、7 月 24 日至 27 日，调查机关分别赴本案申请人浙江鸿盛化工有限公司和国内生产企业南通建民化工有限公司进行了初裁前实地核查。实地核查期间，调查机关实地考查了被核查公司的间苯二酚生产现场，对被核查公司在调查问卷答卷中提供的数据和信息等进行了核实，并收集了相关证据材料。实地核查结束后，被核查公司向调查机关提交了调查问卷补充修正材料和有关证据。

7. 公开信息。

根据《产业损害调查信息查阅与信息披露规定》第八条、第十四条的规定，本案所有公开材料均已及时送交商务部贸易救济公开信息查阅室。各利害关系方可以查找、阅览、摘抄、复印全部公开信息。

调查机关对申请书及所附证据材料、调查问卷答卷及所附证据材料、实地核查结果、利害关系方提交的评论意见以及陈述会上的发言材料进行了认真分析，对各利害关系方的意见依法给予了充分考虑。

（四）住友化学株式会社关于终止调查的请求

住友化学株式会社在《关于终止间苯二酚反倾销调查的请求》、住友无损害抗辩和住友陈述会材料中多次提出，2012 年 4 月 22 日，国外生产者三井化学株式会社的间苯二酚生产装置发生爆炸，截至 2012 年 6 月仍未恢复生产。爆炸事件导致亚洲乃至全球的间苯二酚市场供需状况发生了实质性的变化，住友化学株式会社专注供应日本市场，对中国出口下降，中国国内间苯二酚市场将出现供应短缺和价格上涨。住友化学株式会社认为，鉴于出现以上重大情势变迁，调查机关应立即终止本次反倾销调查 。

申请人评论意见认为住友化学株式会社的主张不能成立，原因是：第一，在反倾销调查中，调查机关通常不应考虑调查期之外的信息。第二，三井化学株式会社间苯二酚产能仅占三家应诉企业的 12.7%，占 2011 年全球总产能的比例仅为 7%，且产品主要供应日本国内市场，在全球间苯二酚市场严重供过于求的情况下，其装置停产不足以对中国间苯二酚市场状况带来实质性影响。第三，从 2012 年 1－7 月的进口数据看，被调查产品进口量仍然较大，进口价格未出现暴涨。因此，三井化学株式会社间苯二酚装置爆炸事件并未导致住友化学株式会社所谓“重大情势变迁”的情况，其影响并非是“显而易见、无可置疑的、持续不断的”，调查机关应不予考虑 。

调查机关注意到本案立案后三井化学株式会社间苯二酚生产装置发生爆炸的事实。调查机关认为：第一，本案立案公告已明确产业损害调查期为 2009 年 1 月 1 日至 2011 年 9 月 30 日，调查机关认定国内产业损害和因果关系的依据是调查期内的证据和事实，三井化学株式会社间苯二酚生产装置爆炸发生在调查期之外，并不影响调查机关对于本案的认定结论。第二，根据《反倾销条例》第二十七条的规定，住友化学株式会社所称“重大情势变迁”并非调查机关应当终止反倾销调查的法定情形。住友化学株式会社关于终止本次调查的请求缺乏法律依据。

二、被调查产品

调查机关在立案公告中确定的本案调查范围及被调查产品描述如下：

调查范围：原产于日本和美国的进口间苯二酚

被调查产品名称：间苯二酚，又称1，3－苯二酚、雷琐辛。英文名称：M－dihydroxybenzene 或 Resorcinol。

分子式：$C_6H_6O_2$

化学结构式：(略)

物理化学特征：外观通常呈白色针状结晶体，暴露于空气当中会逐渐变红，易溶于水、乙醇、乙醚，溶于氯仿、四氯化碳，不溶于苯。

主要用途：间苯二酚是一种重要的化学合成中间体和精细化工原料，主要用于橡胶黏合剂和紫外线吸收剂的生产。此外，间苯二酚还可用于生产木材黏合剂、阻燃剂和各种医药、农药的中间体等。

该产品归在《中华人民共和国进出口税则》：29072100。该税则号项下的间苯二酚盐不在本次申请调查产品范围之内。

三、国内同类产品和国内产业

(一)国内同类产品的认定。

根据《反倾销条例》第十二条和《反倾销产业损害调查规定》第十条、第十一条关于同类产品认定的规定，调查机关对国内生产的间苯二酚与被调查产品的物理化学特性、产品用途、产品的可替代性、生产工艺流程、销售渠道、销售区域、消费者评价、价格等因素进行了考察，各方提交的产业损害调查问卷答卷、实地核查材料等证据显示：

1. 国内生产的间苯二酚与被调查产品外观相同，均为白色针状结晶体，暴露于空气当中会逐渐变红；二者的分子式、化学结构式、物理化学特征相同；调查期内，国内生产的间苯二酚均执行《中华人民共和国化工行业标准：间苯二酚(1，3－苯二酚)》(HG/T 3989－2007)，质量指标均达到干品结晶点/度≥108℃，间苯二酚含量≥98.50%，对苯二酚、邻苯二酚和苯酚的含量分别≤0.10%、0.50%和0.20%，与被调查产品无实质区别；国内生产的间苯二酚与被调查产品一般均采用纸塑复合袋等包装，规格以25千克/袋为主。

2. 国内生产的间苯二酚与被调查产品的用途基本相同，均为重要的化学合成中间体和精细化工原料，主要用于生产橡胶黏合剂、紫外线吸收剂、木材黏合剂、阻燃剂和各种医药、农药的中间体等。

3. 国内生产的间苯二酚与被调查产品的生产工艺主要包括磺化碱熔法、间苯二胺水解法和间二异丙苯氧化法三种。其中，国内生产企业采用磺化碱熔法和间苯二胺水解法，被调查产品生产企业采用磺化碱熔法和间二异丙苯氧化法。初步证据表明，三种工艺均以纯苯为基本原材料，且对制成的间苯二酚质量无实质性影响。

4. 国内生产的间苯二酚与被调查产品的销售渠道基本相同，均包括直销和分销，销售区域也均集中在我国沿海地区和各大工业城市；二者的客户群体基本相同，部分客户互相重合，部分客户认为国内生产的间苯二酚和被调查产品质量相当，可以相互替代；调查期内，国内生产的间苯二酚价格与被调查产品进口价格总体变化趋势基本一致。

综上所述，国内生产的间苯二酚与被调查产品之间外观和基本物理化学特性相同，产品包装、产品用途、销售渠道和市场区域、客户群体等基本相同，生产工艺流程不存在实质区别，价格总体变化趋势基本一致，具有相似性和可比性，可以相互替代。因此，国内生产的间苯二酚与被调查产品属于同类产品。

住友化学株式会社在产业损害调查问卷答卷中提出，住友化学株式会社通过严格的质量管理提供高品质的被调查产品，取得了中国国内"高品质用户"的认定，而国内同类产品无法取得"高品质用户"认定，二者差异很大，不存在可替代性及竞争关系 。

调查机关认为，住友化学株式会社仅简单断言其间苯二酚产品与国内同类产品不存在可替代性和竞争关系，并未提供可供核实的证据予以佐证。住友化学株式会社和国内生产企业提供的主要客户名单 和下游用户使用意见反馈报告 等证据显示，被调查产品与国内同类产品的客户群体基本相同，部分客户同时使用被调查产品和国内同类产品，且认为国内同类产品与被调查产品质量相当。因此，被调查产品与国内同类产品存在竞争关系，可以相互替代。

(二)国内产业的认定。

根据《反倾销条例》第十一条和《反倾销产业损害调查规定》第十三条关于国内产业认定的规定，调查机关对本案国内产业范围进行了审查。调查期内的2009年、2010年和2011年1～9月，4家提交国内生产者问卷答卷的国内生产企业的同类产品产量之和占国内总产量的比例均超过50%，占国内同类产品总产量的主要部分，符合《反倾销条例》第十一条和《反倾销产业损害调查规定》第十三条关于国内产业认定的规定，可以代表国内产业。本裁决依据的国内产业数据，除特别说明外，均来自上述4家国内生产者问卷答卷企业。

四、倾销和倾销幅度

(一)正常价值、出口价格及价格调整项目的初步认定。

日本

1. 日本三井化学株式会社和日本住友化学株式会社

日本三井化学株式会社和日本住友化学株式会社为申请书列明的日本生产商，两公司登记应诉后，调查机关向其发放了问卷，但两公司均未提交答卷，没有配合调查机关的调查，调查机关无法获得其倾销调查期内被调查产品的正常价值、出口价格、调整因素等直接数据和证据。依据《反倾销条例》第二十一条，调查机关决定采用可获得的最佳信息对上述公司在调查期内的正常价值、出口价格、影响正常价值和出口价格可比性因素等进行认定。

2. 其他日本公司

如前所述，2012 年 3 月 23 日，本案立案后，调查机关通知了申请书上列明的出口商或生产商，也通知了涉案国驻华使馆，同日，调查机关将立案公告登载在商务部网站上，任何利害关系方均可在商务部网站上查阅本案立案公告。立案后，调查机关给予各利害关系方 20 天的登记应诉期，给予所有利害关系方合理的时间获知立案有关情况。

2012 年 4 月 12 日，调查机关向申请书列明的公司发放了调查问卷，同日，调查机关将调查问卷登载在商务部网站上，任何利害关系方可在商务部网站上查阅本案调查问卷。

申请书未列明的、调查期内可能存在的其他出口经营者未登记应诉，也未提交答卷。调查机关通过查询海关数据、咨询相关行业协会、查阅相关网站、公开刊物，以及申请人提供的相关数据认定了其正常价值、出口价格，并对影响正常价值和出口价格可比因素进行了调整，并在同一贸易环节进行了比较。

①正常价值

经调查，调查机关初步认定相关咨询公司提供的调查期内被调查产品同类产品日本国内市场平均销售价格作为正常价值，为 6885 美元/吨。

②出口价格

经调查，调查机关初步认定调查期内中国海关统计数据计算出的日本对中国出口加权平均价格作为计算其出口价格的基础，为 4993. 75 美元/吨。

③调整项目

根据《反倾销条例》第六条规定，为公平合理比较，调查机关对该公司影响价格可比性的调整项目逐一进行了审查。

第一，正常价值部分。调查机关经初步审查，确定上述日本市场内被调查产品同类产品的销售价格已是出厂价水平，调查机关不再做相应调整。

第二、出口价格部分。经初步审查，调整项目包括海运费、保险费、日本境内环节费用等，为 131. 70 美元/吨。

④关于到岸价格(CIF 价格)

经初步审查，调查机关暂根据中国海关统计的日本对中国出口的加权平均价格作为到岸价格，为 4993. 75 美元/吨。

美国

1. 美国茵蒂斯派克化学公司

美国茵蒂斯派克化学公司为申请书列明的美国生产商，该公司登记应诉后，调查机关向其发放问卷，但该公司未提交答卷，没有配合调查机关的调查，调查机关无法获得其倾销调查期内被调查产品的正常价值、出口价格、调整因素等直接数据和证据。依据《反倾销条例》第二十一条，调查机关决定采用可获得的最佳信息对上述公司在调查期内的正常价值、出口价格、影响正常价值和出口价格可比性因素等进行认定。

2. 其他美国公司

如前所述，2012 年 3 月 23 日，本案立案后，调查机关通知了申请书上列明的出口商或生产商，也通知了涉案国驻华使馆，同日，调查机关将立案公告登载在商务部网站上，任何利害关系方均可在商务部网站上查阅本案立案公告。立案后，调查机关给予各利害关系方 20 天的登记应诉期，给予所有利害关系方合理的时间获知立案有关情况。

2012 年 4 月 12 日，调查机关向申请书列明的公司发放了调查问卷，同日，调查机关将调查问卷登载在商务部网站上，任何利害关系方可在商务部网站上查阅本案调查问卷。

申请书未列明的、调查期内可能存在的其他出口经营者未登记应诉，也未提交答卷。调查机关通过查询海关数据、咨询相关行业协会、查阅相关网站、公开刊物，以及申请人提供的相关数据认定了其正常价值、出口价格，并对影响正常价值和出口价格可比因素进行了调整，并在同一贸易环节进行了比较。

①正常价值

经调查，调查机关初步认定相关咨询公司提供的调查期内美国间苯二酚国内市场平均销售价格作为正常价值，为 7290 美元/吨。

②出口价格

经调查，调查机关初步认定调查期内中国海关统计数据计算出的美国对中国出口加权平均价格作为计算其出口价格的基础，为5766.84美元/吨。

③调整项目

根据《反倾销条例》第六条规定，为公平合理比较，调查机关对该公司影响价格可比性的调整项目逐一进行了审查。

第一，正常价值部分。调查机关经初步审查，确定上述日本市场内被调查产品同类产品的销售价格已是出厂价水平，调查机关不再做相应调整。

第二、出口价格部分。经初步审查，调整项目包括海运费、保险费、美国境内环节费用等，为212.38美元/吨。

④关于到岸价格(CIF价格)

经初步审查，调查机关暂根据中国海关统计的美国对中国出口的加权平均价格作为到岸价格，为5766.84美元/吨。

(二)价格比较。

根据《反倾销条例》第六条的规定，调查机关对被调查产品的出口价格和正常价值进行比较时，考虑了影响价格的各种可比性因素，按照公平、合理的方式进行了比较。

对于已知的未配合调查的公司，根据《反倾销条例》第二十一条的规定，调查机关决定采用已经获得的事实和可获得的最佳信息做出有关倾销和倾销幅度的裁定。

对于申请书未列明的、调查期内可能存在的其他出口经营者，调查机关通过查询海关数据、咨询相关行业协会、查阅相关网站、公开刊物，以及申请人提供的相关数据认定这些公司的正常价值、出口价格，并对影响正常价值和出口价格可比因素进行了调整，在计算倾销幅度时，调查机关将平均正常价值和平均出口价格进行比较，得出倾销幅度。

(三)倾销幅度。

经过调查，各公司的倾销幅度分别为：

1. 日本公司

(1)住友化学株式会社　40.5%

(Sumitomo Chemical Company, Limited)

(2)三井化学株式会社　40.5%

(Mitsui Chemicals, Inc.)

(3)其他日本公司　40.5%

(All Others)

2. 美国公司

(1)茵蒂斯派克化学公司　30.1%

(INDSPEC Chemical Corporation)

(2)其他美国公司　30.1%

(All Others)

五、产业损害及损害程度

(一)累积评估的适当性。

初步调查证据显示，来自日本和美国的被调查产品的倾销幅度均不小于2%，并且来自日本和美国的进口被调查产品数量占中国间苯二酚总进口量的比例均超过3%，不属于可忽略不计的范围。经调查，被调查产品之间以及被调查产品与国内同类产品之间在物理化学特性、技术指标、生产工艺、产品用途、销售渠道、销售市场区域、客户群体、消费者和生产者的评价等方面基本相同，具有相似性和可比性，可以相互替代，在中国国内市场上同时出现，存在相互竞争关系，竞争条件基本相同。根据《反倾销条例》第九条和《反倾销产业损害调查规定》第十五条、第十六条的规定，调查机关认定，对来自日本和美国的进口被调查产品适用累积评估是适当的。

(二)被调查产品进口量及所占中国国内市场份额。

1. 被调查产品进口数量。

根据中国海关统计数据，调查期内，被调查产品进口数量2009年为10131.36吨；2010年为11815.46吨，比2009年上升16.62%；2011年1~9月为7500.45吨，比2010年同期下降17.19%，但比2009年同期上升7.53%。

住友化学株式会社提出，一般贸易之外的其他贸易方式进口的目的在于再出口，并未进入中国商业，与国内同类产品不构成竞争，不应计入被调查产品的进口数量 。

申请人评论意见认为：第一，根据中国法律法规规定，除一般贸易外的其他贸易方式的进口产品均属"进口货物"范畴。第二，世贸规则和中国相关法律法规规定的反倾销调查审查对象为"倾销进口产品"，并未明确要求排除一般贸易以外的其他进口，中国和欧盟等的反倾销调查实践均将加工贸易等进口数量包括在内。第三，通过加工贸易等方式进口的被调查产品与国内产业同类产品存在竞争关系，同样会对国内产业造成影响和冲击，不应从被调查产品进口数量中排除 。

调查机关认为：

第一，根据《反倾销条例》第八条和《反倾销产业损害调查规定》第五条、第六条，调查机关在确定倾销对国内产业造成的损害时，应当对倾销进口产品的数量进行审查。无论以何种贸易方式进口的被调查产品，只要存在倾销，均属于倾销进口产品。

第二，中国海关统计数据显示，除一般贸易进口外，其余90%以上的被调查产品通过加工贸易方式进口，即通过非一般贸易方式进口的间苯二酚绝大部分会被下游企业用于生产产品后出口，而非直接再出口。因此，以非一般贸易方式进口的被调查产品已经进入中国国内间苯二酚市场，并非住友化学株式会社所主张的“未进入中国商业”。

第三，中国国内下游企业可以自行选择通过各种方式采购所需的间苯二酚。各方产业损害调查问卷答卷 和下游用户使用意见反馈报告 等证据显示，部分下游生产企业同时通过一般贸易方式、非一般贸易方式进口被调查产品或购买国内同类产品。因此，以非一般贸易方式进口的被调查产品与国内同类产品在中国国内间苯二酚市场上存在竞争。

综上，调查机关认定，住友化学株式会社关于以非一般贸易方式进口的被调查产品不应计入进口数量的主张缺乏事实和法律依据。调查机关决定仍基于全部倾销进口产品的数量对被调查产品进口的影响进行评估。

2. 被调查产品占中国国内市场份额。

调查期内，被调查产品占中国国内市场份额呈先升后降趋势，2009 年为 58.20%；2010 年为 60.78%，比 2009 年上升 2.58 个百分点；2011 年 1~9月为50.48%，比2010年同期下降13.18个百分点。

(三)被调查产品进口价格和中国国内产业同类产品价格。

1. 被调查产品进口价格。

根据中国海关统计数据，并据中国人民银行公布的同期平均汇率折算，调查期内，被调查产品进口加权平均人民币价格(CIF)2009 年为 32363.34 元/吨；2010 年为 33801.84 元/吨，比 2009 年上涨 4.44%；2011 年 1~9 月为 33297.66 元/吨，比 2010 年同期下降 1.87%。调查期内总体呈上升趋势。

2. 国内产业同类产品销售价格。

调查期内，国内产业同类产品的销售价格 2009 年为 30300.05 元/吨；2010 年为 32020.92 元/吨，比 2009 年上涨 5.68%；2011 年 1~9 月为 32862.62 元/吨，比 2010 年同期上涨 3.26%。调查期内呈上涨趋势。

住友化学株式会社质疑申请人浙江鸿盛化工有限公司仅生产间苯二酚，其销售通过关联公司进行，请求调查机关对本案申请人关联销售同类产品的情况予以调查，并以销售公司的非关联转售价格确定国内同类产品价格 。

申请人评论意见回应称，申请人在 2010 年 7 月之前通过关联公司销售同类产品，但一方面申请人同类产品销售给关联公司的价格与关联公司销售给最终用户的价格基本相当；另一方面申请人同类产品销售给关联公司的价格与其他国内生产企业同类产品销售价格基本相当。此外，在调查期内，申请人的同类产品还销售给另外一家关联公司，但销售量占总销售量的比例较低，且销售价格与申请人销售给其他客户的价格基本相当。因此，申请人同类产品关联销售价格可以作为本案同类产品价格的基础 。

住友化学株式会社还在陈述会上质疑申请人浙江鸿盛化工有限公司从关联公司处高价采购原材料间苯二胺，并提请调查机关关注申请人原材料采购价格是否为市场价格 。

调查机关通过实地核查等方式对申请人同类产品销售和原材料采购情况进行了了解。调查证据显示：

(1)申请人在调查期内共向两家关联公司销售过同类产品。2010 年 7 月以前，申请人仅通过上述两家关联公司销售同类产品；2010 年 7 月以后，申请人向其中一家关联公司销售同类产品，并同时向其他非关联公司销售同类产品。

由于 2010 年 7 月以前申请人仅向关联公司销售同类产品，同期申请人不存在对非关联方的销售，调查机关比较了申请人对关联公司的销售价格、关联公司销售给非关联客户的价格以及其他 3 家国内生产企业同类产品同期销售价格，认为申请人与关联公司之间的销售价格与同期其他国内生产企业的销售价格水平基本相当，未偏离市场价格；且申请人销售给关联公司的价格与关联公司转售给非关联客户的价格之间也并不存在不合理差异。据此，调查机关决定认可上述期间申请人的销售价格。

2010 年 8 月至调查期末，申请人同时存在向关联公司和非关联公司的销售。调查机关对比了申请人向关联公司的销售价格和向非关联公司的销售价格，数据显示，该期间申请人向非关联公司销售价格比向关联公司销售价格平均高 5% 以上。为客观反映国内产业的实际经营状况，调查机关决定以申请人向非关联公司的销售价格为基准，对申请人上述期间的销售收入、销售价格和相关指标进行了调整，并以调整后的数据作为裁决的基础。

(2)调查期内申请人主要原材料确系向关联公司采购。调查机关收集的申请人原材料使用记录和关联公司销售记录显示，关联公司对申请人的销售价格明显低于向其他非关联方的销售价格，且主要原材料在申请人同类产品成本中占比较高，关联采购已对申请人的真实成本状况造成扭曲。为客观反映国内产业的实际经营状况，调查机关按照关联公司对其他非关联方的平均销售价格对申请人的原材料采购价格、对应的同类产品成本和相关指标进行了相应调整，并以调整后的数据作为裁决的基础。

(四)被调查产品进口对国内产业同类产品价格的影响。

调查证据显示，2009 年、2010 年和 2011 年 1 ~ 9 月，被调查产品占中国国内市场的份额分别为 58.20%、60.78% 和 50.48%，处于市场主导地位。被调查产品与国内同类产品的质量不存在实质差别，销售区域、销售渠道和客户群体基本相同，部分下游用户同时使用被调查产品和国内同类产品，下游用户对产品价格的敏感程度高。调查期内，国内同类产品和被调查产品价格变化趋势一致，均呈总体上升趋势。因此，被调查产品进口对国内产业同类产品销售价格具有明显的影响。

调查期内，国内产业生产同类产品耗用的主要原材料和燃料动力等采购价格总体呈上涨趋势，国内同类产品单位销售成本持续上升，2009 年为 29890.85 元/吨，2010 年为 32673.04 元/吨，比 2009 年上升 9.31%；2011 年 1 ~ 9 月为 33983.66 元/吨，比 2010 年同期上升 5.81%。同期，国内间苯二酚表观消费量同比分别增长 11.68% 和 4.43%，市场需求旺盛，国内同类产品销售量和市场份额均保持增长，在这种市场状况下，国内产业理应能够通过适当上调价格消化上升的成本压力，实现合理的利润水平。

然而，被调查产品在调查期内以较高的幅度向中国市场倾销，调查期内进口价格整体涨幅不足 3%。受其影响，国内产业无法通过提高国内同类产品销售价格消化上升的成本，国内同类产品平均销售价格和单位销售成本之间的差额迅速下降，2009 年为 409.20 元/吨，2010 年降为 -652.12 元/吨，成本与价格出现倒挂，至 2011 年 1 ~ 9 月进一步降为 -1121.04元/吨，为调查期内的最低水平。

据此，调查机关初步认定，被调查产品进口对国内同类产品价格产生了明显的抑制作用。

住友化学株式会社在无损害抗辩意见中和陈述会上称，2011 年 1 ~ 9 月，被调查产品进口绝对数量和占中国国内市场份额均出现下降，不满足世贸组织《反倾销协定》第 3.2 条“大幅增加”的规定，不能据此认定实质损害 。

申请人评论意见认为，世界贸易组织规则和中国法律法规未对如何考察进口数量的增长做出规定，也未要求调查期内每个期间进口数量必须总是持续性地呈现肯定状态或指向损害 。

调查机关认为，2011 年 1 ~ 9 月，被调查产品进口数量在 2010 年上升 16.62% 的基础上有所下降，但较 2009 年同期上升了 7.53%，仍占据中国市场 50% 以上的市场份额，同时进口价格下降，导致国内同类产品价格无法实现应有增长。根据《反倾销条例》第八条和《反倾销产业损害调查规定》第五条、第六条的规定，调查机关在对上述因素进行综合评估的基础上得出被调查产品进口对国内同类产品价格产生抑制作用的结论，符合中国法律法规的有关规定。

住友化学株式会社在住友无损害抗辩和住友陈述会材料中提出，调查期内被调查产品价格未大幅削低国内同类产品价格 。调查机关认为，本案申请人并未主张被调查产品对国内同类产品价格造成削减，调查机关也未认定调查期内存在价格削减。

申请人在申请书等材料中主张，被调查产品长期占据着中国市场的主导和支配地位，其进口价格的变化对同类产品的销售价格产生直接且重大的影响。调查期内，被调查产品对华出口价格的涨幅明显低于其主要原材料纯苯的涨幅，相对价格实际上明显下降并处于较低水平。受此影响，调查期内，被调查产品的进口人民币价格与国内产业同类产品加权平均内销价格的差额呈持续大幅缩小趋势。因此，被调查产品压低了国内产业同类产品的内销价格 。

针对申请人上述主张，住友化学株式会社在住友无损害抗辩和住友陈述会材料中提出：第一，被调查产品的市场主导地位并不能够证明被调查产品大幅压低国内同类产品价格；第二，申请人的原材料价格波动理论与价格压低无关，且不能简单假设价格应当与成本一起上涨；第三，申请人未说明纯苯占被调查产品成本的比例；第四，将海关统计的被调查产品进口人民币价格与国内同类产品价格进行比较缺乏可比性；第五，2009 年纯苯价格因经济危机影响而非正常大幅下跌，以 2009 年纯苯价格为基准的比较夸大了变化幅度 。

申请人在申请人评论意见中回应称：第一，调查期及之前，被调查产品占中国间苯二酚市场的主导和支配地位，国内生产企业规模小，起步晚，被调查产品价格的变动直接影响国内同类产品价格，且两者在调查期内整体保持同向变化。第二，在生产成本和市场供求两个因素中，生产成本对于加工制造业产品价格更具有决定作用；而主要原材料的价格上涨必然带动生产成本上涨，如果市场供求稳定，增加的生产成本最终会传导至生产价格。第三，从住友化学株式会社提交的答卷数据看，其原材料成本和生产成本大幅上升，而对华出口价格仅微幅上涨，证明其相对价格呈下降趋势。第四，价格比较应具备可比性的要求适用于价格削减而非价格压低分析，申请人是对被调查产品进口价格和国内同类产品价格之间的差额进行趋势变化分析，是否调整至同一贸易水平不会实质性影响变化趋势。第五，2009年及其后被调查产品成本与价格的同向变化说明原材料及生产成本与被调查产品价格之间存在联动关系，以2009年纯苯价格为比较基准并未夸大变化幅度 。

调查机关认为，调查机关未认定调查期内存在价格压低。

住友化学株式会社还主张：第一，2009年和2011年1~9月，申请人分别因新投产设备导致的高成本及价格成本差相对较小或出现下降，不应被视为被调查产品进口所导致的。第二，国内产业无法将成本苯的价格上涨向下游进行快速、直接的转移，是化工品的特性及市场所决定的，与被调查产品无关。因此，本案不存在价格抑制 。

申请人评论意见认为：第一，2009年后期申请人间苯二酚装置投产，设备尚处于磨合阶段。随着产量增加和需求增长，国内产业同类产品价格和销售成本间的差额理应逐步扩大。但事实恰好相反，2010年和2011年1~9月均出现价格和成本倒挂且逐步加剧，说明正是被调查产品倾销而非国内产业新装置投产等原因导致同类产品的价格抑制。第二，在市场供求稳定的情况下，生产成本的增加最终要传导到产品价格的上涨，这符合化工产品市场的逻辑规律 。申请人评论意见还提供了申请人内部调价记录等材料，描述了下游客户在议价过程中使用被调查产品价格压制申请人同类产品价格的情况 。

调查机关认为：

第一，调查机关评估价格影响的基础是代表国内产业的4家国内生产企业而非仅申请人一家的同类产品加权平均销售价格和销售成本。数据显示，申请人2009年和2011年1~9月的单位销售成本并未出现异常波动，且与其他3家国内生产企业的单位销售成本水平基本相当，不存在“申请人因新投产设备所导致的高成本”。2011年1~9月，申请人新增的2万吨/年的间苯二酚生产装置尚未投产，实地核查情况表明，上述新增产能并未对2011年1~9月的申请人同类产品销售成本造成影响。因此，住友化学株式会社的有关主张与本案已查明的事实不符。

第二，关于成本传导问题，调查机关已经在价格影响分析部分进行了说明。在市场需求上升、国内同类产品销售量和市场份额增长的情况下，国内同类产品理应能够将持续上升的成本向销售价格合理传导，而被调查产品倾销进口抑制了国内同类产品价格的合理上升。住友化学株式会社未提供任何证据证明国内同类产品受到的价格抑制与被调查产品无关的主张。

（五）国内产业相关经济因素和指标的评估。

根据《反倾销条例》第七条、第八条和《反倾销产业损害调查规定》第四条至第七条的规定，调查机关对国内产业的相关经济因素和指标进行了调查，证据显示：

1. 表观消费量。

调查期内，中国国内间苯二酚表观消费量2009年为17408吨；2010年为19441吨，比2009年增长11.68%；2011年1~9月为14859吨，比2010年同期增长4.43%。

2. 产能。

调查期内，国内产业同类产品产能2009年为6783吨；2010年为12200吨，比2009年增长79.85%；2011年1~9月为12900吨，比2010年同期增长40.98%。

3. 产量。

调查期内，国内产业同类产品产量2009年为4002.02吨；2010年为7041.51吨，比2009年增长75.95%；2011年1~9月为6950.28吨，比2010年同期增长43.74%。

4. 销售量。

调查期内，国内产业同类产品销售量2009年为2806.58吨；2010年为8053.32吨，比2009年增长186.94%；2011年1~9月为7075.10吨，比2010年同期增长26.48%。

5. 市场份额。

调查期内，国内产业同类产品占中国国内市场的份额2009年为16.12%；2010年为41.43%，比2009年上升25.30个百分点；2011年1~9月为47.61%，比2010年同期上升8.30个百分点。

6. 销售价格。

调查期内，国内产业同类产品加权平均销售价格2009年为30300.05元/吨；2010年为32020.92元/吨，比2009年上涨5.68%；2011年1~9月为32862.62元/吨，比2010年同期上涨3.26%。

7. 销售收入。

调查期内，国内产业同类产品销售收入2009年为8503.96万元；2010年为2.58亿元，比2009年增长203.24%；2011年1~9月为2.33亿元，比2010年同期增长30.61%。

8. 税前利润。

调查期内，国内产业同类产品税前利润2009年为－719.76万元；2010年为－2433.19万元，亏损额比2009年增加238.05%；2011年1～9月为－3028.05万元，亏损额比2010年同期增加120.99%。

9. 投资收益率。

调查期内，国内产业同类产品投资收益率2009年为－5.97%；2010年为－9.50%，比2009年下降3.53个百分点；2011年1～9月为－6.50%，比2010年同期下降0.51个百分点。

10. 开工率。

调查期内，国内产业同类产品开工率2009年为59.00%；2010年为57.72%，比2009年下降1.28个百分点；2011年1～9月为53.88%，比2010年同期上升1.03个百分点。

11. 就业人数。

调查期内，国内产业同类产品就业人数2009年为386人；2010年为452人，比2009年增加17.25%；2011年1～9月为475人，比2010年同期增加5.48%。

12. 劳动生产率。

调查期内，国内产业同类产品劳动生产率2009年为10.37吨/人；2010年为15.57吨/人，比2009年上升50.07%；2011年1～9月为14.63吨/人，比2010年同期上升36.27%。

13. 人均工资。

调查期内，国内产业同类产品就业人员人均工资2009年为19511元/人；2010年为22359元/人，比2009年上涨14.59%；2011年1～9月为14764元/人，比2010年同期下降12.22%。

14. 期末库存。

调查期内，国内产业同类产品期末库存2009年为1423.24吨；2010年为468.85吨，比2009年减少67.06%；2011年1～9月为374.03吨，比2010年同期减少50.20%。

15. 经营活动现金净流量。

调查期内，国内产业同类产品经营活动现金净流量2009年为－191.10万元，2010年为－326.70万元，净流出额比2009年增加70.96%；2011年1～9月为－331.64万元，净流出额比2010年同期增加1434.58%。

16. 投融资能力。

初步调查证据显示，尚未有直接证据证明调查期内国内产业同类产品投融资能力受到不利影响。

(六)国内产业受到实质损害。

调查期内，国内间苯二酚市场表观消费量保持上升，国内产业也处于发展阶段。为满足国内增长的需求，部分国内生产企业新增和改扩间苯二酚生产装置，国内产业同类产品产能提高，产量增加，销售量和销售收入相应出现增长，期末库存量减少，市场份额上升；在就业人数增加的同时，国内产业努力提高同类产品生产水平，劳动生产率也有所提升。随着主要原材料和燃料动力价格上涨，国内产业同类产品销售价格同比也出现一定上涨，但由于被调查产品倾销进口对同类产品价格产生了抑制作用，国内同类产品价格的上涨不能消化增加的成本，国内产业税前利润始终为负值，且2010年和2011年1～9月的亏损额同比分别扩大2.38倍和1.21倍。受亏损影响，国内产业同类产品产能未获得充分利用，开工率持续处于低位且整体呈下降趋势；投资无法获得预期回报，投资收益率同比分别下降3.53个百分点和0.51个百分点，经营活动现金流持续呈净流出态势，净流出额同比分别扩大70.96%和14.35倍。国内产业生产经营状况呈恶化趋势。

综合考虑上述经济因素和指标，调查机关初步认定，国内产业在调查期内受到了实质损害。

住友化学株式会社根据本案申请书提供的申请人损害指标数据，称调查期内申请人的各项经营指标均呈积极态势，不能得出损害结论。

调查机关认为，经过初裁前调查，调查机关依据国内产业而非申请人一家企业的数据，在综合分析国内产业各项生产经营和财务指标的基础上得出了国内产业受到实质损害的结论，符合《反倾销条例》第八条和《反倾销产业损害调查规定》第七条的有关规定。

住友化学株式会社还主张，申请人浙江鸿盛化工有限公司的母公司浙江龙盛集团股份有限公司(以下称龙盛集团)的年度报告、《重大资产重组暨关联交易报告书》等公开材料证明，申请人的经营状况良好，利润水平较高，且未来能保持可观的回报 。

申请人在申请人评论意见中回应称：第一，申请人母公司年度报告中披露的是申请人整个公司的净利润数据，不能代表同类产品的利润情况；第二，年度报告也显示，申请人整个公司的利润虽有所上升，但净利润率代表的获利能力则出现下降；第三，国内产业相关经济指标中的一个或多个未必能够给予决定性的指导，仅凭单个指标无法否定国内产业存在损害 。

调查机关认为：第一，住友化学株式会社对龙盛集团2012年6月《重大资产重组暨关联交易报告书》的引用有误，根据上下文，实际应为“公司在(间苯二胺)成本控制方面的优势……”，与国内同类产品无关；第二，龙盛集团2009年年度报告仅对未来收益情况进行了预测，而调查机关损害分析的基础是实际发生、可供核实的数据。第三，龙盛集团2008年至2011年年度报告中披露的是申请人整体净利润情况。根据《反倾销条例》第十条和《反倾销产业损害调查规定》第十二条，倾销进口产品对国内产业的影响，应当根据对国内同类产品生产的单独界定进行评估。调查机关已经按照要求对国内产业同类产品的利润情况进行了详细评估。

六、因果关系

根据《反倾销条例》第二十四条，调查机关审查了原产于日本和美国的被调查产品倾销进口与中国国内产业受到实质性损害之间是否存在因果关系。同时审查了除倾销进口之外，可能对中国国内产业造成损害的其他因素。

(一)原产于日本和美国的被调查产品倾销进口造成了国内产业的实质损害。

初步调查证据表明，调查期内，自日本和美国进口的被调查产品是中国间苯二酚市场的主要进口来源，在国内间苯二酚市场占据主要份额，对国内同类产品销售价格具有重大影响。调查期内，被调查产品以较高的幅度向中国国内市场倾销，进口数量总体上升，始终占据中国国内市场50%以上份额。受被调查产品倾销进口影响，国内产业在同类产品成本上升的情况下无法合理提高销售价格，造成国内同类产品销售价格和单位销售成本之间的差额不断减小，国内同类产品税前利润始终为负值，且亏损额持续增加。由于利润水平明显下降，在国内需求持续增长的情况下，国内产业无法充分利用现有产能，投资无法获得预期回报，同类产品投资收益率下降，经营活动现金流呈净流出态势，且流出额迅速增加，同类产品生产经营活动出现困难，国内产业受到了实质损害。

综上，调查机关认为，初步证据显示，调查期内，被调查产品倾销进口造成了国内产业的实质损害。

(二)其他因素分析。

调查机关对可能使国内产业受到损害的其他已知因素进行了初步调查。

1. 自其他国家(地区)进口产品情况。

中国海关统计数据显示，调查期内的2009年、2010年和2011年1~9月，被调查产品进口量占中国总进口量的比例分别为98.03%、97.97%和96.80%，自其他国家(地区)进口间苯二酚数量占同期中国总进口量的比例仅为1.97%、2.03%和3.20%，且自其他国家(地区)进口的间苯二酚平均价格较同期被调查产品进口价格高20%至45%左右。自其他国家(地区)进口不是造成国内产业损害的原因。

2. 国内需求和消费模式的变化。

中国国内间苯二酚表观消费量数据显示，调查期内国内间苯二酚市场需求持续增长。国内没有出现限制间苯二酚产业发展的政策变化，也没有出现其他替代产品等消费模式变化而导致中国国内间苯二酚需求的萎缩。国内需求和消费模式的变化不是造成国内产业损害的原因。

3. 商业流通渠道和贸易政策及国内外竞争状况。

调查显示，目前国内产业同类产品实行市场化的价格机制，生产经营受市场规律调节。国内产业同类产品的销售渠道、销售区域与被调查产品基本相同，在商业流通领域并不存在其他阻碍国内同类产品销售或造成国内产业损害的因素。调查期内国内没有颁布限制间苯二酚产业发展的贸易政策。国内外正当的竞争也没有对国内产业造成损害。商业流通渠道、贸易政策及国内外正当竞争不是造成国内产业损害的原因。

住友化学株式会社称，鉴于除申请人外的3家国内生产企业经营状况不乐观甚至已经停产，而申请人在2009年10月投产后占据了相当的国内产业份额且经营状况良好，提请调查机关审查申请人开业投产与国内产业经营状况之间的关系 。

申请人评论意见认为，调查期内被调查产品占中国国内间苯二酚市场的主导地位，国内产业同类产品供应量与市场需求始终存在较大缺口，国内生产企业之间没有必要进行恶性竞争。申请人装置投产及产能的逐步释放是顺应国内市场需求发展的结果。国内产业遭受的损害不能归因于国内生产企业之间的正常竞争 。

调查机关认为，数据显示，调查期内，中国国内间苯二酚表观消费量持续上升，虽然包括申请人在内的部分国内生产者增加了产能，但并未出现供过于求的情况。调查期内，申请人与其他3家国内生产企业同类产品销售价格水平基本相当，变化趋势一致，税前利润、利润率等指标变化趋势相同。同时调查显示，其他3家国内生产企业在调查期内均有生产。可见，并不存在住友化学株式会社主张的除申请人外的3家国内生产企业经营状况不乐观甚至已经停产，而申请人经营状况良好的情况。

4. 国内产业经营管理的变化和技术发展情况。

如同类产品认定部分所述，国内产业生产的同类产品与被调查产品在产品质量等方面基本相同，客户群体也基本相同，部分客户相互重合。初步证据显示，国内产业在生产工艺、技术装备、产品质量、生产经营管理等方面上都具备良好的市场竞争能力。部分国内生产企业通过了ISO9001质量体系认证及GB/T 28000职业健康安全管理认证等。调查机关未发现因生产工艺及技术落后和管理不善而对国内产业造成负面影响的情况。

住友化学株式会社提出，日本企业采用的间二异丙苯氧化法生产工艺没有污染，成本低，适合大规模生产。还引用论文主张申请人采用的间苯二胺催化水解法生产工艺对设备腐蚀严重，工业化受到限制，且硝化过程对环境污染较大。住友化学株式会社提请调查机关考虑生产技术差异导致的生产成本问题及可能对申请人效益产生的消极影响 。

对此，申请人认为：第一，住友化学株式会社引用的两篇文章内容陈旧滞后，与国内间苯二酚产业及技术发展的现状严重脱节。第二，申请人采用的间苯二胺水解法工艺清洁环保，具有技术优势，获得了多项奖励和证书，污染物排放均符合国家环保标准，并非住友化学株式会社所称的“生产成本高，污染大”。

住友化学株式会社还主张，绝大多数国内间苯二酚企业难以形成规模生产，工艺相对落后导致较大的污染和较高的生产成本，这种由国内产业自身特性导致的消极影响不能归因于被调查产品 。

申请人评论意见则提出：第一，住友化学株式会社所谓“工艺相对落后导致较大的污染和较高的生产成本”仅为简单断言，未提供任何证据证明。第二，除申请人外其他国内企业采用的磺化碱熔法生产工艺与美国茵蒂斯派克化学公司采用的工艺相同，在成本控制方面并无劣势。第三，所谓“工艺相对落后”无法解释国内产业在整个调查期内损害程度不断加深的事实 。

针对住友化学株式会社的上述两项主张，调查机关认为：第一，调查证据显示，国内同类产品与被调查产品的生产工艺主要包括磺化碱熔法、间苯二胺水解法和间二异丙苯氧化法三种。三种工艺均以纯苯为基本原材料，且对制成的间苯二酚质量无实质性影响。第二，部分被调查产品生产企业与国内同类产品生产企业均采取磺化碱熔法生产工艺。根据住友化学株式会社所引《间苯二酚的技术现状和发展趋势》一文，磺化碱熔法具有工艺简单、投资小、技术成熟的特点，且经多年改进，技术水平得到很大提高，生产成本大幅下降，污染问题得到有效控制。实地核查显示，国内生产企业多采取磺化碱熔法改进工艺，不存在工艺落后的情况。第三，实地核查情况显示，申请人采用的间苯二胺水解法工艺具有转化率高、产品收率高、清洁环保等特点，获得了专业技术领域的认可。国内生产企业均建设有较完备的污染物处理设备，污染物排放指标符合国家标准。第四，在国内产业生产工艺保持不变的情况下，国内产业同类产品的利润水平却持续恶化，说明国内产业同类产品利润水平的恶化并非由生产工艺造成。综上，调查机关初步认定，住友化学株式会社关于国内产业生产工艺落后导致生产成本高和污染大的主张缺乏事实基础，国内产业采用的生产工艺并非造成损害的原因。

5. 国内同类产品出口状况。

调查期内，国内产业无同类产品出口。国内同类产品的出口不是造成国内产业损害的原因。

6. 不可抗力因素。

调查机关未发现在调查期内国内产业受到自然灾害或其他严重不可抗力的事件。

7. 申请人自用被调查产品。

住友化学株式会社称，申请人生产的间苯二酚部分自用于生产间苯二胺，提请调查机关在评估损害时将申请人自用与对外销售的同类产品区别对待 。

调查机关经实地核查查明，申请人不存在间苯二酚产品自用的情况。住友化学株式会社对申请人生产工艺流程的理解有误。

8. 申请人新建20kt/a间苯二酚项目。

住友化学株式会社引用龙盛集团2011年度报告披露的申请人委托贷款情况，认为申请人为2万吨间苯二酚扩产而投入的资金以及发生的贷款必然会对申请人的经营状况产生影响，并直接影响申请人的投资收益率 。

申请人在申请人评论意见中称其新建的20kt/a装置在调查期之后投产，其成本尚记录在在建工程项目中，住友化学株式会社的相关质疑不能成立。

调查机关经实地核查了解，申请人新建20kt/a间苯二酚生产装置在调查期内并未投产，针对该项目的投资在调查期内并未计入同类产品的成本或费用。此外，住友化学株式会社所引用的6笔申请人委托贷款并未明确与同类产品生产经营有关，且其中两笔贷款不在调查期内。此外4笔委托贷款绝大部分发生在2011年1~9月，但当期申请人的财务费用却同比明显下降且为负值。由此可见，调查期内申请人新投产项目并未对国内产业造成负面影响。

综上所述，原产于日本和美国的进口被调查产品倾销进口与国内产业遭受的实质损害之间存在因果关系，其他已知因素不是造成国内产业损害的原因。

七、初步裁定

根据上述调查结果，调查机关初步裁定，在本案调查期内，原产于日本和美国的进口间苯二酚存在倾销，国内间苯二酚产业受到了实质损害，而且倾销与实质损害之间存在因果关系。

有关公司的倾销幅度如下：

1. 日本公司

(1)住友化学株式会社　40.5%

(Sumitomo Chemical Company, Limited)

(2)三井化学株式会社　40.5%

(Mitsui Chemicals, Inc.)

(3)其他日本公司　40.5%

(All Others)

2. 美国公司

(1)茵蒂斯派克化学公司　30.1%

(INDSPEC Chemical Corporation)

(2)其他美国公司　30.1%

(All Others)

再讯：中华人民共和国海关总署公告2012年第58号(二〇一二年十一月二十一日)

根据《中华人民共和国反倾销条例》的规定，商务部决定自2012年11月23日起对进口原产于日本和美国的间苯二酚实施临时反倾销措施(详见附件1)。现将有关事项公告如下：

一、自2012年11月23日起，海关对进口原产于日本和美国的间苯二酚(税则号列：29072100)，除按现行规定征收关税和进口环节增值税外，还将区别不同的供货厂商，按照本公告附件2所列的适用征收比率和下述计算公式征收反倾销保证金及相应的进口环节增值税保证金。

反倾销保证金及进口环节增值税保证金合计计算公式为：

保证金总额＝(海关完税价格×反倾销保证金征收比率)×(1＋进口环节增值税税率)

实施临时反倾销措施产品的详细描述详见本公告附件1。

二、进口经营单位在申报进口上述税则号列项下属于反倾销范围内的间苯二酚时，商品编号应填报为2907210001；上述税则号列项下"间苯二酚盐"的商品编号应填报为2907210090。

三、凡申报进口间苯二酚的进口经营单位，应当向海关提交原产地证明。如果原产地为日本或美国的，还需提供原生产厂商发票。对于申报进口时不能提供原产地证明，且经查验也无法确定货物原产地的，海关按照本公告附件2所列的最高反倾销保证金征收比率征收保证金。对于能够确定货物的原产地是日本或美国，但进口经营单位不能提供原生产厂商发票，且通过其他合法、有效的单证也无法确定原生产厂商的，海关将按照本公告附件2所列相应国家中的其他公司适用的反倾销保证金征收比率征收保证金。

四、有关加工贸易保税进口原产于日本和美国的间苯二酚如何征收反倾销保证金等方面的问题，海关按照中华人民共和国海关总署令第111号和海关总署公告2001年第9号的规定执行。

五、对于所征收的反倾销保证金及进口环节增值税保证金的处理，海关总署将根据终裁结果另行公告。

特此公告。

附件：1 中华人民共和国商务部公告2012年第83号(详见《中国对外经济贸易文告》2012年第76期)(略)

2 间苯二酚反倾销保证金征收比率表(略)

(注：间苯二酚用于塑料工业、染料工业、医药、橡胶等。间苯二酚主要用于橡胶粘合剂、合成树脂、染料、防腐剂、医药和分析试剂等，与苯酚、甲酚相似，与甲醛生成缩聚物，可用于制粘胶丝及尼龙用的轮胎帘子线粘结剂，制备木材胶合剂，用于乙烯基材料与金属的粘合等。)

三十、中华人民共和国商务部公告2012年第14号 对原产于欧盟的进口甲苯二异氰酸酯进行反倾销立案调查的公告(二〇一二年三月二十三日)

中华人民共和国商务部于2012年2月3日收到沧州大化TDI有限责任公司、甘肃银光聚银化工有限公司、甘肃银达化工有限公司、辽宁北方锦化聚氨酯有限公司和沧州大化股份有限公司聚海分公司代表国内甲苯二异氰酸酯产业正式提交的反倾销调查申请，申请人请求对原产于欧盟的进口甲苯二异氰酸酯(型号为TDI80/20)进行反倾销调查。

商务部依据《中华人民共和国反倾销条例》有关规定，对申请人的资格、申请调查产品的有关情况、中国同类产品的有关情况、申请调查产品对国内产业的影响、申请调查地区的有关情况等进行了审查。同时，商务部就申请书提供的涉及倾销、损害及倾销与损害之间的因果关系等方面的证据进行了审查。申请人提供的初步证据表明，在将与出口经营者或进口经营者有关联的国内生产者排除在国内产业之外后，申请人沧州大化TDI有限责任公司、甘肃银光聚银化工有限公司、甘肃银达化工有限公司、辽宁北方锦化聚氨酯有限公司和沧州大化股份有限公司聚海分公司甲苯二异氰酸酯产量在2009年、2010年和2011年占同期中国同类产品总产量的50%以上，符合《中华人民共和国反倾销条例》第十一条、第十三条和第十七条有关国内产业提出反倾销调查申请的规定。同时，申请书中包含了《中华人民共和国反倾销条例》第十四条、第十五条规定的反倾销调查立案所要求的内容及有关证据。

根据上述审查结果及《中华人民共和国反倾销条例》第十六条规定，商务部决定自2012年3月23日起对原产于欧盟的进口甲苯二异氰酸酯(型号为TDI80/20)进行反倾销立案调查。现将有关事项公告如下：

一、立案调查及调查期

自本公告发布之日起，商务部对原产于欧盟的进口甲苯二异氰酸酯(型号为TDI80/20)进行反倾销调查，本次调查确定的倾销调查期为2011年1月1日至2011年12月31日，产业损害调查期为2008年1月1日至2011年12月31日。

二、被调查产品及调查范围

调查范围：原产于欧盟的进口甲苯二异氰酸酯(型号为TDI80/20)

被调查产品名称：甲苯二异氰酸酯，英文名称：Toluene Diisocyanate(简称“TDI”)。

规格型号：TDI80/20

分子式：$C_9H_6N_2O_2$

物理和化学特征：属于有机化学中含氮基化合物项下的异氰酸酯类，常温下为白色或浅黄色的液体，有刺激性气味，能与丙酮、醚类混溶，易与包含有活泼氢原子的化合物胺、水、醇、酸、碱发生反应分解，遇热遇火易发生爆炸。

主要用途：甲苯二异氰酸酯是生产聚氨酯产品的主要原料，用于制造软泡、弹性体、涂料、粘合剂等聚氨酯产品，还可以用于乙烯基聚合物的薄膜、天然橡胶的表面加工、涂料的耐药品性添加剂、纺织加工等方面，在石油、化工、矿山、冶金及汽车工业和铁路运输方面都有着广泛的用途。

该产品归在《中华人民共和国进出口税则》：29291010。

三、登记应诉

就倾销调查，任何利害关系方可于本公告发布之日起20天内，向商务部进出口公平贸易局申请参加应诉，参加应诉的涉案出口商或生产商同时应提供2011年1月1日至2011年12月31日向中国出口本案被调查产品的数量及金额。《倾销调查应诉登记参考格式》可在中华人民共和国商务部网站进出口公平贸易局子网站“公告”栏目下载。

就产业损害调查，利害关系方可自本公告发布之日起20天内向商务部产业损害调查局登记应诉，同时应提供产业损害调查期内的生产能力、产量、库存、在建和扩建的计划以及向中国出口该产品的数量和金额等说明材料。

四、不登记应诉

如利害关系方未在本公告规定的时间内向商务部登记应诉，则商务部有权拒绝接受其递交的有关材料，并有权根据所掌握的现有材料做出裁定。

五、利害关系方的权利

利害关系方对本次调查的产品范围、申请人资格、被调查国家及其他相关问题如有异议，可在上述登记应诉期间将意见书面提交商务部。

利害关系方可在上述期间到商务部贸易救济公开信息查阅室(电话：86－10－65197878)查阅本案申请人提交的申请书的非保密文本。

六、调查方式

调查机关可以采用问卷、抽样、听证会、现场核查等方式向有关利害关系方了解情况并进行调查。

七、本次调查自2012年3月23日起开始，通常应在2013年3月23日前结束调查，特殊情况下可延长至2013年9月23日。

八、商务部联系地址(略)

附件：甲苯二异氰酸酯反倾销调查应诉登记表(略)

(注：甲苯二异氰酸酯是生产聚氨酯产品的主要原料，用于制造软泡、弹性体、涂料、粘合剂等聚氨酯产品，还可以用于乙烯基聚合物的薄膜等)。

又讯：中华人民共和国商务部公告2012年第79号 关于对原产于欧盟的进口甲苯二异氰酸酯反倾销调查初裁的公告(二〇一二年十一月十三日)

根据《中华人民共和国反倾销条例》的规定，2012年3月23日，商务部(以下称调查机关)发布2012年第14号公告，决定对原产于欧盟的进口甲苯二异氰酸酯(型号为TDI80/20)(以下称被调查产品)进行反倾销立案调查。该被调查产品归在《中华人民共和国进出口税则》(2012年版)税则号：29291010。

调查机关对被调查产品是否存在倾销和倾销幅度、被调查产品是否对中国甲苯二异氰酸酯产业造成损害及损害程度进行了调查。根据调查结果和《中华人民共和国反倾销条例》第二十四条的规定，调查机关作出初步裁定(见附件)。现将有关事项公告如下：

一、初步裁定

调查机关初步裁定，在本案调查期内，被调查产品存在倾销，中国甲苯二异氰酸酯产业受到实质损害，且倾销与实质损害之间存在因果关系。

二、征收保证金

根据《中华人民共和国反倾销条例》第二十八条和二十九条的规定，调查机关决定采用保证金形式实施临时反倾销措施。自2012年11月13日起，进口经营者在进口被调查产品时，应依据本初裁决定所确定的各公司的倾销幅度向中华人民共和国海关提供相应的保证金。

对被调查产品的具体描述如下：

调查范围：原产于欧盟的进口甲苯二异氰酸酯（型号为 TDI80/20）。

被调查产品名称：甲苯二异氰酸酯，英文名称：Toluene Diisocyanate（简称“TDI”）

规格型号：TDI80/20

分子式：$C_9H_6N_2O_2$

物理及化学特征：属于有机化学中含氮基化合物项下的异氰酸酯类，常温下为白色或浅黄色的液体，有刺激性气味，能与丙酮、醚类混溶，易与包含有活泼氢原子的化合物胺、水、醇、酸、碱发生反应分解，遇热遇火易发生爆炸。

主要用途：甲苯二异氰酸酯是生产聚氨酯产品的主要原料，用于制造软泡、弹性体、涂料、粘合剂等聚氨酯产品，还可以用于乙烯基聚合物的薄膜、天然橡胶的表面加工、涂料的耐药品性添加剂、纺织加工等方面，在石油、化工、矿山、冶金及汽车工业和铁路运输方面都有着广泛的用途。

该产品归在《中华人民共和国进出口税则》（2012年版）税则号：29291010。

对各公司征收的保证金比率如下：

（1）拜耳材料科技公司 19.2%

（Bayer MaterialScience AG）

（2）波兰扎克姆化工股份公司 18.1%

（Zaklady Chemiczne ZACHEM S.A.）

（3）博苏化学有限责任公司 6.6%

（Borsodchem Zrt.）

（4）柏斯托法国公司 37.7%

（Perstorp France）

（5）陶式西班牙公司 37.7%

（Dow Chemical Tarragona）

（6）其他欧盟公司 37.7%

（All Others）

三、征收保证金的方法

自2012年11月13日起，进口经营者在进口被调查产品时，应依据本初裁决定所确定的各公司的倾销幅度向中华人民共和国海关提供相应的保证金。保证金以海关审定的完税价格从价计征，计算公式为：保证金金额＝（海关审定的完税价格×保证金征收比率）×（1＋进口环节增值税税率）。

四、评论

各利害关系方在本公告发布之日起20天内，可向调查机关提出书面评论并附相关证据，调查机关将依法予以考虑。

附件：中华人民共和国商务部关于原产于欧盟的进口甲苯二异氰酸酯（型号为 TDI80/20）反倾销调查的初步裁定

根据《反倾销条例》（以下称《反倾销条例》）的规定，2012年3月23日，商务部（以下称调查机关）正式发布立案公告，决定对原产于欧盟的进口甲苯二异氰酸酯（型号为 TDI80/20）（以下称被调查产品）进行反倾销立案调查。该被调查产品归在《中华人民共和国进出口税则》（2012年版）税则号：29291010。

调查机关对被调查产品是否存在倾销和倾销幅度、被调查产品是否对中国甲苯二异氰酸酯产业造成损害及损害程度以及倾销与损害之间的因果关系进行了调查。根据调查结果和《反倾销条例》的规定，调查机关做出初步裁定如下：

一、调查程序

（一）立案。

2012年2月3日，沧州大化 TDI 有限责任公司、甘肃银光聚银化工有限公司、甘肃银达化工有限公司、辽宁北方锦化聚氨酯有限公司和沧州大化股份有限公司聚海分公司代表国内甲苯二异氰酸酯产业向调查机关提起对原产于欧盟的进口甲苯二异氰酸酯（型号为 TDI80/20）进行反倾销调查的申请。

调查机关审查了申请材料后，认为申请人符合《反倾销条例》第十一条及第十三条和第十七条有关中国国内产业提出反倾销调查申请的规定。同时，申请书中包含了《反倾销条例》第十四条、第十五条规定的反倾销调查立案所要求的内容及有关的证据。

根据上述审查结果及《反倾销条例》第十六条的规定，调查机关于2012年3月23日发布立案公告，决定对原产于欧盟的进口甲苯二异氰酸酯（型号为 TDI80/20）进行反倾销立案调查。倾销调查期为2011年1月1日至2011年12月31日，产业损害调查期为2008年1月1日至2011年12月31日。

（二）倾销及倾销幅度的初步调查。

1. 立案通知

在决定立案调查前，根据《反倾销条例》第十六条规定，调查机关就收到中国甲苯二异氰酸酯产业反倾销调查申请书一事通知了欧洲联盟欧洲委员会驻中国及蒙古国代表团。

2012年3月23日，调查机关发布立案公告，并向欧洲联盟欧洲委员会驻中国及蒙古国代表团正式提供了立案公告和申请书的公开部分。同日，调查机关将本案立案情况通知了本案申请人及申请书中列明的国外企业。

2. 登记应诉

根据公告要求，自公告发布之日起20天的登记应诉期内，博苏化学有限责任公司(Borsodchem Zrt)、拜耳材料科技公司(Bayer MaterialScience AG)、柏斯托法国公司(Perstorp France)和波兰扎克姆化工股份公司(Zaklady Chemiczne ZACHEM S. A.)向调查机关登记倾销应诉。另外，波兰驻华使馆也向调查机关登记应诉。

3. 发放问卷和收取答卷

2012 年 4 月 17 日，调查机关向应诉的和已知的境外生产商发放了倾销调查问卷，并要求其在 37 天内按规定提交准确、完整的答卷。在该期间内，有关应诉公司向调查机关申请延期递交答卷并陈述了相关理由。经审查，调查机关同意给予申请企业适当延期。至答卷递交截止之日，调查机关收到了博苏化学有限责任公司、拜耳材料科技公司和波兰扎克姆化工股份公司的有关倾销部分问卷的答卷。

此后，调查机关就答卷中的有关问题向应诉公司发送补充问卷，应诉公司在规定时间内递交了补充问卷的答卷。

2012 年 4 月 17 日，调查机关向登记应诉的柏斯托法国公司发放了调查问卷，该公司向调查机关表示拒绝提交答卷。

2012 年 4 月 17 日，调查机关向申请书中已列明的陶氏西班牙公司发放调查问卷；同日，调查机关将调查问卷登载在商务部网站上，任何利害关系方可在商务部网站上查阅本案调查问卷。在规定的答卷递交截止之日，调查机关未收到该公司答卷。

(三)产业损害及损害程度的初步调查。

1. 产业损害调查期

根据《反倾销产业损害调查规定》第十八条的规定，调查机关确定的本案产业损害调查期(以下称调查期)为 2008 年 1 月 1 日至 2011 年 12 月 31 日。

2. 参加产业损害调查活动登记

根据《反倾销产业损害调查规定》第十九条、第二十一条的规定，2012 年 3 月 23 日，调查机关发出了《关于参加甲苯二异氰酸酯反倾销案产业损害调查活动登记的通知》(商调查二处函[2012]81 号)。2012 年 4 月 12 日，参加产业损害调查活动登记截止，调查机关共收到有效登记材料 4 份，分别为国外生产者/出口商博苏化学有限责任公司、拜耳材料科技公司、柏斯托法国公司和波兰扎克姆化工股份公司。经审查，调查机关接受了上述利害关系方的登记。

3. 成立产业损害调查组

2012 年 4 月 27 日，调查机关成立了甲苯二异氰酸酯反倾销案产业损害调查组，负责本案的产业损害调查工作，并于当日发出《关于成立甲苯二异氰酸酯反倾销案产业损害调查组的通知》(商调查二处函[2012]143 号)。

4. 发放和收回调查问卷

根据《反倾销条例》第二十条和《反倾销产业损害调查规定》第二十四条、第二十五条的规定，2012 年 4 月 12 日，调查机关向本案利害关系方发放了《甲苯二异氰酸酯反倾销案产业损害调查问卷(国内生产者调查问卷)》(商调查二处函[2012]117 号)(以下称《国内生产者调查问卷》)、《甲苯二异氰酸酯反倾销案产业损害调查问卷(国外 < 地区 > 生产者/出口商调查问卷)》(商调查二处函[2012]118 号)(以下称《国外 < 地区 > 生产者/出口商调查问卷》)和《甲苯二异氰酸酯反倾销案产业损害调查问卷(国内进口商调查问卷)》(商调查二处函[2012]119 号)(以下称《国内进口商调查问卷》)。

2012 年 5 月 3 日，调查机关收到波兰扎克姆化工股份公司《关于对"甲苯二异氰酸酯反倾销案产业损害调查问卷国外(地区)生产者/出口商调查问卷"答卷延迟提交答卷的申请》。该申请提出延期 13 天提交调查问卷答卷，其延迟提交答卷的理由一是答卷期间包含"五一"劳动节假期，二是核对、整理和翻译答卷资料需要额外时间。

调查机关对波兰扎克姆化工股份公司的申请进行了考虑。调查机关认为，答卷期间包含的"五一"劳动节假期仅为一天，规定的答卷期间已包含合理的核对、整理和翻译有关资料时间，波兰扎克姆化工股份公司提出的延期 13 天的理由不充分。调查机关于 2012 年 5 月 9 日向其回复了《关于不同意延期提交甲苯二异氰酸酯反倾销案产业损害调查问卷答卷的函》(商调查二处函[2012]166 号)，不同意其延期申请。

在调查问卷规定的回收期限内，调查机关共收回调查问卷答卷 8 份，分别为沧州大化 TDI 有限责任公司、沧州大化股份有限公司聚海分公司、甘肃银光聚银化工有限公司、甘肃银达化工有限公司和辽宁北方锦化聚氨酯有限公司提交的《国内生产者调查问卷》答卷 5 份；博苏化学有限责任公司、拜耳材料科技公司和波兰扎克姆化工股份公司提交的《国外 < 地区 > 生产者/出口商调查问卷》答卷 3 份。参加产业损害调查活动登记的柏斯托法国公司未提交调查问卷答卷。

5. 听取利害关系方意见陈述

根据《反倾销条例》第二十条的规定，调查机关听取了利害关系方就本案产业损害调查有关事项的意见陈述。2012 年 4 月 12 日，调查机关收到本案申请人提交的《甲苯二异氰酸酯反倾销案关于召开申请人意见陈述会的申请》。调查机关于 2012 年 4 月 27 日发出《关于召开甲苯二异氰酸酯反倾销案申请人意见陈述会的通知》(商调查二处函[2012]148 号)。2012 年 5 月 18 日，调查机关召开了甲苯二异氰酸酯反倾销案申请人意见陈述会，听取申请人陈述提起申请的主要理由及与本案产业损害调查相关问题的陈述。陈述会后，申请人向调查机关提交了《甲苯二异氰酸酯(TDI)反倾销案申请人意见陈述会汇报材料》。

6. 接收利害关系方书面意见

调查机关未收到各利害关系方除调查问卷答卷之外的关于本案的书面评论意见。

7. 初裁前实地核查

根据《反倾销条例》第二十条和《反倾销产业损害调查规定》第二十七条的规定，2012 年 5 月 25 日，调查机关发出了《关于甲苯二异氰酸酯反倾销案初裁前实地核查的通知》(商调查二处函[2012]189 号)。2012 年 7 月至 8 月，调查机关对国内生产者沧州大化 TDI 有限责任公司、沧州大化股份有限公司聚海分公司进行了初裁前实地核查。调查机关对本案的申请书、被核查企业提交的调查问卷答卷中提供的信息及有关证据进行了核查。2012 年 8 月 9 日，被核查企业向调查机关提交了《甲苯二异氰酸酯(TDI)反倾销案产业损害调查初裁前实地核查后补充材料》及相关实地核查证据材料。

8. 接收利害关系方信息保密申请。

2012 年 9 月 12 日，调查机关收到本案申请人提交的《甲苯二异氰酸酯(TDI)反倾销案申请人关于国内产业损害数据保密性问题的进一步说明》。

9. 信息公开

根据《产业损害调查信息查阅与信息披露规定》第八条、第十四条的规定，调查机关将调查过程中收到的本案所有公开材料已及时送交商务部贸易救济措施公开信息查阅室。各利害关系方可以查找、阅览、摘抄、复印有关公开信息。

调查机关对申请书、调查问卷答卷及所附证据材料和实地核查结果进行了认真分析和全面评估，对各利害关系方的意见依法给予了充分考虑。

二、被调查产品及调查范围

(一)被调查产品。

被调查产品名称：甲苯二异氰酸酯，英文名称：Toluene Diisocyanate(简称“TDI”)

规格型号：TDI80/20

分子式：$C_9H_6N_2O_2$

物理及化学特征：属于有机化学中含氮基化合物项下的异氰酸酯类，常温下为白色或浅黄色的液体，有刺激性气味，能与丙酮、醚类混溶，易与包含有活泼氢原子的化合物胺、水、醇、酸、碱发生反应分解，遇热遇火易发生爆炸。

主要用途：甲苯二异氰酸酯是生产聚氨酯产品的主要原料，用于制造软泡、弹性体、涂料、粘合剂等聚氨酯产品，还可以用于乙烯基聚合物的薄膜、天然橡胶的表面加工、涂料的耐药品性添加剂、纺织加工等方面，在石油、化工、矿山、冶金及汽车工业和铁路运输方面都有着广泛的用途。

税则号：该产品归在《中华人民共和国进出口税则》(2012 年版)税则号：29291010。

(二)调查范围。

原产于欧盟的进口甲苯二异氰酸酯（型号为 TDI80/20）。

三、国内同类产品和国内产业

(一)中国国内同类产品的认定。

根据《反倾销条例》第十二条和《反倾销产业损害调查规定》第十、十一条关于同类产品认定的规定，调查机关对国内生产的甲苯二异氰酸酯与被调查产品的物理特征和化学性能、生产设备和工艺、产品用途、产品的可替代性、消费者和生产者的评价、销售渠道、价格等因素进行了考察，初步调查证据显示：

1. 物理特征和化学性能。国内生产的甲苯二异氰酸酯与被调查产品的化学分子式完全相同。两者外观相同，常温下为白色或浅黄色的液体，能与丙酮、醚类混溶。基本物理特征和化学性能无明显区别，主要技术指标如纯度、异构比、可水解率、酸度等相同或类似。

2. 生产设备和工艺。调查机关经过实地核查，并与《国外<地区>生产者/出口商调查问卷》答卷提供的生产设备和工艺相关信息进行了对比，在此基础上初步认定，国内生产的甲苯二异氰酸酯与被调查产品的原材料基本相同，主要生产设备和工艺无明显差异。认定理由如下：

(1)国内生产的甲苯二异氰酸酯与被调查产品主要原材料均包括甲苯与硝酸(或二硝基甲苯(DNT))、液氯、焦炭、氢气等。

(2)国内生产的甲苯二异氰酸酯与被调查产品均采用胺光气化法进行生产。主要生产工艺流程可以概括为：二硝基甲苯(DNT)通过氢化工序加氢，再经过精制工序生成甲苯二胺(MTD)，甲苯二胺与由氯气和一氧化碳通过光气合成反应生成的光气进行光气化反应，生成的甲苯二异氰酸酯经过脱焦、精制等工序产出成品甲苯二异氰酸酯。在前序工段，原料二硝基甲苯(DNT)可以由甲苯与硝酸进行硝化反应生成，也可以直接外购投入生产。调查机关注意到，虽然不同利害关系方在具体工序中所采用的反应方式、循环路线以及采用的反应溶剂等方面存在一定差别，但在上述主要工艺上无明显差异。

(3)实地核查收集的证据材料与《国外 <地区> 生产者/出口商调查问卷》答卷提供的相关信息显示，国内生产的甲苯二异氰酸酯与被调查产品生产设备相同或类似，均主要包括硝化、氢化、精馏、光气合成、光气化等相关设备。

3. 产品用途、产品的可替代性、消费者和生产者的评价、销售渠道及价格 。

《国内生产者调查问卷》答卷和《国外 <地区> 生产者/出口商调查问卷》答卷显示，国内生产的甲苯二异氰酸酯与被调查产品用途基本相同，均用于制造软泡、弹性体、涂料、粘合剂等聚氨酯产品，还可以用于乙烯基聚合物的薄膜、天然橡胶的表面加工、涂料的耐药品性添加剂、纺织加工等方面，在石油、化工、矿山、冶金及汽车工业和铁路运输方面都有着广泛的用途。国内生产的甲苯二异氰酸酯与被调查产品销售渠道基本相同，均为直接销售和代理销售相结合。销售市场区域基本相同，均在全国范围内进行销售。国内生产的甲苯二异氰酸酯与被调查产品的客户群体基本相同，主要是面向下游聚氨酯产品生产企业。部分国内用户既使用国内生产的甲苯二异氰酸酯，又使用被调查产品，二者可以相互替代。国内生产的甲苯二异氰酸酯价格总体的变化趋势与被调查产品进口价格总体的变化趋势基本一致。

综合以上因素，调查机关认定，虽然国内生产的甲苯二异氰酸酯与被调查产品在不同的工艺阶段存在一定差别，但在主要工艺上无明显差异，二者之间的物理特征和化学性能、生产设备和工艺、产品用途、客户群体、消费者和生产者的评价、销售渠道、销售市场区域等方面基本相同，价格总体变化趋势基本一致，具有可替代性。因此，国内生产的甲苯二异氰酸酯与被调查产品属于同类产品。

(二)中国国内产业的认定。

根据《反倾销条例》第十一条和《反倾销产业损害调查规定》第十三条的规定，调查机关对本案国内产业的范围进行了审查。

本案申请人在反倾销调查申请书中提出，国内甲苯二异氰酸酯生产企业上海巴斯夫聚氨酯有限公司、拜耳材料科技(中国)有限公司与本案欧盟出口经营者具有关联关系，应将上述两家企业排除在国内甲苯二异氰酸酯产业之外。

调查机关对上述申请予以了考虑。本案反倾销调查申请书所附证据及拜耳材料科技公司提交的《进口甲苯二异氰酸酯反倾销案产业损害调查问卷》答卷显示，上海巴斯夫聚氨酯有限公司与欧盟出口经营者德国 BASF Schwarzheide GmbH 和比利时出口经营者 BASF Antwerpen N. V. 存在关联关系，拜耳材料科技(中国)有限公司与欧盟出口经营者德国拜耳材料科技公司(Bayer Material Science AG)存在关联关系。

调查机关认为，申请人的主张符合法律规定，应将与欧盟出口经营者存在关联关系的上海巴斯夫聚氨酯有限公司、拜耳材料科技(中国)有限公司排除在本案国内产业之外。

初步证据显示，调查期内，国内生产者答卷企业生产的甲苯二异氰酸酯产量均占国内产业同类产品总产量的50%以上，符合《反倾销条例》第十一条和《反倾销产业损害调查规定》第十三条关于国内产业认定的规定，可以代表国内产业。本裁决所依据的国内产业数据，除特别说明外，均来自以上特定的国内生产者。

四、倾销和倾销幅度

调查机关审查了应诉公司的答卷，对公司的正常价值和出口价格作如下认定：

(一)正常价值、出口价格及价格调整项目的认定。

(1)拜耳材料科技公司(Bayer MaterialScience AG)

①正常价值

该公司在答卷中称其仅生产一种型号 TDI 产品，主张该产品在中国、欧盟和其他国家(地区)市场销售都没有差别。经初步调查，调查机关暂接受该公司关于同类产品与被调查产品的相似性及型号划分的主张。

调查机关初步审查了该公司在欧盟内的销售情况。

调查期内，该公司欧盟内销售数量占同期向中国出口销售数量的比例超过5%，符合作为确定正常价值基础的数量要求。调查期内，该公司部分产品直接销售给非关联客户，部分产品销售其关联公司后再转售给非关联客户。经审查，调查机关发现该公司销售给关联客户的价格较销售给非关联公司的价格差异明显，故调查机关认定该公司与关联客户的交易不能反映正常贸易过程，在确定正常价值时排除关联客户交易。

调查机关对该公司报告的生产成本和销售、管理及财务费用进行了初步审查，经审查，调查机关初步认定该公司报告的成本费用数据反映了被调查产品的生产销售情况，决定暂接受公司报告的成本费用数据。调查机关根据认定的成本数据对非关联内销交易是否存在低于成本销售情况进行了审查，发现调查期内该公司内销交易价格低于成本的销售数量比例超过20%，根据《反倾销条例》第四条的规定，调查机关暂按排除低于成本销售后的正常贸易过程中进行的内销交易作为确定正常价值的基础。

②出口价格

调查机关审查了该公司在调查期内向中国出口被调查产品情况。在调查期内，该公司称其通过多种方式向中国出口被调查产品：(1)通过设立在中国的关联进口商进口后，再转售给非关联客户，经审查，调查机关暂以中国关联进口商与非关联客户的交易价格为基础结构出口价格。(2)通过设立在第三国(地区)的关联客户向中国出口被调查产品。经审查，调查机关暂以该关联客户与非关联中国客户间的交易价格为基础确定出口价格。

③调整项目

根据《反倾销条例》第六条规定，为公平合理比较，调查机关对该公司影响价格可比性的调整项目逐一进行了审查。

第一、正常价值部分。对于被调查产品销售过程发生的包装费用、信用费用、内陆运费、内陆保险费用、提前付款折扣、发票中折扣等调整项目，经审查，调查机关暂采信其提交的数据和材料，暂接受其调整主张。

第二、出口价格部分。对于通过设立在中国的关联贸易商转售的交易，经初步审查，关于进口关税，公司答卷报告的进口关税计算货币单位存在折算错误，调查机关进行了调整；关于设立在中国关联进口贸易商的转售利润，公司答卷中所报告转售利润为负，公司在补充答卷中报告了相似贸易商通常可实现盈利水平，经初步审查，调查机关暂采信该数据进行调整；关于设立在中国的关联贸易商发生的间接费用，公司答卷未将其报告为调整项目，调查机关暂按在中国的关联贸易商发生间接费用比例补充调整。

对于通过设立在第三国(地区)的关联贸易商转售的交易，经初步审查，调查机关认为，该关联公司承担了客户维护、交易定价、售前仓储及销售风险等等职能，发生了多项直接或间接费用。公司答卷报告了各项直接费用，未将间接费用报告为调整项目，故初裁时调查机关暂根据该关联公司的6-5表计算了间接费用占销售收入的比例，并据此对出口价格进行了补充调整。

对于该公司销售给关联公司、设立在中国的关联进口贸易商转售发生以及设立在第三国(地区)的关联贸易商转售发生的回扣、内陆运费-工厂到分销仓库、售前仓储、内陆运费-分销仓库到客户、内陆保险费用、包装费用、信用费用、国际运输费用、国际运输保险费用、港口装卸费和报关代理费等其他调整项目，调查机关暂采信其提交的数据和材料，暂接受其调整主张。

④关于到岸价格(CIF价格)

经审查，对于通过设立在中国的关联客户转售的交易，调查机关暂采用该公司与设立在中国的关联客户间交易价格确定到岸价格(CIF价格)；对于通过设立在第三国(地区)的关联贸易商转售的交易，调查机关采用设立在第三国(地区)的关联贸易商转售交易价格确定到岸价格(CIF价格)。

(2)波兰扎克姆化工股份公司(Zakłady Chemiczne ZACHEM S. A.)

公司答卷称，波兰扎克姆化工股份公司(以下简称扎克姆公司)是生产工厂，仅负责TDI80/20产品的生产，而不承担任何销售职能，该公司生产TDI产品全部由其母公司捷杭化工股份公司(以下简称捷杭公司)负责对外销售，而且捷杭公司仅销售扎克姆公司所生产的TDI产品，而不从事任何外购活动，为此，公司主张，将扎克姆公司和捷杭公司视为同一公司内部的生产车间和销售部门之间的关系(以下如无特指，通称该公司)。经初步审查，在初裁中，调查机关决定暂接受公司主张。以捷杭公司对外销售价格作为确定正常价值和出口价格的基础。

①正常价值

公司答卷称其生产TDI产品，该产品为单一型号，主张该产品在中国、欧盟和其他国家(地区)市场销售都没有差别。经初步调查，调查机关暂接受该公司关于同类产品与被调查产品的相似性及型号划分的主张。

调查机关初步审查了公司在欧盟内销售被调查产品同类产品情况。调查机关发现，在欧盟内销售的被调查产品同类产品数量占同期向中国出口销售数量的比例超过5%，符合作为确定正常价值基础的数量要求。

调查期内，捷杭公司将部分被调查产品同类产品销售给关联的最终用户。公司主张，在销售中，公司将关联的最终用户视为普通客户，在价格和交易条件方面没有特殊安排。经初步审查，调查机关发现，公司与关联最终用户之间存在紧密的关联关系，公司对关联公司和非关联公司之间的销售价格存在明显差异，该公司的关联最终用户未单独填报答卷，该公司也未提供足够证据表明，关联交易是正常贸易过程中的交易。调查机关认定，该公司与关联公司之间的交易不属于正常贸易过程中交易，在初裁中，调查机关决定在确定正常价值时排除这部分关联公司之间的交易。

调查机关初步审查了扎克姆公司和捷杭公司的生产成本和销售、管理及财务费用。关于生产成本，公司主张，在调查期某期间，对被调查产品的生产设备进行了停产维修，考虑这一特殊状况，公司以其他月份的制造成本数据加权平均来替代该期间的制造成本数据。调查机关就此发放补充问卷，要求公司详细解释该停产维修发生的原因。公司解释，产品生产过程复杂，较为危险，因技术原因而造成生产设备正常停产检修是经常发生，只是因为该期间停工时间大大高于其他月份设备停工时间。调查机关认为，该期间停产维修为公司正常停产检修，虽然比其他月份停产时间长，但公司以其他月份的制造成本数据加权平均来替代该期间数据，与公司实际会计记录不符。在初裁中，调查机关决定暂采用公司年加权平均成本对内销交易是否低于成本销售进行审查。对于公司主张的扎克姆公司和捷杭公司合并的销售、管理及财务费用以及扎克姆公司非主营业务收入的数据，在初裁中，调查机关暂予以接受。经审查，调查机关发现调查期内该公司内销交易低于成本的销售量超过20%，根据《反倾销条例》第四条的规定，调查机关暂按排除低于成本销售后的正常贸易过程中进行的内销交易作为确定正常价值的基础。

②出口价格

调查机关审查了该公司在调查期内向中国出口被调查产品情况。在调查期内，该公司或直接对中国非关联客户进行销售，或通过位于新加坡关联公司转售给非关联中国客户。公司主张，将新加坡关联公司与其他非关联公司同等对待，没有给予特殊安排。调查机关经调查发现，两公司存在紧密的关联关系，公司未提供充分证据证明其主张。根据《反倾销条例》第五条的规定，在初裁中，对于直接对中国非关联客户的销售，调查机关暂以对中国客户的销售价格作为其出口价格，对于通过位于新加坡关联公司转售的部分交易，调查机关暂以新加坡公司转售价格作为计算出口价格的基础。

③调整项目

根据《反倾销条例》第六条规定，为公平合理比较，调查机关对该公司影响价格可比性的调整项目逐一进行了审查。

第一，正常价值部分。关于佣金，公司主张对扎克姆公司和捷杭公司之间的销售佣金进行调整。调查机关审查后认为，本案将上述两公司视为同一公司内部的生产车间和销售部门，为公平比较，调查机关将出口价格和正常价值均调整到捷杭公司销售水平，上述两公司内部之间的佣金与确定正常价值无关，也不影响价格的公平比较，因此，在初裁中，调查机关暂不接受公司的主张。

关于该公司所报告的内销交易的其他调整项目，调查机关暂采信其提交的数据和材料，暂接受其提出的内陆运费、包装费等调整的主张。

第二，出口价格部分。关于佣金，公司主张对扎克姆公司和捷杭公司之间的销售佣金进行调整。调查机关审查后认为，本案将上述两公司视为同一公司内部的生产车间和销售部门，为公平比较，调查机关将出口价格和正常价值均调整到捷杭公司销售水平，上述两公司内部之间的佣金与确定出口价格无关，也不影响价格的公平比较，因此，在初裁中，调查机关暂不接受公司的主张。

关于新加坡关联公司间接费用的调整。公司在原始答卷中未按照调查机关要求填报新加坡关联公司的6-5表，调查机关在补充问卷中要求其填报，公司在补充答卷填报了公司调查期全部产品利润表。此外，公司补充答卷中称，该关联公司自主决定价格，承担寻找客户和市场推广的职能，承担销售风险。调查机关认为，该公司承担了客户维护、交易定价等职能并承受交易风险，发生了多项直接费用和间接费用，公司答卷报告了各项直接费用调整，未报告间接费用调整，初裁时调查机关暂根据公司报告的6-5表计算出间接费用占销售收入的比例，并据此对出口价格进行了补充调整。

对于该公司主张的被调查产品销售过程发生的国际运费、信用费用等调整项目，经审查，调查机关暂采信其提交的数据和材料，暂接受对其调整的主张。

④关于到岸价格(CIF价格)

公司在答卷中汇报了CIF价格计算方法，调查机关审查了该公司货物运输保险投保情况，发现该公司在对中国出口销售中，承担了国际保险费用，该公司主张的CIF计算价格不合理。因此，在初裁中，调查机关暂不接受公司主张，以捷杭公司和新加坡关联公司实际报告的出口销售价格作为其实际的到岸价格。

(3)博苏化学有限责任公司(BorsodChem Private Company Limited by Shares, BorsodChem Ltd)

①正常价值

该公司在答卷中称其生产TDI产品，该产品为单一型号，主张该产品在中国、欧盟和其他国家(地区)市场销售都没有差别。经初步调查，调查机关暂接受该公司关于同类产品与被调查产品的相似性及型号划分的主张。该公司在答卷中还报告外购其他生产商TDI产品的销售情况，经审查，调查机关暂决定确定正常价值时排除外购产品。

调查机关初步审查了该公司在欧盟内的销售情况。

调查期内，该公司欧盟内销售数量占同期向中国出口销售数量的比例超过5%，符合作为确定正常价值基础的数量要求。调查期内，该公司部分产品直接销售给非关联客户，部分产品销售其关联公司后再转售给非关联客户。经初步审查，调查机关发现该公司销售给关联客户价格较销售给非关联公司价格差异明显，故调查机关认定该公司与关联客户的交易不能反映正常贸易过程，在确定正常价值时排除关联客户交易。

调查机关对该公司报告的生产成本和销售、管理及财务费用进行了初步审查，经审查，调查机关初步认定该公司报告的成本费用数据反映了被调查产品的生产销售情况，决定暂接受公司报告的成本费用数据。调查机关根据认定的成本数据对非关联内销交易是否存在低于成本销售情况进行了审查，发现调查期内该公司内销交易价格低于成本的销售数量比例超过20%，根据《反倾销条例》第四条的规定，调查机关认为，该部分交易不属于正常贸易过程中进行的销售，故决定在确定正常价值时排除这部分交易。

该公司在答卷中称，其在调查期内仅向中国出口了一笔被调查产品，该笔被调查产品于调查期内的某月份由其关联公司转售给非关联客户，主张仅应采用该月份其在欧盟内销售同类产品的交易数据确定正常价值。经初步审查，调查机关认为，该公司在调查期内仅出口了一笔被调查产品，在该月份没有与该笔交易可比的合适单笔内销，故调查机关在初裁时暂接受公司主张，采用该月份内销同类产品的加权平均数据确定正常价值。

②出口价格

调查机关初步审查了该公司在调查期内向中国出口被调查产品情况。在调查期内，该公司通过位于中国的关联进口商进口后，再转售给非关联客户，经审查，调查机关暂以中国关联进口商与非关联客户的交易价格为基础确定出口价格。

③调整项目

根据《反倾销条例》第六条规定，为公平合理比较，调查机关对该公司影响价格可比性的调整项目逐一进行了审查。

第一、正常价值部分。对于被调查产品销售过程发生的提前付款折扣、回扣、退款及赔偿、包装费用、利息收入、信用费用、内陆运费、内陆保险费用、发票中折扣、佣金等调整项目，经审查，调查机关暂采信其提交的数据和材料，暂接受对其调整的主张。

第二、出口价格部分。对于通过设立在中国的关联贸易商转售的交易，公司答卷未将设立在中国的关联贸易商发生的间接费用报告为调整项目，经初步审查，调查机关暂按在中国的关联贸易商发生间接费用比例对此做了补充调整。

对于该公司销售给关联公司以及在中国关联进口公司转售发生包装费用、信用费用、内陆运费、国际运输费用、国际运输保险费用、报关代理费、其他需要调整的项目－银行费用、港口装卸费、进口关税、转售利润等其他调整项目，调查机关暂采信其提交的数据和材料，暂接受对其调整的主张。

④关于到岸价格(CIF价格)

经审查，调查机关采用该公司与设立在中国的关联客户间交易价格确定到岸价格(CIF价格)。

(4)柏斯托法国公司(Perstorp France)

柏斯托法国公司登记应诉但拒绝提交答卷，根据《反倾销条例》第二十一条的规定，在初裁中，调查机关暂决定采用已经获得的事实和可获得的最佳信息作出裁决。本案申请书的数据来源于中国海关统计数据。为公平比较，申请人在计算倾销幅度时已做相应的调整。调查机关经审查认为申请人提供的信息是可获得的最佳信息，因此，在初裁中，调查机关暂根据申请人主张的倾销幅度确定该公司倾销幅度。

(5)陶氏西班牙公司(Dow Chemical Tarragona)

2012年4月17日，调查机关向已知的陶氏西班牙公司发放调查问卷；同日，调查机关将调查问卷登载在商务部网站上，任何利害关系方可在商务部网站上查阅本案调查问卷。在问卷截止日，调查机关未收到该公司答卷。根据《反倾销条例》第二十一条的规定，在初裁中，调查机关暂决定采用已经获得的事实和可获得的最佳信息作出裁决。本案申请书的数据来源于中国海关统计数据。为公平比较，申请人在计算倾销幅度时已做相应的调整。调查机关经审查认为申请人提供的信息是可获得的最佳信息，因此，在初裁中，调查机关暂根据申请人主张的倾销幅度确定该公司倾销幅度。

(6)其他欧盟公司(All Others)

调查机关在立案之日将立案公告登载在商务部网站上，任何利害关系方均可在商务部网站上查阅本案立案公告。立案后，调查机关给予各利害关系方20天的登记应诉期，给予所有利害关系方合理的时间获知立案有关情况。2012年4月17日，调查机关将调查问卷登载在商务部网站上，任何利害关系方可在商务部网站上查阅本案调查问卷。调查机关已尽最大努力通知所有利害关系方，也已尽最大努力向所有利害关系方提醒不提交答卷的结果。

调查机关注意到，申请书未列明的、调查期内可能存在的其他出口经营者，未登记应诉，也未提交答卷。本案，调查机关通过查询海关数据、咨询相关行业协会、查阅相关网站、公开刊物，以及申请人提供的相关数据认定这些公司的正常价值、出口价格，并对影响正常价值和出口价格可比因素进行了调整，并在同一贸易环节进行了比较。

①正常价值

经调查，调查机关认定调查期内被调查产品同类产品欧盟内市场平均销售价格作为正常价值，为3333.25美元/吨。

②出口价格

经调查，调查机关认定调查期内中国海关统计数据计算出的欧盟对中国出口加权平均价格作为计算其出口价格的基础，为2534.65美元/吨。

③调整项目

根据《反倾销条例》第六条规定，为公平合理比较，调查机关对该公司影响价格可比性的调整项目逐一进行了审查。

第一，正常价值部分。调查机关经初步审查，确定上述欧盟市场内被调查产品同类产品的销售价格已是出厂价水平，调查机关不再做相应调整。

第二、出口价格部分。经初步审查，调整项目包括海运费、保险费、欧盟境内环节费用等，为158.77美元/吨。

④关于到岸价格(CIF价格)

经初步审查，调查机关暂根据中国海关统计的欧盟对中国出口的加权平均价格作为CIF价格，为2534.65美元/吨。

(二)价格比较。

根据《反倾销条例》第六条的规定，调查机关对被调查产品的出口价格和正常价值进行比较时，考虑了影响价格的各种可比性因素，按照公平、合理的方式进行了调整。

对于博苏化学有限责任公司，调查机关在其提交的证明材料基础上，将正常价值和出口价格调整至出厂水平。在计算倾销幅度时，调查机关将加权平均正常价值和出口价格进行比较，得出倾销幅度。

对于其他所有公司，调查机关根据认定的数据，将正常价值和出口价格调整至出厂水平。在计算倾销幅度时，调查机关将加权平均正常价值和加权出口价格进行比较，得出倾销幅度。

(三)倾销幅度。

经过计算，各公司的倾销幅度分别为：

(1)拜耳材料科技公司　19.2%
(Bayer MaterialScience AG)

(2)波兰扎克姆化工股份公司　18.1%
(Zaklady Chemiczne ZACHEM S.A.)

(3)博苏化学有限责任公司　6.6%
(Borsodchem Zrt.)

(4)柏斯托法国公司　37.7%
(Perstorp France)

(5)陶式西班牙公司　37.7%
(Dow Chemical Tarragona)

(6)其他欧盟公司　37.7%
(All Others)

五、产业损害及损害程度

(一)被调查产品进口量及所占国内市场份额。

1.被调查产品进口数量

根据中国海关统计数据，调查期内，被调查产品的进口数量2008年为21482.59吨；2009年为33804.42吨，比2008年增长57.36%；2010年为38463.13吨，比2009年增长13.78%；2011年为28515.26吨，比2010年减少25.86%，比调查期初的2008年增加32.74%。上述数据表明，调查期内，被调查产品进口数量总体呈上升趋势。

2.被调查产品所占国内市场份额

现有证据显示，调查期内，被调查产品所占国内市场份额2008年为6.48%；2009年为8.22%，比2008年上升1.74个百分点；2010年为8.36%，比2009年上升0.14个百分点；2011年为6.04%，比2010年下降2.32个百分点，与调查期初的2008年基本持平。上述数据表明，2008年至2010年，被调查产品占国内市场份额呈增长趋势；2011年，被调查产品占国内市场份额与上年相比有所下降，与调查期初的2008年基本持平。

(二)被调查产品进口价格及对国内同类产品价格的影响。

1.被调查产品进口价格

在中国海关统计数据的基础上，调查机关计算得出被调查产品进口加权平均价格(CIF价格)，调查机关进一步考虑了年度平均汇率和关税税率等因素，对被调查产品进口加权平均价格进行了调整。年度平均汇率根据中国人民银行公布的当年各月度平均汇率算术平均得出。调查期内，调整后的被调查产品进口加权平均价格(以下称被调查产品进口价格)2008年为

31786.85元/吨；2009年为15540.40元/吨，比2008年下降51.11%；2010年为19141.48元/吨，比2009年上升23.17%；2011年为16376.01元/吨，比2010年下降14.45%，比调查期初的2008年下降48.48%，处于调查期内较低水平。

2. 国内产业同类产品价格

调查机关在对《国内生产者调查问卷》答卷汇总的基础上，计算出国内产业同类产品的加权平均价格(以下称国内产业同类产品价格)。国内产业同类产品价格即出厂价，不含增值税、内陆运输费用、保险费和次级销售渠道费用等其他税费。调查期内，国内产业同类产品价格2008年为27705.05元/吨；2009年为19602.43元/吨，比2008年下降29.25%；2010年为19004.71元/吨，比2009年下降3.05%；2011年为15856.08元/吨，比2010年下降16.57%。

3. 被调查产品进口对国内产业同类产品价格的影响

如上所述，调查期内，被调查产品进口价格2009年比2008年下降51.11%，2010年比2009年上升23.17%，2011年比2010年下降14.45%，比调查期初的2008年下降48.48%，呈先下降、上升再下降趋势。

国内产业同类产品价格2009年比2008年下降29.25%，2010年比2009年下降3.05%，2011年比2010年下降16.57%，呈持续下降趋势。

中国海关统计数据显示，调查期内，被调查产品的进口数量总体呈上升趋势。2009年比2008年增长57.36%，2010年比2009年增长13.78%，2011年比2010年减少25.86%，比调查期初的2008年增加32.74%。

证据显示，被调查产品占国内市场份额呈先上升再下降趋势，2008年至2010年持续上升，累计增长1.88个百分点2011年比2010年下降2.32个百分点，与调查期初的2008年基本持平。

综合考虑上述因素，调查机关认为，调查期内，被调查产品进口数量总体上升，且占有一定的国内市场份额，其价格变化对国内产业同类产品的销售价格等指标具有一定影响。2008年至2009年，被调查产品进口价格大幅下降，2009年比2008年下降51.11%，比同期国内产业同类产品价格低4062.03元/吨，比国内产业同类产品价格低20.72%。调查机关在本裁决中已经考虑了年度平均汇率和关税税率等因素，并对被调查产品进口价格进行了调整。调查机关注意到，国内产业同类产品价格与被调查产品进口价格均不包含增值税、内陆运输费用、保险费和次级销售渠道费用。调查机关同时考虑到被调查产品进口港杂费、报关费、商检费等其他费用，上述费用远小于被调查产品与国内产业同类产品间的价差。据此，调查机关初步认定，2009年被调查产品进口对国内产业同类产品价格产生较明显的削减作用。

被调查产品进口价格2010年比2009年提高23.17%，在2009年比2008年下降51.11%的情况下出现一定回升；2011年，被调查产品进口价格再次下降，比2010年下降14.45%。国内产业同类产品价格2010年比2009年下降3.05%，2011年比2010年下降16.57%。调查机关注意到，虽然2010年被调查产品进口价格比上年提高了23.17%，但被调查产品进口价格是在2009年比2008年下降51.11%，并对国内产业同类产品产生价格削减作用情况下产生的回升。被调查产品进口价格2010年为19141.48元/吨，同期国内产业同类产品价格为19004.71元/吨。2010年，被调查产品进口价格对国内产业同类产品价格产生直接影响和作用。2011年，被调查产品进口价格比上年下降14.45%，同期国内产业同类产品价格比上年下降16.57%。调查机关通过对比分析认为，2011年被调查产品进口价格和国内同类产品销售价格下降趋势一致。综合考虑上述因素，调查机关认为，2010年和2011年，被调查产品进口对国内产业同类产品价格产生了压低作用。

(三)国内产业相关经济因素和指标的评估。

根据《反倾销条例》第八条及《反倾销产业损害调查规定》第五条和第七条的规定，调查机关审查了被调查产品对国内产业的相关经济因素和指标的影响。

1. 关于国内产业相关数据问题

本案申请人在其提交的《甲苯二异氰酸酯(TDI)反倾销案申请人关于国内产业损害数据保密性问题的进一步说明》中提出，沧州大化TDI有限责任公司与沧州大化股份有限公司聚海分公司为关联企业，同属于沧州大化集团有限责任公司，甘肃银光聚银化工有限公司、甘肃银达化工有限公司和辽宁北方锦化聚氨酯有限公司为关联企业，同属于中国北方化学工业(集团)有限责任公司。本案申请人虽然为5家企业，但分属沧州大化集团有限责任公司和中国北方化学工业(集团)有限责任公司两家集团公司。沧州大化集团有限责任公司和中国北方化学工业(集团)有限责任公司虽然在本案中共同代表了国内甲苯二异氰酸酯产业，但同时也是互相独立的市场竞争对手。在相关公开对外文件中(包括但不限于信息披露或裁决)对外披露5家申请企业同类产品的合计或加权平均数据，将导致两家集团公司互相知悉对方的经营状况，对任何一方的利益都会造成严重不利影响。

基于上述事实和理由，申请人申请调查机关对国内产业产能、产量、开工率、销售收入、销售数量、市场份额、期末库存、销售成本、毛利润、毛利润率、税前利润、税前利润率、投资总额、投资收益率、现金流、工资和就业人数、劳动生产率等经济指标数据进行保密。

根据《反倾销条例》第二十二条规定，调查机关认为，申请人为了避免资料泄露产生的不利影响而对于保密信息的处理符合法律规定。

2. 国内产业相关经济因素和指标的评估

(1)表观消费量

调查期内，国内甲苯二异氰酸酯表观消费量2008年为331343.69吨；2009年为411248.85吨，2009年比2008年增长24.12%；2010年为460130.43吨，比2009年增长11.89%；2011年为471312.06吨，比2010年增长2.56%。

(2)产能

调查期内，国内产业同类产品产能2009年比2008年增加25.16%，2010比2009年增加103.77%，2011年比2010年增加8.63%。

(3)产量

调查期内，国内产业同类产品产量2009年比2008年增加36.05%，2010年比2009年增加100.21%，2011年比2010年增加18.75%。

(4)销售量

调查期内，国内产业同类产品销售量2009年比2008年增加36.33%，2010年比2009年增加98.61%，2011年比2010年增加16.90%。

(5)市场份额

调查期内，国内产业同类产品所占国内市场份额2009年比2008年增加2.01个百分点，2010年比2009年增加17.4个百分点，2011年比2010年增加5.57个百分点。

(6)销售价格

调查期内，国内产业同类产品销售价格2008年为27705.05元/吨，2009年为19602.43元/吨，比2008年下降29.25%；2010年为19004.71元/吨，比2009年下降3.05%；2011年为15856.08元/吨，比2010年下降16.57%。

调查期内，国内产业同类产品单位销售成本2009年比2008年下降20.99%，2010年比2009年增加0.15%，2011年比2010年下降4.95%。

(7) 销售收入

调查期内，国内产业同类产品销售收入2009年比2008年下降3.54%，2010年比2009年上升92.55%，2011年比2010年下降2.47%。

(8)利润

调查期内，国内产业同类产品毛利率2009年比2008年下降8.51个百分点，2010年比2009年下降2.69个百分点，2011年比2010年下降11.72个百分点。

调查期内，国内产业同类产品单位毛利润2009年比2008年下降51.52%，2010年比2009年下降17.13%，2011年比2010年下降78.25%。

调查期内，国内产业同类产品税前利润2009年比2008年下降65.99%，2010年比2009年下降37.27%，2011年为负值。

(9)投资收益率

调查期内，国内产业同类产品投资收益率2009年比2008年下降11.22个百分点，2010年比2009年下降1.35个百分点，2011年比2010年下降6.55个百分点。

(10)开工率

调查期内，国内产业同类产品开工率2009年比2008年上升6.72个百分点，2010年比2009年下降1.47个百分点，2011年比2010年上升7.68个百分点。

(11)就业人数

调查期内，国内产业同类产品就业人数2009年比2008年上升45.41%，2010年比2009年上升34.02%，2011年比2010年下降10.11%。

(12)劳动生产率

调查期内，国内产业同类产品劳动生产率2009年比2008年下降6.43%，2010年比2009年提高49.37%，2011年比2010年提高32.11%。

(13)人均工资

调查期内，国内产业同类产品人均工资2009年比2008年增加10.78%，2010年比2009年增加10.80%，2011年比2010年增加8.38%。

(14)期末库存

调查期内，国内产业同类产品期末库存2009年比2008年增加3.58%，2010年比2009年增加40.85%，2011年比2010年增加52.56%。

(15)经营活动现金流量净额

调查期内，国内产业同类产品经营活动现金流量净额2009年比2008年减少56.56%，2010年比2009年增加213.17%，2011年比2010年减少77.87%。

(16)投融资能力

沧州大化TDI有限责任公司、沧州大化股份有限公司聚海分公司、甘肃银光聚银化工有限公司、甘肃银达化工有限公司提交的《国内生产者调查问卷》答卷显示，国内生产企业投融资能力未受到影响。

辽宁北方锦化聚氨酯有限公司提交的《国内生产者调查问卷》答卷显示，国内生产企业投融资能力受到一定影响，产能扩展计划被搁置。

（四）国内产业受到实质损害。

上述证据显示，调查期内，在市场需求持续增长的推动下，国内产业同类产品产能不断扩大，产量、销售量、市场份额、开工率、劳动生产率、就业人数、人均工资均呈总体增长趋势，调查期内国内产业同类产品单位销售成本呈下降趋势。在此情况下，国内产业盈利能力本应有所增长。但由于调查期内国内产业同类产品的销售价格持续下降，调查期末比调查期初下降了42.77%，同期国内产业同类产品毛利率和单位毛利润也呈下降趋势，国内产业同类产品盈利能力不断萎缩。

受上述因素影响，国内产业同类产品在产量和销售量都持续大幅增长的情况下，销售收入和经营活动现金净流量不仅没有出现相应的增长趋势，反而呈不稳定状态，期末库存增加明显，国内产业同类产品税前利润和投资收益率急剧下降，部分企业投融资能力受到影响。2011年，国内产业同类产品毛利率、单位毛利润、税前利润和投资收益率降至调查期内的最低水平，国内产业同类产品税前利润、投资收益率均为负值，国内产业同类产品的财务状况和经营状况严重恶化，陷入亏损状态。

综合考虑上述事实，调查机关认定，国内产业受到实质损害。

六、因果关系

（一）被调查产品倾销进口造成了国内产业实质损害。

中国海关统计数据显示，调查期内，被调查产品的进口数量呈总体增长趋势，且增幅明显。2009年和2010年分别比上年增长57.36%和13.78%，2011年比2010年减少25.86%，但仍比2008年增加32.74%；被调查产品占中国甲苯二异氰酸酯总进口数量的比例呈持续上升趋势，2008年为22.21%，2009年为25.98%，2010年为33.51%，2011年为39.87%，调查期末的2011年比调查期初的2008年提高了17.66个百分点。

调查期内，被调查产品进口数量迅速增加，2008年至2010年，被调查产品国内市场份额持续上升，累计增长1.88个百分点。2011年虽比2010年下降2.32个百分点，但仍维持在2008年的水平。

调查期内，被调查产品在进口数量不断增加并保持一定市场份额的同时，被调查产品进口价格总体呈下降趋势，2009年对国内产业同类产品价格产生了削减作用，2010年和2011年对国内产业同类产品价格产生了压低作用。受此影响，国内产业同类产品价格呈持续下降趋势，2009年至2011年，同比下降29.25%、3.05%、16.57%。国内产业在产能、产量和销售量大幅增长的情况下，销售收入并没有得到相应增长，反而呈不稳定趋势，经营活动现金流量状况恶化。

调查期内，甲苯二异氰酸酯产品市场需求持续增长，国内产业同类产品劳动生产率提高，单位销售成本下降。在此情况下，国内产业同类产品盈利水平理应有所增长。但受被调查产品进口的影响，国内产业同类产品被迫下调价格，盈利能力不仅没有增强反而不断萎缩，国内产业同类产品毛利率和单位毛利润持续下降，国内产业同类产品税前利润和投资收益率急剧下降。2011年，国内产业同类产品毛利率、单位毛利润、税前利润和投资收益率等指标均降至调查期内最低水平，其中，税前利润和投资收益率为负值，国内产业严重亏损。

综合考虑上述事实和证据，调查机关初步认定，调查期内，被调查产品的倾销进口造成了国内产业实质损害。

（二）影响国内产业损害状况的其他因素分析。

调查机关对可能使国内产业受到损害的其他已知因素进行了初步调查。初步证据表明：

1. 国内产业生产成本的影响问题。拜耳材料科技公司在其提交的产业损害问卷答卷中提出，国内生产企业的问题在于单厂产能低，导致产品成本高，缺乏竞争性，同时提供了一个亚太地区厂商成本图，并表明相关成本的估算基于拜耳材料科技公司内部预测。调查机关注意到，拜耳材料科技公司提供的国内产业同类产品成本数据估算仅为推测，在此基础上得出的结论缺少客观、充分、可核实的证据支持。《国内生产者调查问卷》答卷和调查机关实地核查收集的证据显示，调查期内，国内产业产能不断扩大，国内产业同类产品劳动生产率提高，单位销售成本下降，产品竞争力不断提高。调查机关初步认为，国内产业所遭受的实质损害不是由于国内产业同类产品生产成本因素造成的，拜耳材料科技公司的主张不能得到支持。

2. 国内产能扩大的影响。调查期内，国内产业同类产品产能有较大幅度扩大。调查机关对国内产能扩大对国内产业的影响进行了调查。调查显示，为满足国内市场对甲苯二异氰酸酯产品持续增长的需求，随着国内自主知识产权技术的开发和应用，国内产业获得了较好的发展机遇，加快了扩大规模的步伐。国外企业基于国内市场的利好，也在中国投资兴建大规模甲苯二异氰酸酯装置。国内甲苯二异氰酸酯产能的扩大经历了循序渐进的过程，部分生产企业生产装置在调查期末才投产。调查期内，国内市场需求迅速增长，且由于对日本、韩国和美国的反倾销复审措施正在实施中，来自日本、韩国和美国的进口甲苯二异氰酸酯数量大幅下降，国内产业产能扩大是上述因素共同作用的结果。调查期内，国内产业生产能力一直小于同期表观消费量，调查机关初步认为，现有证据不能表明国内产能扩大的因素足以否定本案倾销与损害之间的因果关系。

3. 其他国家(地区)相关产品进口情况。中国海关统计数据表明，除自欧盟进口被调查产品之外，国内甲苯二异氰酸酯其他进口来源国主要是日本、韩国和美国，另外有少部分产品从伊朗、台湾地区、越南和马来西亚等进口。调查期内，中国对日本、韩国和美国三国进口甲苯二异氰酸酯产品一直在实施反倾销复审措施，来自上述三国的进口产品数量大幅下降。调查期内，尚无证据显示征收反倾销税后的日本、韩国和美国的进口产品价格对国内产业造成负面影响。目前尚无证据显示来自日本、韩国、美国或其他国家的进口产品对国内产业造成实质性损害。

4. 消费模式变化情况。调查期内，甲苯二异氰酸酯的消费模式未发生变化。调查机关未发现由于其他替代产品的出现导致国内甲苯二异氰酸酯市场萎缩的事实。

5. 商业流通渠道和贸易政策变化及国内外竞争状况。调查期内，国内甲苯二异氰酸酯产品完全实行市场化的价格体制，生产经营完全受市场调节。国内产业同类产品的销售渠道、销售区域与被调查产品基本相同，国内未颁布限制甲苯二异氰酸酯产业贸易行为和其他相关政策。在商业流通领域并不存在其他阻碍国内产业同类产品销售或造成国内产业损害的因素。国内外的正当竞争未对国内产业造成负面影响。

6. 技术发展状况。国内甲苯二异氰酸酯产业应用先进技术，通过严格的质量管理，产品质量不断提高，其产品与进口被调查产品在性能、质量和技术水平上相似。国内甲苯二异氰酸酯产业的技术发展状况没有对国内产业的生产和经营造成严重不良影响。

7. 国内产业出口状况。调查期内，未发现国内产业对外出口同类产品情况，不存在因出口原因对国内产业发展造成负面影响。

8. 国内产业管理水平和生产率情况。调查期内，国内产业经营管理状况良好，相关企业各项管理制度严格，管理水平和技术水平有所提高。调查期内，国内产业同类产品劳动生产率提高，单位销售成本下降，未发现经营管理不善及生产力降低而导致国内产业遭受实质损害的情况。

9. 不可抗力因素。调查期内，国内甲苯二异氰酸酯产业未发生严重自然灾害或其他不可抗力事件，生产设备运行状况正常，生产经营平稳。

七、初步调查结论

根据以上调查结果，调查机关初步裁定，在本案调查期内，原产于欧盟的被调查产品存在倾销，中国甲苯二异氰酸酯产业受到了实质损害，而且倾销与实质损害之间存在因果关系。

各公司的倾销幅度分别为：

(1)拜耳材料科技公司 [WB]19.2%
(Bayer MaterialScience AG)

(2)波兰扎克姆化工股份公司 18.1%
(Zaklady Chemiczne ZACHEM S. A.)

(3)博苏化学有限责任公司 6.6%
(Borsodchem Zrt.)

(4)柏斯托法国公司 37.7%
(Perstorp France)

(5)陶式西班牙公司 37.7%
(Dow Chemical Tarragona)

(6)其他欧盟公司 37.7%
(All Others)

三十一、中华人民共和国商务部公告2012年第20号 关于对原产于美国和日本的进口邻苯二酚反倾销期终复审终裁的决定(二〇一二年五月二十一日)

2006年5月22日，中华人民共和国商务部发布年度第32号公告，决定对原产于美国和日本的进口邻苯二酚征收反倾销税，实施期限为自2006年5月22日起5年。

反倾销措施实施期间，商务部发布2009年第52号公告，依法对措施进行了调整。

2011年5月21日，商务部发布2011年第23号公告，决定对原产于美国和日本的进口邻苯二酚所适用的反倾销措施进行期终复审调查。

本复审调查的被调查产品与原反倾销调查被调查产品相同，即邻苯二酚，该产品归在《中华人民共和国进出口税则》：29072910。该产品英文名称为Catechol。

商务部对终止美国和日本的进口邻苯二酚所适用的反倾销措施，导致倾销和损害继续或再度发生的可能性进行了调查，并根据调查结果向国务院关税税则委员会提出维持反倾销措施的建议。

根据《中华人民共和国反倾销条例》第五十条及国务院关税税则委员会的决定，现将有关事项公告如下：

一、裁定

商务部裁定，如果终止原反倾销措施，原产于美国和日本的进口邻苯二酚对中国的倾销可能继续发生，进口被调查产品对中国邻苯二酚产业造成的损害有可能继续发生。

二、反倾销措施

自2012年5月22日起，继续按照商务部2006年第32号公告、2009年第52号公告，对原产于美国和日本的进口邻苯二酚实施反倾销措施，实施期限为5年。

三、征收反倾销税的方法

自2012年5月22日起，进口经营者在进口原产于美国和日本的邻苯二酚时，应向中华人民共和国海关缴纳相应的反倾销税。反倾销税以海关审定的完税价格从价计征，计算公式为：反倾销税税额 = 海关完税价格 × 反倾销税税率。进口环节增值税以海关审定的完税价格加上关税和反倾销税作为计税价格从价计征。

四、行政复议和行政诉讼

根据《中华人民共和国反倾销条例》第五十三条，对本复审决定不服的，可以申请行政复议，也可以向人民法院提起诉讼。

五、本公告自2012年5月22日起执行。

附件：中华人民共和国商务部关于原产于美国和日本的进口邻苯二酚所适用的反倾销措施的期终复审裁定

2011年5月21日，中华人民共和国商务部（以下称调查机关）发布公告，决定对原产于美国和日本的进口邻苯二酚所适用的反倾销措施进行期终复审调查。

调查机关对如果终止原反倾销措施，原产于美国和日本的进口邻苯二酚对中国的倾销和损害继续或再度发生的可能性进行了调查。根据调查结果，并依据《中华人民共和国反倾销条例》（以下简称《反倾销条例》）第四十八条，作出复审裁定如下：

一、原反倾销措施

2006年5月22日，调查机关发布年度第32号公告，决定对原产于美国和日本的进口邻苯二酚实施最终反倾销措施，实施期限为五年。

2009年7月28日，调查机关发布年度第52号公告，对原产于美国的进口邻苯二酚实施的反倾销措施作出期中复审裁定，依法对该措施进行了调整。

二、期终复审调查程序

（一）到期公告。

2010年11月22日，调查机关发布该年度第83号公告，告知利害关系方原反倾销措施将于2011年5月22日到期。根据《反倾销条例》，经复审确定终止征收反倾销税有可能导致倾销和损害继续或者再度发生的，反倾销税的征收期限可以适当延长。自该公告发布之日起，国内产业可在原反倾销措施终止日60天前，向调查机关提出书面复审申请。

（二）复审申请。

2011年3月21日，连云港三吉利化学工业有限公司代表中国邻苯二酚产业向调查机关提交了期终复审申请。申请人主张，如果终止反倾销措施，原产于美国和日本的进口邻苯二酚对中国的倾销可能继续发生，倾销对中国邻苯二酚产业造成的损害可能再度发生，请求调查机关继续维持该反倾销措施。

（三）立案前通知。

2011年5月12日，调查机关就有关期终复审申请事宜通知了美国和日本驻华使馆。

（四）立案。

根据《反倾销条例》第十一条、第十三条、第十七条和第四十八条规定，调查机关对申请人资格和申请书的主张及相关证明材料进行了审查，认为申请人资格和申请书符合立案要求。

根据审查结果及《反倾销条例》第十六条、第四十八条、第五十一条规定，调查机关于2011年5月21日发布该年度第23号公告，决定对原产于美国和日本的进口邻苯二酚所适用的反倾销措施进行期终复审调查。

（五）复审内容。

本次复审调查的内容为，如果终止原反倾销措施，是否可能导致倾销和损害的继续或再度发生。

（六）立案通知及利害关系方评论。

立案当日，调查机关就立案事宜通知了美国和日本驻华使馆，并提供了立案公告和申请书公开文本。同时，调查机关通知了申请人和已知的涉案国生产商、出口商。有关申请书公开文本，利害关系方可于商务部公开信息查阅室查找、阅览、抄录并复印相关信息。

在规定时间内，没有利害关系方对本次复审立案发表评论意见。

（七）登记应诉。

2011年5月21日，调查机关在立案公告中公布，任何利害关系方可于立案公告发布之日起20天内，向调查机关申请参加应诉。如利害关系方未在立案公告规定的时间内向调查机关登记应诉，调查机关可以根据已经获得的事实和可获得的最佳信息作出裁定。

在规定期限内，没有美国和日本被调查产品生产商、贸易商登记应诉。

(八)倾销调查和损害调查。

1. 倾销调查

(1)调查问卷

立案后，没有涉案国生产商、出口商应诉本次倾销调查。因此，调查机关没有对涉案国生产商、出口商发放调查问卷。

调查机关向申请人发放问卷和补充问卷，要求申请人进一步提供调查期内邻苯二酚的国际国内市场相关信息。在规定时间内，申请人按照要求提交了答卷。

(2)公开信息渠道

调查机关通过查询海关数据、咨询相关行业协会、查阅相关网站、公开刊物等方式，收集了与被调查产品及其同类产品有关的数据、信息。

(3)各利害关系方意见

在调查过程中，没有利害关系方向调查机关提交口头或书面意见陈述。

(4)听证会

在调查过程中，没有利害关系方向调查机关申请召开听证会。

(5)信息公开

根据《反倾销条例》第二十三条规定，本案所有与倾销调查有关的公开信息均已按规定送交商务部贸易救济措施公开信息查阅室。本案所有利害关系方可以查找、阅览、摘抄、复印与倾销调查有关的公开信息。

(6)信息披露

根据《反倾销条例》第二十五条规定，2012 年 3 月 8 日，调查机关向本案有关利害关系方披露了最终倾销裁定所依据的基本事实，并给予其提出评论意见的机会。

在规定时间内，没有利害关系方提交评论意见。

2. 损害调查

(1)参加产业损害调查活动登记

2011 年 5 月 21 日，调查机关发布《关于参加邻苯二酚反倾销措施期终复审产业损害调查活动登记的通知》。在规定的时间内，没有相关利害关系方参加产业损害调查活动登记。

(2)成立产业损害调查组

2011 年 5 月 24 日，调查机关发布《关于成立邻苯二酚反倾销措施期终复审案产业损害调查组的通知》，成立邻苯二酚反倾销措施期终复审案产业损害调查组。

(3)发放和收回调查问卷

2011 年 6 月 10 日，调查机关向已知的利害关系方发放了邻苯二酚反倾销措施期终复审案《国内生产者调查问卷》、《国内进口商调查问卷》和《国外(地区)生产者/出口商调查问卷》。

在规定的时间内，连云港三吉利化学工业有限公司递交了《国内生产者调查问卷答卷》。

(4)听取利害关系方意见陈述

2011 年 6 月 23 日，应本案申请人连云港三吉利化学工业有限公司申请，调查机关听取了申请人的意见陈述。

申请人认为，如果终止反倾销措施，原产于美国和日本的进口邻苯二酚对中国的倾销行为可能继续发生，倾销行为给中国邻苯二酚产业造成的损害可能继续发生。

本案在立案公告规定的时限及产业损害调查过程中，未收到除申请人之外的其他利害关系方提交的书面评论意见。

(5)召开上下游企业意见陈述会

2011 年 11 月 28 日，调查机关召开本案上下游企业意见陈述会，听取了本案申请企业以及部分下游企业的意见陈述。

邻苯二酚下游企业提出，调查期内，国内生产的邻苯二酚与被调查产品的质量不存在差异，可相互替代。同时表示，支持商务部邻苯二酚反倾销措施期终复审调查，希望通过此次调查，进一步改善中国邻苯二酚市场竞争环境，在中国邻苯二酚产业稳定发展的基础上，促进与下游企业的共同和谐发展。

本案申请企业再次表示，如果终止反倾销措施，原产于美国和日本的进口邻苯二酚对中国的倾销行为可能继续发生，倾销行为给中国邻苯二酚产业造成的损害将继续发生，同时表示，中国邻苯二酚产业的发展需要得到下游企业的大力支持，希望在公平的市场竞争环境中发展中国邻苯二酚产业，并与下游企业形成共同发展的良好局面。

(6)实地核查

2011 年 7 月 25 日，调查机关发布《关于邻苯二酚反倾销措施期终复审案实地核查的通知》。2011 年 8 月，调查机关对本案申请企业连云港三吉利化学工业有限公司进行了实地核查。核查期间，调查机关对本案申请书及该公司提交的《国内生产者调查问卷答卷》中的数据和信息进行了核实，并收集了相关证据材料。核查结束后，连云港三吉利化学工业有限公司向调查机关提交了《邻苯二酚反倾销期终复审案实地核查修改资料》。

(7)信息公开

根据《反倾销条例》第二十三条和《产业损害调查信息查阅与信息披露规定》第八条、第十四条的规定，本案所有与产业损害调查有关的公开信息均已按规定送交商务部贸易救济措施公开信息查阅室。本案所有利害关系方可以查找、阅览、摘抄、复印与产业损害调查有关的公开信息。

(8)信息披露

根据《反倾销条例》第二十五条第二款和《产业损害调查信息查阅与信息披露规定》第十八条、第十九条、第二十条和第二十一条的规定，调查机关在最终裁定前向本案利害关系方披露了本案最终裁定所依据的基本事实，并给予其提出评论意见的机会。信息披露期间，没有利害关系方提出评论意见。

调查机关对申请书及所附证据材料、收回的调查问卷答卷和实地核查结果进行了认真分析和全面评估，并收集和补充了相关证据材料。调查机关对利害关系方提出的评论和意见依法予以了充分考虑。本案调查过程中，调查机关未收到《国内进口商调查问卷答卷》和《国外(地区)生产者/出口商调查问卷答卷》，也未收到除申请企业以外的其他利害关系方提交的评论意见。根据《反倾销条例》第二十一条和《反倾销产业损害调查规定》第三十三条规定，并根据已经获得的事实和可获得的最佳信息对终止原反倾销措施，原产于美国和日本的进口邻苯二酚对国内邻苯二酚产业损害继续或者再度发生的可能性进行了调查。

三、被调查产品和调查范围

(一)被调查产品。

本复审被调查产品与原反倾销调查被调查产品一致，即邻苯二酚，该产品归在《中华人民共和国进出口税则》税则号：29072910。该产品英文名称为Catechol。

(二)调查范围。

原产于美国、日本的进口邻苯二酚。

四、国内同类产品和国内产业

(一)同类产品的认定。

商务部2006年5月22日第32号公告发布的邻苯二酚反倾销原审案件最终裁定中认定，“调查机关在考察了产品的基本物理性能和化学性质、制造过程、生产技术和产品用途、产品的替代性和相互竞争性等因素后，认定被调查产品与中国国内生产的邻苯二酚属于同类产品”。

商务部2011年5月21日第23号公告发布的本次复审调查立案公告中认定，复审被调查产品范围与原反倾销被调查产品一致。

在邻苯二酚反倾销措施实施期间，国内生产的邻苯二酚与原审案件调查期内生产的邻苯二酚在物理和化学性能、生产工艺、产品用途、销售渠道等方面未发生实质性变化。

因此，调查机关认定，本次复审的被调查产品与国内生产的邻苯二酚属于同类产品。

(二)国内产业的认定。

申请人提出，2002年至2006年，连云港三吉利化学工业有限公司是国内唯一的邻苯二酚生产商。2007年罗地亚(镇江)化学品有限公司开始生产邻苯二酚，但由于罗地亚(镇江)化学品有限公司与本案涉案企业之一的美国罗地亚公司存在关联关系，应当排除在国内产业之外。

据调查，罗地亚(镇江)化学品有限公司与美国罗地亚公司存在关联关系，但未有证据表明罗地亚(镇江)化学品有限公司的行为与其他非关联的国内邻苯二酚生产者不同。因此，调查机关认定，本案不将罗地亚(镇江)化学品有限公司排除在国内产业之外。

证据显示，2006年、2007年、2008年、2009年和2010年申请企业产量占国内同类产品总产量的主要部分。

根据《反倾销条例》第十一条和《反倾销产业损害调查规定》第十三条的规定，调查机关认定，调查期内，国内申请企业可以代表中国邻苯二酚产业。

五、复审调查期

本次复审的倾销调查期为2010年1月1日至2010年12月31日，产业损害调查期为2006年1月1日至2010年12月31日。

六、倾销继续或再度发生的可能性

(一)倾销调查期内倾销情况。

美国

由于没有美国的生产商、出口商应诉并提交答卷，调查机关无法直接获得其倾销调查期内被调查产品的正常价值、出口价格、调整因素等数据和证据。依据《反倾销条例》第二十一条，调查机关决定采用可获得的最佳信息对美国被调查产品的正常价值、出口价格、影响正常价值和出口价格可比性因素等进行认定。

调查机关认为，申请人提供的信息是可获得的最佳信息，并根据申请人提供的相关数据对美国被调查产品的正常价值、出口价格进行了认定，对影响正常价值和出口价格可比性的因素进行了调整，并在同一贸易环节进行了比较。

经调查，调查机关认定，倾销调查期内，原产于美国的邻苯二酚对中国出口存在倾销。

日本

由于没有日本的生产商、出口商应诉并提交答卷，调查机关无法直接获得其倾销调查期内被调查产品的正常价值、出口价格、调整因素等数据和证据。依据《反倾销条例》第二十一条，调查机关决定采用可获得的最佳信息对日本被调查产品的正常价值、出口价格、影响正常价值和出口价格可比性因素等进行认定。

调查机关认为，申请人提供的信息是可获得的最佳信息，并根据申请人提供的相关数据对日本被调查产品的正常价值、出口价格进行了认定，对影响正常价值和出口价格可比性的因素进行了调整，并在同一贸易环节进行了比较。

经调查，调查机关认定，倾销调查期内，原产于日本的邻苯二酚对中国出口存在倾销。

(二)倾销继续或再度发生的可能性

美国

由于没有美国生产商、出口商应诉并提交答卷，依据《反倾销条例》第二十一条，调查机关决定采用可获得的最佳信息，通过对美国邻苯二酚倾销调查期内的倾销情况、出口能力、对中国的出口、对第三国(地区)的出口的分析，对美国邻苯二酚倾销继续或再度发生的可能性进行审查。调查机关认为，申请人提供的信息是可获得的最佳信息。

1. 存在继续倾销的可能性

前述倾销调查表明，倾销调查期内美国被调查产品对中国出口存在倾销。

同时，调查机关注意到，在原反倾销调查的最终裁定中，美国邻苯二酚对中国出口的倾销幅度为4%至46.81%；在前述期中复审的最终裁定中，美国邻苯二酚对中国出口的倾销幅度为9.7%至46.81%。根据现有材料，调查机关认为美国邻苯二酚对中国倾销出口情况未发生变化。

2. 出口能力

(1)产能、产量和闲置产能

单位：吨

期间	2006年	2007年	2008年	2009年	2010年
产能	6000	6000	6000	6000	6000
产量	4500	4000	3500	3500	3500
产能利用率	75.00%	66.67%	58.33%	58.33%	58.33%
闲置产能	1500	2000	2500	2500	2500

数据来源：申请书附件六《关于全球邻苯二酚生产以及美国、日本邻苯二酚产业及其国内销售价格的报告》

根据申请人提供的材料和数据，2006年至2010年，美国邻苯二酚产能保持在6000吨，产量则由4500吨下降至3500吨，降幅达22.22%。同期产能利用率由75%下降至58.33%，闲置产能大量增加。2010年中国国内同类产品表观消费量为1.74万吨，美国闲置产能数量占中国国内同类产品表观消费量的比例达14.36%。如果美国将其闲置产能全部释放，其邻苯二酚出口能力将进一步增强。

(2)美国国内市场消费情况

单位：吨

期间	2006年	2007年	2008年	2009年	2010年
产能	6000	6000	6000	6000	6000
消费量	4000	4000	3000	1500	1400
消费量占产能比例	66.67%	66.67%	50.00%	25.00%	23.33%
世界市场消费量	23400	23900	24000	26300	26700
消费量占世界比重	17.09%	16.73%	12.50%	5.70 %	5.24%

数据来源：申请书附件六《关于全球邻苯二酚生产以及美国、日本邻苯二酚产业及其国内销售价格的报告》

根据申请人提供的材料和数据，2006年至2010年，在产能保持不变的情况下，美国邻苯二酚国内市场消费量总体大幅下降，由4000t缩减为1400t，降幅达65%。美国邻苯二酚国内消费量远低于其同期产能数量。2010年美国邻苯二酚消费量占产能的比例仅为23.33%。

2006年以来，在世界市场消费量保持基本稳定的情况下，美国邻苯二酚消费量却大幅下降，其占世界市场消费量的比重也大幅降低，从2006年的17.09%下降至2010年的5.24%。这表明美国邻苯二酚市场需求缩减，内需不足。根据现有材料，这种情形短期内不会发生变化。

(3)对国外市场的依赖程度

单位：吨

期间	2006年	2007年	2008年	2009年	2010年
出口量	3700	3400	2700	3300	3000
产量	4500	4000	3500	3500	3500
出口量占产量比例	82.22%	85%	77.14%	94.28%	85.71%

数据来源：申请书附件六《关于全球邻苯二酚生

产以及美国、日本邻苯二酚产业及其国内销售价格的报告》；申请人提供补充材料《调查期内美国、日本邻苯二酚的对外出口情况》

根据申请人提供的材料和数据，2006 年以来，美国邻苯二酚出口量占其产量的比例一直保持在高水平，2006 年至 2010 年该比例的平均水平超过 80%，表明对外出口是美国消化国内邻苯二酚剩余产量的主要渠道。

以上分析说明，2006 年以来，美国邻苯二酚的产量在产能保持不变的情况下出现大幅缩减，产能闲置的比例较大。同期国内市场需求大幅下降，内需不足。美国邻苯二酚出口量占其产量的比例很高，对国际市场依赖程度很高。

3. 对中国出口情况

单位：吨；美元/吨

期间	2006 年	2007 年	2008 年	2009 年	2010 年
对中国出口数量	3136	2682	389	2546	1449
对中国出口平均价格	3129.80	3343.33	3970.11	3425.83	3653.31
中国总进口量	7828.54	6643.63	6621.75	8425.44	7639.18
对中国出口占中国总进口量比例	40.05%	40.36%	5.87%	30.21%	18.96%

数据来源：全国海关信息中心提供《邻苯二酚进出口情况的统计数据》

(1)对中国出口数量

根据我国海关统计数据，2006 年至 2010 年，美国邻苯二酚对中国出口数量出现波动但总体呈下降趋势，2010 年比 2006 年下降了 53.79%。相应的，美国邻苯二酚对中国出口数量占中国总进口量比例也从 2006 年的 40.05% 下降为 2010 年的 18.96%。这体现了反倾销措施良好的制约效果。从贸易方式方面看，2006 年以来，在反倾销措施的制约下，美国邻苯二酚对中国出口中一般贸易方式下出口量所占比例呈下降趋势，而其他方式下出口量所占比例有所增加。

调查机关注意到，美国罗地亚公司与法国罗地亚公司是关联公司，这两家公司同属于罗地亚公司，并且是世界邻苯二酚最主要生产商。据申请人反映，这两家公司是美国和欧盟邻苯二酚主要生产商。

2003 年 8 月 27 日，调查机关发布该年度第 41 号公告，决定对原产于欧盟的进口邻苯二酚实施为期 5 年的最终反倾销措施。在该措施影响下，我自欧盟进口邻苯二酚大幅下降，而自美国进口邻苯二酚增长迅速，从 2002 年的 80 吨上升至 2005 年的 2730.25 吨。2006 年 5 月 22 日，调查机关发布该年度第 32 号公告，决定对原产于美国的进口邻苯二酚实施反倾销措施。自 2006 年以后，我自美国进口邻苯二酚呈下降之势，从 2006 年的 3136 吨下降至 2010 年的 1449.22 吨；而自欧盟进口数量呈上涨之势，从 2006 年的 3419.35 吨上升至 2010 年的 4188.02 吨。

单位：吨

期间	美国	欧盟	合计
2002	80	3400	3480
2003	1900.01	1059	2959.01
2004	3200.29	1989	5189.29
2005	2730.25	2679	5409.25
2006	3136	3419.35	6555.35
2007	2681.97	3160	5841.97
2008	389.01	4480	4869.01
2009	2546.04	3740	6286.04
2010	1449.22	4188.02	5637.24

数据来源：全国海关信息中心提供《邻苯二酚进出口情况的统计数据》

考虑到美国罗地亚公司与法国罗地亚公司的关联关系，以及前述出现的出口转移情况，调查机关认为，在目前对欧盟进口邻苯二酚仍实施反倾销措施的情况下，如终止对自美国进口邻苯二酚实施的反倾销措施，可能导致罗地亚公司实施贸易转移，扩大自美国罗地亚公司低价出口，进而影响到对欧盟进口邻苯二酚反倾销措施的实施效果。

(2)对中国出口价格

在反倾销措施期间，美国对中国出口价格总体略有上升，由 2006 年的 3129.80 美元/吨上升至 2010 年的 3653.31 美元/吨。前述倾销调查表明，倾销调查期内，原产于美国的进口邻苯二酚对中国出口价格仍属倾销价格。

4. 对第三国出口情况

单位：吨

期间	2006 年	2007 年	2008 年	2009 年	2010 年
出口总量	3700	3400	2700	3300	3000
对中国出口数量	3136	2681.97	389.01	2546.04	1449.21
对第三国出口数量	564	718.02	2310.98	753.96	1550.77

续表

期　　间	2006 年	2007 年	2008 年	2009 年	2010 年
对第三国出口占出口总量的比例	15.24%	21.12%	85.59%	22.85%	51.69%

数据来源：申请人补充提供《调查期内美国、日本邻苯二酚的对外出口情况》

根据申请人提供的统计数据，2006 年以来，美国邻苯二酚生产商、出口商还向除中国以外的其他国家和地区出口邻苯二酚产品。除 2008 年和 2010 年以外，美国对第三国出口邻苯二酚的比例均低于 30%，超过 70%的产品均以低于同期国内销售价格向中国出口。2006 年以来中国邻苯二酚市场需求量总体保持增长，2010 年中国邻苯二酚表观消费量较 2006 年增长了 126.74%，快速增长的中国市场对海外生产商、出口商具有很强的吸引力。如果终止反倾销措施，美国邻苯二酚生产商、出口商向第三国(地区)的出口可能会转向中国市场。

上述调查表明：倾销调查期内美国被调查产品对中国出口存在倾销；自 2006 年以来，美国国内邻苯二酚存在大量闲置产能，产能利用率不断下降；其邻苯二酚市场需求逐年缩减，内需不足；其邻苯二酚出口能力较大，对国外市场依赖程度较高，快速增长的中国市场已成为美国邻苯二酚出口的主要目标市场；受反倾销措施制约，美国对中国出口数量、一般贸易方式下出口量所占比例均呈现总体下降的趋势，而其他方式下出口量所占比例有所增加，出口价格略有上升，但仍属于倾销价格，低价出口是其海外市场销售的一种通常价格策略。综上所述，如果终止原反倾销措施，美国邻苯二酚对中国的倾销可能继续，并可能影响到对欧盟的进口邻苯二酚反倾销措施的实施效果。

日本

由于没有日本生产商、出口商应诉并提交答卷，依据《反倾销条例》第二十一条，调查机关决定采用可获得的最佳信息，通过对日本邻苯二酚倾销调查期内的倾销情况、出口能力、对中国的出口、对第三国(地区)的出口的分析，对日本邻苯二酚倾销继续或再度发生的可能性进行审查。调查机关认为，申请人提供的信息是可获得的最佳信息。

1. 存在继续倾销的可能性

前述倾销调查表明，倾销调查期内日本被调查产品对中国出口存在倾销。

同时，调查机关注意到，在原反倾销调查的最终裁定中，日本邻苯二酚对中国出口的倾销幅度为 42.86%。措施实施期间，没有日本生产商、出口商向调查机关申请倾销及倾销幅度期间复审。根据现有材料，调查机关认为日本邻苯二酚对中国倾销出口情况未发生变化。

2. 出口能力

(1)产能、产量和闲置产能

单位：吨

期　　间	2006 年	2007 年	2008 年	2009 年	2010 年
产能	3500	3500	3500	3500	3500
产量	2500	2500	2000	2700	2900
产能利用率	71.42%	71.42%	57.14%	77.14%	82.85%
闲置产能	1000	1000	1500	800	600

数据来源：申请书附件六《关于全球邻苯二酚生产以及美国、日本邻苯二酚产业及其国内销售价格的报告》

根据申请人提供的材料和数据，2006 年到 2010 年，日本邻苯二酚产业的产能保持在 3500 吨，产量略有波动并呈上升之势，从 2006 年的 2500 吨上升至 2010 年的 2900 吨；闲置产能先升后降，但仍维持在一定水平，如果日本将其闲置产能全部释放，其邻苯二酚出口能力有进一步增强的可能性。

(2)日本国内市场消费情况

单位：吨

期间	2006 年	2007 年	2008 年	2009 年	2010 年
产能	3500	3500	3500	3500	3500
消费量	2200	2200	1800	2000	2100
消费量占产能比例	62.85%	62.85%	51.42%	57.14%	60.00%
世界市场消费量	23400	23900	24000	26300	26700
消费量占世界比重	9.40%	9.20%	7.50%	7.60%	7.87%

数据来源：申请书附件六《关于全球邻苯二酚生产以及美国、日本邻苯二酚产业及其国内销售价格的报告》

根据申请人提供的材料和数据，2006 年至 2010 年，在产能保持不变的情况下，日本邻苯二酚国内市场消费量总体略有下降，由 2200 吨缩减为 2100 吨。日本邻苯二酚国内消费量远低于其同期产能数量，2010 年，日本邻苯二酚消费量占产能的比例仅为 60%。

2006 年以来，在世界市场消费量保持增长情况下，日本邻苯二酚消费量却呈下降之势，其占世界市场消费量的比重也在下降，表明日本邻苯二酚市场需求不足。根据现有材料，没有证据表明这种情形短期内会发生变化。

(3)对国外市场的依赖程度

单位：吨

期间	2006年	2007年	2008年	2009年	2010年
出口量	800	700	600	1100	1200
产量	2500	2500	2000	2700	2900
出口量占产量比例	32%	28%	30%	40.74%	41.38%

数据来源：申请书附件六《关于全球邻苯二酚生产以及美国、日本邻苯二酚产业及其国内销售价格的报告》；申请人提供补充材料《调查期内美国、日本邻苯二酚的对外出口情况》

根据申请人提供的材料和数据，2006年以来，日本邻苯二酚出口量占其产量的比例一直保持在28%以上，表明对外出口是日本消化国内邻苯二酚剩余产能的重要渠道。

以上分析说明，2006年以来，日本邻苯二酚的产量波动较大，闲置产能一直维持在一定水平。同期国内市场需求不足。日本邻苯二酚出口量占其产量的比例逐年增加，对国际市场依赖程度较高。

3. 对中国出口情况

单位：吨；美元/吨

期间	2006年	2007年	2008年	2009年	2010年
对中国出口数量	320.02	192.02	50.59	1018.84	1071.79
对中国出口平均价格	2031.14	2032.76	3944.38	2824.26	3025.47
中国总进口量	7828.54	6643.63	6621.75	8425.44	7639.18
对中国出口占中国总进口量比例	4.08%	2.89%	0.76%	12.09%	14.03%

数据来源：全国海关信息中心提供《邻苯二酚进出口情况的统计数据》

(1)对中国出口数量

根据我国海关统计数据，2006年至2010年，日本邻苯二酚对中国出口数量在波动中大幅上涨，从2006年的320.02吨上升至2010年的1071.79吨，增幅达234.91%。日本邻苯二酚对中国出口贸易方式发生重大变化，在反倾销措施的制约下，2006年以来日本邻苯二酚对中国出口一般贸易方式下出口量所占比例大幅下降，而其他方式下出口量所占比例大幅增加。

(2)对中国出口价格

2006年至2010年，日本邻苯二酚对中国出口价格先升后降，2010年较2006年增长了48.95%。前述倾销调查表明，倾销调查期内，原产于日本的进口邻苯二酚对中国出口价格仍属倾销价格。

4. 对第三国出口情况

单位：吨

期间	2006年	2007年	2008年	2009年	2010年
出口总量	800	700	600	1100	1200
对中国出口数量	320.02	192.02	50.59	1018.84	1071.79
对第三国出口数量	479.98	507.97	549.40	81.15	128.21
对第三国出口占出口总量的比例	60.00%	72.57%	91.57%	7.38%	10.68%

数据来源：申请人补充提供《调查期内美国、日本邻苯二酚的对外出口情况》

根据申请人提供的统计数据，日本对第三国出口数量呈下降之势，从2006年的479.98吨下降至2010年的128.21吨；对第三国出口占其出口总量的比例也在大幅下降，从2006年的60%下降至2010年的10.68%，而对中国出口的比例却在大幅增长。自2006年以来，中国邻苯二酚市场需求量总体保持增长，2010年中国邻苯二酚表观消费量较2006年增长了126.74%，快速增长的中国市场对海外生产商、出口商具有很强的吸引力。如果终止反倾销措施，日本邻苯二酚生产商、出口商向第三国(地区)的出口可能会转向中国市场。

上述调查表明：倾销调查期内日本被调查产品对中国出口存在倾销；自2006年以来，日本邻苯二酚闲置产能一直维持在一定水平；其邻苯二酚国内市场需求已基本饱和，内需不足；其邻苯二酚对国外市场依赖程度不断增加，快速增长的中国市场已成为日本邻苯二酚出口的主要目标市场；受反倾销措施制约，日本对中国出口一般贸易方式下出口量所占比例大幅下降，而其他方式下出口量所占比例大幅增加，出口价格仍属倾销价格，低价出口是其海外市场销售的一种通常价格策略。综上所述，如果终止原反倾销措施，日本邻苯二酚对中国的倾销可能继续。

(三)倾销调查结论。

上述调查表明，美国、日本的邻苯二酚在倾销调查期内存在倾销。如果终止对美国、日本的邻苯二酚的反倾销措施，原产于上述国家的进口邻苯二酚对中国的倾销可能继续发生。

七、损害继续或再度发生的可能性

(一)调查期内国内产业状况。

1. 累积评估的适当性

证据显示，调查期内，被调查产品之间及被调查产品与同类产品之间在物理和化学特性、生产工艺流程、产品用途、销售渠道和客户群体、产品可替代性、消费者和生产者评价等方面基本相同，在国内市场上存在相互竞争关系，而且竞争条件基本相同。

根据《反倾销条例》第九条和《反倾销产业损害调查规定》第十五条、第十六条的规定，调查机关认定，调查期内，对被调查产品对国内邻苯二酚产业造成的影响进行累积评估是适当的。

2. 被调查产品进口数量及所占国内市场份额

(1)被调查产品进口数量

据中国海关统计，调查期内，被调查产品进口数量总体呈下降趋势。2006 年、2007 年、2008 年、2009 年和 2010 年，被调查产品进口数量分别为 3456.02 吨、2873.99 吨、439.61 吨、3564.88 吨和 2521.01 吨。2007 年比 2006 年下降 16.84%，2008 年比 2007 年下降 84.7%，2009 年比 2008 年大幅增长 710.92%，2010 年比 2009 年下降 29.28%。

(2)被调查产品占国内市场份额

调查期内，被调查产品占国内市场份额总体呈现下降趋势。2006 年、2007 年、2008 年、2009 年和 2010 年分别为 33.81%、26.85%、3.2%、20.92% 和 14.43%。2007 年比 2006 年下降 6.96 个百分点，2008 年比 2007 年下降 23.65 个百分点，2009 年比 2008 年增长 17.72 个百分点，2010 年比 2009 年下降 6.49 个百分点。

3. 被调查产品进口价格

调查期内，被调查产品进口价格总体呈上升趋势。2006 年、2007 年、2008 年、2009 年、2010 年，被调查产品进口价格分别为 3028.07 美元/吨、3255.76 美元/吨、3967.15 美元/吨、3253.9 美元/吨和 3386.39 美元/吨。2007 年比 2006 年上升 7.52%，2008 年比 2007 年上升 21.85%，2009 年比 2008 年下降 17.98%，2010 年比 2009 年上升 4.07%。

4. 产业相关经济因素和指标的评估

根据《反倾销条例》第七、八条及《反倾销产业损害调查规定》第四、五、六、七条规定，调查机关对调查期内中国邻苯二酚产业的相关经济因素和指标进行了调查。证据显示：

(1)表观消费量

调查期内，中国邻苯二酚产业的表观消费量呈逐年增长趋势。2006 年、2007 年、2008 年、2009 年和 2010 年，中国邻苯二酚产业的表观消费量分别为 10221 吨、10704.36 吨、13723.69 吨、17040.86 吨和 17476.52 吨。2007 年比 2006 年增长 4.73%，2008 年比 2007 年增长 28.21%，2009 年比 2008 年增长 24.17%，2010 年比 2009 年增长 2.56%。

(2)产能

调查期内，中国邻苯二酚产业生产能力总体呈上升趋势。2007 年比 2006 年增长 100%，2007 年至 2010 年产能未发生变化。

(3)产量

调查期内，同类产品产量总体呈上升趋势。2007 年比 2006 年增长 38.96%，2008 年比 2007 年增长 25.05%，2009 年比 2008 年增长 27.63%，2010 年比 2009 年下降 0.65%。

(4)开工率

调查期内，中国邻苯二酚产业开工率总体呈上升趋势。2007 年比 2006 年下降 14.8 个百分点，2008 年比 2007 年上升 8.44 个百分点，2009 年比 2008 年上升 11.64 个百分点，2010 年比 2009 年下降 0.35 个百分点。

(5)销售量

调查期内，同类产品销售量总体呈上升趋势。2007 年比 2006 年增长 23.71%，2008 年比 2007 年增长 18.46%，2009 年比 2008 年增长 35.02%，2010 年比 2009 年下降 18.7%。

(6)市场份额

调查期内，国内同类产品市场份额总体呈下降趋势。2007 年比 2006 年上升 4.41 个百分点，2008 年比 2007 年下降 2.19 个百分点，2009 年比 2008 年上升 2.44 个百分点，2010 年比 2009 年下降 5.67 个百分点。

(7)销售价格

调查期内，同类产品销售价格总体呈下降趋势。2007 年比 2006 年下降 6.58%，2008 年比 2007 年下降 3.58%，2009 年比 2008 年下降 19.13%，2010 年比 2009 年增长 4.07%。

(8)销售收入

调查期内，中国邻苯二酚产业销售收入总体呈上升趋势。2007 年比 2006 年增长 15.57%，2008 年比 2007 年增长 14.22%，2009 年比 2008 年增长

9.19%，2010年比2009年下降15.39%。

(9)税前利润

调查期内，中国邻苯二酚产业税前利润总体呈下降趋势。2007年比2006年下降78.38%，2008年呈亏损状态，2009年虽然扭亏为盈，但2010年继续亏损。

(10)投资收益率

调查期内，中国邻苯二酚产业投资收益率总体呈下降趋势。2007年比2006年下降12.68个百分点，2008年比2007年下降10.51个百分点，2009年比2008年上升32.94个百分点，2010年比2009年下降29.93个百分点。

(11)就业人数

调查期内，中国邻苯二酚产业就业人数呈逐年下降趋势。2007年比2006年下降16.07%，2008年比2007年下降14.18%，2009年比2008年下降14.05%，2010年比2009年下降30.77%。

(12)劳动生产率

调查期内，中国邻苯二酚产业劳动生产率呈逐年上升趋势。2007年比2006年增长65.57%，2008年比2007年增长45.72%，2009年比2008年增长48.5%，2010年比2009年增长43.5%。

(13)人均工资

调查期内，中国邻苯二酚产业人均工资总体呈上升趋势。2007年比2006年增长29.75%，2008年比2007年下降7.67%，2009年比2008年增长17.05%，2010年比2009年增长13.85%。

(14)期末库存

调查期内，同类产品期末库存呈逐年大幅上升趋势。2007年比2006年增长429.42%，2008年比2007年增长504.02%，2009年比2008年增长88.39%，2010年比2009年增长141.35%。

(15)现金净流量

调查期内，同类产品现金净流量总体呈上升趋势。2006年至2008年同类产品现金净流量呈净流出状态，2009年和2010年呈净流入状态，但2010年现金净流量比2009年下降97.88%。

(16)投融资能力

调查期内，国内产业利用有利时机，投入大量资金进行产能扩大、生产工艺改造、产品开发和技术升级。但同类产品税前利润总体呈下降趋势，2008年和2010年处于亏损状态，国内产业投融资能力受到抑制。

上述证据表明，由于实施邻苯二酚反倾销措施，使原产于美国和日本的邻苯二酚对中国的倾销行为得到了一定的遏制，同时，调查期内，生产邻苯二酚的主要原料苯酚的国际价格总体呈上升趋势，其对中国出口邻苯二酚的价格相应地呈现上升趋势。

调查期内，中国邻苯二酚销售价格总体呈下降趋势。国内邻苯二酚产品销售价格2010年比2006年下降24.19%，而同期邻苯二酚单位生产成本却增长了0.57%，中国邻苯二酚销售价格未能达到合理的价格水平。这表明，调查期内，美国和日本继续向中国大量低价出口被调查产品，同类产品价格大幅下降，被调查产品的进口价格抑制了国内邻苯二酚产品的价格。

调查期内，国内邻苯二酚市场需求旺盛，国内邻苯二酚表观消费量2010年比2006年增长了70.99%，年均增长14.35%。随着国内邻苯二酚市场需求的增长，中国邻苯二酚产业陆续新建和扩建了一批生产装置，国内邻苯二酚产业产能、产量都呈增长态势。但由于美国和日本在中国实施邻苯二酚反倾销措施之后，继续向中国大量倾销被调查产品，使得国内邻苯二酚产业在调查期内多项经济指标并未得到明显的好转，国内产业开工率在调查期内一直处于较低水平。虽然同类产品销售量呈上升趋势，但同类产品销售量的增长幅度低于表观消费量的增长幅度，导致同类产品的市场份额呈下降趋势并在调查期内都处于较低水平。

调查期内，虽然国内邻苯二酚产业销售量2010年比2006年增长60.87%，但由于同类产品销售价格2010年比2006年下降24.19%，导致国内邻苯二酚产业销售收入2010年比2006年仅增长21.96%，国内邻苯二酚产业销售收入的增长受到抑制。与此同时，同类产品单位销售成本呈下降趋势，2010年比2006年下降3.9%，由于被调查产品的价格抑制了同类产品的价格，同类产品销售价格2010年比2006年下降了24.19%，导致同类产品单位销售毛利润大幅下降，2010年比2006年下降82.94%，同类产品单位销售毛利和毛利率都处于较低水平。国内邻苯二酚产业的税前利润大幅下降，2010年税前利润处于亏损状态，比2006年下降了150.37%，期末库存则大幅增加了144.4倍。此外，税前利润下降导致投资收益率大幅下降，国内邻苯二酚产业新建和扩建的生产装置，投入的大量资金无法正常回收，企业偿贷压力增加。

因此，调查期内，虽然对原产于美国和日本的进口邻苯二酚实施了反倾销措施，但由于美国和日本继续向中国大量低价倾销被调查产品，国内产业受被调查产品倾销的影响，仍然遭受实质性损害。

5. 其他国家(地区)进口的情况

调查期内，其他向中国出口邻苯二酚产品的国家(地区)主要为欧盟。2006年、2007年、2008年、2009年和2010年原产于欧盟的邻苯二酚的进口数量分别为4370.35吨、3769.52吨、6121.98吨、4800.03吨和5088.07吨，其进口数量占国内总进口量的比例分别为55.83%、56.74%、92.45%、56.97%和66.6%，占国内的市场份额分别为42.73%、35.21%、44.61%、28.17%和29.11%。自2003年8月26日起，中国对原产于欧盟的进口邻苯二酚征收反倾销税，2009年8月25日，商务部决定继续对原产于欧盟的邻苯二酚征收反倾销税。因此，调查期内，原产于欧盟的邻苯二酚的进口数量相对稳定，占国内市场份额则呈大幅下降趋势，2010年比2006年下降13.62个百分点，在国内市场上的销售价格趋于合理，原产于欧盟的邻苯二酚的倾销行为得到遏制。与此同时，未有证据表明，除欧盟外的其他国家(地区)的进口邻苯二酚对国内产业造成了实质性损害。

因此，调查期内，国内邻苯二酚产业受到的实质性损害并非由其他国家(地区)进口邻苯二酚造成的。

(二)中国邻苯二酚市场供求状况。

中国邻苯二酚产业开始于20世纪90年代，随着中国经济的快速发展，中国邻苯二酚产品市场需求急剧增长。邻苯二酚原审调查期内，中国邻苯二酚产业处于成长期，市场需求呈逐年上升趋势。本案调查期内，邻苯二酚产品在农药、医药、香料、合成树脂、橡胶硬化剂、电镀添加剂、毛皮染色显色剂、油漆和清漆抗起皮剂等领域的广泛应用，带动了中国邻苯二酚市场需求继续逐年稳定增长。2006年至2010年，中国邻苯二酚市场需求年均增长幅度达到14%以上，高于同期世界邻苯二酚需求平均增长幅度，中国已成为全球邻苯二酚需求量最大的国家。

调查期内，中国邻苯二酚市场需求稳定增长，同时，中国对原产于美国和日本的进口邻苯二酚实施反倾销措施，改善了中国邻苯二酚产业市场环境，国内邻苯二酚产业生产经营状况与原审调查期相比有所改善，但由于原产于美国和日本的进口邻苯二酚继续大量低价倾销，国内邻苯二酚产业仍然受到实质性损害。

预计在未来几年内，随着国内邻苯二酚下游香兰素等行业的进一步发展以及新应用领域的开拓，我国邻苯二酚的需求量仍将继续保持在较高的水平，达到每年1.8万吨左右的市场需求水平。同时，随着国内邻苯二酚新建和改扩建装置的陆续投产，国内邻苯二酚的供需状况基本达到平衡。

(三)被调查产品进口大量增加的可能性。

据中国海关统计，调查期内，被调查产品进口数量总体呈下降趋势。由2006年的3456.02吨下降到2010年的2521.01吨，下降了27.05%。被调查产品占中国市场份额总体也呈下降趋势。由2006年的33.81%下降到2010年的14.43%，下降了19.38个百分点。

调查期内，美国和日本向中国出口邻苯二酚合计数量占中国邻苯二酚总进口量的比例较大。2006年、2007年、2008年、2009年和2010年，美国和日本向中国出口邻苯二酚合计数量占中国邻苯二酚总进口量的比例分别为44.15%、43.26%、6.64%、42.31%和33%，表明美国和日本是中国邻苯二酚产品的主要进口国。

美国邻苯二酚市场状况

调查期内，美国邻苯二酚产能保持相对稳定。2006年至2010年美国邻苯二酚生产能力均为6000吨。美国邻苯二酚产量总体呈下降趋势，2006年和2007年美国邻苯二酚产量分别为4500吨和4000吨，2008年至2010年均为3500吨。调查期内，美国邻苯二酚闲置产能总体呈增长趋势。2006年和2007年美国邻苯二酚闲置产能分别为1500吨和2000吨。2008年至2010年均为2500吨，占当年产能的41.67%。以上数据表明，调查期内，美国邻苯二酚闲置产能保持在较高水平。

调查期内，美国邻苯二酚国内消费量呈大幅下降趋势。2006年、2007年、2008年、2009年和2010年，美国邻苯二酚国内消费量分别为4000吨、4000吨、3000吨、1500吨和1400吨。2010年比2006年大幅下降了65%。美国邻苯二酚可供出口的生产能力总体呈大幅增长趋势。2006年、2007年、2008年、2009年和2010年，美国邻苯二酚可供出口的生产能力分别为2000吨、3000吨、4500吨和4600吨。2010年比2006年大幅增长了130%，2010年可供出口的生产能力占当年产能的比例为76.67%。证据显示，调查期内，虽然美国邻苯二酚出口数量总体呈下降趋势，由2006年出口邻苯二酚3700吨下降至2010年出口3000吨，2010年比2006年出口数量下降了18.92%，但是美国邻苯二酚出口数量占其国内产量比例在调查期内都达到75%以上。以上数据表明，美国邻苯二酚具有较强的出口能力，对国际市场依赖程度较高，对外出口是美国邻苯二酚生产企业销售产品的重要方式。

据中国海关统计，调查期内，美国向中国出口邻苯二酚数量总体呈下降趋势。2006年、2007年、2008年、2009年和2010年，美国向中国出口邻苯二酚数量分别为3136吨、2681.97吨、389.01吨、2546.04吨和1449.22吨。2007年比2006年下降14.48%，2008年比2007年下降85.5%，2009年比2008年增长554.49%，2010年比2009年下降43.08%。证据显示，调查期内，美国在各年度出口邻苯二酚的众多国家之中，对中国出口的邻苯二酚数量均位居前列，2006年、2007年、2008年、2009年和2010年，对中国出口邻苯二酚数量占其总出口量的比例分别为84.76%、78.88%、14.41%、77.15%和48.31%，中国是美国邻苯二酚的主要出口国。

日本邻苯二酚市场状况

调查期内，日本邻苯二酚生产能力保持相对稳定。2006年至2010年日本邻苯二酚生产能力均为3500吨。2006年、2007年、2008年、2009年和2010年，日本邻苯二酚产量分别为2500吨、2500吨、2000吨、2700吨和2900吨，2010年比2006年增长16%。2006年和2007年日本邻苯二酚闲置产能均为1000吨，占当年产能的28.57%。2008年、2009年和2010年日本邻苯二酚闲置产能分别为1500吨、800吨和600吨，分别占当年产能的42.86%、22.86%和17.14%。以上数据表明，日本邻苯二酚闲置产能较大。

调查期内，日本邻苯二酚国内消费量总体呈下降趋势。2006年、2007年、2008年、2009年和2010年，日本邻苯二酚国内消费量分别为2200吨、2200吨、1800吨、2000吨和2100吨。2010年比2006年下降了4.55%。日本邻苯二酚可供出口的生产能力变化不大。2006年、2007年、2008年、2009年和2010年，日本邻苯二酚可供出口的生产能力分别为1300吨、1300吨、1700吨、1500吨和1400吨。2010年比2006年增长了7.69%，2010年可供出口的生产能力占当年产能的比例达到40%。证据显示，调查期内，日本邻苯二酚出口数量总体呈增长趋势，由2006年出口邻苯二酚800吨增长至2010年出口1200吨，增长了50%，日本邻苯二酚出口数量占其国内产量比例在调查期内总体呈增长趋势，由2006年的32%增长到2010年的41.38%。以上数据表明，日本邻苯二酚对国际市场依赖程度很高，其大量闲置产能需要通过寻求国外市场来消化。

据中国海关统计，调查期内，日本向中国出口邻苯二酚数量呈大幅增长趋势。2006年、2007年、2008年、2009年和2010年，日本向中国出口邻苯二酚数量分别为320.02吨、192.02吨、50.6吨、1018.84吨和1071.79吨。2007年比2006年下降40%，2008年比2007年下降73.65%，2009年比2008年增长1913.52%，2010年比2009年增长5.2%。证据显示，调查期内，日本在各年度出口邻苯二酚的众多国家之中，对中国出口的邻苯二酚数量均位居前列，2006年、2007年、2008年、2009年和2010年，对中国出口邻苯二酚数量占其总出口量的比例分别为76.8%、70.1%、13.32%、81.02%和60.02%，中国是日本邻苯二酚的主要出口国。

上述证据表明，调查期内，美国和日本的邻苯二酚生产能力保持平稳，维持在9500吨左右，产量总体呈小幅下降趋势，装置开工率较低，2010年装置开工率合计为67.37%，美国和日本邻苯二酚闲置产能较大。美国和日本邻苯二酚国内消费量大幅下降，由2006年的6200吨下降到2010年的3500吨，2010年比2006年下降了43.55%，美国和日本邻苯二酚国内消费量始终维持在较低水平。表明上述两国邻苯二酚具有较强的出口能力，对国际市场依赖度较高，需要通过对外出口的方式来消化其国内消费的剩余产品。中国实施邻苯二酚反倾销措施以后，虽然美国和日本向中国出口邻苯二酚数量趋于减少，但上述两国对中国出口邻苯二酚数量占本国总出口数量的比例均较大，中国是上述两国邻苯二酚的主要出口国。

如果终止反倾销措施，原产于美国和日本的邻苯二酚向中国出口邻苯二酚的数量将可能大量增加。

（四）被调查产品进口价格对国内产业的影响。

据中国海关统计，调查期内，被调查产品进口价格总体呈上升趋势。由2006年的3028.07美元/吨上升到2010年的3386.39美元/吨，增长了11.83%。

调查期内，原产于美国和日本的邻苯二酚对中国的倾销行为得到了一定的遏制，上述两国向中国出口邻苯二酚价格有所上升。同时，调查期内，生产邻苯二酚的原材料价格上升导致邻苯二酚生产成本也随之增加，被调查产品的价格相应地呈现上升趋势。

调查期内，中国邻苯二酚销售价格总体呈下降趋势。国内邻苯二酚产品销售价格2010年比2006年下降24.19%，而同期邻苯二酚单位生产成本却增长了0.57%，中国邻苯二酚销售价格未能达到合理的价格水平，被调查产品的进口价格抑制了国内邻苯二酚产品的价格。另外，美国和日本继续向中国大量低价出口被调查产品，同类产品价格大幅下降，被调查产品的降价将会对国内产业造成不利的影响。

随着中国邻苯二酚产业的快速发展，反倾销措施实施前中国邻苯二酚产品供不应求的局面开始得到改善，市场竞争日趋激烈。被调查产品与同类产品在生产成本、产品质量、销售渠道上基本一致的情况下，产品价格成为企业营销的决定因素，对下游用户选择产品也起着重要的作用。如果终止反倾销措施，被调查产品将存在较大的降价空间并可能转化为实际的降价幅度，很可能通过压低销售价格来扩大对中国出口，以恢复和扩大其在中国的市场份额。

(五)产业损害调查结论。

1. 中国实施邻苯二酚反倾销措施之后，美国和日本继续向中国大量低价倾销被调查产品，中国邻苯二酚产业继续受到实质损害。

2. 美国和日本的邻苯二酚国内消费量呈下降趋势，产品严重依赖出口市场，中国是美国和日本邻苯二酚的主要出口国。如果终止原反倾销措施，来自上述两国的邻苯二酚产品可能继续向中国大量低价倾销，可能造成国内产业继续受到实质损害。

八、复审裁定

根据调查结果，调查机关裁定：如果终止原反倾销措施，原产于美国和日本的进口邻苯二酚对中国的倾销有可能继续发生；原产于美国和日本的进口邻苯二酚对中国国内产业造成的损害有可能继续发生。

根据《反倾销条例》第四十八条的规定，调查机关决定维持对原产于美国和日本的进口邻苯二酚实施的原反倾销措施，将原反倾销措施的实施期限自2012年5月22日起延长五年。

(注：邻苯二酚产品在合成树脂、橡胶硬化剂、农药、医药、香料、电镀添加剂、毛皮染色显色剂、油漆和清漆抗起皮剂等领域的广泛应用。)

三十二、中华人民共和国商务部公告 2012 年第32 号 关于环氧氯丙烷反倾销措施期终复审裁决的公告(二〇一二年六月二十七日)

中华人民共和国商务部于2006年6月28日发布该年度第44号公告，决定对原产于美国、韩国、日本、俄罗斯的进口环氧氯丙烷征收反倾销税，实施期限自2006年6月28日起5年。

2011年6月27日，商务部发布该年度第34公告，决定对原产于美国、韩国、日本、俄罗斯的进口环氧氯丙烷所适用的反倾销措施进行期终复审调查。

本次复审调查产品范围与商务部2006年第44号公告中列明的产品范围一致，该产品归在《中华人民共和国进出口税则》：29103000。

商务部对如果终止原反倾销措施，导致倾销和损害继续或再度发生的可能性进行了调查，并根据调查结果向国务院关税税则委员会提出维持原反倾销措施的建议。

根据《中华人民共和国反倾销条例》第五十条及国务院关税税则委员会的决定，现将有关事项公告如下：

一、裁定

商务部裁定，如果终止原反倾销措施，原产于美国、韩国、日本和俄罗斯的进口环氧氯丙烷对中国的倾销有可能继续发生。如果终止原反倾销措施，原产于美国、韩国、日本和俄罗斯的进口环氧氯丙烷对国内产业造成的损害有可能再度发生。

二、反倾销措施

自2012年6月28日起，继续按照商务部2006年第44号公告公布的征税范围和反倾销税税率征收反倾销税，实施期限为5年。

三、征收反倾销税的方法

自2012年6月28日起，进口经营者在进口原产于美国、韩国、日本和俄罗斯的进口环氧氯丙烷时，应向中华人民共和国海关缴纳相应的反倾销税。反倾销税以海关审定的完税价格从价计征，计算公式为：反倾销税税额＝海关完税价格×反倾销税税率。进口环节增值税以海关审定的完税价格加上关税和反倾销税作为计税价格从价计征。

四、行政复议和行政诉讼

根据《中华人民共和国反倾销条例》第五十三条，对本复审决定不服的，可以申请行政复议，也可以向人民法院提起诉讼。

五、本公告自2012年6月28日起执行。

附件：中华人民共和国商务部关于原产于美国、韩国、日本和俄罗斯的进口环氧氯丙烷所适用的反倾销措施的期终复审裁定

2011年6月27日，中华人民共和国商务部(以下简称调查机关)发布公告，决定对原产于美国、韩国、日本和俄罗斯的进口环氧氯丙烷所适用的反倾销措施进行期终复审调查。

调查机关对如果终止原反倾销措施，原产于美国、韩国、日本和俄罗斯的进口环氧氯丙烷对中国的倾销和损害继续或再度发生的可能性进行了调查。根据调查结果，并依据《中国反倾销条例》(以下简称《反倾销条例》)第四十八条，做出复审裁定如下：

一、原反倾销措施

2006年6月28日，调查机关发布公告，决定对原产于美国、韩国、日本和俄罗斯的进口环氧氯丙烷征收0%～71.5%的反倾销税。

原反倾销措施实施期间，没有利害关系方向调查机关申请过任何形式的复审调查。

二、期终复审调查程序

(一)到期公告。

2010年12月28日，调查机关发布该年度第97

号公告，告知原反倾销措施即将到期。根据《反倾销条例》规定，经复审确定终止征收反倾销税有可能导致倾销和损害的继续或者再度发生的，反倾销税的征收期限可以适当延长。自该公告发布之日起，国内产业可在原反倾销措施终止日60天前，向调查机关提出书面复审申请。

（二）复审申请。

2011年4月13日，山东海力化工股份有限公司代表中国环氧氯丙烷产业向调查机关提交了期终复审申请。中国石油化工股份有限公司齐鲁分公司、天津渤天化工有限责任公司和江苏扬农化工集团有限公司表示支持申请人的复审申请。

申请人主张，如果终止原反倾销措施，原产于美国、韩国、日本和俄罗斯的进口环氧氯丙烷对中国的倾销行为可能继续或再度发生，倾销对中国环氧氯丙烷产业造成的损害有可能再度发生，请求调查机关继续维持原反倾销措施。

（三）立案前通知。

2011年6月20日，调查机关就有关期终复审申请事宜通知了涉案国驻华使馆。

（四）立案。

根据《反倾销条例》第十一条、第十三条、第十七条和第四十八条规定，调查机关对申请人资格和申请书的主张及相关证明材料进行了审查，本案申请人及其支持企业同类产品的产量超过国内同类产品总产量的50%，符合产业代表性要求，申请人资格和申请书符合立案要求。

根据审查结果及《反倾销条例》第十六条、第四十八条、第五十一条规定，调查机关于2011年6月27日发布该年度第34号公告，决定对原产于美国、韩国、日本和俄罗斯的进口环氧氯丙烷所适用的反倾销措施进行期终复审调查，倾销调查期为2010年1月1日至2010年12月31日，产业损害调查期为2006年1月1日至2010年12月31日。复审调查内容为，如果终止对原产于美国、韩国、日本和俄罗斯的进口环氧氯丙烷实施的反倾销措施，是否可能导致倾销和损害的继续或再度发生。

（五）立案通知及利害关系方评论。

立案当日，调查机关就立案事宜通知了美国、韩国、日本和俄罗斯驻华使馆，并提供了立案公告和申请书公开文本。

立案当日，调查机关就立案事宜通知了申请人及已知的涉案国生产商和出口商。利害关系方可到商务部贸易救济公开信息查阅室查阅有关申请书公开文本。

在规定时间内，没有利害关系方就本次复审立案发表评论意见。

（六）登记应诉。

调查机关在该年度第34号公告中公布，任何利害关系方可于公告发布之日起20天内，向调查机关申请参加应诉。如利害关系方未在立案公告规定的时间内向调查机关登记应诉，调查机关可以根据已经获得的事实和可获得的最佳信息做出裁定。

在规定期限内，没有生产商、出口商和进口商登记应诉，俄罗斯政府作为利害关系方登记应诉本次复审倾销调查。

（七）倾销调查与损害调查。

1. 倾销调查

（1）收集证据

立案后，调查机关通过以下方法和渠道，收集了相关证据：

向已知7家生产商发放了调查问卷，在规定期限内，没有企业提交答卷。

要求申请人进一步提供倾销继续或再度发生可能性等方面的相关证据。调查机关对申请书和申请人补充提交的材料进行了审查核实。

调查机关通过查询海关数据、咨询相关行业协会、查阅相关网站、公开刊物，了解与被调查产品及其同类产品有关的数据和信息。

俄罗斯政府作为利害关系方在本案调查过程中通过来函方式表示关注，调查机关通过回函方式予以答复。

（2）听证会和意见陈述

调查机关向利害关系方告知提请召开听证会的权利，复审调查期间，没有利害关系方申请召开听证会。2011年8月24日，调查机关会见了俄罗斯政府代表，听取了俄罗斯政府对本案的意见陈述。

（3）披露

根据《反倾销条例》第二十五条和《反倾销调查信息披露暂行规则》第十条、第十一条的规定，调查机关于2012年5月23日向利害关系方披露了本案倾销部分裁定所依据的基本事实，并给予其提出评论意见的机会。

2. 损害调查

（1）参加产业损害调查活动登记

2011年6月27日，调查机关发布《关于参加环氧氯丙烷反倾销措施期终复审产业损害调查活动登记的通知》（商调查函［2011］192号）。在规定的时间内，没有相关利害关系方参加产业损害调查活动登记。

（2）成立产业损害调查组

2011年7月12日，调查机关发布《关于成立环氧氯丙烷反倾销措施期终复审案产业损害调查组的通知》(商调查函[2011]206号)，成立环氧氯丙烷反倾销措施期终复审案产业损害调查组。

(3)发放和收回调查问卷

2011年7月18日，调查机关向已知的利害关系方发放了环氧氯丙烷反倾销措施期终复审案《国内生产者调查问卷》(商调查函[2011]202号)、《国内进口商调查问卷》(商调查函[2011]203号)和《国外(地区)生产者/出口商调查问卷》(商调查函[2011]204号)。

在规定的时间内，山东海力化工股份有限公司、中国石油化工股份有限公司齐鲁分公司和天津渤天化工有限责任公司递交了《国内生产者调查问卷答卷》。调查机关未收到《国外(地区)生产者/出口商调查问卷》答卷和《国内进口商调查问卷》答卷。

(4)听取利害关系方意见陈述

2011年7月11日，调查机关收到本案申请人山东海力化工股份有限公司提交的《关于召开环氧氯丙烷反倾销措施期终复审国内产业意见陈述会的申请》。调查机关于同日发布《关于召开环氧氯丙烷反倾销措施期终复审案国内产业意见陈述会的通知》(商调查函[2011]208号)。

2011年7月20日，调查机关召开了环氧氯丙烷反倾销措施期终复审案申请人意见陈述会，听取申请人及支持企业陈述申请理由及对本案产业损害调查的相关意见。

申请人及支持企业认为，如果终止反倾销措施，原产于美国、韩国、日本和俄罗斯的进口环氧氯丙烷对国内产业造成的损害可能再度发生。

(5)召开上下游企业意见陈述会

2012年2月7日，调查机关发布《关于召开环氧氯丙烷反倾销措施期终复审案上下游企业意见陈述会的通知》(商调查函[2012]42号)。

2012年2月15日，调查机关召开本案上下游企业意见陈述会，听取了本案申请企业、支持企业以及部分下游企业的意见陈述。

本案申请企业及支持企业表示，对原产于美国、韩国、日本和俄罗斯的进口环氧氯丙烷产品所适用的反倾销措施进行期终复审调查并继续采取措施，不会影响下游用户的正常生产经营。国内环氧氯丙烷产业的发展需要得到下游企业的支持，希望上下游企业在公平的市场竞争环境中共同发展，形成多赢的良好局面。如果终止反倾销措施，国内环氧氯丙烷产业可能再度受到实质损害，因此，希望继续维持原反倾销措施，维护国内产业的合法权益，保障国内环氧氯丙烷产业以及下游产业的健康发展。

下游企业提出，调查期内，国内生产的环氧氯丙烷产品与进口被调查产品在质量上不存在差异，可相互替代，且完全能够满足国内市场需求。同时表示，一个相对公平、健康、稳定的市场环境有利于企业的正常生产经营活动，有利于上下游企业的共同发展，下游企业支持此次期终复审调查。

(6)接收书面陈述材料

2011年7月20日，申请人向调查机关提交了《环氧氯丙烷反倾销措施期终复审案国内产业意见陈述会汇报材料》。

2012年2月15日，申请人向调查机关提交了《环氧氯丙烷反倾销措施期终复审案上下游企业意见陈述会申请人发言稿》。

(7)实地核查

2011年12月15日，调查机关发布《关于环氧氯丙烷反倾销措施期终复审案实地核查的通知》(商调查函[2011]426号)。2012年2月，调查机关对本案申请企业山东海力化工股份有限公司、本案支持企业中国石油化工股份有限公司齐鲁分公司和天津渤天化工有限责任公司进行了实地核查。核查期间，调查机关对本案申请书及《国内生产者调查问卷答卷》中的数据和信息进行了核实，并收集了相关证据材料。核查结束后，以上三家企业分别向调查机关提交了《环氧氯丙烷反倾销期终复审案实地核查汇报材料》和《环氧氯丙烷反倾销期终复审案产业损害调查实地核查后补充资料》。

(8)信息公开

根据《反倾销条例》第二十三条和《产业损害调查信息查阅与信息披露规定》第八条、第十四条的规定，本案所有与产业损害调查有关的公开信息均已按规定送交商务部贸易救济措施公开信息查阅室。本案所有利害关系方可以查找、阅览、摘抄、复印与产业损害调查有关的公开信息。

(9)信息披露

根据《反倾销条例》第二十五条第二款和《产业损害调查信息查阅与信息披露规定》第十八条、第十九条、第二十条和第二十一条的规定，调查机关在裁定前向本案利害关系方披露了本案最终裁定所依据的基本事实，并给予其提出评论意见的机会。信息披露期间，没有利害关系方提出评论意见。

调查机关对申请书及所附证据材料、收回的调查问卷答卷和实地核查结果进行了认真分析和全面评估，并收集和补充了相关证据材料。调查机关对利害关系方提出的评论和意见依法予以了充分考虑。

三、被调查产品及调查范围

(一)被调查产品。

复审被调查产品与原反倾销措施所适用的被调查产品一致。

中文名称：环氧氯丙烷，又名1-氯-2，3-环氧丙烷、表氯醇

英文名称：Epichlorohydrin（简称ECH）

分子式：C_3H_5OCl

化学结构式：（略）

税则号：该被调查产品归在《中国海关进出口税则》：29103000。

物理及化学特征：在常温下是一种透明、有刺激性气味的低黏度、易挥发、不稳定的无色油状液体，可混溶于乙醇、乙醚、氯仿、三氯乙烯等。

主要用途：环氧氯丙烷主要用于生产环氧树脂，还可用于生产合成甘油、硝化甘油炸药、玻璃钢、电绝缘品、表面活性剂、医药、农药、涂料、胶料、离子交换树脂、增塑剂、（缩水）甘油衍生物、氯醇橡胶等多种产品。此外，环氧氯内烷还用作纤维素脂、树脂、纤维素醚的溶剂。

（二）调查范围。

原产于美国、韩国、日本和俄罗斯的进口环氧氯丙烷。

四、国内同类产品和国内产业

（一）同类产品。

商务部2006年6月28日第44号公告发布的环氧氯丙烷反倾销原审案件最终裁定中认定，“国内生产的环氧氯丙烷与被调查产品的物理和化学特性相同，生产工艺和采用的原料相同，用途相同且相互可替代，销售渠道和客户群体基本相同。国内生产的环氧氯丙烷与被调查产品属于同类产品。”

2011年6月27日，商务部发布第34号立案公告认定，复审被调查产品范围与原反倾销被调查产品范围一致。

在环氧氯丙烷反倾销措施实施期间，国内生产的环氧氯丙烷与原审案件调查期内生产的环氧氯丙烷在物理和化学性能、生产工艺、产品用途、销售渠道等方面未发生实质变化。

因此，调查机关认定，本次复审的被调查产品与国内生产的环氧氯丙烷产品属于同类产品。

（二）国内产业。

调查机关对本案提交答卷的3家企业的产业代表资格进行了审查。证据显示，2006年、2007年、2008年、2009年和2010年，提交答卷企业环氧氯丙烷产量占同期国内同类产品总产量的59.43%、51.78%、64.63%、73.29%和60.10%。

根据《反倾销条例》第十一条、第五十一条和《反倾销产业损害调查规定》第十三条规定，调查机关认定，调查期内，国内上述3家提交答卷企业可以代表国内环氧氯丙烷产业。本裁定所依据的国内产业数据，除特别注明外，均来自以上3家企业。

五、复审调查期

本次复审的倾销调查期为2010年1月1日至2010年12月31日，损害调查期为2006年1月1日至2010年12月31日。

六、倾销继续或再度发生的可能性

调查机关在立案之口通知申请书上列明的出口商、生产商和美国、韩国、日本和俄罗斯驻华使馆；同日，调查机关将立案公告登载在商务部网站上，任何利害关系方均可在商务部网站上查阅本案立案公告。立案后，调查机关给予各利害关系方20天的登记应诉期，给予所有利害关系方合理的时间获知立案有关情况。

2011年7月25日，调查机关向登记应诉公司发放了调查问卷；同日，调查机关将调查问卷登载在商务部网站上，任何利害关系方可在商务部网站上查阅本案调查问卷。

调查机关已尽可能通知所有利害关系方，也已尽可能向所有利害关系方提醒不登记应诉或不提交答卷的结果。

调查机关注意到，美国、韩国、日本和俄罗斯的生产商、出口商未参加应诉，也未提交答卷，调查机关无法直接获得倾销调查期内被调查产品的正常价值、出口价格、调整因素以及出口国出口能力、国内消费、对中国出口和对第三国出口等方面的数据和证据。依据《反倾销条例》第二十一条，调查机关决定采用可获得的最佳信息进行认定。

本案申请书的数据来源于中国海关统计数据和涉案国海关统计数据以及其他公开渠道。调查机关审查认为，申请人提供的证据和信息是可获得的最佳信息，调查机关同时核实了有关海关数据。

（一）倾销调查期内的倾销情况。

美国

调查机关根据申请人提供的数据以及经核实的海关数据，对美国被调查产品的正常价值、出口价格进行了认定，对影响正常价值和出口价格可比性因素进行了调整，并在同一贸易环节进行了比较。

经调查，调查机关认定，倾销调查期内，原产于美国的环氧氯丙烷对中国出口存在倾销。

韩国

调查机关根据申请人提供的数据和经核实的海关数据，对韩国被调查产品的正常价值、出口价格进行了认定，对影响正常价值和出口价格可比性因素进行了调整，并在同一贸易环节进行了比较。

经调查，调查机关认定，倾销调查期内，原产于韩国的环氧氯丙烷对中国出口存在倾销。

日本

调查机关根据申请人提供的数据和经核实的海关数据，对日本被调查产品的正常价值、出口价格进行了认定，对影响正常价值和出口价格可比性因素进行了调整，并在同一贸易环节进行了比较。

经调查，调查机关认定，倾销调查期内，原产于日本的环氧氯丙烷对中国出口存在倾销。

俄罗斯

调查机关根据申请人提供的数据和经核实的海关数据，对俄罗斯被调查产品的正常价值、出口价格进行了认定，对影响正常价值和出口价格可比性因素进行了调整，并在同一贸易环节进行了比较。

经调查，调查机关认定，倾销调查期内，原产于俄罗斯的环氧氯丙烷对中国出口存在倾销。

(二)倾销继续或再度发生的可能性。

美国

1. 调查期内的倾销情况

根据原反倾销措施，美国被调查产品所适用的反倾销税税率为4.3%~71.5%。前述倾销调查表明，倾销调查期内，美国被调查产品对中国出口存在倾销的事实。

2. 出口能力

(1)产能、产量

本案申请人提供了有关数据。根据申请人提供的数据，美国是全球环氧氯丙烷的主要生产国，反倾销措施实施期间，美国产能大并稳定在46万吨，而产量总体有所下降，开工率总体呈下降趋势，2006~2010年开工率分别为78.72%、70.67%、63.63%、51.61%和60.52%，累计降幅18个百分点，闲置产能由2006年的9.79万吨上升到2010年的18.61万吨，闲置产能大。

(2)国内消费情况

根据申请人提供的数据，相对于较大的产能，美国环氧氯丙烷的国内消费需求明显不足，2006~2010年国内消费量分别为23.60万吨、24.30万吨、22.70万吨、21.50万吨和23.70万吨。

(3)对国际市场的依赖程度

根据申请人提供的数据和经核实的海关数据，在反倾销措施实施期间，美国环氧氯丙烷对国外市场的出口量占总产量的比例平均为26.95%左右，对国外市场的依赖程度较高。

3. 对中国出口情况

根据中国海关统计数据，2006~2010年，美国环氧氯丙烷对华出口数量总体呈下降趋势，占中国总进口比例也呈下降趋势，但年平均比例仍高达28%。为了保持对中国出口，美国出口商改变了出口贸易方式，加工贸易占美国环氧氯丙烷对中国出口数量的比例从2006年的5.77%上升至2010年的47.74%。

反倾销措施实施后，美国环氧氯丙烷对华出口价格总体呈上升趋势，这不仅归因于反倾销措施以及主要原材料丙烯的价格总体上涨共同作用。而且如上文所述，美国环氧氯丙烷对华出口价格仍然属于倾销价格。

4. 对第三国(地区)出口情况

根据申请人提供的数据，2010年美国环氧氯丙烷生产商、出口商同时向除中国以外的其他国家低价出口环氧氯丙烷产品。2010年美国向除中国以外的其他国家低价出口环氧氯丙烷产品数量合计为60931吨，占同期其环氧氯丙烷对第三国(地区)总出口量的比例为99.64%，占同期环氧氯丙烷总产量的22%，说明其低价寻求国外市场的需求较强。如果终止反倾销措施，该情形可能发生在对中国的出口中。

综合上述调查分析，美国国内环氧氯丙烷产能大，出口能力强，国内消费需求不足，对国际市场依赖程度高，没有证据表明上述情况会发生变化。此外，美国大量低价向第三国(地区)出口环氧氯丙烷，说明其低价寻求国外市场的需求较强。中国环氧氯丙烷需求增长迅速且潜力大，可能成为美国环氧氯丙烷对外出口的主要目标市场。在采取反倾销措施的情况下，倾销调查期内，美国环氧氯丙烷对中国出口仍然存在倾销。如果终止原反倾销措施，其可能会加大低价倾销的力度。综上所述，如果终止原反倾销措施，美国环氧氯丙烷对中国的倾销可能继续发生。

韩国

1. 调查期内的倾销情况

根据原反倾销措施，韩国被调查产品所适用的反倾销税税率为3.8% ~71.5%。前述倾销调查表明，倾销调查期内，韩国被调查产品对中国出口存在倾销的事实。

2. 出口能力

(1)产能、产量

本案申请人提供了有关数据。根据申请人提供的数据，反倾销措施实施期间，韩国产能稳定，保持在6.8万吨，产量有所下降，开工率呈下降趋势，2006~2010年开工率分别为90.44%、87.50%、84.56%、80.88%和81.62%，累计降幅达8.82个百分点，闲置产能有所增加。

(2)国内消费情况

根据申请人提供的数据，韩国环氧氯丙烷的国内消费需求相对稳定并略有下降，2006 年国内消费量约为 6.32 万吨，2010 年国内消费量约为 5.90 万吨。

(3)对国际市场的依赖程度

根据申请人提供的数据和经核实的海关数据，在反倾销措施实施期间，韩国环氧氯丙烷对国外市场的出口量占总产量的平均比例在 34% 左右，对国外市场的依赖程度较高。

3. 对中国出口情况

根据中国海关统计数据，2006 ~ 2010 年，韩国环氧氯丙烷对华出口数量总体呈下降趋势，但占中国进口总量比重总体呈上升趋势，占韩国对外出口量的比重年均高达 57% 以上。为了保持对中国出口，韩国出口商改变了出口贸易方式，加工贸易占韩国环氧氯丙烷对中国出口数量的比例从 2006 年的 16.54% 上升至 2010 年的 63.08%。

反倾销措施实施后，韩国环氧氯丙烷对华出口价格总体呈下降趋势，2010 年比 2006 年下降了 12.61%。这不仅与主要原材料丙烯的价格总体上升的走势相反，而且如上文所述，韩国环氧氯丙烷对华出口价格仍然属于倾销价格。

4. 对第三国(地区)出口情况

根据申请人提供的数据，2010 年韩国环氧氯丙烷生产商、出口商同时向除中国以外的 18 个国家低价出口环氧氯丙烷产品数量合计为 6371 吨，占同期其环氧氯丙烷对第三国(地区)总出口量的比例为 98.68%，说明其低价寻求国外市场的需求较强。如果终止反倾销措施，该情形可能发生在对中国的出口中。

综合上述调查分析，韩国国内环氧氯丙烷产能较大，出口能力较强，国内消费稳定并略有下降，对国际市场依赖程度较高，中国是其最主要的目标市场，没有证据表明上述情况会发生变化。此外，韩国大量低价向第三国(地区)出口环氧氯丙烷，说明其低价寻求国外市场的需求较强。在全球环氧氯丙烷产能严重过剩、除中国外其他消费市场需求低迷的情况下，中国作为环氧氯丙烷需求增长迅速且潜力大的国家，邻近韩国，是韩国环氧氯丙烷对外出口的主要潜在目标市场。在采取反倾销措施的情况下，倾销调查期内，韩国环氧氯丙烷对中国出口仍然存在倾销。如果终止原反倾销措施，其可能会加大低价倾销的力度。综上所述，如果终止原反倾销措施，韩国环氧氯丙烷对中国的倾销可能继续发生。

日本

1. 调查期内的倾销情况

根据原反倾销措施，日本被调查产品所适用的反倾销税税 0% ~ 71.5%。前述倾销调查表明，倾销调查期内，日本被调查产品对中国出口存在倾销的事实。

2. 出口能力

(1)产能、产量

本案申请人提供了有关数据。根据申请人提供的数据，反倾销措施实施期间，日本产能略有增长并相对稳定，保持在 12.1 万吨，而产量总体下降明显，开工率总体呈下降趋势，2006 ~ 2010 年开工率分别为 95.74%、91.98%、88.43%、62.56% 和 62.31%，累计降幅 33 个百分点，闲置产能大幅增加了 8.3 倍。

(2)国内消费情况

根据申请人提供的数据，日本环氧氯丙烷的国内消费需求呈大幅下降趋势，2006 - 2010 年其国内消费量分别为 11.21 万吨、11.60 万吨、10.95 万吨、6.72 万吨、6.73 万吨，2010 年比 2006 年大幅下降了 39.96%。

(3)对国际市场的依赖程度

根据申请人提供的数据和经核实的海关数据，在反倾销措施实施期间，日本环氧氯丙烷对国外市场的出口量占总产量的比重分别为 15.17%、11.23%、15.51%、24.83% 和 30.37%，累计升幅达 15 个百分点，对国外市场的依赖程度在逐年增强，对外出口是日本环氧氯丙烷企业销售的重要方式。

3. 对中国出口情况

根据中国海关统计数据，2006 ~ 2010 年，日本环氧氯丙烷对华出口数量总体呈下降趋势，但是占中国总进口量的比重基本保持稳定。为了保持对中国出口，日本出口商改变了出口贸易方式，加工贸易占日本环氧氯丙烷对中国出口数量的比例从 2006 年的 23.53% 上升至 2010 年的 74.77%。

反倾销措施实施后，日本环氧氯丙烷对华出口价格总体呈下降趋势，这不仅与主要原材料丙烯的价格总体上升的走势相反，而且如上文所述，日本环氧氯丙烷对华出口价格仍然属于倾销价格。

4. 对第三国(地区)出口情况

根据申请人提供的数据，2010 年日本环氧氯丙烷生产商、出口商同时向除中国以外的其他国家低价出口环氧氯丙烷产品。2010 年日本向除中国以外的其他国家低价出口环氧氯丙烷产品数量合计为 20298 吨，占同期其环氧氯丙烷对第三国(地区)总出口量的比例为 99.11%，说明其低价寻求国外市场的需求较强。如果终止反倾销措施，该情形可能发生在对中国的出口中。

综合上述调查分析，日本国内环氧氯丙烷产能大，出口能力强，国内消费呈不断萎缩态势，国际市场依赖程度高，没有证据表明上述情况会发生变化。此外，日本大量低价向第三国(地区)出口环氧氯丙烷，说明其低价寻求国外市场的需求较强。中国环氧氯丙烷需求增长迅速且潜力大，可能成为日本环氧氯丙烷对外出口的主要目标市场。在采取反倾销措施的情况下，倾销调查期内，日本环氧氯丙烷对中国出口仍然存在倾销。如果终止原反倾销措施，其可能会加大低价倾销的力度。综上所述，如果终止原反倾销措施，日本环氧氯丙烷对中国的倾销可能继续发生。

俄罗斯

1. 调查期内的倾销情况

根据原反倾销措施，俄罗斯被调查产品所适用的反倾销税税率为5.4% -71.5%。前述倾销调查表明，倾销调查期内，俄罗斯被调查产品对中国出口存在倾销的事实。

2. 出口能力

(1)产能、产量

本案申请人提供了有关数据。根据申请人提供的数据，反倾销措施实施期间，俄罗斯产能稳定，保持在9.6万吨，而产量总体下降明显，开工率总体呈下降趋势，2006 - 2010 年开工率分别为75.94%、76.56%、76.04%、59.38%和63.54%，累计降幅12个百分点，闲置产能大幅增加。

(2)国内消费情况

根据申请人提供的数据，俄罗斯环氧氯丙烷的国内消费需求较小并总体呈下降趋势，2006年国内消费量约为1.23万吨，占当年产量的16.87%，2010年国内消费量约为1.12万吨，占当年产量的18.39%。

(3)对国际市场的依赖程度

根据申请人提供的数据和经核实的海关数据，在反倾销措施实施期间，由于国内消费规模小且呈下降趋势，俄罗斯环氧氯丙烷对国外市场的出口量占总产量的比例平均为65%左右，对国外市场的依赖程度较高。

3. 对中国出口情况

根据中国海关统计数据，2006 ~ 2010 年，俄罗斯环氧氯丙烷对华出口数量和占进口总量比重总体呈下降趋势，但2010年占进口总量的比重有所反弹，对华出口量占其总出口量的比重较高。为了保持对中国出口，俄罗斯出口商改变了出口贸易方式，加工贸易占俄罗斯环氧氯丙烷对中国出口数量的比例从2006年的53.25%上升至2010年的95.05%。

反倾销措施实施后，俄罗斯环氧氯丙烷对华出口价格总体呈下降趋势，这不仅与主要原材料丙烯的价格总体上升的走势相反，而且如上文所述，俄罗斯环氧氯丙烷对华出口价格仍然属于倾销价格。

4. 对第三国(地区)出口情况

根据申请人提供的数据，2010年俄罗斯环氧氯丙烷生产商、出口商同时向除中国以外的其他国家(地区)低价出口环氧氯丙烷产品。2010年俄罗斯向除中国以外的其他国家(地区)低价出口环氧氯丙烷产品数量合计为4310吨，占同期其环氧氯丙烷对第三国总出口量的比例为100.00%，说明其低价寻求国外市场的需求较强。如果终止反倾销措施，该情形可能发生在对中国的出口中。

综合上述调查分析，俄罗斯国内环氧氯丙烷产能大，出口能力强，国内消费呈不断萎缩态势，对国际市场依赖程度高，没有证据表明上述情况会发生变化。此外，俄罗斯大量低价向第三国(地区)出口环氧氯丙烷，说明其低价寻求国外市场的需求较强。在全球环氧氯丙烷产能严重过剩、除中国外其他消费市场需求低迷的情况下，中国作为环氧氯丙烷需求增长迅速且潜力大的国家，可能成为俄罗斯环氧氯丙烷对外出口的主要目标市场。在采取反倾销措施的情况下，倾销调查期内，俄罗斯环氧氯丙烷对中国出口仍然存在倾销。如果终止原反倾销措施，其可能会加大低价倾销的力度。综上所述，如果终止原反倾销措施，俄罗斯环氧氯丙烷对中国的倾销可能继续发生。

(三)倾销调查结论。

如果终止原反倾销措施，原产于美国、韩国、日本和俄罗斯的进口环氧氯丙烷对中国的倾销有可能继续发生。

七、损害继续或再度发生的可能性

依据《反倾销条例》第五十一条、第二十一条和《反倾销产业损害调查规定》第三十三条的规定，调查机关根据已经获得的事实和可获得的最佳信息，对如果终止反倾销措施，国内产业损害再度发生的可能性进行了审查。

(一)调查期内国内产业状况。

根据《反倾销条例》第七、八条及《反倾销产业损害调查规定》第四、五、六、七条规定，调查机关对调查期内国内产业的相关经济因素和指标进行了调查。证据显示：

1. 表观消费量

调查期内，国内环氧氯丙烷产业的表观消费量呈逐年增长趋势。2006年、2007年、2008年、2009年、2010年，国内环氧氯丙烷产业的表观消费量分别为25.47万吨、32.37万吨、33.76万吨、34.29万吨和42.44万吨。

2007年比2006年增长27.09%，2008年比2007年增长4.29%，2009年比2008年增长1.57%，2010年比2009年增长23.77%。

2. 产能

调查期内，国内环氧氯丙烷产业的生产能力逐年增长。2006年、2007年、2008年、2009年、2010年，国内环氧氯丙烷产业的生产能力分别为9.87万吨、18.53万吨、29.20万吨、33.20万吨和37.20万吨。

2007年比2006年增长87.84%，2008年比2007年增长57.55%，2009年比2008年增长13.70%，2010年比2009年增长12.05%。

3. 产量

调查期内，国内同类产品产量呈逐年上升趋势。2006年、2007年、2008年、2009年、2010年，国内同类产品产量分别为6.54万吨、12.94万吨、18.10万吨、21.26万吨和24.04万吨。

2007年比2006年增长98.02%，2008年比2007年增长39.81%，2009年比2008年增长17.45%，2010年比2009年增长13.09%。

4. 开工率

调查期内，国内环氧氯丙烷产业开工率呈总体下降趋势。2006年、2007年、2008年、2009年、2010年，国内环氧氯丙烷产业开工率分别为66.25%、69.84%、61.98%、64.02%和64.62%。

2007年比2006年增长3.59个百分点，2008年比2007年下降7.87个百分点，2009年比2008年增长2.05个百分点，2010年比2009年增长0.60个百分点。

5. 销售量

调查期内，国内同类产品销售量呈逐年上升趋势。2006年、2007年、2008年、2009年、2010年，国内同类产品销售量分别为63598吨、122330吨、173985吨、214038吨和228521吨。

2007年比2006年增长92.35%，2008年比2007年增长42.23%，2009年比2008年增长23.02%，2010年比2009年增长6.77%。

6. 市场份额

调查期内，国内同类产品市场份额总体呈现上升趋势。2006年、2007年、2008年、2009年、2010年，国内同类产品市场份额分别为24.97%、37.79%、51.54%、62.42%和53.85%。

2007年比2006年上升12.82个百分点，2008年比2007年上升13.74个百分点，2009年比2008年上升10.88个百分点，2010年比2009年下降8.57个百分点。

7. 销售价格

调查期内，国内同类产品销售价格总体呈下降趋势。2006年、2007年、2008年、2009年、2010年，国内同类产品销售价格分别为18881.35元/吨、14334.38元/吨、11081.40元/吨、8108.29元/吨和12468.95元/吨。

2007年比2006年下降24.08%，2008年比2007年下降22.69%，2009年比2008年下降26.83%，2010年比2009年上升53.78%。

8. 销售收入

调查期内，国内环氧氯丙烷产业销售收入总体呈现上升趋势。2006年、2007年、2008年、2009年、2010年，国内环氧氯丙烷产业销售收入分别为12.01亿元、17.54亿元、19.28亿元、17.35亿元和28.49亿元。

2007年比2006年增长46.03%，2008年比2007年增长9.95%，2009年比2008年下降9.99%，2010年比2009年上升64.19%。

9. 税前利润

调查期内，国内环氧氯丙烷产业税前利润总体呈大幅下降趋势，甚至出现亏损。2006年、2007年、2008年、2009年、2010年，国内环氧氯丙烷产业税前利润分别为2.96亿元、2.29亿元、亏损2.93亿元、亏损2.78亿元和亏损0.12亿元。

2007年比2006年下降22.88%，2008年出现亏损，2009年比2008年减少亏损4.88%，2010年比2009年减亏95.63%。

10. 投资收益率

调查期内，国内环氧氯丙烷产业投资收益率总体呈现大幅下降趋势。2006年、2007年、2008年、2009年、2010年，国内环氧氯丙烷产业投资收益率分别为54.59%、18.56%、-18.96%、-20.20%、和-0.73%。

2007年比2006年下降36.03个百分点，2008年比2007年下降37.52个百分点，2009年比2008年下降1.24个百分点，2010年比2009年上升19.47个百分点。

11. 就业人数

调查期内，国内环氧氯丙烷产业就业人数呈逐年上升趋势。2006年、2007年、2008年、2009年、2010年，国内环氧氯丙烷产业就业人数分别为735人、1542人、1790人、1837人和2145人。

2007 年比 2006 年上升 109.80%，2008 年比 2007 年上升 16.08%，2009 年比 2008 年上升 2.63%，2010 年比 2009 年上升 16.77%。

12. 劳动生产率

调查期内，国内环氧氯丙烷产业劳动生产率总体呈上升趋势。2006 年、2007 年、2008 年、2009 年、2010 年，国内环氧氯丙烷产业劳动生产率分别为 88.91 吨/人、83.95 吨/人、101.10 吨/人、115.69 吨/人和 112.06 吨/人。

2007 年比 2006 年下降 5.58%，2008 年比 2007 年上升 20.43%，2009 年比 2008 年上升 14.43%，2010 年比 2009 年下降 3.14%。

13. 人均工资

调查期内，国内环氧氯丙烷产业人均工资总体呈上升趋势。2006 年、2007 年、2008 年、2009 年、2010 年，国内环氧氯丙烷产业人均工资分别为 21746.59 元、21953.35 元、21652.85 元、23886.33 元和 28355.25 元。

2007 年比 2006 年上升 0.95%，2008 年比 2007 年下降 1.37%，2009 年比 2008 年上升 10.31%，2010 年比 2009 年上升 18.71%。

14. 期末库存

调查期内，国内同类产品期末库存总体呈大幅增加趋势。2006 年、2007 年、2008 年、2009 年、2010 年，国内同类产品期末库存分别为 2521 吨、8093 吨、11520 吨、7826 吨和 11009 吨。

2007 年比 2006 年增加 221.02%，2008 年比 2007 年增加 42.34%，2009 年比 2008 年减少 32.06%，2010 年比 2009 年增加 40.67%。

15. 现金净流量

调查期内，国内同类产品经营活动产生的现金净流量呈现波动且总体下降趋势。2006 年、2007 年国内同类产品现金净流量为现金净流入 2.05 亿元和 1.19 亿元。2007 年比 2006 年下降 41.95%；2008 年、2009 年国内同类产品现金净流量为现金净流出 1.13 亿元和 3.02 亿元，2009 年比 2008 年下降 167.26%；2010 年国内同类产品现金净流量为现金净流入 0.67 亿元。

16. 投融资能力

调查期内，虽然国内产业产能不断扩大，但同类产品税前利润逐年大幅下降，2008 年至 2010 年处于亏损状态，对资金的回收及下一步投融资活动产生不利影响。

上述证据表明，调查期内，由于实施环氧氯丙烷反倾销措施，原产于美国、韩国、日本和俄罗斯的进口环氧氯丙烷对国内的倾销行为受到一定的遏制。同时，国内环氧氯丙烷市场需求持续增长，2010 年比 2006 年增长了 66.63%。国内环氧氯丙烷产业陆续新建和扩建了一批生产装置，国内产业生产能力得到明显提高，国内产业同类产品产量、销售量均有较大幅度的增长，国内环氧氯丙烷市场份额总体呈现上升趋势，2010 年比 2006 年上升了 28.88 个百分点。国内环氧氯丙烷销售收入、就业人数、人均工资、劳动生产率等经济指标出现了不同程度的好转。与此同时，调查期内，由于国内同类产品的销售价格逐年下降，导致国内产业税前利润总体呈大幅下降趋势，由 2006 年盈利 2.96 亿元，下降至 2010 年亏损 0.12 亿元，其中，2008 年和 2009 年亏损分别达到 2.93 亿元和 2.78 亿元。国内环氧氯丙烷产业投资收益率也相应呈现总体大幅下降趋势。国内环氧氯丙烷产品期末库存大幅增加，2010 年比 2006 年增加了 336.69%，产品积压严重。此外，调查期内，国内环氧氯丙烷产业新建和扩建的生产装置投入了大量的资金，企业效益下降导致企业偿贷压力增加。

因此，调查期内，由于实施环氧氯丙烷反倾销措施，使原产于美国、韩国、日本和俄罗斯的进口环氧氯丙烷对国内的倾销行为受到一定的遏制。国内环氧氯丙烷市场环境有所改善，国内环氧氯丙烷产业得到初步恢复和发展，但仍然容易受到低价进口产品的冲击和影响。

(二)损害再度发生的可能性。

1. 国内环氧氯丙烷市场状况

国内环氧氯丙烷产业开始于二十世纪六十年代，二十世纪九十年代以来，国内多家生产企业陆续引进国外先进生产技术和生产装置生产环氧氯丙烷产品。由于环氧氯丙烷的生产技术较为复杂，且装置所需的前期投资巨大，国内环氧氯丙烷产业的发展滞后于国内市场需求的增长。自 2000 年以来，来自美国、韩国、日本和俄罗斯的进口环氧氯丙烷产品大量向中国市场倾销，给国内环氧氯丙烷产业造成了严重的实质损害。2006 年 6 月 28 日，商务部决定对美国、韩国、日本和俄罗斯向中国出口的环氧氯丙烷产品征收反倾销税，使得被调查产品的倾销行为得到一定程度的遏制，国内环氧氯丙烷市场环境得到改善。

调查期内，随着中国经济的快速发展，带动了下游环氧树脂等行业及相关应用领域的进一步拓展，国内环氧氯丙烷产品市场需求持续增长，2006 年至 2010 年，国内环氧氯丙烷年均表观消费量呈现持续增长趋势。2007 年比 2006 年增长 27.09%，2008 年比 2007 年增长 4.29%，2009 年比 2008 年增长

1.57%，2010年比2009年增长23.77%。预计2012年国内环氧氯丙烷表观消费量将达到55万吨左右。与此同时，国内产业投入资金建设新产能，以适应快速增长的国内需求。预计在未来几年内，随着国内环氧氯丙烷市场需求的增长，国内环氧氯丙烷的产能也将相应地稳步增长。届时，国内环氧氯丙烷的供应将完全能够满足国内市场需求。

2. 被调查产品进口数量增加的可能性

调查期内，被调查产品之间及被调查产品与同类产品之间在物理和化学特性、生产工艺流程、产品用途、销售渠道和客户群体、产品可替代性、消费者和生产者评价等方面基本相同，在国内市场上存在相互竞争关系，而且竞争条件基本相同。

根据《反倾销条例》第九条和《反倾销产业损害调查规定》第十五条、第十六条的规定，调查机关认定，调查期内，就被调查产品对国内产业造成的影响进行累积评估是适当的。

环氧氯丙烷原审调查期内，美国、韩国、日本和俄罗斯向中国大量低价出口环氧氯丙烷，出口数量及占国内环氧氯丙烷市场份额均呈大幅上升趋势。

根据中国海关统计，调查期内，被调查产品进口数量呈下降趋势。2006年至2010年，被调查产品进口数量分别为12.01万吨、5.97万吨、5.72万吨、4.12万吨和2.21万吨，2007年比2006年下降了50.28%，2008年比2007年下降了4.16%，2009年比2008年下降了27.97%，2010年比2009年下降了46.40%。

调查期内，被调查产品占国内市场份额呈下降趋势，分别为47.16%、18.45%、16.95%、12.02%和5.21%。2007年比2006年下降了28.71个百分点，2008年比2007年下降了1.5个百分点，2009年比2008年下降了4.93个百分点，2010年比2009年下降了6.81个百分点。

调查期内，被调查产品进口数量占中国环氧氯丙烷总进口量的比例总体呈下降趋势，分别为82.59%、74.41%、88.75%、72.81%和51.66%。2007年比2006年下降了8.18个百分点，2008年比2007年上升了14.34个百分点，2009年比2008年下降了15.94个百分点，2010年比2009年下降了21.15个百分点。上述证据表明，与原审调查期相比，2006年至2010年，尽管原产于美国、韩国、日本和俄罗斯的被调查产品进口数量总体有所下降，但被调查产品进口数量占中国总进口量的比例一直保持在较高水平，上述四国仍是中国环氧氯丙烷的主要进口来源。

(1)美国

本案申请人提供的数据显示，调查期内，美国环氧氯丙烷产能基本保持稳定，2006年至2010年，美国环氧氯丙烷产能均保持在46万吨。2006年至2010年，美国环氧氯丙烷产量呈总体下降趋势，分别为36.21万吨、32.51万吨、29.27万吨、23.74万吨和27.84万吨。调查期内，美国环氧氯丙烷产业闲置产能总体呈快速增长趋势。2006年到2010年闲置产能分别为9.79万吨、13.49万吨、16.73万吨、22.26万吨和18.16万吨，闲置产能占当年产能的比例分别为21.28%、29.33%、36.37%、48.39%和39.48%。以上数据表明，调查期内，美国环氧氯丙烷闲置产能一直保持在较高水平且总体呈快速增长趋势。

2006年至2010年，美国环氧氯丙烷消费量基本稳定，分别为23.60万吨、24.30万吨、22.70万吨、21.50万吨和23.70万吨。2006年至2010年，美国环氧氯丙烷可供出口的能力一直保持在较高水平，分别为22.40万吨、21.70万吨、23.30万吨、24.50万吨和22.30万吨，占其同期产能的比例分别为48.70%、47.17%、50.65%、53.26%和48.48%。上述数据表明，在调查期内，虽然美国环氧氯丙烷产业产能和消费量比较稳定，但却严重供大于求，产能远大于消费量，导致其可供出口的产能一直维持在较高水平，具有较强的出口能力。

本案申请人提供的数据显示，2006年至2010年，美国环氧氯丙烷出口数量总体呈下降趋势，分别为13.52万吨、9.55万吨、8.19万吨、4.27万吨和6.14万吨。2006年至2010年，美国环氧氯丙烷出口数量占其产量的比例分别为37.34%、29.38%、27.98%、17.99%和22.05%。上述数据表明，2006年至2010年，虽然美国环氧氯丙烷出口数量呈下降趋势，但其出口数量占其产量的比例一直维持在较高水平，美国环氧氯丙烷对国外市场的依赖程度较强，对外出口仍是美国环氧氯丙烷产业销售产品的重要渠道。

根据中国海关统计，2006年至2010年，美国环氧氯丙烷产品对中国出口数量分别为5.87万吨、2.25万吨、2.41万吨、1.26万吨和0.44万吨。2006年至2010年，美国环氧氯丙烷对中国出口数量占同期中国环氧氯丙烷总进口量的比例分别为40.38%、28.09%、37.33%、22.26%和10.24%。美国环氧氯丙烷对中国出口数量占其总出口量的比例分别为43.42%、23.56%、29.43%、29.51%和7.17%。上述数据表明，调查期内，美国环氧氯丙烷对中国出口数量虽然呈下降趋势，但其占中国总进口量的比例一直较高，是向中国出口环氧氯丙烷的主要国家，其对中国出口量占当年总出口量的比例也较高，年均比例为26.62%，中国仍然是美国环氧氯丙烷对外出口的重要市场。

上述证据表明，调查期内，虽然美国环氧氯丙烷市场消费量和产能基本稳定，但美国环氧氯丙烷产业有较高的闲置产能和较强的出口能力，对国外市场的依赖程度也很高。随着中国国内市场需求的持续增加，中国仍将是美国环氧氯丙烷对外出口的重要市场。如果终止原反倾销措施，美国环氧氯丙烷产品对中国的出口数量将可能大量增加。

(2)韩国

本案申请人提供的数据显示，调查期内，韩国环氧氯丙烷产能保持相对稳定，2006年至2010年，韩国环氧氯丙烷产能一直保持在6.8万吨。2006年至2010年，韩国环氧氯丙烷产量总体呈下降趋势，分别为6.15万吨、5.95万吨、5.75万吨、5.50万吨和5.55万吨。调查期内，韩国环氧氯丙烷闲置产能总体呈增长趋势。2006年到2010年闲置产能分别为0.65万吨、0.85万吨、1.05万吨、1.30万吨和1.25万吨，闲置产能占当年产能的比例分别为9.56%、12.50%、15.44%、19.12%和18.38%。以上数据表明，调查期内，韩国环氧氯丙烷闲置产能保持在较高水平。

2006年至2010年，韩国环氧氯丙烷消费量分别为6.32万吨、6.08万吨、6.33万吨、5.86万吨和5.90万吨，总体呈下降趋势。2006年至2010年，韩国环氧氯丙烷可供出口的能力呈增长趋势，分别为0.48万吨、0.72万吨、0.47万吨、0.94万吨和0.90万吨，占其同期产能的比例分别为7.06%、10.59%、6.91% 、13.82%和13.24%。上述数据表明，在调查期内，韩国环氧氯丙烷产业具有较强的出口能力。

本案申请人提供的数据显示，2006年至2010年，韩国环氧氯丙烷出口数量呈先升后降趋势，分别为2.11万吨、2.89万吨、1.82万吨、2.23万吨和1.01万吨。2006年至2010年，韩国环氧氯丙烷出口数量占其产量的比例分别为34.31%、48.57%、31.65%、40.55%和18.20%。上述数据表明，2006年至2010年，尽管韩国环氧氯丙烷出口数量总体呈下降趋势，但其环氧氯丙烷出口数量占其产量的比例较高，对国外市场的依赖程度仍然较高，对外出口仍是韩国环氧氯丙烷产业消化其过剩产量的重要方式。

根据中国海关统计，2006年至2010年，韩国环氧氯丙烷产品对中国出口数量分别为1.53万吨、1.25万吨、1.24万吨、1.30万吨和0.47万吨。2006年至2010年，韩国环氧氯丙烷对中国出口数量占同期中国环氧氯丙烷总进口量的比例分别为10.52%、15.54%、19.20%、22.96%和11.10%。韩国环氧氯丙烷对中国出口数量占其总出口量的比例分别为72.51%、43.25%、68.13%、58.30%和46.53%。上述数据表明，调查期内，韩国环氧氯丙烷对中国出口数量虽然总体呈下降趋势，但其对中国出口量占当年总出口量的比例一直维持在较高水平，且其对中国出口数量占同期中国环氧氯丙烷总进口量的比例也较大，中国仍然是韩国环氧氯丙烷对外出口的重要市场。

上述证据表明，调查期内，韩国环氧氯丙烷消费市场持续低迷，消费量总体呈下降趋势，韩国环氧氯丙烷产业有较高的闲置产能，拥有较强的出口能力，对国外市场的依赖程度也较高。随着中国国内市场需求的持续增加，中国仍将成为韩国消化其过剩产能和产量的重要市场。如果终止原反倾销措施，韩国对中国出口环氧氯丙烷的数量将可能大量增加。

(3)日本

本案申请人提供的数据显示，调查期内，日本环氧氯丙烷产能基本保持稳定，2006年日本环氧氯丙烷产能为11.5万吨，2007年至2010年，日本环氧氯丙烷产能均保持在12.1万吨。2006年至2010年，日本环氧氯丙烷产量呈快速下降趋势，分别为11.01万吨、11.13万吨、10.70万吨、7.57万吨和7.54万吨。调查期内，日本环氧氯丙烷产业闲置产能相应呈快速增长趋势。2006年到2010年闲置产能分别为0.49万吨、0.97万吨、1.40万吨、4.53万吨和4.56万吨，闲置产能占当年产能的比例分别为4.26%、8.02%、11.57%、37.44%和37.69%。以上数据表明，调查期内，日本环氧氯丙烷闲置产能增长到了较高水平。

2006年至2010年，日本环氧氯丙烷消费量快速下降，分别为11.21万吨、11.60万吨、10.95万吨、6.72万吨和6.73万吨。2006年至2010年，日本环氧氯丙烷可供出口的能力呈快速增长趋势，分别为0.29万吨、0.50万吨、1.15万吨、5.38万吨和5.37万吨，占其同期产能的比例分别为2.52%、4.13%、9.50%、44.46%和44.38%。上述数据表明，在调查期内，日本环氧氯丙烷产业的出口能力快速增加，其占产能的比例在2009年以后维持在40%以上，具有较强的出口能力。

本案申请人提供的数据显示，2006年至2010年，日本环氧氯丙烷出口数量呈上升趋势，分别为1.67万吨、1.25万吨、1.66万吨、1.88万吨和2.29

万吨。2006年至2010年，日本环氧氯丙烷出口数量占其产量的比例分别为15.17%、11.23%、15.51%、24.83%和30.37%。上述数据表明，2006年至2010年，日本环氧氯丙烷出口数量总体增加，其出口数量占其产量的比例总体增加，日本环氧氯丙烷对国外市场的依赖程度总体增强，对外出口是日本环氧氯丙烷产业销售产品的重要渠道。

根据中国海关统计，2006年至2010年，日本环氧氯丙烷产品对中国出口数量分别为0.84万吨、0.35万吨、0.69万吨、0.45万吨和0.25万吨。2006年至2010年，日本环氧氯丙烷对中国出口数量占同期中国环氧氯丙烷总进口量的比例分别为5.77%、4.35%、10.66%、7.87%和5.76%。日本环氧氯丙烷对中国出口数量占其总出口量的比例分别为50.30%、28.00%、41.57%、23.94%和10.92%。上述数据表明，调查期内，日本环氧氯丙烷对中国出口数量虽然总体呈下降趋势，但其对中国出口量占当年总出口量的比例一直维持在较高水平，中国是日本被调查产品对外出口的重要市场。

上述证据表明，调查期内，日本环氧氯丙烷市场消费量快速下降，日本环氧氯丙烷产业有较大的闲置产能，出口能力不断增强，对国外市场的依赖程度也很高。随着中国国内市场需求的持续增加，中国仍将成为日本消化其过剩产能和产量的重要市场。如果终止原反倾销措施，日本对中国出口环氧氯丙烷的数量将可能大量增加。

(4)俄罗斯

据本案申请人提供的数据显示，调查期内，俄罗斯环氧氯丙烷产能保持相对稳定。2006年至2010年俄罗斯环氧氯丙烷生产能力均为9.6万吨。2006年至2010年，俄罗斯环氧氯丙烷产量总体呈下降趋势，分别为7.29万吨、7.35万吨、7.30万吨、5.70万吨和6.10万吨。调查期内，俄罗斯环氧氯丙烷闲置产能总体呈增长趋势。2006年到2010年闲置产能分别为2.31万吨、2.25万吨、2.30万吨、3.90万吨和3.50万吨，闲置产能占当年产能的比例分别为24.06%、23.44%、23.96%、40.62%和36.46%。俄罗斯环氧氯丙烷闲置产能较大。

调查期内，俄罗斯环氧氯丙烷消费量呈下降趋势，2006年至2010年分别为1.23万吨、1.21万吨、1.38万吨、1.10万吨和1.12万吨。2006年至2010年，俄罗斯环氧氯丙烷可供出口的能力呈增长趋势，分别为8.37万吨、8.39万吨、8.22万吨、8.50万吨和8.48万吨，占其同期产能的比例分别为87.19%、87.40%、85.63%、88.54%和88.31%。上述数据表明，在调查期内，俄罗斯环氧氯丙烷产业出口能力占其产能的比例均在80%以上，具有很强的出口能力。

2006年至2010年，俄罗斯环氧氯丙烷出口数量总体呈下降趋势，分别为6.06万吨、6.14万吨、5.92万吨、3.34万吨和1.08万吨，2006年至2010年，俄罗斯环氧氯丙烷出口数量占其总产量的比例分别为83.13%、83.54%、81.10%、58.60%和17.70%。俄罗斯环氧氯丙烷对国外市场的依赖程度高，对外出口仍是俄罗斯环氧氯丙烷企业销售产品的重要方式。

根据中国海关统计提供的数据，2006年至2010年，俄罗斯环氧氯丙烷对中国出口数量呈下降趋势，分别为3.77万吨、2.12万吨、1.39万吨、1.12万吨和1.05万吨。2006年至2010年，俄罗斯环氧氯丙烷对中国出口数量占同期中国环氧氯丙烷总进口量的比例分别为25.92%、26.44%、21.55%、19.72%、和24.56%，俄罗斯环氧氯丙烷对中国出口数量占其总出口量的比例分别为62.21%、34.53%、23.48%、33.53%和97.22%。上述数据表明，2006年至2010年，尽管俄罗斯环氧氯丙烷对中国出口数量呈下降趋势，但其对中国出口数量占其总出口量的比例保持在较高水平，2010年达到97.22%，中国是俄罗斯环氧氯丙烷的主要出口国。

上述证据表明，调查期内，俄罗斯环氧氯丙烷产业有较大的闲置产能，及较强的出口能力，对国外市场的依赖程度也较高，中国是其主要的出口国。如果终止原反倾销措施，俄罗斯对中国出口环氧氯丙烷的数量将可能大量增加。

上述证据表明，美国、韩国、日本和俄罗斯环氧氯丙烷市场供大于求，产能过剩，闲置产能较高，拥有较大的出口能力，对国外市场的依赖度高。近年来中国环氧氯丙烷市场需求总体保持较快增长，中国是上述四国环氧氯丙烷对外出口的重要市场，如果终止反倾销措施，上述四国对中国环氧氯丙烷的出口数量将可能大量增加。

(三)被调查产品对国内同类产品价格的影响。

调查期内，被调查产品对国内的倾销行为虽然受到一定程度的遏制，但被调查产品进口价格仍然较低，且先降后升趋势，总体呈下降趋势。2006年至2010年，原产于美国、韩国、日本和俄罗斯的被调查产品进口完关税后价格分别为16631.87元/吨、15761.56元/吨、14237.16元/吨、8065.01元/吨和13737.76元/吨。

调查期内，国内产业同类产品的价格先降后升，总体呈下降趋势，其中，2007年比2006年下降

24.08%，2008年比2007年下降22.69%，2009年比2008年下降26.83%，2010年的价格虽比上年上升53.78%，但仍比2006年下降33.96%。

上述数据表明，调查期内，国内产业同类产品的价格与被调查产品进口价格走势基本一致。2006年到2009年，被调查产品进口价格出现持续下降，受其影响，同期国内产业同类产品的价格出现快速下降；由2006年的18881.35元/吨迅速下降至2009年的8108.29元/吨。2010年，被调查产品进口价格有所上升，国内同类产品价格相应回升，但仍低于2006年、2007年的价格水平。国内产业同类产品对被调查产品进口价格变动敏感，容易受到被调查产品进口价格变化的影响。

上述证据表明如果终止反倾销措施，原产于美国、韩国、日本和俄罗斯的被调查产品有可能大量进入中国市场，被调查产品的价格存在进一步下降的可能性，国内产业将进一步受到被调查产品的影响，国内产业同类产品价格存在进一步下降的可能性。

(四)产业损害调查结论。

1. 调查期内，由于实施环氧氯丙烷反倾销措施，原产于美国、韩国、日本和俄罗斯的进口环氧氯丙烷对中国的倾销行为得到一定遏制，国内环氧氯丙烷产业生产经营状况有所改善，国内环氧氯丙烷产业得到了初步恢复和发展。

2. 国内环氧氯丙烷产业仍然很脆弱。国内产业同类产品对进口产品的数量和价格变化反应敏感，国内产业容易受到低价进口产品的冲击和影响。

3. 美国、韩国、日本和俄罗斯环氧氯丙烷闲置产能较大，对国外市场的依赖程度较高，而中国是上述四国环氧氯丙烷对外出口的主要市场。在全球环氧氯丙烷消费市场需求进一步低迷甚至萎缩的情况下，中国市场需求的增长对被调查国家来说具有较大的吸引力。如果终止反倾销措施，被调查产品对中国的出口数量将可能大量增加。

4. 如果终止反倾销措施，被调查产品向中国的出口价格有可能大幅下降，中国国内同类产品的价格有可能进一步下降，对国内环氧氯丙烷产业造成的损害可能再度发生。

八、复审裁定

根据以上调查，调查机关裁定如下：

如果终止原反倾销措施，原产于美国、韩国、日本和俄罗斯的进口环氧氯丙烷对中国的倾销有可能继续发生，对中国国内产业造成的损害可能再度发生。

(注：主要用途是用于制环氧树脂，也是一种含氧物质的稳定剂和化学中间体、环氧基及苯氧基树脂的主要原料；制造甘油、熟化丙烯基橡胶、纤维素酯及醚之溶剂等。)

三十三、中华人民共和国商务部 公告2012年第42号 关于原产于美国和欧盟的进口乙二醇和二甘醇的单丁醚反倾销调查初裁的公告(二〇一二年七月二十七日)

根据《中华人民共和国反倾销条例》(以下简称《反倾销条例》)的规定，商务部(以下称调查机关)于2011年11月18日正式发布立案公告，决定对原产于美国和欧盟的进口乙二醇和二甘醇的单丁醚(以下称被调查产品)进行反倾销立案调查。该被调查产品归在《中华人民共和国进出口税则》税则号：29094300。

调查机关对被调查产品是否存在倾销及倾销幅度、国内乙二醇和二甘醇的单丁醚产业是否受到损害及损害程度、以及倾销与损害之间的因果关系进行了调查。根据调查结果和《反倾销条例》第二十四条的规定，调查机关作出初步裁定(见附件)，并就有关事项公告如下：

一、初步裁定

调查机关初步裁定，在本案调查期内，原产于美国和欧盟的进口被调查产品存在倾销，中国乙二醇和二甘醇的单丁醚产业受到了实质损害，而且倾销与实质损害之间存在因果关系。

二、征收保证金

根据《反倾销条例》第二十八条和二十九条的规定，调查机关决定采用保证金形式实施临时反倾销措施。自2012年7月28日起，进口经营者在进口原产于美国和欧盟的被调查产品时，应依据本初裁决定所确定的各公司的倾销幅度向中华人民共和国海关提供相应的保证金。

本案征收保证金的产品归在《中华人民共和国进出口税则》：29094300，具体描述如下：

调查范围：原产于美国和欧盟的进口乙二醇和二甘醇的单丁醚。

被调查产品名称：乙二醇和二甘醇的单丁醚，英文名称：Ethylene Glycol Monobutyl Ether(乙二醇的单丁醚)，Diethylene Glycol Monobutyl Ether(二甘醇的单丁醚)。

分子式：乙二醇的单丁醚：$C_6H_{14}O_2$

二甘醇的单丁醚：$C_8H_{18}O_3$

化学结构式：

乙二醇的单丁醚：(略)

二甘醇的单丁醚：(略)

物理化学特征：

乙二醇的单丁醚：无色透明液体，微有香味，接触明火、高热和强氧化剂有燃烧的危险。能溶于水、乙醇、丙酮、苯等有机溶剂，低毒。能溶解油脂、天然树脂、硝基纤维素等。

二甘醇的单丁醚：无色透明液体，微有香味，接触明火、高热和强氧化剂有燃烧的危险。能溶于水、乙醇、丙酮、苯等有机溶剂，低毒。能溶解油脂、天然树脂、硝基纤维素等。

主要用途：乙二醇和二甘醇的单丁醚是广泛应用于水基涂料中的溶剂，也是硝化纤维素、醇酸树脂和用顺酐改性的酚醛树脂的溶剂。一般用做涂料特别是硝基喷漆，可以防雾、防皱，提高涂膜的光泽性和流动性；也用作金属清洗剂，脱漆剂，脱润滑油剂，汽车引擎洗涤剂，干洗溶剂，环氧树脂溶剂，药物萃取剂，农药分散剂，印刷油墨、切削油和纤维油剂的油分散互溶剂；也用作硝化纤维素、清漆、印刷油墨、图章用印台油墨、油脂和树脂等的溶剂，乳胶漆的稳定剂，飞机涂料的蒸发抑制剂，高温烘烤瓷漆的表面加工改进剂。

对各公司征收的保证金比率如下：

美国公司

1. 伊士曼化工公司

(Eastman Chemical Company) 10.1%

2. 陶氏化学公司

(The Dow Chemical Company) 12.5%

3. 益科斯达化工产品有限公司

(Equistar Chemicals, LP) 11.5%

4. 其他美国公司

(All others) 15.1%

欧盟公司

1. 沙索德国有限责任公司

(Sasol Germany GmbH)

沙索溶剂德国有限责任公司

(Sasol Solvents Germany GmbH) 13.0%

2. 英力士化学拉瓦拉有限公司

(INEOS Chemicals Lavera SAS) 9.3%

3. 巴斯夫欧洲公司

(BASF SE)18.8%

4. 其他欧盟公司

(All others) 14.9%

三、征收保证金的方法

自2012年7月28日起，进口经营者在进口原产于美国和欧盟的被调查产品时，应依据本初裁决定所确定的各公司的倾销幅度向中华人民共和国海关提供相应的保证金。保证金以海关审定的完税价格从价计征，计算公式为：保证金金额 =（海关审定的完税价格 × 保证金征收比率）×（1 + 进口环节增值税税率）。

四、评论

各利害关系方在本公告发布之日起20天内，可向调查机关提出书面评论并附相关证据，调查机关将依法予以考虑。

附件：中华人民共和国商务部对原产于美国和欧盟的进口乙二醇和二甘醇的单丁醚反倾销调查的初步裁定

根据《中华人民共和国反倾销条例》（以下简称《反倾销条例》）的规定，商务部（以下称调查机关）于2011年11月18日正式发布立案公告（商务部公告2011年第83号），决定对原产于美国和欧盟的进口乙二醇和二甘醇的单丁醚（以下称被调查产品）进行反倾销立案调查。该被调查产品归在《中华人民共和国进出口税则》税则号：29094300。

调查机关对被调查产品是否存在倾销及倾销幅度、国内产业是否受到损害及损害程度以及倾销与损害之间的因果关系进行了调查，初步调查结论如下：

一、调查程序

（一）立案及立案通知。

1. 立案

2011年10月8日，调查机关收到德纳（南京）化工有限公司代表国内乙二醇和二甘醇的单丁醚产业提交的反倾销调查申请，申请人请求对原产于美国和欧盟的进口乙二醇和二甘醇的单丁醚进行反倾销调查。

经审查，调查机关认为申请人符合《反倾销条例》第十一条、第十三条和第十七条有关中国产业提出反倾销调查申请的规定。同时，申请书中包含了《反倾销条例》第十四条、第十五条规定的反倾销调查立案所要求的内容及有关证据。

根据上述审查结果及《反倾销条例》第十六条的规定，调查机关于2011年11月18日发布立案公告，决定对原产于美国和欧盟的进口乙二醇和二甘醇的单丁醚进行反倾销立案调查。调查机关确定的倾销调查期为2010年7月1日至2011年6月30日，产业损害调查期为2009年7月1日至2011年6月30日。

2. 立案通知

在决定立案调查前，根据《反倾销条例》第十六条规定，调查机关就收到中国乙二醇和二甘醇的单丁醚产业反倾销调查申请书一事通知了美国驻中国大使馆和欧洲联盟欧洲委员会驻中国及蒙古国代表团。

2011年11月18日，调查机关发布立案公告，并向美国驻中国大使馆和欧洲联盟欧洲委员会驻中国及蒙古国代表团正式提供了立案公告和申请书的公开文本，请其通知其所在国家(地区)的相关出口商和生产商。同日，调查机关将本案立案情况通知了本案申请人及申请书中列明的美国和欧盟生产商、出口商。

(二)倾销及倾销幅度的初步调查。

1. 登记应诉

根据公告要求，自公告发布之日起20天的登记应诉期内，被调查产品生产商/贸易商伊士曼化工公司(Eastman Chemical Company)、陶氏化学公司(The Dow Chemical Company)、美国益科斯达化工产品有限公司(Equistar Chemicals, LP)、沙索德国公司(Sasol Germany GmbH)、英力士化学拉瓦拉有限公司(INEOS Chemicals Lavera SAS)、巴斯夫欧洲公司(BASF SE)、英力士欧洲有限公司，氧化物集团(INEOS Europe AG, Division Oxide)、沙索溶剂德国有限责任公司(Sasol Solvents Germany GmbH)、沙索化工太平洋有限公司(Sasol Chemicals Pacific Ltd.)等有关公司向调查机关登记倾销应诉。

2. 企业抽样

考虑到本案登记应诉企业数量和工作量，调查机关根据《反倾销条例》第二十条和《反倾销调查抽样暂行规则》的相关规定，决定对登记应诉的生产商采用随机抽样方式进行调查。2011年12月8日，调查机关向案件各利害关系方发出通知，要求在规定时限内对有关抽样问题发表意见。在规定期间内，伊士曼化工公司、陶氏化学公司、英力士欧洲有限公司、英力士化学拉瓦拉有限公司、沙索德国公司、沙索溶剂德国有限责任公司、沙索化工太平洋有限公司、巴斯夫欧洲公司和欧洲联盟欧洲委员会驻中国及蒙古国代表团向调查机关递交了对抽样的意见。经审查，调查机关决定维持原抽样决定。

2012年12月26日，调查机关在商务部举行现场抽样会，有关利害关系方出席了抽样会。经过随机抽样，陶氏化学公司和伊士曼化工公司被确定为美国抽样选取公司，美国益科斯达化工产品有限公司为调查备选公司；沙索德国公司和巴斯夫欧洲公司被确定为欧盟抽样选取公司，英力士欧洲有限公司为调查备选公司。

由于巴斯夫欧洲公司未在规定时限内提交答卷，2012年2月1日，调查机关通知英力士欧洲有限公司，决定递补该公司为欧盟抽样选取公司。

3. 发放问卷和收取答卷

2011年12月15日，调查机关向上述抽样选取公司和备选公司发放了反倾销调查问卷，并要求其在37天内按规定提交准确、完整的答卷。在该期间内，有关应诉公司向调查机关申请延期递交答卷并陈述了相关理由。经审查，调查机关同意给予申请公司适当延期。至答卷递交截止之日，调查机关收到了美国3家应诉公司和欧盟沙索德国公司、英力士欧洲有限公司的答卷，巴斯夫欧洲公司未在规定时限内提交答卷。

2012年3月8日，调查机关针对应诉公司提交的倾销部分答卷中存在的问题，向应诉公司发放了反倾销调查补充问卷。有关应诉公司向调查机关申请延期递交答卷并陈述了相关理由。经审查，调查机关同意给予申请公司适当延期。在规定的时间内，调查机关收到了反倾销调查补充问卷的答卷。此后，调查机关还分别要求有关应诉公司对答卷有关内容进行解释澄清，在规定的时间内，调查机关收到了有关应诉公司提交的补充答卷资料。

4. 有关利害关系方发表的意见

调查期间，有关利害关系方分别就本案调查中的有关问题发表了意见。

(1)国内产业代表和有关应诉公司负责人约见调查机关，对本案调查表示关注

国内产业代表和陶氏化学公司相关负责人分别拜会了调查机关相关人员，对本案调查表示关注。

(2)乙二醇和二甘醇的单丁醚进口商致函调查机关，对本案调查表示关注

国内4家乙二醇和二甘醇的单丁醚进口商致函调查机关，对本案调查表示关注。

调查机关对以上有关利害关系方发表的意见均依法予以了考虑。

(三)产业损害及损害程度的初步调查。

1. 产业损害调查期

调查机关在立案公告中明确，本案的产业损害调查期(以下简称调查期)为2009年7月1日至2011年6月30日。

陶氏化学公司在其提交的《进口乙二醇和二甘醇的单丁醚反倾销案无损害抗辩书》中提出，2009年7月之前已存在中国国内产业，以2009年7月作为两年调查期起点的做法违反了世贸组织准则。

申请人在提交的《乙二醇和二甘醇的单丁醚反倾销案对陶氏公司无损害抗辩的评论意见》中主张，世贸组织反倾销措施委员会发布的“关于反倾销调查数据收集期间的建议”中提到损害调查的数据收集期间一般不应少于三年，但数据来源一方存在不到三年的情况除外。《反倾销产业损害调查规定》第十八条规定“反倾销案件的产业损害调查期通常为立案调查开始前的三至五年”，但不排除因特定情形对损害调查期作出调整。2009年7月之前，我国并没有规模

化生产乙二醇丁醚，也没有专门用于生产乙二醇丁醚的装置，仅仅是所有醇醚生产企业的生产装置理论上都可以切换生产乙二醇丁醚。

调查机关分析后认定，申请人提供的证据显示，申请人2009年7月建成投产的装置是国内首套规模化专门生产乙二醇和二甘醇的单丁醚的装置，因此国内产业建立时期应从2009年7月算起。本案产业损害调查期符合法律规定，也符合国内产业的实际情况。

2. 参加产业损害调查活动登记

根据《反倾销产业损害调查规定》第十九条、第二十一条的规定，2011年11月18日，调查机关发出了《关于参加乙二醇和二甘醇的单丁醚反倾销案产业损害调查活动登记的通知》(商调查函[2011]327号)。截至2011年12月8日，调查机关共收到9家利害关系方参加反倾销产业损害调查活动登记的申请，分别为：国外生产者/出口商巴斯夫欧洲公司(BASF SE)、陶氏化学公司(The Dow Chemical Company)、益科斯达化工产品有限公司(Equistar Chemicals, LP)、伊士曼化工公司(Eastman Chemical Company)、英力士欧洲有限公司，氧化物集团(INEOS Europe AG, Division Oxide)、英力士化学拉瓦拉有限公司(INEOS Chemical Lavera SAS)、沙索德国有限责任公司(Sasol Germany GmbH)、沙索溶剂德国有限责任公司(Sasol Solvents Germany GmbH)、沙索化工太平洋有限公司(Sasol Chemicals Pacific Ltd)。调查机关经审查后接受了上述利害关系方的登记。

3. 成立产业损害调查组

2011年11月30日，调查机关成立了乙二醇和二甘醇的单丁醚反倾销案产业损害调查组，负责本案的产业损害调查工作，并于当日发出《关于成立乙二醇和二甘醇的单丁醚反倾销案产业损害调查组的通知》(商调查函[2011]390号)。

4. 发放和收回调查问卷

根据《反倾销条例》第二十条和《反倾销产业损害调查规定》第二十四条、第二十五条的规定，2011年12月12日，调查机关向本案利害关系方发放了《乙二醇和二甘醇的单丁醚反倾销案产业损害调查问卷(国内进口商调查问卷)》(商调查函[2011]391号，以下简称《国内进口商调查问卷》)、《乙二醇和二甘醇的单丁醚反倾销案产业损害调查问卷(国内生产者调查问卷)》(商调查函[2011]392号，以下简称《国内生产者调查问卷》)和《乙二醇和二甘醇的单丁醚反倾销案产业损害调查问卷(国外<地区>生产者/出口商调查问卷)》(商调查函[2011]393号)，以下简称《国外<地区>生产者/出口商调查问卷》)。

2012年1月5日，沙索德国有限责任公司、沙索溶剂德国有限责任公司、沙索化工太平洋有限公司、伊士曼化工公司、英力士欧洲有限公司分别通过代理律师事务所向调查机关申请延期递交《国外<地区>生产者/出口商调查问卷答卷》。2012年1月10日，益科斯达化工产品有限公司通过代理律师事务所向调查机关申请延期递交《国外<地区>生产者/出口商调查问卷答卷》。2012年1月12日，陶氏化学公司通过代理律师事务所向调查机关申请延期递交《国外<地区>生产者/出口商调查问卷答卷》。经审查，调查机关批准了上述利害关系方的延期申请。

在调查问卷规定的回收期限或经批准延期递交的期限内，调查机关共收回了11份调查问卷答卷，包括德纳(南京)化工有限公司提交的1份《国内生产者调查问卷》答卷，巴斯夫欧洲公司、陶氏化学公司、益科斯达化工产品有限公司、伊士曼化工公司、英力士欧洲有限公司、沙索德国有限责任公司、沙索溶剂德国有限责任公司、沙索化工太平洋有限公司提交的8份《国外<地区>生产者/出口商调查问卷答卷》，浙江瓯华化工进出口有限公司、甲基贸易(上海)有限公司提交的2份《国内进口商调查问卷答卷》。

2012年5月10日，应调查机关要求，陶氏化学公司、益科斯达化工产品有限公司、英士力欧洲有限公司、沙索德国有限责任公司、沙索溶剂德国有限责任公司、沙索化工太平洋有限公司向调查机关提交了《国外<地区>生产者/出口商调查问卷补充答卷》。

2012年5月24日，应调查机关要求，伊士曼化工公司向调查机关提交了《国外<地区>生产者/出口商调查问卷补充答卷》。

5. 听取利害关系方意见陈述

2011年12月30日，调查机关收到本案申请人提交的《关于召开乙二醇和二甘醇的单丁醚反倾销案国内生产企业意见陈述会的申请》。根据《反倾销条例》第二十条的规定，调查机关于2012年1月9日发出《关于召开乙二醇和二甘醇的单丁醚反倾销案申请人意见陈述会的通知》(商调查函[2012]2号)。2012年1月16日，调查机关召开了乙二醇和二甘醇的单丁醚反倾销案申请人意见陈述会，听取申请人陈述提起申请的主要理由及对本案产业损害调查的相关意见，并于当日收到本案申请人提交的《乙二醇和二甘醇的单丁醚反倾销案申请人意见陈述会陈述意见》。

6. 接收利害关系方书面意见

2012年5月14日，沙索德国有限责任公司、沙索溶剂德国有限责任公司、沙索化工太平洋有限公司向调查机关提交了《沙索正确中英文名称》，调查机关决定采用其提供的中英文名称。

2012年5月24日，伊士曼化工公司向调查机关提交了《乙二醇和二甘醇的单丁醚反倾销案无损害抗辩书》。

2012年6月5日，陶氏化学公司向调查机关提交了《进口乙二醇和二甘醇的单丁醚反倾销案无损害抗辩书》。

2012年6月7日，南京(德纳)化工有限公司向调查机关提交了《乙二醇和二甘醇的单丁醚反倾销案对伊士曼无损害抗辩的评论意见》。(以下简称《对伊士曼无损害抗辩的评论意见》)

2012年6月18日，南京(德纳)化工有限公司向调查机关提交了《乙二醇和二甘醇的单丁醚反倾销案对陶氏公司无损害抗辩的评论意见》。(以下简称《对陶氏公司无损害抗辩的评论意见》)

2012年7月9日，沙索德国有限责任公司、沙索溶剂德国有限责任公司、沙索化工太平洋有限公司(以下简称沙索)向调查机关提交了《乙二醇和二甘醇的单丁醚反倾销案无损害抗辩意见》。

7. 初裁前实地核查

根据《反倾销条例》第二十条和《反倾销产业损害调查规定》第二十七条的规定，2012年3月2日，调查机关发出了《关于乙二醇和二甘醇的单丁醚反倾销案初裁前实地核查的通知》(商调查函[2012]59号)。2012年5月，调查机关对国内生产者德纳(南京)化工有限公司进行了初裁前实地核查。实地核查期间，调查机关对该企业提交的申请书及调查问卷答卷中提供的信息和企业生产经营情况等进行了核查，并实地查看了生产装置现场。2012年5月21日，申请企业向调查机关提交了《乙二醇和二甘醇的单丁醚反倾销案国内生产者调查问卷补充材料》、《乙二醇和二甘醇的单丁醚反倾销案国内产业实地核查补充证据》、《乙二醇和二甘醇的单丁醚反倾销案国内产业实地核查汇报》相关实地核查证据材料。

8. 信息公开

根据《产业损害调查信息查阅与信息披露规定》第八条、第十四条的规定，本案公开材料均已送交商务部贸易救济措施公开信息查阅室。各利害关系方可以查找、阅览、摘抄、复印公开信息。

调查机关对申请书及所附证据材料、收回的调查问卷答卷和实地核查结果进行认真分析和全面评估，对本案利害关系方提交的意见依法予以考虑。

二、被调查产品

调查机关在立案公告中确定的本案调查范围及被调查产品描述如下：

调查范围：原产于美国和欧盟的进口乙二醇和二甘醇的单丁醚。

被调查产品名称：乙二醇和二甘醇的单丁醚。英文名称：乙二醇的单丁醚：Ethylene Glycol Monobutyl Ether；

二甘醇的单丁醚：Diethylene Glycol Monobutyl Ether

被调查产品的具体描述：

分子结构：

乙二醇的单丁醚：

$CH_3-CH_2-CH_2-CH_2-O-CH_2-CH_2-OH$

二甘醇的单丁醚：

$CH_3-CH_2-CH_2-CH_2-O-CH_2-CH_2-O-CH_2-CH_2-OH$

物理和化学特征：乙二醇的单丁醚：无色透明液体，微有香味，相对密度(20℃/4℃)0.90075，沸点170.2℃，闪点(开口)74℃，接触明火、高热和强氧化剂有燃烧的危险。分子式 $C_6H_{14}O_2$，分子量118.17，能溶于水和乙醇、丙酮、苯等有机溶剂，低毒。能溶解油脂、天然树脂、硝基纤维素等。

二甘醇的单丁醚：无色透明液体，微有香味，相对密度(20℃/20℃)0.9536，沸点230.4℃，闪点(开口)93℃，接触明火、高热和强氧化剂有燃烧的危险。分子式 $C_8H_{18}O_3$，分子量162.2，能溶于水和乙醇、丙酮、苯等有机溶剂，低毒。能溶解油脂、天然树脂、硝基纤维素等。

主要用途：广泛应用于水基涂料中的溶剂，也是硝化纤维素、醇酸树脂和用顺酐改性的酚醛树脂的溶剂。一般用作涂料特别是硝基喷漆，可以防雾、防皱，提高涂膜的光泽性和流动性；也用作金属清洗剂、脱漆剂、脱润滑油剂、汽车引擎洗涤剂、干洗溶剂、环氧树脂溶剂、药物萃取剂、农药分散剂、印刷油墨、切削油和纤维油剂的油分散互溶剂；也用作硝化纤维素、清漆、印刷油墨、图章用印油墨、油脂和树脂等的溶剂，乳胶漆的稳定剂、飞机涂料的蒸发抑制剂、高温烘烤瓷漆的表面加工改进剂。

税则号：该产品归在《中华人民共和国进出口税则》：29094300。

三、国内同类产品和国内产业

(一)国内同类产品的认定。

根据《反倾销条例》第十二条和《反倾销产业损害调查规定》第十条、十一条关于同类产品认定的规定，调查机关对国内生产的乙二醇和二甘醇的单丁醚(以下简称国内产品)与被调查产品的物理和化学特征，外观、生产工艺流程、原材料、生产设备、用途、销售渠道、销售市场区域、客户群体、价格等因素进行了考察，初步调查证据显示：

1. 物理和化学特征。调查机关经比较后认定，国内产品与被调查产品的熔点、沸点、密度、蒸气密度、蒸汽压、折射率、闪点等主要物理和化学特征基本相同。能溶于20倍的水和大多数有机溶剂及矿物油。在空气中或在阳光照射下容易生成爆炸性的过氧化物。其蒸气密度大于空气，能在低处扩散较远，遇明火、高温、强氧化剂可燃，燃烧放出刺激烟雾。若遇高热，容器内压增大，有开裂和爆炸的危险。在储运上需要包装完整、轻装轻卸、库房通风、远离明火和高温、与氧化剂分开存放。

陶氏化学公司在其提交的《国外<地区>生产者/出口商调查问卷答卷》和《进口乙二醇和二甘醇的单丁醚反倾销案无损害抗辩书》中提出，其生产的乙二醇和二甘醇的单丁醚产品在水溶性、含水量和酸性等指标比国内产品更具优势，更符合下游客户需求。

对此，申请人在其提交的《乙二醇和二甘醇的单丁醚反倾销案国内生产者调查问卷补充材料》和《乙二醇和二甘醇的单丁醚反倾销案国内产业实地核查汇报》中主张，申请人生产的国内产品技术指标合格，符合客户要求，某些指标甚至超过了被调查产品，同类产品的质量也获得了下游客户和第三方机构的认可。

调查机关分析后认定，陶氏化学公司所指出的其生产的被调查产品的水溶性、含水量和酸性等指标优于国内产品没有客观证据支持。本案申请人提交的下游客户质量评审材料和第三方机构的质量认证等证据显示，国内产品的上述指标达到了比较高的水平，在陶氏化学公司未出具其他证据的情况下，调查机关不支持其主张。

2. 产品外观。调查机关认定，被调查产品与国内产品外观基本一致，均为无色透明液体，微有香味。《国内生产者调查问卷答卷》和《国外<地区>生产者/出口商调查问卷答卷》中的相关陈述也都支持这一观点。

3. 原材料、生产工艺流程和生产设备。调查机关经比较后认定，被调查产品与国内产品的原材料基本相同，均为环氧乙烷和丁醇。

两者的生产工艺流程基本相同，均为：进料—混合—加热反应—精馏—分离—存储等工序。均采用了管道连续化反应技术和自动控制系统，并充分利用反应热以起到节能降耗效果。

关于两者的生产设备，陶氏化学公司认为本公司拥有整套一体化的生产设备，而申请人却没有整套的生产装置。对此，申请人在《乙二醇和二甘醇的单丁醚反倾销案国内产业实地核查汇报》中主张，2009年7月，申请人的乙二醇丁醚项目竣工投产，就已经拥有了规模化生产装置。

经过实地核查，与《国外<地区>生产者/出口商调查问卷答卷》提供的信息比较，调查机关认定，申请人的主要生产装置已规模化，与国外生产商基本相同，均由反应器、蒸馏塔、回收器、贮罐、加热器等装置组成。

4. 产品用途。调查机关经比较后认定，国内产品与被调查产品的用途基本相同，主要用作涂料、油漆和油墨中的溶剂(如水性涂料的成膜助剂，丝网印刷油墨中的溶剂)；用作工业清洗剂、脱漆剂、脱润滑油剂；用于合成乙二醇丁醚醋酸酯；其他包括制药工业用作药物萃取剂、纺织工业用作纤维润滑剂、农药分散剂、干洗溶剂、切削油溶剂等。二甘醇的单丁醚除上述用途外，还可在机械工业用作液压制动液的稀释剂、高速切削油等。《国内生产者调查问卷答卷》和《国外<地区>生产者/出口商调查问卷答卷》中的相关陈述也符合上述情况。

5. 销售方式和销售市场区域。调查机关经比较后认定，国内产品与被调查产品销售方式基本相同，均为直接销售和代理销售相结合；国内产品与被调查产品销售市场区域主要分布在华南、华东和华北。《国内生产者调查问卷答卷》和《国内进口商调查问卷答卷》中相关陈述也支持这一观点。

6. 客户群体和价格。调查机关根据申请人提交的《对伊士曼无损害抗辩的评论意见》中出示的证据，认定国内产品与被调查产品的客户群体有重合，部分国内用户同时使用国内产品和被调查产品，二者可以相互替代。通过实地核查中获得的证据与中国海关统计数据，国内产品价格总体变化趋势与被调查产品进口价格基本一致。

调查机关通过分析后认为，被调查产品与国内产品的物理和化学特征基本相同，外观、生产工艺流程、原材料、生产设备、用途、销售渠道、销售市场区域、客户群体等方面基本相同，具有相似性和可比性，可以相互替代，价格总体变化趋势基本一致。因此，调查机关初步认定，国内生产的乙二醇和二甘醇的单丁醚与被调查产品属于同类产品。

(二)国内产业的认定。

根据《反倾销条例》第十一条和《反倾销产业损害调查规定》第十三条的规定，调查机关对本案申请人的代表资格进行了审查。

初步证据显示，调查期内，德纳(南京)化工有限公司生产的乙二醇和二甘醇的单丁醚产量占国内同类产品总产量主要部分，符合《反倾销条例》第十一条和《反倾销产业损害调查规定》第十三条关于国内产业认定的规定，可以代表国内产业。本裁决所依据的国内产业数据，除特别说明外，均来自以上特定的国内生产者。

伊士曼化工公司在其提交的《乙二醇和二甘醇的单丁醚反倾销案无损害抗辩书》中提出，从申请人投产以来至2010年上半年的一年时间内，申请人始终未能实现规模生产，且未提供其他国内生产者的信息；2010年下半年，申请人并不存在产能，不具备代表中国国内产业的资格。因此在本案调查期内，申请人代表国内产业的合理性存在疑问。陶氏化学公司在其提交的《进口乙二醇和二甘醇的单丁醚反倾销案无损害抗辩书》、沙索在其提交的《乙二醇和二甘醇的单丁醚反倾销案无损害抗辩意见》中也提出了类似的主张。

对此，申请人在其提交的《对伊士曼无损害抗辩的评论意见》中主张，在申请书附件中，申请人已提供了关于其自身产量和国内总产量的相关证据，伊士曼公司依据乙二醇醚产能大小判断代表性，混淆了产能和产量的概念。关于披露其他国内生产商的信息，申请人了解到，国内主要醇醚生产企业如江苏怡达化工有限公司、江苏华伦化工有限公司在调查期内都没有生产同类产品。

调查机关经分析后认定，根据申请人提交的《对伊士曼无损害抗辩的评论意见》中的证据显示，2009年7月到2011年6月，作为国内生产能力最大的同类产品生产企业，申请人同类产品的产量始终占国内同类产品总产量的主要部分，因此申请人具有代表国内产业的资格。

四、倾销和倾销幅度

调查机关审查了应诉公司的答卷，对应诉公司的正常价值、出口价格及调整项目作出初步认定，并在公平比较的基础上计算出倾销幅度，初步裁决如下：

(一)正常价值、出口价格及价格调整项目的初步认定。

美国公司

伊士曼化工公司

(Eastman Chemical Company)

1. 正常价值

调查机关对该公司出口中国的被调查产品及其国内销售的同类产品的型号进行了审查。调查机关认为，该公司在答卷及补充答卷中提供了型号划分的基本依据，能够反映该公司被调查产品及国内同类产品的实际生产和销售情况，决定在初裁中暂接受该公司在答卷中主张的型号划分方法。

调查机关对该公司国内销售的被调查产品同类产品总量及各型号产品数量占同期向中国出口对应数量的比例进行了审查。经审查，调查机关发现，调查期内该公司国内销售的被调查产品同类产品总量及各型号产品数量占同期向中国出口对应数量的比例均大于5%，符合作为确定正常价值的数量要求。

调查机关审查了该公司国内交易情况。调查期内，该公司各型号产品的国内销售全部是销售给非关联客户。经审查，调查机关决定在初裁中暂以该公司销售给国内非关联客户的各型号产品的价格作为确定正常价值的基础。

调查机关对该公司调查期内国内销售是否低于成本进行了审查。关于生产成本，该公司在答卷中报告了倾销调查期内的生产成本明细，包括直接材料、直接人工、燃料动力、制造费用、其他成本等。关于费用及分摊情况，公司在答卷中报告了倾销调查期内发生的销售、管理和财务费用及分摊方法。调查机关审查了该公司提交的生产成本和费用数据。经审查，调查机关决定在初裁中暂接受该公司填报的生产成本和费用数据。

调查机关对该公司国内销售的同类产品是否低于成本销售进行了测试。经审查，调查机关发现，该公司各型号产品内销交易均高于成本。根据《反倾销条例》第四条规定，调查机关决定在初裁中暂以该公司各型号产品的全部内销交易作为确定其正常价值的基础。

2. 出口价格

调查机关审查了该公司调查期内向中国出口被调查产品情况。经初步审查，调查机关发现，在调查期内该公司被调查产品直接销售给中国非关联客户。根据《反倾销条例》第五条的规定，调查机关决定暂以该非关联交易价格作为确定出口价格的基础。

3. 调整项目

根据《反倾销条例》第六条规定，为公平合理比较，调查机关对该公司影响价格可比性的调整项目逐一进行审查。

(1)关于正常价值

关于该公司报告的内销交易的调整项目，经审查，调查机关决定在初裁中暂接受数量折扣、内陆运费、售前仓储费、包装费用、信用费用等调整主张。

关于退款及赔偿调整项目，经审查，调查机关认为该公司提供的付款贷项通知函等证据材料未能证明哪些内销交易存在退款及赔偿情况，调查机关无法根据上述证据材料进行公平价格比较。调查机关决定在初裁中暂不接受该公司退款及赔偿项目调整主张。

关于广告费用调整项目，经审查，调查机关认为该公司主张调整的广告费用并非专门针对被调查产品，同时该公司未证明上述广告费用直接影响了产品价格确定并影响了价格公平比较，调查机关决定在初裁中暂不接受该公司广告费用调整主张。

关于售后服务费用，该公司主张在国内销售中对部分研发费用和技术服务费用进行调整。经审查，调查机关认为该公司未提供充分证据证明该项费用的发生与具体内销交易直接相关并影响了价格的公平比较，调查机关决定在初裁中暂不接受该公司售后服务费用调整主张。

关于其他需要调整项目，该公司主张在国内销售中对部分客户提供的专职人员工资等费用进行调整。经审查，调查机关认为该公司未提供充分证据证明该项费用的发生与具体内销交易直接相关并影响了价格的公平比较，调查机关决定在初裁中暂不接受该公司其他需要调整项目调整主张。

(2)关于出口价格

关于该公司报告的出口交易的调整项目，经审查，调查机关决定在初裁中暂接受内陆运费、售前仓储费、国际运费、信用费用等调整主张。

4. 关于到岸价格(CIF 价格)

经审查，现有证据表明该公司所报告的 CIF 价格是合理的，调查机关决定在初裁中暂接受该公司报告的 CIF 价格数据。

陶氏化学公司

(The Dow Chemical Company)

1. 正常价值

该公司在答卷中主张其在国内生产销售的同类产品和出口中国大陆的被调查产品相同，产品分为两种型号。调查机关经初步调查，暂接受该公司关于被调查产品和同类产品的相似性以及型号划分的主张。

调查机关对该公司国内销售被调查产品同类产品总量占同期向中国大陆出口数量的比例进行了审查。调查期内，公司被调查产品同类产品的国内销售数量占同期向中国大陆出口销售数量大于5%，符合作为确定正常价值基础的数量要求。

调查机关审查了该公司国内交易情况。调查期内，该公司国内销售全部是销售给非关联最终用户。经审查，调查机关决定暂以该公司销售给国内非关联最终用户的价格作为确定正常价值的基础。

调查机关对该公司调查期内国内销售是否低于成本进行了审查。关于生产成本，公司在答卷中报告了倾销调查期内的生产成本明细，包括直接材料、直接人工、燃料动力、制造费用、其他成本等。经初步审查，调查机关决定暂接受公司填报的生产成本。关于费用及分摊情况，公司在答卷中报告了倾销调查期内发生的销售、管理和财务费用，但提交的分摊方法有待进一步澄清。经初步审查，调查机关决定暂接受公司填报的费用数据。

调查机关对该公司国内销售的同类产品是否低于成本销售进行了测试。经审查，调查机关发现，调查期内该公司国内销售中低于成本的销售数量占其国内销售数量的比例不足20%，根据《反倾销条例》第四条规定，调查机关决定暂以该公司各型号产品的全部国内销售作为确定其正常价值的基础。

2. 出口价格

调查机关审查了该公司在调查期内向中国大陆出口被调查产品情况。经初步审查，公司对中国大陆出口被调查产品大部分通过位于香港的关联贸易商进行，再由该贸易商销售给中国非关联客户；仅有少数直接销售给该公司在上海的关联公司，再由该关联公司请代工厂加工成其他产品销售。根据《反倾销条例》第五条的规定，对于通过香港关联贸易公司向中国大陆出口的交易，调查机关暂依据香港贸易公司销售给中国大陆非关联用户的价格作为确定出口价格的基础；对于该公司直接销售给上海关联公司的交易，由于该公司在答卷中未提交上海关联公司加工费用等信息，同时考虑到该部分交易数量很小，调查机关决定暂接受被调查公司与上海关联公司的交易价格。

3. 调整项目

根据《反倾销条例》第六条规定，为公平合理比较，调查机关对该公司影响价格可比性的调整项目逐一进行了审查。

(1)关于正常价值

关于该公司报告的内销交易的调整项目，经审查，调查机关决定暂接受公司填报的内陆运费、售前仓储费(内部/分销仓库)、内陆保费、包装费用、信用费用等调整主张。

关于该公司主张的提前付款折扣和回扣调整项目，由于该公司未提交相关证明文件，调查机关决定在初裁中暂不予接受。

(2)关于出口价格

关于该公司报告的出口交易的调整项目，经审查，调查机关决定暂接受公司填报的内陆运费-工厂到分销仓库、售前仓储费用(内部/分销仓库)、内陆保险费、包装费、国际运费、国际保险费、装卸费、信用费用等调整主张。

对于通过香港关联贸易公司向中国大陆的出口交易，调查机关发现关联贸易公司在销售过程中主要负责联系客户、处理文件、安排物流等中间职能，且关联贸易公司在转售交易中获得一定收益。调查机关发现该公司计算倾销幅度的表格中未填写实际发生的费用，因此决定在初裁中对这部分交易进行其他销售费用项目调整。

4. 关于到岸价格(CIF 价格)

经审查，现有证据表明该公司所报告的 CIF 价格是合理的，调查机关决定暂采信公司报告的 CIF 价格数据。

益科斯达化工产品有限公司

(Equistar Chemicals, LP)

根据《反倾销条例》及商务部《反倾销调查抽样暂行规则》的规定，调查机关决定采用美国抽样选取公司的加权平均幅度，确定参加应诉但未被抽中的美国益科斯达化工产品有限公司的税率。

其他美国公司

(All Others)

本案于 2011 年 11 月 18 日立案，当日，调查机关通知了申请书上列明的出口商或生产商，也通知了涉案国驻华使馆，同日，调查机关将立案公告登载在商务部网站上，任何利害关系方均可在商务部网站上查阅本案立案公告。立案后，调查机关给予各利害关系方 20 天的登记应诉期，给予所有利害关系方合理的时间获知立案有关情况。

2011 年 12 月 15 日，调查机关向登记应诉公司发放了调查问卷，同日，调查机关将调查问卷登载在商务部网站上，任何利害关系方可在商务部网站上查阅本案调查问卷。

调查机关尽最大能力通知了所有利害关系方，也尽最大能力向所有利害关系方提醒不登记应诉或不提交答卷的结果。对于其他未应诉的美国公司，调查机关根据《反倾销条例》、《反倾销调查抽样暂行规则》和《反倾销问卷调查暂行规则》确定其正常价值和出口价格。

欧盟公司

沙索德国有限责任公司

(Sasol Germany GmbH)

沙索溶剂德国有限责任公司

(Sasol Solvents Germany GmbH)

1. 正常价值

调查机关初步审查了沙索溶剂德国有限责任公司(以下简称溶剂公司)在调查期内被调查产品同类产品的国内销售情况。调查期内，该公司委托其关联公司沙索德国有限责任公司生产乙二醇和二甘醇的单丁醚，并向其支付加工费。委托加工所生产的乙二醇和二甘醇的单丁醚所有权属于溶剂公司，溶剂公司负责欧盟内销售。经初步审查，调查期内该公司国内销售被调查产品同类产品数量占同期向中国出口销售数量的比例大于 5%，符合作为确定正常价值的数量要求。

调查期内，该公司只有乙二醇的单丁醚对中国出口，调查机关决定以之为基础确定正常价值。经审查，该公司与出口乙二醇的单丁醚相一致的欧盟内销售的被调查产品同类产品数量占同期向中国出口销售数量的比例大于 5%，符合作为确定正常价值的数量要求。

在审查溶剂公司欧盟内销售过程中，调查机关发现，该公司除委托生产并销售被调查产品外，还在调查期内向其他德国生产商采购少量被调查产品的同类产品在欧盟内销售。调查机关认为，在外购产品过程中，溶剂公司的角色发生了变化，由被调查产品同类产品的委托方变成了外购产品的贸易商。因此，调查机关决定在初裁决定中暂排除这部分交易，将这部分外购产品排除在计算正常价值之外。

根据溶剂公司的报告，该公司调查期内在欧盟内的销售存在关联及非关联销售。公司称：欧盟内销售给非关联客户和关联客户执行统一的定价政策，不因销售给关联客户而有所不同，没有特殊价格安排，不应排除在计算正常价值之外。调查机关对公司欧盟内销售中的关联交易进行了审查，发现公司与关联客户的销售价格与非关联客户的销售价格相差不大，调查机关认为，这部分关联交易反映了正常市场交易状况，属于正常贸易过程中的交易，调查机关决定在确定正常价值时暂不排除这部分关联交易。

调查机关对溶剂公司报告的成本数据进行了初步审查和调查。

溶剂公司对委托加工被调查产品的同类产品生产成本进行了计算，并分摊了主要管理费用、销售费用，但对公司的财务费用和管理费用中的“资产减值损失”、“其他费用”没有分摊，该公司认为上述费用与被调查产品同类产品无关。调查机关认为，反倾销中的成本是完全成本概念，除生产成本、委托加工成本外，还包括管理费用、销售费用、财务费用等三项费用的分摊额，将公司管理费用中的“资产减值损失”和“其他费用”排除在分摊被调查产品同类产品之外，否定了公司管理费用由公司所有产品承担和补偿的基本属性，不符合管理费用的性质；同时作为汇兑损益的财务费用是整个公司财务费用，需要由包括公司委托加工产品在内的所有产品来承担和补偿，应当分摊至被调查产品同类产品之中而不是排除在被调查产品同类产品之外。因此，在初裁决定中，调查机关暂决定将公司未分摊至被调查产品同类产品管理费用中的“资产减值损失”和“其他费用”以及公司的财务费用，按销售收入比例对被调查产品同类产品的相关费用进行了调整。

根据上述调整，调查机关重新核算了该公司被调查产品同类产品欧盟内销售成本，并对调查期内出口中国相应的被调查产品同类产品的欧盟内销售进行了低成本测试，发现其中低于成本销售数量占全部销售的比例超过20%。调查机关认定这部分交易属于非正常贸易过程中的交易。因此，根据《反倾销条例》第四条的规定，调查机关在初裁决定中，依据排除低于成本销售后的被调查产品同类产品欧盟内销售作为确定正常价值的基础。

2. 出口价格

调查机关初步审查了溶剂公司在调查期内被调查产品对中国出口销售情况。调查期内，该公司委托其关联公司沙索德国有限责任公司生产乙二醇和二甘醇的单丁醚，并向其支付加工费，由溶剂公司销售给沙索化工太平洋有限公司，再由沙索化工太平洋有限公司销售给中国非关联贸易商，调查期内，该公司只有乙二醇的单丁醚对中国出口。

对公司通过关联贸易商向中国非关联贸易商销售被调查产品的情形，根据《反倾销条例》第五条的规定，调查机关决定在初裁中依据销售给中国非关联贸易商的价格作为确定出口价格的基础。

3. 调整项目

调查机关对公司主张正常价值的价格调整部分逐一审查和调查。

(1)关于正常价值

公司主张在欧盟内销售被调查产品同类产品过程中，对公司所发生的附加费、分析、计算延迟费等其他需要调整项目进行调整，理由是这些费用不包括在出厂环节价格中，应在确定正常价值时进行调整。

经初步审查，调查机关认为，尽管公司在欧盟内销售被调查产品同类产品过程中可能发生了上述费用，但公司在答卷中并没有说明这些费用是如何发生又是如何计算的，在调查机关两次补充问卷中，公司也没有回答调查机关的所提问题，只是提出根据公司SAP系统数据填报，没有提交任何有关上述费用发生和计算依据。因此调查机关决定，在初裁中对公司“其他需要调整的项目”的主张暂不予接受。

经初步审查，在初裁中，调查机关暂接受了提前付款折扣、回扣、内陆运输-工厂/仓库至客户、佣金等调整项目。

(2)关于出口价格

该公司主张在计算倾销幅度时应将中国客户以进料加工贸易方式进口的交易排除在外。

经初步审查，调查机关认为，计算倾销幅度时并不必然排除加工贸易方式的进口；此外，公司补充答卷时并没有回答在出口到中国时，是如何知道这些交易和业务是加工贸易，也没有提供相关证明文件。因此，调查机关决定，在初裁中对公司将加工贸易方式进口的交易排除在倾销幅度计算之外的主张暂不予接受。

经初步审查，在初裁中，调查机关暂接受了售前仓储费用、内陆运输-工厂/仓库至出口港、国际运费、国际运输保险费、港口装卸费等相关费用、佣金等调整项目。

4. 关于到岸价格(CIF价格)

经初步审查，在初裁中，调查机关暂接受该公司报告的CIF价格数据。

英力士化学拉瓦拉有限公司

(INEOS Chemicals Lavera SAS)

据公司答卷，倾销调查期内，英力士氧化物公司委托其关联公司英力士制造法国有限公司(INEOS Manufacturing France SAS)生产被调查产品，并对中国出口；调查期内英力士集团发生业务重组，倾销调查期后，英力士氧化物公司被位于瑞士的英力士欧洲公司取代，而英力士制造法国公司被英力士化学拉瓦拉公司取代。

1. 正常价值

该公司在答卷中主张其在欧盟内生产销售的同类产品和出口中国的被调查产品相同，产品分为两个型号。调查机关经初步调查，暂接受该公司关于被调查产品和同类产品的相似性以及型号划分的主张。

调查机关分型号对该公司欧盟内销售被调查产品同类产品总量占同期向中国出口数量的比例进行了审查。调查期内，公司两种型号被调查产品同类产品的欧盟内销售数量占同期向中国出口销售数量均大于5%，符合作为确定正常价值基础的数量要求。

调查机关审查了该公司欧盟内交易情况。调查期内，该公司欧盟内销售的一个型号全部为公司直接向非关联客户销售，关联交易审查通过。另一个型号向关联客户销售的价格与向非关联客户销售的价格相比存在明显差异，初步认定公司与关联客户之间的交易不属于正常贸易过程中的交易。经审查，调查机关决定对前一型号暂以欧盟内全部交易作为确定正常价值的基础，后一型号暂以销售给欧盟内非关联客户的价格作为确定正常价值的基础。

调查机关对该公司倾销调查期内欧盟内销售是否低于成本进行了审查。关于生产成本，公司在答卷中报告了倾销调查期内的生产成本明细，包括直接材料、直接人工、燃料动力、制造费用、其他成本等。经初步审查，调查机关发现，关联采购的原材料价格与公司提供的同类产品欧盟公开市场价格相比，关联交易价格不可信，调查机关决定暂以公司提供的调查期内欧盟市场的原材料平均价格作为原材料价格；关于包装费用，公司未按问卷要求进行填报，调查机关作了相应调整。关于费用及分配情况，公司在答卷中报告了倾销调查期内发生的销售、管理和财务费用，但未按调查机关的要求提交分摊方法的证明材料。经初步审查，调查机关决定暂接受公司填报的费用数据。

根据调整后的生产成本和费用，经审查，调查期内该公司欧盟内销售两个型号低于加权平均成本的销售数量占其欧盟内销售数量的比例均高于20%，根据《反倾销条例》第四条规定，调查机关决定暂以高于加权平均成本的内销交易作为确定两个型号正常价值的基础。

2. 出口价格

调查机关审查了该公司在倾销调查期内向中国出口被调查产品情况。经初步审查，公司在倾销调查期内对中国出口被调查产品全部销售给中国非关联客户。根据《反倾销条例》第五条的规定，调查机关决定暂以公司销售给非关联客户的交易价格作为确定出口价格的基础。

3. 调整项目

根据《反倾销条例》第六条规定，为公平合理比较，调查机关对该公司影响价格可比性的调整项目逐一进行了审查。

(1)关于正常价值

关于该公司报告的内销交易的调整项目，经审查，调查机关决定暂接受公司填报的提前付款折扣、回扣、内陆运费、内陆保费、包装费用、信用费用等调整主张。

(2)关于出口价格

关于该公司报告的出口交易的调整项目，经审查，调查机关决定暂接受公司填报的运费及运输相关费用、运输保险费、回扣、包装费用、信用费用等调整主张。

4. 关于到岸价格(CIF价格)

关于CIF价格，经审查，现有证据表明该公司所报告的CIF价格是合理的，调查机关决定暂采信公司报告的CIF价格数据。

巴斯夫欧洲公司

(BASF SE)

巴斯夫欧洲公司在规定时间内向调查机关登记应诉，其提出的延期提交反倾销答卷的申请也经调查机关部分许可，但该公司在延期后的截止日期前未提交答卷。调查机关根据《反倾销条例》、《反倾销调查抽样暂行规则》和《反倾销问卷调查暂行规则》有关规定确定其正常价值和出口价格。

其他欧盟公司

(All Others)

本案于2011年11月18日立案，当日，调查机关通知了申请书上列明的出口商或生产商，也通知了涉案地区驻华使馆，同日，调查机关将立案公告登载在商务部网站上，任何利害关系方均可在商务部网站上查阅本案立案公告。立案后，调查机关给予各利害关系方20天的登记应诉期，给予所有利害关系方合理的时间获知立案有关情况。

2011年12月15日，调查机关向登记应诉公司发放了调查问卷，同日，调查机关将调查问卷登载在商务部网站上，任何利害关系方可在商务部网站上查阅本案调查问卷。

调查机关尽最大能力通知了所有利害关系方，也尽最大能力向所有利害关系方提醒不登记应诉或不提交答卷的结果。对于其他未应诉的欧盟公司，调查机关根据《反倾销条例》、《反倾销调查抽样暂行规则》和《反倾销问卷调查暂行规则》有关规定确定其正常价值和出口价格。

(二) 价格比较。

根据《反倾销条例》第六条的规定，调查机关对进口产品的出口价格和正常价值，考虑了影响价格的各种可比性因素，按照公平、合理的方式进行了比较。调查机关在当事人提交的证明材料基础上，将应诉公司的正常价值和出口价格在出口国出厂价的基础上予以比较。在计算倾销幅度时，调查机关将加权平均正常价值和加权平均出口价格进行比较，得出倾销幅度。

对于应诉但未提交答卷的公司，根据《反倾销条例》第二十一条的规定，调查机关决定采用已经获得的事实和可获得的最佳信息作出有关倾销和倾销幅度的裁定。

(三)倾销幅度。

经过计算，各公司的倾销幅度分别为：

美国公司

1. 伊士曼化工公司

(Eastman Chemical Company) 10.1%

2. 陶氏化学公司

(The Dow Chemical Company) 12.5%

3. 益科斯达化工产品有限公司

(Equistar Chemicals, LP) 11.5%

4. 其他美国公司

(All others) 15.1%

欧盟公司

1. 沙索德国有限责任公司

(Sasol Germany GmbH)

沙索溶剂德国有限责任公司

(Sasol Solvents Germany GmbH) 13.0%

2. 英力士化学拉瓦拉有限公司

(INEOS Chemicals Lavera SAS) 9.3%

3. 巴斯夫欧洲公司

(BASF SE) 18.8%

4. 其他欧盟公司

(All others) 14.9%

五、产业损害及损害程度

(一)累积评估的适当性。

根据《反倾销条例》第九条和《反倾销产业损害调查规定》第十五条、第十六条的规定,调查机关认定,调查期内,来自美国和欧盟的被调查产品倾销幅度均在2%以上;根据海关统计数据,原产于美国和欧盟的被调查产品进口量占国内总进口量的比例均超过3%,不属于微量或可以忽略不计的范围。原产于美国和欧盟的倾销进口产品之间以及原产于美国和欧盟的倾销进口产品与国内同类产品之间物理和化学特征、外观、原材料、生产设备、生产工艺流程、用途、销售渠道、销售市场区域、客户群体等方面相同或基本相同,价格总体变化趋势基本一致,具有可替代性,存在相互竞争关系,竞争条件基本相同。

综合以上因素,调查机关认定,对原产于美国和欧盟的被调查产品对国内产业造成的影响进行累积评估是适当的。

(二)被调查产品进口量及所占国内市场份额。

1. 被调查产品进口量

本案调查期为2009年7月到2011年6月,调查机关将其分为4个时间段来进行数据比较:2009年7~12月、2010年1~6月、2010年7~12月、2011年1~6月。根据中国海关统计,调查期内被调查产品进口量呈先微降后上升趋势,2009年7~12月为4.28万吨;2010年1~6月为4.26万吨,比2009年7~12月下降0.46%;2010年7~12月为4.36万吨,比2010年1~6月上升2.35%。2011年1~6月,被调查产品进口量为4.73万吨,比2010年7~12月上升8.61%,比期初上升10.51%。

2. 被调查产品所占国内市场份额

根据调查机关实地核查所获得的证据显示,2009年7~12月至2011年1~6月,被调查产品占国内市场份额分别为58.15%、61.03%、64.88%、65.45%,2010年1~6月比2009年7~12月上升2.88个百分点,2010年7~12月比2010年1~6月上升3.85个百分点;2011年1~6月比2010年7~12月上升0.57个百分点,比调查期初上升7.3个百分点。

伊士曼化工公司在其提交的《乙二醇和二甘醇的单丁醚反倾销案无损害抗辩书》中提出,一般贸易并不占被调查产品进口数量的主要部分,占全部进口数量的比例大多低于50%,因此,被调查产品进口数量的增长,实质上是其他贸易方式进口的增长,没有必要对仅占有较小比例的一般贸易进口征收反倾销税。沙索在其提交的《乙二醇和二甘醇的单丁醚反倾销案无损害抗辩意见》中也有类似主张。

伊士曼化工公司还提出,被调查产品在绝对数量上增长并不大,不存在世贸组织《反倾销协定》第3.2条中所定义的"大幅"增长。陶氏化学公司在其提交的《进口乙二醇和二甘醇的单丁醚反倾销案无损害抗辩书》和沙索提交的《乙二醇和二甘醇的单丁醚反倾销案无损害抗辩意见》中也有类似主张。

对此,申请人在提交的《对伊士曼无损害抗辩的评论意见》中主张,伊士曼化工公司提出的应排除"一般贸易"以外的其他形式的进口的主张缺乏世贸组织规则或中国国内反倾销法律上的依据,也不符合调查机关在反倾销实践中的一贯做法。

关于被调查产品进口量,申请人认为,被调查产品的绝对和相对进口量都发生了较明显增长,2011年1~6月被调查产品进口量相比2009年7~12月进口量上升了10.51%,市场份额上升了7.3个百分点。

调查机关认为,伊士曼化工公司并未提供肯定性的证据来证明一般贸易形式的被调查产品占全部进口数量低于50%,且不能排除不同贸易形式的被调查产品与国内产品的竞争关系。被调查产品进口量和所占市场份额均持续上升,增长是客观事实。

(三)被调查产品进口价格。

根据中国海关统计数据计算,调查期内,原产于美国和欧盟的被调查产品进口价格(CIF价)呈上升趋势,2009年7~12月为8700元/吨;2010年1~

6月为9691元/吨，比2009年7~12月上升11.39%；2010年7~12月为10262元/吨，比2010年1~6月上升5.89%；2011年1~6月为11981元/吨，比2010年7~12月上升16.75%。

为使被调查产品价格与国内同类产品价格具有可比性，调查机关在被调查产品CIF价格基础上，进行了适当调整。考虑了中国海关5.5%的关税，调查机关还考察了被调查产品的港口建设费、卸货费、报关费、商检费等相关信息，但是在不同港口上述费用没有统一的征收标准，调查机关无法获得一个准确、客观的数据。但经调查机关初步测算，上述费用相对进口价格而言数量较小，不会对价格比较和分析造成影响。

按照上述方法调整后的被调查产品进口价格为，2009年7~12月为9179元/吨；2010年1~6月为10224元/吨；2010年7~12月为10826元/吨；2011年1~6月为12640元/吨。

陶氏化学公司在其提交的《进口乙二醇和二甘醇的单丁醚反倾销案无损害抗辩书》中提出，乙二醇的单丁醚和二甘醇的单丁醚不是一样的产品，定价方式也不同，将乙二醇的单丁醚和二甘醇的单丁醚的价格以平均单价来计算不具合理性。

对此，申请人在《对陶氏公司无损害抗辩的评论意见》中主张，陶氏的主张所涉及的实质法律问题主要包括，一是被调查产品的范围是否可以包括具有差异性的子类别产品；二是当被调查产品中的各子类别产品具有差异性时，这是调查机关在进行损害评估时的义务和方法。对于第一个问题，当被调查产品由不同类别的产品构成时，《反倾销协定》中第2.1和2.6条并未要求调查机关确保各个类别的产品之间具有“相似性”从而构成一种单一的产品。第二个问题，调查机关的审查义务仍是《反倾销协定》第3.1条所规定的“对肯定性结论的客观审查”，并未限制调查机关在评估损害所应采取的具体方法。即使不考虑法律和规则问题，陶氏的主张也缺乏实践中的可行性。乙二醇的单丁醚和二甘醇的单丁醚同属一个海关税则号，中国海关未对这两种产品分别进行统计。

调查机关分析后认为，乙二醇的单丁醚与二甘醇的单丁醚的物理、化学特征以及外观、用途基本相同，由同一生产装置相同的生产工艺同时产出。另外，根据申请人在《乙二醇和二甘醇的单丁醚反倾销案国内生产者调查问卷补充材料》提供的证据显示，调查期内，二者的国内市场销售价格很接近，且互有高低，最大差距不超过5%，因此将乙二醇的单丁醚和二甘醇的单丁醚以平均单价合并计算，符合被调查产品的实际情况。

(四)进口被调查产品对国内产业同类产品价格的影响。

调查证据显示，调查期内，国内产业同类产品国内销售价格2010年1~6月比2009年7~12月上升15.78%，2010年7~12月比2010年1~6月下降0.23%，2011年1~6月比2010年7~12月上升16.84%。

调查期内，被调查产品进口量呈先降后升趋势，其占国内市场份额呈稳定上升趋势，市场份额维持在60%左右。实地核查中获得的证据显示，国内同类产品定价受到了进口产品的影响。

由于部分国内同类产品销售时采取了送货上门的方式，为更客观地评估被调查产品进口价格对国内产业同类产品价格的影响。调查机关根据申请人提供的原始销售记录等证据材料，测算出了运费在销售价格中的平均占比，并在价格比较时，在国内同类产品销售价格中剔除了运费。

2010年1~6月相比2009年7~12月，国内同类产品单位销售成本上升了27.29%，而销售价格仅上升了15.78%，单位毛利润由正变负，下降幅度247.29%；2010年7~12月相比2010年1~6月，国内同类产品单位销售成本上升了4.40%，而销售价格却下降了0.23%，单位毛利润继续下降，下降幅度91.23%。

此外，调查机关将经调整后的被调查产品进口价格与剔除运费后的同类产品国内销售价格进行比较后发现，调查期内，被调查产品进口价格低于同类产品国内销售价格。

综合考虑上述因素，调查机关认为，调查期内被调查产品进口量呈上升趋势，其国内市场份额处于较高水平，对国内产业同类产品的销售价格具有较大的影响力。被调查产品对国内同类产品价格产生了抑制和削减作用。

(五)国内产业相关经济因素和指标的评估。

根据《反倾销条例》第八条及《反倾销产业损害调查规定》第五条和第七条的规定，调查机关审查了被调查产品对国内产业的相关经济因素和指标的影响。

1. 表观消费量

调查期内，国内乙二醇和二甘醇的单丁醚表观消费量呈先下降后微升的趋势，该数据在2009年7~12月、2010年1~6月、2010年7~12月、2011年1~6月分别为：7.36万吨、6.98万吨、6.72万吨和7.23万吨。2010年1~6月比2009年7~12月下降5.12%，2010年7~12月比2010年1~6月下降

3.81%，2011 年 1～6 月比 2010 年 7～12 月增长 7.66%。

2. 产能

调查期内，国内产业同类产品产能保持稳定，在 2009 年 7～12 月、2010 年 1～6 月、2010 年 7～12 月、2011 年 1～6 月，国内产业同类产品产能均为固定值。

伊士曼化工公司在其提交的《乙二醇和二甘醇的单丁醚反倾销案无损害抗辩书》中主张，根据其可获得的资料显示，2011 年 3 月申请人国内同类产品的年产能已经增长至 90000 吨，调查期内申请人的产能实际呈现增长趋势。沙索在其提交的《乙二醇和二甘醇的单丁醚反倾销案无损害抗辩意见》中也提出了类似主张。

对此，申请人向调查机关提交了其产能扩大项目的相关材料，以及该项目扩大产能计划贷款请求被银行拒绝的证据。

调查机关经分析后认定，尽管国内产业同类产品产能在调查期内有扩大计划，但是因其未能正常获利，经营风险增加，导致其投融资能力下降，从而使产能扩大计划未能实施，调查期内申请人产能并未增长。

3. 产量

调查期内，国内产业同类产品产量先降后升，总体呈增长趋势，2010 年 1～6 月比 2009 年 7～12 月下降 35.01%，2010 年 7～12 月比 2010 年 1～6 月下降 98.93%，2011 年 1～6 月比 2010 年 7～12 月增长 14771.26%。

4. 销售量

调查期内，国内产业同类产品国内销售量先降后升，总体呈下降趋势，2010 年 1～6 月比 2009 年 7～12 月下降 60.14%，2010 年 7～12 月比 2010 年 1～6 月下降 26.41%，2011 年 1～6 月比 2010 年 7～12 月增长 85.61%。

5. 市场份额

调查期内，国内产业同类产品市场份额，2010 年 1～6 月比 2009 年 7～12 月减少 2.75 个百分点，2010 年 7～12 月比 2010 年 1～6 月增加 0.63 个百分点，2011 年 1～6 月比 2010 年 7～12 月增加 0.08 个百分点。

6. 销售价格

调查期内，国内产业同类产品国内销售价格呈先上升再下降再上升趋势，总体呈上升趋势。2010 年 1～6 月比 2009 年 7～12 月上升 15.78%，2010 年 7～12 月比 2010 年 1～6 月下降 0.23%，2011 年 1～6 月比 2010 年 7～12 月增长 16.84%。

7. 销售收入

调查期内，国内产业同类产品国内销售收入先降后升，总体呈下降趋势。2010 年 1～6 月比 2009 年 7～12 月下降 53.85%，2010 年 7～12 月比 2010 年 1～6 月下降 26.58%，2011 年 1～6 月比 2010 年 7～12 月增长 116.86%。

8. 税前利润

调查期内，国内产业同类产品税前利润始终为负值，2010 年 1～6 月比 2009 年 7～12 月增亏 168.50%，2010 年 7～12 月比 2010 年 1～6 月增亏 10.90%，2011 年 1～6 月比 2010 年 7～12 月减亏 89.39%。

9. 投资收益率

调查期内，国内产业同类产品投资收益率始终为负，呈先降后升趋势，2010 年 1～6 月比 2009 年 7～12 月减少 3.30 个百分点，2010 年 7～12 月比 2010 年 1～6 月减少 0.59 个百分点，2011 年 1～6 月比 2010 年 7～12 月增加 5.34 个百分点。

10. 开工率

调查期内，国内产业同类产品开工率先降后升，但始终维持在 25% 以下的较低水平，2010 年 1～6 月比 2009 年 7～12 月减少 7.83 个百分点，2010 年 7～12 月比 2010 年 1～6 月减少 14.38 个百分点，2011 年 1～6 月比 2010 年 7～12 月增加 23.07 个百分点。

11. 就业人数

调查期内，国内产业同类产品就业人数先降后升，总体呈下降趋势。2010 年 1～6 月比 2009 年 7～12 月下降 19.23%，2010 年 7～12 月比 2010 年 1～6 月下降 33.33%，2011 年 1～6 月比 2010 年 7～12 月增长 57.14%。

12. 劳动生产率

调查期内，国内产业同类产品劳动生产率先降后升，总体呈上升趋势，2010 年 1～6 月比 2009 年 7～12 月下降 19.53%，2010 年 7～12 月比 2010 年 1～6 月下降 98.39%，2011 年 1～6 月比 2010 年 7～12 月增长 9363.53%。

13. 人均工资

调查期内，国内产业同类产品年人均工资呈先升后降再上升的趋势，总体呈上升趋势，2010 年 1～6 月比 2009 年 7～12 月上升 22.38%，2010 年 7～12 月比 2010 年 1～6 月下降 0.94%，2011 年 1～6 月比 2010 年 7～12 月增长 12.41%。

伊士曼化工公司在其提交的《乙二醇和二甘醇的单丁醚反倾销案无损害抗辩书》中提出，调查期内申请人员工人均工资总体呈现积极的上升趋势；就业人数基本保持稳定，排除申请人在投产初期的 2009

年第四季度以及2010年7~12月停产的特殊情况外，在调查期内的其他期间内，申请人均能实现积极良好的劳动生产率。沙索在其提交的《乙二醇和二甘醇的单丁醚反倾销案无损害抗辩意见》中也提出了类似主张。对此，根据申请人提交的《乙二醇和二甘醇的单丁醚反倾销案国内产业实地核查补充证据》，调查机关认定，调查期内，受人力成本上升影响，员工人均工资呈增长趋势；虽然2011年1~6月，国内产业就业人数、劳动生产率有所上升，但2009年7~12月到2010年7~12月，国内产业就业人数和劳动生产率持续下降，应诉方提出的申请人均能实现积极良好的劳动生产率不符合客观事实。

14. 期末库存

调查期内，国内产业同类产品期末库存呈先升后降再上升趋势，2010年1~6月比2009年7~12月上升211.05%，2010年7~12月比2010年1~6月下降86.27%，2011年1~6月比2010年7~12月增长965.78%。

伊士曼化工公司在其提交的《乙二醇和二甘醇的单丁醚反倾销案无损害抗辩书》中提出，根据申请人在《申请书》中披露的库存数量指数，调查期内申请人的库存数量变动很明显，不能据此得出申请人库存压力大的结论。沙索在其提交的《乙二醇和二甘醇的单丁醚反倾销案无损害抗辩意见》中也提出了类似主张。

对此，申请人提交的《乙二醇和二甘醇的单丁醚反倾销案国内产业实地核查补充证据》显示，调查期内，国内产业库存量一直保持在较高水平，从2009年7~12月到2011年1~6月，库存量占产量比重每半年分别为13.18%、63.07%、806.34%、57.79%，因此调查机关认定，申请人库存压力大是客观的事实。

15. 经营活动现金净流量

调查期内，国内产业同类产品经营活动现金流量净额均为净流出，2010年1~6月比2009年7~12月增加49.32%，2010年7~12月比2010年1~6月增加65.35%，2011年1~6月比2010年7~12月减少263.41%。

16. 投融资能力

调查期内，由于国内产业同类产品盈利能力持续下降，经营状况明显恶化，企业投融资能力出现下降。申请人向调查机关提供的产能扩大项目投资规划书和银行出具的证明显示，调查期内，银行拒绝向申请人投资计划授信，国内产业产能扩大投资项目受阻搁置。

伊士曼化工公司在其提交的《乙二醇和二甘醇的单丁醚反倾销案无损害抗辩书》中提出，国内产业的投融资能力并不仅仅取决于是否能够成功申请贷款，申请人并未提供有关国内产业“筹资或投资能力”的相关数据，只是引用申请人贷款请求被拒的例子来主张申请人的投融资能力“严重受挫”。沙索在其提交的《乙二醇和二甘醇的单丁醚反倾销案无损害抗辩意见》中也提出了类似主张。

对此，申请人在提交的《对伊士曼无损害抗辩的评论意见》中主张，获得贷款是企业融资的主要渠道之一。申请人在立项阶段顺利获得贷款后，因经营状况恶化而无法继续融资取得运营资金，是融资能力受挫的直接证据。

调查机关分析后认定，银行在评估申请人贷款请求时必然要参照税前利润、投资收益率、现金净流量等指标，而申请人在调查期内税前利润、投资收益率均为负值，现金净流量均为净流出，申请人贷款请求被拒绝是投融资能力受损的直接体现。

综上分析并根据现有调查证据，调查期内，国内市场乙二醇和二甘醇的单丁醚表观消费量总体平稳并略有下降，国内产业同类产品的产能保持稳定不变，产量总体略有增长，就业人数略有下降，带动劳动生产率有所上升，但是，由于国内同类产品销售不畅，导致库存压力加大，国内产业开工不足，开工率始终维持在25%以下的较低水平，与此同时，期末库存呈上升趋势，国内产业市场份额呈下降趋势；国内产业同类产品国内销售量呈下降趋势，尽管受销售成本上升的影响，国内产业同类产品国内销售价格呈上升趋势，但由于销量下降幅度较大，国内销售收入呈下降趋势；国内产业同类产品国内销售价格和单位销售成本之间的差额呈先降后升趋势；受此影响，国内产业同类产品税前利润、经营活动现金净流量总体呈先降后升趋势，现金流始终为净流出；受税前利润大幅下降的影响，国内产业同类产品投资收益率在调查期内始终为负值；由于国内产业同类产品盈利能力持续下降，经营状况明显恶化，银行拒绝申请人的贷款请求，国内产业投融资能力显著下降。尽管2011年1~6月国内产业产量、销量、销售收入等指标有所上升，但税前利润、投资收益、同类产品现金流量净额等指标依然为负值，经营处于亏损状态。

综上，调查机关认定，国内产业受到了实质损害。

(六)被调查产品出口国家(地区)的生产能力、出口能力及对国内产业可能产生的进一步影响。

本案国外生产者在《国外<地区>生产者/出口

商调查问卷》中提供的数据显示，美国和欧盟拥有世界上最大的被调查产品产能和产量。调查期内，美国被调查产品年均生产能力在38万吨左右，年均产量约为30万吨；欧盟被调查产品年均生产能力在39.5万吨左右，年均产量约为24.7万吨。由此可见，调查期内，被调查产品出口国家(地区)仍维持着较大的生产能力，且产能利用率较低。

根据《国外<地区>生产者/出口商调查问卷》中提供的数据显示，调查期内，欧盟被调查产品年均产量约24.7万吨，其国内需求量约为15.25万吨；美国被调查产品年均产量约为30万吨，其国内需求量约为18.2万吨。美国和欧盟被调查产品产量中，有38.87%依赖出口。

由此可见，调查期内，被调查产品出口国家(地区)的出口能力较大，对国外(地区外)市场的依赖程度较高。

根据上述测算结果和中国海关数据统计，调查期内，美国和欧盟被调查产品的富余产量中，约有41.19%出口到中国。由此可见，调查期内被调查产品对中国市场的依赖程度较高，中国是其最主要的出口市场之一。

综上，美国和欧盟被调查产品具有较强的生产能力和出口能力，对国外(地区外)市场依赖程度较高，且中国市场对其具有较强的吸引力，调查期内，原产于美国和欧盟的被调查产品进口量占中国总进口量比重，2009年7~12月到2011年1~6月，4个半年分别为65.70%、65.81%、64.82%、74.70%。中国的乙二醇和二甘醇的单丁醚市场在全球的重要地位短期内不会改变。因此，调查机关认为，美国和欧盟乙二醇和二甘醇的单丁醚生产企业可能会进一步向中国出口被调查产品，并继续对国内产业造成不利影响。

六、因果关系

(一)被调查产品大量低价进口造成了国内产业实质损害。

调查期内，原产于美国和欧盟的被调查产品进口量呈上升趋势。2009年7~12月年为4.28万吨；2010年1~6月为4.26万吨，比2009年7~12月下降0.46%；2010年7~12月为4.36万吨，比2010年1~6月上升2.35%。2011年1~6月，被调查产品进口量为4.73万吨，比2010年7~12月上升8.61%，比期初上升10.51%。

调查期内，被调查产品占国内市场份额呈上升趋势。2009年7~12月至2011年1~6月，被调查产品占国内市场份额分别为58.15%、61.03%、64.88%、65.45%，2010年1~6月年比2009年7~12月上升2.88个百分点，2010年7~12月比2010年1~6月上升3.85个百分点；2011年1~6月比2010年7~12月上升0.57个百分点，比期初上升7.3个百分点。

2010年1~6月相比2009年7~12月，国内同类产品单位销售成本上升了27.29%，而销售价格仅上升了15.78%，单位毛利润由正变负，下降幅度247.29%；2010年7~12月相比2010年1~6月，国内同类产品单位销售成本上升了4.40%，而销售价格却下降了0.23%，单位毛利润继续下降，下降幅度91.23%，对国内产业同类产品价格产生了抑制作用；调查期内，被调查产品进口价格低于同类产品国内销售价格，对国内产业同类产品价格有削减作用。国内销售收入呈下降趋势；国内产业同类产品国内销售价格和单位销售成本之间的差额呈先降后升趋势；受此影响，国内产业同类产品税前利润始终为负值，经营活动现金净流量始终为净流出，国内产业同类产品投资收益率在调查期内始终为负值；同期国内产业同类产品开工率始终维持在25%以下的较低水平，期末库存呈上升趋势，国内产业市场份额呈下降趋势；由于国内产业同类产品盈利能力持续下降，经营状况明显恶化，银行拒绝批准申请人的贷款请求，国内产业投融资能力显著下降。尽管2011年1~6月国内产业产量、销量、销售收入等指标有所回升，但税前利润、投资收益、同类产品现金流量净额等指标依然为负值，未能扭转亏损状态。

综上，根据初步证据，调查机关认定，原产于美国和欧盟的被调查产品大量低价进口已经造成了国内产业的实质损害，原产于美国和欧盟的被调查产品的倾销进口与国内产业的实质损害之间存在因果关系。

(二)其他已知因素分析。

调查机关对可能使国内产业受到损害的其他已知因素进行了初步调查。初步证据表明：

1. 国内同类产品表观消费量的变化和消费模式变化因素。国内表观消费量总体呈平稳态势，存在市场潜力，国内没有限制使用乙二醇和二甘醇的单丁醚的政策变化，也未出现由于其他替代产品导致消费模式变化，进而导致国内产业同类产品市场严重萎缩。

2. 国内产业经营管理情况。实地核查情况表明，在生产经营管理方面，申请人不断加强经营管理，提高产品质量，建立健全了生产、经营、成本和质量等各项企业管理制度，企业还通过了ISO9001质量体系认证和ISO14001环境管理体系认证。因此，国内产业受到的实质损害并非由经营管理不善等因素造成。

3. 国内产业技术进步情况。申请人同类产品的生产工艺和设备获得我国多项发明和实用新型专利，还参与了《中华人民共和国化工行业标准——工业用乙二醇正丁醚》的起草。江苏省产品质量监督检验研究所等多家第三方科研机构和下游企业出具的技术评审材料和认证也表明国内产业同类产品的生产工艺和产品质量符合国内外标准和客户要求，国内产业同类产品的生产工艺技术与国外先进技术不存在实质差距。因此，国内产业受到的实质损害并非由生产工艺和技术落后等因素造成。

4. 商业流通渠道和贸易政策变化。目前国内产业同类产品实行市场化的价格机制，生产经营受市场规律调节。国内产业同类产品的销售渠道、销售区域基本与被调查产品相同，国内没有颁布限制乙二醇和二甘醇的单丁醚产业贸易行为和其他相关政策。调查期内，在商业流通领域并不存在其他阻碍国内产业同类产品国内销售或造成国内产业损害的因素。因此，国内产业受到的实质损害并非由商业流通渠道和贸易政策等因素造成。

5. 国内同类产品出口情况。调查数据显示，调查期内，国内产品仅有极少出口，出口量最大时也仅有当期总销量的 2.54%。因此，国内产业受到的实质损害并非国内产品出口造成。

6. 不可抗力的影响。调查期内，国内产业生产装置运行正常，未发生安全生产事故，未受到自然灾害及其他不可抗力事件影响。因此，国内产业受到的实质损害并非由不可抗力因素造成。

7. 调查期内原材料成本上涨的影响。伊士曼化工公司在其提交的《乙二醇和二甘醇的单丁醚反倾销案无损害抗辩书》中提出，申请人在调查期内始终承受着原材料成本方面的压力，在申请人正式开工前，在原材料方面已经承担了大量前期成本，申请人需要时间来消化成本；调查期内主要原材料之一丁醇的价格变化远远超出了申请人的预期，对申请人的经营指标也产生消极的影响，上述影响不应归咎于被调查产品。陶氏化学公司提交的《进口乙二醇和二甘醇的单丁醚反倾销案无损害抗辩书》和沙索提交的《乙二醇和二甘醇的单丁醚反倾销案无损害抗辩意见》中也提出了相似的意见。

对此，申请人在提交的《对伊士曼无损害抗辩的评论意见》中主张，从时间角度看，申请人的乙二醇丁醚项目是 2009 年 7 月正式开工的，而作为原材料的环氧乙烷项目在本案调查期结束后的 2011 年 9 月才建成。乙二醇丁醚项目不会提前承担未来项目的成本；从财务会计的角度，乙二醇丁醚和环氧乙烷是两个完全独立核算的项目，不存在项目间承担成本的问题。此外，另一种原材料丁醇不仅在国内，在欧美也同样大幅度上涨，对被调查产品与国内产品有同等程度的影响。

调查机关分析后认定，尽管环氧乙烷是生产乙二醇丁醚的原材料，但环氧乙烷项目和乙二醇丁醚项目不属于同一个项目，目前没有证据显示上述两个项目间的成本存在转嫁，不支持环氧乙烷项目成本上升导致乙二醇丁醚项目经营状况恶化的主张。关于丁醇价格成本的问题，丁醇价格的上涨在被调查产品的价格中也有所体现，但被调查产品价格仍然低于国内同类产品，且实地核查中获取的证据显示，原材料成本上升的幅度并未明显高出同类产品单位生产成本上升的幅度。在应诉方未出示肯定性证据的情况下，调查机关不支持将损害归因于丁醇价格成本上升的观点。

8. 投产期和相关费用折旧摊销对利润的影响。伊士曼化工公司在其提交的《乙二醇和二甘醇的单丁醚反倾销案无损害抗辩书》中提出，申请人在投产初期承担的巨大的相关费用和折旧的摊销影响了申请人在投产初期的利润；调查期内，与被调查产品相关的三项费用都对申请人同类产品的利润状况产生了重大的消极影响。陶氏化学公司在其提交的《进口乙二醇和二甘醇的单丁醚反倾销案无损害抗辩书》中也提出了类似的主张。

对此，申请人在提交的《对伊士曼无损害抗辩的评论意见》中主张，申请人德纳(南京)化工有限公司成立于 2004 年，到 2009 年 7 月同类产品生产线投产时，企业前期的开办费用已经摊销完毕；申请人调查期内采用了平均摊销法的财务会计准则，在调查期内对设备折旧和其他费用进行平均摊销，并未出现初期摊销多、后期摊销少的情况。

调查机关认定，在实地核查中获得的证据显示，申请人对调查期内的期间费用进行了平均摊销，在应诉方未提供肯定性证据的情况下，调查机关不支持投产初期相关费用和折旧摊销对申请人同类产品的经营产生重大消极影响的观点。

9. 其他国家(地区)进口产品影响。中国海关统计数据显示，调查期内，还有来自马来西亚、日本、韩国、中国台湾等国家(地区)的乙二醇和二甘醇的单丁醚(以下简称其他进口产品)，其他进口产品在中国市场占有一定份额，但从绝对数量和相对数量两方面，其他进口产品都在下降。2011 年 1 ~ 6 月其他进口产品进口量比 2009 年 7 ~ 12 月下降了 22.68%，其占中国市场的份额也从 2009 年 7 ~ 12 月的30.38%下降到2011年1～6月的26.41%。关于价格影响，调查机关注意到，调查期内其他进口产品的价格始终低于国内同类产品的价格。这种价格差异有可能会对国内同类产品造成不利的价格影响。但是，调查期内其他进口产品的价格一直整体高于来自美国和欧盟的进口产品，2009年7～12月至2011年1～6月的四个半年里，前者高出后者的幅度分别为7.45%、6.32%、2.54%、4.95%，整个调查期内，其他进口产品的价格平均高出被调查产品5.35%。因此，调查机关认为，无论从市场份额还是从价格来看，被调查产品在国内市场中都占据着主导地位，比其他进口产品更有优势，对国内产业的影响比其他进口产品要更大，因此国内产业所受到的价格影响主要来自于被调查产品。在本案中，综合考虑被调查产品和其他进口产品的数量、市场份额和价格的变化情况，调查机关认为，虽然其他进口产品与国内产业所遭受的实质性损害有可能在一定程度上有所关联，但这种关联并不能否认被调查产品与国内产业损害之间的因果关系。

10. 申请人内部使用同类产品。伊士曼化工公司在其提交的《乙二醇和二甘醇的单丁醚反倾销案无损害抗辩书》中提出，申请人内部大量使用乙二醇单丁醚产品。一方面，在评估申请人是否代表国内产业时，应当相应地排除申请人自用的部分产品；另一方面，申请人自用的部分国内同类产品，不会与被调查产品之间发生竞争关系。沙索在其提交的《乙二醇和二甘醇的单丁醚反倾销案无损害抗辩意见》中也提出了类似主张。

对此，申请人在提交的《对伊士曼无损害抗辩的评论意见》中主张，生产同类产品的目的主要是用于销售，以获得利润。由于被调查产品的倾销，申请人生产的同类产品的销售不畅，亏损严重。为了减少亏损，申请人只能将部分自产的乙二醇的单丁醚用于生产下游产品乙二醇丁醚醋酸酯。自用是申请人迫不得已的选择，是倾销造成的损害结果。

调查机关认为，在认定申请人的国内产业代表性时，以总产量作为主要的判定指标，而产品自用与否、自用量多少并非制约性、决定性的因素，对国内产业代表性的认定不具备实质性影响。关于自用产品与被调查产品竞争的问题，根据实地核查中得到的证据显示，申请人在销售不畅的前提下，将同类产品用作自用弥补亏损，本身就是与被调查产品竞争的结果，且部分自用产品来源于外购，在市场上势必要与被调查产品产生一定的竞争，调查机关不支持自用产品与被调查产品无竞争关系的观点。

11. 申请人停产。陶氏化学公司在其提交的《进口乙二醇和二甘醇的单丁醚反倾销案无损害抗辩书》中主张，产品质量问题和原材料供应问题导致了申请人在2010年下半年的停产。

申请人在提交的《对陶氏公司无损害抗辩书的评论意见》中主张，关于产品质量，申请人已提交证据证明申请人生产的乙二醇丁醚的产品纯度大于等于99.5%，高于进口产品通常的大于等于99%，在水分、馏程、酸度、比重等方面的技术指标甚至高于被调查产品。关于原材料供应问题，申请人指出，巴斯夫－扬子石化停产时间与申请人停产时间并不吻合，二者之间无必然联系，陶氏化学公司主张的申请人的原材料来源高度依赖于巴斯夫－扬子石化没有客观依据，且调查期内申请人并未受到原材料短缺的影响，停产是由被调查产品倾销造成。

调查机关分析后认定，申请人提供的证据材料已充分证明国内产品的质量是符合市场和用户需求的，且实地核查中的得到的证据显示，申请人停产是因销售不畅、库存加大，进而导致库容量饱和引起，而不是因原材料供应不足引起，调查机关不支持陶氏化学公司的主张。

基于以上证据事实和分析，原产于美国和欧盟的被调查产品大量低价倾销与国内产业遭受实质损害之间存在因果关系，调查期内其他已知因素可能造成的影响不足以影响该因果关系的认定。

七、初步裁定

根据上述调查结果，调查机关初步裁定，在本案调查期内，原产于美国和欧盟的进口乙二醇和二甘醇的单丁醚存在倾销，国内乙二醇和二甘醇的单丁醚产业受到了实质损害，而且倾销与实质损害之间存在因果关系。

有关公司的倾销幅度如下：

美国公司

1. 伊士曼化工公司
(Eastman Chemical Company)　　10.1%

2. 陶氏化学公司
(The Dow Chemical Company)　　12.5%

3. 益科斯达化工产品有限公司
(Equistar Chemicals, LP)　　11.5%

4. 其他美国公司
(All others)　　15.1%

欧盟公司

1. 沙索德国有限责任公司
(Sasol Germany GmbH)
沙索溶剂德国有限责任公司

(Sasol Solvents Germany GmbH)　13.0%

2. 英力士化学拉瓦拉有限公司

(INEOS Chemicals Lavera SAS)　9.3%

3. 巴斯夫欧洲公司

(BASF SE)　18.8%

4. 其他欧盟公司

(All others)　14.9%

(注：乙二醇和二甘醇的单丁醚可应用于醇酸树脂和用顺酐改性的酚醛树脂的溶剂等，也用作环氧树脂溶剂等。)

(中国塑料加工工业协会　郭齐)

政策法规

2012年国家与塑料行业相关的政策法规

一、中华人民共和国商务部令2012年第1号(二〇一二年二月四日)

修订后的《进出口许可证证书管理规定》已于2011年12月22日经中华人民共和国商务部2011年第58次部务会议审议通过，现予以公布，自2012年3月5日起施行。原《进出口许可证证书管理规定》(外经贸配字[1999]第87号)同时废止。

进出口许可证证书管理规定

第一章 总则

第一条 为加强对各类进出口许可证证书(以下简称许可证书)的管理，建立健全规章制度，特制定本规定。

第二条 本规定所称许可证书是指由商务部监制完成且尚未发放的各类具有许可进、出口性质的证明、文件、原产地证书等。

第三条 商务部配额许可证事务局(以下简称许可证局)受商务部委托，管理各类许可证书，并监督、检查地方商务主管部门和商务部驻各地特派员办事处(以下简称特办)所属进出口许可证签发机构(以下简称发证机构)对本规定的执行情况。

第四条 发证机构对许可证书的管理实行主要领导负责制，并指定专人承担具体管理工作。

发证机构应建立许可证书的内部管理制度，并认真执行。

第二章 许可证书的征订

第五条 为提高许可证书的使用率，发证机构须认真核算下一年度的许可证书需求量，合理上报征订数量。

第六条 许可证书的征订分为年度征订和补充征订。

许可证书一般一年集中征订一次，特殊情况下可安排多次集中征订。商务部每年10月下发通知征订下年度许可证书，发证机构按照通知要求填写《商务部进出口许可证书需求量报送单》(见附件1，以下简称报送单)，并报许可证局。

年度征订后如仍有不足，发证机构应至少提前20个工作日向许可证局提出补充征订申请，并按要求填写报送单，并报许可证局。许可证局审核后，根据核实情况予以补充或调剂。

第七条 发证机构上报报送单，须同时在商务部空白证书管理系统(以下简称空白证书管理系统)中填报相关征订信息。

第三章 许可证书的印制与发运

第八条 许可证局本着科学规划、确保用证、节约高效的原则，统一计划、合理安排许可证书的印制工作。

第九条 许可证局应按照中央国家机关政府采购的相关要求，通过规定程序，从中央国家机关定点印刷厂中选择质量信誉好、技术力量强、证书安全有保障的印制单位。

除许可证局委托的印制单位外，其他任何单位和个人不得擅自印制许可证书。

第十条 许可证局负责监督印制单位按其提供的许可证书样式、数量等要求，在规定时间内印制各类许可证书。

第十一条 许可证局根据发证机构报送的各类许可证书的征订数量，结合印制单位实际库存量、发证机构实际使用量、剩余量等情况，制定许可证书印制与发运计划。

第十二条 许可证书一般一年集中印制一次。集中印制数量不能满足实际发证需求的，许可证局可以根据实际情况及时安排追加印制。

第十三条 每批次印制完毕，许可证局应组织检查验收，验收合格后方可入库。许可证局负责在空白证书管理系统中进行入库登记。

经检查不合格的许可证书，印制单位应及时销毁。

第十四条 对年度征订的许可证书，许可证局应在征订通知规定的时限内发运至各发证机构。补充征订的许可证书，应自收到报送单之日起20个工作日内发运至相应的发证机构。

第十五条 许可证局确定发运明细后通知其委托的发运单位组织发运，发运后发运单位应在空白证书管理系统中进行发运登记。

第四章 许可证书的验收与保管

第十六条 发证机构对许可证书实行专人、专柜、专库统一保管。

第十七条 发证机构须在收到许可证书当日组织现场验收。验收工作应由两名以上工作人员同时在场，按货运单数量认真清点无误后予以签收，并填写《商务部进出口许可证书签收单》(一式三份，见附件2)，签收单应于次日寄送发运单位和许可证局，签收单须存档三年。

第十八条　发证机构在验收许可证书时，发现有单证不符、包装损坏和许可证书缺失等情况，应立即封存，作出书面检验记录，由验收人员及主要负责同志签字后连同检验记录报许可证局处理。

第十九条　发证机构在验收许可证书后，应将检验无误的证书及时存入专用库房，并按证书的种类、箱号、流水号分类整理，有序存放，同时在空白证书管理系统中进行接收登记。

第二十条　存放许可证书的库房须具备防火、防潮、防盗等安全设施。库房、专柜的钥匙须由专人负责保管。库房内不得存放其他物品，无关人员不得进入库房。

第五章　许可证书的进、出库台账登记与使用

第二十一条　发证机构应建立各类许可证书的进、出库台账登记制度。

第二十二条　发证机构原则上应分设许可证书保管人员与许可证书领用人员。

第二十三条　领取许可证书时，保管人员和领用人员应同时在场对许可证书逐一清点，并填写《商务部进出口许可证书进、出库台账登记表》(见附件3，以下简称登记表)，经保管人员和主要负责同志签字后方可使用。登记表应由许可证书保管人员妥善保管。

第二十四条　领取许可证书时，如发现有缺号、错号、纸张缺页、流水号不连续、无防伪标记等印制错误，应立即封箱，报告主要负责同志，并对检验情况进行书面记录，由保管人员及主要负责同志签字后，连同该箱许可证书一同报许可证局处理。

第二十五条　发证机构在启用各类许可证书时，须在空白证书管理系统中进行使用登记。

第二十六条　对印制错误且已发运到发证机构的许可证书，发证机构应退回许可证局，由许可证局按废证予以登记处理。

对库存期间因火烧、水浸、蛀蚀等造成许可证书损毁的，发证机构应立即书面报许可证局，并将受损证书按废证予以登记处理。

对打印错误和签发之日起20个工作日内未领取的许可证书，发证机构应予撤销，并按废证予以登记处理。

第二十七条　对在保管、使用过程中产生的废证，发证机构须在空白证书管理系统中进行废证登记。

第六章　许可证书的调剂与遗失的处理

第二十八条　地方商务主管部门或特办之间不得擅自相互借用各类许可证书。特殊情况下，确需临时借用许可证书，须由申请使用方向许可证局提出书面申请，许可证局审核并协商双方同意后统一安排调剂，并在空白证书管理系统中登记调剂信息。

第二十九条　同一地方商务主管部门设立的延伸打印终端间的许可证书调剂由该商务主管部门自主安排，并在空白证书管理系统进行相应登记。

第三十条　许可证书在仓储、运输、保管、使用过程中发生遗失的，相关部门均应立即将有关情况书面报许可证局。

第七章　许可证书的核查

第三十一条　发证机构每季度应对许可证书进行清点核对，核查许可证书的种类、数量等出入库登记与实际使用情况是否相符。

第三十二条　发证机构发现许可证书出入库登记与实际使用情况不符的，应立即查找原因，追究相关责任，采取必要防范和整改措施，同时书面报许可证局。

第三十三条　发证机构应于每年一月底前填写上一年度《商务部进出口许可证书使用情况登记表》(见附件4)，并报许可证局。

第八章　许可证书的销毁

第三十四条　对因改版而过期的空白许可证书，发证机构须在《商务部过期空白进出口许可证书封存/销毁登记表》(见附件5)上登记，经主要负责同志审核无误后封存。

新版许可证书启用当年，经报上级主管部门分管负责同志批准，旧版空白许可证书按保密文件销毁规定予以销毁，并在《商务部过期空白进出口许可证书封存/销毁登记表》上如实登记。有关销毁的请示签批件及销毁清单须留存备查。销毁情况报许可证局。

第三十五条　发证机构应将废证在《商务部进出口许可证书废证封存/销毁登记表》(见附件6)上登记，经主要负责同志审核后封存。废证保存期为两年。

保存期满的许可证书废证，经报上级主管部门分管负责同志批准，按保密文件销毁规定予以销毁，并在《商务部进出口许可证书废证封存/销毁登记表》上如实登记。有关废证销毁的请示签批件及销毁清单须留存备案。销毁情况报许可证局。

第九章　检查与处罚

第三十六条　许可证局对发证机构执行本规定的情况定期组织检查或抽查，并将检查结果纳入年

度考核范围。

第三十七条　许可证局对发证机构检查或抽查内容包括：

（一）发证机构许可证书内部管理制度制定与执行情况；

（二）许可证书的征订、验收情况；

（三）许可证书的保管及专库、专柜的安全措施情况；

（四）许可证书的进、出库台账登记情况；

（五）许可证书的使用情况；

（六）过期空白许可证书和废证的封存/销毁登记情况；

（七）按规定在空白证书管理系统进行登记的情况。

第三十八条　对未执行本规定的发证机构，许可证局视情节轻重给予警告或通报批评，并限期整改。

对不执行本规定造成许可证书丢失、被盗的发证机构，商务部将按照《进出口商品许可证发证机构管理办法》的有关规定进行处罚。

第十章　附则

第三十九条　本规定由商务部负责解释。

第四十条　本规定自2012年3月5日起施行，原《进出口许可证证书管理规定》（外经贸配字［1999］第87号）同时废止。

附件：（略）

二、中华人民共和国商务部令2012年第5号（二〇一二年五月八日）

《商务领域标准化管理办法（试行）》已经2012年3月14日商务部第62次部务会议审议通过，现予发布，自2012年7月1日起施行。《国内贸易部标准化管理实施办法》（内贸科字〔1997〕第135号）和《外经贸行业标准化管理办法》（外经贸技发〔1999〕第103号）同时废止。

商务领域标准化管理办法（试行）

第一章　总则

第一条　为加强商务领域标准化工作，提高商务领域经营、管理、服务及安全保障水平，根据《中华人民共和国标准化法》及相关规定，制定本办法。

第二条　本办法所称商务领域标准化工作，包括制定和修订商务领域标准，组织实施商务领域标准，对商务领域标准的实施进行监督。

第三条　在商务领域内需要统一规范的技术要求，应当制定标准。

第四条　对需要在全国范围内统一的商务领域技术要求，应当制定国家标准。

对没有国家标准而又需要在全国商务领域统一的技术要求，可以制定行业标准。

对国家标准、行业标准未作规定或规定不全的技术要求，省级商务主管部门可依法向本级标准化行政主管部门提出制定商务领域地方标准的建议。

第五条　商务领域国家标准、行业标准分为强制性标准和推荐性标准。

强制性标准依据国家标准化法律法规确定，强制性标准以外的标准是推荐性标准。

第六条　符合下列情形之一的，可以制定商务领域标准化指导文件：

（一）技术尚在发展中，需要有相应的标准文件引导其发展或者具有标准化价值，尚不能制定为标准的项目；

（二）采用国际标准化组织、国际电工委员会或者其他国际组织的技术报告的项目。

第七条　商务部有计划地发展商务领域标准化事业。

县级以上商务主管部门以及商务领域企事业单位应当将商务标准化工作纳入本部门、本单位发展规划，普及标准化知识，增强标准化意识。

第八条　鼓励商务领域行业组织及有关机构参与相关国际标准化活动，参加国际标准的研究、制定。

鼓励商务领域企事业单位采用国际标准和国外先进标准。

第二章　标准化工作的管理

第九条　商务部负责管理全国商务领域标准化工作。负责编制全国商务领域标准化工作规划和体系纲要，组织拟定商务领域国家标准和制定行业标准，组织实施和推广应用商务领域标准，组织管理商务领域相关专业标准化技术委员会，建立商务领域产品、服务质量检验和认证机构，统一管理商务领域国际标准化活动，指导地方商务主管部门的标准化工作。

第十条　省、自治区、直辖市商务主管部门负责管理本行政区域内商务标准化工作。主要职责是：

（一）贯彻执行国家标准化法律、法规、方针、政策和商务领域标准化规定，制定具体实施办法，并组织实施；

（二）制定商务领域行业标准化工作规划和计划，并组织实施；

（三）协助督促、检查单位或个人承担的商务领域国家标准和行业标准的起草工作；

（四）组织拟订商务领域地方标准；

（五）宣传贯彻商务领域国家标准、行业标准和地方标准，并对实施情况进行监督检查；

（六）组织、指导商务领域标准推广应用工作；

（七）承办商务部委托的其他商务领域标准化工作。

第十一条　商务领域相关专业标准化技术委员会由用户、生产经营单位、行业协会、科学技术研究机构、学术团体及有关部门专家组成，是专门从事该专业标准化的技术组织，负责在批准的专业范围内开展标准化技术工作。主要职责是：

（一）制定本专业标准体系目录；

（二）提出制定本专业国家标准、行业标准年度计划的建议；

（三）协助组织本专业标准的制定和复审工作，协调解决有关技术问题；

（四）承担相应的国际标准化技术工作；

（五）参与审查本专业标准草案，对标准草案提出审查意见并对标准涉及的技术问题负责；

（六）开展本专业标准宣传、推广和技术咨询服务等工作；

（七）承办其他商务领域标准化工作。

第十二条　商务领域相关专业标准化技术归口单位，由商务部根据需要确定，参照商务领域相关专业标准化技术委员会的职责承担相应的标准化技术工作。

第十三条　商务部根据国家财政管理规定，组织商务领域标准化工作经费的预算申报，并按相关资金管理办法实施。

第三章　标准的计划

第十四条　任何单位和个人均可向商务部提出标准项目申请，并填写《商务领域标准项目建议书》和《商务领域标准项目计划汇总表》。申请国家标准项目的，应同时提交标准草案。

必要时，商务部可以依法直接下达编制标准项目计划任务。任务承担人依据前款规定提交相关材料。

第十五条　商务部经汇总、审查、协调，形成商务领域标准项目年度计划。

申请国家标准项目的，由商务部提交国务院标准化行政主管部门或其他有关主管部门批准，并依据相关国家标准管理办法实施。

申请行业标准项目的，商务部批准后向项目申请人下达《商务领域标准项目任务计划书》(下称《任务计划书》)。《任务计划书》应载明标准项目名称、归口单位、承担单位、期限等内容。

第十六条　有下列情形之一的，可以对已经确定的标准计划项目申请进行调整：

（一）商务发展急需的标准项目可以申请增补；

（二）特殊情况，对标准计划项目的内容，包括项目名称、标准内容、起草单位和起草人等，可以申请调整；

（三）不宜制定标准的计划项目可以申请撤销。

第十七条　国家标准计划项目需调整的，由项目申请人填写《商务领域国家标准计划项目调整申请表》报商务部，经审查同意后，由商务部报国务院标准化行政主管部门批准；需要调整的行业标准计划项目由项目申请人填写《商务领域行业标准计划项目调整申请表》，报商务部批准。

调整的标准计划项目未获批准时，应当按照原定计划执行。

第四章　标准的制定

第十八条　制定商务领域标准应遵循以下原则：

（一）有利于建立统一开放、竞争有序的现代市场体系；

（二）有利于方便群众生活；

（三）有利于保证商品和服务的质量；

（四）有利于促进商务领域产业发展；

（五）有利于采用国际标准和国外先进标准；

（六）严格限定强制性行业标准的范围。

第十九条　收到《任务计划书》的项目申请人或行业标准任务承担人(以下统称标准起草方)应当按照《标准化工作导则》(GB/T1. 1—2009)的规定起草标准征求意见稿，编写编制说明及有关附件。

第二十条　标准起草方应采取有效措施保证按计划完成任务，并定期向商务部报告标准起草进展情况。

第二十一条　标准起草方不能按期完成起草任务的，应提前3个月向商务部提出延期申请。同一项目可申请延期1次，经批准同意的，最长可延期1年。

超过期限项目未完成也未提出延期申请的，或申请延期后仍未完成的，项目自动撤销。

第二十二条　标准起草方应当就标准征求意见稿征求生产、管理、科研、检验(认证)、质量监督、经销、使用等单位的意见。强制性标准的反馈意见一般不少于40份，推荐性标准的反馈意见一般不少于30份。同一单位专家的意见不应多于2份。

标准征求意见稿应当公开征求意见，法律法规另有规定除外。

第二十三条　标准起草方应当根据征集的意见对标准征求意见稿进行修改，形成标准送审稿、标准编制说明及有关附件。

第二十四条　商务部负责审查行业标准送审稿。审查具体组织工作可委托商务领域相关专业标准化技术委员会、协会(商会或学会)或其他组织承担。

第二十五条　参加审查的人数不得少于9人，应包括相关专业领域的生产、经销、使用、科研、检验(认证)等方面的代表，其中使用方面的代表不少于参加审查人员的1/4。

第二十六条　行业标准审查可采用会议审查或函审方式。对于技术、经济、群众生活影响大，涉及面广的标准应当采用会议审查方式。

采用会议审查方式，组织者应当在会议前1个月将标准送审稿及有关材料提交给参加标准审查会议的人员。采用函审方式，组织者应当在函审表决日前2个月将函审通知、标准送审稿及有关文件提交给参加函审的人员。

会议审查和函审的表决按照国家有关行业标准管理相关规定进行。

会议审查应当形成会议纪要，会议纪要应包括专家意见并由专家签字认可。

第二十七条　行业标准送审稿经审查通过后，由标准起草方修改完善并形成标准报批稿报送商务部。

第二十八条　行业标准的修订按照本章有关规定进行。

第五章　标准的审批、发布与复审

第二十九条　国家标准由国务院标准化行政主管部门审批、编号、发布。

行业标准由商务部审批、编号、发布，并报国务院标准化主管部门备案。

第三十条　强制性行业标准的代号为SB或WM，推荐性行业标准的代号为SB/T或WM/T。

第三十一条　商务部委托出版单位负责行业标准的出版发行，其他单位未经批准不得擅自印刷发行。

第三十二条　行业标准发布实施后商务部应当适时复审。

商务领域相关专业标准化技术委员会或专业标准化技术归口单位，受商务部委托，组织对标龄三年以上的行业标准进行复审，分别提出确认现行标准继续有效、予以修订或废止的意见，报商务部审核。

第三十三条　经复审，发现相关技术内容存在问题，影响标准继续使用，或需对原标准少量技术内容进行增减的，由商务领域相关专业标准化技术委员会或专业标准化技术归口单位提出该标准的修改建议，并填写行业标准修改单。

第三十四条　行业标准修改单由商务部批准，统一编号后以公告形式发布。

第三十五条　行业标准再版时应将标准和相应的标准修改单共同编辑出版，并在封面上注明。行业标准复审的，应将已发布的行业标准修改单一并复审。行业标准修订的，应将已发布的行业标准修改单 并修订。

第六章　标准的实施与监督

第三十六条　强制性标准必须执行。不符合强制性标准的产品或服务，禁止生产、销售和进口。

法律、行政法规规定强制执行的推荐性标准，在该法律、行政法规效力范围内强制执行。

第三十七条　企业申请产品质量认证，应当依据《中华人民共和国标准化法》第十五条规定办理。

第三十八条　企业所提供的产品和服务没有国家标准、行业标准和地方标准的，应当制定相应的企业标准。

已有商务领域国家标准、行业标准或地方标准的，鼓励企业制定严于国家标准、行业标准或地方标准要求的企业标准，在企业内部使用。

鼓励行业组织、企业自愿采用推荐性行业标准。

第三十九条　各级商务主管部门、专业技术委员会、相关行业协会应当加强商务领域标准的贯彻实施工作。

第四十条　任何单位或个人在商务领域标准实施过程中发现问题，及时向标准归口单位咨询，重大问题应及时向商务部报告。

第四十一条　标准起草方无正当理由未按时完成或未按规定完成项目制定工作的，商务部责令其限期改正；逾期不改正的，5年内不得承担商务领域标准化任务。

第四十二条　任何单位或个人均可向商务主管部门举报违反商务领域强制性标准的行为。商务主管部门依据有关法律、法规及部门规章的规定予以处罚，或移送有关部门予以处罚。

第七章　附则

第四十三条　本办法中有关表格的样式、提交文件的要求由商务部另行制定。

第四十四条　本办法自2012年 月 日起施行。《国内贸易部标准化管理实施办法》(内贸科字[1997]第135号)和《外经贸行业标准化管理办法》(外经贸技发[1999]第103号)同时废止。

三、中华人民共和国环境保护部 中华人民共和国发展和改革委员会 中华人民共和国商务部 公告2012年第55号(二〇一二年八月二十四日)

为贯彻落实《国务院办公厅关于限制生产销售使用塑料购物袋的通知》(国办发〔2007〕72号)、《国务院办公厅关于建立完整的先进的废旧商品回收体系的意见》(国办发〔2011〕49号)，加强废塑料加工利用的污染防治，保护人民群众身体健康，保障环境安全，促进循环经济健康发展，环境保护部、发展改革委、商务部联合制定《废塑料加工利用污染防治管理规定》。此规定自2012年10月1日起执行。

特此公告。

附件：废塑料加工利用污染防治管理规定

第一条　为贯彻落实《国务院办公厅关于限制生产销售使用塑料购物袋的通知》(国办发〔2007〕72号)、《国务院办公厅关于建立完整的先进的废旧商品回收体系的意见》(国办发〔2011〕49号)，加强废塑料加工利用的污染防治，保护人民群众身体健康，保障环境安全，促进循环经济健康发展，制定本规定。

第二条　在中华人民共和国境内废塑料加工利用活动必须遵守本规定要求。

本规定所称废塑料加工利用，是指将国内回收的废塑料(包括工业边角料、废弃塑料瓶、包装物及其他塑料制品、农膜等)及经批准从国外进口的各类废塑料等进行分类、清洗、拉丝、造粒的活动；以及将废塑料加工成塑料再生制品或成品的活动。

第三条　废塑料加工利用必须符合国家相关产业政策规定及《废塑料回收与再生利用污染控制技术规范》，防止二次污染。

禁止在居民区加工利用废塑料。禁止利用废塑料生产厚度小于0.025mm的超薄塑料购物袋和厚度小于0.015mm超薄塑料袋。禁止利用废塑料生产食品用塑料袋。禁止无危险废物经营许可证从事废塑料类危险废物的回收利用活动，包括被危险化学品、农药等污染的废弃塑料包装物，废弃的一次性医疗用塑料制品(如输液器、血袋)等。

无符合环保要求污水治理设施的，禁止从事废编织袋造粒、缸脚料淘洗、废塑料退镀(涂)、盐卤分拣等加工活动。

第四条　废塑料加工利用单位应当以环境无害化方式处理废塑料加工利用过程产生的残余垃圾、滤网；禁止交不符合环保要求的单位或个人处置。

禁止露天焚烧废塑料及加工利用过程产生的残余垃圾、滤网。

第五条　进口废塑料加工利用企业应当符合《固体废物进口管理办法》以及环境保护部关于进口可用作原料的固体废物和废塑料环境保护管理相关规定。

禁止进口未经清洗的使用过的废塑料。

禁止将进口的废塑料全部或者部分转让给进口许可证载明的利用企业以外的单位或者个人，包括将进口废塑料委托给其他企业代为清洗。

进口废塑料分拣或加工利用过程产生的残余废塑料应当进行无害化利用或者处置；禁止将上述残余废塑料未经清洗处理直接出售。

进口废纸加工利用企业应当对进口废纸中的废塑料进行无害化利用或者处置；禁止将进口废纸中的废塑料，未经清洗处理直接出售。

第六条　进口废塑料加工利用企业发现属于国家禁止进口类或者不符合环境保护控制标准的进口废塑料，应当立即向口岸海关、检验检疫部门和所在地环保部门报告并配合做好相关处理工作。

第七条　废塑料加工利用集散地应当建立废塑料加工利用散户产生的残余垃圾和滤网集中回收处理机制。鼓励废塑料加工利用集散地对废塑料加工利用散户实行集中园区化管理，集中处理废塑料加工利用产生的废水、废气和固体废物。

鼓励有条件的废塑料加工利用集散地申请开展国家"城市矿产"示范基地建设，申请开展废旧商品回收体系建设试点工作。

第八条　省级环保、商务主管部门应当组织核查并公布合格的废塑料加工利用企业名单；对核查发现问题的，应当依法处理并将处理结果向社会公布。

自2013年1月1日起，未经环保核查合格的企业，不予批准进口废塑料。

第九条　本规定自2012年10月1日起实行。

四、中华人民共和国商务部、中华人民共和国海关总署公告2012年第94号，公布《2013年自动进口许可管理货物目录》(二〇一二年十二月十日)

根据《中华人民共和国对外贸易法》、《货物进出口管理条例》和《货物自动进口许可管理办法》，现发布《2013年自动进口许可管理货物目录》，自2013年1月1日起执行。《2012年自动进口许可管理货物目录》同时废止。

附件：2013 年自动进口许可管理货物目录

机电类商品

一、以下商品编码的产品由商务部签发

类别	海关商品编号	商品名称	备注	计量单位
光盘生产设备	8477101010	用于光盘生产的精密注塑机	加工塑料的	台

二、以下商品编码的产品由地方、部门机电产品进出口办公室签发

类别	海关商品编号	商品名称	备注	计量单位
化工装置	8417809010	平均温度>1000℃的耐腐蚀焚烧炉	为销毁管制化学品或化学弹药用	台
	8417809090	其他非电热的工业用炉及烘箱	包括实验室用炉、烘箱和焚烧炉	台
	8419409010	氢－低温蒸馏塔	温度≤－238℃，压力为0.5－5兆帕，内径≥1米等条件	台
	8419409020	耐腐蚀蒸馏塔	内径大于0.1米，接触表面由特殊耐腐蚀材料制成	台
	8419409090	其他蒸馏或精馏设备		台
	8419500010	热交换器	专用于核反应堆的一次冷却剂回路的	台
	8419500040	冷却气体用热交换器	用耐 UF6 腐蚀材料制成或加以保护的	台
	8419500050	耐腐蚀热交换器	0.15平方米<换热面积<20平方米	台
	8419609010	液化器	将来自级联的 UF6 气体压缩并冷凝成液态 UF6	台
	8419609090	其他液化空气或其他气体用的机器		台
	8419899010	带加热装置的发酵罐	不发散气溶胶，且容积大于20升	台
	8419899021	凝华器（或冷阱）	从扩散级联中取出 UF6 并可再蒸发转移	台
	8419899023	UF6 冷阱	能承受－20℃或更低的温度	台

（其他略）

五、中华人民共和国工业和信息化部公告 2012 年第 64 号（二〇一二年十二月二十一日）

为加快产业结构调整，加强环境保护，综合利用资源，规范行业投资行为，制止盲目投资和低水平重复建设，促进合成氨行业健康发展，依据国家有关法律法规和产业政策，特制定《合成氨行业准入条件》，现予以公告。

附件：合成氨行业准入条件

为促进合成氨行业结构优化和产业升级，规范市场竞争秩序，依据国家有关法律法规和产业政策要求，按照"总量平衡、优化存量、节约能（资）源、保护环境、合理布局"的可持续发展原则，特制定本准入条件。

一、生产企业布局

（一）根据资源、能源状况和市场需求情况，各合成氨主要生产省（自治区、直辖市）应严格控制合成氨行业产能扩张，引导本地区合成氨行业有序发展。

（二）原则上不得新建以天然气和无烟块煤为原料的合成氨装置（按照区域规划搬迁、综合利用项目除外）；三年内，煤炭调入省区原则上不得新建合成氨产能（以高硫煤为原料除外）；引导东部地区合成氨生产装置有序转移，在西部地区煤炭产地，按照煤化电热一体多联产模式，建设大型煤制合成氨基地。新建项目须符合国家产业政策及有关政策规定。

（三）严禁在依法设定的生态保护区、风景旅游区、自然保护区、文化遗产保护区、饮用水源保护区内和国家及地方所规定的区域内新建合成氨生产装置，已在上述区域内投产运营的合成氨装置，地方政府应根据该区域规划，依法通过关闭、搬迁、转产等方式要求企业逐步退出。

（四）新建、改扩建项目应建设在依法设立、环保设施齐全的化工园区或集聚区内，项目规划必须符合国家和省、自治区、直辖市区域规划、化肥行

业发展规划、城市建设发展规划、土地利用规划、节能减排规划、环境保护和污染防治规划等要求。

二、装置规模及技术装备

(一)新建合成氨生产装置，单系列生产规模应不低于1000吨/日(综合利用和联产项目除外)，造气炉按需设置。

(二)新建合成氨生产装置应采用先进技术和装备，鼓励采用具有自主知识产权的国产化技术。以煤为原料的新建合成氨装置应采用连续气化工艺。

(三)鼓励现有企业开展以原料结构调整、产品结构调整、节能、环保和安全为目的的技术改造。现有固定层间歇式煤气化工艺应全部配套建设吹风气余热回收、造气炉渣综合利用装置。淘汰天然气常压间歇转化工艺。

三、资源能源消耗和综合利用

现有生产企业合成氨单位产品能耗应符合现行的《合成氨单位产品能源消耗限额》(GB21344)国家标准规定的限定值(见表1)，新建生产企业合成氨单位产品能耗应符合现行的《合成氨单位产品能源消耗限额》(GB21344)国家标准规定的准入值(见表2)。表1、表2所列能耗限额随最新标准(GB21344)的发布更新。

表1　合成氨单位产品能耗限额限定值(GB21344)

原料类型	合成氨单位产品综合能耗限额限定值 (千克标准煤/吨)(kgce/t)
优质无烟块煤	≤1900
非优质无烟块煤、焦炭、型煤	≤2200
天然气、焦炉气	≤1650

备注：标准以外煤种参照非优质无烟块煤、焦炭、型煤类

表2　合成氨单位产品能耗限额准入值(GB21344)

原料类型	合成氨单位产品综合能耗限额准入值 (千克标准煤/吨)(kgce/t)
优质无烟块煤	≤1500
非优质无烟块煤、焦炭、型煤	≤1800
天然气、焦炉气	≤1150

备注：标准以外煤种参照非优质无烟块煤、焦炭、型煤类

现有企业应在三年内达到“表2合成氨单位产品能耗限额准入值(GB21344)”的要求，新建或改扩建合成氨项目须进行节能评估和审查。

现有生产企业合成氨单位产品水耗应符合《取水定额第8部分：合成氨》(GB/T18916.8－2006)规定的取水定额值，新建生产企业合成氨单位产品水耗应达到行业最先进指标，合成氨企业造气渣应100%利用。

四、环境保护

(一)合成氨生产企业应严格执行《合成氨工业水污染物排放标准》(GB13458)、《大气污染物综合排放标准》(GB16297)、《锅炉大气污染物排放标准》(GB13271)和固体废物污染防治法律法规、危险废物处理处置的有关要求，做到达标排放。企业污染物排放须达到地方污染物排放标准要求和主要污染物排放总量控制规定。

(二)新建合成氨项目必须严格执行环境影响评价制度并按规定取得主要污染物排放总量指标。企业环境保护设施必须与主体工程同时设计、同时施工、同时投入生产和使用。

(三)新建合成氨企业应达到《氮肥行业清洁生产评价指标体系(试行)》中规定的“清洁生产先进企业水平”；支持和鼓励现有合成氨企业积极开展清洁生产，依法进行清洁生产审核，大力推广清洁生产技术，不断提高企业清洁生产水平。

(四)企业应当按照国家或地方污染物排放标准，结合行业特点以及主要污染物总量减排工作的需要，制定自行监测方案，对污染物排放状况和污染防治设施运行情况开展自行监测和监控，保存原始监测和监控记录，建立废气废水排放量、固体废物产生量和处理处置量等台账。定期向社会公布监测结果。

五、安全、消防及职业卫生

(一)企业必须严格执行安全生产法律、法规，生产条件必须符合有关标准的规定，并建立健全安全生产责任制。

(二)企业必须严格执行《危险化学品建设安全监督管理办法》和《建设项目职业卫生“三同时”监督管理暂行办法》，认真开展建设项目安全条件审查、安全设施设计审查、试生产备案和竣工验收工作。建设项目安全生产防护设施和职业卫生防护设施必须与主体工程同时设计、同时施工、同时投入使用。

(三)企业严格执行《危险化学品重大危险源监督管理暂行规定》，建立健全监测监控体系，完善控制措施，制定重大危险源应急预案。

(四)企业必须严格执行《危险化学品生产企业安全生产许可证实施办法》，依法取得安全生产许可证。

六、监督与管理

（一）合成氨建设项目应在投产十二个月内达到本准入条件中规定的能源消耗和污染物排放指标。逾期未达到本准入条件规定的，相关行政主管部门要根据国家有关法律、法规的要求责令其限期整改或停产。

（二）加快落后产能退出，发生以下情况之一的现有合成氨企业，由省级工业、安全、环保等有关部门依法对其进行重点监控，限期整改仍达不到相关规定的，应作为落后产能退出。

1、三废排放不达标。

2、发生重大安全、环保事故。

3、年平均吨氨综合能耗高于现行的《合成氨单位产品能源消耗限额》（GB21344）国家标准规定的限定值。

七、附则

（一）本准入条件适用于中华人民共和国境内（台湾、香港、澳门特殊地区除外）各类新建、改扩建、现有的合成氨生产企业。

（二）本准入条件中涉及的国家和行业标准若进行了修订，则按修订后的新标准执行。

（三）本准入条件自2013年1月1日开始实施，由国家工业和信息化部负责解释，并根据行业发展情况和宏观调控要求进行修订。

（注：合成氨主要用于制造氮肥和复合肥料，各种含氮有机中间体、聚氨酯、聚酰胺纤维和丁腈橡胶等都需直接以氨为原料。）

六、中华人民共和国财政部 中华人民共和国国家发展和改革委员会 中华人民共和国海关总署 国家税务总局公告2012年第83号 关于调整《国内投资项目不予免税的进口商品目录》的公告（二〇一二年十二月二十四日）

为加快转变经济发展方式、推动产业结构调整和优化升级，积极鼓励企业引进国内不能生产的先进技术设备，统筹兼顾对外开放和国内发展，促进先进技术引进和企业自主创新，财政部、国家发展改革委、海关总署、国家税务总局在广泛收集、整理各地方、有关部门、行业协会、企业意见的基础上，针对《国内投资项目不予免税的进口商品目录（2008年调整）》（以下简称《2008年目录》）执行中存在的问题，对《2008年目录》中的部分条目进行了调整，形成了《国内投资项目不予免税的进口商品目录（2012年调整）》（以下简称《2012年目录》），现将有关事项公告如下：

一、根据近年来国内装备制造水平和相关产业发展的变化，对《2008年目录》中部分条目所列技术规格进行了相关调整。另外，根据《中华人民共和国进出口税则》对《2008年目录》中部分条目所列税则号列进行了相应调整和修正，同时对部分商品的名称等内容进行了调整和修正，调整后形成的《2012年目录》详见附件。

二、《2012年目录》自2013年1月1日起执行，即2013年1月1日及以后新批准的国内投资项目（以项目的审批、核准或备案日期为准，下同），其进口设备一律按照《2012年目录》执行。

为保证老项目顺利实施，对2013年1月1日以前批准的国内投资项目，其进口设备在2013年6月30日及以前申报进口的，仍按照《2008年目录》执行。但对于有关进口设备按照《2008年目录》审核不符合免税条件的，而按照《2012年目录》审核符合免税条件的，自2013年1月1日起，可以按照《2012年目录》执行。货物已经征税进口的，不再予以调整。

自2013年7月1日起，国内投资项目项下申报进口的设备一律按照《2012年目录》执行。

三、现行政策对国内投资项目项下进口设备的免税条件另有规定的，有关进口设备仍需执行相关规定。但此前公布实施的《进口不予免税的重大技术装备和产品目录（2012年修订）》中相关装备和产品的技术指标与《2012年目录》不一致的，以《2012年目录》所列技术规格为准，并自2013年1月1日起一并调整。

附件：国内投资项目不予免税的进口商品目录（2012年调整）

编号	税则号列	设备名称	技术规格	备注
十五		包装机械		
6	84223010	聚酯瓶饮料灌装设备	能力≤48000瓶/h（瓶容积以550ml计）	技术规格调整
9	84412000	纸塑复合水泥袋生产成套设备	能力≤300袋/min	设备名称调整
10	84418010	纸塑铝软包装制袋设备	所有规格	

续表

编号	税则号列	设备名称	技术规格	备注
13	847740 84223010 84223030	塑料杯成型充填包装机	能力≤48000件/h(容积以250ml计)	新增条目
十七		模具		新增类别
11	84807190 848007900	塑料模具	所有规格(为锁紧力>3000t的注塑机配套的注塑模具和精度<±0.003mm的塑料模具除外)	新增条日
二十五		化工设备		
1	84198910	加氢反应器、精制反应器	所有规格	
2	84178090	轻质纯碱煅烧炉	$\phi \leq 3600$mm	
3	84178090	重质纯碱煅烧炉	$\phi \leq 3200$mm	
4	84193990	磷铵造粒机	240000t/年及以下	
5	84193990	回转干燥器	240000t/年及以下磷铵装置用	
6	84198990 84798999	高压冷凝器	所有规格	税号调整，重大技术装备进口不予免税目录同类税号一并调整
7	84195000	块孔石墨换热器	所有规格	
8	84198990 84798999	阳极保护冷却器	200000t/年及以下硫酸生产线用	税号调整，重大技术装备进口不予免税目录同类税号一并调整
9	84195000 84778000	胶片冷却装置	密炼机用≤400L	
10	84198990	氨合成塔	合成塔直径$\leq \phi 2800$mm	
11	84198990	尿素合成塔(CO_2汽提法)	内径×壁厚×总长$\leq \phi 2800 \times 122 \times 36118$mm	
12	84198990	尿素合成塔(氨气提法)	内径×壁厚×总长$\leq \phi 2200 \times 109 \times 46880$mm	
13	84198990	二氧化碳汽提法工艺汽提塔	内径×壁厚×总长$\leq \phi 2350 \times 28 \times 11815$mm	
14	84198990	碳化塔	所有规格	
15	84198990	PVC及烯烃聚合釜	所有规格	
16	84223030 84223090	纯碱包装机	所有规格	
17	84223030 84223090	颗粒体物料包装机	≤800包/单秤＊每小时(50公斤/包)	技术规格调整，重大技术装备进口不予免税目录指标一并调整
18	84772010	混炼挤压造粒机组	产量≤25万吨/年	设备名称变更，技术规格调整，重大技术装备进口不予免税目录同类指标一并调整

续表

编号	税则号列	设备名称	技术规格	备注
19	84772090	橡胶螺杆挤出机	单螺杆直径≤250mm；双螺杆单根直径≤200mm；三复合螺杆及以上单根最大直径≤150mm	技术规格调整，重大技术装备进口不予免税目录同类指标一并调整
20	84775900	机械式轮胎定型硫化机	模腔直径≤150英寸	技术规格调整，重大技术装备进口不予免税目录指标一并调整
21	84775900	平板硫化机	热板规格＜2200mm×10000mm	
22	84775900	液压硫化机	模腔直径≤2400mm	技术规格调整
23	84775900	斜胶轮胎成型机	所有规格	
24	84778000	密闭式炼胶机	密炼室容积≤400L	
25	84778000	双辊开放式炼胶机、压片机	直径≤660mm	
26	84778000	橡胶压延机	辊长＜1730mm的四辊、三辊、二辊压延机	
27	8424 84798999	高压洗涤器	容器外壳直径≤2830mm	税号调整
28	84198990 84798999	磷酸生产设备（包括塔、罐、动设备、静设备等）	所有规格	税号调整
29	85433000	离子膜电解槽	所有规格	
30	90248000	耐久性能试验机	载重胎最高时速≤150km，轿车胎时速≤240km	
31	84148090 840681 84068200	乙烯裂解气压缩机及配套工业汽轮机	年产量≤120万吨	技术规格调整
32	84148090 840681 84068200	乙烯制冷压缩机及配套工业汽轮机	年产量≤120万吨	技术规格调整
33	84148090 840681 84068200	丙烯制冷压缩机及配套工业汽轮机	年产量≤120万吨	技术规格调整
34	84186920 84148090 84798999	聚乙烯配套用循环气压缩机（离心式）及其膨胀机	年产量≤40万吨	税号调整
35	84148090	聚乙烯配套用往复式压缩机（迷宫密封式）	年产量≤45万吨	技术规格调整
36	84137010	离心式急冷油泵	所有规格	
37	84137010	离心式急冷水泵	所有规格	
38	84195000	板翅式换热器冷箱（含乙烯冷箱）	所有规格	设备名称变更，税号调整，技术规格调整
39	8418 84195000	电站和石化空冷器（含加氢装置空冷器）	所有规格	设备名称变更，税号调整

续表

编号	税则号列	设备名称	技术规格	备注
40	84068200 84143014 84148090	硝酸装置四合一机组(包括汽轮机、空气压缩机、尾气透平、氮氧合物压缩机)	年产量≤60 万吨	技术规格调整
41	84198990	PTA 氧化反应器	单机年产≤120 万吨	技术规格调整，税号调整，重大技术装备进口不予免税目录同类指标一并调整
42	84068200 84148090	PTA 工艺空气压缩机机组(包括蒸汽轮机、离心压缩机)	单机年产≤100 万吨	技术规格调整
43	84193990	PTA 蒸汽回转干燥机	单机年产≤120 万吨	技术规格调整
44	84798200	PTA 搅拌机	单机年产≤100 万吨	新增条目
45	84148090	循环氢离心压缩机组	所有规格	新增条目
46	84148090 84183	二、四、六列往复式新氢压缩机组	轴功率≤8000kW	新增条目
47	84148090	长输管道压缩机组	轴功率≤30MW	新增条目
48	85015300	管道压缩机用高速变频防爆电机	输出功率≤25MW	新增条目
49	84148090	炼油用大型原油原料气往复压缩机	所有规格	新增条目
50	84137010 84137090	加氢进料泵	所有规格	新增条目
51	84068200 84068110	工业汽轮机	输出功率≤100000kW	新增条目
52	8481	地面安装高压大口径全锻焊管道球阀	公称通径≤48 英寸(48″)、压力等级≤900 磅(class900LB)	新增条目
53	8481	埋地安装高压大口径大锻焊管道球阀	公称通径≤48 英寸(48″)、压力等级≤900 磅(class900LB)	新增条目
54	84714991	千万吨级炼油装置 DCS 集散控制系统	所有规格	新增条目
三十		塑料加工设备		
(一)		塑料制品液压机		
1	8477	塑料制品液压机	所有规格	
(二)		注塑(射)机		
1	84771010	注塑(射)机	锁模力≤6000t(制品重量的重复误差<0.3%的精密注塑机、4 色及以上注塑机、锁模力>550t 的电动注塑机除外)	技术规格调整
(三)		塑料挤出机		
1	84772010	同向平行双螺杆混炼造粒机	螺杆直径≤320mm	技术规格调整

续表

编号	税则号列	设备名称	技术规格	备注
2	84772010	异向平行双螺杆混炼造粒机	螺杆直径≤450mm	技术规格调整
3	84772090	异向平行双螺杆挤压成型机	螺杆直径≤100mm	
4	84772090	吹塑薄膜挤出机	薄膜层数≤9 层	技术规格调整
5	84772090	单螺杆异型材塑料挤出成型机	所有规格	
6	84772090	锥形双螺杆异形塑料挤出成型机(含排气式)	螺杆大端直径≤92mm	
7	84772090 84778000	平膜塑料挤出机	薄膜层数≤7 层	设备名称变更，技术规格调整
8	84772090	单螺杆挤管机	螺杆直径≤200mm	
9	84772090	塑钢门窗挤出机	螺杆直径≤200mm	
10	84772090	锥形双螺杆排气式塑料挤出机	螺杆大端直径≤92mm	
11	84772090	单螺杆排气式塑料挤出机	螺杆直径≤150mm	
12	84772090	塑料发泡挤出机	所有规格	新增条目
13	84772090	塑料网材挤出机	所有规格	新增条目
14	84772090 847740	塑料土工格栅挤出成型机组(包括挤出机、机头，冷却成型机)	所有规格	新增条目
15	84772090 847740	塑料双壁波纹管挤出成型机组(包括挤出机、机头、冷却成型机)	双壁波纹管直径≤2m	新增条目
16	84772010 84772090	其他未列名的塑料挤出机(含造粒机)	所有规格	
17	84198990 85437099	废塑料杀菌机	所有规格	
18	84778000	废塑料颜色分选机	所有规格	
19	84778000	废塑料杂质分选机	所有规格	
(四)		塑料中空吹塑成型机		
1	84774010	塑料中空吹塑成型机	产量≤48000 瓶(件)/h(瓶容积以550mL 计)	技术规格调整，税号调整
2	84774010	塑料多层中空吹塑成型机	≤6 层	技术规格调整，税号调整
3	84774010	塑料一步法注拉吹中空吹塑成型机	容量≤50L	税号调整
(五)		其他塑料加工机械		
编号	税则号列	设备名称	技术规格	备注

续表

编号	税则号列	设备名称	技术规格	备注
1	84193990 84211990 84772010 84772090 84774010 84774020 84774090 84775900 84778000 84798999	木塑复合材料生产及成型机组	所有规格	税号调整
2	84211990 84772010 84772090 84774010 84774020 84774090 84775090 84778000 84193990 84798999	废塑料回收与利用机组	所有规格	税号调整
3	84223030 84223090 84224000	塑封机	所有规格(半导体行业用塑封机除外)	设备名称变更，技术规格调整
4	84223030 84223090 84224000 84798999	复膜机	所有规格	税号调整

(其他略)

七、中华人民共和国商务部 中华人民共和国海关总署 中华人民共和国国家质量监督检验检疫总局公告2012年第98号，公布2013年进口许可证管理货物目录(二○一二年十二月二十七日)

根据《中华人民共和国对外贸易法》、《中华人民共和国货物进出口管理条例》和《重点旧机电产品进口管理办法》，现发布《2013年进口许可证管理货物目录》，自2013年1月1日起执行。《2012年进口许可证管理货物目录》同时废止。

附件：2013年进口许可证管理货物目录

重点旧机电产品进口目录

货物种类	海关商品编号	商品名称及备注	单位
一、化工设备	8419409090	其他蒸馏或精馏设备	台
	8419609010	液化器(将来自级联的UF6气体压缩并冷凝成液态UF6)	台
	8419899010	带加热装置的发酵罐(不发散气溶胶，且容积>20升)	台

消耗臭氧层物质

	海关商品编号	商品名称及备注	单位
	2903191010	1，1，1-三氯乙烷(甲基氯仿)，用于清洗剂的除外	千克
	2903191090	1，1，1-三氯乙烷(甲基氯仿)，用于清洗剂的	千克

续表

	2903399020	溴甲烷（甲基溴）	千克
	2903710000	一氯二氟甲烷	千克
	2903720000	二氯三氟乙烷	千克
	2903730000	二氯一氟乙烷	千克
	2903740000	一氯二氟乙烷	千克
	2903750010	1，1，1，2，2－五氟－3，3－二氯丙烷	千克
	2903750020	1，1，2，2，3－五氟－1，3－二氯丙烷	千克
	2903750090	其他二氯五氟丙烷	千克
	2903760010	溴氯二氟甲烷	千克
	2903760020	溴三氟甲烷	千克
	2903771000	三氯氟甲烷	千克
	2903772011	二氯二氟甲烷	千克
	2903772012	三氯三氟乙烷，用于清洗剂除外（CFC－113）	千克
	2903772014	二氯四氟乙烷（CFC－114）	千克
	2903772015	一氯五氟乙烷（CFC－115）	千克
	2903772016	一氯三氟甲烷（CFC－13）	千克
	2903791011	一氟二氯甲烷	千克
	2903791012	1，1，1，2－四氟－2－氯乙烷	千克
	2903791013	三氟一氯乙烷	千克
	2903791014	1－氟－1，1－二氯乙烷	千克
	2903791015	1，1－二氟－1－氯乙烷	千克
	2903791090	其他仅含氟和氯的甲烷、乙烷及丙烷的卤化衍生物	千克
	2903799021	其他仅含溴、氟的甲烷、乙烷和丙烷	千克
	3824710011	二氯二氟甲烷和二氟乙烷的混合物（R－500）	千克
	3824710012	一氯二氟甲烷和二氯二氟甲烷的混合物（R－501）	千克
	3824710013	一氯二氟甲烷和一氯五氟乙烷的混合物（R－502）	千克
	3824710014	三氟甲烷和一氯三氟甲烷的混合物（R－503）	千克
	3824710015	二氟甲烷和一氯五氟乙烷的混合物（R－504）	千克
	3824710016	二氯二氟甲烷和一氟一氯甲烷的混合物（R－505）	千克
	3824710017	一氟一氯甲烷和二氯四氟乙烷的混合物（R－506）	千克
	3824710018	二氯二氟甲烷和二氯四氟乙烷的混合物（R－400）	千克
	3824740011	二氟一氯甲烷、二氟乙烷和一氯四氟乙烷的混合物（R－401）	千克
	3824740012	五氟乙烷、丙烷和二氟一氯甲烷的混合物（R－402）	千克
	3824740013	丙烷、二氟一氯甲烷和八氟丙烷的混合物（R－403）	千克
	3824740014	二氟一氯甲烷、二氟乙烷、一氯二氟乙烷和八氟环丁烷的混合物（R－405）	千克
	3824740015	二氟一氯甲烷、2－甲基丙烷（异丁烷）和一氯二氟乙烷的混合物（R－406）	千克

续表

	3824740016	五氟乙烷、三氟乙烷和二氟一氯甲烷的混合物(R-408)	千克
	3824740017	二氟一氯甲烷、一氯四氟乙烷和一氯二氟乙烷的混合物(R-409)	千克
	3824740018	丙烯、二氟一氯甲烷和二氟乙烷的混合物(R-411)	千克
	3824740019	二氟一氯甲烷、八氟丙烷和一氯二氟乙烷的混合物(R-412)	千克
	3824740021	二氟一氯甲烷、一氯四氟乙烷、一氯二氟乙烷和2-甲基丙烷的混合物(R-414)	千克
	3824740022	二氟一氯甲烷和二氟乙烷的混合物(R-415)	千克
	3824740023	四氟乙烷、一氯四氟乙烷和丁烷的混合物(R-416)	千克
	3824740024	丙烷、二氟一氯甲烷和二氟乙烷的混合物(R-418)	千克
	3824740025	二氟一氯甲烷和八氟丙烷的混合物(R-509)	千克
	3824740026	二氟一氯甲烷和一氯二氟乙烷的混合物	千克
	3824740090	其他含甲烷、乙烷或丙烷的氢氯氟烃混合物(不论是否含甲烷、乙烷或丙烷的全氟烃或氢氟烃，但不含全氯氟烃)	千克
	2903191010	1，1，1-三氯乙烷(甲基氯仿)，用于清洗剂的除外	千克
	2903191090	1，1，1-三氯乙烷(甲基氯仿)，用于清洗剂的	千克
	2903399020	溴甲烷(甲基溴)	千克
	2903710000	一氯二氟甲烷	千克
	2903720000	二氯三氟乙烷	千克
	2903730000	二氯一氟乙烷	千克
	2903740000	一氯二氟乙烷	千克
	2903750010	1，1，1，2，2-五氟-3，3-二氯丙烷	千克
	2903750020	1，1，2，2，3-五氟-1，3-二氯丙烷	千克
	2903750090	其他二氯五氟丙烷	千克
	2903760010	溴氯二氟甲烷	千克
	2903760020	溴三氟甲烷	千克
	2903771000	三氯氟甲烷	千克
	2903772011	二氯二氟甲烷	千克
	2903772012	三氯三氟乙烷，用于清洗剂除外(CFC-113)	千克
	2903772014	二氯四氟乙烷(CFC-114)	千克
	2903772015	一氯五氟乙烷(CFC-115)	千克
	2903772016	一氯三氟甲烷(CFC-13)	千克
	2903791011	一氟二氯甲烷	千克
	2903791012	1，1，1，2-四氟-2-氯乙烷	千克
	2903791013	三氟一氯乙烷	千克
	2903791014	1-氟-1，1-二氯乙烷	千克
	2903791015	1，1-二氟-1-氯乙烷	千克
	2903791090	其他仅含氟和氯的甲烷、乙烷及丙烷的卤化衍生物	千克
	2903799021	其他仅含溴、氟的甲烷、乙烷和丙烷	千克

续表

	3824710011	二氯二氟甲烷和二氟乙烷的混合物(R－500)	千克
	3824710012	一氯二氟甲烷和二氯二氟甲烷的混合物(R－501)	千克
	3824710013	一氯二氟甲烷和一氯五氟乙烷的混合物(R－502)	千克
	3824710014	三氟甲烷和一氯三氟甲烷的混合物(R－503)	千克
	3824710015	二氟甲烷和一氯五氟乙烷的混合物(R－504)	千克
	3824710016	二氯二氟甲烷和一氟一氯甲烷的混合物(R－505)	千克
	3824710017	一氟一氯甲烷和二氯四氟乙烷的混合物(R－506)	千克
	3824710018	二氯二氟甲烷和二氯四氟乙烷的混合物(R－400)	千克
	3824740011	二氟一氯甲烷、二氟乙烷和一氯四氟乙烷的混合物(R－401)	千克
	3824740012	五氟乙烷、丙烷和二氟一氯甲烷的混合物(R－402)	千克
	3824740013	丙烷、二氟一氯甲烷和八氟丙烷的混合物(R－403)	千克
	3824740014	二氟一氯甲烷、二氟乙烷、一氯二氟乙烷和八氟环丁烷的混合物(R－405)	千克
	3824740015	二氟一氯甲烷、2－甲基丙烷(异丁烷)和一氯二氟乙烷的混合物(R－406)	千克
	3824740016	五氟乙烷、三氟乙烷和二氟一氯甲烷的混合物(R－408)	千克
	3824740017	二氟一氯甲烷、一氯四氟乙烷和一氯二氟乙烷的混合物(R－409)	千克
	3824740018	丙烯、二氟一氯甲烷和二氟乙烷的混合物(R－411)	千克
	3824740019	二氟一氯甲烷、八氟丙烷和一氯二氟乙烷的混合物(R－412)	千克
	3824740021	二氟一氯甲烷、一氯四氟乙烷、一氯二氟乙烷和2－甲基丙烷的混合物(R－414)	千克
	3824740022	二氟一氯甲烷和二氟乙烷的混合物(R－415)	千克
	3824740023	四氟乙烷、一氯四氟乙烷和丁烷的混合物(R－416)	千克
	3824740024	丙烷、二氟一氯甲烷和二氟乙烷的混合物(R－418)	千克
	3824740025	二氟一氯甲烷和八氟丙烷的混合物(R－509)	千克
	3824740026	二氟一氯甲烷和一氯二氟乙烷的混合物	千克
	3824740090	其他含甲烷、乙烷或丙烷的氢氯氟烃混合物(不论是否含甲烷、乙烷或丙烷的全氟烃或氢氟烃，但不含全氯氟烃)	千克
	2903191010	1，1，1－三氯乙烷(甲基氯仿)，用于清洗剂的除外	千克
	2903191090	1，1，1－三氯乙烷(甲基氯仿)，用于清洗剂的	千克
	2903399020	溴甲烷(甲基溴)	千克
	2903710000	一氯二氟甲烷	千克
	2903720000	二氯三氟乙烷	千克
	2903730000	二氯一氟乙烷	千克
	2903740000	一氯二氟乙烷	千克
	2903750010	1，1，1，2，2－五氟－3，3－二氯丙烷	千克
	2903750020	1，1，2，2，3－五氟－1，3－二氯丙烷	千克
	2903750090	其他二氯五氟丙烷	千克

续表

	2903760010	溴氯二氟甲烷	千克
	2903760020	溴三氟甲烷	千克
	2903771000	三氯氟甲烷	千克
	2903772011	二氯二氟甲烷	千克
	2903772012	三氯三氟乙烷，用于清洗剂除外(CFC－113)	千克
	2903772014	二氯四氟乙烷(CFC－114)	千克
	2903772015	一氯五氟乙烷(CFC－115)	千克
	2903772016	一氯三氟甲烷(CFC－13)	千克
	2903791011	一氟二氯甲烷	千克
	2903791012	1，1，1，2－四氟－2－氯乙烷	千克
	2903791013	三氟一氯乙烷	千克
	2903791014	1－氟－1，1－二氯乙烷	千克
	2903791015	1，1－二氟－1－氯乙烷	千克
	2903791090	其他仅含氟和氯的甲烷、乙烷及丙烷的卤化衍生物	千克
	2903799021	其他仅含溴、氟的甲烷、乙烷和丙烷	千克
	3824710011	二氯二氟甲烷和二氟乙烷的混合物(R－500)	千克
	3824710012	一氯二氟甲烷和二氯二氟甲烷的混合物(R－501)	千克
	3824710013	一氯二氟甲烷和一氯五氟乙烷的混合物(R－502)	千克
	3824710014	三氟甲烷和一氯三氟甲烷的混合物(R－503)	千克
	3824710015	二氟甲烷和一氯五氟乙烷的混合物(R－504)	千克
	3824710016	二氯二氟甲烷和一氟一氯甲烷的混合物(R－505)	千克
	3824710017	一氟一氯甲烷和二氯四氟乙烷的混合物(R－506)	千克
	3824710018	二氯二氟甲烷和二氯四氟乙烷的混合物(R－400)	千克
	3824740011	二氟一氯甲烷、二氟乙烷和一氯四氟乙烷的混合物(R－401)	千克
	3824740012	五氟乙烷、丙烷和二氟一氯甲烷的混合物(R－402)	千克
	3824740013	丙烷、二氟一氯甲烷和八氟丙烷的混合物(R－403)	千克
	3824740014	二氟一氯甲烷、二氟乙烷、一氯二氟乙烷和八氟环丁烷的混合物(R－405)	千克
	3824740015	二氟一氯甲烷、2－甲基丙烷(异丁烷)和一氯二氟乙烷的混合物(R－406)	千克
	3824740016	五氟乙烷、三氟乙烷和二氟一氯甲烷的混合物(R－408)	千克
	3824740017	二氟一氯甲烷、一氯四氟乙烷和一氯二氟乙烷的混合物(R－409)	千克
	3824740018	丙烯、二氟一氯甲烷和二氟乙烷的混合物(R－411)	千克
	3824740019	二氟一氯甲烷、八氟丙烷和一氯二氟乙烷的混合物(R－412)	千克
	3824740021	二氟一氯甲烷、一氯四氟乙烷、一氯二氟乙烷和2－甲基丙烷的混合物(R－414)	千克
	3824740022	二氟一氯甲烷和二氟乙烷的混合物(R－415)	千克
	3824740023	四氟乙烷、一氯四氟乙烷和丁烷的混合物(R－416)	千克

续表

	3824740024	丙烷、二氟一氯甲烷和二氟乙烷的混合物(R－418)	千克
	3824740025	二氟一氯甲烷和八氟丙烷的混合物(R－509)	千克
	3824740026	二氟一氯甲烷和一氯二氟乙烷的混合物	千克
	3824740090	其他含甲烷、乙烷或丙烷的氢氯氟烃混合物(不论是否含甲烷、乙烷或丙烷的全氟烃或氢氟烃，但不含全氯氟烃)	千克
	2903191010	1，1，1－三氯乙烷(甲基氯仿)，用于清洗剂的除外	千克
	2903191090	1，1，1－三氯乙烷(甲基氯仿)，用于清洗剂的	千克
	2903399020	溴甲烷(甲基溴)	千克
	2903710000	一氯二氟甲烷	千克
	2903720000	二氯三氟乙烷	千克
	2903730000	二氯一氟乙烷	千克
	2903740000	一氯二氟乙烷	千克
	2903750010	1，1，1，2，2－五氟－3，3－二氯丙烷	千克
	2903750020	1，1，2，2，3－五氟－1，3－二氯丙烷	千克
	2903750090	其他二氯五氟丙烷	千克
	2903760010	溴氯二氟甲烷	千克
	2903760020	溴三氟甲烷	千克
	2903771000	三氯氟甲烷	千克
	2903772011	二氯二氟甲烷	千克
	2903772012	三氯三氟乙烷，用于清洗剂除外(CFC－113)	千克
	2903772014	二氯四氟乙烷(CFC－114)	千克
	2903772015	一氯五氟乙烷(CFC－115)	千克
	2903772016	一氯三氟甲烷(CFC－13)	千克
	2903791011	一氟二氯甲烷	千克
	2903791012	1，1，1，2－四氟－2－氯乙烷	千克
	2903791013	三氟一氯乙烷	千克
	2903791014	1－氟－1，1－二氯乙烷	千克
	2903791015	1，1－二氟－1－氯乙烷	千克
	2903791090	其他仅含氟和氯的甲烷、乙烷及丙烷的卤化衍生物	千克
	2903799021	其他仅含溴、氟的甲烷、乙烷和丙烷	千克
	3824710011	二氯二氟甲烷和二氟乙烷的混合物(R－500)	千克
	3824710012	一氯二氟甲烷和二氯二氟甲烷的混合物(R－501)	千克
	3824710013	一氯二氟甲烷和一氯五氟乙烷的混合物(R－502)	千克
	3824710014	三氟甲烷和一氯三氟甲烷的混合物(R－503)	千克
	3824710015	二氟甲烷和一氯五氟乙烷的混合物(R－504)	千克
	3824710016	二氯二氟甲烷和一氟一氯甲烷的混合物(R－505)	千克
	3824710017	一氟一氯甲烷和二氯四氟乙烷的混合物(R－506)	千克
	3824710018	二氯二氟甲烷和二氯四氟乙烷的混合物(R－400)	千克

续表

	3824740011	二氟一氯甲烷、二氟乙烷和一氯四氟乙烷的混合物(R-401)	千克
	3824740012	五氟乙烷、丙烷和二氟一氯甲烷的混合物(R-402)	千克
	3824740013	丙烷、二氟一氯甲烷和八氟丙烷的混合物(R-403)	千克
	3824740014	二氟一氯甲烷、二氟乙烷、一氯二氟乙烷和八氟环丁烷的混合物(R-405)	千克
	3824740015	二氟一氯甲烷、2-甲基丙烷(异丁烷)和一氯二氟乙烷的混合物(R-406)	千克
	3824740016	五氟乙烷、三氟乙烷和二氟一氯甲烷的混合物(R-408)	千克
	3824740017	二氟一氯甲烷、一氯四氟乙烷和一氯二氟乙烷的混合物(R-409)	千克
	3824740018	丙烯、二氟一氯甲烷和二氟乙烷的混合物(R-411)	千克
	3824740019	二氟一氯甲烷、八氟丙烷和一氯二氟乙烷的混合物(R-412)	千克
	3824740021	二氟一氯甲烷、一氯四氟乙烷、一氯二氟乙烷和2-甲基丙烷的混合物(R-414)	千克
	3824740022	二氟一氯甲烷和二氟乙烷的混合物(R-415)	千克
	3824740023	四氟乙烷、一氯四氟乙烷和丁烷的混合物(R-416)	千克
	3824740024	丙烷、二氟一氯甲烷和二氟乙烷的混合物(R-418)	千克
	3824740025	二氟一氯甲烷和八氟丙烷的混合物(R-509)	千克
	3824740026	二氟一氯甲烷和一氯二氟乙烷的混合物	千克
	3824740090	其他含甲烷、乙烷或丙烷的氢氯氟烃混合物(不论是否含甲烷、乙烷或丙烷的全氟烃或氢氟烃,但不含全氯氟烃)	千克
	2903191010	1,1,1-三氯乙烷(甲基氯仿),用于清洗剂的除外	千克
	2903191090	1,1,1-三氯乙烷(甲基氯仿),用于清洗剂的	千克
	2903399020	溴甲烷(甲基溴)	千克
	2903710000	一氯二氟甲烷	千克
	2903720000	二氯三氟乙烷	千克
	2903730000	二氯一氟乙烷	千克
	2903740000	一氯二氟乙烷	千克
	2903750010	1,1,1,2,2-五氟-3,3-二氯丙烷	千克
	2903750020	1,1,2,2,3-五氟-1,3-二氯丙烷	千克
	2903750090	其他二氯五氟丙烷	千克
	2903760010	溴氯二氟甲烷	千克
	2903760020	溴三氟甲烷	千克
	2903771000	三氯氟甲烷	千克
	2903772011	二氯二氟甲烷	千克
	2903772012	三氯三氟乙烷,用于清洗剂除外(CFC-113)	千克
	2903772014	二氯四氟乙烷(CFC-114)	千克
	2903772015	一氯五氟乙烷(CFC-115)	千克
	2903772016	一氯三氟甲烷(CFC-13)	千克

续表

2903791011	一氟二氯甲烷	千克
2903791012	1，1，1，2－四氟－2－氯乙烷	千克
2903791013	三氟一氯乙烷	千克
2903791014	1－氟－1，1－二氯乙烷	千克
2903791015	1，1－二氟－1－氯乙烷	千克
2903791090	其他仅含氟和氯的甲烷、乙烷及丙烷的卤化衍生物	千克
2903799021	其他仅含溴、氟的甲烷、乙烷和丙烷	千克
3824710011	二氯二氟甲烷和二氟乙烷的混合物(R－500)	千克
3824710012	一氯二氟甲烷和二氯二氟甲烷的混合物(R－501)	千克
3824710013	一氯二氟甲烷和一氯五氟乙烷的混合物(R－502)	千克
3824710014	三氟甲烷和一氯三氟甲烷的混合物(R－503)	千克
3824710015	二氟甲烷和一氯五氟乙烷的混合物(R－504)	千克
3824710016	二氯二氟甲烷和一氟一氯甲烷的混合物(R－505)	千克
3824710017	一氟一氯甲烷和二氯四氟乙烷的混合物(R－506)	千克
3824710018	二氯二氟甲烷和二氯四氟乙烷的混合物(R－400)	千克
3824740011	二氟一氯甲烷、二氟乙烷和一氯四氟乙烷的混合物(R－401)	千克
3824740012	五氟乙烷、丙烷和二氟一氯甲烷的混合物(R－402)	千克
3824740013	丙烷、二氟一氯甲烷和八氟丙烷的混合物(R－403)	千克
3824740014	二氟一氯甲烷、二氟乙烷、一氯二氟乙烷和八氟环丁烷的混合物(R－405)	千克
3824740015	二氟一氯甲烷、2－甲基丙烷(异丁烷)和一氯二氟乙烷的混合物(R－406)	千克
3824740016	五氟乙烷、三氟乙烷和二氟一氯甲烷的混合物(R－408)	千克
3824740017	二氟一氯甲烷、一氯四氟乙烷和一氯二氟乙烷的混合物(R－409)	千克
3824740018	丙烯、二氟一氯甲烷和二氟乙烷的混合物(R－411)	千克
3824740019	二氟一氯甲烷、八氟丙烷和一氯二氟乙烷的混合物(R－412)	千克
3824740021	二氟一氯甲烷、一氯四氟乙烷、一氯二氟乙烷和2－甲基丙烷的混合物(R－414)	千克
3824740022	二氟一氯甲烷和二氟乙烷的混合物(R－415)	千克
3824740023	四氟乙烷、一氯四氟乙烷和丁烷的混合物(R－416)	千克
3824740024	丙烷、二氟一氯甲烷和二氟乙烷的混合物(R－418)	千克
3824740025	二氟一氯甲烷和八氟丙烷的混合物(R－509)	千克
3824740026	二氟一氯甲烷和一氯二氟乙烷的混合物	千克
3824740090	其他含甲烷、乙烷或丙烷的氢氯氟烃混合物(不论是否含甲烷、乙烷或丙烷的全氟烃或氢氟烃，但不含全氯氟烃)	千克

(其他略)

八、中华人民共和国商务部　中华人民共和国海关总署公告2012年第96号《两用物项和技术进出口许可证管理目录》(二〇一二年十二月三十一日)

根据《两用物项和技术进出口许可证管理办法》(商务部 海关总署令2005年第29号)和2013年《中华人民共和国进出口税则》，商务部和海关总署对《两用物项和技术进出口许可证管理目录》进行了调整，现将调整后的《两用物项和技术进出口许可证管理目录》(见附件)予以公布。

进口放射性同位素须按《放射性同位素与射线装置安全和防护条例》和《两用物项和技术进出口许可证管理办法》有关规定，报环境保护部审批后，在商务部配额许可证事务局申领两用物项和技术进口许可证。进口经营者持两用物项和技术进口许可证向海关办理进口手续。

本公告自2013年1月1日起正式实施，商务部、海关总署2011年第101号公告公布的《两用物项和技术进出口许可证管理目录》同时废止。

附件：两用物项和技术进出口许可证管理目录

说明：

一、本目录分为《两用物项和技术进口许可证管理目录》与《两用物项和技术出口许可证管理目录》。

二、本目录所列物项和技术是指《中华人民共和国核出口管制条例》、《中华人民共和国核两用品及相关技术出口管制条例》、《中华人民共和国导弹及相关物项和技术出口管制条例》、《中华人民共和国生物两用品及相关设备和技术出口管制条例》、《中华人民共和国监控化学品管理条例》、《中华人民共和国易制毒化学品管理条例》、《中华人民共和国放射性同位素与射线装置安全和防护条例》和国务院批准的《有关化学品及相关设备和技术出口管制办法》等相关行政法规所附清单和名录以及国家依据相关法律、行政法规予以管制、临时管制或特别管制的物项和技术。

三、进出口本目录的物项和技术，不论该物项和技术是否在本目录中列明海关商品编号，均应依法办理两用物项和技术进出口许可证。

四、本目录所列物项和技术及其商品名称和描述与相关法律规定不一致时，以相关法律规定为准。

Ⅰ、两用物项和技术进口许可证管理目录

一、监控化学品管理条例监控名录所列物项

序号	商品名称	描述	海关商品编号	单位
1	氮芥气 HN1：N，N－二(2－氯乙基)乙胺	第一类 可作为化学武器的化学品	2921193000	千克
2	氮芥气 HN2：N，N－二(2－氯乙基)甲胺	第一类 可作为化学武器的化学品	2921194000	千克
3	氮芥气 HN3：三(2－氯乙基)胺	第一类 可作为化学武器的化学品	2921195000	千克
4	硫芥气：2－氯乙基氯甲基硫醚	第一类 可作为化学武器的化学品	2930909013	千克
5	芥子气：二(2－氯乙基)硫醚	第一类 可作为化学武器的化学品	2930909014	千克
6	二(2－氯乙硫基)甲烷	第一类 可作为化学武器的化学品	2930909015	千克
7	倍半芥气：1，2－二(2－氯乙硫基)乙烷	第一类 可作为化学武器的化学品	2930909016	千克
8	1，3－二(2－氯乙硫基)正丙烷	第一类 可作为化学武器的化学品	2930909017	千克
9	1，4－二(2－氯乙硫基)正丁烷	第一类 可作为化学武器的化学品	2930909018	千克
10	1，5－二(2－氯乙硫基)正戊烷	第一类 可作为化学武器的化学品	2930909019	千克
11	二(2－氯乙硫基甲基)醚	第一类 可作为化学武器的化学品	2930909021	千克
12	氧芥气；二(2－氯乙硫基乙基)醚	第一类 可作为化学武器的化学品	2930909022	千克
13	烷基(甲基、乙基、正丙基或异丙基)硫代膦酸烷基(氢或少于或等于10个碳原子的碳链，包括环烷基)－S－2二烷(甲、乙、正丙或异丙)氨基乙酯及相应烷基化盐或质子化盐 例如： VX：甲基硫代膦酸乙基－S－2－二异丙氨基乙酯	第一类 可作为化学武器的化学品	2930909026	千克

续表

序号	商品名称	描述	海关商品编号	单位
14	路易氏剂1：2－氯乙烯基二氯胂	第一类 可作为化学武器的化学品	2931909011	千克
15	路易氏剂2：二(2－氯乙烯基)氯胂	第一类 可作为化学武器的化学品	2931909012	千克
16	路易氏剂3：三(2－氯乙烯基)胂	第一类 可作为化学武器的化学品	2931909013	千克
17	烷基(甲基、乙基、正丙基或异丙基)氟膦酸烷(少于或等于10个碳原子的碳链，包括环烷)酯 例如： 沙林：甲基氟膦酸异丙酯 梭曼：甲基氟膦酸频那酯	第一类 可作为化学武器的化学品	2931901913	千克
18	二烷(甲、乙、正丙或异丙)氨基氰膦酸烷(少于或等于10个碳原子的碳链，包括环烷)酯 例如： 塔崩：二甲氨基氰膦酸乙酯	第一类 可作为化学武器的化学品	2931901914	千克
19	烷基(甲基、乙基、正丙基或异丙基)膦酰二氟 例如： DF：甲基膦酰二氟	第一类 可作为化学武器的化学品	2931901915	千克
20	烷基(甲基、乙基、正丙基或异丙基)亚膦酸烷基(氢或少于或等于10个碳原子的碳链，包括环烷基)－2－二烷(甲、乙、正丙或异丙)氨基乙酯及相应烷基化盐或质子化盐 例如： QL：甲基亚膦酸乙基－2－二异丙氨基乙酯	第一类 可作为化学武器的化学品	2931901911	千克
21	氯沙林：甲基氯膦酸异丙酯	第一类 可作为化学武器的化学品	2931901912	千克
22	氯梭曼：甲基氯膦酸频那酯	第一类 可作为化学武器的化学品	2931901912	千克
26	PFIB：1，1，3，3，3－五氟－2－三氟甲基－1－丙烯(又名：全氟异丁烯；八氟异丁烯)	第二类：可作为生产化学武器前体的化学品	2903391000	千克
27	频哪基醇：3，3－二甲基丁－2－醇	第二类：可作为生产化学武器前体的化学品	2905191000	千克
28	2，2－二苯基－2－羟基乙酸：二苯羟乙酸；二苯乙醇酸	第二类：可作为生产化学武器前体的化学品	2918191000	千克
29	二烷(甲、乙、正丙或异丙)氨基乙基－2－氯及相应质子化盐	第二类：可作为生产化学武器前体的化学品	2921196000	千克
30	二烷(甲、乙、正丙或异丙)氨基乙－2－醇及相应质子化盐 例如：二甲氨基乙醇及相应质子化盐二乙氨基乙醇及相应质子化盐	第二类：可作为生产化学武器前体的化学品	2922192900	千克

续表

序号	商品名称	描述	海关商品编号	单位
31	二烷(甲、乙、正丙或异丙)氨基膦酰二卤	第二类：可作为生产化学武器前体的化学品	2929902000	千克
32	二烷(甲、乙、正丙或异丙)氨基膦酸二烷(甲、乙、正丙或异丙)酯	第二类：可作为生产化学武器前体的化学品	2929903000	千克
33	胺吸膦：硫代磷酸二乙基－S－2－二乙氨基乙酯及相应烷基化盐或质子化盐)	第二类：可作为生产化学武器前体的化学品	2930909023	千克
34	二烷(甲、乙、正丙或异丙)氨基乙－2－硫醇及相应质子化盐	第二类：可作为生产化学武器前体的化学品	2930909024	千克
35	硫二甘醇：二(2－羟乙基)硫醚；硫代双乙醇	第二类：可作为生产化学武器前体的化学品	2930909025	千克
36	含有一个磷原子并有一个甲基、乙基或(正或异)丙基原子团与该磷原子结合的化学品，不包括含更多碳原子的情形，但第一类名录所列者除外 例如： 1. 甲基膦酰二氯 2. 甲基膦酸二甲酯 3. 丙基膦酸 4. 甲基膦酸 5. 乙基膦酸二乙酯 6. 甲基膦酸甲基、5－(5－乙基－2－甲基－2－氧代－1，3，2－二氧磷杂环已基)甲基酯　化学文摘登记号：41203－81－0 7. 甲基膦酸二[5－(5－乙基－2－甲基－2－氧代－1，3，2－二氧磷杂环已基)甲基酯]　化学文摘登记号：42595－45－9 8. 甲基膦酸的混合物(化合物6和7的混合物)化学文摘登记号：170836－68－7 9. 甲基膦酸二聚乙二醇酯　化学文摘登记号：294675－51－7 例如：地虫磷：二硫代乙基膦酸－S－苯基乙酯	第二类：可作为生产化学武器前体的化学品	2930909027	千克
37	BZ：二苯乙醇酸－3－奎宁环酯(＊)	第二类：可作为生产化学武器前体的化学品	2933391000	千克
38	奎宁环－3－醇	第二类：可作为生产化学武器前体的化学品	2933392000	千克
40	亚硫酰氯：氯化亚砜；氧氯化硫	第三类：可作为生产化学武器主要原料的化学品	2812101000	千克
41	磷酰氯：三氯氧磷；氧氯化磷	第三类：可作为生产化学武器主要原料的化学品	2812102000	千克

续表

序号	商品名称	描 述	海关商品编号	单位
42	光气：碳酰二氯	第三类：可作为生产化学武器主要原料的化学品	2812103000	千克
43	一氯化硫	第三类：可作为生产化学武器主要原料的化学品	2812104100	千克
44	二氯化硫	第三类：可作为生产化学武器主要原料的化学品	2812104200	千克
45	三氯化磷	第三类：可作为生产化学武器主要原料的化学品	2812104300	千克
46	五氯化磷	第三类：可作为生产化学武器主要原料的化学品	2812104500	千克
47	五硫化二磷	第三类：可作为生产化学武器主要原料的化学品	2813900010	千克
48	氰化钠	第三类：可作为生产化学武器主要原料的化学品	2837111000	千克
49	氰化钾	第三类：可作为生产化学武器主要原料的化学品	2837191000	千克
50	氯化氰	第三类：可作为生产化学武器主要原料的化学品	2853002000	千克
51	氯化苦；三氯硝基甲烷	第三类：可作为生产化学武器主要原料的化学品	2904903000	千克
53	二苯乙醇酸甲酯	第三类：可作为生产化学武器主要原料的化学品	2918199010	千克
54	亚磷酸三甲酯	第三类：可作为生产化学武器主要原料的化学品	2920901100	千克
55	亚磷酸三乙酯	第三类：可作为生产化学武器主要原料的化学品	2920901200	千克
56	亚磷酸二甲酯	第三类：可作为生产化学武器主要原料的化学品	2920901300	千克
57	亚磷酸二乙酯	第三类：可作为生产化学武器主要原料的化学品	2920901400	千克
58	二甲胺	第三类：可作为生产化学武器主要原料的化学品	2921110010	千克
60	三乙醇胺	第三类：可作为生产化学武器主要原料的化学品	2922131000	千克
61	三乙醇胺盐酸盐	第三类：可作为生产化学武器主要原料的化学品	2922132020	千克
62	乙基二乙醇胺	第三类：可作为生产化学武器主要原料的化学品	2922193000	千克
63	甲基二乙醇胺	第三类：可作为生产化学武器主要原料的化学品	2922194000	千克

二、易制毒化学品

序号	商品名称	描 述	海关商品编号	单位
26	1－苯基－2－丙酮（苯丙酮）	可用于制造毒品	2914310000	千克
27	*N*－乙酰邻氨基苯酸（*N*－乙酰邻氨基苯甲酸、2－乙酰氨基苯甲酸）	可用于制造毒品	2924230010	千克
28	3，4－亚甲基二氧苯基－2－丙酮	可用于制造毒品	2932920000	千克

续表

序号	商品名称	描　述	海关商品编号	单位
29	高锰酸钾	可用于制造毒品	2841610000	千克
30	醋酸酐(乙酸酐)	可用于制造毒品	2915240000	千克
32	苯乙酸	可用于制造毒品	2916340010	千克
33	盐酸(氯化氢)	可用于制造毒品	2806100000	千克
34	硫酸	可用于制造毒品	2807000010	千克
35	甲苯	可用于制造毒品	2902300000	千克
36	乙醚	可用于制造毒品	2909110000	千克
37	丙酮	可用于制造毒品	2914110000	千克
38	甲基乙基酮(丁酮)	可用于制造毒品	2914120000	千克
39	邻氨基苯甲酸(氨茴酸)	可用于制造毒品	2922431000	千克
40	哌啶(六氢吡啶)	可用于制造毒品	2933321000	千克
41	三氯甲烷(氯仿)	可用于制造毒品	2903130000	千克

三、放射性同位素(略)

Ⅱ、两用物项和技术出口许可证管理目录

一、核出口管制清单所列物项和技术

7、专门设计或制造用于化学交换或离子交换浓缩工厂的系统、设备和部件

序号	商品名称	描　述	海关商品编号	单位
94	液－液交换柱(化学交换)	为使用化学交换过程的铀浓缩工厂专门设计或制造的有机械动力输入的逆流液－液交换柱(即带有筛板的脉冲柱、往复板柱和带有内部涡轮混合器的柱)。为了耐浓盐酸溶液的腐蚀，这些交换柱及其内部构件一般用适宜的塑料(例如氟碳聚合物)或玻璃制作或保护。交换柱的级停留时间一般被设计得很短(30秒或更短)。		台
95	液－液离心接触器(化学交换)	为使用化学交换过程的铀浓缩工厂而专门设计或制造的液－液离心接触器。此类接触器利用转动来达到有机相与水相的分散，然后借助离心力来分离开这两相。为了耐浓盐酸溶液的腐蚀，这些接触器一般用适当的塑料(例如碳氟聚合物)来制造或作衬里，或衬以玻璃。离心接触器的级停留时间被设计得很短(30秒或更短)。	8421199020	台
99	供料准备系统(化学交换)	专门设计或制造的用来为化学交换铀同位素分离工厂生产高纯氯化铀供料溶液的系统。这些系统由进行纯化所需的溶解设备、溶剂萃取设备和(或)离子交换设备，以及用来将U+6或U+4还原为U+3的电解槽组成。这些系统产生只含几个ppm的铬、铁、钒、钼和其他两价或价态更高的阳离子金属杂质的氯化铀溶液。处理高纯度U+3系统的若干部分的建造材料包括玻璃、碳氟聚合物、聚苯硫酸酯或聚醚砜塑料衬里的石墨和用树脂浸过的石墨。		台
104	离子交换柱(离子交换)	为以离子交换过程进行铀浓缩而专门设计或制造的用于容纳和支撑离子交换树脂/吸附剂填充床层的直径大于1000mm的圆柱。这些柱一般用耐浓盐酸溶液腐蚀的材料(例如钛或碳氟塑料)制成或保护，并能在100－200℃的温度范围内和高于0．7MPa(102psi)的压力下操作。		台

二、核两用品及相关技术出口管制清单所列物项和技术

三、生物两用品及相关设备和技术出口管制清单所列物项和技术

四、监控化学品管理条例名录所列物项

序号	商品名称	描 述	海关商品编号	单位
6	二(2－氯乙硫基)甲烷	第一类 可作为化学武器的化学品	2930909015	千克
7	倍半芥气：1，2－二(2－氯乙硫基)乙烷	第一类 可作为化学武器的化学品	2930909016	千克
8	1，3－二(2－氯乙硫基)正丙烷	第一类 可作为化学武器的化学品	2930909017	千克
9	1，4－二(2－氯乙硫基)正丁烷	第一类 可作为化学武器的化学品	2930909018	千克
10	1，5－二(2－氯乙硫基)正戊烷	第一类 可作为化学武器的化学品	2930909019	千克
11	二(2－氯乙硫基甲基)醚	第一类 可作为化学武器的化学品	2930909021	千克
12	氧芥气；二(2－氯乙硫基乙基)醚	第一类 可作为化学武器的化学品	2930909022	千克
13	烷基(甲基、乙基、正丙基或异丙基)硫代膦酸烷基(氢或少于或等于10个碳原子的碳链，包括环烷基)－S－2二烷(甲、乙、正丙或异丙)氨基乙酯及相应烷基化盐或质子化盐 例如： VX：甲基硫代膦酸乙基－S－2－二异丙氨基乙酯	第一类 可作为化学武器的化学品	2930909026	千克
17	烷基(甲基、乙基、正丙基或异丙基)氟膦酸烷(少于或等于10个碳原子的碳链，包括环烷)酯 例如： 沙林：甲基氟膦酸异丙酯 梭曼：甲基氟膦酸频那酯	第一类 可作为化学武器的化学品	2931901913	千克
18	二烷(甲、乙、正丙或异丙)氨基氰膦酸烷(少于或等于10个碳原子的碳链，包括环烷)酯 例如： 塔崩：二甲氨基氰膦酸乙酯	第一类 可作为化学武器的化学品	2931901914	千克
19	烷基(甲基、乙基、正丙基或异丙基)膦酰二氟 例如： DF：甲基膦酰二氟	第一类 可作为化学武器的化学品	2931901915	千克
20	烷基(甲基、乙基、正丙基或异丙基)亚膦酸烷基(氢或少于或等于10个碳原子的碳链，包括环烷基)－2－二烷(甲、乙、正丙或异丙)氨基乙酯及相应烷基化盐或质子化盐 例如： QL：甲基亚膦酸乙基－2－二异丙氨基乙酯	第一类 可作为化学武器的化学品	2931901911	千克
21	氯沙林：甲基氯膦酸异丙酯	第一类 可作为化学武器的化学品	2931901912	千克
22	氯梭曼：甲基氯膦酸频那酯	第一类 可作为化学武器的化学品	2931901912	

续表

序号	商品名称	描 述	海关商品编号	单位
26	PFIB：1，1，3，3，3－五氟－2－三氟甲基－1－丙烯(又名：全氟异丁烯；八氟异丁烯)	第二类：可作为生产化学武器前体的化学品	2903391000	千克
27	频哪基醇：3，3－二甲基丁－2－醇	第二类：可作为生产化学武器前体的化学品	2905191000	千克
28	2，2－二苯基－2－羟基乙酸：二苯羟乙酸；二苯乙醇酸	第二类：可作为生产化学武器前体的化学品	2918191000	千克
29	二烷(甲、乙、正丙或异丙)氨基乙基－2－氯及相应质子化盐	第二类：可作为生产化学武器前体的化学品	2921196000	千克
30	二烷(甲、乙、正丙或异丙)氨基乙－2－醇及相应质子化盐 例外：二甲氨基乙醇及相应质子化盐二乙氨基乙醇及相应质子化盐	第二类：可作为生产化学武器前体的化学品	2922192900	千克
31	二烷(甲、乙、正丙或异丙)氨基膦酰二卤	第二类：可作为生产化学武器前体的化学品	2929902000	千克
32	二烷(甲、乙、正丙或异丙)氨基膦酸二烷(甲、乙、正丙或异丙)酯	第二类：可作为生产化学武器前体的化学品	2929903000	千克
33	胺吸膦：硫代磷酸二乙基－S－2－二乙氨基乙酯及相应烷基化盐或质子化盐)	第二类：可作为生产化学武器前体的化学品	2930909023	千克
34	二烷(甲、乙、正丙或异丙)氨基乙－2－硫醇及相应质子化盐	第二类：可作为生产化学武器前体的化学品	2930909024	千克
35	硫二甘醇：二(2－羟乙基)硫醚；硫代双乙醇	第二类：可作为生产化学武器前体的化学品	2930909025	千克
36	含有一个磷原子并有一个甲基、乙基或(正或异)丙基原子团与该磷原子结合的化学品，不包括含更多碳原子的情形，但第一类名录所列者除外 例如： 1. 甲基膦酰二氯 2. 甲基膦酸二甲酯 3. 丙基膦酸 4. 甲基膦酸 5. 乙基膦酸二乙酯 6. 甲基膦酸甲基、5－(5－乙基－2－甲基－2－氧代－1，3，2－二氧磷杂环己基)甲基酯　化学文摘登记号：41203－81－0 7. 甲基膦酸二[5－(5－乙基－2－甲基－2－氧代－1，3，2－二氧磷杂环己基)甲基]酯　化学文摘登记号：42595－45－9 8. 甲基膦酸的混合物(化合物6和7的混合物)　化学文摘登记号：170836－68－7 9. 甲基膦酸二聚乙二醇酯　化学文摘登记号：294675－51－7 例外：地虫磷：二硫代乙基膦酸－S－苯基乙酯	第二类：可作为生产化学武器前体的化学品	2930909027	千克

续表

序号	商品名称	描　述	海关商品编号	单位
37	BZ：二苯乙醇酸－3－奎宁环酯（＊）	第二类：可作为生产化学武器前体的化学品	2933391000	千克
42	光气：碳酰二氯	第三类：可作为生产化学武器主要原料的化学品	2812103000	千克
43	一氯化硫	第三类：可作为生产化学武器主要原料的化学品	2812104100	千克
44	二氯化硫	第三类：可作为生产化学武器主要原料的化学品	2812104200	千克
51	氯化苦；三氯硝基甲烷	第三类：可作为生产化学武器主要原料的化学品	2904903000	千克
53	二苯乙醇酸甲酯	第三类：可作为生产化学武器主要原料的化学品	2918199010	千克
54	亚磷酸三甲酯	第三类：可作为生产化学武器主要原料的化学品	2920901100	千克
55	亚磷酸三乙酯	第三类：可作为生产化学武器主要原料的化学品	2920901200	千克
56	亚磷酸二甲酯	第三类：可作为生产化学武器主要原料的化学品	2920901300	千克
57	亚磷酸二乙酯	第三类：可作为生产化学武器主要原料的化学品	2920901400	千克
58	二甲胺	第三类：可作为生产化学武器主要原料的化学品	2921110010	千克
60	三乙醇胺	第三类：可作为生产化学武器主要原料的化学品	2922131000	千克
62	乙基二乙醇胺	第三类：可作为生产化学武器主要原料的化学品	2922193000	千克
63	甲基二乙醇胺	第三类：可作为生产化学武器主要原料的化学品	2922194000	千克

五、有关化学品及相关设备和技术出口管制清单所列物项和技术

六、导弹及相关物项和技术出口管制清单所列物项和技术

序号	商品名称	描　述	海关商品编号	单位
34	聚酰亚胺复合材料	结构复合材料，包括各种复合材料结构件、层压板和制品，以及以树脂或金属为基体的用纤维和丝材增强而制成的各种预浸件和预成形件，其中增强材料的比拉伸强度大于7.62×10^4米和比模量大于3.18×10^6米	3926909010	千克
35	聚酰胺基复合材料	结构复合材料，包括各种复合材料结构件、层压板和制品，以及以树脂或金属为基体的用纤维和丝材增强而制成的各种预浸件和预成形件，其中增强材料的比拉伸强度大于7.62×10^4米和比模量大于3.18×10^6米	3926909010	千克
36	聚碳酸脂复合材料	结构复合材料，包括各种复合材料结构件、层压板和制品，以及以树脂或金属为基体的用纤维和丝材增强而制成的各种预浸件和预成形件，其中增强材料的比拉伸强度大于7.62×10^4米和比模量大于3.18×10^6米	3926909010	千克

七、易制毒化学品(一)

序　号	商品名称	描　述	海关商品编号	单位
27	*N*－乙酰邻氨基苯酸(*N*－乙酰邻氨基苯甲酸、2－乙酰氨基苯甲酸)	可用于制造毒品	2924230010	千克
28	3，4－亚甲基二氧苯基－2－丙酮	可用于制造毒品	2932920000	千克
29	高锰酸钾	可用于制造毒品	2841610000	千克
30	醋酸酐(乙酸酐)	可用于制造毒品	2915240000	千克
32	苯乙酸	可用于制造毒品	2916340010	千克
34	硫酸	可用于制造毒品	2807000010	千克
35	甲苯	可用于制造毒品	2902300000	千克
41	三氯甲烷(氯仿)	可用于制造毒品	2903130000	千克

八、易制毒化学品(二)

序号	商品名称	描　述	海关商品编号	单位
5	乙醇	可用于制造毒品	2207100000 2207200010 2207200090	升/千克
7	碳酸钠(纯碱)	可用于制造毒品	2836200000	千克
10	乙酸	可用于制造毒品	2915211100 2915211910 2915211920 2915211990 2915219000	千克
11	乙酸乙酯	可用于制造毒品	2915310000	千克
12	异丙醇	可用于制造毒品	2905122000	千克
14	氢碘酸	可用于制造毒品	2811199010	千克

(其他略)

九、中华人民共和国商务部2012年第100号 关于公布《2013年进口许可证管理货物分级发证目录》的公告(二〇一二年十二月三十一日)

根据《货物进口许可证管理办法》(商务部令2004年第27号)、《重点旧机电产品进口管理办法》(商务部、海关总署、质检总局令2008年第5号)和《2013年进口许可证管理货物目录》(商务部、海关总署、质检总局公告2012年第98号),现发布《2013年进口许可证管理货物分级发证目录》(见附件),并就有关问题公告如下:

一、2013年实行进口许可证管理的货物共2种,由商务部配额许可证事务局(以下简称许可证局)和商务部授权的地方商务主管部门发证机构(以下简称地方发证机构)负责签发相应货物的进口许可证。

(一)许可证局负责签发重点旧机电产品的进口许可证。

(二)地方发证机构负责签发消耗臭氧层物质的进口许可证。二、在京中央企业的进口许可证由许可证局签发。

二、消耗臭氧层物质的进口许可证实行"一批一证"制。

三、发证机构应严格按照《货物进口许可证管理办法》、《重点旧机电产品进口管理办法》、《2013年进口许可证管理货物目录》和《进口许可证签发工作规范》(商配发〔2007〕360号)等有关规定签发进口许可证。

本目录自2013年1月1日起执行。《2012年进口许可证管理货物分级发证目录》同时废止。

附件:2013进口许可证管理货物分级发证目录

货物种类	海关商品编号	商品名称及备注	单位
许可证局负责签发以下货物的进口许可证			
重点旧机电产品			
一、化工设备	8419409090	其他蒸馏或精馏设备	台
	8419609010	液化器(将来自级联的 UF6 气体压缩并冷凝成液态 UF6)	台
	8419899010	带加热装置的发酵罐(不发散气溶胶，且容积>20 升)	台
地方发证机构负责签发以下货物的进口许可证			
消耗臭氧层物质			
	2903191010	1，1，1－三氯乙烷(甲基氯仿)，用于清洗剂的除外	千克
	2903191090	1，1，1－三氯乙烷(甲基氯仿)，用于清洗剂的	千克
	2903399020	溴甲烷(甲基溴)	千克
	2903710000	一氯二氟甲烷	千克
	2903720000	二氯三氟乙烷	千克
	2903730000	二氯一氟乙烷	千克
	2903740000	一氯二氟乙烷	千克
	2903750010	1，1，1，2，2－五氟－3，3－二氯丙烷	千克
	2903750020	1，1，2，2，3－五氟－1，3－二氯丙烷	千克
	2903750090	其他二氯五氟丙烷	千克
	2903760010	溴氯二氟甲烷	千克
	2903760020	溴三氟甲烷	千克
	2903771000	三氯氟甲烷	千克
	2903772011	二氯二氟甲烷	千克
	2903772012	三氯三氟乙烷，用于清洗剂除外(CFC－113)	千克
	2903772014	二氯四氟乙烷(CFC－114)	千克
	2903772015	一氯五氟乙烷(CFC－115)	千克
	2903772016	一氯三氟甲烷(CFC－13)	千克
	2903791011	一氟二氯甲烷	千克
	2903791012	1，1，1，2－四氟－2－氯乙烷	千克
	2903791013	三氟一氯乙烷	千克
	2903791014	1－氟－1，1－二氯乙烷	千克
	2903791015	1，1－二氟－1－氯乙烷	千克
	2903791090	其他仅含氟和氯的甲烷、乙烷及丙烷的卤化衍生物	千克
	2903799021	其他仅含溴氟的甲烷、乙烷和丙烷	千克
	3824710011	二氯二氟甲烷和二氟乙烷的混合物(R－500)	千克
	3824710012	一氯二氟甲烷和二氯二氟甲烷的混合物(R－501)	千克
	3824710013	一氯二氟甲烷和一氯五氟乙烷的混合物(R－502)	千克
	3824710014	三氟甲烷和一氯三氟甲烷的混合物(R－503)	千克
	3824710015	二氟甲烷和一氯五氟乙烷的混合物(R－504)	千克
	3824710016	二氯二氟甲烷和一氟一氯甲烷的混合物(R－505)	千克

续表

货物种类	海关商品编号	商品名称及备注	单位
	3824710017	一氟一氯甲烷和二氯四氟乙烷的混合物(R－506)	千克
	3824710018	二氯二氟甲烷和二氯四氟乙烷的混合物(R－400)	千克
	3824740011	二氟一氯甲烷、二氟乙烷和一氯四氟乙烷的混合物(R－401)	千克
	3824740012	五氟乙烷、丙烷和二氟一氯甲烷的混合物(R－402)	千克
	3824740013	丙烷、二氟一氯甲烷和八氟丙烷的混合物(R－403)	千克
	3824740014	二氟一氯甲烷、二氟乙烷、一氯二氟乙烷和八氟环丁烷的混合物(R－405)	千克
	3824740015	二氟一氯甲烷、2－甲基丙烷(异丁烷)和一氯二氟乙烷的混合物(R－406)	千克
	3824740016	五氟乙烷、三氟乙烷和二氟一氯甲烷的混合物(R－408)	千克
	3824740017	二氟一氯甲烷、一氯四氟乙烷和一氯二氟乙烷的混合物(R－409)	千克
	3824740018	丙烯、二氟一氯甲烷和二氟乙烷的混合物(R－411)	千克
	3824740019	二氟一氯甲烷、八氟丙烷和一氯二氟乙烷的混合物(R－412)	千克
	3824740021	二氟一氯甲烷、一氯四氟乙烷、一氯二氟乙烷和2－甲基丙烷的混合物(R－414)	千克
	3824740022	二氟一氯甲烷和二氟乙烷的混合物(R－415)	千克
	3824740023	四氟乙烷、一氯四氟乙烷和丁烷的混合物(R－416)	千克
	3824740024	丙烷、二氟一氯甲烷和二氟乙烷的混合物(R－418)	千克
	3824740025	二氟一氯甲烷和八氟丙烷的混合物(R－509)	千克
	3824740026	二氟一氯甲烷和一氯二氟乙烷的混合物	千克
	3824740090	其他含甲烷、乙烷或丙烷的氢氯氟烃混合物(不论是否含甲烷、乙烷或丙烷的全氟烃或氢氟烃，但不含全氯氟烃)	千克

(其他略)

十、中华人民共和国商务部公告2012年第101号 关于公布《2013年出口许可证管理货物分级发证目录》的公告(二〇一二年十二月三十一日)

根据《货物出口许可证管理办法》(商务部令2008年第11号)和《2013年出口许可证管理货物目录》(商务部、海关总署公告2012年第97号)，现发布《2013年出口许可证管理货物分级发证目录》(见附件)，并就有关问题公告如下：

一、2013年实行出口许可证管理的货物共48种，由商务部配额许可证事务局(以下简称许可证局)、商务部驻各地特派员办事处(以下简称特办)及商务部授权的地方商务主管部门发证机构(以下简称地方发证机构)负责签发相应货物的出口许可证。

(一) 许可证局负责签发以下6种货物的出口许可证：玉米、小麦、棉花、煤炭、原油、成品油。

(二) 特办负责签发以下25种货物的出口许可证：大米、玉米粉、小麦粉、大米粉、锯材、活牛、活猪、活鸡、焦炭、稀土、锑及锑制品、钨及钨制品、锡及锡制品、白银、铟及铟制品、钼、磷矿石；蔺草及蔺草制品、碳化硅、滑石块(粉)、镁砂、矾土、甘草及甘草制品；铂金(以加工贸易方式出口)、天然砂(含标准砂)。

(三) 地方发证机构负责签发以下17种货物的出口许可证：冰鲜牛肉、冻牛肉、冰鲜猪肉、冻猪肉、冰鲜鸡肉、冻鸡肉、消耗臭氧层物质、石蜡、部分金属及制品、汽车(包括成套散件)及其底盘、摩托车(含全地形车)及其发动机和车架、钼制品、柠檬酸、青霉素工业盐、维生素C、硫酸二钠、氟石。

二、在京中央企业的出口许可证由许可证局签发。

三、为维护正常的经营秩序，对部分出口货物实行指定发证机构发证或指定口岸报关出口。企业出口此类货物，须向指定发证机构申领出口许可证，并在指定口岸报关出口；发证机构须按指定口岸签发出口许可证。

(一) 锑及锑制品指定黄埔海关、北海海关、天津海关为报关口岸。

(二) 镁砂项下产品"按重量计含氧化镁70%以上的混合物"(HS编码为3824909200)的出口许可证由各特办签发，不再指定报关口岸；镁砂项下其他产品的出口许可证由大连特办签发，指定大连(大窑湾、营口、鲅鱼圈、丹东、大东港)、青岛(莱州海关)、天津(东港、新港)、长春(图们)、满洲里为报关口岸。

(三) 甘草的报关口岸限定为天津海关、上海海关、大连海关；甘草制品的报关口岸限定为天津海关、上海海关。

(四) 稀土的报关口岸限定为天津海关、上海海关、青岛海关、黄埔海关、呼和浩特海关、南昌海关、宁波海关、南京海关和厦门海关。

(五) 以陆运方式出口的对港澳地区活牛、活猪、活鸡出口许可证由广州特办、深圳特办签发。

(六) 进口原木加工锯材复出口的许可证签发：黑龙江省商务厅负责签发本省企业的出口许可证，报关口岸限定为大连和绥芬河海关；内蒙古自治区商务厅负责签发本自治区企业的出口许可证，报关口岸限定为满洲里、二连浩特、大连、天津和青岛海关；新疆维吾尔自治区商务厅负责签发本自治区企业的出口许可证，报关口岸限定为阿拉山口、天津和上海海关；福建省外经贸厅负责签发本省企业的出口许可证，报关口岸限定为福州、厦门、莆田和漳州海关。

(七) 广州特办、海南特办负责签发本省企业对台港澳地区天然砂出口许可证，福州特办负责签发本省企业对台天然砂出口许可证，报关口岸限定于企业所在省的海关；福州特办负责签发标准砂出口许可证。

四、按照2001年国家林业局、原外经贸部、海关总署联合发布的《进口原木加工锯材出口试点管理办法》(林计发〔2001〕560号)的规定，有经营资格的试点企业进口原木加工锯材复出口的，须凭《进口原木加工锯材出口证明》向本公告第三条第(五)项列明的发证机构申领出口许可证，发证机构须在许可证备注栏注明"进口原木加工锯材"。

五、消耗臭氧层物质的出口许可证实行“一批一证”制。

六、发证机构应严格按商务部公布的《货物出口许可证管理办法》、《2013年出口许可证管理货物目录》和《出口许可证签发工作规范》(商配发〔2008〕398号)等有关规定签发出口许可证。

本目录自2013年1月1日起执行。《2012年出口许可证管理货物分级发证目录》同时废止。

附件：2013出口许可证管理货物分级发证目录

地方发证机构负责签发以下货物的出口许可证

1	消耗臭氧层物质	2903140010	非用于清洗剂的四氯化碳	千克
		2903191010	1，1，1－三氯乙烷(甲基氯仿)，用于清洗剂的除外	千克
		2903399020	溴甲烷(甲基溴)	千克
		2903710000	一氯二氟甲烷	千克
		2903720000	二氯三氟乙烷	千克
		2903730000	二氯一氟乙烷	千克
		2903740000	一氯二氟乙烷	千克
		2903750010	1，1，1，2，2－五氟－3，3－二氯丙烷	千克
		2903750020	1，1，2，2，3－五氟－1，3－二氯丙烷	千克
		2903750090	其他二氯五氟丙烷	千克
		2903760010	溴氯二氟甲烷(halon－1211)	千克
		2903760020	溴三氟甲烷(halon－1301)	千克

续表

1	消耗臭氧层物质	2903771000	三氯氟甲烷(CFC－11)	千克
		2903772011	二氯二氟甲烷(CFC－12)	千克
		2903772012	三氯三氟乙烷，用于清洗剂除外(CFC－113)	千克
		2903772014	二氯四氟乙烷(CFC－114)	千克
		2903772015	一氯五氟乙烷(CFC－115)	千克
		2903772016	一氯三氟甲烷(CFC－113)	千克
		2903791011	一氟二氯甲烷	千克
		2903791012	1，1，1，2－四氟－2－氯乙烷	千克
		2903791013	三氟一氯乙烷	千克
		2903791014	1－氟－1，1－二氯乙烷	千克
		2903791015	1，1－二氟－1－氯乙烷	千克
		2903791090	其他仅含氟和氯的甲烷、乙烷及丙烷的卤化衍生物	千克
		2903799021	其他仅含溴氟的甲烷、乙烷和丙烷	千克
		3824710011	二氯二氟甲烷和二氟乙烷的混合物(R－500)	千克
		3824710012	一氯二氟甲烷和二氯二氟甲烷的混合物(R－501)	千克
		3824710013	一氯二氟甲烷和一氯五氟乙烷的混合物(R－502)	千克
		3824710014	三氟甲烷和一氯三氟甲烷的混合物(R－503)	千克
		3824710015	二氟甲烷和一氯五氟乙烷的混合物(R－504)	千克
		3824710016	二氯二氟甲烷和一氟一氯甲烷的混合物(R－505)	千克
		3824710017	一氟一氯甲烷和二氯四氟乙烷的混合物(R－506)	千克
		3824710018	二氯二氟甲烷和二氯四氟乙烷的混合物(R－400)	千克
		3824740011	二氟一氯甲烷、二氟乙烷和一氯四氟乙烷的混合物(R－401)	千克
		3824740012	五氟乙烷、丙烷和二氟一氯甲烷的混合物(R－402)	千克
		3824740013	丙烷、二氟一氯甲烷和八氟丙烷的混合物(R－403)	千克
		3824740014	二氟一氯甲烷、二氟乙烷、一氯二氟乙烷和八氟环丁烷的混合物(R－405)	千克
		3824740015	二氟一氯甲烷、2－甲基丙烷(异丁烷)和一氯二氟乙烷的混合物(R－406)	千克
		3824740016	五氟乙烷、三氟乙烷和二氟一氯甲烷的混合物(R－408)	千克
		3824740017	二氟一氯甲烷、一氯四氟乙烷和一氯二氟乙烷的混合物(R－409)	千克
		3824740018	丙烯、二氟一氯甲烷和二氟乙烷的混合物(R－411)	千克
		3824740019	二氟一氯甲烷、八氟丙烷和一氯二氟乙烷的混合物(R－412)	千克
		3824740021	二氟一氯甲烷、一氯四氟乙烷、一氯二氟乙烷和2－甲基丙烷的混合物(R－414)	千克
		3824740022	二氟一氯甲烷和二氟乙烷的混合物(R－415)	千克

续表

1	消耗臭氧层物质	3824740023	四氟乙烷、一氯四氟乙烷和丁烷的混合物(R-416)	千克
		3824740024	丙烷、二氟一氯甲烷和二氟乙烷的混合物(R-418)	千克
		3824740025	二氟一氯甲烷和八氟丙烷的混合物(R-509)	千克
		3824740026	二氟一氯甲烷和一氯二氟乙烷的混合物	千克
		3824740090	其他含甲烷、乙烷或丙烷的氢氯氟烃混合物(不论是否含甲烷、乙烷或丙烷的全氟烃或氢氟烃,但不含全氯氟烃)	千克
17	▲氟石(萤石)	2529210000	按重量计氟化钙含量在97%及以下	千克
		2529220000	按重量计氟化钙含量在97%以上	千克

(其他略)

(中国塑料加工工业协会 郭齐)

2013年合成树脂及塑料制品海关关税、税则税率

商品编码	附加编号	商品名称(点击查询商品进出口统计数据)	进口税率		出口税率	增值税	消费税	计量单位	监管条件
			优惠	普通					
39011000	01	初级形状比重<0.94的聚乙烯	6.5	45.0	0.0	17.0	0.0	千克	A
39011000	90	初级形状比重<0.94的聚乙烯	6.5	45.0	0.0	17.0	0.0	千克	A
39012000	01	初级形状比重≥0.94的聚乙烯	6.5	45.0	0.0	17.0	0.0	千克	A
39012000	90	初级形状比重≥0.94的聚乙烯	6.5	45.0	0.0	17.0	0.0	千克	A
39013000		初级形状乙烯-乙酸乙烯酯共聚物	6.5	45.0	0.0	17.0	0.0	千克	A
39019010		乙烯-丙烯共聚物(乙丙橡胶)	6.5	45.0	0.0	17.0	0.0	千克	A
39019020		线型低密度聚乙烯	6.5	45.0	0.0	17.0	0.0	千克	A
39019090		其他初级形状的乙烯聚合物	6.5	45.0	0.0	17.0	0.0	千克	A
39021000	10	电工级初级形状聚丙烯树脂	6.5	45.0	0.0	17.0	0.0	千克	A
39021000	90	其他初级形状的聚丙烯	6.5	45.0	0.0	17.0	0.0	千克	A
39022000		初级形状的聚异丁烯	6.5	45.0	0.0	17.0	0.0	千克	AB
39023010		乙烯-丙烯共聚物(乙丙橡胶)	6.5	45.0	0.0	17.0	0.0	千克	
39023090		其他初级形状的丙烯共聚物	6.5	45.0	0.0	17.0	0.0	千克	
39029000	10	端羧基聚丁二烯,CTPB	6.5	45.0	0.0	17.0	0.0	千克	3
39029000	20	端羟基聚丁二烯,HTPB	6.5	45.0	0.0	17.0	0.0	千克	3
39029000	90	其他初级形状的烯烃聚合物	6.5	45.0	0.0	17.0	0.0	千克	
39031100		初级形状的可发性聚苯乙烯	6.5	45.0	0.0	17.0	0.0	千克	A
39031900		初级形状的其他聚苯乙烯	6.5	45.0	0.0	17.0	0.0	千克	A
39032000		初级形状苯乙烯-丙烯腈共聚物	12.0	45.0	0.0	17.0	0.0	千克	
39033000		丙烯腈-丁二烯-苯乙烯共聚物	6.5	45.0	0.0	17.0	0.0	千克	A
39039000		初级形状的其他苯乙烯聚合物	6.5	45.0	0.0	17.0	0.0	千克	
39041010		聚氯乙烯糊树脂	6.5	45.0	0.0	17.0	0.0	千克	A
39041090	01	聚氯乙烯纯粉	6.5	45.0	0.0	17.0	0.0	千克	A

续表

商品编码	附加编号	商品名称(点击查询商品进出口统计数据)	进口税率		出口税率	增值税	消费税	计量单位	监管条件
			优惠	普通					
39041090	90	其他初级形状的纯聚氯乙烯	6.5	45.0	0.0	17.0	0.0	千克	A
39042100		初级形状未塑化的聚氯乙烯	6.5	45.0	0.0	17.0	0.0	千克	
39042200		初级形状已塑化的聚氯乙烯	6.5	45.0	0.0	17.0	0.0	千克	
39043000		氯乙烯-乙酸乙烯酯共聚物	9.0	45.0	0.0	17.0	0.0	千克	
39044000		初级形状的其他氯乙烯共聚物	12.0	45.0	0.0	17.0	0.0	千克	
39045000		初级形状的偏二氯乙烯聚合物	6.5	45.0	0.0	17.0	0.0	千克	
39046100		初级形状的聚四氟乙烯	10.0	45.0	0.0	17.0	0.0	千克	
39046900		初级形状的其他氟聚合物	6.5	45.0	0.0	17.0	0.0	千克	
39049000		初级形状的其他卤化烯烃聚合物	10.0	45.0	0.0	17.0	0.0	千克	
39051200		聚乙酸乙烯酯的水分散体	10.0	45.0	0.0	17.0	0.0	千克	
39051900		其他初级形状聚乙酸乙烯酯	10.0	45.0	0.0	17.0	0.0	千克	
39052100		乙酸乙烯酯共聚物的水分散体	10.0	45.0	0.0	17.0	0.0	千克	
39052900		其他初级形状的乙酸乙烯酯共聚物	10.0	45.0	0.0	17.0	0.0	千克	
39053000		初级形状的聚乙烯醇	14.0	45.0	0.0	17.0	0.0	千克	AB
39059100		其他乙烯酯或乙烯基的共聚物	10.0	45.0	0.0	17.0	0.0	千克	
39059900		其他乙烯酯或乙烯基的聚合物	10.0	45.0	0.0	17.0	0.0	千克	
39061000		初级形状的聚甲基丙烯酸甲酯	6.5	45.0	0.0	17.0	0.0	千克	
39069010		聚丙烯酰胺	6.5	45.0	0.0	17.0	0.0	千克	AB
39069090	01	聚丙烯酸钠	6.5	45.0	0.0	17.0	0.0	千克	
39069090	90	其他初级形状的丙烯酸聚合物	6.5	45.0	0.0	17.0	0.0	千克	
39071010		初级形状的聚甲醛	6.5	45.0	0.0	17.0	0.0	千克	
39071090		其他初级形状的聚缩醛	6.5	45.0	0.0	17.0	0.0	千克	
39072010		聚四亚甲基醚二醇	6.5	45.0	0.0	17.0	0.0	千克	
39072090		初级形状的其他聚醚	6.5	45.0	0.0	17.0	0.0	千克	
39073000	01	初级形状溴质量≥18%或进口CIF价	6.5	45.0	0.0	17.0	0.0	千克	
39073000	90	初级形状的环氧树脂	6.5	45.0	0.0	17.0	0.0	千克	
39074000		初级形状的聚碳酸酯	6.5	45.0	0.0	17.0	0.0	千克	
39075000		初级形状的醇酸树脂	10.0	45.0	0.0	17.0	0.0	千克	
39076011		高粘度聚对苯二甲酸乙二酯切片	6.5	45.0	0.0	17.0	0.0	千克	A
39076019		其他聚对苯二甲酸乙二酯切片	6.5	45.0	0.0	17.0	0.0	千克	A
39076090		其他初级形状聚对苯二甲酸乙二酯	6.5	45.0	0.0	17.0	0.0	千克	A
39077000		初级形状的聚乳酸	6.5	45.0	0.0	17.0	0.0	千克	
39079100		初级形状的不饱和聚酯	6.5	45.0	0.0	17.0	0.0	千克	

续表

商品编码	附加编号	商品名称(点击查询商品进出口统计数据)	进口税率		出口税率	增值税	消费税	计量单位	监管条件
			优惠	普通					
39079910	01	未经增强或改性的初级形状PBT树	6.5	45.0	0.0	17.0	0.0	千克	
39079910	90	其他聚对苯二甲酸丁二酯	6.5	45.0	0.0	17.0	0.0	千克	
39079990		初级形状的其他聚酯	6.5	45.0	0.0	17.0	0.0	千克	AB
39081011		聚酰胺-6，6切片	6.5	45.0	0.0	17.0	0.0	千克	
39081019	10	尼龙11、尼龙12切片	6.5	45.0	0.0	17.0	0.0	千克	
39081019	90	聚酰胺-6切片等	6.5	45.0	0.0	17.0	0.0	千克	
39081090		其他初级形状的聚酰胺-6，6等	6.5	45.0	0.0	17.0	0.0	千克	
39089000		初级形状的其他聚酰胺	10.0	45.0	0.0	17.0	0.0	千克	
39091000		初级形状的尿素树脂及硫尿树脂	6.5	45.0	0.0	17.0	0.0	千克	
39092000		初级形状的蜜胺树脂	6.5	45.0	0.0	17.0	0.0	千克	
39093010		聚(亚甲基苯基异氰酸酯)(聚合MDI	6.5	35.0	0.0	17.0	0.0	千克	
39093090		其他初级形状的氨基树脂	6.5	45.0	0.0	17.0	0.0	千克	
39094000		初级形状的酚醛树脂	6.5	45.0	0.0	17.0	0.0	千克	
39095000		初级形状的聚氨基甲酸酯	6.5	45.0	0.0	17.0	0.0	千克	
39100000		初级形状的聚硅氧烷	6.5	45.0	0.0	17.0	0.0	千克	
39111000		初级形状的石油树脂等	6.5	45.0	0.0	17.0	0.0	千克	
39119000	01	芳基酸与芳基胺预缩聚物	6.5	45.0	0.0	17.0	0.0	千克	
39119000	03	改性三羟乙基脲酸酯类预缩聚物	6.5	45.0	0.0	17.0	0.0	千克	
39119000	04	聚苯硫醚	6.5	45.0	0.0	17.0	0.0	千克	
39119000	05	偏苯三酸酐和异氰酸预缩聚物	6.5	45.0	0.0	17.0	0.0	千克	
39119000	90	其他初级形状的多硫化物、聚砜等	6.5	45.0	0.0	17.0	0.0	千克	
39121100	01	未塑化二醋酸纤维素等	6.5	40.0	0.0	17.0	0.0	千克	
39121100	90	初级形状的未塑化醋酸纤维素	6.5	40.0	0.0	17.0	0.0	千克	
39121200		初级形状的已塑化醋酸纤维素	6.5	40.0	0.0	17.0	0.0	千克	
39122000		初级形状的硝酸纤维素	6.5	45.0	0.0	17.0	0.0	千克	
39123100		初级形状的羧甲基纤维素及其盐	6.5	45.0	0.0	17.0	0.0	千克	
39123900		初级形状的其他纤维素醚	6.5	45.0	0.0	17.0	0.0	千克	
39129000		初级形状的其他未列名的纤维素	6.5	45.0	0.0	17.0	0.0	千克	
39131000		初级形状的藻酸及盐和酯	10.0	45.0	0.0	17.0	0.0	千克	AB
39139000		初级形状的其他未列名天然聚合物	6.5	50.0	0.0	17.0	0.0	千克	
39140000		初级形状的离子交换剂	6.5	45.0	0.0	17.0	0.0	千克	

续表

商品编码	附加编号	商品名称(点击查询商品进出口统计数据)	进口税率		出口税率	增值税	消费税	计量单位	监管条件
			优惠	普通					
39151000		乙烯聚合物的废碎料及下脚料	6.5	50.0	0.0	17.0	0.0	千克	AP
39152000		苯乙烯聚合物的废碎料及下脚料	6.5	50.0	0.0	17.0	0.0	千克	AP
39153000		氯乙烯聚合物的废碎料及下脚料	6.5	50.0	0.0	17.0	0.0	千克	AP
39159010		聚对苯二甲酸乙二酯废碎料及下脚	6.5	50.0	0.0	17.0	0.0	千克	AP
39159090		其他塑料的废碎料及下脚料	6.5	50.0	0.0	17.0	0.0	千克	AP
39161000		乙烯聚合物制单丝，条，杆及型材	10.0	45.0	0.0	17.0	0.0	千克	
39162000		氯乙烯聚合物制单丝，条，杆及型材	10.0	45.0	0.0	17.0	0.0	千克	
39169010		聚酰胺制的单丝，条，杆及型材	10.0	45.0	0.0	17.0	0.0	千克	
39169090		其他塑料制单丝，条，杆及型材	10.0	45.0	0.0	17.0	0.0	千克	
39171000		硬化蛋白或纤维素材料制人造肠衣	10.0	50.0	0.0	17.0	0.0	千克	A
39172100		乙烯聚合物制的硬管	10.0	45.0	0.0	17.0	0.0	千克	
39172200		丙烯聚合物制的硬管	10.0	45.0	0.0	17.0	0.0	千克	
39172300		氯乙烯聚合物制的硬管	10.0	45.0	0.0	17.0	0.0	千克	
39172900		其他塑料制的硬管	10.0	45.0	0.0	17.0	0.0	千克	
39173100		塑料制的软管	10.0	45.0	0.0	17.0	0.0	千克	
39173200		其他未装有附件的塑料制管子	6.5	45.0	0.0	17.0	0.0	千克	
39173300		其他装有附件的塑料管子	6.5	45.0	0.0	17.0	0.0	千克	
39173900		塑料制的其他管子	6.5	45.0	0.0	17.0	0.0	千克	
39174000		塑料制的管子附件	10.0	45.0	0.0	17.0	0.0	千克	
39181010		氯乙烯聚合物制糊墙品	10.0	45.0	0.0	17.0	0.0	千克	
39181090		氯乙烯聚合物制的铺地制品	10.0	45.0	0.0	17.0	0.0	千克	
39189010		其他塑料制的糊墙品	10.0	45.0	0.0	17.0	0.0	千克	
39189090		其他塑料制的铺地制品	10.0	45.0	0.0	17.0	0.0	千克	
39191010		丙烯酸树脂类为主的自粘塑料板等	6.5	45.0	0.0	17.0	0.0	千克	
39191091		宽度≤20cm 的胶囊型反光膜	6.5	45.0	0.0	17.0	0.0	千克	
39191099		其他宽度≤20cm 的自粘塑料板片等	6.5	45.0	0.0	17.0	0.0	千克	
39199010		其他胶囊型反光膜	6.5	45.0	0.0	17.0	0.0	千克	
39199090		其他自粘塑料板，片，膜等材料	6.5	45.0	0.0	17.0	0.0	千克	
39201010		乙烯聚合物制电池隔膜	6.5	45.0	0.0	13.0	0.0	千克	
39201090	01	乙烯－四氟乙烯膜(四氟乙烯单体含	6.5	45.0	0.0	13.0	0.0	千克	

续表

商品编码	附加编号	商品名称(点击查询商品进出口统计数据)	进口税率		出口税率	增值税	消费税	计量单位	监管条件
			优惠	普通					
39201090	10	农用非泡沫聚乙烯薄膜	6.5	45.0	0.0	13.0	0.0	千克	
39201090	90	其他非泡沫乙烯聚合物板，片，膜，	6.5	45.0	0.0	17.0	0.0	千克	
39202010		丙烯聚合物制电池隔膜	6.5	45.0	0.0	13.0	0.0	千克	
39202090	10	农用非泡沫聚丙烯薄膜	6.5	45.0	0.0	13.0	0.0	千克	
39202090	90	非泡沫丙烯聚合物板，片，膜，箔及	6.5	45.0	0.0	17.0	0.0	千克	
39203000		非泡沫苯乙烯聚合物板，片，膜，箔，	6.5	45.0	0.0	17.0	0.0	千克	
39204300	10	农用软质聚氯乙烯薄膜	6.5	45.0	0.0	17.0	0.0	千克	
39204300	90	氯乙烯聚合物板，片，膜，箔及扁条	6.5	45.0	0.0	17.0	0.0	千克	
39204900	10	其他农用软质聚氯乙烯薄膜	6.5	45.0	0.0	13.0	0.0	千克	
39204900	90	其他氯乙烯聚合物板，片，膜，箔及	6.5	45.0	0.0	17.0	0.0	千克	
39205100		聚甲基丙烯酸甲酯板片膜箔及扁条	6.5	45.0	0.0	17.0	0.0	千克	
39205900		其他丙烯酸聚合物板片膜箔及扁条	6.5	45.0	0.0	17.0	0.0	千克	
39206100		聚碳酸酯制板，片，膜，箔，扁条	6.5	45.0	0.0	17.0	0.0	千克	
39206200	01	9≤厚≤15.9 微米聚酯薄膜	6.5	45.0	0.0	17.0	0.0	千克	
39206200	02	5≤厚≤8.9 微米聚酯薄膜	6.5	45.0	0.0	17.0	0.0	千克	
39206200	03	16≤厚≤29.9 微米聚酯薄膜	6.5	45.0	0.0	17.0	0.0	千克	
39206200	04	50≤厚≤99.9 微米聚酯薄膜	6.5	45.0	0.0	17.0	0.0	千克	
39206200	09	其他聚对苯二甲酸乙二酯板片膜等	6.5	45.0	0.0	17.0	0.0	千克	
39206300		不饱和聚酯板，片，膜，箔及扁条	10.0	45.0	0.0	17.0	0.0	千克	
39206900		其他聚酯板，片，膜，箔及扁条	10.0	45.0	0.0	17.0	0.0	千克	
39207100		再生纤维素制板，片，膜，箔及扁条	6.5	45.0	0.0	17.0	0.0	千克	
39207300		醋酸纤维素制板，片，膜，箔及扁条	6.5	45.0	0.0	17.0	0.0	千克	
39207900		其他纤维素衍生物制板，片，膜箔及	10.0	45.0	0.0	17.0	0.0	千克	
39209100	01	聚乙烯醇缩丁醛膜	6.5	45.0	0.0	17.0	0.0	千克	
39209100	90	聚乙烯醇缩丁醛板，片，箔，扁条	6.5	45.0	0.0	17.0	0.0	千克	
39209200		聚酰胺板，片，膜，箔，扁条	10.0	45.0	0.0	17.0	0.0	千克	
39209300		氨基树脂板，片，膜，箔，扁条	6.5	45.0	0.0	17.0	0.0	千克	
39209400		酚醛树脂板，片，膜，箔，扁条	10.0	45.0	0.0	17.0	0.0	千克	

续表

商品编码	附加编号	商品名称(点击查询商品进出口统计数据)	进口税率		出口税率	增值税	消费税	计量单位	监管条件
			优惠	普通					
39209910		聚四氟乙烯制非泡沫塑料板,片,箔	6.5	45.0	0.0	17.0	0.0	千克	
39209990		其他非泡沫塑料板,片,膜,箔,扁条	6.5	45.0	0.0	17.0	0.0	千克	
39211100		泡沫聚苯乙烯板,片,带,箔,扁条	10.0	45.0	0.0	17.0	0.0	千克	
39211210		泡沫聚氯乙烯人造革及合成革	9.0	70.0	0.0	17.0	0.0	千克	5
39211290		泡沫聚氯乙烯板,片,带,箔,扁条	6.5	45.0	0.0	17.0	0.0	千克	5
39211310		泡沫聚氨酯制人造革及合成革	9.0	70.0	0.0	17.0	0.0	千克	5
39211390		泡沫聚氨酯板,片,带,箔,扁条	6.5	45.0	0.0	17.0	0.0	千克	5
39211400		泡沫再生纤维素板,片,膜,箔,扁条	10.0	45.0	0.0	17.0	0.0	千克	
39211910		其他泡沫塑料制人造革及合成革	9.0	45.0	0.0	17.0	0.0	千克	
39211990		其他泡沫塑料板,片,膜,箔,扁条	6.5	45.0	0.0	17.0	0.0	千克	
39219020		以聚乙烯为基本成分的板片	6.5	45.0	0.0	17.0	0.0	千克	
39219030		聚异丁烯为基本成分的板片卷材	6.5	45.0	0.0	17.0	0.0	千克	
39219090	01	离子交换膜	6.5	45.0	0.0	17.0	0.0	千克	5
39219090	10	敏感物项管制结构复合材料的层压	6.5	45.0	0.0	17.0	0.0	千克	35
39219090	90	未列名塑料板,片,膜,箔,扁条	6.5	45.0	0.0	17.0	0.0	千克	5
39221000		塑料浴缸,淋浴盘,洗涤槽及盥洗盆	10.0	80.0	0.0	17.0	0.0	千克	
39222000	10	含濒危动物成分的塑料马桶座圈及	10.0	80.0	0.0	17.0	0.0	千克	EF
39222000	90	其他塑料马桶座圈及盖	10.0	80.0	0.0	17.0	0.0	千克	
39229000		塑料便盆,抽水箱等类似卫生洁具	10.0	80.0	0.0	17.0	0.0	千克	
39231000		塑料制盒,箱及类似品	10.0	80.0	0.0	17.0	0.0	千克	
39232100		乙烯聚合物制袋及包	10.0	80.0	0.0	17.0	0.0	千克	
39232900		其他塑料制的袋及包	10.0	80.0	0.0	17.0	0.0	千克	
39233000		塑料制坛,瓶及类似品	6.5	80.0	0.0	17.0	0.0	千克	
39234000		塑料制卷轴,纡子,筒管及类似品	10.0	35.0	0.0	17.0	0.0	千克	
39235000		塑料制塞子,盖子及类似品	10.0	80.0	0.0	17.0	0.0	千克	
39239000		供运输或包装货物用其他塑料制品	10.0	80.0	0.0	17.0	0.0	千克	
39241000		塑料制餐具及厨房用具	10.0	80.0	0.0	17.0	0.0	千克	AB
39249000		塑料制其他家庭用具及卫生或盥洗	10.0	80.0	0.0	17.0	0.0	千克	B

续表

商品编码	附加编号	商品名称(点击查询商品进出口统计数据)	进口税率		出口税率	增值税	消费税	计量单位	监管条件
			优惠	普通					
39251000		塑料制囤，柜，罐，桶及类似容器	10.0	80.0	0.0	17.0	0.0	千克	
39252000		塑料制门，窗及其框架，门槛	10.0	80.0	0.0	17.0	0.0	千克	
39253000		塑料制窗板，百叶窗及类似制品	10.0	80.0	0.0	17.0	0.0	千克	
39259000		其他未列名的建筑用塑料制品	10.0	80.0	0.0	17.0	0.0	千克	
39261000		办公室或学校用塑料制品	10.0	80.0	0.0	17.0	0.0	千克	
39262011		聚氯乙烯制手套(包括分指手套、	10.0	90.0	0.0	17.0	0.0	双	
39262019		其他塑料制手套(包括分指手套、	10.0	90.0	0.0	17.0	0.0	双	
39262090		其他塑料制衣服及衣着附件	10.0	90.0	0.0	17.0	0.0	千克	
39263000		塑料制家具，车厢及类似品的附件	10.0	80.0	0.0	17.0	0.0	千克	
39264000		塑料制小雕塑品及其他装饰品	10.0	100.0	0.0	17.0	0.0	千克	
39269010		塑料制机器及仪器用零件	10.0	35.0	0.0	17.0	0.0	千克	
39269090	10	敏感物项管制结构复合材料的预成	10.0	80.0	0.0	17.0	0.0	千克	3
39269090	90	其他塑料制品	10.0	80.0	0.0	17.0	0.0	千克	

注释说明：

本目录所称“塑料”，是指品目 39.01 至 39.14 的材料，这些材料能够在聚合时或聚合后在外力(一般是热力和压力，必要时加入溶剂或增塑剂)作用下通过模制、浇铸挤压、滚轧或其他工序制成一定的形状，成形后除去外力，其形状仍保持不变。本目录所称“塑料”，还应包括钢纸，但不包括第十一类的纺织材料。二、本章不包括：(一)品目 27.12 或 34.04 的蜡；(二)单独的已有化学定义的有机化合物(第二十九章)；(三)肝素及其盐(品目 30.01)；(四)品目 39.01 至 39.13 所列的任何产品溶于挥发性有机溶剂的溶液(胶棉除外)，但溶剂的重量必须超过溶液重量的 50%(品目 32.08)；品目 32.12 的压印箔；(五)有机表面活性剂或品目 34.02 的制剂；(六)再熔胶及酯胶(品目 38.06)；(七)附于塑料衬背上的诊断或实验用试剂(品目 38.22)；(八)第四十章规定的合成橡胶及其制品；(九)鞍具及挽具(品目 42.01)；品目 42.02 的衣箱、提箱、手提包及其他容器；(十)第四十六章的缏条、编结品及其他制品；(十一)品目 48.14 的壁纸；(十二)第十一类的货品(纺织原料及纺织制品)；(十三)第十二类的物品(例如，鞋靴、帽类、雨伞、阳伞、手杖、鞭子、马鞭及其零件)；(十四)品目 71.17 的仿首饰；(十五)第十六类的物品(机器、机械器具或电气器具)；(十六)第十七类的航空器零件及车辆零件；(十七)第九十章的物品(例如，光学元件、眼镜架及绘图仪器)；(十八)第九十一章的物品(例如，钟壳及表壳)；(十九)第九十二章的物品(例如，乐器及其零件)；(二十)第九十四章的物品(例如，家具、灯具、照明装置、灯箱及活动房屋)；(二十一)第九十五章的物品(例如，玩具、游戏品及运动用品)；(二十二)第九十六章的物品(例如，刷子、纽扣、拉链、梳子、烟斗的嘴及柄、香烟嘴及类似品、保温瓶的零件及类似品、钢笔、活动铅笔)。三、品目 39.01 至 39.11 仅适用于化学合成的下列货品：(一)温度在 300℃时，压力转为 1013 毫巴后减压蒸馏出的液体合成聚烯烃以体积计小于 60% 的货品(品目 39.01 及 39.02)；(二)非高度聚合的苯并呋喃——茚式树脂(品目 39.11)；(三)平均至少有五个单体单元的其他合成聚合物；(四)聚硅氧烷(品目 39.10)；(五)甲阶酚醛树指(品目 39.09)及其他预聚物。四、所称“共聚物”，包括在整个聚合物中按重量计没有一种单体单元的含量在 95% 及以上的各种聚合物。在本章中，除条文另有规定的以外，共聚物(包括共缩聚物、共加聚物、嵌段共聚物及接枝共聚物)及聚合物混合体应按聚合物中重量最大的那种共聚单体单元所构成的聚合物归入相应品目。在本注释中，归入同一品目的聚合物的共聚单体单元应作为一种单体单元对待。如果没有任何一种共聚单体单元重量为最大，共聚物或聚合物混合体应按号列顺序归入其可归入的最末一个品目。五、化学改性聚合物，即聚合物主链上的支链通过化学反应发生了变化的聚合物，应按未改性的聚合物的相应品目归类。本规定不适用于接枝共聚物。六、品目39.01至39.14所称“初级形状”，只限于下列各种形状：(一)液状及糊状，包括分散体(乳浊液及悬浮液)及溶液；(二)不规则形状的块，团、粉(包括压型粉)、颗粒、粉片及类似的散装形状。七、品目39.15不适用于已制成初级形状的单一热塑材料废碎料及下脚料(品目39.01至39.14)。八、品目39.17所称“管子”，是指通常用于输送或供给气体或液体的空心制品或半制品(例如，肋纹浇花软管、多孔管)，还包括香肠用肠衣及其他扁平管。除肠衣及扁平管外，内截面如果不呈圆形、椭圆形、矩形(其长度不超过宽度的1.5倍)或正几何形，则不能视为管子，而应作为异型材。九、品目39.18所称“塑料糊墙品”，适用于墙壁或天花板装饰用的宽度不小于45厘米的成卷产品，这类产品是将塑料牢固地附着在除纸张以外任何材料的衬背上，并且在塑料面起纹、压花、着色、印制图案或用其他方法装饰。十、品目39.20及39.21所称“板、片、膜、箔、扁条”，只适用于未切割或仅切割成矩形(包括正方形)(含切割后即可供使用的)，但未经进一步加工的板、片、膜、箔、扁条(第五十四章的物品除外)及正几何形块，不论是否经过印制或其他表面加工。十一、品目39.25只适用于第二分章以前各品目未包括的下列物品：(一)容积超过300升的囤、柜(包括化粪池)、罐、桶及类似容器；(二)用于地板、墙壁、隔墙、天花板或屋顶等方面的结构件；(三)槽管及其附件；(四)门、窗及其框架和门槛；(五)阳台、栏杆、栅栏、栅门及类似品；(六)窗板、百叶窗(包括威尼斯式百叶窗)或类似品及其零件、附件；(七)商店、工棚、仓库等用的拼装式固定大型货架；(八)建筑用的特色(例如，凹槽、圆顶及鸽棚式)装饰件；(九)固定装于门窗、楼梯、墙壁或建筑物其他部位的附件及架座，例如，球形把手、拉手、挂钩、托架、毛巾架、开关板及其他护板。子目注释：一、属于本章任一品目项下的聚合物(包括共聚物)及化学改性聚合物应按下列规则归类：(一)在同级子目中有一个“其他”子目的：1. 子目所列聚合物名称冠有“聚(多)”的(例如，聚乙烯及聚酰胺-6，6)，是指列名的该种聚合物单体单元含量在整个聚合物中按重量计必须占95%及以上。2. 子目号3901.30、3903.20、3903.30及3904.30所列的共聚物，如果该种共聚单体单元含量在整个聚合物中按重量计占95%及以上，即应归入上述子目。3. 化学改性聚合物如未在其他子目具体列名，应归入列明为“其他”的子目内。4. 不符合上述(一)、(二)、(三)款规定的聚合物，应按聚合物中重量最大的那种单体单元(与其他各种单一的共聚单体单元相比)所构成的聚合物归入该级其他相应子目。为此，归入同一子目的聚合物单体单元应作为一种单体单元对待。只有在同级子目中的聚合物共聚单体单元才可以进行比较。(二)在同级子目中没有“其他”子目的：1. 聚合物应按聚合物中重量最大的那种单体单元(与其他各种单一的共聚单体单元相比)所构成的聚合物归入该级相应子目。为此，归入同一子目的聚合物单体单元应作为一种单体单元对待。只有在同级子目中的聚合物共聚单体单元才可以进行比较。2. 化学改性聚合物应按相应的未改性聚合物的子目归类。聚合物混合体应按单体单元比例相等、种类相同的聚合物归入相应子目。二、子目3920.43所称增塑剂，包括次级增塑剂。

(刘均科)

全国塑料工业生产、经营情况统计

2012 年塑料制品行业经济运行情况分析

2012 年，面对国内外复杂多变的经济形势，塑料制品行业认真贯彻中央“稳中求进”的方针政策，坚持以国内外市场需求为导向，加大结构调整力度与转型升级速度，实现了发展速度与经济效益同步增长、进出口贸易规模进一步扩大的良好成绩，行业经济运行总体上保持着稳定态势。但一些行业和地区也出现了企业用工需求不足、盈利能力下降等问题，行业发展速度有所减缓，未来行业发展将由跨越式高速发展回归稳健，进入平稳发展阶段。

一、新国家标准《国民经济行业分类》的实施对塑料制品行业数据口径的影响

新国家标准《国民经济行业分类》(GB/T 4754—2011)已经国家质量监督检验检疫总局和国家标准化管理委员会批准发布，并于 2011 年 11 月 1 日起实施。根据国家统计局国统字〔2011〕69 号文件《国家统计局关于执行新国民经济行业分类国家标准的通知》，新《国民经济行业分类》从 2012 年定报统一开始使用。

因此，2012 年的统计数据是按照新的国民经济行业汇总的。在新的国民经济行业分类中，原属塑料制品行业的“塑料鞋”行业被划分到“制鞋业”中，也就是说塑料制品行业从 2012 年的统计数据开始，就不在包含“塑料鞋”行业数据。中国轻工业信息中心根据 2011 年塑料制品行业经济运行数据计算出塑料鞋行业主要经济指标占塑料制品行业的比重(详见表 1)，据此可以估算出 2012 年塑料制品行业主要经济运行数据与往年相比在统计口径上的差异。

表 1　2011 年塑料鞋行业主要经济指标占塑料制品行业比重

指标名称	单　位	塑料制品行业总计	塑料鞋行业	占比/%
企业数	个	12963	438	3.38
从业人员	万人	247.1	12.0	4.87
工业总产值	亿元	16079.8	426.1	2.65
工业销售产值	亿元	15764.8	420.0	2.66
其中：出口交货值	亿元	2276.7	169.5	7.44
主营业务收入	亿元	15583.7	415.3	2.67
利税总额	亿元	1293.0	22.0	1.70
其中：利润总额	亿元	882.3	12.3	1.40
资产总计	亿元	9445.0	146.6	1.55

同时，海关进出口数据统计口径也有所调整，由于塑料鞋占塑料制品出口比重比较大，进口额相对较小，因此，调整后对塑料制品行业出口总额影响较大。2011 年塑料鞋出口 145.6 亿美元，如果 2011 年塑料制品海关出口数据如剔除塑料鞋及相关产品数据后，塑料制品行业出口总额将减少 25%。

二、2012 年塑料制品行业经济运行情况概述

2012 年，塑料制品行业规模以上企业 1.3 万个，累计完成工业总产值 16757.3 亿元，同比增长 15.04%，增速比去年同期(下同)下降 12.5 个百分点。实现销售产值 16450.2 亿元，同比增长 14.95%，增速下降 12.6 个百分点。其中，出口交货值 2140.9 亿元，同比增长 2.7%，下降 7.1 个百分点。累计产销率为 98.2%，保持较高水平。塑料制品产量 57819kt，同比增长 8.99%，降低 13.4 个百分点。可以看出塑料制品行业产销基本顺畅，但增速趋缓。

2012 年，塑料制品行业规模以上企业完成主营业务收入 16310.1 亿元，同比增长 11.79%。实现利税 1431.3 亿元，同比增长 17.12%。其中：利润总额为 963.3 亿元，同比增长 15.94%。行业资产总计为 10412.1 亿元，同比增长 13.03%，资产负债率 51.5%。

2012 年，塑料制品行业规模以上企业中：亏损企业 1490 个，亏损面 11.2%。比去年同期提高 1.6 个百分点。从业人员 233.2 万人，同比下降 1.55%。

据海关总署统计数据汇总整理，2012 年，塑料制品行业进出口总额为 696.24 亿美元，同比增长 15.08%，其中进口额 184.84 亿美元，同比增长 -0.42%，出口额 511.4 亿美元，同比增长 21.95%。贸易顺差 326.56 亿美元。

2012 年橡胶和塑料制品业共完成固定资产投资 4344.68 亿元，投资总额居主要轻工行业中前列。同比增长 16.7%，投资增速较往年有所降低。

三、塑料制品行业产、销总值完成情况

(一) 工业总产值完成情况

2012年，塑料制品行业工业总产值16757.3亿元，同比增长15.04%。其中：12月份完成工业总产值1648.31亿元，为年内单月最高值，同比增长14.58%，增速比11月有小幅降低。但行业生产形势总体是正常的。

2012年轻工重点行业中，塑料制品行业总产值位居第二位，占全部轻工行业总产值的9.3%塑料制品行业产值增幅低于轻工行业平均发展水平3.2个百分点。

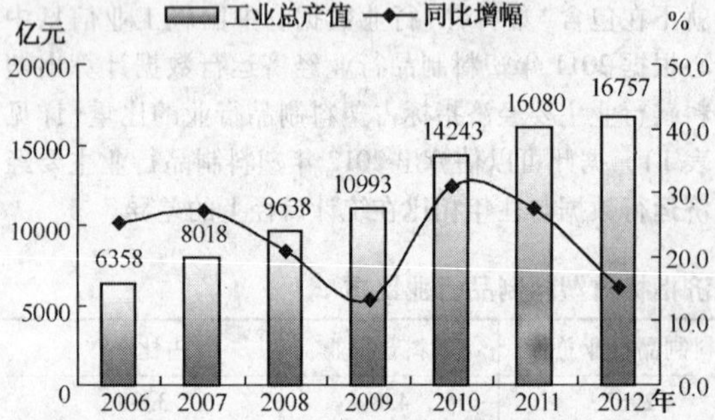

图1　2006~2012年塑料制品行业工业总产值完成情况

分子行业看，2012年，塑料板、管、型材制造业工业总产值4133.52亿元，居首位，同比增长18.64%；塑料薄膜制造业工业总产值2222.93亿元，同比增长14.23%；塑料丝、绳及编织品制造业工业总产值2188.23亿元，同比增长19.13%；上述3个行业工业总产值合计占行业的比重超过50%。

从总产值分地区完成情况看，2012年，比重主要集中在广东省、浙江省、山东省、江苏省、辽宁省、福建等省。其中：广东省累计完成工业总产值3161.01亿元，同比增长9.65%；浙江省工业总产值值2061.53亿元，同比增长9.19%；山东省工业总产值1557亿元，同比增长17.44%；江苏省工业总产值1539.45亿元，同比增长5.78%。

以上四省总产值合计占全国的近50%，除山东省外，其他三省总产值增速低于全国平均水平。安徽产值增速达到27.8%，继续保持领先位置。上海市总产值仍然为负增长，同比下降1.85%，增幅居末位。

(二) 工业销售产值完成情况

2012年，全国塑料制品行业销售产值16450.19亿元，同比增长14.95%。其中：12月份完成销售产值1625.19亿元，为单月最高值，同比增长14.59%。销售产值走势与工业总产值走势一致，季节性因素明显，产销率保持较高水平，表明行业产销基本顺畅。

2012年，产销率基本保持着在98%左右，高于轻工行业平均产销率水平。1~12月份累计产销率为98.17%，居轻工主要行业第11位。但产销率增幅比去年同期下降0.08%。除塑料丝、绳及编织品、塑料包装箱及容器、日用塑料行业外，其他子行业产销率均比去年同期有所下降。其中：塑料丝绳及编织品制造业累计产销率达到98.6%，为行业最高值。

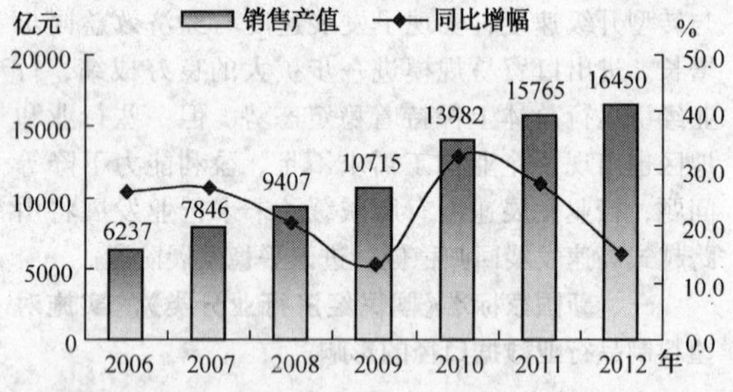

图2　2006~2012年塑料制品行业销售产值完成情况

(三) 出口交货值完成情况

近年来，塑料制品行业出口交货值占销售产值的比重呈下降走势。2012年出口交货值2140.9亿元，同比增长2.7%，比去年降低6.7个百分点。出口交货值增幅及占销售产值的比重呈现逐步走低的态势，2012年出口交货值占销售产值的比重为13%，比去年同期的比重降低1.4个百分点。

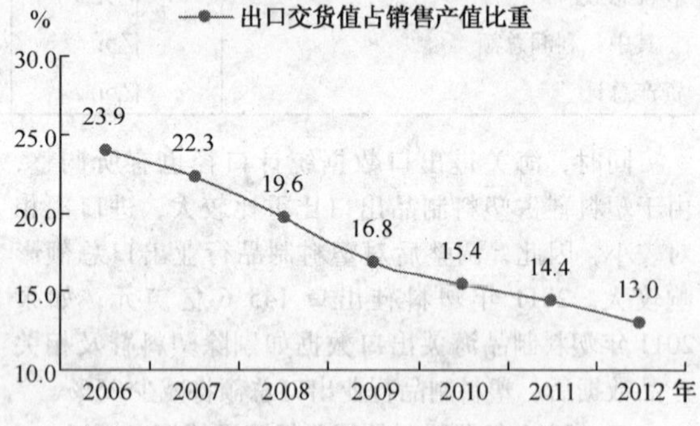

图3　2006~2012年塑料制品行业出口交货值占比变化情况

出口交货值占销售产值比重最大的子行业为日用塑料制造业，比重为33.2%，其次为塑料零件制造业，比重为28.6%。塑料薄膜制造业出口交货值占销售产值比重为11.8%，居第三位(不包括其他塑料制品)。

(四) 产品产量完成情况

2012年，塑料制品行业规模以上企业累计完成产量57819kt，同比增长8.99%。增速比去年降低13.36个百分点。其中，12月份塑料制品产量

5578kt，为年内月度最高值，但月度产量已连续两月出现负增长。2012 年前 7 个月产量走势基本正常，从 8 月份起月度产量低于去年且增幅也有所下降。

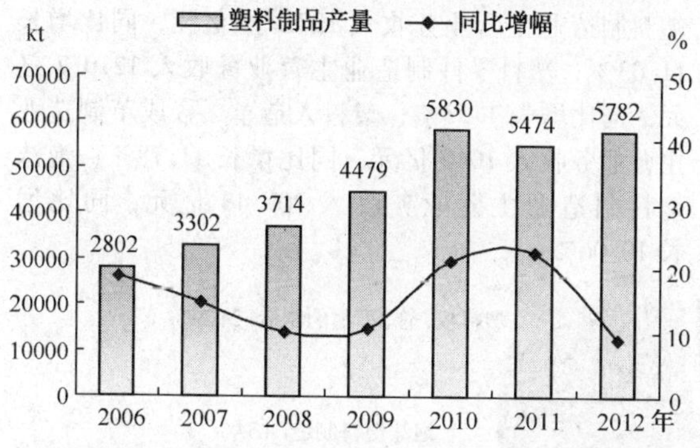

图 4　2006 ~ 2012 年塑料制品产量完成情况

1. 产量分地区完成情况

塑料制品产量主要集中在浙江省、广东省、山东省、江苏省、辽宁省等地区。我国塑料制品产业格局虽没有发生根本改变，但由于内陆省份发展速度较快，与传统产业大省间的差距在逐步缩小，广东省、浙江省、山东省等产业大省所占比重呈现缓慢下降走势。2012 年，全国塑料制品完成累计产量 57819kt，同比增长 8.99%。其中：浙江省塑料制品产量 9485.4kt，超过广东省居首位，同比增长 13.02%；广东省产量 9193.1kt，同比增长 7.45%；山东省产量 4531.2kt，同比增长 18.39%；江苏省产量 3492.6kt，同比增长 -2.29%；辽宁省产量 3239kt，同比增长 10.93%。以上五省产量合计占总产量的 51.8%。

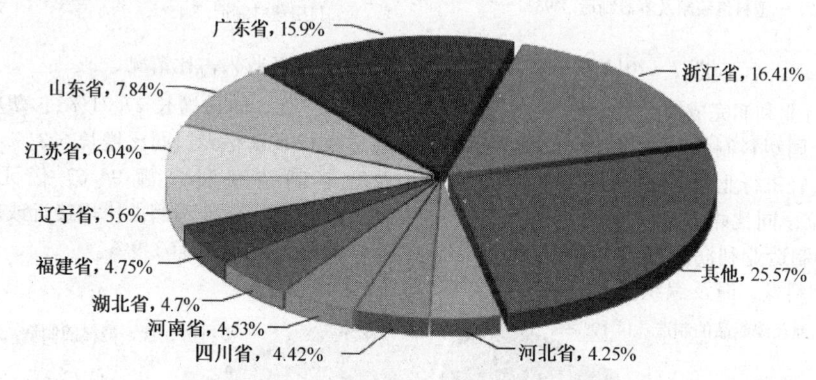

图 5　2012 年主要地区塑料制品产量占比情况

2012 年，塑料制品主产区广东、江苏两省产量增速低于全国平均水平，其中江苏省产量为负增长。广东省产量占全国的比重比去年同期下降 3.72 个百分点。四川省产量增速达到 37.3%，居首位。

2. 产量分品种完成情况

分品种产量看，2012 年，塑料薄膜产量 9703kt，同比增长 9.33%，其中，农用薄膜 1627kt，同比增长 7.74%。泡沫塑料 1721kt，同比增长 23.1%。塑料人造革、合成革 3143kt，同比增长 15.55%。日用塑料制品 4618kt，同比增长 14.43%。其他塑料制品 38634kt，同比增长 7.26%。

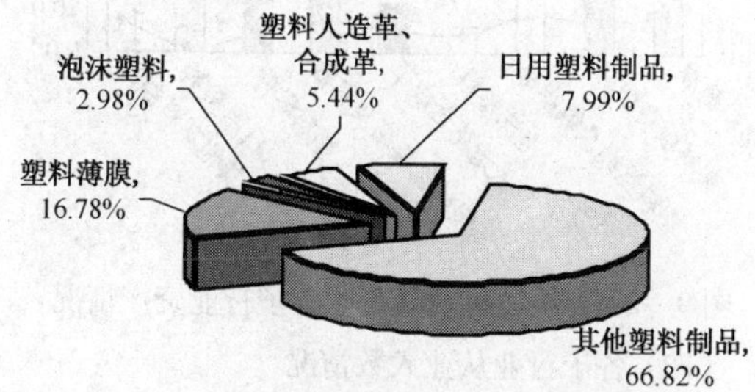

图 6　2012 年分品种塑料制品产量占比情况

由于国家统计制度调整，从 2011 年起占塑料制品产量比重较大的塑料板管型材以及塑料编织品、塑料包装箱及容器等产品未列入统计目录，其产量包含在其他塑料制品中，保留的品种除塑料薄膜以外，占比均较小，致使其他塑料制品比重过大，不能完全反映塑料制品行业发展现状，建议国家统计目录中尽快恢复“塑料板片”“塑料管及其附件”、“塑料条棒型材”“塑料丝绳及编织品”、“塑料包装箱及容器”等品种的产量统计。

四、塑料制品行业主要经济效益指标完成情况

2012 年，塑料制品行业主要经济效益指标保持平稳增长，但增速逐步趋缓。塑料制品行业规模以上企业 1.32 万个，其中：亏损企业 1490 个，亏损面 11.2%。从业人员 233.2 万人，同比下降 1.55%。

完成主营业务收入 16310.1 亿元，同比增长 11.79%。实现利税 1431.3 亿元，同比增长 17.12%。其中：利润总额为 963.3 亿元，同比增长 15.94%。

2012 年，塑料制品行业资产总计 10412.1 亿元，同比增长 13.03%，资产负债率 51.5%。

（一）各子行业主营业务收入情况

2012 年，全国塑料制品行业累计完成主营业务收入 16310.1 亿元，占轻工行业总计的 9.2%，居第二位，同比增长 11.79%。今年 2 月份以来，主营业务累计增速呈回落走势。全年主营业务增速比去年同期降低 15.73 个百分点。

其中，塑料板、管、型材制造业主营业务收入 3960.93 亿元，同比增长 14.59%；塑料薄膜制造业主营业务收入 2179.51 亿元，同比增长 10.93%；塑料丝、绳及编织品制造业主营业务收入 2172.79 亿元，同比增长 18.42%；塑料包装箱及容器制造业主营业务收入 1461.45 亿元，同比增长 13.11%；日用塑料制造业主营业务收入 1377.94 亿元，同比增长 11.03%；塑料零件制造业主营业务收入 1210.7 亿元，同比增长 1.53%；塑料人造革、合成革制造业主营业务收入 1040 亿元，同比增长 11.78%；泡沫塑料制造业主营业务收入 707.48 亿元，同比增长 10.06%。

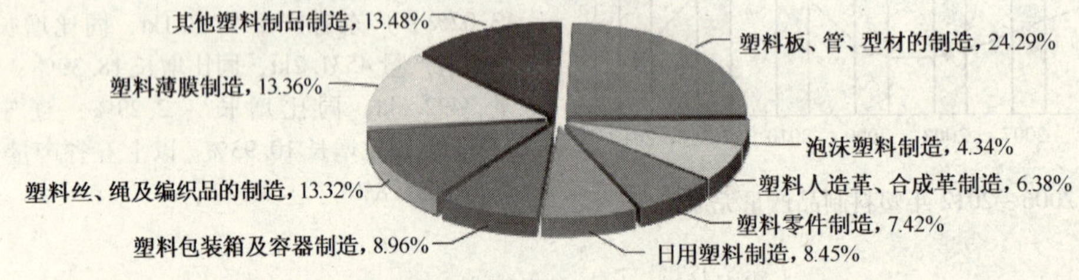

图 7　2012 年塑料制品行业子行业主营业务收入占比情况

（二）各子行业利润完成情况

2012 年，全国塑料制品行业累计完成利润总额 963.27 亿元，占轻工行业利润总额的 8.5%，居轻工主要行业第四位，同比增长 15.94%。其中，塑料板、管、型材的制造业利润总额 264.45 亿元，同比增长 19.2%；塑料丝、绳及编织品的制造利润总额 136.71 亿元，同比增长 27.31%；；塑料薄膜制造利润总额 120.02 亿元，同比增长 6.31%；塑料包装箱及容器制造利润总额 94.67 亿元，同比增长 11.68%。以上行业利润占比均接近或超过 10%，利润合计占行业比重为 63.9%。

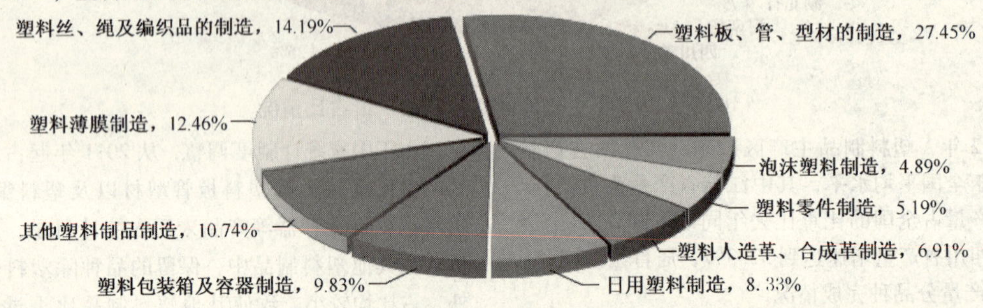

图 8　2012 年塑料制品行业子行业利润占比情况

各子行业的盈利能力参差不齐，塑料薄膜、塑料零件、塑料包装箱及容器、塑料零件利润增幅低于行业平均水平，其中塑料零件利润总额增幅仅为 1.6%，下降幅度较大。

（三）各子行业资产情况

2012 年，全国塑料制品资产总计 10412.05 亿元，同比增长 13.03%。其中，塑料板、管、型材制造业资产总计 2676.82 亿元，同比增长 13.74%；塑料薄膜制造业资产总计 1635.14 亿元，同比增长 17.46%；塑料包装箱及容器制造业资产总计 1049.5 亿元，同比增长 14.59%；以上行业资产占比超过 10%。

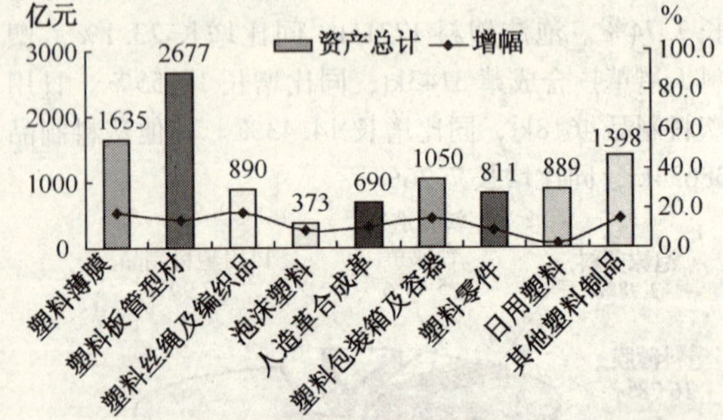

图 9　2012 年塑料制品行业各子行业资产情况

（四）各子行业从业人数情况

2012 年，全国塑料制品行业规模以上企业从人数233.18万人，同比下降1.55%。子行业中：塑料零件、日用塑料、塑料薄膜、泡沫塑料制造业从业人数同比均为负增长。

其中：塑料板、管、型材制造业39.42万人（占16.91%），同比增长4.37%；塑料丝、绳及编织品制造业32.38万人（占13.89%），同比增长4.36%；塑料零件制造业29.44万人（占12.62%），同比增长-8.89%；日用塑料制造业27.76万人（占11.9%），同比增长-1.73%；以上行业从业人员占比超过10%（不包括其他塑料制品行业）

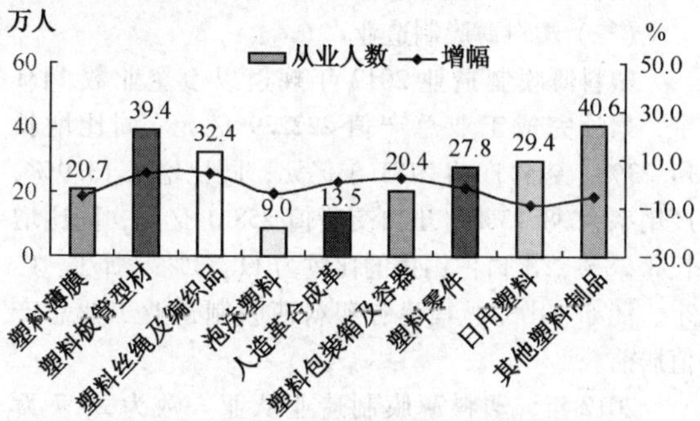

图10　2012年塑料制品各子行业从业人数情况

五、塑料制品主要产区经济运行情况

我国塑料制品主要产区集中在东南沿海一带，广东省、浙江省、山东省、江苏省、辽宁省是塑料制品产业大省，数据表明五省产值合计占行业总产值的比重达到56.4%，经过多年的发展，已形成各具特色的产业区域。以下对总产值居前三位的地区进行分析。

（一）广东省

1. 产、销总值完成情况

2012年，广东省塑料制品行业规模以上企业2830个，累计完成工业总产值3161亿元，占全行业比重为18.86%，同比增长9.65%。销售产值3107.63亿元，占全行业比重为18.89%，同比增长9.1%。累计产销率为98.3%。出口交货值921.1亿元，占全行业比重为43.02%，同比增长4.37%

2. 主要塑料制品产量完成情况

2012年，广东省塑料制品总产量为9193kt，同比增长7.45%，占行业总产量比重为15.9%。在列入统计目录的产品中，除其他塑料制品外，广东省塑料薄膜产量最高，为1404kt，同比增长10.18%，占广东省塑料制品总产量的15.24%。其次为日用塑料制品，产量为1032kt，同比增长22.03%。泡沫塑料产量709kt，同比增长21.78%。塑料人造革、合成革产量为186kt，同比增长11.19%。

3. 主要经济效益指标完成情况

2012年，广东省塑料制品企业累计实现主营业务收入3101.8亿元，同比增长34%，占行业总计的占19.02%。利润总额为135.55元，同比增长1.39%，占行业总计的14.1%。资产总计为2173.5亿元，同比增长8.46%，从业人数为69.22万人，同比增长-8.86%。

4. 进出口情况

2012年，广东省塑料制品进出口总额228.40亿美元，同比增长22.73%。其中：进口额53.08亿美元，同比增长6.59%，占进口总额的28.72%。出口额175.32亿美元，同比增长28.63%，占出口总额的34.28%。

（二）浙江省

1. 产、销总值完成情况

2012年，浙江省塑料制品行业规模以上企业1845个，累计完成工业总产值2061.5亿元，同比增长9.19%，占全行业比重为12.3%。销售产值1999.7亿元，同比增长8.36%，占全行业比重为12.16%。累计产销率为97%。出口交货值397.7亿元，占全行业比重为18.58%，同比增长6.36%。

2. 主要塑料制品产量

2012年，浙江省塑料制品总产量为9485kt，同比增长13.02%，占行业总产量比重为16.41%。在列入统计目录的产品中，除其他塑料制品外，塑料薄膜产量最高，为3045kt，同比增长20.63%，占浙江省塑料制品总产量的32.1%。塑料人造革、合成革产量为1339kt，同比增长10.58%。日用塑料制品产量1029kt，同比增长6.78%。泡沫塑料产量为163kt，同比增长-1.63%。

3. 主要经济效益指标完成情况

2012年，浙江省塑料制品行业规模以上企业累计实现主营业务收入1858.56亿元，同比增长15.82%；亿元，占行业总计的11.93%。利润总额为102.77亿元，同比增长10.98%，占行业总计的11.65%。资产总计为1654.86亿元，同比增长13.9%，资产负债率为62.66%。从业人数为28.24万人，同比增长1.73%。

4. 进出口情况

2012年，浙江省塑料制品进出口总额为123.69亿美元，同比增长9.07%。其中：进口额9.97亿美元，占行业进口总额的5.4%，同比增长-0.54%，累计完成出口额113.71亿美元，占行业出口总额的22.24%，同比增长9.89%。

（三）山东省

1. 产、销总值完成情况

2012年，山东省塑料制品行业规模以上企业1177个，累计完成工业总产值1557亿元，占行业比重为9.29%，同比增长17.44%。销售产值1539.7亿元，占全行业比重为9.36%，同比增长17%。出口交货值113.7亿元，占全行业比重为5.31%，同比增长-4.74%。

2. 主要塑料制品产量

2012年，山东省塑料制品行业规模以上企业塑料制品总产量为4531kt，同比增长18.39%，占行业总产量比重为7.84%。在列入统计目录的产品中，除其他塑料制品外，产量最大的产品为：塑料薄膜708kt，同比下降0.14%，占山东省塑料制品总产量的15.62%。日用塑料制品161kt，同比下降15.57%。塑料人造革、合成革，产量62.3kt，同比增长10.31%。泡沫塑料46.9kt，同比增长142.7%。

3. 主要经济效益指标完成情况

2012年，山东省塑料制品行业规模以上企业累计实现主营业务收入1528.5亿元，占行业总计的9.37%，同比增长15.87%。利润总额为105.95亿元，占行业总计的11%，同比增长24.21%。资产总计为620.4亿元，同比增长19.28%，占行业总计的5.96%。从业人数为14.33万人，同比下降2.63%，占行业总计的6.14%。

4. 进出口情况

2012年，山东省塑料制品进出口总额39.59亿美元，同比增长5.85%。其中：进口额11.01亿美元，占行业进口总额的5.96%，同比增长4.49%。累计完成出口额28.58亿美元，占行业出口总额5.59%，同比增长6.38%。

六、塑料制品行业主要子行业分析

从国民经济行业分类来看，塑料制品行业下分塑料薄膜制造；塑料板管型材制造；塑料丝绳及编制品制造；泡沫塑料制造；塑料人造革合成革制造；塑料包装箱及容器制造；塑料零件制造；日用塑料制造及其他塑料制品制造9个子行业。

2012年，除泡沫塑料制造业外，其他塑料制品子行业工业总产值均超过千亿元。塑料板管型材、塑料薄膜、塑料丝绳及编织品、塑料包装箱及容器行业总产值居前，四个行业合计占塑料制品行业产值总计的60%。

(一) 塑料板、管、型材制造业

塑料板管型材制造业经过近年的高速发展已成为塑料制品行业第一大子行业，2012年规模以上企业数2504个，累计完成总产值4133.5亿元，同比增长18.64%。销售产值4048.5亿元，同比增长18.46%，产销率为97.94%。出口交货值191.9亿元，同比增长0.16%，出口占销售的比重为4.74%。广东、山东、辽宁、浙江、江苏省塑料板管型材制造业工业总产值居前五位。

2012年，塑料板管型材制造业从业人数为39.4万人，同比增长4.37%。资产总计2676.8亿元，同比增长13.74%。主营业务收入3960.9亿元，同比增长14.59%。实现利税388.7亿元，同比增长21.3%，其中：利润总额264.45亿元，同比增长19.2%。资产负债率47.5%，行业亏损面为9.7%，亏损企业亏损额11.54亿元，较同期有大幅上升，同比增长19.95%。广东、山东、河南、辽宁、湖北省塑料板管型材制造业利润总额居前。

(二) 塑料薄膜制造业

塑料薄膜制造业2012年规模以上企业数1431个，累计完成工业总产值2222.9亿元，同比增长14.23%。销售产值2181.3亿元，同比增长13.9%，产销率为98.13%。出口交货值258.1亿元，同比增长3.28%，出口占销售的比重为11.83%。浙江、广东、江苏、山东、福建省塑料薄膜制造业工业总产值居前。

2012年，塑料薄膜制造业从业人数为20.7万人，同比下降5.55%。资产总计1635.1亿元，同比增长17.5%。主营业务收入2179.5亿元，同比增长10.93%。实现利税172.3亿元，同比增长10.23%，其中：利润120亿元，同比增长6.31%。资产负债率51.02%，行业亏损面为13.5%，亏损企业亏损额12亿元，同比大幅增长78.8%。浙江、广东、山东、江苏、福建省塑料薄膜制造业利润总额居前。

(三) 塑料丝绳及编织品制造业

2012年塑料丝绳及编织品制造业规模以上企业数1836个，累计完成总产值2188.2亿元，同比增长19.13%。销售产值2157.6元，同比增长19.39%，产销率为98.6%。出口交货值93.5亿元，同比增长5.36%，出口占销售的比重为4.33%。山东、辽宁、河南、江苏、湖北省塑料丝绳及编织品制造业总产值居前。

2012年，塑料丝绳及编织品制造业从业人数为32.38万人，同比增长4.36%。资产总计889.65亿元，同比增长17.76%。主营业务收入2172.78亿元，同比增长18.42%。实现利税203.6亿元，同比增长23.98%，其中：利润136.7亿元，同比增长27.3%。资产负债率47.72%，行业亏损面为5.83%，亏损企业亏损额1.77元，同比下降3.9%。山东、河南、辽宁、江苏、河北省塑料丝绳及编织品制造业利润总额居前。

(四) 塑料包装箱及容器制造业

塑料包装箱及容器制造业2012年规模以上企业数1450个，累计完成总产值1497.1亿元，同比增长

16.78%。销售产值1472.7亿元，同比增长17.21%，产销率为98.37%。出口交货值122.48亿元，同比增长18.7%，出口占销售的比重为8.32%。广东、浙江、山东、江苏、辽宁省塑料包装箱及容器制造业工业总产值居前。

2012年，塑料包装箱及容器制造业从业人数为20.4万人，同比增长2.57%。资产总计1049.5亿元，同比增长14.59%。主营业务收入1461.4亿元，同比增长13.11%。实现利税141.9亿元，同比增长12.89%，其中：利润94.6亿元，同比增长11.68%。资产负债率51.41%，行业亏损面为11.53%，亏损企业亏损额7亿元，同比增长83.72%，亏损额增幅居行业第一位。浙江、广东、山东、江苏、安徽省塑料包装箱及容器制造业利润总额居前。

七、塑料制品海关进出口贸易情况

据海关总署统计数据整理，2012年，塑料制品行业进出口总额为696.24亿美元，同比增长15.08%，其中，出口额511.4亿美元，同比增长21.95%。进口额184.84亿美元，同比增长-0.42%，贸易顺差326.56亿美元。2012年塑料制品对外贸易贸易总额增速有所降低。

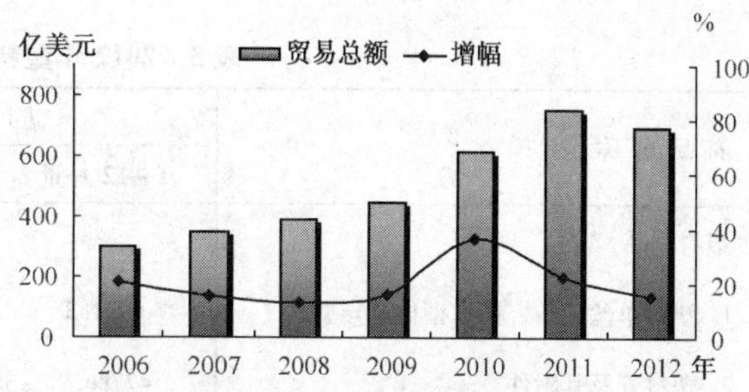

图11　2006~2012年度中国塑料制品进出口贸易总额情况

（一）出口情况

2012年，全国塑料制品行业累计出口额511.40亿美元，同比增长21.95%。增幅比去年同期下降4.52个百分点。2012年塑料制品出口形势虽不及去年同期强劲，年初累计出口额出现了负增长情况，但从一季度末开始，出口呈现企稳回升态势，自5月份以来，累计出口额增速均保持在20%以上。

出口商品中，日用塑料制品累计出口额152.89亿美元，占比接近30%，同比增长46.01%，占比及增幅均居子行业出口首位（详见表2）

表2　2012年塑料制品海关出口统计

商品名称	出口量/t		出口额/万美元	
	1~12月量	同比/%	1~12月额	同比/%
塑料制品	—	—	5114015.0	21.95
1. 塑料单丝、条、杆、型材及异型材	147810.3	2.92	32417.1	10.53
2. 塑料管及其附件	489185.7	9.02	186691.8	24.55
3. 塑料板、片、膜、箔、带及扁条	2407397.9	10.45	756129.9	10.42
4. 塑料人造革、合成革	574463.7	0.88	266634.0	-12.27
5. 塑料包装箱及容器及其附件	2194879.9	2.27	720903.9	19.91
6. 塑料零件	41681.9	1.25	44451.9	3.47
7. 建筑用塑料制品	1959611.3	13.39	352168.7	24.50
8. 日用塑料制品	—	—	1528936.9	46.01
9. 其他塑料制品	—	—	1225680.8	16.57

（二）进口情况

2012年塑料制品累计进口额184.84亿美元，同比增长-0.42%。进口额占全国轻工行业主要商品进口总额的16.02%，居第二位。全年各月度累计进口额均为负增长，年末比年初降幅有所减小，但与去年相比下降幅度较大。其中：12月份完成进口额15.29亿美元，同比增长-2.46%。

进口商品中，塑料板.片.膜.箔.带及扁条所占比重最大，占进口总额的60.62%。高于2011年0.22个百分点。

进口商品中有6种进口额增幅为负增长，其中进口比重最大的塑料板.片.膜.箔.带及扁条进口额下降0.83%，对行业总体进口影响较大。2012年塑料零件、建筑用塑料制品进口额增幅相对较高，但比去年同期下降幅度较大。（见表3）

表3　2012 年塑料制品海关进口统计

商品名称	进口量/t		进口额/万美元	
	1～12 月量	同比%	1～12 月额	同比%
塑料制品	—	—	1848400.2	-0.42
1. 塑料单丝、条、杆、型材及异型材	8901.3	-8.11	9111.5	1.12
2. 塑料管及其附件	47786.9	-6.83	71280.0	-2.16
3. 塑料板、片、膜、箔、带及扁条	1113030.3	-2.20	1120468.3	-0.83
4. 塑料人造革、合成革	54864.3	-15.46	57119.4	-4.18
5. 塑料包装箱及容器及其附件	214796.6	3.68	139192.8	-0.89
6. 塑料零件	31266.0	-4.25	111512.3	5.28
7. 建筑用塑料制品	68542.8	-10.89	21501.2	3.87
8. 日用塑料制品	—	—	20805.2	-0.80
9. 其他塑料制品	—	—	297409.4	0.20

八、行业固定资产投资规模继续扩大，增速趋缓

近年来，塑料制品行业投资规模持续扩大，年均增长速度超过 30%，这也是促进塑料制品行业近年来持续快速发展的一个重要原因，2012 年行业投资总额仍保持稳定增长，但增速有所放缓。

2012 年橡胶和塑料制品业共完成固定资产投资 4344.68 亿元，投资总额居主要轻工行业中前列。同比增长 16.7%，投资增速较往年有所降低。

表4　2012 年轻工主要行业固定资产投资完成情况

主要轻工行业	投资额	
	自年初累计/亿元	比去年同期增长/%
农副食品加工业	6906.62	32.0
食品制造业	3080.04	28.1
酒、饮料和精制茶制造业	2601.92	36.2
皮革、毛皮、羽毛及其制品和制鞋业	1337.58	14.3
木材加工及木、竹、藤、棕、草制品业	2494.97	31.3
家具制造业	1557.25	30.2
造纸及纸制品业	2220.91	15.5
文教、工美、体育和娱乐用品制造业	1148.16	20.8
橡胶和塑料制品业	4334.68	16.7
金属制品业	5955.01	9.9

近年来，塑料制品行业固定投资规模稳步扩大，是未来塑料制品行业经济增长的基础和上行动力。

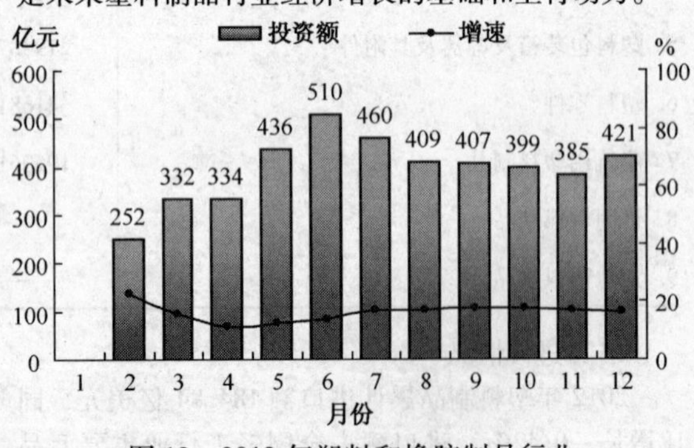

图 12　2012 年塑料和橡胶制品行业月度固定资产投资完成情况

（中国轻工业信息中心　张涌涛）

附表 1　2012 年 1～12 月份全国塑料制品行业规模以上工业企业产销总值

指标名称	计量单位	汇总企业数/个	工业总产值(现价)			工业销售产值(现价)				其中：出口交货值			
			本月止累计/千元	同比增长/%	占行业比重/%	本月止累计/千元	同比增长/%	占行业比重/%	产销率/%	本月止累计/千元	同比增长/%	占行业比重/%	出口占销售比重/%
塑料制品业	千元	13246	1675728508	15.04	100.00	1645018531	14.95	100.00	98.17	214091770	2.71	100.00	13.01
塑料薄膜制造	千元	1431	222292548	14.23	13.27	218134129	13.99	13.26	98.13	25809644	3.28	12.06	11.83
塑料板、管、型材的制造	千元	2504	413351902	18.64	24.67	404849943	18.46	24.61	97.94	19191392	0.16	8.96	4.74
塑料丝、绳及编织品的制造	千元	1836	218822930	19.13	13.06	215765147	19.39	13.12	98.60	9351298	5.36	4.37	4.33
泡沫塑料制造	千元	747	73275286	15.56	4.37	71704519	14.38	4.36	97.86	4729202	5.72	2.21	6.60
塑料人造革、合成革制造	千元	549	108576811	17.23	6.48	105894105	16.98	6.44	97.53	8700695	-2.93	4.06	8.22
塑料包装箱及容器制造	千元	1405	149717405	16.78	8.93	147272165	17.21	8.95	98.37	12248410	18.70	5.72	8.32
塑料零件制造	千元	1335	141052064	13.26	8.42	138413736	13.49	8.41	98.13	45978797	5.40	21.48	33.22
日用塑料制造	千元	1249	123480483	3.55	7.37	121559775	3.15	7.39	98.44	34807399	-2.33	16.26	28.63
其他塑料制品制造	千元	2190	2251597079	11.52	13.44	221425012	11.54	13.46	98.34	53274933	1.66	24.88	24.06

注：1. 数据来源：国家统计局。

2. “规模以上”是指年主营业务收入 2000 万元及以上全部工业法人企业。

附表 2　2012 年 1～12 月份全国塑料制品行业规模以上工业企业主要经济指标

指标名称	汇总企业个数/个	其中：亏损企业数		亏损企业亏损额		主营业务收入		主营业务成本		利税总额	
		本月止累计/个	累计同比/%	本月止累计/千元	累计同比/%	本月止累计/千元	累计同比/%	本月止累计/千元	累计同比/%	本月止累计/千元	累计同比/%
塑料制品业	13245	1490	16.59	6725403	37.54	1631012782	11.79	1398440571	11.49	143134563	17.12
塑料薄膜制造	1431	193	20.63	1200545	78.80	217950648	10.93	190892214	11.32	17231820	10.23
塑料板、管、型材	2504	243	24.62	1154302	19.95	396092951	14.59	333578338	14.38	38872897	21.29
塑料丝、绳及编织品	1835	107	0.00	177433	-3.90	217278534	18.42	187993216	18.09	20361335	23.98
泡沫塑料制造	747	67	4.69	131401	-8.83	70748114	10.06	60609556	9.23	6720288	17.36
塑料人造革、合成革	549	57	29.55	174823	36.13	103999668	11.78	91986294	10.93	9502817	29.65
塑料包装箱及容器	1405	162	20.00	700009	83.72	146144765	13.11	122600340	12.14	14191617	12.89
日用塑料制造	1335	151	9.42	412604	8.43	137793904	11.03	116256930	10.38	11843580	21.66
塑料零件制造	1249	217	12.44	1432333	31.10	121070342	1.53	104926705	0.94	8254015	5.22
其他塑料制品制造	2190	293	21.07	1341953	42.05	219933856	8.10	189596978	8.36	16156194	8.46

续表

指标名称	汇总企业个数/个	其中：利润总额		资产总计		负债合计		流动资产合计		应收账款净额		产成品存货		全部从业人员平均人数	
		本月止累计/千元	累计同比/%	本月止累计/千元	累计同比/%	本月止累计/千元	累计同比/%	本月止累计/千元	累计同比/%	本月止累计/千元	累计同比/%	本月止累计/千元	累计同比/%	本月止累计/人	累计同比/%
塑料制品业	13245	96327442	15.94	1041205057	13.03	536376706	10.67	600573947	11.01	170379145	11.95	56207707	9.05	2331784.00	-1.55
塑料薄膜制造	1431	12001893	6.31	163514362	17.46	83420603	17.07	91169524	13.78	20095603	17.17	7726465	15.76	207169.00	-5.55
塑料板、管、型材	2504	26445222	19.20	267681939	13.74	127244261	5.24	151210068	9.55	40115093	18.03	17516927	11.05	394219.00	4.37
塑料丝、绳及编织品	1835	13671391	27.31	88965429	17.76	42455230	15.20	46035397	19.19	11258587	11.16	4963543	13.02	323786.00	4.36
泡沫塑料制造	747	4713677	18.67	37250532	8.94	19721290	12.08	22910063	11.38	8597185	14.62	1913322	6.07	89558.00	-4.07
塑料人造革、合成革	549	6656149	32.42	68981636	10.65	42259876	10.32	42409443	8.26	8705845	11.64	3302208	16.31	134940.00	0.68
塑料包装箱及容器	1405	9467216	11.68	104950297	14.59	53954201	15.46	56683330	16.82	17114279	16.85	3968835	-1.99	204129.00	2.57
日用塑料制造	1335	8023452	22.75	81139482	9.18	42377695	7.42	47695244	10.35	13623442	11.34	4177359	1.24	277569.00	-1.73
塑料零件制造	1249	4998429	1.57	88906195	2.32	50013841	1.73	57320430	2.20	20208551	-5.45	5023341	6.74	294375.00	-8.89
其他塑料制品制造	2190	10350013	4.16	139815186	14.86	74929709	16.34	85140448	11.04	30660560	12.03	7615707	6.11	406039.00	-5.42

注：1. 资料来源：国家统计局。
2. “规模以上”是指年主营业务收入2000万元及以上全部工业法人企业。

附表3　2012年1～12月份全国塑料制品业主要产品产量总表

产品名称	单　位	本月止累计	同比增长/%	占行业比重/%
塑料制品总计	t	57818647	8.99	100.00
其中：塑料薄膜	t	9702505	9.33	16.78
其中：农用薄膜	t	1627391	7.74	2.81
泡沫塑料	t	1720622	23.13	2.98
塑料人造革、合成革	t	3142678	15.55	5.44
日用塑料制品	t	4618427	14.43	7.99
其他塑料制品	t	38634415	7.26	66.82

注：1. 数据来源：国家统计局。
2. “规模以上”是指年主营业务收入2000万元及以上全部工业法人企业。

附表 4　2012 年 1 ~ 12 月份全国塑料制品业主要产品产量

地区	塑料制品			1. 塑料薄膜			其中：农用薄膜		
	本月止累计/t	同比增长/%	占全国比重/%	本月止累计/t	同比增长/%	占全国比重/%	本月止累计/t	同比增长/%	占全国比重/%
全国	57818647	8.99	100.00	9702505	9.33	100.00	1627391	7.74	100.00
北京	389878	-1.68	0.67	37028	-5.10	0.38	14328	-6.43	0.88
天津	1421398	38.44	2.46	285865	5.92	2.95	67038	14.02	4.12
河北	2454633	21.23	4.25	160503	10.68	1.65	31488	-9.29	1.93
山西	247349	12.07	0.43	19533	-23.86	0.20	16227	-21.06	1.00
内蒙古	259337	9.25	0.45	24892	7.64	0.26	24892	7.64	1.53
辽宁	3238998	10.93	5.60	258884	25.91	2.67	99641	1.18	6.12
吉林	790785	16.28	1.37	138301	14.05	1.43	123412	10.80	7.58
黑龙江	637843	18.28	1.10	43086	32.36	0.44	24693	53.43	1.52
上海	1847549	-2.32	3.20	314945	-5.82	3.25	40684	1.63	2.50
江苏	3492566	-2.29	6.04	916768	-14.54	9.45	42797	-0.17	2.63
浙江	9485401	13.02	16.41	3045216	20.63	31.39	126487	28.24	7.77
安徽	2117729	16.76	3.66	210676	-1.58	2.17	11022	-73.78	0.68
福建	2745337	14.79	4.75	467908	8.43	4.82	7791	-7.91	0.48
江西	1224194	62.27	2.12	12136	4.26	0.13			
山东	4531200	18.39	7.84	708108	-0.14	7.30	365488	0.69	22.46
河南	2618627	13.49	4.53	531297	7.12	5.48	238328	11.34	14.64
湖北	2720014	25.15	4.70	182192	14.35	1.88	15725	37.40	0.97
湖南	1228524	29.87	2.12	121300	7.19	1.25	40866	63.90	2.51
广东	9193123	7.45	15.90	1404162	10.18	14.47	51306	43.94	3.15
广西	1618576	-61.00	2.80	128685	-0.27	1.33	13982	8.53	0.86
海南	33464	80.34	0.06	20579	291.16	0.21			
重庆	904814	19.11	1.56	210475	30.97	2.17	8258	-16.09	0.51
四川	2556047	37.30	4.42	216916	37.29	2.24	65814	22.15	4.04
贵州	341455	18.92	0.59	4787	15.26	0.05	2570	-19.04	0.16
云南	333016	-4.43	0.58	97226	10.57	1.00	61610	19.47	3.79
西藏									
陕西	421364	110.95	0.73	18594	-9.55	0.19	18594	-9.55	1.14
甘肃	190300	32.34	0.33	43324	38.07	0.45	43324	38.07	2.66
青海	19360	5242.46	0.03						
宁夏	107802	11.17	0.19	9999	4.34	0.10	9999	4.34	0.61
新疆	647963	29.97	1.12	69121	6.35	0.71	61030	5.09	3.75

续表

地区	2. 泡沫塑料			3. 塑料人造革、合成革			4. 日用塑料制品			5. 其他塑料制品		
	本月止累计/t	同比增长/%	占全国比重/%	本月止累计/t	同比增长/%	占全国比重/%	本月止累计/t	同比增长/%	占全国比重/%	本月止累计/t	同比增长/%	占全国比重/%
全国	1720622	23.13	100.00	3142678	15.55	100.00	4618427	14.43	100.00	38634415	7.26	100.00
北京	2382	-8.56	0.14	8657	60.56	0.28	33885	9.18	0.73	307926	-1.31	0.80
天津	29801	56.96	1.73	7900	-26.98	0.25	203985	115.10	4.42	893847	41.40	2.31
河北	39204	-59.04	2.28	200722	67.28	6.39	242151	6.70	5.24	1812053	26.09	4.69
山西										227816	16.80	0.59
内蒙古	172	-49.32	0.01							234273	9.52	0.61
辽宁	55939	159.04	3.25	90826	1.44	2.89	24307	-5.16	0.53	2809043	8.99	7.27
吉林	19391	56.22	1.13	3746	19.71	0.12	78287	27.71	1.70	551060	14.33	1.43
黑龙江							12963	-47.11	0.28	581793	20.65	1.51
上海	69226	-9.91	4.02	51622	17.13	1.64	134453	4.83	2.91	1277304	-2.34	3.31
江苏	145627	130.54	8.46	374823	-13.07	11.93	360087	-20.87	7.80	1695261	9.21	4.39
浙江	163188	-1.63	9.48	1339745	10.58	42.63	1028616	6.78	22.27	3908636	10.80	10.12
安徽	38148	15.46	2.22	45479	23.99	1.45	73434	21.78	1.59	1749992	19.08	4.53
福建	36655	6.46	2.13	672182	39.48	21.39	287818	3.91	6.23	1280774	9.77	3.32
江西	10132	-1.29	0.59				34127	15.93	0.74	1167799	66.10	3.02
山东	46907	142.68	2.73	62306	10.31	1.98	160609	-15.57	3.48	3553270	24.58	9.02
河南	115761	45.64	6.73	59355	76.42	1.89	86517	20.83	1.87	1825697	12.24	4.73
湖北	32712	-39.88	1.90	36909	56.47	1.17	271785	18.01	5.88	2196416	28.77	5.69
湖南	9015	17.61	0.52	1039	-77.19	0.03	100483	12.43	2.18	996687	36.30	2.58
广东	708881	21.78	41.20	185944	11.19	5.92	1032927	22.03	22.37	5861208	3.10	15.17
广西	91066	55.06	5.29				88810	38.83	1.92	1310016	-66.49	3.39
海南										12885	-3.08	0.03
重庆	40411	17.37	2.35	1423		0.05	46597	13.98	1.01	605908	15.71	1.57
四川	33501	451.52	1.95				278794	192.45	6.04	2026836	26.50	5.25
贵州	13696	14.02	0.80				9238	51.46	0.20	313735	18.45	0.81
云南	13841	97.90	0.80							221948	-12.45	0.57
西藏												
陕西	4096		0.24				12540	68.05	0.27	386134	124.86	1.00
甘肃	870	-3.97	0.05							146106	31.02	0.38
青海										19360	5242.46	0.05
宁夏							8853	-27.04	0.19	88950	18.20	0.23
新疆							7162	52.97	0.16	571680	33.30	1.48

注：1. 数据来源：国家统计局。

2. 统计口径：规模以上企业。

附表5　2012年1~12月份塑料制品海关出口统计

产品名称	出口量/t		出口额/万美元	
	1－当月量	同比增长/%	1－当月额	同比增长/%
塑料制品	—	—	5114015.0	21.95
1. 塑料单丝、条、杆、型材及异型材	147810	2.92	32417.1	10.53
2. 塑料管及其附件	489186	9.02	186691.8	24.55
3. 塑料板、片、膜、箔、带及扁条	2407398	10.45	756129.9	10.42
4. 塑料人造革、合成革	574464	0.88	266634.0	-12.27
5. 塑料包装箱及容器及其附件	2194880	2.27	720903.9	19.91
6. 塑料零件	41682	1.25	44451.9	3.47
7. 建筑用塑料制品	1959611	13.39	352168.7	24.50
(1) 塑料糊墙品和铺地制品	1154459	12.41	186386.6	27.00
(2) 塑料门、窗、窗板(帘)及类似品	315407	5.45	79106.9	15.49
(3) 其他建筑用塑料制品	489746	21.80	86675.2	28.20
8. 日用塑料制品	—	—	1528936.9	46.01
(1) 塑料制餐具及厨房用具	763793	5.37	249444.2	12.34
(2) 塑料卫生设备、洁具及其配件	665030	10.27	260888.7	39.79
(3) 塑料制办公室或学校用品	359277	-7.13	119558.6	5.72
(4) 其他日用塑料制品	—	—	899045.4	71.13
9. 其他塑料制品	—	—	1225680.8	16.57

注：数据来源：海关总署。

附表6　2012年1~12月份塑料制品海关进口统计

产品名称	进口量/t		进口额/万美元	
	1－当月量	同比增长/%	1－当月额	同比增长/%
塑料制品	—	—	1848400.2	-0.42
1. 塑料单丝、条、杆、型材及异型材	8901	-8.11	9111.5	1.12
2. 塑料管及其附件	47787	-6.83	71280.0	-2.16
3. 塑料板、片、膜、箔、带及扁条	1113030	-2.20	1120468.3	-0.83
4. 塑料人造革、合成革	54864	-15.46	57119.4	-4.18
5. 塑料包装箱及容器及其附件	214797	3.68	139192.8	-0.89
6. 塑料零件	31266	-4.25	111512.3	5.28
7. 建筑用塑料制品	68543	-10.89	21501.2	3.87
(1) 塑料糊墙品和铺地制品	62994	-10.65	16229.0	-1.60
(2) 塑料门、窗、窗板(帘)及类似品	2889	-35.10	1682.7	-11.71
(3) 其他建筑用塑料制品	2660	35.20	3589.5	55.88
8. 日用塑料制品	—	—	20805.2	-0.80
(1) 塑料制餐具及厨房用具	5122	-10.59	4595.6	-16.05
(2) 塑料卫生设备、洁具及其配件	30562	28.77	10230.4	15.24
(3) 塑料制办公室或学校用品	1635	-0.55	684.8	1.95
(4) 塑料鞋及塑料制鞋底、鞋跟	—	—	5294.4	-11.02
9. 其他塑料制品	—	—	297409.4	0.20

注：本表据海关总署统计数据汇总整理。

（中国轻工业信息中心　张涌涛）

调查与浅析我国 BOPET 的行情

综观近年我国的 BOPET 市场，普通类包装膜的售价已经连续 26 个月都停滞在成本线以内。面对逐渐趋恶的经营环境和可能重新整合的行业预景，本专委会开展了一次行业内外的深度调研，组织行业同仁“适应国内外经济形势新变化，加快形成新的经济发展方式，把推动发展的立足点转变到提高质量和效益上来”，增强长期发展的后劲。

本次调查资讯的来源：①行业内部的调查问卷和实地走访联系的情况；②互联网与股市证券界的信息；③相关咨询机构的分析资料。

一、国内 BOPET 的产能与市场需求

1. 生产能力

截止 2012 年 12 月底的不完全统计，国内已经建成 BOPET 大小生产线 117 条，其中：小于 8μm 超薄膜线 8 条、8 ~ 75μm 薄膜线 77 条、75 ~ 250μm 中厚膜线 23 条、150 ~ 400μm 厚膜和超厚膜线 9 条；国内 BOPET 生产企业共有 77 家(包括在建尚未投产的企业)，产能(包括在建)：10kt 以下企业 17 家，15 ~ 50kt 企业 47 家，50kt 以上企业 13 家(已建成 50kt 以上规模的有双星、浙江欧亚、绍兴欧亚、翔宇、无名、杜邦；新增生产线后即将突破 50kt 的有富维、大东南，首次新建就超过 50kt 的有宁波金源、绍兴日月集团、恒力集团、江阴兴业、健元春)。

2013 年之后，有生产线 73 条在建设中（详见后附表）。

1）各地区产能汇总

地区	企业（家）	至 2012 年底已建		在建设中的		2013 年预期释放		已建产能占全国的/%
		条	kt	条	kt	条	kt	
江苏	18	350	66.15	190	45.3	10	188	39.38%
浙江	19	350	58.1	150	37.5	12	335	34.59%
广东	8	110	9.34	40	6.7	1	20	5.56%
山东	13	120	8.65	100	24.4	6	134	5.15%
上海	2	50	7.1	/		/		4.23%
安徽	3	40	5.38	20	2.4	2	24	3.20%
天津	2	30	3.16	/		/		1.88%
河南	5	40	3.1	20	4.6	2	46	1.85%
福建	1	10	3.0	60	18	3	90	1.79%
湖北	1	10	1.8	/		/		1.07%
四川	1	30	1.5	10	2.0	1	20	0.89%
河北	1	10	0.54	/		/		0.32%
辽宁	3	20	0.15	140	42			0.09%
合计	77	1170	167.97	730	182.9	37	857	100%

预计 2013 年底产能将达 2536.7kt，现有在建设备投产后将达 3508.7kt。

2）各地区产能情况对比如下：

地　区	2010 年占国内产能比例	地　区	2012 年占国内产能比例
浙江省	42.9%	江苏	39．38%
江苏省	19.9%	浙江	34．59%
上海市	7.5%	广东	5．56%
山东省	7.1%	山东	5．15%
安徽省	7.0%	上海	4．23%

续表

地　区	2010 年占国内产能比例	地　区	2012 年占国内产能比例
广东省	6.2%	安 徽	3．20%
天津市	3.0%	天 津	1．88%
河南省	1.9%	河 南	1．85%
湖北省	1.9%	福 建	1．79%
四川省	1.6%	湖 北	1．07%
河北省	0.5%	四 川	0．89%
辽宁省	0.4%	河 北	0．32%
合计	100%	辽 宁	0．09%
		合 计	100%

3）2013 年产能释放预期（2013.4 修改补充）

企业名称	条数	新增产能/kt	产品厚度/μm	预计投产时间
青州富翔塑业有限公司	1 条	30	2～75	2012 年 12 月已试车
广东汕头树业环保科技股份有限公司	1 条	20		2012 年 12 月已试车
恒力集团（14 条已付定金，12 条直熔，2 条厚膜）	7 条	210 直熔		5 月第一套聚合试车，拉膜要 2014 年初。8 月第二套聚合
江苏江阴兴业聚化（三房巷）	8 条	240 直熔		3 季度聚合试车
福建百宏实业（据悉 20 万吨切片 6 条直熔 +1 条切片）	3 条	90 直熔		2012 年已经投产 1 条，2013 年 2 季度聚合及另 3 条试车
宁波金源（可人）	4 条	120		3 月底聚合及 2 条开车（其中 1 条 2012 年试车过），1～1.5 月后另两条试车
浙江大东南	2 条 1 条	60 25	12～75 50～250	2 条计划 3 月开车。1 条厚膜计划 7 月安装，年底开车
江苏双星彩塑	2 条 1 条	60 未定	12～100 厚膜	2 条已安装，4 月初开车 1 条，预计 5 月再开一条（总共 15 条）。另 1 条厚膜预计年底（200～400μm）
绍兴日月集团	3 条	90	8～75	计划 7 月底 8 月初 1 条试车，年底 2 条。
河南银金达彩印股份有限公司	2 条	46	PETG 热收缩膜	1 线已试车，2 线计划 6 月安装，后续计划还有 4 条（100kt PETG 切片直熔）
潍坊乐港食品股份有限公司塑胶厂（国产）	1 条	10	36～120	计划 6 月
国风塑业	1 条	4	1.2～12	计划 6～7 月
山东寿光健元春有限公司	2 条	60		计划 8 月试车
青岛顺德塑料机械有限公司	1 条	11	75～450 土工膜	
江苏裕兴	1 条	10	100～350	上半年

续表

企业名称	条数	新增产能/kt	产品厚度/μm	预计投产时间
仪化东丽5线(新)	1条	15	75~350	
富维山东	1条	23	38~250	
四川东材	1条	20	50~300	
合肥乐凯	1条	18~20	38~250	
常州百佳薄膜科技有限公司	1条	15	75~400	
SKC(江苏)尖端塑料	2条	33	35~350	
日本三菱树脂(苏州)	1条	20	150~350	5月
张家港康得新光电材料有限公司	1条	15	50~350	
宁波长阳科技有限公司	2条	15+25	75~350	4月、8月安装
合 计：37条(15条直熔拉膜线未计入，预计先出切片拉膜到2014年)；857kt(直熔450kt拉膜未计入)；其中厚膜15条，257kt。				

注：双星的厚膜线暂按20kt/a计算。

4)不同厚度生产线产能情况

	2012年		在建设中的		2013年预期增加	
	条	kt	条	kt	条	kt
小于8μm	8	33.8	2	9	1	4
8~75μm	77	1318.9	50	1421	21	581
75~250μm	23	263	4	93	3	68
150~400μm	9	64	17	306	12	204

上表显示，中厚膜和超厚膜生产线的再一波投资，需警惕重蹈普通包装膜过剩的复辙。

2. 市场需求量

1) 国内2012、2013年需用量的测算

与其他商品一样，BOPET需要量会出现上下的弹性变化，这变化受制于本身的价格和收益变化，以及BOPP、BOPA、CPP(替代商品)的价格变化。

2012年国内的需用量测算约在1300kt;

2013年国内的需用量测算约在1480kt。

2) 需求量测算的依据:

① 以2010年的表观需用量(内外销量+进口量)作推算的基础。

2010年国内产销两旺，2009年末产能量+2010年实际新增产能量(剔除年中、年末投产的因素)，约1060kt，当年产能释放165kt，考虑到实际产能释放时间及实际开工等因数，行业预估2010年当年国内市场需求在1000kt左右。

② 以权威部门统计的塑料薄膜产量增长率作参考。

商务部(前对外经贸部)1999年5月的反倾销调查报告认为，本行业之前几年的需用量增长率在10%左右。根据中商情报网的资讯，2012年12月份，我国生产塑料薄膜919.5kt，同比增长6.74%。中商情报网监测数据显示：2012年1~12月，全国塑料薄膜的产量达9702.5kt，同比增长9.33%。

由国家统计局获悉我国最近五年塑料薄膜产量逐年递增的数据：

项目\年份	2008	2009	2010	2011	2012	平均值
产量/kt	5901	6944.3	7588.4	8436	9702.5	7714.4
增长/%		17.7	9.3	11.2	15	13.3

按以上权威部门的意见和业间的运行情况，本行业需用量的逐年递增率在 13.4%，市场可以容纳消化每年 80～100kt 的递增量(往年可消化 80kt/a 左右的递增量，见陈勇的撰文；13.4% 平均递增率见中国市场的供需矛盾表)。

3) BOPET 供需矛盾是不容争辩的事实

(1) 全球及主要国家产量、消费量的数据比较

总产能：

kt

国家和地区 \ 年份	2007	2008	2009	2010	2011	2012	2013	2014～2015
全球总产能	2880	3032	3147	3312	3602	3946	4826	5842
北美	334	334	349	356	331	344	357	357
南美	38	38	38	38	38	38	58	58
欧洲	310	313	329	329	329	339	349	349
中东/非洲	79	155	172	172	176	196	196	220
远东/亚洲	2118	2192	2252	2417	2728	3029	3866	4858

需用量：

kt

年份	用途	胶片/成像	磁　录	包　装	电气/电子	复合印刷	热转印	其他工业	总计
2008	需用	97	52	1207	211	54	80	514	2215
	增长	-8.50%	-16.10%	9.10%	10.50%	-16.80%	2.60%	5.80%	5.80%
2009	需用	87	45	1305	227	49	82	542	2337
	增长	-10.30%	-13.50%	8.10%	7.60%	-9.30%	2.50%	5.40%	5.50%
2010	需用	79	35	1404	245	41	86	571	2461
	增长	-9.20%	-22.20%	7.60%	7.90%	-16.30%	4.90%	5.40%	5.30%
2011	需用	74	28	1529	268	39	96	602	2636
	增长	-6.30%	-20%	8.90%	9.40%	-4.90%	11.60%	5.40%	7.10%
2012	需用	70	24	1665	286	36	103	634	2818
	增长	-5.40%	-14.30%	8.90%	6.70%	-7.60%	7.30%	5.30%	6.90%
2013	需用	61	21	1812	311	32	108	664	3009
	增长	-12.90%	-12.50%	8.80%	8.70%	-11.10%	4.90%	4.70%	6.80%
2014	需用	53	21	1944	338	29	112	691	3188
	增长	-13.10%	0%	7.30%	8.70%	-9.40%	3.70%	4.10%	5.90%

由上表可以看出，全球的聚酯膜生产企业主要集中在亚洲，占到世界生产能量的 77.48%(3302kt)，其中远东区域就占 66.4%；全球的聚酯膜的需求量虽然有 5%～6% 的年增长率，但是，总供给量仍大于总需求量，其中胶片/成像、磁录、复合印刷的需求量呈负增长，电气/电子、包装和其他新型工业的需求量呈正增长。

(2) 中国市场在全球总体供需矛盾中凸显严峻

年　份	2010 年	2011 年	2012 年	2013 年	2014 年 2015 年(预计)
设计产能/(kt/a)	1057.7	1368.7	1669.7	2506.7	3498.7
产能增长量/kt	165	311	301	837	992
产能增长率/%	—	29.4	22.0	50.1	39.6(两年)
需求/(kt/a)	1000	1150	1300	1480	1900
需求增长率/%	—	11.5	13.04	13.84	28.38(两年)

注：产能数据已根据最新数据调整。2015 年的预计只是目前在建生产线的数字。

在全球大市场中求生存的背景下，本行业继续沉浸在“寒冬”里，不少企业度日如年。时至今日(2012～2013年)，国内的产能和需求之间有370～1020kt的不平衡，主要表现在普通类产品的严重供大于求。加上，国内富余的产品受贸易保护的限制难以外销。导致普通类薄膜连续28个月的膜料差价的下跌不起(差价下跌的分析见下)。同时，产品出售不畅时就引来两个现实问题：库存品大量积压和生产线被迫停机。消息反映，已有5条生产线按期安装完毕，鉴于市场压力而不正式投产；有2条生产线或转让或搁置海关码头。

面对现实，促使业间不得不去理性地思考缩减生产能量的问题。

3. 由开机率和库存量看供需矛盾的严峻性

开机率＝当年产量/设计产能　　库存量＝(产量－销量)

根据行业内既有资金和仓储的特点，小型生产企业的仓储积压不适宜超越15天；中型企业的仓储积压不适宜超越20天；大型企业的仓储积压不适宜超越30天。按照pci的分析意见，企业或行业的开机率在85%～95%表示经营状态优秀；75%～85%表示良好；75%以下是已经陷入危机状态。

2012年3月初步调查，19家反馈单位所统计的当月份库存量就在50750t，相当于5条上万吨的生产线。按调查反馈单位的统计情况，2012年1月以来，行业内部分企业因多种原因而发生停产时间有187天，已经实际减少产量30194t，相当于3条上万吨的生产线。调查反映，1～2月80.7%的开工率大于同期60%的产销率(由于反馈数据的不完全，实际情况肯定更严重)。据了解，2012年上半年大型普通膜生产企业的开工率与2011年相比无明显降低，造成企业库存增加严重，约上升30%～40%的库存量；下半年有众多生产线出现间断停机待产的现象，由此造成不同程度的亏损。

2013年3月调查情况显示：各企业开机率参差不齐，低的只有50%左右的开机率，高的开工率则超过90%。最高的和最低的都不是生产规模大型的企业。个别6.7m宽的单条生产线及生产品种类较多的企业维持了较高的开工率；一些小型企业在市场行情低迷的情况下，由于灵活调整市场需要的产品种类反而降低了开工率。调查还显示一些开工率并不高的企业反而“异军突出”是效益较好的企业。

二、国内BOPET企业的生产技术管理状况

企业之魂是产品，而不在企业规模的大小，企业发展的终极目的是提升产品的获益价值。检验企业发展成败的唯一标准就是企业所生产产品的品质高低和让市场满足的程度，而不是由企业规模的大小等其他外在因素来作衡量标准。

物竞天择，影响企业产品品质的决定因素在于，行业人的思想境界与素质、管理能力与水平、技术进步与发展、项目立案与建设能否跟得上市场需要。如果企业的发展与建设状态能与企业的规模扩大相适应，当然是企业越大收益越高；如果企业的发展与市场需要不相适应甚至远远跟不上，固然，随着企业规模的不断扩大，各种矛盾和问题众生，收益也会急剧下降。

1）企业的主要产品种类(见生产线一览表)

2）产品标准衬托行业实际运行的状况

目前，本行业仅有国际标准ISO 15988：2003塑料－薄膜及薄片－双向拉伸聚酯薄膜(译文)；食品容器及包装材料用聚对苯二甲酸乙二醇酯成型品标准(1992.3.1)；电气设备中电容器用双轴取向聚酯薄膜标准规范(2000.1.1)；包装用双向拉伸聚酯薄膜(GB/T 16958—2008讨论稿)共四项。

2012年11月，合肥乐凯科技产业有限公司制定“模内装饰(IMD)用薄膜油墨粘接性能测定方法”、“模内装饰(IMD)用硬化薄膜耐湿热老化性能测定方法”。这两项行业标准获得了国家标准化管理委员会批准并发布，将于2013年8月1日起实施。这两个方法用薄膜产品质量的重要指标控制模内装饰(IMD)产品性能和健全了光学功能薄膜标准体系。

产品种类和生产标准体现行业水准；产品生产标准偏少、标准偏低，或说明行业的产品规范管理滞后或说明行业存在产品同质化竞争的事实。

3）行业间存在不同的生产技术管理模式

国内区别生产技术管理水准的企业分类：享有国外技术管理扶持的合资企业；具有相关研发能力的内资企业(组织管理机构设立单独的市场部和技术开发所或中心，专门划拨研发经费，制定新产品上市目标等)；自行研制零星产品的内资企业(有专职岗位人从事产业资讯和生产技术改良的具体工作等)；专事传统生产，缺乏产品更新规划的内资企业。

薄膜的整个生产过程着实体现原料、设备、配方及工艺三个方面的技术管理经验。目前，本行业产品展开创新生产的难点：①薄膜生产要与原料研究开发和生产单位协同配合；②薄膜的研发过程中缺乏具有调试工艺的中试设备；③鲜有薄膜专业殷实并且意识超前的领军人才。

4）不同的生产技术管理有不同的收益

调查显示，不同企业的生产交货周期、品种切换时间、产品执行标准(国标行标企标)、市场信息与产品研发等先行指数的不同，所产生的经营效果也不同。这些不同，归终到底是在企业的生产要以市场需求为导向，而不是单纯以供应为立足点。

比较不同管理方式的市场收获

a企业：投入新品的研发经费达到2125万元，近年上市销售的产品基本都是企业以往没有的，不仅销量大，出口量大，而且客户流失小到只有2%。

f企业：小型企业，长年来重视产品开发、重视产品生产的监控管理，产品管控文件达23项。虽然，近年的研发经费递减，新品产值减少；但是，年产值总体向上；客户流失小，老客户增加，说明品质可控，生产稳定，产品已被市场认可。

企业	生产周期	品种切换时间	研发经费	新品上市量	技术管理文件
a公司	15天	4~24/h	2125	10/年	编制15件
b公司	30天	4~48/h	1500	3/年	编制9件
d公司	5~7天	1~2/h	30	0	编制6件
c公司	25~30天	2~24/h	1480	1/年	编制17件
f公司	10天	12~120/h	180	1/年	编制23件
e公司	10~20天	1~7/h	—	—	—
g公司	15天	1~2/h	—	—	—
h公司	15天	1~6/h	200	3/年	编制4件

部分企业当年产品研发经费占年产值比较：

单位：万元

	a公司	b公司	f公司	d公司	c公司	h公司
2009年	629	3582	210	30	1443	/
2010年	1329	3969	190	5	1712	/
2011年	1875	3084	160	5	1673	/
2012年	2125	1500	180	30	1480	200

本行业的收益启示与其他行业雷同：防止产品通用化是获得产业高利润和持续盈利能力的关键。在竞争市场上，只有那些具有较强科研能力和创新能力、客户关系密切、敏锐发现细分市场和产品的公司才能保持领先地位。

三、通用类产品严重过剩阻滞行业的发展

1. 过剩造成和进一步造成的祸害

①产品价格大幅下跌。②产成品库存量增多。③企业利润大幅下降，出现亏损企业。④信贷风险增加。⑤内外贸易摩擦加大。⑥阻滞经济增长，浪费资源，污染环境。⑦影响就业和社会稳定。

2. 产品已基本丢失经济收益

（1）各种通用类薄膜与原料切片的差价对照（《聚酯薄膜资讯NO.04》）

价差/(元/t)	2008年	2009年	2010年	2011年	2012年
BOPP	2000~2500	1500~2000	1500~2500	2000~2500	1400~2000
BOPET	—	3500	10500	4500	2000
BOPA	—	—	12251	7600	7400
CPP	—	—	2170	2430	1970

上表与下表比较有全年与逐月的区别，一致反映行业的产品价值在逐渐减少，使企业的利润率成为个位数或负数，更大的销售量无法转化为更多的利润。

据镀铝膜专委会提供的资讯，2011年国内聚酯镀铝膜的市场主流加工费为2500元/t（淡季2000元/t，旺季3000元/t）；复合膜的加工费一般在1.8~2.0元/m^2。

按商务国际贸易经济合作研究院提供的资讯，2012年聚酯膜经涂层加工、压铸模加工、磨砂涂层加工后(扩散膜、增亮膜等)的市场价是2000~4000元/m²，窗贴膜、液晶屏保护的市场价是1000~2000元/m²；而彩印企业提供的资讯：2012年一般的复合+彩印包装膜的市场价是2.5~5.5元/m²。

以上资讯表明，光学、光伏类聚酯薄膜虽然对技术管理的要求颇高，但是顺应当今社会经济的发展需要，其附价值相比普通类包装膜要大不少；普通类包装膜固有市场刚需的一面，可是市场交涉的回旋空间非常小，尤其是用在复合+彩印方面。聚酯薄膜作为包装材料的重要基材之一，投资金额和经营付出都远远高过镀铝、复合彩印，如今行业的加工差价是非常落魄的。

(2) 2012年市场通用类产品的差价

2012年行业通用类产品的主流差价有6个月达不到1700元/t；11个月达不到2500元/t；2个月甚至落在1150元/t。

时间	平均价格/(元/t)	中石化膜级切片结算价/(元/t)	原料价差/(元/t)
2012年1月	13000	11200	1800
2012年2月	13300	11400	1900
2012年3月	12800	10700	2100

续表

时间	平均价格/(元/t)	中石化膜级切片结算价/(元/t)	原料价差/(元/t)
2012年4月	12300	10650	1650
2012年5月	11800	10600	1200
2012年6月	11600	9100	2500
2012年7月	11100	9950	1150
2012年8月	12300	10100	2200
2012年9月	12600	10600	2000
2012年10月	11800	10500	1300
2012年11月	11300	10150	1150
2012年12月	11600	10550	1050

通用类薄膜差价直线下跌的三大因素：供需、成本和技术管理水准，其中供需矛盾是主要矛盾。硬性调控，调控不了产品售价，只能调控供需量，这才符合市场经济规律；生产设施不作大改进的前提下，各生产线的成本消耗是不会出现大的差别；长时间积累的技术管理经验，才能对产品价格的扬挫起到推助的作用。

(3) 不同产品的差价比较(b、c、d、e、i公司)

2011年

项　目	a公司	c公司	d公司	e公司	i公司
薄膜单价	18450	15007/ 18809	17150 /40132	19058/	16000 /28500
原料单价	11106	11411/ 11411	9218 / 12337	13117/	9800 /14500
加工差价	7344	3595/ 7398	3869 /13146	5941/	6200 /14000

2012年

项　目	b公司	c公司	d公司	e公司	i公司
薄膜单价	14200	11113/ 15486	11874 /24474	14027/	13000 /21000
原料单价	9200	9666/ 9666	9762 /11478	10599/	10500 /15500
加工差价	5000	1447/ 5819	3170 /11054	3428/	2500 /5500

调查显示：同一公司(c、d、i公司)不同产品的差价就有2~3倍，不同公司的不同产品的差价有最少1~2倍，最多3~8倍。

3. 低于成本的销售即是无序竞争的典型

1) 企业部分产品的成本解剖

① 制造、销售、管理、财务费所占全部经营费用的比例(按2012年情况)。

各项费用	A公司	B公司	C公司	D公司	E公司	平均值
制造费用	83.8	77.97	76.64	81.97	79.42	79.96
销售费用	1.88	3.42	4.28	2.15	1.16	2.58
管理费用	10.0	6.32	3.42	6.27	2.20	5.64
财务费用	0.6	2.35	4.99	0.37	7.47	3.16
小　计	96.28	90.06	89.33	90.76	90.25	91.34

② 生产制造费用所占生产价值的比例(按 2011 和 2012 年情况)

制造费用	A 公司	B 公司	C 公司	D 公司	E 公司	平均值
直接材料	84.3	84.8	89.0	71.5	87.4	83.4
包装材料	2.2	3.5	1.99	2.7	2.3	2.54
直接人工	3.0	2.0	1.43	3.4	2.8	2.53
水、电、煤	5.9	9.7	4.48	22.3	7.5	9.98
生产价值额	13400	12308	25877	15239	10364	/

以上调查显示：本行业的生产制造费用占全部经营费用的 79.96%，其中的原料消耗和能源消耗又占绝对的大比值，充分说明本行业具有“料重工轻、能耗量大”的特点，这也是行业控制成本支出的关键环节。

2）经商的铁板定律：“千做万做，亏本生意不做”；“谷贱伤农，物贱伤业”

低价倾销，能起到暂时的“损人利己”效果，但终究是“损人损己”的。在行业产能严重过剩的形势下，竞相的逐低销售只会产生“逐烂”的结果。调查反映，大比例销量产品的售价走势对市场的影响面非常大。用户在聚酯薄膜使用中，除了有外观厚度差异的认识外，对产品性能的判断大都不明确；一般的用户处于成本的考虑特别看重价格，容易混淆品质而迁就使用。12μm 普通类薄膜为例，它作为包装材料(印刷复合膜、真空镀铝膜、激光防伪膜、转移膜、证件护卡膜、亚光膜、高亮膜等)大约占到市场需求的 63%，它的售价影响到其他厚膜和功能性薄膜的售价，2010 年的行情攀升是这样牵动的，而今直线下跌也是这样全面牵动的。

典型的不当竞争可能是满足一时的开机需要(银行还贷、股市交易、政府业绩)，以低于成本的价格进行销售，但是，这会带来市场经营秩序的混乱，带来市场产品的声誉下降；更重要的是经营空间被严重挤压后，让企业失去必要的财力来源、不得已的削减新技术新装备的投放能量，进而妨碍到整个产业的长远发展。

3）探询部分企业产品的成本构成项目

费用项目	A 公司	B 公司	C 公司	D 公司	E 公司	销售底限（红）	销售底限（黄）
包装材料	300	431	514	413	235		
直接人工	400	248	370	525	293		
水、电、煤、油	800	1188	1159	3402	777	1460 × 1.17 ≈ 1700 元/t	
销售费用	300	541	676	400	151		
小　计					1460 元/t		
100% 管理费用 40% 管理费用	1600 800	998 499	541 271	1166 583	287 115		2084 × 1.17 ≈ 2500 元/t(40% 的管理费和设备折旧)
100% 设备折旧 40% 设备折旧	600 300	1568 784	1684 842	1717 859	1273 509		
					+624		
财务费用	400	371	790	68	975		

注：考虑设备条件和产品品种的关系，选择 E 企业的经营成本做底线界限相比较有代表性。

4. 目前，国内 BOPET 加工费的最低界限

由上表，结合 BOPET 的消耗并比较 BOPP、BOPA、CPP 膜的应市价格，聚酯薄膜产品 ≥3000 元/t 的价格可为市场合理的售价。

通过上表可得知，国内 BOPET 目前加工费的最低界限：薄膜产品的当月售价 - 当月原料价 ≤1700 元/t 为不可触犯的红线，≤2500 元/t 为不可触犯的黄线。大型或直熔一体企业以此底线 -200 元/t 作为最低成本的界限相对比较恰当。曾记得，2012 年 3 月展开的业间调查，有不少企业自报的 12μm 通用类

薄膜产品的基本加工成本就是2500元/t，但是，当年年末的市场售价却直线下跌到不足1500元/t。这对产品单一的企业来说是致命的。

供需不平衡留给我们的市场警示：控制住平均售价底限的关键在于控制住最低售价的金额和数量(水桶的盛水效应全在最低哪块桶板的盛水位置)。

四、事在人为，行业人塑造行业自身的发展

1. 行业迅猛发展突显的规模与盛衰

20多年来，我国聚酯薄膜生产企业由初期的几家拓展到今天的76家；产品种类由2～3个逐渐变成几十种，我国的聚酯薄膜从紧缺商品变成世界上最大的生产基地和需求市场。但是，好景不长，短短二三年的时间行业就由盛转衰，其原因有技术和政策两方面因素。技术上，企业缺乏核心竞争力的准备，在市场环境突变时应对失措；政策上，地方政府与企业一哄而上、盲目跟风，中央政府又对本行业缺少给力的协调和长远规划。

迅猛发展给行业带来结构性和素质性的缺陷：①发展迅猛后的产能过剩；②自主创新的活力偏弱；③企业竞争能力不强；④生产过程的能源消耗比较大；⑤生产规模与经济收益不相称。

2. 行业意识必须适宜变化的行情

2010年的“旺势”与其后遗症：膜价从4月9日的14000元/t一路飚升到11月的28500元/t，期间还不断传出排队提货和先收预款再发货的消息。其原因主要①受国外大幅调整产品的影响，国内普通类膜的出口量猛增，全年同比上年增加了93.3kt②在“膜慌”心理的驱动下，用户买涨不买跌，唯恐断了货，把膜厂30～40kt的正常储备量都转移到自己库房里。当年末正逢节假期，出口猛势逐减，国内需要量又减弱，整个市场形势衰变至今。“旺势”带来的后遗症：①吸引更多的国内游资，掀起一股非理性投资的新潮，酿成无序竞争的祸患；②业界忽略了培养市场的必要耐心，出货颓势的心理承受显得十分脆弱；③不得不自尝“旺势”时期或许有过“不重信誉”的苦果。

亟需改善当前行业人的认识问题：

①建立商业互信的基础需要彼此间应有宽容；②投资人或经营人需要提高市场的前瞻眼光；③企业在投资前或经营中需要有技术管理方面的准备

3. 借鉴国外解决产能过剩问题的几点做法

①建立行业产能过剩预警机制。让企业及时了解宏观信息，正确判断市场供求变化趋势，减少投资的盲目性。②尽量做好“有保有压”工作。防止行业产能过剩继续恶化，特别是要防止出现资金链断裂。“保”，支持企业研发体系建设，支持整体水平的技术改造。“压”，有力反击低价倾销的行为，适当关停、淘汰部分生产能力，减少过剩产品的应市。③引导和扩大需求，尽可能多地利用和消化过剩产能。④“腾笼换鸟”，提升产业层次，富裕的生产能力加速向相比薄弱地区转移。产业资本有退有进，实行“错位发展”。⑤建立实施救助的办法和机制，确保社会的和谐稳定。

企业在加大自主创新力度、加大自主创新方面投入的同时，尚须得到政府政策的支持——建议政府、银行界不能再采取“抱薪救火”的方式，而应当放手让缺乏性的企业倒闭或被兼并，然后，重点扶持几家企业，以银行和大客户的名义注资或提供市场的形式获取企业的部分控制权，重点放在专业队伍经营、新技术新工艺研发上和培养完整的海内外销售力量。

4. 国内2013～2015年的市场预测

在冷酷的市场面前，本行业同其他产业相似，原先由投资和外贸推动的经济模式正向以终端客户消费为基础的经济结构转变。

本行业资产大投放的火爆增长期已经过去，2013～2014年是业间产能、产值量的调整期，2015年之后的几年，将是行业经济平衡增长时期。

目前产品市场与细化分类后的发展

(1) 既有的行业产品种类：包装、普通工业、电子、光学、光伏、特种功能、化学涂覆。

既有的产品市场：华东、华南地区为主要，依次为华北、其他地区及出口(只有小部分企业的中低端产品)。

(2) 追寻市场发展需要进行细化分类的产品(日本经济综合研究院推定)

包装类：复合、印刷、镀铝、收缩、透明蒸镀(SIO，Al_2O_3)；

电气电子类：电线遮盖、绝缘胶布、电动机蕊绝缘、电容器、膜开关、干式成像胶片、可卷印刷电路板、透明导电体(ITO)、太阳能电池背板；

光学类：面罩保护、棱镜、扩散、反射、彩色过滤、电波遮蔽、隔热保温；

涂硅离型类：陶瓷电容器、液晶屏、半导体晶片、电路板工程纸、医用胶贴、粘着标签、窗膜粘贴；

磁录类：数据储存、影象、音频、热敏打印、热敏洞版、LC卡、复合卡；

内模转印类(IMO或TOM)：家电、电脑、手机和箱包产品外壳；

金属化蒸镀类：多色装饰、金银线、交通标示；

护卡类：证卡保护、防伪识别、制图、制版等。

(3) 产品的终端应用和竞争替代

一般的聚酯薄膜，具有力学性能高、耐化学药品性好、防潮防水性优、耐热防水性优、绝缘性能优、使用时间和使用温度的范围比较广的优异特点，同时，存在着不易热封合，不耐水解，耐热性不够高和气体阻隔性稍差的不足。但是，它通过共聚改性、共混改性、表面涂层改性等方法，对聚酯原料本身或薄膜表层进行改性，重新获得高阻隔性、高耐热性、高透光率、高光泽度、低雾度、抗紫外线辐射、阻燃、可热封等之类的特异性能。

所以，具有特异性能的薄膜大多与全球亟需发展的产业保持一致，其中需求增长比较快的有液晶屏用光学薄膜、光伏电池用薄膜、高阻隔性的金属镀膜；增长最快的依次是电子电器用膜、包装用膜和其他工业用膜。

同 BOPP、PVC、PE 膜相比，BOPET 膜所具有的良好性能并有持续的改进，能够相当程度地替代其他包装材料。目前，引作软包装材料的薄膜都把高性能、多功能的薄膜作为开发的热点方向，具体追求高阻隔性、无菌抗菌性、高耐热性，以及再封性和易开封性。热收缩膜则在饮料包装上拓展。

根据《塑料加工工业技术进步指导意见(2013～2015 年)》(讨论稿)重点产品发展方向的项目内容：BOPET 扭结膜等环保型软包装薄膜；保温、隔热、防暴、遮蔽私密及安全防护等功能窗贴膜；太阳能 TPT 背材用聚酯薄膜；耐候性聚酯薄膜；高介电强度电容膜；耐热抗老化聚酯绝缘薄膜；可回收利用的热收缩膜等。

总结语：行情表明，迅猛发展的产业投资，已在短时间内将我国比较紧缺的聚酯薄膜变成世界上最大的生产基地和需求市场。2013 年，国内的生产能力即将达到 2507kt/a，大大高于 1480kt/a 的需要量；明显过剩的产能已经造成普通类产品积压和价格的下跌不起，造成生产单一产品的生产线被迫停产。为此，在全球产能出现过剩的背景下，维护行业加工费的最低界限乃在于坚守住最低的售价和数量(≤1700 元/t 和≤2500 元/t 是当前交易不可触犯的红黄警戒线)。不计成本的竞相逐低只会产生“逐烂”、产生无序竞争的结果，其终究是“损人损己”的。同时，聚酯薄膜行业事实存在着“料重工轻、能耗量大”的显明特点，促使行业人务必注意控制这些关键环节。

物竞天择，企业产品依赖自身生产技术经验的持续积累和突变性的提升，企业发展的成败在于企业所生产产品的品质高低和让市场满足的程度，行业发展的生命在于有以技术和创新为导向的企业。水无定势、水无定形，真正持久的商业成功属于把创新、经营能力与资本市场有机整合在一起的企业家。

(说明：各项资讯本身需要有个去伪存真、不断完善的过程，加上受视角的限制所解析的资讯或许有谬误之处。以上所列示的调查资讯仅供企业参考使用。)

(中国塑料加工工业协会 BOPET 专委会　王德钧)

2012 年废塑料进口量升价升

第一节　中国废塑料进口分析综述

1. 2012 年废塑料进口量价同时小幅上升。

从海关资料来看，2012 年废塑料总进口量比 2011 年上升 5. 87%，多进口了 491，919t，突破 8800kt 大关(表 1)。

2012 年乙烯聚合物的废塑料及下脚料进口 3691981t，同比增长 12. 32%；

2012 年苯乙烯聚合物的废塑料及下脚料进口 241661t，同比增长 63. 69%；

2012 年氯乙烯聚合物的废塑料及下脚料进口 691000t，同比下降 41. 76%；

2012 年聚对苯二甲酸乙二酯的废塑料及下脚料进口 2045430t，同比增长 22. 81%；

2012 年其他废塑料进口 2207531t，同比增长 5. 17%；

2007～2012 年总废塑料进口增长 28. 45%，平均年增长 5. 13%。

表 1　2007～2012 年中国废塑料进口统计

年　份	2007	2008	2009	2010	2011	2012
PE 废料进口量/t	2260700	2143928	2206162	2634785	3286996	3691981
PE 废料进口金额/万美元	100686. 09	132568. 88	110387. 26	168636. 82	218424. 22	247256. 45
进口年平均单价	445. 38	618. 35	500. 36	640. 04	664. 51	669. 71
PS 废料进口量/t	203200	97001	137126	243370	147634	241661

续表

年　份	2007	2008	2009	2010	2011	2012
PS 废料进口金额/万美元	9760.13	5846.28	7874.58	16998.61	12428.84	20021.46
进口年平均单价	480.32	602.70	574.26	698.47	841.87	828.49
PVC 废料进口量/t	1155486	1829191	1969611	1718493	1186502	691000
PVC 废料进口金额/万美元	50542.90	99913.22	79686.86	91125.94	76187.84	45090.49
进口年平均单价	437.42	546.22	404.58	530.27	642.12	652.54
聚酯废料进口量/t	1108150	1060483	1360974	1650816	1665555	2045430
聚酯废料进口金额/万美元	62522.86	73818.92	73280.08	117761.38	158905.08	171379.35
进口年平均单价	564.21	696.09	538.44	713.35	954.07	837.86
其他废塑料进口量/t	2183909	1944566	1652024	1761957	2098997	2207531
其他废塑料进口金额/万美元	97675.70	119341.00	83384.46	114148.44	145061.26	156574.72
进口年平均单价	447.25	613.72	501.74	647.85	691.10	709.28
废塑料总进口量/t	6911445	7075169	7325897	8009421	8385684	8877603
年增长率/%	17.83	2.37	3.54	25.97	4.70	5.87

2. 私营企业占据进口主导。

从海关统计中可看出，2007 ~ 2012 年，广东省、浙江省、江苏省等省市私营企业进口废塑料进口总量的 80.00% 左右。

3. 进口贸易方式以一般贸易为主

从海关统计中可看出，2012 年乙烯聚合物的废塑料进口贸易方式主要为一般贸易（占进口量 99.81%），其次为来料加工装配贸易（占进口量 0.18%），进料加工贸易（占进口量 0.0.01%），边境小额贸易（占进口量 0.00%）（表 2）。

表 2　2012 年乙烯聚合物的废塑料及下脚料进口交易类型统计

进口交易类型	进口金额/美元	进口数量/kg	占比例/%
一般贸易	2468702101	3685262143	99.81
来料加工装配贸易	3721525.00	6503582	0.18
进料加工贸易	97813	143481	0.01
边境小额贸易	43074	71790	0.00
进口总计	2472564513	3691980996	100.00

从海关统计中可看出，2012 年苯乙烯聚合物的废塑料进口贸易方式主要为一般贸易（占进口量 84.83%），其次为进料加工贸易（占进口量 13.66%），来料加工装配贸易（占进口量 1.51%）（表 3）。

表 3　2012 年苯乙烯聚合物的废塑料及下脚料进口交易类型统计

进口交易类型	进口金额/美元	进口数量/kg	占比例/%
一般贸易	172285947.00	205009069	84.83
进料加工贸易	25260167.00	33006982	13.66
来料加工装配贸易	2668479.00	3644985	1.51
进口总计	200214593.00	241661036	100.00

从海关统计中可看出，2012 年氯乙烯聚合物的废塑料进口贸易方式主要为一般贸易（占进口量 99.86%），其次为进料加工贸易（占进口量 0. 14%）（表 4）。

表4 2012年氯乙烯聚合物的废塑料及下脚料进口交易类型统计

进口交易类型	进口金额/美元	进口数量/kg	占比例/%
一般贸易	450513027	690060319	99.86
进料加工贸易	391908	939632	0.14
进口总计	450904935	690999951	100.00

从海关统计中可看出，2012年聚对苯二甲酸乙二酯的废碎料及下脚料进口贸易方式主要为一般贸易(占进口量85.35%)，其次为进料加工贸易(占进口量14.63%)，边境小额贸易(占进口量0.02%)(表5)。

表5 2012年聚对苯二甲酸乙二酯的废碎料及下脚料进口交易类型统计

进口交易类型	进口金额/美元	进口数量/kg	占比例/%
一般贸易	1444285726	1745678085	85.35
进料加工贸易	269333032	299179008	14.63
边境小额贸易	174716	572730	0.02
进口总计	1713793474	2045429823	100.00

从海关统计中可看出，2012年其他塑料的废塑料进口贸易方式主要为一般贸易(占进口量99.20%)，其次为进料加工贸易(占进口量0.78%)，来料加工装配贸易(占进口量0.02%)(表6)。

表6 2012年其他塑料的废碎料及下脚料进口交易类型统计

进口交易类型	进口金额/美元	进口数量/kg	占比例/%
一般贸易	1547844975	2189942928	99.20
进料加工贸易	17679767	17249708	0.78
来料加工装配贸易	222497	338520	0.02
进口总计	1565747239	2207531156	100.00

第二节 2012年废塑料进口分析

从海关统计中可看出，2012年废塑料主要进口地为中国香港，其次为德国、美国、日本、中国台湾省、加拿大、比利时、马来西亚，进口量占总进口量的八成~八成半。

1. 乙烯聚合物的废塑料及下脚料进口

从海关统计中可看出，2012年乙烯聚合物的废塑料及下脚料进口地有95个，比上年92个进口地增加3个进口地，主要进口地为德国(占15.05%)，其次为美国(14.63%)、中国香港(10.60%)、日本(8.82%)、法国(6.94%)、比利时(5.19%)、英国(5.00%)、马来西亚(4.93%)，八进口地进口量占总进口量的71.16%，比上年增加9.44%(表7)。

表7 2012年乙烯聚合物的废碎料及下脚料十大进口国家/地区统计

排 序	原产进口地	进口金额	进口数量/kg	占比例/%
1	德国	368130126	555823232	15.05
2	美国	363490018	540105120	14.63
3	中国香港	271266488	391354930	10.60
4	日本	227407561	325636680	8.82
5	法国	169904637	256318483	6.94
6	比利时	126393089	191443153	5.19
7	英国	115596734	184432531	5.00
8	马来西亚	125150633	182196069	4.93
9	加拿大	97793903	145197900	3.93
10	韩国	87046615	143128139	3.88
进口总计		2472564513	3691980996	100.00

2. 苯乙烯聚合物的废塑料及下脚料进口

从海关统计中可看出，2012 年苯乙烯聚合物的废塑料及下脚料进口地有 56 个，比上年 53 个进口地增加 3 个进口地，主要进口地为中国香港（占 22.14%），其次为中国台湾省（9.65%）、法国（9.30%）、美国（8.13%）、德国（7.88%）、马来西亚（7.55%）、加拿大（4.99%）、西班牙（2.83%），八进口地进口量占总进口量的 72.47%，比上年下降 11.45%（表 8）。

表 8　2012 年苯乙烯聚合物的废碎料及下脚料九大进口国家/地区统计

排　序	原产进口地	进口金额/美元	进口数量/kg	占比例/%
1	中国香港	42979825	53509248	22.14
2	中国台湾省	17793660	23317527	9.65
3	法国	18250262	22480336	9.30
4	美国	16779087	19653275	8.13
5	德国	16478369	19052845	7.88
6	马来西亚	15129211	18243838	7.55
7	加拿大	9709642	12050964	4.99
8	西班牙	6199997	6845598	2.83
9	中国澳门	5233018	6607279	2.73
进口总计		200，214，593	241661036	100.00

3. 氯乙烯聚合物的废塑料及下脚料进口

从海关统计中可看出，2012 年氯乙烯聚合物的废塑料及下脚料进口地有 52 个，比上年 54 个减少 2 个进口地，主要进口地为德国（18.49%），其次为马来西亚（15.77%）、中国香港（占 13.63%）、美国（12.56%）、法国（9.01%）、泰国（13.07%）、澳大利亚（7.35%）、加拿大（4.94%）、日本（3.92%），八进口地进口量占总进口量的 85.67%，比上年增加 1.58%（表 9）。

表 9　2012 年氯乙烯聚合物的废碎料及下脚料十大进口国家/地区统计

排　序	原产进口地	进口金额/美元	进口数量/kg	占比例/%
1	德国	83503801	127757187	18.49
2	马来西亚	71194613	108971954	15.77
3	中国香港	62336915	94153433	13.63
4	美国	56291010	86786574	12.56
5	法国	40455380	62236945	9.01
6	澳大利亚	33172599	50809796	7.35
7	加拿大	21930729	34102910	4.94
8	日本	17412655	27074427	3.92
9	中国台湾省	15126991	23126247	3.35
10	英国	6421856	9758997	1.41
进口总计		450，904，935	690999951	100.00

4. 聚对苯二甲酸乙二酯的废塑料及下脚料进口

从海关统计中可看出，2012 年聚对苯二甲酸乙二酯的废塑料及下脚料进口地有 161 个，比上年 158 个进口地增加 3 个进口地，主要进口地为日本（占 16.25%），其次为美国（10.14%）、泰国（7.88%）、印度尼西亚（6.54%）、中国香港（6.10%）、墨西哥（5.09%）、德国（4.97%）、越南（3.98%），八进口地进口量占总进口量的 60.95%，比上年下降 0.25%（表 10）。

表 10　2012 年聚对苯二甲酸乙二酯的废碎料及下脚料十大进口国家/地区统计

排　序	原产进口地	进口金额/美元	进口数量/kg	占比例/%
1	日本	277022136	332454965	16.25
2	美国	152249748	207457935	10.14
3	泰国	166522669	161086683	7.88
4	印度尼西亚	133389392	133833864	6.54
5	中国香港	87614713	124723350	6.10
6	墨西哥	76712880	104049681	5.09
7	德国	78751350	101719770	4.97
8	越南	79161816	81444473	3.98
9	马来西亚	65483225	67921998	3.32
10	韩国	50079609	64550883	3.16
进口总计		1713793474	2045429823	100.00

5. 其他塑料的废塑料及下脚料进口

从海关统计中可看出，2012 年其他塑料的废塑料及下脚料进口地有 121 个，比上年 102 个增加 19 个进口地，主要进口地为中国香港（占 16.25%），其次为日本（10.14%）、德国（7.88%）、美国（6.54%）、马来西亚（6.10%）、法国（5.09%）、加拿大（4.97%）、菲律宾（3.98%），八进口地进口量占总进口量的 60.95%，比上年减少 5.05%（表 11）。

表 11　2012 年其他塑料的废碎料及下脚料十大进口国家/地区统计

排　序	原产进口地	进口金额/美元	进口数量/kg	占比例/%
1	中国香港	267524962	378697878	16.25
2	日本	227793903	314678836	10.14
3	德国	188466355	261684984	7.88
4	美国	170674612	242625872	6.54
5	马来西亚	112289919	162667926	6.10
6	法国	94047596	134767458	5.09
7	加拿大	72114012	104010107	4.97
8	菲律宾	64427011	93436493	3.98
9	中国台湾省	51139534	70301615	3.32
10	澳大利亚	47761641	68957998	3.16
进口总计		1565747239	2207531156	100.00

第三节　2012 年废塑料进口商分析

1. 2012 年乙烯聚合物的废碎料及下脚料进口商以贸易商为主

从海关资料来看，2012 年乙烯聚合物的废塑料及下脚料进口商有 691 家，比上年 695 家进口商减少 4 个进口商。

2012 年乙烯聚合物的废塑料及下脚料前十位进口商进口量占总进口量的 12.90%。

福清冠威塑料工业有限公司、福州嘉裕华进出口有限公司、厦门元瀚进出口有限公司、深圳市安缘通化工材料有限公司、漳州市程盛再生资源有限公司、深圳市乐天世纪科技有限公司、日照欧申贸易有限公司、天津金正纯金属制品有限公司、日照亚信工贸有限公司、天津树茂金属制品有限公司，分别位居 2012 年乙烯聚合物的废塑料及下脚料进口量 1～10 位，进口量分别占总进口量的 2.90%、2.23%、1.37%、1.12%、0.96%、0.93%、0.87%、0.86%、0.84% 和 0.82%。

从资料分析，乙烯聚合物的废塑料及下脚料进口生产使用企业以塑料制品工业为主。

2012 年乙烯聚合物的废碎料及下脚料进口商以贸易商为主，前三十六位进口商中二十三位为贸易商，进口量占总进口量的 18.62%（表 12）。

表 12　2012 年乙烯聚合物的废碎料及下脚料三十六大进口商统计

排　序	进口商	所属行业	进口数量/kg	占比例/%
1	福清冠威塑料工业有限公司	塑胶工业	107045125	2.90
2	福州嘉裕华进出口有限公司	贸易商	82339803	2.23
3	厦门元瀚进出口有限公司	贸易商	50444663	1.37
4	深圳市安缘通化工材料有限公司	贸易商	41235377	1.12
5	漳州市程盛再生资源有限公司	贸易商	35350667	0.96
6	深圳市乐天世纪科技有限公司	塑胶工业	34434172	0.93
7	日照欧申贸易有限公司	贸易商	32116347	0.87
8	天津金正纯金属制品有限公司	塑胶工业	31885436	0.86
9	日照亚信工贸有限公司	贸易商	31123985	0.84
10	天津树茂金属制品有限公司	塑胶工业	30213414	0.82
11	福建华厦塑胶有限公司	塑胶工业	29874892	0.81
12	莱州市泰华工贸有限公司	贸易商	29305451	0.79
13	青岛博亿惠进出口有限公司	贸易商	29055569	0.79
14	天津华禹诚国际贸易有限公司	贸易商	28925765	0.78
15	广州市和远进出口有限公司	贸易商	28573134	0.77
16	福州友峰塑胶有限公司	塑胶工业	27078472	0.73
17	青岛汇恩名峻进出口有限公司	贸易商	26645811	0.72
18	佛山市南海里水里塑塑料有限公司	塑胶工业	25693210	0.70
19	河北福发塑胶有限公司	塑胶工业	25078359	0.68
20	山东滨州鲁闽塑料制品有限公司	塑胶工业	25008260	0.68
21	高要市龙宝塑料制品有限公司	塑胶工业	23479320	0.64
22	深圳市港进利国际货运代理有限公司	贸易商	23453267	0.64
23	天津政鑫盛源国际贸易有限公司	贸易商	22834555	0.62
24	天津威尔德国际贸易有限公司	贸易商	22304307	0.60
25	河北嘉裕塑胶有限公司	塑胶工业	22210047	0.60
26	广州恒通和顺进出口有限公司	贸易商	22204740	0.60
27	福州瀛福塑业进出口贸易有限公司	贸易商	21349210	0.58
28	佛山市欧达同人贸易发展有限公司	贸易商	21211409	0.57
29	天津圣锦昊进出口贸易有限公司	贸易商	20937615	0.57
30	辽宁斯达派克塑料有限公司	塑胶工业	20754581	0.56
31	天津市天塑科技集团有限公司	塑胶工业	20732444	0.56
32	大城县弘亚再生资源利用有限公司	贸易商	20185429	0.55
33	厦门合力成进出口有限公司	贸易商	20130348	0.55
34	青岛富昌龙国际贸易有限公司	贸易商	19391258	0.53
35	北方国际集团有限公司	贸易商	19095656	0.52
36	深圳市裕鑫兴进出口贸易有限公司	贸易商	18739163	0.51
	进口总计		3691980996	100.00

2012年乙烯聚合物的废塑料及下脚料进口商三十六大进口商，其中十三大进口商为进口生产使用企业，进口量占总进口量的11.47%；六大进口生产使用企业以塑料制品工业为主。

2. 2012年苯乙烯聚合物的废碎料及下脚料进口贸易商与进口生产使用企业平分秋色。

从海关资料来看，2012年苯乙烯聚合物的废塑料及下脚料进口商有265家，比上年261家进口商增加4个进口商。

2012年苯乙烯聚合物的废塑料及下脚料前十位进口商进口量占总进口量的36.95%；

广州广钢MBA塑料新技术有限公司、东莞联记塑胶原料有限公司、佛山市三水南威塑胶电子制品有限公司、上海英科实业有限公司、中轻建材进出口公司、淄博英科框业有限公司、佛山市海庆源贸易有限公司、清远市开泰贸易有限公司、盛兴环保资源(太仓)有限公司、深圳市大广宏进出口有限公司，分别位居2012年苯乙烯聚合物的废塑料及下脚料进口量1~10位，进口量分别占总进口量的6.73%、5.24%、5.21%、4.67%、3.84%、2.52%、2.45%、2.21%、2.10%和1.98%。

2012年苯乙烯聚合物的废碎料及下脚料进口贸易商与进口生产使用企业平分秋色，前三十四大进口商中十六大进口商为贸易商，进口量占总进口量的30.29%(表13)。

表13　2012年苯乙烯聚合物的废碎料及下脚料三十四大主要进口企业统计

排　序	进口企业	所属行业	进口数量/kg	占比例/%
1	广州广钢MBA塑料新技术有限公司	塑胶工业	16258470	6.73
2	东莞联记塑胶原料有限公司	贸易商	12657106	5.24
3	佛山市三水南威塑胶电子制品有限公司	家用电器工业	12586895	5.21
4	上海英科实业有限公司	贸易商	11291017	4.67
5	中轻建材进出口公司	贸易商	9277357	3.84
6	淄博英科框业有限公司	建材工业	6093176	2.52
7	佛山市海庆源贸易有限公司	贸易商	5914448	2.45
8	清远市开泰贸易有限公司	贸易商	5340648	2.21
9	盛兴环保资源(太仓)有限公司	回料加工	5081211	2.10
10	深圳市大广宏进出口有限公司	贸易商	4795081	1.98
11	东莞建德塑胶原料制品有限公司	塑胶工业	4681635	1.94
12	佛山市赞佳贸易有限公司	贸易商	4629330	1.92
13	福建全通资源再生工业园有限公司	回料加工	4448331	1.84
14	揭东县利丰塑胶制品有限公司	塑胶工业	3494514	1.45
15	东阳市德进塑胶有限公司	塑胶工业	3174051	1.31
16	广州恒通和顺进出口有限公司	贸易商	3142330	1.30
17	台州东泰塑胶有限公司	塑胶工业	3042518	1.26
18	佛山市南海里水里塑塑料有限公司	塑胶工业	2635420	1.09
19	广州市君懋进出口贸易有限公司	贸易商	2609980	1.08
20	惠州市佳祥塑料制品有限公司	塑胶工业	2601540	1.08
21	佛山市南海融佳进出口贸易有限公司	贸易商	2440770	1.01
22	佛山市欧达同人贸易发展有限公司	贸易商	2296970	0.95
23	佛山市顺德区杏坛镇森玛实业有限公司	贸易商	2174220	0.90
24	高要市龙宝塑料制品有限公司	塑胶工业	2003809	0.83
25	佛山市瀚联贸易有限公司	贸易商	1967780	0.81
26	飞跃(台州)塑胶实业有限公司	塑胶工业	1957487	0.81

续表

排　序	进口企业	所属行业	进口数量/kg	占比例/%
27	兰溪市乐福进出口有限公司	贸易商	1808647	0.75
28	罗定市协成再生资源有限公司	回料加工	1799720	0.74
29	南京杰达塑业有限公司	建材工业	1698314	0.70
30	佳顺工程塑胶(太仓)有限公司	塑胶工业	1627226	0.67
31	惠州市加太塑料制品有限公司	塑胶工业	1625700	0.67
32	深圳市金银岛贸易有限公司	贸易商	1575830	0.65
33	肇庆市信业塑料有限公司	塑胶工业	1369630	0.57
34	揭阳市安展进出口有限公司	贸易商	1281040	0.53
进口总计			241661036	100.00

从资料分析，苯乙烯聚合物的废塑料及下脚料进口生产使用企业以塑料制品工业、家用电器工业、建材工业、回料加工、薄膜包装工业为主，2012年苯乙烯聚合物的废塑料及下脚料进口商三十四大进口商，其中十八大进口商为进口生产使用企业，进口量占总进口量的31.52%。

3.2012年氯乙烯聚合物的废碎料及下脚料进口进口生产使用企业首次超过贸易商

从海关资料来看，2012年氯乙烯聚合物的废塑料及下脚料进口商有332家，比上年363家进口商减少31个进口商。

2012年氯乙烯聚合物的废塑料及下脚料前十位进口商进口量占总进口量的25.54%。

深圳市乐天世纪科技有限公司、深圳市安缘通化工材料有限公司、广州市和远进出口有限公司、深圳市港进利国际货运代理有限公司、深圳市裕鑫兴进出口贸易有限公司、深圳市金银岛贸易有限公司、广州市君懋进出口贸易有限公司、河北福发塑胶有限公司、惠州市加太塑料制品有限公司、河北嘉裕塑胶有限公司，分别位居2012年氯乙烯聚合物的废塑料及下脚料进口量1~10位，进口量分别占总进口量的4.14%、4.09%、3.21%、2.76%、2.30%、2.13%、1.96%、1.72%、1.70%和1.53%。

2012年氯乙烯聚合物的废塑料及下脚料前十位进口商八位为广东省企业；

2012年氯乙烯聚合物的废碎料及下脚料进口前三十四大进口商中二十大进口商为贸易商，进口量占总进口量的29.52%(表14)。

表14　2012年氯乙烯聚合物的废碎料及下脚料三十四大主要进口企业统计

排　序	进口商	所属行业	进口数量/kg	占比例/%
1	深圳市乐天世纪科技有限公司	回料加工	28594102	4.14
2	深圳市安缘通化工材料有限公司	回料加工	28271656	4.09
3	广州市和远进出口有限公司	贸易商	22203362	3.21
4	深圳市港进利国际货运代理有限公司	贸易商	19069440	2.76
5	深圳市裕鑫兴进出口贸易有限公司	贸易商	15868469	2.30
6	深圳市金银岛贸易有限公司	贸易商	14686500	2.13
7	广州市君懋进出口贸易有限公司	贸易商	13524660	1.96
8	河北福发塑胶有限公司	贸易商	11908382	1.72
9	惠州市加太塑料制品有限公司	贸易商	11776936	1.70
10	河北嘉裕塑胶有限公司	贸易商	10541906	1.53
11	汕头市丰盈实业有限公司	贸易商	10523312	1.52
12	揭东县利丰塑胶制品有限公司	贸易商	9090518	1.32
13	佛山市南海里水里塑塑料有限公司	塑料制品工业	8977610	1.30

续表

排 序	进口商	所属行业	进口数量/kg	占比例/%
14	深圳市永柏盛进出口有限公司	贸易商	8374370	1.21
15	邯郸市嘉裕塑胶有限公司	塑料制品工业	7444429	1.08
16	佛山威明塑胶有限公司	塑料制品工业	7188990	1.04
17	惠州市佳祥塑料制品有限公司	塑料制品工业	7080530	1.02
18	佛山市欧达同人贸易发展有限公司	贸易商	7046460	1.02
19	普宁市美利安塑料制品有限公司	塑料制品工业	6905630	1.00
20	清远市开泰贸易有限公司	贸易商	6530436	0.95
21	飞跃(台州)塑胶实业有限公司	塑料制品工业	6476125	0.94
22	广州市泽天橡塑制品有限公司	塑料制品工业	6274610	0.91
23	惠州市科信达实业有限公司	塑料制品工业	6186050	0.90
24	东阳市德进塑胶有限公司	塑料制品工业	6115780	0.89
25	深圳市宁信达进出口有限公司	贸易商	6064250	0.88
26	广州恒通和顺进出口有限公司	贸易商	6049480	0.88
27	博罗县龙华镇金峰塑胶原料加工厂	回料加工	5848560	0.85
28	佛山市南海融佳进出口贸易有限公司	贸易商	5847503	0.85
29	揭阳市安捷进出口有限公司	贸易商	5806380	0.84
30	天津东海晟英进出口贸易有限公司	贸易商	5751184	0.83
31	深圳市环欧进出口有限公司	贸易商	5726024	0.83
32	海丰县新洲塑料制品有限公司	塑料制品工业	5623074	0.81
33	广州市鑫铸贸易有限公司	贸易商	5412133	0.78
34	宁波和诚塑化有限公司	塑料制品工业	5408092	0.78
进口总计			690999951	100.00

从资料分析，氯乙烯聚合物的废塑料及下脚料进口生产使用企业以塑料制品工业为主，2012 年氯乙烯聚合物的废塑料及下脚料三十四大进口商中，其中十四大进口商为进口生产使用企业，进口量占总进口量的 19.75%。

4. 2012 年聚对苯二甲酸乙二酯的废碎料及下脚料进口商仍以化纤工业为主

从海关资料来看，2012 年聚对苯二甲酸乙二酯的废塑料及下脚料进口商有 368 家，比上年 362 家进口商增加 6 个进口商。

2012 年聚对苯二甲酸乙二酯的废塑料及下脚料前十位进口商进口量占总进口量的 30.20%。

宁波大发化纤有限公司、濠锦化纤(福州)有限公司、浙江振邦化纤有限公司、慈溪市江南化纤有限公司、慈溪市三泰化纤实业有限公司、江阴市南阳彩色纤维母粒有限公司、宁波振邦进出口有限公司、宁波舜象科技实业有限公司、杭州贝斯特化纤有限公司、浙江华盛化纤有限公司，分别位居 2012 年聚对苯二甲酸乙二酯的废塑料及下脚料进口量 1 ~ 10 位，进口量分别占总进口量的 6.77%、4.17%、3.97%、 3.89%、 2.47%、 2.42%、 1.74%、1.72%、1.54% 和 1.51%。

2012 年聚对苯二甲酸乙二酯的废塑料及下脚料前十位进口商中，有八家属于浙江省；进口量占总进口量的 23.61%。

2012 年聚对苯二甲酸乙二酯的废塑料及下脚料进口商前三十八大进口商中仅有七大进口商为贸易商，进口量占总进口量的 6.76%(表 15)。

表15 2012年聚对苯二甲酸乙二酯的废碎料及下脚料三十八大主要进口企业统计

排序	进口商	所属行业	进口数量/kg	占比例/%
1	宁波大发化纤有限公司	化纤工业	138551037	6.77
2	濠锦化纤(福州)有限公司	化纤工业	85374773	4.17
3	浙江振邦化纤有限公司	化纤工业	81176752	3.97
4	慈溪市江南化纤有限公司	化纤工业	79478960	3.89
5	慈溪市三泰化纤实业有限公司	化纤工业	50460437	2.47
6	江阴市南阳彩色纤维母粒有限公司	化纤工业	49496357	2.42
7	宁波振邦进出口有限公司	贸易商	35643404	1.74
8	宁波舜象科技实业有限公司	回料加工	35204849	1.72
9	杭州贝斯特化纤有限公司	化纤工业	31492449	1.54
10	浙江华盛化纤有限公司	化纤工业	30911513	1.51
11	宁波海曙罡阳进出口有限公司	贸易商	28998507	1.42
12	福州隆诚实业有限公司	回料加工	27419892	1.34
13	杭州汉邦化纤有限公司	化纤工业	26463544	1.29
14	天津慧能塑料工贸有限公司	回料加工	26354908	1.29
15	张家港成兴化纤有限公司	化纤工业	24065870	1.18
16	肇庆天富新合纤有限公司	化纤工业	22107002	1.08
17	福建鑫华股份有限公司	化纤工业	21847582	1.07
18	龙福环能科技股份有限公司	回料加工	20837173	1.02
19	江西省赣鑫纺织有限公司	化纤工业	20249624	0.99
20	慈溪市三盛化纤有限公司	化纤工业	19789074	0.97
21	宁波鑫驰进出口有限公司	贸易商	19403345	0.95
22	杭州奔马化纤纺丝有限公司	化纤工业	18807775	0.92
23	江苏中再生投资开发有限公司	回料加工	18274177	0.89
24	慈溪市新兴化纤厂	化纤工业	16817196	0.82
25	上海奖南国际贸易有限公司	贸易商	16194077	0.79
26	杭州三星纸业有限公司	纸工业	15971359	0.78
27	苏州思成化纤有限公司	化纤工业	15615271	0.76
28	浙江安顺化纤有限公司	化纤工业	15213940	0.74
29	高密市宏泰化纤有限公司	化纤工业	15143886	0.74
30	嘉兴市富达化学纤维厂	化纤工业	14168786	0.69
31	佳利塑业(太仓)有限公司	塑料工业	14017614	0.69
32	广州市泽天橡塑制品有限公司	塑料工业	13945290	0.68
33	湖南贝裔贸易有限公司	贸易商	13684389	0.67
34	杭州吉成化纤有限公司	化纤工业	13602598	0.67
35	江阴市新南洋纺织科技有限公司	化纤工业	13147709	0.64
36	宁波新纶化纤有限公司	化纤工业	12911529	0.63
37	宁波港豪进出口有限公司	贸易商	12467552	0.61
38	宁波亚聚进出口有限公司	贸易商	11787175	0.58
	进口总计		2045429823	100.00

从资料分析，聚对苯二甲酸乙二酯的废碎料及下脚料进口生产使用企业仍以化纤工业为主，2012年聚对苯二甲酸乙二酯的废塑料及下脚料进口商前三十八大进口商中二十三大进口商为化纤工业，进口量占总进口量的41.01%。

5.2012年其他塑料的废碎料及下脚料进口商以贸易商为主

从海关资料来看，2012年其他塑料的废塑料及下脚料进口商有571家，比上年577家进口商减少了6家进口商。

2012年其他塑料的废塑料及下脚料前十位进口商进口量占总进口量的12.70%。

深圳市安缘通化工材料有限公司、深圳市乐天世纪科技有限公司、长沙鑫煜进出口贸易有限公司、广州市和远进出口有限公司、佛山市南海里水里塑塑料有限公司、福州宏伟兴业化纤有限公司、深圳市港进利国际货运代理有限公司、广州恒通和顺进出口有限公司、佛山市欧达同人贸易发展有限公司、福建三宏再生资源科技有限公司，分别位居2012年其他塑料的废塑料及下脚料进口量1～10位，进口量分别占总进口量的1.90%、1.55%、1.34%、1.33%、1.24%、1.14%、1.12%、1.00%、0.98%和0.90%。

2012年其他塑料的废塑料及下脚料前十位进口商中七家为属于广东省企业，进口量占总进口量的9.32%。

2012年其他塑料废塑料及下脚料三十二大进口商中，有十八家属于广东省，进口量占总进口量的17.32%。

2012年聚对苯二甲酸乙二酯的废塑料及下脚料进口商前三十二大进口商中十七大进口商为贸易商，进口量占总进口量的13.72%（表16）。

表16　2012年其他塑料的废碎料及下脚料三十二大主要进口企业统计

排序	进口商	所属行业	进口数量/kg	占比例/%
1	深圳市安缘通化工材料有限公司	包装工业	41980183	1.90
2	深圳市乐天世纪科技有限公司	化学工业	34177773	1.55
3	长沙鑫煜进出口贸易有限公司	贸易商	29509325	1.34
4	广州市和远进出口有限公司	贸易商	29323692	1.33
5	佛山市南海里水里塑塑料有限公司	塑料制品工业	27293790	1.24
6	福州宏伟兴业化纤有限公司	化纤工业	25123963	1.14
7	深圳市港进利国际货运代理有限公司	贸易商	24823335	1.12
8	广州恒通和顺进出口有限公司	贸易商	22013970	1.00
9	佛山市欧达同人贸易发展有限公司	贸易商	21600695	0.98
10	福建三宏再生资源科技有限公司	回料加工	19846150	0.90
11	汕头市丰盈实业有限公司	包装工业	19578176	0.89
12	深圳市裕鑫兴进出口贸易有限公司	贸易商	18501590	0.84
13	晋江市龙湖峰华贸易有限公司	贸易商	18351915	0.83
14	厦门利洲贸易有限公司	贸易商	18197386	0.82
15	河北福发塑胶有限公司	塑料制品工业	16909768	0.77
16	海丰县新洲塑料制品有限公司	塑料制品工业	16395062	0.74
17	福建全通资源再生工业园有限公司	回料加工	16153754	0.73
18	湖南泰亨经贸有限公司	贸易商	15846811	0.72
19	惠州市加太塑料制品有限公司	塑料制品工业	15419138	0.70
20	高要市龙宝塑料制品有限公司	塑料制品工业	15145258	0.69
21	清远市开泰贸易有限公司	贸易商	14955351	0.68
22	天津云祥通金属制品有限公司	塑料制品工业	14619182	0.66
23	佛山市南海融佳进出口贸易有限公司	贸易商	14156274	0.64

续表

排序	进口商	所属行业	进口数量/kg	占比例/%
24	泉州嘉佳利纤维发展有限公司	化纤工业	14035463	0.64
25	深圳市金银岛贸易有限公司	贸易商	13789805	0.62
26	骏业金属制品(太仓)有限公司	塑料制品工业	13671110	0.62
27	厦门元瀚进出口有限公司	贸易商	13183692	0.60
28	广州市君懋进出口贸易有限公司	贸易商	12638863	0.57
29	广州祥莱进出口贸易有限公司	贸易商	12183990	0.55
30	佛山市赞佳贸易有限公司	贸易商	12118216	0.55
31	河北嘉裕塑胶有限公司	塑料制品工业	12101408	0.55
32	广州弘亿贸易有限公司	贸易商	11694020	0.53
	进口总计		2207531156	100.00

从资料分析，其他塑料的废碎料及下脚料进口生产使用企业以包装工业、塑料制品工业、化纤工业、回料加工为主，2012 年其他塑料的废碎料及下脚料进口商三十二大进口商中十五大进口商为进口生产使用企业，进口量占总进口量的 12.99%。

第四节　2012 年废塑料进口消费地区流向分析

从海关资料来看，2012 年废塑料及下脚料主要进口流向为广东省、山东省、福建省、河北省、天津市、江苏省、辽宁省和浙江省，进口量占总进口量的 95.33% 以上。

从海关资料来看，2012 年乙烯聚合物的废塑料及下脚料进口消费省市有 21 个，比上年 22 个进口消费省市减少 1 个进口消费省市。

主要进口流向为广东省、山东省和福建省，广东省、山东省和福建省进口量分别占总进口量的 26.00%、17.89% 和 17.48%(表 17)。

表 17　2012 年乙烯聚合物的废碎料及下脚料八大进口省市统计

排　序	进口省市	进口金额/美元	进口数量/kg	占比例/%
1	广东省	665745873.00	960028544	26.00
2	山东省	420336849.00	660373321	17.89
3	福建省	419387219.00	645339031	17.48
4	河北省	346375585.00	513480517	13.91
5	天津市	262543125.00	392327058	10.63
6	江苏省	103217503.00	148621503	4.03
7	辽宁省	65398080.00	103233887	2.80
8	浙江省	67296873.00	95470339	2.59
进口总计		2472564513	3691980996	100.00

从海关资料来看，2012 年苯乙烯聚合物的废塑料及下脚料进口消费省市有 13 个，比上年 14 个进口消费省市减少 1 个进口消费省市。。

主要进口流向为广东省、江苏省和浙江省，前八位 2012 年苯乙烯聚合物的废塑料及下脚料进口消费省市进口量占总进口量的 98.14%，广东省、江苏省和山东省进口量分别占总进口量的 61.31%、9.17% 和 8.54%(表 18)。

表 18　2012 年苯乙烯聚合物的废碎料及下脚料八大进口省市统计

排　序	进口省市	进口金额/美元	进口数量/kg	占比例/%
1	广东省	119591741.00	148157722	61.31
2	江苏省	19701829.00	22165673	9.17
3	浙江省	17107547.00	20638326	8.54
4	山东省	14605953.00	17203480	7.12
5	上海市	13396077.00	16163616	6.69
6	福建省	7812007.00	7905812	3.27
7	安徽省	2087250.00	2537251	1.05
8	广西壮族自治区	1985558.00	2403073	0.99
进口总计		200214593.00	241661036	100.00

从海关资料来看，2012年氯乙烯聚合物的废塑料及下脚料进口消费省市有16个，与上年持平。

主要进口流向为广东省、河北省和天津市，2012年氯乙烯聚合物的废塑料及下脚料前八位进口消费省市进口量占总进口量的97.01%，广东省、河北省和天津市进口量分别占总进口量的73.60%、4.79%和5.73%（表19）。

表19　2012年氯乙烯聚合物的废碎料及下脚料八大进口省市统计

排　序	进口省市	进口金额/美元	进口数量/kg	占比例/%
1	广东省	332914163.00	508554126	73.60
2	河北省	25897825.00	39992839	5.79
3	天津市	25465926.00	39569194	5.73
4	浙江省	22478415.00	34639133	5.01
5	江苏省	11003183.00	17337142	2.51
6	上海市	8290026.00	12604490	1.82
7	湖南省	5848422.00	9055103	1.31
8	广西壮族自治区	5664816.00	8564291	1.24
进口总计		450904935.00	690999951	100.00

从海关资料来看，2012年聚对苯二甲酸乙二酯的废塑料及下脚料进口消费省市有21个，比上年22个进口消费省市减少1个进口消费省市。

主要进口流向为浙江省、江苏省和福建省，2012年聚对苯二甲酸乙二酯的废塑料及下脚料前八位进口消费省市进口量占总进口量的95.76%，浙江省、江苏省和广东省进口量分别占总进口量的43.96%、24.69%和14.19%（表20）。

表20　2012年聚对苯二甲酸乙二酯的废碎料及下脚料八大进口省市统计

排　序	进口省市	进口金额/美元	进口数量/kg	占比例/%
1	浙江省	827749659.00	899219007	43.96
2	江苏省	423093841.00	504960958	24.69
3	福建省	197498471.00	290238925	14.19
4	广东省	60124550.00	74811448	3.66
5	山东省	45756907.00	58806751	2.88
6	上海市	42268594.00	52984058	2.59
7	湖南省	32101745.00	41375919	2.02
8	天津市	23100095.00	36180550	1.77
进口总计		1713793474.00	2045429823	100.00

从海关资料来看，2012年其他塑料的废塑料及下脚料进口消费省市有19个，比上年21个进口消费省市减少2个进口消费省市。

主要进口流向为广东省、福建省和江苏省，2012年其他塑料的废塑料及下脚料前八位进口消费省市进口量占总进口量的92.95%，广东省、福建省和江苏省进口量分别占总进口量的44.19%、14.31%和8.28%（表21）。

表21　2012年其他塑料的废碎料及下脚料八大进口省市统计

排　序	进口省市	进口金额/美元	进口数量/kg	占比例/%
1	广东省	681469031.00	975504516	44.19
2	福建省	221291435.00	315966824	14.31
3	江苏省	134244001.00	182839377	8.28
4	天津市	99089045.00	146958469	6.66
5	浙江省	100607618.00	132031411	5.98
6	上海市	87756796.00	118299115	5.36
7	河北省	67797249.00	100613148	4.56
8	湖南省	59383956.00	79754739	3.61
进口总计		1565747239.00	2207531156	100.00

第五节　中国废塑料价格分析

2002 年废塑料进口价仅 202～240 美元/t；

2004 年废塑料进口价跃过 300 美元/t 大关，达到 314～360 美元/t；

2009 年废塑料进口价回落，跌破 600 美元/t 大关，PE 废塑料进口年平均单价达到 500.36 美元/t，比 2008 年下降 19.08%；

2012 年 PE 废塑料进口价又进一步上升，达到 669.71 美元/t，比 2011 年上升 0.78 百分点；

2012 年 PS 废塑料进口价回落，下降到 828.49 美元/t，比 2011 年下降 1.59 百分点；

2012 年 PVC 废塑料进口价又进一步上升，又突破 650 美元/t 大关，达到 652.54 美元/t，比 2011 年上升 1.62%；

2012 年聚酯废塑料进口年平均单价跌降较大，跌破 840 美元/t 大关，跌到 837.86 美元/t，比 2011 年下降 12.18%。

2012 年其他废塑料进口年平均单价又进一步上升，又突破 700 美元/t 大关，达到 709.28 元/t，比 2011 年上升 2.63%(表 22)。

表 22　中国 2007～2012 年废塑料进口平均单价统计　　美元/t

年　份	2007	2008	2009	2010	2011	2012
PE 废塑料进口年平均单价	445.38	618.35	500.36	640.04	664.51	669.71
PS 废塑料进口年平均单价	480.32	602.70	574.26	698.47	841.87	828.49
PVC 废塑料进口年平均单价	437.42	546.22	404.58	530.27	642.12	652.54
聚酯废塑料进口年平均单价	564.21	696.09	538.44	713.35	954.07	837.86
其他废塑料进口年平均单价	447.25	613.72	501.74	647.85	691.10	709.28

2007～2012 年 PE 废塑料进口年平均单价年均增长 8.50%；

2007～2012 年 PS 废塑料进口年平均单价年均增长 11.52%；

2007～2012 年 PVC 废塑料进口年平均单价年均增长 8.32%；

2007～2012 年聚酯废塑料进口年平均单价年均增长 8.23%；

2007～2012 年其他废塑料进口年平均单价年均增长 9.66%。

第六节　废弃塑料政策和回收利用

中国对进口废塑料的需求近年来不断扩大。凭借低成本的人工分拣和宽松的监管控制，再生行业蓬勃发展起来。

但政府开始采取措施对该行业实施更严格的管控。

首先在 2011 年出台政策，从海关方面加强对废料进口和流通的控制。现在，政府又公布了一项新的法规，取缔一切可能造成环境污染的不当的再生操作。

中国国家环境保护总局、发改委和商务部联合发布《废塑料加工利用污染防治管理规定》，新规定在 2012 年 10 月 1 日正式生效，将严格禁止一些不负责任的废料再生加工，包括：

禁止在居民区加工利用废塑料；

禁止利用废塑料生产食品用塑料袋；

禁止露天焚烧废塑料及加工利用过程产生的残余垃圾、滤网；

禁止进口未经清洗的使用过的废塑料；

禁止将进口的废塑料全部或者部分转让给进口许可证载明的利用企业以外的单位或者个人，包括将进口废塑料委托给其他企业代为清洗；

禁止将进口废塑料分拣或加工利用过程产生的残余废塑料未经清洗处理直接出售；

禁止将进口废纸中的废塑料，未经清洗处理直接出售。

新规定要求再生企业一旦发现属于国家禁止进口类或者不符合环境保护控制标准的进口废塑料，立即向口岸海关、检验检疫部门和所在地环保部门报告并配合做好相关处理工作。

此外，还鼓励废塑料加工利用集散地对废塑料加工利用散户实行集中园区化管理，集中处理废塑料加工利用产生的废水、废气和固体废物。

规定要求省级环保、商务主管部门组织核查并公布合格的废塑料加工利用企业名单；对核查发现问题的，应当依法处理并将处理结果向社会公布。

从 2013 年 1 月 1 日开始，只有通过监管机构检查的再生企业才允许进口废旧塑料。

据介绍，今后 3 年内，国家将针对资源蕴涵量大的废塑料和橡胶等大宗固体废旧物资，开发综合高效利用新工艺、新方法及新设备，发展相应技术规范与标准。

我国将通过技术集成，建立工程化应用示范线和技术集成示范园区，为提高再生资源综合回收利用效率与再生资源产品质量，减少大宗固体废弃物及其控制再利用过程的环境污染提供技术支撑。

目前全球每年约产生废弃聚苯乙烯(PS)泡沫塑料 5800kt，其中中国每年产生约 1800kt，除少数发达国家外，其他国家的废弃 PS 泡沫材料并未得到有效回收。

据不完全统计，目前北欧国家和日本PS泡沫塑料回收再生利用率为72%，韩国PS泡沫塑料回收再生利用率为64%，而其余国家和地区的PS泡沫塑料回收再生利用率仅为10%～30%。

在我国，由于回收机制还不够完善，导致70%被掩埋或者焚烧，仅有30%左右被回收利用，大多数废弃聚苯乙烯材料并未得到有效的回收与利用，造成了严重的环境污染。

严峻资源危机和环境污染，迫使我们必须加大资源的回收与再利用，走循环回收利用的绿色发展道路。

1. 全球首家一站式电子用废旧塑料精炼厂昆山投运

一捆捆来自电子产品的废旧塑料，经过粉碎、分选、纯化、精炼，变成一颗颗晶莹黑透的胶粒，重新成为可利用的“宝贝”。

2013年1月10日，记者在由纬创资通新设的纬润高新材料有限公司产线上见证了这一系列神奇的变化。

由世界排名前三的笔记本电脑生产巨头纬创资通投资6.08亿元设立的纬润公司，成为全球首家一站式电子废弃物塑料精炼厂，纬创也成为全球笔电巨头中首家进军“绿资源”事业、将企业社会责任体现在资源循环利用上的企业。

2. 加拿大用可再生塑料沥青铺路

加拿大温哥华市正在尝试利用一种沥青材料铺设道路，该材料所使用的沥青可用从塑料制品中回收提取的蜡制成。

温哥华市将这种用混合沥青铺路的过程称之为“温式混合”。该方法可以在较低的温度下生产和运输沥青，从而可将由于加热搅拌沥青所导致的碳排放减少近20%。

3. 废旧塑料环保再利用市场成为新宠儿

2012年7月6日，再生资源生产厂的工人在包装带生产线上工作。山东滨州市邹平县九户镇的再生资源生产厂，用回收来的废旧塑料生产出60余种打包带，生产工艺环保无污染，产品广受厂家欢迎。

4. 澳大利亚用废塑料废橡胶炼钢获得双赢成效

澳大利亚新南威尔士大学教授维娜·萨哈吉瓦拉研发出一种将废橡胶、废塑料用于钢铁生产的新方法——聚合物注入工艺。不仅可以大大减少废橡胶、废塑料造成的环境污染，还可以有效降低钢铁生产成本。

废橡胶和废塑料中含有很多碳，将废弃橡胶和塑料作为碳元素的替代品投入电弧炼钢炉中，原来被“锁”在废弃塑胶中的碳在超高温度下就会发生反应，与煤一起燃烧成为洁净的燃料，从而减少温室气体排放量，同时也缓解了将它们作为垃圾填埋对环境造成的污染问题。

聚合物注入工艺的好处是，通过注入聚合物与焦炭或无烟煤的混合物，可以增大熔渣的体积并提高起泡度，这样可以延长弧长、增加从电弧到钢的传热量、减少经过熔渣及侧边墙的热损耗，进而可提高用电效率。

这样一来，可减少大约3%的耗电量。每炼1t钢，有大约24%的成本都来自于用电成本。采用聚合物注入技术后，每炼一炉钢，平均所需要注入的碳总量可减少10%～20%，再加上聚合物的潜在价格要低于焦炭，碳注入物的总成本可节省15%～35%。

目前，聚合物注入技术在第一钢铁公司的工厂已成为一项常规技术，在澳大利亚很多炼钢炉都采用了这项技术，相当于每年消耗100万只废旧轮胎。在国外的发展势头也非常良好。测试表明，使用这项技术不会对钢的质量或环境产生负面影响。第一钢铁公司集团也因此获得了新南威尔士政府2011年绿色地球奖。

2010年，全球钢产量超过了14亿吨，其中有超过4亿吨是采用电弧炉工艺炼制而成的。因此，这一技术的应用空间很大。

5. 日本帝人拟在华开拓聚酯产品回收业务

据日经新闻报道，日本帝人公司计划在中国扩大聚酯产品的回收利用业务。该公司明年将委派专门负责人常驻中国，推动当地服装厂商等参与聚酯产品回收计划。目前，在中国回收的废旧衣料将被运往日本用于生产再生纤维，然后作为布料和纱线出口到中国，今后该公司将讨论在中国建设回收利用设施。

帝人旗下子公司帝人纤维将希望参与回收利用计划的企业组织在一起，建立了“ECO CIRCLE”机构。该机构与合作企业从商品开发阶段起展开合作，在店铺柜台回收旧衣服，然后制成再生纤维销售给参加合作的企业，再制造为纺织产品。参与该计划的企业包括在工装回收利用方面提供合作的企业在内，已经超过150家。

在中国回收的废旧衣物将运往帝人集团旗下的日本的松山工厂，制成纱线和布料后出口中国，布匹和布料的染色工艺的一部分由中国帝人工厂负责。今后还将讨论与中国化学纤维工业协会展开合作，在中国国内建设生产再生纤维的设施。

帝人拥有将聚酯产品在分子水平上分解为原料、然后制成聚酯纤维的最尖端技术。

（柴国樑）

2012 年 BOPP 行业企业经济指标数据

根据2013年3月中国塑协双向拉伸聚丙烯薄膜(BOPP)专委会的统计数字，2012年BOPP薄膜总产能3947259t，总产量为3119202t，比2011年2808855t产量增长11.05%。2012年全国共有90家BOPP生产企业。其中南亚分南通、惠州两地，昆岭分云南和苏州两地。详细数据如下。

公司名称	产能/t	产量/t	销售额/万元
天津天塑科技有限公司新型包装材料分公司	10000	10000	16000
天津阳光塑料有限公司	14000	12000	
天津市华恒包装材料有限公司	32000	未投产	
宝硕富太塑料包装材料公司	14000	13000	
中国石油抚顺石油化工公司合成洗涤剂厂	23000	18000	21600
山西迎太塑料有限公司	3000	未投产	
大连天成包装材料有限公司	12000	停产	
大连三荣化学有限公司	18000	停产	
黑龙江庆港塑料有限公司	12000	停产	
大庆市龙兴塑胶制品有限责任公司	3000	3000	
上海光乾塑胶有限公司(改做电容膜)	4000	3400	
维龙(上海)包装工业有限公司	15000	14000	20000
上海金浦塑料包装材料公司	28000	21000	28000
上海高昌包装材料有限公司高龙分公司	4000	停产	
宝燕工业科技(上海)有限公司	25000	20000	40000
桂林集琦包装有限公司	3500	停产	
苏州瑞泰包装材料有限公司	8000	8000	10000
江苏恒创包装材料有限公司	120000	105000	139090

续表

公司名称	产能/t	产量/t	销售额/万元
苏州昆岭薄膜工业有限公司	20000	18000	
常州金氏集团金海塑业有限公司	50000	40000	39000
常州越浩软塑新材料有限公司	25000	20000	28000
江苏中达新材料集团股份有限公司	150000	60000	
南亚塑胶(南通)公司	25000	20000	
浙江伊美薄膜工业集团有限公司	120000	110000	
浙江百汇包装有限公司	138000	65000	
浙江绍兴富陵控股集团有限公司	50000	60000	70000
瑞安市东威塑胶有限公司新型包装材料公司	55000	60000	70000
浙江奔多实业有限公司(包含江苏奔多)	100000	100000	130000
宁波大榭开发区金源复合材料有限公司	50000	36000	
浙江华滨包装材料有限公司	48000	48000	50000
泉州利昌塑胶有限公司	60000	60000	
浙江凯利包装材料有限公司(包含大连凯威)	140000	140000	200000
浙江杭宝集团公司	35000	未投产	
浙江大东南包装股份有限公司	50000	42500	
宁波大东南万象科技有限公司	10000	8000	25000
金田集团塑业有限公司	320000	280000	300000
浙江权威软塑新材料有限公司	30000	37000	
温州康达包装材料有限公司	4000	4200	4600
海宁长盛包装有限公司	60000	67000	90000
杭州萧山华益塑料有限公司	180000	98000	150000
宁波亚塑科技有限公司	80000	54000	
福建时代包装材料有限公司	272000	254174	

续表

公司名称	产能/t	产量/t	销售额/万元
合肥金菱里克塑料有限公司	75000	70000	100000
烟台世昊塑业有限公司	4000	3000	
青岛庆昕塑料有限公司	25000	21000	
济南康雅薄膜有限公司	25000	15000	18000
山东群力塑胶有限公司	50000	50000	70000
烟台恒源包装有限公司	5000	5000	
青岛英诺包装科技有限公司	16000	15000	20000
中塑投资集团	30000	25000	30000
山东宝利特包装材料有限公司	5000	5000	7000
聊城中塑塑业有限公司	35000	30000	42000
山西斯瑞林包装材料有限公司(山西鸿基)	11000	9400	
洛阳石化吉润化工有限责任公司	20000	10046	
湖北狮虹材料科技有限公司	12000	12000	24000
中山新亚洲胶粘制品有限公司	25000	23000	
广东德冠双轴拉伸薄膜有限公司	85000	64000	90000
广东华业包装材料有限公司	64000	54856	76274
汕头丰兴盛包装材料有限公司	50000	42500	
汕头冠华薄膜工业有限公司	28800	30000	
揭阳市运通塑料包装有限公司	100000	80000	120000
永宁塑料制品有限公司	70000	60000	70000
广东普宁市威孚包装材料厂	37000	35000	
湛江包装材料有限公司	11000	11035	23144
南亚塑胶胶膜(惠州)有限公司	30000	25500	
中港合资顺德美嘉思食品有限公司	10000	停产	
赛诺国际有限公司(包括珠海华诺和海南赛诺)	16000	12000	30000
潮州市展鹏塑胶制品有限公司	15000	10000	10000

续表

公司名称	产能/t	产量/t	销售额/万元
汕头市雄伟塑料包装材料公司	20000	8000	6000
佛山塑料集团股份有限公司(东方分公司、无锡环宇、成都东盛、湖南东林、经纬分公司)	100059	74777	114205.6
贵州西众塑胶股份有限公司	6000	3000	6000
云南昆岭薄膜工业有限公司	10000	10000	
云南红塔塑胶有限公司(包括成都)	56000	55000	
河北海伟集团电子材料有限公司	35000	15000	
丹东申海塑业有限责任公司	1500	停产	
南通百正电子材料有限公司	13000	7000	21000
浙江南洋科技股份有限公司	12000	10000	
泉州嘉德利电子材料有限公司	7500	6400	
安徽铜峰电子股份有限公司	12000	10914	33600
黄冈龙辰电子科技有限公司	6000	5100	
江门市润田实业投资有限公司	2400	2400	10000
四川东材企业集团公司	4500	4500	15000
江苏首义薄膜有限公司	64000	47000	62000
福融辉工业集团(中国)有限公司(包括广州宏铭、广州宏顺、福融辉实业(福建)、福建兰天无锡分公司	175000	158000	210240
广东中炬塑胶有限公司	10000	8500	
江苏中立方实业有限公司	8000	未投产	
青岛嘉泽包装有限公司	6000	未生产	
康得新复合材料有限公司	60000	12000	
山东冠贸包装材料有限公司	28000	24000	
霸州市胜芳福兴彩印包装有限公司	35000	30000	50000
合计	3947259	3119202	

由于我们国家 BOPP 薄膜生产线发展速度过快，导致市场供大于求的局面剧演剧烈。下图可以看到薄膜与原料的价格差，从年初到目前在一步步缩小，利润在一步步降低。从下图我们不难看出，加工差价在年初到年尾一直呈现出缩减的态势。

2012 年全年，薄膜全行业，无论是生产商，还是经销商，都深感市场的艰难和出货的困难，因此产品质量和售后服务越来越提到议程上来。2013 ~ 2015 年市场产能产量仍将是一个不断释放的过程，供求关系仍将继续紧张中度过。2012 年，随着许多新线的投产，价格和利润空间受到压缩，原料与薄膜差价的平均值很低，对于普通膜来说，全年平均价约为 1200 ~ 1600 元/t 左右。大部分企业处于微利或微亏状态。

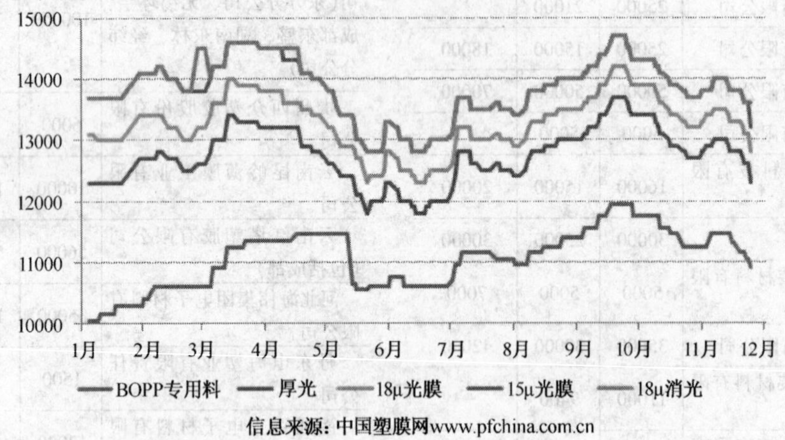

2012 ~ 2013 年度 BOPP 专用料与薄膜价格差趋势图

尽管 2012 年利润空间很低，仍然有 21 条线签约，其中包装膜 19 条，电容膜 2 条，新增产能超过 50 万吨，这些产能将于 2014 至 2015 年形成实际产能，除非市场需求出现大的增加，否则今后几年全行业将进入亏损期。

值得警惕的是，目前还有多家企业有意上线，建议各有关企业谨慎小心，控制风险。

（中国塑料加工工业协会 BOPP 薄膜专委会　孙冬泉）

2012 年 BOPA 行业企业经济指标数据

根据中国塑料加工工业协会 2013 年 3 月的调查数据，2012 年 BOPA 薄膜总产能 105300t，比 2011 年总产能 80300 增长 31.13%，2012 年 BOPA 薄膜产量为 95596t，比 2011 年 73878t 产量增长 29.40%。目前全国共有 8 家 BOPA 生产企业，其中运城分为天津、湛江、昆山三地；东鸿分为沧州、德州两地；长塑分为厦门、无锡、温州 3 地。本次统计全部填报。详细数据如下：

公司名称	生产能力/t	总产量/t	销售额/万元
天津运城塑业有限公司（包含昆山运城和湛江明）	14000	13000	37800
沧州东鸿包装材料有限公司（包含德州东鸿）	18000	19000	60000

续表

公司名称	生产能力/t	总产量/t	销售额/万元
上海紫东化工材料有限公司	5000	4600	
上海九天塑料薄膜有限公司	4500	3600	
尤尼吉可高分子科技（中国）有限公司	4800	4700	16000
晓星化纤（嘉兴）有限公司	8000	7000	
厦门长塑实业有限公司（包含无锡、温州）	40000	37400	139763.8
佛山塑料集团股份有限公司	11000	6296	21933.4
合　计	105300	95596	

2012 年处于所有产能均得到释放的状态，行业企业出现两极分化局面，厦门长塑、沧州东鸿、天津运城三家企业继续扩张，厦门长塑增加投产 2 条布鲁克纳新线，沧州东鸿 2 条自主设计生产线 2013 年投产，昆山运城公司新线 2012 年初投产，其余企

业处于苦苦支撑的状态。

本年度 BOPA 价格自年初小幅调涨后价格便进入下滑通道。进入 5 月后，特别是刚过中旬，来自下游的订单突然减少，彩印包装企业本月开机率降至 2012 年最低谷，许多大型彩印企业仅维持最低的生产负荷，缺乏订单是近期下游加工企业最主要的表现，至于资金方面倒不是很大的问题，现阶段造成这种现象的主要原因还是外围宏观造成的，一方面是市场商家对宏观经济的担忧，生产的缩量是主要经营思路，一方面又是居民消费信心的下降，高企的物价和一系列的食品安全使尼龙膜库存居高不下，终端彩印包装工厂开机率持续低迷，6～7 月新接订单数量较少，主要包装基地开机率继续下滑。8 月开始，市场略有恢复，BOPA 行业第八次会议再次在上海召开：鉴于 BOPA 良好的产销形势，为巩固膜厂的利润现状，BOPA 指导价格在行业会议后大幅上涨 2000 元/t。

三季度前期，BOPA 市场整体表现为周期性的波动，尼龙膜厂家降低设备运行负荷、低价出货等市场竞争手段在淡季表现得淋漓尽致。但当旺季来临时，BOPA 又表现得如火如荼，膜厂满负荷运行，库存短时间消化殆尽，膜价快速的从低谷拉涨到高位，完全没有供应过剩的迹象。这就是国内 BOPA 市场鲜明的特点，今年三季度的热销局面一方面得益于尼龙膜市场刚性需求的增长，另外向沧州东鸿、天津运城等企业在外销上有了跨越性的突破，加大的缓解了国内市场销售压力。

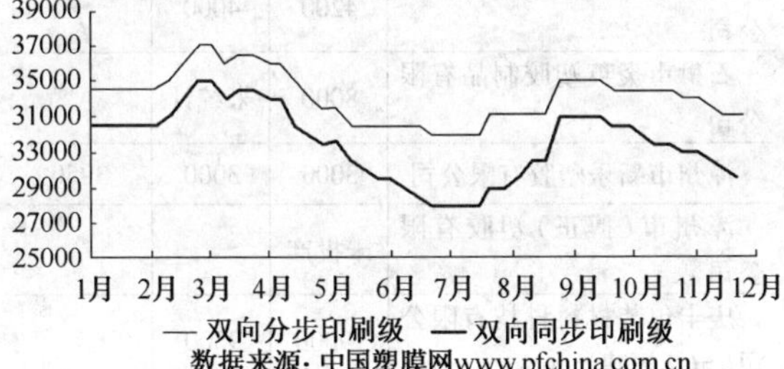

2012～2013 年度 BOPA 价格趋势图

在 BOPA 行业，技术决定你的成本，怎样更好地降低分步线复合级产品比重、提高印刷级产品的品质仍将是后期我们的 BOPA 企业要坚持的生产路线。

2012 年 BOPA 行业企业处于微利或亏损的边缘，2013 年产能过剩，经济效益可能比 2012 年还要困难。BOPA 行业未来发展重点要把控制产能扩张、拓宽应用领域作为一个重要课题，才能保证行业健康发展。

（中国塑料加工工业协会　孙冬泉）

2012 年 CPP 行业企业经济指标数据

根据 2013 年 4 月中国塑协流延薄膜专委会的统计数字，2012 年 CPP 实际总产能约为 873700t，实际产量约为 564120t，开机率 64.6%。产能比 2011 年的 818100t 增长了 6.8%；产量比 2011 年的 526424.2t 增长了 7.2%。目前全国共有约 142 家 CPP 生产企业，本次统计共有 111 家企业填报，约 31 家企业未填报。详细数据如下：

公司名称	产能/t	产量/t	销售额/万元
上海紫藤包装材料有限公司	20000	停产	
上海美丰包装材料有限公司	15000	11300	19000
上海亿中塑料制品有限公司	4000	5000	
上海金午实业有限公司	3000	卖掉了	
上海大汇塑业有限公司	12000	6200	8680
上海三宜包装有限公司	未统计	未统计	
天津星达塑料包装有限公司(包括津泽)	34000	28000	
天津市华恒包装材料有限公司	7000	刚刚投产	
天津北洋塑料包装材料有限公司	未统计	未统计	
保定宝来塑料包装材料公司	3000	停产	
雄县立亚包装材料有限公司	3500	3200	3800
东光县楚天塑料有限公司	3500	3300	4190
河北沧州佳创塑业公司	2000	1800	2200
河北雄县盛世佳铝塑包装材料有限公司	6000	5400	7100
河北雄县华中塑胶制品有限公司	3000	2500	
河北泰达包装材料有限公司(3 条线)	15000	10000	14000
河北海伟集团电子材料有限公司	7000	4200	
河南许昌浩达塑胶有限公司	5500	5000	6800
山西迎太塑料有限公司	11500	7000	
大连天成包装材料有限公司	7000	停产	

续表

公司名称	产能/t	产量/t	销售额/万元
哈尔滨光宇电源有限公司	1000	停产	
丹东申海塑业有限责任公司	1000	停产	
徐州润彭塑料制品有限公司	2000	卖掉了	
无锡环亚包装材料公司	6000	5800	1100
江阴市通利包装材料有限公司	8000	6000	11000
常州海企塑业有限公司	6000	3500	
张家港昊隆制膜有限公司	4000	1900	
张家港市华鑫彩印包装有限公司	14000	13500	16000
美塑化科技(苏州)有限公司	5000	3000	
徐州润田塑业有限公司	2500	1970	2758
无锡南方包装新材料科技有限公司	5500	2000	
江苏宝丽鑫文具有限公司	未统计	未统计	
扬州华坤塑料制品有限公司	3000	2000	3000
金华汇源塑胶有限公司	未统计	未统计	
浙江百汇包装有限公司	6000	3150	
浙江绍兴富陵塑料纺织有限公司	5000	3000	
杭州新光塑料有限公司	7000	5800	10540
浙江大东南包装股份有限公司	32000	19200	
龙港盛华软包装材料厂	未统计	未统计	
金田集团永安包装材料有限公司	5000	3600	4896
富阳天纬塑胶有限公司	1000	900	1300
浙江和和塑胶有限公司(金华塑料总厂)	1200	停产	
温州远大塑胶有限公司	24000	18000	43200
浙江九洲印务有限公司	4800	4500	6075
温州华夏包装材料有限公司	3000	2200	2900
浙江光华化工有限公司	7000	7750	10686
宁波佳仁塑料有限公司	4000	3900	
杭州东恒塑胶有限公司	1100	停产	
宁波瑞成包装材料有限公司	3500	2500	
浙江世嘉包装材料有限公司	4000	4000	

续表

公司名称	产能/t	产量/t	销售额/万元
杭州永正吹塑彩印包装有限公司	4800	3850	5775
浙江嘉禾印刷有限公司	6300	未统计	
海宁海欣真空包装有限公司	6000	未统计	
安徽宁国双津(集团)实业有限公司	14000	15000	26000
安徽双永包装装饰材料有限公司	2500	停产	
安徽凌云包装材料有限公司	2500	停产	
安徽松泰包装材料有限公司	3500	1400	1820
安徽金泽信环保材料有限公司	11000	未统计	
黄山永新股份有限公司	16000	13000	15000
福州佳通第一塑料有限公司	6500	6300	9460
福州乐尔佳塑胶有限公司	3000	停产	
厦门顺峰包装材料有限公司	9000	5400	
福建晋江市新达塑料制品有限公司	1200	停产	
福州市航升塑料包装厂	4000	3200	4200
鹏达包装材料有限公司	10500	9600	13980
福建省南安环球塑胶有限公司	4200	4000	
石狮市炎英塑胶制品有限公司	8000	未统计	
漳州市新乐塑胶有限公司	3000	3000	3950
漳州市(搏正)塑胶有限公司	未投产		
庆丰包装材料科技有限公司(包括福建)	19000	9500	
山东省青州市金诺尔塑胶有限公司(青州市星达塑料包装材料有限公司)	8500	8000	10770
青州泰欣包装材料有限公司	3500	3000	4500
潍坊鸿昌塑胶有限公司	6000	3800	5100
山东烟台兴德包装材料有限公司	3000	未统计	
烟台世昊塑业有限公司	3000	2000	2600
烟台恒源包装有限公司	6000	3000	
山东振鲁塑料制品有限公司	1800	停产	

续表

公司名称	产能/t	产量/t	销售额/万元
山东临沂塑料制品厂	1100	停产	
山东临沂金洲工贸企业集团公司	2500	未统计	
临沂市中钢塑业有限公司（原通达）	2500	未统计	
青岛凯姆拓塑胶工业有限公司	18000	18000	24000
湖北慧狮塑业股份有限公司	20000	16000	27500
湖北江裕塑料工业发展有限公司	2000	停产	
武汉鑫鸣塑料制品有限责任公司	3000	停产	
武汉天兴双马塑料包装有限公司	7000	7200	9739
武汉斯德隆科技发展有限公司	6000	2000	2600
佛山塑料集团股份有限公司	11000	7026	7862
广东华业包装材料有限公司	18000	8152	11327
汕头市惠业食品包装实业有限公司	2000	停产	
汕头市澄海区东大峰包装材料有限公司（汉钊塑料薄膜厂）	6000	5000	67500
佛山东美包装材料有限公司	2000	停产	
广州市华富包装材料有限公司	2000	停产	
广东艺美包装工业有限公司	1000	停产	
金宇达实业有限公司	1200	停产	
庵埠南新塑料工艺厂	4600	停产	
潮安县庵埠镇佳阳塑料材料厂（卖掉一条线到义乌）	3000	2000	
佛山市万田塑料有限公司（几年前就不生产了）	4500	停产	
汕头从泰塑料薄膜有限公司（原广东省包装总公司汕头包装材料公司）	1500	停产	
深圳市大仓和实业发展有限公司	300	倒闭	
汕头双润包装材料有限公司	3500	停产	
广东江门市新会区奥特塑料制品厂	3000	停产	

续表

公司名称	产能/t	产量/t	销售额/万元
汕头市德福包装材料公司	10000	5600	7840
潮安县宏辉工贸有限公司	3200	2500	
广东潮安县雅格利实业有限公司	8000	5000	
潮安县利群包装有限公司	13000	未统计	
汕头市新达橡塑制品有限公司	2000	停产	
广东威孚包装材料有限公司	15000	14200	
长盛达包装塑料包装材料有限公司	2500	停产	
佛山市富兴塑料材料厂	2000	1000	
广州普洛夫尔薄膜有限公司	5000	4500	
阳江明轩实业有限公司	2000	停产	
广州三华塑料有限公司	3000	1000	
汕头东丽包装材料有限公司	6000	5000	
揭东县地都镇弘正塑料薄膜厂	3500	3200	
广东省潮安县和生包装材料有限公司	3500	2000	2800
东莞金友信包装材料有限公司	5500	3200	4300
鹤山山友软塑包装材料有限公司	20000	12000	16200
汕头市江虹包装材料有限公司	2000	300	
中山市美誉塑料包装材料有限公司	3800	3000	3820
潮州市南华塑料实业有限公司	12000	10500	
天虹包装材料有限公司	7000	5500	
潮安县金美工贸有限公司	未统计	未统计	
潮安县民辉包装有限公司	600	400	
广东东盛包装材料有限公司	11000	10000	
佛山市高明海能科技有限公司	7000	未统计	
汕头市利民食品包装有限公司	未统计	未统计	
佛山市蓝月亮包装材料有限公司	2000	停产了	
广州三达塑业包装有限公司	2500	900	

续表

公司名称	产能/t	产量/t	销售额/万元
成都双流东莲长虹塑料制品有限公司	3500	3200	
四川海联达包装材料有限公司	7000	6000	8400
除以上已统计的112家企业外，全国还有15家左右企业，合计估算产能	90000		
未统计单位总产能，按照以统计产能产量比例(开机率)估算产量		96448	
合　计	873700	564120	

受到外部经济环境和产能过剩的影响，CPP行业2012年全年的价格有小范围的浮动。价差基本保持在1200～2000元。对进口线来讲，大部分企业处于薄利或者成本与利润持平的状态。相对国产线生产企业来讲，生存状况更严峻一些。随着国产线和进口线在产品质量上面的差距越来越小，进口线的优势已经越来越微弱了，较高的加工成本，相差不大的售价水平使得进口线企业的经营情况更加困难，基本上都处于持平甚至亏本的状态。

虽然形式并不乐观，但去年还是有十多条生产线投产，这部分增长的产能大部分来自原来的CPP企业，也有几家行业外企业的投产，如金田集团、上海创发、中炬公司等。此外，在调查中我们发现，还有约十几条线将会在2013年内试投产，而原有的产能少于2000t的生产线，由于装备水平、成本和产品质量等问题已经大部分处于停产状态。

虽然大部分企业的效益仅仅持平，但行业中也有一些做的好的企业榜样。比如浙江远大近几年的发展比较迅速，而且在企业经营理念和节电降耗方面有自己独特的经验和心得。另外，上海美丰和海宁光华出口业务的增长比较快，其中美丰的出口量已经达到了产能的40%，高端膜的开发，使得他们的经济效益明显高于行业的其他企业。因此我们流延薄膜专委会也呼吁企业在新产品研发、节能降耗和扩大出口方面加大力度。我们流延薄膜专委会也会每年为大家提供交流的平台，欢迎企业来沟通交流好的经验和心得。

（中国塑料加工工业协会流延薄膜专委会　孙冬泉）

综　述

合成树脂

第一章 合成树脂综述

一、2007~2012 年国内合成树脂产量分析

到 2012 年底，合成树脂的产能达到 62Mt 左右，产量约 50.8Mt。

2007~2012 年国内合成树脂产量年均增长率为 10.60%(表 1)。

表 1 2007~2012 年国内合成树脂产量统计 kt

项 目	2007	2008	2009	2010	2011	2012
合成树脂全计	30735.53	31295.91	36870.29	43907.67	47981.64	50860.54
年增长率/%	21.69	1.82	17.81	19.09	9.28	6.00
其中：PE 产量	6924.70	6894.70	8128.54	9856.84	10050.0	10450.0
PP 产量	7126.49	7332.06	8128.54	9167.28	9956.0	11216.00
PS 产量	2056.80	2061.00	2100.00	2300.00	2029.58	2124.00
PVC 产量	9716.78	8816.42	9155.18	11511.15	12951.81	13261.50
ABS 产量	1630.00	1130.00	1320.00	1410.00	1488.78	1513.35

注：资料来源：历年国家统计局统计数；2007~2008 年 PS，ABS 为估算。

二、进出口总述

据海关统计，2012 年我国合成树脂产品进口 29985.87kt，同比增长 3.43%，其中聚苯乙烯、ABS 树脂、聚氯乙烯、聚酰胺(PA)、PBT 的进口量同比下降；聚乙烯、聚丙烯、聚碳酸酯(PC)、聚甲醛(POM)、聚苯硫醚和塑料下脚料进口上升。

2012 年五大通用塑料进口同比下降 6.98%。

从整体看，国际油价和人民币汇率等仍将是决定塑料原料进口数量和价格的主要因素。2012 年塑料原料进口保持量降价升局面。

2007~2012 年间合成树脂进口量年均增长为 7.91%，低于 2007~2012 年同期国内产量年均增长率 2.66%。

2012 年我国合成树脂产品出口 3146.68kt，同比下降 2.56%，其中聚乙烯、聚丙烯、聚碳酸酯(PC)、聚甲醛(POM)、聚苯硫醚、聚苯乙烯、ABS 树脂、PBT 的出口量同比下降；仅聚酰胺(PA)、聚氯乙烯和塑料下脚料出口上升(表 2)。

表 2 2007~2012 年合成树脂进出口统计 kt

产品	2007	2008	2009	2010	2011	2012
1. 合成树脂合计，进口	20463.10	20868.90	28323.14	29304.83	28963.46	29985.87
出口	3582.65	3295.20	3056.65	2646.78	2889.64	3146.68
其中：1、PE 进口	5051.43	4950.796	8066.22	8024.47	8177.11	8768.70
出口	174.71	210.303	217.43	374.96	570.21	545.59
LDPE 进口	772.60	708.22	1349.55	1383.98	1460.30	1571.14
出口	15.58	16.97	24.01	78.83	79.76	69.90
HDPE 进口	2091.23	2312.59	3859.12	3495.71	3526.40	4009.78
出口	37.95	39.86	30.63	61.00	175.96	134.96
LLDPE 进口	1670.56	1475.75	2200.89	2478.39	2457.08	2306.86
出口	6.86	9.85	7.30	18.23	66.35	82.86
2. PP 进口	3070.06	2788.92	4162.46	3868.09	3777.71	3909.31
出口	31.13	41.66	44.77	82.90	165.83	141.60

续表

产品	2007	2008	2009	2010	2011	2012
3. PS 进口	1214. 12	1066. 25	1107. 44	1151. 99	1038. 54	979. 88
出口	308. 01	323. 44	274. 74	358. 26	355. 67	335. 27
改性的 PS 进口	—	—	195. 59	276. 79	243. 10	236. 65
出口	—	—	8. 72	14. 44	17. 16	20. 36
其他聚苯乙烯进口	1214. 12	1066. 25	911. 85	799. 29	719. 44	682. 46
出口	32. 60	29. 01	7. 25	14. 19	16. 44	16. 40
EPS 进口	109. 56	85. 25	77. 47	75. 91	75. 99	60. 77
出口	275. 43	294. 43	258. 77	329. 63	322. 07	298. 51
4. ABS 共聚物进口	217. 275	195. 186	253. 49	258. 96	204. 70	166. 54
出口	32. 36	43. 26	93. 10	94. 60	64. 250	41. 59
改性的 ABS 树脂进口	—	—	183. 38	210. 09	194. 30	169. 10
出口	—	—	21. 64	20. 74	21. 12	20. 55
ABS 共聚物进口	217. 275	195. 186	235. 15	237. 95	185. 27	149. 63
出口	32. 36	43. 26	71. 46	74. 47	43. 13	21. 04
5. PVC 进口	1410. 80	1148. 47	1971. 90	1530. 46	1336. 03	1228. 90
出口	752. 99	651. 59	278. 53	275. 24	451. 76	465. 85
聚氯乙烯糊树脂进口	—	63. 24	85. 54	98. 35	97. 11	119. 22
出口	—	7. 61	3. 29	6. 37	18. 23	8. 93
纯 PVC 进口	1014. 33	797. 54	1629. 92	1199. 12	1050. 87	940. 42
出口	711. 70	599. 56	235. 65	218. 28	367. 63	385. 63
未塑化 PVC 进口	183. 75	176. 47	167. 06	125. 10	88. 12	69. 89
出口	12. 86	5. 75	6. 34	5. 20	9. 86	9. 97
已塑化 PVC 进口	105. 80	89. 53	72. 65	88. 65	80. 34	80. 24
出口	28. 43	33. 38	29. 79	35. 93	45. 82	49. 50
以上五大通用塑计进口	13028. 72	10925. 30	18713. 48	18053. 70	16182. 09	15053. 33
出口	1299. 20	1226. 99	887. 31	1179. 13	1583. 61	1529. 90
聚酰胺(PA)进口	786. 93	854. 36	921. 99	896. 68	341. 50	336. 19
出口	102. 78	127. 28	96. 01	125. 64	94. 74	96. 74
聚碳酸酯(PC)进口	1020. 76	1017. 45	1026. 86	1264. 25	1227. 91	1374. 51
出口	306. 13	278. 59	214. 71	295. 24	237. 99	211. 75
聚甲醛(POM)进口	184. 86	178. 85	165. 95	222. 95	211. 01	213. 09
出口	39. 03	42. 98	31. 17	57. 37	65. 96	57. 52
PBT，进口	155. 10	147. 30	127. 17	163. 17	154. 30	141. 40
出口	27. 10	43. 10	51. 73	81. 81	93. 40	87. 30
聚苯硫醚进口	47. 42	49. 43	41. 79	53. 04	51. 00	52. 32
出口	6. 19	9. 35	10. 67	21. 05	26. 54	26. 32

续表

产品	2007	2008	2009	2010	2011	2012
塑料下脚料进口	5871.51	7075.17	7325.90	8009.42	8385.7.	8877.60
出口	29.06	23.60	33.29	25.97	26.98	27.98

注：资料来源：历年国家海关统计。

聚氯乙烯糊树脂2008年才单独新列出代码，无历年数据，因此无法同比。

改性的ABS树脂2009年才单独新列出代码，无历年数据，因此无法同比。

改性的聚苯乙烯2009年才单独新列出代码，无历年数据，因此无法同比。

三、消费结构

2012年PE、PP、PS、PVC、ABS五大通用塑料产量为38564.9kt，比2011年增长4.28%，占2012年合成树脂总产量的75.83%左右，比2011年减1.24%；

2012年我国合成树脂表观消费量为776997.3kt，比2011年增长4.92%。

2007～2012年间合成树脂表观消费量年均增长率为10.29%，低于同期产量年均增长率0.31%（表3、表4）。

表3　2007～2012年国内合成树脂表观消费量统计　　kt

产品	2007	2008	2009	2010	2011	2012
合成树脂	47615.58	48869.61	58339.54	70257.22	74055.46	77699.73
年增长率/%	7.17	2.63	19.38	20.42	5.41	4.92
国内总自给率/%	64.55	64.04	61.76	62.07	64.79	65.46
其中：PE	11801.42	11635.19	15977.33	17506.34	18312.55	18673.12
年增长率/%	5.40	−1.41	37.32	9.57	4.61	1.97
国内自给率/%	58.68	59.26	50.88	56.30	58.46	55.96
PP	10165.42	10079.33	12322.87	12952.47	13417.20	14983.71
年增长率/%	15.69	−0.85	22.26	5.11	3.59	11.68
国内自给率/%	70.11	72.74	66.58	70.78	73.08	74.85
PS	3072.47	2888.90	3008.10	3102.30	2958.50	3006.30
年增长率/%	6.77	−5.97	4.13	3.13	−4.64	1.59
国内自给率/%	66.94	71.34	69.81	74.41	68.60	70.65
PVC	10374.59	9313.30	10848.65	12546.44	13836.08	14024.55
年增长率/%	12.71	−10.23	16.49	15.65	10.28	1.36
国内自给率/%	93.66	94.66	84.39	90.07	93.61	94.55
ABS	3770.39	3038.60	3438.24	3650.38	3298.40	3137.19
年增长率/%	15.17	−19.41	13.15	6.17	−9.64	−4.89
国内自给率/%	43.23	37.19	38.39	42.08	45.14	48.24

注：由于改性聚苯醚无海关独立统计和产量统计，POM、PS、ABS无较完全的产量统计，故上述表中数据均为资料积累估算，仅供参考。

表 4　国内合成树脂消费结构

消费结构	比例 / %	
	2016 年	2013 年
建筑材料	33.00	32.00
包装材料	30.00	31.00
农业	9.30	9.60
家用电器	8.20	7.80
家庭用品	5.80	5.60
服装鞋帽	2.20	2.40
汽车工业	2.50	2.40
工矿配件	2.00	1.80
家具	3.00	3.20
玩具娱乐用品	2.90	3.10
医疗器械	0.90	1.00
其他	0.20	0.10
合计	100.00	100.00

在国民经济持续快速发展推动下，如今我国塑料消费量一年超过60Mt，超过美国居世界第一。

如今，中国已成为世界重要的塑料加工中心和消费大国，仅中国农用薄膜产量就居世界首位，是其它所有国家总和的2倍。

经过了2011年和2012年前三个季度的新产能消化之后，从2012年10月开始塑料又进入了新产能投放阶段。先是2012年10月大庆石化的300kt产能投产，接着10月底11月初“难产”的抚顺石化也投产了，产能是450kt。

根据计划，2013年上半年还有武汉石化和四川炼化，各300kt。原计划四川炼化明年1月投产，武汉石化2月份投产，但是目前笔者掌握的信息是武汉石化要推迟到6月份了。

虽然需求端分为国内需求和塑料直接出口两部分，但是塑料直接出口量较少。

下游需求的估算较为困难，主要原因是下游制成品中原料并不单一而且公布的产量数据也不以原料为标准来区分。

从过去12年的数据看，农膜产量2005年之前出现了负增长，特别是2004年下滑得比较严重。2005年突然爆发，产量大幅增长18.4%。之后增速下滑仍然是正增长，直到2011年再次出现小幅负增长。

但是这一年的负增长与2010年的12月份地膜产量过高有关。2012年农膜产量较2011年略有增长。

自然灾害的频发和国内消费能力的提升是农膜需求的推动力，同时考虑到农产品价格波动较大和农膜目前的消费规模，农膜的需求在2013年较2012年持平或略高，存在略低于2012年的可能性，但是不存在大幅下降的可能性。

而塑料薄膜在过去12年中除了2008年受到金融危机的冲击小幅萎缩0.2%外，其他年份都保持增长。保持增长的年份中除了2011年增速为6%外，其他年份增速均超过10%，更有7年增速超过15%。

我国汽车和家电制造商正在积极推动创新，而这将给塑料行业带来巨大商机。我国汽车行业正在开发成本较低的加工工艺和新型成型工艺，并且已经将此类工艺投入量产。

比如，汽车内饰在汽车总重量中约占到130～150kg，而目前亚洲的汽车内饰重量比欧美产的汽车要轻大约20kg。塑料约占汽车总质量的10%，占内饰质量的75%，因此在减轻内饰重量上有“很大的潜力可挖”。

将塑料与互补型材料结合起来，既能大大减轻车重，又能使功能性得到提升。

与此同时，今年以来，我国家电产业继续保持高速增长势头。作为家电产品创新和规模生产中起到极其重要作用的家电塑料模具行业，也得到快速发展。有关数据显示，家电行业塑料每年的需求量达百万吨。

未来4年全球汽车用塑料市场规模预计将以13.7%的复合年增长率继续增长，从2011年的221.55亿美元增至2016年时的421.35亿美元。

各种汽车塑料中，聚丙烯仍将是主导品种，消费量将占到总量的36%；其次是聚氨酯，占17%；ABS占12%；复合材料占11%；高密度聚乙烯占10%；聚碳酸酯占7%；聚甲基丙烯酸树脂占7%。

亚太地区将继续引领汽车塑料消费量，消费量将占到全球需求量的52%，欧洲占29%，北美占10%，其他地区占9%。

四、全球发展合成树脂发展趋势

1. 生物塑料2016年产量将达6Mt

欧洲生物塑料协会在其最新发布的年度报告中称，全球生物塑料市场的增长速度超出预期。

从现在起到2016年，目前1.2Mt的产量数字可能将翻五倍。其中生物基PET所占比例可能最大，预计未来四年这部分产能将猛增10倍。推动这一产能增长的将是生物基的非生物可降解生物塑料类，“特别是所谓的‘直接替代’解决方案”，如生物基的聚乙烯和PET。“其中占据先导部分的将是生物基PET，现已占到全球生物塑料产能的大约40%。到2016年的产能将超过4.6Mt。”这将占到生物塑料总产能的80%。排在PET之后的是生物基聚乙烯，产能数为250kt，占总产能的比例超过4%。

2. 全球聚烯烃生产能力正在逐步转移

20年前，西欧和北美的聚乙烯(PE)产能几乎占了全球产能的三分之二，但是预计到2015年，西欧和北美的聚乙烯产能将只占全球差能的三分之一，取而代之的是这些地区将会成为主要的进口国。

2015年，尽管中国仍然是一个进口大国，但是中东，中国以及亚洲/太平洋地区的市场份额将会有三倍的增长，聚乙烯产能的市场占有率会超过一半。同时，全球的总产能将会翻两番，聚丙烯的产能数据也与聚乙烯的相似。CBI的统计数据显示，2010年中国大陆有324万吨/年的新建PE和PP产能将陆续投产。

随着中东越来越多的聚烯烃产能的投产，预计2015年供需平衡将会更加的日趋恶化。2015年，聚丙烯/聚乙烯的处境将更为艰难。由于供需平衡状况的不理想，来年全世界的PE和PP开工率远远低于100%。

虽然预测声明2015年亚洲的需求将增长5%～6%，但是，在欧洲和美国预计需求增长将会趋于平缓。

而造成PE/PP产能过剩的“剩余因素”之一就是聚烯烃供应的产业健康状况不佳。许多企业装置都已经过了最佳的生产期了，但是仍然在开工运作。

PE/PP装置产能的盈余期大概是十年，抑或可以持续到十二年左右。据统计，实现一个PE或PP产业供应链需要十年甚至二十年的时间。

2012年国内外陆续有几百万吨乙烯装置投产。

尤其是中东PE/PP产能的激增给全球市场带来更大的竞争压力。由此还衍生出一系列问题，产品单一、高端产品缺失，产业发展不平衡，产能过剩，开工率低，库存积压等。

3. 全球聚合物市场竞争加剧

A. 需求增速放缓产能持续扩增

全球聚合物行业目前再次陷入困境，成熟经济体的聚合物市场需求还远没有恢复到危机前的水平，欧洲债务危机恶化、资本市场的波动以及全球经济增速减缓令市场信心受挫。一方面中印两国需求增速放缓，另一方面美国和中东的出口不断增多，全球聚合物市场竞争再度加剧。

B. 中印需求增速放缓

中国是全球最大的聚合物消费市场。2011年中国聚合物市场需求达到4900万吨，占全球总需求的27%。

受政府实施积极的经济刺激措施影响，2008年后中国聚合物消费市场快速复苏。2009年和2010年中国聚乙烯(PE)和聚氯乙烯(PVC)需求连续两年实现两位数的增长，但是2011年中国聚合物需求估计增长5.6%，比2010年11%的增速将回落5.4%。

步入2012年中国政府将GDP增长目标调低，投资和需求将有所下滑。此外，受欧洲债务危机和美国经济前景堪忧的影响，中国塑料成品和半成品出口也将下降。受这两方面因素影响，2012年中国的聚合物需求增速将放缓，从而影响全球聚合物市场。

快速增长的印度聚合物市场在2011年也受到了冲击。自2011年第二季度起，工业生产放缓以及政府为抑制通货膨胀采取了紧缩的信贷政策，导致通用合成树脂需求增速减慢。受国内下游市场需求疲软以及出口美国、欧洲和中国市场需求下降的影响，印度聚合物生产商不得已下调了开工率。这种状况在2012年仍将持续。

C. 美国出口竞争力增强

页岩气革命令美国裂解生产商陆续转向使用更为廉价的乙烷作为原料，从而增强了美国PE和PVC生产商的出口竞争力。乙烷的价格优势令美国乙烯产业链的盈利表现抢眼，刺激了石化生产商们进一步加大原料轻质化的投资力度，提高了石化产品的出口竞争能力。

2011年美国PE出口量估计达到4.3Mt，PVC出口量估计为2.9Mt。其中PVC出口量估计比上年增长6.4%，出口至墨西哥、巴西、智利、委内瑞拉、俄罗斯、中国、中东和北非国家的聚合物出现强劲增长，而出口至加拿大、欧洲和东南亚地区的量减少。

美国还是PP主要出口国，2011年出口了1.8Mt，但因丙烯原料缺乏，PP出口前景堪忧。这是因为石脑油裂解装置转而使用更为轻质的乙烷原料，同时一些炼油厂关闭导致炼油厂丙烯供应的减少。2011年美国聚苯乙烯(PS)净出口量约为350kt，主要是受到苯市场波动的冲击。

D. 中东产能继续扩张

中东竞争者给亚洲PE和PP生产商带来的压力日趋增加。今年1月沙特朱拜勒工业园区的电力供应中断，刺激远东市场PE和PP价格暂时反弹。不过未来几个月，受该工业园区的电力供应恢复正常以及中东地区新增产能投产的影响，聚合物生产利润将受到挤压。

沙特聚合物有限公司位于朱拜勒的聚合物项目将在2012年正式投产，该项目包括两套550kt/a高密度聚乙烯(HDPE)/线型低密度聚乙烯(LLDPE)装置、一套400kt/a PP装置和两套100kt/a聚苯乙烯(PS)装置。沙特卡扬石化的一套300kt/a低密度聚乙烯(LDPE)装置将在2012年中期投产。卡塔尔石化公司也将开启位于梅萨伊德的一套300kt/a LDPE装置。

此外，美国埃克森美孚化学位于新加坡裕廊岛上的两套650kt/a PE装置将在2012年开始投产。

印度的印度斯坦石油和米塔尔能源公司(HMEL)将在2013年4月份开启位于Punjiab的一套440kt/a均聚PP装置。

印度芒格洛尔炼化公司(MRPL)位于芒格洛尔的一套440kt/a PP装置也将在今年内投产。

4. 中国聚烯烃需求增长 亚洲出口国获益

随着中国对聚烯烃的需求持续增长，泰国和新加坡将从对华聚烯烃出口中获得丰厚利润。

东南亚国家对中国的出口在过去十年里已经增加了三倍，GlobalData公司预期，亚洲各国之间现有的贸易协定将促进塑料业务的进一步增长。

聚烯烃是全球消费量最大的聚合物，其中聚乙烯和聚丙烯是两种最常见的类型，被用于包装、建筑和汽车等领域。

东南亚国家生产的很大一部分聚烯烃被出口到中国市场，中国是全球最大的聚烯烃进口国和消费国。

中国对聚烯烃的需求预计将从2011年的每年31.5Mt增至2016年的41.1Mt，年增长率达到5.5%。

东盟的缔结使得成员国占据了彼此贸易往来的有利位置，因为根据东盟自由贸易协定，成员国之间的贸易可以免征进口税。

新加坡和泰国都是东盟成员国，而中国已经签订了中国-东盟自由贸易协定，同样也采取零进口税机制，这有助于增加这些国家之间的经济贸易。

泰国是对中国最大的聚烯烃出口国，也是东南亚聚烯烃行业中聚乙烯和聚丙烯消费量和产量最大的国家。

泰国湾大量的天然气储备为泰国带来了充足的原料，而位于东部沿海的罗勇府的聚烯烃工厂占据了靠近海运路线的地理优势。

新加坡也在逐步扩大其作为石化产品出口国的影响力。新加坡本身对聚烯烃的需求不是太大，已经成为对其他亚洲国家重要的聚烯烃出口国，凭借其理想的地理位置和健全的石化产品出口基础设施，吸引了出口企业的关注。新加坡还是中东对亚洲进口的全球转运枢纽，以发挥其零进口税的优势。

其他亚洲国家也进口聚合物，给泰国和新加坡带来了更多的业务。印度尼西亚是东南亚第二大的聚烯烃树脂消费国，但因其国内产能增长不足而依赖进口。越南也缺乏足够的生产基础设施来满足国内的聚烯烃需求，在过去十年里，其需求量保持着每年15%以上的高速增长。

东南亚的聚乙烯需求预计将从2011年的4.9Mt增至2016年的6.2Mt，而同一时期的产量预计将从6.3Mt增至9.3Mt。

该地区对聚丙烯的需求预计将从2011年的3.6Mt增至2016年的4.7Mt，同一时期的产量预计将从3.72Mt持续增长至6.18Mt，主要是因为有多座新厂将投产。

第二章 2012年聚乙烯产量进口增长出口下降

一、2012年国内生产发展概况

A. 国内生产

2012年抚顺石化年产750kt和大庆石化年产600kt聚乙烯新增装置已经建成，在9月正式投产(表5、表6)。

表5 2006~2012年聚乙烯产量统计表

项 目	2006年	2007年	2008年	2009年	2010年	2011年	2012年
生产能力/kt	6820	7685	7850	9300	13000	14000	14500
产量/kt	5993.00	6924.70	6894.70	8128.54	9856.84	10050.00	10450.00
开工率%	87.87	90.11	87.83	87.40	75.82	71.78	72.07
年产量增长率/%	13.28	15.55	-0.43	17.90	21.26	1.96	3.98

2006~2012年，聚乙烯产量年均增长率为9.71%。

表6 2013年1~12月聚乙烯产量统计表

聚乙烯产品种类	产量/kt	同比增长/%
低密度聚乙烯 LDPE	1959.44	5.68
高密度聚乙烯 HDPE	3068.34	-5.43
线性低密度聚乙烯 LLDPE	3355.10	-0.89
中密度聚乙烯 MDPE	31.68	-18.99
超高分子量聚乙烯 UHMW	143.45	6.52

2013年2月中国石油化工股份有限公司齐鲁分公司总投资8.77亿元新建的250kt/a聚乙烯装置一次投料成功。

据介绍，此装置既能生产高密度聚乙烯专用料产品，也可根据市场需要随时调整生产低密度和中密度树脂产品，从而实现中低高多种密度聚乙烯产品生产。这一项目的挤压造粒机组和循环气压缩机组首次实现国产化，填补了国内空白。

B. 工艺技术发展

1. 燕化形成高附加值新型工程塑料聚乙烯生

产链

2012 年，燕山石化聚乙烯专用料储存与包装设施项目完成联动试车，至此，燕化多种聚乙烯高端产品形成完整生产链。

目前，随着国内新建项目不断上马，聚乙烯装置盈利能力下降，而国内高端聚乙烯树脂又依赖进口。面对国内竞争加剧的不利局面，燕山石化依靠企业技术优势，重点转向开发聚乙烯高附加值高端产品，成功开发出聚乙烯瓶盖专用料、橡胶型氯化聚乙烯电缆专用料、过氧化物交联聚乙烯管材料等新产品。这些新产品不仅填补了国内空白，而且生产能耗大幅降低，市场售价比普通产品每吨高出千余元。

燕山石化此次批量生产的是分子量为 150 万～350 万超高分子量聚乙烯（UHMW－PE）9100CG、9200CG、9300CG 系列产品，经过检验，各项指标均达到质量要求，且下游用户在进行生产试用以后，对该产品性能和质量较为满意，表示愿意建立长期合作关系。

为了满足密封要求，国内不少瓶盖和瓶盖内衬使用添加了增塑剂的塑料制品，由此带来增塑剂迁移污染隐患，燕化开发的聚乙烯瓶盖专用料省去了造粒和添加剂环节，达到了环保卫生要求。

2. 交联聚乙烯专用料批量生产

经过 5 年的开发研究，先后完成了小试、中试和工业化实验，由辽阳石化公司自主研发的高密度聚乙烯（HDPE）新产品——交联聚乙烯专用树脂 J0253P 开始批量生产。截至 2012 年 12 月 3 日，该产品已累计生产 2282t。

该产品的成功量产，打破了国外公司技术和产品垄断，填补了国内空白，推动了中国石油聚乙烯新产品的产业化进程，成为企业新的效益增长点。

据了解，交联聚乙烯专用料开发项目是辽阳石化承担研发的中国石油重点新产品开发项目之一，于 2007 年 9 月立项。该产品是地暖塑料管材生产主要原料之一，具有产品粒度均匀、大小适宜、相对分子质量分布较窄的特点。其制品内外表面光滑，流动阻力小，不易霉变，不易滋生细菌，同时，具有较强的抗溶剂、化学药品腐蚀能力和抗冲击性，并具有较强的耐磨性、耐老化性，在 70℃的水温和 1 兆帕的流体压力下使用寿命可达 50 年。

3. 茂石化开发高挺高强 PE 膜料

2012 年，茂名石化研发的高挺度、高强度聚乙烯（PE）薄膜料 HXF5107 新产品在其高密度聚乙烯装置实现工业化生产，第一批产品产量 1540t。

据了解，该牌号是高密度聚乙烯薄膜料 TR144 的改进型产品，部分关键指标优于 TR144，密度达到 951kg/m^3，可有效提高制成品强度，主要用于制作购物袋、复合包装膜、衬垫、重包装膜、农膜、食品袋、箱子内衬等，也可与其他工艺生产的聚乙烯掺混用于管材和中空容器。目前，国内市场对高强、高挺聚乙烯膜料的需求量逐年上升，市场需求缺口较大，很大部分依赖进口。

4. 钢管防腐专用料有望规模生产

2012 年，宝鸡石油钢管有限责任公司正式展开埋地钢质管道聚乙烯防腐专用料装置改造，以期早日实现万吨级规模化生产。据悉，该专用料将应用于西气东输等国内工程的建设。

据介绍，该产品由中国石油独山子石化公司、宝鸡石油钢管有限责任公司、西南化工销售公司共同开发。

2012 年 10 月 18 日该产品通过中国石油组织的产品鉴定后，开始进行万吨级装置改造。

埋地钢质管道聚乙烯防腐专用料以独山子石化公司开发生产的聚乙烯管材料 TUB121N3000 和 DGDZ2400 为基础树脂，经过 3PE 聚乙烯防腐专用料配方改性及其制备工艺技术研究，由宝鸡石油钢管公司生产出两种 3PE 聚乙烯防腐专用料 BSG－PE01 和 BSG－PE02。该产品主要性能指标（包括拉伸强度、3PE 防腐层整体性能等）满足国标要求，其中拉伸强度、断裂伸长率、维卡软化点、氧化诱导期等主要技术指标优于国内同类产品，达到国内领先水平。

该防腐专用料研发项目为中国石油科技项目，2011 年 4 月 1 日立项，在项目承担方的相互配合下，产品顺利完成工业化试生产以及第三方检测，实现了中国石油内部资源的上下游优化。

5. 高熔指线型聚乙烯试产成功

2012 年 9 月 21 日，茂名石化研发的高熔指线型聚乙烯新产品在化工分部全密度装置首次实现工业化试产，产量达到 500t。

该产品熔融指数高达 50g/10min，耐环境应力开裂性好，主要用于生产热塑性粉末涂料，还可用于注塑产品。茂名石化近期已与部分聚烯烃改性、粉末涂料等下游厂家达成试用意向，待产品完成测试后将送厂试用。

6. 上海石化成为国内首家生产医用聚乙烯树脂专用料企业

目前，上海石化 Q281D 高压低密度聚乙烯新产品通过上海市食品药品包装材料测试所权威检测，符合国家食药监局颁布的国家药品包装膜、袋材料标准。

这标志着国内首款可安全使用于医药包装的低

密度聚乙烯树脂专用料在上海石化诞生，并可以实现工业化生产。

这也是中国石化系统内高压低密度聚乙烯产品在医药包装领域中首次达标并满足用户需求。

据了解，在国家药品包装膜、袋材料标准中，对聚乙烯材料的检测标准包括外观、隔阻性能、机械性能、重金属含量等，其中，最重要的标准是正己烷溶出物。

上海石化塑料部2号聚乙烯装置生产的Q281D高压低密度聚乙烯产品所制成的薄膜的正己烷溶出物为24mg，低于国家药品包装膜、袋材料标准值30mg，其他各项性能指标也均满足标准要求。

7. 技术开发——超高分子量聚乙烯树脂工艺技术开发成功

由齐鲁石化研究院承担的“超高分子量聚乙烯技术开发”荣获科技进步一等奖，是齐鲁石化唯一的获奖项目。

该项目从小试、中试到万吨级以上工业装置实现全流程开发，形成了具有自主知识产权集成创新的国际先进水平的超高分子量聚乙烯(UHMWPE)树脂工艺技术。利用该技术在齐鲁公司建成了3000t/a UHMWPE生产装置，产销量均达到每年2000t以上。

超高分子量聚乙烯(UHMWPE)其分子结构与普通聚乙烯基本相同，但物理机械性能却极为出色，具有广阔的市场发展前景。研究院科研人员通过充分的技术调研，设计建成了流程合理、功能完备的聚乙烯催化剂配制装置和采用先进DCS控制的具有聚合反应动力学研究功能的乙烯聚合小试装置。

开发出了UHMWPE纤维专用树脂，经检测和纺丝试验验证，其主要性能达到甚至超过了国外专用树脂水平。

鉴于迅速增长的市场需求，该院将原1500t/a UHMWPE工业化生产装置扩能到3000t/a。在该装置上开发生产的纤维和管材专用树脂满足了用户的特殊要求。

同时产品用于多规格的板材、管材和异型材生产，质量得到进一步提升，产生了显著的社会效益和经济效益。

该院又通过工业化数据采集和工程放大研究，自主完成了万吨级以上连续生产工业装置工艺包的基础设计，为形成国内集成创新的UHMWPE树脂全流程工艺技术打下了基础。其投资和生产成本与国外相比有明显优势。

近年来，随着市场对UHMWPE性能认识的提高和加工技术的进步，UHMWPE在高附加值的制品领域也得到了快速发展。尤其是新产品特种纤维专用树脂的开发成功，不仅拓宽了产品应用领域，提高了产品的附加值，还可降低特种纤维行业对国外产品的依赖程度，有利于促进行业发展，具有良好的社会效益。

8. 聚乙烯淋膜专用料工业化生产

2012年，茂名石化研究院与化工分部共同开发的高压聚乙烯淋膜专用料666－000在1号高压聚乙烯装置实现工业化生产，首批产品达到1057t。

据了解，该产品熔指为4.0g/10min，不含爽滑剂、开口剂，流动性优于旧牌号产品，在下游主要用于涂覆在纸张、薄膜、无纺布、编织布等柔性基材表面形成复合材料。

二、2012年国内聚乙烯树脂出口生产省市集中在东部沿海地区

1. 2012年初级形状的聚乙烯(相对密度小于0.94)出口同比下降

2012年初级形状的聚乙烯(相对密度小于0.94)出口省市有22家，比上年20家增加2个出口省市，出口6990228879758179kg，同比下降12.26%。

初级形状的聚乙烯(相对密度小于0.94)出口生产企业主要集中在上海市，出口数量17596103kg，占总出口数量的25.172%，比上年减少出口数量22.47%；

其次为广东省，出口数量14788868kg，占总出口数量的21.156%，比上年减少出口数量35.46%；

上海市，广东省，江苏省，山东省和浙江省五省市出口数量占初级形状的聚乙烯(相对密度小于0.94)2012年总出口数量的83.024%，比上年减少1.707%(表7)。

表7　2012年初级形状聚乙烯(相对密度小于0.94)20大出口省市统计

排序	出口省市	出口金额/美元	出口数量/kg	占比例/%
1	上海市	27531186.00	17596103	25.172
2	广东省	24305131.00	14788868	21.156
3	江苏省	21306471.00	11714549	16.758
4	山东省	9627220.00	8133680	11.636
5	浙江省	10843868.00	5802502	8.301
出口总计		110555319.00	69902288	100.00

2. 2012年初级形状的聚乙烯(相对密度在0.94及以上)出口同比下降

2012年初级形状的聚乙烯(相对密度在0.94及以上)出口省市有22家，与上年24家出口省市减少2家出口省市，出口134956984kg，出口同比下降23.30%。

2012年初级形状的聚乙烯(相对密度在0.94及以上)出口生产企业主要集中在广东省，出口数量

92116652kg，占总出口数量的 68.256%%，比上年增加出口数量 14.90%；

其次为上海市出口数量 22977912kg，占总出口数量的 33.32%，比上年出口下降 60.81%；

江苏省出口数量 5815570kg，占总出口数量的 4.309%，比上年出口数量下降 16.40%。

广东省，上海市，江苏省，山东省和河北省五省市出口数量占初级形状的聚乙烯(相对密度在 0.94 及以上)2012 年总出口数量的 95.484%，比上年上升 0.264%(表 8)。

表 8 2012 年初级形状的聚乙烯(HDPE) 24 大出口省市统计

排序	出口省市	出口金额/美元	出口数量/kg	占比例/%
1	广东省	136326239.00	92116652	68.256
2	上海市	33613799.00	22977912	17.026
3	江苏省	8137921.00	5815570	4.309
4	山东省	7785202.00	4962082	3.677
5	河北省	3536869.00	2990488	2.216
出口总计		199685243.00	134956984	100.00

3. 2012 年初级形状的线型低密度聚乙烯(LLDPE)出口同比上升

2012 年初级形状的线型低密度聚乙烯(LLDPE)出口省市有 22 家，与上年 16 家增加 6 家，出口 82861210kg，同比上升 24.89%。

2012 年初级形状的线型低密度聚乙烯出口生产企业主要集中在广东省出口数量 44014265kg，占总出口数量的 53.118%，比上年出口数量上升 61.04%；

其次为上海市，出口数量 29402028kg，占总出口数量的 35.483%，比上年出口数量下降 3.65%；

天津市出口数量 2664300kg，占总出口数量的 3.215%，比上年出口数量下降 12.18%。

广东省，上海市，天津市，山东省和浙江省五省市出口数量占初级形状的线型低密度聚乙烯 2012 年总出口数量的 96.324%，比上年下降 0.159%(表 9)。

表 9 2012 年线型低密度聚乙烯 LLDPE 5 大出口省市统计

排序	出口省市	出口金额/美元	出口数量/kg	占比例/%
1	广东省	65188314.00	44014265	53.118
2	上海市	40874522.00	29402028	35.483
3	天津市	3803352.00	2664300	3.215
4	山东省	2678025.00	1900140	2.293
5	浙江省	2515884.00	1834512	2.214
出口总计		119651001.00	82861210	100.00

三、2012 年初级形状聚乙烯出口商以改性聚乙烯树脂为主

1. 初级形状聚乙烯(相对密度小于 0.94)LDPE

2012 年初级形状聚乙烯(相对密度小于 0.94)出口商共计有 436 家，比上年 445 家减少 9 家出口商。

出口额最高的十大出口商有六家为生产企业，余四家为贸易商，十大出口商出口数量占总出口数量的 46.886%。

2012 年初级形状聚乙烯(相对密度小于 0.94)二十大出口商中大生产企业仅占六家，出口数量占总出口数量的 26.906%，仅有一家为聚乙烯树脂原料生产厂，余均为改性聚乙烯树脂(即 PE 合金)生产企业。

2012 年初级形状聚乙烯(相对密度小于 0.94)二十大出口商中大贸易商占十四家，出口数量占总出口数量的 33.863%(表 10)。

表 10 2012 年初级形状聚乙烯(相对密度小于 0.94)二十大出口商统计

排序	出口商	所属行业	出口数量/kg	占比例/%
1	赛拉尼斯(上海)国际贸易有限公司	改性聚乙烯	6057125	8.665
2	上海虹丹物流有限公司	贸易商	5709325	8.168
3	淄博广龙塑料工贸有限公司	贸易商	3401625	4.866
4	上海合冠仓储有限公司	贸易商	3275900	4.686
5	常州盖亚材料科技有限公司	改性聚乙烯	2821830	4.037
6	广州番禺光耀星瀚塑料有限公司	改性聚乙烯	2728000	3.903
7	浙江远大高分子材料有限公司	改性聚乙烯	2668100	3.817
8	中国石化化工销售有限公司广州经营部	聚乙烯树脂	2510000	3.591
9	浙江万马高分子材料股份有限公司	改性聚乙烯	2022100	2.893
10	珠海保税区好利工贸有限公司	贸易商	1579500	2.260
11	青岛保税区中启联合物流有限公司	贸易商	1441000	2.061

续表

排序	出口商	所属行业	出口数量/kg	占比例/%
12	东莞市对外加工装配服务公司	贸易商	1085375	1.553
13	广州保税区玮骏国际贸易有限公司	贸易商	1083500	1.550
14	丹东诚通贸易有限公司	贸易商	1076075	1.539
15	不详	贸易商	996550	1.426
16	上海旌凯贸易发展有限公司	贸易商	966000	1.382
17	上海泽林物流有限公司	贸易商	792750	1.134
18	大连保税区盛泉国际工贸有限公司	贸易商	771000	1.103
19	青岛泺亨物流有限公司	贸易商	750500	1.074
20	广州畅浩货运代理有限公司	贸易商	742500	1.062
	出口总计		69902288	60.769

2. 初级形状聚乙烯相对密度在 0.94 及以上(HDPE)

2012 年初级形状聚乙烯(HDPE)出口商共计有 371 家，比上年 389 家出口商减少 18 家出口商；

出口额最高的十位出口商仅二家为生产企业，八家为贸易商，十大出口商出口数量占总出口数量的 81.255%。

2012 年初级形状聚乙烯(HDPE)四十大出口商中生产企业仅占九家，出口数量占总出口数量的 4.917%，无聚乙烯树脂原料生产厂，均为改性聚乙烯树脂(即 PE 合金)工业生产企业。

2012 年初级形状聚乙烯(HDPE)四十大出口商中贸易商占三十一家，出口数量占总出口数量的 86.801%(表 11)

表 11　2012 年初级形状的聚乙烯(HDPE)四十大出口商统计

排序	出口商	所属行业	出口数量/kg	占比例/%
1	广东合捷国际供应链有限公司	贸易商	87721536	65.000
2	上海雅胜物流有限公司	贸易商	5308475	3.933
3	不详	贸易商	3352516	2.484
4	上海合冠仓储有限公司	贸易商	3158500	2.340
5	上海虹丹物流有限公司	贸易商	2042000	1.513
6	浙江中大新佳贸易有限公司	贸易商	1909500	1.415
7	珠海保税区好利工贸有限公司	贸易商	1829325	1.355
8	常州市登峰塑料有限公司	改性 PE 树脂	1600000	1.186
9	苏州康斯坦普工程塑料有限公司	改性 PE 树脂	1467120	1.087
10	青岛保税区中启联合物流有限公司	贸易商	1271000	0.942
11	上海贝莱特塑胶有限公司	改性 PE 树脂	1131800	0.839
12	隆控物流(上海)有限公司	贸易商	940500	0.697
13	丹东诚通贸易有限公司	贸易商	798600	0.592
14	上海林达塑胶化工有限公司	改性 PE 树脂	795600	0.590
15	上海仓吉物流有限公司	贸易商	721500	0.535
16	上海天隆五金有限公司	贸易商	702000	0.520
17	威海东韩机械设备有限公司	贸易商	663010	0.491
18	上海黎仓物流有限公司	贸易商	652500	0.483
19	中国燕山联合对外贸易有限公司	贸易商	612000	0.453
20	青岛太平洋海洋工程有限公司	贸易商	540000	0.400
21	上海联成国际有限公司	贸易商	486800	0.361
22	广州保税区新纪元物流有限公司	贸易商	470250	0.348
23	丹东科华经贸有限公司	贸易商	465000	0.345
24	沙提(上海)热熔胶有限公司	改性 PE 树脂	417884	0.310

续表

排序	出口商	所属行业	出口数量/kg	占比例/%
25	淄博新塑化工有限公司	改性PE树脂	364450	0.270
26	不详	贸易商	346500	0.257
27	中国水电建设集团国际工程有限公司	贸易商	330000	0.245
28	舒尔曼塑料(东莞)有限公司	改性PE树脂	324800	0.241
29	上海外联发物流有限公司	贸易商	318125	0.236
30	不详	贸易商	303750	0.225
31	中国机械设备进出口总公司	贸易商	300000	0.222
32	上海遨翔物流有限公司	贸易商	292500	0.217
33	广州保税区玮骏国际贸易有限公司	贸易商	283250	0.210
34	山东省梁山县全兴塑料有限公司	改性PE树脂	281750	0.209
35	不详	贸易商	273800	0.203
36	宁波保税区广盛物流有限公司	贸易商	272000	0.202
37	常州皇博进出口有限公司	贸易商	270000	0.200
38	不详	贸易商	265000	0.196
39	常州双欧板业有限公司	改性PE树脂	249530	0.185
40	广州捷飞物流有限公司	贸易商	247500	0.183
出口总计			134956984	91.718

3. 线型低密度聚乙烯 LLDPE

2012 年线型低密度聚乙烯 LLDPE 出口商共计有 175 家，比上年 LLDPE 出口商 178 家域少 3 家，出口额最高的十位出口商中九家为贸易商，出口数量占总出口数量的 64.650%。

2012 年线型低密度聚乙烯 LLDPE 二十大出口商中十九为贸易商，出口数量占总出口数量的 73.313%(表 12)。

表 12　2012 年线型低密度聚乙烯 LLDPE1 二十大出口商统计

排序	出口商	所属行业	出口数量/kg	占比例/%
1	广东合捷国际供应链有限公司	贸易商	26606584	32.110
2	上海虹丹物流有限公司	贸易商	5891250	7.110
3	上海合冠仓储有限公司	贸易商	5851750	7.062
4	中化国际贸易股份有限公司	贸易商	4235000	5.111
5	珠海保税区好利工贸有限公司	贸易商	3708175	4.475
6	上海泽林物流有限公司	贸易商	1666500	2.011
7	丰顺正通高分子材料有限公司	改性PE树脂	1609225	1.942
8	隆控物流(上海)有限公司	贸易商	1479250	1.785
9	上海遨翔物流有限公司	贸易商	1287000	1.553
10	不详	贸易商	1235275	1.491
11	天津天保国际物流有限公司	贸易商	1204500	1.454
12	上海雅胜物流有限公司	贸易商	1074325	1.297
13	天保名门(天津)国际货运代理有限公司	贸易商	990000	1.195
14	上海经贸物流有限公司	贸易商	982500	1.186
15	广州保税区玮骏国际贸易有限公司	贸易商	950750	1.147
16	宁波保税区太平仓储有限公司	贸易商	816750	0.986
17	上海金港实业有限公司	贸易商	742500	0.896
18	广州保税区新纪元物流有限公司	贸易商	715500	0.863
19	上海仓吉物流有限公司	贸易商	660500	0.797
20	青岛保税区中启联合物流有限公司	贸易商	649500	0.784
出口总计			82861210	75.255

四、2012年国内聚乙烯树脂总进口小幅增长出口大幅上升

2012年，我国共进口聚乙烯8768.7kt，同比增长7.23%；

2012年出口聚乙烯545.6kt，同比下降4.32%。

2012年国内聚乙烯对外依存度为44.04%，比2011年我国聚乙烯对外总依存度上升2.50%(表13)。

表13　2007～2012年PE进出口统计　t

产　品		2007年	2008年	2009年	2010年	2011年	2012年
PE(相对密度≤0.94)	进口	772597	708216	1349546	1383982	1460299	1571136
	出口	15575	16970	24007	78832	79758	69902
PE(相对密度≥0.94)	进口	2091227	2312588	3859125	3495708	3526400	4009781
	出口	37946	39862	30633	61003	175958	134957
LLDPE	进口	1670555	1475755	2200894	2478394	2457079	2306862
	出口	6857	9948	7302	18228	66349	82861
乙烯－乙酸乙烯酯共聚物	进口	427368	363573	505635	478865	500754	607547
	出口	24127	34469	39335	45904	48669	53587
其他乙烯聚合物	进口	89679	90664	151022	187522	232581	273375
	出口	90202	109056	116148	171001	199474	204279
合计	进口	5051426	4950796	8066222	8024471	8177113	8768701
	出口	174707	210303	217425	374968	570208	545586
净进口合计		4876719	4740493	7848797	7649503	7606905	8223115
年增长率/%		－6.11	－2.79	65.57	－2.54	－0.56	8.10

注：上述数据均摘自海关进出口统计，其他非正常进出口均不包括在上述。

2007～2012年间，PE进口增长73.59%；年均增长11.66%；

2007～2012年间，PE出口增长212.29%；年均增长25.58%；

2007～2012年间，PE净进口增长68.62%；年均增长11.02%。

分析显示，沙特阿拉伯、伊朗、韩国、泰国和新加坡依然是中国进口PE前五大产地，2012年五大产地进口量占中国进口总量的60.56%，比2011年增长6.88%。

中东、泰国、马来西亚、俄罗斯等周边国家近年来也在大规模扩建聚乙烯生产装置，除了满足他们本国需求外，主要是为向中国出口。

2012年，从中东沙特阿拉伯、伊朗、卡塔尔、科威特、阿拉伯联合酋长国八国进口聚乙烯超过411万吨，比2011年269.14万吨增加进口数量52.22%；占中国进口总量的50.12%。

2012年中东仍为世界上最大的聚乙烯出口地区。

1. 初级形状的聚乙烯(相对密度小于0.94)LDPE进口上升出口下降

从海关统计中可看出，2012年初级形状的聚乙烯(相对密度小于0.94)进口地有53个，比上年55个减少2个进口地，进口量为1571135604kg，同比增加7.59%。

主要进口地为伊朗，进口数量422353060kg，占总进口数量的26.882%，比上年增加进口数量41.82%；

其次为韩国，进口数量161878299kg，占总进口数量的10.303%%，比上年增加进口数量0.60%；

马来西亚进口数量132273455kg，占总进口数量的8.419%，比上年减少进口数量6.50%；

沙特阿拉伯进口数量121164856kg，占总进口数量的7.712%，比上年增加进口数量3.28%；

卡塔尔进口数量106087058kg，占总进口数量的6.752%，比上年减少进口数量16.31%；

五原产进口地进口数量占初级形状的聚乙烯(相对密度小于0.94)2012年总进口数量的60.068%，比上年增加2.258%。

2012年，从中东伊朗、卡塔尔、沙特阿拉伯、阿拉伯联合酋长国、以色列、科威特、约旦七国进口初级形状的聚乙烯(相对密度小于0.94)超过82万吨，比上年增加超过26万吨，占中国初级形状的聚乙烯(相对密度小于0.94)进口总量的52.321%，比上年增加13.511%。

2012 年中东仍是世界上最大的聚乙烯出口地区（表 14）。

表 14 2012 年初级形状聚乙烯（相对密度小于 0.94）五大进口国家/地区和中东进口国家/地区统计

排序	原产进口地	进口金额/美元	进口数量/kg	占比例/%
1	伊朗	548796761.00	422353060	26.882
2	韩国	231958628.00	161878299	10.303
3	马来西亚	177674387.00	132273455	8.419
4	沙特阿拉伯	162613811.00	121164856	7.712
5	卡塔尔	146512397.00	106087058	6.752
进口总计		2245723103.00	1571135604	100.00

从海关统计中可看出，2012 年初级形状的聚乙烯（相对密度小于 0.94）出口地有 108 个，比上年 107 个出口地增加 1 个出口地，出口 69902288kg，同比下降 12.36%。

主要出口地为韩国出口数量 8745646kg，占总出口数量的 12.511，比上年增加出口数量 37.79%；

其次为越南，出口数量 7170160kg，占总出口数量的 10.257%，比上年减少出口数量 21.86%；

泰国，出口数量 5171096kg，占总出口数量的 7.398%；

沙特阿拉伯出口数量 3861550kg，占总出口数量的 5.524%；

朝鲜出口数量 3463892kg，占总出口数量的 4.955%；

五出口地 2012 年初级形状的聚乙烯（相对密度小于 0.94）出口量占总出口量的 40.646%，比上年增加 2.085%（表 15）。

表 15 2012 年初级形状聚乙烯（相对密度小于 0.94）五大出口国家/地区统计

排序	出口目的地	出口金额/美元	出口数量/kg	占比例/%
1	韩国	14205128.00	8745646	12.511
2	越南	8702949.00	7170160	10.257
3	泰国	9963724.00	5171096	7.398
4	沙特阿拉伯	7085973.00	3861550	5.524
5	朝鲜	4970204.00	3463892	4.955
出口总计		110555319.00	69902288	100.00

2. 初级形状的聚乙烯（相对密度在 0.94 及以上）进口上升出口下降

从海关统计中可看出，2012 年初级形状的聚乙烯（相对密度在 0.94 及以上）进口地有 61 个，比上年 62 个减少 1 个进口地，进口量为 4009781076kg，同比增加 13.71%。

主要进口地为沙特阿拉伯，进口数量 702364396kg，占总进口数量的 17.516%，比上年增加进口数量 24.26%；

其次为韩国，进口数量 651616275kg，占总进口数量的 16.251%，比上年进口数量下降 0.86%；

伊朗进口数量 645527445kg，占总进口数量的 16.099%，比上年增加少进口数量 57.55%；

阿拉伯联合酋长国进口数量 435014694kg，占总进口数量的 10.849%，比上年增加进口数量 7.34%；

泰国进口数量 309487389kg，占总进口数量的 7.718%，比上年增加进口数量 0.40%；

五进口地进口量占 2012 年初级形状的聚乙烯（相对密度在 0.94 及以上）总进口量的 68.433%，比上年增加 13.531%。

2012 年，来自中东地区的初级形状的聚乙烯（相对密度在 0.94 及以上）供应大幅增加。

其中，沙特阿拉伯跃居中国第一大 HDPE 进口国，伊朗、阿拉伯联合酋长国、卡塔尔、科威特分列中国 HDPE 进口国分列第三、四、六、八位。

2012 年，从中东沙特阿拉伯、伊朗、阿拉伯联合酋长国、卡塔尔、科威特、埃及、阿曼、苏丹八国进口初级形状的聚乙烯（相对密度在 0.94 及以上）超过 248.03 万吨、占中国初级形状的聚乙烯（相对密度在 0.94 及以上）进口总量的 61.857%（表 16）。

表 16 2012 年初级形状的聚乙烯（HDPE）五大进口国家/地区统计

排序	原产进口地	进口金额/美元	进口数量/kg	占比例/%
1	沙特阿拉伯	940605867.00	702364396	17.516
2	韩国	965655697.00	651616275	16.251
3	伊朗	851945626.00	645527445	16.099
4	阿拉伯联合酋长国	539321055.00	435014694	10.849
5	泰国	425908755.00	309487389	7.718
进口总计		5516815241.00	4009781076	100.00

从海关统计中可看出，2012 年初级形状的聚乙烯（相对密度在 0.94 及以上）出口地有 114 个，比上年 115 个减少 1 个出口地，，出口 134956984kg，同比减少 23.30%。

主要出口地为中国香港，出口数量 93025646kg，占总出口数量的 68.930%%，比上年增加出口数量 25.31%。

2012 年 HDPE 五出口地出口量占总出口量的 79.462%，比上年增加 15.280%（表 17）。

表17 2012年初级形状的聚乙烯(HDPE)
五大出口国家/地区统计

排序	出口目的地	出口金额/美元	出口数量/kg	占比例/%
1	中国香港	137154640.00	93025646	68.930
2	韩国	9940508.00	6736684	4.992
3	中国台湾省	4048141.00	2986225	2.213
4	尼日利亚	2463049.00	2408500	1.785
5	朝鲜	3082851.00	2082409	1.543
出口总计		199685243.00	134956984	100.00

3.2011年初级形状的线型低密度聚乙烯进口下降出口上升(表18)

表18 2012年初级形状的线型低密度
聚乙烯月进口数量统计 kg

一月	二月	三月	四月	五月	六月
150774947	203507344	198493302	151704550	145384611	162225621
七月	八月	九月	十月	十一月	十二月
213561281	244618118	219796439	181429238	202413619	232953088

从海关统计中可看出，2012年初级形状的线型低密度聚乙烯进口地有41个，与上年41个持平，进口量为2306862158kg，同比进口数量减少6.11%。

主要进口地为沙特阿拉伯，进口数量578265471kg，占总进口数量的25.41%，比上年进口数量减少10.89%。

五进口地进口量占总进口量的72.771%，比上年增加0.31%。

2012年，来自中东地区的初级形状的线型低密度聚乙烯供应大幅增加。

其中，沙特阿拉伯仍位居中国初级形状的线型低密度聚乙烯进口国首位，阿拉伯联合酋长国、科威特、伊朗、卡塔尔、以色列分列中国LLDPE进口国分列第五、七、八、十一、二十八位。

2012年，从中东沙特阿拉伯、阿拉伯联合酋长国、科威特、伊朗、卡塔尔、以色列亚六国进口初级形状的线型低密度聚乙烯超过965.1kt、占中国初级形状的线型低密度聚乙烯进口总量的41.837%，比上年增加进口数量1.26%(表19)。

表19 2012年线型低密度聚乙烯LLDPE
五大进口国家/地区统计

排序	原产进口地	进口金额/美元	进口数量/kg	占比例
1	沙特阿拉伯	745046042.00	578265471	25.067%
2	泰国	554061068.00	388395227	16.837%
3	新加坡	529980952.00	377359639	16.358%
4	韩国	271556467.00	184288382	7.989%
5	阿拉伯联合酋长国	167365981.00	150408638	6.520%
进口总计		3167406331.00	2306862158	100.00

从海关统计中可看出，2012年初级形状的线型低密度聚乙烯出口地有92个，比上年88个增加4个出口地，出口82861210kg，同比增加24.89%。

主要出口地为中国香港，出口数量31466544kg，占总出口数量的37.975%，比上年增加出口数量77.19%；

2012年五出口地初级形状的线型低密度聚乙烯出口量占总出口量的62.466%，比上年增加7.856%(表20)。

表20 2012年线型低密度聚乙烯LLDPE
五大出口国家/地区统计

排序	出口目的地	出口金额/美元	出口数量/kg	占比例
1	中国香港	42028760.00	31466544	37.975%
2	印度	11048601.00	6796541	8.202%
3	越南	9048418.00	6164560	7.440%
4	印度尼西亚	7519186.00	4186283	5.052%
5	中国台湾省	4445365.00	3146035	3.797%
出口总计		119651001.00	82861210	100.00

五、表观消费量增长

2012年聚乙烯树脂表观消费量为18673.12kt，同比增长1.97%。

2012年聚乙烯树脂国内自给率为55.96%，同比下降2.50%(表21)。

表21 2006~2012年国内聚乙烯树脂表观消费量统计

产品	2006	2007	2008	2009	2010	2011	2012
表观消费量/kt	11196.42	11801.42	11635.19	15977.33	17506.34	18312.55	18673.12
年增长率/%	2.84	5.40	−1.41	37.32	9.57	4.61	1.97
国内自给率/%	53.53	58.68	59.26	50.88	56.30	58.46	55.96

2006~2012年间聚乙烯树脂表观消费量年均增长率为8.90%，低于同期产量年均增长率0.81%。

1.2011年初级形状聚乙烯进口商以贸易商为主

A. 初级形状聚乙烯(相对密度小于0.94)

2012年初级形状聚乙烯(相对密度小于0.94)进口商共计有2551家，比上年2569家减少18个进口地，进口额最高的十位进口商进口数量占总进口数量的19.036%，比上年增加3.436%；

中化国际贸易股份有限公司、爱施开国际贸易(上海)有限公司、宁波晶海工贸有限公司、上海虹丹物流有限公司、浙江前程石化有限公司、江苏荣尚国际贸易有限公司、不详、上海合冠仓储有限公司、利乐包装(呼和浩特)有限公司、利乐包装(北京)有限公司，分别位居2012年初级形状聚乙烯(相对密度小于0.94)进口量1~10位，进口量分别占总进口量的4.196%、2.815%、1.945%、1.741%、1.694%、1.670%、1.405%、1.272%、1.174%和1.124%。

2012年初级形状聚乙烯(相对密度小于0.94)十大进口商中有生产使用企业三家，进口贸易商七家，分别占总进口量的3.992%和15.043%。

从资料分析，初级形状聚乙烯(相对密度小于0.94)进口生产使用企业以塑料工业、包装工业、五金工业、塑料改性工业为主。

2012年初级形状聚乙烯(相对密度小于0.94)四十大进口商中仅有九家为进口生产企业，进口量占总进口量的8.367%。

2012年初级形状聚乙烯(相对密度小于0.94)四十大进口商中有三十一家为进口生产企业，进口量占总进口量的29.262%(表22)。

表22 2012年初级形状聚乙烯(相对密度小于0.94)四十大进口商统计

排序	进口商	所属行业	进口数量/kg	占比例
1	中化国际贸易股份有限公司	进口贸易商	65925250	4.196%
2	爱施开国际贸易(上海)有限公司	进口贸易商	44233000	2.815%
3	宁波晶海工贸有限公司	进口贸易商	30552000	1.945%
4	上海虹丹物流有限公司	进口贸易商	27348500	1.741%
5	浙江前程石化有限公司	塑料改性工业	26621625	1.694%

续表

排序	进口商	所属行业	进口数量/kg	占比例
6	江苏荣尚国际贸易有限公司	进口贸易商	26235000	1.670%
7	不详	进口贸易商	22071050	1.405%
8	上海合冠仓储有限公司	进口贸易商	19989325	1.272%
9	利乐包装(呼和浩特)有限公司	包装工业	18438316	1.174%
10	利乐包装(北京)有限公司	包装工业	17659216	1.124%
11	辽宁华塑实业集团有限公司	塑料工业	16075275	1.023%
12	康美包(苏州)有限公司	包装工业	15378908	0.979%
13	新会市会城飞马贸易有限公司	进口贸易商	15235000	0.970%
14	宁波柏森国际贸易有限公司	进口贸易商	14574500	0.928%
15	埃克森美孚化工商务(上海)有限公司	进口贸易商	13897900	0.885%
16	群星集团公司	进口贸易商	13502250	0.859%
17	陶氏化学(上海)有限公司	进口贸易商	11315434	0.720%
18	临沂市华扬进出口有限公司	进口贸易商	11187225	0.712%
19	利乐包装(昆山)有限公司	包装工业	11049496	0.703%
20	广州保税区新纪元物流有限公司	进口贸易商	9966750	0.634%
21	重庆普润石化有限公司	塑料改性工业	9556500	0.608%
22	睿铂(上海)贸易有限公司	进口贸易商	9382544	0.597%
23	宁波远大国际贸易有限公司	进口贸易商	9198750	0.585%
24	广州金发科技股份有限公司	塑料改性工业	9057475	0.576%

续表

排序	进口商	所属行业	进口数量/kg	占比例
25	青岛保税区中启联合物流有限公司	进口贸易商	9048250	0.576%
26	汕头市金园区金源昌贸易有限公司	进口贸易商	8783500	0.559%
27	不详	进口贸易商	8759650	0.558%
28	广州保税区精卫国际贸易有限公司	进口贸易商	8398950	0.535%
29	宁波聚雄进出口有限公司	进口贸易商	8201500	0.522%
30	上海海天龙国际物流有限公司	进口贸易商	7722000	0.491%
31	达鼎塑胶(河源)有限公司	塑料工业	7643000	0.486%
32	天津天保国际物流有限公司	进口贸易商	7433750	0.473%
33	广州旭翔国际贸易有限公司	进口贸易商	7424650	0.473%
34	厦门国贸集团股份有限公司	进口贸易商	7375000	0.469%
35	宁波经济技术开发区中基进出口有限公司	进口贸易商	7294885	0.464%
36	宁波保税区长荣国际贸易有限公司	进口贸易商	7230500	0.460%
37	青岛泺亨物流有限公司	进口贸易商	7103250	0.452%
38	满洲里盛世华强贸易有限公司	进口贸易商	7000000	0.446%
39	佛山市创造材料进出口有限公司	进口贸易商	6740200	0.429%
40	上海东鼎国际贸易有限公司	进口贸易商	6599609	0.420%
进口总计			1571135604	37.629%

B. 初级形状的聚乙烯相对密度在0.94及以上

2012年初级形状的聚乙烯相对密度在0.94及以上(HDPE)进口商共计有2971家，比上年2985家减少14家进口商，进口额最高的十位进口商进口数量占总进口数量的26.866%。

广东合捷国际供应链有限公司、上海雅胜物流有限公司、临沂市华扬进出口有限公司、

不详、浙江前程石化有限公司、辽宁华塑实业集团有限公司、杭州科利化工有限公司、上海泽林物流有限公司、宁波晶海工贸有限公司、上海外联发物流有限公司，分别位居2012年初级形状的聚乙烯(HDPE)进口量1~10位，进口量分别占总进口量的5.581%、5.170%、2.849%、2.412%、2.018%、1.952%、1.930%、1.765%、1.640%和1.549%。

初级形状聚乙烯(HDPE)十大进口商中进口生产使用企业三家，进口贸易商七家，分别占总进口量的5.900%和21.961%。

从资料分析，初级形状聚乙烯(HDPE)进口生产使用企业以塑料制品工业、汽车部件工业、塑料改性工业为主。

2012年初级形状聚乙烯(HDPE)进口商四十大进口商中有十九大为进口生产企业，进口量占总进口量的17.450%。

2012年初级形状聚乙烯(HDPE)进口商四十大进口商中有二十一大为进口贸易商，进口量占总进口量的33.502%(表23)。

表23　2012年聚乙烯(HDPE)四十大进口商统计

排序	进口企业名称	所属行业	进口数量	占比例
1	广东合捷国际供应链有限公司	贸易商	133226234	5.581%
2	上海雅胜物流有限公司	贸易商	123414495	5.170%
3	临沂市华扬进出口有限公司	贸易商	68011850	2.849%
4	不详	贸易商	57593938	2.412%
5	浙江前程石化有限公司	塑料改性工业	48179000	2.018%
6	辽宁华塑实业集团有限公司	塑料制品工业	46593975	1.952%
7	杭州科利化工有限公司	塑料改性工业	46068000	1.930%
8	上海泽林物流有限公司	贸易商	42136500	1.765%
9	宁波晶海工贸有限公司	贸易商	39154875	1.640%

续表

排序	进口企业名称	所属行业	进口数量	占比例
10	上海外联发物流有限公司	贸易商	36983755	1.549%
11	潍坊亚星乐天化工有限公司	塑料改性工业	33550000	1.405%
12	青岛保税区中启联合物流有限公司	贸易商	33256750	1.393%
13	江苏荣尚国际贸易有限公司	贸易商	33016500	1.383%
14	中化国际贸易股份有限公司	贸易商	32298750	1.353%
15	来福太（厦门）塑胶制品有限公司	塑料制品工业	31584637	1.323%
16	扬州亚普汽车塑料件有限公司	汽车工业	30764270	1.289%
17	上海卜力国际贸易有限公司	贸易商	30504763	1.278%
18	宁波远大国际贸易有限公司	贸易商	30211750	1.266%
19	亚大塑料制品有限公司	塑料制品工业	29823650	1.249%
20	上海合冠仓储有限公司	贸易商	27688825	1.160%
21	不详	贸易商	15576250	0.652%
22	山东资润化工有限公司	塑料改性工业	15451500	0.647%
23	淄博洁林塑料制管有限公司	塑料建材工业	15134975	0.634%
24	农夫山泉股份有限公司	包装工业	14864785	0.623%
25	珠海世韬金属有限公司	汽车工业	14331654	0.600%
26	厦门航开保税贸易有限公司	贸易商	14303375	0.599%
27	营口东盛实业有限公司	贸易商	14057175	0.589%
28	临沂飞扬塑料有限公司	塑料制品工业	13790446	0.578%

续表

排序	进口企业名称	所属行业	进口数量	占比例
29	广州金发科技股份有限公司	塑料改性工业	13545775	0.567%
30	上海紫日包装有限公司	包装工业	13165900	0.551%
31	威海金泓高分子有限公司	塑料改性工业	12725000	0.533%
32	骏业塑胶（深圳）有限公司	塑料制品工业	12582000	0.527%
33	恒隆胶品（深圳）有限公司	塑料制品工业	12546600	0.526%
34	爱施开国际贸易（上海）有限公司	贸易商	12027750	0.504%
35	天津远大天一化工有限公司	塑料改性工业	11885250	0.498%
36	厦门象屿股份有限公司	贸易商	11490250	0.481%
37	浙江文德进出口有限公司	贸易商	11363325	0.476%
38	山东华鲁国际贸易有限公司	贸易商	11265000	0.472%
39	宁波晟宇国际贸易有限公司	贸易商	11135500	0.466%
40	佛山市创造材料进出口有限公司	贸易商	11093250	0.465%
	进口总计		2387322555	50.952%

C. 初级形状的线型低密度聚乙烯

2012年初级形状的线型低密度聚乙烯进口商共计有1，788家，比上年1，813家减少25家进口商，进口额最高的十位进口商进口数量占总进口数量的15.855%。

广东合捷国际供应链有限公司、上海雅胜物流有限公司、广州金发科技股份有限公司、上海泽林物流有限公司、浙江前程石化有限公司、重庆普润石化有限公司、山东省塑料工业总公司、上海外联发物流有限公司、中国食品工业（集团）公司、新会市会城飞马贸易有限公司，分别位居2012年初级形状的线型低密度聚乙烯进口量1～10位，进口量分别占总进口量的2.809%、1.955%、1.761%、

1.563%、1.444%、1.436%、1.426%、1.176%、1.160%和1.125%。

初级形状的线型低密度聚乙烯十大进口商中有四家生产使用企业和六家进口贸易商，分别占总进口量的5.801%和10.054%。.

从资料分析，初级形状的线型低密度聚乙烯进口生产使用企业以塑胶工业、塑料改性工业包装工业为主。

2012年初级形状的线型低密度聚乙烯进口商四十大进口商中有十一家为进口生产企业，进口量占总进口量的10.701%。

2012年初级形状的线型低密度聚乙烯进口商四十大进口商中有二十九家为进口贸易商，进口量占总进口量的27.130%(表24)。

表24　2012年线型低密度聚乙烯LLDPE四十大进口商统计

排序	进口商	所属行业	进口数量/kg	占比例
1	广东合捷国际供应链有限公司	进口贸易商	64789305	2.809%
2	上海雅胜物流有限公司	进口贸易商	45109565	1.955%
3	广州金发科技股份有限公司	塑料改性工业	40631800	1.761%
4	上海泽林物流有限公司	进口贸易商	36066750	1.563%
5	浙江前程石化有限公司	塑料改性工业	33304500	1.444%
6	重庆普润石化有限公司	塑料改性工业	33132275	1.436%
7	山东省塑料工业总公司	进口贸易商	32899500	1.426%
8	上海外联发物流有限公司	进口贸易商	27136500	1.176%
9	中国食品工业(集团)公司	包装工业	26758875	1.160%
10	新会市会城飞马贸易有限公司	进口贸易商	25960745	1.125%
11	埃克森美孚化工商务(上海)有限公司	进口贸易商	25141500	1.090%
12	易便世(上海)贸易有限公司	进口贸易商	25031650	1.085%

续表

排序	进口商	所属行业	进口数量/kg	占比例
13	厦门建发化工有限公司	进口贸易商	23504175	1.019%
14	辽宁华塑实业集团有限公司	塑胶工业	23339300	1.012%
15	天津港保税区中轻腾发实业有限公司	进口贸易商	23095720	1.001%
16	上海合冠仓储有限公司	进口贸易商	20906669	0.906%
17	中化塑料公司	进口贸易商	19556025	0.848%
18	厦门象屿股份有限公司	进口贸易商	19360060	0.839%
19	威海联桥国际经济技术合作有限公司	进口贸易商	19051300	0.826%
20	深圳市永德丰实业有限公司	进口贸易商	19025100	0.825%
21	浙江明日控股集团有限公司	塑胶工业	17813850	0.772%
22	不详	进口贸易商	17635640	0.764%
23	浙江众成包装材料股份有限公司	包装工业	16832675	0.730%
24	不详	进口贸易商	16697675	0.724%
25	中普科贸有限责任公司	进口贸易商	16476475	0.714%
26	不详	进口贸易商	16001975	0.694%
27	深圳市光明新区经济发展有限公司	进口贸易商	15939100	0.691%
28	骏业塑胶(深圳)有限公司	塑胶工业	14964793	0.649%
29	青岛泰达瀚信国际贸易有限公司	进口贸易商	14725500	0.638%
30	临沂市华扬进出口有限公司	进口贸易商	14694450	0.637%
31	中化国际贸易股份有限公司	进口贸易商	14610225	0.633%

续表

排序	进口商	所属行业	进口数量/kg	占比例
32	淄博天鹤塑胶有限公司	塑胶工业	14468975	0.627%
33	润华农水（天津）国际贸易有限公司	进口贸易商	13479999	0.584%
34	深圳市恒中化工有限公司	塑胶工业	13016250	0.564%
35	通源塑料包装（苏州）有限公司	包装工业	12601500	0.546%
36	山东资润化工有限公司	进口贸易商	12549000	0.544%
37	上海虹丹物流有限公司	进口贸易商	12343900	0.535%
38	青岛保税区中启联合物流有限公司	进口贸易商	11734750	0.509%
39	新会市华翔塑料化工有限公司	进口贸易商	11177730	0.485%
40	汕头海湾物资有限公司	进口贸易商	11145700	0.483%
进口总计			2306862158	37.831%

2. 进口消费省市集中流向东部沿海地区

A. 初级形状的聚乙烯（相对密度小于0.94）

从海关资料来看，2012 年初级形状的聚乙烯（相对密度小于0.94）进口消费省市有 27 个，比上年 27 个持平；

2012 年初级形状的聚乙烯（相对密度小于 0.94）前五位进口消费省市进口量占总进口量的 76.694%，比上年减少 1.616%。

2012 年初级形状的聚乙烯（相对密度小于 0.94）主要进口流向为上海市，进口数量 332780438kg，占总进口数量的 21.181%，比上年进口增加 2.433%（表 25）。

表 25　2012 年初级形状聚乙烯（相对密度小于 0.94）五大进口省市统计

排序	进口省市	进口金额/美元	进口数量/kg	占比例
1	上海市	486998109.00	332780438	21.181%
2	广东省	465644048.00	331228845	21.082%
3	浙江省	322192079.00	238278799	15.166%
4	山东省	219453760.00	167619308	10.669%
5	江苏省	197526233.00	135057093	8.596%
进口总计		2245723103.00	1571135604	100.00

B. 初级形状的聚乙烯（相对密度在 0.94 及以上）

从海关资料来看，2012 年初级形状的聚乙烯（相对密度在 0.94 及以上）进口消费省市有 27 个，比上年 25 个增加 2 个进口消费省市；

2012 年初级形状的聚乙烯（相对密度在 0.94 及以上）前五位进口消费省市进口量占总进口量的 76.694%，比上年进口减 3.996%；

2012 年初级形状的聚乙烯（相对密度在 0.94 及以上）主要进口流向上海市，进口数量 332780438kg，占总进口数量的 21.181%（表 26）。

表 26　2012 年初级形状聚乙烯（相对密度小于 0.94）五大进口省市统计

排序	进口省市	进口金额/美元	进口数量/kg	占比例
1	上海市	486998109.00	332780438	21.181%
2	广东省	465644048.00	331228845	21.082%
3	浙江省	322192079.00	238278799	15.166%
4	山东省	219453760.00	167619308	10.669%
5	江苏省	197526233.00	135057093	8.596%
进口总计		2245723103.00	1571135604	100.00

C. 初级形状的线型低密度聚乙烯

从海关资料来看，2012 年初级形状的线型低密度聚乙烯进口消费省市有 26 个，比上年 23 个增加 3 个进口消费省市；

2012 年初级形状的线型低密度聚乙烯前五位进口消费省市进口量占总进口量的 77.615%，比上年进口减少 1.565%。

2012 年初级形状的线型低密度聚乙烯主要进口流向为广东省，进口数量 652762930kg，占总进口数量的 28.297%，比上年进口增加 5.28%（表 27）。

表 27　2012 年线型低密度聚乙烯 LLDPE 五大进口省市统计

排序	进口省市	进口金额/美元	进口数量/kg	占比例
1	广东省	866106002.00	652762930	28.297%
2	上海市	574360973.00	425075373	18.427%
3	山东省	397801472.00	292972042	12.700%
4	浙江省	321927487.00	234203522	10.152%
5	天津市	253155267.00	185456189	8.039%
进口总计		3167406331.00	2306862158	100.00

六、2012 年聚乙烯价格分析

2012 年上半年，国内聚乙烯市场大涨大落行情较为明显。现货市场在经历了 1 月到 2 月中旬的盘整阶段后，2月下旬到4月中旬期间在原油价格高企、石化限产保价政策和季节性需求等利好刺激下快速上涨。然而从4月下旬至今，在需求淡季、原油暴跌和宏观经济环境不明朗等利空因素作用下，现货市场进入下行通道。

展望下半年，三季度通常为我国塑料制品行业集中囤货备料的高峰期，随着需求好转，聚乙烯市场迎转机。

三季度为我国聚乙烯企业停车检修和需求反弹的集中期。近两年，国内石化企业7月份集中检修计划陆续增多，虽然上半年由于石化行业经营压力较大，石化库存长期维持高位，但随着三季度装置检修计划的陆续实施，石化库存有望回落，市场压力将得到缓解。

2012年抚顺石化年产750kt和大庆石化年产600kt聚乙烯新增装置已经建成，在9月正式投产；

齐鲁石化年产250kt装置目前也在紧锣密鼓建设之中，在12月份投产运行。

三季度末四季度初国内共计1600kt产能得以释放，这对四季度国内市场供应产生一定冲击。

聚乙烯进口6月以后风险因素依然较多，市场信心难以获得稳定支撑。国外廉价货源不断出现，依然对国内市场走势形成压力。

三季度通常进口聚乙烯总量将呈现上行趋势，四季度伴随国内装置稳定正常生产和下游需求走淡，整体进口量将逐渐减少。

合成树脂的亚洲现货价格正在进一步上涨。用于加工塑料袋等的聚乙烯价格创约9个月、水管原料聚氯乙烯树脂价格创3个月来的新高。

数据显示，2012年12月低密度聚乙烯的亚洲现货价格为每吨1430美元左右，比2011年12月上旬上涨了10%，聚氯乙烯树脂的现货价格为每吨1020美元左右，与创出近期最低价的去年11月下旬相比，上涨了11%。

从下列六产品月均价走势来分析，六产品中有四产品低开高走，仅一产品低开高走，但跌幅度有限。

如上海石化LDPE -Q281 12月月均价比1月月均价高出2.30%；

大庆石化产HDPE -5000S 12月月均价比1月月均价高4.17%；

上海石化产HDPE－MH602 12月月均价仅比1月月均价高2.27%；

扬子石化LLDPE－DFDA－7042 12月月均价比1月月均价高出18.15%；

上海赛科LLDPE－LL0220KJ 12月月均价比1月月均价高出17.64%；

而燕山石化LDPE－1C7A 12月月均价比1月月均价低出8.28%；

由下表看出，2012年国内PE市场行情弱势盘整为主，LDPE和HDPE价格持续小幅波动，据中国塑料城统计，LDPE－Q281价格1~12月份的波动幅度在10%内；

LLDPE－DFDA－7042价格由1月份的1~12月份的波动幅度较大，在18%内；

HDPE受市场整体货源偏少因素影响，价格变动不大，涨幅在6%内(表28~表33)。

表28 LDPE－Q281上海石化2012年中国塑料城月均价走势 元/t

1月	2月	3月	4月	5月	6月
11306	11238	11556	11423	10734	10505
7月	8月	9月	10月	11月	12月
10686	10695	11288	11013	11390	11566

表29 LDPE－1C7A燕山石化2011年中国塑料城月均价走势 元/t

1月	2月	3月	4月	5月	6月
13140	13428	13552	13547	12672	12275
7月	8月	9月	10月	11月	12月
12400	12363	12690	12269	12095	12052

表30 HDPE－5000S大庆石化2012年中国塑料城月均价走势 元/t

1月	2月	3月	4月	5月	6月
11000	10950	11243	11705	11397	11470
7月	8月	9月	10月	11月	12月
11684	11550	11440	11169	11190	11459

表31 HDPE－MH602上海石化2012年中国塑料城月均价走势 元/t

1月	2月	3月	4月	5月	6月
11300	11228	11256	11315	11152	11050
7月	8月	9月	10月	11月	12月
11200	11286	11414	11500	11500	11557

表32 LLDPE－DFDA－7042 扬子石化2012年中国塑料城月均价走势 元/t

1月	2月	3月	4月	5月	6月
9766	10095	10839	10731	10200	10100
7月	8月	9月	10月	11月	12月
10600	10763	11371	11266	11309	11538

表 33 LLDPE－LL0220KJ 上海赛科 2012 年中国塑料城月均价走势 元/t

1 月	2 月	3 月	4 月	5 月	6 月
9676	10076	10752	10736	10177	9932
7 月	8 月	9 月	10 月	11 月	12 月
10304	10581	11223	10988	11277	11383

七、国内外发展趋势

1. 全球 PE 需求 5 年新增 20Mt

IHS 化学公司最新发布的《2013 年聚乙烯全球分析报告》显示，全球聚乙烯（PE）消费增长速度在 2010 年达到 8.4% 之后出现明显回落，2012 年的增速估计为 3.4%。该公司预计，全球聚乙烯需求量将从 2012 年的 79Mt 增加至 2017 年的 99Mt，主要是受到亚太、中欧、中东和南美地区需求增长的刺激。

据预计，2016 年 PE 市场产能将达 105.1Mt。其主要产品类型有 LDPE、EVA 共聚物、薄膜挤出技术以及挤压吹塑成形。

在全球范围内，高密度聚乙烯（HDPE）和低密度聚乙烯（LDPE）共占市场份额近 69.8%，这也是推动塑料行业继续向前的主要驱动力。

包装应用行业市场的地理分析显示，2011～2016 年间欧洲地区的最高年复合增长率将达到 8.8%，亚太地区其次，达 8.2%，而美国预计可达 6.0%。

在未来的聚合物市场，PE 将起主导作用。

廉价的页岩基原料正在令北美地区的聚乙烯工业重新焕发生机。沃菲阿迪斯称，北美聚乙烯的大多数目标出口地区正在投资新建出口导向型的塑料加工产能，这将有助于刺激聚乙烯需求增长。

卡塔尔石化公司（Qapco）2012 年 11 月 21 日宣布，其在卡塔尔麦赛义德的低密度聚乙烯（LDPE）装置建成投产。这是 Qapco 的第三套 LDPE 装置，年产能力 300kt。该装置的投产使卡塔尔石化公司 LDPE 总年产能力达到 700kt。

该新装置采用利安德巴赛尔公司技术，由伍德公司负责工程、采购和施工。

沃菲阿迪斯称，美国页岩气革命带来充裕的廉价乙烷原料，从而刺激北美地区几乎所有大型聚烯烃生产商进行乙烯或聚乙烯扩能，这些产能将在未来 5 年陆续投产。北美地区这些新项目以及中东地区新增产能将令欧洲和亚洲的高成本生产商所面临的竞争压力日趋增加。按当前公布的数据，至 2022 年全球将新增逾 47000kt 的聚乙烯产能。

沃菲阿迪斯指出，在西欧等成熟市场，产业的整合、业务的优化以及向高附加值高性能产品的战略转型将不可避免，因为在大宗商品方面，他们难以与北美和中东地区的生产商进行竞争，只有通过产品的差别化战略，出口高附加值树脂产品才能够赢得一线生机。

2. 三井化学将建茂金属 LLDPE 装置

日本三井化学公司日前表示，三井化学旗下子公司 Prime 聚合物公司将在新加坡与三井商事公司合作组建一家公司（Prime 聚合物公司持有 80% 股权，三井商事持有 20% 股权），新建一套设计产能为 300kt/a 茂金属线型低密度聚乙烯（LLDPE）生产装置，预计 2014 年年底投产。

3. 埃克森美孚计划投建乙烯和聚乙烯扩能项目

受美国低廉的天然气价格吸引，埃克森美孚化学公司 6 月初宣布，计划投资数十亿美元在美国海湾沿岸实施乙烯和聚乙烯扩能项目。这是继雪佛龙菲利普斯化学、陶氏化学、壳牌化学、沙索及台塑后，最近一年第六家对外宣布将在美实施乙烯裂解计划的公司。

埃克森美孚化学计划在美国得克萨斯州贝敦市建设一套年产能达 1500kt 的乙烯裂解装置，同时在该公司的蒙贝韦（MontBelvieu）基地套配建设两套聚乙烯装置（每套年产能为 650kt）。该项目将在 2013 年 3 月动工建设，2016 年下半年将建成投产。

4. 南非沙索计划在美新建 LDPE 工厂

沙索北美公司计划在路易斯安娜州查尔斯湖新建一套年产能达 420kt 低密度聚乙烯（LDPE）装置，将使用埃克森美孚公司的管状工艺技术，预计 2016 年年底建成。该工厂产能将达 420kt/a。

5. 中国 PE 需求 5 年新增 8000kt

IHS 化学公司最新发布报告显示，全球聚乙烯（PE）消费增长速度在 2010 年达到 8.4%之后出现明显回落，2012 年的增速估计为 3.4%。

预计全球 PE 需求量将从 2012 年的 79000kt 增加至 2017 年的 99000kt，主要是受到亚太、中欧、中东和南美地区需求增长的刺激。

其中，中国将占到新增需求的 40%。中国 PE 需求量将从 2012 年的 19000kt 增加至 2017 年的 27000kt，年均增速超过 7%。

尽管未来几年中国将新增大量的聚乙烯产能，但是到 2017 年中国的聚乙烯进口量仍将超过 8Mt。而到 2035 年，中国 PE 需求量将达到 35Mt，人均消费量将达到发达国家的水平。

全球最大的聚乙烯进口国中国将占到新增需求的 40%。中国聚乙烯需求量将从 2012 年的 19Mt 增加至 2017 年的 27Mt，年均增速超过 7%。

尽管未来几年中国将新增大量的聚乙烯产能，但是到 2017 年中国的聚乙烯进口量仍将超过 8Mt。

到2035年，中国聚乙烯需求量将达到35Mt，人均消费量将达到发达国家的水平。亚太和中东地区及美国的主要出口商将继续受益于中国市场的增长。

八、进出口贸易方式分析

1. 初级形状的聚乙烯相对密度小于0.94

从海关统计中可看出，2012年初级形状的聚乙烯相对密度小于0.94进口贸易方式主要为一般贸易(占进口量61.453%)，其次为保税区仓储转口货物(占进口量18.808%)，进料加工贸易(占进口量13.584%)，来料加工装配贸易(占进口量4.192%)，边境小额贸易(占进口量1.367%)，保税仓库进出境货物(占进口量0.595%)，其他(占进口量0.002%)，合计为总进口量的100.00%(表34)。

表34　2012年初级形状的聚乙烯相对密度小于0.94进口交易类型统计

进口交易类型	进口金额/美元	进口数量/kg	占比例
一般贸易	1405415109.00	965515760	61.453%
保税区仓储转口货物	398820116.00	295497357	18.808%
进料加工贸易	304448301.00	213416893	13.584%
来料加工装配贸易	96679486.00	65865967	4.192%
边境小额贸易	28391097.00	21470215	1.367%
保税仓库进出境货物	11886875.00	9345620	0.595%
其他	82，119.00	23792	0.002%
进口总计	2245723103.00	1571135604	100.00

从海关统计中可看出，2012年初级形状的聚乙烯相对密度小于0.94出口贸易方式主要为保税区仓储转口货物(占出口量39.849%)，其次为一般贸易(占出口量37.222%)，进料加工贸易(占出口量12.128%)，来料加工装配贸易(占出口量6.578%)，保税仓库进出境货物(占出口量2.458%)，边境小额贸易(占出口量1.555%)，对外承包工程出口货物(占出口量0.151%)，其他(占出口量0.060%)，合计为总出口量的100.00%(表35)。

表35　2012年初级形状的聚乙烯相对密度小于0.94出口交易类型统计

出口交易类型	出口金额/美元	出口数量/kg	占比例
保税区仓储转口货物	40526826.00	27855574	39.849%
一般贸易	43647770.00	26018941	37.222%
进料加工贸易	15890538.00	8477599	12.128%
来料加工装配贸易	5749553.00	4597824	6.578%
保税仓库进出境货物	2741950.00	1718055	2.458%
边境小额贸易	1719532.00	1087118	1.555%
对外承包工程出口货物	186825.00	105555	0.151%
其他	92325.00	41622	0.060%
出口总计	110555319.00	69902288	100.00

2. 初级形状的聚乙烯相对密度在0.94及以上

从海关统计中可看出，2012年初级形状的聚乙烯相对密度在0.94及以上进口贸易方式主要为一般贸易(占进口量59.537%)，其次为进料加工贸易(占进口量19.433%)，保税区仓储转口货物(占进口量15.602%)，来料加工装配贸易(占进口量5.166%)，保税仓库进出境货物(占进口量0.252%)，其他(占进口量0.007%)，边境小额贸易(占进口量0.003%)，外商投资企业作为投资进口的设备、物品(占进口量0.001%)，合计为总进口量的

100.00%(表36)。

表36 2012年初级形状的聚乙烯相对密度在0.94及以上进口交易类型统计

进口交易类型	进口金额/美元	进口数量/kg	占比例
一般贸易	3356777182.00	2387322555	59.537%
进料加工贸易	1095205123.00	779211483	19.433%
保税区仓储转口货物	815947752.00	625598363	15.602%
来料加工装配贸易	234267164.00	207162055	5.166%
保税仓库进出境货物	13816536.00	10088875	0.252%
其他	611588.00	266855	0.007%
边境小额贸易	140580.00	106500	0.003%
外商投资企业作为投资进口的设备、物品	49316.00	24390	0.001%
进口总计	5516815241.00	4009781076	100.00

从海关统计中可看出，2012年初级形状的聚乙烯相对密度在0.94及以上出口贸易方式主要为保税区仓储转口货物(占出口量79.662%)，其次为一般贸易(占出口量10.510%)，来料加工装配贸易(占出口量3.979%)，进料加工贸易(占出口量3.204%)，边境小额贸易(占出口量1.041%)，对外承包工程出口货物(占出口量0.870%)，保税仓库进出境货物(占出口量0.702%)，其他(占出口量0.032%)，合计为总出口量的100.00%(表37)。

表37 2012年初级形状的聚乙烯相对密度在0.94及以上出口交易类型统计

出口交易类型	出口金额/(美元	出口数量/kg	占比例
保税区仓储转口货物	157713997.00	107509892	79.662%
一般贸易	20160820.00	14183898	10.510%
来料加工装配贸易	7579977.00	5369835	3.979%
进料加工贸易	8171203.00	4324167	3.204%
边境小额贸易	1987847.00	1404282	1.041%
对外承包工程出口货物	2617168.00	1173500	0.870%
保税仓库进出境货物	1365787.00	948005	0.702%
其他	88444.00	43405	0.032%
出口总计	199685243.00	134956984	100.00

3. 初级形状的线型低密度聚乙烯

从海关统计中可看出，2012年初级形状的线型低密度聚乙烯进口贸易方式主要为一般贸易(占进口量57.512%)，其次为进料加工贸易(占进口量18.450%)，保税区仓储转口货物(占进口量17.837%)，来料加工装配贸易(占进口量6.065%)，保税仓库进出境货物(占进口量0.134%)，其他(占进口量0.002%)，合计为总进口量的100.00%(表38)。

表38 2012年初级形状的线型低密度聚乙烯进口交易类型统计

进口交易类型	进口金额/美元	进口数量/kg	占进口量比例
一般贸易	1890975637.00	1326717988	57.512%
进料加工贸易	582387206.00	425626062	18.450%
保税区仓储转口货物	521341588.00	411473587	17.837%
来料加工装配贸易	167974783.00	139901390	6.065%
保税仓库进出境货物	4624278.00	3100659	0.134%
其他	102839.00	42472	0.002%
进口总计	3167406331.00	2306862158	100.00

从海关统计中可看出，2012 年初级形状的线型低密度聚乙烯出口贸易方式主要为保税区仓储转口货物(占出口量81.488%)，其次为一般贸易(占出口量15.411%)，来料加工装配贸易(占出口量1.237%)，保税仓库进出境货物(占出口量1.136%)，边境小额贸易(占出口量0.417%)，对外承包工程出口货物(占出口量0.241%)，进料加工贸易(占出口量0.060%)，其他(占出口量0.009%)，合计为总出口量的100.00%。

表39　2012 年初级形状的线型低密度聚乙烯出口交易类型统计

出口交易类型	出口金额/美元	出口数量/kg	占出口量比例
保税区仓储转口货物	91，692，758.00	67521689	81.488%
一般贸易	24，176，578.00	12769752	15.411%
来料加工装配贸易	1，506，586.00	1024825	1.237%
保税仓库进出境货物	1，363，151.00	941550	1.136%
边境小额贸易	510，986.00	345820	0.417%
对外承包工程出口货物	343，077.00	200000	0.241%
进料加工贸易	47，280.00	50000	0.060%
其他	10，585.00	7574	0.009%
出口总计	119，651，001.00	82861210	100.00

第三章　聚氯乙烯糊树脂 2012 年进口量升价降消费升

一、中国聚氯乙烯糊树脂工业

1. 聚氯乙烯糊树脂产能高发展，装置负荷运行率仍处于较低水平。

2012 年底国内 PVC 糊树脂总装置能力在1000kt/a，正常情况下实际市场供应量在 65 ~ 70kt/月，国内 PVC 糊树脂市场供应与需求大致平衡(表40)。

表40　2008 ~2012 年中国 PVC 糊树脂产能与产量增长统计

项目	2008	2009	2010	2011	2012
产能/kt	592.0	652.0	685.0	700.0	1000.0
产量/kt	约380.0	约440.0	约510.0	约530.0	约560.0
年增长/%	52.00	15.80	15.91	3.92	5.66
开工率/%	64.19	67.48	74.45	75.71	56.00

2008 ~2012 年产能增长了 68.92%，年均增长率为 14.00%；

2008 ~2012 年产量增长了 47.37%，年均增长率为 10.18%；

2012 年 12 月山东中联化学年产 40kt 糊树脂项目试生产，经过近 3 个月投料试生产，于 2013 年 3 月生产出一级品率达到 100% 的合格产品。

由内蒙古伊东集团东兴化工有限责任公司投资建设的年产 10 万吨高端 PVC 糊树脂项目目前进入紧张的设备安装调试阶段，标志着内蒙古首个 PVC 糊树脂项目即将投产。

据介绍，伊东集团东兴化工糊树脂项目是该公司大型氯碱项目的一部分，投资 8.7 亿元。项目依托乌兰察布市当地丰富的石灰石资源和便利的交通条件，采用国际先进技术。

年产 10 万吨糊树脂装置由 3 条生产线组成，可以生产 4 个牌号的产品，产品质量及价格在国内具有显著的比较优势，同时可实现全公司聚氯乙烯生产能力的平衡。

一期项目于 2011 年 4 月破土动工，于 10 月竣工投产。

2. 聚氯乙烯糊树脂出口省市分析

从海关统计中可看出，2012 年聚氯乙烯糊树脂出口生产企业主要集中在天津市，出口数量 1859640kg，占总出口数量的 20.815%，比上年下降 63.83%(表41)。

2012 年五省市聚氯乙烯糊树脂出口量占 2012 年总出口数量的 75.53%。

表 41 2012 年聚氯乙烯糊树脂九大出口省市统计

排序	出口省市	出口金额/美元	出口数量/kg	占比例
1	天津市	2，726，627.00	1859640	20.815%
2	浙江省	4，659，876.00	1675237	18.751%
3	宁夏回族自治区	1，397，393.00	1102675	12.342%
4	辽宁省	1，428，813.00	989120	11.071%
5	上海市	822，404.00	674886	7.554%
6	山东省	1，332，977.00	580144	6.493%
7	福建省	623，821.00	528256	5.913%
8	河北省	428，381.00	455535	5.099%
9	湖南省	670，561.00	454000	5.082%
出口总计		15，077，367.00	8934297	100.00

3. 聚氯乙烯糊树脂出口商以贸易商为主

聚氯乙烯糊树脂出口商以贸易商为主，2012 年聚氯乙烯糊树脂出口商中七成为贸易商。

2012 年聚氯乙烯糊树脂出口商共计有 77 家，比上年 78 家减少 1 家，2012 年聚氯乙烯糊树脂出口量最高的十位出口商有五家为聚氯乙烯糊树脂生产企业，五家为贸易商，出口数量占总出口数量的 66.218%。

2012 年聚氯乙烯糊树十八大出口商中生产企业有五家，出口数量占总出口数量的 40.836%；而贸易商占十三家，出口数量占总出口数量的 36.532%（表 42）。

表 42 2012 年聚氯乙烯糊树脂十八大出口商统计

排序	出口商	所属行业	出口数量/kg	占比例
1	杭州远远化工贸易有限公司	贸易商	1371830	15.355%
2	宁夏英力特化工股份有限公司	聚氯乙烯糊树脂生产企业	1077675	12.062%
3	天津渤化化工进出口公司	聚氯乙烯糊树脂生产企业	1043000	11.674%
4	沈阳化工股份有限公司	聚氯乙烯糊树脂生产企业	781520	8.747%
5	郴州华湘化工有限责任公司	聚氯乙烯糊树脂生产企业	417000	4.667%
6	上海氯碱化工股份有限公司	聚氯乙烯糊树脂生产企业	329280	3.686%
7	海宁市二轻贸易有限公司	贸易商	306000	3.425%
8	东莞市虎门保税仓	贸易商	211600	2.368%
9	温州市精锐电器有限公司	贸易商	192000	2.149%
10	上海新宇田国际贸易有限公司	贸易商	186212	2.084%
11	青岛新宇田化工有限公司	贸易商	175982	1.970%
12	南通百事威国际贸易有限公司	贸易商	127000	1.421%
13	厦门渊英商贸有限公司	贸易商	127000	1.421%
14	厦门广投贸易有限公司	贸易商	121675	1.362%
15	天津市财宇贸易有限公司	贸易商	121500	1.360%
16	丹东天顺贸易有限公司	贸易商	115000	1.287%
17	北京瑞华纺织有限公司	贸易商	108000	1.209%
18	温州市登泰贸易有限公司	贸易商	100000	1.119%
	出口总计		8934297	100.00

二、2012 年聚氯乙烯糊树脂进口量升价降，出口量价同降

聚氯乙烯糊树脂 2008 年才单独新列出代码。

2012 年，我国共进口聚氯乙烯糊树脂 119223t，同比增长 22.77%；2012 年出口聚氯乙烯糊树脂 8934t，同比下降 50.99%，出口减少近万吨。

2012 年国内聚氯乙烯糊树脂对外依存度为 16.45%，比 2011 年我国聚氯乙烯糊树脂对外总依存度上升 3.49%(表 43)。

表 43　2009～2012 年聚氯乙烯糊树脂进出口统计

	2009 年	2010 年	2011 年	2012 年
进口数量/kg	85539413	98346390	97111528	119223177
进口金额/美元	90029981	135830066	168951611	178360178
平均进口价/(美元/kg)	1.05250	1.38114	1.7398	1.4960
出口数量/kg	3293118	6365348	18229895	8934297
出口金额/美元	4360238	9569955	32893682	15077367
平均出口价/(美元/kg)	1.32405	1.50345	1.8044	1.6876
净进口合计	82246295	91981042	78881633	110288880
年增长率/%	47.85	11.84	-14.24	39.82
对外依存度	16.27	16.16	12.96	16.45

1. 2012 年聚氯乙烯糊树脂进口上升

从海关统计中可看出，聚氯乙烯糊树脂 2011 年进口地有 18 个，比上年 17 个增加 1 个进口地。

主要进口地为中国台湾省进口数量 55603150kg，占总进口数量的 46.638%，比上年增加进口数量 25.68%；

其次为韩国进口数量 41929426kg，占总进口数量的 35.169%，比上年增加进口数量 43.00%；

马来西亚进口数量 7460640kg，占总进口数量的 6.258%，比上年增加进口数量 8.31%；

泰国进口数量 3816600kg，占总进口数量的 3.201%，比上年增加进口数量 38.19%；

德国进口数量 8796941kg，占总进口数量的 9.06%；

五原产进口地进口数量占聚氯乙烯糊树脂 2012 年总进口数量的 94.772%，比上年减少 0.25%(表 44)。

表 44　2012 年聚氯乙烯糊树脂十大进口国家/地区统计

排序	原产进口地	进口金额/美元	进口数量/kg	占比例
1	中国台湾省	80970265.00	55603150	46.638%
2	韩国	61525575.00	41929426	35.169%
3	马来西亚	10689051.00	7460640	6.258%
4	泰国	6359964.00	4180300	3.506%
5	德国	6828948.00	3816600	3.201%
6	日本	5388486.00	3171794	2.660%
7	美国	2765736.00	1196244	1.003%
8	瑞典	2558772.00	1138500	0.955%
9	法国	387712.00	231000	0.194%
10	斯洛文尼亚共和国	190282.00	115000	0.096%
进口总计		178360178.00	119223177	100.00

2. 2012 年聚氯乙烯糊树脂出口下降

从海关统计中可看出，2012 年聚氯乙烯糊树脂出口地有 53 个，比上年 55 个减少 2 个出口地。

主要出口地为印度出口数量 1974616kg，占总出口数量的 22.102%，比上年减少出口数量 69.06%；

其次为俄罗斯出口数量 1369530kg，占总出口数量的15.329%，比上年减少出口数量3.21%；

巴基斯坦出口数量1178130kg，占总出口数量的13.187%，比上年减少出口数量54.82%；

中国香港出口数量640100kg，占总出口数量的7.165%，比上年减少出口数量46.30%；

伊朗出口数量480290kg，占总出口数量的5.736%，比上年减少出口数量71.00%；

五出口地出口数量占初聚氯乙烯糊树脂2012年总出口数量的63.159%，比上年减少出口数量10.851%(表45)。

表45　2012年聚氯乙烯糊树脂十大出口国家/地区统计

排 序	出口目的地	出口金额/美元	出口数量/kg	占比例
1	印度	2744950.00	1974616	22.102%
2	俄罗斯	4135780.00	1369530	15.329%
3	巴基斯坦	1654871.00	1178130	13.187%
4	中国香港	897977.00	640100	7.165%
5	伊朗	951425.00	480290	5.376%
6	厄瓜多尔	433307.00	407850	4.565%
7	印度尼西亚	370075.00	380000	4.253%
8	朝鲜	582063.00	371720	4.161%
9	韩国	428079.00	280520	3.140%
10	加纳	230534.00	192000	2.149%
出口总计		15077367.00	8934297	100.00

三、2012年聚氯乙烯糊树脂进出口交易类型分析

从海关统计中可看出，2012年以聚氯乙烯糊树脂进口贸易方式主要为进料加工贸易(占进口量83.811%)，其次为一般贸易(占进口量14.244%)，保税仓库进出境货物(占进口量1.47%)，来料加工装配贸易(占进口量0.507%)，保税区仓储转口货物(占进口量0.291%)，其他(占进口量0.001%)，合计为总进口量的100.00%(表46)。

表46　2012年聚氯乙烯糊树脂进口交易类型统计

进口交易类型	进口金额 /美元	进口数量/kg	占比例
进料加工贸易	145126477.00	99921590	83.811%
一般贸易	29729196.00	16982027	14.244%
保税仓库进出境货物	2004276.00	1367000	1.147%
来料加工装配贸易	905555.00	604301	0.507%
保税区仓储转口货物	592799.00	347263	0.291%
其他	1875.00	996	0.001%
进口总计	178360178.00	119223177	100.00

从海关统计中可看出，2012年以聚氯乙烯糊树脂出口贸易方式主要为一般贸易(占出口量94.240%)，其次为保税仓库进出境货物(占出口量4.083%)，边境小额贸易(占出口量1.599%)，其他(占出口量0.045%)，保税区仓储转口货物(占出口量0.034%)，合计为总出口量的100.00%。

表47　2012年聚氯乙烯糊树脂出口交易类型统计

出口交易类型	出口金额/美元	出口数量/kg	占比例
一般贸易	14255300.00	8419693	94.240%
保税仓库进出境货物	554649.00	364800	4.083%
边境小额贸易	253475.00	142820	1.599%
其他	7090.00	3984	0.045%
保税区仓储转口货物	6853.00	3000	0.034%
出口总计	15077367.00	8934297	100.00

四、消费结构分析

我国PVC糊状树脂主要用于制造装饰材料(壁纸、地板卷材)、人造革、浸渍手套、蓄电池隔板、玩具、金属涂层、软管、汽车内饰材、箱包、鞋子、瓶盖内衬、油墨、胶黏剂等产品。

在国内，华东和华南是PVC糊状树脂的主要加工区，占PVC糊状树脂应用消费比例的70%以上。

2012年聚氯乙烯糊树脂表观消费量为670.29kt，同比增长10.09%。

2012年聚氯乙烯糊树脂国内自给率为88.55%，同比下降3.49%(表48)。

表48　2009~2011年国内聚氯乙烯糊树脂表观消费量统计

年份	2009年	2010年	2011年	2012年
表观消费量/kg	525.21	601.98	608.88	670.29
年增长率/%	18.70	14.62	1.15	10.09
国内自给率/%	83.78	84.72	87.04	83.55

2008~2012年间聚氯乙烯糊树脂表观消费量年均增长率为9.74%，低于同期产量年均增长率4.26%。

在消费结构方面，总体来看中国与世界差异不大。特别是由于高端产品应用差距正在快速缩小。

2012年，中国聚氯乙烯糊树脂产量约560kt，进口119.2kt，出口8.9kt，表观消费量670.29kt。

中国聚氯乙烯糊树脂年消耗量的30%~35%经加工制品(如人造革、浸渍手套、壁纸、地板卷材等产品)后出口。

1. 进口生产使用企业以塑胶工业为主

2012年聚氯乙烯糊树进口商共计有155家，比上年158家减少3家进口商，进口额最高的十位进口商进口数量占总进口数量的57.39%，比上年减少9.45%。

从资料分析，聚氯乙烯糊树进口生产使用企业以塑胶工业、医疗制品工业、建材工业、劳保用品工业、塑料制品工业、汽车用品、改性塑料、料电线电缆工业为主，2012年聚氯乙烯糊树五十四大进口商其中四十一大进口生产企业进口量占总进口量的76.070%(表49)。

表49　2012年聚氯乙烯糊树脂五十四大进口商统计

续表

排序	进口商	所属行业	进口数量/kg	占比例/%
1	淄博蓝帆塑胶制品有限公司	塑胶制品	15347600	12.873
2	徐州富山医疗制品有限公司	医疗制品	14495000	12.158
3	山东蓝帆新材料有限公司	改性塑料	13114400	11.000
4	来百利(惠州)手套有限公司	劳保制品	5575000	4.676
5	来士达劳保(惠州)有限公司	劳保制品	3774200	3.166
6	淄博恒昌塑胶制品有限公司	塑胶制品	3575600	2.999
7	淄博鸿烨上勤塑胶有限公司	塑胶制品	3513000	2.947
8	河源嘉太医保用品有限公司	医疗制品	3188400	2.674
9	石家庄鸿业塑胶制品有限公司	塑胶制品	3136000	2.630
10	江苏华源手套有限公司	劳保制品	2705000	2.269
11	隆基(厦门)塑胶有限公司	塑胶制品	2680000	2.248
12	石家庄九源塑业有限公司	塑胶制品	2570000	2.156
13	东莞市领会进出口有限公司	贸易商	2459400	2.063
14	淄博英科医疗制品有限公司	医疗制品	1989600	1.669
15	长春汉高表面技术有限公司	改性塑料	1439950	1.208
16	东莞市虎门保税仓	贸易商	1216000	1.020
17	广州市柏拉图塑胶有限公司	塑胶制品	1165000	0.977
18	石家庄骏飞塑料制品有限公司	塑胶制品	1142400	0.958
19	桑巴蒂(保定)墙纸有限公司	装饰材料	880000	0.738
20	吴江创源玩具有限公司	玩具制品	875000	0.734%
21	张家港西一新型汽车配件有限公司	汽车用品	810300	0.680%
22	无锡康龙橡塑制品有限公司	塑胶制品	750000	0.629
23	南亚塑胶工业(惠州)有限公司	塑胶制品	748000	0.627
24	高密市星宇劳保用品有限公司	劳保制品	745200	0.625
25	厦门建发股份有限公司	贸易商	674400	0.566
26	江门市中塑进出口有限公司	贸易商	670900	0.563

续表

排序	进口商	所属行业	进口数量/kg	占比例/%
27	山东淄博山川医用器材有限公司	医疗制品	600000	0.503
28	石家庄鸿升塑料制品有限公司	塑胶制品	534400	0.448
29	韩华贺化贸易(上海)有限公司	贸易商	517500	0.434
30	南通荣威塑胶工业有限公司	塑胶制品	481000	0.403
31	石家庄鸿锐集团鸿迪塑胶制品有限公司	塑胶制品	470400	0.395
32	苏州 PPG 包装涂料有限公司	装饰材料	467533	0.392
33	广州昊夫物流服务有限公司	贸易商	421500	0.354
34	深圳市同益佳实业发展有限公司	贸易商	414750	0.348
35	青岛能善高新材料有限公司	改性塑料	408200	0.342
36	上海荣威塑胶工业有限公司	塑胶制品	384000	0.322
37	深圳市康飞仕进出口有限公司	贸易商	380000	0.319
38	凯碧塑胶制品(惠州)有限公司	塑胶制品	372160	0.312
39	中山崇高玩具制品厂有限公司	玩具制品	341200	0.286
40	上海和氏壁化工有限公司	改性塑料	324000	0.272
41	昆山阿基里斯人造皮有限公司	建材工业	292000	0.245
42	圣戈班高功能塑料(上海)有限公司	改性塑料	268942	0.226
43	西卡(中国)建筑材料有限公司	建材工业	264000	0.221
44	江门市新会区发达橡胶工业有限公司	塑胶制品	264000	0.221

续表

排序	进口商	所属行业	进口数量/kg	占比例/%
45	东莞市对外加工装配服务公司	贸易商	251150	0.211
46	澄海市振丰工贸有限公司	贸易商	247500	0.208
47	高密市正丰贸易有限公司	贸易商	227700	0.191
48	上海聚茂塑胶制品有限公司	塑胶制品	216000	0.181
49	佛山市南海时利和汽车用品有限公司	汽车用品	208800	0.175
50	宁波和富塑胶实业有限公司	塑胶制品	201700	0.169
51	唐山川欧森塑料制品有限公司	塑胶制品	189600	0.159
52	东莞市永竹化工有限公司	改性塑料	187500	0.157
53	深圳市华汉城贸易发展有限公司	贸易商	175200	0.147
54	广东省东莞机械进出口有限公司	贸易商	175000	0.147
	进口总计		119223177	100.00

2. 进口消费省市主要集中在长江三角洲及珠江三角洲

从海关资料来看，2012 年聚氯乙烯糊树脂进口消费省市有 13 个，与上年增加 1 个。

2012 年聚氯乙烯糊树脂主要进口流向为山东省，进口数量 44306170kg，占总进口数量的 37.16%，比上年进口数量增加 54.81%；

其次为广东省，进口数量 24523398kg，占总进口数量的 20.57%，比上年进口数量减少 0.54%；

江苏省，进口数量 21638455kg，占总进口数量的 18.15%，比上年进口数量增加 11.97%；

河北省，进口数量 20132640kg，占总进口数量的 16.89%，比上年进口数量增加 49.74%；

福建省，进口数量 3845450kg，占总进口数量的 3.23%，比上年进口数量增加 21.42%。

2012 年聚氯乙烯糊树脂五大进口省市进口数量占总进口数量的 95.99%；比上年进口数量增加 2.32%（表 50）。

表 50　2012 年聚氯乙烯糊树脂十大进口省市统计

排序	进口省市	进口金额/美元	进口数量/kg	占比例/%
1	山东省	64941410.00	44306170	37.16
2	广东省	36881316.00	24523398	20.57
3	江苏省	33395679.00	21638455	18.15
4	河北省	29308784.00	20132640	16.89
5	福建省	5602785.00	3845450	3.23
6	上海市	4002304.00	2319883	1.95
7	吉林省	2515030.00	1447630	1.21
8	浙江省	507948.00	331226	0.28
进口总计		178360178.00	119223177	100.00

中国聚氯乙烯糊树脂需求市场在东部沿海地区，主要分布在长江三角洲及珠江三角洲。

2012 年聚氯乙烯糊树脂进口消费省市 13 个，有 7 个在东部沿海地区，长江三角洲及珠江三角洲八省市进口量占总进口数量的 81.33%

五、2012～2013 年价格走势及原因分析

自 2011 年下半年以来，国内糊树脂下游企业受资金紧缩、订单量下降等因素制约，开工率明显不足，部分地区甚至停产倒闭，从一定程度上导致糊树脂需求量萎缩，造成企业出货量大幅减少，市场成交量进一步受到压缩。

2012 年 9 月份国内糊树脂市场虽已摆脱了上半年的低迷，销售情况有所好转，皮革料送到报价在 10800～11000 元/t，手套料送到报价在 10500～10600 元/t，但 2011 年上半年的行情仍相距甚远。

2012 年 9 月份 PVC 糊树脂出现了上涨行情。9 月 17 日华东市场通用 PVC 糊树脂价格达到 10200～10400 元/t，比 8 月上涨了 300 元，厂家销售情况基本良好。由于前几个月国内 PVC 糊树脂企业或停产检修，或压低负荷等原因，国内厂家库存较低，这也为市场价格上涨打下了基础。

此外，近期 PVC 糊树脂出口量也有所上升，俄罗斯、乌克兰等国家需求的增加对国内市场也是利好。目前，PVC 糊树脂厂家已经普遍提高生产负荷。

10 月份 PVC 糊树脂市场将有所变化。内蒙古伊东化工新建 100kt/aPVC 糊树脂装置预计将竣工开车。沈阳化工 8 月 31 日宣布 130kt/aPVC 糊树脂装置 3 年搬迁新区计划，搬迁后 PVC 糊树脂装置能力将达到 200kt/a。

2008 年中国聚氯乙烯糊树脂进口月平均价/(美元/t)	1 月	2 月	3 月	4 月	5 月	6 月
	1235.65	1291.91	1264.17	1268.06	1349.70	1386.28
	7 月	8 月	9 月	10 月	11 月	12 月
	1418.86	1422.98	1512.69	1548.26	1405.45	1266.87
2009 年中国聚氯乙烯糊树脂进口月平均价/(美元/t)	1 月	2 月	3 月	4 月	5 月	6 月
	1107.20	1037.35	954.53	960.95	952.28	1017.48
	7 月	8 月	9 月	10 月	11 月	12 月
	972.46	1080.85	1121.41	1187.86	1159.01	1169.25
2010 年中国聚氯乙烯糊树脂进口月平均价/(美元/t)	1 月	2 月	3 月	4 月	5 月	6 月
	1169.70	1210.29	1282.17	1407.07	1408.75	1420.28
	7 月	8 月	9 月	10 月	11 月	12 月
	1430.07	1416.19	1434.28	1454.87	1435.96	1495.21

续表

2011年中国聚氯乙烯糊树脂进口月平均价/(美元/t)	1月	2月	3月	4月	5月	6月
	1556.46	1619.08	1609.46	1668.43	1738.48	1794.67
	7月	8月	9月	10月	11月	12月
	1864.24	1848.30	1852.68	1806.16	1784.76	1714.62
2012年中国聚氯乙烯糊树脂进口月平均价/(美元/t)	1月	2月	3月	4月	5月	6月
	1640.74	1553.02	1504.24	1551.42	1555.86	1563.81
	7月	8月	9月	10月	11月	12月
	1508.76	1413.44	1399.69	1458.28	1449.42	1463.67
2008年中国聚氯乙烯糊树脂出口月平均价/(美元/t)	1月	2月	3月	4月	5月	6月
	948.10	1010.40	1101.75	1246.18	1213.48	1288.25
	7月	8月	9月	10月	11月	12月
	1308.04	1405.56	1556.14	1410.11	1663.14	1148.84
2009年中国聚氯乙烯糊树脂出口月平均价/(美元/t)	1月	2月	3月	4月	5月	6月
	1202.27	1296.41	1093.31	1553.44	1190.41	1417.62
	7月	8月	9月	10月	11月	12月
	1203.31	1370.48	1213.44	1484.14	1373.85	1558.96
2010年中国聚氯乙烯糊树脂出口月平均价/(美元/t)	1月	2月	3月	4月	5月	6月
	1440.67	1835.20	1689.44	1.719.98	1547.01	1506.42
	7月	8月	9月	10月	11月	12月
	1857.78	1676.35	1285.66	1508.67	1223.30	1320.72
2011年中国聚氯乙烯糊树脂出口月平均价/(美元/t)	1月	2月	3月	4月	5月	6月
	1299.87	1415.00	1816.79	1807.09	1635.62	1905.19
	7月	8月	9月	10月	11月	12月
	1946.14	1845.01	1855.51	2082.56	2230.72	1808.09
2012年中国聚氯乙烯糊树脂出口月平均价/(美元/t)	1月	2月	3月	4月	5月	6月
	2483.25	1419.69	1523.44	1814.32	1758.63	1672.16
	7月	8月	9月	10月	11月	12月
	1643.88	1865.76	1640.74	1561.08	1746.74	1714.78

六、后言

法国KEM ONE(原阿科玛乙烯工业分部)宣布扩大其位于西班牙的PVC糊树脂装置产能，扩能幅度为7000t/a，届时该装置产能将达42kt/a。新增产能于2013年全面投产后，KEM ONE位于法国Saint－Auban和西班牙Hernani的两个生产基地的整体产能将达112kt/a。

国内受宏观经济形势、聚氯乙烯市场持续低迷及下游需求不振等因素的影响，国内糊树脂产业已呈现供应不断增加、需求疲软的状态。

而目前国内企业在建或准备扩建的糊树脂装置累计总产能近100kt/a。若全部实施，将加重供过于求的态势。

这主要是因为，糊树脂产业供需结构依然存在问题。目前宏观经济环境不佳，国内房地产市场不景气，糊树脂产品应用于壁纸、软管方面的需求大幅度减少。尤其是国内普通糊树脂的最大用途人造革的应用，出现了很大萎缩，主要原因是人造革应用中糊树脂的替代品——聚氨酯人造革用量越来越大。

由于目前下游需求的增速低于糊树脂产能的增速，且糊树脂产品种类单一，因此短期内市场总体供求矛盾已十分突出。

再加上下游制品行业对国际出口市场依赖性较强，国际经济环境恶化，对国内糊树脂市场也产生了较大影响。

在需求萎缩的同时，未来国内企业在建或准备扩建糊树脂装置的态势却愈加明显，扩能高潮正在到来。据不完全统计，目前新扩建年总产能累计近百万吨。

有消息称，中盐红四方公司年产100kt项目，目前已进入设备安装阶段，计划2013年6月正式开车；

内蒙古伊东化工新建100kt/a PVC糊树脂装置2013年竣工开车。

沈阳化工2012年8月31日宣布130kt/a PVC糊树脂装置3年搬迁新区计划，搬迁后PVC糊树脂装置能力2015年将达到200kt/a。

另外，内蒙古晨宏力二期60kt/a PVC糊树脂装置和西安热电化工新建的40kt/a PVC糊树脂装置，预计都在2013年内竣工。

山东朗盛石油化学有限公司年产60kt特种糊树脂项目动工，计划2013年竣工；

而台塑公司将把在中国台湾的年产70kt糊树脂搬迁到宁波，计划2014年投产。

如果这些项目全部实施，国内糊树脂产能过剩的局面将进一步加剧。

虽然项目众多，产能巨大，但我国糊树脂牌号依旧较少，特别是高端产品稀缺。在汽车行业等应用领域，国内生产的糊树脂产品大多数还不能完全满足全部质量指标要求，受到很大制约，特别是抗石击涂料糊树脂专用料，还需要大量进口以满足后加工需求。

另外，其他相关的改性产品如掺混树脂、氯醋树脂、抗静电糊树脂等，由于具有独特的性能，在汽车塑熔胶、PVC方块地毯、印花油墨等制品中的用量不断增加。

在汽车、医疗等领域，由于国内产品尚不能完全满足实际需求，导致每年还需进口将近100kt的同类产品。

对此，有专家提醒，中国糊树脂行业应建立科学的发展规划，而非盲目扩大产能。准备涉足糊树脂的生产厂家要谨慎行事，避免市场风险，新厂家除非准备生产共聚高档糊树脂，否则对于目前糊树脂市场不宜盲目进入。

今后行业应侧重扩大对中高端糊树脂的科研、开发与生产，以减少高端专用料的进口需求，力求尽可能生产具有自己特色的专用树脂品种，以满足不同用户对糊树脂的需求，不断拓宽产品的应用范围，使我国糊树脂的生产向高品质、低成本方向发展，提升其在国内外市场的竞争能力。

第四章　2012年聚氯乙烯树脂产量增长进口下降出口上升

一、2012年聚氯乙烯产量实现同比增长

2012年全国PVC总产能突破23000kt大关，比2011年增长1530kt。

2006~2012年产能增长了95.08%，年均增长率为11.78%；

2006~2012年产量增长了60.97%，年均增长率为8.26%；

2006~2012年期间产能增长大于产量增长，年均增长率高出3.52%。

1.2012年聚氯乙烯开工率仍低于六成

2012年底国内聚氯乙烯(含糊树脂，不含停产转产)产能共计23410kt/a，增速有所放缓，同比增长6.99%。

2012年国内聚氯乙烯月产量继续维持在1070~1170kt左右，月产量超过1100kt的月份，仅3，5，6，9，12月五个月，2012年国内聚氯乙烯开工率仍低下，最高月份也仅刚过六成，最低月份仅刚过五成。

统计数据显示，2012年12月份全国聚氯乙烯产量为1122kt，1~12月份的累计产量为13261.5kt，与2011年同期累计相比增加了2.39%(表51)。

表51　2006~2012年中国PVC产能产量统计

项目	2006	2007	2008	2009	2010	2011	2012
产能/kt	12000	15200	16000	18000	20690	21880	23410
年增长/%	31.87	26.67	5.26	12.50	14.94	5.75	6.99
产量/kt	8238.0	9716.78	8816.42	9155.28	11301.00	12951.81	13261.50
年增长/%	23.29	17.95	-9.27	3.84	23.44	14.61	2.39
开工率/%	68.65	67.15	55.10	50.86	49.13	59.91	56.65

目前国内聚氯乙烯产能几乎过剩一半，2012 年聚氯乙烯生产企业出现大面积亏损。

据广东塑交所对 73 家重点聚氯乙烯生产企业统计，普遍利润大幅下降，甚至亏损，如上海氯碱化工股份有限公司 2012 年利润大幅下降 50%；

2012 年聚氯乙烯亏损企业达 36 家，亏损比例几乎近一半，是近年来最为严重的一年。

2012 年，由河北盛华化工有限公司自主研发生产的高抗冲 PVC 复合树脂获得国家发明专利。盛华化工年产 10kt 高抗冲 PVC 复合树脂工业化生产线已经投产，聚合釜生产装置达到了 $30m^3$。

到 2012 年底，公司建成年产 50kt/a 的高抗冲 PVC 复合树脂工业化生产线，聚合釜装置扩大到 $70m^3$。

国内一些大型 PVC 生产企业开始加大在特种、专用 PVC 树脂领域的研发投资力度，并向高抗冲 PVC 复合树脂这一高端产品发起攻关，但一直没有取得成功。

2. 我国聚氯乙烯新增产能正向西北部地区转移

我国七大区域聚氯乙烯产能分布如下：

西北地区占 36.00%；华北地区占 29.00%；华东地区占 13.00%；华中地区占 8.00%；西南地区占 7.00%；东北地区占 4.00%；华南地区占 300%。

从生产大区划分来看，聚氯乙烯树脂产地已由东部地区向中西部地区转移，2008 年前东部地区聚氯乙烯树脂产能达 75% 以上，2010 年降到 54.36%，2011 年降到 47.19%，中西部地区聚氯乙烯树脂产能首次超过东部地区聚氯乙烯树脂，2012 年中西部地区聚氯乙烯树脂产能首次超过全国产能五成，占全国聚氯乙烯树脂产能一半江山。

从 2013 年以及以后的新增产能来看，新增产能主要集中在中西部地区，尤其是新疆、内蒙古两地，主要因为中西部地区丰富的矿产资源和低廉的成本，新增产能装置多为 40 万吨以上大装置。

电石法聚氯乙烯装置正集中向西部地区扩展，其多向上下游产业链靠拢，并涌现出新疆中泰化学股份有限公司、新疆天业化学股份有限责任公司等百万吨级以上规模企业，电石法聚氯乙烯成本正向最小化发展，市场竞争压力进一步增加。

二、2012 年出口生产省市分析

1. 2012 年国内聚氯乙烯树脂出口生产省市分析

2012 年初级形状的聚氯乙烯（未掺其他物质）出口省市有 25 家，比上 24 家出口省市增加 1 家出口省市。

2012 年初级形状的聚氯乙烯（未掺其他物质）出口生产企业主要集中在新疆维吾尔自治区，出口数量 216479356kg，占总出口数量的 56.136%，比上年出口增加 44964276kg，比上年上升 26.22%；

其次为天津市出口数量 95759525kg，占总出口数量的 24.832%，比上年出口增加 28757750kg，比上年上升 42.92%；

江苏省出口数量 21575918kg，占总出口数量的 5.595%，比上年出口减少 8450090kg，比上年减少 28.14%；

河北省出口数量 18120480kg，占总出口数量的 4.699%，比上年出口增加 6087561kg，比上年增加 50.59%；

山东省出口数量 10395597kg，占总出口数量的 2.696%，比上年出口减少 18618850kg，比上年减少 64.17%；

五省市出口数量占初级形状的聚氯乙烯（未掺其他物质）2012 年总出口数量的 93.957%，比上年增加 9.564%（表 52）。

表 52　2012 年初级形状的聚氯乙烯（未掺其他物质）五大出口省市统计

排序	出口省市	出口金额/美元	出口数量/kg	占比例/%
1	新疆维吾尔自治区	198547936.00	216479356	56.136
2	天津市	90243949.00	95759525	24.832
3	江苏省	20826371.00	21575918	5.595
4	河北省	17028724.00	18120480	4.699
5	山东省	9956914.00	10395597	2.696
出口总计		364205012.00	385633252	100.00

2012 年初级形状的未塑化聚氯乙烯出口省市有 20 家，与上年 16 家出口省市增加 4 个出口省市。

初级形状的未塑化聚氯乙烯出口生产企业主要集中在山东省，出口数量 2072124kg，占总出口数量的 20.794%，比上年出口增加 1048279kg，比上年上升 102.39%；

其次为新疆维吾尔自治区，出口数量 1304384kg，占总出口数量的 13.090%，比上年出口减少971156kg，比上年减少42.68%；

广东省，出口数量1229475kg，占总出口数量的12.338%，比上年出口减少1026292kg，比上年减少45.50%；

江苏省，出口数量1162983kg，占总出口数量的11.674%，比上年出口增加30041kg，比上年上升2.65%；

辽宁省，出口数量1059106kg，占总出口数量的10.628%，比上年出口增加787081kg，比上年上升289.34%。

2012年五省市出口数量占初级形状的未塑化聚氯乙烯总出口数量的68.521%，比上年减少8.68%(表53)。

表53　2012年初级形状的未塑化的聚氯乙烯五大出口省市统计

排序	出口省市	出口金额/美元	出口数量/kg	占比例/%
1	山东省	3，215，217.00	2072124	20.794
2	新疆维吾尔自治区	1，703，138.00	1304384	13.090
3	广东省	1，675，919.00	1229475	12.338
4	江苏省	2，959，672.00	1162983	11.671
5	辽宁省	1，167，611.00	1059106	10.628
	2012	14，664，423.00	9964884	100.00

2012年初级形状的已塑化聚氯乙烯出口省市有24家，比上年22家出口省市增加2家出口省市。

2012年初级形状的已塑化聚氯乙烯出口生产企业主要集中在广东省，出口数量21160160kg，占总出口数量的42.745%，比上年出口数量减少2.81%；

其次为浙江省，出口数量9131014kg，占总出口数量的18.445%，比上年出口数量上升4.82%；

上海市出口数量5986772kg，占总出口数量的12.094%，比上年出口数量上升98.72%；

江苏省出口数量4752745kg，占总出口数量的9.601%，比上年出口数量上升88.76%。

福建省出口数量2988572kg，占总出口数量的6.037%，比上年出口数量上升95.28%；

五省市2012年出口数量占初级形状的已塑化聚氯乙烯总出口数量的88.921%，比上年出口数量上升4.159%(表54)。

表54　2012年初级形状的已塑化的聚氯乙烯五大出口省市统计

排序	出口省市	出口金额/美元	出口数量/kg	占比例/%
1	广东省	32，058，634.00	21160160	42.745
2	浙江省	14，227，109.00	9131014	18.445
3	上海市	12，953，018.00	5986772	12.094
4	江苏省	9，974，196.00	4752745	9.601
5	福建省	3，546，370.00	2988572	6.037
出口总计		83，362，585.00	49503564	100.00

2. 国内聚氯乙烯出口商

2012年其他初级形状的聚氯乙烯未掺其他物质出口商共计有331家，出口额最高的十位出口商九家为生产企业，仅一家为贸易商，十大出口商出口数量占总出口数量的65.275%。

新疆中泰化学股份有限公司、天津大沽化工股份有限公司、苏州华苏塑料有限公司、唐山氯碱有限责任公司、天津乐金大沽化学有限公司、山东东岳化工有限公司、新疆天业对外贸易有限责任公司、内蒙古三联化工股份有限公司、中化物产股份有限公司、唐山三友国际贸易有限公司，分别位居2012年其他初级形状的聚氯乙烯未掺其他物质出口量1~10位，出口量分别占总出口量的24.874%、21.167%、5.432%、3.555%、3.263%、2.122%、1.613%、1.428%、1.023%和0.797%。

2012年其他初级形状的聚氯乙烯未掺其他物质三十八大出口商中生产企业占十六大，十六大生产企业出口数量占总出口数量的65.950%，均为聚氯乙烯树脂原料生产厂。

2012年其他初级形状的聚氯乙烯未掺其他物质三十八大出口商中贸易商占二十二大，二十二大贸易商出口数量占总出口数量的3.259%(表55)。

表55 2012年其他初级形状的聚氯乙烯未掺其他物质三十八大出口商统计

排序	出口商	所属行业	出口数量/kg	占比例/%
1	新疆中泰化学股份有限公司	聚氯乙烯树脂原料	95922500	24.874
2	天津大沽化工股份有限公司	聚氯乙烯树脂原料	81628775	21.167
3	苏州华苏塑料有限公司	聚氯乙烯树脂原料	20947746	5.432
4	唐山氯碱有限责任公司	聚氯乙烯树脂原料	13710500	3.555
5	天津乐金大沽化学有限公司	聚氯乙烯树脂原料	12583000	3.263
6	山东东岳化工有限公司	聚氯乙烯树脂原料	8185000	2.122
7	新疆天业集团对外贸易有限公司	聚氯乙烯树脂原料	6220000	1.613
8	内蒙古三联化工股份有限公司	聚氯乙烯树脂原料	5508000	1.428
9	中化物产股份有限公司	贸易商	3945000	1.023
10	唐山三友国际贸易有限公司	聚氯乙烯树脂原料	3072000	0.797
11	上海氯碱化工股份有限公司	聚氯乙烯树脂原料	2462600	0.639
12	广州东江汇诚国际贸易有限公司	贸易商	1666500	0.432
13	宜宾天原股份有限公司	聚氯乙烯树脂原料	1020000	0.265
14	内蒙古君正化工有限责任公司	聚氯乙烯树脂原料	840000	0.218
15	青岛海晶化工集团有限公司	聚氯乙烯树脂原料	725500	0.188
16	中平能化国际贸易有限公司	贸易商	717500	0.186
17	昆明汉声经贸有限公司	贸易商	553000	0.143
18	上海海螺国际投资发展有限公司	贸易商	544500	0.141
19	韩华化学(宁波)有限公司	聚氯乙烯树脂原料	517075	0.134
20	SUPER乐运(天津)国际物流发展有限公司	贸易商	510000	0.132
21	湖北宜化化工股份有限公司	聚氯乙烯树脂原料	510000	0.132
22	广州江枫物流有限公司	贸易商	506000	0.131
23	惠州市致远国际贸易有限公司	贸易商	505235	0.131
24	新疆天业集团(上海)销售中心	聚氯乙烯树脂原料	472500	0.123
25	湖南金环化工进出口有限公司	贸易商	406000	0.105
26	郑州宏润进出口贸易有限公司	贸易商	378175	0.098
27	上海申缆科技贸易公司	贸易商	352000	0.091
28	新疆野马经贸有限公司	贸易商	348000	0.090
29	宁波显龙国际贸易有限公司	贸易商	306000	0.079
30	上海中昌树脂有限公司	贸易商	288000	0.075
31	新疆黄金中亚工程技术有限公司	贸易商	232000	0.060
32	丹东鼎泰贸易有限公司	贸易商	220000	0.057
33	广州保税区精卫国际贸易有限公司	贸易商	210000	0.054
34	上海对外经济贸易实业浦东有限公司	贸易商	184000	0.048
35	深圳仁锐实业有限公司	贸易商	182000	0.047
36	福州布罗森进出口有限公司	贸易商	178150	0.046
37	长沙诚瑞化工机械有限公司	贸易商	170000	0.044
38	丹东茂兴经贸有限公司	贸易商	165000	0.043
	出口总计		385633252	100.00

2012年初级形状未塑化的聚氯乙烯烯出口商共计有216家，出口额最高的十位出口商全部为为贸易商，十大出口商出口数量占总出口数量的57.014%。

潍坊高信化工科技有限公司、丹东大同江贸易有限公司、乌鲁木齐美利得进出口有限公司、江苏利思德化工有限公司、浙江天博进出口有限公司、新疆未来型材有限公司、佛山億石建材有限公司、上海川投进出口有限公司、宁波浩航进出口有限公司、黑龙江佳进国际贸易有限公司，分别位居2012年初初级形状未塑化的聚氯乙烯出口量1～10位，出口量分别占总出口量的15.623%、8.578%、8.093%、7.534%、4.027%、3.249%、3.131%、2.470%、2.302%和2.007%。

2012年初级形状未塑化的聚氯乙烯十八大出口商全部为贸易商，占总出口量的66.732%(表56)。

表56　2012年初级形状未塑化的聚氯乙烯十八大出口商统计

排序	出口商	所属行业	出口数量/kg	占比例/%
1	潍坊高信化工科技有限公司	贸易商	1556800	15.623
2	丹东大同江贸易有限公司	贸易商	854743	8.578
3	乌鲁木齐美利得进出口有限公司	贸易商	806500	8.093
4	江苏利思德化工有限公司	贸易商	750780	7.534
5	浙江天博进出口有限公司	贸易商	401307	4.027
6	新疆未来型材有限公司	贸易商	323789	3.249
7	佛山億石建材有限公司	贸易商	312000	3.131
8	上海川投进出口有限公司	贸易商	246100	2.470
9	宁波浩航进出口有限公司	贸易商	229360	2.302
10	黑龙江佳进国际贸易有限公司	贸易商	200000	2.007
11	佛山市联塑进出口贸易有限公司	贸易商	156131	1.567
12	青岛格鲁博进出口有限公司	贸易商	146300	1.468
13	丹东金三源贸易有限公司	贸易商	136000	1.365
14	厦门物资集团有限公司	贸易商	120000	1.204
15	北京瑞华纺织有限公司	贸易商	109000	1.094
16	丹东市远达商务公司	贸易商	101000	1.014
17	深圳市智勇光贸易有限公司	贸易商	100000	1.004
18	郑州市杰德大通商贸有限公司	贸易商	100000	1.004
	出口总计		9964884	100.00

2012年初级形状已塑化的聚氯乙烯出口商共计有236家，出口额最高的十位出口商九家为生产企业，仅一家为贸易商，十大出口商出口数量占总出口数量的47.810%。

东莞银禧塑胶有限公司、上海理研塑料有限公司、科铨塑胶(深圳)有限公司、飞佛特种纺织品(宁波)有限公司、大连JMS医疗器具有限公司、桐乡市小老板特种塑料制品有限公司、东莞普立万氯乙烯聚合体有限公司、爱普科精细化工(苏州)有限公司、新疆立爱普贸易有限公司、冠德塑胶(深圳)有限公司，分别位居2012年初级形状已塑化的聚氯乙烯出口量1～10位，出口量分别占总出口量的9.213%、8.995%、8.267%、4.727%、3.381%、3.088%、2.739%、2.542%、2.432%和2.426%。

2012年初级形状已塑化的聚氯乙烯三十八大出口商中生产企业占二十三大，二十三大生产企业出口数量占总出口数量的59.679%，均为改性聚氯乙烯树脂(即PVC合金)，PVC电缆料生产企业。

2012年初级形状已塑化的聚氯乙烯三十八大出口商中贸易商占十五大，十五大贸易商出口数量占总出口数量的 14.083%(表 57)。

表 57　2012 年初级形状已塑化的聚氯乙烯三十八大出口商统计

排序	出口商	所属行业	出口数量/kg	占比例/%
1	东莞银禧塑胶有限公司	PVC 改性	4560926	9.213
2	上海理研塑料有限公司	PVC 改性	4452994	8.995
3	科铨塑胶(深圳)有限公司	PVC 改性	4092403	8.267
4	飞佛特种纺织品(宁波)有限公司	医疗器具	2340024	4.727
5	大连 JMS 医疗器具有限公司	医疗器具	1673637	3.381
6	桐乡市小老板特种塑料制品有限公司	PVC 电缆料	1528865	3.088
7	东莞普立万氯乙烯聚合体有限公司	PVC 改性	1355852	2.739
8	爱普科精细化工(苏州)有限公司	PVC 改性	1258601	2.542
9	新疆立爱普贸易有限公司	贸易商	1203720	2.432
10	冠德塑胶(深圳)有限公司	PVC 改性	1200720	2.426
11	江阴中卡新材料有限公司	PVC 改性	1097934	2.218
12	台州市金康进出口有限公司	贸易商	1064000	2.149
13	保荣利塑胶原料(深圳)有限公司	贸易商	863215	1.744
14	亮军塑胶(深圳)有限公司	PVC 改性	863000	1.743
15	大电塑料(上海)有限公司	PVC 改性	851662	1.743
16	东莞大通电线有限公司	PVC 改性	723775	1.462
17	浙江中大新佳贸易有限公司	贸易商	674500	1.363
18	镒胜电子科技(昆山)有限公司	PVC 改性	537860	1.087
19	增城金太源塑胶有限公司	PVC 改性	511335	1.033
20	安徽进出口股份有限公司	贸易商	474650	0.959
21	深圳市龙岗区对外经济发展有限公司	贸易商	442228	0.893
22	东莞佳凯塑胶制品有限公司	PVC 电缆料	426948	0.862
23	广州金发科技股份有限公司	PVC 改性	364500	0.736
24	东莞启东电线电缆有限公司	PVC 电缆料	354100	0.715
25	福州布罗森进出口有限公司	贸易商	343325	0.694
26	福泰克(连云港)电线有限公司	PVC 电缆料	335456	0.678
27	深圳市二善进出口有限公司	贸易商	305450	0.617
28	江阴长江磁卡有限公司	PVC 改性	289412	0.585
29	杭州美亚三福塑料有限公司	PVC 电缆料	279718	0.565
30	上海中大康劲国际贸易有限公司	贸易商	279100	0.564
31	友谊县兴旺达对外贸易有限责任公司	贸易商	278075	0.562
32	佛山市南海奇镭鞋材有限公司	PVC 改性	252000	0.509
33	深圳中外运物流有限公司	贸易商	224936	0.454
34	深圳市宝安外经发展有限公司	贸易商	220423	0.445
35	无锡凯嘉经贸发展有限公司	贸易商	200000	0.404
36	东莞荣泰塑化材料有限公司	贸易商	200000	0.404
37	浙江经协国际经贸有限公司	贸易商	197800	0.400
38	杭州乐荣电线电器有限公司	PVC 电缆料	180570	0.365
	出口总计		49503564	100.00

三、2012 年仍进口下降出口上升

根据海关数据显示，2012 年 1～12 月份 PVC 纯粉进口量累计为 940.42kt，累计同比减少 10.51%。

2012 年 1～12 月份 PVC 纯粉累计出口 385.63kt，累计同比增加 4.90%。

随着我国聚氯乙烯(PVC)行业的快速发展，我国聚氯乙烯进出口格局发生了重大变化，进口逐年减少，出口量上下波动大，根据海关统计的六个 VCM 聚合物出口数据显示，2012 年除聚氯乙烯糊树脂出口下降 51.01% 外，其余五个 VCM 聚合物出口均小幅增长。

2012 年 VCM 聚合物合计进口 1228.9kt，累计同比减少 8.02%。

2012 年 VCM 聚合物合计出口 465.85kt，累计同比增加 3.12%(表 58)。

表 58　2007～2012 年 PVC 树脂进出口统计　kt

项　目		2007	2008	2009	2010	2011	2012
初级状 PVC，不掺其他物质	进口	1014.33	797.54	1629.92	1199.12	1050.87	940.42
	出口	711.70	599.56	235.65	218.28	367.63	385.63
聚氯乙烯糊树脂	进口	—	63.24	85.54	98.35	97.11	119.22
	出口	—	7.61	3.29	6.37	18.23	8.93
初级状未塑化的 PVC	进口	183.75	176.47	167.06	125.10	88.12	69.89
	出口	12.86	5.75	6.34	5.20	9.86	9.97
初级状已塑化 PVC	进口	105.80	89.53	72.65	88.65	80.34	80.24
	出口	28.43	33.38	29.79	35.93	45.82	49.50
氯乙烯—乙酸乙烯酯共聚物	进口	11.61	9.24	9.20	10.98	12.24	12.56
	出口	1.15	1.20	0.32	9.18	9.75	10.71
其它氯乙烯共聚物	进口	7.34	8.93	8.50	8.31	7.35	6.57
	出口	2.12	2.50	0.10	0.28	0.47	1.11
合　计	进口	1410.80	1148.47	1971.90	1530.46	1336.03	1228.90
	出口	752.99	651.59	278.53	275.24	451.76	465.85
净进口	合计	567.63	496.88	1693.37	1255.22	884.27	763.05
年增长	%	-41.27	-12.46	240.80	-25.87	-29.55	-13.71

2007～2012 年间，中国 VCM 聚合物进口量下降 12.89%，年均进口量下降 2.27%；

2007～2012 年间，中国 VCM 聚合物出口量下降 38.13%，年均下降 7.69%。

1. 2012 年初级形状的聚氯乙烯(不掺其他物质)进口下降出口上升

从海关统计中可看出，2012 年初级形状的聚氯乙烯(不掺其他物质)进口地有 33 个，与上年 42 个进口地减少 9 个进口地，进口 940416013kg，同比减少 10.51%。

主要进口地为美国，进口数量 345783426kg，占总进口量的 36.769%，同减少 4.88%；

其次为中国台湾省进口数量 313895456kg，占总进口量的 33.378%，同比增加 17.75%；

日本进口数量 165106646kg，占总进口量的 17.557%，同比减少 42.23%；

韩国进口数量 43666073kg，占总进口量的 4.643%，同比增加 98.56%；

泰国进口数量 24492911kg，占总进口量的 3.23%，同比减少 27.81%；

五进口地进口数量占初级形状的聚氯乙烯(不掺其他物质)2012 年总进口数量的 94.952%，比上年增加 1.370%(表 59)。

表59　2012年初级形状的聚氯乙烯(未掺其他物质)五大进口国家/地区统计

排序	原产进口地	进口金额/美元	进口数量/kg	占比例/%
1	美国	314553643.00	345783426	36.769
2	中国台湾省	308322547.00	313895456	33.378
3	日本	169361064.00	165106646	17.557
4	韩国	49152468.00	43666073	4.643
5	泰国	26776905.00	24492911	2.604
进口总计		922933114.00	940416013	100.00

从海关统计中可看出，2012年初级形状的初级形状的聚氯乙烯(不掺其他物质)出口地有87个，比上年100个出口地减少13个出口地，出口385633252kg，同比增加4.90%。

主要出口地为俄罗斯联邦出口数量97491749kg，占总出口数量的25.281%，比上年出口数量减少15.29%；

其次为向印度出口84382148kg，占总出口数量的21.881%，比上年出口数量增加228.23百分点；

向乌兹别克斯坦出口数量38587650kg，占总出口数量的10.006%，比上年增加出口数量22.72%；

向韩国出口33227725kg，占总出口数量的8.616%，比上年增加出口数量13.32%；

向马来西亚出口29789672kg，占总出口数量的7.725%，比上年出口数量增加138.64%；

五出口地出口数量占初级形状的初级形状的聚氯乙烯(不掺其他物质)2012年总出口数量的73.510%，比上年增加13.782百分点(表60)。

表60　2012年初级形状的聚氯乙烯(未掺其他物质)五大出口国家/地区统计

排序	出口目的地	出口金额/美元	出口数量/kg	占比例/%
1	俄罗斯联邦	88627126.00	97491749	25.281
2	印度	81709588.00	84382148	21.881
3	乌兹别克斯坦	34827657.00	38587650	10.006
4	韩国	31450034.00	33227725	8.616
5	马来西亚	27602234.00	29789672	7.725
出口总计		364，205，012.00	385633252	100.00

2.2012年初级形状未塑化的聚氯乙烯进口下降出口上升

从海关统计中可看出，2012年初级形状的未塑化聚氯乙烯进口地有39个，比上年34个进口地增加5个进口地，进口69885499kg，同比下降20.70%。

主要进口地为韩国进口数量24930960kg，占总进口量的35.674%，比上年进口量下降40.80%；

其次为中国台湾省进口数量21162795kg，占总进口量的30.282%，比上年进口量下降0.19%；

日本进口数量11927395kg，占总进口量的17.067%，比上年进口量增加9.56%；

马来西亚进口数量5143140kg，占总进口量的7.359%，比上年进口量减少1.69%；

美国进口数量2307450kg，占总进口量的3.302%，比上年进口量减少28.46%；

五原产进口地进口数量占初级形状的未塑化聚氯乙烯2012年总进口数量的93.684%，比上年增加1.352%(表61)。

表61　2012年初级形状的未塑化的聚氯乙烯五大进口国家/地区统计

排序	原产进口地	进口金额/美元	进口数量/kg	占比例/%
1	韩国	31658682.00	24930960	35.674
2	中国台湾省	29117483.00	21162795	30.282
3	日本	14514466.00	11927395	17.067
4	马来西亚	7479820.00	5143140	7.359
5	美国	4167721.00	2307450	3.302
进口总计		95237774.00	69885499	100.00

从海关统计中可看出，2012年初级形状的未塑化聚氯乙烯出口地有59个，比上年71个出口地减少12个出口地，出口9964884kg，同比增加1.05%。

主要出口地为朝鲜出口数量1253799kg，占总出口数量的12.582%，比上年进口量增加127.27%；

其次为向巴林出口942600kg，占总出口数量的9.459%；

向印度出口881713kg，占总出口数量的8.848%；

向吉尔吉斯出口数量817200kg，占总出口数量的8.201%，比上年进口量减少30.74%；

向印度尼西亚出口694410kg，占总出口数量的6.969%，比上年进口量增加21.88%；

五出口地出口数量占初级形状的未塑化聚氯乙烯2012年总出口数量的46.059%，比上年增加0.497%(表62)。

表62 2012年初级形状的未塑化的聚氯乙烯五大出口国家/地区统计

排序	出口目的地	出口金额/美元	出口数量/kg	占比例/%
1	朝鲜	1，474，781.00	1253799	12.582
2	巴林	1，619，816.00	942600	9.459
3	印度	1，268，474.00	881713	8.848
4	吉尔吉斯	928，190.00	817200	8.201
5	印度尼西亚	1，297，451.00	694410	6.969
出口总计		14，664，423.00	9964884	100.00

3.2012年初级形状已塑化的聚氯乙烯进口下降出口增长

从海关统计中可看出，2012年初级形状的已塑化聚氯乙烯进口地有44个，比上年47个进口地减少3个进口地。

初级形状的已塑化聚氯乙烯2012年总进口80239968kg，同比下降0.12%。

主要进口地为中国台湾省进口数量13207204kg，占总进口量的16.460%，比上年进口量减少4.27%；

其次为美国进口数量12668084kg，占总进口量的15.788%，比上年进口量增加20.33%；

中华人民共和国进口数量9278254kg，占总进口量的11.563%，比上年进口量增加8.72%；

日本进口数量9249534kg，占总进口量的11.527%，比上年进口量减少18.50%；

中国香港进口数量8964863kg，占总进口量的11.173%，比上年进口量增加44.09%；

五原产进口地进口数量占初级形状的已塑化聚氯乙烯2012年总进口数量的66.510%，比上年进口量增加0.420%(表63)。

表63 2012年初级形状的已塑化的聚氯乙烯五大进口国家/地区统计

排序	原产进口地	进口金额/美元	进口数量/kg	占比例/%
1	中国台湾省	19，752，972.00	13207204	16.460
2	美国	28，199，848.00	12668084	15.788
3	中华人民共和国	16，027，015.00	9278254	11.563
4	日本	34，023，582.00	9249534	11.527
5	中国香港	13，520，854.00	8964863	11.173
进口总计		171，412，800.00	80239968	100.00

从海关统计中可看出，2012年初级形状的已塑化聚氯乙烯出口地有101个，比上年101个出口地持平，出口49503564kg，同比上升8.05%。

主要出口地为中国香港出口数量11706485kg，占总出口数量的23.648%，比上年出口数量减少10.50%；

其次为向菲律宾出口数量4334518kg，占总出口数量的8.756%，比上年出口数量增加40.56%；

向泰国出口数量2986612kg，占总出口数量的6.033%，比上年出口数量增加220.57%；

向越南出口数量2818714kg，占总出口数量的5.694%，比上年出口数量增加2.89%；

向新加坡出口数量2762683kg，占总出口数量的5.581%，比上年出口数量增加42.73%。

五出口地出口数量占初级形状的已塑化聚氯乙烯20112年总出口数量的49.712%，比上年出口数量减少 1.060%(表 64)。

表 64 2012 年初级形状的已塑化的聚氯乙烯五大出口国家/地区统计

排序	出口目的地	出口金额/美元	出口数量/kg	占比例/%
1	中国香港	19792034.00	11706485	23.648
2	菲律宾	5895229.00	4334518	8.756
3	泰国	6572570.00	2986612	6.033
4	越南	4927030.00	2818714	5.694
5	新加坡	6469832.00	2762683	5.581
出口总计		83362585.00	49503564	100.00

四、消费

2006~2012 年间 PVC 树脂总表观消费量年均增长 7.27%，低于同期产量年均增长率 0.99%。2012 年国内自给率 94.55%，同比增长 0.94%(表 65)。

表 65 2006~2012 年国内 PVC 表观消费量统计资料

项目	2006	2007	2008	2009	2010	2011	2012
表观消费量/kt	9204.59	10374.59	9313.30	10848.65	12546.44	13836.08	14024.55
年增长率/%	14.81	12.71	-10.23	16.49	15.65	10.28	1.36
国内自给率/%	89.50	93.66	94.66	84.39	90.07	93.61	94.55

2011 年我国 PVC 表观消费量为 140245.5kt，同比增长 1.36%。

表 66 2013 年 PVC 消费结构预测

消费行业	占比例/%	消费行业	占比例/%
管材管件	29.00	薄膜	11.00
型材	26.00	电线电缆	9.00
片材管材	9.00	其他软制品	700
人造革	5.00	其他硬制品	4.00

注：其他 PVC 软制品包括墙纸、发泡、材料以及地板革材。

1. PVC 进口消费省市集中流向东部沿海地区

从海关资料来看，2012 年初级形状的聚氯乙烯(未掺其他物质)进口消费省市有 19 个，比上年 24 个进口消费省市减少 5 个进口消费省市，前五位 2012 年初级形状的聚氯乙烯进口消费省市进口量占总进口量的 96.977%，比上年增加 12.87%；

2012 年初级形状的聚氯乙烯(未掺其他物质)主要进口流向为广东省，进口数量 605032003kg，占总进口数量的 64.337%，比上年进口增加 46.7211 倍；

其次为福建省，进口数量 116853784kg，占总进口数量的 12.426%%，比上年进口增加 43.00 倍；

上海市，进口数量 90608859kg，占总进口数量的 9.635%，比上年进口增加 7.148 倍；

江苏省，进口数量 81662705kg，占总进口数量的 8.684%%，比上年进口增加 171.97%；

浙江省，进口数量 17828848kg，占总进口数量的 1.896%，比上年进口增加 69.80%(表 67)。

表 67 2012 年初级形状的聚氯乙烯(未掺其他物质)五大进口省市统计

排序	进口省市	进口金额/美元	进口数量/kg	占比例/%
1	广东省	594288939.00	605032003	64.337
2	福建省	103996850.00	116853784	12.426
3	上海市	90113230.00	90608859	9.635
4	江苏省	82076857.00	81662705	8.684
5	浙江省	17776857.00	17828848	1.896
进口总计		922933114.00	940416013	100.00

从海关资料来看，2012 年初级形状的未塑化聚氯乙烯进口消费省市有 16 个，比上年 14 个进口消费

省市增加2个进口消费省市，主要进口流向为江苏省、河北省、广东省、上海市和山东省，前五位2012年初级形状的未塑化聚氯乙烯进口消费省市进口量占总进口量的96.459%，比上年减少1.041%。

2012初级形状的未塑化聚氯乙烯主要进口流向为江苏省，进口数量37455943kg，占总进口数量的53.596%，比上年进口增加1.37%；

其次为河北省，进口数量21499300kg，占总进口数量的30.764%，比上年进口减少38.88%；

广东省，进口数量5386860kg，占总进口数量的7.708%，比上年进口减少41.73%；

上海市，进口数量19403111716142kg，占总进口数量的2.776%，比上年进口增加13.06%；

山东省，进口数量1128674kg，占总进口数量的1.615%，比上年进口增加7.96%(表68)。

表68　2012年初级形状的未塑化的聚氯乙烯五大进口省市统计

排序	进口省市	进口金额/美元	进口数量/kg	占比例/%
1	江苏省	45013997.00	37455943	53.596
2	河北省	31379522.00	21499300	30.764
3	广东省	6413246.00	5386860	7.708
4	上海市	4087220.00	1940311	2.776
5	山东省	3374961.00	1128674	1.615
进口总计		95237774.00	69885499	100.00

从海关资料来看，2012年初级形状的已塑化聚氯乙烯进口消费省市有20个，比上年210个进口消费省市持平。

主要进口流向为广东省、江苏省、福建省、山东省和浙江省，前五位2012年初级形状的已塑化聚氯乙烯进口消费省市进口量占总进口量的82.164%，比上年增加0.884%。

2012初级形状的已塑化聚氯乙烯主要进口流向为广东省，进口数量35839417kg，占总进口数量的44.665%，比上年进口增加3.10%；

其次为江苏省，进口数量15079066kg，占总进口数量的18.792%，比上年进口增加11.73%；

福建省进口数量5904253kg，占总进口数量的7.358%，比上年进口减少14.15%；

山东省进口数量5618494kg，占总进口数量的7.002%，比上年进口减少18.31%；

浙江省进口数量3487324kg，占总进口数量的4.346%，比上年进口减少1.94%(表69)。

表69　2012年初级形状的已塑化的聚氯乙烯五大进口省市统计

排序	进口省市	进口金额/美元	进口数量/kg	占比例/%
1	广东省	63454180.00	35839417	44.665
2	江苏省	34281502.00	15079066	18.792
3	福建省	13495619.00	5904253	7.358
4	山东省	11348002.00	5618494	7.002
5	浙江省	10742302.00	3487324	4.346
进口总计		171412800.00	80239968	100.00

2.2012年初级形状的聚氯乙烯(未掺其他物质)大进口商

2011年初级形状的聚氯乙烯进口商共计有799家，比上年818家减少19家进口商，进口额最高的十位进口商进口数量占总进口数量的29.937%，比上年增加3.577%，九家为进口生产使用企业，一家为贸易商。

从资料分析，2012年初级形状的聚氯乙烯(未掺其他物质)进口生产使用企业以塑胶工业、装饰材料工业、塑料改性、建材工业、制鞋工业为主。

2012年三十八大初级形状的聚氯乙烯进口商中有三十七大为进口生产企业进口量占总进口量的51.238%，三十八大初级形状的聚氯乙烯进口商中仅有一家贸易商(表70)。

表 70　2012 年初级形状的聚氯乙烯(未掺其他物质)三十八大进口商统计

排序	进口商	所属行业	进口数量/kg	占比例/%
1	明达塑胶(厦门)有限公司	塑胶工业	54774500	5.824
2	广州宏信塑胶工业有限公司	塑胶工业	48067229	5.111
3	太平洋塑胶(福建)有限公司	塑胶工业	35010000	3.723
4	东莞怡昌塑胶制品有限公司	塑胶工业	22284448	2.370
5	力升树灯(河源)有限公司	装饰材料工业	21926360	2.332
6	澄海市华翔塑胶有限公司	塑胶工业	21342943	2.270
7	东莞泛昌窗帘制品有限公司	装饰材料工业	21227750	2.257
8	上海荣威塑胶工业有限公司	塑胶工业	21020707	2.235
9	宇达(中国)投资有限公司厦门分公司	贸易商	18268000	1.943
10	南通荣威塑胶工业有限公司	塑胶工业	17603300	1.872
11	广州宏纶新型材料有限公司	装饰材料工业	15675650	1.667
12	东莞银禧塑胶有限公司	塑胶工业	15332500	1.630
13	东莞百信塑胶制品有限公司	塑胶工业	14500049	1.542
14	太仓敬富塑胶制品有限公司	塑胶工业	14325000	1.523
15	科铨塑胶(深圳)有限公司	塑胶工业	14265415	1.517
16	东莞保利文塑胶制品有限公司	塑胶工业	13973359	1.517
17	上海吉龙塑胶制品有限公司	塑胶工业	13181271	1.402
18	上海劲嘉建材科技有限公司	建材工业	11203550	1.191
19	佛山市高明亿阳塑胶有限公司	塑胶工业	11187875	1.190
20	南亚硬质胶布(广州)有限公司	建材工业	10648000	1.132
21	中山守强塑胶工业有限公司	塑胶工业	5452500	0.580
22	佛山唯尔塑胶制品有限公司	塑胶工业	5214800	0.555
23	东莞宇光鞋业有限公司	制鞋工业	5104000	0.543
24	东莞美哲塑胶制品有限公司	塑胶工业	5088500	0.541
25	从化市铠硕塑胶有限公司	塑胶工业	4989750	0.531
26	东莞金波罗电业科技有限公司	建材工业	4987800	0.530
27	元鼎饰材实业(镇江)有限公司	装饰材料工业	4963000	0.528
28	东莞普隆塑胶制品有限公司	塑胶工业	4787140	0.509
29	上海守强家饰有限公司	装饰材料工业	4776000	0.508
30	佛山高明骏腾塑胶有限公司	塑胶工业	4579500	0.487
31	嘉森塑胶(深圳)有限公司	塑胶工业	4458000	0.474
32	冠德塑胶(深圳)有限公司	塑胶工业	4399500	0.468
33	增城金太源塑胶有限公司	塑胶工业	4354150	0.463
34	东莞普立万氯乙烯聚合体有限公司	塑料改性	4287225	0.456
35	大洋塑胶(惠州)有限公司	塑胶工业	4282085	0.455
36	广州金发科技股份有限公司	塑料改性	4241500	0.451
37	上海长隆塑胶制品有限公司	塑胶工业	4048000	0.430
38	上海鼎丰塑料有限公司	塑胶工业	4000000	0.425
	进口总计		940416013	100.00

2012年初级形状的未塑化的聚氯乙烯进口商共计有291家，比上年282家增加9家进口商，进口量最高的十位进口商进口数量占总进口数量的73.483%，比上年进口增加8.713%，十大进口商均为进口生产使用企业。

从资料分析，初级形状的未塑化的聚氯乙烯进口生产使用企业以塑料制品工业、塑胶工业、手套工业、包装工业、汽车工业、医疗器械工业、建材工业、玩具工业为主。

2012年三十八大初级形状的未塑化的聚氯乙烯进口商中有三十二大为进口生产企业进口量占总进口量的87.957%。

三十八大初级形状的未塑化的聚氯乙烯进口商中仅有六家贸易商，进口量占总进口量的3.289%(表71)。

表71 2012年初级形状的未塑化的聚氯乙烯三十八大进口商统计

排序	进口商	所属行业	进口数量/kg	占比例/%
1	石家庄万力塑胶制品有限公司	塑料制品工业	9687000	13.861
2	张家港市易华塑料有限公司	塑料制品工业	7376000	10.554
3	宿迁市彩塑包装有限公司	包装工业	6953100	9.949
4	宿迁格林手套有限公司	手套工业	5982800	8.561
5	顶级手套(兴化)有限公司	手套工业	5379200	7.697
6	江苏尤佳手套有限公司	手套工业	5008800	7.167
7	石家庄鸿业塑胶制品有限公司	塑料制品工业	3579600	5.122
8	石家庄博仁塑料制品有限公司	塑料制品工业	2815000	4.028
9	张家港顶级手套有限公司	手套工业	2718000	3.889
10	张家港华源塑胶有限公司	塑胶工业	1855800	2.655
11	江苏杰盛手套有限公司	手套工业	1798800	2.574
12	深圳市宝安外经发展有限公司	贸易商	1289825	1.846
13	西默塑品(上海)有限公司	塑料制品工业	952951	1.364
14	东莞泛昌窗帘制品有限公司	装饰材料	933205	1.335
15	青岛大同体系汽车配件有限公司	汽车工业	814918	1.166
16	石家庄鸿锐集团鸿迪塑胶制品有限公司	塑料制品工业	604800	0.865
17	浙江汇锋新材料有限公司	建材工业	519200	0.743
18	石家庄鸿升塑料制品有限公司	塑料制品工业	500000	0.715
19	珠海驰力灯饰电子有限公司	电子工业	472500	0.676
20	石家庄鸿鹰塑料制品有限公司	塑料制品工业	455800	0.652
21	石家庄九源塑业有限公司	塑胶工业	420000	0.601
22	克林尼科医疗器械(南昌)有限公司	医疗器械工业	411271	0.588
23	中山崇高玩具制品厂有限公司	玩具工业	370380	0.530
24	深圳市兴宝工贸有限公司	贸易商	360000	0.515
25	安姆科怀特瓶盖(上海)有限公司	包装工业	323553	0.463
26	上海瑞斯达防护制品有限公司	防护制品	270300	0.387
27	石家庄联合顺达塑胶制品有限公司	塑胶工业	246400	0.353
28	浙江瓯华化工进出口有限公司	贸易商	198800	0.284
29	泛太医疗器械(珠海)有限公司	医疗器械工业	182412	0.261
30	深圳市光明新区经济发展有限公司	贸易商	169030	0.242
31	铜陵市耐科科技有限公司	建材工业	160454	0.230
32	满洲里康盛贸易有限公司	贸易商	159600	0.228
33	新益塑胶制品(深圳)有限公司	塑料制品工业	152150	0.218
34	天津鸿泰塑胶管业有限公司	建材工业	137688	0.197
35	宁波和富塑胶实业有限公司	塑胶工业	136000	0.195
36	中山霖扬塑料有限公司	塑料制品工业	128759	0.184
37	威海韩浩电子有限公司	电子工业	123763	0.177
38	旭有机材商贸(上海)有限公司	贸易商	120000	0.172
	进口总计		69885499	100.00

2012年初级形状的已塑化的聚氯乙烯进口商共计有911家，比上年947家减少36家进口商，进口额最高的十位进口商进口数量占总进口数量的28.071%，比上年进口减少2.029%。

从资料分析，初级形状的已塑化的聚氯乙烯进口生产使用企业以医保用品工业、电线电缆工业、医保用品工业、塑胶工业、改性树脂、装饰材料工业、家用电器工业、制鞋工业、汽车工业为主，2012年三十九大初级形状的已塑化的聚氯乙烯进口商中有三十二大为进口生产企业进口量占总进口量的43.339%。

三十九大初级形状的已塑化的聚氯乙烯进口商中仅有七家贸易商，进口量占总进口量的8.101%（表72）。

表72 2012年初级形状的已塑化的聚氯乙烯三十九大进口商统计

排序	进口商	所属行业	进口数量/kg	占比例/%
1	苏州百特医疗用品有限公司	医保用品工业	4951183	6.170
2	大大电子实业（深圳）有限公司	电子工业	2810809	3.503
3	加铝（天津）铝合金产品有限公司	装饰材料工业	2188439	2.727
4	东莞市创业发展总公司	贸易商	2128775	2.653
5	大连爱丽思生活用品有限公司	装饰材料工业	2119258	2.641
6	惠州住润汽车线业有限公司	汽车工业	1900900	2.369
7	威海金元电线有限公司	电线电缆工业	1806000	2.251
8	青岛京信新材料有限公司	改性树脂	1667700	2.078
9	广州市番禺区口岸实业公司莲花山公共保税仓库	贸易商	1542050	1.922
10	宁波和富塑胶实业有限公司	塑胶工业	1409975	1.757
11	四国电线（东莞）有限公司	电线电缆工业	1239180	1.544
12	东莞市对外加工装配服务公司	贸易商	1216235	1.516
13	古河汽车配件（东莞）有限公司	汽车工业	1193075	1.487
14	东莞中豪鞋材有限公司	制鞋工业	1160050	1.446
15	崇仁（厦门）医疗器械有限公司	医保用品工业	1158296	1.444
16	张家港爱丽塑料有限公司	塑胶工业	1124784	1.402
17	正规电线电缆（东莞）有限公司	电线电缆工业	1098278	1.369
18	莱尼电气线缆（常州）有限公司	电线电缆工业	1074207	1.339
19	泰尔茂医疗产品（杭州）有限公司	医保用品工业	1069764	1.333
20	安徽博西华制冷有限公司	家用电器工业	1051340	1.310
21	北京英特迈进出口有限公司	贸易商	503232	0.627
22	亨特制造（中国）有限公司	汽车工业	482328	0.601
23	惠州市日成塑胶有限公司	改性树脂	473655	0.590
24	耀邦行贸易（深圳）有限公司	贸易商	443000	0.552
25	南海市中美玩具厂	玩具工业	431975	0.538
26	苏州特雷卡电缆有限公司	电线电缆工业	413212	0.515
27	德尼培橡胶塑料科技（苏州）有限公司	塑胶工业	409518	0.510
28	法福来（厦门）医疗器具有限公司	医保用品工业	398699	0.497
29	广州市韦士泰医疗器械有限公司	医保用品工业	397656	0.496
30	大连JMS医疗器具有限公司	医保用品工业	377200	0.470
31	新海洋精密组件（赣州）有限公司	电子工业	365747	0.456
32	东莞建达制造有限公司	电子工业	354125	0.441
33	广州保税区拓新物流服务有限公司	贸易商	350875	0.437
34	安费诺－泰姆斯（常州）通讯设备有限公司	电子工业	348556	0.434
35	大连通世泰建材有限公司	装饰材料工业	326500	0.407
36	东莞联立电器实业有限公司	家用电器工业	326291	0.407
37	北京威卡威汽车零部件有限公司	汽车工业	324787	0.405
38	东莞新光电线有限公司	电线电缆工业	322848	0.402
39	深圳市罗诚投资服务有限公司	贸易商	317710	0.396
进口总计			80239968	100.00

五、2012～2013 年价格走势

2012 年以来国内 PVC 市场整体呈现无趋势震荡性行情为主，PVC 市场价跌破 7500 元大关，在 7400 元下盘整。

从统计数据分析，2012 年齐鲁石化产 PVC S－700 粉料仅 4、5、9、10 月四个月月均价在 7350－7390 元/t，其余八个月均在 7300 元/t 以下，12 月月均价破 7000 元大关，仅 6833 元/t，比最高 5 月月均价跌 7.54%(表 73)。

表 73 PVC S－700 齐鲁石化 2012 年中国塑料城月均价走势 元/t

1 月	2 月	3 月	4 月	5 月	6 月
7150	7185	7278	7384	7390	7217
7 月	8 月	9 月	10 月	11 月	12 月
7077	7179	7352	7333	7036	6833

从统计数据分析，2012 年天津乐金产 PVCLS－100 粉料仅 5 月一个月月均价在 7500 元/t 以上，其余十一个月均在 7300 元/t 以下，7、11、12 月三个月月均价破 7000 元大关，12 月仅 6861 元/t，比最高 5 月月均价跌 8.98%(表 74)。

表 74 PVCLS－100 天津乐金 2011 年中国塑料城月均价走势 元/t

1 月	2 月	3 月	4 月	5 月	6 月
7200	7285	7208	7289	7538	7135
7 月	8 月	9 月	10 月	11 月	12 月
6954	7118	7328	7288	6968	6861

从统计数据分析，2012 年上氯沪峰产 PVC－EB101(专用粒料)6 月一个月月均价过 13500 元/t，其余十一个月均在 13500 元/t 以下，11 月月均价破 13000 元大关，仅 12590 元/t，比最高 6 月月均价跌 7.43%(表 75)。

表 75 PVC－EB101(专用粒料)上氯沪峰 2012 年中国塑料城月均价走势 元/t

1 月	2 月	3 月	4 月	5 月	6 月
13200	13200	13200	13200	13436	13600
7 月	8 月	9 月	10 月	11 月	12 月
13290	13200	13380	13400	12590	13200

六、进出口交易类型分析

1. 其他初级形状的聚氯乙烯未掺其他物质

从海关统计中可看出，2012 年其他初级形状的聚氯乙烯未掺其他物质进口贸易方式主要为进料加工贸易(占进口量 86.363%)，其次为来料加工装配贸易(占进口量 6.627%)，一般贸易(占进口量 3.337%)保税区仓储转口货物(占进口量 72.752%)，保税仓库进出境货物(占进口量 0.921%)，其他(占进口量 0.000%)，合计为总进口量的 100.00%(表 76)。

从海关统计中可看出，2012 年其他初级形状的聚氯乙烯未掺其他物质出口贸易方式主要为一般贸易(占出口量 68.954%)，其次为进料加工贸易(占出口量 29.862%)，保税区仓储转口货物(占出口量 0.805%)，边境小额贸易(占出口量 0.338%)，保税仓库进出境货物(占出口量 0.024%)，其他(占出口量 0.017%)，对外承包工程出口货物(占出口量 0.00%)，合计为总出口量的 100.00%(表 77)。

表 76 2012 年其他初级形状的聚氯乙烯未掺其他物质进口交易类型统计

进口交易类型	进口金额 /美元	进口数量/kg	占比例/%
进料加工贸易	785525841.00	812167215	86.363
来料加工装配贸易	65385949.00	62323270	6.627
一般贸易	39254532.00	31382016	3.337
保税区仓储转口货物	24313811.00	25875633	2.752
保税仓库进出境货物	8423406.00	8664000	0.921
其他	29575.00	3879	0.000
进口总计	922933114.00	940416013	100.00

表 77 2012 年其他初级形状的聚氯乙烯未掺其他物质出口交易类型统计

出口交易类型	出口金额/美元	出口数量/kg	占比例/%
一般贸易	250665394.00	265908018	68.954
进料加工贸易	108869832.00	115159225	29.862
保税区仓储转口货物	2913915.00	3105035	0.805
边境小额贸易	1539848.00	1303288	0.338
保税仓库进出境货物	92227.00	91825	0.024
其他	119701.00	65273	0.017
对外承包工程出口货物	4095.00	588	0.000
出口总计	364205012.00	385633252	100.00

2. 初级形状未塑化的聚氯乙烯

从海关统计中可看出，2012 年初级形状未塑化的聚氯乙烯进口贸易方式主要为进料加工贸易（占进口量 90.737%），其次为来料加工装配贸易（占进口量 5.189%），一般贸易（占进口量 3.625%），其他（占进口量 0.342%%）保税区仓储转口货物（占进口量 0.106%），保税仓库进出境货物（占进口量 0.001%），合计为总进口量的 100.00%（表 78）。

表 78 2012 年初级形状未塑化的聚氯乙烯进口交易类型统计

进口交易类型	进口金额/美元	进口数量/kg	占比例/%
进料加工贸易	83331435.00	63412199	90.737
来料加工装配贸易	5141314.00	3626395	5.189
一般贸易	5903958.00	2533278	3.625
其他	444577.00	239081	0.342
保税区仓储转口货物	415053.00	73956	0.106
保税仓库进出境货物	1437.00	590	0.001
进口总计	95237774.00	69885499	100.00

从海关统计中可看出，2012 年初级形状未塑化的聚氯乙烯出口贸易方式主要为一般贸易（占出口量 84.253%%），其次为边境小额贸易（占出口量 14.196%），进料加工贸易（占出口量 0.914%），其他（占出口量 0.374%），保税仓库进出境货物（占出口量 0.221%），保税区仓储转口货物（占出口量 0.041%），合计为总出口量的 100.00%（表 79）。

表 79 2012 年初级形状未塑化的聚氯乙烯出口交易类型统计

出口交易类型	出口金额/美元	出口数量/kg	占比例/%
一般贸易	12798056.00	8395731	84.253
边境小额贸易	1637463.00	1414643	14.196
进料加工贸易	148093.00	91104	0.914
其他	43086.00	37304	0.374
保税仓库进出境货物	22424.00	22015	0.221
保税区仓储转口货物	15301.00	4087	0.041
出口总计	14664423.00	9964884	100.00

3. 初级形状已塑化的聚氯乙烯

从海关统计中可看出，2012 年初级形状已塑化的聚氯乙烯进口贸易方式主要为进料加工贸易（占进口量 46.455%），其次为一般贸易（占进口量 34.630%），来料加工装配贸易（占进口量 14.977%），保税仓库进出境货物（占进口量 2.145%），保税区仓储转口货物（占进口量 1.750%），其他（占进口量 0.043%），合计为总进口量的 100.00%（表 80）。

表80 2012年初级形状已塑化的聚氯乙烯进口交易类型统计

进口交易类型	进口金额/美元	进口数量/kg	占比例/%
进料加工贸易	76904504.00	37275411	46.455
一般贸易	67247181.00	27787157	34.630
来料加工装配贸易	20964910.00	12017163	14.977
保税仓库进出境货物	2145180.00	1721182	2.145
保税区仓储转口货物	4022535.00	1404375	1.750
其他	128490.00	34680	0.043
进口总计	171412800.00	80239968	100.00

从海关统计中可看出，2012年初级形状已塑化的聚氯乙烯出口贸易方式主要为进料加工贸易(占出口量52.865%)，其次为一般贸易(占出口量42.471%)，来料加工装配贸易(占出口量2.696%)，边境小额贸易(占出口量0.925%)，保税仓库进出境货物(占出口量0.518%)，保税区仓储转口货物(占出口量0.300%)，其他(占出口量0.124%)，对外承包工程出口货物(占出口量0.101%)，合计为总出口量的100.00%(表81)。

表81 2012年初级形状已塑化的聚氯乙烯出口交易类型统计

出口交易类型	出口金额/美元	出口数量/kg	占比例/%
进料加工贸易	47717398.00	26170005	52.865
一般贸易	31989628.00	21024523	42.471
来料加工装配贸易	1725773.00	1334617	2.696
边境小额贸易	808779.00	457925	0.925
保税仓库进出境货物	478919.00	256217	0.518
保税区仓储转口货物	331757.00	148737	0.300
其他	132098.00	61440	0.124
对外承包工程出口货物	178233.00	50100	0.101
出口总计	83362585.00	49503564	100.00

七、聚氯乙烯产能远远供大于求

2012年来，受国家抑制通胀以及楼市低迷等因素影响，PVC期现价格承压较大，行情走势较为疲弱。

1. 产能过剩，需求不足，扩能不停

国内聚氯乙烯产能近年来高速扩张，导致产能出现过剩局面，国内市场竞争激烈，产品价格偏低，企业进口意愿不高，进口量出现下降。

2001~2008年，我国聚氯乙烯产能由3200kt迅猛增长到16000kt，8年增长了5倍，其中高达42%的产能过剩。

2008~2012年，我国聚氯乙烯产能由160000kt迅猛增长到234100kt，4年增长了46.31%，其中高达45%的产能仍过剩。

2012年以来，聚氯乙烯扩产还在继续。

另外，国家对房地产业的调控政策不断出台，房地产市场处于调整期。而国内建筑和民用工程是聚氯乙烯的主要需求来源，房地产业进入“冷静期”对聚氯乙稀进口需求起到抑制作用。

a. 安徽华塑PVC一期工程投产

2013年1月24日，安徽华塑股份年产1000kt聚氯乙烯(PVC)项目一期工程第一釜PVC产品顺利下线，产品各项指标合格，这标志着华塑股份循环经济产业链全线贯通。

该项目2005年4月开始立项准备，2010年3月28日开工建设。

2012年，该项目主体工程无为矿山、热电厂、机械动力厂、水泥厂、电石厂相继投产。PVC装置采用国内首次引进的法国阿克玛悬浮聚合技术，其138m^{3}的聚合釜单釜生产能力在国内首屈一指。

b. 鄂托克旗打造聚氯乙烯/PVA及深加工产业集群

以鄂尔多斯西部沿黄沿线地区为重点建设全国重要的焦化、聚氯乙烯生产加工基地的整体规划。鄂托克旗着力打造以PVC/PVA及深加工为核心的产业集群，目前已出初具雏形。

2013年1月，在棋盘井工业园建设的鄂尔多斯电力冶金集团有限公司400kt PVC/300kt 烧碱/775kt 水泥熟料循环经济产业链项目已单体试车，即将投产；

在蒙西工业园建设的君正能源化工有限公司年产1200kt PVC/烧碱综合项目一期600kt PVC，内蒙古中谷矿业有限责任公司600kt PVC/600kt烧碱综合项目电石项目，内蒙古双欣环保材料股份有限公司330kt/a可降解高分子聚乙烯醇及深加工项目(二期110kt PVA，三期220kt PVA)土建和设备已经完成，逐步进入单体试车阶段。

c. 2012年10月12日，金牛化工40万吨/年聚氯乙烯项目主体工程开工建设。

d. 新疆祥运60万吨PVC项目奠基

由浙江企业投资的新疆祥运工贸有限公司年产600kt PVC生产建设项目，2012年5月30日在新疆库车县奠基。该项目占地2500亩，总投资86.7亿元，除PVC项目外，还计划配套4×15万千瓦自备电厂、烧碱厂、水泥厂等项目，明年建成投产。投产后，预计年均销售收入53.7亿元。

e. 新疆将形成570万吨PVC生产规模

新疆3月5日发布《新疆化工行业安全发展规划(2011～2015年)》。“十二五”期间，新疆将进一步提高油、气、煤、盐资源在区内加工的数量和深度，最大限度地延伸石油、天然气和煤炭产业链，建设一批大型化工项目。

依托新疆煤炭和原盐资源优势，大力发展煤—电—高载能产业一体化，有力地支持盐化工以及精细加工产业的发展。新疆的氯碱、电石等盐化工进入高速发展期，十二五期间将建成罗布泊、吐鲁番-哈密、乌鲁木齐-昌吉、石河子、库车-拜城五大盐化工基地。将形成5700kt聚氯乙烯、600kt硝酸钠(钾)、3000kt钾肥的生产规模。

2. 氯碱行业亏损严重

聚氯乙烯由于产能过剩和下游加工业开工不足，2012年氯碱业出现全行业亏损，亏损面接近50%。

据氯碱协会对73家重点氯碱企业月度统计分析显示，2012年1～9月合计亏损3.37亿元，亏损企业达36家，亏损面达到近50%，为近几年来最为严重的情况。

此外，38家氯碱及相关行业上市公司半年报也显示，18家企业出现不同程度亏损，部分亏损严重。

统计显示，在产烧碱开工率降至72%，在产聚氯乙烯装置开工率降至60%。业界提醒，国家安全准入、环保核查步伐加快，目前的局面应引起全行业高度重视。

2012年氯碱行业的运行呈现两大特点：一是行业规模有所扩大，但扩张速度明显降低。从产能看，据中国氯碱工业协会统计，2011年底烧碱产能34120kt，2012年1～9月新增产能2560kt，退出产能390kt，净增2170kt；

2011年底聚氯乙烯(PVC)产能21630kt，2012年1～9月新增产能1320kt，同时退出580kt，净增740kt。

从产量上看，据国家统计局统计，2012年前9个月，国内烧碱产量为19599kt，同比增长4.1%，在产烧碱装置的开工率为72%；PVC产量为10025kt，同比增长1.9%，目前在产PVC装置的平均开工率为60%以下。

第五章　2012年聚丙烯树脂表观消费量小幅增长国内对外依存度下降

一、2012年聚丙烯生产能力不断提升，产量也不断增长。

从2012年底国内聚丙烯装置产能的最新统计来看，中石化装置产能5264.1kt，占总产能41.03%；

中石油产能3512.7kt，占总产能27.38%；

非中石化、中石油煤制烯烃装置产能2752.2kt，占总产能221.45%，；

其他聚丙烯装置产能1301.0kt，占总产能221.45%，后二者合计聚丙烯装置产能超过中石油产能540.5kt，超过15.39%。

而且聚丙烯未来扩能很大一部分不在两大石化手上，主导格局呈现碎片化趋势，企业对价格控制能力正在分散。

也就是说，未来聚丙烯竞争加剧趋势化已经形成。

2012年成为聚丙烯产能扩张的又一高峰。

2012年国内产能达到1283万吨，年增长产能超过2100kt(表82)。

表82　2006～2012年国内PP产量统计表

项目	2006	2007	2008	2009	2010	2011	2012
产量/kt	5842.00	7126.49	7332.06	8205.18	9167.28	9956.0	11216.00
年增长率/%	11.71	21.99	2.88	11.61	11.73	8.60	12.66

2006～2012年PP产量年均增长率为11.48%。

2012年8月30日22时28分，伴随着合格的HP500N均聚物产品的涌出，标志着中国石油重点建设工程项目——大庆炼化公司年300kt聚丙烯二套装置工程，经过工程建设者600多个日夜的辛勤努力，实现一次投产成功。

至此，大庆炼化公司聚丙烯生产能力可由原来的年300kt增至年600kt，成为中国石油最先进的聚丙烯生产基地。

2012年11月18日，洛阳石化140kt/a聚丙烯装置建成，顺利实现中间交接。装置投产后，洛阳石化聚丙烯年产量将超过200kt。

140kt/a聚丙烯装置是洛阳石化做精做优化工的重要项目。该装置可行性研究报告于2010年3月得到总部批复，2010年12月30日批复基础设计，批复总投资5.68亿元。

表83 2012年聚丙烯装置新增扩能统计

新增聚丙烯装置	产能/kt	投产日期
宁夏石化	100.0	2012年3月
北海炼厂	400.0	2012年4月
大唐多伦	500.0	2012年4月
山东玉皇	100.0	2012年6月
大庆炼化公司二期	300.0	2012年8月30日
抚顺大乙烯	300.0	2012年10月

产能快速增长必将导致供求矛盾的加剧。

由于煤制烯烃主要集中在通用料领域，行业未来的竞争将更加白热化。而传统油制烯烃会将重心转向专用料的研发和生产。

不过，聚丙烯扩能对于行业来说是个好消息。扩能不仅只是新装置投产，同时伴随着落后产能的淘汰，以及石化行业转型和结构调整，是我国经济发展的大势所趋。

随着神华300kt、宁煤500kt、大唐500kt煤制烯烃装置的投产，作为后起之秀的煤制烯烃有望打破国内中石油、中石化油制烯烃“两分天下”的行业格局。

二、2012年国内聚丙烯树脂出口生产省市仍集中于东部沿海地区

2012年国内聚丙烯树脂出口生产省市有28家，仍主要集中于东部沿海地区。

从海关统计中可看出，2012年初级形状的聚丙烯出口生产企业主要集中在广东省，出口数量77837104kg，占总出口数量的54.968%，比上年出口减8596518kg，比上年下降9.95%；

2012年五省市初级形状的聚丙烯出口数量占2012年总出口数量的89.076%，比2011年增加1.233%(表84)。

表84 2012年初级形状的聚丙烯十大出口省市统计

排序	出口省市	出口金额/美元	出口数量/kg	占比例/%
1	广东省	122651167.00	77837104	54.968
2	上海市	31241852.00	19833507	14.006
3	浙江省	19145156.00	12638357	8.925
4	江苏省	20652228.00	8096372	5.718
5	河北省	10739178.00	7731794	5.460
6	海南省	6050200.00	4200000	2.966
7	山东省	5392666.00	3240246	2.288
8	辽宁省	3110675.00	1910991	1.350
9	新疆维吾尔自治区	3197143.00	1843156	1.302
10	安徽省	1861540.00	951977	0.672
出口总计		231，406，804.00	141603186	100.00

三、国内聚丙烯（PP)出口商以改性聚丙烯树脂为主

2012年初级形状的聚丙烯出口商共计有341家，出口额最高的前十位出口商六家为生产企业，四家为贸易商，十大出口商出口数量占总出口数量的58.50%。

2012年初级形状的聚丙烯三十八大出口商中生产企业占十九大，十九大生产企业出口数量占总出口数量的22.45%，仅有中国石化化工销售有限公司为聚丙烯树脂原料生产厂，其它均为改性聚丙烯树脂(即PP合金)生产企业(表85)。

表 85 2012 年初级形状的聚丙烯三十八大出口商统计

排序	出口商	所属行业	出口数量/kg	占比例/%
1	广东合捷国际供应链有限公司	贸易商	50454476	35.631
2	中国石化化工销售有限公司广州经营部	改性聚丙烯树脂	6342000	4.479
3	广州金发科技股份有限公司	改性聚丙烯树脂	4901319	3.461
4	上海雅胜物流有限公司	贸易商	4103400	2.898
5	上海大赛璐塑料工业有限公司	改性聚丙烯树脂	3921364	2.769
6	廊坊佳世化工有限公司	改性聚丙烯树脂	3397100	2.399
7	巴赛尔聚烯烃工程塑料(苏州)有限公司	改性聚丙烯树脂	2886776	2.039
8	宁波保税区高新货柜有限公司	贸易商	2694600	1.903
9	LG 化学(广州)工程塑料有限公司	改性聚丙烯树脂	2261110	1.597
10	前程物流有限公司	贸易商	1876000	1.325
11	肇庆市大旺嘉升电子产品有限公司	改性聚丙烯树脂	1512650	1.068
12	东莞大日化工厂有限公司	改性聚丙烯树脂	1466575	1.036
13	宁波保税区海盛仓储有限公司	贸易商	1315500	0.929
14	宁波保税区上善仓储有限公司	贸易商	1180000	0.833
15	博禄塑料(上海)有限公司	改性聚丙烯树脂	1091850	0.771
16	中海物流(深圳)有限公司	贸易商	1091040	0.770
17	合肥杰事杰新材料有限公司	改性聚丙烯树脂	894513	0.632
18	青岛保税区中启联合物流有限公司	贸易商	792000	0.559
19	普立万聚合体(深圳)有限公司	改性聚丙烯树脂	784005	0.554
20	宁波保税区太平仓储有限公司	贸易商	396000	0.280
21	上海天隆五金有限公司	改性聚丙烯树脂	396000	0.280
22	青岛中新华美塑料有限公司	改性聚丙烯树脂	380000	0.268
23	广州保税区玮骏国际贸易有限公司	贸易商	370750	0.262
24	深圳市宝安外经发展有限公司	贸易商	338005	0.239
25	上海本田贸易有限公司	贸易商	324000	0.229
26	广州东思国际贸易有限公司	贸易商	321750	0.227
27	上海鹏益物流有限公司	贸易商	297000	0.210
28	上海保税商品交易市场第二市场有限公司	贸易商	290300	0.205
29	苏州恒润进出口有限公司	贸易商	285780	0.202
30	江苏连连超微细化工有限公司	改性聚丙烯树脂	277500	0.196
31	淄博艾福迪塑料包装有限公司	改性聚丙烯树脂	274730	0.194
32	保定市力达塑业有限公司	改性聚丙烯树脂	267229	0.189
33	上海金发科技发展有限公司	改性聚丙烯树脂	255500	0.180
34	宁波兰羚钢铁实业有限公司	改性聚丙烯树脂	247500	0.175
35	宁波保税区广盛物流有限公司	贸易商	247500	0.175
36	广东聚石化学股份有限公司	改性聚丙烯树脂	229000	0.162
37	广州萃杰科贸有限公司	贸易商	225000	0.159
38	泰兴市天舟贸易有限公司	贸易商	223625	0.158
	出口总计		141603186	100.00

四、2012 年国内聚丙烯树脂进出口同步增长

2002～2012 年九年中聚丙烯进口量四年跌七年升，2010～2011 年二年进口量连降，2012 年世界聚丙烯产能增长，而价格下降，促使进口量再次反弹

上涨，。

2012 年聚丙烯进口量为 3909.31kt，同比增长3.48%。

2006～2011 年五年中聚丙烯出口量年年增长，年均增长为 44.59%，而 2012 年因人民币升值出口下降(表 86)。

表 86　2006～2012 年 PP 进出口统计

项目	2006	2007	2008	2009	2010	2011	2012
进口/kt	2944.74	3070.06	2788.92	4162.46	3868.09	3777.71	3909.31
出口/kt	26.24	31.13	41.66	44.77	82.90	165.83	141.60
净进口量/kt	2918.50	3038.93	2747.27	4117.69	3785.19	3611.88	3767.71
年增长率/%	-2.74	4.12	-9.60	49.88	-8.07	-4.58	4.31

2006～2012 年间，聚丙烯进口量年均增长为4.84%。

2006～2012 年间，聚丙烯净进口量年均增长为4.35%。

1. 2012 年聚丙烯进口量升价升

尽管产能逐年递增，但我国聚丙烯目前仍然呈现供不应求的局面，自给率为 74.85%，缺口依然靠进口弥补，进口量由 2002 年的 2240kt 增加到 2012 年的 3909.3kt，我国成为全球最大的聚丙烯净进口国。

2012 年韩国、沙特阿拉伯和印度为我国聚丙烯进口前三大市场，2012 年韩国、沙特阿拉伯和印度三大市场进口聚丙烯数量分别为 912030t、842715t 和 330792t，分别占进口总量的 23.330%、21.557% 和 8.462%。

2012 年韩国、沙特阿拉伯和印度三进口地进口数量占全部进口数量的 53.349%，比 2011 年增加 3.70%；

从海关统计中可看出，2012 年初级形状的聚丙烯进口地有 68 个，与 2011 年 68 个持平，进口 3909.31kt，同比增长 3.48%。

主要进口地为韩国进口数量 912030t，比上年进口数量增加个 3.98 百分点；

其次为沙特阿拉伯进口数量 842715t，比上年增加进口数量 19.75%；

印度进口数量 330792t，占总进口数量的 8.462%，比上年进口数量增加 17.90%，超过中国台湾省进口数量居第三位；

而中国台湾省进口数量 330603t，比上年进口数量下降 24.57%，比印度进口数量少 188.34t 而退居第四；

阿拉伯联合酋长国进口数量 264775t，占总进口数量的 6.773%，比上年进口数量增加 11.79%；

五原产进口地进口数量占聚丙烯 2012 年总进口数量的 68.579%，比上年增加 1.379%(表 87)。

表 87　2012 年初级形状的聚丙烯十大进口国家/地区统计

排序	原产进口地	进口金额/美元	进口数量/kg	占比例/%
1	韩国	1387512773.00	912030474	23.330
2	沙特阿拉伯	1165388202.00	842715226	21.557
3	印度	459014520.00	330791526	8.462
4	中国台湾省	506580643.00	330603185	8.457
5	阿拉伯联合酋长国	318444568.00	264774642	6.773
6	新加坡	385738457.00	247463282	6.330
7	泰国	298232542.00	200535391	5.130
8	日本	281904062.00	147629306	3.776
9	美国	221339773.00	139047044	3.557
10	巴西	102135645.00	74570308	1.908
进口总计		5794697159.00	3909310387	100.00

2. 2012 年聚丙烯出口量价同步下降

从海关统计中可看出，2012 年初级形状的聚丙烯出口地有 118 个，比 2011 年 114 个增加 4 个出口地，出口数量 141603t，比 2011 年出口数量下降

14.61%，出口平均价格为 1634.19 美元/t，同比下降 2.38%。

中国香港地区仍为我国聚丙烯最主要出口市场，2012 年向中国香港地区出口数量达 7245165314t，同比增长 10.93%，出口数量占同期全部出口数量的 51.165%。

其次为越南，出口数量 12188 吨，占总出口数量的 8.607%，比上年出口数量减少 55.42%；

出口泰国数量 7287t，占总出口数量的 5.146%，比上年出口数量增加 38.33%；

出口俄罗斯联邦出口数量 4636t，占总出口数量的 3.274%，；

出口印度数量 3949t，占总出口数量的 2.78%；

五出口地出口数量占聚丙烯 2012 年总出口数量的 70.981%，比上年增加 3.821%（表 88）。

表 88　2012 年初级形状的聚丙烯十大出口国家/地区统计

排序	出口目的地	出口金额/美元	出口数量/kg	占比例/%
1	中国香港	106530110.00	72451293	51.165
2	越南	21025823.00	12188480	8.607
3	泰国	15223769.00	7286989	5.146
4	俄罗斯联邦	7154585.00	4636414	3.274
5	印度	6135831.00	3948887	2.789
6	日本	6269971.00	3204346	2.263
7	韩国	5619744.00	3067606	2.166
8	印度尼西亚	6953249.00	2937075	2.074
9	马来西亚	5596648.00	2827553	1.997
10	美国	5703810.00	2099152	1.482
出口总计		231406804.00	141603186	100.00

五、聚丙烯表观消费小幅上升，低于同期产量年均增长

1. PP 消费概述

2006～2012 年间，中国 PP 表观消费量年均增长达 9.30%，低于同期产量年均增长率 2.18%。

2012 年 PP 表观消费量为 14983.71kt，同比增长 11.68%。

2012 年 PP 国内自给率为 74.85%，同比上升 1.77%（表 89）。

表 89　2006～2012 年国内 PP 表观消费量统计资料

项　目	2006	2007	2008	2009	2010	2011	2012
表观消费量/kt	8786.74	10165.42	10079.33	12322.87	12952.47	13417.20	14983.71
年增长/%	6.76	15.69	－0.85	22.26	5.11	3.59	11.68
国内自给率/%	66.49	70.11	72.74	66.58	70.78	73.08	74.85

目前我国聚丙烯产品结构不均衡，存在结构性过剩和短缺现象。结构性过剩产品主要是以拉丝料为主的通用型产品。国内聚丙烯生产企业拉丝、低融共聚等通用型聚丙烯产品比重大；国内煤制烯烃迅速发展，初期以拉丝级产品为主；同时中东产能大幅扩张，低成本产品涌入国内市场，这些产品也以拉丝等通用产品为主。

结构性短缺产品主要是指高抗冲注塑料、高熔指纤维料、高档 BOPP 专用料、CPP、管板材等在内的专用料。这是由于国内对高端专用料的需求不断增加，而且我国高端专用料开发力度偏弱，生产能力有限。

目前，聚丙烯市场出现的结构性问题已引起行业许多有识之士的重视，不少企业已将结构调整作为重点，开始加大专用产品的研究与开发。

2. PP 进口消费省市集中流向东部沿海地区

从海关资料来看，2012 年初级形状的聚丙烯进口消费省市有 28 个，比 2011 年 25 个增加 3 个进口消费省市，五进口消费省市 2011 年初级形状的聚丙烯进口消费省市进口量占总进口量的 86.862%，比上年减少 0.038%。

2012 年初级形状的聚丙烯主要进口流向为广东

省，进口数量 1755011418kg，占总进口数量的 44.893%，比上年进口增加 34204050kg，增加 1.99%；

其次为浙江省，进口数量 759701776kg，占总进口数量的 19.433%，比上年进口增加 67340026kg，上升 9.73%；

上海市，进口数量 338814195kg，占总进口数量的 8.667%，比上年进口减少 31111021kg，下降 8.41%；

江苏省，进口数量 281706237kg，占总进口数量的 7.206%，比上年进口增加 26706134kg，上升 10.47%；

山东省，进口数量 260302431kg，占总进口数量的 6.659%，比上年进口增加 15612007kg，上升 6.38%(表 90)。

表 90　2012 年初级形状的聚丙烯十大进口省市统计

排序	进口省市	进口金额/美元	进口数量/kg	占比例/%
1	广东省	2573618784.00	1755011418	44.893
2	浙江省	1090603233.00	759701776	19.433
3	上海市	512793333.00	338814195	8.667
4	江苏省	444310280.00	281706237	7.206
5	山东省	377694769.00	260302431	6.659
6	福建省	245869483.00	166227976	4.252
7	辽宁省	95070439.00	60196818	1.540
8	湖北省	87075835.00	56121979	1.436
9	天津市	75191001.00	44680195	1.143
10	河北省	64833971.00	42378646	1.084
进口总计		5794697159.00	3909310387	100.00

3. 聚丙烯消费结构分析

2012 年我国 PP 最大的消费领域是编织袋、捆扎绳等编织制品，约占消费总量的 42.00% 左右；

注塑制品是我国 PP 的第二大消费领域，约占消费总量的 19.00% 上下，主要消耗 PP 专用料；

我国 PP 的另外一个主要消费领域是薄膜，约占消费总量的 16.00%，其中以双向拉伸 PP 薄膜为主。

此外，我国 PP 还用于生产纤维、管片板材等制品，广泛应用于生产和生活的各个领域。

我国聚丙烯消费结构见表 91。

表 91　我国聚丙烯消费结构预测

应用领域	预测 2015 年		2013 年	
	消费量/(kt/a)	所占比例/%	消费量/(kt/a)	所占比例/%
BOPP 薄膜	2500.0	13.1579	2050.0	12.8125
CPP 薄膜	600.0	3.1579	580.0	3.6250
纤维制品	2750.0	14.4737	2150.0	13.4375
编织制品	7300.0	38.4211	6200.0	38.7500
注塑制品	3800.0	20.5262	3100.0	19.3750
管材制品	1300.0	6.8421	860.0	5.3750
其他制品	650.0	3.4211	1060.0	6.6250
合计	19000.0	100.00	16000.0	100.00

4. 聚丙烯进口生产使用企业分析

从海关资料来看，2012 年初级形状的聚丙烯进口商有 4，502 家，比 2011 年 4，513 家减少 11 家进口商，前八位初级形状的聚丙烯进口商进口量占总进口量的 10.54%。

从资料分析，初级形状的聚丙烯进口生产使用企业以塑料制品工业、塑料改性工业、薄膜包装工业、化学工业、化纤工业、家用电器工业为主，

2012年初级形状的聚丙烯进口商三十九大进口商，其中二十一大进口商为贸易商，进口量占总进口量的15.53%；

另十八大进口生产企业以塑料制品工业、薄膜包装工业、塑料改性工业、家用电器工业、化纤工业为主，进口量占总进口量的10.166%（表92）。

表92 2012年初级形状的聚丙烯三十九大进口商统计

排序	进口商	所属行业	进口数量/kg	占比例/%
1	广东合捷国际供应链有限公司	进口贸易商	84140245	2.152
2	上海雅胜物流有限公司	进口贸易商	81838124	2.093
3	浙江前程石化有限公司	塑料改性工业	49225575	1.259
4	广州市合诚化学有限公司	化学工业	44943025	1.150
5	深圳市宝安外经发展有限公司	进口贸易商	41478839	1.061
6	爱施开国际贸易（上海）有限公司	进口贸易商	37664000	0.963
7	宁波柏森国际贸易有限公司	进口贸易商	37019000	0.947
8	广州保税区精卫国际贸易有限公司	进口贸易商	35706600	0.913
9	东丽高新聚化（南通）有限公司	塑料改性工业	32131560	0.822
10	汕头市柯士达商贸有限公司	进口贸易商	29558670	0.756
11	宁波保税区高新货柜有限公司	进口贸易商	28614275	0.732
12	深圳市龙岗区对外经济发展有限公司	进口贸易商	28135446	0.720
13	浙江凯利包装材料有限公司	薄膜包装工业	26920250	0.689
14	东莞市对外加工装配服务公司	进口贸易商	25638520	0.656
15	湖北金龙非织造布有限公司	化纤工业	23613760	0.604
16	宁波杉杉物产有限公司	进口贸易商	21328235	0.546
17	顺德市新宝电器有限公司	家用电器工业	21187150	0.542
18	宝豪塑胶五金制品（江门）有限公司	家用电器工业	21103025	0.540
19	普杰无纺布（中国）有限公司	化纤工业	20857800	0.534
20	上海嘉博国际贸易有限公司	进口贸易商	19872125	0.507
21	宁波保税区上善仓储有限公司	进口贸易商	19825000	0.507
22	廊坊佳世化工有限公司	化学工业	18723137	0.479
23	佛山市创造材料进出口有限公司	进口贸易商	17602500	0.450
24	广东联塑科技实业有限公司	塑料制品工业	17280750	0.442
25	泉州利昌塑胶有限公司	塑料制品工业	16787250	0.429
26	东莞三星道达尔工程塑料有限公司	塑料制品工业	16651850	0.426
27	汕头丰兴盛包装材料有限公司	薄膜包装工业	15796370	0.404
28	宁波亚朔科技股份有限公司	塑料改性工业	15719910	0.402
29	宁波保税区海盛仓储有限公司	进口贸易商	15478100	0.396
30	湖石化学贸易（上海）有限公司	进口贸易商	15477000	0.396
31	四川科伦大药厂有限责任公司	薄膜包装工业	15450000	0.395
32	澄海市对外加工装配服务公司	进口贸易商	14259310	0.365
33	宁波晶海工贸有限公司	进口贸易商	14122500	0.361
34	佳施加德士（苏州）塑料有限公司	塑料改性工业	13925950	0.356
35	深圳市宁信达进出口有限公司	进口贸易商	13700576	0.350
36	广州宏顺塑胶工业有限公司	塑料制品工业	13558500	0.347
37	普宁市威孚包装材料有限公司	薄膜包装工业	13494000	0.345
38	上豪贸易（深圳）有限公司	进口贸易商	13002550	0.333
39	爱思开能源（广州）国际贸易有限公司	进口贸易商	12745000	0.326
进口总计			3909310387	100.00

六、2012～2013年PP树脂行情可谓跌宕起伏

目前聚丙烯市场已经具有较高的透明度和成熟度，贸易环节的议价能力将继续处于最弱环节，买方市场格局将进一步明显。

从中国塑料城统计看出，2012年国内PP市场行情-在2011年收盘低位弱势小幅盘整为主，上海石化PP- T300价格由1月份的10613元/t升至12月的11342元/t，升幅在729元/t，上升幅度6.87%(表93)。

表93 PP-T300上海石化2012年中国塑料城月均价走势 元/t

1月	2月	3月	4月	5月	6月
10613	10985	11613	11889	11415	10907
7月	8月	9月	10月	11月	12月
11138	11418	12471	12377	11913	11342

上海赛科PP-S1003价格由1月份的10446元/t跌至12月的10350元/t，跌幅在96元/t，下降幅度0.92%(表94)。

表94 PP-S1003上海赛科2011年中国塑料城月均价走势 元/t

1月	2月	3月	4月	5月	6月
10446	10721	11489	11618	10916	10807
7月	8月	9月	10月	11月	12月
11161	11363	11973	11572	11340	10350

埃克森美孚PP- AP03B价格由1月份的11463元/t升至12月的12090元/t，升幅在627元/t，上升幅度5.47%(表95)。

表95 PP-AP03B埃克森美孚2011年中国塑料城月均价走势 元/t

1月	2月	3月	4月	5月	6月
11463	11547	11719	11800	11772	11707
7月	8月	9月	10月	11月	12月
11554	11420	12011	12433	12340	12090

韩国晓星PP-R R200P(热水管，0.2~0.4)价格由1月份的12193元/t升至12月的13000元/t，升幅在807元/t，上升幅度6.62%(表96)。

表96 PP-R R200P(热水管，0.2~0.4)韩国晓星 2011年中国塑料城月均价走势 元/t

1月	2月	3月	4月	5月	6月
12193	12800	13373	13568	13459	13215
7月	8月	9月	10月	11月	12月
13400	13340	13261	13088	13068	13000

从中远期来看，聚丙烯与聚乙烯之间的差价仍有扩大的空间和预期，理由主要来自两方面。

一是聚丙烯洛阳石化140kt/a的新装置、宁波禾元30万吨/年的新装置、徐州海天200kt/a的新装置陆续投产，在未来一个季度内，聚丙烯市场将面临与适应至少640kt新产能释放压力。

二是春节后至清明节左右的农膜旺季即将启动，对聚乙烯将起到直接的带动作用，虽然也会间接的对聚丙烯市场产生一定提振作用，但力度会小于直接上游聚乙烯品种。

七、世界PP新技术应用现状

1. 透明聚丙烯

聚丙烯也就是我们生活中常见的材料(pp)，在饭盒、矿泉水瓶等一些塑料制品中都能看见它的影子，而它也以无毒、耐热、价格低在市场上建立了新优势，透明PP与其他一些常用的透明材料相比，具有透明度、光泽度优异，质轻价廉，刚度及综合性能好，可回收及有较高的热变形温度(一般大于110℃)，使之获得了广泛的应用。

目前，已工业化的透明PP生产技术主要有3种：

(1) 在PP树脂中加入透明成核剂；

(2) 利用Z-N催化剂生产无规共聚PP；

(3) 采用茂金属催化剂生产高透明PP。

随着市场对透明PP的认同，PP的透明改性是目前改性的热点之一，由于具有成本低，能在传统的成型设备上进行加工等优点，透明PP和传统的透明材料聚对苯二甲酸乙二醇酯(PET)等相比有较大的优势，其需求量不断上升。

国内目前通用低性能PP品种较多，市场趋于饱和，但高附加值的高透明性PP产量较少，这与国内透明成核剂的研究及开发较为落后，与国外先进水平相比有很大的差距有密切的关系，因此立足于我国的国情，开发一些高效、多功能化且成本低廉的透明成核剂有着重大的现实意义。

随着市场对透明PP的认同，PP的透明改性是目前改性的热点之一，由于具有成本低，能在传统的成型设备上进行加工等优点，透明PP和传统的透明材料聚对苯二甲酸乙二醇酯(PET)等相比有较大的优势，其需求量不断上升。

A. 透明聚丙烯添新品

2012年，齐鲁石化与Milliken公司合作，采用该公司最先进的Millad NX 8000K透明成核剂，开发出了两款新型透明聚丙烯产品——QPT91N和QPT93N。据悉，这两款产品在透明性、加工稳定性、美观性方面优势突出。

QPT91N透明聚丙烯产品的熔融指数为30，是中国市场上第一款商业化的氢调法高熔指透明聚丙烯。其生产工艺中没有添加过氧化物，所以气味和黄色指数比其他使用过氧化物的产品低，可应用于大型贮藏容器和食品容器。该产品能给终端用户带来高透明度、高光泽度、刚性和韧性的良好平衡等一系列优点，并可提高生产效率。

QPT93N是中国石化企业首个针对医疗市场并采用Milliken公司的NX 8000K技术的透明聚丙烯产品，无论在透明度还是加工适用性上都领先国内外其他同类树脂。除了医用注射器外，这款熔融指数为12的透明聚丙烯也可用来生产食品保鲜盒以及婴儿奶瓶。

据了解，这两款产品均符合美国食品和药物管理局(FDA)、欧盟RoHS指令及REACH法规、中国GB 9693－88食品包装用聚丙烯树脂卫生标准中的相关规定。

B. 兰州石化推出透明聚丙烯专用料

兰州石化2012年成功开发出首批975.8t无规透明聚丙烯专用料RP340R新产品，填补了中国石油高熔融指数无规透明聚丙烯生产的空白。

无规透明聚丙烯专用料RP340R可应用于热成型聚丙烯食品包装容器。该产品的研发成功，可使之取代聚苯乙烯材料。

在新产品开发过程中，兰州石化制定了新产品开发方案、产品质量标准，优化生产组织和工艺操作，通过采取调整催化剂体系、环管氢气浓度、乙烯结合量等攻关措施，使产品的熔融指数、弯曲模量、冲击强度均优于同类产品。

C. 台塑PP宁波公司强力打造突破性的透明聚丙烯树脂

2012年，台塑PP宁波公司，中国台湾地区最大石化生产商中国台湾塑胶公司旗下的分公司，采用米丽肯(Milliken)公司最先进的技术开发出了新型透明聚丙烯(PP)5200XT。

台塑PP宁波公司的这款新型透明聚丙烯树脂5200XT是由位于中国宁波的工厂生产，将为广大塑料加工商提供出众的外观、稳定性和质量，同时能耗可降低30%，从而有效的降低成本和提高可持续性发展。

2. 扬子石化聚丙烯车用新材料开发

目前国内聚丙烯生产企业普遍采用的聚丙烯釜内合金催化剂是第四代球形高效齐格勒－纳塔丙烯聚合催化剂。这种催化剂共聚能力较弱，受原料中乙烯浓度的影响和生产工艺的制约，难以生产出高端的汽车专用料。飞驰的汽车在呼唤高性能的塑料产品。

与传统聚丙烯相比，2012年扬子石化开发的聚丙烯汽车用新产品具有成本低、能耗小、质量稳定等优点，且抗低温冲击强度高，刚性和韧性平衡性好，达到了国际先进水平，填补了国内高档聚丙烯汽车专用料的空白，成功替代进口产品。

其中K9015成为国内首个通过德国大众公司实验的聚丙烯汽车专用料，并成为德国大众在中国唯一指定用料，用于奥迪等高档车型。

3. 锦西石化耐热注塑聚丙烯树脂成功研发

2012年10月30日，经质检部门检测，锦西石化公司生产的246吨1040L牌号耐热注塑聚丙烯树脂9项技术指标均符合标准，标志着锦西石化成为中国石油首家成功研发生产耐热注塑聚丙烯树脂的炼化企业。此次生产填补了中国石油在此领域的空白，为打破国外产品垄断，扩大中国石油聚丙烯产品的市场份额创造了有利条件。

耐热注塑聚丙烯树脂具有硬度高、弯曲模量高、光泽度好等特点，广泛用于热水器、咖啡壶和风扇等小家电外壳生产。

目前，耐热注塑聚丙烯树脂在国外已形成系列产品。

我国仅有中国石化开发的HC9006BM和HC9012BM牌号产品，还没有形成规模。我国大型家电外壳生产厂家主要依赖韩国聚丙烯树脂。

4. 上海石化研发出BOPP电工膜料

2012年经过中试环管装置多次试验后，符合要求的低灰分电容器介质用双向拉伸聚丙烯(BOPP)膜专用料日前在上海石化塑料部研发成功。该新产品灰分控制在40ppm左右，达到电工膜对聚丙烯原料的灰分要求。目前，该产品已开始进行工业化生产准备。

BOPP电工膜是一种满足电力电容器固体介质要求的优良材料，对击穿强度有特殊要求，且对膜洁净度要求很高。因而其所用的聚丙烯原料灰分指标非常严格，必须低于50ppm。

5. 中原石化开发高端双向拉伸聚丙烯膜料

2012年8月3日，中原石化2号聚丙烯装置造粒线生产出高端双向拉伸聚丙烯膜料——BOPP(PPH－F03D)。新产品的成功开发将进一步优化产品结构。高端双向拉伸聚丙烯膜料——BOPP(PPH－F03D)新产品市场前景广阔。

6. 合成杜仲胶与聚丙烯等共混的合金新材料

合成杜仲胶与聚丙烯等共混的合金新材料，具有超高韧性，可用于汽车保险杠、仪表盘、内饰件等。杜仲胶还可用于制造高速火车、汽车的减震材料等。具有吸收声波功能的环氧化杜仲胶可用于潜艇、舰船的隐身材料。

7. 独石化开发PE注塑包装桶专用料

2012年6月7日，独山子石化公司承担的聚丙烯高档注塑包装桶专用料开发项目在北京通过中国石油炼油与化工分公司组织的专家验收。

聚丙烯高档注塑包装桶专用料项目克服了SPHERIPOL I 工艺聚丙烯装置生产高乙丙胶相含量抗冲树脂的工艺控制难点，成功生产出聚丙烯高档注塑包装桶专用料新产品 K445R，产品技术指标满足要求，生产过程平稳可控，产品加工性能得到塑料加工企业的一致认可。

8. 美国沙特企业合建 100kt PP 混配物项目

2012 年 6 月 10 日，沙特阿拉伯 Alujain 集团的子公司国家石化工业有限公司（NatPet）与美国 A. Schulman 公司合资组建聚丙烯(PP)混配物企业。

合资企业双方各持股 50%，将在 NatPet 公司位于沙特延布的聚丙烯(PP)生产装置附近建设 PP 混配物装置。合资企业将分两个阶段建设 100kt/a 混配物项目，第一阶段将需投资 2.66 亿里雅尔(约合 7090 万美元)。

9. SABIC 推出新型无规聚丙烯

沙特基础工业公司(SABIC)近日宣布推出无规共聚聚丙烯产品 PP651H。

据了解，该聚丙烯新产品具有较高的相对分子质量，可为有较高压力要求的管道提供良好的热稳定性和抗抽提性能，尤其适用于运输高温热水的管道。在长期耐腐蚀方面，PP651H 也具有相当的优势。

10. 沙特基础扩充高清晰度 PP 种类

为了满足客户需求，沙特基础工业公司已开发两种新的高清晰度 PP。这两种用于注射模塑的无规 PP 共聚物具备独特的流动性能，使生产更加高效节能。

SABIC PP QR674K，熔体流动速率（MFR）为 40g/min，其感官性能有所提高，更适用于食品接触应用。

典型目标应用包括瓶盖、外壳、家居用品、厨具、食品/非食品容器。

11. 铃木开发出易显色的轻量车用 PP 树脂材料

据日本媒体报道，日本铃木汽车公司开发出了一种与以往聚丙烯(PP)相比轻了 10% 左右且在材料着色方面十分出色的树脂材料——“Suzuki Super Polypropylene”(以下简称为 SSPP)，并已将其用于了在 2012 年 7 月 11 日发售的“Escudo”的底部滑动保护板(skid plate)中。这是 SSPP 在全球范围内首次用于量产车。

此次铃木“Escudo”的底部滑动保护板采用的 SSPP 通过其优异的显色性能，在无涂饰的情况下呈现出了高亮度的银金属色。而且，因为没有涂膜，刮痕等瑕疵不会太引人注目，也不会产生挥发性有机化合物(VOC，Volatile Organic Compound)，可以减少环境负荷。

目前，SSPP 正在专利申请中。今后，铃木将在内部装饰零部件及保险杆等外部装饰零部件方面不断扩大其用途。

12. 新型抗菌 PP 专用料试产成功

2012 年，扬子石化成功生产出了新型抗菌聚丙烯(PP)专用料 YPJ－630KJ 产品，新产品各项质量指标均达到聚丙烯树脂优级品标准，满足了高端用户的需求，标志着该产品在国内首次工业化试生产获得成功。

这一专用料产品改变了以往在塑料专用料生产出来之后再加入抗菌母粒来制备抗菌产品的方法，在塑料聚合过程加入纳米化抗菌助剂，直接生产抗菌聚丙烯专用料。这一新品的开发，提升了抗菌塑料的使用效率，稳定了质量，进一步适应了家电企业的市场需求。

13. 蔗渣纤维增强 PP 复合材料问世

日本企业小岛冲压工业与旗下的内浜化成开发出了高性能环保纤维增强聚丙烯(PP)，用甘蔗渣中提取的纤维(蔗渣纤维)作为 PP 的增强材料，提高了 PP 的强度和耐热性。

甘蔗渣的纤维块首先被分解为长 10～15mm、宽(直径)1mm 左右的蔗渣纤维，再染成黑色，然后与 PP 混合制成颗粒，最后使用注射成型机和模具成型，制成部件。当 PP 材料中蔗渣纤维的质量比达到 40% 时，其强度指标——弯曲弹性模量为 2750MPa，比滑石粉填充型 PP 的 2500MPa 高 10%，质量则减轻了 20%，耐热性也更优良，成本降低了约 20%。

14. 高熔指抗冲共聚 PP 工业化生产

2012 年，茂名石化和北京化工研究院共同开发的高熔指抗冲共聚聚丙烯 PPB－MM35－S 实现工业化生产，首批产品产量达到 530.75t，并已检验合格。

该牌号是茂名石化首次采用非对称外给电子体技术直接聚合法生产的高熔指抗冲共聚聚丙烯新产品。

与降解法相比，直接聚合法优势在于生产出来的产品具有高熔指、高抗冲和低异味等特点，在下游加工过程中充模快而平稳，可减少注射缺陷和废品率，降低能耗，缩短成型周期，提高工作效率，并可进行特定制品的生产，减少原材料的使用，具有较高的附加值。

15. 扬子石化开发三元无规共聚 PP

北京化工研究院和扬子石化共同开发的三元无规共聚聚丙烯(PP)树脂，2012 年成功实现工业化生产。

经过检测，扬子石化生产的三元共聚塑料产品各项性能指标均达到进口料标准。

三元无规共聚聚丙烯产品是聚丙烯高端产品之一，其材料的透明度、冲击性能、热封性能相对于普通聚丙烯产品均有很大提升，被广泛应用于热密封、食品包装膜等行业。该产品生产难度大、性能优良，因此具有较高的经济附加值高，每吨产品售价高出通用料1000元以上。长期以来，国内三元共聚产品作为热封料在市场一直处于供不应求的态势。

八、进出口贸易方式分析

从海关统计中可看出，2012年初级形状的聚丙烯进口贸易方式主要为一般贸易（占进口量40.898%），其次为进料加工贸易（占进口量35.360%），来料加工装配贸易（占进口量11.163%），保税区仓储转口货物（占进口量11.090%），保税仓库进出境货物（占进口量1.277%），边境小额贸易（占进口量0.158%），其他（占进口量0.053%），外商投资企业作为投资进口的设备、物品（占进口量0.000%），出口加工区进口设备（占进口量0.00%），合计为总进口量的100.00%（表97）。

表97　2012年初级形状的聚丙烯进口交易类型统计

进口交易类型	进口金额/美元	进口数量/kg	占比例/%
一般贸易	2435586461.00	1598864259	40.899
进料加工贸易	2107659583.00	1382325212	35.360
来料加工装配贸易	580497310.00	436393542	11.163
保税区仓储转口货物	591968622.00	433544367	11.090
保税仓库进出境货物	66703958.00	49938570	1.277
边境小额贸易	6775767.00	6185625	0.158
其他	5492425.00	2054512	0.053
外商投资企业作为投资进口的设备、物品	11100.00	3000	0.000
出口加工区进口设备	1933.00	1300	0.000
总计	5794697159.00	3909310387	100.00

从海关统计中可看出，2012年初级形状的聚丙烯出口贸易方式主要为保税区仓储转口货物（占出口量52.911%），其次为一般贸易（占出口量27.181%），进料加工贸易（占出口量13.388%），来料加工装配贸易（占出口量3..257%），边境小额贸易（占出口量1.568%），保税仓库进出境货物（占出口量1.272%），其他（占出口量0.372%），对外承包工程出口货物（占出口量0.070%），合计为总出口量的100.00%（表98）。

表98　2012年初级形状的聚丙烯出口交易类型统计

出口交易类型	出口金额/美元	出口数量/kg	占比例/%
保税区仓储转口货物	104605919.00	74923937	52.911
一般贸易	71818150.00	38461331	27.161
进料加工贸易	39434735.00	18957558	13.388
来料加工装配贸易	6470587.00	4612455	3.257
边境小额贸易	4435083.00	2220384	1.568
保税仓库进出境货物	3237187.00	1800801	1.272
其他	1180918.00	527017	0.372
对外承包工程出口货物	224225.00	99703	0.070
出口总计	231406804.00	141603186	100.00

九、发展趋势

1. 全球聚丙烯产能持续扩张 中国成为增长引擎

IHS化学公司的最新报告显示，尽管成本越来越高，替代产品所占市场份额也在增加，但是受新兴经济体需求强劲增长的刺激，未来几年，全球聚丙烯（PP）产能将持续扩张。

据IHS化学发布的数据，2011年全球PP产量为51418kt，需求为50705kt。其中，亚太地区的PP产量为20982kt，需求为22879kt；欧洲产量为10415kt，需求为10204kt；北美地区产量为7447kt，需求为7634kt；中东地区产量为593kt，需求为3422kt。

俄国最大的石化公司西布尔公司2013年4月10日宣布其在托博尔斯克的500kt/a聚丙烯（PP）厂已经建成。

经俄国监管机构现场检查完成后，很快将开始运营。投产初期，丙烯原料将由西布尔公司在Kstovo的裂解装置提供。该公司在托博尔斯克的丙烷脱氢工厂预计2013年5月或6月建成。该聚丙烯装置预计2014年将全面达产，主要生产PP均聚物。

巴西石化在其位于Marcus Hook的聚丙烯(PP)生产装置附近收购一个工厂，用于精制丙烯，为其PP生产装置提供350kt/a的丙烯原料。预计，2013年巴西石化在Marcus Hook的投资将达到3000万美元，2014年将再增2600万美元。

此外，巴西石化还将在巴西新建一个以甘蔗为原料的“绿色丙烯”的商业化项目，目前已完成工程设计，预计一期产能达到30kt/a以上。

印度在建PP项目产能为1500kt/a。其中，HMEL公司采用Novolen工艺在印度Bathinda建设440kt/a的装置。ONGC公司采用Ineos工艺在Dahej建设340kt/a的装置。

印度公司正致力于研发使用创新技术PP替代传统材料。信实公司生产一种新的高透明无规共聚PP产品，满足迅速增长的包装材料领域需求。

该公司还与汽车和电器领域的设备制造商(OEM)共同研发PP替代元件材料，包括长玻纤填充PP，可以降低元件重量，提高燃油效率。

俄罗斯和独联体的PP生产商也正在增加PP产能。

2011年全球PP市场价格波动显著，尤其是在北美地区，替代产品尤其是高密度聚乙烯和聚苯乙烯消费增长明显，使该地区的PP市场波动尤甚。

PP工业面临的一个主要问题是丙烯原料的短缺，这已经造成业界对长期供应的担忧。要克服这一问题，必须增加炼油厂以及专门生产丙烯的生产设施，如丙烷脱氢装置、烯烃歧化装置以及甲醇制烯烃装置的丙烯供应，而丙烯生产专用技术的应用反过来又会刺激PP成本上涨。

2. 国内聚丙烯发展趋势

聚丙烯高峰扩能阶段依然在持续。煤制烯烃产品在国内市场已经成为常态，丙烷脱氢工艺系列今年起开始作用市场，贸易壁垒频现的情况下进口政策将有哪些转变，进口未来变化形势对国内聚丙烯市场影响度如何?

另一方面，原料来源多元化将令聚丙烯生产成本的竞争继续加剧，而聚丙烯粉料淘汰步伐或将加快。当然，聚丙烯粉料企业众多，行业的淘汰并非一日之事，如何寻求新的发展机遇是业者考虑的重点(表99)。

表99　2013~2015年聚丙烯装置新增扩能统计

新增聚丙烯装置	产能/kt	投产日期
洛阳石化扩能	140.0	2013年2月19日投产
中石油呼尔浩特	150.0	2013年6月
中化泉州炼厂	200.0	2013年8月
徐州海天石化	200.0	2013年4月
中石油四川石化(彭州)	400.0	2013年9月
宁波禾元石化有限公司	300.0	2013年
宁波天圣有限公司	300.0	2013年
陕西延长石化集团	300.0	2013年
中石化武汉分公司	400.0	2013年4月
中石化中原分公司	100.0	2013年
广州石化20万/年聚丙烯装置	200.0	2014年5月
宁波福基石化有限公司	400.0	预计2015年6月
张家港扬子江石化有限公司	400.0	预计2015年6月
青海大美煤业股份有限公司	400.0	预计2015年8月
九台能源公司(格尔旗)	350.0	预计2015年
华亭煤集团(甘肃省华亭工业发展区)	200.0	预计2016年
总计/万吨	4440.0	

由中化二建集团承建的中化泉州石化200kt/a聚丙烯项目脱气、造粒钢结构于2013年3月5下午全部吊装就位，至此，高96m的脱气、造粒钢结构圆满封顶。该钢结构长10m、宽10m，坐落在脱气、造粒3层混凝土平台上，分6段安装。其安装难度、精度、高度都开创了中化泉州石化工地钢结构安装之最。图为聚丙烯脱气造粒钢结构封顶时的情景。

2013年3月3日下午，广州石化200kt/a聚丙烯装置建成中交，标志着该项目正式转入生产准备阶段。

200kt/a 聚丙烯装置是广州石化在化工区的第一个重点建设项目，该项目总投资7.4亿元，由上海工程公司EPC总承包，中石化五建公司、中石化四建公司总施工。

200kt/a 聚丙烯装置于2011年7月8日正式动工兴建，项目从建设到中交，仅历时19个月零25天，较目前国内同类聚丙烯装置最短21个月的建设工期又提前了1个多月。

2013年东华能源股份有限公司发布公告，将在浙江宁波和江苏张家港各建一个400kt聚丙烯项目。

东华能源将以独资设立的宁波福基石化有限公司为主体，投资建设1320kt/a 丙烷脱氢制丙烯装置、400kt/a 聚丙烯装置，以及下游配套项目等，项目总投资预计不超过50亿元人民币。

项目计划分两期建设，第一期规划建设一套660kt/a 丙烷脱氢装置，一套400kt/a 聚丙烯装置，并根据项目需要配套异丙醇等下游项目。预计一期项目建设期为一年半，总投资额为30亿元人民币。

此外，东华能源还将以控股子公司张家港扬子江石化有限公司为主体，在张家港新增投资建设400kt/a 聚丙烯项目。项目建设投资预计不超过10亿元人民币。

2012年11月8日，青海大美煤业股份有限公司与陶氏化学公司（"陶氏"）的全资子公司联合碳化物化学品及塑料技术有限公司，签署了UNIPOL/聚丙烯工艺技术的许可协议。

这一位于中国青海省西宁经济技术开发区的煤基聚烯烃项目计划于2015年建成投产。其400kt/a 聚丙烯装置，将生产聚丙烯均聚物、无规共聚物和抗冲共聚物。

陶氏和青海大美的代表于2012年9月28日举行了400kt/a 聚丙烯装置的签字仪式。

这是自2006年以来，陶氏在中国签署的第12项UNIPOL/聚丙烯技术许可协议。

陶氏 UNIPOL/聚丙烯技术生产的树脂，已占全球聚丙烯产量的17%。

目前，全球已有47套转让自陶氏功能塑料技术转让和催化剂业务部的UNIPOL/聚丙烯装置投入生产运行。

CB&I 表示其鲁玛斯技术部门已获华亭煤集团合约，为其中国甘肃省华亭工业发展区的一座聚丙烯（PP）工厂提供许可、基本工程及相关服务。

这座PP工厂年产量达20万公吨，预计于2014年启动。该工厂将采用纳瓦伦先进的气相聚合技术，生产一系列的PP均聚物、无规共聚物和耐冲击共聚物。

此外，这座工厂也是煤转甲醇项目的一部分，该项目年产量可达60万公吨，并于2010年年底开始生产。

北京九台集团子公司九台能源公司与美国联合碳化物化学品及塑料技术公司签订协议，九台能源公司的甲醇制烯烃的聚丙烯（PP）工厂将获得Unipol聚丙烯技术授权。

据悉，九台能源公司将采用Unipol聚丙烯技术生产聚丙烯，年产量将达35万公吨。新建工厂将生产聚丙烯系列产品。该工厂预计于2015年在内蒙古投入运营。

第六章 国内聚苯乙烯树脂进口量降价升，出口量跌价升

一、2012年聚苯乙烯生产小幅增长

2006~2012年间PS产量增长了21.58%，年均增长3.31%（表100）。

表100 2006~2012年国内PS生产能力和产量统计表

项 目	2006	2007	2008	2009	2010	2011	2012
生产能力/kt	2800.0	2950.0	2950.0	3100.0	3100.0	3100.0	3100
产量/kt	1747.0	2056.1	2061.0	2100.0	2300.0	2029.6	2124.0
开工率/%	62.50	69.70	69.86	67.74	74.19	65.47	68.52
年增长率/%	12.18	17.69	0.24	1.89	9.52	-11.76	4.62

从统计资料来看，PS树脂生产厂主要集中在广东省，浙江省，天津市，江苏省和上海市五省市，合计产量占总产量的95.60%。

国内主要发泡聚苯乙烯（EPS）生产商有宁波新桥化工有限公司，江阴新和桥化工有限公司，无锡兴达泡塑新材料有限公司，江苏嘉盛化学品工业有限公司，东莞新长桥塑料有限公司，江苏诚达石化工业有限公司，江苏利士德化工有限公司，江阴倪家巷新材料有限公司，台达化工（天津）有限公司，苏州常乐泡塑有限公司，江苏丽天新材料有限公司，

新疆蓝山屯河新材料有限公司等。

受市场需求疲软的影响，中国大型发泡聚苯乙烯(EPS)生产商江苏无锡兴达集团于2011年11月底将装置的开工率从75%下调至50%。

兴达集团拥有4套EPS装置，总产能为1110kt/a，公司在无锡的装置拥有450kt/a产能，在常州的装置拥有360kt/a产能，在新疆的装置拥有120kt/a产能，在惠州的装置拥有180kt/a产能，是中国专业生产EPS的龙头企业，年产能力为1150kt，约占全国的40%，拥有全球单体产能最大的EPS专业生产基地。

2011年10月份，该公司4套EPS装置的平均开工率水平为80%，11月份降至75%，12月已进一步大幅下调至50%，2012年1月份开工率仍保持在40%～50%，2012年开工率仍保持在55%左右。

国内PS树脂生产厂不多，国内主要聚苯乙烯(PS)生产商有雪佛龙菲利普斯化工(中国)有限公司，道达尔石化(佛山)有限公司，扬子石化，镇江奇美化工有限公司等。

而从事改性PS品种生产的厂家和产能大大超过了基础树脂生产厂。近年来我国PS改性发展较快，主要由于双螺杆混炼挤出机的引进和国产双螺杆混炼挤出机的推出，给改性PS创造了有利条件。

国内主要PS工程塑料改性厂有广州金发科技股份有限公司，青岛海尔新材料研发有限公司，优利(东莞)塑胶材料有限公司，珠海科杰高分子材料有限公司，星际塑料(深圳)有限公司，鸿富锦精密工业(深圳)有限公司，东进塑料(烟台)有限公司，出光复合工程塑料(广州)有限公司，南京利佳塑料发展有限公司，日超工程塑料(深圳)有限公司，积水化成品(苏州)科技有限公司，上海金发科技发展有限公司，山阳稻田复合塑料(东莞)有限公司，上海锦湖日丽塑料有限公司，深圳市科聚新材料有限公司，漂莱特(中国)有限公司，厦门昭伟塑胶工业有限公司，广东锦湖日丽高分子材料有限公司，青岛国恩科技发展有限公司，济南裕鲁科技有限公司，山东兄弟科技股份有限公司，宁波长桥工程塑料有限公司，LG化学(天津)工程塑料有限公司，山东润科化工股份有限公司，普立万聚合体(深圳)有限公司，潍坊裕鑫化工有限公司，常熟聚和化学有限公司，南通艾德旺化工有限公司，广州广钢MBA塑料新技术有限公司，深圳市亿利丰塑料有限公司，佛山市三水南威塑胶电子制品有限公司，越谷化成工程塑料(上海)有限公司，星际塑料(深圳)有限公司，康准精密模具(昆山)有限公司，无锡华利特金属塑料制品有限公司，青岛海尔新材料研发有限公司，吴江东永材料科技有限公司，天津松井塑料有限公司，吴江东永材料科技有限公司。

二、2012年国内聚苯乙烯树脂出口生产省市仍集中于东部沿海地区

1. 可发性聚苯乙烯仍集中于江浙二省

2012年可发性聚苯乙烯出口生产企业主要集中在江苏省、浙江省二省，江浙二省2012年可发性聚苯乙烯出口量占总出口数量的89.738%，比上年出口增加5.526%。

江苏省，出口数量167026090kg，占总出口数量的55.954%，比上年出口减少16.16%；

其次为浙江省，出口数量100845835kg，占总出口数量的33.784%，比上年出口增加40.02%；

广东省，出口数量21012156kg，占总出口数量的7.039%，比上年出口减少46.19%；

天津市，出口数量5677000kg，占总出口数量的1.902%，比上年出口减少39.02%；

河北省出口数量1496820kg，占总出口数量的0.501%，比上年出口增加532.37%。

2012年五省市可发性聚苯乙烯出口数量占总出口数量的99.180%，比上年出口减少0.77百分点(表101)。

表101　2012年初级形状的可发性聚苯乙烯五大出口省市统计

排　序	出口省市	出口金额/美元	出口数量/kg	占比例/%
1	江苏省	274834109.00	167026090	55.954
2	浙江省	171296460.00	100845835	33.784
3	广东省	33794504.00	21012156	7.039
4	天津市	9709328.00	5677000	1.902
5	河北省	1758922.00	1496820	0.501
出口总计		495748708.00	298504724	100.00

2. 改性的初级形状聚苯乙烯出口仍集中于广东、江苏二省

2012年改性的初级形状聚苯乙烯出口省市有12个，与上年12个出口省市持平。

改性的初级形状聚苯乙烯出口主要集中于广东，江苏二省，二省2012年改性聚苯乙烯出口量占总出口数量的80.431%，比上年出口增加5.010%。

2012年改性的初级形状的聚苯乙烯广东省，出口数量11580530kg，占总出口数量的56.887%，比上年出口增加15.27%；

其次为江苏省，出口数量4792812kg，占总出口数量的23.544%，比上年出口增加64.13%；

山东省，出口数量2528937kg，占总出口数量的12.423%，比上年出口增加57.82%；

上海市，出口数量839412kg，占总出口数量的4.123%，比上年出口减少55.53%；

新疆维吾尔自治区，出口数量182450kg，占总出口数量的0.896%。

2012年五省市改性聚苯乙烯出口数量占总出口数量的97.874%，比上年出口增加0.893%（表102）。

表102 2012年改性的初级形状的非可发性聚苯乙烯五大出口省市统计

排 序	出口省市	出口金额/美元	出口数量/kg	占比例/%
1	广东省	27130039.00	11580530	56.887
2	江苏省	10347649.00	4792812	23.544
3	山东省	5757525.00	2528937	12.423
4	上海市	2229468.00	839412	4.123
5	新疆维吾尔自治区	282717.00	182450	0.896
出口总计		47680245.00	20356975	100.00

3. 其他初级形状聚苯乙烯出口主要集中于广东、江苏省二省

2012年其他初级形状聚苯乙烯出口省市有14个，比上年12个出口省市增加2个出口省市。

2012年初级形状的其他聚苯乙烯出口生产企业主要集中于广东、江苏省二省，二省2012年改性聚苯乙烯出口量占总出口数量的87.105%，比上年出口增加0.335%。

广东省2012年初级形状的其他聚苯乙烯出口数量12355508kg，占总出口数量的75.319%，比上年出口减少7.64%；

其次为江苏省出口数量1933410kg，占总出口数量的11.786%，比上年出口增加131.60%；

安徽省，出口数量5543053kg，占总出口数量的3.379%；

河北省出口数量384600kg，占总出口数量的2.345%；

上海市出口数量368784kg，占总出口数量的2.248%，比上年出口减少54.85%；

2012年五省市其他聚苯乙烯出口数量占总出口数量的95.077%，比上年出口减少2.263%（表103）。

表103 2012年其他初级形状的聚苯乙烯五大出口省市统计

排 序	出口省市	出口金额/美元	出口数量/kg	占比例/%
1	广东省	21229544.00	12355508	75.319
2	江苏省	3262622.00	1933410	11.786
3	安徽省	228475.00	554305	3.379
4	河北省	456518.00	384600	2.345
5	上海市	1546583.00	368784	2.248
出口总计		28775253.00	16404140	100.00

三、2012年国内聚苯乙烯树脂出口商以生产企业为主

1. 2012年国内可发性聚苯乙烯树脂出口商以生产企业为主

从海关资料来看，2012年其他初级形状的可发性聚苯乙烯出口商有118家，比上年132家出口商减少14家出口商，前十位其他初级形状的可发性聚苯乙烯出口商出口量占总出口量的95.933%。

二十大出口商中有十二家为可发性聚苯乙烯生产企业，八家可发性聚苯乙烯贸易商，分别占总出口量的94.994%和3.787%；

前十位其他初级形状的可发性聚苯乙烯出口商改性九家为非可发性聚苯乙烯生产企业，占总出口量的92.682%

宁波新桥化工有限公司2012年其他初级形状的可发性聚苯乙烯出口100601150kg，占总出口量的33.702%，比上年出口增加39.86%；

江阴新和桥化工有限公司2012年其他初级形状的可发性聚苯乙烯出口61893950kg，占总出口量的20.735%，比上年出口上升减少11.26%；

无锡兴达泡塑新材料有限公司2012年其他初级形状的可发性聚苯乙烯出口34940600kg，占总出口数量的11.705%，比上年出口减少35.77%；

江苏嘉盛化学品工业有限公司2012年其他初级形状的可发性聚苯乙烯出口23594375kg，占总出口量的7.904%，比上年出口增加33.02%；

东莞新长桥塑料有限公司2012年其他初级形状的可发性聚苯乙烯出口20792425kg，占总出口量的6.966%，比上年出口减少46.69%。

江苏诚达石化工业有限公司2012年其他初级形状的可发性聚苯乙烯出口12051900kg，占总出口量的4.037%，比上年减少45.21%；

江苏利士德化工有限公司司2012年其他初级形状的可发性聚苯乙烯出口12051900kg，占总出口量的3.716%，比上年出口增加101.67%；

江苏省对外经贸股份有限公司2012年其他初级形状的可发性聚苯乙烯出口8414000kg，占总出口量的3.251%，比上年出口增加28.80%；

江阴倪家巷新材料有限公司2012年其他初级形状的可发性聚苯乙烯出口6565000kg，占总出口量的2.199%，比上年出口减少22.34%；台达化工(天津)有限公司2012年其他初级形状的可发性聚苯乙烯出口5127200kg，占总出口量的1.718%，比上年出口增加45.49%(表104)。

表104　2012年初级形状的可发性聚苯乙烯二十大出口商统计

排　序	出口商	所属行业	出口数量/kg	占比例/%
1	宁波新桥化工有限公司	EPS生产企业	100601150	33.702
2	江阴新和桥化工有限公司	EPS生产企业	61893950	20.735
3	无锡兴达泡塑新材料有限公司	EPS生产企业	34940600	11.705
4	江苏嘉盛化学品工业有限公司	EPS生产企业	23594375	7.904
5	东莞新长桥塑料有限公司	EPS生产企业	20792425	6.966
6	江苏诚达石化工业有限公司	EPS生产企业	12051900	4.037
7	江苏利士德化工有限公司	EPS生产企业	11092000	3.716
8	江苏省对外经贸股份有限公司	贸易商	9704100	3.251
9	江阴倪家巷新材料有限公司	EPS生产企业	6565000	2.199
10	台达化工(天津)有限公司	EPS生产企业	5127200	1.718
11	苏州常乐泡塑有限公司	EPS生产企业	5086000	1.704
12	江苏丽天新材料有限公司	EPS生产企业	1497000	0.501
13	丹东市进出口有限责任公司	贸易商	330000	0.111
14	新疆蓝山屯河新材料有限公司	EPS生产企业	320000	0.107
15	黑河和兴经贸有限公司	贸易商	294875	0.099
16	北京时代华通国际贸易有限公司	贸易商	238476	0.080
17	不详	贸易商	216000	0.072
18	江苏省茂源进出口有限公司	贸易商	180200	0.060
19	不详	贸易商	170000	0.057
20	天津市郎威国际贸易有限公司	贸易商	170000	0.057
出口总计			298504724	98.781%

2. 2012 年国内改性聚苯乙烯树脂出口商以生产企业为主

从海关资料来看，2012 年其他初级形状的可发性聚苯乙烯出口商有 95 家，比上年 101 家出口商减少 6 家出口商，前十位其他初级形状的可发性聚苯乙烯出口商出口量占总出口量的 74. 242%，比上年出口上升 6. 370%。

前十位其他初级形状的改性非可发性聚苯乙烯出口商中八家为改性聚苯乙烯生产企业，二家为为贸易商。

四十大出口商中有二十家为改性聚苯乙烯生产企业，二家为聚苯乙烯生产企业，十八家为改性聚苯乙烯贸易商，分别占总出口量的 64. 798%，8. 127% 和 23. 121%；

广州金发科技股份有限公司 2012 年其他初级形状的改性聚苯乙烯出口 5052975kg，占总出口量的 24. 822%，比上年出口增加 61. 98%；

青岛海尔新材料研发有限公司 2012 年其他初级形状的改性聚苯乙烯出口 1733200kg，占总出口量的 8. 514%，比上年出口增加 134. 98%；

昆山市鑫明对外贸易有限公司 2012 年其他初级形状的改性聚苯乙烯出口 1456479kg，占总出口量的 7. 155%；

上海新域信息系统有限公司 2012 年其他初级形状的改性聚苯乙烯出口 1265088kg，占总出口量的 6. 215%；

优利(东莞)塑胶材料有限公司 2012 年其他初级形状的改性聚苯乙烯出口 1244100kg，占总出口数量的 6. 111%，比上年出口减少 57. 58%；

雪佛龙菲利普斯化工(中国)有限公司 2012 年其他初级形状的改性聚苯乙烯出口 1129500kg，占总出口量的 5. 548%，比上年出口减少 46. 42%；

珠海科杰高分子材料有限公司 2012 年其他初级形状的改性聚苯乙烯出口 1112701kg，占总出口量的 5. 466%；

星际塑料(深圳)有限公司 2012 年其他初级形状的改性聚苯乙烯出口 570278kg，占总出口量的 5. 031%，比上年出口上升 2. 78%；

鸿富锦精密工业(深圳)有限公司 2012 年其他初级形状的改性聚苯乙烯出口 570278kg，占总出口量的 2. 801%，比上年出口上升 0. 05%；

道达尔石化(佛山)有限公司 2012 年其他初级形状的改性聚苯乙烯出口 525000kg，占总出口量的 2. 579%，比上年出口减少 29. 27%(表 105)。

表 105　2012 年改性的初级形状的聚苯乙烯四十大出口商统计

排　序	出口商	所属行业	出口数量/kg	占比例/%
1	广州金发科技股份有限公司	改性 PS	5052975	24. 822
2	青岛海尔新材料研发有限公司	改性 PS	1733200	8. 514
3	昆山市鑫明对外贸易有限公司	贸易商	1456479	7. 155
4	上海新域信息系统有限公司	贸易商	1265088	6. 215
5	优利(东莞)塑胶材料有限公司	改性 PS	1244100	6. 111
6	雪佛龙菲利普斯化工(中国)有限公司	PS 树脂生产厂	1129500	5. 548
7	珠海科杰高分子材料有限公司	改性 PS	1112701	5. 466
8	星际塑料(深圳)有限公司	改性 PS	1024181	5. 031
9	鸿富锦精密工业(深圳)有限公司	改性 PS	570278	2. 801
10	道达尔石化(佛山)有限公司	PS 树脂生产厂	525000	2. 579
11	东进塑料(烟台)有限公司	改性 PS	399715	1. 964
12	出光复合工程塑料(广州)有限公司	改性 PS	379575	1. 865
12	深圳市宝安外经发展有限公司	贸易商	349978	1. 719
13	不详	贸易商	307620	1. 511
14	南京利佳塑料发展有限公司	改性 PS	255000	1. 253
15	日超工程塑料(深圳)有限公司	改性 PS	226393	1. 112
16	积水化成品(苏州)科技有限公司	改性 PS	219072	1. 076
17	上海金发科技发展有限公司	改性 PS	209625	1. 030

续表

排　序	出口商	所属行业	出口数量/kg	占比例/%
18	不详	贸易商	200000	0.982
19	理光通运(深圳)仓储有限公司	贸易商	193975	0.953
20	山阳稻田复合塑料(东莞)有限公司	改性 PS	190685	0.937
21	上海兰生文体进出口有限公司	贸易商	186500	0.916
22	上海锦湖日丽塑料有限公司	改性 PS	181700	0.893
23	上海稻田产业贸易有限公司	贸易商	140375	0.690
24	深圳市鸿宇威贸易有限公司	贸易商	113900	0.560
25	深圳市科聚新材料有限公司	改性 PS	111050	0.546
26	漂莱特(中国)有限公司	改性 PS	91127	0.448
27	江阴市顶一工贸有限公司	贸易商	75020	0.369
28	不详	贸易商	73000	0.359
29	厦门昭伟塑胶工业有限公司	改性 PS	64361	0.316
30	青岛海杰尔进出口有限公司	贸易商	64000	0.314
31	宇航物流(大连保税物流园区)有限公司	贸易商	62100	0.305
32	深圳市飞业伟贸易有限公司	贸易商	54000	0.265
33	博州阿拉山口盛坤贸易有限公司	贸易商	52000	0.255
34	广东锦湖日丽高分子材料有限公司	改性 PS	46750	0.230
35	青岛国恩科技发展有限公司	改性 PS	42000	0.206
36	不详	贸易商	39000	0.192
37	不详	贸易商	38000	0.187
38	广州保畅国际物流有限公司	贸易商	36000	0.177
40	吴江东永材料科技有限公司	改性 PS	36000	0.177
	出口总计		20356975	100.00

3.2012 年国内其他初级形状聚苯乙烯树脂出口商以生产企业为主

从海关资料来看，2012 年其他初级形状的聚苯乙烯出口商有 143 家，比上年 141 家出口商增加 3 家出口商，前十位其他初级形状的聚苯乙烯出口商出口量占总出口量的 82.426%，比上年增加 5.356%。

二十大出口商中有道达尔石化(佛山)有限公司(占总出口量的 9.979%)、雪佛龙菲利普斯化工(中国)有限公司(占总出口量的 7.472%%)和镇江奇美化工有限公司(占总出口量的 0.390%)三家是聚苯乙烯原料生产集团，均为外商投资企业，占总出口量的 17.841%；

二十大出口商中其余为改性聚苯乙烯专用产品粒料生产企业(11 家)及聚苯乙烯贸易商(6 家)，分别占总出口量的 45.270% 和 25.931%；

鸿富锦精密工业(深圳)有限公司 2012 年其他初级形状的聚苯乙烯出口 3594455kg，占总出口数量的 21.912%%；

东莞联记塑胶原料有限公司司 2012 年其他初级形状的聚苯乙烯出口 3298800kg，占总出口数量的 20.110%；

广州广钢 MBA 塑料新技术有限公司 2012 年其他初级形状的聚苯乙烯出口 1807250kg，占总出口数量的 11.01%；

深圳市亿利丰塑料有限公司 2012 年其他初级形状的聚苯乙烯出口 738000kg，占总出口数量的 4.499%(表 106)。

表 106　2012 年其他初级形状的聚苯乙烯二十大出口商统计

排　序	出口商	所属行业	出口数量/kg	占比例/%
1	鸿富锦精密工业(深圳)有限公司	改性 PS 粒料	3594455	21.912
2	东莞联记塑胶原料有限公司	贸易商	3298800	20.110
3	广州广钢 MBA 塑料新技术有限公司	改性 PS 粒料	1807250	11.017
4	道达尔石化(佛山)有限公司	PS 树脂生产厂	1636950	9.979
5	雪佛龙菲利普斯化工(中国)有限公司	PS 树脂生产厂	1225650	7.472
6	深圳市亿利丰塑料有限公司	改性 PS 粒料	738000	4.499
7	不详	贸易商	539056	3.286
8	佛山市三水南威塑胶电子制品有限公司	改性 PS 粒料	257500	1.570
9	越谷化成工程塑料(上海)有限公司	改性 PS 粒料	235000	1.433
10	星际塑料(深圳)有限公司	改性 PS 粒料	188242	1.148
11	康准精密模具(昆山)有限公司	改性 PS 粒料	180565	1.101
12	无锡华利特金属塑料制品有限公司	改性 PS 粒料	165500	1.009
13	漂莱特(中国)有限公司	贸易商	128600	0.784
14	东莞毅兴塑胶原料有限公司	贸易商	114000	0.695
15	深圳市北方实业发展有限公司	贸易商	96000	0.585
16	青岛海尔新材料研发有限公司	改性 PS 粒料	96000	0.585
17	吴江东永材料科技有限公司	改性 PS 粒料	91000	0.555
18	东莞建德塑胶原料制品有限公司	贸易商	77645	0.473
19	天津松井塑料有限公司	改性 PS 粒料	72400	0.441
20	镇江奇美化工有限公司	PS 树脂生产厂	64000	0.390
出口总计			16404140	100.00

4. 2012 年国内初级形状其他苯乙烯树脂出口商以生产企业为主

从海关资料来看，2012 年初级形状其他苯乙烯树脂出口商有 136 家，比上年 142 家出口商减少 6 家出口商，前十位初级形状其他苯乙烯树脂出口商出口量占总出口量的 69.239%，比上年减少 7.171%(表 107)。

表 107　2012 年初级形状其他苯乙烯树脂二十大出口商统计

排序	出口商	所属行业	出口数量/kg	占比例/%
1	石家庄市永昌利进出口有限公司	贸易商	1351952	13.862
2	济南裕鲁科技有限公司	改性 PS 粒料	1143030	11.720
3	威海金泓罗门哈斯化工有限公司	改性 PS 粒料	1106380	11.344
4	山东兄弟科技股份有限公司	改性 PS 粒料	930890	9.545
5	珠海东洋油墨有限公司	改性 PS 粒料	610000	6.254
6	宁波长桥工程塑料有限公司	改性 PS 粒料	447811	4.592
7	潍坊优博化学品有限公司	改性 PS 粒料	353050	3.620
8	LG 化学(天津)工程塑料有限公司	改性 PS 粒料	319000	3.271
9	上海铁联国际储运有限公司	贸易商	315451	3.234
10	山东润科化工股份有限公司	改性 PS 粒料	175300	1.797

续表

排序	出口商	所属行业	出口数量/kg	占比例/%
11	普立万聚合体(深圳)有限公司	改性 PS 粒料	162125	1.662
12	潍坊裕鑫化工有限公司	改性 PS 粒料	148000	1.517
13	常熟聚和化学有限公司	改性 PS 粒料	122726	1.258
14	南通艾德旺化工有限公司	改性 PS 粒料	119500	1.225
15	不详	贸易商	108370	1.111
16	上海罗门哈斯化工有限公司	改性 PS 粒料	93552	0.959
17	海尔集团电器产业有限公司	改性 PS 粒料	90704	0.930
18	上海东方明珠国际贸易有限公司	贸易商	86000	0.882
19	浙江省机械设备进出口有限责任公司	贸易商	84100	0.862
20	不详	贸易商	79000	0.810
	出口总计		9752993	100.00

四、国内可发性聚苯乙烯树脂进口逐年下降出口量价同升

随着我国可发性聚苯乙烯行业的发展，我国可发性聚苯乙烯由进口国发展到净出口国，2005 年前我国可发性聚苯乙烯进口大于出口，2006 年起我国可发性聚苯乙烯出口超过进口，成为净出口国。

2005 ~ 2010 年，可发性聚苯乙烯出口继续保持大幅增长，2011 年出口量小幅回落，比上年回落 2.29%；2012 年出口量再回落，比上年回落 7.32%；出口年平均价格为 1660.77 美元/t，同比上升 2.41%。

2012 年进口可发性聚苯乙烯数量 60.8kt，同比下降 20.03%，进口年平均价格为 1709.07 美元/t，同比上升 7.07%。

我国出口产品价一般均低于进口价，但可发性聚苯乙烯少见——2000 ~ 2008 年出口价均远高于进口价；2009 ~ 2010 年出口价低于进口价 10.99% 和 2.07%；2011 年出口价又高于进口价 1.59%，但 2011 年出口价低于进口价 2.73%(表 108)。

表 108　2007 ~ 2012 年初级形状的可发性聚苯乙烯进出口统计

项　目	2007	2008	2009	2010	201	2012
进口量/t	109560	85246	77468	75913	75991	60767
年增长率/%	-9.21	-22.19	-9.12	-2.01	0.10	-20.03
进口金额/万美元	13927.31	11997.93	9763.65	10521.64	12130.15	10385.59
年平均进口单价/(美元/t)	1271.20	1407.45	1260.35	1386.01	1596.26	1709.07
年增长率/%	15.48	10.72	-10.45	9.97	15.17	7.07
出口量/t	275426	294427	258773	329631	322067	298505
年增长率/%	84.37	6.90	-12.11	27.38	-2.29	-7.32
出口金额/万美元	42173.88	45502.20	29028.50	44742.74	52229.40	49574.87
年平均出口单价/(美元/t)	1531.22	1545.45	1121.78	1357.36	1621.69	1660.77
年增长率/%	10.09	0.93	-27.41	21.00	19.47	2.41
净出口量/t	165866	209181	181305	253718	246076	237738
年增长率/%	477.59	26.11	-13.33	39.94	-3.01	-3.39

注：资料来源——历年国家海关统计。

2007 ~ 2012 年间初级形状的可发性聚苯乙烯国内出口量增长 8.38 倍，年均增长率为 1.62%，平均出口单价年均上升 1.64%；

2007 ~ 2012 年初级形状的可发性聚苯乙烯国内

进口量下降44.54%，年均下降11.09%，平均进口单价年均增长率为6.10%。

1. 可发性聚苯乙烯进口逐年下降，进口单价逐年上升

2012年可发性聚苯乙烯进口小幅下降，进口单价上升。

从海关统计中可看出，2012年初级形状的可发性聚苯乙烯进口地有30个，比上年31个进口地减少1个进口地。

主要进口地为韩国，进口19113765kg，占总进口数量的31.454%，比上年进口数量减2.24%；

其次为中国台湾省，进口18436930kg，占总进口数量的30.340%，比上年减少进口数量42.60%；

美国进口4909287kg，占总进口数量的8.079%，比上年减少进口数量14.92%；

中国香港进口4229800kg，占总进口数量的6.961%，比上年增加进口数量10.83%；

日本进口3544103kg，占总进口数量的5.832%，比上年进口数量减少21.30%；

五进口地进口数量占可发性聚苯乙烯2012年总进口数量的82.666%，比上年减少4.084%（表109）。

表109　2012年初级形状的可发性聚苯乙烯五大进口国家/地区统计

排　序	原产进口地	进口金额/美元	进口数量/kg	占比例/%
1	韩国	32708859.00	19113765	31.454
2	中国台湾省	28894115.00	18436930	30.340
3	美国	12705400.00	4909287	8.079
4	中国香港	5980508.00	4229800	6.961
5	日本	5977328.00	3544103	5.832
进口总计		103855892.00	60767386	100.00

2. 可发性聚苯乙烯出口量减价升

海关统计数据显示，我国可发性聚苯乙烯出口市场相对分散，2012年我国共向全世界107个国家（地区）出口了可发性聚苯乙烯，比上年102个出口地增加5个出口地，其中，伊朗、俄罗斯和巴西仍是2012年中最主要的三个出口市场。

2012年，我国向伊朗市场出口可发性聚苯乙91211350kg，同比下降24.85%，出口数量占全部出口数量的30.556%，出口平均价格1721.62美元/t,，同比上升5.72%；

其次为向俄罗斯联邦出口3944697531039646kg，同比上升27.09%，出口数量占全部出口数量的13.215%，出口平均价格1634.09美元/t,，同比上升1.21%；

向巴西出口22949500kg，同比大幅上升13.11%，出口数量占全部出口数量的7.688%，出口平均价格1641.98美元/t，同比上升1.10%；

向土耳其出口22345025kg，同比大幅上升13.69%，出口数量占全部出口数量的7.486%，出口平均价格1620.29美元/t，同比上升2.42%；

向澳大利亚出口11748840kg，出口数量占全部出口数量的3.936%。

五出口地出口数量占可发性聚苯乙烯2012年总出口数量的62.881%，比2011年减少1.549%（表110）。

表110　2012年初级形状的可发性聚苯乙烯五大出口国家/地区统计

排　序	出口目的地	出口金额/美元	出口数量/kg	占比例/%
1	伊朗	157031703.00	91211350	30.556
2	俄罗斯	64460017.00	39446975	13.215
3	巴西	37682643.00	22949500	7.688
4	土耳其	36205483.00	22345025	7.486
5	澳大利亚	19146819.00	11748840	3.936
出口总计		495748708.00	298504724	100.00

五、国内聚苯乙烯树脂进口量跌价升，出口量价同升

随着我国聚苯乙烯行业的发展，我国2012年聚苯乙烯(PS)国内自给率上升到70%以上，小部份PS资源靠进口。

2012年，我国共出口聚苯乙烯36.8kt，比上年

同期(下同)增长 9.37%。

2012 年，进口聚苯乙烯数量达 919.1kt，同比下降 4.81%(表 111)。

表 111　2007～2012 年聚苯乙烯(PS)进出口统计

项　目	2007	2008	2009	2010	2011	2012
其他聚苯乙烯						
进口量/t	1214121	1066247	911845	799290	719438	682463
年增长率/%	1.31	-12.18	—	-12.34	-9.99	-5.14
进口金额/万美元	159450.74	153421.02	108774.99	111899.25	113280.83	110058.84
年平均进口单价/(美元/t)	1313.30	1438.89	1192.91	1399.98	1574.57	1612.67
年增长率/%	17.83	9.56	-17.10	17.36	12.47	2.42
出口量/t	32598	29013	7254	14187	16435	16404
年增长率/%	-16.39	-11.00	-75.00	95.57	15.85	-0.19
出口金额/万美元	4543.94	5223.80	1205.35	2462.33	3076.14	28775253
年平均出口单价/(美元/t)	1393.91	1800.50	1661.58	1735.63	1871.70	1754.16
年增长率/%	9.67	29.17	-7.72	4.46	7.84	-6.28
改性的聚苯乙烯						
进口量/t	—	—	195591	276794	243107	236646
年增长率/%	—	—	—	41.52	-12.17	-2.66
进口金额/万美元	—	—	26024.34	43711.78	43710.21	43763.56
年平均进口单价/(美元/t)	—	—	1330.55	1579.22	1797.98	1849.33
年增长率/%	—	—	—	18.69	13.85	2.86
出口量/t	—	—	8718	14438	17162	20357
年增长率/%	—	—	—	65.61	18.87	18.62
出口金额/万美元	—	—	1529.93	3176.56	4017.05	4768.02
年平均出口单价/(美元/t)	—	—	1754.83	2000.14	2340.66	2342.20
年增长率/%	—	—	—	25.38	17.03	0.07
总计净进口量/t	1181523	1037234	1091134	1047459	928945	882348
年增长率/%	1.90	-12.21	5.20	-4.00	-11.31	-5.02

注：1. 资料来源——历年国家海关统计

2. 改性的聚苯乙烯 2009 年才单独新列出代码，无历年数据，因此无法同比。

2007～2012 年聚苯乙烯净进口量年均增长率为下降 5.67%。

1. 2012 年聚苯乙烯进口下降，进口单价增长

从海关统计中可看出，2012 年其他聚苯乙烯进口地有 42 个，比上年 40 个进口地增加 2 个进口地。

主要进口地仍为中国台湾省进口数量 258761641kg，占总进口数量的 37.916%，比上年进口数量减少 0.31%；

其次为中国香港进口数量 129797725kg，占总进口数量的 19.019%，比上年进口数量减少 14.77%；

韩国进口数量 106763673kg，占总进口数量的 15.644%，比上年进口数量减少 13.16%；

新加坡进口数量 76236847kg，占总进口数量的 11.171%，比上年进口数量增加 10.73%；

泰国进口数量 3918358038790067kg，占总进口数量的 5.741%，比上年进口数量增加 1.01%；

五原产进口地进口数量占其他聚苯乙烯2012年总进口数量的89.491%，比上年增加0.180%(表112)。

表112　2012年其他初级形状的聚苯乙烯五大进口国家/地区统计

排　序	原产进口地	进口金额/美元	进口数量/kg	占比例/%
1	中国台湾省	397269949.00	258761641	37.916
2	中国香港	211457339.00	129797725	19.019
3	韩国	179525208.00	106763673	15.644
4	新加坡	120158121.00	76236847	11.171
5	泰国	57461850.00	39183580	5.741
进口总计		1100588391.00	682462729	

2. 2011年聚苯乙烯出口量价同升

海关统计数据显示，我国聚苯乙烯出口市场相对分散，2012年我国共向全世界57个国家(地区)出口了聚苯乙烯，比上年49个出口地增加8个出口地。

2012年中国香港地区、日本和西班牙是其中最主要的三个出口市场，2012年，我国向中国香港出口聚苯乙烯8345881kg，同比下降11.79%，出口数量占全部出口数量的50.877%，出口平均价格为1930.33美元/t，，比上年上升下降7.73%；

其次向日本出口2861381kg，同比增加54.28%，占总出口量的17.443%，出口平均价格为1582.21美元/t，比上年下降10.04%；

向西班牙出口1197760kg，同比增加36.19%，占总出口量的7.302%；

向印度出口391380kg，占总出口量的2.386%，同比下降29.82%；

向越南出口385094kg，占总出口量的2.348%。

五出口地出口数量占初级形状的其他聚苯乙烯2012年总出口数量的80.355%，比上年下降0.235%(表113)。

表113　2012年其他初级形状的聚苯乙烯五大出口国家/地区统计

排　序	出口目的地	出口金额/美元	出口数量/kg	占比例/%
1	中国香港	16110301.00	8345881	50.877
2	日本	4527298.00	2861381	17.443
3	西班牙	1187952.00	1197760	7.302
4	印度	382114.00	391380	2.386
5	越南	846200.00	385094	2.348
出口总计		28775253.00	16404140	100.00

3. 2012年改性的聚苯乙烯进口量跌价升

从海关统计中可看出，2012年改性聚苯乙烯进口地有28个，比上年29个进口地减1个进口地。

主要进口地为中国台湾省进口数量75472512kg，占总进口数量的31.893%，比上年进口数量上升32.08%；

其次为中国香港进口数量60865428kg，占总进口数量的25.720%，比上年进口数量下降17.60%；

韩国进口数量59619830kg，占总进口数量的25.194%，比上年进口数量下降13.26%；

日本进口数量13010023kg，占总进口数量的5.498%，比2011年进口数量下降35.60%；

泰国进口数量8478141kg，占总进口数量的3.583%，比上年进口数量上升41.90%。

五原产进口地进口数量占改性聚苯乙烯2012年总进口数量的91.887%，比上年下降5.083%(表114)。

表114　2012年改性的初级形状聚苯乙烯五大进口国家/地区统计

排　序	原产进口地	进口金额/美元	进口数量/kg	占比例/%
1	中国台湾省	130485300.00	75472512	31.893
2	中国香港	102825593.00	60865428	25.720
3	韩国	109429444.00	59619830	25.194
4	日本	38818572.00	13010023	5.498
5	泰国	13725829.00	8478141	3.583
进口总计		437635597.00	236645782	100.00

4. 2012 年改性的聚苯乙烯出口量价同时上升

海关统计数据显示，我国改性聚苯乙烯出口市场相对分散，2012 年我国共向全世界 44 个国家(地区)出口了改性聚苯乙烯，比上年 42 个出口地增加 2 个出口地。

2012 年中国香港地区、土耳其和美国是其中最主要的三个出口市场。

2012 年，我国向中国香港出口改性聚苯乙烯 6931967kg，出口数量占全部出口数量的 34.052%，比上年下降 9.70%；

其次向土耳其出口 3127000kg，占总出口量的 15.361%，比上年上升 52.02%；

向美国出口 1746863kg，占总出口量的 8.581%，比上年上升 205.18%；

向泰国出口 1532530970245kg，占总出口量的 7.528%，比上年上升 58.00%；

向中国台湾省出口 1524981kg，占总出口量的 7.491%。

五出口地出口数量占初级形状的改性聚苯乙烯 2012 年总出口数量的 73.014%，比上年下降 0.196%(表 115)。

表 115　2012 年改性的初级形状的非可发性聚苯乙烯五大出口国家/地区统计

排　序	出口目的地	出口金额/美元	出口数量/kg	占比例/%
1	中国香港	15528010.00	6931967	34.052
2	土耳其	8581943.00	3127000	15.361
3	美国	5044789.00	1746863	8.581
4	泰国	3372496.00	1532530	7.528
5	中国台湾省	2110538.00	1524981	7.491
出口总计		47680245.00	20356975	100.00

六、PS 表观消费量增长下降

2006 ~ 2012 年国内 PS 表观消费年均增长率为 0.73%，低于同期 PS 产量年均增长率 2.58%。

表 116　2006 ~ 2012 年国内 PS 表观消费量统计资料

项　目	2006	2007	2008	2009	2010	2011	2012
表观消费量/kt	2877.76	3072.47	2888.90	3008.10	3102.30	2958.50	3006.30
年增长率/%	0.77	6.77	-5.97	4.13	3.13	-4.64	1.59
国内自给率/%	60.71	66.94	71.34	69.81	74.41	68.60	70.65

1. PS 进口消费省市流向集中于东部沿海地区

A. 可发性初级形状的聚苯乙烯

从海关资料来看，2012 年可发性初级形状的聚苯乙烯进口消费省市有 17 个，比上年 12 个进口消费省市增加 5 个进口消费省市，主要进口流向为广东省、上海市、天津市、浙江省和山东省，五进口消费省市 2012 年初级形状的可发性聚苯乙烯进口消费省市进口量占总进口量的 87.889%，比上年进口增加 0.399%。

2012 年可发性初级形状的聚苯乙烯主要进口流向为广东省，进口数量 32226298kg，占总出口量的 53.032%，比上年进口量减少 26.36%；

其次为上海市，进口数量 6545658kg，占总出口量的 10.772%，比上年进口量减少 10.21%；

天津市，进口数量 5934300kg，占总出口量的 9.766%，比上年进口量上升 33.14%；

浙江省，进口数量 4539947kg，占总出口量的 7.471%，比上年进口量减少 20.80%；

山东省，进口数量 4161756kg，占总出口量的 6.849%，比上年进口量减少 20.66%(表 117)。

表 117　2012 年初级形状的可发性聚苯乙烯五大进口省市统计

排　序	进口省市	进口金额/美元	进口数量/kg	占比例/%
1	广东省	54210339.00	32226298	53.032
2	上海市	8705566.00	6545658	10.772
3	天津市	13860765.00	5934300	9.766
4	浙江省	5713837.00	4539947	7.471
5	山东省	4948872.00	4161756	6.849
进口总计		103855892.00	60767386	100.00

B. 改性初级形状的聚苯乙烯

从海关资料来看，2012 年改性初级形状的聚苯乙烯进口消费省市有 19 个，比上年 18 个进口消费省市增加 1 个进口消费省市，主要进口流向为广东省、江苏省、上海市、辽宁省和山东省，五进口消费省市 2012 年初级形状的改性聚苯乙烯进口消费省市进口量占总进口量的 86.732%，比上年减少 2.418%。

2012 年初级形状的改性聚苯乙烯主要进口流向为广东省，进口数量 148349313kg，占总进口数量的 62.688%，比上年进口数量减少 12.44%；

其次为江苏省，进口数量 21971393kg，占总进口数量的 9.285%，比上年进口数量增加 75.02%；

上海市，进口数量 17368899kg，占总进口数量的 7.340%%，比上年进口数量增加 13.44%；

辽宁省，进口数量 8828297kg，占总进口数量的 3.731%，比上年进口数量减少 22.72%；

山东省，进口数量 8728787kg，占总进口数量的 3.689%（表 118）。

表 118　2012 年改性的初级形状的聚苯乙烯五大进口省市统计

排　序	进口省市	进口金额/美元	进口数量/kg	占比例/%
1	广东省	258112090.00	148349313	62.688
2	江苏省	39170683.00	21971393	9.285
3	上海市	36242452.00	17368899	7.340
4	辽宁省	23578860.00	8828297	3.731
5	山东省	16725102.00	8728787	3.689
进口总计		437635597.00	236645782	100.00

C. 初级形状的聚苯乙烯

从海关资料来看，2012 年初级形状的聚苯乙烯进口消费省市有 19 个，与上年 19 个进口消费省市持平，主要进口流向为广东省、浙江省、江苏省、上海市和山东省，五进口消费省市 2012 年初级形状的聚苯乙烯进口消费省市进口量占总进口量的 94.091%，比上年减少 0.949%。

2012 年初级形状的聚苯乙烯主要进口流向为广东省，进口数量 437970043kg，占总进口数量的 64.175%，比上年减少 8.12%；

其次为浙江省，进口数量 85834371kg，占总进口数量的 12.577%，比上年增加 22.48%；

江苏省，进口数量 58789383kg，占总进口数量的 8.614%，比上年减少 27.39%；

上海市，进口数量 34851510kg，占总进口数量的 5.107%，比上年减少 1.09%；

山东省，进口数量 24688947kg，占总进口数量的 3.618%，比上年增加 18.86%（表 119）。

表 119　2012 年其他初级形状的聚苯乙烯五大进口省市统计

排　序	进口省市	进口金额/美元	进口数量/kg	占比例/%
1	广东省	685407474.00	437970043	64.175
2	浙江省	131064602.00	85834371	12.577
3	江苏省	98616388.00	58789383	8.614
4	上海市	68478424.00	34851510	5.107
5	山东省	45965111.00	24688947	3.618
进口总计		1100588，391.00	682462729	100.00

2. 初级形状的聚苯乙烯 2012 年进口生产使用企业分析

A. 初级形状的可发性聚苯乙烯

从海关资料来看，2012 年初级形状的可发性聚苯乙烯进口商有 314 家，比上年 326 家进口商减少 12 家进口商，前十位初级形状的可发性聚苯乙烯进口商进口量占总进口量的 45.422%，比上年进口量增加 3.732%。

初级形状的可发性聚苯乙烯十大进口商中有三家生产使用企业和七家进口贸易商，分别占总进口量的 11.013% 和 34.409%。

五十九大进口商有三十五大进口商是进口生产使用企业，主要分布于塑胶工业，包装工业，建材工业，电子工业，装饰材料工业，玩具工业，鞋材工业等行业，占总进口量的37.402%。

五十九大进口商有二十四大进口商是进口贸易商，占总进口量的48.290%。(表120)

表120　2012年初级形状的可发性聚苯乙烯五十九大进口商统计

排　序	进口商	所属行业	进口数量/kg	占比例/%
1	上海英科实业有限公司	进口贸易商	5092987	8.381
2	深圳市宝安外经发展有限公司	进口贸易商	3758532	6.185
3	海盐恒达塑业有限公司	塑胶工业	3274470	5.389
4	深圳市龙岗区对外经济发展有限公司	进口贸易商	2611876	4.298
5	北京富汇通轻工进出口公司	进口贸易商	2607450	4.291
6	不详	进口贸易商	2506600	4.125
7	天津市化轻贸易有限公司	进口贸易商	2300000	3.785
8	不详	进口贸易商	2032000	3.344
9	佛山市三水南威塑胶电子制品有限公司	电子工业	1799500	2.961
10	长荣玩具(东莞)有限公司	玩具工业	1618500	2.663
11	淄博英科框业有限公司	装饰材料	1516899	2.496
12	东莞市对外加工装配服务公司	进口贸易商	1475100	2.427
13	东莞新航包装材料有限公司	包装工业	1392856	2.292
14	深圳市宜盛实业有限公司	进口贸易商	1150000	1.892
15	不详	进口贸易商	1120000	1.843
16	惠阳东亚电子制品有限公司	电子工业	1100000	1.810
17	昌邑市大华木业有限公司	建材工业	1003000	1.651
18	苏州市宝成实业有限公司	建材工业	875000	1.440
19	政星塑料制品(河源)有限公司	塑胶工业	776000	1.277
20	福清永大塑胶有限公司	塑胶工业	750000	1.234
21	不详	进口贸易商	706662	1.163
22	广州长城木业有限公司	建材工业	659000	1.084
23	深圳怡丰宝环保包装品有限公司	包装工业	612920	1.009
24	东莞恒新包装材料有限公司	包装工业	528450	0.870
25	肇庆童星玩具厂有限公司	玩具工业	502000	0.826
26	东莞市锦茂进出口有限公司	进口贸易商	500000	0.823
27	东莞联兴发泡胶碗厂有限公司	包装工业	453200	0.746
28	上海大道包装隔热材料有限公司	建材工业	414160	0.682
29	不详	进口贸易商	400000	0.658
30	东莞利达运动用品有限公司	鞋材工业	399406	0.657
31	东莞远展包装制品有限公司	包装工业	375000	0.617
32	中国江苏国际经济技术合作公司	进口贸易商	368000	0.606
33	汉池电子(深圳)有限公司	电子工业	352000	0.579
34	青岛瑞普化工有限公司	建材工业	351450	0.578
35	惠州市惠信发泡胶制品有限公司	建材工业	343125	0.565

续表

排 序	进口商	所属行业	进口数量/kg	占比例/%
36	松泽化妆品(深圳)有限公司	化妆品工业	342000	0.563
37	上海植信化工有限公司	建材工业	336000	0.553
38	余姚市华伦进出口有限公司	进口贸易商	332000	0.546
39	森绍荣实业(深圳)有限公司	进口贸易商	321500	0.529
40	深圳市光明新区经济发展有限公司	进口贸易商	317625	0.523
41	不详	进口贸易商	288000	0.474
42	东莞虎门创颖包装制品有限公司	包装工业	284000	0.467
43	不详	进口贸易商	283495	0.467
44	佛山市南海奇镭鞋材有限公司	鞋材工业	277000	0.456
45	升鑫包装材料(中山)有限公司	包装工业	275000	0.453
46	宁波卓艺家纺有限公司	装饰材料	275000	0.453
47	宁波天旗科技有限公司	建材工业	268200	0.441
48	苏州合欣进出口贸易有限公司	进口贸易商	258398	0.425
49	青岛保税区格力特国际贸易有限公司	进口贸易商	256000	0.421
50	余姚中一进出口有限公司	进口贸易商	249000	0.410
51	海尔集团大连电器产业有限公司	电子工业	224000	0.369
52	必佳半导体包装制品(深圳)有限公司	包装工业	220000	0.362
53	佛山市南海方维贸易有限公司	进口贸易商	217880	0.359
54	惠州市惠阳东威发泡胶制品有限公司	包装工业	206000	0.339
55	北京爱王塑料制品有限公司	塑胶工业	200000	0.329
56	正升(英德)塑胶制品有限公司	塑胶工业	193467	0.318
57	江苏开元国际集团外经有限公司	进口贸易商	191450	0.315
58	东莞新长桥塑料有限公司	塑胶工业	191050	0.314
59	广州市意华塑料包装有限公司	包装工业	179400	0.295
60	天旗运动用品(宁波)有限公司	鞋材工业	160000	0.263
进口总计			60767386	100.00

B. 初级形状的改性聚苯乙烯

从海关资料来看，2012 年初级形状的改性聚苯乙烯进口商有 588 家，比上年 603 家进口商减少 25 家进口商，前十位初级形状的改性聚苯乙烯进口商进口量占总进口量的 38.904%，比上年增加 6.954%。

初级形状的改性聚苯乙烯十大进口商中有七家生产使用企业和三家进口贸易商，分别占总进口量的 25.542% 和 13.362%。

八十大进口商有五十一家进口商是进口生产使用企业，主要分布于家用电器工业，塑料改性工业，电子工业，塑胶工业，装饰材料，食品包装工业，玩具工业等行业，占总进口量的 43.831%。

八十大进口商有二十九家进口商是进口贸易商，占总进口量的 25.103%（表 121）。

表 121　2012 年改性的初级形状的聚苯乙烯八十大进口商统计

排 序	进口商	所属行业	进口数量/kg	占比例/%
1	广州金发科技股份有限公司	改性 PS	22838500	9.651
2	厦门昌和贸易发展有限公司	进口贸易商	16978100	7.174
3	常州丰盛塑料有限公司	塑胶工业	10987800	4.643

续表

排 序	进口商	所属行业	进口数量/kg	占比例/%
4	上海金发科技发展有限公司	改性 PS	9697667	4.098
5	深圳市宝安外经发展有限公司	进口贸易商	9692381	4.096
6	东莞美泰电子有限公司	电子工业	5008000	2.116
7	不详	进口贸易商	4949485	2.092
8	中山奥马电器有限公司	家用电器工业	4375000	1.849
9	广州松下空调器有限公司	家用电器工业	4018000	1.698
10	广东科龙冰箱有限公司	家用电器工业	3519500	1.487
11	恒康电子(深圳)有限公司	电子工业	3027164	1.279
12	广州益力多乳品有限公司	食品包装工业	2880000	1.217
13	上海伊藤忠商事有限公司	进口贸易商	2784153	1.177
14	普拉材料贸易(大连)有限公司	进口贸易商	2783772	1.176
15	东莞市对外加工装配服务公司	进口贸易商	2630748	1.112
16	合肥美菱股份有限公司	家用电器工业	2590000	1.094
17	中山志和家电制品有限公司	家用电器工业	2483011	1.049
18	大连金门物流有限公司	进口贸易商	2443000	1.032
19	宇航物流(大连保税物流园区)有限公司	进口贸易商	2352100	0.994
20	惠阳东亚电子制品有限公司	电子工业	2262425	0.956
21	惠州大亚湾汇利日用制品有限公司	日用制品	1207000	0.510
22	东莞市常平盈景塑胶制品有限公司	塑胶工业	1206800	0.510
23	佛山市赛兴商贸有限公司	进口贸易商	1095000	0.463
24	合肥华凌电器有限公司	家用电器工业	1076000	0.455
25	深圳市龙岗区对外经济发展有限公司	进口贸易商	1044525	0.441
26	上海稻田产业贸易有限公司	进口贸易商	1023004	0.432
27	三捷科技(厦门)有限公司	电子工业	1021675	0.432
28	威海朝光电子有限公司	电子工业	992850	0.420
29	中山市中山港对外加工装配服务公司	进口贸易商	992093	0.419
30	吴江市朝鑫塑胶制品有限公司	塑胶工业	992000	0.419
31	太仓中航塑业有限公司	塑胶工业	974000	0.412
32	山东东鑫电子有限公司	电子工业	973700	0.411
33	浙江星星家电股份有限公司	家用电器工业	962500	0.407
34	基达玩具(深圳)有限公司	玩具工业	949750	0.401
35	东莞市大朗外资引进公司	进口贸易商	948500	0.401
36	广东高乐玩具制造股份有限公司	玩具工业	940000	0.397
37	三菱商事(大连)有限公司	进口贸易商	909600	0.384
38	深圳粤发材料包装实业有限公司	包装工业	886000	0.374
39	凯硕电脑(苏州)有限公司	电子工业	879000	0.371
40	珠海市衡丰塑料有限公司	塑胶工业	866000	0.366

续表

排 序	进口商	所属行业	进口数量/kg	占比例/%
41	东莞市长安福翔塑胶五金有限公司	塑胶工业	860000	0.363
42	出光复合工程塑料(广州)有限公司	改性 PS	849961	0.359
43	华登(河源)玩具制品有限公司	玩具工业	848750	0.359
44	利民(番禺南沙)电器发展有限公司	家用电器工业	841000	0.355
45	金电实业(深圳)有限公司	电子工业	839000	0.355
46	TCL 集团有限公司	家用电器工业	830900	0.351
47	不详	进口贸易商	813000	0.344
48	天长实业(深圳)有限公司	进口贸易商	795300	0.209
49	东莞益卓电子科技有限公司	电子工业	750139	0.205
50	不详	进口贸易商	715841	0.302
51	常州富敬塑胶有限公司	塑胶工业	700800	0.296
52	东莞宏华塑胶制品有限公司	塑胶工业	698000	0.295
53	不详	进口贸易商	697000	0.295
54	东莞定嘉橡塑材料有限公司	塑胶工业	669000	0.283
55	汕头市佳纬塑料制品有限公司	塑胶工业	664825	0.281
56	广东省东莞五金矿产进出口有限公司	进口贸易商	660000	0.279
57	TCL 海外电子(惠州)有限公司	家用电器工业	646000	0.273
58	汕头市金信达贸易有限公司	进口贸易商	612000	0.259
59	优利(东莞)塑胶材料有限公司	装饰材料	606500	0.256
60	东莞铂联电子制品有限公司	电子工业	600440	0.254
61	佛山市顺德区东亚电器有限公司	家用电器工业	595000	0.251
62	合肥会通新材料有限公司	改性 PS	594000	0.251
63	淄博英科框业有限公司	装饰材料	588000	0.248
64	不详	进口贸易商	575900	0.243
65	福建省晋江市进出口有限公司	进口贸易商	570000	0.241
66	东莞市亿阳信通集团有限公司	电子工业	558000	0.236
67	广耀电子塑胶(深圳)有限公司	塑胶工业	557500	0.236
68	深圳市昌红五金制造有限公司	家用五金工业	552425	0.233
69	丰田通商(上海)有限公司	进口贸易商	552375	0.233
70	京大物流(大连保税物流园区)有限公司	进口贸易商	550250	0.233
71	深圳市同益实业有限公司	进口贸易商	533550	0.225
72	东莞市石碣镇经济发展总公司	进口贸易商	525100	0.222
73	上海吉列有限公司	家用五金工业	520700	0.220
74	菏泽好达实业有限公司	进口贸易商	520000	0.220
75	广州普乐包装容器有限公司	包装工业	516260	0.218
76	东莞兴发玩具厂有限公司	玩具工业	511250	0.216
77	东莞信柏塑胶有限公司	塑胶工业	498015	0.210

续表

排　序	进口商	所属行业	进口数量/kg	占比例/%
78	不详	进口贸易商	494000	0.209
79	浙江嵊州佰音电子有限公司	电子工业	485000	0.205
80	中山市德勤贸易有限公司	进口贸易商	460000	0.194
进口总计			236645782	100.00

C. 初级形状的聚苯乙烯

从海关资料来看，2012 年初级形状的聚苯乙烯进口商有 2，143 家，比上年 2，151 家进口商减少 8 家进口商。

前八位初级形状的聚苯乙烯进口商进口量占总进口量的 19.947%，比上年进口减少 5.093%。

一百大进口商有六十五大进口商是进口生产使用企业，主要分布于家用塑料改性工业，电器工业，电子工业，塑胶工业，装饰材料等行业，进口量占总进口量的 36.711%。

一百大进口商有三十五大进口商是进口贸易商，进口量占总进口量的 23.145%（表 122）。

表 122　2012 年其他初级形状的聚苯乙烯一百大进口商统计

排　　序	进口商	所属行业	进口数量/kg	占比例/%
1	深圳市宝安外经发展有限公司	贸易商	25240121	3.698
2	厦门昌和贸易发展有限公司	贸易商	25173900	3.689
3	深圳永合科技化工有限公司	改性 PS 粒料	23840000	3.493
4	永塑(东莞)塑料有限公司	改性 PS 粒料	15737000	2.306
5	东莞市对外加工装配服务公司	贸易商	13753588	2.015
6	富华杰工业(深圳)有限公司	改性 PS 粒料	11664981	1.709
7	宁波家联塑料科技有限公司	改性 PS 粒料	10868735	1.593
8	深圳市龙岗区对外经济发展有限公司	贸易商	9857551	1.444
9	吴江东永材料科技有限公司	改性 PS 粒料	8737000	1.280
10	上海夏普电器有限公司	电器工业	7102075	1.041
11	鸿富锦精密工业(深圳)有限公司	改性 PS 粒料	6670355	0.977
12	GE 塑料上海有限公司	改性 PS 粒料	6431692	0.942
13	宁波杉杉物产有限公司	贸易商	6356000	0.931
14	宁波东升包装材料有限公司	包装工业	6270000	0.919
15	苏州市三鑫塑业有限公司	塑胶工业	5918600	0.867
16	惠州大亚湾汇利日用制品有限公司	日用制品	5492500	0.805
17	星际塑料(深圳)有限公司	改性 PS 粒料	5250189	0.769
18	天津三协塑料有限公司	塑胶工业	5160025	0.756
19	宝豪塑胶五金制品(江门)有限公司	五金制品	5121000	0.750
20	昆山銓錸科技有限公司	改性 PS 粒料	5096700	0.747
21	余姚市天都贸易有限公司	贸易商	4995000	0.732
22	烟台阳光物流有限公司	贸易商	4989125	0.731
23	台州富岭塑胶有限公司	塑胶工业	4764000	0.698
24	不详	贸易商	4724831	0.692
25	宁波晶圆贸易有限公司	贸易商	4457750	0.653

续表

排　序	进口商	所属行业	进口数量/kg	占比例/%
26	日超工程塑料(深圳)有限公司	改性PS粒料	4428198	0.649
27	惠阳市对外加工装配服务公司	贸易商	4267243	0.625
28	苏州惠业塑胶工业有限公司	塑胶工业	4200200	0.615
29	宝星磁电工业(惠州)有限公司	电器工业	4170600	0.611
30	浙江华鸿工艺品有限公司	装饰材料	4121548	0.604
31	陶氏丁苯胶乳(张家港)有限公司	合成橡胶工业	4104000	0.601
32	深圳市恒中化工有限公司	改性PS粒料	3960000	0.580
33	深圳市顺安外资实业发展有限公司	贸易商	3746325	0.549
34	东莞丽骏塑胶制品有限公司	塑胶工业	3497850	0.513
35	朗诗德电气有限公司	电子工业	3479000	0.510
36	金育塑胶电子(吴江)有限公司	电子工业	3350000	0.491
37	茂瑞电子(东莞)有限公司	电子工业	3144000	0.461
38	深圳市当凌实业发展有限公司	贸易商	3102875	0.455
39	广州金发科技股份有限公司	改性PS粒料	3088950	0.453
40	沙伯特(中山)有限公司	改性PS粒料	3019742	0.442
41	中山市美图塑料工业有限公司	塑胶工业	3015000	0.442
42	优利(苏州)科技材料有限公司	改性PS粒料	2977200	0.436
43	深圳市光明新区经济发展有限公司	贸易商	2806541	0.411
44	东莞大日化工厂有限公司	改性PS粒料	2707300	0.397
45	青岛海尔新材料研发有限公司	改性PS粒料	2691500	0.394
46	广州市白云区富强塑胶实业有限公司	贸易商	2638650	0.387
47	东莞市建筑材料进出口有限公司	贸易商	2634610	0.386
48	大日精化(深圳)有限公司	改性PS粒料	2564050	0.376
49	上海益力多乳品有限公司	食品包装工业	2528000	0.370
50	上海伊藤忠商事有限公司	贸易商	2473750	0.362
51	东莞金百升塑胶电子有限公司	电子工业	2446500	0.358
52	青岛海尔国际贸易有限公司	贸易商	2426000	0.355
53	不详	贸易商	2391000	0.350
54	东莞金荣塑胶制品有限公司	塑胶工业	2370000	0.347
55	丰田通商(上海)有限公司	贸易商	2355000	0.345
56	佳比塑胶制品(通州)有限公司	塑胶工业	2346500	0.344
57	山阳稻田复合塑料(东莞)有限公司	改性PS粒料	2342472	0.343
58	伟成盒带厂(深圳)有限公司	包装工业	2333360	0.342
59	汕头市富旺贸易有限公司	贸易商	2315000	0.339
60	东莞美泰电子有限公司	电子工业	2282375	0.334
61	威海朝光电子有限公司	电子工业	2279175	0.334
62	宁波艺博恒辉进出口有限责任公司	贸易商	2228402	0.327

续表

排　序	进口商	所属行业	进口数量/kg	占比例/%
63	浙江前程石化有限公司	改性 PS 粒料	2220000	0.325
64	珠海市金贸塑料制品有限公司	塑胶工业	2214250	0.324
65	上海西野贸易有限公司	贸易商	2174175	0.319
66	东莞益盛胶片有限公司	包装工业	2123500	0.311
67	汕头市天辰经贸有限公司	贸易商	2100000	0.308
68	中裕电器(深圳)有限公司	家用电器工业	2020000	0.000
69	东芝家用电器制造(南海)有限公司	家用电器工业	2008400	0.294
70	伟易达(东莞)塑胶制品有限公司	塑胶工业	1897525	0.278
71	利民(番禺南沙)电器发展有限公司	家用电器工业	1880575	0.276
72	不详	贸易商	1877550	0.275
73	浙江星星家电股份有限公司	家用电器工业	1874500	0.275
74	东莞联记塑胶原料有限公司	贸易商	1820311	0.267
75	歌乐电磁(深圳)有限公司	家用电器工业	1784881	0.262
76	惠州市对外加工装配服务公司	贸易商	1760935	0.258
77	昆山固品工程塑料有限公司	改性 PS 粒料	1759000	0.258
78	上海稻田产业贸易有限公司	贸易商	1756700	0.257
79	宁波双马无纺地毯厂	装饰材料	1741000	0.255
80	因塔思(威海)电子有限公司	电子工业	1716525	0.252
81	广东省东莞畜产进出口有限公司	贸易商	1696125	0.358
82	惠城区对外加工装配服务公司	贸易商	1681717	0.246
83	万景塑胶制品(深圳)有限公司	塑胶工业	1646988	0.241
84	芜湖帮的贸易有限公司	贸易商	1615000	0.237
85	台州黄岩海普工贸有限公司	贸易商	1592000	0.233
86	上海英科实业有限公司	贸易商	1588000	0.233
87	大隆饰品玩具(惠州)有限公司	玩具工业	1580000	0.232
88	前程物流有限公司	贸易商	1571000	0.230
89	深圳市汇众进出口有限公司	贸易商	1553393	0.228
90	宁波田丰日用品制造有限公司	塑胶工业	1508000	0.221
91	合一电器(深圳)有限公司	家用电器工业	1508000	0.221
92	广东锦湖日丽高分子材料有限公司	改性 PS 粒料	1494000	0.219
93	天津松井塑料有限公司	改性 PS 粒料	1483000	0.217
94	宁波联合埃希物流有限公司	贸易商	1472000	0.216
95	东莞兴华玩具有限公司	玩具工业	1453000	0.213
96	东莞恒骏吸塑制品有限公司	装饰材料	1446000	0.212
97	海尔集团大连电器产业有限公司	家用电器工业	1435000	0.210
98	东莞恒力塑胶制品有限公司	塑胶工业	1409250	0.206
99	深圳永淦电子有限公司	电子工业	1407400	0.206
100	城高(增城)塑胶五金有限公司	装饰材料	1392169	0.204
进口总计			682462729	100.00

D. 初级形状的其他苯乙烯

从资料分析，2012 年初级形状的其他苯乙烯聚合物进口商有 1228 家。

初级形状的其他苯乙烯聚合物十大进口商中有生产使用企业六家和进口贸易商四家，分别占总进口量的 48.691% 和 6.412%。

陶氏丁苯胶乳(张家港)有限公司 2012 年初级形状的其他苯乙烯聚合物进口 118283675kg，占总进口量的 43.578%，比上年进口增加 25.13%；

宁波杉杉物产有限公司 2012 年初级形状的其他苯乙烯聚合物进口 6431000 0kg，占总进口量的 2.369%；

不详公司(原始统计中仅有代码，下同)2012 年初级形状的其他苯乙烯聚合物进口 4958000kg，占总进口量的 1.827%；

浙江星星家电股份有限公司 2012 年初级形状的其他苯乙烯聚合物进口 44675000kg，占总进口量的 1.646%。

浙江新长城进出口有限公司 2012 年初级形状的其他苯乙烯聚合物进口 3493250kg，占总进口量的 1.287%，比上年进口增加 30.63%；

浙江前程石化有限公司 2012 年初级形状的其他苯乙烯聚合物进口 3081000kg，占总进口量的 1.135%；

罗门哈斯国际贸易(上海)有限公司 2012 年初级形状的其他苯乙烯聚合物进口 2502015kg，占总进口量的 0.922%，比上年进口增加 58.37%；

宁波长桥工程塑料有限公司 2012 年初级形状的其他苯乙烯聚合物进口 2306555kg，占总进口量的 0.850%，比上年进口增加 35.52 个百分；

积水化成品(苏州)科技有限公司 2012 年初级形状的其他苯乙烯聚合物进口 2024400kg，占总进口量的 0.746%；

东莞百瑞立塑胶五金有限公司 2012 年初级形状的其他苯乙烯聚合物进口 2003900kg，占总进口量的 0.738%。

五十九大初级形状的其他苯乙烯聚合物进口商有三十一大进口商是进口生产使用企业，主要分布于合成橡胶工业，塑料改性工业，电子工业，塑胶工业，装饰材料，包装材料工业，文具工业，染料化工，汽车工业等行业，占总进口量的 58.442%。

初级形状的其他聚苯乙烯五十九大进口商中有贸易商二十八家，占总进口量的 15.724%(表 123)。

表 123 2012 年初级形状的其他苯乙烯聚合物五十九大进口商统计

排 序	进口商	所属行业	进口数量/kg	占比例/%
1	陶氏丁苯胶乳(张家港)有限公司	合成橡胶工业	118283675	43.578
2	宁波杉杉物产有限公司	贸易商	6431000	2.369
3	不详	贸易商	4958000	1.827
4	浙江星星家电股份有限公司	电子工业	4467500	1.646
5	浙江新长城进出口有限公司	贸易商	3493250	1.287
6	浙江前程石化有限公司	塑料改性工业	3081000	1.135
7	罗门哈斯国际贸易(上海)有限公司	贸易商	2502015	0.922
8	宁波长桥工程塑料有限公司	塑料改性工业	2306555	0.850
9	积水化成品(苏州)科技有限公司	塑料改性工业	2024400	0.746
10	东莞百瑞立塑胶五金有限公司	塑胶制品	2003900	0.738
11	广州金发科技股份有限公司	塑料改性工业	1670000	0.615
12	上海外电国际贸易有限公司	贸易商	1588595	0.000
13	不详	贸易商	1550950	0.571
14	广州保税区拓新物流服务有限公司	贸易商	1542000	0.568
15	雪佛龙菲利普斯化工贸易(上海)有限公司	贸易商	1537275	0.566
16	昆山固品工程塑料有限公司	塑料改性工业	1519000	0.560
17	帝人化成复合塑料(上海)有限公司	塑料改性工业	1480040	0.545
18	余姚市翌升经贸有限公司	贸易商	1430750	0.527

续表

排 序	进口商	所属行业	进口数量/kg	占比例/%
19	宁波联合埃希物流有限公司	贸易商	1359000	0.501
20	东莞怡昌塑胶制品有限公司	塑胶制品	1334000	0.491
21	上海锦湖日丽塑料有限公司	塑料改性工业	1313652	0.484
22	宁波晶圆贸易有限公司	贸易商	1312500	0.484
23	中化塑料公司	贸易商	1285881	0.474
24	上海日绵有限公司	塑料改性工业	1282600	0.473
25	巴斯夫(中国)有限公司	塑料改性工业	1282220	0.472
26	深圳永合科技化工有限公司	塑料改性工业	1266750	0.467
27	宁波雨时化工有限公司	塑料改性工业	1210200	0.446
28	上海稻田产业贸易有限公司	贸易商	1199050	0.442
29	邯郸汉光办公自动化耗材有限公司	贸易商	1140500	0.420
30	优利(苏州)科技材料有限公司	塑料改性工业	1128000	0.416
31	宁波保税区高新货柜有限公司	贸易商	1114000	0.410
32	杜邦中国集团有限公司	贸易商	1112500	0.410
33	旭化成医疗器械(杭州)有限公司	医疗器械	1083657	0.399
34	LG化学(天津)工程塑料有限公司	塑料改性工业	1013600	0.373
35	上海宇菱通贸易有限公司	贸易商	974315	0.359
36	麦格纳唐纳利(上海)汽车系统有限公司	汽车工业	964175	0.355
37	上海源理国际贸易有限公司	贸易商	958500	0.353
38	上海罗门哈斯化工有限公司	塑料改性工业	926684	0.341
39	三井化学(上海)有限公司	塑料改性工业	924910	0.341
40	深圳市龙岗区对外经济发展有限公司	贸易商	919261	0.339
41	上海礼紫仓储有限公司	贸易商	866500	0.319
42	天津积水化成品有限公司	塑料改性工业	862200	0.318
43	上海裕佳塑料有限公司	塑料改性工业	861100	0.317
44	上海伊藤忠商事有限公司	贸易商	848925	0.313
45	帝斯曼工程塑料(江苏)有限公司	塑料改性工业	838000	0.309
46	南亚硬质胶布(广州)有限公司	建材工业	835200	0.308
47	上海和氏璧化工有限公司	塑料改性工业	830418	0.306
48	慈溪市华美达进出口有限公司	贸易商	818000	0.301
49	建发物流(上海)有限公司	贸易商	816975	0.301
50	汇成塑胶制品(江门)有限公司	塑胶制品	792000	0.292
51	泰怡凯电器(苏州)有限公司	电子工业	787723	0.290
52	巴斯夫染料化工有限公司	染料化工	773551	0.285
53	北京市塑化贸易有限公司	贸易商	773150	0.285
54	深圳市华富洋进出口有限公司	贸易商	772000	0.284
55	苏州巨丰塑料有限公司	塑胶制品	770000	0.284

续表

排 序	进口商	所属行业	进口数量/kg	占比例/%
56	余姚市对外贸易有限公司	贸易商	755500	0.278
57	浙江前浪进出口有限公司	贸易商	748125	0.276
58	爱宇隆贸易(上海)有限公司	贸易商	730650	0.269
59	上海住友商事有限公司	贸易商	724915	0.267
60	南海市中美玩具厂	玩具工业	716500	0.264
	进口总计		271427521	100.00

七、进出口贸易方式分析

1. 2012 年初级形状的可发性聚苯乙烯

从海关统计中可看出，2012 年初级形状的可发性聚苯乙烯进口贸易方式主要为进料加工贸易(占进口量 55.861%)，其次为一般贸易(占进口量 25.575%)，来料加工装配贸易(占进口量 18.919%)，保税区仓储转口货物(占进口量 0.355%)，其他(占进口量 0.021%)，出口加工区进口设备(占进口量 0.002%)，国家间、国际组织无偿援助和赠送的物资(占进口量 0.000%)合计为总进口量的 100.00%(表 124)。

表 124 2012 年初级形状的可发性聚苯乙烯进口交易类型统计

进口交易类型	进口金额 /美元	进口数量/kg	占比例/%
进料加工贸易	52412636.00	33945407	55.861
一般贸易	37595476.00	15540992	25.575
来料加工装配贸易	13268867.00	11054036	18.191
保税区仓储转口货物	505400.00	212680	0.350
其他	45510.00	12972	0.021
出口加工区进口设备	27744.00	1266	0.002
国家间、国际组织无偿援助和赠送的物资	259.00	33	0.000
进口总计	103855892.00	60767386	100.00

从海关统计中可看出，2012 年初级形状的可发性聚苯乙烯出口贸易方式主要为进料加工贸易(占出口量 97.602%)(表 125)。

表 125 2012 年初级形状的可发性聚苯乙烯出口交易类型统计

出口交易类型	出口金额 (美元)	出口数量/kg	占比例/%
进料加工贸易	484275336.00	291346250	97.602
一般贸易	5899689.00	3684238	1.234
边境小额贸易	2936296.00	1799512	0.603
来料加工装配贸易	2340810.00	1497000	0.501
保税区仓储转口货物	155360.00	96000	0.032
其他	97710.00	61740	0.021%
保税仓库进出境货物	9201.00	9014	0.003
对外承包工程出口货物	31212.00	8370	0.003
国家间、国际组织无偿援助和赠送的物资	3094.00	2600	0.001
出口总计	495748708.00	298504724	100.00

2. 2011 年改性的初级形状的聚苯乙烯

从海关统计中可看出，2012 年改性的初级形状的聚苯乙烯进口贸易方式主要为进料加工贸易(占进口量58.836%)(表126)。

表126　2012 年改性的初级形状的聚苯乙烯进口交易类型统计

进口交易类型	进口金额 /美元	进口数量/kg	占比例/%
进料加工贸易	249140880.00	139233208	58.836
一般贸易	96963368.00	48953437	20.686
来料加工装配贸易	49246143.00	33113598	13.993
保税区仓储转口货物	41864195.00	15148193	6.401
其他	115856.00	31286	0.013
保税仓库进出境货物	303436.00	166060	0.070
进口总计	437635597.00	236645782	100.00

从海关统计中可看出，2012 年改性的初级形状的聚苯乙烯出口贸易方式主要为进料加工贸易(占出口量52.198%%)(表127)。

表127　2012 年改性的初级形状的聚苯乙烯出口交易类型统计

出口交易类型	出口金额/美元	出口数量/kg	占比例/%
进料加工贸易	26295931.00	10625929	52.198
一般贸易	16106568.00	6901918	33.904
来料加工装配贸易	3854703.00	2248158	11.044
保税区仓储转口货物	1252204.00	461940	2.269
保税仓库进出境货物	28186.00	11832	0.058
边境小额贸易	109970.00	88300	0.434
其他	32683.00	18898	0.093
出口总计	47680245.00	20356975	100.00

3. 2012 年其他初级形状的聚苯乙烯

从海关统计中可看出，2012 年其他初级形状的聚苯乙烯进口贸易方式主要为进料加工贸易(占进口量60.626%)(表128)。

表128　2012 年其他初级形状的聚苯乙烯进口交易类型统计

进口交易类型	进口金额 /美元	进口数量/kg	占比例/%
进料加工贸易	687468279.00	413748023	60.626
一般贸易	202752297.00	123104333	18.038
来料加工装配贸易	166008418.00	122272907	17.916
保税区仓储转口货物	42098946.00	22487543	3.295
保税仓库进出境货物	2130776.00	822450	0.121
其他	126435.00	27472	0.004
出口总计	1100588391.00	682462729	100.00

从海关统计中可看出，2012 年其他初级形状的聚苯乙烯出口贸易方式主要为进料加工贸易(占出口量64.813%)(表129)。

表129 2012 年其他初级形状的聚苯乙烯出口交易类型统计

出口交易类型	出口金额/美元	出口数量/kg	占比例/%
进料加工贸易	17689038.00	10632082	64.813
一般贸易	9675213.00	5058535	30.837
来料加工装配贸易	874962.00	441679	2.692
保税区仓储转口货物	273258.00	144278	0.880
边境小额贸易	167082.00	90800	0.554
其他	72450.00	21082	0.129
保税仓库进出境货物	20108.00	11184	0.068
对外承包工程出口货物	3142.00	4500	0.027
出口总计	28775253.00	16404140	100.00

八、2012 年价格走势

2007～2012 年间初级形状的可发性聚苯乙烯平均出口单价年均上升 6.10%；

2007～2012 年初级形状的可发性聚苯乙烯平均进口单价年均增长率为 1.64%。

2007～2012 年聚苯乙烯平均进口单价年均增长率为 4.19%；

2007～2012 年聚苯乙烯平均出口单价年均增长率为 4.70%。

2009～2012 年改性的初级形状的非可发性聚苯乙烯平均进口单价年均增长率为 11.60%；

2009～2012 年改性的初级形状的非可发性聚苯乙烯平均出口单价年均增长率为 5.94%(表130)。

表130 2007～2012 年初级形状的聚苯乙烯进出口年平均单价统计

项 目	2007	2008	2009	2010	2011	2012
可发性聚苯乙烯						
年平均进口单价/(美元/t)	1271.20	1407.45	1260.35	1386.01	1596.26	1709.07
年增长率/%	15.48	10.72	-10.45	9.97	15.17	7.07
年平均出口单价/(美元/t)	1531.22	1545.45	1121.78	1357.36	1621.69	1660.77
年增长率/%	10.09	0.93	-27.41	21.00	19.47	2.41
其他聚苯乙烯						
年平均进口单价/(美元/t)	1313.30	1438.89	1192.91	1399.98	1574.57	1612.67
年增长率/%	17.83	9.56	-17.10	17.36	12.47	2.42
年平均出口单价/(美元/t)	1393.91	1800.50	1661.58	1735.63	1871.70	1754.15
年增长率/%	9.67	29.17	-7.72	4.46	7.84	-6.28
改性的初级形状的非可发性聚苯乙烯						
年平均进口单价/(美元/t)	—	—	1330.55	1579.22	1797.98	1849.33
年增长率/%	—	—	—	18.69	13.85	2.86
年平均出口单价/(美元/t)	—	—	1754.83	2000.14	2340.66	2341.21
年增长率/%	—	—	—	25.38	17.03	0.07

从 2012 年中国塑料城月均价统计分析，GPPS (GPS－525 江苏莱顿)1～5 月小幅盘，6 月份又出现明显的下滑，破 11000 元大关，八月份又回到上半年高位，九月份反弹冲上 12000 元大关，月均价达 12516 元，比六月份月均价增长 17.85%，十月份又反弹冲上 13000 元大关，月均价达 13386 元，比九月份月均价又增长 6.95%，十一月份月均价又增长 2.21%，十二月份月均价达全年最高价 13652 元(表131)。

表 131　GPPSGPS－525 江苏莱顿 2012 年中国塑料城月均价走势　元/t

1月	2月	3月	4月	5月	6月
11386	11573	11756	11678	11443	10620
7月	8月	9月	10月	11月	12月
11177	11631	12516	13386	13586	13652

从 2012 年中国塑料城月均价统计分析，GPPS(GP5250 宁波台化)1～5 月小幅盘，6 月份又出现明显的下滑到 11300 元，创全年之底；八月份又回到上半年高位，九月份反弹冲上 12000 元大关，月均价达 12669 元，比六月份月均价增长 12.12%，十月份又反弹冲上 13000 元大关，月均价达 13355 元，比九月份月均价又增长 5.41%，十一月份月均价又增长 2.21%，十二月份月均价达全年最高价 13852 元(表 132)。

表 132　GPPS GP5250 宁波台化 2012 年中国塑料城月均价走势　元/t

1月	2月	3月	4月	5月	6月
11813	12000	12052	11847	11665	11300
7月	8月	9月	10月	11月	12月
11543	11900	12669	13355	13650	13852

从 2012 年中国塑料城月均价统计分析，HIPS(PH－88 镇江奇美)1～5 月幅盘，6 月份又出现明显的下滑到 13355 元；八月份又回到上半年高位，九月份反弹冲上 14000 元大关，月均价达 14023 元，比六月份月均价增长 5.00%，十月份月均价达 14211 元，比九月份月均价又增长 1.34%，十一月份月均价又回落 2.22%，十二月份月均价又冲上 14000 元达 14164 元(表 133)。

表 133　HIPS PH－88 镇江奇美 2012 年中国塑料城月均价走势　元/t

1月	2月	3月	4月	5月	6月
13240	13702	13971	13984	13995	13355
7月	8月	9月	10月	11月	12月
13531	13722	14023	14211	13895	14164

从 2012 年中国塑料城月均价统计分析，HIPS(－622 上海赛科)1－5 月幅盘，六月份又出现明显的下滑到 12610 元，破 13000 元大关，创全年之底；七、八月份又回到上半年高位，九月份反弹冲上 13971 元，创全年最高价，比六月份月均价增长 10.79%，十月份月均价达又回落，比九月份月均价下降 1.21%，十一月份月均价又回落 1.25%，十二月份月均价又冲上 13900 元达 13954 元，比十一月份月均价增长 2.38%(表 134)。

表 134　HIPS－622 上海赛科 2011 年中国塑料城月均价走势　元/t

1月	2月	3月	4月	5月	6月
12766	13011	13815	13615	13227	12610
7月	8月	9月	10月	11月	12月
13231	13554	13971	13802	13629	13954

九、发展趋势

非洲地区首个苯乙烯和 PS 工厂将在亚历山大 Dekheila 港口建立，产能为 200kt/a。此项目的投资金额达 4.08 亿美元。

乌克兰 2012 年 5 月聚苯乙烯产量为 1925t，较 2011 年同期的 1596t 增长了 20.6%，较今年 4 月的 1916t 微增 0.5%。

2012 年 1～5 月，乌克兰聚苯乙烯产量总计达 6375t，同比下跌了 13.3%。

Stirol 公司是乌克兰唯一的聚苯乙烯生产商，年产聚苯乙烯约 50kt，大多数产品用于出口。2011 年，乌克兰聚苯乙烯产量达 20675t，较 2010 年增长了 24.5%。

总投资 3 亿美元的阿贝尔化学项目工程，2012 年 4 月 25 日在江苏省泰兴市经济开发区开工。该项目采用国际先进的工艺技术，生产苯乙烯、聚苯乙烯、环已酮、已内酰胺等化工产品。其中，苯乙烯年产能将达到 500kt。

阿贝尔化学项目分二期实施，一期主要建设年产 500kt 苯乙烯、50kt 级化工码头以及 17 万立方米化工仓储项目；二期主要建设年产 300kt 的聚苯乙烯、110kt 环已酮和 100kt 已内酰胺项目。

第七章　2012 年 ABS 国内消费下降自给率上升

一、2012 年 ABS 树脂生产

2006～2012 年间 ABS 产量增长了 28.34%，年均增长约为 4.25%(表 135)。

表 135 2006～2012 年 ABS 近年产量统计

项 目	2006 年	2007 年	2008 年	2009 年	2010 年	2011 年	2012 年
生产能力/t	1800000	2000000	2000000	2000000	2350000	2450000	2500000
产量/t	1320000	1630000	1130000	1320000	1345954	1488778	1513342
开工率/%	71.03	81.50	56.50	66.00	57.27	60.77	60.53
年产量增长率/%	10.22	23.48	－30.67	16.81	11.97	10.61	1.65

资料来源：2004～2009 年为笔者估算。

国内的镇江奇美公司因在 2012 年 4 月 27 日发生爆炸，700kt 年产能停工检修大致 20 天，同时 LG 甬兴共 700kt/a 产能 ABS 装置自 5 月初开始检修，大致 20 天。

2012 年上半年 ABS 厂家平均开工率约为 40% 左右，日产量 6000 吨左右；7～8 月 ABS 厂家平均开工率不足 70%，日产量仅 3800t 左右。

宁波 LG 甬兴 8 月 14 日第二批装置检修（4 条线），开工率维持 60% 左右。下半年 ABS 厂家平均开工率约为 55% 左右，产量上升。

二、2012 年国内 ABS 树脂出口商和出口生产地主要分布在广东省和上海市

1. 改性初级形状的 ABS 树脂

2012 年，改性初级形状的 ABS 树脂出口生产企业主要集中在广东省，出口数量 15910992kg，占总出口数量的 77.409%，比上年出口数量减少 2.86%；

其次为上海市，出口数量 2654457kg，占总出口数量的 12.914%，比上年出口数量减少 6.29%；

江苏省，出口数量 1098116kg，占总出口数量的 5.343%，比上年出口数量增加 35.65%；

山东省，出口数量 366312kg，占总出口数量的 0.812%，比上年出口数量减少 4.80%；

天津市，出口数量 166452kg，占总出口数量的 2.19%，比上年出口数量减少 63.96%；

2012 年改性初级形状的 ABS 树脂五省市出口商小计出口数量占总出口数量的 98.258%，比上年出口数量减少 0.562%（表 136）。

表 136 2012 年改性初级形状的 ABS 树脂出口省市统计

排 序	出口省市	出口金额/美元	出口数量/kg	占比例/%
1	广东省	42，313，325.00	15910992	77.409
2	上海市	7，429，531.00	2654457	12.914
3	江苏省	4，032，460.00	1098116	5.343
4	山东省	790，260.00	366312	1.782
5	天津市	493，093.00	166452	0.810
6	辽宁省	365，904.00	124390	0.605
7	浙江省	270，489.00	104416	0.508
8	河北省	92，289.00	72000	0.350
9	福建省	82，500.00	25000	0.122
10	安徽省	37，519.00	18003	0.088
11	河南省	47，843.00	13500	0.066
12	黑龙江省	1，350.00	500	0.002
13	陕西省	2，200.00	200	0.001
出口总计		55，958，763.00	20554338	100.00

2. 其他初级形状的 ABS 树脂

2012 年，其他初级形状的 ABS 树脂出口生产企业主要集中在广东省，出口数量 7484694kg，占总出口数量的 35.580%，比上年出口减少 14.38%；

其次为浙江省，出口数量 6154546kg，占总出口数量的 29.257%，比上年出口减少 7.64%；

江苏省，出口数量 3371154kg，占总出口数量的 16.026%，比上年出口增加 97.30%；

上海市出口数量 3123023kg，占总出口数量的 14.846%，比上年出口减少 17.73%；

辽宁省，出口数量 376419kg，占总出口数量的 1.789%，比上年出口减少 6.15%。

2012 年其他初级形状的 ABS 树脂五省市出口小计出口数量占总出口数量的 97.498%，比上年增加 0.298%(表 137)。

表 137 2012 年其他初级形状的 ABS 树脂五大出口省市统计

排 序	出口省市	出口金额/美元	出口数量/kg	占比例/%
1	广东省	15632056.00	7484694	35.580
2	浙江省	12194617.00	6154546	29.257
3	江苏省	7192144.00	3371154	16.026
4	上海市	8416035.00	3123023	14.846
5	辽宁省	996350.00	376419	1.789
	2012	45844026.00	21036084	100.00

三、ABS 树脂出口商以 ABS 改性生产企业为主

1. 改性初级形状的 ABS 树脂

从海关资料来看，2012 年改性 ABS 出口 20554338kg，比上年减少 2.66%。

2012 年改性 ABS 出口商有 125 家，比上年 131 家出口商减少 6 家出口商。

2012 年前十位出口商统计出口量占总出口量的 80.616%，全部为出口生产企业。

三十七大出口商中出口企业有二十四家生产企业，均为 ABS 改性；ABS 贸易商(13 家)，分别占总出口量的 90.486% 和 4.635%；

出口主要以 ABS/PP、ABS/PA 合金为主；

出口企业以外商独资、合资和私企为主；

出口口岸以广东省口岸为主，其次为上海口岸。

LG 化学(广州)工程塑料有限公司 2012 年 ABS 出口 8006825kg，占总出口量的 28.973%，同比出口减少 25.62%；

广州金发科技股份有限公司 2012 年 ABS 出口 3293975kg，占总出口量的 16.026%，同比出口增加 79.53%；

深圳市星光塑胶原料有限公司 2012 年 ABS 出口 1600000kg，占总出口量的 7.784%；

上海矶野塑胶有限公司 2012 年 ABS 出口 1407792kg，占总出口量的 6.849%，同比出口增加 129.48%；

大日精化(深圳)有限公司 2012 年 ABS 出口 1030450kg，占总出口量的 5.013%；

星科工程塑料(深圳)有限公司 2012 年 ABS 出口 1009137545082kg，占总出口量的 4.910%，同比出口增加 85.13%；

上海锦湖日丽塑料有限公司 2012 年 ABS 出口 838525kg，占总出口量的 4.080%，同比减少出口 27.84%；

山阳稻田复合塑料(东莞)有限公司 2012 年 ABS 出口 544445kg，占总出口量的 2.649%；

日超工程塑料(深圳)有限公司 2012 年 ABS 出口 509077kg，占总出口量的 2.477%，同比出口减少 32.26%；

康准精密模具(昆山)有限公司 2012 年 ABS 出口 381317kg，占总出口量的 1.855%，同比出口减少 13.95%(表 138)。

表 138 2012 年改性初级形状的 ABS 树脂三十七大出口商统计

排 序	出口商	所属行业	出口数量/kg	占比例/%
1	LG 化学(广州)工程塑料有限公司	ABS 改性	5955200	28.973
2	广州金发科技股份有限公司	ABS 改性	3293975	16.026
3	深圳市星光塑胶原料有限公司	ABS 改性	1600000	7.784
4	上海矶野塑胶有限公司	ABS 改性	1407792	6.849
5	大日精化(深圳)有限公司	ABS 改性	1030450	5.013
6	星科工程塑料(深圳)有限公司	ABS 改性	1009137	4.910
7	上海锦湖日丽塑料有限公司	ABS 改性	838525	4.080

续表

排　序	出口商	所属行业	出口数量/kg	占比例/%
8	山阳稻田复合塑料(东莞)有限公司	ABS 改性	544445	2.649
9	日超工程塑料(深圳)有限公司	ABS 改性	509077	2.477
10	康准精密模具(昆山)有限公司	ABS 改性	381317	1.855
11	常州塑料集团新材料有限公司	ABS 改性	327000	1.591
12	丽碧复合塑料(深圳)有限公司	ABS 改性	278117	1.353
13	上海长伟锦磁工程塑料有限公司	ABS 改性	249550	1.214
14	新疆百可途物流有限公司	ABS 贸易商	232000	1.129
15	安特普工程塑料(苏州)有限公司	ABS 改性	231605	1.127
16	普立万聚合体(深圳)有限公司	ABS 改性	227448	1.107
17	佛山市南海拓迪文进出口贸易有限公司	ABS 贸易商	204000	0.992
18	青岛海尔新材料研发有限公司	ABS 改性	149600	0.728
19	深圳市科聚新材料有限公司	ABS 改性	142000	0.691
20	沙伯基础创新塑料(中国)有限公司	ABS 改性	138100	0.672
21	喀什安喀斯国际贸易有限公司	ABS 贸易商	71875	0.350
22	LG 化学(天津)工程塑料有限公司	ABS 改性	55873	0.272
23	伊新(大连)物流有限公司	ABS 贸易商	54000	0.263
24	岸本工贸(大连保税区)有限公司	ABS 贸易商	54000	0.263
25	上海日绵有限公司	ABS 改性	52246	0.254
26	南京利佳塑料发展有限公司	ABS 改性	50151	0.244
27	深圳福汉兴国际运输有限公司	ABS 贸易商	49000	0.238
28	清远市建德工程塑料有限公司	ABS 改性	48000	0.234
29	天津利得国际贸易有限公司	ABS 贸易商	45339	0.221
30	中航技(天津)机械设备有限公司	ABS 贸易商	43000	0.209
31	深圳市宝安鸿彬实业有限公司	ABS 贸易商	42971	0.209
32	上海大赛璐塑料工业有限公司	ABS 改性	42300	0.206
33	青岛海杰尔进出口有限公司	ABS 贸易商	42000	0.204
34	深圳能源物流有限公司	ABS 贸易商	40000	0.195
35	淄博东聚化工有限公司	ABS 改性	39100	0.190
36	深圳市福汉兴业国际货运代理有限公司	ABS 贸易商	39000	0.190
37	深圳中外运物流有限公司	ABS 贸易商	35340	0.172
出口总计			20554338	100.00

2. 其他初级形状的 ABS 树脂

从海关资料来看，2011 年 ABS 出口商有 327 家，比上年 331 家出口商减少 4 家出口商。

2012 年国内前十位 ABS 出口商出口商统计出口量占总出口量的 76.333%，其中出口生产企业八家，ABS 贸易商二家，分别占总出口量的 71.649% 和 4.684%；

2012 年国内 ABS 前三十八大出口商中生产厂商占二十家，其中仅有宁波乐金甬兴化工有限公司(占总出口量的 26.924%)，镇江奇美化工有限公司(占总出口量的 8.144%)，中石化国际事业上海有限公司(占总出口量的 3.946%)等三家是 ABS 树脂原料生产厂，其余十七家均为 ABS 改性；三十八大出口商中 ABS 贸易商有十八家；出口商中生产厂商和

ABS 贸易商分别占总出口量的 77.880% 和 11.904%；

出口企业以外商独资、合资和私企为主；

出口口岸以浙江省口岸为主，其次为广东省口岸(表 139)。

表 139　2012 年其他初级形状的 ABS 树脂三十八大出口商统计

排　序	出口商	所属行业	出口数量/kg	占比例/%
1	宁波乐金甬兴化工有限公司	ABS 树脂原料	5663775	26.924
2	鸿富锦精密工业(深圳)有限公司	ABS 改性	3204104	15.231
3	镇江奇美化工有限公司	ABS 树脂原料	1713175	8.144
4	康准精密模具(昆山)有限公司	ABS 改性	1412955	6.717
5	中国金山联合贸易有限责任公司	ABS 树脂原料	925175	4.398
6	中石化国际事业上海有限公司	ABS 树脂原料	830100	3.946
7	丽碧复合塑料(深圳)有限公司	ABS 改性	728650	3.464
8	大日精化(深圳)有限公司	ABS 改性	594338	2.825
9	上海实寓贸易有限公司	ABS 贸易商	517000	2.458
10	深圳市宝安外经发展有限公司	ABS 贸易商	468189	2.226
11	上海电视电子进出口有限公司	ABS 贸易商	306000	1.455
12	广州广钢 MBA 塑料新技术有限公司	ABS 改性	269150	1.279
13	肇庆嘉裕国际贸易有限公司	ABS 贸易商	240000	1.141
14	优利(东莞)塑胶材料有限公司	ABS 改性	221975	1.055
15	深圳市亿利丰塑料有限公司	ABS 改性	170000	0.808
16	帝人化成复合塑料(上海)有限公司	ABS 改性	165000	0.784
17	岸本工贸(大连保税区)有限公司	ABS 贸易商	162200	0.771
18	宁波联合埃希物流有限公司	ABS 贸易商	133000	0.632
19	鸿富泰精密电子(烟台)有限公司	ABS 改性	101960	0.485
20	丹东诚通贸易有限公司	ABS 贸易商	101850	0.484
21	青岛保税物流园区怡港国际物流有限公司	ABS 贸易商	92000	0.437
22	青岛海尔新材料研发有限公司	ABS 改性	75000	0.357
23	丹东市远达商务公司	ABS 贸易商	70300	0.334
24	尚志化工(吴江)有限公司	ABS 改性	60000	0.285
25	山阳稻田复合塑料(东莞)有限公司	ABS 改性	58506	0.278
26	深圳市瑞广宏进出口有限公司	ABS 贸易商	57000	0.271
27	大科能树脂(上海)有限公司	ABS 改性	54000	0.257
28	上海合冠仓储有限公司	ABS 贸易商	54000	0.257
29	深圳市友安进出口发展有限公司	ABS 贸易商	52605	0.250
30	天津松井塑料有限公司	ABS 改性	48900	0.232
31	上海锦湖日丽塑料有限公司	ABS 改性	48425	0.230
32	温州元晟贸易有限公司	ABS 贸易商	45800	0.218
33	深圳市恒祥新进出口有限公司	ABS 贸易商	45622	0.217
34	深圳市建和科技发展有限公司	ABS 贸易商	42000	0.200
35	烟台北明储运有限公司	ABS 贸易商	40561	0.193
36	佛山能和进出口贸易有限公司	ABS 贸易商	38200	0.182
37	苏州永辉高分子材料科技有限公司	ABS 改性	38000	0.181
38	理光通运(深圳)仓储有限公司	ABS 贸易商	37475	0.178
	出口总计		21036084	100.00%

四、国内ABS树脂2012年进出口同比增长

依照数据显示，中国2007～2012年间ABS进口量如过山车，起伏波动较大，2008年进口量跌了10.17%，2009年进口量又暴增了20.48%，2011年全球经济危机，需求不旺，出口受阻，国内产量上升，进口量又大幅下降20.95%，2012年全球经济继续低迷，国内产能增长，进口量又进一步下降18.64%（表140）。

表140　2007～2012年我国ABS树脂进出口量统计

产　品	项　目	2007	2008	2009	2010	2011	2012
ABS树脂	进口/10^4t	217.275	195.186	235.15	237.95	185.27	149.63
同比增长	/%	7.84	-10.17	0.48	2.16	-22.14	-19.24
ABS树脂	出口/t	32357	43264	71459	74472	43133	21043
同比增长	/%	65.26	33.71	115.20	4.22	-42.08	-51.21
改性的ABS树脂	进口/10^4t	—	—	18.34	21.01	19.43	16.91
	出口/t	—	—	21643	20125	21117	20554
ABS共聚物	进口/10^4t	217.275	195.186	253.49	258.96	204.70	166.54
	出口/t	32357	43264	93102	94597	64250	41590
ABS净进口	10^4t	214.04	190.86	244.18	249.50	198.27	162.385
同比增长	/%	7.28	-10.83	27.94	2.18	-20.53	-18.10

注：1. 资料来源——历年国家海关统计。
2. 改性的ABS树脂2009年才单独新列出代码，无历年数据，因此无法同比。

2007～2012年间ABS进口量年均增长率为负5.18%；

2007～2012年间ABS出口量年均增长率为5.15%。

1. 2012年ABS树脂进口量价同降

虽然中国ABS树脂产能和产量均增长很快，但仍不能满足国内实际生产需求，每年都需要大量进口。

中国ABS树脂的需求量和进口量均已居全球第一，并成为世界ABS树脂第一大进口国。

随着国内产量的大幅度增长及技术水平的提高，未来几年ABS树脂进口量会有下降的趋势。随着生产能力的增加，自给率不断增加，2012年其自给率达到48.24%，比2011年上升2.99%。

我国ABS共聚物进出口均以进料加工贸易方式为主。

A. 改性初级形状的ABS树脂量价同降

从海关统计中可看出，2012年改性初级形状的ABS树脂进口地有36个，比上年33个进口地增加3个进口地；中国台湾和韩国仍为我国ABS树脂进口主要市场。

2012年，自韩国进口93904261kg，占总进口量的55.535%，比上年进口下降16.85%，进口平均价格2449.34美元/t，比上年进口均价下降6.37%；

自中国台湾省进口44091360kg，占总进口量的26.075%，比上年进口下降10.00%；进口平均价格2448.95美元/t，比上年进口均价上升0.62%；

自上述两大主要市场改性初级形状的ABS树脂进口数量之和占全部进口数量81.61%，比上年进口数量下降1.74%；

其次为日本进口11333176kg，占总进口量的6.702%，比上年进口下降1.63%，进口平均价格3470.01美元/t，比上年进口均价下降5.10%；

中华人民共和国进口8737572kg，占总进口量的5.167%，比上年进口下降14.43%，进口平均价格2806.32美元/t，比上年进口均价下降5.25%；

马来西亚进口6082754kg，占总进口量的3.597%，比上年进口增加26.14%，进口平均价格2497.29美元/t，比上年进口均价下降4.33%；

五原产进口地进口数量占改性初级形状的ABS树脂2012年总进口数量的97.077%，比上年进口增加0.087%（表141）。

表141　2012年改性初级形状的ABS树脂七大进口国家/地区统计

排　序	原产进口地	进口金额/美元	进口数量/kg	占比例/%
1	韩国	230003797.00	93904261	55.535
2	中国台湾省	107977600.00	44091360	26.075
3	日本	39326230.00	11333176	6.702
4	中华人民共和国	24520425.00	8737572	5.167
5	马来西亚	15190398.00	6082754	3.597
进口总计		432234102.00	169091422	100.00

B. 其他初级形状的ABS树脂进口量价同降

从海关统计中可看出，2012年其他初级形状的ABS树脂进口地有52个，比上年51个进口地增加1个进口地，中国台湾省和韩国仍为我国ABS树脂进口主要产地。

2012年，自中国台湾进口802243888kg，同比下降9.54%，占总进口量的53.616%；进口平均价格2053.28美元/t，比上年同期进口均价下降1.12%；

自韩国进口472660081492172306kg，同比下降3.96%，占总进口量的31.589%；进口平均价格2104.05美元/t，比上年同期下降5.96%；

自上述两大主要市场进口数量之和占全部进口数量的85.205%，比上年同期增加2.055%。

其次为马来西亚进口77815646kg，同比进口减少23.19%，占总进口量的5.201%；

日本进口61958493kg，同比减少21.89%，占总进口量的4.141%；

泰国进口36988000kg，同比减少21.66%，占总进口量的2.472%；

五原产进口地进口数量占其他初级形状的ABS树脂2012年总进口数量的97.019%，比上年增加0.129%(表142)。

表142　2012年其他初级形状的ABS树脂五大进口国家/地区统计

排　序	原产进口地	进口金额/美元	进口数量/kg	占比例/%
1	中国台湾省	1647228506.00	802243888	53.616
2	韩国	994498887.00	472660081	31.589
3	马来西亚	168664014.00	77815646	5.201
4	日本	182260159.00	61958493	4.141
5	泰国	81009631.00	36988000	2.472
进口总计		3190376829.00	1496265127	100.00

2. 2012年ABS树脂出口量价同降长

与其他几大通用塑料原料相比，中国ABS树脂的出口一直处于较低水平，随着我国合成树脂工业的发展，2006年，我国ABS树脂出口出现止跌回升，出口数量取得了大幅跃进，但绝对数量仍处于较低水平，仍以进口为主。

A. 改性初级形状的ABS树脂出口量价同降

从海关统计中可看出，2012年改性初级形状的ABS树脂出口地有45个，比2011年44个出口地增加1个出口地。

中国中国香港地区仍为中国内地改性初级形状的ABS树脂最主要的出口目的地，2012年中国内地共向中国中国香港地区出口改性初级形状的ABS树脂14212522kg，同比下降2.86%，占全部出口量的69.146%；出口平均价格2660.31美元/t，比上年出口均价下降1.83%。

其次为日本出口改性初级形状的ABS树脂1321270kg，同比下降15.54%，占全部出口量的6.428%；出口平均价格2463.47美元/t，比上年出口均价增加1.34%。

向泰国出口改性初级形状的ABS树脂678682kg，占全部出口量的3.302%；

向越南出口改性初级形状的ABS树脂636270kg，占全部出口量的3.096%，比上年出口下降10.86%；

向俄罗斯联邦出口改性初级形状的ABS树脂554300kg，占全部出口量的2.697%。

五出口地出口数量占改性初级形状的ABS共聚物2012年总出口数量的84.669%，比上年下降2.892%(表143)。

表 143 2012 年改性初级形状的 ABS 树脂五大出口国家/地区统计

排 序	出口目的地	出口金额/美元	出口数量/kg	占比例/%
1	中国香港	37809685.00	14212522	69.146
2	日本	3254914.00	1321270	6.428
3	泰国	1842077.00	678682	3.302
4	越南	2311430.00	636270	3.096
5	俄罗斯	1706452.00	554300	2.697
出口总计		55958763.00	20554338	100.00

B. 其他 ABS 树脂出口量价同降

有关数据显示，从海关统计中可看出，2012 年其他 ABS 共聚物出口地有 52 个，比上年 45 个出口地增加 7 个出口地。

中国中国香港地区为中国内地其他 ABS 树脂最主要的出口目的地，2012 年中国内地共向中国香港地区出口其他 ABS 树脂 14112065kg，同比下降 7.95%，占全部出口量的 67.085% 以上，出口平均价格 2084.45 美元/t，比上年出口平均价格下降 4.45%。

其次为出口中国台湾省其他改性初级形状的 ABS 树脂 19521591517191kg，同比大幅上升 28.67%，占全部出口量的 9.280%；出口平均价格 2023.34 美元/t，比上年出口平均价格下降 14.17%；

出口越南其他初级形状的 ABS 树脂 1352179kg，同比大幅上升 66.80%，占全部出口量的 6.628%；出口平均价格 2224.23 美元/t，比上年出口平均价下降 3.65%。

出口泰国其他初级形状的 ABS 树脂 959278kg，同比大幅下降 28.38%，占全部出口量的 4.560%；出口平均价格 2644.70 美元/t，比上年出口平均价下降 4.28%；

出口日本其他初级形状的 ABS 树脂 536602930475kg，同比大幅上下降 42.33%，占全部出口量的 2.551%；出口平均价格 2855.32 美元/t，比上年出口平均价上升 1.17%；

五出口地出口数量占其他 ABS 共聚物 2012 年总出口数量的 89.904%，比上年下降 0.60%（表 144）。

表 144 2012 年其他初级形状的 ABS 树脂五大出口国家/地区统计

排 序	出口目的地	出口金额/美元	出口数量/kg	占比例/%
1	中国香港	29，415，884.00	14112065	67.085
2	中国台湾省	3，949，886.00	1952159	9.280
3	越南	3，007，559.00	1352179	6.428
4	泰国	2，537，000.00	959278	4.560
5	日本	1，532，170.00	536602	2.551
出口总计		45，844，026.00	21036084	100.00

五、2012 年 ABS 国内消费下降自给率上升

2012 年 ABS 表观消费量 3137.2kt，同比下降 4.89%。

2006～2012 年间 ABS 表观消费量年均增长率为 -0.19%，低于同期产量年均增长率 2.49%（表 145）。

表 145 2006～2012 年国内 ABS 表观消费量统计资料

项 目	2006	2007	2008	2009	2010	2011	2012
表观消费量/kt	3273.66	3770.39	3038.60	3438.24	3650.38	3298.40	3137.19
年增长率/%	4.50	15.17	-19.41	13.15	6.17	-9.64	-4.89
国内自给率/%	39.05	43.23	37.19	38.39	42.08	45.14	48.24

在一些传统的应用领域，ABS 树脂正面临着越来越多的竞争，市场份额已经开始降低。我国必须针对市场需求，围绕现有生产装置，大力发展抗冲击、耐热、耐候、高流动、电镀、阻燃、高光泽、抗静电、激光标识、抗电磁屏蔽、抗振动阻尼、气体阻隔等专用 ABS 树脂品种以及电冰箱、头盔、板

材以及汽车仪表板表皮等各种专用料的开发。

另外，近年来ABS树脂与其它高价性能的工程树脂的合金/共混物发展很快。其中最主要的品种有ABS/PC、ABS/PVC、ABS/PBT、ABS/PA以及TUP/ABS等。

ABS/PC合金是为改进ABS阻燃性，且具有良好的机械强度、韧性，用于建材，汽车和电子工业，如做电视机、办公自动化设备外壳和电话机。ABS/PC合金中PC贡献耐热性、韧性、冲击强度、阻燃性，ABS优点为良好加工性、表观质量和低密度，以汽车工业零部件为应用重点。

ABS/PA合金是耐冲击、耐化学品、良好流动性和耐热性材料，用于汽车内件装饰伯，电动工具、运动器具、割草机和吹雪机等工业部件，办公室设备外壳等；

ABS/PBT合金有良好的耐热性，强度、耐化学品性和流动性、适于做汽车内饰件，摩托车外垫件等；

添加抗静电剂的永久抗静电性牌号用途有：复印机、传真机等的传递纸张机构、IC片支座、录像和高级音频磁带等；另外还有ABS/PSU、ABS/EVA、ABS/PVC/PET、ABS/EPDM、ABS/CPE、ABS/PU等合金。

我国也应加大ABS树脂共混合金的开发力度，尽快大规模推出自己的ABS树脂共混合金产品，以改变我国ABS树脂产品品种单一、产品质量档次低的现状，满足国内实际生产对不同品质产品的需求。

ABS一直在汽车部件生产中起着重要作用。PP虽然在汽车配件生产中后来居上，但是ABS在高档轿车部件中的贵族地位是PP无法撼动和完全取代的。ABS的贵族地位是与ABS良好的特性相关的：热塑性ABS树脂被广泛认可为是一种可以自由设计的工程材料，具有突出的美学、流动、韧性、尺寸稳定性和高耐热性。

改性ABS可以提供宽范围的牌号选择，包括低气味ABS、耐热ABS、消光ABS、电镀级ABS和耐候ABS，ABS在汽车的内外饰部件上有广泛的应用。在内饰上，ABS可以用于生产门板、仪表板饰框、手套箱、中控仪表板、空调出风口等。在外饰上，ABS用于制造散热格栅、镜框、牌照板、饰标等。

在国外ABS树脂产品向高性能化、功能化、多品种化方向发展，各种专用料已系列化，可满足不同层次、不同用户的需求，而我国大多数ABS生产企业还只能生产通用型产品。而我国改性ABS质量水平还较低的现状。

要加快引进技术的吸收利用和国产化技术的开发，加大研发力度，积极开辟新的市场领域。我国大型ABS树脂的生产装置都是引进国外技术和生产工艺，但在消化吸收引进技术方面的步伐却比较缓慢，难以按照市场的需求及时调整产品结构，造成高性能ABS树脂产品主要依赖进口的局面。因此急需加快对引进技术的消化吸收和国产技术的开发工作，以保证我国ABS行业健康稳定发展。

1. 2012年ABS进口消费省市仍主要流向珠江三角洲和长江三角洲

从海关资料来看，2012年改性初级形状的ABS树脂进口消费省市有19个，与上年持平。

主要进口流向为广东省、福建省、江苏省、上海市和浙江省，前五位2012年改性初级形状的ABS树脂进口消费省市进口量占总进口量的77.784%，比上年增加2.623%。

2012年ABS共聚物主要进口流向为广东省，进口数量56067045kg，同比增加4.43%，占总进口数量的33.15%(表146)。

表146　2012年改性初级形状的ABS树脂五大进口省市统计

排　序	进口省市	进口金额/美元	进口数量/kg	占比例/%
1	广东省	137144319.00	56067045	33.158
2	福建省	58770534.00	25782690	15.248
3	江苏省	53468858.00	21088985	12.472
4	上海市	43365802.00	15479207	9.154
5	浙江省	40226942.00	13108502	7.752
进口总计		432234102.00	169091422	100.00

从海关资料来看，2012年其他初级形状的ABS树脂进口消费省市有22个，比上年22个进口消费省市持平。

主要进口流向为广东省、江苏省、浙江省、上海市和福建省，前五位2012年其他初级形状的ABS树脂进口消费省市进口量占总进口量的92.902%，比上年进口减少1.218%。

2012年ABS共聚物主要进口流向为广东省，进口数量948438388kg，占总进口数量的63.387%，比上年进口减少10.45%。

其次为江苏省，进口数量162354742kg，占总进口数量的10.851%，比上年减少20.36%；

浙江省，进口数量140439493kg，占总进口数量的9.386%，比上年进口减少1.85%；

上海市，进口数量102052235kg，占总进口数量的6.820%，比上年进口减少4.58%；

福建省，进口数量36781386kg，占总进口数量的2.458%，比上年进口增加26.22%(表147)。

表147 2012年其他初级形状的ABS树脂五大进口省市统计

排 序	进口省市	进口金额/美元	进口数量/kg	占比例/%
1	广东省	1928490977.00	948438388	63.387
2	江苏省	391675393.00	162354742	10.851
3	浙江省	290090451.00	140439493	9.386
4	上海市	244826728.00	102052235	6.820
5	福建省	79519413.00	36781386	2.458
进口总计		3190376829.00	1496265127	100.00

2. ABS共聚物进口商以生产使用企业为主

A. 改性初级形状的ABS树脂

从海关资料来看，2012年改性初级形状的ABS树脂进口商有904家,，比上年915家进口商减少11家进口商。

前十位改性初级形状的ABS树脂进口商进口量占总进口量的20.200%。

2012年改性初级形状的ABS树脂十大进口商中有生产使用企业八家和进口贸易商二家，分别占总进口量的16.10%和4.10%。

三十九大进口商有二十六大进口商是进口生产使用企业，主要分布于塑胶工业，电子工业，玩具制品，机械配件，电线电缆，运动器材，改性塑料，塑料制品等行业，进口量占总进口量的29.770%(表148)。

表148 2012年改性初级形状的ABS树脂三十九大进口商统计

排 序	进口商	所属行业	进口数量/kg	占比例/%
1	福清福捷塑胶有限公司	塑胶工业	5551523	3.28
2	优利(苏州)科技材料有限公司	电子工业	4607950	2.73
3	上海伊藤忠商事有限公司	进口贸易商	3724934	2.20
4	武汉五邦塑胶金属有限公司	塑胶工业	3571625	2.11
5	浙江前浪进出口有限公司	进口贸易商	3216000	1.90
6	福建日新塑料制品有限公司	塑胶工业	2844875	1.68
7	福清华森塑胶有限公司	塑胶工业	2768050	1.64
8	福捷(武汉)电子配件有限公司	电子工业	2698950	1.60
9	福建冠华精密模具有限公司	机械工业	2597700	1.54
10	福清泳贸塑胶有限公司	塑胶工业	2563050	1.52
11	雅美工业（惠阳）有限公司	家用电器	2542083	1.50
12	苏州隆登电子科技有限公司	电子工业	2294800	1.36
13	东莞玮丰实业有限公司	进口贸易商	2270150	1.34
14	宁波晶圆贸易有限公司	进口贸易商	2270000	1.34
15	东莞市对外加工装配服务公司	进口贸易商	2102369	1.24
16	华登(河源)玩具制品有限公司	玩具制品	1961000	1.16
17	安徽博西华制冷有限公司	家用电器	1867600	1.10
18	合联胜利光电科技(厦门)有限公司	电子工业	1636750	0.97

续表

排　序	进口商	所属行业	进口数量/kg	占比例/%
19	常州富敬塑胶有限公司	塑胶工业	1617625	0.96
20	东莞市凯远进出口有限公司	进口贸易商	1516854	0.90
21	上海夏普电器有限公司	家用电器	1049625	0.62
22	天隆电脑配件(苏州)有限公司	电子工业	1040000	0.62
23	威海朝光电子有限公司	电子工业	1024700	0.61
24	伊新(大连)物流有限公司	进口贸易商	1010726	0.60
25	广州番禺对外贸易有限公司	进口贸易商	976339	0.58
26	威海三元塑胶科技有限公司	塑胶工业	975424	0.58
27	威海成宇硒鼓有限公司	电子工业	969825	0.57
28	天津凡振电子有限公司	电子工业	955300	0.56
29	塑科贸易(上海)有限公司	进口贸易商	954948	0.56
30	苏州茂群电子有限公司	电子工业	916000	0.54
31	山东东鑫电子有限公司	电子工业	911200	0.54
32	深圳市宝安外经发展有限公司	进口贸易商	911037	0.54
33	东莞汇景塑胶制品有限公司	塑胶工业	910843	0.54
34	宁波开创贸易有限公司	进口贸易商	893000	0.53
35	LG 化学(天津)工程塑料有限公司	改性塑料	887046	0.52
36	北海万利通供应链管理有限公司	进口贸易商	875000	0.52
37	通用电气百龙特塑料国际贸易(上海)有限公司	进口贸易商	812482	0.48
38	厦门光莆显示技术有限公司	家用电器	792000	0.47
39	京都电工(东莞)有限公司	家用电器	763144	0.45
	进口总计		169091422	100.00

B. 初级形状的 ABS 树脂

从海关资料来看，2012 年 ABS 共聚物进口商有 4289 家，比上年 4311 家进口商减少 22 家进口商；

前十位 ABS 共聚物进口商进口量占总进口量的 16.015%，比上年减 3.93%，前十位 ABS 共聚物进口商中分别有四家进口生产企业和六家进口贸易商，分别占总进口量的 5.841%，10.174%。

从资料分析，2012 年其他初级形状的的 ABS 树脂进口生产使用企业以改性塑料，塑胶工业，电子工业，清洁设备，塑料制品等行业为主，前二十二大进口生产企业进口量占总进口量的 12.968%(表 149)。

表 149　2012 年其他初级形状的 ABS 树脂三十八大进口商统计

排　序	进口商	所属行业	进口数量/kg	占比例/%
1	深圳市宝安外经发展有限公司	进口贸易商	41938655	2.803
2	广州金发科技股份有限公司	ABS 改性	32374750	2.164
3	东莞市对外加工装配服务公司	进口贸易商	27767919	1.856
4	深圳市龙岗区对外经济发展有限公司	进口贸易商	22653859	1.514
5	宁波晶圆贸易有限公司	进口贸易商	22289700	1.490
6	富华杰工业(深圳)有限公司	电子工业	22113672	1.478
7	镇江奇美化工有限公司	ABS 改性	20795770	1.390

续表

排 序	进口商	所属行业	进口数量/kg	占比例/%
8	中化塑料公司	进口贸易商	17982103	1.202
9	宁波信升化工有限公司	ABS 改性	17104000	1.143
10	建生裕科(上海)贸易有限公司	进口贸易商	14589950	0.975
11	鸿富锦精密工业(深圳)有限公司	ABS 改性	12107965	0.809
12	浙江前浪进出口有限公司	进口贸易商	11794000	0.788
13	永塑(东莞)塑料有限公司	ABS 改性	11046200	0.738
14	上海鹏益物流有限公司	进口贸易商	10635000	0.711
15	开平对外加工装配服务公司	进口贸易商	9592750	0.641
16	丽碧复合塑料(深圳)有限公司	ABS 改性	9303390	0.622
17	莱克电气股份有限公司	家用电器工业	9262200	0.619
18	伟易达(东莞)塑胶制品有限公司	塑胶工业	9128000	0.610
19	青岛海尔国际贸易有限公司	进口贸易商	8787000	0.587
20	上海高信国际物流有限公司	进口贸易商	4890991	0.327
21	伟易达(清远)塑胶电子有限公司	家用电器工业	4848000	0.324
22	广东省东莞畜产进出口有限公司	进口贸易商	4712850	0.315
23	青岛海尔新材料研发有限公司	家用电器工业	4516000	0.302
24	大日精化(深圳)有限公司	ABS 改性	4398207	0.294
25	新玛基(清远)实业有限公司	电子工业	4301000	0.287
26	山阳稻田复合塑料(东莞)有限公司	ABS 改性	4052096	0.261
27	大科能树脂(上海)有限公司	ABS 改性	3910327	0.261
28	东莞峰达电子有限公司	家用电器工业	3777912	0.252
29	东莞美泰电子有限公司	家用电器工业	3669500	0.245
30	宁波开创贸易有限公司	进口贸易商	3645000	0.244
31	建生裕科贸易(深圳)有限公司	进口贸易商	3620000	0.242
32	深圳市光明新区经济发展有限公司	进口贸易商	3593059	0.240
33	广州和氏璧化工材料有限公司	ABS 改性	3590000	0.240
34	苏州三星电子有限公司	电子工业	3528700	0.236
35	苏州爱普电器有限公司	家用电器工业	3521000	0.235
36	深圳市宝安鸿彬实业有限公司	进口贸易商	3465850	0.232
37	吴江东永材料科技有限公司	ABS 改性	3426000	0.229
38	镇泰(中国)工业有限公司	ABS 改性	3420200	0.229
	进口总计		1496265127	100.00

六、2012~2013 年价格走势

2012 年新年之后，受原油飙升以及上游原料持续走高引领，国内 ABS 市场维持上涨走势。5 月 ABS 市场整体需求偏淡，商家信心缺失，多以出货为主，局部价格继续小幅下滑，但下游接受度依然不高，市场走货仍较一般。6 月后 ABS 市场行情阶梯状下滑，十一月跌至全年低谷。

由于货源充足，削弱上涨动能，为了避免成本倒挂，ABS 厂家多采取下调开工率的做法，减少市场供应量(表 150～表 155)。

表 150　ABS750A 大庆石化 2012 年中国塑料城月均价走势　元/t

1 月	2 月	3 月	4 月	5 月	6 月
15333	15933	16178	15823	15504	14570
7 月	8 月	9 月	10 月	11 月	12 月
15059	15095	15476	15277	14822	15026

表 151　ABS　HI－121H LG 甬兴 2012 年中国塑料城月均价走势　元/t

1 月	2 月	3 月	4 月	5 月	6 月
15753	16309	16347	15997	15350	14590
7 月	8 月	9 月	10 月	11 月	12 月
15040	15240	15757	15580	14997	15238

表 152　ABS PA－757 中国台湾奇美 2012 年中国塑料城月均价走势　元/t

1 月	2 月	3 月	4 月	5 月	6 月
16086	16652	17104	16952	16140	15150
7 月	8 月	9 月	10 月	11 月	12 月
15454	15659	16064	15750	15436	15461

表 153　ABS FR－500 LG(阻燃)甬兴 2012 年中国塑料城月均价走势　元/t

1 月	2 月	3 月	4 月	5 月	6 月
22933	23000	23278	22900	22059	20890
7 月	8 月	9 月	10 月	11 月	12 月
21977	22000	22414	22622	22195	22133

表 154　ABS920 透明，19－23 日本东丽 2012 年中国塑料城月均价走势　元/t

1 月	2 月	3 月	4 月	5 月	6 月
24200	24200	24200	23768	24200	24040
7 月	8 月	9 月	10 月	11 月	12 月
24000	23800	23800	23800	23622	23457

表 155　ABS 650SK(耐热 104℃)上海锦湖 2012 年中国塑料城月均价走势　元/t

1 月	2 月	3 月	4 月	5 月	6 月
26000	26000	26000	26000	26000	26000
7 月	8 月	9 月	10 月	11 月	12 月
26000	26000	26000	26000	26000	26000

七、贸易方式分析

1. 改性的初级形状的 ABS

从海关统计中可看出，2012 年改性的初级形状的 ABS 进口贸易方式主要为进料加工贸易(占进口量 60.994%)，其次为一般贸易(占进口量 18.115%)，保税区仓储转口货物(占进口量 11.484%)，来料加工装配贸易(占进口量 9.056%)，保税仓库进出境货物(占进口量 0.316%)，其他(占进口量 0.034%)，外商投资企业作为投资进口的设备、物品(占进口量 0.001%)，合计为总进口量的 100.00%(表 156)。

从海关统计中可看出，2012 年改性的初级形状的 ABS 出口贸易方式主要为进料加工贸易(占出口量 77.112%)，其次为一般贸易(占出口量 17.764%)，来料加工装配贸易(占出口量 3.398%)，保税区仓储转口货物(占出口量 1.436%)，保税仓库进出境货物(占出口量 0.199%)，边境小额贸易(占出口量 0.049%)，其他(占出口量 0.042%)，合计为总出口量的 100.00%(表 157)。

表 156　2012 年改性的初级形状的 ABS 进口交易类型统计

进口交易类型	进口金额 /美元	进口数量/kg	占比例/%
进料加工贸易	256775973.00	103136454	60.994
一般贸易	87047577.00	30631664	18.115
保税区仓储转口货物	56564297.00	19418630	11.484
来料加工装配贸易	29848789.00	15312749	9.056
保税仓库进出境货物	1732892.00	533755	0.316
其他	261622.00	57170	0.034
外商投资企业作为投资进口的设备、物品	2952.00	1000	0.001
进口总计	432234102.00	169091422	100.00

表 157 2012 年改性的初级形状的 ABS 出口交易类型统计

出口交易类型	出口金额/美元	出口数量/kg	占比例/%
进料加工贸易	43709175.00	15849892	77.112
一般贸易	9690075.00	3651182	17.764
来料加工装配贸易	1299401.00	698482	3.398
保税区仓储转口货物	1078852.00	295225	1.436
保税仓库进出境货物	133462.00	40840	0.199
边境小额贸易	24127.00	10000	0.049
其他	23671.00	8717	0.042
出口总计	55958763.00	20554338	100.00

2. 其他初级形状的 ABS 树脂

从海关统计中可看出，2012 年其他初级形状的 ABS 树脂进口贸易方式主要为进料加工贸易（占进口量 52.003%），其次为一般贸易（占进口量 26.893%），来料加工装配贸易（占进口量 14.564%），保税区仓储转口货物（占进口量 5.678%），保税仓库进出境货物（占进口量 0.850%），其他（占进口量 0.012%），合计为总进口量的 100.00%（表 158）。

表 158 2012 年其他初级形状的 ABS 树脂进口交易类型统计

排 序	进口贸易方式	进口美元	进口数量/kg	占比例/%
1	进料加工贸易	1676842726.00	778102567	52.003
2	一般贸易	916451601.00	402389981	26.893
3	来料加工装配贸易	372614751.00	217912232	14.564
4	保税区仓储转口货物	195374134.00	84950545	5.678
5	保税仓库进出境货物	28138040.00	12725335	0.850
6	其他	955577.00	184467	0.012
进口总计		3190376829.00	1496265127	100.00

从海关统计中可看出，2012 年其他初级形状的 ABS 树脂出口贸易方式主要为进料加工贸易（占出口量 71.434%），其次为一般贸易（占出口量 19.876%），保税区仓储转口货物（占出口量 4.349%），来料加工装配贸易（占出口量 2.800%），保税仓库进出境货物（占出口量 0.738%），边境小额贸易（占出口量 0.658%），其他（占出口量 0.144%），合计为总出口量的 100.00%（表 159）。

表 159 2012 年其他初级形状的 ABS 树脂出口交易类型统计

排 序	出口贸易方式	出口美元	出口数量/kg	占比例/%
1	进料加工贸易	33120942.00	15026963	71.434
2	一般贸易	8540461.00	4181084	19.876
3	保税区仓储转口货物	2471412.00	914914	4.349
4	来料加工装配贸易	954775.00	589109	2.800
5	保税仓库进出境货物	345537.00	155292	0.738
6	边境小额贸易	345314.00	138500	0.658
7	其他	65585.00	30222	0.144
出口总计		45844026.00	21036084	100.00

（柴国樑）

工程塑料

2012/2013 年工程塑料综述

一、工程塑料产业的发展机遇

随着科技的进步和人民生活水平的不断提高，传统的塑料制造行业正发生着一场深入的变革。引领这场变革力量来自于一种先进高分子材料——工程塑料。

工程塑料的出现给塑料制造行业带来了更高性能的产品和更广阔的应用领域。

塑料产品按照性能和价格递增的顺序，可以分为通用塑料、通用工程塑料和特种工程塑料三大类，并呈现金字塔状分布。

位于金字塔底部的通用塑料性能单一，相对廉价，在日常生活中也最为常见。

通用塑料包含五大品种，即聚乙烯(PE)、聚丙烯(PP)、聚氯乙稀(PVC)、聚苯乙烯(PS)和丙烯腈-丁二烯-苯乙烯共聚物(ABS)。

而位于金字塔中部和顶部的通用工程塑料和特种工程塑料则具备更优异的性能和更高的经济附加值，拥有巨大的市场潜力。

通用工程塑料包括聚碳酸酯(PC)、聚酰胺(PA)、聚甲醛(POM)、聚对苯二甲酸丁二醇酯(PBT)和聚苯醚(PPO)；特种工程塑料则包括聚苯硫醚(PPS)、液晶聚合物(LCP)、聚砜(PSF)、聚酰亚胺(PI)、聚芳醚酮(PEEK)和聚芳酯(PAR)等。

相比通用塑料，工程塑料在性能上有很大的提高，如机械强度高、刚性大、尺寸稳定性好、耐热性好、电绝缘性优异等。

因此，工程塑料是一种可以用做结构材料并承受机械应力，在较宽的温度范围和较苛刻的化学及物理环境中使用的塑料材料。

工程塑料在汽车行业的应用就是体现其优异性能很好的例子。

首先，采用工程塑料能降低汽车传动件之间的摩擦力，增加耐磨性，提高密封性，使汽车在安全性，舒适度和燃油效率等方面获得更大的突破。

其次，工程塑料以其重量轻、可塑性强、制造成本低的特点，大幅提高了汽车的零部件集成度和内外型设计空间，同时降低了整车重量和制造成本。

工程塑料不仅应用在汽车保险杠、仪表盘面板、车门内饰中，还成为发动机空气管道、节气门阀体、中冷器等关键部件中的主要材料。截至 2011 年，国内工程塑料下游需求的 14% 来自汽车制造行业，而欧美国家该比例已经接近 50%。

工程塑料已经成为 21 世纪汽车工业最好的材料选择。同样的，工程塑料在航空航天、电子电气、汽车、石化、国防军工等领域也都有广泛的运用。

当前，国内工程塑料产业正处在快速发展时期。继“十一五”期间成为化学工业最强劲的经济增长点之后，工程塑料作为战略新兴产业再一次被列入新材料产业“十二五”发展规划。去年国内工程塑料消费总量达到 2737kt，同比增长 11.8%，需求量增速全球最快。预计今后 10 年工程塑料的需求量仍将以每年 8% 至 11% 的速度增长。

尽管发展迅速，国内工程塑料的年产量仍然远远不能满足下游的需求。

举例来说，2010 年全国聚碳酸酯消费总量约为 1611.7kt(包括出口 210.17kt)，其中 1374.5kt 来自进口，自给率尚不足 14.72%。

“十二五”规划则明确指出，到 2015 年国内工程塑料市场满足率将力争超过 50%。

在工程塑料产业的发展和进口替代过程中，掌握核心技术的企业将能够充分受益技术壁垒和产品高附加值带来的可观回报，并与工程塑料产业一同实现持续快速的增长。

二、2012~2013 年国内工程塑料总述

目前，国内主要厂家的产品技术指标和装置水平已经向国际标准靠拢，有些甚至超过了国外装备水平。使部分国内产品能够在市场上具有相当的竞争能力并占据一定的市场份额，同时培育了一批有代表性的、年产值在十亿元以上，依靠自主知识产权发展起来的骨干企业。

到 2012 年底，国内工程塑料(包括外资公司在大陆工厂)树脂生产能力已达到 150 万吨，产量将近 1100kt；

共混、改性能力超过 7000kt，其中改性工程塑料产量 1800kt；已基本形成了初具规模的工程塑料生产体系。

随着我国国民经济的高速发展，中国工程塑料行业已进入高速发展时期，用量仅次于美国，居世界第二位；产业规模继美国、德国、日本之后居世界第四位。

工程塑料行业所属的企业有近千家，职工总数有几万人，已逐步形成了具有基础树脂合成、塑料改性与合金、助剂生产、塑机模具制造、加工应用

等相关配套能力的产业链。

由河北开滦集团、北京化工大学联合组建的开滦—北化大工程塑料改性研究中心在北京化工大学科技楼正式挂牌成立。该中心旨在建立产学研用联合体，围绕聚甲醛、尼龙等工程塑料改性相关领域开展研究工作，为开滦集团提供技术储备和技术支撑，同时促进北京化工大学理论研究的深入和技术的工程转化。

北京化工大学在塑料改性研究方面先后承担了多项国家科技攻关项目，改性品种包括聚甲醛、聚酰胺6等通用塑料和工程塑料。在聚甲醛改性方面，北京化工大学拥有多个相关发明专利，在聚甲醛的无卤阻燃、增强和增韧耐磨研究方面达到了国际先进水平，在塑料替代金属的汽车轻量化研究方面也有多年的技术积累。

目前，国内虽有企业已在生产聚甲醛，但尚未形成完善的聚甲醛改性体系，产品质量始终没有实质性突破。

开滦—北化大工程塑料改性研究中心近期将主要围绕聚甲醛的增强、阻燃、增韧、耐磨和耐候五个方面开展研究工作，具体由开滦煤化工研发中心负责组织实施，北京化工大学提供人才、技术、仪器设备等。改性材料年产量7000kt（其中工程塑料1800kt），净产值超过1200亿元人民币。

由于国外企业一致看好中国市场，近年来在华投资逐年增加；特别是共混改性领域，几乎所有国际知名企业都建立了生产装置。

日本工程塑料生产商——宝理塑料在中国江苏南通的宝泰菱工程塑料（南通）有限公司工程塑料混料工厂也将于2013年秋季投用，成为宝理塑料第4个工程塑料生产基地。

聚酰胺66聚合物生产商英威达公司，向中国及亚太市场推出优质工程塑料品牌TORZEN。公司计划在华投资建立自有的改性工厂，此举标志着英威达在亚洲地区加紧了优质工程塑料的市场布局。

由于国外大牌公司的不断涌入，使原本竞争十分激烈的市场更加白热化。他们凭借着资金、技术、品牌和服务的优势，同国内企业争夺市场。我们所面临的是国际化竞争：原料竞争、市场竞争、技术竞争、服务竞争、成本竞争、贸易方式竞争。在诸多竞争中，国内企业并不具备优势，从某种意义上讲劣势却十分明显。

目前，外资树脂合成装置的生产能力占国内工程塑料树脂合成总体能力的60%，在共混改性市场占有率则高达50%以上，而且占据的都是高端市场。

一些下游合资企业、独资企业也都不同程度设置门槛，使国内企业很难进入。因此目前仍有近50%的树脂和改性材料需要依靠进口，国内产品基本上集中在中、低端市场。近年来国外企业非常重视国内市场，看好中国国内巨大的市场需求，外国公司近来纷纷加强在中国进行本土化开发并不断扩大生产规模。

2010年12月，拜耳材料科学公司宣布投资10亿欧元对其上海工厂的聚碳酸酯和MDI进行大规模扩能。扩能后高性能聚碳酸酯年产能将达到50万吨。并将其聚碳酸酯业务的总部迁往上海，确保更进一步靠近快速发展的亚洲聚碳酸酯市场。

2011年1月12日，巴斯夫宣布，其浦东基地的工程塑料改性装置产能将在现有年4.5万吨基础上新增65kt。巴斯夫在华聚酰胺和聚对苯二甲酸丁二醇酯（PBT）工程塑料产能将达11万吨，占巴斯夫亚洲总产能的50%以上。

2012年1月7日，阿科玛公司宣布，始建于2007年的阿科玛常熟材料，将于3月投产。同时，决定追加投资，加速常熟工厂二期建设进程，计划于2012年中期将常熟工厂产能提高50%。此次扩产将使阿科玛常熟工厂达到世界级规模，并能够为各应用领域的亚洲客户提供全方位的本地服务，以进一步加强我们在聚合物领域的领先地位。

美国因维达公司在上海建立200kt/a已二腈和100kt/a尼龙66装置，将于2014年前投产。这些消息的发布并不是个别企业的个体行为——扩大产能已经成为业内大企业的基本共识。而且企业的发展速度超越整体行业的发展速度。

固有的市场份额已经无法满足企业需求，市场格局被打乱的概率逐渐增大。这种共识所带来的将是一种巨人间的搏斗——大企业对行业份额的重新瓜分。虽然整个市场还未走到这一步，但这种可能性已经越来越明确，因此我们必须做好迎接新挑战的准备。

预计到2013年中国工程塑料总体市场的年增长速度将达到10.2%，届时年需求量将接近3000kt。销售额增长的速度则略快（未来5年销售额保持11.2%的年均增长率），到2013年销售额约为115.6亿美元。

三、消费分析

随着人民生活水平的大幅提升和技术手段的改进，国内“以塑代钢”、“以塑代木”将成为一种趋势。改性塑料行业作为塑料加工行业类中发展最快而且发展很具潜力的一个子类行业，预计在未来5年，我国总的市场需求量仍将保持10%以上的增长率（表1）。

表1 近年来我国工程塑料的消费量 10^4t

产品	2005年	2006年	2007年	2008年	2009年	2010年	2011年	2012年	2015年预测
PA	21.7	25.64	29.4	33.7	38.1	41.5	43.5	48.0	61.00
PC	70	79.8	96.6	106.2	107.9	121	130	140	183.00
POM	19.2	22.23	29.58	29.09	29.98	37.561	40.51	43.5	55.00
PBT	11	18.2	22.1	24.9	27.4	30.3	32.8	36.5	48.00
MPPO	4	4.96	6.2	7.4	7.6	8	8.5	9.20	11.50
特种工程塑料	—	3.17	5.4	6.8	9.5	10.5	12.0	13.5	17.50
合计	125.9	154	186.4	206.8	221.1	243.3	262.8	290.7	376.00

注：产品均按本体料计，不含改性产品。

塑料在汽车工业中的应用已经有50多年的历史。随着汽车向轻量、节能方向的发展，给材料提出了更高的要求。由于1kg塑料可以替代2~3kg钢等更重的材料，而汽车自重每下降10%，油耗可以降低6%~8%。所以增加改性塑料在汽车中的用量可以降低整车成本、重量，并达到节能效果。乘用车和商用车的不同塑料用量也有所不同。

2011年改性PP、PC合金及改性ABS的需求分别约为1146.3kt、151.3kt和149.7kt。我国家电用改性塑料市场主要被国外企业所占据，国内改性塑料企业占有不到1/3的市场份额。由于国内企业的产品大多局限于低技术含量、低标准的层面，因此对那些具有高性能需求的领域开拓能力明显不足。

四、工程塑料发展趋势

对于工程塑料行业今后的发展，国内始终保持着乐观的态度。尽管有来自国外商品和在华外资企业的双重压力，但是我们坚信：国内企业一定能够寻求一条自我发展之路。

重点解决行业存在的技术与产品创新能力不足，和“低、小、散”的结构性问题。加速产业升级和结构调整，狠抓产品的更新换代。

到2015年基本做到：产业结构比较合理，发展方式更加科学，综合实力、发展后劲显著增强，为2020年全行业实现基本现代化打下坚实基础。

1. 发展目标中国工程塑料行业“十二五”期间的整体发展目标是：深入贯彻落实科学发展观，以国际视野和战略思维，大力推进国内工程塑料的应用与发展，以技术创新和产业创新为引领，促进产业结构升级，提高自给率，推动行业走上新型可持续的健康发展之路。

目前宏观形势正在发生深刻的调整变化，新一轮产业革命和科技革命将加快进行。

我国工业化、信息化、城镇化、市场化进程的深入发展和经济结构加快转型，以及国际化、扩大内需等政策深入实施，都将为工程塑料行业创新发展、转型发展提供积极稳定的政策环境。

2010年发改委和工信部联合公布的《石化产业振兴规划指导意见》中明确指出：高端化学品是石化行业重点发展领域，化工新材料和精细化工产品成为了推动产业结构调整的重要组成部分。并将工程塑料定位到新材料范畴，成为了国家重点发展的七大战略性新兴产业。

当前，随着我国经济快速发展，高端塑料产品的国内需求正处于快速增长期；特别是电子电气、通讯IT、交通运输、航空航天等产品的刚性需求将长期存在，高端市场潜力巨大。因此可以肯定的说：中国工程塑料行业在“十二五”期间必然还会有一个跨越，并通过发展方式的转变，促进实现行业可持续的发展。

2. 发展原则

A. 是坚持科技创新与产业振兴相结合。

B. 是坚持解决当前问题与着眼长远发展相结合，标本兼治。

C. 是加强技术改造与自主创新。

D. 是坚持企业为主体、市场为导向、产学研相结合。

E. 是增强资源节约和环境保护意识。

工程塑料是化工新材料中最具活力和发展前景的领域，是国家七大战略性新兴产业之一，是今后一段时期重点扶持和发展的产业。近年来随着我国高新技术产业和制造业的快速发展，对工程塑料领域提出了迫切的高性能化与国产化的技术要求。

我国工程塑料原料树脂对外依存度超过70%，严重影响了行业的发展。

“十二五”期间要着重解决国内树脂的供应问题，加大投资力度，鼓励国企、民企、外资等多元化投资，加快树脂原料的生产，逐步提高的自给率，预计2015年的树脂需求：PA树脂800kt、PC树脂

850kt、POM 树脂 500kt、PBT 树脂 420kt、PPO 树 80kt、特种工程塑料树脂 110kt，工程塑料树脂原料总需求量 3760kt。

到 2015 年国内(包括外资公司)五大工程塑料树脂生产能力预计达到 2600kt，产量达到 2000kt；国内工程塑料改性能力 10000kt/a，产量预计可达 9000kt/a 以上。

树脂自给率达到 70% 以上，国内改性塑料企业市场占有率达到 80%；进一步满足国民经济发展对化工新材料的需求。

第一章 聚碳酸酯树脂 2012 年进口上升出口下降

聚碳酸酯产品是综合性能优异的热塑性工程材料，广泛应用于汽车、家电、医疗、光学、机械等领域，迅速扩展到航空航天、电子、计算机等高新技术行业。

聚碳酸酯是五大通用工程塑料中唯一具有良好透明性的品种，抗冲击强度高，自身具有阻燃性。

一、2012/2013 年聚碳酸酯生产

中石化三菱化学合资建设的 60kt/a 聚碳酸酯装置，2012 年 2 月 18 日在燕山石化开车成功。

终端需求急剧萎缩，出口企业受欧洲危机等影响，2012 年订单普遍下滑，开工率不足 50%；同时国内需求亦不温不火，板材、注塑等市场尤其不景气，光盘应用基本缺失，水桶应用大幅减少，厂商出货十分缓慢。为了减少亏损、维持正常营业利润，聚碳酸酯企业 2012 年大多维持低负荷开工、限量保价。

从事改性聚碳酸酯品种生产的厂家和产能大大超过了基础树脂生产厂。

近年来我国聚碳酸酯改性发展较快，主要由于双螺杆混炼挤出机的引进和国产双螺杆混炼挤出机的推出，给改性聚碳酸酯创造了有利条件。

2012 年国内主要聚碳酸酯工程塑料改性厂有拜耳(上海)聚氨酯有限公司，沙伯基础创新塑料(中国)有限公司，帝人化成复合塑料(上海)有限公司，帝人聚碳酸酯有限公司，日超工程塑料(中山)有限公司，广州拜耳材料科技有限公司，LG 化学(广州)工程塑料有限公司，东莞大日化工厂有限公司，珠海东洋油墨有限公司，GE 塑料上海有限公司，山阳稻田复合塑料(东莞)有限公司，普立万聚合体(深圳)有限公司，鸿富锦精密工业(深圳)有限公司，出光复合工程塑料(广州)有限公司，三养工程塑料(上海)有限公司，东莞建德塑胶原料制品有限公司，日超工程塑料(深圳)有限公司，大日精化(深圳)有限公司，新生赞记塑胶原料(惠州)有限公司，广州金发科技股份有限公司，上海菱宇贸易有限公司，深圳福保赛格实业有限公司，菱翔光电(苏州)有限公司，深圳市宝安鸿彬实业有限公司，LG 化学(天津)工程塑料有限公司，星际塑料(深圳)有限公司，广东锦湖日丽高分子材料有限公司，东莞乐帝乐塑料有限公司，银禧工程塑料(东莞)有限公司，庆鸿塑胶(深圳)有限公司，深圳市科聚新材料有限公司，越谷化成工程塑料(上海)有限公司，安特普工程塑料(苏州)有限公司，鸿富锦精密工业(武汉)有限公司，常州大湖工程塑料有限公司，厦门昭伟塑胶工业有限公司，寿光卫东化工有限公司，力又实业(深圳)有限公司等。

二、2012 年聚碳酸酯出口

1. 出口生产省市分布分析

2012 年初级形状的聚碳酸酯出口省市有 18 家，比 2011 年持平。

2012 年初级形状的聚碳酸酯出口生产企业主要集中在广东省，出口数量 115978194kg，比 2011 年同比出口减少 14.16%，占总出口数量的 54.77%(表 2)。

五省市出口商出口数量占 2012 年初级形状的聚碳酸酯总出口数量的 99.41%，比 2011 年减少 0.17%。

表 2　2012 年初级形状的聚碳酸酯八大出口省市统计

排　序	出口省市	出口金额/美元	出口数量/kg	占比例/%
1	广东省	378245825.00	115978194	54.77
2	上海市	202240771.00	71874533	33.94
3	浙江省	47657992.00	18989154	8.97
4	江苏省	8863393.00	2600775	1.23
5	天津市	3208915.00	1063095	0.50
6	山东省	1766497.00	402210	0.19
7	福建省	1047104.00	310109	0.15
8	湖北省	878299.00	211464	0.10
出口总计		644986831.00	211749967	100.00

2. 聚碳酸酯出口生产商分析

从海关资料来看，2012 年初级形状的聚碳酸酯出口商有 525 家，比 2011 年 536 家出口商减少 11 家聚碳酸酯出口商。

2012 年前十位初级形状的聚碳酸酯出口商出口量占总出口量的 75.59%，比 2011 年下降 0.37%。

2012 年拜耳(上海) 聚合物有限公司初级形状的聚碳酸酯出口量超过帝人聚碳酸酯有限公司连续二年位居首位，出口量占 2012 年总出口量的 28.55%。

2012 年初级形状的聚碳酸酯五十八大出口商出口量中有三十八家为生产企业，仅有拜耳(上海)聚合物有限公司和帝人聚碳酸酯有限公司二家是 PC 树脂原料生产厂，其余均为 PC 改性(即 PC 合金)生产企业，合计出口量占总出口量的 84.34%(表 3)。

2012 年初级形状的聚碳酸酯五十八大出口商出口量中有二十家为贸易商业，合计出口量占总出口量的 84.34%(表 3)。

表 3　2012 年初级形状的聚碳酸酯五十八大出口商统计

排　序	出口商	所属行业	出口数量/kg	占比例/%
1	拜耳(上海)聚氨酯有限公司	PC 树脂原料	46584645	22.00
2	沙伯基础创新塑料(中国)有限公司	PC 改性	39547027	18.68
3	帝人化成复合塑料(上海)有限公司	PC 改性	14754238	6.97
4	帝人聚碳酸酯有限公司	PC 树脂原料	13863550	6.55
5	广州保畅国际物流有限公司	贸易商	12302914	5.81
6	日超工程塑料(中山)有限公司	PC 改性	9996675	4.72
7	广州拜耳材料科技有限公司	PC 改性	6854325	3.24
8	LG 化学(广州)工程塑料有限公司	PC 改性	5916150	2.79
9	东莞大日化工厂有限公司	PC 改性	5541375	2.62
10	奉化旭日进出口有限公司	贸易商	4687800	2.21
11	珠海东洋油墨有限公司	PC 改性	3965300	1.87
12	东莞联记塑胶原料有限公司	PC 改性	3933600	1.86
13	GE 塑料上海有限公司	PC 改性	2825127	1.33
14	山阳稻田复合塑料(东莞)有限公司	PC 改性	2676486	1.26
15	普立万聚合体(深圳)有限公司	PC 改性	2376631	1.12
16	鸿富锦精密工业(深圳)有限公司	PC 改性	2365266	1.12
17	出光复合工程塑料(广州)有限公司	PC 改性	2348075	1.11
18	三养工程塑料(上海)有限公司	PC 改性	2256850	1.07
19	东莞建德塑胶原料制品有限公司	PC 改性	1906350	0.90
20	日超工程塑料(深圳)有限公司	PC 改性	1747483	0.83
21	大日精化(深圳)有限公司	PC 改性	1649550	0.78
22	新生赞记塑胶原料(惠州)有限公司	PC 改性	1584000	0.75
23	广州金发科技股份有限公司	PC 改性	1579875	0.75
24	上海菱宇贸易有限公司	贸易商	1311117	0.62
25	深圳福保赛格实业有限公司	贸易商	1040110	0.49
26	菱翔光电(苏州)有限公司	PC 改性	989500	0.47
27	深圳市宝安鸿彬实业有限公司	PC 改性	748062	0.35
28	LG 化学(天津)工程塑料有限公司	PC 改性	690250	0.33
29	中海物流(深圳)有限公司	贸易商	632200	0.30

续表

排 序	出口商	所属行业	出口数量/kg	占比例/%
30	上海华长贸易有限公司	贸易商	609732	0.29
31	通用电气百龙特塑料国际贸易(上海)有限公司	贸易商	561562	0.27
32	星际塑料(深圳)有限公司	PC改性	495921	0.23
33	三井塑料贸易(上海)有限公司	贸易商	481211	0.23
34	深圳泰合威储运有限公司	贸易商	392020	0.19
35	深圳能源物流有限公司	贸易商	390250	0.18
36	深圳市立扬货物运输有限公司	贸易商	384175	0.18
37	广东锦湖日丽高分子材料有限公司	PC改性	379000	0.18
38	东莞乐帝乐塑料有限公司	PC改性	329000	0.16
39	太松国际贸易(上海)有限公司	贸易商	302800	0.14
40	银禧工程塑料(东莞)有限公司	PC改性	288000	0.14
41	庆鸿塑胶(深圳)有限公司	PC改性	281000	0.13
42	深圳市科聚新材料有限公司	PC改性	273250	0.13
43	上海经贸山九物流有限公司	贸易商	268847	0.13
44	越谷化成工程塑料(上海)有限公司	PC改性	237500	0.11
45	天津天保世纪贸易发展有限公司	贸易商	232238	0.11
46	深圳市友安进出口发展有限公司	贸易商	230584	0.11
47	安特普工程塑料(苏州)有限公司	PC改性	218522	0.10
48	鸿富锦精密工业(武汉)有限公司	PC改性	211464	0.10
49	上海稻田产业贸易有限公司	贸易商	207025	0.10
50	常州大湖工程塑料有限公司	PC改性	201870	0.10
51	佛山中外运物流有限公司	贸易商	183550	0.09
52	厦门昭伟塑胶工业有限公司	PC改性	182247	0.09
53	寿光卫东化工有限公司	PC改性	177550	0.08
54	上海港时捷物流有限公司	贸易商	157100	0.07
55	力又实业(深圳)有限公司	贸易商	155075	0.07
56	上海明宝工程塑料贸易有限公司	贸易商	151119	0.07
57	上海华英仓储有限公司	贸易商	147425	0.07
58	上海豫峰国际贸易有限公司	贸易商	132000	0.06
出口总计			211749967	100.00

三、2012年进口增长出口下降

2007～2012年间PC进口量增长34.66%，年均增长率6.13%。

2012年PC进口量比上年增长11.94%；

2012年PC出口量比上年下降11.02%；

2012年PC净进口量比上年增长17.46%(表4)。

表4 2007～2012年PC进出口统计

年 份	2007	2008	2009	2010	2011	2012
PC进口量/t	1020757	1017451	1026863	1264253	1227908	1374506
年增长率/%	13.51	-0.32	0.93	23.12	-2.87	11.94
PC出口量/t	306129	278586	214706	295243	237985	211750
年增长率/%	65.09	-9.00	-22.93	37.51	-19.39	-11.02
PC净进口量/t	714628	738865	811147	969010	989923	1162756
年增长率/%	0.11	3.39	9.78	19.46	2.16	17.46

注：资料来源：历年海关资料汇总。

从海关统计中可看出，2012 年初级形状的聚碳酸酯进口地有 53 个，比 2012 年持平。

主要进口地为韩国，进口数量 293326605kg，占总进口数量的 21.34%，比 2011 年增加进口数量 15.93%；

其次为中国台湾省，进口数量 202598984kg，占总进口数量的 14.74%，比 2011 年增加进口数量 9.67%；

泰国进口数量 179614037kg，占总进口数量的 13.07%，比 2011 年增加进口数量 5.11%；

中国大陆进口数量 150592283kg，占总进口数量的 10.96%，比 2011 年减少进口数量 4.62%；

美国进口数量 144590194kg，占总进口数量的 10.52%，比 2011 年进口数量增加 3.65%；

日本进口数量 106318262kg，占总进口数量的 7.74%，比 2011 年进口数量增加 3.50%；

新加坡进口数量 83818631kg，占总进口数量的 6.10%，比 2011 年进口数量增加 5.88%；

沙特阿拉伯进口数量 71011322kg，占总进口数量的 5.17%，比 2011 年进口数量增加 22.65%；

2012 年初级形状的聚碳酸酯八进口地进口量占总进口量的 89.64%，比 2011 年减少 2.73%（表 5）。

表 5　2012 年初级形状的聚碳酸酯十大进口国家/地区统计

排　序	原产进口地	进口金额/美元	进口数量/kg	占比例/%
1	韩国	815536391.00	293326605	21.34
2	中国台湾省	579852465.00	202598984	14.74
3	泰国	514904722.00	179614037	13.07
4	中国	520746482.00	150592283	10.96
5	美国	464039207.00	144590194	10.52
6	日本	397858318.00	106318262	7.74
7	新加坡	237414791.00	83818631	6.10
8	沙特阿拉伯	159348653.00	71011322	5.17
9	荷兰	123750933.00	40212047	2.93
10	西班牙	96022181.00	35339351	2.57
进口总计		4115434711.00	1374506262	100.00

从海关统计中可看出，2012 年初级形状的聚碳酸酯出口地有 62 个，比 2011 年 64 个出口地减少 2 家出口地，出口 211749967kg，同比减少 11.02%（表 6）。

表 6　2012 年初级形状的聚碳酸酯十大出口国家/地区统计

排　序	出口目的地	出口金额/美元	出口数量/kg	占比例/%
1	中国香港	490993802.00	157396029	74.33
2	中国台湾省	39160429.00	12783256	6.04
3	韩国	27456786.00	9308783	4.40
4	日本	18023588.00	6223490	2.94
5	印度尼西亚	11676786.00	5086902	2.40
6	越南	13593609.00	4895660	2.31
7	泰国	10179242.00	3971153	1.88
8	澳大利亚	5700950.00	2410375	1.14
9	比利时	5081722.00	2242860	1.06
10	马来西亚	5006326.00	1616579	0.76
出口总计		644986831	211749967	100.00

四、聚碳酸酯消费

聚碳酸酯是一种无味、无毒、透明的无定形的综合性能优异的热塑性工程塑料，具有突出的抗冲击、耐蠕变性能；具有较好的耐热性和耐寒性；绝缘性能优良、吸水率低、透光性好；其与 ABS(丙烯腈-丁二烯-苯乙烯)、PBT(聚对苯二甲酸丁二醇酯)等材料共混制成塑料合金，可提高综合应用性能。

聚碳酸酯主要应用以下领域：

汽车：高端品牌的车灯、天窗、保险杠、防弹玻璃、仪表盘。

建筑材料：用于生产防紫外线辐射，抗冲击力强的阳光板。

日常用品：旅行箱、豆浆机、冰箱冷冻室抽屉、吸尘器、眼镜片。

电子：蓝光光碟、苹果手机和 ipad 的屏幕、外壳，笔记本电脑屏幕和外壳。

医疗器械：注射器、血液分离器、牙科用具。

航空航天：飞机座椅、飞机眩窗、仪表盘，航天服(表 7)。

表 7 国内 2012~2015 年 PC 消费结构分配

消费领域	2015 年消费量/kt	消费比例/%	2012 年消费量/kt	消费比例/%
VCD、CD、DVC 等用光盘片和镜片	570	31.60	510	36.41
阳光板、屏障等的中空板	480	26.61	370	26.43
饮用水桶、瓶等包装用	350	19.40	250	17.85
板材、管材	98	5.43	85	6.07
汽车工业用	70	3.88	60	4.29
安全玻璃	50	2.77	40	2.86
仪表、电子电器用	32	1.77	26	1.86
工矿配件	26	1.44	18	1.29
各类照明灯具用	25	1.39	15	1.07
医疗器械用	16	0.89	15	1.07
其他用途	83	4.82	11	0.79
合计	1800	100.00	1400	100.00

聚碳酸酯广泛用于汽车零件，家居用品，医疗设备等领域，目前主要依赖进口。

初步预测，2015 年我国聚碳酸酯需求量将达到 183 万吨，中沙聚碳酸酯项目投产后将部分缓解进口压力。

1. 进口消费流向分析

从海关资料来看，从 2012 年 PC 树脂出口流向来看，仍主要集中在广东省、上海、浙江省三省市，广东省、上海市和浙江省进口量分别占总进口量的 50.30%、19.09% 和 11.12%。

2012 年初级形状的聚碳酸酯进口消费省市有 26 个，比 2011 年 25 个进口消费省市增加 1 个进口消费省市。

2012 年初级形状的聚碳酸前八位进口消费省市进口量占总进口量的 96.51%，比 2011 年减少 0.18%(表 8)。

表 8 2012 年初级形状的聚碳酸酯十大进口省市统计

排 序	进口省市	进口金额/美元	进口数量/kg	占比例/%
1	广东省	2109986832.00	691398129	50.30
2	上海市	798995910.00	262348861	19.09
3	浙江省	371762360.00	152841445	11.12
4	江苏省	363313916.00	115105696	8.37
5	天津市	110553426.00	35325637	2.57
6	北京市	65903643.00	25804985	1.88
7	福建省	74338084.00	24031928	1.75
8	山东省	69201285.00	19627126	1.43
9	辽宁省	42357452.00	10490178	0.76
10	河南省	18505291.00	7301635	0.53
进口总计		4115434711.00	1374506262	100.00

2. 2012 年初级形状的聚碳酸酯进口商以外商独资企业为主

2012 年初级形状的聚碳酸酯进口商共计有 3732 家，比 2011 年 3751 家进口商减少 19 家进口商，进口额最高的十位进口生产使用企业进口数量占总进口数量的25.92%,,比2011年减少0.69%。

2012年初级形状的聚碳酸酯七十七大进口商中有五十家进口生产使用企业，主要为聚碳酸酯改性(即PC合金)生产企业，其次为电子工业(手机外壳、电脑外壳等)，多媒体CD，工矿配件，塑胶工业，

五十家进口生产使用企业合计进口量占2012年总进口量的32.04%。

2012年初级形状的聚碳酸酯进口商中美国通用电器塑料旗下二家进口商进口量占2011年总进口量的3.21%。

2012年初级形状的聚碳酸酯七十七大进口商中有二十七 家贸易商 合计进口量占2012年总进口量的13.65%(表9)。

表9　2012年初级形状的聚碳酸酯七十七大进口商统计

排　序	进口商	所属行业	进口数量/kg	占比例/%
1	沙伯基础创新塑料(中国)有限公司	PC改性	140816169	10.24
2	拜耳(上海)聚氨酯有限公司	PC改性	41708521	3.03
3	帝人化成复合塑料(上海)有限公司	PC改性	33357475	2.43
4	GE塑料上海有限公司	PC改性	27297772	1.99
5	中化塑料公司	PC改性	23632700	1.72
6	塑科贸易(上海)有限公司	贸易商	22506225	1.64
7	上海明宝工程塑料贸易有限公司	贸易商	17440313	1.27
8	通用电气百龙特塑料国际贸易(上海)有限公司	贸易商	16764874	1.22
9	广州稻烟产业贸易有限公司	贸易商	16638324	1.21
10	广州金发科技股份有限公司	PC改性	16130283	1.17
11	宁波科固国际贸易有限公司	贸易商	15523733	1.13
12	广东华维科技有限公司	(多媒体CD)	14934910	1.09
13	宁波瑞源贸易有限公司	贸易商	14780750	1.08
14	深圳市宝安外经发展有限公司	贸易商	14201925	1.03
15	LG化学(广州)工程塑料有限公司	PC改性	12600310	0.92
16	宁波茂林进出口有限公司	贸易商	12020250	0.87
17	菱优工程塑料(上海)有限公司	PC改性	11641606	0.19
18	广州和氏璧化工材料有限公司	PC改性	11107200	0.81
19	上海和氏璧化工有限公司	PC改性	11099750	0.81
20	上豪贸易(深圳)有限公司	贸易商	10582221	0.77
21	东莞大日化工厂有限公司	PC改性	3820775	0.28
22	广东奥林磁电实业有限公司	电子工业	3751750	0.27
23	广州香林电子产品有限公司	电子工业	3671623	0.27
24	东莞市健宇塑胶原料有限公司	贸易商	3659224	0.27
25	宁波明仁国际贸易有限公司	贸易商	3621300	0.26
26	宁波中得进出口有限公司	贸易商	3613400	0.26
27	上海天增国际贸易有限公司	贸易商	3529750	0.26
28	安迈特提箱(东莞)有限公司	塑胶工业	3513794	0.26
29	理光(深圳)工业发展有限公司	工矿配件	3392475	0.25
30	中山皇冠皮件有限公司	工矿配件	3388605	0.25

续表

排 序	进口商	所属行业	进口数量/kg	占比例/%
31	珠海东洋油墨有限公司	PC 改性	3382650	0.25
32	厦门金泰化工有限公司	塑胶工业	3369725	0.25
33	绵阳龙华薄膜有限公司	塑胶工业	3362295	0.24
34	天马精密注塑(深圳)有限公司	电子工业	3214494	0.23
35	讯维数码科技(中山)有限公司	(多媒体 CD)	3177500	0.23
36	昆山彩德塑料有限公司	塑胶工业	3141094	0.23
37	上海经贸山九物流有限公司	贸易商	3070127	0.22
38	常熟市汇邦新材料有限公司	PC 改性	3031000	0.22
39	南京川和进出口有限公司	贸易商	2966387	0.22
40	江门市天粤科技工业有限公司	工矿配件	2959800	0.22
41	富泰华工业(深圳)有限公司	PC 改性	2904519	0.21
42	三进光电(苏州)有限公司	PC 改性	2813989	0.20
43	宁波天伦万宜贸易有限公司	贸易商	2803000	0.20
44	浙江前程石化有限公司	贸易商	2796475	0.14
45	深圳能源物流有限公司	贸易商	2732100	0.20
46	浙江新长城进出口有限公司	贸易商	2629575	0.19
47	纬立资讯配件(昆山)有限公司	电子工业	2627300	0.19
48	群星集团公司	工矿配件	2519944	0.18
49	绿点科技(深圳)有限公司	电子工业	2496600	0.18
50	深圳市名商实业有限公司	贸易商	2478608	0.18
51	普立万聚合体(深圳)有限公司	PC 改性	2447771	0.18
52	湖石化学贸易(上海)有限公司	贸易商	2420400	0.18
53	上海普利特复合材料有限公司	PC 改性	2371000	0.17
54	广州拜耳材料科技有限公司	PC 改性	2314155	0.17
55	康准精密模具(昆山)有限公司	工矿配件	2300740	0.17
56	潮阳市益邦贸易有限公司	贸易商	2286000	0.17
57	新玛基(清远)实业有限公司	工矿配件	2275260	0.17
58	圣美树脂制品(昆山)有限公司	塑胶工业	2260624	0.16
59	威斯康工程塑料(无锡)有限公司	PC 改性	2249890	0.16
60	苏州奥美材料科技有限公司	PC 改性	2196000	0.16
61	宁波开创贸易有限公司	贸易商	2190642	0.16
62	天马精密工业(中山)有限公司	电子工业	2159900	0.16
63	顺德市新宝电器有限公司	电子工业	2145000	0.16
64	海宁市正兴耐力板有限公司	建材工业	2119360	0.15
65	北京保利星数据光盘有限公司	(多媒体 CD)	2106000	0.15
66	东莞定嘉橡塑材料有限公司	塑胶工业	2077550	0.15
67	建生裕科贸易(深圳)有限公司	贸易商	2069000	0.15

续表

排序	进口商	所属行业	进口数量/kg	占比例/%
68	句容华叶新技有限公司	工矿配件	1985800	0.14
69	深圳泰合威储运有限公司	贸易商	1980700	0.14
70	佛山中外运物流有限公司	贸易商	1979950	0.14
71	优利(苏州)科技材料有限公司	塑胶工业	1972247	0.14
72	伟创力精密注塑(珠海)有限公司	电子工业	1969025	0.14
73	汕头市立德光盘科技有限公司	(多媒体 CD)	1948000	0.14
74	余姚市鑫晶磊塑料有限公司	塑胶工业	1947200	0.14
75	慈溪市合创塑料制品有限公司	塑胶工业	1947025	0.14
76	东莞市新广联数码科技有限公司	电子工业	1936000	0.14
77	南京纺织品进出口股份有限公司	贸易商	1931500	0.14
	进口总计		1374506262	100.00

五、2012年国内聚碳酸酯(PC)价格走势

2012年元旦后PC现货市场延续节前坚挺行情，主流报盘继续推高，2012年1月份低端料重心接近20000元/t关口，中高档市场推高至20800~23000元/t，场内气氛微妙。相比于节前市场供应面，新货虽略有补充，但整体吃紧局面继续。

1月份年关临近，考虑到PC下游工厂以劳动密集性的出口企业为主，多数工厂面临停工放假，市场有效需求不多，而到1月中旬为止工厂普遍未表现出备货需求，由此来看市场供需相对节前暂无明显改观。

自2012年2月以来，PC再生市场有价无市行情延续：因节前相关厂家整体库存水平不高，加之年后多开工较晚以及海关严查持续进行，场内流通领域供货较少；

此外节后运费、报关费用以及工人成本大幅上调等利好支撑，进而带动部分报盘上调，其中优质毛料、破碎料上调300~500元/t。但外围经济环境低迷，终端需求释放有限，需求弱势持续困扰市场，采购商多操盘谨慎，接货意向不高。整体来看，场内利好利空多方博弈，市场陷入上下两难的尴尬境地。

2012年国内聚碳酸酯价格下半年不断下跌，市场低迷。

2012年国内聚碳酸酯行业低迷分析

1. 工程塑料领域的产品附加价值较高，在整个经济面表现低迷之际，下游领域能省则省；

2. 工程塑料领域的产品，大多依赖进口，近期，有闻外国两家PC生产企业扩大了产能，全球聚碳酸酯市场供需不平衡；

3. 工程塑料行业，除少数品种外，多出产品长期维持市场清淡的局面。

六、进出口贸易方式

从海关统计中可看出，2012年初级形状的聚碳酸酯进口贸易方式主要为一般贸易(占进口量44.927%)(表10)。

表10 2012年初级形状的聚碳酸酯进口交易类型统计

进口交易类型	进口金额/美元	进口数量/kg	占比例/%
一般贸易	1723780609.00	617519011	44.927
进料加工贸易	1749897761.00	546593726	39.767
保税区仓储转口货物	376923367.00	112894337	8.213
来料加工装配贸易	165724898.00	65559260	4.770
保税仓库进出境货物	91886513.00	29448895	2.143
边境小额贸易	4856390.00	2040000	0.148
其他	2356343.00	450572	0.148
出口加工区进口设备	8830.00	461	0.000
进口总计	4115434711.00	1374506262	100.00

从海关统计中可看出，2012 年初级形状的聚碳酸酯出口贸易方式主要为进料加工贸易(占出口量79.256%)(表 11)。

表 11　2012 年初级形状的聚碳酸酯出口交易类型统计

出口交易类型	出口金额/美元	出口数量/kg	占比例/%
进料加工贸易	503518557.00	167823817	79.256
保税区仓储转口货物	90263960.00	26935040	12.720
来料加工装配贸易	34585280.00	10410932	4.917
一般贸易	15012028.00	6081567	2.872
保税仓库进出境货物	1512250.00	465233	0.220
其他	66713.00	21378	0.010
边境小额贸易	24472.00	7000	0.003
对外承包工程出口货物	3571.00	5000	0.002
出口总计	644986831.00	211749967	100.00

七、聚碳酸酯发展趋势

我国最大的聚碳酸酯项目——中国沙特年产260kt 聚碳酸酯项目，2012 年 12 月 10 日在天津滨海新区中沙(天津)石化有限公司奠基。

中国石化公司与沙特基础工业公司共同投资 110 亿元用于这一项目，预计 2015 年建成，包括 2 套130kt/a 非光气法聚碳酸酯联合生产装置，配套建设公用工程及辅助设施，工艺处于世界先进水平，共有设备 1976 台(套)，其中进口设备 218 台(套)，是中沙双方继百万吨乙烯项目投产后，在津兴建的又一个大型石化项目。

上海菱优 80kt/a 装置、中石化三菱 60kt/a 装置预计 2013 年建成投产。

在“十二五”期间，我国 PC 的表观需求量将维持在 10% ~15% 左右的增长速度，到 2015 年需求量将达到 2000kt 左右。

2011 年全球 PC 产能为 4695kt。其中沙特 SABIC 年产 1315kt，占全球产能 28%，位居世界第一。德国拜耳集团年产 1300kt，屈居第二。中国 2011 年 PC 产能仅为 436kt，不到全球产能的一成。因此中国 PC 产业具有良好的发展前景。“十二五”末我国力争 PC 产能达到 1100kt 左右，届时国内的年需求量为 170 ~2000kt，本土化供应率达到 50% ~60%。

据相关统计显示，截至 2015 年底前新增 600kt 左右的 PC 产能。

近年来，下游企业对聚碳酸酯的需求旺盛，国内外市场依然被看好，聚碳酸酯仍将维持增长态势。

我国 2012 年对聚碳酸酯产品的年消费量大约1400kt，已占全球消费总量的 33% 左右，大大超过产量所占比例。

我国“十二五”期间，聚碳酸酯的表观需求量增速将维持在 10% ~15%，2015 年需求量将达到1800kt 左右，预计届时聚碳酸酯产能将达 1100kt，本土化供应率达到 50% ~55%。

第二章　2012 年 PBT/PET 树脂进口下降出口增长

聚对苯二甲酸丁二醇酯，英文名 polybutylece terephthalate(简称 PBT)，PBT 为乳白色半透明到不透明、结晶型热塑性聚酯。具有高耐热性、韧性、耐疲劳性，自润滑、低摩擦系数，耐候性、吸水率低，仅为 0.1%，在潮湿环境中仍保持各种物性(包括电性能)，电绝缘性，但体积电阻、介电损耗大。耐热水、碱类、酸类、油类、但易受卤化烃侵蚀，耐水解性差，低温下可迅速结晶，成型性良好。缺点是缺口冲击强度低，成型收缩率大。

一、国内 PBT/PET 树脂生产

国内 PBT 工程塑料基础树脂生产厂不多，目前国内主要有 5 家 PBT 树脂生产企业：星新材料控股69% 的子公司南通星辰合成材料有限公司(15kt/a PTA 直接酯化法、6kt DMT 酯交换法)和仪化集团公司工程塑料厂(80kt/a，PTA 直接酯化法)，长春化工(常熟)年产 60kt PBT，江阴和时利工程塑胶科技发展有限公司 20kt/a，蓝山屯河化工有限公司(60kt/a，PTA 直接酯化法)。

而从事改性 PBT 品种生产的厂家和产能大大超过了基础树脂生产厂。

近年来我国 PBT 改性发展较快，主要由于双螺杆混炼挤出机的引进和国产双螺杆混炼挤出机的推

出，给改性 PBT 创造了有利条件。

2012 年国内主要 PBT 工程塑料改性厂有 丽碧复合塑料(深圳)有限公司、佛山明宝复合塑料有限公司、帝斯曼工程塑料(江苏)有限公司、GE 塑料上海有限公司、宝理塑料(上海)有限公司、宝理工程塑料贸易(上海)有限公司、长春化工(江苏)有限公司、上海怡康化工材料有限公司、吉祥塑料科技(苏州)有限公司、LG 化学(广州)工程塑料有限公司、长春化工(江苏)有限公司、丽碧复合塑料(深圳)有限公司、新疆蓝山屯河聚酯有限公司、江阴和时利工程塑胶科技发展有限公司、广州金发科技股份有限公司、佛山明宝复合塑料有限公司、GE 塑料上海有限公司、温州市立邦塑粉有限公司、山阳稻田复合塑料(东莞)有限公司、南亚塑胶工业(惠州)有限公司、沙伯基础创新塑料(中国)有限公司、新光工业(杭州)有限公司、帝斯曼工程塑料(江苏)有限公司、南通中蓝工程塑胶有限公司、吉祥塑料科技(苏州)有限公司、上海金发科技发展有限公司、日超工程塑料(深圳)有限公司、LG 化学(广州)工程塑料有限公司、上海大赛璐塑料工业有限公司、舒尔曼塑料(东莞)有限公司、深圳市科聚新材料有限公司等，从沿海到内地、从国有企业、合资企业发展到乡镇企业，以外商独资、合资和私企为主。

PBT 由于生产技术问题以及市场开发等众多因素影响，中国 PBT 开工率还很低，详见表 12。

表 12 2007～2012 年中国近年 PBT 树脂产量统计

项 目	2007	2008	2009	2010	2011	2012
生产能力/t	120000	170000	220000	242000	241000	241000
产量/t	56000	61500	95200	113000	136000	158000
开工率/%	46.67	36.18	43.27	43.13	56.43	65.56

从上表可看出，由于众多原因，我国 PBT 树脂产量虽然在逐年上升，但开工率仍在 70% 以下。(表中数据为业内人士估测，仅供参考)

PBT 树脂在国内的年需求量大约在 20 至 22 万吨，仪征化纤年产 6 万吨 PBT 树脂工厂的投产进一步刺激国内树脂市场供大于求的局面，各生产厂商之间的成本的竞争和压力也将更大。

国内聚酯产能约 1900 万吨，实际产量在 1300 万吨上下，用于工程塑料仅 1% 左右。

二、国内聚对苯二甲酸丁二酯(PBT)出口生产省市分布分析

2011 年聚对苯二甲酸丁二酯出口省市有 16 家，比上年 15 家出口省市增加 1 个出口省市，2012 年聚对苯二甲酸丁二酯前五位出口省市出口量占总出口量的 92.761%(表 13)。

表 13 2012 年初级形状的聚对苯二甲酸丁二酯五大出口省市统计

排 序	出口省市	出口金额/美元	出口数量/kg	占出口数量%
1	江苏省	99262092.00	43498946	49.807
2	广东省	55684224.00	18013353	20.626
3	福建省	22012507.00	8642214	9.896
4	上海市	22675564.00	6077704	6.959
5	新疆维吾尔自治区	10131821.00	4779950	5.473
出口总计		226122795.00	87334351	100.00

三、2012 年聚对苯二甲酸丁二酯(PBT)海关进出口同步下降

2012 年聚对苯二甲酸丁二酯(PBT)进口量，比 2011 年进口数量下降 8.36%；

2012 年聚对苯二甲酸丁二酯(PBT)出口量，比 2011 年出口数量下降 6.53%；

2008～2012 年间聚对苯二甲酸丁二酯(PBT)进口量年均增长率为下降 1.02%；

2008～2012 年间聚对苯二甲酸丁二酯(PBT)出口量年均增长率为 19.30%；

2008～2012 年间聚对苯二甲酸丁二酯(PBT)出口年均增长率大于进口年均增长率。

详见统计表14。

表14　2008～2012年聚对苯二甲酸丁二酯（PBT）进出口统计

产品	2008	2009	2010	2011	2012
进口/10^4t	14.73	12.72	16.32	15.43	14.14
出口/10^4t	4.31	5.71	8.18	9.34	8.73
净进口，/10^4t	10.42	7.01	8.17	6.09	5.41
年增长/%	-18.59	-32.26	16.55	-25.46	-11.17

海关统计从2007年起将聚对苯二甲酸丁二酯（PBT）从“初级形状的其他聚酯”代码分离出来独立。

PBT树脂需求的扩大带动了国内PBT树脂生产规模的不断扩大，同时也推动PBT树脂进口量的不断上升。尽管国内PBT树脂生产能力受市场需求拉动逐年增长，但是仍低于国内市场需求的增长；国内PBT树脂产业产量和销售量总体上呈增长趋势，但是增长速度远低于中国大陆市场需求的增长速度。

1. PBT树脂2012年进口下降

从海关统计中可看出，PBT树脂2012年进口地有40个，比上年38个进口地增加2个进口地。

主要进口地为中国台湾省，进口数量50606337kg，占总进口数量的35.777%，比上年进口量减少6.66%；

其次为马来西亚，进口数量27032994kg，占总进口数量的19.112%，比上年进口量减少8.80%；

日本进口数量19701079kg，占总进口数量的13.928%，比上年进口量减少11.04%；

中国进口数量19417512kg，占总进口数量的13.728%，比上年进口数量减少10.88%；

韩国进口数量10499203kg，占总进口数量的7.423%，比上年进口数量增加18.61%。

五原产进口地进口数量占PBT树脂2012年总进口数量的89.967%，比上年增加1.417%（表15）。

表15　2012年初级形状的聚对苯二甲酸丁二酯五大进口国家/地区统计

排　序	原产进口地	进口金额/美元	进口数量/kg	占比例/%
1	中国台湾省	143173709.00	50606337	35.777
2	马来西亚	78298157.00	27032994	19.112
3	日本	90176951.00	19701079	13.928
4	中国	64098469.00	19417512	13.728
5	韩国	41108738.00	10499203	7.423
进口总计		485204277.00	141448438	100.00

2. PBT树脂2012年出口下降

从海关统计中可看出，PBT树脂2012年出口地有54个，比上年57个出口地减少3个出口地。

主要出口地为韩国出口数量23943196kg，占总出口数量的27.416%，比上年出口量减少9.89%；

其次为中国中国香港出口数量22150083kg，占总出口数量的25.362%，比上年出口量下降12.39%；

印度出口数量7251237kg，占总出口数量的8.303%，比上年出口量增加17.20%；

日本出口数量5103912kg，占总出口数量的5.844%，比上年出口量下降28.60%。

中国台湾省出口数量5103912kg，占总出口数量的5.202%，比上年出口量增加135.70%。

五出口地出口数量占PBT树脂2012年总出口数量的72.127%，比上年下降3.313%（表16）。

表16　2012年初级形状的聚对苯二甲酸丁二酯五大出口国家/地区统计

排　序	出口目的地	出口金额/美元	出口数量/kg	占比例/%
1	韩国	52435010.00	23943196	27.416
2	中国中国香港	68841403.00	22150083	25.362
3	印度	16408621.00	7251237	8.303
4	日本	15184026.00	5103912	5.844
5	中国台湾省	9789748.00	4542966	5.202
出口总计		226122795.00	87334351	100.00

四、聚对苯二甲酸丁二酯进口消费省市集中于东部沿海地区

从海关资料来看，2012 年 PBT 树脂进口消费省市有 16 个，比上年 18 个进口消费省市减少 2 个进口消费省市，2012 年 PBT 树脂前五位进口消费省市进口量占总进口量的 90.569%，比上年进口量减少 1.011%。

2012 年 PBT 树脂主要进口流向为广东省，进口数量 68030506kg，占总进口数量的 48.096%；

其次为上海市，进口数量 34665164kg，占总进口数量的 24.507%，比上年进口量增加 5.56%；

江苏省，进口数量 15401294kg，占总进口数量的 10.888%，比上年进口量减少 4.73%；

福建省，进口数量 5094788kg，占总进口数量的 3.602%，比上年进口量减少 48.49%；

山东省，进口数量 4916713kg，占总进口数量的 3.476%，比上年进口量减少 1.38%(表 17)。

表 17　2012 年初级形状的聚对苯二甲酸丁二酯五大进口省市统计

排　序	进口省市	进口金额/美元	进口数量/kg	占比例/%
1	广东省	217276693.00	68030506	48.096
2	上海市	112496976.00	34665164	24.507
3	江苏省	68130217.00	15401294	10.888
4	福建省	14867479.00	5094788	3.602
5	山东省	18965041.00	4916713	3.476
进口总计		485204277.00	141448438	100.00

五、聚对苯二甲酸丁二酯(PBT)出口商以外资企业为主

从海关资料来看，2012 年聚对苯二甲酸丁二酯(PBT)出口商有 198 家，比上年 202 家出口商减少 4 个出口商，2012 年聚对苯二甲酸丁二酯(PBT)前十位出口商出口量占总出口量的 76.753%，比上年增加 2.723%，全部为生产企业。

2012 年聚对苯二甲酸丁二酯(PBT)三十八大出口商中有二十九家为生产企业，仅有南通星辰合成材料有限公司和江阴和时利工程塑胶科技发展有限公司及南通中蓝工程塑胶有限公司三家是 PBT 树脂原料生产厂，其余二十六家均为 PBT 改性(即 PBT 合金)，食品包装和粉末涂料生产企业，三十五家生产企业合计出口量占总出口量的 92.051%。

2012 年聚对苯二甲酸丁二酯(PBT)三十八大出口商中有九家为贸易商，合计出口量占总出口量的 3.385%。

2012 年初级形状的其他聚酯二十九大出口生产企业主要集中在江苏省、福建省、浙江省、广东省四省。

2012 年聚对苯二甲酸丁二酯(PBT)出口商以外资企业和私营企业为主(表 18)。

表 18　2012 年初级形状的聚对苯二甲酸丁二酯三十八大出口商统计

排　序	出口商	所属行业	出口数量/kg	占比例/%
1	长春化工(江苏)有限公司	PBT 改性	27150700	31.088
2	龙海莉丰成食品有限公司	食品包装	8590239	9.836
3	南通星辰合成材料有限公司	PBT 树脂原料	7816375	8.950
4	丽碧复合塑料(深圳)有限公司	PBT 改性	4954700	5.673
5	新疆蓝山屯河聚酯有限公司	PBT 改性	4783950	5.478
6	江阴和时利工程塑胶科技发展有限公司	PBT 树脂原料	3439328	3.938
7	广州金发科技股份有限公司	PBT 改性	2865273	3.281
8	拜耳无锡皮革化工有限公司	皮革化工	2661219	3.047
9	佛山明宝复合塑料有限公司	PBT 改性	2466900	2.825
10	GE 塑料上海有限公司	PBT 改性	2303372	2.637
11	温州市立邦塑粉有限公司	粉末涂料	2079858	2.381
12	山阳稻田复合塑料(东莞)有限公司	PBT 改性	2069486	2.370

续表

排 序	出口商	所属行业	出口数量/kg	占比例/%
13	中国北方车辆公司	粉末涂料	1500000	1.718
14	杜邦贸易(上海)有限公司	贸易商	1391869	1.594
15	南亚塑胶工业(惠州)有限公司	PBT 改性	1344525	1.540
16	沙伯基础创新塑料(中国)有限公司	PBT 改性	966600	1.107
17	新光工业(杭州)有限公司	PBT 改性	788525	0.903
18	浙江鑫富生化股份有限公司	生物化学	556150	0.637
19	帝斯曼工程塑料(江苏)有限公司	PBT 改性	544720	0.624
20	巴斯夫染料化工有限公司	染料化工	510500	0.585
21	南通中蓝工程塑胶有限公司	PBT 改性	486150	0.557
22	吉祥塑料科技(苏州)有限公司	PBT 改性	459350	0.526
23	上海金发科技发展有限公司	PBT 改性	442250	0.506
24	三运物流(上海)有限公司	贸易商	422075	0.483
25	日超工程塑料(深圳)有限公司	PBT 改性	348486	0.399
26	LG 化学(广州)工程塑料有限公司	PBT 改性	315150	0.361
27	上海大赛璐塑料工业有限公司	PBT 改性	285600	0.327
28	深圳能健恒商贸发展有限公司	贸易商	274225	0.314
29	舒尔曼塑料(东莞)有限公司	PBT 改性	202150	0.231
30	深圳市科聚新材料有限公司	PBT 改性	158000	0.181
31	稻 田工贸(大连保税区)有限公司	贸易商	153975	0.176
32	温州华特热熔胶有限公司	胶粘剂工业	151470	0.173
33	广州保畅国际物流有限公司	贸易商	150445	0.172
34	老虎粉末涂料制造(太仓)有限公司	粉末涂料	150082	0.172
35	东丽商事(上海)有限公司	贸易商	147575	0.169
36	上海机械国际贸易有限公司	贸易商	140000	0.160
37	新兴物流(深圳)有限公司	贸易商	138875	0.159
38	深圳福保赛格实业有限公司	贸易商	138400	0.158
总计			87334351	95.436%

六、聚对苯二甲酸丁二酯生产使用企业以改性PBT为主

PBT(增强、改性 PBT)主要用于汽车、电子电器、工业机械和聚合物合金、特混工业。如作为汽车中的分配器、车档部件、点火器线圈骨架、绝缘盖、排气系统零部件、摩托车点火器、电子电器工业中如电视机的偏转线圈，显象管和电位器支架，伴音输出变压器骨架，适配器骨架，开关接插件、电风扇、电冰箱、洗衣机电机端盖、轴套。

另外还有运输机械零件，缝纫机和纺织机械零件、钟表外壳、镜筒、电熨斗罩、水银灯罩、烘烤炉部件、电动工具零件、屏蔽套等。

2012 年聚对苯二甲酸丁二酯进口商共计有 1576 家，比上年 1585 家进口商减少 9 个进口商，进口额最高的十大进口商进口数量占总进口数量的 26.157%，比上年减少 1.083%。

十大进口商中有八家为生产使用企业，占总进口数量的 21.159%。

2012 年聚对苯二甲酸丁二酯五十八大进口商中有三十三家为生产使用企业，主要集中在广东省、上海市、江苏省三省市，三十三家生产使用企业合计进口量占 2012 年总进口量的 34.744%。

五十八大进口商中有二十五家为贸易商合计进口量占 2012 年总进口量的 19.167%。

五十八大进口商中有三十四家为生产使用企业分别属改性 PBT、电子工业、塑胶制品、包装工业、汽车部件、家用电器、五金制品行业，以改性 PBT 为主(表 19)。

表 19　2012 年初级形状的聚对苯二甲酸丁二酯五十八大进口商统计

排　序	进口商	所属行业	进口数量/kg	占比例/%
1	丽碧复合塑料(深圳)有限公司	改性 PBT	4941000	3.493
2	巴斯夫染料化工有限公司	染料化工	4690119	3.316
3	杜邦贸易(上海)有限公司	贸易商	4321075	3.055
4	佛山明宝复合塑料有限公司	改性 PBT	3970320	2.807
5	帝斯曼工程塑料(江苏)有限公司	改性 PBT	3884185	2.746
6	威海新凯帝电子有限公司	电子工业	3588518	2.537
7	GE 塑料上海有限公司	改性 PBT	3098890	2.191
8	宝理塑料贸易(上海)有限公司	改性 PBT	3036517	2.147
9	上海高信国际物流有限公司	贸易商	2748490	1.943
10	台达电子(东莞)有限公司	电子工业	2718750	1.922
11	中海物流(深圳)有限公司	贸易商	2681650	1.896
12	龙海莉丰成食品有限公司	包装工业	2577425	1.822
13	深圳市宝安外经发展有限公司	贸易商	2540272	1.796
14	惠州住润汽车部品有限公司	汽车部件	2521669	1.783
15	宝理工程塑料贸易(上海)有限公司	改性 PBT	2366315	1.673
16	上海特维碧贸易有限公司	贸易商	2292750	1.621
17	长春化工(江苏)有限公司	改性 PBT	1996000	1.411
18	赛拉尼斯(上海)国际贸易有限公司	贸易商	1790798	1.266
19	东莞市对外加工装配服务公司	贸易商	1618680	1.144
20	深圳能源物流有限公司	贸易商	1547404	1.094
21	深圳市龙岗区对外经济发展有限公司	贸易商	781096	0.552
22	上海怡康化工材料有限公司	粉末涂料	769245	0.544
23	佛山市建准电子有限公司	电子工业	713375	0.504
24	东莞辰达电器有限公司	家用电器	708563	0.501
25	北京市塑化贸易有限公司	贸易商	708525	0.501
26	吉祥塑料科技(苏州)有限公司	改性 PBT	614375	0.434
27	东莞市东盈进出口有限公司	贸易商	603121	0.426
28	深圳市塑电通科技有限公司	五金制品	591300	0.418
29	深圳市路迪斯达传输设备有限公司	装备工业	586000	0.414
30	东莞市创汇塑胶五金制品有限公司	五金制品	564650	0.399
31	深圳正佳物流有限公司	贸易商	517048	0.366
32	深圳仁锐实业有限公司	贸易商	462814	0.327
33	上海帛众化工国际贸易有限公司	贸易商	453225	0.320
34	东莞建通电子五金有限公司	电子工业	450895	0.319
35	珠海珍迎机电有限公司	五金制品	439567	0.311

续表

排 序	进口商	所属行业	进口数量/kg	占比例/%
36	东莞骏伟塑胶五金有限公司	塑胶制品	429711	0.304
37	浙江杭州出口加工区国际物流有限公司	贸易商	422400	0.299
38	上海庆华物流有限公司	贸易商	414925	0.293
39	东丽合成纤维(南通)有限公司	合成纤维	408000	0.288
40	杭州裕安贸易有限公司	贸易商	394975	0.279
41	南宁富宁精密电子有限公司	电子工业	373150	0.264
42	瀚兴国际贸易(上海)有限公司	贸易商	372000	0.263
43	厦门台松精密电子有限公司	电子工业	371675	0.263
44	中国出版对外贸易总公司	贸易商	369880	0.261
45	LG 化学(广州)工程塑料有限公司	改性 PBT	363650	0.257
46	文登珍迎机电有限公司	五金制品	360700	0.255
47	宁波晶圆贸易有限公司	贸易商	359200	0.254
48	强竣电子科技(深圳)有限公司	电子工业	352000	0.249
49	大连泰达阿尔卑斯物流有限公司	贸易商	350726	0.248
50	上海古产国际贸易有限公司	贸易商	350300	0.248
51	上海新长征国际贸易有限公司	贸易商	344875	0.244
52	创乐电子实业(惠州)有限公司	电子工业	343763	0.243
53	广州长濑贸易有限公司	贸易商	341020	0.241
54	东莞利峰塑胶制品有限公司	塑胶制品	340960	0.241
55	深圳巴鑫储运贸易有限公司	贸易商	325496	0.230
56	中江湧德电子有限公司	电子工业	324875	0.230
57	凯德机械制品(东莞)有限公司	装备工业	323400	0.229
58	上海合辉电子元件有限公司	电子工业	320900	0.229
进口总计			141448438	53.911%

七、价格趋势

2012 年初大宗商品市场仍笼罩在欧债危机、国内资金紧张等利空因素的阴霾当中，本已利润微薄的下游中小企业则普遍面临年底巨大的还贷压力。

尽管目前国家已出现相关货币政策，适时适度进行预调微调，巩固好宏观调控的成果，但继续坚持稳健的货币政策基调并未改变，后期下游中小企业生存压力过大仍为对我国 PBT 行业发展的一大挑战。

2012 年中国塑料城月均价走势来分析，PBT2012 年月均价在平盘，无大波动。

八、进出口贸易方式分析

从海关统计中可看出，2012 年初级形状的聚对苯二甲酸丁二酯进口贸易方式主要为进料加工贸易(占进口量 42.683%)，其次为一般贸易(占进口量 22.741%)，保税区仓储转口货物(占进口量 22.436%)，来料加工装配贸易(占进口量 9.653%)，保税仓库进出境货物(占进口量 2.458%)，其他(占进口量 0.025%)，外商投资企业作为投资进口的设备、物品(占进口量 0.003%)，合计为总进口量的 100.00%(表 20)。

表 20　2012 年初级形状的聚对苯二甲酸丁二酯进口交易类型统计

进口交易类型	进口金额 /美元	进口数量/kg	占比例/%
进料加工贸易	211652464.00	60375101	42.683
一般贸易	113935274.00	32166864	22.741
保税区仓储转口货物	108388450.00	31735809	22.436
来料加工装配贸易	40313420.00	13654476	9.653
保税仓库进出境货物	10646368.00	3476190	2.458
其他	254945.00	35998	0.025
外商投资企业作为投资进口的设备、物品	13356.00	4000	0.003
总计	485204277.00	141448438	100.00

从海关统计中可看出，2011 年初级形状的聚对苯二甲酸丁二酯出口贸易方式主要为进料加工贸易(占出口量 74.343%)，其次为一般贸易(占出口量 17.503%)，保税区仓储转口货物(占出口量 4.806%)，来料加工装配贸易(占出口量 3.071%)，保税仓库进出境货物(占出口量 0.220%)，边境小额贸易(占出口量 0.057%)，其他(占出口量 0.001%)，合计为总出口量的 100.00%(表 21)。

表 21　2012 年初级形状的聚对苯二甲酸丁二酯出口交易类型统计

出口交易类型	出口金额/美元	出口数量/kg	占比例/%
进料加工贸易	165690680.00	64926744	74.343
一般贸易	38949838.00	15285967	17.503
保税区仓储转口货物	14322903.00	4197039	4.806
来料加工装配贸易	6238987.00	2681811	3.071
保税仓库进出境货物	773570.00	191820	0.220
边境小额贸易	139876.00	50100	0.057
其他	6941.00	870	0.001
出口总计	226122795.00	87334351	100.00

九、发展趋势

巴斯夫 2011 年 1 月 12 日在上海宣布，其浦东基地的工程塑料改性装置产能将在现有年 45kt 基础上新增 65kt。该扩建项目一期工程增产 39kt，预计 2013 年完工；二期工程增产 26kt，计划于 2015 年完成。该扩建项目耗资逾千万欧元，可提供 50 多个新岗位。届时，巴斯夫在华聚酰胺和聚对苯二甲酸丁二醇酯(PBT)工程塑料产能将达 110kt，占巴斯夫亚洲总产能的 50% 以上。

朗盛与杜邦计划将其聚对苯二甲酸丁二醇酯(PBT)的合资企业产能扩大一倍。两家公司将向该生产线追加投资 1000 万欧元，扩建工程计划 2012 年投产。这一举措同样是对全球 PBT 合成材料需求激增所做的反应。

河南省义煤集团开祥化工有限公司年产 100kt 级聚对苯二甲酸丁二醇酯(PBT)装置上周实现机械竣工，2013 年 4 月进入投料试车阶段。

PBT 项目是该公司依托甲醇、1，4－丁二醇两个主厂区公用工程及辅助设施，进一步延伸产业链条的产品升级项目，PBT 是 1，4－丁二醇的下游产品。该项目由该公司和扬州普利特共同研发，南京扬子石化研究院设计，采用世界先进的 PTA 直接酯化、连续缩聚工艺。该项目分两期建设，工程概算投资 4.75 亿元。

一期工程于 2012 年 8 月开工。目前，该公司正积极进行整个装置的设备联调联试工作，有望在 4 月底打通全流程。

第三章　2012 年尼龙树脂进出口同步大幅下降

尼龙无论在产量和产能上或者在消费数量上，都位居五大工程塑料之首，其主要有两种不同的类型——尼龙 6 和尼龙 66。

尼龙 6 切片主要用于生产纤维与工程塑料产品，全球来看，其中约 55% 用于生产各种民用和工业用纤维，约 45% 用于汽车、电子电气、铁路和包装材料等领域。

分区域看，欧美地区以生产工程塑料和薄膜为主，而包括中国在内的亚太地区则以生产纤维为主。随着国内汽车产量的不断提高，工程塑料和膜用领域正在成为尼龙6切片的主要需求增长点。

未来随着人们生活水平的继续提高、尼龙应用领域的扩大以及更有针对性措施的推广，尼龙产品的需求量还会进一步上升，中国尼龙行业将迎来新增长。

一、2012年尼龙生产概况

自2009年商务部对部分进口尼龙6切片征收反倾销保证金起，国内新增及扩建尼龙6产能不断上升。2012年，我国尼龙6切片产能约为1680kt。预计到2013年底，国内产能或将突破1900kt。无论是原料供应还是下游需求，国内尼龙6行业未来发展都蕴藏新的动力。

从上游来看，长期制约中国尼龙6行业发展的原料己内酰胺供应瓶颈未来几年将逐步得到缓解。甚至到2015年以后，中国可能由己内酰胺净进口国变为净出口国。尽管受生产技术、原料等因素制约，己内酰胺国产化进程未必会像想象中那么顺利，较高的进口依存度还将维持一段时间，但对于尼龙行业的利好是明显的。

由于尼龙切片和己内酰胺的生产有较大重合性，国际上己内酰胺供应商也基本是尼龙6切片的主要生产商。而在国内，除了巴陵石化、石家庄化纤和南京帝斯曼等仅有的几家外，其余的都是非一体化的生产商。这一局面在未来有望得到改善，如长乐力恒，不仅大力扩大尼龙生产，还决定向上游延伸发展。

巴陵石化己内酰胺事业部以年产55kt"尼龙6"切片规模，居中南地区同类产品之首。2012年，该部累计销售51.6kt，产销率为102%，销售网络覆盖国内30多个地区。

2012年巴陵石化己内酰胺事业部共有3套聚合装置，其中两套装置于1996年建成后陆续投产，产量质量连年攀升。

2011年7月，巴陵石化在该事业部动工新建一套年产15kt的聚合切片装置，利用原料自供和自有技术的优势，全部采用国产化设备，促进降低成本，也改变了以往产品品种调整不便的情形。

我国长碳链尼龙生产已成功跃上万吨规模。

国产长碳链尼龙的问世，打破了进口产品一统天下的局面，对我国高性能工程塑料的发展具有重要的示范意义。

山东东辰工程塑料有限公司是国内首家专门从事长碳链尼龙1212合成、改性开发及销售的企业，同时合成尼龙612、610、1010。现年生产长碳链树脂2000t，改性尼龙工程塑料3000t及PP、PE、PVC、ABS改性产品8000t。

在全国独家开发的尼龙1212、1313，填补国内空白，其性能指标经国家权威机构鉴定，达到国外同类产品标准，部分性能超过进口尼龙11、12，为国家重点推广产品。

无锡市嘉禾橡塑有限公司是国内首家专门从事长碳链尼龙1212合成、改性开发及销售的企业，同时合成尼龙612、610、1010。

现年生产长碳链树脂2000t，改性尼龙工程塑料3000t及PP、PE、PVC、ABS改性产品8000t。

自2009年推出工程塑料业务以来，英威达已利用其改性工厂网络来支持这项业务的运营。使用第三方改性工厂可加快英威达产品的上市，并帮助其业务在短时间内快速壮大。在北美、南美、欧洲、亚洲市场成功发展相关业务后，英威达目前正计划第二阶段的发展：投资建立自有的改性工厂。而中国快速增长的尼龙市场，已成为其优先的投资对象。

英威达是全球最大己二腈生产及供应商，占全球己二腈产能约60%的份额。虽然英威达将部分己二腈用于自有的聚酰胺6，6聚合物生产，但大部分出售给外部客户。

生产己二腈所用的主要原料是丁二烯，但该材料的市场价格持续大幅波动。过去两三年，全球丁二烯市场出现了前所未见的价格波动。这种情况在亚洲尤其是中国更为明显。为此，英威达决定实现原材料的本土化生产。

把最先进工厂建在中国，目前，英威达正在上海化学工业区建设一座聚酰胺6，6中间体和聚合物生产厂(表22)。

表22 中国PA树脂改性装置规模和产量统计

年份	PA混炼装置规模/kt	改性PA产量/kt	市场需求量/kt
2002	150	120	180
2003	180	140	220
2004	220	160	280
2005	250	180	350
2006	300	220	400
2007	400	290	480
2008	450	320	515

续表

年份	PA 混炼装置规模/kt	改性 PA 产量/kt	市场需求量/kt
2009	480	330	530
2010	620	450	610
2011	680	510	650
2012	800	550	720

注：由于 PA 改性混炼装置同时改性混炼 PP、PC、ABS、PBT 等产品，很难确切分割规模，改性混炼 PA 数据仅为业内人士估算。上表数据包括 PA/PP、PA/PC，PA/ABS 等产品产量。

2012 年 8 月 21 日，中国平煤神马集团年产 250kt 己二酸及 200kt 己内酰胺项目开工仪式在平顶山市化工产业集聚区举行。这标志着我国建设世界领先的尼龙化工生产基地拉开序幕，将增强我国在该产业中的竞争力和话语权。平煤神马集团是亚洲最大、世界第四的尼龙化工产品生产基地。作为全球尼龙 66 系列产品供应商，目前尼龙 66 系列产品年生产能力达 300kt，己二酸年生产能力 200kt，产品远销 30 多个国家和地区，与 40 多家世界 500 强企业及跨国集团建立了战略合作关系。

国内尼龙工程塑料基础树脂生产厂不多，而从事改性尼龙品种生产的厂家和产能大大超过了基础树脂生产厂。

近年来我国尼龙改性发展较快，主要由于双螺杆混炼挤出机的引进和国产双螺杆混炼挤出机的推出，给改性尼龙创造了有利条件。

2012 年国内主要尼龙工程塑料改性厂有帝斯曼工程塑料(江苏)有限公司，艾曼斯(苏州)工程塑料有限公司，苏威(上海)有限公司，江苏阜宁伊士曼化工有限公司，山东汇金化工有限公司，日超工程塑料(深圳)有限公司，广州金发科技股份有限公司，福洛塑胶(昆山)有限公司，江苏三木集团有限公司，南京聚隆科技股份有限公司，罗地亚(上海)工程塑料有限公司，普立万聚合体(深圳)有限公司，南通兴鑫化工有限公司，江西省宜春远大化工有限公司，丽碧复合塑料(深圳)有限公司，杭州色彩化工有限公司，深圳市泰塑塑化材料科技有限公司，山东东辰工程塑料有限公司，深圳市科聚新材料有限公司，苏州翰普高分子材料有限公司，启东博文工程塑料有限公司，平顶山神马工程塑料有限责任公司，丽碧复合塑料(深圳)有限公司，宁波敏特尼龙工业有限公司，天津碧美特工程塑料有限公司，屹立(苏州)工程塑料科技有限公司，上海耐特复合材料制品有限公司，华峰集团有限公司，深圳市泰塑塑化材料科技有限公司，旭化成(苏州)复合塑料有限公司，深圳市科聚新材料有限公司，沙伯基础创新塑料(中国)有限公司，福洛塑胶(昆山)有限公司，星际塑料(深圳)有限公司，舒尔曼塑料(东莞)有限公司，古道尔工程塑胶(深圳)有限公司，东莞市朗普工程塑料科技有限公司，中山市华业塑料有限公司，安特普工程塑料(苏州)有限公司，兰蒂奇工程塑料(苏州)有限公司，晋伦塑料科技(东莞)有限公司等。

从沿海到内地、从国有企业、合资企业发展到乡镇企业，以外商独资、合资和私企为主。

二、2012 年 PA 树脂出口生产省市分布分析

1. 2012 年其他初级形状的聚酰胺出口上升

其他初级形状的聚酰胺 2012 年出口省市有 18 家，比上年 16 家增加 2 家出口省市，出口 37815294kg，同比上升 22.14%。

其他初级形状的聚酰胺 2012 年出口生产企业仍主要集中在江苏省出口数量 13482251kg，占总出口数量的 35.653%，比上年出口数量增加 11.64%；

其次为广东省，出口数量 10867157kg，占总出口数量的 28.737%，比上年出口数量减少 38.92%；

上海市，出口数量 10117502kg，占总出口数量的 26.755%，比上年出口数量增加 16.74%；

山东省出口数量 1661735kgkg，占总出口数量的 4.394%，比上年出口数量增加 117.29%；

浙江省出口数量 552054kg，占总出口数量的 1.460%，比上年出口数量减少 25.93%；

五省市出口数量占其他初级形状的聚酰胺 2012 年总出口数量的 97.000%，比上年增加 0.27%（表 23）。

表 23　2012 年其他初级形状的聚酰胺五大出口省市统计

排　序	出口省市	出口金额/美元	出口数量/kg	占比例/%
1	江苏省	96392078.00	13482251	35.653
2	广东省	52727469.00	10867157	28.737
3	上海市	75442410.00	10117502	26.755
4	山东省	4186825.00	1661735	4.394
5	浙江省	1438387.00	552054	1.460
出口总计		234021015.00	37815294	100.00

2. 聚酰胺-6，6切片出口上升

聚酰胺-6，6切片2012年出口省市有14家，与上年15家减少1家出口省市，出口49949853kg，同比上升11.30%。

聚酰胺-6，6切片2012年出口生产企业主要集中在广东省，出口数量20050973kg，占总出口数量的40.142%，比上年出口数量增加34.33%；

其次为上海市出口数量10363107kg，占总出口数量的20.747%，比上年出口数量增加9.34%；

河南省，出口数量9802235kg，占总出口数量的19.624%，比上年增加出口数量1.09%；

江苏省出口数量6930122kg，占总出口数量的13.874%，比上年出口数量减少17.11%；

浙江省出口数量1736520kg，占总出口数量的3.477%，比上年出口数量增加9.62%。

五省市出口数量占聚酰胺-6，6切片2012年总出口数量的97.864%，比上年减少0.283%(表24)。

表24 2012年聚酰胺-6，6切片五大出口省市统计

排 序	出口省市	出口金额/美元	出口数量/kg	占比例/%
1	广东省	76509796.00	20050973	40.142
2	上海市	40569499.00	10363107	20.747
3	河南省	29919792.00	9802235	19.624
4	江苏省	26515828.00	6930122	13.874
5	浙江省	3838928.00	1736520	3.477
出口总计		182294738.00	49949853	100.00

3. 2012年聚酰胺-6、聚酰胺-11、聚酰胺-12、聚酰胺-6，9等切片出口下降

初级形状的聚酰胺-6等切片2012年出口省市有13家，比上年14家出口省市减少1家出口省市，出口5275831kg，同比增加0.33%。

初级形状的聚酰胺-6切片等2012年出口生产企业主要集中在江苏省，出口数量2728351kg，占总出口数量的51.714%，比上年出口数量增加28.58%；

其次为山东省出口数量1506908kg，占总出口数量的28.562%，比上年出口数量增加130.10%；

上海市，出口数量688088kg，占总出口数量的13.042%，比上年出口数量减少28.06%；

广东省出口数量302443kg，占总出口数量的5.733%，比上年出口数量减少67.89%；

河南省出口数量20000kg，占总出口数量的0.379%。

五省市出口数量占其他初级形状的聚酰胺-6等切片2012年总出口数量的99.431%%，比上年增加4.659%。

表25 2012年聚酰胺-6、-11、-12、-6，9、-6，10、-6，12聚酰胺切片五大出口省市统计

排 序	出口省市	出口金额/美元	出口数量/kg	占比例/%
1	江苏省	22217123.00	2728351	51.714
2	山东省	14353476.00	1506908	28.562
3	上海市	8383744.00	688088	13.042
4	广东省	1069104.00	302443	5.733
5	河南省	101300.00	20000	0.379
出口总计		46425665.00	5275831	100.00

三、2012年进口出口同下降

2012年PA总进口量回落到34万吨下，比2011年总进口量减少1.55%。

2012年PA总出口量回落到10万吨，比2011年总进口量减少6.84%。

2007~2012年间PA年总进口年均下降0.49%。

2007~2012年间PA年总净进口年均下降1.21%(表26)。

表 26　2006～2011 年国内 PA 树脂进出口统计

项　目		2007	2008	2009	2010	2011	2012
聚酰胺－6，6 切片		205513	223996	174111	224679	230732	239557
	出口	26763	25096	29348	43491	44877	49950
PA－6、聚酰胺－11、聚酰胺－6，12 聚酰胺－12、聚酰胺－6，10 等切片	进口	491495	551207	681699	580439	19304	11646
	出口	41643	72154	40533	45451	5259	5276
其他形状聚酰胺－6，6、聚酰胺－11、聚酰胺－12、聚酰胺－6、聚酰胺－6，10 等	进口	23943	21523	18492	18227	17058	13791
	出口	7613	5875	4293	3316	3073	3695
其他初级状态的聚酰胺	进口	65974	57638	47690	72332	74408	71198
	出口	26763	24150	21840	33383	41528	37815
聚酰胺总进口量/t		786925	854364	921992	895677	341502	336192
聚酰胺总出口量/t		102782	127275	96013	125641	94737	96736
聚酰胺净进口量/t		684143	727086	825979	770036	246765	239456
年增长率/%		28.54	6.28	13.60	－6.77	－67.95	－2.96

聚酰胺－6、聚酰胺－11、聚酰胺－6，12、聚酰胺－12、聚酰胺－6，10 等切片 2011～2012 年进口大幅缩量，比 2010 年进口大跌 96.67%～65.17%；

主要因素有二个：一是国内产能过剩；二是这二产品市场主要是服装业，全球经济衰退造成服装出口大减。由此造成聚酰胺－6、聚酰胺－11、聚酰胺－6，12、聚酰胺－12、聚酰胺－6，10 等切片聚酰胺产品 2011～2012 年进口量大跌，由此造成聚酰胺 2011～2012 年总进口量大跌。

1. 2012 年其他初级形状的聚酰胺进口增加出口减少

从海关统计中可看出，其他初级形状的聚酰胺 2012 年进口地有 36 个，比上年 38 个进口地减少 2 个进口地，进口 71197558kg，同比减少 4.31%。

主要进口地为中国，进口数量 13531613kg，占总进口数量的 19.006%，比上年进口数量减少 12.74%；

五原产进口地进口数量占其他初级形状的聚酰胺 2012 年总进口数量的 73.694%，比上年减少 1.828%(表 27)。

表 27　2012 年其他初级形状的聚酰胺五大进口国家/地区统计

排　序	原产进口地	进口金额/美元	进口数量/kg	占比例/%
1	中国	102672188.00	13531613	19.006
2	美国	74571515.00	12932293	18.164
3	日本	90237056.00	11110270	15.605
4	荷兰	62601934.00	8408230	11.810
5	韩国	25932036.00	6486089	9.110
进口总计		480139001.00	71197558	100.00

从海关统计中可看出，其他初级形状的聚酰胺 2012 年出口地有 66 个，与 2011 年 64 个出口地增加 2 个出口地，出口 37815294kg，同比减少 8.94%。

主要出口地为中国香港出口数量 13178031kg，占总出口数量的 34.848%，比上年出口数量减少 32.13%；

五原产出口地出口数量占其他初级形状的聚酰胺2012年总出口数量的71.791%，比上年减少9.272%（表28）。

表28 2012年其他初级形状的聚酰胺五大出口国家/地区统计

排　序	出口目的地	出口金额/美元	出口数量/kg	占比例/%
1	中国香港	87428275.00	13178031	34.848
2	日本	29088982.00	5156309	13.636
3	韩国	28853204.00	3826593	10.119
4	中国台湾省	17689787.00	3081271	8.148
5	印度	12825929.00	1905828	5.040
出口总计		234021015.00	37815294	100.00

2.2012年聚酰胺-6，6切片进口出口同步增长

从海关统计中可看出，聚酰胺-6，6切片2012年进口地有45个，比2011年42个进口地增加3个进口地，进口239557235kg，同比增长3.82%。

主要进口地为美国进口37956180kg，占总进口数量的15.844%，比上年进口数量减少11.12%；

五原产进口地进口数量占聚酰胺-6，6切片2012年总进口数量的59.826%，比上年减少3.424%（表29）。

表29 2011年聚酰胺-6，6切片五大进口国家/地区统计

排　序	原产进口地	进口金额/美元	进口数量/kg	占比例/%
1	美国	132370379.00	37956180	15.844
2	韩国	111692729.00	29148270	12.168
3	德国	115623362.00	29044656	12.124
4	日本	123498012.00	25174698	10.509
5	中国	99482390.00	21993040	9.181
进口总计		921283483.00	239557235	100.00

从海关统计中可看出，聚酰胺-6，6切片2012年出口地有45个，与2011年45个出口地持平，出口49949853kg，出口同比上升11.30%。

主要出口地为中国香港出口数量21484446kg，占总出口数量的43.012%，比上年出口数量减少0.94%；

五原产出口地出口数量占聚酰胺-6，6切片2011年总出口数量的88.464%，比上年减少1.567%（表30）。

表30 2012年聚酰胺-6，6切片五大出口国家/地区统计

排　序	出口目的地	出口金额/美元	出口数量/kg	占比例/%
1	中国香港	85580424.00	21484446	43.012
2	韩国	27078611.00	8009937	16.036
3	中国台湾省	19871076.00	6737335	13.488
4	日本	22173662.00	5847904	11.708
5	印度	6766603.00	2108104	4.220
出口总计		182294738.00	49949853	100.00

3.2012年其他初级形状的聚酰胺-6，6等进口下降出口上升

从海关统计中可看出，其他初级形状的聚酰胺-6，6等2012年进口地有41个，比2011年41个进口地增加1个进口地，进口13790855kg，同比进下降19.15%。

主要进口地为中国进口数量2893462kg，占总进口数量的20.981%，比上年进口数量减少11.30%；

五原产进口地进口数量占其他初级形状的聚酰胺－6，6等2011年总进口数量的66.989%，比上年进口数量减少1.744%(表31)。

表31　2012年其他初级形状的聚酰胺－6，6等五大进口国家/地区统计

排　序	原产进口地	进口金额/美元	进口数量/kg	占比例/%
1	中国	7617916.00	2893462	20.981
2	日本	17050999.00	1791969	12.994
3	美国	8638601.00	1769621	12.832
4	中国台湾省	6381825.00	1588311	11.517
5	泰国	3481428.00	1194988	8.665
进口总计		73706847.00	13790855	100.00

从海关统计中可看出，其他初级形状的聚酰胺－6，6等2012年出口地有43个，比上年41个出口地增加2个出口地，出口3695235kg，同比出口增加20.24%。

主要出口地为中国香港，出口数量1942922kg，占总出口数量的52.579%，比上年出口数量增加32.04%；

五出口地出口数量占其他初级形状的聚酰胺－6，6等2012年总出口数量的79.703%，比上年增加1.17%(表32)。

表32　2012年其他初级形状的聚酰胺－6，6等五大出口国家/地区统计

排　序	出口目的地	出口金额/美元	出口数量/kg	占比例/%
1	中国香港	7337183.00	1942922	52.579
2	印度尼西亚	1067444.00	315050	8.526
3	马来西亚	654967.00	290675	7.866
4	中国台湾省	611701.00	275407	7.453
5	墨西哥	335551.00	121175	3.279
出口总计		13314824.00	3695235	100.00

4.2012年聚酰胺－6、聚酰胺－11、聚酰胺－12、聚酰胺－6，9等切片进口下降出口增长

从海关统计中可看出，2012年聚酰胺－6、聚酰胺－11、聚酰胺－12、聚酰胺－6，9、聚酰胺－6，10、聚酰胺－6，12切片进口地有33个，比2011年27个进口地增加6个进口地，进口11645829kg，同比进口下降39.67%。

主要进口地为美国，进口数量2163486kg，占总进口数量的18.577%，比上年进口数量减少38.24%；

五原产进口地进口数量占2012年聚酰胺－6、聚酰胺－11、聚酰胺－12、聚酰胺－6，9、聚酰胺－6，10、聚酰胺－6，12切片总进口数量的70.513%，比上年进口增加9.845%。

表33　2012年聚酰胺－6、聚酰胺－11、聚酰胺－12、聚酰胺－6，9、聚酰胺－6，10、聚酰胺－6，12切片五大进口国家/地区统计

排　序	原产进口地	进口金额/美元	进口数量/kg	占比例/%
1	美国	21550614.00	2163486	18.577
2	日本	22284053.00	1960514	16.834
3	瑞士	21809719.00	1508809	12.956
4	德国	14052620.00	1303509	11.193
5	中国台湾省	4723890.00	1275884	10.956
进口总计		116388412.00	11645829	100.00

从海关统计中可看出，2012年聚酰胺－6、聚酰胺－11、聚酰胺－12、聚酰胺－6，9、聚酰胺－6，

10、聚酰胺-6，12切片出口地有40个，比上年48个出口地减少8个出口地，出口5275831kg，同比出口增长0.33%。

主要出口地为向美国，出口数量867668kg，占总出口数量的16.446%，比上年出口数量增加227.08%；

五原产出口地出口数量占2012年聚酰胺-6、聚酰胺-11、聚酰胺-12、聚酰胺-6，9、聚酰胺-6，10、聚酰胺-6，12切片总出口数量的60.890%,，比上年出口增加10.610%（表34）。

表34 2012年聚酰胺-6、聚酰胺-11、聚酰胺-12、聚酰胺-6，9、聚酰胺-6，10、聚酰胺-6，12切片五大出口国家/地区统计

排 序	出口目的地	出口金额/美元	出口数量/kg	占比例/%
1	美国	8729405.00	867668	16.446
2	印度	6781504.00	746778	14.155
3	比利时	5202930.00	741656	14.058
4	韩国	4048367.00	506787	9.606
5	日本	2033861.00	349544	6.625
出口总计		46425665.00	5275831	100.00

四、消费

随着我国汽车工业、电子电气工业的发展，PA工程塑料消费呈快速上升趋势。

2010年本体树脂和改性PA的实际消耗已超过800kt。

2012年本体树脂和改性PA的实际消耗已超过1000kt。

PA工程塑料消费2008～2012年年均增长达11.47%（表35）。

表35 国内PA非纤维产品（含改性PA）消费分配

用 途	2015		2012	
	需求量/(kt/a)	占比例/%	需求量/(kt/a)	占比例/%
电器电子产品	420.00	32.31	330.00	31.43
交通运输	335.00	25.77	250.00	23.81
机械工业	192.00	14.77	137.00	13.05
日用五金	98.00	7.45	76.00	7.24
尼龙薄膜	55.00	4.23	43.00	4.10
单丝、棕丝	38.00	2.92	31.00	2.95
尼龙粉末	41.00	3.15	35.00	3.33
其 他	121.00	9.31	148.00	14.10
合 计	1300.00	100.00	1050.00	100.00

1. 聚酰胺塑料进口消费地区流向分析

1.1. 其他初级形状的聚酰胺集中流向东部沿海地区

从海关资料来看，其他初级形状的聚酰胺2012年进口消费省市有21个，比上年19个进口消费省市增加2个进口消费省市。

主要进口流向为广东省，进口数量22918358kg，占总进口数量的32.190%，比上年进口数量减少17.13%；

上海市，进口数量20274046kg，占总进口数量的28.476%，比上年进口数量减少11.54%；

江苏省，进口数量19053374kg，占总进口数量的26.761%，比上年进口数量增加21.55%；

山东省，进口数量2804504kg，占总进口数量的3.939%，比上年进口数量增加43.07%；

福建省，进口数量1508175kg，占总进口数量的2.11%，比上年进口数量减少33.23%。

2011年其他初级形状的聚酰胺前五位进口消费省市进口量占总进口量的94.67%,，比上年进口减少1.187%（表36）。

表 36　2012 年其他初级形状的聚酰胺五大进口省市统计

排　序	进口省市	进口金额/美元	进口数量/kg	占比例/%
1	广东省	139797152.00	22918358	32.190
2	上海市	141396320.00	20274046	28.476
3	江苏省	130862405.00	19053374	26.761
4	山东省	25099541.00	2804504	3.939
5	福建省	13257778.00	1508175	2.118
合计		480139001.00	71197558	100.00

1.2. 聚酰胺 -6，6 切片集中流向东部沿海地区

从海关资料来看，聚酰胺 -6，6 切片 2012 年进口消费省市有 20 个，比上年 22 个进口消费省市减少 2 个进口消费省市。

主要进口流向为上海市，进口数量 90082122kg，占总进口数量的 37.604%，上年进口数量增加 10.32%；

其次为广东省，进口数量 84132050kg，占总进口数量的 35.120%，比上年进口数量增加 2.22%；

江苏省，进口数量 20577996kg，占总进口数量的 8.590%，上年进口数量增加 0.73%；

浙江省，进口数量 19737520kg，占总进口数量的 8.239%，比上年进口数量减少 17.29%；

北京市，进口数量 5177566kg，占总进口数量的 2.161%，比上年进口数量减少 14.57%。

2012 年聚酰胺 -6，6 切片前五位进口消费省市进口量占总进口量的 91.714%，比上年减少 0.166%（表 37）。

表 37　2012 年聚酰胺 -6，6 切片五大进口省市统计

排　序	进口省市	进口金额/美元	进口数量/kg	占比例/%
1	上海市	321421702.00	90082122	37.604
2	广东省	350773312.00	84132050	35.120
3	江苏省	76308304.00	20577996	8.590
4	浙江省	67506277.00	19737520	8.239
5	北京市	19791102.00	5177566	2.161
进口总计		921283483.00	239557235	100.00

1.3. 2011 年聚酰胺 -6、聚酰胺 -11、聚酰胺 -12、聚酰胺 -6，9、聚酰胺 -6，10、聚酰胺 -6，12 切片集中流向东部沿海地区

从海关资料来看，2012 年聚酰胺 -6、聚酰胺 -11、聚酰胺 -12、聚酰胺 -6，9、聚酰胺 -6，10、聚酰胺 -6，12 切片进口消费省市有 14 个，比上年 18 个进口消费省市减少 4 个进口消费省市。

主要进口流向为广东省，进口数量 3427991kg，占总进口数量的 29.435%，比上年进口数量下降 26.24%；

上海市，进口数量 2904522kg，占总进口数量的 24.940%，比上年进口数量下降 25.99%；

江苏省，进口数量 1354654kg，占总进口数量的 11.632%，比上年进口数量下降 56.19.%；

河北省，进口数量 1119275kg，占总进口数量的 9.611%，比上年进口数量下降 47.05%；

浙江省，进口数量 980355kg，占总进口数量的 8.418%，比上年进口数量下降 64.17%。

2012 年聚酰胺 -6、聚酰胺 -11、聚酰胺 -12、聚酰胺 -6，9、聚酰胺 -6，10、聚酰胺 -6，12 切片前五位进口消费省市进口量占总进口量的 84.037%，比上年下降 1.515%（表 38）。

表 38　2011 年聚酰胺 -6、聚酰胺 -11、聚酰胺 -12、聚酰胺 -6，9、聚酰胺 -6，10、聚酰胺 -6，12 切片五大进口省市统计

排　序	进口省市	进口金额/美元	进口数量/kg	占比例/%
1	广东省	25441769.00	3427991	29.435
2	上海市	31496379.00	2904522	24.940
3	江苏省	13694116.00	1354654	11.632
4	河北省	14434494.00	1119275	9.611
5	浙江省	10789171.00	980355	8.418
进口总计		116388412.00	11645829	100.00

2. 2012 年聚酰胺进口企业

2.1. 聚酰胺-6，6 切片进口以外商独资企业为主

聚酰胺-6，6 切片 2012 年进口商共计有 1588 家，比上年 1626 家进口商减少 38 个进口商，进口额最高的十家进口生产使用企业进口数量占总进口数量的 32.760%，比上年增加 2.02%。

聚酰胺-6，6 切片 2012 年五十六大进口商中有三十五家为生产使用企业主要为聚酰胺改性(即聚酰胺合金)、玩具制品、化纤工业、电子工业(手机外壳、电脑外壳等)染料化工、汽车工业、家用电器、皮革化工等生产企业，三十五大进口生产使用企业合计进口量占 2012 年总进口量的 37.605%。

聚酰胺-6，6 切片 2012 年五十六大进口商中有二十一家为贸易商，合计进口量占 2012 年总进口量的 23.314%(表 39)。

表 39　2012 年聚酰胺-6，6 切片五十六大进口商统计

排　序	进口商	所属行业	进口数量/kg	占比例/%
1	上海青浦出口加工区物流有限公司	贸易商	11903642	4.969
2	杜邦中国集团有限公司	聚酰胺改性	11011080	4.596
3	旭化成塑料(上海)有限公司	聚酰胺改性	10786183	4.503
4	上海浦贸国际货运代理有限公司	贸易商	10294356	4.297
5	杜邦贸易(上海)有限公司	贸易商	8650771	3.611
6	罗地亚(上海)工程塑料有限公司	聚酰胺改性	6871027	2.868
7	巴斯夫染料化工有限公司	染料化工	6315493	2.636
8	拜耳无锡皮革化工有限公司	皮革化工	4485362	1.872
9	杭州帝凯工业布有限公司	化纤工业	4219228	1.761
10	深圳市宝安外经发展有限公司	贸易商	3946570	1.647
11	广州金发科技股份有限公司	聚酰胺改性	3845105	1.605
12	叶水福临江物流(上海)有限公司	贸易商	3583006	1.496
13	温州龙华日用电子有限公司	电子工业	2971653	1.496
14	上海和氏璧化工有限公司	聚酰胺改性	2952180	1.232
15	屹立(苏州)工程塑料科技有限公司	聚酰胺改性	2923199	1.220
16	承茂国际贸易(上海)有限公司	贸易商	2578675	1.076
17	深圳能源物流有限公司	贸易商	2540971	1.061
18	日超工程塑料(深圳)有限公司	聚酰胺改性	2463295	1.028
19	上海毅塑兴塑胶原料商贸有限公司	贸易商	2440125	1.019
20	上海新龙塑料制造有限公司	聚酰胺改性	2413006	1.007
21	丽碧复合塑料(深圳)有限公司	聚酰胺改性	1214250	0.507
22	上海三立汇众汽车零部件有限公司	汽车工业	1199000	0.501
23	中山市美捷时喷雾阀有限公司	汽车工业	1143000	4.596
24	中海物流(深圳)有限公司	贸易商	1142690	0.477
25	东莞华伟配线器材有限公司	家用电器	1089999	0.455
26	思瑞克斯(广州)电器有限公司	家用电器	1069750	0.447
27	舒尔曼塑料(东莞)有限公司	聚酰胺改性	966575	0.403
28	湖南长丰环球经贸有限公司	贸易商	949299	0.396
29	上海庆华物流有限公司	贸易商	869975	0.363
30	上海耐特复合材料制品有限公司	聚酰胺改性	862169	0.360

续表

排　序	进口商	所属行业	进口数量/kg	占比例/%
31	泉州天宇化纤织造实业有限公司	化纤工业	836000	0.349
32	广州和氏璧化工材料有限公司	聚酰胺改性	829105	0.346
33	温州市永昌尼龙销售有限公司	贸易商	828685	0.346
34	天津认知汽车配件有限公司	汽车工业	815000	0.340
35	广州番禺对外贸易有限公司	贸易商	797493	0.333
36	兰蒂奇工程塑料(苏州)有限公司	聚酰胺改性	788025	0.329
37	番禺得意精密电子工业有限公司	电子工业	780400	0.326
38	宁波宝翔国际贸易有限公司	贸易商	780361	0.326
39	广州市合诚化学有限公司	精细化工	777400	0.325
40	淮安新宁公共保税仓储有限公司	贸易商	770475	0.322
41	深圳市通捷利物流有限公司	贸易商	698580	0.292
42	上海海棕榈进出口有限公司	贸易商	688525	0.287
43	威海新凯帝电子有限公司	电子工业	677953	0.283
44	温州华东塑料有限公司	塑料工业	660000	0.276
45	烟台华润锦纶有限公司	化纤工业	660000	0.276
46	嘉里物流(上海外高桥)有限公司	贸易商	625750	0.261
47	东莞永常兴工程塑料有限公司	聚酰胺改性	613006	0.256
48	北京市塑化贸易有限公司	贸易商	604875	0.252
49	浙江裕鑫化纤有限公司	化纤工业	600000	0.250
50	强竣电子科技(深圳)有限公司	电子工业	586750	0.245
51	伟光联仓储运输(深圳)有限公司	贸易商	581500	0.243
52	广州市汇辰工程塑料有限公司	聚酰胺改性	577162	0.241
53	大通物流(深圳)有限公司	贸易商	574000	0.240
54	伟世通汽车空调(北京)有限公司	汽车工业	553000	0.231
55	世洋伟业树脂(北京)有限公司	聚酰胺改性	531050	0.222
56	聚威工程塑料(上海)有限公司	聚酰胺改性	519733	0.217
进口总计			239557235	100.00

2.2. 聚酰胺－6、聚酰胺－11、聚酰胺－12、聚酰胺－6，9、聚酰胺－6，10、聚酰胺－6，12 切片等

其他初级形状的聚酰胺－6，6 等 2012 年进口商共计有 1，306 家，比上年 1，341 家进口商减少 35 家进口商；进口额最高的十家进口生产使用企业进口数量占总进口数量的 41.300%。

其他初级形状的聚酰胺－6，6 等 2012 年四十大进口商中二十八家为生产使用企业主要为汽车工业、化纤工业、聚酰胺改性(即聚酰胺合金)、电子工业(手机外壳、电脑外壳等、制鞋工业、塑胶工业、塑料制品、眼镜化工生产企业，二十八大进口生产使用企业合计进口量占 2012 年总进口量的 50.251%。

其他初级形状的聚酰胺－6，6 等 2012 年四十大进口商中十二家为贸易商，合计进口量占 2012 年总进口量的 28.149%(表 40)。

表40 2012年聚酰胺－6、聚酰胺－11、聚酰胺－12、聚酰胺－6，9、聚酰胺－6，10、聚酰胺－6，12切片四十大进口商统计

排 序	进口商	所属行业	进口数量/kg	占比例/%
1	河北亚大汽车塑料制品有限公司	汽车工业	830496	7.131
2	杜邦贸易(上海)有限公司	贸易商	646175	5.549
3	东芝货物管理(杭州)有限公司	贸易商	548075	4.706
4	德固赛特种化学(上海)有限公司	精细化工	546015	4.689
5	东莞中塑塑胶制品有限公司	塑料制品	543730	4.669
6	出光复合工程塑料(广州)有限公司	聚酰胺改性	434008	3.727
7	德州东鸿制膜科技有限公司	工矿配件	352000	3.023
8	阿托菲纳(上海)物流有限公司	贸易商	321450	2.760
9	宇部兴产(上海)有限公司	贸易商	296770	2.548
10	深圳市永德丰实业有限公司	贸易商	290960	2.498
11	临海市铁马制管有限公司	工矿配件	280427	2.408
12	易力声科技(深圳)有限公司	贸易商	251200	2.157
13	连云港宇研鞋业有限公司	制鞋工业	250896	2.154
14	上海玫洛国际贸易有限公司	贸易商	248618	2.135
15	邦迪管路系统有限公司	汽车工业	245652	2.109
16	恩佳升(连云港)电子有限公司	电子工业	215000	1.846
17	福州富拉马斯塑胶有限公司	塑料制品	187761	1.612
18	弗兰科希管件系统(上海)有限公司	汽车工业	166607	1.431
19	北京市塑化贸易有限公司	贸易商	162029	1.391
20	艾伦(无锡)商用车部件有限公司	汽车工业	155933	1.339
21	深圳市龙岗区对外经济发展有限公司	贸易商	145760	1.252
22	长春亚大汽车零件制造有限公司	汽车工业	140975	1.211
23	陆逊梯卡华宏(东莞)眼镜有限公司	眼镜工业	138976	1.193
24	阿雷蒙紧固件(镇江)有限公司	工矿配件	135275	1.162
25	武汉荟普化学新材料有限公司	聚酰胺改性	134401	1.154
26	上海森村贸易有限公司	贸易商	133914	1.150
27	北京百科新特科技发展有限公司	贸易商	121465	1.043
28	东莞上顺塑胶制品有限公司	塑料制品	119290	1.024
29	上海亚大汽车塑料制品有限公司	汽车工业	117086	1.005
30	漳州东利光学科技有限公司	眼镜工业	113760	0.977
31	东莞市对外加工装配服务公司	贸易商	111787	0.960
32	杜邦兴达(无锡)单丝有限公司	化纤工业	106726	0.916
33	艾曼斯(苏州)工程塑料有限公司	聚酰胺改性	105254	0.904
34	创意塑胶工业(苏州)有限公司	塑料制品	93522	0.803
35	百科塑料(上海)有限公司	聚酰胺改性	77880	0.669
36	东特(浙江)有限公司	聚酰胺改性	76100	0.653

续表

排　序	进口商	所属行业	进口数量/kg	占比例/%
37	世洋伟业树脂(北京)有限公司	聚酰胺改性	75000	0.644
38	东莞新溢眼镜制造有限公司	眼镜工业	71102	0.611
39	北京京燃凌云燃气设备有限公司	工矿配件	69500	0.597
40	霓达摩尔科技(常州)有限公司	工矿配件	68700	0.590
	进口总计		11645829	100.00

2.3. 其他初级形状的聚酰胺-6，6等

其他初级形状的聚酰胺-6，6等2012年进口商共计有896家，比上年902家进口商减少6个进口商，进口额最高的十家进口生产使用企业进口数量占总进口数量的31.060%。

其他初级形状的聚酰胺-6，6等2012年四十大进口商中有二十八家为生产使用企业主要为聚酰胺改性(即聚酰胺合金)、汽车工业、工矿配件、电子工业(手机外壳、电脑外壳等)、家用电器、渔具丝网、塑胶制品生产企业，二十八大进口生产使用企业合计进口量占2012年总进口量的35.135%。

其他初级形状的聚酰胺-6，6等2012年四十大进口商中有十二家为贸易商，合计进口量占2011年总进口量的22.655%(表41)。

表41　2012年其他初级形状的聚酰胺-6，6等四十大进口商统计

排　序	进口商	所属行业	进口数量/kg	占比例/%
1	深圳市宝安鸿彬实业有限公司	贸易商	989573	7.176
2	苏威特种聚合物(常熟)有限公司	聚酰胺改性	651000	4.721
3	深圳市宝安外经发展有限公司	贸易商	498675	3.616
4	户田塑磁材料(浙江)有限公司	工矿配件	421670	3.058
5	汕头金园工贸有限公司	贸易商	344225	2.496
6	雅美工业(惠阳)有限公司	工矿配件	327675	2.376
7	深圳市永德丰实业有限公司	贸易商	278800	2.022
8	惠阳亚伦塑胶电器实业有限公司	电子工业	266100	1.930
9	顺德美的洗碗机制造有限公司	工矿配件	254312	1.844
10	深圳市龙岗区对外经济发展有限公司	贸易商	251106	1.821
11	东莞长明复合材料有限公司	聚酰胺改性	223164	1.618
12	广东柏亚进出口有限公司	贸易商	221000	1.603
13	武汉荟普化学新材料有限公司	聚酰胺改性	195905	1.421
14	广州市律韵贸易有限公司	贸易商	192145	1.393
15	汕头市金园区奇乐丝网实业有限公司	渔具丝网	190000	1.378
16	江洋散热器(苏州)有限公司	工矿配件	176000	1.276
17	深圳市光明新区经济发展有限公司	贸易商	165018	1.197
18	昆山中发六和机械有限公司	工矿配件	160580	1.164
19	新东江塑胶(深圳)有限公司	塑料制品	143894	1.043
20	东海精工(张家港)有限公司	聚酰胺改性	140000	1.015
21	崇达电子五金(深圳)有限公司	工矿配件	136000	0.986

续表

排 序	进口商	所属行业	进口数量/kg	占比例/%
22	东莞市对外加工装配服务公司	贸易商	128895	0.935
23	汕头祥发渔具有限公司	渔具丝网	128000	0.928
24	屹立(苏州)工程塑料科技有限公司	聚酰胺改性	123305	0.894
25	东莞玮丰实业有限公司	贸易商	122075	0.885
26	厦门海投物流有限公司	贸易商	112537	0.816
27	广州长欣塑胶有限公司	塑料制品	112537	0.816
28	青柏塑胶电子(深圳)有限公司	电子工业	111977	0.812
29	联辉泰塑胶制品(深圳)有限公司	塑料制品	108421	0.786
30	艺莱创电子元器件(深圳)有限公司	电子工业	105497	0.765
31	鸿利达塑胶制品(深圳)有限公司	塑料制品	102785	0.745
32	东莞市旷鸿电子塑胶制品有限公司	塑料制品	101900	0.739
33	河源天裕电子塑胶有限公司	汽车工业	100850	0.731
34	深圳市泰塑塑化材料科技有限公司	工矿配件	98571	0.715
35	奥仕达主力电器(深圳)有限公司	家用电器	98525	0.714
36	荣丰电器(深圳)有限公司	电子工业	97000	0.703
37	江苏斗星汽车配件有限公司	汽车工业	96643	0.701
38	深圳市怡亚通供应链股份有限公司	贸易商	96000	0.696
39	江苏金岛塑化有限公司	塑料制品	89247	0.647
40	金进精密泵业制品(深圳)有限公司	工矿配件	83926	0.609
	进口总计		13790855.0	59.790

2.4. 其他初级形状的聚酰胺

其他初级形状的聚酰胺2012年进口商共计有902家，比上年936家进口商减少34个进口商，进口额最高的十家进口生产使用企业进口数量占总进口数量的39.909%。

其他初级形状的聚酰胺2012年四十大进口商中有二十九家为生产使用企业主要为家用电器、聚酰胺改性(即聚酰胺合金)、汽车工业、工矿配件、电子工业(手机外壳、电脑外壳等)、家纺工业、塑胶制品、玩具工业生产企业，二十九大进口生产使用企业合计进口量占2012年总进口量的318.403%。

其他初级形状的聚酰胺2012年四十大进口商中有十一家为贸易商，合计进口量占2011年总进口量的19.427%(表42)。

表42 2011年其他初级形状的聚酰胺四十大进口商统计

排 序	进口商	所属行业	进口数量/kg	占比例/%
1	帝斯曼工程塑料(江苏)有限公司	聚酰胺改性	7622626	10.706
2	苏威(上海)有限公司	聚酰胺改性	5767973	8.101
3	杜邦贸易(上海)有限公司	贸易商	4669255	6.558
4	富泰华工业(深圳)有限公司	工矿配件	2397158	3.367
5	日超工程塑料(中山)有限公司	聚酰胺改性	1894838	2.661
6	杜邦中国集团有限公司	聚酰胺改性	1661446	2.334

续表

排序	进口商	所属行业	进口数量/kg	占比例/%
7	艾曼斯(苏州)工程塑料有限公司	聚酰胺改性	1261319	1.772
8	盐城东国汽车配件有限公司	汽车工业	1095882	1.539
9	中海物流(深圳)有限公司	贸易商	1026375	1.442
10	上海怡康化工材料有限公司	聚酰胺改性	1017072	1.429
11	张家港保税区允拓应用材料有限公司	工矿配件	1016475	1.428
12	江苏斗天汽车配件有限公司	汽车工业	980042	1.377
13	通用电气百龙特塑料国际贸易(上海)有限公司	贸易商	932828	1.310
14	烟台北明储运有限公司	贸易商	829575	1.165
15	深圳仁锐实业有限公司	贸易商	767687	1.078
16	绿点科技(无锡)有限公司	精细化工	704813	0.990
17	深圳泰合威储运有限公司	贸易商	621995	0.874
18	太松国际贸易(上海)有限公司	贸易商	599650	0.842
19	亚什兰(中国)投资有限公司	贸易商	591650	0.831
20	烟台富泰通国际物流有限公司	贸易商	577285	0.811
21	北京市塑化贸易有限公司	贸易商	302635	0.425
22	中化塑料公司	贸易商	302500	0.425
23	广州挚翔国际货运代理有限公司	贸易商	300000	0.421
24	深圳市宝安外经发展有限公司	贸易商	287795	0.404
25	艾曼斯(上海)化学贸易有限公司	贸易商	282068	0.396
26	东莞市对外加工装配服务公司	贸易商	277406	0.390
27	天津华铁隆津泰储运有限公司	贸易商	274900	0.386
28	浙江新中和羊毛有限公司	纺织工业	272000	0.382
29	星晨实业(河源)有限公司	工矿配件	258968	0.364
30	上海海棕榈进出口有限公司	贸易商	256150	0.360
31	江苏海外集团国际技术工程有限公司	贸易商	255000	0.358
32	中涂化工(上海)有限公司	装饰材料	247791	0.348
33	苏州九海化工有限公司	装饰材料	241007	0.339
34	上海毅塑兴塑胶原料商贸有限公司	贸易商	240550	0.338
35	广州市合诚化学有限公司	精细化工	240000	0.337
36	法马通连接器(东莞)有限公司	家用电器	239400	0.336
37	江门市盈正进出口有限公司	贸易商	224300	0.315
38	日东纺(中国)有限公司	贸易商	213120	0.299
39	和晋高新装饰材料(昆山)有限公司	装饰材料	211500	0.297
40	思瑞克斯(广州)电器有限公司	家用电器	210850	0.296
	进口总计		71197558	57.830

五、聚酰胺塑料出口生产商分析

1. 聚酰胺-6，6 切片

从海关资料来看，2012 年聚酰胺-6，6 切片出口商有 238 家，前十位聚酰胺-6，6 切片出口商出口量占总出口量的 79.785%。

聚酰胺-6，6 切片 2012 年四十大出口商中有二十七家为出口生产企业，二十七家为聚酰胺改性(即聚酰胺合金)，皮革化工一家，合计出口量占总出口量的 89.541%。

聚酰胺-6，6 切片 2012 年四十大出口商中有十三家为贸易商，合计出口量仅占总出口量的 4.90%(表 43)。

表 43 2012 年聚酰胺-6，6 切片四十大出口商统计

排 序	出 口 商	所属行业	出口数量/kg	占比例/%
1	杜邦中国集团有限公司	聚酰胺改性	9926725	19.873
2	平顶山神马工程塑料有限责任公司	聚酰胺改性	9802160	19.624
3	拜耳无锡皮革化工有限公司	皮革化工	4941915	9.894
4	罗地亚(上海)工程塑料有限公司	聚酰胺改性	4853405	9.717
5	日超工程塑料(深圳)有限公司	聚酰胺改性	4010661	8.029
6	巴斯夫染料化工有限公司	聚酰胺改性	2758958	5.523
7	丽碧复合塑料(深圳)有限公司	聚酰胺改性	1104475	2.211
8	宁波敏特尼龙工业有限公司	聚酰胺改性	975000	1.952
9	天津碧美特工程塑料有限公司	聚酰胺改性	768125	1.538
10	广州金发科技股份有限公司	聚酰胺改性	711050	1.424
11	屹立(苏州)工程塑料科技有限公司	聚酰胺改性	695725	1.393
12	上海耐特复合材料制品有限公司	聚酰胺改性	595050	1.191
13	华峰集团有限公司	聚酰胺改性	521250	1.044
14	深圳市泰塑塑化材料科技有限公司	聚酰胺改性	501300	1.004
15	旭化成(苏州)复合塑料有限公司	聚酰胺改性	446050	0.893
16	中海物流(深圳)有限公司	贸易商	378525	0.758
17	深圳市锦旺发贸易有限公司	贸易商	308635	0.618
18	上海外联发物流有限公司	贸易商	267400	0.535
19	深圳市科聚新材料有限公司	聚酰胺改性	266350	0.533
20	上海三凯进出口有限公司	贸易商	240500	0.481
21	沙伯基础创新塑料(中国)有限公司	聚酰胺改性	237842	0.476
22	普立万聚合体(深圳)有限公司	聚酰胺改性	230445	0.461
23	福洛塑胶(昆山)有限公司	聚酰胺改性	216000	0.432
24	星际塑料(深圳)有限公司	聚酰胺改性	196984	0.394
25	叶水福临江物流(上海)有限公司	贸易商	190087	0.381
26	上海浦贸国际货运代理有限公司	贸易商	180352	0.361
27	舒尔曼塑料(东莞)有限公司	聚酰胺改性	173340	0.347
28	古道尔工程塑胶(深圳)有限公司	聚酰胺改性	167750	0.336
29	承茂国际贸易(上海)有限公司	贸易商	156000	0.312
30	三运物流(上海)有限公司	贸易商	150300	0.301
31	东莞市朗普工程塑料科技有限公司	聚酰胺改性	150000	0.300

续表

排序	出口商	所属行业	出口数量/kg	占比例/%
32	中山市华业塑料有限公司	聚酰胺改性	137200	0.275
33	安特普工程塑料(苏州)有限公司	聚酰胺改性	136518	0.273
34	拉题工程塑料贸易(上海)有限公司	贸易商	127184	0.255
35	森六(上海)贸易有限公司	贸易商	127050	0.254
36	上海铁联国际储运有限公司	贸易商	123925	0.248
37	兰蒂奇工程塑料(苏州)有限公司	聚酰胺改性	110867	0.222
38	深圳中外运物流有限公司	贸易商	98875	0.198
39	中基宁波对外贸易股份有限公司	贸易商	98000	0.196
40	晋伦塑料科技(东莞)有限公司	聚酰胺改性	91075	0.182
	出口总计		49949853	94.441

2. 初级形状的聚酰胺-6等

从海关资料来看，2012年初级形状的聚酰胺-6等出口商有198家，前十位其他初级形状的聚酰胺-6等出口商出口量占总出口量的81.485%。

初级形状的聚酰胺-6等2012年十八大出口商中有十一家为出口生产企业，杜邦兴达(无锡)单丝有限公司，无锡市兴达尼龙有限公司和无锡殷达尼龙有限公司三家为化纤尼龙切片生产企业，余下十家分别为聚酰胺改性(即聚酰胺合金)，工矿配件，精细化工，汽车工业生产企业，合计出口量占总出口量的74.826%。

初级形状的聚酰胺-6等2012年十八大出口商中有七家为贸易商，合计出口量占总出口量的12.944%(表44)。

表44　2012年聚酰胺-6、聚酰胺-11、聚酰胺-12、聚酰胺-6，9、聚酰胺-6，10、聚酰胺-6，12切片十八大出口商统计

排序	出口商	所属行业	出口数量/kg	占比例/%
1	杜邦兴达(无锡)单丝有限公司	化纤工业	1413601	26.794
2	山东东辰工程塑料有限公司	聚酰胺改性	1123647	21.298
3	章丘市友贵机械锻造有限责任公司	工矿配件	366025	6.938
4	德固赛特种化学(上海)有限公司	精细化工	291179	5.519
5	阿托菲纳(上海)物流有限公司	贸易商	282485	5.354
6	深圳市科聚新材料有限公司	聚酰胺改性	231500	4.388
7	常州昌瑞汽车部品制造有限公司	汽车工业	179386	3.400
8	无锡尚之敬贸易有限公司	贸易商	165000	3.127
9	无锡市兴达尼龙有限公司	化纤工业	133920	2.538
10	苏州翰普高分子材料有限公司	聚酰胺改性	112325	2.129
11	苏州国信集团旺顺进出口有限公司	贸易商	110863	2.101
12	宁波宝腾进出口有限公司	贸易商	51391	0.974
13	无锡殷达尼龙有限公司	化纤工业	46135	0.874
14	深圳市利德源进出口有限公司	贸易商	35000	0.663
15	弗兰科希管件系统(上海)有限公司	汽车工业	29000	0.550
16	启东博文工程塑料有限公司	聚酰胺改性	21000	0.398
17	广州润盈贸易有限公司	贸易商	20000	0.379
18	深圳中外运物流有限公司	贸易商	18150	0.344
	出口总计		5275831	100.00

3. 其他初级形状的聚酰胺-6，6等

从海关资料来看，2012年其他初级形状的聚酰胺-6，6等出口商有106家，前十位其他初级形状的聚酰胺-6等出口商出口量占总出口量的83.692%。

其他初级形状的聚酰胺-6，6等2012年十三大出口商中有十家为出口生产企业，均为聚酰胺改性（即聚酰胺合金），工矿配件生产企业，合计出口量占总出口量的82.889%。

其他初级形状的聚酰胺-6，6等2012年十三大出口商中有十家为出口贸易商，合计出口量占总出口量的2.642%（表45）。

表45 2012年其他初级形状的聚酰胺-6，6等十三大出口商统计

排 序	出 口 商	所属行业	出口数量/kg	占比例/%
1	罗地亚(上海)工程塑料有限公司	聚酰胺改性	1909200	51.667
2	普立万聚合体(深圳)有限公司	聚酰胺改性	232820	6.301
3	南通兴鑫化工有限公司	聚酰胺改性	224000	6.062
4	江西省宜春远大化工有限公司	聚酰胺改性	212800	5.759
5	丽碧复合塑料(深圳)有限公司	聚酰胺改性	112300	3.039
6	杭州色彩化工有限公司	聚酰胺改性	102950	2.786
7	德氏连接器制造(上海)有限公司	工矿配件	102182	2.765
8	中涂化工(上海)有限公司	聚酰胺改性	89640	2.426
9	厦门利通洋物流有限公司	贸易商	57692	1.561
10	深圳市泰塑塑化材料科技有限公司	聚酰胺改性	49000	1.326
11	东莞华伟配线器材有限公司	工矿配件	28000	0.758
12	深圳市依特斯贸易有限公司	贸易商	20000	0.541
13	深圳市飞翔创富贸易有限公司	贸易商	20000	0.541
出口总计			3695235	100.00

4. 其他初级形状的聚酰胺

从海关资料来看，其他初级形状的聚酰胺2012年出口商有261家，比上年252家出口商增加9家聚酰胺出口商，前十位其他初级形状的聚酰胺出口商出口量占总出口量的71.575%。

其他初级形状的聚酰胺2011年三十八大出口商中有二十二家为出口生产企业，十一家为聚酰胺改性（即聚酰胺合金），六家精细化工，四家工矿配件，一家化纤工业生产企业，合计出口量占总出口量的57.473%。

其他初级形状的聚酰胺2011年三十八大出口商中有十六家为贸易商，合计出口量占总出口量的34.182%（表46）。

表46 2012年其他初级形状的聚酰胺三十八大出口商统计

排 序	出 口 商	所属行业	出口数量/kg	占比例/%
1	杜邦贸易(上海)有限公司	贸易商	6896443	18.237
2	帝斯曼工程塑料(江苏)有限公司	聚酰胺改性	5048693	13.351
3	杜邦中国集团有限公司	聚酰胺改性	4393182	11.617
4	广州保畅国际物流有限公司	贸易商	2216550	5.862
5	艾曼斯(苏州)工程塑料有限公司	聚酰胺改性	2153304	5.694
6	苏威(上海)有限公司	聚酰胺改性	1486813	3.932
7	江苏阜宁伊士曼化工有限公司	聚酰胺改性	1454725	3.847
8	山东汇金化工有限公司	聚酰胺改性	1310750	3.466

续表

排　序	出　口　商	所属行业	出口数量/kg	占比例/%
9	张家港保税区允拓应用材料有限公司	工矿配件	1099637	2.908
10	德固赛特种化学(上海)有限公司	精细化工	1006148	2.661
11	空气化工产品(南京)特种胺有限公司	油墨涂料	713550	1.887
12	日超工程塑料(深圳)有限公司	聚酰胺改性	646874	1.711
13	迪辰仓储服务(深圳)有限公司	贸易商	562225	1.487
14	无锡市兴达尼龙有限公司	化纤工业	518320	1.371
15	江门市新轻出进出口有限公司	贸易商	497429	1.315
16	深圳能源物流有限公司	贸易商	462625	1.223
17	江西省宜春远大化工有限公司	工矿配件	448780	1.187
18	张家港保税区中融物流有限公司	贸易商	447475	1.183
19	伟光联仓储运输(深圳)有限公司	贸易商	390700	1.033
20	中海物流(深圳)有限公司	贸易商	331675	0.877
21	江苏永林油脂化工有限公司	精细化工	241000	0.637
22	广州金发科技股份有限公司	聚酰胺改性	211350	0.559
23	埃亚尔化工(上海)有限公司	精细化工	210725	0.557
24	艾曼斯(上海)化学贸易有限公司	贸易商	209711	0.555
25	深圳泰合威储运有限公司	贸易商	196875	0.521
26	福洛塑胶(昆山)有限公司	聚酰胺改性	162000	0.428
27	捷高科技(苏州)有限公司	工矿配件	139950	0.370
28	上海兆辰物流有限公司	贸易商	137600	0.364
29	泉州市瑞通贸易有限公司	贸易商	133000	0.352
30	日通国际物流(深圳)有限公司	贸易商	126450	0.334
31	浙江永在进出口有限公司	贸易商	124000	0.328
32	江苏三木集团有限公司	聚酰胺改性	114820	0.304
33	式卡(上海)贸易有限公司	贸易商	112261	0.297
34	宁波三彩化工有限公司	油墨涂料	96000	0.254
35	张家港大塚化学有限公司	油墨涂料	94175	0.249
36	南京聚隆科技股份有限公司	聚酰胺改性	92500	0.245
37	中国石油集团长城钻探工程有限公司	工矿配件	90000	0.238
38	东莞市虎门保税仓	贸易商	81270	0.215
出口总计			37815294	100.00

六、2012年价格走势——PA价格由高走低

2012年1月国内PA66市场在外围向好及库存骤降支撑下迎来开门红行情，截止2月国内神马EPR27上涨500元/t至26000元/t，PA66走高可谓千呼万唤始出来。

虽然目前国内PA6市场现货存量处于低位，但厂家库存多数较高，出货不畅局面仍难以打破。需求仍然疲弱，国内PA6生产厂家目前承受巨大压力。

下游锦纶抽丝行业三季度进入传统生产旺季，相比较一二季度的淡季，有所放大，但据业内人士反映，综合多方面消息，需求量无大幅放大的趋势。

行业分析：

1. 目前，工程塑料领域，各产品整体表现清淡，市场缺乏炒作情绪。

2. 工程塑料产品附加值较高，在整体环境表现低迷的时刻，下游能省则省，需求大幅减少。

后市预测：综合来看，业者对于市场预期信心不足，并且上游行情持续清淡，下游也持续疲软，因此生意社橡塑分社 PA6 分析师范婷璐预计，PA6 仍将保持低位盘整。

然而低迷经济环境增加大宗商品市场的不确定性，2012 年 PA 市场好景不长，六月份起又全面下跌，以最低位收尾。

PA1010 （09 - 12 上海赛璐珞）一月份78000 元/t，六月份跌至 75750 元/t，跌幅 2.88%，下半年 PA1010 维持在 75000 元/t，直至年末。

七、进出口贸易交易类型分析

1. 其他初级形状的聚酰胺 PA

从海关统计中可看出，2012 年其他初级形状的聚酰胺 PA 进口贸易方式主要为进料加工贸易（占进口量 33.199%）（表 47）。

表 47　2012 年其他初级形状的聚酰胺 PA 进口交易类型统计

进口交易类型	进口金额/美元	进口数量/kg	占比例/%
进料加工贸易	166853841.00	23636722	33.199
保税区仓储转口货物	160228582.00	22090408	31.027
一般贸易	122512027.00	19996502	28.086
来料加工装配贸易	24274899.00	4580173	6.433
保税仓库进出境货物	5995961.00	867367	1.218
其他	273691.00	26386	0.037
合计	480139001.00	71197558	100.00

从海关统计中可看出，2012 年其他初级形状的聚酰胺 PA 出口贸易方式主要为保税区仓储转口货物（占出口量 36.374%）（表 48）。

表 48　2012 年其他初级形状的聚酰胺 PA 出口交易类型统计

出口交易类型	出口金额/美元	出口数量/kg	占比例/%
保税区仓储转口货物	85760057.00	13754769	36.374
进料加工贸易	91730597.00	12646093	33.442
一般贸易	49585087.00	10073114	26.638
来料加工装配贸易	5630708.00	1103587	2.918
保税仓库进出境货物	1016083.00	114101	0.302
对外承包工程出口货物	215334.00	91100	0.241
其他	81309.00	32109	0.085
边境小额贸易	1840.00	421	0.001
出口总计	234021015.00	37815294	100.00

2. 聚酰胺 6，6 切片

从海关统计中可看出，2012 年初级形状的聚酰胺 6，6 切片进口贸易方式主要为一般贸易（占进口量 34.143%）（表 49）。

表 49　2012 年聚酰胺 6，6 切片进口交易类型统计

进口交易类型	进口金额/美元	进口数量/kg	占比例/%
一般贸易	310747047.00	81790990	34.143
进料加工贸易	300295772.00	71879035	30.005
保税区仓储转口货物	226023780.00	63289809	26.419
来料加工装配贸易	62091550.00	16625202	6.940
保税仓库进出境货物	21659101.00	5920948	2.472
其他	466233.00	51251	0.021
进口总计	921283483.00	239557235	100.00

从海关统计中可看出，2011 年初级形状的聚酰胺 6，6 切片出口贸易方式主要为进料加工贸易（占出口量 70.436%）（表 50）。

表 50　2012 年聚酰胺 6，6 切片出口交易类型统计

出口交易类型	出口金额/美元	出口数量/kg	占比例/%
进料加工贸易	133678013.00	35182507	70.436
一般贸易	36952025.00	11787485	23.599
保税区仓储转口货物	10370996.00	2658944	5.323
保税仓库进出境货物	734026.00	179170	0.359
来料加工装配贸易	484039.00	104452	0.209
边境小额贸易	42218.00	28303	0.057
出料加工贸易	24530.00	6750	0.014
其他	8891.00	2242	0.004
出口总计	182294738.00	49949853	100.00

3. 初级形状的聚酰胺 - 6，6 等（包括聚酰胺 - 6、聚酰胺 - 6，9、聚酰胺 - 6，10、聚酰胺 - 6，12）

从海关统计中可看出，2012 年初级形状的聚酰胺 - 6，6 等进口贸易方式主要为一般贸易（占进口量 41.921%）（表 51）。

表51　2012年初级形状的聚酰胺-6，6等进口交易类型统计

进口交易类型	进口金额/美元	进口数量/kg	占比例/%
一般贸易	60041327.00	4882051	41.921
进料加工贸易	26539135.00	3800443	32.634
保税区仓储转口货物	24568437.00	2270685	19.498
来料加工装配贸易	4631957.00	619042	5.316
保税仓库进出境货物	486930.00	68525	0.588
其他	120626.00	5083	0.044
进口总计	116388412.00	11645829	100.00

从海关统计中可看出，2012年初级形状的聚酰胺-6，6等出口贸易方式主要为一般贸易(占出口量77.815%)(表52)。

表52　2012年初级形状的聚酰胺-6，6等出口交易类型统计

出口交易类型	出口金额/美元	出口数量/kg	占比例/%
一般贸易	36878153.00	4105375	77.815
进料加工贸易	5120249.00	831381	15.758
保税区仓储转口货物	4253340.00	314445	5.960
保税仓库进出境货物	153539.00	21880	0.415
来料加工装配贸易	19334.00	2425	0.046
其他	1050.00	325	0.006
出口总计	46425665.00	5275831	100.00

4. 其他初级形状的聚酰胺-6，6等(包括聚酰胺-6、聚酰胺-6，9、聚酰胺-6，10、聚酰胺-6，12)

从海关统计中可看出，2012年其他初级形状的聚酰胺-6，6等进口贸易方式主要为进料加工贸易(占进口量44.754%)(表53)。

表53　2012年其他初级形状的聚酰胺-6，6等进口交易类型统计

进口交易类型	进口金额/美元	进口数量/kg	占比例/%
进料加工贸易	38670131.00	6171919	44.754
来料加工装配贸易	8657682.00	3740341	27.122
一般贸易	25118011.00	3730583	27.051
保税区仓储转口货物	689612.00	96976	0.703
保税仓库进出境货物	376129.00	27563	0.200
其他	195282.00	23473	0.170
进口总计	73706847.00	13790855	100.00

从海关统计中可看出，2012年其他初级形状的聚酰胺-6，6等出口贸易方式主要为进料加工贸易(占出口量62.396%)(表54)。

表54　2012年其他初级形状的聚酰胺-6，6等出口交易类型统计

出口交易类型	出口金额/美元	出口数量/kg	占比例/%
进料加工贸易	8698008.00	2305687	62.396
一般贸易	4447350.00	1366424	36.978
保税仓库进出境货物	105746.00	10220	0.277
边境小额贸易	33771.00	8000	0.216
保税区仓储转口货物	29937.00	4874	0.132
对外承包工程出口货物	12.00	30	0.001
出口总计	13314824.00	3695235	100.00

第四章　2012年聚甲醛(POM)进口下降出口消费上升

一、2012年聚甲醛生产小幅上升

2012年国内聚甲醛的生产能力超过540.0kt。

国内聚甲醛生产企业有云天化、神华宁夏煤业、上海蓝星、杜邦-旭化成张家港公司、新疆香梨股份等，产能合计510kt，拟建和在建的产能合计达到520kt，未来产能增速显著。

神华神宁煤业集团煤化工分公司聚甲醛厂60kt级生产线环保项目进行验收。

中海化学天野公司聚甲醛项目共有3条生产线，可年产聚甲醛约60kt。

开封龙宇化工有限公司100kt级聚甲醛生产基地的原料优势，延长聚甲醛产业链条，提高产品附加值，实现产业结构优化升级。该项目总投资1亿元，产品规模为年产20kt高端改性聚甲醛和1000t晶核剂，预计年产值3.9亿元。MC025具有高强度、高韧性等特点，主要应用于板、棒材料加工领域。由于MC025生产工艺、技术要求严格，国内聚甲醛生产企业很少涉足，因此，国内优质MC025多为进口产品。

开封龙宇已经掌握5类聚甲醛产品生产技术，可通过调整各类产品产能适应市场需求，避免与国内其他企业在同类产品上产生恶性竞争(表55)。

表55 2001~2012年中国聚甲醛产能产量统计

年 份	生产能力/t	产量/t
2001年	13000	680
2002年	13000	2500
2003年	13000	3200
2004年	63000	26000
2005年	120000	65000
2006年	170000	90000
2007年	230000	150000
2008年	280000	155000
2009年	280000	165000
2010年	420000	210000
2011年	540000	260000
2012年	580000	280000
2013年预计	600000	320000

注：表中产量数据为业内人士估测，仅供参考。

国内POM工程塑料基础树脂生产厂不多，而从事改性POM品种生产的厂家和产能大大超过了基础树脂生产厂。近年来我国POM改性发展较快，主要由于双螺杆混炼挤出机的引进和国产双螺杆混炼挤出机的推出，给改性POM创造了有利条件。

中国聚甲醛企业亟待突破技术瓶颈，但当前的技术基本在大学里，处于试验阶段，真正突破尚需时日。由于技术水平不过关，我国进口的是改性聚甲醛，而出口的是初级聚甲醛，普通的价格相差几倍，特殊的相差20~30倍。

开封龙化一期年产6000t改性聚甲醛装置近日顺利产出玻璃纤维增强型改性聚甲醛合格产品，产品质量达到配方设计要求，这标志着装置转入试生产阶段。

开封龙化先后与国内13所著名高校和科研院所建立了合作关系，在聚甲醛增强、增韧、耐候性能研究及汽车专用料、煤矿井下材料、尼龙等工程塑料替代等研究领域取得了较大突破。

2012年10月23日，改性聚甲醛项目一次通过河南煤化集团公司组织的机械竣工及投料前工程验收。

兖矿集团鲁南化工公司推出了聚甲醛及改性产品。

2012年国内主要POM工程塑料改性厂还有山阳稻田复合塑料(东莞)有限公司，旭化成(苏州)复合塑料有限公司，日超工程塑料(深圳)有限公司，普立万聚合体(深圳)有限公司，东莞大日化工厂有限公司，塞拉尼斯(南京)多元化工有限公司，张家港大塚化学有限公司，沙伯基础创新塑料(中国)有限公司，上海怡康化工材料有限公司，安特普工程塑料(苏州)有限公司，天津松井塑料有限公司，深圳市科聚新材料有限公司，巴斯夫(中国)有限公司，宝理工程塑料贸易(上海)有限公司，山阳稻田复合塑料(东莞)有限公司，塞拉尼斯(南京)多元化工有限公司，旭化成塑料(上海)有限公司，旭化成(苏州)复合塑料有限公司，上海怡康化工材料有限公司，富华杰工业(深圳)有限公司，旭化成塑料(广州)有限公司，普立万聚合体(深圳)有限公司，镇泰(广州)实业有限公司，上海和氏璧化工有限公司，珠海斗门超毅科技有限公司，东莞大日化工厂有限公司等，从沿海到内地、从国有企业、合资企业发展到乡镇企业，以外商独资、合资和私企为主。

二、2012年出口生产省市分布集中于东部沿海地区

2012年初级形状的聚甲醛出口省市有19家，与2011年17家出口省市增加2家出口省市。2012年初级形状的聚甲醛出口生产企业主要集中在江苏省出口数量24877065kg，比2011年出口数量增加17.06%，占总出口数量的43.251%；

五省市出口数量占2012年初级形状的聚甲醛总出口数量的97.837%，比上年出口数量下降1.743%(表56)。

表56 2012年初级形状的聚甲醛五大出口省市统计

排序	出口省市	出口金额/美元	出口数量/kg	占比例/%
1	江苏省	47941942.00	24877065	43.251
2	广东省	38685370.00	16178443	28.128
3	云南省	10487703.00	7100825	12.345
4	上海市	10114529.00	6120464	10.641
5	重庆市	2955803.00	1996575	3.471
出口总计		112388408.00	57517706	100.00

三、出口生产商以外资企业为主

从海关资料来看，2012年初级形状的聚甲醛出口商有158家，比2011年163家出口商减少5家聚甲醛出口商。

2012年前十位初级形状的聚甲醛出口商出口量占总出口量的91.478%，比2011年聚甲醛出口量增加0.328%。。

2012年初级形状的聚甲醛出口商中杜邦集团属下3家出口商出口量占总出口量的22.52%,，比2011年聚甲醛出口量减少2.05%。

2012 年初级形状的聚甲醛三十八大出口商中有二十一家为贸易商，合计出口量占总出口量的 23.146%(表 57)。

表 57　2012 年初级形状的聚甲醛三十八大出口商统计

排序	出　口　商	所属行业	出口数量/kg	占比例/%
1	宝泰菱工程塑料(南通)有限公司	聚甲醛原料生产厂	16667625	28.978
2	天盟农资连锁有限责任公司	贸易商	9117400	15.851
3	杜邦中国集团有限公司	POM 改性	8063891	14.020
4	上海蓝星聚甲醛有限公司	聚甲醛原料生产厂	5082110	8.836
5	杜邦－旭化成聚甲醛(张家港)有限公司	聚甲醛原料生产厂	4841150	8.417
6	山阳稻田复合塑料(东莞)有限公司	POM 改性	3876765	6.740
7	旭化成(苏州)复合塑料有限公司	POM 改性	1828238	3.179
8	赛拉尼斯(上海)国际贸易有限公司	贸易商	1210375	2.104
9	日超工程塑料(深圳)有限公司	POM 改性	1038234	1.805
10	深圳市新宁现代物流有限公司	贸易商	890294	1.548
11	普立万聚合体(深圳)有限公司	POM 改性	565398	0.983
12	余姚市周佳塑料进出口有限公司	贸易商	436000	0.758
13	东莞大日化工厂有限公司	POM 改性	374000	0.650
14	中海物流(深圳)有限公司	贸易商	351775	0.612
15	塞拉尼斯(南京)多元化工有限公司	POM 改性	341468	0.594
16	深圳泰合威储运有限公司	贸易商	206685	0.359
17	厦门太松进出口贸易有限公司	贸易商	199775	0.347
18	天津渤化红三角国际贸易有限公司	贸易商	160000	0.278
19	深圳市宝安鸿彬实业有限公司	贸易商	158334	0.275
20	张家港大塚化学有限公司	POM 改性	141818	0.247
21	沙伯基础创新塑料(中国)有限公司	POM 改性	132600	0.231
22	西努沃(上海)家电贸易有限公司	贸易商	100000	0.174
23	上海怡康化工材料有限公司	POM 改性	80000	0.139
24	深圳综合信兴物流有限公司	贸易商	63385	0.110
25	安特普工程塑料(苏州)有限公司	POM 改性	62640	0.109
26	天津松井塑料有限公司	POM 改性	55975	0.097
27	上海铁联国际储运有限公司	贸易商	54750	0.095
28	上海品泊国际贸易有限公司	贸易商	54000	0.094
29	深圳市科聚新材料有限公司	POM 改性	53000	0.092
30	巴斯夫(中国)有限公司	POM 改性	48900	0.085
31	天津利得国际贸易有限公司	贸易商	48000	0.083
32	杜邦贸易(上海)有限公司	贸易商	47600	0.083
33	天津市沃兰国际贸易有限公司	贸易商	44051	0.077

续表

排序	出 口 商	所属行业	出口数量/kg	占比例/%
34	厦门锦集进出口贸易有限公司	贸易商	38000	0.066
35	港塑塑料贸易(上海)有限公司	贸易商	37450	0.065
36	广州市番禺区口岸实业公司莲花山公共保税仓库	贸易商	34800	0.061
37	深圳中外运物流有限公司	贸易商	30673	0.053
38	深圳福保赛格实业有限公司	贸易商	30350	0.053
	出口总计		57517706	100.00

四、2012 年聚甲醛(POM)海关进口下降出口上升

2007～2012 年间聚甲醛进口量年均上升 2.88%，比 2005～2010 年间聚甲醛进口量年均增长率下降 2.41%。

因世界经济衰退等原因，2012 年聚甲醛总出口量萎缩至 60kt 下，比 2011 年聚甲醛出口量减少达 12.80%。

2007～2012 年间聚甲醛出口量年均增长 8.06%，比 2005～2010 年间聚甲醛进口量年均增长下降 13.87%(表 58)。

表 58　2007～2012 年聚甲醛进出口统计

项　目	2007 年	2008 年	2009 年	2010 年	2011 年	2012 年
进口量/t	184861	178846	165951	222951	211014	213092
进口金额/万美元	35262.32	36906.93	33568.49	46038.88	46500.93	47549.86
出口量/t	39032	42979	31167	57370	65960	57518
出口金额/万美元	6662.47	8053.56	5774.12	10364.07	12884.82	11238.84
净进口量/t	145829	135867	135478	165581	145054	155574
年增长率/%	4.38	-6.83	-0.80	22.22	12.40	7.25

从进出口量方面来看，2012 年我国聚甲醛进口变化可分三阶段：

第一阶段 2012 年 1～2 月，是我国聚甲醛需求的传统淡季，进口量明显下降，1 月份仅进口 11.3kt，这主要是因为我国传统节日春节的来临，大部分企业放假，因此下游对聚甲醛的需求速度减少。

出口量也是全年最低，仅 3000 余吨。

第二阶段 2012 年 3～6 月，进口量由上升—萎缩—回升—萎缩，由 1 月份的 11.5kt 迅速上升至 3 月份的 19.1kt，增幅达 69.55%，并且在随后 4 月内进口量又回落 17.6kt，5 月份进口量再次回升达到 19.8kt，6 月份进口量再次萎缩到 17.7kt，降幅达 10.59%。

3～5 月出口量是全年高位，均在 5kt 以上，但六月份又跌到 4803t，跌幅达 13.57%。

第三阶段 2012 年 7～12 月，进口量再次回升—萎缩—回升—萎缩，8 月份进口量升到 20.5kt；9 月份进口量升到 21.5kt，创全年之最。但市场萎缩，10 月份进口量跌到 16.6kt，11 月份进口量又回跌到 16.3kt，比 9 月份进口量降幅达 24.12%。

受全球经济危机影响，使得我国制品出口受到严重打击，出口受阻，以加工出口贸易为主的下游塑料制品企业生存环境受到巨大打压，由此聚甲醛的进口量也随之递减。

7～10 月出口量是全年高位，均在五 kt 以上，但 11 月份又跌到 3633t，比 9 月份进口量降幅达 35.94%(表 59)。

表 59　2012 年聚甲醛月进出口统计　　kg

	一月	二月	三月	四月	五月	六月
进口数量	11275561	17667698	19118071	17583685	19817165	17718283
出口数量	3067023	3167427	5384397	5745199	5557278	4803290

续表

	七月	八月	九月	十月	十一月	十二月
进口数量	18310475	20460257	21453252	16566485	16279421	16841714
出口数量	5528040	5240454	5671202	5153305	3633492	4566599

从海关统计中可看出，2012年初级形状的聚甲醛进口地有44个，比2011年49个进口地减5个(表60)。

表60　2012年初级形状的聚甲醛十大进口国家/地区统计

排序	原产进口地	进口金额/美元	进口数量/kg	占比例/%
1	中国台湾省	78564142.00	40817799	19.155
2	韩国	64324177.00	34608295	16.241
3	中国	72042069.00	30558656	14.341
4	美国	59943482.00	27883959	13.085
5	日本	82667229.00	26124531	12.260
6	泰国	36994771.00	21871862	10.264
7	荷兰	33100168.00	13647974	6.405
8	德国	29136490.00	10807374	5.072
9	马来西亚	13222889.00	5154441	2.419
10	中国香港	1402075.00	515060	0.242
进口总计		475498563.00	213092067	100.00

2012年初级形状的聚甲醛出口量占总出口量的85.707%，比上年增加1.867%(表61)。

表61　2012年初级形状的聚甲醛十大出口国家/地区统计

排序	出口目的地	出口金额/美元	出口数量/kg	占比例/%
1	中国香港	71，625，003.00	34756057	60.427
2	土耳其	5，019，143.00	3262861	5.673

续表

排序	出口目的地	出口金额/美元	出口数量/kg	占比例/%
3	日本	5924387.00	2187839	3.804
4	意大利	2854277.00	1790090	3.112
5	中国台湾省	2986254.00	1789514	3.111
6	巴西	1992710.00	1357902	2.361
7	德国	1757132.00	1182480	2.056
8	越南	1970290.00	1131550	1.967
9	俄罗斯联邦	1512843.00	974025	1.693
10	印度	1330660.00	864263	1.503
出口总计		112388408.00	57517706	100.00

五、消费

近几年聚甲醛的市场增长不是特别快，因为其产品应用领域非常分散，市场空间有限。聚甲醛在塑料大件产品上应用得较少，主要用于小件产品。

此外，聚甲醛销售费用高，在余姚塑料交易商城购买聚甲醛的客户，一般只是买几吨甚至不到1t，一般人不愿意代理销售这种产品。

此外，聚酰胺等工程塑料与聚甲醛具有相互替代性，且用户已经形成了使用习惯，要更换成聚甲醛比较困难，这导致聚甲醛使用量不高(表62)。

表62　2007～2012年国内聚甲醛表观消费量统计资料

项　　目	2007	2008	2009	2010	2011	2012
表观消费量/t	295829	290867	299784	375581	405054	435130
年增长率/%	28.78	－1.68	3.07	25.28	7.85	7.43
国内自给率/%	50.70	53.29	55.04	55.91	64.19	64.43

随着航天航空工业、汽车工业和电子电气等的快速发展，全世界需求量每年以5%左右的速度增长，具有广阔发展前景。但聚甲醛生产主要集中在美国、日本、德国和波兰等国家，这些国家长期对中国实施技术封锁。国内技术与国外相比仍有较大差距，国内需求的聚甲醛主要依赖进口。

1.2012年初级形状的聚甲醛进口商

2012年初级形状的聚甲醛进口商共计有2088家，比2011年2220家减132家进口商，进口额最高的十位进口商进口数量占总进口数量的28.907%。

2012 年初级形状的聚甲醛十大进口商中有三家为生产使用企业，均为 POM 改性（即 POM 合金）生产企业。

2012 年初级形状的聚甲醛七十五大进口商中有三十五家为生产使用企业，主要为 POM 改性（即 POM 合金）生产企业，其次为电子工业（手机外壳、电脑外壳等），卫浴工业，家用电器，五金配件，工矿配件，汽车工业，服饰制品，合计进口量占 2012 年总进口量的 22.648%。

2012 年初级形状的聚甲醛七十五大进口商中有四十家为贸易商，占 2012 年总进口量的 32.073%（表 63）。

表 63 2012 年初级形状的聚甲醛七十五大进口生产使用企业所属行业

排序	进 口 商	所属行业	进口数量/kg	占比例/%
1	杜邦中国集团有限公司	POM 改性	13283389	6.234
2	余姚市周佳塑料进出口有限公司	贸易商	9106000	4.273
3	赛拉尼斯（上海）国际贸易有限公司	贸易商	8263808	3.878
4	浙江新长城进出口有限公司	贸易商	7624000	3.578
5	宝理工程塑料贸易（上海）有限公司	POM 改性	4942668	2.319
6	山阳稻田复合塑料（东莞）有限公司	POM 改性	4168885	1.956
7	东莞市对外加工装配服务公司	贸易商	4151269	1.948
8	宝理塑料贸易（上海）有限公司	贸易商	3565016	1.673
9	中海物流（深圳）有限公司	贸易商	3261575	1.531
10	深圳市东荣贸易有限公司	贸易商	3232675	1.517
11	深圳市宝安外经发展有限公司	贸易商	3154370	1.480
12	杜邦贸易（上海）有限公司	贸易商	2950625	1.385
13	塞拉尼斯（南京）多元化工有限公司	POM 改性	2925596	1.373
14	旭化成塑料（上海）有限公司	POM 改性	2749005	1.290
15	深圳市新宁现代物流有限公司	贸易商	2459236	1.154
16	旭化成（苏州）复合塑料有限公司	POM 改性	2164400	1.016
17	禹鹤贸易（上海）有限公司	贸易商	2138675	1.004
18	深圳市龙岗区对外经济发展有限公司	贸易商	2099695	0.985
19	上海怡康化工材料有限公司	POM 改性	1977125	0.928
20	富华杰工业（深圳）有限公司	POM 改性	1891162	0.887
21	佑珉国际贸易（上海）有限公司	贸易商	923000	0.433
22	明达塑胶（厦门）有限公司	塑胶工业	918000	0.431
23	三井塑料贸易（上海）有限公司	贸易商	897326	0.421
24	穗晔（上海）国际贸易有限公司	贸易商	891975	0.419
25	有信制造（中山）有限公司	家用电器	884591	0.415
26	东莞明门幼童用品有限公司	幼童用品	801138	0.376
27	建生裕科贸易（深圳）有限公司	贸易商	792500	0.372
28	穗晔（广州）贸易有限公司	贸易商	724125	0.340
29	太松国际贸易（上海）有限公司	贸易商	710000	0.333
30	礼兴塑胶（深圳）有限公司	塑胶工业	702984	0.330
31	旭化成塑料（广州）有限公司	POM 改性	699422	0.328

续表

排序	进 口 商	所属行业	进口数量/kg	占比例/%
32	群升国际贸易(上海)有限公司	贸易商	697000	0.327
33	深圳泰合威储运有限公司	贸易商	686100	0.322
34	吉田拉链(深圳)有限公司	服饰制品	664119	0.312
35	上海毅塑兴塑胶原料商贸有限公司	贸易商	659800	0.310
36	上海华长贸易有限公司	贸易商	613028	0.288
37	普立万聚合体(深圳)有限公司	POM 改性	602410	0.283
38	南京纺织品进出口股份有限公司	贸易商	602000	0.283
39	深圳市学志供应链管理有限公司	贸易商	600000	0.282
40	厦门象屿通富物流有限公司	贸易商	594000	0.279
41	东莞伟嘉塑胶电子制品有限公司	家用电器	588000	0.276
42	天津长濑国际贸易有限公司	贸易商	577966	0.271
43	上海三凯进出口有限公司	贸易商	556500	0.261
44	烟台北明储运有限公司	贸易商	545229	0.256
45	镇泰(广州)实业有限公司	POM 改性	540320	0.254
46	东莞市金马经贸有限公司	贸易商	529150	0.248
47	深圳市捷瑞时佳科技有限公司	贸易商	518972	0.244
48	福建佳昌化学工业有限公司	精细化工	507549	0.238
49	余姚市大禹进出口有限公司	贸易商	488496	0.229
50	珠海铭祥汽车工业有限公司	工矿配件	474950	0.223
51	威海韩信电子有限公司	家用电器	473605	0.222
52	深圳市旗丰供应链服务有限公司	贸易商	465125	0.218
53	丰田通商(天津)有限公司	贸易商	462094	0.217
54	上海和氏璧化工有限公司	POM 改性	459450	0.216
55	宁波茂忠塑料有限公司	塑胶工业	456000	0.214
56	顺德市新宝电器有限公司	家用电器	450000	0.211
57	科迅塑胶制品(深圳)有限公司	塑胶工业	442751	0.208
58	珠海斗门超毅科技有限公司	POM 改性	434336	0.204
59	深圳市永德丰实业有限公司	贸易商	430510	0.202
60	宁波双林精密模具有限公司	工矿配件	423500	0.199
61	高精科技(深圳)有限公司	工矿配件	421028	0.198
62	珠海市格力物流有限公司	贸易商	417462	0.196
63	东莞克模实业有限公司	工矿配件	413450	0.194
64	东莞利富高塑料制品有限公司	塑胶工业	411025	0.193
65	深圳市宝安鸿彬实业有限公司	贸易商	408150	0.192
66	宁波松洋塑胶有限公司	工矿配件	408000	0.191

续表

排序	进 口 商	所属行业	进口数量/kg	占比例/%
67	树研塑胶科技(惠州)有限公司	工矿配件	406650	0.191
68	浙江嘉联精密五金配件有限公司	工矿配件	402000	0.189
69	宁波杉杉物产有限公司	贸易商	400000	0.188
70	深圳市汇众进出口有限公司	贸易商	395418	0.186
71	珠海珍迎机电有限公司	工矿配件	391033	0.184
72	东莞大日化工厂有限公司	POM 改性	390275	0.183
73	天津大荣精工有限公司	工矿配件	387961	0.182
74	厦门航空开发股份有限公司	贸易商	380000	0.178
75	易妥发仓储服务(深圳)有限公司	贸易商	376975	0.177
进口总计			213092067	54.721

2. 进口消费地区流向分析

2012 年初级形状的聚甲醛进口省市有 23 家(与上比年增加 1 家)。

2012 年级形状的聚甲醛进口商主要集中在广东省，进口数量 111006818kg，比上年减少 1.94%，占总进口量的 52.093%；

五省市进口数量占 2012 年初级形状的聚甲醛总进口数量的 91.524%，比上年增加 0.374%(表 64)。

表 64　2012 年初级形状的聚甲醛五大进口省市统计

排序	进口省市	进口金额/美元	进口数量/kg	占比例/%
1	广东省	245436550.00	111006818	52.093
2	上海市	105033712.00	42249977	19.827
3	浙江省	36136944.00	22307866	10.469
4	福建省	19205885.00	10706166	5.024
5	江苏省	19164162.00	8759871	4.111
总计		475498563.00	213092067	

六、2012 年价格走势

(图表内所例的价格系中国塑料城交易价的月平均价)

从中国塑料城统计看出，2012 年国内聚甲醛市场行情以小幅波动为主，美国杜邦 POM－100P 价格由 1 月份的 31000 元/t 跌至 12 月的 31000 元/t，无波动。

七、进出口贸易方式分析

从海关统计中可看出，2012 年初级形状的聚甲醛进口贸易方式主要为一般贸易(占进口量 38.573%)(表 65)。

表 65　2012 年初级形状的聚甲醛进口交易类型统计

进口交易类型	进口金额/美元	进口数量/kg	占比例/%
一般贸易	169153982.00	82195926	38.573
进料加工贸易	165001695.00	66691814	31.297
保税区仓储转口货物	98364165.00	41639722	19.541
来料加工装配贸易	39425372.00	21336993	10.013
保税仓库进出境货物	3292356.00	1184857	0.556
其他	260993.00	42755	0.020
进口总计	475498563.00	213092067	100.00

从海关统计中可看出，2012 年初级形状的聚甲醛出口贸易方式主要为进料加工贸易(占出口量 58.173%)(表 66)。

表 66　2011 年初级形状的聚甲醛出口交易类型统计

出口交易类型	出口金额/美元	出口数量/kg	占比例/%
进料加工贸易	71066906.00	33459760	58.173
一般贸易	26861529.00	17354732	30.173
来料加工装配贸易	8330325.00	4091074	7.113
保税区仓储转口货物	5738864.00	2495316	4.338
保税仓库进出境货物	225567.00	85848	0.149
对外承包工程出口货物	162920.00	30000	0.052
边境小额贸易	1178.00	525	0.001
其他	1119.00	451	0.000
出口总计	112388408.00	57517706	100.00

八、发展趋势

1. 亚洲聚甲醛扩能速度快供需天平将失衡

众多亚洲聚甲醛项目将于今后两年投产，产能将增加约35%。但全球经济不景气导致需求增速远低于预期，只有4% ~5%。

因需求增长远不及扩能的速度，亚洲聚甲醛目前供需基本平衡的局面将不复存在。

据业界估计，目前亚洲地区的聚甲醛年生产能力约810kt，该地区的聚甲醛年需求接近800kt，表面上看供求比较平衡。

从已经公布的项目来看，未来两年，该地区将有约280kt/a聚甲醛新能力将投运，即产能将增加35%。

这其中包括：中国河南开封龙宇化工公司的60kt/a新装置2013年将投产，届时该公司的聚甲醛产能增加到120kt/a。

从亚洲地区的整体经济增长情况来推算，其聚甲醛的年均增长率在4% ~5%。需求增速远不及扩能的速度，供应过剩将不可避免且短期难以消除，这一切无疑让业界对聚甲醛的消费难言乐观。

2. 蒙能国际32万吨聚甲醛项目开建

蒙能国际能源开发有限公司年产320kt聚甲醛项目2012年10月在内蒙古阿拉善盟开工建设。

蒙能国际能源开发有限公司与阿拉善盟今年2月签订框架式协议，计划总投资800亿元。其中，新型高端煤化工项目预计投资500亿元，铁路建设项目预计投资300亿元。作为高端煤化工项目的年产32万吨聚甲醛项目一期工程投资102亿元。

第五章　2012年聚苯硫醚PPS出口上升进口下降

聚苯硫醚简称PPS，被称为第六大工程塑料，具有优秀的热稳定性、耐强酸耐强碱的化学稳定性、绝缘性以及阻燃性，在各个行业应用范围极为广泛。

聚苯硫醚(PPS)因具有耐高温、耐辐射、耐腐蚀、耐磨、阻燃、高模量、高尺寸稳定性、电性能优良等特点，广泛应用于环保、汽车、电子、石化、制药等行业，其生产技术及产品长期以来被少数国家把持，加之涉及军工，我国该产品的进口受限。

近年来，随着我国成为亚洲第一塑料消费大国，对聚苯硫醚的需求缺口加大，聚苯硫醚随之被列为国家“十二五”重点发展项目。

一、国内聚苯硫醚(PPS)生产

国内聚苯硫醚工程塑料基础树脂生产厂不多，仅有得阳科技股份有限公司和山西福思特，而从事改性聚苯硫醚品种生产的厂家和产能大大超过了基础树脂生产厂。

近年来我国聚苯硫醚改性发展较快，主要由于双螺杆混炼挤出机的引进和国产双螺杆混炼挤出机的推出，给改性PBT创造了有利条件。

国内主要聚苯硫醚(PPS)工程塑料改性厂有拜耳(上海)聚氨酯有限公司，巴斯夫化工有限公司，丽碧复合塑料(深圳)有限公司，上海卡耐尔化工有限公司，孟州市泰利杰有限责任公司，上海亨斯迈聚氨酯有限公司，黄山市德邦粉体材料有限公司，苏威(上海)有限公司，科莱恩(天津)有限公司，广州金发科技股份有限公司，东莞大日化工厂有限公司，清远市建德工程塑料有限公司，来泰祥化工(江苏)有限公司，日邦聚氨酯(上海)有限公司，丽碧复合塑料(深圳)有限公司，上海和氏璧化工有限公司，LG化学(天津)工程塑料有限公司，诺誉化工(上海)有限公司，上海怡康化工材料有限公司，广州和氏璧化工材料有限公司等、从沿海到内地、从外商独资、合资企业发展到乡镇企业、以外商独资、合资和私企为主。

二、聚苯硫醚PPS出口生产省市分布分析

2012年聚苯硫醚出口省市有20家，比2011年18家出口省市增加2家；2012年聚苯硫醚出口生产企业主要集中在上海市，出口数量12491363kg，比上年同比减少7.26%，占总出口数量的47.465%%；其次为广东省，出口数量6300938kg，比上年同比减少8.10%，占总出口数量的23.943%；

五省市出口商出口数量占2012年初级形状的聚甲醛总出口数量的88.344%，比上年同比减少0.146%(表67)。

表67　2012年初级形状的多硫化物五大出口省市统计

排序	出口省市	出口金额/美元	出口数量/kg	占比例/%
1	上海市	76209187.00	12491363	47.465
2	广东省	30012723.00	6300938	23.943
3	浙江省	2260752.00	2044760	7.770
4	山东省	4356181.00	1391637	5.288
5	河南省	1594588.00	1020525	3.878
出口总计		127171923.00	26316752	100.00

三、2012年聚苯硫醚PPS进口上升出口下降

2007 ~2012年间聚苯硫醚进口增长了10.33%，年均增长1.99%。

2007～2012 年间聚苯硫醚出口增长了 325.15%，年均增长 33.57%。

2012 年聚苯硫醚进口量 52.3kt，同比增长 2.59%。

2012 年聚苯硫醚出口量 26317t，比 2011 年下降 0.84%（表 68）。

表 68 2007～2012 年聚苯硫醚进出口统计

项 目	2007 年	2008 年	2009 年	2010 年	2011 年	2012 年
进口量/t	47424	49426	41792	53040	51003	52324
进口金额/万美元	23630.57	26463.66	21874.42	31751.08	35403.61	41032.62
出口量/t	6190	9345	10669	21052	26539	26317
出口金额/万美元	2828.24	3980.92	4742.45	9784.45	13051.48	12717.19
净进口量/t	41234	40081	31123	31988	24464	26007
年增长率/%	17.38	-2.80	-22.35	2.78	-23.52	6.31

从进口量方面来看，2012 年我国聚苯硫醚进口变化可分三阶段：

第一阶段 2012 年 1～2 月，是我国聚苯硫醚需求的传统淡季，进口量明显下降，这主要是因为我国传统节日春节的来临，大部分企业放假，因此下游对聚苯硫醚的需求速度减少，1 月份进口量仅 2764t，是全年月进口量最低一个月，二月开始上升，2 月份进口量比 1 月份增长 53.47%。

第二阶段 2012 年 3～8 月，进口量逐步上升—萎缩—上升，由 2 月份的 4241 吨迅速上升至 3 月份的 4624t，增幅达 9.03%，并且在随后 4 月份进口量小幅下降，降幅 2.75%；5 月份进口量达到 4581t，比 4 月又增长 1.87%，6 月份进口量又下降 6.35%；7～8 月份进口量又上升 10.68%，进口量维持在 4740t 以上。

第三阶段 2010 年 7～12 月，进口量再次回升—萎缩—回升—萎缩，9 月份进口量上升到 5190t，比 8 月又上升 9.26%，成为全年月进口量最高一个月；10 月份进口量大幅下降，比 9 月进口量萎缩达 21.25%；11 月份进口量又上升到 48310kt，比 10 月增幅 18.20 百分点；12 月份进口量又下降到 3722t，比 11 月降幅 22.96%。

1. 2012 年聚苯硫醚年进口量上升

从海关统计中可看出，2012 年聚苯硫醚进口地有 30 个，比 2011 年 29 个增 1 个。聚苯硫醚进口地，2012 年聚苯硫醚进口量 52324t，同比增长 2.59%（表 69）。

表 69 2012 年初级形状的多硫化物八大进口国家/地区统计

排序	进口目的地	进口金额/美元	进口数量/kg	占比例/%
1	日本	177842257.00	18821705	35.972
2	美国	111230078.00	11415923	21.818
3	韩国	18178996.00	6195384	11.840
4	德国	43700898.00	4967548	9.494
5	中国台湾省	10974849.00	2766415	5.287
6	中国	13001108.00	2330271	4.454
7	马来西亚	10139341.00	1567521	2.996
8	法国	7359194.00	1278401	2.443
进口总计		410326205.00	52323748	100.00

2. 2012 年聚苯硫醚年出口量下降

从海关统计中可看出，2012 年聚苯硫醚出口地有 63 个，比 2011 年 52 个出口地增加 11 个聚苯硫醚出口地。

2012 年聚苯硫醚出口量 26317t，比 2011 年下降 0.84%（表 70）。

表 70 2012 年初级形状的多硫化物八大出口国家/地区统计

排序	出口目的地	出口金额/美元	出口数量/kg	占比例/%
1	中国香港	34164153.00	6496224	24.685
2	韩国	16006757.00	3411257	12.962
3	日本	14962488.00	2349422	8.927
4	中国台湾省	8703038.00	1703629	6.474
5	泰国	8759892.00	1572073	5.974
6	印度尼西亚	6771988.00	1286653	4.889
7	马来西亚	5890759.00	1123900	4.271
8	新加坡	5908442.00	1051976	3.997
出口总计		127171923.00	26316752	100.00

四、聚苯硫醚 PPS 进口集中于东部沿海地区

2012 年聚苯硫醚 PPS 进口省市有 21 家，比 2011 年 24 家进口省市减少 3 家聚苯硫醚 PPS 进口消费省市。2012 年聚苯硫醚 PPS 进口商主要集中在广东省，进口数量 21028767kg，比上年同比减少 1.81%，占总进口数量的 40.190%；其次为上海市，进口数量 20021099kg，比上年同比增加 5.44%，占总进口数量的 38.264%；

江苏省进口商进口数量 68054495224103kg，比上年同比增加 30.27%，占总进口数量的 13.006%；

山东省进口商进口数量 1213883kg，比上年同比减少 43.39%，占总进口数量的 2.320%；

天津市进口商进口数量 698032812965kg，比上年同比减少 14.77%，占总进口数量的 1.334%。

五省市进口商进口数量占 2011 年聚苯硫醚 PPS 总进口数量的 95.115%，比 2011 年减少 0.135%(表 71)。

表 71　2012 年初级形状的多硫化物八大进口省市统计

排序	进口省市	进口金额/美元	进口数量/kg	占比例/%
1	广东省	150320893.00	21028767	40.190
2	上海市	135596587.00	20021099	38.264
3	江苏省	57032213.00	6805449	13.006
4	山东省	7957166.00	1213883	2.320
5	天津市	5409294.00	698032	1.334
6	辽宁省	4550811.00	480439	0.918
7	北京市	5435836.00	459625	0.878
8	福建省	4229752.00	444459	0.849
进口总计		410326205.00	52323748	100.00

五、聚苯硫醚 PPS 出口商以外资企业为主

从海关资料来看，2011 年聚苯硫醚 PPS 出口商有 133 家，比 2011 年 136 家减少 3 家聚苯硫醚 PPS 出口商。

2012 年前十位聚苯硫醚 PPS 出口商出口量占总出口量的 40.244%，比 2011 年下降 41.726%。

聚苯硫醚 PPS 出口商以外资企业为主，2012 年前三位聚苯硫醚 PPS 出口商均为外资企业，出口量占总出口量的 29.709%。

2012 年初级形状的多硫化物(聚苯硫醚(PPS))三十八大出口商中有二十四家为生产企业，仅有四川得阳特种新材料有限公司一家是聚苯硫醚 PPS 原料生产厂，其余均为聚苯硫醚改性(即 PPS 合金)，电子工业与精细化学等生产企业，合计出口量占总出口量的 42.527%。2012 年初级形状的多硫化物(聚苯硫醚(PPS))三十八大出口商中有十四家为贸易商，合计出口量占总出口量的 5.651%。

从 2012 年聚苯硫醚 PPS 出口生产企业分布来看，主要集中在广东省、上海市、江苏省、山东四省市(表 72)。

表 72　2012 年初级形状的多硫化物(聚苯硫醚(PPS))三十八大出口生产企业所属行业

排　序	出口企业名称	所属行业	出口数量/kg	占比例/%
1	拜耳(上海)聚氨酯有限公司	PPS 改性	5785313	11.057
2	巴斯夫化工有限公司	PPS 改性	5072193	9.694
3	丽碧复合塑料(深圳)有限公司	PPS 改性	4687178	8.958
4	上海卡耐尔化工有限公司	精细化学	1458650	2.788
5	吉林市兴运润滑油经销有限公司	贸易商	892400	1.706
6	孟州市泰利杰有限责任公司	PPS 改性	850825	1.626
7	山东泰和化工进出口有限公司	贸易商	737510	1.410
8	上海亨斯迈聚氨酯有限公司	PPS 改性	639185	1.222
9	四川得阳特种新材料有限公司	PPS 原料生产厂	476987	0.912
10	青岛和兴精细化学有限公司	精细化学	455700	0.871
11	烟台信谊化工有限公司	精细化学	453110	0.866

续表

排 序	出口企业名称	所属行业	出口数量/kg	占比例/%
12	肇庆大旺奇昌化工有限公司	精细化学	422400	0.807
13	广州华懿物流有限公司	贸易商	299200	0.572
14	黄山市德邦粉体材料有限公司	PPS 改性	294000	0.562
15	苏威(上海)有限公司	PPS 改性	248775	0.475
16	纳尔科工业服务(南京)有限公司	贸易商	242204	0.463
17	空气化工产品(南京)特种胺有限公司	精细化学	212000	0.405
18	杭州天宇化工有限公司	精细化学	210910	0.403
19	亨斯迈纺织染化(中国)有限公司	精细化学	207560	0.397
20	旭化成精细化工(南通)有限公司	精细化学	196336	0.375
21	鹤壁市海富商贸有限公司	贸易商	136000	0.260
22	杭州邦化进出口有限公司	贸易商	116000	0.222
23	科莱恩(天津)有限公司	精细化学	108935	0.208
24	巴斯夫染料化工有限公司	精细化学	99630	0.190
25	广州金发科技股份有限公司	PPS 改性	95350	0.182
26	上海兆辰物流有限公司	贸易商	92975	0.178
27	青岛市益诺泰和国际贸易有限公司	贸易商	92050	0.176
28	东莞大日化工厂有限公司	PPS 改性	88900	0.170
29	雪佛龙菲利普斯化工贸易(上海)有限公司	贸易商	74950	0.143
30	深圳中外运物流有限公司	贸易商	69125	0.132
31	赛拉尼斯(上海)国际贸易有限公司	贸易商	68503	0.131
32	南京泰尔圣贸易有限公司	贸易商	64850	0.124
33	岳阳东润化工有限公司	精细化学	55450	0.106
34	罗地亚(镇江)化学品有限公司	精细化学	54750	0.105
35	清远市建德工程塑料有限公司	PPS 改性	40000	0.076
36	来泰祥化工(江苏)有限公司	PPS 改性	37800	0.072
37	吉林市物资进出口有限公司	贸易商	36000	0.069
38	广西汉都仪进出口有限公司	贸易商	35000	0.067
出口总计			52323748	100.00

六、聚苯硫醚(PPS)工程塑料进口消费以改性(即 PPS 合金)为主

从海关资料来看，2012 年聚苯硫醚 PPS 进口商有 1178 家，比 2011 年 1193 家进口商减少 15 家聚苯硫醚 PPS 进口商。

2012 年聚苯硫醚(PPS)进口额最高的十位进口生产使用企业进口数量占总进口数量的 37.570%，比 2011 年增加 2.89%。聚苯硫醚 PPS 进口商也以外资企业为主，2012 年前六位聚苯硫醚 PPS 进口商均为外资企业，出口量占总出口量的 28.867%。

2012 年初级形状的多硫化物(聚苯硫醚(PPS))五十六大进口商中有二十九家为生产使用企业，主要为聚苯硫醚改性(即 PPS 合金)生产企业，其次为建材工业、电子工业(手机外壳、电脑外壳等)，家用电器、工矿配件、精细化学，合计进口量占 2012 年总进口量的 36.765%。

2012 年初级形状的多硫化物(聚苯硫醚(PPS))五十六大进口商中有二十七家为贸易商，合计进口量占 2012 年总进口量的 24.242%(表 73)。

表73　2012年主要进口生产使用企业所属行业

排　序	进口企业名称	所属行业	进口数量/kg	占比例/%
1	日邦聚氨酯(上海)有限公司	PPS改性	4619532	8.829
2	丽碧复合塑料(深圳)有限公司	PPS改性	3037421	5.805
3	科思泰半导体配件(苏州)有限公司	电子工业	2734843	5.227
4	泰莱贸易(上海)有限公司	贸易商	1664525	3.181
5	拜耳(上海)聚氨酯有限公司	PPS改性	1586457	3.032
6	深圳中电投资股份有限公司	贸易商	1461600	2.793
7	上海亘杰物流有限公司	贸易商	1319625	2.522
8	巴斯夫(中国)有限公司	PPS改性	1095460	2.094
9	深圳市宝安外经发展有限公司	贸易商	1075735	2.056
10	上海高信国际物流有限公司	贸易商	1062713	2.031
11	雪佛龙菲利普斯化工贸易(上海)有限公司	贸易商	877661	1.677
12	台光电子材料(昆山)有限公司	电子工业	808220	1.545
13	上海礼紫仓储有限公司	贸易商	748350	1.430
14	深圳市龙岗区对外经济发展有限公司	贸易商	696192	1.331
15	苏威(上海)有限公司	PPS改性	655558	1.253
16	凡一半导体材料(苏州)有限公司	电子工业	623600	1.192
17	上海迪艾希国际贸易有限公司	贸易商	610421	1.167
18	深圳市轩羽实业有限公司	贸易商	577640	1.104
19	宝理工程塑料贸易(上海)有限公司	PPS改性	564905	1.080
20	肇庆大旺奇昌化工有限公司	精细化学	528000	1.009
21	上海和氏璧化工有限公司	PPS改性	229077	0.438
22	河源市对外加工装配服务公司	贸易商	226700	0.433
23	广州高露洁棕榄有限公司	精细化学	226314	0.433
24	爱森(中国)絮凝剂有限公司	精细化学	222454	0.425
25	东莞极盛电子有限公司	电子工业	216150	0.413
26	北京市塑化贸易有限公司	贸易商	214400	0.410
27	深圳市新宁现代物流有限公司	贸易商	206013	0.394
28	纳尔科工业服务(南京)有限公司	贸易商	201552	0.385
29	巴斯夫特性产品有限公司	精细化学	184245	0.352
30	罗姆集成电路设计(天津)有限公司	电子工业	168900	0.323
31	杜邦中国集团有限公司	贸易商	168080	0.321
32	LG化学(天津)工程塑料有限公司	PPS改性	163200	0.312
33	东莞大宝化工制品有限公司	精细化学	160000	0.306
34	佛山市三水弘溢贸易有限公司	贸易商	159250	0.304
35	佛山飞马化纤有限公司	化纤工业	158800	0.303
36	大连泰达阿尔卑斯物流有限公司	贸易商	155500	0.297
37	诺誉化工(上海)有限公司	PPS改性	152568	0.292

续表

排 序	进口企业名称	所属行业	进口数量/kg	占比例/%
38	惠州市逸睿贸易有限公司	贸易商	149608	0.286
39	镇江河长电子有限公司	电子工业	142050	0.271
40	科昵西贸易(上海)有限公司	贸易商	139350	0.266
41	深圳泰合威储运有限公司	贸易商	138116	0.264
42	佛山市顺德区淘金者贸易有限公司	贸易商	137450	0.263
43	上海怡康化工材料有限公司	PPS 改性	130275	0.249
44	互太(番禺)纺织印染有限公司	印染工业	129625	0.248
45	广州和氏璧化工材料有限公司	PPS 改性	129275	0.247
46	广州番禺纺织品进出口有限公司	贸易商	124400	0.238
47	广州市昂联贸易有限公司	贸易商	124400	0.238
48	蓝星东丽膜科技(北京)有限公司	膜工业	121096	0.231
49	广东省外贸开发公司	贸易商	120000	0.229
50	青岛大成精密塑料有限公司	工矿配件	118000	0.226
51	广东省外运进出口有限公司	贸易商	114020	0.218
52	青岛澳东化工有限公司	精细化学	112000	0.214
53	库尔兹压烫科技(合肥)有限公司	精细化学	111758	0.214
54	上海繁纳旭进出口有限公司	贸易商	109600	0.209
55	深圳市路迪斯达传输设备有限公司	工矿配件	105620	0.202
56	丹尼斯克(中国)有限公司	贸易商	103000	0.197
进口总计			52323748	100.00

七、聚苯硫醚(PPS)价格走势

由于聚苯硫醚(PPS)本体法生产世界上仅有少数几家公司能生产，故市场价格居高不下，近几年市场价一直维持在55000元/t(普通级)，80000元/t(耐高温级)水平上。

八、进出口贸易方式分析

从海关统计中可看出，2012年聚苯硫醚PPS进口贸易方式主要为一般贸易(占进口量51.764%)(表74)。

表74 2012年聚苯硫醚PPS进口交易类型统计

进口交易类型	进口金额/美元	进口数量/kg	占比例/%
一般贸易	183953717.00	27085019	51.764
进料加工贸易	130524709.00	10370177	19.819
保税区仓储转口货物	63126992.00	8264929	15.796
来料加工装配贸易	30846358.00	6578861	12.573
保税仓库进出境货物	1593265.00	15745	0.030
其他	281164.00	9017	0.017
进口总计	410326205.00	52323748	100.00

从海关统计中可看出，2012年聚苯硫醚PPS出口贸易方式主要为进料加工贸易(占出口量53.649%)(表75)。

表75 2012年聚苯硫醚PPS出口交易类型统计

出口交易类型	出口金额/美元	出口数量/kg	占比例/%
进料加工贸易	77875802.00	14118596	53.649
一般贸易	38598362.00	11134743	42.310
保税区仓储转口货物	10108934.00	950272	3.611
保税仓库进出境货物	240000.00	71123	0.270
对外承包工程出口货物	261145.00	31610	0.120
来料加工装配贸易	77650.00	9250	0.035
边境小额贸易	9500.00	1000	0.004
其他	530.00	158	0.001
出口总计	127171923.00	26316752	100.00

九、发展趋势

总投资约4亿元的聚苯硫醚生产线日前在甘肃省敦煌市工业园首期建设完工，这是甘肃省首条聚苯硫醚生产线。投建这条生产线的敦煌西域特种新材股份有限公司，拥有10.5274平方千米的敦煌西湖千万芒硝矿储量，成功构建了从芒硝、元明粉、硫化钠、聚苯硫醚等基本产品，到涂料、纤维、注塑等多级产品的循环经济产业链。依据自身资源和技术优势，从2006年开始实施芒硝尾矿资源开采工艺技术研究、硫化钠焙烧尾气余热利用工艺研究、聚苯硫醚合成工艺研究三项技术课题，所取得成果被认定达到国内领先水平。目前在建的聚苯硫醚项目即采用了多项国家发明专利和企业自主科技成果。

(柴国樑)

塑料机械

2012年我国塑机行业经济运行分析和前景展望

2012年，面对复杂多变的国内外形势，全行业牢牢把握主题主线，坚持稳中求进的总基调，坚持又好又快发展的导向，坚定发展信心，把握有利条件，同心合力，逆势奋进，克服了诸多困难挑战，取得了来之不易的新成绩，交出了令人欣慰的“塑机答卷”。

一、2012年塑机行业经济发展概况

2012年塑机行业经济发展情况，可以用四句话来概括，即：“形势十分严峻，成绩来之不易，发展亮点不少，经济反弹明显”。总的来看，我们遇到的困难比预料的要多，经过全行业的共同努力，经济运行呈现出“稳中有进、总体健康”的良好态势，各项经济指标的完成情况比预期要好。

(一)形势十分严峻

1. 从国际看：环境复杂多变，出口形势严峻。

2012年以来，国际金融危机的深层次影响不断显现，欧债危机仍处高危阶段，非经济因素对世界经济复苏的干扰和影响加大，并通过多种渠道传导给我国经济。世界舞台上新问题、新挑战层出不穷，国际市场竞争加剧，形形色色的保护主义明显抬头并愈演愈烈，突出的表现是，一些国家的贸易保护范围正从传统产业向新兴产业扩展。此外，在南海问题、钓鱼岛问题等涉及中国领土、领海、海洋权益的问题上，中国不断遭受到外来挑衅，日本等传统出口市场受阻。外部环境的复杂严峻，给我国塑机产品的出口带来了较大的困难和挑战。

2. 从国内看：发展困难增多，下行压力加大。

2012年以来，影响经济平稳运行的不利因素较多，不仅一些长期制约经济可持续发展的结构性矛盾尚未根本解决，而且受国际市场需求萎缩、房地产市场低迷等因素的影响，经济下行压力加大，部分企业出现生产经营困难，国际资本也显示流入放缓和流出加快的迹象。内需市场总体不旺，投资增长受到多重制约，转方式调结构压力继续增大。凡此种种，给我国塑机行业经济发展带来诸多不利影响。

3. 从行业看：市场需求不振，增长明显放缓。

面对外需疲软与内需收缩双重叠加、国内外经济增速普遍下滑的严峻形势，我国塑机行业经济发展困难较多，各项经济指标总体上呈现回落趋势。

4. 从企业看：新增订单明显减少，生产经营困难重重。

一方面，国外市场持续低迷，且贸易壁垒不断增多，贸易保护主义愈演愈烈，国际市场竞争更加激烈。同时，国内市场需求不振，经济下行压力加大，居民消费信心走弱，因而企业新增订单明显减少，出厂价格持续走低。另一面，市场开拓难度加大，要素成本不断上升，盈利空间大为缩小，部分企业生产经营困难、举步维艰。不少企业反映，当前的情况与2008年国际金融危机相比，形势更为严峻。

(二)成绩来之不易

根据国家统计局和中国海关对我国塑机行业365家规模以上企业的数据统计，2012年我国塑机行业主要经济指标运行情况如下：

1. 工业总产值完成462.06亿元，与上年同比下降1%。其中第1季度为97.65亿元，同比增长0.15%；第2季度126.46亿元，同比下降1.15%，环比增长29.5%；第3季度118.43亿元，同比下降4.02%，环比下降6.35%；第4季度119.52亿元，同比增长3.31%，环比增长0.92%。

2. 工业销售产值达到444.73亿元，与上年持平。其中第1季度为94.32亿元，同比下降2.03%；第2季度为119.22亿元，同比下降1%，环比增长26.4%；第3季度115.78亿元，同比下降1.17%，环比下降2.89%；第4季度115.41亿元，同比增长4.34%，环比下降0.32%。

3. 出口交货值达到75.66亿元，同比下降6%。其中第1季度为17.88亿元，同比增长6.18%；第2季度17.96亿元，同比下降11.44%，环比增长0.45%；第3季度20.13亿元，同比下降5.89%，环比增长12.08%；第4季度19.69亿元，同比下降10.82%，环比下降2.19%。

4. 塑机产量约 27 万台，同比减少 7%。其中第 1 季度为 52362 台，同比减少 21%；第 2 季度 75481 台，同比下降 12%，环比增长 31%；第 3 季度 69891 万台，同比下降 11%，环比下降 8%；第 4 季度 72654 台，同比增长 20%，环比增长 4%。

5. 从经济效益指标来看，2012 年我国塑机行业主营业务收入利润率为 8.83%，高于全国机械行业 6.81% 的平均水平，位居机床、工程机械、农机、重型等 22 个主要机械分行业的第 2 位，仅略低于印刷机械行业 8.93% 的主营业务收入利润率水平。

综合 2012 年我国塑机行业经济运行情况，应该看到在世界经济低迷、国内经济下行压力较大的背景下，我国塑机行业出现小幅回落，并不让人感到意外。能够取得如此成绩，实属来之不易。

2012 年我国塑机行业主要经济指标统计及产量分布详见表 1、图 1 和图 2。

表 1　2012 年我国塑料机械制造工业主要经济指标统计

月份	塑机产量		工业总产值		工业销售产值		出口交货值		主营业务收入		利润总额	
	台数	同比增长/%	金额/亿元	同比增长/%	金额/亿元	同比增长/%	金额/亿元	同比增长/%	金额/亿元	同比增长/%	金额/亿元	同比增长/%
1	10832	-54	24.82	-21	23.89	-21	5.23	-13	57.48	3	3.38	-31
2	16160	-11	31.4	20	31.54	20	5.64	32				
3	25370	-21	41.43	4	38.89	-2	7.01	7	40.93	4	2.73	-28
4	23957	-22	41.13	-4	37.81	-4	5.82	-6	38.2	7	3.92	3
5	25066	-8	40.9	-0.3	39.01	2	5.95	-2	40.74	-6	3.57	-8
6	26458	-4	44.43	1	42.4	-0.3	6.19	-23	43.13	-1	3.26	-1
7	22711	-14	39.52	-6	38.96	-3	6.6	-3	37.45	-2	2.48	-36
8	23075	-13	39.43	-1	37.5	-1	6.53	-6	37.3	-7	3.41	7
9	24105	-5	39.48	-4	39.32	0	7	-9	38.89	-7	2.89	-22
10	20549	-10	36.13	-4	35.24	1	5.33	-25	26.59	-29	3.45	21
11	25232	45	38.26	-1	37.16	0	6.1	-17	37.79	1	3.66	10
12	26873	34	45.13	15	43.01	11	8.26	7	45.44	10	6.44	52
合计	270388	-7	462.06	-1	444.73	0	75.66	-6	443.94	-2	39.19	-4

注：数据来源于国家统计局。

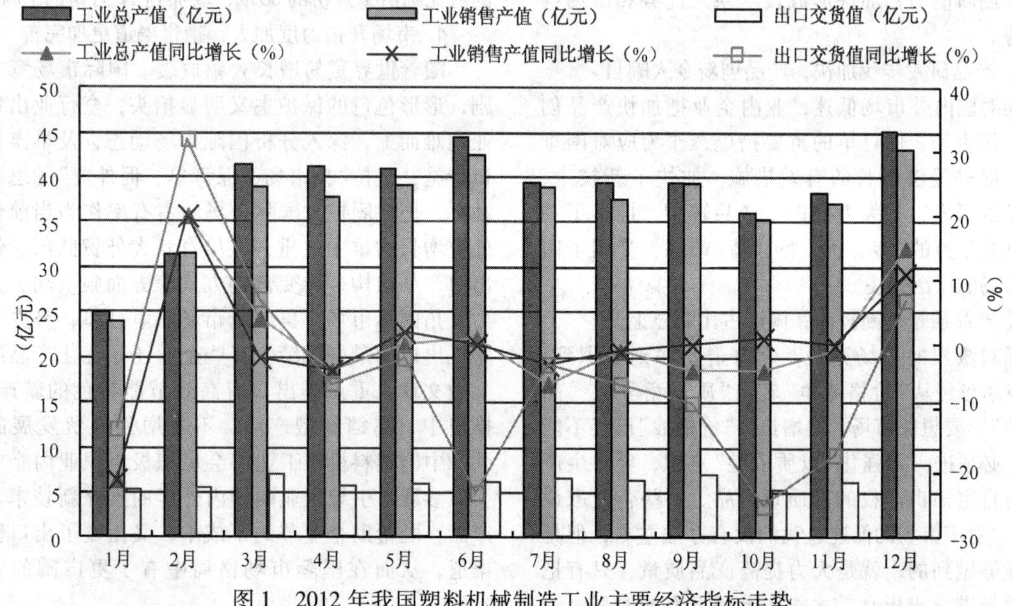

图 1　2012 年我国塑料机械制造工业主要经济指标走势

注：数据来源于国家统计局。

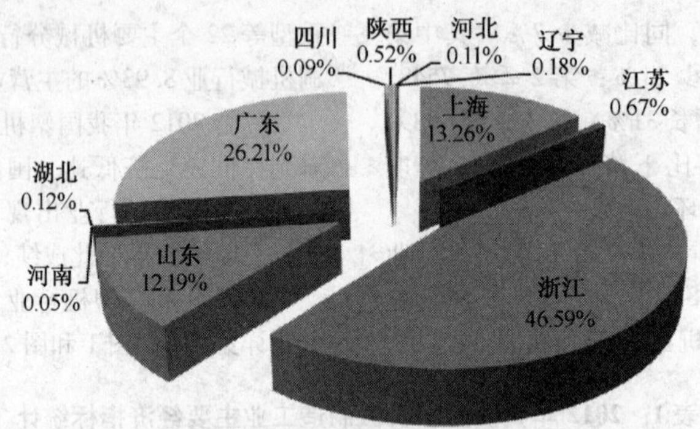

图2 2012年我国塑机产量分布

注：数据来源于国家统计局。

(三)发展亮点不少

尽管2012年主要经济指标出现不同程度的回落，但是我们还应该看到塑机行业经济发展的亮点不少。

1. 创新投入不断加大，创新能力不断增强

2012年以来，业内企业都有这样一个共识，只有利用经济下行的倒逼机制，加大科技投入，才能渡过难关；只有着力提升自主创新能力，才能实现经济可持续发展。于是，业内企业致力于转型升级，在科技创新方面"舍得花钱"，加强技术进步和技术改造，引进先进技术和设备，推进以企业为主体的技术创新体系建设，积极实施科技创新工程，深入实施知识产权战略，着力建设技术研究中心等研究平台，并与知名高校和科研院所加强产学研结合，共同开展新技术、新工艺的研发。同时，十分注重科技人才的培育，大力开展职工技术培训，努力提升科技创新能力，加快形成技术领先优势和市场竞争优势。

2. 产品研发步伐加快，产品创新令人瞩目

面对国内外市场低迷，业内企业把加快产品创新作为保市场、保订单的重要措施，作为应对困难挑战、促进经济增长的有效措施，加快了新技术、新产品的研发，并大力推进了产品转型，推出了一批独具竞争力的"专、优、特、精"产品，受到了国内外市场的广泛关注。

3. 产品质量不断提高，国产占比明显上升

面对激烈的市场竞争，业内企业深刻认识到，市场竞争已经从"价格竞争"转向"质量竞争"、"品质竞争"。要想保市场、促增长，"价格战"已经不能奏效，必须进一步强化"以质取胜"意识，努力生产出具有自主知识产权的高质量产品。一些企业家说得好，"对于市场的低迷，我们没有办法左右，但是我们能够做到的，就是大力提高产品质量，只有把产品质量进一步提高，才能在市场下滑的时候，让国内外客户看好我们的产品，选择我们的产品。"

业内企业认真学习贯彻国务院印发的《质量发展纲要(2011~2020年)》，积极实施质量兴企战略，牢固树立全面、全程和全员的质量意识，进一步加强企业质量管理。不少企业还积极实施质量提升工程，坚持把质量视为产品的生命，对产品设计、生产、制造、营销、服务等实施全过程质量管理，全面提升产品的质量水平，培育形成以技术、标准、品牌、服务为核心的质量新优势，大力提升"塑机质量"。有的企业摒弃了以追求产量为中心的粗放发展模式，走质量效益型的道路，大力增强创新能力，积极开发新产品，努力提高技术含量和附加值，着力提高产品档次和质量。在全行业的共同努力下，我国塑机产品的质量水平进一步提升，市场竞争力有了较大的提高，取得令人可喜的成效。据国家统计局和中国海关数据显示，2012年进口塑机设备的占比由1月份的40%，下降到12月份的27%，而国产塑机设备的占比则由1月份的60%，增加到12月份的73%。

4. 市场开拓力度加大，销售渠道更加完善

随着世界贸易增长大幅放缓、国际市场竞争加剧，形形色色的保护主义明显抬头，全行业出口企业迎难而上，深入分析国际市场动态，及早谋划出口措施，坚持"拓市场、保订单、促外贸"的思路不动摇，把巩固扩大国际市场的占有率作为当前促进外贸增长的重中之重，在培育壮大外贸队伍、优化出口产品结构、转变营销方式等方面狠下功夫，大力开拓国际市场，勇于抢市场、争订单，努力争取塑机出口的最好成绩。有些企业还在优化产品结构上做文章，重点推出具有高效节能特色的新产品，推出中、高档新型产品，不断增强外贸发展的后劲。中国塑料机械工业协会也积极组织业内企业参会、参展，引导企业向国内外客商推介新技术、新产品，既帮助企业节约了成本，又拓宽了出口销售渠道，从而在国际市场格局中有了更广阔的发展空间。

与此同时，在国内需求不足和经济增速放缓的

情况下，业内企业立足国内市场，着力扩大内需，不断更新观念，推进营销创新，全方位、多层次地分析和挖掘客户的需求，着力建设更加完善的销售渠道，发扬勤于跑市场、善于闯市场、勇于拓市场的精神，实施服务内容、服务方式的创新，坚持诚信为本、质量至上、以客为尊的原则，加大产品推介和销售力度，做好引导消费节能型塑机的文章，努力提高服务质量和用户满意度，不仅巩固了老客户，而且赢得了新客户，取得了良好的业绩。

5. 管理水平不断提升，降本增效积极推进

针对新增订单减少、企业成本上升、盈利空间缩小等问题，业内企业采取多种措施，苦练内功，应对市场变化，强化管理能力，加强费用成本控制。不少企业还进一步确立了向管理要效益的理念，加强管理创新，不断健全现代企业制度，推进企业精细化管理，坚持诚信经营和规范经营，加强管控水平和全面风险管理能力，深化节支降耗，深入挖潜增效，降低企业经营管理成本，努力提高企业经济效益和发展质量。

6. 企业文化发挥作用，引领职工攻坚克难

面对比以往更加复杂多变的经济环境，业内企业顺应时代发展需要，更加重视先进企业文化的作用，积极采取各种措施，切实加强企业文化建设，团结引领职工同舟共济、攻坚克难。例如，有的企业搭建了职工学习和交流平台、职工思想动态及时反馈平台、企业民主管理平台、增进职工友谊和丰富文化生活平台、为职工服务和为职工办实事平台，弘扬企业精神，提高职工素质，加强人文关怀，引导职工认清形势，坚定信心，逆势奋进，使企业克服了一个个困难，呈现出经济企稳回升的势头。

目前，行业发展的亮点正在增多，积极因素不断积累，有利条件正在集聚，从而为经济运行聚积了能量，打下了良好基础。

(四)经济反弹明显

2012 年，由于国内外市场持续低迷，我国塑机行业经济运行承受了巨大压力。但是从逐月经济指标的走向来分析，传递出反弹明显的积极信号。特别是进入 2012 年 12 月份以来，行业产销、出口和效益指标全面恢复快速增长，当月的利润总额超过第 1 季度的利润总和，实现 52% 的同比增速。行业经济“稳”的基础有所巩固，“好”的态势明显。

二、2012 年塑机产品进出口概况

(一)塑机市场容量分析

特点：进口塑机占比明显下降，国产塑机占比明显上升。

根据国统局和海关数据统计，2012 年国内塑料机械市场容量为 493.85 亿元，其中进口塑料机械为 133.96 亿元，占国内塑料机械市场容量的 27%，国产塑料机械为 359.89 亿元，占国内塑料机械市场容量的 73%。2012 年我国塑料机械市场容量、我国塑机市场份额占比走势详见表 2 和图 3。

表 2　2012 年我国塑料机械市场容量

月份	国内塑料机械市场容量/亿元	其中：进口/亿元	国内/亿元	进口占比/%	国产占比/%
1	24.54	9.72	14.82	40	60
2	37.13	10.84	26.29	29	71
3	45.84	12.6	33.24	27	73
4	45.54	12.29	33.26	27	73
5	43.48	12.41	31.07	29	71
6	48.34	12.6	35.74	26	74
7	41.92	11.47	30.45	27	73
8	43.02	12.41	30.61	29	71
9	43.07	12.22	30.85	28	72
10	37.89	9.95	27.94	26	74
11	37.95	8.13	29.82	21	79
12	45.13	9.32	35.81	21	79
合计	493.85	133.96	359.89	27	73

注：数据来源于国家统计局和中国海关。

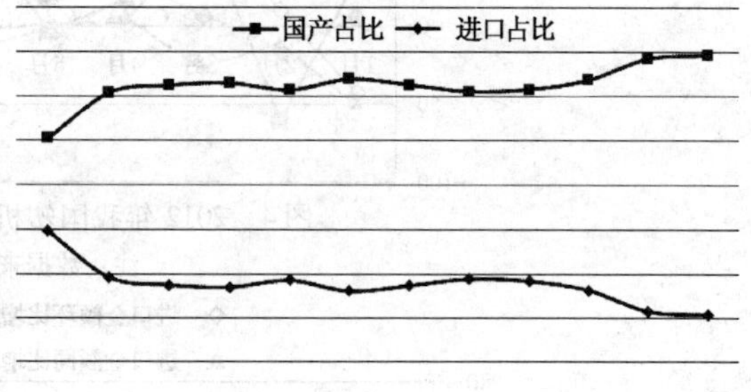

图 3　2012 年我国塑机市场份额占比走势

注：数据来源于国家统计局和中国海关。

(二)塑机产品进出口总量分析

特点：进口数量和金额明显减少，出口数量和金额明显增加。

数据显示，2012 年我国进口塑料机械的数量为 10482 台，同比下降了 24%；进口塑料机械的金额为 212635 万美元，同比下降 3%。国产塑料机械出口的数量为 69693 台，同比增长了 35%；出口金额为 161886 万美元，同比增长了 11%。2012 年我国塑机产品进出口总量、进出口增速走势详见表 3、图 4、图 5 和图 6。

表 3　2012 年我国塑机产品进出口总量

月份	进口					出口					贸易逆差	
	数量/台	金额/万美元	平均单价/(万美元/台)	数量同比增长/%	金额同比增长/%	数量/台	金额/万美元	平均单价/(万美元/台)	数量同比增长/%	金额同比增长/%	金额/万美元	同比增长/%
1	542	15427	28	−48	−24	6099	15867	3	6	30	−440	−105
2	603	17206	29	−11	32	2448	8111	3	−14	12	9095	57
3	990	20016	20	−24	−26	3984	12722	3	9	16	7294	−54
4	999	19507	20	6	5	4708	12456	3	32	11	7051	−3
5	1016	19665	19	−1	7	4590	15606	3	16	30	4059	−37
6	984	20009	20	−15	17	7803	13757	2	81	2	6252	78
7	1131	18184	16	−64	−7	6825	14436	2	55	23	3748	−52
8	849	19698	23	−13	8	4351	14030	3	4	9	5668	5
9	1026	19392	19	16	17	5866	13669	2	2	−2	5723	118
10	827	15822	19	15	2	11445	13024	1	177	3	2798	−3
11	724	12934	18	−18	−16	5027	13428	3	15	−4	−494	−133
12	791	14775	19	−15	−19	6547	14780	2	39	5	−5	−100
合计	10482	212635	20	−24	−3	69693	161886	2	35	11	50749	−29

注：数据来源于中国海关。

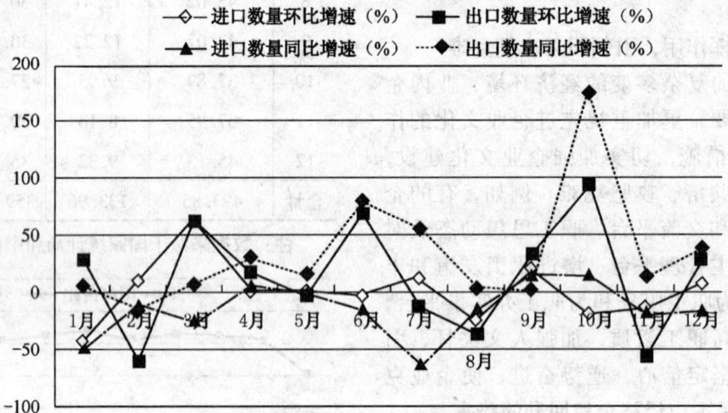

图 4　2012 年我国塑机产品进出口数量增速走势

注：数据来源于中国海关。

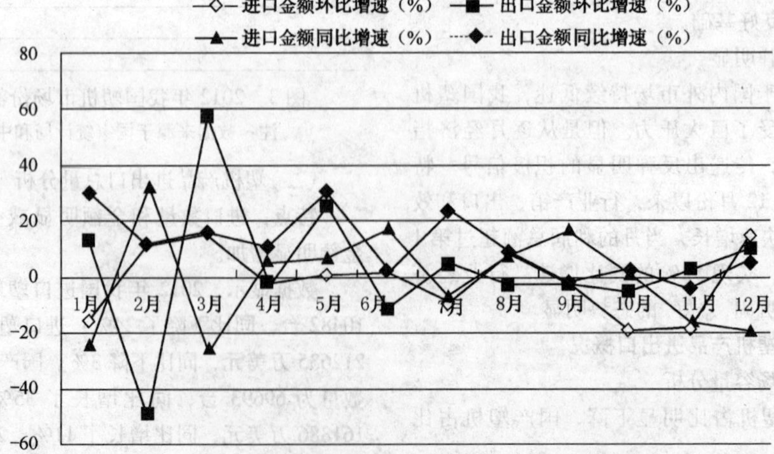

图 5　2012 年我国塑机产品进出口金额增速走势

注：数据来源于中国海关。

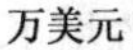

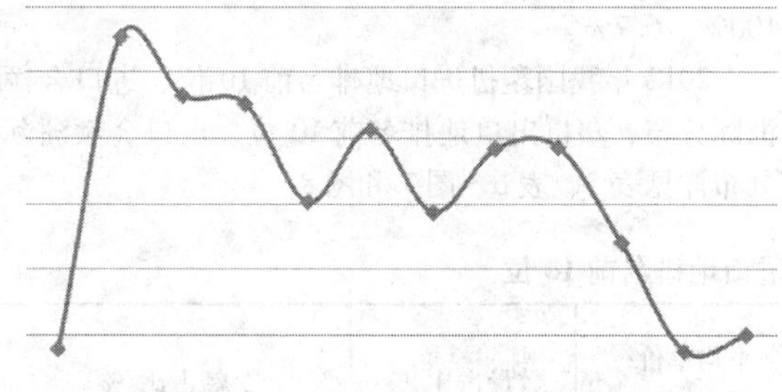

图6　2012 年我国塑机产品贸易逆差金额走势

注：数据来源于中国海关。

（三）塑机产品进出口分税号分析

1. 与塑机整体贸易逆差形势不同，注塑机、塑料中空成型机为贸易顺差。根据中国海关数据，2012 年注塑机进口数量为 6622 台，出口数量为 24839 台，进口数量小于出口数量；注塑机进口金额为 80929 万美元，出口金额为 89963 万美元，贸易顺差 9034 万美元。塑料中空成型机进口 89 台，金额 2091 万美元；出口 914 台，出口金额 4236 万美元，贸易顺差 2145 万美元。

2. 注塑机、挤出机和吹塑机是塑机出口的三大品种。其中注塑机出口数量占 35.64%，出口金额占 55.57%。

3. 挤出机、吹塑机和塑料压延成型机出口增幅较大。其中挤出机出口数量和金额分别同比增长 32%、24%；吹塑机出口数量和金额分别同比增长 159%、8%；塑料压延成型机出口数量和金额分别同比增长 57%、38%。2012 年我国塑机产品进出口分税号统计详见表 4。

表 4　2012 年我国塑机产品进出口分税号统计

序号	税号	名　称	进口				出口			
			数量/台	数量占比/%	金额/万美元	金额占比/%	数量/台	数量占比/%	金额/万美元	金额占比/%
1	84771010	注塑机	6622	63.17	80929	38.06	24839	35.64	89963	55.57
2	84771090	其他注射机	407	3.88	6318	2.97	1110	1.59	2198	1.36
3	84772010	塑料造粒机	275	2.62	20207	9.50	3538	5.08	6536	4.04
4	84772090	其他挤出机	889	8.48	43574	20.49	8542	12.26	27381	16.91
5	84773010	挤出吹塑机	98	0.93	6771	3.18	1847	2.65	5311	3.28
6	84773020	注射吹塑机	58	0.55	2542	1.20	774	1.11	874	0.54
7	84773090	其他吹塑机	140	1.34	15326	7.21	16772	24.07	9428	5.82
8	84774010	塑料中空成型机	89	0.85	2091	0.98	914	1.31	4236	2.62
9	84774020	塑料压延成型机	97	0.93	4440	2.09	2098	3.01	2391	1.48
10	84774090	其他真空模塑机及其他热成型机器	654	6.24	12948	6.09	5072	7.28	4726	2.92
11	84775900	其他模塑或成型机器	1153	11.00	17489	8.22	4187	6.01	8843	5.46
合计			10482	100	212635	100	69693	100	161886	100

注：数据来源于中国海关。

（四）进出口地域分布统计

进口方面，2012 年我国从日本、德国、意大利和美国这几个主要来源国家进口的数量和金额均有不同程度的降低。其中从日本进口数量和金额分别同比减少 13.84%、8.37%；从德国进口数量和金额分别同比减少 5.56%、1.47%；从意大利进口数量和金额分别同比减少 28.98%、18.47%；从美国进口数量和金额分别同比减少 81.72%、16.63%；从欧洲进口数量和金额分别同比减少 3.09%、4.3%；从亚洲进口数量和金额分别同比减少 11.88%、1.14%。

出口方面，泰国、印度尼西亚、美国、俄罗斯成为我国塑机增长最快的出口市场。从整体而言，出口到各大洲的数量和金额均全面增长。其中出口至亚洲的数量和金额分别同比增长 29.15%、

8.41%；出口至非洲的数量和金额分别同比增长18.93%、15.02%；出口至欧洲的数量和金额分别同比增长109.05%、12.8%；出口至拉丁美洲的数量和金额分别同比增长13.06%、1.82%；出口至北美洲的数量和金额分别同比增长20.84%、69.43%；出口至大洋洲的数量和金额分别同比增长100%、6.7%。

2012年我国塑机进口地排名前10位、进口金额洲际分布、塑机出口地排名前10位、出口金额洲际分布详见表5、表6、图7和图8。

表5 2012年我国塑机进口地排名前10位

序号	名称	进口数量/台	进口金额/万美元	平均单价/(万美元/台)	数量占比/%	金额占比/%
1	日本	4244	71015	17	40.49	33.4
2	德国	1071	61763	58	10.22	29.05
3	中国台湾	2669	28885	11	25.46	13.58
4	韩国	801	11620	15	7.64	5.46
5	意大利	201	10926	54	1.92	5.14
6	瑞士	142	8421	59	1.35	3.96
7	美国	473	5207	11	4.51	2.45
8	奥地利	137	4373	32	1.31	2.06
9	法国	73	3287	45	0.7	1.55
10	加拿大	60	2045	34	0.57	0.96
合计		9871	207541	21	94.17	97.6

注：数据来源于中国海关。

表6 2012年我国塑机出口地排名前10位

序号	名称	出口数量/台	出口金额/万美元	平均单价/(万美元/台)	数量占比/%	金额占比/%
1	泰国	2900	13778	5	4.16	8.51
2	印度尼西亚	3916	12308	3	5.62	7.60
3	巴西	2300	8650	4	3.30	5.34
4	土耳其	1523	8521	6	2.19	5.26
5	越南	2798	7719	3	4.01	4.77
6	俄罗斯	3986	7704	2	5.72	4.76
7	印度	2117	7064	3	3.04	4.36
8	美国	1840	6750	4	2.64	4.17
9	马来西亚	1999	4872	2	2.87	3.01
10	伊朗	1576	4825	3	2.26	2.98
合计		24955	82192	3	35.81	50.77

注：数据来源于中国海关。

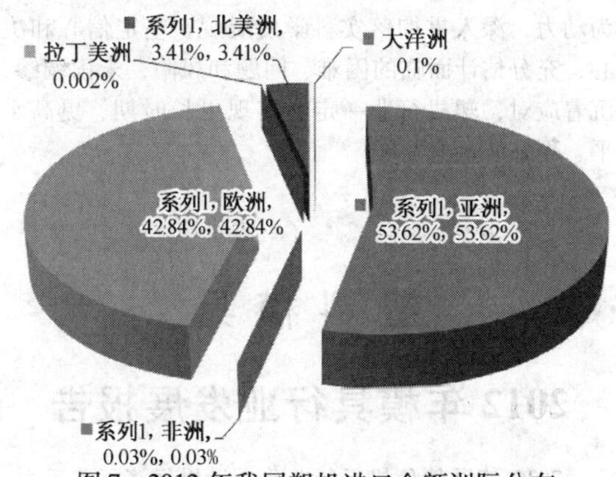

图7　2012年我国塑机进口金额洲际分布

注：数据来源于中国海关。

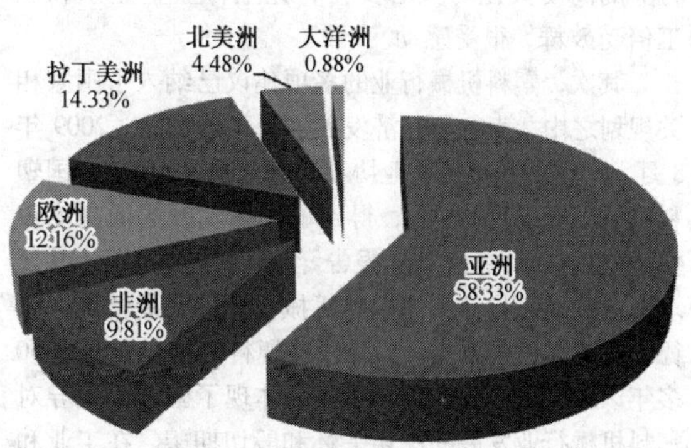

图8　2012年我国塑机出口金额洲际分布

注：数据来源于中国海关。

三、当前和今后一段时期我国塑机行业经济发展前景展望

当前，国内外形势依然错综复杂，经济运行所面临的不稳定、不确定因素较多，保持工业经济稳定增长的基础尚不牢固，情况不容乐观。展望今后一段时期，我国塑机行业既面临着严峻的挑战，又面临诸多良好的机遇，我们对行业经济的未来抱有信心，一个崭新的发展春天定会来到。

(一)国际经济形势分析

从总体上看，当前和今后一段时期，世界经济形势仍将十分严峻复杂。一是发达国家经济面临多重困境。美国经济总量虽然基本恢复到金融危机前的水平，但增长迟缓、复苏乏力；欧洲主权债务危机仍在发酵，欧元区经济已陷入整体衰退；日本挣扎在维持微弱正增长的边缘，居高不下的沉重债务使其也有可能陷入危机。二是发展中国家经济面临严重问题。在国际金融危机期间，相对于发达国家经济的不景气，发展中国家经济增长较为强劲。但目前受发达国家危机日益严重的影响，以及本国经济刺激政策的逐步退出，特别是自身结构性问题暴露的影响，发展中国家经济增长明显减速。三是随着世界贸易增长大幅放缓、国际市场竞争加剧，形形色色的保护主义愈演愈烈，并有可能导致全球经济继续恶化。当前我国已成为他国贸易保护的“重灾区”。国际经济环境的动荡，使得外需乏力的局面可能会延续，各种保护主义又在打压中国企业，出口形势仍然严峻。凡此种种，给我国塑料机械产品出口，仍会带来诸多不利和困难。

与此同时，我们还应该看到，世界多极化、经济全球化的大趋势没有变，和平、发展、合作的时代潮流没有变，国际大环境总体上有利于我国和平发展的局面没有变。世界经济将出现结构调整，特别是新科技革命正孕育重大突破，全球范围内新能源、新材料、生物经济方兴未艾，既给我们既带来挑战，又给我们带来机遇。

(二)国内经济形势分析

虽然影响经济平稳运行的不利因素仍然较多，但是应该看到，我国经济发展长期向好的趋势没有发生改变，我国经济发展的潜力和动力仍然较大，处于重要战略机遇期的基本条件没有发生变化。其中，需求潜力尤为明显。一是城镇化带来的巨大需求，从而持续释放出巨大的内需潜能。二是消费需求的巨大潜力。随着收入分配改革的深化、城乡居民收入的进一步增加，居民消费水平必将有一个更快的提升。

据国家工业和信息化部党组成员、总工程师朱宏任分析，当前我国工业经济运行正处在筑底企稳的紧要关口，有利因素正在集聚，随着企业稳增长政策效应的进一步显现，企稳的势头将得到进一步巩固。总体来看，我国工业经济运行朝着企稳方向发展，生产增势缓中见稳，面临的下行压力正逐步减缓。

(三)行业经济形势分析

2012年行业经济虽然出现小幅回落，仍然取得了来之不易的成绩，并继续出现积极变化，呈现诸多向好迹象。随着中央一系列稳增长政策逐步显现效应，随着国家支持塑机行业发展的政策措施的逐步发挥作用，以及全行业各项应对举措的逐步落实，经济向好趋势将进一步明显。

(四)行业发展的机遇和有利条件

当前，我国塑料机械行业仍然面临着前所未有的发展机遇。

首先，党中央、国务院领导的高度重视，使全行业受到巨大鼓舞和鞭策，为行业经济发展注入强大的活力和动力。继2011年4月中共中央政治局常委、国务院总理温家宝亲临海天塑机集团公司视察之后，2012年8月又亲临广东伊之密精密机械股份有限公司调研，充分体现了党中央、国务院对塑机行业的高度关注与关心支持，让全行业企业家和职工倍受鼓舞、很受感动。

其次，塑料机械行业的多项建议已纳入了国家相关规划之中，为行业经济发展插上飞翔翅膀。2009年8月，中国塑料机械工业协会向国务院提交了《中国塑料机械工业发展报告》，得到了国务院领导的高度重视。张德江副总理在该《报告》上作了重要批示，并要求工业和信息化部关注塑料机械行业的发展情况。张德江副总理的重要批示，是我国塑料机械行业诞生50多年以来层次最高的领导批示，体现了国务院领导对塑料机械行业发展的深切关怀和殷切期望。在工业和信息化部、国家发展和改革委员会等有关部委的重视和支持下，塑料机械行业的多项建议已纳入了国家相关规划之中，行业的主张上升为国家意志，成为中国装备制造业发展中的一个亮点，从而为塑料机械行业提供了千载难逢的历史机遇。

其三，国家部委的重视关心和倾力支持，形成了激发塑料机械行业持续发展的不竭动力。几年来，工业和信息化部等国家有关部委对塑料机械行业的支持，既有政策的推动，也有项目的安排，还有资金的扶持，政策环境的逐步改善，给全行业带来新的希望，有力地推动着塑机行业的又好又快发展。

其四，塑料机械行业作用和地位的提升，为行业持续快速发展开辟了广阔空间。塑料机械作为高分子复合材料加工的“工作母机”，其地位和作用日益显现，不仅每年带动塑料制品产业实现了2万多亿元的产值，而且成为航空航天、国防、家电、汽车等国民经济各行业的重要技术装备，成为战略性新兴产业的配套专用设备，为塑料机械行业的发展创造了有利条件。

其五，我国塑机装备具有较高的性价比，在国内外市场依然有巨大需求。

其六，相关产业的稳中有进，加大了对塑料机械产品的需求。据相关产业资料显示，在我国经济出现积极变化的大背景下，家电产业的经济运行，呈现出逐月好转迹象，我国自有品牌汽车出口再创新高，未来几个月仍将快速增长。相关产业的稳中有进，工业景气总体趋稳，将会释放出巨大的市场潜力，拉动着塑料机械的稳步增长。

总之，展望今后一段时期，尽管国内外经济环境依然复杂严峻，但是我国塑机行业经济发展长期向好的趋势没有改变，大有作为的重要战略机遇仍然存在。国家重视和支持塑机行业发展的措施正在发挥作用，国内外市场对我国塑机装备依然有着巨大需求，塑机行业经济发展的潜力和动力仍然较大。只要我们以学习贯彻党的十八大和全国“两会”精神为动力，深入贯彻落实科学发展观，坚定信心和决心，充分估计面临的困难、问题和风险，未雨绸缪，沉着应对，塑机行业一定会实现更长时期、更高水平、更好质量的发展。

（中国塑料机械工业协会）

塑料模具

2012年模具行业发展报告

2012年欧债危机反复恶化、世界经济复苏乏力，市场需求疲软，国际形势复杂多变，经济发展低迷。受国内外诸多不利因素影响，我国经济也结束了多年来的高速增长期，发展速度有较大回落。受此影响，2012年模具市场也呈现需求不旺，行业经济运行情况要差于预期的状况。由于汽车、电子、轻工、机械等模具主要用户行业的低速增长，因此国内模具市场也呈现低速增长景象。世界模具市场虽然疲软，但由于我国模具的比较优势还在，再加上积极开拓市场和努力提高服务水平，因此模具出口情况要好于预期，“出口带动”战略成果显著。

一、行业经济运行总体概况

2012年对模具行业来说，是困难的一年，综合来看，我国模具行业发展增长水平要低于上年，根据中国模具工业协会预计，2012年全国模具总销售额比上年增长10%左右，达到1365亿元。在这约10%左右的增长率中，技术含量高的中高档产品的增长率要高于总体水平，技术含量低的中低档产品增长率要低于总体水平。我国模具出口额达到37.31亿美元，创出了历史新高。整个行业在技术进步、转型升级和结构调整方面也都取得了可喜成绩。

根据国家统计局资料，模具制造业主营业务收入2000万元以上的企业经济运行情况虽差于预期，但仍有发展，增长速度虽有所回落，但企业数和产值、主营收入、利润总额、劳动生产率等指标都高于上年，创历史新高。一些主要指标发展情况见表1。

国家统计局数据还显示了不同所有制企业数比例及相应产值比例变化情况(见图1)，与上年相比，三资企业和国有企业数量及其产值比例比上年都略有减少，民营企业数量及其产值比例数都比上年略有增多。

表 1 2012 年主营收入 2000 万元以上模具企业主要指标

年份	企业数/个	工业总产值/亿元	工业销售产值/亿元	利润总额/亿元	亏损企业数/个	亏损企业亏损总额/亿元	资产总计/亿元	职工人数/万人	人均年产值/（万元/人）
2012	1688	1892.69	1840.04	115.79	248	9.13	1597.71	37.29	50.26
同比增长率/%	6.23	15.37	14.93	12.63	27.83	11.88	15.86	-3.0	8.69

注：1. 表中工业总产值和产品销售收入等不完全是模具产品，包括了模具制品及其他产品。

2. 由于年报数据尚未发布，因此表中 2012 年数据是国家统计局 1～12 月份的统计数据，今后会与年报数据有出入。

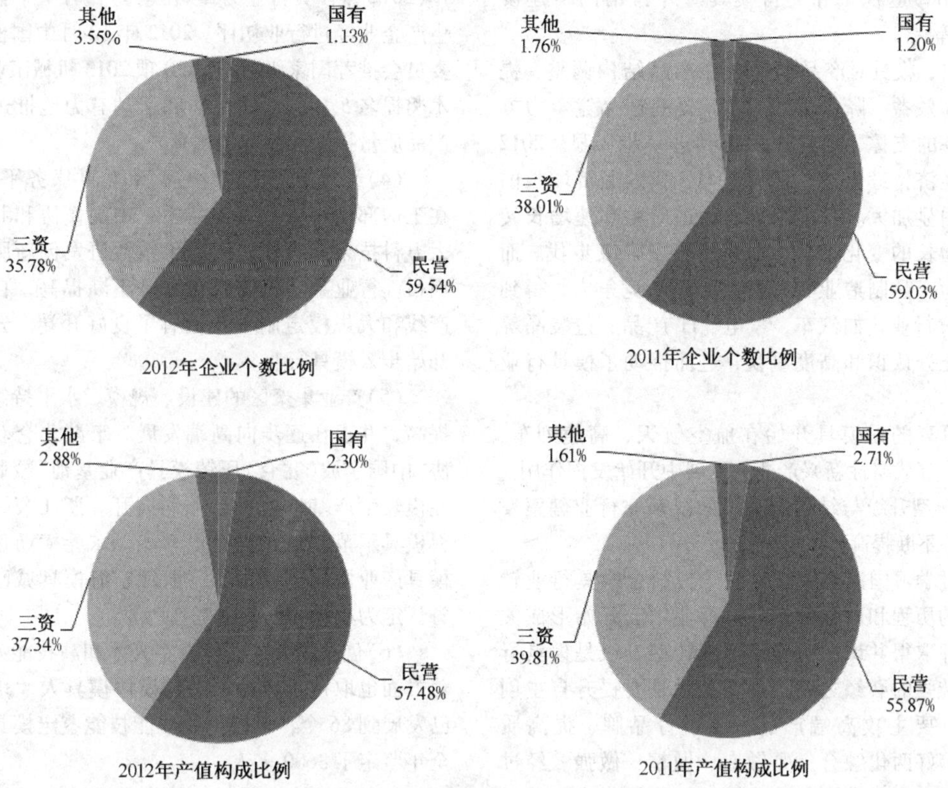

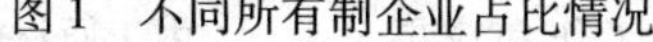

图 1 不同所有制企业占比情况

2012 年我国模具行业经济运行主要有如下特点：

1. 行业总体发展速度有所放缓，出口高速增长，行业地位稳步提升

充满挑战的 2012 年过去了，我国模具工业克服了世界经济复苏动力不足和持续的欧债危机对我国经济增长的冲击，全年实现了 10% 增长，模具出口保持了高速增长，全年出口额达到 37.31 亿美元，同比增长 24.16%，比年初预计要好。如果按季度分析，则 1～3 月、1～6 月、1～9 月、1～12 月，与上年同比的增长率分别是 25.98%、23.92%、26.42%、24.16%，表现为高速平稳发展走势。之所以有如此骄人的成绩，主要有三条原因：一是我国模具行业技术水平提高很快，模具产品性价比进一步提高；二是模具企业开拓国际市场的步伐加快，措施得力，成效显著；三是工业发达国家为了降低生产成本，所需模具向我国转移态势进一步发展。与此同时，模具对制造业转型升级的支撑作用被广泛认可，行业地位稳步提升。首先，模具在国民经济，特别是制造业发展中的作用和地位进一步得到政府主管部门的重视和支持。例如工信部制定的“三基规划”开始落实，列入国家和地方支持的模具项目大大增加：以提高高档模具技术水平和生产能力为主的 8 项技术改造项目年初通过评审，被列入国家项目，投资强度超过 10 亿元，在规模上是

模具行业近三个“五年计划”以来的第一次；据不完全统计，2012年各级政府对模具研发项目的经费支持超过1亿元，用于奖励和补贴模具新产品研制、标准制修订、科技成果和市场开拓的费用超过3000万元。又如为支持模具出口，财政部制定的新的模具进出口税号于2012年1月开始施行，模具产品增加了3个税号，这是近20年来第一次调整模具进出口税号。再如商务部在模具行业第一次授牌“科技兴贸模具出口基地”，并着手研究提高精密模具出口退税率和支持模具海外营销网络建设的政策等。

同时，模具对产品制造业在产品结构调整、提升质量和效益、降低生产成本，提高产品竞争力方面所发挥的支撑、保障作用得到进一步彰显。2012年全球经济持续低迷、增长乏力，我国经济增长的压力也明显加大。我国制造业为适应由高速增长转向稳定增长的变化形势，加快了转型升级步伐。而模具作为产品制造业转型升级的核心竞争力，得到模具用户行业，如汽车、家电、IT产品、包装品等行业的充分认识和高度重视，进而推动了模具行业发展。

更可喜的是模具开始在航空航天、高速列车、船舶制造等战略性新兴产业的发展中开始发挥作用。

2. 转型升级与结构调整成效显著，行业健康发展，水平不断提高

通过学习国家有关文件政策，结合模具行业转型升级的历程和面临的挑战，行业中已开始形成关注氛围并取得共识：明确了不断转型升级是模具行业由大转强的必经之路，主要手段是要提升自主创新能力，要主攻高端产品，要培育品牌、提高质量，要搞好两化融合，要做专、做精、做强。经过多次研讨，中国模协制定了模具行业转型升级的量化指标体系，并做了许多工作，主要工作和成果如下：

(1)根据全球金融危机以来模具行业骨干重点企业的情况好于一般企业，大企业好于小企业，高水平企业好于低水平企业的发展特点，中国模协修订了《中国重点骨干模具企业评定细则》：提高了评定标准；明确了每两年评定一次；取消终身制，四年进行一次复审。根据新的《评定细则》，对原授牌的110家重点骨干企业进行了复审(通过103家)，对新申报48家企业进行了评定(通过30家)。5月30日，中国模协发布了133个模具行业重点骨干企业名单。这有利于转型升级，在行业中产生很好反响。

(2)注重科研开发，成果显著。模具行业2012年获得机械工业科学技术奖6项，其中二等奖3项，三等奖3项。在2012年上海国际模展上，评定“精模奖”146项，其中27项一等奖达到或接近国际先进水平。这些成果的研发和应用，推动了模具行业的技术进步和总体水平的提升。

(3)中国模协召开了“模具行业推进质量提升与品牌建设交流会”，工信部科技司和中小企业司领导到会解读国家政策、指导模具行业推进质量提升与品牌建设；按计划参加“机械工业优质品牌”培育工作(2012年模具行业为塑料模具)，有9个塑料模具生产企业经过行业初评。2012年12月中国模协技术委员会推荐国家级新产品20项2013机械工业科学技术奖提名5项。这些工作和活动有力地推进了行业产品质量提升和品牌的培育。

(4)继续推进信息化建设和公共服务平台建设，在工信部中小企业司支持下，中国模协和北京数码大方科技公司合作，启动了精益研发创新服务平台项目。行业数字化信息化水平不断提高，自动化生产线和大规模定制生产已有了良好开端。云计算已开始步入模具行业。

(5)产业集聚区的建设、规模、水平持续发展和提高，并正在逐步向高端发展。宁波北仑获中国模协“中国宁波(北仑)压铸模具产业基地”授牌，其高端模具生产基地建设已顺利展开。浙江余姚高端塑料模具示范基地建设也已开始。东莞横沥正在建设模具产业协同创新中心，浙江宁海模具城已被浙江省认定为小企业创业示范基地等。

(6)创新型人才、复合型人才和高技能人才的培养方面也取得了成绩，中国模协模具人才培训基地已发展到86个，机械工业职能技能鉴定模具分中心全年鉴定了3600多人。

3. 模具企业产业链延伸势头不断发展

由于原材料和能源价格上涨以及人工成本大幅上升等原因，2012年模具产品利润率进一步下滑。为了生存与发展，有越来越多的企业延伸了产业链。这一趋势的发展对模具行业的结构产生了影响。其一是整个行业的产能产值和投资的增长中，非模具占比不断上升；其二是模具的产能产值中，自产自用的内配比例相对提高，销售额的占比相对减少。2012年模具行业规模以上企业工业总产值和工业销售产值同比上年分别增长15.37%和14.93%，而全国模具销售总额只增长10%，这也反映出产业链延伸所造成的结构变化。

在回顾取得成绩的同时，我们还应该重视困难和问题，也必须认清差距，明确目标与任务。困难和问题有一些是长期以来一直存在的，有一些是新

形势下产生的，综合起来大致有如下几点：

(1)我国模具工业与国际先进水平相比，仍旧存在较大差距，缩短差距任重道远。

(2)国际经济低迷，国内制造业增速降低，模具市场总体来看仍是需求不旺。

(3)生产成本持续提高，主要是原材料价格上涨和劳务成本提高；行业税负较重：模具行业平均税负达到8～10%，高出机械制造业平均税负(4.5%)约一倍；增值税返还政策停止后，新的扶植政策至今未落实。

(4)企业同质化现象严重，中低档模具产能过剩，不正当竞争加剧，导致模具价格和经营利润率不断下降，亏损企业增多。

(5)创新能力薄弱，高水平人才严重匮乏。

(6)中小企业融资困难、应收款增多、资金紧张、成本上升、利润率下降现象不但仍旧存在，得不到较好解决，而且还在不断发展。

二、科技创新与新产品开发

增强自主创新能力，努力提高企业核心竞争力，向专、精、特、新方向发展已成为行业共识。经过全行业共同努力，2012 年新获授权的模具方面的专利有 2000 多个，其中三分之一以上为发明专利。为广大中小企业服务和各地公共服务平台及产学研用相结合的技术创新联盟继续发挥作用，促进了模具行业科技创新和新产品开发。2012 年模具行业部分科技成果见表2。2012 年模具行业部分重大新产品见表3。

2012 年 12 月，中国模具工业协会对全国各地拟上报申请国家级新产品和中国机械工业科学技术奖的模具项目进行了专家评审，对其中 25 项写出了推荐意见，认为这些项目都达到了国内领先水平，有的还达到或接近国际水平，基本上体现了我国模具工业不断进步的发展趋势。

第十四届中国国际模具技术和设备展览会于 2012 年5 月31 日至6 月3 日在上海举办，中国模具工业协会组织专家对 223 个申报参评的模具项目进行了评定，最终评出“精模奖”一等奖 27 项、二等奖 46 项、三等奖 73 项，现将一等奖和二等奖分别列于表4、表5。

表2　2012 年模具行业部分科技成果

序号	项 目 名 称	主要完成单位	成果水平及获奖情况
1	大型铝合金型材挤压成套工模具设计制造技术与应用	沈阳新鑫模具有限公司	国家科技进步奖二等奖
2	轿车齿轮净成形工艺与模具制造关键技术及应用	江苏太平洋精锻科技股份有限公司	中国机械工业科学技术奖二等奖
3	精密多腔饮料盖模具开发及应用	四川省宜宾普什模具有限公司	中国机械工业科学技术奖二等奖
4	移动式半导体激光强化与修复汽车模具的装备与工艺	湖南大学湖南湖大三佳车辆技术装备有限公司	中国机械工业科学技术奖二等奖
5	五轴数控精密子午线轮胎模具电火花加工技术及设备	苏州电加工机床研究所有限公司	中国机械工业科学技术奖三等奖
6	振锤模具制造技术	上海交通大学长春轨道客车股份有限公司	中国机械工业科学技术奖三等奖
7	高品质模具设计与制造关键技术及应用	浙江大学、浙江金典模具有限公司、浙江精诚模具机械有限公司	中国机械工业科学技术奖三等奖

表3 2012年模具行业部分重大新产品

序号	项目名称	主要完成单位	水平
1	59/80R63巨型子午线轮胎模具	山东豪迈机械科技股份有限公司	国家重点新产品
2	机电气一体化自动多功能连续模	昆山飞宇精密模具有限公司	国家火炬计划
3	汽车点烟器摩擦壳连续冲压模具	昆山荣腾模具部品制造有限公司	国家火炬计划
4	车用大型复杂精密注塑模具	苏州万隆汽车零部件股份有限公司	国家火炬计划
5	HD-141型数控转塔冲床重载翻边模具	扬州恒德模具有限公司	国家火炬计划
6	具有超大角度双导杆斜顶的汽车仪表板模具	浙江模具厂	国家火炬计划
7	96腔热流道PET瓶坯模具	浙江德玛克机械有限公司	国家火炬计划
8	光学级精密轿车反射镜注塑模具	浙江赛豪实业有限公司	国家火炬计划
9	外拉脱模大型精密汽车保险杠注塑模具	浙江凯华模具有限公司	国家火炬计划
10	新型快速装卸式桥梁钢芯模	浙江永峰模具制造有限公司	国家火炬计划
11	汽车门板低压发泡注塑模具	滨海模塑集团有限公司	国家火炬计划
12	连接器端子精密连续注塑成型模具	杭州嘉力讯电子科技有限公司	国家火炬计划
13	节能环保型汽车覆盖件模具	瑞鹄汽车模具有限公司	国家火炬计划
14	基于阻燃型纸基覆铜板的高密冲模	莆田市城厢区星华电子模具有限公司	国家火炬计划
15	高性能轴承滚动体镦压组合模具	洛阳卫创轴承模具有限公司	国家火炬计划
16	精冲模具用氮气弹簧	湖北兴升科技发展有限公司	国家火炬计划
17	大容量双筒循环注塑机及模具	湖北鄂丰模具有限公司	国家火炬计划
18	高铬耐磨耐热玻璃模具	常熟市精工模具制造有限公司	国家火炬计划
19	冲头压块组件	北京永茂机电科技有限公司	专利产品
20	静音斜楔		
21	倾斜式旋转凸轮		

表4 "精模奖"一等奖

序号	模具名称	单位名称
1	大型导光板注射压缩成型模	四川长虹模塑科技有限公司
2	手机B壳多种大面积嵌件注塑模具	北京东明兴业科技有限公司
3	90克PET瓶胚64腔两面旋转模具	四川宜宾普什模具有限公司
4	K1汽车前车门窗框内外一次压合模具	山东潍坊福田模具有限责任公司
5	D312双色前大灯注塑模	浙江赛豪实业有限公司
6	EA211MPI缸盖重力铸造模具	宁波合力模具科技股份有限公司
7	ϕ112.2空调电机铁芯高速冲级进模(三列)	宁波震裕模具有限公司
8	汽车类弹簧盖冷冲级进模	无锡微研有限公司
9	汽车地图袋双规格叠层注塑模具	青岛海尔模具有限公司

续表

序号	模 具 名 称	单 位 名 称
10	64 腔扁平滴头模具	天津市津荣天河机电有限公司(天津市中环三峰电子有限公司)
11	双轴倾斜式旋转斜楔	北京永茂机电科技有限公司
12	翼子板冲孔修边整形模	东风模具冲压技术有限公司模具分公司
13	轿车后桥副车架压铸模具	广州市型腔模具制造有限公司
14	成形与淬火一体化热冲压专用模具	机械科学研究总院先进制造技术研究中心 烟台泰利汽车模具制造有限公司
15	自动填装陶瓷插芯法兰芯底座模具	宁波贝隆精密模塑有限公司
16	保时捷汽车中控支架镁合金压铸模具	宁波市北仑辉旺铸模实业有限公司
17	BP31 叶片模内组装模具	宁波舜宇模具有限公司
18	SⅡ汽车仪表板本体注塑模具	宁波远东制模有限公司
19	盒式导板吊装斜楔机构	盘起工业(大连)有限公司
20	LC－42X77 电视前面框模	厦门海盛模具有限公司
21	SSOP024 引线框架模具	厦门市特克模具工业有限公司
22	中控排挡面板模具	上海超日精密模具有限公司
23	高强钢冲压成形智能化加工测试通用模具	上海工程技术大学 上海信适智能科技有限公司
24	SGMG60 侧围外板模具	上海赛科利汽车模具技术应用有限公司(SSDT)
25	婴儿车底座支架模具	唯科(厦门)精密塑胶模具有限公司
26	涡轮风扇叶片注塑模	余姚市福莱达模塑厂(普通合伙)
27	FORD－CD391 仪表板微发泡注塑模	浙江凯华模具有限公司

表 5 “精模奖”二等奖

序号	模 具 名 称	单 位 名 称
1	日产发动机油底壳压铸模具	广州市型腔模具制造有限公司
2	手机镜头镜筒内进胶精密外螺纹模具	宁波贝隆精密模塑有限公司
3	东风 2.0T 缸体压铸模	宁波合力模具科技股份有限公司
4	重卡变速箱壳体压铸模具	宁波市北仑辉旺铸模实业有限公司
5	货箱左/右边板外板翻整侧翻整侧冲孔模	山东潍坊福田模具有限责任公司
6	深腔厚板不锈钢件拉延模	四川宜宾普什模具有限公司
7	72 腔 29/25 瓶盖模具	四川宜宾普什模具有限公司
8	D338 三色三工位灯具模	浙江赛豪实业有限公司
9	江淮星锐多功能商用车－左右翼子板模具	安徽江淮福臻车体装备有限公司
10	大型精密 V 开口自动可调下模	安徽联盟模具工业股份有限公司
11	LED 支架注塑模	安徽铜陵中发三佳科技股份有限公司
12	照相机镜头支撑圈模具	北京电子科技职业学院 北京莱比德精密模具有限责任公司
13	电脑射频连接器多工位精密级进模	成都宏明双新科技股份有限公司

续表

序号	模具名称	单位名称
14	大型双色注塑模具	东莞康佳模具塑胶有限公司
15	汽车内饰门板模具	福州蓝卡潞工业有限公司
16	新型节能定位模架系列	杭州萧山精密模具标准件厂
17	GMX352(美国原厂通用)顶盖整形侧整形模具	河北金环模具有限公司
18	Y-TEC-J53R 项目下控制臂连续模具	湖北十堰先锋模具股份有限公司
19	空调翅片高速精密级进模[φ5.2×72 列×2 步进]	黄山三佳谊华精密机械有限公司
20	全球同步开发高档汽车(一体式 3D)加油管模具	宁波方正汽车模具有限公司
21	浴缸注塑模具	宁波锦隆电器有限公司
22	美国日立 H300/H301 支架砂型铸造模具	宁波强盛机械模具有限公司
23	汽车中央通道饰板模具	宁波如强模塑有限公司
24	一出二安全气囊盖模具	宁波双林模具有限公司
25	奔驰新开发 X204 项目尾门窗框注塑模	宁波跃飞模具有限公司
26	奥迪轿车 B 下立柱注塑模具	宁海县第一注塑模具有限公司
27	空调面板模内贴膜模具	青岛英联精密模具有限公司
28	原子印章滑壳顺序顶出塑料模具	厦门捷信达模具塑胶有限公司
29	多腔侧面热流道模	厦门精卫模具有限公司
30	点钞系统主体上盖模具	厦门市超日精密模具有限公司
31	旋转型芯橡胶模具	厦门市驰杰模具工业有限公司
32	汽车类精密电容器塑胶壳模具(2.5×6.5×7.2)	厦门市松竹精密科技有限公司
33	PBF&AK2 型腔测压自动分解模	上海戈冉泊精密模塑有限公司
34	集水盒	深圳市乐华行模具有限公司
35	可变进气格栅单腔双色模具	深圳市银宝山新科技股份有限公司
36	大型骨架内腔定位加热分体式管件模具	台州市黄岩炜大塑料机械有限公司
37	全自动合盖旋转脱模牙膏盖注塑模	台州市黄岩西诺模具有限公司
38	福特汽车二次燃烧控制器注塑模	天津轻工职业技术学院
39	大型汽车成型结构件的级进模具	天津市津兆机电开发有限公司
40	双动压合机构	天津鑫茂天和机电科技有限公司
41	125 双 V 导向系列斜楔	武汉东风科尔模具标准件有限公司
42	左右支架多工位连续模	烟台泰利汽车模具制造有限公司
43	44×24SELF BASE 托板叠层模	余姚市宏硕模具制造有限公司
44	雷诺车门中立柱注塑模	浙江亨达塑料模具有限公司
45	汽车车门本体注塑模	浙江黄岩美多模具厂
46	C520-104141-OP10 拉延模	重庆平伟汽车模具股份有限公司

表2~表5 所列的科技新产品成果只是行业中的一部分，此外尚有许多成果也值得重视。例如被列入国家04科技重大专项的“特种材料复杂型面加工的五轴联动精密数控电火花成形机床”(由北京电加工机床研究所承担)获得了CCMT2012“春燕奖”，连云港杰瑞模具技术有限公司“压铸生产线智能化工业机器人产业化”项目和“高效节能自锁式两模板注塑机”项目都列入了2012年国家火炬计划。这些项目都与模具休戚相关。

三、固定资产投资情况

由于受全球经济不景气和我国经济发展放缓影响，国内固定资产投资增速也放缓了。模具行业全年投入只比上年略有增加，总数略超250亿元，其中投向于模具产业链延伸和模具集聚生产基地的建设占多数。

模具集聚生产基地建设进一步活跃：总投资20亿元的宁波北仑大碶高档模具及汽配产业基地、总投资15亿元的华中模具产业园、总投资10亿元的天津辰东模具产业园和苏州角直模具产业园都已开工建设；总投资15亿元的滁州(国际)家电模具城和总投资14亿元的宁海模具城工贸区建设自上年开工以来顺利续建；黄岩模具博览中心和余姚中模国际大厦都已完成2亿元投资；广东东莞横沥模具产业科技园已完成投资11亿元；河北泊头汽车模具产业基地完成投资近2亿元；广东南海联沙模具城、福州模具产业园、沈阳近海模具产业基地都在建设中；浙江萧山精密模具产业基地、河北南皮模具园区、浙江宁海宁东模具园区和四川遂宁金桥模具产业园都已开始筹建招商；广东、浙江、江苏等地的许多原有模具城(园、区)在由大变强方面都有较大投入。

模具企业部分亿元以上的项目情况：总投资8亿元的一汽模具制造有限公司新工厂项目已竣工；亿和精密工业控股有限公司10亿元项目已完成4亿多元；武汉重冶集团6亿元的模架模坯项目已竣工投产，10亿元的汽车覆盖件模具项目已开工；上海华普汽车模具制造有限公司3亿元项目已投产；上海同捷科技股份有限公司无锡模具分公司已完成投资3亿多元；浙江凯华模具有限公司台州工厂、广东百年科技、杭州龙记、福田潍坊模具厂、东莞钜升塑胶电子制品有限公司智能化精密模具柔性制造生产线等都已竣工投产；广东新宝电器股份有限公司1亿多元模具自动化项目、江苏成功数字化科技有限公司1500万美元丹徒模具项目、唐山德丰科技有限公司2亿元模具及机械项目、富伟精机股份有限公司2.5亿元江苏新厂项目等都已开工建设；宁波合力模具科技股份有限公司1.1亿元项目已完成大半；广东巨轮模具股份有限公司印度工厂已顺利投产，揭阳自动化模具车间项目已开始建设；泊头市京泊汽车模具有限责任公司1亿多元技改项目已开始建设。鉴于中高档及新型模具材料供不应求大量进口的状况，不少特钢企业陆续开始投资模具钢项目，如江苏天工国际5亿元模具新材料项目等。

四、对外贸易情况

2012年我国模具进出口总额为62.15亿美元，比2011年增加了18.62%。其中进口总额为24.84亿美元，比上年增加11.14%；出口总额为37.31亿美元，比上年增加24.16%。有关情况如下：

1. 按模具种类分，进出口最高的仍是塑料橡胶模具，分别占了进出口总额的53.78%和71.68%；其次是冲压模具，分别占了进出口总额的32.74%和10.12%。具体如表6。

2. 按进口货源地分，进口模具主要来自日本、韩国和德国，其次是我国台澎金马关税区、加拿大、美国、意大利、瑞士、新加坡和西班牙。具体如表7。

3. 按出口目的地分，我国出口模具的市场主要是中国香港、美国和日本，其次是印度、德国、巴西、泰国、法国、我国台澎金马关税区和越南。具体如表8。

4. 按进口目的地分，进口最多的是广东、江苏和上海，其次是天津、北京、山东、辽宁、吉林、重庆和福建。具体如表9。

5. 按出口货源地分，出口模具主要来自广东、江苏和浙江，其次为上海、山东、天津、福建、辽宁、安徽和河北。具体如表10。

表6 各类模具2012年进出口情况表

模具种类	进口		出口	
	金额/万美元	所占比例/%	金额/万美元	所占比例/%
塑料橡胶模具	133617.36	53.78	262360.85	70.32
冲压模具	81338.02	32.74	44611.53	11.95
压铸模具	12214.90	4.92	10919.83	2.93
轮胎模具	1691.61	0.68	438.99	0.12
玻璃模具	908.51	0.37	8143.10	2.18
粉末冶金模具	308.27	0.12	212.41	0.06
其他模具及模具标准件	18371.07	7.39	46421.54	12.44

注：压铸模具、轮胎模具、玻璃模具是2012年才新列出其相应税号，因此尚有部分企业未按新税号而仍按老税号报关，所以本表所列数据尚不能完全反映实际情况，实际数据当大于表列数据。

表7　2012年进口模具主要货源地情况表

货源地	日本	韩国	德国	我国台澎金马关税区	加拿大	美国	意大利	瑞士	新加坡	西班牙
进口量/万美元	79061.23	56673.87	24009.67	21261.79	9134.20	8542.08	5436.67	1984.37	1733.14	1270.53
所占比例/%	31.82	22.81	9.66	8.56	3.68	3.44	2.19	0.80	0.70	0.51

表8　2012年出口模具主要目的地情况表

目的地	中国香港	美国	日本	印度	德国	巴西	泰国	法国	我国台澎金马关税区	越南
出口量/万美元	63330.15	43416.94	30318.83	19953.61	19110.99	10792.9	10208.01	9158.84	8683.30	6044.31
所占比例/%	16.97	11.64	8.13	5.35	5.12	2.89	2.74	2.45	2.33	1.62

注：表中出口到中国香港的部分，由于中国香港多为转口贸易，其最终目的地并非都是中国香港。

表9　2012年进口模具最多的10个省市情况表

目的地	广东	江苏	上海	天津	北京	山东	辽宁	吉林	重庆	福建
进口量/万美元	62570.63	48711.24	27853.00	16527.92	14858.07	14398.07	13934.62	6671.95	4532.28	3338.72
所占比例/%	25.18	19.61	11.21	6.65	5.98	5..80	5.61	2.69	1.82	1.34

表10　2012年出口模具最多的10个省市情况表

货源地	广东	江苏	浙江	上海	山东	天津	福建	辽宁	安徽	河北
出口量/万美元	159466.67	56272.30	54882.96	29829.38	15605.61	14836.49	10337.20	7043.14	3533.18	2734.55
所占比例/%	42.74	15.08	14.71	7.99	4.18	3.98	2.77	1.89	0.95	0.73

从今年1至4季度我国模具进出口数据看，不但每个季度进出口都表现为正增长，而且全年模具出口的增长幅度一直高于进口的增长，全年外贸顺差额达到了11.76亿美元，比上年增加了4.06亿美元。

按逐季出口情况来看，1～3月、1～6月、1～9月、1～12月与上年同比的增长率分别为25.98%、23.92%、26.42%、24.16%，基本上表现为高速平稳增长的态势，但4季度增速明显放缓，预示2012年增速可能会继续下滑。

再从进出口模具价格进行分析：从海关提供的各类模具进出口的数量和金额可以看出，2012年出口冲压模具平均每吨价为9940美元，比上年下降3.14%；进口冲压模具平均每吨价为18301美元，比上年下降10.48%；进出口平均单价之比为1.84:1，差距有所缩小。进出口单价都有下降，尤其是进口单价降幅更大，这一方面是由于国际市场的疲软对模具出口企业造成的竞争加剧所致，另一方面是人民币汇率升高所造成。我国模具制造水平提高和技术进步致使进口模具价格下降也是一个重要原因。出口产品价格走低，成本上涨，致使企业效益下滑，生产经营较为困难，这是一个值得注意的问题。与此同时，我国出口塑料橡胶模具的每套平均价格有大幅上升。这说明我国出口的塑料橡胶模具的技术含量和附加值都有明显提升。进口塑料橡胶模具的每套平均单价变化不大，进出口平均单价比缩小到了2.95:1，但差距仍旧很大。

出口的逐年增长，促进了行业技术水平的提高，但差距仍旧明显。今后企业不但要在转型升级、调整出口产品结构上下功夫，还要利用政策优势和企业自身的优势，在各专业领域、高端产品制造、高新技术上下功夫，缩短与国际先进水平的差距，不断提高企业在国际市场的竞争力。

今年海关资料统计显示中国模具已出口到了181个国家和地区，比上年有增加，说明开拓市场已见成效。

2012年不少国家出台了量化宽松的货币政策，尤其是日本使日元大幅贬值已累及周边，也正在冲击着我国的对日外贸。今后如果日元再大规模贬值，则不但将挤占我国的海外市场，而且也会挤占我国的国内市场。有关汇率变化情况应引起我们的高度警惕。

五、2013年发展形势预测与展望

2013年全球经济仍将处于金融危机后的调整期中，形势仍将复杂多变，世界经济形势虽然缓慢复苏的趋势已然明显，但总体上仍将十分严峻。2013年也是我国“十二五”规划承上启下的重要一年，国家将保持宏观调控稳中求进主基调不变，将继续实施积极的财政政策和稳健的货币政策，经济将保持平衡较快发展，制造业大国的基本格局不会改变，迈向制造业强国的步伐将加快，总体情况可能会略好于上年。中国经济正处在增长阶段转换和寻求新平衡的关键期，从2012年四季度开始，发展向好态势日渐明朗，但落后产能过剩、生产经营成本上升、利润率继续下滑情况仍旧存在，因此发展增长预期只能是谨慎乐观。模具制造业是制造业的重要组成部分，2012年及今后一段时期内，可能会随着国民经济一起进入中速增长期。这一时期产能扩张已退居次要位置，创新能力将较快增强，转型升级将加快，产品水平的提升也将加快。由于模具主要用户行业如汽车、电子、轻工、机械等预期将低速增长，因此模具市场总体情况也将是在低速增长的情况下略好于上年。预计将会有10%左右的增长率。由于中国模具在国际市场中比较优势仍旧存在，因此在“出口带动”战略的进一步实施和广大企业积极努力奋斗之下，增速虽然可能会有所回落，但全年达到20%左右的增长率还是有可能的。

结构优化和转型升级是一个庞大的系统工程，是“十二五”期间发展的主旋律，也是模具行业由大转强的必经之路，整个模具市场和行业运行也必然会伴随着这个主旋律前进。从市场适应于这个主旋律出发，在2013年发展不快的模具市场中，预计有些模具发展会快一些、好一些。

科学发展、结构调整、开拓创新、改变发展方式、转型升级、提升核心竞争力，在以数字化制造及新能源、新材料的广泛应用为主要代表的第三次工业革命浪潮悄然来临之际，这些词语已成为工业界的热门话题。在此情景下，模具行业今后会如何发展？应该如何发展？粗略展望如下：

1. 模具产需可能会恢复到二位数增长

扩大内需战略的实施，会推动我国制造业发展。其中汽车、家电、IT产业、包装、建材、日用品等模具大用户行业的发展，仍将为模具发展提供大的市场空间。例如汽车制造工艺中90%以上使用模具，汽车相关模具已占我国模具总量的三分之一以上（德、日、美占到40%以上），汽车模具的发展主要依赖新车型的推出；塑料制品90%以上由模具成形，因此塑料模具将随塑料工业的发展而有较快发展，我国塑料制品2012接近60Mt，年增长将在15%以上。由于国外工业发达国家制造成本等原因，中低档模具（包括部分中高端模具）需求主要通过对外采购解决。我国模具水平和出口能力完全可以满足需要，因此模具出口市场空间巨大。

我国模具经过30年发展，模具工业体系基本完整、技术水平大幅提高、经营管理能力不断进步。展望2013，通过加快转型升级、增强创新能力、提升产品水平，模具产业增长10%是有把握的，同时由于我国模具在国际市场中的比较优势仍旧存在，全年出口额达到20%左右的增长率还是有可能的。

2. 数字化信息化将引领发展

模具行业的数字化信息化主要包括数字化设计制造、柔性自动化生产和信息化管理等。信息化发展到今天，模具行业不但已离不开数字化信息化，而且今后的发展还有赖于数字化信息化向深度和广度的不断发展。现在数字化信息化在模具行业的应用已可以显著缩短模具的生产周期、提高产品质量、降低成本以及改善服务，它们正向着集成化、网络化、智能化方向不断发展。

3. 专业化生产和集聚生产基地将不断发展并推进转型升级

模具行业专业化生产已有几十年历史，随着其渐进式的发展，现在已经有了多种形式。按模具种类、大小、精度、服务对象、工艺工序等分工进行专业化生产已被证明是有效的。专业化与标准化通用化相结合，零件式大规模定制生产将不断发展。专业化生产将有效提升企业的核心竞争力，并将催生一大批具有强大生命力的“高、精、特、新”企业。

模具集聚生产基地从20世纪90年代开始不断诞生和发展，今后还会得到更好更快发展。有一些基地已开始向高端发展。专业化生产和集聚生产基地的不断发展必将推进企业和行业的转型升级。

4. 智能模具及大型、精密、高效、高性能模具将会快速发展

智能模具具有良好的发展前景。我国现在已经能够生产的智能模具的智能水平还比较低，大都还处于初级阶段，但最终将会发展成为具有感知、分析、决策和执行功能的具有高度智能化水平的智能成形装备。为各种智能制造及战略性新兴产业服务的智能模具和大型、精密、高效、高性能模具将不断扩展其用途和功能，提高其附加值和可靠性。

5. 为低碳经济和新的成形技术服务的新型模具将稳步发展

各种复合材料和高分子材料代替金属在汽车等工业产品中的应用越来越多，轻金属和高强度材料的应用也已越来越多，它们已在轻量化、提高性能、节能减排等方面有了卓越的表现，今后还将会

起到更大作用。各种新型材料由于其优异的性能而使其应用将越来越广泛。包括各种复合材料在内的各种新材料大都要有新的成形技术和新型模具为其服务才能体现和提升其价值。因此，适应潮流的为低碳经济和新的成形技术服务的新型模具必将稳步发展。

6. 模具将向满足成形件未来发展方向和多样性个性化需求方向不断发展

鉴于人们对美好生活和快速低成本生产的追求，模具成形未来的发展方向主要有轻、薄、环保、无缺陷、强度高、性能好以及高品质的外观等，整体成形、精密成形、智能成形、快速成形、模内装配、经济绿色等都是需要追求的。为此，必须有相应的模具来予以满足。模具制造本身也必然会发生有利于满足这些要求的变革。多样性和个性化需求越来越突出将是社会发展的必然，大规模定制的生产方式将得到发展。这必将给模具工业的发展带来福音。

7. 现代制造服务业将进一步发展

制造业要提高竞争力和提高附加值必须要有生产性服务业来支撑和配套。这在低成本优势正在不断减弱的现在尤为重要。因此，生产型企业要向生产服务型企业转变的命题也就出来了，服务外包和服务性企业也就迎来了发展契机，为广大中小企业服务的各种公共服务平台必将日渐展示其强大生命力而得到快速发展。

8. 模具企业长期以来被动接受模具订单进行生产的方式将逐渐向主动开发和为用户提供整体解决方案的方向逐步发展。

市场需求已越来越广泛，不少企业已开始主动进入产品开发领域，积极参与产品生产企业的研发、设计和生产，有些企业甚至已开始自主研发产品并发展产业链。以模具为核心延伸产业链为用户提供一体化整体解决方案将是模具行业今后重要发展方向之一。

六、政策建议

(1)模具工业是基础装备制造业，也是技术、资金、人才密集行业，政府应在技术开发、技术改造方面给予支持。

(2)应采取措施降低模具行业税负，尽快落实新的扶持政策。

(3)模具是高技术高附加值产品，生产过程低耗材、低耗能、无污染，建议提高精密复杂模具出口退税率。

（中国模具工业协会　周永泰）

科技进步

2012～2013 年国内外塑料新材料、新产品、新技术发展概况

新材料部分：

1. 木塑复合材料项目获国家科技进步奖

1 月 18 日，2012 年度国家科学技术进步奖在北京人民大会堂揭晓。由东北林业大学组织、国家林业局推荐，以中国工程院李坚院士领衔、长江学者王清文教授总负责的研究、推广团队申报的“木塑复合材料挤出成型制造技术及应用”，获国家科学技术(二等)奖。

“十一五”以来，我国木塑产业进入一个高速发展时期，现在年总产量已达到 1000kt，成为全球最大的木塑材料生产国和出口国。未来 10 年，我国木塑产业还将充分展现自己资源化和环保化优势，在政府的帮助和支持下，向可持续发展方向不断攀登，在具有战略意义的新兴材料领域一显身手。

2. 重庆引进“863”项目西南最大塑料新材料产业基地将落成

重庆双桥经开区将引进国际领先、国内一流的技术和设备，研制生产国家战略急需的“863”项目——液晶高分子工程塑料，新建西南地区最大的塑料新材料产业基地。

这种液晶高分子工程塑料目前只有美国、日本、德国等少数工业发达国家才能工业化生产，我国尚属空白。此项目还将生产重庆急需的笔电专用材料——聚碳酸脂特种工程复合材料，高阻隔加纤阻燃吹塑尼龙复合材料。用于替代美国 GE 公司和德国巴斯夫公司产品。该产业基地占地 1500 亩，主要进行改性塑料、工程塑料、高分子材料等战略新兴新材料的研制、生产、销售和废旧塑料循环利用。该项目将投资 45 亿元，于年底启动，三年全部建成。

3. 高熔指线型聚乙烯试产成功

9 月 21 日，茂名石化研发的高熔指线型聚乙烯新产品在化工分部全密度装置首次实现工业化试产，产量达到 500t。该产品熔融指数高达 50g/10min，耐环境应力开裂性好，主要用于生产热塑性粉末涂料，还可用于注塑产品。茂名石化近期已与部分聚烯烃改性、粉末涂料等下游厂家达成试用意向，待产品完成测试后将送厂试用。

4. 大庆石化成功开发高密度聚乙烯新产品

大庆石化公司新建年250kt全密度装置首次使用铬系催化剂成功生产出DMDA-6143高密度聚乙烯新产品。1月1日至5日，大庆石化共生产1000多吨合格的DMDA-6143高密度聚乙烯。该产品的成功研发，打破了国外垄断，提升了大庆石化的创效能力。

5. 茂名石化油箱专用料首次配套轿车

茂名石化研发成功的HBX4505M是国内生产的首个汽车油箱专用料，具有质量轻、安全性高、防腐性强、抗冲击性能优良、成型简便等优点，属于市场高端产品，每吨价格比通用料高约500元，广泛应用于汽车多层燃油箱和单层燃油箱的生产。经过几年的推广，已有数家厂商采购该牌号专用料生产出商业产品，同时，该牌号的试制品还通过了十多家欧美系、日系和国内主流汽车厂家的严格测试，有望在下一阶段进入这些汽车厂家的采购名单。

6. 茂名石化开发高熔指线型PE粉末涂料

茂名石化公司研发的高熔指线型聚乙烯(PE)粉末涂料新产品MLPE-8250首次工业化试产，生产新产品382t。该新产品各项主要性能与进口同类产品相当，熔指达到50g/10min，流动性好，比高压聚乙烯粉末涂层料具有更好的耐环境应力性能。产品按粉料形态生产，并简化了生产工艺流程，降低了能耗，重点应用在粉末涂层行业以及色母料、注塑制品生产，价格比通用料高600多元/吨。

7. 中原石化开发高端PP膜料

中原石化2号聚丙烯装置造粒线成功生产出600t高端双向拉伸聚丙烯膜料BOPP，实现了向高端产品的跨越，新产品市场前景广阔。长期以来，由于装置结构问题无法实现牌号切换，中原石化聚丙烯产品单一、没有特色、应对市场能力弱。随着中国石化首套煤化工示范项目——中原石化600kt/a甲醇制烯烃(MTO)项目的成功投产，中原石化新产品开发迎来了难得的机遇。2号聚丙烯装置造粒线于2011年9月份正式投用，是MTO项目的配套装置，这也是首次在2号聚丙烯装置造粒线上进行牌号切换。

8. 无规共聚PP管材专用树脂实现量产

5月30日，经独山子石化公司研究院测试评价，独山子石化量产的无规共聚聚丙烯(PP)管材专用树脂T4401各项性能指标优异，完全可替代进口料。

独山子石化公司在引进国外专利商工艺包基础上，通过性能改进以及添加剂的国产化，提升了产品性能并摆脱了对国外添加剂的依赖。5月20日，独山子石化公司聚烯烃装置转产一次成功，产品实现规模化生产。通过与国内外同类产品的对比剖析，新产品具备突出的耐水抽提性能，冲击性能和耐压强度良好。公司计划年产无规共聚聚丙烯管材专用树脂T4401产品40kt，以有效缓解国内目前依赖进口的局面。

无规共聚聚丙烯管材具有优异的耐高温蠕变性和耐水抽提性，主要用于家庭冷热水输送、地暖热水输送等，其对原料性能尤其是加工和冲击性能要求苛刻。

9. 吉林石化量产新牌号ABS

5月3日，吉林石化公司200kt/aABS专用料装置成功进行新牌号切换，新牌号产品——H816ABS产品正式投入批量生产，这标志着该公司实现了由低端ABS通用料向高端ABS通用料的过渡。

H816牌号ABS产品是吉林石化公司科研人员在韩国三星ABS工艺技术基础上，自主开发的一种新型高端ABS通用料，不但熔体质量流动速率、冲击强度、拉伸强度、弯曲弹性等物性指标比原有牌号GE-150有全面提高，黄色指数和产品白度也都有明显改善，适用于机械、汽车、电子电器、仪器仪表、纺织和建筑等工业领域，市场覆盖面很大。

10. 金轮塑业研发纳米隔热复合材料

由河北衡水金轮塑业有限公司承担的纳米隔热复合材料研发项目日前获得成功。其研发的纳米隔热复合材料热传导系数U值比国际知名公司同类产品低30%，节能率提高近30%。

11. 苏州纳米所碳纳米管功能复合材料研究获新进展

单根碳纳米管具有优异的力、电、性能，开发超强多功能碳纳米管宏观材料一直是材料领域研究热点之一。受限于传统碳纳米管分散和取向技术的限制，碳纳米管优异的性能至今未能在材料中得以充分发挥。

中国科学院苏州纳米技术与纳米仿生研究所李清文课题组以可纺丝碳纳米管阵列为基础材料，发展了干法制备高性能碳纳米管功能复合材料，为实现碳纳米管在复合材料中的高负载、高取向及定向电子传递探索了新的制备思路。主要的研究成果包括：

(1)通过取向碳纳米管薄膜的层层固态组装制备了高强度、高导电及可折叠的碳纳米管膜。

(2)与美国北卡罗来纳州立大学YT Zhu教授课题组合作，在碳纳米管薄膜缠绕的过程中，通过喷雾法引入聚合物，得到高碳纳米管含量的聚合物复合材料。

(3)利用取向碳纳米管薄膜定向的电子输运特点，首次报道了具有梯度变色的碳纳米管/氧化钨复合柔性薄膜。

12. 纳米技术在聚氨酯氨纶纤维应用取得突破

插层复合纳米技术，就是将单体或聚合物插进层状无机物片层之间，再将厚1nm，宽100nm左右的片状结构基体元剥离，使其均匀分散于聚合物中。从而实现聚合物与无机层状材料在纳米尺度上的复合。此种纳米技术已由中科院化学所孙贤育研究员、孔克健研究员和北京大学化学与分子工程学院吴瑾光教授等科技人员在干法氨纶应用中研究成功，并已获得了发明专利。

13. 复旦大学研发新材料：可穿上身发电

复旦大学高分子科学系彭慧胜教授课题组的最新研究成果："纳米最直观的概念就是头发丝的十万分之一，如果用一纳米直径的小球堆积起一毫米直径的小球，它的表面积可以提高10的5次方"。这是一种"由小变大"的方法，道理跟石油化工中的催化作用相同，催化剂的表面积越大，效果就越好。彭慧胜将这一设计运用到了碳纳米管的光电转化中。

根据实验结果，新研制的太阳能电池最高光电转化效率超过9%，但是白天发电，晚上怎么办呢?"我们就在想能不能把发电和储能集成起来，想用的时候用它，不想用就放到那里，把剩下的储存下来。"于是，利用同一纤维材料，彭教授课题组构建出微型线状超级电容器，成功地实现了这一设想。

14. 浙江大学研制世界最轻材料：仅为空气密度1/6

约8cm^{3}的"碳海绵"立在桃花花蕊上

浙江大学高分子系高超教授的课题组制备出了一种超轻气凝胶——它刷新了目前世界上最轻材料的纪录，弹性和吸油能力令人惊喜。这种被称为"全碳气凝胶"的固态材料密度为每立方厘米0.16mg，仅是空气密度的1/6。这一进展被《自然》杂志在"研究要闻"栏目中重点配图评论。

15. 国内首片15in单层石墨烯在重庆问世

采用石墨烯材料，就可能用上屏幕可以来回弯曲折叠的手机。采用可折叠屏幕后，即使手机屏变得更大了，但携带起来还是很方便。1月22日，中科院重庆绿色智能技术研究院已经成功制备出国内首片15in的单层石墨烯，这样的大尺寸，达到了国内最高水平。它或将为手机、电脑等电子产品带来一场革命。

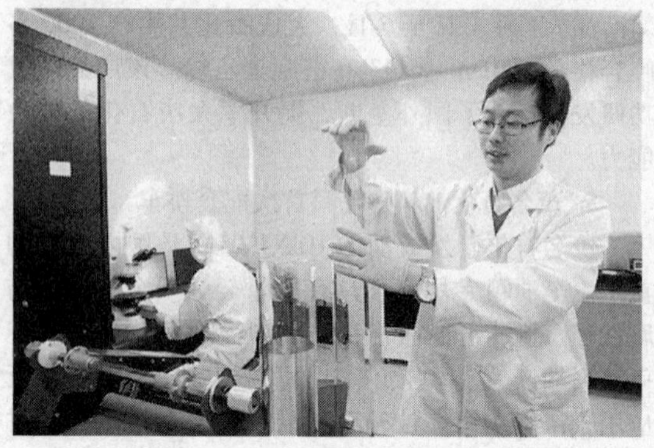

技术人员正在展示15in单层石墨烯

16. 拜耳推出交通领域用轻质PU材料

拜耳材料科技公司研制出一种提高汽车能源效率的聚氨酯材料，公司在2012UTECH展上展出这种名为Bayflex的轻质聚氨酯系统。Bayflex聚氨酯系统是一种创新的填料集成系统，有助于材料轻量化设计，并具有优异的力学性能，通过该系统，成品部件的质量可减少高达30%。这种材料密度比水还轻，为0.9g/cm^3。

17. 科聚亚推出双组份聚氨酯组合料

科聚亚公司正推出Adiprene Duracast双组份聚氨酯组合料，一种相分离后拥有优质性能的预聚物。产品不含有MOCA或者BDO固化剂，贮存期相当长，而脱模时间很短，方便生产商们更精确地控制比例和材料消耗，低成本创造高生产率。不含有TDI和MOCA同时也意味着对环境和安全的保障，工作人员不需要处理任何灰尘或熔融的问题，短流程降低了人为失误的几率，提高了质量水平。

18. 尼龙6树脂基高导热复合材料将问世

中国科学院宁波材料技术与工程研究所所属先进制造技术研究所复合材料研究团队在热塑性树脂基高导热复合材料研究中取得进展。

通过双螺杆挤出机开发了以尼龙6为树脂基的高导热复合材料。尼龙6树脂基高导热复合材料的密度为1.504g/cm^3(20℃)，远低于铝合金材料(2.7g/cm^3)。

19. 巴斯夫推出聚酰胺新产品

3月15日，巴斯夫宣布已推出针对水辅注塑成型技术(WIT)优化升级后的聚酰胺(PA)新产品Ultramid A3HG6 WIT Balance和Ultramid A3WG7 WIT。两种新材料已全面上市。由于耐水解性能提高，聚酰胺Ultramid A3HG6 WIT Balance特别适于承载冷却剂或与水接触的零部件。考虑到严格的耐盐要求，PA610的成分也确保了材料对氯化钙具有较高的耐应力开裂性能，该材料已成为冷却水管等WIT多种应用的首选。Ultramid A3WG7 WIT则采用35%玻璃纤维增强，特别适合量油计等原油传输管道或其他对耐油性、刚性和尺寸稳定性有较高要求的零部件。

20. 车用聚甲醛专用料研发取得成果

河南煤化集团研究院与北京化工大学合作实施的车用聚甲醛专用料的开发与研究项目通过中期审查，该项目开发的产品质量达到或超过国外同类产品水平，性价比高。

该项目主要研究内容包括增强聚甲醛、增韧聚甲醛、耐磨与耐候聚甲醛等9个配方及相关工艺的开发。目前，项目组已成功开发3个增韧聚甲醛配方，并在开封龙化顺利通过中试验证，具备了工业化生产的条件，现已销售出9t产品，比普通聚甲醛产品增效约3倍。同时，项目组还开发出两个增强聚甲醛小试配方，正在准备中试验证。

21. 上海石化成功开发吸湿改性聚酯新品

一种吸湿快干性能良好的新型聚酯切片在上海石化研制成功，填补了国内吸湿改性聚酯生产技术和产品的空白。已生产吸湿型聚酯切片1239余吨，创造了良好的经济效益和社会效益。纯棉制品以其优良的吸湿透气性带给人们舒适感，但其保水率较高，导湿性能较差，而传统聚酯纤维吸水性差。因此，市场呼唤具有吸湿、快干特性的纤维及面料问世。

上海石化自2011年开始，与中国纺织科学研究院合作进行吸湿快干聚酯及纤维的开发。项目组通过研究吸湿改性共聚单体分子量、添加方式、添加量以及聚合工艺等对聚酯产品性能的影响，开发了有效抑制降解的聚酯吸湿改性共聚技术，并在连续式聚酯中试和工业化生产装置上实现了批量生产，产品质量稳定，可纺性好，其吸湿快干性能达国家标准要求，不仅成功应用于新一代武警训练服，并逐渐延伸到运动服、毛巾、袜子等民用领域。

22. 中国生物医用高分子材料制备获新进展

由中科院长春应用化学研究所承担、长春圣博玛生物材料公司和东北师范大学参与的吉林省“双十”重大科技攻关项目“生物可降解医用高分子材料及其制品开发”通过吉林省科技厅的鉴定。

生物可降解医用高分子材料作为用于诊断、治疗和器官再生的材料，由于无须二次手术，可减轻病人痛苦，简化手术程序，具有提高治疗效果、延长病人生命并提高病人生存质量等作用。近年来，该种材料被广泛应用于药物控制释放载体、手术缝合线、骨固定和修复器件以及组织工程支架等领域，其相关研究在生物技术、生命科学和医学等领域均占有重要地位。

中科院长春应化所等单位的科研人员从可生物降解高分子材料的结构设计出发，制备了不同种类的生物医用高分子材料，并对其基本性能、功能化、靶向性、生物学评价和临床应用进行了研究，取得了一系列进展。

23. 新型塑料抗冲击超钢铁

合肥杰事杰新材料股份有限公司，通过技术创新研发出抗冲击力超过钢铁的塑料板。一个1kg的铁球，从1.5m的高度垂直落下，砸到同是1毫米厚的钢板和新材料塑料板上。“砰”的一声响后，铁球落到钢板上，钢板被砸得凹进去一块，而同样的铁球落在新材料塑料板上，塑料板却安然无恙。

24. 杜邦推出耐300℃线缆氟塑料

杜邦公司推出杜邦ECCtreme氟树脂产品。该系列产品的首个成员ECCtreme ECA 3000采用了形态学控制技术，可耐受300℃高温且保持优异的电性能和化学性能。这项技术打破了氟塑料通常只能在260℃以下环境中持续使用的局限。此外杜邦还展示了拥有超高弹性模量和抗拉强度的新产品KevlarAP、无卤产品Hytrel和可再生资源材料系列新产品等。这些产品可帮助用户设计兼具高性能、环保安全及轻量化等特点的整体线缆解决方案。

25. 中美合作开发新型高端墙体保温材料

无锡捷阳节能科技有限公司联手美国麻省理工学院研发成功一种新型高端墙体保温材料JY保温复合板。与普通复合板相比，JY保温复合板不仅施工更快捷、安装更简便，而且保温性能更优越，阻燃效果更好，使用寿命比普通复合板延长一倍以上。

26. 杜邦第四代发泡剂问世

杜邦公司研发出第四代发泡剂产品FEA－1100，该产品具有环境可持续性和卓越的隔热保温性能。

该发泡剂室温下为稳定液体，通过调整在配方中的含量可以达到满意的发泡性能，与金属材料、塑料、弹性体材料以及与主要类型的聚醚多元醇(如曼尼希基聚醚、蔗糖型聚醚、聚芳酯等)生产聚氨酯泡沫时都表现出了良好的性能。与目前应用的发泡剂相比，该产品环保、隔热保温特性显着，不易燃、不消耗臭氧，可以低转换成本取代其它液体发泡剂，具有广泛的应用前景。

新产品部分：

27. 透明塑料真空保鲜缸问世获国家专利

上海交通大学教授孙企达发明的真空保鲜米缸

近日获得国家专利。该产品有两种类型。一种采用聚丙烯透明塑料制成，结合具有较强吸力且可单手操作的手动抽气泵和截止放气阀等，使用方便，成本较低，更贴近百姓需求，现已批量投放市场。另一种采用不锈钢材料，结合无油清洁低真空、安全密封等技术，可使米缸处于低压、低氧和隔潮的状态，保持大米新鲜的同时还可防止虫蛀。

据悉，我国居民家庭粮食因后续保存不力，每年损失在10%左右，国内外多数国家均未解决这一问题。

28. 我国PE－RT塑料管材年产量100kt

随着我国经济的快速发展，耐热聚乙烯(PE－RT)塑料管材近年来在国内得到了迅速的发展。年产量达到100kt左右，生产线近千条。这种耐热聚乙烯(PE－RT)塑料管材主要用于低温地板辐射采暖系统，用于隐蔽工程。随着耐热聚乙烯(PE－RT)塑料管材的发展，耐热聚乙烯(PE－RT)塑料管材的产品质量问题受到用户和同行的关注，而影响产品质量的因素主要有原材料、设备、模具、生产工艺等。

29. 茂名石化高压聚乙烯高透明薄膜新产品问世

茂名石化开发的高压聚乙烯高透明薄膜新产品M300在2号高压聚乙烯装置实现首次工业化试产，首批产品产量达到350t。

该新产品密度达到0.925g/cm^3，熔融指数达到2.8g/10min，雾度达到5.2%，具有良好的加工性能、较好的开口性、柔软性能、力学强度和较高的透明性及表面光泽性等特点，下游主要用作生产高档包装薄膜，市场上当前的同类型产品主要以进口产品为主，进口料的最大竞争力就在薄膜的浊度。

30. 国内实现碳纳米管触控屏产学研结合量化

富士康旗下的天津富纳源创科技有限公司通过与清华大学团队的产学研结合，成功实现了全球首个碳纳米管触控屏产业化，已生产碳纳米管触控屏700万片，月产规模达到150万片，成功地为华为、酷派、中兴等手机配套。

31. 浙江大学造出纳米纸

浙江大学的科学家用滤纸和二氧化钛薄膜制作出一种新型“纳米纸”，这种材料能继续与多种化学分子结合并展现不同特性，实现材料应用上的“百搭”。

通过前体物溶液浸润再水解的方式，可以让二氧化钛薄膜包裹在滤纸的纳米纤维上，之后再用含有其他化学分子的溶液继续浸润纳米纸，就能制造出不同用途的新材料。肉眼看来，纳米纸的外观与普通滤纸没有差别，但功能却有了极大差异。滤纸由无数的纤维素纤维组成，自然形成的精细结构非人力所及，而二氧化钛水解后产生的羟基具有足够的化学活性，能够和绝大多数的分子相结合，这两个材料的特性共同决定了纳米纸‘万金油’的特点。

32. 巴斯夫开发出三聚氰胺树脂泡沫新品

巴斯夫在三聚氰胺树脂泡沫巴数特(Basotect)的清洁擦洗应用领域又开发出了新一代产品BasotectW。与之前的产品相比，其清洁效率更高，颜色更白。该产品现已通过ko－Tex Standard100生态纺织品标准的Ⅱ类产品认证，确保使用和加工BasotectW不会对人体健康造成伤害，即不会释放出任何可以通过皮肤吸收的有害物质。

33. 青岛能源所开发出高安全性阻燃生物质复合材料动力锂电池隔膜

在中科院“百人计划”、科技部“863”储能电池重大专项、山东省杰青基金和青岛市重点实验室等攻关项目支持下，中国科学院青岛生物能源与过程研究所仿生能源与储能系统团队历经3年多的科研攻关，在动力锂离子电池隔膜领域取得突破性进展，成功开发出具有自主知识产权的高安全性阻燃生物质复合材料的动力锂电池隔膜，并达到中试生产规模。

新技术部分：

34. 我国掌握生物降解二氧化碳基塑料产业化技术

中科院长春应用化学研究所承担的中科院知识创新工程重要方向项目“二氧化碳基塑料的产业化关键技术”通过验收，同时该所已建成万吨级二氧化碳基塑料生产线，并完成3万吨/年生产线工艺包的设计。

二氧化碳基塑料是以二氧化碳和环氧化物为主要原料，经化学方法制得的绿色高分子材料，既可高效利用二氧化碳，变废为宝，又具有良好的阻气性、透明性，并可完全生物降解，有望广泛应用在一次性医疗和食品包装领域。

中科院长春应化所于2001年在国内较早地开展了该领域的研发，并在2004年与蒙西集团合作建成了世界上第一条具有完全自主产权的年产千吨级二氧化碳共聚物生产线。为加速推进二氧化碳基塑料的产业化，长春应化所于2008年承担了中科院知识创新工程重要方向项目“二氧化碳基塑料的产业化关键技术”的研究。

35. 深圳先进院与香港中大合作在新一代太阳能电池研究获重要进展

6月初，由中国科学院深圳先进技术研究院与香港中文大学合作成功研发出了光电转换效率达17%的铜铟镓硒(CIGS)薄膜太阳能电池，领先全国，比肩世界顶级水平。

该工作由先进院集成所光伏太阳能中心团队和香港中文大学共同完成。CIGS电池以价格低廉的玻璃、塑胶、金属箔片作为基底，再镀上1/200mm的多层薄膜材料组成，可在阴天及散射光下发电，适用于高楼林立的城市环境，比传统的晶体硅太阳能电池薄50倍，成本降低一半，被称为“下一代非常有前途的新型薄膜太阳能电池”。

36. 废旧塑料变能源新技术已研制出来

我国废旧塑料分类杂、产量大、回收难，污染很严重，华南再生资源(中山)有限公司研究研制的废旧塑料通过逆转工程制造液、气、固态能源项目，将降低我国废旧塑料的产量，保护国家环境。

华南再生资源(中山)有限公司研究研制的废旧塑料通过逆转工程制造液、气、固态能源项目，通过逆转工程可将废旧塑料生产出高剂量标准的固、液、气三大可储存性战略能源，且无二次污染，无残余物转移。

37. 一种可控制降解的聚乳酸/淀粉全生物分解塑料制备方法

该方法添加亚磷酸酯作为降解控制剂，以由淀粉或其改性衍生物、聚乳酸、扩链剂、降解控制剂制成的塑料母粒为原料，通过真空热处理，与助剂连续共挤出，辅以单轴或双轴热拉伸增强，制得全生物分解塑料。本发明的方法路线简单，易于操作，使用的原料价格低廉、来源广泛、天然可再生，制得的产品性能好，在拉伸强度、断裂伸长率、杨氏模量上均优于现有相关全生物分解塑料。该方法与传统高分子聚乳酸生产方法相比能耗低、成本低。

38. 塑料光纤批量生产技术取得突破性进展

4月27日，由中国科学院理化技术研究所研究员甄珍、刘新厚领导的有机光波导材料及器件研究中心，经过多年的努力，攻克了从本体聚合法直接生产PMMA光纤(塑料光纤)的技术难关，提出了单分子扩散转移原材料提纯新技术和平推式薄层本体聚合新技术制备高纯度光纤级PMMA原料以及与之相配套的包层材料，形成了具有自主知识产权的高纯度光纤级PMMA光学模塑料(芯层材料)以及皮层材料制备的核心技术，成功地解决了产业化途径中的关键技术问题和批量生产设备与工艺。在其自行研制的日生产10万米PMMA光纤的全自动流水线上已连续数月生产出光衰减在170～200dB/km的PMMA光纤，并已基本形成了光衰减在150dB/km的PMMA光纤的批量生产的潜能力，产品技术指标达到国际同类产品的最好水平。

39. 纤维增强热塑性塑料管材卷制成型技术公开专利

由合肥华宇橡塑设备有限公司公开了其发明的纤维增强热塑性塑料管材卷制成型技术，其技术路线是，先将纤维编织的网清洗、干燥，并进行偶联处理，热塑性塑料预制成带状片材，把纤维网与加热软化的热塑性塑料片材压延迭合成带状复合片材，再将带状热塑性塑料片材、带状复合片材叠放在加热旋转的管材内模上，再次缠绕压延卷制，经冷却定型形成纤维增强热塑性塑料管材。该发明工艺简单，设备投资成本少，生产效率高，产品易大型化，纤维网纵、横向纤维使管材的纵、横向性能都得到了提高，调整纤维网纵、横向纤维的比例，可以生产出满足不同工程要求的管材。

(中国塑料加工工业协会专家委员会　葛存良　高坤光　王德禧)

3D打印在模具制造中的应用

3D打印技术是材料成型方法中增材制造的一种。主要包括光固化立体成形(Stereo Lithography Apparatus，SLA)、分层实体制造(Laminated Object Manufacturing，LOM)、金属粉末选择性激光烧结(Selective Laser Sintering，SLS)、熔积成形(Fused Deposition Modeling，FDM)、激光熔覆(Laser Engineered Net Shaping，LENS)等技术。其原理是使用不同的材料做“墨”，使用激光或者电子束作为热源，通过计算机的控制把材料融化堆积成实体零件。其特点是可以实现无模成型，同时成型零件无需或少量加工后即可使用，可以大幅度的缩短生产周期、提高生产效率。在模具制造行业，受传统加工方法的限制，很多优秀的设计难以实现，这在很大程度上限制了模具行业的发展。随着科技的发展进步，3D打印技术的出现，利用3D打印技术完全可以实现设计师的优秀创意，极大的推进了模具行业的进步。

1　3D打印在模具制造方面的应用

1.1　在随形水路模具制造中的应用

在注塑成型过程中，模具的冷却效果不仅直接影响着注射成型时间，同时还影响着制品的性能和模具的使用寿命。冷却效果好的模具可以缩短注射成型时间、降低产品翘曲变形率、提高模具的使用寿命，一方面提高了生产效率，另一方面节约资源，降低生产成本。模具的冷却效果很大程度上取决于模具内部的冷却水路分布，若冷却水路分布不均衡，则模具型腔温度也会出现不均衡，从而导致冷却效果不理想。理想的冷却水路是均匀的分布在成型型腔周围，高效率的带走模具内的热量，精确的控制模具的温度，这种理想的水路称作“随形水路”或“异形水路”，水路形状随型腔变化而变化。图1就是使用3D打印方法制作出的异形水路模具成形实例。

图1　不同冷却水路模具成型对比

图1所示为制作儿童饮水杯的例子，目标是保证杯子完全无毒性，必须采用安全级别为食品级材料，该种材料的流动性能远低于ABS等常用塑料，必须通过提高注射温度的方法提高材料的流动充型性能，提高注射温度又会增加注射成型冷却时间，从而降低了生产效率、增加了成本。左边模具凸模即为传统方法加工的直进直出的冷却水路，这种水路与凸模接触面积小，散热效果不理想，无法缩短注射成型时间。右侧为使用3D打印方法建造出的具有随形水路的模具，为了降低模具成本，底座部分利用传统加工方法制作，上部随形水路部分利用3D打印方法制作。打印完成后进行简单的抛光和热处理后即可投入使用。可以看出，冷却水路均匀的环绕在凸模型腔周围。事实证明，使用环形的水路设计更加合理高效、减少了产品翘曲变形的废品率、缩短40%的注射成型时间、提高生产效率、节约成本。

图2是随形冷却结合最新模具技术运用的又一个例子：这是一个高尔夫赠品球的模具，量大而成本极低。该产品生产工艺为PP挤吹模塑成型结合弹性体的注塑成型。避免球的变形和困气缺陷并保证圆度是非常重要的，这在吹塑成型中好的排气是必须的。

(a)为模腔的随形冷却水路，(b)中绿色小槽为模腔上的排气通道，(c)右为实际模腔剖切图。这种模具结合了不带任何外观痕迹的排气槽和冷却水路，依靠改变材料及工艺参数来制造完成。它可以使模仁部分的体积做得非常小且非常紧凑，因此也节省了时间和成本。8个这样的模仁组成一副4腔的模具，达到生产2000万的需求，而这副4腔模具仅仅只需要50小时的加工量，有随形冷却可以提高20%的生产效率。

图3为模具应用冷却水路实例。(a)左为PE吹塑瓶模，由于瓶的颈部壁较厚，传统的冷却限制着生产周期和生产效率，而采用金属粉末激光烧结工艺制造一个小镶件来快速冷却颈部镶件，这样就可以使生产周期从15s降到8s或9s，提高了近70%的生产效率，但不会造成任何质量上的牺牲。(b)中为一个从后模顶出结构上考虑冷却的镶件，旨在带走浇口附近的大量的热，这样也降低了三分之二的生产周期。(c)右为包含了一种螺旋形状的随形冷却的模芯，比较起来模芯相应地在尺寸上也减小了一半。加工这样较小的零件是很经济的，先放在EOSINT M270系统上加工，胶位顶部留下0.3mm的余量再用传统抛光等精加工方法达到所要求的表面光洁度。

1.2　在难加工模具中的应用

在模具制造中，模具的制造成本随精密程度或形状的复杂程度增加而增加。精密模具制造需要昂贵的加工设备及专业技术人员经过多种步骤才能完成，耗费大量的人力及物力，即使只是简单的1模2腔结构的注射模，也需要CNC铣床及配合电火花机床(EDM)加工来完成，其中CNC铣床加工会产生金属废屑且需经过粗、精加工步骤进行，而对于深槽或小转角处则需以电加工方式进行处理。对于结构复杂的模具，其内部往往设有滑块、插销或相关零部件，类似的模具制作时更耗时、耗经费。图4中(a)、(b)、(c)为使用3D打印方法制作的模具，都是直接3D打印无后加工的例子，(a)、(b)图中包含倒扣的软胶模具，不用耗费太多的人力和物力就可以很容易地完成制作，这些倒扣在按传统机加工时会增加许多难度。(c)图是手提式电动工具外壳的模仁，按照传统加工手法，需要分割成20个组件，制造100种电极(分成粗加工100个，精加工100个)，工期大致需要35~40天。可是，利用复合加工技术(激光烧结配合高速切削加工)，不需要分割，也不需要电极，就可以一步到位地把模仁加工成形，工期可以缩短到15天甚至10天。可见，越是复杂程度高的难加工模具，利用3D打印方法制造就越具有优势。

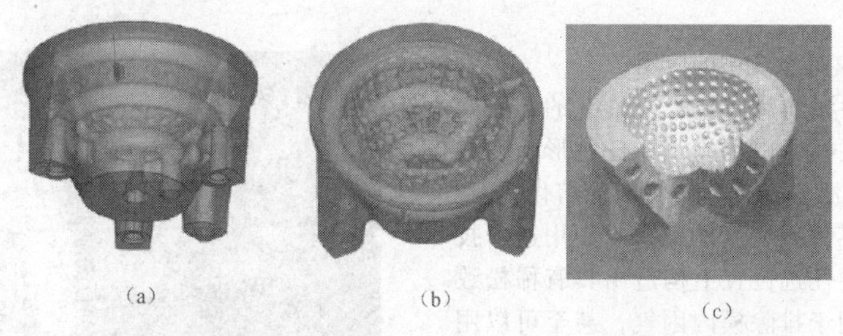

（a）（b）（c）

图2 高尔夫球模具随形水路冷却实例

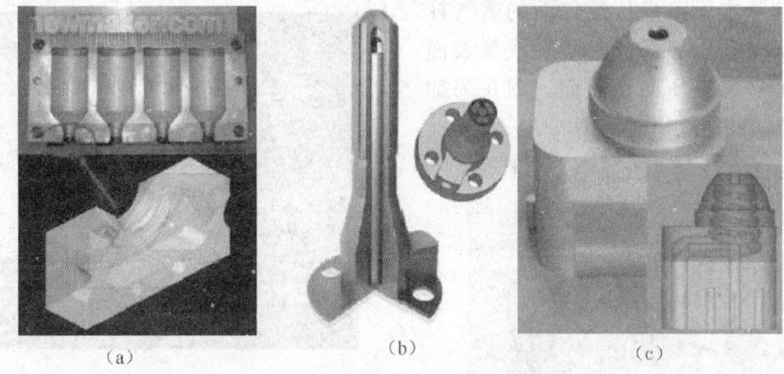

（a）（b）（c）

图3 模具随形水路冷却实例

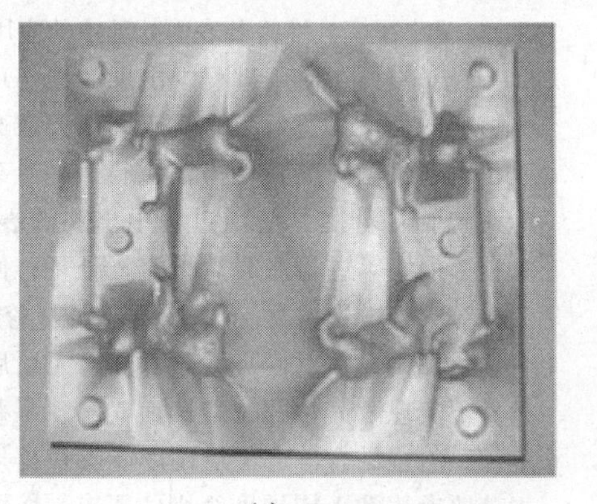

(a)

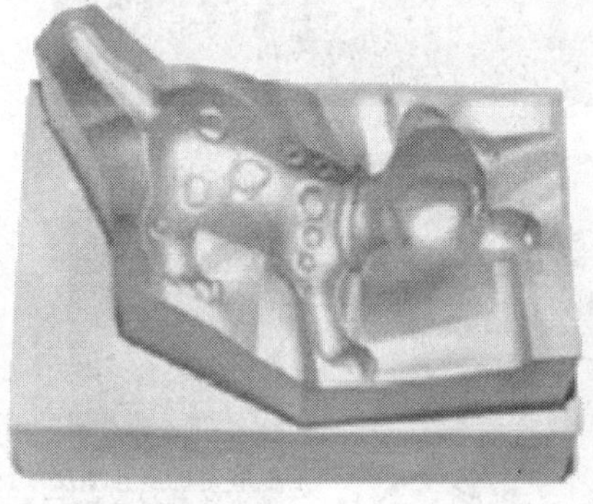

(b)

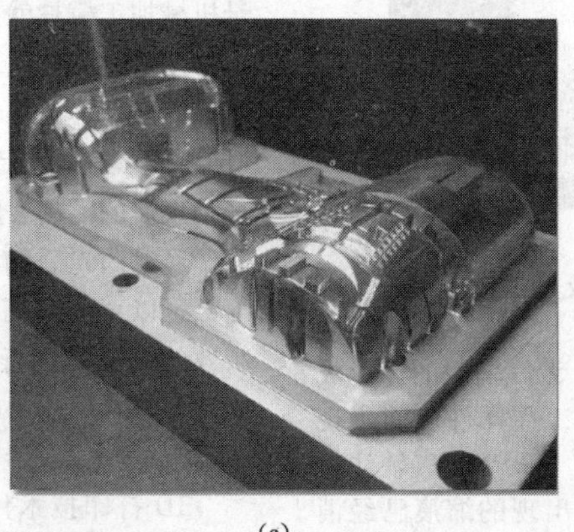

(c)

图4 难加工模具的应用实例

1.3　在排气及气辅系统中的应用

金属粉末选择性激光烧结技术所具有的加工柔性，使其不但可以在模具内部构筑起任意形状的异型水路，还可以通过激光控制金属粉末的熔化程度，以求达到控制造型零件致密度的效果。利用这一技术，就可以在模具的任选位置上构造出具有稀松致密度的多孔质层，用于排除模内困气，甚至可以用作气辅成型时的腔内进气部位。图5就显示了一种具多孔质表面层的透气杆被装入模腔内，用于模内排气和气辅进气。其基本思路是从模仁面的透气杆顶端面以及筋板底部多孔质层部分向塑料成型表面施加气体压力使注塑产品被压向型腔面。图6为加气体辅助与不加气体辅助的效果对比图。

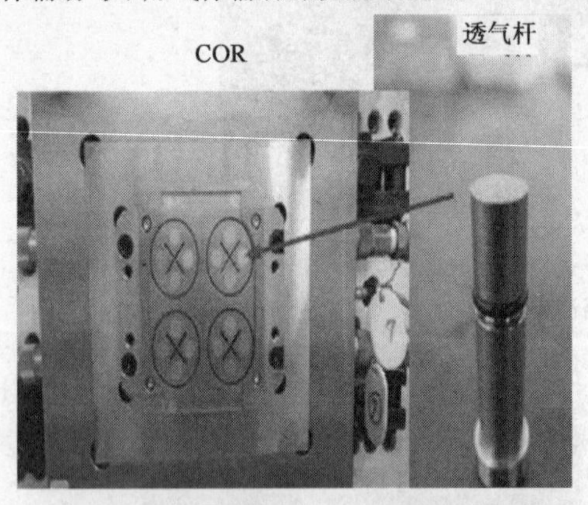

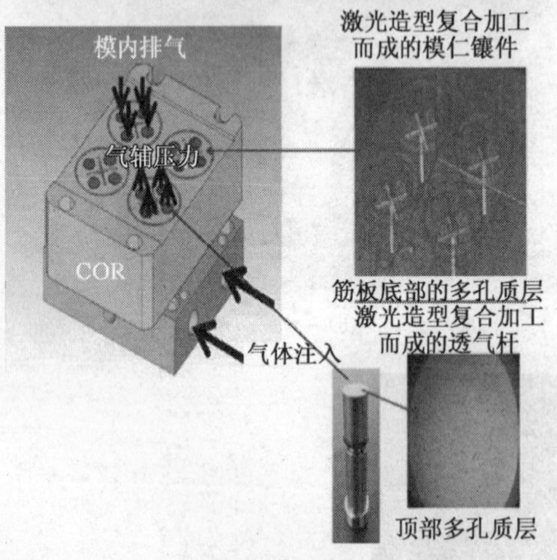

图5　安装透气杆的模腔及其工作原理

图6上为保压为350kg/cm²，无气辅时的注射成型样件，可以从图中红框中看出，在样件表面出现了缩痕。下图为保压为350kg/cm² +30MPa气辅注射成型样件，从图中可以看出表面出现的缩痕已经消除。所以，利用3D打印的方法制作多孔件镶嵌于模具中可以显著的改善注射成型件的质量。

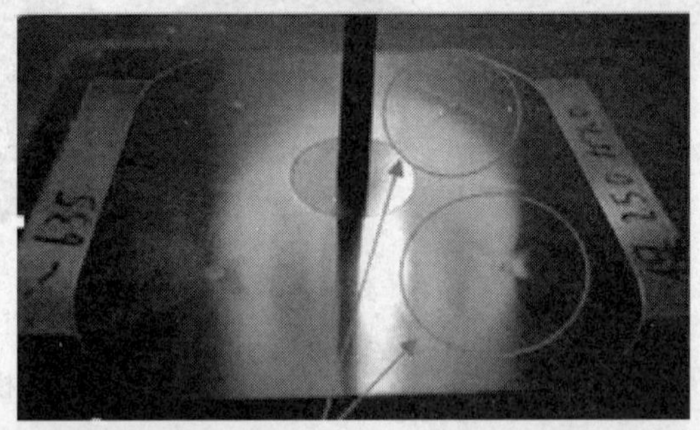

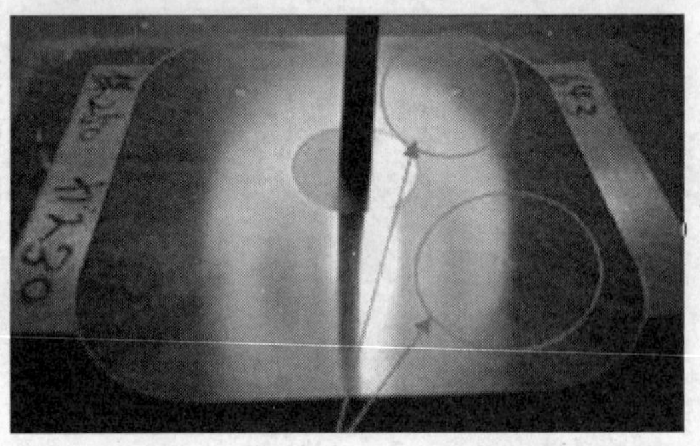

图6　有无气辅时注塑效果对比

1.4　在模具维修及表面处理中的应用

针对模具在使用过程中出现的损伤可以使用激光熔覆的方法进行修复，对于表面要求高硬度的模具也可通过激光熔覆的方法进行表面处理。其具体应用包括：对模具使用过程中出现的裂纹、划伤、磨损、崩塌等进行激光熔覆修复处理；使模具实现激光淬火、激光熔凝淬火、激光熔覆(修复)与激光合金化加工；在对模具无须预热、无须后续热处理条件下实现激光熔覆，熔覆面光滑、平整，与模具本体呈冶金结合，熔覆层硬度能够根据用户模具的工艺要求达到不同硬度级别的要求，熔覆后只要少量机械加工模具就可以直接投入使用。

图7中(a)~(d)为使用激光熔覆修复模具表面磨损的过程。图(a)为表面磨损待修复的模具，图(b)为模具表面正在进行激光熔覆，图(c)为激光熔覆结束后的模具表面，图(d)为经过抛光后的模具表面。经过抛光后的模具表面具有高的光洁度和高硬度，可以直接应用。使用激光熔覆的方法可以快速高效的对模具进行修复、处理，提高模具的重复利用率，有效的节约成本。

2　结论

3D打印技术代表了快速制造领域的发展方向，运用该技术能直接成型高复杂结构、高尺寸精度、高表面质量的致密金属零件，减少制造金属零件的

(a)

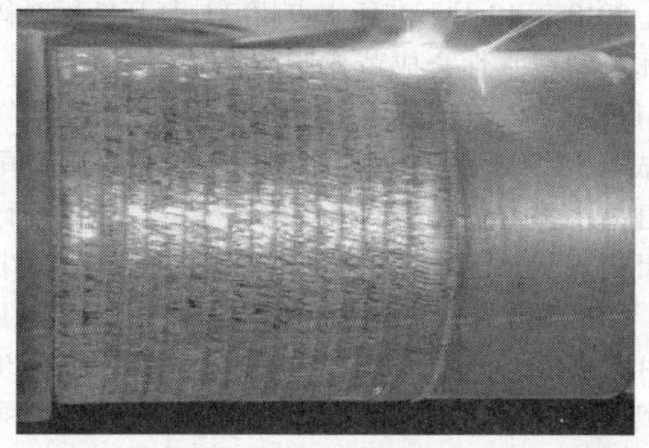

(b)

(c)

(d)

图 7　激光熔覆修复模具表面过程

工艺过程，为产品的设计、生产提供更加快捷的途径，进而加快产品的市场响应速度，更新产品的设计理念和生产周期[15]。3D 打印技术在未来将会得到更好、更快的发展。但是，由于巨大的市场价值与商业机密，目前 3D 打印技术的发展与推广还存在一些问题，主要是耗材及成型设备十分昂贵，这无疑会大大增加生产成本，使其应用领域受到限制，暂时还仅应用在航空航天及医疗等高利润行业。只有研发出可靠性和技术指标达到国际先进水平、价格低廉、具有自主知识产权的金属粉末激光成型设备、成型材料和配套的工艺路线等，这项技术才能得到广泛的推广。

（青岛中科昊泰新材料科技有限公司、中国塑料加工工业协会专家委员会　曹广元　车忠良　刘毅　王德禧）

人造革合成革工业生态化建设

一、低碳排放 - 转型升级取得突破性的发展

1. 工业生产实现低排放，推进生态化建设的启程

从 2010 年国家公布的《第一次污染源调查报告》数据反应塑料普查对象 8.08 万个，占了工业源普查对象的 5.58%，调查数量为工业源的第五位，但是所有污染源站的比例微乎其微，从国家环保部公布的各项能源消耗，如煤电消费占全国消费总量的不过千分之一，但是为工业总产值的贡献率达到 5%。《第一次污染源调查报告》数据反应农业（COD、总氮、总磷）总量排放占全国的 46%，超过了工业和生活污染而成为全国最大的污染源，机动车排放污染物对城市大气污染影响大，工业污染主要集中在少数行业，我国采取了主要污染物总量强制控制措施，在“十二五”还将继续实行主要污染物总量控制计划，并扩大控制污染物的种类，在低于发达国家污染峰值时，环境质量将会逐步得到提前改善。

从污染源普查数据和环统计数据充分显示，塑料制品是低碳排放，加工低能耗、效率高、无污染排放，可再生循环利用。以“十一五”末期的国家统计局公布数据位分析看到：2010 年塑料制品全部国有及规模以上非国有工业企业主要指标万元工业总产值为 0.1512t 标准煤，比“十一五”初期 0.2441t 标准煤降低 30% 以上。在塑料供应链系统上综合能耗最低。塑料制品作为聚合材料，可替代金属、橡胶、木材以及一些无机材料，2010 年塑料万元工业总产值吨标准煤为金属制品的 83%、为橡胶制品的 61%。

塑料制品同时为汽车轻量化减少燃油消耗、为建筑提供保温节能材料、为农业提供节水器材等方面，塑料制品材料循环利用无疑是节能型产品。从整个产业碳足迹研究看，塑料产业链的碳足迹要比橡胶制品、金属制品少1/3。2010年塑料产量5000多万吨，其消耗煤炭总量3779.6kt，相比橡胶加工消耗5081.0kt、木材加工4326.4kt，低25%、12.6%；其电力消费量为533亿千瓦小时，占全国的千分之一，除比木制品加工电力能耗相对高7.9%以外，要比金属制品低近一倍，按照万元产值电力消费量，比橡胶制品、金属制品是低31%、19.49%。

人造革合成革是塑料重要组成部分，由于工艺复杂，相对于其他塑料制品加工生产装备条件要求高，蒸汽加热定型工艺燃煤能耗比重大，但相对于同类应用领域的其他面料综合能耗比较低，单位综合能耗比牛羊革加工能耗低20%。目前人造革合成革全行业固定资产投资已经从粗放经营扩产逐步转向节能环保、生态绿色制品，新建企业的生态化投资占固定资产投资总额的10%～20%与前期科技投入并驾齐驱。目前，全行业所有合成革企业的工业废气得到有效治理，废水治理设施全面采用生化处理工艺升级改造。根据对合成革重点大中型企业的统计，"十一五"末合成革行业实现节能总量376kt标煤，一般企业吨综合能耗下降12.5%，先进企业吨综合能耗下降25%，与"十五"规划末期相比，2010年工业废气DMF排放量仅温州地区减少14kt，工业废水循环利用，新开合成革项目综合能耗已经达到0.55t/万元产值。"十一五"期间涌现了一批清洁生产环境友好型企业，大中型企业已经全部获得清洁生产审核，节能减排取得了显著成效。

2. 产业集群与大型骨干企业在节能减排起到引领作用

丽水市大力支持推进水性生态合成革发展，为节约资源和环境保护，提升产业专业升级速度，起到积极地示范作用。丽水经济开发区管委会认为，"解决合成革的发展问题，不能只抓末端治理，更不能关停企业，而要从源头上采用国际先进技术，以水性聚氨酯原料替代油性原料"。在市政府全力支持下，开发区开始走水性生态合成革发展的探索道路。1)建立"中国合成革循环经济示范基地"。2007年开发区管委会突出成革循环经济示范工程，企业万元产值能耗水平下降较快，其中浙江力帆革业有限公司同比下降46.32%、丽水市富泰革基布有限公司同比下降45.23%、浙江豪登合成革有限公司同比下降18%；2)建立"合成革绿色生产工艺及品质提升关键技术开发与示范项目"。浙江优耐克、浙江德美博士达两家合成革用水性聚氨酯树脂生产企业落户园区，年生产能力达到5万吨水性聚氨酯规模；其中优耐克水性聚氨酯应用合成革获得国家环保部科技进步奖，3项省级重大科技专项取得进展。3)建立"中国水性树脂应用与生态合成革研发中心"。与四川大学、安徽大学开展聚氨酯革后整理水性材料应用工艺研发与推广；建立国内第一条自主研发的水性合成革红外中波干法生产线，为区内企业提供水性树脂研发、生产组织的基础开发工作。4)第一家政府与国外跨国公司签署已合成革项目为内容的合作协议。2010年12月浙江丽水市政府与拜耳新材料科技有限公司就水性合成革树脂合作签订框架协定后，2011年在浙江五洲公司、方源公司投产水性聚氨酯合成革生产线，成为全行业首批与国外跨国公司合作建立水性生态合成革出产线，标记着合成革行业从此迈入一个新时期。5)第一家建立煤改气集中供热。园区实施集中供热后，用煤总量下降，多生产出4亿多度电，使二氧化硫的去除率从目前的30%达到90%左右，节能效果将十分明显。6)建立"丽水市水性生态合成革研究院"，开展以生态合成革的研究组织，也是第一家获得省级合成革产业联盟单位，纳入国家级产业联盟项目；同时也第一家组织水性聚氨酯技术培训班，对园区内企业进行水性聚氨酯应用技术裴玄，奠定人才基础。7)首次组织国际性的水性生态合成革产业大会。在2011年组织水性生态合成革及产业安全论坛会基础上，2013年再次组织召开"中国国际水性生态合成革产业大会"，水性聚氨酯生产线全面对外开放展示。各国从事水性聚氨酯应用合成革专家云集丽水，再次推动全行业水性生态合成革发展。丽水市青田县质监局加大合成革行业节能减排控制，积极引导企业开展ISO 14000环境管理体系认证，促进生态文明建设和循环经济发展，培育凯乐科技和联侨合成革两家企业为省级能源计量示范单位。8)建立"中国水性生态合成革示范基地"。开发区管委会政策引导、服务企业到位，先后编制了《合成革行业清洁生产暂行管理办法》、《水阁工业区生态改造规划》、《水阁工业区循环经济规划》、《合成革行业循环经济示范与建设大纲》、《合成革行业循环经济关键技术研发与示范》等规范性文件。2011年在水性生态合成革各项基础示范工程的基础上，制定了《丽水市合成革产业集群转型升级实施方案》从宏观指导开发区合成革行业循环经济建设，并在实践中有效的加强督促和落实规划的实施。明确了鼓励措施：①水性树脂的用量与扩大产能挂钩的鼓励措施。用环境空间换产能扩张。对年度使用水性树脂400t，给予在现有合成革厂区内审批一条湿法生产线指标。②水性树脂的应用程度与安排生产用地挂钩的鼓励措施。将在东扩区块，安排2000～3000亩用地，用于建设水性生态合成革园区。对水性树脂生产工艺掌握、产品销售的较好企业，将优先给予安排。③水性树脂使用量与资金奖励挂钩。在水性树脂用量达到一定数量（如前段企业达到年用量达到200t，后段企业达到50吨以上）的企业，给予一定的资金奖励（如每吨奖励1000元左右）。④鼓励水性树脂的研发与生产。帮助水性树脂生产和研发企业向上级科技及宏观管理部门申报课题，同时，开发区自身也拿出一定的科技基金来扶持水性树脂的研发与应用。政府服务于企业，形成了水性生态合成革生产规模，在行业起到了积极引导作用，经中国轻工业联合会批准授予“中国水性生态合成革示范基地”。

温州合成革工业自温州建立“中国合成革之都”以来，率先走出粗放经营模式，在生态化建设方面寻求突破。温州合成革行业共投入5亿元，用于节约资源、环境治理、清洁生产工艺改造，在节能与环保工作方面不断创造奇迹。1）率先实现干法生产线安装DMF回收装置：2002年温州人造革有限公司和上海同济大学联合攻克“废气净化回收”技术难题。通过推广回收技术，仅温州地区节约资源价值近2亿元。干法生产线投资DMF回收装置，实现节约资源消耗，为全行业实施干法生产线回收起到了带动作用。近几年温州企业率先实施多塔高效回收装置：温州金大利、温州新兄弟等公司积极投入各项治理硬件设施，一个企业在碱性法脱硫脱氨新设备就投入100多万元。隆兴皮革公司，研发“新型管式高压静电DOP收受接管装置”，一天就可收挥发的废气150kg。2）率先建立合成革固废处置中心：温州民间资本参与环保建设，投入4500万元完成全国首个合成革固废处置中心，完成一期、二期工程建设，温州地区所有合成革企业的精馏残渣得到妥善处置。3）实施工业废水纳入联网在线监测，率先突氨氮生化处理工艺。在第一次全国产排污调查后，发现废水处理过程中产生大量氨氮，严重超国家标准，由此温州组织专家攻克难关，在污水处理过程中产生的氨氮指标完全达到饮用水标准。浙江力邦制革有限公司的工业废水经物理和生化处理再利用，一年节约用水36kt；4）率先采取生产线封闭系统，解决无组织排放问题。PU干法生产线的封闭，一直是全国同行的难题，温州金大利公司2008年开始研究风量风压的调整，从源头上捕集回收废气有了新的突破，达到降低排风量对电能的消耗，同时解决了VOC气体回收问题。为此2009年温州市市、区环保部门充分肯定节能环保成果，召开了现场会并组织对合成革企业生产线和配料车间的封锁工作进行专项检查。5）温州开展燃煤锅炉脱硫工程试点工作，其中6家为合成革企业，燃煤锅炉脱硫工程采用双碱法，辅以PLC自动控制系统，实行自动加药工艺，对锅炉排出的烟气中的二氧化硫进行分解，为深化节能减排效益提供实践经验。6）率先建立废气检测室：2011年12月温州经济技术开发区合成革13家合成革企业拿出启动资金78万元，购置总价值约60万元的设备，包括一套价值40多万元的进口气相色谱仪，实施自检自查，及时了解废气处理设备的运行情况。温州经济技术开发区合成革废气检测室运行，成为第一家由企业自行投资成立废气检测室的区域。7）率先开发水性聚氨酯浆料：温州寰宇公司2001年开发合成革水性聚氨酯环保材料、2010年6月温州宏得利树脂有限公司牵手世界500强企业美国陶氏集团，共同开发水性聚氨酯生产项目、长丰公司2011年与中国科学技术大学建立合作关系，成功研发出水性聚氨酯人造革贝斯，经干法贴面后，成为环保型的绿色人造革。温州企业生态化建设社会责任意识不断提高，温州合成革商会率先大规模的组织以环境友好为内容的培训班业技术培训，260名员工参加了培训。温州经济技术开发区内永达利合成革、长江合成革、一都合成革、亚展人造革等12家合成革企业，向社会发出《开发区合成革企业公开承诺书》；

大型骨干企业引领作用突出。目前人造革合成革工业上市公司五家以及大型骨干企业在节能减排、环境保护以及推进生态化制品，投入科研力量以及科研经费比重很大，在关键性技术、具有前沿技术方面，在行业的起到了支撑引领作用。如安利等五家上市公司大力实施节能减排，加大环保投入，实现减少工业用水210kt左右，减少3000吨标准煤左右，减少烟尘排放23.128t，减少SO_2排放20t左右；2009年实现综合能耗0.463t标煤/万元，同比上年下降7.49%；90%以上的工业废水循环使用，大大低于全国工业企业平均水平。清洁生产推进实施期间，企业在环保管理、“三废”处理、节能减排等方面取得了良好的效果，实现了空气、噪声、烟尘检测结果也均达到了国家相关标准要求。华伦皮塑2008年以来，就围绕锅炉节能减排，实施了余热利用、燃煤分层燃烧、利用热管技术增加锅炉进气温度、淘汰普通的导热油循环泵改用新型泵等等，实行这些技改项目后，可实现年节约燃煤10%以上。

3. 环境标注认证以及标准化建设形成框架体系，为生态化建设提供规范污染源调查提供节约资源支撑。根据中国塑协落实中国轻工业联合要求，中国塑料加工工业协会人造革合成革专业委员会与大专院校研究所2008年先后对近17家企业进行污染源因子函调，经甄别筛选获得12家有效数据，实测企业数为12家，获得污染物指标数4个，原始产污系数32个，原始排污系数32个，个体产污系数13个，个体排污系数13个。通过对这些数据的专家评审和企业反馈，最后确定出针对不同情况的原始系数和个体系数的权重和表达方式，得出人造革、合成革制造行业产排污系数，确定了生产吨产品排放的COD、NH3－N、工业废水量以及工业废气量。这是人造革、合成革行业第一次开展产排污系数核算，产排污系数能够全面涵盖各种不同的产品、工艺、规模、原材料以及末端治理技术设备等因素组合，科学地反映污染物产生和排放的客观规律，实测和收集了大量关于人造革、合成革制造行业产排污的数据，产排污系数基本代表了行业企业污染物产生与排放的总体情况，客观地体现了塑料人造革、合成革制造工业的资源利用和产排污状况，不仅为全国第一次工业污染源普查工作提供依据，而且通过核算产排污系数，为合理分析污染源提供了依据。比如按照2012年聚氨酯合成革产量，结合产排污系数核算，如果不进行处理将造成工业废水排放18000kt，但是厌氧/好氧生物组合工艺＋脱氮工艺，并经过生化处理循环利用，污水排放很小。《合成革制造业产排污系数核算》填补了我国合成革行业基础数据的空白，为国家对合成革行业环境领域规划、统计、核算、科研和节能减排等工作提供了重要科技支撑和数据依据。

逐步形成节能减排与环境保护管理标准体系。目前全国涉及节能与环保方面的标准数量已经上千项，塑料行业环保标准主要有《进口废塑料环境保护管理规定》、《废塑料加工利用污染防治管理规定》，《废塑料回收与再生利用污染控制技术规范》；塑料行业环境标志产品标准有《环境标志产品技术要求——再生塑料制品》、《环境标志产品技术要求——泡沫塑料》、《环境标志产品技术要求——塑料门窗》、《环境标志产品技术要求——一次性餐饮具》、《环境标志产品技术要求——建筑用塑料管材》、《环境标志产品技术要求——再生塑料制品》、《环境标志产品技术要求——合成革》、《环境标志产品技术要求——木塑制品》。人造革合成革专业委员会在实践中不断强调行业节能环保标准体系建设，依据系统理论，梳理环节，形成人造革合成革工业节能环保工作的标准化、体系化、系统化的概念；在能耗限额标准、生产工艺能耗水平等各方面，对分析企业进行节能环保改造的节能潜力、实施节能改造工程，提高能源利用效率起到了积极地作用。专委会围绕转变发展方式和淘汰落后产能、产品、生产技术和生产工艺，重点协调各方加强节能减排、清洁生产标准、产品安全、检测方法标准的研制。从安全与卫生、环保产品方面比较早的就开始研究，历经五年的时间完成了《聚氯乙烯人造革有害物质限量》标准，于2008年国家质检总局发布实施。这两年完成了《服装用聚氨酯合成革安全要求》、《聚氨酯超细纤维合成革通用安全技术条件》、《家居用聚氨酯合成革安全技术条件》、《汽车用聚氨酯合成革安全技术条件》、《家居用聚氯乙烯人造革安全技术条件》等标准的起草、审核以及报批、发布程序。从清洁生产工艺、环境治理方面，2006年国家环保部发布《合成革工业污染物排放标准》、2009年国家环保部发布《清洁生产标准合成革工业》、2010年国家环保部发布《清洁生产审核指南合成革工业》标准。《聚氨酯合成革清洁生产工艺技术规范》纳入工业和信息化部2010年第二批行业标准制修订计划》。从节能减排方面，人造革合成革行业已经着手进行《聚氨酯合成革节能降耗技术要求》标准的起草制定工作。

从标准入手推动行业节能减排纳入规范化随着国家行业标准的制定发布，合成革行业的地方环境标准这两年也随之而动，作为地方标准，及时引导本地区规范环境治理与节能减排工作。如浙江省2010年10月28日发布的强制地方标准DB 33/762—2009《合成革单位产量可比电耗、综合能耗限额及计算方法》，2012年福建省发布了《福建省合成革与人造革行业环境准入条件》。国家清洁生产标准对于合成革综合能耗分为三级，12～16t综合能耗，浙江省按照产品性质实施节能减排，限定浙江省的合成革企业可比单位产量综合能耗限额限定值≤11000.00kgce/万米，按照浙江的标准，实际上是达到国家综合能耗的一级标准，补充了现有标准，如提出：可比单位产量电耗限额限定值/合成革≤8000.00kWh/万米、DMF回收≤750.00kgce/t。合成革生产企业制定能耗限额标准，对合成革生产企业做好节能、减排、低碳工作，进一步挖掘节能潜力起到指导作用，并将对地方的节能降耗工作起到积极推动作用。节能减排标准颁布后各行业协会和机构通过组织宣传、贯标活动，促进实施工作。如：广东省鞋类产品质量监督检验站组织《聚氯乙烯人造革有害物质限量》标准培训、温州合成革商会组织《合成革单位产量可比电耗、综合能耗限额及计算方法》培训，起到积极地引导作用。

二、绿色工业革命——产业生态建设仍需前行

人造革、合成革、超纤革制造装备自动化程度高，工艺复杂系数高，作为新型聚合材料，既是工业中间品，也是人们生活的必需品。进入本世纪以来人造革合成革工业，应用各种纺织基材、高分子材料以及各种功能助剂聚合为高物性、高品质、高稳定性新型合成面料；涉及面广，用量大、主要包括鞋里鞋面、箱包面料、服装面料、汽车内饰、文化体育用品以及各类日用生活用品等。人造革合成革是支撑民生产业十分重要的工业，与各行各业同样面临在第三次工业技术革命中围绕低碳经济和新能源发展。在当前金融危机后时代经济形势下，人造革合成革工业盈利水平下降，部分节能环保指标与零排放仍存在一定差距。随着国家环境容量制约和环境标准不断提高，走低消耗、低排放、高效益、高产出的转型升级工业化发展道路的必然要求。

1. 国家政策明确、节能环保形势紧迫、转型升级任务艰巨

当前，国家对节能减排与环境保护工作的重视已达到空前的程度。在“十一五”期间，国务院做出了《关于落实科学发展观加强环境保护的决定》的重大决策，并将节能减排作为国民经济发展和改善生态环境的重要举措和约束性考核指标。进入十二五以来各项规划也相继出台，如《“十二五”节能环保产业发展规划》、《国家环境保护标准“十二五”规划》、《节能减排“十二五”规划》、《工业转型升级规划》、《战略性新兴产业发展“十二五”规划》。

《“十二五”节能环保产业发展规划》明确了：“水、气、固、土和重金属”污染防治立体推进发展，既包括烟气脱硝问题，也包括一些危险化学品处理问题；既包括产品、材料的发展，也包括环保服务业的发展。政策的意图是从治理水、固、气三层面立体推进发展。制定了包括税收、绿色信贷、金融等一系列产业扶持政策，确定了产业鼓励和限制的技术、产品，强调要以经济杠杆来撬动节能与环保市场。《战略性新兴产业发展“十二五”规划》把节能环保产业作为未来5年国民经济四大支柱产业（新一代信息技术、生物和高端装备制造业）之首。拟定24个重点支持方向中，涉及污水处理、固废无害化处理和大气污染物防治3个。《国家环境保护标准“十二五”规划》计划在未来5年新立项450项标准，完成600项环境保护标准计划项目，涵盖环境空气质量标准、重点行业污染物排放标准和环境管理规范等。还将研究出台各行业污染物达标治理的工程技术规范，完成环境保护标准体系构建，形成8大类标准簇。环境保护标准五大类：水、气、土、生态、声与振动；增设PM2.5平均浓度限值和臭氧8h平均浓度限值，收紧PM10等污染物的浓度限值。在生态环境方面，构建包含生态环境质量标准、生态保护与恢复标准、生态监测与评价标准三大类别的生态环境标准体系；政策上意图通过提高环保门槛促进产业升级换代，加速各产业领域的“优胜劣汰”进程。《节能减排“十二五”规划》提出：到2015年全国万元国内生产总值能耗下降到0.869t标准煤，比2010年的1.034t标准煤下降16%。全国化学需氧量和二氧化硫排放总量分别控制在23476kt、20864kt，分别减少8%；全国氨氮和氮氧化物排放总量分别控制在2380kt、20462kt，分别减少10%。到2015年，单位工业增加值能耗比2010年下降21%左右，主要产品单位能耗指标达到先进节能标准的比例大幅提高，部分行业和大中型企业节能指标达到世界先进水平。《“十二五”环境保护规划》：在化学需氧量、二氧化硫的基础上又增加了两项即氨氮和氧氧化物；解决涉及民生安全的危险废物、有机污染物、危险化学品、重金属的侵害。在进出口环境关税、市场准入环节、投资环节、上市环节等四大环节把控，实施国家监察，考核审批等硬手段；淘汰化工、印染、制革等八个行业落后产能；提高印染化工制革等八个行业污染物排放标准和清洁生产评价指标。全面推行排污许可证制度，严格控制长三角、珠三角等区域的印染、制革等行业新建单纯扩大产能项目。鼓励使用水性、低毒或低挥发性的有机溶剂，推进精细化工行业有机废气污染回收利用。重点对挥发性有机污染物和有毒废气监测，减少二恶英等有毒有害废气排放。限制生产和使用高环境风险化学品。《工业转型升级规划（2011～2015年）》指出：要按照建设资源节约型、环境友好型社会的要求，以推进设计开发生态化、生产过程清洁化、资源利用高效化、环境影响最小化为目标，增强工业的可持续发展能力。其中重点支持发展包括水性聚氨酯合成革技术、定岛和不定岛超细纤维合成革技术、合成革、涂料、粘合剂用聚氨酯水分子分散液工业生产技术。工信部《关于进一步加强中小企业节能减排工作的指导意见》提出了在年综合能耗10kt标准煤以上的中小企业及各省指定的年综合能耗5kt标准煤以上不满10kt标准煤重点用能企业中的中小企业，争取用3～5年时间，培育和形成一批中小企业节能减排示范企业（产业基地、集聚区），较大幅度提升中小企业能源资源利用水平和清洁生产水平，重点用能行业的中小企业单位能耗下降25%左右，使中小企业单位

产品能耗、主要污染物排放、清洁生产等指标有显著提高。

国家各个规划节能减排方案目标分解落实到各省市区县，从人造革合成革企业特别是产业集群已经分别接到相关通知，提出要在规定的时间内逐步在采取各项措施，有的地区明确提出减少燃煤锅炉，减少二氧化硫、二氧化碳排放。如此大的力度，强化环境保护，节能减排，确实取得了实效，从这两年国家统计公报看，全国万元国内生产总值能耗下降3.6%，万元国内生产总值用水量129m^3，下降7.2%，二氧化碳年排放总量一定将低于美国、俄罗斯、印度、日本。

2. 实施节约资源与环境保护法律效力机制，加快生态建设势在必行

关于节约资源与环境保护从国家政策方面，通过建立良性循环机制包括强化资源有偿使用和污染者付费政策，综合运用经济杠杆等手段，解决经济发展与环境保护的矛盾。通过建立问责制，开展绩效考评纳入各级干部政绩考核体系以及合理确定排污费征收标准、限制高耗能、高耗材、高污染产品出口，推动企业成为节能环保的投入主体，实施市场化、社会化运作。

目前针对建设生态文明、资源节约、环境保护实践中的问题，修订原有法律，发动群众监督，实施联合执法机制，推进资源节约和环境保护的法治化建设。2013年6月18日《最高人民法院、最高人民检察院关于办理环境污染刑事案件适用法律若干问题的解释》，对有关环境污染犯罪的定罪量刑标准作出了新的规定，污染环境罪等罪名的入罪要件认定标准都有所降低，体现了从严打击环境污染犯罪的立法精神。“重大环境污染事故罪”：一是扩大了污染物的范围，将原来规定的“其他危险废物”修改为“其他有害物质”；二是降低了入罪门槛，将“造成重大环境污染事故，致使公私财产遭受重大损失或者人身伤亡的严重后果”修改为“严重污染环境”。修改后，罪名由原来的“重大环境污染事故罪”相应调整为“污染环境罪”《解释》认定“严重污染环境”的14项标准、非法排放危险废物3吨构成犯罪、致使一人以上重伤、中度残疾或者器官组织损伤导致严重功能障碍的都要判罪。

3. 淘汰落后、突破新关口，全面提升民生生态产品发展水平

目前部分地区很严重的环境污染，很高的工业污染排放、很多的污染事故突发事件，“很严重、很高、很多”水、气、土以及重金属污染环境引发社会矛盾日益突出。但在中国仍处于工业化中期，又难以限制对资源、环境压力较大的产业的发展。未来我国环境与发展的矛盾将更加突出，工业排放日趋复杂，控制环境污染和防治生态退化的难度也在加大。近年来从世界各国不断推出各种生态治理措施，我国也不断加大环境治理，从国家层面看采取：正面积极引导，通过鼓励各类节能减排与环境治理政策支持、实现推进工业技术进步。同时两个重要倒逼措施，第一是采取限制淘汰，公布淘汰落后生产能力(包括企业名单、产品名单)、制定限制措施；第二进入法制管理，提出污染环境罪，采取强大的舆论环境、社会监督推进生态文明建设。中央连续多年在各大区派出环境督察员，确保“十二五”期间国家对于环境保护目标实现。

人造革合成革工业面临着转型升级，进一步提高先进生产力，实施绿色革命、生态化建设的关键时期。十八大报告第一次提出来要合理控制能源消耗总量，我们认为：在节能减排问题上，人造革合成革工业在生态合成革、清洁生产基础上要突出能源和资源消耗的总量控制，研发和推进适于合成革燃煤锅炉推进工程，煤改气工程以及余热余能利用工程；通过采用红外加热、微波加热、UV加热等技术进一步实施扩大清洁能源利用；在环境友好基础上，进一步提升二甲基甲酰胺精(蒸)馏残渣危险废物的处理技术水平、提升DMF的高效回收率，提高环保发展水平面；在生态制品方面，积极推进绿色产品、环保产品，卫生产品，禁用各类重金属，实现表面无残留物。稳步推进全行业生态化进程，全面提升生态产品发展水平和发展速度。

三、产业发展—推进节约资源，生态化进程目标与方向任务

1. 继续稳定企业发展，提升效益质量是节能环保生态化建设的基础

中国塑料行业有着稳固的工业基础，规模以上企业13414家，233万职工，大中型企业13.3%、民企55.69%、外资以及港澳台企业3068家占了22.87%。2012年我国塑料制品规模以上企业总产量达5781万吨，工业总产值近1.7万亿元，其中民企占了50%，国企、民企、港台与外资企业产值平均分别为2.086亿、1亿、1.4亿。塑料行业固定资产投资为发展奠定基础，2011年投资总额2630亿元，其中港台与外商企业投资分别占了4.1%、3.8%；国有控股占了5%、集体控股1.8%、民营企业占了83.7%。从第二次工业普查反应：人造革合成革技术改造经费年支出2.32亿元，占塑料行业总技改支

出的7.98%，次于管道行业和编织行业，其中消化吸收经费支出246万元，占技改经费支出的1.1%。技术引进经费支出和购买国内技术经费支出92万元，所占比重很小，说明人造革合成革行业技术改造来源主要是自主知识产权创新以及科研院所科技转化生产力比重高。中国塑料—人造革合成革工业2012年549家企业，实现工业总产值1085.77亿元，同比增长17.23%．主营业务收入1040亿元，同比增长11.78%；从业人员13.49万，人均产值83万高于塑料平均水平。2012年人造革合成革产量3142.7kt，同比增长15.55%。浙江企业占了47%，产量42.67%；福建企业与产量占全国的比重分别都为21%；江苏占了全国的11.9%。进入"十二五"以来浙江临海合成革工业全区稳定发展继续保持增长，全省2011年产量突破1000kt，占全国的44%；2012年产量达到1330kt，同比增长10.6%；福建福鼎合成革产业基地的崛起为全省突破600kt奠定了实力基础，增长速度39.5%，占全国比重从2008年的2%跃居21.3%，从2010年的第四位跃居第二位；江苏合成革374.8kt，下降13.1%，占全国的11.9%。2012年我国人造革合成革行业经济、技术形势发生了新的变化，行业总资产689亿增加10%，主营业务成本继续上涨，同比增长10.93%；负债率61%比2011年增长10.32%；资产利润率提高了9.65%。老企业举步维艰：成本压力、过剩经竞争、通胀环境、市场萎缩，亏损企业57家，亏损额1.7亿，两项同比都有所增加；新企业起步艰难：环境保护、融资市场、投资预期的影响较大。外贸出口风险加大，削弱了企业产品出口的竞争力，2012年全国人造革合成革企业出口量出口额49.86亿美元，占塑料行业的15.5%，出口量占了总销售量的18%，占全部工业总产值的31%，去年出口量增长1.83%，但是出口额同比下降6.08%；出口交货值87亿，同比出现负增长为2.93%。

2. 继续开创"生态合成革—中国创造—企业品牌"，推进跨越发展步伐

生态合成革是在2002年中国塑协人造革合成革专委会在广州召开"中国合成革企业家峰会"上意大利克莱斯皮专家首次提出，"生态合成革"定义，至今已经十年的历程。人造革合成革工业发展最关键的是选择了正确的生态发展发展道路。第一、巩固生态型高端技术为行业先进生产力科研成果。一批重大科技成果，极大地提升了中国人造革合成革在国际市场的行业竞争力。以特种功能性、水性生态型品牌为代表的中国新型合成革生产技术已成为国际上"中国制造合成革"形象，受到许多外国应用市场以及国内消费者的高度评价。优耐克水性生态合成革亮相国际最具规格行业展会期间引起国外官渡关注，纷纷报道。科研创新成果缩小了与世界先进水平的差距，合成革科技技术成果已经占据世界先进水平，可以说目前听到和了解到的国外新技术已经甚少，各类新技术报道都是来自中国技术。第二、巩固清洁生产技术创新为生态化建设支撑作用。科技创新和技术进步为行业节能减排、循环经济、生态化发展提供了重要支撑。浙江优耐克、安徽科天、浙江博士达等公司开发的水性聚氨酯应用技术成果，在行业中得到广泛应用，极大地加快了行业生态化建设进程，为此浙江优耐克获得环保部科技奖；以温州企业为代表的DMF回收技术，全面提升了节能减排水平；以南平合成革产业园为代表的污水处理技术，提升了污水集中处理发展水平。第三、巩固大型科研基地，培育中小企业科研中心。行业技术创新基础建设拓取得较大进步，产学研紧密合作，创办了不同形式的研发机构。目前安利、禾欣、双象、国信、华峰、温革、万华等公司建成了国家和省市合成革工程技术中心，大型骨干企业建立了独立的重点实验室。在未来几年要在中小型企业继续拍于涉及汽车革、家具革、超细纤维革以及助剂、涂饰材料等研发中心。在不同的产业集群建立不同的生态合成革产业平台、生态合成革研究院、生态合成革中试基地。要发挥大型企业在自主创新，推进行业技术进步中的带头和引领作用。在每个特色区域建设国家级和行业工程技术中心、重点实验室、检测中心、新技术开发中心。在中部地区继续培育"水性生态合成革产业化示范基地"等不同形式的创新平台，逐步完善多层次科技创新体系。建立川大、安大、陕科大等五所大学联席制度，完善合成革专业人在培养基地。促进大学、企业和行业协会合作开展职业教育工程，培养高层次技术人才和高级技能型人才。在适当时机召开工程师大会，表彰一批为行业发展做出贡献的科技人才，形成行业技术创新项目的申报和管理组织体系。第四、巩固现有标准体系，推进生态化标准体系建设。积极将生态化示范企业实践成果，上升到行业标准、推荐标准体系，在现有26项行业标准基础上，完善标准框架，建立国家、行业、地方以及企业突出以生态合成革产品标准、节能减排标准、环境保护标准、术语、检测等标准研发、立项、推广工作，着手做好生态工艺标准的研究工作。三以科技为先导，实现企业成长目标，推进产业革命，

在“十二五”后确定人造革合成革工业未来产业方向，在彩色卫生产品、生态制品、节能减排以及资源节约、环境友好等领域要通过自主创新，转变经济发展方式，实现产业革命性的发展。以解决行业生态绿色、多功能、复合型产品的重大科技需求为导向；以突破生态化、绿色制造、环境影响的共性关键技术为主攻方向，实施以水性生聚氨酯、无溶剂聚氨酯、热缩弹性体、聚烯烃等环保材料、环保工艺的生态化建设重点工程。发展绿色制造、新型低环境复合材料和高性能复合人造革合成革制品，开发纳米级复合涂层面料，为高档品牌箱包、品牌鞋、高档服装提供时尚化新型民生资源；开发多功能性化高端产品，推进抗菌防霉、防紫外线、阻燃、透气透湿、发光变色、自洁防污、耐刮、耐候性等功能性产品发展；开发超宽超厚消音耐磨型聚氯乙烯人造革地板，应用公共场所以及大型交通工具地板市场，满足不断提高的绿色节能家装市场要求；开发新型超细纤维合成革，在海岛型的基础上，开发定岛型、菊掰型以及木纹型等多种超细纤维合成革；开发环保型具有透气功能的聚氨酯壁纸，用于高档装修新材料；开发合成革天然植绒产品，提升的合成革产品质感。为战略性产业发展提供新材料，为新能源、信息产业、国防军工、民航交通业等高端产业领域提供高端产品。超细纤维合成革产量超越1亿米；生态型高端产品占生产量的20%。实现人造革合成革工业领域的科学技术全面达到或超过国际先进水平，引领世界人造革合成革工业技术的发展。打造“生态合成革－中国创造－企业品牌”新一代新型科学技术国际品牌。

以行业绿色生态化工艺发展的需求为科技创新方向，以科技创新成果引领和支撑行业生态化发展。开发干湿法应用水性聚氨酯生产工艺技术、挤压热塑性聚氨酯合成革生产工艺、烯烃弹性体人造革生产；推进自动配色、上浆上料系统工艺发展；开发印刷着色、压花工、揉纹、植绒、UV定性等表面后处理新工艺技术。推进无溶剂型聚氨酯合成革新工艺技术；VOC无组织排放回收工艺；DMF高效回收工艺；DOP静电除尘二次喷淋回收新工艺；污水COD/BOD以及氨氮处理新技术；开发固渣处理新技术；开发节能型导热系统，研究和解决部分地区燃煤集中，有计划实施煤改气工程；开发发泡炉热系统循环利用技术、浆料与色浆自动供料系统。年减少有机溶剂使用量70kt，减少DMF有机气体排放量，无组织排放有机气体回收技术普及50%，大型企业水性聚氨酯应用覆盖面达到30%。形成具有中国特色、国际先进水平的节能体系，在丽水、福鼎、南平通过建设集中供热系统、集中污水处理系统示范基地，实现更绿色环保的发展方式。

要充分利用国内生产资料，不断开发新型环保合成材料，促进新型超细纤维革基布、环保型助剂、水性色浆、水性聚氨酯、无溶剂聚氨酯、聚氨酯弹性体、烯烃弹性体开发与应用，扩大新型环境友好新材料的应用覆盖面，将各类环保材料作为行业主流材料，始终保持我国人造革合成革超纤革新聚合材料低排放行业地位。扩展生物基高分子、环保材料的的应用，促进产品生态化升级。重点发展水性聚氨酯替代DMF溶剂型聚氨酯，开发应用环保型DOP、稳定剂、环氧大豆油等各类环保骨料的应用比重，提高环保材料的应用比例达到30%。水性面层聚氨脂：水性黏合层聚氨酯：水性发泡性聚氨酯：水性色浆以及着色剂：

充分发挥塑料行业规划指导意见的引导和保障作用。以《中国塑料“十二五”发展规划指导意见》为指导，与各级政府主管部门、各行业协会的产业技术政策衔接，积极组织申报国家科技创新计划，组织实施科技创新重点工程。加大生态化建设宣传、社会责任宣传，每年召开行业科技工作会议，表彰并发布行业重大科研成果和企业创新发展成就；组织技术交流活动，宣传科技创新成果。加大国际科技合作与交流，推动与其他国家科技交流，组织参与合成革国际活动工作。加快人造革合成革经济数据库、科技成果数据库、专利数据库，知识产权数据库，着手研究人造革合成革价格指数信息系统，培育合成革工业市场价格风向标体系，建立迅速反应机制，开展多种贸易平台建设，实现增值服务。开设大型“中国国际合成革网站”的建设，举办合成革工业展览会，加快网络化建设，形成较为完善的科技信息资源共享平台。

在“十二五”期间我们要通过品牌建设提升行业社会信誉，进一步推进我行业标准战略、专利战略、品牌战略实施，创造具有自主知识产权的核心技术；创造知识产权文化，形成自主知识产权。以生态合成革建设为中心的去DMF化污染物、煤改气工程是一项持久而复杂系统工程。企业要有计划的做好技术准备、人才准备、结合各自的企业特点和市场产品定位需求，进一步确定在当前经济形势下的企业发展战略和经营模式。进一步开发和研究解决生态合成革难点，运用体系集成和资本化运作经验，在实践中须要进一步解决。在企业内部要．研究企业生产生态链，实现企业资源能量代谢，从采购环保原料、清洁生产管理、节约能源等各能量，有机结合，形成企业内部节约资源的平衡、生产环节生态链。从行业层面进一步力促．落实优惠政策，引导企业运用有利于生态合成革发展的投资政策、税收政策、信贷政策等，比如对于连续三年降低三废、节能减排突出给予政策补贴、贷款贴息等支持等。“十二五”期间是我国人造革合成革工业由生产大国向科技强国迈出重要步伐的时期，也是企业生存与发展的更加艰苦的阶段，只有通过科技创新和技术进步，实现人造革合成革绿色环保型、生态化、高端产品全面发展。

（中国塑料加工工业协会人造革合成革专业委员会　冯庶君）

硬聚氯乙烯管道的技术进步

1　PVC－U 管道行业的整体情况

中国的 PVC 管材加工产业始于 20 世纪 50 年代，开始产品主要应用于化工防腐等领域。在 20 世纪 80 年代以来，随着原料性能和加工设备水平的提高，制品性能也得到提高，产品的应用领域越来越多。

目前 PVC－U 管材在结构上有实壁管；单壁波纹管、双壁波纹管、加筋管等结构壁管；多孔管；多层管等。在材料上有 PVC、PVC－C、PVC－M、复合材料等。加工方式有挤出、缠绕、内螺旋、发泡、复合挤出等。PVC－U 管材的连接方式主要为刚性的粘接和柔性的承插接口。产品一般公称口径为 16～1000mm，结构壁管公称直径达到 1.2m 以上。

目前 PVC－U 管材主要应用领域为建筑物内的排水管、常温的供水管、电工护套管、消防用管、户外建筑落雨管；市政供水管、排水管、电力和通讯等设施护套管；给水、灌排等农业用管；化工防腐、矿山及输送其他介质等工业用管道。

按重量来区分，其中约 45% 用于各种排水用途，并以建筑物内为大部分；30% 用于供水领域；20% 用于各种护套；5% 左右用于其他领域。主要应用领域见图 1。PVC 管道中硬制品为绝大部分，此外还有极小比例用于医用、介质输送等方面的软管和复合软管。

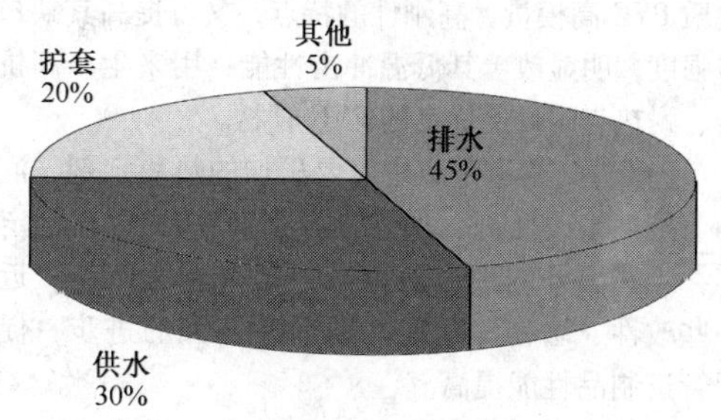

图 1　PVC－U 管材主要应用领域

在中国目前较大规模 PVC－U 管材生产企业约有 1000 家，行业年生产能力约为 10000kt 左右。2010 年各种塑料管道应用量约在 8400kt 以上，分析其中 PVC－U 管道 4600kt 左右；2011 年各种塑料管道应用量约在 10000kt 左右，分析其中 PVC－U 管道 5000kt 左右。可见在所有的塑料管道中，PVC－U 是最大材料种类，并将在今后的几年中仍占主导地位。主要的原因是：PVC－U 管道以其相对低廉的价格和良好的性能，具有较高的性价比。其高模量、高强度、耐腐蚀和安装相对容易使用户愿意接受。

在中国，PVC－U 塑料管道生产和应用技术已基本完善。在产品的开发、生产、工程应用等方面，均积累了许多成功的经验。相关产品、设计、施工、验收等国家及行业标准、规程、规范均已制定，并在实践中不断完善，在中国 PVC 管道产业的发展已经进入了成熟期，仍具有十分广阔的市场前景，还有很大的发展空间。

2　PVC 树脂及加工助剂

作为 PVC－U 管道的基础材料，中国的 PVC 树脂行业近年有较快发展，满足市场需求的供给量和相对低廉的价格，为 PVC－U 管道生产创造了条件。原料性能稳定提高，和价格相对较低也使得 PVC－U 管道的市场价格与其他管道相比有一定的优势。下表为近年中国聚氯乙烯树脂产能和实际产量统计。

2005～2010 年中国聚氯乙烯产能和实际产量统计　　10^4t/a

年份	2005 年	2006 年	2007 年	2008 年	2009 年	2010 年
产能	972	1158	1520	1581	1781	2043
产量	670	823	971	882	915	1130

在树脂产量不断增加的同时，原料的技术进步也在进行中，在中国改性 PVC 专用料的研发相对较晚，尽管已经有较多的理论研究成果，但工业化批量生产只是近期才实现。该技术采用接枝共聚方法，向 PVC

中添加高分子弹性体，以核－壳结构的聚丙烯酸酯弹性体为基质，与VC单体进行原位聚合后形成具有互穿网络结构的改性聚氯乙烯树脂。共混体系既可保持硬质PVC高模量，高刚性的特点，又可提高其缺口冲击强度，明显改善其低温冲击性能，用来生产高抗冲击、耐热与耐候性优良的PVC管材。

PVC－U管道生产中需要添加的热稳定剂、润滑剂、抗冲击改性剂、加工助剂等，中国均有稳定生产，一些国外的生产商也在中国有较大市场。近年一些改性、增韧等功能性助剂有较大的进步，促进了管道制品性能提高。

随着人们生活水平、健康要求的提高，环保意识增强，铅污染日益受到人们的关注，因此PVC加工业逐渐禁铅是大势所趋。近年热稳定剂在绿色环保、可持续发展等方面取得较大进步，锌基类、有机锡类、有机基类等无铅热稳定剂的研发、应用水平有较大提高。在2006年中国发布的国家标准中提出了给水用PVC－U管材卫生性能要符合相关的卫生标准和法规要求，并要求饮水用PVC－U管材、管件必须采用非铅盐热稳定剂，还严格控制了PVC树脂中VCM(氯乙烯单体)含量。CPPA还在2012年发布的行业发展建议中提出，希望在2015年末尽可能实现所有PVC管材含铅盐热稳定剂的替代工作。

3　建筑用排水管道的进步

建筑排水是目前PVC－U管道的最大应用领域，由于耐腐蚀、重量轻、容易安装而受到好评，在目前中国建筑排水领域占有80%以上的市场份额。

由于室内排水噪音给应用者生活带来影响，因此生产企业做了大量的工作，采取增加密度、使用多层材料、发泡等方法加大隔声量，增加管内内螺旋结构改变水流状态，从隔声、降噪等多角度出发，改善建筑排水用PVC－U管材的消音性能，并且在管件的设计和施工技术的改进、采用同层排水技术等方面，充分考虑了降低噪音的要求。图2列出了芯层发泡管(PSP)、实壁内螺旋管、芯层发泡内螺旋管、中空壁管、中空壁内螺旋管的剖面图从中我们不难发现其进步过程。

4　压力管道的进步

PVC－U管道强度较高，但其韧性较差，为克服其缺陷，行业一直以来重视高强度、高韧性的产品研发。经过共混改性、接枝改性生产的改性聚氯乙烯(PVC－M)管材和通过拉伸方法使分子结构取向排列的双向拉伸聚氯乙烯(PVC－O)管材等产品在中国也在不断进步中，并分别有不同程度的生产和应用。

4.1　PVC－M管材

聚氯乙烯的改性方法一般为物理改性和化学改性两种方法。

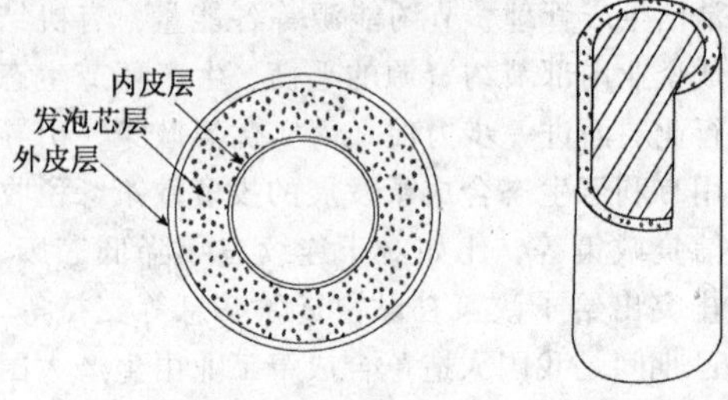

实壁内螺旋管立体剖面图　芯层发泡内螺旋管立体剖面图

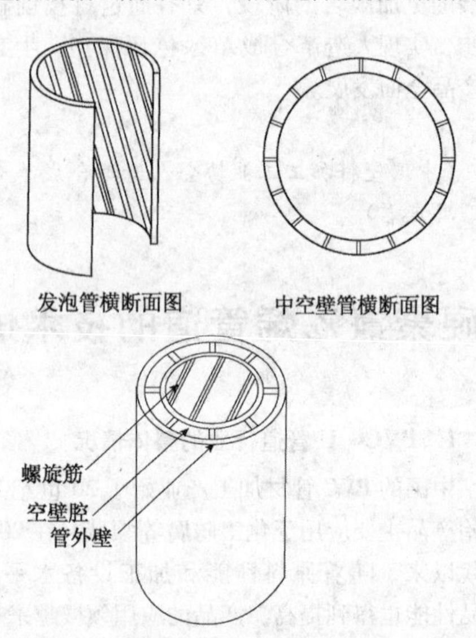

图2　不同结构PVC－U排水管材剖面图

物理改性是在PVC基体中加入其他的无机、有机材料或一些有特殊功能的助剂等，经过混合混炼而制得具有优异性能的PVC复合材料，分为填充改性、共混改性和功能性改性等。

共混是指采用其它高聚物与聚氯乙烯树脂充分混合，改进PVC的加工性能，提高管材制品的物理机械性能，达到改性目的。这是目前在中国普遍采用的方法。

PVC压力管道要解决脆性问题，主要方法之一就是将适量的增韧改性剂，在合适的工艺条件下，采用共混改性的方法，使各组分相容或形成相界面(phase interface)，受到外力冲击时，界面处吸收冲击动能，从而提高复合材料的抗冲击、抗开裂及抗点载荷性能(图3为管道破坏试验照片)。在中国已经有几十家企业能够生产PVC－M管材，在中国已经有大量成功应用的经验(图4为一些工程照片)，产品标准是参考澳大利亚/新西兰、南非和英国的相关标准在2008年制定的。

品牌企业风采介绍

辽宁华塑实业集团有限公司

江门市辉隆塑料机械有限公司

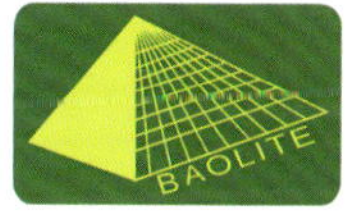

福建宝利特集团有限公司

苯领高分子材料（上海）有限公司

三斯达（福建）塑胶有限公司

顾地科技股份有限公司

普立万集合体（上海）有限公司

甘肃瑞盛.亚美特科技农业有限公司

中山环宇实业有限公司

聚合你我，共塑美好生

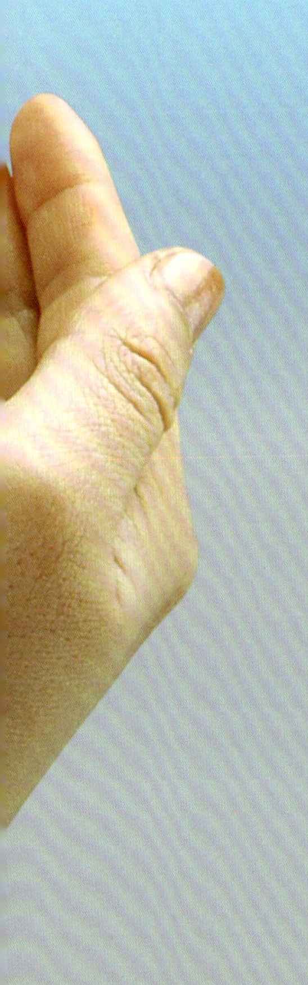

辽宁华塑集团董事长 孙晓军

华塑集团坐落于经济发达、风景秀丽、素有"湿地之都"、"鹤乡"美誉的海滨城市——辽宁•盘锦，占地面积310亩，总投资10亿元，现有员工1500余人。旗下拥有近20家企业，年销售收入近百亿元，是一家专业从事石油化工产品销售、塑料原料贸易、塑料制品生产、仓储物流、电子商务、融投资为一体的大型民营企业集团。

2012年6月，投资60亿元建设的华塑（营口）高分子新材料产业园项目破土动工，成为集团发展的重要里程碑。

经过10多年发展，集团与盘锦石化、燕山石化、大庆石化、抚顺石化、天联石化、齐鲁石化、上海赛科、吉林石化等大型石化企业建立了密切的合作关系，同时与日本伊藤忠商社、美国埃克森、日本住友、美国陶氏、韩国三星等国外知名石化企业展开多方面合作，营销网络覆盖东北三省、华北、华东、华南地区。华塑集团致力于发展塑料产业，以全球化的视野和思维，以合作、共赢的胸怀，不断聚合各个利益相关者，凝聚所有人力量，共同努力，为人们塑造高品质的生活，同时保护环境、关注生态，积极承担社会责任。

打造全球最具影响力的塑料产业生态领导者

集团公司以“塑料产业生态的领导者”为战略定位，以全球化的视野和思维，以合作、共赢的胸怀，不断聚合各个利益相关者，凝聚所有人力量，共同努力，为人们塑造高品质的生活，同时保护环境、关注生态，积极承担社会责任。

辽宁华塑集团（盘锦）塑料产业园区实景

华塑集团（盘锦）塑料产业园

盘锦大晴精密塑料模具有限公司
盘锦美佳塑料彩印有限公司
盘锦天衣塑业有限公司
辽宁华森塑料制品有限公司
盘锦瀚格管业有限公司
盘锦华恒水织布有限公司
辽宁喜爱农塑料有限公司
盘锦华塑兴贸物流有限公司

2009年7月辽宁华塑实业集团投资10亿元建设了以发展塑料制品加工为主的华塑集团（盘锦）塑料产业园，该园区是盘锦市人民政府和北方华锦化学工业集团有限公司重点支持的园区，是规划建设中的中国北方塑料城的核心组成部分。

目前，华塑集团（盘锦）塑料产业园已完成建筑面积12万平方米的标准化厂房，并投入使用，拥有员工近千人，设备总投资2亿元，年加工能力近20万吨，可以向市场提供塑料管材管件、农用棚膜地膜、塑料彩印包装膜袋、基材膜、收缩膜、水织布、注塑制品、塑料模具等系列产品。目前已有6家子公司产品投放市场，部分产品出口日本、俄罗斯、韩国、朝鲜等国家和地区。

辽宁华塑实业集团有限公司
地址：辽宁盘锦精细化工产业园区
电话：400 - 811 - 0333
传真：0427 - 3126906
邮箱：huasu@lnhuasu.cn

辽宁华塑集团（盘锦）塑料产业园区鸟瞰图

华塑集团（营口）高分子新材料科技园

营口海星新材料有限公司
营口海洋新型包装材料有限公司
海翔新材料有限公司
大晴模塑（营口）有限公司
营口金海彩印有限公司
营口蓝海高新农业装备有限公司
营口海斯特管业有限公司
营口海塑兴贸物流有限公司

华塑集团（营口）高分子新材料科技园项目总投资60亿元人民币，占地2050亩。其中包括商业服务中心、物流产业园、高分子新材料科技园三大主体部分。

三大主体建成后，每年可加工各种高端塑料制品50万吨、原料贸易超过100万吨，物流配送200万吨，预计工业产值将超100亿元。塑料原料及产品将覆盖国内各地市场及部分国外市场；运输网络辐射东北、华北、华东、华南等省市地区。

营口园区先进设备

辽宁华塑集团（营口）高分子新材料科技园

辽宁华塑实业集团有限公司
Liaoning Huasu Industrial Group Co., Ltd.

福建宝利特集团有限公司

FUJIAN POLYTECH GROUP CO.,LTD.

电话：0591-85698818 传真：0591-85698828 网址：www.cnpolytech.com

福建宝利特集团有限公司系外商独资企业，地处福州市江阴工业集中区。前身为福建宝利特制革工业有限公司，创办于1994年。宝利特集团注册资本4000万美元，总投资额10000美元，下属拥有福建宝利特纺织涂层有限公司、福建宝利特新材料科技有限公司、福建宝利特合成材料有限公司、利达化工（福建）有限公司。宝利特集团总占地面积442亩，现拥有五条国际先进水平的PU/PVC人造革生产线、一条压延生产线和一条纺织涂层生产线以及整厂配套设备，并拥有十余套生产各种高分子材料的专用设备，专业生产各种中高档PU/PVC人造革系列产品、高档织物涂层面料、油性/水性PU树脂、各种特殊高分子材料、处理剂及环保增塑剂等产品，年产值达15亿元。产品主要物性指标符合GB/T8948-2008、GB/T8949-2008国家标准，并达到欧盟EN-71、ROHS、REACH及美国ASTM等各项标准，质量达到国内外同类产品的先进水平。

福建宝利特集团通过ISO9001质量管理体系认证、ISO14001环境管理体系、ISO28001职业健康安全管理体系，连续多年获得各级政府及有关部门授予："全国外商投资双优企业"、"福建省百家明星侨资企业"、"全国明星侨资企业"、"省级花园式单位"、"纳税信用A级企业"、"福州市产品质量奖"、"福州市级企业技术中心"、"福州市知识产权示范企业"、"福建省技术创新工程创新型试点企业"、"福建名牌产品"、"福建省著名商标"、"福建省高新技术企业"、"福建省装饰革企业工程技术研究中心"等荣誉称号。截至2013年5月，集团总共申请发明专利12项，其中4项获得国家发明专利证书；申请实用新型专利9项，其中7项获得国家实用新型专利证书。

企业荣誉 Company / HONOR

★ 高新技术企业 ★

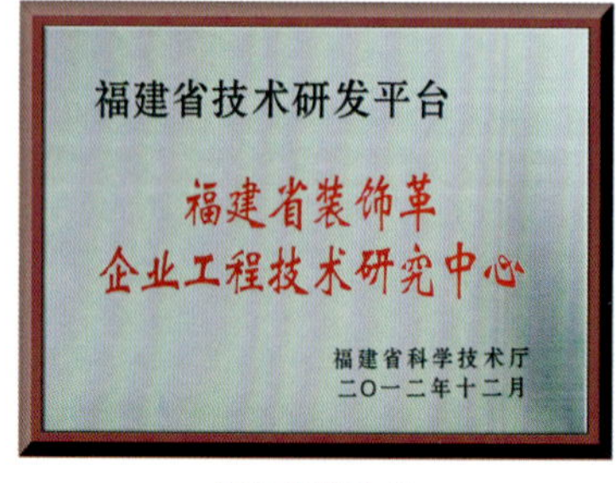

★ 福建省装饰革企业工程技术研究中心 ★

★ 福建省著名商标 ★

PATENT/ 专利证书 Certificate

- “水性聚氨酯色浆的制备方法”发明专利证书。
- “革用胶粘剂、其制备方法及在制革工艺中的应用”发明专利证书。
- “一种应用水性聚氨酯制造仿真人造革的方法”发明专利证书。
- “一种印刷图案PU/PVC干法人造革制造方法及PU/PVC人造革”发明专利证书。
- “模拟负载测试仪”实用新型专利证书。
- “一种人造革生产线的冷却装置”实用新型专利证书。
- “一种发泡人造革生产线”实用新型专利证书。

⋮

★ 发明专利证书 ★

★实用新型专利证书★

企业展示 Enterprise / SHOW

荣誉证书

福建宝利特集团有限公司

2011年度质量管理先进企业

福建省质量技术监督局

二〇一二年八月

★ 质量管理先进企业 ★

福建宝利特集团有限公司

2011年度

福州市守合同重信用企业

福州市工商行政管理局

二〇一三年二月

★ 守合同重信用企业 ★

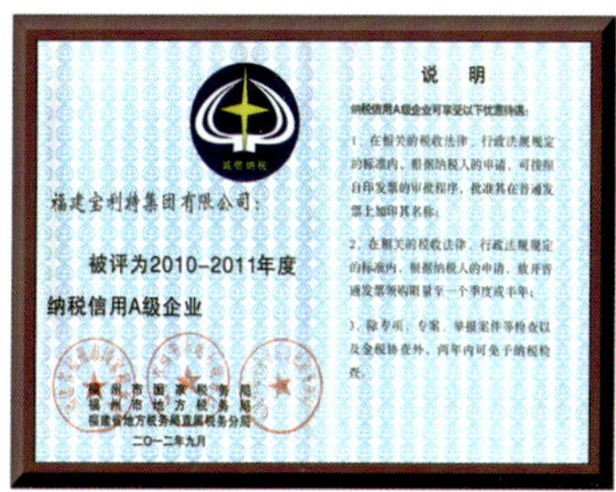

福建宝利特集团有限公司：

被评为2010-2011年度

纳税信用A级企业

二〇一二年九月

说 明

★ 纳税信用A级 

苯领是全球领先的苯乙烯系列产品供应商， 在不同的行业和区域拥有超过80年的经验。苯领为各种行业提供苯乙烯系列产品，这些行业包括包装、家用电器、电气与电子、汽车、建筑与建材、玩具与休闲、医疗保健与诊断。

包装

食品包装要求严格，远高于其他各行各业。维持货架吸引力的同时，必须满足极为苛刻的物理性要求，确保产品安全无忧。

在多用途性方面，Styrolution® PS 真正做到了无与伦比，它可以根据具体的应用进行调整，并拥有良好的节能效果。

Styrolux® 热塑性薄膜具有出色的机械强度、卓越的热成型性以及较高的热变形温度。同时，对气味和气体的渗透率非常低，尤其是氧气。

Styrolution® PS 和 Styrolux® 不仅透明度较高，操作处理过程中还能维持稳健可靠的性能，对于包装外观要求较高的食品而言不啻为黄金组合。

化妆品包装则是一个竞争激烈的领域，其视觉效应往往直接决定着产品的成与败。不少制造商都选择使用 NAS® 和 Zylar®，来注塑成型具有高透明度的容器。

PACKAGING

家用电器

一件家居用品中常常包含多种聚合物，或者是为了延长使用寿命或抗化学作用，或者仅仅是为了让商品看上去更具吸引力。

苯领可以就各种各样的材料为您提供建议，并且能提供多种产品系列来帮助您解决几乎所有的产品难题。

Novodur®、Terlux®、Luran®、Luran® S，Styrolution® PS和Terluran®等均深受家居用品制造商们的青睐，通过微调材料特性来吸引更多消费者。而最终产品通常都具有出色的高光泽度表面、耐候性、耐热性、明艳色彩和色牢度。

NAS® 和Zylar®是滤水器、吸尘器部件、平底杯和办公用品等产品的最佳解决方案，可实现极高的透明度。

HOUSEHOLD

电气与电子

非同寻常的工作要求需要非同寻常的材料来实现。电气和电子产品所要求的属性众多，包括尺寸稳定性、耐候性和耐冲击性、耐刮擦性以及抗静电性等。

当然，美观性也非常重要：消费者需要并且期望材料在外观和手感方面都能有出色表现。无瑕疵的表面光泽度和精准度会决定整个产品线的成败。

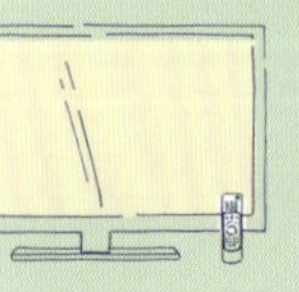

苯领针对这一领域提供的材料非常易于加工，包括Luran® S，Styrolution® PS和Terluran®。

从移动电话到坚固耐用的割草机外壳，从户外微波天线到冰箱，这些产品可以满足几乎所有您能想到的应用的需求。

ELECTRICAL & ELECTRONICS

汽车

创新性和定制化是苯领产品的核心理念。作为汽车行业的全球最大苯乙烯系列产品供应商，我们的材料在各种各样的应用中都展现出极佳的效果。

我们与汽车制造商及其零部件供应商密切合作，为实现全新性能并满足美观要求提供材料上的解决方案，包括对色彩进行微调、改进耐刮擦性以及增强 UV 稳定性。同时，尽可能降低零部件成本及重量，例如用注塑成型的免喷漆染色零部件替换喷漆零部件。

苯领提供广泛的特种ABS, ASA，及其合金产品系列：

AUTOMOTIVE

- Novodur® 耐高温 (HH) ABS 品级
- Luran® S 和Luran® SC：ASA和 ASA/PC合金
- Terblend® N 和Terblend® S： ABS/PA 和 ASA/PA 合金

苯领的产品系列包括许多重要的"第一"。2003 年，苯领发明了Luran® S 778 T Q42，适合用于免喷漆,抗 UV 的外饰部件。然而，我们的开发从未停歇！正如 2011 年生产的Luran® S 778 T SPF30，它进一步改善了耐光性，拓展了新的外饰部件应用并使其拥有更深厚浓郁的优质色彩。

继 2010 年推出了具有极高流动性的 ABS/PA 材料 Terblend® N NM-21 EF 后，苯领又带来具有高流动性的全新ASA/PA 混合产品系列，在浅色稳定性方面作出了进一步改善。这为汽车设计师带来开创浅色内饰设计的全新机遇。

建筑与建材

在全球各地，苯领聚合物在提升建筑物长期价值，提高住宅区和商业区居民的生活质量方面发挥着重要的作用。

对于需要经历多年日晒雨淋，温度变化及物理风化的建筑产品来说，耐久性是建材选择的关键标准。苯领建筑材料能为您提供可靠的坚固性。我们的建筑材料具有出色的耐刮擦/抗冲性，尺寸稳定性及耐黄变性，随着时间的推移仍能维持优良的延展性。

Luran® S 具有无与伦比的耐候特性，是户外用途/标志等需要长期保持精美外观应用的理想材料。

BUILDING & CONSTRUCTION

玩具与休闲

为休闲设备或玩具用品选择最适合的材料意味着需要面临真正的技术挑战。苯领能够提供最为顶尖的技术支持，为您的最佳解决方案开发过程排忧解难。

以下是我们帮助客户开发改良的或全新的休闲产品的几个示例：

婴儿玩具
Terluran® 提供高冲击效能，以满足於玩具安全标准。我们的ABS产品深受各大玩具品牌和生产商的欢迎。

最具价值玩具用品
ABS 是一种应用很广泛的玩具塑料材料。Playmobil 玩具中便使用了我们的 ABS 产品，此外，在一款可作为馈赠佳品的知名品牌巧克力彩蛋中也使用了我们的 ABS 产品。

坚固耐用，颇受欢迎
对于需要在儿童的玩耍过程中仍保持坚固耐用的高透明度玩具来说，Zylar® 展现出了良好的效果。

LEISURE & TOYS

雪橇和滑雪板
Novodur® ABS 的性能适合与 Terlux® 薄膜一起用于装饰。

医疗保健与诊断

医疗保健和诊断 (HD) 行业必须遵守众多最严格的法规，因而也会伴随一些最高昂的开发成本。

即使面临这些挑战，制造商也不能在产品性能上作出任何妥协，因为医疗保健产品不仅要符合行业标准，还要能够吸引购买者，具有合适的单位成本。

苯领的深厚经验可以帮助医疗保健和诊断市场实现更快的开发周期和优异的材料性能。我们还专门针对医疗保健和诊断应用推出了 Novodur® 全系列材料，同时提供远超行业标准的服务套餐。

此外，我们还承诺不断维护医疗保健和诊断材料配方（除非法规要求发生变化），并且对相应产品进行各种测试，确保适用性。

- **苯领东亚有限公司**
  香港九龙尖沙咀弥敦道 132 号
  美丽华大厦 8 楼 816 室
  电话：+852 3926 2333
- **苯领高分子材料（上海）有限公司**
  上海市普陀区岚皋路 567 号
  品尊国际中心2304 室
  电话：+86 21 2226 9999
- **苯领高分子材料（上海）有限公司广州分公司**
  广州天河区天河路 208 号
  粤海天河城大厦 3406 室
  电话：+86 20 3896 3666

www.styrolution.com

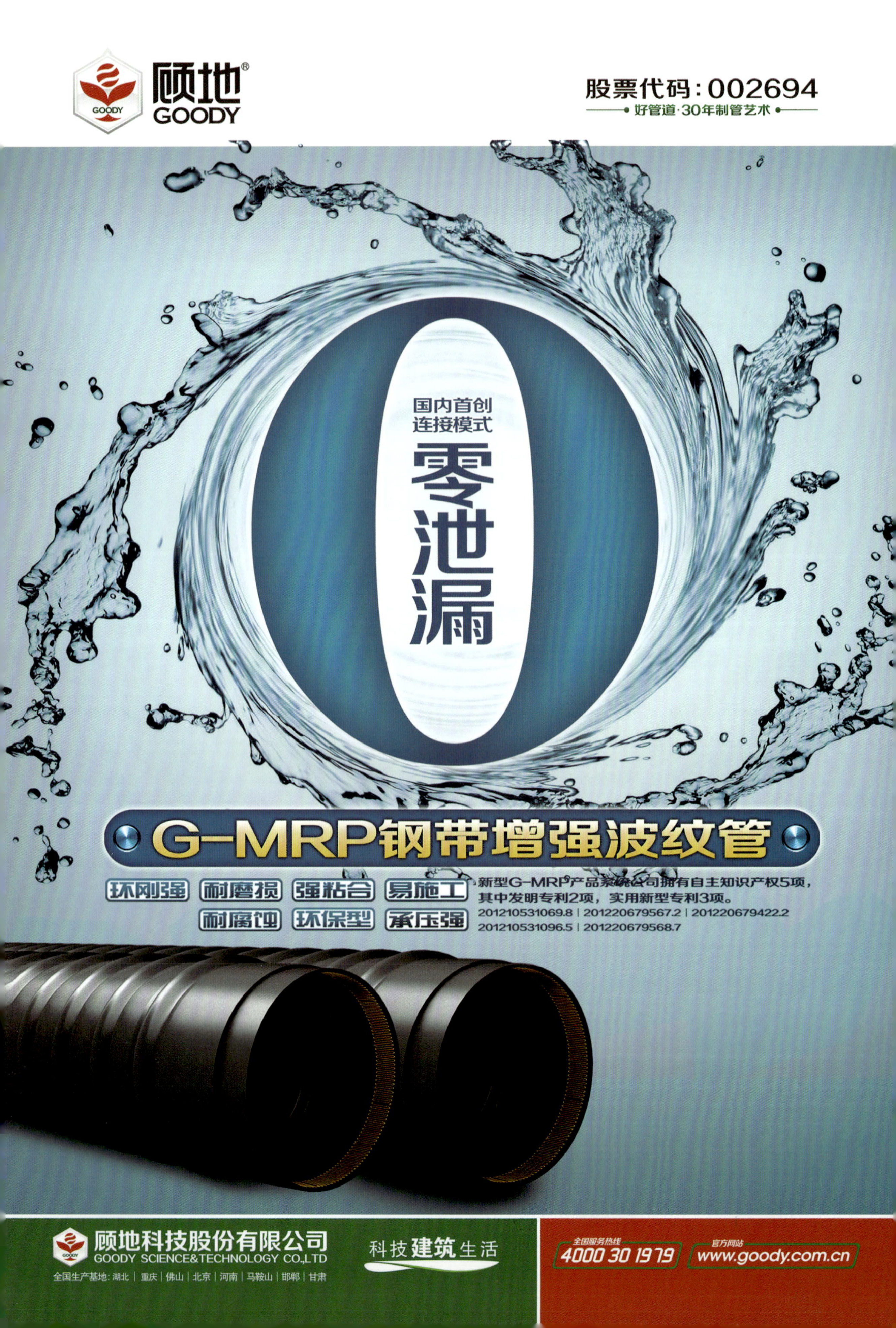
顾地®
GOODY
股票代码：002694
好管道·30年制管艺术
国内首创
连接模式
零泄漏
G-MRP钢带增强波纹管
环刚强
耐磨损
强粘合
易施工
耐腐蚀
环保型
承压强
新型G-MRP®产品系统公司拥有自主知识产权5项，
其中发明专利2项，实用新型专利3项。
201210531069.8 | 201220679567.2 | 201220679422.2
201210531096.5 | 201220679568.7
顾地科技股份有限公司
GOODY SCIENCE&TECHNOLOGY CO.,LTD
全国生产基地：湖北 | 重庆 | 佛山 | 北京 | 河南 | 马鞍山 | 邯郸 | 甘肃
科技建筑生活
全国服务热线
4000 30 1979
官方网站
www.goody.com.cn

普立万特种工程塑料

创新、方案、价值

特种热塑性工程塑料

- Stat-Tech™ & Stat-Tech™ NT 静电耗散和导电材料
- LubriOne™ 润滑和耐磨材料
- Edgetek™ AMX 耐高温材料
- Trilliant™ HC 医用材料
- Edgetek™ 工程材料
- Maxxam™ & Maxxam™ FR 阻燃聚烯烃材料
- Nymax™/Bergamid™ 聚酰胺材料

高性能金属替代材料

- Therma-Tech™ 导热塑料
- Gravi-Tech™ 高密度材料
- OnForce™ LFT 长玻纤增强材料

阻燃方案

- FireCon™ 氯化聚乙烯阻燃材料
- Maxxam™ FR 阻燃聚烯烃
- ECCOH™ 低烟无卤阻燃（LSFOH）材料
- ECCOH™ PF 低烟无卤阻燃（LSFOH）材料
- Syncure™ 交联聚乙烯线缆材料

www.polyone.com

甘肃瑞盛·亚美特高科技农业有限公司由甘肃农垦集团所属上市公司甘肃亚盛实业(集团)股份有限公司与以色列亚美特滴灌综合设备有限公司共同投资兴办，是集滴灌管线生产、滴灌系统整体设计、配套安装的节水灌溉企业。目前公司在兰州新区、内蒙古通辽市、吉林省松原市有三大滴灌设备生产基地，拥有先进的滴灌管生产线10条，滴灌带生产线70条，4条PVC管材生产线及其配套设施，年产滴灌管（带）16亿米，PVC管材5000吨以上，可生产壁厚0.16–1.0八大系列32种规格的滴灌管线，年产值6亿元。公司现有职工500余名，拥有硕士、高级工程师、科技带头人在内的200余名科技人才队伍。几年来公司先后获得ISO9001 国际质量体系认证，中国灌溉企业甲级等级证书，高新技术企业证书，中国质量监督检验协会AAA级信用会员单位荣誉证书；“瑞盛·亚美特”牌滴灌管被中国质量监督检验协会授予“中国优质名牌”荣誉证书和“中国驰名品牌”荣誉证书。

公司设备先进，技术领先，是国内生产中高端滴灌设备能力较强的企业之一。主要生产工艺由以色列亚美特滴灌综合设备有限公司引进，并以各大专院校、科研单位为依托，建立起集产、学、研一体化的经营模式，研发了一系列适应中国国情的滴灌产品，并获得自主知识产权。自主研发“内镶式扁平滴头”，成功申报了国家实用新型专利，结束了该产品长期依赖国外进口的局面；自主研发“水流泥沙过滤系统”，获得国家发明专利，在节水滴灌工程中得到很好的推广与应用；自主研发并申报了国家发明专利“引河滴灌首尾改装新技术成套设备技术”，打破了在黄河灌区（高泥沙河流，水质复杂）不能推广使用滴灌技术的禁锢，为我国在北方地区黄河流域及有地表水的地区推广节水技术开辟了新的道路，成为在高泥沙河流上推广节水灌溉的里程碑；自主开发采用“雨水集流、太阳能发电”的滴灌新技术，解决了西北干旱缺水、缺电地区的灌溉问题，为干旱缺水地区推广滴灌开辟了一条新路径。

公司结合国内不同地区的地形地理条件、降雨量、蒸发量、土壤成分、水质水源、种植作物及株行距等实际，形成独有的设计方案，将高效节水滴灌技术推广至全国十六个省份，产品远销澳大利亚、韩国、哈萨克斯坦等国，成功铺设农田节水面积230多万亩。高效水肥一体化滴灌技术广泛应用于马铃薯、玉米、棉花、葡萄、番茄、啤酒花、哈密瓜、蔬菜、中药材、果树、甘蔗、经济林带、绿化、生态治理等项目，产生了良好的经济效益和社会效益。据统计，玉米成功实施滴灌节水技术后平均每亩可实现节水49%、节肥54%、增产58%，每亩净增经济效益706元；马铃薯实施滴灌后平均每亩可实现节水58%、节肥65%、增产86%，每亩净增经济效益1800元；其它果蔬等经济作物实施滴灌后节水、节肥、增产效果更为明显并可大大改善作物品质，商品率由68%提高到96%以上。高效滴灌技术的应用和推广，对促进农民增收、作物增产、节约水资源、改善环境、带动地方经济发展起到了很好的作用，成为支农战线上的一面旗帜。

公司地址：甘肃省兰州新区纬七路经三支路交界处
邮编：730087
网址：www.ruisheng-yamit.com
销售电话：0931-8256203
传真：0931-8555722
邮箱：946913994@qq.com

图3 PVC－M管道破坏试验

图4 PVC－M管道工程

除增韧要求外，还可以通过选择不同的改性聚合物达到不同的改性目的，如提高管材热变形温度、阻燃性、耐油性等。

化学改性是通过化学反应使聚氯乙烯结构发生变化，分子内部化学键破裂与重组，通过分子链的变化使PVC内部结构发生变化，达到改性目的。化学改性方式有共聚合、氯化改性和交联等。

共聚合是指VCM与其他单体或高聚物进行的聚合反应，是PVC改性的主要方法之一，一般只能在树脂厂完成。按聚合原理，共聚合的方法主要有无规共聚、接枝共聚等。在中国目前只有接枝共聚PVC生产。

4.2 PVC－O管材

近年来PVC－O管材生产技术日趋成熟，已在多个国家生产和应用。在中国则是起步不久，尽管有一些科研院校和加工企业一直关注该产品，并有科研成果的报道，但到目前止只有一家生产企业有批量生产，口径也限制在250mm以下。图5为PVC－O管材照片，图6为PVC－O管材破坏试验照片。

胚管图

管材扩口图

图5　PVC－O管材

图6　PVC－O管材破坏试验

PVC－O 管材是通过取向加工工艺生产的管材。是把挤出的 PVC－U 管材在线或离线进行轴向和径向拉伸，使 PVC 分子链在轴向和径向规整排列，获得高强度、高韧性，由于技术已经成熟，产品标准 ISO 16422 在 2006 年正式发布。

PVC－O 管材对树脂稳定性、配方设计、生产设备与模具的要求较高，拉伸温度、拉伸倍率、拉伸速率等取向工艺条件都要控制好，才可能生产出合格的 PVC－O 管材。

该工厂开发了可实现在线双向取向拉伸的模具，进行了配方和挤出生产工艺设计，生产的管材的强度、韧性大幅度提升。但在配方研究、分子链取向的表征、配套技术等方面还有待研究，管材规格偏小。

5 存在的主要问题和差距

PVC－U 管道行业发展的同时也存在着一些问题和差距，主要有以下几个方面：

a. 由于中国目前小的生产企业较多，技术水平、产品更新速度等方面有待提高，市场上一般产品多，高技术产品少，因此希望加强与先进国家的交流，合作研发 PVC－O 等技术先进的产品。

b. 由于竞争的压力，少部分小的生产企业生产的 PVC－U 管材中过量添加碳酸钙和回收料，以此来降低成本，造成有的产品质量不符合标准要求，使用户担心 PVC－U 管材的质量不符合标准要求。

c. PVC－U 管材产品、应用等标准、规程、规范还相对滞后，目前中国给水用 PVC－U 管材产品标准还是 2006 年参照 ISO 4422：1996 制定的，我们要加快向 ISO 1452：2009 转换的速度。

d. 原料、助剂尚不能满足需求。牌号不全，高性能、高效、高附加值类产品不多等问题限制了 PVC－U 管材性能的进一步提高。材料长期性能的评价还基本属于空白。

e. 用户对环保、饮用水安全、长期使用的可靠性更关注，担心 PVC 管道的卫生安全，已经影响到实际应用。

由于以上的问题和其他原因，尽管 PVC－U 管材仍是最大的塑料管道材料，但目前在中国聚烯烃管材的增长速度确实是已超过了 PVC－U 管道的增长速度。因此我们更要加快技术进步，发挥 PVC 材料优势，以促进 PVC－U 管道的稳步增长。

6 PVC－U 管道发展重点

——充分发挥中国 PVC 树脂产能的优势，大力推进 PVC 管道生产的规范化和技术进步。加强通过各种改性方式提高 PVC 管材综合性能的技术研究，如接枝改性复合材料（PVC－M 等）和定向改性（取向）材料（PVC－O 等）等，以进一步扩展 PVC 管道应用领域，扩大市场份额。

——进一步提高建筑物同层排水塑料管道系统、中水雨水回收利用塑料管道系统、室内通风塑料管道系统等建筑领域应用产品的技术水平和配套水平。

——努力扩大工业领域用塑料管道市场，大力开发用于中、高压力石油输送、耐磨、耐腐蚀、耐热等特种介质输送以及矿山用阻燃和抗静电双抗管道。

——完善塑料管道系统的配套技术，在管件、阀门、检查井等产品上加强研发、推广力度，以提高管道系统的安全性和可靠性。

——继续推进完成 PVC－U 管道中采用环保型热稳定剂替代铅盐稳定剂的禁铅工作。

——加强超高聚合度（分子量）聚氯乙烯树脂、（交联）耐热聚氯乙烯树脂、高表观密度大口径管材用聚氯乙烯树脂等专用料的研发、应用。

（中国塑料加工工业协会塑料管道专业委员会 王占杰）

石墨烯的特性及其复合材料应用进展

一、石墨烯特性介绍

石墨烯英文 Graphene，是一种由 C 原子经 sp^2 电子轨道杂化后形成的蜂巢状的二维结构，是 C 元素的另外一种同素异形体。他是包括零纬富勒烯、一维碳纳米管、三维石墨在内的碳的同素异形体的基本组成单元。它具有超强的机械强度、高导热率、高透光率、高比表面积和奇特的电学性能等特点。2008 年，美国麻省理工学院的《技术评论》中，将石墨烯列为十大新兴技术之一。2009 年 12 月 18 日出版的《Science》杂志中，“石墨烯研究取得新进展”被列为 2009 年十大科技进展之一。2010 年，英国曼彻斯特大学物理学家安德烈·盖姆和康斯坦丁·诺沃肖洛夫继其 2004 年成功在实验中从石墨中分离出石墨烯以来仅仅 6 年时间，因其“在二维石墨烯材料的开创性实验”，共同获得了 2010 年诺贝尔物理学奖，从另一方面证明了石墨烯材料的价值，从此石墨烯以其超强的优异性能向工业化应用走来。

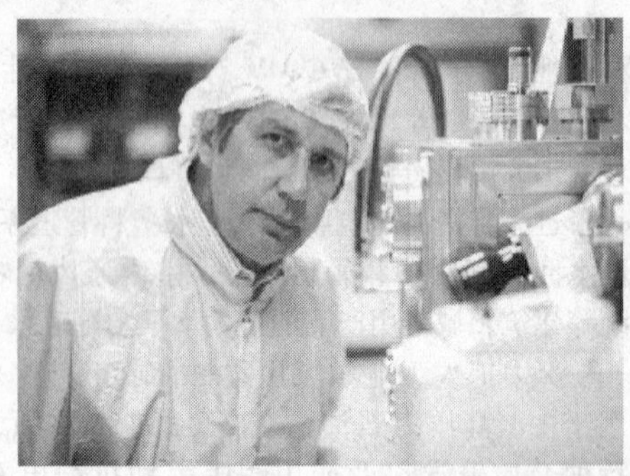

图1 康斯坦丁·诺沃肖洛夫
和安德烈·海姆

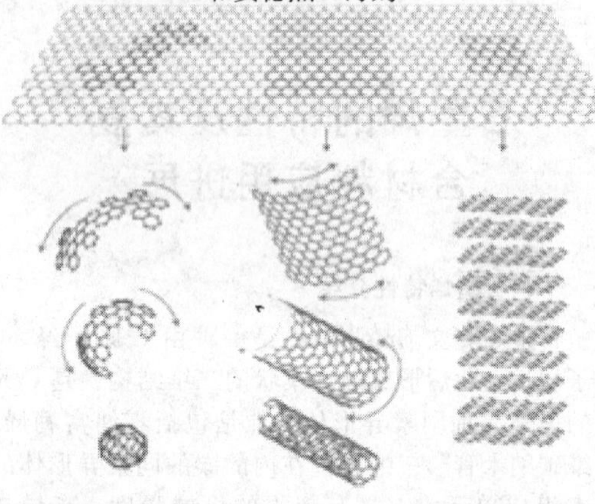

图2 石墨烯构成零维、二维、三维材料的示意图

单层石墨烯厚度只有一个碳原子厚，为0.335nm。是目前已知的最薄的一种材料，其拥有许多碳材料所不具备的特性。通常所说的石墨烯为单层石墨烯、双层石墨烯和少层石墨烯（<10层），超过10层的石墨烯通常称为石墨烯微片（Graphene Nanosheets）或者纳米石墨微片，即碳原子层数多于10层、厚度在5~100nm范围内的超薄的石墨烯层状堆积体。石墨烯微片保持了石墨原有的平面型碳六元环共轭晶体结构，具有优异的机械强度、导电、导热性能，以及良好的润滑、耐高温和抗腐蚀特性，成本较低。石墨烯的特性如下：

(1)导电性极强：石墨烯是能隙为零的半导体，电子的运动速度能够达到光速的1/300，远远超过其他金属导体或半导体的运动速度。常温下其载流子迁移率最高，而电阻率只有约$10^{-6}\Omega\cdot cm$，比铜或银更低，为目前世界上电阻率最小的材料。因为它的电阻率极低，电子迁移的速度极快，因此被期待可用来发展出更薄、导电速度更快的新一代电子元件或晶体管，同时少量石墨烯添加到聚合物中，即可强化复合材料的电子输送功能；

(2)超大比表面积：由于石墨烯的单层二维结构，使其拥有超大的比表面积，理想的单层石墨烯的比表面积高达$2630m^2/g$，远高于普通活性炭的$1500m^2/g$，超高比表面积使石墨烯在储能材料的应用方面具有巨大的潜力；

(3)高热导率：石墨烯的导热能力出众，高于碳纳米管和金刚石，单层石墨烯在室温下热导率能达到5300W/(m·K)，是金刚石的5倍；

(4)超高强度：石墨烯是迄今为止强度最高的物质，同时又拥有很好的韧性，可以弯曲，杨氏模量达到1060GPa，被证明为当代最牢固的材料，比最好的钢都要坚硬100倍，其硬度比金刚石还高，可以用来制备超强力膜并具有制备“太空电梯”的潜力；

(5)高透光率：几乎是完全透明的，单层石墨烯有相当高的透明度，仅吸收大约2.3%的可见光。

石墨烯特殊的结构形态，使其具备目前世界上最硬、最薄的特征，同时也具有很强的韧性、导电性和导热性。这些极其特殊的特性使其拥有无比巨大的发展空间，未来可以应用于电子、航天、光学、储能、生物医药、日常生活等大量领域。国家《2012年科学发展报告》称石墨烯集合世界上最优质的各种材料品质于一身，故有业内人士如此评价：如果说20世纪是硅的世纪，石墨烯则开创了21世纪的新材料纪元，将给世界带来实质性变化。

二、石墨烯及其复合材料的应用进展

全球针对石墨烯的研究非常火热，截至2012年，全球有17361篇被SCI收录的关于石墨烯研究的论文，其中前两位的中国和美国占据了其中的半壁江山，中国的论文数量虽居首位，但中国的论文整体质量不如美国，美国的石墨烯论文被引用数量远远领先。同时各国均在积极进行石墨烯相关专利申请，如IBM、DOW、SAMSUNG等均在积极推进石墨烯产业的研究和专利布局，截至2013年6月，国内机构共申请3000余项相关发明专利，456项已获得授权，另外还有2000余篇尚在审查中。除了国内外积极进行石墨烯的专利布局外，石墨烯的产业化进程日趋激烈，研究人士一直致力于其商业用途，市场对其关注度也日趋升温。

石墨烯以其精妙的结构，无以伦比的性能，使之在应用方面具有广阔的前景。如利用其超高的电子迁移率应用于电子芯片、晶体管等电子行业领域，超高的透光率、导电性应用于触摸屏，柔性显示以及太阳能电池领域，其超高的比表面积应用于新能源领域如超级电容器、锂离子电池以及生物探测器领域，超高导热系数应用于导热复合材料，石墨烯表面能够容许缺陷从而利用此性质应用于海水淡化，此外，石墨烯在生物器件、抗菌材料等方面也有非常广泛的应用前景。

1　石墨烯在新能源领域中的应用

1.1　石墨烯超级电容器

美国《探索》杂志2007年将超级电容器列为2006年世界十大科技发现之一，认为超级电容器是能量储存领域的一项革命性发展。碳质材料是目前研究和应用最为广泛的超级电容器材料，主要有活性炭，活性碳纤维，碳气凝胶，碳纳米管等。自从石墨烯成功制备以来，业界积极探索这种碳质新材料在超级电容器中的应用。石墨烯具有极高的比表面积，石墨烯片层的两边均可以富集电荷形成双电层，此外石墨烯皱褶及叠加效果，可以形成纳米孔道和纳米空穴，利于电解液的扩散，所以石墨烯基超级电容器具有良好的功率特性。

基于石墨烯独特的2D结构和优异的内在物理特性，例如超高导电性能和巨大的比表面积，石墨烯基材料在超级电容器应用中展现出巨大的应用潜力。依照美国国家能源局的数据预测，超级电容器在全球市场的规模预计将从2007年的40亿美元发展到2013年的120亿美元。石墨烯作为电极制成的超级电容器将在性能上有极大的提高，未来随着超级电容器的逐步推广，石墨烯也将面临巨大的市场空间。

2012年4月，美国加州大学洛杉矶分校(UCLA)研究人员利用DVD刻录机发明出微型超级电容器，这种超级电容器只需数秒时间即可使手机或汽车充满电，其充电和放电速度是标准电池的100～1000倍。20美元的CD/DVD刻录机(光驱)是制作石墨烯电极的出色“制造装置”，使用波长为788nm的激光进行照射，氧化石墨烯被激光照射后还原并剥离，变成多层石墨烯片重叠的状态，颜色也会由金黄色变成黑色。最后将附有石墨烯的薄膜基板从光盘上剥离下来，便可使用于电容器或充电电池。UCLA用这种方法试利用廉价材料仅不足30分钟制出了面积为1cm^2，厚度仅为68～82μm的柔性100多个微型电化学电容器。

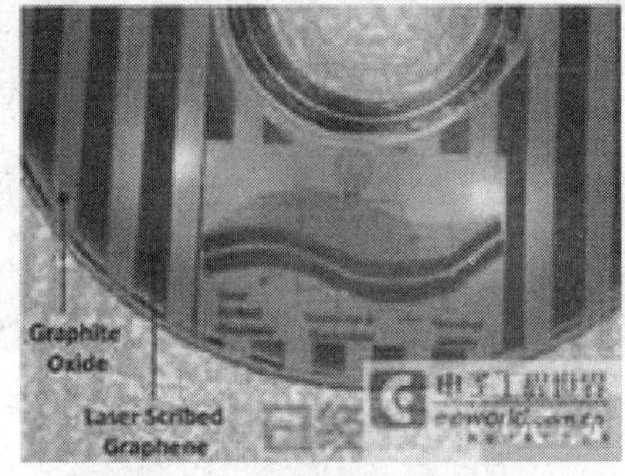

图3　DVD激光刻录制备的石墨烯膜

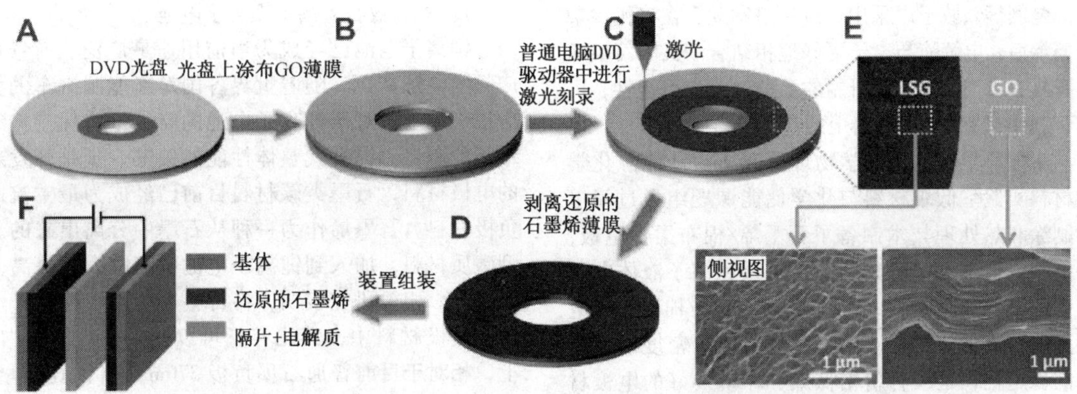

图4　DVD激光刻录制备石墨烯超级电容器的示意图

美国 Nanotek Instruments 公司研制的石墨烯基超级电容器，此超级电容器采用了石墨烯，混合5%的乙炔黑，通过弯曲和卷曲石墨烯片，电解液可以更大比例地和石墨烯表面进行接触，从而提高储存电量。据报道室温下可以达到85.6Wh/kg的能量密度，相当于镍氢电池的能量密度，充放电仅需要几分钟，甚至几秒钟。这意味新一代的超级电容器作为储能器件将逐步取代具有环境污染的铅酸电池和具有安全隐患的锂离子电池成为了可能，并在储能和动力电池领域带来重大进步。

图5　弯曲和卷曲的石墨烯堆叠结构

美国莱斯大学研究人员在石墨烯薄片上快速生长出碳纳米管，长度可以达到120μm，以形成大量的表面积，更重要的是看起来类似储能超级电容器。研制的这种石墨烯/碳纳米管复合材料，或可作为最好的电极界面材料，在诸多储能和电子器件得到应用，相关研究成果发表在《自然－通讯》上。

据韩国教育科技部透露，韩国科学技术院(KAIST)研究团队成功研制出大容量、可挠式(Flexible)下一代蓄电池超级电容器。该电池的成功研制基于石墨烯的应用。此次研制的超级电容器有望在电动汽车和智能电网等领域予以采用。研究组发现，在将氮掺杂石墨烯后，电解液与离子更好地相结合。又因石墨烯本身具有可挠性，此次研制的蓄电池具有可挠性，可用于制作携带在衣服或身上的蓄电产品。

中国科学院兰州化学物理研究所清洁能源化学与材料实验室低维材料与化学储能课题组通过简单的刷涂和热处理技术制备了石墨烯/棉布柔性电极，并组装成电容器，研究了其在水系和离子液体电解液中的电化学性能。结果表明，石墨烯/棉布柔性电极具有较高的比容量、功率密度、能量密度以及良好的稳定性，是一种价格低廉、环境友好的电极材料。同时，该研究小组采用简单的火焰还原法将氧化石墨烯纸快速还原为石墨烯纸，结果表明石墨烯纸在不同体系电解液中均具有良好的电容性能。

图6　石墨烯/棉布柔性电极

此外国内外学者还进行了石墨烯水凝胶、活化石墨烯、炭黑、碳纳米管等纳米粒子插层石墨烯制备石墨烯超级电容器电极的研究，以及聚吡咯、PANI等导电聚合物与石墨烯的混合物制备石墨烯超级电容器电极，以及石墨烯与金属氧化物(MnO_2，RuO_2等)复合制备石墨烯超级电容器电极材料等的研究。目前国内外石墨烯基超级电容器大多处于研发阶段，相信随着石墨烯成本的降低和石墨烯基复合电极技术的进步，石墨烯超级电容器会逐步走向产业化。

1.2　高效石墨烯基锂离子电池

锂离子电池已经成为当前用途最广泛、前景最广阔的电池能源，随着世界各国对新能源汽车的大力推广，未来对于锂离子电池的需求量将保持持续增长的态势。提升其整体性能的关键一步是开发新的电极材料，石墨类碳材料目前已经成为最主流的负极材料。石墨烯作为一种从石墨中分离出来的新型碳质材料，加入到锂离子电池中能够大幅提高其导电性。相关研究表明，将石墨烯应用于锂离子电池的负极材料中，其比容量可以达到540mAh/g以上，相对于目前普通石墨负极370mAh/g的比容量，可大幅提高锂离子电池性能。

锂离子电池能量密度大、循环寿命长，是目前消费电子领域应用最为广泛的电池，但功率密度还不够大，电池满充时间需要几个小时，超级电容器功率密度高但能量密度低，无法满足续航要求，限制了其在电动车和储能设备中的应用。石墨烯锂离子电池解决了能量密度和功率密度两者的要求，是石墨烯最有可能实现产业化应用的方向之一。石墨烯在锂离子电池中的应用一个方向是石墨烯复合电极材料，包括正极和负极，另一个方向是石墨烯作为锂离子电池的导电添加剂，冉一个就是石墨烯功能涂层(图7)。

图7　石墨烯在锂离子电池中的应用

石墨烯优异的导电性能可以提高电极材料的电导率，进而提高锂离子电池的充放电速度，同时石墨烯柔韧的二维结构有效抑制了电极材料在充放电过程中引起的电极材料粉化，并增强与集流体间的导电接触。石墨烯包覆磷酸铁锂作为锂离子电池正极材料是目前无论是学术，还是产业化研究方面报道最多的，通过石墨烯的包覆，磷酸铁锂正极材料的导电性提高，进而提高正极的容量特性，功率特性和循环稳定性。

中科院宁波所材料所刘兆平团队采用石墨烯构建包覆磷酸铁锂纳米颗粒的高效三维导电网络，突破国外关于磷酸铁锂碳包覆的专利壁垒，显著提高磷酸铁锂正极材料的电化学性能，据报道已在宁波艾能锂电材料科技有限公司建成相关中试线。此外，采用石墨烯涂层铝箔、铜箔作为锂离子电池的集流体，代替传统炭黑涂层，涂层厚度小于1um，不影响电池容量的前提下，降低并稳定电池内阻，同时还能提高电池的散热能力，延长电池寿命。据报道，年产200万平方米的石墨烯涂层铝箔中试线在宁波墨西新材料有限公司已经建成。

据报道，清华大学康飞宇教授团队与东莞鸿纳新材料公司合作开发的石墨烯作为锂离子电池导电添加剂项目已有小批量产品试用。

中国宝安旗下的深圳贝特瑞新能源材料股份有限公司、四川金路集团等报道已具备石墨烯材料中试生产石墨烯用于锂离子电池电极材料中。东莞新能源科技有限公司，青岛乾运高科新材料股份有限

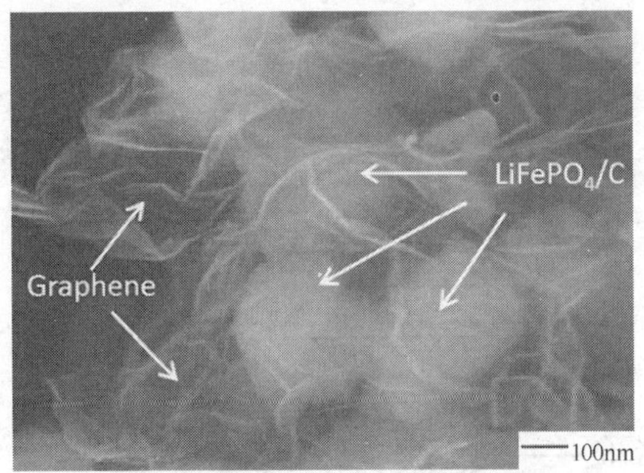

图8　石墨烯/C/磷酸铁锂电极 SEM 图

公司等传统锂离子电池、锂离子电池电极生产厂家等均对石墨烯在锂离子电池中的应用研究也有相关涉足。美国 Vorbeck Materials 公司、美国能源部下属的研究所－西北太平洋国家实验室(PNNL)以及美国普利斯顿大学的研究小组 2010 年 7 月宣布，通过向锂离子充电电池的电极中添加少量石墨烯，不仅可以保持原来的能量密度，还能大幅度提高输出功率密度。日本住友电木株式会社尝试将石墨烯用作锂离子电池的负极材料，制备的锂离子电池目前在能量密度上还比不上石墨，但却在低温下的放电特性和反复充放电方面显示出了超越石墨的出色特性。

2013 年 2 月，加利福尼亚锂电池研究小组与美国阿贡国家实验室联合推出了第三代硅－石墨烯复合阳极材料，采用先进的阴极材料和电解液溶剂，其能量密度达到 525Wh/kg，电池负极容量为 1250mAh/g。

日本物质材料研究机构通过在石墨烯中添加碳纳米管来制作电极，使输出功率密度与能量密度达到了前所未有的水平。在石墨烯中添加 CNT 之后，CNT 会通过自组织方式自然地进入石墨烯中，这制造了适当的间隙，使电流及离子的密度增加。电极单位重量的输出功率密度达到了 58.5kW/kg，单位重量的能量密度达到了 62.8Wh/kg，是采用活性炭电极时的 10 倍。在采用离子液体作为电解液时，能量密度进一步提高到了 155.6Wh/kg。

石墨烯在锂离子电池负极中应用的研究主要集中在如下方向，石墨烯直接作为锂离子电池的负极，石墨烯/SnO_2 复合材料，石墨烯/Si 复合材料以及石墨烯与 Fe_2O_3、TiO_2、Co_3O_4 等复合作为锂离子电池的负极材料，石墨烯作为正极材料方面的研究集中在石墨烯与磷酸铁锂、磷酸钴理、磷酸钒锂等正极材料复合上，其中与磷酸铁锂复合的报道最多。石墨烯作为一种性能优异的活性材料大规模的应用于锂离子电池中是时间的问题，目前的关键在于如何

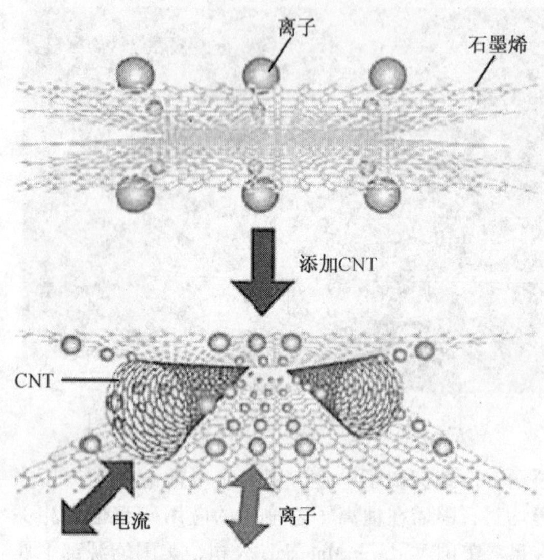

图9 碳纳米管石墨烯复合电极

降低石墨烯的成本，以及解决石墨烯与电解液及电极材料相互作用问题。

1.3 光伏太阳能电池

光伏太阳能电池是石墨烯被寄予厚望的应用实例之一，石墨烯在太阳能电池中应用主要有三个方面：替代ITO电极、作受体材料、染料敏化太阳能电池光阳极材料。

富士电机控股株式会社目前正在新能源产业技术综合开发机构的“革新性太阳能发电技术研究开发”项目中，积极开发采用石墨烯的太阳能电池用透明导电膜。富士电机放弃了迄今一直在研发的使用氧化石墨烯制作石墨烯片的工艺，同时作为替代方法导入了三星公司等也采用的CVD法。通过一系列自主改进得到的2层石墨烯片的导电率将高达ITO的几倍，并且能够确保90%的光透射率等，已经达到能够充分满足性能指标的水平。

石墨烯在太阳能电池用途方面被寄予厚望的不仅仅是透明电极。插入半导体层之间的中间电极方面的应用目前也正在探讨之中。在太阳能电池中使用石墨烯作为中间电极的优点是透明且与半导体层的相容性较高。特别是中间电极材料要求同时兼具这两个性质。在这一方面，石墨烯中电子和空穴的载流子迁移率相等这一性质也作出了一定贡献。以前，中间电极一般重叠使用n型和p型两种材料。由于石墨烯既有n型又有p型，因此仅需1层石墨烯就能替代原来的材料。

美国麻省理工学院及哈佛大学的研究人员发现，石墨烯可以对光产生不同寻常的反应，在室温和普通光照射下，就可以发生热载流子效应，产生电流。这一发现不仅为石墨烯再添新奇属性，更有希望使其在太阳能电池、夜视系统、天文望远镜及半导体传感器等应用领域发挥作用。该研究发表在近期出版的《科学》杂志上。研究人员在实验室制造了复杂的石墨烯纳米P－N结，利用850纳米的激光照射石墨烯P－N结介面，并测量激光照射点产生的光电流。结果发现，随着激光强度的增加，特别是在低温的条件下，可取得最大为5mA/W的光电流，这一数值比以前的石墨光电器件高6倍。

美国南加州大学的研究人员开发了一种柔性碳原子薄膜透明材料，并用它制作出有机太阳电池。这种石墨烯有机太阳电池的光电转化效率还比不上硅太阳电池，但石墨烯有机太阳电池造价低，而且柔韧性好，研究人员看好这种石墨烯有机太阳电池在家用窗帘，甚至可以做成会发电的衣服。

石墨烯材料因其优异的材料性能而广泛应用于电子、信息、能源、生物医学等各个领域，其在太阳电池领域的应用是重要的研究领域之一，但目前石墨烯在太阳能电池领域的应用和研究还处于初期阶段，石墨烯的制备技术仍处于工艺较复杂，成本较高的阶段，且现有制备方法所制得的石墨烯薄膜都存在较多的缺陷。未来对石墨烯薄膜材料进一步的研究应集中在改进石墨烯薄膜的制备工艺，寻求简单、环保、成本较低的制备方法等，在此基础上，实现与其他材料复合，掺杂其他物质，得到复合涂层，从而提高太阳电能池光电转换效率。

2 高性能复合材料领域

2.1 石墨烯导热、散热材料

目前石墨散热片已大量应用于通讯工业、笔记本、手机等领域。消费电子向超薄化、智能化和多功能化发展，功率的日益增加和产品的越做越薄日益显现出热量散射的重要性。因其在导热方面的突出特性，石墨导热片受到了越来越多的关注，在智能手机、超薄的PC和LED灯具、电视等等方面有着广泛的应用。目前的苹果手机，Samsung，国产小米手机等的散热膜均为石墨片制成。

石墨烯制备的散热膜散热性能要大大优于石墨片。另外在散热片中嵌入石墨烯或石墨烯微片可使得局部热点温度大幅下降。美国加州大学一项研究显示，石墨烯的导热性能优于碳纳米管。普通碳纳米管的导热系数可达3000W/m·K以上，而单层石墨烯的导热系数可达5300W/m·K。优异的导热性能使得石墨烯有望成为未来超大规模纳米集成电路的散热材料。

常州碳元科技发展有限公司采用高取向聚合物碳化、石墨化等工艺制备的石墨散热膜 eCARBON，最薄 12um，导热系数最高 1900W/m · k，为电子产品的薄型化发展提供了可能。eCARBON 高导热石墨膜具有良好的再加工性，可根据用途与 PET 等其他薄膜类材料复合或涂胶，可裁切冲压成任意形状，可多次弯折；适用于将点热源转换为面热源的快速热传导。eCARBON 高导热石墨膜广泛应用于高功率 LED，智能手机，液晶面板，平板电脑、笔记本电脑等产品。据报道，Samsung 是其下游客户之一。

2012 年 9 月，松下新开发出了厚度为 10μm 的"PGS 石墨膜"，主要用作智能手机等移动终端的散热膜。导热率高达 1950W/m · K，这同样为业界最高水平，该公司原来最薄的产品厚度为 17μm。

2013 年 4 月，贵州新碳高科有限责任公司推出柔性石墨烯散热薄膜。该产品采用了上海新池能源科技有限公司的石墨烯粉末原料，制备石墨烯溶液利用辊对辊技术形成有良好取向性的石墨烯微片层状结构，然后在高温特定气氛下还原，热导率在800 ~ 1600W/m · K。其散热效果比常用的散热材料铜要提高 2 ~ 4 倍，而且具有良好的可加工性能。薄膜厚度控制在 25μm 左右，相当于普通 A4 纸的三分之一厚，能帮助现有电脑、智能手机、LED 显示屏等大大提高散热性能。

此外，厦门凯纳石墨烯技术有限公司、南京科孚纳米技术有限公司也有相关石墨烯微片散热产品。

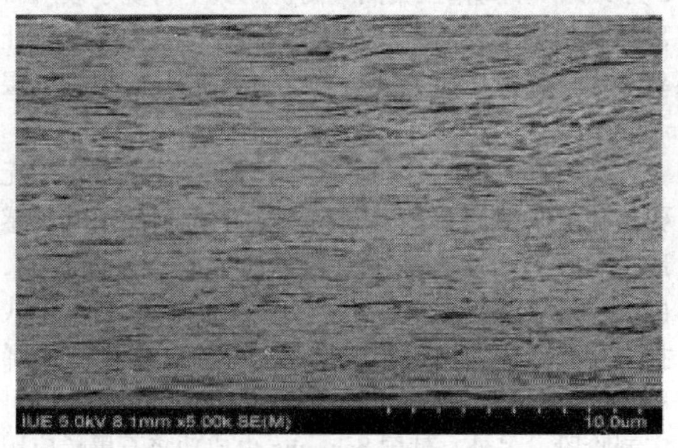

图 10　石墨散热片 SEM 图

2.2　石墨烯导电添加剂

石墨烯与聚合物的复合可以有效地提高聚合物的功能性，能经济有效地利用石墨烯独特的性能。针对不同的聚合物基体和不同的需求，石墨烯/聚合物导电复合材料的制备方法主要有三种：溶液混合、熔融共混、原位聚合法。其中熔融混合法因为成本较低是工业化最常见的方法。2006 年，从事石墨烯研究的著名的美国教授 Ruoff 课题组首次报道了聚苯乙烯/石墨烯导电复合物的制备。

美国 Vorbeck Materials 公司开发的"Vor - x"石墨烯导电添加剂，据介绍天然橡胶添加 4% 的"Vor - x"后的导电性能达到 0. 3S/m。厦门凯纳石墨烯技术有限公司开发的导电石墨烯微片，在 PC 中加 5wt% 石墨烯微片后，体积电阻为 $10^5\,\Omega \cdot cm$，达到抗静电等级；添加 10wt% 石墨烯微片，体积电阻 $10^3\,\Omega \cdot cm$，达导电级别，与价格昂贵的(20 多万元/吨)的超导炭黑在 10% 添加量时性能相当，而石墨烯微片成本更低。此外，美国 XG Science 公司也提供各种规格的石墨烯导电微片产品。据报道，美国的 Ovation Polymers 公司已经推出了基于石墨烯的石墨烯热塑性色母料和复合母料。

石墨烯导电添加剂可减少导电填料在聚合物中的用量，增强聚合物力学性能，这方面的应用很多如飞机的抗静电轮胎，以及航海航天用增强导电塑料等，据报道美国 Cabot 公司已经将石墨烯应用于航天航空复合材料中。另外增加石墨烯用量可以制备高强度的石墨烯电磁屏蔽材料。

2.3　石墨烯导电油墨

石墨烯油墨适用于网印、凹印、柔印、胶印和喷墨印刷等方式，可以应用于印刷线路板(PCB)、射频识别(RFID)、显示设备(如 OLED)、电极传感器等方面，能潜在应用于有机太阳能电池、印刷电池和超级电容器上面。因此石墨烯油墨有望在射频标签、智能包装、薄膜开关、导电线路以及传感器等下一代轻薄、柔性电子产品中得到广泛应用，市场前景巨大。与现有的纳米金属(如纳米银粉、纳米铜粉等)导电油墨相比，石墨烯油墨具有巨大成本优势。

2012 年 6 月，英国剑桥大学的 F. Torrisi 等利用石墨烯的 *N* - 甲基吡咯烷酮溶液，首次使用普通的喷墨打印机打印出由石墨烯制成的柔性电路，最新研究突破有助于科学家们大规模廉价制造出可穿戴的电子设备。随着石墨烯神奇墨水的发明，今后的电路图可以从网络上下载后，用自家的打印机喷涂在纸上。这就使电子爱好者的创意更容易验证了。另一方面，石墨烯应用于墨水，使电路能够大规模迁移到柔软的材料上。给人们留下硬邦邦印象的"电路板"，今后可能会被"电路布"取代。

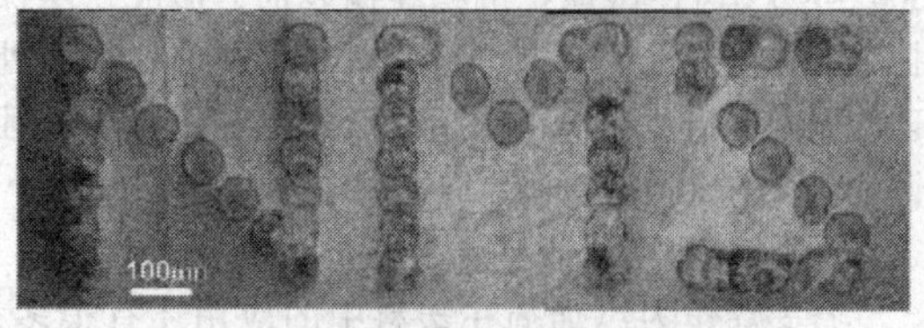

图 11　喷墨打印机打印的石墨烯图案

美国 Vorbeck Materials 公司开发的“Vor－ink”是首个得到美国环保署批准的石墨烯产品，该油墨导电性好，价格远低于银基油墨，已经用于 Topflight、CT、MWV 等美国包装公司行业的隐形电子条码安全系统中，以及用于射频识别商标上的电磁波定向屏蔽层。美国 Fulton 富尔顿公司的 e－Couple 使用石墨烯纳米印刷感应线圈来实现笔记本电脑和手机的无线充电。

2013 年 5 月，美国西北大学材料科学与工程学院研究人员使用含有微小石墨烯薄片油墨，以喷墨打印模式，打印出导电性能提高 250 倍、折叠时电导率仅有轻微下降的柔性电极，未来有可能生产低廉、大幅、可折叠且精美细致的电子设备。先前的研究已经喷墨打印出晶体管、太阳能电池、发光二极管、传感器等各种元器件，但打印高导电电极仍是一个挑战，因其要求非常精细的分辨率。该研究成果表明，喷墨打印可低成本、大面积地打印出柔性基底，是生产电子元件的一个有吸引力的方法。

2013 年 1 月，一直从事以凹印油墨为主的各类印刷包装油墨的珠海乐通化工股份有限公司与宁波墨西科技签订《石墨烯油墨项目合作协议》，合作开发石墨烯导电油墨。此外据报道，台湾力准国际企业有限公司也有石墨烯导电油墨销售，属于喷墨打印，打印材料透过率≥88%，导电率达 300S/cm。

2.4　石墨烯防腐涂料

美国阿贡国家实验室科学家领导的研究小组发现，在钢材的接触表面吸附上一层石墨烯将大幅减小其摩擦系数和磨损率，并能有效防止其生锈。这一工序成本很低、操作简单，只需把含有少量石墨烯的溶液滴到两个接触面之间即可。随着接触面之间的相对运动，石墨烯会均匀并且牢牢地附着在整个接触表面。

美国布法罗大学的研究人员制备的不锈钢采用石墨烯复合材料，可作为无毒的替代涂料，原先的涂层含有六价铬。澳大利亚莫纳什大学和美国莱斯大学研究人员合作，石墨烯薄膜作为涂层，使铜的耐腐蚀性增强近百倍，为恶劣环境下的金属防洪提供了巨大潜力。研究小组通过化学气相沉积，在 800～900℃时使碳原子沉积在铜表面，形成一层保护膜，并在盐水中对其进行测试。腐蚀性比未经处理的铜慢 7 倍；沉积在镍上，形成保护膜，耐腐蚀性是裸镍的 20 倍。

2.5　其他复合材料

石墨烯作为添加剂在塑料中的应用还有很多，如制备石墨烯复合材料的石墨烯/聚丙烯母粒，石墨烯/聚丙烯片材，石墨烯/超高分子量聚乙烯纤维等。关于石墨烯应用的例子还有很多，如石墨烯在人造骨关节耐磨层的应用，石墨烯在防弹衣中的应用等。值的注意的一个例子是奥地利 Head 公司推出石墨烯增强的网球拍产品。石墨烯作为增强填料的潜力非常巨大，据欧洲 NanoMaster 项目的参与方们表示，添加 5% 的石墨烯能把 TPO 和 PP 的机械性能增强一倍，而当把 1% 的石墨烯与 PMMA 混合时，可把拉伸弹性模量提高 80%。石墨烯增强的热塑性复合料和色母料将能适应现有的生产链，为注塑、挤吹和吹膜挤出大批量生产的零部件赋予新的特性。

三、石墨烯在电子行业中的应用

3.1　石墨烯柔性透明电极及应用

在铜箔或镍箔上化学气相沉积法(CVD)是目前制备大尺寸、高质量石墨烯透明导电薄膜最重要的方法，然后将石墨烯转移到柔性基材(如 PET)或者硬质材料(玻璃)上。国内外很多研究机构用此法已制备出石墨烯柔性透明导电电极，如韩国成均馆大学与 Samsung 合作实现了 30 寸石墨烯到 PET 的转移。另外，日本索尼和产综研，美国斯坦福大学，中国科学院沈阳金属所，中国科学院重庆研究院等分别利用 CVD 法制备出高质量石墨烯薄膜。

2013 年 1 月 24 日，中科院重庆研究院推出国内第一款 15 寸单层石墨烯薄膜，并成功将其完整地转移到 PET 柔性衬底和其他基底上，并且通过进一步应用制备了 7 英寸的石墨烯触摸屏(图 13)。2013 年 2 月 9 日，上海南江集团继高价购买中科院宁波所石墨烯制备技术之后，又一次性以 2.1 亿元技术转让费与中科院重庆研究院合作共同推进大面积、单层石墨烯项目产业化。

2013 年 5 月，常州二维碳素科技有限公司、无锡格菲电子薄膜科技有限公司、深圳力合光电传感股份有限公司联合江南石墨烯研究院在常州宣布，国内首条年产 3 万平方米的石墨烯薄膜生产线正式投产，有望成功用于手机电容触摸屏，实现石墨烯触摸屏手机的小批量生产。据了解，目前仅处于可定制阶段。另外，韩国 Samsung 也成功将石墨烯应用于柔性触摸平板显示器，此前报道 2012 年将实现量产，但目前仍未见其石墨烯触摸屏平板显示设备推向市场。

3.2　石墨烯芯片

利用石墨烯高的电子迁移率的特点，制备石墨烯集成电路可以有效地提高处理器的性能。2010 年 IBM 公司托马斯·沃森研究中心科学家林育明领导的团队制备了首块基于石墨烯的晶体管，这块集成电路建立在一块碳化硅上，并且由一些石墨烯场效应晶体管组成，其能在 100G 赫兹的频率上运行，其

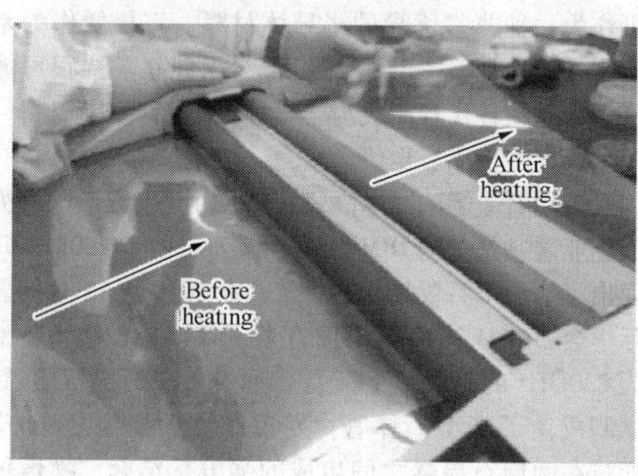

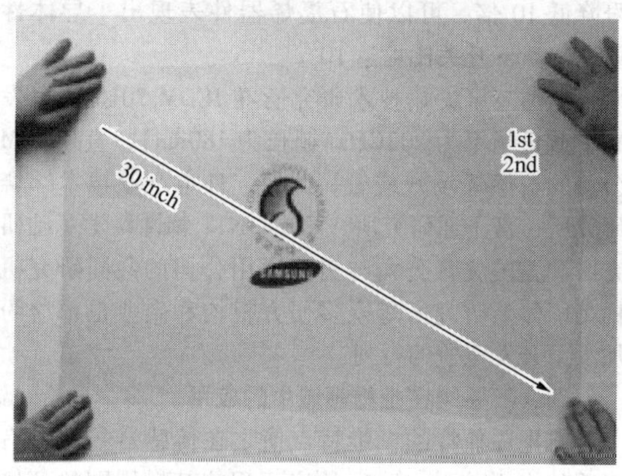

图 12 CVD 法制备并转移至 PET 的 30 寸石墨烯薄膜

无以伦比的性能使之具有代替硅材料的潜能。

2012 年 5 月，三星电子成功开发出可生产比原有半导体芯片速度快百倍以上的石墨烯芯片，三星电子研究组实现了“在石墨烯上附上半导体”的创意，在石墨烯上结合硅制成“萧特基(Schottky)屏障”，该屏障的高度像水坝一样时涨时降，以此来实现不断反复捕获与释放电子，使石墨烯处理器有了实际价值。

2012 年 7 月美国哥伦比亚大学一项新研究证明石墨烯具有卓越的非线性光学性能，并据此开发出一种石墨烯 - 硅光电混合芯片。这种硅与石墨烯的结合，让人们离超低功耗光通信近了一步，让该技术在光互连以及低功率光子集成电路领域具有广泛的应用价值。

图 13 中科院重庆研究院制备的石墨烯透明导电膜

3.3 石墨烯轻质导线和碳海绵

2011 年，浙江大学高超课题组利用石墨烯溶致液晶制备了石墨烯导电纤维(图 14)，研究人员还通过引入二价金属离子交联结构将石墨烯纤维强度提升 0.5GPa，单根纤维的长度可达到数十米，也可形成多根纤维缠绕而成的纱线；这种石墨烯纤维在具有超高强度的同时还兼具良好的导电性和柔韧性，其导电能力在弯曲 - 伸直 1000 次后没有任何减弱，预示着石墨烯纤维这一新品种高性能纤维材料在多功能织物、柔性可穿戴传感器、超级电容器、石墨炸弹、轻质导线等领域有广泛的应用前景。

2013 年 3 月，高超课题组用冷冻干燥制备的“碳海绵”密度仅 0.16mg/cm^3，是目前世界上最轻纪录保持者(图 15)。石墨烯气凝胶具有高弹性，被压缩 80% 后仍可恢复原状；对有机溶剂具有超快、超高的吸附力，是已报道的吸油力最高的材料(900 倍自身重量的吸油量)；“碳海绵”作为催化载体，吸音、保温材料、导电、高效复合材料等的产业化应用有待进一步研究推广。

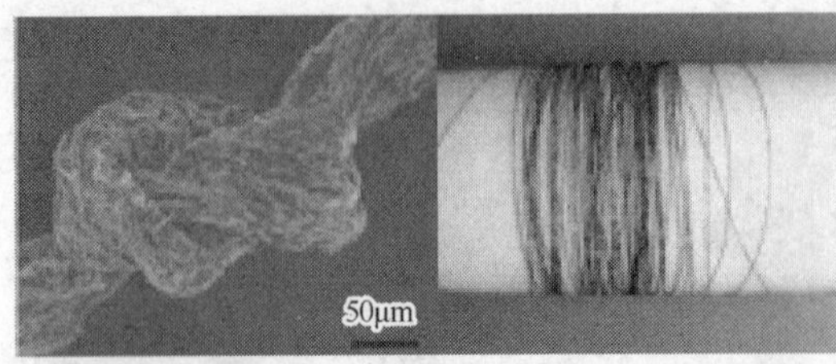

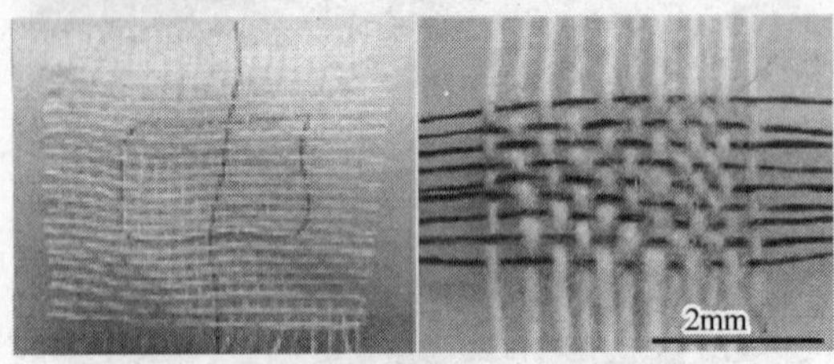

图14　石墨烯导电纤维

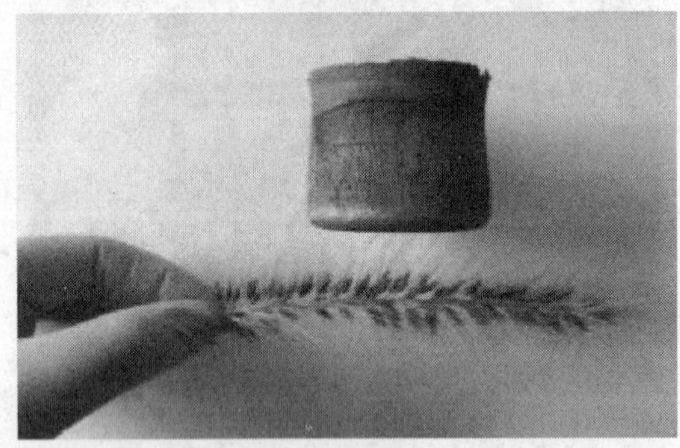

图15　石墨烯导电气凝胶

3.4　石墨烯光传感器

2013年新加坡南洋理工大学学者研发出了一个以石墨烯作为感光元件材质的新型感光元件，可望透过其特殊结构，让感光元件感光能力比起传统CMOS或CCD要好上1000倍，而且损耗的能源也仅需原本的1/10；这项技术初期将率先被应用在监视器与卫星影像领域之中。但研究也指出，此技术终将应用在一般的数码相机/摄影机之上，这个以石墨烯打造的最新感光元件，还可让制造成本压到现今的1/5低。

2011年10月，IBM的一个研究小组首次披露了他们研制的石墨烯光电探测器；2011年2月诺基亚向美国专利商标局申请的石墨烯光传感器专利，专利已经于2014年6月11日获得了授权。该光传感器采用两层石墨烯，光吸收层和前置放大器用FET通道层都采用了石墨烯，能够检测到微弱光线。主要是可吸收光的多层石墨烯和金属电极共同构成了光检测层，单层或双层石墨烯纳米带则作为了前置放大器FET通道。

3.5　石墨烯晶体管

有“微电子大厦的基石”之称的多晶硅是半导体产业的基础原料，被大量应用于集成电路，目前硅基芯片的运行速度已经达到GHz的级别。石墨烯拥有比硅更高的载流子迁移率，且产生的热量很少，可作为一种非常优异的半导体材料。石墨烯作为基质制备的处理器能够达到1THz，因此石墨烯很可能将作为硅的替代者而成为半导体产业新的基础材料，使集成电路更小、更快。

采用石墨烯的高速晶体管(FET)开发方面最积极的企业之一是美国IBM公司。该公司曾于2008年开发出了第一个石墨烯晶体管，并在2010年12月的国际学会“IEDM 2010”上发布了栅长240nm、截止频率为230GHz的石墨烯FET等，通过重叠两层石墨烯，试制成功了新型晶体管，发现能够大幅控制噪音。通过在两层石墨烯之间生成的强电子结合，噪声信号降低10倍，可以使石墨烯器件表现出半导体性质，室温下开关比可达10^7。

韩国三星尖端技术研究所在IEDM 2010上也发布了截止频率为202GHz(栅长为180nm)，直逼IBM公司的石墨烯场效应管。此外，日本产业技术综合研究所、富士通研究所、NEC、NTT物性科学基础研究所和美国波音公司与美国通用公司的共同研究机构美国休斯研究所等众多研究机构和企业也都纷纷加入了开发竞争的行列。

四、石墨烯在生物领域中的应用

石墨烯独特的二维特点使之在传感器领域具有光明的应用前景。巨大的表面积使其对周围的环境非常敏感，即使是一个气体分子吸附或释放都可以被检测到。石墨烯气体检测的高灵敏性来自于石墨烯电学上的低噪音特性，机制主要是石墨烯吸附气体后引起了电荷输运的改变。另外石墨烯在生物小分子传感器、酶传感器、DNA化学传感器以及医药传感器(如乙酰氨基酚)等方面具有较大潜力，目前处于基础研发阶段。

石墨烯具有单原子层结构，其比表面积很大，非常适合于做为药物载体。通过制备具有生物相容性的聚乙二醇功能化的石墨烯，使石墨烯具有很好的水溶性，且能在血浆等生理环境中保持稳定分散。

但石墨烯的生物毒性是首先需要研究的焦点之一。石墨拥有巨大的比表面积，能与核酸和芳香族药物产生 π－π 堆积和疏水等相互作用，在药物输送上具有显著优势，但目前基础研究主要集中在体外的细胞，体内研究较少。此外，石墨烯应用于催化领域也具有较好的应用前景，目前也主要出于研究阶段。

五、国际国内相关政策及石墨烯产业发展动向

目前石墨烯相关项目在国内外得到了相关政策的大力扶持。尽管欧洲是石墨烯的发源地，但世界其他地方尤其是远东地区在石墨烯创新上占据领先。韩国、中国、日本以及美国在石墨烯的创新研究上处于领先。

NanoMaster 是一项由欧盟框架计划 7（FP7）资助的项目，旨在“开发出以知识为基础的加工方法来让石墨烯和膨胀石墨增强热塑性色母料和复合料的生产更上一个档次，并最终实现在欧洲的产业商用化。”NanoMaster 项目的目标在于，把零部件中的塑料用量减少 50%，进而减重 50%，同时保留石墨烯的导电和传热性能。项目在 2011 年 12 月发起，将在 2015 年 11 月结束。

欧盟委员会 2013 年 1 月 28 日宣布了“未来和新兴技术（FET）旗舰项目”的竞赛结果，两个代表未来前沿科技的多国联合科研项目－石墨烯和人脑工程从 21 个候选项目中最终胜出，将在今后 10 年中各获 10 亿欧元的科研资助。石墨烯项目的研究团队包括来自欧盟 17 个国家的 176 个研究小组。其中石墨烯的生产是这个项目的中心之一。

美国已完结的相关石墨烯项目有石墨烯晶体管、石墨烯超级电容器（得州大学奥斯汀分校承担）、锂离子电池用纳米石墨烯复合材料电极的商业化生产（Nanotek Instruments 公司承担）以及以石墨烯为基质的高灵敏度 NO_x 探测器的研发（美国结构材料工业公司与康奈尔大学，南卡罗来纳大学合作）。英国德国主要资助的项目为石墨烯基电子产品的研发。

国内“十二五”发展规划中石墨烯作为纳米材料提及，但未作为专项重点扶持。目前石墨烯的价值和前景已经得到了国际上许多科学家的认可，我国也和发达国家同处于起跑阶段，但是产业化的步伐却已经落于人后，国外的科技巨头们正在加快推进石墨烯的产业化和应用。IBM、三星等已经紧锣密鼓地开始了石墨烯的应用研究，国内的国家政策扶持力度还不够，需要政府出台相关政策，为应用创新创造条件。

总结

目前国内外石墨烯产业仍处于专利的布局期，仍处于产业化研发阶段。困扰石墨烯产业的发展的瓶颈，一是低成本高质量石墨烯的产业化制备，另外是石墨烯下游产业对石墨烯的需求的产业链的打开，即产业的发展需要进一步开发石墨烯的产业化应用。石墨烯产业的大门已经慢慢开启，随着产业链的逐步成熟必将得到巨大的发展。

（青岛中科昊泰新材料科技有限公司、中国塑料加工工业协会专家委员会　郭金明　王梦媚　昝立伟　王德禧）

各地区塑料工业

北　京　市

【塑料企业基本情况】

北京塑料工业企业500家左右，其中生产能力万吨以上的企业不足30家。中塑协的统计数据显示，北京塑料制品1～12月产量合计389.9kt，累计比同期增长-1.68%。其中塑料薄膜累计产量37kt，累计比同期增长-5.10%、其中农用薄膜占14.3kt，累计比同期增长-6.43%；泡沫塑料累计产量2.3kt，累计比同期增长-8.56%，塑料人造革、合成革累计产量8.7kt，累计比同期增长60.56%；日用塑料制品累计产量33.4kt，累计比同期增长9.18%；其他塑料制品累计产量307.9kt，累计比同期增长-3.31%；北京市塑料制品占全国比例为0.67%。

对房山和昌平地区的调研情况是：房山现有塑料企业21家，其中北京燕山和成橡塑新材料有限公司、北京聚菱燕塑料有限公司、北京伊士通新材料发展有限公司、北京大正伟业塑料厂、北京中能环科科贸发展有限公司，是生产汽车改性料、管材料、纺丝专用料、填充母粒的专用料生产企业。北京嘉德福塑料制品有限公司、北京燕山集联石油化工有限公司是生产高档聚乙烯薄膜，无菌包装袋和FFS膜的专业薄膜生产厂。

昌平地区塑料企业主营业务收入2000万元以上的企业10家，其中北京海科华昌新材料技术有限公司，具有年产各类改性工程塑料和抗菌母料8，000t的生产能力；北京伏尔特技术有限公司是生产高质量精密过滤器的系列产品；韩华综化(北京)塑料有限公司．公司主要生产GMT、EPP等汽车零部件以及建筑模板；北京正奇塑料制品有限公司为“北京市学生营养餐专用餐具”供应商。公司主要产品有一次性塑料餐具及吸管等

【经营情况】

2012年北京塑协对协会的部分会员单位进行了调研，根据对塑协几家规模较大的企业调研表明；2012年塑料制品主要呈现以下特点：利润低、市场竞争激烈、一些小企业为市场竞争，采用劣质原料，冲击了正规产品。企业反馈的情况是：人工成本不断增加，制品价格涨幅低于原料，原辅材料价格趋高。

【大事记】

1. 发挥协会作用，做好上级部门下达的调研工作

北京塑协于2012年2月接到市经信委传真，要求调研北京市昌平城南旧县村铝塑彩印厂的废气排放污染问题。

北京塑协及时安排，由常务副理事长刘济组织秘书处人员和行业相关技术专家到北京富昌铝塑彩印厂调研，通过实地调研和该公司提供的文件，我们及时提出调研建议。

2. 北京地区塑料企业调研

北京塑协对房山和昌平地区塑料企业做了调研。房山现有规模以上塑料企业21家，昌平地区塑料企业主营业务收入2000万元以上的企业10家。

3. 第六届会员(换届)大会的筹备工作，具体落实现有会员单位现状及今后发展规划。

【企业选介】

1. 北京华盾雪花塑料集团有限责任公司

2012年北京市塑料企业中，我们认为北京华盾雪花塑料集团有限责任公司的农用塑料制品，是北京市塑料行业的拳头产品，也是北京市“十二五”时期都市产业发展规划中，作为资源型都市产业体系的重点发展项目。目前北京华盾雪花塑料集团有限责任公司塑料新材料产业基地(固安)项目已通过评审，预计在近二年内将投产。公司将继续对农膜进行产品研发、设备更新投入，进一步提升高档功能膜比例，保持功能性农膜技术、品牌、规模的行业领先地位；土工膜重点向高附加值的环卫领域发展，从以环卫应用为主，向尾矿治理、路桥遂道建设领域延伸；中空产品中容器托盘从以化工、食品等市场为主，重点向高附加值的港口、物流领域扩展；扩大包装产品生产规模。长寿命、可循环利用的农膜、土工材料、容器托盘等产品必将成为产品发展的方向。项目的实施将为企业发展规划的实施发挥关键作用。

北京绿源塑料有限责任公司隶属于华盾雪花塑料集团有限责任公司，成立于1994年，通过引进国外先进的微灌生产技术和设备，不断地消化吸收，加强技术开发，已经成为国内最著名、最具规模的节水灌溉企业之一，成为中国节水灌溉行业的龙头企业。主要提供产品包括：内镶式滴灌管、管上补偿式滴灌管、微喷头、过滤施肥设备、管材、管件、园林喷头等。产品广泛应用于果树、蔬菜、瓜果、花卉、棉花、甘蔗以及保护地作物等经济作物，还大量应用于沙漠、丘陵改造、城乡园林绿化、道路防护林工程等。产品主要销往全国29个省、市、自治区、直辖市，并出口西班牙、加拿大、伊朗等地。

绿源公司新开发产品：内镶补偿式滴灌带(管)，

内镶式滴灌管及配套管件，年出口200t左右，大部分销往中亚、南非及欧洲等地，从国外引进内镶式滴灌管生产线管上式滴灌管生产线各二条

2. 北京北泡塑料集团公司

北泡塑料集团公司组建于2000年，前身为北京泡沫塑料厂(始建于1964年)，生产泡沫塑料制品已有近40年的历史，是国有大型二类企业。是我国生产聚氨酯泡沫塑料制品品种最全、规模最大的企业之一。主要生产基地位于通州区张家湾工业区。

经过多年的产业结构及产品调整，北泡塑料集团公司已发展成为一个以塑料建材为主的企业集团。主要产品有：软质聚氨酯泡沫塑料、聚苯乙烯泡沫塑料、聚乙烯泡沫塑料、气垫膜、注射制品、聚苯乙烯泡沫夹芯板及系列产品、轻钢结构。软质聚氨酯泡沫塑料蹭获国家银质奖，聚苯乙烯泡沫塑料蹭获全国评比第一名，聚苯乙烯泡沫夹芯板荣获“新型环保节能夹芯板质量可靠称号”。

集团公司目前已拥有独资经营企业7家、控股公司6家，参股公司3家、第三产业16家，集团所属国家划拨土地近80亩，注册资金2.40亿元。现有职工1829人，各类工程技术人员284人，中级以上技术职称65人。2002年末资产总额2.668亿元。

集团所属轻钢有限公司，1987年从澳大利亚引进聚苯乙烯泡沫塑料夹芯板生产线，在此基础上又研制开发了相关系列产品；1998年引进钢结构生产线，年生产能力为6000t，1998年通过ISO 9000标准质量体系认证。实现设计、生产、销售、安装四位一体。2002年4月被评为“重合同、守信用”单位称号。星月公司2002年引进聚氨酯发泡生产线，质量体系认证工作正在进行中。

开发新产品：低密度汽车装饰用阻燃泡沫塑料。

3. 北京禧天龙塑料制品有限公司

北京禧天龙塑料制品有限公司2002年在北京注册成立，公司目前拥有50多台国内最先进的节能型“海天”全自动注塑机、1200套模具，以及拥有90000m^{2}的办公区。公司注册资金1500万元，年产量达8000t，资产总额近5000万元。公司的生产线涵盖了几乎所有的塑料家居日用产品：整理箱、整理柜、衣架、塑料凳、脸盆、桶、密封容器、保鲜盒、垃圾桶、烫衣板等。是国内较大的家庭日用品生产、销售商之一。

新产品开发：以收纳系列、保鲜系列为主要产品，包括整理箱、整理柜、保鲜盒等。

4. 北京燕山和成橡塑新材料有限公司

北京燕山和成橡塑新材料有限公司，将成为北京塑料行业新的经济增长点。该公司成立于2010年2月，主营业务为橡胶制品、塑料制品、化工产品的生产、研发、销售等。一期规划为2011年7月份前建成15条改性专用料生产线，产能为30kt/a。产品主要为管材料、熔喷料、瓶盖料及其他食品药品容器专用料系列。到2015年底完成三期年总产能100kt的整体规划，预计建成80条橡塑改性专用料生产线。

5. 北京市鑫华亨塑料用品厂

北京市鑫华亨塑料用品厂是一家专业生产塑料周转箱、塑料托盘、塑料中空桶、薄膜等塑料制品的企业，并在北方塑料制品市场中占有较大份额。地处京南四环外五环内，地势优越、交通便利。公司汇聚了大量专业技术人员及高级工程师。积累了丰富的塑料制品生产加工经验，拥有2800t大型注塑机及诸多注塑设备、全自动吹塑设备，产品种类繁多。在多年的生产过程中，建立了一整套严格的质量保障体系，拥有完善的检测系统，产品通过了ISO 9001：2000质量体系认证，QS生产许可证等权威机构的质量检测。

6. 北京北化高科新技术有限公司

成立于2003年，是由年轻博士们创办，注册于北京海淀科技园高薪企业，公司致力于各种高分子材料的研究、开发、生产及销售。经过几年的快速发展，在产品方面，公司目前有黑色母粒、白色母粒、彩色母粒、抗老化母粒、加工母粒、填充母粒、专用料7大系列产品，广泛用于管材、土工、农业生产、产品包装、模塑成型、彩色共挤、纤维纺丝、电缆护套8大领域；在设备方面，公司已拥有产品生产线12条、产品研发线3条、质量检测设备25个，这同时保证了生产和研发速度，产品质量定性以及技术与服务的快速反应性；在研发创新方面，公司已有专利65个，在请专利21个，创新产品检测检验方法12种，大量的科技创新使公司一直处于国内同行业产品研发检测技术领先地位。

新产品开发：塑料重包装用高浓度高分散钛白粉母粒、ASA彩色型材共挤专用料料。

引进设备：德国WP ZSK58双螺杆挤出机一台。

7. 福建亚通新材料科技股份有限公司北京分公司

福建亚通新材料科技股份有限公司是一家专业从事高分子材料及其制品的研究开发和生产制造的国家级重点高新技术企业，现系中国塑料加工工业协会塑料管道专委会理事长单位，建设部全国唯一塑料管道科技产业化基地，全国化学建材骨干企业，全国化学建材工作先进集体，国家博士后科研工作站，科技部、建设部联合定点的国家科技成果推广示范基地。

公司创立于1994年，现已发展成为拥有资产5.3亿多元、职工近2000人(其中具有大专以上学历的员工占职工总数的35%以上)的高新技术企业。公司研发和生产具有国际先进、国内领先水平的工程塑料管道系列产品、新型高分子功能复合材料、高效农业节水灌溉系统等，产品广泛应用于建筑、高速公路、水利、通信、电力、农业排灌、城市给水、排水、污水处理、现代园艺等领域，产品种类及配套之全居全国同行业之首。

亚通北京公司是亚通科技的全资子公司，公司位于北京市通州区张辛庄工业园区，创立于2002年，目前拥有职员70人，8条生产线，年生产能力达10kt。公司依托福建总部，研发，生产并销售塑料管道系列、塑料节水器材产品等，产品广泛应用于建筑、高速公路、水利、通信、电力、农业排灌，城市给(排)水、污水处理、现代园艺等领域。

8. 北京聚菱燕塑料有限公司

北京聚菱燕塑料有限公司成立于1998年10月，是生产和销售汽车用聚丙烯共混合金材料的合资企业。由日本三菱化学株式会社、日本丰田通商株式会社以及北京燕山石油化工集团有限公司共同出资建立。有北京、佛山二个生产基地。

聚菱燕采用燕化集团公司优质的聚丙烯基础树脂，结合三菱化学株式会社下属的日本聚化株式会社和日本智索株式合资之日本聚丙烯株式会社之先进技术，制造汽车用聚丙烯共混合金材料产品。以中国为拓展销售对象。

产品汽车用PP共混合金材料生产能力大于50kt/a，2012年产量48.3kt，实现产值7019.5万元，实现利润5172.7万元，生产设备：包括世界先进水平的TEX65高速双螺杆挤出造粒生产线在内的八条进口生产线。目前正在开发高流动高冲击性聚丙烯材料。

9. 燕山集联石化公司

北京燕山集联石油化工有限公司，简称为燕山集联石化。坐落于北京市房山区，地处京广线旁边，具有十分便利的陆路、铁路运输条件。

伴随着中国第一座石油化工城中国石油化工股份公司燕山分公司及其前身：北京东方红炼油厂、北京石油化工总厂、北京燕山石油化学总公司、北京燕山石油化工有限公司四十年的创业与发展，北京燕山集联石油化工有限公司及其前身北京燕山石油化工总厂“五七连”、北京燕山石化厂办大集体企业，燕山石化“十大直属集体企业”走过了三十五年的成长历程，目前形成了以服务燕山石化主体，面向国内外市场的石油化工、精细化工与环保产业、塑料加工(编织袋、重包装袋)、清洁燃料、物流、工程与服务、机织地毯、进出口贸易等多种业务，年收入达15亿元、利税4000多万元、净资产1.5亿元的产业群体。公司注册资金5000万元。

公司以北京燕山石化公司为基础，涉足产业包括：石油化工、塑料深加工、精细化工与环保产业、清洁能源、物流、汽车检测、工程与服务、地毯生产、进出口贸易、合资合作等。

集联公司拥有危险化学品安全生产许可证、危险化学品包装物生产许可证、煤加工生产经营许可证及乳胶生产的“十环”认证、危险化学品运输许可证等多项政府许可认证，为推进集联公司在政府限定性行业的生产经营开通了“绿色通道”，同时也为集联公司服务于燕山石化主体和外部企业创造了先决条件。

开发的新产品：抗静电性FFS重包装膜、减薄型FFS重包装膜

引进设备：德国W&H公司VAREX三层共挤吹膜生产线　2条

德国W&H公司CONVERPRINT六色印刷线　1条

10. 北京雷诺丽特北京医疗事业部

2012年4月，香港奥星集团的医疗耗材事业部合并至雷诺丽特集团，成为雷诺丽特医疗事业部的成员。由此，北京奥星医药耗材有限公司更名为北京雷诺丽特北京医疗事业部，这样大大增强生产及研发能力。RENOLIT SOLMED产品线非常丰富，提供全系列、多种类以PVC，PP，PE及EVA为基材的医用级塑料薄膜及软管等相关组件。产品广泛用于医疗、技术和药品领域，包括血液系统、肠外营养输液系统、透析及分离系统、细胞培养及生物技术应用等。包括提供输液产品包装用零配件耗材，针对制药、日化、饮料、医疗等行业的特殊情况及需求提供工业和医疗用耗材等的全面服务。

新产品开发：各种共混改性医用树脂

各种医用包装产品出口：亚洲、欧洲

引进设备：3条挤出生产线

11. 北京顾地塑胶有限公司

顾地塑胶股份有限公司分别在广东省佛山市顺德区、高明区，重庆市璧山县、湖北省鄂州市、北京市通州区建立了五个大型现代化生产基地，下属控股了佛山高明顾地塑胶有限公司、佛山高明顾地新材料科技企业有限公司、湖北顾地塑胶有限公司、重庆顾地塑胶电器有限公司、北京顾地塑胶有限公司。北京顾地塑胶有限公司1979年成立，最早生产穿线管，目前是一家建筑、建材的企业，是经国家相关部门批准注册的企业。是中国难燃PVC电工管

和线槽的发明者和制造者，公司主要生产 PVC－U 给排水管、PVC－M 高抗冲给水管、抗菌 PP－R 冷热水管、PP－R 铝塑稳态管、PE－RT 地暖管、PE 给水及燃气管、PVC－C 高压电力护套管、PVC－U 双壁波纹管、HDPE 双壁波纹管、钢带增强 HDPE 螺旋波纹管等产品，广泛应用于建筑内给排水、市政给水、燃气、建筑采暖、市政排水排污等领域。

12. 北京诚联恺达科技有限公司

北京诚联恺达科技有限公司成立于2007 年，其前身是成立于1986 年的北京长城玻纤增强材料厂的改性塑料事业部。诚联恺达是一家主营高性能改性塑料、热塑性弹性体、橡塑密封条三大产品的研发、生产和销售的高新技术公司。改性工程塑料包括改性 PA66、PA6、PP、PE、PBT、PC、ABS 等百余个品种，广泛应用于汽车、电子、铁路、家电、通讯、纺机、电器、机械、体育休闲用品等众多领域，橡塑密封条产品目前也已经广泛应用于北京及其周边地区的众多建筑中，具有较好的市场影响力和知名度。

公司具备年产一万吨改性塑料、热塑性弹性体以及两千吨橡塑密封条的生产能力。多年来公司视质量为企业的生命，先后通过了 ISO9001 质量管理体系认证、TS16949 汽车产品质量管理体系认证。雄厚的技术实力和完善的质量体系为产品质量的稳步提升提供了可靠的保障。

诚联恺达现为中国工程塑料协会及中国阻燃协会的理事单位。公司是北京及周边地区最大的改性塑料、热塑性弹性体、橡塑密封条生产企业。经过多年的发展，公司已经和国内多家建筑厂家以及汽车配套厂家合作，阻燃系列产品也获得美国 UL 黄卡认证。"科技创新、品质精良、优质服务、信誉至上"—诚联恺达全体员工以此立志为每一位客户提供最佳的产品及服务。

13. 北京伊士通新材料发展有限公司

北京伊士通新材料发展有限公司创建于 2005 年 5 月，目前总资产近亿元，主要从事各种改性塑料的产品设计、研发与生产 2009 年 6 月，工厂一期工程建成投产，产能达到 30kt/a，其中改性 PP 特种纤维料系列产品产能为 20kt/a，改性工程塑料系列产品产能为 10kt/a。公司立足自主研发，并依托众多国内外著名石化企业的科研机构及高等院校的研究力量，在改性 PP、改性 PET 和其他改性工程塑料领域取得了令人瞩目的成果，产品畅销国内外，被广泛应用于汽车零部件、照明电器、医用纺织、电动工具、家电通讯等领域。公司肩负"开发环保新材料，为客户提供增值服务"的光荣使命，不断提供满足客户需求的各类高品质、高附加值的产品。开发的新产品：改性 PET 节能灯、改性 PP 防火墙。

14. 福润(北京)塑业有限公司

福润(北京)塑业有限公司是2011 年建厂的新的塑料制品生产企业，现有注射机大的 2 台 SA7000 6800u 螺杆 Φ110 注射容量 4467；PL3000 1800JΦ65；PL6500Φ90 注射容量 2576，200L 桶中空设备一台，小中空设备 8 台，开工率较高。

15. 北京海科华昌新材料技术有限公司

北京海科华昌新材料技术有限公司，是由中国科学院理化技术研究所和海尔科化工程塑料国家工程研究中心股份有限公司于 2002 年合资成立，1993 年被国家计委正式批准成立的工程塑料国家工程研究中心。海科华昌公司配备了从科学实验到材料测试所需的全套仪器和设备；拥有配套齐全的多条挤出造粒生产线，具有年产各类改性工程塑料和抗菌母料 8000t 的生产能力，是国内高水平的高分子材料产业化基地之一。

【发展趋势】

北京地区的塑料工业发展减缓，主要原因是缺乏地区性的统一发展规划和行业的政府指导，列入政府指导性的产品安排也仅仅有农业薄膜和回收塑料；其次进入上世纪九十年代以后，塑料产品的配套性越来越突出，故塑料加工逐步渗透到汽车、电子、医药、食品、纺织服装等等行业，自行配套，自成体系，地区性的塑料工业肯定会发展但是很难形成行业规模。

目前北京地区塑料制品需求主要应该是建筑塑料类的各种管道、建筑保温材料及特殊农业薄膜产品。

对原料的需求主要是聚乙烯、聚丙烯及少数量的 PVC 原料，来源以中石化北京燕山分公司产品为主。

（北京塑料工业协会　苏一凡）

天　津　市

【大事记】

2012 年天津市塑料行业协会本着为振兴天津市塑料工业的发展，为社会和经济发展服务的意愿，做了如下的工作。

1. 召开了 2013 年塑料天津塑协工作会议，对 2012 年天津塑协工作进行了总结并制定出了 2013 年天津塑协的工作要点和工作安排。

2. 根据天津市塑料制品行业人力资源和企业人才现状，2013 年天津市塑料行业协会对会员单位进行了调研。了解会员单位人力资源的状况，制定出了解决企业人力资源的方案。由于注塑企业占天津市塑料制品企业 57.5%，因此天津塑协积极和天津劳动部门联合组织制定了天津市注塑工(初、中级)考级标准。

考级标准如下：

一、对报考人员制定了报考条件：

具备下列条件之一的，可申请报考初级工：

(1)在同一职业(工种)连续工作二年以上或累计工作四年以上的；

(2)经过初级工培训结业。

具备下列条件之一的，可申请报考中级工：

(1)取得所申报职业(工种)的初级工等级证书满三年；

(2)取得所申报职业(工种)的初级工等级证书并经过中级工培训结业；

(3)高等院校、中等专业学校毕业并从事与所学专业相应的职业(工种)工作。

二、制定出了考核大纲

(一)基本要求

1　职业道德

1.1　职业道德基本知识

1.2　职业守则

(1)遵守法律、法规和有关规定。

(2)爱岗敬业、具有高度的责任心。

(3)严格执行工作程序、工作规范、工艺文件和安全操作规程。

(4)工作认真负责，团结合作。

(5)爱护设备及工具、夹具、刀具、量具、模具。

(6)着装整洁，符合规定；保持工作环境清洁有序，文明生产。

2　基础知识

2.1　基础理论知识

(1)识图知识。

(2)公差与配合。

(3)常用金属材料及热处理知识。

(4)常用非金属材料

2.2　机械基础知识

(1)机械传动知识。

(2)模具的基础知识。

(3)工具、夹具、量具使用与维护知识。

(4)气动和液压知识

(5)设备润滑知识

2.3　塑料及成型基础知识

(1)塑料的基础知识。

(2)塑料添加剂的基础知识。

(3)塑料注射成型知识。

2.4　电工知识

(1)通用设备常用电器的种类及用途。

(2)电力拖动及控制原理基础知识。

(3)安全用电知识。

2.5　安全文明生产与环境保护知识

(1)现场文明生产要求。

(2)安全操作与劳动保护知识。

(3)环境保护知识。

2.6　质量管理知识

(1)企业的质量方针。

(2)岗位的质量要求。

(3)岗位的质量保证措施与责任。

2.7　相关法律、法规知识

(1)劳动法相关知识。

(2)合同法相关知识。

(二)各级别要求

1　初级

职业功能	工作内容	技 能 要 求	相 关 知 识
一、工艺准备	(一)读图	1. 能够读懂包含孔、槽、台阶、柱、斜面的多面体等简单零件图。	1. 简单零件的表示方法
	(二)塑料材料准备	1. 能根据常用包括丙烯腈－丁二烯－苯乙烯(ABS)、聚苯乙烯(PS)、聚丙烯(PP)、聚乙烯(PE)、聚氯乙烯(PVC)、聚碳酸酯(PC)等热塑性塑料的名称、代号对塑料进行区分。 2. 能操作辅助设备，准备待加工成型的塑料	1. 常用热塑性塑料及其特性知识 2. 常用辅助设备的用途、操作方法

续表

职业功能	工作内容	技能要求	相关知识
一、工艺准备	(三)模具、辅助工具准备	1. 能进行模具日常维护、保养。 2. 能正确选择使用剪钳、修整刀具等辅助工具。	1. 常用模具金属材料的知识 2. 辅助工具的种类、结构和安全使用方法
	(四)设备调整和维护保养	1. 能正确操作注塑机安全保护装置 2. 能正确识别注塑机动作、仪表显示。 3. 能进行注塑机的日常维护、保养和润滑	1. 注塑机安全装置的用途、操作方法。 2. 注塑机结构的基础知识。 3 设备清洁、点检知识。
二、加工操作	(一)模具的安装	1. 能安全、正确装夹模具。 2. 能正确操作注塑机,检查包括二板式、三板式、侧抽芯等模具的动作是否正常。	1. 注塑成型塑料模具的基本结构。 2. 注塑机的基本操作方法
	(二)注射工艺调校	1. 能完成简单型腔模具的产品成型 2. 能正确清理型腔中的残余塑料 3. 能正确使用脱模剂 4. 能读懂产品工艺卡	1. 常用塑料的成型条件 2. 常用塑料的成型工艺过程 3. 产品工艺卡的知识
	(三)产品后加工、处理	能按产品工艺要求完成产品后加工。	产品工艺要求
三、质量检验	(一)产品尺寸检验	能准确测量产品各要素尺寸。	常用量仪(例如:游标卡尺、内径千分尺、内径千分表、千分表等)的结构、工作原理和使用方法
	(二)产品质量分析	1. 能准确检查产品外观缺陷 2. 能判断常见缺陷产生的原因	1. 塑料产品的一般检验项目和检验方法 2. 常见塑料制品缺陷的判别方法

2 中级

职业功能	工作内容	技能要求	相关知识
一、工艺准备	(一)读图	能够读懂包含多柱、孔、筋和多复杂曲面联结的零件图。	复杂零件的表示方法
	(二)塑料材料准备	1. 能正确选用包括增塑剂、润滑剂、染色剂等常用塑料添加剂。 2. 能正确完成包括性能测试等热塑性塑料的预处理	1. 注塑材料组成、分类、特性的知识。 2. 热塑性塑料的预处理的知识。
	(三)模具准备	1. 能正确校准模具与注塑机包括安装尺寸、开模行程等参数的匹配。 2. 能正确完成包括更换顶针等工作的模具简单维修。	1. 注塑模具的结构知识。 2. 注塑机的工艺参数知识。
	(四)设备调整	1. 能检定注塑机安全保护装置的工作状态。 2. 能正确操作注塑机完成所有动作。 3. 能正确清洗注塑机料筒	常用注塑机的种类、结构、操作方法。

续表

职业功能	工作内容	技能要求	相关知识
二、加工操作	(一)塑料性能调校	1. 能准确完成塑料试件收缩率、表面纹路、色度等的工艺调校。 2. 能编制产品工艺卡	1. 注塑成型条件 2. 注塑成型工艺过程、工艺参数。 3. 注塑机调校知识。 4. 成型工艺辅助设备的调校
	(二)注射工艺调校	能完成包括长螺丝柱、长片状筋、多孔等形状的型腔模具的产品成型	
	(三)产品后加工、处理	能完成包括退火、调湿等产品后处理。	塑料制品后处理方法
三、质量检验	(一)产品质量检验	能正确检查包括色度、密度、强度等内容的产品内在质量。	塑料制品测试、分析仪器的原理和使用方法
	(二)产品质量分析	1. 能根据产品外观缺陷产生的原因调整工艺参数 2. 能正确判断模具对塑料产品内在、外观质量的影响。	1. 塑料制品缺陷的产生原因和处理方法。 2. 注塑模具设计、制造基本知识。

2012年5月天津塑协组织部分会员单位，参加了第二十六届雅式国际橡塑展。为推动企业提升自身的技术水平、产品质量，掌握塑料行业现状和发展前景、开拓视野起到了积极的促进作用。

积极配合中国塑料加工工业协会年鉴编制工作，2012年天津塑协调研了天津市塑料加工企业的现状并结合天津市塑料行业的发展方向编制了2012年天津市地区塑料行业的年鉴，并发表在中国塑协的文献上。

3. 2012年中国包装联合会塑料制品包装专委会在津举办塑料包装、注塑、改性原料展。天津塑协组织了20家企业参加了在天津滨海新区举办的国际展会。

4. 为了推动企业经济发展，针对中小企业融资困难的问题，2012年12月天津塑协组织了有融资要求的32家企业和多家银行进行了座谈。银行方面就2013年金融政策和银行经营的产品对企业进行了讲解和宣传，有多家企业根据自身的情况与银行达成了融资协议。

5. 为助力天津塑料企业“健康成长工程”，加快培养和造就更多具有全球视野，精通现代化管理，崇尚自主创新，善于开拓市场的优秀企业家，全面提升企业主要管理者领导力和创新能力，促进其尽快实现转型升级，高速成长。天津市塑料行业协会与清华大学继续教育学院合作，举办了“高级工商管理课程(EMBA)研修班。”

6. 为了在环渤海地区打造一个集塑料设备展示和原料、相关设备配件的塑料卖场。2012年天津塑协与天津南马路五金城研讨合作建立北方地区塑料卖场项目并定于2013年启动。

7. 2012年塑化剂风波使人们对塑料制品产生了疑虑。天津市塑料行业协会受天津电视台“有嘛别有病”栏目组邀请，讲解了塑化剂的科普知识，宣传了如何安全使用塑料制品和如何辨别塑料制品存在不安全因素等相关知识。

8. 天津国丰塑料模具有限公司在汽车塑料模具行业中已经跻身为全国第三名。

【基本情况】

天津市的塑料产业涉及领域广泛，初级形态树脂有HDPE、LLDPE、PVC、PP、PS、ABS等。二次加工改性树脂围绕天津电子通讯、汽车、航空、家电行业所需材料进行开发生产，一些耐侯性强、耐高温、耐刚性、阻燃等专用材料已经被相关企业认可。塑料制品的应用覆盖到了农业、工业、包装、建材、市政、汽车、航空、电子电器、机械、军工等领域。

2012年天津地区共有主营塑料制品加工企业841户，非主营塑料制品加工企业约661户。主营从业人员4.32万人，非主营从业人员约6万人。2012年天津市塑料初级形态树脂产量3228kt，比去年同期降低5.28%。二次加工树脂产量435kt，比去年同期降低4.3%。塑料制品产量1940kt，比去年同期增长17.6%。主营业务收入317.2亿元，比去年同期增长26.9%。

2012年天津市塑料制品产品结构分别占塑料制品产量比重是：

塑料薄膜327kt占天津市塑料制品总产量的16.8%；泡沫塑料34.8kt，占天津市塑料制品总产量的1.79%；人造革111.9kt，占天津市塑料制品总产量的0.6%；日用塑料制品237.9kt，占天津市塑料制品总产量的12.35%；塑料板片材条棒型材257kt占天津市塑料制品总产量的13.2%；塑料管及附件157kt，占天津市塑料制品总产量的8.1%；塑料丝绳编制品79kt，占天津市塑料制品总产量的4.1%；包装、容器制品181kt，占总天津市塑料制品产量的9.32%；配套等注塑制品等654.4kt，占天津市塑料制品总产量的33.73%。

天津市合成树脂及共聚物产量3229kt，占全国合成树脂及共聚物产量的6.19%，比同期下降5.28%。

【企业经营】

2012年天津市塑料行业的总体规模稳步发展。在汽车配套领域出现增长缓慢的情况下，电子通讯配套、包装、出口加工贸易出现了新的增长。部分重点企业塑料制品规模进一步扩大，技术创新能力得到了进一步增强。2012年天津市规模以上塑料加工企业完成塑料制品产量142.1万吨，与去年同期增长38.4%，规模以上企业保持了快速的发展趋势。一些在天津在建的大项目例如：壳牌50万吨油脂、丰田汽车新车型项目等为天津塑料制品的发展奠定了良好的市场基础。

2012年天津市塑料产品表观消费量约252万吨，其中塑料建材、工业、食品包装，汽车、电子行业占天津市塑料产品消费量的81.2%。

【存在问题】

1. 产业结构调整困难；

由于天津市塑料行业摆不上天津市经济活动的议事日程，行业天津塑协对塑料行业的产业结构进行调整出现了较大的障碍，产品技术含量低、盲目发展、恶性竞争的现象仍有发生。

2. 工厂成本上升压力加大；

随着天津市最低工资水平的提高，工厂成本上升压力加大。大部分塑料制品加工企业利润较低，经济运行艰难。

3. 塑料产业体系不完善；

天津市塑料制品涵盖了各个领域，但是在加工设备、模具制造、专用改性塑料、复合高分子材料等开发应用方面发展滞后。不适应天津地区高新技术产业配套的能力和发展需求。

4. 产品结构有待提高；

为汽车、电子等产业配套的产品未能随市场需要提升配套水平。技术含量高，有市场发展前景的产品发展缓慢。

5. 产品研发经费投入不足；

行业研发力量薄弱，企业研发经费投入不足，使塑料加工工业的技术升级，产品换代艰难。

【发展趋势】

1. 推动产业集群化，树立环渤海地区塑料产业中心地位

推动天津塑料示范园区的建设，协助有关部门开展园区招商工作．把园区打造成集塑料相关产品的销售、展示、交易、物流、仓储为一体的环渤海地区塑料产业中心。

2. 培育骨干企业产业转型升级

利用天津市产业优势和市场的需求，在拓展石油、海洋、汽车、航空、电子通讯、医疗器具等高新技术领域的市场需求的同时。发展环保、节能、低碳、多功能、附加值高的产品。

3. 加快发展研发、实验室平台建设

充分利用现有政策推动在津建立高分子材料研发中心、塑料模具技术鉴定中心等平台，为天津市塑料行业的发展做好技术储备工作。

4. 改性材料前景广阔

开发研制耐高温性、耐候性、耐磨性、阻燃、超导电、高电磁性合金材料以及具有屏蔽功能的材料及产品将是天津地区高新技术产业和先进制造业的需求。

5. 提高包装材料的技术含量和配套

提高包装材料和产品技术含量，在开发有市场发展的包装材料和制品的同时，做好天津市新增500kt油脂项目的包装配套工作。

6. 医用塑料

建立医用高分子材料和制品孵化器基地，瞄准世界前沿科学技术和应用材料，发展技术含量高、高附加值的高分子材料的人体器官。

开拓各类医疗器具和药品包装制品的市场并推广应用。

7. 加强人员的培训

加强专业人员和从业人员的培训，组织行业管理、产品检验、加工工艺、高分子材料、模具加工及设计、操作人员等培训。提高行业的整体水平。

天津市塑料行业协会将继续推动天津市塑料行业的发展，引领天津市塑料行业落实科学发展观，以围绕着天津市总体经济发展和加快塑料产业经济增长方式转变为主线，强化企业自主创新和科技创新能力，开拓新的应用领域和需求市场，实现天津市塑料产业新的发展。

（天津塑料行业协会　郑天禄）

山 西 省

【大事纪】

1. 2012山西省塑料工业发展较快，不仅塑料企业的数量和产品品种增加较快，而且出现了一批发展速度很快的企业和特色产品。山西省的塑料企业450个，生产能力月850kt，产能约750kt。规模以上企业33个，产量达到630kt，占到全省塑料总产量的85%左右。目前已形成以大型企业为龙头、中小型企业为主体的发展格局，行业内实现了良性的竞争和循环。

2. 2012年《山西省塑料行业协会网站》和《山西塑协通讯录》继续完善和改进，逐步形成了网络新媒体和传统媒体并行的宣传平台。十年来网站先后在2002年、2009年和2011年经过三次全新全面改版。今天的网站图文并茂，内容更加丰富多彩。山西中德、香港雅式展览有限公司、中国(台州)塑料交易会、国际(泰国)塑料展。晋城凤凰、榆化漳河等单位刊登了旗帜广告，不但大力宣传了企业，而且充分展示了模范企业的风采。现在网站设有：关于协会、行业新闻、政策法规、质量标准、塑协动态、联系我们、旗帜广告、协会大事记、网站会员登录、协会公告、模范企业及会员单位展示、友情链接等栏目和内容。网站和中国塑协及全国主要省市协会的网站都进行了链接。扩大了信息量，提高了信息质量，点击率更高。《山西塑协通讯录》也增刊发行，相比于2011年发行量增加了一半，成为省内塑料行业最具权威性的杂志，赢得了企业的一致好评，两个媒体的融合逐渐打造成山西塑料行业交流、宣传、学习平台。

3. 2012年全国能博会在太原召开，新疆在会上举办了一个招商引资项目合作洽谈会，山西中德、晋城凤凰、太原杰森、青科恒安、阳煤集团、山西华龙等十多个企业的领导及工程技术人员都踊跃参加，受到了省经信委的表扬。各种国内外行业活动，不但使企业的领导及工程技术人员开阔了眼界，增长了见识，增进了友谊和感情，而且交流学习了新产品、新技术；各单位选择采购了先进适用的设备仪器。大家一致反映行业的集体活动很好、很有意义；为我省塑料工业走出山西、走向世界，转型跨越发展奠定了良基。

4. 组团参观“第二十六届国际橡塑展”

第二十六届中国国际塑料橡胶工业展览会(以下简称《2012上海国际橡塑展》)的规模居世界第二，亚洲第一。于2012年4月18日至4月20日在上海(浦东)新国际博览中心举行。《2012上海国际橡塑展》展场面积将扩大约20万平方米，有35个国家2600家企业参展，奥地利、加拿大、法国、德国、意大利、日本、韩国、台湾、英国、美国等12国家和地区的展团，展示新的化工原料及超过2500台机械设备，力争为观众带来多元化的解决方案，从而提升竞争力和产品的性能。“绿色科技”与“创新设计”将成为未来的关键词，也是这次展览会的热点。今年展会的主题是：《塑料科技，成果未来》。为此，协会组织我省塑料行业的董事长、总经理、厂长、总工程师、企业高级管理人员和科技人员参观了这次展览会。参观这次展览会的有：山西中德集团、山西乾通塑胶有限公司、太原龙通塑料有限公司、山西华龙塑料有限公司、山西翼城泰鑫塑胶有限公司、山西民生塑料制品有限公司、太原杰森实业有限公司、山西东盛塑胶有限公司、山西青科恒安矿业新材料有限公司、阳泉市方大塑胶有限公司、介休市塑料有限公司、山西方园塑业有限公司、太原市塑料研究所、龙通塑料有限公司、山西省塑料行业协会等二十二个单位35人参观了这次国际塑胶展。参展的人员都是有备而来，达到了各自的目的，有的订购了急需要的设备仪器，有的学到最先进技术，中德集团公司与有关国际化工企业，签约了一级直接供货合同。大家一致认为收获很大，新的塑料产品对改善未来生活至关重要，塑料工业也有助于其它产业在节约能源和保护环境有重要的意义，要加快产业结构调整，为振兴我省的塑料行业加快发展共同努力！

5. 中国塑料加工工业协会第六届二次理事扩大会暨塑料加工应用与发展论坛会》于2012年4月16日至4月17日在上海召开。出席会议代表有协会理事、各专业委员会主任和秘书长、各省市协会负责人、大专院校和科研单位代表以及企业家等180多人参加了这次会议。山西塑协张玉英会长出席了这次会议。理事会由中国塑料加工工业协会副会长、上海市塑料行业协会常务副会长刘景芬主持。中国塑料加工工业协会常务副会长曹俭作了《中国塑料加工工业协会第六届二次理事会工作报告》；中国轻工联合会副会长、中国塑料加工工业协会会长钱桂敬作关于《塑料加工工业“十二五”发展规划指导意见(征求意见稿)》的编制说明；马占峰秘书长作了《中国塑料加工工业协会财务工作报告》和有关人事变动说明。

6. 2012年5月，山西中德塑钢型材公司荣获“中国驰名商标”荣誉称号，实现了品牌道路上的一次新飞跃，给山西同行企业极大的信心和勇气。山西中德塑钢型材有限公司品牌建设的成功，得益于以下几个方面：一是做大做强实现规模化经营。截至目前，山西中德拥有最先进的型材挤进生产线200余条，年产值近16亿元，员工1500余人，下辖5个全资子公司(即山西中德塑钢型材有限公司、山西通达建材有限公司、四川中德塑钢型材有限公司、山西中德管业有限公司和山西中德科技有限公司)，在国内塑料建材行业排名前五。二是强劲的国际化发展势头。公司产品九大系列200余个品种不仅覆盖山西，同时还辐射华北、东北、西南、西北等地区。产品继2003年出口蒙古国后，又以自主身份成功打入泰国、韩国、印度尼西亚、危地马拉、俄罗斯、乌克兰、比利时、埃及等国家，使用范围越来越广。三是科技化和多元化战略取得重大进展。不仅注重传统产品的生产经营和关联产品的开发营销，而且注重产品的设计制造和品牌的开发保护，以自主知识产权创新为基础的科技化和多元化战略取得了重大进展。

7. 组织会员单位学习参加《塑料机械关键技术系列培训》

由中国塑料机械工业协会、中国塑料机械行业专家委员会联合举办的《塑料机械关键技术系列培训》，经国家人力资源和社会保障部、中国机械工业联合会批准列为现代制造领域(“653工程”)继续教育培训项目，目的是为了促进企业技术创新和产品结构调整，为企业提供更多的人才储备。经研究，决定山西塑料行业协会积极组织塑料机械制造、塑料制品成型及使用相关企业的工程技术人员或企业技术负责人，以及研发、制造和售后服务等技术人员，于2012年8月22~26日在北京化工大学参加了《塑料机械关键技术系列培训—先进挤出工艺技术及理论》高级研修班，为山西塑料企业的发展培养高素质人才。

8. 编写了2011年《中国塑料工业年鉴山西篇》

《中国塑料工业年鉴》由中国塑料加工工业协会主办。年鉴全面反映中国塑料工业发展状况。为从事和涉及塑料工业的生产、销售和科研单位全方位提供行业动态、市场和技术信息。年鉴的组稿、编辑和出版工作得到中国轻工业联合会，各省市塑料协会的关心和支持。全国31个省市自治区和直辖市，多年来参与编写的有：北京、天津、山西、上海、广东、浙江、江苏、福建、新疆等15个地区。为了反映山西塑料工业的现状和学习赶超先进，我们协会每年都认真总结和编写《中国塑料工业年鉴—山西篇》，受到了各级领导和业界同仁的赞扬。

9. 组团参加第十届中国塑料交易会和第二十届亚洲塑料论坛

第十届中国塑料交易会于9月3~5日在台州举行。台州素有“塑料制品王国”的美誉，交易会是全面展示中国塑料制品、原料、机械模具及相关技术，强力吸引国际采购的重要平台。设展位1200个参展企业500家，展出面积3万平方米。国外组团有：欧盟、西班牙、马来西亚、新加坡、日本、印度、缅甸等20多个国家和地区。期间举办了第二十届亚洲塑料论坛会。论坛以可持续发展带来的挑战为主题，以各国塑料工业现状和需求、世界塑料行业热点和塑料绿色包装三大主题为核心，各国代表作了发言。山西塑协组团参加了交易会和塑料论坛，代表团有：山西明坤集团、山西泰鑫塑胶有限公司、芮城金牛建材有限公司、太原塑信科贸公司、晋特塑料有限公司等15个单位23位代表。台州塑协张小赧会长和山西塑协张玉英会长，都是全国劳动模范和人大代表，彼此友谊很深；张小赧会长热情设宴，招待了山西塑协代表团全体。张玉英会长应邀出席了第十届中国塑料交易会的开幕剪彩仪式。

10. 评出2012年度名优产品，表彰模范企业和先进个人

为了把我省塑料行业的品牌做大做强。更好的实施品牌建设与企业产业发展相结合的方针，提高企业的科级创新能力和技术水平，使企业逐步向高端发展，协会努力为企业搭建平台，推进行业名优品牌评选与高新技术产业化有机结合，激励企业向新兴产业发展。根据《山西省塑料行业协会名优产品评选办法》的有关规定，2012年11月17日召开了山西塑料行业名优产品评委会，经过专家的认真审核评定，评出了山西中德塑钢型材有限公司等15个单位的15种产品，为2012年度的名优产品。

11. 2012年12月，山西中德塑钢型材有限公司四川公司收到成都市质量管理协会文件通知及证书，成为“2012年度成都市用户满意企业”。为激励先进，树立典型，发挥先进企业的模范作用，成都市质量协会用户委员会办公室紧紧围绕放心产品工程、优质服务示范单位活动中，在全川范围内组织多家生产(经销)企业作为“成都市用户满意企业”，以产品知识进市场、示范挂牌树榜样、质检专家送技术相结合的模式，以此进一步推动全社会加强质量诚信建设工作。据悉，四川省数百家企业参与了本次申报，经相关政府部门审核，在初选的几百家企业中又再次精选出了几十家企业，作为“用户满意企业单位”。作为川内塑钢型材产业重点企业的中德集团，拥有雄厚的科研开发和自主创新实力，拥有一流的科研队伍和研发体系，其技术水平已经达到了国际

水平，部分还达到了国际领先水平。目前，中德集团四川公司拥有遍布全国各地的400余家经销机构，生产塑钢型材管材近两百个品种，年生产能力逾180kt，位居全国行业前列。

12.12月27日，山西省塑料行业协会成立十周年暨理事会换届大会在长治市隆重召开，中国塑料加工工业协会秘书长马占峰，长治市政府副市长陈鹏飞，山西省经信委处长李正峰，四川塑料行业协会秘书长隋佩侠，以及来自省内的20多家塑料行业企业代表参加了会议。会议选举产生了山西省塑料行业协会第三届理事会，中德集团公司董事长程田青当选为新一届理事会会长。

【基本情况】

截至2012年，塑料制品行业规模以上企业1.30万个，占全国规模以上工业企业数4.15%；从业人数247.12万人，占全国工业从业人员总数2.75%；塑料制品加工业年产值就达到1.61万亿元，占到全国工业总产值的1.89%；塑料制品出口总额为565.03亿美元，占全国出口总额的2.98%。据不完全统计：山西省的塑料企业约有450个左右，生产能力约750kt，产量约600kt。规模以上企业30个左右，产量500kt左右，占到总产量的85%左右。

【企业经营】

山西省的塑料工业起步很早，20世纪60年代在全国名列前茅，如塑料地膜最早就是我们研发的、硬质PVC板材等国标是我们组织起草的，而且我们也荣获过很多国家、省部级科技成果奖，我们在塑料加工行业有着悠久的历史和良好的传统。

目前，山西省的塑料企业约450个左右，涵盖了国有企业、集体企业、合资企业、民营企业，其中民营企业居多，占总数的57%左右。主要以生产塑料型材（含板、片材）、塑料棒、管材、塑料农地膜、矿用塑料、部分塑料丝及编织制品和塑料包装箱及容器、日用塑料制品等为主，部分企业几年也开始生产塑料行业上下游的相关延伸产品。山西的塑料企业以中小企业为主，规模以上或接近规模的企业有30余家，其中塑料制品企业规模以上的有：山西中德塑钢型材有限公司、山西万士达工程塑料有限公司、长治清华永腾建材有限公司、山西新派塑胶有限公司、山西新超管业公司、山西乾通塑胶有限公司、太原明坤工贸公司、山西焕德塑钢工贸有限公司、介休市塑料有限公司、山西迎太塑料制品厂、山西塑料总厂、太原民生塑料厂等。我省的塑料工业在国内占的份额较小，与先进发达省份还有不小差距。

【重点企业】

序号	企业名称	产量	加工能力	主要产品名称
1	山西中德塑钢型材有限公司	120000	180000	PVC型材、彩色仿木型材、双色共挤型材
2	长治清华永腾建材有限公司	50000	65000	铝塑、PPR、PE－RT、PE－X、PE矿用管、PE给水管材、UPVC排水管及管件、UPVC型材
3	山西中德管业有限公司	30000	50000	PE管材、PPR管材、PE－RT管材、中空螺旋管、穿线管
4	晋城凤凰实业有限责任公司	40000	50000	各种煤矿用聚乙烯管材、管件；聚氨酯筛板、燃气用埋地管材、管件；给水用PPR管等
5	山西万士达工程塑料有限公司	15000	15000	PE燃气管、PE管材、PE矿用管材及管件
6	山西华鹏铝塑型材有限公司	10000	15000	各种铝塑、木塑共挤型材
7	山西东盛塑胶管道有限公司	15000	15000	各种煤矿用阻燃抗静电聚乙烯管材、管件
8	山西新超管业公司	15000	18000	纳米抗菌不锈钢复合管、PPR、PE－RT管、PEX
9	青科恒安矿业新材料有限公司	8000	10000	煤矿用阻燃抗静电PVC管材，管件；PVC软管
10	山西惠丰塑料型材有限公司	80000	90000	PVC塑钢型材、管材等
11	山西迎太塑料有限公司	25000	30000	塑料管材、农用地膜、10m宽幅双防无滴膜、保鲜袋、PVC型材等
12	山西塑料总厂	8000	10000	PE波纹管、给水管
13	山西乾通塑胶有限公司	4000	4000	PPR、PE－RT管材、管件
14	太原市杰森实业有限公司	6000	8000	矿用钢丝网骨架PE复合管等

续表

序号	企业名称	产量	加工能力	主要产品名称
15	晋城市晋韩塑料有限公司	13000	15000	UPVC 型材、PE 管材、高分子环保免漆板
16	山西晋特塑料制品有限公司	3000	5000	各类塑料周转箱
17	山西民生塑料制品厂	4000	5500	农地膜、发泡片材
18	太原市料四厂	3000	12000	钢塑共挤型材
19	山西众和金牛新型建材有限公司	5000	6000	PEX、PPR、PE－RT 管材、管件
20	山西明坤科工贸集团	3000	4000	PP、PE、PPR、PE－RT 管材、管件、矿用管材
21	山西祁县旺中塑料制品有限公司	3000	4000	PP、PE、PPR、PE－RT 管材、管件
22	山西泰鑫塑料制品有限公司	3000	4000	PVC 给水管、PE 管材、PP－R 管材
23	山西方圆塑业有限公司	3000	10000	BOPP 包装薄膜
24	运城鸿基包装材料有限公司	20000	21000	PVC 树脂
25	山西省榆社化工股份有限公司	250000	500000	PVC 树脂
26	太化股份公司氯碱分公司	60000	100000	PVC 树脂
27	山西省阳煤集团 PVC 树脂厂	80000	200000	
28	山西华星塑料有限公司	7000	10000	超高分子量 PE 大口径特种耐磨管材
29	山西汾西机电有限公司	注射机		合模力 600kN 到 40000kN 注射量 80g 到 60000g

【塑料制品进出口】

本省 2012 年塑料制品出口量达 565.03 亿美元，进口原辅材料约 1100t 左右，山西中德管材有限公司、山西万士达公司塑料有限公司、长治清华永腾建材公司、山西明坤科工贸集团、山西乾通塑胶有限公司等单位生产的 PE 燃气管、PP－R 管，大多是进口韩国和北欧的原料。中德塑钢型材有限公司在原料上采用美国的钛白粉、英国的稳定剂、瑞士的抗紫外线吸收剂、西班牙的群青等；山西华星塑料有限公司生产的超高分子量 PE 管材，原材料大部分由德国进口。中德塑钢型材有限公司的塑钢型材出口蒙古、泰国、俄罗斯、乌克兰等国，少部分彩色型材出口美国。山西万士达工程塑料有限公司生产的燃气管出口新加坡等东南亚国家。山西华龙塑料有限公司生产的阻燃抗静电塑料拉伸网出口俄罗斯等。

【新产品开发】

塑料在我省已成为国民经济发展的支柱产业。为了加快我省塑料工业的发展，要扶持环保、节能及高科级产业及产品，促进塑料工业发展，为加快我省国民经济发展作出新贡献。重点开发和研制方向：

1. 新型建材塑料制品

今后 5～15 年塑料建材将成为新的消费热点和经济增长点。随着塑料建筑制品的品种逐步系列化、配套化和标准化，环保节能的要求和推广应用的力度加大，需要各种塑料管、门窗、高分子防水材料、装饰装修材料、保温材料及其它建筑用塑料制品将有较大幅度增加。我省除了自已的建筑特色产品外，今后还要鼓励开发低噪音的芯层发泡、内壁螺旋构造 PVC 排水管道，重点发展塑料埋地排水管、新型防水卷材、隔热保温材料、塑料装饰材料。研制生产表面具有木材纹理或其他具装饰效果的低发泡 PVC 型材、板材等，以推动以塑代木战略，适应经济建设的快速发展。

2. 农用塑料制品及包装塑料

国情决定了应把农用塑料放在塑料工业重中之重切实抓好。我省是严重缺水的地区，也是农、地膜研发和应用最早的省份，今后农膜要向薄型长寿化方向发展，重点要开发多功能、耐老化、易吸收、易降解农、地膜、大棚膜等农用材料及制品；节水灌溉用各种类型喷灌、滴灌管道、管件、喷头等配套件、塑料井管、防渗膜、水利用土工编织布等。另外，塑料软包装、纺织袋、中空容器、周转箱等，是塑料制品应用中的最大领域之一。我国塑料包装材料约占包装总产量的 1/3，居各种包装材料之首。我省在包装塑料制品方面应加强开发。

3. 再生及降解塑料制品

环境保护因素，总的要求是调整后的塑料产业，应随着科技的进步和相关法规的建立，对某些消费后或消费过程存在综合治理、对环境造成影响的产品，从生产技术、应用材料等方面进行改造和提高，这一类产品包括包装袋、农用薄膜、医用包装和一次性用具、PS泡沫制品白色污染等塑料废弃处理等问题。要资源再生—产品材料能多次回收再用、循环使用。高效处理——包括产品材料降解性能的研发、应用。

4. 加大原辅材料研发的力度

要解决制约我国成为塑料强国的"瓶颈"问题，首先是原材料短缺严重，价格不稳定，技术创新不足，恶性竞争。我国目前原材料的一半需进口，同时还要进口大量废旧塑料。我省"十二五"期间，除PVC树脂产量要力争达到1000kt左右外，对其他原辅材料、助剂也要加强自主研发。充分利用本省资源，缓解原材料短缺，推动我省塑料工业的发展。

5. 开发具有山西特色的矿用塑料

山西省是煤炭重化工基地，仅山西煤焦集团目前年产原煤4160万吨，煤矿的安全生产已提到重要议程。仅太原西山煤电集团2011年就需各种钢管道8185t，折合成长度约100万米，而矿用塑料管材等在煤矿应用还处于起步阶段。为了发展地方特色，推动区域经济发展，开发各种多功能阻燃抗静电的矿用管材、管件；矿用顶柱、矿用假顶网、矿用塑料拉伸网、矿工帽、矿用茅杆等以塑代钢，以塑代木的矿用产品是我省塑料行业发展的重点。

6. 塑料日用品及医用高分子材料

塑料日用品与人民生活十分密切，今后应努力在花色、品种、降低成本上进行开发。另外，医用高子材料是与医学生命科学与生命体直接或间接接触的材料，目前市场需求规模达(120～150)亿元。"十二五"期间将步入高速发展时期，未来市场需求将提升至(200～250)亿元。我省在这方面应加强开发。

【市场需求】

塑料制品主要是塑料型材(含板、片材)、塑料棒、管材、管件、塑料农地膜、矿用塑料、超高分子量聚乙烯的发口径特种耐磨管材、部分塑料丝及编织制品和塑料包装箱及容器、日用塑料制品等，由于受山西省地方特色经济影响，近几年矿用塑料需求量及发展都很快。同时，随着城中村改造和新农村建设的推行，高质量大壁厚的PE给水管和穿线管的需求量也正在逐步增多。受铝材影响，普通型材的销量收到一定冲击。

【存在问题】

1. 人才的溃乏，特别是高分子塑料专业人才短缺

每年中北大学、太原理工大学都有相当数量的高分子材料专业的本科和硕士研究生毕业，但由于环境不够宽松，几乎全部外流，甚至从事多年的本专业技术人员也调离岗位或远去发达地区，所以我省企业专业技术人员占职工总数的比例，要比发达地区小得多，而且技术人员中大多数是中初级职称，高级职称的技术人员为数更少。

2. 产品结构、生产工艺技术及装备问题

行业中由于缺乏宏观引导，产品生产中的中低档产品重复、盲目发展现象仍时有发生。而特殊工程塑料产品很少。对新开发、效益好的品种如、各种异型材、管材、管件制品，存在省内企业一哄而上，市场开发跟不上的状况。

3. 科研投入和开发能力不足

塑料虽然是国民经济中必不可少的重点行业，但政府在政策优惠、特殊支撑方面及政府主管部门或行业协会协调等方面仍显不足，高等院校、科研院所与企业携手引进高新技术或共同开发技术含量高的产品不力，很多企业的品牌意识不强。企业间相互沟通交流不够，没有形成强强联手，资源共享、共同打造山西品牌，提升竟争力的芬围，更没形成具有一定规模的产业链或产业区。

4. 原料生产发展滞后，产品技术进步受限

塑料产业是综合行业，其制品的研发、生产涉及轻工、化工、机械等多个行业，具体涉及到原料、助剂、设备、模具等多个产业。而塑料原料是最重要的环节，而我省除PVC树脂外，其它均不生产，所用原材料主要靠国内外进口。

5. 政府支持力度不够

在沿海及发达省市，塑料行业已作为政府的支柱产业给以重点支持，我省的塑料工业政府虽然也给了一定的支持，但力度还很不够。众多中小企业正处于快速发展时期，政府的政策倾斜和扶持，对他们发展壮大很有必要。

【发展趋势】

"十二五"期间，我省国民经济发展将发生新的飞跃，一些热点、重点行业、支柱产业的崛起和发展将带动塑料产业的提升和发展。在总结我省塑料工业发展的经验和问题基础上，根据我国塑料发展动向和市场需求、预测，结合我省实际情况，及时对塑料产业、产品结构进行调整，从而推进塑料行业新的发展。以国内外市场需求为导向，以"品种、质量、效益"为调整中心，以行业骨干企业为依托，全力推动企业的技术进步。在继续推进总产量增长的同时，着重增强塑料产品的经济效益和科技含量。要更加注重高、精、特殊用途产品的引进、消化、吸收，及具有本省特色产品的自主研发。我省塑料行业产品结构调整应分为鼓励发展类产品、改造提

高类产品和限制淘汰类产品。要大力开发符合产业和环保政策的产品。围绕当前世界塑料材料和产品发展方向，即“高性能化、复合化、环保化、信息化”，大力发展与国民经济支柱产业密切相关的新型材料和制品，用高新技术大力改造传统塑料材料和产品。

今后协会要加强自身建设，充分用好党和政府给我们的各项政策，更好的发挥纽带和桥梁作用，组织更多、更好的各种行业考察、培训等活动。把塑协通讯、塑协网站办的更好，真正办成为企业服务的平台，让我们的企业走出去，让更多的国内外企业进入我省、为我们引进、消化、吸收国际先进技术、先进设备开辟绿色通道。同时我们要培育一批代表我省形象、水平、实力的在国内国际有竞争能力的代表性企业和优秀企业家。这批企业，技术上应具备或接近届时国际先进水平和国内领先水平，逐步形成自已的特色和优势。我们必须努力打造更多的名企和名牌产品，赶超国内外先进水平。

今后协会更要坚持以人为本，树立和落实全面协调、可持续的科学发展观，更好地开展“双向服务”活动，搞好“塑料通讯”和塑协网站建设，传播更多更好的信息，让全国和世界了解山西的塑料企业，了解我们的产品，推动我省塑料行业的发展。让全国和世界了解山西的塑料企业，了解山西的塑料产品，为提高我省塑料行业整体水平而努力！

（山西省塑料行业协会　程田青　赵　军）

黑龙江省

【基本情况】

黑龙江省目前塑料制品综合加工能力大约是70多万吨，规模企业塑料制品的年产量仅为64多万吨，占全国的1.10%，在全国31个省市自治区中名列第20位。

根据黑龙江省统计部门2012年对全省塑料制品主营业务收入在2000万元以上91户企业的快报统计，其中：国有企业3户，股份合作制企业2户，股份制企业77户，外商及港澳台投资企业1户，其它企业8户。从业人数11777人，制品产量637843t，产值1344806万元，利税108099万元，出口交货值5980万元。

我省年销售额在5000万元以上的塑料企业有53家：大庆庆港塑料有限公司、大庆林港塑胶有限公司、哈尔滨哈轻塑胶公司、哈高科绥棱二塑有限公司、黑龙江齐塑塑料制品有限公司、哈尔滨塑五有限公司、五常塑料有限公司、穆棱市塑料有限责任公司、哈尔滨工业大学五塑实业有限公司、北安市进发塑料制品有限责任公司、黑龙江双峰塑料制品有限公司、哈尔滨华加新型材料有限公司、哈尔滨兰根塑料门窗有限公司、哈尔滨特种塑料制品有限公司等。

【主要产品及重点企业概况】

1. 农用塑料薄膜：主要生产企业有哈尔滨塑五有限公司、五常塑料有限公司、穆棱市塑料有限责任公司、哈尔滨工业大学五塑实业有限公司。

2. 塑料门窗及节能膜：黑龙江省塑料门窗行业的发展较早，为我省的建设事业做出了很大的贡献。目前已经形成以塑料型材、组装门窗、配套五金件等完整产业链。其中规模较大的有中大集团、哈尔滨蓝根塑料门窗有限公司、黑龙江美城集团公司、齐齐哈尔鲁宏塑窗型材厂、牡丹江市华安塑料型材有限公司、哈尔滨华加新型建材有限公司和大庆威泰型材有限公司、黑龙江成才塑胶改性新材料总厂。

目前我省的门窗已打进了俄罗斯远东地区，全球经济一体化的大趋势将不断促使我省企业扩大在整个俄罗斯市场的销售渠道，未来产品出口必然呈上升趋势。

节能膜，就目前典型的建筑围护部件而言，建筑外门窗的能耗约占建筑物全部热损失的30%～40%，其中玻璃的热辐射散热占70%，渗漏占15%，窗框占15%。因而增强外门窗的保温隔热性能，减少门窗能耗的同时必须考虑玻璃的能耗，是改善室内热环境质量和提高建筑节能水平的重要环节。建筑玻璃节能膜的应用将赋予普通中空玻璃更高的保温、安全、隔音、消除霜露等功能，是一种多功能性、高技术产品，对于有效利用能源、节约能源、保护环境等方面意义重大，是建筑玻璃应用的发展趋势。主要生产企业有黑龙江成才塑胶改性新材料总厂。

3. 塑料管材：塑料管材的应用领域很大，我省塑料管材生产企业有60多家，生产的管材主要可以分为以下四大方面：

(1)建筑用方面：建筑用塑料管材包括室内、外水管和室内外排水管。管材的材质主要有PE、PP－R、PEX、PE－RT、PVC－U、铝塑复合管、玻璃钢管等；室外排水管材包括排污水管材和排雨水管材，管材的材质有PVC－U、PP、PE等。

(2)市政建设方面：包括埋地排水管材和燃气管材。埋地排水管材包括排污水管材和排雨水管材，管材的材质有PVC－U、PE、PP实壁和结构壁管，玻璃钢管材。燃气管材主要是城镇燃气管网用管材，材质是 MDPE。

(3)工业用方面：包括电力和通讯用的护套管，工业生产中使用的输送液体、气体和液固混合物体的管道。工业用塑料管道繁多，其材质也较繁杂，主要有 PE、PP、PVC－U、ABS、UHMWPE 和钢塑复合管等。

(4)农业用方面：包括水井、滴灌、微喷灌、渗灌等用管，管材的材质有 PE、PP、PVC－U。

目前，我省塑料管材生产能力一直保持高速增长，品种和规格不断丰富，质量不断提高，并呈现向规模化、系列化方向发展。先后开发出了硬质聚氯乙烯管(PVC－U)、聚乙烯管(PE)、铝塑复合管(PAP)、交联聚乙烯管(PE－X)、共聚聚丙烯管(PP－R、PP－B)、钢塑复合管(SP)、ABS 工程塑料管等。

主要生产企业有哈尔滨市阿城金大管材厂、哈尔滨特种塑料制品有限公司、哈尔滨百富通、大庆铝塑复合管厂、肇东华澳钢建材有限公司、哈尔滨建筑塑料厂、哈尔滨东光直埋保温管厂、齐齐哈尔佳昌塑料制品有限公司、明水塑料厂、哈尔滨市塑料四厂、黑龙江省兴业管材厂、华诚塑料厂、黑龙江成才塑胶改性新材料总厂。

4. 汽车塑料配件制品：东北是我国的汽车工业重地，汽车占全国的1/4，有我国最大的汽车企业一汽集团，此外，还有哈飞、华晨等重量级企业。而一批为其配套的零部件厂商紧紧分布在主企周围，形成集群式布局，使与之配套的汽车零部件企业获得了巨大的市场空间，带动了我省汽车零部件(包括汽车塑料零部件)的飞速发展。

我省生产汽车用塑料制品的企业有几十家，主要集中在哈尔滨平房汽车零部件产业园区及其周围，其中较有规模的只有哈尔滨哈轻塑胶公司、黑龙江齐塑塑料制品有限公司、北安进发塑料制品有限公司等三、四家。其中哈尔滨哈轻塑胶公司、黑龙江齐塑塑料制品有限公司是为哈飞"松花江"、"赛马"、"中意"、"民意"等车型提供配件，主要产品有保险杠、仪表板、内饰件等；北安进发塑料制品有限公司是为一汽"捷达"、"奥迪"、"高尔夫"等提供配件。这些企业除生产汽车用塑料制品以外，还生产其他塑料产品。其中塑料进气歧管以其重量轻、成本低、性能好等特点迅速取代了金属进气歧管，成为新型发动机的首选，生产企业有黑龙江成才塑胶改性新材料总厂。

5. 塑料包装材料：塑料包装方面具备注塑成型、挤出成型、中空成型、吹塑成型、压延成型、发泡成型、流延成型、复合成型等十几种塑料成型工艺。产品有：编织系列产品、吹塑膜袋产品、共挤复合软包装类产品、干式复合软包装和中空容器等包装用塑料制品。主要生产企业有：哈尔滨隆华彩印厂、牡丹江彩印总厂、黑龙包装公司、北大荒包装公司、哈尔滨塑五公司等。

6. 建筑隔热保温材料：黑龙江省是我国最北部的一个省份，属高寒地区，采暖期长达180天，采暖能耗在全国居于前列。近几年来，我省加大了保温节能住宅建设的力度，外墙保温聚苯乙烯发泡板的用量逐年增加，硬质发泡聚氨酯保温技术刚刚开始推广。目前我省模塑聚苯乙烯发泡板(EPS)生产企业约80家左右，产量约5000t(25万立方米)。挤出发泡苯板(XPS)的企业有大庆石化总厂塑料制品厂(年产6万立方米)、大庆绿福建筑材料有限公司(年产8万立方米)等近十家，硬质发泡聚氨脂有哈尔滨天硕建材工业有限公司等。

【存在问题】

1. 发展速度缓慢。近十年来我省已开始加大对塑料工业的投入力度，引进了一些国内外先进的技术和设备，但是行业的总体装备水平仍然偏低、工艺技术相对落后，产品结构不合理，中低档产品偏多；科技投入不足、开发能力薄弱、具有自主知识产权自行研制的塑料制品较少。

2. 二十年来在激烈的市场竞争中，省内一大批国有、集体企业及后来的个体企业纷纷倒闭，失去了当年的繁荣景象。

3. 在改革大潮中，我省也新建立了不少塑料企业，其性质都是股份制和私有制企业，其特点都是规模小，其产品只能立足本省市场，缺少走出去参与全国竞争的实力和勇气，这与我省是经济属于欠发达地区有直接关系，塑料生产企业规模小、资金积累少，上新项目产品缺少资金，大环境吸引外资能力又较差，尤其塑料行业更是如此。

4. 关于产业链问题。塑料作为一种新材料，在国计民生的许多方面都有大量应用。如汽车等现代运输工具、农业、家电、电子产品等方面的应用量都很大。塑料制品在产业链中，为别人所需，是带动不了别人的句号，因而不能带动其它产业。在我省的经济结构中，汽车工业、大家电，甚至小家电、电子工业、包装行业等领域和南方发达地区相比差距较大，因此影响了塑料制品工业的发展。

5. 市场不规范。外省产品严重冲击我省塑料产品市场，如日用塑料制品，几乎已被外省产品所占领。外省产品有的以水货或废旧塑料为原料，有的在质量上打折扣，价格低廉，对我省冲击很大，尤其塑料建材市场混乱。

6. 全省塑料行业处于无序状态，行业协会管理近乎瘫痪，对于规范企业行为，加强行业管理等无能为力。

【发展趋势及建议】

我省塑料行业也面临更多发展机遇，随着国家西部大开发战略实施，我省经济增长将会长期保持较高水平，加上即将实施的农村土地流转所带来的小城镇化建设，拉动我省城镇基础建设、农业水利、环境保护等领域的投资增长，为我省塑料工业的发展提供了巨大市场空间。鉴于目前我省塑料工业总体处于国内下游水平，加上运输成本、地理劣势等限制条件，未来我省塑料行业发展应立足本省及周边省份市场需求，突出市场导向作用，产品开发应以具有较好市场前景、附加值高的产品为主，形成多品种、小批量、高附加值的多元化的发展模式，避免激烈竞争，同时也要重视新产品应用市场开发，逐步扩展应用领域。发挥我省大庆石化聚烯烃等树脂产品和我省城镇建设及全国粮食基地等方面优势，重点发展农用塑料、塑料建材、塑料包装材料及大型塑料容器、绿色可降解塑料等大类产品，同时希望政府着力治理白色污染，健全塑料回收体系建设，提高废塑料资源利用水平，促进我省塑料回收产业全面升级；大力扶持业内知名企业进行资源整合，向集约化、规模化、名牌化发展，增强抗风险能力，推动我省塑料工业健康可持续发展。

（黑龙江省塑料制品行业协会　邹　奇；黑龙江省塑料研究所　姜振生）

上　海　市

【大事记】

2月1日，上海塑料行业协会秘书长刘建国出席由上海普利特复合材料股份有限公司承担的上海市重点技术改造项目“年产5万吨汽车用高性能低气味低散发聚丙烯技术改造”项目验收会议，充分肯定了该技术改造项目的创新性和带来的经济效益、社会效益，并代表全体验收小组成员在一致通过的“验收小组意见”上签字。

2月16日下午，在电信世界第五会议室由上海投资咨询公司组织召开对上海晓宝增强塑料有限公司落地长兴岛项目可行性研究报告专家评估会议。上海塑料行业协会副秘书长钮贤圭应邀出席本次专家评估会议。

2月29日下午，2011年度上海市“企业诚信创建”活动总结表彰会议暨上海市企业诚信建设宣传教育活动启动仪式在华亭宾馆二楼宴会厅举办。大会向获得2011年度上海市“企业诚信创建”活动优秀组织单位和个人颁奖。会上，“上海市企业诚信建设宣传教育活动”正式启动。上海塑协秘书长刘建国、信息部副主任李思倩同全市近200家行业协会领导、各委办局主要领导、各区县文明办主要领导逾300人出席会议。协会行业诚信创建网络管理平台建设人员李思倩被授予“优秀行业诚信平台管理奖”。

3月9日下午，“上海塑料行业协会企业诚信创建工作培训暨表彰会议”在新华社区青年中心三楼会议室召开，此次培训会吸引了行业内众多企业的积极参与。会上，上海塑协秘书长刘建国对于上一年度获得各级别诚信创建企业荣誉的企业授予了荣誉证书，并进行表彰。

3月13日下午，在上海保健品行业协会会议室召开了市工经联党委第四联合党支部和上海塑料行业协会党支部联合活动。会上大家分别交流了各自协会的情况，并一致认为通过“结对”形式密切双方党支部间的交流，促进双方党支部党建工作，“创先争优”活动的开展也会推进兄弟行业协会间的交流与合作。

3月15日下午，在上海古象大酒店三楼古象厅，雅式展览服务有限公司举行了“「CHINAPLAS2012国际橡塑展」‘未来概念展示区’新闻发布会”。上海塑协副会长刘景芬、秘书长刘建国及受主办方委托上海塑协邀请的上海市汽车行业协会、上海电器行业协会、上海仪器仪表行业协会、上海橡胶工业同业公会等协会领导、各方媒体记者出席了本次新闻发布会。

3月29日上午，由副会长兼支部书记刘景芬带队，协会一行四人去浦东七灶拜访了业内单位——上海舜川塑胶新材料有限公司；下午，由陈铭会长带队，协会一行五人前往金山分别拜访了新会员单位——上海海湾石化有限公司、上海晟海塑业有限公司，均受到公司领导的热情接待，双方就协会职能、工作开展，公司情况、经营发展等进行了很好的沟通。

由雅式展览服务有限公司主办，中国轻工业联合会－中国塑料加工工业协会、中国塑料机械工业协会、杜塞尔多夫(中国)有限公司、上海塑料行业协会、上海外经贸商务展览公司、北京雅展展览服务有限公司共同协办的世界第二、亚洲第一的国际塑料橡胶展——“第二十六届中国国际塑料橡胶工业展览会(「Chinaplas2012」)”于2012年4月18～21日在上海新国际博览中心盛大举行。

4月18日下午，在「Chinaplas2012国际橡塑展」隆重举行的同期，由雅式展览服务有限公司、深圳市塑胶行业协会、上海塑料行业协会和低碳生物材料产学研创新联盟联合主办的"第四届中国国际生物塑料应用研讨会"在上海新国际博览中心M17号会议室举办。雅式展览服务有限公司梁雅琪副总经理、深圳市塑胶行业协会刘绍然会长、王文广秘书长、上海塑料行业协会刘建国秘书长等出席会议并致辞。

由深圳市塑胶行业协会、上海塑料行业协会、上海三承高分子材料科技有限公司、深圳市沃特新材料股份有限公司、雅式展览服务有限公司联合主办，阿科玛(中国)投资有限公司、卡博特(中国)投资有限公司等协办的「CHINAPLAS 2012国际橡塑展」同期研讨会—《2012高分子导电－抗静电第二届国际研讨会》4月20～21日在「CHINAPLAS 2012国际橡塑展」展会M17会议室成功举行。

上海市工商业联合会(商会)第十三次会员代表大会于5月6日至7日在上海展览中心举行，全国政协副主席、全国工商联主席黄孟复，中共上海市委副书记殷一璀分别代表全国工商联与中共上海市委出席会议并讲话。大会通过无记名投票的方式选举产生了上海市第十三届执行委员会，选举产生王志雄为上海市工商联(商会)第十三届执行委员会主席(会长)的新一届领导班子。上海塑料行业协会/上海市工商联塑料行业商会应邀出席大会。上海塑协/商会副会长单位上海日之升技术发展有限公司陈晓东总经理、上海普利特复合材料股份有限公司周文董事长、理事单位上海杰事杰新材料(集团)股份有限公司杨桂生董事长、会员单位上海亚虹塑料模具制造有限公司谢亚明董事长当选为上海市工商业联合会(商会)第十三届执行委员会委员。

5月27日，在广东东莞常平，中国塑料加工工业协会举行了全国塑料行业协会峰会。上海塑协会长陈铭、副会长刘景芬与全国31家行业协会10余家专业委员会、业内龙头企业的领导出席了大会。上海塑协陈铭会长代表上海塑料行业协会围绕协会工作进行了大会交流发言。

5月31日下午，由上海塑料行业协会、上海市国际展览有限公司联合举办的《模具与塑料制品行业技术、装备对接会》在上海新国际博览中心E6馆M34会议室召开。会议由上海塑料行业协会秘书长刘建国主持，协会会长陈铭到会并致辞。协会组织了近50家会员单位及业内相关企业参加会议，并组织、偕同了7家会员单位/业内企业参加了「第十四届中国国际模具技术和设备展览会」用户专区的展示。

5月31日~6月1日，上海塑协副会长刘景芬、副秘书长钮贤圭和信息部主任杨忠民赴京出席了《"创新、发展、责任、影响力"赛日科技、慧聪网2011年度第六届塑料行业十佳颁奖典礼》；同期，出席了由中国合成树脂协会秘书长郑垲主持的《汽车及家电行业塑料应用创新发展研讨会》。

6月14日，在上海塑料行业协会驻所会议室召开了上海塑料行业专业技术人员2012年度技术职称评审申报工作专题会议。协会副会长、上海塑料行业专业技术人员职称资格认证工作委员会主任刘景芬就近三年上海塑料行业协会组织开展上海塑料行业专业技术人员技术职称评审工作情况作了总体回顾；协会副秘书长钮贤圭宣讲上海塑料行业专业技术人员职称资格认证办法、申报表的填写要求、今年职称申报工作的概况及具体的工作流程和时间安排；上海塑料行业专业技术人员职称评审专家委员会主任杨忠民就如何撰写技术总结、个人业绩报告和专业技术论文向与会人员作了具体讲解；与会人员和协会方面就此项工作的一些具体细节进行了热烈的质、答询互动。

6月18日，在上海塑协驻所会议室召开了协会秘书处与各专委会秘书长联席会议。陈铭会长、刘景芬副会长到会。改性塑料/工程塑料专委会秘书长孟庆国、PVC制品专委会秘书长钮贤圭、塑料包装专委会秘书长翁维志和上海塑协秘书处全体人员参加会议。

6月19日，协会党支部在"七一"前夕，进行革命传统教育。协会全体党员、秘书处工作人员走进了"浙东小延安"——梁弄。教育活动使大家倍受鼓舞，进一步激发了工作热情，在工作中把延安精神与学习贯彻落实科学发展观紧密结合起来，不断创新，确保在实践中取得实效。

6月28日下午，在市政协文化俱乐部四楼礼堂，中共上海市工业经济联合会委员会召开了"纪念建党91周年暨创先争优表彰大会"。会上，上海塑协党支部被授予"2012年市工经联党委系统创先争优先进党支部"，秘书长刘建国被授予"2012年市工经联党委系统创先争优优秀党员"。

6月29日，上海塑协陈铭会长携刘建国秘书长、钮贤圭副秘书长和杨忠民主任一行四人前往副会长单位——上海新上化高分子材料有限公司拜访，受到该公司总经理、上海塑协副会长徐永卫的热情接待。

7月12日，上海塑料行业协会节能减排新技术现场交流会在上海金浦塑料包装有限公司会议厅召开。上海塑协陈铭会长、刘景芬副会长亲临会议，连同到会的相关会员单位共计30人出席会议。会议的出发点是“创新驱动转型发展”，以节能减排措施和手段，帮助企业可持续发展，并吸引企业技术人员多关注企业自身的技术改造，以提高企业竞争力。

8月21日，在上海塑协理事单位—上海英科实业有限公司会议室召开了该公司承担的上海市特色产业项目——“高分子仿木框条技术改造项目”验收专家评审会。验收小组组长宣布该项目圆满完成，同意验收。上海塑协副会长刘景芬应邀担任项目验收组专家。

8月23日，2012年上海塑料行业技术职称专家评审委员会会议在上海塑协会议室召开。会上，上海塑协副会长、上海塑料行业专业技术职称资格认证工作委员会主任刘景芬对2012年上海塑料行业协会开展业内技术职称申报工作情况作介绍；协会秘书长刘建国代表认证工作委员会作上海塑料行业初、中级职称预审工作情况汇报，并完成了相应评审工作；职称评审专家委员会主任杨忠民就2012年高级职称各申报人员的主审论文和业绩报告、个人总体情况、申报资格审查等作介绍，与会专家按照评审办法、评审的各项标准和程序进行了严格审定；上海塑协会长陈铭到会，并对协会开展此项工作提出了更高的要求。

8月28~31日，在上海市浦东新区惠南镇衡山度假村，上海市民政局、上海市社会团体管理局主办，上海人才服务行业协会承办的“上海市社会组织高级管理人员(CEO班)培训”如期举办。上海塑协会长陈铭、副会长刘景芬、秘书长刘建国与全市近200家兄弟行业协会、商会会长/副会长/秘书长等同仁参加。

9月4日，为对上海汇宇精细化工有限公司申请认定其“lesutan”商标为上海市著名商标提出负责任的征询意见，上海塑协副会长刘景芬、副秘书长钮贤圭和信息部主任杨忠民三人去该公司拜访考察，受到该公司技术部经理沈美云的热情接待。

9月5日上午，上海塑协秘书长刘建国、副秘书长钮贤圭、信息部副主任李思倩一行三人前往位于嘉定区的业内企业—上海嘉倍德塑胶机械有限公司，针对该公司申请认定其“嘉倍德”商标为“上海市著名商标”出具协会征询意见进行现场调访，受到公司副总经理陈华斌、总经理助理黄新平的热情接待。

9月6日，为对上海永超真空镀铝有限公司申请认定其“永超”、“RADIX”商标为上海市著名商标提出负责任的征询意见，上海塑协副会长刘景芬、副秘书长钮贤圭和信息部主任杨忠民三人去该公司拜访考察，受到该公司董事长洪晓冬、总经理江谷和董事长助理曹梅的热情接待。

9月19日下午，2012年度上海塑料行业名优品牌专家评审会议在上海塑协驻地会议室召开。协会副会长、上海塑料行业名优品牌评选工作组组长刘景芬在会上作《上海塑料行业名优品牌评选工作组2012年度工作报告》；上海塑料行业名优品牌专家评审组组长杨忠民依据工作组的初审结果提请与会专家组成员通过了2012年度申报重新认定为上海塑料行业名优品牌企业的申请，以及对其中八家企业的“上海塑料行业名优品牌企业”的命名，并依次重点介绍申请新认定为2012年度上海塑料行业名优品牌的企业情况；依据评选程序和评审标准，到会专家依次予以打分评估。

9月22~25日，「第12届中国塑料交易会」在浙江台州市国际会展中心隆重举行。上海塑协作为支持单位，副会长刘景芬、秘书长刘建国带队，协会秘书处及协会所属PVC制品专业委员会、塑料包装专业委员会的秘书长一同前往参加「第12届中国塑料交易会」开幕式、参观展会，并与参展的会员单位、业内企业及参会的全国各地协会和业界同仁进行了沟通与交流。

10月10~11日，上海塑协假座苏州国嘉高分子科技有限公司会议室召开了2012上海塑料行业协会工作会议。陈铭会长、刘景芬副会长以及协会秘书处全体人员出席会议。秘书处人员对协会工作畅所欲言、各抒己见，提出了许多有益的意见和建议。

10月19日下午，为加强长三角地区同业协会之间的交流，上海塑协秘书长刘建国、副秘书长钮贤圭会应邀出席了在苏州市万隆汽车零部件股份有限公司三楼会议室举行的苏州市塑胶化工行业协会二届四次理事(扩大)会议暨苏州市塑胶化工行业协会与上海市塑料行业协会的合作签约仪式。

11月1日下午，由上海市金山区经济委员会组织对上海海湾石化有限公司申报的国家重点产业振兴和技术改造项目竣工专家验收会议在金山宾馆举行。与会专家认为该项目已完成了预期的目标，一致同意验收。上海塑料行业协会副秘书长钮贤圭参加了评审会议。

11月8日下午，上海塑料行业协会/上海市工商联塑料行业商会五届二次会员大会暨理事会在上海龙门和一大酒店三楼多功能会议厅举行。会上，对荣获2012年度上海塑料行业名优品牌(或企业)的单位及2012年度上海市诚信企业颁发了铭牌和证书，并进行了行业名优品牌、职称资格评定、诚信创建企业代表交流发言。

11月20日上午，由雅式展览服务有限公司主办、上海塑料行业协会协办的“「2013 CHINAPLAS 国际橡塑展」上海推介会”在上海古象大酒店三楼宴会厅举行。雅式展览服务有限公司董事长朱裕伦先生携公司高管；上海塑料行业协会；19家上海市塑料用家和相关行业协会；以及由上海塑协和有关协会推荐的业内10余家终端产品生产企业的老总或代表；华东六省一市及二级市的同业协会领导等100余人出席会议。

11月20日下午，在上海古象大酒店召开了华东六省一市(含台州市)塑料行业协会会长、秘书长工作会议。雅式展览服务有限公司董事长朱裕伦先生携雅式高管亲临会议。上海塑料行业协会副会长刘景芬、副秘书长钮贤圭，华东六省一市塑协领导出席会议。

上海塑协与上海市化学建材行业协会、苏州国嘉高分子科技有限公司经过精心筹备，于11月24日在江苏吴江湖之景大酒店会议室，举办了“特种炭黑母粒在聚乙烯压力管及工程塑料中的应用研讨会”。协会会长陈铭、副会长刘景芬、秘书长刘建国，及会员单位上海普利特复合材料股份有限公司、上海俊尔新材料有限公司、上海日之升新技术发展有限公司、上海锦湖日丽塑料有限公司，中国化工报、慧聪塑料网社会媒体等40余人参加了会议。

12月6日下午，在上海麦特密封件有限公司会议室，受上海市经济和信息化委员会委托，奉贤区经济委员会主持召开了上海市高新技术产业化重点项目——上海麦特密封件有限公司承担的“聚氨酯切削密封件”验收会议。上海塑协副会长、高工刘景芬应邀担当验收会专家。

12月7日下午，在上海金发科技发展有限公司会议室，受上海市经济和信息化委员会委托，青浦区经济委员会主持召开了由上海金发科技发展有限公司承担的上海市高新技术产业化重点项目“5万吨汽车用环境友好型改性塑料产业化”验收会。上海塑协副会长、高工刘景芬应邀担任验收会专家。

12月21日，原秘书长刘建国因个人原因向会长提出辞呈。经会长单位推荐，协会书面征询各理事单位意见，一致同意会长聘任秦建旺同志为上海塑协秘书长。

【基本情况】

2012年，上海塑料工业与全国同行业一样，经历了国内外经济下行带来的巨大挑战，经受了激烈的市场竞争带来的严峻考验。在迎接党的十八大召开和学习贯彻党的十八大精神的过程中，上海塑料行业在上海市委、市府提出的“创新驱动转型发展”指引下，推动技术进步、产品结构调整、节能减排、绿色环保，整个行业取得较好的业绩。具体情况如下：

表1　2012年上海塑料制品业主要经济指标(规模以上工业企业)　　亿元

制造行业名称	塑料薄膜	塑料板/管/型材	塑料丝/绳及编织品	泡沫塑料	塑料人造革/合成革	塑料包装箱及容器	日用塑料制品制造	塑料零件制造	其他塑料制品制造	合计
单位数	80	82	26	50	7	89	46	88	144	612
主营业务收入	83.08	89.85	15.60	41.94	10.32	88.69	84.60	117.65	146.48	678.2
同比增减/%	−8.4	−1.2	−3.0	−6.4	14.4	−2.2	8.3	−15.7	7.5	−2.6
出口交货值	15.59	5.76	2.90	3.49	2.21	13.96	18.70	61.38	31.50	155.5
同比增减/%	−7.3	−13.4	−20.9	−6.7	47.5	−2.7	−6.2	−19.9	8.9	−9.7
工业总产值	82.02	81.87	14.71	42.83	10.76	91.61	84.51	117.03	145.30	670.6
同比增减/%	−8.8	−2.9	−6.9	−4.8	24.0	0.5	6.8	−13.4	8.4	−1.9
利润总额	3.175	4.270	0.706	3.014	1.141	3.997	11.141	2.782	4.350	34.576
增减额	−1.886	0.182	0.345	0.282	0.063	−1.035	1.717	−6.636	−0.836	−4.804
应收账款净额	17.58	17.62	3.00	10.56	1.15	25.91	11.70	24.82	35.04	147.4
同比增减/%	18.0	7.9	15.3	−5.5	32.6	54.8	8.3	−18.3	14.0	9.6
产成品存货	4.36	7.30	0.63	1.58	1.12	3.38	2.92	7.65	9.21	38.1
同比增减/%	−2.1	2.7	−43.3	−7.6	33.1	−32.3	−8.4	11.1	19.7	0.4

表2 上海塑料制造业主要经济指标

产品名称	产量/t	比去年同期/±%	占全国同类产品比例/%
初级形态的塑料	3151808	-3.76	6.05
聚氯乙烯树脂	227911	-29.11	1.73
聚苯乙烯树脂	305770	18.45	11.55
聚酯	1307830	-5.39	11.47
塑料加工专用设备	34233(台)	13.19	11.28

【企业经营】

2012年上海塑料行业、塑料原料生产方面，聚乙烯树脂由于市场原因全年产量仅227911t，比去年同期下降29.11%，占全国比中1.73%；聚苯乙烯树脂产量为305770t，比去年同期增加18.45%，占全国同类产品比例14.6%；聚酯产量1307830t，比去年同期下降5.4%，占全国同类产品比重为11.5%；塑料加工专用设备34233台，比去年同期增加13.2%，占全国同类产品比例11.3%；塑料制品产量为1847549t，比去年同期下降2.3%，占全国同类产品比例为3.2%。

第一、塑料新材料企业发展快

上海工程塑料、改性塑料、高分子新材料发展比较快，其中代表性的企业有：上海普利特复合材料股份有限公司、上海日之升新技术发展有限公司、上海俊尔新材料有限公司、上海新上化高分子材料有限公司均是上海塑协副会长单位。这些企业经营情况，见表：

单位名称	2012年销售额/与2011年比	2012年产量/与2011年比	实现利润/与2011年比
上海普利特复合材料股份有限公司	12亿元/+30%	70kt/+20%	1.45亿元/+60%
上海日之升新技术发展有限公司	18356.6万元/+14.8%	11637t/+25.7%	3235.7万元/+74.55%
上海俊尔新材料有限公司	1.2亿元/+53%	7500t/+25%	630万元/2011年：110万元
上海新上化高分子材料有限公司	31407万元/-9.2%	28175t/与去年同期持平	300万元/+5.3%

第二、塑料制品中为汽车配套的企业总体情况良好

随着汽车产业的发展，汽车轻量化，用非金属即工程塑料、改性塑料替代，带动了本市塑料制品企业中为汽车配套的企业，即汽车塑料零部件制造业发展。华德塑料制品有限公司2012年工业产值达6.5亿元，同比增长4.8%；××汽车饰件有限公司(公司要求保密)2012年工业产值为418.4亿元，同比增长8.5%，实现利润33.4亿元，比2011年同比增长8.1%。

第三、塑料托盘企业发展较快

随着物流业的发展，近年来塑料托盘发展很快，全国产量前三位的塑料托盘制造企业均在上海，例如：上海力卡塑料托盘制造有限公司，2012年产量为1637kt，主营业务收入为78500万元，产销率为98%，净利润为3194万元，产品出口欧洲(德国、西班牙)、亚洲(马来西亚、日本等)

第四、高分子聚合物改性产品发展势头喜人

上海三承高分子材料科技有限公司是集研发、生产和经营于一体的高分子聚合物改性材料产品的专业公司。作为新材料-高分子聚合物改性产品的专业公司，产品广泛供应国内外的环保产业、IT行业、电子电器、农业科技、日用卫生用品、汽车塑料合金和特种电缆电线等的行业市场。目前产品市场范围包括江、浙、沪、粤、闽、冀、京、津、辽、鲁等经济发达地区和部分出口北美，欧盟，东南亚和日本，至2012年度，公司已具备10000t/a的产能规模和产品研发和测试中心。其销售额可达1.2亿元(人民币)。

至2012年度，在公司现有的产品结构中，具有21世纪初期国际先进水平和国内领先水平产品的销售额已经占到年度销售总额的89.70%。其中主要产品系列是：

·数码广告纸基涂覆材料，医疗，卫生，食品用材料产品占年度销售总额的41.8%；

·多功能(阻燃-导电-高强度)特种管道材料占年度销售总额的25.5%；

·高性能聚烯烃抗静电粒料系列产品占年度销售总额的10.2%；

·特种电线、电缆材料系列产品占年度销售总额的14.2%；

公司其它产品(包括新开发和试销产品)占年度

销售总额10.3%。

2012年度具有国际先进和国内领先技术水平的产品市场销售比例的份额占到了公司全年产品销售额的绝大部分。主要科技产品：低热值环保聚烯烃填充产品系列；高性能聚烯烃抗导电－抗静电粒料产品系列；农用多功能母粒系列产品；特种电线、电缆材料系列产品。

【重点企业】

序　号	单位名称	主要产品
1	中石化上海高桥分公司	合成树脂
2	上海天原集团胜德塑料有限公司	塑料制品
3	上海心尔新材料科技股份有限公司	新材料、助剂
4	上海尼邦高分子材料有限公司	塑料新材料
5	上海双树塑料厂	酚醛塑料
6	中石化上海石化股份有限公司塑料部	聚乙烯、聚丙烯
7	上海爱平塑胶有限公司	PVC功能膜、血袋膜、尿袋
8	上海英科实业有限公司	塑料镜框、家装材料
9	上海欧亚合成材料有限公司	热固性塑料
10	上海安诺塑胶制品有限公司	PP－R给水管、UPVC排水管
11	上海金山星星塑料有限公司	塑料包装袋
12	上海仪表塑料件有限公司	精密塑料件
13	上海华谊聚合物有限公司	ABS
14	上海南翼包装有限公司	吨装包装袋
15	维卡塑料(上海)有限公司	PVC门窗
16	上海派瑞特塑业有限公司	塑料托盘、周转箱
17	上海杰事杰新材料有限公司	工程塑料、改性塑料
18	华德塑料制品有限公司	车用塑料制品
19	延锋伟世通汽车饰件系统有限公司	轿车方向盘、仪表盘、座椅总成
20	上海上塑控股(集团)有限公司	塑料管道
21	中石化化工销售华东分公司树脂部	塑料树脂销售
22	上海爱思塑料制品有限公司	为箱包配套塑料件
23	上海日之升新技术发展有限公司	工程塑料、改性塑料
24	上海中山市场经营管理有限公司	塑料树脂销售
25	上海海外化工有限公司	塑料材料
26	上海氯威塑料有限公司	PVC塑料制品
27	上海普利特复合材料股份有限公司	工程塑料、改性塑料
28	上海永超真空镀铝有限公司	镀铝塑料膜
29	上海国嘉塑化有限公司	黑色母料
30	上海白蝶管业科技股份有限公司	塑料管道
31	上海至正道化高分子材料有限公司	塑料新材料
32	上海金菲石油化工有限公司	中空级、管道级HDPE、聚乙烯
33	上海申德精密注塑有限公司	精密塑料件
34	上海海湾石化有限公司	重包装膜、袋

续表

序　号	单位名称	主要产品
35	上海金浦塑料包装材料有限公司	BOPP 双向拉伸膜
36	上海力卡塑料托盘制造有限公司	塑料托盘
37	上海塑料制品公司	塑料制品
38	上海海棠头盔厂	安全帽
39	上海紫日包装有限公司	塑料防盗瓶盖
40	上海长伟锦磁工程塑料有限公司	塑料新材料
41	上海华伟塑胶有限公司	尼龙扎带
42	上海欣禾包装有限公司	塑料包装制品
43	上海宝山迦南塑料厂	PVC 制品
44	上海新上化高分子材料有限公司	塑料新材料
45	上海俊尔新材料有限公司	改性塑料
46	雅式展览服务有限公司	承办展览、展示
47	上海三承高分子材料科技有限公司	高分子聚合物改性材料
48	上海达凯塑胶有限公司	复合塑料材料
49	上海人民塑料印刷厂	塑料印刷包装材料
50	美利肯商贸(上海)有限公司	塑料助剂
51	上海金昌工程塑料有限公司	工程塑料、改性塑料
52	上海天马精塑有限公司	精密塑料件(日用)
53	上海晓宝增强塑料有限公司	电缆加强芯

【塑料制品进出口】

1. 上海石化成功开发出低二甘醇含量的工业丝专用聚酯切片外销土耳其1160t。

2. 上海华德塑料制品有限公司塑料制品出口主要是：美国、北美 GM 公司，销售人民币 6500 万元，总体情况良好，稳中有升。

3. 上海力卡塑料托盘制造有限公司 2012 年出口额 614 万美元，产品出口主要销售在欧洲(德国、西班牙等)、亚洲(马来西亚、日本等)。

4. ×××汽车饰件系统有限公司——中国汽车零部件百强企业排名第四位，在中国汽配行业 10 大知名品牌中列第二。2012 年出口 28 亿，相比 2011 年呈增长趋势。主要出口产品：汽车座椅、电子、仪表板、门板内饰产品。

5. 上海三承高分子材料科技有限公司产品广泛供应国内外的环保产业、IT 行业、电子电器、农业科技、日用卫生产品、汽车塑料合金和特种电缆电线等行业市场。其中部分产品出口美国、欧盟、东南亚和日本等。

【新产品开发】

1. 上海普利特复合材料股份有限公司承担的上海市重点技术改造项目“年产 50kt 汽车用高性能低气味低散发聚丙烯改造”项目于 2012 年 2 月 1 日召开的验收会议上顺利通过验收。

2. 2 月 16 日，由上海投资咨询公司组织召开对上海晓宝增强塑料有限公司落地长兴岛项目可行性研究报告通过专家评估。

3. 8 月 21 日，上海英科实业有限公司承担的上海市特色产业项目——“高分子仿木框条技术改造”项目通过专家评审同意验收。

4. 11 月 1 日，上海海湾石化有限公司申报的国家重点产业振兴和技术改造项目“年产 1200t 多层共挤 FFS 重包装膜技术改造”项目通过验收。

5. 12 月 6 日，上海麦特密封件有限公司承担的上海高新技术产业化重点项目“聚氨酯切削密封件”通过评审验收。

6. 12 月 7 日，上海金发科技发展有限公司承担的上海市高新技术产业化重点项目“5 万吨汽车用环境友好型改性塑料产业化”项目经过专家评审验收。

7. 中石化上海石化塑料事业部首产医用聚乙烯专用料，经上海食品药品包装材料测试报告，符合国家食品药品监督管理局颁布的国家药品包装容器材料标准。这标志着国内首款可安全使用与医疗器具和食品包装的聚乙烯树脂产品在上海石化诞生并可以实现工业化生产。

8. 中石化上海石化成功开发出适用性广泛的NEP型聚酯，继完成1000t/a中试试验，成功推广应用于10kt/a生产线，顺利投产放到150kt/a生产装置，实现了工业化稳定生产。

9. 上海金浦包装材料有限公司首制成功国内最薄的镀铝基膜。国内最薄的BOPP薄膜(双向拉伸聚丙烯薄膜—8μm镀铝基膜)具有良好的牢度及极佳的金属光泽、优异的发射性、阻气性、阻湿性、遮光性、保香性和导电性，能够消除静电反应，保持稳定的尺寸和复合性能。

10. 上海日之升新技术发展有限公司在新产品研发方面重点是在环境友好型功能高分子改性材料，主要类别有PP、PA、相容剂。新产品对该公司的净利润增长贡献度达到50%以上，仅2012年该公司申请发明专利80项，获授权的发明专利14项，并被上海市6部委评为“上海市知识产权优秀企业”。

【市场需求】

2012年，上海塑料制品主要产品“塑料薄膜制造，塑料板、管、型材制造，塑料丝、绳及编织品制造，泡沫塑料制造，塑料人造革、合成革制造，塑料包装箱及容器制造，塑料零部件制造，塑料托盘制造及其他塑料制品制造等。

其中，塑料托盘全国制造此产品的前三大户均在上海，不仅满足上海、全国乃至出口。塑料在汽车方面的应用随着汽车为了节能减排减少自重，塑、料件代替金属件发展很快。上海塑料制造业中，为汽车配套的塑料制品企业随着汽车行业的发展也得到了相应的发展。

他们对塑料原料的需求：通用料主要来源于上海石化、高化公司，上海华谊集团下属的上海氯碱化工股份有限公司、上海聚合物有限公司，上海金菲石油化工有限公司、上海赛科石油化工有限责任公司等。

工程塑料改性塑料主要由以下企业制造供应：上海普利特复合材料股份有限公司、上海日之升新技术发展有限公司、上海锦湖日丽塑料有限公司、上海金昌工程塑料有限公司、上海杰事杰新材料股份有限公司、华东理工大学华昌聚合物有限公司、上海欧亚合成材料有限公司、上海俊尔新材料有限公司、上海尼邦高分子材料有限公司、上海长伟锦磁工程塑料有限公司等。

【存在问题】

1. 产品结构需调整

尽管企业自主创新的意识在不断提升，但自主开发的能力仍然不足，产品结构的调整仍要继续向技术含量、产品经济附加值高的方向发展。

2. 经济效益下降

在原油价格持续振荡的大环境下，塑料加工业已经进入了“高成本时代”。当前中小企业普遍面临一个尴尬环境：产销两旺，利润下降，生产成本全面提高(原材料价格、人工成本等)。

3. 节能减排仍有潜力

为了降低企业生产成本，为了推进低碳循环经济，企业在节能减排方面、在加强内部管理等方面仍有潜力可挖。

4. 制品出口受阻、订单减少

出口市场低迷的局面，受世界经济部景气及人民币升值等影响，一些塑料制品企业由于订单减少，出口企业没有满负荷生产，或在开发国内的市场。

5. PVC生产处于亏损状态

氯碱企业因受液氯出路的困扰，装置开工率始终维持在较低水平。聚氯乙烯受原料乙烯价格上涨拉动，有成本助推价格上升的内在要求，但受制于电石法聚乙烯价格影响，难有良好表现。下游行业受房地产调控影响需求萎缩，使PVC企业受到影响，PVC生产处于亏损状态。PVC产品价格长期徘徊在历史地位。

【发展趋势】

随着全球经济的高速发展和一体化进程的加速，以及资源、能源和环境问题受到世界各国越来越多的关注，近年来，上海由于受到土地、人工等商务成本的不断增长，塑料产品在产业结构调整方面向技术含量高、技术附加值高的方面倾斜。总体上海塑料业发展趋势概况如下：

1. 塑料新材料发展引起各方高度重视

随着科学技术的进步和新兴产业快速发展，对塑料新材料需求的种类和数量大大增加，以塑料新材料、工程塑料改性的新兴产业，如汽车、计算机、家电、通讯等对塑料新材料的种类和数量需求也将进一步扩大。

塑料新材料随着高新技术的发展，使得塑料新材料与信息能源、交通、建筑等产业结合越来越密切，而激烈的市场竞争、优胜劣汰的自然规则、经济效益的强烈驱动，又使得塑料新材料产业不断的整合和重组，大量的研发投入、产业技术及市场标准制定并控制知识产权，产业蓬勃发展期指日可待。

在塑料新材料的研究中，更加注重资源的高效和重复利用，更加注重环保，使塑料新材料的发展有效地纳入到循环经济的模式，同时更加大力开发清洁生产新工艺、大力发展新型的节能减排工程应用材料。

2. 塑料制品企业应注重调整产品结构

塑料制品企业应根据市场需求调整产品结构，提高产品质量与档次，提高产品的技术含量和经济附加值，着力推进产业转型升级，改造提升优势产业，引导企业加强技术改造与技术开发、技术引进与消化吸收再创新结合，大力推进企业自主创新能力。

3. 推进节能减排工作和循环经济

引导企业对节能技术和技术改造的投入，推广节能技术、推进节能技术、工艺，实施节能重点工程，开展清洁生产、创建绿色企业和节能企业的典型。倡导企业科学用能、合理用能、节约用能的良好氛围。全国推行清洁生产、推进循环经济。

上海塑料行业将继续按照上海市委、市府提出的“创新驱动转型发展”；坚持“服务企业、规范行业、发展产业”的总要求，积极推进上海塑料产业新一轮发展。

（上海塑料行业协会　刘景芬）

重　庆　市

【发展方向】

重庆直辖以后，西部大开发给重庆塑料工业带来了新的发展机遇。以塑料加工与应用为核心。整体产业蓬勃发展，令人瞩目。企业为适应市场经济的需求。进行了调整、招商引资、转换经营机制。吸收了一系列改革措施政策，加快了改革的步伐。一批外资、合资、民营等不同所有制性质的企业迅猛崛起，蓬勃发展。规模以上的企业数量增长迅速。产业结构向规模化集约化方向发展。一批大中型企业经济增长迅速。去年，塑料工业产值已超过300多亿。

“十二五”期间，塑料工业年均增长26%左右，塑料制品达到300余万吨。

1. 发展思路：抓住重庆工业迅猛发展、工程建设突飞猛进、农业现代化建设稳步推进的机遇，建立以企业为主体的产、学、研相结合的技术创新体系，推动塑料制品工业向“多功能、复合型、环保型、高科技”方向发展，实现塑料制品工业的快速发展。

2. 发展重点：大力发展塑料建材(塑料管材、板材、型材)、工业配件及工程塑料、日用塑料、塑料包装和容器类，研究开发废旧塑料再生利用技术、提高循环经济再利用、研究开发降解塑料制品的推广应用，提高产品质量，抓好节能减排。

3. 西部大开发战略：西部大开发战略实施10周年之际，党中央、国务院召开了西部大开发工作会议，指出下一个十年西部大开发的总体目标是“上三个大台阶”，即今后十年要通过努力使西部地区的经济综合实力上一个大台阶，使人民群众的生活水平和质量上一个大台阶、使西部地区的生态环境上一个大台阶。初步规划到2015年西部地区经济生产总值比2008年翻一番，今后几年西部地区经济年均增长达10%以上；“十二五”期间，中央将在重大基础建设项目上继续向西部地区倾斜，在转移支持和投资安排上也将继续向西部地区倾斜。国家计划西部大开发新开工23项重点工程，投资总规模为6822亿元。23个新开发项目主要是基础设施建设，无疑将为包括塑料行业在内的相关行业带来新的投资机遇。

4. 两江新区战略：重庆两江新区作为我国第三个国家级新区，于2010年6月正式获国务院批准成立，体现了中国开发战略从沿海到内陆、从东到西的战略大转移。两江新区将构成增长极内核、带动区域协同发展。1200km^2 的两江新区，力争促进“西三角”(重庆—成都—西安)乃至680万 km^2，3亿多人口的西部开放开发。“西三角”物质丰富，人口众多。据测算：两江新区将拉动“成渝经济带”制造业年均增长提高10个百分点，云南和贵州能源产业增速提高5个百分点。湖南、湖北、陕西、广西制造业和交通运输业增速提高5个百分点。设立重庆两江新区，有利于探索内陆地区开发开放新模式，对于推动西部大开发，促进区域协调发展具有重要意义，两江新区成为国家推进新十年西部大开发的突破口和新引擎。

5. 城乡统筹战略：“十二五”期间，随着重庆城市化进程的持续推进，城市建设和改造规模的不断扩大，建筑及房地产产业的发展，将为塑料产品提供巨大的需求市场。

6. 中心城市战略：继国务院3号文件后，又一重要规划将重庆发展提升到国家战略。在城乡统筹建设部编制的《全国城镇体系规划》中，重庆与北京、天津、上海、广州，被确定为国家五大中心城市，这对重庆经济和社会发展具有重大意义。作为国家中心城市，重庆在区域经济发展中肩负着五个方面的使命：“突出的区域辐射功能，在中国西部乃至中国的物流、交通和人流门户与枢纽；肩负着更重要的产业职能和经济职能；成为国际改革开放的重要试验区。"未来10年，重庆将建成在全国具备引领、辐射、集散功能的中心城市之一。

7. 按照重庆市总体规划，主城区将由过去的600多平方公里扩展为3000余平方公里，工业产品、民用产品将会迅速发展。重庆是中国汽车生产基地，在近年内，汽车年生产达到400万余辆；摩托车年生产1000万余辆；笔记本电脑、智能电子仪器仪表年产量达到2亿台之多；形成重型车、轻型车、微型车、轿车多系列的研发生产格局，成为中国汽车名城、摩托车之都；笔电行业、电子仪器仪表将成为世界级的信息产业高地．这就需要大量的汽车、摩托车上用的塑料配件。塑料建材、工业配件、日用商品以及包装类产品等，将会更加带动提升塑料加工工业向多品种、高质量方向发展。

【大事记】

2012年重庆市塑料行业协会在市委、市府的关怀下，在市经信委、市民政局的具体指导下，我们全行业认真学习邓小平理论，以"三个代表"主要思想为指导，深入贯彻落实科学发展观，按照"稳增长、调结构"的总体要求，以企业为主体，以市场为导向，开拓市场、技术创新、技术交流，努力提高产品质量以及在市场中的影响力和盈利的能力。在全行业中的广大职工，团结奋斗，战胜困难，促使重庆塑料工业持续快速发展。协会以服务会员、服务企业为宗旨，不断学习，加强自身建设，提高服务能力，认真调查研究，广交朋友，树立了良好的形象。会员队伍也得到了不断的壮大和发展。

1. 积极参加市政府有关部门组织的各项活动和交办的事项，宣传贯彻市委市府政策和会议精神，反应企业意愿，发挥了政府与企业间桥梁和助手作用。

①宣传贯彻2012年可持续发展工作思路、振兴工业经济座谈讨论会议精神。

2012年一季度协会先后多次参加市经信委召开的2012年可持续发展的工作思路："稳增长、调结构，促转型、抓活动"，重视民生工程等座谈会，在会上，协会介绍了重庆塑料工业发展的概况，阐述了塑料工业更需要政府的支持，和加强提高对民生工业产品的监管引起了市经信委领导和相关部门重视。

②贯彻扶持民营企业振兴工业经济座谈会议精神。

二季度多次参加市经信委支持民营企业振兴重庆工业经济的讨论学习，积极宣传贯彻市委、市府、市经信委5月3日、6月8日、6月28日振兴工业经济座谈学习和动员大会，根据市经信委的要求，协会秘书处工作人员，会同协会技术顾问，深入到企业与企业领导、工程技术人员，进行座谈、了解情况，共同探讨、征求意见，就塑料工业发展的未来、产品开发工程，重大技术攻关工程、重大设备提升工程等项目汇总之后，形成书面材料，以表格的形式已报送给市经信委，在市政府出台的《振兴重庆工业经济三年规划》和出台扶持民营经济发展的政策，提供了具有价值的参考意见，引起了政府相关部门的重视，起到了献计献策的帮助作用。

③参加市经信委工业品消费处、民营专项资金办组织的民营经济发展专项资金项目投资指南座谈会。在座谈讨论中，除了文件规定的条款外，我们根据重庆市塑料行业协会的具体情况，提出了增加和补充意见：

同时在会上也提出了轻工与重工(机械行业)在投入和产出也应有所区别对待，政府在制定出台的相关政策也给予了考虑。

④参加市政府有关部门组织的对新产品、新技术、新项目、扶持民营专项资金的评审、验收等工作。

2. 2012年3月29日在南坪国际会展中心会议厅召开2012中国(重庆)塑料产业合作对接会(技术交流)暨重庆市塑料行业协会年会。到会单位的领导有：重庆市塑料行业协会会长、常务副会长、常务理事、理事和会员单位以及市内相关企业，市外企业和相关单位领导：深圳、余姚、安徽、山东、广东、浙江等省市协会的企业单位代表共200余人出席了会议。

市经信委工业品消费处张处长到会、市经信委艾主任出席会议并作了题为"重庆塑料工业发展与未来"的报告。还有相关院校的领导出席会议并作了重庆塑料产业发展的演讲，10余家企业单位在大会上进行了技术交流与演讲。塑料行业协会作了2012年的工作总结。这次会议开得很好很成功。同期在重庆南坪国际会议展览中心举办第八届西部国际塑料工业展，影响大、评价高，收到了很好的效果，为企业营造技术交流、新产品交流平台，促进重庆塑料工业可持续发展。

3. 2013年9月18日召开的三届四次常务理事会议，刘汉龙秘书长主持会议，传达了市委市政府《关于推进新型工业化的若干意见》和黄市长关于推进新型工业化的讲话主要精神。汇报了到区县各工业园区多次考察了解的情况，提出了建立工业园区的设想。

会上，重庆捷成塑胶(集团)公司陈杰总经理、重庆溯联塑胶有限公司韩宗俊总经理、重庆一龙管道有限公司叶正茂总经理、重庆工友塑料有限公司黄冠文总经理、重庆鸿岱科技有限公司夏浩籍总经理、重庆皇华碳酸钙有限公司谈勇总经理、重庆光能汽车配件有限公司李书记、重庆瑞琦塑胶管道有限公司李总经理、重庆巴王矿产品有限公司、重庆巨翁塑料制造有限公司毋永清总经理、重庆太岳科技有限公司谭光明总经理、澳彩化工魏子斌总经理、象屿重庆有限责任公司唐夏总经理、重庆科跃化工建材公司陈天淑董事长等单位领导就塑料行业发展方向以及如何抱团征地进入园区展开了激烈讨论，支持协会提出的思路，付志敏会长进行了小结：这次会议开得很好很成功，同志们发言积极踊跃，对建立塑料工业园很感兴趣，工作继续往前推进。

4. 坚持编辑出刊《重庆塑料产业》建立信息平台，为企业提供信息、宣传企业的美誉度和知名度。

为了更好的服务于会员，服务于企业，服务于行业，秘书处在人员少、资金不足的情况下客服困难，积极想办法，广泛收集整理国内外有关信息资料，坚持出刊《重庆塑料产业》。在杂志中采用了彩页，使内容更加丰富多彩。这样及联络沟通了与企业的往来关系，也反映了协会的形象。发挥了通讯的宣传作用，及时传达各种信息，其主要反映在以下几个方面：一是传达了国家和政府的有关政策和相关会议的主要精神；二是及时报道了业内的重大活动事件；三是逐步介绍了会员单位的主要产品、企业规模以及联系方式；四是及时给会员单位介绍和提供塑料工业发展方向、领先的信息和国家要求逐步淘汰的产品等信息。

【重点企业】

1. 顾地科技股份有限公司

“顾地”品牌创建于1979年，成长于广东，发展于全国，是中国难燃PVC电工管和线槽的发明者和制造者，作为推动中国塑胶管道“以塑代钢”的先行者，顾地自创业以来，秉承“追求卓越品质，尽显顾地精华”的经营理念和“勇于创新、追求更高”的信念，引领了塑胶界一系列改革浪潮，为国家的建设和社会的繁荣做出了巨大贡献。

顾地科技股份有限公司(深交所A股上市企业，股票代码：002694)于2010年整体改制设立，目前公司在湖北、重庆、佛山、北京、河南、马鞍山、邯郸、甘肃拥有八大生产基地。公司主要生产PVC－U给排水管、PVC－M高抗冲给水管、抗菌PP－R冷热水管、PP－R铝塑稳态管、PE－RT地暖管、PE给水及燃气管、PVC－C高压电力护套管、PVC－U双壁波纹管、HDPE双壁波纹管、钢带增强HDPE螺旋波纹管等产品，广泛应用于建筑内给排水、市政给水、燃气、建筑采暖、市政排水排污等领域。近几年来公司产品的产量和销售额均呈快速增长趋势，公司营销网络遍布华北、华东、西南、西北、华南、华中各区域，产品畅销全国30个省(市)、自治区，同时远销中亚、东南亚、非洲等国家和地区，公司是目前国内最具规模和影响力的塑胶建材制造商之一。

公司是中国塑料加工工业协会副理事长单位、中国塑协塑料管道专委会副秘书长单位，同时也是全国塑料制品标准化技术委员会塑料管材、管件及阀门分技术委员会的核心成员单位，在行业内具有较高的知名度和美誉度。

公司拥有一支强大的科研团队，拥有近百名高学历、高水平的专业科研技术人才，近年来在国内外公开发表学术论文近400余篇，著书三本，获得省部级科技成果奖两项。公司拥有多项发明专利及实用新型专利，技术实力雄厚。最近几年，公司先后通过了ISO9001国际质量体系认证、ISO14001环境体系认证、ISO18001职业安全认证、压力管道元件制造许可认证及国家节水产品认证等多种准入制度，公司曾荣获“中国名牌产品”等称号。“山前有路，山外有山”，为适应时代的发展，顾地科技将加快创新的脚步，在不断加强规范管理的同时，积极开拓市场，寻求环保建材领域的发展机会，把公司建设成为中国最具规模、最具实力也最具魅力的现代化企业。

2. 重庆捷泰塑胶工业有限公司

重庆捷泰塑胶工业有限公司成立于2006年6月，注册资本1800万元人民币，总投资额1.6亿元，主要从事EPP珠粒料、EPP成型制品及PP无纺布的研发、生产。公司生产设备主要从德国引进全套先进PP发泡珠粒料挤出生产线和一次成型设备，引领了发泡剂出技术发展的新方向，属于目前最为先进的新型环保材料。EPP(聚丙烯)珠粒材料、成型制品及PP无纺布已在交通运输、军工、航空航天、日用品及包装业等领域获得了广泛应用，尤其是在汽车配件、电子产品外包装等方面的市场前景广阔。

3. 重庆光能公司

重庆光能公司座落在重庆市高新技术产业开发区，地理环境优越，交通便捷。公司始建于2003年，总投资1.5亿元，占地3.5万平方米，建筑面积4万余平方米，是生产汽车塑料内外饰件和功能件，重型汽车暖风装置、军用产品塑料零部件和摩托车塑料覆盖件的专业公司。是长安福特马自达、长安铃木、重庆英特公司、建设集团、建设雅马哈、嘉陵集团、铁马集团的优秀供应商。

重庆光能公司自创建以来，不断引进先进的管理。先后通过 ISO 9002、ISO 9001：2000、QS 9000、TS 16949、ISO 14001 等质量管理体系和环境管理体系评审。建有塑料制品及其涂装质量、性能检测试验中心试验室，具备完整的质量保证能力。

重庆光能公司有与客户同步工程能力。公司拥有学科结构合理的强大的开发和工程队伍，建有模具厂、涂装厂。长期以来以主机厂导向，与主机厂紧密合作，充分展示出新产品开发、试制、开模、注塑、后加工、涂装、装配一条龙的生产优势，在激烈的市场竞争中实现以新取胜的战略，不断为主机厂赢得时间，赢得市场。

重庆光能公司在销售管理、物流管理、技术管理、生产管理和质量管理等方面，逐渐形成了自己的特色，在双色注塑工艺、精密发泡工艺和塑料制品后加工工艺等方面都取得了重要突破，形成了生产能力，年产销近 2 亿元。

4. 重庆市一龙管道有限公司

重庆市一龙管道有限公司成立于 2004 年，公司座落于重庆市南岸区茶园新城区，是一家集高科技、高性能、绿色环保为一体的新型塑料管材、管件生产和销售企业。

公司注册资金 6016 万元人民币，占地面积 10 万平方米。现有员工 300 余人，其中工程技术人员约占 20%。

公司总投资达 3.5 亿元人民币，拥有 20 多条国内先进的 PE 直壁管、PE 双壁波纹管、PE 钢带缠绕管等生产设备，产品规格 dn20 - dn2000mm（其中给水压力管道规格 dn20 - dn800mm），检测手段齐全，年生产能力可达 50kt 以上。

公司自创立以来，坚持以“科技为先导，视质量为生命”的经营理念，积极走“借脑办厂”的发展道路，大胆改革创新，注重“品牌经营”，相继与国内重点大学合作成立创新研发中心，成为新一代最具生命力的管道企业之一。凭着科学的生产工艺、严格的质量管理、先进的服务理念、合理的产品价格，在短时间内，一龙迅速占领了重庆市场的半壁江山，并积极向云南、贵州、四川、湖南、湖北、甘肃、内蒙古、山西、东北等地发展，不断延伸市场空间，扩大市场占有率。如今，一龙已进入快速健康发展轨道，呈现出强劲的发展势头！

企业要发展，人才是关键。公司坚持“以人为本”，实施人才战略，积极引进包括中国塑料加工工业协会专家委员会专家、塑料管道专业委员会专家组专家、全国塑料制品标准化技术委员会委员在内的众多塑料制品行业的资深专业技术人员加盟，并与国内及世界知名厂商进行多方面技术合作与交流。与北京化工大学、四川大学、重庆大学、华东理工大学等高校建立了长期紧密的合作关系，与上海石化研究院、山东齐鲁石化研究院建立了技术情报共享关系。

公司成立至今，从项目开发起步到产品标准化生产，制定了一整套严格的质量管理体系及保证模式，并贯穿于开发、生产、销售、后期安装服务的全过程，不断加强和完善公司质量管理，产品性能完全达到国家、行业和企业标准的要求，出厂合格率达到 100%，并顺利通过国家 ISO 9001 质量体系及 ISO 14001 环境体系的认证。

展望未来，塑料管道行业前景灿烂。“固本、立新、见远”是我们不变的企业宗旨，更是我们制胜的法宝。我们将以一流的产品和优质的服务来树立企业品牌形象，以合理的价格去赢得市场，力争使一龙发展成为西南乃至全国塑料管道行业的领跑者！

5. 重庆百联塑胶有限公司

重庆百联塑胶有限公司成立于 2001 年 3 月，生产基地坐落在中国著名的龙乡重庆铜梁工业园，占地 3 万余平方米，引进国内外先进技术和设备，先后投资近亿元，年产塑胶管道可达 180kt，是一家专业生产“百联”牌塑胶管材管件的大型民营企业。

公司注重质量，视质量为企业生命，遵循“高起点、严管理，守信诺、诚服务，勤奋发、求进取，创名牌、显声威”的质量方针和“顾客满意率 100%”的质量目标，建立了完整的质量保证体系，并先后通过了 ISO 9001 质量管理体系和 ISO 14001 环境管理体系认证。

公司以“立足重庆、面向西南、辐射全国”的销售战略方针，于 2001 年组建了“百联”品牌营销中心（位于重庆南岸区南坪珊瑚大厦 26 - 9），下辖贵州贵阳、贵州遵义、贵州安顺、云南昆明、四川成都、四川南充、四川达州、四川绵阳、陕西西安、重庆万州、重庆黔江 11 个直销中心；创业十年，“百联”品牌系列产品得到相关主管部门及众多合作客户的认可，先后获得“重庆名牌产品”、“重庆市著名商标”、“重庆品牌 100 强”，并和众多企事业单位建立了良好的合作关系。主导产品 PVC - U 双壁波纹管、

HDPE 双壁波纹管、PVC－U 排水管、PVC－U 螺旋消音排水管、PVC－C 高压电力套管、PVC 电线槽管、PP－R 环保卫生饮用水管、PE 燃气、饮用水管、HDPE 缠绕管、HDPE 钢带增强缠绕波纹管、钢丝网骨架增强塑料复合管、热镀锌衬塑复合钢管，已成功应用在家装、民建、市政三大领域，为数以千万的客户及众多国家级重点工程项目提供了优质的产品和服务！

公司注重人才的引进和培养，现有员工 300 多人，其中高级管理人才 15 人，中级技术人才 48 人，2008 年，公司针对家装市场成功开发了 WP-PR 银离子抗菌管并应用于家装管道市场，为公司填补了高档家装管道市场的空白；公司将一如既往的加大科技研发投入力度，力促企业向更高层次迈进！

为了保证重庆工程产品的供应和提供良好的售后服务，2009 年，公司在茶园新区建立了 1000 多平米的物流配送中心，配置了 10 辆大型配送车，库存量保持在 600～800 万元，在重庆本土市场月供货能力可达 3000 万元，实现了在重庆区域销售的一站式服务！

2012 年，公司又拆巨资在铜梁新建生产厂房 27000 平方，引进新型管材 PSP 生产线，结束重庆地区无 PSP 管材生产线的历史。届时，重庆百联塑胶公司将成为西南地区塑胶管道产品最齐全的生产厂家之一！

不断开拓，努力进取！这是“百联人”十年如一日的行事准则，公司将以“团结、勤奋、进取”的企业精神，不断为中国现代民用建筑、农业、水利、电力、交通、通信等产业和新型建材事业做出应有的贡献。

6. 重庆太岳科技有限公司

重庆太岳科技有限公司成立于 2006 年 2 月，是一家专注于聚氯乙烯(PVC)加工用复合铅盐稳定润滑剂系列产品(简称复合铅稳定剂)的生产经营企业。目前，公司建有年产 20000 吨的复合铅稳定剂生产线，有 30 多个品种，“御象”、“太岳”、“御象牌”三个商标，其中的“御象”商标为九龙坡区著名商标并在业内享有很高知名度。

公司成立至今，秉承了原重庆长江化工厂在市场、生产、技术研发长达数十年的沉淀，其公司法人、技术部、市场部和生产系统主管分别是原长江厂总工程师、市场和生产技术主管。

原重庆长江化工厂在 2003 年前属国有中型企业，成立于 1927 年，是中国最早从事 PVC 加工用稳定剂的厂家，为上世纪八十年代和九十年代国内稳定剂行业协作组组长厂；原业内享有盛誉的《热稳定剂》季刊杂志是原重庆化工局主办和重庆长江化工厂协办的产物；其生产规模、品种及质量冠于全国，“川江”牌稳定剂系列产品覆盖国内 30 余个省市自治区，并出口欧美东南亚等国家和地区，该公司在 2003 年因改制失败而解散，但其精华在重庆太岳科技有限公司中得以保存和延续。

“以人为本，科技创新”是公司企业的文化精髓，特别是 PVC 稳定剂行业和 PVC 加工行业资深专家的加盟，公司的创新能力较同业有非常明显的优势；目前，公司拥有多项国家发明专利，并已通过 ISO 9001—2008 质量认证。

（重庆市塑料行业协会　付志敏　刘汉龙）

浙　江　省

【基本情况】

2012 年是抗击国际经济风波、稳定经济发展大局、加快经济转型升级的关键一年，面对能源成本、资金成本、用人成本不断上涨等诸多挑战，浙江省塑料制品行业坚持以科学发展为主题，以加快转变发展方式为主线，加快产品结构调整和企业转型升级，提升科技、管理和营销水平，实现了经济平稳增长。

1. 行业规模

据浙江省统计局统计，2012 年全省塑料制品行业规模以上企业 1845 家(其中亏损企业 229 家，同比增长 34.7%，亏损面 12.41%)，占全国塑料制品行业规模企业总数的 13.9%(其中亏损企业占全国塑料制品行业亏损企业总数的 15.4%)，从业人员 27.5 万，同比下降 3.3%，占全国塑料制品行业从业人员总数的 11.8%。

2. 塑料制品产量

2012 年，全省规模以上企业完成塑料制品总产量 948.54 万吨，同比增长 13.02%，占全国同期塑料制品总产量的 16.41%，居全国第一位，增幅较上年同期上涨了 6.1 个百分点，其中：塑料薄膜产量 304.52 万吨，同比增长 20.63%，占全国同期塑料薄膜总产量的 31.39%(居第一位)；塑料薄膜中农用薄膜产量 126.5kt，同比增长 28.24%，占全国同期农用薄膜总产量的 7.77%(居第三位)；泡沫塑料制品产量 163.2kt，同期下降 1.63%，占全国同期泡沫塑料制品总产量的 9.48%(居第二位)；塑料人造革、合成革产量 1339.7kt，同比增长 10.58%，占全国同期塑料人造革、合成革产量的42.63%(居第一位);日用塑料制品产量1028.6kt,同比增长6.78%,占全国同期日用塑料制品总产量的22.27%(居第二位);其它塑料制品3908.6kt,同比增长10.80%,占全国同期其它塑料制品总产量的10.12%(居第二位)。在五大类塑料制品中,除泡沫塑料制品产量比上年同期略有下降外,其余四大类产品的产量比上年同期均有不同程度的增长,其中薄膜中农用薄膜增长幅度居第一位(增长28.24%),这说明经济类农作物的产量在大幅度增加,对农用薄膜的需求量呈现大幅增长的态势。

3. 主要经济指标

2012年浙江省塑料制品行业规模以上企业完成工业总产值2061.5亿元,同比增长9.2%,占全国塑料制品行业同期工业总产值的12.30%;主营业务收入1987.3亿元,同比增长5.7%,占全国塑料制品行业同期主营业务收入的12.18%;产销率达96.40%,增幅较上年同期回落了了0.98个百分点,实现利税147.8亿元,同比下降0.1%,占全国塑料制品行业同期利税总额的10.33%,其中利润97.9亿元,同比下降2.3%,占全国塑料制品行业同期利润总额10.16%;亏损企业亏损额7.1亿元,同比增长66.5%,亏损额占全国全国塑料制品行业同期亏损额的10.56%。出口交货值397.7亿元,同比增长6.4%。

4. 技术创新步伐加快,名牌产品、著名商标产品平稳增长

全行业不断依靠科技进步,加大科技开发力度,加快企业高新技术成果的产业化,推动产品结构调整和产业升级。2012全行业科技活动经费支出总额达16.9亿元,同比增长17.9%,新产品产值436.1亿元,同比增长31.8%,新产品产值率为21.15%。

2012年,浙江省塑料行业共有11个产品获"浙江省名牌产品"称号,其中:新增6个,到期复评5个;4个产品获2012年度"浙江出口名牌"名单;23个产品获2012年度浙江省著名商标产品,其中新增17个,复评7个;22家企业获2012年度浙江省高新技术企业称号。

5. 食品用塑料包装、容器、工具等制品生产企业逐步规范

随着国内《食品安全法》及有关法律法规的相继颁布实施,对塑料制品行业提出了新的要求,特别是对食品包装用塑料制品生产企业实施了市场准入制度,对企业使用的原辅材料、生产设备设施、各项管理制度提出了严格要求,许多小企业在该项准入制度的实施中被淘汰。截止2012年底止,全省共有1115家(含非规模企业)食品用塑料包装、容器、工具等制品生产企业获得QS证。

6. 2012年度"浙江出口名牌"名单

浙江省商务厅2012年12月30日公布(新增105个,复核94个,其中塑料复核4个)

序号	企业名称	品牌	备注
1	浙江海利得新材料股份有限公司	海利得	复核
2	浙江铭仕管业有限公司	铭仕	复核
3	伟星集团有限公司	伟星	复核
4	浙江大东南股份有限公司	绿海 LUHAI	复核

【技改情况】

2012年浙江省重点技术改造项目(塑料行业相关项目)

序号	项目名称	企业名称	项目内容	总投资/万元
1	年产30kt多功能薄膜项目	绍兴翔宇绿色包装有限公司	项目采用全球薄膜技术最领先的德国道尼尔公司的双向拉伸共挤改良技术,引进具有国际先进水平的多功能改良BOPET薄膜生产线设备,项目建成后形成年产30kt多功能薄膜(光学、光伏、锂电池隔离膜)的生产能力,产品替代进口,提升光伏产品性能,拓展光学薄膜领域,投产后实现销售收入55000万元,,利税8500万元,创汇4500万美元。	30000

续表

序号	项目名称	企业名称	项目内容	总投资/万元
2	28kt/a 新型食品包装材料	浙江巨化股份有限公司	项目主要采用氯乙烯氯化法技术工艺，引进具有国际先进水平的沉降式离心机设备，购置板式换热器、皂化釜、流化床、、循环水泵、拌和机、压缩机系统等国产设备，项目建成后，形成年产年产 80kt VDC 单体、2.8 吨 PVDC 新型食品包装材料的生产能力。产品具有技术含量高、填补市场短期、替代进口等特点，实现销售收入 59113 万元，利税 6139 万元。	19802
3	新建年产 80kt 塑料管道投资项目	永高股份有限公司	项目主要采用自动化和立体成型技术，引进具有国际先进水平的 IPT 液压试验机、Prointralink 数据管理软件和 PE 挤出生产线等设备，项目建成后形成新建年产 80kt 塑料管道生产能力，产品具有核心自主知识产权，实现销售收入 132462 万元，利税 19069 万元。	52110
4	年产 2500 台伺服节能高效精密注塑机	浙江申达机器制造股份有限公司	年产 2500 台伺服节能高效精密注塑机，适用 IT 和汽车行业的高速、高效、薄壁注塑机。	27010
5	年产 15kt 再生塑料改性 PE 管材生产线	浙江东管管业有限公司	年产 15kt 利用废弃塑料包装物改性再生新型 PE 管材生产线就是改造项目。	2850
6	年产 8000t 多功能农膜项目	浙江陈佳塑料包装有限公司	年产 8000t 高强度、防流滴、特大、多功能农膜生产线技术改造。	2600
7	年产 10000t 塑料改性及综合利用项目	台州利丰洁具有限公司	年产 10000t 塑料改性及综合利用项目	2380
8	年产 1000t 新型免喷涂、环保塑料软管项目	浙江沪天胶带有限公司	年产 1000t 新型免喷涂、环保 LDPE 塑料软管技术改造项目。	1860
9	年产 5000 万米新型合成革项目	绍兴东泰聚合材料有限公司	年产 5000 万米新型 PU 合成革项目。	55000
10	年产 10000t 特种膜项目	浙江汉高新材料有限公司	年产 10000t 纳米透气复合膜技改项目。	8500
11	年产 5000t PVB 及 5700t 制品项目	湖州鑫富新材料有限公司	年产 5000t PVB 及 5700t PVB 胶片项目	12000
12	年产 4000 台智能型注塑机机械手项目	金华凯力特自动化科技有限公司	年产 4000 台智能型注塑机机械手技改项目	4182
13	年产 50000t 多功能膜项目	浙江大东南集团有限公司	年产 50000t 镀铝和涂布型多功能新型包装材料技改项目。	57000
14	新增年产 5000t 汽车、轨道交通用 GMT 新型轻质复合材料技改项目	浙江华江科技发展有限公司	项目主要采用自主研发的以 PP 纤维和玻璃纤维为原料，经开松、混合、交叉铺网，再经针刺成毡，通过复合机模压成型技术，引进具有国际领先水平的非织造布针刺复合生产线、平板复合机设备，购置抽吸装置、收卷机、压板机等国产设备。项目建成后形成年产 5000t 汽车、轨道交通用 GMT 新型轻质复合材料生产能力，产品具有抗冲击强度高、抗蠕变性能和尺寸稳定性好等特点，实现销售收入 10000 万元，利润 1300 万元，税金 500 万元，创汇 300 万美元。	4130

续表

序号	项目名称	企业名称	项目内容	总投资/万元
15	年产135kt新型包装材料技改项目	温州市金田塑业有限公司	项目主要采用双螺杆主挤出机和副挤出机多层共挤平膜法技术，引进具有国际先进水平的原料处理及挤出系统、铸片机、纵拉机、横拉机、牵引系统、收卷系统、分切机、易损件等设备，购置回收造粒系统、钢卷芯、料仓罐风管、高低压配电室、生产用供热系统、纸管生产设备、水净化设备等国产设备，项目建成后形成年产135kt新型包装材料生产能力。产品具有透明度高、印刷性好、应用范围广等特点，实现销售收入184615万元，利税20093万元。	63970
16	投资兴建年产8000t易揭安全型铝箔封口膜系列产品产业化推进技术改造项目	浙江金石包装有限公司	项目主要采用新技术、新材料、新工艺进行创新优化设计技术，购置树脂强力搅拌机组、宽幅干复机、制动控温热封仪、热封强度分析仪、剥离强度测试仪、熔融指数测试仪等总计260套国产设备，项目建成后形成年产8000t易揭安全型铝箔封口膜系列产品的生产能力，产品具有低温热封性好、易揭、安全等特点，实现销售收入32200万元，利税5330万元。	8475
17	年新增5000万只模内注塑家电面板、手机机壳系列产品生产线技术改造	浙江国泰电子有限公司	项目主要采用自主创新研发技术，引进具有国际先进水平的自动化丝印、信息注塑设备，购置自动化丝印、数控冲床、注塑机、红外线隧道烘干机、数控电火花加工机、信息集成管理系统等国产设备。项目建成后，新增5000万只模内注射家电面板及手机机壳系列产品的生产能力，实现销售收入25000万元，利税2989万元，创汇1100万美元。	7448
18	年产50kt钢塑复合管项目	浙江金州管道科技有限公司	项目主要采用中频替代煤、油等一次性能源加热钢管本体和双面内外立式涂敷等具有自主知识产权的授权发明、实用新型专利技术，购置具有国内领先水平的节能环保型喷砂、钢管滚塑机、涂敷、衬塑等国产设备，项目建成后形成年产50kt涂/衬塑新型钢塑复合管生产能力。项目建成后实现销售收入37038万元，利税4853万元，创汇1000万美元。	21307
19	年产60kt饱和聚酯树脂、5000t塑粉生产线	浙江中法新材料有限公司	新建厂房及办公用房70288m²，新增反应釜、冷却钢带机、磨粉机等国产设备，形成年产60kt饱和聚酯树脂、5000t塑粉的生产能力。	13601
20	年产100kt高性能高分子塑料复合材料技术改造项目	浙江普利特新材料有限公司	项目主要采用本公司自有的专利技术，本公司已有授权专利项目4项，其母公司上海普利特新材料有限公司将继续注入专利技术，母公司目前已有授权专利技术117项，能保证公司具有国内领先、国际的技术和工艺，引进具有国际或代表国外同类仪器设备水平的研究开发用主要仪器，项目建成后形成年产100kt高性能高分子塑料复合材料的生产能力，产品具有低、抗划擦、抗紫外线及良好的加工性。实现销售收入180500万元，利税34375万元，创汇18万美元。	29700

续表

序号	项目名称	企业名称	项目内容	总投资/万元
21	年产 30kt 高吸水性树脂技改项目	浙江卫星石化股份有限公司	项目在对国内外现有生产工艺进行分析和研究得基础上，通过公司技术人员攻关，开发具有自主知识产权的连续化工业化生产工艺，引进具有国内先进水平的干燥粉碎设备，购置管道反应器、管道配料器、聚合反应器等国产设备。项目建成后可形成年产 30kt 高吸水性树脂的生产能力，实现销售收入 45230 万元，利税 12860 万元。	31853
22	年产 9000t 新型 3.4m 聚烯烃热收缩膜新建项目	浙江众成包装材料股份有限公司	项目主要采用“三泡法五层共挤”生产技术，项目建成后形成年产 9000t 新型 3.4m 聚烯烃热收缩膜的生产能力，产品具有厚度最薄可达 7.5μm，能更好地满足市场需求，符合包装材料轻薄化的复杂趋势，和节约用材的环保理念，实现销售收入 21150 万元，利税 6205 万元，创汇 2300 万美元。	21133
23	年产 30ktBOPET 生产线技改项目	浙江绍兴华东包装有限公司	项目主要采用双向拉伸技术，引进具有国际先进水平的宽幅(8.7m)BOPET 生产设备(生产线、分切机、塑料再生机等设备)，购置配套国产设备(空压机、冷冻机等)，项目建成后，形成年产 30kt BOPET 生产能力，其中热封膜 15kt、高透明膜 5kt、烫金膜 0.3t、转移膜 4kt、亚光膜 3kt，实现销售收入 60000 万元，利税 20000 万元。	30000
24	年产 2500 万米功能性复合材料项目	浙江布兰卡复合新材料有限公司	项目主要采用公司自主研发的高分子聚合、复合技术，购置具有国际先进水平的涂层机、定型机、压光机、复合机等国产设备，项目建成后形成年产 2500 万米功能性复合材料，产品具有透湿、透气、、防水、阻燃、抗紫外线、抗静电、防电磁辐射的特点，实现销售收入 32500 万元，利税 2900 万元，创汇 2000 万美元。	12000
25	年产 30kt 高分子材料和 50 万米纳米塑料管材项目	上虞市精亮工贸有限公司	项目主要采用高分子材料复合技术，引进具有国际先进领先水平的德国 Leistritz 挤出机、美国 Gala 造粒机组等设备，购置国产管材生产等主辅机，项目建成后形成年产年产 30kt 高分子材料和 50 万米纳米塑料管材生产能力，产品具有高强度、高韧性、耐环境应力好等特点，实现销售收入 8000 万元，利税 1600 万元。	5680
26	年产 16kt 新型高阻隔金属化膜包装材料技改项目	浙江凯利包装材料有限公司	项目主要采用先进的真空镀膜技术，引进具有国际先进水平的真空镀膜机、数控分切机、各类先进测试仪器等进口设备，购置冷冻机、空压机、行车、叉车等国产设备。项目建成后形成年产 16kt 新型高阻隔金属化膜包装材料的生产能力，产品具有高阻隔、易回收等特点，实现销售收入 35400 万元，利税 4231 万元，创汇 3000 万美元。	4980

续表

序号	项目名称	企业名称	项目内容	总投资/万元
27	年产400万平方米防火保温墙体板、600万只电池塑料外壳、6000t汽车免维护电池外壳专用料建设项目	浙江永通新材料股份有限公司	项目主要采用公司自主研发的防火节能复合专用料生产技术，购置具有国内先进水平的注塑机、双螺杆造粒机等国产设备，项目建成后形成年产400万平方米防火保温墙体板、600万只电池塑料外壳、6000t汽车免维护电池外壳专用料的生产能力，实现销售收入73200万元，利税26278万元。	21000
28	新建年产20kt BOPET薄膜项目	浙江华清新材料有限公司	项目主要采用平膜法工艺，引进具有国际先进水平的BOPET生产设备，购置干燥机、辅助挤出机、铸片装置、纵横拉伸装置等国产设备。项目建成后形成年产20kt BOPET薄膜生产能力，产品具有优良的物理和化学性能，实现销售收入50000万元，利税5000万元，创汇1500万美元。	25000
29	年产24万条环保型塑料涂覆布正压风筒项目	浙江天地塑业有限公司	项目采用热熔—涂覆—卷筒热压成型新工艺，并采用导热电碳黑、丙烯酸类树脂为原料的导电涂层材料等关键技术，研制超宽幅的风筒布，制作整体风筒，解决风筒的漏风、吹开等问题，引进具有国际先进水平的宽幅复膜机等设备，购置宽幅织布机等国产设备，项目建成后形成年产24万条环保型塑料涂覆布正压风筒的生产能力，产品具有防漏风、吹开、耐寒、耐高温、阻燃、抗静电等特点，实现销售收入15300万元，利税3450万元。	10700
30	年产5000t膨胀型阻燃剂阻、耐分解环保ABS技改项目	浙江富丽新材料有限公司	项目主要采用本公司与浙江大学联合研发的环保阻燃ABS树脂技术，购置双螺杆生产线、注塑机、锥形量热仪、电子万能试验机、垂直水平燃烧实验仪等国产设备，项目建成后形成年产5000t膨胀型阻燃剂阻燃耐分解环保ABS的生产能力，产品具有无卤环保、耐分解、易加工、阻燃级别高等特点，实现销售收入11000万元，利税1600万元。	3500
31	年产25000t太阳能电池背材膜项目	浙江南洋科技股份有限公司	项目主要采用引进的PET膜及感受自有的生产技术，引进具有国际先进水平的分切机等设备，购置原料干燥配重系统、再造粒回收系统、热媒加热系统等国产设备。项目建成后形成年产25000t太阳能电池背材膜的生产能力。产品具有高耐热性、难燃性、绝缘性和稳定性，通过特性电晕处理可增加太阳能电池使用寿命，实现销售收入50000万元，利税8024万元。	21000
32	年产10kt高强度、耐热、耐寒塑料垃圾桶及新建厂房技改项目	台州市中天塑业有限公司	项目主要采用注塑成型技术，引进具有国际领先水平的塑料注塑成型机，购置塑料注塑成型机、模具等国产设备，项目建成后形成年产10kt高强度、耐热、耐寒塑料垃圾桶的生产能力，产品具有外形美观、强度高、耐热、耐寒等特点，实现销售收入15000万元，利税1200万元，创汇1100万美元，项目新建厂房等总建筑面积11140平方米。	13660

续表

序号	项目名称	企业名称	项目内容	总投资/万元
33	年产32kt节能环保型PP－R系列管材、管件扩建项目	浙江伟星新型建材股份有限公司	项目主要采用单螺杆挤出成型技术，购置PP－R管材专用单螺杆挤出机、管件注塑机、电熔管件布线机等国产设备。项目建成后形成年产32kt节能环保型PP－R系列管材、管件的生产能力，产品具有耐热、耐腐蚀、绝热、卫生无毒等特点，实现销售收入86661万元，利税22120万元。	23577
34	年产12kt PVB中间膜生产项目	浙江普利金塑胶有限责任公司	项目主要采用与浙江大学合作研发的技术，引进具有国际先进水平的在线厚度检测及控制系统设备，购置挤出机、混料机、除湿机、流延机、粉丝机等国产设备。项目建成后形成年产12kt PVB中间膜的生产能力，产品具有抗冲击、抗穿刺、耐高低温、隔音隔热等特点。实现销售收入36000万元，利税7200万元，创汇2600万美元。	10106
35	年产30万条改性TPU拉带护理床垫生产线加工项目	浙江大自然旅游用品有限公司	项目主要采用自动热熔技术，引进热熔接带机设备，购置过胶机、复合机等国产设备。项目建成后形成年产30万条改性TPU拉带护理床垫的生产能力，产品具有国内首创、成本低等特点，实现销售收入6000万元，利税1000万元，创汇925万美元。	2500
36	年产50kt合成革用PU树脂及2000万米水性生态合成革项目	丽水优耐克水性树脂科技有限公司	项目主要采用中波红外干燥技术，购置合成革用水性PU树脂合成流水线、混料斧、水性合成革干法生产线等国产设备。项目建成后形成年产50kt合成革用PU树脂及2000万米水性生态合成革生产能力，产品填补国内空白、替代进口、节能降耗。	15000
37	年产70kt BOPP薄膜多功能薄膜及高阻隔包装薄膜项目	浙江云塑薄膜工业有限公司	项目主要采用双向拉伸技术，引进具有国际先进水平的8.2M高速多层共挤薄膜生产线、分切机等设备，购置原料输送系统、空压机等国产设备。项目建成形成年产70kt BOPP薄膜多功能薄膜及高阻隔包装薄膜的生产能力，产品具有透明、高阻隔等特点，可实现销售收入100000万元，利税13086万元。	52000

2012浙江省重点技术创新项目(塑料相关行业项目)

序号	项目名称	承担单位	项目主要内容	总投资/万元
1	汽车、轨道交通用玻璃纤璃纤维增强PP新型轻质复合材料(GMT)	浙江华江科技发展有限公司	玻璃纤维增强PP新型轻质复合材料采用短切改性无碱玻璃纤维表面处理技术、短切PP纤维改性技术及两者共混制造毛毡片材技术。片材产品中PP纤维和长玻璃纤维分布均匀、浸渍性好、拉伸强度高、尺寸稳定性优良。采用复合纳米抗菌与光催化技术，使片材具有优良的抗菌与污染物降解环保效果。主要用于汽车顶棚等内饰及保温结构件、轨道交通列车车厢内饰及保温结构件的制造。	1300

续表

序号	项目名称	承担单位	项目主要内容	总投资/万元
2	无卤阻燃光伏封装材料研究	杭州福特斯光伏材料光伏有限公司	本想买利用改性后的EVA基体树脂，加入改性及复配的无卤阻燃剂、交联剂、抗老化剂等经熔融挤出、流延成膜，最终制成无卤阻燃型EVA胶膜	970
3	3.4M宽幅聚烯烃热收缩膜关键制造技术产业化	浙江众成包装材料股份有限公司	在公司现有专利技术的基础上，研制3.4M宽幅聚烯烃热收缩膜生产设备，提高分切、对折机速度至500~600m/min，改善设备的生产效率，采用三泡法生产工艺，并于管膜处安装高能电子束交联机，实现在线辐射交联，研究电子束辐射剂量和膜层材料组成比例对薄膜成膜稳定性、机械性能和热收缩率的影响规律，使薄膜的机械强加工性及热收缩率达到最佳值；优选弹性体作共混改性剂，研究弹性体种类、用量及在膜层位置的变化对聚烯烃热收缩膜成膜能力、机械性能和热收缩性能的影响，降低薄膜的收缩应力和起始收缩温度；优化薄膜外层材料，采用有效的复配技术，研究不同密度的PE对薄膜外层热封性的影响规律，提高薄膜热封强度，减少封口破包率。	1815
4	大口径高性能衬塑复合钢管关键技术开发及产业化应用	浙江金洲管道科技股份有限公司	我国衬塑复合钢管产业化生产起步于上世纪九十年代末，限于生产工艺等因素，公称口径219mm及以上的大中口径衬塑复合钢管关键工艺技术始终没有突破，项目以本公司的授权发明专利技术再创新，通过内衬塑料、黏结剂重新设计选型、复合关键技术、工程应用接头性能、以及大中口径衬塑复合钢管开发等系统性研究，确定控制主要影响衬塑结合强度因素的方法和生产工艺，在大中口径衬塑复合钢管的生产中采用中频电阻加热替换传统的油气加热系统，改进内衬塑管生产加工艺和钢塑复合工艺，实现产业化生产。	1675
5	有机化无机颗粒改性聚合物复合材料制备关键技术研究	华之杰塑料建材有限公司	使用国家科技进步二等奖——“有机化无机颗粒改性聚合物复合材料制备关键技术研究”技术，通过原位聚合制备无机纳米颗粒复合PVC树脂，实现了无机颗粒在PVC树脂中的均匀分散，将纳米尺寸效应、大比表面积以及较强的界面相互作用、较好的尺寸稳定性和热稳定性与PVC较好的韧性、加工性及电性能完美地结合起来，提升PVC复合材料的整体物理机械性能。	876
6	LED照明用滤蓝光防眩光阻燃PC材料制备关键技术	浙江俊尔新材料股份有限公司	优选合适分子量的PC基体树脂，复配以有机交联微球为主的防眩光剂以及特殊的蓝光吸收剂、阻燃剂、抗氧剂、光稳定剂等适当的分散体系，使用特定的螺杆挤出机和特定的混合工艺来制造滤蓝光、高透光、高阻燃等综合性能优异的LED照明用滤蓝光防眩光阻燃PC材料。	1830

续表

序号	项目名称	承担单位	项目主要内容	总投资/万元
7	环保型生物基鞋底用PU树脂的开发	浙江华峰新材料股份有限公司	项目利用从玉米等植物中提炼生物基多元醇和多元酸原材料设计并构建特殊的聚酯多元醇分子链结构，合成生物基聚酯多元醇，进而生产环保型生物基鞋底用PU树脂。	1300
8	聚四氟乙烯中空纤维膜制备及产业化应用	浙江东大水业有限公司	项目研制了一种新型的聚四氟乙烯中空纤维膜制作方法，所制备的PTFE中空纤维膜具有强度高、柔韧性好、孔隙率高、与PVDF、PP和PVC等其他膜相比具有耐酸碱、耐高低温、耐微生物侵袭、抗氧化性优异、表面摩擦系数低等特点，特别适用于膜蒸馏模生物反应器。可广泛用于化工、制药、中水回用、海水淡化等领域，尤其对高浓度有机物、高含盐、高酸碱等废水及有机溶液废液等的处理有较好效果。项目符合国家产业政策，经济和社会效益明显。	8000
9	超疏水BOPP薄膜关键技术研究及产业化	昌源集团有限公司	根据“荷叶效应”研究经验并结合现有科研和生产条件，拟在模压机滚筒上安装微(纳)米结构镍模板，在加热加压的条件下通过滚筒的连续运转和持续的模压方法在BOPP薄膜表面构建合适的大面积微(纳)米结构，从而获得超疏水性。	2085
10	横走式注塑机智能机械手的研发	金华凯力特自动化科技有限公司	项目采用伺服电机驱动，通过振动与共振控制技术及同步传动机构的研究，优化可满足时间控制要求又能减少振动的运动机构升降速方案及机械整体结构，进行控制系统、人机界面的开发，通过操作面板，可以轻松设定各种控制参数，通过示教程序，可以方便地设定机械手的运行模式，界面更加人性化。产品具有高速、平稳、定位精准、操作方便及“快拿轻放”等优点，广泛应用于包装、电子器件、机械制造等领域。	410
11	带编织护套波纹管	金华市春光橡塑软管有限公司	针对现有波纹管存在的扭曲和弯曲性较差、耐磨性薄弱、使用寿命较低等缺点，将PET编织护套技术运用于波纹管，创新性地使用渗塑结构接头，解决了PET编织材料无法进行注塑加工的难题，实现PET编织层与EVA波纹管壁的有效连接，使带编织护套波纹管的弯曲、扭曲、耐踩压性能大幅提高，同时耐磨指标提高200%以上，从而提高产品的使用寿命和元，扩大其应用领域。产品可广泛用于家用吸尘器、各种抽吸系统、通风系统等领域。	1054

[企业荣誉]

1. 2012 年中国民营企业五百强

排位	企业名称	所属行业	营业收入总额/万元
239	浙江大东南集团有限公司	橡胶和塑料制造业	1191948
286	利时集团股份有限公司	橡胶和塑料制造业	1043614
353	浙江明日控股集团股份有限公司	批发和零售业	871000
500	伟星集团有限公司	综合	656858

2. 2012 年浙江省综合百强企业

排位	企业名称	营业收入总额/万元
75	浙江大东南集团有限公司	1191948
88	利时集团股份有限公司	1043614
90	海天塑机集团有限公司	1018049

3. 2012 年浙江省制造业百强企业

排位	企业名称	营业收入总额/万元
49	浙江大东南集团有限公司	1191948
58	利时集团股份有限公司	1043614
60	海天塑机集团有限公司	1018049
88	浙江富陵控股集团有限公司	640081
91	浙江赐富化纤集团有限公司	601053.23

【重点企业】

序号	企业名称	企业简介	2012 年主要指标	企业获得的主要荣誉
1	浙江明日控股集团股份有限公司	公司创建于 1998 年，经销 PE、PP、PVC、PS、ABS、弹性体等合成树脂及甲醇、橡胶、乙二醇、片碱等化工产品，并生产 CPP 薄膜、农地膜、液体包装用 PE 吹塑薄膜、包装用 PE 吹塑薄膜、复合膜及袋。注册资本 3 亿元。	2012 年经销合成树脂及化工产品 1032kt，塑料薄膜产量 30kt。经营收入 949000 万元，利税总额 10176 万元。	中国塑料加工工业协会副理事长单位、浙江省塑料行业协会会长单位、全国“守合同重信用”单位(国家工商总局)、2011～2012 年中国民营企业 500 强企业(全国工商联)、重合同守信用 AAA 级单位(浙江省工商局)、信用等级 AAA 级企业(浙江省人行、农行)、浙江省高新技术企业(杭州新光)、浙江名牌产品(杭州新光)。
2	永高股份有限公司	公司创建于 1993 年，主要生产 PVC－U、PP－R、PE、PE－RT、CPVC 等 3500 余不同规格、品种的管材及管件，年生产能力 600kt。2011 年在深圳证券交易所上市，股票代码 002641	主营收入 251427.79 万元。	中国塑料加工协会副理事长单位、浙江省塑料行业协会副会长单位、全国塑料制品标准化委员会委员单位、建立省级高新技术企业研发中心和博士后科研工作站、2012 年公司获得国家授权专利 32 项(其中：发明专利 2 项，实用新型专利 30 项)、浙江省专利示范企业、“浙江省工业行业龙头骨干企业”、“中国驰名商标”、浙江省名牌产品。

续表

序号	企业名称	企业简介	2012 年主要指标	企业获得的主要荣誉
3	浙江伟星新型建材股份有限公司	公司创建于 1999 年，企业注册资本 25340 万元，主要产品：PP-R、PERT、PB 等塑料管材及管件，广泛应用于给水、排水、排污、燃气、采暖、电力、矿山等领域。2010 年在深圳证券交易所上市，股票代码 002372	产量 12 万吨，主营收入 185730.1 万元。利税 40600 万元，其中利润总额 29600 万元。	中国塑料加工工业协会理事会副理事长单位，中国塑料加工工业协会塑料管道专业委员会副理事长单位，中国塑料行业先进单位、全国塑料制品标准化委员会塑料管材管件及阀门分技术委员会委员单位、浙江高新技术企业、浙江省专利示范企业、浙江省创新型企业、重合同守信用 AAA 级单位(浙江省工商局)、浙江省首批标准创新型企业、浙江省绿色企业，“冷热水用聚丙烯管道系统”国家标准主要的起草单位之一，省级科技推广项目 15 项，主持起草 35 项国家和行业标准，率先开发的高性能 F-PPR 复合管填补了国内空白。
4	浙江禾欣实业集团股份有限公司	公司是一家集生产经营 PU 合成革、超细纤维合成革、合成革基布、浆料、色料为一体的国内产业链配套最完整的企业之一。专业生产干湿法 PU 革基布、PU 树脂、PU 色料、聚氨酯合成革、高档超纤皮面料、绒面超纤等产品，公司于 2010 年在深圳证券交易所上市，股票代码 002343	主营收入 135588.08 万元	“国家认定企业技术中心”，浙江省“五个一批”重点骨干企业、国家高新技术企业、银行信用“AAA”企业、中国驰名商标。
5	杭州萧山华益塑料有限公司	公司创建于 2000 年，主要产品：各种用途的 BOPP 薄膜，产能 14 万吨，总资产 5 亿元	产量 136967 吨，产值 16020 万元，销售额 148000 万元，利税 9242 万元，其中利润 7507 万元。	浙江省名牌产品
6	浙江伊美薄膜工业集团有限公司	公司创建于 2001 年，产品：双向拉伸聚丙烯薄膜，产能 120kt。注册资本 3700 万美元	产量 89097t，销售收入 113907 万元，产值 113555 万元，利税 2707 万元，其中利润 905 万元。	浙江省名牌产品
7	浙江大东南股份有限公司	公司创建于 1975 年，主要产品：BOPP、BOPET、CPP、PE 薄膜及袋，生产能力 150kt，2008 年在深圳证券交易所上市，股票代码 002263	主营收入 80869.77 万元。	中国塑料加工工业协会副理事长单位、浙江省塑料行业协会常务副会长单位、浙江省工业行业重点骨干企业、国家高新技术企业、全国塑料行业排头兵企业、2012 年度中国民营企业 500 强、中国塑料包装行业龙头企业、浙江省名牌产品、浙江省著名商标、浙江省出口名牌、2012 年浙江省综合百强企业、2012 年浙江省制造业百强企业。

续表

序号	企业名称	企业简介	2012年主要指标	企业获得的主要荣誉
8	南塑集团有限公司	公司创建于1991年，主要产品：塑料编织布及袋、PVC压延薄膜，塑料制品生产能力80kt。资产总额5.26亿元。	工业销售收入75500万元，出口总额2823万元。产量68447t，产值7.76亿，利税9251万元，其中利润5991万	浙江省塑料行业协会副会长单位、中国塑料十强企业（排名第六名）、"浙江名牌产品"、"浙江省著名商标"、浙江省纳税信用AAA级单位、省农行AAA级资信企业，省"三优"企业、省成长型工业企业、省清洁型生产企业，GB/T 8946—2011第一起草单位。
9	瑞安市东威塑胶有限公司	公司创建于1997年，产品：双向拉伸聚丙烯（BOPP）薄膜、PVC压延膜，生产能力66kt。注册资金10080万元。	产量69366t，销售额72656万元，产值77693万元，利税1572万元。	浙江省塑料行业协会副会长单位。
10	浙江俊尔新材料有限公司	公司创建于1995年，改性尼龙、改性聚碳酸酯、改性聚酯、改性聚烯烃、特种工程塑料和热塑性弹性体六大系列产品，广泛应用于汽车、电子、机械、航空等领域，注册资本7500万元。	产量29340t，营业收入51219万元，利税5017万元，其中利润3667万元。	浙江省塑料行业协会副会长单位、国家高新技术企业、国家火炬计划重点高新技术企、中国化工行业技术创新示范企业、国家认可实验室、浙江省创新型示范企业、浙江省产学研合作示范企业、浙江省著名商标。
11	浙江众成包装材料股份有限公司	公司创建于2001年，是一家集科研、设计生产、销售及售后服务于一体的全过程制造企业，是全球知名的高品质POF热收缩膜制造商和国内优秀的POF热收缩膜整体包装解决方案提供商，POF热收缩膜生产能力25kt，目前是全球第二、中国第一的POF热收缩膜生产企业。2010年在深交所中小板上市，股票代码：002522。	产量21143t，主营收入45380.30万元，利税25320万元，其中利润10264万元，出口交货值3962万美元。	公司已获授权专利20余项、浙江省高新技术产品、"浙江省著名商标"、"浙江名牌产品"、"浙江省知名商号"、"浙江出口名牌"、浙江省转型升级引领示范企业、浙江省绿色企业、中国轻工业塑料行业十强企业、国家高新技术企业、国家火炬计划重点高新技术企业。
12	三友控股集团有限公司	公司创建于1971年，主要产品：纺织用各种类别的塑料纱管、摩托车配件、摩托车、毛纺等。	营业收入总额42800万元，利税2405万元，其中利润1425万元。	中国塑料加工工业协会副理事长单位、中国纺织器材行业协会副理事长单位、浙江省塑料行业协会常务副会长单位、中国纺织器材行业50强、全国纺织行业先进集团、浙江省著名商标。
13	台州富岭塑胶有限公司	公司创建于1992年，主要产品：塑料餐具及厨房用具，产品90%出口，在美国设有二个分公司、澳洲设有一个分公司，市美国五大快餐连锁企业之一。总资产26803万元。年生产能力30000t。	产量18000t，销售总额31716万元，利税2885万元，其中利润2121万元。	中国塑料加工工业协会副理事长单位、中华人民共和国海关A类企业、国家高新技术企业、浙江省科技术型中小企业、浙江省绿色企业、浙江省守法诚信进出口企业、浙江省工商信誉AAA级单位、浙江省名牌产品、浙江省出口名牌

续表

序号	企业名称	企业简介	2012 年主要指标	企业获得的主要荣誉
14	浙江德斯泰塑胶有限公司	PVB 中间膜、EVA 太阳能电池封装膜、PVB 树脂粉，企业注册资金 2037.46 万	产量：PVB 中间膜、EVA 太阳能电池封装膜 10000t，PVB 树脂粉 4000t，产值 30000 万元，销售收入 26000 万元，利税 3800 万元，其中利润 2000 万元。	浙江省高新技术企业、银行资信等级为 AAA 级，有国家发明专利 4 项。
15	宁波色母粒有限公司	公司创建于 1985 年，产品：PP、PE、ABS、PS、PA 色母料，年生产能力：色母料 20000t，染色造粒 15000t。	色母料产量 8000t，染色造粒产量 6000t，产值 24000 万元，利税 3500 万元，其中利润 2500 万元	全国塑料制品标准化委员会塑料制品分技术委员会委员单位、浙江省塑料行业协会副会长单位、浙江省著名商标、色母料行业标准主要起草单位、拥有 5 项发明专利。
16	升阳控股有限公司	公司创建于 2002 年，产品：塑料编织布及袋，注册资金 5000 万元。	产量 16000t，产值 20000 万元。	中国塑编制品行业 20 强(排名第十四位)。
17	浙江锦盛包装有限公司	公司创建于 1989 年，产品：化妆品用塑料瓶，年生产能力 6000 万套，70% 产品外销。总资产 18406 万元。	实现销售 18500 万元，出口创汇 1756 万美元，技改投入 829 万元，利税 4137 万元，其中利润 1949 万元	浙江省知名商号、浙江省科技型中小企业、浙江省著名商标。
18	浙江龙士达塑业有限公司	公司创建于 1996 年，主要产品：日用塑料制品。注册资金 3206 万元。	产量 5600t，销售收入 14000 万元，利税 1200 万元。	浙江省科技中小型企业、浙江省著名商标。
19	浙江天梯橡塑有限公司	公司创建于 1994 年，产品：涂塑水带、钢丝增强管、纤维增强管、透明单管，以及花园管系列、煤气管、空气管、塑筋螺旋管等。注册资金 1580 万元。生产能力 20000t。	产量 10000t，产值 14000 万元，利税 800 万元，其中利润 400 万元。	浙江省著名商标
20	浙江远大塑胶有限公司	公司创建于 2003 年，产品：CPP 薄膜，5 条 CPP 薄膜生产线，产能 20kt，资产 1 亿元。	产量 12kt，产值 10000 万元，主营业务收入 8000 万元，利税 428 万元，其中利润 103 万元。	CPP 食品包装行业贡献奖
21	浙江步步乐箱包有限公司	公司创建于 1997 年，主要产品：PP、PC、PE 塑料拉杆、儿童箱包。能力 10000t。	产量 4000t，产值 7000 万元，利税 703 万元，利润 394 万元。	浙江省中小型企业技术中心；浙江省重合同守信用企业。

【行业优势】

1. 有一批大中型企业(集团)

经过五十余年的不懈努力，浙江省塑料行业发展迅猛，涌现出一批大中型骨干企业，这些企业拥有世界一流的塑料加工设备，这些大中型企业对行业的发展起到了积极的促进作用，是行业的中流砥柱，其中产量、产值、利润占全行业60%以上，目前全省塑料行业有五家上市公司。

2. 形成了一批优势产品

全省塑料制品中薄膜(BOPET、BOPP、CPP、聚烯烃收缩薄膜)和人造革、合成革在产量和质量上均处于国内领先地位，水性生态合成革已在浙江省小规模生产；BOPS片材、塑料管材及管件、异型材、日用塑料制品、塑料编织袋、塑料纱管、薄膜在全国也占有相当份额。

3. 区域优势明显

浙江省塑料加工业主要集中在台州、温州、宁波和绍兴，台州地区主要以生产塑料管材及配件、汽车和摩托车配件、日用塑料制品为主，温州地区主要以生产塑料编织制品、人造革、合成革及塑料薄膜为主，宁波地区主要以生产各种塑料注塑件(家用电器配件、办公用品配件等)、改性塑料为主，绍兴地区主要以生产各种双向拉伸薄膜(设备均为进口)为主。

4. 有较强的塑料机械和模具设计制造力量

2012年全省塑料加工专用设备产量120259台，同比下降15.12%，占全国同期塑料加工专用设备总产量的39.64%(居第一位)。宁波地区现已成为中国最大的注塑机生产基地，被誉为“中国塑机之都”，舟山地区是国内最大的塑料机械用螺杆制造基地，有“中国塑机螺杆之都”之称，黄岩、余姚的模具加工产业在国内知名度也很高，特别是黄岩近几年来发展相当迅速，有“中国模具之乡”之称。塑料机械和模具设计制造业的发展推动了浙江省塑料工业的发展。

5. 合成树脂产量迅速增长

2012年浙江省塑料树脂及共聚物产量5013.39kt，同比增长15.69%，占全国同期塑料树脂及共聚物总产量的9.62%，居全国第三位，其中：PVC树脂362.5kt，同比下降4.04%，占全国同期PVC树脂总产量的2.75%(居第十二位)；PS树脂238.2kt，同比增长21.05%，占全国同期PS树脂总产量的11.34%(居第五位)；聚酯4399.1kt，同比增长7.91%，占全国同期聚酯总产量的38.59%(居第一位)，合成树脂材料的迅速增长为浙江省塑料行业的发展提供了强有力的支撑。

【存在问题】

浙江省塑料行业在过去的几年里积极应对金融危机的挑战，取得了一定的成绩，但同时行业发展中结构性矛盾和问题也很突出：

1. 重复建设、过度扩张问题日益突出

目前盲目投资、重复建设和过度扩张的现象在行业内仍然很严重，以双向拉伸薄膜产品为例，“十五”、“十一五”期间，浙江省双向拉伸薄膜行业规模不断扩大，生产设备都是引进国外先进设备，目前BOPP、BOPET、薄膜产能在全国占有相当比例，已相对过剩，在这种状况下还有企业在投资上设备雷同、产品品种雷同的双向拉伸薄膜项目，还有一些企业准备投资上双向拉伸薄膜项目，人造革、合成革、编织袋产能也相对过剩，由此造成产品库存增加，引发行业的无序竞争，使得行业利润大幅下滑，出现了同样的产品相互压价，严重阻碍了行业的良性发展。

2. 投资呈下滑趋势

浙江省塑料行业近几年来投资呈下滑趋势，下滑的原因主要有以下几个方面：(1)企业创新能力较弱，缺乏高科技含量、高附加值项目；(2)土地制约因素突出，土地紧缺，且成本越来越高；(3)投资大量外流，浙江省塑料行业已将许多塑料制品项目向省外转移，主要向新疆、宁夏、安徽、东北等地转移。没有有效投入就没有有效产出，没有高质量投入就没有高质量产出。“十一五”时期浙江塑料行业投入明显不足，将在较大程度影响“十二五”时期的行业发展。

3. 节能减排工作进展缓慢

全省复合塑料膜生产企业中普遍存在小企业多，且以凹版印刷、干式复合为主，大量使用有机溶剂甚至苯类溶剂，对环境、对工人身体健康及被包装食品都会造成危害；PVC制品企业仍在使用含铅热稳定剂；合成革生产企业DMF吸收率、污水回用率不够高，氨氮处理技术进展缓慢；行业内大多数塑料机械尚未应用电磁替代电阻加热、变频等节能技术。

4. 贸易摩擦多发，出口难度增大

受国际贸易保护主义势力的影响，贸易摩擦将继续呈现出常态化特征，表现为贸易摩擦案件数量多、形式多样的特点。从贸易摩擦的手段看，“两反两保”是主要的贸易壁垒手段，多种贸易保护措施并用将更广泛、具有更大的杀伤力，特别是反补贴和保障措施渐成贸易壁垒的焦点。技术性贸易壁垒的形式将更加多样，贸易摩擦将会从“显性”向“隐性”扩展，环境保护等因素会更多的体现在摩擦中，由于浙江省塑料制品出口具有量大价廉的优势，由此可能会产生更多的贸易摩擦。

5. 面临“低端陷阱”和“三明治陷阱”的风险

当前，浙江塑料行业面临两个陷阱：一是低端陷阱。塑料行业结构调整步伐不快，以低技术含量、低附加值产品为主的结构特征明显，由于产业结构没有重大变化，增长潜力受到较大制约，行业长期处于低层次而难以升级。二是“三明治陷阱”。“三明治”的两边分别是成本和售价，中间层是企业利润。在成本明显提高和售价不断下跌的双向挤压下，企业利润迅速变薄。这两个陷阱是当前浙江塑料行业面临的突出问题。

6. 低成本低价格的竞争优势不断削弱

浙江塑料制品加工企业大多采用低成本低价格的竞争方式。随着生产要素供需矛盾增大，国际大宗商品价格持续高位震荡，国内要素价格改革步伐加快，制度性廉价资源逐步缩减，行业发展面临全方位的高成本约束。特别是企业用工成本持续较快上升，劳动密集型为主的产业结构面临着越来越大的转型压力。

除上述问题外，全行业还存在总体装备水平低、工艺技术相对落后；科技开发和创新能力薄弱；产品结构不尽合理，低档产品产能相对过剩；大中型企业少，小企业多；区域发展不平衡；废旧塑料二次加工污染严重等问题。

【应对措施】

未来全行业仍将面临严峻而复杂的国内外经济形势，面对宏观调控的新动向，生产经营将出现许多新情况和新问题，需要扎实应对。

1. 坚持把结构性调整作为加快转变行业经济发展方式的主攻方向

抓住机遇，加快转变经济发展方式，淘汰落后产能、优化生产工艺，推动产业结构优化升级，推进产品结构调整。

2. 重视人才培养

人才是科技进步和经济发展的重要资源、是企业立业之本，以人为本是企业发展的根本。要积极培养和吸纳知识面广、既懂生产经营又懂技术的高素质人才，建立有利于人才的培养使用和成长的激励机制。

3. 坚持把科技进步和创新作为加快行业发展的重要支撑

采用高新技术和先进工艺，推进行业科技进步；依靠科技进步，加快产品更新；不断扩大塑料制品的应用领域。

4. 坚持把建设资源节约型、环境友好型企业作为加快行业发展的重要着力点

大力推进废旧塑料的回收再利用，减少废旧塑料的二次污染；严格工艺配方、确保产品使用的安全性和卫生性；在复合膜行业大力推广应用无苯无酮油墨，实现清洁生产。

5. 规范行业道德和行业行为

要解决行业无序竞争的关键是要规范市场，要营造良好的市场环境，不仅靠政府的宏观调控政策，更重要的是企业不能靠拼价格来赢得市场，而是要以提高产品技术含量来赢得市场。要以诚信为本，以质取胜。要提倡行业团结、互助、协调、自律，共同维护和发挥行业整体优势，对行业内出现的矛盾和问题共同探讨，友好协商，以维护企业的共同利益。

6. 重视信息化建设，要充分利用信息化提高企业综合竞争力

信息化建设在建立现代化企业制度、有效降低成本、加快技术进步、促进技术创新、改善管理体制等方面起着重要作用并产生深远影响，企业需要打好信息化建设的基础，以提高企业在产品生产、销售等各个环节的信息化水平，要充分利用信息资源促进企业发展。

7. 关注国家政策，用心采取发展对策

塑料制品行业是“十二五”期间国家扶持的新兴产业之一，国家已先后出台了一系列政策：加强技术创新鼓励政策，改革科研投入体制，把专项资金支持和技术改造作为塑料加工产业升级的重要手段，设立新产品研发和产业化的扶持资金，支持并推广一批技术创新示范项目；企业享受国家有关支持技术改造、节能节水、技术进步及研发费用扣除等税收优惠政策；建立技术创新战略联盟，支持完善产、学、研、用相结合的行业技术创新体制，建立行业公共服务平台；支持企业建立国家认定企业技术中心、国际工程研究中心、国家工程实验室，开展共性、关键技术研发。企业要利用好这些政策，以增强发展后劲。

【大事记】

1. “2012 中国塑料产业”大会在宁波举行

由大连商品交易所、中国石化联合会和中国轻工业联合会举办的2012 中国塑料产业大会5月30～31日在宁波开幕。本次会议重点研讨在严峻的国内外经济形势下，塑料产业面临的市场形势和未来的发展方向，同时探讨期货市场与塑料现货市场相互促进的方式。共有塑料产业链上各领域生产企业及从事塑料期货的相关人士600多人与会，协会韩新伟会长应邀出席大会，并作为聚烯烃论坛的特邀嘉

宾对 2012 年下半年聚烯烃原料走势进行了分析和预测。

2. 浙江省塑料行业协会四届三次理事会顺利召开

协会四届三次理事会议于 7 月 12 日在杭州召开，有三十四个理事单位的理事出席了会议，会议审议通过了：协会 2011 年工作总结和 2012 年工作思路的报告、2011 年度浙江省塑料行业协会财务收支情况报告、人事调整议案（协会会长人选的调整的议案、协会秘书长人选调整的议案）、关于发展新会员的议案

3. 举办“浙江省塑料产业高峰论坛”

由浙江省塑料行业协会主办，台州市塑料行业协会和台州市国际会展中心有限公司协办的“浙江省塑料产业高峰论坛”于 2012 年 9 月 22 日在台州隆重举行，浙江省经济和信息化委员会、浙江省商务厅、中国塑料加工工业协会、台州市人民政府及台州市经济和信息化委员会、路桥区政府有关领导出席会议，会议着重研讨浙江省工业经济运行情况、塑料行业经济运行情况、2012 年塑料原料走势分析、贸易壁垒法律法规及应对等议题。总之，企业要增强忧患意识和风险意识，激发进取精神和创新活力。要把面临的形势估计得严峻一些，把困难和风险考虑得充分一些，把应对措施准备得扎实一些，牢牢把握主动权。采取稳健的经营方针，拓市场、避风险、强内功、增后劲，交出较好的企业经营业绩，以确保全省塑料行业健康发展。

4. 第十二届中国塑料交易会在台州举办

9 月 22 ~ 25 日，第十二届中国塑料交易会在浙江台州举办，本届塑交会设展位 1600 个，有 500 多家企业、3 万余人参展。

相比往年，本届塑交会展览面积增加 30%，展区划分更加清晰。展览分为机械馆、模具机床馆、原料馆、制品馆。原料、制品展区分别由上年的 5000m^2 增加到 10000m^2。

5. “2012 中国汽车用塑料及安全技术高峰论坛”在台州举行

9 月 23 日至 24 日，“2012 中国汽车用塑料及安全技术高峰论坛”在台州市会展中心报告厅举行，工信部消费品司、中国塑料加工工业协会、台州市经济和信息化委员会、中石化、宁波华翔集团、浙江大学、上海一汽大众、上海通用汽车、奥托立夫中国汽车方向盘有限公司等单位的领导和专家以及全国各地的汽车用塑料企业及相关的原料、零部件、设备、科研院所等各方面的单位代表，共计 112 位。

会上有关专家就“生物塑料载汽车上的应用”、“汽车零部件模具设计对材料性能的影响”、“私营汽车零部件企业的挑战与机遇”、“激光烧结技术在汽车配件中的应用”、“车用聚合物发泡材料：产业界现状和学术界技术进展”、“模具设计与注塑工艺”、“无味环保型相容剂在车用塑料中的应用”等作了精彩的报告，受到与会代表的欢迎与好评。

6. 举办新版“职业病防治法”和“环保政策法规”解读讲座

近年来国家对职业病防护和环境保护越来越重视，不断的修正和出台有关法律法规，为使广大企业更深入地了解今年国家修正和颁布的“中华人民共和国职业病防治法”及新版“环保政策法规”，我会联合浙江省橡胶工业协会、浙江省化学试剂工业协会、浙江省有机硅材料行业协会和浙江省氟化学工业协会于 11 月 29 日在杭州联合举办了新版“职业病防治法”和“环保政策法规”解读讲座，讲座邀请浙江省医学科学院、浙江省环保评估中心有关专家重点解读“中华人民共和国职业病防治法”（修正版）中企业在职业病防护中承担的责任、“环保政策及污染防治”、“职业卫生”等内容；对促进企业遵守国家有关法律法规，做好职业病防护和环保工作，有效避免不必要的经济损失具有重要作用。

7. 开展标准查阅服务

协会与浙江省技术监督局标准化研究院合作，在“浙江塑料网”上推出了为企业提供标准阅览、标准打印、标准翻译、标准跟踪、标准确认、技术水平对比等一系列标准服务。数据库标准主要结构为：国内标准有国家标准、行业标准、台湾标准；国外标准主要为 ISO、IEC、ITU 三大国际标准组织的部分标准以及美、欧、日等国和 CSA 标准、ANSI 标准、ASME 标准、ASTM 标准、UL 标准等主要国外组织标准的部分先进标准。

8. 一批企业获中国塑料行业企业信用 AAA 等级

中国塑料加工工业协会根据商务部信用工作办公室、国资委行业协会联系办公室有关文件精神，结合中国塑料行业企业实情，本着“诚信、自愿、公平、公正、科学、严谨”的原则，由企业自愿申报，经第三方专业评价机构评价，有 66 家获中国塑料行业（第一批）企业信用 AAA 级企业通过了复评，其中浙江省有 9 家企业（温州市华康合成革有限公司、义乌市大大箱包材料有限公司、温州人造革有限公司、义乌市鑫挺人造革有限公司、浙江经纬集团环保工程有限公司、浙江龙跃科技有限公司、浙江中财管道科技股份有限公司、浙江中财型材有限责任公司、

浙江中元枫叶管业有限公司)。19家企业中国塑料行业(第四批)企业信用等级评价结果,其中浙江有4家(浙江伟星新型建材股份有限公司、浙江华庆集团有限公司、浙江众成包装材料股份有限公司、台州市希尔家庭用品有限公司)。

9. 中国第六届国际塑木论坛在宁波举行

"中国第六届国际塑木论坛"于2012年11月3~5日在宁波慈举行,本届论坛以"资源有限、发展无限"为主题,与会演讲者围绕世界塑木发展的新动向、新技术以及塑木产品运用的新领域展开研讨,大会邀请了多位来自世界知名企业、科研院校、行业协会、专业研究机构的代表和高级专家,介绍行业发展情况及前景,共同交流介绍最新科研成果、生产技术以及应用技术的发展,加强企业核心竞争力,提高企业产品质量和管理能力,为企业提供一个高端的技术交流平台,和新产品推介平台。

10."浙江省塑料行业协会暨台州市塑料行业协会2012年理事扩大会议"在台州隆重召开

12月21日,"浙江省塑料行业协会暨台州市塑料行业协会2012年理事扩大会议"在台州隆重召开,浙江省塑料行业协会、台州市塑料行业协会会长及秘书长、台州市经济和信息化委员会、台州市民间组织管理局、台州市出入境检疫检疫局、台州市海关、台州市各县(市)经济和信息化局及浙江省和台州市塑协理事单位的100余名代表出席了会议。

会议分别听取了省、市塑协会长作的工作报告及省塑协秘书长对全省塑料行业现状及存在问题的简要分析。台州市经济和信息化委员会叶国敏副主任就台州市工业经济及塑料行业的情况在会上作了简要介绍,同时对台州市塑料行业协会的工作给予了充分的肯定,他希望省塑协能一如既往地关心和支持台州的塑料工业。

(浙江省塑料行业协会 汪建萍)

温州市

【概况】

2012年温州市塑料制品工业全社会完成工业总产值623亿元,同比下降5%,塑料制品总产量4080kt,同比下降4%。其中规模企业193家,完成工业总产值267.36亿元,同比下降4.96%;出口交货值29.62亿元,同比下降9.88%;塑料行业规模企业总产值占全市工业企业总产值的6.42%;列在全市33个行业中列第5位。规模企业塑料制品产量1290.2kt,同比下降3.86%(塑料制品各品种产量、各县市区产量详见表1、2,工业总产值超亿元企业见表4)。

截至2012年底,全市塑料制品行业规模企业资产总计258.86亿元,同比增长1.51%;主营业务收入250.07亿元,同比下降11.60%;实现利润总额5.61亿元,同比下降28.16%;完成利税总额12.12亿元,同比下降24.12%;其中亏损企业39家,比上年增加19家;亏损金额1.01亿元,同比增加7.74%。从业人员平均数为47980人,同比下降9.62%;应付职工薪酬137573万元,同比下降0.05%(各项财务指标详见表3)。在国际金融危机和欧债危机造成国际市场疲软及国内经济宏观调控,经济增速放缓双重影响下,全市塑料行业步履艰难,多项铄指标出现十几年来未曾出现的负增长,但从4季度开始触底有所好转。

表1 2012年全市规模企业塑料制品各品种产量

品 种	企 业 数	全年产量/t	同比增长/±%	年市产量/%
塑料制品总计	193	1290187	-3.86	100
其中:塑料薄膜	33	462969	1.80	35.88
泡沫塑料	4	28349	-25.98	2.20
塑料人造革合成革	59	240135	-14.20	18.61
日用塑料制品	4	10765	-3.20	0.84
其他塑料制品	93	547969	-7.14	42.47

注:以上数据由市统计局提供。

表2　2012年各县(市)区规模企业塑料制品产量

序号	地区	企业数	产量/t	同比/±%	占全市/%	序号	地区	企业数	产量/t	同比/±%	占全市/%
1	瑞安	33	359452	-3.07	27.86	6	开发区	4	17245	-6.80	1.34
2	苍南	36	334747	4.07	25.95	7	泰顺	1	6500	1.17	0.5
3	平阳	53	308179	0.52	23.89	8	鹿城	1	3562	-1.55	0.27
4	龙湾	56	236282	-17.90	18.31	9	瓯海	1	2336	-17.66	0.18
5	乐清	8	21883	-7.63	1.70						

表3　2012年温州市规模企业主要财务指标　　万元

指标名称	1~12月累计	同比/±%	指标名称	1~12月累计	同比/±%
资产总计	2588628.5	1.51	财务费用	54903.2	-4.84
流动资产合计	1783604.4	0.11	其中：利息收入	17856.5	112.86
应收账款	450836.2	4.42	利息支出	64018.9	8.53
存货	314271.8	6.03	本年折旧	58262.4	-8.74
其中：产成品存货	124341.3	16.34	科技活动经费支出总额	8854	4.86
银行贷款余额	721227.9	-0.32	周围技术成果费用	1107.3	-42.03
负债合计	1790974.2	2.66	应付职工薪酬	137573	-0.05
主营业务收入	2500705.2	-11.60	应交增值税	55370	-20.98
主营业务成本	2266829.3	-11.56	利润总额	56091.6	-28.16
主营业务税金及附加	9735.8	-15.86	利税总额	121197.4	-24.12
销售费用	31744.9	-6.22	税金总额	65105.8	-20.25
管理费用	91128.1	1.91	亏损企业	39	129.41
			亏损企业亏损额	10942.6	7.74
			从业人员平均数	47980	-9.62

表4　温州市2012年工业总产值亿元以上企业

序号	企业名称	工业总产值/万元	备注
1.	金田集团有限公司	3558600	双向拉伸聚丙烯薄膜(BOPP)
2.	温州市亚泰进出口有限公司	141491	销售收入(塑料原料经营)
3.	温州晨光集团有限公司	102186	编织袋
4.	瑞安市东威塑胶有限公司	72542	BOPP薄膜 PVC压延薄膜
5.	浙江强盟实业股份有限公司	69667	BOPET薄膜
6.	金田塑业有限公司	52997	BOPP薄膜
7.	浙江俊尔新材料有限公司	52218	工程塑料
8.	南塑集团有限公司	42354	编织袋 PVC压延薄膜
9.	浙江华滨包装材料有限公司	41917	BOPP薄膜
10.	浙江华庆集团有限公司	34224	编织袋

续表

序 号	企业名称	工业总产值/万元	备 注
11.	温州银泰化工有限公司	34112	聚丙烯树脂(粉料)
12.	温州市朗顺进出口有限公司	31000	销售收入(塑料原料经营)
13.	华泰塑胶集团有限公司	28493	PVC 压延薄膜
14.	长虹塑料集团有限公司	27423	PA 扎带
15.	佑利控股集团有限公司	24500	CPVC、PVC 硬管
16.	浙江经纬集团有限公司	23851	PE、PP 管
17.	华正塑料集团有限公司	23503	编织袋
18.	浙江中宇节能科技有限公司	22853	编织袋
19.	浙江贤超包装有限公司	19024	编织袋
20.	浙江建新塑胶股份有限公司	18821	PVC 压延薄膜
21.	瑞安市塑料薄膜厂	17789	PVC 压延薄膜
22.	温州升阳塑业有限公司	16084	编织袋
23.	广天集团有限公司	15792	编织袋
24.	浙江佰通防腐设备有限公司	15116	聚四氟乙烯管材
25.	浙江宏泰电器有限公司	14798	PA 扎带
26.	浙江金石包装有限公司	13481	彩印复合软包装
27.	温州华利集团有限公司	13465	编织袋
28.	煌盛集团有限公司	13608	钢丝增强 PE 复合管
29.	瑞安市奥华塑胶有限公司	13481	PVC 硬片
30.	浙江南方塑胶制造有限公司	12091	酚醛电木粉

一、大事要事

1. 温州塑协七位企业家当选市人大代表

在温州市2012年度人大换届选举中煌盛集团有限公司董事长邵泰清、温州市亚泰进出口有限公司董事长林永森、南塑集团有限公司董事长林增标、浙江白马包装厂厂长林宣朗、温州佳利包装厂厂长林国产、温州赵氟隆有限公司副总经理陈国龙、温州嘉田电雕制版有限公司董事长蔡景烛当选温州市第十二届人大代表。

2. 温州塑协六企业入“温州百强企业”榜

由温州市企业联合会温州市企业家协会温州市工业经济联合会评选的2012年温州百强企业，温州塑协六企业上榜，它们是：

(29)温州市亚泰进出口有限公司

(64)温州晨光集团有限公司

(74)瑞安市东威塑胶有限公司

(75)金田集团有限公司

(79)浙江强盟实业股份有限公司

(92)华泰塑胶集团

3. 中共温州市塑料行业协会党支部成立

经市工商联机关常委研究同意，中共温州市塑料行业协会支部于6月15日成立，周肇枢同志任党支部书记。

4. 俊尔公司田际波获市职工“金捶奖”

由市委宣传部、市总工会、温州日报报业集团、温州广播电视传媒集团联合举办的温州市“金捶奖”杰出职工评选活动日前揭晓，浙江俊尔新材料有限公司田际波获第三届“金捶奖”杰出职工称号(全市十个)。

5. 温州市65人参加全国塑编大会，六家企业获塑编二十强

2012年全国塑编产业链与市场对接会暨沈阳康平塑编经贸会于8月28日在沈阳市辽宁大厦多功能厅召开，中国塑料加工工业协会常务副理事长曹俭主持开幕式，中国轻工业联合会副会长、中国塑料加工工业协会理事长钱桂敬、工业和信息化部消费品司司长高延敏、国务院国有资产监督管理委员会研究室行业协会处梁方处长，沈阳市市长陈海波，副市长王翔坤参加开幕式并作重要讲话，参加会议

有关省温州塑协领导，塑编生产企业代表，塑机制造企业代表，原料、助剂生产企业代表，大专院校、研究机构代表1190余人，温州市有65人参加会议，会上中国塑协塑编专委会会长浙江华庆集团有限公司董事长姜集康作2011年专委会工作报告，专委会常务副会长南塑集团有限公司董事长林增标作关于塑料编织袋国家标准制订工作总结，专委会高级顾问宋云鹤作塑编产业现状及提升调整的建议。会议表彰2011年塑编行业二十强。并颁发奖牌，温州晨光集团有限公司(第一名)、南塑集团有限公司(第六名)浙江华庆集团有限公司(第七名)、华正塑料集团有限公司(第十三名)、温州升阳塑业有限公司(第十四名)、广天集团有限公司(第十八名)等六家温州企业获此殊荣。

6. 温州塑协组织参观[CHINAP2012国际橡塑展]

温州市塑料行业协会组团46人前往上海参观4月18~21日第二十六届国际塑料橡胶工业展览会，本届展会有36个国家和地区2729家知名展商，设25个展馆，参观人数近110000人，本届展会主题是“橡塑科技，成就未来”。参观展会为我市塑料企业创新和调整提供宝贵的信息。

7. 俊尔公司陈晓敏荣获首届魅力女温商荣誉称号

温州市女企业家协会四届五次会员大会上，浙江俊尔新材料股份有限公司董事长陈晓敏荣获首届魅力女温商荣誉称号，表彰她奋力拼搏勇于创新精神。

8. 聚酰胺扎带行业标准评审会在乐清召开

8月2日长虹塑料集团有限公司负责起草的《聚酰胺扎带》行业标准评审会在乐清召开，会议由中国塑料制品标准化技术委员会秘书长陈家琪主持，参加会议的有中国塑料加工工业协会常务副理事长曹俭，中国塑协综合部主任田岩，乐清市经信局、质检局领导有有关专家30多人。会上首先由负责起草的长虹公司毛维琴副总经理介绍了标准说明、检测报告、征求意见处理情况及标准内容，到会专家进行了逐条讨论并提出来不少改进建议，会议开了一天，中午都没有休息会议最后由陈秘书长作总结，会议一致通过本标准，并认为本标准国际上未见报导，具有国际先进水平。国内生产聚酰胺著名企业神马集团和华峰集团公司都派有关专家参加，温州市塑料行业协会名誉会长宋云鹤高工、常务副会长周肇枢、秘书长余正光高工参加评审。

9. 长虹塑料集团有限公司起草聚酰胺扎带加工贸易单耗标准

为了加强加工贸易单耗管理，规范和完善海关和商务主管部门对加工贸易单耗的审批、申报、核销，根据《海关总署办公厅，国家发展改革委办公厅下达2010年度加工贸易单耗标准制订计划和单耗管理研究课题项目的通知》(署办函[2010]3号)，特制定聚酰胺扎带加工贸易单耗标准。该标准由海关部署办公厅、国家发展改革委办公厅委托中国轻工业联合会负责制订工作，由中国塑料加工工业协会、长虹塑料集团有限公司负责起草。

10. 温州塑协进行2012年职称培训和评审

温州塑协在市人保局支持下，开展2012年塑料加工成型专业职称培训和评审，经协会申报请市职称改革领导小组批准，2012年职称培训于6月4日开始报名，经动员全市有25人报名参加培训，其中申报工程师18人、助工6人、技术员1人，本年度报名人员中有大学本科高分子专业毕业2人、大专10人、文化和专业水平都较历年高。在8月27日、28日、29日3天培训、考试、答辩，本年培训特请温州大学刘建平副教授博士讲课，学员反映良好，在培训期间市人力资源和社会保障局陈瑶琴处长亲临指导。考试时陈瑶琴处长、考试中心黄正鹏主任到场监督指导。评审结果工程师18人，降级4人，助工降级1人，授工程师14人、助工9人、技术员1人，评审时陈瑶琴再次来协会指导。

经公示后上报市人力资源和社会保障局。2012年10月11日，温州市人力资源和社会保障局以温人社发[2012]248号文下达“关于公布倪任林等25位同志具有塑料加工成型中、初级专业技术职务任职资格的通知”批准倪任林等14人具有塑料加工成型专业工程师职务任职资格；姜曙等9人具有塑料加工成型助理工程师任职资格；蒋义庆等2人具有塑料加工成型技术员职务任职资格。上述同志任职资格时间从2012年9月26日开始计算。

11. 瑞安温州塑协举办“塑料薄膜行业现状及发展”讲座

瑞安市塑料行业协会于2012年12月12日下午在瑞安市国际大酒店举办《瑞安市塑料薄膜行业的现状及今后发展的建议》专题讲座，由温州市塑料行业协会名誉会长宋云鹤高级工程师主讲。

塑料薄膜制品是全国十大塑料制品中列第二位的产品，而瑞安市是《中国塑料薄膜生产基地》，塑料薄膜是瑞安市三大支柱产业之一，近几年来，在国际金融危机、欧洲债务危机及国内经济增速放缓、市场需求疲软，塑料行业增速也随之下滑，特别是2012年呈现负增长，如何破解薄膜产业发展瓶颈，已成为全行业的当务之急，为此瑞安温州塑协十分重视，组织了50多家企业参与了讲座，温州温州塑协常务副会长周肇枢同志也到会聆听。

二、技改、投资、升级

1. 平阳藉企业家回归投资建新厂

平阳藉企业家山东利邦塑业有限公司林宣厂、林国产投资6.5亿元，其中固定资产投资5.8亿元，征地87亩，建厂房及辅助用房9.6万平方米，引进德国布鲁克纳机械公司二条特种双向拉伸聚丙烯薄膜生产线。项目建成后，将形成7万吨多层共挤双向拉伸聚丙烯薄膜的生产能力，年销售收入约10.5亿元，销售税金约3850万元，该项目列入省、市技术改造"双千工程"重点项目计划。目前厂房基建已在进行，项目对平阳的塑编产业的转型提升具有非常重要的示范和带头作用，有利于塑编产业的产品结构调整、提高核心竞争能力。

2. 俊尔公司磨砺亮剑，滨海新区建新厂

在全国经济增速放缓，面临国内外诸多严峻挑战之时浙江俊尔新材料股份有限公司练好内功磨砺以待，才能选准时机亮出制胜之剑在滨海园区投资22481万元征地77亩，设计年生产高级工程塑料能力6万吨，是目前生产能力的2倍，厂房设计已近收尾，厂房建设就要动工。

浙江俊尔新材料股份今年被告评为"2012年浙江省创新型示范企业"公司建厂以来以磨技术、储人才、磨内功、储能量，以不断创新、开拓市场，把企业做强做大。

【协会活动】

1. 温州塑协召开四届二次常务理事会

2012年5月10日，州市塑料行业协会在温州煌盛集团会议室召开四届二次常务理事会，参加会议的有会长、常务副会长、副会长、常务理事36人。

会上通报了2012年一季度塑料行业运行情况；通报了筹建温州市塑料市场进展情况；审议通过了吸收5个新会员及增设一个常务副会长；布置了2012年人才工作站职称申报、培训及评审工作及协会有关工作事宜。

2. 瑞安市塑料行业协会召开第三届一次会员大会暨协会成立十周年庆典大会

2012年8月8日在瑞安市国际大酒店国际厅召开瑞安市塑料行业协会第三届第一次会员大会暨协会成立十周年庆典大会，大会由卢文忠主持，会上尤作虎会长作"再接再厉、不断前进"的第二届理事会工作报告，常务副会长余建勇作第二届理事会财务收支报告，由工作人员宣读协会章程修改报告及新章程，到会会员一致通过三个报告。大会以举手表决的方式选出了第三届理事会，第三届理事会选出会长、常务副会长12人、副会长9人、秘书长1人，瑞安市塑料薄膜厂董事长周育兴当选第三届会长，瑞安市塑料协会林锡洪当选为秘书长。会上还通报表彰塑料行业"优秀新居民员工"。

3. 温州塑协召开会长办公会议商议"市场"大事

温州市塑料行业协会于2012年9月7日在温州市亚泰进出口有限公司会议室召开会长办公(扩大)会议，参加会议有会长、常务副会长、副会长、秘书长，各县(市)协会会长、秘书长及部分重点企业负责人30人。会议专题研究筹建温州市塑料市场有关问题，会议由余正光秘书长主持，邵泰清会长作主题发言，宋云鹤名誉会长阐述了市场的历史原因和现实意义，介绍了项目可行性报告内容，周肇枢常务副会长通报了筹建温州塑料市场的前期工作进展情况。与会同志一致认为市场建设十分必要且完全可行，会议同意该项目由温州市塑料行业协会牵头主办，由温州市亚泰进出口有限公司、温州市朗顺进出口有限公司承办，并欢迎会员企业共同参股。

4. 温州市塑料行业协会召开第四届第二次会员大会

温州市塑料行业协会于2012年12月18日下午在国贸大酒店召开第四届第二次会员大会，与会人员130人，会议由余正光秘书长主持，邵泰清会长作《温州市塑料行业协会2012年工作总结和2013年工作计划》的报告，常务副会长林增标作《审议2012年协会财务收支》的报告，常务副会长周育兴宣读市人力资源和社会保障局[2012]248号文件《关于公布倪任林等25位同志具有塑料加工成型中、初级专业技术职务任职资格的通知》，浙江俊尔新材料股份有限公司常务副总经理朱春光、金田集团有限公司副总经理范志勇、瑞安市东威塑胶有限公司总经理王辉煌在会上作典型发言，温州晨光集团有限公司作书面发言，温州塑协常务副会长周肇枢作《温州塑料行业的昨天、今天和明天》的发言。温州市统战部副部长、市工商联党组书记陈芳铭最后作重要讲话，市经信委调研员游聚森向获中、初级技术职称的25位同志颁发证书。大会通过新增补常务副会长1个，新增理事单位2个，新增会员企业6个。

5. 平阳县塑料包装协会召开五届一次会员大会

平阳县塑料包装协会于2012年12月27日在萧江大酒店召开平阳县塑料包装协会五届一次会员大会，会议由林宣朗秘书长主持，姜集康会长代表第四届理事会作工作报告，执行副会长吴美秋作财务工作报告，执行副会长温积考作章程修改说明，到会人员一致通过三个报告。会议以举手表决方式选举产生第五届理事会理事，第五届第一次理事会选举产生会长、执行副会长、副会长、秘书长，浙江中宇科技有限公司董事长陈积博当选第五届会长，浙江旭光塑料有限公司董事长毛芳钧当选为秘书长(兼执行副会长)。

(温州市塑料行业协会　宋云鹤)

温州市合成革行业

【概况】

2012年，受国内外经济大环境的影响，合成革企业的生产经营面临市场冷，订单少，成本高，融资难等困难与挑战。面对困境，各企业提振信心，攻坚破难，开拓奋进，全行业经济状况比预计得要好。全市合成革会员企业工业总产值为103.79亿元，同比下降13.51%，季度工业产值环比向稳平进趋势明显，二季度比一季度、三季度比二季度、四季度比三季度产值环比增长分别为23.5%、1.68%、13.3%。有21%企业年产值实现正增长，13%的企业年产值与去年持平，其余企业产值下行。据统计，年工业产值超亿元企业44家，超2亿元7家，超6亿元1家，有17家企业停产和外迁。2012年，温州人造革有限公司实现工业总产值6.76亿元，评为温州市综合评价百佳企业，获龙湾区区长质量奖；龙湾区(高新区)功勋企业。

【出口贸易工作】

2012年国际需求疲软，世界贸易增速下滑，金融危机、欧债危机、美国财政悬崖等外部因素对国内经济发展产生较大影响。温州合成革外贸出口在连续11年同比增幅高位运行的情况下，也受到严重影响。全年外贸出口为4.699亿美元，约合人民币29.4亿元，同比减少11.01%，占全年销售总额的四分之一强。主要出口到亚洲、非洲、南美、北美和欧洲。出口交货值亚洲占50.09%，占合成革出口的半壁江山。合成革出口产终国排名前十位的国家和地区为：印度、墨西哥、伊朗、埃及、韩国、哥伦比亚、叙利亚、土耳其、印度尼西亚、摩洛哥，其中印度尼西亚、摩洛哥首次进入前十位。

外贸出口产终国为106个，比2011年增加6个。温州人造革有限公司全年出口交货值达3.06亿元，同比增长4.0%，再居行业出口龙头；温州合力革业有限公司、浙江龙跃科技有限公司出口交货值均超亿元人民币。

【2012中国(温州)国际合成革展会】

2012年8月30日至9月1日，商会与中国塑协合成革专委会、德纳公司共同承办的2012中国(温州)国际合成革展，与17届中国国际皮革展、中国箱包皮具材料及设备展等共四个展会在温州同期举行。本届合成革展会汇聚了近200家来自山东、江苏、浙江、福建、广东等地区的合成革企业参展，我商会组织一批企业组团参展，为合成革行业搭建一个集展示、交流、合作、共赢为一体的商贸平台。展会上，参展企业亮出了各自的新产品，为市场注入了新的吸引力。展会期间，还组织了近20多名国内外客商(分别来自马来西亚、印度、斯里兰卡等国家)到合成革企业进行实地考察，以感受“中国合成革之都”风采。

【承办2012中国合成革峰会】

8月30日下午，由中国塑协主办，中国塑协人造革合成革专委会和我商会等单位承办的2012中国合成革峰会在温州万和豪生大酒店举行，中国塑协领导，国内合成革行业巨头及上下游产业链上专家200多人参会，会议围绕着“创新与发展”的主题，采用主题演讲、领导报告、嘉宾对话等形式，为中国合成革行业的发展建言献策，共同探索合成革产业的创新发展之路。峰会上，还邀请建筑装饰行业专家就家居装饰、时尚壁纸市场和技术情况进行对话，和国内家居界、装饰界建立交流机制，为拓展新市场而努力。在峰会上，温州市有9家合成革企业获得中国塑协颁发的“高端品牌奖”、“科技创新奖”、“绿色企业奖”等11个奖项，提高企业产品竞争力。

【品牌建设】

我商会申报的集体商标经国家工商局商标局于2012年2月核准，获得了集体商标注册证。今后业内规模较小尚无拥有自主商标的企业可使用集体商标，提高企业国际市场竞争力。2012年商会继续深入开展“家家争名牌，百家创品牌“活动，市级以上品牌又增加了两个，分别是温州新华迪合成革有限公司华革(图形)商标，温州市日利制革有限公司RIL(图形)商标获温州市知名商标称号。至12月底止，全市合成革企业累计已取得各类品牌56个，品牌产品销售占全行业销售总额的38%以上。

【安全生产和环境保护】

2012年，商会根据省安监局《关于进一步做好危险化学品溶剂回收企业安全许可的意见》要求，结合企业的实际，对安全生产许可条件提出建议和意见并被采纳。商会还坚持督促企业按照标准进行整改。经企业努力，全市已有62家企业已经获得省安监局颁发的危化品安全生产许可证。

商会积极配合市政府和各级环保部门做好合成革行业整治提升工作，商会分别召开理事会、会长办公会议和各类座谈会，技术交流会等进一步提高治理效果。商会与温大合作研究二甲胺废气治理新工艺，中试已取得重大进展；同时商会还通过各种途径向政府各个功能区管委会建议继续进行排污许可证的颁发工作，以进一步加大环境治理的力度。商会还专题召开会长办公会议，就深化环境整治，提升企业作深入讨论，找出薄弱环节，有针对性提出整改意见实现环境质量进一步提高。

2012 年 10 月 8 日，市环保局《关于要求确保合成革企业污染防治设施正常运行的通知》下达后，商会立即行动，及时将文件转发给企业，要求企业继续提高认识，抓好硬件设施建设。温革、金大利、正大利、新大力公司等企业依托技术创新，投入大量资金改进环保设施和技术改造，如将塔顶水温度降至常温(30°C 以下)回用至生产线，取得良好经济效益和社会效益，为企业转型升级开辟了新途径。

【扶贫济困】

商会多年来一直践行扶贫济困，奉献爱心的社会责任。春节前，商会组织 17 家企业捐款 9 万多元，走访慰问瑶溪、海滨、永中等 80 户贫困户，为他们送去一份温暖。2012 年，龙湾合成革企业通过扶贫、助学、拥军、公益事业等活动共慷慨解囊捐赠 200 多万元，显现了一片赤诚之心。

【商会工作】

行业遇到的困难越多，商会的工作量越大，2012 年商会继续主动服务，如积极帮助企业解决融资难，把企业融资难，融资成本高的情况积极向政府和银行反映，并引导企业实行信用互保，使企业融资难得到些缓解。商会还积极主动向有关部门反映协调企业生产经营活动中遇到的困难。如 8 月初，商会接到会员企业关于 COD 在线监测设备建设问题很多反映，主要是提供龙湾区和高新区 COD 在线监测设施产品和运行维护某单位的报价大大高于其他中标单位，企业无法接受。商会向市环保部门如实反映企业的呼声，经多次洽谈，最后为企业降低了 400 多万元的费用；商会还积极参与危化品安全生产许可证颁发过程中有关设备测试收费的洽谈，全力为企业讲话，为企业降低了 100 多万元的费用，减轻了企业的负担。

6 月底，商会召开党员会议，选举产生党支部委员会，常务副会长、温州华都皮革有限公司董事长王会弟当选为党支部书记。12 月 19 日，商会在香格里拉大酒店召开五届一次会员大会，总结四届理事会工作，选举产生了第五届理事会成员、温州华康合成革有限公司董事长王永康再次当选为会长，温州华都皮革有限公司董事长王会弟当选为监事会监事长，换届工作圆满成功。

11 月，中国轻工业联合会召开“全国轻工业特色区域和产业集群发展工作会议”，研究和部署轻工业特色区域和产业集群发展思路和主要任务，表彰先进。在会上，温州市合成革商会被授予“十一五轻工业特色区域和产业集群先进集体”荣誉称号，成为全国 59 个受表彰的单位之一。

(温州市合成革商会　童人本)

江　苏　省

合成高分子材料是 20 世纪全球经济发展中增长最快的行业之一，塑料又是三大合成高分子材料中比例最大的最重要的行业，进入 21 世纪以来更是以强劲的发展势头迅猛推进。塑料的原料合成树脂与合成橡胶、合成纤维三大类合成高分子材料与钢铁、木材、水泥一起构成现代社会中的四大基础材料，是支撑现代高科技发展的重要新型材料之一，是信息、能源、工业、农业、交通运输乃至航空航天和海洋等国民经济各重要领域都不可缺少的生产资料，人类的生存和发展离不开这四大类基础材料，这是最基本的生产资料和消费资料。

江苏是我国最主要的塑料加工工业基地之一，改革开放给江苏的塑料加工工业发展带来了巨大的生机和活力，随着改革开放的不断深入而有了突飞猛进的发展。通过引进国外的先进设备与技术，兴办三资企业，改造了一大批中小企业，涌现了大批的具有新的形象和活力的高新企业和龙头企业；产品质量和档次显著提高，产品品种不断增多，应用领域不断扩大，出口创汇逐年增加，全行业整体水平上了历史新台阶。

江苏塑料加工工业始于 60 年代初，是当时的新兴行业。初期的产量仅 1200 多吨，1969 年产量才超过 10kt。1979 年，江苏塑料制品总量在全国同行业中率先突破 100kt，并连续十一年位据全国同行业第一。改革开放三十年以来，特别是进入 2010 年以后，江苏的塑料加工业按总吨位计算已退居全国第四，但是按经济总量计算仍位列广东浙江之后，约占全国总量的十分之一，是中国为数不多的、主要的塑料加工业基地之一。包括原料、塑料机械、模具和助剂，按照塑料产业链计算，江苏的塑料工业综合水平仍然位列全国前茅。

江苏的塑料产品涉及领域广泛，从农业，工业和消费品包装，到建材、汽车、机械、军工、电子通讯等；几乎当前国内外塑料界所有的塑料产品都有生产，近十年来的发展和调整，江苏的塑料高档次产品的比例有了很大提升；普通塑料机械的进口比例大大减少，普通塑料机械的出口逐年增加。从品种上分析，农用薄膜的产量随着宽辐大蓬膜的推广应用和长寿无滴膜的新型多功能膜的兴起，无论在品质、档次上还是在总量上都有了显著的提高和增长。工业用膜（包括收缩膜、双向拉伸膜、缠绕膜、内衬膜、食品、服装、玩具日用品包装膜、锂电池隔膜等）占薄膜总量的80%以上。板材中的ABS、PS复合板、铝塑复合板、PC板、PET板以及为家电、室内外装饰装潢用板、汽车配套内饰用板，大型客机内饰片板材等的产量逐年上升。塑料编织袋及其他编织产品进过多年的调整和发展，在品质上有了很人改善，品种上有了新的发展，应用领域有了进一步的拓展，其产量仍然保持着增长的趋势，但塑料编织袋，尤其是小型塑料编织袋吨位总量已被山东超越。编织吨装袋的直接和间接出口量都在逐年增长，但由于受国际经融危机影响而逐步显现的工农业产品出口不力，也导致塑料编织袋的出口显现下降趋势。管材和型材以惊人的速度在发展，已出现不少大型的生产厂家，凸现该类产品对规模经济的要求和品牌效应的威力，但该类产品的经济效益不很明显，企业之间的差异很大。而普通泡沫制品和普通桶类包装容器的产量增长速度较缓。

江苏曾经是全国塑料编织产品的发源地，第一台塑料圆织机就是江苏常州成功开发和推向市场的，在现在看来视乎很平常的四梭圆织机革命性的使塑料行业淘汰了落后的平织机。第一台双色注射剂也是江苏开发和最早推向市场的，第一条国产双向拉伸聚丙烯薄膜生产线的开发投产也是在江苏。聚氯乙烯异型材的最早开发和生产也是在江苏，聚丙烯加工母料的开发和推广也是在江苏开始的，如此等等，很多开创塑料发展的历史先河都有着江苏塑料战线组织领导者和科技工作者的艰辛努力。

现阶段江苏的塑料企业主要以民营企业和股份制企业为绝大多数，按统计局规模企业制品生产能力达4Mt以上，估计全行业消费总吨位应该在6Mt以上。由于全球金融危机对塑料行业的危及影响，许多为汽车工业、食品工业配套以及出口型企业在明显滑坡的后续，艰难中拓展新的市场领域。

近十年内，江苏的塑料企业重组和格局的变化相当大，原来占主导地位的国有企业、集体企业份份改制后，真正的国有企业或国有控股企业所占比重已很小。加上近年来不断涌现出的新的民营塑料企业，发展迅速、面貌一新。起点高，管理新，观念新、效益佳是现阶段江苏塑料企业的几个主要特点。改制后的各企业都投入了大量的资金，谨慎地选择时代热点项目，进行技术提升改造和新产品开发和引进。为数不少的民营化企业都实施了工厂的整体搬迁，以土地的区位优势换资金、换发展后劲。使整个塑料加工行业从质和量两个方面的取得了突飞猛进的发展。全省各类技改项目的成功实施，大大提高了企业新产品的开发能力和市场竞争力，先后开发出一批技术含量高、紧跟市场热点的新产品，近年来除了为汽车工业，高速铁路等交通新热点配套的项目外，江苏已有为数不少的塑料企业在为航空航天的发展做积极的配套工作。江苏的塑料行业继续在汽车燃油箱、保险扛、仪表板、大巴内饰、小轿车内饰、民用航空内饰、城市和农村供水用塑料件、大口径管材管件、多功能复合膜和多功能农膜、双向拉伸聚酯、双向拉伸聚丙烯、双向拉伸聚苯乙烯、共挤复合膜、聚碳酸酯板、光导板、铝塑复合板、信用卡基材、身份证材料、装饰广告用材料、防水材料、手机、电视、冰箱、音响、电器电气用材等方面，为包装、电子、交通、机械、通讯、航空航天等领域的发展作出巨大贡献。

随着改革开放的深入发展，技术装备的引进和自身技术开发能力的提高，江苏塑料工业已形成成型工艺齐全、产品品种繁多、生产规模持续趋大、社会效益和经济效益较好的基本格局，成为全省经济发展的重要支柱行业之一，尽管江苏塑料已从计划经济时代的全国第一位被广东、浙江超越，仍然位居全国塑料工业经济总量的的第三位。广东浙江江苏山东四省占据全国塑料总量的65%，江苏继续保持着在中国塑料界举足轻重的塑料工业基地的地位。

江苏的塑料工业另一个值得注意的特点，塑料工业上游的石化产业和塑料机械装备业都相当地发达，有塑料原料和塑料装备大省之号称。PP、PE、PS类的大型石化企业有扬子石化及扬巴石化、金陵石化等在全国享有盛名；仪征化纤、申龙高科、安得利化工等的塑料级和瓶级PET原料不紧在全国负有盛名，而且已成功打开出口市场。坐落于镇江大港的国亨化工、奇美化工的PS、ABS以及太仓港的氯碱化工和遍布徐州、新沂、镇江、南通、常州无锡等地的PVC树脂在全国享有很高的知名度。苏、锡、常的塑料机械尤其是张家港的塑料机械非常发达，在全国具有一定的知名度。这几年来在行业发展的思路上，立足于消化吸收和提高控制水平，在加工设备的节能降耗上倍加关注。

仅仅从产品的种类和配套服务面来看，江苏的塑料工业无论从品种种类还是规模上都已经达到一相当高的水平，尤其是产品品种种类，几乎能提供世界上所有的已有产品。但是在整体水平上升的大趋势下，江苏塑料工业仍然存在一些共性的问题。产品结构的不合理性仍然困扰着江苏的塑料工业，高精尖产品开发仍显不够充足，较低水平产品重复交叉，没有一个权威机构能够协调和真正做到适应性调整；企业间盲目模仿相当普遍，企业的自我创新意识在不断上升，可开发能力仍然不足，自主知识产权的拥有和自主知识产权自我保护能力很差。重量级塑料加工企业所占比例仍然有待提高。尽管涌现出了中达股份、江阴申龙高科、江南模塑集团、常州巨力集团、江苏琼花集团、常州创佳型材、连云港中金医药包装、昆山彩华包装、江阴龙山集团、江阴龙奇包装、无锡环宇包装、无锡环亚包装、无锡国泰包装、常州海企塑业、无锡巨龙、苏州富事达、江苏华信塑业等重量级企业，在江苏新建地级市的宿迁市也已出现了很有分量的重量级塑料企业。这些新塑料工业企业的出现，加之原来的龙头企业如：中达股份、申龙高科、江苏琼花等的的崛起，极大地改变了江苏的塑料包装面貌，极大地影响了江苏塑料包装的发展进程，某种意义上将改变江苏乃至全国的塑料包装历史进程。但除此而外，大多数塑料加工企业规模不大，原材料消耗和能源消耗偏高，大部分企业的经济效益偏低。

江苏塑料工业的发展应在以下几个方面做好基础工作：

新型塑料建材和多功能塑料复合包装材料仍将是江苏塑料制品工业的重点发展和快速增长的主要领域；农用塑料不但继续占据重要位置，而且将会随着农业种植结构的优化调整出现新的发展机遇；科技含量高的高附价值的工程塑料、工业配套塑料件及其它改性复合材料的应用领域将不断扩大。重点大类塑料产品如工业配套件、管材、建材、软/硬压延制品、薄膜、片材、及高档包装材料的生产将朝着规模经济的方向发展，为减少对环境的污染，将加大塑料回收利用和降解塑料应用。功能性塑料的开发和研究将是今后的发展重点。

塑料管材的主要发展领域是各种规格(尤其是大口径)、多材质和多种结构的管材管件；燃气管已进入发展的大机遇时期，已成为将持续一相当长发展期的热点产品。塑料建材的发展将要超出仅仅是型材的格局，型材也应朝着优化结构的方向发展，增加品种，提高档次。结构发泡材料、轻型墙体、隔断材料将进入活跃期。懂塑料不懂建筑设计和懂建筑不懂塑料是塑料建材发展的制约因素。应加强设计和应用的研究，加强塑料人才和建筑艺术人才的多学科人才的培养，推进建材产品快速健康。在发展的过程中必须同步考虑标准化、系列化、适用化、配套化、美感化等新型建材发展的几大要素。

塑料包装广阔的市场前景，使塑料包装行业的规模随着随着市场需求的快速增长和品种、品质的不断涌现而不断扩大。骨干塑料包装企业的崛起、新型高阻隔材料的成功开发，改变着江苏的塑料包装行业面貌，改变着塑料包装的形象。骨干塑料包装企业主要依靠引进先进设备、以及和国外同行一流企业建立技术合作开发纽带，加速了与国际塑料包装行业技术水平的靠拢，加快了塑料包装进入国际市场的步伐。塑料包装材料的发展经历了简单塑料包装、复合塑料包装阶段，当今的市场需求正向着塑料包装的多功能化发展。塑料包装的复合化、多功能化、环保化是江苏今后发展的重点方向。塑料包装应按食品药品等包装物的要求，努力开发多功能性包装材料，提供被包装物性能保护功能；开发延长货物保质保鲜寿命的高阻隔、防渗透包装材料，无菌包装材料，热灌装材料，保味包装材料，耐蒸煮包装材料；开发水果、蔬菜等的气调环境保鲜包装材料以及粮食等储存、运输的防霉防蛀包装材料。尽管就整体而言，高技术含量、高附加值的塑料包装产品目前所占的比例仍然不高，未能满足日益增长的市场要求。但是，随着社会进步和人们生活质量要求的持续提高，塑料包装作将随着食品、饮品、药品、生物制品等朝阳行业的发展而大发展。随着这些行业对塑料包装的要求不断提高，塑料包装始终存在很大的发展空间。塑料包装可持续发展的前景广阔，一个大发展的时机已经成熟。

农用塑料的发展重点是果蔬、花卉、经济作物、育苗等用途的长寿、无滴、防雾、高强度高透明、保温等多功能塑料棚膜及其相关配件制品，除草、防虫等多功能地膜。深入发展农田水利建设用的各类塑料管道、管槽、管件、节水型微灌、渗灌、滴灌以及水利建设中的水渠、大坝建设用土工材料。农用塑料应引入现代农业的概念，农用塑料的研究开发应着眼于现代农业的目标、着眼于农业科技的发展和新技术的应用。

工业配套件的开发重点是工程塑料、汽车、家电、电子信息产品的配套件。邮电通讯用新型电缆、穿线管。信息、通讯、机械、国防工业配套的各种科技含量较高、附加值较高的配套产品。汽车工业中的塑料比重将大幅度增长，十年后的汽车塑料件将有一半以上采用复合材料和回收利用材料。航空航天工业技术进步的着眼点之一是减轻自重，高分子复合材料将大有作为，塑料将担当非常重要的角色。电子电器工业的配套将围绕节能省料的方针，对高电磁性能塑料合金、超导电塑料、电磁屏蔽材料、光机能性材料、光学纤维复合材料、新型传感高分子材料、信息处理用各种计录、储存材料、CAD静电记录膜、微缩用胶片等的需求将急剧上升。塑料工业要继续当好热点行业的配角，为朝阳行业服务，塑料行业将随着朝阳行业的发展而获得新的发展机遇，将随着朝阳行业的大发展而大发展。

日用塑料制品的发展仍然有着不可估量的前景。关键是设计理念的突破，能否侧重以人为中心，追求现代美学设计观，朝便捷、舒适、适用、经济、美观的方向发展，提高质量和降低成本是这一领域极其重要的行业发展要素。江苏的日用消费品开发和推新的速度和规模都远远落后于浙江广东，有很大的发展潜力，理应奋起直追，创照出日用消费塑料制品的未来新天地。

轻量化、节材、安全可靠的塑料工程材料、塑料医疗领域一次性可靠材料、易弯曲材料以及胰岛素笔针以及吸入器用微量泵等配药辅助用具的发展和应用趋势值得我们关注。包装材料发展趋势值得业内有识之士的高度关注，建筑领域的绝缘绝热材料及新型铺地材料的发展也值得我们去研究和开拓市场。各种体育休闲用品、运动器材、运动系列产品、和运动有关的人造草皮等的需求量的不断增长也值得我们去关注。由于具有很高的发光效率很低的能耗效应，发光二级管（LED）的发展非常迅速，从手电到汽车等的车灯，无处不在的广泛推开应用趋势很猛，目前和此有关的塑料的开发速度也很迅猛。LED周围的反光镜可控制灯光的偏转并将光源集中起来，目前正在开发的耐温、传热、可任意成型的此类材料的开发对推动下一家用节能光源有着基础性铺垫的不可估量的发展前途，我们必须要高度关注。合成纤维塑料的应用近几年有了更大的发展。可制成抗压性强但结构非常轻量化的的元件的开发已市场化多年。将玻璃纤维嵌入热固性基体中、或将用环形纤维制成的模制件嵌入热固性基体中的产品市场化已是指日可待，这将是外科手术中的假肢、假臂以及涵盖到风涡轮转动叶片的一系列配套产品的工业化也是展望之中了。对纳米技术在塑料中的应用研究和关注已经很多年了，如今的现状是已有很大的迈进，纳米填料盒基于纳米技术的添加剂是的塑料的特性有了质的飞跃，使得塑料能提供更多更新的特性。甚至可以将原来不可实现的表面上看起来互相矛盾的特性要求互相结合起来。透明性和随机性、折射率和硬度、表面功能和材料机械性能、材料的绝缘性能和传导性能等等都可以通过纳米技术友好的共存和同时提供。纳米技术在塑料领域的应用可以使塑料具有高级流变学特性和高的电传导性，前者可以使塑料变得更易于加工成型，后者可以更好的防止静电问题的干扰。塑料的表面自动清洁也将在纳米技术的应用中得以实现。

塑料制品工业经历了从计划经济向市场经济转变的历程，企业在从计划经济模式转向市场经济的过程中，遇到许多困难，面临许多问题，为数不少的企业步履艰难，原有的历史烙印仍然影响着企业的发展和管理模式。因此，解决塑料企业今后发展中的矛盾和问题的根本出路在于真正的现深化改革。已经实施了企业股份之改造的新的活力和发展机遇，但是我们的管理模式还很落后，有的甚至停留或倒退在家族式管理模式，不能适应新的发展了的新形势，必须引入新的管理思想和模式。

塑料制品企业应根据市场需求调整产品结构，加速发展短线、三高产品，根据不同品种适度掌握产品规模。下决心停掉一批低档产品和长线产品。坚持市场决定生产的导向原则，坚决从数量主导型过渡到质量、品种、出口、效益主导型。地方政府应重点扶持一批大型企业、特大型企业、重点企业、明星企业。以名优产品为龙头，以经济效益为中心，以资本投入为纽带，以市场发展为导向，组建具有实力的、符合经济规律的、有利于企业发展的企业集团，实现适应市场需求产品的规模效应。继续改变和直至结束老、小、散、差的落后状况。

随着技术装备的不断升级提高以及产品精度和档次的提高，江苏的出口塑料逐年在增加，但相对于江苏庞大的塑料总量，全省的塑料制品的出口量占总量的比例相对较低，制品技术含量不高。出口总量中间接配套出口占主大多数。应继续研究国际市场的需求情况，研究国际市场新产品，在提高原有出口产品质量、巩固和扩大原有产品的出口量的同时，重点开发热点产品，重点发展新市场。应鼓励和引导有条件的企业跨出国门，直接参与国际竞争。可将国内渐趋饱和的产品生产移到其它仍然有着较大需求的国家，境外办企业应从输出技术和设备为主。尽管国际金融危机在短期内获得全球性回暖的可能性预期不大，国际市场的需求目前看不到活力，但我们从长远看，经济全球化的势头仍然不可逆转。而风险往往伴随着机遇，经济低潮时期未必不是我们出击的最佳时机，等所有的人都看到了光明时，我们再启动投资往往就要付出加倍的代价，尤其是在投资时效上不能获得最大收益。在汇率发生了较大变化的新形势下，要研究我们的出口方向和调整出口品种，是我们的出口能继续保持一定范围的优势。

当今世界的经济发展显著特点之一，是技术已成为推动企业发展和经济增长的极其重要的因素，更是企业能得以持续发展的基本要素，技术含量低的产品和企业不可能有持续的生存空间。所以重视产品的技术含量，以新技术促进企业的持续、快速发展，是塑料行业能保持持续发展的核心竞争力。塑料加工业的技术发展非常迅速，出现了许多新技术新工艺，许多新产品的出现本身就伴随着新技术的开发和应用。计算机辅助注射成型、新型异型吹塑成型、超微孔塑料、受控低压注射成型、多相聚合物片状注射成型、可熔芯技术注射成型、挤出浸渍复合成型、熔体挤拉成型、多元材料复式加工技术、壳芯注射成型、双注射成型、模内背衬注射成型、液-气辅助成型等新技术的开发和应用推广，将为塑料产品的开发和设计提供更为广阔的空间。企业应格外重视技术，尤其是新技术工作。应根据自身的条件和发展需要，选择开发研究、综合吸收、引进消化、技术合作、购买软件等各种方式，积极采用高新技术。在引进先进装备的同时注重引进软件和技术。

实现现代化，人是决定因素。企业和产品的竞争，越来越表现为人才的竞争。人才是任何企业发展宝贵的财富，企业应从制度、分配机制上解放思想，引入激励机制、股份机制，高薪用人才、创造条件留住人才，用好人才，确保塑料工业的持续高速发展。为此，江苏塑料界应加强和大学的合作和沟通，在继续重视高科技人才培养、重视工艺和设备的结合性培养、重视塑料工程类人才的培养的同时，更应注重第一线实用型技术人才的培养，重视高职高专类人才的培养。进一步提高职工队伍的素质，注重职工技术的培训，大力培养和吸引人才，在培养实用性技术人才中要注重和生产性企业的衔接和沟通，尽量缩短高职类人才到达岗位后的适应期和过渡期。

塑料作为一门新兴的材料工业，与传统工业相比，其发展历史不长，但发展速度相当快。新项目的上马已从计划经济式的逐级审批制转向市场经济体制下的市场主导化。企业对项目的实施与否具有绝对的决定权。社会主义市场经济体制下的集体企业投资风险主要由投资单位而非经营者或单位领导，对投资项目的可行性研究存在诸多不踏实因素和投资项目的目的不明确性。这是上一轮投资热潮中为数不少的项目失败的主要原因，也是造成不少企业效应严重滑坡的不良因素。盲目投资、盲目发展不仅对单位本身造成重大损失，也对金融界构成严重风险威胁，最大的伤害是国家利益的受损。一哄而上，不仅使投资单位在一开始就步履艰难，也对原来生产销售较能维持的单位构成严重威胁。因此，呼吁政府重视行业的管理和协调。

节约能源、资源，建立节约型社会是当代中国经济和社会发展的一个鲜明主题。塑料加工是通过塑料加工机械和使用塑料原料成型出市场所需制品的过程，在加工过程中消耗电能和原料，能源和材料的节约使用一直是塑料行业降低成本努力奋斗的目标。随着科技日新月异不断发展，通过变频伺服等电子自动化先进技术和新型装备降耗节能比以往得到了很大提高，提高生产率的同时还节约劳动力资源。在材料节约方面通过塑料制品合理用材设计、材料科学选用、材料改性、多功能材料开发等多种方式减薄制品壁厚、增加应用功能达到节约材料的目的，通过机头、边角料的直接回用、使用后塑料循环利用实现省资源化，成效显著。

降低能耗是塑料机械行业一直在努力追求的目标。从过去的流量比例和压力比例控制，发展到变量控制、变频控制和伺服控制。注塑机的高效率主要体现在工作节拍快，制品周期短。这方面的努力和工作仍需要继续深入和推广。

在塑料制品加工领域，节能降耗不但需要从塑料加工机械方面着手，还应该深入到塑料原料及加工技术的节能领域。如高熔体流动指数树脂在较低的温度下获得较好的流动性，在加工中可显著减少能耗，并能明显地缩短成型周期。合理选择材料或添加增强材料、填充物等以达到提高性能、节约树脂用量等目的，如复合塑料、纤维增强塑料、塑木复合材料等都属于节能型原料。利用化学或物理发泡的方式能够制得质轻、保温性好的发泡塑料制品，它的密度低、机械性能较好，可以大大降低树脂的使用量。

除了上述几个重要的方面江苏塑料界将持续努力攀登外，江苏塑料界将按照中国塑协“十二五”发展规划的指导意见去认真思考和落实，调整我们的战略，完善我们的规划，提升我们的水平。并按照江苏省有关塑料领域的十二五发展规划要求，在塑料制品行业加强改性、合金化、再生利用技术推广应用，推进节能性加热技术和元件的应用，加快引进技术和装备的消化吸收，推进先进塑料成型装备的国产化，进一步扩大工程塑料、多功能塑料、配套塑料件、环保型塑料、在日用、电器、交通工具、军工、农业、医药、环保和包装等领域的应用。

在做好上述各项工作的同时，更应加大重视废旧塑料的回收利用工作的力度，应加强宏观指导与管理，建立切实可行的回收激励机制，建立回收利用体系。建议尽快制定有关塑料回收利用的法律法规，规范回收利用的工作，杜绝不良形象的发生。提供条件设立塑料回收利用基金，从税收政策等方面鼓励塑料回收利用工作。

关于塑料饭盒的话题和争论一直没有停顿过，虽然从国家层面对发泡饭盒有了理性的回归，但是由于多年来许多伪科学的宣传，少数小报为了吸引眼球过多地做了些添油加醋，混淆了视听，至今仍然没有真正科学理性的对待塑料饭盒。如何真确使用塑料饭盒的科技知识普及工作做得不够，媒体的宣传还没有从正面去引导，

闹得沸沸扬扬的塑料袋的废弃与使用话题，目前仍然有着伪科学响亮话语，看似很慷慨激昂，仔细推敲，很有哗众取宠的内影。塑料的废弃物处理是个很大课题，应科学地对待，应体现实事求是，把贯彻科学发展观融入其中。人们使用塑料袋是因为塑料袋能满足他们需求，就使用量来说比其他购物袋、包装袋占压倒性优势，如果不使用塑料袋换用其他材质的袋如布袋、纸袋。如果仍被人们随意地丢弃，类似性质的“白色污染”同样存在，非但并不能减轻环境压力，而且浪费的资源和造成的污染可能更大。使用布袋、纸袋同样也浪费资源，而且浪费的是深林资源，因为造纸需要砍伐大量木材，加工过程的对水资源和土质的污染迫在眉睫，远远甚于所谓的白色污染对我们日常生活的危害。塑料袋回收后还可再生他用，能够实现循环再利用，是典型的资源节约型和环境友好型材料。实践证明，不管使用任何材质的购物袋、包装袋，回收再利用或者循环使用是解决问题有效的途经。滥用包装袋、购物袋是指人们滥用这种行为，滥用塑料袋会影响生态环境。关键要做的是解决滥用和随意丢弃，而不是禁用。塑料袋回收后再制造成垃圾袋和其他性能要求不高的包装袋，是很有现实意义的，实现了资源循环利用。塑料袋的过量使用、或者无节制使用会给生态环境造成危害，应当采取措施规范人们乱扔的恶习和加强回收利用加以解决。禁止”和“弃用”塑料袋的提法不符合我国国情。应当加强回收利用、减少和循环使用塑料袋。要为塑料包装袋和塑料包装盒正名，造成视觉污染的所谓“白色污染”的问题所在不在塑料本身，问题出在使用塑料袋和塑料盒的人身上，是人们的不良习惯让塑料背上了悲剧色彩的误解。

建议加强治理白色污染工作，加强相关立法，从优化人们的良好消费习惯，提高人的行为素质入手，变废为宝。在找到更经济有效、更有利于环保的新型替代材料成功研制之前，切忌因噎废食。

塑料是能源依赖性极强的一大类化工产品，今年来塑料原料的价格随着石油的价格暴涨飞速上涨，塑料加工企业的原料成本已超过其承受极限。进口原料的关税在很大程度上影响着国内塑料原料的价格，中石化企业在大量消耗国家资源的同时在谋取近乎暴利的高额经济效益，而中石化又是在海外上市的公司，在让海外投资者获益匪浅的同时让国内的塑料加工企业承受了巨大的成本压力。继续呼吁国家调整塑料和石化原料的进口关税税则，逐步取消塑料原料的进口关税。

根据目前的能源态势，呼吁国家在制定政策鼓励塑料原料的进口，把有限的、宝贵的资源尽可能多的留给子孙后代。

（江苏省塑料加工工业协会　韦华）

山　东　省

一、行业规模持续扩大，综合实力逐步增强

1. 2012 年山东省塑料行业综合情况

2012 年山东省塑料制品行业主营业务收入完成 2010 亿元，同比增长 15.67%，塑料制品总产量累计完成 13400kt，同比增长 16.19%，主营业务收入和制品总产量均居全国第三位；出口主营业务收入完成 145 亿元；实现利润总额 130 亿元，同比增长 11.75%；产值利润率为 6.68%，高于全国同行业平均水平 1.47 个百分点；全行业累计产销率 99.00%，同比增长 0.97%；职工总数 62 万人。

2012 年山东省生产各种塑料原材料 4278.7kt，占全国总量的 8.21%。

2012 年山东省塑料加工专用设备完成 34416 台，比上年降低 9.8%，占全国总量的 10.37%。这也是山东省塑料加工专用设备连续第二年下降，占全国总量的比重连续第二年缩小。

在主要塑料制品中，农用薄膜、编织制品、一次性塑料手套、塑料安全绳网、塑料土工材料、管材型材等大类产品在全国都占有重要位置。

截至 2012 年底，山东省塑料行业保持“中国驰名商标”5 个；保持“山东省著名商标”72 个；“山东名牌”产品 81 个。

2. 2012 年山东省塑料行业规模以上企业情况

截至2012年底，山东省塑料制品行业规模以上企业统计1218个，约占全部企业总数的15%，其生产规模和生产总量约占全行业总数的75%~80%。

2012年山东省塑料制品行业规模以上企业实现主营业务收入1600.7亿元，增长18.39%。其中塑料板管型材占26.53%(同比增长26.77%)、塑料丝绳及编织品占23.04%(同比增长25.57%)、塑料薄膜占13.36%(同比增长21.94%)，其他品种所占比重均不超过9%，同比增长均超过26%。

2012年山东省塑料制品行业规模以上企业累计完成制品总产量4531kt，增长18.4%，其中销往外省的为1010kt。以产品销售收入计算，销往外省的占10.75%，出口110亿元，占6.87%。

2012年山东省塑料制品行业规模以上企业累计完成工业总产值1557亿元，同比增长17.44%。

2012年山东省塑料制品行业规模以上企业累计实现利润总额93.46亿元，增长27.03%，居全国第二位。

二、科技创新持续发力，将带动产业技术升级

近几年，山东塑料行业继续加大科研开发力度，规模以上企业科研经费投入持续增加，已超过经营费用的2%；省塑料协会力促行业内外产学研携手发力，并重点在循环利用、环保经济、增加新资源、扩大新利用领域等方面下功夫。

2011-2012年度，山东省塑料研究开发中心(聚乙烯醇淀粉高岭土纳米复合全降解材料、新型环保汽车纤维内饰件用粘合剂及成型工艺研究、聚乳酸/聚乙烯醇/多面体齐聚硅倍半氧烷/热塑性弹性体纳米复合材料)、山东春潮色母料有限公司(纳米有机-无机层状杂化阻燃新材料开发及应用、汽车内饰专用纳米改姓复合新材料)、山东道恩集团(新型阻燃热塑性弹性体材料的研发、抗柔顺剂增强聚丙烯洗衣机专用料研发)、泰安现代塑料有限公司(300kN单向拉伸塑料格栅、矿用双向拉伸塑料格栅、多维塑料格栅)、淄博正华发泡材料有限公司(该公司与山东理工大学联合研发的绿色环保型聚氨酯化学发泡剂)等科研项目均已研发成功或获得项目鉴定。山东清田塑工有限公司研究开发的“表面涂覆型长效流滴消雾复合膜”荣获2012年度中轻联科学技术奖二等奖。

在2012年全省工业转方式调结构1000个重点技术改造项目中，塑料制品工业占29项，总投资469318万元(见表1)；列入2012年全省工业转型升级导向计划重点项目的9项，总投资184974万元，其中建设投资154661万元(见表2)。

表1　2012年全省工业转方式调结构重点技术改造项目表(塑料)　　万元

序号	企业名称	项目名称	总投资	建设地点
1	山东慧科助剂股份有限公司	年产10kt聚氯乙烯用环保PVC复合热稳定剂技改项目	2900	沂源县
2	山东东大一诺威新材料有限公司	120kt/a聚氨酯产品搬迁扩建项目	43184	临淄区
3	淄博新塑化工有限公司	600t/a聚乙烯催化剂项目	27000	张店区
4	山东联创节能新材料股份有限公司	$10^7m^2/a$硬质聚氨酯高效防火保温复合板	45000	高新区
5	山东中塑泰富科技有限公司	POF环保热收缩膜建设项目	14964	高新区
6	山东华奥斯新型建材有限公司	同步印刷木纹亚光膜项目	32000	滕州市
7	枣庄拓怡新型材料科技有限公司	新型木塑节能保温墙体材料	6003	薛城区
8	山东鑫迪家居装饰有限公司	PVC亚光膜	4320	滕州市
9	山东胜通集团股份有限公司	60kt/aBOPET光学薄膜项目	122721	垦利县
10	山东道恩集团有限公司	5000t级聚氨酯热塑性弹性体材料生产项目	6200	龙口市
11	山东龙口特种胶管有限公司	钢丝缠绕胶管技术改造项目	8225	龙口市
12	烟台中科金泰电子有限公司	注塑机节能改造专用伺服控制系统产业化	280	开发区
13	山东寿光龙兴农膜有限公司	年产50kt高档农用多层薄膜项目	31988	寿光市
14	山东通佳机械有限公司	高效节能挤出机产业化	12000	高新区
15	山东春潮色母料有限公司	纳米有机-无机层状杂化阻燃新材料生产项目	5000	新泰市

续表

序号	企业名称	项目名称	总投资	建设地点
16	泰安鲁普耐特塑料有限公司	三维编织管状复合材料技术改造项目	2000	岱岳区
17	泰安路德工程材料有限公司	矿用阻燃抗静电经编格栅技改项目	4500	肥城市
18	山东浩然特塑有限公司	千吨级聚砜树脂生产线技术改造项目	1300	工业新区
19	威海市文峰管业有限公司	耐高温纳米复合管材项目	3920	工业新区
20	威海威鹰塑胶有限公司	风力发电叶片制备用同步张力成型支撑膜技术改造项目	2000	工业新区
21	乳山昌盛环保餐具有限公司	环保餐具新材料研发项目	1100	乳山市
22	山东广顺物资有限公司	年产8亿只可降解便当盒项目	6374	莱城区
23	莱芜市精诚塑料机械有限公司	高速内镶贴片式滴灌管生产线	2600	高新区
24	山东雷华塑料工程有限公司	年产10kt高强度宽幅智能型土工布项目	12000	临沭县
25	山东玉和磨具制造有限公司	年产10000t树脂磨具生产项目	4150	莒南县
26	山东浩阳新型工程材料股份有限公司	高档多功能土工复合新材料项目	59379	禹城市
27	齐河县联成塑料编织厂	年产1000t塑料编织丝项目	910	齐河县
28	山东大丰生物科技有限公司	绿色环保钙锌塑料热稳定剂项目	3800	博兴县
29	山东滨州安惠绳网集团有限责任公司	化纤绳网小企业创业辅导基地项目	3500	惠民县
合计		—	469318	—

表2　2012年工业转型升级导向计划重点项目表(塑料)

序号	企业名称	项目名称	主要建设内容	投资		
				总投资	建设投资	铺底流动资金
1	枣庄市天禾宇信新型材料科技有限公司	年产12kt木塑复合制品技改项目	新建主体工程20000m^2，其他辅助工程、公用工程、服务工程，新购置主要设备260套。新增产能12kt木塑复合材料。	11592	11212	380
2	山东神州翔宇科技集团有限公司	年产100kt多聚复合材料	采用高压热压技术，引进木塑专用锥形双螺杆挤出机，购置挤出型材模具、四立柱气动夹紧牵引机、锥形双螺杆挤出机粒机、破碎机、磨粉机等设备，建设中试车间等配套设施。建设仓房、厂房、办公楼、产品研发中心、产品展示中心等土建工程30000m^2，购买年产100kt多聚复合材料1套。	13000	8600	4400
3	山东东宝钢管有限公司	年产260万米钢-塑复合管建设项目	项目采用钢丝、钢带为增强体的独特的符合方式，新增生产线及配套设备、检测及辅助配套设备等180套，达到260万米的钢塑复合管生产能力；配备新建车间、仓库、检验中心，研发大楼等，总建筑面积85000m^2	90000	78000	12000
4	泰安路德工程材料有限公司	高密度聚乙烯单向拉伸格栅生产项目	利用现有厂房，新上3条生产线，购置单螺杆挤出机、板材冲孔机床等设备50台套，提高产品的产能和质量。	4000	3000	1000

续表

序号	企业名称	项目名称	主要建设内容	投资		
				总投资	建设投资	铺底流动资金
5	山东春潮色母料有限公司	纳米有机－无机层状杂化阻燃材料开发及利用	该项目拟建车间、仓库、办公室等各一座，总建筑面积14000m^2，拟购置生产设备30台，相关实验设备10台，设备购置费用1000万元。	5000	3500	1500
6	山东蓝景膜技术工程有限公司	渗透汽化透水膜、膜组件及其产业化	1000台渗透汽化膜组件生产线建设，包括土建、设备设施、仪器等	16241	15490	751
7	山东新巨丰科技包装有限责任公司	纸铝塑无菌包材二期工程项目	项目总建筑面积11000m^2。新增生产能力无菌包装纸基复合包材50亿，按其匹配、组合、选择设备。进口意大利柔版印刷机、美国收放卷机、德国流延复合机、意大利分切机、国产配置检品机、包装机、配套设备等。	21941	18659	3282
8	山东鲍尔浦实业有限公司	超高分子量聚苯乙烯航标	公司将建设生产车间30000m^2；现代化生产线26条；航标试验池2000m^2；科研楼3000m^2(含省级实验室)；	18000	12000	6000
9	山东亚新塑料包装有限公司	年产万吨塑料彩印包装袋生产项目	购置十色印刷机、高速制袋机等设备36台套，占地32250m^2，其中产房17500m^2。投产后形成20kt彩印包装袋生产能力。	5200	4200	1000
合计				184974	154661	30313

经过多年的发展，山东塑料工业已形成门类比较齐全的工业体系，并建立起以专业研究开发机构、大学专业院系和科研机构、企业所属科研机构等共同参与的专业科研力量。

三、产学研结合、专业基地培育取得新成效

1. 山东省塑料研究开发中心/山东省塑料协会与山东轻工业学院共同建立战略合作关系

为了加强高校与行业间的协作，促进高等教育与行业的共同发展，本着优势互补、互惠互利、长期合作的原则，山东省塑料研究开发中心、山东省塑料协会与山东轻工业学院材料科学与工程学院共同建立战略合作关系。2012年11月14日在济南正式签约。

双方坚持以加强高校与行业的协作，实现高校与行业共同成长、发展的“双赢”；探索高等教育与行业协同发展的新型合作模式，实施适应行业发展需求的人才培养、人力资源开发、技术服务、科研成果转化等全方位一体化链接服务为合作目的。

双方商定，为充分发挥各自优势，山东轻工业学院(注：根据国家教育部批复，山东轻工业学院于2013年3月份正式更名为齐鲁工业大学)根据人才培养计划每年选派一定数量的学生到山东塑料行业内有关生产企业进行岗位实训；省塑料研究中心与行业协会可根据行业实际需求，委托山东轻工业学院进行人才定向培养；同时双方还将就行业技术革新、项目开发、员工培训、文化建设、产业发展以及在校大学生岗位实训指导、创业教育和职业指导等进行深度合作。

2. 山东省工程塑料工程技术研究中心批准建立

根据山东省科技厅关于申报山东省工程技术研究中心的具体要求，山东省塑料研究开发中心根据单位实际需求及国内外技术、产业发展状况和趋势，积极策划了工程塑料工程技术研究中心的组织框架、管理模式、发展目标及任务等申报内容。山东省工程塑料工程技术研究中心以山东省塑料研究开发中心为依托，山东省轻工业学院(2013年3月份已更名为齐鲁工业大学)为协办单位。2012年底前工程技术研究中心已得到山东省科技厅批准，目前正处于三年的组建期中。

组建本中心的目的旨在充分发挥产学研结合，推动科研机构、大学与企业间的交流与合作，促进科技成果的转化，尤其是具有自主知识产权的核心技术，增强对引进技术的消化、吸收及二次开发。研究开发工程塑料高性能多功能化以及低成本化制备与加工技术，加速其产业化进程，不断推进产品和产业的升级，跟上世界工程塑料产业的发展步伐。

3. 加强行业品牌建设和特色区域及产业基地的培育

为使山东塑料产业继续保持更快、健康的发展势头，增强企业核心竞争力，进一步加强和培养产业集群和制造业基地建设，实现生产力空间布局上的优化和生产要素的有效集中，促进区域经济的发展，提高山东塑料制造业大省在全国乃至在国际上的整体竞争力，协会积极开展塑料产业集群和制造业基地的培育活动。行业品牌建设和特色区域及产业基地建设取得新进展。

淄博市桓台县被授予“山东省塑料管材(管件)研发生产基地”称号。2012 年 10 月，山东省轻工集体企业联社与山东省塑料协会联合授予淄博市桓台县“山东省塑料管材(管件)研发生产基地”称号；授予山东汇丰管业有限公司为“山东省塑料管材(管件)研发生产龙头企业”荣誉称号；授予山东万吉塑胶有限公司、山东瑞泰管业有限公司、淄博富佳珅塑料管材有限公司等三家企业为“山东省塑料管材(管件)研发生产骨干企业”荣誉称号。桓台县拥有 104 家塑料管材(管件)生产加工企业，其中规模以上企业 54 家，年产各类管材、管件 97 万吨。2011 年，全县塑料管材、管件行业实现销售收入人民币 85.5 亿元。桓台县塑料管材(管件)研发生产企业有较高集中度，具备较大的生产规模，工艺装备先进，在全省居领先地位。

滨州市惠民县塑料安全绳网生产基地、日照市莒县塑料小包装产品和日照市岚山区橡塑制品生产基地等其他产业集群和专业生产基地正在积极培育过程中。

中国驰名商标、山东省著名商标和山东省名牌产品申报与评审工作积极稳妥。2012 年新增“中国驰名商标”1 个；新增山东省著名商标 11 个，续展 13 个；46 个塑料及相关产品获得 2012 年度山东省名牌产品(包括复审)称号。

4. 一批新的企业荣获“山东省塑料行业十佳企业”荣誉称号

在 2012 年的工作中，山东省塑料协会继续发挥自己的业务优势，通过协会掌握有关企业信息，利用熟悉生产企业的优势，在山东省塑料行业内开展“山东省塑料行业十佳企业”评比活动，共有 19 家企业获得 2012 年度“山东省塑料行业十佳企业”荣誉称号。

5. 青岛市塑料行业协会正式成立

2012 年 12 月 28 日，青岛市塑料行业协会举行成立大会。青岛市塑料行业属于传统产业，2011 年塑料行业主营业务收入 215.7 亿元，总产值 231 亿元，行业总体规模呈上升趋势。目前，青岛市具有一定规模的塑料制品生产企业 230 多家(不含塑料原材料、助剂、塑料机械等企业)，从业人员 2.9 万人。由青岛宏达塑胶总公司筹备并牵头的青岛市塑料行业协会共有 86 家规模型企业组成。

四、努力进取，成就铸就辉煌

1. 山东清田塑工有限公司荣获中国轻工联合会科学技术奖

在 2013 年 3 月中旬召开的中国轻工联合会三届三次理事会暨全国轻工行业工作座谈会上，山东清田塑工有限公司研究开发的“表面涂覆型长效流滴消雾复合膜”荣获 2012 年度中国轻工联合会科学技术奖二等奖。

2. 山东省轻工联社综合竞争力品牌、最具潜力品牌、行业品牌典范企业及卓越贡献带头人

2013 年 1 月 17 日，在济南召开的全省轻工联社工作会议暨四届四次常务理事(扩大)会议上，公布表彰了获得 2012 年度全省轻工联社系统综合竞争力十佳品牌、最具潜力品牌、行业十佳品牌典范企业及品牌卓越贡献带头人等荣誉称号的名单，我省塑料行业部分品牌、企业及负责人上榜。

(1)山东省轻工联社综合竞争力十佳品牌：“春潮”—山东春潮色母料有限公司。

(2)山东省轻工联社最具潜力品牌：“蓝帆”—山东蓝帆塑胶股份有限公司。

(3)山东省轻工联社行业十佳品牌典范企业：山东汇丰管业有限公司、山东清田塑工有限公司、潍坊现代塑胶有限公司、青岛海威集团有限公司、山东泰峰塑料土工材料有限公司、聊城华塑工业有限公司、山东企鹅塑胶集团有限公司、淄博庄园塑料制品公司、荣成兴达塑料制品有限公司、山东三塑集团有限公司。

(4)山东省轻工联社品牌卓越贡献带头人(10 人)：王士禄(山东汇丰管业有限公司董事长)；王长青(山东企鹅塑胶集团有限公司董事长、书记)；田开生(山东三塑集团有限公司总经理)；刘培模(荣成兴达塑料制品有限公司董事长)；刘衍红(山东清田塑工有限公司董事长)；杨延洪(淄博庄园塑料制品公司董事长)；张利(潍坊现代塑胶有限公司董事长)；武庆东(聊城华塑工业有限公司董事长)；郭元生(山东泰峰塑料土工材料有限公司董事长)；郝世恩(青岛海威集团有限公司董事长)。

五、影响行业健康持续发展的因素分析

我省塑料工业在保持快速发展的同时，在国际国内综合因素的影响下，当前在其发展过程中出现许多制约进一步发展的问题，面临着许多新的挑战，同时也带来许多新的机遇。

1. 保持行业均衡健康发展，急需调整产业结构。

产业结构不合理是影响我省塑料行业发展的重要因素。我省塑料企业多数处于产业链的低端，盈利能力低，大多数产业只有3% ~5%的利润率，缺乏创新的动力和能力。应加大行业“转型升级”的工作力度，加快技术改造步伐，逐步淘汰落后产能，大力推广高附加值、高性能的产业，提升我省塑料行业的水平。

(1)企业组织规模小而散，国际竞争力不强

由于企业过去追求“大而全”、“小而全”，专业化协作水平低，没有形成合理的分工协作关系。绝大多数企业规模过小，产业集中度低，资金和技术投入分散，资产负债率高，在生产、市场、研究与开发等方面难以形成规模经济的优势。2012年我省万余家塑料制品生产企业中，列入国家统计范围的规模以上企业仅1218家，约占10%左右。

与企业组织结构不合理相关的是企业社会化分工、专业化协作水平不高，没有形成以大企业为主导、中小企业为支撑的产业体系。专业化协作水平低，规模经济效益得不到有效发挥，中小企业没有形成“专、精、特、新”的优势，发展后劲不足。

(2)产品结构层次低，高附加值产品少

我省产品结构不合理的矛盾十分突出，一般产品相对过剩与技术含量高、附加值大的产品短缺同时并存。在主要塑料产品中，有80%以上的产品生产能力利用不足或严重不足，但是由于产品结构不合理，产品差别化不足、档次不高、附加值较低，许多高档塑料制品(特别是高档日用品)仍然需要从外省市或外国调入，以满足人们的日常需要。

山东塑料行业制品总量超过江苏，但销售收入却不及江苏，说明我们产品的附加值低；我省规模以上企业2012年生产农用薄膜365kt，居全国第一位，但其他高附加值的包装类薄膜仅为342.6kt，而浙江省的包装类薄膜却高达2918.7kt(农用薄膜126.5kt)，是我们的8.52倍；广东省的包装类薄膜为961kt，是我们的2.81倍；江苏省的包装类薄膜也达到874kt，是我们的2.55倍。以注塑产品为主的附加值比较高的日用塑料制品，我省仅为160.6kt，而广东省1032.9kt，浙江省1028.6kt，江苏省360.1kt。这些都说明山东塑料行业产品结构存在问题，必须加以引导。

(3)技术水平低，创新能力不足，急需提升工艺装备水平。

我省塑料产品结构层次低的根源在于技术水平落后。

一是企业技术改造投入不足，企业的落后设备不能及时得到改造或更新，不少企业(主要是尚未改制的国有或国有控股企业和集体企业)设备陈旧、老化，带病运转，甚至一些七、八十年代的设备还在超期服役，造成多数产品单耗高、浪费大，资源利用率低。

二是企业创新能力不足。受各种压力的综合影响，塑料行业科研开发经费投入比重低，我省大中型工业企业研发费支出占销售收入比例不足2%，有的甚至更低。2012年我省塑料行业1218家规模以上企业共投入研究开发费用5000多万元，虽比上年略有增加，但也仅占整个管理费用的2.0%左右。

三是高技术产业发展缓慢。从反映产业核心竞争力的高新技术产业发展看，我省塑料行业目前尚处于起步阶段，产业规模小，技术基础薄弱。高新技术产业增加值占整个行业生产总值的比重仅为3.5%左右，远低于发达国家和新兴工业化国家以及个别发达省份水平。

四是人才结构不合理，高级技术人才短缺。山东塑料行业有万余家生产企业，员工62万人。现有技术员工只占全部员工的1/3左右，而且多数是初级工。技工、技术员、工程师和高级工程师仅占4%左右。许多企业引进世界上先进的技术和设备往往是把工人送到国外培训后才能投入生产，仅少数企业技术和管理人才较雄厚，这直接影响到尽快使塑料制品业缩小与先进国家的差距。

(4)区域结构趋同，地区发展差距仍在拉大

由于在传统的计划经济体制下，各地长期追求自成体系，重复建设十分严重，造成地区产业结构趋同，近年来虽有改善，但特色经济、比较优势和协作效益不明显，特别是中东部工业基础好的优势和西部地区的潜在优势均未发挥出来，生产要素在区域间合理流动和配置的体制和机制没有形成。东中西部塑料工业发展不平衡，差距不断拉大，地区产业结构严重趋同。由于区域发展的不平衡，在近几年每年各地上报的1000项工业技术改造项目塑料部分中，地区间的趋同性甚至低水平的重复性比较明显。

2. 塑料废弃物的回收利用急需规范和政策扶持

塑料制品在日常使用后大部分能够回收再利用，但仍有一部分(约为塑料废弃物的10%左右)完全进入城市垃圾系统，成为目前传统意义上的垃圾；同

时，由于部分个人的不良习惯随意丢弃(特别是超薄包装袋和一次性塑料快餐盒)，而形成视觉污染，也就是人们所说的"白色污染"问题。其实，对于这一部分被彻底丢弃而成为垃圾的塑料废弃物，只要技术成熟、成本合理、措施得当，它完全可以成为新的社会资源。

(1)塑料回收产业的规范问题。

目前塑料制品所用原料95%以上是可塑性塑料，可回收利用，既节约资源、又利于环保节能。现主要问题是缺乏规范管理、产品不能开据发票，无法正常进入流通领域，但目前我省每年有(100～150)亿元以上的市场需求。应对塑料回收企业进行规范化管理，纳入常规的市场流通。

(2)塑料垃圾及医疗塑料废弃物的回收利用问题。

我国现行的医疗塑料废弃物的处理方式是强制焚烧，这种方式虽然简单，但对资源是极大的浪费。山东省每年产生的医疗塑料废弃物有几十万吨，这对石油资源短缺的中国来说是一笔巨大的财富。国际上有些发达国家已经对其再回收利用，例如：废塑料炼油技术。目前国内也有类似技术，并且相对成熟。

根据我们的实施方案，对医疗塑料废弃物先行处理、消毒，再由专业回收企业进行后续加工，纳入常规的市场流通。对回收企业来讲，医疗塑料废弃物是免费的，成本主要是物流成本和企业运行成本，经济上可行。如果加上目前作为不可回收进入填埋场的塑料废弃物进行再利用，全省可以额外增加一座年产150多万吨汽油、柴油及其他化工原料和副产品、产值达(120～150)亿元人民币的现代石化企业，从而为减少塑料纯粹废弃物、增加社会资源、减少环境污染等提供更加积极的技术和物质基础。

现在的主要问题是突破政策瓶颈，尽快建立实验基地，积累经验，逐步推广。

3. 农用薄膜发展中遇到升级换代和政策瓶颈的制约

(1)农用薄膜的升级换代问题

我省是农膜生产和应用大省，生产和使用总量均占全国总量的三分之一。近几年在日韩发展起来的PO膜是农膜行业的高端产品，我省部分农膜生产企业有意向上PO膜项目，鉴于自身资金实力和技术水平，该类项目发展缓慢，政府有关部门应给予大力支持。

(2)现行政策对农用薄膜生产和应用的制约作用比较明显，急需突破瓶颈促发展。

山东省既是农用薄膜生产大省，也是消费大省，2012年规模以上企业共生产销售各种农膜365kt，同比增长仅为0.55%。为更好地落实国家"三农"政策，支援农业发展，切实保护农民的积极性，让农民得到实惠，应该实施"农膜下乡"活动，对种粮农民实施补贴。

现行的政策是对农膜生产企业生产的农用薄膜税收不征也不退，企业采购塑料原料时可以要发票也可以不要发票，正规企业必须要发票，多数企业不要发票，在整个农膜行业造成不正当竞争。同时，农膜生产企业对当地财政贡献不大，享受不到当地政府的扶持政策。

我们已向政府有关部门提出建议，国家对塑料农用薄膜生产企业正常征税，支农的税收部分直接补贴给购买农用薄膜的农民，由农民持购货发票到财政部门领取补贴，使得农膜行业的惠农政策真正起到惠农作用。

4. 中小企业融资困难问题短时难以解决

融资难仍是制约塑料行业中小企业发展的突出问题。山东省塑料企业有一万多家，其中85%以上的是小微型企业，由于长期受国家政策的影响，我省塑料制品行业普遍存在融资难问题，严重制约了塑料加工企业的发展及产业水平的提高，特别是对于小微型企业，融资难已成为制约其生存和发展的关键问题。按照现在的实际情况，银行针对小微型企业贷款的成本和风险确实高于大型企业，期望银行主动给小微型塑料企业贷款也不太现实，积极主动地开展行业互助是解决小微型企业融资难的有效途径。我们建议：建立山东省塑料行业互助基金。

5. 具有一定劳动技能的劳动力供求矛盾愈发严重

塑料行业所使用的生产操作工人大多为临时人员，同时生产过程对操作人员又有一定的技术要求，因此，虽然我省劳动力资源丰富，但从行业调查情况看，具有一定技术基础或经过专业培训的人员仍十分紧缺。同时，新的《劳动合同法》颁布实施后，对企业的约束进一步加大，使劳动力成本增幅较大，且价格呈逐年上涨趋势，使企业成本增加，进而影响企业的经济效益。

劳动力的短缺是相对的，缺的是有一定劳动技能的人才，特别是高技能人才更缺。山东省塑料协会下步的重要工作就是积极开展职工培训，通过一系列的培训工作，提高塑料行业从业人员的劳动技能及管理水平。

6. 国内外政策影响塑料制品的对外贸易

多种因素影响我省塑料制品对外贸易。尽管塑料制品出口实现稳步增长，但诸多因素仍然成为制约出口扩大的主要问题。2012年年初我省塑料制品出口增幅就已出现回落态势。以塑料小包装、塑料编织制品为代表的出口产品也只维持上年水平。

人民币升值对塑料制品出口的影响。人民币升值显然会导致出口产品价格的提高，这就在一定程度上抑制出口的增长。而我省目前的出口产品基本上是技术含量低，附加值低的制造业产品，加上出口竞争的激烈，平均利润率仅为3%~5%，塑料制品更是如此，对以出口为主的塑料下游企业的影响十分巨大！从长远来说，人民币升值将迫使企业进行产品结构的调整，但就近期来说将会导致塑料制品出口增幅的回落。

原油价格对塑料行业出口的影响。由于国际原油价格持续高涨，塑料原料价格随之跃升，下游的塑料制品加工企业面临高价原料冲击。塑料制品出口价格虽有所上升，但依然远远低于原材料价格涨速，利润日趋微薄。原油价格的大起大落对我省塑料行业对外贸易所造成的影响将是长期的。

贸易摩擦、技术壁垒对塑料行业的影响。我省塑料制品加工企业中小企业占绝大比例。多数塑料制品企业技术装备落后、产品档次低，出口产品主要为日常生活用品和工艺品，特殊工程塑料制品比重过低，高技术含量和高附加值产品极少，企业出口量不少，但利润却难以增加。面临世界经济发达地区以及其他一些经济共同体的反倾销措施和贸易壁垒，我省塑料制品加工企业受到程度不同的影响。

7. 中小企业面临倒闭风险的程度越来越严重

事实上，融资难仅仅是当前中小企业生存困境的一个缩影。更令人担忧的是，在原材料成本上涨、劳动力短缺、工资上涨、市场萎缩、税负过重等因素的多重挤压下，中小企业的营商环境在整体上趋于恶化。就拿劳动力成本来说，“用工荒”、“涨薪潮”现象的出现，表明我国的人口红利逐渐式微，廉价劳动力时代即将结束，这意味着相当多的中小企业可能由此陷入困境。因为，目前我国大部分中小企业的核心竞争力，仍然是低成本延伸的低价优势，处于产业链的低端，利润相当微薄，加薪对他们来说无疑是雪上加霜。

中小企业是推动国民经济发展、构造市场经济主体、促进社会稳定的基础力量，在确保国民经济适度增长、缓解就业压力、优化经济结构等方面，均发挥着越来越重要的作用。由于中小企业的人员规模、资产规模与经营规模都比较小，抗风险能力与大企业相比较弱，中小企业发展尤其需要正确指导与大力扶持。

六、促进行业健康持续发展的措施和建议

(一)以市场为导向，着力调整企业组织结构

我国工业结构的战略性调整，是适应两个根本性转变的要求，朝着社会化大生产和专业化协作的方向发展的，其中企业组织结构的调整是核心和关键。从企业组织结构调整入手，产品、技术、区域、劳动力等结构的调整才有实施的载体。就山东省塑料行业企业组织结构的调整，大体可以分四种情况：

一是关闭破产一批。主要是解决两类企业的问题：第一类是要依法关闭那些产品质量低劣、浪费资源、污染严重的小企业，这主要是小作坊式的废旧塑料加工厂。第二类是长期亏损、资不抵债、扭亏无望的企业，要实施破产。对这两类企业，要建立一个退出市场的机制和通道，加快其退出市场的步伐。

二是限制新上一批。对于生产能力相对过剩的塑料编织制品、一般农地膜大棚膜产品、普通塑料管材、低档塑料小包装等产品应适当限制新上。

三是做大做强一批。对那些符合国家产业政策、有发展前景的重点企业，要通过重点技术改造等措施，提高整体素质。为此，要以市场为导向，以资本为纽带，以优势企业为龙头，推进强强联合，培育若干拥有名牌产品、先进技术、竞争力强的大型企业和企业集团，具备条件的要向跨国公司发展。重点放在高效支农产业、塑料建材、高档塑料包装、汽车配套等主要行业，形成能代表山东塑料工业水平、能与国际大公司相抗衡的企业实力，成为行业的主力、支柱和行业排头兵。

四是搞专搞精一批。积极扶持中小企业特别是科技型中小企业，使它们向“专、精、特、新”的方向发展；建立小企业同大中型企业合理的分工协作关系，形成小企业对大中型企业的专业化配套和专业化服务，提高生产的社会化水平；发挥中小企业在活跃城乡经济、满足社会各方面需要、吸纳劳动力就业等方面的作用。

调整企业组织结构要根据不同行业的特点，分类指导，区别对待。经过企业组织结构的调整，最终形成以大企业为主导，大中小企业合理分工、有机联系、协调发展的格局。

(二)出台并落实有关加快结构调整的政策措施

要加强结构调整规划的导向性作用，并针对结构调整的难点和重点，制定具体的实施细则。对于三年调整振兴规划中涉及到的特色区域建设、名牌产品称号企业等的物质奖励问题、塑料行业高级技工培训基地的建立以及废旧塑料回收再利用的试点等所需资金的落实，这些都是当前贯彻落实调整振

兴规划所最为迫切的。

建议进一步加大财税金融等政策扶持力度。积极推动财税、金融等方面的扶持政策尽快落实到位，帮助企业解决困难。一是加大对暂时出现经营和财务困难企业的支持力度，鼓励担保机构提供信用担保和融资服务。二是由于部分塑料制品的出口政策尚未得到改善，因此，建议省政府有关部门向国家有关部门积极反映，应实施适度灵活的进出口税收政策，支持企业扩大产品出口，增加出口信贷额度。

（三）有序推进塑料产业区域结构调整，促进区域经济合理布局和协调发展。

区域经济结构的调整，主要是发展特色经济和优势产业，形成地区之间分工合作、协调发展的生产力布局。近年来，我省东部地区的塑料产业已开始向我国中西部地区和我省经济相对落后地区转移，这是市场经济条件下企业的自主选择。为推进塑料产业转移有序进行，目前迫切需要加强政府搭台、行业指导、规划和规范的力度。

（四）积极发展新兴产业和高技术产业，培育新的经济增长点

高新技术及其产业化是21世纪企业技术进步的方向和市场竞争的制高点，同时也将成为经济增长的重要支撑。对具备商品化条件的高新技术要加速产业化，以培育新的经济增长点，这也应当成为工业结构调整的一个重要内容。从我省塑料行业的实际情况出发，未来一定时期内，应当不失时机地有选择地加快高新技术产业的发展，发挥后发优势，力争实现跨越式发展。

1. 加快特色区域和专业基地建设。积极培育以滨州市惠民县“塑料安全绳网专业生产基地”、泰安莱芜为中心的“塑料合成土工材料生产基地”、日照市莒县刘官庄镇的“塑料小包装专业生产基地”、淄博市的“一次性塑胶手套生产基地”和“医用塑料专业生产基地”、菏泽市单县的“聚乙烯软管生产基地”、郓城县的“农用塑料薄膜生产基地”、“临沂塑料小商品专业批发城”等具有区域特色的专业生产基地，使其充分发挥特色区域和专业生产基地的带动示范作用。

2. 努力提升行业整体素质。为使“十二五”规划能够落实到实处，整体提高山东塑料工业的水平和在全国同行业的位次，将在主管部门的领导下，继续加快实施山东塑料行业名牌战略、行业重点产品重点企业培育、行业内诚信企业和消费者满意企业等重点活动的步伐。鼓励企业积极参与山东名牌、山东著名商标和驰名商标的申报和评选；引到企业积极申报有关国际认证体系；同时，加强行业协会建设，积极为企业提供优质服务，修订和完善行业自律公约，推进行业自律。

3. 注重技术创新和环境保护，节约能源和资源，对塑料节能环保产品采取特殊政策。

随着国家对发展环境友好型、资源节约型、社会和谐型经济作出的战略部署，要求塑料行业必须更加注重环境保护和资源的节约再利用。要重视环境保护工作，推行清洁生产，大力节约能源和资源，创建清洁生产、节约高效企业；完善塑料再生资源回收利用体系，强化对废弃塑料产品的回收利用；应在回收技术的引进、开发和应用方面加大投入，努力提高再生利用产品的档次及拓宽应用范围，在保护环境的同时，节省更多的能源和资源，不断提升行业的整体综合素质，形成节约型增长方式。

（1）对降解塑料减免企业所得税。积极贯彻国务院办公厅的通知精神，大力提倡生产和使用可降解塑料。由于降解塑料成本明显高于普通塑料（如纯光降解地膜成本比普通地膜高60%左右），单纯依靠生产企业很难得到普及和推广，应在一定时期内给予一定政策支持。可对生产企业按降解塑料的生产量三年内免征企业所得税。

另外，如果扶持政策到位，新的降解塑料的研发与投产将得到快速发展。如聚烯烃类可控性全降解塑料研究项目、利用植物秸秆研发全降解塑料包装材料等重点项目均已成功，其示范作用和社会效益将难以估量。

（2）加快对塑料废弃物回收再利用的研究与开发。

2009年省政府批准的《山东省轻工业调整振兴规划》和《山东省塑料工业调整振兴指导意见》都将医疗塑料废弃物进行必要的灭菌回收再利用和废旧塑料回收再利用列入其中，并要求山东省塑料协会、山东省塑料研究开发中心及相关企业加快研究，尽早列入国家级试点，省府有关部门给予必要的扶持。

“对医疗塑料废弃物进行必要的灭菌回收再利用”项目中的塑料医疗废弃物回收技术已经突破（山东省塑料研究开发中心负责），项目进行中涉及塑料、卫生、环保、石化、科技、财政等行业和政府部门，需省政府统筹协调。

（3）建立非降解塑料购物袋义务回收制度。可以借鉴国外经验和做法，生产不可降解塑料袋的厂商义务回收塑料袋或征收一定比例的回收处理费。对生产可再生材料的企业给予很多政策优惠支持，允许生产降解塑料的厂商一定期限内不需回收其旧塑料袋循环使用，而目前生产不可降解塑料袋的厂商均有义务回收塑料袋或按生产量征收一定比例的回

收处理费。这一措施如得以实施，一方面可以使得厂家生产成本得以降低，另一方面可以减少非降解塑料的生产量。

七、塑料行业发展前景分析

当前的塑料产业面临三大困境：资源、市场和环境，要想崛起就必须打破这些桎梏。经过近几年的快速发展，国内塑料制品的市场不断趋向饱和，国外市场也由于金融危机开始萎缩；生产塑料的原材料－石油也在不断减少；而塑料制品的最终归宿及其引发的环境问题和食品安全问题，也逐渐被世界各国所重视。

1. 塑料制品业具有很大的发展潜力

经济技术创新能力的提升推动了塑料制品工业的进步和发展。科技创新和制度管理方面的创新发展大大激发了市场活力；为满足国内外市场需求，我国塑料制造业基地规模化、高科技化发展进一步拓展了塑料制品的应用领域；塑料行业通过新的资本运营和资源配置的调整，形成企业新的发展动力。

区域经济战略升级转移为我国塑料行业发展新增市场空间。塑料加工行业将随着国家经济发展大趋势而实现战略升级，逐步实现区域性战略转移。随着新农村建设、城市化进程的加快，对塑料管道、异型材、人造革合成革等塑料建材一系列的塑料制品对经济增长的提升作用带来巨大发展空间。

随着人们生活水平提高和国际市场需求稳步增长，塑料制品生活必需品升级换代成为新的增长空间。

2. 自主创新、产业升级需向深度和广度进军

塑料行业正面临国内市场国际化，跨国公司在我国这个极具发展前景的巨大市场已经占有优势，企业间的竞争也日益激烈。

塑料消费持续扩大，废塑料产生量越来越大，政策、环境、投入、成本、技术进步、质量标准等多种因素制约整体发展的速度和质量。新材料、新成果、新技术、新工艺应用进程加快推动力塑料行业技术进步与发展，丰富了塑料应用领域，逐步推进高科技领域向更高层次进步，逐步拉近与发达国家的距离。随着现代制造业的发展，我国塑料加工也将从现在的塑料加工大国向强国迈进。原始创新、自主品牌、高附加值产品推动塑料加工企业向深度和高度进军，将成为今后该领域发展的总体趋势。

3. 全球经济持续低迷，未来出口存在不确定性

欧美等国家经济的缓慢复苏制约了我国塑料制品出口规模的快速上升；国际贸易保护主义频频发生，提高进口产品门槛成为当前贸易保护主义的常见形式，给我国塑料制品出口带来一定威胁；在国内原材料价格上涨和能源、劳动力成本上升的因素共同带动下，行业出口企业的生存环境更加困难。

但也应看到，我国出口产品类型和价格优势，有利于保证出口增速的基本稳定。近年来，我国塑料制品主要出口品种中，日用塑料制品占近一半的份额，而日用塑料制品的国际需求波动相对较小。同时，出口价格优势有利于带动我国塑料制品出口规模的上升。

（山东省塑料协会　刘丰田）

江　西　省

【基本情况】

江西省是革命老区，是农业大省，工业基础相对薄弱。经济发展较慢，在华东地区是欠发达省份，塑料工业同样如此，与全省经济发展同步，不论总量和规模都相对较小。但是进入新世纪以来，江西坚持以新型工业化为核心，以大开放为主战略，加快工业园区建设，主动对接长珠闽，联结港粤台，融入全球化，经济社会发生前所未有的深刻变化。截止2012年底，我省拥有省级以上工业园区94家，其中国家级高新技术产业开发区3家，经济技术开发区6家，出口加工区4家。有效地推动塑料行业快速发展，2012年全省塑料制品规模以工业企业实现工业增加值73亿元，同比增长27.6%，实现利税总额32亿元，同比增长46%，实现利润总额22亿元，同比增长51.1%。塑料制品产量1220kt，同比增长62.3%，占全国总量的2.12%。其中塑料薄膜1.2kt，同比增长4.26%。占全国总量的0.13%，日用塑料制品3.4kt，同比增长15.93%，占全国总量的0.74%，其他塑料1167kt，同比增长66.1%，占全国总量3.02%。塑料行业在全国排位不断前移。

随着江西塑料行业这几年快速发展，形成了有一定特色的产业基地，如进贤县医疗器械生产基地，该基地所生产的医疗器械在全国有一定影响力和知名度，带动相连企业快速发展。宜黄县塑编产业基地，年产量在300kt以，安义县的型材生产基地，樟树的医用包装产业相对发展较快。而且形成一定规模和配套。

【重点企业】

1. 瑞金市金和塑业发展有限公司

瑞金市金和塑业发展有限公司成立于2006年，注册资金2100万元，厂区占地面积12000多平方米。是一家集研发、生产、销售、服务于一体的现代高

新塑料管材企业。

公司专业生产“欧美瑞、江雄”牌 PVC－U 给水管、排水管、电工套线管、螺旋消音管、HDPE 给水管、燃气管、硅芯管(非开挖用管)，PP－R 冷热给水管及配套的管材配件。产品通过国家塑料制品监督检验中心检验，江西省产品质量监督检测院检测，产品卫生安全性通过江西省疾病预防控制中心检测，各项检测指标均符合国家和行业标准。

企业通过 ISO 9001：2008 质量管理体系认证、ISO 14001：2004 环境管理体系认证，通过江西省卫生厅涉及饮用水卫生安全产品许可审批。欧美瑞、江雄品牌商标获得赣州市知名商标，企业获得中国环境标志产品认证(十环认证)、中国塑料加工工业协会授予“AAA”级资信等级。

2. 江西得康管业有限公司

江西得康管业有限公司成立于 2004 年，注册资金 8000 万元，占地面积 24000m^2，地处九江市瑞昌工业园南区。

公司主要产品为建筑给排水用 PVC 管材、管件、电气穿线管材、管件给水用无规共聚三型聚丙烯 PP－R 管材、管件，高密度聚乙烯(PVC－C)套管；聚乙烯塑钢缠绕管等。公司拥有国内先进的生产设备及模具、精良的制造工艺和齐全的检查设备。是建设部“以塑代钢、节约能源”产业化江西示范基地，公司致力于新型建材管道的研发生产、年生产能力 12kt。

公司已通过 IS9001 中国质量认证中心认证，拥有“得康”、“得惠”系列商标。“得康”牌系列产品先后获得了“国家建设部推荐产品”，“江西省消费者信得过产品”，“九江市著名商标”公司正积极申报江西省著名商标及中国驰名公司，严格依据质量体系的要求管理和控制产品质量，建立了以品管部为龙头，从原料—生产系统—成品检验—销售服务的一整套严格控制的生产经营体系，努力打造优质品牌、名牌。

3. 南昌天高新材料股份公司

南昌天高新材料股份公司成立于 1998 年、地处南昌市昌北国家经济开发区，厂区占地面积 30 多万平方米，注册资金 8700 万元，2012 年公司总资产 2.6 亿元。

公司主要产品是双向拉伸塑料土工格栅，年生产能力为 3500 万平方米。单向拉伸塑料土工格栅，年生产能力为 4500 万平方米。拥有防渗施工资质，土工膜年生产能力为 4000 万平方米。而且具有专业的防渗膜施工队伍和设备。公司拥有发明专利及实用新型专利多项、并且注重自主创新，提升核心竞争力。2000 年通过 ISO 9001 质量体系认证，陆续参与制定《土工合成、塑料土工格栅》等国家、行业标准的修订工作。2009 年通过国家高新技术企业资格审查，承担了国家级火炬计划项目及省、市级科技攻关项目，项目产品获评省级自主创新产品，省级重点新产品等。创立了土工合成材料的市级工程技术研究中心。已经参与了国内如南水北调、兰新铁路、大西铁路、杭长铁路、大广高速等重大工程，属国内高强度格栅及防渗膜生产的龙头企业。

2012 年江西省塑料制品产量企业名单

序号	企业名称	产量/t	主要产品
1	江西康乐塑胶有限公司	10000	管材、管件
2	万年县中信塑业有限公司	10000	编织袋
3	江西建大实业有限公司	10000	塑料线
4	江西旺族投资发展有限公司	10000	编织袋
5	江西昌九生化赣北分公司	4000	管材
6	江西联创塑业发展有限公司	3500	管材
7	江西省樟树市赣通塑胶制品有限公司	3000	管材
8	南昌关联塑业有限公司	2600	PVC 电缆料
9	南昌市三星吹膜厂	1300	薄膜
10	江西旭辉塑业有限公司	1200	塑料杯

【存在问题】

1. 江西省塑料行业里是一个以塑料制品加工为主，产业整体不配套的产业，但是地处中部，交通便捷，也是一个大有发展潜力的产业。

2. 江西省塑料行业产业结构不合理，先进设备相对较少，加工工艺落后，中低产品多，产品结构单一。有的子行业在省内是空白，与发达省份比较差距大。

3. 中小企业多，大型企业少，全省主营收入规模以上塑料加工企业只有 50 多家，产值过亿的企业只有十几家。产业集中度不高。产品附加值低，市场竞争力不强，特别小型企业，由于缺乏规模，经济效益不佳。

4. 整个行业专业技术人员匮乏，特别是高尖端技术人才少。企业与专业院所对接不够，有些先进技术在企业没有得到很好运用，企业技术创新与开发能力差，导致整个行业在发展过程不能做到创新发展。

【目标任务】

今后五年是江西经济社会发展的关键时期。综观未来发展趋势，尽管世界经济低速增长态势仍将延续，但世界多极化、经济全球化的大势没有变。我国发展仍处于可以大有作为的重要战略机遇期，经济社会发展基本面长期向好。江西省处于工业化、城镇化加速发展期，多年来高强度投入积累的能量正在加速释放，将有力支撑经济增长。必须始终坚持抢抓机遇、加快发展、科学发展。将全面贯彻落实党的十八大和省第十三次党代会精神，适应国内外形势新变化，抓住用好发展机遇期，以科学发展为主题，以加快转变经济发展方式为主线，围绕建设富裕和谐秀美江西的奋斗目标，进一步解放思想，深化改革，扩大开放。

2013 年是全面深入贯彻落实党的十八大精神的开局之年，是实施“十二五”规划承前启后的关键一年，是为全面建成小康社会奠定坚实基础的重要一年。江西省经济社会发展的总体要求是：深入学习、全面贯彻落实党的十八大和中央经济工作会议精神，以邓小平理论、“三个代表”重要思想、科学发展观为指导，紧紧围绕建设富裕和谐秀美江西的奋斗目标，深入实施三大国家战略，突出主题主线，坚持稳中求进，深化改革开放，强化创新驱动，优化生态环境，保障改善民生，同步推进新型工业化、信息化、城镇化和农业现代化，不断提高经济增长质量和效益，努力实现经济持续健康较快发展和社会和谐稳定，为全面建成小康社会奠定坚实基础

江西省经济社会发展的主要预期目标是：生产总值增长 10% 以上，财政总收入和公共财政预算收入均增长 15% 以上，规模以上工业增加值增长 14.5%，固定资产投资增长 20% 以上，社会消费品零售总额增长 15% 以上，外贸出口总额力争增长 10% 左右，实际利用外商直接投资增长 10% 以上，节能减排完成国家下达的计划任务。

（江西省塑料工业协会　邹文云）

湖　南　省

【大事记】

1、2012 年 4 月，湖南塑协组织部分会员单位参加了在上海浦东新国际博览中心举办的第二十六届雅式国际橡塑展。

2、2012 年 5 月，湖南省塑料行业协会会长蒯建政、副秘书长黄钧出席参加了在广东东莞常平举行的全国塑料行业协会峰会。

出席本次会议的有中国轻工业联合会副会长、中国塑料加工工业协会理事长钱桂敬，中国塑料加工工业协会常务副理事长曹俭、名誉会长廖正品、秘书长马占峰以及全国 17 个省、市、自治区的塑料行业协会代表和 49 家企业代表。本届峰会的主题为“交流合作，优势互补，共同发展”，峰会由曹俭常务副理事长主持，与会省市地方协会会长、秘书长重点介绍了各自地方的行业形势和企业发展状况、介绍了各自行业组织的会员管理、会员结构以及协会自身建设的经验以及面临的问题。本次峰会是全国塑料行业协会的一次形势分析会、经验交流会、是一次团结的盛会，对于行业团结和发展必将产生积极的影响。

3、2012 年 7 月，湖南塑协参加了中国塑协塑料技术协作委员会在黑龙江哈尔滨举办的第七届中国塑料工业高新技术及产业化研讨会暨 2012 中国塑协塑料技术协作委员会年会·技术交流会/中国塑协注塑制品专委会二届六次年会，会上进行了 2011 年和 2012 年上半年工作报告，湖南塑协作为副理事长单位参与讨论了关于换届工作的方案，并做了重要的学术报告。

4、2012 年 9 月，湖南塑协组员参加了浙江台州第十二届中国塑料交易会及浙江省塑料行业发展论坛。中国塑料交易会自 2001 年开始在浙江台州已连续举办了 11 届，并且连续 8 年被商务部列为塑料行业重点支持的展会。中国塑料交易会已成为强力吸引国际商家进入中国塑料市场，了解中国塑料市场的一个重要平台。

5、协助中国塑协完成《2012 年中国塑料工业年鉴—湖南篇》的编辑工作。《中国塑料工业年鉴》是由中国塑料加工工业协会主办，全面反映我国塑料工业的发展情况。湖南塑协作为中国塑协副理事长单位，从协会大事记、基本情况、重点企业介绍、存在问题及市场前景的各个方面认真总结全面介绍了湖南省塑料行业发展情况。

6、2012 年 10 月，按照湖南省民政厅行业管理办公室的要求，湖南塑协成立了第一届“中共湖南省塑料行业协会支部委员会”，并荣获中共湖南省社会组织工作委员会授牌。

7、2012 年底，参加了由湖南省轻工行业管理办公室主持的 2012 年行业运行情况及 2013 年行业发展

趋势的汇报座谈会。湖南塑协蒯建政会长出席会议，对湖南省2012年塑料行业发展情况做了总结报告，并对2013年湖南省塑料行业的发展提出了意见和建议。

【基本情况】

2011年是“十二五”开局之年，是我国塑料加工行业重点发展的机遇期。2011年度湖南省塑料工业发展迅速，湖南省塑料产业园产值达14亿元，2011年全年湖南省规模以上企业(年销售收入2000万元以上)塑料制品产量已达703.4kt，累计同比增长24.49%，占全国总比例的1.28%。

2012年是我国塑料加工工业转型跨越、扎实推进的关键一年，我国塑料加工行业在经历“十一五”、“十二五”以及2011年高速增长之后，2012年湖南省乃至全国塑料发展都遭受到了严重的考验，面对复杂多变的国内外经济形势，湖南省塑料工业企业积极深入贯彻落实科学发展观、国家《轻工业调整和振兴规划》和中国塑料加工工业协会《中国塑料加工工业“十二五”发展规划指导意见》，继续推进湖南省塑料产业的结构调整，加快湖南省塑料工业企业的转型发展，使得湖南省塑料产品制品产量仍保持较快增长。据不完全统计，2012年全年湖南省规模以上企业(年销售收入2000万以上)塑料制品产量达122.85万吨，累计比同期增长29.87%，占全国总比例的2.12%。2012年1~12月湖南省塑料行业塑料产品产量表和塑料树脂及共聚物、塑料加工专用设备产量表分别如表1所示。

表1　2012年1~12月湖南省塑料行业塑料产品产量

产品名称	产量/t	比同期/±%
塑料制品合计	1228524	29.87
塑料薄膜	121300	7.19
其中：农用薄膜	40866	63.90
泡沫塑料	9015	17.61
塑料人造革、合成革	1039	-77.19
日用塑料制品	100483	12.43
其他塑料制品	996687	36.30

注：以上统计为规模以上企业(年销售收入2000万元以上)。

表2　2012年1~12月塑料树脂及共聚物、塑料加工专用设备产量

产品名称	产量/t(台)	比同期/±%
塑料树脂及共聚物	604776	0.97
1. 聚氯乙烯树脂	254714	-12.32
2. 聚苯乙烯树脂		
3. 聚酯	52591	44.43
塑料加工专用设备	45287	-63.75

【重点企业】

湖南省有3000余家塑料行业企业，但大多数企业规模过小，产业集中度低，规模以上塑料加工及配套企业仅226家，下表是湖南省部分影响力大、实力雄厚的重点企业：

序号	企业名称	主要产品	产能/(t/a)
1	湖南路路通塑业股份有限公司	C-PVC、U-PVC管材等	35000
2	湖南神塑科技有限公司	PVC、PPR、PE管材、管件	60000
3	湖南五祥新材料科技有限公司	管道产品、型材门窗	170000
4	株洲湘瑞塑料建材有限公司	PVC异型材、UPVC、PP-R管材等、塑料门窗	25000
5	株洲时代工程塑料制品有限公司	注塑产品、工程塑料	20000
6	湖南省塑料研究所	工程塑料、塑料改性专用料	10000
7	湖南五强新材料有限公司	PVC型材	15000
8	湖南省坤源塑化有限公司	U-PVC管材、管件	12000
9	长沙天卓塑胶有限公司	HDPE双壁波纹排水管	30000
10	长沙双龙塑料型材实业有限公司	PVC异型材	10000
11	湖南万容包装有限公司	食品包装	10000
12	湖南晶鑫科技股份有限公司	复合膜食品软包装袋	10亿只
13	益阳市湘衡塑业有限公司	编织袋等	20000

续表

序号	企业名称	主要产品	产能/(t/a)
14	湖南长丰汽车塑料制品有限公司	汽车用塑料制品	10000
15	汨罗平桂制塑实业有限公司	PVC 板材、PVC 胶粒	20000
16	长沙日松管业有限公司	PP-R、CPVC、HDPE	10000
17	湖南省宏通实业有限公司	U-PVC 管材、电力管材等	8000
18	常德七星泰塑业有限公司	U-PVC 系列管材、管件、电缆套管	20000
19	株洲塑料有限公司	PVC 软、硬板、PVC 管材、件，氟塑料	25000
20	株洲晶昱实业有限责任有限公司	橡胶、塑料改性胶粒	6000
21	湖南光顺管材有限公司	PVC、PPR 给排水管	5000
22	浏阳市塑料厂	农地膜	10000
23	湖南振云塑胶公司	塑料管道	20000

湖南五祥新材料科技有限公司：

湖南五祥新材料科技有限公司以“五强”牌管道和型材为推广品牌，公司产品及服务涵盖：管道产品、型材门窗领域。产品广泛应用于建筑给排水、建筑门窗、电力、通信、市政给排水等领域。是中南地区最大的建筑配套新材料生产基地。是湖南省专业从事废旧塑料资源回收与综合再利用的高新技术企业，是全国区域循环经济示范基地的龙头企业。

2010 年 11 月湖南五祥新材料科技有限公司成功收购湖南五强产业集团股份有限公司新型材料分公司，使整体实力大幅增强。公司先后成为中塑协管道专委会的会员单位，湖南省涉水产品卫生学会主任委员单位，湖南省政府采购协会理事单位，湖南省新材料产业协会理事单位。先后通过了 ISO 9001 质量管理体系、ISO 14001 环境管理体系、OHSAS 18001 职业健康安全管理体系、节水产品等认证。公司荣获湖南省“著名商标”、湖南名牌产品，企业信用 AAA 等级、质量信用 AAA 等级、品牌信誉 AAA 等级等资质。

公司先后投入 1 亿多元，引进了具有国际一流水平的生产线 30 条，年生产能力达 170kt。公司为严格执行质量管理标准，通过引进国内最先进的生产设备和技术力量，并坚持以“未经检验合格的原材料不采购、未经检验合格的产品不入库、出库检验有瑕疵的产品不出库”的三不准原则，严格把好各个关口，确保了产品质量。在废旧塑料资源回收再利用方面具有丰富的经验，曾与美国、加拿大、日本、韩国、英国等国家的再生资源机构多次研发探讨废旧塑料的再生利用，曾先后承担过国家及省部级科研项目 10 余项，目前已经获得 6 项实用新型专利证书、2 项发明专利证书、2 个科技成果鉴定，2 项实用新型专利和 1 项发明专利正在申请。

公司非常注重企业高端品牌形象的打造，于 2013 年 1 月 1 日起在湖南经济电视台和潇湘电影频道进行了企业品牌宣传片的投放，并对加盟的经销商统一进行店面的装修和宣传。

公司的发展带动了汨罗地区再生塑料行业的良好趋势，不仅取得了较好经济效益，同时也成为了汨罗市财税收入的一个亮点和支柱企业，公司目前解决了 400 余人的就业问题。多年来一直热忠于社会公益事业的发展，先后为市公益活动、新农村建设、资助贫困生、捐助村老年院的基础设施建设等公益事业捐款 150 多万元。公司作为一个拥有高度社会责任感的企业，将以领先新型塑料环保建材事业为目标，崇尚科技、珍惜人才、追求创新，不懈不怠，努力打造企业核心竞争力，为中国新型塑料环保节能建材行业的发展增砖添瓦。

【存在问题】

2012 年湖南省塑料工业在保持快速增长的同时，受国内外经济形势发展变化的影响，省内塑料工业发展可谓喜忧参半，尽管湖南省塑料工业规模以上企业塑料制品总产量相比去年增加近三成，但全省塑料行业产业结构不合理、科技创新能力低、生产力成本不断攀升等仍是制约着湖南省塑料行业发展的重要因素。

1. 科技创新能力偏低、缺乏竞争力

湖南省塑料工业整体状况相对落后，科技创新的能力有限，缺乏自主知识产权技术，特别是缺乏企业和高等院校、科研院所的有效结合，共同开发产品的技术创新能力偏低，同时湖南省塑料工业生产装备水平不高，大量高能耗、低产能的加工设备仍在使用，导致企业加工工艺技术相对落后，市场竞争能力弱。

2. 人力成本上涨，劳动力短缺

随着劳动力成本不断增加，使得企业成本增加，用工缺口增大，直接影响到企业的经济效益。用工缺口和用工成本上升，是企业面临的双重压力。用工的缺口特别是高专业技术水平人才的缺乏，对湖南省塑料行业的发展影响巨大。

3. 中小企业融资困难，资金短缺

中小企业作为湖南省经济的重要组成部分，在实施中部崛起战略中的作用日益加大。湖南省塑料企业3000余家，绝大部分是中小型企业，而湖南省塑料中小企业融资的现状是：融资渠道狭窄，主要靠企业自身内部积累，同时中小企业获得银行贷款的难度很大。目前湖南省中小企业仍居中下水平，发展速度偏低，效益低下，其进一步发展仍然面临着资金短缺的难题，因此极大地制约中小企业的快速发展和做强做大。

4. 生产成本上升，企业压力加大

原材料价格上涨，劳动力成本上升，企业生产成本逐年加大，湖南省企业原材料购进与产品出厂价格"高进低出"明显，导致企业压力不断加大。同时湖南省塑料行业中小企业普遍负税较高，导致企业盈利减少而加剧了企业的资金紧张状况，企业的技术改进受到了更大程度的限制，进而加大了企业的经营风险，甚至对下游行业的产量和质量带来隐患，最终可能陷入恶性循环，使企业缺失竞争力。

5. 产业结构不够合理

产业结构不够合理也是影响湖南省塑料行业发展的一个重要因素。湖南省塑料企业以中小企业为主，小微型企业、家庭作坊式企业数量众多，技术力量薄弱，产品都是以中低档次产品、老产品为主，缺乏高档次、高技术含量的产品，且产品的种类类同、质量良莠不齐，很大程度上制约着湖南省塑料行业的发展。

【市场前景】

塑料行业是一个朝阳产业，随着我国和湖南省国民经济的快速发展，一些重点行业、支柱产业的崛起和发展以及对塑料产品的需求，推动了湖南省塑料行业向绿色生态、节能低碳、多元化、高端化不断发展。根据湖南省塑料工业发现现状和市场行情，今后湖南省塑料行业发展的主要趋势表现在以下几个方面。

1. 农村市场

湖南省是一个农业大省，拥有5750万亩耕地，4200多万农村人口。随着经济的发展，农用塑料制品已成为湖南省现代农业发展中不可缺少的生产资料，特别是近年来，湖南省认真贯彻落实中央"三农"工作方针政策，围绕农业增效和农民增收两大目标，以农业结构战略性调整为主线，大力推进农业产业化经营，农业经济运行质量有了明显提高。因此，在发展现代农业、建设社会主义新农村的新形势下，我们要大力推广农用薄膜、农用沼气管、农用塑料节水器材等农用塑料的应用，支持湖南省自主农用塑料品牌的生产与销售，把提升湖南省塑料农业技术水平作为研发重点，以推进湖南省农业的结构调整、农民增收。

2. 汽车工业

中国汽车行业的良好发展给汽车相关产品带来了巨大的市场需求，据有关资料显示，汽车工业大量使用的材料中，塑料占7%～10%，近年来，汽车轻量化的要求使其塑料用量的增长正在快速增长，而且全塑车神是未来汽车的发展方向。随着湖南省新型工业化进程的不断推进，汽车工业在湖南省已成为支柱产业并作为重点扶持产业在发展，据统计湖南全省规模以上列入国家汽车生产企业及产业公告的35家，产能已达到约30万辆。预计到2015年，湖南省汽车产能将达到100余万辆，汽车塑料零部件材料的需求将达到80kt左右，其市场前景是非常巨大的。

3. 家电行业

在家电行业中，产品塑料化已经成为家电行业中重要发展方向发展之一，塑料已成为家电领域应用量增长速度最快的材料，近几年每年平均增长速度达到29.5%。目前塑料在家电中用量已占重量比的40%，并随着新型环保、绿色健康材料的研发生产和应用，国内家电市场必将迎来新一轮消费结构的快速升级，从而带动塑料行业的整体发展。

4. 基础设施类建设

"十二五"期间，湖南省委省政府将"一化三基"战略调整为"两化三基"，即在原来的新型工业化的基础上增加"新型城镇化"提法，而城镇化进程的加快，推动了湖南省塑料管道行业的快速发展，城市给排水、市政排污管道等基础设施用塑料管道市场需求旺盛，预计"十二五"期间，塑料管道生产量将保持在10%左右的增长速度，塑料管道在全国各类管道中市场占有率超过60%。随着湖南省高铁、长沙地铁工程的建设，高性能化工程塑料需求量明显增多，如特种结构泡沫材料、塑料轴承、电子电器用塑料元件等，因此，湖南省塑料企业应加大科研投入，依托技术，实现自主创新，推动湖南省工程塑料技术发展，为湖南省支柱产业做好配套服务。

（湖南省塑料行业协会　龙洁）

广 东 省

【概况】

1　行业规模

2012，广东省塑料制品行业规模以上企业2830个，(统计数据比上年统计数减少162家)。占全国塑料制品规模以上企业统计数比重21.36%，比上一年降低1.64%；规模以上企业从业人员69.2万人，同比-8.86%。自2011年国家统计局将规模以上工业统计范围内的工业企业起点标准从年主营业务收入500万元调整到2000万元之后，广东省塑料制品规模以上企业数及从业人员数连续两年减少。自2012年又实行新国家标准《国民经济行业分类》(GB/T 4754—2011)统计办法，2012年统计数据将“塑料鞋”数据列入“制鞋业”。受此影响，广东省塑料制品规模企业各项统计数据相应变化。塑料鞋参考数据：2011年广东省塑料鞋制造企业统计数210家，占规模企业数比重7.02%；塑料鞋制造从业人员5.3万人，占规模企业从业人员数比重约6.58%，塑料鞋产值194.6亿元，占规模企业产品产值比重5.23%；塑料鞋出口交货值81.26亿元，占规模企业产品出口交货值比重7.77亿元；塑料鞋企业资产总计67.32亿元，占规模企业资产比重3.25%；塑料鞋企业利润总额3.09亿元，占规模企业利润总额比重2.09%。

2　主要塑料制品产量

2012年，广东省塑料制品总产量9193kt，同比增长7.45%，占全国产量比重15.9%，比上年下降3.7%。其中：塑料薄膜产量1404kt，同比增长10.18%，占全省塑料制品总产量15.24%，占全国同类产品产量比重24.5%，比上年上升8.26%。泡沫塑料产量709kt，同比增长21.78%，占全省塑料制品总产量7.71%，占全国同类产品产量比重41.20%，比上年降低0.3%。塑料人造革合成革产量186kt，同比增长11.19%，占全省塑料制品总产量2.02%，占全国同类产品产量比重5.92%，比上年降低1.78%。日用塑料产量1033kt，同比增长22.03%，占全省塑料制品总产量11.24%，占全国同类产品产量比重22.3%，比上年降低5.93%。其他塑料制品5861kt，同比增长3.1%，占全省塑料制品总产量63.76%，占全国同类产品产量比重15.17%。比上年降低3.13%。其中，日用塑料和其他塑料制品产量占全省塑料制品总产量的75%。2012年广东省塑料制品总产量同比增幅低于全国增幅，占全国比重继续下降，但总量规模仍居全国省份前列，为我国塑料工业大省。

3　主要塑料制品产值销售值

2012年，广东省塑料制品规模以上企业总产值3161.8亿元，同比增长9.65%，占全国比重18.87%，比上年降低4.25%。销售产值3107.6亿元，同比增长9.11%，产销率为98.29%。主要产品分类产值中：塑料薄膜制品统计企业305家，产值425.41亿元，同比增长6.61%，占全国同类产品产值比重19.14%。塑料板、管、型材制品统计企业276家，产值515.3亿元，同比增长11.95%，占全国同类产品产值比重12.71%。塑料丝、绳及编织制品统计企业92家，产值100.88亿元，同比增长12.89%，占全国同类产品产值比重4.41%。泡沫塑料制品统计企业169家，产值143.14，同比增长27.81%，占全国同类产品产值比重19.53%。塑料人造革合成革制品统计企业69家，产值110.83亿元，同比增长11.05%，占全国同类产品产值比重10.21%。塑料包装箱及容器制品统计企业245家，产值223.23亿元，同比增长16.33%，占全国同类产品产值比重14.91%。日用塑料制品统计企业418家，产值430.15亿元，同比增长11.07%，占全国同类产品产值比重30.50%。塑料零件制品统计企业377家，产值357.68亿元，同比增长2.02%，占全国同类产品产值比重28.97%。其他塑料制品统计企业879家，产值854.14亿元，同比增长7.96%，占全国同类产品产值比重37.93%。2012年广东省塑料制品增幅连续二年高于产量增幅，原因与行业加快产品结构调整，产品向高端高附加值和配套于多个行业方向发展，以及原料价格、用工成本、生产成本等因素有关。但2012年广东塑料制品产值增幅低于全国产值增幅。产值占全国比重降至20%以下。塑料薄膜、泡沫塑料产值增幅高于全国增幅。

4　主要塑料制品出口交货值

2012年广东省塑料制品出口交货值921.09亿元，同比增长4.37%，占全国比重43.07%。其中：塑料薄膜86.64亿元，占全省出口交货值9.41%，同比-7.98%，占全国比重33.57%。塑料板、管、型材制品80.15%，占全省出口交货值8.70%，同比增6.94%，占全国比重41.76%。塑料丝、绳及编织制品20.83亿元，占全省出口交货值2.26%，同比增长31.33%，占全国比重22.28%。泡沫塑料20.82亿元，占全省出口交货值2.26%，同比增长17.76%，占全国比重44.03%。塑料人造革合成革24.17亿元，占全省出口交货值2.62%，同比-5.95%，占全国比重27.89%。塑料包装箱及容器

35.86 亿元，占全省出口交货值 3.89%，同比增长 16.58%，占全国比重 29.29%。日用塑料制品 182.71 亿元，占全省出口交货值 19.84%，同比增长 4.83%，占全国比重 39.74%。塑料零件 154.60 亿元，占全省出口交货值 16.78%，同比增长 5.14%，占全国 44.42%。其他塑料制品 315.31 亿元，占全省出口交货值 34.23%，同比增长 3.93%，占全国比重 59.19%。

2012 年，广东省塑料制品出口交货值占产品产值 29.13%，比上一年增加 1.46%，增幅也高于全国增幅，总交货值占全国比重仍在 40% 以上，占全国比重最低的是人造革合成革制品 27.89% 和塑料丝、绳及编织制品 22.28%，而其他塑料制品占全国比重达到 59.19%。在全国塑料制品出口交货值中，广东省占非常重要份量。

5　产品进、出口

2012 年，广东省塑料制品累计进、出口额 228.4 亿美元。其中进口额 53.08 亿美元，同比增长 6.59%，占全国塑料制品进口总额 28.72%。出口额 175.32 亿美元，同比增长 28.63%，占全国塑料制品出口额 34.28%。2012 年广东省塑料制品出口额增幅高于全国增幅，仍保持较高增长，产品出口额占全国比重已超三分之一，是我国塑料制品出最大的省份。从塑料制品出口交货值产品分类比重可看出，出口产品结构以普通塑料制品为主。

6　行业经济效益、企业资产

2012 年，广东省塑料制品企业累计实现主营收入 3101.8 亿元，同比增长 34%，增长幅度大于全国增长幅度，主营收入占全国比重 19.2%，比上年降低 2.65%。利润总额 135.55 亿元，同比增长 1.39%，低于全国增幅，产值利润率 4.29%。利润总额占全国比重 14.07%，比上年降低 2.7%。企业资产总计 2173.5 亿元，同比增长 8.46%，规模以上企业平均资产 7680 万元，同比增长 10.9%。亏损企业数 437 个(含塑料鞋企业)，企业亏损面 14.34%(按含塑料鞋企业 3047 家计)，比上年增加 34 个，亏损企业亏损总额 17.68 亿元(含塑料鞋企业)，比上年增亏 4.29 亿元，亏损企业平均亏损额 405 万元，亏损额占全国比重 25.96%，比上年降低 1.9%。

2012 年广东省塑料制品企业平均资产增加幅度大，基本接近全国平均水平，产值利润比上年略有提高，但仍低于全国平均水平，企业亏损面较上年略有增大。塑料制品企业资产偏少，塑料制品整体产品结构利润偏低，亏损企业及亏损额仍占全国较大比重。

【存在问题】

1、2012 年，广东省塑料制品产量发展继续趋于平缓，产量增速首次在 10% 以下，总产量已略少于浙江省，占全国比重仍在下降。大规模的产量增长模式转为平稳发展态势将在较长一个时期成为广东省塑料加工业的发展趋势。

2、国家调整规模企业统计标准后，塑料制品统计数据不再统计塑料鞋相关数据，而塑料鞋是日用塑料主要的产品之一，也是广东传统的日用塑料制品之一，故 2012 年，塑料行业部份数据比上年再度下降，反映出塑料制品企业偏中、小型，在广东省塑料制品结构中日用塑料制品类比重较大。

3、行业效益比上一年有所提高，但仍较低。除受企业运营成本高等一系列原因外，产业、产品结构调整仍有待推进，塑料制品中普通日用、民用消费品要向高端、高附加值方向调整和发展，塑料做为新型材料的功能要进一步强化，塑料制品做为新型材料的应用领域和市场开发力度要加大，塑料配套于更多的行业的力度也要加大。产业和产品结构合理、上档次才能有效地提高行业经济效益。

4、塑料制品出口是广东省塑料行业的优势，出口额一直占全国三分之一，出口产品货值也占产值较大比重，但整体上还是以低端低值产品为主，同类产品进、出口价差仍很大，产品出口额仍靠数量支撑。

5、国际、国内针对安全、环境、卫生等方面的法规越来越多，标准越来越严格，塑料制品在展现自身“绿色环保”的同时，也由于材料、添加剂等自身问题，以及使用观念、回收利用等因素，影响到部分产品发展和应用领域的拓展。

【大事记】

1、全国塑料行业协会峰会在广东东莞召开

2012 年 5 月 27 日，由中国塑料加工工业协会召集，广东省塑料工业协会协办的全国塑料行业协会峰会在广东省东莞市常平镇召开。这是全国塑料行业协会首次峰会，中国塑协及各省、市(区)和地方的 45 个塑料行业协会的会长和秘书长以及近 50 家重点企业的董事长、总经理参加了本次会议。会议围绕“交流合作、优势互补、共同发展”及“十二五”我国塑料产业发展等议题进行交流，有效地增进了全国塑料行业的交流和合作。

2、广东省塑料工业协会换届

2012 年 8 月，广东省塑料工业协会召开四届会员代表大会进行换届。137 个理事单位的 197 位代表参加了会议。会议通过了“广东省塑料工业协会三届理事会工作报告”、“广东省塑料工业协会章程”、“广东省塑料工业协会三届理事会财务报告”等一系列议案，并选举产生广东省塑料工业协会四届理事会。符岸当选为会长，佛塑科技王磊、广东联塑左满伦等44人当选为副会长。聘任何树强为秘书长。

3、2012年(第七届)中国塑料工业新材料、新工艺、新装备行业峰会举行

2012年11月8日，由中国塑协、广东省塑协、广东南海狮山镇政府联合主办、广东仕诚塑料机械有限公司承办的2012年(第七届)中国塑料工业新材料、新工艺、新装备行业峰会在佛山市南海区南国桃园举行。本届峰会对会议主题做了调整，增加了“新装备”内容，增加了管理类的报告内容，峰会整体水平更高、内容更充实。主报告人邀请到了中国工程院院士等一些行业著名专家，参会企业及各类机构代表超500人，成为年内有影响的塑料专业会议。

4、节能推广、改造系列工作铺开

广东省塑料工业协会及省塑协节能改造服务中心继续积极推广塑料机械节能改造，广东联塑、广东雄塑、广东顾地、广东海兴、深圳永高等一批注塑机应用大企业与省塑协节能改造服务中心合作，已开始注塑机节能改造。

5、塑料行业推广能源管理体系认证工作

广东省塑料工业协会牵头在全省塑料行业企业推进能源管理体系认证工作，塑料行业被省经信委批准为能源管理体系建设及认证试点行业。部份骨干塑料企业已参与首批能源管理体系认证。后续工作将继续在全省塑料行业中推广展开。

6、广东省塑料工业协会获具备承接政府职能转移和购买服务资质

广东省民政厅根据《关于确定具备承接政府职能转移和购买服务资质的社会组织目录的指导意见》(粤民民【2012】135号)文件精神，发文通告(粤民民【2013】55号)《广东省本级社会组织具备承接政府职能转移和购买服务资质目录》(第二批)，广东省塑料工业协会被确定为“广东省本级社会组织具备承接政府职能转移和购买服务资质”的社会组织。

7、“中国塑料积木科普教玩具研发生产基地”挂牌

2012年5月，中国塑料加工工业协会授予广东邦领塑模实业有限公司“中国塑料积木科普教玩具研发生产基地”称号，并在汕头市向该公司授牌。

8、“广东省塑料工业协会塑料循环利用专业委员会”成立

经广东省民政厅批准“广东省塑料工业协会塑料协会利用专业委员会”于12月正式成立。该专业委员会设于汕头市。

同年10月，广东省塑料工业协会成立协会工作机构“广东省塑料工业协会创新经营服务中心”。

9、“美吉特塑料中心”项目启动

2012年5月，“美吉特塑料中心”项目启动仪式在东莞常平镇举行。全国塑料行业协会峰会、广东省塑料工业协会会长(扩大)会议同期举行。“美吉特塑料中心”规划建成大型综合、具备多功能现代物流服务设施的塑料交易中心。规划建筑面积30万平方米。

另一大型塑料原料交易所“海西塑料交易中心”在汕头启动。该项目是粤东地区首个大型塑料原料交易项目。规划建成具备仓储保税、电子商务、金融服务、塑料现货交易市场、现货、期货业务培训等功能的大型塑料交易所。

10、高明塑料制品国际采购中心项目启动

2012年12月，佛山“高明塑料制品国际采购中心项目在高明区奠基，该项目计划建成大型新材料综合性批发交易市场。

(广东省塑料行业协会　符岸)

福　建　省

【大事记】

1、2012年，福建越特新材料科技有限公司与中科院福建物质结构研究所合作开发的透气抗菌防臭高性能MDI聚氨脂鞋垫材料项目、福建山里人木塑科技有限公司与福建农林大学合作开发的竹粉/聚乙烯复合材料及其户外装饰地板的研发项目获福建省经贸委、省财政厅资金补助金。

2、2012中国塑料管道十大顶级品牌在京揭晓，福建亚通新材料科技股份有限公司名列前茅。

3、2012年福建思嘉环保材料科技有限公司的清洁能源沼气工程用红泥复合材料(PVC/纤维/红泥/高岭土复合材料)、福建正大集团有限公司的改性聚丙烯发泡鞋用中底材料、福建亚通新材料科技股份有限公司的钢带增强聚乙烯(PE)螺旋波纹管(ϕ600mm～ϕ2000mm)分别被省政府授予2012年度福建省优秀新产品一等奖、二等奖、三等奖。

【工业发展情况】

初步统计，2012年全省生产总值19701.78亿元，增长11.4%；公共财政总收入3008.91亿元，增长15.9%，其中，地方公共财政收入1776.21亿元，增长18.3%；全社会固定资产投资12709.66亿元，增长25.5%；外贸进出口总额1559.27亿美元，增长8.6%，其中，出口978.36亿美元，增长5.4%；实际利用外商直接投资63.38亿美元，增长2.2%；社会消费品零售总额增长15.9%；居民消费价格总水平上涨2.4%；节能减排年度目标可以实现。

过去五年，福建综合实力大幅提升，城乡面貌显著变化，人民生活持续改善，改革开放不断深化，发展后劲有效增强。

【行业发展情况】

2012 年，福建省塑料制品加工业规模以上企业 567 家、从业人员 14.3 万人；产量 2745kt，增长 14.8%；实现工业总产值 1003 亿元，增长 22.5%；出口交货值 150.9 亿元，增长 11.3%；实现利税 94 亿元，增长 50.9%；行业发展呈以下特点：

1、综合实力不断提高。多年来，福建省塑料制品产值、出口、利税始终呈两位数增长趋势，塑料制品产值多年来均保持全国第 6 位。其中：塑料合成革、日用塑料制品、塑料薄膜的产值分别居全国同行业第 2、3、4 位。福建亚通新材料科技股份有限公司、福建振云塑业股份有限公司、福建恒杰塑业新材料有限公司、福清市祥龙塑胶有限公司在国内塑料管件、管材市场知名度较高，福建思嘉环保材料科技有限公司在国内大型充气玩具类产品市场上保持较强竞争力。

2、产品呈特色化、多样化。福建省塑料制品已经不再以简单的、初级的消费品为主，而是已成为众多新兴产业离不开的核心配套材料，这部分产品不仅产品档次高、加工技术难度大，而且在塑料制品总量中的比重也越来越大，随着科技进步的加快和工业化进程的深入，其应用范围越来越广。2012 年值塑料制品加工业产值 100 亿元以上的品种有塑料薄膜、塑料板、管、型材、日用塑料制品、塑料人造革、合成革。

3、科技创新能力不断提高。通过设立福建省环境友好高分子材料工程技术研究中心、福建省改性塑料行业技术开发基地、福建省功能材料技术开发基地、福建省管材行业技术开发基地、福建省制鞋行业技术开发基地以及福建省石化下游高分子材料技术转移中心、福州市塑胶行业技术创新中心等关键技术研发及技术推广平台，推进了全省塑胶产业的产学研结合和科技成果转化。

4、行业发展呈区域性。福建省塑料制品加工业主要在福州、厦门、宁德、泉州四个设区市，四个设区市塑料制品加工业产值占全省同行业产值 81%。其中福州以塑料膜、塑料鞋、塑料管材及配件、日用制品为主，厦门以塑料包装膜、卫生洁具、改性材料、电子电器塑料和日用塑料为主，宁德以合成革材料料为主，泉州以塑料鞋、鞋用材料、日用塑料制品、密胺餐具和塑料管材等为主。

【问题和不足】

存在的问题和不足，主要是：经济总量不够大，大企业大项目不多，自主创新能力不足，外贸出口竞争力不强；节能减排、生态环境保护压力较大；要高度重视这些问题，采取更为有力的措施切实加以解决。

【今后主要任务】

今后五年是深入贯彻落实党的十八大精神，全面建成小康社会的关键时期。综观国内外形势，世界经济已由国际金融危机前的快速发展期进入深度转型调整期，我国发展仍然具备难得的机遇和有利条件，经济社会发展基本面长期趋好，海峡西岸经济区建设全面推进，福建科学发展、跨越发展保持强劲态势。我们要抓住机遇，乘势而上，全力推动我省经济、政治、文化、社会、生态文明建设迈上新台阶。

今年经济社会发展的主要预期目标是：全省生产总值增长 11% 左右；地方公共财政收入增长 12%；全社会固定资产投资增长 20%；外贸出口增长 5%，实际利用外商直接投资增长 5%；完成单位生产总值能耗、化学需氧量、二氧化硫、氨氮、氮氧化物等年度节能减排任务。

促进产业转型升级。一是深入实施企业技术改造等专项行动。实施重点行业能效对标，强化合同能源管理，推动以升级淘汰落后、以改造代替关停。二是推进“两化”深度融合。加快信息化集约建设，完善新型信息技术类基础设施，建立产业服务云计算平台。三是促进战略性新兴产业倍增发展。加快培育重点骨干企业。四是强化科技创新。突出企业主体，深化产学研结合，进一步提升和拓展高新区、开发区和产业园区。五是实施人才强省战略。推进重大人才工程建设，创新完善人才政策，大力培育核心人才，注重发挥企业家才能，支持企业、高校、研发机构引进人才。

（福建省塑料行业协会　许榕）

云　南　省

【大事记】

1、积极参加省民政厅组织的省级行业协会商会评估工作，荣获省民政厅授予的 4A 级评估等级荣誉

云南省塑料行业协会根据云南省民政厅下发的云民民[2011]87 号《云南省民政厅关于开展省级行业协会商会评估工作的通知》要求及安排，于 2011 年 11 月 21 日向云南三方社会组织评估服务中心评估委员会递交了评估申请表。经申报、参评资格审核、公告参评资格、自评、评估专家小组初评、评估委

员会评审、向社会公告评审等程序，2012年6月5日，云南省民政厅以(云民民[2012]37号)文件，宣布了对45家行业协会商会评估等级的决定，云南省塑料行业协会荣获4A级评估等级。

2、开展农膜产品质量行业自律活动，促进产品质量稳定提高

为贯彻落实云南省塑料行业协会塑料薄膜专委会第三届一次会议决议，云南省塑协从云南省农膜行业实际出发，继续开展以微膜为主要对象的农膜产品质量自我检查、自我监督、自我整改的行业自律活动，保障2012年春耕期间微膜产品质量保持在高水平，让农民放心使用。

2012年农膜行业自律活动于2011年12月份开始第一阶段工作，首先是企业自查、自我整改；第二阶段工作从2012年1月开始，由省塑协派出专人，在事先不通知企业，也不通报时间的情况下到生产企业随机抽取微膜样品送省产品质量监督检测研究院接受检验。抽查监督工作已于2012年1月底结束，被抽检的17家企业18个样品经检验均符合标准要求，详见表1。

表1　2012年春耕年度云南省塑协抽样检验合格的微膜产品名单

产品名称	注册商标	厚度规格/mm	生产企业	备注
聚乙烯微膜	腾飞	0.006	大理市民族塑料厂有限公司	微膜抽检连续五年合格
聚乙烯微膜	新花	0.005	大理兴隆塑料地膜厂	微膜抽检连续五年合格
聚乙烯微膜	五朵金花	0.005	大理博云塑料有限公司	微膜抽检连续二年合格
聚乙烯微膜	勐巴娜西	0.006	芒市民族塑料薄膜厂	微膜抽检连续五年合格
聚乙烯微膜	山茶	0.005	楚雄广利塑料有限公司	微膜抽检连续六年合格
聚乙烯微膜	春叶	0.005	昆明春叶塑料制成品有限公司	微膜抽检连续五年合格
聚乙烯微膜	昆鑫	0.005	昆明新鑫润丰塑料有限公司	微膜抽检连续五年合格
聚乙烯微膜	迎春花	0.005	云南塑料厂	微膜抽检连续五年合格
聚乙烯微膜	杜鹃花	0.005	宣威市中博塑料有限公司	微膜抽检连续五年合格
聚乙烯地膜		0.008		
聚乙烯微膜	金叶	0.005	曲靖市麒麟金叶塑料有限公司	微膜抽检连续六年合格
聚乙烯微膜	小康	0.005	曲靖市寥廓鑫源工贸有限公司	微膜抽检连续三年合格
聚乙烯微膜	文笔	0.005	师宗县文昌塑料厂	微膜抽检连续六年合格
聚乙烯微膜	旭日	0.005	玉溪市旭日塑料有限责任公司	微膜抽检连续五年合格
聚乙烯微膜	塑友	0.006	个旧市老杨塑料厂	微膜抽检连续四年合格
聚乙烯微膜	神膜	0.005	马龙县佳誉塑料制品有限责任公司	
聚乙烯地膜	龍廷	0.008	丽江市古城区金龙塑料有限公司	
聚乙烯微膜	春花	0.005	昆明市宜良薪馨塑料制品有限责任公司	

3、召开云南省塑料行业协会塑料薄膜专业委员会第三届二次会议，修订云南省塑料行业协会农用薄膜行业自律规定

2012年7月2日，云南省塑料行业协会塑料薄膜专委会第三届二次会议在嵩明县福朗里休闲山庄召开，塑料薄膜专委会主任委员玉溪市旭日塑料有限责任公司总经理王明显主持会议。

会议首先由万达期货杨文云讲解了有关期货知识；省塑协詹家驹传达了云南省生物可降解地膜试验示范项目会议情况；王明显总经理传达了在北京召开的农用地膜回收利用座谈会相关信息。

会议进行塑料薄膜行业自律修改草案和对农膜抽查检验的讨论，大家认为农膜行业自律抽样工作必须坚持，这对市场对企业都有好处。在对塑料薄膜行业自律草案进行讨论时，企业代表提出了各自的修改意见，最后形成了正式的行业自律规定，并签字认可。最后，王明显总经理对此次会议作了总结发言，会议圆满完成了各项议程。

4、召开云南省塑协塑料管道、塑料门窗、工程塑料专委会第三届一次会议

2012年9月4日，云南省塑料行业协会塑料管道、塑料门窗、工程塑料专委会第三届一次会议在昆明沙朗西翥温泉田庄召开，专委会主任委员单位云南金恒实业有限公司办公室主任宋志颖主持会议。

会议首先由中国石油西南化工销售云南分公司介绍独山子石化聚乙烯管材专用料新产品；深圳发展银行昆明分行介绍融资贷款产品和服务；省质监局特种设备处高杰主任科员向到会企业详细讲解燃气管道生产许可的要求和条件；昆明普尔顿管业有限公司总工程师童薇向与会代表传达今年中国塑协塑料管道专委会会议精神，近几年国内塑管产品产量发展很快，推陈出新也很多，但生产、应用、销售混乱，应该通过行业自律，保证塑管质量，避免恶性竞争；省住建厅城建处李平辉副处长讲话指出，十一五化学建材发展规划中，大量采用新型管材替代传统管材，省住建厅要求新型管材应用比例达到90%，云南省塑料建材市场得到较快发展，云南省十二五城市建设发展规划要求进一步完成各县、市城市供排水管网建设，预计总投资90亿元。中缅油气输送管道建成后，燃气供应管道也将大幅增长，云南省塑料管材生产企业应抓住机遇，保证产品质量，树立信誉，加强品牌建设，规范市场行为。省塑协理事长詹家驹分析了国内及省内塑料管道行业的形势，对专委会下一步工作提出了建议和安排。与会代表根据詹理事长提出的下步工作安排进行了询问和表决，大家一致以热烈的掌声通过，作为本次会议决议。宋志颖主任对本次会议进行了总结，会议圆满完成了各项议程。

5、召开塑料包装专委会饮料包装材料组第三届一次会议，制定了云南省塑料行业协会聚碳酸酯(PC)饮用水桶生产和使用的行业自律规定

云南省塑料行业协会塑料包装专委会饮料类包装材料组于8月17日下午2时在云南省塑协办公室召开三届一次会议，塑料包装专委会饮料类包装材料组组长昆明鑫慧新包装材料有限公司总经理杨延忠主持本次会议。为了提高饮用水桶的卫生、安全水平，保障消费者健康，认真履行饮用水桶生产和使用企业的社会责任，云南省塑料行业协会组织有关会员企业对聚碳酸酯(PC)饮用水桶生产和使用的行业自律草案逐条逐句进行讨论，形成正式的行业自律规定以便共同遵守执行，并向社会公布接受广大消费者监督。会议就下阶段大家关心的问题进行讨论，达成了共识。

6、对云南省聚乙烯微膜企业标准进行复审和备案工作

云南省塑料行业协会根据云质监函(2005)175号文件精神，组织薄膜专委会有关专家于2011年12月16日召开了云南省《聚乙烯微膜》企业示范标准技术审查会。专家组认真审查了这个标准，认为它总结了各生产企业多年生产和科技进步的经验，也总结了六来行业自律的经验，经过集思广益的研审讨论，又有新的提高，它符合国家有关法规要求，整体具有较高的技术水平和比较完善的内容，检验规则是科学的，可靠的，是一个好的标准，并把这个标准作为全省生产及销售聚乙烯微膜产品的最低标准执行，以履行全行业对省质监局的承诺、保障微膜产品质量。协会以云塑协(2011)30号文件通知农膜企业开展微膜企业标准复审、备案工作，各农膜企业积极响应，标准到期的企业都到当地质监部门完成备案工作。

7、主持《氧化生物降解聚烯烃塑料袋》标准评审会

2012年3月20日下午，云南省地方标准《氧化生物降解聚烯烃塑料袋》审查会在昆明市桂花大厦召开，会议由云南省塑料行业协会理事长詹家驹主持。与会专家认真审核了由昆明鑫鑫大壮降解塑料技术有限公司、国家环保产品质量监督检验中心负责起草，红河州质量技术监督综合中心参与起草的《氧化生物降解聚烯烃塑料袋》地方标准并针对此标准提出了修改意见，要求标准起草单位严格按专家组的修改意见进行修改报中华人民共和国国家质量监督检验检疫总局备案。此标准经中华人民共和国国家质量监督检验检疫总局备案，备案号为：34754—2012，云南省质量技术监督局于2012年07月25日发布，2012年09月01正式实施，标准号为：DB 53/412—2012。

8、召开三届一次常务理事会

2012年9月18日以通讯方式召开云南省塑料行业协会第三届一次常务理事会。9月18日，协会秘书处以云塑协(2012)34号《关于召开云南省塑料行业协会第三届一次常务理事会的通知》及附件一、附件二、附件三：附件四寄发给38位常务理事进行审议、表决、建议。截止11月30日，秘书处共收到36位常务理事填写的《云南省塑协第三届一次常务理事会审议、表决、建议回复表》，通过了三届一次常务理事会需要审议、表决的决议，圆满完成了各项会议议程。

9、积极组织企业参加国际会展、交流

2012年8月29~31日，举办2012第三届昆明国际给排水水处理展览会。由云南省城镇供水协会、云南省市政工程协会、云南省塑料行业协会、云南省建筑业协会、昆明市再生水协会主办，云南省城市排水与污水处理委员会、云南省塑料行业协会、昆明风向标会展有限公司承办的2012第三届中国(昆明)国际给排水及水处理展览会在昆明国际会展中心举办。云南普尔顿集团、昆明创辉塑胶科技有

限公司、昆明通全球管业有限公司等15家省内外塑料管道生产企业参家本次会议，本次展览会为生产企业和使用单位搭建了良好的交流平台，充分展示了企业的产品和企业形象。

2012年3月29~31日，组织了6家企业12名负责人参加在重庆国际会展中心举办的第八届西部国际塑胶工业展览会。

2012年4月18至21日，组织了18家塑料企业35名管理人员和技术人员参加在上海新国际博览中心举行的第二十六届中国国际塑料橡胶工业展览会。

2012年5月27日，参加在广东省东莞召开的全国塑料行业协会峰会，和全国十七个省市级塑料行业协会理事长、秘书长进行交流、沟通，寻求合作机遇。

10、接受省、市电视台三次采访

分别向社会公众介绍塑料袋安全使用问题，塑化剂和看标识正确使用塑料制品等知识，通过这些工作，消除了因公众不明真相的恐慌心理及这些负面风波造成塑料行业损失。同时，协会和媒体也建立了良好的互动合作关系，正确引导消费者认识、使用塑料制品。

11、筹备建立云南省塑料行业融资信息平台

为帮助会员企业解决资金紧张的问题，协会在众多银行中选择与深圳发展银行昆明分行作为筹资融资合作伙伴，在双方共同努力下，于2012年9月下旬完成云南省塑料行业融资信息平台工作，接受有流动资金贷款需求的会员企业申请，协助九家会员企业以优惠的条件取得贷款，解决了部分企业融资难问题。

12、进行2012年云南省轻纺行业塑料专业技术职务评审工作

根据云轻纺职改[2012]1号文件《关于2012年云南省轻纺工程专业和工艺美术专业技术职务任职资格评审工作的通知》要求，于2012年3月18日下发《关于开展云南省轻纺行业塑料专业技术职务评审工作的通知》到各会员企业，经材料申报、初审及云南省轻纺工程评审委员会评审，对4名具备轻纺工程中级专业技术职务任职资格和11名初级专业技术任职资格的工程技术人员的申报资料进行评审，并于2012年9月29日颁发了相应的职称证书。

13、开展行业统计、发布行业信息

云南省塑协首次对全省塑料管材产量进行统计；每月对全省生产的塑料薄膜产量进行行业统计，每个季度对全省塑料制品生产情况进行统计并在《云南塑料信息》内部月刊、《云南塑料》网站塑胶市场栏目发表。

14、以每月定期的《云南塑料信息》开展行业信息交流

根据会员单位的需求及时在《云南塑料》网站上发表行业新闻、技术信息、及供求、人才信息；为会员单位牵线搭桥，介绍经贸合作信息。

15、向有关部门推荐专家

推荐绿色建筑评价标识专家2名(经省住建厅批准)和推荐云南省轻纺工程技术职务评审委员会专家1名。

16、协办质量检验人员专业技术培训

为帮助企业提高质量管理和质量检验水平，及时学习并掌握新的质量检验标准和方法，加强企业质量检验工作，帮助企业建立健全质量检验制度，提高企业质检人员的技术水平和专业能力，协会分别于今年3月、7月、12月组织会员单位质量管理和质量检验员参加中质协在昆明市举办的两期质量检验人员专业技术人员培训。

【基本情况】

2012年，云南省生产总值(GDP)完成103909.8亿元，比上年增长13.0%，高于全国5.2个百分点。全省人均生产总值GDP达到22195元(折合3531美元)，比上年增长12.3%。

2012年，全省塑料行业生产塑料制品333kt，比上年减少4.43%，占全国比例0.58%。其中，塑料薄膜97.2kt，比上年增加10.57%，占全国比例1.0%；农用薄膜61.6kt，比上年增加19.47%，占全国比例3.79%；泡沫塑料13.8kt，比上年增加97.9%，占全国比例0.8%；其他塑料制品221.9kt，比上年减少12.45%，占全国比例0.57%。初级形态的塑料(塑料树脂及共聚物)247.7kt，比上年增加22.47%，占全国比例0.48%；聚氯乙烯树脂246.6kt，比上年增加22.54%，占全国比例1.87%。目前，云南省发展速度较快的塑料产品主要是塑料管道及附件，塑料薄膜，塑料丝绳及编织品，塑料包装及容器。

【重点企业】

云南省重点企业详见表2。

表2　2011年云南省塑料制品产量在3000t以上的企业名单

序　号	企业名称	产量/t	主要产品
01	云南金恒实业有限公司	34600	管材、管件
02	玉溪市旭日塑料有限责任公司	26466	塑料薄膜

续表

序　号	企业名称	产量/t	主要产品
03	昆明特瑞特塑胶有限公司	18230	管材、管件
04	云南普尔顿企业集团有限公司	11500	管材、管件
05	昆明仙织塑业有限公司	10000	塑料编织袋
06	昆明创辉塑胶科技有限公司	8000	管材、管件
07	昆明傲远管业有限公司	8000	管材、管件
08	宣威市中博塑料有限公司	6781	塑料薄膜
09	大理博云塑料有限公司	6727	塑料薄膜
10	昆明春叶塑料制成品有限公司	5847	农用薄膜、包装材料
11	昆明金连山塑胶化工工贸有限责任公司	5739	管材、管件
12	昆明耀龙塑胶有限公司	4894.30	管材、管件
13	昆明海午塑胶科技有限公司	5000	管材、管件
14	昆明通全球管业有限公司	6000	管材、管件
15	云南恩典塑业有限公司	5000	塑料编织袋
16	玉溪红塔新型建材有限公司	4254	塑钢型材
17	云南新同基塑料工程有限责任公司	4000	管材、管件
18	云南师宗县文昌塑料厂	3605	塑料薄膜
19	澄江恺达塑胶有限公司	3554	管材、管件
20	云南龙塑实业有限公司	3000	管材、管件
21	昆明俊兴塑胶科技有限公司	3000	管材、管件
22	云南塑料厂	3000	农用薄膜、管材
23	昆明鑫慧新包装材料有限公司	3000	PC 饮水罐
24	曲靖麒麟海绵有限责任公司	3000	聚氨酯泡沫塑料
25	昆明民族塑料化工有限公司	3000	注塑产品
26	云南铭信塑胶有限公司	3000	管材、管件
27	昆明瑞业塑料制品有限责任公司	3000	塑料包装及容器
28	昆明东方塑纸包装有限公司	3000	塑料包装袋

（云南省塑料行业协会　韩简吉）

安　徽　省

【大事记】

一、协会主要活动

安徽省塑料协会第二届第三次理事会议于 2013 年 7 月 20 日在安徽建筑大学化学化工学院召开。会议实到理事 70 名，超过应到理事 99 名的三分之二，符合本会《章程》的议事表决规定。

协会顾问夏传友、省轻工协会行业联络处张卫平处长及其他有关人员应邀参加了会议。会议由常务副会长兼秘书长翟光景主持。

会议的主要任务是，听取和审议安徽省塑料协会会长韦明关于 2012 年工作回顾及 2013 年工作安排意见；听取和审查秘书长翟光景提交的 2011 年财务决算和 2012 年财务预算草案；讨论常务副会长宣华荣提交的关于推荐增选会员、理事、常务理事、副会长人员建议名单等议案。

1. 会议一致通过了韦明会长所作的《2012 年工作总结和 2013 年工作安排意见》的报告。会议认为：韦会长的报告内容翔实、比较全面。既报告了 2012 年协会所做的主要工作，又分析了当前塑料行业的现状和形势，并对今年的工作提出了具体的安排意见。

2. 会议一致通过了翟光景秘书长所作的《2012年财务决算和2013年财务预算》的报告。会议认为：2012年协会的财务收支符合《章程》的有关规定；2013年的预算符合实际情况。

3. 会议一致同意常务副会长宣华荣提议：增补安徽中鼎橡塑制品有限公司、安徽伊亚格管业有限公司、安庆盛峰化工股份有限公司为副会长单位；合肥恒创塑料机械有限公司为理事单位，并颁发了牌匾。

4. 会议听取了合肥安丰电器塑胶有限公司、安徽中鼎橡塑制品有限公司、宣城福美达新材料有限公司、合肥恒创塑料机械有限公司、安徽省轻工设计院有限公司等单位的负责人介绍本企业的基本情况和经营状况。

5. 会议听取了兴业银行合肥分行的负责人介绍的小企业联保、增级贷等贷款业务的情况，为银企间相互认识，加强联系搭建了平台。会议还听取了省科协负责人介绍的引进海外盖塑胶工业新技术、人才、资金、合作等战略的情况。听取了省贸促会关于受省政府委托组团参加西部博览会后的情况介绍。

6. 会议要求各会员单位积极参加由我会为支持单位的在国内外具有重要影响力的：中国国际塑胶工业展览会、中国塑料交易会、中国西部国际塑胶工业展览会和杜塞尔多夫「2013国际塑料及橡胶工业展」。

7、会议组织与会人员参观了安徽建筑大学化学化工学院的实验设备和测试仪器等。

8、会议重点是总结2012年塑料行业工作。探讨和研究2013的安徽省塑料行业形势和面临的困难，提出了工作方向。

本次理事会在各位理事的共同努力下，在安徽建筑大学材化学院的大力支持下，取得了圆满成功，开成了一个团结、和谐、务实、奋进的会议。

二、协会组团参加展会，广泛开展交流活动

一是组团参观了第二十六届中国国际塑胶工业展览会；二是组团参观了第十二届中国塑料交易会；三是参观了第八届中国西部国际塑胶工业展览会；四是参加(中国蚌埠)电子信息产业合作对接会；五是参加了慧聪塑料网举办的第六届塑料行业十佳颁奖典礼及汽车、家电行业塑料应用创新发展研究会；六是参加雅式展览服务有限公司及上海塑料协会举办的第二十七届中国国际塑胶工业展览会的新闻发布会。通过观展参会，使安徽省有关塑料企业的负责人大开眼界，不仅了解到各地塑料工业发展的趋势，获得了市场信息和未来市场的需求及远景，而且为本企业的发展打开了联系的窗口。

三、成功主办第二届中国·合肥塑胶工业展览会

协会与中国塑料加工工业协会改性塑料专业委员会、省信息家电行业协会联合主办了第二届中国·合肥塑料工业展览会。此次展会吸引了南京聚力化工机械有限公司、宁波海波机械制造有限公司、张家港亿利机械有限公司等100多家参展商。展出产品有：生产设备，原、辅材料，测量仪器等上千种产品。展会为业内企业创造了相互交流的服务平台，为安徽省塑料工业的发展作出了应有的贡献。

【热点问题】

2012年是实施“十二五”发展规划的第二年，安徽省塑料行业形势严峻，在政府主管部门和监督管理部门的领导和指导下，协会认真贯彻党和国家的方针、政策，按照协会章程的有关规定，开展了一系列活动，主要做了以下几项工作。

一、认真开展调研活动

为了掌握行业的基本情况，我们通过发放《企业调研表》了解企业2011年以来的生产经营状况、存在的困难和需要协会协调解决的主要问题，协会秘书处向60多家企业发放了《企业调研表》。从反馈的情况来看，工业经济形势对企业生产经营的影响较大。

走出去调研。先后赴肥西富光塑胶有限公司、兴奇塑料制品有限公司、舒城玉发塑业有限公司、全椒欧波塑料有限责任公司、华星塑料有限公司、淮南众意工程塑料制品有限公司、芜湖国风塑胶有限公司、顺达(芜湖)汽车饰件有限公司、芜湖瑞明汽车部件有限公司等单位进行调研，认真听取企业负责人介绍情况，参观生产现场、询问生产经营状况。通过企业调研，主要表现为：

经济下滑，市场疲软，恢复缓慢，用工成本增加，开工不足等，资金困难等热点问题等。

二、掌握影响企业热点问题后，采取措施

1. 主动在有关政府部门的会议上反映了塑料行业困难和企业的诉求。

2. 协会与招商银行合肥分行等银行成功举办了专场金融产品推介会。有17户企业的负责人参加了会议。会上，招商银行合肥分行分别介绍了小企业订单贷、联保贷等融资产品和小微企业助力贷、生意贷等贷款产品。参会的企业负责人纷纷与招商银行的领导互动交流，并商讨适合本企业情况的贷款事宜。招商银行的领导表示：将为有关企业设计出针对性、个性化、量身定制的融资服务方案，会议收到了良好的效果。为企业解决贷款难的困难。

3. 为有关企业进行注塑机节能改造。已为富光塑胶有限公司、淮南众意工程塑料制品有限公司等企业改造了多台注塑机，节电效果明显。为安徽美螺建材有限等公司出具推荐函，后经评审，该公司的“美螺”牌商标入选为省著名商标。

4. 认真参加政府部门的行业会，为有关企业申报问题提出专业性的意见，努力获得认可。

5. 积极组织专家组成员参加有关部门组织的各类评审活动，争取有利于行业、企业发展的项目支持，并为企业申报项目牵线搭桥，做好协调服务工作。对会员企业申请支持解决在发展中遇到的技术难题、发展瓶颈等问题积极组织专家进行诊断、指导和攻关。

经过协会不懈努力，帮助行业解决实际困难，行业一致认为：安徽省塑料协会为安徽省塑料行业真正办了好事。

【基本情况】

2012年安徽省塑料工业继续呈现出平稳增长、逆市上扬的态势。

安徽省塑料制品业实现工业总产值726.3亿元，同比增长27.8%；

工业总产值位居安徽省轻工17个行业的第三位。

尽管塑料行业的发展存在一些不利因素，但从整体上而言，推动塑料行业上升的动力仍然强劲。塑料行业向上增长的趋势没有改变，只不过是增长率将由过去的30%下降为15%左右。

【企业经营】

2012年安徽省塑料制品销售产值708.3亿元，同比增长27.4%；

出口交货值18.8亿元，同比增长9.2%。

全年完成塑料制品2120kt，同比增长16.8%。

2012年安徽省塑料企业没有发现亏损。但是，由于安徽省塑料产业集中度低、生产力分散、专业化生产程度低、深加工比率低、自主品牌终端产品少、利润率低仍是塑料制品行业所面临的突出问题。

【重点企业】

1. 安徽华猫软包装有限公司

企业基本情况：安徽华猫软包装有限公司成立于2006年，地处安徽省省级开发区—安庆市怀宁县经济开发区，主要生产食品用塑料包装，多层复合食品膜袋、塑料制品加工、销售、塑料原料及辅助材料、复合卷膜袋销售。

2012年，随着国民经济的增长，我国食品行业对包装需求逐步向多元化、高档次、安全性方向发展。目前公司研发的耐高温蒸煮膜产品工艺要求高，我们遇到的最大难题是：蒸煮时在高温高压难以保证高的热封强度；蒸煮时，在高温高压下的抗穿刺和抗破包能力不强，为解决这一问题，我公司特聘请了艾克森美孚的技术专家为公司的技术顾问，一起研发，现场指导实验，终于研制成了高温蒸煮膜，我们有理由相信，高温蒸煮膜将逐步占领市场，进入一个飞速发展时期，必将对食品包装产生深远的影响，在食品、医药、化工等领域获得广泛的应用。

华猫公司成立短短几年，各项日程有序进行，到2012年底公司实现产值1.7亿元，实现利税1100万元，生产经营连续稳步提升，公司销售收入逐年以80%速度增长。

公司拥有员工155人，组织机构健全，其中专业技术人员45人，本科达近20人，高级职称人员8名，一线骨干人员大多具有8~10年以上软包装行业生产经营和管理经验。技术熟练、经验丰富，是一支非常富有活力和现代企业的创新团队。

企业经营：安徽华猫软包装有限公司是塑料复合软包装产品的专业生产商，以塑料软包装专业生产为主体。主要产品：食品包装、日用化工、种子、农药等产品，同时有外包装(膜)的研发、生产与销售。计划今年拟建一幢建筑面积为6000m^2 的十万级净化车间，用于医药包装生产线。

公司生产主要以塑料食品包装为主，生产新型高档环保PVC、BOPP、PE、CPP等各类包装卷膜包装材料，产品广泛用于种子包装、食品包装、医药包装等。同时与许多上市公司建立良好的业务伙伴关系，众多国内知名品牌企业：如美国杜邦、先峰种业(中国)公司、江苏克胜集团、安徽真心、郑州思念、莲花味精、上海白味林等知名企业，产品畅销全国各地。

公司目前全套引进国内最先进的技术装备和生产工艺，2012年公司实现年产塑料制品7000t，现有生产线17条，实现年产高压3000t、底压2600t、印刷膜26383200m，到十二五末公司年综合生产能力达到15000t以上软包装。

设备技术引进：2012年公司引进两套日立全自动电脑喷码机和自动贴标机、条形码防伪技术及各种防伪标识等功能。

外资利用：2012年10月公司增设注册为中美合资九九收益软件(安徽)有限公司，公司注册资本1020万元，其中中方占注册资本的49%，外方投资占注册资本的51%，资金主要用于公司主营业务，收益管理软件系统开发与销售，未来软包装高档环保塑料制品自主研发与生产销售。

新产品开发：2012年公司开拓未来市场，为满足不同客户需求，公司自主研发自立袋、拉链袋、异形袋生产工艺，积极开发新产品、新工艺，产品技术创新能力取得新提高。为即将合作的欧洲市场打下坚实基础。

2012年，年产6000t塑料制品项目已正式启动生产，同时被列入“861”计划项目，引领未来的华猫公司多次荣获省、市、县级荣誉称号。

企业发展趋势：随着软包装行业的高速发展，包装在人们生活当中越来越重要，消费观念的转变，对食品包装也提出了更高要求、产品品质的提高和消费人群的增大，从软包装行业角度发展空间看，提升产品档次，走高端市场路，会有一个很好的利润空间。

2. 黄山永新股份有限公司

企业基本情况：黄山永新股份有限公司成立于1992年5月，主要生产经营塑料彩印复合软包装材料、真空镀铝膜、药品包装材料、多功能薄膜等高新技术产品，是中国包装龙头企业、国家创新型企业、中国创新型企业100强、国家高新技术企业、全国企事业知识产权试点企业、第一批“国家资源节约型、环境友好型”试点企业。

2004年7月，公司在深圳证券交易所中小企业板发行上市，2007年7月完成公开增发。通过两次融资，实现了公司快速发展，在此期间，公司完成了在珠三角和环渤海两大经济圈的实体投资，扩大了在国内的业务覆盖范围，进一步巩固了公司在行业内的领先地位。

公司现有员工1608人，其中具有中专以上学历的人员占职工总数的80%，科技人员占员工总数的35%，从事高新技术产品研究、开发专职技术人员超过10%。

永新股份老厂区占地150亩，又在黄山市经济开发区购置300亩。公司硬件设备处于国内领先水平。建有10万级、30万级全封闭洁净车间及无菌多功能生产厂房。各生产厂房均依据科学的流程设计，配备恒温、恒湿、高效空气过滤、消毒、灭菌等装置，优良的生产环境从根本保障包装生产全过程的环保、卫生、消防、安全等要求。公司拥有从美国、日本、德国等地引进的具有国际领先水平的十一条彩色凹版印刷生产线、一条彩色柔版印刷生产线、四条无溶剂复合生产线、四条镀膜生产线、十四条多功能薄膜生产线等先进生产设备，具备年产塑料彩印软包装制品42000t（其中：医药包装产品6000t），真空镀铝膜11000t的生产能力，多功能包装薄膜24000t生产能力。是目前全国最大的塑料软包装生产企业之一，具备强大的年生产能力，能充分满足客户大批量、高质量、及时供货的需求。通过了ISO9001、HACCP、ISO14000等质量、食品安全和环境保护体系认证，同时，公司引进国内领先的气相色谱仪、透湿透氧检测仪等质量检测设备，为产品品质提供可靠的保障。

公司先后荣获“全国五一劳动奖状”、“全国先进包装企业”、中国“医药包装优秀单位”、“全国守合同重信用企业”等荣誉称号。

公司二十年从事彩印复合软包装材料的研发和生产，有着雄厚的经验和技术积累。公司紧随国际行业发展潮流，重视技术创新，与中国科学技术大学、合肥工业大学等高校建立长期合作关系，设立了国家认定企业技术中心、博士后工作站、国家地方联合工程实验室、安徽省软包装材料工程技术研究中心等研发机构，具有良好的检测、研发、服务、技术推广能力，充分保障了公司持续的研发能力。

产品客户覆盖食品、医药、日化、农化、电子等多个领域的宝洁、雀巢、卡夫、拜耳、亨氏、美赞臣、喜之郎、伊利、百事、三九、洽洽、箭牌、贝因美、旺旺、太太乐、徐福记等50多家跨国公司和200多家国内知名企业、上市公司。2012年共实现营业收入15亿元，利润总额2.1亿，塑料彩印软包装制品42000t，真空镀铝膜11000t，多功能包装薄膜24000t，各项经济指标均居全国同行业前列。计划未来3~4年，形成年产值达到30亿元、年利税超过3.2亿元的生产经营能力，打造世界一流、中国第一的绿色软包装制造业知名品牌公司。

科技成果和新产品开发情况：通过自主创新，近几年来，黄山永新股份有限公司获授权专利51项，共承担各类计划项目近百项，其中国家技术创新计划项目1项，国家火炬计划项目4项，国家重点新产品计划项目4项，安徽省科技攻关计划项目10多项，安徽省861计划项目5项；获得省部级以上科技奖7项，高新技术产品31项，中国包装名牌产品2项，中国包装行业优质产品1项，安徽省名牌产品1项。通过自主创新，企业的整体竞争力大幅提升，近一步巩固了领头羊地位，经济效益和各项经营指标连续三年名列前茅。对我国软包装行业的发展、产品的升级换代起到巨大的推动作用，加快了软包装行业的技术进步。中国包装联合会塑料制品包装委员会作了如此评价：黄山永新股份有限公司是中国包装龙头企业，规模、产能和市场占有率位居塑料复合软包装行业第一，科研投入较大，具有较强的产品创新能力，各项主要经济指标在同行业均名列前茅。

企业财务状况：截至2012年底，永新股份总资产突破18亿元，公司负债率为23%，银行信用等级

AAA 级。

公司近三年主要经营指标情况表 万元

指标名称	2010 年	2011 年	2012 年
总资产	110393.86	131373.97	183158.25
销售收入	127639.22	151308.61	152101.32
利润总额	14313.16	17387.60	21222.09
上缴税金	7506	9656	11958
固定资产	36378.05	48406.85	54038.75

在国内及省内同行业所处地位等：永新股份有限公司是中国包装产品定点生产企业、中国包装龙头企业，在彩印软包装行业排名全国第一。2004 年 7 月“永新股份”成功上市，成为安徽省首家在深圳中小企业板块上市的企业。2007 年再次增发成功。永新股份在软包装应用领域的技术研发和创新能力不断加强，拥有很多国内第一家研发的产品、工艺和技术（详见《永新领先的技术/产品/工艺表》，其中“高阻隔真空镀铝膜、镀氧化硅膜和在线一次成型计量农药包装膜”，填补国内空白。高阻隔奶粉包装膜，其阻隔性能较普通奶粉包装提高了 10 倍以上，解决了长期困扰国内奶粉行业的结块问题，将奶粉产品的保质期延长了一倍以上，促进了奶粉尤其是高档奶粉行业的发展。

部分领先的产品/工艺/技术表

产品	生产高阻隔镀铝膜	国内第一家
	生产透明高阻隔氧化硅蒸镀膜	国内第一家
	高速高阻隔配方奶粉包装膜	国内第一家
	生产站立式液体包装膜	国内第一家
	在线一次成型计量农药包装膜	国内第一家
工艺	合作开发出低浓度有机气体排放回收工艺	国内第一家
	应用高镀铝生产工艺	国内第一家
技术	引进宽幅高速柔版印刷	国内第一家

经过多年的行业积累和发展，公司经营规模和资产规模不断扩大，与其他同行业企业相比，不论是在企业规模、资金实力、技术水平、管理经验上等方面，均具有明显的优势。进一步巩固了永新在软包装行业领头羊地位，经济效益与各项经营指标均位居同行业前茅。

1. 近三年进口额和出口额

	2010 年	2011 年	2012 年	2013 年预计
进口额	1740	1600	2100	2500
出口额	1020	1260	1100	1300
进出口额	2760	2860	3200	3800

2. 出口市场占比和市场占有率

出口市场占比稳居高位。在越南，公司出口液洗包装产品占据某跨国公司在当地 70% 以上的市场份额；而对菲律宾的出口近三年来我司一直占据 70% ~80% 的镀铝膜市场。

3. 安徽安利合成革股份有限公司

安徽安利合成革股份有限公司成立于 1994 年，地处国家级安徽省合肥市经济技术开发区，主要生产经营生态功能性聚氨酯合成革，下有一家控股子公司合肥安利聚氨酯新材料有限公司，主要生产经营聚氨酯树脂，所生产的产品是高分子复合材料，属新材料产业。

2011 年，安利股份在深交所上市。

企业大事记：2012 年 3 月，由公司主持制定的“运动鞋用聚氨酯合成革安全要求”行业标准起草项目启动会在肥召开。

2012 年 6 月，由公司主持起草的国家标准《人造革合成革术语》初稿审查工作会在肥举行。

此外，公司主持起草的《休闲鞋用聚氨酯合成革》、《人造革合成革试验方法透气性的测定》等 2 项国家行业标准和参与起草的《人造革合成革用颜色色卡》等 1 项国家行业标准已经国家工信部批准立项。

截至 2012 年底，公司累计主持、参与制定国家及行业标准 22 项、其中主持制定国家及行业标准 7 项，参与制定国家及行业标准 15 项，是行业内主持参与制定标准最多的企业，行业地位及行业话语权进一步加强。

2012 年，公司牵头承担的公安部“特警战训靴环境自适应复合材料技术课题”获得国家“十二五”科技支撑项目立项

企业基本情况：2012 年底，公司实现产值 18 亿元，利税 1.43 亿元，出口创汇 8887.36 万美元，生产经营业绩连续多年保持稳定增长。

公司拥有员工 2000 余人，平均年龄 29 岁，其中，硕士、博士 33 人，高级职称人员 19 名，享受国务院政府特殊津贴专家 1 人、安徽省政府特殊津贴专家 1 人。骨干员工大多具有 10 年以上的合成革生产经营和管理经验，技术娴熟，经验丰富，富有活力和创新精神。

企业经营：公司主营业务为中高档聚氨酯合成革产品的研发、生产、销售与服务，主要产品为生态功能性聚氨酯合成革。产品广泛应用于中高档鞋类（男女鞋、童鞋、运动休闲鞋、工作鞋、劳保鞋等）、沙发家具、手袋、箱包、文具证件、球和体育用品、汽车内饰等的加工制作。

众多国内外知名的品牌企业，如阿迪达斯（adidas)、锐步(REEBOK)、彪马(PUMA)、乐途(LOTTO)、斐乐(FILA)、茵宝(UMBRO)、斯凯捷(SKECHERS)、匡威(Converse)、爱斯克斯(asics)、美津浓(MIZUNO)、蔻驰(COACH)、迪斯尼(DISNEY)、安踏、特步、贵人鸟、匹克、德尔惠、乔丹、双星、达芙妮、森达、富贵鸟、红蜻蜓、意尔康、奥康、欧美尔、蒙努、永艺、联邦、芝华士、欧意美、蒙发利、澳瑞特、皇朝家俬、奇瑞、比亚迪、上汽名爵、厦门金龙、众泰等,与公司建立了良好的合作关系;

公司产品深受全球中高端客户青睐,用于北京人民大会堂和上海虹桥机场、韩国首尔机场等公共场所座椅和国家卫星定位系统;产品畅销全国各地,并直接出口到50多个国家和地区,连同制成品出口,可以说"安利合成革,全球都在用",是国内出口额最大且出口发达国家最多的合成革企业。

2012年,受欧债危机持续,发达经济体陷入低迷,全球经济增长明显放缓,我国经济减速、进出口下降,制造业景气度走低等因素影响,公司实现营业收入111096.33万元,较上年同期增长12.07%;公司实现利润总额5752.10万元,较上年同期减少17.81%。

2012年,公司实现聚氨酯合成革产量4829万米、聚氨酯树脂35178吨。公司现有12条干法生产线10条湿法生产线,具有年产聚氨酯合成革6500万米、聚氨酯树脂50kt的生产经营能力。

塑料制品进出口:2012年,公司聚氨酯合成革出口量为2680万米,同比增长20%左右,实现创汇额8887.36万美元,同比增长20.45%,产品远销东欧、东南亚、南美、北美等50多个国家和地区,出口量、出口创汇额、出口发达国家数量均居国内同行业前列。

企业外资利用:公司注册类型为港澳台商投资股份有限公司,境外股东为香港敏丰贸易有限公司[S. &F. TRADING CO. (H. K.) LIMITED]和香港劲达企业有限公司(REAL TACTENT ERPRISE LIMITED),注册资金21120万元,其中中方投资13833.6万元,占比65.5%,外方投资7286.4万元,占比34.5%。资金主要用于公司主营业务,即聚氨酯合成革的生产、研发、销售,以及相关配套项目建设。

企业新产品开发:2012年,公司坚持产品技术创新,积极开发新产品新工艺,创新能力取得新提高。2012年,公司全年投入5313.57万元用于产品及工艺技术研发创新,占全年营业收入的比重为4.78%,相继成功开发出湿法单涂浸清水工艺、一刀贴零涂刮逆涂工艺、无皱镜面革、弹力高剥革、弹力揉纹革、背涂镜面革、反贴鞋里革、高固鞋里革、压花抛焦系列革、耐水解弹力冷压树脂、不黄变镜面树脂、弹力冷压一刀贴用树脂、耐水解高撕裂含浸系列树脂等10余项新产品新工艺,为公司未来市场开拓打下坚实基础。

2012年,公司"高剥离耐水解无纺布聚氨酯合成革"被列入安徽省"十一五"技术创新优秀项目,"年产2200万米生态功能性聚氨酯合成革建设项目"被列入安徽省财政专项资金项目,"生态功能性聚氨酯合成革搬迁技改项目"等5项项目被列入合肥市"双千工程"项目;自主承担建设的"安徽省聚氨酯合成革与树脂工程技术研究中心"项目顺利通过合肥市科技局验收。

2012年,公司再次被国家科技部认定为"国家火炬计划重点高新技术企业",并荣列"安徽省百强高新技术企业";拥有的"国家级企业技术中心"被安徽省经信委评为"2012年优秀省级企业技术中心";先后获得国家重点新产品认定1项,获得安徽省高新技术产品认定4项,获得安徽省新产品认定3项;获得全国工商联科技进步二等奖1项。

2012年,公司新增授权专利24项,其中发明专利8项,实用新型专利7项,外观设计专利9项;公司累计拥有有效专利84项,其中发明专利22项,实用新型专利21项,外观设计专利41项,是业内拥有专利权最多的企业,显现出公司持续、良好的技术创新能力。

市场需求:公司主营产品聚氨酯合成革属于塑料制品,所属行业是塑料制品行业下的子行业人造革合成革行业。人造革合成革是塑料工业的一个重要组成部分,作为天然皮革的替代材料,已被广泛应用于国民经济各个行业之中。根据原料不同,人造革合成革可以分为PVC人造革和PU合成革,目前PU合成革占据市场主导地位。

随着人们消费水平的不断提升,环保意识的加强,公司生态功能性聚氨酯合成革逐步成为未来人造革合成革行业的发展重点,代表市场主流产品之一,市场对生态革的需求将会持续增长。

企业发展趋势:随着人们消费观念的转变和下游制品业的要求提高,许多应用领域内的消费需求也将随着人造革合成革产品品质的提高和差异化功能的增加而越来越大。从人造革合成革行业技术发展的角度来看,高物性PU合成革及超细纤维PU合成革将成为未来市场主导产品。

4. 安徽中鼎橡塑制品有限公司

企业概况:安徽中鼎橡塑制品有限公司位于安徽省宁国经济技术开发区河沥园区,系国家大型企业——安徽中鼎控股(集团)股份有限公司下属全资企业，公司创立于1999年，占地面积30万平方米，注册资本14600万元，现有员工1100余人，主要从事汽车用塑料制品、OA办公机器用胶辊以及其他橡塑制品、机械零件产品的研发、生产与销售。

公司为中国塑料加工工业协会理事单位、安徽省塑料协会副会长单位、宁国市骨干企业。近年来，公司通过不断加大研发投入，不断扩大生产规模，公司生产经营各项指标保持了年均22%以上的增速。公司先后被认定为安徽省高新技术企业、安徽省创新型试点企业。公司总经理夏玉洁为十二届全国人大代表、宣城市政协常委、宣城市工商联副主席。

企业主营业务及产品情况：公司主营业务包括塑料制品、办公机器用胶辊两大主营业务。塑料制品以汽车用功能件为主，产品还配套与工程机械、家电等领域。

1）主要汽车用塑料制品

（1）防尘罩类（转向机防尘罩、转向柱防尘罩、护套等）

（2）管件类（进气管、干净进气管、中冷管、滴水管、空调水管、排水管等）

（3）壶类（动力转向油壶、制动油壶、储液罐、水箱、副水箱等）

（4）冷凝器用塑料滤筒

（5）汽车限位器固定座

（6）塑料轴承

（7）其他汽车用塑料零件

2）其他行业用塑料制品

（1）工程机械用塑料制品：工程机械操控面板、履带密封圈

（2）家电用塑料制品：密封圈

公司生产的塑料制品主要配套于汽车行业，公司生产的汽车用塑料制品，为中鼎橡塑的核心业务产品，产品广泛配套于汽车发动机系统、车身系统、电气系统、底盘系统，公司依托中鼎集团三十多年以来在国内外汽车零部件市场的技术优势和市场优势，目前已经具备了国内外知名主机厂同步研发的能力，逐渐成为国内外一级汽车主机厂的第一选择。产品不仅配套于比亚迪、江淮、奇瑞、上海大众、广州本田等国内汽车生产企业，更与美国福特、日本日产、克莱斯勒、德国大众、韩国现代等世界知名汽车整机厂商构建了稳定的战略协作伙伴关系。自2007年以来，公司汽车用塑料制品业务飞速发展，自主研发设计能力和生产销售规模均位居国内同行业前列，公司自主研发的三维中空吹塑成型技术、两步法吹塑技术以及双色注塑技术均达到国际先进水平。2012年汽车用塑料制品产值突破3亿元。中鼎橡塑汽车用塑料制品业务的健康快速发展，不仅为企业创造了良好的经济效益，与此同时，公司汽车用塑料零部件业务的技术升级和产能扩张，更是顺应了汽车整车轻量化的潮流，对于节能减排、发展循环经济，具有非常积极的促进意义。

近年来，在汽车用塑料制品等核心业务健康快速成长的基础上，为优化企业产业结构，延伸产业链，公司逐步进军家用电器、电子、工程机械、高铁、航空航天、军工等领域。凭借着从事塑料制品研发与生产多年来建立的技术优势，公司非汽车用塑料零部件的研发与批产工作进展顺利，目前公司已顺利开发了工程机械用履带密封圈、航天军工用插座绝缘体等产品，未来几年将保持快速增长。

3）办公机器用胶辊等橡胶制品

（1）OA机器用胶辊（搬送辊、打印辊、转写辊、充电辊、搓纸辊等）

（2）其他橡胶制品

公司生产的OA机器用胶辊主要为苏州佳能、上海施乐、上海惠普、福建实达、大连斯大、福建爱普生等国内主要打印机、复印机生产厂家配套，并出口到美国、欧洲、日本等国家或地区。

企业经营状况：2012年，公司生产各类塑料制品1.5亿件，产值2.8亿元，利税总额0.42亿元。

质量保证：质量是企业的生命，是企业得以生存和发展的基础。自创办以来，中鼎橡塑中鼎橡塑就本着“持续改进，不断满足和超越客户需求”的质量方针，力求产品质量精益求精。公司先后通过了ISO14001，ISO9001：2000，ISO/TS16949等体系认证，建立了完善的质量控制和管理体系，产品实物质量达到国际先进水平，取得了进军高端产品市场、海外市场的通行证。

5. 宣城福美达新材料有限公司

公司基本情况：宣城福美达新材料有限公司成立于2008年，位于安徽宣州经济开发区东山路6号，是专业生产各种塑胶材料和木塑复合材料的民营科技企业。公司占地面积20000m^2，建筑面积12000m^2。公司经济实力雄厚，具有先进的生产设备、完善的科学管理制度、齐全的检测装备、成熟的生产工艺，集科研（安徽大学高分子材料研究中心设在我公司）、生产、销售于一体。

公司拥有员工150余人，平均年龄30岁左右，其中，硕士、博士10人，高级职称人员30人，享受国务院政府特殊津贴专家1人、安徽省政府特殊津贴专家1人。骨干员工大多具有10年以上的木塑生产加工和管理经验，技术娴熟，经验丰富，富有活力和创新精神。

企业经营：福美达公司是皖东南最大的从事木塑生产与销售的民营企业之一，公司主要从事木塑材料、人造草坪、各种塑胶板材和铝材整体护栏的生产、销售；塑料制品、建筑材料加工与销售。

2012年底，公司实现产值2395万元，利税192万元，出口总额为900万美金，生产经营业绩连续多年保持稳定增长。

企业主营业务及产品情况：自成立来，福美达公司先后被认定为“安徽省高新技术企业”、“宣城市农业产业化龙头企业”和“资源综合利用企业”等称号；福美达公司长期注重企业创新能力、关键技术研发的培养，2010年通过了ISO 9001质量管理体系认证和ISO 14001环境管理体系，获得“宣城市重点实验室”荣誉；拥有安徽省高新技术产品4件；授权实用新型专利8件；授理中的发明型专利2件。公司已与上海华东理工大学材料学院、安徽大学化学院建立产学研合作，将公司作为产学研基地，年研发经费500余万元。

设备技术引进：2012年我公司引进PE木粉碎机、高温混料机、造粒机、挤出机组、打磨机、万能试验机等高新技术设备。

塑料制品进出口：2012年公司木塑装饰材料出口额900万美金，同比增长30%左右，实现创汇额8885万美金，同比增长30%，产品远销东欧、东南亚、南美、北美等50多个国家和地区，出口量、出口创汇额、出口发达国家数量均居国内同行业前列。

新产品开发：2012年，公司坚持产品技术创新，积极开发新产品新工艺，创新能力取得新提高。2012年，公司全年投入500万元用于产品及工艺技术研发创新，占全年营业收入的比重为5%，相继成功研发出环保型装饰装修木塑复合材料和玻纤增强PVC新型复合材料等新产品，为公司未来市场开拓打下坚实基础。2012年公司自主承担“年产4200t木塑地板技术改造”项目顺利通过宣城市经信委验收。

市场需求：自2008年以来，公司在开拓托板市场的同时，也密切关注着国内建材市场新型材料，发现中国木塑复合材料在国外市场占有率极高，该产品不但环保，而且科技含量高，既节约能源，且使用范围广、产品附加值高。木塑材料兼具了塑料、木材和竹材各自的良好物化性能和机械加工性能，适用于建筑、通讯、包装、仓储、家具等行业。木塑材料的原料来源广泛，木塑制品的加工机械化程度高、生产效率高、成本低、性能良好、物美价廉、使用广泛，具有较好的市场前景。木塑复合材料的主要特点和优点可概括为：原料再生资源化、产品可塑化、使用环保化、成本经济化、可回收再生化，因此木塑材料极具工业价值、应用前途广阔。

21世纪是人类追求绿色环保的时代，木塑等复合材料的特点正迎合了时代的这种需求。但是木材受生长期的限制，远不能满足需求，而竹子是速生植物，繁殖迅速。木塑复合材料完全可以替代木材，而且其性价比还优于它们，附加值高。因此，木塑复合材料具有广阔的市场应用前景和较强的市场竞争与抗风险能力。

企业发展趋势：近年来，由于大量的外资进入我国的地板行业，加上各省市、各地方在承接国际产业转移方面比拼优惠政策，产生了较严重的内耗，加剧了我国地板市场的竞争。我国地板产业集群与国际发达地区相比，还处于发展初期，难以在国际上立足，利用市场低迷期进行产业调整、升级，才是国内地板行业的出路。虽然目前国内已有不少的规模化企业，但总体上来看，我国地板行业还是一个散、杂、乱的产业。它注定要被规模化发展模式取代，而规模化、规范化是企业走向完善、逐渐成熟的必由之路。

【存在的问题】

2012年，受欧债危机持续，发达经济体陷入低迷，全球经济增长明显放缓，安徽省塑料行业经济减速、进出口下降，塑料行业的生产销售形势，仍将面临着四大双重压力：

一是工业品价格下降和制造成本上升带来的压力；

二是融资困难和财务成本上升带来的压力；

三是产能落后和产业转型升级困难带来压力；

四是国内外市场萎缩和产能过剩带来的压力。

目前，产业集中度低、生产力分散、专业化生产程度低、深加工比率低、自主品牌终端产品少、利润率低仍是塑料制品行业所面临的突出问题，特别是高科技产品、高技术装备、专业技术人才及专业管理人才严重缺乏给安徽省塑料行业的发展形成了较大的掣肘。随着国家宏观调控力度和密度的不断加大，塑料行业的波动频率也会越来越快。

【发展趋势】

在发现问题和存在的不利因素的同时，我们也看到机遇和积极因素。

一是党的“十八大”报告，明确提出了我国经济发展的总任务、总目标，到2020年要实现“两个”翻番，必然会出台一系列有利于工业经济发展的方针政策，必将带来新的发展机遇。中央经济工作会议提出的：今年继续保持宏观政策的连续性和“稳中求进”的总基调，必将带来企稳回升的好势头。

二是我国仍处在现代化、工业化、城镇化的历史时期。繁荣市场、建设城镇、扩大就业、服务“三农”，离不开塑料工业。特别是塑料建材在建筑工程、市政工程、工业建设中用途广泛。随着我国经济逐步进入全面小康社会，居民改善住房状况的强大需求仍然旺盛，塑料建材产品有巨大的市场空间。

三是安徽省塑料工业的发展，已形成了一定特色：骨干企业起到了支撑作用；四大类的塑料制品形成了格局；一批成长性的企业不断涌现；塑料制品企业遍及各地，各有优势，各有亮点。各企业应坚定信心，克服困难，为促进安徽省塑料工业的快速发展作出应有的贡献。

安徽省塑料协会2013年工作基本思路是：

认真学习贯彻国家的经济方针政策，努力创新工作方法，不断开拓服务范围，积极维护会员合法权益；增强会员企业的互动平台，提高会员企业的合作意识和共同盈利能力，互生互荣，努力把协会办得有声有色，努力保持安徽省塑料工业总体呈现持续、稳定和健康的良好发展态势。

（安徽省塑料协会　翟光景）

海　南　省

【大事记】

1. 组织“渤海商品交易所——茂名石化产品交易中心”与海南省塑料行业企业交流，并于2012年团拜会时组织召开了“渤海商品交易所——茂名石化产品交易中心”推介会，协助成兴塑胶、金煌塑胶、琳雄物资工贸等企业完成了银行绑定等企业开户手续，有效地拓展了企业购买原料的渠道及投资保值空间。

2. 组团赴上海参加了第二十六届中国国际塑料橡胶工业展览会

2012年4月17日~4月19日，协会组团参加上海参加雅式会展，了解新的信息、动态，观看设备、洽谈购买事宜；拜会参展的武汉丽华公司董事长一行，共议生物基塑料落户海南日程；参观、拜访了远东国际租赁有限公司，远东国际租赁有限公司中的塑料包装设备融资租赁，可通过企业自主选择设备、厂商负责供货、远东负责付款的方式，三方各司其责，合作共赢，有效解决企业设备更新所需的融资问题。

3. 召开了“塑料行业企业与海大塑料专业学生座谈会”

2012年5月18日，由海南省塑料行业协会与海南大学材料及化工学院主办的“海南省塑料行业企业家与塑料专业学生座谈会”在海大举行。本次座谈会，企业家代表就企业概况、专业人才引进使用等情况进行发言，学生们就感兴趣的问题，涉及到工作、生活、人才使用、创业筹划等问题，相互提问，交换意见，相互学习，取得了良好效果，今后将共选择主题继续组织。

4. 优化行业信息交流平台建设，完善协会信息服务功能。

逐步完善协会网站，坚持每天更新行业新闻、行业知识、会展信息、会议活动等版块，力求把第一手的塑料行情、塑料价格传递给会员企业，会员企业有任何供求信息和咨询，协会也会在第一时间及时反馈给企业，为企业带来了极大的便利。

5. 组织海南科技考察团赴苏州中科院实地考察

11月16日，海南科技考察团前往苏州，拜访苏州中科院绿色建筑与城市科学研究院的陈天地院长，学习其成功经验。在会议中，双方进行了深入探讨，陈天地院长就海南科技考察团提出的在发展中遇到的问题，给出了明确的指导建议，为正在筹备的“海南省木薯淀粉改性—生物基环保塑料产业创新联盟”的工作确立了目标。

服务企业是协会的职责，协调解决企业遇到的问题是协会的义务，传递信息是协会服务职能的有效延伸，有效地促进行业的发展是协会的生命力。

【企业选介】

1. 海南兴伟塑胶科技有限公司

海南兴伟塑胶科技有限公司前身为海口金煌塑胶，创立于1998年，生产加工PE PVC PPR等塑管及喷灌滴灌微灌节水器材，并具有农业节水工程的施工能力；生产的主打产品，质量稳定，逐步赢得了客户信任，企业得到稳步发展。

2004年在海口扶贫开发区购地建厂，顺利完成企业扩张与产品升级；公司始终重视生产节能与环保，积极履行企业社会责任，依靠质量与信誉及海南鼓励设施农业发展的政策支持，建立了稳定的销售网络，企业得到快速发展。由于生产场地已不能满足需要，于2012年在老城开发区购地45亩，2013年更名为海南兴伟塑胶科技有限公司，建造标准厂房、购置新设备、建立实验室，累计投资2500万元，预计6月份搬迁完毕，7月初全面投产，主要产品为PVC管材管件、PPR冷热供水管、复合高分子节水器材等，设计年产能15000t，预计销售额12000万元。

2. 海南南宝塑料制品有限责任公司

海南南宝塑料制品有限责任公司前身为海南无线电五厂，1988年改为海南电子塑料配件厂，为海南电子产品提供配件及包装；2000年在海南海口桂林洋开发区购地扩建，进入高速发展时期，开发的水果包装箱、水产养殖箱等领跑海南注塑行业；为新大洲摩托研发的配套塑料制品，款式新颖、质量可靠，赢得用户认同。

2002年胡安涛总经理带领全体员工，完成公司股份制改造，改名为海南南宝塑料制品有限责任公司，在上海、广西、云南及海南昌江设立分厂，服务三农，并积极会同科研机构研发新产品，寻求企业稳定发展之路。

3. 海口琳雄物资工贸有限公司

海口琳雄物资工贸有限公司前身为琼山琳雄塑料彩印厂，成立于1989年，是海南最早进入塑料行业的企业之一，主要生产塑编制品、包装膜袋、复合膜袋；

1995年更名为海口琳雄物资工贸有限公司，扩展了原料销售业务；诚实守信，各项业务稳定发展，2010年通过了QS认证，2005年在龙桥购地建厂，建筑面积约3000m^2，今年扩建厂房至8000m^2，设计产能11000万元。

2012年综合销售收入已过亿元，厂房扩建后，产能、销售将增长25%。

4. 儋州宝强塑料制品有限公司

儋州宝强塑料制品有限公司前身为儋州耿丰实业有限公司，创办于1995年，专业生产水泥、矿产品包装用塑编产品，2001年更名为儋州宝强塑料制品有限公司，扩建厂房，增置生产线，年生能力约15000万条标准水泥包装袋；同时涉足资源回收领域，在全省主要市县设立废旧塑料收购点，购置先进的机械手给料破碎清洗造粒生产线，变废为宝，也保证了生产用部分原料的供给与质量。

在生产加工过程中，利用厂区边采石形成的巨坑，对清洗用水进行多次物理沉淀，重复利用，实现了污水零排放，为资源回收加工企业保护环境积累了值得借鉴的经验。

董事长方耿丰先生作为儋州市第七、八、九届政协委员，积极参政议政，同时以企业家的实际行动保护环境。

5. 海口成兴塑胶有限公司

海口成兴塑胶有限公司成立于1998年，拥有先进的吹膜设备，专业生产热收缩膜、包装膜、基材膜，年生产加工能力约8000t。

2010年取得国家质检总局颁发的QS认证，同年复合膜生产线投产。

设置试验室，配备齐全的检验检测设备、仪器，在保证主营业务发展的同时，致力于木薯淀粉生物基塑料研发与产业化尝试。

6. 海南南塑塑料制品有限公司

海南南塑塑料制品有限公司的生产经营团队，1999年开始进入发泡塑料生产领域，坚持不懈；2004年增置设备，扩大规模，更名为海南南塑塑料制品有限公司，专注于ERS系列产品的生产与改进，年生产能力5000t，销售额7000万元，同时涉足农业、旅游，构建多元化经营平台。

7. 海南宝秀节水灌溉设备工程有限公司

1999年进入农业节水灌溉领域，2002年成立公司专业生产、研发节水灌溉系统，2004年更名为海南宝秀节水灌溉设备工程有限公司，拥有节水系统工程的施工团队，年生产PE喷水带、滴灌、微喷等节水灌溉器材3000t。

技术先进、生产规范、经营诚信，通过ISO9001国际质量体系认证，取得海南省农业厅的推广证书，列入政府农机补贴采购目录，已申报10项专利，为向东南亚推广做准备。

8. 海南佳昕塑料包装有限公司

海南佳昕塑料包装有限公司成立于1998年，主要为海南椰树集团及其他食品饮料公司配套各种塑瓶等包装用品，年产3600t。

2010年在海口狮子岭开发区购地扩建，在稳步发展原有产品的同时，研发、引进的科技含量高的产品，将于今年投产。

9. 海口民创塑料制品有限公司

前身为振东塑料厂，1983已开始从事塑料瓶等容器的加工，是海南最早进入塑料行业的企业，多年来，自行摸索模具设计、改进设备、诚信经营，取得了稳步发展。

2011年搬迁至海口港澳工业区，购进设备，扩大规模，改名为海口民创塑料制品有限公司。

2012年捕鱼笼项目取得国家专利，目前正在有序的进行该项目的专利技术转让及规模生产工作。

10. 海南同德管业有限公司

成立于2010年，同年，购置海南首条聚丙烯大口径双臂波纹管生产线，设备先进、配套齐全，专业生产市政工程、房地产用排水管道，年生产能力约4000t，销售额约5000万元。

11. 海南中海石油塑编有限公司

海南中海石油塑编有限公司位于海南省西部东方工业园区，是中国海洋石油总公司旗下中海石油化学股份有限公司的全资子公司。

2002年底动工，2003年8月22日投产，总投资2572万元，占地40亩，建筑面积13000m^2；设计产能5000t，采用国内先进的内粘式制袋设备及工艺，产品主要为基地两套大型尿素装置配套包装，部分外销。

沈俊斌总经理自2009年就位后，倡导与坚持“作风扎实　本领过硬　执行有力”的企业精神，加强技改研发投入，提高产质量，保证企业的健康稳定发展。

【发展趋势】

2013年，塑料行业应不断加强创新力度，尽快实现行业结构的调整，不断适应市场需求的转变，加快新产品的研发，重视产品质量的提升，促进塑料行业持续、稳定、健康发展。

围绕行业发展方向，2013年协会主要工作计划如下：

一、继续协助企业落实工业用地的申请、报建、环评等事宜。

二、配合商务厅推荐组织5~8家企业参加东盟博览会，拓展东南亚市场。此项工作从4月份开始，8月份截止，10月份参展。

三、联合中科院海南办事处，落实“木薯淀粉改性——生物基环保塑料产业创新战略联盟”向科技厅的申报工作，实现产业升级与持续发展，争取下半年成立，首批加盟企业6~8家。预计11月成立。

四、向商务厅申报参加2013年德国K展事宜，争取5~10家企业享受相关优惠政策。

五、协助企业向工信厅申报企业技改资金等。

六、加强与中科院海南办事处的联系，争取取得中科院广东分院的技术支持，向科技厅、组织部申请，争取在两年内在具备条件的企业成立院士工作站，为行业的持续、健康、科学发展储备科技支撑。

七、加强与海大化工与材料学院的交流，解决企业的技术与人才培养难题。

八、与甘肃、贵州两省进行劳务合作，由海大化工与材料学院进行基本技能培训，为企业输送掌握基本技能的员工。

九、进一步加强行业与光大银行迎、交通银行的联系，争取一定额度的行业授信，增加企业融资渠道。

（海南省塑料行业协会　周鸿勋）

新疆维吾尔自治区

【大事记】

（一）借助政府平台，——承办“塑料产洽会”

借助政府搭建的平台，在做好为政府服务的同时，唱好行业的戏，这是新疆塑料协会工作的定位点之一。

2012年7月9~10日新疆维吾尔新疆维吾尔自治区政府组织举办“2012年新疆产学研洽谈会暨院士企业行活动”，新疆塑料协会具体承办了“塑料专场”活动。为保证此项工作的顺利进行，新疆塑料协会根据新疆维吾尔自治区经信委和轻工行办的安排做了大量工作，专门研究、制订“筹备工作方案”。先后向骨干企业、科研院校等单位发出邀请；并将征集的塑料类29个项目成果汇集成会议材料进行了专题资料汇编。活动期间还为中油管业、西部节水、通利塑业等有关企业与到会的科研院校牵线搭桥，陪同专家到实地考察。

在活动期间，“塑料专场”有四川大学等高校发布了17个成果项目，来自全国60多个单位、共计100余名塑料行业的企业负责人、技术人员参加了本次活动。

（二）服务重点工程——土工膜监造

复合土工膜具有抗拉、抗顶破、抗撕裂，强度高，延伸性能好，变形模量大，耐老化、防渗性能好，使用期长等特点，应用在渠道铺设中具有防渗、排水、隔离、加强、抗拉防护等特点。应新疆额河建管局的要求，根据新疆维吾尔自治区经信委和轻工行办的批示，塑料协会承担了该局所承建的重点水利工程之关键材料——土工膜的产品质量监造。为此专门修订了《土工合成材料驻厂监造管理制度》，筛选6名行业内塑料专业质量技术工程师组成土工膜监造组，实施驻厂监造。监造协议于2012年4月份签订，经过4个月工作，累计监造复合土工膜81.7万m^2。

（三）关注热点产业——做好“塑料管材产业研究”课题

了解行业政策动态，关注行业发展变化，着重关注热点产业、最新技术等是协会工作的核心之一。在新疆维吾尔自治区高效节水相关政策的刺激下，高效节水事业得到快速发展，新增节水面积以每年(350~400)万亩增加，农地膜、管材及其滴灌带产品呈持续稳定增长。新疆的塑料节水器材在内地的影响力增大，一些名牌产品已进入东北、内蒙古及甘肃等全国大部分省区并深受用户欢迎、订单量逐步增加。为适应产品发展的要求，新疆塑料协会成立以专门调查、系统分析塑料管材在新疆及全国的发展情况为目的的《塑料管材产业研究》课题组。这个项目也列入了今年轻工行办考核的研究课题。

（四）塑料行业标准化建设工作稳步推进

一直以来，新疆塑料协会一直重视企业及行业标准化建设。在地方标准化管理部门的组织下，积极开展行业标准化推进工作。

1. 配合行办与技术监督局完成“新疆塑料节水器材标准化委员会(国家分会)”相关工作。

2. 配合行办和技术监督局完成向国家提出“关于国标 GBT 19812.3《塑料节水器材内镶式滴灌带、管》在执行中的若干问题与修改意见”申报工作——此修改意见提出前已进行了专门的验证试验和实验。

根据目前国标尚未修改而影响企业生产和法定检验与质量监督等实际情况，向行办和技术监督局提议：允许企业备案符合实际情况、严于国标水平的企业标准。此建议已获准，有关企业的标准备案工作已经展开。

3. 宣传标准化工作对企业经营发展，尤其是技术进步的重要作用。经过多年的努力，已有越来越多的企业重视此项工作，今年内累计备案的塑料类新疆维吾尔自治区级企业标准 40 余项。

(五) 借科技东风、促企业发展

新疆维吾尔自治区仅经信委系统内的各类科技工作和项目就很多，新疆塑料协会主要参与了科技项目调查、征集、行业汇总和初步审查等工作。

今年的科技项目基本涵盖了新疆塑料行业的骨干、新产业或技术，反应了行业发展的方向。涉及了 30 余家企业的 100 多个项目，累计投资 20 多亿元，预计年产值达 30 亿元以上。

(六) 治理污染、变废为宝

上世纪八十年代的一场“白色革命”为新疆的农业增产、农民增收带来了巨大的效益。近三十年过去了，新疆地膜平均残膜量达到 17kg/亩，是全国平均水平的 4 ~5 倍，减产量达 12%。“白色污染”严重影响到了农业可持续发展和农民持续增收。

为治理“白色污染”，国家补助资金 5117 万元在全疆 17 个县市开展地膜回收利用项目示范工作。废旧地膜回收造粒后市场售价可达 6000 元/t 以上，按 80% 的回收率计算，全疆年使用 150kt 地膜，可回收 120kt，将产生 7 亿元以上的价值。

(七) 积极与内地同行交流，及时把握行业形势

1. 2012 年 5 月 27 ~30 日率会员企业代表组团参加中塑协在东莞召开的 2012 年各省及地方塑料协会(商会)工作会议和广东省塑料工业协会组织的各省塑料协会联谊活动，

2. 2012 年 9 月 21 ~25 日，塑料协会组织了 12 名行业代表参加了在台州召开的“第 12 届中国塑料制品交易会”等全国性行业活动。

(八) 走出国门，介绍企业

落实新疆维吾尔自治区经信委新贸促发字【2012】1 号文件精神，新疆塑料协会配合轻工行办组织企业参加 2012 年 5 月 3 ~5 日在塔什干举办“2012 乌兹别克中国商品展”通知有出口业务和发展潜力的企业参展。

(九) 组织骨干企业和专家开展产业发展研究

针对新疆地区塑料行业在近年来发展较快的特点，及时了解新疆地区塑料市场的动态。今年组织骨干单位以地区为主的进行行业热点及产业问题的研究工作，为企业经营和行业管理提供科学的决策参考。

【地区热点】

新疆维吾尔自治区要求推进农业高效节水标准化规范化建设

2012 年 5 月 24 日，中央政治局委员、新疆维吾尔自治区党委书记张春贤来到昌吉州呼图壁、玛纳斯两县，就农业高效节水建设进行专题调研。

新疆远离海洋和高山环抱的综合地理环境下，形成了典型的干旱气候。目前，新疆水资源的总量是 832 亿立方米，而现状用水量已达 518 亿立方米。新疆绿洲农业用水占总用水量的 95%，远远高于全国 62% 的平均值。新疆资源丰富，由于水资源不足，严重阻碍了新疆资源开发、工业发展和生态建设。

根据新疆的地理特点，为发展新疆的特色农业，新疆已成为最大的农业节水产品的生产区和使用区，并启动了《新疆绿洲灌区节水关键技术和用水安全研究与示范》课题研究。

目前，新疆维吾尔自治区已累计建设高效节水灌溉面积 2500 万亩以上，并以每年 300 万亩的速度发展。并制定目标确保到 2020 年新疆农业用水比重降到 90% 以下。据统计，新疆是我国最早进行滴灌实验的地区，取得多项国内领先的研究成果，特别是在棉花、番茄、辣椒、甜瓜、小麦、水稻等农作物创造高产纪录。应用滴灌技术节约用水，有力支持当地工业和经济发展，综合效益明显；应用滴灌节水技术后，增加了农民的收入，降低劳动强度。全疆广泛开展农业高效节水建设后，亩均减少灌溉水量 $100m^3$ 以上，粮食作物平均每亩增产 50kg，棉花等经济作物平均每亩增收 700 元，设施农业平均每亩可增收 1500 元。

经济效益的提高和政府节能补贴的增加，激励了农民对滴灌带(管)、农地膜需求的增加，同时也为节水产品的生产厂家提供了扩大再生产的机遇。催生全疆新增节水器材生产厂家 300 家、拥有滴灌带生产线 3000 条，新增滴灌工程服务公司 130 家。地方节水器材使用也超过兵团，农地膜、滴灌带(管)年产销量增幅超 10%，新疆成为全国最大的节

水器材生产地和使用地.

节水灌溉不仅在疆内产销两旺，而且骨干企业依托塑料协会这个平台，积极与科研机构产学研紧密合作，滴灌集成技术和节水材料不断创新，新材料、新产品和新技术研究成果转化，加快了节水灌溉技术革命性转变，使自己的产品走向了全国，走出了国门。新疆天业节水灌溉股份有限公司不仅在国内29个省、市、新疆维吾尔自治区建立了滴灌技术示范基地，累计推广5387万亩，而且在亚、非洲13个国家推广应用4.67万亩，扩大了天业滴灌技术在国外的应用，提高了天业节水的国际知名度。

【基本情况】

（一）2012年基本情况

据统计，2012年1~11月，全疆85家规模以上企业累计生产各类塑料制品55.7万吨，比去年同期增长28.1%；实现工业产值75.6亿元，同比增长37.5%，在轻工各行业中规模和增幅位居第一。1~11月实现销售收入73.3亿元，同比增长29.3%；实现利润4.6亿元，同比增长69.8%。行业经济效益大幅提升，行业形势继续呈现强劲增长态势。其中管材类产品占总比重为41.4%，位居大类第一，比上一年度增长了3个百分点。

表1　2012年1~11月份各类塑料制品产量分析

制品大类	1~11月累计	比重/%	同比增减/%
全部制品合计	557，232.35	100.00	28.11
塑料薄膜	60，087.13	10.78	9.83
农用薄膜	52，158.83	9.36	8.70
塑料板、片及类似型材	37，919.28	6.80	95.90
塑料制管子及其附件	230，959.96	41.45	10.09
其中：滴灌带	48，610.69	8.72	
塑料编织袋	43，474.67	7.80	23.09
塑料包装箱及容器	40，843.32	7.33	43.04
日用塑料制品	6，478.00	1.16	73.51

在各类塑料制品中，除“塑料薄膜”和“管子及附件”的增幅在10%左右外，其他各类产量均较2011年同期增长20%以上。其中增幅位居前列的有：“塑料板、片及类似型材”为95.9%、“日用塑料”为73.51%、“塑料包装箱及容器”为43.04%。塑料制品产量的高速度增长，主要得益于基础设施建设热潮和产业援疆引发的新疆经济大发展。而周边国家经济形势的逐步回暖，对各类塑料制品的需求也日渐旺盛，使处于对外贸易前沿的新疆各口岸塑料制品出口形势向好，同时出口产品的疆内本地化生产比重逐步加大。

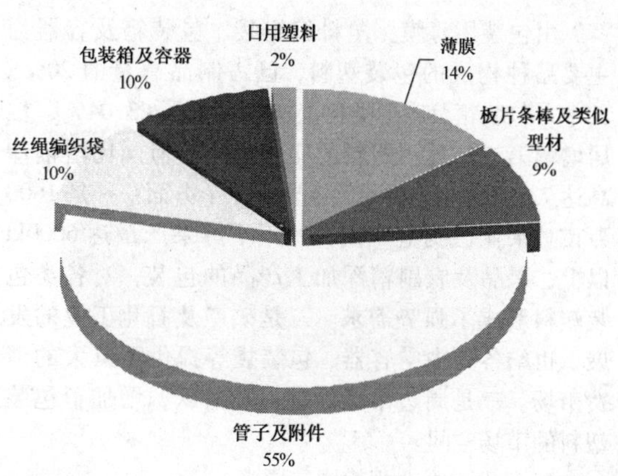

图1　2012年塑料制品产量大类分析

（二）行业特点

1. 塑料节水器材持续快速增长

在“大力发展节水农业”的政策指导下，特别是“节水农田改造补贴资金”的有效落实，确保了新疆维吾尔自治区农业节水灌溉面积以每年300万亩以上的增幅持续增长，有效拉动了滴灌带及其配套的管材管件、农地膜等产品的需求，其产量增幅均保持在10%左右。

2. 塑料建材迎来发展新机遇

近年来，在城市化建设和产业援疆等政策的引领下，新疆经济社会进入了一个新的全面发展时期，给包括塑料建材在内的各类建筑材料创造了新的消费市场和发展机遇。新疆维吾尔自治区塑料协会统计显示，近年来各类塑料建材产销量年增长率均保持在20%以上，这种高速增长幅度还将持续相当一段时间。

目前在比较热销的塑料建材产品，主要有：PVC门窗型材、装饰型材，PVC建筑物通风管、上下水管道，PE或PP耐热管道（热水管、地暖管）；PVC或HDPE埋地管道、PE或PVC油田管道、煤矿井下管道；EPS、XPS泡沫板材等等。其中主导品种是PVC（门窗）型材，其产量增幅较上年翻了一番。

3. 包装和日用塑料制品异军突起

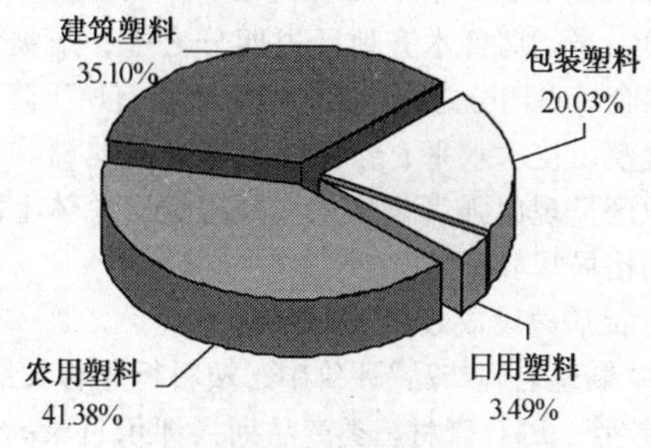

图2　按用途分类分析

由包装用薄膜、塑料编织袋、包装箱及容器为主要品种构成的包装塑料，已占制品总量的20%。其中，包装箱及容器类比上一年增长了43.04%，位居增幅第三。日用塑料的比重虽小，但同比增幅却高达73.51%。分析原因主要有三个方面：一是1600万亩林果业已到盛产期，每年干鲜果产量达6000kt以上；果品及农副精深加工产品的包装，对各类包装塑料形成了强势需求。二是矿产及石化工业的发展，也给各类中空容器、包装袋等提供了巨大的消费市场。三是周边市场的进一步活跃，增加了包装塑料的市场空间。

4. 行业与企业规模同步增大

今年进入新疆维吾尔自治区统计口径的规模以上企业为85家，较上年的72家增加了13家，增幅为18.1%，如图3。规模以上企业户均产值为8，899.46万元/户，比2011年的6，472.04万元/户增长了37.51%。总产量过5万吨的企业有：新疆中石油管业工程有限公司和新疆天业节水灌溉股份有限公司，较上年增加1家。随着产业转移的深入，一批进疆的国内知名企业产能逐步形成，正对新疆地区塑料工业形成新的支撑。

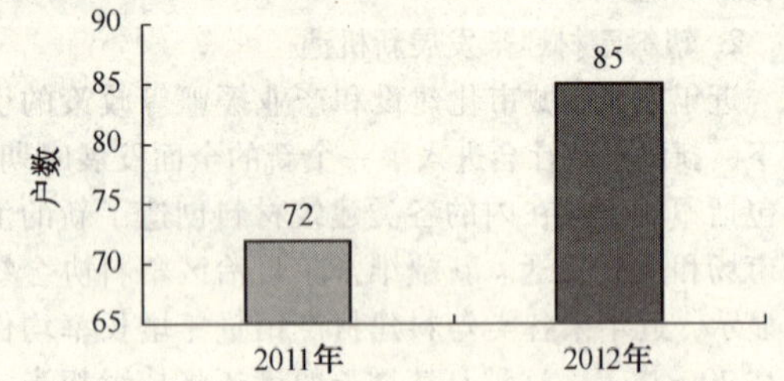

图3 2011～2012年规上企业数分比较

5. 区域发展快慢各异，北强南弱格局未变

经过近几年的快速发展，特别是塑料节水器材、包装塑料生产的普及和废旧塑料回收利用的推广，在全疆县以上行政区域内基本上结束了无塑料制品生产的历史，但企业规模、产品档次、加工水平差异很大。在区域结构上，疆内的万吨级以上企业和进疆的知名企业多集中在乌昌地区。北疆地区占整体规模一半，乌鲁木齐地区占四分之一，南疆和东疆地区合计占四分之一(如图4)，比重有所下降。从企业规模、技术水平、综合能力等方面北疆和乌鲁木齐地区呈现出强者恒强的发展态势，总体上北强南弱的格局基本未变。

6. 品牌建设成效显著

在"新疆名牌产品"评价中，塑料行业有农地膜、滴灌带/管、PVC管材三类产品列入评价目录。经过评审，新疆天业股份有限公司的"天业牌"、新疆通利塑业有限公司的"同历牌"、新疆联塑节水设备有

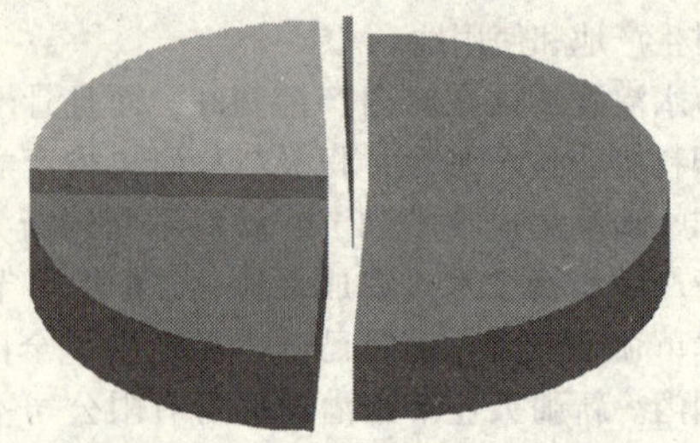

图4 2012年1～11月塑料制品产量大区分析

限公司的"志强牌"、新疆双吉塑业有限公司的"双吉牌"、新疆独山子天利高新技术股份有限公司的"雄鹰牌"、新疆龙盛祥农业发展有限责任公司的"西域白浪牌"、新疆天业节水灌溉股份有限公司的"天业牌"、新疆芳草湖益民塑料化工有限公司的"益民牌"、塔农节水器材有限公司的"新农牌"共计8家企业的9个品牌和产品获得"新疆名牌产品"称号。至此全疆塑料行业已有20家企业的21个品牌、12种产品获得"新疆名牌"称号。

在"驰名商标"和"著名商标"的培育方面也有相当的成就，目前已有新疆天业集团、新疆中油管业工程有限公司等一批企业的商标分别获得"驰名商标"和"著名商标"称号。

在向中国轻工业联合会主持的《全国轻工企业绩效先进评比》活动中，新疆天业节水灌溉股份有限公司和新疆未来型材有限公司获奖。在中轻联主持的"2011年度全国轻工业十强企业"的评选活动中，新疆天业(集团)有限公司获得"2011年度塑料行业十强企业称号"、新疆蓝山屯河型材有限公司获得"2011年度型材行业十强企业称号"。

7. 企业创新和技改投入力度加大

新疆地区塑料行业的技术创新能力集中在农地膜、塑料节水器材、型材及材料改性等几个主要产业领域。中型以上骨干企业均设有专门的企业研发机构，建立了技术创新激励机制，以企业为主体的技术创新已是行业创新活动的主流，每年向国家相关部委和新疆维吾尔自治区申报或获得批准立项的各项创新项目都有数十项，也有多项成果获得相关部门的奖励。今年，塑料行业列入新疆维吾尔自治区经信委系统的重点技术创新、重点技术改造和产业升级、重点新产品、中小企业专项、民生工程专项等各类科技项目多达几十项，累计投入项目资金超过30.7亿元，占轻工业的16.2%。其中部分技术改造、技术创新、节能减排项目已完成或投产，并初见成效。

8. 走出疆外开拓市场空间

新疆"膜下滴灌"技术成功推广应用后，新疆地区成为国内高效节水灌溉农业和农用塑料节水器材

产业高地，为加速国内外市场拓展，新疆天业节水灌溉设备股份有限公司等一批企业，先后走出新疆推广技术、开拓市场。去年在东北的吉林省、黑龙江省、内蒙古新疆维吾尔自治区等地为100多万亩农田进行了高效节水灌溉工程改造，取得了良好的效果。

【设备技术引进】

新疆首家超高分子量聚乙烯管材项目落户北方化工

新疆北方化工塑料有限责任公司为适应市场需求及提升公司产品在市场中竞争力，投资2600万元，引进高超分子量聚乙烯管材项目及生产技术，开发出具有超高分子聚乙烯耐磨管、超高分子量聚乙烯钢塑复合管、煤矿井下用管道、超高分子量聚乙烯钢丝骨架复合管、超高分子聚乙烯板材等。新建10条生产线，年产3000t超高分子量聚乙烯管道，产品广泛应用于石油、化工、电力、煤炭、煤电、煤化工、冶金焦化、海水处理、清淤工程、污水处理等。

超高分子量聚乙烯管材作为一种综合性能优异的新型塑料管材，在代替钢管、铸铁管应用于上述行业，进行各种粉粒体、浆体、液体、气体的耐磨、耐腐蚀输送方面具有其他管材无可比拟的优越性，在国内外都刚刚起步，甚至空白，却备受人们的青睐。

目前，世界上能够制造超高分子量聚乙烯原料及制品的国家有美国、德国、日本、意大利、俄罗斯和中国。我国超高分子量聚乙烯原料及制品特别是挤出技术的成熟与发展已引起广泛的重视。

【塑料制品进出口】

据乌鲁木齐海关的资料，2012年各口岸塑料类商品进出口表现比2011年呈现较快增长态势。各口岸全年累计出口各类塑料制品101.9kt，同比增长40.1%；出口总值5.47亿美元，同比增长49%。

从商品类别分析：

1. 初级形状塑料商品的情况是：进出口总量为231.4kt，同比增长18%；进出口总值为2.2亿美元，同比增长12%。其中：出口（聚氯乙烯）总量218.9kt，同比增长27%；出口总值2.02亿美元，同比增长8.9%；进口总量为12.5kt，同比下降53%；进口总值1782万美元，同比下降59%。

2. 塑料编织袋(周转袋除外)出口总量32717万条，同比增长28.5%；出口总值7637万美元，同比增长62.1%。

【新产品开发】

研发新产品、填补西北五省空白

新疆蓝山屯河化工有限公司研发的生物降解PBS树脂产品研制成功，此产品不仅环保、对人体也无毒害，填补了生物降解树脂PBS产品在西北五省区的空白。

与其他生物降解塑料相比，生物降解PBS树脂是目前降解塑料加工性能最好的材料，可在堆肥、水体等接触微生物条件下发生降解，在正常储存和使用过程中性能稳定。

【存在的问题】

塑料工业产、销均取得了历史的新高，发展形势总体乐观，同时也还存在着一些突出的矛盾和问题，应着重从以下几个方面寻求突破。

（一）推行“塑料节水器材行业准入”制度

滴灌带、农用薄膜(地膜和大棚膜)属重要的农业生产资料，国家对其实行了免增值税政策，目前以节水为主题的补贴、鼓励政策很多，而这些政策执行部门不统一，其效果没有达到“扶优扶强”和“淘汰落后”的目的，市场秩序混乱、产品质量良莠不齐日益突出。如何继续保持新疆节水器材的优势，应当引起高度重视。新疆维吾尔自治区实行“塑料节水器材行业准入”制度，采取认证认可或备案制度已势在必行。

（二）引导企业整合，提高综合能力

目前新疆地区塑料制品的整体表现为产业集中度低、生产力分数、专业化生产程度低、深加工比率低。没有进行高质量的改革、兼并、重组，而是随塑料行业实施了更加粗放型的管理。导致地方企业基本设备投资过度，低值产品不理性增长。尤其是部分塑料产品过度集中导致竞争也过度。要引导这些企业通过市场机制，重组整合，形成特色和规模，增强抗风险能力，避免盲目的生产和恶性竞争。

（三）鼓励企业技术创新，提升科技素质

当前多数企业不具备自主创新能力，鼓励和引导企业通过“产学研”、产业联合体等多种途径走联合开发、引进吸收的路线，提升创新能力。塑料协会发挥行业协会的桥梁纽带作用，组织企业走出去、请进来，在创新实践中提升企业的科技素质。

（四）加快专业技术人才队伍建设

有效发挥塑料协会的专家委员会作用，集中行业力量开展一些专业技术活动，在有效解决行业中的技术难题的同时，提升企业专业技术人员的创新能力。发挥“国家第39号职业技能鉴定站”和“新疆塑料制品行业生产力促进中心”的作用，加大面向中小微企业的专业技术岗位培训和职业技能鉴定，培养一批操作技术能手。

塑料工业既是一个应用广泛的制品加工业，也是一个与其他行业紧密联系和配套的材料工业，与地区经济结构和水平密切相关，随着新疆跨越式发展的步伐新疆塑料行业将进一步发展壮大。

【发展趋势】

随着农业政策支持力度加大、重点工程建设项目实施等举措的逐步深入，在政策引导和市场空间上为新疆的塑料工业打造了良好的上升通道。特别是近年来的一批重点技术改造和创新项目将于年内达产见效；另外，南疆的部分合成树脂项目相继建成投产，对南疆塑料工业形成拉动等。综上所述，2013 年塑料工业仍延续 2012 年的高速增长态势，增长率将保持在 20% 以上；2013 年全疆各类塑料制品的总产量将突破 1600kt、工业总产值将突破 200 亿元，双双再创造历史新高。

从产品门类方面看，以滴灌带、管材、农地膜等为主的“塑料节水器材”产品；以门窗型材、外墙保温材料、室内装饰材料为主的各类塑料建材；以塑料托盘、中空容器、编织袋等为主要产品的包装塑料制品；以出口为目的的各种厨卫制品、装饰装修材料、日用塑料制品等，仍将是 2013 年及今后几年内的热门产品。其中，各种复合材料、工矿及特殊性能和大口径管材及其配套的管件；大型或异型结构、多层复合或高阻隔性能中空容器、包装箱框；用于工程项目的功能性结构材料、对通用树脂改性等新产品，将是最热门的内容。

从技术应用方面看，以企业为主体、主动性的节能减排、降耗增效、提升品质、创新应用领域等为目的的新产品开发、技术创新和改造升级活动，将继续成为企业经营活动的主要内容。其中以电磁加热技术、智能伺服控制技术、CAD 及 CAM 辅助设计制造等为代表的节能降耗和优化制造为目的“先进适用型”技术将日益受到重视。受此影响，疆内企业的各类出访、参观、参展活动会更加频繁；与各类科研院所的“产学研”联合行动、合作项目；疆外各方面围绕塑料行业的投资融资、产业与技术转移活动也会层出不穷。

从地域优势方面看，未来几年新疆确定在乌鲁木齐、独山子、库尔勒 3 个重点地区延伸石化产业链。其中，乌鲁木齐周边以乌石化百万吨芳烃项目为支撑向下延伸芳烃产业链；独山子周边依托中石油大乙烯项目延伸烯烃产业链；南疆库尔勒、库车一线充分利用塔里木盆地的天然气资源重点发展天然气下游加工产业。

从产业结构方面看，产品结构将由清一色的“终端制品”逐步变为“材料型制品”，行业整体上由纯“加工型”逐步表现为“加工制造型”，产业水平进一步提升和优化。

从产业趋势方面看：绿色、低碳、环保的可持续发展与成为塑料行业未来发展的主基调，塑料行业中各细分子行业根据特点纷纷规划出低碳发展的线路图。

（新疆塑料协会　孔德海、李显贵、陈项）

主要制品行业情况

农用薄膜

【行业现状】

2012年是我国农膜行业较为困难的一年，在经历了连续三年高速增长(2009～2011年，全国规模以上农膜企业农膜产量增长率分别为18.4%、27.7%、14.5%)之后，进入2012年受国内外大环境制衡，农膜产量增速逐季下滑，企业利润空间不断被挤压，近九成农膜企业挣扎在亏损边缘线上，农膜行业遭遇严重困境。2012年一季度全国规模以上农膜企业产量累计同比增长率尚在16.96%，二季度降至9.32%，三季度为7.38%，1～10月累计同比增长率则降为5%，而1～11月降到了最低点3%。通常情况下考虑到物价上涨，劳动力成本加大以及其他因素，对于大多数农膜企业，产量增长率能达到5%，企业才有钱可赚，下跌到3%，可以想见处境何等艰难。好在12月份出现转机，1～12月增长率回升到7.74%，下行止跌，走出谷底，企业看到曙光。尽管如此，相比2011年，2012年的增长率回落了6.76个百分点。在整个塑料加工行业增长率比较低，回落量比较高。

2012年农膜产量增速大幅下滑的原因，与国际金融危机深层次影响凸现和我国经济下行压力加大，不无关联。除了国际原油价格持续不稳，以及国内收紧信贷规模外，一些大宗农产品出口受挫或价格走低，种植面积减少，导致对农膜的需求旺势减弱。特别是农业大省种植面积的波动，对农膜产量的影响更大。2012年全国规模以上农膜企业农膜产量为1627.4kt。全国总产量、总购买量约为2200kt，其中棚膜1000kt，地膜1200kt。

目前我国农膜生产企业有千家左右，其中年产量在万吨以上的大型骨干企业有35家，他们产量的总和占到全国规模以上农膜企业农膜产量的50%，占全国总产量的三分之一，产量最高的企业可以达到50～60kt/年。年产量在3000～10000t之间的大中型企业将近百家，其产量之和占到全国总产量的近三成。其余约870家企业为中、小、微企业。可见农膜行业产量的60%以上集中在前130余家大型企业中，随着市场经济的深化发展，优胜劣汰、兼并重组，农膜的集中度还会进一步提高。近几年伴随农膜行业快速发展出现的最大变化，一是高端产品的研发取得突破进展，以涂覆型PO膜为代表的一批高端产品在研发、应用、检测等方面达到世界先进水平，某些方面甚至跃居世界前列。涂覆型PO膜实现工业化生产打破了国外垄断地位，为我国农膜在高端市场的竞争，打下坚实基础。二是产品结构得到优化。《农膜行业“十二五”规划》提出到2015年中高档功能膜在市场上的份额提高到50%，据农塑制品分会测算，50%的目标已经提前完成。到“十二五”末，中高档功能膜在市场上的份额将达到60%。三是由于农膜产量和性能的提高，带动了农业栽培技术的升级，为农业集约化、规模化经营提供了条件，使农产品工厂化生产成为现实。

【存在问题】

农膜行业虽然发展较快，但存在先天不足：一是农膜生产可以单机运行，产品适宜分散、小批量、多品种投入，准入门槛低，所以形成大多数规模小，产量低的企业，技术、设备、检测手段不完善，致使市场上低档农膜产品份额达50%之多。二是长期以来，农膜被列为“支农”产品，受农民购买力限制，产品定价不能太高，农膜企业一直处于微利水平，抽不出更多资金用于研发与技改，产品更新换代迟缓。三是均衡生产与季节性供货之间矛盾突出。农膜需求旺季主要集中在春播与秋种两个时间段，此时订单多，需抓紧生产，其余时间则为淡季，企业多停工、停产，多数企业生产工人系季节工，人员流动性大，难以正规培训达到业务素质的稳步提高。从设备运行、产品质量和生产管理角度考虑，企业的理想状态应该是常年均衡生产，然而淡季生产的产品卖不出去需入库储存，资金不能回笼，企业本来就贷款难，故难以做到均衡生产。以上不足造成行业存在的突出问题：一是产能过剩，全行业目前产能为4000kt，利用率不到60%。二是多数企业抗御风险能力低，一旦外部环境条件恶劣，就无法维持生产，处境堪忧。三是一些企业为挤占市场，甚至采用不正当手段，以次充好、偷税漏税、相互压价、恶意竞争，干扰了正常生产经营秩序，既损害农民复兴又损害农膜产品的声誉。

为改变农膜行业自主创新能力薄弱，转型升级缓慢的局面，除了农膜行业和企业自身努力外，我们建议：

1. 享受同化肥、种子、农药等行业同等优惠政策

我国化肥等支农产品在生产用电、绿色通道和淡季仓储等方面，都享有较多的优惠政策。例如化肥产业用电每年可降低成本60多亿元，化肥仓储享受财务贴息政策，化肥优惠运价每吨成本可降低80元，每年政府补贴50亿元。作为与化肥、种子、农药同等重要的农资产品的农膜，也应得到国家在电价、旺季产品运输和淡季仓储等方面的政策优惠，

享受到同等待遇。

2. 适度降低农膜原料进口关税

目前农膜原料进口关税为6.5%，而化肥原料进口关税都在4%以下，建议对需要进口的部分农膜专用原材料适当减免进口关税，以降低国内企业的成本压力。同时引导国内石化、化工企业积极开发国产农膜用原材料。以缓解进口带来的压力。

3. 加大对农膜新产品开发和设备更新改造的支持力度，使创新型企业能获得相关研发经费和资金支持。另外农膜企业、特别是中、小企业普遍感到贷款难、贷款贵、手续繁杂，感到税赋重，企业无利可图，希望能在融资、税收等方面予以政策倾斜。

【开展活动】

1. 为农膜专委会顺利换届做好准备

中国塑协农膜专委会第三届理事会2003年底组成，2008年任期届满，由于当时条件不成熟，经中国塑协同意，会员代表大会通过准予延期换届。农膜专委会2011年年会上，中国塑协曹俭常务副理事长就换届事宜做了重要指示，使换届工作正式纳入议事日程，进入2012年准备工作全面铺开，包括新一届(即第四届)农膜专委会常委会主任单位的摸底排队筛选，换届领导小组的组建，换届方案的起草，常委会组成名单的确定，第三届理事会在换届大会上的工作报告和财务报告，《中国塑协农膜专委会工作条例》的修改与修改说明报告，换届大会的议程与整个会务工作安排等等。在中国塑协精心指导严格把关下，农膜专委会秘书处全力以赴投入各项准备工作中，于2012年6月底全部准备工作安排就绪。应该强调的是中国塑协领导与有关同志为之付出了艰辛努力，是换届工作顺利完成的重要保证。

2. 换届工作圆满成功

中国塑协农膜专委会2012年年会暨第四届常委会换届选举大会于2012年7月17日在吉林省白山市拉开序幕。先召开换届领导小组会议，由中国塑协秘书长马占峰主持，通过了换届方案与选举原则与办法、常委会委员推荐名单、三届五次理事会全议程。接着召开农膜专委会三届五次理事会会议，由三届理事会理事长韩连贵主持，通过换届选举办法，换届选举大会议程，四届常委会委员候选名单，大会主席团组成名单。2012年7月18日中国塑协农膜专委会2012年年会暨第四届常委会换届选举大会隆重召开，由马占峰秘书长主持，白山市陈耀辉副市长致欢迎词，国家工信部谢立安调研员做重要讲话，大会审议通过第三届理事会《工作报告》和《财务报告》，审议通过《农膜专委会工作条例》，审议通过农膜专委会第四届常委会委员名单，之后召开农膜专委会四届一次常委会委员全体会议，选举产生了四届常委会主任、副主任和秘书长。

新当选的第四届常委会主任、白山市喜丰塑料(集团)股份有限公司董事长曹志强做就职演说，对专委会今后工作做了阐述。中国塑协常务副理事长曹俭做大会总结讲话，他对新一届专委会工作提出了希望与要求，对农膜行业发展提出宝贵建议。与会代表参观了白山喜丰公司后，大会转入技术交流，宣读十二篇论文，对当前行业发展、市场状况，产品研发和技术创新进行了精辟分析，受到好评。

3. 认真编制《农膜行业技术进步“十二五”发展建议》

为推动农膜行业在“十二五”期间更好更快发展，引领农膜企业走技术创新、节能降耗、品牌效益之路，按照中国塑协要求，农膜专委会秘书处在广泛征求企业领导与技术人员意见基础上，对本行业“十一五”科技进步取得的成绩，行业发展现状，存在问题，与国外先进水平的差距等进行了认真总结，并提出“十二五”期间科技进步发展思路和重点发展方向，经过近一个月的企业基本情况收集汇总于2012年9月中旬完成《农膜行业技术进步“十二五”发展建议》，全文近万字，包括四大部分，第一部分从高端产品研发、产品升级品种扩大、装备工艺改进、产品质量稳步提高和节能降耗设备的应用等五方面总结了“十一五”期间农膜行业技术进步取得的成绩；第二部分从产品结构、产品功能、生产装置、科技投入和管理水平等方面阐明行业存在的差距；第三部分分析了农膜行业面临的机遇与挑战，未来发展趋势；第四部分提出“十二五”期间农膜行业科技发展的总体思路、基本原则、发展目标、主要任务、重点发展方向以及有关政策建议。《发展建议》凝结了农膜行业的集体智慧，对今后发展具有指导作用。

4. 落实2012年年会上议定事项

① 制订、颁发、收集、汇总《农膜吨产品成本分析表》

为规范农膜生产管理、降低生产成本、提高产品质量，专委会秘书处根据年会上领导指示精神、集思广益制订出《农膜吨产品分析表》并下发各企业填报，通过收集与汇总，为制订农膜行业先进生产指标和产品标准做好资料准备和打好基础，这项工作正在进行中，对提高行业的管理水平会将起到积极作用。

② 起草《农膜行业准入条件实施细则》和《农膜行业管理规定》

2012年年会上代表普遍反映《农膜行业准入条件》颁布2年来由于缺乏具体监管手段，没能得到有效执行。为切实贯彻落实《准入条件》，使其具有一定的可操作性，便于具体监管。农膜专委会秘书处于8月份起草了《农膜行业准入条件实施细则》和《农膜行业管理规定》，为有关职能部门实施《准入条件》提供参考。

③ 根据2012年年会座谈会反映的问题，专委会秘书处起草了行业目前困境及争取扶持政策的建议，上报中国塑协，以中国塑协名义向有关上级部门反映。

5. 积极宣传农膜，努力扩大影响

抓住机遇，积极主动宣传农膜，扩大农膜的影响力，让更多人了解农膜、关注农膜，从而支持农膜是农膜专委会每一个工作人员应尽的职责，也是一分责任。

① 积极向媒体投稿，宣传农膜的作用与贡献，介绍农膜行业、农膜产品现状。2012年初向化工报投稿，题目是《优化农膜品质，为农业科技上水平助力》，刊登在《中国化工报》2012年第15期。向《现代塑料工业》杂志投稿，题目是《农膜应用与发展情况介绍》，该文刊登于该杂志2012年第一季刊第53页上。

② 为落实温家宝总理批示精神，工信部会同财政部、农业部、商务部于2012年4月25日在北京召开研究地膜回收利用、传统地膜应用及可降解环保地膜的开发应用座谈会，农膜专委会应邀出席座谈，并要求介绍地膜应用及建议等。接到通知后，按要求进行了准备，并打印书面材料向与会领导分发，以加深对发言内容的了解，受到领导、与会代表的重视。

③ 撰写农膜行业2011年年鉴，纳入塑料加工工业年鉴，向社会广泛宣传农膜行业的发展与进步、今后趋势、开展的重大活动以及重点企业的介绍，扩大农膜的影响力。

6. 组织农膜企业参加第26届国际橡塑展，并出席中国塑协六届二次理事会。

经过精心组织，参加2012年4月份在上海举办的橡塑展的企业有40多家，共115人，庞大的参展团受到主办方的好评。利用参会的机会，农膜专委会工作人员广泛同企业交流，加深了解。农膜专委会受经费限制，不可能经常到各地走访企业了解情况，为了弥补这一不足，我们充分利用一切机会，如大会、小会、参展、参观等各种场合有意识地多与企业代表交流，了解企业生产、销售情况，存在哪些困难，并通过电邮、书信、通讯以及信息平台等方式，联系企业，征集意见，咨询难题，听取建议，为上级需要了解的问题提供素材。我们深深体会到农膜专委会的根基在企业，农膜专委会的活力来自基层，今后仍需加强同生产一线企业的联系与交流，不断充实和改进自己的工作。

【发展趋势】

今年农膜市场将持续稳中略进，农膜产量的增长率将在8%～10%之间。2013年有利的因素，其一是全球经济尽管复苏乏力的走势不会改变，但受大国经济刺激政策驱动，预计2013年全球经济增速3.3%左右，比上年度略有加快，呈现缓慢复苏的预期。国际经济形势的转暖，对我国经济的拉升无疑是利好消息。其二我国经济增速从2012年9月结束探底下滑，开始出现回升态势，而且还具有一定的回升空间，中央经济工作会议确定稳中求进总基调，对巩固和发展已出现的适度回升，起到保驾护航作用。其三是今年中央一号文件明确继续加大对“三农”的支持力度，强调创新农业生产经营体制，稳步提高农民组织化程度，扶持联户经营、农业大户、家庭农场，支持新型农民合作组织，培育壮大龙头企业。内需拉动是经济增长最直接最可靠的动力。土地流转集中，趋向规模经营，势必提升对农膜品质和数量的需求，所以2013年农膜产量不会出现2012年的增速下滑的局面，保持8%～10%的增长率是完全可能的。也应该看到，随着农膜产量的不断提高，基数越来越大，增长率继续象过去一样保持两位数的高速度，难度越来越大，将会逐渐小幅度降低。到2020年农膜产量的增长率会保持在7%的水平。同时农膜的品质会有较大提高，品种也进一步扩大，中高档农膜产品在市场上所占的份额有较高的水平。要实现上述目标，必须做艰苦扎实的努力。今后工作重点是培育驰名商标，实施品牌战略，注重人才培养，鼓励引进人才，加大科技投入，提高技术水平，制订产品标准和定额指标，强化企业管理，在“十二五”期间行业综合素质有较大提高。具体如下：

1. 落实准入监管，整顿生产秩序规范

农膜行业经营行为，防止盲目投资和重复建设，加快产业结构调整，加强对农膜生产、经营和使用的监督管理，保证农膜质量降低能耗，保护农业生产和生态环境，促进我国农膜行业、持续协调健康发展，工业和信息化部于2009年12月17日发布了工消费【2009】第73号公告，公告附件《农用薄膜行业准入条件》的规定中，对新建农膜企业及改扩建农膜项目的规模、资源消耗、产品质量、环境保护等方面做出了细致的规定。但从实际执行情况来看，由于缺乏有效的监管手段及涉及到多个政府部门职能的原因，三年来这些规定没能有效地得到执行，造成一些不符合条件的、小的农膜生产企业生产的假冒伪劣农膜产品在市场上泛滥，严重损害了广大消费者及农膜专委会会员企业的利益。因此，农膜专委会要将落实准入监管、整顿生产秩序，作为今后重点工作来抓，配合工信、工商、质监等各有关职能部门，将《农用薄膜行业准入条件》的规定落到实处；另外，农膜专委会还应建立行业准入证书制度，新建或已建的农膜生产企业在符合国家关于市场准入规定的同时，还应取得农膜专委会及当地工信局颁发的资质证书，才能从事生产、经营等活动。通过以上两条措施，保证国家整体发展战略的实施，保护广大消费者及农膜专委会会员企业的利益不受侵害。

2. 规范市场秩序，防止恶意、无序竞争

目前，由于中国农膜市场供大于求，一些新进入农膜行业的小企业为挤占销售市场，采取不正当竞争的方式和“坑农”的手段，以劣质农膜冒充优质农膜，采用极低的销售价格冲击市场；有的企业使用国外进口的聚乙烯废料，加工生产劣质农膜低价销售，扰乱市场，使国内一些大中型农膜生产企业陷入困境。另外，由于经销商的资金状况、销售能力和农业技术水平的差异，普遍存在相互压价、以次充好、售后技术服务跟不上等现象，这也给一些不正规的小农膜生产企业提供可滋生的土壤和环境。部分小的农膜经销商和生产企业缺斤短两、以次充好，坑农害农现象时有发生，严重损害了农民利益，同时也严重影响了农膜行业的正常生产经营。因此，农膜专委会将会配合有关部门对以上不正当竞争行为进行整顿，规范生产企业及经销商的经营行为；鼓励企业自发地开展技术改造及科技创新，以提高自身产品质量、完善产品功能及售后服务水平的方式参与竞争，为广大农民提供更加优质的产品及更周到的服务。

3. 培育驰名商标，实施品牌战略

品牌是企业的标志、品牌是企业的灵魂、企业的生命线。中国的农膜生产企业要想做大、做强，在激烈的市场竞争中生存，就必须加强自身的品牌建设，把品牌战略作为保证企业持久发展的重要工作来抓。树立自己企业的品牌形象，让消费者认同企业的产品，进而购买和使用。这样才能促进企业积极主动地搞好生产和经营，维护自身的利益。因此，农膜专委会将会把积极推进农膜企业品牌建设工作作为“十二五”期间的重点工作来抓。支持企业把争创中国驰名商标、省著名商标作为管理和发展的重要目标，推动企业积极开展ISO9001质量管理体系认证工作。发挥典型示范和带动作用，积极推进实施品牌战略示范企业创建工作。推进企业实行先进的质量和产品标准，积极开展质量、环境、职业安全健康等认证工作，不断完善质量管理和保证体系。推动出口企业提高使用和注册自主商标的比例。

4. 注重人才培养，提高国内农膜行业科技及管理水平

我国农膜产品与国外先进水平相比较，存在品种少，高档产品比例低、流滴及耐老化功能时间短等缺点。除了生产设备落后老化等原因，主要的还是科技水平及管理上的差距。在竞争全球化的今天，中国农膜生产企业若要参与到国际市场的竞争，就必须提高科技及管理水平。而提高科技及管理水平，就必须注重人才的培养和引进。因此，农膜专委会鼓励农膜生产企业培养和引进高级技术和管理人才，鼓励企业针对产品质量及企业管理方面的改革与创新，支持企业通过内、外招聘的方式加强职工队伍素质建设，并以技术交流的方式，提高行业内科技人员的业务素质，为提高国内农膜行业科技及管理水平培养人才。

5. 积极推动行业内各项指标及产品标准的制定工作，争取达到国际先进水平

目前，国内农膜企业所制定的各项指标，包括原料消耗、能源消耗、制造费用、管理费用等，存在混乱、落后等现象，不利于企业降低生产成本；农膜产品标准与国际先进水平相比，落后的程度更大，聚乙烯地覆薄膜标准GB/13735—92已经20年没有修订。这些都严重制约了中国农膜产业的健康发展因此，农膜专委会将组织企业间进行交流活动，介绍先进经验，以达到降低生产成本、提高产品质量的目的。积极推动农膜行业各项先进指标及先进的产品标准制定工作，争取达到国际先进水平。

【重点企业介绍】

白山市喜丰塑料股份有限公司

白山市喜丰塑料（集团）股份有限公司是全国农膜行业排头兵企业，主要生产农用薄膜、节水器材、汽车零部件、化工制品、纸制品等七大系列200多种产品。公司占地面积30万平方米，现有职工1650人，通过多年的内外招聘，使专业技术人员达到490人，占员工总人数的30%。喜丰公司年产农膜能力120kt，产值12亿元，2012年农膜产量60kt，其中pvc农膜23kt，农膜产销量连续多年居全国第一，是目前亚洲最大的农用薄膜生产企业。曾先后荣获全国五一劳动奖状和全国首批“重合同、守信用”企业、全国文明单位等荣誉称号。喜丰农膜荣获中国名牌产品、吉林省名牌产品，“喜丰”牌商标荣获中国驰名商标。喜丰公司始终以振兴民族工业为已任，以

"让喜丰产品为亿万农民带来最大收益"为企业宗旨，坚持"一切服从质量、一心为了用户"的质量方针，在全国农膜企业率先通过ISO9001质量体系认证，喜丰农膜已成为广大农民心中的知名品牌。

喜丰节水器材产品自投放市场以来深受广大农民用户欢迎，产品供不应求，并已经出口到美国、西班牙、泰国、洪都拉斯、突尼斯等20多个国家和地区，2012年出口创汇共计200万美元。在吉林省十二五期间新增1000万亩玉米膜下滴灌工程当中，喜丰公司2012年承揽了20万亩的总体安装工程并圆满地完成了工程设计、施工等工作，收到了巨大的社会效益和经济效益，为农民致富做出重要贡献。

天津市天塑集团有限公司第二塑料制品厂

天津市天塑集团有限公司第二塑料制品厂始建于1956年，是国家轻工系统大型农用薄膜专业生产企业，主要产品"兰花"牌农用薄膜，年综合生产能力50kt。企业现拥有专业工程技术人员124人，占全部职工总数24.8%，现有各类专业设备162台(套)，建有省级企业技术中心，固定资产总额3亿元。企业是中国塑料加工协会理事、农用薄膜专委会副理事长单位、中国农用塑料应用技术学会副理事长单位。与国际、国内多家著名公司合作，企业竞争力、综合实力始终保持在国内同行业领先位置。

作为国家定点农用薄膜制造企业，第二塑料制品厂一直是我国农用薄膜产品国家标准制定主要参与单位。经历了计划经济向市场经济变革，作为国内几大农用薄膜制造企业之一，承担着我国农业建设的历史重任，确保粮经作物保障供给发挥了不可替代的作用。"兰花"牌农用薄膜被广泛应用到全国20多个省、市、自治区，产品深受广大用户的好评。相继荣获国家和相关部委颁发多项荣誉："兰花"牌产品荣获国家银质奖，企业通过了ISO9000质量保证体系国际认证，国家免检产品称号，被国家商务部认定为应急物资供应单位，少数民族用品定点生产企业、并先后被评为亿万农村消费者信得过产品、天津市著名商标、天津市名牌产品、中国名牌、中国驰名商标等荣誉。

2008年11月由于市政快速路工程，企业整体搬迁到天津北辰区西堤头塑料工业园区。企业认真研究国外、国内的农膜生产形式，结合自身的硬件和软件水平，提升IE、IT管理、加大技术改造、生产设备改造。2011年企业产销量达55kt，创历史最好水平。

企业下一步发展方向："十二五"期间企业定位以服务"三农"为主线，以产业政策为导向，加快企业科技进步，努力提高整体水平，加快农膜产品结构调整，通过技术研发、加快产品升级换代，在"十二五"期间高档农膜产销量争取占全国60%达到全国第一，综合能力达到行业龙头地位。

山东清田塑工有限公司

山东清田塑工有限公司隶属山东清源集团有限公司，成立于1998年，是一家集科研开发、产品生产、技术服务于一体的农用塑料薄膜生产企业。现有职工300人，注册资本8000万元，拥有吹塑生产设备80余台套，年生产加工能力50kt。现为中国塑料加工工业协会副理事长单位、中国农用塑料应用技术学会副会长单位、中国农用塑料专委会副会长单位。2011年被认定为"高新技术企业"，2012年又被国家科技部认定为"国家火炬计划重点高新技术企业"。

主要产品有"清田"牌微地膜和功能膜两大系列。微地膜系列产品包括：普通聚乙烯地面覆盖薄膜、黑色除草地膜、化学除草地膜、无滴地膜、银灰地膜、配色地膜、红外增温地膜。功能膜系列产品包括：长寿膜、耐候流滴膜、多功能膜、转光膜、紫光膜、防雾型三层复合高保温日光温室专用膜、PE缠绕膜、热收缩膜等产品。产品覆盖全国29个省、市、自治区，是国内农用塑料薄膜行业的龙头企业。公司率先在同行业通过了ISO9001质量管理体系、ISO14001环境管理体系和OHSAS18001职业健康安全管理体系三体系认证。"清田"牌农用塑料薄膜为"国家免检产品"、"中国名牌产品"、"山东名牌产品"，"清田牌"商标为"中国驰名商标"。

公司注重科研开发，同大专院校、科研院所建立了密切的合作关系，聘请了高级工程师、农艺师为技术顾问，建立了省级企业技术中和省内唯一的功能性塑料薄膜工程技术研究中心。拥有国家发明、实用新型和外观设计专利34项。"表面涂覆型长效流滴复合膜"等三项科研成果通过省级科技成果鉴定。承担了多项"国家重点新产品计划"和"国家火炬计划"。每年都有3～5个新产品的上市，确保企业的可持续发展。

公司一直坚持"清田产品、如同人品；以心血炼精品，以人品铸品牌"的"以质取信"经营理念，不断调整产业结构和经营模式，秉承"品行天下"的发展理念，为农业提供更多更好的优质产品，为"三农"服好务，为发展民族经济作出应有的贡献。

四川省犍为罗城忠烈塑料有限责任公司

四川省犍为罗城忠烈塑料有限责任公司是国家民委、财政部、中国人民银行指定的"全国少数民族特需用品"定点生产企业、是中国塑料加工工业协会副会长单位、是四川省名牌产品、也是四川省农业生产资料总公司超薄强力微膜定点生产厂家。

公司经过20多年的拼搏努力，产品现已远销全国各地，年销售率已达80%，拥有广阔的市场发展空间、稳定的销售网络和极强的市场竞争力。产品主要有农膜、地膜、微膜、超强微膜、大棚膜、黑膜等。2011年农膜产量达30kt。

公司被中国塑料加工工业协会评为首批“AAA”信用等级企业、被中国农行乐山市分行评为“AA”信誉企业。公司生产的“麒麟”牌产品，通过四川省产品质量监督检验院检验，各项指标均超过省标准，“麒麟”牌注册商标被四川省工商行政管理局评为四川省“著名商标”被乐山市工商行政管理局评为“嘉州人民最喜爱的产品”。

北京华盾雪花塑料集团有限责任公司

北京华盾雪花塑料集团有限责任公司始建于1965年，主要生产农膜、土工防渗材料、容器托盘、包装制品、塑料管材、微喷滴灌等产品，主导产品功能性农膜自1980年起保持产销量国内第一，土工防渗材料、吹塑托盘和中空容器的市场占有率也名列前茅。

集团技术力量雄厚，拥有多项自主知识产权，成功研发了从普通棚膜，到长寿棚膜、流滴保温长寿棚膜、高保温流滴长寿棚膜、高保温日光温室膜等第一、二、三代系列产品。经过几代职工的共同努力，企业培育了华盾知名品牌，形成了核心能力，也是今天华盾人共享的财富和荣誉。

集团1999年在业内率先通过ISO9001质量体系认证，2000年建成一流的检测中心，并荣获“北京市质量管理先进单位”和“行业用户满意企业”称号，现为中国塑料加工工业协会副理事长单位和中国农用塑料应用技术学会农用塑料制品分会理事长单位。2009年公司荣获中国轻工业联合会“科学技术进步奖”，并被中国塑协评为“中国塑料行业先进单位”。集团拥有完善的市场信息、市场销售系统，产品销往全国各27个省区、直辖市及俄罗斯、日本、东南亚、美国等国家和地区。

山东天鹤塑胶股份有限公司

山东天鹤塑胶股份有限公司是国内大型塑料加工企业，拥有20年薄膜产品的生产开发经验，占地面积100000m²；现为中国塑料加工工业协会副会长，农膜专委会副会长、中国农用塑料应用技术学会农塑制品分会理事、中国土工合成材料工程协会会员，省、市级“重合同、守信用”企业，2005年度外贸出口先进单位，山东省塑料行业综合实力50强企业。2005年“天鹤牌”工业工程膜被评为山东名牌，2006年“齐大牌”农用塑料薄膜被评为“国家免检产品”和“山东名牌”。公司2004年已通过ISO9001质量管理体系认证，2006年通过ISO14000环境管理体系认证。2009年5月评为中国塑料行业先进单位，2010年获国家高新技术企业称号，2012年获轻工系统卓越绩效先进企业，2012年11月被认定为山东省技术中心企业。公司现有员工239人，其中各类专业人员60余人，从事研究开发的技术人员42人，其中包括硕士以上和国家级农膜专家、高级工程师14人。公司拥有各种塑料加工设备78台套，其中有引进国际先进技术水平意大利道尔奇公司的三层共挤农膜专用生产设备，另有三套国产大型三层共挤设备其关键装置IBC自动控制系统和冷却定型系统是从加拿大引进的，全部装备及试验检测设备技术水平国内领先，年加工能力70000吨。现有三大系列主导产品：一是农用PE、EVA吹塑棚膜系列产品；二是土工合成材料系列产品；三是聚烯烃包装膜系列产品。2010年开始进行“年产20kt涂覆型持久流滴消雾膜项目”的建设，2011年底完成投产，成为国内“涂覆型持久流滴消雾膜”产能最大、产量最高、质量最好、销量第一的企业。

2004年参与了GB 4455—2006“农业用聚乙烯薄膜”、GB/T 20202—2006“农业用乙烯-醋酸乙烯酯共聚物薄膜”两个国家标准的修订、制定项目；2010年参加了GB/T 17643—2010土工合成材料聚乙烯土工膜标准制定，并于2012年正式发布，主持起草了两个行业标准，“集装箱运输用聚乙烯袋内衬膜”“涂覆持久型聚乙烯棚膜”两个标准的制定，2013年6月专家审定会通过。公司自主研制开发的国内外最大幅宽土工合成材料厚型聚乙烯土工膜、工程施工配套产品土工膜连接锁畅销国内外市场，产品的技术性能达到并超过了美国土工合成材料学会GRIGM13/GM17的标准要求，出口量居行业第一；2005年被中国塑料工业协会授予“土工合成材料生产出口基地”。公司自主开发的聚乙烯热收缩膜专供青岛啤酒集团使用，聚乙烯拉伸缠绕膜和多层复合高阻隔保鲜包装膜远销北美和东南亚市场。2011年“齐大”“天喜”牌农膜的国内市场占有率2%以上，农地膜市场占有率及总量、聚乙烯土工膜市场占有率及总量均名列同行业前茅。

公司坚持以科技求发展，以质量求生存，依靠过硬的产品质量和完善的售后服务体系赢得了广大用户的信赖。

聊城华塑工业有限公司

聊城华塑工业有限公司成立于1996年，现拥有总资产1.1亿元，占地面积7万m²，年加工多种功能农用大棚膜能力80kt。现已发展成为集科研、生产、贸易和技术服务为一体的国内最大农用薄膜生产企业之一。

公司是中国塑料加工工业协会常务理事单位，山东省文明诚信标兵单位，山东省政府轻工业规划重点支持企业，产品获得山东省名牌称号，并承担了多项山东省科技发展计划项目、创新基金项目。

近年来，公司投入巨额资金开发新技术新产品，对涂覆液体、涂覆装备和涂覆型镜面温室膜产品、工艺配方进行了全面研究与开发，共申报了22项国家专利，已获专利证书13项，其中发明专利9项。

目前，华塑公司涂覆型镜面温室膜技术研发处于国内外领先地位，是第一家集研制涂覆液体、自制涂覆装置、并生产成品的企业。华塑独创专利技术——聚合物基纳米复合材料，是国内外唯一不用电晕就能在线涂覆的液体；华塑在线涂覆装置生产流程最短，可以做到常温固化，最大限度减少皱折和粘连；由于不用电晕，华塑镜面温室膜具有更优异的亲水性、高透明性、更高的强度。产品自2010年投放市场以来深受客户好评，2011年，该系列产品获得科技部国家重点新产品荣誉称号。

公司还率先将光催化杀菌技术应用到农用薄膜生产，试验出杀菌除臭禽畜养殖专用大棚膜；并最早实施利用大棚膜全面优化自然界光波(含生物防治)，国内第一家采用内添加和表面处理两种工艺试验出生物防害农用大棚膜，为大棚种植绿色蔬菜提供了条件。

追求永无止境，发展没有终点。聊城华塑公司将始终以“抓质量、重科研、树品牌”为发展宗旨，为“三农”服务，为中国农膜赶超世界先进水平作出应有的贡献。

杭州新光塑料有限公司

杭州新光塑料有限公司(前身杭州新光塑料厂)，创建于1964年，是国内塑料行业的骨干企业。公司总资产2.8亿元，占地126亩，建筑面积3.5万m^2，拥有专业生产线60余条，现拥有年生产各类塑料薄膜4万多吨(农用大棚膜20kt)的能力，年销售额达6亿元。

公司大股东——浙江明日控股集团有限公司为国内塑料界知名企业，浙江省塑料贸易龙头企业，年销售各类塑料原料100余万吨，年经营规模100亿元，总资产逾10亿元，为大型综合性企业集团，实力雄厚。

新光凭借近四十年从事塑料加工的经验和二十年成功引进国内外一流的专业设备和技术经验。充分发挥工贸结合的优势，依靠创新的意识、科学的管理造就了品质一流的各类产品，始终以“精益求精、尽善尽美”为质量宗旨，严格执行ISO9001等认证工业体系，被中国质量诚信促进会评为浙江省质量诚信消费者信得过单位，公司是中国塑料加工协会农用薄膜专业委员会副理事长单位，企业资信3A级和纳税信誉3A级企业。公司拥有市级企业技术中心，以雄厚的技术实力不懈致力于新产品的开发，并为用户量身定制各种性能卓越的特种农膜，不断延伸农膜的内涵、功能和应用领域。公司产品荣获轻优、省优称号，省市“科技进步奖”，被评为浙江省著名商号。

现有主要产品：包装材料系列产品如流延CPP蒸煮级、镀铝级、复合级、餐巾纸包装及各特殊要求产品用膜；吹膜的牙膏片材、性能优异的热封膜等；软包装系列产品如食品包装膜、液体包装膜、脱氧剂、干燥剂包装等；农膜产品系列是长寿膜，蔬菜、西瓜、葡萄等瓜果及花卉专用膜，食用菌隔热膜，高保温EVA长寿流滴消雾膜，多功能地膜，黑地膜，反光膜，和宽幅集装箱袋膜和收缩膜等二十多种产品。

山东寿光龙兴农膜有限公司

山东寿光龙兴农膜有限公司是山东寿光健元春有限公司的子公司，公司综合实力强，技术力量雄厚，是五层共挤复合EVA日光温室大棚膜、EVOH/PA复合土壤杀菌消毒熏蒸膜、牧草青储膜、粮食熏蒸膜、水产养殖膜、液体包装膜等高档农用薄膜的大型专业生产企业，是中国塑料加工工业协会农用薄膜专业委员会副主任单位，公司生产的“龙兴”牌大棚膜是山东名牌产品，“龙兴”商标为中国驰名商标。

公司拥有自营进出口权，获得“出口产品质量许可证”、“出口危险货物包装容器生产企业质量许可证”，通过了ISO9001：2008质量管理体系认证、美国AIB认证、HACCP认证、英国皇冠体系标志认证，成立了潍坊市功能性农用大棚薄膜工程技术研究中心和市级企业技术中心。

公司拥有从意大利引进的具有当今世界先进水平的五层共挤复合膜设备、国产三层共挤复合膜设备和单层农地膜、包装膜生产设备20余台，农地膜年生产能力60kt，其中五层共挤复合膜生产线是目前国内唯一一条可以生产五层共挤宽幅高档农膜的生产设备。

公司注重技术创新，加大先进装备的投入和各类专业技术人才的引进，与中国农科院、山东农业大学等全国多所知名院校、科研院所都建立了长期的产学研联合关系。

山东寿光龙兴农膜有限公司近几年发展迅猛，

是农膜行业发展潜力较大的企业。

保定宝理塑研塑料有限公司

保定宝理塑研塑料有限公司是一家集农地膜、包装膜研发、生产、销售于一体的大型塑料制品加工生产企业，其前身为国有河北宝硕集团下属骨干企业，2008年因河北宝硕集团破产改制发展而成。公司秉承了原河北宝硕集团优良的资产，良好的工作作风，精湛的加工技艺，主要生产1～16m LDPE、LLDPE、mLLDPE、EVA、PO高中档农膜、地面覆盖膜、功能性大棚膜及各种三层、五层、七层PE、PA、EVOH等阻隔包装膜、收缩膜等系列产品，年生产能力60kt。公司研发的EVA系列日光膜和PO系列光生态长效日光温室采用世界一流的美国三层共挤机组制造，产品性能居国内领先。

公司汇集了一批锐意创新的优秀塑料挤出专业化人才，拥有博士、研究生导师1人，中国塑料加工工业协会专家委员会委员、中国包装联合会特聘专家各一人，硕士研究生2人，高级工程师2人，工程师15人，大专以上专业技术人员占员工总数的70%，公司积20余年的专业生产经验，凭借雄厚的技术力量以及与高等院校、科研单位产学研合作平台，推陈出新、引进技术、不断开发新技术产品，完善产品设计，公司本着“扎根农业、服务农户、追求质量、不断进取”的经营理念，秉承"制度创新，技术创新，管理创新，市场创新"的企业精神，致力于研发、生产一流质量的产品，努力打造中国名牌，争做行业龙头，牢固树立产品质量和服务质量意识，为广大农民提供优质的产品和满意的服务，以高度的社会责任感和使命感，雄厚的实力、成熟的魄力，为中国农膜行业的技术进步和事业的发展贡献自己的力量。

公司拥有国际、国内先进水平的生产设备，完善的检测手段以及成熟的工艺，产品质量稳定可靠。公司目前拥有各种先进吹膜、印刷、复合设备近百余台套，包括引进世界最先进水平的美国七层共挤吹膜生产线一条、巴登菲尔三层共挤生产线四条、德国Alpine公司三层共挤生产线两条，国内最先进的进口8.5m五层涂覆型大棚膜生产线一条、国内知名品牌功能性地膜设备20余台套、输水膜设备两台套、三层共挤包装膜设备十余套、德国W&H八色柔版印刷机一台、陕西北人九色、八色凹版印刷机两台、其他辅助设备数十套。所有农用大棚膜、包装膜设备均采用IBC自动膜泡控制，采用超声波传感器自动控制膜径宽度。引进的美国巴登菲尔公司PO膜设备配置水平国内领先：自动风环及在线自动测厚系统有效地控制薄膜的厚薄均匀度，带制冷装置的IBC系统提高了产品的光学性能。

公司不仅拥有国内外一流的农地膜、包装膜生产、控制设备，还拥有大批的产品检验仪器：全自动万能拉力机，水分测试仪，雾度仪，快速流滴实验仪，高倍分层显微镜，密度仪等，为产品质量起到了保驾护航的积极作用。

公司占地面积110亩，拥有现代化标准厂房面积达25000m^{2}以上。拥有数千万元固定资产和精良设备，致力于为客户提供一流的产品服务。雄厚的综合实力保证了宝理产品技术、质量、价格方面的优势，产品深受市场欢迎。

河南省银丰塑料有限公司

河南省银丰塑料有限公司始建于2004年，以生产塑料制品为主导产品，是一家科、工、贸一体的综合型民营企业，企业拥有大中型吹塑膜机制袋生产线，分切生产线，彩印生产线，各种功能型母粒、色母粒生产线、复合膜生产线及完备的塑料制品的化验检测设备。主要生产各种规格的农、地膜，功能膜，长寿无滴膜，缠绕膜，包装彩印膜，管材等几十个品种。

公司始终坚持“诚信、质优、惠农、利民”的经营理念，优化管理，强练内功，外树形象，扩大市场占有率。自公司成立以来，不断发展壮大，每年一个新台阶，每天都有新变化，先后被授于“河南省优秀民营企业”、“河南省高成长型民营企业”、“河南省百高企业”。公司生产的“增产牌”“华丰牌”塑料薄膜系列产品被评为“河南省优质产品”，“河南省名牌产品”和“河南省著名商标”。被省质量技术监督局评为“质量诚信AAA级企业”；企业还被河南省银行协会评为优良信用客户，被郑州海关评为A类进出口企业。优质的产品和完善的服务得到了全国各地经销商和农民的一致好评，产品畅销全国各地。企业拥有自营进出口权。公司出口产品分三大类四十多个品种，出口到美国、法国、西班牙、澳大利亚，荷兰、日本等几十个国家，广泛应用于建筑、医药、航空等领域。凭借良好的信誉，公司成为世界500强企业“埃克森美孚”在中国的“核心战略合作伙伴”。现在银丰公司已经发展成河南省最大的塑料薄膜生产企业。

安徽华驰塑业有限公司

安徽华驰塑业有限公司成立于2007年，系安徽省2007年度徽商大会工业企业签约项目单位。公司坐落在风景秀丽、交通便捷的安徽省合肥市蜀山新产业园区，占地25.6亩，总投资近亿元。现有员工160余人，其中大专以上学历占30%。作为中国塑业加工工业协会副会长单位、中国降解塑料专委会副会长单位、中国农用薄膜专委会副主任单位、行业内首批企业信用评价 AAA 级信用企业，我公司拥有烟用农地膜 50kt、塑料购物袋、连卷袋 30kt 的年产能，产品热销四川、江西、河南、湖北、安徽、湖南等地。2011 年，我公司因为成绩突出获得合肥市经委及市财政专项资金奖励。至诚守信、追求卓越，我公司将一如既往发挥自身规模优势，致力于打造国内塑料薄膜行业第一品牌。

（中国塑料加工工业协会农用薄膜专业委员会　刘敏）

改性塑料

【行业动态】

2012 年世界经济形势面临诸多变数，下行压力不断增大，美国经济增长势头不明朗，欧洲主权债务危机短期内很难解决，加之种种摩擦争斗带来不利影响，要想在短时间内让世界经济走出低谷是很难的，复苏前景不容乐观。世界经济萎靡不振给我们带来的直接作用是就是外需不旺，特别是直接出口或间接出口为主要业务的我国众多塑料加工企业都面临着出口萎缩、订单减少、开工率不足的严峻形势。另一方面，靠政府投资拉动经济的传统模式弊病甚多，不宜频繁使用，而内需不振又是国内长期存在的客观事实。在国内外经济发展遇到困难的时刻，党和政策及时提出调结构、保增长的重大决策，做为新材料重要领域之一的塑料加工工业在科学发展观的引领下，注重科技创新和转变经济增长模式，在过去的一年里仍然取得较好的成绩。改性塑料行业做为塑料加工行业的重要方面军也不负重望，虽然整体利润下滑，但倒闭企业很少，仍然维持着较高的增长，究其原因仍然是改性塑料企业得益船小好调头，技术创新和投入容易，市场应变能力强。

2012 年改性塑料行业呈现几大特点：

1. 大力开拓非金属矿物粉体材料在塑料中应用，据粉体行业提供的数字以及我们自行推算的结果，在各种塑料制品中使用碳酸钙、滑石粉等非金属矿物粉体材料的数量有望达到 15Mt 以上，占塑料制品总产量的 12% 左右。

2. 大力强度科学地、合理地使用废旧塑料。做为一种资源再生利用，废旧塑料已不可回避地摆在社会面前，关键问题不在于要不要利用，而是如何在利用过程中实现绿色加工和高值化应用。

3. 大力研发改性塑料配方及加工艺，实现降低成本、改善性能和增加功能三大目标，不仅增强了产品市场竞争力，而且还能够以高性能价格比和高性能多功能的姿态为各行各业服务。

4. 大力开拓国内外应用市场，为改性塑料和找到更加理想的用武之地。如江苏一家公司为美国某箱包公司生产行销全球的箱包塑料配件，年需求量达 10 亿个，意味着仅此一项就是 10 亿元的产值。这说明做为世界制造基地，我们的企业仍然具备着劳动力以及能源方面的优势，同时也和我们企业科技人员的聪明才智密切相关。

5. 大力争取国家和地方政府对发展改性塑料的支持。资源节约与环境保护领域，每年都有国家的大力支持，其总投资达数百亿元。很多改性塑料企业都努力争取列入国家支持的队伍，不仅企业形象有所提升，而且在国家拨款总投资 10%，地方政府全力配套和提供土地、贷款等政策的扶持下，企业可以迈上新的台阶。

6. 加大环保方面的投入，不仅取得良好的经济效益，而要在生产过程中减少或避免对环境的污染，同时注重能源的高效利用、节能减排，努力打造经济效益和社会效益相统一的局面，为建设环境友好型社会做出贡献！

7. 科技成果推广和技术创新成为推动企业及行业发展的强大动力

在过去的一年时在，有很多科技成果得到肯定和推广，有的正在研发之中的科技项目不久将绽放出耀眼光芒。

（1）聚酯（PET）瓶片的高值化利用，从共混合金到薄膜，编织制品和工业零部件的制造，都体现出 PET 材料的优势。

（2）沉淀硫酸钡的新应用。实际应用结果表明，沉淀硫酸钡在塑料薄膜中使用较滑石粉、碳酸钙、元明粉等有更好的透明性与力学性能，其外感和手感也非常理想。

（3）木丝和废塑料制成的复合材料较之木粉有更好的性能，加之使用挤出成型工艺和设备可以制作建筑模板、物流托盘等大面积制品。

（4）无机粉体填充塑料轻量化技术可利用可控发泡工艺使塑料制品在保持良好性能的前提下，密度有较大幅度下降，可以达到 $0.8g/cm^3$ 以下。

（5）免干燥节能型 PET 挤出加工设备及大面积熔体在线过滤器的研制和应用已将 PET 瓶片的加工提到新的高度，实现节约干燥所需热能和确保 PET 分子不发生严重水解和降解。

（6）全新环保型粉体混合处理设备打造清洁生产环境，本项技术与装备已在“地球卫士”（石头纸制造企业)公司大面积应用，粉体处理车间粉尘飞扬的现象已不复存在。

【专委会工作】

1. 召开2012年年会暨改性塑料新技术、新设备、新产品展示交流大会

2012年10月19日至23日，专委会在四川省成都市石棉县西昌市召开年会，同期举办“改性塑料新技术、新设备、新产品展示交流大会”。来自全国各地二十多年省市的二百多位企业家、专家和科技管理人员出席了会议。中国塑料加工工业协会曹俭常务副理事长出席了会议开幕式并做了题为“增强行业组织凝聚力，提高服务水平，引导行业健康发展”的报告。他指出中国塑协自2011年5月换届后，在新一届领导的带领下，协会自身建设和引领行业发展两方面都取得显著成绩。在今年4月上海召开的协会六届二次理事会上，《塑料加工业十二五发展规划指导意见》获得与会代表好评，将成为今后一段时间塑料加工行业的行动指南。该规划的主要内容是依靠科技创新，大力推进技术进步，推动产业升级，着力构建现代化产业体系，推动产业结构调整，加快转变发展方式，优化产品结构、区域布局和企业组织结构，突出绿色、保环，着力实现循环和可持续发展、突出品牌战略，着力提高产业素质，着力推进由单纯依靠扩能发展向注重技术进步、优化结构、提高发展质量方向转变。他希望改性塑料专委会秉承凝聚企业、热心服务的一贯作风，在塑料加工业“十二五”发展规划的指引下，认真倾听企业呼声，研究解决行业发展的共性问题，开创改性塑料企业与行业蓬勃发展的新局面！专委会赵安赤理事长致开幕辞，他指出：改性塑料行业自20世纪80年以来迅速成长壮大，如今已成为塑料加工产业的一支最具活力和发展前景的方面军，实现了专业化、规模化和功能化的目标，形成了主营企业上千家、相关助剂、添加剂和配混加工机械制造企业数百家，从业人员数十几万人的产业大军，为塑料加工产业和国民经济建设做出了重要贡献！在回顾了改性塑料专委会自20世纪80年代由“填充塑料技术经济协作组”演变而来所走过的历程后，他强度在“广泛性、权威性、代表性”的原则指导下，专委会始终与企业团结在一起，战斗在一起，得到业内外的普遍认可和赞许。本届年会暨交流大会得到大家的热烈响应和积极参与就是专委会兴旺、行业兴旺的最有力的证明！他要求大家继续发挥改性塑料在行业中的先锋作用，发挥改性塑料在节约降耗、绿色环保和功能改性三大优势，为建设资源节约型、环境友好型、高性能价格比型的新型材料产业而奋斗！他在介绍了本届年会和交流会的主要内容和日程安排后，表示对出席会议的协会领导和各位代表，对本次活动的东道主——石棉巨丰粉体有限公司及各协办单位、支持单位表示衷心感谢！

在年会开幕式之后举办的改性塑料新技术、新设备、新产品展示交流大会上，与会专家、企业家就大家所关心的“石塑纸”、“PET瓶片高效利用”、“填充塑料减重”、“废旧塑料高值化利用”、“塑筋复合材料及大容量挤注成型机”、“新型配混与加工设备”、“免干燥节能型挤出机”、“不停机连续在线大面积过滤器”、“打造粉体处理清洁环境”等众多内容进行了详细讲解并展开热列讨论，为大家开阔眼界、明确方向和目标提供了机会和条件，也为大家沟通有无、广结挚友、扩展业务搭建了平台。

应本届会议东道主——四川石棉巨丰粉体有限公司的盛情邀请，全体代表前往石棉巨丰粉体有限公司参观考察，走进石棉、走近巨丰，大家对巨丰粉体有限公司在短短几年时间就达到年产200kt优质功能碳酸钙粉的成绩以及产销两旺的强劲发展势头表示祝贺，留下了深刻的印象。

四川是风景如画、人杰地灵的宝地，会议代表不仅收获颇丰，还欣赏了四川大自然多姿多彩的风光，特别是大会安排代表们参观了举世闻名的西昌卫星发射基地，经受了一次深刻的爱国主义教育，鼓舞了克服困难的勇气，坚实了勇往直前的信心！

大会考察期间石棉县政府举办了欢迎大会，介绍了石棉县经济发展形势及招商活动，欢迎企业家到石棉投资建厂，一展身手。

交流大会上浙江余姚中国塑料城管委会的领导向代表们介绍了正在大力建设的涉塑产业园和改性塑料交易区，热烈欢迎大家到余姚建功立业。

会议编辑印制了40多万字的“论文资料集”，不仅刊登了数十篇科技论文，而且收集整理编排了大量信息资料，为代表们提供了丰富的知识和多方位的商机，成为业内人士的新“助手”和“朋友”。

本届年会和交流、参观考察活动得多家企业的鼎力支持，除东道主石棉巨丰粉体有限公司为代表们提供了奔波一千多公里的舒适大客车并赠送极富石棉地方特色的纪念品——汉白玉熊猫和松茸外，深圳市新彩再生材料科技有限公司独家赞助冠名为“金秋新彩”的专委会欢迎酒会；重庆可益荧新材料有限公司为酒会抽奖活动独家赞助了一百多份奖品；福建龙岩市亿丰粉碎机械有限公司和石棉巨丰粉体有限公司联手赞助了在西昌市举行的欢送酒会——彝族风情共享，双丰助你前行！这些企业的慷慨解囊，为本次会议的成功，始终处于欢乐气氛之中奠

定了坚实的物质基础，对此专委会和全体代表表示由衷的感谢！

2. 对行业和企业的共性问题和科技进步的动向进行调研，协助企业做好科技成果鉴定及各类项目的申报工作

为企业服务，引导行业依靠科技进步健康发展是专委会的职责和义务。专委会几位主要领导应邀到会员单位进行考察，并给予必要的指导和建议。一年来曾到如下企业进行考察，实行面对面服务。

(1) 去内蒙古大唐国际再生资源开发有限公司参加“第一届高铝粉煤灰综合利用技术交流会”，就活性硅酸钙在塑料中的应用前景发表意见。

(2) 去江西(南昌)恒大高新技术股份有限公司就塑料行业所需非矿产品的要求与资源形势发表意见。

(3) 为海城金昌技术有限公司起草“30Mt 宿松滑石矿开采及深加工项目可行性研究报告”及“宿松滑石矿及产业链开发建议方案”。

(4) 参观在北京新国际展览中心举办的“第十九届中国(北京)国际建筑装饰及材料博览会”暨“第十三届中国(北京)国际墙纸布艺家居软装博览会”，就“地球卫士”环保科技有限公司和辽宁华兴新材料纸业有限公司的“石塑纸”产品的市场反应和发展前景进行考察了解。

(5) 参加中国国际咨询公司组织的国家发改委下达的“资源节约与环境保护 2012 年国家预算项目复审会”，对部分有关废旧塑料综合利用项目的水平进行评审。

(6) 在上海国际橡塑工业展览会期间，组织数十位改性塑料专委会会员单位代表参观专委会副理事长单位——上海心尔新材料科技有限公司。

(7) 参加中国国际工程咨询公司组织的“重庆大足循环经济园区项目”调研考察活动，对废旧塑料综合利用的新模式和新要求提供建议。

(8) 协助石家庄德倍隆科技有限公司申请高新技术企业，提供指导意见和建议。

(9) 赴辽宁本溪华兴新材料纸业有限公司和海城金昌滑石粉实业有限公司进行走访考察，了解“石塑纸”的加工设备及工艺，并就石塑纸的定位和应用前景进行讨论。

(10) 赴大连忠益塑筋机械有限公司考察新型木塑复合材料的特点及大型挤注加工设备，就其建筑模板产品的性能如何改进发表意见。

(11) 参观大连聚兴塑胶材料有限公司，对该公司的成立历程和目前的生产与科技动态进行了解并提出建议。

(12) 应广西梧州苍梧县人民政府邀请，组织五人专家组前往考察，对苍梧县再生塑料循环经济产业园区筹建献计献策。

(13) 前往河南驻马店嘉石新材料科技有限公司就正在建设的重钙粉体加工项目发表意见。

(14) 参加中国无机盐工业协会钙镁盐分会组织的专家组赴湖北荆门市参观考察“凯龙化工集团股份有限公司的”纳米碳酸钙工程，就其生产设备、工艺及纳米碳酸钙在塑料中的应用前景发表意见。

(15) 赴武汉参观中塑联新材料科技湖北有限公司，对该公司近年来取得的超常发展表示祝贺，并就在北京成立公司并与专委会进行合作进行了讨论。

(16) 中塑联(北京)新材料科技有限公司举办开业典礼，邀请中国塑协曹俭常务副理事长及协会各部门工作人员参加庆典。该公司为改性塑料专委会提供至少 $25m^2$ 的办公面积，同时也成为专委会副理事长单位，为专委会举办小型活动提供了最适宜的场所。

(17) 应江西省永丰县人民政府邀请，参加由清华大学化工系牵头的专家组前往考察，为永丰县碳酸钙产业链起草十年百亿的发展规划。

(18) 应邀参加常州市永明机械制造有限公司的科技成果鉴定会，鉴定委员会对该公司研发的编织袋产品涂膜所必须使用的单机双面同步涂膜、复膜机给予了很高评价，认为已达到国际先进水平。

(19) 参观南京创博机械设备有限公司，对该公司的新技术应用和新设备的研发制造留下深刻印象，对多方合作研制 PET 瓶片改性并制造薄膜、编织制品及注塑制品的可行性进行了探讨。

(20) 参观南京橡塑机械厂有限公司新建并投入使用的生产基地，该公司是我国小型平行同向双螺杆挤出机的创始单位，多年来为改性塑料行业提供了大量装备，做出了巨大贡献！如今生产厂区从闹市搬到工业园区，重新焕发出青春的光芒。

(21) 前往重庆巴王矿业有限公司考察，该公司地处乌江江边，距长江主航道仅 2km，因此从长江上游一路下行到长三角地区十分便利。该公司的自有方解石资源十分丰富，相信不久后将成为我国非金属矿的重要加工生产和销售基地，该公司也正在为不久将来迈上重钙加工与应用重点单位的台阶而积极开展立项、合资开发等工作。

(22) 组成专家组前往湖北省咸丰县瀑源化工有限公司考察。该公司地处的咸丰县拥有目前全国范围内质地最优的方解石矿山，而且储量极为丰富，我们一方面为优质资源不当利用造成浪费而痛心，一方面又对咸丰地区的碳酸钙产业走上兴旺发展之

路抱有信心。

(23) 组织专家组应邀前往上海优珀斯特材料科技有限公司，对该公司研制生产的交叉复合薄膜产品性能和加工工艺设备及产品特点做了详尽的了解，认为该产品性能及加工工艺设备都颇具特色，建议尽快做好准备，由中国轻工业联合会组织进行科技成果鉴定，专家组对其准备工作提出了指导性意见和建议。

(24) 组织专家组前往黄岩誉隆工贸有限公司进行考察。该公司计划用废旧塑料经改性成为专用料用于电动自行车外塑料覆盖件的生产，当地政府对该企业给予了大力支持，正在争取列入资源节约与环境保护方面的发改委 2013 年中央投资预算项目，专家组给予了充分肯定并做了申报项目的具体指导。

(25) 组织专家组前往浙江荣新工贸有限公司，该公司使用废旧塑料制作物流托盘，年产量达 20kt 以上，是浙江省最大的注塑塑料托盘生产企业。该公司为了保证托盘质量，在大量使用废旧塑料的情况下，而对社会上收购来的废旧塑料颗粒无法确保其性能稳定，固要自已上 50kt/a 的废旧塑料改性项目，对此专家组全力以赴支持并为其出谋划策，并建议在申报国家预算投资项目的同时，积极寻找物美价廉稳定的废旧塑料资源。

(26) 参观浙江通力改性工程塑料有限公司，该公司从一个废旧塑料加工街道小厂，如今成为填海造地几十亩，盖起数座现代化标准厂房的大型改性塑料加工厂，足以说明改性塑料行业的生命力之旺盛。该公司最稀缺的就是申报各种成果、专利及科技项目的材料撰写能力，缺乏申请经验和渠道。为了培育行业骨干企业，打造名牌，专委会可以在这方面加强服务，为企业做出有益有贡献!

(27) 组织专家组前往宁波宇龙塑料机械有限公司参观考察。该公司是通过改性技术将废旧塑料加工成几乎和全新树脂一样性能的颗粒料方面做得最好的企业之一，目前已完成全新厂区的建设，企业将登上新的台阶。该公司最需要的是专利的申报、科技成果的总结提升，各类科技项目材料的撰写和上报渠道，对此专家组提出了中肯的建议并给予必要的帮助。

(28) 参观考察位于祖国西南边陲的南宁市的科易德贸易有限公司，在长期从事贸易业务的基础上，该公司决定自已从事填充母料和色母料的生产，在产品品种和生产关键技术方面急需给予帮助和指导，专委会可在这方面提供全方位的服务。

(29) 组织专家组参观昆山科信橡塑机械有限公司，对该公司在混炼设备设计、制造和应用方面的进展做了详尽的了解。该公司曾于 2010 年专委会举办成立二十周年纪念活动时接待过会议代表，与当时相比，企业已搬入全新的厂房，设备销售形势大好，企业管理水平也进一步提升，其发展过程所取得的宝贵经组十分值得总结和推广。

(30) 率领部分企业领导参观阜新鑫克机械制造有限公司，了解粉体处理设备在保护清洁生产环境方面的新理念和新设计思路。该公司的数十套粉体处理设备已运行数年，其生产环境没有出现粉尘飞扬的情况。这对解决目前许多企业处理碳酸钙粉体而出现的粉尘飞扬污染周围环境问题树立了样板，带来了希望。

(31) 应广西投资集团有限公司邀请，中国无机盐工业协会钙镁盐分会组织专家组到文本南宁对文本碳酸钙产业的发展规划进行调研。广西的重钙和轻钙都已成为改性塑料的重要原料基地，但广西不满足于低值原料供应商的地位，希望重新整合区内碳酸钙产业并重视深加工应用行业的发展。专家组为此进行了论证并提出了建议。

3. 参加兄弟专委会和上下游行业的技术交流和经贸洽谈活动，汲取经验、互通情况，宣传改性塑料行业所取得的科技进步，提出对其他行业的希望和要求，携手共进，共创多赢!

主要会议和活动有：

中国塑协六届二次理事会(上海)

中国无机盐工业协会钙镁盐分会 2012 年年会(大连)

中国国际生物降解塑料应用研讨会(上海)

2012 高分子导电——抗静电第二届国际研讨会(上海)

2012 全国塑编产业链技术交流与市场对接会暨沈阳康平塑编经贸展洽会(沈阳)

2012 塑料新材料、新技术、新成果交流会暨中国塑协专家委员会二届四次会议(成都)

4. 召开骨干会员单位参加的专委会理事长办公会议，传达于 2011 年年底召开的专委会工作会议等上级协会的精神，商讨 2012 年年会会议地点及内容和当年的各项工作。

5. 参与由全国塑料标准化技术委员会改性塑料分会(SAC/TC15/SC10)组织的“改性塑料的环保要求和标识”、“改性塑料用阻燃剂黑点和异色点的测定”、“塑料丙烯腈 - 丁二烯 - 苯乙烯/聚甲基丙烯酸甲酯合金”三项国家标准的编写和评审工作，此三个标准已于 2012 年 11 月初召开的年会上获得通过，正式报批之中。

6. 根据上级协会的要求，对专委会工作进一步

规范化，为争创五A级协会创造条件

(1) 停办会刊《塑料改性通讯》

自1987年起，经当时的轻工业部塑料工业局批准成立中国塑料工程学会塑料改性专业委员会，创办会刊《塑料改性通讯》，后又经中国轻工总会信息中心同意做为内部资料免费交流。至2011年底，共编辑印刷71集，共计100多万字。会刊深受企业欢迎，为众多企业家所珍藏，并成为企业领导和科技人员的助手与朋友。该会刊不登载广告，不在市面上出售，经税务局审查也未提出任何异议。时至今日，书面交流已被电子信息冲击而趋于消沉，我们也应当审时度势，与时俱进，故决定坚决贯彻上级协会指示，停止编辑此会刊。

(2) 遵照会员部要求在吸收新会员时将协会会员登记表同时发给申请单位，做到专委会理事单位入会时同时也成为中国塑协会员单位。

(3) 规范财务制度。

7. 积极推进专委会组织建设，不断吸纳有经济实力和重大影响力的企业为专委会会员单位，团结广大企业家、专家、科技人员和管理营销人员，把专委会建成行业发展的核心力量。

8. 坚决执行国家有关规定，谢绝社会上一切与改性专委会的合作意向洽谈，表明必须先与中国塑协商谈的立场。

(中国塑料加工工业协会改性塑料专业委员会　刘英俊)

中空制品

一、塑料中空制品(瓶、桶、箱、托盘等)发展现状及趋势

三十年来，随着我国市场经济的发展，塑料中空制品发生了很大的变化，新原料、新技术、新设备层出不穷，产品结构也发生了很大的变化，从单一小型包装桶、瓶向多品种、多样化、大型化、功能化方面迅速发展。根据有关数据显示，2012年，全国塑料中空制品(塑料瓶、塑料桶、塑料箱、塑料托盘等)总产量超过7Mt。饮料、啤酒、矿泉水、药品、化工、日用化妆品、汽车等广阔市场持续增长，促进了塑料中空制品的发展，现简要分述如下。

(一) 塑料饮料瓶市场潜力诱人

塑料包装容器应用市场广阔，其中，饮料行业有着诱人商机，汽水、果汁、蔬菜汁、饮料所需的塑料容器需求量与日俱增。近年来我国软饮料消费持续快速增长，年均增长率达到20%，预计未来几年，我国软饮料产量仍可维持15%～20%的增速，至2017年产量将超过2.5亿吨。

2012年1～12月，全国软饮料的产量达130240kt，同比增长11.99%。其中，全国包装饮用水类的产量达55627kt，同比增长19.2%。占软饮料总产量的43%；2012年全年果汁和蔬菜汁饮料类产量22291686t，同比增长14.23%；全国碳酸饮料的产量达13112.9kt，同比下降1.49%。从各省市的产量来看，2012年1～12月，广东省软饮料的产量达21035kt，同比增长11.56%，占全国总产量的16.15%。紧随其后的是河南省、浙江省和吉林省，分别占总产量的6.98%、6.94%和5.86%。中国成为世界第二大饮料生产国，如80%使用塑料瓶装盛，至少需塑料瓶1085亿只。

饮料行业的激烈竞争也将使吹瓶、灌装技术的发展显得更为迫切，这为以PET瓶为主要材料的软饮料包装机械制造行业提供了广阔的市场空间。初步估计，2011年我国PET瓶软饮料包装机械的市场需求量在312台套，同比增长17%，预计未来几年我国对PET瓶软饮料包装机械的市场需求量将保持年均15%的增长率，至2017年其市场需求量将超过700台套。

1. 碳酸饮料包装中PET瓶的应用比例占57.4%，市场前景看好。

目前行业中PET聚酯瓶产量较大的企业有珠海中富和上海紫江集团，分别占有国内PET瓶30%和20%的市场份额。

聚酯瓶在塑料包装行业的起步较晚。大量的注拉吹技术设备的引进，促进了PET瓶大幅度生产，并以其优良的性能，获得用户的欢迎，短短几年里，成为食用油、饮料瓶等包装的主流包装材料。同时，在化妆品、医药等行业的需求也在增加。

目前健康型饮料比重上升、而碳酸类饮料份额呈下降趋势，2012年碳酸饮料占软饮料的市场份额已经下降到21.9%，落后于饮用水25.7%以及果汁品类22.2%。而昔日风光无限的饮料界大佬可口可乐公司也在罐装饮料市场上也让出头把交椅，以10.3%的份额排于加多宝凉茶之后。

即便如此，碳酸饮料市场份额的持续下滑已是不争的事实。相关公开资料显示，2000年时，碳酸饮料在国内市场份额占比可达36%，而后的2006～2010年，其份额由30.96%下降到22.34%，今年前3季度继续下滑至21.9%。而茶饮料、果汁饮料产量在近几年却以逾3倍的速度递增。

2. 茶饮料包装瓶市场良好。

到2012年中国茶饮料产量已达到11700kt，茶饮

料在全国市场的增长幅度达到了30%，国内饮料市场上五大品类的市场份额茶饮料占15%，茶饮料行业成为中国传统茶产业的支柱，茶饮料也成为消费者最喜欢的饮料品类之一。

2012年茶饮料用聚酯瓶约134亿只，可用塑料市场容量约540kt。

3. 聚丙烯透明包装瓶的开发是近几年国内外塑料包装的一个热点。

随着透明改性剂－成核剂的开发成功，在普通PP中加入0.1%～0.4%山梨醇缩二甲苯(苯甲醛)成核剂(美国米利肯，新日本理化，二井东亚、牌号Mil－lad3988等)，高透明PP可广泛用于注射、吹挤、吹拉、挤压、热型容器、食品、药品瓶等，其价格适宜，是PS、ABS、PET、PE瓶的竞争对手，有着广阔的市场前景。

(二) 饮水包装瓶(桶)的市场

目前，包装饮用水已经取代碳酸饮料长期垄断的地位，连续多年以40%以上的比重稳居十大饮料头把交椅。根据统计数据显示，2012年1～12月，全国包装饮用水类的产量达55627kt，同比增长19.2%。占软饮料总产量的43%，康师傅、娃哈哈、农夫山泉、华润怡宝、景田五巨头占据包装饮用水市场近半份额。每年需要超过1011亿只塑料瓶。

目前，市场的5加仑饮水桶以PC、PET为主。2012年全国PC桶生产线已超过600条，每条生产线生产能力约20万个，全国饮用水桶年生产能力约为12000多万个，实际产量约10000万个。

中投顾问发布的《中国饮用水市场投资分析及前景预测报告》显示，我国瓶装饮用水行业进入稳步成长阶段，目前形成了纯净水、矿物质水、矿泉水和天然水各领风骚的局面。未来，以康师傅为代表的矿物质水，以娃哈哈、华润怡宝为代表的纯净水，以农夫山泉为代表的天然水，四强之间的竞争将更加激烈。

(三) 啤酒塑料包装瓶的应用已经开始推广

啤酒包装业国际上近几年采用的耐热聚酯瓶(PET)的发展迅速，特别是PET瓶涂层技术(等离子技术)的应用，内涂0.21mm的碳层，它的阻透性几乎与玻璃一样，同时，能承受高温灭菌处理，使其应用范围扩大，适应热灌装茶饮料等包装。

引起包装界注目的聚萘二甲酸乙二醇酯(PEN)新型聚酯瓶，正在步入啤酒业，引起啤酒包装的革命(克服啤酒瓶爆炸事件的良策)。由于PEN与PET分子结构相似，以萘环代替苯环，使PEN比PET更具有优异的阻透性、防紫外线性、耐热性、耐高温(非晶态PEN热变温度达100℃而PET仅为70℃)。由于萘是从煤焦油分离出来，我国有丰富来源，工业化生产即将实现。不久的将来，PEN将大量进入包装领域，引发继PET之后，又一次包装革命。目前，国内少量进口，但价格是PET的5倍，阻碍了PEN的应用。

2012年，全国饮料酒的产量达638.16亿升，同比增长5.96%。全国啤酒的产量达490.2亿升，同比增长3.06%。需用包装瓶(598～721)亿个；全国白酒(折65度，商品量)的产量达115.3亿升，同比增长18.55%。增速较去年同期下降12.15个百分点；全国葡萄酒的产量达13.8亿升，同比增长16.9%。

近几年来塑料包装行业多次进行技术交流，引导有关企业进行开发。从技术方面，啤酒不同于一般的碳酸饮料，即使是微量的氧气进入包装容器也会使啤酒的口味发生变化，而啤酒中CO_2的流失会影响泡沫特性，因此，如何满足保鲜度和保存期的要求，对阻隔性能要求很高。同时，在我国95%的啤酒通过巴氏灭菌方式生产，要求包装瓶的使用要耐62～67℃。这些要求成为塑料啤酒瓶开发中的关键问题。

长久以来，啤酒一直以玻璃瓶包装为主，尤其在我国，玻璃啤酒瓶的使用率达80%以上。但玻璃瓶存在的先天缺陷引发了全球寻求廉价而适用的替代品的热潮，我国也陆续出现了新型饮料酒包装容器，特别是PET啤酒包装容器，不过由于目前酿酒企业玻璃瓶灌装设备的退出成本仍然较高以及我国消费者的消费习惯等因素，PET瓶包装的啤酒发展较为缓慢。随着我国液态食品行业的快速发展及PET瓶在液态食品包装领域应用比例的不断提高，预计未来几年我国对PET瓶软饮料包装机械的市场需求量将超过700台套。

(四) 药品固体剂型包装发展前景广阔

2012年，从行业未来发展趋势来看，中国医药市场容量越来越大，规模将以14%～17%速度增长。随着医药需求和医保体系健全，我国将成为全球药品消费增长最快的地区之一，有望成为仅次于美国的药品市场。据有关资料统计，2011年中国医药包装市场容量已达到400亿元。目前，药品包装正在成为我国包装领域重要分支。随着我国医疗体制的改革，药品种类增加，药品包装形式也在发生变化。由原来的纸袋包装、塑料袋包装、玻璃瓶到现在的聚乙烯瓶、聚丙烯瓶、聚酯瓶、铝塑包装、条形包装。扭转了药品包装落后的局面。

国外药品包装已大量采用汽罩PTP包装及条形SP包装，应用于片剂、胶囊等圆体剂型包装。在国内我国药品汽罩包装以及条形复合膜包装也将成为主流并有着广阔的发展前景。

（五）大型化工液体包装容器成为新的发展热点

适用于化工液体、润滑油、涂料、化妆品等工业用桶是近几年发展起来的新型大包装容器。已成为新的发展热点，一些公司先后从国外引进200升L环塑料桶，齐鲁石化和金陵石化塑料厂从德国Mauser公司引进BM－201型吹塑机，生产国际通用危险货物、运输包装用200L自承式L型闭口刚性塑料桶，系第二代产品。1993年秦川机械厂自行设计和制造出首台国产化大型吹塑机，并在江苏吴江青云塑料厂投入运行，取得了较好的效果，以后又有多家公司与德国、台湾厂商以合作生产和合资生产方式生产大中型吹塑机，如广东金明塑料设备有限公司，利用国外技术，可生产容积达230L大桶的吹塑机，秦川机床集团有限公司(原秦川机床厂)控股的秦川未来塑料机械有限公司，现可生产不同规格8种型号吹塑机，另外张家港也有几家能生产大中型中空容器的机械厂，例如上海帆顺实业有限公司在上海化工区投资1.2亿元建造的工厂所用设备即为张家港华丰公司生产。

（六）塑料托盘在物流运输中前景广阔

中国现拥有塑料托盘制造企业1000多家，已经形成了一个快速发展的行业。随着中国现代物流的快速发展，预计中国塑料托盘也将继续保持快速成长态势。

2012年以来，塑料托盘行业产销两旺，很多塑料托盘企业反应市场销售状况良好，一季度同比增长幅度在30%以上，二季度、三季度产销量有所下降，全年产销量增长速度达到20%以上，仅上半年社会消费托盘产品达到3.26亿元，和去年相比较增长了将近14%，但是幅度降低了5%，特别是天津地区，随着滨海新区的逐步建立，大量产业链的投入，塑料托盘在天津地区进入一个旺盛的时期。河南郑州地区塑料托盘的使用也在增加，食品行业的规定拉动了河南塑料托盘的使用率。在整个2012年随着中央“东厂西移”的战略方针，内地对塑料托盘的需求量进入一个饥渴的阶段并继续发展的趋势。预估明年及2013年在河北，河南，天津，北京等地对塑料托盘的需求量还将至少翻一翻。

塑料托盘由于符合环保、循环再生、综合利用及坚固耐用的特点，一直以来深受客户欢迎，2012年塑料托盘产销量在托盘总产销量中有所上升，但是随着石油价格的上涨，塑料托盘生产成本上升，带动塑料托盘价格上升，将给塑料托盘市场需求带来影响，给其他材料托盘带来市场机遇。

近些年我国的塑料托盘拥有量增长很快，据统计国内现有托盘保有量超过8亿个，并且还在以每年20%的速度增长。

塑料托盘的生产和销售处于最佳状态，订单量快速扩大，销售渠道骤然变宽，机器不停转，员工加班干，尤其是“中国十大明星托盘企业”，诸如上海力卡、上海庆豪订单压力更大。山东力扬、上海派瑞特、上海鑫鹏等大型塑料托盘生产企业情况相差无几。塑料托盘涨幅大一是因为塑料托盘结实耐用、洁净美观；二是因为塑料托盘通过加入钢件等方法进行工艺改革，承载量增加，作用范围拓宽，使用价值提升；三是因为啤酒、饮料、奶制品等重量大、包装规范的产品使用托盘的必要性逐步显现，青岛啤酒、燕京啤酒、汇源、康师傅、娃哈哈、蒙牛、伊利等大型生产企业对塑料托盘的需求都在增大。

（七）塑料汽油箱方兴未艾

燃油箱塑料化是现代汽车油箱塑料化的趋势。塑料油箱比金属油箱有优越性能，随着汽车工业的发展，各国对塑料油箱的使用越来越广泛，福特公司的使用率达100%，欧美发达国家塑料油箱的使用率已经占到90%多的市场份额。

我国全年累计生产汽车1927.18万辆，同比增长4.6%，销售汽车1930.64万辆，同比增长4.3%，产销同比增长率较2011年分别提高了3.8和1.8个百分点。随着环保和轻量化的推行，车用塑料的普及程度将在未来得到进一步提升，车用塑料应用领域将进一步扩大。

按目前130kg/辆的平均用量来算，2012年中国汽车塑料件市场用量为2345.8kt；以单车塑料价值2800～4000元/t来计算，汽车塑料件市场规模约为(650～900)亿元。为全球最大的汽车产销市场和汽车零部件市场，预计中国汽车塑料市场占有率约为30%，即2015年中国汽车塑料市场为3800kt。

2012年，受世界经济增速放缓的影响，我国经济增速也出现了明显回落。与此同时，摩托车工业在经济下行压力加大的情况下也呈低位运行态势，全年摩托车产销量分别为2362.98万辆和2365.07万辆，同比分别下降12.50%和12.17%，其中出口摩托车893.59万辆，同比下降16.83%，高于行业总销量降幅4.66个百分点。全年产销量为2007年以来新低。

目前，国内塑料燃油箱的使用率已达到了70%左右。据中国汽车工业协会统计，2012年，乘用车产销1552.37万辆和1549.52万辆，同比分别增长7.2%和7.1%；商用车产销374.81万辆和381.12万辆，同比分别下降4.7%和5.5%。

据预计,"十二五"期间,我国国内汽车产量将达2500万辆,占世界汽车产量的30%左右。据此预测,未来我国乘用车对汽车塑料燃油箱的市场需求将达到千万只以上。同时,由于环保、节能的需要,我国中型、轻型货车使用塑料燃油箱的比例也将越来越高,这也将带来对汽车塑料燃油箱更大的市场需求。

(八)汽车保险杠

随着汽车工业的不断发展,人们对汽车轻量化和环保性的要求越来越高,塑料作为新型零部件材料,在汽车上的应用前景也越来越广阔。塑料的应用提高了汽车的轻量化和环保性,塑料质轻,可使汽车轻量化以达致节能目标,而塑料更赋予汽车生产商较高的零件设计和造型自由度。时至今日,塑料材料已大大改变了汽车的内外设计,从ABS刹车系统、前后保险杠到车门镶钣等,不少汽车内装和车身部件都已采用了高质量的塑料作为主要材料。

选择塑料作为汽车材料,除可为汽车设计带来突破外,对可持续发展及环境保护也有一定贡献。塑料不但可减少汽车的废气排放量,还可降低天然资源如石油的消耗,有助达到可持续性的环保目的。以塑料取代传统金属部件,可大大减轻汽车重量,并降低汽车能耗。100kg的塑料在功能上等同公斤的金属部件,由此推论,汽车平均走150000km,便可节省750L的燃油。聚丙烯与聚烯烃材料成为车身内外饰的主要原料,聚丙烯材料因为具有密度小、成本低、产量大、性价比高、化学稳定性好和易于加工成型等特点,已经广泛应用于汽车保险杠、防擦饰条、门内柱及车门护板等汽车部件。

近来,一些保险杠生产商开始采用TPO材料来替代反应注塑成型的PUR或PC/PBT材料。此外,采用发泡PP做芯层,TPO做表皮的仪表板,以及用TPO材料制作车顶棚及安全气囊装置的表皮逐渐成为主流设计的趋势,PVC/ABS压延表皮由于在品质和环保等方面存在局限,其应用在逐渐减少。当此类聚烯烃材料用于生产各种内外饰件的时候,配件厂商都要保证成品达到一定耐刮擦的标准。目前,某些世界级汽车生产商已经开始要求部件表面在经受10N或者15N刮擦力的情况下,仍能表现出优异的耐刮擦效果。塑料在汽车零部件的使用范围正在扩大塑料在汽车中的应用范围正在由以内装饰件为主转向外装饰件和功能结构件、由通用塑料为主转向工程塑料、复合材料或塑料合金等,今后的重点发展方向是开发结构件和外装件。塑料汽车内装饰件主要有仪表板、车门内板、副仪表板、杂物箱盖、座椅、后护板等,仪表板是主要的汽车内装饰件之一。而塑料汽车外装饰件主要有保险杠、挡泥板、车轮罩、导流板等。目前汽车保险杠是塑料用量最大的部件之一。

现时,国外汽车用塑料约占汽车重量的15%,预计10年此数字将提高至超过20%。中国汽车用塑料目前占汽车重量的7%~8%。汽车塑料化将是未来汽车发展的大趋势,而首当其冲的是车身内饰件塑料化。目前,世界主要的汽车生产国的汽车内饰塑料化已基本完成,今后的重点发展方向将是扩展塑料在车身外装件和结构件上的应用,最后可望推进到全塑车身。

2012年我国轿车产量1073.8万辆,其中自主品牌轿车销售304.96万辆,同比增长3.5%,占轿车市场的28.4%,市场份额同比下降0.7个百分点,如全部使用塑料保险杠,每辆车用两副,每副保险杠重量在4~6kg,则需用塑料85904~128856t,其中聚丙烯用量占到1/2,其中聚丙烯用量占到1/2,则需50000t左右,可见市场是比较大的。

(九)化妆品、洗涤用品包装用量越来越大

2012年1~12月全国规模以上日用化学产品制造行业企业数量为1332.00家,日用化学产品制造行业资产合计213908716.00千元,同比增加6.98%;实现销售收入348094196.00千元,同比增加11.06%;完成利润总额34127133.00千元,同比增加17.44%,对塑料包装容器的需求量越来越大。

随着人们消费水平的提高和消费能力的增强,化妆品、洗涤用品的生产和销售得到了空前的发展,市场竞争也越来越激烈,商家在化妆品、洗涤用品的包装上下足工夫,向规格形状多样化,塑料选材多样化方向发展。

对于中低档化妆品,包装容器的容量大小呈现多样化,以方便消费者的选择;对于高档产品,采取小容量容器进行包装,以满足低收入者的需求。相对来说,洗发水和淋浴露的用量较多,500~750mL的家庭装也就很常见。

普通的化妆品、洗涤用品包装容器,绝大部分采用聚乙烯PE制造。由于透明容器能让消费者清楚的看到内容物,因此消费者对透明容器的要求越来越广,而透明聚丙烯PP正是满足这一要求的主要材料,与其他透明塑料相比,PP是一种质优价廉,极具竞争优势的包装用材料。

透明的聚对苯二甲酸乙二醇酯PET塑料瓶同样已成为今日化妆品、洗涤用品受欢迎的包装容器,由它制造的产品透明度、光泽度好,化学性能稳定,阻气性好,手感好。

另外,模内标贴技术的应用也提高了化妆品、洗涤用品包装的档次。目前绿色包装材料、纳米材料改性、抗菌材料的开发也正被用于化妆品、洗涤用品包装。

（十）塑料软包装容器

塑料软包装容器在我国经过了二十多年的历程，虽然每一个产品都有它的成长期和衰落期，但塑料软包装容器其生命周期仍在成长期，为什么在当今包装容器不断更新、不断蓬勃发展的时代，塑料软包装容器还是不衰呢？这是因为（以同容量25L为例）塑料软包装容器可以折叠，运输中可以重叠，减少运输成本，它的运输成本是一般塑料桶的1/3；塑料软包装容器产品重量轻，生产用原料成本低，产品重量是一般的塑料桶的1/3.6；由于塑料软包装容器产品重量轻，装载同容量的物品所废弃的塑料比一般的塑料桶少，减少白色污染。

塑料软包装容器主要用低密度聚乙烯LDPE为原料制造，产品有两种：

1）热压式软塑折叠包装容器——口部与箱体采用热压成型；

2）装配式软塑折叠包装容器——口部与箱体采用装配成型。

二、塑料中空制品成型技术的进步

近几年，我国塑料中空容器成型技术有了长足的进步，中空吹塑机增长较快，2012年中空吹塑机产量已经接近16000台；除原料的发展，品种的增加，也促进了塑料包装容器的发展。

吹塑成型技术的进步（包括挤吹、注吹、注拉吹等工艺）特别是大型中空成型设备，多层共挤中空成型工艺设备的发展，带动了其他中空成型技术的发展，包括气体辅助注射成型、半壳注射技术（shell-technology）、旋转成型、吸塑成型的技术发展。现简述如下：

1.挤吹中空成型技术

挤吹中空塑料成型机是中空容器成型的主要设备，世界上80%至90%的中空容器是采用挤吹成型的。在我国中空塑料成型机的发展历程中，挤吹中空塑料成型机是发展最快最完善的中空塑料成型机。近几年来，挤吹成型工艺技术的发展主要体现在三维（3D）吹塑复杂中空成型容器和大型包装容器。

（1）三维（3D）吹塑成型工艺

三维（3D）吹塑成型也称为少废料或者无飞边的吹塑成型。近年来，市场对复杂、曲折的输送管材制件的需求推动了这一技术的进步。3D吹塑成型工艺通常是使用6～8轴的机械手来运送型坯并将其放置在吹塑模具内进行吹胀。

（2）大型吹塑成型技术

目前，大型吹塑成型的容器主要有IBC桶，200L双L全塑桶。IBC容器已形成500～2000L的系列产品。而200L双L全塑桶成型技术的发展也很好。

200L双L全塑桶所用原料是平均分子量在30万左右的高密度聚乙烯（HMWHDPE），熔体流动速率MI（HLMI：190℃、21.6kg）2～6g/10min，原料特性及制品工艺特点决定了其成型设备的特点和要求。200L储料式中空机在200L双L全塑桶生产中得到广泛应用。能稳定生产该桶的设备，国内共计约45台，其中秦川未来塑料机械有限公司占32台。

大型中空机一般包括：挤出机、机头、合模装置、吹胀装置、制品取出装置、液压站、强弱电控制系统。一般的外辅设备包括：混送料系统、余料粉碎回收系统等。按其挤出型坯的方式，大型中空机可分为储料式和连续挤出式，而按型坯的结构又可分为单层或多层。目前，国内的200双L全塑桶绝人多数采用单层储料式中空机吹制。随着技术发展及市场要求提高，此类设备将朝着高效、节能、提高产品质量、功能齐全的方向发展。

挤出机

大型中空机所配置的挤出机，其加工的原料一般主要是HMWPE，若采用常规设计，则其塑化效率明显不足。国内生产的ϕ150/25挤出机在加工HMWPE粉料时，其塑化能力仅为250kg/ho。在国外，尤其是在德国，许多大的中空机制造企业早已采用带强迫喂料结构、强制冷却段结构的单螺杆挤出机，被称为IKV结构。IKV结构的挤出机在相同长径比条件下，其塑化量较常规设计提高50%以上，且挤出量稳定，加之合理的屏障段和混炼段设计，能获得高的塑化质量。

储料式机头

储料式机头的流道主要有3种形式：单层心型包络流道、双层心型包络流道和螺旋流道。

早期的中空机机头较多采用单层心型包络流道，这主要是因为当时对成型制品要求不高。随着用户对容器质量要求不断提高，尤其在大型容器方面，因为熔合缝的强度问题，单层心型包络就显出弱点，转而出现了双层心型包络和螺旋流道设计。如果是单层心型包络流道，挤出的型坯圆周上存在明显的熔合缝区，而在双层心型包络流道挤出的型坯被完整的熔料层所覆盖，因此融合缝区的强度得以提高。双层螺旋流道，内外层分别有两台挤出机供料，并同时储料。由于制品的内层不用着色，在市场上非常有竞争力，有逐步替代单层200L全塑桶的趋势。

对储料式中空机机头来讲，衡量其水平的一个重要方面是其换料的速度。对于使用者来讲，希望是更换速度越快越好。但实际上是很难的。一个好的机头设计其换料时间往往仍需几个小时，因此除了在设计流道时充分注意，减少滞留区外，也出现过某些采用辅助动作的方法来解决这个问题，但其带来的问题是机头结构复杂、故障率高和零件寿命降低。近几年，又出现了一种采用液压提升流道，实现外部工人清理，用以加速换料的方法。由于其带来机头结构庞大、制造、装配精度要求高、实际清理时工人的劳动环境差等问题，主要还是采取好的流道设计。

合模装置

大型中空成型机的合模装置，近年来的主要变化是进一步向节能化发展。早期的合模装置大都采用四板液压直动式，能耗较大。以后发展为液压节能型合模装置，即使在使用较广泛的四拉杆三板联动式。过去十年，市场上的大型中空机的合模装置，无论其外部形状如何，实质上几乎都可归入到三板联动式，它的主要特点是将快速移模缸与增压缸分开，用较小的油缸推动三块范本的联动快移，在较小油泵站的条件下获得更高的移模速度。

近年来，大型中空机的合模装置逐步趋向于采用两板销锁式机构，该装置的移模运动由油缸或伺服电机通过滚珠丝杆来实现，运动付采用了滚柱直线导轨，具有刚性高，运动精度高，运动轻快的特点，实际上是把机床制造技术向塑机制造方面的移植。这种两板式合模装置的合模力是由两对或三对位置可调的销锁缸来实现。

为了方便模具安装，这些销锁缸可以简单地从模板上取下来，并通过沿轴向的调整来适应不同的模具厚度。与此相类似的还有一种被称为“胡氏机构”的锁模装置，它的原理同销锁式机构基本相同，只是可以用在要求锁模力更大的合模机构上。

另外，合模装置液压控制方面，一般都采用比例液压阀，精确地控制合模速度，有利于制品的成型。

型坯壁厚控制

中空机机头的型坯壁厚控制是中空成型的关键技术之一，其作用在全塑桶成型方面尤其显著。型坯壁厚控制分为轴向控制(AWDS)和径向控制(PWDS)两种形式。目前的大型中空机一般都具有轴向型坯控制功能，其控制点由从24点到256点不等。轴向壁厚控制的作用是使得注出的料坯根据制品不同的吹胀比沿轴向获得不同的厚度，从而保证最终制品有比较均匀的壁厚分布，它是通过使芯模根据预设位置作轴向运动而改变模头的开口量来达到改变坯厚的目的。

2. 多层共挤中空成型技术

多层共挤中空成型技术发展前景看好。多层吹塑高阻隔性中空制品必将在中空制品领域内占的比例越来越大。多层吹塑制品不仅在食品包装工业发展很快，而且在化学品、化妆品、医疗卫生及其它工业包装方面也迅速增长。

多层共挤中空塑料成型机在我国是一个薄弱环节。多层共挤中空制品的发展促进了多层共挤出中空塑料成型机的发展。国际上，近年来，多层共挤中空塑料成型机发展的速度很快，同时技术进步也很快。国内也有一些品种推出，但存在一定差距，需要从下列几个方面加强研究开发：研究一定范围的共挤出机头(模头)，以满足不同材料、不同层次、机头直径等要求；研究组合包装系统，它能根据不同的原料特制出可能允许的组合数的机头；研究基础机械程序，它可用不同数量的模塑工位和包括生产速度和制品设计的平台尺寸。

3. 气辅助塑与水辅注塑

气体辅助注塑技术(GIT)通过把厚壁的内部掏空，能够成功地生产出厚壁、偏壁制品，在生产形状复杂介质导管方面具有一定的优势。由于气辅技术可使制品的外观表面性质优异、内应力低、轻质高强，因此非常适合于家电、家具、汽车、办公用品、日用品以及玩具等领域的制品，其中包括管道状制件、大型扁平结构零件和由不同厚度截面组成的制作，具有节省材料、缩短生产周期、提高制件的刚性和表面质量的优点。

为了缩短冷却时间并获得比较小的管子壁厚，用水代替气体来成型中空结构的注塑技术，通常称为水辅注塑(Water assisted in jection molding，简称WAIM)。除此之外，目前世界上还有很多机构在进行与该项技术有关的研究开发。利用水辅注塑的产品，其壁厚更小，壁面更光滑。

在水辅助注射成型过程中，水像柱塞一样推动熔体迅速向前移动，在这个过程中，要求水不会蒸发，水前面的熔体也不会冻结固化。为此，要求水的流量达到20～80L/min，甚至更高。刚开始注水时，为了避免水的流速过高和压力过大，以避免注水口附近产生漩涡而导致制品壁面缺陷，通常要对注水压力实行分级控制，刚开始时，压力较低，然后迅速提高到所需的注水压力。

4. 半壳注塑技术

半壳注塑技术实际上就是两种工艺过程的结合，即先用注塑的方法生产两个半壳，然后将两个半壳焊接起来成为中空制品。为了保证这两种工艺流程能够很好匹配，要求注塑的两个半壳的焊接面必须非常平整、毫无翘曲。一般是利用计算机辅助工程(CAE)设计软件进行优化设计，以尽量消除因制件冷却不均匀而产生的内应力，保证焊接完好。

目前，使用半壳注塑技术生产的产品有汽车仪表板上的各种气管、发动机进气管和汽车油箱等。

5. 模具滑动注射成型

模具滑动注射成型法是由日本制钢所开发的一种制造中空制品两步注射成型法。其原理是：首先将中空制品一分为二，对两部分分别注射形成半成品，然后将两部分半成品和模具滑动至对合位置。二次合模，在制品两部分结合缝处再注入塑料熔体(2 次注射)最后得到完整的中空制品。与吹塑制品相比，该技术所成型的产品具有表面质量好、尺寸精度高、壁厚均匀且设计自由度大等优点。

在制造形状复杂的中空制品时，模具滑动注射成型法与超声波焊接相比的优点是：不需要将半成品从模具中取出，因而可以避免半成品在模具外因冷却而造成的制品形状和精度下降的问题，此外，还可以避免焊接工艺中因产生局部应力而引起的熔接强度降低问题。

6. 旋转模塑

旋转模塑时，模具在加热的炉子内沿 2 个轴旋转，装在模具内的塑料熔结在模具表面，冷却后即可以得到与模具形状相仿的中空制品。旋转模塑的优点是成型过程没有压力，从而使制品没有内应力，壁厚比较均匀(与吹塑和热成型相比)，同时，模具也比较简单。因此，该技术特别适合于小批量生产大型制品。

最初用于旋转模塑的主要材料是 PVC 塑料，目前则更多地使用聚乙烯、聚丙烯和尼龙。常见的旋转模塑产品有玩具、功能性家具、容器和储槽、汽车零部件、体育休闲用品、交通隔离标志等。目前，用旋转模塑制造的储槽容积可达 $80m^3$。近几年，旋转模塑产品的增长速度较快，平均年增长率约 20%，远远高于其他塑料制品的增长率。

旋转模塑的主要缺点是可适用的塑料品种很少，其原因是：要求塑料受热时间比较长，从而要求塑料的热稳定性非常好；由于需要将塑料磨成粉，使材料价格有所提高；很难用成型加强肋的方法来提高产品的刚度。

7. 热成型工艺技术

热成型指的是对挤出热塑性片材通过一系列的成型或拉伸得到制品的方法，具体来说就是通过加热软化片材，然后借助真空或低的压力使软化的片材压向整个模面，从而得到简单又经济的制品。这种成型的主要优点是模具费用低、模具研制周期短、厂房投资费用低、设备投资小且短时间里就可运转，聚合物的热成型极相似于金属板的成型。

(1) 热成型方法

有很多热成型技术包括烘箱、模具及串联的辅助设备。真空辅助包模成型也许是最简单的一种。在单级设备里，切好的片材夹在一个框架上，通过幅射(红外)加热使它软化。压紧在框架中的热片材被向下拉(预拉伸)到冷凸模上，上面受大气压，下面抽真空，强压软化的片材紧贴向模型。

在压力成型中，用加热的空气穿过多孔板吹向片材，将片材压向凹模里，然后该片材受真空的拉伸并紧贴向模壁，在一般生产加工过程中空气的压力可以高达 1MPa。在两级设备里，加热装置在成型区的外面，热片材夹在框架上来回输送。通常，凸模比凹模有较大的拉伸度，但脱模较难些，因而制件的外表面清晰度差些，而制件紧贴模具的内表面清晰度大些。

(2) 双片热成型

双片热成型特点是成型快、壁厚均匀，可以制作双色和厚度不同的制品，甚至材料不同的制品。在工艺上可分为两种：一种是双片压力热成型，另一种是双片真空热成型。其中，双片真空热成型工艺是：当 2 个片材分别在模具内真空成型以后，再将 2 个模具合并，并用压力使制品熔合成为中空制品，如有必要，甚至可以在空腔内放入其它构件。典型产品有冲浪板、油箱、小船、门、管道、玩具等。

与吹塑相比，用这种方法生产小型或中型产品时，效率更高；与旋转模塑相比，这种方法不仅生产效率更高，而且可以适用更多的塑料，包括多层共挤出片材。

总之，我国中空制品行业最近几年发展良好，“十二五”期间发展前景广阔。

(中国塑料加工工业协会　孙冬泉)

人造革合成革

一、行业经济运行情况

中国塑料—人造革合成革工业 2012 年 549 家企业，实现工业总产值 1085.77 亿元，同比增长 17.23%. 主营业务收入 1040 亿元，同比增长 11.78%；从业人员 13.49 万，人均产值 83 万高于塑料平均水平。2012 年人造革合成革产量 3142.7kt，同比增长 15.55%。浙江企业占了 47%，产量

42.67%；福建企业与产量占全国的比重分别都为21%；江苏占了全国的11.9%。进入“十二五”以来浙江临海合成革工业全区稳定发展继续保持增长，全省2011年产量突破1000kt，占全国的44%；2012年产量达到1330kt，同比增长10.6%；福建福鼎合成革产业基地的崛起为全省突破600kt奠定了实力基础，增长速度39.5%，占全国比重从2008年的2%跃居21.3%，从2010年的第四位跃居第二位；江苏合成革374.8kt，下降13.1%，占全国的11.9%。2012年我国人造革合成革行业经济、技术形势发生了新的变化，行业总资产689亿增加10%，主营业务成本继续上涨，同比增长10.93%；负债率61%比2011年增长10.32%；资产利润率提高了9.65%。老企业举步维艰：成本压力、过剩经竞争、通胀环境、市场萎缩，亏损企业57家，亏损额1.7亿，两项同比都有所增加；新企业起步艰难：环境保护、融资市场、投资预期的影响较大。外贸出口风险加大，削弱了企业产品出口的竞争力，2012年全国人造革合成革企业出口量出口额49.86亿美元，占塑料行业的15.5%，出口量占了总销售量的18%，占全部工业总产值的31%，去年出口量增长1.83%，但是出口额同比下降6.08%；出口交货值87亿，同比出现负增长为2.93%。

临海·中国合成革创新产业基地。临海有18家合成革企业2012年产值36亿多元，实现税收1.8亿元，合成革产业以生态、环保、高科技为目标，不断引进先进技术，转变生产方式，推进废水、废气治理，推行清洁化生产。合成革企业将接入园区集中供热系统，将减少年均用煤30%，二氧化硫减排40%，为合成革产业的发展铺出了“绿”的底色。浙江南泰合成革有限公司在国内合成革产业中率先引进膜分离技术处理二甲胺废水，90%可以直接回用于生产用水，其水质达到车间用水要求，2012年底通过环保部门验收。浙江强丰革业有限公司针对二甲胺废水，与温州环科院合作，采用强化生化法，废水经处理后，达到排放标准再回用于车间用水。园区合成革企业将投入1800多万元全面推进二甲胺废水处理工程，而整个废水整治设施改造总计投入1.23亿元，该项目已列入医化园区的国家循环化改造示范试点内容。园区启动投资3.7亿元的临港热电公司建设，集中供热即将实施：集中供热系统较之传统的锅炉，不仅节约标煤三分之一左右，大大降低了产品能耗，而且还能保证产品质量的稳定性和生产的安全性。绿色能源金太阳工程启动：高盛合成革有限公司与金太阳工程实施方签订了合作协议，金太阳工程施工人员将通过测量、勘察，在企业屋顶上安装太阳能电池板，金太阳工程实施后，企业都将用上绿色能源。

2012年4月在上海世博展览馆，中国塑料加工工业协会授予福鼎市“中国合成革产业示范基地”牌匾。福鼎合成革产业发展于2005年，至2012年福鼎市共引进合成革及配套企业48家，产值达150亿元，超亿元企业36家，已逐步形成区域经济规模和集聚效应优势，成为宁德市产值规模超百亿元的产业集群，产品在国内占有率达25%以上，同时还远销美国、俄罗斯、欧洲、非洲、中东、东南亚等国家和地区，出口贸易值占总销售额的20%。目前福鼎已形成革基布—聚胺树脂—合成革—制革品等“一条龙”的合成革产业链。福建省宁德市政府正式下文同意福鼎市政府组建合成革质量检测机构，合成革检测机构的成立，将对进一步提高福鼎市合成革产品质量水平和产业研发能力，促进宁德市合成革产业的健康发展起到重要推动作用。

二、做好行业政策层面的研究服务工作

在中国塑协的领导下，注重做好人造革合成革行业发展调查研究，掌握发展状态，关注政策形势，做好服务工作。针对关税问题开展工作，对于国家关税调整提出了积极的建议，例如：针对合成革服装面料的问题，积极与会员单位、地方商会、协会加强沟通研究，组织项目申报，及时反映会员诉求。3月份与相关行业协会共同向国家财政部关税司反映行业情况，在国家出台与韩国经济合作框架协议中涉及合成革服装面料进出口关税税率问题，提出保持原关税的要求并取得59系列税号仍保持原税率的结果。6月份参与海关总署关于59系列外贸加工的“PVC涂层织物”海关标准的起草工作。专委会有效的开展了为企业做好上市提供行业资讯、高新技术企业申报、新产品鉴定。如在塑协指导下，积极申报无溶剂革技术创新项目、推荐烟台万华超纤股份有限公司申报中国轻工业联合会科技项目评审。积极为企业上市做好服务工作，其中山东同大海岛新材料股份有限公司5月份成功上市，目前行业内共有5家上市公司。

三、组织“中国人造革合成革特色区域市区县长座谈会”

针对合成革特色区域十年来发展中的问题，开展特色区域转型升级发展研究。专委会在调查研究的基础上，于4月19日在上海组织召开了“中国人造革合成革特色区域市区县长座谈会”，全面总结了2002年以来十年的合成革特色区域建设成果，来自十大特色区域的市区县长以及地方商协会领导和企业家100多人，参加了特色区域政策研究以及经验交流活动。

四、组织军民融合与政府采购政策交流会议

针对企业参与政府采购与军需采购问题开展服务工作。针对企业提出的企业产品如何进入政府采购系统、军需采购的问题，4 月 20 日下午在上海组织召开了“合成革军需与政府采购会议”，请总后勤部领导、国务院发展研究中心、国际采购组织专家为企业讲授了国家有关采购政策以及程序，参会企业 60 多家，会议期间开展对接活动。

五、组织“合成革英文标准术语——中欧座谈会”

针对合成革进出口遇到的技术壁垒与贸易壁垒问题，开展国际交流研究。经过近一年的准备，首先确定从合成革英文标准术语开始，逐步进入技术贸易与国际组织的交流沟通机制。4 月 22 日在上海组织召开了“合成革英文标准术语——中欧座谈会”，国际制革协会秘书长保罗参加了会议开展了交流活动。这是第一次组织有国际高级专家参加的合成革英文术语方面的会议，是一个具有与国际接轨的前瞻性的课题。

六、完成“中国水性生态合成革产业示范基地”建设工作

随着环境保护日益突出，以及消费者对于生态产品的日益需求的增长，专委会在 2012 年继续力促行业大量应用环保材料和环保工艺作。在完成水性合成革产业联盟建设的基础上，继续抓重点企业，积极推广应用开发。比如：促进合肥市科天化工的水性树脂推广与应用也取得突破，先后在温州、广东潮州、江苏泰兴等地建成水性生态合成革干、湿法生产线，受到当地政府的大力支持。鼓励水性聚氨酯应用开发从南方向北方转移，在河北省建立“水性聚氨酯合成中试基地”。在中国塑协领导下下，我专委会协助浙江丽水市开发区管委会初步完成了成“中国水性生态合成革产业示范基地”建设方案，同时完成向中国轻工业联合会申报“中国水性生态合成革产业示范基地”的申报，并经过专家组考察，进一步明确了示范基地任务，确立了一丽水市为全行业生态合成革发展示范基地。

七、组织协调推进广清洁化生产技术与节能技术标准工作

为了更好的实施《合成革清洁生产标准》，全面实施蒸馏塔回收装置，同时更重要的是向深度开发。在通用标准的基础上，开展清洁生产技术规范的研究工作。在 2012 年 2 月份和 8 月份在丽水和温州召开《合成革工业清洁生产技术规范》和《聚氨酯合成革节能降耗技术要求》两项行业标准的制定工作会，通过讨论明确，吸取先进企业经验，为制定出符合实际的清洁生产标准奠定基础。

八、组织协调完成人造革合成革行业的安全技术标准工作

积极稳妥推进行业标准化工作，促进并规范行业可持续发展。2012 年先后完成《足球用聚氨酯合成革》、《鞋面用聚氨酯超细纤维合成革》、《合成革用抗菌剂》、《合成革用聚氨酯表面处理剂》、《沙发用聚氨酯合成革》和《家居用聚氨酯合成革》、《软体沼气池用聚氯乙烯涂层膜材》、《软体聚氯乙烯涂层织物沼气池》、《自洁型聚氯乙烯涂层织物建筑结构膜材》等 8 项行业标准的全部报批工作。2012 年发布的 7 项行业标准有 QB/T 4340—2012《服装用聚氨酯合成革安全要求》、QB/T 4341—2012《抗菌聚氨酯合成革—抗菌性能试验方法和抗菌效果》、QB/T 4345—2012《防护鞋底用聚氨酯树脂》、QB/T 4346—2012《织物复合用干法聚氨酯薄膜》、QB/T 4344—2012《裙腰带用聚氯乙烯人造革》、QB/T 4347—2012《汽车用聚氯乙烯薄膜和片材》行业标准的发布。2012 年申报行业标准项目 15 项，已获立项批准的行业标准项目 10 项。同时积极协调两项强制性国家标准的 WTO 征询意见处理工作，力争早日完成《汽车用聚氨酯合成革安全技术》和《家居用聚氯乙烯人造革安全技术要求》两项国家标准的发布前的全部协调工作。

九、举办第二届中国(上海)国际人造革合成革工业展览会

2012 年 4 月 19 ~ 22 日在上海市世博主题馆成功举办《第二届中国(上海)国际人造革合成革工业展览会》，展会面积 10000m^2，参展企业 200 多家。本次展会规格高、规模大、产品丰富、全面展示了中国合成革世界水平，在行业内外引起震动。浙江临海、义乌市、高明市、福建福鼎、浙江丽水等组团参展，同时国内外知名企业均参加展览，展览面积比上届扩大一倍，参观人员超过 15000 人，对宣传行业、协会和企业取得显著效果。

十、举办“2012 中国国际合成革展览会”

中国塑料加工工业协会主办的“2012 中国国际合成革展览会”于 2012 年 8 月 30 ~ 9 月 1 日在温州国际会展中心隆重开展。本次展会汇集了“中国合成革之都”和国内外知名企业 200 多家参展，展会在拓市场、增实效、求合作、谋发展的原则指导下，展示产业新成就，营销合成革新产品，展现和引领产业及市场变化新趋势、新需求，吸引了海内外专业贸易商前来参观采购，为参展企业打造集促进贸易与品牌建设功能为一体的商贸盛宴！展会还进行了采购商－温州厂商联谊、深入企业参观洽谈等项活动。

十一、组织"2012年专委会年会暨第二中国届生态合成革论坛"

2012年4月20日上午在上海举办"2012年专委会年会暨第二中国届生态合成革论坛"、本次会议是再次推动合成革向生态化、环保型方向发展的重要会议。冯庶君秘书长主持了会议，中国塑料加工工业协会常务副理事长曹俭做了重要讲话。中国皮革协会理事长苏超英到会做了讲话，介绍了中国皮革行业发展形势，就欧盟提出合成革英文术语问题发做了科学的分析。到会人员200多人，来自欧洲皮革协会、美国陶氏公司、德国巴斯夫、德国拜耳、美国文泰离型纸、天祥技术、丽水优耐克和陕西科技大学等院校专家以及国内9家合成革公司的专家做了主题发言。会议紧扣当前形势，内容丰富，主题突出。

十二、举办"第二届中国合成革高峰"

2012年8月30日在温州成功举办了"第二届中国合成革高峰"，250多名代表出息了会议，冯庶君秘书长主持了会议。中国塑协人造革合成革专委会理事长孙福荣、温州市合成革商会会长王永康致辞；中国塑料加工工业协会常务副理事长曹俭做了重要讲话。浙江梅盛实业集团股份有限公司、烟台万华超纤材料股份有限公司做了经验介绍；中国室内装饰协会等也介绍了合成革在装饰装修行业的应用；温州市政府顾问谢浩先生就温州市金融改革与发展做了生动的发言。最后对安徽安利合成革股份有限公司、上海华锋超纤材料股份有限公司、浙江禾欣实业集团股份有限公司、温州人造革有限公司、无锡双象超纤材料股份有限公司等56家企业进行了表彰，分别授予了"2011～2012年度高端品牌"奖、"2011～2012年度科技创新"奖和"2011～2012年度绿色企业"奖。

十三、在广东和丽水举办水性生态合成革培训班

1. 丽水班：2012年4月首届水性生态合成革制造工程技术培训班在丽水开班。"首届水性生态合成革制造工程技术培训班"于2012年4月6日在丽水顺利开班。该培训班由丽水市经济开发区管委会，中国合成革用水性树脂及水性生态合成革研发中心联合举办。丽水市多家合成革企业的技术总工，生产主管及研发中心全体人员计100多人参加了本次培训。本次培训班采取了理论学习和组织现场参观相结合的培训教学方法。首先，由中国合成革用水性树脂及水性生态合成革研发中心常务副主任谢镇铭作了水性生态合成革制造基本知识的讲解，着重介绍了生态合成革的概念，水性生态合成革制造基本原材料、设备的选用以及水性贝斯的发展。随后，由水性生态合成革研发办主任王峰讲解了水性生态合成革工艺技术和水性生态合成革制造中常见的问题，最后由水性生态合成革研发中心孙涛介绍了水性生态合成革实验室的建设要求及进行了水性电脑配色仪介绍。在培训休息期间还组织观看了多款用丽水市优耐克水性树脂科技有限公司的水性树脂制作的生态合成革样品。最后，在开发区工作人员的带领下，参加培训班的全体学员还参观了优耐克武义生态合成革专用生产线。

2. 广东班："2012年中国(广东)水性生态合成革生产技术培训班"由中国塑料加工工业协会人造革合成革专业委员会和合肥市科天化工有限公司合作举办的于2012年7月28日在广东圆满举行。专家和企业家共65位代表参加了此次培训会，会后中国塑协领导为每位学员颁发了结业证书。本次培训班承办单位合肥科天化工有限公司董事长戴家兵博士和潮州金山塑胶董事长黄文强先生对各位参加培训的代表表示了热烈的欢迎。安徽大学王武生教授对水性聚氨酯的基本原理等方面进行了讲解。昆山世名的市场总监石一磊先生为参加培训的学员介绍了水性色浆的理论及应用知识，安徽大学教授、合肥科天化工有限公司高级技术顾问张启衔先生介绍了水性助剂相关知识。由合肥科天化工有限公司董事长戴家兵博士全面介绍了水性合成革生产工艺(包括水性贝斯工艺、水性(仿)超纤合成革工艺、水性半PU革工艺、水性干式服装革工艺、压延PVC革水性直涂工艺)，并重点讲述了水性合成革贝斯制作的工艺等。学员乘坐金山塑胶班车赶往金山塑胶生产基地，实地参观了金山塑胶刚刚投产的水性贝斯生产线。

十四、成立南平市合成革产业协会

南平市合成革产业协会于2012年2月20日成立，郑建华先生当选为会长。协会设常务副会长6人，副会长10人，秘书长1人。南平市合成革产业协会是地级市协会，目前拥有会员单位51家。涉及领域以合成革产业为主，物流、酒店等行业兼而有之。协会成立后，创办内部刊物《南平合成革产业资讯》，展示会员风采。目前，荣华山新型轻纺专业园合成革企业有生产线56条，其中干法24条、湿法30条、压延2条。2011年协会所属会员企业实现工业产值9亿元，2012年实现工业产值32亿元。随着国家海西开发进程的逐步深入，在不断的探索与前进中，南平市合成革产业协会作为闽北合成革产业一个重要的服务交流平台，将为合成革产业的发展壮大起到积极的推动作用。协会成立后，积极开展各项工作，规范会员企业的生产经营，协调企业办好相关手续和环保测评的报批。引导企业增强环保意识，保护好闽江源头的生态环境，树立企业家们的社会责任感；引领企业加强技术创新，提升产品的附加值，增加产品的多样性，不断挖掘企业的经济效益；规范企业良性互动，有序竞争，倡导企业之间优势互补，共同构建团结一心、和谐共赢的轻纺专业园。

（中国塑料加工工业协会
人造革合成革专业委员会　冯庶君）

塑料异型材及门窗制品

【中国塑料行业"十二五"规划指明了行业发展方向】

一、关于中国塑料行业"十二五"规划

"十一五"期间是塑料行业发展最快也是最好的黄金时期。产量每年增长20.1%，产值平均每年增长22.34%。2010年，我国塑料行业总产值占国内生产总值GDP的3.55%，在轻工中已经占到10.27%，是轻工第一大行业。利润翻了两番多。出口达14620kt，出口额是360亿美元，占轻工出口10%左右。目前我国已经成为世界上最大的塑料制品生产、消费国家。2010年塑料制品的表观消费量占到全球的四分之一，人均46kg，已略超世界平均40kg的水平。节能工作也取得很大的成绩，提前完成了国家要求的单位GDP能耗平均降低20%的要求。但应清醒地看到存在的问题：(1)自主创新的能力不强，特别是中小企业多，技术力量薄弱。(2)装备水平还不能适应生产发展需要。(3)产品结构不合理，中低档产品比例比较高。尤其是像塑编等几个行业这个问题尤其突出。(4)区域布局也不合理，中西部地区在"十一五"时期虽然发展很快，但东、中西部地区发展差距仍然较大。

"十二五"是塑料加工行业承上启下实现跨越式发展的关键时期。是转变发展方式、调整优化产业结构、提升发展质量、全面提升塑料加工行业的整体水平，向产业的高端化发展的重要阶段。因此"十二五"必须把握历史发展机遇，依靠技术进步，大力提升技术创新水平，开创塑料加工业发展的新局面，为实现世界先进大国目标打好基础。关于"十二五"规划内容，重点说明三个问题。

（一）"十二五"规划中明确提出了塑料加工业的定位。

"十二五"规划中明确提出塑料加工业是以塑料制品加工为核心，涵盖原料、机械、模具、助剂为一体的一个新兴制造业，是为工业、农业、建筑、交通、运输、航空航天等国民经济各行各业提供重要配件和特种材料的国民经济基础性产业，也是为广大消费者提供安全可靠消费品的民生产业。塑料加工业提供的是人类社会经济与生活都不可缺少的生产资料和生活资料，"十二五"规划把这个定位明确了。这里需作两点说明：

第一，关于"新兴制造业"，主要考虑：一是塑料加工业已从传统初级消费品正快速向高层次消费需求过渡，产品档次高，技术难度大。二是合成树脂、合成橡胶、合成纤维三大合成高分子材料是构成现代社会的基础材料之一，是支持现代高科技发展的新型材料。目前塑料加工业已成功进入工业、农业、交通运输、电子信息、建筑、国防军工等领域，在高科技领域得到广泛应用。在未来新材料技术革命中，塑料加工业将发挥更加重要的作用。因此塑料加工业不仅是传统制造业，更是科技含量高的"新兴制造业"。

第二，关于快速成长的国民经济新的支柱产业之一，2010年塑料加工业总产值已占GDP3.35%，离5%通常标准还有一定距离，很显然还不能视为国民经济支柱产业。但国内巨大的市场需求和发展空间，将使塑料加工业继续保持较快增长，作为二十一世纪新材料的塑料，随着科技进步的加快和工业化进程的深入，其应用范围越来越广；虽然国际金融危机尚未走出阴影，但这场危机并未能从根本上改变世界经济长期发展趋势，我国塑料加工业比较优势将继续得以加强，将有利于进一步拓展国际市场。塑料加工业作为朝阳产业，具有快速发展的特点，进一步提升了在国民经济中的地位。塑料加工业理应受到高度重视，应加大培育力度，使之更快成长为国民经济支柱产业之一。

"十二五"规划给塑料加工业定位是实事求是的，是准确的。其目的是号召全行业进一步坚定信心，更加重视塑料加工业在国民经济中占有的重要地位，更加坚定不移地走新兴制造业的发展路子，促其加快成为国民经济新兴支柱产业。

（二）"十二五"规划中强调大力推进技术进步，加快技术创新体系的建设，大力提升产业素质。

提高行业的技术进步和创新能力也是我们"十二五'期间需要解决的一个关键问题。"十二五"期间，塑料加工业要大力实施专利、品牌、标准战略，加大人才、资金等技术创新要素向有条件企业聚集的力度，加快以企业为主体，产、学、研、用紧密结合的塑料加工业技术创新体系和服务平台建设。为"十二五"塑料加工业快速发展提供强大的技术支撑。

塑料是未来材料技术革命的重要领域，要紧紧抓住国家重点支持新兴战略产业发展机遇，依靠技术进步，加快新技术、新工艺、新产品的开发。要紧紧围绕"功能化"这一核心，开发新型材料，新的功能产品。功能化是塑料行业下一步发展的方向和希望。需要高度关注并大力开展研究，特别是开展纳米技术研究。当前要重点关注高阻隔性多层共挤纳米微层复合材料及相关的微层复合材料；纤维功能增强复合材料、聚合物合金材料等现代制造业高性能工程塑料；熔体静电纺丝纳米过滤材料、纳米抗菌、阻燃、降解等功能性材料；太阳能光伏发电配套材料、锂离子电池隔膜、节能保温、超高分子量合成树脂等材料以及农用多功能材料等，这里特别强调一下要加大对各种离子膜材料的攻关力度，解决功能膜发展瓶颈。同时要加强与石化行业合作开发急需的新材料。

"十二五"要通过技术进步和技术创新，不断提高产业素质，提高产业核心竞争力，为全力建设塑料加工业现代化产业体系打好基础。

（三）加快转变发展方式、加快结构调整和优化区域布局。

既然我们是一个新兴的制造业，就要有现代产业体系作支撑，要大力开发新材料、新产品，实现产业向高端化发展。"十二五"规划中提出，中高档产品的比率要提高。企业组织结构调整，"十二五"规划提出要创造条件在行业中能形成一批销售收入300亿以上的企业和企业集团，以便进一步提高生产集中度，进而促进企业的发展能力、科研能力、市场开拓能力的提升。

关于优化区域布局，"十二五"规划明确提出，要在充分发挥优势的基础上，实现差异性发展战略，沿海地区要加强品牌建设，加快产业高端化进程，形成新的竞争优势。中部地区要抓住机遇，发挥承东启西的地缘优势，积极主动承接产业转移。西部地区要根据资源禀赋的特点，发挥后发优势，形成具有自身特色的塑料加工业。通过"十二五"调整，努力形成布局合理各具特色的产业布局，促进塑料加工健康发展。

二、认真贯彻中央经济会议的精神，确保塑料加工业继续保持平稳快速发展

认真学习，深刻领会，认真贯彻落实中央经济工作会议精神。"十二五"期间经济工作主基调就是稳中求进。"稳"就是要保持国家宏观政策稳定，保持经济平稳较快增长、物价稳定和社会大局稳定。"进"就是要抓住并利用好重要的发展机遇期，在转变发展方式上取得新的进展；在深化改革开放上取得新的突破；在改善民生上取得新的突破。一个"新进展"两个"新突破"。总的方针是：稳增长、控物价、调结构、惠民生、抓改革、促和谐。要重点处理好速度、结构和物价的关系，强调要把扩大内需作为战略基点，把发展实体经济作为坚实的基础。工业是实体经济是主体，充分体现了党中央、国务院对工业的重视。这句话来之不易，这是这次全球金融危机以及温州问题出现之后得出的结论，中国的发展还是必须走实体经济这条路。塑料加工业必须抓住发展不放松，要把实体经济办好、办强、办大。

【钱会长对塑料异型材行业在"十二五"期间发展的指示】

1. 坚持"环境友好型、资源节约型、科技创新型"的战略方向，坚持绿色、环保、节能低碳发展。这是异型材及门窗产业的发展方向。住房和城乡建设部在《建筑业发展"十二五"规划》中明确提出，"十二五"建筑业的发展要以建筑节能减排为重点，坚持节能减排和科技创新相结合，发展绿色建筑，使节能减排成为建筑业发展新的增长点。异型材及门窗作为绿色节能建筑的重要配套产品，必须真正成为绿色产品、节能产品。当前要把淘汰含铅热稳定剂作为重点，同时积极开发推广应用新型环保的各种助剂和填充料，使异型材及门窗在绿色环保、节能低碳方面实现新的突破，以满足绿色节能建筑的新要求。

2. 加大结构调整力度，努力提升产业素质，促进产业升级。当前要努力提高高档异型材和标准异型材的市场份额。要研究提高行业进入门槛，以限制落后产能的增加，要淘汰质量不达标、使用安全风险大、节能效果差的低档产品。要加大企业兼并重组力度，提高生产集中度，逐步形成一批具有核心自主竞争力的企业集团。要进一步整合和完善产业链，要形成专业化分工更加合理，大、中、小企业协调发展的格局，进一步改善和提高行业组织结构。当前建设部门正推行节能标志认证，北京市也正启动绿色建筑评审活动。《绿色建筑设计标准》将于明年起全面实施。今年将开展绿色建筑评价标识试点活动。塑料异型材及门窗产业要把握有利时机，寻找切入点，积极参与此项工作。紧紧围绕绿色环保、节能减碳要求和绝热系数、气密性等主要指标，研究节能标志认证和绿色标识评审方法，创造条件在行业积极稳妥开展此项工作，为绿色节能建筑设计和市场采购提供可靠依据，向消费市场推出绿色、节能的名牌产品。

3. 加大技术研发力度，进一步提高自主创新能力。要紧紧围绕建筑节能设计标准对门窗节能技术指标的新要求，瞄准国际先进水平，加大新产品开发力度。要根据市场需求，大力开发整窗保温系数 K 值小于2.0的高保温性能的产品、高效隔声窗、高气密性节能推拉窗等产品。要针对不同气候区域门窗结构特点大力实施“差异化”发展。要按产品功能多元化和艺术化的要求，开发抑烟、抗菌、抗静电等新功能和色彩鲜艳、艺术性强的新产品，提高附加值。要大力推进新工艺、新装备、新材料、新助剂、新填充料的研究。要发挥企业作为技术创新的主体作用，引领行业技术进步，希望有条件的企业加快国家级、省级和企业技术中心的建设，努力提高创新水平和新产品研发能力，充分发挥大型企业技术创新示范作用，推动行业发展转型升级。

4. 加强诚信建设。行业诚信体系建设需要行业共同行动和共同维护，需要企业及从业人员以职业道德和行业自律为基础。当前要重点打击假冒伪劣和以次充好的行为，反对超量填加填料和以牺牲节能效果和使用安全性而随意降低异型材截面面积的行为。要大力改进市场营销，努力开拓市场，要规范市场秩序、反对不正当竞争，共同维护良好的市场秩序。特别在塑料建材下乡活动中要严把质量关，严防伪劣产品败坏行业信誉。希望异型材及门窗产业要加强行业自律，以诚信为本，共同维护产业信用和良好的社会形象，为行业健康发展打好基础。

随着绿色、节能建筑业的蓬勃发展，异型材及门窗作为最具节能优势和高性价比的产品，在绿色节能建筑中将会发挥更大的作用。在未来旺盛的市场需求推动下一定会得到更大的发展。

【行业现状】

2012年是“十二五”规划的初始年。在年会上钱桂敬会长对我们塑料异型材及门窗行业的稳步发展做出了四点重要指示，指示内容：(1)坚持“环境友好型、资源节约型、科技创新型”的战略方向，坚持绿色、环保、节能低碳发展。这是异型材及门窗产业的发展方向。(2)加大结构调整力度，努力提升产业素质，促进产业升级。(3)加大技术研发力度，进一步提高自主创新能力。(4)加强诚信建设。(5)专委会将带领会员企业认真贯彻落实钱会长的指示精神，为行业实现“十二五”规划目标落实各项工作。

受全球经济深陷金融债务危机泥潭的严重影响，我国的发展方式转变也正处在举步维艰的关键时期，国家放缓、放稳了发展步伐，近年对房地产的大力调控起到了显著作用。抑制过度的的购房需求，推动楼市的优胜劣汰已初见成效，房价过速上涨，超市场需求的房屋供应均已受到一定的扼制。

伴随楼市放缓，建材需求总量也必然放缓，增速消减成必然，塑料门窗异型材市场受到波及。行业总体市场供应受影响情况是一、二、三线城市逐次影响减弱，由东向西、由沿海向内陆、由经济发达区域向经济欠发达地区逐次减弱。需求量的区域变化除南北方向外和十年前相比正好相反。十年前是房地产发展的癫狂时期，抬头见塔吊处处有工地，房地产市场由狂热到癫狂再到冷静是发展的必然。众多早期发展较快区域内大中城市的建设规模和城市建设率已经接近80%，建设速度放缓也是必然。

我们国家是发展中国家，工业化进程还有很长的路要走，和发达国家相比我们还有很大的差距，我们有80%的人口处于低收入水平，还有许多贫瘠、偏远地段还处在温饱线上，从地域上看，经济发展的快慢具有显著差距。就是这种差距大大弥补了原有固定市场总需量的急速削减而造成的影响，使我们行业市场总需求量与去年相比基本持平或略有增加。

2012年各类塑料异型材产量据不完全统计年产量在5000~5200kt左右。行业总产能略有增加大约在8000~8500kt左右。规模以上门窗应用塑料异型材大约在3000~3100kt左右。拥有各种型号的挤出设备生产线大约在13000条左右。塑料门窗约占市场年需求总量的35%~40%左右。目前，塑料异型材伴随我国的经济发展状况以其更适用于寒冷地区、冬冷夏热地区、更适合经济性需求的特点，产品基本覆盖了中低端消费市场，在我国半数以上的三、四线城市、农村县乡市场已广泛应用，目前在欠发达地区的中小城市、农村的应用势头仍在不断扩展中。

我们行业基本上都是中小型企业，去年以来，行业面临诸多困境：专业技术人员和熟练技术工人严重不足，职业经理人欠缺，用工难及工资上涨，中小企业税赋重，贷款难、原辅材料成本上涨，总产能过剩形成的无利或微利使企业生存艰难形成巨大压力等。

今年上半年，诸多塑料异型材应用设备、模具制造企业呈现供不应求的局面，间接反映了主产品的市场仍需求强劲。高填充模具的订货量急速下降，新断面模具不断增加反映了低端市场对劣质材料的判知能力增强和需求水平在逐步提高。

近年来，原有异型材生产企业在产能布局和产能规模上基本趋于理性，业外仍有大踏步跨进者，虽然数量不多但步伐较大不能不令人担忧。这些新生力量会对行业今后的发展、企业格局、市场份额等诸多方面产生什么样的影响我们只能拭目以待。新建、扩建企业的增加，必将促使各方面人才流动，尤其是行业内一些较有影响力的企业内的优秀人才可能成为人才争夺的目标。

近一年以来，专委会会同会员骨干企业认真落实钱桂敬会长对我们塑料异型材及门窗行业的的四条工作指示并取得了一定的成绩。

1. 落实坚持“环境友好型、资源节约型、科技创新型”的战略方向，坚持绿色、环保、节能低碳发展，加大技术研发力度，进一步提高自主创新能力，是异型材及门窗产业的发展方向。

(1) 经过专委会和全国塑料标准化技术委员会的共同努力，“塑料异型材有害物质限量”的国家标准编制工作即将完成，报批后我国塑料异型材成为真正绿色环保产品将进入倒计时。

(2) 为了配合并落实“塑料异型材有害物质限量”的国家标准颁布的顺利实施，促进、落实“钙锌热稳定剂”的产业配套体系已见成效。

(3) 具有世界先进水平的“有机基热稳定剂”研发工作处于研发工作的后期，批量实验已经进行，热稳定效果良好、稳定，不久即可在行业大范围推广。

(4) 我国的塑料门窗装饰效果绝大部分处于较低水平，受价格承受能力的影响，高端“通体彩色表面覆膜”的装饰功能始终在市场上没有大范围应用，在专委会多年来大力支持下的：“塑料异型材表面装饰用彩色粘覆膜”即将投入工业化生产。其性能和效果将与世界先进制品相媲美，其价格将有极大的市场竞争力，为塑料异型材及门窗制品进军中高端市场奠定一定的基础。

(5) “高气密性保温塑料推拉窗”的研制工作已有基本定型产品，市场效果非常好。其他几种款式还在继续研制中。

2. 落实第二条：加大结构调整力度，努力提升产业素质，促进产业升级。改造黄石模具企业群体，促进黄石模具群体向中高端转化的产业升级已初见成效。

3. 落实第四条：加强诚信建设。在骨干会员的共同努力下，主产品质量在稳步提升，行业产品信誉、形象在稳步提升，上下游制品之间的纠纷逐渐喊少，拖欠现象逐步缓和，企业内部劳资双方也更合谐，AAA信誉单位在逐渐增多。

【重大发展态势】

一、中原大经济区是今后我国经济发展的重要区域

在2011年年会工作报告中提出的“围绕华北平原腹地的河北省南部、河南省区、安徽北部、山西山东部分区域将是今后我国经济发展中快速发展的区域即‘中国中原大经济区’概念。而伴随经济发展，城乡建设是发展中的重要环节，这些便于进行“新农村建设”、“农业现代化”的平原腹地，在农村社区化改造方面也会走在我国新农村改造的前列，也为保障13亿亩耕地红线做出示范和贡献。我们建材行业必将为今后的经济发展，为低碳环保，为节能减排做出更重大贡献。从多方迹象表明，“中原大经济区”是目前我国最具发展潜力的地方，基本建设、农村发展改造(包括住宅建设)、经济年度增速等变化最显著的区域，这一判断基本准确。

二、黄河几字湾将是现在和未来考虑的重要发展区域

黄河自甘肃省兰州逐渐北上进宁夏过蒙古，途经包头后逐渐转向南成山西、陕西两省分界线，这一段被称为：黄河几字湾。自古有：黄河百害，唯富后套的名言，黄河几字湾所经过的地方是我国西北部地区人口聚集之地，是西北边陲极为重要的战略腹地，是中国乃至世界罕见的能源富集区，被誉为中国腹地的“乌金三角”，从多方发展角度分析将是我国今后重要经济建设发展区域。

黄河“几”字湾区域状况分折

黄河经由甘肃、宁夏、内蒙古、陕西、山西5省区形成“几”字湾流域，包括5省区接壤地带的白银、平凉、庆阳、石嘴山、中卫、吴忠、银川、呼和浩特、二连浩特、阿拉善左旗、鄂尔多斯、包头、乌海、巴彦淖尔、延安、榆林、大同、朔州、忻州、吕梁、临汾等21市(县)和宁东能源化工基地，总面积50多万平方公里。目前，黄河“几”字湾流域煤炭已探明储量808397Mt，约占全国总储量的66.5%，国家确定的13个大型煤炭基地中，有6个集中在此区域；天然气已探明储量2.88亿立方米，约占全国总储量的37.8%；原油已探明储量2160Mt，约占全国总储量的7.5%；钠盐保有储量885400Mt，约占全国总储量的70%；铁矿石、铝土矿、硅石等资源的储量也相当丰富。

得益于丰富的资源禀赋，西部大开发10年来，这一区域的基础设施建设取得突破性进展，经济增长速度明显高于中西部其他地区，是中国经济甚至全球经济增速最快的地区之一。

与此同时，这一区域又是同蒙古、俄罗斯、东北亚地区以及阿拉伯国家交流、合作的重要窗口，也是西煤东运、西气东输、西电东送的重要基地。仅“十一五”期间，这一区域就以不足全国6%的国土面积，调出了占全国能源总调出量一半以上的能源。

罕见的能源富集使黄河“几”字湾区域被誉为中国腹地的“乌金三角”。但是，由于这一区域资源禀赋相近，产业结构趋同，且分属5个省区，条块分割、无序竞争严重，制约了这一区域整体效益的发挥，导致了诸多不良后果。

产业结构单一，极大地增加了产业运行成本和风险，抑制了企业的创新能力，资源的综合与循环利用举步维艰。这里煤炭企业普遍存在技术开发经费严重不足的问题，技术创新投入不及企业销售额的1%，高新技术人才缺乏。其次，难以形成合理的分工协作体系。企业受利益驱动，追求短期效益，资源破坏和浪费严重，安全生产问题突出。此外，极易导致市场剧烈波动，增加国家宏观调控的难度和国家运行成本，给资源的可持续利用、经济社会的可持续发展带来严重隐患。若干利益群体之间的无序竞争，致使成本与价格难以控制。作为能源富集区，没能形成强劲的国际话语权，经济总体发展水平低。与全国相比，尤其是与东部沿海地区相比，该区域属经济欠发达边缘地区。这与该区域长期以资源开发为主、加工业不发达、尚未形成良好的发展机制有密切关系。正在加剧生态环境的恶化。黄河“几”字湾地带地处半干旱地区，又是黄河泥沙的集中输出区，需要加速统筹规划，实现水资源高效利用，才能优化本区域及下游生态环境。

这一系列问题仅靠一地的努力无法从根本上得到解决。只有从国家层面建立跨行政区域的统一协调机制，才能确保该区域经济社会的持续稳定和健康协调发展。

黄河“几”字湾区域正迎来蓄势突破的难得机遇。一方面，随着国家扩大内需政策的持续发力，这一区域可以发挥能源富集、市场广阔的优势，在新的起点上拓展发展空间；另一方面，国内外产业调整和跨区域重组不断深化，也为这一区域承接沿海地区和国际产业转移，促进产业结构优化升级带来机遇。

要抓住机遇，蓄势破题。尽快建立黄河“几”字湾经济合作机制，研究制定5省区区域合作协调机制，协调区域发展中的重大问题，由国家牵头制定中长期发展规划和有关重大政策，并从政策、资金等方面给予支持，打造一个中国腹地经济圈。

黄河“几”字湾区经济圈的战略可定位于四个方面：

一是中西部快速发展的又一“增长极”。以新型工业化、农牧业现代化、城镇化为引领，以发挥综合比较优势为主线，大力优化产业结构，实现经济社会跨越式发展，将这一区域建设成为中西部大开发新的“增长极”和全国区域协调发展的腹心战略支撑点。

二是扩大开放的重要窗口。充分发挥黄河湾作为向西、向北开放的桥头堡和廊道的作用，深化中国——中亚经济合作，着力推进面向中亚、西亚乃至欧洲国家的出口加工基地和区域性国际商贸中心建设，加快承接国内产业转移步伐，形成东联西出、北融南通的创新平台和向西向北开放的战略基地。

三是全国重要的能源原材料供应基地。有序加强煤炭和石油天然气产业链建设以及新能源开发力度，把这一区域建设成为集煤炭、电力、煤制天然气、天然气、成品油、风电和光伏发电为一体的综合性能源供应基地。积极利用我国西北部及中亚地区丰富的矿产资源，把这一区域建设成为以合成材料为主的原材料工业基地和新能源研发与供应基地。

四是保障国家安全的战略要地。以新一轮西部大开发为契机，以多民族文化融合共生为核心，通过加快对外开放和经济社会发展，促进黄河湾区域经济大发展，将其建设成为中亚、西亚、东北亚地区和平发展的“稳定器”和经济发展的“发动机”，为我国中西部边疆的安全建立战略屏障。

三、“第三次工业革命”与中国塑料工业

国外学者提出了“第三次工业革命”的概念和理论，国内展开了热议并掀起了波澜。第一次工业革命是蒸气机带动着机械化的发展；第二次工业革命是自动化的发展，现在热议的“第三次工业革命”正处在萌芽时期，它不是一个纯粹的机械或者单个的技术突破，而是带动了一批技术在研究方向上的改变。这正是“第三次工业革命”和前两次不一样的地方。它以原子能、电子计算机、空间技术和生物工程的发明和应用为主要标志，涉及信息技术、新能源技术、新材料技术、生物技术、空间技术和海洋技术等诸多领域的一场信息控制技术革命。这次科技革命不仅极大地推动了人类社会经济、政治、文化领域的变革，而且也影响了人类生活方式和思维方式，使人类社会生活和人的现代化向更高境界发展。

“第三次工业革命”过程中我们塑料加工行业的主要关注与行动点：

第一点两化融合(信息化与工业化融合)。

“第三次工业革命”是进入信息化的标志，发达国家是在工业化完成或基本完成的情况下进入信息化的，并把信息化作为国家发展的优先战略，而我国则在工业化还没有完成的情况下又遭遇信息化，使得我国工业化进程必需与信息化同时开展并考虑与信息化的充分融合，走出一条与发达国家不同的实现工业化的发展道路，即有中国特色的新型工业发展之路。我国塑料加工各行业应在信息化的大数

据时代走出我们自己的自主创新发展战略之路。

(1) 数据分析可以发现创新机遇。从盲目到主动，也可能是未来新的开端。对已知的数据进行分析就能了解趋势并能做出判断，对我们来讲数据分析将成为机遇与挑战。挑战是怎样从海量信息中找出规律，机遇是我国拥有世界上最多的人，最多的个体，最多的数据，不是追求某某的隐私，而是了解整个群体的趋势。

(2) 信息技术与行业结合可以改变工业生产方式。信息相当于延伸了大脑的智力，使我们做到了以前难以想象的事情，随着处理技术的提高，信息会更广泛地渗透到各方面的应用。随着新兴信息技术的产生和应用，不少传统行业的生产方式，以及商业模式都在悄然发生着变化，随着信息技术与各行各业结合的更加紧密，未来工业的生产方式也将发生显著变化。

第二点新材料技术是中国塑料工业在“第三次工业革命”中无可替代的基础和支撑。

新材料涉及领域广泛，一般指新出现的具有优异性能和特殊功能的材料，或是传统材料改进后性能明显提高和产生新功能的材料，主要包括新型功能材料、高性能结构材料和先进复合材料，其范围随着经济发展、科技进步、产业升级不断发生变化。新材料既是现代化的一种高新技术，又代表现代化的高新技术产业。新材料有两方面内涵：一方面是指运用新概念、新方法和新技术，合成或制备出具有高性能或具有特殊功能的新材料。如碳纤维可以说是一种全新概念的新材料，用聚丙烯腈原丝经过专门的碳化工艺制备而成；另一方面是指对传统材料的再开发，使性能获得重大的改进和提高，如纳米改性、稀土改性、工程塑料改性等目前较活跃，品种增多，性能不断提高。中国塑料工业在新材料技术方面占据得天独厚的优势。

新材料是一种基础性和支柱性战略产业，是现代高新技术和产业的基础和先导。任何一种高新技术的突破都必须以该领域的新材料技术突破为前提。材料方面的突破将有可能引发新的产业性革命。中国塑料工业实现颠覆性自主创新，中国塑料工业步入世界先进强国之列，必将寄希望于新材料技术。

新一轮产业变革是一种建立在互联网和新材料、新能源相结合上的新经济发展模式。材料工业是国民经济的基础产业，新材料是材料工业发展的先导，新材料已被列入国家七大战略性新兴产业之一。

(1) 新材料是攻关新科技革命的物质基础，它在第三次工业革命的地位和作用主要表现在以下方面：

第一，新材料本身就是一种高新技术，又是现代高新技术和产业的基础和先导。在第三次工业革命中，将出现高新技术的大量开发和应用，任何一种高新技术的突破都必须以该领域的新材料技术突破为前提。就我国而言，某些重大工程和项目中出现的问题和困难都可以归结为材料技术还没有取得突破。而新材料的突破往往会引发人类划时代的变革，因此新材料在第三次工业革命中将起到无可代替的基础和支撑作用。

第二，新材料与现代科学技术深度融合，是现代科学技术的组成部分，也是制约现代科学技术发展的瓶颈。第三次工业革命将以新能源、信息和新材料结合为特征，这样的话将有大量的各种新材料得到开发应用，如果新材料的性能和质量不能突破，将直接影响到其它高新技术的应用和产业发展。

第三，新材料对实现可持续发展的作用非常重要，大有作为。第三次工业革命的背景是资源、能源问题的全球性紧迫，目标是可持续发展。新材料的作用非常重要，大有作为。例如：新能源材料是新能源、可再生能源开发利用的基础。环境友好材料对节约资源、保护环境、维持生态平衡将起到重要作用。轻质高强的新型结构材料将体现节能降耗的巨大效益。生物医用材料将提高人类生活质量和健康水平。新型绿色建材关系到资源充分利用。

(2) 全球新材料产业发展趋势

新材料技术与纳米技术、生物技术、信息技术相互融合，结构功能一体化、功能材料智能化趋势明显，材料的低碳、绿色、可再生循环等环境友好特性备受关注。

从全球来看，新材料的发展趋势可归纳为：

第一，新材料与其他新技术深度融合，形成跨学科、跨领域、跨部门的发展态势。

第二，新材料上、下游产业结合更加紧密。新材料具有跨学科、领域、部门的特征，与信息、能源、医疗、交通、建筑等产业结合越来越紧密，新材料产业呈横向扩散和互相包融趋势。新材料与器件制造一体化，上下游产业纵向联合，产业链向下游应用延伸。产品高性能化、功能化和多功能化，开发和应用联系更加紧密。

第三，新材料更加注重可持续发展。发展绿色、高效、低能耗、可回收再用的新材料以及发展先进的数字化制造技术是新材料发展的主要方向。未来新材料的发展将加强注重与资源、能源、环境协调发展，注重资源再生利用，发展低能高效、无污染或少污染制造技术，提高产品人性化、环保化。以绿色建材为例，未来新材料在建材领域的目标是：抗菌、防霉、隔热、阻燃、调温、调湿、消磁、防射线、抗静电等。

第四，经济需求成为主要发展动力。当前的世界，谁能在新技术及产品上发展更快，谁就能占领未来经济新增长的主动权。

(3) 我国新材料产业发展现状

虽然我国新材料的发展取得了巨大成绩，但是总体发展水平仍与发达国家有较大差距，新材料产业尚未实现由资源密集型向技术密集型的跨越，产业发展面临一些亟待解决的问题，这主要表现在：

第一，新材料自主开发能力薄弱。关键新材料保障能力不足，许多关键产品还依赖进口，受到国外制约。

第二，产业发展缺乏科学规划、统筹规划和政策引导，产业结构不甚合理，产业规模小，较分散、同一水平重复多，形成国内同行竞争。

第三，大型材料企业创新动力不强，研发投入少，关键新材料保障能力不足；产学研用相互脱节，产业链条不完美，新材料推广应用困难，新材料产业研发投入少且分散。

第四，新材料产业总体仍处在高投入、高消耗、低效益的粗放型阶段。新材料的高产值以高能耗换取。

(4) 发展新材料的对策

第一，应加速产业结构调整，促进新材料由资源型向集约型转变。完善产业发展的政策体系，加快资源整合，优化产业布局，根据各地优势资源及产业基础，重点培育和发展一批新材料产业骨干企业；通过支持企业强强联合、兼并重组，促进产业集聚和资源整合，培育一批具有国际竞争力的大型新材料企业集团，构建产学研用协调发展的产业模式。

第二，加强企业技术创新及技术改造。鼓励支持上下游企业和科研院所建立各种模式的创新联盟，由企业、研究机构和大学共同参与，强化技术开发的实用性、先进性和集成性，通过知识产权的约定保障各自利益。

培育一批有典型示范效应的产业基地和园区，搭建产学研用一体化创新平台，加快技术研发、成果推广和产业化步伐。鼓励国外研究机构和公司参与产学研用联盟，在互惠互利及产权保护协议的基础上，开展合作研究、人才培训和技术交流。

第三，健全和完善新材料产品国家标准体系。根据我国新材料产品的特点和发展趋势，健全和完善新材料产品的国家标准体系。积极参与新材料国际标准的制定。

第四，建立和完善高效的投融资体系。建立有利于新材料产业发展风险投资扶持政策，积极引导风险资本与成长型新材料企业对接，完善市场退出机制。加大财政、金融、税收、土地等方面对新材料产业的扶持力度，设立新材料产业发展专项资金，确保对新材料产业连续、稳定的支持。

第五，营造使用我国自主开发的新材料的机制和环境。鼓励优先使用我国自主开发的新材料，加大支持力度，对于战略性的重要新材料，可成立专门的工程应用研究中心，开展高端应用研究，在应用中实现改进和提高。

第六，争取和创造良好的国际环境，保证国内企业健康发展。高度重视利用反专利、反倾销手段，为我国新材料的发展创造公平的市场环境，保护我国新材料产业健康发展。严格控制稀缺资源和资源型初级产品出口，强化我国具有资源优势的新材料的比较优势，构建良好的供应体系，共同培育国内材料产业发展的市场环境。

第七，实施专业人才培养战略。加大新材料领域创新型人才的培养力度，建立适合创新人才发展的激励和竞争机制，吸收国外高水平的技术和管理人才，为推动我国新材料产业科技创新体系的建设提供保障。

新材料是材料工业发展的先导，新材料已被列入国家七大战略性新兴产业之一。中国塑料工业应该在“第三次工业革命”中充分利用国家政策的支持，整合社会与行业的资源，建立重大新材料研发项目，促使我国塑料工业实现颠覆性、革命性改变，将我国的塑料工业推向世界先进最前沿。

四、塑料异型材将成为“环境友好型”材料

钱桂敬会长在2011年行业年会上的第一条工作指示内容：坚持“环境友好型、资源节约型、科技创新型”的战略方向，坚持绿色、环保、节能低碳发展。这是异型材及门窗产业的发展方向。什么是环境友好型？初步认为：我们的塑料异型材产品应该具备资源节约型、制造能源低耗型、应用节约能源型、环境保护型、可再生利用型、性能优良型等条件可称为环境友好型材料。

第一条、资源节约型

塑料异型材其主要用途为建筑门窗和其他用途的建材，这些用途材料的材质主要是铝、塑、木三种。木：木材主来源是森林，减少木材消耗是保护森林，保护大自然、保护人类生存环境，森林是宝贵不可缺的资源。铝：铝是由铝土矿经电解而成，目前铝土矿虽然不是紧缺资源但也不是取之不尽用之不竭。塑：主原料 PVC 树脂，PVC 树脂可通过石油法和电石法两种途径获得，两种途径生产的 PVC 树脂品质基本相同。电石法生产 PVC 树脂的主要原材料是石灰石和食盐，石灰石就是碳酸钙，我国大多山脉都是这种山石，不存在资源问题；食盐即氯化钠，海水中富含此物，不存在资源问题。以塑代木，以塑代铝节约资源。

第二条、制造能源低耗型

据资料介绍：“塑料门窗比铝合金门窗节约生产能耗 87%，根据我协会了解的情况：生产一吨塑料异型材比生产一吨铝型材(均从初始原料算起，塑料异型材采取耗电量最大的电石法计算)可节约用电 10000 度左右。根据网上查询：发一度电用煤 0.36kg，多生产一吨塑料异型材少生产一吨铝型材，可节约煤炭 3.6 吨，少排放 CO_2 气体 9.43 吨、少排放 SO_2 气体 30.6kg、少排放氮氧化物气体 26.64kg。以塑代铝是制造能源低耗型，同时节约了煤碳不可再生资源，减少了大量有害气体排放，尤其是可有效大量减少二氧化碳气体排放，延缓温室效应造福人类，利及子孙。

第三条、应用节约能源型

据资料介绍：“塑料门窗比铝合金门窗节约采暖能耗 30% ~50%”；

目前我国塑料异型材及门窗制造应用水平 U_W = 1.6 ~1.8W/m^2·K；

我国目前断桥铝合金门窗制造应用水平 U_W = 2.2 ~2.4W/m^2·K；

如图所示德国塑料门窗制造水平 U_W = 0.73W/m^2·K。

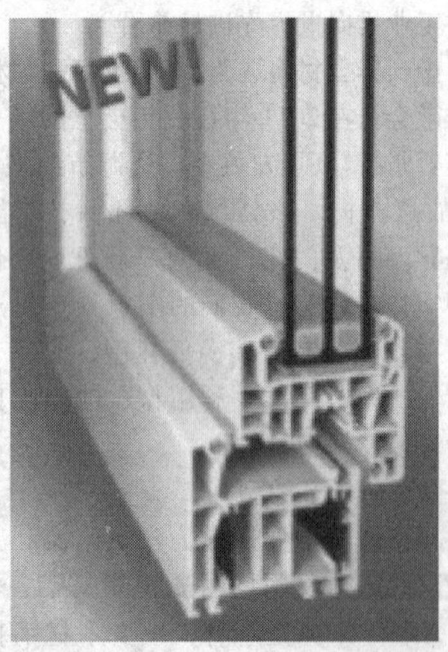

塑料门窗是世界上目前保温、节能效果最好的产品。用于制造塑料门窗的主原料：塑料异型材是应用节约能源型材料。

第四条、环境保护型

如第二条、第三条所述，在大量节约制造与应用节能的同时即节约了不可再生资源，又可大量减少有害气体排放，有效保护了人类生存环境。“塑料异型材有害物质限量”的国家标准即将颁布，届时塑料异型材制品将成为百分之百的绿色产品，成为环境保护型产品。

第五条、可再生利用型

塑料异型材主原材料为 PVC 树脂，而 PVC 树脂具有可反复塑化性能，这种性能成就了它可反复被重新加工的特性，废旧料可重新加工成全新制品。塑料异型材具有可再生利用型。

第六条、性能优良型

在塑料门窗的发源地德国，早期制造的塑料门窗距今已经 70 多年，很多早期制品仍在完好的应用。多年来塑料门窗在建筑物上的应用除玻璃幕墙外应用到世界各地各种建筑和各种恶劣环境中，均体现了其优异的性能、顽强的生命力和应用发展前景。用塑料异型材制作的塑料门窗具有优良的高抗风压性能，在高层建筑和台风频发地区展现了其无可替代的优势；在北方干旱高风沙地区展示了其高气密防尘功能；只要我们严格按应用环境要求合理选择适用的塑料异型材及相匹配的各种附配件，即能体现出其优良的机械物理性能。塑料异型材有其他材质无法相比的更优良的“可装饰性”。塑料异型材是性能优良型材料。

塑料异型材是环境友好型材料。

五、中国住宅消费趋势

近年来，中国的住宅市场呈现了向两极分化的明显态势，呈“M 形消费”。著名经济学家郎咸平在“2012 名家高峰论坛”上提出了“M 型消费”态势。郎咸平说：所谓“M 型消费”，即 14% 的老百姓只买高端产品，使得高端产品一片火爆，而 84% 的老百姓比较贫穷，购买不起中档产品，他们转而纷纷购买低档产品，这样就使得中档产品逐渐萎缩。郎咸平说：目前中国特殊的市场环境使房地产产品具有保值的功能堪比国际上公认的保值工具黄金。郎咸平提醒说：如今中国的“M 型消费”态势又使得房地产投资应该紧跟市场的消费态势。

我们行业内的企业应密切关注市场变化、需求变化、长远发展态势，及时调整产品方案、主要市场方向、研发方向、企业发展战略等，争取走在变化与发展的前列。

【存在的问题】

一、2011 年年会工作报告中曾提出了九个方面的问题，如下：

1. 行业向高端消费市场发展形成了瓶颈；

2. 低利润环境的困扰；

3. 产能增速过快；

4. 企业领导者的综合素质；

5. 专业技术人才匮乏；

6. 产品核心竞争力需要提升；

7.“企业诚信”尚显不足，行业自律仍需加强；

8. 科技研发投入不足、自主创新能力薄弱；

9. 上下游制品间战略合作关系、协作进行科研、开发等尚未有效实现。

上述九个方面的问题仍均不同程度的存在，我们仍要继续努力尽快、尽早改善或解决。今年二季度后期以来PVC树脂价格走低，型材企业利润点有所回升，应格外珍惜期待以久的局面。多年来，低利润空间的困扰失掉了发展后劲，损失了研发力量，只为温饱生存，我们行业应在今后一段时间内抓紧积蓄能量，做好创新发展的基础准备。

二、去年年会工作报告中曾对“培育自主品牌是‘十二五’期间的重要战略之一”较详细的进行了阐述，培育自主品牌是一个长期的战略措施，也是我们行业重要欠缺与不足且很重要的一面，我们要持久的坚持下去。

三、许多企业的领导存在“领导意识”不足。

现存企业领导的“领导意识”应注重以下二个方面：

第一，着眼于对企业领导者观念进行重塑；

第二，建立、改进企业战略的架构

1. 重塑观念，改变领导的经营管理思想，是迈向成功的先决条件。这并不意味着要对过去的成功企业家所言所行亦步亦趋，而是指企业领导者要打破看待事物和他人的固有的狭隘思维。企业领导者要优化自我认知，对经营管理领域所经历的危机、所克服的恐惧、所秉承的立场、所汲取的教训都有清晰了解；在此基础上积极拓展改进，寻求并积累诀窍，以事业而非个人成见为出发点，始终关注目标确保不放过任何一条有助于实现目标的好点子，找到知识的拥有者和来源；同样重要的是要同工作团队、伙伴、客户等人群建立互信。

2. 领导企业上规模并确保掌控局面，必然需要对战略、文化等方面做好规划和计划。做好企业战略部署，关键在于企业领导者及其团队认清顾客及其需求、企业内部现状、行业竞争等现实情况，基于此制定长远却不脱离现实的远景目标，确保企业战略每一步，在企业内每一层级都能达成共识。企业领导者必须警惕各层级员工“消极抵触”情绪，为此需要更明确、更耐心地完成远景等战略叙述，保障员工的参与渠道并汲取其良好建议。

战略共识形成，就需要细化为资源、组织、流程等架构。在这一转化过程中，常常出现两种危险情况：第一，缺乏实现远景目标所需的资源，员工建议也不被企业领导者采纳，导致员工对于实现目标失去兴趣；第二，企业领导者频频更改远景目标，让员工每每觉得领导者又开始了新一轮空谈。企业领导者需要针对核心业务制定配套程序、规章与资源分配办法，更加清晰地定义岗位职责，确保战略与架构不出现脱节。

四、我们行业内企业领导较普遍存在两种较大的认识误区：团队创新和企业文化。

谈到创新很多人的概念局限在技术与产品创新的局部层面上，对企业团队创新还比较模糊，认识不够全面，“企业团队”是现代组织的结构形式和现代组织活动的方式，是当代管理的最重要环节之一，通过创新，可以使企业团队个体成员的能力得到极大的释放和发挥，可以使企业团队的任务较好地完成，从而可以使团队的绩效大大提高。此外，创新还是一种文化，它在平等、协力的“企业团队”氛围中使企业团队成员能够更好的生存发展不断受到鼓励，它也可以使团队成员之间更加和谐。关于“企业团队创新”，在本工作报告的后面的参考资料中有较详细的阐述。

谈到企业文化，不少人认为，企业的核心思想、标语、口号、宣传册等一些表象，没有理解企业文化的真正内涵，关于“企业文化”在2012年工作报告的后面的参考资料中有较详细的阐述。

希望我们行业内企业领导能认真领会“企业团队创新”，“企业文化”的真正内涵，并逐步改善现有不良状况。

【重点企业】

西安高科建材科技有限公司

高科建材是西安大型国由西安大型国有企业西安高科(集团)公司投资组建的现代化新型建材企业，是国家火炬计划重点高新技术企业，中国有机锡环保型材创新示范基地。总资产超10亿元，员工2000多人。

经过十余年发展壮大，高科建材已成长为中国塑料型材行业领先企业、西部管道龙头企业。高科建材品牌影响力位列行业三甲。旗下拥有三个生产基地，两个控股公司。产业横跨型材、管道、门窗、楼宇智能及电子元器件五大门类，形成了产业化、规模化、集约化、现代化、高端化、国际化的新型建材产业集群。

高科建材拥有各类专利技术二十多项，是西安市技术中心和陕西省技术中心。先后通过了

ISO9001、ISO14001、ISO18001 国际质量、环境和安全体系认证，先后获得西安市名牌、陕西省名牌、陕西省著名商标和中国驰名商标，在全国建有 100 多个销售部、500 多家经销商，产品同时出口美国、德国、加拿大、俄罗斯、澳大利亚、巴西、韩国、印度等 19 个国家和地区。

2013 年开始，高科建材着眼于长远和更大的发展，按照"总体规划，分步实施"的原则，规划建设高科集团新型建材产业园，到"十二五"末将形成高科集团新型建材产业集群。

高科建材将本着"创造绿色人居空间"的企业使命，以"领先新型建材业，做最值得信赖的国际品牌"为愿景，坚持"锲而不舍、勇于超越"的企业精神，奉献环保节能建材产品，顺应低碳经济的国际化潮流，积极推动行业进步，引领中国新型建材业走上绿色健康产业之路!

【专委会工作】

专委会在 2012 年的工作除例行延续的《塑料异型材》杂志、塑料异型材网站等方面工作外，重点开展了以下各方面工作：

1. 进行行业调查，为指导行业发展建立数据支持

2. 筹备并召开"2012 年全国塑料异型材及门窗行业年会"；(河南省焦作市召开)

3. 为了促进黄石模具企业产业升级，开展了诸多相关工作；

4. 布置落实去年年会中钱桂敬会长的四点指示。

5. 在中国塑料加工工业协会的领导下开展各项工作，认真落实中国塑料加工工业协会布置的评选和其他方面工作；

6. 为 2010 年《中国塑料工业年鉴》撰稿；

7. 为《塑料异型材专用钛白粉》行业标准的编制进行大量基础工作，目前已经完成审查，争取今年完成报批；

8. 正在编制的四个助剂行业标准编制工作已经进入审查阶段，争取今年完成报批；

9. 为行业今后产品实现真正的环保、绿色，成为环境友好环产品进行诸多相关工作；

10. 专委会高度关注、支持、协助以企业为主体的科技创新工作，及时做好各项服务；

11. 继续推进科技创新项目："高气密节能塑料推拉窗"研制工作；

12. 为众多企业排忧解难，在生产、技术、人才、市场等方面给予企业帮助；

13. 针对今年市场变化现状，专委会多次向行业内企业提出：及时调整各方面工作的建议，以创新求发展，以变化求生存；

14. 认真研究、学习，洞察国际国内政治经济形势和状况，分析发展态势，为行业发展提供参考意见；

15. 促进企业在"企业诚信"、行业自律，建立行业良好的形象和秩序；

16. 为保证行业快速健康发展，在提高与培养企业高管人员的自身管理水平、领导艺术，胸襟、胆识、魄力等综合素质方面，专委会做了大量的工作；

17. 以创新求发展，培育创新型专业技术人才，打造行业内高水平专业技术队伍，专委会一直在孜孜不倦的努力着。

(中国塑料加工工业协会异型材及门窗专业委员会　王存吉)

注塑制品

【行业现状】

2012 年行业生产经营情况

2012 年国内外经济形势依然复杂多变，对我国塑料加工行业生产发展也产生了较大的影响，我们注塑行业在"迎难而上保平稳，开拓创新求增长"方针的指导下，行业加快转变发展方式，加快结构优化调整，把工作着力点放在细分市场和实施差异化战略上来，放到依靠创新技术进步，优化产品结构调整和开发新产品上来，保持了行业生产经营平稳发展。根据纳入中国塑协注塑专委会统计的二十五家企业完成工业总产值 15.0 亿元。其中周转箱产值 4.45 亿元；汽车配件产值 5.4 亿元；家电配件产值 1.33 亿元；日用制品产值 0.81 亿元；其他制品产值 3.01 亿元。同比工业总产值增长 -3.3%，其中周转箱增长 -2.6%；汽车配件增长 -5.2%；家电配件增长 234%；日用制品增长 1.7%；其他制品增长 -25.8%。完成工业总产量 67050 吨。其中周转箱产量 28713t；汽车配件产量 12321t；家电配件产量 1527t；日用制品产量 5514t；其他制品产量 18956t。同比工业总产量增长 -0.8%。周转箱产量增长 -1.4%；汽车配件产量增长 -6.9%；家电配件产量增长 -13.3%；日用制品产量增长 13.1%；其他制品产量增长 2%。工业增加值 2.06 亿元，同比增长 4.4%。固定资产净值平均余额 4.99 亿元，同比增长 -1.8%。2012 年行业完成产品销售收入 14.2 亿元，实现利润 6376 万元。同比销售收入增长 -4.8%，利润增长 11.8%。行业中 7 家企业销售收

入超5000万元，5家企业销售收入超亿元。12家企业利润超百万元，行业仍有1家企业亏损，亏损额27万元，明显下降。行业职工平均人数3920人，同比增长-6.6%，行业职工年平均收入32071元/人，同比增加6785元/人。

【行业重点企业产能】

2012年度中国塑协注塑制品行业企业完成技经指标排行榜
（1～10名）

排行名次	销售收入/万元		实现利润/万元		工业总产值/万元		工业总产量			
							总产量/t		其中：周转箱产量/t	
1	浙江远翅控股集团有限公司	51419	浙江远翅控股集团有限公司	2822	浙江远翅控股集团有限公司	54443	广州洛民塑料有限公司	11677	广州洛民塑料有限公司	4799
2	广州洛民塑料有限公司	20102	广州洛民塑料有限公司	706	广州洛民塑料有限公司	18156	浙江远翅控股集团有限公司	9745	顺德大良塑料二厂有限公司	4786
3	苏州富事达塑业有限公司	12026	新疆珠江塑料有限公司	566	苏州富事达塑业有限公司	13179	天津市津英达塑料制品有限公司	6789	苏州富事达塑业有限公司	3500
4	天津市津英达塑料制品有限公司	10092	杭州万里塑胶有限公司	462	哈尔滨哈轻塑胶有限公司	12064	顺德大良塑料二厂有限公司	5982	大连七塑塑料有限公司	2887
5	哈尔滨哈轻塑胶有限公司	9127	哈尔滨哈轻塑胶有限公司	396	天津市津英达塑料制品有限公司	10200	苏州富事达塑业有限公司	5870	山西晋特塑料制品有限公司	2200
6	顺德大良塑料二厂有限公司	7454	天津市津英达塑料制品有限公司	312	顺德大良塑料二厂有限公司	7383	威海市海鹰塑胶有限公司	4865	威海市海鹰塑胶有限公司	2015
7	威海市海鹰塑胶有限公司	5058	威海市海鹰塑胶有限公司	260	威海市海鹰塑胶有限公司	5180	新疆珠江塑料有限公司	3300	烟台一塑科技发展有限公司	1800
8	大连七塑塑料有限公司	4316	苏州富事达塑业有限公司	183	新疆珠江塑料有限公司	4520	哈尔滨哈轻塑胶有限公司	3032	无锡市巨龙塑化有限公司	1432
9	新疆珠江塑料有限公司	4266	山西晋特塑料制品有限公司	180	大连七塑塑料有限公司	4385	大连七塑塑料有限公司	2887	杭州万里塑胶有限公司	1117
10	无锡市巨龙塑化有限公司	3672	大连七塑塑料有限公司	161	无锡市巨龙塑化有限公司	3723	山西晋特塑料制品有限公司	2500	昆明市民族塑料化工有限公司	1083

【专委会活动】

一、继续认真做好创建行业协会品牌建设年的各项工作

2012年是中国塑协创建行业协会品牌建设年，专委会按国家民政局5A级评估等级要求，扎扎实实做好专委会秘书处各项基础工作，提高为行业、企业、政府服务能力。规范会员登记管理；加强刊物、网站管理、财务管理；明确分支机构（专委会）管理办法；为专委会今后工作铺好路，打好基础。

二、组织召开2012年中国塑协注塑专委会年会

2012年7月25日至30日，在哈尔滨市召开中国塑协注塑制品专委会二届六次年会。

进入2012年，国内国外经济形势复杂多变，对行业发展也产生较大影响。在此背景下，中国塑料加工工业协会塑料技术协作委员会和注塑制品专委会于2012年7月25～30日，在哈尔滨市联合召开第七届中国塑料工业高新技术及产业化研讨会暨2012中国塑协塑料技术协作委员会年会·技术交流会/中国塑协注塑制品专委会二届六次年会，发表最新科研成果、进行技术交流、开展协作开发，引导成果产业化，促进科技创新，推进行业技术进步。

会议开幕式上，中国塑料加工工业协会曹俭常务副理事长对大会召开表示祝贺并作了"当前中国塑料工业运行情况与对策"的报告、黑龙江省塑料公司吴勇总经理致辞并简介黑龙江塑料工业概况、中国塑协注塑制品专委会顾大全秘书长致辞并作了"中国塑协注塑制品专委会2012年年会工作报告"、中国塑协塑料技术协作委员会包建成理事长致辞并汇报了委员会一年的工作、哈尔滨哈轻塑胶有限公司总经理贾丽萍简介了公司简况并致辞、哈尔滨理工大学材料学院周浩然主任致辞并简介学院概况、北京工商大学材料与机械工程学院黄志刚院长致辞并简介学院概况。

除3篇报告外，大会共收到论文44篇，其中大会报告了32篇，有：浙江远翅控股集团有限公司哈尔滨分公司王海波总经理的"稳中求进，以技术优化推进企业发展”、清华大学化工系高分子研究所于建教授的“聚合物纳米合金制备技术”、中包联塑料委专家委员会副主任兼秘书长/上海市包装技术协会绿色包装委员会秘书长陈昌杰的“中国塑料包装现状及发展趋势论略”、江西南昌大学黄兴元教授的“气体辅助挤出成型技术及其在塑料异型材挤出中的应用”、沈阳市塑料机械研究所金世源所长的“同心双螺杆挤出成型机”、赛默飞世尔科技(中国)有限公司张铭的“Haake转矩流变仪在聚合物加工中的应用”、鲁谷(北京)科技有限公司刘忠诚总裁的“变频高效加热节电系统在塑料机械中的应用”、博创机械有限公司黄土荣技术经理的“伺服微发泡技术为客户提供新的塑料成本解决方案”、佛山市步明精密机器有限公司黄步明董事长的“注射成型加工的成本和价值分析”、北京化工大学金晓明的“机筒开槽单螺杆挤出机研究进展”、北京化工大学教授谢鹏程的“一种新型微型注射成型技术”、北京理工大学化工与环境学院王建的“数值研究螺筒结构对挤出机性能的影响”、科倍隆(南京)机械有限公司经理王彦军的“ZSK Mc18 -配混挤出的最新里程碑”、天华化工机械及自动化研究设计院李世通教授级高工的“万吨级PE - HD燃气管专用料配混造粒装置技术开发”、华东理工大学联合化学反应工程研究所辛忠教授的“基于超支化的高熔体强度聚丙烯的制备及发泡性能”、北京工商大学材料与机械工程学院刘本刚的“PET发泡材料挤出成型关键技术”、北京工商大学材料与机械工程学院温变英教授的“聚合物基导电梯度功能材料研究”、吉林省塑料研究院孟立新副院长的“碳纤维/矿物填料/聚合物复合材料在摩擦材料中的应用”、哈尔滨理工大学韩志东教授的“氮化硼在PE/EVA中的选择性分布及其介电性能的研究”、北京天罡助剂有限公司陈祖欣高工的“光稳定剂给塑料带来活力”、福州市福塑科学技术研究所有限公司彭超所长的“螺杆清洗剂的流变性能研究”、巴斯夫亚太增塑剂实验中心桂国球博士的“世界增塑剂发展趋势——环保与安全”、哈尔滨理工大学韩宝忠教授的“电缆材料新技术”、艾迪科(上海)贸易有限公司树脂添加剂薛顺德技术经理的“水滑石在PVC热稳定剂的应用”、哈尔滨理工大学郝广平副教授的“转矩流变仪应用”、塑料助剂专委会热稳定剂分会施珣若会长的“有机碱复合稳定剂在管道管件加工中的应用”、北京阿科玛化学有限公司侯志芬研发经理的“PVC加工无铅化热稳定剂的解决途径”、浙江海普顿新材料股份有限公司高尔金总经理的“硬质聚氯乙烯(PVC - U)管材专用热稳定剂应用性能研究”、上海思尔达科学仪器有限公司姚汉樑董事长的“热变形实验关键技术及其新进展”、北京化工大学任冬云教授的“一种粉体材料动摩擦系数的测试方法”、中国塑协塑料技术协作委员会丁常楷高工的“中国塑料工业技术水平初探”、清华大学环境学院只艳的“废弃电器电子产品塑料分选与资源化技术研究进展”等。

另外，作为书面发言的12个报告有：北京工商大学材料与机械工程学院翁云宣副教授的“食品包装用塑料制品相关法规和标准介绍”、北京市化学工业研究院贾义军院长助理的“PBT工程塑料技术和市场分析”、北京加成助剂研究所李杰所长的“邻羟基苯并三唑类紫外线吸收剂的结构与作用特点及发展趋势”、哈尔滨理工大学张文龙教授的“氯化聚氯乙烯的性能及应用”、北京崇高纳米科技有限公司李毕忠总经理的“PET工程塑料注射成型技术”、浙江诸暨七色鹿色母粒料有限公司董事长王仲文的“工程塑料着色用色母粒”、北京化工大学苑会林教授的“含氟塑料薄膜的加工与应用”、中国塑协塑料技术协作委员会杨惠娣秘书长的“塑料注射成型技术进展”、中国塑协塑料技术协作委员会/苏州塑料研究所丁常楷总工的“国内各种混炼设备比较”、福建师大环境科学与工程学院陈庆华教授级高工的“膨胀型阻燃剂超支化聚合物的设计及其在高分子材料加工中的应用”、福州大学材料科学与工程学院郑玉婴教授的“无胶热压PTFE覆膜高温滤料”、丹阳力博聚源树脂应用有限公司杨小东总经理的“江苏丹阳地区塑料回收再生行业概况”等。

会议发表论文内容包括新材料、新产品、新工艺、新技术、新设备，以及检测仪器开发和应用等，其中有不少创新点，包括：气体辅助挤出成型技术、新型同心双螺杆挤出成型机、国产伺服微发泡技术设备、国产万吨级同向双螺杆挤出机等；在检测仪器方面对Haake转矩流变仪在电性能、发泡材料性能方面的应用，以及粉体材料动摩擦系数的测试方法引起了代表的兴趣；在推进节能新技术方面，会议积极推荐变频高效加热节电系统在塑料机械上的应用以及气体辅助注射成型、微发泡注射成型、两板注射成型机等新技术。

对于当前聚氯乙烯行业中禁用铅稳定剂及其替代方案也进行了集中研讨，认为行业禁铅是必然趋势，而且，目前也已经有多种铅稳定剂替代品出现，包括钙锌复合稳定剂、复合型多功能有机锡和有机稳定剂等，但是，从经济和技术两方面还存在需要进一步解决的问题，在一些应用领域，如大规格管材挤塑和管件注塑方面还需要有所突破。

会议期间还专门安排了一单元时间进行各学科自由交流、创造深入探讨机会，推进各方技术协作。

会议期间代表还参观了哈尔滨哈轻塑胶有限公司，对企业先进的管理印象深刻。

会议得到哈尔滨哈轻塑胶有限公司、哈尔滨理工大学材料学院大力支持和精心安排，在此表示衷心感谢！对于会议的各支持单位也在此一并致谢！

三、年会优秀发言稿：中国塑协注塑专委会副理事长单位，浙江远翅控股集团有限公司"稳中求进，以技术优化推进企业发展"

浙江远翅控股集团有限公司总部设于中国杭州，于1984年进入汽车塑料配件行业。1997年增资，2002年由集体企业转制为民营企业。截至2011年12月底，公司总资产7.4亿元，目前在国内设有浙江远翅、昌河远翅、重庆远翅、柳州远翅、南京远翅、九江远翅、哈尔滨远翅七家生产型企业和杭州正远机电公司贸易型企业。总占地面积为20.3万平方米，建筑面积为10.4万平方米。公司现有员工1733余人，从事科技活动人员80余人，直接从事研发人员60余人。主要生产汽车塑料内饰件、前后保险杠、汽车仪表板、方向盘等汽车配件。2010年获得中国机械500强荣誉，市场占有率比较高。2011年企业总产值63524万元，税收2185万元，利润3644万元。至此，2012年已经走完了一半的里程，回首过去，让我们感触最深的就是那股寒潮，远胜于2008年的那场危机。由于汽车行业在国家优惠政策取消的影响下，小排量车的市场销量明显降缓，我公司配套的各大主机厂的产量受到一定的冲击，直接影响到集团的新产品项目开发以及新产品所创造的经济效益。为此集团公司在年初就积极应对，在集团会议上就提出了"稳中求进，以技术优化推进企业的发展"的理念，在稳定企业正常生产的过程中，延伸企业技术中心的开发及管理，优化生产制造工艺，以此推进整个集团的稳定发展。

远翅集团技术中心承担了整个远翅集团的新产品开发工作，在2007年12月被浙江省经济技术委员会授予"省级企业技术中心"称号。中心下设七个部门，项目管理部、产品开发部、工装工艺部、业务部、办公室、实验室、市场开发部。依照项目的开发流程和要求进行分工协作，保证产品开发的有序进行。同时推行规范化、标准化的管理模式，在自身不断向前发展的同时，带动供应商同步前进、提升，期间仍不断汲取新知识，提升整个技术中心整体水平和能力，更进一步的发挥自身优势，主动推进自主创新，加快科技成果向现实生产力的转变，不断提高企业发展的质量和效益，增强企业在国内国际市场的竞争力。

由于集团公司的生产企业大部分建立在主机厂附近，同时主机厂对供应商的管理能力、开发能力、应对能力、质量控制及服务等也提出了更高的要求，这就使原来集团技术中心单一的研发全部在总部进行，各子分公司负责装车、跟进、反馈这一模式已经显出了各种各样的弊端：沟通不畅、信息传递不及时、信息传递错位、时间滞后、管控风险加大等。为了加强集团技术中心整体水平，让流程统一化，管理标准化，信息平台化，提升同级化，整个集团的技术中心管理必须进行延伸，向一线拓展。因此，在新年伊始，中心就根据集团提出的新理念，按照一下几方面进行了拓展、延伸：

新产品业务整体化：技术中心成立市场开发部，主要针对新产品市场的拓展。以前各分公司方面的市场基本上由分公司进行联系及洽谈，而客户源了解的也仅仅是单一分公司的经营及发展情况，缺乏对整个集团的了解。成立市场开发部后，由技术中心市场开发部连同分公司同时推进与客户的沟通与交流，让客户全面的了解远翅集团的生产、开发能力。同时市场开发部对整个集团的市场信息进行管理，定期进行回访，在年末进行整理、对比、分析，以便提供给集团一份详尽的市场分析报告。同时中心对各子分公司的新产品开发管理实行双重管理，一方面各子分公司的产品部/技术质量部从属于公司主管新产品开发的主管经理的领导，做好公司各方面的工作，另一方面同时归属于集团技术中心的领导，对于总部技术中心下达的各项工作任务应及时圆满完成，并积极配合集团技术中心，对新产品的管控做到一线。

开发流程统一化：技术中心的向前延伸不仅仅是人员、部门、框架的延伸，同时还是管理模式的延伸，一方面由于各子分公司技术力量的不统一性而造成的技术能力参差不齐，另一方面没有系统的进行各项流程的培训，造成各子分公司对新产品开发的流程理解不一，都不能按照流程去完成工作，在思想上就存在的差异，这对新产品开发的管控是极其不利的。开发流程的统一，是中心管理延伸的基础，只有打好了这个基础，集团技术中心与各子分公司产品部/技术质量部的思想才能统一，才能有效的完成相关工作，快速推进开发进程。

部门管理标准化：有了统一的流程，就为我们夯实了基础，开发管理工作才能进入正轨，真正做到标准化管理。中心会同各子分公司的产品部/技术质量部将各种技术管理制度积极推进运行，对各子分公司的技术部门采用集团技术中心的统一管理的模式，包含规范的文件格式，清晰的看板制度，有序的进度管控。

信息畅通平台化：目前，各子分公司与集团技术中心之间的沟通存在信息不畅通，信息错位、延后等问题，在今后的管理中，集团技术中心与各子分公司的产品部/技术质量部之间会在信息沟通上对平台进行升级管理，采用视频会议系统、规范的会议制度以及定期的项目例会制度，一方面更多时候的问题交流可以通过视频呈现，更加直接的看到问题，使得沟通效果更佳，对问题的讨论也形象化，另一方面各子分公司的技术人员直接参与到整个项目开发过程中，真正做到 PDT 小组成员应尽的职责。

检测共享化：集团技术中心现有实验室已经不断增加试验设备，目前两台大型设备(高低温试验箱、氙灯老化箱)均能满足各种不同标准的相关试验，可以为各分公司的新产品以及常规产品进行相关试验项目的检测。而且实验室在推进认证工作，更多项目的检测将得到国家认可，为今后整个集团公司的产品检测提供更多的帮助，也为集团的新产品开发成本的降低提供支持。

技术中心的管理延伸是整个集团发展的需要，通过将技术管理延伸到各子分公司的前沿，可以将整个集团的技术力量凝聚起来，不仅仅只依靠单方面总部技术中心的整体开发平台，还结合了各分公司产品部小而专的特殊优势，更全面的将整个集团的开发能力及技术水平展现在客户面前，保质、保时的开发出客户满意的产品，为公司创造良好的经济效益。

在目前汽车市场低迷的情况下，稳定是企业的重点，而如何在稳定中求前进，又是放在企业管理者面前的一道难题。现在对我们企业来说，稳定的市场是前提，而稳定的产品质量是创造经济效益的根本，所以集团公司在 2011 年初就提出了降本增效的要求，并且一直贯穿在整个集团公司的生产经营过程中。技术优化也作为其中一项重要的工作，列在工作目标的前列。中心在技术优化工作中起到了领头羊的作用，负责牵头分公司，对新产品开发及正常生产过程中的重点、难关组织攻关小组，进行技术攻关及优化，提升产品质量，创造良好的经济效益。下面简单列举几项技术优化给企业带来的优势。

1. 模具采用三次顶出，达到机械手取件要求

目前我公司开发出来的产品，产品供货批量都是非常大，月产量可达到2.5 万台份，尤其是前后保险杠及仪表板产品，都在为公司创造良好的经济效益。但在这些大件的生产过程中，若采用人工取件，一方面生产周期无法控制，人为因素影响到班产量，另一方面一旦出现操作人员疲劳生产，在安全上就存在很大的隐患。因此我们在设计模具时考虑到产品供货量及取件自动化的要求，确定在原模具的顶出上再增加一次顶出，在不影响开发进度与不增加费用的前提下，完成了顶出机构的改进，使得机械手取件平稳运行，产品的班产量也有了比较明显的提高。也许很多人会说，机械手取件很普通，但由于我公司原来一直匹配微车及家轿产品的企业，产品附加值较低，原来一直采用人工取件的方式，所以在这次技术优化过程中尝到了班产量明显提升，产量大幅提高所带来的甜头，为今后的新产品开发增添了新的经验积累。

2. 内分型类型模具抽芯新结构方式的选用

内分型产品在模具第一次顶出时，产品相对型腔是不动的，根据这个原理，我们将原油缸抽芯结构的孔改成斜导柱滑块结构，只需将滑块设计在模具型腔一侧，锁模块设计在模具型芯一侧。相对油缸抽芯来讲，机械机构费用低，生产时不需要做油缸抽芯动作，可以有效减短生产周期，提高班产量。内分型模具我们原来一般都是在较高附加值产品上设计使用，但根据集团公司对相关产品整个生产过程中合格率的调查，外分型产品后续修边、打磨、抛光所带来的工作量远远超过内分型模具增加的费用。所以近年来，技术中心开发新模具时，首先分析产品内分型的可行性，在可行性分析达到内分型要求的产品，都按照内分型的要求进行模具设计及制作，以确保产品在后期生产过程中保质保量，减少报废率，提高合格率，以创造更高的经济效益。

3. 气体辅助注射成型技术的推广

气体辅助注射成型技术是源于 20 世纪 70 年代，主要生产中空产品，目前我公司主要应用于家电产品及汽车产品上，尤其对于大型平板塑料件及厚薄不均匀的产品。对于平板塑料件，产品质量要求高，采用传统注射成型工艺生产极易变形，而采用气体辅助成型供以后，既保证了产品刚性、强度和外观质量，又减小了制品翘曲变形的风险。而厚薄不均匀的产品，传统的生产工艺需要多副模具然后将几个零件组装在一起，经过组装在一起的零件不仅仅精度差，累积误差大，强度也会大受影响。在采用气体辅助注射成型工艺后，一方面可以通过零件合并来简化成型工艺，减少生产成本，同时可以通过气道设计形成各种气体加强筋或凸台增加制品的刚度和强度。现在在公司生产的产品中，采用气体辅助注射工艺后，降低了注射压力和锁模力，对机台的要求降低，仅为普通注射压力的 50% ~75%，相应成型同样投影面积制品的锁模力也只需 50% ~75%，降低生产成本，提高经济效益。同时还可消除由于

壁厚不均匀带来的缩痕，提高制品表面质量，提升产品合格率，也拓宽了产品设计思路。

气体辅助注射技术目前在汽车领域使用也越来越广泛，它所具备的优点也越来越多的被人们认可，尤其是产品尺寸稳定性的提高、制品残余应力的减少以及翘曲变形量的降低都是它无所厚非的优势所在。

以上简单介绍了一些目前在我公司运用的工艺、技术优化给企业带来的优势。只有从细微之处发现持续改进的目标，从细节做起，才能在目前低迷的汽车市场中抢占先机，求稳定，求发展。

简单粗略的介绍了一下我公司在技术中心管理示范及技术优化给企业带来的推动力，也即将结束我在此次会议上的发言。不到之处，请在坐各位予以指出。同时也希望对我公司配套业务感兴趣的同仁，可以有个交流和沟通的机会。

四、做好行业技术经济信息交流平台建设

1. 坚持做好一年一度全行业经济技术指标的统计汇总，交流发行到各成员单位；

2. 继续做好《中国塑协注塑专委会通讯》出版发行工作；

3. 每年组织有关人员编写《中国塑料工业年鉴》注塑制品章节，宣传扩大注塑行业在国内外塑料行业的影响力以及注塑产业在国民经济中的地位和作用。

五、认真做好中国塑协布置的各项工作，协助协会各职能部门开展工作

例如：产品质量标准，产品创优，市场调查决策咨询，技术信息交流等；配合兄弟行业和上、下游行业的产业调查、技术咨询，应北京(美国)科勒有限公司和丹佛斯(天津)有限公司招聘要求开展技术人才信息交流和寻找加工单位等活动；支持帮助成员单位申报地方驰名商标、先进企业、专项创优等工作，提供信息资料、发挥行业优势，提高专委会的公信力。

【重点企业】

1. 无锡市巨龙塑化有限公司

中国塑协注塑制品专业委员会理事长单位，2010年中国塑料行业先进单位。

无锡市巨龙塑化有限公司(原无锡市塑料一厂)，始建于1956年，半个世纪以来，公司从小到大，从生产塑料发夹、鞋底等日用小商品，发展形成拥有国内外先进80g至20000g注塑机群、塑料制品年加工能力8000t的专业化公司。2010年公司注塑制品销售收入超亿元，利润超千万元。年生产销售200万只/4922吨八个系列，一百多个品种规格塑料周转箱，系列大型塑料托盘和配套生产汽车、家电、电子、电器塑料配件以及高新技术工程塑料制品。获得上海大众、一汽集团、美的、小天鹅、春兰、松下等配套企业的好评。公司现有员工200余人，其中工程技术人员占17%。有一支文化水平高、技术管理好、团结求实、创新高效的员工队伍。产品荣获国家银奖质量，公司于1998年通过ISO9000质量认证。

公司引进建立注塑模具CAD辅助设计系统和CAD/CAM模具加工中心，模具设计制造能力达到国内模具行业的先进水平。

公司是中国塑料加工行业的骨干单位。1990年被列为中国轻工总会和江苏省重点企业，1994年以来连续被评为江苏省明星企业。1990年以来一直担任中国塑料加工工业协会注塑制品专业委员会理事长和中国包协塑料制品的包装委员会箱包组组长的职务。是两个行业组织的所在驻地，为行业发展作出贡献，评为“中国塑协优秀专委会”、“2009年度中国塑料行业先进单位”。

2. 杭州万里塑胶有限公司

中国塑协注塑制品专业委员会副理事长单位，2010年中国塑料行业先进单位。

杭州万里塑胶有限公司是专业生产各种塑料制品的中型企业。现为中国塑料加工工业协会注塑制品专业委员会副理事长单位，浙江省塑料工业协会理事单位。公司地处杭州莫干山路方家塘路，紧邻杭州汽车北站，交通十分便利。公司拥有固定资产原值2882万元，土地面积22582m^2，建筑面积13573m^2，职工人数170人，其中各类专业技术人员59人。公司有从45g到6300g注塑机和从ϕ45到ϕ150的挤出机等塑料加工专用设备23台(套)，塑料制品年生产能力8930t。各种塑料烫金、印刷、制版、加工辅助设备6台(套)。各种塑料性能检测和产品检测设备18台(套)。各种金加工设备15台(套)。

2010年公司工业总产值3800万元，塑料制品总产量3000t，产品销售收入3800万元，实现利税300万元。主要产品有24瓶啤酒箱、12瓶啤酒箱、食品周转箱、饮料周转箱、活塞专用周转箱、扑克专用周转箱、各种规格的通用周转箱和多种规格的异型周转箱、周转筐等；各种规格的高发泡聚乙烯(EPE)片材、复合片材、管材、棒材；各种汽车和工业配套件；高档家电塑料件；中空制品和日用塑料制品等500余种。为杭州松下电器公司、可口可乐公司和南京依维柯汽车有限公司指定塑料制品合格供应厂家。

公司质量检测手段齐全，质量管理体系完善，取得由“万泰认证”颁发的ISO9001：2000《质量管理体系》认证证书和ISO14001：2004《环境管理体系》认证证书。公司生产的产品在历年国家、省、市质量监督检查中所有指标全部合格，其中塑料饮料周转箱和食品周转箱多次被评为轻工部优质产品和浙江省优质产品。公司的“万里”商标是杭州市著名商标。公司信用等级AAA级。

公司十分重视技术进步和产品开发。近年来，公司加快设备更新换代，引进了6台全电脑控制的塑料注塑成型机。2006年公司开发了符合现代商业概念的塑料周转箱和工业专用周转箱6只，汽车工业和其他工业新产品2只。这些产品进入市场后，深受用户欢迎，并取得了很好的社会效益和经济效益。

公司努力按社会主义市场经济要求完善内部管理，建立灵活、快速、以人为本的反应机制，提高生产效率，降低生产成本，提高产品质量，提供优质服务、增加经济效益。公司将积极努力加强与大专院校和科研单位的联合；重视和完善信息交流工作、完善公司网络平台；积极引进先进技术、加大技术投入、引进各类人才；不断调整产品结构、努力向高科技含量、高附加值、产品深加工和精加工的方向发展；积极寻求与社会各方面、多层次、多方位、多种形式的合作；为用户提供更加优质的多种类型的服务，真正使公司成为用户可信任的朋友。

3. 浙江远翅控股集团有限公司

中国塑协注塑制品专业委员会副理事长单位，2010年中国塑料行业先进单位，中国轻工百强企业。

浙江远翅控股集团有限公司是一家汽车内外饰件生产企业，集团总部地处杭州萧山区。公司现有职工1900余人，总资产约8亿元人民币，总占地面积21万平方米，建筑面积17.2万平方米，2011年公司销售额达6.1亿元人民币。

公司是国内最早开发、配套汽车塑料仪表板、保险杠、门内板、方向盘等汽车内外饰件的企业之一。企业一直以来坚持走技术创新、产品创新之路，新产品开发投入占公司全年销售额的3%左右。2011年共生产仪表板75万套、保险杠148万支、方向盘20.5万只、门板52.4万块。主要配套车型有轿车、微车、轻卡、大客车、重型车等；主要客户有一汽、东风、长安、上海通用五菱、昌河汽车、哈飞汽车、福田汽车等二十多家主机厂。

公司于1998年通过ISO 9000体系认证，2006年3月通过ISO/TS 16949质量体系认证，2006年6月通过CCC质量体系认证。

公司2005年被评为省科技创新优秀单位。2005年远翅商标获“浙江省著名商标”；2007年公司技术中心被授予“省级企业技术中心”；2008年远翅产品获杭州市名牌产品；2009年至2010年连续2年获得杭州市专利示范企业；2009年至2011年连续3年获“中国机械五百强”企业。

随着公司发展战略需要，集团已分别在南京、柳州、景德镇、九江、重庆、哈尔滨等地建立了子公司，构建30分钟配套服务圈。为主机厂提供模块化、准时制供货服务，逐步走上汽车塑料产业化的发展之路。

4. 苏州工业园区富事达塑业有限责任公司

中国塑协注塑制品专业委员会副理事长单位，2010年中国塑料行业先进单位。

苏州工业园区富事达塑业有限责任公司(苏州塑料一厂)专业生产工程注塑制品、波纹管、片板材和改性材料，积累了50年的塑料加工专业技术经验。是江苏省高新技术企业，拥有自营进出口权，名列国家统计局公布的中国塑料加工企业的前列。

公司现有员工250人，各类专业技术人员100多人，工厂占地面积3.7万平方米，建筑面积2.5万平方米，固定资产3900万元。注塑生产基地位于苏州工业园区，挤出生产基地位于相城区。

追求质量零缺陷，满足并超越顾客的期望，是我们孜孜以求的目标，也是公司持续发展的基石之一。目前已通过了TUV公司的ISO 9001：2000、DVA6.1、QS 9000的质量体系认证，2006年完成TS16949体系的转变。

公司实验室拥有研究分析测试设备近40台(套)，能按ISO、DIN、ASTM、GB等标准进行塑料理化性能测试。目前实验室通过了CMA认证，并被授权为江苏省塑料质量监督检测站苏州分站。

公司注重新品开发能力提升，引进了美国UG公司的CAD/CAM/CAE，实现了设计无纸化，成型过程演示化，制模程序电脑化。同时不断完善创新机制，加入新品开发投入力度。特别是加强特种工程塑料制品的开发。研究所被批准为苏州市工程塑料应用和开发技术中心，是首批市政府批准的10家技术中心之一。

企业将逐步建成在工程塑料行业中规模适度、技术领先、管理先进、装备精良、员工优秀、产品适销，拥有自身核心竞争力众多比较优势的塑料加工企业，办成一个蕴含公司经营哲学及企业文化有相当个性特点的优秀企业。

公司研发部门根据市场需求的变化不断研发新

产品，满足不同客户的要求。如各系列的围板箱，欧标 VDA 箱系列，日系 DP 箱系列，物流箱内材系列(用于汽车另部件、电子行业等领域)新产品总计已远远超过老产品。公司注重知识产权的保护，每年对物流箱均有实有新型和外观设计的专利申请，并有专人对专利管理、创造、保护和运用等工作的开展进行责任制，使专利产品进入销售状态，推动了专利新产品向市场的转型，专利新产品的销售动态十分喜人。

5. 天津市永濠天塑塑料有限公司

中国塑协注塑制品专业委员会副理事长单位，2010 年中国塑料行业先进单位。

天津市永濠天塑塑料有限公司(原天津市塑料制品模具厂)建于一九六五年一月，是国内著名的注塑机加工专业厂和塑料模具制造专业厂。现任中国模协理事长单位和中国塑料加工工业协会注塑制品专业委员会副理事长单位，中国包协塑料制品包装会箱包组副理事长单位。主要生产经营注塑、挤出、模具制造三大产品系列。

公司是在七十年代全国最早生产塑料周转箱的厂家，“冰山”牌塑料周转箱系列产品曾多次荣获市级及国家级优质产品称号。

公司开发的塑料保温箱属于专利产品，这项产品的开发，当时填补了国内空白。多年来为公司创造了稳定的经济效益，目前正致力于将该产品规格化、系列化。

近年来，公司致力于外向型发展，在站稳内地市场的同时，积极拓展国外市场，通过各种渠道，与国外客户接洽，相继开发了晒鱼盘及大型花盆两项产品，在产品开发研制过程中，倾注了全体职工大量心血，使产品顺利进入国外市场，并为公司争取了长年订单，成为新的经济增长点。

天津市塑料制品模具厂完成改制，更名为天津市永濠天塑塑料制品有限公司。改制后计划在原设备基础上重新购置设备 1600t、1100t、650t 注塑机，继续开发汽车配件、电动自行车配件，抓住开发滨海新区的机遇，开发大型捕捞容器。渔业配套设施。

6. 天津市津英达塑料制品有限责任公司

中国塑协注塑制品专业委员会理事会单位。

天津市津英达塑料制品有限责任公司是 1995 年天津钢管公司和汉沽春光塑料厂合资组建的联营企业，是中国塑料加工协会会员单位，2009 年中国塑料行业先进单位，主要产品是石油套管、油管用钢塑螺纹保护器。

公司位于天津市汉沽区东风北路，占地面积 14869.3m^2，厂房占地 10880.43m^2，办公楼及附属设施占地 459.81m^2，公司现有员工 400 多名，科技人员 15 名。

目前公司总资产 6000 万元，投入巨资进行基础建设，更新全部生产设备，选用世界先进水平的德国 DEMAG 和日本全电脑控制系统注塑机，从 125—3600T 不同型号 22 台，45T—200T 液压机 9 台，CNC 数控机床 20 余台，还拥有模具加工的全套设备，车、铣、刨、磨、钻床、线切割等共计 15 台，使用的中小型模具完全由企业自行设计制作。有一条金属喷涂生产线，能完成各种金属件的表面涂层处理。

公司已于 2000 年通过了 ISO9001/2000 版国际质量体系认证，2003 年公司获取了中华人民共和国进出口企业资格证书。

十几年来，自行开发研制了螺纹保护器 10 大系列 300 多个品种，填补了多项国内外同类产品的空白，其中有 16 种产品获得国家发明专利，并有几项产品多次荣获国际大奖。

2012 年，完成工业总产值 10200 万元，年实现利润 312 万元，被命名为纳税大户，为了促进企业的发展，适应市场的需求，确立了以钢管公司为依托，开发自己的产品，开拓广阔的塑料制品市场的经营思路，在 2003 年 5 月份又与天津钢管公司组建了鑫广塑料制品有限责任公司(劳服企业)，投资 920 万元，主要生产塑料托盘，目前已开发了 10 种不同规格的托盘，同时还开发了不同规格的卫生垃圾桶以及家电、汽车配件等产品的制造。其中塑料托盘先后开辟了工业、医药、食品等行业的市场。

2006 年 4 月份又组建了广达石油制管有限公司，投资 1500 万元，主要生产石油套管和油管用接箍，目前正在准备开发二期工程，到今年 11 月底二期工程正式投入生产，生产产品最大规格为 20″，生产能力为 60 万只/年。

公司塑料制品市场在不断的开拓，产品品种在不断的增加。产品不仅仅局限于螺纹保护器、塑料托盘和垃圾桶，还逐步向家电和汽车配件等产品发展，以三个方面作为首要的技术攻关点；一是：新型原材料的使用与改性助剂的选择，二是：新型的注塑工艺，三是：塑模设计、制作及试模结果检验水平的提高。

公司奉行“追求科学管理，坚持质量第一，满足客户需求”的质量方针，视产品质量为生命，不断融合国内外先进的质量方针和技术手段，产品质量的可靠性和稳定性得到充分的保障，公司现有专业质量管理人员 20 名，从班组操作工开始层层把关，形成立体的质量管理体系，确保产品出厂合格率为 100%。

几年来，津英达塑料制品有限责任公司被评为国家级“守合同、重信用”单位，被市政府命名为“优秀企业”“三星级企业”“明星企业”，被市精神文明办命名为“精神文明单位”，被市总工会命名为“十五”立功先进单位，被评为区级“绿色企业”。

7. 哈尔滨哈轻塑胶有限公司

中国塑协注塑制品专业委员会副理事会单位，中国塑协注塑行业先进单位。

哈尔滨哈轻塑胶有限公司，国有控股企业。黑龙江省从事塑料成型加工的龙头企业，注册资本6252万元，是黑龙江省内最大的汽车塑料零部件系统供应商，是哈飞汽车、东安动力、奇瑞汽车等公司的重要零部件供应商。已从原生产单一的电器附件小厂，发展成为生产多品种，涉及多领域的综合性塑料加工企业。注塑加工制品注塑量从100g到50000g成系列配套，注塑锁模力80t至4000t，年注塑加工能力18000t。

公司员工总数424人，退休职工323人。现有专业技术人员103人(高级专业技术人员10人，中级专业技术人员31人，初级专业技术人员62人)，占在岗员工总数的23%；公司为提高产品研发能力和强化质量保证体系，近年已培养一批能够熟练应用AUTOCAD软件、PRO/ECATIA/UG软件，从事产品三维设计的研发队伍，在研发手段，技术技能，实验检测，经验积累，工作流程方面基本与国外先进国家同步，并拥有专利多项。

近几年获得荣誉及体系认证情况：

1. 公司曾荣获哈尔滨市第二十八届、第二十九届、第三十届劳模大会“先进单位”、“先进集体”称号；

2. 2008年公司被评为黑龙江省企业技术中心及哈尔滨市第一批企业技术中心；

3. 荣获2007年黑龙江省和谐劳动关系优秀企业称号；

4. 荣获2004年哈尔滨市纳税A级企业称号；

5. 企业连续十几年荣获哈尔滨市“守信用、重合同”优秀企业称号；

6. 1999年通过ISO 9002：1994版国际质量管理体系认证；

7. 2003年10月又通ISO 9001：2000版国际质量管理体系换版认证；

8. 2006年6月通过ISO/TS 16949认证；

9. 2006年12月通过3C认证；

10. 2009年9月，企业获得黑龙江省注塑行业唯一一家“高新技术企业”称号。

公司主要产品有八大类：

类别	产品系列	产品名称
第一类	汽车内外饰件装饰件	仪表盘、同色保险杠、门内护板、门槛立柱类
第二类	塑料物流产品	注塑叉车托盘、各种塑料周转箱、环保卫生清洁箱
第三类	塑料防护用品	塑料安全帽、防护箱等
第四类	日用塑料小商品	塑料盆、塑料桶、整理箱
第五类	塑料材料共混改性	聚丙烯、ABS
第六类	挤出成型产品	双壁波纹管、大口径缠绕排水管、异型材
第七类	墙体保温材料	XPS保温板
第八类	电器附件	灯头、开关、排插

企业始终秉承“注入新理念，塑出好品质”的企业文化，即以好的人品，注塑出好的产品、乃至精品。企业始终坚持以发展为宗旨，以经济效益为中心，以市场为导向，以科技为动力，不断推动企业向更高的目标迈进。

8. 佛山市顺德区大良塑料二厂有限公司

中国塑协注塑制品专业委员会副理事会单位，中国塑协注塑行业先进单位。

佛山市顺德区大良塑料二厂有限公司的前身是始建于1968年的大良镇民办塑料厂(1972年正名为大良镇塑料二厂)。公司是一个综合性塑料制品生产企业，主要生产大中型系列塑料周转箱、周转萝、塑料货架，以及生产大中型的中空异型制品、各类中空瓶罐制品并兼生产及出口钢制品。

公司是国家塑料制品加工协会副理事长单位，已获ISO 9001：2000国际质量体系认证，取得中国食品用塑料包装容器QS认证。同时取得多家知名国际品牌的饮料集团的质量认证，并在1984年已注册使用“高山牌”商标。

公司占地2万平方米，年产塑料制品可达10kt，生产设备先进，技术力量雄厚，能设计和研发具有工艺技术含量高，结构较复杂，质量要求严的模具和塑料制品。

9. 四川广汉锐星塑胶有限公司

中国塑协注塑制品专业委员会理事会单位。

四川广汉锐星塑胶有限公司是由四川省广汉塑料厂改制成立的塑胶产品和模具制造的民营股份制企业，是中国塑料加工工业协会会员，与四川大学、西南科技大学、西南石油大学建立了“产学研实习基地”。

公司位于古蜀文化三星堆遗址发源地——广汉市，距成都30km，交通运输条件十分便捷。从德国、日本引进的中空容器吹塑生产线，大型注塑机、宽规格塑胶挤出板材和大型热成型机等先进设备，为提供质量稳定优良的塑胶制品奠定了技术装备基础。形成了挤出、吹塑成型、注塑成型和热成型、模具机械制造的产业结构、具有较强竞争能力的综合性塑料加工企业。

公司按照 ISO 9001：2000《质量管理体系要求》建立的质量保证体系，取得了《食品质量安全许可证》、《危险化学品包装物容器生产许可证》、《出口商品包装质量许可证》，保证了公司产品质量和服务质量的高标准，“鱼跃牌”商标连续多年获得德阳市知名商标称号。

公司产品主要系列有：中空吹塑容器（容积 2 ~ 200L）、周转箱及日用品、塑料板材（ABS、聚乙烯、聚丙烯）及家电塑料配件等，广泛应用和服务于国民经济各领域。

10. 昆明民族塑料化工有限公司

中国塑协注塑制品专业委员会理事会单位。

昆明民族塑料化工有限公司（原昆明民族塑料厂），属省级先进企业，系集体企业改制重组的有限责任公司，是云南最大的注塑专业厂。现有职工 160 人，注册资本 1228 万元，资产总值 4500 万元。主要设备有日本东芝公司的二万克大型注塑机，日本三菱公司的一万克，日本钢制所四千克等各种中、小型注塑机，年生产能力达 7500t。公司已通过 ISO9001：2008、GB/T 19001—2008 质量体系认证，内部实行微机处理，产品以汽车配件、塑料周转箱、工矿配件为主。微机械制造、农业、啤酒、饮料、烟草、食品、环卫等行业配套服务，公司连续十二年荣获“云南省昆明市重信用、守合同”先进单位，是云南省“放心产品”生产单位，多年被昆明市盘龙区政府授予“纳税先进”单位。随着昆明市现行的城市发展总体规划，为提高城市品质，打造宜居城市，主城区拟实行搬迁改造，进入园区，是企业有条件进行产品结构调整，扩大现有生产规模，加快产业升级换代改造，实现科学发展。为本省经济建设作出了一份贡献。同时公司的知名度也在扩大，品牌效应在强化。

11. 西安泓涛塑业有限公司

中国塑协注塑制品专业委员会理事会单位。

西安泓涛塑业有限公司，2010 年中国塑料行业先进单位（原西安市塑料制品四厂）始建于 1955 年，是由建厂初期的 5 人刻章小组逐步发展起来的，尤其是近几年来迅速发展，到目前为止，已拥有总资产 600 万元，2003 年产值首次突破 1000 万元；主要设备已全部更换为先进的电脑控制注射成型机（规格为 200t 至 850t）。主要产品有各类塑料周转箱、工业配件。民用产品三大类，上百个品种，公司的注册商标“丽丽”，“丽丽”牌塑料周转箱在西北地区有较高的知名度，1985 年通用周转箱产品获得陕西省优质产品称号；2000 年乳制品周转箱系列产品获西安市优秀新产品奖。

近年来，凭借雄厚的技术力量和先进的设备，不断的开发出适销对路的新品种，使产品多样化，系列化，满足广大用户的需求。2003 年开发新品种十多个（储物、整理系列箱；各种规格的桶产品等）2013 年计划增加 5 ~ 10 个新品种（工位器具等）。

随着国家对西部政策的倾斜，西部大开发为西部塑料制品包装、储运业提供了更加广阔的发展前景，但市场竞争也会更为激烈，为了更多的占领市场份额，计划增添 1200 ~ 2000t 大型注塑机，开发规格较大的周转箱及工业配件。

12. 山西晋特塑料制品有限公司

中国塑协注塑制品专业委员会理事会单位。

山西晋特塑料制品有限公司，2010 年中国塑料行业先进单位，是在 2000 年原太原塑料制品三厂和太原塑料模具机械厂合并的基础上成立的塑料制品专业生产企业。现企业占地面积约 30 亩，其中生产建筑面积 10000 余平方米。现有职工 200 余人，其中各类专业技术人员 40 人。

公司拥有固定资产 3000 余万元，下设注塑分厂等生产、管理机构，现有主要塑料机械设备 20 余台，已形成较完善的大型和精密系列注塑产品规模生产线，产品以各类塑料周转箱为主。现已有适用于冷饮、乳制品、禽蛋、蔬菜、水果、肉食、食品及工业专用箱系列和塑料办公用品、酒店餐饮用品和家居用品等系列产品，年综合加工塑料能力达 4000 余吨。

公司产品均执行国家标准和企业内控标准，符合国家通用尺度堆码标准，企业采用科学的营销的战略和战术，经过几年的努力，已形成”了一个依托，三个中心“：即以本省为依托，以”环渤海区域的北京为中心，以长江三角洲区域的上海为中心，以珠江三角洲区域的广州为中心“的产品销售网络，产品辐射到全国 20 余个省、市，在国内同类产品中占有一定的市场份额。

13. 威海市威鹰塑胶有限公司

中国塑协注塑制品专业委员会理事会单位。

威海市威鹰塑胶有限公司位于胶东半岛东端威海工业新区苘山镇镇区，是胶东半岛塑料制品种类最全、生产规模较大的生产厂家。始建于 1985 年，厂区占地 100000m^2，建筑面积 28000m^2，拥有固定资产 4800 万元，是一家致力于挤塑、注塑加工的专业企业，产品涉及汽车、电子、农场、化工等众多领域。公司拥有挤塑设备40余台，员工200多人，是一座大型现代化企业。现已成为国内北方地区最大的仓储物流产品制造商。

工厂拥有一支多年从事产品设计与制造的高级工程师组成的专业设计队伍，多年来工厂以客户的需要为导向，依靠先进的物流技术、科学的管理经验和理念，逐步开发出物流容器、工位器具、仓储设施、搬运设备等四大系列的产品。基本上满足了制造企业生产现场对零配件、半成品、成品以及相关的信息流动达到7R的要求(即：正确的产品、正确的质量、正确的条件、正确的客户、正确的地点、正确的时间和正确的成本)。

威海市威鹰塑胶有限公司是中国塑协注塑制品专业委员会会员，连续多年被评为“重合同，守信用”企业，AAA级信誉企业，省级先进企业，全国500家最佳经济效益福利企业，市级文明单位和工业先进企业，并率先在全国同行业获得ISO 9001国际质量体系认证。

以“追求卓越，执着创新”为宗旨，几年来，公司从专业生产物流箱、管材的基础上新增了农场使用养殖设备、与国外几大客户建立了长期合作关系，并以一流的质量和服务赢得了客户的认可。公司除发展自己的主导产品外还承接各种模具制造及自身加工业务，在精密模具设计加工方面实力雄厚、经验丰富。已经和韩国、日本、东南亚以及欧美等多家该类业务的贸易公司进行合作配套，为其提供了优质的产品和超值的服务，在业界赢得了一致的肯定。

14. 烟台一塑科技发展有限公司

中国塑协注塑制品专业委员会理事会单位。

烟台一塑科技发展有限公司其前身为烟台塑料一厂，2009年中国塑料行业先进单位，是主要从事塑料注塑制品生产加工的股份制企业，拥有从原料进厂到产品出厂一整套管理体系和质量检测设备。先进的设备、工艺和丰富的生产经验，使企业具备了相当的规模和实力，在全国同行业中享有很高的声誉。

公司以促进塑料行业的发展和为社会作贡献为已任，努力为客户提供高质量服务。一次性通过ISO 9000质量体系认证，并取得美国可口可乐、百事可乐公司的严格质量认证，产品远销俄罗斯、韩国等国家，年产量6000t。公司将依靠设备更新、技术进步，不断提高产品质量，以价格低、质量优、守信用竭诚为广大客户提供优质服务。

15. 义乌市一切塑料有限公司

中国塑协注塑制品专业委员会理事会单位。

义乌市一切塑料有限公司是专业生产迪风牌发动机配件企业。主要产品有潍柴、重汽、一汽等主机厂配套用发动机冷却风扇及发动机油气分离器等配套产品。同时生产各类工业用工位器具周转箱和民用各类生产用塑料制品。

公司有三十余年生产历史。拥有国内最先进200～6000g注塑成型机，并通过ISO 9000：2001质量认证及TS 16949国际汽车质量管理体系认证。2009年中国塑料行业先进单位。

16. 宁波东海塑料有限公司

中国塑协注塑制品专业委员会理事会单位。

宁波东海塑料有限公司地处浙江宁波东海之滨，是中国塑协注塑制品专业委员会理事单位，专业生产塑料周转箱和工程塑料制品。产品有：液压动力单元用塑料油箱、工程塑料部件、家用电器配件、外贸塑料件、工业配件、日用塑料制品及各种系列塑料周转箱。

公司拥有大、中、小注塑机及塑料制品模具，配有塑料热转印、丝网印刷、热熔塑料焊接等专用设备，能广泛满足塑料加工的各种特殊要求。公司宗旨“诚信为本，精益求精”，公司理念：“用户需求高于一切”，公司产品广销国内外市场。

17. 新疆珠江塑料有限责任公司

中国塑协注塑制品专业委员会理事会单位。

新疆珠江塑料有限责任公司是新疆塑料制品行业的综合企业，是新疆区域最具竞争力的塑料制品企业之一。年生产能力23kt。公司注册地址为：乌鲁木齐市珠江路48号，注册资金1000万元。

公司从成立之际，本着“以农为本，服务新疆农业，为新疆人民造福”的原则，积极开发与农业及林果业息息相关的产品，经过多年的发展，公司生产的农用地膜、水果发泡网、塑料周转箱及滴灌节水器材等产品都有了相当大的市场份额。公司的“丑小鸭”注册商标是新疆的著名商标，拥有良好的社会信誉和公众形象。尤其是“丑小鸭”牌农用地膜和塑料周转箱深受用户的信任和好评，产品被评为“用户满意产品”；企业获得“重合同、守信用”称号，并拥有完善的售后服务体系。

主要产品：1、聚乙烯农用塑料薄膜；2、10～220L系列中空桶、200LL环桶，主要用于盛装各类液态化工原料、防冻液等；3、各类塑料周转箱，主要用于新疆的香梨、苹果、葡萄、大枣等水果的转运和储存；4、涂料桶、油品桶及高级乳胶漆桶；5、节水滴管带；6、PE发泡网；7、拟开发的产品有组合托盘。

公司控股的库尔勒珠江塑料有限公司位于库尔

勒市经济技术开发区工业园区内，2010年新建一个贮存量为5000t的水果保鲜冷库。当年已投入使用。

【新产品开发】

1. 包装物流仓储产品

新产品名称	开发研究单位
300L塑料周转箱 垃圾分类和大型垃圾桶，塑料托盘	昆明民族塑料化工实业总公司
系列塑料托盘、物流箱系列	无锡市巨龙塑化有限公司
Z043型超强可口可乐箱 雪花啤酒12瓶箱 F118型超市周转箱、梅匾 酒瓶折叠架 豆腐干、豆制品货架、海鲜、家禽塑料模板	杭州万里塑胶有限公司
塑料保温箱、电力系统电表专用箱、电池箱 晒鱼箱、大型捕捞容器、建筑配件、方便面、水果等各类专用周转箱	天津市永濠天塑制品有限公司
大型塑料托盘	天津市津英达塑料制品有限公司
系列塑料托盘、军用周转箱、汽车件专用箱系列	苏州富事达塑业有限公司
多用周转箱	四川锐星塑胶有限公司
畜牧专用箱	威鹰塑胶有限公司
叉车托盘、环保清洁箱、食品、鸡蛋箱	哈尔滨哈轻塑胶有限公司

2. 汽车塑料配套件

新产品名称	开发研究单位
CH7146外饰件总成(昌河铃木亚纳) CH7146仪表板总成(昌河铃木亚纳) F202前后保险杠总成(重庆长安金牛星) GP50前后保险杠蒙皮(通用五菱宝骏630) N109仪表板总成(新五菱之光)	浙江远翅塑料有限公司
长安B501仪表板 M－201－H微型客车 前后保险杠、仪表板 电动车仪表板 仪表盘、同色保险杆、门内护板、门槛立柱类	哈尔滨哈轻塑胶有限公司
一汽红塔汽车配件 二汽云南汽车配件	昆明民族塑料化工实业总公司
汽车发动机冷却风扇、油气分离器	义乌一切塑料制品有限公司

3. 家用电器、日用制品

新产品名称	开发研究单位
药品食品、南天电子配件包装	昆明民族塑料化工实业总公司
出口料理板、小推车、座椅	苏州富事达塑业有限公司
电动自行车塑料配件、新能源配件	无锡市巨龙塑化有限公司
滑雪用具、XPS保温板	哈尔滨哈轻塑股有限公司
大型花盆、电动自行车配件	天津市永濠天塑塑料制品公司
螺丝保护器(石油管道)	天津市津英达塑料制品公司

【存在的问题】

目前行业注塑制品专业化生产企业，大多数是由20世纪六、七十年代轻工业创办国有集体塑料制品企业经改制成为民营、私营和合资企业，绝大多数为中小型企业，主要集中在东部沿海地区。虽然经过改革开放几十年已取得较大发展，但总体水平仍然跟不上国民经济快速发展的要求，与国外先进国家比存在着一定差距，主要存在以下问题：

1. 国内注塑制品企业整体技术装备、工艺技术、生产管理水平、产品标准、质量与国外先进水平比还处于相对落后状态，产品档次处于末端，产品开发、自主创新能力、深度加工跟不上市场需求。

2. 我国注塑制品行业企业以配套加工产品为主，行业整体创新能力薄弱，自主开发最终产品品种少；中低档产品偏多，高档配套产品少；通用技术产品多，高技术高附加值产品少；产品标准不能适应商业市场需求，缺少自主知识产权制品和国家知名品牌产品，针对市场需要的产品设计方面总体研发力量较薄弱。

3. 注塑设备模具产业发展不平衡，总体水平偏低。虽然个别企业的产品已达到相当高的水平，已达到或接近国际水平，但总体看来，与国外先进水平相比尚有差距。由于信息不对称，缺乏对市场需求研究等原因，还存在盲目投资，重复建设现象。

4. 企业营运成本不断上升，阻碍企业生存和发展。近年来金融危机对经济实体冲击、油价、电价、运输价、人工费的不断提高，增加企业的运行成本；能源、原材料等的上游产品价格上涨挤占了企业的大部分效益；同时企业安全生产、低碳、低耗、绿色环境保护费用投入升高；人力资源用工成本提高；给企业生存带来挑战，目前国内注塑加工企业以中小型企业为主体，再融资发展生产仍存在不少困难，希望能得到国家产业政策上的支持和各地区政府相关部门人力、财力上的支持，调整产业结构，否则只能退出市场，寻求出路。

【发展形势】

“十二五”期间，注塑制品行业要围绕加快体制创新，科技创新、产品创新、经营模式创新，推进行业绿色低碳经济发展模式，着力扩大新材料、新技术、新工艺的推广应用，开拓新兴市场，保持行业经济平稳发展。

1. 调整产业结构，发展规模经济，实现规模效益，切实做大做强一批注塑制品产业龙头企业。“十二五”将打造一批年销售超亿元，产量超万吨骨干企业，使优势企业在自主开发，规模性和市场竞争力上再上一个新台阶，培育1~2只国家名牌产品。

2. 遵照中国塑料工业未来重点发展方向要求，企业从过去“三低两高”(低附加值、低质量、低价值和高污染、高耗能)向高质量和高附加值的增长方式转变，走绿色发展道路。鼓励注塑制品企业开发无污染的绿色制品，节能环保组织生产，有条件的企业积极采用国际先进的环保、节能全电动注塑机。行业构建绿色制品评价体系，总体交流、表彰先进、营造绿色环保社会氛围，推动绿色产品的发展。

3. 根据中央“十二五”期间进一步扩大内需，确保经济稳定增长的重要决策，行业重点开拓市场，抓住产业发展信息，跟上形势，做好服务配套工作，服务国内有发展潜力的大企业、行业和朝阳产业，积极采用信息技术、网络技术和电子商务在销售经营管理中的应用。

4. 搭建产学研结合平台，推进知识产业结构转型升级。积极开发新技术产品，保持行业先进生产力持续发展。

5. 加强注塑制品行业与其他行业(上游行业中国塑料模具工业协会、中国塑料机械工业协会和中国石油化工工业协会；下游行业工业汽车行业协会、家电行业协会、建筑建材企业协会、物流包装工业协会)的交流与合作，共同建设一个社会化、网络化、开放式的服务体系，为注塑制品行业的企业技术创新和高新技术产业化的各种需求提供全方位服务，帮助上下游行业企业新产品开发，科技成果产业化提供服务平台。

6. 广泛开展职业培训，努力提高员工素质。当今注塑加工业技术水平体现一个国家塑料现代化的水平。注塑行业新技术、新装备、新材料、新工艺不断推陈出新，需要大量能掌握先进设备和加工工艺技术的员工，才能保证产品的高质量，满足需求，因此广泛开展职工培训，提高员工技术水平，建立行业培训基地，加快产业发展，适应新一轮的发展需要。由条件的企业积极筹建企业技术中心，提高自主创新能力，满足高分子材料，先进成型工艺、高性能的结构设计和市场需求产品设计。

(中国塑料加工工业协会注塑制品专业委员会　顾大全)

聚氨酯制品

【行业情况】

1. 产量：中国2012年聚氨酯总产量达到7800kt。其中，聚氨酯泡沫塑料3200kt，聚氨酯纤维(氨纶)350kt，聚氨酯弹性体600kt(包括CPU、TPU、防水铺装材料)，聚氨酯合成革浆料和聚氨酯鞋底原液1950kt，涂料1300kt，聚氨酯胶黏剂密封剂400kt。中国已经成为聚氨酯生产和消费大国。

2. 产业集中度加强，产业布局趋于合理。目前聚氨酯的生产应用已经形成以上海为中心的长江三角洲地区，以烟台和天津为中心的黄河三角洲和环渤海地区，以广州为中心的珠江三角洲地区，以福建泉州为中心的西海岸地区，以兰州为中心的西北地区，以锦州为中心的东北地区和以重庆为中心的西南地区。使聚氨酯应用更加合理与方便。

3. 产业升级稳步加快，技术创新水平逐步提高，生产规模逐渐扩大，产品质量稳定提升。现在，烟台万华生产的MDI产品，华峰鞋革树脂、氨纶等产品产量已经达到世界第一。水性鞋用聚氨酯胶黏剂，非黄变异氰酸酯，HPPO技术都在快速发展。

4. 因为环保和市场的原因，聚氨酯生产逐步向亚洲转移，以TDI为例，2005年，中国产量只占全球7%，而到2012年我国产量已经占到全球30%，而欧洲、美洲产量在减少。另外，我国聚氨酯原材料产能市场由于扩产迅速，产能已经出现过剩苗头，如聚醚多元醇产品、异氰酸酯产品等。

表1　2011~2012年中国大陆聚氨酯生产情况

10^4t

年　份	聚氨酯原料	聚氨酯制品
2011	336	700
2012	392	780
增长率	16%	11%

表2　2011~2012年中国大陆聚氨酯泡沫生产状况

产品名称	2011	2012	增长率
软泡	140	150	7%
硬泡	150	170	13%
合计	290	320	10.34%

【原材料生产情况】

1. MDI

MDI的生产、技术、工艺、设备都比较复杂，生产行业集中度很高。烟台万华2012年大陆地区总产能已经达到1400kt，居全球第二。全球MDI消费主要集中在亚洲（40%）、西欧（35%）、北美（20%）、其他（5%）。中国大陆2012年MDI总产能1990kt，产量1400kt，开工率70%。

表3　2012年MDI中国大陆生产情况

序号	单位名称	区域	产能/10^4t	产量/10^4t
1	烟台万华	华东	140	100
2	拜耳上海	华东	35	24
3	上海联恒	华东	24	16
总计			199	140

表4　2012年中国大陆聚合MDI消费情况

领　域	2012年/10^4t	占比/%
冰箱、冰柜	38	40
冷链物流	5.5	5.79
管道保温	8	8.42
板材	4.5	4.74
太阳能、电热水器	7	7.37
喷涂	6	6.32
其他	26	27.37
聚合MDI合计	95	

2. TDI

因环保和市场问题，全球TDI生产和消费向中国大陆转移，中国成为全球第一消费大国。2012年全球总产能的情况是：中国大陆TDI总产量为830kt、美国总产能380kt、韩国总产能300kt、日本总产能260kt。2012年大陆TDI产量为600kt，设备开工率约为72%。

表5　中国大陆TDI主要生产企业

序号	公司名称	区域	产能/10^4t	产量/10^4t
1	拜耳/上海	华东	25	20
2	上海BASF	华东	16	13
3	甘肃银达	西北	10	7
4	沧州大化	华北	15	11
5	烟台巨力	华东	8	6
6	北方锦化	东北	5	3
7	蓝星化工	华北	4	0
合计			83	60

表6　2011年至2012年中国大陆TDI消费领域

领　域	2011年/10^4t	2012年/10^4t	增长率
聚氨酯软泡	38	42	10.5%
聚氨酯涂料	6.6	7	6%
弹性体	7	8	14%
胶黏剂	2.8	3	7%
其他	1.2	1.1	-8%
合计	56	60	7%

3. PPG

聚醚生产技术含量相对较低，产品同质化严重，现有生产企业40多家，年产100kt的企业有十几家。2012年硬泡聚醚增长幅度较大，未来几年增长趋势看好，聚氨酯软泡聚醚占41%，聚氨酯硬泡聚醚占46%。2012年聚醚总产能3340kt/a，未来5年新增产能1250kt。中国2012年聚醚总产量2200kt/a，开工率为65.8%，产能已经明显过剩。

表7　2012年中国聚醚多元醇消费结构

聚醚多元醇领域	2012年	比例/%
聚氨酯软泡	90	41.86
聚氨酯硬泡	95	44.19
其他	30	13.95
合计	215	100

【发展前景】

“十二五”规划中提出“在十二五末，中国聚氨酯工业，不仅要在产业规模上达到9~10Mt，居世界第一。而且要在技术水平上有显著的提升。”主要通过自主科技创新开发，使重要基本原料、助剂，主要类型产品的生产技术、产品质量达到或接近国际水平。加快产业结构调整，提高产品高端化水平，淘汰落后产能。初步形成布局合理、绿色环保、低碳高效的聚氨酯原料工业体系，为聚氨酯制品的生产和消费提供可靠的保证。

1. 未来聚氨酯保温材料市场看好

尽管2012年中国整体的经济增速放缓，但是聚合MDI消费还是呈现了较好的发展态势。截止到2012年底，电器行业仍然是中国聚合MDI主要的消费领域，这一行业的冷暖直接影响到总体消费量。2012年12月3日我国公安部消防局下文通知，不再执行65号文，回到原来的46号文，也就是说不再强制要求使用A级材料，而屋面可以正常使用B1和B2级材料，这对于聚氨酯外墙保温来说，是一个特大利好消息。政府对于建筑物消防条例的修改，使得PU保温材料在未来几年的发展有乐观预期。PU

材料优越的保温性能，是建筑节能领域无法忽视的。我国用于建筑领域的聚合MDI消费量占比不到20%，而美国用于建筑领域的需求占比超过55%。我国建筑节能市场空间巨大，既有建筑(500～600)亿平方米，多数为高耗能建筑，每年新建建筑达20亿平方米，建筑能耗占总能耗比例接近35%，未来该领域的发展空间巨大。电器行业未来几年的增速将逐步放缓，但是庞大的基数足以保证其在中国市场的地位。另外矿山填充、密封剂等新兴领域在2012年的表现可谓靓丽，预计未来几年国内聚合MDI增长再次出现新的亮点。

2. 异氰酸酯项目正在加快产业结构调整

脂肪族和脂环族二异氰酸酯(ADI)作为一类特殊有机二异氰酸酯，因其制品具有优良的机械性能、突出的化学稳定性和优秀的耐光耐候性，近年来得到广泛关注。其产品广泛应用于航空、航天、船舶、涂料等领域。与其他芳香族异氰酸酯产品相比，具有更高经济含量与附加值，由于该产品的特殊地位，其生产工艺、技术一直受到西方发达国际的封锁和限制。

大陆地区的ADI的年需求量不断增长，目前全部依赖进口，巨大的市场需求，超常的增长速度以及高额的生产利润，吸引了世界异氰酸酯巨头的极大关注，纷纷在华投资建厂，积极参与市场竞争。大陆地区相关企业也积极研发技术或寻求技术来源，加快研发和生产包括HDI、HMDI、IPDI为主的更多类型的异氰酸酯产品，谋求在异氰酸酯行业的更大市场和发展空间。

3. 水性聚氨酯产品技术发展加快

水性聚氨酯产品应用十分广泛，可用于织物涂层整理，皮革涂饰剂，胶黏剂，涂料，鞋用树脂，人造革用树脂，油墨等。但由于水性聚氨酯分散体(PUD)链段上含有亲水基团或链段，降低了漆膜耐水性、耐沾污性、物理机械性和化学性能；同时制备工艺和成膜过程也决定了PUD漆膜的耐溶剂性、耐热性和力学强度等性能不及相应的溶剂型制品。此外，由于水的蒸发潜热高，造成水性产品干燥时间长的问题。因此，提高水性聚氨酯性能以及优化制备和施工工艺，使水性聚氨酯朝着多品种，高固含，高清洁，低消耗，优品质等方向发展依然是科研的重点。近年来，围绕水性聚氨酯的研究技术逐步深入，材料不断提高，优秀人才辈出，生产企业迅速增加。

【专委会工作】

2012年聚氨酯行业和全国其他行业一样，受国际经济运行回调和国家政策调控的影响，发展速度变缓。企业用工成本增高、利润下滑，行业发展速度回落。聚氨酯软泡主要用于家具，家具行业受国家房地产调控影响，出口受制国际经济形势低迷影响，行业销售下滑约在15%～20%状态。聚氨酯硬泡建筑板材增长较快，其他子行业也全面回落。针对行业的具体情况和协会全年整体工作安排，聚氨酯制品专委会主要从以下几个方面开展工作。

1. 聚氨酯制品专委会的2012年工作主要是围绕协会的工作开展的。根据年初协会编制“十二五”规划的具体要求，依据专委会的特点，积极配合协会的各项工作，及时保质保量的提供各种材料和相关数据，确保协会的规划编制科学、合理并可持续执行。考虑行业存在的具体问题我们聚氨酯制品专委会将2012年的工作重点确定为协调硬泡产品阻燃实验和淘汰HCFC－141b工作。根据国家节能减排的要求，做好聚氨酯保温板材的应用和推广。同时做好专委会的日常工作，积极为聚氨酯制品企业提供相关技术、政策咨询。

2. 针对聚氨酯外墙外保温行业遇到的问题，积极工作寻找突破口。2012年3月，北京市消防局下发391号文，规定北京新建及旧房改造建筑外墙保温不能使用有机保温材料，只能使用阻燃达到复合A级的制品材料，其芯材达到B1级的热固型材料。北京的部分政府建设的保障房和政府主导的旧房保温改造项目开始使用聚氨酯保温板。南京的保障房建设的外墙保温也开始部分使用聚氨酯保温板，各大房地产开发商，也开始尝试使用聚氨酯保温板，这无疑对聚氨酯在外墙外保温方面是一重大利好。受政策面利好刺激，2011年下半年和2012年全年，全国新增聚氨酯板材生产线保守估计2012超过150余条，主要分布在江苏、浙江、山东、北京、东北等地。新增产能在技术和管理上缺乏足够的专业人员。聚氨酯制品专委会在各类行业会上上，倡导企业抓质量、练内功，为建筑保温市场提供优质的聚氨酯保温板。同时我们根据国家标准和部分聚氨酯泡沫生产企业的要求，积极和消防局防火所主动联系，继续进行大型聚氨酯泡沫制品火灾实验，以积累数据，验证聚氨酯泡沫制品的阻燃性。

3. 协助环境保护部环境保护对外合作中心做好HCFC－141b淘汰项目管理相关工作。2012年配合环境保护部环境保护对外合作中心核查了32家PU泡沫生产企业，这32家企业于2013年3月年初与环境保护部环境保护对外合作中心签署淘汰HCFC－141b合同。

4. 聚氨酯制品专委会2012年5月份在北京组织召开了聚氨酯硬泡发展论坛、参加了协会在上海召开的年会、家具协会在绍兴的年会、在北京国举办的新型绿色建材展览会等活动。2012 年 7 月与住建部建科技发展促进中心在南京组织召开了全国外墙保温与节能结构技术交流推广会、参加了聚氨酯工业协会在深圳举办的展览会和年会、在北京举办的房博会、对部分聚氨酯板材企业进行了走访和调研。以上就是专委会今年的主要工作和简单回顾。

【存在的问题】

1. 今年聚氨酯板材企业上生产线较多，多处在调试和试生产状态，产能处于饱和，企业间竞争激烈，现在已经出现价格战。部分新进入的企业，很可能出现在试生产结束后，产品滞销，无利润而倒闭。

2. 受行业管理和企业管理的影响，今年发展会员较少。

聚氨酯制品涵盖面非常广，涉及行业比较多，专委会重点围绕着聚氨酯软泡和硬泡行业开展工作。在软泡和硬泡行业关注影响行业发展的重点问题，了解相关产业政策，在此基础上引导企业应对行业发展问题，聚拢行业企业，为我国聚氨酯制品行业的健康有序发展而努力。

附录：聚氨酯制品专委会重点会员企业

1. 江苏绿源新材料有限公司

中国塑料加工工业协会副理事长单位、聚氨酯制品专委会理事长单位。主要产品涉及聚氨酯原料、聚氨酯建筑保温板、聚氨酯软泡。产量 30kt，产值 5.7 亿。产品销往华东、华北及东北地区。

2. 宁波万华容威聚氨酯有限公司

中国塑协聚氨酯制品专委会副理事长单位。主要产品组合聚醚。产量 60kt，产值 12 亿。产品主要销往华东、华南地区。

3. 常州晶雪冷冻设备有限公司

中国塑协聚氨酯制品专委会副理事长单位。主要产品为聚氨酯冷库保温板。产量 120 万平方米，产值 3.9 亿。产品销往全国。

4. 江苏恒康家居科技有限公司

中国塑协聚氨酯制品专委会副理事长单位。主要产品家具制品，枕头 360 万个、床垫 120 万条、其他 63 万个产值 7.01 亿。产品主要出口。

5. 山东东大聚合物有限公司

中国塑协聚氨酯制品专委会副理事长单位。主要产品为组合聚醚。产量 27kt，产值 4.5 亿。产品主要销往华北、华东地区。

6. 圣诺盟控股集团有限公司

中国塑协聚氨酯制品专委会副理事长单位。主要产品海绵制品。产量 32kt，产值 6.5 亿。产品主要出口。

7. 多维联合集团有限公司

中国塑协聚氨酯制品专委会副理事长单位。主要产品建筑保温板。产量 180 万平方米，产值 3.6 亿。产品主要销往华北、东北、内蒙古。

8. 上海馨源新材料有限公司

中国塑协聚氨酯制品专委会常务理事单位。主要产品软泡海绵。产量 15kt，产值 3 亿。产品主要销往华东地区。

9. 济宁市宁宇聚氨酯有限公司

中国塑协聚氨酯制品专委会副理事长单位。主要产品家居海绵。销往山东等地。

10. 浙江海利士电器有限公司

中国塑协聚氨酯制品专委会副理事长单位。主要产品冰箱、冰柜。年产量约 70 万台，产值 5 亿。销往全国、部分出口。

11. 营口双信聚氨酯有限公司

中国塑协聚氨酯制品专委会常务理事单位。主要产品组合聚醚，产量 15kt，产值 3 亿。产品主要销往东北地区。

12. 沈阳国盛防腐保温有限公司

中国塑协聚氨酯制品专委会常务理事单位。主要产品聚氨酯保温管。产值 7000 万，是东北地区最大的保温管生产企业。

13. 山东万事达建筑钢品科技有限公司

中国塑协聚氨酯制品专委会会员单位。主要产品聚氨酯复合板，产量 100 万平方米，产值 2 亿。产品销往山东地区。

14. 绍兴市恒丰聚氨酯实业有限公司

中国塑协聚氨酯制品专委会副理事长单位。主要产品聚醚多元醇，聚氨酯复合板，产值 4 亿。产品销往全国及土耳其。

15. 聊城市三力保温材料有限公司

中国塑协聚氨酯制品专委会会员单位。主要产品聚氨酯冷库板，产量 30 万平方米，产值 6000 万。产品销往全国各地。

（中国塑料加工工业协会聚氨酯制品专业委员会 刘卫东）

塑料编织制品

【概况】

塑料丝、绳及编织制品业 2012 年规模以上企业 1835 多家，塑编制品产量约 9829 千吨（年销售收入

2000万元以上企业)同比增长15%，增幅下滑6个百分点。塑编产量占全部塑料制品产量17%，比去年提高2个百分点。工业总产值2188.23亿元，同比增长19.13%；工业销售产值2157.65亿元，同比增长19.39%；累计出口交货值93.51亿元，同比增长5.36%；主营业务收入2172.79亿元，同比增长18.42%；利税总额203.61亿元，同比增长23.98%；其中利润总额136.71亿元，同比增长27.31%；销售利润率6.29%。主要经济指标都是二位数增长，亏损企业107个，累计亏损额1.77亿元，同比减少3.90%；全部从业人员平均323786人，同比增加4.36%。

全社会塑编制品产量约139000kt，同比增长15%左右；产值约3000亿元。2012年全国增加圆织机1万台左右，全国到2012年底拥有各种圆织机约31万台，全国具有塑编制品生产能力约160000kt，从业人员比去年略有增加约50万人。

国际金融危机、欧洲债务危机，使国际市场对我国塑料制品的需求急剧下降，我国塑料制品出口量大幅下降，塑编制品同样受其影响，加上印度越南以低价在国际市场上与我国塑编制品竞争，对我国塑编制品出口亦有一定影响，近年国家采用调控措施主动放缓我国经济发展速度，使国内市场对塑编制品的需求有所减少，2012年全国规模以上企业塑料制品总产量为59818647t，同比增长8.99%，与2011年增幅22.35%相比降低13.36个百分点，而2012年塑编制品产量增幅为15%，虽比2011年增幅21.06%，下滑6.06个百分点，但仍比全国塑料制品产量增幅高6.01个百分点。塑编制品在国内外经济十分复杂的条件的双重压力下，塑编制品仍能获得高于全国GDP增幅近一倍的发展速度说明塑编制品市场需求和潜力仍然很大，具有扎实、稳定、高速发展的基础，其发展前景是良好的。

【行业发展特点】

1. 企业规模不断壮大，龙头企业越显优势

2012年塑编行业广大职工努力拼搏，深入贯彻科学发展观，坚决执行中央的调整产品结构，调整企业结构的新的经济发展精神，全行业取得高速发展的业绩，特别是业内一些龙头企业业绩更为显著，2012年塑编行业中已出现年产值超十亿的3家企业，他们是山东寿光健元春、天津华今集团和温州晨光集团(详见附表1)。

山东省寿光健元春除不继扩大塑编生产外，还发展了聚丙烯(PP)粉料生产，2012年引进了德国8.7m阔双向拉伸聚酯(BOPET)薄膜设备及配套分切机，使企业在不断延长产业链的同时，在生产装备上引进具有国际一流先进水平的大型塑料薄膜生产设备，生产技术和产品档次上了一个新台阶，使企业跃居塑编行业龙头企业；天津华今集团公司在自身大幅度扩大塑编生产的同时在江西收购了2个企业成立了2个分公司，在江苏收购了一家公司成立了化工分公司，使集团规模迅速壮大，跃居成为塑编行业的龙头企业；温州晨光集团有限公司，一贯致力于发展塑编生产，2012年产值销售同时超10亿元，并且塑编制品产量达85666t，在产品结构上积极发展高档的透明编织袋生产，由于企业一贯注重产品质量和诚信服务，在全国不少企业呈现负增长的情况下仍取得较大幅度增长，更可喜的是其2012年利润总额销售利润率和人均利润跃居全行业第一位；山东广庆集团在原来以生产塑料编织袋为核心的同时发展了聚丙烯粉料生产和塑编机械生产，近年又引进德国布鲁克纳公司双向拉伸聚丙烯(BOPP)薄膜设备并已顺利投产，还在黑龙江发展双向拉伸薄膜生产，使集团拥有塑编机械、塑编原料、塑编配套材料和塑编制品生产的较为完整的产业链，使集团公司在生产规模、生产装备、生产技术、产品档次上上了一个新台阶。

另一方面不少原来全年主营业务收入不到亿元企业迅速发展，年主营业务收入纷纷超亿元，挤身全国塑编生产经营超亿元大户行列，如温州地区的浙江中宇节能科技有限公司(温州市平阳县)、温州市中际化纤有限公司(温州市苍南县)、温州共和包装有限公司(温州市苍南)使温州市塑编行业年主营业务收入超亿元的企业从原来8个增加到11个。

2. 产品档次有所提升，低档次产品还有一定份额

近年来，塑编产品档次有所提升，从调查的29家会员企业中，塑编产品吨售价在12000元以上的有14家，占48.28%，且有2家企业每吨塑编产品售价在15000元以上，最高的是江苏万乐复合材料有限公司每吨塑编产品平均售价为16093元，其次浙江中宇节能科技有限公司每吨塑编制品平均售价为15560元。但是，低档次塑编产品还有不少企业仍在生产，在这次调查中还有4家企业塑编制品每吨售价低于1万元，占13.79%。可喜的是在调查中发现一些企业已成功地大批生产耐老化编织袋，不少企业放弃了使用低档次母粒、回料加粉料的三合一塑编生产，开始大批生产透明编织袋和半透明编织袋(无碳酸钙母粒和回炉料)，在产品档次提高的同时极大地改善了生产环境，使生产车间粉尘飞扬的状况获得极大地改善，防止了生产工人职业病(尘肺)的发生，如温州晨光集团有限公司由此获省绿色企业的荣誉称号。江苏万乐复合材料有限公司与华中科技大学合作，新产品获江苏省著名品牌证书，获省资金50万

元，并正在申报中国驰名商标。

3. 积极淘汰落后设备引进国内外先进设备

2012年许多企业积极淘汰落后设备引进国内外先进设备，山东寿光健元春有限公司基本完成了塑编设备的更新换代，拉丝机主要为主机直驱，后缠绕单锭变频高速拉丝机，圆织机主要为大十梭、十二梭，生产食品集装袋，同时引进意大利五层共挤农膜设备，从德国引进8.7m阔BOPET薄膜生产设备及配套分切机，由于生产装备性能大大提高使企业人均产值达148.44万元，居全行业第一位，2012年利润总额比上年同期提高113%。

4. 节能降耗成绩显著

经多年努力，许多企业通过淘汰落后设备，引进先进节能设备，行业内塑编袋生产能耗普遍下降，在本年调查的29个企业中每吨编织袋能耗在1000kW·h以下的有17家，占58.62%；在850 kW·h以下有13家，占44.83%；天津华今集团有限公司2012年每吨编织袋平均电耗达到700kW·h，接近国际先进水平。但是仍有6家企业每吨编织袋电耗在1000~1200kW·h之间，占20.69%；还有2家企业每吨编织袋电耗超过1400kW·h，少数企业在能耗降低后又有所反弹。塑编袋产品的经济效益不是很高，2012年全国1835个规模企业的平均销售利润率为6.29%，若每吨编织袋电耗降低200 kW·h，即可提高销售利润率1.15个百分点，降低400kW·h即可提高销售利润率2.25个百分点，若年产10kt编织袋，则可增加利润280万元。

5. 园区建设日新月异

(1) 冲刺500亿产业，打造中国塑编示范城

辽宁康平经济开发区2002年12月成立，2006年5月经省人民政府批准为省级开发区，规划面积52.6km²，由朝阳工业园高性能纤维新材料产业基地及苇塘、陆港两个经济区组成。康平县塑编产业集群位于朝阳工业园内，2005的始建军，规划面积10km²，已建成面积5.5km²，落户塑编及配套企业170余家，是沈阳市确立的33个重点产业集群之一，已成为东北地区规模最大的塑编产业集群，自2008年以来，康平塑编制品产量在东北三省以及华北地区县级塑编产业集群中的第一位，2011年完成产值126亿元，2012年将实现产值200亿元。

康平县塑编产业集群的发展得到省、市政府的高度关怀和支持，提出了“要在现有基础上，切实加快产业规模提速、加快产业结构调整提速，力争实现500亿元产业规模”的新要求。康平县为此通过五项措施全力打造“中国塑编示范城”。聘请专家高标准编制了《辽宁康平塑编集群发展规划》争取政策支持，已争取到产业技改资金和公共研发服务平台补助5000万元；加大招商力度，三位副县长各率一支招商队伍，分赴温州、聊城、大庆等招商，吸引100余家塑编及配套企业来康平考察，签约项目30个，总投资达8亿元；促进集群技术创新与沈阳大学签订产学研战略合作协议，促进塑编产业集群技术创新，提升集群知名度和影响力，经申请，在2012年全国塑编产业链技术交流与市场对接暨沈阳康平塑编经贸洽谈会上，由中国轻工业联合会和中国塑协批准授予康平县“中国塑编示范城”荣誉称号，集群中三家企业获“2011年度塑编行业二十强企业”荣誉称号。

(2) 萧江塑编产业转型升级谋突围

据萧江镇经济发展办提供的信息，去年萧江镇工业总产值近80亿元，塑编产业就占了近8成，达60多亿元，为全国最大的塑编生产基地。萧江塑编产业起步于上世纪80年代中后期，产业得益于数千名在外闯荡的营销大军而迅速发展壮大，如今已拥有包括塑料编制袋生产及相关复合、彩印、盖光、制版等配套企业300多家，年产值2000万元以上企业35家，塑编产品畅国内市场并运销欧美、东南亚等国际市场。1999年，中国地区开发促进会正式命名萧江镇压为“中国塑料编织城”、“中国塑料编织第一镇”2002年经温州市人民政府申请，由中国轻工业联合会和中国塑协审查批准授予温州市“中国塑编之都“荣誉称号。

以温州晨光集团有限公司、浙江华庆集团有限公司牵头的萧江镇塑编产业集群已声名远扬，温州晨光集团2012年产值、销售双双突破十亿元，浙江华庆集团有限公司董事长姜集康二次被推选为中国塑协塑料编织专业委员会会长，晨光、立天为副会长。但近年来，因土地制约产业整体提升缓慢，萧江塑编产量由原来占全国14%，逐步下降到13%、9%、8%、7%，而山东、辽宁迅速上升后来居上发展速度大大超过了萧江。“中国塑编城”身陷重围，为了突破，萧江塑编企业正在积极转型升级，正一塑业投资1200万从奥地利史格林格公司引进具有世界一流水平的阀口袋制袋机，为了使该设备顺利投产又投入500万元用于配套技术设备与相关人员的培训，这台设备可一次性完成阀口袋子热合、贴底、烘干和印刷等多道工序，仅需5名工人，每天可“吐”成品塑料编织袋2.5t，而用传统方法至少需要350名工人。产品正逐渐走进美国、加拿大等高端国际市场。

立天集团从2004年开始涉及棉纱纺纱，2009年正式进军家纺行业，并在新疆设立了3万亩棉花基

地，从2009年每年投入技改资金2000多万元，现有5条纺纱生产线，车间工人不足10人，年纺纱产值可达3亿元。

华庆集团利用成本优势进军国际市场，董事长姜集康二次赴美国考察，了解到美国人均工资大约是中国的10倍，塑编袋的价格是国内的2.5倍，华庆就盯着劳动力成本优势做好产品进军国际市场，公司塑编袋产能从1天1t，扩大到1天5t，公司年产值从几千万元增长到5亿元。

萧江塑编产业以规模、技术、产品档次的提升以求突围。

(3)“借口岸光，打俄罗斯牌”创建穆棱塑编产业城

穆棱毗邻俄罗斯，靠近绥芬河、东宁、密山、珲春等6个口岸的距离均不超过100km，拥有公路、铁路、航空、陆海联运、铁海联运“五位一体”的物流网络，区位优势十分明显。近年来提出了“借口岸光、打俄罗斯牌”的发展思路，积极发展塑编袋生产，创建穆棱塑编产业城，来自温州的企业家叶友焕，2004年，在招商引资优惠政策的吸引下，组建了黑龙江万事达塑料制品有限公司，经8年发展，现拥有圆织机1000台，年产各类塑料编织袋6亿条，拥有8个子公司，成为全国出口名列前茅的塑编企业。来自浙江的升华(温州苍南)、惠尔森等塑编企业相继在穆棱落户，并迅速发展壮大。山东广庆集团(董事长温州苍南龙港人)投资4亿元引进德国布鲁克纳公司双向拉伸聚丙烯BOPP薄膜生产线，填补了东北三省空白，为塑编行业提供重要生产配套材料。目前，穆棱塑编产业城共有5家大企业入驻，已成为东北地区较大的塑料编织生产基地，2012年，圆织机扩大到2000台，年产各种塑编制品10亿条以上，形成了强大的产业集聚效应。2013年BOPP引进、万事达年生产40kt聚酯纤维项目、升华新上的彩条防雨布生产线……一个个项目、一条条生产线，正在使穆棱的“塑编产业之路”迈向高端，编织着全省对俄出口加工基地塑编产业城的锦绣未来。

6. 经济效益普遍下降

国内外复杂因素的影响，塑编袋在国内处市场的需求都有所下降，不少企业为了获得订单纷纷开展降价竞争，2012年全国塑编袋售价普遍下降，据我们对重点重点企业的监测利润总额下降60%以上的有7家占24.14%，29家企业中出现了3家亏损企业。

【大事要事】

1. 孙冬泉秘书长、赵克武副秘书长应邀访问辽宁康平

2月24日到25日中国塑协副秘书长，塑料编织制品专委会秘书长孙冬泉、副秘书长赵克武应康平县人民政府的邀请，专程到辽宁省康平经济开发区考察塑编产业集群全面情况。中共康平县委书记王一兵、康平县政府县长李晓航、中共康平县委副县长慈鸿钢、辽宁省康平经济开发区康平县级主任高原等分别热情接待孙冬泉秘书长和赵克武副秘书长。王一兵书记在介绍了康平塑编产业集群时说：康平县塑编产业的发展得到辽宁省委、省政府、沈阳市委、市政府的高度重视，时任辽宁省委书记的李克强同志曾3次视察康平塑编产业发展情况，对塑编产业发展做出了重要指示。康平全县投资5亿多元开展园区建设，组织干部发扬“千辛万苦、千言万语、千方百计、千山万水”的“四千精神”到温州、大庆、海城招商，第一批温州来康平投资的华康、华泰、国大、时代、康荣等25家企业落户康平，几年来到康平落户塑编企业138家，固定资产投资32亿元，拥有塑编生产线390条，圆织机13650台，造粒机203召，切袋机1090召、缝合机1510台、印刷机203台、涂膜机86台、打包机312台、从业人员近2万人。2011年实现销售收入126亿元，其中塑编制品产量890kt，产值110亿元，实现利税12亿元，塑编产量跃居辽宁第一位，占全省塑编产量70%，产品畅销国内15个省市，外销美、英、法等30多个国家和地区，按照本市县“十二五”规划，到2015年塑编生产及配套企业200家，年产值200亿元。欢迎“2012年全国塑编产业链技术交流与市场对接会”在康平县开，并提出申报“中国塑编示范城”的要求。

25日上午孙冬泉秘书长、赵克武副秘书长，在慈鸿钢副县长、高原主任及沈阳市康平县塑编协会秘书长李普阳等陪同下，考察了康平县开发区塑编产业集群，分别参观了友谊、时代、国大、华泰、惠彬、健康、拓源等7家企业。

孙冬泉秘书长在考察后，认为康平地域广阔，人杰地灵，投资环境具有磁性效应，抓住机遇，建设了塑编产品集群，并对康平塑编产业的今后发展提出希望和要求，为全国塑编年会打了前站。

2. 辽宁省康平县获“中国塑编示范城”荣誉称号

中国轻工业联合会、中国塑协于2012年8月22日，以中轻联科技[2012]250号下达“关于授予辽宁省康平县“中国塑编示范城”称号的通知。通知指出：据你县申请，根据中国轻工业联合会《关于共建和授予中国轻工业特色区域称号的行业规范》和中国塑协《关于授予中国塑料加工行业特色区域荣誉称号的管理办法》的要求，中国轻工业联合会委托中国塑协组织考评组，对你县进行了实地考评，认为你县塑编行业的发展在全国塑编行业中具有典型示范作用，

建议授予你县《中国塑编示范城》称号，中国轻工业联合会轻工行业特色区域和产业集群审核委员会进行了审核，基本符合要求。经研究中国轻工联合会和中国塑协同意并正式授予你县《中国塑编示范城》称号。

3. 中国塑协塑编专委会制订《中国塑料编织行业自律公约》

近几年来由于行业投资过剩等因素的影响，塑料编织行业出现了持续困难的局面，最为突出的是市场行为不规范、价格竞争不合理、产品质量参差不齐等。严重破坏了行业的竞争秩序，影响行业的整体形象，阻碍行业的健康发展。为了促进中国塑编行业的健康发展，创造和维护公平的塑料编织市场环境，保障中国塑料编织生产企业和广大用户的合法权益，依据国家有关法规和国家部门《关于加强行业自律的有关规定》和《中国塑协塑料编织制品专委会工作条例》之规定，中国塑协塑编专委会特制订了《中国塑料编织行业自律公约》本公约业经中国塑协塑编专委会三届三次理事会讨论通过。并在辽宁沈阳召开的“2012 年全国塑编产业链技术交流与市场对接会暨沈阳康平塑编经贸展洽会”上公布。

自律公约共五章四十九条，第一章为总则，第二章自律条款，第三章公约的执行，第四章奖励与惩处，第五章为附则，本公约自 2012 年 9 月 1 日起施行。

4. 中国塑协塑编专委会召开第三届三次理事会

2012 年 8 月 27 日晚，中国塑协塑编专委会在沈阳辽宁举行中国塑协塑编专委会第三届三次理事会。会议由孙冬泉主持，在会议主席台就座的有中国塑协塑编专委会会长、浙江华庆集团有限公司董事长姜集康，中国塑协副秘书长、中国塑协塑编专委会秘书长孙冬泉，中国塑协塑编专委会常务副会长、南塑集团有限公司董事长林增标，中国塑协塑编专委会常务副会长、广庆集团有限公司董事长傅广星，中国塑协副秘书长、中国塑协塑编专委会副秘书长田岩，中国塑协塑编专委会高级顾问、温州市塑料行业协会名誉会长宋云鹤，天津华今塑业有限公司董事长助理韩忠锋。

参加会议的还有中国塑协塑编专委会副秘书长、苍南县塑料行业协会秘书长许良然，中国塑协塑编专委会副秘书长、平阳塑料包装协会林成伟，山东新宇包装股份有限公司董事长魏传平，江苏中乾塑业有限公司总经理王崇保，江苏常编塑业有限公司党委书记陈普建，雁峰集团有限公司董事长陈志淡，兖矿集团福兴实业公司总经理丁云富，安徽省锦翔塑编包装实业有限公司董事长孟凡杰等 50 多家理事会成员单位。

会议讨论通过了姜集康会长的《专委会工作总结报告》；赵克武副秘书长宣布 2011 年塑编行业二十强企业名单；孙冬泉秘书长向参加会议代表介绍了《中国塑料编织行业自律公约》实施的必要性和紧迫性，会议经过热烈讨论后通过。林增标常务副会长介绍了塑编新国标的报批情况；宋云鹤高级顾问介绍了《再生塑料编织袋》行业标准的前期制定情况，田岩副秘书长就《农用塑料经编遮阳网》批复进行了说明；赵克武副秘书长作了《塑编专委会 2012 年工作计划》报告，与会代表进行了广泛讨论后通过。嵊州市德利经编网业有限公司副总经理丁云富对《农用塑料经编遮阳网》行业标准进行全面介绍。

与会代表还对 8 月 28 日、29 日《2012 年全国塑编产业链技术交流与市场对接会暨沈阳康平塑编经贸展洽会》会议议程进行了讨论并获得一致通过。会议内容充实丰富、气氛热烈，与会代表还对专委会今后工作提了不少建设性意见和建议，九点半会议完成各项议程，圆满结束。

5. 2012 年全国塑编产业链技术交流与市场对接会暨沈阳康平塑编经贸展洽会在沈阳召开

由中国塑协和沈阳市人民政府共同主办的，中国塑协塑编专委会和康平县人民政府承办的“2012 年全国塑编产业链技术交流与市场对接会暨沈阳康平塑编经贸展洽会”于 2012 年 8 月 28 ~ 29 日在沈阳市辽宁大厦多功能厅召开，开幕式由中国塑协常务副理事长曹俭主持。出席本次会议在主席台就座的领导和嘉宾有沈阳市人民政府市长陈海波、中国轻工业联合会副会长、中国塑协理事长钱桂敬、工业和信息化部消费品司副司长高延敏、沈阳市人民政府副市长王翔坤、辽宁省经信委副主任蔺晓刚、沈阳化工大学校长逄玉俊、国务院国有资产监督管理委员会研究局处长梁方、中国塑协常务副理事长曹俭、沈阳市人民政府秘书长阎秉哲、中国塑协名誉理事长廖正品、中国塑协塑编专委会会长浙江华庆集团有限公司董事长姜集康、中共康平县书记王一兵、康平县人民政府县长李晓航、中国塑协副秘书长中国塑协塑编专委会秘书长孙冬泉、广东省塑料工业协会会长符岸、江苏省塑料加工工业协会会长韦华、山东省塑料工业协会常务副会长刘路兴、浙江省塑料工业协会常务副秘书长汪建萍、中国塑协塑编专委会高级顾问、温州市塑料行业协会名誉会长宋云鹤、中国塑协塑编专委会常务副会长、南塑集团有限公司董事长林增标；中国塑协塑编专委会常务副会长、广庆集团有限公司董事长傅广伟；中国塑协塑编专委会常务副会长、天津华今塑业有限公司董事长陈宗敏；中国塑协塑编专委会副会长、常州市永明机械制造有限公司总经理何敏；中国塑协塑编专委会副会长、雁峰集团有限公司董事长陈志淡、烟台永太机械有限公司副总经理蔡煜建；奥地利史太林格有限公司北京代表处首席代表王二明。

开幕式上，首先由中共康平县委书记王一兵致辞，王书记简单介绍了康平塑编集群的情况和今后发展的规划目标。国务院国有资产管理委员会研究局梁方处长代表行业协会管理办公室讲话，他对塑编专委会工作提出了新的更高要求和殷切希望，工业和信息化部消费品司副司长高延敏在会上提出建议塑编行业要在六个方面进行产业升级，产业要生产集中度低向生产集中度高转变；要由老旧设备淘汰慢向淘汰快转变；要由区域品牌影响力小向区域品牌影响力大转变；要由新产品开发力度小向新产品开发力度大转变；要由国标、行标数量少向国标、行标数量多转变；要由诚信及社会责任弱向诚信及社会责任强转变。

会议进行了2011年度塑编行业二十强企业授牌仪式，由孙冬泉秘书长宣读二十强企业名单，陈海波市长、钱桂敬理事长、高延敏司长、王延坤副市长、蔺晓刚副主任、逢玉俊校长、梁方处长、曹俭常务副理事长、廖正品名誉会长、姜集康会长给塑编二十强企业颁发奖牌。

会议进行了康平县“中国塑编示范城”揭授牌仪式。由钱桂敬理事长和陈海波市长共同为“中国塑编示范城”揭牌，全休代表热烈鼓掌表示祝贺。钱桂敬理事长发表重要讲话，指出塑编行业在“十一五”期间发展迅速，成绩显著，但与先进国家相比还有较大差距，需要我们去正视、去缩小、去赶超。塑编行业比较突出的问题是：一是生产集中度低、小企业多、规模偏小；二是产品结构不合理，中低档比例大；三是产能过剩，低水平、同质化倾向越来越突出；四是技术力量薄弱，创新能力不强部分企业工艺技术装备落后。因此，在“十二五”期间塑编行业要不失时机加快转变发展方式，加快调整优化结构，加快技术进步和科技创新，促进塑编行业健康、可持续发展。钱理事长还要求塑编专委会继续发扬为会员服务、为行业服务、为企业服务的优良传统，加强专委会自身建设，加强塑编行业行规行约建设，较好反映行业诉求，研究行业发展重大问题，大力促进技术创新、深化节能降耗、团结和带领塑编行业夺取改革和发展的新胜利，开创行业新局面。

这次大会得到辽宁省委、省政府，沈阳市委、市政府，关心和大力支持，陈海波市长在百忙中来参加会议，并作了重要讲话。

会上还举行了战略合作与投资合作签约仪式，康平县经济开发区与沈阳化工大学、广东省塑料工业协会、江苏省塑料加工工业协会、山东省临邑县塑料工业协会、浙江省苍南县塑料行业协会、平阳县塑料包装协会签署了战略合作协议。康平经济开发区还与莱阳金开塑业有限公司、温州晨光集团有限公司、天津华今塑业有限公司、雁峰集团有限公司等20家企业签署了投资意向。本次会议共有30多个意向投资项目签约，项目总投资超过15亿元。

会议期间有关领导还参观了展洽会的塑编机械设备和原辅料展区。本届展会上有国内著名的常州永明机械有限公司、雁峰集团有限公司、烟台永太机械有限公司、奥地利史太林格有限公司等国内外30多家企业设备，原辅材料展出。许多公司展出了实物，还现场开机操作获得到会代表的好评，获得了很好收益。

九点四十分，会议进入了主题发言，由孙冬泉主持。由姜集康作“2011年塑编专委会工作总结汇报”的报告，并提请大会审议，与会代表一致鼓掌通过。由林增标作“关于塑编新国标制订工作的总结汇报”，塑料编织袋的新的国家标准《塑料编织袋通用技术要求》已于2011年10月28日在北京铁道大厦召开的专家评审会上获得通过，已由中国轻工业联合上报国家标准化委员会审核批复。慈鸿钢作了“辽宁康平塑编产业投资环境介绍”，并欢迎各企业到康平考察投资。会上江苏中乾、常州永明、雁峰集团、奥地利史大林格先后作了发言。会后全体代表在辽宁大厦集体合影留念。

下午，全体代表前往沈阳康平经济区塑编产业集群基地参观，代表们先后参观了沈阳佳康塑编厂、沈阳拓源塑编厂、沈阳恒辰彩布厂、沈阳惠杉塑业有限公司、沈阳万益达塑编厂、沈阳华泰塑业有限公司、沈阳时代塑编包装公司、沈阳友谊塑业有限公司、沈阳国大塑业有限公司等企业。

晚上，在沈阳辽宁大厦第一宴会厅，康平县委、县政府举行了“2012年全国塑编产业链技术交流与市场对接会暨沈阳康平塑编经贸展洽会”的答谢酒会，宴请全体参加会议代表。

29日上午，继续进行主题交流，由中国塑协塑编专委会高级顾问宋云鹤、《再生塑料编织袋》制标组曾焕、中国塑协改性委员会秘书长刘英俊等10多位代表进行发言，交流了塑编生产技术、介绍了塑编机械、原辅材料，发言内容丰富，深受与会代表欢迎。

29日下午，大会进行塑编行业“十二五”创新发展座谈会，由孙冬泉主持，嵊州市德利经编网业有限公司副总经理丁云富对《农用塑料经编遮阳网》行业标准的制订和批复作了介绍。还进行了与会专家针对企业在生产经营中遇到的难题进行答疑交流，宋云鹤顾问和兖矿集团福兴实业公司朱开文工程师对企业提出的问题进行了答复，受到了企业的欢迎和好评。

大会加强了行业交流，探讨了塑编行业的未来发展趋势，研讨了下游企业的需求情况，促进了塑编企业更多地采用新技术、新设备、新工艺和新材料，加强和促进了行业的节能工作，为提高我国塑编产品质量，增强企业竞争能力促进我国塑编技术创新和发展方式转变，推动我国塑编产业健康持续发展起到了重要作用，受到了与会代表的一致欢迎。

本次大会盛况空前是一次成功的大会上，是一个继往开来的大会，参加大会有700多家企业的1190名代表，除西藏、青海没有代表外，全国28个省市都有代表参加，其中辽宁代表358人，山东省152人，浙江省103人，江苏省92人，河北省73人、河南省66人，温州市代表有65人，还有一家国外企业参加会议。本次会议在国内外具有深远影响。本次大会规模之宏大，人数众多，会议内容丰富，气氛热烈和谐，必将推动我国乃至全球塑编产业的持续健康发展，大会在祥和的气氛中圆满结束。

6. 2011年度塑编行业二十强企业名单

2011年塑编行业二十强经企业自我申报，专委会秘书处初评后经中国塑协塑编专委会第三届三次理事会讨论通过，并在"2012年全国塑编产业链技术交流与市场对接会暨沈阳康平塑编经贸展洽会"大会开幕式上予以公布，在大会上进行授牌仪式，由参加会议领导颁发了奖牌。

温州晨光集团有限公司、天津华今塑业有限公司、山东新宇包装股份有限公司、江西金沙包装集团有限公司、广庆集团有限公司、南塑集团有限公司、浙江华庆集团有限公司、洛阳市强胜实业有限公司、山东寿光健元春有限公司、龙岩市宏祥工业包装有限公司、江西亚美达科技有限公司、昌邑市海美塑品有限责任公司、华正塑料集团有限公司、温州升阳塑业有限公司、沈阳华泰塑业有限公司、沈阳时代塑编包装有限公司、江苏乾申塑业有限公司、广天集团有限公司、兖州市宏泰塑料制品有限公司、沈阳佳康塑编厂。

7. 塑编专委会编制"十二五"期间塑编行业技术创新与产品发展方面(征求意见稿)

为了推进我国塑编行业稳定、健康发展，促进全行业技术创新和产品升级换代，加速产品结构调整步伐，加快发展塑编行业发展，中国塑协塑编专委会编制了"十二五"期间塑编行业技术创新和产品发展方向(征求意见稿)。规划共有七章，内容包括塑编机械创新发展方向、塑编工艺改进方向、塑编产品发展方向、原料改性方向、印刷油墨发展方向、胶黏剂发展方向和产学研结合是实现创新的良好途径。

目前初稿正在广泛征求业内外专家意见，力争修改完善后供全行业生产发展中参考。

8. 温州塑编业改造升级项目快速推进

目前，温州市平阳首个传统塑编产业改造升级项目——温州晨光塑胶有限公司项目被告列入省、市、县技术改造"双千工程"重点项目计划。目前，厂房打桩工作已基本完成，工程总体进展顺利。该项目于平阳县萧江镇标准园区，用地约87亩，总投资约6.5亿元，项目建成后，将形成70kt/a多层共挤双向拉伸聚丙烯薄膜生产能力，年销售收入约10.5亿元。

9. 中国塑协塑编专委会成立塑料编织行业技术顾问小组

中国塑协塑料编织制品专业委员会为了更好地做好会员服务，帮助企业解决工艺、技术、设备等方面的疑难问题，加强塑编行业技术交流，共同促进技术水平提高，决定成立塑料编织行业技术顾问小组，第一批塑料行业技术顾问小组成员有宋云鹤、朱开文、刘友、王振保、陈志淡、王林、孙书适、丁云富、杨玉文、罗之超、陈祖欣等人。

10. 山东塑编制品质检中心在临淄开建

2012年10月，作为傅山经济开发区的新"地标"，投资1个多亿的国家泵类产品质量检测中心，省级机电产品检测中心大楼拨地而起，淄博高新区山东省电光源类产品检测中心和功能玻璃检测中心也与企业"零距离"对接，今年，山东塑料及编织制品质检中心已在临淄开始建设，并于年底投入运行。质监给力，正助推县域经济加速崛起。

11. 全国塑编企业有318家获食品包装生产许可证

从12月19日在北京举行的2012年食品包装行业交流发布会上获悉，全国塑编企业约有12000家，目前取得食品包装许可证的有318家，占全国塑编企业总数的2.645%。

虽然，我国塑编产业规模产值在不断扩大，但产品质量让人担忧。国家质检总局于2006年7月18日颁布了《食品用包装、容器、工具等制品生产许可通则》和《食品用塑料包装、容器、工具等制品生产许可证审查细则》，可6年来，全国取得生产许可证的塑编企业总共只有318家。部分企业的产品质量比认证质量差的状况有所反弹，包括生产环境不能保持认证时的状态，有的企业厂门大开，任凭外界尘土吹刮，甚至风淋消毒室，洗手设施根本不用，操作人员进出根本不更衣消毒，粉尘积满生产设备，过多地添加碳酸钙母料，过渡追求降低成本，蒸发残渣超标等。

12. 孙冬泉秘书长、赵克武副秘书长走访山东新宇包装股份有限公司

2012 年 12 月 4 日至 5 日，塑编专委会秘书长孙冬泉、副秘书长赵克武专程走访了山东新宇包装股份有限公司，新宇公司创建于 2002 年，位于山东临邑临盘工业园，注册资本 5100 万元，占地 20 万平方米，是山东省先进民营企业、主营塑料编织袋和布衣工艺品，主导产品有集装袋、阀口袋、包装袋等 5 大系列 150 多个品种，企业拥有自营进出口权，产品远销韩国、俄罗斯、日本、马来西亚、美国、以色列、南非等 20 多个国家和地区。年产量超过 5 亿条，是中国塑编之乡的支柱企业，是中国塑协塑编专委会的副会长单位，2012 年在全国塑编行业生产经营遇到极大困难的境况下，全年预计可实现销售收入 3.5 亿元，比 2011 年增长 50% 以上，预计净利润 4000 万元以上，出口创汇 3600 万美元，公司“十二五”规划要初步形成原料经营、塑料制品、物流服务为主的产业链，到 2015 年实现销售 8 亿元，净利润 8500 万元。

十年来，新宇打造了“六力”发展能力，竞争力 1：旗舰力——行业排名第三，竞争力 2：市场力——国内国际双轨驱动，竞争力 3：产品力——产品层次高，竞争力 4：管理力——柔性制造能力强，竞争力 5：区位力——综合经济带，竞争力 6：政策力——符合“十二五”规划年复合增长率不低于 15%。新宇公司以谋求更好发展，正积极筹划上市，以更加开放的姿态进入资本市场，公司股份改造已完成，战略投资者引进工作在紧张进行中。

孙秘书长认为：新宇的发展具有借鉴意义，值得行业内企业学习。

附表 1　2012 年产值超亿元企业

企业名称	工业总产值/万元	主营业务收入/万元	塑编制品产量/t	利税总额/万元	利润总额/万元
山东寿光健元春有限公司	167400	164432	44858	5696	3178
天津华今集团有限公司	123800	129800	120000	7800	7800
温州晨光集团有限公司	102182	104078	85666	17700	9489
广庆集团有限公司	94025	88259	56663	8834	7216
南塑集团有限公司	80255	82028	70132	8637	4509
洛阳市强胜实业有限公司	82500	66000	68000	1573	551
龙岩市宏祥工业包装有限公司	62138	58965	52000	11566	7886
江苏森帝塑业有限公司	45000	48000	36000	3700	1600
江苏万禾复合材料有限公司	43500	41600	25850	3650	1500
浙江华庆集团有限公司	34224	34377	36976	3489	2183
新疆蓝德精细石油化工股份有限公司		27755.17			
浙江中宇节能科技有限公司	22855	22562			
淄博新力塑编有限公司	21157	19975	15238	580	509
华正塑料集团有限公司	23503	18855	17000	137	−932
浙江贤超包装有限公司	19024	18480	17926	756.5	275.5
温州升阳塑业有限公司	16084	16911	13623	710	175
广天集团有限公司	15792	15781	17160	1270	380
温州华利集团有限公司	13465	14925	13060	686	52
温州市中标化纤有限公司	11893	10612		547	127
兖矿集团福兴实业公司	12287.04	10501.74	2100	198.25	162.48
温州共和包装有限公司	9527	10088		404	35
沈阳友谊塑业有限公司	10835	9102	9850	720	240

（中国塑料加工工业协会塑料编织制品专业委员会　宋云鹤　孙冬泉）

塑料管道

【行业现状】

在经历了多年的高速发展后，我国塑料管道行业进入了相对稳定、成熟发展时期。行业在不断进步中，更加注重技术、创新和产品质量水平的提高。

1. 生产能力强，产业集中度提高

统计 2012 年塑料管道生产量 11000kt，较 2011 年同比增长 10%。尽管一些地域的小企业有减少的现象，但目前国内塑料管道生产企业仍超过 5000 家。其中超过 20 家企业的年生产能力已经大于 150kt，统计 20 家的产品产量超过全行业总产量的 35%。近年产量情况见表 1。

表 1　近年塑料管道产量和增长速度

年份	2008	2009	2010	2011	2012
产量/kt	4593	5804	8402	10000	11000
增长率/%	28.2	18.9	31.1	19.0	10.0

2. 各种塑料管道材料比例变化不大

以聚氯乙烯(PVC)、聚乙烯(PE)和聚丙烯(PP)材料为主的塑料管道加工产业在材料结构上变化不大，分析 PVC 材料约占塑料管道总量的 50% 左右，PE 材料约占 30%，PP 材料约占 10%。塑料基和塑料基金属增强材料管道发展速度加快，耐热聚乙烯(PE－RT)、超高分子量聚乙烯(UHMWPE)以及改性、复合、增强等材料用量有较大增加。行业更加关注一些特种性能材料的技术进步。

3. 应用领域进一步拓宽

市政及建筑给、排水管道和农用(饮用水、灌排)管道目前仍是塑料管道的主要用途，污水处理、供暖、城市非开挖施工等领域的应用比例也在不断提高。最近的市场走势表明，建筑用塑料管道市场需求趋稳，市政建设用以及特殊用途管道的应用比例进一步增加。

4. 重视技术进步，整体技术水平提升

越来越多的企业重视新产品的开发和新技术的引进，塑料管道的新品种、新结构、新材料、新技术、新工艺及专利项目越来越多。

行业更加关注加工设备的生产效率、节能以及自动化程度的提高。整体技术水平的不断提升，带来了塑料管道新产品不断出现，既完善了使用性能，又扩大了产品的应用领域。

5. 生产企业逐步追求规模化，骨干企业加快地域布局步伐

与前期情况不同的是，尽管新进塑料管道行业企业的数量下降，但新上企业的实力一般较强，更追求经济规模，年生产能力超过 30kt 以上居多。

以往塑料管道生产企业主要集中在广东、浙江等沿海和经济发达地区，近年一些大企业在东北、华北、中部、西部等地区投资或增加规模，异地布点建厂，带动行业地域布局逐步趋于合理。

6. 用户和生产企业的品牌意识进一步提高，骨干企业的产品质量水平整体上升

由于工程质量的问题出现和市场的逐步规范，用户也越来越关注塑料管道的产品质量。工程指定标准、材料，以及要求专项检测、产品标记等现象也越来越多。尽管市场上质量水平参差不齐，但合格产品是市场的主流，骨干企业的产品质量水平整体上升。

7. 出口产品增加，尤其是单价增长较快

近年塑料管道产品出口持续增长，2012 年出口量接近 500kt，更加可喜的是在出口单价呈上升趋势。近年塑料管道产品的出口情况见表 2。

表 2　近年塑料管道出口情况

	出口量/kt	增长率/%	占总产量比例/%	出口额/亿美元	增长率/%	平均单价/(美元/t)
2008 年	356.3	22.0	7.7	10.02	31.0	2862.76
2009 年	318	－12.4	5.5	8.63	－14.5	2714.13
2010 年	396.2	20.0	5.0	11.59	26.0	2930.00
2011 年	448.7	13.2	4.5	14.99	29.3	3340.76
2012 年	489.2	9.0	4.4	18.67	24.5	3816.00

【专委会活动】

2012 年专委会的主要活动：

1. 加强专委会自身建设，做好行业服务工作

增强行业力量，扩大行业影响力，是专委会工作的重要任务之一，2012 年专委会新增加 2 家理事单位及 50 多家会员单位，同时也清理了部分未完成义务的会员单位。专委会凝聚力不断增强，不断有新的相关单位提出入会要求。

2012 年专委会尽量及时收集并向会员单位传递相关产业政策、行业动态、新技术和新工艺等方面情况，还积极参加房地产、市政排水等用户行业的相关活动、会员单位的用户推介、企业标准制定及审查、企业发展战略评审等活动，为企业生产、技术创新、市场推广和发展提出建议和帮助。

专委会还积极向相关部门提出有利于行业发展的相关意见和建议，完成有关行业规划、发展、技术进步等方面相关建议工作，对国家相关部门税收、政府采购等政策的调整提出合理建议，维护行业的

正当利益。

专委会还与北京、上海、天津、重庆等地区的塑料管道相关协会开展常态化联谊活动，共同做好促进塑料管道行业健康发展的服务工作。

2. 努力作好杂志和网站建设工作，加强行业宣传

信息咨询、产品推广是塑料管道专委会的重要职能之一。目前，塑料管道专委会拥有专业网站及《中国塑料管道资讯》杂志两大交流平台。

专委会以《中国塑料管道资讯》为基础，从政策、法规、行业动态、专委会平台、会员风采、市场信息等方面传递信息，并加大了向相关的设计单位、研究院、自来水公司、燃气公司、相关协会及媒体等单位的发放力度，扩大了行业的影响力。2012 年全年完成了 6 期《中国塑料管道资讯》杂志的编辑、发行工作，2003 年以来共出刊 54 期。作为专委会的内部刊物，《中国塑料管道资讯》既是行业交流、沟通的桥梁，也是专委会服务会员单位的一个主要平台，得到了行业内相关人士的支持、帮助与认可。专委会也将努力提高专业知识和编辑水平，争取把杂志办得更出色，更好地为行业和会员单位服务。

网站作为专委会两大交流平台之一，2012 年在为行业及会员单位提供信息共享、形象宣传等方面也取得了进步，专委会计划在 2013 年对网站进行全新改版，扩大信息量，及时更新和发布信息。

3. 开展技术交流，促进行业技术进步

为促进塑料管道行业技术水平和创新能力的提高，加强行业及企业间的交流与合作，促进行业的健康发展，2012 年中国塑协塑料管道专业委员会成功的组织开展了一系列相关活动。

塑料管道专委会于 3 月 2 日在北京组织召开了“塑料管道 2012 年技术工作会议”，邀请相关领导、专家以及塑料管道企业代表，讨论《塑料管道行业“十二五”期间(2011 ~2015)发展建议》及行业技术发展方向，为行业的科学发展献计献策。专家们建议“十二五”期间行业应以 PVC – U 管道、PE 管道、PP 管道为发展重点，并大力发展改性、复合以及其他新型塑料管道，尽快完善应用的配套技术和质量保证体系。同时还应进一步加大产品创新力度，适应市场需求，重点开发、生产新材料类塑料管道、改性与复合类塑料管道、环境友好型塑料管道、新型塑料管道系统。

为促进塑料检查井市场的健康发展，2012 年 6 月 14 日，塑料管道专委会与北京市建设工程物资协会管材管件分会在北京共同主办了“塑料检查井交流会”，80 多位代表参加了会议。会议内容涉及塑料检查井相关产品标准、应用技术规程、技术发展、市场推广等多方面内容，提出加工企业应根据市场需求，通过发挥本身独有的优势来提高竞争力，避免产品同质化及恶性竞争。

专委会还在上级协会的领导下参与了推荐轻工行业重点推广技术工作，塑料管道企业多个项目列入其中，为行业技术水平的提升创造了条件。

专委会还参与了多项塑料管道、检查井等相关的产品标准、应用规程的制定、审查、交流等工作，为制品生产和管道应用打下好的基础。

4. 加强行业自律，努力提高产品质量意识和水平

塑料管道产品质量水平参差不齐的现象已严重影响行业的健康发展，专委会已多次呼吁并在一定范围内采取办法开展行业自律工作，以提高行业的产品质量意识和品牌意识。

专委会在 2012 年通过杂志、报纸、网站等媒体共发布了 4 期不同品种塑料管材的行业指导价格，分析原料价格、行业企业加工成本的情况，制定符合标准要求的相关产品的建议市场价格，为加工企业、用户单位及相关机构提供参考数据。

2012 年 3 月召开的专委会理事会上还重点讨论了塑料管道行业产品质量参差不齐的问题，会议纪要提出应加强企业自律，建立行业诚信体系，并通过相应途径加大产品质量监管，以减少低价竞标、恶性竞争等不良现象。

国家质检总局和水利部在 2012 年联合开展了 PP – R管材等节水产品质量国家监督抽查与质量提升活动，活动的主要目的之一是督促生产企业严格执行产品标准，提高产品质量。专委会高度重视该工作，积极响应并配合此次活动，还从行业现状和发展角度提出了促进产品质量水平提升的工作建议，利用网站、杂志等方式进行报道，促进塑料管道产品质量不断提升，为行业的健康发展尽到应尽的社会责任和义务。

在大家的共同努力下，我们高兴的看到，目前塑料管道行业不只关注价格，更重视产品质量，注重品牌和服务的生产企业和用户越来越多。

5. 加强与上、下游行业的交流，提高塑料管道的加工和应用水平

为加强行业间的交流，密切行业间的联系，促进塑料管道更好加工、更广泛应用，专委会积极参与了上、下游行业的相关工作和交流活动。

上游行业的进步，为塑料管道产品性能的提高和更好应用提供了良好条件。专委会积极支持原料、助剂、加工装备等行业的技术进步与质量提升工作，

在PVC－M、HDPE混配料、非铅盐热稳定剂等产品的研发、应用等技术进步中做好配合工作。

2012年专委会积极参与了水利部农村饮水安全中心主办的"全国农村水利工程材料设备产品信息年报"的相关工作，为水利行业用户选好、用好塑料管道提出合理建议。专委会还参加了由住房和城乡建设部科技发展促进中心和全国化学建材协调组塑料管道专家组主办的"第14届全国塑料管道生产和应用技术推广交流会"，积极参加了中国城市燃气协会、中国城镇供水排水协会排水专业委员会和设备材料委管道部、中国建筑金属结构协会辐射供暖供冷委员会、全国房地产总工之家、北京建委建设工程物资协会等相关活动。

根据住建部《城市供水行业2010年技术进步发展规划和2020年远景目标》"管道材料的选择与应用部分"内容的要求，中国水协设备材料委管道部组织编制了《城市供水钢塑复合管材及管配件的选择与应用》。专委会积极配合，参与了编写工作，为供水行业更好的选择相关产品提出建议。

专委会还积极关注用户行业的市场动向，参加了中国水工业互联网等相关单位主办的"新形势下的城市排水系统与技术发展研讨会"，参与研讨北京等城市排水系统存在的主要问题，建议高质量的大口径塑料排水管道应为城市排水系统和地下蓄水系统的良好应用发挥作用。

7月26～28日，在枫叶集团的协助下，塑料管道专委会与中国城市燃气协会在贵阳共同主办了"2012年PE燃气管道应用技术交流培训班"，100多位燃气设计、施工、应用等相关人员参加了培训。培训内容涉及到PE燃气管材及管件的产品标准、原料、质量鉴别及控制、检测方法、加工工艺、生产技术、市场推广、设计和应用等多个方面。通过培训与交流，更多燃气用户深入了解了PE燃气管道加工、质量控制、施工、应用等相关知识，便于选择好、设计好、应用好PE燃气管道，该工作对塑料管道行业的健康发展和燃气行业的放心使用起到了很好的促进作用，专委会今后将继续与给水、排水、燃气、石油等行业合作共同举办这类相关活动。

为更好的提供宣传和展示平台，塑料管道专委会与中国石油天然气管道局等单位在6月中旬共同举办了"2012中国国际油气储运技术与装备展览会"，与中国建筑金属结构协会给水排水设备分会等单位于9月下旬在上海联合举办了"2012上海建筑给排水、水处理技术及设备展览会"。通过展示行业产品，为企业与用户提供良好的交流平台，为塑料管道市场拓展提供新的机遇。

通过与下游相关行业的交流与合作，进一步拓宽了塑料管道行业的发展空间，延伸了塑料管道的应用领域。

6. 加强国际交流，加大中国塑料管道行业走向国际的步伐

在促进与国外塑料管道行业间的交流，加强与国际相关协会联系等方面，中国塑协塑料管道专委会也做了一些工作。

2012年4月初，塑料管道专委会参加了由中国塑料加工工业协会组织的赴美参加2012年美国NPE展会及交流活动。考察期间，中国塑料加工工业协会与美国塑料协会(SPI)签订了合作协议，还与美国塑料工程师协会(SPE)等单位进行了交流。

为加大行业开拓国际市场的力度，专委会还于5月14日在上海参加了由西班牙AENOR认证机构及CEIS检测服务中心主办的认证研讨会，了解了塑料管道产品的相关检测标准和认证要求等新资讯。

塑料管道专委会组织国内相关单位20余人参加了9月24～26日在西班牙举办的第十六届国际塑料管道会议。会议内容涉及塑料管道行业的发展进程；塑料管道、新型塑料管道及管件的发展；新型结构壁管和多层复合管材；管道在燃气、供水、排水等系统中的应用；新型塑料管道设计和测试方法；传统材料的衰退、标准与规范；塑料管道工程案例分析；管道修复、环保建材、生命周期评估等方面内容。

我国共有7个专题报告和2个海报发言。在国际会议上，国家建材测试中心(材料部)博士熊志敏作了《测试HDPE管材料点荷载的新方法》的报告，亚大集团经理王志伟作了《PE管在工业领域的应用及生产质量控制程序》的报告，上海奉贤自来水公司工程师张志浩作了《环境温度对给水用PE管道在应用中的影响》的报告，天津盛象公司副总经理李洪山作了《排水管道工程设计、计算及实验—天津市武清区雍阳东道》的报告，中国塑协塑料管道专委会秘书长王占杰作了《PVC－U管道的技术进步》的报告，常州河马公司副总经理周敏宏作了《排水用塑料检查井在中国的推广与应用》的报告，浙江中财公司副总经理陈增贵作了《高温天气下给水用PE管耐压验证》的报告。还有沧州明珠公司经理池永生作了《浅析管材挤出过程中鲨鱼皮症与口模长径比的关系》的报告，浙江双林塑料机械公司经理李星作了《大口径缠绕增强聚乙烯管生产技术》的报告，另有5个书面论文分别来自福建亚通公司陈鹊的《大口径钢塑复合排水管在中国的应用及进展》、杭州鸿雁电器有限公司盛仲夷的《新型PP－R熔接式管件的研究》、塑料管道专

委会王占杰的《中国塑料管道行业五年总结与下一个五年发展展望》、天津军星集团夏成文的《高导热系数聚乙烯管》和大庆油田设计院张丽的《油田非金属管道应用技术现状及建议》。通过这些报告，使国际同行了解了中国塑料管道行业的技术进步与行业现状，受到了会议组织者的好评。

代表团在会议期间还与有关国家的行业协会、机构、企业就技术、信息、合作等方面展开了交流。并分别对西班牙 AENOR 认证机构、CEIS 检测机构和德国费亚泰克集团进行了考察和交流。

专委会还接待了国际同行、相关协会、机构、企业的来访与交流。通过参加国际会议及交流、考察活动，应充分认识到中国塑料管道行业与世界先进水平还存在差距，中国塑料管道行业要真正走出国门，应不断加强交流与合作，学习先进的经营及服务理念，加强科技创新，注重细节管理，提高塑料管道行业的生产和应用水平，提高产品质量水平，提高行业整体竞争力。

7. 组织理事会、年会等重要活动，促进行业交流

2012 年 3 月 23 日，在南京协和公司的协助下，塑料管道专委会在南京召开了第八届六次理事会议。会议对 2011 年塑料管道专委会工作进行了总结，并通过了 2012 年工作计划，表决通过了 2 家理事单位及 54 家会员单位的申请。

5 月 24 ~ 26 日，在顾地科技股份有限公司的支持下，“中国塑料加工工业协会塑料管道专委会 2012 年年会”在重庆召开。来自国内外相关单位领导、专家、会员单位、塑料管道生产企业、上下游企业、行业协会、检测机构、认证单位、相关媒体等单位代表 540 余人参加了会议。年会主题为“巩固‘十一五’成就规划‘十二五’发展”。

中国轻工业联合会副会长、中国塑协理事长钱桂敬在会议上详细介绍了塑料加工行业“十二五”发展规划指导意见。钱理事长指出，塑料加工业“十二五”期间要紧紧围绕体制创新、科技创新、质量模式创新推进绿色低碳发展。规划总体思路突出了依靠科技创新，大力推进技术进步，推动产业升级，构建现代产业体系；要突出结构调整，加快转变发展方式，优化产品结构，区域布局和企业组织结构的调整；突出品牌战略，提高产业发展质量。

钱会长表示，塑料管道是塑料加工业中重要组成部分，目前已成为塑料加工业中第一大产业，在肯定管道行业取得辉煌成就的同时，也应清醒认识到当前存在的问题。产能过剩，产品同质化程度严重、产品标准化缺失和滞后、专用料不能满足生产需要等问题，都需要认真解决。他强调，行业应该牢牢把握转变发展方式，调整产业结构，提升发展质量，加强人才引进，大力推进技术创新、科技进步，新产品研发，提高中高档产品比重，大力推进塑料管道行业安全工程建设、重视产品及工程质量、完善标准化体系建设，全面提升塑料管道的整体水平。

围绕会议主题，会议提出今后一段时间内，行业的重点工作是调整产品结构，优化产品定位策略，满足市场需求；研发新产品、新技术，进一步拓宽应用领域；加强品牌建设，提高产品质量水平；促进行业间的交流，进一步加强与上、下游相关单位的合作；加强国际交流，互通有无，缩小与发达国家的差距。

会议还安排了塑料管道原料、助剂、设备、新技术、检测、应用、质量管理及行业发展等方面 23 个专题交流。

8. 加快产业结构调整，促进行业稳步健康发展

为了能够科学、合理的制定行业发展规划，调整产业布局，推动塑料管道行业的健康发展，塑料管道专委会在对会员单位和行业企业调查研究的基础上，制定出《中国塑料管道行业“十二五”期间(2011 ~ 2015)发展建议》，经会议多次讨论、交流，并在广泛征求专家、生产企业、相关行业的意见后，于 2012 年正式发布，为规划、指导塑料管道行业健康发展，合理调整产业结构提供了重要的参考。

塑料管道行业发展迅速，但这种高速增长是基于我国经济高速增长和管网建设相对落后而带动的高速增长，不可能一直持续增长，塑料管道行业正由快速成长期逐步向成熟期过渡。行业应抓住机遇，优化结构调整，大力推进科技创新和技术进步。

【存在的问题】

塑料管道行业虽取得了较大的进步，但还存在一些不足和问题需要进一步解决。行业还存在关注增长速度，忽视综合效益；关注产量增加，忽视质量控制；关注产品生产，忽视工程质量；关注传统应用，忽视技术创新等老问题，尽管其中部分问题不只是塑料管道行业独有的，在一些发达国家也有不同程度的经历。

1. 生产能力已出现较严重的供大于求现象

经统计目前国内塑料管道年生产能力超过 25000kt，总体设备利用率较低，已经出现较严重的供大于求现象，更加剧了行业的竞争。

2. 部分企业产品质量低劣，影响行业声誉

市场上产品质量是长期困扰行业的问题。个别企业的质量意识、诚信意识、品牌意识、服务意识

不强，市场上的产品质量水平参差不齐。有的企业产品质量达不到标准要求，损害了消费者权益，影响了行业的信誉。

造成产品质量水平参差不齐的主要原因之一是市场不规范，低价竞争、不合理价格中标等现象更助长了低质量产品的流通。

3. 原材料制约行业的发展

尽管近年国内树脂行业有较大进步，尤其聚氯乙烯行业更加明显。但一些品种树脂依然存在着规格、数量的不足，有的品种质量尚不十分稳定，有的需大量依靠进口，管道制品进一步提高性能受到制约，一些领域的下游用户也担心国产原料的质量保障的现象。

4. 产品创新方面还有待加强

由于有的小企业科技研发水平不够，有的企业不愿过多科技投入，有的高水平管道受到市场接受价格的制约等原因，相对而言，市场上相类似的通用产品较多，中低档产品占大部分，而高技术、高附加值的产品相对较少。行业应通过不断的自主开发，加快科技创新，开发新产品，进一步提高产品的精度、可靠性、稳定性和配套水平。

5. 工程施工质量应进一步完善

有的企业注重塑料管道生产，忽视应用技术的研究，有的工程技术标准、施工技术不配套。有的用户、设计、施工、监理等部门对塑料管道产品的性能、特点、设计、安装等技术还了解不够，影响了塑料管道合理的设计、使用。

行业应加强技术培训，建立专业培训基地，组织编写教材，有计划的对生产和施工人员开展技术培训，加强标准、规范的学习与宣贯。

6. 标准化工作应进一步加强

标准化工作目前还存在产品标准覆盖不全；有的产品标准水平相对不高；一些标准修订速度太慢；原料、工程技术等相关标准、规程、规范还不配套；标准宣贯工作过慢和宣贯面过小；尤其是标准实施的监督工作不完善等需要进一步解决的问题，限制了行业的更好发展。

7. 理念创新更加重要

我们一段时间以来偏重于技术引进、消化吸收、仿制产品，注重硬件的投入和产品的创新，但往往忽视软件的作用，忽视思想的转变。我们应更加注重理念的创新，学习先进国家的市场竞争、产品创新、质量意识、百年企业的观念。中国塑料管道行业不乏大的企业，但我们应更深层次研究如何把行业和企业做强。

【发展趋势与规划】

塑料管道在节能、节地、节水、节材等方面优势突出，符合国家相关产业政策，是其发展很快的主要原因之一。分析今后几年中塑料管道生产量将保持在10%左右的速度增长，到2015年，预期全国塑料管道产量将超过13200kt。塑料管道在全国各类管道中市场占有率超过50%。

近年塑料管道行业发展迅速，但这种高速增长是基于我国经济高速增长和管网建设相对落后而带来的增长，不可能一直持续高速。我们要正视行业存在的困难和问题，在行业总生产能力较严重供大于求、竞争加剧的情况下，产业结构需要进一步调整、技术水平和产品质量需要进一步提高。建议行业企业应抓住机遇，优化产业结构调整，大力推进科技创新和技术进步，提高产品质量，提升行业发展质量。

1. 发展重点建议

根据我国塑料管道行业的现状与产品特点，应进一步加强高性能、高附加值的新产品开发；在以PVC管道、PE管道、PP管道为发展重点的基础上，加大改性、复合以及其他新型塑料管道的研发，尽快完善管道生产和应用配套技术体系，提高产品性能，以适应新的应用领域的开拓。

——重点开发、生产新材料类塑料管道、改性与复合类塑料管道、环境友好型塑料管道和新型塑料管道系统。注重高性能、高附加值产品的研发，满足不同用途塑料管道产品在环保、节能、防火、防菌、保温、阻氧、增强、抗震、降噪等特殊领域的性能要求。

——充分发挥我国PVC树脂产能的优势，大力推进PVC管道生产的技术进步于与推广应用。加强通过各种改性方式提高PVC管材综合性能的技术研究，如接枝改性复合材料(PVC－M等)、定向改性(取向)材料(PVC－O等)、可熔接(FPVC)材料、无机纳米改性PVC材料、PVC－C材料等，推进完成PVC－U管道中采用环保型热稳定剂替代铅盐稳定剂工作，以进一步扩展PVC管道应用领域，扩大市场份额。

——进一步提高建筑物同层排水塑料管道系统、地板采暖塑料管道系统、地源热泵塑料管道系统、太阳能热水塑料管道系统、中水雨水回收利用塑料管道系统、室内通风塑料管道系统等建筑领域应用产品的技术水平和配套水平。

——积极关注市镇排水、排污管网系统的建设，推进高模量PP双壁波纹管、复合缠绕增强等大口径排水用结构壁塑料和复合管道；雨水回收储存、利用系统；大口径压力塑料管道、城镇集中供热二次管网用复合塑料管道等市政塑料管道系统的研究、生产与应用。

——在埋地管道工程建设中积极推广非开挖施工技术，包括非开挖施工和旧管道修复。促进HDPE、耐应力开裂PE－RC等材料管道品种管道加强研发、更好应用。

——努力扩大工业领域用塑料管道市场，大力开发用于中、高压力石油输送、耐磨、耐腐蚀、耐热等特种介质输送以及矿山用阻燃和抗静电双抗管道，如高压增强热塑性塑料管道(RTP)、分子量超过200万的UHMW－PE、大口径PEX、特种材料、复合管道等工业领域有特殊需求的塑料管道品种。

——完善塑料管道系统的配套技术，在管件、阀门、检查井等产品上加强研发、推广力度，以提高管道系统的安全性和可靠性。

——推进降低塑料管道加工能耗和提高生产效率、加工自动化的工作。

2. 实施措施建议

2.1 加强行业科技创新和技术进步，提高塑料管道系统的配套水平

引导企业积极研发新技术、开发新产品，提高产品附加值，走出低价竞争的误区，逐步实现产业升级换代。制定鼓励政策，加强国际交流，促进企业与科研机构合作，加强新材料、改性材料、复合材料、新型管道的研究、生产和配套工作，提高塑料管道整体或某方面性能，以满足特殊领域或特殊环境下应用的塑料管道系统需求，形成多样化的产品市场

2.2 完善质量保证体系，引导市场健康发展

要加强行业自律，完善质量保证体系，健全质量认证和监督制度。对企业的工艺装备、生产规模、检测手段和质量保证体系等提出合理化建议，配合相关单位加强对行业产品质量的监督抽查。企业应加强对用户的服务，协助用户选择最佳的产品。相关产品及工程项目建议实行质量承诺及保证制度。

对于涉及公共安全、人身安全的产品，应逐步建立、健全强制性的管理办法。

生产企业不应采取以低价作为进入市场的手段，要有长期的市场意识，注重产品质量、技术创新和后续服务与改进，为用户提供合格产品与服务。

建议应用领域制定合理的招投标管理办法，完善管理体制，能够通过合理的竞争机制，选用符合标准要求、价格合理的塑料管道产品。

2.3 注重与上游行业的协调发展，促进行业发展质量提升

建议原料行业加快塑料管道专用树脂及混配料的研发和稳定生产，促进PE压力管道用混配料的国产化和多样化；开发PVC功能化树脂、接枝改性PVC树脂；推进大口径排水用高模量PP管道专用料的研发，尽快扭转我国专用树脂及混配料生产与供需失衡的局面。

促进助剂行业的技术进步，提高功能化助剂的技术水平，制定相关政策，加速推进PVC管道制品铅盐热稳定剂的替换工作。

促进装备业企业与加工企业间的合作，推进生产装备的技术改造，提高生产效率、自动化水平和塑料管道生产的稳定性。采用先进技术，降低加工能耗。

2.4 加强对应用市场的服务，便于用户选好、用好塑料管道产品

行业应组织编制产品应用手册，积极培训工程技术人员，促进用户完善施工技术，提高塑料管道工程质量。要加强与用户行业的交流，普及塑料管道产品相关知识，利于用户选好、用好塑料管道产品。

生产企业还应成为整个管道系统的供应商，提供整体应用方案和全套技术服务。

2.5 防止行业过热发展，鼓励形成大型产业集群

塑料管道行业目前的总体产能已经供大于求，因此不应过热发展、盲目扩大产能。

建议企业分析自身优势和市场方向，根据自身资源科学发展。特别是一些中小企业更应择优发展适宜产品，主动淘汰落后产能。鼓励行业企业合理兼并，逐步形成合理的大型产业集群，发挥规模化经营的优势，提高产业集中度，提高综合竞争能力。

(中国塑料加工工业协会塑料管道专业委员会　王占杰)

双向拉伸聚丙烯薄膜

锂离子电池隔膜发展概况与加工技术发展趋势探讨

一、锂离子电池及隔膜产业发展概况

1.1 锂离子电池产业发展概况

1.1.1 锂电池产业总体情况

韩国企业，通过材料、零部件等产业链的资源优化，经过近几年的努力，于2011年超越了传统的锂电池生产大国日本，一跃成为锂电池生产巨头。中国与韩、日两国相比，拥有原材料及成本优势，但在技术上的差距较大(具体对比详见图1)。如何整合资源，突破技术瓶颈，提高产品附加值是我们当前急需解决的问题。

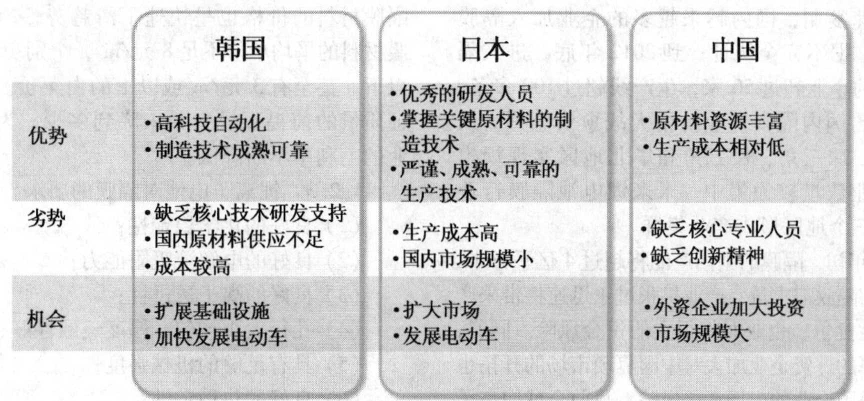

图1　中国和韩国、日本锂电池产业情况对比

2012年，全球和中国锂离子电池需求继续保持增长。市场驱动力主要来自消费类电子产品和小型动力电池，包括笔记本电脑(含平板)、智能手机、电动自行车等。

虽然锂电池的需求量增速较大，但日本、韩国厂家占有率依然很高，其中韩国的2家公司份额增长明显。中国厂家的份额也在逐步增长，但是格局变化大，部分厂家的变化比较极端。未来的几年，总体电池市场会保持稳步的增长，但笔记本电脑用圆柱电池的出货在下降，智能手机用途的聚合物电池在大幅增长(图2)。

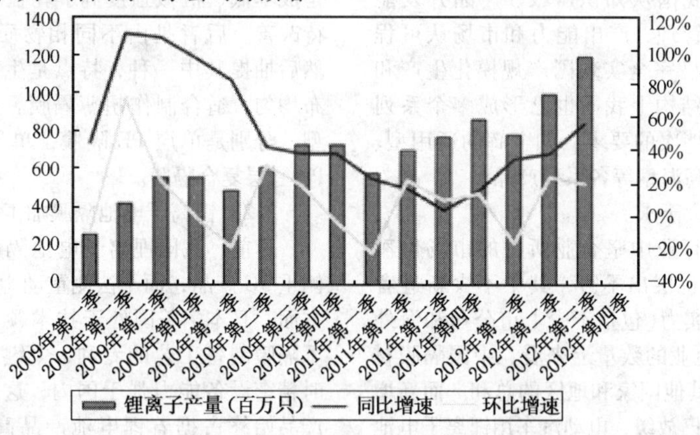

图2　我国锂电池季度产量及增速图

1.1.2　锂电池产业增长点

(1) 随着智能手机和平板电脑的快速增长，聚合物电池的市场将不断扩大，我国聚合物电池份额将进一步扩大；

(2) 我国是世界上最大的电动自行车生产国和消费市场，电动自行车升级换代，为锂离子电池在电动自行车上的应用提供了巨大的市场需求；

(3) 随着锂离子电池成本的下降，国内通信后备电源用锂离子电池的年新增市场容量潜力大。通信后备电源领域将是锂离子电池的又一新的应用领域；

(4) 电动汽车是未来锂离子电池的最大市场(预计2015～2020年，电动汽车的年增长率约为20%)，目前世界各国都在加紧研发；

(5) 市场发展新热点：规模储能。在未来电网，包括发电、配电、再生能源发电中具有关键地位。

1.1.3　锂电池的应用趋势。

目前，锂离子电池主要应用于3C、平板电脑、电动工具中，也正在往动力汽车、动力自行车应用方向发展。未来，锂电池将在储能系统中发挥重要的作用。

1.2　锂离子电池隔膜产业发展概况

1.2.1　锂离子电池隔膜现状

隔膜是锂离子电池四大关键材料之一，作用是将正极与负极材料隔开，容许离子通过而不能让电子通过。由于技术壁垒高，它是最后实现国产化的锂离子电池材料，国内中、高端隔膜需求依然绝大部分依赖进口。隔膜国产化技术壁垒在于起步晚、技术及生产设备受外国少数厂商封锁，国内自主研发需时长、成本高、投资金额大、周期长、技术风险高，最初国内企业的投资热情并不高，但是随着干法工艺快速复制，国内越来越多的企业加入隔膜研发生产中。据不完全统计，到2012年底，进入隔膜生产领域的企业超过50家，生产线超过100多条。2012年开始，国内隔膜行业价格大战愈演愈烈。从分布区域看，珠三角、长三角和华北地区实现规模产业化的企业数量较为集中，未来锂电池隔膜行业有望在上述三个地区形成产业集群。

到2013年初，隔膜的国内产能将超过4亿平方米，超出我国目前隔膜需求量。产业扩张过于迅速将带来产能过剩、恶性竞争，企业面临很大的资金风险。同时，大量实力雄厚的外资企业加大对中国隔膜市场的开拓也加剧了国内隔膜企业的市场竞争风险。目前全球锂离子电池隔膜主要来自日本旭化成、美国Celgard、韩国SKInnovation、日本东燃及日本宇部，约占全球隔膜销量的60%，主要面向国际一线电池厂商。

1.2.2　我国锂电池隔膜产业呈现出以下特点：

(1) 产品研发自主化、产品结构系列化

目前，我国干法、湿法两种工艺生产的隔膜均已实现了市场化，产能急剧扩大，质量也在不断提升。总体来说，目前我国从知识产权、产品开发能力、生产技术、质量管理、产出能力和市场认可程度等方面国产隔膜都已完全实现国产规模化生产和应用。另外，在产品结构上我国也已形成多个系列满足不同市场和不同挡次的要求，如金辉的通用型、高透型、超薄型、耐高温型等各系列产品。

(2) 市场渐显供大于求。

目前，我国隔膜行业中坚企业所占的市场份额越来越大，新进企业也层出不穷，其中不少新进者颇具资金实力或技术实力(包括不少上市公司和海外技术力量)。从隔膜企业的数量上来看，中国隔膜材料企业数量远超全球其他国家和地区的总和。而新增3C锂电池市场的增速已放缓，电动汽车用锂离子电池的发展远滞于各界预期，这就导致产能的增加远大于市场需求的增加。而且，大的锂电池厂和动力汽车厂都纷纷加入到锂电隔膜生产项目，实施产业链延伸策略，使到原本容量较小的隔膜市场需求更少。

(3) 同质化竞争日益激烈

隔膜生产技术已从日本扩散到韩国、中国，加上国内大量隔膜项目的上马，隔膜技术已从垄断技术向公知技术方向转化，这将加剧国内隔膜行业的同质化竞争。目前我国已涌现了一大批锂电池生产企业，将会出现投资过热，进而导致竞争愈演愈烈。

(4) 毛利率逐渐降低。

目前，在3C小电池用中高端材料产品市场，国际巨头采购量越来越大的同时，价格也越压越低，这使得材料企业的利润率越来越低。目前，相对于其他材料领域，隔膜材料领域的情况稍好，这是因为国际巨头刚开始采购，量还不大，但即便如此，隔膜材料的价格也呈快速下滑趋势，2012年中国隔膜材料的平均单价不足8元/m^2，个别卖到了5元/m^2以下，甚至有3元/m^2或以下的白菜价。而企业在保证质量的前提下成本并未降到多少，为此，隔膜行业的毛利率不断降低。

1.2.3　锂离子电池对隔膜的要求

(1) 良好的化学稳定性；

(2) 良好的电解液吸附能力；

(3) 良好的离子透过性；

(4) 孔径大小均匀，厚度一致性好；

(5) 具有足够的机械强度；

(6) 良好的热稳定性；

(7) 不含有害物质。

二、锂离子电池隔膜加工技术的现状与发展趋势

2.1　锂离子电池隔膜的制造工艺

锂离子电池隔膜的生产工艺按照干法和湿法分为两大类：即干法工艺和湿法工艺。前者是机械外力造成结晶缺陷处破裂形成微孔的加工方法，特点是成本低、机械强度高、孔径均匀性及厚度均匀性待改善。后者是由不同相物质混合成均相混合物，然后抽提其中一种，特点是生产成本较高，孔径分布均匀，适合制作超薄隔膜。产品有三种常见的类型，分别是单层PE隔膜，单层PP隔膜，PP、PE、PP三层复合隔膜。

2.2　锂离子电池隔膜加工技术总体情况

目前，我国锂离子电池隔膜加工技术中，湿法侧重3C产品，而干法侧重动力类电池。在技术水平方面，日本、美国处于技术领先地位，基本上垄断了隔膜制备工艺的专利、关键材料技术及配方，同时精密设备能力强于国内，这些因素，使美日隔膜产品始终占据着锂电池产品高端市场，在储能站、电动汽车等能源、交通、航空领域得到应用，技术水平高。而我国由于受技术专利、研发水平、精密设备等条件限制，国内企业隔膜技术水平仍与国外企业存在很大差距，产品一致性较差，市场主要为中低端电池产品、电动工具、低端动力电池方面。

由此可见，我国国产加工技术与国外技术相比，还存在较大的差距，产品价格只有进口隔膜的1/3～1/2甚至更低。而我们非但没有加紧追赶技术，却还在疯狂扩张产能，复制生产线，造成低端产品产能严重过剩，产品价格差距更加拉大。但市场的要求在不断变化，国外同行的水平在不断提高，我们的隔膜工艺技术水平却发展滞后。另外，国内厂家的研发基础和研发投入都比较薄弱，仅仅是在市场上寻找一些即将成熟的技术进行复制，市场盈利有限。由于技术实力薄弱，快速的市场机会难以扑捉，促使公司产品技术总滞后于市场。

2.3　锂离子电池隔膜加工技术发展趋势

今后电池隔膜将往薄(3C市场)和厚(动力电池市场)两个方向发展，同时电池隔膜性能呈现多样化特点，以适用不同市场需求。具体如下表所示：

编号	类型	应用	优点	缺点
1	超薄隔膜	3C电池	厚度薄，电池能量密度提高等	安全性下降
2	聚合物电池隔膜(注)	软包电池	优异的吸液和保液性能，提高电池循环性能等	成本提高，耐热性有待提高
3	陶瓷涂覆隔膜	动力电池	耐热性能优异、改善隔膜浸润性等	成本提高
4	新型隔膜	动力电池	耐热性能优异、改善隔膜浸润性等	孔径大小和均匀性有待提高

注：聚合物电池隔膜：如PVDF覆合隔膜。

未来动力电池隔膜主要是往高透气、强耐热、高安全性方向发展。具体如下表所示：

类　型	技术特点	代表公司	优　点	缺　点
多层隔膜	PP/PE/PP三层复合膜	美国Celgard公司等	兼具低闭孔温度(PE层)和高破膜温度(PP层)	耐热性能有待提高，机械强度相对湿法为差
有机/无机复合膜	无机纳米材料增强湿法PE隔膜	日本旭化成、东丽等	耐热性好、内阻低	工业化生产困难
陶瓷涂层隔膜	聚烯烃等隔膜表面涂覆陶瓷涂层	日本旭化成、韩国三星等	耐热性好、内阻低	成本提高
新型隔膜	PET无纺布隔膜	德固赛(Degussa)的Separion隔膜	熔点高，耐热性能优异，电解液亲润性好等	闭孔温度无或太高，机械强度较差，孔径分布、孔径和厚度均匀性较差
	聚酰亚胺(PI)纳米纤维隔膜	美国杜邦(DuPont)		
	聚酰胺(PA)隔膜	日本三菱树脂的“SUPERNYL”系列隔膜		

三、我国锂离子电池隔膜行业面临的机遇与挑战

1. 国家《节能与新能源汽车产业发展规划(2012～2020年)》中对电动汽车的明确目标，将拉动隔膜的巨大需求；

2. 国际高端锂电池制造商扩大对中国生产基地的投资，为了降低成本，他们将加快对国产隔膜的引进，对国产隔膜的技术、品质提高起积极的推动作用；

3. 国产隔膜虽然在低端市场可以取代进口隔膜，但是在品质上的差距造成还没能进入高端客户群，而面临产能过剩的国产隔膜，会在无序的、残酷的价格战中丧失竞争力；

4. 国产隔膜有重复国产廉价3C电池发展道路的倾向。当国产隔膜越做越低端，厂家一味盲目扩产，没有创新，打价格战，那么巨大的国内市场可能被外国产品占据。

5. 中国锂电池隔膜产业需创新自强

(1) 加强行业引导。

(2) 提高企业的自主创新水平，确保产品质量的稳定一致性。

(3) 注重隔膜专用原料的研发。

(4) 自主创新建自己特色的隔膜生产线

(中国塑料加工工业协会双向拉伸聚丙烯薄膜专业委员会　吴耀根)

泡沫塑料EPS

【行业现状】

2012年是中国EPS产业备受防火问题影响的一年。在65号文件的影响之下，全国外墙保温工程EPS板材用量增速明显降缓，除既有建筑物改造持续给力外，新建建筑、彩钢板用量均有不同程度的下降。东北地区仍是EPS应用的主力地区，用量基本稳定，受防火要求影响较小。西北地区新疆市场尚可，内蒙受房地产影响严重，用量减少约1/3，其余地区基本维持用量。华北地区防火问题一定程度上受北京地区影响，彩钢板问题，尤为严重，今年整体用量一般。华东地区各保温材料百花齐放，竞争激烈，重点城市已开始淘汰非A材料的使用，山东尚可，江苏影响严重。

包装方面，用量始终不温不火。全球经济持续低迷，东部沿海出口市场、家电及小家电等均难以翻身，国外礼品、家电包装制品订单减少，沿海地区经济模式转型，一系列问题使 EPS 泡沫包装受到明显威胁。部分应用领域纸浆模、EPP 等对 EPS 的冲击较明显。

根据 EPS 专委会统计，2012 年国内 EPS 制品用量为 2128kt，仅比去年同期增长 1.9%。2012 年 EPS 树脂产量达到 2433kt，出口量 320kt，原材料产能达到 5825kt，占全球总产能的一半以上。EPS 企业数量近万家。

【专委会活动】

一、深入行业调研工作，积极开展地区性座谈会

针对行业发展需求，专委会积极组织专家赴各地了解企业生存状况，在 EPS 企业集中的区域，以召开地区座谈会的形式，同企业近距离沟通交流，为企业发展出谋划策。

自去年底《建筑设计防火规范》征求意见后，专委会多次和工作组企业赴北京就标准制定一事走访消防局、住建部、质检局以及原料主要企业负责人，沟通专家与相关领导。邀请住建部领导到 EPS 产业集中区参观考察、交流意见。同时就灰色料是否应写入国家标准一事，专委会在山东寿光召集原料企业座谈会，汇总企业意见，上报相关部门。通过开展相关工作，专委会为及时传达标准最新进展，引导企业正确面对文件的冲击提供助力。

二、加强国际合作交流，提升中国 EPS 产业影响力

作为 EPS 行业对外交流的窗口之一，专委会积极开展形式多样的工作，提升中国 EPS 产业在全球的影响力。越来越多的外资企业通过专委会，了解中国 EPS 产业并进入中国市场。在吸引国外资金与先进技术的同时，专委会与亚洲 EPS 联盟等国际 EPS 行业组织建立起了广泛的联系，组织人员参与国际会议，参观国外企业，举行全方位的学术交流等，引起从业者的积极反响。

在专委会的努力之下，一年一度的亚洲 EPS 行业论坛 12 月在中国无锡举行，来自全球的几十名企业、行业组织代表齐聚一堂，介绍全球 EPS 产业发展状况，将新的技术与应用引进到国内，加快国内 EPS 产业同国际接轨步伐。

三、强化信息集成，开展形式多样的宣传工作

作为一个时刻为行业服务的团体，EPS 专委会通过展会、网站等多种途径，为广大企业发布市场、科技等行业信息，提供交流平台，对 EPS 产业健康发展起到了积极的导向作用。

作为每年 EPS 行业年会的重要组成部分，EPS 展览会汇集了同时期国内 EPS 原料、制品、设备、应用等方面的最新科研成果和技术。除此之外，专委会又与上海展业展览有限公司合作，每年组织企业参加“保温材料与节能技术展览会”，为企业寻求商机提供可靠平台。

四、推进行业标准的制定及审核工作

近年来，越来越多的企业对规范行业市场、制定行业标准的呼声越来越高。通过抓标准不仅可以凝聚企业对于专委会的向心力，起到规范市场，促进 EPS。

产业升级的作用，也是依靠优秀企业带动行业发展的可行之路。在这样的背景下，专委会投入了大量的精力积极参与到标准的制、修订过程中，取得了较好的成果。

随着防火问题对 EPS 板的考研，添加石墨的灰黑色 EPS 开始在国内市场绽露头角，其更高的阻燃特性以及更好地防火性能受到了业界广泛推崇，并已在行业内大量使用，有鉴于此，针对石墨 EPS 标准的制定就提上了议事日程。经过专委会同企业的不懈努力，住建部已会同相关机构制定石墨聚苯保温板的国家标准。目前该标准已完稿，有望近期发布。

五、完善组织建设，开展评优推先工作，提高龙头企业声誉

专委会在自身建设过程中，不断吸取其他行业组织的经验与方法，完善工作条例，细化工作流程。通过定期召开常委会，充分发挥民主监督的作用，对本行业的重要问题形成决议，有效保障了 EPS 产业的健康发展。此外，专委会经过认真考察、筛选，将一批热心行业事业、积极为行业服务的企业加入到常委会中来，免去了一些长期不参加专委会工作的常委，使常委会保持应有的活力，以满足行业发展需要。

中国 EPS 产业历经 20 余年的发展，目前已成为全球产量、用量最大的国家。EPS 应用已经渗透到生产生活的方方面面，不可或缺。但同时我们也应理性的看到，目前国内 EPS 产业发展正处于一个瓶颈期，原有的生产、发展模式亟待调整，而能否解决好这些问题，则是行业下一步发展的关键。产能持续增加，产品同质化严重，对 EPS 材料本身的性能升级及新应用的开发速度缓慢。市场增长速度低于预期，各种新材料对 EPS 传统应用的冲击使企业盈利困难。产品质量参差不齐，严重影响 EPS 的市场声誉。国际上对于 EPS 性能的探索为我们国内企业技术革新提供了思路，各原料企业能够重视对技术的研发。生产企业要从产品质量做起，多向地区龙头企业学习，抵制恶意竞争，开发现有EPS的新用途。对EPS材料本身的性能升级及新应用的开发将是整个行业面临的挑战。

【重点企业】

见龙机构始建于1973年，1976年确立核心产品——可发性聚苯乙烯，并在高雄建立年产40ktEPS工厂。上世纪90年起，见龙机构陆续在宁波、江阴、东莞、天津、克拉玛依、盘锦建立EPS生产基地，至2012年底总年产能力将达到2000kt，见龙机构也将因此成为全球最大EPS制造商。

无锡兴达集团创建于1992年，是专业生产可发性聚苯乙烯树脂(EPS)的大型民营塑化企业集团。旗下"锡发牌"商标为中国驰名商标，产品畅销全国30多个省、市、自治区，远销欧洲、美洲、大洋洲等20多个国家和地区。现在兴达集团总产能已达到年产EPS800kt的规模。生产规模雄居"世界前三、中国前列"。

中国海景控股有限公司专注于为电子信息行业提供包装服务，在青岛、合肥、惠州等地设有主要生产基地。公司主要业务是为国内大型家电集团(海尔集团、美的集团、TCL集团、长虹集团、澳柯玛集团、海信集团、长虹美菱等)提供包装制品和结构件制品的配套服务，在中国家电缓冲包装行业中具有市场领导地位。

上海大道属新加坡上市公司——大道工业集团在中国的旗舰公司，主要经营业务为包装、隔热、汽车零部件及其他发泡塑料的应用，Apple、HP、松下等国际知名的企业均为大道客户。公司在行业中一直以优质产品及领先技术著称，成功服务于多个领域，诸如建筑保温、工业保温、电子产品、包装、物流和汽车行业等。

山东秦恒科技有限公司成立于2004年1月，注册资本1000万元，高新技术企业，山东省名牌产品、山东省著名商标企业。中国建筑节能协会副会长单位、中国塑协EPS专业委员会常委单位，山东省建设科技协会墙材革新与建筑节能专业委员会副主任委员单位。公司已通过ISO9001质量管理体系、ISO14000环境管理认证。

【新产品开发】

江苏利士德化工有限公司EPS分公司研发了新型高阻燃HF系列EPS，该系列EPS具有高阻燃性能、较低的导热系数以及良好的导电性能。因此HF系列制成的EPS保温板在建筑领域有良好的市场前景。

【存在问题】

1. 产能盲目扩张，行业内部竞争过度。据不完全统计，仅今年一年EPS行业新增释放产能扩充了近1000kt，继去年西北地区布局后，今年东北、华北又成为树脂产能新的增长点。新增百万吨产能为历年之最，2013年预计仍有400kt以上的产能释放，总产能超6000kt，企业面临空前压力。许多新加入这一行业的企业，因为没有做充分的市场调查，加上本身对EPS行业的运营管理不熟悉，投产后不久就面临严重的经营危机。据统计，近年来全行业的平均开工率呈逐渐下滑趋势，今年原料企业的平均开工率仅为50%左右，少数企业已面临停产。

2. EPS防火问题如不能得到有效解决，必对行业前景产生严重影响。作为近年来拉动EPS产业快速发展的重要因素，2012年全年EPS板材用量没有明显增长，进而整个行业进入冬天。随着年底65号文件的解禁，预计2013年EPS用量会有较大反弹。

【发展趋势】

最新应用一：Insulation Concrete Form(保温混凝土模块)是将工厂标准化生产的EPS模块经积木式插接组合成现浇混凝土剪力墙的内外两侧免拆模板，通过连接桥将两侧模板连接成截面尺寸准确的空腔构造，经支护在其内浇筑混凝土，混凝土成型后，拆除内外两侧的支撑，所形成的现浇混凝土复合墙体。该系统采用EPS作为模块取代了传统的建筑模板，实现了保温模板一次完成，适用于工业与民用建筑混凝土剪力墙结构的节能建筑工程。目前在三北地区应用较多。

最新应用二：EPS自上世纪60年代起被用作土工材料，EPS土工泡沫重量只有土壤的1%，并且只相当于其他轻质填充物重量的10%。作为土工材料，EPS土工泡沫对调节土壤结构，减轻负荷提供了有力的帮助。EPS在道路工程中的应用始于1965年。国内如浙江省的沪杭、杭宁、甬台温、杭金衢、杭州绕城等高速上应用EPS处理桥头台背回填；沪宁高速上海安亭段拓宽工程中应用EPS作为路基拼接段的主要填料；江苏段扩建工程中也采用EPS作为软土地基的路基填料。

最新应用三：空心楼盖是一种现浇钢筋砼空心楼盖；也叫现浇空心大板，是由高强薄壁管芯模现浇而成的空心无梁楼盖。其特征在于薄壁管内填充EPS泡沫塑料。空心楼盖(板)技术是我国建筑结构领域的一项重大创新，它为21世纪建筑现代化提供了技术支撑，是一种性能价格比较优越，更符合人性的高技术水平的结构体系。

(中国塑料加工工业协会泡沫塑料EPS专业委员会 王庆圆)

硬质PVC发泡制品

【行业现状】

1. 总体情况

2012年硬质PVC发泡制品行业仍未完全摆脱全球金融危机的影响，延续去年市场较为低迷的态势，大部分产品市场回升速度并不明显，一方面由于国内外的政策因素影响使市场竞争更为激烈，另一方面由于国内劳动力成本不断上升，本身处于微利的一些产品受到了较大影响，部分企业不得不靠减产、减人来减亏。当然，一些符合国家发展政策的产品却并未受到影响，特别是一些新兴的产品还保持了较快的发展速度。

2. 市场主要影响因素

硬质PVC发泡制品行业的主要产品是发泡板材、型材，用于满足室内外建筑装饰材料、家具、橱柜等行业的大量需求。无论是出口还是内销，都和房地产相关，所以硬质PVC发泡制品行业的兴与衰始终伴随房地产而起伏。2012年政府控制房价、调整住房供应结构、加强土地控制、信贷控制等一系列宏观调控政策继续加强的背景下，地方政府过度的投资冲动受到一定程度的抑制，对土地与房屋开发投资的增速也相应减缓。与此同时，加息、提高存款准备金率等措施所导致的房地产开发贷款与消费贷款增速的放缓都直接影响房地产开发的规模和施工、竣工速度。因此从整体上看，建筑装饰材料行业也相应减速。

3. 硬质PVC发泡制品行业目前的主要产品

行业目前产量较大的品种有硬质PVC发泡建筑模板、硬质PVC实心发泡板系列、硬质PVC发泡中空格子板系列、室内外装饰材料系列。

1）建筑模板：硬质PVC发泡建筑模板生产工艺技术来源于普通硬质PVC发泡实心板的工艺技术，并此其基础上改进了配方及成型工艺，提高了产品的性能。由于该产品具有防腐、防水、强度高、重量轻、可回收等特点，其用于建筑模板时具有不用脱模剂，混泥土成型表面质量高、可重复使用等优点，随着在建筑领域应用得到了很好效果，去年硬质PVC发泡建筑模板产量保持了30%增长速度，全年产量达到100kt以上。

2）普通硬质PVC发泡实心板方面：该产品从工艺来分可分为：自由发泡板、结皮发泡（CELUKA法）板及共挤发泡板，产品的厚度从3～30mm，部分先进水平可生产40mm以上。该类产品发展历史较长，生产技术较成熟。其中的结皮发泡及共挤发泡产品由于产品质量好，市场需求比较平稳，各主要企业产量与去年持平。其中的自由发泡实心板领域由于进入门槛较低，生产企业众多，且80%的企业年产量都低于5000t，产品质量参差不齐，加之国内外竞争日益激烈，不少企业都陷入了低价竞争，部分企业产品质量越做越差，最终走向了减产或停产的境地，有能力的企业通过技术改造，转向了其他工艺的硬质PVC实心板生产。

3）中空格子板方面：硬质PVC发泡中空格子板由于其采用中空结构及内外结皮发泡技术，使其具有光洁平整的外观及良好的机械性能，同时还具有重量轻的特点，可以用于替代木材用于门、窗、家具、厨柜、卫浴柜、隔断等领域。该技术经过引进、消化吸收及发展，生产技术日臻完美，同时也带动了国内的相关模具及设备快速发展。目前具备生产该类产品的企业已经超过50家，总产能超过300kt。但是，其中有部分生产硬质PVC发泡中空格子板的企业为了拓展市场，采取低价策略，使得其产品质量起来越差，在使用过程中出现了一些较严重的质量问题，从而使得该产品的推广受到了较大影响。鉴于此，专委会组织了相关企业制定了该产品的行业标准，随着去年12月该标准批准实施，将改变该产品质量参差不齐的状况。

4）室内外装饰材料方面：PVC发泡型材不但具有木材的优点，又克服了木材易变形、易虫蛀、易燃烧、需要油漆等缺点，目前PVC发泡型材已经广泛用于室内外各种装饰装修等领域。但由于该类产品品种多，低档次产品加工技术难度不大，没有严格的质量标准，所以生产该类产品的企业较多，企业规模大多较小，产品质量参差不齐。2012年该类产品的产量与2011年基本持平。

【行业活动】

对于PVC发泡中空格子板来说，由于其发展快，真正投产时间也比较短，目前该类产品既无国家标准也无行业标准，只有一些相关的企业标准，有的生产企业甚至连企业标准都没有，导致市场上同类产品的质量差别较大，非常不利于行业发展。为了促进该类产品健康发展，在行业标准制定计划得到国家有关单位批准后，专委会组织了相关企业进行《硬质PVC低发泡中空格子板》行业标准的制定，并于2012年12月通过国家发改委批准正式发布，该标准将于2013年6月1日正式实施。

1. 提高行业整体技术，大力发展环保产品

由于硬质PVC发泡产品重量只有普通硬质PVC产品的一半，可大量替代木材的使用，同时其隔热、

隔音性能非常好，其使用时不但可以节约材料，减少森林的砍伐，还可大幅降低能耗，符合国家对建筑节能减排的要求。特别是该产品无毒无味，在使用过程中无任何对人体有害的物质释放，用作室内装饰材料时可以极大改善室内环境。再者，由于其可回收性，也符合国家发展循环经济的政策要求。因此，PVC发泡产品是一类极为环保的产品，值得大力推广及发展。为此，专委会加强了其在行业的宣传力度，同时，还组织一些规模不断扩大的企业进行技术改造项目进行申报，争取在国家政策及资金上获得支持。

2. 加强专委会建设，提升专委会服务质量

1）充分利用协会及专委会的资源优势，为企业提供全面服务

由于专委会熟悉行业情况，能及时掌握国家相关政策信息，专委会不断为行业内的企业提供硬质PVC发泡制品相关标准及生产技术等方面的服务，也帮助相关企业开发新产品、建设新项目。

2）完善专委会网站，提升行业宣传力度

专委会网站可以快捷方便的为行业相关企业服务，也是广大会员的交流平台。为了提高网站的服务质量，专委会及时对网站的“重点报道”及“行业动态”等项目进行更新，以便会员单位能及时了解到相关信息，同时还利用网站的“产品介绍”、“推荐产品”及“广告宣传”等栏目为会员单位的产品进行宣传。并且，还收集国内外相关技术资料补充到网站的“技术资料”、“行业标准”等栏目内，为广大会员单位和技术人员服务。

3. 积极发展会员，壮大专委会队伍

通过网络宣传、行业走访、提供专业技术支持、提供政策及信息服务等多方面来积极发展会员，2012年本专委会一共新增加了8个成员，为本专委会逐渐壮大，促进整个行业健康发展打下了坚实的基础。

【重点企业】

硬质PVC发泡制品生产企业主要分布在广东、山东等地区，硬质PVC发泡实心板产品生产技术成熟，广东广洋高科技股份公司等公司是该产品的代表企业；PVC发泡中空板是最两年才开始大批量投产，主要分布在上海、江浙一带，规模较大的企业设计产能都在20kt/a，产值可达人民币2亿元/年；PVC发泡建筑模板经过两年发展，2012新增50条左右生产线，新增产能约100kt。

1. 广东广洋高科技股份公司

广东广洋高科技股份公司于1995年3月成立，是由企业家与科技人员共同创建，集科、工、贸于一体的新型高科技企业。拥有雄厚的技术和充足的资金，致力于新技术、新产品的开发和生产。广洋公司是国家重点高新技术企业，1998年公司成为中国塑料加工工业协会常务理事单位、中国塑料加工工业协会微发泡板材专业委员会副理事长单位，1999年被国家外经贸部授予进出口经营权，2000年通过了ISO9001质量体系认证，同年7月份通过了中国科技部和中国科学院的高新技术企业"双高认证"，2001年12月份，广洋公司经广东省人民政府批准，整体变更成为股份公司，为公司的进一步发展创造了良好的条件。

广洋公司下设化工新材料厂、宝力威化学建材有限公司，并在湛江设立了湛江分公司。公司研制生产的REC系列稀土多功能稳定剂，它以我国丰富资源轻稀土为主要原料，经计算机辅助优化设计，与一种或数种阴离子基络合并与协同剂调优复配而成，它是一种无毒、无味，除具有优良的热稳定性和长期耐热性外，兼具有改善加工、偶联、增韧、增艳等作用的PVC用新一代稳定剂。该产品填补了国内外空白，产品性能及生产工艺具有独创性、新颖性、实用性。先后被列入国家、广东省、广州市"火炬"计划。

宝力威化学建材公司引进国外最先进的1.6m、1.2m硬聚氯乙烯板材发泡生产线四条，塑木板是一种新型的化学建材，广泛应用于装修、装璜、广告、建筑、汽车、火车、船舶、家具等各行各业。对推动以塑代木、保护国家森林资源、消防安全、节约能源等具有深远意义，是一种理想的绿色环保产品。塑料家具以广洋公司自行生产的U－PVC微发泡板材为原料，进行深度加工，充分发挥U－PVC板材难燃、低烟、防水、防潮、耐酸、耐碱、耐油和易清洗的特点，首先自主开发了厨房、高级浴室梳妆柜等专用的家具制品，倡导"尊贵，高雅，舒适"的现代家居理念，深受用户青睐。

公司2011年产值2亿，2011年广洋公司出口0.7亿，占总产值35%，2012年产值2.2亿，出口约9800万，出口占总产值约45%。

2. 海宁市海创塑胶电器有限公司

海宁市海创塑胶电器有限公司位于中国长三角经济圈中心位置——浙江海宁，专业从事室内外装饰材料研发与生产已达10年之久，在行业内享有盛誉，产品远销国内外300多个国家及地区。企业拥有德国全自动双螺杆热挤出生产线30余条，依据完善的ISO9001质量管理体系与ISO14001环境管理体系，为产品的卓越品质提供了强有力的保证。企业独有研发队伍，拥有163多项产品专利，用科技与生活演

绎全新的产品理念，创造了实用价值和审美价值的完美统一。该公司2010年产值达到1.5亿元，2011年产值1.7亿元，增幅13%。2011年公司利税达到3500万元以上。

3. 济南海富塑胶有限公司

海富塑胶是由海富公司与美国福安投资公司共同投资建立的中美合资企业。本公司现有员工200余人，占地面积17000m²，主要以生产PVC系列板材为主。目前公司共有6条生产线，全部进口于德国和奥地利。本公司依靠先进的设备，严格的企业管理，先后开发了宽幅PVC发泡板和超厚PVC挤出硬板，PVC挤出硬板厚度可达50mm，并于2011年成功开发生产出了CPVC板，高光亮PVC板材和永久抗静电PVC板材。2012年公司累计生产PVC系列板材12000t，实现产值11600万元，出口创汇1500万美元。产品畅销国内，并远销东南亚、中东、北美、中南美、欧洲等世界各地。

4. 山东博拓塑业股份有限公司

山东博拓塑业股份有限公司始建于2006年，2010年9月在原沂源县伟锋橡塑有限公司基础上改制为股份有限公司，公司总占地面积100000m²，注册资金500万元人民币，固定资产4500万元，是一家集研发、生产、营销为一体的现代化PVC发泡板材的生产企业。

公司生产的PVC微发泡板材，产品规格品种齐全，是以塑代木、以塑代钢的新型绿色环保材料，具有防潮、阻燃、隔音、隔热、吸音、保温、不变型、无毒、美观、抗老化、能力强等优点。并具有同木材一样的加工性能，可锯、可刨、可开孔、可钉、可上螺丝、可粘接，而且具有木材没有的热粘合、塑料焊接等加工方法，是一种符合国际标准的新型装修装饰材料。

公司现有职工230余人，其中大中专毕业生150多人，拥有一支高素质、事业型的管理团队，秉承“敬业、创新、务实、严谨”的企业精神，不断加强内部企业管理，完善全面质量管理体系，推行“5S”管理法。在国外，产品已辐射美国、印度、俄罗斯、欧洲、南美、中亚、非洲等国家和地区；在国内，产品辐射各省区市。未来的山东博拓，将成为集研发、生产、营销、国际贸易为一体的大型专业PVC发泡板材生产基地。

公司2010年与青岛科技大学开展产学研一体化合作，建立了“教学实践基地”和“工程技术科研中心”，2012年组建“青岛科技大学博拓实验室”，为公司的科研创新提供了人才保障。

公司2012年成为国家高新技术企业，公司已申报专利35项，其中已授权发明专利2项，实用新型专利22项，11项发明专利全部初审合格进入实审阶段。公司已通过ISO9001：2008质量管理体系认证、GB/T 24001—2004/ISO14001：2004环境管理体系认证和OHSMS18001职业健康安全管理体系认证。

公司2012年实现产值约10196万，利税1690万。

【新产品开发】

硬质PVC发泡制品新产品开发主要从配方、加工设备模具、工艺技术等方面进行。去年行业主要推进发展了以下新产品：

1. 硬质PVC发泡外墙装饰板

该产品由海宁市海创塑胶电器有限公司组织牵头，经过半年左右时间研发成功的新产品。产品主要用于建筑物的外墙装饰，产品采用共挤方式，基层为PVC自由发泡层，面层为ASA(或耐候PVC)共挤层。基层可以采用PVC回收料进行高倍率发泡，不但可以减少PVC废料对环境的污染，还可以减小产品重量，提高产品的保温隔热作用。ASA面层主要为产品提供了良好的耐候性及美观的装饰效果，其使用寿命可达到50年以上。该产品具有优良的保温性能，可以有效防止室内外的热量交换，从而减少冬季取暖时的热损失，减少夏季空调制冷时的工作时间，属于目前国家大力发展的节能产品之一。项目计划投资3000万元，预计每年可生产PVC发泡外墙装饰板材约10000t，产值可达1.5亿。若这些外墙装饰板全部应用于墙砖外层，保守计算每年可节约10000kW的能量，折合标准煤约11000t。

2. 硬质PVC低发泡建筑模板

该产品由黄石鸿泰板业有限公司等企业研究开发，由于PVC发泡建筑模板可以使用回收原料，不但降低了产品生产成本，还有效利用每年产生的大量PVC废旧材料，并且，多次使用后的PVC发泡模板还可以再次回收用于生产新的模板。虽然其一次成本较木模板高，但由于其可重复使用30次以上，而木模板一般只能重复使用5次左右，因此，从整个使用周期来看PVC发泡模板成本远低于木模板。该产品于2010年开始小批量试用以来，经过配方及工艺改进，2012年迎来了快速增长期。据统计，2011年仅房屋建筑用模板就达到8亿平方米，若其中1/5使用木模板也需要1.6亿平方米的木模板，以常用厚度中最薄的12mm计算，约需要192万立方米的木材，约合576万立方米的原木，需要砍伐大约180万亩的森林。若其中1/3采用PVC发泡建筑模板，则可有效减少60万亩的森林砍伐。因此，该产品具有非常好的经济及社会效益和发展前景。

【存在问题】

PVC 发泡制品是 PVC 成员中较为年轻的一员，其发展历史较晚，技术上还有待进一步提高，市场开发也不太成熟，目前总体规模也还较小。

1. 规模化方面的问题

由于 PVC 发泡制品进入门槛低，初期投资可以很小，使得行业内的几百家企业年产量大多在 5000 吨以下，年产量上万吨的企业仅不到 10 家。使得企业不具备规模化经济生产，企业的创新能力及市场竞争力也较弱。

2. 技术先进性方面的问题

我国大约是在 20 世纪 60 年代开始 PVC 发泡制品的研发及试生产，由于成本及环保意识等方面原因，在研发初期，该技术并没有得到足够重视，研发投入也非常有限。随着我国经济不断发展，人们的生活水平不断提高，以及对环境保护的重视，在近十年该技术受到了较大重视，研发的人力物力明显增加了，生产技术及产量都得到了快速提升。尽管如此，同欧美等地区相比，我国的 PVC 发泡技术仍然存在较大差距。国外研发方向更注重产品质量，我国更注重降低产品成本。

3. 行业标准方面的问题

对于 PVC 发泡制品中产量最大的实心板，现行行业标准是 1999 年制定的，限于当时的生产技术水平，部分指标要求较低，导致该行业充斥着大量低档次产品，影响着该类产品健康发展，因此，该标准急需进行修订。

对于近年发展非常迅速的 PVC 发泡建筑模板，由于是新兴的一个产品，目前还没有相应行业标准或国家标准，虽然目前处于市场开拓阶段，生产企业大多对产品质量有较严要求，但随着进入的企业增加，竞争的加剧，若没有相应标准来约束，容易形成恶性竞争，不利于该产品长期健康稳定的发展。

【发展趋势】

PVC 发泡产品不但具有许多与木材相同或相近的性能，还具有木材不具备的防水、防腐、防蛀、阻燃、易于着色的基本优点；因无需油漆保护，在使用过程中不会产生任何有害物质，具备环保的优势；密度低，使用寿命长，可回收利用，具有节约材料和环境友好的优势。众多优良性能决定 PVC 发泡产品是木材的最佳替代品，因此发展 PVC 发泡制品在应用木材的众多领域的替代工作将大有作为，重点包括在室内外装饰装修领域的应用等等。从发达国家 PVC 发泡制品发展来看，PVC 发泡配方主要朝着无铅化发展，工艺方式主要朝着共挤及微孔发泡方向发展。结合我国国情及行业发展的实际现状，行业将重点发展无铅化产品及节能微孔发泡产品。如钙锌配方、硬质 PVC 低发泡建筑模板。

总之，我们将充分利用 PVC 发泡制品的保温、隔音、防潮、防水、防蛀、防腐、阻燃、无毒、力学性能优良、可回收利用等等突出优势，不断研发出国内外需求量大的新产品种类，推进行业不断快速发展。

（中国塑料加工工业协会硬质 PVC 发泡制品专业委员会　黄勇）

滚　塑

中国滚塑行业的历史、现状及研究状况

滚塑是大型和复杂中空塑料制品的重要的加工成型方法，自 1855 年诞生世界上第一个旋转成型的专利以来，滚塑的发展极其缓慢，这个现象到 20 世纪 60 年代后才有所缓解。到 2011 年为止，全世界的滚塑企业约有 3000 家，滚塑材料的使用量至少 1530kt。中国作为全世界的塑料加工大国，滚塑行业的整体状况比较模糊，许多数据已经极度落后于现实。因此，了解中国滚塑行业的最新情况，为今后的发展和趋势判断提供基本的参考，已经是业内迫切的愿望。

1. 中国滚塑行业的历史

从现有可查询到的资料来看，我国的滚塑研究并不很晚。1970 年，上海塑料三厂应贵州汞矿要求，研制烘箱式滚塑机，使用聚乙烯粉末试制钢衬塑汞罐，是目前公开文献中可查到的最早的开展滚塑研究的报道。70 年代中期，北京玻璃钢研究所开发成功滚塑尼龙容器并在森林灭火器等产品中得到应用。1982 年，大连塑料研究所的“双轴滚塑成型工艺和设备”通过技术鉴定，这是可查到的滚塑得到国家层面的关注的开始。

1983 年，佳木斯二塑引进了国内第一台进口滚塑机——德国恩斯特莱茵哈特的滚塑试验机组，1986 年，江苏省东台县塑料总厂引进了日本 ATMO 的穿梭式滚塑机组和磨粉机组，这是我国聚乙烯滚塑大规模工业化的开始。1989 年 9 月，福建省三明市达发科研所引进了全塑船专利技术，建立了滚塑生产线，批量生产全塑船等专利产品。11 月，该所研制的“4.1M 全塑工作艇”通过福建省级第Ⅰ类新产品技术鉴定，经专家论证，属国内首创。1990 年 1 月，齐鲁石化为了开发滚塑级的 LLDPE 材料，成立的烟台齐鲁联合塑料制品厂正式投产，引进了美国

大型三臂三工位滚塑机组，主要产品为船和大型储罐。20 世纪 90 年代初期，在江苏无锡、浙江慈溪、广东珠海等地，涌现出一批如无锡海溪、慈溪远东、珠海波利玛等优秀的企业，二十多年来带动当地形成了相当规模的产业集群。

中国滚塑行业的快速发展起始于 20 世纪末和 21 世纪初，目前我国滚塑行业的大部分龙头企业，都是在这个时候成立的，如做军品箱的河北金后盾，做医教模型的天津天堰，做游乐设施的温州永浪，南京万德，做全塑储罐的台州仁生，做工程机械部件的宁国天亿，做滚塑模具的上海春旭，做滚塑设备的烟台方大等。

随着滚塑工艺和滚塑产品逐渐被社会接受，国内滚塑同行也逐渐增加了和世界其他国家的沟通交流，2005 年，由中国塑协滚塑专委会主办了第一届国际滚塑论坛，使得国内滚塑同行逐步认识到滚塑工艺的延展性和产品的多样性。2005 年后，中国滚塑行业迎来了至今仍在持续的高速扩张时期，这期间，滚塑厂家不断增加，新型滚塑产品层出不穷，应用领域不断扩大，就目前掌握的资料来看，中国有可能是全世界滚塑企业数量最多的国家。

2. 中国滚塑行业现状

自 2004 年开始接触滚塑行业，由于业务关系走遍了全国大部分地区，联系和接触了很多的滚塑企业。根据这八、九年的整理，基本摸清了中国滚塑行业的状况。

到 2012 年底为止，中国滚塑相关企业一共有 900 多家，主要分布在浙江、江苏、上海、广东、山东等地，这一情况和我国塑料生产的地区分布类似，其中浙江宁波地区、温州台州地区、江苏无锡地区、广东广州佛山地区，都是滚塑企业最为集中地区域，另外，作为直辖市的上海、北京和天津，滚塑企业也较为集中(表 1)。

表 1　中国滚塑企业的省市分布

名称	数量	名称	数量	名称	数量
浙江	260	湖北	10	海南	2
江苏	218	江西	7	黑龙江	2
上海	84	新疆	6	宁夏	2
广东	82	福建	5	青海	2
山东	56	湖南	5	云南	2
天津	34	香港	5	内蒙古	1
河北	28	重庆	5	山西	1
北京	24	甘肃	4	台湾	1
安徽	19	广西	4	澳门	0
四川	15	吉林	3	西藏	0
河南	14	陕西	3		
辽宁	12	贵州	2		

中国滚塑行业产业规模约 89 亿人民币，整体呈小而散的局面，目前尚没有大型企业，中型企业也不足 50 家，最大的滚塑制品企业 2012 年年产值约 3 亿元左右。全国滚塑制品企业材料使用量约为 250kt/a(表 2)。

表 2　中国滚塑企业规模及材料用量

年产值规模	数量/家	总产值预估/亿元	年材料用量预估/kt
1 亿元以上	10	25	32
5000 万 ~1 亿元	20	15	26
1000 万 ~5000 万元	100	25	75
500 万 ~1000 万元	250	19	88
500 万以下	532	5	29
合计	912	89	250

中国滚塑行业的主要产品集中在游乐设施、防腐管道、防腐设备、储罐等方向，这个和国外有较大区别。在美国，游乐设施和储罐占到滚塑产品应用的 60% 左右，我国仅有 28%，而在国外数量很少的防腐方面的应用，在我国却占到近四成。按照国家统计局的标准分类方法，我国的滚塑制品已经在至少 46 个行业中得到应用(表 3)。

表 3　中国滚塑行业主要产品应用方向

产品应用	制造商数量/家	行业产值/(亿元/年)
游乐设施	150	20
防腐管道	100	20
防腐设备	130	15
储罐	70	5
包装箱	20	5
皮划艇	20	2
交通设施	20	1.5
灯饰	30	1
车辆配件	15	1

3. 中国滚塑技术的研究状况

中国开始滚塑技术研究较早，但受重视程度远远不够，多年来很少有高质量的研究成果出现，乐观估计，中国的滚塑技术水平还落后欧美 20 年左右。

2005 年后，中国滚塑技术申请的国家专利数量呈迅速发展势头，几乎每 2 年就增长一倍。到 2012 年底，我国公开的滚塑技术专利总数为 436 篇(图 1)。

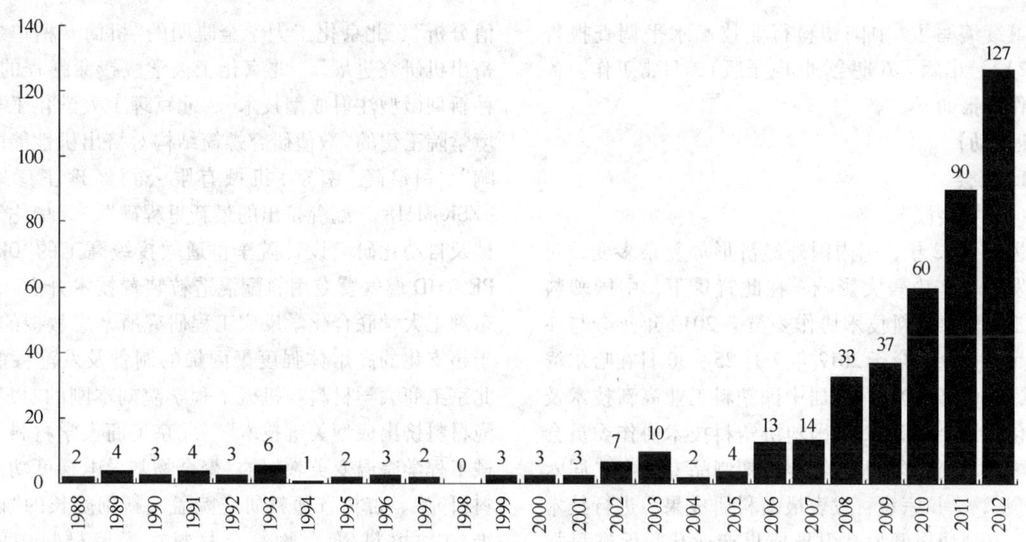

图 1　1988 ~ 2012 年中国滚塑技术专利公开数量

从 1979 年到 2012 年 33 年间，我国滚塑技术公开文献发表的很少，只有 2005 年中国塑协滚塑专委会成立后，带动了一个小高峰，近 3 年来，年文献数量又日渐减少，到 2012 年底，公开发表的滚塑文献总数量仅有 358 篇，而其中介绍性的和综述性的文献就占到 2/3 左右(图 2)。

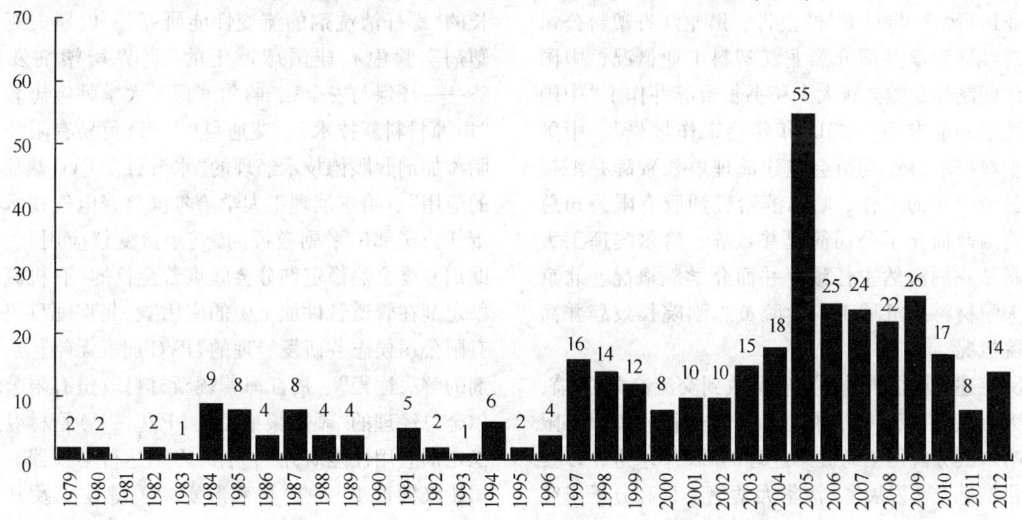

图 2　1979 ~ 2012 年中国滚塑技术公开文献数量

我国有 115 所高校具备高分子或塑料专业的研究生和博士招生资格，到 2012 年，仅有 6 所高校进行了 11 次滚塑方面的研究工作。这么多年来，我国仅有 6 本滚塑方面的专著出版，其中还有 2 本译著。以上情况说明，我国的滚塑技术基础研究还异常薄弱，行业技术人员对滚塑技术的关注度、参与度远远不够，这是我国滚塑产业落后于世界发展水平的真实写照，也是制约我国滚塑行业发展的瓶颈所在。

（中国塑料加工工业协会滚塑专业委员会　史春才）

塑料技术协作委员会

塑料技术协作委员会 2012 年开展了以下几项活动：召开了“塑料混炼先进技术和设备应用研讨会”、“第七届中国塑料工业高新技术及产业化研讨会暨 2012 中国塑协塑料技术协作委员会年会 · 技术交流会/中国塑协注塑制品专委会二届六次年会”；理事会及换届工作；组织了几次《中国塑料工业发展史》座谈会和调研访谈；聚氯乙烯用热稳定剂的订标工作；继续编写了《中国塑料行业技术水平调查报告(2012)》；出版了6期会刊(电子版)；日常工作。各项工作汇报如下。

【行业活动】

1. 年会

(1) 年会概况

进入2012年，国内国外经济形势复杂多变，对行业发展也产生较大影响。在此背景下，中国塑料加工工业协会塑料技术协作委员会2012年年会与注塑制品专委会联合于2012年7月25~30日在哈尔滨召开，会议名称为"第七届中国塑料工业高新技术及产业化研讨会暨2012中国塑协塑料技术协作委员会年会·技术交流会/中国塑协注塑制品专委会二届六次年会"，会议宗旨：发表最新科研成果、进行技术交流、开展协作开发，引导成果产业化，促进科技创新，推进行业技术进步。会议得到哈轻塑胶有限公司和哈尔滨理工大学的大力支持。

会议开幕式上，中国塑料加工工业协会曹俭常务副理事长对大会召开表示祝贺并作了"当前中国塑料工业运行情况与对策"的报告、黑龙江省塑料公司吴勇总经理致辞并简介黑龙江塑料工业概况、中国塑协注塑制品专委会顾大全秘书长致辞并作了"中国塑协注塑制品专委会2012年年会工作报告"、中国塑协塑料技术协作委员会包建成理事长致辞并汇报了委员会一年的工作、哈尔滨哈轻塑胶有限公司总经理贾丽萍简介了公司简况并致辞、哈尔滨理工大学材料学院周浩然主任致辞并简介学院概况、北京工商大学材料与机械工程学院黄志刚院长致辞并简介学院概况。

除上述3篇报告外，大会共收到交流论文45篇，其中大会报告了32篇，有：浙江远翅控股集团有限公司哈尔滨分公司王海波总经理的"稳中求进，以技术优化推进企业发展"、清华大学化工系高分子研究所于建教授的"聚合物纳米合金制备技术"、中包联塑料委专家委员会副主任兼秘书长/上海市包装技术协会绿色包装委员会秘书长陈昌杰的"中国塑料包装现状及发展趋势论略"、江西南昌大学黄兴元教授的"气体辅助挤出成型技术及其在塑料异型材挤出中的应用"、沈阳市塑料机械研究所金世源所长的"同心双螺杆挤出成型机"、赛默飞世尔科技(中国)有限公司张铭的"Haake转矩流变仪在聚合物加工中的应用"、鲁谷(北京)科技有限公司刘忠诚总裁的"变频高效加热节电系统在塑料机械中的应用"、博创机械有限公司黄土荣技术经理的"伺服微发泡技术为客户提供新的塑料成本解决方案"、佛山市步明精密机器有限公司黄步明董事长的"注射成型加工的成本和价值分析"、北京化工大学金晓明的"机筒开槽单螺杆挤出机研究进展"、北京化工大学教授谢鹏程的"一种新型微型注射成型技术"、北京理工大学化工与环境学院王建的"数值研究螺筒结构对挤出机性能的影响"、科倍隆(南京)机械有限公司经理王彦军的"ZSK Mc18 -配混挤出的最新里程碑"、天华化工机械及自动化研究设计院李世通教授级高工的"0kt级PE-HD燃气管专用料配混造粒装置技术开发"、华东理工大学联合化学反应工程研究所辛忠教授的"基于超支化的高熔体强度聚丙烯的制备及发泡性能"、北京工商大学材料与机械工程学院刘本刚的"PET发泡材料挤出成型关键技术"、北京工商大学材料与机械工程学院温变英教授的"聚合物基导电梯度功能材料研究"、吉林省塑料研究院孟立新副院长的"碳纤维/矿物填料/聚合物复合材料在摩擦材料中的应用"、哈尔滨理工大学韩志东教授的"氮化硼在PE/EVA中的选择性分布及其介电性能的研究"、北京天罡助剂有限公司陈祖欣高工的"光稳定剂给塑料带来活力"、福州市福塑科学技术研究所有限公司彭超所长的"螺杆清洗剂的流变性能研究"、巴斯夫亚太增塑剂实验中心桂国球博士的"世界增塑剂发展趋势——环保与安全"、哈尔滨理工大学韩宝忠教授的"电缆材料新技术"、艾迪科(上海)贸易有限公司树脂添加剂薛顺德技术经理的"水滑石在PVC热稳定剂的应用"、哈尔滨理工大学哈尔滨哈普电气技术有限责任公司郝广平副教授的"转矩流变仪应用"、塑料助剂专委会热稳定剂分会施珣若会长的"有机碱复合稳定剂在管道管件加工中的应用"、北京阿科玛化学有限公司侯志芬研发经理的"PVC加工无铅化热稳定剂的解决途径"、浙江海普顿新材料股份有限公司高尔金总经理的"硬质聚氯乙烯(PVC-U)管材专用热稳定剂应用性能研究"、上海思尔达科学仪器有限公司姚汉樑董事长的"热变形实验关键技术及其新进展"、北京化工大学任冬云教授的"一种粉体材料动摩擦系数的测试方法"、中国塑协塑料技术协作委员会丁常楷高工的"中国塑料工业技术水平初探"、清华大学环境学院只艳的"废弃电器电子产品塑料分选与资源化技术研究进展"等。

另外，作为书面发言的报告有13篇：北京工商大学材料与机械工程学院翁云宣副教授的"食品包装用塑料制品相关法规和标准介绍"、北京市化学工业研究院贾义军院长助理的"PBT工程塑料技术和市场分析"、北京加成助剂研究所李杰所长的"邻羟基苯并三唑类紫外线吸收剂的结构与作用特点及发展趋势"、哈尔滨理工大学张文龙教授的"氯化聚氯乙烯的性能及应用"、北京崇高纳米科技有限公司李毕忠总经理的“PET工程塑料注射成型技术”、浙江诸暨七色鹿色母粒料有限公司董事长王仲文的“工程塑料着色用色母粒”、北京化工大学苑会林教授的“含氟塑料薄膜的加工与应用”、中国塑协塑料技术协作委员会杨惠娣秘书长的“塑料注射成型技术进展”、中国塑协塑料技术协作委员会/苏州塑料研究所丁常楷总工的“国内各种混炼设备比较”、广州市普同实验分析仪器有限公司总经理张成耀的“高分子材料动态流变工作站及其应用”、福建师大环境科学与工程学院陈庆华教授级高工的“膨胀型阻燃剂超支化聚合物的设计及其在高分子材料加工中的应用”、福州大学材料科学与工程学院郑玉婴教授的“无胶热压PTFE覆膜高温滤料”、丹阳力博聚源树脂应用有限公司杨小东总经理的“江苏丹阳地区塑料回收再生行业概况”等。

会议发表论文内容包括新材料、新产品、新工艺、新技术、新设备，以及检测仪器开发和应用等，其中有不少创新点，包括：气体辅助挤出成型技术、新型同心双螺杆挤出成型机、国产伺服微发泡技术设备、国产万吨级同向双螺杆挤出机等；在检测仪器方面对Haake转矩流变仪在电性能、发泡材料性能方面的应用，以及粉体材料动摩擦系数的测试方法引起了代表的兴趣；在推进节能新技术方面，会议积极推荐变频高效加热节电系统在塑料机械上的应用以及气体辅助注射成型、微发泡注射成型、两板注射成型机等新技术。

对于当前聚氯乙烯行业中禁用铅稳定剂及其替代方案也进行了集中研讨，认为行业禁铅是必然趋势，而且，目前也已经有多种铅稳定剂替代品出现，包括钙锌复合稳定剂、复合型多功能有机锡和有机稳定剂等，但是，从经济和技术两方面还存在需要进一步解决的问题，在一些应用领域，如大规格管材挤塑和管件注塑方面还需要有所突破。

会议期间还专门安排了一单元时间进行各学科自由交流、创造深入探讨机会，推进各方技术协作。会议期间代表还参观了哈尔滨哈轻塑胶有限公司，对企业先进的管理印象深刻。

对于哈尔滨哈轻塑胶有限公司、哈尔滨理工大学材料学院和哈尔滨哈普电气技术有限责任公司对会议的大力支持和精心安排，在此表示衷心感谢！对于会议其他各支持单位也在此一并致谢！

(2) 主要报告和内容

◆稳中求进，以技术优化推进企业发展

浙江远翅控股集团有限公司/孔小炎

主要内容：介绍两方面内容，一是技术中心开发延伸发展及取得的优势，二是技术优化给企业带来的成效。前者从新产品业务整体化、开发流程统一化、部门管理标准化、信息畅通平台化、检测共享化等方面进行拓展、延伸，加强了集团技术中心整体水平；后者包括模具采用三次顶出达到机械手取件要求、内分型类型模具抽芯新结构方式的科学选用、气体辅助注射成型技术应用给企业带来优势和成效。

◆中国塑料包装现状及发展趋势论略

中国包联塑料委专家委员会副主任兼秘书长·上海市包装技术协会绿色包装委员会秘书长/陈昌杰

主要内容：以塑料软包装材料、塑料编织袋、中空容器和泡沫塑料类包装材料为主介绍了我国塑料包装产业现状；对值得关注的若干问题，提到了塑料包装的卫生安全性、生产中的高消耗和高污染、缺乏足够的创新意识，以及塑料包装废弃物的处理问题；对于问题的解决，提到：塑料包装材料的卫生安全性，已引起了国家有关职能部门的高度重视；中华人民共和国国家质量监督检验检疫总局，在2006年第133号公告——关于对食品用塑料包装、容器、工具等制品实施市场准入制度的公告中，确立了在全国范围内实施食品包装材料准入制度，包括：严格的生产许可制度、强制检验、市场准入标志、监督管理制度等。报告也提到节能减排、清洁化生产以及生产过程中的废弃物的回收利用工作取得的进展。

◆中国塑料工业技术水平初探

中国塑协塑料技术协作委员会/丁常楷，杨惠娣

主要内容：从合成树脂(通用塑料、工程塑料和生物基塑料)、塑料助剂、塑料机械几方面介绍了中国塑料工业一般科技水平。

◆聚合物纳米合金制备技术

清华大学化工系高分子研究所/姚雪蓉，郭朝霞，于建

主要内容：介绍一种利用聚合物基体中自由体积对单体的扩散和聚合行为的限制作用，建立通过扩散-聚合制备纳米合金的技术方法。

◆基于超支化的高熔体强度聚丙烯的制备及性能研究

华东理工大学联合化学反应工程研究所/周帅，辛忠*，赵世成

主要内容：系统的研究了乙烯基硅烷(VS)和苯乙烯(St)双单体接枝聚丙烯(PP-g-VS/St)的制备及性能。结果表明，长支链的引入使PP-g-VS/St的结晶峰值温度和熔融峰值温度相对于线性等规聚丙烯(iPP)分别提高了10℃和2℃，且球晶得到了细化。PP-g-VS/St在10℃/min的降温速率下结晶产

生的晶型为α晶型与少量γ晶型的混合物；在注塑条件下结晶产生的晶型为α晶型与β晶型的混合物。利用莫志深法研究PP－g－VS/St的非等温结晶动力学过程发现，在结晶的早期和后期，长支链对PP－g－VS/St的结晶分别起到了加速成核和阻碍生长两种相反的作用；同时，Kissinger法的研究结果表明长支链结构的引入使非等温结晶活化能有所增加。相对于iPP，PP－g－VS/St的拉伸强度、弯曲模量和冲击强度分别提高了29%、29%和453%。

◆PBT工程塑料技术和市场分析

北京市化学工业研究院/贾义军，钱志国，徐新民

北京科方创业科技企业孵化器有限公司/朱慧琼

主要内容：作为热塑性工程塑料，主要用于电子电器、汽车和机械等领域。本文主要总结并分析和比较了聚对苯二甲酸丁二醇酯(PBT)工程塑料近年国内外市场发展变化、应用发展趋势及产能分布状况，并对改性PBT工程塑料近年来的技术研究和发展情况作了总结。结论表明：过去5年PBT工程塑料从树脂的合成到改性后的应用在国内取得了快速的发展，但就改性PBT工程塑料与国外先进企业相比，国内企业生产的PBT工程塑料规模和技术开发的系统性、可配套性和先进性还有一定差距。

◆光稳定剂给塑料带来活力

北京天罡助剂有限公司/陈炜，陈祖欣

主要内容：介绍各类光稳定剂的性能特点，以及在农膜、聚丙烯汽车件和管材中的应用。

◆膨胀型阻燃剂超支化聚合物的设计及其在高分子材料加工中的应用

福建师大环境科学与工程学院·环境材料开发研究所/陈庆华，姜明，陈荣国，肖荔人，钱庆荣，刘欣萍，许兢

主要内容：本研究从商品化原料出发，经过富水相绿色合成途径先合成单体2，4，6－三(*N*，*N*－二羟乙基)胺基－1，3，5－三嗪(TEAT)，进而使TEAT与亚磷酸酯发生酯交换聚合反应，获得NP－HBP，为解决长久合成NP－HBP使用高毒性的卤磷类化合物的问题建立了新方法；并将TEAT、NP－HBP用于阻燃聚丙烯(PP)，在系统表征与测试阻燃PP性能的基础上，重点探讨TEAT、NP－HBP协效膨胀阻燃的机制，为设计新型IFR体系提供科学依据和理论指导。

◆氮化硼在PE/EVA中的选择性分布及其介电性能的研究

哈尔滨理工大学材料科学与工程学院/韩志东，王永亮，王春锋

主要内容：本文以PE和EVA为基体树脂，研究了PE/EVA共混物的形貌结构，以BN为填料，通过熔融法制备了PE/EVA/BN复合材料，采用SEM研究了BN在PE/EVA共混物中的选择性分布，探讨了复合材料的结构与介电和拉伸性能。研究结果表明，PE/EVA共混物在混合比为1/1时具有两相连续结构，添加BN后，BN选择分布在PE相，PE/BN相与EVA相形成两相连续结构；与PE/BN和EVA/BN相比较，PE/EVA/BN复合材料的体积电阻率和介电损耗与EVA/BN相近，介电常数与PE/BN相近，PE/EVA/BN的介电性能可用复合模型预测；PE/EVA/BN复合材料的断裂伸长率较PE/BN有所提高，但由于两相间界面结构的存在，拉伸强度显著降低。

◆碳纤维/矿物填料/聚合物复合材料在摩擦材料中的应用

吉林省塑料研究院/魏忠良，孟立新，王周翔，刘震宇

主要内容：介绍了刹车片的发展历程、碳纤维矿物质及树脂复合材料刹车片及其在汽车、列车、飞机等方面的应用。

◆电缆材料新技术

哈尔滨理工大学/韩宝忠，王暄，赵洪

主要内容：介绍了紫外光各种交联技术及优劣比较，各种高压交流电缆料的生产现状、开发面临的问题、科研和开发进展、关键技术；高压和超高压直流电缆料的研究重点。

◆世界增塑剂发展趋势

巴斯夫(中国)有限公司/桂国球

主要内容：介绍国内外各种增塑剂市场及用途，涉及增塑剂的国内外相关法规，重点介绍了BASF公司的安全增塑剂Hexamoll DINCH和C10醇增塑剂DPHP的性能和应用。

◆气辅挤出成型技术及其在塑料异型材挤出中的应用

南昌大学聚合物加工研究室/黄兴元，柳和生；上饶师范学院/黄益宾

主要内容：在建立的聚合物气辅辅助挤出成型实验装置上对圆形截面口模和T型截面口模挤出成型进行了研究，通过建立气辅挤出成型的机理模型，对两种口模的气辅挤出过程进行了数值模拟研究，研究结果表明，对比传统挤出成型，采用气辅挤出成型技术，不仅基本消除了挤出胀大现象，而且能够精确控制挤出物的截面形状和尺寸，表明气辅挤出成型技术非常适合于在异型材挤出成型中的应用。

◆PET挤出发泡关键技术

北京工商大学材料与机械工程学院/刘本刚，王

向东

主要内容：介绍了发泡 PET 性能特点和应用，并从 PET 结晶速率慢和熔体强度低等成型难点入手，介绍了树脂选择、发泡剂选择，以及对设备的要求等方面介绍了研发思路。

◆塑料注射成型技术进展

中国塑协塑料技术协作委员会/杨惠娣

主要内容：介绍塑料注塑成型开发方向和各种新技术，包括超高速注射成型、薄壁成型－超薄壁成型、微型和大型成型、塑料汽车玻璃成型、精密成型－超精密成型、流体辅助注射成型、气体辅助注射成型、外气成型、水辅助注射成型、泡沫塑料成型、结构泡沫成型、Mucell 技术、液态硅树脂成型、粉末注射成型、热固性塑料成型、反应注射成型、复合成型等。

◆注射成型加工的成本和价值分析

佛山市步明精密机器有限公司/黄步明

主要内容：本文通过实例对各种不同结构型式的注塑机的性能指标如：精密度，效率，能耗，洁净度，耗材，可靠性、耐用性等折化成可以比较的货币形式进行分析处理，从而比较各种不同结构型式的注塑机所创造的价值的大小，进而找到最合适注塑产品的设备，使注塑企业的投资价值最大化。

◆伺服微发泡注射成型技术——为客户提供新的塑料成本解决方案

博创机械有限公司/黄土荣

主要内容：介绍了伺服微发泡注射成型机的原理、技术特点、节能效果、应用实例与发展方向。

◆新一代二板直压式注塑机的性能特点介绍

佛山市步明精密机器有限公司/黄步明

主要内容：介绍一种全液压新型二板直压式注塑机，具有机身长度最短、结构最简单、开合模速度最快、能耗最低的特点。

◆一种新型微型注射成型技术

北京化工大学机电工程学院/杨卫民，谢鹏程

主要内容：介绍一种利用大型设备实现微型注射成型的方法——微分注射成型的原理和技术。

◆国内各种混炼设备比较

中国塑协塑料技术协作委员会/苏州塑料研究所等/丁常楷

主要内容：介绍国内各种混炼设备的现状，包括平行同向双螺杆挤出机，锥形同向双螺杆挤出机，以及特殊设计挤出机（三螺杆挤出机、往复式单螺杆挤出机（BUSS－KNEADER）、FCM（LCM）连续混炼机、KCK 连续混炼机、混沌塑化挤出机、电磁动态塑化挤出机、超切变塑化挤出机、行星螺杆挤出机）；提出了混炼设备的开发和应用中的问题，以及对混炼设备发展的建议。

◆万吨级 PE－HD 燃气管专用料造粒装置技术开发

天华化工机械及自动化研究设计院/李世通，马永金

主要内容：针对高密度聚乙烯（PE－HD）燃气管专用料的双螺杆挤压机配置与工艺技术开发，从设备构成、配置技术、对工艺的影响进行了探讨，并通过装置的运行生产对配置及工艺技术进行了验证。

◆有机碱复合稳定剂在管道管件加工中的应用

塑料助剂专委会/浙江传化华洋化工联合研究中心/施珣若

主要内容：中塑协管道专委会秘书长在 2011 年助剂专委会年会报告中，从重视环境保护和可持续发展的角度出发再次公开对热稳定剂提出了要求：淘汰铅盐稳定剂用于 PVC 饮用水管；全部的 PVC 管道禁铅时间表；热稳定剂的品种不应只有铅盐类产品。尤其是第三句话意味深长，指出了目前替代产品在应用中的缺陷和不足，希望热稳定剂行业顺应潮流迎头追赶，尽早解决铅盐产替代物产品的品质和应用等问题。不能应铅盐影响 PVC 管道行业的高速、健康发展。其实铅盐替代产品种类不少，品质质量各有千秋，国内外都有报道。本文对含有机碱类化合物及其复配成品在 PVC 管道、管件加工中应用为例，分析论证了含有机碱类热稳定剂替代铅盐产品在 PVC 硬质制品加工中应用的可行性。

◆PVC 各类稳定剂及发展方向

北京阿科玛化学有限公司/侯志芬

主要内容：介绍各类稳定剂概况，国内外禁铅法律法规，以及非铅稳定剂应用概况。

◆PVC 用热稳定剂的无重金属化探讨——水滑石在 PVC 热稳定剂中的应用

艾迪科（ADEKA）精细化工（上海）有限公司/石塚秀博，薛顺德

主要内容：具有良好性能的 PVC 产量大，用途广泛，但热稳定性差，我公司经多年的研究和不断学习，并主张无重金属，环保的 PVC 热稳定剂研制和推广，本公司研制的无重金属 PVC 热稳定剂已在全世界被广泛应用和得到了社会的认可。为未来 PVC 热稳定剂产业奠定了良好的发展方向。另外，2015 年欧洲将全面禁止使用丁基锡，但是锡亦属重金属类，也正在研究讨论今后能否完全禁用有机锡类热稳定剂。

◆硬质聚氯乙烯（PVC－U）管材专用热稳定剂应用性能研究

浙江海普顿新材料股份有限公司/瞿英俊，唐

伟，陈森方，孟建新，高尔金

主要内容：测试了甲基锡热稳定剂 HTM2012 和钙锌热稳定剂 HCZ1086F 在 PVC 硬质管材制品中的静态、动态热稳定性能以及流变性能。结果表明，与国内外同类产品相比，使用 HTM2012 和 HCZ1086F 的 PVC 硬质管材体系具有较优的静态、动态热稳定性和优秀的加工流变性能，且产品不含铅、镉等重金属，是绿色环保型热稳定剂。

◆氯化聚氯乙烯的性能及应用

哈尔滨理工大学材料科学与工程学院/张文龙，韩克伟；

哈尔滨中大型材科技股份有限公司/冯伟刚，胡森；

工程电介质与及其应用教育部重点实验室·国家重点实验室培育基地/张文龙

主要内容：简要介绍了 PVC-C(氯化聚氯乙烯)的性能、生产方法、用途和发展前景。

◆螺杆清洗剂流变行为的研究

福州市福塑科学技术研究所有限公司/彭超

主要内容：利用转矩流变仪研究了固体螺杆清洗剂和液体螺杆清洗剂的转矩流变行为。通过试验分析对比了几种不同清洗效果的固体螺杆清洗剂的流变行为及液体螺杆清洗剂加入到 PP 中的流变行为。结果表明平衡扭矩越大的固体螺杆清洗剂清洗效果越好；而液体螺杆清洗剂在降低了 PP 的平衡扭矩的同时还提高了 PP 的清洗效果。

◆聚合物基导电梯度功能材料研究

北京工商大学材料与机械工程学院/温变英，宦春花，刘鹏

主要内容：运用 Stokes 法则，借助于悬浮液流延法制备了一系列 PVB/金属粉体导电梯度功能材料，并对其梯度结构和材料的电性能进行了表征。电性能测试结果表明，材料一侧的表面电阻率保持在 $10^{15}\Omega$ 数量级，另一侧的表面电阻率降为 $10^{5}\Omega$ 数量级，逾渗转变发生在金属粉含量 3% ~4.5%(v)之间。实验事实证明，悬浮液流延法是一种制备组分呈连续梯度分布的填充复合型聚合物基梯度材料的有效方法。

◆子母式内排气高效挤出机原理

沈阳市塑料机械研究所/金世源

主要内容：介绍一种新型挤出机，其螺杆的结构特点是，在主螺杆的压缩段之后增加了一条附加螺纹，但附加螺纹的螺距与主螺纹螺距相等，这就给螺杆的加工带来了很大方便。主螺杆中有一深孔，深孔中有一内螺杆，内螺杆安装在固定不动的分流板上，内螺杆的螺纹方向与外螺杆螺纹方向相反。这种结构的螺杆挤出机，其产量很高，且能用于含水量大的物料挤出。

◆机筒开槽单螺杆挤出机研究进展

北京化工大学塑料机械及塑料工程研究所/金晓明，薛平，贾明印，潘龙，蔡建臣

主要内容：开槽机筒单螺杆挤出机具有产量高、挤出稳定性好等优异性能，在塑料聚合物加工等领域已经得到越来越广泛地应用。本文比较了轴向开设直槽机筒单螺杆挤出机和螺旋沟槽机筒单螺杆挤出机的结构、输送机理及工业应用等，深入分析了开槽机筒单螺杆挤出机的存在的问题和发展趋势。

◆ZSK Mc18 配混挤出的最新里程碑

科倍隆(南京)机械有限公司/王彦军

主要内容：介绍 ZSK Mc18 配混挤出机的设计基准、剪切率、功率密度、能量密度、结构特点和性价比等。

◆锥形同向双螺杆超高分子聚乙烯挤出机

舟山市通发机械有限公司/吴汉民

主要内容："锥形同向双螺杆超高分子聚乙烯挤出机"从结构上进行了重大创新，在整机设计上综合目前国际上两类双螺杆挤出机—"锥形异向双螺杆挤出机"和"平行同向双螺杆挤出机"的功能优势，创新研制成功国内首台锥形同向双螺杆挤出机。该产品具有高混炼、高挤出压力、低挤出温度、塑化性能好等特点，挤出力大，塑化性能好，效率高，比功率小等特点，同时针对超高分子量聚乙烯流动性极差、摩擦因数小容易在加料段发生打滑、成型温度范围窄等特点，对机筒、螺杆进行特殊设计，机筒螺杆出料段采用分段压力控制，通过优化螺杆各段结构参数，克服物料打滑，增大了输送能力，提高了挤出压力，并通过对物料挤出实行全流程温度精确控制，实现了超高分子量聚乙烯低温挤出，并达到提高产量、降低能耗的目标。

◆废弃电器电子产品塑料分选技术研究进展

清华大学环境学院·巴塞尔公约亚太地区协调中心/只艳，董庆银，刘丽丽，李金惠；

东江环保股份有限公司/任玉森

主要内容：目前我国废弃电器电子产品报废量日益增加，本文阐述了目前国内废弃电器电子产品拆解塑料的主要种类以及相应的分选技术，详细阐述了传统分选技术和现代识别分选技术的适用范围和优缺点，并提出了我国废塑料自动分选技术面临的主要问题，为我国废弃电器电子产品塑料的分选和回收利用产业提供参考。

◆变频高效加热节电系统在塑料机械中的应用

鲁谷(北京)科技有限公司总裁　刘忠诚

主要内容：介绍了变频高效加热节电技术的工作原理和具体应用成果。

◆数值研究螺筒结构对挤出机性能的影响

北京理工大学化工与环境学院/王建，郭迪，陈晋南

主要内容：为了进一步改进单螺杆挤出机的性能，本文数值模拟研究了机筒内壁开螺槽的螺筒结构对单螺杆挤出机性能的影响。使用 POLYFLOW 软件，数值模拟了硬质聚氯乙烯(PVC－R)熔体在单螺杆螺筒挤出机中的三维等温流场及混合过程。统计计算了五种结构流道中粒子的混合指数 λ、分离尺度 $S(t)$和累计停留时间分布 $F(t)$，比较研究了五种结构混合挤出 PVC－R 的性能，重点研究了螺筒深度对单螺杆螺筒挤出机的影响。研究表明，相对于传统单螺杆挤出机，在机筒上加工螺旋沟槽的结构形成单螺杆螺筒挤出机，有助于提高挤出机的混合性能；在螺筒与螺杆之间间隙不变的情况下，大的螺筒槽深更有利于混合。

◆转矩流变仪在聚合物加工中的应用

赛默飞世尔科技(中国)有限公司/张铭

主要内容：介绍了转矩流变仪结构组成、新旧产品的异同、测试原理和技巧、不同类型流变仪，各种具体应用以及对结果数据的评估等。

◆一种粉体材料动摩擦系数的测试方法

北京化工大学塑料机械及塑料工程研究所/任冬云

主要内容：通过测定塑料粉体的摩擦特性，达到更合理地设计螺杆和机筒的目的。但现有粉体材料动摩擦系数的测试装置一般只能测试常温，常压下粉体材料的摩擦系数。本研究开发了一种专利(国家发明专利申请号：201110382368.5，2011－11－28)的能精确测量粉料在不同温度、压力和转速下的动摩擦系数的方法和测量装置。申请国家发明专利：一种测量粉体物料动摩擦系数的装置及方法。

◆热变形测试的关键技术及实验自动化

上海思尔达科学仪器有限公司/姚汉樑

主要内容：热变形测试定义、保证实验进行和保证精度的三个关键问题、温度控制、最小施加力的问题、试样架自身热变形的问题，以及热变形的自动测试技术。

◆新一代无胶热压 PTFE 覆膜高温滤料的研究

福州大学材料科学与工程学院/郑玉婴；

厦门三维丝环保股份有限公司/蔡伟龙，罗祥波，郑锦森；

福州大学化学化工学院/汪谢；福建超级计算中心/林锦贤

主要内容：采用自主研发的聚四氟乙烯(PTFE)发泡涂层剂对聚苯硫醚(PPS)滤料基材进行前处理，通过高温热压覆膜法制备了 PTFE 覆膜滤料。SEM 观察发现该覆膜滤料的除尘机理为表面过滤，牢度测试及过滤性能研究得出 PTFE 薄膜与滤料基材结合牢固，覆膜滤料具有除尘效率高、过滤精度高、运行阻力低、易清灰、寿命长等特点，能有效控制 PM2.5 等超细粉尘的排放，是一种新型高性能环境友好滤料，可广泛应用于燃煤电厂、水泥行业、垃圾焚烧、化工厂及其他相关领域的高温烟气粉尘的治理。

(以下为书面报告)

◆我国食品包装用塑料制品相关法规和标准

北京工商大学材料与机械工程学院/翁云宣

从包装材料，定义、术语、标志、标签、印刷，环境安全和过度包装等方面介绍了我国食品有关法规，包括包装材料相关的食品安全法及实施条例(食品卫生法废止、食品卫生行政处罚办法)、产品质量法、标准化法、计量法、进出口商品检验法、进出口食品安全管理办法、商标法、卫生部门有关食品包装材料和添加剂公告、包装资源回收法、中华人民共和国工业产品生产许可证管理条例及实施办法(生产许可 QS)和其他行政法规等。

◆邻羟基苯并三唑类紫外线吸收剂的结构与作用特点及发展趋势

北京加成助剂研究所/李杰，隋昭德，夏飞

主要内容：详细分析了邻羟基苯并三唑类紫外线吸收剂的结构特点，以紫外吸收最大峰及摩尔消光系数(摩尔吸收系数)数据，说明邻羟基苯并三唑类紫外线吸收剂有着更高的紫外线吸收效率。国内邻羟基苯并三唑类紫外线吸收剂的现有消费量较低，因而有较好的市场发展趋势。

◆氟塑料薄膜在光伏电源和燃料电池中的应用

北京化工大学材料科学与工程学院/苑会林

主要内容：简述了氟塑料薄膜在光伏电源和燃料电池中的应用。分别论述了太阳能电池背板用 PVDF 膜和全氟磺酸离子交换膜的制作、应用以及国内外的研究现状，以及本科研室在相关领域的最新研究成果。

◆工程塑料着色用色母粒

浙江七色鹿色母粒有限公司/王仲文，王执中，汤志龙，傅琪斌

主要内容：常规的 PE 色母粒已无法适应中高档制品的要求，特别是工程塑料的要求。色母粒的生产者需针对现实，跳出低价竞争的怪圈，从塑料制品生产者与使用者的角度出发，不但给予制品特定

要求的色泽而且保证塑料树脂的性能尽量少的损害、最好是能加强。知识、技术——究竟因何而存在?答案似乎是今后的社会更强调发展与应用，从生产好产品升级到提供“令人满意的服务”!

◆纳米PET树脂及其工程塑料应用

北京崇高纳米科技有限公司/李毕忠，吴坤，李泽国

主要内容：本文通过双螺杆挤出机熔融共混技术，将蒙脱土以纳米尺度分散在聚对苯二甲酸乙二醇酯(PET)基体树脂中制得纳米复合PET树脂。蒙脱土在与PET树脂结合前，先经过了有机化处理。X射线衍射结构分析表明，蒙脱土层间距依次按照纯蒙脱土、有机化蒙脱土、PET复合蒙脱土的顺序从1.3nm增大到2.3nm，直至3.1nm。透射电子显微镜图象显示，纳米分散的层状硅酸盐的片层厚度平均在30nm左右。纳米复合PET具有良好的熔体强度、快速结晶、良好机械强度等性能，是开发耐热、增强、阻燃工程塑料的良好基础树脂。

◆流变仪应用技术

广州市普同实验分析仪器有限公司/张成耀，江太君

主要内容：近年来高分子材料的应用日益深入，作为其重要研究内容的高分子材料流变学越来越受到人们的重视，流变特性测试的方法、设备也因此得到迅猛发展。基于广州市普同实验分析仪器有限公司高分子材料动态流变工作站详细阐述了高分子材料加工流变性能测试与成型的完整解决方案及具体应用，同时介绍了流变性能测试设备制造及应用的发展趋势。

◆丹阳地区回收塑料的现状与发展前景

丹阳力博聚源树脂应用有限公司/杨小东

主要内容：介绍了丹阳地区塑料汽车零部件和眼镜片加工企业，以及塑料回收再生概况和问题。

2. 塑料混炼先进技术和设备应用研讨会

中国塑料工业协会塑料技术协作委员会于2012年4月15日在上海喜游天大酒店召开了“塑料混炼先进技术和设备应用研讨会”，主旨：积极推广近年国内研发的各种新型混炼设备和技术，加强混炼设备生产厂家、科研机构和塑料改性造粒生产厂家之间的技术交流，用好新型设备，推进该领域的技术进步，该领域各方专业人士40人参加了会议。

会议的主题发言有：浙江舟山通发塑料机械有限公司吴汉民董事长的“锥双同向双螺杆挤出机的开发和应用技术”、科倍隆(南京)机械有限公司经理位永喜代表沈君技术总监的“同向混炼双螺杆挤出机的技术进展”、上海心尔新材料有限公司王梓刚董事长的“配混料生产厂应如何选用不同的混炼设备”、南京科亚化工成套装备有限公司潘志荣工程总监的“国内同向双螺杆技术新进展”、南京科亚化工成套装备有限公司潘志荣工程总监代王秀娟的“往复式混炼机市场和技术进展”、石家庄德倍隆公司郭彦力总工代表崔鹏总经理的“三螺杆混炼设备应用特点与优势”、华东理工大学化工机械研究所谢林生教授的“双转子连续混炼造粒系统的开发及应用”、鲁谷科技(北京)有限公司张红中总经理的“变频感应加热在混炼造粒机上的应用进展”，以及北京理工大学化工与环境学院陈晋南教授的“计算机模拟技术在塑料螺杆混炼中的应用”等共9项内容。会议邀请了塑料混炼设备和应用方面的资深专家北京化工大学耿孝正教授、塑料技术协作委员会专家丁常楷高工等进行点评，主题发言者和参会人士进行了互动研讨，交流充分而深入，得到全体与会代表的热烈欢迎。

短短一天的会议使代表对各种类型混炼设备有了进一步的认识，特别对于近年开发成功的具有我国自主知识产权并产业化的锥形同向双螺杆挤出机从不知到知之，了解了其特点，对于三螺杆挤出机、连续混炼机等混炼设备也有进一步新的认识。变频电磁感应加热器是近年发展起来的节能设备，但不少代表对其应用心存疑虑，通过介绍和互动讨论，澄清了一些模糊概念，提高了认识。特别要指出的是北京理工大学化工与环境学院陈晋南教授的“计算机模拟技术在塑料螺杆混炼中的应用”的介绍，深入浅出、联系实际，揭开了模拟技术的神秘面纱，使企业了解到其并不是高深莫测的理论，而是一项具有解决实际问题功能的应用技术，一些企业当场表示了要开展合作的意向。

3. 理事会及换届工作

借“第七届中国塑料工业高新技术及产业化研讨会暨2012中国塑协塑料技术协作委员会年会·技术交流会中国塑协注塑制品专委会二届六次年会”召开之机，中国塑料加工业协会塑料技术协作委员会于2012年7月24日晚，在哈尔滨天植大酒店召开了理事扩大会。会议根据“中国塑料加工工业协会塑料技术协作委员会工作条例”就理事会换届工作进行了讨论，对新一届理事会人选进行讨论，对于换届工作，经讨论有以下几点意见：

(1) 提议包建成继续担任理事长;

(2) 按照行业，会后协商产生5~7名常务副理事长，并提议杨惠娣担任常务副理事长兼秘书长;

(3) 出席年会的代表单位均应作为会员单位;

(4) 按照上报中国塑协的换届方案，做好各项换届工作，鉴于当前经济形势、企业经营较为困难，

拟以通讯方式进行换届各项程序，并完成换届工作。

（5）计划在取得塑料加工工业协会批准后，在4季度以通讯方式开始进行换届选举工作。

4. 组织了多次《中国塑料工业发展史》座谈会和访谈

接受中国塑协关于组织编写《中国塑料工业发展史》(以下简称“《发展史》”)的工作后，在协会领导的支持下，利用“2012塑料新材料、新技术、新成果交流会暨中国塑协专家委员会二届四次会议”在成都召开、“2012塑料助剂与应用技术信息交流会”在青岛召开、“第五届生物基和生物分解材料技术与应用国际研讨会暨中国塑协降解塑料专业委员会2012年年会”在广东东莞召开的机会，组织相关人员开了《中国塑料工业发展史》编辑工作座谈会，以及会下访谈，就如何组织编写，书稿的结构和内容等展开了讨论，也提出了一些撰写人选，几次参加座谈会和访谈的意见归纳如下：

（1）编写宗旨、原则等指导思想要明确，可参考其他类似志书，制订编辑思想。

（2）组织编写《中国塑料工业发展史》是一件很有意义的好事，但也是一件难事，首先经费就是一个大问题；鉴于行业中的一些知情人年事已高，编写工作具有紧迫性，从某种意义上，需要积极抢救。

（3）《中国塑料工业发展史》可以按照3条线编写：一是整个行业，可从科技、新产品、生产管理、标准化、制度等方面编写，且涉及整个行业的部分，必须由协会来写；二是分地区，如北京、天津、上海、广东…，包括港澳台地区；三是从行业应从树脂、助剂、制品、机械和模具等涉及全行业的领域编写；四是按照制品，如板、管、丝、膜……各类制品不要平均着力，要有重点。

（4）对于入史的企业标准一要早，二要大(对行业影响大)，三是各种第一，如产量、质量、出口量、创新性、设备先进性等多方面考虑，具有特点的重点企业；对一些历史上一段时间对行业产生过积极影响，但现在不存在了的企业，从尊重历史的原则，应编入本发展史。

（5）入选人物也是要对行业有较大影响者，有一些人对一个地区塑料工业的发展影响较大，但不一定对全国整个行业有较大影响，是否就写到地区篇；对有争议的人士，是否要写、是否能写，没有展开，但存不同看法，原则是尊重历史，这还需进一步订出一些选择的原则。

（6）编写《中国塑料工业发展史》是一项很大的工程，工程量极大；所写事件等均要有出处，有证据，查实资料是必须的；如查阅档案，就很费时费力，没有专人，难于完成，建议组织专门班子，由专职人员来写。

（7）编写工作各环节均会发生费用，建议协会立项，向有关部门申请经费，申请可在编写工作开展到一定程度时进行；部分经费也可请企业赞助。

（8）关于资料征集，收集的面尽可能宽一些，以便于撰写，还可通过网络进行，广泛发动；最好在协会成立内部专门机构，以方便向各有关方面发公函征集资料或委托撰写《中国塑料工业发展史》；重要企业的厂志可发函收集；港澳台可发函请相关地区同业公会等机构提供；有些资料是否可通过各地轻工联合会获取，也需要发正式函。

（9）具体编写是按照时间，还是按照事件，应该视行业具体情况、具体特点决定。

（10）鉴于行业规模虽大，但企业规模不大，资料保存等基础工作较差，有些内容尽量写，尽量挖，但也只能写到哪算到哪。

5. 聚氯乙烯用热稳定剂的订标工作

（1）制作了制样钳。

（2）进一步修订“聚氯乙烯热稳定性试验方法——静态烘箱法”和“聚氯乙烯热稳定性试验方法——动态双辊法”文本

（3）对热稳定剂方法标准的精确度组织实验室间验证试验，具体工作包括收集样品、集中混料和分发试样。

6. 继续编写了《中国塑料行业技术水平调查报告(2012)》

7. 出版了6期会刊(电子版)

8. 日常工作

完成各类咨询工作，重点推进产业化项目，包括气辅挤出技术、导热塑料开发、锥形同向双螺杆挤出机用于超高分子量聚乙烯技术、电磁加热技术、计算机模拟在配方开发上的应用等。

【新会员介绍】

单位名称：广州市普同实验分析仪器有限公司

地址：广州市番禺节能科技园天安科技发展大厦208

邮政编码：511400

电话：020－39283061

传真：020－39283062

网址：www. Potop－lab. com

法人代表：张成耀

电子邮箱：thdzcy@ qq. com

手机：13928858930

联系人：饶毅

电子邮箱：419602672@ qq. com

手机：13640826195

职工人数：30 人　　　技术人员：20 人

注册资本(万元)：300 固定资产(万元)：13

主要业务：

流变仪、高分子材料实验室设备、橡塑机械开发和生产。

主要技术和开发方向：

高分子材料流变工作站，具有自主知识产权，拥有 4 项世界首创技术与 10 项发明专利，可进行挤出毛细管流变仪性能测试、密炼转矩流变性能测试以及挤出、吹膜、压片、流延、造粒、配混、密炼、注塑等成型加工实验。

成立至今先后成功研制了薄膜"鱼眼"测试仪、色母分散性测色仪、小型精密挤出流延实验机、小型精密挤出吹膜实验机、高分子材料薄膜单向/双向拉伸实验设备、1.5 螺杆混炼机等新产品。可广泛应用于聚合物流变性能测试、配方研发、工艺优化、质量控制、创新研究、设计指导，是从事高分子材料(塑料、橡胶)研究的高等院校实验室、塑料原材料行业技术支持部门实验室、塑料加工行业研发部门实验室的必备设备。

【存在问题】

经费、人力不足，今后通过更多发挥理事会成员作用，加强与企业联系，发挥企业在创新技术产业化过程中的主体作用，以加速推进新技术的产业化工作的展开。

(中国塑料加工工业协会塑料技术协作委员会　杨惠娣)

塑料再生利用

2012 年中国塑料回收再生利用行业现状与发展趋势

2012 年是"十二五"我国经济发展关键的一年，也是国际局势剧烈变动的一年。国际经济低速增长的形势没有改变，欧债危机没有完全消除，影响我国产品出口贸易形势更加严峻，经济环境更加复杂。我国经济增长形势进入低速增长阶段，按国家统计局数据显示，塑料加工业在满足国民经济多方面配套需求仍取得合理的常态增长，但受国际经济形势低迷和国内成本要素抬升的影响行业利润大幅下挫，经营状况不佳，扩展内需压力增大。废塑料受严格管控和国内需求不足的影响下滑很大。

1. 2012 年塑料加工业基本现状与塑料消费情况

1.1　塑料制品产量稳步增长，经济运行状况回暖

据国家统计局数据，2012 年塑料制品行业规模以上企业(销售收入 2000 万元及以上)13246 个，累计完成工业总产值 16757.29 亿元，同比增长 15.04%。塑料制品产量 57818.6kt，比上年同期增长 8.99%。2012 年塑料加工业规模以上企业完成主营业务收入 16310.13 亿元，同比增长 11.79%；实现利税总额 1431.35 亿元，同比增长 17.21%，其中利润 963.27 亿元，同比增长 15.94%。规模以上企业从业人员 233.18 万人，同比下降 1.55%。主营业务收入、利税、利润均保持稳步增长(表 1)。

表 1　2012 年规模以上企业塑料制品产量及增长情况

产品名称	产量/kt	同比增长/%
塑料制品	57818.6	8.99
塑料薄膜	9702.5	9.33
其中：农用薄膜	1627.4	7.74
泡沫塑料	1720.6	23.13
塑料人造革、合成革	3142.7	15.55
日用塑料制品	4618.4	14.43
其他	38634.4	7.26

注：数据来源：国家统计局

1.2　塑料制品进出口保持稳步增长

据海关数据，2012 年塑料制品出口量 13821.6kt，同比增长 5.79%，出口额 491.85 亿美元，同比增长 24.55%；占轻工出口额的 9.69%。进口量 1798.7kt，同比下降 3.46%；进口额 184.75 亿美元，同比下降 0.46%。进口产品平均单价是出口的 3.3 倍，显示我出口塑料制品是以附加值较低的日用品居多，满足国外一般性消费需求。

1.3　塑料表观消费量保持增长，人均塑料消费创历史新高

2012 年中国合成树脂产量比上年增长 8.7%，自给率达到 73.8%，比上年增加了 1.3 个百分点；进口量增加了 802kt，比上年增长 3.5%；表观消费量达到 70633kt，比上年增加了 4492kt，增长 6.8%。从表观消费量的增长可以看出，改变了上年增幅为负的状况，实现了近 3% 的增幅。可以判断出市场开始回暖，逐步走出市场低迷状况。

据测算，2012 年国内相对实际的塑料消费量大约为 54673.7kt，废塑料回收再利用量为 24878kt，塑料助剂消费量约为 4450kt。除助剂以外的添加剂因为无法统计可忽略不计，那么上述三项合计即为

2011 年中国塑料消费量计约 84000kt。这样可以计算出中国(不含港澳台)人均消费塑料为 62.7kg。(根据中国第六次人口普查登记的全国总人口为 1339724852 人)。

五大通用树脂表观消费量比上年增长 6.6%，表明我国一般消费品品社会需求仍保持稳定增长，但失去了以往强劲增长势头。塑料加工业生产、产值、利润增幅下滑影响了废塑料市场需求增长，2012 年塑料回收再生利用行业需求不足进入调整阶段。因而可以做出判断，国内塑料回收再生利用量增幅将下滑，但仍可保持适当增长。

1.4　经济发达国家和经济增速较快的发展中国家是废塑料的主要来源地

塑料与经济发展程度密切相关，塑料消费持续增长造就大量废塑料产生。全球塑料消费主要集中于经济发达地区和经济增速较快的如中国、印度等发展中国家，是废塑料的主要产生地。我们初步了解到美国年消费合成树脂 5000 多万吨，德国约 16000kt，日本约 9000kt，印度约 8000kt，整个欧洲消费约有 60000kt 左右，其余国家消费量情况还需进一步摸清。按这个数据可以测算出北美、欧洲、中国、日本、印度等地区和国家的塑料消费量约 2 亿多吨，约占全球塑料消费总量的 77%。

中国当年塑料制品的废弃率大约在 45% ~55% 之间，发达国家应该有更高比例的废弃率，这样可测算全球年塑料废弃量大约有 100Mt 左右。由于塑料消费在很多领域的多种产品，因收集难度大其回收率均不是很高。一国回收率的计算通常是当年回收再生的废塑料量对该国相对实际消费塑料量的比率。这样按照 25% 的相对平均的回收率测算全球回收再生废塑料量应该在 25Mt 左右。一般情况是发达国家的废塑料出口到诸如中国、印度、越南等塑料消费需求得不到充分满足的经济发展较快的国家，由于全球范围内区域经济失衡和需求增长差异增大，于是废塑料贸易作为新料的补充而日益扩大。

2. 废塑料再生利用行业概况

“十一五”期间得益于我国经济快速发展，废弃塑料循环利用产业得到迅猛发展，塑料行业消费水平、技术进步、应用领域进一步得到提升。五年来废塑料再生技术进步明显，含废旧塑料的再生制品由于其绿色低碳内涵获得相关环保认证得到推广使用，如废塑料可以制造外墙美观、屋顶防雨防晒、相框、画框等装饰材料；可以制造外墙保温材料、窨井盖、涂料、油漆等建筑上的应用；以及在园林、公园、湿地户外等领域替代木材的走廊、拱桥等铺地和防护等结构性材料。塑木材料及产品日臻成熟已获得市场青睐，废塑料改性技术不仅提升了废塑料使用性能，还扩展其市场需求，实现技术和市场双赢效果。废塑料在显著降低产品成本方面发挥了突出作用，只要按照标准科学合理使用废塑料，不会对产品质量造成影响，如在塑料管道、型材、薄膜产品得到有效利用。

目前全球合成树脂消费量约 250Mt，相当于 1950Mt 钢铁的体积，而 2012 年全球钢铁消费量仅 1422Mt，可以看出从体积上计算全球合成树脂消费量远高于钢铁的消费量。2012 年中国钢铁产量近 700Mt，略高于 2012 年 84000kt 的塑料体积，可见中国塑料消费潜力巨大，前景广阔。

2.1　塑料再生利用产业已成长为经济发展中不可或缺的资源型环保产业

据测算，用于降低塑料产品成本的再生塑料约占废塑料回收再生总量的 60% 以上。随着塑料的大量使用，废塑料对环境科学合理的安全处置课题始终是困扰人们的一个难题。迄今为止，解决塑料废弃物的最好途径是物理机械式再生利用，对不易分类的混合废塑料进行化学裂解回收单体材料或者焚烧回收能量，塑料被填埋是最不可取的办法。改革开放 30 年来，塑料再生利用产业从回收利用总量、从业人员规模、分选技术进步、加工装备革新、产品应用范围、公众认知等方面均发生了不同程度的变化，已经形成资源型环保产业，成为发展循环经济的重要内容。根据 2012 年塑料消费、塑料加工业发展状况不难测算出塑料回收再利用基本情况。据估算，2012 年我国相对实际的塑料应用量约 54673.7kt，按往年经验值测算为 53.5% 的废弃量比率可计算出废弃量约 34130kt，测算出的回收再生量约为 16000kt，那么回收再生率应为 29.3%(详见表 2)。

表 2　2008 ~2012 年塑料废弃量、回收再生量和回收再生率测算表　10^4t

项　目	2008	2009	2010	2011	2012
国内相对实际塑料消费量(测算)	3500.86	4170.68	4693.6	5229.5	5467.37
塑料废弃量(测算)	1805	2353	2800	2871	3413
国内回收再生量(测算)	900	1000	1200	1350	1600
进口量	707.4	732	800.9	838.4	887.8
再生利用量	1607.4	1732	2000.9	2188.4	2487.8
回收率	25.7%	24.0%	25.6%	25.8%	29.3%

2.2　废塑料行业已经形成大中型塑料回收再生利用企业为主体，废塑料专业交易市场为辅助的格局

我国废塑料产业从来源可分为进口废塑料和国内回收再生废塑料两部分，但市场流通过程中没有明显的分界线，已形成一个相互融合的整体。因废弃塑料的社会累计量庞大，废弃量将不会随消费量减少而明显降低，反而可能会有所增长。每年废塑料产生量随着塑料消费量增长和累积量增大而持稳步增长态势，回收再利用的负担加重。

长期以来，废塑料回收再生利用企业随着我国经济发展而不断壮大，成为废塑料行业的主体。这些大中型企业尤其以进口废塑料企业居多，已经形成规模经营，其再生利用量占总再生量的40%以上，大多分布在沿海塑料加工发达地区。这部分企业因有相对稳定的废塑料货源和销售渠道，资源集中，利润较高，效益良好，市场竞争力强。其分类技术及装备较先进，成本低，效率高，可规模化、集中化处理废塑料，环保设施较完善，废水能够达标排放，可有效避免二次污染。还有一些规模企业分布在中西部地区，以国内回收再生为主，从事国内废塑料回收再利用事业，为环境保护和再生资源产业发展做出很大贡献。

更多的是国内废塑料回收再生中小企业，其中绝大多数属于家庭作坊式的个体户，规模普遍较小，在大城市周边及城乡结合部扎堆经营。他们采用技术简单实用，加工交易利润空间小，物流成本很低，环保意识薄弱；通过市场要素集结与整合作用逐步形成自发性的交易集中、流通顺畅的集散市场，加工交易集约化，专业分工细化，其物流配送和走向完全市场化，具有强大生存和竞争能力，基本实现产业细化和延伸。经过多年发展在全国各地形成几十个类似的废塑料专业加工交易市场。这些市场一般分别有200~500、500~1000、1000~2000家左右不等数量的小企业构成。

2.3　塑料再生利用产业技术进步明显，应用更新加快，规模化发展条件日渐成熟

随着我国市场经济发展，废塑料回收再生利用产业规模持续扩大，转型升级加快；废塑料再生利用新技术、新产品得到持续开发应用，技术人员素质有所提升；随着环境治理政策深化，产业集群逐步得到规范发展，成为循环经济领域的重要组成部分。近年来，很多废塑料产品由于其绿色低碳内涵成为社会和市场推崇的新亮点，代表着先进性和发展趋势。如惠东美新利用废塑料和废木屑添加所需助剂经共混而成的塑木材料及制品年产1万多吨，并且远销海外。目前该产品国内市场需求已达700kt，催生了100多家关联企业。上海英科实业有限公司年回收利用废弃聚苯乙烯泡沫塑料达到60kt，利用废弃聚苯乙烯泡沫塑料生产的画框、相框产品全部出口供不应求，是变废为宝发展循环经济的典型企业。塑料再生利用产业正在由低质量、高能耗向高质量、低能耗、多品种、精细分类、高技术应用的方向发展，塑料回收利用加工交易市场逐步走向规范经营，产业聚集度在增加，规模化发展条件日渐成熟。

3. 进口废塑料基本情况

3.1　废塑料进口的战略性意义

全球性的资源、能源紧缺形势正在促进再生资源产业的发展，其回收成本远比开发原生资源或能源低，在发展中国家有巨大的市场需求。目前中国进口废塑料规模居世界首位，其不断增长的市场需求正在影响全球塑料再生产业的发展趋势。据悉，世界70%的废旧物资被运到中国，进而也说明我国自有再生资源远不能满足市场需求，需要国际市场的有益补充，以缓减我国资源紧缺的局面，保持我国低成本制造业在全球的竞争优势。从发展趋势看，我国塑料进口依存度仍保持在26.2%，对进口再生塑料市场需求仍将保持稳定增长，将对开拓再生塑料应用领域、塑料加工技术进步和产业结构调整起到一定的促进作用。

3.2　废塑料进口量及增长情况

中国是全球进口废塑料最大地区，对全球塑料再生利用市场需求和价格走势有着决定性的影响。从海关统计中可看出，2012年废塑料主要进口地为中国香港，其次为德国、美国、泰国、日本、中国台湾省、加拿大、比利时、澳大利亚、菲律宾、马来西亚，进口量占总进口量的八成。

表3　2008~2012年进口废塑料及增长

10^4t

项　目	2008	2009	2010	2011	2012	年均增长/%
PE废塑料	214.4	220.6	263.5	328.7	369.3	14.56
PS废塑料	9.7	13.7	24.3	14.8	24.2	25.68
PVC废塑料	182.9	196.9	171.8	118.6	69.1	-21.60
PET废塑料	106.1	136.1	165.1	166.5	204.5	17.83
其他废塑料	194.4	165.2	176.2	209.8	220.7	3.22
进口废塑料总量	707.5	732.6	800.9	838.4	887.8	5.84

注：来源：海关数据。

3.3　进口废塑料企业状况

目前，登记注册的向中国大陆地区出口废塑料

的境外企业总数有3561家，分布在88个国家和地区，其中美国667家、中国香港553家、日本512家、韩国239家、中国台澎金马关税区181家，占注册企业总数的60%。登记注册的国内废塑料进口、加工企业总数则有3000余家。

3.4 中国塑料回收再生利用行业的环保贡献

2012年我国回收再生利用废塑料总量约24878kt，与当年合成树脂消费总量70633kt的1/3相当，等于节约或减少进口24878kt原料，或等于节约或减少进口大约50～70Mt的原油，同时减少垃圾填埋16Mt，还减少炼制乙烯大量的CO_2、SO_2排放。与从原油制造塑料相比，还可节省70%的能耗，节能减排成效显著。

可见进口再生塑料是塑料原料重要的有益的补充，可有效缓减资源紧缺。目前，塑料再生利用在促进环境保护、扩大就业、增加税收和区域循环经济发展也发挥着巨大作用，有力推进节能减排工作，有利于塑料行业自身的稳定持续健康发展，巩固中国制造低成本竞争优势，为中国经济建设、循环经济发展和环境保护事业做出贡献。

4. 发展趋势简析

4.1 随着经济发展技术进步进程加快，塑料再生利用产业发展前景看好

随着我国经济稳步增长，废塑料应用技术不断被开发，其应用领域逐步扩展，用量直线上逐步升，成为塑料原料重要补充。目前已经占到塑料消费总量84Mt的29.6%。目前经济转型之际，塑料新材料、新产品日新月异，在高端领域的应用案例越来越多，成为产业结构调整转型升级的推手，可见其发展前景之广阔。

目前废塑料的品种主要是五大通用塑料，还有聚酯瓶片，使用量基数大，回收再生渠道多，再生技术成熟，一般从业人员很容易掌握。主要应用于较低层次的消费领域，如塑料包装、日用品等。也有很多性能高、品质好的工程塑料，特别是进口废塑料中的如尼龙、聚碳酸酯、有机玻璃、聚甲醛、PVB薄膜、氟塑料等市场紧缺，需求旺盛。

4.2 低成本造就了废塑料逐步扩大的应用市场，发展潜力很大

塑料的发展历史实质上是不断向着高性能化与多功能化的方向发展。在塑料制品制造过程中添加适量的同类型废塑料可有效降低成本而不降低性能和功能。废塑料制造的产品如上海英科实业有限公司全部用聚苯乙烯泡沫制品回收再生后制作的画框、相框等系列产品畅销海外，成本低，性能高，利润高，走出了一条废塑料再生利用高值化利用的典型案例。还有些废塑料制早的诸如下水道井盖、马路街边座椅、塑木材料及制品均有实例应用，用量也是越来越大。国家应当出台政策鼓励废塑料产品的使用，不仅体现了当前国家倡导的节能减排、绿色低碳产业转型之路，也是鼓励人们不乱丢弃废弃物，加强废弃物回收利用，物尽其用，以实现社会可持续发展，为子孙后代留下一片蓝天和一方净土。

塑料改性技术赋予废塑料强大市场需求和生命力，废塑料改性技术已经得到包括金发科技在内的广大改性商开发与重视。可大量使用废塑料的塑木材料及产品国内需求已经达到700kt，在国内已经形成100多个塑木产业关联企业的规模，广泛应用于园林美化、室外装饰，对北美、欧洲的出口需求量也很大。还有很多废塑料产品得到政府鼓励

作为21世纪新材料，塑料在包装、日用品、塑料鞋、地板等低端应用市场有着稳定增长的需求，在高端应用领域不断被开发并获得更快的增长需求。不论经济增长快与慢，对塑料的需求将是稳步增长，这对废塑料应用市场提供了稳定增长的保证。

5. 废塑料行业存在的主要问题和建议措施

目前我国已超过美国成为全球最大的塑料消费国，巨大的需求造成了原材料的巨大缺口。废塑料回收再生量已经超过原生料进口量填补了大约30%的原料缺口，从而有效地减少环境污染和能源消耗，有利于国家的可持续发展战略。但是我国塑料回收行业起步较早，整体规模也比较大，从行业发展看，还存在很多问题。

5.1 再生资源产业发展作为国家重大发展战略缺乏统筹规划，政策环境有待深化和改善

5.1.1 适合于再生资源产业发展的税费改革政策不到位

改革开放以来促进了再生资源从特种行业转向市场化得到繁荣发展，近几年来国家对废物回收再利用行业税收优惠政策不断调整逐渐脱离实际，可操作性不高，废塑料回收再生利用企业大多为中小企业，基本上享受不到减免税或者先征后返乃至2011年新政策返50%税率的优惠政策。这种可操作性差的税收政策实质上没有减轻再生利用企业的税赋，从而制约行业发展。

5.1.2 塑料废弃物回收产业的污染治理要从源头上抓起

经济迅猛发展以及城市化水平提升产生了大量垃圾，大大增加了塑料废弃物排放，增加环境负担浪费资源。在城市周边和城乡结合部拾荒者担负起这个重大责任，同时在再生利用的处理过程中存在二次污染。特别是长期以来形成的塑料废弃物集散

市场发展到今天成为污染治理的重点。媒体曝光引发关注，地方政府在治理过程中难有作为。严厉治理过后即是产业重新洗牌，从业人员转移别处生存。所以治理塑料废弃物污染要从源头上抓起，没有授权或资质的公司和个人应不允许从事回收与再生利用行业。

5.1.3　扶持再生资源产业与治理污染并重

如何在发展经济的同时实现资源再生和环境保护良性发展成为重大课题。在政府决策、行业协会和企业参与、社会各界关注下取得进步和阶段性成果的同时，新的问题接踵而来。尽管我国已经发布了《循环经济促进法》，相继出台了减免税等优惠政策和新管理法规，但是归根结蒂，我国还没有形成适合于我国特色的塑料废弃物回收再生利用的有效运行机制。有的政策脱离实际，未能满足废弃物物尽其用循环发展的市场化需求。

鉴于不同地区经济发展水平的巨大差异以及市场需求的巨大差异，再生资源产业分布与发展程度有着很大不同，对政策有着不同的需求。科学的管理法规应当是促进再生资源发展与环境保护并重，针对不同地域再生资源产业实际进行差异化管理，可能是一个不错的选择。

5.1.4　推进适合于废塑料产业实际的园区化管理模式

圈区管理不仅要降低入园门槛，还需要相配套的减免税费等优惠扶持政策，制订符合实际操作的行业规范和标准，建立和完善信息、物流配送、技术支撑、质量检测等服务体系，对从业人员进行专业培训等。

探索建立以再生利用企业为主体，以市场为导向的循环经济运作机制，突出以人为本，提升产业素质，整治与扶持相结合，最终达到资源再生、环境保护目标，实现再生资源的物尽其用以及高值化利用。

5.2　企业是再生资源再生利用行业主体，鼓励从事再生资源产业的企业发展可有效促进环保增效

我国经济经过入世以来的迅猛发展，以大中型企业为主导的塑料再生产业市场化进程加快，环保增效显著，做出了巨大贡献。废塑料再生利用行业尽管以小企业占据大多数，但行业龙头企业在环保技术处理、废塑料分类技术应用以及高值化利用方面上引导行业发展，同时也是废塑料处理量集中、能效发挥最佳、环保设施齐全的典范。现行政策应当扶持大中型塑料再生利用企业发展，创造有利环境促进这些企业在推动再生资源循环发展、绿色低碳发展和我国经济的可持续发展做出更大贡献。

5.3　加强宣传与科技投入，应把废塑料产品列入政府采购目录

应该加强塑料再生利用正面宣传，引导社会、媒体正确看待废塑料。废塑料行业被一些媒体渲染成污染根源，形象不好，其实在我们生活中、工业品中很多产品都含有废塑料，回收后的PET瓶片可以制造涤纶纤维，是我国化纤产品、服装等产品低成本制造的基本保障。

加强科技投入，增加废塑料产品的科技含量，实现高值化利用与物尽其用。提升从业人员专业水平，提高产业发展素质，彻底改变废塑料面貌，赋予其新的内涵、新的意义和开始一个新的起点。

把一些包括废塑料的再生资源产品列入政府采购目录作为一项长期政策引导全社会重视勤俭节约风尚，倡导绿色低碳之风，深入开展保护环境、节约资源的公益性活动，赋予再生资源产品新的内涵。

（中国塑料加工工业协会　马占峰）

医用塑料

医用塑料制品产业是随着现代医学而发展的新型产业，它以其高科技、高附加值、高增长进度和拥有广阔的市场而备受瞩目。20多年来，随着医疗器械的发展，医用塑料制品在医疗事业中起着越来越重要的作用。据统计2010年中国医疗器械市场规模达到1644亿元人民币，同比增长16.2%。随着我国国民经济的稳步发展和医疗技术的不断创新，医疗器械市场成为发展最为迅猛的市场之一。医疗器械的朝阳性已不言而喻。随着经济的发展和卫生水平的提高，及新医改政策的影响。十二、五期间医疗器械行业仍将保持高速的发展势头，平均复合增长率能达到20.19%。

作为医疗器械产品，首先要求是产品的安全性及有效性，而且有效性也必须是在产品的安全性保证的基础上有效。医用高分子材料同样必须循序这样的原则。医用塑料产品的安全性，主要是针对产品对医疗人员、患者以及产品的用后处理方法是否安全。

医用塑料最大的优点是价格便宜，加工性能优良，可用注塑或挤出吹塑等常规工艺生产，随着医学科学技术的不断发展，生物技术的突破性研究以及人们对健康的日益关注，医用塑料的应用已遍及整个医学领域，并将越来越多地替代传统材料。医用塑料产品使用的高分子材料有90多种。塑料以其

优良的性能、可靠的品质、方便的成型工艺在医疗领域获得越来越广泛的应用。典型医用塑料包括聚氯乙烯(PVC)、聚乙烯(PE)\聚丙烯(PP)\聚四氟乙烯(PTFE)、热塑性聚氨酯(TPU)、聚碳酸酯(PC)、聚酯类(PET)等。

目前，我国把医疗器械分为三类，实行分类管理制度。第一类是指通过常规管理足以保证其安全性、有效性的医疗器械；第二类是指对其安全性、有效性应当加以控制的医疗器械；第三类是指植入人体，用于支持、维持生命。对人体具有潜在的危险，对其安全性、有效性必须严格控制的医疗器械。医疗器械分类目录由国务院药品监督管理部门依据医疗器械分类规则、商国务院卫生行政部门制度调整、公布。现行的《医疗器械分类目录》中，一类器械108种；二类器械127种；三类器械71种。

2000年《医疗器械监督管理条例》的出台，是我国医疗器械监管真正进入一个依法行政、依法监督的新时期。《医疗器械监督管理条例》初步建立了以产品上市前审批、上市后监督和警戒以及对生产企业监管为核心的医疗器械监管体系。其中，警戒主要包括不良事件监测、日常监管、专项检查和生产质量管理体系检查等。国家对医疗器械实施注册管理、注册审查。包括产品检测、临床试验、生产质量管理体系现场审查等内容。中国医疗器械工业蓬勃发展，自20世纪90年代以来一直保持了两位数的发展速度，在国民经济中所占比例不断提高，由2006年的0.22%(456亿元)上升到2010年0.32%(1011亿元)，主要集中在江苏、广东、山东、上海、北京等地。2010年这5个省市的销售产值占了全国产值的64.14%。

卫生部部长陈竺在“2012中国卫生论坛”上发布了《健康中国2020战略研究报告》。

1.“健康中国2020”战略研究报告提出了健康中国这一重大战略思想。

“健康中国”战略是一项旨在全面提高全民健康水平的国家战略，是在准确判断世界和中国卫生改革发展大势的基础上，在深入医药卫生体制改革实践中形成的一项需求牵引型的国民健康发展战略。“健康中国”战略思想的提出，是科学发展观在国民健康领域的具体体现，是卫生系统探索中国特色卫生改革发展道路集体智慧的结晶，是卫生战线对中国特色卫生事业发展理论体系的丰富发展。

“健康中国2020”战略是以科学发展观为指导，以全面维护和增进人民健康，提高健康公平，实现社会经济与人民健康协调发展为目标，以公共政策为落脚点，以重大专项、重大工程为切入点的国家战略。实施“健康中国2020”战略，是构建和谐社会的重要基础性工程，有利于全面改善国民健康，确保医改成果为人民共享，也有利于促进经济发展方式转变，充分体现贯彻落实科学发展观的根本要求。

2.“健康中国2020”战略研究对卫生事业发展所遵循的指导思想与原则。

关于卫生事业发展的指导思想，“健康中国2020”战略研究提出，卫生事业发展要以邓小平理论和“三个代表”重要思想为指导，深入贯彻落实科学发展观，把健康摆在优先发展的战略地位，将“健康强国”作为一项基本国策；坚持以人为本，以社会需求为导向，把维护人民健康权益放在第一位，以全面促进人民健康，提高健康的公平性，实现社会经济与人民健康协调发展为出发点和落脚点；强调“预防为主”，实现医学模式的根本转变，以公共政策、科技进步、中西医结合、重大行动为切入点，着力解决长期(或长远)威胁我国人民生命安全的重大疾病和健康问题；实施综合治理，有机协调部门职能，充分调动各方面积极性，共同应对卫生挑战，实现“健康中国，多方共建，全民共享”。

关于卫生事业发展的基本原则，“健康中国2020”战略研究提出，卫生事业发展要坚持以下四个方面的原则，一是坚持把“人人健康”纳入经济社会发展规划目标，二是坚持公平效率统一，注重政府责任与市场机制相结合，三是坚持统筹兼顾，突出重点，增强卫生发展的整体性和协调性，四是坚持预防为主，适应并推动医学模式转变。

3.“健康中国2020”战略研究提出“到2020年，主要健康指标基本达到中等发达国家水平”，具体包括的目标。

为实现卫生事业与国民健康的发展目标，“健康中国2020”战略研究构建了一个体现科学发展观的卫生发展综合目标体系，将总体目标分解为可操作、可测量的10个具体目标和95个分目标。这些目标涵盖了保护和促进国民健康的服务体系及其支撑保障条件，是监测和评估国民健康状况、有效调控卫生事业运行的重要依据。

10个具目标是：国民主要健康指标进一步改善，到2020年，人均预期寿命达到77岁，5岁以下儿童死亡率下降到13‰，孕产妇死亡率降低到20/10万，减少地区间健康状况的差距；完善卫生服务体系，提高卫生服务可及性和公平性；健全医疗保障制度，减少居民疾病经济风险；控制危险因素，遏制、扭转和减少慢性病的蔓延和健康危害；强化传染病和地方疾病防控，降低感染性疾病危害；加强监测与监管，保障食品药品安全；依靠科技进步，适应医学模式的转变，实现重点前移、转化整合战略；继承创新中医药，发挥中医药等我国传统医学在保障国民健康中的作用；发展健康产业，满足多层次、多样化卫生服务需求；履行政府职责，加大健康投入，到2020年，卫生总费用占GDP的比重达到6.5%～7%，保障“健康中国2020”战略目标实现。

4.“健康中国2020”战略研究提出的今后一个时间卫生工作的战略重点。

“健康中国2020”战略研究依据危害的严重性、影响的广泛性、明确的干预措施、公平性及前瞻性的原则，筛选出了针对中重点人群、重大疾病及可控健康危险因素的三类优先领域，并进一步提出了分别针对上述三类优先领域以及实现“病有所医”可采取的21项行动计划作为今后一个时期的重点任务，包括针对重点人群的母婴健康行动计划、改善贫困地区人群健康行动计划、职业健康行动计划；针对重大疾病的重点传染病控制行动计划、重点慢性病防控行动计划、伤害监测和干预行动计划；针对健康危险因素的环境与健康行动计划、食品安全行动计划、全民健康生活方式行动计划、减少烟草危害行动计划；促进卫生发展，实现“病有所医”的医疗卫生服务体系建设行动计划、卫生人力资源建设行动计划、强化基本医疗保险制度行动计划、促进合理用药行动计划、保障医疗安全行动计划、提高医疗卫生服务效率行动计划、公共安全和卫生应急行动计划、推动科技创新计划、国家健康信息系统行动计划、中医药等我国传统医学行动计划、发展健康产业行动计划。

5. 为保障各项指标的实现，“健康中国2020”战略研究在政策措施方面所提出的建议。

“健康中国2020”战略研究提出了推动卫生事业发展的8项政策措施。一是建立促进国民健康的行政管理体制，形成医疗保障与服务统筹一体化的“大卫生”行政管理体制；二是健全法律支撑体系，依法行政；三是适应国民健康需要，转变卫生事业发展模式，从注重疾病诊疗向预防为主、防治结合转变，实现关口前移；四是建立与经济社会发展水平相适应的公共财政投入政策与机制，通过增加政府卫生投入和社会统筹，将个人现金卫生支出降低到30%以内；五是统筹保障制度发展，提高基本医疗保险筹资标准和补偿比例，有序推进城乡居民医保制度统一、管理统一；六是实施“人才强卫”战略，提高卫生人力素质；七是充分发挥中医药等我国传统医学优势，促进中医药继承和创新；八是积极开展国际交流与合作。

目前行业现状全球十大医疗器械公司

1. Johnson&Johnson(强生)美国
2. GEMS(通用医疗)美国
3. Baxter(百特)美国
4. Tyco(泰科)美国
5. Medtronic(美敦力)美国
6. AbbottLaboratories(雅培)美国
7. PhieipsMedicalSystem(飞利浦医疗)荷兰
8. SiemensMedical(西门子医疗)德国
9. BectonDichinson(碧迪)美国
10. FreseniusMdeicalCare(费森尤斯)德国

从我国医疗器械生产企业的情况看：国有企业占1%的比重，非公有制经济类型占99%以上；其中民营企业占61%，中外合资企业占38%。

到目前为止，我国目前已形成了三大医疗器械生产区，珠江三角洲——广东、深圳；长江三角洲——江苏、浙江、上海；京津环渤海湾——京、津、鲁、冀、辽。根据相关统计：截止2012年6月，生产企业共计14862家，Ⅰ类4168家，Ⅱ类8249家，Ⅲ类2445家，经营企业170742家。至2011年统计全国共批准医疗器械产品注册证18623件，批准国产器械1399件，批准进口器械注册4632件。

截止到2012年10月我国医疗器械生产企业挂牌上市30家，境内18家，境外12家(纽约所3家，纳斯达克2家，港交所5家，新加坡、台湾各1家)。已申报尚未上市共10家。8家申请登陆创业版，2家申请中小版。

纽约所上市：迈瑞公司、泰和诚公司、康辉医疗公司。

纳斯达克上市：德海尔医疗公司、稳健医疗公司。

香港联交所上市：金卫医疗公司、威高公司、创生控股公司、微创医疗公司、先健科技公司。

新加坡交易所上市：三瑞控股。

台湾证券交易所上市：金卫医疗公司。

上交所主板上市：新华医疗公司、山东药玻公司、华润万东公司、航天长峰公司。

深交所——中小版上市：九安医疗公司、鱼跃医疗公司。

深交所——创业版上市：凯利泰公司、博晖创新公司、三诺生物公司、和佳股份公司、宝莱物公司、冠昊生物公司、理邦仪器公司、阳普医疗公司、乐普医疗公司。

我国医疗器械产业与发达国家相比仍然有较大距离，特别是在具有产业战略高度的持续技术创新能力建设方面落差巨大。

现在政府管理由几部分组成：

行业政策：药监局、发改委、法制办

安全监管：药监局、卫生部、质监局

生产发展：药监局、工信部

流通渠道：药监局、商务部

产业整体前景：机遇与挑战并存

行业持续快速发展与扩容，成为医院主要收入来源

今后若干产品将成为发展方向：重离子、质子加速器等粒子治疗设备，采用X线的直线加速器治疗设备。

新型介入产品：

微创诊疗技术产品

高端体外诊断设备与技术

肿瘤热疗仪器设备

透析设备及消耗品

今后医疗器械产业的发展空间巨大，政府将更加重视。2013年3月5日第十二届全国人民代表大会第一次会议上，温家宝总理在政府工作报告上指出：

深入医药卫生体制改革，建立新型农村合作医疗制度和城镇居民基本医疗保险制度，全民基本医保体系初步形成，各项医疗保险参保超过13亿人，加强城乡基层医疗卫生服务体系建设，建立基本药物制度并在基层医疗机构实施，公立医院改革试点稳步推进。国民健康水平进一步提高，人均预期寿命达到75岁。

深入医药卫生事业改革发展。巩固完善基本药物制度和基层医疗卫生机构运行新机制，加快公立医院改革，鼓励社会办医。扶持中医药和民族医药事业发展。健全全民医保体系，建立重特大疾病保障和救助机制，全面开展儿童白血病等20种重大疾病保障试点工作。

食品药品安全是人们关注的突出问题，要改革和健全食品药品安全监管体制，加强综合协调联动，落实企业主体责任，严格从生产源头到消费的全程监管，加快形成符合国情、科学合理的食品药品安全体系，提升食品药品安全保障水平。

深入科技体制改革。推动科技与经济紧密结合，着力构建以企业为主体、市场为导向、产学研相结合的技术创新体系。瞄准关系全局和长远发展的战略必争领域，加强基础研究、前沿先导技术研究。健全科技资源开放共享机制，完善支持科技发展和成果应用转化的财税、金融、产业技术和人才政策，创造公平开放的创新环境，最大限度地调动广大科技工作者的积极性、主动性，激发社会的创新活力，为医疗器械产业的发展描绘出光明的前景。

天津市塑料研究所有限公司自上世纪70年代开始，从事医用塑料的研发、生产和销售，有着雄厚技术和产品储备。是中国塑料加工工业协会医用塑料专业委员会的理事长单位，是全国标准化技术委员会分会主任委员单位。现产品涵盖心外科用体外循环类、呼吸麻醉类、神经外科类、透析类以及其他五种系列产品。产品通过直接和间接的销售网络销往全国各大中城市的400余家医院。

产品质量和技术居国内领先水平，其中自行研制的一管多腔、变径、复合挤出等专有技术，能为国内外客户加工各类特种导管、插管。

（中国塑料加工工业协会医用塑料专业委员会　陈俊尧　关平平）

降解塑料

中国降解及生物基塑料现状分析

2012年，我国生物基材料及降解制品总产量约500kt，比2011年增长约10%。淀粉基塑料制品供不应求，尤其是一次性五件套餐饮具市场发展迅速，在国内已经有2千多个超市已经有产品上架销售，一些著名酒店如香格里拉、新开元等开始使用淀粉基酒店易耗品。

聚乳酸和聚羟基烷酸值的产能稳中有升，聚乳酸(PLA)的使用量有所上升，美国 NatureWorks 公司已开始在泰国投产新的100kt规模工厂，并利用木薯淀粉为原料生产PLA。聚乳酸国内表观消费量已在18kt左右，国家发改委专项支持浙江海正公司的产能已在5kt以上。

丁二酸、丁二醇二元或多元共聚酯产量逐渐上升，其中对苯二甲酸/已二酸/丁二醇共聚酯产能已经超过70kt。国内已投产生产企业已经超过4家，其中浙江杭州鑫富药业股份有限公司产能10kt、安徽安庆和兴化工有限公司产能10kt、山东汇盈新材料有限公司等单位的产能已在15000t/a以上，新疆蓝山屯河化工有限公司产能已经完成5000t年产能建设。植物纤维模塑制品产量增加，其他生物聚合物如尼龙等已经有中试生产。淀粉基塑料产量逐渐提高，其中武汉华丽等发改委专项支持的企业销售增加迅速，武汉华丽公司产能已在40kt以上。

一、发展降解塑料的必要性和意义

大量塑料的使用不仅消耗了大量的石油和能源，而且因为不能自然降解，燃烧时又释放出大量二氧化碳，部分地造成和加重了“白色污染”和“温室效

应”。2012年，我国塑料表观消费量已在60Mt以上，其中塑料包装材料的发展最迅速。塑料包装材料占生活垃圾的41%，而这种垃圾实际上是“永久性”的不能被降解。怎样面对及如何处理塑料垃圾已成为世界性的环保问题。为净化周围环境，消除塑料废弃物，人们努力地做好以下工作来减少污染：一是卫生填埋(用土掩埋垃圾)，二是废物利用。卫生填埋虽可明显地缓解环境污染，但是却将环保的重任推到下一代人身上。废物利用是较可行的办法，世界上相继出现了焚烧利用热能、回收再利用、自然降解等三种主要的解决塑料废弃物方法。回收再利用是从垃圾中回收塑料，要经过分拣、冲洗、干燥、粉碎等过程，最后加工成制品，虽然会耗费一定的人力和物力，但一定程度上能使环境有所改善。但是对一次性、不易回收的制品，专家建议生产可自然降解塑料。

无论是从能源替代、二氧化碳减少，还是从环境保护以及部分解决“三农”问题，发展降解塑料都是必要，也是十分有意义的。

(一) 利用可再生能源，替代石化资源，可持续发展

我国石油消费量是世界第二，在我国，能源的多元化、可持续、与环境友好以及降低进口依存度已是大势所趋。生物基降解塑料其原料主要来源于以阳光和二氧化碳为能源和碳源的可再生资源，如淀粉和纤维素等。相对于普通塑料，生物基降解塑料可降低30%～50%石油资源的消耗，减少我们对石油资源的依赖。

(二)减少二氧化碳排放，防治温室效应

我国二氧化硫和二氧化碳的排量分居世界第一和第二位，每年燃烧和填埋处理的塑料废弃物释放的二氧化碳在百万吨以上。而生物基降解塑料在生产过程中，其原料主要以消耗二氧化碳和水(植物光合作用将其变成淀粉)来生产，可以减少二氧化碳排放，是“绿色塑料”理念的完美体现。

(三)促进环境保护，减少白色污染

据有关部门统计，由于塑料地膜较薄，用后破碎在农田中并夹杂了大量的沙土，很难回收利用；一次性日用杂品和医疗材料中一部分也是难以收集或不宜回收利用的，由此引发的环境问题日益严重。若其中50%采用降解塑料替代的话，则降解塑料的需求量将超过百万吨，因此降解塑料在中国具有较大的市场潜力。

(四)部分解决三农问题

目前生物基降解塑料多以淀粉、秸秆等可再生资源为原料生产，其大量推广后会拉动国内玉米、土豆等农副产品的需求，促进玉米、土豆等农产品种植、农副产品加工业的发展，提高农民收入。

(五)突破贸易壁垒

现在一些发达国家对一些进口物品的包装提出了一些更新要求，即规定不能使用不可降解的材料进行包装货物，而降解塑料的出现有利于突破这些贸易壁垒。

(六)改善企业形象

可降解包装材料作为传统聚合物的环保型替代物将不断获得进展，一些零售商正在着力使用生物分解包装材料来提高他们自己的形象。

二、降解塑料和生物基塑料

(一) 降解塑料

降解塑料根据降解途径可以分为光降解塑料、热氧降解塑料和生物分解塑料。

光降解塑料，由自然日光作用下，经过一段时间和包含一个或更多步骤，导致材料化学结构的显著变化而损失某些性能(如完整性、分子质量、结构或机械强度)和/或发生破碎的塑料。光降解塑料由于其降解需要光的条件，而塑料废弃物废弃后，要么是被搁在封闭的垃圾处理系统(焚烧、填埋、堆肥等)中，要么就是曝露在条件不固定的自然环境中，很难保证光降解塑料所需要的固定条件。因此，在大多数情况下，光降解塑料因为受条件限制无论是在垃圾处理系统中还是在自然环境而不能全部降解。

热氧降解塑料，在热和/或氧化作用下，经过一段时间和包含一个或更多步骤，导致材料化学结构的显著变化而损失某些性能(如完整性、分子质量、结构或机械强度)和/或发生破碎的塑料。热氧降解塑料因为受条件限制，大多数情况下也很难彻底降解。

生物分解塑料是指，在自然界如土壤和/或沙土等条件下，和/或特定条件如堆肥化条件下或厌氧消化条件下或水性培养液中，由自然界存在的微生物作用引起降解，并最终完全降解变成二氧化碳(CO_2)或/和甲烷(CH_4)、水(H_2O)及其所含元素的矿化无机盐以及新的生物质的塑料。生物分解塑料按照其原料来源和合成方式可以分为三大类，即利用石化资源合成得到的生物分解塑料、可再生材料衍生得到生物分解塑料以及以上两类材料共混加工得到的塑料。

生物分解塑料因为在一定条件下可以生物分解，不增加环境负荷，是解决白色污染的有效途径。普通塑料如常用的聚乙烯(如塑料袋)、聚丙烯(如塑料餐具)、聚酯(如饮料瓶)等不能生物分解，在目前常用的垃圾处理方式即卫生填埋条件下，普通塑料将

存在上百年以上，而生物分解塑料在堆肥条件下几周内就可以完全分解，回归自然。

生物分解塑料可以和有机废弃物(如厨余垃圾)一起堆肥处理，因此和一般塑料垃圾相比，省去了人工分拣的步骤，大大方便了垃圾收集和处理，从而使城市有机垃圾堆肥化和无害出处理变得极为现实。

(二) 生物基塑料

生物基塑料是指由生物体(包括动物、植物和微生物)或其他再生资源如二氧化碳直接合成的具有塑料特性的高分子材料，如聚羟基烷酸酯(PHA，包括PHB、PHBV等)，或从天然高分子或生物高分子(淀粉、纤维素、甲壳素、木质素、蛋白质、多肽、多糖、核酸等)出发，或从它们的结构单元或衍生物出发，通过生物学或化学的途径而获得的具有塑料特性的高分子材料，或者以这些高分子材料为主要成分的共混物或复合物，如聚乳酸、聚氨基酸、可热塑型淀粉、淀粉基塑料、植物纤维模塑制品、改性纤维素、改性蛋白质、生物基聚酰胺、二氧化碳共聚物等。

由可再生的天然生物质资源，如淀粉、植物秸秆、甲壳素等衍变得到的生物基塑料(biobasepolymer)是一类绿色塑料，具有良好的生物分解性，并因原材料丰富易得，其研究开发更是受到各国的重视。开发生物基塑料的根本出发点，是因为目前大量使用的石化资源是有限的，而可再生资源却是可持续发展的。相对于普通塑料，生物基降解塑料可降低30%~50%石油资源的消耗，减少我们对石油资源的依赖。

(三) 降解塑料、生物分解塑料、可堆肥塑料与生物基塑料之间的区别

1. 降解性能的区别

(1) 降解塑料和生物分解塑料之间的区别。

从第一节的定义上可以看出，降解塑料是一个大类，包括了光降解、热氧降解塑料和生物分解塑料，生物分解塑料只是其中一种，只是它在自然环境、堆肥等条件下可以生物分解成二氧化碳(或甲烷)和水等。因此，降解塑料包括了生物分解塑料，而生物分解塑料是降解塑料中的一种，只是它能在自然条件下能被完全降解。

(2) 生物分解塑料和可堆肥塑料的区别。

生物分解塑料是指在自然环境或堆肥化条件或土壤条件或高固态等条件下可以生物分解的一类塑料，而可堆肥塑料指在堆肥化条件下可以分解成二氧化碳和水的一类塑料，后者除了材料要求变成二氧化碳和水外，还要求在堆肥周期内塑料能变成小于2cm大小的小块，并要求堆肥产生的堆肥的重金属含量要满足各国的标准要求，并且堆肥与传统堆肥比较不会对植物的生长产生不良影响。国际上对生物分解性能要求虽不全一样，但基本类同，检验方法主要为ISO 14855堆肥条件下生物分解性能测定(我国标准为GB/T 19277，等同采用ISO)，对单一聚合物生物分解率要求在50%以上(180d内)，对共混物要求成分在1%以上的每种材料生物分解率在60%以上。欧洲的要求直接要求相对生物分解率或绝对生物分解率在90%以上。我国的降解性能要求国家标准为GB/T 20197。可堆肥塑料要求的标准美国主要为ASTMD6400、ASTMD6868，欧盟的标准为EN13432、14995，我国在GB/T 20197中也作了类似的规定。目前，ISO17088正在颁布阶段，其基本在ASTMD6400和EN13432基础上制定。关于生物分解塑料的降解性能要求，目前国际上各国要求基本接近，但是必须要搞清楚检验的条件和依据标准。

(3) 生物基塑料、降解塑料及生物分解塑料之间的区别。

根据降解塑料的定义，在一定条件下具有降解性能的塑料都可以称作降解塑料，而生物基塑料由于其成分中有很大一部分为生物质材料，所以生物基塑料可以称作为降解塑料。但是根据生物分解塑料的定义，生物分解塑料应该是在一定条件下能被降解成二氧化碳或甲烷、水以及生物死体的一类降解塑料，所以生物基塑料就不能简单地称为生物分解塑料，只有当其降解性能满足生物分解性能要求或其所有组分均为生物分解塑料时，才可以称作为生物分解塑料。

(4) 生物基和生物分解之间的区别。

生物分解主要是从塑料废弃后它对环境消纳性能出发提出的概念，而生物基则是从原材料来源角度出发提出的概念。生物分解塑料在使用废弃后在一定条件下可以变成二氧化碳和水，而生物基塑料它的原材料来源主要为可再生资源如淀粉、纤维素等。虽然大多数生物基塑料能够生物分解，但生物基塑料不一定能生物分解，而生物分解塑料也不一定是生物基塑料。换句话说，生物基塑料是降解塑料，但不一定是生物分解塑料；生物分解塑料是降解塑料，但降解塑料不一定是生物分解塑料；生物分解塑料也不一定是生物基塑料。

三、行业现状

由于光降解塑料和氧化降解塑料主要是添加型降解塑料，在本文不作具体描述，这里主要介绍生物分解塑料和淀粉基塑料现状。

(一) 生物分解塑料

1. 化石基生物分解塑料

化石基生物分解塑料是指主要以石化产品为单体，通过化学合成的方法得到的一类聚合物，如聚己内酯(PCL)、聚丁二酸丁二醇酯(PBS)(也可归于“可再生材料基生物分解塑料)、聚对二氧环己酮(PPDO)、聚乙烯醇(PVA)、聚对苯二甲酸/己二酸/丁二酯(PBAT)、二氧化碳共聚物(PPC)等。

(1) 脂肪族二元醇、二元酸二元或多元共聚物

① 安庆和化工有限公司

1998年3月组建的民营股份制企业，属生物化工制业，是目前国内最大的丁二酸及系列产品生产企业。从2007起就获安徽省省级高新技术企业至今，公司有外贸自营进出口权。并拥有多项发明专利及科研成果。现有资产6000万元，年销售收入亿元。现正在实施“十二五”(863计划“重大化工产品的先进生物制造”一万吨聚丁二酸丁二醇酯项目)。项目完成后形成年销售3.8亿元。

② 杭州鑫富药业股份有限公司

2004年在深交所上市，是全球维生素B5第一大生产供应商，国家级高新技术企业。公司是一家以泛酸系列为主导产品的出口生产型企业，已实现年产“D-泛酸钙”5000t、“D-泛醇”1000t的生产能力。公司占地面积220亩，总资产达4亿多元。目前PBS的产能是年产13kt。生物分解树脂PBS、PBSA、PBAT以二元酸与二元醇为原料，采用高效无毒催化剂，按一步缩聚法直接合成，该材料符合EN13432、ASTMD6400等国际标准，系列有2003、1803、1903等牌号，满足吹塑、挤塑、注塑、纺丝及发泡等不同用途的加工需求，公司还开展生物分解材料的改性和制成品的研发。

③ 山东汇盈新材料科技有限公司

成立于2008年4月，占地330亩，主要致力于完全生物降解塑料及精细化工类产品的生产、经营和研发，主要产品包括PBS、PBAT及其共聚物，BDO等。公司于2012年建成年产55kt1，4-丁二醇(简称BDO)和年产25kt可完全降解塑料(PBS、PBAT)产品一期项目。1，4-丁二醇项目工艺技术和核心设备引进英国DAVY公司第四代技术，达到世界先进水平。一期年产25ktPBS项目已于2012年6月投产，二期年产80ktPBS项目正在建设中，计划于2013年底投产。目前，PBS、PBAT项目已累计完成投资12亿元，综合产能位居全球第一。全部建成投产后，将达到年产105kt的生产规模，预计可实现年销售收入40亿元、利税13.3亿元、利润9.7亿元。

④ 新疆蓝山屯河化工股份有限公司

是一家依托新疆本土资源优势，以化工高分子材料制造为主导产业的高科技化工新材料企业。公司注册资本2.58亿元，拥有员工1000余人。公司是新疆自治区百户“优强企业”之一，主要产品PBT、EPS、PET、PBS、PVC型材等综合生产能力达310kt/a。公司是国家认定的高新技术企业、国家创新型试点单位。荣获了54项国家专利，三个新疆名牌产品称号。公司已有年产5000t薄膜级PBS及PBAT生产装置。

⑤ 广州金发科技有限公司

上市公司，对外宣称建立了年产35000t的生产线。

⑥ 常茂生物化学工程股份有限公司

江苏省高新技术企业，主要产品有L-苹果酸、DL-苹果酸、L(+)-酒石酸、L-天冬氨酸、富马酸、马来酸、丁二酸等有机酸产能达30000t以上，是目前世界上独具特色的四碳系列有机酸制造商。公司已建年产10000t生物发酵法丁二酸生产线。

(2) PCL

PCL由七元环的ε-己内酯在辛酸烯锡等催化剂作用下开环聚合而成，其中一个简单反应式如图2所示。PCL熔点较低，只有60℃，所以很少单独使用。但PCL与许多树脂有较好的相容性，可与其他生物分解性聚脂共混加工。国内从事PCL生产的单位主要为深圳光华伟业公司等。

(3) 聚对二氧环己酮(PPDO)

PPDO由单体对二氧环己酮(PDO)在催化剂的作用下开环聚合而成。PPDO的玻璃化温度为-17~-10℃，熔点为110℃，热变形温度在90℃左右，其最大特点是兼具高强度和优良的韧性，是一种极具应用前景的可生物分解塑料。该聚合物最早由美国Ethicon公司在20世纪70年代成功合成出来，并开发出商品名为PDS的手术缝合线。但由于其成本很高，一直未能进入通用材料领域。近几年，我国四川大学在PPDO的低成本和高性能化方面进行了大量的研究，取得了突破性进展，特别是其生产成本在合成生物分解塑料中具有很强的竞争力，并且其具有较高的相对分子质量，能进行吹塑等加工。该产品另一个突出特点是，通过热化学回收，可回收其原料PDO单体，并且回收率高达93%~96%，回收的单体可以直接用于合成PPDO。目前四川大学开发的PPDO的拉伸强度≥29MPa，断裂伸长率≥200%，开发的PPDO纳米复合材料的拉伸强度和断裂伸长率分别高达50MPa和500%以上，目前正与企业合作进行产业化。

(4) 二氧化碳共聚物

二氧化碳共聚物目前主要以生物化工生产时的副产物二氧化碳废气为原料，与环氧丙烷或环氧乙烷催化合成得到的聚合物。

① 内蒙古蒙西高新技术集团有限公司

公司成立于1994年，是一家集水泥、新型建材、高岭土、粉煤灰提取氧化铝、LED光电、二氧化碳基全降解塑料及置业开发等多领域集团化运作的国家高新技术企业。PPC是利用从工业废气中捕集、提纯的CO_2和环氧丙烷聚合而成。蒙西集团采用长春应化所的技术于2002年建成3000t/aPPC中试线，产品在医用敷材、一次性日用品及防尘固沙等领域得到应用。公司计划在天津滨海新区建设100kt/aPPC生产装置，十二五期间建成30kt/aPPC生产线。

② 浙江台州邦丰塑料有限公司

从2010年6月开始，浙江台州邦丰塑料有限公司利用长春应化所的专利技术，投资1.5亿元，在浙江温岭市上马工业区建设30kt二氧化碳基塑料生产线。2012年一期10kt/a生产线试车成功。目前已经实现连续稳定生产，成为世界上第一条连续稳定生产的万吨级二氧化碳基塑料生产线。

③ 河南天冠集团有限公司

天冠集团已拥有全球独一的具自主知识产权的二氧化碳捕获技术和成套装备技术，获得了10多项专利及专有技术，开发了数个系列的技术平台，建成了千吨级PPC工业化生产线，在该领域中已成为国际领先者。天冠集团计划在2015年，建成形成年产100ktPPC的生产能力。

④ 江苏中科金龙化工股份有限公司

利用生物基来源的CO_2制备新型高分子材料的省高新技术企业，主要产品有CO_2合成的聚碳酸亚丙酯(PPC)多元醇化工中间体及延伸产品全生物降解塑料改性母粒、阻燃外墙保温材料、高分子共聚生物材料、环保型水性聚氨酯分散体。已建成年产22kt二氧化碳基聚碳酸亚丙酯多元醇生产线，累计形成销售8000t。已建成年产160万平方米高阻燃保温材料生产线。水性分散体产能为10000t，生物降解及阻隔材料产能为2000t。

⑤ 南通华盛高聚物科技发展有限公司

是国内著名的塑料包装薄膜的专业生产商，每年出口美国、日本和欧盟的塑料薄膜超过20kt，从2007年12月开始与长春应化所合作开发全生物降解二氧化碳基塑料改性和膜加工技术，并于2010年建立了企业院士工作站。突破了二氧化碳基塑料的抗冲击强度差和耐温差的难题，制备了二氧化碳塑料改性树脂(商品名PCO2)，实现了二氧化碳基塑料在食品包装领域的应用，并在2011年3月份通过了美国生物分解塑料协会的认证，由此取得了产品进入美国和欧洲的通行证。

(5) 其他

其他化学合成聚合物也有一部分市场，如改性聚乙烯醇等。PVA类材料经改性后才具有良好的生物分解性能。国内从事PVA改性加工的单位有北京工商大学等，四川大学也成功研制出一种可热塑性加工吹塑成膜的PVA/PLA复合材料。北京工商大学的干法吹膜得到聚乙烯醇薄膜的拉伸强度≥60MPa，断裂伸长率≥100%，透光率≥91%，氧气透过系数为$2.64\times10^{-17}cm^3\cdot cm/cm^2\cdot s\cdot Pa$。

2. 可再生材料基生物分解塑料

(1) 天然材料基生物分解塑料

天然生物分解塑料是指以天然聚合物为原料，可通过各种成型工艺制成的生物分解塑料。这类材料包括淀粉、纤维素、甲壳素、大豆蛋白等天然聚合物及其各种衍生物和混合物。

其中，热塑性淀粉和植物纤维模塑已经产业化，植物纤维模塑是指将植物纤维粉末通过热塑成型办法制得的制品。其他天然材料尚处于基础研究阶段。例如，四川大学研究开发的基于纤维素的天然高分子复合膜，是通过易于回收再利用的绿色室温离子液体作为共溶剂，使纤维素分别与淀粉、木质素、大豆蛋白等天然高分子中的一种或两种在不添加任何其他助剂的情况下复合成膜，获得光学透明性和阻隔性好的完全生物分解的天然高分子复合膜。武汉大学张俐娜教授在溶液中将纤维素溶解，然后再将其处理后来制作纤维、薄膜等，目前也正在产业化中试过程中。

(2) 生物基生物分解塑料

利用可再生天然生物质资源如淀粉等，通过微生物发酵直接合成聚合物，如聚羟基烷酸酯类(PHA，包括PHB，PHBV等)；或通过微生物发酵产生乳酸等单体，再化学合成聚合物，如PLA等。

① 聚乳酸

PLA是以淀粉发酵法制得的L-乳酸为原料，再经化学合成得到。所以是介于微生物产生类和化学合成类之间的高分子。PLA是无色、透明的热塑性聚合物，熔点为175℃，可采用通用热塑性塑料的加工方法加工，挤出成型可将板材制成托盘，还可制成薄膜、纤维、食品包装材料、医用导入管等。

我国PLA的生产仍属起步阶段，建成的生产线较少，到目前为止，国内PLA总产能约为10kt/a，2012年表观消费量约18kt。目前产业化的有中科院长春应用化学所与浙江海正生物材料有限公司，已经实现5kt/a的生产能力。正在中试的单位有上海同杰良生物材料有限公司、江苏九鼎集团。其中上海同杰良生物材料有限公司2006年完成了百吨级中试，生产状态稳定，正在筹建万吨级生产线。据报道，中粮公司正在筹建万吨级规模的生产线。为提高PLA的热性能、韧性和加工性能，四川大学采用共聚的方法对PLA进行改性，改性后的PLA断裂伸长率可提高到300%，并显著改善了加工性能，特别是吹塑加工性能。目前已与五粮液集团的一个全资子公司签订了合作中试开发协议。

a. 浙江海正生物材料有限公司

由海正集团、中科院长春应化所及其他投资者共同组建于2004年，公司于2008年建成年产5000t聚乳酸PLA生产线，为世界上第二条商业化生产线，产品应用领域包括注塑、挤出、纤维和薄膜等领域，制品耐热温度100度以上。“十二五”，海正集团计划以现有5kt生产线为基础，开工建设万吨级生产线，一期产能50kt/a，二期达到100kt/a，相应配套乳酸由海正与合作伙伴共同建设。

b. 上海同杰良生物材料有限公司

公司已开发纤维级聚乳酸专用树脂，目前规划建设万吨级乳酸与聚乳酸生产工厂。

c. 浙江南益生物科技有限公司

是南龙集团全资子公司。经本公司技术团队近五年的努力，已在聚乳酸改性和聚乳酸余废料直接改性应用方面取得阶段性成果，并已有两项发明专利授权。其中低成本高性能全降解农业地膜用改性料、高耐候性片材用改性料已中试成功。现将着手以改性聚乳酸为基材，与其他生物基降解材料(PBAT、PBS、PPC、木薯淀粉)共混或共聚物的研发，成本大幅度降低。现有规模PLA专用树脂生产能力7000t，正计划建设PLA专用树脂50kt/a生产线。

d. 厦门协和环保科技有限公司

是一家主要从事环保型纸质食品包装的研发、生产以及销售，公司现有拥有四万多平方米的功能完善厂房以及配套设施。目前产能30kt，正拟建设20ktPLA片材包括吹膜/吸塑/注塑产品、一次性包装以及淋膜纸杯与纸餐具等。与国内外研发团队和科研机构一起共同研究，例如中国科学院长春应用化学研究所，北京工商大学。同时，还有北京工商大学建立了生物基降解塑料产学研基地。同时，2012年，公司又被授予高新技术企业的称号。2011年，公司被中国轻工企业投资发展协会授予中国包装-绿色包装品牌。

e. 安徽恒鑫新材料有限公司

专业纸杯生产企业，目前纸杯出口十几个国家。由合肥恒鑫环保科技有限公司收购了罗宾生化科技汕头有限公司后重组成立的。其技术发展可追述至2002年开始研发改性PLA及PLA制品，现已形成热成型、注塑、吹塑、淋膜、型材等几大系列产品及对应的专用改性PLA树脂的工业化生产，其产品市场主要全部出口至国外，现在合肥正在建设5万平米的生产厂房，拟建成PLA的集中研发、生产的大型工业园区，今年至明年要在PLA发泡、双拉及无纺布的工业转化上落实实施。

f. 四川柯因达生物科技有限公司

对聚乳酸改性后，其熔体质量流率2~3g/10min，熔融温度范围140~145℃，拉伸强度≥20MPa，断裂伸长率≥130%，直角撕裂强度≥110N/mm，生产的产品有PLA收缩薄膜、日用塑料袋、垃圾袋等。

② 聚羟基烷酸酯

自然界中许多微生物都用PHA贮藏能量。PHA具有良好的生物相容性能、生物分解性和塑料的热加工性能，因此可将其同时作为生物医用材料和生物可降解包装材料，已经成为生物材料领域最为活跃的研究热点。我国在PHA研究方面介入较早，处于世界先进水平。

国内规模化生产的单位有宁波天安生物材料有限公司，已经达到2kt/a的生产能力，目前正准备筹建年产万吨的生产线，该公司也是目前全世界生产PHA规模最大的企业。

天津国韵生物科技有限公司在天津已完成年产10kt/a规模的PHA(P(3HB，4HB)，3HB和4HB的共聚物)生产线建设。

3. 共混生物分解塑料

共混生物分解塑料是指利用上述几种生物分解材料共混加工得到的产品。国内已产业化或已中试的单位有武汉华丽、浙江华发、南京比澳格、河北昭和、浙江天禾、广东上九、肇庆华芳、福建百事达、博事雅高分子、烟台万利达等公司。

其中武汉华丽公司目前年产能已经达到30kt以上，熔体流动速率0.5~1.0g/10min，密度1.20~1.30g/cm^3，拉伸强度9~11MPa，产品包括了粒料、薄膜、片材、注塑品等。最近，四川大学通过原位合成脂肪族聚酯，与天然高分子，特别是淀粉和大豆蛋白共混，成功地制备出相容性与成型加工性能好、耐水性好和力学性能优异的淀粉/脂肪族聚酯和大豆蛋白/脂肪族聚酯复合材料。该产品中天然高分子物质可以不经过改性、且含量高，生产工艺简单，因此复合材料的成本低廉。

北京工商大学以共混为主的生物分解塑料已开发片材、餐具、薄膜袋，并在多个企业进行规模化生产。

4. 生物分解塑料入市前准备工作

生物分解塑料产业直面我国“三农”、能源和环境三大主题，是世界发展之大势和新兴的产业，在宏观和战略上是可行的。战术层面上，原料及其来源特别是生物质生物分解塑料其资源的丰度与成本，原料生产与转化技术，以及产品市场等都是可行的。但问题在于当前成本与价格尚难与石油基产品竞争，瓶颈是如何通过技术进步以降低生产成本。虽然生物分解塑料经过多年的研发，在欧洲和北美已经多有商业应用，但国外大公司在成本问题上也和我们一样面临着同样的问题。

因此，如何对生产企业来讲，如何做好产品上市前的准备就显得尤为重要。

首先，生产者应该全面了解国内外产品生产、应用和销售现状，即应该了解国际市场需求到底有多大、各类原料的价格到底有多大的区别、原料的生产能力到底有多大。在目前以供应为主的国内市场背景下，生产者应根据实际情况来选择适合自己投资规模的项目。

其次，要根据降解塑料的定义，正确定位生产产品，有效进行宣传。从降解塑料降解机理上，降解塑料可以分为热氧降解塑料、光降解塑料、生物分解塑料。从原料来源角度，降解塑料可以分为生物基塑料和石化基塑料，生物基塑料是强调其原料来源的可再生性，生物基塑料可以是100%来自于可再生材料，也可以是部分来自于可再生材料。石化基的生物分解其原料来源主要是石油，但却具有生物分解性能。因此，生物基塑料不一定是生物分解塑料，而生物分解塑料也不一定是生物基的，生物基概念主要强调其原料来源，生物分解概念主要强调其产品使用废弃后的环境可处理性。从垃圾处理角度上看，生物分解塑料如果用于可堆肥有机材料的盛装，则可以叫做可堆肥塑料。所以在产品上市前，应该正确定位产品，进行合理的宣传。另外，不管是生物基的生物分解塑料，还是化石基的生物分解塑料，因为其具备了碳绿色循环的概念，因此，它的广泛应用对促进低碳经济有重要的意义。

再次，要完善产品质量保证的证书工作。生产企业不管生产何种产品，应当首先确保产品的物理力学性能能满足使用的要求，如果是食品接触包装材料，其卫生性能应该满足相关国家的卫生要求。在此基础上，应该进行生物分解性能的检验，对出口产品的生物分解性能，目前美国认证的依据标准主要为 astm d 6400（纸类产品主要为 astm d 6868），欧盟主要为 en 13432。对生物基含量的测试主要为 astm d 6866。目前，国家塑料质量监督检验中心（北京）的生物分解检验能力已经得到美国、欧盟和日本等国的认可，也是国内唯一被认可的实验室，生产企业可以凭借该实验室的检验报告到美国、欧盟和日本进行生物分解塑料的相关认证及标志许可。

最后，生产企业在入市前还应根据需要做好原料的储备、流动资金的准备工作，对出口型的企业还应该注意知识产权保护等。

（二）淀粉基塑料

近年来，随着国际原油价格的持续攀升和石油资源的日渐趋紧，生物基材料经济和环保意义日渐显现，产业发展的内在动力不断增强。淀粉基塑料作为生物基材料的一类产品，近些年在生产技术上取得了一些重大突破，基本克服了工业化生产过程中的成本和性能制约问题，得到了快速发展。按照中国塑协降解塑料专业委员会初步统计，截至2013年6月，从事淀粉基塑料的研究单位和生产企业约100家，年生产能力约250kt，实际年生产约150kt。

1. 淀粉基本性质

淀粉是一种天然的多聚葡萄糖高分子，以颗粒的形式广泛存在于植物的果实、根、茎及叶中。目前生产淀粉的农作物主要有玉米、木薯、马铃薯、小麦等。淀粉的密度 1.449 ~ 1.513g/cm^3，有吸湿性。

淀粉由直链淀粉和支链淀粉两部分组成，不同来源的淀粉，所含的直链淀粉和支链淀粉的含量不同。玉米淀粉中直链淀粉含量约为26%左右，高直链玉米淀粉可达到70%，只有极少数的淀粉，如黏玉米是由支链淀粉组成而不含直链淀粉。[8] 直链淀粉是由葡萄糖以α-1，4-糖苷键结合而成的链状聚合物，高度结晶结构，能溶于热水而不成糊状，遇碘显蓝色；支链淀粉中，除α-1，4-糖苷键相连外还有以α-1，6-糖苷键相连的葡萄糖分子，无定形结构，带有分支，在冷水中不溶，与热水作用则膨胀而成糊状，遇碘呈紫色或红紫色。通常情况下，淀粉的直链部分与支链部分按辐射形式排列，支链分子的线性片段和直链分子平行排列在一起。邻近的片段产生氢键，形成微晶体，使淀粉能以淀粉颗粒的形式存在，以及呈现双折射现象。一般地，高直链含量的淀粉较易塑化。

2. 淀粉与塑料共混

（1）淀粉改性

天然淀粉用途广泛，但天然淀粉性质存在一些缺陷，例如糊黏度不具热稳定性、抗剪力稳定性不够、冻融稳定性较差、不具冷水溶解性，分支结构较多，单独并没有塑料的特性。为了满足工业上各种特定需要，需要对天然淀粉进行改性。淀粉改性处理方式一般有(1)物理改性，包括烟熏改性、预糊化、油脂改性、金属离子改性、超高压辐射改性等；(2)酶法改性，包括抗消化、糊精等；(3)化学改性，包括极限糊精、酸改性、氧化、酯化、醚化、交联、阳离子淀粉、接枝共聚等；另外还可以应用遗传技术和精选技术培育出具有特殊用途的改性淀粉。淀粉及改性淀粉被广泛应用于纺织浆料、造纸助剂、食品添加剂、药品崩解剂、塑料添加剂、石油钻井助剂、铸造粘合剂、饲料添加剂、建筑粘合剂、工业污水剂、表面活性剂、吸水剂、药物释放囊等。

上世纪末，随着石油资源短缺和环境污染加重，作为可再生资源的淀粉逐渐被应用于塑料加工中，但用于塑料的淀粉往往需要改性处理。

① 物理改性

物理改性包括淀粉微细化、通过挤压机破坏淀粉结构或添加偶联剂、增塑剂、结构破坏剂(如水、尿素、碱金属氢氧化物或碱土金属氢氧化物)等以增强淀粉和聚合物之间的相容性。

淀粉的粒度直接影响它在基材中的分散均匀性，尤其是薄膜制品。淀粉粒径越细，则分散得越均匀，材料的力学性能就越好。目前多采用气流粉碎技术和球磨粉碎技术，可得到超细淀粉。

偶联剂主要是对淀粉进行表面改性，从其改性原理上看，它不仅仅是单纯的物理改性，还具有化学键合作用的化学改性。如淀粉与LDPE共混时，淀粉表面用铝酸酯偶联剂改性后，淀粉羟基与偶联剂发生络合作用。对淀粉进行偏磷酸钠交联改性和硅烷偶联剂表面处理，得到的疏水性淀粉再经多元醇塑化处理后，可与聚己内酯混合制得全降解淀粉塑料膜。

增塑剂有利于淀粉与塑料热塑化共混加工，加入增塑剂后，在热和剪切力的作用下，淀粉分子间的氢键作用被削弱破坏，分子链热运动加剧，扩散力提高，材料的玻璃化温度降低，实现了分解前的微晶熔融。淀粉分子在热分解前就因增塑作用破坏其内部的结晶和有序结构，由双螺旋结构转变为无规线团结构，从而使淀粉具有热塑加工性。增塑剂可以是小分子，也可以是高分子聚合物。常用的小分子增塑剂一般含有能与淀粉羟基形成氢键的基团，如甘油等多元醇类、水和小分子糖类等。但小分子增塑剂与淀粉之间相互作用的稳定性较差，制备的热塑性淀粉易重结晶，导致材料老化变脆，而失去其实际应用的价值。使用疏水性的可生物降解聚合物(脂肪族聚酯、脂肪族与芳香族聚酯等)为增塑剂，可以避免在热塑性淀粉熔体中有可迁移的增塑剂，使淀粉在熔融、塑炼过程中形成的是热塑性淀粉而非解体淀粉。有时也可以增塑剂混合使用方式，来增加增塑效果，含酰胺基团小分子塑化热塑性淀粉，与甘油等增塑剂相比，酰安基团能与淀粉形成更稳定的氢键，从而更有效地抑制热塑性淀粉的老化。适当采用含羟基如甘油、乙二醇、山梨醇、聚乙烯醇等高相对分子质量的增塑剂和低相对分子质量的增塑剂混合增塑，有利于提高制品的力学性能。

② 化学改性

由于淀粉中含有大量的非极性基团 - OH，使其与非极性聚合物的相容性受到影响。通过使淀粉发生氧化、氨基化、酯化、醚化及交联等反应，使反应产物具有疏水基团，可改善淀粉的疏水性能，从而提高它与高聚物的相容性。

淀粉的接枝反应措施，可进一步提高淀粉与高聚物的相容性。淀粉可以接枝亲水性或疏水性单体而使改性后的淀粉具亲水性或疏水性。接枝共聚化学反应有自由基共聚、离子共聚、官能团共混。与淀粉共聚的单体有丙烯酸酯、乙酸乙烯酯、丙烯酰胺等。将淀粉接枝共聚物与可生物降解聚酯(PLA、PCL)共混，一方面改善了淀粉与生物降解聚酯的相容性，同时降低了生产成本。

(2) 淀粉与塑料共混

用于共混的淀粉可以是原淀粉、物理改性或化学改性淀粉，也可以是与单体反应形成的共聚物。用于共混时主要通过淀粉改性，破坏淀粉分子双螺旋结构和直链分子的对称性，降低结晶度，使其在高温下分子链的运动加强，从而具有热塑性。用于与树脂共混的变性淀粉一般结晶度低、与高分子树脂相容性好，具有一定的分子柔顺性。

与淀粉共混的传统合成树脂有聚乙烯、聚乙烯醇、聚氯乙烯、聚苯乙烯等，生物分解树脂有聚乳酸、聚丁烯酸琥珀酸酯、聚乙烯醇、聚羟基烷酸酯类(如聚羟基丁酸戊酸酯等)、聚己内酯、二氧化碳共聚物等，淀粉也可与其他天然材料(包括纤维素、甲壳质等)进行共混加工。通过共混加工，可以得到片材、薄膜以及制成的包装制品等。

挤出加工时，将处理过的淀粉与聚合物等一起在排气式同向旋转双螺杆挤出机中混炼，制成母料。母料按所需比例添加到通用塑料中，在通常的成型设备上加工成制品。也可以用于挤出熔融接枝改性等方法对淀粉进行改性，并与聚合物共混加工。华南理工大学瞿金平等将塑料动态塑化挤出机，用于淀粉热塑化加工及其淀粉基塑料的加工生产，取得了很好的效果。

冲压成型时，原料可以全部是天然产物，如淀粉及少量的纤维素和天然食用胶等助剂，制成一次性餐具等。

通过发泡工艺，也可制作淀粉泡沫塑料，例如采用纯天然材料淀粉及农作物秸秆制备绿色泡沫塑料，不仅成本低廉而且产品又能生物分解。

另外，淀粉也有被用于制作聚氨酯和脲醛树脂等。淀粉制备聚氨酯的主要途径是使淀粉液化，合成含有多羟基的物质，再用于合成聚氨酯泡沫。淀粉制备聚氨酯的第二条途径是淀粉不经液化直接和聚醚、发泡剂等反应。[41] 氧化淀粉带有较多的醛基及羧基，能在脲醛树脂聚合物反应过程中，生成缩醛及半缩醛结构，从而提高脲醛树脂的耐老化性能，同时氧化淀粉能与树脂中的游离甲醛结合，可减少游离甲醛含量，且能降低脲醛树脂的生产成本。氧化淀粉在制革工业中同样存在复鞣填充的效果。

3. 淀粉基塑料现状

近二十年来，我国在淀粉基塑料研究方面，江西科学院应用化学研究所、华南理工大学、四川大学、兰州大学、天津大学、中科院长春应用化学研究所、北京工商大学、浙江大学等高校和科研机构取得了一些进展。

淀粉基塑料目前包括了淀粉共混传统塑料如聚乙烯、聚丙烯等，也包括了淀粉共混生物降解的树脂如聚乳酸、聚丁二酸丁二酯等。和传统塑料共混不具备生物降解性能，和生物降解树脂共混可以生物降解。

生产方面，许多企业已由中试阶段进入产业化生产阶段，产品也逐渐由试制品变为商品，并在逐渐推广应用。已实现规模化生产的单位有武汉华丽环保科技有限公司、浙江天禾生态科技有限公司、浙江华发生态科技有限公司、比澳格(南京)环保材料有限公司、河北昭和生态科技有限公司、广东上九生物降解塑料有限公司、苏州汉丰新材料有限公司、北京新华联生物材料有限公司、烟台阳光澳州环保材料有限公司、常州龙骏实业发展有限公司、安徽德琳环保发展(集团)有限公司、上海心尔新材料科技股份有限公司、深圳虹彩新材料科技有限公司等。

市场方面，从2008年开始，淀粉基塑料制品市场需求逐渐增加，一度出现供不应求局面。除国外市场持续增长外，国内市场也有较大起色，尤其是一次性五件套餐饮具市场发展迅速。武汉华丽、浙江华发、广东上九等发改委专项支持的企业，其中武汉华丽公司产量已在40kt以上。武汉华丽环保科技有限公司对淀粉进行了热塑化改性，并利用反应挤出，拥有多个淀粉基塑料的专利，可用于一次性餐饮具、塑料购物袋、垃圾袋、酒店用品、厨房用品、化妆品包装瓶、衣架等日用品的加工制造。苏州汉丰公司开发了非主粮植物淀粉改性的全生物分解专用树脂及其制备方法，可以生产多种淀粉基塑料一次性餐盒、刀叉勺，并且开发了耐低温冷冻食品包装用塑料制品。浙江天禾公司开发了多种淀粉基的刀叉勺及餐具，年产能约万吨。常州龙骏和安徽德琳公司均以淀粉基的餐具为主，产品主要在国内市场销售。

十二五期间，淀粉基塑料行业目标是重点培育出10家以上、拥有自主知识产权、产品性能优良、年产50kt规模以上的生产企业。

4. 淀粉基塑料环保性能

淀粉基塑料，如果是淀粉和传统塑料如聚乙烯、聚苯乙烯等塑料共混，制得的塑料制品其降解性能达不到目前国家标准规定的生物分解性能要求；而与其他可生物分解聚合物共混加工，制得的制品一般都是可以生物分解的。

从防治环境污染角度，淀粉共混了生物分解树脂制得的制品可以完全降解，最终分解为二氧化碳和水，从而使得一次性包装制品或者垃圾袋可以与有机垃圾一起堆肥化处理，也可以在自然环境中生物分解，不仅方便了垃圾处理，而且部分地解决了白色污染问题。另外，在焚烧处理时，添加了淀粉后的塑料制品其释放的二氧化碳等温室气体要比普通塑料少得多，是名副其实的低碳产品。

从节约石化资源角度，由于淀粉是可再生的生物质资源，所以淀粉基塑料很大程度地节约了石化资源，在石油储备和替代竞赛的当今世界，具有极重要战略意义。

5. 淀粉基塑料存在问题

添加淀粉后，增加了塑料成型加工工艺的复杂性，淀粉改性及其与塑料共混技术领域还有很多问题没有得到较好的解决。尽管淀粉本身价格很低，但共混加工时，需要通过复杂的化学改性和物理改性等方法的综合运用以实现最终产品的性能满足日常需求。繁杂过程导致成本增加，使得最终制品的价格仍不利于商业应用推广。因此，如何继续降低产品的价格，仍是重点研究的课题，也是是否能够大规模推广的关键。

其次，淀粉基塑料制品普遍程度上比不添加淀粉的塑料制品的性能要差，例如耐水性能、物理力学性能等。到目前为止，产业化生产淀粉基塑料的生产设备、配方等均需进一步深入研究，水平有待进一步的提高。

再次，淀粉基塑料的环保意义需要进一步得到正确的宣传，淀粉基塑料意义首先是其生物基概念，即其原料应用了或部分地使用了生物质资源，从而节约了石油资源；其次是和其他可生物分解的树脂或天然高分子共混时，可以完全降解，也只有在这种情况下，最终的制品可以生物分解，起到治理白色污染的作用。而当淀粉和非生物分解的传统塑料共混时，最终制品是不能完全降解。因此，如何在适当场合、正确地运用淀粉基塑料的“生物基”和“降解”的概念，显得非常重要。

另外，目前多数生产企业的淀粉仍是玉米淀粉，为避免与人争粮，应研究如何采用非粮食类淀粉如木薯淀粉作为原料。今后还应在如何采用环境友好的、绿色的化学改性过程、减少改性步骤和反应时间等淀粉化学改性方式与方法上取得突破，使得生产可以可持续发展。

最后，还应该加强知识产权的保护。国外一些企业已经申请了许多有关淀粉基塑料的专利，国内企业应该在加强技术研发同时，注意专利申请等知识产权保护的工作。

四、产业发展面临的主要问题

(一) 成本仍偏高，投资跟不上，造成后面市场被垄断风险

到目前为止，尚无法达到规模性成本效益和市场推广力度，形成产品成本过高，在国内推广较难，主要从国外寻求出路进行销售。由于产品成本高，产品销量增加相对缓慢，投资者很难下决心来扩大原料生产规模，如浙江海正5kt规模生产线目前销售已经超过过半，而且国际市场需求也远远超过100kt(美国NatureWorks公司已和泰国化学公司合作，开始建设另一条100kt生产线)，但因为考虑到投资风险，到目前仍没有投产30kt规模生产线。由于错过前期最佳规模放大时机，从而面临市场和价格被前面规模企业垄断的风险。

(二)合成技术、成型加工机械及配套设施有待提高

首先是生物基材料的性能还无法完全满足各种消费者需求。尽管目前市场上已有众多品种，但每种材料本身的机械和加工性能只是某一方面有突出的特性，综合性能还存在这样或那样的不足，这一点将是制约其市场应用推广的瓶颈之一；其二是目前国内从事制品加工研究的力量尚显薄弱，大部分企业将关注的重点集中在材料合成上，而忽略了制品加工开发，一些制品在耐热、耐水及机械强度方面与传统塑料制品相差较远，而这一点恰恰是生物基材料能否大规模市场化的关键。

(三)缺乏应用推广方面政策支持

虽然我国有面上鼓励政策，但是没有具体推动材料发展的具体细则出台，也没有专门有关强制推进某一领域发展的政策措施。在进出口方面，除聚乳酸原料，其他原料和制品均没有单独的税则编号，这就很难对这类优先发展材料给予相关政策进行鼓励出口或进口。

(四)盲目上线苗头开始出现

由于生物基材料目前行业正处快速发展阶段，许多风险投资公司或一些大的公司，纷纷介入到这个行业中，引起了一股投资热。许多投资公司在前期均会深入调研和论证，但也不乏一些投资公司和魄力大的企业家可能因看好前景而忽视了实际操作细节，从而对一些品种产品重复建设或者盲目迅速上线。最终使行业在尚未进入产供销良性循环过程，却已经投入了过于庞大的前期资金，最终使得行业处于不健康发展。

(五)人才缺乏

随着近几年的市场逐渐起色，一些公司纷纷扩大规模，于是人才紧缺的问题开始凸现。人才缺乏也已经成为抑制行业发展的另外一个瓶颈了。

五、2013年产业发展的基本趋势

(一) 市场需求仍具旺盛态势

虽然存在一定困难，但整个生物基材料产业开始显现出快速发展态势。2012年，生物基材料预计将继续增加，随着欧美发达国家有关环保政策出台，出口也将成倍增加。淀粉基塑料将继续供不应求，聚乳酸原料市场需求将成倍增加。木塑产品的产量将成倍增加。

(二) 工艺技术进步，装备水平不断提高，原料生产规模被迫迅速增加

材料合成与工艺技术进步，装备水平不断提高，原料生产规模被迫迅速增加。由于市场需求增加，目前万吨级新生产线正在江苏建设，预计聚乳酸的产能在年底有所增加；二元酸和二元醇共聚酯的产能已超过70kt，另有一条25kt生产线正在建设；二氧化碳共聚物的产能已达到40kt。

(三) 降解地膜逐渐得到国家重视

农业覆盖膜主要包括指棚膜、地膜、畜牧养殖用膜等，在农业增产增收中发挥着不可替代的巨大作用。自20世纪80年代以来，农膜覆盖栽培技术在我国得到了大力推广，目前我国地膜覆盖面积在3.0亿亩以上，用量在1000kt以上。但是随着地膜广泛使用，其残留地膜对土壤的污染问题也逐渐显现。残留地膜污染问题，引起了国家有关部门的重视，如何加强地膜回收及在利用，如何合理推广降解地膜使用，已成为当今热点。

但是由于地膜使用情况的复杂性，加上成本因

素等，建议生产企业在确保产品性能与质量的前提下，加强研发，降低成本，缩小与常规普膜价格的差距，提高农户应用生物可降解地膜的积极性。

由于不同品种、不同规格的生物降解地膜在农作物上的应用差异性和生态适应性不同，需要经过严谨的试验示范、筛选、扩大推广等循序渐进的科学评价利用程序。科学筛选出适宜不同作物和不同生态区域的最佳性能质量、最好增产效果、最佳降解效果的生物可降解地膜。通过连续科学试验和客观评价，筛选出适应性较广、降解速度与作物生育进程相对吻合、增产潜力相对较大、各地表现一致的生物降解膜，并逐步扩大示范面积。

（四）多个城市垃圾分类逐渐推进将推动降解垃圾袋的使用。随着广州、南京、北京等发达城市垃圾分类措施的逐步落实，像余姚等中小城市的垃圾袋招标文书中规定政府采购有机垃圾袋要采用生物降解垃圾袋。目前全国垃圾袋总需求量在300kt以上。

六、政策措施建议

（一）加大专项资金支持力度

确立一批重点支持生产企业，对重点企业的生产和销售实施资金补贴，以解决前期阶段成本较高的问题。

对一些重点项目，以产业化专项资金的方式进行资助。

建立知识产权培育基金。扶持专利发展，鼓励生产企业在国内外申请专利等。

（二）加大推广应用方面政策

可以强制推进一些生物基材料制作一次性包装，如酒店客房用易耗品、民航飞机上使用制品、购物袋、有机生活垃圾袋等。

（三）税收政策

在税收政策上对生物降解塑料进行调整。

1. 调整出口退税和关税率

我国目前尚没有对生物降解塑料给予产品海关编号，从而造成生物降解塑料进出口中没有对应的类别，只能填写其他类。因此设立单独的海关编码，将生物塑料的出口退税率调整至15%或更高；在3年内零关税。

2. 所得税和增值税

为鼓励和扶持一些企业的发展，可以按照新的企业所得税条例规定减免优惠政策如：一是民族区域自治地方的企业需要照顾和鼓励的，经省级人民政府批准，可以实行定期减免和免税；二是法律、行政法规和国务院有关规定给予减税免税的企业依照规定执行。重点支持的生物降解塑料高新技术企业自投产年度起免征所得税五年，五年后所得税调整至10%；企业利用废气、废水、废渣等废弃物为主要原料进行生产的，可在五年内减征或免征所得税等。

3. 争取将生物基材料作为碳交易的一部分。

4. 完善标识体系，能让普通消费者通俗易懂，易于识别，从而加快推广的速度。

（中国塑料加工工业协会降解塑料专业委员会　翁云宣）

氟塑料加工

【行业现状】

中国氟塑料加工行业在经历了10年的高速发展后，进入了前所未有的转型期。十二五期间，国家调整和优化产业结构，重点发展战略新兴产业，给氟塑料制品业的发展带来了机遇与挑战。2012年，尽管放缓了发展的步伐，但整个行业还是呈现常态化平稳增长的趋势。

中国现拥有七家国内和三家外资氟树脂生产企业，PTFE树脂的生产能力超过80kt/a。2012年国内生产PTFE树脂64kt。目前，中国PTFE原料的基本性能已接近国外先进企业大宗产品的指标，完全可以满足一般工业产品的要求。但对电性能有较高要求的制品，仍需使用国外优质原料。

中国现有氟塑料加工企业1500家左右，以中小企业为主。2012年中国国内PTFE树脂消耗量47kt，部分制品企业PTFE的树脂消耗量超过千吨。2012年聚四氟乙烯制品的构成如图1所示。

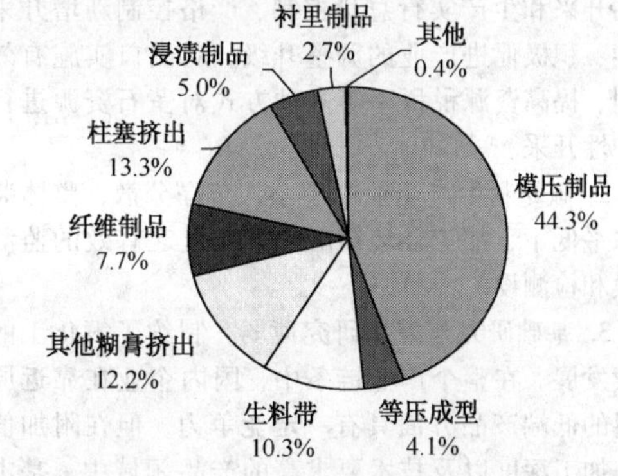

图1　2012年聚四氟乙烯制品构成

根据进出口数据统计，2012年聚四氟乙烯树脂、可熔性氟塑料和聚四氟乙烯制品进口量比上年都大幅下跌，而聚四氟乙烯制品出口量比上年明显上涨。截止到2012年12月底，聚四氟乙烯树脂进口量

4206t，同比下降25.70%，进口平均价格同比上涨2.62%；出口量20923t，同比下降7.48%，出口平均价格同比下降22.08%。可熔性氟聚合物进口量8411t，同比下降4.37%，进口平均价格同比上涨4.86%；出口量8194t，同比上涨1.78%，出口平均价格同比下降4.82%。聚四氟乙烯制品进口量4586t，同比下降47.46%，进口平均价格同比上涨8.57%；出口量18283吨，同比上涨45.07%，出口平均价格同比下降15.62%。聚四氟乙烯制品进口单价是出口单价的2.6倍，说明我国出口的聚四氟乙烯制品仍然是以中低端产品为主，出口产品结构急需调整。分析原因，进口量大幅下降和制品出口量大幅上涨，与国产原材料供应的变化和市场需求密切相关。一方面，2011年上半年国产原材料严重短缺，价格暴涨，对进口原料的需求自然增长，原料与制品出口量受原料供应的制约自然就会减少，2012年以来，国产原料价格持续下跌，对进口的需求必然减少；另一方面，2012年太阳能、电子和机械行业市场情况不是很乐观，高端产品需求降低，对进口的需求也会相应减少。综上所述，2012年原材料进出口市场的变化仅能分析为恢复正常水平。具体数据见表1、表2：

表1　2012年1~12月氟塑料进口量及与上年比较表

产　　品	进口总量/t	累计比同期/%	进口总金额/美元	进口平均价格/(美元/t)	累计比同期/%
初级形状的聚四氟乙烯	4206	-25.70	66841718	15892	2.62
其他初级形状的氟聚合物	8411	-4.37	185417726	22045	4.86
聚四氟乙烯制非泡沫板、片、膜、箔及扁条	4586	-47.46	128926591	28113	8.57

表2　2012年1~12月氟塑料出口量及与上年比较表

产　　品	出口总量/t	累计比同期/%	出口总金额/美元	出口平均价格/(美元/t)	累计比同期/%
初级形状的聚四氟乙烯	20923	-7.48	243984177	11661	-22.08
其他初级形状的氟聚合物	8194	1.78	129760182	15836	-4.82
聚四氟乙烯制非泡沫板、片、膜、箔及扁条	18283	45.07	193279498	10571	-15.62

【存在问题】

1. 萤石是氟化工的基础原料，作为不可再生资源被无序开采和浪费，这一问题已引起国家重视。从1999年起，国家将萤石作为战略资源进行保护。2010年仍有保护萤石开发政策出台，提出对萤石资源的开采和生产实行总量控制、严格控制新增开采产能、积极促进产业的调整升级、对出口实施有效控制、提高资源税税率等多种方式对萤石资源进行保护性开采。

2. 氟塑料生产企业规模小，布局分散，整体装备水平低下，加工环境简陋，企业缺乏有效的监测手段和检测设备。

3. 基础研究与应用研究薄弱，制约了氟化工的后续发展。在整个产业链条中，国内企业在靠近原材料的低端产品方面具有一定竞争力，但在附加值高、加工深度以及技术要求高的产品领域中，基本上被国外企业占据。很多企业技术投入不足，专业技术人员缺乏。因此在高端产品方面，国内企业只在少数产品上实现了工业化生产。

4. 区域发展不平衡，企业两级分化。销售利润过低，利润中没有后续的开发基金。产品有以次充好现象，再生原料使用无法可依。

【专委会活动】

1. 开展标准化工作

(1)《聚全氟乙丙烯薄膜》行业标准已获批准

2012年3月30日，全国塑料制品标准化技术委员会在北京主持召开了《聚全氟乙丙烯薄膜》行业标准审查会。会议对标准起草工作给予充分肯定，会议认为标准的编制原则和主要内容制定的依据技术先进、合理可行；主要验证项目和数据能指导标准制定；本标准与现行法律、法规和强制性标准无抵触并且协调一致；标准制定过程中无重大分歧意见。

根据中华人民共和国工业和信息化部2012年第70号文件公告，《聚全氟乙丙烯(FEP)薄膜》行业标准已批准公布，标准编号为QB/T 4398—2012，实施日期为2013年6月1日。

(2) 氟塑料的4项行业标准计划已批准制定

2012年通过申报、答辩，《聚全氟乙丙烯管材》(项目编号2012—1208T—QB)、《聚四氟乙烯薄膜》(2012—1209T—QB)、《聚四氟乙烯管材》(2012—1210T—QB)和《聚四氟乙烯双向拉伸薄膜》(2012—1211T—QB)4项行业标准计划已于6月批准制定，4

项行标的主要起草单位分别为北京市塑料研究所、上海市塑料研究所和上海市凌桥环保设备厂有限公司担任。

2. 开展行业先进评选工作

为了总结和交流氟塑料加工企业在发展过程中的典型经验，推动我国氟塑料加工行业可持续发展，提升专委会的凝聚力和企业核心竞争力，氟塑料专委会在会员单位中开展了“中国氟塑料先进企业和先进个人”的评选活动。

经企业自行申报，根据2012年7月19日召开的“先进企业专家评审会”评审意见，经四届十二次常务理事会审议，评选出了中国氟塑料行业先进企业和先进个人。

3. 换届选举筹备工作

为配合换届需要，专委会组织全体会员单位进行了重新登记审核工作，并备案至上级协会。为增加专委会领导层的决策能力，在第五届领导班子中增设副主任，在原理事单位中进行了副主任的提名工作。为适应行业发展新形势，优化专家成员的专业结构，进行了新一届专家需重新推荐选举工作。

4. 编辑出版专委会成立20周年纪念专刊

为庆祝中国塑协氟塑料加工专业委员会成立20周年，专委会印制了20周年纪念专刊。反映了氟塑料专委会发展历程，以及氟塑料行业的发展变化。宣传表彰了为行业发展做出杰出贡献的企业和个人，有力的提升氟塑料专委会在行业中的影响力和凝聚力。

5. 召开常务理事会

(1) 召开四届十一次常务理事会

“中国塑协氟塑料加工专业委员会第四届十一次常务理事会”于2012年4月17日在浙江省嘉善县举行，北京市塑料研究所等十余家常务理事单位的代表参加了会议，会议讨论了有关专委会换届和专委会成立20周年庆典的筹备工作。

(2) 召开四届十二次常务理事会

中国塑协氟塑料专委会第四届十二次常务理事会于2012年8月15日在北京达园宾馆召开。北京市塑料研究所等12家常务理事单位参加了会议。国家工业和信息化部规划司王建忠处长出席会议。会议审议了中国塑协氟塑料加工专业委员会工作条例和工作细则初稿，形成讨论稿提交四届十次理事会讨论；初步拟定了新一届理事单位提名单；审议通过了中国塑协氟塑料加工专业委员会第五届理事会领导机构选举程序；讨论通过了第五届理事会将组建中国氟塑料行业专家组，新一届专家需重新推荐选举产生，确定了专家的评选标准；审议了2012年7月19日召开的专家评审会意见，通过2008~2012年中国氟塑料行业先进企业和先进个人评选名单。

6. 召开常委会

(1) 召开四届十次理事会

中国塑协氟塑料加工专业委员会第四届十次理事会于2012年11月5日在北京举行。北京市塑料研究所等50家理事单位和11家会员单位参加了会议。国家工业和信息化部规划司王建忠处长和中国塑料加工工业协会许琳副秘书长出席了会议。会议听取并审议了陈生秘书长作的2012年专委会工作报告和和下一步工作建议；讨论并修改了中国塑协氟塑料加工专业委员会工作条例和工作细则，提交第五届会员代表大会审议；根据第四届十二次常务理事会决议产生的提名单，选举产生了第五届常委会委员候选名单。

(2) 召开五届一次常委会

中国塑协氟塑料加工专业委员会第五届一次常委会于2012年11月6日在北京举行。国家工业和信息化部规划司王建忠处长和中国塑料加工工业协会许琳副秘书长出席了会议。常委会由许琳副秘书长主持。会上选举产生了主任、副主任和秘书长以及专家组成员。北京市塑料研究所当选为本届主任单位，庄甦当选为本届主任，上海上化氟材料有限公司等15家单位当选为副主任单位，陈生当选为本届秘书长，许琳当选为本届副秘书长，王建忠、王倩等42位同志被聘任为本届常委会专家组成员。

7. 举办“氟塑料专委会成立二十周年庆典活动”

“中国塑协氟塑料加工专业委员会成立二十周年庆典”于2012年11月6日上午在北京隆重举行。中国轻工业联合会陶小年副会长、国家工业和信息化部规划司王建忠处长、国家工业和信息化部中小企业司胡阳辉处长、中国塑料加工工业协会许琳副秘书长、中国轻工业联合会综合业务部李英处长、氟塑料专委会第一、二届秘书长李明武等领导出席本次庆典活动。氟塑料专委会的近二百余名代表以及部分特邀嘉宾欢聚一堂，共庆中国塑协氟塑料加工专业委员会成立二十周年。

陶小年副会长、王建忠处长、许琳副秘书长和庄甦理事长在大会上致辞，李英处长宣读了原中国轻工总会军工办公室主任、氟塑料专委会名誉理事长王桂芬的贺信，还有部分会员单位代表发表了讲话。会上进行了先进企业和先进个人的表彰活动。

8. 召开“氟塑料专委会第五届会员代表大会”

中国塑协氟塑料加工专业委员会第五届会员代表大会于2012年11月6日下午在北京举行。国家工业和信息化部规划司王建忠处长、国家工业和信息化部中小企业司胡阳辉处长、中国塑料加工工业协会许琳副秘书长以及专委会100余家会员单位的近200名代表出席了会议。

会上审议通过了专委会第四届理事会工作报告和财务报告、第五届常委会工作条例、工作细则和第五届常委会选举办法。选举产生了"中国塑协氟塑料专委会第五届常委会"，北京市塑料研究所等65家会员单位当选为专委会第五届常委会委员。

与会代表听取了国家工业和信息化部中小企业司政策处胡阳辉处长关于《促进中小企业发展的主要政策》的报告和国家氟材料工程技术研究中心王树华主任关于《2015年中国氟树脂展望》技术报告。

【发展建议】

1. 加快产业结构调整，促进行业可持续发展

加强企业管理，建立现代化管理模式。调整产业结构，鼓励规模企业的发展，促进行业内企业重组联合，打造行业航母企业，逐步形成规模企业和区域集群相结合发展效应。

2. 提高科技创新能力

着力提升企业自主创新能力，加强企业技术改造，实施质量和品牌战略。加快开发和推广应用低碳技术、清洁生产技术、节能减排技术和循环经济技术，促进优化升级。

3. 加快行业相关标准的制修订工作

借助于行业协会的力量，联合相关企业，尽快建立我国氟塑料制品的标准体系，应首先完成涉及企业较多的制品标准。

（中国塑料加工工业协会氟塑料加工专业委员会　庄甦　吕方　陈生）

多功能母料

"十二五"我国塑料母料行业发展新趋势

一、后金融危机下的全球形势

2012年，不断恶化的欧债危机对全球经济产生重大冲击和重创，各国经济实体和各项重要经济指标迅速下滑，经济危机给全球各国带来了异常严峻的挑战。货币升值以及环境、卫生、安全、标准、资源、反倾销、国际贸易壁垒等瓶颈问题限制，中国经济经过30年的高速增长后，在2012年遭遇了严重超出预期的外需疲弱形势，国内房地产调控及其他关联影响和内外交困的共同作用下，使2012年以来中国经济增长率加速下滑、PMI持续走软，进出口贸易增速更是显著放缓。前三个季度，GDP增速逐季回落，分别为8.1%、7.6%和7.4%，也创下2008年金融危机后的最低增速。

2013年，全球经济仍将处于深度结构调整之中，经济增长动力不足，但有利因素正在逐渐增多，预计比2012年有所改善。从2012年第4季度开始逐渐出现向好的趋势，原因：一是生产状况开始好转；二是货币投放开始加快；三是人民币贬值压力开始缓解；四是出口好转有望延续。同时世界高端制造业发展也比较迅猛，以能源为原料的产业和新兴的智能工业成为引领经济加快复苏的新增长点。美国和德国等欧盟成员国都正在加速推进"再工业化"战略，试图强化经济增长的动力，欲通过促进产业资本回流重组全球产业链，因此预计美国和欧盟经济将延续温和复苏的势头。

二、"十二五"母料行业发展新机遇

2012年是"十二五"规划的第二年，也是国家进入投资项目集中建设阶段重点投入的一年，政府加快了投资项目的审批，新开工项目计划总投资197119亿元，同比增长24.9%，国家对重点在建及续建项目投资以及"十二五"规划重大项目开工给予信贷以及财政配套等方面积极支持，在重大规划项目建设投入的带动下，将在一定程度上带动投资及经济保持较快增长，也将形成各行各业一个巨大的市场发展前景。

2013年我国中央领导新旧班子的成功交接，标志着我国进入一个新的历史发展时期。在习近平主席为首的党中央领导下，提出了坚持走科学发展观之路，深化改革带动科技创新，加快转型升级，淘汰落后产能，坚持绿色环保，安全，低碳，富国强军等一系列国策，在新的发展形势下，必将掀起一场工业革命和经济革命，各行各业将形成一个巨大的市场需求，随着国家重大投资项目集中建设的投入，将迎来一个巨大的市场发展前景和空间，"十二五"发展期间母料行业也将迎来一个历史发展的新时期和新机遇。

三、塑料及母料行业的发展前景

（1）塑料及母料行业发展前景

21世纪，我国合成树脂行业进入高速发展期，中国成为世界合成树脂生产和消费大国。2011年我国合成树脂产能达到55Mt，产量达到48Mt，表观消费量达到74056kt，更为重要的是，合成树脂产业作为新材料产业的重要组成部分，肩负着石油和化学工业结构调整和战略性新兴产业材料支撑的双重重任，化工新材料已被国家认定为"十二五"期间重点支持的支柱产业，地位和作用将越来越重要，随着塑料产业和新材料产业的巨幅增长，母料行业在塑

料及新材料行业的应用范围将会越来越广，发展空间和市场潜力巨大。

国家已明确认定：

国家重点支持的化工新材料种类：

1. 有机硅材料

2. 有机氟材料

3. 工程塑料及塑料合金

4. 高性能纤维及复合材料

5. 纳米材料

6. 功能高分子材料及功能膜

7. 特种合成橡胶

发展新材料的意义：

1. 新材料是带动传统产业升级的革命性力量

2. 新材料是事关国家安全的战略性新兴产业

3. 新材料具有广阔的市场前景

4. 新材料产业是“创新驱动”的重要体现

新材料发展现状：

我国新材料研发和应用发端于国防科工领域，在国民经济各领域的应用不断扩大，2010 年我国新材料产业规模超过 6500 亿元，“十一五”年均增长约 20%。化工新材料主要应用于去汽车、建筑、电子、电器、通讯 IT、航天航空等行业，我国是全球最大的汽车生产国，电子电器的生产国和出口国，也是全世界最大的建筑市场，发展化工新材料具有突出的市场优势。

中国塑料市场竞争优势

1. 稳定的经济与政策环境；

2. 全球金砖国家最高的 GDP 增长速度；

3. 优异的基础设施条件；

4. 快捷决策能力与巨大购买力；

5. 占据全球塑料工业约 1/4 的表观消费量；

6. 未来较长时间将持续保持全球塑料市场最高年增长量；

7. 从树脂、设备、加工、应用最全面的供应、加工与消化能力。

（2）多功能母料优异的竞争优势

塑料工业水平是反映国力强弱的重要因素之一，推动塑料工业快速优质发展，将是我国化工现代化进程的重要内容。随着塑料工业的高速发展，塑料以塑代钢、以塑代木、以塑代藤、以塑代石等应用范围越来越广，塑料所应用的广泛领域涉及各行各业，用量非常巨大，而母料行业由原来单一的色母料着色已逐步向满足各种塑料制品不同功能的要求转变，母料功能化是母料行业在“十二五”发展期间的大势所趋，各类高技术含量和高附加值的多功能母料发展速度迅猛，已成为取代部分改性塑料的最佳替代品。以多功能母料生产出的高性能、多功能、环保、节能等高技术含量和高附加值的各类塑料制品，广泛应用于民用、医用、工业、农业、汽车、包装、建材、机械、纺织、交通、航天、航空、国防科技等诸多领域，具有广阔的市场前景和巨大的发展空间。

四、母料行业发展新趋势

在新的历史发展时期，母料行业各企业将面临很多挑战和机遇：普遍存在劳动力等生产制造和经营等成本不断上升，原材料持续涨价，通胀威胁、货币升值以及环境、卫生安全、资源、反倾销、国际贸易壁垒等瓶颈限制，大部分企业缺乏高端核心技术、自主知识产权和自主品牌，再加上剧烈的市场竞争，全球各国标准化的实施，造成了种种难以回避的发展问题，因此母料行业各企业当务之急的是：提升科技创新能力，推动绿色环保，安全低碳，转型和产业升级，并加强上下游产业链互动，实现共赢。

1. 剧烈的市场竞争

国际市场上的竞争，早已经是建立在非价格优势基础上的价格竞争。这种竞争，主要是针对满足消费者在产品质量、品种、品牌、技术水平、售后服务、企业形象、个人感受等差异化的消费需求，而进行定价的价格竞争。非价格竞争优势主要体现在产品差异化，主要体现在产品的技术创新、质量内涵、服务内容、分销渠道、培养消费群体等方面。实施产品差异化的目的，是通过扩大产品的非价格方面的特征，来拉大与竞争对手产品的距离，从而增加产品优势。这种策略有助于开拓市场、树立品牌形象、持续发挥竞争优势。

市场的供求关系不断变化，产能过剩带来相互倾轧，市场无序的恶性竞争，“错误投资”、“重复建设”和“低技术水平运作”等，使原本已经白热化的市场竞争变得更加激烈。企业目前存在的诸多问题包括缺乏核心技术和自主知识产权，企业发展面临着“中等收入陷阱”——当劳动力成本不断上升的同时，企业发展却没有本质性的突破；从而造成劳动生产率和盈利能力的下降。加上原来劳动力成本不断攀升的情况下，人们期待值过高，甚至超过了企业发展速度，造成企业发展中存在的种种问题，应迅速引起各企业的重视和共识，不断预防、改善和提升，才能确保企业持续性高速发展。

2. 科技创新

目前的科技创新范围广泛，它涵盖了自主知识产权、配方研发、技术改造与提升、新材料应用、营销模式、管理模式等全方位各层面的创新。如果我们不能真正建立起自己科技创新的完善体系，危机的阴影就有可能与我们的经济如影随形。其结果，可能最终导致低端制造和高端制造优势的双重流失。这将是我国母料行业未来发展最大的隐患！

把自主创新作为产业发展的战略基点和结构调整的主要支撑，大力提高原始创新能力、集成创新能力和引进消化吸收再创新能力。充分发挥科技是第一生产力和人才是第一资源的作用，以产业创新推动科技创新、以科技创新支撑产业创新。在全行业推动创新技术领先、创新载体优良、创新人才富集、创新体系健全的企业创新思维。

营销创新。因为营销创新的核心是要赢得消费者的信赖，只有赢得消费者信赖的产品才是有市场的产品，只有满足消费者需要的技术创新才是能够得到价值回报的创新。市场营销的创新，是推动和促进技术创新与产品创新的根本力量。

母料企业要关注新材料技术发展和应用市场变化，及时调整产品结构，顺应市场，满足客户需求。发挥先进技术，特别是拥有自主知识产权的技术优势，促进科研成果的转化与产品的升级，增强企业综合核心竞争能力。我们推崇办好企业的六字要素：势准、道正、术精。

3. 母料行业的转型与产业升级

自“十二五”以来，中国的发展模式已由投机性向投资性转变，原来倾向于投机性的泡沫经济已逐渐向投资性的实体经济发展，产业结构调整是我国目前重点改变的发展模式之一，把增长模式从出口和房地产相关投资主导型，转变为由消费为核心的内需主导型，内需的发展将会为塑料及母料行业的需求量带来大幅增长，在母料产业发展过程中，其中最突出的特点是：效率与成本已经成为制造业竞争的核心。在现在转型中，提高效率比成本控制更加重要！这次的结构调整和产业升级主要是建立在淘汰落后产能、提高效率的基础上进行的，核心内容就是：科学改革与创新、转型与产业升级。

母料行业普遍存在“量有余而质不足”的缺陷。国内企业多而不大，大而不强，缺乏核心竞争力，特别在经营理念上缺乏战略意识，销售策略上缺乏理论指导，产品技术含量不高，自主品牌缺失、结构失衡、行业集中度差，开工率低、盈利水平差，市场面临着价格竞争。因此，在这次产业结构调整的大形势下，迫切要求母料行业各企业必须进行产业升级，竞争中寻求发展，制定一个适合自身实力和环境要求的发展战略，并有效地加以实施，是企业保持竞争优势的关键。

母料行业的发展应坚持解决当前问题与着眼长远发展相结合，标本兼治，坚持低碳经济、清洁生产、绿色发展的概念，发挥科技引领和支撑作用，加快转变增长方式，促进产业升级。以市场需求为导向，注重结构、质量和效益，提高中高档产品比重，促进产品升级换代。提高高端产品自给率以满足国民经济发展需求。加大引进技术的消化吸收力度，推动产业技术进步；强化技术改造，促进产业技术的系统化和集成化；增强自主创新对产业发展的支撑能力，加快转型和产业升级。

塑料母料行业应密切配合各行业塑料制品的升级换代，加强以新技术、新工艺、新材料、功能化、标准化、轻量化、专用化、环保、节能、安全、低碳、高性能、低成本等综合核心技术优势，与各行业的塑料制品企业共同转型、创新和产业升级。

4. 标准化——不可回避的发展趋势

历史已进入标准化发展时期，全球环保指令及安全标准等法律法规已深入到全球各国市场各领域，很多企业产品由于不达标而影响出口，甚至被巨额罚款屡见不鲜，在国内市场的销售也受到严重影响，使企业发展受阻，因此各企业、行业、国家乃至全球各国纷纷制定各种不同层面的相关标准，规范产业的正常有序运作和发展，如企业的产品质量保证体系标准、环境体系标准、安全标准、企业标准、行业标准、国家标准、国际标准等现已逐渐普及化，有些标准甚至是强制性执行，在新的历史发展时期，我们应深刻认识到从产品质量层面、制造及管理层面，经济贸易等层面，各种标准无处不在，对每个企业，上下游产业各企业，最终产品不达标将会影响整个产业链的发展，可谓一荣俱荣，一辱俱辱。因此，企业要生存和发展，必须做好各方面的工作，顺应经济全球化的要求，适应标准化的时代潮，广泛学习标准、认识标准、制定标准、掌握标准、善用标准，标准化已成为企业高速发展的一种能源和新动力，“标准化”是“十二五”期间母料行业发展的大势所趋。

5. 绿色科技

全球各国对绿色环保、安全低碳的产业发展，在国际社会已经提高到一个非常明确和实质性的议题，达标企业将受到市场青睐并得到高速发展，不达标企业将会发展缓慢，减产被罚，官司不断，最终被市场淘汰，因此塑料母料行业各企业应崇尚绿色科技，关爱自然，我们深知维系一个美好的生态环境，需要我们全球人类共同努力，环保节能，安全低碳，是我们全球人类愉快生活，愉快工作的基本保证，我们推崇“当代人类创造财富自享并传给下一代的同时，还应保留更美好的生态环境和资源传给下一代”，我们秉承“企业、人、环境和美共同发展”的环保理念，力争创造科技、环境与产业完美的融合。

6. 上下游产业链互动共赢

抓源头环节和源头材料是达标的关键：使用符合国际环保指令及安全标准要求的高性能功能性助剂和着色剂等源头材料，是各种母料实现功能化和达标的关键，将卫生安全控制融入到上下游产业链中各环节，从源头开始对产品各生产环节进行控制，从配方设计开始，严格控制源头材料的选材、符合环保、卫生安全、添加使用量等相关标准，如何从源头材料上控制接触物不被意外或故意污染，从根本上规范产品生产，减少安全问题的发生，对产品的预防、监控、问题及时寻根等三方面问题予以重视，加快安全问题的分析和解决，可以在生产过程中的各环节精确地有效控制质量事故的发生，建立完善可控的质保体系。

加强上下游产业链沟通和协作，努力改善现存实质性问题，生产出更多符合全球环保指令和安全标准的优质助剂，确保塑料母料产品符合相关质量标准，才能满足各行业塑料制品符合全球环保指令和安全标准要求，是保持上下游产业保持高速发展的关键。通过加强上下游产业链互动交流，最终提升整体的综合核心竞争能力，2013 年是一个充满生机之年，市场需求前景美好，发展空间潜力巨大，母料行业及上下游产业链各企业同仁共同携手、共享商机、共创繁荣、共赢共发展。

五、结论

2013 年受后经济危机的深远影响下，欧美各国经济逐渐复苏，再加上“十二五”发展期间国家的重点项目投入等有利因素不断增加的大形势下，我国塑料和母料行业市场，必将带来新的挑战与机遇，我国进入了新一轮的高速发展历史时期，母料行业各企业应乘势而上，把握机遇，在新形势下加强自身科技创新能力、转型和产业升级，向功能化、标准化、轻量化、环保、节能、安全、低碳、高性能、低成本等高端核心技术发展，努力发展拥有自主知识产权和高端技术产品，加强上下游产业链互动，以高技术含量、高附加值的高端技术产品支撑塑料及新材料行业的可持续性高速发展，塑料及母料行业市场需求潜力巨大，发展前景无限广阔。

（中国塑料加工工业协会多功能母料专业委员会　罗崇远）

工程塑料

塑料是电子信息、交通运输、航空航天、机械制造业的上游产业，在国民经济中占据着重要的地位，塑料表观消费量的增长与 GDP 增长的弹性系数为(1.1～1.5)：1。其发展不仅对国家支柱产业和现代高新技术产业起着支撑的作用，同时也推动传统产业改造和产品结构的调整。近年来，随着我国制造业的快速发展，塑料的应用领域日趋广泛，用量不断增加，特别是加入 WTO 以后，为塑料行业带来了前所未有的发展机遇。近年来，中国工程塑料工业虽然一直在快速发展，生产能力不断提高，品种也在增加，但仍然满足不了市场需求，大部分中高档产品仍然采用进口原料。

工程塑料市场的特点，大致有如下几个方面：

1. 在汽车领域的应用目前社会正朝着注重环保、安全、健康的方向发展，节能与环保成为了汽车工业的两大课题。轻量化、舒适化、节能化是汽车发展的最新趋势，这一趋势加速了汽车塑料化的进程。塑料以其重量轻、设计空间大、制造成本低、性能优异、功能广泛，最终能使汽车在轻量化、安全性和制造成本几方面获得更多的突破，从而成为了 21 世纪汽车工业最好的选择。国家发改委已制定相关政策，加速汽车零部件的国产化进程，同时也限定了汽车的燃油消耗标准，加之由于去年的原材料涨价，许多整车厂为了降低成本已放开了指定材料的限制。这无疑给零配件生产厂商和塑料供应商提供了一个绝好的发展机遇。国内汽车零部件的加工水平正在迅速提高，新的加工设备、加工工艺被大量的采用，从而使工程塑料的应用水平和用量得以不断的提升。今后工程塑料行业不再只是单纯迎合汽车工业的发展，而是作为参与者要在汽车工业发展中发挥更重要的作用。

2. 在电子电气领域的应用电子电气例来是工程塑料的主要应用领域，其消耗量占到总用量的 40% 以上，随着中国电器产品出口量的逐年增加，工程塑料的用量呈上涨趋势。中国是世界制造业大国，尽管中国产品的技术含量和附加值都还很低，但这并不影响中国制造业对工程塑料的巨大需求，特别是迫于成本压力，市场对材料本土化的要求越来越明显，这为工程塑料提供了广阔的应用前景。

3. 市场竞争更加白热化和国际化。到目前为止，几乎所有国际上的大牌公司都在国内建立了改性工厂和树脂厂，大量跨国公司登陆使市场竞争进一步加剧。由于看好中国国内巨大的市场需求，外国公司近来纷纷加强在中国进行本土化开发并不断扩大生产规模。这些举措都是跨国公司以强化市场地位、优化资源配置为目的的国际化运营。因此国内工程塑料行业面临的是日益激烈的国际化竞争，这就迫使国内生产厂要整合资源，不断提升产品技术含量，加强服务意识与市场开发力度，增加研发力量的投入，避免由于低水平的重复投入与低价无序竞争造成的有限资源的极大浪费。

4. 用量增加，但盈利水平有限近年来，中国工程塑料市场需求火爆而企业利润微薄，能源和原材料涨价幅度大大超过了工业品出厂价格指数，影响了大部分加工工业的盈利能力。加之部分下游行业回款形势不好，使企业产成品资金占用增长幅度过大。2012 年中国工程塑料消耗量同比增长低于前几年的增长幅度，主要原因在于原材料涨价。许多加工企业被迫减少了低利润的定单，同时也使用了部分再生料。尼龙和 PBT 使用再生料的情况较为普遍，而用于制作光盘的 PC 量也显著降低。

5. 废旧塑料的回收利用成了热门话题一是为了降低成本而采用再生原料，这块市场不容忽视，几乎占到了工程塑料总用量的五分之一，但产品质量良莠不齐，亟待规范，否则会造成工程塑料的非正规使用和声誉的败坏，也会对下游产品的内在质量产生严重影响，最终导致国内工程塑料行业不能健康发展。另一方面则是为落实循环经济理念，为了减少环境污染、节约能源与资源，这是国家鼓励支持的。总之，废旧塑料的回收利用将成为整个行业必须重视的问题。

6. 国内行业状况国内工程塑料市场前景广阔，有着巨大的发展潜力。劳动成本低于发达国家，人员素质高于其他发展。

专委会对工程塑料行业发展的观点

工程塑料是当今世界塑料工业中增速最快的领域，因其优异的性能，被广泛应用于汽车工业、电子电气、机械设备、建筑材料等行业。随着我国经济的发展，我国已然成为全球工程塑料需求增长最快的国家。

2011 年我国工程塑料的消费量约 2720kt，同比 2010 年增长 10.93%，2012 年我国虽然由于金融危机的影响国内外市场需求不景气，但由于汽车工业等领域的快速发展，国内工程塑料增长速度仍然很快。预计接下来几年其增速均会保持在 10% 以上。但另一方面，从目前整个国内的工程塑料行业来看，我国的工程塑料仍落后于欧美等国家的先进水平。主要表现在：产业化程度低，研发和创新能力不强，品牌意识相对较低。目前国内工程塑料中低端产品多，且竞争激烈，而高端产品少，特别是高端工程塑料的研发和生产明显不足，对高端设备制造，国防工业及航空航天发展产生了一定影响。对此国内企业应当注重产品创新，完善产品结构和产业结构，同时加强公司的科学管理及品牌建设，以实现中高端产品市场的跨越式发展。

另外，工程塑料行业发展，必须注重行业人才的储备。产、学、研之间的密切合作，将是推动我国工程塑料转型升级的有效途径，通过培养行业的优秀人才以促进产业科学合理的发展。“十二五”规划中国家已明确将工程塑料归为新材料，是国家将重点发展的七大新兴战略产业之一，这也更迫切的要求工程塑料行业有更多优秀的人才去参与其中。国内企业应注重打造创新技术团队，合理的利用内部资源和社会资源，通过各类技术人员的交流合作，以提升企业乃至行业的水平。

在立足于国内市场的基础上，我国工程塑料企业应当准备好开拓国际市场的准备。多年来我国工程塑料出口份额相对较低，对国际市场的开拓仍具有非常大的空间。当然，这就需要国内企业提升自身的品牌影响力。

工程塑料作为当前国民经济建设中不可或缺的材料，不仅对国家支柱产业和现代高新技术产业起着重要作用，同时对传统行业的转型升级及产业改造起着深远影响。因此工程塑料行业在未来的发展中仍具备非常大的潜力。

专委会活动：

2012 年工程塑料专委会除了进行日常秘书处工作还开展了一系列活动：

1. 进一步加强与塑协旗下其他专委会的合作与交流，联合兄弟协会，在浙江台州塑交会期间成功举办“2012 中国汽车用塑料及安全技术高峰论坛”，邀请国内外相关专家、企事业单位共聚一堂，10 余位工程塑料应用开发及相关领域的专家做专题报告，内容包括生物塑料在汽车上的应用、S + 激光数字成型技术与制造技术的革命、私营汽车零部件企业的挑战与机遇、塑料前端模块优化设计及 CAE 分析等，参会代表有来自全国各地产业界的企业家也有来自高校和研究院所的专家代表，共计 100 余人。此次论坛获得与会人员的一致好评；相关 PPT 专家报告整理后供会员专享下载；

2. 召开专委会三届三次理事会会议，听取秘书处工作报告及下一步重点工作，着重听取了副理事长和塑协领导对专委会工作的建议和意见；

3. 2012 年 9 月 23 日晚，中塑协领导与工信部消费品司轻工一处处级调研员谢立安处长就车用塑料与相关企业召开专项调研会，与会各个企业代表及专家畅所欲言，获得与会人员一致好评；

积极宣传专委会，推销专委会，制作完成专委会介绍宣传视频，继续发送专委会宣传册近 300 册。

电子期刊制作并发送会员企业及相关单位；

4. 增强专委会与科研院所、地方政府的公共关系，拜访了宁波市利时集团、宁波海关、巨化集团、宁波长城精工等企业，走访了余姚塑料城、慈溪汽车摩配协会、甬赣经济发展促进会等。双方就如何进行合作展开了交流等。

今后的发展"十二五"依然"发展是硬道理"，科学发展也是硬道理。转变发展观念，创新发展模式，提高发展质量，切实把经济社会发展转入全面协调可持续发展的轨道，使增长方式由粗放型向集约型转变。增长方式的转变意味着要从过度依赖资金、自然资源和环境的投入，以量扩张实现增长，转向依靠提高劳动生产率和技术进步，提高效率获取经济增长。从目前看，解放以来一直推动中国经济增长的高投入、高消耗、低产出的老路已经走到尽头，它不可能使中国的经济实现可持续性发展。全球性的人口、资源、环境的矛盾日益尖锐，使我们的现代化面临着严峻的挑战。提高自主创新能力，转变经济增长方式，发展循环经济，建设资源节约型、环境友好型社会，走新型工业化道路，将成为今后发展的主要战略目标。

（中国塑料加工工业协会工程塑料专业委员会　郑静）

专家委员会

面对通胀和企业转型的时机，中国塑协专家委员会应该在先进制造技术领域多做工作，用先进制造技术推动企业产品技术的更新换代，用新兴产业带动塑料产业的提升和发展，针对国内塑料产业的现实情况，2012 年专家委员会主要完成如下工作。

一、为"全国发展改革试点小城镇"授牌和为"西部塑料化工产业商贸总部基地"授牌

2012 年 10 月 18 日，中国塑协专家委员会在成都市新都区木兰镇中塑 · 成都国际贸易中心举办了"全国发展改革试点小城镇"授牌仪式和中塑 · 成都国际贸易中心"西部塑料化工产业商贸总部基地"荣誉称号的授牌仪式。出席大会庆祝活动的有中国轻工业联合会党委副书记、副会长兼中国塑加工工业协会理事长钱桂敬；中国塑协常务副会长曹俭及中国塑协名誉会长廖正品；国家发改委城市和小城镇改革发展中心领导、新都区政府、木兰镇镇政府及中塑集团的各位领导及来宾 300 多人。中国塑协钱桂敬部长和国家发改委领导分别向中塑 · 成都国际贸易中心和木兰镇政府进行了授牌仪式。

二、召开中国塑协专家委员会二届四次会议暨 2012 年塑料新材料、新技术、新成果交流会

2012 年 10 月 18 ~ 20 日，中国塑协专家委员会二届四次会议暨 2012 年塑料新材料、新技术、新成果交流会在成都召开。

中国塑协曹俭副理事长主持了开幕仪式并讲话。

清华大学于建教授、北京航空航天大学詹茂盛教授和北京理工大学的陈晋南教授分别主持了交流活动。

中国塑协钱桂敬理事长出席会议并做了重要讲话。他支出：中国塑料加工工业协会专家委员会，聚集了我们最优秀的专家，要发挥我们专家作为学科领头人的作用；同时，应该鼓励和发挥专家为行业发展提供技术咨询服务，专家委员会要起到培养人才的作用，要注意形成一支老中青结合的专家团队；在一些科研攻关项目中，能凝聚和培养更多的拔尖人才，使我们这个行业的人才队伍建设更加广泛；人才既是我们从事塑料加工业未来竞争优势的关键，也是我们实现塑料加工，由大到强的第一要素，我们应该把培养发现人才放在首位，这是我们塑料加工业最好、最大的人才库，充分发挥我们专家委员会的作用，是我们"十二五"科技进步当中一个重要的措施之一。

会议论文集收录论文 57 篇，精心选择安排了 24 位专家进行了内容丰富、高水平的演讲，不少内容涉及了当前塑料产业共同关注的关键性、共性技术问题，如四川大学王琪教授的新型无卤阻燃高分子泡沫材料的研究，解决了 XPS 板材的阻燃问题。北京化工大学苑会林教授的酚醛泡沫塑料保温板材在建筑外墙外保温中的应用演讲引起了广泛的关注，苑教授介绍酚醛发泡板材满足了当今建筑外墙保温材料的所有性能的要求，是一个值得推广的保温材料。在塑机节能减排方面瞿金平院士的论文，回顾了塑料塑化输运方法从纯剪切形变加工到振动剪切形变加工再到体积拉伸形变加工的演变过程、论证了这种新型塑料加工设备能耗降低，在多相多组份复合材料、生物质复合材料等物料体系的加工方面具有独特优势，有利于实现塑料加工成型过程节能降耗。塑料微成型技术我国处于刚刚起步阶段，被认为是继 IT、生物之后，21 世纪最具发展潜力的高新技术，是未来十年高增长的新型产业，也是当前高科技发展的重要领域之一。中科院宁波材料科学与工程研究所的翟文涛研究员的超薄石墨烯高导热膜的制备、北京化工大学吴大鸣教授的聚合物微尺度成型模具设计制造技术、北京化工大学杨卫民教

授的熔体静电纺丝微纳米纤维制备技术进展及德国弗劳恩霍夫学会北京技术代表张洪波先生的柔性材料的真空镀膜技术，涉及的都是微纳米材料及微纳米加工技术，是功能高分子复合材料制备的最新技术，充分体现了我国科学家勇于把高端技术和创新技术的研发有机的结合起来，这对提高我国塑料制造业的总体水平是大有好处的。

三、聘任专家

2012 年继续做好专家的遴选工作，通过 9 月 13 日通过评审的专家评审，共聘任 78 位专家。

2012 聘任专家表

编　号	姓　名	专家类别	英　　文	工作单位
1.	赵永生 Yongsheng Zhao	塑料异型材	Plastic Profiles	北新建塑有限公司
2.	常素芹 Suqin Chang	功能型鞋用材料	Functional Shoe to Use Material	中国皮革和制鞋工业研究院
3.	高衡 Gao Heng	塑料管道	Plastic Pipe	上海瑞好管业有限公司
4.	江林 Jiang Lin	塑料管道	Plastic Pipe	上海佑逸管业有限公司
5.	李学庆 Xeuqing Li	塑料管道	Plastic Pipe	惠升管业有限公司
6.	陈友标 Youbiao Chen	管理与投资	Management and Investment	广东华业包装材料有限公司
7.	王宝生 Baosheng Wang	降解塑料	Degradable Plastics	辽宁宇森降解塑料有限公司
8.	王刚 Wang Gang	塑料薄膜	Plastic Film	营口永胜降解塑料有限公司
9.	刘忠诚 Zhongcheng Liu	企业管理、法律	Enterprise Management，Law	鲁谷(北京)科技有限公司
10.	陈光岩 Guangyan Chen	高分子合成与改性	Polymer Synthesis and Modification	吉林石化研究院
11.	李志刚 Zhigang Li	碳纤维复合材料	Carbon Fiber Composite Mmaterials	余姚市特种塑料科技有限公司
12.	温殿辉 Dianhui Wen	塑料管道	Plastic Pipe	辛辛那提(山东)管道有限公司
13.	彭兴亭 Xingting Peng	PVC 挤出及注塑制品	PVC Extrusion and Injection Products	威海金泓高分子有限公司
14.	咸旭胜 Xusheng Xian	高分子材料	Polymer Materials	重庆可益荧新材料有限公司
15.	黄惠发 Huifa Huang	聚酯薄膜	Polyester Film	汕头市鑫瑞纸品有限公司
16.	王国华 Guahua Wang	工程塑料	Engineering Plastic	天台县国邦工程塑料有限公司
17.	王军 Wang jun	塑料管道	Plastic Pipe	山西乾通塑胶有限公司副
18.	郭炳胜 Bingsheng Guo	PVC 型材挤出	PVC Profile	保定宝硕新型建筑材料有限公司
19.	张学全 Xuequan Zhang	塑料改性	Plastics Modification	天津玉泉工贸有限公司
20.	杨爱平 Aiping Yang	企业管理	Business Management	成都中塑投资集团有限公司
21.	王德川 Dechuan Wang	企业管理	Business Management	成都中塑投资集团有限公司
22.	王俊霄 Junxiao Wang	企业管理	Business Management	河北精信化工集团有限公司

续表

编号	姓名	专家类别	英文	工作单位
23.	张广辉 Guanghui Zhang	企业管理	Business Management	河北精信化工集团有限公司
24.	杨拥民 Yongmin Yang	塑料型材制造、加工	Plastic Material Manufacturing and Processing	力尔铝业股份有限公司
25.	蒯一希 Yixi Kuai	复合塑料管道及设备	Composite Plastic Piping and Equipment	四川金石东方新材料设备股份有限公司
26.	陈绍江 Shaojiang Chen	复合塑料管道及模具	Composite Plastic Piping and Die	四川金石东方新材料设备股份有限公司
27.	林世凯 Shikai Lin	资深管理师	Senior Management Division	台湾台塑集团南亚塑胶有限公司
28.	胡连生 Liansheng	塑料加工	Plastic Processing	介休市塑料工业有限公司
29.	梁东文 Dongwen Liang	企业管理	Business Management	太原市杰森实业有限公司
30.	马四平 Siping Ma	企业管理	Business Management	山西榆化漳河塑材有限公司
31.	周先俊 Xianjun Zhou	塑料型材	Plastic Profiles	山西榆化漳河塑材有限公司
32.	郄卫东 Weidong Qie	塑料薄膜	Plastic Film	山西民生塑料制品有限公司
33.	马建军 Jianjun Ma	企业管理	Business Management	山西永腾建材股份有限公司
34.	闫玉亮 Yuliang Yan	塑料管道	Plastic Pipe	山西泰鑫塑胶制品有限公司
35.	杨绍华 Shaohua Yang	塑料管道	Plastic Pipe	祁县旺中塑料制品厂
36.	张辉 Zhang Hui	塑料制品加工	Plastic Products Processing	山西新派塑胶有限公司
37.	常榆江 Yujiang Chang	塑料注塑	Plastic Injection Molding	晋中市塑力达塑胶制品有限公司董事长
38.	刘芳兴 Fangxing Liu	塑料加工	Plastic Processing	天津中财型材有限责任公司
39.	王建志 Jianzhi Wang	型材加工	Plastic Profiles	天津凯德瑞塑料异型材制造有限公司
40.	秦旭红 Xuhong Qin	塑料异型材及门窗	Plastic Different Profile and Doors and Windows	济南方信集团有限公司
41.	朱国才 guncai Zhu	滚塑技术研发	Research and Development of Rotational Moulding Technology	温岭市旭日滚塑科技有限公司
42.	姜小强 Xiaoqiang Jiang	滚塑设备设计制造	Roll - Plastic Equipment Design and Manufacture	浙江安吉天洋滚塑设备有限公司
43.	王钦兔 Qintu Wang	滚塑加工工艺	Roll - Plastic Processing Technology	浙江兴邦塑胶科技有限公司董事长
44.	孙如川 Ruchuan Sun	滚塑加工工艺	Roll - Plastic Processing Technology	广东佛山山大塑料厂
45.	林日昇 Risheng Lin	滚塑模具制造	Roll - Plastic Mould Manufacturing	宁波市镇海金鸿模具机械厂
46.	奕玉利 Yuli Yi	滚塑材料与翻译	Roll - Plastic Materials and Translate	慈溪市德顺容器有限公司

续表

编 号	姓 名	专家类别	英 文	工作单位
47.	冯立新 Lixin Feng	设备制造	Equipment Manufacturing	无锡市侨诺塑机有限公司
48.	马大庆 Daqing Ma	检测设备	Testing Equipment	石家庄开发区中实检测设备公司
49.	章立志 Lizhi Zhang	滚塑设备制造	Roll – Plastic Equipment Manufacturing	杭州本凡机械有限公司
50.	李彦平 Yanping Li	企业管理	Enterprise Management	金后盾专用装备制造集团
51.	秦国良 Gunliang Qin	生产管理	Production Management	河北金后盾塑胶有限公司
52.	宋洪锁 Hongsuo Song	滚塑模具设计和制造	Roll – Plastic Mould Design and Manufacturing	河北金后盾塑胶有限公司
53.	翟志彬 Zhibin Zhai	产品设计及工艺	Product Design and Process	河北金后盾塑胶有限公司
54.	黄明 Huang Ming	滚塑工艺	Roll – Plastic Processing	安徽省宁国市天亿滚塑有限公司
55.	张春华 Chunhua Zhang	双向拉伸及流延膜设备	Equipment of Two – Way Stretch and Flow film	广东仕诚塑料机械有限公司
56.	陈叔安 Shuan Chen	技术开发	Development of Technology	上海上塑控股(集团)有限公司
57.	周宁琳 Ninglin Zhou	纳米技术及生物功能材料	Nano Technology &Biological Function Material	南京师范大学化学与材料科学学院/南京周宁琳新材料科技有限公司
58.	姜海鹏 Haipeng Jiang	高分子材料	Polymer Materials	上海振华园锯片厂
59.	米永存 Yongcun Mi	高分子材料	Polymer Materials	北京诚联恺达科技有限公司
60.	张立华 Lihua Zhang	科技开发与管理	Scientific Technology Development and Management	甘肃瑞盛·亚美特高科技农业有限公司
61.	罗伟 LuoWei	阻燃聚碳酸酯薄膜	Flame Retardant Polycarbonate Film	苏州奥美材料科技有限公司
62.	杜献超 Xianchao Du	光学聚碳酸酯薄膜	Optical Polycarbonate Film	苏州奥美材料科技有限公司
63.	任月璋 Yuezhang Ren	聚碳酸酯薄膜加工	Polycarbonate Film Processing	苏州奥美材料科技有限公司
64.	王金立 Jinli Wang	塑料期刊编审	Plastic Journal Editor	中国兵器工业集团第五三研究所
65.	祖国富	高分子材料	Polymer Materials	宏岳塑胶集团有限公司
66.	张磊 Zhang Lei	质量检验	Quality Inspection	秦皇岛市产品质量监督检验所
67.	吴锡盾 Xidun Wu	小家电器研发、制造、销售	Research, Development, Manufacturing, Sales of Small Home Appliances	广东天际电器股份有限公司
68.	张辉旋 Huixuan Zang	高分子材料改性	Polymer Materials Modified	本科汕头卜高通美实业有限公司
69.	盛修業 Xiuye Sheng	生产经营管理	Production and Operation Management	南亚塑胶工业(南通)有限公司
70.	邱朝雄 Chaoxiong Qui	生产经营管理	Production and Operation Management	南亚塑胶工业(南通)有限公司

续表

编　号	姓　名	专家类别	英　文	工作单位
71.	陈卫国 Weiguo Chen	高分子材料	Polymer Materials	山东鲁燕色母粒有限公司
72.	姚汉樑 Hangliang Yao	测试技术	Testing Technology	上海思尔达科学仪器有限公司
73.	温变英 Bianying Wm	高分子材料	Polymer Materials	北京工商大学
74.	毕宏海 Honghai Bi	高分子材料	Polymer Materials	上海邦中新材料有限公司
75.	储江顺 Jiangshun Chu	高分子材料	Polymer Materials	上海邦中新材料有限公司
76.	薛明生 Mingsheng Xue	高分子材料	Polymer Materials	北京中联建诚建材有限公司
77.	巫志国 Zhigun Wu	技术及企业管理	Technology and Enterprise Management	四川煌盛管业有限公司
78.	李世通 Shitong Li	聚合物加工装备	Polymer Processing Equipment	天华化工机械及自动化研究设计院

（中国塑料加工工业协会　许琳）

塑 料 助 剂

1. 2012 年行业状况

2012 年是实施"十二五"规划承上启下的重要一年，我国经济运行总体平稳，以加快转变经济发展方式为主线，按照稳中求进的工作总基调，及时加强和改善宏观调控，把稳增长放在更加重要的位路，经济社会发展呈现稳中有进的良好态势。一年来，塑料助剂行业绝大部分企业能较好地适应宏观经济的发展趋势，根据市场需求的变化，调整、优化产品结构，重视提高自主创新能力，积极开发新产品、新技术不少企业加大了专用产品及高附加值产品的研发力度；根据产品工艺特点，努力搞好节能减排、推进清洁生产；依靠科技创新和管理创新，降低生产成本；使整个行业在 2012 年取得了新的进步。2012 年国内塑料助剂的消费量为 5122kt。2012 年塑料助剂各主要品种的消费量见表 1。

表 1　2012 年塑料助剂消费量统计　　kt

品　种	消费量
增塑剂	3045
热稳定剂	500
阻燃剂	410
冲击改性剂与加工改良剂	320
着色剂	387
润滑剂	135
发泡剂	190
抗氧剂	88
抗静电剂	6.5
光稳定剂	8
偶联剂	16
其他	17
合计	5122.5

2. 专委会活动

2.1　举办年会和技术研讨会

塑料助剂专委会于 2011 年 11 月 1 日 ~11 月 4 日在浙江杭州组织召开了"塑料助剂专业委员会年会暨 2011 年塑料助剂生产与应用技术信息交流会"，来自全国各地的塑料助剂生产企业、塑料加工企业、大专院校、科研院所的 230 多位代表参加了会议。会议发表论文 60 篇，在大会上宣读论文 20 篇，向参会企业传达了助剂行业的新技术、新成果。年会期间还组织了专题讨论与交流，加强了同行间的交流与合作。2011 年 5 月与中国电器科学研究院有限公司合作，在广州举办了“2011年塑料制品老化与防老化技术研讨会”，来自全国各地的塑料助剂生产企业、塑料加工企业、大专院校、科研院所的60多位代表参加了会议。

2011年8月上旬，热稳定行业的18家骨干企业共聚内蒙，就热稳定剂行业的发展及当前面临的问题展开讨论并达成一定共识。在2011年塑料助剂年会期间进行了进一步的讨论。

2.2 组织编写了塑料助剂行业“十二五”规划

塑料助剂专委会秘书处在增塑剂、热稳定剂、阻燃剂、抗氧剂和光稳定剂、偶联剂起草人提供的材料的基础上进行了汇总、整理、加工，并发给各理事单位征求意见，形成了塑料助剂行业“十二五”规划，在年初上报给中国塑料加工工业协会。

2.3 参加展会和日常工作

专委会派员参加了“第二十五届中国国际塑料橡胶工业展览会”、“第十二届中国塑料博览会”、“第七届中国国际工程塑料工业展览会”，宣传了专委会及《塑料助剂》杂志，加强了横向交流。

继续办好《塑料助剂》杂志，充实“塑料助剂信息网”的内容。

专委会秘书处利用掌握的信息资源，为企业提供业务和技术咨询，或推荐有关专家帮助解决问题，向应用企业推荐会员单位品质优良的产品。专委会秘书处还根据会员单位的要求为他们提供了相关资料，包括文献、国内外专利以及有关证明材料等。

3. 产品结构调整与技术进步

3.1 增塑剂

由于PVC制品行业的发展，2012年，国内增塑剂的表观消费量继续保持增长。国内增塑剂产能不断扩大，达到了4600kt，生产品种不断丰富，进口量继续下降，从2011年的进口300kt减为200kt。

2012年，国内外对邻苯类增塑剂的限制使用范围仍在继续扩大，面对这种形势，我国增塑剂生产企业加大了环保增塑剂的研发力度，努力扩大非邻苯类增塑剂的产量，环氧类达到200kt，对苯类为550kt，偏苯类为55kt，此外，偏苯三酸酯类、柠檬酸酯类等环保型增塑剂的产量也有增长。

随着国内增塑剂上游原料装置投产，2012年，国内增塑剂生产企业的装置规模、技术水平以及产品质量均有提高。

3.2 热稳定剂

近几年来，我国热稳定剂的消费量随着PVC工业的快速发展而大幅度增加。目前我国稳定剂的生产能力已超过600kt，2012年消耗量约500kt，生产的厂家超过1000家，能够生产制品行业所需的所有热稳定剂品种。2012年，热稳定剂各品种的产量见表2。

表2 2012年热稳定剂产量统计 kt

品 种	产 量
含铅/镉类产品	350
复合稳定剂	100
含锡类产品	50
合计	500

近年来，热稳定剂行业在朝着无毒、环保、高效的方向取得了长足的进步，产品结构日益优化，产品性能不断提升。2012年钙锌类环保型热稳定剂的产能、品种比2011年有较大增长，铅盐的比例逐步减少，有机化合物基热稳定剂的研发和生产取得了可喜的进展，我国特有的稀土掺杂热稳定剂推广应用进步明显。尿嘧啶、β-二酮、水滑石等辅助热稳定剂品种的生产和应用取得了显著成绩；新材料、新技术、新工艺的应用促进了和提升了热稳定剂行业的整体水平。2012年，热稳定剂行业在推动产品无铅镉化方面做了大量工作，促进了热稳定剂的环保化进程。

3.3 阻燃剂

2012年，溴系阻燃剂上半年产量下降了近1/3，下半年有所好转。在十溴联苯醚限制使用后，一些较为新型的性能优良的阻燃剂得到较快发展，如十溴二苯乙烷、溴化环氧树脂、溴化聚苯乙烯、聚溴代苯乙烯、四溴双酚A碳酸酯低聚物、三溴苯氧基氰脲酸酯等，不但产量增加，质量也有大幅提高，出现了产销两旺的可喜情景。

近几年，有机磷类阻燃剂以较快的速度增长，例如，去年有机磷酸酯阻燃剂产量达到11万余吨，出口量达5万余吨。

无机阻燃剂具有稳定性好，低毒或无毒，贮存过程中不挥发，不析出，原料来源丰富，价格低廉等优点，是目前高分子材料中应用最为广泛的阻燃剂之一。2012年，无机阻燃剂中金属氢氧化物在改进造粒技术，向超细化方向发展，采用偶联剂对其进行表面处理，采用大分子键合的方式对其进行改性等方面都取得了一定进展。另外，阴离子型层状功能材料作为阻燃剂得到了迅速发展。

另外，膨胀型阻燃剂和硅系阻燃剂等也得到了长足的发展。

3.4 抗氧剂和光稳定剂

2012年，由于国内、国际市场需求依然不旺，国内塑料抗氧剂、光稳定剂主要产品的产品价格和原材料价格相对稳定，平均价格低于2011年。塑料抗氧剂、光稳定剂的产量比2011年增加10%左右，出口量比2011年增加20%左右。2012年抗氧剂和光稳定剂的产能、产量、出口量见表3、表4。

表3　2011年抗氧剂产能、产量、出口量统计

$10^4 t$

品种	产能	产量	出口量
受阻酚类	6	4.8	0.6
亚磷酸酯类	4.8	4.3	0.2
含硫类	1.1	0.7	0.4
合计	11.9	9.8	1.2

表4　2011年光稳定剂产能、产量、出口量统计

$10^4 t$

品种	产能	产量	出口量
受阻胺类	1.2	1.1	0.7
苯并三唑类	0.6	0.4	0.3
二苯甲酮类	0.6	0.4	0.25
合计	2.4	1.9	1.25

去年，抗氧剂、光稳定剂系列产品数目有所增加，如亚磷酸酯抗氧剂618、高温受阻酚抗氧剂1330、光稳定剂123等已经实现稳定的工业生产和销售。同时，塑料抗氧剂、光稳定剂企业向自主主导市场方向发展，由单一性能或单一功能产品，向多性能、多功能方向发展。另外，塑料抗氧剂、光稳定剂企业在走出国门，扩大国际市场的影响方面取得了新进展。

3.5　其他

2012年，其他塑料助剂，如冲击改性剂与加工改良剂、发泡剂、润滑剂、偶联剂、抗静电剂、抗菌剂、成核剂、扩链剂、防雾剂等在开发新产品和技术进步方面也都取得了不同程度的进展。

4. 存在问题

塑料助剂企业大多数为中小企业，大中型骨干企业少，绝大部分产品未形成规模经营；产品结构不尽合理，高端产品少，专用品种不多，部分产品质量不够稳定；和国外先进企业相比，我国塑料助剂企业的技术工艺水平不高，装备相对落后；部分企业的科技投入不足、自主创新能力不强，缺少高水平的专业人才；部分产品还存在着高排放、高污染的问题。

4.1　增塑剂

(1) 产品结构不尽合理，品种较少

世界上已商品化的增塑剂达100多种，而我国目前生产的约30多个品种，其中大部分的产量为邻苯类产品，环保类高效品种所占比例较小，许多专用和高性能品种还不能生产，依赖进口。

(2) 我国增塑剂市场面临环保压力加大

随着世界各国环保意识的提高，医药及食品包装、日用品、玩具等塑料制品对主增塑剂提出了更高的纯度及卫生要求，国际社会对DOP等邻苯二甲酸酯类产品的限用范围进一步扩大，而我国增塑剂生产企业对新型环保增塑剂的开发和推广力度还跟不上法规和市场对生产企业的要求。

(3) 生产工艺参差不齐，总体水平比较低

4.2　热稳定剂

热稳定剂行业存在的主要问题是：原始创新不足(主要体现在研发经费投入少、高瑞人才严重缺乏、尤其是推扩应用工程技术人才严重短缺和重视不够)；环保产品的推扩应用滞后，含铅、镉等重金属产品仍然占据市场主要份额；产品技术标准相对落后，产品质量波动较大；企业品牌意识薄弱、缺乏长远规划，没有形成具有较强竞争力的国际知名品牌；产品标准落后、应用标准缺失；90%以上企业生产规模偏小、产品质量偏差、导致同行业无序竞争现象严重，一些客户恶意拖欠货款的现像依旧存在。

4.3　阻燃剂

阻燃剂行业存在的主要问题是：

(1) 产品结构不尽合理，无论生产销售仍以溴系阻燃剂为主，虽然一些无卤阻燃剂产品的发展较为迅速，但是依然没有改变溴系阻燃剂为主的总体格局；

(2) 生产工艺、产品质量与国外产品有差距，产品质量的稳定性不高；

(3) 自主研发的力量和投入不够；

(4) 大部分阻燃剂生产企业的规模不大，竞争力不强。

(5) 目前阻燃剂在国内的使用仍不普及。

4.4　抗氧剂和光稳定剂

(1) 国内塑料抗氧剂、光稳定剂企业在新产品、新工艺、新应用等持续发展方面投入过低。仍然以扩大单一产品产能、产量和销售量为提高企业销售额和利润的主要方式。

(2) 市场开发能力薄弱，在国内市场和国际市场(特别是国际市场)，仍然以降价为主要竞争方式，致使国内全行业平均销售价格和利润率降低。

(3) 国内仍然缺少工程塑料、改性塑料的专用型或特殊类型抗氧剂、光稳定剂品种，尚不能满足工程塑料及改性塑料行业发展和质量、档次提高的

需求。

(4) 抗氧剂、光稳定剂企业安全生产问题、环境保护问题严峻。亚磷酸酯类抗氧剂、苯并三唑类和二苯甲酮类紫外线吸收型光稳定剂、硫化钠法硫代酯抗氧剂工艺的三废排放量依然很高、污染程度严重。

(5) 没有通用光稳定剂国家标准。

5. 发展趋势

(1) 随着我国总体经济的持续健康发展，随着塑料工业的快速发展，今后一段时间，我国塑料助剂行业将保持平稳较快的发展态势。

(2) 塑料助剂行业要根据形势对塑料助剂产品提出的新要求，积极开发“绿色、环保、无毒、高效”的产品，替代对人类健康和环境有害的品种；要细分市场，增加品种，满足不同层次用户的需求，扩大专用产品和高端产品和高附加值产品的比重；要加大工程塑料、特种塑料、可降解塑料用的各种助剂产品的研发力度；要紧跟塑料助剂复合多功能化的发展趋势，加大对复配技术的研究开发，推出更多综合性能好、性价比高、使用方便的复配产品。

(3) 要把提升自主创新能力作为增强行业竞争力的战略基点，加大对技术创新的投入，重视技术人才的引进与培养，注重开发拥有自主知识产权的产品和专有技术，努力突破关键核心技术，提升企业竞争力。要重视标准化、专利、企业工程技术中心、产学研合作等方面的工作。

要根据产品特点，积极开发应用低碳技术，搞好清洁生产，淘汰落后工艺和落后设备，减少三废排放，努力做好工业废弃物的回收利用工作。

(4) 加强同行业交流与合作，以求得取长补短，共同提高。积极探索企业之间的各种合作和联合的方式，支持骨干企业做大做强，促进塑料助剂产品规模化经营，加快提高行业的集中度。

(中国塑料加工工业协会塑料助剂专委会秘书处)

新材料研究开发工作委员会

2012 年，新材料研究开发工作委员会在中国塑料加工工业协会的领导下，在各有关单位的协助下，面对我国经济增长明显回落，出口增速回落，贸易顺差下降，贸易利益减少；工业企业增速减缓，企业融资困难，中小企业经营困难，尤其对出口依赖程度相对较高的东部地区企业、民营企业所受影响首当其冲如此的困难局面，通过增加科研设备，加大科研投入，联合一切力量，积极应对危机影响。

一、进一步加大科技投入，完善研究开发基础

在国际金融危机扩散和国家加大房地产调控力度，国际竞争环境恶劣形势下，为了提高塑料加工行业和企业的自主创新能力和研发水平，增强市场竞争力，今年新材料研究开发工作委员会的依托企业山东日科化学股份有限公司投入 4180 万元，建设建筑面积 7500m^2 新的研发中心大楼，增添新的研发设备，完善中试设备，科技研发投入由 2011 年的 3385 万元增加到 3850 万元，已签订购买合同的设备仪器有核磁共振波谱仪、全自动真密度分析仪、低温摆锤试验机，成为目前国内同行业实验仪器设备最为齐全的科研中心，为搞好研究开发创造了条件。

二、加大研发力度

在加大科技投入，完善研究开发基础上，先后承担的 2 项科技计划按照计划顺利进行。列入“十二五”国家支撑计划《节能门窗用耐候高性能塑料型材的研究开发与应用示范》项目；按照项目进度计划，针对 4 种塑料改性剂的研究做了大量试验分析工作，完成了实验室小试，进入到了中试；已申请发明专利 4 项；已经建成年产 20kt 耐候塑料抗冲改性剂生产线 1 条。

AMB 树脂产品项目已经建成投产，并通过国家科技部、商务部、质量监督检测总局、国家环保总局评审，列入国家 2011 年重点新产品计划，成为国家重点新产品；

获得发明专利授权：

1. 国家发明专利：透明性、抗冲击、耐候性优良的聚氯乙烯混合物，专利号：Zl201010291380.0；

2. 美国发明专利：聚氯乙烯加工塑化改性剂及其制备方法及其应用，专利号：00004747USU，代理机构已经通知授权。

获得奖励：

1. 工程塑料专用低温高效增韧剂(AMB 树脂)的研制项目获得山东省技术发明三等奖 1 项、获得国家轻工业联合会技术发明三等奖 1 项。

2. 理事长赵东日博士 2012 年 5 月被山东省政府聘为泰山学者。

三、积极开展技术交流、展览等各项工作

1. 积极参加了协会组织的各项活动；

2. 与协会异型材专委会组织的未增塑聚氯乙烯(PVC－U)型材专用加工助剂标准制定工作；

3. 先后参加了上海和美国国际橡塑展。

(中国塑料加工工业协会新材料研究开发工作委员会　徐贵一)

流延薄膜

PVC保鲜膜市场分析与生产技术

一、保鲜膜介绍及分类

保鲜膜主要用于超市、家庭、菜市场、酒店等场所，是用来包装水果、蔬菜及其他食品或物品的一种包装制品，便于水果、蔬菜等食品的保鲜并起到分类、美化物品等作用，以促进产品的销售。目前市场上使用的保鲜膜主要有三大类：PVC保鲜膜、PE保鲜膜、PVDC保鲜膜，在这三种保鲜膜中，PVC保鲜膜凭借其特有的优点，如：粘度好、透明度好、记忆性好、透氧性佳、透湿度高，以及包装出的产品美观、价格低廉等特点，深受人们喜欢，因此国际及国内市场上80%的食品保鲜包装都采用PVC保鲜膜。PE保鲜膜则主要用于肉食或高温场合使用，而PVDC保鲜膜主要用于一些熟食、火腿等产品的包装。

二、PVC保鲜膜安全性及其在国内外情况介绍

在日本，食品包装用的PVC保鲜膜是从20世纪60年代后半期开始使用的，那时正值自助贩卖超市兴起之时。这种商场的出现给我们的日常生活以及购物带来了巨大的变化，其中尤以生鲜食品买卖方式的变化最为显著。在自助贩卖的情况下，生鲜食品被按一定的数量和重量包装并陈列后提供给顾客，所以这样一来，PVC保鲜膜和托盘就变得不可或缺了。

为什么要选用PVC保鲜膜，那是因为它具备适合包装生鲜食品的各种优质特性(如气体透过性、透明性、伸缩性、粘着性等)，以及合理的市场价格。

在那之后，超市迎来了多店铺展开的兴盛期，同时生鲜食品的包装也被安排到具备高速包装机等设备的中央场所统一进行。包装领域的机械适应性、配送运输时的商品保护以及温度管理等方面对保鲜膜提出了更多的性能要求。在这一过程中，PVC保鲜膜随着其品质的不断提高，较好地满足了市场的大部分要求，由此也成为了这一领域不可或缺的食品包装用保鲜薄膜。

关于PVC保鲜膜与健康、环境等相关的问题，大多是由于宣传不够而引起的误解，而且其中大部分问题已得到解决。

1. 关于PVC单体

关于产品中残留单体的问题，现在使用的原材料为基准残留单体1ppm以下的材料，完全符合欧洲EPFMA和美国FDA标准，也符合我国《食品用塑料自粘保鲜膜》的GB 10457—2009国家标准，所以PVC保鲜膜产品是完全符合国际及国家标准的，是安全的。

2. 关于DEHA(DOA)

随着技术的不断开发，已经研制和推出环保无毒PVC增塑剂作为传统增塑剂邻苯二甲酸酯最安全的替代产品。

三、PVC保鲜膜产业的发展现状及趋势

自2005年以来，我国民众对PVC保鲜膜的使用产生了误导性的恐慌，使PVC保鲜膜需求也出现了大的滑坡，此时PE保鲜膜市场份额大幅度上升。虽然欧洲EPFMA和美国的FDA的都制定了针对PVC保鲜膜的严格标准，但是他们仍都在使用PVC保鲜膜，并没有禁止PVC保鲜膜在食品包装方面的使用。中国国家质检总局颁布了《食品用塑料自粘保鲜膜》新国家标准，只要严格按照国家标准生产及正确使用，PVC保鲜膜是安全的，不会对人体健康造成影响。随着人民生活水平的不断提高，食品保鲜膜的需求量也越来越大。现在国内及国际上生产PVC保鲜膜企业不多，产量也不大。在国内的每年的产量大约在2万多吨，国内每年的需求量3万多吨，加上出口到欧洲、美国、南美洲、非洲及中东等地区，世界总需求量在100～150kt左右。国内使用进口设备生产企业主要有6家企业(台湾南亚、杭州恩希爱、日本理研、大连三荣、上海郡是和法国林帕克)和使用国产新乐华宝设备的企业6家(北京永夏旗舰、沧州金三洋、无锡新迪和江阴阿拉等)。

四、PVC流延保鲜膜设备的生产技术与研发状况

PVC流延保鲜膜的生产工艺和加工技术

采用流延生产工艺：

PVC食品级原料(粉料树脂、各种助剂等)—高速搅拌热混—低速搅拌冷混—真空自动上料—螺杆塑化挤出—PVC专用流延模头部分—冷却定型部分—切边及分切装置—全自动上纸管和三轴自动收卷、自动卸卷部分—自动气泡去除机—自动切边机—熟化包装。

PVC保鲜膜生产线的最新技术应用：

1. 混料系统：原来PVC粉料与辅助液体原料一般采用人工称重配混，现在充分利用最新自动化技术，采用全自动称重计量配混系统，提高了计量准确，减少了配料带来的误差和对产品质量的影响，并且省工省力，大大降低了原料和用工成本。

2. 挤出塑化流延系统。本系统由真空料斗、螺杆机筒、换网装置、流延模头等组成，主要作用是把原料进行充分塑化，从流延模头模唇处定量、定压均匀挤出。此部分是生产高品质PVC保鲜膜的技术核心部分，关键是螺杆的设计、高精度的温度控制系统、特殊的换网部分和模头设计等。因此本系统要保证原料良好的塑化，原料挤出时的温度一致性，又不能产生分解，所以机器设计时的加温及冷却系统控制方式及精度尤为重要，如果有控制不好或操作不当出现分解就有可能造成含氯气体的挥发。

3. 流延定型冷却系统。本系统接收从模头挤出一定幅宽的熔融透明薄膜，使之定型、冷却，并把膜进行引取，向后道工序输送。在本系统中薄膜在输送过程中要平稳，要有一定的拉伸，避免出现抖动现象，减少薄膜的褶皱。

4. 分切、切边及边料回收系统。本系统采用特殊的分切结构设计，保证分切后的超薄薄膜在高速运行下稳定、薄膜平整和分开宽度均匀，以及边料100%在线破碎后回原料配混系统回收利用，可有效降低生产成本和消耗。

5. 三轴全自动卷取系统。本系统把分切后的成品薄膜按设定的速度、张力、压力进行自动卷取，到达设定米数后自动切断并完成上卷、卸卷、穿纸管等全套动作。PVC保鲜膜生产环节中卷取的质量非常重要，因为PVC膜卷在收卷时压力要一致均匀，这样膜卷不会出现摺皱，保证了膜卷平整、美观等，并且三轴全自动收卷系统可有效减少膜卷外层的尾料、减少消耗、降低工人劳动强度。

6. 膜卷在线自动排气装置。从收卷部分卸下来的膜卷自动输送到排气机内，通过自动冲气，采用高压原理，把膜卷内存留的空气排出，使膜卷更紧、更实，增加了膜卷的透明度，以及膜卷的美观度，使膜卷更有卖相。

7. 自动膜卷切边机。采用最新的伺服驱动设计，通过把膜卷的两个端面不整齐部分切掉，使膜卷两端形成特别整齐的效果，既美观又利于使用时顺利开卷。

综上所述，使用合理且环保的产品配方，严格执行生产工艺，就可以生产出质量合格、环保达标的PVC保鲜膜。

（清华大学　赵安赤）

塑料配线器材

2012年是实施“十二五”规划的承启之年，也是我国加快经济转型升级步伐，促进社会和谐发展的关键之年，11月又迎来了十八大的胜利召开。专委会根据上级文件精神，不断加强自身建设，认真履行专委会职责，积极拓展协会服务领域，为促进行业经济又好又快发展等方面做了一些有益的工作。在2012年里我们硕果累累：塑料配线器材专委会两家企业被评为2011年度乐清市明星企业，两家企业荣获“2011年度柳市镇百强企业”奖，四家企业荣获“2011年度柳市镇明星企业”奖，郑元和理事长也被中国轻工业联合会授予：“轻工业特色区域和产业集群先进个人”、被柳市镇政府评选为“慈善工作先进个人”称号。

2012年由于受世界经济持续低迷的影响，全市工业总产值有所下降，据统计2012年1～10月，乐清市工业总产值818.39亿元，同比下降6.1%，轻工行业2012年1～10月实现工业总产值44.56亿，同比只下降1.8%，而塑料配线器材行业1～10月份，据不完全统计产量基本上与上年同期持平。

一、建立健全组织，充实会员队伍

根据专委会年度工作计划安排，我们定期召开各类会议和举办各种活动，全局工作朝着制度化、规范化发展。今年专委会共召开会员大会1次，理事会3次，理事长办公会议5次，传达上级精神和商讨行业发展方向。专委会在坚持标准的前提下，会员结构也得到进一步优化，激活了会员的向心力，增强了专委会凝聚力，提升了专委会影响力。同时，坚持积极谨慎发展新会员的原则，2012年专委会新增会员7家，使专委会注入了新的活力，充实了会员队伍。

二、积极为企业服务，增强企业知名度和影响力

为了充分展示塑料配线器材专委会的良好形象，提升专委会会员企业整体素质，增强企业业务交流，专委会认真做好宣传舆论导向方面的工作。

1. 利用简讯、网站，汇集会员企业荣誉广泛宣传。为了加强会员之间的联系，便于彼此之间的交流，专委会充分利用QQ群和移动E管家信息平台为会员提供更快捷的信息服务。在市、乡镇的经济工作会议和有关部门的表彰会议上，会员企业获得了诸多的荣誉，为了更广泛地宣传先进，激励其他企业学习，专委会办公室将有关表彰内容进行收集汇总，刊登在专委会网站和行业资讯上，以增强对会员企业的宣传力度，从而提高会员的知名度。发布最新行业信息，整合力量，定期编印行业资讯或者通过网站及时发布专委会工作动态，加强和促进会员之间的横向沟通联系，促进相互学习和交流，促进行业共同发展。

2. 发动会员单位参加各类评选活动。塑料配线器材专委会积极组织具有影响力的会员企业参评中国塑协开展的2011年度轻工塑料行业十强企业、轻工百强企业评价工作。为更好组织实施节能降耗重点项目，推动全市节能降耗工作，塑料配线器材专委会积极发动会员单位参评市经信局组织的“2012年乐清市节能降耗重点项目”申报项目活动。

此外，专委会还发动符合条件的会员企业申报乐清市人民政府在全市范围内开展的“2011年度乐清市明星企业、成长型中小企业评选”、“2012年柳市镇镇长质量奖”等活动。如：2012年2月15日召开的乐清市经济工作暨大投资推进大会，塑料配线器材专委会理事长单位：长虹塑料集团有限公司，理事单位：浙江永兴塑料有限公司被评为“2011年度乐清市明星企业”。长虹塑料集团有限公司还被评为“2011年度乐清市开放型经济工作先进单位即外贸出口30强企业”、自锁式捆扎带顺利通过了“浙江名牌产品”的复审；2012年3月6日召开柳市镇经济工作暨表彰会议，塑料配线器材专委会理事长单位：长虹塑料集团有限公司，副理事长单位：浙江万沙电气有限公司被评为“2011年度柳市镇百强企业”。塑料配线器材专委会副理事长单位：乐清市新光塑料有限公司、浙江金星电器开关厂、乐清市海泰塑料制造有限公司，及理事单位：中国爱克斯电气有限责任公司均被评为“2011年度柳市镇明星企业”。长虹塑料集团有限公司还被评为“2011年度柳市镇十佳出口创汇企业”、“2011年度柳市镇慈善工作先进单位”等称号。

三、关爱会员，提升专委会的凝聚力和向心力

为更有效地开展走访、联络会员企业，专委会有计划地开展以“访企业、明需求、谋发展”为主题的走访活动，收集企业运营中出现的重点和难点问题。由别旭辉副秘书长带队的理事会成员分别对会员企业进行走访，召开座谈会，了解企业运行情况，倾听企业领导对公司生产经营、发展前景、遇到困难和面临难点问题的汇报，并为多家企业解决了设备、技术等方面的难题，共同为企业出谋划策、排忧解难，取得了显著成绩。

为分享会员们红喜事的快乐和分担白喜事的忧愁，专委会成立了联谊会，安排专人负责联谊会的资金管理和事情通报、组织工作。会员企业有红白喜事时，专委会组织安排领导和会员到现场送上心意和温暖。联谊会活动增进了会员之间的友谊，使会员关系更加密切，成为推动专委会工作一股不可或缺的力量。

四、上下联动，积极配合职能部门全面开展专委会工作

1. 积极配合中国塑协工作，发挥助手作用。专委会秘书处积极传达和完成中国塑协下发的各项通知及任务。4月16～17日，专委会代表出席了在上海召开的第六届理事扩大会议暨塑料加工业应用与发展论坛。会议审定了第六届二次理事扩大会议议程；审定2012年工作要点；审议理事、会员增减情况的报告；审议塑料加工业“十二五”发展规划指导意见(征求意见稿)等相关事项。

4月份，按中国塑协要求，上报推荐乐清市为“轻工业先进特色区域和产业集群”，这项工作受到了乐清市政府的极力支持。11月份，在广州中山市召开的“全国轻工业特色区域和产业集群”工作会议上，本人也被评选为“轻工业特色区域和产业集群先进工作者”；推荐浙江亚泰塑料有限公司、浙江可易塑料有限公司等10余家企业作为塑料配线器材行业的重点企业，上报中国塑协。

专委会秘书处还积极完成填写2012中国塑协活动明细，分支机构会员名册报送，中国塑协及各分支机构下半年工作安排明细表，重点产业竞争力评价企业调查问卷等各项工作。

2. 成立行业质量专家库。为了推动我行业产品质量进步，提升质量管理水平，增进质量工作经验交流，切实推进品牌战略和质量强市工作，为政府职能部门科学决策，为产业、企业转型升级提供技术支撑。我专委会配合乐清市质量协会工作，决定成立为行业为基础单位的专业专家组。塑料配线器材专委会委派毛维琴、潘逸龙、黄鑫森、周书兰4位专家入选乐清市产品质量专家库。

五、开展技术研讨与培训活动，积极打造学习型社会团体

为了提升会员单位的综合素质和管理水平，专委会努力整合相关培训资源和信息，通知组织会员参加各种培训学习。

为了进一步深入开展节能降耗活动，专委员及时总结和交流各企业在节能降耗活动中的先进经验和先进设备的采用，使会员企业基本上都完成了今年我市下达万元工业产值能耗下降5%的目标任务。专委会还积极引导行业中的企业参加乐清市经信局组织的“2012年节能降耗财政专项资金补助项目”，争取政府资金补助，为企业解决资金困难问题。另一方面，为了加强会员单位内人才培训工作，今年四月份专委会与温州市人事局密切合作，积极组织会员单位有关技术人员参加塑料高级工程师、助理工程师职称评审。

5月下旬，组织会员单位积极参加乐清市质量协会举办的“企业标准化人员培训班”。6月中旬，通知各会员参加由周培玉教授主讲的“中小企业的创新策略—透视企业创新成败”讲座。与此同时，我们多次参加和协助兄弟协会换届和召开年会、讲座，取长补短，使专委会工作人员的能力得到了锻炼和提升。

六、组织考察访问，开拓会员视野与经营理念的提升

为促进与亚洲同行的交流，专委会根据需要部分会员单位参加今年4月18~21日，在上海举行的第二十六届中国国际塑料橡胶工业展览会，来自各个国家和地区的绿色橡塑科技供应商，提供的先进环保橡塑产品及科技，和先进的生产设备及工艺。

7月22日专委会理事会一行8人赴江苏考察。与江苏华洋尼龙有限公司的相关负责人召开了座谈会，分析了市场的发展前景及同行业的技术交流。另外还参观了我专委会在江苏的会员企业——副理事长单位海安永达塑料新材料有限公司。

8月12~17日，我专委会30多家会员企业一行52人，由华峰集团带队赴云南丽江、玉龙雪山和香格里拉一带参观游览。一路上，各企业代表谈笑风生，不仅交流各自的生产经验，管理技巧，而且还探讨着塑料配线器材行业的总体发展方向，各会员企业不仅在融洽、和谐的氛围中度过了快乐的云南之旅，同时也有效地促进了会员间的相互交流、相互学习，不断提升和增强了会员间的凝聚力。

七、加强行业自律，制定行业标准，规范行业发展秩序

为了规范行业行为，协调同行利益关系，维护行业间的公平竞争和正当利益，今年以来，专委会多次不定期地召开行业自律会议，有效地促进了行业健康有序发展，达成和谐共处的局面。

为引导本行业的健康发展，按照国家工信部《聚酰胺扎带行业标准》的计划要求，专委会制标小组2012年按部就班地实施着这项工作：

1. 5月份完成了行业标准征求意见稿。2012年1~4月份，由标准起草小组牵头企业长虹塑料集团有限公司，收集了专委会企业及会员以外的共13家企业，200多种3000多根聚酰胺扎带，送到专业检测机构进行了检测。针对检测结果，应用了统计技术对样品的检测数据进行汇总和分析。针对聚酰胺扎带产品的特点和我国现有的生产水平，及GB/T 191、GB/T 2423、GB/T 5169.5—2008、GB 13140.1—2008等相关标准要求，对《聚酰胺扎带行业标准》做了进一步的修改和规定。

标准起草小组在对标准的技术指标进行充分验证后，并在工作组中进行多次讨论，标准起草小组针对各项检测结果，并多次征求中国标准化委员会、及中国塑料加工工业协会领导的意见和建议，于2012年5月完成了《聚酰胺扎带》行业标准的征求意见稿的编制工作，并完成了《聚酰胺扎带行业标准编制说明》、《聚酰胺扎带行业标准测试分析报告》，并把征求意见稿发放给生产企业、使用企业、专业检测机构三十多家企业征求意见。

2. 8月份顺利通过了行业标准审查会，形成行标报批稿。由长虹塑料集团有限公司牵头起草的自锁式聚酰胺扎带行业标准审查会，于2012年8月2日在浙江省乐清市柳市镇举行。出席本次会议的有：中国塑料加工工业协会副理事长曹俭；国家塑料制品质量监督检验中心常务副主任、国家塑料制品标准化技术委员会秘书长陈家琪；中国塑料加工工业协会副秘书长综合业务部主任田岩；国家塑料制品标准化技术委员会工程师李田华；乐清市质量技术监督局局长王守根；乐清市质量技术监督局质量科科长叶阿建以及浙江省塑料行业协会、温州市塑料行业协会的领导。

会议由国家塑料制品标准化技术委员会秘书长陈家琪担任了《聚酰胺扎带》行业标准审查组组长并主持了会议。起草组介绍了标准主要内容、编制情况及主要意见处理情况；专家就上述介绍的情况进行详细提问，起草组一一作出了解释；专家组逐条对标准内容进行了审查；专家组在认真听取了标准主要起草人对该标准编制情况的说明与标准内容的讲解后，对标准文本条款逐项进行研讨和审查，最终形成审查意见：专家组一致认为该行业标准具有较好的科学性、前瞻性和实用性，顺利通过了本次审核。

目前，该标准已形成了《聚酰胺扎带行业标准》报批稿，已报送到国家工信部，等待批复发行！

下一年度工作思路和要点：

在新的一年里，我们将认真学习贯彻十八大精神，深入贯彻落实科学发展观，坚持面向塑料行业，创新务实，全心全意为企业和会员单位服务。同时，为了强化“中国塑料配线器材工贸基地”建设，努力克服国际金融危机带来的不利影响，加大内销、扩大出口，进一步提升企业的经济效益，新的一年里我们将扎实有效地做好以下各项工作：

一、引导行业企业适应经济发展形势，为会员企业保驾护航

今年以来，全球经济形势复杂多变，和其他产业一样，全球性的经济不景气，成为了专委员发展的焦点问题。预计明年上半年或者更长时间内经济不会有太大的复苏，未来企业间的竞争将愈发激烈，各企业仍将面临严峻的挑战，希望行业中的各企业能从产品质量入手，夯实管理，扩大销售区域，拓展销售领域，以适应新环境的要求。专委会将持续关注未来塑料配线器材产业发展的走势，为企业发展保驾护航。

二、利用多种渠道，推动行业企业产业升级转型

专委会将积极推动产业升级，应对塑料配线器材行业国际化发展需求。推进行业内科技进步和技术创新，提倡节约资源，推行清洁生产，提高可持续发展能力。规范国内塑料配线器材市场秩序，实现行业的良性竞争和健康发展，产品品质高端化，地区产业均衡化的发展目标。明年专委会将着手申请制定，塑料配线器材行业其他产品的国家标准或行业标准，进一步促进塑料配线器材行业稳步发展。

三、依靠科技技术升级，提升企业综合素质

依靠科技进步，推动行业自主创新，以增强企业自主创新能力为出发点，积极利用国内外科技资源，帮助企业在引进技术的基础上，加强消化吸收再创新和集成创新；积极开展合作创新，提高研发水平；从目前塑料配线器材产业发展的趋势来看，企业仅靠增加资金投入、扩大生产规模的粗放式经营已不能满足形势发展的需要，塑料配线器材生产已进入调整产品结构、提高开发能力、提高产品附加值的新时期。因此，专委会将引导企业在产品技术升级、换代上下功夫。

四、做好发展工作，扩大专委会规模

发展会员是一个组织具有生命力的重要表现，做好会员发展和管理工作，既要发展规模较大的企业，也要发展中小型企业，以增强专委会的广泛性和代表性，增强专委会的凝聚力和影响力。专委会仍将通过一系列举措，扩大自身在行业内的影响力，吸纳更多会员，进一步壮大专委会的队伍，发挥专委会常委的作用，使塑料配线器材行业发展成一个有凝聚力、向心力的强大团体。

在新的一年里，我们将站在新的起点，迎接新的挑战，深入贯彻落实科学发展观，在中国塑料加工工业协会的正确领导下，围绕乐清市委、市政府的总体发展思路和工作思路，结合本行业的发展要素，在专委会理事会的带领下，精诚合作，锐意创新，科学发展，为塑料配线器材行业转型升级、快速发展而努力奋斗！

（中国塑料加工工业协会配线器材专业委员会　侯芳放）

塑料配线器材行业特色区域与产业集群情况——中国塑料配线器材工贸基地

一、2011 年塑料配线器材行业基本情况

塑料配线器材生产企业在全国范围内有 100 多家，其中有 80% 的企业聚集在浙江省乐清市，是一个成熟、多元化的产业。塑料配线器材产品主要包括：尼龙扎带、压线帽、接线端子、线卡、配线槽等产品，其中尼龙扎带为主导产品，其主要原料为尼龙 PA66。

现在本行业已形成了专业化分工细、区域规模经济优势明显、技术含量和市场占有率高等产业优势。塑料配线器材已成为电器设备、工程、建筑、汽车行业中不可缺少的重要组成部分，其发展水平和产业兴衰直接关系到我国塑料工业和电器工业的发展。随着国内经济的飞速发展，国内对配线器材市场的需求每年呈现 30% 以上的增长速度。产品不仅销往全国各地，而且行业中 50% 以上企业都从事国际贸易，产品销往欧洲、北美洲、南美洲、大洋洲、非洲、亚洲等 200 多个国家和地区。

塑料配线器材行业经过长足的发展，已经形成完整的工业体系和门类，但与国际发达国家相比，与社会发展和国民经济增长不断变化和升级的要求相比，在质量品种、新产品技术含量、技术开发水平及产品规模布局、人才等多方面与国外的差距还较大，仍有许多不足。

目前都是国内众多中小型企业占据很大一部分市场份额，但从以后竞争将趋向品牌化、规模化来看，中小型企业的生存空间将被压缩。特别是加入 WTO 后，由于塑料配线器材行业市场的开放，国际上的尼龙扎带公司会有更多的机会参与国内的项目建设，国内的尼龙扎带市场的产品销售将会更注重产品质量，市场会更加规范化，现有的一些小生产线无论是在质量上还是在生产水平上，都不能适应市场上对产品高水平的要求，势必要被淘汰。

整体上来说，供需还算平衡，在供给能力增长的同时，需求量也在快速增长，所以在未来几年内供需之间的摩擦不会太激烈。但生产企业在扩大生产规模时也要注意市场供需的变化，在细分市场中的供需变化会随着企业投入的具体产品而变化，所以企业在决定扩大何种产品产量时要尤其关注该类产品的市场动态。

二、2011 年塑料配线器材行业特色区域和产业集群发展概况

随着社会经济的飞速发展，形形色色的塑料产品已装点着不同的社会领域，丰富着人们的生产和生活。据不完全统计，浙江省乐清市塑料制品的生产企业有 300 多家，塑料行业是乐清经济的支柱产业之一，年产值达 260 多亿元。乐清塑料行业的发展大致经历了起步、形成、发展三个阶段。20 世纪 70 年代末为起步阶段。1979 年，乐清塑料产业企业不上十家，塑料制品产量不足千吨，其产值仅占工业总产值的 5% 左右。80 年代期间，随着乡镇企业的蓬勃发展，个体工业如雨后春笋般地发展起来，塑料产业得到了一定的发展，企业数发展到50来家，塑料制品产量已达40kt。90年代以后工业经济的高速增长，推动了塑料产业的发展壮大。到2007年，塑料产业企业发展至300多家，实现销售收入200亿元，占乐清市全年工业销售收入的25%以上。

2011年，乐清市工业总产值达到1503.33亿元，同比增长16.1%。据不完全统计，乐清2011年生产塑料配线器材达320kt，实现工业总产值超110亿元，占全国总产量的70%以上。经过30多年的发展，乐清现在形成了专业化分工细、区域规模经济优势明显、技术含量和市场占有率高等产业优势。长虹塑料、海泰塑料、新光塑料、亚泰塑料、华达塑料、惠华电子、可易塑料等一批规模龙头企业，不仅年产值过亿，而且不断提升自身产品质量，使产品一次成形合格率达到了98%以上，出厂合格率达到100%，为我市塑料配线器材发展奠定了坚实的基础。在乐清市，塑料配线器材销售网点达100多个，产品不仅销往全国各地，且销往欧洲、北美州、南美州、大洋州、非州、亚州等200多个国家和地区。

2008年初，以长虹塑料有限公司为发起单位，吸纳了70多家生产企业成立了塑料配线器材专业委员会，理事长郑元和在乐清柳市繁华路段——新市中街，打造出一个塑料配线器材专销基地，让所有生产塑料配线器材厂家的销售网点，集中在一条街、一片区域进行销售，既方便客户的采购，又便于企业提升产品质量，扩大了销售规模，增加企业效益，形成协会统一管理、集中销售、规模经营的新局面，使塑料配线器材行业成为乐清市经济增长的新亮点。柳市低压电器、虹桥电子元器件专业市场分别被称为“低压电器之都”、“电子元器件基地”，作为电器的配套产品塑料配线器材行业也茁壮成长起来了。

三、特色区域和产业集群发展特点

乐清市打造塑料配线器材工贸基地，带动了区域经济。与国外厂家相比：我们的产品品种多、规格型号齐全、质量好、价格低，所以产品远销欧洲、北美州、南美州、大洋州、非州、亚州等，几乎是遍布全球。

塑料配线器材行业的快速发展，一方面得益于该行业产业链覆盖了整个行业的三个领域，包括塑料原料、塑料加工机械以及塑料制品领域。也得益于这三个领域的协同合作，塑料配线产业不断发展以满足国内及出口市场的需求，为这些产业提供了高品质、低成本的运营环境，给企业带来了更高的利润。

另一方面，塑料配线器材产业市场相对稳定，市场需求量大。例如，面对国际经济危机严峻挑战，塑料配线器材的多数公司对市场进行“两手抓”：国内、国外齐抓共管，在放眼世界的同时也积极开发国内市场，使得订单不减、生产不停。另一方面，狠抓节能减排工作，倡导清洁生产，降低生产成本，增强产品竞争力。以过硬的产品质量和夯实的管理基础和组织建设，与全球性的经济危机打了一次大胜仗。

乐清塑料产业显示了典型产业集群特征，形成了不易为其他地区所比拟的核心竞争力。成立基地有三大优势：一是竞争优势。大量塑料制品生产企业在空间上高度集中，使得竞争更加激烈。有效竞争的结果，促进了企业对市场的快速反应和应对能力，推动了技术改造和管理创新。二是专业化分工优势。企业间处于既竞争又合作的状态，明显降低了制造成本和交易成本，增强了竞争力。三是区域规模经济优势。规模经济是一个大企业生产两种或多种类似产品所具有的生产成本和营销成本优势。乐清众多的塑料制品中小企业，正是通过产业集聚，形成专业化合作网络，获得与大企业同样的规模经济，构成“无形大工厂”式的区域产业规模。

乐清塑料配线器材产业坚持走产、学、研之路，充分利用新型材料和先进技术，不断开发市场需求的具有环保生态功能的新产品。例如塑料配线器材专委会会长单位：长虹塑料有限公司采用了世界先进水平的智慧型500T富强鑫注塑机以及热流道模具、机械手等先进设备，使企业由原来的半自动生产，改为全自动匀速流水线作业，不仅大大提高了生产能力，而且更好地保证了产品的性能特点，稳定了产品质量，增强了企业的竞争力!

为了实现行业自我管理、自我约束、自我监督和自我发展，在乐清市委市政府以及中国塑料加工工业协会的大力支持和帮助下，2008年5月12日由中华人民共和国民政部批准成立了：中国塑料加工工业协会塑料配线器材专业委员会! 协会组织生产企业率先在尺寸规格、性能指标等核心评价指标上制定统一标准，通过标准来对整个行业的规范起到推动作用，协助有关部门开展产品质量监测、评定工作，提高企业的技术素质和管理水平，协调和服务全市塑料配线器材生产企业，从而形成了行业自我管理、自我约束、自我监督、自我完善和自我发展的良好发展势态!

四、特色区域和产业集群发展中存在的问题

由于大部分塑料配线器材生产企业，都在浙江省乐清市柳市这个工业重镇设立了自己的销售中心，但这些销售机构分布散杂，而且没有行业标准，各企业都使用自己的企业标准，因而难免出现产品良莠不均、品质参差不齐的现象。

自专委会成立以来，我们时刻关注这一重点工作，在这种情况下，专委会决定号召塑料配线器材领域内的领军企业率先在尺寸规格、性能指标等核心评价指标上制定统一标准，希望通过标准来对整个行业的规范起到推动作用，这样还能够协助有关

部门开展产品质量监测、评定工作，提高企业的技术素质和管理水平。协调和服务全市塑料配线器材生产企业，形成了行业自我管理、自我约束、自我监督、自我完善和自我发展的良好发展势态！

由于“聚酰胺(尼龙)扎带”国内尚无国家标准和行业标准，为了规范企业行为，保障产品质量安全，促进塑料配线器材行业产业结构调整和优化升级，2010年长虹塑料有限公司根据产业发展需求，向国家工信部提出申请制定“自锁式聚酰胺(尼龙)扎带”行业标准，2011年元月7日获得国家工信部批准，并通过了公示。目前，长虹塑料集团有限公司正在为行业标准《自锁式聚酰胺(尼龙)扎带》的制定而进行各项准备工作。

我国塑料配线器材行业在快速发展的同时，长期的积累矛盾和问题逐步显现，一些企业产品质量不高的问题比较突出。自主创新能力不强、产品附加值低，关键技术装备主要依赖进口；产业结构亟待调整，出口市场未形成多元化格局；出口产品以贴牌加工为主，中低端产品多，高质量、高附加值产品少；低水平重复建设和盲目扩张严重，节能减排压力巨大；产品质量保障体系不完善，企业质量安全意识不强。

塑料配线器材产业在未来的两三年内可能面临以下四大压力：一是原材料价格暴跌暴涨和利润微薄带来的压力；二是融资困难和财务成本上升带来的压力；三是产业升级和结构调整带来的压力；四是国外市场萎缩和产能过剩带来的压力。

五、2012年及“十二五”期间特色区域和产业集群发展思路和方向

目前，国内塑料配线器材生产企业大部分属于中小企业，生产技术力量较为薄弱，信息交流及科技开发力度差，产品优级品率低、制造成本高，直接影响企业生产效益。故应进一步加强塑料国内配线器材行业的管理，加强行业自律，提高行业的技术创新水平，扩大产品的出口创汇，提升产品质量安全、品牌形象和市场竞争力，满足消费需求。塑料配线器材产品的可靠性、使用寿命要求达到国际同类产品水平。因产品质量安全问题造成的外贸争端、消费者投诉和重大突发事件明显减少。

制定国家标准或行业标准，在尺寸规格、性能指标等核心评价指标上，制定统一标准，通过标准来对整个行业的规范起到推动作用。第一步制定尼龙(PA聚酰胺)扎带标准，通过不断的研究和探讨，下一步将把塑料配线器材全部产品(如接线端子、线帽、线卡等产品)规范化标准化管理，进一步引导行业健康有序发展。另一方面，为配合环保发展的大方向，塑料配线器材行业将在“十二五”期间，从不同方面加大投入，全力推进绿色制造和低碳经济，使行业可持续发展。在当前国家大力发展循环经济、建设节约型社会的政策环境下，塑料配线器材行业的发展趋势为：大力发展多种规格塑料配线器材产品，继续努力自主创新，以技术降低成本，提高产品竞争力，向节材、节能、节水方向发展，提高塑料的再生利用率，实现可持续发展。

乐清未来塑料产业的发展，要以塑料配线器材为核心，带动原料贸易及塑模、塑机研发和贸易，形成完整的产业链，加快塑料配线器材的升级和换代，向专业化、规模化、国际化方向发展。

六、措施与政策建议

乐清塑料配线器材产业坚持走产、学、研之路，充分利用新型材料和先进技术，不断开发市场需求的具有环保生态功能的新产品。维护生态平衡，保护环境是关系到人类生存、社会发展的根本性问题。因而塑料配线器材协会要求各生产企业的绿色制造要从原材料抓起。要求选择原材料时，设计人员要改变传统的选材方法，不能依据传统的制造业思想，需要在满足基本功能的前提下，考虑使用符合标准、良好的环保材料。要求各企业以提高国内产品的环保水平为已任，增强社会责任感，从而使乐清的塑料配线器材制造业提升到新的管理层面。具体建议为以下几个方面：

1. 制定行业标准，采纳各企业好的建议，做好咨询服务工作。

2. 举办行业研讨会等专题会议，加强行业规划发展工作。

3. 产品开发

A、追求产品质量

B、促进产品多元化发展

4. 拓宽渠道销售

A、销售模式分类，分析市场投资理性化

B、市场投资建议

5. 品牌营销

A、不同品牌经营模式

B、切入开拓品牌

C、应对全球经济危机

D、把握扩大内需保增长，提前应对全球经济危机

（中国塑料加工工业协会塑料配线器材专业委员会　侯芳放）

镀铝膜

在2010年火爆的镀铝膜行情刺激下，到2012年镀铝膜产能又迎来了一个新的大增长。目前国内超

过2m的生产线在70条以上，设备年产能约450～500kt，粗略统计单月产能过千吨的企业约12家。这其中还不包括一些做镭射、卡纸等自产自销不进入社会流通的设备产能。新增长主要分布在山东、浙江、安徽、潮汕等地区。但从今年1～9月份的市场情况来看，行业产能利用率不足五成，供求关系严重失衡。以8月份为例，除海宁长宇镀铝膜单月销售超过4500t以外，其他单月销售超过1000t的企业不超过两家。

进入2012年，包装膜需求总量的增长几乎停滞。据中国塑膜网统计：下游彩印开机率方面，今年第三季度：湖南/西南5～7成、华南/华北地区4～6成、华东地区5～7成，较第二季度略有回升；而就在二季度，华北地区彩印镀铝仅1～2成开机率。就目前来看，今年第四季度的情况，依然不容乐观。外部经济没有达到大家预期的增长，包装行业产能同时又在急剧扩张，直接加剧市场无序竞争。

2012年镀铝膜及镀铝基材全年价格波动不大，近两年来行业自身已经失去价格主导权，薄膜价格基本尾随专用料成本的变化而变化，很长时间材料加工费维持在成本线以下，以典型的PET镀铝膜及基材为例：

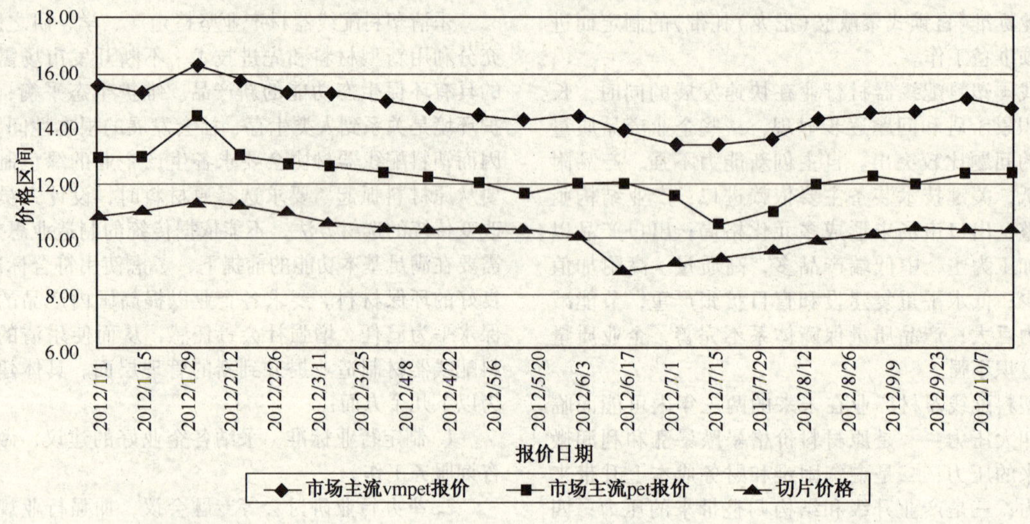

2012年VMPET价格走势图

从以上价格走势图可以看出：

1. 全年镀铝膜主流加工费维持在2300元/t左右，在6月下旬到7月的近一个月时间里，平均加工费2000元/t。

2. PET基材加工费维持在2000元/t左右，在7月底有几天与同期切片差价仅1400元/t。

CPP镀铝膜加工费情况也差不多，下面是2012年CPP镀铝膜主流价格走势：

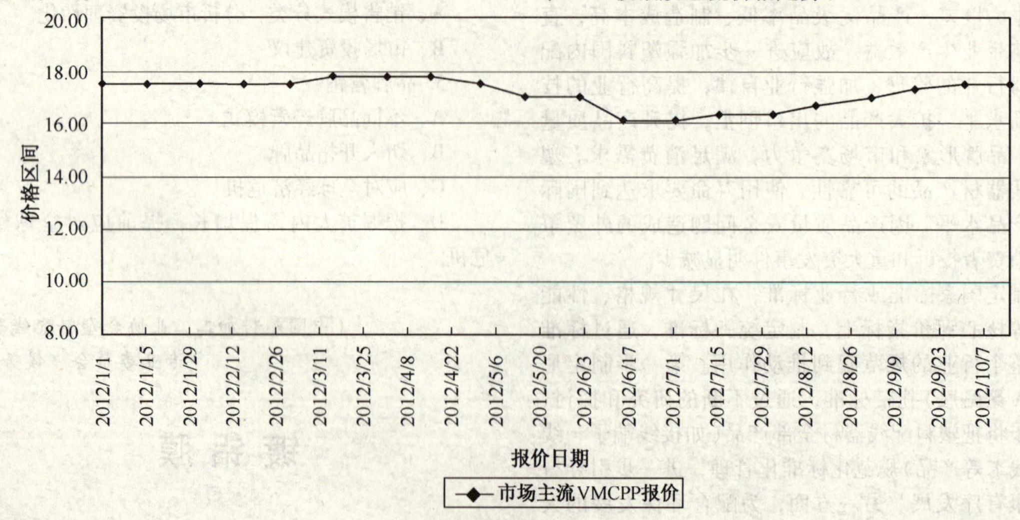

2012年VMCPP价格走势图

由于行业中镀铝膜的质量、基材的品质以及采购的渠道都有很大的差异性，镀铝加工成本也存在一定的差距，因此对于极高质量要求产品的加工费可以会到达8000～10000元/t，但最低加工费也有仅1000～1200元/t的。这几个方面的因素也导致同样用途的VMPET或VMCPP，市场上的销售价格有较大的区间。一方面是持续低迷的市场需求，另一方面是快速扩充的生产产能，同时还伴随着不断增加的人工、管理及财务成本，种种因素考验着我们每个企业的经营者。

就目前的情况来看，大部分企业是在艰难中谋求生存而不是发展。但正是在这种大的环境下，通过镀铝膜行业这十几年来不断的发展成熟和完善，一些企业逐渐摸索出适合自身发展的方向，在残酷的市场环境中保持强有力的竞争力，同时也给我们镀铝膜行业后期的发展提供了一些启示：

一、产品品质的多样化发展

随着人们对食品安全和包装效果的日益重视，以及下游厂家包装设备的不断升级，从而对镀铝膜阻隔性和功能性的要求更加明确和加强。我们只有顺应这种发展趋势，力求走在行业前列，避免产品同质化，以增加产品附加值和企业竞争力。比如长宇公司在几年前就开始根据产品阻隔性及产品用途进行分级销售，从11年下半年开始，又对高雾膜、CPP加强型膜、超低温膜、低摩擦膜等加强了研发和推广，目前这些产品都已在批量生产，取得了比较好的效益。

二、产品类型的多元化转型

早期的镀铝膜主要用于食品软包装及镭射标签，近几年已逐步向其他领域拓展。比如电子膜及目前还基本依赖进口的太阳膜；用于标签及高档礼品盒包装的消光镀铝膜；利用其反光、遮光效果的镀铝膜、镀铝布；以及主要用于出口的丝线级、绣片级镀铝膜等等。目前有几家镀铝企业在这些领域分别做的比较专业，具有相对较高的市场竞争力。

三、销售渠道的拓展

对于行业的发展这是一个不得不提的话题。前面所讲到的产品类型的转型和产品品质的多样化也是渠

道拓展的方向，另外一个很重要的是出口贸易的增长。长宇公司自11年初正式开始出口贸易，到现在出口可以达到总销售额的10%～15%，特别是今年第二季度，曾一度达到20%。在这里需要提请注意的是，外贸不等于高利润，它只是产品销售的一个途径，只是意味着产品质量控制及企业管理更加严谨。

因此镀铝行业要稳定良性的发展要从三个方面努力：

1. 通过装备的改良、管理的创新及技术的突破来降低成本，使镀铝产品更经济，在各种包装材料中更有竞争力。

2. 提高客户对产品的认知度，扩宽产品的用途，使镀铝膜应用更广泛，以提高镀铝膜的用量。

3. 提高客户对产品的认可度。正是由于目前镀铝膜产品质量的参差不齐，导致镀铝膜两个极好的固有特性——阻隔性和美观性得不到市场广泛的认可，因为镀铝质量得不到保障，影响客户使用和镀铝膜产品的推广。

我相信通过我们大家的努力镀铝行业一定能更加快速健康的发展。

（中国塑料加工工业协会镀铝膜专业委员会　曾祥平）

密胺塑料制品

一、密胺专委会成立情况

1、筹备阶段

密胺，也叫密胺树脂，英文名称为melamine，中文译名美耐皿。密胺树脂制成的餐具和脲醛树脂加表面密胺粉制成的餐具合称密胺(仿瓷)餐具。我国于20世纪60年代引进密胺(仿瓷)餐具制造技术，经过50年的不断发展，取得了长足的进步，成为世界主要密胺(仿瓷)餐具生产国。近年来，随着我国塑料工业的迅猛发展，共有1000多家出口密胺餐具的生产企业，遍布全国20多个省市。

2009年8月11日，中国塑料加工工业协会向中国轻工业联合会、国资委和民政部等相关业务主管部门递交了申请成立密胺塑料制品专业委员会的报告等相关材料。中国轻工业联合会等主管部门对成立密胺塑料制品专业委员会一事给予了高度重视，经过研究后，下发了准予筹备成立密胺塑料制品专业委员会的批复文件。

在中国塑料加工工业协会廖正品会长的指导下，密胺塑料制品专业委员会筹备工作就此展开。2010年4月，美加美餐具股份有限公司、恒盛仿瓷餐具有限公司、台州希尔家庭用品有限公司、华美塑胶制品有限公司、三恒密胺制品有限公司、莆田金景餐具有限公司等6家发起单位，在泉州市举行了密胺塑料制品行业发展座谈会，就密胺塑料制品行业未来发展方向问题，展开讨论，在求同存异、共谋

发展的思路上，一致明确了成立专委会的必要性和重要性。期间，成立了密胺塑料制品专业委员会筹委会。在美加美餐具股份有限公司的积极支持下，落实了专委会筹建工作的办公场所，专委会筹委会秘书处的办公地点确定在美加美餐具股份有限公司。

2010年7月，在泉州召开了有美加美、恒盛、希尔、华美、三恒、金景等6家企业参加的发起人会议，对《工作条例(草案)》、机构组织和会费标准等有关事项进行了认真的讨论，求同存异，共谋发展，达成了一致的意见。

2010年9月5日，在浙江台州召开专委会筹备会议，会议由中国塑料加工工业协会马占峰秘书长主持。

2、正式成立

从积极筹备到得到正式同意筹建的批复，再到积极筹备，最后到确定日期召开成立大会，历经几个月。中国塑料加工工业协会密胺塑料制品专业委员会成立大会暨第一届理事会议于2010年10月15日在泉州市举行。本次大会应到会员单位35家，实到会员单位33家。

成立大会议程严格按照既定程序有条不紊地进行，通过全体与会代表的共同努力，按照民主协商，共谋思路，协调平衡的原则，会议通过表决，审议、通过了《中国塑料加工工业协会密胺塑料制品专业委员会工作条例(草案)》，审议、通过了《中国塑料加工工业协会密胺塑料制品专业委员会会费管理办法》。

大会以无记名投票的方式进行等额选举，选举产生了密胺塑料制品专业委员会第一届理事会，选举产生了密胺塑料制品专业委员会第一届理事长、副理事长、秘书长以及副秘书长。

二、密胺专委会大事记

中国塑料加工工业协会密胺塑料制品专业委员成立后，进行密胺塑料制品行业的自律管理，团结广大会员，为行业发展积极开展相关活动，主要如下：

1、2010年4月，美加美餐具股份有限公司、恒盛仿瓷餐具有限公司、台州希尔家庭用品有限公司、华美塑胶制品有限公司、三恒密胺制品有限公司、莆田金景餐具有限公司等6家发起单位，在泉州市举行了密胺塑料制品(仿瓷餐具)行业发展座谈会，成立了密胺塑料制品专业委员会筹委会。

2、2010年9月5日，在浙江台州召开专委会筹备会议，会议由中国塑料加工工业协会马占峰秘书长主持。

3、2010年10月15日，中国塑料加工工业协会密胺塑料制品专业委员会正式成立。

4、2010年10月15日，在美加美餐具股份有限公司的会议室里，举行“密胺塑造制品质量安全卫生研讨会”，参加密胺专业委员成立大会的代表与应邀的专家学者就密胺塑料制品质量安全卫生问题开展了研讨，会议由密胺专业委员会会长吴家福主持。

5、2010年11月，密胺专委会网站(www. chinamelamine. cn)正式开通，上传密胺塑料制品行业相关法规政策、有关部门对密胺塑料制品的新要求新规、会员单位资讯以及密胺塑料制品供销信息。

6、2010年12月，编印专委会宣传资料《中国密胺》，积极介绍、宣传密胺专委会。

7、2011年5月，密胺专委会部分理事单位、会员单位参与福建省泉州市出入境检验检疫局组织的“欧盟塑料食品接触产品安全卫生法规解读”“欧盟塑料食品接触产品技术法规应对策略及建议”，并编写《应对欧盟塑料制食品接触产品技术法规材料汇编》。

8、2011年6月10日，密胺专委会部分理事单位、会员单位参与Intertek天祥集团在厦门举办“欧盟塑料食品容器最新法规解读专场研讨会”，以期帮助相关企业单位的产品安全进入国外市场，降低产品风险。

9、2011年11月18日，中国轻工业联合会副会长、中国塑料加工工业协会理事长钱桂敬、中国塑料加工工业协会副理事长曹俭、中国塑料加工工业协会主任刘姝等来泉州视察中国塑协密胺塑料制品专业委员会，召开座谈会。

10、2012年1月，整理、汇编密胺专委会行业相关信息资料《密胺参考》(第一期)。

11、2012年6月，整理、汇编密胺专委会行业相关信息资料《密胺参考》(第二期)。

12、2012年7月22日，天祥集团部分领导到我会副秘书长单位恒盛密胺餐具有限公司参观，并就密胺塑料制品检验检测相关问题进行座谈，探讨密胺行业发展事宜。

13、2012年11月18日在福建出入境检验检疫局(福州市)三楼会议室召开密胺专委会副理事长会议。主要内容：①传达、学习上级有关文件；②研讨当前密胺塑料制品(密胺餐具)生产、出口所面临的问题；③与商检相关部门领导讨论企业商检分类方式相关事宜；④讨论进一步加强专委会内部管理、存在问题与建议；⑤讨论2013年专委会相关工作开展的有关事宜。

14、2013年1月，整理、汇编密胺专委会行业相关信息资料《密胺参考》(第三期)。

15、2013年6月，整理、汇编密胺专委会行业相关信息资料《密胺参考》（第四期）。

16、2013年8月9日～2013年8月11日，组织专委会理事单位、部分会员单位参观、考察广东省部分密胺行业龙头企业和机器设备、材料供应企业等单位。2013年8月11日下午召开"2013年密胺餐具行业发展"座谈会，内容包括：①市场与技术交流；②会员代表经验交流。

三、行业展望

（一）密胺塑料制品行业风险时刻存在

1、欧美出口市场形势严峻。自2008年以来，我国密胺餐具遭遇了较大的挑战，欧盟委员会通过了法规（EU）No 284 / 2011，进一步提高了技术门槛，订单减少、超标通报等，对我国密胺塑料制品出口造成影响。

2、生产成本不断上升，无序竞争影响行业合力形成。近些年来，密胺塑料制品的原料价格不断上升，物流、人力成本等价格也水涨船高，给出口密胺塑料制品企业造成很大的经济压力，密胺塑料制品出口难度进一步增大；而我国密胺塑料制品企业，除了少数一部分的企业在生产、管理等方面较为规范之外，大部分密胺塑料制品企业的生产技术、质量管理体系十分不健全，尚未通过相关管理认证，很多企业仍以家庭作坊式生产为主，产品品质的关注度尚未提升至企业的核心层面，未树立正确的质量安全意识观。为了降低成本，不少企业把降低原料等级、缩减工艺流程作为市场竞争的主要手段，导致整个行业呈现出相互压价、无序竞争的恶性循环，无法形成行业合力。这使得国内密胺塑料制品生产企业出口雪上加霜。

3、研发能力薄弱，产品附加值低，缺乏规模效应。我国虽然成为世界主要密胺餐具生产国，加工企业众多，但是大部分都是中小企业，技术水平相对比较落后，自主研发产品较少，企业在产品研发方面依附性强、自主创新能力差。大部分密胺产品的生产企业，产品多走低端路线，我国用于出口的密胺塑料制品大都是日常生活用品和工艺品，而具有高技术含量和高附加值的特殊工程塑料制品出口相对较少，产品附加值不高，从而导致企业出口量虽然不少，但利润却难以增加，制约着出口竞争力的提升。

（二）密胺行业发展机遇

1、密胺塑料制品行业经过多年的发展，中国密胺行业无论是产品数量还是质量都有了很大的发展，并跻身国内大行业领域。尤其是密胺（仿瓷）餐具因其颜色鲜艳、造型美观、价格低廉受到越来越多国外消费者的喜爱，加上近来来密胺（仿瓷）餐具质量有了很大提升，出口外贸保持在7%～10%的增长。因此，密胺（仿瓷）餐具在今后依然是欧美等地餐具的主流品种，行业前景依然广阔。

2、随着了国内国外产品质量标准越来越严格的严峻考验，密胺塑料制品（仿瓷餐具）相关的技术、原材料、机器设备的改进，生产技术的提高，以及自动化程度的提高，尤其是部分密胺制品企业增强产品的原创性技术，强化自主品牌战略，使得密胺塑料制品（仿瓷餐具）在国内外市场的竞争力逐渐上升，助推我国密胺塑料制品（仿瓷餐具）品牌国际化，扩大了影响力。这必然有利于推动我国密胺塑料制品（仿瓷餐具）的发展，为密胺行业带来新的发展机遇。

3、据统计，我国密胺（仿瓷）餐具已占全球产量的80%以上份额，每年出口总额超10亿美元，其中厂家大多集中在福建省、广东潮汕地区和浙江台州等地，形成了相对集中的产业集群，出现了有交互关联性的服务供应商、相关产业的厂商及其他相关机构等组成的群体，对我国密胺塑料制品（仿瓷餐具）行业，走产业集群化发展，有利于降低企业的制度成本（包括生产成本、交换成本），提高规模经济效益和范围经济效益，进一步整合行业合力，提升行业的综合竞争力。

4、随着网络技术的发展，电子商务越来越深入社会，电子商务产品给中小口企业提供了新的发展机会，不仅能节省大量减少人力、物力，降低交易成本，更为中小企业进入国际市场创造了一个自由平等的竞争环境和更为广泛的合作空间。如阿里巴巴推出的专门用于出口贸易的电子商务产品"出口通"，又如天祥集团研发的ISI，帮助买家在作出采购决策的过程中获取可靠的工厂资讯，包括厂商基本资料、生产能力和合规方案等。电子商务新平台为密胺塑料制品（仿瓷餐具）企业在当今全球商业环境的发展提供了又一机遇。

2008年以来，密胺塑料制品（仿瓷餐具）行业的发展经历艰辛，对于行业的发展既是挑战，也是机遇。密胺塑料制品（仿瓷餐具）行业只有抓住机遇，以强烈的社会责任感，积极应对各种看似不利的事件，在推进整个行业的发展的同时，获得企业的发展。

（中国塑料加工工业协会密胺塑料制品专业委员会　赖汉文）

挤出聚苯乙烯泡沫板材行业

一、2012 年我国挤塑板产量及行业形势

受国家房地产调控、提高建筑外墙保温材料阻燃要求影响，2012 年我国挤塑板行业发展速度继续在低速徘徊，预计产量约 1200 万立方米，略高于 2010 年水平。行业内产量较大的企业有欧文斯科宁(南京)建筑材料公司、可耐福保温材料(中国)有限公司、北京北鹏新型建材有限公司、南京法宁格节能科技有限公司、上海上福塑料制品有限公司、广州市孚达五金制品有限公司、西安中兆新型材料有限公司、廊坊美佳塑胶制品有限公司、大连甘子井区革镇堡鑫乾程挤塑板材厂、青岛欧克斯新型建材有限公司、张家港市天晟塑胶有限公司、北京五洲泡沫塑料有限公司、包头市中通化工防腐保温材料有限公司、南京天运塑业有限公司、唐山万兴化工建材有限公司、山东冰轮工程有限公司、吉林省华恒节能科技有限公司、杭州希尔特节能保温材料有限公司等。

受国家控制含氢氯氟烃(HCFC)发泡剂等因素影响，2012 年 XPS 生产设备有了可喜的变化，过去的只能使用 HCFC 发泡剂的低价、简陋的挤出生产设备逐渐不被市场接受，能够使用 HCFC 替代品、具有高度自动控制水平的挤出生产线获得了市场认可，将成为今后挤塑板行业的发展方向。提高挤出生产线技术水平、提高产品环保性能有利于提升产业集中度，促进行业健康发展。

二、挤塑板行业 HCFC－22/142b 替代

在 2011 年 7 月召开的蒙特利尔多边基金第 64 次执委会上，中国挤塑板行业 HCFC 淘汰计划获得批准。我国挤塑板行业将在 2015 年前淘汰 HCFC－22/142b 共 10031t(折合 592ODPt，其中 HCFC－22 约占 60%)，获得多边基金赠款 5000 万美元。联合国工业发展组织作为主要国际执行机构，德国技术合作公司(GIZ)作为辅助国际执行机构；轻工业塑料加工应用研究所作为国内执行机构。

2012 年，环境保护部环境保护对外合作中心组织编写了 XPS 泡沫行业 HCFC 淘汰计划项目实施手册，聘请了会计师事务所和专家共同对申报企业进行了考察。共有 11 家 XPS 企业通过了考察，这些企业都是 2007 年 9 月之前投产并能够提供有效证据的企业：上海新兆塑业有限公司、南京法宁格节能科技有限公司、广州孚达保温隔热材料有限公司、成都科文保温材料有限公司、天津市天德橡塑机械有限公司、南京天运塑业有限公司、杭州希尔特节能保温材料有限公司、青岛欧克斯新型建材有限公司、烟台长城磨具磨料有限公司、北京五洲泡沫塑料有限公司、唐山万兴化工建材有限公司。

这 11 家企业已经于 2013 年初与环境保护部环境保护对外合作中心签署了 HCFC 淘汰项目合同，根据企业的 HCFC 消费量的多少获得相应的资助。这些企业均选择二氧化碳技术替代 HCFC，赠款主要用于采购二氧化碳发泡生产线、安全改造和试车费用等。

(中国塑料加工工业协会　孟庆君)

塑料行业淘汰消耗臭氧层物质工作

一、泡沫塑料行业含氢氯氟烃淘汰工作进展

2011 年 7 月，我国聚氨酯和挤出聚苯乙烯(XPS)泡沫行业含氢氯氟烃(HCFCs)淘汰计划活动蒙特利尔多边基金执委会第 64 次会议批准，其中，聚氨酯泡沫行业获得多边基金资助 7300 万美元，计划淘汰HCFC－141b14685t；挤出聚苯乙烯泡沫行业获得资助5000 万美元，计划淘汰 HCFC－22 和 HCFC－142b 共 10，031t。

两个行业计划批准以后，环境保护部环境保护对外合作中心随即组织行业计划的实施工作。首先，两个行业都开展了项目实施手册编制工作，建立一系列规章制度规范各相关方的责任和义务、项目实施程序、财务制度、采购程序、监督核查机制和政策措施等。其次，通过公开招标选择国内执行机构，协助环境保护部环境保护对外合作中心管理和实施行业计划；选择会计师事务所协助开展项目企业获得赠款资格和 HCFCs 消费量的核查；第三，根据项目实施手册相关规定，发布项目申报通知，组织开展项目现场核查；第四，组织通过考察的企业编制项目执行计划；第五，签署 HCFCs 淘汰合同，开展 HCFCs 淘汰活动。

其中，聚氨酯泡沫行业 2012 年主要在冷藏集装箱、冰箱冰柜和小家电三个子行业以及适合使用水替代 HCFC－141b 的泡沫产品，如聚氨酯管中管等产品企业中开展 HCFC－141b 淘汰活动。有青岛中集冷藏箱制造有限公司等 32 家聚氨酯泡沫企业通过了环境保护部环境保护对外合作中心组织的考察，基准年(2011 年)HCFC－141b 消费量合计 8760. 69t。挤出聚苯乙烯泡沫行业主要在年 HCFC－22/142b 消费量大于 100t 的企业开展淘汰活动。有上海新兆塑业有

限公司等 11 家 XPS 企业通过考察，基准年 HCFCs 消费量合计 3296.8t。

二、中国塑料加工工业协会参与的 ODS 淘汰活动

中国塑料加工工业协会多年来一直积极支持环境保护事业，在环境保护部环境保护对外合作中心的领导下，积极参与我国泡沫塑料行业淘汰消耗臭氧层物质（ODS）活动。

2012 年，中国塑料加工工业协会在环境保护部环境保护对外合作中心组织的聚氨酯泡沫行业 HCFC－141b 淘汰国内执行机构招标中中标，成为国内执行机构，协助执行首批通过核查的 32 家聚氨酯泡沫企业 HCFC－141b 淘汰项目。国内执行机构合同于 2012 年 12 月签订。

另外，中国塑料加工工业协会于 2011 年获得的聚氨酯泡沫行业项目实施手册编写项目和聚氨酯泡沫行业全氯氟烃（CFC－11）淘汰计划完成报告编制项目在 2012 年也取得了很大进展，基本完成了项目规定工作内容，正在做作后的完善工作。

（中国塑料加工工业协会　孟庆君）

专 利 技 术

2012年专利

【名称】 顶开窗型单栋塑料大棚
【公开(公告)号】 CN102301927A
【公开(公告)日】 2012.01.04
【申请(专利权)人】 杭州市农业科学研究院
【地址】 浙江省杭州市转塘镇杭新路东1号
【发明(设计)人】 柴伟国；俞永华；卢如国
【摘要】 顶开窗型单栋塑料大棚，属于塑料大棚技术领域。其特征在于长拱杆、短拱杆通过连接件连接构成单榀拱架，两侧不等长的长拱杆、短拱杆在其顶部形成垂直顶通风窗，各个单榀拱架通过主纵杆在长拱杆顶部进行纵向连接构成大棚主体拱架，大棚主体拱架上覆盖塑料薄膜构成塑料大棚，大棚下部两侧设置侧通风窗。上述顶开窗型单栋塑料大棚，通过在大棚顶部设置垂直顶通风窗，与下部的侧通风窗相配合，形成较好的热压通风，即使在外界无风的状态下仅利用热压，也能实现自然通风。在日常生产中，由于增加了热压通风能力，在风压热压两者共同叠加作用下，显著提高了单栋大棚的自然通风性能，棚内温度不会过高，满足作物生长要求。

【名称】 酚醛模塑料热态粉碎工艺
【公开(公告)号】 CN102303378A
【公开(公告)日】 2012.01.04
【申请(专利权)人】 浙江嘉化集团股份有限公司
【地址】 浙江省海盐县经济开发区杭州湾大桥新区滨海大道1号
【发明(设计)人】 沈文明
【摘要】一种酚醛模塑料热态粉碎工艺，将酚醛模塑料生料经双辊开炼机加热辊压炼塑成片，用铲刀将料片从辊筒表面剥离，经切片装置切成小料片后，立即用高压风机将热态料片负压吸入经改装的横宽形振动筛锤片式粉碎机粉碎，在粉碎的同时，利用输送风边粉碎边冷却，粉碎后的粉料吸入料仓即为成品，酚醛模塑料切成小料片后的输送、粉碎、冷却过程均处在密封负压状态的管道和设备内进行。由于料片在热态下受锤片打击时不易产生细粉末，料片边粉碎边冷却，细粉末明显减少，80目以上细粉含量在10%以下，产品颗粒均匀，能耗降低；并且，由于输送、粉碎、冷却过程均处在密封负压状态的管道和设备内进行，生产环境得到优化。

【名称】 塑料造粒机用的振动筛选机构
【公开(公告)号】 CN102303379A
【公开(公告)日】 2012.01.04
【申请(专利权)人】 常熟市中联光电新材料有限责任公司
【地址】 江苏省苏州市常熟市沙家浜镇常昆工业园区中利路1号
【发明(设计)人】 周建新；袁文新；姚国清；陆文龙；张健；朱卫星
【摘要】 一种塑料造粒机用的振动筛选机构，属于造粒机的配套设施技术领域。包括机架，一粒末引出槽，安装在机架上；一合格粒料筛网，叠置在粒末引出槽内，并且该合格粒料筛网的底部与粒末引出槽之间保持有第一隙道；一不合格粒料筛网，叠置在合格粒料筛网内，并且该不合格粒料筛网的底部与合格粒料筛网之间保持有第二隙道；一振动电机，固定在所述的粒末引出槽的底部的外壁上，其中：在机架的左端并且位于粒末引出槽的下方设置有一用于对进入到所述不合格粒料筛网和进入到合格粒料筛网内的塑料粒子进行冷却的冷却装置。优点：避免塑料粒子粘结，减少返回造粒机重新造粒的量，保障造粒机造粒效率和节约能源；确保出自第二隙道的塑料粒子的质量。

【名称】 一种用于垃圾塑料的免水洗回收方法及专用设备
【公开(公告)号】 CN102303381A
【公开(公告)日】 2012.01.04
【申请(专利权)人】 阳文皇
【地址】 湖南省湘潭市雨湖区先锋工业园区吉祥路30号赛普公司
【发明(设计)人】 阳文皇；毕育鸣
【摘要】 一种用于垃圾塑料的免水洗回收方法及专用设备，它属于一种垃圾塑料的回收方法。它主要是解决现有水选工艺用水量大，运行成本高、对环境污染较大等技术问题。其技术方案要点是：它包括塑料与杂质分离、塑料风干、造粒工序；先将垃圾塑料原料送入破碎设备中破碎成片状料，然后将破碎后的垃圾塑料片料送入风选设备中，塑料片料及其中的杂质随着热风气流的螺旋推进，因在推进过程中会产生振动，且由于塑料与杂质的密度差异，从而使塑料与杂质完全脱离并分别飘落在不同位置而选出塑料片料并去除杂质，同时由于水份在热风的作用下加速汽化，再将风选出来的干燥干净塑料片料送至造粒设备制成可以再利用的颗粒。本发明能对垃圾塑料进行回收再利用，且工艺方法相对简单，对环境污染较少。经处理的回收塑料包括垃圾塑料均可用于制造现浇钢筋砼芯模、或用于制造工业、建筑、及日用品等，也可用于制作成生产原料如造粒料等。

【名称】 一种垃圾塑料的收回再利用方法及专用设备

【公开(公告)号】 CN102303382A

【公开(公告)日】 2012.01.04

【申请(专利权)人】 阳文皇

【地址】 湖南省湘潭市雨湖区先锋工业园区吉祥路30号赛普公司

【发明(设计)人】 阳文皇；毕育鸣

【摘要】 一种垃圾塑料的收回再利用方法及专用设备，它属于一种垃圾塑料的回收方法。它主要是解决现有水选工艺用水量大，运行成本高、对环境污染较大等技术问题。其技术方案要点是：它包括塑料与杂质分离、塑料风干、造粒、塑料改性、再造粒工序；先将垃圾塑料原料送入破碎设备中破碎成片状料，然后将破碎后的垃圾塑料片料送入风选设备中，塑料片料及其中的杂质随着热风气流的螺旋推进，因在推进过程中会产生振动，且由于塑料与杂质的密度差异，从而使塑料与杂质完全脱离并分别飘落在不同位置而选出塑料片料并去除杂质，同时由于水份在热风的作用下加速汽化，再将风选出来的干燥干净塑料片料送至造粒设备制成可以再利用的颗粒；在垃圾塑料颗粒中添加具有相容与偶联性能的改性剂混合后，再制成塑料粒料用于生产产品。本发明能对垃圾塑料进行回收再利用，且工艺方法相对简单，对环境污染较少。经处理的回收塑料包括垃圾塑料均可用于制造现浇钢筋砼芯模、或用于制造工业、建筑、及日用品等，也可用于制作成生产原料如造粒料等。

【名称】 塑料滚轮组件

【公开(公告)号】 CN102309286A

【公开(公告)日】 2012.01.11

【申请(专利权)人】 天佑电器(苏州)有限公司

【地址】 江苏省苏州市工业园区亭融街8号

【发明(设计)人】 孔钊；田玮；杨菲菲；江仁宝

【摘要】 本发明提供一种塑料滚轮组件，其包括有滚轮、连接于其上的旋转臂以及装配件。其中装配件包括用于卡扣在旋转臂上的配接部及其上设置的销棒，而旋转臂上设置有用于与销棒配接的孔。本发明涉及的滚轮组件可安装到吸尘器等电动工具的底座上使用。相比于现有技术，本发明涉及的滚轮组件在安装的方便性、结构的可靠性以及使用寿命等方面均有较大程度的提高，同时还降低了制造成本。

【名称】 一种塑料压滤板便携式铣槽装置

【公开(公告)号】 CN102310219A

【公开(公告)日】 2012.01.11

【申请(专利权)人】 三门峡市盛源材料工程有限公司

【地址】 河南省陕县三门峡西站

【发明(设计)人】 李自安；阴朝阳；张林

【摘要】 本发明公开了一种塑料压滤板便携式铣槽装置。主要由底板、支架、支撑柱、固定和活动导柱、牵引支架、定心支架构成，在底板上设置固定和活动导柱，在底板上对称设置支撑柱，支撑柱外侧设置支架，支架上设置动力头和深度调节器，支架底部两侧设置锁紧手柄，动力头主轴下端设置铣卡头，底板一侧设置链条连接座，底板上设置定心轴。链条连接座通过链条与牵引支架上设置的链轮连接，牵引支架上设置轴承座总成、链轮及摇把，牵引支架下边设置牵引支架压紧器。定心轴通过定心板与定心支架连接，定心支架两端设置定心支架压紧器。具有结构简单，造价低廉，使用方便、安全，加工效率高，便与携带的优点。

【名称】 一种塑料条冲切装置

【公开(公告)号】 CN102310428A

【公开(公告)日】 2012.01.11

【申请(专利权)人】 上海新必工贸有限公司

【地址】 上海市闵行区纪翟路1525弄

【发明(设计)人】 吕建荣

【摘要】 本发明涉及一种塑料条冲切装置，该装置包括框架、定位板及冲切刀模，框架内部设置加强撑，定位板经固定螺丝固接设在框架的左侧，冲切刀模设在框架前侧及内侧的后部。与现有技术相比，本发明简单易用，只要将产品卡于下切刀口上，左端紧靠定位板，就可以进行冲压，质量易控制，塑料条上端开口卡在下切刀上，并紧贴在框架壁上，不会发生冲缺偏移，生产效率高，一次冲压，同时完成两个零件的冲切，替代了以前用手工逐一划切生产方式。

【名称】 一种塑料条冷冲模具

【公开(公告)号】 CN102310430A

【公开(公告)日】 2012.01.11

【申请(专利权)人】 上海新必工贸有限公司

【地址】 上海市闵行区纪翟路1525弄

【发明(设计)人】 吕建荣

【摘要】 本发明涉及一种塑料条冷冲模具，包括上模和下模，上模经设置的导套与下模上设置的导柱套设连接，凸模设置在上模上，上模由导套、模柄、上模座、凸模固定板及凸模构成，下模由导柱、定位板、凹模及下模座构成。与现有技术相比，本发明中的凸模是采用斜面设计，凸模为锋利的刀片，冲模刀口与冲压件接触面积减小，塑料条断切面光洁平齐，模具在无需很大负载的情况下完成了冲切，不但冲切的产品的断切质量得以提高，而且延长了模具的使用寿命。

【名称】 一种带防护板的塑料条冷冲装置

【公开(公告)号】 CN102310431A

【公开(公告)日】 2012.01.11

【申请(专利权)人】 上海新必工贸有限公司

【地址】 上海市闵行区纪翟路1525弄

【发明(设计)人】 吕建荣

【摘要】 本发明涉及一种带防护板的塑料条冷冲装置，该冷冲装置由上模和下模组成，上模由上模座、模柄、导套、凸模及凸模固定板组成，下模由凹模、导柱、防护板及下模座组成，上模及下模经导套与导柱进行配合连接。与现有技术相比，本发明中的凸模是采用斜面设计，凸模成为锋利的刀片，冲模刀口与冲压件接触面积减小，使塑料条断切面光洁平齐，模具在无需很大负载的情况下完成了冲切，延长了模具的使用寿命，下模的凹模上增设的防护板可防止操作人员的手指滑动误入到冲模工作区内，增加了设备运行的安全性。

【名称】 电线电缆塑料粒子振动筛分机

【公开(公告)号】 CN102310497A

【公开(公告)日】 2012.01.11

【申请(专利权)人】 常熟市中联光电新材料有限责任公司

【地址】 江苏省苏州市常熟市沙家浜镇常昆工业园区中利路1号

【发明(设计)人】 周建新；袁文新；姚国清；陆文龙；张健；朱卫星

【摘要】 一种电线电缆塑料粒子振动筛分机，属于造粒机的配套设施技术领域。包括机架，一粒末引出槽，该粒末引出槽浮动地安装在机架上；一合格粒料筛网，该合格粒料筛网叠置在所述粒末引出槽内，并且该合格粒料筛网的底部与粒末引出槽之间保持有第一隙道；一不合格粒料筛网，该不合格粒料筛网叠置在所述的合格粒料筛网内，并且该不合格粒料筛网的底部与合格粒料筛网之间保持有第二隙道；一振动电机，该振动电机固定在所述的粒末引出槽的底部的外壁上。优点：由于配置了粒末引出槽，从而能使夹杂于合格的塑料粒子中的细碎粒末和杂质由合格粒料筛网筛剔至第一隙道中，确保出自第二隙道的塑料粒子的质量。

【名称】 一种塑料型条复合共挤模具

【公开(公告)号】 CN102310537A

【公开(公告)日】 2012.01.11

【申请(专利权)人】 上海新必工贸有限公司

【地址】 上海市闵行区纪翟路1525弄

【发明(设计)人】 吕建荣

【摘要】 本发明涉及一种塑料型条复合共挤模具，包括主挤出模、前挤出模、流道模、口模，主挤出模设在流道模的一侧，前挤出模设在流道模的前部，口模设在流道模的另一侧，将主挤出模头和前挤出模头自成一体，分别在前挤出机模头和主挤出机模上安装加热套，对其单独加热，充分发挥材料的各自的使用性能。与现有技术相比，本发明结构简单，易于安装，使不同材料不再受相同加热温度的制约，对材料复合挤出质量有明显效果且操作简单。

【名称】 双层复合塑料网材成型机头

【公开(公告)号】 CN102310538A

【公开(公告)日】 2012.01.11

【申请(专利权)人】 张建群

【地址】 山东省济宁市高新区327国道96号山东通佳机械有限公司

【发明(设计)人】 张建群；李勇；侯立新

【摘要】 一种双层复合塑料网材成型机头，在机头体的内孔中装置中间层芯棒，中间层芯棒的内孔中装置内芯棒，内芯棒和中间层芯棒有通往下出口的流道，机头体侧壁装置与流道相通的双料机头连接器；机头体下端装置口模，内芯棒的下端装置经线成型模，口模的口边与经线成型模圆台锥面形成间隙流道，在中间层芯棒下端安装分隔料环，经线成型模内端面开有若干经线流槽；口模的前端外周设置纬线成型模，纬线成型模与推拉装置连接。本发明结构简单、紧凑、合理、生产效率高，可以生产不同规格尺寸的塑料方格网，实现双层双色的精密塑料方格网的生产。

【名称】 注塑机开合式自动取胚装置

【公开(公告)号】 CN102310529A

【公开(公告)日】 2012.01.11

【申请(专利权)人】 浙江宏振机械模具集团有限公司

【地址】 浙江省台州市黄岩区西城黄轴路47－1号

【发明(设计)人】 蔡业

【摘要】 注塑机开合式自动取胚装置，包括安装在注塑机上的注塑模具和安装在注塑机一侧的取胚装置，所述的注塑模具有模头和模孔，所述的取胚装置包括取料板，取料板中制有取料孔，取料板由往复运动装置带动，往复运动装置安装在机架上，其特征在于所述的取料板包括甲模板和乙模板，甲模板上制有半爿甲取料孔，乙模板上制有半爿乙取料孔，甲取料孔与乙取料孔相对应，甲模板与乙模板有打开装置和闭合装置。本方案采用哈夫方式，取出塑料瓶胚后无需翻转动作，由打开装置将甲模板和乙模板分开，塑料瓶胚自由落下，动作简单、可靠，工作效率高。

【名称】 一出八塑料管材生产设备中的真空定型装置

【公开(公告)号】 CN102310546A

【公开(公告)日】 2012.01.11

【申请(专利权)人】 张家港市杰达机械制造有限公司

【地址】 江苏省苏州市张家港市锦丰镇锦南路A19幢市杰达机械制造有限公司

【发明(设计)人】 季湘杰

【摘要】 本发明公开了一种一出八塑料管材生产设备中的真空定型装置，包括机架，机架上设置有内设真空室的真空室箱体，真空室内设置有定径套，真空室箱体的两侧分别设置有管材入口和管材出口，在每个管材入口的正上方设置有一个喷淋水管；所述的管材出口均与冷却水槽装置连接；所述的机架上还设置有真空泵，所述的真空室箱体内设置有八个独立的真空室，所述的真空泵通过一个集中真空包将八个真空室分别抽真空；所述的竖向相邻的管材入口与喷淋水管间设置有导流挡板，所述的导流挡板能阻止导流挡板上方的水流至导流挡板下方的管材上。本发明的优点是：结构简单，大大提高了生产的效率，进而大大提高了产能，同时提高了产品质量。

【名称】 一出八塑料管材生产设备中的挤出模具

【公开(公告)号】 CN102310539A

【公开(公告)日】 2012.01.11

【申请(专利权)人】 张家港市杰达机械制造有限公司

【地址】 江苏省苏州市张家港市锦丰镇锦南路A19幢市杰达机械制造有限公司

【发明(设计)人】 季湘杰

【摘要】 本发明公开了一种一出八塑料管材生产设备中的挤出模具，包括：模腔体和模头，所述的模腔体内设置有流道，流道上设置有流道进口和流道出口，所述的模头连接在流道出口处，所述的流道为三级分叉型流道，其结构为：主干流道的末端分叉出两个一级次流道，每个一级次流道的末端分叉出两个二级次流道，每个二级次流道的末端分叉出两个三级次流道，每个三级次流道的末端均设置有流道出口，每个流道出口处均连接有模头。本发明的优点是：结构简单，采用三级分叉型流道，使物料能均匀地分配到各级流道中，一个流道进口对应八个流道出口，这样大大提高了生产的效率，进而大大提高了产能。

【名称】 塑料异型材挤出用牵引机履带架

【公开(公告)号】 CN102310543A

【公开(公告)日】 2012.01.11

【申请(专利权)人】 铜陵中发三佳科技股份有限公司

【地址】 安徽省铜陵市铜官山区石城路电子工业区

【发明(设计)人】 李治军；程文姣；李朋；杨亚萍

【摘要】 本发明公开了一种塑料异型材挤出用牵引机履带架，包括机架、固接在机架上的杠杆机构和置于机架上的上履带架，上履带架与杠杆机构及机架之间设有自动平衡装置，所述自动平衡装置包括连接板、拉杆、支座、蝶形弹簧，所述的连接板的下端固定在上履带架的侧面，拉杆的两端分别通过带圆通孔的轴、蝶形弹簧与连接板上端、固定在机架上的支座活动连接。采用这种技术方案，由于蝶形弹簧具有一定的弹性变形，且弹性变形量不大，所提供的平衡力基本维持不变，因此能够有效地调节上履带架的平衡，并且结构简单。

【名称】 自动塑料吹瓶机进管胚导向架

【公开(公告)号】 CN102310550A

【公开(公告)日】 2012.01.11

【申请(专利权)人】 林明茫

【地址】 浙江省台州市黄岩区黄椒路528号台州市黄岩亚力塑机有限公司

【发明(设计)人】 林明茫

【摘要】 自动塑料吹瓶机进管胚导向架，包括进料机构，进料机构有进管胚滑道，所述进管胚滑道上安装导向架，所述导向架包括由多根金属条间隔构成的导滑槽，导滑槽上端的每根金属条通过平面连接板固定，导滑槽下端的每根金属条通过弯曲形连接片固定。管胚在进管胚滑道的导滑槽中滑动时与导向架的金属条之间为线接触，接触面积小，散热慢，而且金属条表面光滑、摩擦系数小，因此管胚滑动速度快，能及时到达合模机构，保证生产效率，导滑槽的上端通过平面连接板固定使导向架呈平面，有利于管胚进入导滑槽，导滑槽的下端两侧卷起呈槽，起到很好的导向作用，再由于管胚在进管胚滑道内滑动顺畅，因此避免了管胚发生来回碰撞而变形，确保了产品的质量。

【名称】 塑料瓶管加热器自身插管链条

【公开(公告)号】 CN102310551A

【公开(公告)日】 2012.01.11

【申请(专利权)人】 林明茫

【地址】 浙江省台州市黄岩区黄椒路528号台州市

黄岩亚力塑机有限公司

【发明(设计)人】 林明茳

【摘要】 本发明涉及一种塑料瓶管加热器自身插管链条，包括机架，机架上安装瓶管输送机构，瓶管输送机构由动力带动转轴，转轴上安装主动链轮，主动链轮经过输送链条带动从动链轮，输送链条带动瓶管支承座，所述的输送链条包括内链片和外链片，内链片与外链片由链销相连，所述的链销包括长管链销和短管链销，长管链销两头各自与外链片相固定，短管链销套在长管链销外，并且两头各自与内链片相固定，其特征在于所述的长管链销内安装瓶管支承轴，瓶管支承轴外有上轴承和下轴承，上轴承与外链片之间有上轴承垫圈，下轴承与外链片之间有下轴承垫圈，瓶管支承轴的上头安装瓶管支承插头，瓶管支承轴的下头安装自转齿轮。

【名称】 全自动塑料吹瓶机平移自动上胚装置

【公开(公告)号】 CN102310552A

【公开(公告)日】 2012.01.11

【申请(专利权)人】 浙江德玛克机械有限公司

【地址】 浙江省台州市黄岩区经济开发区西工业园区新前片

【发明(设计)人】 王巍植

【摘要】 全自动塑料吹瓶机平移自动上胚装置，包括直线移动固定板和安装在一边的直线移动气缸，另一边安有直线轴，直线轴另一头连接直线轴固定板，直线轴上安装直线移动滑板，直线移动气缸的活塞杆与直线移动滑板相配合，直线移动滑板上安装上下移动气缸，并连接上下移动滑板，上下移动滑板上安装上下轴，上下轴与直线移动滑板相配合，在上下移动滑板下端两侧安装左、右固定板，左固定板上安装左气缸，右固定板上安右气缸，左气缸连接左轴固定板，左轴固定板上安左轴，左轴穿过各移动条，通过螺钉与乙、丁移动条相固定，右气缸连接右轴固定板，右轴固定板上安右轴，右轴穿过各移动条，通过螺丝与甲、丙移动条相固定，在各移动条下端连有夹口钳。

【名称】 塑料吹瓶机拉伸杆螺旋式带动机构

【公开(公告)号】 CN102310553A

【公开(公告)日】 2012.01.11

【申请(专利权)人】 浙江德玛克机械有限公司

【地址】 浙江省台州市黄岩区经济开发区西工业园区新前片

【发明(设计)人】 王巍植

【摘要】 塑料吹瓶机拉伸杆螺旋式带动机构，包括机架，在机架上安装动力，动力带动拉伸杆，其特征在于所述的动力包括安装在机架上的伺服电机，伺服电机经过减速机构带动滚珠丝杆，在滚珠丝杆外安装滚珠丝套，滚珠丝套与滚珠丝杆相配合，滚珠丝套带动连接板，连接板下安装拉伸杆，机架的两侧有导轨，连接板的两头部与导轨相接触。与已有技术相比：具有工作可靠性高，运行平稳，速度快，使用寿命长；伺服电机等安装方便，控制系统简单，调试、维修容易。

【名称】 全生物降解塑料树脂

【公开(公告)号】 CN102311617A

【公开(公告)日】 2012.01.11

【申请(专利权)人】 蔡大武；蔡正星

【地址】 湖北省武汉市江夏区工业联社大院2栋3楼3号

【发明(设计)人】 蔡大武；蔡正星

【摘要】 本发明是属于一种全生物降解塑料树脂的制作方法：其特征：树脂由下列材料组成：脂肪族聚酯、淀粉、滑石粉、硬脂酸、抗氧剂、环保增塑剂、复合改性剂、其中各成份的重量份数比例为：脂肪族聚酯(pbs)：30~70份；淀粉35~50份；滑石粉：5~10份；抗氧剂：0.3~0.6份；硬脂酸0.5~1份；甘油：2~5份；增塑剂2~5份；改性剂2~5份。玉米淀粉价格低又是可再生资源，经改性后与PBS共聚的树脂可制作价格低廉的各种包装薄膜、一次性水杯、快餐盒、包装材料、注塑成各种制品的全生物降解塑料。

【名称】 PPO复合材料、其制备方法和应用

【公开(公告)号】 CN102311634A

【公开(公告)日】 2012.01.11

【申请(专利权)人】 深圳市科聚新材料有限公司

【地址】 广东省深圳市宝安区福永街道桥头富桥第三工业区二期C2、A19栋

【发明(设计)人】 徐东；徐永；周兵

【摘要】 本发明适用于工程塑料技术领域，提供了一种PPO复合材料、其制备方法和应用。该PPO复合材料，包括如下的组分：聚苯醚、聚苯乙烯、双酚A双(二苯基磷酸酯)、SEBS、三甘醇双-3-(3-叔丁基-4-羟基-5-甲苯苯基)丙烯酸酯、硫代二丙酸二月桂酯、亚磷酸三(壬基苯酯)、氧化锌、抗紫外线剂、炭黑、润滑剂%。本发明PPO复合材料，通过选用上述组分及其含量，使得PPO复合材料的具有优异的力学性能，优异的抗老化，抗紫外，耐水解特性能；本发明PPO复合材料制备方法，操作简单、成本低廉、适于工业化应用。

【名称】 一种塑料成型用吸水增韧材料

【公开(公告)号】 CN102311656A

【公开(公告)日】 2012.01.11

【申请(专利权)人】 大连方盛塑料有限公司
【地址】 辽宁省大连市金州区站前街道吴屯机场
【发明(设计)人】 梁继鹏
【摘要】 本发明公开了一种塑料成型用吸水增韧材料，其原料及其质量份数为：增韧剂10－20份，无机硅酸盐材料50－60份，偶联剂0.5－1.5份，树脂20－30份；所述增韧剂为丁二烯－苯乙烯、苯乙烯－丁二烯或者丙烯晴－苯乙烯共聚物；所述补强剂为滑石粉或者蒙脱土；所述无机硅酸盐为硅酸镁、硅酸钙、硅酸钠或者硅酸钡中的一种或多种；所述偶联剂为硅烷偶联剂。本发明提供了一种既能吸水又能增加韧性，提高产品质量的用于塑料成型加工中的吸水增韧材料，解决了现有塑料成型加工中因原料原因交脆、受潮而影响产品质量的问题，在塑料管材、注塑成型、中空吹塑成型等多种塑料成型工艺中使用能达到增韧、消除水泡的功能。
【名称】 利用塑料和橡胶制取混合油的方法
【公开(公告)号】 CN102311752A
【公开(公告)日】 2012.01.11
【申请(专利权)人】 苏华山
【地址】 山东省济南市历下区文化东路29号D楼3单元1102室
【发明(设计)人】 苏华山；苏华阳；孙稼霖；魏豪；苏同兴
【摘要】 本发明属于石油化工炼制领域，特别公开了一种利用塑料和橡胶制取混合油的方法。该方法以废塑料或橡胶、钯催化剂、环己胺、N－甲基吗啉和羟基丁二酸二乙酯为原料，加热至120～430℃，反应1～4h热效分解得到混合油。本发明工艺简便、容易操作、成本低、产品收率高、充分利用了废物，变废为宝，实现了资源再利用，有助于保护环境。
【名称】 一种预硬态塑料模具钢钢板及其制造方法
【公开(公告)号】 CN102312168A
【公开(公告)日】 2012.01.11
【申请(专利权)人】 山西太钢不锈钢股份有限公司
【地址】 山西省太原市尖草坪街2号
【发明(设计)人】 陈建礼；张晓琨；田培凤；王之香
【摘要】 本发明涉及一种预硬态塑料模具钢钢板及其制造方法，钢板的成分的重量百分比为：C：0.28～0.40；Si：0.20～0.80；Mn：0.60～1.0；Cr：1.40－2.2；Mo：0.30～0.50；P≤0.030；S≤0.030；Al：0.01～0.08；Ti：0.01～0.05；B：0.0010～0.0050；其余为Fe和不可避免的杂质。制造方法包括下述依次的步骤：第一步冶炼钢水的成分达到要求出钢浇注成钢锭；第二步热轧将钢锭轧制成厚60～200mm×宽300～1500mm×长2000～8000mm的钢板；第三步冷却将钢板冷却到550℃以下，缓冷时间不少于24小时；第四步回火钢板装在回火炉中400－600℃回火，保温4－12个小时，出炉并在空气中冷却到室温。本发明制造的预硬态塑料模具钢的钢板表面硬度差在20HB之内。
【名称】 电磁波防护层及其制备于塑料外壳的方法
【公开(公告)号】 CN102312195A
【公开(公告)日】 2012.01.11
【申请(专利权)人】 向熙科技股份有限公司
【地址】 中国台湾台北县
【发明(设计)人】 洪崇喜；郑兆希
【摘要】 本发明提供一种电磁波防护层(electromagnetic interference)及其制备于塑料外壳的方法。该电磁波防护层用于制备一电子产品的塑料外壳，以保护该电子产品内部电子元件不受电磁波干扰，本发明的电磁波防护层仅包括单层金属层，以溅射或蒸发的方式来制备，其中金属层表面会形成一致密氧化层。金属层的材料可以选自铝、钛、锌、铬及其任意组合的群组其中的一种，或选自铜锡、铜锌或铜铝合金。
【名称】 由塑料瓶构成的潜水坝
【公开(公告)号】 CN102312415A
【公开(公告)日】 2012.01.11
【申请(专利权)人】 俞小明
【地址】 江西省南昌市经济开发区志敏大道1101号12区13栋一单元501室
【发明(设计)人】 俞小明；胡菊华；周利华
【摘要】 由塑料瓶构成的潜水坝，涉及水利工程领域，用于抬升河流湖泊水体水位。由大量回收塑料瓶作为构建水坝的主要材料，水坝节能环保，建造成本低。防洪时，拆除速度快。用绳，网，钢架等连接塑料瓶，瓶子开口可进水下沉。可建若干固定桩，把部件联接在固定桩上，水在瓶间缝隙流过，流速降低，节流而不断流。坝顶离水面可有一段距离，方便航运。为降低生态负面影响，可保留部分靠岸浅滩河道不拦截。建坝要注意减少对河道的冲刷。
【名称】 连体塑料网固沙栅栏及其固沙施工方法
【公开(公告)号】 CN102312423A
【公开(公告)日】 2012.01.11
【申请(专利权)人】 娄志平
【地址】 浙江省嵊州市浦口街道新浦路40号
【发明(设计)人】 娄志平
【摘要】 本发明旨在提供一种结构简单，造价低廉、可以直接在工厂里加工成成品的连体塑料网固沙栅栏及其固沙施工方法，属于治沙工程技术领域，构成连体塑料网固沙栅栏的固沙塑料网的孔隙度可在45%～55%之间选择，宽幅可在15cm至25cm之间选择，固沙塑料网的底边间隔25cm割裂一道深度5cm的裂缝，构成宽度25cm深度5cm的压沙网。连体塑料网固沙栅栏是由许多条间隔1m，纵、横垂直相交成十字形的固沙塑料网通过割开的裂缝嵌接构成。在沙漠施工现场，把连体塑料网固沙栅栏摊开绷紧，使固沙塑料网上的竹、木条与沙漠垂直，然后从每个固沙栅栏的中间用工具向四边的固沙塑料网铲沙，使沙堆埋至固沙栅栏网一半以上的高度，最后在塑料网固沙栅栏中心的低凹处栽种上固沙植物。

【名称】 注塑拼块组合建筑模板

【公开(公告)号】 CN102312568A

【公开(公告)日】 2012.01.11

【申请(专利权)人】 缪巍

【地址】 浙江省台州市黄岩区西城模具城浙江亨达塑料模具有限公司

【发明(设计)人】 缪巍

【摘要】 注塑拼块组合建筑模板，包括至少两块以上由塑料材料制成的建筑模板，其特征在于所述各块建筑模板的四周制有边框，边框中制有连接孔，各连接孔由连接销相连接，连接销的头部制有紧固锁头。本方案所述的建筑模板由塑料材料所制成，重量轻、不腐蚀，使用寿命长，成本低，不与混凝土粘合，可多次重复使用。使用时将各块建筑模板放置平整，各块建筑模板上的连接孔互相对应，再将连接销插入连接孔中，旋转连接销，使连接销头部的紧固锁头卡在边框内壁上，达到固定作用，将各块建筑模板互相连接在一起。本方案采用销孔配合方式，将各块建筑模板互相拼接组合在一起，结构简单，安装方便，拆卸容易。

【名称】 一种塑料光纤网络电力抄表系统

【公开(公告)号】 CN102314765A

【公开(公告)日】 2012.01.11

【申请(专利权)人】 中国电力科学研究院

【地址】 北京市海淀区清河小营东路15号

【发明(设计)人】 田世明；张海亮

【摘要】 本发明提供一种塑料光纤网络电力抄表系统，属于电力线上信息的传输领域。本发明抄表系统抗电磁干扰和抗核辐射能力强，性能可靠；采集数据实时性强，实现低成本及数据的高速传输。塑料光纤网络电力抄表系统由电表、抄表模块、塑料光纤、塑料光纤网络交换机和数据处理中心组成；抄表系统的信号流向为：抄表模块的光发送器将电表信号转化为网络型光信号，光信号被耦合到塑料光纤中，抄表模块的光接收器接收信号并将光信号还原为网络电信号，塑料光纤网络交换机进行数据处理，数据处理中心处理数据后完成抄表全过程。本发明抄表系统具有优异的抗电磁干扰性能，保密性强、高灵敏度和较小的体积，且制备简单、成本低，系统防水防潮，使用寿命长。

【名称】 一种钢塑复合电缆挤出模具

【公开(公告)号】 CN102314976A

【公开(公告)日】 2012.01.11

【申请(专利权)人】 成都营门电缆有限责任公司

【地址】 四川省成都市外西土桥工业区1号

【发明(设计)人】 潘生安；潘准；曾庆兵

【摘要】 本发明涉及电线电缆的加工领域，具体为一种钢塑复合电缆挤出模具。一种钢塑复合电缆挤出模具，包括模芯和模套，模具为圆柱体结构，模芯为中空结构，模忎和模套成一角度，模套为两层结构，外表层的材质为钢，靠近模芯一侧的内层为改性聚四氟乙烯塑料模套，钢外表层沿斜角延伸出去，呈开口状，钢外表层与塑料模套靠近模芯一侧的变向段位设置无锐边。采用钢塑复合电缆挤出模具可提高塑料挤出速度，模具且不易清洁和护理，在挤出塑料制品时，模口塑料流动变拖拽为滑移，电缆表面光洁度好，解决了钢质挤出模具的生产缺点。

【名称】 一种塑料薄膜

【公开(公告)号】 CN102320172A

【公开(公告)日】 2012.01.18

【申请(专利权)人】 大连方盛塑料有限公司

【地址】 辽宁省大连市金州区站前街道吴屯机场

【发明(设计)人】 梁继鹏

【摘要】 本发明公开了一种塑料薄膜，其特征在于，由基层(1)和镀层(2)组成，所述基层(1)上镀有镀层(2)，所述基层(1)是由聚烯烃或聚苯二甲酸乙二醇制成。所述基层(1)的厚度有10－100m。本发明的有益效果是：该塑料薄膜不光质量好、耐用，而且外表也很美观，特别适合用于礼品的包装。

【名称】 一种异形塑料袋下料机

【公开(公告)号】 CN102320490A

【公开(公告)日】 2012.01.18

【申请(专利权)人】 重庆南岸区江山塑料制品厂

【地址】 重庆市南岸区鸡冠石盘龙工业园区

【发明(设计)人】 金峰；申华全；张大彬

【摘要】 本发明提出一种异形塑料袋下料机，其包括机架、放料装置、涨力控制器、卷取装置、尺寸调节装置、切取定位装置、传动装置、检测装置和控制系统。放料装置设置在机架尾部，涨力控制器与放料装置的放料装置轴的端头的放料轴端齿轮相联，卷取装置设置在机架中间并与放料装置的主轴平行，尺寸调节装置与卷取装置两端的限位条相联，切取定位装置设置在尺寸调节装置的其中一根调节杆上，传动装置设置在卷取装置的下方，检测装置设置在卷取装置的主轴端的机架上，控制系统设置在机架前端的控制箱内。此设备生产效率高、操作安全、维护方使、生产质量稳定、操作人性化，具有同类设备许多不具备的优点。

【名称】 泡沫塑料用多元醇及采用这种多元醇的聚异氰脲酸酯泡沫塑料

【公开(公告)号】 CN102321237A

【公开(公告)日】 2012.01.18

【申请(专利权)人】 南京红宝丽股份有限公司

【地址】 江苏省南京市高淳县太安路128号

【发明(设计)人】 邢益辉；黄东平；付振华；周国庆

【摘要】 本发明涉及泡沫塑料用多元醇和采用上述多元醇的聚异氰脲酸酯泡沫塑料，所述泡沫塑料用多元醇的制备方法包括以下步骤：将高度羟甲基化三聚氰胺与单元醇进行醚化反应；其中，所述高度羟甲基化三聚氰胺的羟甲基化度不小于5.5；单元醇为甲醇、乙醇、丙醇、丁醇中的一种或两种以上任意比例的混合物；聚异氰脲酸酯泡沫塑料用多元醇的羟值为160~650mgKOH/g。作为改进，本发明多元醇的制备还包括以下步骤：将醚化反应产物和含-NH基团的醇胺化合物混合，发生脱水反应，并通过抽真空除去反应所产生的水。再加入过量氧化烯烃，发生开环反应。以本发明所述泡沫塑料用多元醇为原料制备聚异氰脲酸酯泡沫塑料，可有效提高聚异氰脲酸酯泡沫塑料的阻燃性能。

【名称】 一种塑料用防霉剂及其制备方法

【公开(公告)号】 CN102321275A

【公开(公告)日】 2012.01.18

【申请(专利权)人】 吴江市天源塑胶有限公司

【地址】 江苏省苏州市吴江市黎里镇工业园区牌楼桥堍

【发明(设计)人】 肖伟荣

【摘要】 本发明公开一种塑料用防霉剂。本发明涉及塑料的辅料领域。本发明内容是：一种塑料用防霉剂，其特征在于：所述防霉剂由40%~60%替硝唑，40%~60%酮康唑组成。所述替硝唑和酮康唑根据比例，按照倍比递增原则混匀，溶于氯仿中，在220℃，与塑料聚合物1:(5~10)混合，制成有活性的防霉母粒。本发明是一种低毒，高效，热稳定性好的塑料用防霉剂。

【名称】 一种能够快速锁紧定型块的塑料异型材挤出模水箱

【公开(公告)号】 CN102328424A

【公开(公告)日】 2012.01.25

【申请(专利权)人】 铜陵中发三佳科技股份有限公司

【地址】 安徽省铜陵市铜官山区石城路电子工业区

【发明(设计)人】 张家权；吕华军；孙晓峰；杨亚萍

【摘要】 本发明公开了一种能够快速锁紧定型块的塑料异型材挤出模水箱，它包括水箱，前挡板(6)和后挡板(2)上设有滑槽，定型块位于滑槽内，并能够沿滑槽前后滑动，所述的水箱上设有凸轮锁紧装置挤压定型块(7)实现锁紧。本发明方便定型块的锁紧，大大提高了生产效率。

【名称】 一种塑料芯轴的后处理工装

【公开(公告)号】 CN102328420A

【公开(公告)日】 2012.01.25

【申请(专利权)人】 阔丹-凌云汽车胶管有限公司

【地址】 河北省保定市涿州市开发区

【发明(设计)人】 李凯；曹红恩；齐辉

【摘要】 本发明公开了一种塑料芯轴的后处理工装，属橡胶挤出产品技术领域。包括带有中心孔的套式拉刀和带有加热装置的芯轴锁套；所述套式拉刀的中心孔与该中心孔端面形成刮削刃角；所述套式拉刀与芯轴锁套固定。本发明可改变作为橡胶产品胎具的塑料芯轴的表面粗糙度，使其与橡胶管子内壁存在缝隙，在橡胶管子挤压成型后方便退出，可提高劳动效率，减少脱模剂污染，保护环境。

【名称】 一种用于注塑模具中防止顶出过程出现“抽真空”的机构

【公开(公告)号】 CN102328405A

【公开(公告)日】 2012.01.25

【申请(专利权)人】 北京英特塑料机械总厂

【地址】 北京市通州区果园北京英特塑料机械总厂

【发明(设计)人】 焦新军

【摘要】 本发明涉及一种用于注塑模具中防止顶出过程出现“抽真空”的机构，它通过在中空壳体制品内部设置进气顶杆的机构来抵制顶出时中空现象的发生，适用于薄壁、高型腔和小的脱模斜度类软质塑料壳体制品的模具成型结构，本发明克服了传统通过调整注塑工艺来避免“抽真空”现象，设计加入进气顶杆机构，不再需要重复调试注塑工艺流程，使注塑生产过程简单且易操控，缩短了成型周期，提高了生产效率，使生产制造成本显著降低。

【名称】 一种V法铸造用的砂箱铸型塑料覆膜加热器
【公开(公告)号】 CN102335722A
【公开(公告)日】 2012.02.01
【申请(专利权)人】 泰州市美鑫铸造有限公司
【地址】 江苏省泰州市兴化市安丰镇工业园区
【发明(设计)人】 陈文美；胡兆坤；张九银
【摘要】 一种V法铸造用的砂箱铸型塑料覆膜加热器，砂箱为箱体结构，包括加热元件和绝缘板，绝缘板放置在砂箱的内底部，加热元件放置在砂箱的内底部和绝缘板之间，加热元件布设在砂箱的整个内底部；使大小不等的塑料覆膜受热均匀，提高覆膜效率。

【名称】 一种用于制造抗菌纤维和塑料的功能切片的制备方法
【公开(公告)号】 CN102336957A
【公开(公告)日】 2012.02.01
【申请(专利权)人】 上海亿金纳米科技有限公司
【地址】 上海市文汇路1128号310室
【发明(设计)人】 唐晓峰；赵宏鑫
【摘要】 本发明涉及一种功能树脂切片的制造方法，尤其涉及一种分散性好，能耗低，工艺简单的用于制造抗菌纤维和塑料的抗菌切片的制备方法，本发明包括以下步骤：1)将浓度为10～50000ppm的无机抗菌剂粉搅拌分散于0.01%～5%的分散剂中；2)选择适当的原始树脂切片，与1)得到的共混物充分搅拌混合；3)干燥后通过双螺杆进行挤出造粒；本发明制备的切片不仅可以用来作为抗菌树脂母粒，还可以直接用来制造抗菌塑料和纤维。

【名称】 一种负离子塑料板的制备方法
【公开(公告)号】 CN102336945A
【公开(公告)日】 2012.02.01
【申请(专利权)人】 惠州市鼎晨新材料有限公司
【地址】 广东省惠州市惠城区小金口街道九龙村C栋厂房
【发明(设计)人】 林春涛
【摘要】 本发明涉及一种负离子塑料板的制备方法。以塑料为主原料，添加托玛琳矿石粉、锗石粉、砭石粉，以植物纤维素、粘合剂、润滑剂、偶联剂为辅料，将上述材料在搅拌器中混合，搅拌、铸压成型塑料板。其制备方法简单，本发明产品具有净化空气效果，可用于居室装饰材料。

【名称】 一种高阻燃性可膨胀石墨的制备方法
【公开(公告)号】 CN102336403A
【公开(公告)日】 2012.02.01
【申请(专利权)人】 华南理工大学
【地址】 广东省广州市天河区五山路381号
【发明(设计)人】 刘定福
【摘要】 本发明涉及一种高阻燃性可膨胀石墨的制备方法，采用浓硫酸与硝酸的混酸、硝酸与磷酸的混酸、发烟硝酸或浓硫酸，和用量为石墨质量的5%～60%的固体强氧化剂一起氧化石墨，反应温度为15～50℃，反应10～100min后，过滤水洗至pH为4～7，得到初级可膨胀石墨；而后将初级可膨胀石墨与胍盐溶液，在20～80℃的温度下反应，反应20～200分钟后，反复抽滤、水洗至pH为6～7，然后在40～80℃下烘干10～72小时，制得高阻燃性可膨胀石墨。本发明方法的优点在于将胍盐插层到可膨胀石墨层间，提高了其膨胀率和阻燃性，可广泛用于塑料、橡胶、涂料、泡沫等多种材料的阻燃。

【名称】 一种利用废油脂制备聚氨酯聚醚多元醇的方法
【公开(公告)号】 CN102336901A
【公开(公告)日】 2012.02.01
【申请(专利权)人】 句容宁武新材料发展有限公司
【地址】 江苏省镇江市句容边城镇句陈公路杨庄段
【发明(设计)人】 应珏；张悦凡；翟洪金；盛恩善；郑磊；倪小明；陈杰；蔡敏俊；于文超
【摘要】 本发明公开了一种利用废油脂制备聚氨酯聚醚多元醇的方法，该方法在碱性催化剂作用下，由共起始剂与氧化烯烃反应制得。首先将废油脂加热升温，控制在110～130℃抽真空，时间为3～6h，然后加入吸附剂，搅拌1～3h，吸附杂质，经过滤后得到精制的废油脂；然后将废油脂或废油脂与植物油的混合物与多元醇或胺类化合物或两者的混合物作为共起始剂加入反应器中，加入催化剂和氧化烯烃，在催化剂的存在下共起始剂与氧化烯烃在一定温度、压力下反应制得聚醚多元醇。本发明制备聚醚多元醇的方法原料便宜、易得，产品质量稳定，使用性能良好，且用其制备的聚氨酯泡沫塑料可降解性好。

【名称】 一种汽车用木塑材料零件的制作方法
【公开(公告)号】 CN102336024A
【公开(公告)日】 2012.02.01
【申请(专利权)人】 上海新安汽车隔音毡有限公司
【地址】 上海市嘉定区宝安公路5355号
【发明(设计)人】 庄健
【摘要】 本发明涉及一种汽车用木塑材料零件的制作方法，将两层木塑材料放入烘箱内加热软化，上模具及下模具内放置表面材料，烘软的两层木塑材料平铺在下模具内后控制合模并在两层木塑材料中间吹气，最后去除得到零件的边料，然后在零件上粘接塑料件并安装限位绳即得到产品。与现有技术相比，本发明制作得到的零件与普通的单层结构零件相比，一方面可以保证相同强度，另一方面，由于采用双层中空结构，因此能够节省材料，并且降低零件的重量。

【名称】 异种材料与塑料注塑结合的方法

【公开(公告)号】 CN102336022A

【公开(公告)日】 2012.02.01

【申请(专利权)人】 汉达精密电子(昆山)有限公司

【地址】 江苏省苏州市昆山市出口加工区第二大道269号

【发明(设计)人】 郭俊映

【摘要】 一种异种材料与塑料注塑结合的方法，其包括如下步骤：(1)确认异种材料需涂黏胶的位置；(2)在异种材料需涂黏胶位置对应的注塑模具区域增设水路；(3)在异种材料上涂黏胶，并使黏胶固化；(4)将异种材料放入注塑模具中注塑成型；(5)对注塑模具进行冷却处理；(6)注塑模具开模顶出产品，并对产品进行打磨及喷涂处理。本发明的异种材料与塑料注塑结合的方法采用高低模温成型方式及异种材料涂黏胶后再注塑塑料的制程，使得注塑后的产品能够达到一体成型的外观效果。

【名称】 塑料射出机的锁模方法

【公开(公告)号】 CN102336009A

【公开(公告)日】 2012.02.01

【申请(专利权)人】 昆山榕增光电科技有限公司；刘忠男

【地址】 江苏省苏州市昆山市巴城镇石牌中华路299号

【发明(设计)人】 张祐严；刘忠男

【摘要】 本发明公开了一种塑料射出机的锁模方法，包含下列步骤：(a)至少取一定位体及一具有卡榫的定位单元固设在活动模座上；(b)至少取一导杆穿置于固定模座、活动模座及各定位体，且使各导杆的一端固设在固定模座上；(c)当活动模座与固定模座合模后，控制定位单元，使卡榫沿导杆径向卡抵在导杆及定位体之间，当活动模座与固定模座开模前，控制定位单元，使卡榫沿导杆径向脱离导杆及定位体之间。使用该锁模方法后，当需要获得较大的锁模力时，只要选取结构强度较强的定位体、卡榫及导杆，就可以在不变更锁模所需的空间下，获得较大的锁模力，完成锁模作业。

【名称】 电动落料机

【公开(公告)号】 CN102335995A

【公开(公告)日】 2012.02.01

【申请(专利权)人】 陈会希

【地址】 广东省佛山市顺德区容桂街道环山路4座201号之1

【发明(设计)人】 陈会希

【摘要】 电动落料机，它涉及一种塑料工业领域的落料机。它由上座、上套、外套、底座、中板、上旋体、下旋体、波箱左挡块、波箱右挡块和波箱压盖组成，上座与上套相连，上套通过中板与外套相连，上套套接在上旋体的外圈，上旋体通过中板与下旋体相连，下旋体的外圈套接有外套，底座与下旋体相连，下旋体底端的齿轮通过数个齿轮轴传动带动波箱压盖底部的齿轮，波箱压盖上左右两侧设置有波箱左挡块和波箱右挡块。它能使注塑机和挤出机使用的二次废料顺利下料，提高了机器的生产效率。

【名称】 塑料制品成型颜色的自动调色装置

【公开(公告)号】 CN102335987A

【公开(公告)日】 2012.02.01

【申请(专利权)人】 陈鹤亭

【地址】 辽宁省沈阳市浑南新区富民南街8号金水花城2-2-31-4

【发明(设计)人】 陈鹤亭

【摘要】 塑料制品成型颜色的自动调色装置，包括计算机、变频电机或电机调速器、调色箱、色料盒、色料供给器。色料供给器由色料斗和色料推进螺杆组成，色料推进螺杆通固定连接在色料斗下端出口与色料斗相连通，调色箱上周围设有多个供色料供给器安装的托架，色料盒设在调色箱中，托架穿装在调色箱上，托架一端与色料盒固定连接相通，色料供给器装在托架上，色料推进螺杆的进料端通过连轴器连接变频电机输出轴，变频电机与计算机或点机调速器信号连接，当色料推进螺杆与连轴器连接后，通过托架法兰盘和连轴器法兰盘连接，构成色料供给器可拆装结构。本发明装在塑料制品成型机，由计算机程序控制或手动电机调速器调整颜色，在制作制品过程中可更换色料供给器，操作方便简单，生产效率高，塑料制品色泽好。

【名称】 植物纤维与热塑性塑料复合粒料的生产方法及设备

【公开(公告)号】 CN102335977A

【公开(公告)日】 2012.02.01

【申请(专利权)人】 张毅

【地址】 福建省福州市晋安区茶园路99号河滨花园3座203

【发明(设计)人】 彭建新；陈云范；彭建成

【摘要】 本发明提供一种植物纤维与热塑性塑料复合粒料的生产方法和设备，该方法包括气流过程、液滴化过程以及混合粘结过程；气流总体作上升运动，依次上升穿过冷却区预热、加热区加热至工作温度、预热区与塑粉进行热交换，然后再次进入预热区和冷却区形成循环热气流，热塑性塑料粉总体做下降运动，植物纤维由循环热气流带入冷却区顶部与塑液滴相遇，在气流的作用下充分均匀粘入塑液滴形成纤维塑液滴而下落，冷却形成复合粒料。本发明方法和设备采用悬浮粘结技术通过控制气流速度、温度、进料位置，达到植物纤维与热塑性塑料的充分分散，均匀粘结的效果，所生产的复合粒料有效克服了植物纤维在基体中聚结成团的问题复合材料的力学性能得到有效改善。

【名称】 一种塑料工具箱
【公开(公告)号】 CN102335915A
【公开(公告)日】 2012.02.01
【申请(专利权)人】 陆火英
【地址】 江苏省启东市惠丰镇小效村五组5号
【发明(设计)人】 陆火英
【摘要】 本发明涉及一种塑料工具箱，包括箱体，所述箱体的一侧具有凸条，另一侧具有凹槽，所述箱体底部有一斜面，所述斜面可方便工具箱纵向组合时在该斜面形成一取件口，可以方便的使使用者的手伸进伸出，横向相接时只要把工具箱的凸条镶嵌进另一工具箱的凹槽内就可以进行横向组合；纵向连接时，上下层相叠，凸条通过螺杆来连接，螺杆可用于调节箱体之间的距离，这样工具箱重量及盒内物品的重量可以被四根金属质的螺杆承受，上层重量通过四根螺杆传递到下层，可使货架不易翻到，很稳定。本发明的有益效果为：本发明使用方便、结构简单、制作方便，便于储藏、运输。

【名称】 PVC木塑发泡木纹型材及其制备方法
【公开(公告)号】 CN102336989A
【公开(公告)日】 2012.02.01
【申请(专利权)人】 北京欧尼克新型材料有限公司
【地址】 北京市通州区漷县镇漷县四街1号
【发明(设计)人】 韩伟；黄振海
【摘要】 本发明公开了一种PVC木塑发泡木纹型材及制备方法，该木塑发泡木纹型材由以下重量份数的塑料、有机填料、助剂、改性剂、发泡剂、木纹色母粒等原料制成。所述木塑发泡木纹型材是在锥形双螺杆挤出生产线上按一步法的工艺路线，将可发泡混合料与木纹色母粒混合并从挤出机中共同挤出，经发泡模具发泡成型，由定型模冷却定型后得到所述PVC木塑发泡型材。本发明所提供的PVC木塑发泡地板具有质轻、比强度高、防水、防腐、保温的优点，并且具有木材可钉、可锯、可刨的加工特点；此外，其具有高度仿真的实木外观，纹路清晰自然，表面色泽亮丽，是一种理想的仿木木塑产品，可广泛用于建筑、运输、包装、家庭装饰及日用品市场。

【名称】 一种含氟塑料薄膜专用料的制备方法
【公开(公告)号】 CN102336992A
【公开(公告)日】 2012.02.01
【申请(专利权)人】 刘波
【地址】 上海市松江区横港路49弄36号301
【发明(设计)人】 刘波
【摘要】 本发明涉及一种含氟塑料薄膜专用料的制备方法。专用料配方是：聚偏氟乙烯50～85重量份、增强树脂5～30重量份、无机填料5～15重量份、纳米级填料5～15重量份、流动性改性剂0.5～5重量份、热稳定助剂0.1～2重量份，加入至混合搅拌机中，在室温下以每分钟50～1000转的转速混合10～40分钟，然后通过双螺杆挤出机在170～230℃下熔融挤出、冷却、干燥、切粒，得到专用料粒子。以此专用料为原料的后续成膜加工具有熔体流动性好、生产产量高、设备适用性强等优点；同时生产得到的氟塑料薄膜的水汽阻隔性能优异、撕裂强度高、耐候性优异、耐酸碱，完全满足太阳能电池封装背板中保护层膜的性能要求。

【名称】 SMC高性能环氧树脂组合物
【公开(公告)号】 CN102337007A
【公开(公告)日】 2012.02.01
【申请(专利权)人】 蓝星(北京)化工机械有限公司
【地址】 北京市大兴区经济技术开发区兴业街5号
【发明(设计)人】 杨刚；孟秀青；胡伟；陈伟明；刘欣彤
【摘要】 本发明涉及一种适合SMC成型的高性能的环氧基体树脂组合物，由下述成分制成：100质量份的混合环氧树脂；20～60质量份的固化剂；10～40质量份的增稠剂；0.5～5.0质量份的内脱模剂；50～120质量份的填料。本发明中环氧基体树脂分别选自缩水甘油醚类环氧树脂和缩水甘油胺类环氧树脂或缩水甘油酯类环氧树脂，它们的组成物对纤维有良好的浸润性和粘接强度，固化产物具有良好的耐热性和机械强度，采用本发明环氧树脂组合物制成的环氧片状模塑料适用于耐温性、耐腐蚀性、绝缘性要求严格的场合。

【名称】 一种高强度P34HB/长玻纤复合材料及其制备方法
【公开(公告)号】 CN102337012A
【公开(公告)日】 2012.02.01
【申请(专利权)人】 华南理工大学

【地址】 广东省广州市天河区五山路381号
【发明(设计)人】王小萍；李文锋
【摘要】 本发明提供了一种高强度P34HB/长玻纤复合材料及其制备方法。所述复合材料由下述重量百分比的原材料配置而成：P34HB40~90，成核剂0~3，长玻纤5~40，填料0~30，偶联剂0~0.5。所述复合材料的制备方法为：将P34HB、成核剂、填料、偶联剂在高速混合机中混合，将混合均匀的原料投置于双螺杆挤出机加料口，长玻纤由玻纤口进入，物料熔融挤出，造粒，得到具有生物降解性能的高强度P34HB/长玻纤复合材料。该复合材料表面没有浮纤，具有很高的光滑度和力学强度，可以用传统的塑料加工方法加工成注塑制品、挤出制品、薄膜以及泡沫制品，大量替代石油基塑料在工业、农业、医疗和包装等领域的使用。

【名称】一种无卤素高效阻燃剂组合物及其制备方法
【公开(公告)号】 CN102337034A
【公开(公告)日】 2012.02.01
【申请(专利权)人】东华大学
【地址】 上海市松江区新城区人民北路2999号
【发明(设计)人】 彭治汉；游丽华；惠银银；付金鹏；穆俊迁；黄烈迁
【摘要】 本发明公开了一种无卤素高效阻燃剂组合物及其制备方法。本发明的无卤素阻燃剂组合物的组分和质量百分比包括：苯代三聚氰胺羧乙基苯基次膦酸缩合物10%~80%、三聚氰胺和/或其衍生物15%~70%、有机磷酸酯5%~20%。本发明的无卤素阻燃剂组合物，可用于各种聚烯烃、尼龙、聚氨酯和聚酯等合成材料和纺织品的阻燃，尤其适用于聚酯和尼龙工程塑料，在PBT树脂中添加12%(wt)其阻燃等级即可达到UL94V-0级(1.6mm)。本发明的阻燃剂复合物具有阻燃效率高、流动性好、不析出等特点，可满足电器外壳和支架、电子电器接插件等用阻燃树脂的使用要求。

【名称】废旧塑料改性沥青及其制备方法
【公开(公告)号】 CN102337035A
【公开(公告)日】 2012.02.01
【申请(专利权)人】 交通运输部公路科学研究所
【地址】北京市海淀区西土城路8号
【发明(设计)人】 曹东伟；张玉贞；唐国奇；孔宪明；张海燕
【摘要】 本发明提供一种储存稳定性良好，成本较低的废旧塑料改性沥青，以及工艺简单，便于操作的废旧塑料改性沥青的制备方法。所述废旧塑料改性沥青由基质沥青、废旧塑料、相容助剂以及无机填料的混合物制成，且基于100重量份所述基质沥青，所述废旧塑料为4-12重量份，所述相容助剂为2-5重量份，所述无机填料为2-20重量份。

【名称】 塑料组合物及其应用以及塑料表面选择性金属化的方法
【公开(公告)号】 CN102337038A
【公开(公告)日】 2012.02.01
【申请(专利权)人】比亚迪股份有限公司
【地址】 广东省深圳市坪山新区比亚迪路3009号
【发明(设计)人】 宫清；周良；苗伟峰；张雄
【摘要】 本发明提供了一种塑料组合物，该塑料组合物含有塑料基材组分和催化剂组分，其中，所述催化剂组分为选自除铜以外的元素周期表第9、10和11列金属元素的氧化物，元素周期表第9、10和11列金属元素的硅酸盐、硼酸盐和草酸盐，含有元素周期表第9、10和11列金属元素的加氢催化剂以及具有铜铁矿结构的ABO2型复合氧化物中的一种或两种以上；所述A为选自元素周期表第9、10和11列金属元素中一种，B为Ni、Mn、Cr、Al或Fe，且A与B不同。本发明还涉及本发明提供的塑料组合物在塑料表面选择性金属化中的应用。本发明还提供了一种塑料表面选择性金属化的方法。使用该方法后，可以进一步容易地形成电路。

【名称】一种塑料基材电镀的方法
【公开(公告)号】 CN102337571A
【公开(公告)日】 2012.02.01
【申请(专利权)人】 厦门建霖工业有限公司
【地址】福建省厦门市莲前路859号莲前大厦12楼1208室
【发明(设计)人】 余水；柯学标；乔永亮；李明仁
【摘要】 一种塑料基材电镀的方法，涉及一种塑料表面处理方法。提供一种可以实现塑胶材料的表面金属化，简化电镀工艺流程，大幅度减少废水排放量，减少对环境和人类的污染，适合多种塑胶表面要求的塑料基材电镀的方法。对塑料基材进行预处理；对处理的塑胶基材进行物理气相沉积金属化，并依次进行物理气相沉积等离子体改性，镀金属底层、金属过渡层和金属导电层；对处理的塑胶基材直接进行电镀铜，或电镀铜和电镀镍；对处理的塑胶基材的电镀铜层表面进行拉丝处理或对处理的塑胶基材的电镀铜电镀镍层上进行拉丝处理；对处理的塑胶基材转挂入PVD炉进行等离子体处理后，进行铬层的沉积，或对处理的塑胶基材干式除尘除静电后进行有机涂层保护处理。

【名称】轻卡前桥塑料密封销盖
【公开(公告)号】 CN102338219A

【公开(公告)日】 2012.02.01
【申请(专利权)人】 诸城市义和车桥有限公司
【地址】 山东省潍坊市诸城市泰薛路王家铁沟村南侧
【发明(设计)人】 陈忠义
【摘要】 本发明公开了一种轻卡前桥塑料密封销盖，其特征在于，在球弧形顶面的下部设有带有多条圈筋的圆柱面。通过以上设置，将本发明扣合在转向节的上端，能明显改善转向节销密封性，降低了汽车前桥的市场故障率，而且大大降低了工人的劳动强度，降低了产品成本及服务费用。

【名称】 预承插感应加热熔接塑料管件
【公开(公告)号】 CN102338254A
【公开(公告)日】 2012.02.01
【申请(专利权)人】 杨蒙
【地址】 广东省东莞市塘厦镇湖柏山庄湖光阁204
【发明(设计)人】 杨蒙
【摘要】 本发明公开了一种预承插感应加热熔接塑料管件，是一种全新的适合塑料和金属复合成的复合管道安装的新型管件。本发明所述的预承插感应加热熔接塑料管件，包括塑料套和至少一个连接端，塑料套与待热熔紧固的复合管的管口适配，塑料套与待热熔紧固的复合管相互套装形成复合套，各连接端通过设置于管件内的通道彼此连通，连接端的端口与复合套的套口连接适配。本发明的预承插感应加热熔接塑料管件，连接牢固，抗压力性强，密封性好，安装效率高，适用范围广泛。

【名称】 塑料光纤耦合器及其制作方法
【公开(公告)号】 CN102338907A
【公开(公告)日】 2012.02.01
【申请(专利权)人】 上海康阔光通信技术有限公司
【地址】 上海市浦东新区蔡伦路255号9号楼
【发明(设计)人】 黄勇；黄生
【摘要】 本发明公开了一种塑料光纤耦合器及其制作方法，包括：一根光混合管和N根环形分布的塑料光纤束，N为大于等于6的正整数。本发明可以有效地减少光耦合过程中所产生的光损耗；另外还可以有效解决分光均匀性问题。

【名称】 一种新型光学塑料偶次非球面液晶投影镜头
【公开(公告)号】 CN102338925A
【公开(公告)日】 2012.02.01
【申请(专利权)人】 无锡艾德里安科技有限公司
【地址】 江苏省无锡市滨湖区锦溪路100号
【发明(设计)人】 马捷
【摘要】 本发明涉及投影显示领域，尤其涉及一种新型光学塑料偶次非球面液晶投影镜头，包括：前组、光阑、后组、LCD液晶平板、保护玻璃平板，画面经投影镜头后，投影到屏幕上；投影镜头的孔径光阑置于前组和后组之间；LCD液晶平板置于后组后，采用单片设计，光线不用分离。后组中光学塑料非球面透镜采用光学塑料—PMMA制作而成，而且做成偶次非球面。本发明实现了液晶投影镜头的小型化，高质量化与低成本化，最后实现的液晶投影镜头最大处直径20mm，总长度90mm。

【名称】 氟塑料轻质阻燃电缆
【公开(公告)号】 CN102339661A
【公开(公告)日】 2012.02.01
【申请(专利权)人】 上海永进电缆(集团)有限公司
【地址】 上海市奉贤区金汇镇金钱公路1468号
【发明(设计)人】 陈存华；陈智；陈浩
【摘要】 本发明涉及电缆。氟塑料轻质阻燃电缆，包括外绝缘层、内绝缘层、缆芯，外绝缘层和内绝缘层之间设有阻燃层，内绝缘层和缆芯之间设有阻燃填充物，阻燃层内填充有压缩的阻燃性气体。外绝缘层内含有氟塑料成分，内绝缘层内含有氟塑料成分。由于采用了上述技术方案，本发明具有自身重量轻、阻燃能力强等优点。

【名称】 小型塑料外壳式断路器
【公开(公告)号】 CN102339694A
【公开(公告)日】 2012.02.01
【申请(专利权)人】 北京翠祥电器元件有限公司
【地址】 北京市大兴区中关村科技园区生物医药产业基地天华街25号
【发明(设计)人】 南寅；刘立改；彭世春
【摘要】 本发明涉及小型塑料外壳式断路器，包括绝缘塑料外壳及置于其中的进出线端子、热脱扣系统、磁脱扣系统、动静触头、操作机构及灭弧系统，操作机构带动动触头实现电路闭合和断开；磁脱扣系统由磁扼、铁芯、套管和线圈组成，线圈一端经磁扼与静触头连接或直接与静触头连接；另一端与热脱扣连接或与接线端子连接，磁脱扣系统的线圈为非圆圈形结构。磁脱扣系统的铁芯由一非圆柱形的导磁材料制成。磁脱扣系统的套管为一非圆圈形结构。本发明对磁脱扣系统与热脱扣系统进行了优化设计，提出了一种9mm宽度的超薄型小型断路器。相对于传统的18mm宽度的产品此断路器宽度减小了50%具有操作可靠性高、结构简单、成本低等优点。

【名称】 塑料光纤墙面交换机
【公开(公告)号】 CN102340403A
【公开(公告)日】 2012.02.01
【申请(专利权)人】 四川汇源塑料光纤有限公司

【地址】 四川省成都市崇州市工业集中发展区
【发明(设计)人】 宋昌林；唐波；储九荣；刘中一
【摘要】 本发明塑料光纤墙面交换机，包括供电电路，与供电电路的直流电压输出端连接的滤波电路，有88E6063控制芯片的控制芯片电路，分别与控制芯片电路连接的抗干扰电路、有25HMz晶振集成块的晶振电路、有EDL300T集成电路的塑料光纤接口电路、分别有RJ45集成电路的第一、第二、第三网络电缆接口电路。本发明安装、使用方便、应用范围广、外形小巧美观，占用空间极小。

【名称】 抗摔碰型显微塑料玻片标本
【公开(公告)号】 CN102342271A
【公开(公告)日】 2012.02.08
【申请(专利权)人】 路思谦；路鸥；高红
【地址】 山东省日照学苑路669号济宁医学院
【发明(设计)人】 路思谦；路鸥；高红；路明钧
【摘要】 一种具有抗摔碰功能的显微塑料玻片标本制作方法，在载玻片两面、盖玻片朝向标本的一面覆盖抗化学药品腐蚀功能的透明薄膜，使玻片标本既能耐受制片过程中化学药品的腐蚀，又有塑料的抗摔碰功能，对不易取得的标本；价格中等到昂贵的标本保存、使用有积极有益的效果。

【名称】 一种塑木复合板材
【公开(公告)号】 CN102343610A
【公开(公告)日】 2012.02.08
【申请(专利权)人】 南通绿恒新型建材科技有限公司
【地址】 江苏省南通市通州区三余镇环西路98号
【发明(设计)人】 梁为民
【摘要】 本发明公开了一种塑木复合板材，其特征在于：由以下组分按质量配比制成：木材60%~90%，塑料5%~38%，助剂2%~5%。木材70%~85%，塑料10%~25%，助剂2%~5%。所述的助剂为氯化聚乙烯。与发明在塑料与木头中添加2%~5%的氯化聚乙烯助剂，加工出来的板材性能好，板面平整，生产效率高。

【名称】 一种耐磨塑木复合板材
【公开(公告)号】 CN102343611A
【公开(公告)日】 2012.02.08
【申请(专利权)人】 南通绿恒新型建材科技有限公司
【地址】 江苏省南通市通州区三余镇环西路98号
【发明(设计)人】 梁为民
【摘要】 本发明公开了一种耐磨塑木复合板材，具有塑料和木材，其特征在于：还添加有石粉和金属粉，所述的塑料、木材、石粉与金属粉的质量比为：1:(2~5):(0.3~0.5):(0.2~1)。所述的塑料、木材、石粉与金属粉的质量比为：1:(4~5):0.5:1。与发明在塑木板材中添加石粉和金属粉，石粉和金属粉不仅增加了复合板材的强度和硬度，同时耐磨性能也大大提升，满足特定场合对于耐磨性要求高的需求。

【名称】 一种塑木复合材料
【公开(公告)号】 CN102343612A
【公开(公告)日】 2012.02.08
【申请(专利权)人】 南通绿恒新型建材科技有限公司
【地址】 江苏省南通市通州区三余镇环西路98号
【发明(设计)人】 梁为民
【摘要】 本发明公开了一种塑木复合材料，由木材和塑料构成，其特征在于：所述的木材所占的质量百分比为80%~90%，所述的塑料所占的质量百分比为20%~10%。所述的木材所占的质量百分比为86%，所述的塑料所占的质量百分比为14%。本发明将木粉与塑料按照本发明的配比配置，其中木材所占比例为80%~90%，而塑料所占比例为20%~10%，所以复合材料的强度高。

【名称】 一种带有颜色的塑木复合板
【公开(公告)号】 CN102343613A
【公开(公告)日】 2012.02.08
【申请(专利权)人】 南通绿恒新型建材科技有限公司
【地址】 江苏省南通市通州区三余镇环西路98号
【发明(设计)人】 梁为民
【摘要】 本发明公开了一种带有颜色的塑木复合板，具有塑料、木材以及少量助剂，其特征在于：还具有质量比为2%~10%的色素。还具有少量石粉。与现有技术相比，与发明在塑木板材中色素，从而根据需要，将不同颜色的色素添加到板材中形成不用颜色的塑木复合板材，不仅颜色不会退掉，而且表面颜色一致，内板材内外颜色也一致，加工成家具或其他产品，无需另行上漆。

【名称】 一种农作物秸秆塑料复合人造板的加工方法
【公开(公告)号】 CN102343641A
【公开(公告)日】 2012.02.08
【申请(专利权)人】 南通绿恒新型建材科技有限公司
【地址】 江苏省南通市通州区三余镇环西路98号
【发明(设计)人】 梁为民
【摘要】 本发明公开了一种农作物秸秆塑料复合人造板的加工方法，其步骤如下：第一步、将农作物秸秆切段干燥；第二步、粉碎烘干：将干燥的农作物秸秆粉碎成粉状，并烘干到含水率5%～10%；第三步、包裹：用PVC树脂将上述烘干的秸秆粉包裹成颗粒；第四步、造粒：将上述包裹的颗粒与塑料混合造粒，粒径为3～5mm，其中秸秆粉颗粒含量为60%～70%，助剂为0.5～1.5%，余量为塑料；第五步、挤出发泡、冷却定型、出料。本发明农作物秸秆切段干燥后粉碎，然后经脱水、包裹、造粒、挤出发泡、冷却定型及出料工序加工出来，不仅将农作物加以利用，同时还减少了农作物燃烧后烟气的排放。

【名称】 塑料产品的制作系统及方法

【公开(公告)号】 CN102343642A

【公开(公告)日】 2012.02.08

【申请(专利权)人】 汉达精密电子(昆山)有限公司

【地址】 江苏省苏州市昆山市出口加工区第二大道269号

【发明(设计)人】 郭雪梅；吴政道；郭俊映

【摘要】 本发明提供一种塑料产品的制作系统，其包括：一模具成型机台，其上设有一注塑模具，且该注塑模具中设有加热及冷却功能元件；一薄膜供给装置，其设于上述模具成型机台上；一薄膜供给装置控制器，其设于上述模具成型机台上与上述薄膜供给装置连接；一高低温控制装置，其与上述注塑模具连接；一注塑机，其与上述注塑模具连接。本发明所提供的塑料产品的制作系统，使塑料产品达到高光无结合线的要求并保证焕彩效果产品表面具有一定的硬度之外，而且还具有夜光效果。

【名称】 用型料与废弃纸塑铝软包装复合材料共挤制造型材的方法

【公开(公告)号】 CN102343656A

【公开(公告)日】 2012.02.08

【申请(专利权)人】 青岛人民印刷有限公司

【地址】 山东省青岛市李沧区兴华路15号

【发明(设计)人】 王渊博；窦中华；滕奇元

【摘要】本发明公开了一种用型料与废弃纸塑铝软包装复合材料共挤制造型材的方法，其内容为：型材的复合材料内芯与外覆层分别配料，用生产线主机和辅机双机共挤的方式生产型材，调整二机的转速与压力比使型材的复合材料内芯的内或外表面覆盖一层厚度均匀密实的覆盖层。应用本发明的方法生产的型材，具有复合材料内芯与覆盖层。其为将废弃的软包装复合材料制成型材，并用全新的塑料均匀地覆盖该型材的内或外表面，从而使型材外表一致强度提高，使用范围扩大，具有显著的经济和社会效益。

【名称】 回收塑料在线循环清网、不断料超大滤网面积熔体过滤器

【公开(公告)号】 CN102343658A

【公开(公告)日】 2012.02.08

【申请(专利权)人】 南京创博机械设备有限公司；张宏革

【地址】 江苏省南京市江宁区谷里工业集中区安康路16号

【发明(设计)人】 张宏革；罗江

【摘要】 本发明涉及的是一种回收塑料在线循环清网、不断料超大滤网面积熔体过滤器，其结构是包括液压油缸、大柱塞、过滤器本体、滤网、环柱状流道、内流道、小柱塞、限位板架；优点：在同样单位空间内的过滤面积可加大4～20倍，单机产能可达到1.5t/h以上；滤网采用螺旋狭缝、梯形截面滤隙、多边形柱面结构，可反复在线清理循环使用，大幅降低相应消耗；过滤器具有预充填与排气通道，清网过程不断料，生产过程连续不中断，避免了物料损耗；每个滤网柱塞体仅用一个液压油缸驱动，实现大小柱塞联动，结构大为简化，众多功能过程一气呵成；采用两个(或两个以上)柱塞体并联设置，实现过滤与生产过程的长期连续稳定运行。

【名称】 半自动塑料瓶胚加热吹瓶机

【公开(公告)号】 CN102343663A

【公开(公告)日】 2012.02.08

【申请(专利权)人】 林明茳

【地址】 浙江省台州市黄岩区黄椒路528号台州市黄岩亚力塑机有限公司

【发明(设计)人】 林明茳

【摘要】 半自动塑料瓶胚加热吹瓶机，包括并列安装的拉吹机组件和加热器组件，拉吹机组件包括模具和开合模机构，模具的上方安装拉吹机构，加热器组件包括由链轮带动的环形传动链条，链条带动瓶胚支承座，模具上设置进胚导向装置，包括在机架上安装导向筒，模具模口上安装托胚叉，托胚叉与瓶胚相接触；所述链条包括内、外链片，内、外链片由链销相连，所述链销包括长、短胚链销，长胚链销两头各自与外链片相固定，短胚链销两头各自与内链片相固定，长胚链销内安装瓶胚支承轴，瓶胚支承轴外有上、下轴承，上、下轴承与外链片之间分别有上、下轴承垫圈，瓶胚支承轴的上头安装插头，并与瓶胚相配合，下头安装自转齿轮，并与自转齿条相接触。

【名称】 塑料制品热成型机的接标装置

【公开(公告)号】 CN102343666A

【公开(公告)日】 2012.02.08

【申请(专利权)人】 浙江宏华机械塑胶有限公司

【地址】 浙江省温州市瑞安市东山街道办事处经济开发区发展区

【发明(设计)人】 张华林；孙超超

【摘要】 本发明公开了一种塑料制品热成型机的接标装置，其特征在于：所述接标装置包括接标座、剪式连杆、接标模和接标模安装板，剪式连杆连接在接标座上，剪式连杆的伸缩由驱动元件驱动，接标模安装板连接在剪式连杆的中心铰点的铰接轴上，接标模在接标模安装板上固定安装，接标模的周面设有吸气孔，接标座上设有滑轨，接标模安装板上设有滑块，滑块在滑轨上滑动设置。本发明用于塑料制品热成型机上，能够完成快速接标，使贴标速度与塑料制品热成型速度同步，从而实现同一设备的制品成型和贴标的全自动化生产，大大提高生产效率，减轻劳动成本。

【名称】 一种复合防辐射塑料

【公开(公告)号】 CN102343696A

【公开(公告)日】 2012.02.08

【申请(专利权)人】 常熟市慧丰塑料制品有限公司

【地址】 江苏省苏州市常熟市辛庄镇(杨园)双浜村

【发明(设计)人】 张根庆

【摘要】 本发明揭示了一种复合防辐射塑料，包括基层以及表层，所述的基层为塑料层，表层为防辐射涂层，由于采用了掺锑二氧化锡的防辐射涂层，而其本身有很好的导电、防静电辐射、放紫外线等特点，在与塑料复合后能够很好的阻挡紫外线、红外线等对人体的伤害，而塑料本身在燃烧过程中也不会产生有毒有害气体污染环境，具有很好的环保效果，作为绿色环保型防辐射塑料在市场有很好的前景。

【名称】 塑料包装袋的印刷方法

【公开(公告)号】 CN102343731A

【公开(公告)日】 2012.02.08

【申请(专利权)人】 扬州科信包装印刷有限公司

【地址】 江苏省扬州市广陵区连运西路8号

【发明(设计)人】 陆新楠

【摘要】 本发明公开了一种塑料包装袋的印刷方法。该塑料包装袋的印刷方法包括如下步骤：安装印版滚筒、调试刮刀、调专色、电脑套印、核对样品、印刷、烘干、缠绕成卷、固化，将成卷的塑料薄膜放在室温条件下固化24h，使油墨充分的固化。采用该技术方案的塑料包装袋的印刷方法，印刷质量好、可以如实还原设计的图案，加快了印刷准备，提高刻生产效率，适合规模化生产。

【名称】 壁挂式塑料托架

【公开(公告)号】 CN102343996A

【公开(公告)日】 2012.02.08

【申请(专利权)人】 杨春龙

【地址】 四川省绵竹市东北镇广和村3组

【发明(设计)人】 杨春龙

【摘要】 本发明公开了壁挂式塑料袋托架，涉及生活用品，意在解决现有的塑料袋托架不能直接挂在墙壁上，且不用的时候将袋口合上不方便这个问题，其包括紧固件、固定座、支架、压条及吸盘，固定支座呈形，紧固件将支架相对固定在固定座的形凹槽内的两端，支架上设置有压条，吸盘设置在固定座上，本发明壁挂式塑料袋托架，其设计简单，易于制造，使用方便。

【名称】 一种循环使用废塑料生产纸塑复合袋的一体化工艺

【公开(公告)号】 CN102344008A

【公开(公告)日】 2012.02.08

【申请(专利权)人】 温州晨光集团晨亮塑业有限公司

【地址】 浙江省温州市平阳县萧江镇工业园区(长兴路江边)

【发明(设计)人】 周上来；胡茂林；彭希金；萧金爱；林德峰

【摘要】 本发明公开了一种循环使用废塑料生产纸塑复合袋的一体化工艺，包括收集废旧塑料，将废旧塑料用洗涤剂清洗，并将废塑料进行分类，再利用节能用电机进行熔化，对熔体进行冷却、切粒，制得造粒料，在造粒料加入专用料，并添加增白剂，并混合均匀进行拉丝，制得拉丝，将拉丝支撑半成品编织袋和半成品编织布，将半成品编织布与牛皮纸利用中缝、边缝复合机进行复合，然后自动抽边、裁片，制得纸塑复合编织袋，在纸塑复合编织袋中加入内衬袋，制成纸塑复合内衬编织袋。与现有技术相比，本发明的循环使用废塑料生产纸塑复合袋的一体化工艺循环利用废塑料，降低了生产成本，利用本发明工艺制得的纸塑复合袋具有强度好、防水防潮的优点。

【名称】 粉煤灰泡沫塑料颗粒保温防水材料及制作方法

【公开(公告)号】 CN102344268A

【公开(公告)日】 2012.02.08

【申请(专利权)人】 新疆生产建设兵团第五建筑安装工程公司

【地址】 新疆维吾尔自治区石河子市北五路164号

【发明(设计)人】 刘绍明；李呈坤；陈翠萍；郭雪芳；谢长林；高新民；张为华；蔡新疆；马国防；刘俊芳；唐冬萍；方拥政

【摘要】 一种粉煤灰泡沫塑料颗粒保温防水材料及制作方法，由以下原料组成：水泥、检测合格的32.5普通硅酸盐水泥、含CaO80%～85%生石灰、粒度为4～8mm聚苯乙烯泡沫塑料颗粒、粉煤灰，将上述的粉煤灰、生石灰、水泥，按比例放入搅拌机内混合0.5～5min，制成胶凝材料，向上述胶凝材料内加入适当的胶凝材料、聚苯乙烯泡沫塑料颗粒，和水：向上述混合后的材料内加入泡沫剂、防水剂，搅拌0.5～5min使其成泡沫料浆；在30～60min内浇注，表面拍实抹平，保持湿润12～72h，制成保温防水板：用憎水剂间隔1～3h，表面喷洒处理3～5次。本发明具有密度低、强度高、保温隔热、防水性能好，且制造成本低的优点，同时为粉煤灰、泡沫塑料颗粒等废弃物提供了再利用机会，节约了大量的粘土。

【名称】 中温快速固化无色透明环氧树脂固化剂及其制备方法

【公开(公告)号】 CN102344545A

【公开(公告)日】 2012.02.08

【申请(专利权)人】 舒城金泽信环保材料有限公司

【地址】 安徽省六安市舒城县杭埠镇杭埠工业园区

【发明(设计)人】 郝玉龙；吴月荣

【摘要】 本发明公开了一种中温快速固化无色透明环氧树脂固化剂，其各组分的重量份为：三乙醇胺55～65、碳酸丙烯酯25～35、乙二胺10～15。将三种原料物质混合反应后生成本发明的固化剂，将所得的固化剂同环氧树脂按比例调胶后，可加热快速固化，生成无色透明高韧性的环氧树脂固化塑料。可以广泛应用在电子和非电子产品的灌注密封或高温粘结修补中。

【名称】 一种离子膜的生产方法

【公开(公告)号】 CN102344578A

【公开(公告)日】 2012.02.08

【申请(专利权)人】 深圳市金钒能源科技有限公司

【地址】 广东省深圳市南山区中山园路1001号TCL国际E城D1栋202单元

【发明(设计)人】 郑东冬

【摘要】 本发明涉及一种离子膜的生产方法。所述离子膜生产方法包括步骤：将磺酸树脂与二甲基甲酰胺进行混合处理，并进行搅拌；对混合液进行过滤处理；将滤液放置在塑料容器中进行沉淀处理；将经沉淀处理的滤液倒入烘干装置内，在120℃的恒温下进行烘干处理90分钟，在恒温烘干的同时进行抽真空处理；将烘干成型的离子膜取出进行冷却处理。根据本发明所公开的技术方案所生产的离子膜表面非常平整，而且离子膜的韧性和气密性非常好，离子膜的使用寿命大大增加，从而也增加了钒液流电堆的使用寿命，提高了钒液流电堆的工作效率。

【名称】 一种PVA废塑料再生胶棉制备方法

【公开(公告)号】 CN102344580A

【公开(公告)日】 2012.02.08

【申请(专利权)人】 博罗县业鸿塑胶制品有限公司

【地址】 广东省惠州市博罗县罗阳镇小金村四角楼

【发明(设计)人】 林创喜

【摘要】 本发明涉及一种PVA废塑料再生胶棉制备方法，包括方法步骤：取PVA废塑料除杂、清洗、烘干后粉碎，与淀粉搅拌均匀混合，加水后加热，并加环氧树脂粘合剂，搅拌得物料倒入喷浆絮棉块内，冷却后脱水，切成所需胶棉块。本发明产品可适用于地面擦拭。吸水性强，去污效果好。有利于PVA废塑料再生推广应用。

【名称】 一种硬脂酸铅类复合稳定润滑剂的非水生产方法

【公开(公告)号】 CN102344582A

【公开(公告)日】 2012.02.08

【申请(专利权)人】 南京协和助剂有限公司；南京协和化学有限公司

【地址】 江苏省南京市六合区化学工业园区方水路90号-98

【发明(设计)人】 黄艳

【摘要】 本发明属于聚氯乙烯塑料加工助剂领域，涉及一种硬脂酸铅类复合稳定润滑剂的非水生产方法。本发明将硬脂酸和催化剂先投入捏合机料斗中，启动捏合机，并加热升温，捏合搅拌一定时间至物料熔化并混合均匀后，再加入氧化铅，继续捏合，搅拌物料进行充分反应，放料冷却，得到硬脂酸铅类复合稳定润滑剂产品。本发明所述的非水合成方法，生产过程中不采用水作为反应介质，没有废水排放，且硬脂酸铅类复合稳定润滑剂的生产反应体系为粘性膏状物，解决了产品生产过程中的粉尘污染问题，且在捏合机中完成非水合成操作，充分利用了捏合机搅拌动力大、剪切力强、捏合效果好等优点。

【名称】 新型石粉塑料塑化剂的制作方法

【公开(公告)号】 CN102344584A

【公开(公告)日】 2012.02.08

【申请(专利权)人】 吕大龙

【地址】 山东省青岛市延安三路105号楼1002室

【发明(设计)人】 吕大龙

【摘要】 新型石粉塑料塑化剂的制作方法涉及化工技术领域。制作方法是，采用原料为石粉、皮革化工下角料、邻苯二甲酸二丁酯、聚乙烯树脂、聚丙烯树酯。各原料的重量百分比为85%~90%、3%~8%、2%~5%、2%~5%、2%~5%，且满足各原料重量百分比之和为100%。其制作步骤为：把皮革化工下角料加入粉碎机粉碎；将石粉和粉碎后的皮革化工下角料加入炒罐内加热干炒，并陆续加入邻苯二甲酸二丁酯、聚乙烯树酯和聚丙烯树酯，干炒温度为120~180℃，干炒时间为5~20min；将干炒混合料倒入研磨机研磨成细面；将研磨料加入造粒机造粒。本制作方法加大了填充料石粉的量，采用皮革化工下角料变废为宝，可降低生产成本，产品质量好。

【名称】 一种热塑性动态硫化橡胶制备方法

【公开(公告)号】 CN102344593A

【公开(公告)日】 2012.02.08

【申请(专利权)人】 冯波

【地址】 广东省东莞市大岭山镇杨屋管理区卓林五金厂

【发明(设计)人】 冯波

【摘要】 本发明公开了一种热塑性动态硫化橡胶的制备方法，包括：将橡胶和热塑性塑料的混合物在硫化助剂和有机过氧化物的存在的条件下动态硫化；还包括：在上述步骤之后，再添加自由基吸收剂和热稳定剂，并熔融混合，以获得热塑性动态硫化橡胶。本发明的制备方法能降低热塑性动态硫化橡胶的制备成本，同时还提高了热塑性动态硫化橡胶的交联密度，改善热塑性动态硫化橡胶的加工流动性。

【名称】 一种塑料的加工方法

【公开(公告)号】 CN102344602A

【公开(公告)日】 2012.02.08

【申请(专利权)人】 常熟市慧丰塑料制品有限公司

【地址】 江苏省苏州市常熟市辛庄镇(杨园)双浜村

【发明(设计)人】 张根庆

【摘要】 本发明揭示了一种塑料的加工方法，所述该塑料加工步骤如下：(1)调节注塑机温度至200~350℃；(2)将聚乙烯塑料与阻燃剂放在一起进行搅拌混合；(3)将混合好的塑料混合物放入注塑机中进行凝练加工；(4)把从注塑机中加工好的聚乙烯塑料进行冷却处理；(5)把冷却处理的聚乙烯塑切成粒状塑料，并打包存放。在聚乙烯塑料中添加了阻燃剂十溴二苯醚后，能够使塑料具有很好的阻燃性能，而且该塑料混合物在燃烧后容易分解，并且产生的气体不会对空气造成污染，具有很好的环保效果，塑料混合物具有很好的热稳定性，能够长时间的保存，发挥阻燃效果。

【名称】 高填充硬质聚氯乙烯地板

【公开(公告)号】 CN102344618A

【公开(公告)日】 2012.02.08

【申请(专利权)人】 苏州富通电器塑业有限公司

【地址】 江苏省吴江市芦墟镇国赵路8号

【发明(设计)人】 陈健；张建光；杨文乾；徐建辉

【摘要】 本发明属于PVC地板，特别涉及高填充硬质聚氯乙烯地板。一种高填充硬质聚氯乙烯地板，其特征在于由如下配方组成，按重量份数其配方为：聚氯乙烯树脂100~120份，二甲基二巯基乙酸异辛酯锡8~10份，碳酸钙200~250份，膨胀珍珠岩200~250份，邻苯二甲酸二辛酯25~30份，石蜡10份，AC发泡剂20~25份。该地板的冲击强度等各种性能均能满足使用要求，深受乘客和驾、售人员欢迎。通常，公共汽车、电车每天停运后必须用水冲洗车厢，过去车厢地板均为木质材料，木料经不起水腐蚀，每隔1年甚至半年就要更新一次。自采用该PVC地板后这种PVC塑料地板一直完好无损。

【名称】 抗静电PVC塑料地板

【公开(公告)号】 CN102344619A

【公开(公告)日】 2012.02.08

【申请(专利权)人】 苏州富通电器塑业有限公司

【地址】 江苏省吴江市芦墟镇国赵路8号

【发明(设计)人】 陈健；张建光；杨文乾；徐建辉

【摘要】 本发明属于PVC地板，特别涉及抗静电PVC塑料地板。一种抗静电PVC塑料地板，其特征在于由如下配方组成，按重量份数其配方为：聚氯乙烯树脂100~120份，二甲基二巯基乙酸异辛酯锡8~10份，高岭土200~250份，邻苯二甲酸二辛酯25~30份，乙氧基化脂肪族烷基胺11~15份，石蜡10份。可以有效地减少静电产生，防止静电带来的危害。

【名称】 阻燃PVC塑料地板

【公开(公告)号】 CN102344621A

【公开(公告)日】 2012.02.08

【申请(专利权)人】 苏州富通电器塑业有限公司

【地址】 江苏省吴江市芦墟镇国赵路8号

【发明(设计)人】 陈健；张建光；杨文乾；徐建辉

【摘要】 本发明属于PVC地板，特别涉及阻燃PVC塑料地板。一种阻燃PVC塑料地板，其特征在于由如下配方组成，按重量份数其配方为：聚氯乙烯树脂100~120份，二甲基二巯基乙酸异辛酯锡8~10份，邻苯二甲酸二辛酯25~30份，乙氧基化脂肪族烷基胺11~15份，氢氧化铝5~10份、氢氧化镁5~10份，抗老化剂2~4份。本发明提供一种新型阻燃PVC地板，其阻燃性能卓著。

【名称】 户外高分子环保地板

【公开(公告)号】 CN102344623A

【公开(公告)日】 2012.02.08
【申请(专利权)人】 苏州富通电器塑业有限公司
【地址】 江苏省吴江市芦墟镇国赵路8号
【发明(设计)人】 陈健；张建光；杨文乾；徐建辉
【摘要】 本发明涉及一种户外高分子环保地板，其制备方法是：首先按比例混合聚氯乙烯、稳定剂、发泡剂、润滑剂，将混合物在160～200℃高温下，在20～40MPa的高压下分子链进行断链重组，形成新的分子结构链；然后按比例加入其余原材料后，降温至120℃成型，由发泡塑料挤出机高压挤出、经模具挤压定型、再经冷却牵引，切割检验，最后包装产品。本产品具有防水、防蛀、阻燃、抗老化、不褪色、免维护、表面强度高、内部韧性好等优点，能替代木材作为户外的建筑材料，且无毒、加工无污染、属节能环保型产品。

【名称】 邻苯二甲酸酯类增塑剂测定用标准样品的制备方法
【公开(公告)号】 CN102344624A
【公开(公告)日】 2012.02.08
【申请(专利权)人】 福建出入境检验检疫局检验检疫技术中心
【地址】 福建省福州市湖东路312号国检广场
【发明(设计)人】 吕水源；唐熙；李小晶；石坚；许才明；唐泓；梁鸣
【摘要】 本发明提供一种邻苯二甲酸酯类增塑剂测定用标准样品的制备方法，将目标化合物邻苯二甲酸酯类增塑剂与稳定剂、润滑剂等混合均匀，形成混合物，并将该混合物与基体材料进行高速搅拌，搅拌冷却后进行挤出吹膜获得膜厚度25～30μm的薄膜，并将该薄膜进行系列处理后以获得标准样品。本发明的优点在于：通过操作简单方便的制备方法获得邻苯二甲酸酯类增塑剂测定用标准样品，有助于提高实验室间塑料中邻苯二甲酸酯类增塑剂检测数据的可比性和一致性，为统一检测塑料中邻苯二甲酸酯类增塑剂的标准奠定了基础、提供了可能。

【名称】 一种阻燃塑料配方
【公开(公告)号】 CN102344626A
【公开(公告)日】 2012.02.08
【申请(专利权)人】 常熟市慧丰塑料制品有限公司
【地址】 江苏省苏州市常熟市辛庄镇(杨园)双浜村
【发明(设计)人】 张根庆
【摘要】 本发明揭示了一种阻燃塑料配方，所述的阻燃塑料配方由聚氯乙烯树脂，添加剂，热稳定剂，改质剂，填充剂其中各组成所占重量比例分别为聚氯乙烯树脂占65%～80%，添加剂占4%～5%，热稳定剂占6%～10%，改质剂占5%～10%，填充剂占5%～10%。该阻燃塑料配方中加入各种成分后，使生产的塑料具有很强的阻燃效果，而且塑料本身的延展性、抗压性等性能都得到了很大的提高，使生产出来的塑料更加凝练，该塑料中各种成分在高温燃烧的情况下不会造成有害气体，具有很好的环保效果，而且生产成本低，使用户能够获得更大的利润。

【名称】 一种阻燃塑料的加工工艺
【公开(公告)号】 CN102344627A
【公开(公告)日】 2012.02.08
【申请(专利权)人】 常熟市慧丰塑料制品有限公司
【地址】 江苏省苏州市常熟市辛庄镇(杨园)双浜村
【发明(设计)人】 张根庆
【摘要】 本发明揭示了一种阻燃塑料的加工工艺，其特征在于：所述的加工工艺步骤如下：(1)将塑料混合物与阻燃剂剂放一起混合均匀；(2)将混好的塑料放入注塑机中凝练加工，调节注塑机的温度；(3)将生产出来的塑料通过冷却水冷却，并通过切粒机切成粒状；(4)将切好的塑料城中打包，并进行存放。由于在聚氯乙烯和聚乙烯的混合物中添加了三氧化二锑阻燃剂，塑料混合物就具有了很好的阻燃性能，而且具有良好的难燃性和自熄性，使该塑料混合物生产的产品能够起到很好的阻燃效果，而且塑料中添加阻燃剂后使塑料在燃烧过程中不会产生有毒气体污染空气，起到了很好的环保效果。

【名称】 复合型导电塑料及制备工艺
【公开(公告)号】 CN102344634A
【公开(公告)日】 2012.02.08
【申请(专利权)人】 吴江市天源塑胶有限公司
【地址】 江苏省苏州市吴江市黎里镇工业园区牌楼桥堍
【发明(设计)人】 肖伟荣
【摘要】 本发明公开了一种复合型导电塑料及制备工艺。本发明属于塑料材料制备领域。一种复合型导电塑料，其特征在于：所述导电塑料由30%～60%共聚合物，掺杂20%～35% $AsSO_4$ 和20%～35% $ZnCl_2$ 组成，所述的共聚合物为聚乙炔，聚吡咯，聚苯硫醚，聚萘乙烯，聚乙烯吡啶衍生物。复合型导电塑料制备工艺，包括(1)将30%～60%共聚合物和导电填料20%～35% $AsSO_4$ 和20%～35% $ZnCl_2$ 在开炼机上熔融共混，熔融温度为320～350℃，混合均匀后，挤出，冷却制粒。本发明在常压下制备得到复合型导电塑料，简化制备工艺，降低制备成本。

【名称】 一种耐电击穿环保型氨基模塑料及生产工艺

【公开(公告)号】 CN102344644A
【公开(公告)日】 2012.02.08
【申请(专利权)人】 南京化工职业技术学院；南京湘宝钛白制品实业有限公司
【地址】 江苏省南京市六合区葛关路625号
【发明(设计)人】 许宁；关琦；刘山；伍凯飞；杨小燕；杨玉明；苏建华
【摘要】 本发明是提供一种耐电击穿环保型氨基模塑料及生产工艺，聚合工序控制甲醛与尿素摩尔比1.1～1.2，按计量一次性投入甲醛溶液，分4～6批次投入尿素，体系控制pH为8～9，温度控制在58～60℃，得到脲醛树脂产物；捏合工序同时加入脲醛树脂产物、纸浆、复配固化剂，氧化锌、绝缘增强剂以及色粉，控制捏合温度为60～65℃，捏合时间为1～1.5h；干燥工序对捏合产物进行干燥，控制干燥温度为90～95℃，含水量为4%。应用本发明制备得到的氨基模塑料制品残余甲醛迁移量为2.089～2.479mg/dm^2，耐电击穿强度为16.5～17.2kV/mm。

【名称】 一种高增韧团状模塑料
【公开(公告)号】 CN102344656A
【公开(公告)日】 2012.02.08
【申请(专利权)人】 江苏兆鋆新材料科技有限公司
【地址】 江苏省镇江市句容市华阳镇东昌南路20号兆鋆公司
【发明(设计)人】 鲁平才；阮诗平
【摘要】 本发明公开了一种高增韧团状模塑料，该团状模塑料由如下重量份的原料经聚合反应得到，其中：不饱和树脂60～80，低收缩剂10～40、固化剂1～2、脱模剂2～5、增韧剂4～20、晶须30～80、偶联剂2～5、填料100～250、玻璃纤维50～150。本发明采用端活性基团液态橡胶和晶须来增韧BMC材料。通过端乙烯基液态丁腈橡胶提高BMC材料的韧性，通过经活性端苯乙烯偶联剂处理的碳酸钙晶须提高BMC材料的强度，抵消液态橡胶加入使材料强度下降的趋势。从而得到强度不下降的高增韧BMC材料。

【名称】 PC/ABS工程塑料、其制备方法和应用
【公开(公告)号】 CN102344661A
【公开(公告)日】 2012.02.08
【申请(专利权)人】 惠州市沃特新材料有限公司
【地址】 广东省惠州市惠城区小金口镇科技产业园
【发明(设计)人】 杨永佳；陶德良；何征
【摘要】 本发明适用于工程塑料技术领域，提供了一种PC/ABS工程塑料、其制备方法和应用。该PC/ABS工程塑料包括PC、ABS、固态间苯二酚－双(二苯基磷酸酯)、苯乙烯－马来酸酐共聚物、抗氧剂及紫外光吸收剂。本发明PC/ABS工程塑料，通过使用苯乙烯－马来酸酐共聚物作为相容剂，使得PC/ABS工程塑料的力学性能显著提升；通过使用固态间苯二酚－双(二苯基磷酸酯)一方面提高了PC/ABS工程塑料的阻燃性能，另一方面简化了生产程序。本发明PC/ABS工程塑料制备方法，操作简单、成本低廉，经济效益高，非常适于工业化生产。

【名称】 无卤环保高温尼龙
【公开(公告)号】 CN102344667A
【公开(公告)日】 2012.02.08
【申请(专利权)人】 苏州工业园区鑫丰林塑料科技有限公司
【地址】 江苏省苏州市苏州工业园区扬东路277号晶汇大厦3幢918室
【发明(设计)人】 王志凤
【摘要】 本发明涉及一种有机高分子复合材料，更具体地说，是涉及一种无卤环保高温尼龙，是由以下成分按重量比组成，高温尼龙：35.5%～75%，无卤无碱玻纤：5%～25%；填充剂：0.1%～8%，热稳定剂：0.1%～3.0%，玻纤处理剂：0.1%～3.0%，润滑剂：0.2%～2.5%，其他助剂：0.1%～0.5%，活性炭：1%～5%。本发明的无卤环保高温尼龙的有益效果：采用无卤环保技术，减少了塑料中的卤素，焚烧时也不会产生有毒气体，对人体和环境都不构成污染，绿色环保。

【名称】 具有金属外壳的尼龙66
【公开(公告)号】 CN102344679A
【公开(公告)日】 2012.02.08
【申请(专利权)人】 苏州工业园区鑫丰林塑料科技有限公司
【地址】 江苏省苏州市苏州工业园区扬东路277号晶汇大厦3幢918室
【发明(设计)人】 王志凤
【摘要】 本发明涉及一种有机高分子复合材料，更具体地说，是涉及一种具有金属外壳的尼龙66，是由以下成分按重量比组成，尼龙66：49.5%～90%，金属纤维：0～45%；合成树脂：0～35%；增塑剂：0～30%；热稳定剂：2%～5%；偶联剂：0.2%～1.0%；其他助剂：0.3%～5.5%，活性炭：0.3%～5.3%，本发明的具有金属外壳的尼龙66的有益效果：通过独特的加工工艺，添加相关试剂，使塑料原料替代金属生产产品成为现实，具有优异的机械强度，良好的外观，较高的耐热性。

【名称】 一种耐火塑木复合板材
【公开(公告)号】 CN102344688A
【公开(公告)日】 2012.02.08

【申请(专利权)人】 南通绿恒新型建材科技有限公司

【地址】 江苏省南通市通州区三余镇环西路98号

【发明(设计)人】 梁为民

【摘要】 本发明公开了一种耐火塑木复合板材，具有塑料和木材，其特征在于：还添加有质量比为2%～5%的耐火材料。所述的耐火材料为氧化硅、硅砖或者粘土砖酸性耐火材料。所述的耐火材料为氧化镁、氧化钙或镁砖碱性耐火材料。所述的耐火材料为氧化铝、氧化铬中性耐火材料。与发明在塑木板材中添加耐火材料，比如氧化硅、氧化镁、氧化铝、氧化铬等，通过添加这些耐火材料，提高塑木复合板的防火性能，从而满足特定防火等级高的要求。

【名称】 一种塑木复合板的加工方法

【公开(公告)号】 CN102344687A

【公开(公告)日】 2012.02.08

【申请(专利权)人】 南通绿恒新型建材科技有限公司

【地址】 江苏省南通市通州区三余镇环西路98号

【发明(设计)人】 梁为民

【摘要】 本发明公开了一种塑木复合板的加工方法，其特征在于：步骤如下：第一步、烘干：将木粉烘干到含水率5%～20%；第二步、包裹：用PVC树脂将上述烘干的木粉包裹成颗粒；第三步、造粒：将上述包裹的颗粒与塑料混合造粒，粒径为3～5mm，其中木粉颗粒含量为60%～90%，助剂为0.5%～1.5%，余量为塑料；第四步、挤出发泡、冷却定型、出料。所述的助剂为不饱和聚酯树脂和或氯化聚乙烯。本发明将木粉与塑料按照本发明的配比配置，然后经脱水、包裹、造粒、挤出发泡、冷却定型及出料工序加工出来，塑木复合板强度高，塑料具有防水性，所以复合板材防水性能也好。

【名称】 聚氯乙烯管道系统用胶粘剂的配方及制备方法

【公开(公告)号】 CN102344770A

【公开(公告)日】 2012.02.08

【申请(专利权)人】 福建振云塑业股份有限公司

【地址】 福建省福清市镜洋镇上店村

【发明(设计)人】 严立万；莫晨杰；陈远贞；黄千顷；方斌

【摘要】 本发明提供的聚氯乙烯塑料管道系统用胶粘剂配方体系及其制备的一般方法，通过采用SG－5型聚氯乙烯(PVC)树脂、四氢呋喃、环已酮、丁酮等四种组分的质量配比，以及水浴加热溶解、冷却封存等生产工艺，形成粘结强度大、挥发时间短，粘结强度大，气味性弱，低温抗冻性好等优点的胶粘剂。

【名称】 一种温和条件下使煤与废塑料共液化的方法

【公开(公告)号】 CN102344823A

【公开(公告)日】 2012.02.08

【申请(专利权)人】 六盘水师范学院

【地址】 贵州省六盘水市明湖路育才巷19号

【发明(设计)人】 杜琨；范志芳；李志

【摘要】 本发明为一种温和条件下使煤与废塑料共液化的方法，在高压釜中加入煤、废塑料、木质素磺酸盐、催化剂以及溶剂，通入氢气冲压至1.0～10.0Mpa，然后升温至300～450℃进行液化反应，高压釜加氢液化试验后的气体收集后用气相色谱仪进行气相组成分析，其它液化产物全部收集于滤纸筒中，并在索氏萃取装置上按顺序进行正已烷和四氢呋喃溶剂萃取，正已烷可溶物为油；溶于四氢呋喃而不溶于正已烷的为沥青烯和前沥青烯，利用四氢呋喃不溶物的量计算出液化的全部转化率，本发明使煤在较低温度下发生解聚反应，同时和废塑料共液化，提高吡啶等溶剂对煤的抽提率，加速煤液化过程，既可大幅度降低煤液化氢耗量和生产成本，又可解决废塑料所产生的白色污染。

【名称】 一种螺杆的制作方法

【公开(公告)号】 CN102345006A

【公开(公告)日】 2012.02.08

【申请(专利权)人】 周建军

【地址】 浙江省舟山市定海区金塘镇沥港欣工路26－28号

【发明(设计)人】 周建军

【摘要】 一种螺杆的制作方法，其特征在于：包括以下步骤：一、选料，选取公知材料FDAC或SLD或DC53的金属棒，按给定的规格和长度下料；二、粗磨，至各部位按图纸规格的正公差1mm；三、螺杆制作，按图纸要求铣螺槽和铣键槽；四、真空淬火处理，使硬度达到HRC48～52，校正，打磨各部外圆至图纸要求的精度；五、放入气体氮化炉中进行氮化处理；六、精磨、抛光，直至图纸要求的尺寸。本发明的优点在于将螺杆经过本工艺的真空淬火和氮化处理，整体硬度达到HRC52～60表面硬度达到HV900，这使螺杆有很高的耐磨性能，能满足添加35%以下玻纤的腐蚀程度工程塑料，螺杆的使用寿命是现有双金属螺杆的三倍以上。

【名称】 一种高亮度塑料型材定型模

【公开(公告)号】 CN102366992A

【公开(公告)日】 2012.03.07

【申请(专利权)人】 黄石市通达塑料模具有限公司

【地址】 湖北省黄石市黄石港区工业园

【发明(设计)人】 胡拥军;吕文强;菖幼标;涂文珍;周炎平

【摘要】 本发明涉及塑料制品的加工模具,是一种高亮度塑料型材定型模,它具有三套依次连接的组合模,每套组合模包括有上盖板和底板,两板之间装有型腔模板,且在上盖板和底板中均设置有真空吸附系统及水冷却系统,所述水冷却系统包括有进、出水咀以及冷却水路,其特征是:所述水冷却系统中的冷却水路为轴向多个连续布置的S形循环水路,本发明解决了现有塑料定型模加工中对产品表面冷却不均匀,产品表面光亮度不理想的问题,广泛用于加工塑料门窗等建材制品以及塑料日用制品。

【名称】 塑料管材生产辅助定型装置

【公开(公告)号】 CN102366997A

【公开(公告)日】 2012.03.07

【申请(专利权)人】 浙江金洲管道工业有限公司

【地址】 浙江省湖州市经济开发区杨家埠

【发明(设计)人】 顾苏民;姚爱国;钱慧良;张淮;徐泽旋

【摘要】 本发明公开了一种塑料管材生产辅助定型装置,包括框架,所述框架通过左转轴、右转轴安装有可旋转的左辊轮、右辊轮。所述的左辊轮与右辊轮为从两端向中间逐渐变细的形状。所述框架上安装有上直线导轨、下直线导轨,所述上直线导轨与下直线导轨的滑块上固定有左移动件、右移动件,所述左转轴、右转轴安装在所述的左移动件、右移动件上,所述的框架上安装有推动所述左移动件与右移动件在所述的上直线导轨、下直线导轨上前进/后退的推进装置。本发明的辅助定型装置,能够使得塑管既能够以较快的速度进行生产,也能保证塑管的圆度,结构简单、造价低廉。

【名称】 连续长纤维增强热塑性塑料的浸渍设备和方法

【公开(公告)号】 CN102367003A

【公开(公告)日】 2012.03.07

【申请(专利权)人】 四川大学

【地址】 四川省成都市武侯区一环路南一段24号

【发明(设计)人】 杨杰;吴玉倩;王孝军;张刚;龙盛如

【摘要】 本发明公开了一种浸渍设备和方法,尤其是一种连续长纤维增强热塑性塑料的浸渍设备和方法。本发明提供了一种纤维束之间不互相影响的连续长纤维增强热塑性塑料的浸渍设备和方法,包括设备外体、所述设备外体的上游端设置有熔体入口,所述设备外体的下游端设置有挤出口,所述设备外体的内部设置有浸渍流道,所述浸渍流道的两端分别与所述熔体入口和所述挤出口连通,所述浸渍流道至少并列设置有两条,所述设备外体的侧壁上设置有与浸渍流道数量相同的长纤维加入口,所述长纤维加入口分别与各个浸渍流道连通。由于每个浸渍流道是独立设置的,使得纤维可以独立浸渍前进而不相互干扰,保证了稳定生产。

【名称】 一种串联型连续长纤维增强热塑性塑料的浸渍设备及方法

【公开(公告)号】 CN102367004A

【公开(公告)日】 2012.03.07

【申请(专利权)人】 四川大学

【地址】 四川省成都市武侯区一环路南一段24号

【发明(设计)人】 王孝军;吴玉倩;杨杰;龙盛如;张刚

【摘要】 本发明公开了一种浸渍设备及方法,尤其是一种串联型连续长纤维增强热塑性塑料的浸渍设备及方法。本发明提供了一种具有良好通用性的串联型连续长纤维增强热塑性塑料的浸渍设备,包括设备外体、所述设备外体的上游端设置有熔体入口,所述设备外体的下游端设置有挤出口,所述设备外体的内部设置有浸渍流道,所述浸渍流道的两端分别与所述熔体入口和所述挤出口连通,所述设备外体的侧壁上至少设置有两个长纤维加入口,所述长纤维加入口沿熔体流动方向排布并且与所述浸渍流道连通。由于采用多个长纤维加入口分别入纤维,并且长纤维加入口设置在侧壁,从而长纤维加入口与浸渍流道的转角处顶散纤维,使得每束纤维分别浸渍后重新聚集,提高了浸渍效果。

【名称】 一种导电炭黑改性PP材料及其制备方法

【公开(公告)号】 CN102367310A

【公开(公告)日】 2012.03.07

【申请(专利权)人】 深圳市科聚新材料有限公司

【地址】 广东省深圳市福永街道桥头富桥第三工业区二期A19栋

【发明(设计)人】 徐东;徐永;王刚

【摘要】 本发明公开了一种导电炭黑改性PP材料及其制备方法,该导电PP材料按重量份数,其组成:PP树脂55~75份,导电炭黑15~25,增韧剂6~10份,相容剂4~8份,抗氧剂0.2~0.4份,酸吸收剂0.1~0.3份。本发明通过在PP树脂中加入炭黑共混改性得到一种电阻率可调永久性导电的塑料材料,该复合材料具有持久稳定的导电性,电阻率可在较大范围内调节,并且具有热塑性塑料的性能优良,价格较为低廉,是理想的抗静电材料,能广泛的应用于集成电路、晶片、传感器护套等精密电子元件生产过程的防静电周转箱、托盘、晶片载体、薄膜袋等及电讯、电脑，自动化系统、工业用电子产品、消费电子产品、汽车用电子产品等领域中的电子产品EMI屏蔽外壳等行业中。

【名称】 一种通用白色母粒及其制备方法
【公开(公告)号】 CN102367320A
【公开(公告)日】 2012.03.07
【申请(专利权)人】 深圳市科聚新材料有限公司
【地址】 广东省深圳市宝安区福永镇富桥工业区三区二期A19栋
【发明(设计)人】 徐东；徐永；凌源
【摘要】 本发明公开了一种通用白色母粒及其制备方法。通用白色母粒按重量百分比由以下组分组成：载体树脂16%～23%；颜料50%～75%；加工助剂0%～3%；热稳定剂0%～2.5%；分散剂4%～7%；偶联剂0.1%～3%；填充剂0%～40%。本发明通用白色母粒分散性好、白度高，可以用于为聚乙烯、聚丙烯、聚苯乙烯、高抗冲聚苯乙烯、丙烯晴－丁二烯－苯乙烯共聚物等多种塑料着色，与被着色塑料的相容性良好，最终产品没有流纹、白度高、冲击性能优良，特别适合应用于对白度、表面光泽度要求高的白色家电产品。

【名称】 一种丙烯酸底漆基料及丙烯酸底漆的制备方法
【公开(公告)号】 CN102367341A
【公开(公告)日】 2012.03.07
【申请(专利权)人】 深圳市美丽华油墨涂料有限公司
【地址】 广东省深圳市宝安区福永镇凤塘大道243号
【发明(设计)人】 鲁春风
【摘要】 本发明公开了一种丙烯酸底漆基料及丙烯酸底漆基料制备方法，以聚苯乙烯改性甲基丙烯酸甲酯、80－200秒硝基纤维素液为本发明丙烯酸底漆基料配方主要成份，同时含有溶剂和流平剂组成。本发明的丙烯酸底漆基料配方符合手机行业对涂料无卤素的要求(配方中溴含量小于900ppm，氯含量小于900ppm，溴和氯总含量小于1500ppm)；将本发明的基料配方生产的丙烯酸底漆配套喷涂稀释剂和紫外线辐射固化面漆使用，喷涂于聚碳酸酯塑料上，干燥固化后的涂层具有优异的耐水煮性能，涂层经过100℃沸水煮30分钟后，涂层不起泡、不开裂、不变色。

【名称】 一种直壁式塑料检查井
【公开(公告)号】 CN102367683A
【公开(公告)日】 2012.03.07
【申请(专利权)人】 江苏通全球工程管业有限公司
【地址】 江苏省苏州市张家港市锦丰镇合兴工业园江苏通全球工程管业有限公司
【发明(设计)人】 陈鹤忠；姚军
【摘要】 本发明公开了一种直壁式塑料检查井，其包括：由塑料制成的井底座、安装于井底座上方的管体及安装于管体上方的井盖，所述井盖为由钢纤维制成的井盖。该种直壁式塑料检查井结构简单、施工方便、制造成本较低。

【名称】 一种超大孔隙聚氨酯网状泡沫塑料的制备方法
【公开(公告)号】 CN102372854A
【公开(公告)日】 2012.03.14
【申请(专利权)人】 深圳市国志汇富高分子材料股份有限公司
【地址】 广东省深圳市福田区八卦二路旭飞花园C座1209室
【发明(设计)人】 汪洋
【摘要】 本发明公开了一种超大孔隙聚氨酯网状泡沫塑料的制备方法，包括以下步骤：(1)准备由以下组份组成的原料：多元醇，异氰酸酯，有机硅泡沫稳定剂，水，辅助发泡剂，交联剂，开孔剂，凝胶催化剂，着色剂；(2)将原料用配有恒温冷冻装置的贮罐贮存；(3)将除异氰酸酯之外的原料同时加入拌合装置在3秒内拌合均匀，得到混合物料；(4)开启异氰酸酯加料阀，加入混合物料中高速搅拌，得到混合料；(5)将混合料注入发泡腔内进行发泡，150～200秒后关闭发泡腔，开启气阀进行抽真空；(6)从发泡腔内取出已经形成的带有反光状膜的超大孔聚氨酯网状泡沫体，经过网化处理后形成超大孔聚氨酯网状泡沫塑料。本发明可制备出具有超大孔隙的聚氨酯网状泡沫塑料。

【名称】 一种塑料用加工助剂及其制备方法
【公开(公告)号】 CN102372857A
【公开(公告)日】 2012.03.14
【申请(专利权)人】 青阳县三宝塑业有限责任公司
【地址】 安徽省池州市青阳县丁桥镇马塘工业集中区
【发明(设计)人】 吴跃强
【摘要】 本发明公开了一种塑料用加工助剂及其制备方法，各原料组分按重量份比为：轻质碳酸钙粉90～100、氯化钙3～5、云母粉2～2、秸秆灰烬1～2、活性氧化锌3～5、气相二氧化硅3～5、甲基丙烯酸酯的聚合物1～2、聚乙烯蜡1～2、烷基磺酸钠1～2、硅油1～2。制备方法：将轻质碳酸钙烘干至水份含重量为0.3%以下，加入高速捏合机中，然后按重量份比添加其它配方材料，再升温至100～

130℃，保温搅拌8~10min后，出料得成品。本发明所制备的塑料用加工助剂降低了颗粒间的表面能，增强了塑料的相容性和分散性；促进了高分子材料塑化，降低熔体粘度，改善加工流动性；提高制品冲击度、刚度、耐热性及尺寸稳定性，具有节能降耗、环保、无毒、无“三废”的特点。

【名称】 淀粉基生物降解塑料的制备方法
【公开(公告)号】 CN102372858A
【公开(公告)日】 2012.03.14
【申请(专利权)人】 陈天云
【地址】 江苏省淮安市楚州区城东乡汤朱村5-22号
【发明(设计)人】 陈天云
【摘要】 本发明公开了一种淀粉基生物降解塑料的制备方法中的配方和重量比为热塑性淀粉树脂50~80，纤维为8~28，可生物降解材料为15~50，树脂0~35，增容剂为2~8，润滑剂为1~6，无机材料超细粉为5~20，发泡剂为1~6。淀粉基生物降解塑料的生产方法是将：树脂、增容剂、润滑剂、无机材料超细粉、纤维，热塑性淀粉树脂、生物降解材料、发泡剂，分别依次投入控温混合机中，低速混合料温60℃至高速混合到料温120℃，混合时间10分钟，放料备用或料送入双螺杆挤出机中，120℃，170℃下熔融造粒，即成为淀粉基生物降解塑料备用材料。该材料可用设备挤出拉片、中空、吸塑、注塑、模塑等方法成型，本材料能生物降解友好环境，其产品一次性餐具、防震减压包装、薄膜片材等一次性器材，具有无毒、卫生、环保、成本低、品质性能高等特点，可二次加工。

【名称】 一种抗低温聚乙烯塑料及其制造锁具的方法
【公开(公告)号】 CN102372866A
【公开(公告)日】 2012.03.14
【申请(专利权)人】 苏州泰盾施封设备有限公司
【地址】 江苏省吴江市经济开发区出口加工区11号厂房
【发明(设计)人】 雒朋康；王江平
【摘要】 本发明涉及一种聚乙烯塑料及其制造锁具的方法。本发明所提供的聚乙烯塑料材料中高密度聚乙烯与线性低密度聚乙烯混合质量比为60:(40~80):20。将原料以此质量比混合压制得到的塑料，不仅具有良好的抗低温冲击性能，而且其抗伸强度、抗撕裂性能都达到与聚乙烯产品相当的水平。利用本发明生产的聚乙烯塑料材料制作的锁具，同时具有良好的抗拉性、抗撕裂性以及抗低温冲击性和柔韧性，刚性强的同时又不易被折断，能够适应低温条件下对锁具的使用要求，保证低温不失效。其机械性能与使用PP作为原料生产的锁具相似，同时具有PP所不能实现的抗低温性能，扩展了锁具的使用范围，增强了锁具使用的安全性。

【名称】 一种塑料土工格栅专用增强母料
【公开(公告)号】 CN102372868A
【公开(公告)日】 2012.03.14
【申请(专利权)人】 泰安现代塑料有限公司
【地址】 山东省泰安市岱岳区泰山青春创业开发区创业路北首
【发明(设计)人】 卜爱华；王学文；王勇；王鹏
【摘要】 本发明公开了一种塑料土工格栅专用增强母料，由合理配比的聚烯烃、专用炭黑、改性纳米增强材料、加工助剂、抗氧剂组成，本发明制得的增强母料在格栅中添加量少，分散性好，提高了格栅生产的稳定性和拉伸强度，抗老化性能好，生产成本低。

【名称】 一种矿用无卤阻燃塑料土工格栅母料
【公开(公告)号】 CN102372869A
【公开(公告)日】 2012.03.14
【申请(专利权)人】 泰安现代塑料有限公司
【地址】 山东省泰安市岱岳区泰山青春创业开发区创业路北首
【发明(设计)人】 卜爱华；王学文；王勇；王鹏
【摘要】 本发明公开了一种矿用无卤阻燃塑料土工格栅母料，由一定配比的聚烯烃、专用炭黑、复合阻燃剂、相容剂、改性纳米增强材料、加工助剂、抗氧剂组成，其中复合阻燃剂为纳米无机阻燃剂、微胶囊红磷、磷酸酯类阻燃剂的复合物。本发明制得的母料添加到格栅中性能稳定，阻燃性能好，环保效果好。

【名称】 沥青氯乙烯抗静电塑料地板
【公开(公告)号】 CN102372878A
【公开(公告)日】 2012.03.14
【申请(专利权)人】 苏州富通电器塑业有限公司
【地址】 江苏省吴江市芦墟镇国赵路8号
【发明(设计)人】 陈健；张建光；杨文乾；徐建辉
【摘要】 本发明属于PVC地板，特别涉及一种沥青聚氯乙烯抗静电塑料地。一种沥青聚氯乙烯抗静电塑料地板，其特征在于由如下配方组成，按重量份数其配方为：聚氯乙烯树脂100~120份，沥青50~60份，导电炭黑20~30份，稀土稳定剂R108A8-10份，双季戊四醇25~30份，乙氧基化脂肪族烷基胺5~10份。本发明具有铺装方便，价格低廉等优点。

【名称】 CPE改性PVC塑料地板

【公开(公告)号】 CN102372879A
【公开(公告)日】 2012.03.14
【申请(专利权)人】 苏州富通电器塑业有限公司
【地址】 江苏省吴江市芦墟镇国赵路8号
【发明(设计)人】 陈健;张建光;杨文乾;徐建辉
【摘要】 本发明属于PVC地板,特别涉及一种CPE改性PVC塑料地板。一种CPE改性PVC塑料地板,其特征在于由如下配方组成,按重量份数其配方为:聚氯乙烯树脂100~120份,碳酸钙35~40份,CPE8-10份,二甲基二巯基乙酸异辛酯锡8~10份,邻苯二甲酸二辛酯10~20份,硬脂酸5~8份。在聚氯乙烯(PVC)树脂中添加适量的CPE,可降低树脂的熔融粘度、提高流动性、改善塑料的加工性能;还可以提高PVC的冲击强度、耐低温性能、耐侯性能、延长制品的使用寿命。CPE添加在钙塑材料中,不仅可以代替增塑剂DBP,还有助于碳酸钙与PVC树脂的均匀分散。

【名称】 粉煤灰高填充聚氯乙烯塑料地板
【公开(公告)号】 CN102372880A
【公开(公告)日】 2012.03.14
【申请(专利权)人】 苏州富通电器塑业有限公司
【地址】 江苏省吴江市芦墟镇国赵路8号
【发明(设计)人】 陈健;张建光;杨文乾;徐建辉
【摘要】 本发明属于PVC地板,特别涉及一种粉煤灰高填充聚氯乙烯塑料地板。一种粉煤灰高填充聚氯乙烯塑料地板,其特征在于由如下配方组成,按重量份数其配方为:聚氯乙烯树脂100~120份,粉煤灰400~500份,二甲基二巯基乙酸异辛酯锡8~10份,邻苯二甲酸二辛酯25~30份,硅烷偶联剂4~5份。本发明提供一种粉煤灰高填充聚氯乙烯塑料地板,其制品的耐磨性和尺寸稳定性好,均达到国家塑料地板标准。

【名称】 一种新型防腐塑料涂布地板
【公开(公告)号】 CN102372881A
【公开(公告)日】 2012.03.14
【申请(专利权)人】 苏州富通电器塑业有限公司
【地址】 江苏省吴江市芦墟镇国赵路8号
【发明(设计)人】 陈健;张建光;杨文乾;徐建辉
【摘要】 本发明属于PVC地板,特别涉及一种新型防腐塑料涂布地板。一种新型防腐塑料涂布地板,其特征在于由如下配方组成,按重量份数其配方为:聚氯乙烯树脂100~120份,纳米级石英砂50~100份,稀土稳定剂R108A8~10份,双季戊四醇25~30份。本发明提供一种新型防腐塑料涂布地板,具有防腐,耐磨等优点。

【名称】 改性PVC泡沫吸声材料的制备方法
【公开(公告)号】 CN102372883A
【公开(公告)日】 2012.03.14
【申请(专利权)人】 程阿新
【地址】 浙江省湖州市德清县新市镇南汇街44号
【发明(设计)人】 程阿新
【摘要】 本发明公开了一种改性PVC泡沫吸声材料的制备方法,按照质量份数计,首先将2~3份的硅烷偶联剂和10~12份的EPR在100℃、3000转速条件下混合处理10min;将1~2份的润滑剂、3~5份的复合稳定剂和100份的聚氯乙烯在25℃、3000转速条件下混合6min;最后将已经混合均匀的PVC/EPR混合物与AC等发泡助剂再双螺杆挤出机中进行熔融挤出发泡,最终得到PVC泡沫吸声改性材料。本技术方案改善聚氯乙烯泡沫塑料的成型加工性,大幅度提高吸声性能。

【名称】 一种阻燃绿色环氧模塑料
【公开(公告)号】 CN102372899A
【公开(公告)日】 2012.03.14
【申请(专利权)人】 江苏中鹏新材料股份有限公司
【地址】 江苏省连云港市海州区开发区振兴路18号
【发明(设计)人】 封其立;孙波;张德伟;周佃香;吕秀波;王岚;刘旭光
【摘要】 一种阻燃绿色环氧模塑料,包括阻燃性环氧树脂、酚醛树脂、硅微粉、咪唑类固化促进剂、脱模剂、着色剂、硅烷偶联剂。所用的环氧树脂,是含有萘环的环氧树脂,两个苯环之间有一个萘环,并且萘环上还有烷烃基,这样大大减少了环氧树脂的自由体积数,因此可以改善环氧树脂的耐热性和耐水性,降低模塑料的吸水率,提高弹性模量,降低线膨胀系数。本发明具有低粘度、低膨胀系数、高导热性而且耐260℃回流焊性能好,可用于大规模集成电路的封装。此塑封料不含溴、锑等阻燃剂,燃烧的过程中不会产生有毒气体,同时不添加P系、金属氧化物阻燃剂,达到UL-94V-0级的阻燃标准,同时使环氧模塑料流动性、操作性及可靠性能满足封装的要求。

【名称】 一种高效的生物降解塑料专用色母组合物及其制备方法
【公开(公告)号】 CN102372911A
【公开(公告)日】 2012.03.14
【申请(专利权)人】 金发科技股份有限公司;上海金发科技发展有限公司;珠海万通化工有限公司
【地址】 广东省广州市高新技术产业开发区科学城科丰路33号
【发明(设计)人】 焦建;苑仁旭;钟宇科;赵葳;徐依斌;曾祥斌;蔡彤旻;夏世勇

【摘要】 本发明公开了一种高效的生物降解塑料专用色母组合物及其制备方法，该色母组合物以质量百分比计，包含生物降解聚酯10.0%~80.0%、颜料1.0%~80.0%、润滑剂0.1%~10.0%、耐高温剂0.1%~5.0%和抗水解剂0.1%~5.0%，其制备方法是将各组分在高速混合机中混合后加入到熔融混炼设备进行混炼塑化并挤出、造粒、干燥即得。本发明提供的色母组合物不仅具有完全的生物降解性能，而且具有易分散，耐高温和抗水解的高效着色能力，在应用于生物降解塑料着色过程中能保持原有材料的物理机械性能。

【名称】 植物纤维与塑料合成的地板

【公开(公告)号】 CN102372926A

【公开(公告)日】 2012.03.14

【申请(专利权)人】 苏州富通电器塑业有限公司

【地址】 江苏省吴江市芦墟镇国赵路8号

【发明(设计)人】 陈健；张建光；杨文乾；徐建辉

【摘要】 本发明属于PVC地板，特别涉及植物纤维与塑料合成的地板。一种植物纤维与塑料合成的地板，其特征在于由如下配方组成，按重量份数其配方为：聚氯乙烯树脂100~120份，木纤维100~200份，二甲基二巯基乙酸异辛酯锡8~10份，邻苯二甲酸二辛醋25~30份，乙氧基化脂肪族烷基胺11~15份，石蜡10份。本发明提供一种新型植物纤维与塑料合成的地板，具有环保、低成本、高韧性、良好的热学性能等优点。

【名称】 一种利用废聚苯乙烯泡沫塑料生产防锈漆的方法

【公开(公告)号】 CN102372955A

【公开(公告)日】 2012.03.14

【申请(专利权)人】 张启美

【地址】 山东省烟台开发区泰山路美食村40号

【发明(设计)人】 张启美

【摘要】 本发明具体涉及一种利用废聚苯乙烯泡沫塑料生产防锈漆的方法。使用废弃的废聚苯乙烯泡沫塑料，通过净化、粉碎、溶制、调漆等方法，生产出优质的防锈漆。该方法生产的防锈漆不仅可以在防水、防锈、绝缘等方面取得显著的效果，而且还能够为保护生态环境、减少白色污染找到了一条较好的利用途径，是一种变废为宝、化害为利好方法。

【名称】 塑料中六价铬的提取方法

【公开(公告)号】 CN102373334A

【公开(公告)日】 2012.03.14

【申请(专利权)人】 北京吉天仪器有限公司

【地址】 北京市朝阳区酒仙桥东路1号6座西4层

【发明(设计)人】 刘霁欣；肖融；秦德元；那星

【摘要】 本发明公开了一种塑料中六价铬的提取方法。该方法包括如下步骤：将塑料和提取液混合，得到混合物；密闭环境中，混合物在温度80~160℃持续混匀若干时间；静置回收无机相，无机相离心分层，得到含有六价铬的无机层清液；所述提取液为有机溶剂与碱性溶液的混合物。本发明的塑料中六价铬的提取方法，从塑料中提取的总Cr和六价铬的回收率高，能够准确检测塑料制品中的Cr(Ⅵ)。

【名称】 合金与塑料的结合方法

【公开(公告)号】 CN102373499A

【公开(公告)日】 2012.03.14

【申请(专利权)人】 可成科技股份有限公司

【地址】 中国台湾台南县

【发明(设计)人】 张正武；谭家彦；胡少刚

【摘要】 本发明涉及一种合金与塑料的结合方法，其首先对合金进行电化学处理，使其表面形成微孔洞，随后将塑料以射出成形方式成形在合金的表面，由于熔融状的塑料可进入微孔洞内，因此待塑料冷却固化后，塑料便能够附着于合金表面上。

【名称】 通电(低压直流电)快速打设塑料排水板方法

【公开(公告)号】 CN102373707A

【公开(公告)日】 2012.03.14

【申请(专利权)人】 中交天津港湾工程研究院有限公司；中交第一航务工程局有限公司；天津港湾工程质量检测中心有限公司

【地址】 天津市河西区大沽南路1002号

【发明(设计)人】 叶国良；李树奇；李一勇；刘天韵；曹永华；侯晋芳；刘爱民；梁萌；杨京方

【摘要】 一种通电(低压直流电)快速打设塑料排水板方法，首先采取措施保证桩管与振动锤的绝缘，然后在桩管上端连接低压直流电源，打设时接通直流电源，带电打设桩管。采用蓄电池组提供低压直流电源，与塑料排水板打设桩管上端连接，打设过程中，接通直流电源，降低粘性土的摩阻力，提高塑料排水板的打设效率，减少电力消耗。

【名称】 一种塑料拉伸双筋网状结构材料及其制造方法

【公开(公告)号】 CN102373769A

【公开(公告)日】 2012.03.14

【申请(专利权)人】 范雯丽

【地址】 山东省泰安市长城路中段岱岳花园5号楼6单元601

【发明(设计)人】 范雯丽

【摘要】 本发明公开了一种塑料拉伸双筋网状结构

材料及其制作方法，所述的双筋网状结构材料包括多个节点，节点之间设有筋带，其特征在于：每个节点连接四组筋带，每组料条筋带，共八条筋带，使得相邻的四个节点和此节点之间的筋带连接形成方形、矩形或菱形单元孔，所述的网格结构为此多个方形、矩形或菱形单元孔组成，相邻两个单元邻边重合；所述的制作方法为先在塑料板上制出孔单元，所述孔单元包括呈方形或菱形排列的八个孔，其中有四个孔位于菱形的顶点，另四个孔分别位于菱形的四个边上；菱形的每个顶点重合有四个方形或菱形顶点、相邻孔单元邻边重合；然后再对塑料板进行纵横向拉伸即可。本发明能够同时承受多向载荷，节点受到撕裂破坏的几率减少，同时其整体的结构强度增强，受力状态更为合理。

【名称】 双层植物纤维与塑料合成的地板

【公开(公告)号】 CN102373782A

【公开(公告)日】 2012. 03. 14

【申请(专利权)人】 苏州富通电器塑业有限公司

【地址】 江苏省吴江市芦墟镇国赵路 8 号

【发明(设计)人】 陈健；张建光；杨文乾；徐建辉

【摘要】 本发明属于 PVC 地板，特别涉及双层植物纤维与塑料合成的地板。一种双层植物纤维与塑料合成的地板，其特征在于由双层结构构成，辅料组成表层，主料构成底层；按重量份数，主料配方为：聚氯乙烯树脂 100 ~ 120 份，木纤维 100 ~ 200 份，二甲基二巯基乙酸异辛酯锡 8 ~ 10 份，邻苯二甲酸二辛醋 25 ~ 30 份，乙氧基化脂肪族烷基胺 11 ~ 15 份，石蜡 10 份；辅料的配方为：聚氯乙烯树脂 100 ~ 120 份，MBS 树脂 10 ~ 12 份，硬脂酸锌 3 ~ 5 份，邻苯二甲酸二丁酯 4 ~ 6 份，三盐基硫酸铅 5 ~ 8 份，二叔丁基对苯二酚树脂 2 ~ 4 份。具有环保、低成本、高韧性、良好的热学性能等优点。

【名称】 双层 CPE 改性 PVC 塑料地板

【公开(公告)号】 CN102373790A

【公开(公告)日】 2012. 03. 14

【申请(专利权)人】 苏州富通电器塑业有限公司

【地址】 江苏省吴江市芦墟镇国赵路 8 号

【发明(设计)人】 陈健；张建光；杨文乾；徐建辉

【摘要】 本发明属于 PVC 地板，特别涉及一种双层 CPE 改性 PVC 塑料地板。一种双层 CPE 改性 PVC 塑料地板，其特征在于由双层结构构成，辅料组成表层，主料构成底层；按重量份数其中，主料配方为：聚氯乙烯树脂 100 ~ 120 份，碳酸钙 35 ~ 40 份，CPE8 ~ 10 份，二甲基二巯基乙酸异辛酯锡 8 ~ 10 份，邻苯二甲酸二辛酯 10 ~ 20 份，硬脂酸 5 ~ 8 份。辅料的配方为：聚氯乙烯树脂 100 ~ 120 份，MBS 树脂 10 ~ 12份，硬脂酸锌 3 ~ 5 份，邻苯二甲酸二丁酯 4 ~ 6份，三盐基硫酸铅 5 ~ 8 份，二叔丁基对苯二酚树脂 2 ~ 4 份。CPE 添加在钙塑材料中，不仅可以代替增塑剂 DBP，还有助于碳酸钙与 PVC 树脂的均匀分散。

【名称】 双层粉煤灰高填充聚氯乙烯塑料地板

【公开(公告)号】 CN102373791A

【公开(公告)日】 2012. 03. 14

【申请(专利权)人】 苏州富通电器塑业有限公司

【地址】 江苏省吴江市芦墟镇国赵路 8 号

【发明(设计)人】 陈健；张建光；杨文乾；徐建辉

【摘要】 本发明属于 PVC 地板，特别涉及一种双层粉煤灰高填充聚氯乙烯塑料地板。一种双层粉煤灰高填充聚氯乙烯塑料地板，其特征在于由双层结构构成，辅料组成表层，主料构成底层；按重量份数其中，主料的配方：聚氯乙烯树脂 100 ~ 120 份，粉煤灰 400 ~ 500 份，二甲基二巯基乙酸异辛酯锡 8 ~ 10 份，邻苯二甲酸二辛酯 25 ~ 30 份，硅烷偶联剂 4 ~ 5份；辅料的配方为：聚氯乙烯树脂 100 ~ 120 份，MBS 树脂 10 ~ 12 份，硬脂酸锌 3 ~ 5 份，邻苯二甲酸二丁酯 4 ~ 6 份，三盐基硫酸铅 5 ~ 8 份，二叔丁基对苯二酚树脂 2 ~ 4 份。本发明提供一种粉煤灰高填充聚氯乙烯塑料地板，其制品的耐磨性和尺寸稳定性好，均达到国家塑料地板标准。

【名称】 带导电层的聚氯乙烯塑料地板

【公开(公告)号】 CN102373792A

【公开(公告)日】 2012. 03. 14

【申请(专利权)人】 苏州富通电器塑业有限公司

【地址】 江苏省吴江市芦墟镇国赵路 8 号

【发明(设计)人】 陈健；张建光；杨文乾；徐建辉

【摘要】 本发明属于 PVC 地板，特别涉及带导电层的聚氯乙烯塑料地板。一种带导电层的聚氯乙烯塑料地板，其特征在于包括导电层，PVC 层，复合增强层；由上到下依次为导电层，PVC 层，复合增强层；所述的导电层由膜和金属丝网构成；所述的 PVC 层中含有导电炭黑。所述的复合增强层由无纺布层和粘合剂层构成；所述的膜由聚全氟乙丙烯组成。本发明在传统防静电 PVC 塑料地板的基础上，还添加了导电层，即设有金属网，使得导电性能大大增强，并且防止电磁泄漏，尤其适用于核磁共振等高电磁场所。

【名称】 一种新型双层防腐塑料涂布地板

【公开(公告)号】 CN102373793A

【公开(公告)日】 2012. 03. 14

【申请(专利权)人】 苏州富通电器塑业有限公司

【地址】 江苏省吴江市芦墟镇国赵路 8 号

【发明(设计)人】 陈健；张建光；杨文乾；徐建辉

【摘要】 本发明属于PVC地板，特别涉及一种新型双层防腐塑料涂布地板。一种新型双层防腐塑料涂布地板，其特征在于由双层结构构成，辅料组成表层，主料构成底层；按重量份数其中，主料的配方为：聚氯乙烯树脂100~120份，纳米级石英砂50~100份，稀土稳定剂R108A8~10份，双季戊四醇25~30份。辅料的配方为：聚氯乙烯树脂100~120份，MBS树脂10~12份，硬脂酸锌3~5份，邻苯二甲酸二丁酯4~6份，三盐基硫酸铅5~8份，二叔丁基对苯二酚树脂2~4份。本发明提供一种新型防腐塑料涂布地板，具有防腐，耐磨等优点。

【名称】 双层沥青氯乙烯抗静电塑料地板

【公开(公告)号】 CN102373794A

【公开(公告)日】 2012.03.14

【申请(专利权)人】 苏州富通电器塑业有限公司

【地址】 江苏省吴江市芦墟镇国赵路8号

【发明(设计)人】 陈健；张建光；杨文乾；徐建辉

【摘要】 本发明属于PVC地板，特别涉及一种双层沥青聚氯乙烯抗静电塑料地板。一种双层沥青聚氯乙烯抗静电塑料地板，其特征在于由双层结构构成，辅料组成表层，主料构成底层；按重量份数其中，主料的配方为：聚氯乙烯树脂100~120份，沥青50~60份，导电炭黑20~30份，稀土稳定剂R108A8~10份，双季戊四醇25~30份，乙氧基化脂肪族烷基胺5~10份；辅料的配方为：聚氯乙烯树脂100~120份，MBS树脂10~12份，硬脂酸锌3~5份，邻苯二甲酸二丁酯4~6份，三盐基硫酸铅5~8份，二叔丁基对苯二酚树脂2~4份。本发明具有铺装方便，价格低廉等优点。

【名称】 双层结构抗静电聚氯乙烯塑料地板

【公开(公告)号】 CN102373795A

【公开(公告)日】 2012.03.14

【申请(专利权)人】 苏州富通电器塑业有限公司

【地址】 江苏省吴江市芦墟镇国赵路8号

【发明(设计)人】 陈健；张建光；杨文乾；徐建辉

【摘要】 本发明属于PVC地板，特别涉及双层抗静电聚氯乙烯塑料地板。一种双层结构抗静电聚氯乙烯塑料地板，其特征在于由双层结构构成，辅料组成表层，主料构成底层；按重量份数其中，主料配方为：聚氯乙烯树脂100~120份，三盐基硫酸铅8~10份，高岭土200~250份，双季戊四醇25~30份，炭黑5~10份，邻苯二甲酸二丁酯4~6份，乙氧基化脂肪族烷基胺5~10份，石蜡10份；辅料的配方为：聚氯乙烯树脂100~120份，MBS树脂10~12份，硬脂酸锌3~5份，邻苯二甲酸二丁酯4~6份，三盐基硫酸铅5~8份，二叔丁基对苯二酚树脂2~4份。本发明提供一种双层结构抗静电聚氯乙烯塑料地板，应用高聚物增塑体系，极大地减少VOC的释放，符合环境保护的要求，并且采用双层结构，表层结构抗磨等性能优良。

【名称】 一种塑料门窗型材与塑钢门窗钢衬同步焊接方法

【公开(公告)号】 CN102373868A

【公开(公告)日】 2012.03.14

【申请(专利权)人】 朱惠芬

【地址】 山东省济南市历下区闵子骞路80号

【发明(设计)人】 朱惠芬

【摘要】 本发明提供一种塑料门窗型材与塑钢门窗钢衬同步焊接方法，其结构是由塑料门窗型材和钢衬组成，钢衬设置在塑料门窗型材的空腹之中，钢衬的两端连接有塑料型材接头，塑料型材接头的端部加工有与塑料门窗型材端部相平行的断面，纵向和横向的塑料门窗型材连同钢衬在平行的断面处同步焊接在一起。该塑料门窗型材塑钢门窗钢衬同步焊接方法和现有技术相比，具有设计合理、结构简单、有效提高塑料门窗型材在拐角部位的连接强度，提高塑钢门窗的使用寿命等特点，因而，具有很好的推广使用价值。

【名称】 宽内圈轴承塑料保持架装配模具及其装配方法

【公开(公告)号】 CN102374238A

【公开(公告)日】 2012.03.14

【申请(专利权)人】 浙江八环轴承有限公司

【地址】 浙江省台州市路桥区新安西街889号

【发明(设计)人】 戴学利；王苏平；周云；牛建平；陈振林；郑牧

【摘要】 本发明提供一种宽内圈轴承塑料保持架装配模具，它包括上模、分球器和下模；下模包括底座、多根支承杆、调节螺钉和弹簧；所述底座具有轴承外圈的承接座；支承杆固定在底座上；所述分球器套在支承杆上，由所述弹簧支撑，轴向可运动地与下模连接在一起，所述分球器具有能穿入轴承外圈和轴承内圈之间的分球部位，所述分球部位具有排列方式与宽内圈轴承保持架上的钢球球兜相一致的钢球球兜；所述上模用于连接轴承保持架，所述上模具有可套在轴承内圈外的内孔。本发明还提供一种利用上述宽内圈轴承塑料保持架装配模具的宽内圈轴承装配方法。本发明结构简单，操作方便，能反复使用，提高装配效率和装配质量，减少保持架损坏造成的损失。

【名称】 植物纤维与塑料合成的地板

【公开(公告)号】 CN102372926A
【公开(公告)日】 2012.03.14
【申请(专利权)人】 苏州富通电器塑业有限公司
【地址】 江苏省吴江市芦墟镇国赵路8号
【发明(设计)人】 陈健;张建光;杨文乾;徐建辉
【摘要】 本发明属于PVC地板，特别涉及植物纤维与塑料合成的地板。一种植物纤维与塑料合成的地板，其特征在于由如下配方组成，按重量份数其配方为：聚氯乙烯树脂100~120份，木纤维100~200份，二甲基二巯基乙酸异辛酯锡8~10份，邻苯二甲酸二辛醋25~30份，乙氧基化脂肪族烷基胺11~15份，石蜡10份。本发明提供一种新型植物纤维与塑料合成的地板，具有环保、低成本、高韧性、良好的热学性能等优点。

【名称】 一种利用废聚苯乙烯泡沫塑料生产防锈漆的方法
【公开(公告)号】 CN102372955A
【公开(公告)日】 2012.03.14
【申请(专利权)人】 张启美
【地址】 山东省烟台开发区泰山路美食村40号
【发明(设计)人】 张启美
【摘要】 本发明具体涉及一种利用废聚苯乙烯泡沫塑料生产防锈漆的方法。使用废弃的废聚苯乙烯泡沫塑料，通过净化、粉碎、溶制、调漆等方法，生产出优质的防锈漆。该方法生产的防锈漆不仅可以在防水、防锈、绝缘等方面取得显著的效果，而且还能够为保护生态环境、减少白色污染找到了一条较好的利用途径，是一种变废为宝、化害为利好方法。

【名称】 塑料中六价铬的提取方法
【公开(公告)号】 CN102373334A
【公开(公告)日】 2012.03.14
【申请(专利权)人】 北京吉天仪器有限公司
【地址】 北京市朝阳区酒仙桥东路1号6座西4层
【发明(设计)人】 刘霁欣;肖融;秦德元;那星
【摘要】 本发明公开了一种塑料中六价铬的提取方法。该方法包括如下步骤：将塑料和提取液混合，得到混合物；密闭环境中，混合物在温度80~160℃持续混匀若干时间；静置回收无机相，无机相离心分层，得到含有六价铬的无机层清液；所述提取液为有机溶剂与碱性溶液的混合物。本发明的塑料中六价铬的提取方法，从塑料中提取的总Cr和六价铬的回收率高，能够准确检测塑料制品中的Cr(Ⅵ)。

【名称】 合金与塑料的结合方法
【公开(公告)号】 CN102373499A
【公开(公告)日】 2012.03.14
【申请(专利权)人】 可成科技股份有限公司
【地址】 中国台湾台南县
【发明(设计)人】 张正武;谭家彦;胡少刚
【摘要】 本发明涉及一种合金与塑料的结合方法，其首先对合金进行电化学处理，使其表面形成微孔洞，随后将塑料以射出成形方式成形在合金的表面，由于熔融状的塑料可进入微孔洞内，因此待塑料冷却固化后，塑料便能够附着于合金表面上。

【名称】 一种塑料拉伸双筋网状结构材料及其制造方法
【公开(公告)号】 CN102373769A
【公开(公告)日】 2012.03.14
【申请(专利权)人】 范雯丽
【地址】 山东省泰安市长城路中段岱岳花园5号楼6单元601
【发明(设计)人】 范雯丽
【摘要】 本发明公开了一种塑料拉伸双筋网状结构材料及其制作方法，所述的双筋网状结构材料包括多个节点，节点之间设有筋带，其特征在于：每个节点连接四组筋带，每组料条筋带，共八条筋带，使得相邻的四个节点和此节点之间的筋带连接形成方形、矩形或菱形单元孔，所述的网格结构为此多个方形、矩形或菱形单元孔组成，相邻两个单元邻边重合；所述的制作方法为先在塑料板上制出孔单元，所述孔单元包括呈方形或菱形排列的八个孔，其中有四个孔位于菱形的顶点，另四个孔分别位于菱形的四个边上；菱形的每个顶点重合有四个方形或菱形顶点、相邻孔单元邻边重合；然后再对塑料板进行纵横向拉伸即可。本发明能够同时承受多向载荷，节点受到撕裂破坏的几率减少，同时其整体的结构强度增强，受力状态更为合理。

【名称】 双层粉煤灰高填充聚氯乙烯塑料地板
【公开(公告)号】 CN102373791A
【公开(公告)日】 2012.03.14
【申请(专利权)人】 苏州富通电器塑业有限公司
【地址】 江苏省吴江市芦墟镇国赵路8号
【发明(设计)人】 陈健;张建光;杨文乾;徐建辉
【摘要】 本发明属于PVC地板，特别涉及一种双层粉煤灰高填充聚氯乙烯塑料地板。一种双层粉煤灰高填充聚氯乙烯塑料地板，其特征在于由双层结构构成，辅料组成表层，主料构成底层；按重量份数其中，主料的配方：聚氯乙烯树脂100~120份，粉煤灰400~500份，二甲基二巯基乙酸异辛酯锡8~10份，邻苯二甲酸二辛酯25~30份，硅烷偶联剂4~5份；辅料的配方为：聚氯乙烯树脂100~120份，MBS树脂10~12份，硬脂酸锌3~5份，邻苯二甲酸二丁酯4~6份，三盐基硫酸铅5~8份，二叔丁基对苯二酚树脂2~4份。本发明提供一种粉煤灰高填充聚氯乙烯塑料地板，其制品的耐磨性和尺寸稳定性好，均达到国家塑料地板标准。

【名称】 双层沥青氯乙烯抗静电塑料地板
【公开(公告)号】 CN102373794A
【公开(公告)日】 2012.03.14
【申请(专利权)人】 苏州富通电器塑业有限公司
【地址】 江苏省吴江市芦墟镇国赵路8号
【发明(设计)人】 陈健；张建光；杨文乾；徐建辉
【摘要】 本发明属于PVC地板，特别涉及一种双层沥青聚氯乙烯抗静电塑料地板。一种双层沥青聚氯乙烯抗静电塑料地板，其特征在于由双层结构构成，辅料组成表层，主料构成底层；按重量份数其中，主料的配方为：聚氯乙烯树脂100~120份，沥青50~60份，导电炭黑20~30份，稀土稳定剂R108A8~10份，双季戊四醇25~30份，乙氧基化脂肪族烷基胺5~10份；辅料的配方为：聚氯乙烯树脂100~120份，MBS树脂10~12份，硬脂酸锌3~5份，邻苯二甲酸二丁酯4~6份，三盐基硫酸铅5~8份，二叔丁基对苯二酚树脂2~4份。本发明具有铺装方便，价格低廉等优点。

【名称】 双层结构抗静电聚氯乙烯塑料地板
【公开(公告)号】 CN102373795A
【公开(公告)日】 2012.03.14
【申请(专利权)人】 苏州富通电器塑业有限公司
【地址】 江苏省吴江市芦墟镇国赵路8号
【发明(设计)人】 陈健；张建光；杨文乾；徐建辉
【摘要】 本发明属于PVC地板，特别涉及双层抗静电聚氯乙烯塑料地板。一种双层结构抗静电聚氯乙烯塑料地板，其特征在于由双层结构构成，辅料组成表层，主料构成底层；按重量份数其中，主料配方为：聚氯乙烯树脂100~120份，三盐基硫酸铅8~10份，高岭土200~250份，双季戊四醇25~30份，炭黑5~10份，邻苯二甲酸二丁酯4~6份，乙氧基化脂肪族烷基胺5~10份，石蜡10份；辅料的配方为：聚氯乙烯树脂100~120份，MBS树脂10~12份，硬脂酸锌3~5份，邻苯二甲酸二丁酯4~6份，三盐基硫酸铅5~8份，二叔丁基对苯二酚树脂2~4份。本发明提供一种双层结构抗静电聚氯乙烯塑料地板，应用高聚物增塑体系，极大地减少VOC的释放，符合环境保护的要求，并且采用双层结构，表层结构抗磨等性能优良。

【名称】 一种塑料门窗型材与塑钢门窗钢衬同步焊接方法
【公开(公告)号】 CN102373868A
【公开(公告)日】 2012.03.14
【申请(专利权)人】 朱惠芬
【地址】 山东省济南市历下区闵子骞路80号
【发明(设计)人】 朱惠芬
【摘要】 本发明提供一种塑料门窗型材与塑钢门窗钢衬同步焊接方法，其结构是由塑料门窗型材和钢衬组成，钢衬设置在塑料门窗型材的空腹之中，钢衬的两端连接有塑料型材接头，塑料型材接头的端部加工有与塑料门窗型材端部相平行的断面，纵向和横向的塑料门窗型材连同钢衬在平行的断面处同步焊接在一起。该塑料门窗型材塑钢门窗钢衬同步焊接方法和现有技术相比，具有设计合理、结构简单、有效提高塑料门窗型材在拐角部位的连接强度，提高塑钢门窗的使用寿命等特点，因而，具有很好的推广使用价值。

【名称】 宽内圈轴承塑料保持架装配模具及其装配方法
【公开(公告)号】 CN102374238A
【公开(公告)日】 2012.03.14
【申请(专利权)人】 浙江八环轴承有限公司
【地址】 浙江省台州市路桥区新安西街889号
【发明(设计)人】 戴学利；王苏平；周云；牛建平；陈振林；郑牧
【摘要】 本发明提供一种宽内圈轴承塑料保持架装配模具，它包括上模、分球器和下模；下模包括底座、多根支承杆、调节螺钉和弹簧；所述底座具有轴承外圈的承接座；支承杆固定在底座上；所述分球器套在支承杆上，由所述弹簧支撑，轴向可运动地与下模连接在一起，所述分球器具有能穿入轴承外圈和轴承内圈之间的分球部位，所述分球部位具有排列方式与宽内圈轴承保持架上的钢球球兜相一致的钢球球兜；所述上模用于连接轴承保持架，所述上模具有可套在轴承内圈外的内孔。本发明还提供一种利用上述宽内圈轴承塑料保持架装配模具的宽内圈轴承装配方法。本发明结构简单，操作方便，能反复使用，提高装配效率和装配质量，减少保持架损坏造成的损失。

【名称】 一种防反射塑料薄膜及其制备方法
【公开(公告)号】 CN102375164A
【公开(公告)日】 2012.03.14
【申请(专利权)人】 素塔电子科技(上海)有限公司
【地址】 上海市嘉定区回城南路1982号
【发明(设计)人】 朴赞镐
【摘要】 本发明公开了一种防反射塑料薄膜，由基材、硬质涂覆层、沉积层和湿法层依次层叠组成，硬质涂覆层覆盖在基材的上层或下层或上下层，沉积层由依次交替层叠的高折射率沉积层和低折射率沉积层多次交替沉积形成，且最上层为高折射率沉积层。该薄膜的制备方法为：(a)制备硬质涂覆层组成物；(b)将上步制备的硬质涂覆层组成物涂覆在基材的一面或两面上，进行光聚合形成硬质涂覆层；(c)使用真空沉积法、溅射法或离子镀金法在硬质涂覆层依次交替涂覆高折射率沉积层和低折射率沉积层；(d)制备聚硅氧烷低聚物；(e)将上步制备的聚硅氧烷低聚物以湿法沉积涂覆在最上层的高折射率沉积层上。本发明技术方案制备的薄膜，耐磨性、耐水性、耐化学性强，具有优秀的防止反射的效果，而且还具有优秀的物理化学性质，能够适用于各种光学部件。

【名称】 有控制芯片的塑料光纤墙面交换机

【公开(公告)号】 CN102377575A

【公开(公告)日】 2012.03.14

【申请(专利权)人】 四川汇源塑料光纤有限公司

【地址】 四川省成都市崇州市工业集中发展区

【发明(设计)人】 宋昌林；唐波；储九荣；刘中一

【摘要】 本发明有控制芯片的塑料光纤墙面交换机，包括供电电路，与供电电路的直流电压输出端连接的滤波电路，有IP178CH控制芯片的控制芯片电路，分别与控制芯片电路连接的抗干扰电路、有25HMz晶振集成块的晶振电路、有EDL300T集成电路的塑料光纤接口电路、分别有RJ45集成电路的第一、第二、第三网络电缆接口电路。本发明安装、使用方便、应用范围广、外形小巧美观，占用空间极小。

【名称】 一种塑料光纤接入层以太网交换机

【公开(公告)号】 CN102377642A

【公开(公告)日】 2012.03.14

【申请(专利权)人】 西安飞讯光电有限公司

【地址】 陕西省西安市高新区新型工业园信息大道17号

【发明(设计)人】 缪德俊；缪立山；彭新玲

【摘要】 本发明涉及一种650nm塑料光纤接入层以太网交换机，以填补现有技术的空白。包括电源管理单元电路以及分别与电源管理单元电路相连的嵌入式通信处理器控制单元电路和以太网交换单元电路。具有的抗干扰能力、防雷击能力、防泄密能力等优点。

【名称】 废塑料催化裂解用固体超强酸催化剂及其制造方法、应用

【公开(公告)号】 CN102380401A

【公开(公告)日】 2012.03.21

【申请(专利权)人】 浙江国裕资源再生利用科技有限公司

【地址】 浙江省杭州市富阳市场口镇东梓村

【发明(设计)人】 凌国余；戚新军；凌明杰；裴文；吴成功

【摘要】 本发明公开了一种废塑料催化裂解用固体超强酸催化剂及其制造方法、应用，其目的在于解决废纸回收再利用产生的造纸废渣得不到有效利用，给环境带来巨大压力的问题。本发明所述固体超强酸催化剂为过渡金属改性的锡系固体超强酸，所述的过渡金属改性的锡系固体超强酸的表达式为以下表达式中的一种：$SO_4^{2-}/SnO_2-Fe_2O_3$、$S_2O_8^{2-}/SnO_2-Fe_2O_3$、$SO_4^{2-}/SnO_2-ZnO$、$S_2O_8^{2-}/SnO_2-ZnO$、$O_4^{2-}/SnO_2-TiO_2$、$S_2O_8^{2-}/SnO_2-TiO_2$。本发明生产成本低、制造容易，能有效将造纸废渣主成分废塑料催化裂解制备成燃料油。

【名称】 一种复杂形状塑料件的加工夹具

【公开(公告)号】 CN102380782A

【公开(公告)日】 2012.03.21

【申请(专利权)人】 江苏申模数字化制造技术有限公司

【地址】 江苏省镇江市丹徒新城瑞山东路106号

【发明(设计)人】 梁建光；王芳芳；张壮志；颜震；孔啸

【摘要】 本发明提出一种复杂形状塑料件的加工夹具，其特征在于包括：胎膜件，真空吸盘，传感器安装板以及真空泵接口；胎膜件适当部位开有凹槽，真空吸盘放置于该凹槽中，通过真空泵接口与真空泵相连。本发明的加工夹具有效的提高了复杂塑料件加工过程中的定位精度和定位速度，由于在胎膜吸附的同时采用真空吸盘进行夹紧，吸附力稳定且分布均匀，在完成夹紧的同时，还能避免夹紧过程中零件的变形。

【名称】 一种纤维织物增强树脂基复合材料预浸料的孔加工方法

【公开(公告)号】 CN102380892A

【公开(公告)日】 2012.03.21

【申请(专利权)人】 北京新风机械厂

【地址】 北京市海淀区永定路52号

【发明(设计)人】 刘漪涛；王和峰

【摘要】 本发明提供了一种纤维增强树脂基复合材料预浸料的孔加工方法，该方法具体为：将纤维增强树脂基复合材料预浸料剪裁后，铺叠压平；用塑料薄膜封装后，将包裹好的预浸料坯料，冷冻至-14～-24℃之间；使用薄板钻头或开孔器在叠放的预浸料坯料上钻孔。本发明提高预浸料的钻孔工艺性，降低孔壁粗度，孔壁无飞边、毛刺等缺陷提高加工尺寸精度(达到IT9)，提高生产效率，降低废

品率，无需专用设备。

【名称】 一种聚氟乙烯薄膜边角料回收技术

【公开(公告)号】 CN102380918A

【公开(公告)日】 2012.03.21

【申请(专利权)人】 中化蓝天集团有限公司；浙江蓝天环保高科技股份有限公司

【地址】 浙江省杭州市经济技术开发区5号大街27号

【发明(设计)人】 张艳中；张昱喆；张羽标；陈伟；马培良

【摘要】 本发明提供了一种PVF薄膜边角料回收技术，按照如下步骤进行：(1)将聚氟乙烯薄膜边角料粉碎成碎片；(2)将所述碎片与潜溶剂搅拌成混合均匀浆料；(3)将浆料直接流延制备聚氟乙烯薄膜或者返回至聚氟乙烯薄膜生产过程，与聚氟乙烯树脂混合均匀后经双向拉伸制备聚氟乙烯薄膜。本发明所述回收技术克服了常规热塑性塑料薄膜边角料回收技术上的不足，不但回收工艺简单易操作，而且消除污染，降低了生产成本。经本发明回收技术制备的PVF薄膜边角料完全可以用于PVF薄膜生产，制备的PVF薄膜与双向拉伸法制备的PVF薄膜性能一致。

【名称】 泡沫塑料板材机水循环式冷却真空系统

【公开(公告)号】 CN102380926A

【公开(公告)日】 2012.03.21

【申请(专利权)人】 杭州方圆塑料机械有限公司

【地址】 浙江省杭州市富阳市新登工业园区

【发明(设计)人】 袁国清；袁健华；姜良君；樊晓帅

【摘要】 一种泡沫塑料板材机水循环式冷却真空系统，涉及一种真空泡沫板材机的水循环式真空系统。它包括机架、真空泵、水泵、真空桶、真空冷凝桶、热水箱、冷水箱、用于连接的阀和管路、用于信号传递的温度传感器和水位传感器、外接的冷却塔等，其主要技术特征是，抽真空时热气直接从真空冷凝桶底部的冷凝水通过，真空结束后，排出冷凝水到热水箱，冷水箱则为真空冷凝桶补充冷凝水，同时热水箱的水通过水泵再次补充到冷水箱。本发明采用直接通过水冷凝和水循环利用的方式，提高了真空效果，减少了水资源的浪费。

【名称】 一种用于塑料制件和注塑模具之间气体密封的注塑模具成型结构

【公开(公告)号】 CN102380930A

【公开(公告)日】 2012.03.21

【申请(专利权)人】 青岛海信模具有限公司

【地址】 山东省青岛市经济技术开发区团结路218号

【发明(设计)人】 张明磊；王小新；邵振；鲁韶磊；王启亮

【摘要】 一种用于塑料制件和注塑模具之间气体密封的注塑模具成型结构，在注塑模具上对应塑料制件的边缘的区域内具有锯齿状或波浪纹状凸起，所述凸起沿所述边缘连续均匀设置，形成塑料模具上对应塑料制件的边缘的区域内的凸起环，在注塑过程中，当用于形成塑料制件的塑料熔体流动到所述凸起环时会快速凝固并包紧在凸起环上，从而确保注入到塑料制件和模具之间的气体不会泄露到塑料制件以外。

【名称】 一种塑料注射成型机的自动开模装置

【公开(公告)号】 CN102380936A

【公开(公告)日】 2012.03.21

【申请(专利权)人】 金孝禹

【地址】 浙江省温州市乐清市白石镇东浃村

【发明(设计)人】 金孝禹

【摘要】 本发明公开一种塑料注射成型机的自动开模装置，针对现有技术中存在的上述问题，本发明的目的在于设计提供一种塑料注射成型机的自动开模装置的技术方案，该装置提升了工作效率，降低了人工成本。所述的塑料注射成型机的自动开模装置，包括圆盘，所述圆盘同轴穿设在立柱上，所述圆盘上设有一组由上模和下模组成的模具，其特征在于所述立柱上设有一自动开模装置，所述自动开模装置包括一固定在立柱上的支架，所述支架上端设置第一液压缸以及推动第一液压缸向前运动的第二液压缸，所述第一液压缸顶端设置拉模钩，所述上模和下模一端铰接设置，另一端设置一模锁，所述模锁上端与上模铰接，下端与下模扣接，模锁侧壁设有一个与拉模钩相配合的锁钩，所述立柱中下端设有一靠模板，所述模板顶端设置一磁铁，所述磁铁吸住翻转过来的上模。

【名称】 一种水冷圆盘塑料注射成型机

【公开(公告)号】 CN102380940A

【公开(公告)日】 2012.03.21

【申请(专利权)人】 金孝禹

【地址】 浙江省温州市乐清市白石镇东浃村

【发明(设计)人】 金孝禹

【摘要】 本发明公开一种塑料注射成型机，针对现有技术中存在的上述问题，本发明的目的在于设计提供一种水冷圆盘塑料注射成型机的技术方案，其具有节能、无噪音、冷却效果好等优点。所述的一种水冷圆盘塑料注射成型机，包括圆盘，所述圆盘同轴穿设在立柱上，所述圆盘上设有一组由上模和下模组成的模具，其特征在于还包括一水冷装置，所述水冷装置包括内圈、外圈，所述内圈与立柱固定，所述外圈与圆盘固定，所述内圈上设有第一进水道、第一出水道，所述外圈上设有第二进水道、第二出水道，所述上模上设置第一冷却通道，下模上设置第二冷却通道，所述第一冷却通道的出水口端与第二冷却通道的进口端通过水管连通，当完机器完成一工位时，所述第一进水道、第二进水道、第一冷却通道、第二冷却通道、第二出水道、第一出水道连通。

【名称】 一种塑料吹瓶机合模机构

【公开(公告)号】 CN102380948A

【公开(公告)日】 2012.03.21

【申请(专利权)人】 董爱华

【地址】 广东省佛山市禅城区祖庙路33号百花广场1129室

【发明(设计)人】 董爱华

【摘要】 本发明属于一种塑料吹瓶机，主要包括动力驱动，铰链组合件，互动机构和底模机构，互动机构主要包括互动支撑板，齿轮和齿条。本发明主要优点是：动力驱动完全不用露在模板外面，模板也就不用掏空，减少加工工时，加强模板强度，整套模架采用滑动座固定，整体降低了模架高度，滑动定位更精确，互动支撑板直接安装在模架底板的平面上，模架底板不用再加工缺口，加宽了两个螺丝的固定点，这样加工与安装更简单，互动支撑板也受力更大，互动齿条采用齿条，能起到防转功能，避免齿条在推动过程中发生卡死现象，定位托叉定位也准确。

【名称】 一种玻纤布增强热塑性材料的制备方法

【公开(公告)号】 CN102380955A

【公开(公告)日】 2012.03.21

【申请(专利权)人】 宁波华业材料科技有限公司

【地址】 浙江省宁波市北仑区纬三路79号

【发明(设计)人】 金一平；周伟

【摘要】 本发明涉及一种玻纤布增强热塑性材料的制备方法，包括：将玻纤布预热至180～200℃，同时辊压，将聚丙烯淋膜到玻纤布的一面或二面；再将淋膜好的玻纤布放入200℃的压机，同时加0.2～0.8MPa的压力，将所得材料再进行冷压，得玻纤布增强热塑性材料。本发明工艺简单，成本低，将粘稠状态的聚丙烯包覆到玻纤表面，包覆面积大，包覆均匀，强度大，克服了热塑性塑料原有的缺点，具有良好的应用前景。

【名称】 一种印花塑料板

【公开(公告)号】 CN102380990A

【公开(公告)日】 2012.03.21

【申请(专利权)人】 苏州潮盛印花制版实业有限公司

【地址】 江苏省苏州市吴江市盛泽镇荷花村工业园区东茂集团

【发明(设计)人】 钟钊伟；黄锡坚；张硕

【摘要】 本发明公开了一种印花塑料板，包括塑料板基材(1)，涂覆在塑料板基材(1)上表面的粘接层(2)，粘接在粘接层(2)上的印花薄膜(3)。本发明提供的印花塑料板，结构设计合理，坚固耐用，尤其在塑料板表面粘接有印花薄膜后，印花可以是平面或立体印花，且颜色可调不易褪色，美观度好，能满足人们高要求的生活标准，且印花塑料板成本低，用途广泛。

【名称】 一种环保型耐高温PVC硬挺复合布

【公开(公告)号】 CN102380995A

【公开(公告)日】 2012.03.21

【申请(专利权)人】 上海三川塑料有限公司

【地址】 上海市浦东新区合庆镇跃丰路68号

【发明(设计)人】 王嘉明

【摘要】 本发明涉及一种环保型耐高温PVC硬挺复合布，包括上层布料、中层PVC塑料及下层布料，所述中层PVC塑料的主要成分按重量百分比为：聚氯乙烯树脂40%～50%、碳酸钙20%～30%、聚己二醇0.5%～1%、PVC稳定剂0.5%～1.5%、邻苯二甲酸二壬酯(DINP)10%～20%及环保增塑剂5%～15%；本发明的中层PVC塑料添加的增塑剂使用DINP来替换DOP，及UN488来替换DBP，所以非常环保，而且这种PVC硬挺复合布所制成的劳动防护用品不仅穿戴柔软、舒适，而且具有耐酸碱、耐高温、高强度、安全性能可靠的优点；此外，本发明制作简单，成本低，还可以作为纺织面料投放市场，具有广阔的应用前景。

【名称】 一种食品包装塑料基材薄膜及其生产工艺

【公开(公告)号】 CN102380996A

【公开(公告)日】 2012.03.21

【申请(专利权)人】 大连方盛塑料有限公司

【地址】 辽宁省大连市金州区站前街道吴屯机场

【发明(设计)人】 梁继鹏

【摘要】 本发明涉及一种食品包装塑料基材薄膜，包括内层、中间层和外层三层结构；所述的内层、中间层和外层均采用低密度聚乙烯LDPE和茂金属线性低密度聚乙烯mLLDPE制成混合制成。其生产工艺包括混合进料挤出、吹膜、定型、牵引切割等步骤。本发明设计的食品包装塑料基材薄膜提供一种高阻隔性、高气密性、抗污染性、热封强度高、热封性能好，有一定的耐压性和耐冲击性，符合食品安全认证的食品包装袋料基材薄膜。

【名称】 一种多功能边封机
【公开(公告)号】 CN102381499A
【公开(公告)日】 2012.03.21
【申请(专利权)人】 无锡市伟丰印刷机械厂
【地址】 江苏省无锡市新区硕放工业园新农路
【发明(设计)人】 吴伟平
【摘要】 一种多功能边封机，包括传动装置和封口带，传动装置包括主动带轮、传送带和被动带轮，且所述主动带轮和被动带轮分别为两个，分别设置在所述传送带的两侧，所述主动带轮通过所述传送带与所述被动带轮连接，在所述主动带轮和被动带轮之间位置位于所述传送带两侧分别设有一个冷却块和一个加热块，所述主动带轮分别通过引导带与引导轮连接，所述封口带在所述主动带轮和被动带轮之间传动，所述封口带夹持待封口的塑料袋的封口部分进行封口。本发明中的边封机通过电子恒温控制器能够实现对传动装置的自动控制，另外，印花轮的设置可以实现在包装袋上印制花纹或文字，简单方便，不用二次加工，该装置结构简单，操作方便，效率提高，同时也节约了成本。

【名称】 折叠式抗菌塑料杯
【公开(公告)号】 CN102396879A
【公开(公告)日】 2012.04.04
【申请(专利权)人】 王崇高
【地址】 江苏省泰州市海陵区八字桥南小街3号楼503室
【发明(设计)人】 王崇高
【摘要】 本发明公开了一种折叠式抗菌塑料杯的生产方法，该折叠式抗菌塑料杯是由耐折叠抗菌树脂经注塑成型加工制作而成，折叠式抗菌塑料杯的注塑成型模进行了不等厚设计，折叠式抗菌塑料杯折叠处的厚度比杯体要薄，注塑成型后的产品要立即趁热折叠2~3次。折叠式抗菌塑料杯具有抗菌、重量轻、耐撞击、耐折叠、耐腐蚀、耐老化，体积小、便于储运和携带方便以及生产成本低的特点，广泛适用于军事、救援、野外考察、出差和旅游。

【名称】 旋转模塑精密成型机
【公开(公告)号】 CN102398340A
【公开(公告)日】 2012.04.04
【申请(专利权)人】 张家港市亿利机械有限公司
【地址】 江苏省苏州市张家港市锦丰镇沿江路9号张家港市亿利机械有限公司
【发明(设计)人】 陈鹤忠；姚军
【摘要】 本发明公开了旋转模塑精密成型机，包括用于固定模具的模具安装盘，模具安装盘活动设置在模头座上，模头座固定在外轴的一端，外轴的外部设置有外轴链轮，外轴链轮通过外轴链条与外轴驱动电机相连接，外轴驱动电机固定在机架上，外轴设置在轴承座的内部，轴承座设置在机架的上方；模具安装盘与旋转轴相连接，旋转轴位于模头座的内部，旋转轴上固定有纵向锥齿轮，纵向锥齿轮与横向锥齿轮相啮合，横向锥齿轮固定在内轴上，内轴独立设置在外轴的内部，内轴的一端伸出外轴，内轴的伸出部分上固定有内轴链轮，内轴链轮通过内轴链条与内轴驱动电机相连接，内轴驱动电机固定在机架上。本发明适用于生产塑料窨井。

【名称】 台面板注塑模具及台面板注塑工艺
【公开(公告)号】 CN102398345A
【公开(公告)日】 2012.04.04
【申请(专利权)人】 海尔集团公司；青岛海尔模具有限公司
【地址】 山东省青岛市崂山区高科园海尔路1号海尔工业园
【发明(设计)人】 黄俊；史允岭；刘军；徐丽丽
【摘要】 本发明公开了一种台面板注塑模具及台面板注塑工艺，涉及模具技术领域，为使所述台面板具有较高的强度和生产效率而发明。所述台面板注塑模具，包括相互配合使用的前模和后模，在所述前模的型腔内设有用于吸附所述内嵌件的第一吸盘；和/或，在所述后模的型腔内设有用于吸附所述内嵌件的第二吸盘。所述台面板注塑工艺包括：将用来制作台面板的内嵌件放置在前模的第一吸盘上或后模的第二吸盘上，并使所述第一吸盘或第二吸盘吸附所述内嵌件；将所述前模和所述后模合模，并向合模后的型腔中注射塑料熔体，以便在所述内嵌件的周围直接注塑成型塑料件后形成台面板；开模并取出注塑成型的台面板。本发明可用于制作台面板。

【名称】 塑料挤出机中抽真空系统中的分腔真空排气室
【公开(公告)号】 CN102398359A
【公开(公告)日】 2012.04.04
【申请(专利权)人】 张家港市贝尔机械有限公司
【地址】 江苏省苏州市张家港市经济开发区振兴路6号张家港市贝尔机械有限公司
【发明(设计)人】 何德方；马德生
【摘要】 本发明公开了一种塑料挤出机中抽真空系统中的分腔真空排气室，包括：由若干侧板围成的真空排气室腔体，真空排气室腔体的侧板上设置有抽气口和进气口，真空排气室腔体内设置有能阻挡由进气口进入真空排气室腔体内的气流的隔板，所述的隔板挡在抽气口与进气口之间、并将真空排气室腔体分隔成两个相对独立的腔体，隔板的里端与真空排气室腔体的内侧板固定，隔板的外端与真空排气室腔体的外侧板之间留有间隙，所述的真空排气室腔体的外侧板能够开启，且外侧板与相连接的侧板密封连接。本发明结构简单，有效避免了物料堵塞抽气管路的现象发生，保证了隔板上方腔体内气流的通畅流动，使抽真空系统能长期稳定、正常地工作。

【名称】 多功能塑料修补机

【公开(公告)号】 CN102398368A

【公开(公告)日】 2012.04.04

【申请(专利权)人】 江门市保值久机电有限公司

【地址】 广东省江门市新会区江咀村塘子坑工业区新厂房3座2号

【发明(设计)人】 翁良轩

【摘要】 本发明公开了一种多功能塑料修补机，包括电源模块、用于执行工序操作的操作手柄，所述操作手柄采用导线与电源模块相连接，所述操作手柄端部设置有两根用于通电发热的熔焊头，所述熔焊头外套接有金属连接套，所述熔焊头上细下粗使金属连接套在套接时紧固在熔焊头上，所述金属连接套上设置有用于连接工装头的连接孔，本设计的多功能塑料修补机结构简便，虽然只有一个电源模块，一把操作手柄，却具有植钉机与加热抹平工具的功能，携带方便；在进行塑料修补时，可以进行植钉，植钉后套上连接有工装头的金属连接套，切换电流大小，可以用于进行塑料的抹平，使用方便。

【名称】 桶盖联体塑料桶

【公开(公告)号】 CN102398725A

【公开(公告)日】 2012.04.04

【申请(专利权)人】 李新波

【地址】 湖南省浏阳市洞阳镇宝升塑料制品厂

【发明(设计)人】 李新波

【摘要】 本发明为解决塑料桶盖丢失的技术问题，提供一种防止桶盖丢失的桶盖联体塑料桶，其包括桶体[1]、内盖[4]、外盖[2]，在桶体[1]口部和外盖[2]之间设置一软体细长连接件[3]，所述连接件[3]一端可360度回转套接在外盖[2]上，所述内盖[4]和外盖[2]可以为整体结构，也可以是单独设置。设计科学、方便实用，有效解决了桶盖容易丢失的问题。

【名称】 一种玻纤增强热塑性材料的加工工艺

【公开(公告)号】 CN102399065A

【公开(公告)日】 2012.04.04

【申请(专利权)人】 佛山市顺德区威林工程塑料有限公司

【地址】 广东省广州市天河区中山大道西491号棠利大厦东2楼801室

【发明(设计)人】 胡琛；黄达成；黄慧；郭小会

【摘要】 本发明公开一种玻纤增强热塑料材料的加工方法，与传统的加工方法相比，玻纤在进入螺筒前先经过除电加热管，去除玻纤中的残余水分，以避免玻纤中残余水分对材料的降解，玻纤在经过干燥处理后再经过胶辊，胶辊的上方有一个偶联剂容器，偶联剂可通过胶辊均匀的涂覆在玻纤表面，玻纤在涂覆完偶联剂后再进入螺筒，由于偶联剂均匀的涂覆在材料表面，偶联剂与玻纤浸润较好，材料的外观性能可得到改善，机械性能可得到提高。

【名称】 塑料加工复合功能助剂及其制备方法

【公开(公告)号】 CN102399377A

【公开(公告)日】 2012.04.04

【申请(专利权)人】 安徽省忠宏管业科技有限公司

【地址】 安徽省池州市经济技术开发区金安工业园

【发明(设计)人】 刘忠斌

【摘要】 本发明公开了一种塑料加工复合功能助剂及其制备方法，各原料组分按重量份比为：轻质碳酸钙粉90~100、云母粉1~2、焙烧沸石粉3~5、秸秆灰烬1~2、氧化锌3~5、气相二氧化硅3~5、甲基丙烯酸酯的聚合物1~2、聚乙烯蜡1~2、烷基苯磺酸钠1~2、硅油1~2。制备方法：将轻质碳酸钙烘干至水份含重量为0.3%以下，加入高速捏合机中，然后按重量份比添加其它配方材料，再升温至100－130℃，保温搅拌8－10min后，出料得成品。本发明所制备的塑料加工复合功能助剂降低了颗粒间的表面能，增强了塑料的相容性和分散性；促进了高分子材料塑化，降低熔体粘度，改善加工流动性；提高制品冲击度、刚度、耐热性及尺寸稳定性，具有节能降耗、环保、无毒、无“三废”的特点。

【名称】 高性能阻燃抗静电聚丙烯塑料的制备方法

【公开(公告)号】 CN102399389A

【公开(公告)日】 2012.04.04

【申请(专利权)人】 李天辉

【地址】 安徽省宿州市埇桥区芦岭煤矿中学

【发明(设计)人】 李天辉

【摘要】 本发明提供了一种高性能的阻燃抗静电聚丙烯塑料，是在聚丙烯中加入一定量聚氯乙烯，三氧化二锑，硬脂酸，硬脂酸钙，芥酸酰胺，超导石墨，受阻酚类抗氧化剂1010，混合，经过螺杆挤出机熔融挤出即得；试验证明，本发明制备的阻燃抗静电聚丙烯塑料的性能：氧指数达到29，表面电阻达到103~108Ω，抗拉强度50MPa；成本远低于市场销售的双抗网。

【名称】 一种耐热、抗冲、玻璃纤维增强黑色丙烯腈-丁二烯-苯乙烯改性塑料及其制备方法
【公开(公告)号】 CN102399408A
【公开(公告)日】 2012.04.04
【申请(专利权)人】 上海纳米技术及应用国家工程研究中心有限公司
【地址】 上海市闵行区江川东路28号
【发明(设计)人】 吴娟娟；陈超；盛小海；洪月蓉
【摘要】 本发明涉及一种耐热、抗冲玻璃纤维增强黑色丙烯腈-丁二烯-苯乙烯改性塑料及其制备方法，主要解决玻璃纤维增强复合材料抗冲击性能差的问题，同时，提高复合体系的耐热性。本发明通过添加耐热的苯乙烯、马来酰亚胺等多单元无规共聚物提高耐热性和相容性，通过添加无碱玻璃短纤维来提高其刚性，降低材料的线胀系数和成型收缩率，同时，添加对力学性能和耐热性影响较小的硅丙烯酸系类抗冲击改性剂来改善整个体系的抗冲击性能。较好地解决了在提高耐热性和刚性同时，抗冲击急剧下降的问题。本发明技术方案简单明了，可以进行规模化生产。

【名称】 一种生物降解材料及其制备方法和应用
【公开(公告)号】 CN102399417A
【公开(公告)日】 2012.04.04
【申请(专利权)人】 中国科学院宁波材料技术与工程研究所
【地址】 浙江省宁波市镇海区庄市大道519号
【发明(设计)人】 汤兆宾；朱锦；杨勇；张传芝
【摘要】 本发明公开了一种生物降解材料，由以下重量份的原料组成：20~90份碳酸二甲酯-丁二醇共聚物、0~70份聚乳酸、0.1~30份天然植物油、0.5~20份增塑剂和0.5~20份反应促进剂，可用于制备生物降解薄膜，制备出的薄膜既具有普通塑料的各种优良性能，又能被土壤中的微生物完全分解快速吸收。本发明还公开了一种生物降解材料的制备方法，制备方法简单，易于控制，可操作性强，生产成本低廉，并可将制备的生物降解材料再经简单的处理就可以得到生物降解薄膜，易于工业化生产并具有很好的经济效益，具有广阔的应用前景。

【名称】 一种抗菌聚对苯二甲酸乙二酯组合物及其制备方法
【公开(公告)号】 CN102399419A
【公开(公告)日】 2012.04.04
【申请(专利权)人】 中国石油化工股份有限公司；中国石油化工股份有限公司北京化工研究院
【地址】 北京市朝阳区朝阳门北大街22号
【发明(设计)人】 尹华；张师军；李杰；刘涛；张丽英等
【摘要】 本发明涉及一种抗菌聚对苯二甲酸乙二酯组合物及其制备方法。该组合物包含有共混的以下组分：聚对苯二甲酸乙二酯，100重量份；聚胍/聚硅酸盐复合抗菌剂，0.1~2.0重量份；纳米丁苯吡粉末橡胶，0.5~10重量份。该组合物只需要较低的抗菌剂添加量，即可达到99%的抗菌效果，并且该组合物在经过一定的水洗之后，仍然具有较好的抗菌功能，可应用于制备纤维以及其他塑料制品。

【名称】 以人的头发做为塑料原料制做器物
【公开(公告)号】 CN102399448A
【公开(公告)日】 2012.04.04
【申请(专利权)人】 汪砚秋
【地址】 天津市经济技术开发区第四大街泰丰家园二期10门601室
【发明(设计)人】 汪砚秋
【摘要】 以人的头发做为塑料原料制做器物，涉及一种塑料原料。本发明公开了一种塑料原料，它就是人的头发。先用塑料造粒机将人的头发造成塑料颗粒，再用注塑机将这些颗粒原料注塑成各种器物。

【名称】 塑料排水带的生产设备
【公开(公告)号】 CN102400457A
【公开(公告)日】 2012.04.04
【申请(专利权)人】 宁波广宏工程塑料有限公司
【地址】 浙江省宁波市宁海县长街工业区
【发明(设计)人】 陈敏莲；徐大斌
【摘要】 本发明公开的了一种塑料排水带的生产设备，包括驱动装置，它还从头至尾依次包括送料装置、压合装置和收卷装置，所述的送料装置中平行排列装有多组原料，每组原料包括芯板卷(5)、上滤膜卷(7)和下滤膜卷(21)；所述的驱动装置与压合装置连接并驱动压合装置。采用以上结构后，由于送料装置中平行排列装有多组原料，换句话说，一次生产时可以安排多条排水带同时进行，这样，大大提高了生产效率。

【名称】 钢塑复合供水压力罐
【公开(公告)号】 CN102400482A
【公开(公告)日】 2012.04.04
【申请(专利权)人】 张本照
【地址】 山东省日照市莒县安庄镇坪上村201号
【发明(设计)人】 张本照
【摘要】 本发明提供了一种钢塑复合供水压力罐的技术方案，包括有支架，在支架上方安装一个钢制罐体，罐体两端设为弧型，罐体内表面用化学处理，产生一层保护膜，罐体上方设有电接点压力继电器和压力表的安装螺孔，罐体下端一侧为进水管，另

一侧为出水管，罐体底部有安全阀螺口和排污阀螺口，在罐体内注塑，让塑料均匀贴覆在钢制罐体的内表面上，形成1～2毫米的注塑防腐层，达到永远不腐蚀的目的。

【名称】 局部加厚塑料软管

【公开(公告)号】 CN102401200A

【公开(公告)日】 2012.04.04

【申请(专利权)人】 马庆礼

【地址】 新疆维吾尔自治区昌吉市健康西路14001号(昌吉市园艺工作站)

【发明(设计)人】 马庆礼

【摘要】 本发明公开了一种与普通塑料软管不同的局部加厚塑料软管，其特点是：局部加厚塑料软管的管壁厚度各部位是不同的，在特定的部位，在管壁圆周的内侧面上或外侧面上或在管壁圆周同部位内、外侧面上、在一定宽度(与插接式管件相适应的宽度)内，设有一条或多条局部加厚长条体(2)，其长边与局部加厚塑料软管纵轴方向平行，或设有一排以上(包括一排)不连续加厚块状体(13)，并使其厚度、硬度符合插接式管件的要求，加厚长条体横截面或局部加厚块状体横截面边缘包络线(14)可以是任意形。局部加厚塑料软管的主要优点：保持了普通塑料软管的柔软性；生产容易；易于安装；使用成本大幅下降；可以广泛应用于农业、林业等节水灌溉领域。局部加厚软管的制造材料为塑料类材料，例如PE或PVC等。

【名称】 废旧塑料造粒机用的气液两级分离器及分离方法

【公开(公告)号】 CN102407027A

【公开(公告)日】 2012.04.11

【申请(专利权)人】 洛阳骏腾能源科技有限公司；周强

【地址】 河南省洛阳市高新技术开发区丰华路银昆科技园5号楼105室

【发明(设计)人】 周强；周仁福；陶然

【摘要】 废旧塑料造粒机用的气液两级分离器及分离方法，由气体分离器和液体静置分离器组成，一个倾斜的分离板将液体静置分离器分隔为静置分离室和溢流室两部分，气体分离器为竖直设置的管状结构，废气从气体分离器下部的高温混合气体入口进入气体分离器的蛇形管气道，在上升过程中与气体分离器的冷却水通道进行热交换，冷却的气体从气体分离器顶部的排气口排出，冷却凝结的混合液体通过导流管进入静置分离室，静置分层后，不同比重的组分分别通过静置分离室和溢流室侧壁上的液体溢出口或液体静置分离器的底部的排污口排出。通过简单的结构方式，完成了废旧塑料造粒过程中高温混合废气中个组分的有效分离，实现了气体的净化、分离和资源的回收利用。

【名称】 一种PPO塑料空调壳体注塑工艺

【公开(公告)号】 CN102407587A

【公开(公告)日】 2012.04.11

【申请(专利权)人】 上海浦东美灵塑料制品有限公司

【地址】 上海市浦东新区合庆镇向阳村

【发明(设计)人】 张志林

【摘要】 本发明公开了一种PPO塑料空调壳体注塑工艺，该工艺包括如下步骤：(1)原料预处理；(2)注塑系统和注塑模具预处理；(3)塑化；(4)注射；(5)保压；(6)冷却成型；(7)脱模。该工艺实施步骤简单，有效的降低成型周期和生产成本，同时通过相应的工艺条件，有效提高该工艺的成品质量。

【名称】 一种ABS塑料空调壳体注塑工艺

【公开(公告)号】 CN102407588A

【公开(公告)日】 2012.04.11

【申请(专利权)人】 上海浦东美灵塑料制品有限公司

【地址】 上海市浦东新区合庆镇向阳村

【发明(设计)人】 张志林

【摘要】 本发明公开了一种ABS塑料空调壳体注塑工艺，该工艺包括如下步骤：(1)原料预处理；(2)注塑系统和注塑模具预处理；(3)塑化；(4)注射；(5)保压；(6)冷却成型；(7)脱模。该工艺实施步骤简单，有效的降低成型周期和生产成本，同时通过相应的工艺条件，有效提高该工艺的成品质量。

【名称】 一种ABS塑料洗衣机盖板注塑工艺

【公开(公告)号】 CN102407589A

【公开(公告)日】 2012.04.11

【申请(专利权)人】 上海浦东美灵塑料制品有限公司

【地址】 上海市浦东新区合庆镇向阳村

【发明(设计)人】 张志林

【摘要】 本发明公开了一种ABS塑料洗衣机盖板注塑工艺，该工艺包括如下步骤：(1)原料预处理；(2)注塑系统和注塑模具预处理；(3)塑化；(4)注射；(5)保压；(6)冷却成型；(7)脱模。该工艺实施步骤简单，有效的降低成型周期和生产成本，同时通过相应的工艺条件，有效提高该工艺的成品质量。

【名称】 一种塑料管材的成型用挤出模具

【公开(公告)号】 CN102407598A
【公开(公告)日】 2012.04.11
【申请(专利权)人】 湖南路路通塑业股份有限公司
【地址】 湖南省长沙市枫林三路418号麓谷基地
【发明(设计)人】 戴毅明；戴愈
【摘要】 本发明公开了一种塑料管材的成型用挤出模具，包括进料端和挤出端。进料端用于塑料管的制造原料的进入，塑料管的制造原料在挤压作用下通过挤出端挤出成型。本发明所提供的塑料管材的成型用挤出模具，其挤出端为耐高温、耐磨的高分子材料挤出端。在融熔状态下的塑化材料被挤入到模具并被从模具挤出的过程中，经过了两种热学性能完全不同的材料，融熔态的塑化材料通过模具的流道时，在流经两种材料构成的最后段塑料管材的内外壁表层受到材料的影响，导致成型的塑料管的表层分子排列改变，使得管材内外壁非常光滑。因此，本发明所提供的塑料管材的成型用挤出模具能够实现在不使用润滑剂的前提下提高塑料管材的内壁光滑程度的目的。

【名称】 一种钢丝骨架塑料复合管的封口方法及设备
【公开(公告)号】 CN102407601A
【公开(公告)日】 2012.04.11
【申请(专利权)人】 广东东方管业有限公司
【地址】 广东省佛山市顺德区杏坛镇东村工业大道南9号
【发明(设计)人】 林津强
【摘要】 本发明公开了一种钢丝骨架塑料复合管的封口方法及设备，其特征在于，在方法上，它是采用管材自身塑料封口的方式，先对复合管的端口加热，再通过外力作用令复合管加热后内外翻出来的塑料包裹住钢丝；在设备上，它包括封口机架及其上设置的固定复合管的模具，模具外设置有与复合管端口对应的加热板。本发明能将管材的塑料包裹住钢丝，起到封口的作用，具有良好的推广价值。

【名称】 钢塑复合材料的加工工艺
【公开(公告)号】 CN102407629A
【公开(公告)日】 2012.04.11
【申请(专利权)人】 任立蓬
【地址】 辽宁省沈阳市铁西区南九中路51号定名轩
【发明(设计)人】 任立蓬
【摘要】 目前的钢塑复合大多用对钢基电加热或火加热，受热面不均匀，温度不好控制，钢基表面易受污染，影响塑料附着。本发明将低熔点金属如锡、锌、铅、铝等放入一池内加热至熔化后，放入待复合的钢基，调控适量温度后取出，与塑料复合。

【名称】 塑料杯封口机放膜装置
【公开(公告)号】 CN102407957A
【公开(公告)日】 2012.04.11
【申请(专利权)人】 胡敏
【地址】 江苏省无锡市锡山经济开发区芙蓉中三路99号
【发明(设计)人】 胡敏
【摘要】 本发明公开一种塑料杯封口机放膜装置，包括机架，所述机架上一侧设置升降机构，另一侧设置膜纸盛放装置，所述升降机构下部设置连接轴，所述连接轴上设置不完全齿轮，所述机架上设置与不完全齿轮相啮合的齿条，所述不完全齿轮的一侧设置转环，所述转环连接有吸盘，所述吸盘位于膜纸盛放装置的下方，且位于塑料杯输送线的上方。通过在连接轴上设置不完全齿轮，机架上设置与不完全齿轮相啮合的齿条，可以实现连接轴的转动；通过在连接轴上设置吸盘，可以实现将膜纸吸住，并将膜纸压在塑料杯上，此装置能够自动对塑料杯饮料进行放膜，降低工人劳动强度，提高生产效率，还避免了手工操作对膜纸的污染。

【名称】 腰果酚丁基醚组合物的合成方法
【公开(公告)号】 CN102408315A
【公开(公告)日】 2012.04.11
【申请(专利权)人】 中国林业科学研究院林产化学工业研究所
【地址】 江苏省南京市锁金五村16号
【发明(设计)人】 夏建陵；黄坤；李梅；陈瑶；杨小华；万厉；张燕
【摘要】 本发明公开了一种腰果酚丁基醚组合物的合成方法，腰果酚和氯代正丁烷在碱性催化剂存在下，无氧条件反应，反应结束减压蒸馏，过滤除去生成的盐得到产物腰果酚丁基醚组合物，所述的碱性催化剂为碱金属碳酸盐或碱金属氢氧化物。本发明用于合成腰果酚丁基醚的方法简单，产率较高。而且反应过程中不加入水，不产生废水。由于腰果酚的酚羟基被烷氧基所替代，使得该产物具有很好的颜色稳定性，并且大大降低了腰果酚对于皮肤的腐蚀性。该产物可以用来制备具有良好的颜色稳定性的环氧固化剂。在涂料、胶黏剂、橡胶、塑料、弹性体、复合材料和油墨中可以用作改性剂。

【名称】 低烟无卤阻燃电缆料的相容剂的制备方法
【公开(公告)号】 CN102408522A
【公开(公告)日】 2012.04.11
【申请(专利权)人】 宝应宝洲电缆材料厂
【地址】 江苏省扬州市宝应县安宜镇机场路
【发明(设计)人】 杨永泉

【摘要】 低烟无卤阻燃电缆料的相容剂的制备方法，涉及电线电缆用低烟无卤阻燃塑料的生产技术领域。先将双二五硫化剂与马来酸酐丙酮溶液混合形成接枝混合体，然后在抽气的状态下，将所述接枝混合体与塑化后的 EVA 树脂在挤塑机内进行接枝反应，最后经造粒、冷却，制成粒状相容剂。将本发明产品与常规低烟无卤阻燃电缆料生产其它原料共混后，经常规方法制成低烟无卤阻燃电缆料，能降低两相间界面能，在聚合物共混过程中促进相的分散，阻止分散相的凝聚，强化相间粘结，因此增加了高分子树脂间及氢氧化镁材料的相容及分散，最大程度上保证拉伸强度和断裂伸长率的性能。

【名称】 植物纤维增强的硬质聚氨酯泡沫塑料

【公开(公告)号】 CN102408535A

【公开(公告)日】 2012.04.11

【申请(专利权)人】 吴江明峰聚氨酯制品有限公司

【地址】 江苏省苏州市吴江北厍镇玩字村

【发明(设计)人】 费近峰

【摘要】 本发明涉及一种植物纤维增强的硬质聚氨酯泡沫塑料，其特征在于包括以下组份：阻燃聚醚多元醇 50 ~ 60 份、聚醚二醇 10 ~ 20 份、阻燃剂 5 ~ 15 份、发泡剂 5 ~ 10 份、泡沫稳定剂 1 ~ 2 份、植物纤维 10 ~ 50 份、催化剂 1 ~ 2.5 份、水 0.01 ~ 0.15 份、多异氰酸酯 20 ~ 30 份，是采用一步发泡工艺制备得到。本发明得到的植物纤维增强的硬质聚氨酯泡沫塑料，易于加工，泡沫表面致密，具有良好的物理力学性能，阻燃性良好。

【名称】 环保型可控降解农用地膜及其制备方法

【公开(公告)号】 CN102408587A

【公开(公告)日】 2012.04.11

【申请(专利权)人】 宁夏绿环生物降解制品开发有限公司

【地址】 宁夏回族自治区银川市贺兰县全民创业基地富兴北街 7 号

【发明(设计)人】 杨建军；侯世荣

【摘要】 本发明公开的环保型可控降解农用地膜，该农用地膜按重量份计是由以下的原料经熔融共混挤出吹膜而成：聚乙烯醇 25 ~ 50 份，淀粉 72 ~ 87 份，小分子增塑剂 10 ~ 20 份，改性无机纳米助剂 0.2 ~ 2 份，抗氧化剂 0.5 ~ 1.5 份，增容剂 0.5 ~ 1.5 份，紫外线吸收剂 0.2 ~ 1.5 份。本发明还公开了上述农用地膜的制备方法。本发明提供农用地膜中所含的纳米复合改性剂在采用了易与淀粉形成氢键的小分子增塑剂的同时，又添加一定量的经表面处理过的无机纳米助剂，因而当用其改性 PVA 后，不仅可大大减少小分子增塑剂的用量，降低成本，避免薄膜后期的力学性能下降的问题，而且还能得到具备塑料薄膜力学性能和后期使用性能均佳的可控完全生物降解农用地膜。

【名称】 一种优质渗透管的制备方法

【公开(公告)号】 CN102408599A

【公开(公告)日】 2012.04.11

【申请(专利权)人】 伪川工业有限公司

【地址】 福建省漳州市漳浦县绥安工业区漳州伪园工业有限公司

【发明(设计)人】 郭文礼

【摘要】 本发明公开了一种优质渗透管的制备方法，属于农业生产中灌溉设施的管道。优质渗透管的组分：40 目的胎面粉，60 目的胎面粉，LDPE(4314)，普通 LDPE，HDPE，PE 改质剂，外滑剂，内滑剂，AC。渗透管的制备方法：把以上九种组分的原料按重量比称重后放进混料机进行充分搅拌，搅拌的温度从常温升至 70℃，即把混合料取出。把取出的混合料放进塑料挤出机进行挤压成型。按规格要求截断挤出管道，并按拟定的要求进行侧孔钻孔加工。由于本发明有效地克服了老化速度快、寿命短、防爆破能力差、进出水不均匀、易折断等不足，能够减少农业生产中灌溉设施的管道投资成本，有利于促进农业科学节水滴灌技术的普及。

【名称】 交联聚乙烯无卤低烟阻燃电缆材料

【公开(公告)号】 CN102408607A

【公开(公告)日】 2012.04.11

【申请(专利权)人】 贵州鸽牌长通电线电缆有限公司

【地址】 贵州省贵阳市国家高新技术产业区

【发明(设计)人】 胡静

【摘要】 本发明公开了一种交联聚乙烯无卤低烟阻燃电缆材料，属于电缆线用塑料；旨在提供一种阻燃性能好、无熔滴、烟雾少、韧性高、便于加工的电缆线用塑料。它由下列重量份原料制成：交联聚乙烯 100 份、氢氧化镁 20 份、氢氧化铝 7 份、三盐基硫酸铅 1.4 份、二盐基亚磷酸铅 0.7 份、石蜡 0.5 份、邻苯二甲酸酯 30 份、纳米蒙脱土 10 份；制备方法是将上述各原料混合均匀投入螺杆挤出机中熔融混炼 2 分钟，该螺杆挤出机的温度控制在 210 ~ 220℃、螺杆转速为 50 转/分钟；然后挤出、冷却、切粒、筛分即可。本发明具有重量轻、韧性好、火焰小、燃烧慢、无熔滴、烟雾少、抗迁移、成炭性好、易于加工等诸多优点；是一种取代 PVC 的电缆塑料。

【名称】 一种吸水母料、其制备方法及其应用

【公开(公告)号】 CN102408608A

【公开(公告)日】 2012.04.11
【申请(专利权)人】 乌鲁木齐聚兴永塑胶有限公司
【地址】 新疆维吾尔自治区乌鲁木齐市七道湾乡七道湾村
【发明(设计)人】 王文其；王英哲；肖梅
【摘要】 一种吸水母料、其制备方法及其应用，涉及一种再生塑料添加剂。本吸水母料由如下重量份的原料制成，600目~800目氧化钙50~75份，树脂5~8份，铝酸酯偶联剂1~1.5份，硬脂酸1~1.5份，聚乙烯蜡2~3份，硬脂酸钙0.5~1份，石蜡1~1.5份。其在再生塑料中的添加比例的质量百分比2%~5%，可有效吸收再生塑料中的水份，并明显提高产品质量和生产效率。
【名称】 一种可光、生物降解的聚乙烯塑料袋
【公开(公告)号】 CN102408612A
【公开(公告)日】 2012.04.11
【申请(专利权)人】 吴江明峰聚氨酯制品有限公司
【地址】 江苏省苏州市吴江北厍镇玩字村
【发明(设计)人】 费近峰
【摘要】 本发明公开一种可光、生物降解的聚乙烯塑料袋，其特征在于包括以下组份：LDPE100份、填料5~10份、增容剂0.1~1.5份、光敏剂0.1~1份、玉米淀粉1~10份、微晶纤维素1~10份、硅烷偶联剂2~11份。制备过程如下：(1)将玉米淀粉、碳酸钙粉末、微晶纤维素粉碎成超细颗粒；(2)将玉米淀粉干燥，加入硅烷偶联剂进行表面处理，加入增容剂，备用；(3)碳酸钙粉磨加入活化剂、分散剂，备用；(4)将步骤(2)、(3)获得的材料混合，加入LDPE，微晶纤维素，光敏剂，二辊混炼，破碎，挤出造粒，获得母料；(5)将可光、生物降解的母料与LDPE混合干燥，吹塑、收卷、制袋，得到可光、生物降解的聚乙烯塑料袋。本发明获得的塑料袋后能在25天左右的时间内裂成碎片，且可被真菌侵蚀崩解，达到光降解、生物降解的复合效果。
【名称】 PP/ABS合金材料、其制备方法和应用
【公开(公告)号】 CN102408633A
【公开(公告)日】 2012.04.11
【申请(专利权)人】 惠州市沃特新材料有限公司
【地址】 广东省惠州市惠城区小金口镇科技产业园
【发明(设计)人】 何征；章驰天；杨永佳
【摘要】 本发明适用于工程塑料技术领域，提供了一种PP/ABS合金材料、其制备方法和应用。该PP/ABS合金材料包括ABS和PP。本发明PP/ABS合金材料，通过含阻燃剂的ABS母粒，实现了阻燃剂在合金材料中的均匀分散，使得合金材料的阻燃性能显著提升；通过上述组分的配合使用，使得所制备的合金材料具有优异的力学性能、刚性抗蠕变性能及尺寸性能。
【名称】 一种塑料型材的成型工艺
【公开(公告)号】 CN102408641A
【公开(公告)日】 2012.04.11
【申请(专利权)人】 大连方盛塑料有限公司
【地址】 辽宁省大连市金州区站前街道吴屯机场
【发明(设计)人】 梁继鹏
【摘要】 本发明公开了一种塑料型材的成型工艺，步骤如下：1)配料：将聚苯乙烯树脂为100份，热稳定剂4~5份，改性剂5~10份，聚磷酸三苯酯0.5份，钛白粉7~9份，润精剂0.5~1份，无机填充料10~30份；2)混合搅拌：将上述各原料投入搅拌机中，温度控制在100~120℃；3)造粒：将上述搅拌料在热分解点以下温度，然后反复熔炼；4)成型：在模具中成型，温度控制在180~200℃左右。应用本发明的工艺制造的塑料型材硬密度高，抗冲击能力强、韧性好、表面光亮如镜，纹路自然高雅、不褪色、不褪光、不老化。
【名称】 一种低铅塑料型材及其制备方法
【公开(公告)号】 CN102408647A
【公开(公告)日】 2012.04.11
【申请(专利权)人】 芜湖海杉型材有限公司
【地址】 安徽省芜湖市芜湖县赵桥工业园
【发明(设计)人】 左胜贵；黄小军；阴其路；朱青松
【摘要】 本发明公开了一种低铅塑料型材及其制备方法，其主要是将组成原料聚氯乙烯树脂、低铅复合稳定剂、凹凸棒土、碳酸钙、丙烯酸酯类抗冲改性剂ACR、钛白粉、硬脂酸、聚乙烯蜡、紫外线吸收剂和颜料按一定重量份依次通过混料反应和加温造型处理得到成品。本发明制备方法简单，配方合理，本发明制备的低铅塑料型材具有良好散热性能、拉伸性能好，可以有效的应用于各行各业中。
【名称】 高填充PVC木塑发泡地板及其制备方法
【公开(公告)号】 CN102408648A
【公开(公告)日】 2012.04.11
【申请(专利权)人】 北京欧尼克新型材料有限公司
【地址】 北京市通州区漷县镇漷兴四街1号
【发明(设计)人】 韩伟；黄振海
【摘要】 本发明公开了一种高填充PVC木塑发泡地板及其制备方法，该木塑发泡地板由以下重量份数的塑料、有机填料、助剂、改性剂、发泡剂等原料制成，所述木塑发泡地板经热成型设备加热熔融后，在特殊结构的成型模具中发泡成为一种带有连续均匀分布泡微孔的新型木塑发泡地板产品。本发明所

提供的PVC木塑发泡地板具有质轻、比强度高、防水、防腐、保温的优点，并且具有木材可钉、可锯、可刨的加工特点；此外，其加工及配方成本低，可广泛用于建筑、运输、包装、家庭装饰及日用品市场。

【名称】 曲棍球注塑料及其制备方法
【公开(公告)号】 CN102408662A
【公开(公告)日】 2012.04.11
【申请(专利权)人】 江苏安格特新材料科技有限公司；常州阻燃材料工程技术研究中心有限公司
【地址】 江苏省常州市武进区遥观镇工业园区长虹路南
【发明(设计)人】 石明东；朱燕勤
【摘要】 本发明涉及热塑性弹性体注塑料及其制备方法，一种曲棍球注塑料，其特征在于，以质量百分数计，该组合物的组分包括：SBS弹性体树脂30%~40%、SEBS弹性体树脂5%~20%、POE5%~12%、填充油20%~45%、固体粉末填料10%~40%、相容剂0.1%~5%、抗氧剂0.1%~2%、加工助剂0.01%~2%。

【名称】 掺杂氮化铝的绝缘导热ABS复合材料及其制备
【公开(公告)号】 CN102408663A
【公开(公告)日】 2012.04.11
【申请(专利权)人】 上海亚明灯泡厂有限公司
【地址】 上海市嘉定区嘉新公路1001号
【发明(设计)人】 陈宇
【摘要】 本发明涉及绝缘导热塑料材料领域，公开了一种掺杂氮化铝的绝缘导热ABS复合材料及其制备方法，ABS复合材料的配方包括如下质量百分数的组分：ABS基体68%~95%，氮化铝粉末1%~30%，偶联剂1%~3%，润滑剂1%~3%。制备方法包括(1)AlN粉末的等离子表面活化处理；(2)制备偶联剂处理的AlN粉末；(3)AlN粉末与ABS基体母粒及润滑剂的混合；(4)注塑；(5)冷却。本发明的有益效果为利用氮化铝的良好的导热性及ABS的韧性、刚性、抗冲击性、抗腐蚀性；通过熔融共混法制得具有较高导热性、绝缘性和耐腐蚀性的氮化铝掺杂的ABS复合材料，作为LED灯具壳体的理想材料。

【名称】 一种粉煤灰纤维改性酚醛模塑料及其制造方法
【公开(公告)号】 CN102408669A
【公开(公告)日】 2012.04.11
【申请(专利权)人】 厦门柯依达工贸有限公司
【地址】 福建省厦门市翔安区内厝开发区324国道244公里处
【发明(设计)人】 林良菽；吴惠生；林丽荣
【摘要】 一种粉煤灰纤维改性酚醛模塑料及其制造方法，涉及一种酚醛模塑料。提供一种无公害、低成本的粉煤灰纤维改性酚醛模塑料及其制造方法。其原料组成和按质量百分比的含量为酚醛树脂25%~50%，固化剂4%~10%，固化促进剂0.5%~4%，粉煤灰纤维5%~25%，有机填料10%~45%，无机填料5%~30%，润滑剂1%~3%，阻燃剂0~10%，色料0~8%。将各原料粉碎后混合，得混合料；将混合料炼胶后，冷却，造粒，得粉煤灰纤维改性酚醛模塑料。

【名称】 一种无氨酚醛模塑料及其制备方法
【公开(公告)号】 CN102408670A
【公开(公告)日】 2012.04.11
【申请(专利权)人】 无锡创达电子有限公司
【地址】 江苏省无锡市新区城南路201-1号
【发明(设计)人】 翁根元
【摘要】 本发明公开了一种无氨酚醛模塑料及其制备方法，其原料组分的配比为：酚醛树脂100份、高岭土30~50份、玻璃纤维140~180份、硬脂酸3~8份、丁腈橡胶10~20份，还可以加入少量固化促进剂、颜料等助剂。把以上各组分配比混合均匀后，通过加热熔融，经过捏合、混炼、粉碎后得到不规则颗粒状的无氨酚醛模塑料。本发明的优点在于利用本发明制备的无氨酚醛模塑料，具有良好的耐热性、高的机械强度、低的成型收缩率和尺寸稳定性；并且在生产和模压成型过程中无氨气释放，具有环保的特点。

【名称】 一种电子器件封装用塑料膜成型工艺
【公开(公告)号】 CN102408674A
【公开(公告)日】 2012.04.11
【申请(专利权)人】 大连方盛塑料有限公司
【地址】 辽宁省大连市金州区站前街道吴屯机场
【发明(设计)人】 梁继鹏
【摘要】 本发明公开了一种电子器件封装用塑料膜成型工艺，将环氧树脂和酚醛树脂按比例混合，加入无机添加料和固化促进剂成型，所述环氧树脂和酚醛树脂的质量比为(45~60)∶(25~30)，所述无机添加料的添加量占树脂总重的0.5%~10%，固化促进剂的添加量占树脂总重的0.03%~0.10%。所述无机添加剂为炭黑或者结晶型硅微粉或者两者的混合物。所述固化促进剂为有机酸酐与咪唑衍生物络合盐。本发明的有益效果是：该封装电子器件用塑料产品具有交联密度高，收缩率小，粘结力强，致密性高，耐热性和电性能好，可靠性高等优点，有机酸酐与咪唑衍生物络合盐制备工艺简单，贮存稳定，无毒，成本低。

【名称】 一种环保型环氧模塑料及其制备方法
【公开(公告)号】 CN102408676A
【公开(公告)日】 2012.04.11
【申请(专利权)人】 无锡创达电子有限公司
【地址】 江苏省无锡市新区城南路201-1号
【发明(设计)人】 马和平
【摘要】 本发明公开了一种环保型环氧模塑料及其制备方法，该塑料原料包括以下组分：二氧化硅100份，环氧树脂10~12份，酚醛树脂5~7份，阻燃剂4~6份，2-甲基咪唑0.15~0.25份，硬脂酸0.6~1.0份，炭黑0.4~0.5份，r-缩水甘油醚三甲氧基硅烷0.4~0.6份。将上述原料混合25分钟，经双螺杆混炼机挤出，然后冷却至20~30℃，即制得环保型环氧模塑料。本发明的优点在于利用本发明得到的环氧模塑料，不含有背景技术所涉及的有害物质，具有环保的特点；并且此种环保型环氧模塑料具有成型性好，高填料低膨胀，并可达到UL94V-0的阻燃效果。

【名称】 高性能双抗片状模塑料及制造方法
【公开(公告)号】 CN102408692A
【公开(公告)日】 2012.04.11
【申请(专利权)人】 青岛润兴高分子材料有限公司
【地址】 山东省青岛市城阳区棘洪滩街道(青岛润兴塑料新材料有限公司2号厂房3楼)
【发明(设计)人】 张明连；李继红；金海木；刘英田
【摘要】 一种强度高，阻燃性能极好、抗静电能力强，从而实现以塑代钢、降低成本的高性能双抗片状模塑料，技术方案是：其特征是由下列重量份的原料组成：不饱和聚酯树脂100份、低收缩树脂30~50份、增强纤维玻璃纤维玄武岩纤维或者碳纤维120~180份、导电炭黑25~50份，氢氧化铝150~250份，氧化镁5~10份、脱模剂硬脂酸锌5~10份，消泡剂1~2份，固化剂1~2份，促进剂异辛酸钴0.5~2份、苯乙烯1~10份，偶联剂1~2份。高性能双抗片状模塑料的制造方法，包括下列步骤：(1)氢氧化铝处理；(2)树脂糊配制；(3)增稠剂配制；(4)浸渍制片；(5)熟化。本发明还公开了高性能双抗片状模塑料材料的制造方法。

【名称】 一种长余辉发光塑料的制备方法
【公开(公告)号】 CN102408700A
【公开(公告)日】 2012.04.11
【申请(专利权)人】 暨南大学
【地址】 广东省广州市天河区黄埔大道西601号
【发明(设计)人】 阳区；刘应亮；马文石；雷炳富；邓苏青；郑明涛；阳运华；崔江虎；胡超凡
【摘要】 本发明公开了一种长余辉发光塑料的制备方法。具体是采用有机改性处理的长余辉发光材料作为发光颜料，以热塑性聚氨酯为基料树脂，经过简单的塑化混合过程，即可得到长余辉发光聚氨酯塑料或发光聚氨酯塑料母粒，并在此基础上进一步通过该发光聚氨酯塑料母粒与其他高分子材料共混得到不同类型的长余辉发光塑料。该方法能解决无机发光粉体与塑料之间的相容性，且能避免发光塑料加工过程中发光粉体的发黑问题，所制备的长余辉发光塑料色泽均匀、力学性能和发光性能良好，可以广泛的应用于各种板材、软管、膜材、汽车零部件、鞋类服饰辅料及各种饰物等，起到弱光指示和装饰美化的作用。

【名称】 铁氧体/聚酰胺复合材料、其制备方法和应用
【公开(公告)号】 CN102408703A
【公开(公告)日】 2012.04.11
【申请(专利权)人】 深圳市科聚新材料有限公司
【地址】 广东省深圳市宝安区福永街道桥头富桥第三工业区二期C2、A19栋
【发明(设计)人】 徐东；徐永；杨海灵
【摘要】 本发明适用于工程塑料技术领域，提供了一种铁氧体/聚酰胺复合材料、其制备方法和应用。该铁氧体/聚酰胺复合材料，包括如下重量份数的组分：铁氧体磁粉72~92；聚酰胺5~17；环状聚酯2~7；偶联剂0.5~2；抗氧剂、润滑剂、分散剂、偶联剂及着色剂的混合物0.5~2。本发明铁氧体/聚酰胺复合材料，通过环状聚酯和偶联剂的改性作用，显著地增加了加工流动性，能够广泛的用于制作注塑产品，所注塑得到的产品具有优异机械性能，磁性能优异且稳定。本发明制备方法，操作简单、成本低廉，对设备要求低，非常适于工业化生产。

【名称】 一种多组分塑料连接器及其制造方法
【公开(公告)号】 CN102408706A
【公开(公告)日】 2012.04.11
【申请(专利权)人】 安徽宜万丰电器有限公司
【地址】 安徽省芜湖市弋江区高新技术产业开发区汽配路中段
【发明(设计)人】 吴康希；仇珍芳；章云；金川人；邵登
【摘要】 本发明公开了一种多组分塑料连接器及其制造方法，其主要是将干燥后的配比完成的原材料加入到已经升温的注塑机里，通过设定注塑机不同段的注射压力、速度、注射时间及注射胶量，同时设定好最后的保压压力及保压速度已达到最佳的注塑工艺，得到最终合格产品。本发明解决了注塑成

型的多组分塑料连接器在成型时产品易出现拉白、断裂、韧性差、强度低等物理性能缺陷，同时本注塑工艺稳定性，所得产品质量稳定，提高了生产效率，降低了生产成本。

【名称】 聚邻苯二甲酰胺长纤包覆增强材料的生产方法

【公开(公告)号】 CN102408708A

【公开(公告)日】 2012.04.11

【申请(专利权)人】 中山市纳普工程塑料有限公司

【地址】 广东省中山市东升镇兆益路

【发明(设计)人】 冯波；冯建棋

【摘要】 本发明涉及高分子材料技术领域，尤其涉及一种高强度、高耐温 PPA 增强材料的制备方法；包括以下步骤：a、按配比称取原辅料：聚邻苯二甲酰胺 36～63、浸润剂 0.3～0.6、抗氧剂 0.4～1.0、加工助剂 1.0～2.0；并进行干燥处理，其中聚邻苯二甲酰胺需用除湿干燥法，露点 -40℃，130～140℃干燥时间 5～6h，长玻纤烘干温度 120～130℃；将干燥好的塑料及辅料加入高混机，进行高速混合 3～5min；将高混好的原辅料加入到长纤包覆机的双螺杆进料口中塑化，再将长纤维经过模头浸润包覆到材料表面，长玻纤重量占总组份的 60～35 份，经拉条、切粒，制得产品。本发明通过选择特定的原材料，控制特定的工艺条件，生产出增强最的 PPA 玻纤增强材料，能够完全替代金属材料广泛应用。

【名称】 阻燃型高木质含量木塑复合材料及其制备方法

【公开(公告)号】 CN102408736A

【公开(公告)日】 2012.04.11

【申请(专利权)人】 东北林业大学

【地址】 黑龙江省哈尔滨市香坊区和兴路 26 号

【发明(设计)人】 宋永明；王清文；贾莹莹；王海刚；张志军

【摘要】 阻燃型高木质含量木塑复合材料及其制备方法，它涉及木塑复合材料及其制备方法。它解决了高木质含量的木塑复合材料易于燃烧且现有阻燃处理技术存在阻燃剂添加量大、阻燃效率不高、成本偏大的问题。材料由木质纤维用阻燃剂、木质纤维材料、热塑性塑料、塑料用阻燃剂、偶联剂、润滑剂、抗氧剂、抑烟剂和助剂制成。方法：称取原料；制阻燃处理液；制阻燃木质纤维材料；热塑性塑料和塑料用阻燃剂进行熔融造粒，得到阻燃热塑性塑料基体颗粒；阻燃木质纤维材料、阻燃热塑性塑料基体颗粒、偶联剂、润滑剂、抗氧剂、抑烟剂和助剂混合，得预混料；预混料进行熔融复合，得熔体材料；熔体材料成型后即得。本发明中阻燃剂用量少，阻燃效率高，成本低。

【名称】 溶剂型木质素或其衍生物改性模塑料及其制备方法

【公开(公告)号】 CN102408740A

【公开(公告)日】 2012.04.11

【申请(专利权)人】 程贤甦

【地址】 福建省福州市西江滨大道 66 号融侨锦江 C 区 7 号楼 701 单元

【发明(设计)人】 程贤甦

【摘要】 本发明提供了一种溶剂型木质素或其衍生物改性模塑料及其制备方法，将溶剂型木质素或其衍生物、塑化剂、填充剂、固化与固化促进剂、增塑剂、增韧剂和润滑剂共混，通过热压固化工艺或注射成型工艺制得溶剂型木质素或其衍生物改性模塑料。本发明采用溶剂型木质素或其衍生物能够部分甚至 100% 替代酚醛树脂，制得与酚醛模塑料性能相似的木质素改性模塑料，既可少用或不用酚、醛等石油化学品，降低石油资源的消耗以及模塑料的生产成本，尤其是用木质素或木质素衍生物完全替代酚醛时，不需要预先合成酚醛树脂，节水节能，减少含酚污水的污染，将会产生重大的社会效益；其加工工艺简单、容易实施，效果良好。

【名称】 塑料薄膜热密封胶带

【公开(公告)号】 CN102408847A

【公开(公告)日】 2012.04.11

【申请(专利权)人】 常熟市富邦胶带有限责任公司

【地址】 江苏省苏州市常熟市支塘镇工业北园区

【发明(设计)人】 沈加平

【摘要】 本发明公开了一种塑料薄膜热密封胶带，包括：基材薄膜层和压敏层，所述基材薄膜层是铁氟龙布薄膜层，所述压敏层是硅酮系列胶层，所述压敏层涂布在所述基材薄膜层的表面。本发明的塑料薄膜热密封胶带，具有良好的耐热性和机械强度、优异的电气特性、耐热性、耐气候性、防腐性、防水性、无毒性等特点，可在 -60～250℃的环境下使用，并达到无残胶，可反复使用，易于更换。

【名称】 利用废旧塑料生产石油产品的方法

【公开(公告)号】 CN102408905A

【公开(公告)日】 2012.04.11

【申请(专利权)人】 中国科学院广州能源研究所

【地址】 广东省广州市天河区五山能源路 2 号

【发明(设计)人】 陈新德；李洁；熊莲；张海荣；黄超；罗彩容；丁飞

【摘要】 本发明公开了一种利用废旧塑料生产石油产品的方法，包括如下步骤：1）将反应原料置于反应釜中，在真空条件下进行热裂解反应；2）热裂解反应结束后，冷却、沉降，脱除产物中的固体杂质，得到聚烯烃蜡；3)步骤2)得到的聚烯烃蜡与未完全裂解的原料，加入催化剂进行非临氢降凝反应；4)非临氢降凝反应得到的产物通过减压蒸馏进行切割分离，得到产品。本方法以废旧塑料为原料，采用热裂解、非临氢降凝两步法生产石油产品，从而提高产品的质量和收率，且非临氢降凝工艺不需要氢气循环系统及抗氢蚀设备，操作简便，节约成本。

【名称】 利用废旧塑料制备润滑油基础油的方法

【公开(公告)号】 CN102408906A

【公开(公告)日】 2012.04.11

【申请(专利权)人】 中国科学院广州能源研究所

【地址】 广东省广州市天河区五山能源路2号

【发明(设计)人】 陈新德；罗彩容；熊莲；张海荣；黄超；李洁；丁飞

【摘要】 本发明公开了一种废旧塑料制备润滑油基础油的方法，该方法以废旧塑料为原料，采用釜式热裂解、加氢异构反应、减压蒸馏等工艺制得高粘度指数润滑油基础油。原料在反应釜中热裂解得到聚烯烃蜡，所得的聚烯烃蜡和氢气在釜式或固定床反应器中进行加氢异构制备高粘度指数润滑油基础油，其中所用的加氢异构催化剂为负载过渡金属活性组分的氢型分子筛催化剂，过渡金属活性组分含量为0.1t% ~10t%，具有较高的加氢异构催化活性。本发明通过常规设备和可行工艺使废旧塑料实现高附加值资源回收利用的目的，适于推广应用。

【名称】 塑料制品的制备方法及塑料制品

【公开(公告)号】 CN102409319A

【公开(公告)日】 2012.04.11

【申请(专利权)人】 比亚迪股份有限公司

【地址】 广东省深圳市坪山新区比亚迪路3009号

【发明(设计)人】 宫清；周良；苗伟峰；张雄

【摘要】 本发明公开一种塑料制品的制备方法，该方法包括：1)成型塑料基体；塑料基体中含有化学镀促进剂；化学镀促进剂为Ni_2O_3、Co_2O_3、$CuSiO_3$、CuC_2O_4、Cu/Fe/Mn或Cu/Fe/Al三元共烧结氧化物、Cu/Fe/Al/Mn四元共烧结氧化物的一种或多种；2)激光气化塑料基体表面，裸露出化学镀促进剂；3)化学镀铜或化学镀镍，继续进行至少一次化学镀和/或电镀，在塑料基体表面形成金属层。本发明提供的制备方法，工艺简单，对能量要求低，成本低廉；另外，化学镀促进剂分布于塑料基体中，所以化学镀后形成的镀层与塑料基体的结合力非常高。本发明进一步公开了由上述方法所制备的塑料制品。

【名称】 一种ABS塑料表面电镀前处理的方法

【公开(公告)号】 CN102409320A

【公开(公告)日】 2012.04.11

【申请(专利权)人】 沈阳工业大学

【地址】 辽宁省沈阳市经济技术开发区沈辽西路111号

【发明(设计)人】 孙硕；徐炳辉；于锦；刘聪颖；温宇；洪文英

【摘要】 本发明涉及一种ABS塑料表面电镀前处理的方法，其电镀前处理工艺流程如下：去除应力，碱洗除油，酸洗，粗化，中和处理，化学活化，常规电镀；其中化学活化是将塑料基材放入活化溶液中，在水浴中升温处理一定时间；活化溶液配方为：硫酸镍10~12g/L，次磷酸钠20~25g/L，柠檬酸钠5~8g/L，pH=9~11，温度为70~75℃。本发明是一种不使用金属钯活化的新方法，还可取代硼氢化钠及甲醇活化工艺，有利于环保；在此前处理的基础上可实现直接电镀，解决了处理过程复杂，使用$PdCl_2$价格昂贵，容易污染镀液等问题。

【名称】 一种高效抗弯折新型塑料排水板

【公开(公告)号】 CN102409661A

【公开(公告)日】 2012.04.11

【申请(专利权)人】 青岛理工大学

【地址】 山东省青岛市四方区抚顺路11号

【发明(设计)人】 耿雪玉；冀言亮；于洁；耿雪川

【摘要】 本发明涉及软土地基处理过程中所用的塑料排水板，是一种新型的纵向排水体。此高效抗弯折新型塑料排水板，其特征在于包括十字形芯板和滤膜。此高效抗弯折新型塑料排水板能够防止在土体中发生弯折堵塞现象、增大与土体接触面积从而加速排水、而且非常环保。即以圆柱状结合点5为中心，粘贴上十字形芯板面2和滤膜，可以增加塑料排水板的强度，防止发生弯折堵塞现象；十字形芯板上粘贴着由许多凸起3一起组成的排水通道4使排水路径增多，有利于水的排出；高效抗弯折新型塑料排水板所使用的材料是可降解的材料，会在一段时间后自行降解消失，有利于土地的再次开发利用。

【名称】 一种三维塑料拉伸网及其制作方法

【公开(公告)号】 CN102409687A

【公开(公告)日】 2012.04.11

【申请(专利权)人】 王奇伟

【地址】 江西省南昌市东湖区一纬路53号3单元102室

【发明(设计)人】 王奇伟

【摘要】 本发明涉及一种三维塑料拉伸网，包括筋条、肋条和由筋条及肋条交叉分隔而成的正方形、矩形、圆形、椭圆形、菱形、直角三角形或正三角形网格孔，在单向、双向、三向或者四向的三维塑料拉伸网的肋条/筋条的交叉节点上或者在肋条/筋条上设有与肋条/筋条熔合为一体的凸缘，凸缘的形状包括半球凸缘、圆锥凸缘、圆锥台凸缘、多边棱锥凸缘、台面为多边形的棱锥台凸缘。其制作方法包括制备带有凸缘的初始料带、冲孔、加热、纵向拉伸、横向拉伸和收卷成品。本发明用于道路拓宽、加筋挡墙、铺设在河道底部或边坡，能提高抗拔力、固土、防冲刷、抗坍滑；比传统的二维平面拉伸网增强固土效果及垂直抗压性能、提高拉伸断裂强度、增加排水通量。

【名称】 小型塑料清洗机

【公开(公告)号】 CN102416676A

【公开(公告)日】 2012.04.18

【申请(专利权)人】 栾清杨

【地址】 辽宁省大连市西岗区双兴街25号

【发明(设计)人】 李晶晶

【摘要】 小型塑料清洗机，属于废旧塑料回收再利用设备技术领域，包括不锈钢机体，机体上部连接进料口，机体内部设置一根螺杆，螺杆由机体外部的电机带动转动，且螺杆分成两部分，靠近进料口的部分设置搅拌杆，另一部分设置宽螺纹，机体下部设置污水管，机体右上部设置出料口，出料口连接导料管，导料管下部连接水管，导料管连接输料管，导料管和输料管的连接处连接一段风筒，风筒的另一端连接一台强力风机，输料管的另一端连接干燥塔，干燥塔的出料口上部连接热风机，热风机向干燥塔内吹热空气。本发明结构简单，操作方便，利用螺杆的搅拌及推动作用，可以节省工序，且使物料清洗干净。

【名称】 塑料的磁性成型方法

【公开(公告)号】 CN102416685A

【公开(公告)日】 2012.04.18

【申请(专利权)人】 中煤科工集团重庆研究院

【地址】 重庆市九龙坡区二郎科城路6号

【发明(设计)人】 刘小林；刘罡；李天明；陈健；李宝鹏；叶淑英；肖利群

【摘要】 本发明公开了一种塑料磁性成型方法，包括磁性功能材料制备-塑化注入-充磁牵引-保压冷却固化工艺，将多磁性功能材料作为母料按既定比例与其它基体树脂(塑料)混合，通过注塑机塑化后注入具有加热功能的模具型腔内，同时利用充磁机对模具型腔内的熔体进行充磁，使得熔体内处于半熔态的磁性功能材料获得磁性，趋向于向产品表面运动，从而使大多数的磁性材料富集于产品表面，然后经保压后冷却固化，经脱模得到制品；该方法对注射机、挤出机和模具均无特殊要求，原材料树脂可随意更换，可在功能助剂添加量较小的情况下达到常规注塑成型制品相同的效果，同时降低了成本和加工难度，较好的保持了树脂本体原有的性能，适合于各种制品。

【名称】 再生料生产内镶贴片式滴灌管的方法及内镶贴片式滴灌管

【公开(公告)号】 CN102416693A

【公开(公告)日】 2012.04.18

【申请(专利权)人】 高利强

【地址】 宁夏回族自治区贺兰县创业基地水源街4号

【发明(设计)人】 高利强

【摘要】 一种内镶贴片式滴灌管，包括输水管、滴头。输水管包括再生料部分、PE原料部分，再生料部分、PE原料部分之间紧密结合构成输水管，滴头安装在输水管的PE原料部分上。本发明还提供了一种利用再生料生产内镶贴片式滴灌管的方法。本发明提供利用再生料生产内镶贴片式滴灌管的方法及内镶贴片式滴灌管，采用二次回收的塑料作为主料、PE原料作为辅料生产滴灌管，滴头贴设在输水管的PE原料部分上，如此滴头能够牢固的贴设在采用二次回收塑料制成的滴灌管，进而降低内镶贴片式滴灌管生产成本及降低环境污染。

【名称】 环保型PET-PBS光亮膜

【公开(公告)号】 CN102416741A

【公开(公告)日】 2012.04.18

【申请(专利权)人】 江苏立霸实业股份有限公司

【地址】 江苏省无锡市宜兴市环保科技工业园画溪路88号

【发明(设计)人】 卢凤仙

【摘要】 环保型PET-PBS光亮膜，涉及一种复合于金属板材或建筑材料上的装饰保护膜，底层塑料膜层、着色层、粘合剂层、印刷层、PET膜层依次层状叠加排布，底层塑料膜层为PBS膜，不会造成白色污染，各种有害气体渗出能力弱，利用膜的密闭性使得金属和空气隔绝起到完全防腐作用，该膜可以根据需要印刷各种图案和颜色，且表面有多种光泽度，展示多姿多彩的装饰效果。

【名称】 基体中埋设有导电纤维毡的塑料制品

【公开(公告)号】 CN102416743A

【公开(公告)日】 2012.04.18

【申请(专利权)人】 上海科斗电子科技有限公司

【地址】 上海市闵行区元江路5500号第2幢577室

【发明(设计)人】 孙倩倩

【摘要】 本发明涉及塑料，基体中埋设有导电纤维毡的塑料制品，包括塑料基体，塑料基体中埋设有导电纤维层，所述导电纤维层是导电纤维织成的导电纤维毡。基体中埋设有导电纤维毡的塑料制品，比目前常用的金属外壳，具有重量轻、易于加工、成本低的优点，由于采用了上述技术方案，本发明既具有塑料产品易于成形的特点，也具有导电材料才具备的电磁屏蔽防辐射的特点。

【名称】 一种食品包装塑料基材薄膜及其生产工艺

【公开(公告)号】 CN102416744A

【公开(公告)日】 2012.04.18

【申请(专利权)人】 大连方盛塑料有限公司

【地址】 辽宁省大连市金州区站前街道吴屯机场

【发明(设计)人】 梁继鹏

【摘要】 本发明涉及一种食品包装塑料基材薄膜，包括内层、中间层和外层三层结构；所述的内层采用低密度聚乙烯LDPE、线性低密度聚乙烯LLDPE和茂金属线性低密度聚乙烯mLLDPE制成，所述的中间层采用低密度聚乙烯LDPE和线性低密度聚乙烯LLDPE制成，所述的外层采用茂金属线性低密度聚乙烯mLLDPE制成。其生产工艺包括混合进料挤出、吹膜、定型、牵引切割等步骤。本发明设计的食品包装塑料基材薄膜提供一种高阻隔性、高气密性、抗污染性、热封性能好，耐压性和耐冲击性好，符合食品安全认证的食品包装袋料基材薄膜。

【名称】 一种食品包装的塑料基材薄膜及其加工工艺

【公开(公告)号】 CN102416745A

【公开(公告)日】 2012.04.18

【申请(专利权)人】 大连方盛塑料有限公司

【地址】 辽宁省大连市金州区站前街道吴屯机场

【发明(设计)人】 梁继鹏

【摘要】 本发明公开了一种食品包装的塑料基材薄膜，由内层、中间层和外层三层共挤吹塑而成，所述内层原料包括LDPE低密度聚乙烯、LLDPE线性低密度聚乙烯和mLLDPE茂金属线性低密度聚乙烯，所述中间层和外层原料均为LDPE低密度聚乙烯和LLDPE线性低密度聚乙烯。本发明的食品包装塑料基材薄膜阻隔性和气密性好，具有好的抗污染性、耐压性和耐冲击性，同时具有热封强度高、热封性能好的特点，符合国家食品安全认证。本发明的食品包装塑料基材薄膜生产工艺，设计合理，流程简单，易于实现。

【名称】 一种食品包装的塑料基材薄膜及其加工工艺

【公开(公告)号】 CN102416746A

【公开(公告)日】 2012.04.18

【申请(专利权)人】 大连方盛塑料有限公司

【地址】 辽宁省大连市金州区站前街道吴屯机场

【发明(设计)人】 梁继鹏

【摘要】 本发明公开了一种食品包装的塑料基材薄膜，由内层、中间层和外层三层共挤吹塑而成，所述内层原料包括LDPE低密度聚乙烯、HDPE高密度聚乙烯和mLLDPE茂金属线性低密度聚乙烯，所述中间层和外层原料均为LDPE低密度聚乙烯和HDPE高密度聚乙烯。本发明的食品包装塑料基材薄膜阻隔性和气密性好，具有好的抗污染性、耐压性和耐冲击性，同时具有热封强度高、热封性能好的特点，符合国家食品安全认证。本发明的食品包装塑料基材薄膜生产工艺，设计合理，流程简单，易于实现。

【名称】 一种食品包装的塑料基材薄膜及其加工工艺

【公开(公告)号】 CN102416747A

【公开(公告)日】 2012.04.18

【申请(专利权)人】 大连方盛塑料有限公司

【地址】 辽宁省大连市金州区站前街道吴屯机场

【发明(设计)人】 梁继鹏

【摘要】 本发明公开了一种食品包装的塑料基材薄膜，由内层、中间层和外层三层共挤吹塑而成，所述内层、中间层和外层中均包括下述原料，LDPE低密度聚乙烯和LLDPE线性低密度聚乙烯。所述内层中LDPE和LLDPE质量比为(65－75)：(25－35)；所述中间层中LDPE和LLDPE质量比为(35－45)：(55－65)；所述外层中LDPE和LLDPE质量比为(30－40)：(60－70)。本发明的食品包装塑料基材薄膜阻隔性和气密性好，具有好的抗污染性、耐压性和耐冲击性，同时具有热封强度高、热封性能好的特点，符合国家食品安全认证。

【名称】 一种食品包装的塑料基材薄膜及其加工工艺

【公开(公告)号】 CN102416748A

【公开(公告)日】 2012.04.18

【申请(专利权)人】 大连方盛塑料有限公司

【地址】 辽宁省大连市金州区站前街道吴屯机场

【发明(设计)人】 梁继鹏

【摘要】 本发明公开了一种食品包装的塑料基材薄膜，包括下述原料：LDPE低密度聚乙烯，LLDPE线性低密度聚乙烯和mLLDPE茂金属线性聚乙烯，其质量比为LDPE: LLDPE: mLLDPE＝(15～25)：(40～45)：(34～40)。本发明的食品包装塑料基材薄膜阻隔性和气密性好，具有好的抗污染性、耐压性和耐冲击性，同时具有热封强度高、热封性能好的特点，符合国家食品安全认证。而且，本发明的食品包装塑料基材薄膜生产工艺，设计合理，流程简单，易于实现。

【名称】 一种无水泥浇注料用酰胺类结合剂

【公开(公告)号】 CN102417319A

【公开(公告)日】 2012.04.18

【申请(专利权)人】 河南省耕生耐火材料有限公司

【地址】 河南省开封市巩义市大峪沟镇工业区耕生大道88号

【发明(设计)人】 郑化；石凯；张顺庆；顾华志；周安宏；张诚

【摘要】 本发明涉及一种无水泥浇注料用酰胺类结合剂。它含有丙烯酰胺88.4%～90.0%、N－N′－亚甲基双丙烯酰胺8.4%～10.0%、过硫酸铵0.8%～1.0%、四甲基乙二胺配合物0.4%～6%。本发明酰胺类结合剂通过溶解于水中的方式加入浇注料中，有效的解决了浇注料表面粉化的问题，大大提高了浇注料的抗折强度和耐压强度；该结合剂适用于高铝质、刚玉质、碳化硅质等无水泥浇注料，也可适用于耐火捣打料、喷补料、喷射料、可塑料、火泥等形式的不定形耐火材料；添加本发明结合剂的耐火材料适用于砌筑冲天炉、铁水沟、混铁炉、钢包等部位；应用本发明酰胺类结合剂的浇注料脱模时间短、易于养护或免于养护，施工效率高，工艺简单。

【名称】 一种制备全降解淀粉塑料母料的方法

【公开(公告)号】 CN102417614A

【公开(公告)日】 2012.04.18

【申请(专利权)人】 河南省南街村(集团)有限公司

【地址】 河南省漯河市临颍县南街村颍松大道

【发明(设计)人】 李盘欣；郭斌；宋伟强；安保杰；黄亚男；李丹阳

【摘要】 本发明涉及一种制备全降解淀粉塑料母料的新方法。将天然淀粉首先在60Coγ射线辐射下进行处理，以此破坏其微观结构，提高可塑性；进一步，将辐照后的淀粉与一定比例的可降解的增塑剂混合，在双螺杆挤出机塑化挤出，冷却后造粒，即得全降解淀粉塑料母料。该母料可用来制备各种全降解塑料制品，如塑料包装制品，一次性快餐盒及农用地膜等。辐射法制备全降解淀粉塑料母料，具有操作简单、可室温进行、易于大批量生产等特点，还可通过控制辐射吸收剂量来调整淀粉分子量、制品的耐水性、稳定性等性能，应用前景十分广阔。

【名称】 生物可降解塑料

【公开(公告)号】 CN102417615A

【公开(公告)日】 2012.04.18

【申请(专利权)人】 吴江市天源塑胶有限公司

【地址】 江苏省苏州市吴江市黎里镇工业园区牌楼桥堍

【发明(设计)人】 肖伟荣

【摘要】 本发明公开一种生物可降解塑料。本发明属于塑料制备技术领域。本发明的生物可降解塑料是由60%～80%几内丁，19.5%～39.5%淀粉和0.5%～10%热聚性聚合物组成。所述生物可降解塑料堆积密度为10～20kg/m^3。所述热聚性聚合物是在淀粉中可溶的聚合物。本发明的有益效果是：生物可降解塑料组成成分为天然大分子，无毒、环保；加工设备简单，反应条件温和；制成的生物可降解塑料，韧性较强，在自然条件下不易霉变。

【名称】 一种防霉塑料及制备工艺

【公开(公告)号】 CN102417647A

【公开(公告)日】 2012.04.18

【申请(专利权)人】 吴江市天源塑胶有限公司

【地址】 江苏省苏州市吴江市黎里镇工业园区牌楼桥堍

【发明(设计)人】 肖伟荣

【摘要】 本发明公开一种防霉塑料及制备工艺，本发明涉及塑料材料的制备领域。一种防霉塑料，所述防霉塑料由1%～2%防霉剂，70%～80%树脂，18%～28%增塑剂组成。所述的防霉剂由20%苯酚，20%8－羟基喹啉铜、30%氯化三乙或三丁基锡，10%已唑醇、10%戊菌唑等组成。所述的树脂由聚乙烯或聚丙烯组成。所述的增塑剂为磷酸酯类。制备工艺包括(1)混合：将防霉剂，树脂，增塑剂按照等比递增方式将各种原料均匀混合。(2)塑炼：温度为200～280℃，剪切时间5小时。(3)切粒。

【名称】 一种可生物降解的聚乙烯塑料膜

【公开(公告)号】 CN102417648A

【公开(公告)日】 2012.04.18

【申请(专利权)人】 吴江明峰聚氨酯制品有限公司

【地址】 江苏省苏州市吴江北厍镇玩字村

【发明(设计)人】 费近峰

【摘要】 本发明涉及一种可生物降解的聚乙烯塑料膜，其特征在于包含以下组份：低密度聚乙烯100份、羟丙基变性淀粉20～50份、填料10～20份、增容剂10～20份、增塑剂10～15份、硅烷类偶联剂1～10份、硬脂酸锌0.5～5份。将羟丙基变性淀粉、碳酸钙颗粒粉碎至粒度为20～200目，加入偶联剂、增容剂，混合均匀，备用；加入低密度聚乙烯以及其他助剂，混合均匀；将原料混合物混炼、造粒、挤出吹胀、冷却、牵引、卷取，获得可生物降解的聚乙烯塑料膜。本发明获得的可生物降解的聚乙烯塑料膜耐水性好，能够在短期内完全降解，是可降解、环保材料。

【名称】 一种用多层石墨作为填料的高导热复合塑

料的制备方法
【公开(公告)号】 CN102417649A
【公开(公告)日】 2012.04.18
【申请(专利权)人】 广东工业大学
【地址】 广东省广州市番禺区广州大学城外环西路100号
【发明(设计)人】 张海燕；涂文英；洪浩群；曾国勋；陈易明；林锦
【摘要】 本发明公开了一种用多层石墨作为填料的高导热复合塑料的制备方法，该方法有如下步骤：先将开炼机或锥形双螺杆挤出机加热到预定温度，将塑料放在开炼机或锥形双螺杆挤出机上搅拌，加入导热填料，待塑料与导热填料混合均匀后，取出混合材料压模制样或注射成型，即得到高导热复合塑料；本发明的导热填料是鳞片形多层石墨，具有超大的形状比和优异的润滑性能、高强度的力学性能以及极佳导热性能；此鳞片多层石墨相对于石墨，在与塑料混炼中更易于形成导热网链；高导热复合塑料基体是聚乙烯或聚乙烯接枝马来酸酐，价格便宜，易加工；本发明的高导热复合塑料具有优良的化学稳定性，热分解温度高，操作简单，导热系数高。
【名称】 一种低烟无卤阻燃注塑料及其制备方法
【公开(公告)号】 CN102417653A
【公开(公告)日】 2012.04.18
【申请(专利权)人】 福建陶金峰新材料有限公司
【地址】 福建省三明市泰宁县上青工业园区
【发明(设计)人】 吴良芳；肖友霞；王喜锋
【摘要】 本发明提供一种低烟无卤阻燃注塑料，由原料共混后挤出制得，所述原料的组分及各组分的重量百分含量为：EVA：40%～60%，氢氧化铝：10%～20%，氢氧化镁：20%～30%，抗氧剂1010：1%～2%，硬脂酸钡：2%～3%，端胺基多元醇酯：5%～7%。所述低烟无卤阻燃注塑料的制备方法是将上述原料混合均匀，然后将混合原料用挤出机挤出造粒制得低烟无卤阻燃注塑料。所述低烟无卤阻燃注塑料不但具有优良的阻燃性能，且材料中不含卤素，燃烧时不会释放出大量的烟雾和卤化氢气体，具有良好的安全和环保性能，同时该低烟无卤阻燃注塑料还具有较好的机械性能和工艺性能，适用于分支电缆、电器设备等领域。
【名称】 一种可完全转移镀铝层的BOPP镀铝基膜
【公开(公告)号】 CN102417655A
【公开(公告)日】 2012.04.18
【申请(专利权)人】 上海金浦塑料包装材料有限公司
【地址】 上海市金山区卫二路140号
【发明(设计)人】 余小双；张金忠；张瑾瑾；陈滨
【摘要】 本发明属于塑料薄膜加工制备领域，具体涉及一种可完全转移镀铝层的BOPP镀铝基膜的功能母料及其制备工艺，其特征在于包括以下组份(重量份)：基础树脂100份；爽滑剂2～3份；防粘连剂1～15份，将爽滑剂和防粘连剂与基础树脂在高混机中进行充分混合均匀，然后经过挤出机熔融塑化后，经过扁长模头挤出，挤出温度为：250～270℃，熔体经过激冷辊以及水浴冷却后形成厚片。随后对厚片进行双向拉伸，最后冷却即得到BOPP镀铝基膜。本发明制备的BOPP镀铝基膜其镀铝层可完全转移到纸张或其他薄膜上，并且可以多次转移，既环保又节约原料。
【名称】 一种聚丙烯汽车保险杠用专用料的制备方法
【公开(公告)号】 CN102417660A
【公开(公告)日】 2012.04.18
【申请(专利权)人】 吴江明峰聚氨酯制品有限公司
【地址】 江苏省苏州市吴江北厍镇玩字村
【发明(设计)人】 费近峰
【摘要】 本发明公开了一种聚丙烯汽车保险杠用专用料的制备方法，该方法包括如下步骤：将160～165质量份PP、30～35质量份聚乙烯、10～15质量份POE、10～15质量份滑石粉、10～20质量份钛酸酯偶联剂、10质量份抗氧化剂和10质量份己二酸搅拌混合，将混合均匀的物料由双杆同向平行塑料挤出机，机身温度：200～210℃，机头温度：204～209℃，挤出后的材料在水温为30～45℃的水中冷却，即得。本发明方法工艺简单，便于大规模生产，且该方法生产出的产品具有较高的流动性、刚性、韧性、耐热性等，还要有良好的尺寸稳定性和抗老化性能。
【名称】 纳米碳酸钙填充的低烟阻燃PS发泡塑料
【公开(公告)号】 CN102417669A
【公开(公告)日】 2012.04.18
【申请(专利权)人】 吴江明峰聚氨酯制品有限公司
【地址】 江苏省苏州市吴江北厍镇玩字村
【发明(设计)人】 费近峰
【摘要】 本发明涉及一种纳米碳酸钙填充的低烟阻燃PS发泡塑料，其特征在于包括以重量份计的以下组份：PS80～90份、LDPE10～20份、填料10～30份、钛酸酯偶联剂1～5份、液体石蜡5～25份、EVA蜡1～5份、抗氧剂0.1～1.5份、光稳定剂0.1～05份、润滑剂0.1～0.5份、司盘601～5份、阻燃剂5～15份、甲基乙烯基硅橡胶1～10份；所述的填料为纳米碳酸钙；润滑剂为硬脂酸；所述的阻燃剂为 Sb_2O_3 与 $Mg(OH)_2$ 的等质量混合物；所述的光稳定剂为炭黑。本发明获得的PS塑料具有良好的阻燃性，且拉伸强度、断裂伸长率、弹性模量良好。

【名称】 一种高强度PVC非开挖管件的制备工艺
【公开(公告)号】 CN102417671A
【公开(公告)日】 2012.04.18
【申请(专利权)人】 上海远洲管业有限公司
【地址】 上海市卢湾区中山南一路500弄丽都大厦一号楼1107室
【发明(设计)人】 张双全；周文忠；王锡臣
【摘要】 本发明公开了：一种高强度PVC非开挖管件的制备工艺，其特点是该管件由100份聚氯乙烯树脂；1～3份丙烯酸树脂；5～10份氯化聚氯乙烯；1～5份精对苯二甲酸—新戊二醇共聚物；3～5份稳定剂；1～8份抗冲改性剂；5～15份工程塑料；1～5份增容剂；0.5～1.5份润滑剂；1～5份填充剂；0.05～1份交联剂；所述组分按重量份配比后经混合搅拌和模具注塑而成。本发明与现有技术相比具制备工艺简单，操作方便，耐低温韧性提高100～200%，常温抗冲强度提高100～150%，拉伸强度提高30～60%，维长软化点提高5～15℃，使用寿命延长10～20年。

【名称】 一种淀粉基可降解塑料母粒及制备和发泡塑料的方法
【公开(公告)号】 CN102417688A
【公开(公告)日】 2012.04.18
【申请(专利权)人】 南昌大学
【地址】 江西省南昌市红谷滩新区学府大道999号
【发明(设计)人】 李建科；杨有仙；高炜丽；赵燕；邓文辉；王俊杰
【摘要】 一种淀粉基可降解塑料母粒及制备和发泡塑料的方法，下列组分按质量份：玉米淀粉50～150份、丙烯酸甲酯5～30份、硝酸铈铵0.5～3份、蒸馏水100～200份。将玉米淀粉烘至恒重，丙烯酸甲酯除去阻聚剂，60～67℃、84.513KPa蒸馏，无水 $NaSO_4$ 干燥；用蒸馏水调玉米淀粉，取20%加入反应器中，排空气、通氮气并搅拌；调pH≤3.0，将硝酸铈铵用稀硝酸配成溶液，取90%加入反应器中，搅拌，再加丙烯酸甲酯，搅拌，再加入剩余的玉米淀粉和硝酸铈铵，通氮气，30～40℃，搅拌反应1～2h；调pH6.5～7.5，终止反应，造粒；按质量份数塑料母粒100份、偶氮二甲酰胺0.5～2份、聚甘油酯2～6份，50℃混合，发泡成型。本发明兼具有合成和天然高分子优良性能，且生物降解速度快，加工性能优越，适应性好，工艺简单，成本低，且不含PP、PE、PS。

【名称】 棉纤维增强注射型酚醛模塑料及其制备方法
【公开(公告)号】 CN102417692A
【公开(公告)日】 2012.04.18
【申请(专利权)人】 桂林电器科学研究院
【地址】 广西壮族自治区桂林市七星区辰山路1号
【发明(设计)人】 王明军；钟立松；陈武荣；刘有龙
【摘要】 本发明公开了一种棉纤维增强注射型酚醛模塑料及其制备方法。该酚醛模塑料由下述重量配比的组分制成：线型酚醛树脂100；六次甲基四胺10～20；无机填料20～90；长度为1～10mm的棉纤维25～65；促进剂0.5～8；润滑剂1～8；染料0～10。本发明所述模塑料以线型酚醛树脂为基体材料，选用特定长度的棉纤维作为增强材料，并仅以六次甲基四胺为固化剂，通过添加适当用量的无机填料和促进剂，使塑料在具有快速固化能力的同时又能保持塑料在注射机料筒中的良好热稳定性，从而使该塑料能够注射成型；产品工艺性好，且成型所得的产品具有较好的耐磨性和力学性能。

【名称】 一种塑料合金材料组合物、塑料合金材料及注塑件
【公开(公告)号】 CN102417699A
【公开(公告)日】 2012.04.18
【申请(专利权)人】 比亚迪股份有限公司
【地址】 广东省深圳市坪山新区比亚迪路3009号
【发明(设计)人】 周翔磊；李江辉；彭程
【摘要】 本发明公开了一种塑料合金材料组合物及由该组合物制备得到的塑料合金材料，以及采用该塑料合金材料经注塑得到的注塑件，该组合物包括聚乳酸、聚碳酸酯、丙烯腈-苯乙烯-丁二烯共聚物、相容剂，所述相容剂为马来酸酐接枝的丙烯腈-丁二烯-苯乙烯三元共聚物和/或马来酸酐接枝的聚丁二烯-乙烯-丁烯三元共聚物，其中，所述聚丁二烯-乙烯-丁烯三元共聚物的封端为聚苯乙烯。通过该组合物制得的塑料合金材料的塑性较好，采用该组合物制备的注塑件的外观较好，可直接作为一些电子产品的表面。

【名称】 相容剂及其制备方法、包含该相容剂的合金、制备方法
【公开(公告)号】 CN102417717A
【公开(公告)日】 2012.04.18
【申请(专利权)人】 上海日之升新技术发展有限公司
【地址】 上海市闵行区沪闵路3078号

【发明(设计)人】 汤俊杰；王尹杰；段浩；齐阳城

【摘要】 本发明提供了一种塑料合金用相容剂及制备方法，尤其涉及一种聚苯醚/聚丙烯合金用相容剂的制备，该相容剂是一种接枝物，由苯乙烯乙烯丁二烯嵌段共聚物、聚苯醚、马来酸酐单体、过氧化物引发剂和加工助剂发生接枝反应得到。将除过氧化物引发剂除外的其它组分如苯乙烯乙烯丁二烯嵌段共聚物、聚苯醚、马来酸酐单体和加工助剂按比例放入高速混合机中混合，然后将过氧化物通过主喂料加入到双螺杆挤出机中，引发剂通过侧喂料加入到挤出机中，经熔融塑化、捏合混炼、机头挤出、拉条、冷却、切粒、干燥，得到相容剂产品。将此相容剂与聚苯醚、聚丙烯、增韧剂和抗氧剂按比例放入混料机中混合，再加入到双螺杆挤出机中塑化挤出得到聚苯醚/聚丙烯合金。

【名称】 一种用于汽车的塑料连接器及其制造方法

【公开(公告)号】 CN102417723A

【公开(公告)日】 2012.04.18

【申请(专利权)人】 安徽宜万丰电器有限公司

【地址】 安徽省芜湖市弋江区高新技术产业开发区汽配路中段

【发明(设计)人】 吴康希；仇珍芳；章云；金川人；邵登

【摘要】 本发明公开了一种用于汽车的塑料连接器及其制造方法，其主要是将干燥后的配比完成的原材料加入到已经升温的注塑机里，通过设定注塑机不同段的注射压力、速度、注射时间及注射胶量，同时设定好最后的保压压力及保压速度已达到最佳的注塑工艺，得到最终合格产品。本发明解决了注塑成型的用于汽车的塑料连接器在成型时产品易出现拉白、断裂、韧性差、强度低等物理性能缺陷，同时本注塑工艺稳定性，所得产品质量稳定，提高了生产效率，降低了生产成本。

【名称】 聚氨酯填充枕保温大棚薄膜

【公开(公告)号】 CN102428848A

【公开(公告)日】 2012.05.02

【申请(专利权)人】 李志鹏

【地址】 黑龙江省哈尔滨市香坊区和兴路26号

【发明(设计)人】 李志鹏；郭艳玲；王海滨；詹长书；王茜

【摘要】 本聚氨酯填充枕保温大棚薄膜，是靠两层膜形成的独立填充枕中“吹入”聚氨酯小球和空气，作为隔冷保温层，以代替传统单层薄膜的塑料大棚薄膜。聚氨酯填充枕保温大棚薄膜由双层塑料薄膜构成充气枕的枕皮，枕芯填充空气和聚氨酯小球的混合物，起到保温作用。充气枕大棚保温膜中聚氨酯小球是循环封闭利用的，不会泄露和污染环境。每个充气枕有单独的通气口，用来向充气枕中吹入或吸出空气。通气口边设有电极，在从充气枕中吸气时，用来回收聚氨酯小球。所有通气口的充吸气、电极的工作由设备并联统一控制。使用本薄膜的塑料大棚，在冬季不再需要使用棉被保温，并且具有更好的抗积雪能力，有广阔的市场。

【名称】 废旧塑料造粒机用的斜体式气液两级分离器及分离方法

【公开(公告)号】 CN102430259A

【公开(公告)日】 2012.05.02

【申请(专利权)人】 洛阳骏腾能源科技有限公司；周强

【地址】 河南省洛阳市高新技术开发区丰华路银昆科技园5号楼105室

【发明(设计)人】 周强；周仁福；陶然

【摘要】 废旧塑料造粒机用的斜体式气液两级分离器及分离方法，由气体分离器和液体静置分离器组成，一个倾斜的分离板将液体静置分离器分隔为静置分离室和溢流室两部分，气体分离器为倾斜的管状结构，废气从气体分离器顶部的高温混合气体入口进入气体分离器的蛇形管气道，并与气体分离器的冷却水通道进行热交换，冷却的气体从气体分离器下部的排气口排出，冷却凝结的混合液体通过导流管进入静置分离室，静置分层后，不同比重的组分分别通过静置分离室和溢流室侧壁上的液体溢出口或液体静置分离器的底部的排污口排出。通过简单的结构方式，完成了废旧塑料造粒过程中高温混合废气中个组分的有效分离，实现了气体的净化、分离和资源的回收利用。

【名称】 连续自动化铝塑分离系统

【公开(公告)号】 CN102430566A

【公开(公告)日】 2012.05.02

【申请(专利权)人】 杭州富伦生态科技有限公司

【地址】 浙江省杭州市富阳市灵桥镇光明村羊家埭路9号

【发明(设计)人】 羊军

【摘要】 一种连续自动化铝塑分离系统，包括储水池、清水泵、回用水泵、排污泵、回水池、电器控制室，其特征在于包括上料输送带连打散器，打散器斜输送带，斜输送带连均料器，均料器连分选台，分选台连反应器，反应器连上料机，上料机连干离心机，干离心机连湿离心机、湿离心机出塑料料膜的出口连漂洗池、磨擦机、挤干机，湿离心机出铝粉的出口连离心过滤机，离心过滤机连1号净化池、2号净化池、3净化池；所述离心机连回酸池，净化池连回水池。本发明与现有技术相比，具有以下明显效果：1. 结构设计合理，自动化程度高；2. 可对铝塑复合膜废料进行连续有效的分离，并在整个系统中回收利用试剂和污水，实现循环利用。

【名称】 塑料异型管裁切机

【公开(公告)号】 CN102430782A

【公开(公告)日】 2012. 05. 02

【申请(专利权)人】 安徽中鼎橡塑制品有限公司

【地址】 安徽省宁国市经济技术开发区东城大道81号

【发明(设计)人】 夏玉洁；谢元喜；徐东法

【摘要】 本发明公开了一种塑料异型管裁切机，包括机架，所述机架上固定有直线导轨，所述直线导轨的滑块上固定有滑动板，所述的滑动板和固定在所述机架上的伸缩装置连接，所述的滑动板上表面固定有固定座，所述的固定座上安装有快速装夹钳，所述的机架上还设有电动机和一根可转动的旋转轴，所述的旋转轴上固定有锯片铣刀，所述的电动机通过连接装置带动所述的旋转轴旋转。其既能够保证使用者的人身安全，在锯片铣刀上方安装冷却水，排除了产品切割部位产生变形、不光滑毛刺严重等不良现象。

【名称】 一种用于在塑料件上粘接橡胶层的模具及运用该模具的生产方法

【公开(公告)号】 CN102431103A

【公开(公告)日】 2012. 05. 02

【申请(专利权)人】 厦门市金汤橡塑有限公司

【地址】 福建省厦门市湖里区禾山镇高殿村高崎五组

【发明(设计)人】 何龙河

【摘要】 本发明公开一种用于在塑料件上粘接橡胶层的模具及运用该模具的生产方法，包括上模、下模，下模上端面设有至少一个与待加工塑料件外形相对应的型腔，上模的下端面设有与下模上端面型腔相对应的型腔，下模上端面所述型腔的周边设有与上模下端面相密封的密封圈，所述下模上端面密封圈围成的空间内设有连通至外部抽真空设备的抽真空管路，上模中设有注入橡胶材料的通道，该通道由上模的外部连通至上模的下端面与下模上端面相对应的型腔中；运用上述模具的生产方法其关键工序在于注入橡胶材料和硫化的过程是在设定的真空状态下进行的；从而省去排气工序，提高硫化速度，进一步提高生产效率，降低模耗，提高产品的良品率。

【名称】 塑料门窗双头 V 型清角的加工设备及方法

【公开(公告)号】 CN102431110A

【公开(公告)日】 2012. 05. 02

【申请(专利权)人】 济南德佳机器有限公司

【地址】 山东省济南市历下区(高新区)齐鲁软件园创业广场 B 座 5 层 511 室

【发明(设计)人】 张修福

【摘要】 本发明公开了一种塑料门窗双头 V 型清角的加工设备及方法，包括固定机头、活动机头、传输机构和机架；活动机头沿导轨移动，通过内置伺服电机带动同步带移动，到位后刹紧和工进；固定机头固定在机架上，包括定位机构和铣削机构，定位机构包括左、右 45°定位装置、后定位装置和压紧装置；铣削机构包括按成窗 V 型焊口的水平方向呈 90°布置的左、右 45°数控轴、竖直数控轴及与其连接的 C 型架、对称并垂直布置的两排刀具；传输机构通过启动传输电机带动同步带实现传动功能。本发明将成窗通过传输机构送到两个机头之间，定位后实现窗框 V 型焊熘自动清理，具有定位准确、调整方便、适用于塑料门窗进行高自动化、高效率以及大批量生产的特点。

【名称】 全自动注拉吹塑料中空容器制品成型装置及方法

【公开(公告)号】 CN102431118A

【公开(公告)日】 2012. 05. 02

【申请(专利权)人】 乳山市五星塑料厂

【地址】 山东省威海市乳山市乳山口工业园

【发明(设计)人】 张守民

【摘要】 本发明属于塑料制品的加工技术领域，具体涉及一种全自动注拉吹塑料中空容器制品成型装置及方法，包括注塑机、机械手、吹瓶机和操控盘，注塑机和吹瓶机均具备自身独立控制系统，机械手在操控盘的控制下进行往复运作，三者联动实现自动化生产。本发明具有整个过程易实现、投资少，见效快，节能，省工等显著优点。

【名称】 大型双色注塑模具和注塑形式转换方法

【公开(公告)号】 CN102431124A

【公开(公告)日】 2012. 05. 02

【申请(专利权)人】 青岛海尔模具有限公司；海尔集团公司

【地址】 山东省青岛市崂山区高科园海尔路 1 号海尔工业园

【发明(设计)人】 张平；李传戈；黄俊；徐丽丽；王涛

【摘要】 本发明提供了一种大型双色注塑模具和注塑形式转换方法，属于塑料加工领域，为解决现有技术中，模具通用性较差，闲置并造成资源浪费的问题而设计。一种大型双色注塑模具，包括：相适应的第一前模顶板和第二前模顶板；与该第一前模顶板和该第二前模顶板相对应，设置有相适应的第一后模底板和第二后模底板；在所述第一前模顶板和所述第二前模顶板的连接边两侧边缘以及所述第一后模底板和所述第二后模底板的连接边两侧边缘相对应的设置有导向槽；所述导向槽内设置有连接所述第一前模顶板和第二前模顶板以及连接所述第一后模底板和所述第二后模底板的导向块。

【名称】 塑料瓶制造方法

【公开(公告)号】 CN102431147A

【公开(公告)日】 2012. 05. 02

【申请(专利权)人】 珠海天威飞马打印耗材有限公司

【地址】 广东省珠海市南屏科技工业园屏北一路32号

【发明(设计)人】 苏健强；汪继忠

【摘要】 本发明公开了一种塑料瓶制造方法，包括：注塑、吹塑、脱模三道工序；第一工位，将瓶坯料精确注塑出瓶嘴部分并对瓶体进行拉伸，得到预制瓶，模芯连同预制瓶转到第二工位；第二工位，在吹塑模具中用吹塑的方法生产出塑料瓶，吹塑模具包括不可吹塑的容腔及可吹塑的空腔，容腔的形状尺寸与瓶嘴部分相适配，瓶身置于空腔中，吹塑完成后再转到第三工位；在第三工位，进行脱模。本发明适用于生产瓶嘴成型精度高、便于与瓶盖实现密封要求的塑料瓶。

【名称】 塑料拉吹机双向同步升降开合模机构

【公开(公告)号】 CN102431154A

【公开(公告)日】 2012. 05. 02

【申请(专利权)人】 浙江宏振机械模具集团有限公司

【地址】 浙江省台州市黄岩区西城黄轴路47-1号

【发明(设计)人】 蔡业

【摘要】 塑料拉吹机双向同步升降开合模机构，包括塑料拉吹机机架底板和机架顶板，机架底板与机架顶板之间安装左定模板和右定模板，机架底板上滑动设置左动模板和右动模板，左定模板与左动模板之间连接左曲臂，右定模板与右动模板之间连接右曲臂，左动模板和右动模板对应的两侧分别安装左、右半爿模具，机架顶板上安装拉伸机构，所述的拉伸机构包括拉伸支架、拉伸杆和带动拉伸杆的拉伸气缸，机架底板中安装底模，底模有升降机构，其特征在于所述的机架底板下安装升降开合模动力，升降开合模动力带动连接座，连接座的两侧分别连接左连杆和右连杆，左连杆连接左曲臂，右连杆连接右曲臂。

【名称】 塑料瓶坯加热器自动上坯和脱坯机构

【公开(公告)号】 CN102431155A

【公开(公告)日】 2012. 05. 02

【申请(专利权)人】 汪祥建

【地址】 浙江省台州市黄岩区后洋模具城科达塑料模具机械有限公司

【发明(设计)人】 汪祥建

【摘要】 塑料瓶坯加热器自动上坯和脱坯机构，包括机架上安瓶坯输送装置，瓶坯输送装置包括主动齿轮和从动齿轮，主动齿轮由电机带动旋转，主动齿轮和从动齿轮上安传动链条，瓶坯输送机构一头安上坯和脱坯机构，上坯和脱坯机构包括机架上安滑轨，滑轨一侧有上坯滑道连拨盘，滑轨另一侧有出坯滑道，滑轨一头制斜面，另一头为直面，传动链条外安插坯装置，所述插坯装置包括壳体中安主杆，主杆上安自转齿轮，壳体中安复位弹簧下有滚轮固定块，壳体侧壁开升降孔，滚轮固定块上安滚轮杆外头安滚轮与滑轨配合，主杆下端安瓶坯插头内制胀紧孔，胀紧孔内安胀紧弹簧和钢珠，钢珠与瓶坯内壁接触。

【名称】 免贴标吸塑产品的加工工艺及所用模具

【公开(公告)号】 CN102431156A

【公开(公告)日】 2012. 05. 02

【申请(专利权)人】 蒋会见

【地址】 河北省石家庄市经济技术开发区清源街8号富强印业

【发明(设计)人】 蒋会见

【摘要】 本发明公开了一种免贴标吸塑产品的加工工艺及所用模具，其工艺包括图案印刷及定位吸塑成型；其中吸塑成型工序中，带有印刷图案的部位在吸塑的同时接受冷却处理；相应地，本发明的模具在相应于制品有图案的部位设有冷却结构。本发明将图案直接于塑料片材上印刷，然后整体吸塑成型，所用模具在吸塑成型时使产品相应部位免受热，从而不会导致图案变形的后果；图案直接以塑料片材为载体，免用纸张，节约森林资源，适于流水线加工与大规模生产，且节约场地、流程、人工，成本降低，易于存放。本发明的加工工艺适用于附有图案的塑料制品，本发明的模具适用于带有图案的塑料制品的加工成型，适用于PVC、PET、PP、PS、PE、PC、PMMA等塑料。

【名称】 一种塑料膜压膜装置

【公开(公告)号】 CN102431162A

【公开(公告)日】 2012. 05. 02

【申请(专利权)人】 吴江市英力达塑料包装有限公司

【地址】 江苏省苏州市吴江市松陵镇高新村(体育路旁)

【发明(设计)人】 倪迪

【摘要】 本发明涉及一种塑料膜压膜装置，包括支架，支架上设置有前压辊和后压辊，所述前压辊和后压辊的两端分别固定在支架两端，所述支架两端的前端各设置有一个用于调节前压辊和后压辊间距的手轮，塑料膜从前压辊和后压辊之间穿过。本发明的优点是，这种塑料膜压膜装置结构简单，能够调节压力大小，防止塑料膜发生褶皱现象，从而提高了产品质量。

【名称】 一种塑料门窗 Y 型焊接设备及方法

【公开(公告)号】 CN102431164A

【公开(公告)日】 2012. 05. 02

【申请(专利权)人】 济南德佳机器有限公司

【地址】 山东省济南市历下区(高新区)齐鲁软件园创业广场 B 座 5－511 室

【发明(设计)人】 安立保

【摘要】 本发明公开了一种塑料门窗 Y 型焊接设备及方法，其设备包括机架、导轨、活动托料架、机头滑块、左机头和右机头，左机头只可微动，到位后左机头刹紧装置对其刹紧，右机头可沿固定在机架上的导轨手动移动，到位后右机头刹紧装置对其刹紧；所述右机头包括定位机构、压紧机构、加热机构、托料架和机头底板；所述定位机构包括 Y 型定位板，所述加热机构包括加热板，所述压紧机构包括位于机头底板中部的中压紧机构、以及位于该中压紧机构左右两侧的左压紧机构和右压紧机构。本发明只需要一次焊接就可以自动完成 Z 型材中挺对其框料的 Y 型的焊接加工，不需要对框料先行焊接锯切 Z 型材形状再焊接，大大节省了加工时间，提高了加工效率，省时省力、高效。

【名称】 制作偏振光隐形图像薄膜的方法及薄膜

【公开(公告)号】 CN102431223A

【公开(公告)日】 2012. 05. 02

【申请(专利权)人】 夏知识

【地址】 浙江省温州市苍南县金乡镇金狮北路 72－8 号

【发明(设计)人】 夏知识

【摘要】 本发明公开提供一种制作偏振光隐形图像薄膜的方法，包括如下步骤：提供具有偏振光介质特性的塑料薄膜，并将所述塑料薄膜制作成偏振光隐形图案载体，提供偏振光片，将所述隐形图案载体黏贴到所述偏振光片的上表面，在所述隐形图案载体的上表面制作图案区，并在所述图案区印刷上油墨层，在所述偏振光片的下表面黏贴反射层，在所述图案区上成型保护层，得到偏振光隐形图像薄膜。本发明制作偏振光隐形图像薄膜的方法成本低廉、制作工艺简单、易于推广应用，此外本发明还公开了一种薄膜。

【名称】 定向麻纤维/塑料复合板材的制造方法

【公开(公告)号】 CN102431241A

【公开(公告)日】 2012. 05. 02

【申请(专利权)人】 东北林业大学

【地址】 黑龙江省哈尔滨市香坊区和兴路 26 号

【发明(设计)人】 王伟宏；张晨夕；王海刚；王清文

【摘要】 定向麻纤维/塑料复合板材的制造方法，本发明属于复合板材领域。本发明解决现有热压法制备麻纤维/塑料复合板材存在力学强度方向控制性差、麻纤维弯曲使复合板材蠕变性能差的技术问题。方法：一、将落地麻或者废弃麻袋片拆分成麻线；二、将聚乙烯连续纤维或聚丙烯连续纤维与麻线轻捻成股，得到混合线；三、根据定向复合板材形状设计钢框后将混合线按横纵方向均匀缠绕在钢框上，然后放在垫板上，去除钢框，再盖上上压板，垫板与上压板之间放置垫块；四、预热；五、热压，得到定向麻纤维/塑料复合板材。本发明的板材具有麻纤维与聚合物混合均匀、粘结牢固、板材幅面大、可二次弯曲成型、加工方便、制造工艺简单、纵横方向强度可设计性强等优点。

【名称】 一种塑竹板材及其生产工艺

【公开(公告)号】 CN102431245A

【公开(公告)日】 2012. 05. 02

【申请(专利权)人】 宁波雄歌进出口有限公司

【地址】 浙江省宁波市江北区槐树路 146 号黄金水岸 1104

【发明(设计)人】 石雄军

【摘要】 本发明公开了一种塑竹板材，包括竹板，竹板的至少一个侧面上附着有塑料层，竹板沿其厚度方向具有若干间隙，间隙内填充有与塑料层一体连接的塑料填充体。同时还公开了一种生产工艺，包括以下步骤：1)选取竹子裁截成需要的长度；2)将竹子压裂并使其形成具有间隙的平直板面，再进行横向拉扯；3)处理得到竹板材原料板；4)使塑料附着在竹板材原料板的表面的同时，将塑料挤入间隙内即得到的塑竹板材。与现有技术相比，本发明的塑料层与竹板表面无论是受到外力或老化影响都将不会出现剥离现象，即使产品出现折损也将不会出现直接断裂，从而有效降低意外伤害的安全系数；本发明的强度较高、生产成本低、产品无污染；本发明还具有木材的二次加工性。

【名称】 一种提高塑料袋抗冲击压力的方法及产品和工具
【公开(公告)号】 CN102431703A
【公开(公告)日】 2012.05.02
【申请(专利权)人】 郑伟春
【地址】 辽宁省营口市鲅鱼圈区卢屯镇汝儿姑村1229号
【发明(设计)人】 郑伟春
【摘要】 本发明公开一种提高塑料袋抗冲击压力的方法，采用热合线的形状为：在塑料袋的折角线与侧边间采用斜线，在折角线间采用直线，所述斜线与直线的过度段采用向塑料袋的上侧凸起型曲线，所述凸起型曲线的位置与折角线的位置相对应。本发明的优点是：①由于采用了特殊的热合线形状，热合的塑料袋封口更加严密，改变了原直线或弧线热合的受力方向，因而提高了封口处的抗冲击能力，使该塑料袋在装料时不容易受物料的冲击而破裂或漏眼。避免杂菌生成或漏气漏水等。②由于在一把刀上加工多个热合刀刃可大大提高生产效率和节约材料，符合节能减排的需要。

【名称】 一种环保塑料保鲜盒的密封装置
【公开(公告)号】 CN102431713A
【公开(公告)日】 2012.05.02
【申请(专利权)人】 陈浠
【地址】 广东省汕头市澄海区澄华街道城西益民路汇璟花园C10幢304号
【发明(设计)人】 陈浠
【摘要】 本发明涉及一种具有外壳的保鲜盒，该外壳可以具有任何结构，用适当处理的环保塑料制造。本发明公开的装置包括形为成层薄片的盖子，该薄片包括外部塑料层和内部塑料层。上述薄片用热合接、粘接或者其它任何方法固定在外壳的开口上。拉片突出于上述薄片，起手作用。构成实际盖子的成层薄片可以直接固定在外壳的开口上，为此适当成形该薄片，或者该盖子可以由周边支架支承，该支架仍然采用环保塑料制作，并具有内周边法兰，该成层薄片固定在该周边法兰上，该盖子组件用标准的卷边系统固定于容器的外壳上。

【名称】 一种塑料安瓿吹灌封一体机
【公开(公告)号】 CN102431946A
【公开(公告)日】 2012.05.02
【申请(专利权)人】 楚天科技股份有限公司
【地址】 湖南省长沙市宁乡县玉潭镇新康路1号
【发明(设计)人】 刘振；王业洲；邓京良；詹文中；刘焱宇
【摘要】 本发明公开了一种塑料安瓿吹灌封一体机，包括机架以及设于机架上的灌封装置、模切装置、挤出制瓶装置、定位组件，模切装置位于灌封装置的正下方，定位组件位于灌封装置的下方并可通过升降运动带着瓶卡到达模切工位或灌封工位。本发明具有结构简单紧凑、成本低廉、占地面积小、输料时间短、定位方便快捷、易于控制调试等优点。

【名称】 一种塑料安瓿的吹灌封一体机
【公开(公告)号】 CN102431947A
【公开(公告)日】 2012.05.02
【申请(专利权)人】 楚天科技股份有限公司
【地址】 湖南省长沙市宁乡县玉潭镇新康路1号
【发明(设计)人】 王业洲；邓京良；詹文中；刘焱宇；唐岳
【摘要】 本发明公开了一种塑料安瓿的吹灌封一体机，包括机架以及设于机架上并按工序沿水平方向依次布置的挤出制瓶装置、灌封装置、模切装置，所述灌封装置上灌封工位的下方设有灌封定位组件，所述挤出制瓶装置通过第一传送组件与灌封装置相连以完成瓶卡的传送，所述灌封装置通过第二传送组件与模切装置相连以完成灌封后瓶卡的传送。本发明具有结构简单紧凑、成本低廉、占地面积小、输料时间短、定位方便快捷、易于控制调试等优点。

【名称】 一种纳米复合塑料涂料的水性合成及其制备方法
【公开(公告)号】 CN102432740A
【公开(公告)日】 2012.05.02
【申请(专利权)人】 刘方旭
【地址】 山东省烟台开发区旭日小区16号楼1单元4号
【发明(设计)人】 刘方旭
【摘要】 本发明一种纳米复合塑料涂料的水性合成及其制备方法，其水性纳米复合塑料涂料是一种有机聚合的混合物；具有硬度高、耐热性强、不回粘、丰满度高和耐水、耐醇性好的性能；是烯基单体在蒸馏水和乳化剂存在下预乳化制成壳层单体混合物；烯基单体和部分引发剂在蒸馏水和乳化剂存在下，进行聚合反应制成种子乳液；向种子乳液中加入预乳化的壳层单体、剩余引发剂和功能单体进行壳聚合反应；在搅拌下向上述核壳乳液中加入纳米二氧化硅分散体、润湿分散剂、消泡剂缓冲剂等助剂，过滤后即得到成品；具有无毒环保、无气味、可挥发物极少、不燃不爆的高安全性、不黄变、耐候性强、硬度高、耐磨、抗冲击、耐化学腐蚀、粘接性好的优点。

【名称】 耐高温高阻燃性聚氨酯发泡塑料
【公开(公告)号】 CN102432819A

【公开(公告)日】 2012.05.02
【申请(专利权)人】 吴江明峰聚氨酯制品有限公司
【地址】 江苏省苏州市吴江北厍镇玩字村
【发明(设计)人】 费近峰
【摘要】 本发明涉及一种耐高温高阻燃性聚氨酯发泡塑料，其特征在于包括以下组份：A 料组合聚醚：蔗糖聚醚 70～80 份、阻燃剂 50～100 份、发泡剂 1～10份、催化剂 2～5 份、泡沫稳定剂 1～2 份、水 0.01～0.15 份；B 料异氰酸酯：多异氰酸酯 20～30 份，多异氰酸酯为多亚甲基多苯基多异氰酸酯。制备方法采用将 A 料和 B 料机械混合后一次浇注发泡的方法。本发明获得的耐高温高阻燃性聚氨酯发泡塑料比传统的阻燃型 PU 硬泡具有更好的阻燃性，提高了产品的防火性，且耐热性良好。

【名称】 一种液态醇酸树脂及其制备方法
【公开(公告)号】 CN102432851A
【公开(公告)日】 2012.05.02
【申请(专利权)人】 天长市开林化工有限公司
【地址】 安徽省天长市天长金集黄庄工业园天长市开林化工有限公司
【发明(设计)人】 王和山
【摘要】 本发明涉及一种液态醇酸树脂及其制备方法，其原料组成为油、松香、苯甲酸、多元醇、废料以及溶剂油等；本发明以回收的废旧塑料以及化纤工业废料为主要原料，加入各种辅料，通过在反应釜中发生聚酯化反应，随后进行兑稀，最后进行过滤制得液态醇酸树脂成品。本发明利用废弃塑料制备醇酸树脂，变废为宝，工艺过程简单易操作，利用导热油进行加热的方式更加安全节能，应用范围广泛。

【名称】 低温改性发泡剂及其制备方法
【公开(公告)号】 CN102432908A
【公开(公告)日】 2012.05.02
【申请(专利权)人】 杭州海虹精细化工有限公司
【地址】 浙江省杭州市余杭区良渚镇大陆七贤桥村海虹新材料科技园
【发明(设计)人】 董梅；谢雪源；陈海贤
【摘要】 本发明涉及一种低温改性发泡剂及其制备方法。该发泡剂以氰尿酸锌为改性剂，向相对于 100 份重量比的发泡剂中添加 1－10 重量份的氰尿酸锌，可有效降低高温发泡剂的分解温度，适应各种橡胶制品的加工条件，同时氰尿酸锌又是多种橡胶的热稳定剂，因此添加氰尿酸锌既可使发泡剂适应橡胶塑料的加工温度，又可对橡胶制品起到热稳定的作用。

【名称】 软泡阻燃聚醚多元醇的合成方法
【公开(公告)号】 CN102432859A
【公开(公告)日】 2012.05.02
【申请(专利权)人】 山东蓝星东大化工有限责任公司
【地址】 山东省淄博市张店区淄博高新区 309 国道以北、热电厂东邻
【发明(设计)人】 段燕芳
【摘要】 本发明涉及一种软泡阻燃聚醚多元醇的合成方法。其所要解决的技术问题是提供一种阻燃性能好、安全无毒、成本低的阻燃软泡聚醚多元醇的合成方法，其以三聚氰胺－甲醛缩合物和多元醇类化合物为混合起始剂，先在胺类催化剂作用下，与氧化烯烃进行聚合得到高羟值聚醚，高羟值聚醚再在碱金属催化剂作用下，补加氧化烯烃进一步聚合得到。本发明提供的方法，制备工艺简单，成本低，对物理机械性能影响较小。利用本发明提供的方法制得的软泡阻燃聚醚多元醇，色泽浅、粘度低，可广泛用于阻燃型聚氨酯软泡的制备。制得的阻燃型软质聚氨酯泡沫塑料制品，氧指数高，阻燃效果好、耐热性高、尺寸稳定性好、强度高。

【名称】 一种硬脂酸铅类稳定润滑剂及其生产方法和热稳定剂组合物
【公开(公告)号】 CN102432916A
【公开(公告)日】 2012.05.02
【申请(专利权)人】 南京协和助剂有限公司；南京协和化学有限公司
【地址】 江苏省南京市六合区化学工业园区方水路 90－98 号
【发明(设计)人】 黄艳
【摘要】 本发明属于聚氯乙烯塑料加工助剂领域，涉及一种硬脂酸铅类稳定润滑剂及其生产方法和热稳定剂组合物。本发明采用以脂肪酸酰胺作为催化剂催化硬脂酸和氧化铅反应。本发明的催化剂脂肪酸酰胺类化合物可催化硬脂酸与氧化铅直接反应生成硬脂酸铅至二盐基硬脂酸铅之间的一系列的产物；催化剂脂肪酸酰胺类化合物还是一种很好的润滑剂。因此，在反应结束后，无需将催化剂与反应体系分离，可直接作为产品的一种成分存在，作为复合稳定剂的高效润滑剂使用；本发明所述的技术方案实质上是非水合成法，没有废水排放，且硬脂酸铅类稳定润滑剂的生产方法中的反应体系是有粘度的料液体系，因此该反应解决了产品生产过程中的粉尘的污染问题。

【名称】 无卤阻燃添加剂和用其阻燃的软硬质聚氨酯泡沫及弹性体
【公开(公告)号】 CN102432917A

【公开(公告)日】 2012.05.02
【申请(专利权)人】 四川大学
【地址】 四川省成都市双流县川大路二段2号
【发明(设计)人】 王玉忠；陈明军；肖守松；苏子秋；贾云；陈力
【摘要】 本发明公开的无卤阻燃添加剂是由8~25重量份的三聚氰胺-2-羧乙基苯基次膦酸盐和0~15重量份的无卤液体磷酸酯和膦酸酯中的至少一种复配而成。本发明还公开了用该无卤阻燃添加剂阻燃的软质聚氨酯泡沫、硬质聚氨酯泡沫和热塑性聚氨酯弹性体。该无卤阻燃添加剂的添加量仅为8重量份时，就能使软质聚氨酯泡沫、硬质聚氨酯泡沫和热塑性聚氨酯弹性体的垂直燃烧分别通过CalT. B. 117A、UL-94V-0测试标准，且添加量高达40重量份时，也能较好地保持聚氨酯泡沫塑料的原有性能。用该无卤阻燃添加剂阻燃的软质聚氨酯泡沫、硬质聚氨酯泡沫和热塑性聚氨酯弹性体可分别适用于具有较高阻燃要求的家具、交通工具、建筑和电缆领域。

【名称】 一种塑料加工复合功能助剂及其制备方法
【公开(公告)号】 CN102432918A
【公开(公告)日】 2012.05.02
【申请(专利权)人】 青阳县三宝塑业有限责任公司
【地址】 安徽省池州市青阳县丁桥镇马塘工业集中区
【发明(设计)人】 吴跃强
【摘要】 本发明公开了一种塑料加工复合功能助剂及其制备方法，各原料组分按重量份比为：轻质碳酸钙粉90~100、云母粉3~5、氯化钙1~2、秸秆灰烬1~2、氧化锌3~5、气相二氧化硅3~5、甲基丙烯酸酯的聚合物1~2、聚乙烯蜡1~2、烷基苯磺酸钠1~2、甘油1~2。制备方法：将轻质碳酸钙烘干至水份含重量为0.3%以下，加入高速捏合机中，然后按重量份比添加其它配方材料，再升温至100~130℃，保温搅拌8~10min后，出料得成品。本发明所制备的塑料加工复合功能助剂降低了颗粒间的表面能，增强了塑料的相容性和分散性；促进了高分子材料塑化，降低熔体粘度，改善加工流动性；提高制品冲击度、刚度、耐热性及尺寸稳定性，具有节能降耗、环保、无毒、无“三废”的特点。

【名称】 一种塑料加工功能助剂及其制备方法
【公开(公告)号】 CN102432919A
【公开(公告)日】 2012.05.02
【申请(专利权)人】 池州市新科建材有限公司
【地址】 安徽省池州市贵池区马衙街道马衙村洪夏村民组
【发明(设计)人】 汪绍春
【摘要】 本发明公开了一种塑料加工功能助剂及其制备方法，各原料组分按重量份比为：轻质碳酸钙粉90-100、煅烧陶土3-5、凹凸棒土2-2、秸秆灰烬1-2、活性氧化锌3-5、气相二氧化硅3-5、甲基丙烯酸酯的聚合物1-2、聚乙烯蜡1-2、烷基苯磺酸钠1-2、甘油1-2。制备方法：将轻质碳酸钙烘干至水份含重量为0.3%以下，加入高速捏合机中，然后按重量份比添加其它配方材料，再升温至100~130℃，保温搅拌8~10min后，出料得成品。本发明所制备的塑料加工功能助剂降低了颗粒间的表面能，增强了塑料的相容性和分散性；促进了高分子材料塑化，降低熔体粘度，改善加工流动性；提高制品冲击度、刚度、耐热性及尺寸稳定性，具有节能降耗、环保、无毒、无“三废”的特点。

【名称】 一种非淀粉类可生物降解的塑料膜
【公开(公告)号】 CN102432942A
【公开(公告)日】 2012.05.02
【申请(专利权)人】 吴江明峰聚氨酯制品有限公司
【地址】 江苏省苏州市吴江北厍镇玩字村
【发明(设计)人】 费近峰
【摘要】 本发明涉及一种非淀粉类可生物降解的塑料膜，其特征在于包括以下组份：HDPE100份、聚乙烯醇、0.5~1.5份、硅烷化偶联剂1.2~5.5份、填料0.5~1.5份、植物纤维1~10份；热氧化降解促进剂B10~20份、增塑剂10~20份、壳聚糖10~15份。填料为轻质活性碳酸钙；所述的植物纤维为木料粉、农作物秸秆粉，如大豆秸秆、小麦秸秆、玉米秸秆，粒度为20~200目。(1)将植物纤维粉碎至20~200目，加入增塑剂、硅烷化的偶联剂，混合均匀，备用；(2)将HDPE、剩余的原料混合，加入步骤(1)的材料，加入告诉混合器内混合均匀出料，用造粒机或者双螺杆制成颗粒，再将颗粒料吹塑成厚度为15~50微米的薄膜，即可获得非淀粉类可生物降解的塑料膜。本发明获得的塑料制品未采用淀粉，但生物降解完全，耐水性好。

【名称】 一种复合纤维增强聚丙烯材料及其制备方法
【公开(公告)号】 CN102432947A
【公开(公告)日】 2012.05.02
【申请(专利权)人】 金发科技股份有限公司；上海金发科技发展有限公司；绵阳东方特种工程塑料有限公司
【地址】 广东省广州市高新技术产业开发区科丰路33号
【发明(设计)人】 刘乐文；郑明嘉；姚程；何浏炜；

李聪；肖鹏；陶四平；杨泽

【摘要】 本发明公开一种复合纤维增强聚丙烯材料及其制备方法。所述复合纤维增强聚丙烯材料由如下按重量百分比计算的组分组成：复合纤维 10%～70%；聚丙烯树脂 28%～88%；接枝聚丙烯 1%～10%；抗氧剂 0.1%～2%；加工助剂 0.2%～2%；所述复合纤维为由连续玻纤和聚合物长丝经过在线复合得到。所述复合纤维增强聚丙烯材料的制备方法为：将除了复合纤维的其它组分混合后通过挤出机混炼；复合纤维在挤出机中段加入，通过螺杆剪切分散得到。本发明所述产品中玻璃纤维与聚丙烯的相容性好，成型工艺简单，材料表面浮纤现象少，即使在高玻纤含量时仍能保持良好的外观；具有良好的加工性能，可以用于取代工程塑料的相关制件和应用于对表面要求高的外观件。

【名称】 无机粉体塑料及制备方法

【公开(公告)号】 CN102432956A

【公开(公告)日】 2012.05.02

【申请(专利权)人】 成都新柯力化工科技有限公司

【地址】 四川省成都市青羊区蛟龙工业港东海路4座

【发明(设计)人】 陈庆；曾军堂；陈兵

【摘要】 无机粉体塑料，由裹覆层包覆的微细化无机粉体颗粒微胶囊与高分子聚合物组成。以重量份计的组成为：无机粉体微胶囊 75～85 份，高分子聚合物成分 15～25 份。其中的无机粉体微胶囊是由粒径为 2.5～5.0μm 的无机粉体与由活性剂、引发剂、界面改性剂、分散剂组成的裹覆层组成；高分子聚合物成分为聚苯乙烯、聚对苯二甲酸乙二醇酯、低密度聚乙烯、高密度聚乙烯、茂金属聚乙烯、线性低密度聚乙烯、丙烯腈－丁二烯－苯乙烯共聚物、聚丙烯等中的至少一种。该无机粉体塑料（俗称石头塑料）具有良好的流动性和可热塑加工性，极大降低了塑料产品成本，减少了塑料制品对石油资源的依赖。

【名称】 聚偏二氟乙烯 OK 线制品使用的色母粒及其制备方法

【公开(公告)号】 CN102432964A

【公开(公告)日】 2012.05.02

【申请(专利权)人】 江苏昊华光伏科技有限公司

【地址】 江苏省苏州市常熟市辛庄镇光环路 28 号

【发明(设计)人】 王海林；王卫国

【摘要】 本发明公开了一种聚偏二氟乙烯 OK 线缆色母粒，这种色母粒由颜料、塑料助剂和载体树脂组成，所述塑料助剂包含 $N-N'$－乙撑双硬脂酸酰胺、聚乙烯蜡、硬脂酸锌、抗静电剂及高级复合润滑剂。按配方将上述物料进行混合，然后在捏合锅中高速捏合，最后将搅拌均匀的混合料投入到主机温度控制在 180～210℃ 的双螺杆挤出机中挤出，经冷却、烘干、切粒制成所需色母粒，该色母粒分散性好、遮盖力强、易搅拌、不渗色、防静电、无环境污染。

【名称】 一种环保型发泡板

【公开(公告)号】 CN102432959A

【公开(公告)日】 2012.05.02

【申请(专利权)人】 无锡天马塑胶制品有限公司

【地址】 江苏省无锡市惠山区惠山经济开发区堰桥配套区堰锦路 21 号

【发明(设计)人】 马新刚

【摘要】 本发明公开一种环保型发泡板。这种环保型发泡板是用废旧 PVC 塑料粉末、木粉、石粉、PVC 树脂、发泡剂、调节剂、稳定剂和润滑剂等原料，经均匀混合、用挤出机及模具挤制成平板状毛坯、对平板状毛坯边沿进行修整等步骤而制成。这种环保型发泡板，不仅可回收、使用寿命长、有利于健康，而且使用前不需进行脱模处理，劳动强度低。可用作建筑模板的，也可用作生产家具的板材。

【名称】 甲基丙烯亚胺泡沫塑料及其制备方法

【公开(公告)号】 CN102432971A

【公开(公告)日】 2012.05.02

【申请(专利权)人】 刘天义

【地址】 河南省许昌市襄城县城关镇东大街 38 号附6号

【发明(设计)人】 刘天义

【摘要】 本发明公开了一种甲基丙烯亚胺泡沫塑料及其制备方法，它是选用甲基丙烯酸、甲基丙烯腈、异丙醇、叔丁醇、甲基丙烯酸烯丙酯、氧化镁、偶氮二异丁腈、过氧化二苯甲酰、过氧苯甲酸叔丁酯为原料，按一定生产工艺制备而成的泡沫塑料制品，本发明所用的原料种类少，制备工艺简单，制出的泡沫产品孔径小，强度高。

【名称】 一种塑料复合油墨用酯醇溶聚氨酯树脂的制备方法

【公开(公告)号】 CN102432993A

【公开(公告)日】 2012.05.02

【申请(专利权)人】 山西省应用化学研究所

【地址】 山西省太原市和平北路 28 号

【发明(设计)人】 马国章；毛祖秋；石红翠；侯彩英；贾金兰；郭晓勇；张博

【摘要】 本发明公开了一种塑料复合油墨用酯醇溶聚氨酯树脂的制备方法，以二聚脂肪酸与二元胺和含羟基的一元胺反应合成数均分子量 400～2000 的端羟基聚酰胺，加入聚酯多元醇、小分子二元醇和脂肪醇聚氧乙烯醚，与二异氰酸酯反应制得端基为异氰酸酯基的聚氨酯/聚酰胺嵌段聚合物，再以二元胺扩链剂扩链，最后以分子量调节剂控制分子量，并加入稀释剂制成塑料复合油墨用酯醇溶聚氨酯树脂。本发明制备得到的聚氨酯树脂数均分子量25000~60000，固含量28%~35%，黏度500~1500mPa·s/25℃，对多种塑料薄膜基材附着力牢度好，颜料润湿分散佳，溶剂残留量低，对环境危害小，环保安全。

【名称】 一种薄状废塑料的挤干脱水机

【公开(公告)号】 CN102435052A

【公开(公告)日】 2012.05.02

【申请(专利权)人】 江苏联冠科技发展有限公司

【地址】 江苏省苏州市张家港市锦丰镇三兴工业区白熊路2号江苏联冠科技发展有限公司

【发明(设计)人】 王国龙；秦小飞

【摘要】 本发明公开了一种薄状废塑料的清洗生产线上使用的薄状废塑料的挤干脱水机，在机架上固定设置有挤出仓，挤出仓内设置有送料螺杆，送料螺杆与减速机相连接；在挤出仓的上方设置有进料斗，挤出仓的出料端通过排水仓与固定压实仓相连接；在所述挤出仓的底部、以及排水仓上分别设置有排水孔，所述的固定压实仓为一个上部半敞开的敞口仓体，在所述固定压实仓的上部铰接有一个下部半敞开的活动压实仓，活动压实仓的上端与油缸的活塞杆相铰接，活动压实仓和固定压实仓可形成一个口径逐渐缩小的锥形口。上述结构的挤干脱水机，脱水效果好，能耗低、噪音小、维修方便，操作也十分方便。广泛适用于薄状废塑料的回收清洗领域。

【名称】 塑料及塑料包装材料中苯乙酮的检测方法

【公开(公告)号】 CN102435701A

【公开(公告)日】 2012.05.02

【申请(专利权)人】 福建出入境检验检疫局检验检疫技术中心

【地址】 福建省福州市湖东路312号国检广场

【发明(设计)人】 李小晶；唐熙；唐泓；陈旻实；江晓芬；吕水源；刘伟；姜晓黎；戴金兰；许才明

【摘要】 本发明提供一种塑料及塑料包装材料中苯乙酮的检测方法，其是将待测塑料或塑料包装制备成均质待测物存储备用，之后对均质待测物进行提取过滤以获得待测液，接着把获得的待测液采用高效液相色谱法进行分析检测，并将高效液相色谱检测所获得分取比例及苯乙酮的峰面积代入计算值中进行计算，以获得各待测样液中苯乙酮的理论测定值，并从该理论测定值中扣除掉空白值即获各待测样液中苯乙酮的实际测定值。本发明的优点在于：填补了我国在塑料及塑料包装材料中苯乙酮的检测上的技术空白，且操作简便、准确灵敏。

【名称】 一种塑料管材无屑切割机

【公开(公告)号】 CN102441906A

【公开(公告)日】 2012.05.09

【申请(专利权)人】 广东联塑机器制造有限公司

【地址】 广东省佛山市顺德区龙洲路龙江段联塑工业村

【发明(设计)人】 蔡炳然；崔鲜霞；李优红；王泽清

【摘要】 本发明涉及管材切割相关技术领域，特别是一种塑料管材无屑切割机，包括机架，在机架上依次设置随动机构和切割机，切割机包括两个夹紧机构和切割机构，所述夹紧机构包括开有夹紧通孔的夹紧底板，切割机构包括开有切割通孔的切割底板，夹紧通孔和切割通孔具有同一轴心，两个夹紧机构平行设置，切割机构设置在两个夹紧机构中间。本发明结构简单、切割可靠、切割管材厚度、管径规格范围大，夹紧适应多规格管径的V型自动夹紧机构的机器，适合所有管径不同型号的无屑切割机应用。

【名称】 一种酚醛模塑料成品细粉料回收利用的加工方法

【公开(公告)号】 CN102441950A

【公开(公告)日】 2012.05.09

【申请(专利权)人】 无锡创达电子有限公司

【地址】 江苏省无锡市新区城南路201-1号

【发明(设计)人】 章志平；邱家会

【摘要】 本发明公开了一种酚醛模塑料成品细粉料回收利用的加工方法，其步骤包括在回收利用的100份酚醛模塑料成品细粉料中加入6.25~10份酚醛树脂、12.5~15份玻璃纤维，再以每分钟400~500转的速度高速混合30~35分钟；把混合好的原料加到螺杆挤出机的加料斗，机器预热并将螺杆挤出机的转速频率设定为25Hz；开启加料，把加料频率从0Hz加到30Hz，当挤出机头开始挤出粉料的时候，开启冷冻水，把三个温区温度重新设定；用红外测温仪测量挤出口的料温，保证料温控制在90~110度之间；压片冷却；粉碎筛选；循环利用。本发明的优点在于：将酚醛模塑料成品细粉料重新造粒利用，减少了浪费，降低了生产成本。

【名称】 油壶塑料材料回收机

【公开(公告)号】 CN102441952A

【公开(公告)日】 2012.05.09

【申请(专利权)人】 安徽中鼎橡塑制品有限公司

【地址】 安徽省宁国市经济技术开发区东城大道81号
【发明(设计)人】 夏玉洁；谢元喜；徐东法
【摘要】 本发明公开了一种油壶塑料材料回收机，包括具有切割室的机架，所述的切割室内设有一转轴，所述的转轴上固定有锯片，所述的机架上安装有一个带动所述转轴旋转的电动机，所述的切割室内固定有直线导轨，所述直线导轨的滑块上固定有一滑动板，安装在机架上的推动气缸的活塞杆伸入所述的切割室和所述的滑动板固定连接，在所述的滑动板上固定有一个用于放置加工件的固定座。本发明针对焊缝进行切割，去除焊缝处的材料，对剩余的两边油壶进行破碎处理，变废为宝，回收再利用。该设备设计时充分考虑切割的危险性，设计安全门防护，封闭式作业；加工件固定座更换快捷，操作简易，并且塑料油壶种类繁多，仅目前就有30多种，适用面广。

【名称】 一种长而薄的金属片的塑料注塑方法
【公开(公告)号】 CN102441963A
【公开(公告)日】 2012.05.09
【申请(专利权)人】 张家港市中南电子有限公司
【地址】 江苏省苏州市张家港市乐余镇东林村
【发明(设计)人】 不公告发明人
【摘要】 本发明公开一种长而薄的金属片的塑料注塑方法，包括如下步骤：①对该金属片进行初注塑：沿该金属片的轮廓边缘进行注塑，并在两侧注塑形成多个凸柱，两侧的所述的凸柱的高度之和再加上金属片的厚度达到成品要求的厚度，形成半成品；②对步骤①中得到的半成品进行终注塑：利用这些的所述的凸柱将半成品定位在所需的注塑模具中进行注塑，得到最终成品。在通过这些凸柱在终注塑的注塑模具中进行定位，从而有效避免了注塑液产生的冲击力对金属片的定位效果的影响，进而大大地提高了成品率，注塑后的成品性能好、便于安装，该方法适于在长而薄的不规则形状的金属片的注塑中推广使用。

【名称】 控制塑料射出制品翘曲的模具结构及其制品
【公开(公告)号】 CN102441966A
【公开(公告)日】 2012.05.09
【申请(专利权)人】 私立中原大学
【地址】 中国台湾中坜市
【发明(设计)人】 陈夏宗；张英
【摘要】 一种控制塑料射出制品翘曲的模具结构及其制品，该模具结构是由第一半模和第二半模组成，而第一、二半模相应设有第一模穴与第二模穴，而第一半模与第二半模其中之一所对应的第一模穴或第二模穴的一面设有至少一突变厚度结构，且所制成的塑料射出制品相应具有突变厚度部位。据此，可通过突变厚度结构改变流动及冷却模式，且局部中断连续收缩，而改变翘曲方向及翘曲量来控制因模温差异或产品结构所产生的翘曲问题。

【名称】 一种塑料边框的注塑方法及成型模具
【公开(公告)号】 CN102441968A
【公开(公告)日】 2012.05.09
【申请(专利权)人】 青岛海信模具有限公司
【地址】 山东省青岛市高新区市北新产业园
【发明(设计)人】 张明磊；王小新；王国琪；刘永存
【摘要】 本发明公开了一种塑料边框的注塑方法及成型模具，注塑方法包括注射步骤，特征是在注射步骤中，采用塑料注塑成型机将熔融塑料通过喷嘴及浇注系统注入型腔，上述浇注系统采用热流道浇注系统，热流道浇注系统中的热流道浇口采取在塑料边框的侧边端面处进料方式。成型模具包括静模、动模、型腔及浇注系统，特征是浇注系统为热流道浇注系统，设置在动模上，热流道浇口位于能在塑料边框的侧边端面处进料的型腔上。本发明在塑料边框注塑成型过程中，既能够实现无冷料把，节省原料，缩短成型周期，提高生产效率；又能够避免在塑件产品(塑料边框)正面产生浇口痕迹，确保产品的外观质量。

【名称】 塑料管材挤出成型装置
【公开(公告)号】 CN102441976A
【公开(公告)日】 2012.05.09
【申请(专利权)人】 束方才
【地址】 江苏省兴化市苏源小区36号楼304室
【发明(设计)人】 束方才
【摘要】 本发明公开了一种塑料挤出成型装置，主要包括动力机构、料斗、料筒、料筒加热器、螺杆、机头、定径装置、冷却装置、牵引装置、和切断装置等，所述的料筒与机头连接处设置有分流板所述的分流板与料筒的连接处设置有过滤网，其具有能过滤熔融物料流中的杂质和未塑化物料，提高混炼或塑化的效果，生产的管材的质量高的优点。

【名称】 共挤热缠绕结构壁管材，加工方法及模具
【公开(公告)号】 CN102441997A
【公开(公告)日】 2012.05.09
【申请(专利权)人】 宁波康润机械科技有限公司
【地址】 浙江省宁波市鄞州区金谷中路(东)9号
【发明(设计)人】 徐新；肖耀云
【摘要】 本发明公开了一种共挤热缠绕结构壁管材，

其由塑料带作为基层在模具芯管上螺旋热缠绕粘结成型的大口径管材，这种管材的管壁是中空薄壁矩形管在模具芯管上螺旋热缠绕粘结成型，中空薄壁矩形管外壁热缠绕粘结共挤包敷相同材料的单壁波纹管，所述的中空薄壁矩形管内设置个加强筋。本发明还公开了一种共挤热缠绕结构壁管材的加工方法和共挤热缠绕结构壁管材的共挤包敷聚乙烯单壁波纹管的加工模具。本发明将钢塑共挤及铝塑共挤模具技术应用于柔软的PP管与聚乙烯共挤，模具专门针对波纹软管设计了有环凸中心释放区的独特流道，以保证PP管在高压共挤时不变形，还可采用复合或改性塑料生产以进一步降低成本。

【名称】 一种表面具有木质感的轻质木塑复合板材及其制备方法

【公开(公告)号】 CN102442035A

【公开(公告)日】 2012.05.09

【申请(专利权)人】 东北林业大学

【地址】 黑龙江省哈尔滨市香坊区和兴路26号

【发明(设计)人】 王伟宏；王海刚；宋永明；王清文

【摘要】 一种表面具有木质感的轻质木塑复合板材及其制备方法，涉及一种木塑复合板材及其制备方法。要解决现有木塑复合材料密度偏大、运输和使用操作不便、表面缺乏木质感的问题。木塑复合板材包括发泡木塑复合材料层，还包括上薄木板和下薄木板，发泡木塑复合材料层设置在上薄木板和下薄木板之间，发泡木塑复合材料层与上薄木板和下薄木板之间固定连接。方法：将植物纤维粉末、热塑性塑料粉末、偶联剂和AC发泡剂混合；将下薄木板铺装在模具内，再铺放发泡木塑复合材料层；覆盖上薄木板，覆盖上盖板；放入热压机中热压；定型，砂光，即得到木塑复合板材。木塑复合板材的密度小、抗弯强度高。用于家具制造、建筑装饰、交通运输等领域。

【名称】 环保型PET-PVF光亮膜

【公开(公告)号】 CN102442039A

【公开(公告)日】 2012.05.09

【申请(专利权)人】 江苏立霸实业股份有限公司

【地址】 江苏省无锡市宜兴市环保科技工业园画溪路88号

【发明(设计)人】 卢凤仙

【摘要】 环保型PET-PVF光亮膜，涉及一种复合于金属板材或建筑材料上的装饰保护膜，底层塑料膜层、着色层、粘合剂层、印刷层、PET膜层依次层状叠加排布，底层塑料膜层为PVF膜，能保护金属板表面不易锈蚀、装饰表面不易褪色或脆化，利用膜的密团性使得金属和空气隔绝起到完全防腐作用，该膜可以根据需要印刷各种图案和颜色，且表面有多种光泽度，展示多姿多彩的装饰效果。

【名称】 ACR改性体系塑料

【公开(公告)号】 CN102443219A

【公开(公告)日】 2012.05.09

【申请(专利权)人】 苏州工业园区鑫丰林塑料科技有限公司

【地址】 江苏省苏州市苏州工业园区扬东路277号晶汇大厦3幢918室

【发明(设计)人】 王志凤

【摘要】 本发明涉及一种有机高分子复合材料，更具体地说，是涉及一种ACR改性体系塑料，包括百分比大于80.5%的PVC、5.0%~8.0%的ACR抗冲击改性剂、0~1.0%的ACR加工剂、4.0%~4.5%的复合铅盐、0.5~0.8的硬脂酸钙、0.5%~1.5%润滑剂、4.0%~6.0%的轻质碳酸钙、以及4.0%~6.0%的金红石。本发明ACR改性体系塑料的抗低温冲击性有所提高，进一步提高了塑料的使用率。

【名称】 废旧塑料的再生利用工艺方法

【公开(公告)号】 CN102443210A

【公开(公告)日】 2012.05.09

【申请(专利权)人】 郧县金龙塑业包装有限公司

【地址】 湖北省十堰市郧县城关镇广场东街35号

【发明(设计)人】 刘情厚；闵云宝

【摘要】 为了避免目前废旧塑料的回收利用存在占用土地资源和污染环境的问题，本发明提出废旧塑料的再生利用工艺方法。其技术方案为：废旧塑料的再生利用工艺方法，步骤如下：(1)废旧聚乙烯塑料破碎后，通过洗料筒清洗，由水池二次漂洗后，烘干，制成废旧聚乙烯塑料颗粒；(2)废旧聚乙烯塑料颗粒与聚乙烯原生料、活化剂、相容剂、增塑剂、抗氧剂、润滑剂搅拌混合，进行塑化过滤，最后切制成颗粒状塑料；废旧聚乙烯塑料与其它原料的配比关系，按重量百分比如下：废旧聚乙烯塑料为60%~65%，聚乙烯原生料为15%~16%，填充料为15%~20%，相容剂为1%，增塑剂为1%，抗氧剂为1%、活化剂为0.5%~1%，润滑剂为0.5%~1%。

【名称】 一种由众多颗粒组成装饰工艺品的制作工艺

【公开(公告)号】 CN102442147A

【公开(公告)日】 2012.05.09

【申请(专利权)人】 彭伟强

【地址】 广东省梅州市梅江区梅州大道21号

【发明(设计)人】 彭伟强

【摘要】 本发明公开了一种由众多颗粒组成装饰工

艺品的制作工艺，包括以下操作步骤：首先选用塑料颗粒，然后制作工艺品成型模具，将选好的塑料颗粒放置于工艺品成型模具的模腔内进行加热使塑料颗粒表面熔解，各塑料颗粒表面部分互相熔接且相邻的多个塑料颗粒之间形成有通孔间隙，再者将工艺品成型模具冷却至常温，使各塑料颗粒熔接固定成型形成装饰工艺品半成品胚体，装饰工艺品半成品胚体拼接成型完成整体的装饰工艺品半成品，再经过喷涂着色处理、安装装饰件及测试工序后得到完整的装饰工艺品，其制作工艺紧凑，突破传统的工艺品制作方法，所制得的工艺品装饰效果好，使人达到耳目一新的装饰效果，而且其制作工艺巧妙，方便实用，适合普遍推广使用。

【名称】 一种 PET 塑料打包带及其加工方法
【公开(公告)号】 CN102442474A
【公开(公告)日】 2012.05.09
【申请(专利权)人】 上海自立塑料制品有限公司
【地址】 上海市南翔工业区美裕路 755 号
【发明(设计)人】 陈存兴；许乾慰
【摘要】 本发明公开了一种 PET 塑料打包带及其加工方法，属于打包带技术领域，该 PET 塑料打包带宽度 9～32mm，厚度 0.5～1.4mm，拉伸强度 380～500MPa，搭接强度大于母带强度的 95%；该打包带的加工方法包括以下步骤：PET 原料经高速搅拌分散，去湿干燥，添加助剂，混炼塑化，挤出型胚，型胚骤冷却，加热拉伸，热处理，冷却定型，收卷制得成品。针对现有技术中 PET 打包带搭接强度低的缺陷，本发明提供了一种低成本、高性能、高搭接拉伸断裂负荷的 PET 塑料打包带，不但搭接强度高，而且耐候性和韧性俱佳。

【名称】 一种塑料膜收放料装置
【公开(公告)号】 CN102442595A
【公开(公告)日】 2012.05.09
【申请(专利权)人】 吴江市英力达塑料包装有限公司
【地址】 江苏省苏州市吴江市松陵镇高新村(体育路旁)
【发明(设计)人】 倪迪
【摘要】 本发明涉及一种塑料膜收放料装置，包括支撑架，支撑架上端设置有收放辊，所述收放辊由连接轴两端连接两片挡板组成，并且连接轴连接挡板的两端突出，设置于支撑架的安装槽内。本发明的优点是，这种塑料膜收放料装置结构简单，收料及放料方便，边缘也整齐，提高了生产效率和产品质量。

【名称】 一种聚全氟乙丙烯树脂的凝聚洗涤方法
【公开(公告)号】 CN102443091A
【公开(公告)日】 2012.05.09
【申请(专利权)人】 中昊晨光化工研究院
【地址】 四川省自贡市富顺县晨光路 135 号
【发明(设计)人】 兰军；张建新；李斌；余金龙；赵少春；高家勇；王先荣；白鲸
【摘要】 本发明涉及一种聚全氟乙丙烯树脂的凝聚洗涤方法，采用乳液聚合方法制备聚全氟乙丙烯树脂聚合乳液，再经过静置、稀释、搅拌凝聚和洗涤即得，搅拌凝聚的过程中还可以辅以化学凝聚的方式。本发明提供的凝聚洗涤方法将机械凝聚和化学凝聚进行结合，凝聚效果优异，明显优于传统凝聚方法，所得的聚全氟乙丙烯树脂粒径大，体积密度大，有利于 FEP 塑料的进一步加工，另外，所述方法操作简便、条件温和，适宜工业化大规模应用。

【名称】 一种聚氨酯硬质泡沫及其制备方法
【公开(公告)号】 CN102443134A
【公开(公告)日】 2012.05.09
【申请(专利权)人】 广东万华容威聚氨酯有限公司；宁波万华容威聚氨酯有限公司；烟台万华聚氨酯股份有限公司
【地址】 广东省佛山市高明区明城镇工业区 508 号
【发明(设计)人】 朱霞林；王林；华卫琦；丁建生
【摘要】 本发明公开了一种聚氨酯硬质泡沫及其制备方法，泡沫塑料由以下原料按照重量份经过高压发泡机制成：组合聚醚 100 份，表面活性剂 1.5～3 份，复合催化剂 1.5～3 份，水 1～3 份，混合发泡剂 16～26 份，聚合异氰酸酯 140～170 份其中，混合发泡剂由甲酸甲酯和 1，1，1，3，3－五氟丙烷(HFC－245fa)组成。制得导热系数低、尺寸稳定性好、成本合适的聚氨酯泡沫。

【名称】 热固性聚苯基喹噁啉树脂及其制备方法与应用
【公开(公告)号】 CN102443170A
【公开(公告)日】 2012.05.09
【申请(专利权)人】 中国科学院化学研究所
【地址】 北京市海淀区中关村北一街 2 号
【发明(设计)人】 杨士勇；李诚；刘金刚
【摘要】 本发明公开了一种聚苯基喹噁啉聚合物及其制备方法与应用。该聚合物的结构通式如式 I 所示。该聚合物是以芳香族四酮化合物、芳香族四胺化合物及芳香族封端剂为原料，通过高温缩聚法制备的。该聚合物材料可通过设计合适的分子量获得良好的熔融性能，通过反应性端基的高温固化反应，获得良好的热性能及力学性能。该材料可作为高性能工程塑料、耐高温胶黏剂、纤维增强树脂基复合材料及其制件等，可应用于航空航天、石油化工和汽车等高技术领域。

【名称】 一种复合塑料加工助剂及其制备方法
【公开(公告)号】 CN102443192A
【公开(公告)日】 2012.05.09
【申请(专利权)人】 安徽省忠宏管业科技有限公司
【地址】 安徽省池州市经济技术开发区金安工业园
【发明(设计)人】 刘忠斌
【摘要】 本发明公开了一种复合塑料加工助剂及其制备方法，各原料组分按重量份比为：轻质碳酸钙粉90~100、高岭土3~5、云母粉2~2、秸秆灰烬1~2、活性氧化锌3~5、气相二氧化硅3~5、甲基丙烯酸酯的聚合物1~2、聚乙烯蜡1~2、十二烷基磺酸钠1~2、硅油1~2。制备方法：将轻质碳酸钙烘干至水份含重量为0.3%以下，加入高速捏合机中，然后按重量份比添加其它配方材料，再升温至100~130℃，保温搅拌8~10min后，出料得成品。本发明所制备的复合塑料加工助剂降低了颗粒间的表面能，增强了塑料的相容性和分散性；促进了高分子材料塑化，降低熔体粘度，改善加工流动性；提高制品冲击度、刚度、耐热性及尺寸稳定性，具有节能降耗、环保、无毒、无“三废”的特点。

【名称】 一种生物降解塑料及制备该生物降解塑料的方法
【公开(公告)号】 CN102443195A
【公开(公告)日】 2012.05.09
【申请(专利权)人】 于瑞德
【地址】 新疆维吾尔自治区乌鲁木齐市河南西路299号
【发明(设计)人】 于瑞德
【摘要】 本发明涉及一种生物降解塑料，以热塑性淀粉、聚烃基脂肪酸酯和辅助性成分为原料，经螺旋挤出设备和制膜设备加工而成。包含：10%~60%(重量)的热塑性淀粉；10%~45%(重量)的聚烃基脂肪酸酯；5%~25%(重量)的丙三醇；2%~5%(重量)的碳酸钙；1%~2%(重量)的硬脂酸钙。本发明还涉及制备该生物降解塑料的方法。

【名称】 一种矿用阻燃塑料土工格栅母料
【公开(公告)号】 CN102443208A
【公开(公告)日】 2012.05.09
【申请(专利权)人】 泰安现代塑料有限公司
【地址】 山东省泰安市岱岳区泰山青春创业开发区创业路北首
【发明(设计)人】 卜爱华；王学文；王勇；王鹏
【摘要】 本发明公开了一种矿用阻燃塑料土工格栅母料，由配比的聚烯烃、专用炭黑、复合阻燃剂、相容剂、改性纳米增强材料、加工助剂、抗氧剂组成，复合阻燃剂采用溴系阻燃剂、协效阻燃剂、纳米无机阻燃剂的复合物。本发明制得的母料添加到格栅中，阻燃效果好，拉伸强度、抗老化性能好，产品性能稳定。

【名称】 废旧塑料的再生利用工艺方法
【公开(公告)号】 CN102443210A
【公开(公告)日】 2012.05.09
【申请(专利权)人】 郧县金龙塑业包装有限公司
【地址】 湖北省十堰市郧县城关镇广场东街35号
【发明(设计)人】 刘情厚；闵云宝
【摘要】 为了避免目前废旧塑料的回收利用存在占用土地资源和污染环境的问题，本发明提出废旧塑料的再生利用工艺方法。其技术方案为：废旧塑料的再生利用工艺方法，步骤如下：(1)废旧聚乙烯塑料破碎后，通过洗料筒清洗，由水池二次漂洗后，烘干，制成废旧聚乙烯塑料颗粒；(2)废旧聚乙烯塑料颗粒与聚乙烯原生料、活化剂、相容剂、增塑剂、抗氧剂、润滑剂搅拌混合，进行塑化过滤，最后切制成颗粒状塑料；废旧聚乙烯塑料与其它原料的配比关系，按重量百分比如下：废旧聚乙烯塑料为60%~65%，聚乙烯原生料为15%~16%，填充料为15%~20%，相容剂为1%，增塑剂为1%，抗氧剂为1%、活化剂为0.5%~1%，润滑剂为0.5%~1%。

【名称】 可热塑化的橡胶组合物及其制备方法
【公开(公告)号】 CN102443218A
【公开(公告)日】 2012.05.09
【申请(专利权)人】 郑勇
【地址】 山东省潍坊市奎文区左岸华庭3-2-501
【发明(设计)人】 郑勇
【摘要】 本发明公开了一种可热塑化的橡胶组合物及其制备方法，将乳液聚合法制备的丙烯酸酯橡胶颗粒和水相悬浮聚合法制备的氯化聚乙烯橡胶颗粒按9:1~1:9的重量比混合，然后加入乳液聚合法制备的丙烯酸酯、甲基丙烯酸烷基酯、苯乙烯和丙烯晴中的一种的均聚物或者两种及两种以上的共聚物颗粒或者乳液，两种橡胶颗粒与均聚物或者共聚物的加入重量比为9:1~7:3，搅拌均匀并干燥得到所述可热塑化的橡胶组合物。本发明采用物理混合得到可热塑化的橡胶组合物，可做为增韧剂来改性尼龙、聚氯乙烯等塑料材料，也可造粒后直接用来加工制品，完全可以替代ABS、ASA或ACS树脂。因此本发明相对于现有技术简化了生产步骤，降低了生产成本。

【名称】 PVC门窗异型材使用改性塑料
【公开(公告)号】 CN102443221A

【公开(公告)日】 2012.05.09
【申请(专利权)人】 苏州工业园区鑫丰林塑料科技有限公司
【地址】 江苏省苏州市苏州工业园区扬东路277号晶汇大厦3幢918室
【发明(设计)人】 王志凤
【摘要】 本发明涉及一种有机高分子复合材料，更具体地说，是涉及一种PVC门窗异型材使用改性塑料，包括百分比大于90.6%的聚氯乙烯以及余量的力学性能改性剂、UV-531、阻燃剂、装饰效果改善剂。本发明的PVC门窗异型材使用改性塑料在保证了塑料本身具备的物理性能之外，还可改善PVC的使用性能，不会因为型材加入其他颜料后，对光线的吸收率加强，亮度而有所下降，较为美观。

【名称】 挤出U-PVC门窗异型材塑料
【公开(公告)号】 CN102443222A
【公开(公告)日】 2012.05.09
【申请(专利权)人】 苏州工业园区鑫丰林塑料科技有限公司
【地址】 江苏省苏州市苏州工业园区扬东路277号晶汇大厦3幢918室
【发明(设计)人】 王志凤
【摘要】 本发明涉及一种有机高分子复合材料，更具体地说，是涉及一种挤出U-PVC门窗异型材塑料，包括PVC、三盐基硫酸铅、氯化聚乙烯(CPE)、复合润滑剂、ACR、硅烷类偶联剂、$CaCO_3$，配比为PVC85%~92.5%、三盐基硫酸铅0.5%~3.1%、氯化聚乙烯(CPE)0.6%~3.8%、复合润滑剂0.5%~1.5%、ACR0.2%~1.8%、硅烷类偶联剂0.2%~1.2%、$CaCO_3$0.5%~1.0%。本发明挤出U-PVC门窗异型材塑料具有良好的力学性能和加工性能，同时具有优良的耐候性，进一步提高了门窗异型材塑料的使用率。

【名称】 PVC门窗异型材加工改性塑料
【公开(公告)号】 CN102443225A
【公开(公告)日】 2012.05.09
【申请(专利权)人】 苏州工业园区鑫丰林塑料科技有限公司
【地址】 江苏省苏州市苏州工业园区扬东路277号晶汇大厦3幢918室
【发明(设计)人】 王志凤
【摘要】 本发明涉及一种有机高分子复合材料，更具体地说，是涉及一种PVC门窗异型材加工改性塑料，包括百分比大于85.6%的聚氯乙烯以及余量的单体铅盐、抗氧化剂、复合稳定润滑剂、以及加工改进型ACR。本发明的PVC门窗异型材加工改性塑料可改善PVC的热仰稳定性、溶体塑化的均匀性和流动性、二次加工的热熔接性能。

【名称】 遇火膨胀塑料
【公开(公告)号】 CN102443227A
【公开(公告)日】 2012.05.09
【申请(专利权)人】 桐乡市小老板特种塑料制品有限公司
【地址】 浙江省嘉兴市桐乡市大麻镇工业园区
【发明(设计)人】 沈建清
【摘要】 本发明所设计的一种遇火膨胀塑料，它主要包括PVC和石墨，所述的遇火膨胀塑料由重量份100份的PVC、30~70份的石墨、1~3份的交联剂、1~6份的PVC用稳定剂、0.5~3份的PVC润滑剂、0~150份的碳酸钙、0~20份的PVC改性剂、0~5份的PVC加工助剂、0~20份阻燃剂和0~12份的PVC增塑剂构成。将上述材料按比例称量，放入搅拌机，搅拌均匀后输送至捏合机在100~150℃下对其进行预塑化后进入挤塑机。挤塑机将产品直接挤出成型，或对产品进行造粒处理。所述的遇火膨胀塑料安装在门、窗的4个边框上，当遇见火灾等灾害时，塑料会预热开始膨胀，具有阻燃，达到密封的效果。

【名称】 一种纤维增强塑料
【公开(公告)号】 CN102443255A
【公开(公告)日】 2012.05.09
【申请(专利权)人】 上海晓宝增强塑料有限公司
【地址】 上海市浦东新区川南奉公路5898号
【发明(设计)人】 裴民
【摘要】 本发明涉及一种通讯网络中光纤接入(FTTx)网络工程的室外系统和室内系统的纤维增强塑料。一种纤维增强塑料，它含有的组分及重量份数为：光固化树脂13~25，纤维纱75~87。本发明提高了通讯设施以及用户终端设备的安全防护性能；尤其是缆径细微，曲率半径小，能满足光纤接入(FTTx)网络工程易分支、易接入、施工方便的特殊要求。

【名称】 一种高耐热PC/ASA合金材料及其制备方法
【公开(公告)号】 CN102443256A
【公开(公告)日】 2012.05.09
【申请(专利权)人】 哈尔滨鑫达高分子材料有限责任公司
【地址】 黑龙江省哈尔滨市经开区哈平路集中区大连北路9号
【发明(设计)人】 代汝军；袁程程；王海波；马俊杰；马庆维；韩杰

【摘要】 本发明公开了一种高耐热PC/ASA合金材料及其制备方法，通过PC与ASA树脂共混可以改善PC的应力开裂性能、加工性，提高PC的耐化学药品性和耐候性。随着PC含量的提高，合金材料的冲击强度和热变形温度显著提高。为提高PC/ASA合金的耐热性，使用α-甲基苯乙烯-丙烯腈共聚物(α-SAN)代替合金中的SAN相，可以使热变形温度提高到大约140℃，PC/ASA合金综合了PC的耐热、高强度、韧性和ASA的耐候性、耐化学性和加工性。因此PC/ASA合金作为一种新型的性能优良的工程塑料不仅能够满足市场多样化的需求，而且其应用前景是很可观的，可广泛的用于电器工程材料、汽车工程材料、建筑塑料制品等领域。

【名称】 一种环保无卤阻燃PC/ABS塑料粒子和制备方法及用途

【公开(公告)号】 CN102443257A

【公开(公告)日】 2012.05.09

【申请(专利权)人】 巨金高分子材料(上海)有限公司

【地址】 上海市浦东新区康桥镇康意路499号2幢A座5015室

【发明(设计)人】 吴敏；黄彦

【摘要】 本发明涉及PC/ABS改性工程塑料及其制备技术领域，具体的说是一种环保无卤阻燃PC/ABS塑料粒子和制备方法及用途，由65~70%的PC(聚碳酸酯)、15%~20%的ABS树脂(丙烯腈-丁二烯-苯乙烯共聚物)、10~15%的无卤阻燃剂、0.5%~1.5%抗滴落剂组成，将称好的PC，ABS，无卤阻燃剂和抗滴落剂等，经过一初混，加入双螺杆挤出机熔融，混炼，充分混合，分散后通过模头进行挤出，经过水浴冷却后，切粒干燥，本发明与现有技术相比解决了PC的流动性问题，又解决了ABS的易燃特性，同时极大改善了其总体的物理性能。

【名称】 一种辐射改性大豆分离蛋白/淀粉塑料及其制备方法

【公开(公告)号】 CN102443269A

【公开(公告)日】 2012.05.09

【申请(专利权)人】 河南工业大学

【地址】 河南省郑州市高新技术产业开发区莲花街

【发明(设计)人】 陈复生；刘伯业；徐卫河；何乐；王红娟等

【摘要】 一种辐射改性大豆分离蛋白/淀粉可生物降解塑料及其制备方法，以大豆分离蛋白和淀粉为主要原料，通过射线辐射改性原料制备而成，在制备所述可生物降解塑料时，各原料组分按照以下重量份混合组成：改性大豆分离蛋白85~95份，改性淀粉5~15份，己内酰胺1~3份，水10~20份，甘油10~25份。本发明的优点是：大豆分离蛋白经过适量的甲醇或乙醇改性，减少了蛋白中的亲水基团，提高了塑料的抗水性能；采用适量的淀粉充当填充剂可以使塑料的柔韧性增强，降低成本后适于工业化生产，并且可以通过调节淀粉的含量和辐照剂量得到不同力学性能的材料，科技含量高，具有创新性；其制备工艺采用常规塑料设备与方法，工艺简单，易于操作；再者本发明是由改性大豆分离蛋白和增塑剂热压后形成的，废弃后很容易被微生物分解成二氧化碳和水，不污染环境；且大豆蛋白是一种可再生的资源，取之不尽用之不竭。

【名称】 带过滤装置的塑料拉丝机

【公开(公告)号】 CN102443862A

【公开(公告)日】 2012.05.09

【申请(专利权)人】 常州普灵仕制衣有限公司

【地址】 江苏省常州市丁堰72号

【发明(设计)人】 张英

【摘要】 本发明涉及一种拉丝机的技术领域，尤其是一种带过滤装置的塑料拉丝机。其包括喂料口、过滤箱、进料管、滤板和滤网，喂料口与过滤箱固定连接，过滤箱与进料管固定连接，过滤箱内设有滤板和滤网，滤板上设有小孔，滤网数量为两个，滤网位于滤板的下方，滤网的材质为不锈钢。这种带过滤装置的塑料拉丝机使用方便，实用性强，在喂料口下方设置过滤箱，对需要拉丝的物料进行过滤，提高了物料的纯度，保证了整个拉丝过程的流畅，提高了工作效率，节省了工作时间，同时也提高了产品的质量。

【名称】 一种适用于空心塑料地板的锁扣结构

【公开(公告)号】 CN102444263A

【公开(公告)日】 2012.05.09

【申请(专利权)人】 上海德克曼地板有限公司

【地址】 上海市松江区佘山工业区天马山天云路198号

【发明(设计)人】 蔡卫东

【摘要】 一种适用于空心塑料地板的锁扣结构，涉及地板技术领域，包括一空心塑料地板本体，所述空心塑料地板本体的两个长边设置有凸榫和凹槽，其特征在于：在所述空心塑料地板本体的两个短边上均设置有向内凹进的固定槽，其中，在一个所述固定槽内设置有嵌条凸榫，在另一个所述固定槽内设置有嵌条凹槽。本发明的有益效果是；通过在空心塑料地板本体的固定槽内胶固嵌条凸榫和嵌条凹槽，并利用嵌条凸榫与嵌条凹槽的卡扣连接，实现相邻两块空心塑料地板的连接，有效规避了空心结构给连接带来的不便。

【名称】 筒式弹性金属塑料轴瓦及其制备方法
【公开(公告)号】 CN102444672A
【公开(公告)日】 2012.05.09
【申请(专利权)人】 柳盛春
【地址】 吉林省辽源市龙山区北寿街八委二组
【发明(设计)人】 柳盛春;王建武;徐俊明;李文山
【摘要】 本发明涉及一种筒式弹性金属塑料轴瓦及其制备方法，它在筒式金属基体圆内焊接2~16块弹性金属塑料瓦面，每块弹性金属塑料瓦面之间设有润滑水槽，经过弹性金属塑料瓦面制作；焊料的配制；弹性金属塑料瓦面预处理；钎焊等工序完成制备方法。本发明具有结构简单，成本低，弹性好，消振能力强，摩擦系数小，承载能力高，自润滑性能及自调节性能好，使用寿命长，不导电，绝缘好，使用异常时，对轴无损伤，维修简便等特点。

【名称】 塑料光纤生产在线监测损耗的方法
【公开(公告)号】 CN102445330A
【公开(公告)日】 2012.05.09
【申请(专利权)人】 四川汇源塑料光纤有限公司
【地址】 四川省成都市崇州市工业发展集中区
【发明(设计)人】 李凯;张用志;储九荣;吴祥君;张海龙;刘中一
【摘要】 本发明塑料光纤生产在线监测损耗的方法，该方法是将塑料光纤通过一个包含有至少一个光敏接收元件构成的接收积分球，将发射光源发射出的被测光线从塑料光纤侧面的包层外注入到塑料光纤中，在塑料光纤中传输的光的一部分从塑料光纤包层外泄漏出，经过接收积分球中的光敏接收元件接收并转换成电信号输出，塑料光纤中的杂质及芯包界面缺陷会导致塑料光纤损耗变化，从而使包层外的散射光能量发生变化，该变化即转作为塑料光纤生产在线即时的监测损耗。本发明可以即时监测到通过仪器的光纤损耗的变化情况，并进行统计，得到完整的整盘光纤的损耗波动情况。

【名称】 一种碳纤维增强塑料层压板孔隙含量的测试方法
【公开(公告)号】 CN102445410A
【公开(公告)日】 2012.05.09
【申请(专利权)人】 哈尔滨飞机工业集团有限责任公司
【地址】 黑龙江省哈尔滨市平房区友协大街15号
【发明(设计)人】 陈国权;马飞亚;金光慧;刘晓政;耿凯;刘宇
【摘要】 本发明是一种碳纤维增强塑料层压板孔隙含量的测试方法，属于理化测试技术，其特征在于：采用扫描电镜进行检验，具体分析步骤如下：制备碳纤维增强塑料试片；试样的镶嵌；试样的磨平与抛光；安放试样；扫描电镜抽真空；调整扫描电镜参数；扫描电镜低真空孔隙含量测量；试验结果的计算。本发明能对碳纤维增强塑料层压板孔隙含量进行准确分析，仪器先进，易操作，满足了科研生产和失效分析的需要。

【名称】 一种垃圾塑料的制作方法
【公开(公告)号】 CN102485461A
【公开(公告)日】 2012.06.06
【申请(专利权)人】 朱秀刚
【地址】 浙江省衢州市龙游县健康路13-2号
【发明(设计)人】 朱秀刚
【摘要】 本发明公开了一种利用垃圾为原料生产可塑性材料的制作方法。利用本方法可杜绝垃圾高温焚烧，显著减少有毒有害物污染环境，节约能耗、节约土地，本发明通过下述技术方案予以实现：将垃圾中含有的纤维、纸张、厨余物等生物质和塑料薄膜、塑料作为原料进行晒烘干、粉碎、热轧及球磨，使其成为干燥的粉碎物，经筛选、磁吸金属物后再和添加剂、润滑剂一并在高速混合机中混合，混合物进入具有强剪切、强磨擦并产生高温、高压的膨化机中挤出，快速失压。再进入挤出机挤出各种型材或粒子。粒子用塑料机械生产出注塑、挤出、泡沫等各种垃圾塑料产品。

【名称】 热合式热收缩套制作工艺流程
【公开(公告)号】 CN102485479A
【公开(公告)日】 2012.06.06
【申请(专利权)人】 青岛华仕达机器有限公司
【地址】 山东省青岛市城阳区棘洪滩街道上崖社区(原金岭工业园3号路东12号)
【发明(设计)人】 黄保东;孙丕寿
【摘要】 本发明涉及一种热合式热收缩套制作工艺流程，包括如下制作步骤：1)取出塑料基料和熔胶，制作出复合为基材层和熔胶层的半成品材料，根据直径要求制备不同宽度，不同长度的热收缩带成品。2)对热缩基材切口，把复合为双层的热收缩带作基材层和熔胶层的剥离。3)将基材/基材两端在设备上进行电热热合，4)热合后的基材部位，进行压合式冷却，使其达到适合下一工序的温度要求。5)将冷却后的基材与第一层溶胶进行风热热合。6)将第一层溶胶与第二层溶胶进行风热热合，7)熔接侧端整理。本发明有效解决了热收缩带的收缩率，极大提高了生产效率，市场前景广阔。

【名称】 无色、低凝胶含量的丁苯嵌段共聚物及其

制备方法
【公开(公告)号】 CN102485762A
【公开(公告)日】 2012.06.06
【申请(专利权)人】 中国石油化工股份有限公司
【地址】 北京市朝阳区朝阳门北大街22号
【发明(设计)人】 王雪；华炜；李传清；徐林；李建成；徐炜；刘天鹤；梁爱民；李伟
【摘要】 本发明涉及一种以有机锂引发剂合成的丁苯嵌段共聚物及其制备方法，其特征在于采用有机锂作为引发剂在惰性溶剂中进行丁二烯－苯乙烯的阴离子聚合反应；随后依次分别进行羟基酸的终止反应及中和反应。所制得的丁苯嵌段共聚物性能如下：(1)单体单元中的结合苯乙烯含量为10－60%重量，乙烯基含量为6－18%重量；(2)数均分子量范围为5×104 －30×104；(3)在100℃下的门尼粘度ML1＋4为20－200；(4)在5%甲苯溶液中的色度低于15APHA；以及(5)在5%甲苯溶液中的不溶物含量低于100ppm。本发明的丁苯嵌段共聚物能应用于塑料改性中，特别是应用于ABS和HIPS的改性。
【名称】 大型容器内衬用聚乙烯组合物
【公开(公告)号】 CN102485781A
【公开(公告)日】 2012.06.06
【申请(专利权)人】 中国石油化工股份有限公司；中国石化扬子石油化工有限公司
【地址】 北京市朝阳区朝阳门北大街22号
【发明(设计)人】 陈枫
【摘要】 本发明涉及一种大型容器内衬用聚乙烯组合物，包括聚乙烯、改性剂、抗氧剂，与现有技术相比，本发明采用多种改性剂，结合传统的抗氧剂，协同改善聚乙烯的性能，通过增加聚乙烯树脂的极性，增加金属骨架和聚乙烯内衬的结合力来提高制品寿命，从源头上解决塑料内衬和金属骨架之间结合较差的问题。
【名称】 竹屑废料再生复合塑料板及其生产工艺
【公开(公告)号】 CN102485787A
【公开(公告)日】 2012.06.06
【申请(专利权)人】 湖南忠悦塑业有限公司
【地址】 湖南省岳阳市汨罗市劳动南路五里墩4号
【发明(设计)人】 涂威忠
【摘要】 本发明为竹屑废料再生复合塑料板及其生产工艺，采用废旧PVC料和竹屑作为原料，经过分类、破碎、清洗、干燥，再经磨粉、预处理、分子改性，最后制取出竹屑废料再生复合塑料板。整个生产过程不产生污染物、能耗低，所生产的再生复合塑料板价格低、质量稳定。
【名称】 农作物废料再生复合塑料板及其生产工艺
【公开(公告)号】 CN102485788A
【公开(公告)日】 2012.06.06
【申请(专利权)人】 湖南忠悦塑业有限公司
【地址】 湖南省岳阳市汨罗市劳动南路五里墩4号
【发明(设计)人】 涂威忠
【摘要】 本发明为农作物废料再生复合塑料板及其生产工艺，采用废旧PVC料和农作物废料作为原料，经过分类、破碎、清洗、干燥，再经磨粉、预处理、分子改性，最后制取出农作物废料再生复合塑料板。整个生产过程不产生污染物、能耗低，所生产的再生复合塑料板价格低、质量稳定。
【名称】 一种碳酸氢钠注射液塑料软袋包装及其制备方法
【公开(公告)号】 CN102488617A
【公开(公告)日】 2012.06.13
【申请(专利权)人】 四川科伦药物研究有限公司
【地址】 四川省成都市新都区卫星城工业开发区南二路520号
【发明(设计)人】 李勇；欧苏；王利春
【摘要】 本发明公开了一种碳酸氢钠注射液塑料软袋包装及其制备方法，包装包括由阻气材料制成的外袋和设置在其内部的医用软塑料内袋，内袋中抽真空后灌装碳酸氢钠注射液或灌装碳酸氢钠注射液后抽真空或灌满碳酸氢钠注射液，内袋和外袋之间的空腔中填充有二氧化碳气体，其中，灌装有碳酸氢钠注射液的内袋经高温灭菌处理后再装入外袋中。本发明制备方法简单、方便，便于生产、加工和存贮，能够有效防止碳酸氢钠注射液的分解，使药液可以处于一个相对平衡的状态，保证了约液的稳定性，保证了输液液体的质量，同时也方便了输液时的操作。
【名称】 一种醇水性塑料凹版调金油的制备方法
【公开(公告)号】 CN102485813A
【公开(公告)日】 2012.06.06
【申请(专利权)人】 成都市新津托展油墨有限公司
【地址】 四川省成都市新津县花源镇工业园区
【发明(设计)人】 付勇；金勇
【摘要】 本发明涉及一种由特定结构多元丙烯酸酯树脂、乙醇、水及酯类溶剂组成的醇水性塑料凹版复合金墨用调金油。其中特定结构多元丙烯酸酯树脂是由丙烯酸酯、醋酸乙烯酯、功能单体聚合而成，具有醇水溶性，对金粉有很好的分散能力和分散稳定性。以特定结构多元丙烯酸酯树脂为连接料制备的调金油，不仅可以有效提高金粉的分散性，减少金粉用量，降低成本；同时还可提高金粉的附着力，改善印刷效果；由于特定结构多元丙烯酸酯树脂的醇水溶性，使其在调配金墨时仅需使用乙醇和水为溶剂，避免了其它有毒有害溶剂及增塑剂的使用，具有很好的安全环保性，非常符合现代塑料复合包装印刷的要求，在塑料凹版复合油墨领域有着广阔的应用前景。

【名称】 一种塑料层压板加盖封装产品组装夹具结构

【公开(公告)号】 CN102490136A

【公开(公告)日】 2012.06.13

【申请(专利权)人】 爱普科斯科技(无锡)有限公司

【地址】 江苏省无锡市新区无锡新加坡工业园新都路2号

【发明(设计)人】 张燕

【摘要】 本发明提供了一种塑料层压板加盖封装产品组装夹具结构，能够保证塑料盖子和基板与胶水的充分接触，并始终保持其粘合时所需的压力不变，保证胶水的粘合效果。其包括载板，层压板置于所述载板上，在所述层压板上铺设塑料盖板，所述塑料盖板与所述层压板通过胶水粘合在一起，其特征在于：其还包括压块、盖板安装导向板，所述压块置于所述塑料盖板上，所述盖板安装导向板套装于所述塑料盖板的外围。

【名称】 一种带旋转轴的数控泡沫塑料切割机

【公开(公告)号】 CN102490200A

【公开(公告)日】 2012.06.13

【申请(专利权)人】 天津理工大学

【地址】 天津市南开区红旗南路延长线天津理工大学主校区

【发明(设计)人】 韩佳颖

【摘要】 数控泡沫塑料切割机以精确高效的特点在近十年来得到了广泛应用。但是至今为止还只限于4个步进电机控制两组倒T型切割架，由于其结构限制，目前还只能加工投影形状为四边形的产品，例如广告字切割，模型飞机机翼切割等，限制了泡沫塑料切割机的应用范围。该方案通过在普通四轴的数控泡沫切割机上添加一个步进电机驱动的第五轴，使泡沫切割机加工三维螺旋曲面零件、旋转多面体和椎体零件成为了可能，极大增强了泡沫塑料切割机的应用范围。

【名称】 一种塑料烘干器

【公开(公告)号】 CN102490284A

【公开(公告)日】 2012.06.13

【申请(专利权)人】 浙江华顺椅业有限公司

【地址】 浙江省湖州市安吉县递铺镇阳光工业三区

【发明(设计)人】 李玉青

【摘要】 本发明涉及机械技术领域，具体是一种塑料烘干器。它包括机架，设置在机架的物料槽、设置在物料槽下端的出料装置以及电控系统，所述物料槽的底部呈弧形，且所述物料槽的底部设置有弧形加热板，所述物料槽内设置有搅拌装置，所述搅拌装置包括横贯所述物料槽中心的转轴，所述转轴一端穿过物料槽与所述电控系统相连，所述转轴上设置有搅拌叶片组。本发明提供的搅拌装置，在对塑料粒加热过程中进行不断搅拌，避免塑料粒相互粘附，保证了塑料制件的机械性能。

【名称】 一种中空板塑料成型机用新型整体真空定型板

【公开(公告)号】 CN102490287A

【公开(公告)日】 2012.06.13

【申请(专利权)人】 余建文

【地址】 湖北省武汉市江汉区江汉路257号

【发明(设计)人】 余建文

【摘要】 本发明提出了一种中空板塑料成型机用新型整体真空定型板，它是按真空定型板尺寸选取整体钢材，内部设有若干用深孔加工的加工出水道和气道，真空定型板正面设置网纹槽和若干直纹槽，其上加工出多个与气道连通的真空吸口，气道两端用丝堵堵死；真空定型板反面设置了若干与真空吸管连接的接口，该接口与气道连通，同时所有真空吸管接口与总集器罐相连，并与真空泵相连。在真空定型板的两端，用设有使水道串联或并联或混合连通的连通槽的侧封板密封连接起来，达到最佳冷却效果。本发明整体结构，不怕变形，冷却效果好，维修量小，真空定型板内的真空分布均匀，真空吸附能力强，真空泵的功率大大下降，大大提高产品质量和生产效率。

【名称】 一种注塑机螺杆

【公开(公告)号】 CN102490327A

【公开(公告)日】 2012.06.13

【申请(专利权)人】 浙江华业塑料机械有限公司

【地址】 浙江省舟山市定海区金塘镇欣港路191号浙江华业塑料机械有限公司

【发明(设计)人】 周秀琴；夏增富；王成学；徐世

【摘要】 一种注塑机螺杆，在进料段(A)、压缩段(B)、均化段(C)上设置有螺棱(1)，其特征在于：所述均化段(C)上设置有能脱卸式与均化段(C)相连接且可为不同结构的镶嵌段(C1)，所述镶嵌段(1)与均化段(C)相连接的一端设置有既起到均化效果又能方便拆卸的锁紧段(C2)。本发明的优点在于：镶嵌段与均化段为脱卸式连接，可更换不同结构的镶嵌段，适用于多种机型，结构简单，经济适用：当塑料加工需添加色粉或/和色母料时，使用带与进料段相同螺棱的镶嵌段；当塑料加工不需添加色粉或/和色母料时，使用带螺棱纹的镶嵌段；镶嵌段的前段设置有多边形的锁紧段，既起到均化效果又方便拆卸。

【名称】 一种模具
【公开(公告)号】 CN102490320A
【公开(公告)日】 2012.06.13
【申请(专利权)人】 常州鑫鹏工具制造有限公司
【地址】 江苏省常州市新北区西夏墅镇镇南西路115-1号
【发明(设计)人】 金震宇
【摘要】 本发明注塑设备技术领域，具体涉及一种注塑设备中的模具，其包括设有注塑通道的上模具、下模具，在上模具、下模具组装到位后，上模具、下模具之间形成注塑模腔，上模具的下端面固定设置有限位柱，限位柱的下端固定设置有限位块，所述限位块的直径大于限位柱的直径，下模具的上端面开设有与限位块配合的限位盲孔，在限位盲孔的一侧设置有与其相贯通的调节槽，调节槽的槽底可供限位块通过，其调节槽的槽口尺寸小于限位块的直径。在注塑过程中，可以旋转调节上模具，使注塑料充分的流到模腔内每个部位，注塑出的产品外观完整，同时在旋转的过程中，注塑料间的气泡被挤出，注塑出的产品内部便不会产生气泡，提高了注塑产品的内部质量。

【名称】 注塑机动模板的调节装置
【公开(公告)号】 CN102490331A
【公开(公告)日】 2012.06.13
【申请(专利权)人】 佛山市顺德区震德塑料机械有限公司
【地址】 广东省佛山市顺德区大良红岗工业区
【发明(设计)人】 张贤宝；陈桂烽
【摘要】 本发明涉及一种二板式注塑料机，具体地说是涉及动模板的精度调节。它包括动模板、入闸螺母、拉杆、定位架、传动齿轮组和楔块，定位架安装于入闸螺母侧的动模板上，传动齿轮安装于定位架上，传动齿轮组又包括主动轮和末端输出轮，主动轮与动模板连动，末端输出轮同轴地设有凸轮，楔块通过弹簧安装于定位架上，弹簧使得楔块具有向定位架运动的趋势。本发明结构设计合理，与拉杆具有联动功能的自动调节齿距机构，能自动调节入闸螺母与拉杆之间的位置，实现二板式注塑机抱闸精度发要求。不需要增加额外的动力装置，节约了相当大的成本，具有明显的经济效益。

【名称】 塑料挤出机机头
【公开(公告)号】 CN102490343A
【公开(公告)日】 2012.06.13
【申请(专利权)人】 四川省资阳市雅之江塑业有限公司
【地址】 四川省资阳市雁江区侯家坪工业园
【发明(设计)人】 马健；杨智勇；周术兵；刘军；郭建军
【摘要】 本发明公开一种塑料挤出机机头，包括外筒体组件以及安装于所述外筒体组件内的滤芯组件，所述外筒体组件包括外筒体(3)，所述滤芯组件包括滤管(4)，所述滤管(4)的出料口和所述外筒体(3)的出料口连通，所述滤管(4)的外周管壁上贴附有过滤网(5)。本发明中，进入外筒体组件的高温塑化物料先由过滤网滤掉较大的杂质，之后再由滤管进行二次过滤，可有效增强过滤效果。

【名称】 塑料模具自动加热装置
【公开(公告)号】 CN102490344A
【公开(公告)日】 2012.06.13
【申请(专利权)人】 阿丽贝(鞍山)塑料防腐设备有限公司
【地址】 辽宁省鞍山市铁西区创业街138号
【发明(设计)人】 郑世义；关玉华
【摘要】 塑料模具自动加热装置，涉及一种模具加热装置，主体框架(1)连接伸缩梁(12)，伸缩梁前端连接中部加热装置(6)；上、下部加热装置通过万向调节器(5)分别固定在中部加热器上；上、下部加热器的传动丝母也固定在中部加热器上；伸缩梁电机(13)、伸缩梁减速机(14)、齿轮(15)、齿条(16)配合呈前后移动状，上下加热装置分别经下部加热装置电机(2)、上部加热装置电机(8)、下部加热装置减速机(3)、上部加热装置减速机(9)连接丝杠、丝母并围绕中部加热装置呈旋转状。本发明装置在加热过程中即不会出现温度不够、也不会出现温度过高的过烧现象，使产品质量有了显著的提高。

【名称】 一种双口容器的吹塑成型方法
【公开(公告)号】 CN102490347A
【公开(公告)日】 2012.06.13
【申请(专利权)人】 东莞佳鸿机械制造有限公司
【地址】 广东省东莞市望牛墩镇金牛路68号东莞佳鸿机械制造有限公司
【发明(设计)人】 李伟宏
【摘要】 本发明涉及吹塑成型技术领域，特指一种双口容器的吹塑成型方法，该方法包括如下步骤：A. 注塑成型双口容器管胚，B. 整理双口容器管胚，C. 双口容器管胚安装于吹塑机中，D. 吹塑机对双口容器管胚进行加热，E. 吹塑机对双口容器管胚进行拉伸与吹塑形成双口容器，该成型方法可以利用聚丙烯、聚对苯二甲酸乙二醇酯或聚乙烯等材料节约、简单、快速地制造出无缝、透明的双口塑料包装容器，该吹塑成型方法制造出来的双口塑料包装容器具有透明度好，产量高，壁厚均匀，重量轻，成本低等优点，更好的满足国内外市场对塑料双口容器的需要。

【名称】 一种吹塑制品成型方法及其设备

【公开(公告)号】 CN102490348A

【公开(公告)日】 2012.06.13

【申请(专利权)人】 广州市中新塑料有限公司

【地址】 广东省广州市增城市中新镇中福北路3号

【发明(设计)人】 石贵初；杨军；吕凡磊

【摘要】 本发明一种吹塑制品成型方法及其设备，通过设置真空吸塑装置，在模具合模时，真空泵通过管道抽取模具型腔内的空气，使模具上、下模侧的料分别与模具充分贴合；型坯吹气成型时，真空泵通过管道抽取模具型腔内的空气，使吹胀后的型坯外表面与模具型腔之间形成负压，使吹胀后的型坯在足够的压力差下延伸成型。本发明不但可以成型一些用普通吹塑成型工艺无法成型的深、窄腔塑料制品，而且加快了型坯成型速度，缩短了型坯成型周期，提高了生产效率。

【名称】 一种发动机塑料进气歧管焊接筋结构

【公开(公告)号】 CN102490356A

【公开(公告)日】 2012.06.13

【申请(专利权)人】 重庆长安汽车股份有限公司

【地址】 重庆市江北区建新东路260号

【发明(设计)人】 刘纯；鄢烈；罗昆；池诚；陈洪文

【摘要】 本发明公开一种发动机塑料进气歧管焊接筋结构，包括设在塑料进气歧管上片上的上焊接筋和设在塑料进气歧管下片上的下焊接筋，其特征是：所述下焊接筋的下末端呈圆弧状，下末端的宽度大于下焊接筋的宽度，在下焊接筋及下末端的边缘设有挡料边；所述上焊接筋的上末端呈圆弧状，上末端的宽度大于上焊接筋的宽度；所述塑料进气歧管上片和塑料进气歧管下片通过焊接机的摩擦振动对应焊接。本发明由于断开式焊接筋末端的宽度较焊接筋其它部位宽，焊接筋末端近似圆弧状结构，从而提高了焊接后焊接筋末端的焊接强度；由于在塑料进气歧管下片上的下焊接筋及下末端的边缘设有挡料边，阻止了焊接溢料进入进气道，避免了对塑料进气歧管性能的影响。

【名称】 一种零件连接于塑料中空体内腔的方法

【公开(公告)号】 CN102490365A

【公开(公告)日】 2012.06.13

【申请(专利权)人】 亚普汽车部件股份有限公司

【地址】 江苏省扬州市扬子江南路508号

【发明(设计)人】 孙岩；姜林；刘亮；朱志勇；刘义虎；苏卫东；王晔

【摘要】 本发明涉及一种零件连接于塑料中空体内腔的方法，包括以下步骤：熔融状的筒状型坯向下流动，被割刀割成相互分离的两片并悬挂在模头下；将内置零件分别安装在芯模机构上并置于预成型框架的内腔；油箱左半模及油箱右半模分别夹着左平面型坯、预成型框架及右平面型坯合模；芯模机构上的吹气头向型坯内腔进行预吹，型坯向外膨胀贴合在油箱左右半模的内壁；将内置零件分别焊接在型坯的内壁，然后芯模机构的夹持装置与各内置零件分离；油箱左右半模打开，预成型框架连同芯模机构移出后重新闭合，左右型坯粘接形成油箱，再对型坯内腔进行高压吹使油箱成型。该方法制成的油箱蒸汽排放量小，制造周期短，焊接质量好。

【名称】 双挤出流延塑料夹网膜产品连续生产成型工艺及设备

【公开(公告)号】 CN102490366A

【公开(公告)日】 2012.06.13

【申请(专利权)人】 大连塑料研究所有限公司

【地址】 辽宁省大连市甘井子区周家街11号

【发明(设计)人】 孙成伦；王善君；李振宇；车广陆；谢明涛；宋春明；贾冰茹

【摘要】 本发明涉及一种双挤出流延塑料夹网膜产品连续生产成型工艺及设备，所述工艺是将由树脂、填料及功能性助剂形成的混合原料搅拌均匀后投入到双螺杆挤出机中，设定挤出机温度及和片模机头的温度，控制模唇温度，开启挤出机，熔融物料经片膜机头流出，被引入流延复合辊；同时将编织布引入两片薄膜之间复合成型；经冷却定型，并在牵引辊的牵引作用下经导辊、切边、展平，最后收卷成夹网膜制品。本发明将熔融原料经双螺杆挤出机挤出塑化后经流延拉伸，膜的表面结构发生变化，基材塑料与填充料之间产生微孔，从而降低了膜的密度。因此，相同配比条件下，双挤出流延成型工艺生产的夹网膜产品比重小，单位重量轻，所述设备结构简单合理，制作成本是贴合法设备的1/4左右，实现了连续生产成型。

【名称】 拼插式玻璃纤维增强塑料托盘

【公开(公告)号】 CN102490967A

【公开(公告)日】 2012.06.13

【申请(专利权)人】 振石集团华美复合新材料有限公司

【地址】 浙江省嘉兴市桐乡市经济开发区发展大道

2133号
【发明(设计)人】 盛江峰；于治东；沈柏林；陈永霞
【摘要】 本发明涉及一种拼插式玻璃纤维增强塑料托盘，特别是一种适用于不同尺寸规格和承载能力又能长期周转使用的托盘。该拼插式玻璃纤维增强塑料托盘，由以下部件组成，长条形的面板，所述面板的上方为平面；交叉放置在面板下方的梁，所述梁与面板卡接，所述梁与面板平行设置；支撑梁的托脚，所述托脚与梁卡接固定；所述的面板、梁、托脚的材质均为玻璃纤维增强塑料。本发明具有承载能力高、能长期周转使用、强度高、防水防腐、可适用尺寸范围大、可适用承载能力范围大、易于维护、安装简单的优点。

【名称】 一种包装袋
【公开(公告)号】 CN102490970A
【公开(公告)日】 2012.06.13
【申请(专利权)人】 常州市银鹭数控刀具厂
【地址】 江苏省常州市新北区西夏墅镇微山湖路83号
【发明(设计)人】 恽益群
【摘要】 本发明涉及一种包装袋，其包括薄膜材料制成的包装袋主体、设置于包装袋主体一端得开口以及设置于开口处的热密封的封口组件，所述的包装袋内设置有若干个分隔密封组件，所述的分隔密封组件为密封条，其包括设置于包装袋主体内部一侧袋体上的塑料凸条和设置于包装袋主体内部与凸条相对位置的塑料凹条。

【名称】 隔离弹壳储存隔离袋的方法
【公开(公告)号】 CN102490986A
【公开(公告)日】 2012.06.13
【申请(专利权)人】 杨惠珠
【地址】 重庆市渝中区双钢路1号重庆钢铁设计研究总院离退处
【发明(设计)人】 杨惠珠
【摘要】 目前，隔离法(用隔离袋把饮用水和包装物隔离开)，问题是怎样把隔离袋迅速的装到桶口里，为此，本发明提供一种隔离弹壳里储存隔离袋的方法。目的是把柔软的塑料薄膜，又没有固定形状的隔离袋，迅速装到桶口里，是难攻克的课题。为此，本发明借助隔离弹这个载体，把隔离袋、隔离弹壳，…,迅速的装到桶口里——然后向隔离袋里灌装饮用水。隔离袋与隔离弹壳的连接是密封性的连接，其特征是：在隔离弹壳里储存隔离袋。有益效果是开发商投资自制，隔离弹只有两件，隔离弹壳和隔离袋，造无难点。投资少、质量难保、用人太多。推荐开发商投资建隔离弹专业制造厂，估算36万颗隔离弹/日产量，隔离弹的质量稳定、满足巨大产量、投资效益高、成本低。

【名称】 一种天然斜发沸石制备白炭黑的方法
【公开(公告)号】 CN102491351A
【公开(公告)日】 2012.06.13
【申请(专利权)人】 沈阳化工大学
【地址】 辽宁省沈阳市经济技术开发区11号
【发明(设计)人】 方庆红；刘晓晨；王娜；杨凤；韩文驰；高雨
【摘要】 一种天然斜发沸石制备白炭黑的制备方法，涉及一种制备白炭黑的制备方法。包括如下步骤：将原料沸石经粉碎加工使其粒径细化，对沸石做焙烧处理；在80~150℃下，用强碱溶液A和沸石反应1~5h，然后过滤获得水玻璃溶液；制备的溶液加水稀释后，加入乙醇和电解质B，用酸C进行沉析、沉淀得含水二氧化硅；沉淀物经陈化、过滤、洗涤、干燥后即得本产品白炭黑。主要用于橡胶及塑料的补强和填充，提高硫化橡胶的抗拉强度、断裂伸长率、耐疲劳性能等。本方法生产工艺简单、成本低廉，环保程度高，可广泛用于各类高分子材料补强剂，造纸、印刷油墨的吸附剂等。

【名称】 一种相容剂及其制备方法和使用该相容剂的工程塑料
【公开(公告)号】 CN102492076A
【公开(公告)日】 2012.06.13
【申请(专利权)人】 深圳市科聚新材料有限公司
【地址】 广东省深圳市宝安区福永镇富桥工业区三区二期A19栋
【发明(设计)人】 徐东；徐永；程必舒
【摘要】 本发明公开了一种相容剂及制备方法以及一种使用该相容剂的工程塑料，所述的相容剂是由甲基丙烯酸缩水甘油酯、苯乙烯、丙烯腈三元聚合物为自主聚合成的三元共聚物GMA-St-AN。所述的工程塑料的原料是70分质量的PA6和30份质量的ABS，加入1到5份质量的GMA-St-AN。在PA6/ABS合金中应用，比较与传统的SMA和ABS-g-MAH效果更好。

【名称】 一种热塑性丙烯酸树脂
【公开(公告)号】 CN102492080A
【公开(公告)日】 2012.06.13
【申请(专利权)人】 江苏三木化工股份有限公司
【地址】 江苏省无锡市宜兴市官林镇三民路85号
【发明(设计)人】 宋坤忠；薛华；吴丽萍
【摘要】 一种热塑性丙烯酸树脂，制备方法如下：(1)将质量比为50%的有机溶剂投入反应容器，搅拌均匀，加热到回流状态；(2)将质量比为38%～42%的甲基丙烯酸甲酯、3%～8%的苯乙烯、1%～2%的特殊功能单体、1%～3%的甲基丙烯酸环己酯、0.5%～1%的引发剂混合均匀，滴加入反应容器，控制反应容器内温度为有机溶剂回流温度，滴料控制时间为3.5～4h；(3)滴完后，保温2～5h，降温至75℃以内，过滤，即得。本热塑性丙烯酸树脂，其特征在于可以应用于制备工程塑料铝粉漆涂料。本发明具有高硬度、耐刮伤、耐乙醇擦拭、耐高温高湿等良好的性能，同时又和铝粉有良好附着力。

【名称】 一种可生物降解高回弹软质聚氨酯泡沫塑料及其制备方法

【公开(公告)号】 CN102492109A

【公开(公告)日】 2012.06.13

【申请(专利权)人】 西安科技大学

【地址】 陕西省西安市雁塔路中段58号

【发明(设计)人】 汪广恒

【摘要】 本发明公开了一种可生物降解高回弹软质聚氨酯泡沫塑料及其制备方法，其塑料由100重量份的多元醇、1～20重量份的大豆蛋白质、2～15重量份的发泡剂、0.05～10重量份的催化剂、0.05～5重量份的泡沫稳定剂和30～70重量份的多异氰酸酯制成；其制备方法包括步骤：一、将大豆蛋白质与多元醇按比例混合后，在常温或低温加热条件下静置；二、将发泡剂、催化剂和泡沫稳定剂按比例加入并混合均匀；三、将多异氰酸酯按比例加入并混合均匀；四、注入发泡模具并在常温下静置，获得固化后的聚氨酯泡沫塑料。本发明经简单搅拌混合原料、冷固化成型即可，生产工艺简单，产品质量稳定且所制备聚氨酯泡沫塑料自然生物降解性能良好。

【名称】 一种软质聚氨酯泡沫塑料及生产工艺

【公开(公告)号】 CN102492114A

【公开(公告)日】 2012.06.13

【申请(专利权)人】 浙江川洋海绵有限公司

【地址】 浙江省嘉兴市海宁市盐官镇园区四路2号

【发明(设计)人】 赵建良；张忠华；李铁虎；陈刚；江良

【摘要】 本发明公开了一种软质聚氨酯泡沫塑料及制备软质聚氨酯泡沫塑料的生产工艺，原料聚醚、异氰酸酯、水、催化剂、匀泡剂的混合物通过一步法连续发泡工艺反应而成，所述聚醚由PPG和POP组成，所述异氰酸酯TDI的异构体比例2，4－TDI:2，6－TDI为75～85:15～25。本发明通过一步法连续块泡工艺下生产出表观密度达到80kg/m^{3}的高密度海绵，该海绵因为使用了连续法发泡工艺，所以具有较模塑海绵生产能力高、开孔性好的特点。通过上述工艺可以较普通块泡海绵在连续生产条件下密度高，达到80kg/m^3，这样就使泡沫的孔茎较粗，所以弹性与承载力要高。

【名称】 一种尼龙/石墨导热塑料及其制备方法和用途

【公开(公告)号】 CN102492134A

【公开(公告)日】 2012.06.13

【申请(专利权)人】 中国科学院宁波材料技术与工程研究所

【地址】 浙江省宁波市镇海区庄市大道519号

【发明(设计)人】 祝颖丹；杨恒；颜春；张笑晴；李建广；张希平；范欣愉

【摘要】 本发明涉及一种尼龙/石墨导热塑料及其制备方法和用途，具体地，公开了一种内酰胺开环聚合制备尼龙/石墨导热塑料的方法，所述方法将石墨等高导热填料高份量、均匀分散在内酰胺聚合体系中，制得高导热塑料。所述塑料既显著提高了热导率，又保持了材料优良的综合性能。该方法解决了现有制备方法存在的高份量石墨填充困难、分散不均等问题，生产方便，制得的尼龙/石墨导热塑料质量稳定，成本低，性能优良，具有广阔的工业化应用前景。

【名称】 一种可熔性聚酰亚胺模塑料及其制备方法

【公开(公告)号】 CN102492141A

【公开(公告)日】 2012.06.13

【申请(专利权)人】 上海市合成树脂研究所

【地址】 上海市徐汇区漕宝路36号

【发明(设计)人】 邱孜学；贺飞峰；包来燕；吕凯

【摘要】 本发明公开了一种可熔性聚酰亚胺模塑料及其制备方法，该方法包含：步骤1，聚酰胺酸溶液制备：采用等摩尔比的2，3，3′，4′－二苯醚四甲酸二酐和二氨基二苯醚在非质子极性溶剂中，室温反应3～5h制备得到聚酰胺酸溶液；步骤2，化学亚胺化：上述聚酰胺酸溶液按100重量份计，向该聚酰胺酸溶液中加入脱水剂40～160重量份、叔胺类有机碱催化剂5～50重量份及非极性芳烃，强烈搅拌0.5～2h，粉末析出，过滤，获得a型聚酰亚胺模塑粉。该方法制备的a型聚酰亚胺与s－型聚酰亚胺相比，成型温度降低70℃，在220℃的机械性能远远高于s－型聚酰亚胺，且该a型聚酰亚胺具有可溶可熔的特性。本发明提供的a型聚酰亚胺模塑粉的制备方法，条件温和，操作安全、方便，收率高，具有市场前景。

【名称】 一种分散石墨填充聚四氟乙烯树脂的制备方法

【公开(公告)号】 CN102492157A
【公开(公告)日】 2012.06.13
【申请(专利权)人】 江苏梅兰化工有限公司
【地址】 江苏省泰州市扬州路460号
【发明(设计)人】 司耀俊；钱厚琴；殷铭
【摘要】 本发明属含氟塑料及其制备方法技术领域，涉及一种以聚四氟乙烯(PTFE)分散液为基材，石墨为填充料采用湿法混合法以及助剂体系，制备分散石墨填充聚四氟乙烯树脂的方法，其特征在于：(1)以1‰聚丙烯酸钠溶液为分散剂，配制固含量为5%石墨分散液；(2)将所述石墨分散液与固含量为12.7%的聚四氟乙烯分散液均匀混合，其中石墨固含量占5%~70%；(3)加入3%的丁二酸溶液为凝聚助剂，搅拌、过滤、洗涤、烘干，得到固体粉末状态树脂。本发明的有益效果是：制备工艺简单，易于工业化，原料损耗少，填充准确性高，填料分布均匀，在保持设备条件不变的情况下，可大范围调整所需要的填充量，制备低填充量，或高填充量的聚四氟乙烯树脂，满足不同的需要。
【名称】 一种新型含磷含硅阻燃剂及其制备方法
【公开(公告)号】 CN102492171A
【公开(公告)日】 2012.06.13
【申请(专利权)人】 上海交通大学
【地址】 上海市闵行区东川路800号
【发明(设计)人】 王立春；霍瑞美；江平开；吴新锋；李雅南；李密
【摘要】 本发明公开了一种新型含磷含硅阻燃剂，具有如下重复结构单元：其中，m为2-4，n为5-8。本发明还公开了该新型含磷含硅阻燃剂的制备方法。本发明得到一种含有双螺环结构、DOPO侧基的含磷含硅的阻燃剂，可用于聚烯烃电缆材料，使其具有非常优异的阻燃性能。另外，与传统的阻燃剂相比，本发明具有无卤、低烟、低毒、环保等特点，适用于塑料、橡胶、纤维等高分子材料。
【名称】 一种低烟无卤光缆阻燃护套料
【公开(公告)号】 CN102492201A
【公开(公告)日】 2012.06.13
【申请(专利权)人】 江苏七宝光电集团有限公司
【地址】 江苏省苏州市吴江市震泽镇八都工业区318国道旁
【发明(设计)人】 崔七宝；陈炳炎
【摘要】 本发明涉及一种低烟无卤光缆阻燃护套料，其主要成分及配比如下：聚乙烯(PE)为58%~62%、阻燃剂为32%~36%、偶联剂为0.8%~1.2%、软化剂为1.0%~1.4%、塑料光亮剂为0.6%~1.0%、润滑剂为0.6%~1.0%、抗氧化剂为0.8%~1.2%、碳黑为1.0%~1.4%。本护套料不会产生浓重的黑烟以及有害物质HCl。
【名称】 废旧PE电缆外皮合成木塑复合板材配方及制造方法
【公开(公告)号】 CN102492209A
【公开(公告)日】 2012.06.13
【申请(专利权)人】 天津鼎升昊科技发展有限公司
【地址】 天津市南开区华苑产业区华天道2号2100室-D1006
【发明(设计)人】 聂莉
【摘要】 本发明涉及一种废旧PE电缆外皮合成木塑复合板材配方及制造方法。将废旧PE电缆外皮颗粒、纯PE粉末、金属皂类稳定剂和润滑剂加入高混机中混合，将硅烷偶联剂进行水解处理，然后将硅烷偶联剂和木粉混合，放入高混机中混合，将上述两组原料放入高混机中混合，将混合好的原料加入双螺杆挤出机中进行混炼挤出，将粉碎的木塑材料于模具中压制成型，即可得到复合板材。木塑复合材料制品因兼有木材和塑料的优点，因而被广泛应用于很多领域，如家具、建筑、工业、车辆船舶、包装运输等国民生产的各个方面。
【名称】 一种利用赤泥复配聚氯乙烯彩色硬质塑料的生产方法
【公开(公告)号】 CN102492234A
【公开(公告)日】 2012.06.13
【申请(专利权)人】 中国铝业股份有限公司
【地址】 北京市海淀区西直门北大街62号
【发明(设计)人】 段光福；刘万超；陈湘清；于延分
【摘要】 一种改性赤泥复配聚氯乙烯彩色硬质塑料的生产方法，其特征在于是将分级后的-800目赤泥采用钛酸酯偶联剂改性，改性赤泥与聚氯乙烯、抗冲改性剂、稳定剂、润滑剂高速混合、熔融挤出、覆膜制得彩色硬质塑料，其中聚氯乙烯：100份；改性赤泥：35~45份；抗冲改性剂：5~10份；稳定剂：3~5份；润滑剂：0.2~0.8份。本方法对赤泥改性处理，显著提高了赤泥和聚氯乙烯的相容性，对塑料进行覆膜处理后，改变了赤泥复配聚氯乙烯基体塑料单调的棕红色，使其具有木质花纹，颜色丰富多彩，非常美观。
【名称】 PVC树脂成型加工用内润滑剂及其制备方法
【公开(公告)号】 CN102492237A
【公开(公告)日】 2012.06.13
【申请(专利权)人】 山东瑞丰高分子材料股份有限公司

【地址】 山东省淄博市沂源县城保丰路26号

【发明(设计)人】 张海瑜；呼建强；刘春信；张振国；葛峰

【摘要】 本发明是一种PVC树脂成型加工用内润滑剂及其制备方法。属于仅用碳-碳不饱和键反应得到的高分子材料预处理有机配料。其特征在于由如下按照重量份数计的原料组成：环氧油酸50～95，脂肪族二元醇4.5～49.5，钛酸丁酯0.1～0.5。其制备方法包括如下步骤：①投料、升温，②缩合反应，③切片、包装。提供了一种润滑性能优异，相容性、分散性好，同时具有一定辅助热稳定性的PVC树脂成型加工用内润滑剂及其制备方法。由于环氧油酸中环氧基团具有化学活性，能吸收氯化氢，从而避免聚氯乙烯塑料加速老化，起到稳定作用。本发明的内滑剂与PVC成型加工配方体系中的其他组分配伍性良好，生产成本低。

【名称】 利用废旧聚氯乙烯电缆料生产木塑复合材料的配方及方法

【公开(公告)号】 CN102492245A

【公开(公告)日】 2012.06.13

【申请(专利权)人】 天津鼎升昊科技发展有限公司

【地址】 天津市南开区华苑产业区华天道2号2100室-D1006

【发明(设计)人】 聂莉

【摘要】 特别是涉及一种利用废旧聚氯乙烯电缆料生产木塑复合材料的配方及加工方法。将废旧聚氯乙烯电缆颗粒、纯聚氯乙烯粉、木粉、金属皂类稳定剂、偶联剂、增塑剂、氯化聚乙烯、甲基丙烯酸多元酯、润滑剂按照配方配制的原料加入高混机中混合，将混合好的原料加入挤出机中进行挤出定型。本方法所采用的聚氯乙烯原料为国内废旧电缆拆解企所拆解出的废旧电缆外皮，价格低廉，且有利于环境保护。本方法所采用的塑料助剂大部分为无毒或低毒产品，在材料生产和使用过程中对人体和环境危害很小。

【名称】 废旧PVC电缆外皮/木粉复合板材的配方及生产方法

【公开(公告)号】 CN102492246A

【公开(公告)日】 2012.06.13

【申请(专利权)人】 天津鼎升昊科技发展有限公司

【地址】 天津市南开区华苑产业区华天道2号2100室-D1006

【发明(设计)人】 聂莉

【摘要】 本发明涉及一种废旧PVC电缆外皮/木粉复合板材的配方及生产方法。将废旧PVC电缆外皮颗粒、纯PVC粉末、金属皂类稳定剂、氯化聚乙烯、甲基丙烯酸多元酯和润滑剂加入高混机中混合，将硅烷偶联剂进行水解处理，然后将硅烷偶联剂和木粉混合，放入高混机中混合，将上述两组原料放入高混机中混合，将混合好的原料加入双螺杆挤出机中进行混炼挤出，将粉碎的木塑材料于模具中压制成型，即可得到复合板材。木塑复合材料制品因兼有木材和塑料的优点，因而被广泛应用于很多领域，如家具、建筑、工业、车辆船舶、包装运输等国民生产的各个方面。

【名称】 一种用于ABS废注塑料的加工改性剂及其使用方法

【公开(公告)号】 CN102492258A

【公开(公告)日】 2012.06.13

【申请(专利权)人】 湖北众联塑业有限公司

【地址】 湖北省武汉市宝丰路1号湖北商务大楼1206室

【发明(设计)人】 邓丽；邓军；邓忠权；陈绪煌

【摘要】 本发明公开了一种用于ABS废注塑料的加工改性剂及其使用方法，所述的加工改性剂包括以下组分及其重量份：氯化聚乙烯1.0～2.0、高胶粉5.0～10.0；本发明所述的ABS废注塑料的加工改性剂的使用方法包括如下步骤：一、ABS废注塑料的处理；二、检测ABS废注塑料的熔体流动指数；三、配料：按ABS废注塑料:氯化聚乙烯:高胶粉=100:1.0～2.0:5.0～10.0；四、投料加工，将上述配制的各组分投入混合机内，在常温条件下开机12～15分钟，停机，卸料包装即可。本发明具有工艺合理、加工简单，可以有效地提高ABS废注塑料的物化性能和产品质量等效益，本发明可以广泛地用于ABS废注塑料的改性加工。

【名称】 一种完全生物降解塑料材料及其制备方法

【公开(公告)号】 CN102492271A

【公开(公告)日】 2012.06.13

【申请(专利权)人】 金发科技股份有限公司；上海金发科技发展有限公司；珠海万通化工有限公司

【地址】 广东省广州市高新技术产业开发区科学城科丰路33号

【发明(设计)人】 钟宇科；焦建；苑仁旭；赵崴；徐依斌；曾祥斌；蔡彤旻；夏世勇

【摘要】 本发明公开了一种完全生物降解塑料材料，按重量百分比计，包含聚乳酸20%～40%；长支链化脂肪族聚酯或长支链化脂肪族-芳香族共聚酯50%～60%；扩链剂0.1%～3%；填充剂1%～10%；增塑剂5%～10%；抗氧剂0.1%～1%；润滑剂0.1%～1%；稳定剂0.1%～1%；成核剂0.1%～1%。其制备方法是将各组分在高速混合机中混合后由计量称精确计量喂料入双螺杆挤出机进行挤出造粒而制得，本发明通过螺杆组合的调整，经过反应性混炼挤出，改善了 PBSA 制品的力学特性，同时改善了聚乳酸的柔韧性和降解速率，得到的完全生物降解塑料材料不仅具有优异的生物降解性能和老化性能，而且具有优良的力学性能和吹膜加工性能。

【名称】 一种聚酰胺塑料用激光标记助剂、制备方法及其应用

【公开(公告)号】 CN102492291A

【公开(公告)日】 2012.06.13

【申请(专利权)人】 上海金发科技发展有限公司；金发科技股份有限公司

【地址】 上海市青浦区朱家角工业园康园路 88 号

【发明(设计)人】 张现军；张永；梁惠强；金雪峰

【摘要】 本发明提供了一种聚酰胺塑料用激光标记助剂、制备方法及其应用。所述的聚酰胺塑料用激光标记助剂其特征在于，包含以重量百分比计的氢氧化物 55% ~75%、氧化锡 10% ~35%、滑石粉 0.5% ~8%、金属锑 0.5% ~4%、无卤阻燃剂 0.5% ~8%、润滑剂 0.5% ~4%。制备方法为：将氧化锡和金属锑在加入润滑剂的情况下通过超声波或高效分散机混合均匀；再将氢氧化物、滑石粉和无卤阻燃剂加入上述混合物中，混合均匀。用于塑料制造时，添加量的重量百分比为 0.5% ~20%。将本发明添加到聚酰胺树脂中后激光打印，即可在浅色的塑料表面形成对比度明显的深色标记，不会产生不良现象，可广泛地应用于低压电器外壳制造等领域。

【名称】 一种粘合聚烯烃塑料的热熔胶

【公开(公告)号】 CN102492375A

【公开(公告)日】 2012.06.13

【申请(专利权)人】 无锡信达胶脂材料有限公司

【地址】 江苏省无锡市新区华友路 6 号

【发明(设计)人】 党渭铭

【摘要】 一种粘合聚烯烃塑料的热熔胶，属于食品包装技术领域。本发明在于提供一种粘合材料，可以作为食品包装的聚烯烃薄膜、聚烯烃与纸张、聚烯烃与铝材的粘合使用。这种材料除其分子结构要与聚烯烃类似以外，还要具有一定的极性，一方面和聚烯烃能够熔合，另一方面，又可以与其它带极性的材料有效粘合，如乙烯 - 醋酸乙烯共聚物，乙烯丙烯酸酯共聚物，乙烯—醋酸乙烯—乙烯醇共聚物等，再加上松香及石油树脂的衍生产品进行增粘，辅以石蜡类产品，以起到浸润和涂布性作用。本发明所制成的热熔胶施工简单、安全卫生，对聚烯烃薄膜、聚烯烃与纸张、铝材等有良好的粘合力和一定的剥离强度。

【名称】 一种塑料制品的制备方法及一种塑料制品

【公开(公告)号】 CN102492940A

【公开(公告)日】 2012.06.13

【申请(专利权)人】 比亚迪股份有限公司

【地址】 广东省深圳市坪山新区比亚迪路 3009 号

【发明(设计)人】 宫清；周良；苗伟峰；张雄

【摘要】 本发明提供了一种塑料制品的制备方法及塑料制品，该方法包括：1)成型塑料基体；塑料基体中含有化学镀催化剂；化学镀催化剂为式Ⅲ所示的化合物；2)去掉塑料基体表面选定区域的塑料，相应区域裸露出化学镀催化剂；3)化学镀铜或化学镀镍，继续进行至少一次化学镀和/或电镀，在塑料基体表面形成金属层。本发明提供的制备方法，工艺简单，对能量要求低，成本低廉；另外，化学镀催化剂分布于塑料基体中，所以化学镀后形成的镀层与塑料基体的结合力非常高。

【名称】 一种基于纤维增强塑料筋锚杆与超高性能水泥基粘结锚固介质的岩锚体系

【公开(公告)号】 CN102493451A

【公开(公告)日】 2012.06.13

【申请(专利权)人】 湖南大学

【地址】 湖南省长沙市岳麓区麓山南路 1 号

【发明(设计)人】 方志；张旷怡；向宇；涂兵；余跃

【摘要】 一种基于纤维增强塑料筋锚杆与超高性能水泥基粘结锚固介质的岩锚体系，该岩锚体系包括以下实施步骤：步骤一、确定锚杆材料及锚固粘结介质；步骤二、设计锚固体系；步骤三、锚具锚固锚杆两端；步骤四、锚杆出厂检验；步骤五、岩锚体系现场安装；步骤六、锚杆张拉；步骤七、封锚。由于本发明岩锚体系采用纤维增强塑料筋作为锚杆、超高性能水泥基材料作为两端粘结介质，采用专门设计的群锚锚具作为地上端锚具、锚杆地下端设计锚具 - 锥形帽组合体，发挥了两种高性能材料的优异特征，克服了现存岩锚体系由于钢筋锈蚀、注浆体老化导致的结构耐久性问题。该岩锚体系结构安全、可靠、高效，且具有优良的物理力学性能和广泛应用前景。

【名称】 一种用于排水的塑料隔渣网

【公开(公告)号】 CN102493546A

【公开(公告)日】 2012.06.13

【申请(专利权)人】 联塑市政管道(河北)有限公司

【地址】 河北省沧州市任丘市北辛庄乡牛村工业园区

【发明(设计)人】 李广权；黄杰伟；宋科明

【摘要】 本发明公开了一种用于排水的塑料隔渣网，包括隔渣网主体和固定装置，所述隔渣网主体由顶面网和侧面网组成，形成倒扣的篮状结构，所述固定装置一端连接隔渣网主体，另一端连接排水管道。本发明提供的隔渣网结构简单，隔渣效果好，排水效率高，且通用性强，可回收再利用。

【名称】 一种多功能用塑料卡子

【公开(公告)号】 CN102494192A

【公开(公告)日】 2012.06.13

【申请(专利权)人】 重庆长安汽车股份有限公司

【地址】 重庆市江北区建新东路260号

【发明(设计)人】 常敬雄；莫利琼；叶情超；张文学

【摘要】 本发明涉及一种多功能用塑料卡子，它包括用于控制线束走向的空腔、防止线索脱出翻边结构、与门槛装饰件卡脚相互卡接的沟槽、通过卡接到门槛内板焊接总成腰型孔的主安装结构，所述的空腔开口向上，沟槽下方水平设置有地毯支撑面，沟槽翻边侧面设置次安装结构。本发明取得的技术效果：结构相对简单、拆装方便、集多种功能于一体，从而减少装配工序，节省工时，起到既可满足功能又可降低成本的作用。

【名称】 检测塑料产品中双酚A的方法

【公开(公告)号】 CN102495145A

【公开(公告)日】 2012.06.13

【申请(专利权)人】 深圳天祥质量技术服务有限公司

【地址】 广东省深圳市南山区蛇口工业三路百盈医疗器械园A座5楼

【发明(设计)人】 杜敬梅；舒文利

【摘要】 本发明公开一种检测塑料产品中双酚A的方法，包括步骤：利用超声萃取法对样品进行前处理；于萃取液中加入有机溶剂及内标物，然后将该混合液经过滤柱制成样品溶液到样品瓶中；用高效液相色谱-紫外/荧光检测器或液相色谱-质谱串联技术分析样品溶液；将上述样品溶液通过流动相进行洗脱处理；所述洗脱处理后的样品溶液经过检测器进行分析检测。本发明的方法检测塑料产品中双酚A的方法检测限低，灵敏度高，检测速度快，能够准确地对样品中双酚A进行定性、定量检测。

【名称】 农用成卷双焊边塑料棚膜和制备工艺及专用双焊边设备

【公开(公告)号】 CN102498977A

【公开(公告)日】 2012.06.20

【申请(专利权)人】 甘肃福雨塑业有限责任公司

【地址】 甘肃省天水市秦安县西川工业园

【发明(设计)人】 陈二虎；何琦峰；刘红军；苏毅

【摘要】 本发明提供一种农用成卷双焊边塑料棚膜及其制备工艺。所述农用成卷双焊边塑料棚膜，具有成卷的棚膜体，其在棚膜体两边侧制有互相平行的供穿固定绳索的焊边。所述的农用成卷双焊边塑料棚膜的制备工艺，其是在塑料薄膜挤出机的塑料热合机后增加第二台塑料热合机，并在第二台塑料热合机前面增加将双层棚膜剖开的剖口刀，将剖开的棚膜另外一个单层边折成双边，再将棚膜撑开的扩口，然后通过第二塑料热合机给棚膜另外一边制作焊边，最后卷取成具有双焊边的成卷棚膜。本发明提供的成卷前一次性双焊边棚膜，有效的解决了农业生产中的要求和运输物流、销售过程中的困难，为农业生产带来了便利。

【名称】 一种塑料袋

【公开(公告)号】 CN102499516A

【公开(公告)日】 2012.06.20

【申请(专利权)人】 陶梦怡

【地址】 江苏省无锡市崇安区锡沪弄108号

【发明(设计)人】 陶梦怡；吴吟燕

【摘要】 本发明公开了一种塑料袋，其包括塑料袋本体，所述塑料袋本体上端设有提物把手，塑料袋内部设有分区的隔离膜。所述提物把手为伞把式。本发明的有益效果是：这种塑料袋，携带方便，不勒手。

【名称】 一种高纯化学品溶解器

【公开(公告)号】 CN102500251A

【公开(公告)日】 2012.06.20

【申请(专利权)人】 瓮福(集团)有限责任公司

【地址】 贵州省贵阳市市南路57号瓮福国际23楼

【发明(设计)人】 刘飞；杨毅；杨正光；陶志；孟文祥

【摘要】 本发明公开了一种高纯化学品溶解器，其特征在于它的上部分为圆柱形，下部分为锥形结构；溶解器内壁有一内衬(10)，采用高纯塑料制作；溶解器内部设置有盘管(8)，盘管(8)上设有进口(1)和出口(6)；溶解器顶部设有液位计插入孔(11)；同时溶解器顶部设有物料加入口(5)；溶解器内设有搅拌器(9)；溶解器的侧壁设置有取样口(3)；溶解器器壁开有密度计插入孔(7)和温度计插入孔(2)。采用本发明的技术方案，可以有效地避免高纯化学品对溶解器的腐蚀，有效避免不同批次的高纯化学品之间的污染。

【名称】 酚醛模塑料细粉分离装置

【公开(公告)号】 CN102527637A

【公开(公告)日】 2012.07.04

【申请(专利权)人】 浙江嘉化集团股份有限公司

【地址】 浙江省海盐县经济开发区杭州湾大桥新区滨海大道1号

【发明(设计)人】 沈文明；宋建平；顾良忠；栾彩霞

【摘要】 一种酚醛模塑料细粉分离装置，包括成品储槽(2)、风力细粉预分离装置(3)、连接管(4)、细粉分级装置(5)和关风卸料器(6)。风力细粉预分离装置和细粉分级装置皆装设在成品储槽的顶部。风力细粉预分离装置包括风道(302)和喷料管(301)，细粉分级装置包括壳体(501)、分级轮(502)、出风管(507)、电机(504)和迷宫密封装置(505)。将喷料管的进口与物料输送管相连，出风管的出口通过排风管与粉尘收集系统相连，酚醛模塑料粉由物料输送管吸入，由风力细粉预分离装置将大部分合格颗粒料分离进成品储槽，余粉经细粉分级装置分离，可将酚醛模塑料粉中的细粉分离，并避免在分离过程中进一步产生细粉。

【名称】 塑料挤出机机筒超大导程内螺旋线加工装置

【公开(公告)号】 CN102528140A

【公开(公告)日】 2012.07.04

【申请(专利权)人】 南京艺工电工设备有限公司

【地址】 江苏省南京市江宁区滨江经济开发区飞鹰路

【发明(设计)人】 杜德鑫；张祖波；单宪民；朱建刚

【摘要】 一种塑料挤出机机筒超大导程内螺旋线加工装置，它包括底板(7)、支承座(8)和动力装置(10)，支承座(8)安装在底板(7)上，其特征是所述的支承座(8)中安装有支撑杆(6)，支撑杆(6)的一端上安装有带轮(11)，带轮(11)一方面通过第一传动带(12)与动力装置(10)的输出轴相连，另一方面通过第二传动带(9)与微型铣头(4)上的动力轮相连，在支撑杆(6)伸入机筒(5)内的一端上对称加工有斜槽，斜角形支撑块(3)安装在所述的斜槽中，斜角形支撑块(3)的大端用于与机筒(5)内壁相抵，斜角形支撑块(3)的小端与调节螺钉(1)相抵，调节螺钉(1)安装在调节支架(2)上，调节支架(2)安装在支撑杆(6)伸入机筒(5)内的一端的端面上。本发明结构简单，制造方便，加工效率高。

【名称】 一种塑料模具电火花精密修复方法

【公开(公告)号】 CN102528376A

【公开(公告)日】 2012.07.04

【申请(专利权)人】 台州学院

【地址】 浙江省台州市椒江区市府大道1139号台州学院157信箱

【发明(设计)人】 高玉新；董晨竹；方志钢；戴晟；程虎

【摘要】 本发明涉及电火花沉积/堆焊合金涂层技术领域，特别涉及一种塑料模具电火花精密修复方法。该塑料模具电火花精密修复方法，采用电火花沉积/堆焊设备，利用自制Fe－Ni－Cr－Re合金电极，在氩气保护气氛中，使电极与模具基体之间产生微弧放电，该微弧将电极端部熔化并沉积到模具基体表面形成堆焊层。该塑料模具电火花精密修复方法，对塑料模具的热输入极少，模具不会产生变形及热裂纹；堆焊层与模具基体呈冶金结合，结合强度高；堆焊层由于采用Fe－Ni－Cr－Re合金，硬度适中，切削性能优异，可实现镜面，适于对塑料模具进行精密修复。

【名称】 一种用于切割塑料薄膜的切割装置及其切割方法

【公开(公告)号】 CN102528832A

【公开(公告)日】 2012.07.04

【申请(专利权)人】 芜湖博耐尔汽车电气系统有限公司

【地址】 安徽省芜湖市经济技术开发区凤鸣湖南路118号

【发明(设计)人】 王文斌；胡傲梅；潘志华；徐炎

【摘要】 本发明公开了一种用于切割塑料薄膜的切割装置及其切割方法，切割装置包括固定架(4)，安装有切割锯齿(2)的切割锯齿安装板(3)的两端分别固定在相互平行的两个固定架(4)上，至少一根固定架(4)上设有量尺(1)；切割装置还包括设置在固定架(4)上且与切割锯齿安装板(3)相互平行的旋转轴(9)，固定架(4)上设有用于安放旋转轴(9)的开口槽，且旋转轴(9)上设有防止旋转轴(9)在开口槽内轴向运动的限位螺母(5)，旋转轴(9)的两端设有防止卷筒式塑料薄膜发生轴向运动的挡盘(10)。具有上述特殊结构的该种用于切割塑料薄膜的切割装置能够快速、准确地切割塑料薄膜，达到保护空调系统免受灰尘等异物的侵扰。

【名称】 塑料加油管溢料修边装置

【公开(公告)号】 CN102528984A

【公开(公告)日】 2012.07.04

【申请(专利权)人】 亚普汽车部件股份有限公司

【地址】 江苏省扬州市扬子江南路508号

【发明(设计)人】 孙岩；姜林；徐松俊；吴陆顺；王昌儒；丛文龙

【摘要】 本发明涉及一种塑料加油管溢料修边装置，机架上安装有下固定板，油管下模固定在下固定板上；下固定板的角部安装有立柱，立柱顶部安装有与下固定板平行的上固定板，上固定板上安装有主气缸，主气缸的活塞杆向下伸出且端部与上模固定板连接，油管上模固定在上模固定板上；上模固定板上安装有管侧修边刀气缸，其活塞杆向下伸出且与管侧修边刀固定板连接，管侧修边刀固定板通过滑块支撑在垂直导轨上并可上下移动，垂直导轨分别固定在立柱上；管侧修边刀固定板上安装有管侧修边刀，管侧修边刀固定板上还安装有管首修边刀及其驱动气缸、管尾修边刀及其驱动气缸。该装置可以自动完成加油管的溢流修边，保证产品的合格率且降低工人的劳动强度。

【名称】 悬索桥主缆防腐用塑料缆套的制造方法

【公开(公告)号】 CN102528993A

【公开(公告)日】 2012.07.04

【申请(专利权)人】 江苏法尔胜缆索有限公司；江苏法尔胜泓昇集团有限公司

【地址】 江苏省无锡市江阴市璜土镇澄常开发区6号

【发明(设计)人】 赵军；宁世伟；薛花娟；徐文雷

【摘要】 本发明涉及一种悬索桥主缆防腐用塑料缆套制造方法，用于悬索桥主缆的防护。所述方法包括以下工艺过程：首先根据塑料缆套的构造，设计并制作塑料缆套的模具，再将塑料粒子磨成粉状注入该模具内，通过对模具的加热及纵向和横向的滚动旋转，使粉状物料借助自身重力作用和离心力的作用均匀地布满模具内腔并且熔融，待冷却后脱模而成，塑料缆套成型后沿分型面分开成两哈夫状结构，并在塑料缆套表面涂刷一层多聚烯烃底漆涂层，利用远红外加热技术将塑料缆套表面加热到120～150℃，使多聚烯烃底漆涂层和塑料缆套表面熔合，再在多聚烯烃底漆涂层表面涂刷一层含固化剂的氟树脂面漆涂层，自然干燥。该制造方法生产成本低、缆套耐老化、使用寿命长。

【名称】 一种塑料外壳热水器及其发泡方法

【公开(公告)号】 CN102529006A

【公开(公告)日】 2012.07.04

【申请(专利权)人】 武汉海尔热水器有限公司；海尔集团公司；青岛经济技术开发区海尔热水器有限公司

【地址】 湖北省武汉市沌口经济技术开发区海尔工业园内

【发明(设计)人】 郑涛；孙强；赵雪森

【摘要】 本发明提供一种对该塑料外壳热水器进行一次性发泡的方法，以及适于一体式发泡的塑料外壳热水器，该热水器包括外壳部件部分、内胆部分、泡沫部分，在塑料外壳和内胆部分之间放置泡沫部分，并安装好其它外部部件，向其中注入发泡料，并进行一次性发泡。该热水器外壳的形状为非规则的几何形状，其截面为异形。本发明能够实现塑料外壳一体式发泡，发泡层无间隙，保温性能提高；具有较高的生产效率；对发泡料的密封，避免出现发泡层气泡、空腔，保温性能提高，同时降低成本；在以上优点的前提下实现外观的差异化。

【名称】 一种塑料水龙头本体的制作方法及产品

【公开(公告)号】 CN102529009A

【公开(公告)日】 2012.07.04

【申请(专利权)人】 深圳成霖洁具股份有限公司

【地址】 广东省深圳市宝安区福永镇桥头村荔园路成霖工业园

【发明(设计)人】 袁家骅

【摘要】 本发明提供一种一体成型塑料水龙头本体的制作方法，包括：第一次塑料射出成型步骤，先备置内部模穴具可取出模块的模具，并在塑料射出及开模后获得内部包覆有模块的塑料水龙头本体粗胚，所述模块至少一端可从粗胚一个阀座部位外侧壁突伸；模块取出步骤，利用模块突出部位将其从塑料水龙头本体的粗胚抽出，使其取出后的内部空间自然形成一中央流道，并在突出部位相对的阀座部位外侧壁上形成一侧边开孔；侧边开孔的封闭步骤，利用密封塞或第二次塑料射出成型等方法，将侧边开孔予以封闭，即可获得一体成型的塑料水龙头本体成品。本发明制作方法大致为单一构件，故毋需使用密封垫圈，可以防止习知组装构件间容易产生泄漏的问题。

【名称】 一种双料筒圆盘注塑成型机

【公开(公告)号】 CN102529012A

【公开(公告)日】 2012.07.04

【申请(专利权)人】 金孝禹

【地址】 浙江省乐清市白石镇东浃村

【发明(设计)人】 金孝禹

【摘要】 本发明公开了一种圆盘注塑成型机。发明要解决的技术问题是提供一种双料筒圆盘注塑成型机。为解决上述问题，本发明采用的技术方案包括转盘装置、送料装置、对模具注射塑料流体的注塑装置和合模装置，所述合模装置包括设置在注塑装置上方的合模油缸，所述合模油缸中的合模油缸活塞作上下运动，同时带动注塑装置作上去运动，其特征在于所述合模装置上端设置有与合模油缸活塞作上下同步运动的活塞，所述活塞上左右对称设置支架，所述支架上设置送料装置，所述注射头内设置2条注料通道，所述送料装置的送料咀与其对应端的注料通道相配合。

【名称】 塑料改性生产装置

【公开(公告)号】 CN102529022A

【公开(公告)日】 2012.07.04

【申请(专利权)人】 河北华强科技开发有限公司

【地址】 河北省衡水市枣强县城东环北路

【发明(设计)人】 王洪君;王帅;王超;夏云广;张文宁;徐文秀

【摘要】 本发明涉及一种塑料改性生产装置,其结构是在本体一端开有用于连通注塑机喷嘴的两条进料流道,在本体另一端开有用于连通注塑模具的两条出料流道,在本体中开有两条活塞运动腔;每条所述活塞运动腔分别与一条所述进料流道和一条所述出料流道相连通;在每条所述活塞运动腔中装有活塞,所述活塞外接活塞驱动装置。本发明可以推动熔体在模具型腔中反复流动,并且不断地在型腔内表面冻结,使得可流动的熔体逐渐变少,直到整个型腔中的熔体完全冷却固化,由此形成多层取向试样,获得在流动方向上性能有较大改善的塑料聚合物制品。

【名称】 用于注塑成型设备的进料装置

【公开(公告)号】 CN102529023A

【公开(公告)日】 2012.07.04

【申请(专利权)人】 鸿富锦精密工业(深圳)有限公司;鸿海精密工业股份有限公司

【地址】 广东省深圳市宝安区龙华镇油松第十工业区东环二路2号

【发明(设计)人】 郭原隆;韩维伦

【摘要】 本发明提供一种用于注塑成型设备的进料装置,其包括一个漏斗状且具有一个中心轴的筒体、收容于该筒体内的一个驱动装置、一个转轴以及多个叶片组。该筒体形成有一个进料端及一个出料端。该转轴沿该筒体的中心轴设置并连接至该驱动装置。每个叶片组包括多个沿该筒体的径向方向连接至该转轴,并且大致位于该转轴的同个轴向横截面上的叶片,每个叶片相对于该转轴的轴向横截面倾斜。该多个叶片组沿该筒体的中心轴方向分层设置。该驱动装置用于驱动该转轴带动该多个叶片组旋转从而形成从该筒体内吹向该进料端的气流。如此,塑料原料中的轻微杂质可被吹出该进料装置,从而减少产品中杂质的含量,提高产品的质量。

【名称】 注塑机用自锁射嘴

【公开(公告)号】 CN102529024A

【公开(公告)日】 2012.07.04

【申请(专利权)人】 东莞市凯昶德电子科技股份有限公司

【地址】 广东省东莞市塘厦镇古寮二路2号凯昶德工业园

【发明(设计)人】 郑友军

【摘要】 本发明涉及一种注塑机用自锁射嘴,包括射嘴主体、射嘴头、针阀、缸体及推杆,射嘴头安装在射嘴主体的前端,射嘴主体上设有滑槽,缸体可滑动地套设于射嘴主体上,缸体与射嘴主体之间形成气腔,缸体上设有连通气腔的进气孔,推杆穿设于滑槽内并与缸体相固定,射嘴主体上设有导向孔,针阀插设于导向孔内,射嘴头设有出料口,使用时,气腔经进气孔充入压缩气体,缸体在压缩气体的作用下带动推杆沿滑槽朝向喷嘴头运动以抵压针阀,针阀在推杆的抵压作用下向出料口移动以封闭出料口而形成自锁。本发明的注塑机用自锁射嘴,能够实现针阀自锁力的无级调节,可满足不同塑料注塑生产的需要,同时具有价格低、适应性广、安全可靠、维护成本低等优点。

【名称】 注塑模具

【公开(公告)号】 CN102529031A

【公开(公告)日】 2012.07.04

【申请(专利权)人】 昆山市华英精密模具工业有限公司

【地址】 江苏省苏州市昆山市望山南路239号

【发明(设计)人】 周有旺;黄义

【摘要】 本发明公开了一种注塑模具,包括剥料板、上模板和下模板,所述下模板固定在模具底座上,所述上料板与上模板之间连接有多根导柱,所述上模板与下模板之间安装有多根限位拉杆。本发明解决了现有技术中在完成开模过程中,需要加四个树脂开闭器和外置拉环。不仅结构复杂,而且操作时很不方便的问题,通过在上、下模板之间安装一个限位装置,通过技术的改进完成了原来两个组件的功能,克服了原来模具因树脂开闭器引起的塑料粉末和普通拉环引起的模具卡模,结构简单,使用方便、提高了产品的质量。

【名称】 塑料盖成型模结构

【公开(公告)号】 CN102529034A

【公开(公告)日】 2012.07.04

【申请(专利权)人】 苏州同大模具有限公司

【地址】 江苏省苏州市张家港市凤凰镇凤凰大道8号

【发明(设计)人】 许卫明;王文斗

【摘要】 一种塑料盖成型模结构,属于塑料成型模具领域。包括上模机构、成型模、底板和盖体顶出机构,成型模设在盖体顶出机构上,特点:盖体顶出机构包括上推板、下推板、第一固定板、上顶板、下顶板、长短顶杆、顶柱、上、下限位螺钉和回位螺钉，长顶杆的一端固定在下顶板上，上端与上推板接触，短顶杆的下端固定在上顶板上，上端与下推板接触，上限位螺钉的下端与下推板连接，上端与上模机构配合，回位螺钉与顶柱连接，而上端与上模组件相配合，顶柱的下端与下顶板连接，上端与第一垫板接触，顶柱配设有上、下滑套，在上滑套外配有上定位套，在下滑套外配有下定位套。优点：避免在顶出过程中损及盖体而确保盖体的质量；齐整性优异，保障配合精度。

【名称】 大口径太阳能塑料镜片拼接模具

【公开(公告)号】 CN102529035A

【公开(公告)日】 2012.07.04

【申请(专利权)人】 厦门大学

【地址】 福建省厦门市思明南路422号

【发明(设计)人】 彭云峰；白志扬；郭隐彪；董之然；徐伟东

【摘要】 大口径太阳能塑料镜片拼接模具，涉及一种镜片拼接模具。设凸模基座、凸模模具、侧面模具、凹模模具、凹模基座、内六角螺栓、螺母；凸模模具由内向外由一级凸模子模具块、二级凸模子模具块、三级凸模子模具块和四级凸模子模具块；凹模模具由一级凹模子模具块、二级凹模子模具块、三级凹模子模具块、四级凹模子模具块中的部分或全部的子模具块拼接而成，侧面模具由小口径的侧面子模具块拼接而成；凸模基座、凹模基座固定在注塑平台上，一级凹模子模具块、二级凹模子模具块、三级凹模子模具块、四级凹模子模具块和燕尾槽结构进行拼接并固定在凹模基座上，侧面子模具块由内六角螺栓和螺母连接成侧面模具并环绕在凸模模具和凹模模具的侧面。

【名称】 高分子塑料隔膜加压真空注塑成型系统及成型法

【公开(公告)号】 CN102529046A

【公开(公告)日】 2012.07.04

【申请(专利权)人】 杭州兴源过滤科技股份有限公司

【地址】 浙江省杭州市余杭区良渚镇良渚路10号

【发明(设计)人】 周立武；徐孝雅

【摘要】 本发明涉及一种能够将熔融塑料中的气泡排出且形成相对真空的高分子塑料隔膜加压真空注塑成型系统及成型法，高分子塑料塑化机的出口与加压装置的进口连通，加压装置的出口料与高分子塑料隔膜注塑模具的进口连通，所述加压装置中的挤出筒壁装有真空吸气嘴，真空吸气嘴出口与电磁阀进口连通，电磁阀出口与真空吸气机吸气口连通；所述加压装置中螺旋挤压机构中活塞头下方装有螺旋搅拌器。优点：一是本申请采用加压抽真空，从根本上解决了塑料隔膜中气穴的产生，确保了塑料隔膜的成型质量及极大地延长了塑料隔膜的使用寿命，极大地降低了用户的使用成本，解决了人们长期以来想要解决而没有解决的难题。

【名称】 一种小体积圆盘注塑成型机

【公开(公告)号】 CN102529048A

【公开(公告)日】 2012.07.04

【申请(专利权)人】 金孝禹

【地址】 浙江省乐清市白石镇东浃村

【发明(设计)人】 金孝禹

【摘要】 本发明公开了一种圆盘注塑成型机，要解决的技术问题是提供一种小体积圆盘注塑成型机。为解决上述问题，本发明采用的技术方案包括转盘装置、送料装置、对模具注射塑料流体的注塑装置和合模装置，所述合模装置包括设置在注塑装置上方的合模油缸，所述合模油缸中的合模油缸活塞作上下运动，同时带动注塑装置作上下运动，其特征在于所述合模装置上端设置有与合模油缸活塞作上下同步运动的活塞，所述活塞右侧设置支架，所述支架上设置送料装置，所述送料装置呈一定角度向上倾斜。

【名称】 注塑机熔塑装置

【公开(公告)号】 CN102529052A

【公开(公告)日】 2012.07.04

【申请(专利权)人】 常州兰喆仪器仪表有限公司

【地址】 江苏省常州市钟楼区永红街道宣塘村委沟南组

【发明(设计)人】 韩金元；谈永建

【摘要】 本发明公开了一种注塑机熔塑装置，在注塑机熔塑料筒外缠绕有至少三个电磁线圈，相邻电磁线圈之间设置防电磁干扰装置，电磁线圈与控制电路电连接，控制电路包括电源开关电路、交流变直流电变压电路、电磁兼容滤波电路、直流变交流变压电路、CPU主控制电路和低压直流电控制电路，所述电源开关电路与交流变直流电变压电路电连接，所述交流变直流电变压电路与电磁兼容滤波电路电连接，电磁兼容滤波电路与直流变交流变压电路电连接，直流变交流变压电路与低压直流电控制电路电连接，直流变交流变压电路与低压直流电控制电路均与CPU主控制电路电连接，低压直流电控制电路与电磁线圈电连接。本发明热利用率高、节电明显且生产安全可靠。

【名称】 一种高质量美式塑料异型材挤出模具

【公开(公告)号】 CN102529059A

【公开(公告)日】 2012.07.04
【申请(专利权)人】 黄石鸿迪塑料模具有限公司
【地址】 湖北省黄石市黄石大道261号
【发明(设计)人】 王忠赤；汤明思；张云霞
【摘要】 一种高质量美式塑料异型材挤出模具，具有模体，模体尾端采用螺钉依次装有过渡板、分流器支架二、分流器支架一、汇流板、口模三、口模二和口模一，并配有分流锥和芯模，其特征是：a. 所述口模二内设有一个主型腔和若干个单腿型腔，每个单腿型腔与主型腔之间间隔一定的距离布置；b. 所述口模一内设有主型腔，主型腔内设有若干个与主型腔连成一体的单腿型腔，单腿型腔外端呈内窄外宽的八字结构，八字结构内端宽度与异型材单腿的设计宽度相等，八字结构外端宽度大于异型材单腿设计宽度；并且口模一的单腿型腔高度比异型材单腿设计高度高；本发明解决了现有美式塑料异型材挤出模具生产的产品尺寸无法保证和质量较差等问题，广泛用于生产各种塑料门窗异型材。

【名称】 塑料拉吹机的直线驱动器拉伸机构
【公开(公告)号】 CN102529073A
【公开(公告)日】 2012.07.04
【申请(专利权)人】 林明莊
【地址】 浙江省台州市黄岩区黄椒路528号台州市黄岩亚力塑机有限公司
【发明(设计)人】 林明莊
【摘要】 塑料拉吹机的直线驱动器拉伸机构，包括支架，支架上设置动力，动力带动拉伸杆，拉伸杆的下方针对着模具，其特征在于所述的动力为直线驱动器，直线驱动器的外壁设置滑道滑块，滑块连接拉伸杆。本技术方案具有如下优点：一是直线驱动器带动的拉伸杆中无润滑油，作为动力带动拉伸杆制成的容器内没有油污，卫生质量高；二是沿着直线驱动器外壁运行的滑块直接带动拉伸杆，使拉伸杆与直线驱动器内的气缸并行移动，拉伸机构的体积大大的缩小，构造十分的简单，机器灵巧；三是直线驱动器能耗省，噪音低，环保节能显著；四是直线驱动器带动拉伸杆运行平稳、可靠，使用寿命长。

【名称】 圆形热塑性塑料熔接设备及方法
【公开(公告)号】 CN102529088A
【公开(公告)日】 2012.07.04
【申请(专利权)人】 昆山市创新科技检测仪器有限公司
【地址】 江苏省昆山市张浦镇俱进路558号
【发明(设计)人】 陶泽成
【摘要】 本发明涉及一种圆形热塑性塑料熔接设备及方法，所述设备包括工作台，所述工作台上设置有下夹具以及两个或四个丝杠副，所述丝杠副上套设有第一平台及第二平台，并且所述第一平台的位置在所述第二平台位置之上，所述第一平台支撑有气缸，所述第二平台支撑有第一电机，所述气缸与所述第一电机动力相连，所述第一电机的输出轴与上夹具相连，所述下夹具与所述上夹具之间的距离可调。据本发明所提供的圆形热塑性塑料熔接设备及方法，可有效解决现有技术中存在的相关问题，避免复杂繁琐的设计过程，无需针对加工产品的尺寸而开发多幅模具，从而节约了人工及生产成本。

【名称】 组合式塑料管材焊接支撑架
【公开(公告)号】 CN102529089A
【公开(公告)日】 2012.07.04
【申请(专利权)人】 华瀚科技有限公司
【地址】 广东省深圳市南山区高新技术产业园北区朗山路16号华瀚创新园
【发明(设计)人】 郑能欢；于洋；杨春江
【摘要】 本发明公开了一种组合式塑料管材焊接支撑架，包括可充气的环形气囊，气囊内侧设有用于支撑气囊保持环形的支撑圈，所述支撑圈由多个支撑组件首尾相接自锁或被锁定形成的环形圈，其中所述支撑组件之间的连接至少在两个位置的连接为可拆卸连接。本发明针对现有技术的支撑装置结构复杂、沉重不便移动、使用范围窄、施压不均、无法针对管材局部变形进行调整的缺陷，提供一种结构简单、施压均匀、适应管道局部变形、重量轻携带方便的组合式塑料管材焊接支撑架。

【名称】 固定式塑料管材焊接支撑架
【公开(公告)号】 CN102529090A
【公开(公告)日】 2012.07.04
【申请(专利权)人】 华瀚科技有限公司
【地址】 广东省深圳市南山区高新技术产业园北区朗山路16号华瀚创新园
【发明(设计)人】 郑能欢；于洋；杨春江
【摘要】 本发明公开了一种固定式塑料管材焊接支撑架，包括可充气的环形气囊，气囊内侧设有用于支撑气囊保持环形的圆环形支撑圈。本发明针对现有技术的支撑装置结构复杂、沉重不便移动、使用范围窄、施压不均、无法针对管材局部变形进行调整的缺陷，提供一种结构简单、施压均匀、焊接密封质量优、对两个管口的同心定位好、重量轻携带方便的固定式塑料管材焊接支撑架。

【名称】 一种环保阻燃型聚氨酯硬质泡沫塑料的制备方法
【公开(公告)号】 CN102532470A

【公开(公告)日】 2012.07.04
【申请(专利权)人】 大连亚泰科技新材料有限公司
【地址】 辽宁省大连市中山路588-3号2单元27层
【发明(设计)人】 孙忠祥
【摘要】 一种环保阻燃型聚氨酯硬质泡沫塑料的制备方法，属于节能环保新材料领域。将阻燃剂与聚醚或聚酯多元醇组合料混合后制得聚氨酯组合料后，再将其与异氰酸酯反应生成聚氨酯，即得到一种环保阻燃型聚氨酯硬质泡沫塑料；其中聚氨酯组合料为聚醚或聚酯多元醇、阻燃剂、催化剂、匀泡剂、发泡剂、改性剂、偶联剂、泡沫稳定剂、增塑剂预混在一起的。其有益效果是：无机阻燃剂分解温度高，除了有阻燃效果外，还有抑制发烟和毒性的作用。发明所使用的异氰酸酯，由于它含有两个苯环，分子量大，产品挥发性较小，蒸气压较低，对人体毒性相对较小，有利于工业安全防护，同时还具有反应速度快、安全系数较高、节能环保、产品多样化等优点。

【名称】 一种分离废旧电子电器产品塑料中阻燃剂的方法
【公开(公告)号】 CN102532588A
【公开(公告)日】 2012.07.04
【申请(专利权)人】 中国科学院生态环境研究中心
【地址】 北京市海淀区双清路18号
【发明(设计)人】 张付申；张聪聪
【摘要】 本发明针对目前我国废旧电子电器产品塑料量大、无害化处理技术匮乏、再生循环利用困难的现状，提供一种废旧塑料中阻燃剂的分离方法。其特征是：采用溶剂热法，在一定的温度和压力条件下，利用有机溶剂快速溶出废旧塑料中的阻燃剂，实现阻燃剂和废旧塑料的有效分离。该方法具有操作简便，流程短，效率高，所需溶剂少、溶剂可以循环利用等优点。同时，处理前后废旧塑料结构变化不大，可以与生活用品塑料一起再生利用，具有良好的应用前景。

【名称】 一种铝塑分离剂及其制备方法
【公开(公告)号】 CN102532592A
【公开(公告)日】 2012.07.04
【申请(专利权)人】 常州化学研究所
【地址】 江苏省常州市常武中路801号常州科教城科技2号大楼五层
【发明(设计)人】 张保坦；李茹；陈修宁；王公应；贾树勇；王红丹
【摘要】 本发明涉及一种铝塑分离剂及其制备方法，该分离剂成分包括水、酸性化合物及有机溶剂，以重量份计各组分配比为：水1~25份，酸性化合物5~50份，有机溶剂25~95份；然后按照配比依次称取相应的组分进行适当的混合，形成均一的相；再将铝塑粉碎物浸泡在所配制的分离液中，搅拌、分离、冲洗，最终可得到80%~90%的塑料，8%~15%的铝。该分离剂不易挥发，对铝塑分离速度快，对铝无氧化腐蚀。此外，该分离剂所采用的原料易得、对环境污染少、可重复利用，生产设备工艺简单，成本低廉。通过本发明制备的产品可广泛地应用于医药、食品、化妆品、日用品、工业品等铝塑包装材料的铝塑分离。

【名称】 一种食品药品包装聚烯烃用高填充母料组合物
【公开(公告)号】 CN102532641A
【公开(公告)日】 2012.07.04
【申请(专利权)人】 广州远华色母厂有限公司
【地址】 广东省广州市增城市新塘镇永和篓元工业区广州远华色母厂有限公司
【发明(设计)人】 曹艳霞；张廷丰；张盛侨
【摘要】 本发明公开了一种食品药品包装聚烯烃用高填充母料组合物，其载体树脂为聚烯烃树脂，所述聚烯烃树脂包括茂金属聚烯烃树脂。所述组合物还包括有填料和功能性助剂，所述功能性助剂包括分散剂、偶联剂、润滑剂和稳定剂，或其至少两者的混合物。本发明通过引入茂金属聚烯烃树脂作为载体树脂，并添加常规的功能性助剂以及填料，得到的填充母料组合物白度高，分散性好，熔体流动性好，加工性能优良，常温及低温抗冲击性能优良，产品符合食品药品接触管控要求，可以作为食品药品包装塑料的专用填充母料，同时可兼着色母料功能。

【名称】 一种光、生物复合降解聚乙烯泡沫塑料及其制备方法
【公开(公告)号】 CN102532647A
【公开(公告)日】 2012.07.04
【申请(专利权)人】 上海杰事杰新材料(集团)股份有限公司
【地址】 上海市闵行区北松路800号
【发明(设计)人】 郭学林
【摘要】 本发明涉及一种光、生物复合降解聚乙烯泡沫塑料及其制备方法，该塑料包含以下组分及其重量分数：低密度聚乙烯(LDPE)70~80份、发泡剂3.5~10份、交联剂0.5~2.5份、相容剂20~30份、改性淀粉25~40份、改性碳酸钙15~25份、促进剂2号2~5份、光降解母料5~8份、复合无机阻燃剂50~70份、润滑剂1~2.5份。与现有技术相比，本

发明采用光、生物复合降解聚乙烯泡沫塑料的方法，使得废弃泡沫塑料通过光、生物复合降解可循环重复利用，无污染对环境友好，而且这种改性泡沫塑料重量轻强度高，阻燃防火性好并且可完全降解，完全适用于工业化产品。该发明的塑料可广泛用于产品包装、塑料建材等众多国民经济领域。

【名称】 太阳能专用塑料管道
【公开(公告)号】 CN102532648A
【公开(公告)日】 2012.07.04
【申请(专利权)人】 福建亚通新材料科技股份有限公司
【地址】 福建省福州市福清市镜洋工业区
【发明(设计)人】 陈鹊；许盛光；任文成；陈黎星；吴亚平；陈建福
【摘要】 太阳能专用塑料管道是由重量份的基本物料组成，耐热聚乙烯树脂100份、紫外线吸收剂1～2份。其中所述的紫外线吸收剂为三(1，2，2，6，6－五甲哌啶基)亚磷酸酯、4－苯甲酰氧基－2，2，6，6－四甲基哌啶、碳黑中的一种。生产时首先将耐热聚乙烯树脂和紫外线吸收剂混合均匀，之后转移到挤出机上并通过挤出机挤出成型为本发明太阳能专用塑料管道。本发明的优点是：连接方便、冷热频繁交替情况下可稳定使用。

【名称】 一种用于高压聚乙烯废注塑料改性成管材专用料的加工改性剂及其使用方法
【公开(公告)号】 CN102532656A
【公开(公告)日】 2012.07.04
【申请(专利权)人】 湖北众联塑业有限公司
【地址】 湖北省武汉市宝丰路1号湖北商务大楼1206室
【发明(设计)人】 邓丽；邓军；邓忠权；陈绪煌
【摘要】 本发明公开了一种用于高压聚乙烯废注塑料改性成管材专用料的加工改性剂，其特征在于：所述的加工改性剂包括以下组分及其重量份：氯化聚乙烯1～2、叔丁过氧基二异丙苯0.3～0.7；本发明所述的使用方法包括如下步骤：一、高压聚乙烯废注塑料的处理；二、检测高压聚乙烯废注塑料的熔体流动指数；三、配料：按高压聚乙烯废注塑料：氯化聚乙烯：叔丁过氧基二异丙苯＝100：(1～2)：(0.3～0.7)；四、投料加工，将上述配制的各组分投入混合机内，在常温条件下开机12～15min，停机，卸料包装即可。本发明具有工艺合理、加工简单，可以有效提高高压聚乙烯废注塑料的物化性能和产品质量。本发明可以广泛地用于高压聚乙烯废注塑料的改性加工。

【名称】 一种塑料焊条
【公开(公告)号】 CN102532659A
【公开(公告)日】 2012.07.04
【申请(专利权)人】 吴江市利达上光制品有限公司
【地址】 江苏省苏州市吴江市黎里镇建新街西南港30号
【发明(设计)人】 凌元若
【摘要】 本发明涉及一种塑料焊条，一种塑料焊条，其特征在于：包括塑料、金属粉和脱氧剂，其中所述塑料、金属粉和脱氧剂按质量百分比为：塑料60%～85%，金属粉12%～38%，脱氧剂1.8%～2.0%，所述塑料为聚乙烯、聚丙烯、聚氯乙烯或酚醛树脂；所述金属粉为铁粉、铝粉或铜粉中的任意一种，以及其任意组合比的混合物，其所述金属粉的粒径为0.2～2.5mm；所述脱氧剂为锰与硅的混合物，其中所述锰与硅所占总质量的比例分别为：1.3%～1.8%，0.2%～0.5%。在制备时，将塑料加热后，加入金属粉和脱氧剂搅拌均匀，然后按照现有的塑料焊条制作工艺成型，本发明塑料焊条造价低廉，具有很大的市场推广力，且具有较好的脱氧效果，提高焊接质量。

【名称】 一种汽车用塑料复合材料的制备方法
【公开(公告)号】 CN102532663A
【公开(公告)日】 2012.07.04
【申请(专利权)人】 潘雪峰
【地址】 江苏省苏州市吴江市盛泽镇南塘村18组
【发明(设计)人】 潘雪峰
【摘要】 一种汽车用塑料复合材料的制备方法，该方法包括如下步骤：将12质量份对苯二甲酸、36质量份偏苯三酸三辛酯和10质量份氧化锌加入反应釜后，在氮气的保护下加热到130～140℃搅拌3h，然后将反应物与90质量份聚乙烯、50质量份聚丙烯、20质量份聚偏氟乙烯、10质量份抗氧化剂、15质量份二氧化钛混合后放入密炼机密炼5h，密练温度为200～205℃、转速为1100～1150rpm；然后经造粒机造粒，得到颗粒，将颗粒放入水槽冷却、干燥。本发明方法制备出的材料没异味、耐划、韧性强、耐热、无毒无污染、加工性能优良，本发明的方法生产工艺简单，降低生产成本，适用于大规模生产。

【名称】 一种低收缩率的复合材料及其制备方法
【公开(公告)号】 CN102532687A
【公开(公告)日】 2012.07.04
【申请(专利权)人】 上海日之升新技术发展有限公司
【地址】 上海市沪闵路3078号
【发明(设计)人】 黄晓明；杨涛；孟成铭
【摘要】 本发明涉及一种低收缩率的复合材料及其

制备方法，复合材料包括以下组分及重量份含量：PP50～80、碳酸钙10～40、POE3～10、相容剂3～10、PE0.5～5、润滑剂0.1～0.5、抗氧剂0.1～0.5、成核剂0.1～1.0，碳酸钙用硅烷偶联剂处理，然后将上述原料混合后放入双螺杆挤出机中，控制双螺杆挤出机的转速为180～600r/min，温度为180～220℃，熔融后进行挤出造粒，即得到产品。本发明制备的低收缩率PP/$CaCO_3$复合材料，具有优异的强度、模量和韧性，碳酸钙本身安全无污染性，在较高强度、刚性及韧性而又要求低收缩率的塑料生产制品中具有优异的应用前景。

【名称】 一种高强、高韧、阻燃聚丙烯材料、制备方法及其应用

【公开(公告)号】 CN102532688A

【公开(公告)日】 2012.07.04

【申请(专利权)人】 合肥杰事杰新材料股份有限公司

【地址】 安徽省合肥市经济技术开发区莲花路2388号

【发明(设计)人】 宋伟华

【摘要】 本发明属于高分子材料改性技术领域和加工技术领域，公开了一种高强、高韧、阻燃聚丙烯材料、制备方法及其应用。本发明的聚丙烯材料包括以下组分和重量份：聚丙烯20～50份，增韧剂0.1～10份，相容剂1～10份，复配阻燃剂16～22份，抗氧剂0.2～0.4份，光稳定剂0.1～0.4份和玻璃纤维30～50份。该聚丙烯材料由以下方法制备：将20～50份聚丙烯，0.1～10份增韧剂，1～10份相容剂，16～22份复配阻燃剂，0.2～0.4份抗氧剂，0.1～0.4份光稳定剂和30～50份玻璃纤维，放入高速混合机中混合3～5分钟，然后将混合物加入挤出机中，挤出切粒得到所需高强、高韧、阻燃聚丙烯材料。本发明制备出的聚丙烯材料具有较高的拉伸强度、弯曲模量以及冲击强度，同时具有良好的阻燃性，是工程塑料建筑模板最适合的材料。

【名称】 一种高熔指的复合材料及其制备方法

【公开(公告)号】 CN102532694A

【公开(公告)日】 2012.07.04

【申请(专利权)人】 上海日之升新技术发展有限公司

【地址】 上海市闵行区沪闵路3078号

【发明(设计)人】 黄晓明；杨涛

【摘要】 本发明涉及一种高熔指的复合材料及其制备方法，复合材料由以下组分及重量份含量的原料制成：PP50～70、滑石粉10～40、POE3～15、相容剂3～10、抗氧剂0.1～0.5、降温母粒0.1～0.5，所有原料混合后放入螺杆机中挤出造粒，控制螺杆机的转速为180～600r/min，温度为190～220℃，熔融后挤出造粒即得到产品。与现有技术相比，本发明具有优异的力学性能和较高的流动性，既满足了产品使用的力学要求，又改善了注塑工艺，在高强度、高韧性而又要求高流动性的塑料生产制品中具有很好的运用前景，可广泛应用于电子电器、汽车、家电等众多领域。

【名称】 快速成型聚丙烯复合材料及制备方法

【公开(公告)号】 CN102532711A

【公开(公告)日】 2012.07.04

【申请(专利权)人】 苏州工业园区润佳工程塑料有限公司

【地址】 江苏省苏州市苏州工业园区葑亭大道698号

【发明(设计)人】 翁永华；汪理文；丁贤麟

【摘要】 本发明属于塑料材料领域，尤其涉及一种快速成型聚丙烯复合材料及其制备方法，由以下重量配比的原料制备成：聚丙烯60%～86%；填料5%～20%；增韧剂5%～25%；成核剂0.3%～0.5%；导热剂2%～5%；热稳定剂0.1%～1.0%；抗氧剂0.1%～1.0%；成核剂为β晶型成核剂Y－619；导热剂为包覆型纳米热导材料，包覆型纳米热导材料由普通矿粉填料层和包覆于矿粉填料表面的纳米热导材料层构成。本发明在在聚丙烯材料的基础配方中加入成核剂和导热剂，成核剂提高PP结晶的温度、加快结晶速度，导热剂将注塑时产生的热量迅速的散去、减少冷却时间，因而提高了聚丙烯复合材料的成型速率；本发明制备工艺简单、提高了生产效率、降低了成本，制得的材料各项物理力学性能优异。

【名称】 珍珠质地的塑料颗粒

【公开(公告)号】 CN102532712A

【公开(公告)日】 2012.07.04

【申请(专利权)人】 何奇伟

【地址】 浙江省诸暨市暨阳街道浣纱北路天成锦江苑9幢1单元501室

【发明(设计)人】 何奇伟

【摘要】 本发明公开了一种珍珠质地的塑料颗粒，包括塑料颗粒，所述的塑料颗粒为聚丙烯或聚乙烯混合粉料制成，粉料为蚌壳粉、珍珠粉中的一种或两种。本发明通过蚌壳粉、珍珠粉中的一种或两种制成的粉料与聚丙烯或聚乙烯混合得到珍珠质地的塑料颗粒，使塑料颗粒以及通过注塑后其制造的产品表面体现出珍珠特有的光泽透明、有宝光、质地坚硬等特性，极大的提高了产品的质感和档次。

（涂红梅）

[illegible] 180～600mm，[illegible] [illegible]

【专利】[illegible]
【公开(公告)号】CN[illegible]
【公开(公告)日】2012.[illegible]
【申请(专利权)人】[illegible]
【发明(设计)人】[illegible]
【摘要】[illegible]

[illegible]
【公开(公告)号】CN[illegible]
【公开(公告)日】20[illegible]
【申请(专利权)人】[illegible]
【发明(设计)人】[illegible]
【摘要】[illegible]

[illegible] 10～20，[illegible] 0.5，[illegible] 180～600mm，[illegible]

【专利】[illegible]
【公开(公告)号】CN10253[illegible]
【公开(公告)日】2012.[illegible]
【申请(专利权)人】[illegible]
【发明(设计)人】[illegible]
【摘要】[illegible]

【公开(公告)号】CN10[illegible]
【公开(公告)日】20[illegible]
【申请(专利权)人】[illegible]
【发明(设计)人】[illegible]
【摘要】[illegible]

塑料标准化

突出重点扎实工作推动轻工业标准化工作新发展

——在全国轻工业标准化工作会议上的讲话

（2012年4月25日）

中国轻工业联合会副会长　钱桂敬

各位代表、同志们：

上午好！今天我们在这里召开2012年全国轻工业标准化工作会议。会议的主要任务是认真贯彻国家标准化管理委员会召开的全国标准化工作会议和工业和信息化部召开的工业标准化工作座谈会的会议精神，总结2011年轻工标准化工作，研究部署今后一个时期轻工标准化发展总体思路和今年重点工作。

这次会议我们荣幸的请到了国家标准化管理委员会于欣丽总工程师，工信部科技司主管行业标准化工作的韩俊副司长，工信部消费品司谢立安处长，四川省经信委李萍副主任等亲自到会并作了重要讲话。在此，我代表中国轻工业联合会对他们的到来，对国家标准委、工信部多年来对轻工标准化工作的支持、帮助表示衷心的感谢！

下面我讲四个方面的问题。

一、2011年轻工标准化工作回顾

2011年，在国家标准委、工信部的正确领导下，在地方政府、行业协会和广大轻工企业的大力支持和帮助下，在全行业标准化工作者的共同努力下，轻工标准化工作取得了一定的成绩，实现了“十二五”的良好开局。

1. 轻工标准体系进一步完善。

经国家标准委批准全年新发布轻工国家标准209项，其中强制性标准17项，推荐性标准192项；新下达轻工国家标准制修订项目95项，其中制定56项、修订39项。经工信部批准全年新发布轻工行业标准218项，全部为推荐性标准；新下达轻工行业标准制修订项目398项，其中制定283项、修订115项。截至2011年底，轻工国家标准、行业标准总数达到4358项，其中国家标准1784项，行业标准2574项。轻工标准体系进一步完善，较好地满足了产业、科技、贸易和社会事业发展需求。

2. 轻工标准化管理工作进一步加强。

2011年8月，为进一步加强轻工标准化管理工作，中国轻工业联合会决定成立标准质量部。2011年9月1日，中国轻工业联合会在北京召开“在京单位轻工业标准化工作座谈会”，向相关行业协会和在京标准化技术委员会传达了8月国家标准委召开的“标准化工作座谈会”及国家标准委工业二部召开的“消费品安全标准座谈会”的会议精神。会议还听取了与会代表对“十二五”和今后一段时间对轻工标准化工作的意见和建议。

3. 标准化技术委员会建设工作进一步规范。

目前，轻工行业标准化技术委员会有122个，其中全国轻工行业标准化技术委员会46个，分技术委员会76个。为了更好地适应产业发展的需要，根据国家标准委对专业标准化技术委员会的管理规定，2011年中国轻工业联合会发布了《全国轻工行业专业标准化技术委员会管理暂行办法》和《全国轻工行业专业标准化技术委员会换届工作暂行办法》。办法的发布使轻工标准化技术委员会工作更加规范，有章可循。

经国家标准委批准，2011年新成立了文具标准化技术委员会；完成了全国衡器标准化技术委员会的调整换届；完成了对家具、家用卫生杀虫用品、口腔护理用品、烟花爆竹、民用装饰镜、制糖、钟表和牙刷、皮革机械分标委会等9个技术委员会的委员调整。

4. 深化工作机制改革创新，促进标准化军民融合。

2011年，按照国家总装备部的要求，我们组织编制了“十二五”军用标准化轻工重点项目论证报告，涉及轻工塑料、玻璃等行业的产品。

组织轻工有关行业标准化管理部门，宣贯了国家军用标准制修订工作有关管理文件、军用标准文本编制要求和军用标准体系表轻工部分。组织实施了总装备部批准的2011年轻工的国家军用标准制修订项目，涉及塑料、玻璃、钟表等行业。

5. 增强发展基础和能力，承担国家质检公益性行业科研专项。

近年来，美国和欧盟先后出台了玩具、文具和鞋类等产品的新技术法规和标准，提出了近乎苛刻的要求。如美国发布了新安全法则《消费品安全改进法案》，对一些有害可迁移元素的控制要求已超过食品量级；又如欧盟发布的新玩具安全指令，涉及到需要控制的有害可迁移元素多达19种（通常为6种），禁用的化学香料达55种。同时，我国的玩具、文具和鞋类生产企业普遍为中小企业，技术力量不足，对新规定理解不够，缺少相应的检测方法标准，导致频繁出现出口产品被召回或通报，影响了我国对外贸易，对中国制造产生不良影响。

为此，我们组织玩具、文具和制鞋行业标准化技术组织，申报国家质检公益性行业科研专项标准项目《欧盟和美国新市场准入指令和法规的玩具、文具和鞋类技术标准研究》，已获批准，获得285万元财政经费支持。为推进国际标准化工作对行业、企业的支持、引领和保护，组织家电标委会申报了《智能家电移动平台及电压力锅等5项国际标准研究》，已获批准，获得115万元财政经费支持。同时，一些轻工标委会还积极争取地方政府的公益性行业科研专项支持，进行相关验证试验，汇总分析试验数据，为制定标准提供了科学依据，如家具标委会。

6. 围绕产品质量提升，促进消费品安全标准化工作。

配合国家标准委制定了化妆品等标准体系规划，发布了家具、家用电器等一批涉及民生的重要产品标准；开展了消费品安全标准体系研究，发布了学生用品、烟花爆竹等安全标准；积极应对儿童玩具等质量安全突发事件，以及电动自行车标准等敏感问题，加强正面宣传和舆论引导，及时消除公众误解，加快标准制修订，发布6项玩具安全标准。配合卫生部参与了有关食品添加剂使用等标准制定工作。

针对社会对“毒玩具”事件的反映，落实国务院领导批示，积极组织玩具标委会加强对欧盟、美国新标准法规中对增塑剂和重金属在玩具中的限定要求的研究，及时修改完善相关国家标准。在国家强制标准《婴儿安抚奶嘴安全要求》中增加了对增塑剂的限定指标要求，对玩具标准中邻苯二甲酸脂的限制与限量要求进行了研讨。组织召开有玩具、塑料标委会和国际化学品制造商协会参加的增塑剂在玩具及塑料制品中应用的专题研讨会，就国际上对增塑剂安全性、国际及国外发达地区在法规和标准中限定情况等信息进行深入的沟通和探讨，为行业组织制定相关标准要求提供了参考。针对“荧光增白剂”事件，全国表面活性剂和洗涤用品标准化技术委员会，配合中国洗涤用品工业协会，积极向国家有关部门汇报，解释了荧光增白剂在洗涤用品中的应用范围、许可品种、安全评价等问题，及时消除了广大消费者的安全质疑。

7. 参与国际标准化活动取得新突破。

参与国际标准化活动是提高我国轻工业国际竞争能力，支撑产业同步参与国际竞争的重要途径。2011年，全国制鞋标准化技术委员会承担了国际标准化组织(ISO)“鞋号标识和标记体系”技术委员会秘书处工作并正式启动；全国照明电器标准化技术委员会积极参与12项国际电工委员会(IEC)半导体照明LED灯具相关标准制定工作，目前已完成7项；全国家用电器标准化技术委员会承担了7项国际标准制定工作；全国玩具标准化技术委员会制定的中国玩具标准《玩具及儿童用品聚氯乙烯塑料中邻苯二甲酸酯增塑剂的测定》被美国消费品安全委员会制定的《美国消费安全改进法案》直接采用。全国钟表标准化技术委员会，第一次作为ISO/TC114/SC14“台钟和挂钟”分委员会主席，在德国柏林主持召开了SC14分委员会会议，由我国提案的第一个时钟国际标准《指针式石英钟—机芯和指针的配合尺寸》即将发布。

2011年全国轻工标准化工作取得了一定成效，是国家有关部门和各级地方政府正确指导、大力支持的结果，是轻工各行业协会、各专业技术委员会、分技术委员会、标准化组织及相关单位的同志们共同努力的结果。在此，我代表中国轻工业联合会向辛勤工作在轻工标准化工作战线上全体同志表示崇高的敬意！向关心支持轻工业改革发展的各级领导、社会各界人士表示衷心的感谢！

在看到成绩的同时，我们也应清醒地认识到存在的不足：一是标准化体系不完善，与轻工行业转型升级需要相比，与广大消费者更多的期盼相比，我们的标准还存在着不适应、跟不上等问题，特别是标龄老化、标准缺失、标准滞后的问题还未得到根本改进；二是标准化制度需要完善，管理需要更规范，标准化顶层设计较为欠缺；三是标准化基础能力比较薄弱，标准化人才较缺乏，标准化信息水平急需提升等。这些还需要我们在今后的工作中认真加以改进。

二、当前轻工标准化工作面临的形势

1. 轻工业整体实力得到进一步提升。

2011年经轻工全行业共同努力，克服外部环境复杂、生产经营成本上升等多重困难，实现了“十二五”良好开局。主要特点：一是轻工业保持平稳较快增长。轻工行业全部工业企业累计实现工业总产值20.14万亿元，利润总额1.25万亿元，其中：规模以上企业实现工业总产值16.47万亿元，同比增长29.30%，利润1.00万亿元，同比增长31.98%。出口4431.1亿美元，同比增长23.0%，轻工累计顺差达全国贸易顺差的2.15倍。二是结构调整步伐加快。企业自主创新能力有所提高，一批在行业有影响的企业由原来主要依靠数量、规模、价格的竞争转为依靠结构调整、技术进步提升竞争力。全行业国家级企业技术中心达到110个，比上年增加15个。随着“十二五”规划的实施，国家支持轻工的科技项目增多。优势集聚和产业有序转移稳步推进，轻工业特色区域和产业集群产值占轻工规模以上企业工业总产值的28.5%，比上年提高1.4个百分点，中西部地区轻工业总产值占全国比重比上年上升3.2个百分点。轻工内外销比重进一步改善，内销占85.7%，比上年提高1.2个百分点。

2. 要适应新形势、新要求，切实发挥标准对轻工业调结构、上质量、上档次、产业升级的支撑和保障作用。

目前，我国轻工业正进入优化结构和产业升级的新的历史发展阶段。新阶段要求我们必须进一步转变发展方式，加快实现科技创新驱动发展；必须进一步优化产业结构，着力质量、档次的提高，向产业链高端发展；必须大力依靠技术进步，科技创新，全面提升轻工业的发展质量和全面提升轻工业的整体素质，为构建轻工业的现代产业体系，实现轻工业强国目标夯实基础。轻工业进入新的历史发展阶段，新形势、新情况对标准化工作提出了更高的要求。一是，消费结构升级，极大推动了消费品生产上质量、上档次的进程，轻工业在保障温饱型消费和小康型消费的同时，正向富裕型消费结构转变，要求标准工作加快适应这种转变，要为产品升级换代提供技术支撑和保证。二是，技术创新、技术进步速度加快，新材料应用更加广泛，产品升级换代周期大大缩短，新产品推出速度空前加快，这对标准修订、升级，新标准制定等工作，提出了新的更迫切的要求，确保不出现标准大量缺失和滞后的压力愈来愈大。三是，轻工业国际化进程加快，与国际市场融合更加紧密，标准工作与国际接轨要求愈来愈迫切，要求愈来愈严，标准成为轻工产品国际通行证的压力愈来愈大。四是，食品卫生及消费品安全工程是社会关注的热点和焦点，标准为食品卫生及消费品安全提供保证的要求愈来愈高，为消费品安全工程建设提供标准支持保障，为广大消费者提供安全消费环境、提振消费信心的要求越来越高。

新形势、新情况也是标准化工作面临的新任务，轻工标准化工作目前的现状，还不能完全适应新要求，一方面，我们要集中力量加快解决标龄老化和标准缺失及滞后的突出问题，另一方面，要迎接新挑战，为轻工业结构调整、产业升级，提供技术含量更高的全方位的标准支撑。因此，必须加强标准化工作队伍建设，多方筹集资金，加强能力建设，要重视加强标准化科研工作。

国家高度重视标准化工作。在国家“十二五”规划中有41处直接提到标准及标准化。今年1月11日国务院常务会议研究部署进一步加强质量工作，2月6日《质量发展纲要》发布实施，明确要求加快标准体系建设，提升标准的先进性、有效性和适用性。同时，党和国家领导人也高度关注工业标准化工作。在今年工信部工作会议上，张德江副总理强调：“要大力实施国家工业标准化战略，增加政府经费投入，完善工业标准制修订机制，加快产业急需、具有创新成果和国际先进水平的重要技术标准制定，积极参与国际标准制定，加大标准实施监督力度，推动建立适应产业发展需要的工业技术标准体系。”标准是工业平稳较快发展的重要技术基础，已成为我国走新型工业化道路，提升产业核心竞争力和综合国力的重要技术支撑。标准化工作内容，已经从单纯的技术领域，逐步扩展到工程建设、安全生产、节能减排等行业管理领域，以及民生、环保等更加广阔的社会领域。我们一定要进一步提高对标准化工作重要性的认识，增强信心，扎实工作，切实发挥标准工作对轻工调整结构、产品升级换代、新产品开发的支撑和保证作用。为食品卫生、消费品安全工作做好基础性工作，提高安全保证。为轻工产品提供国际通行证，为技术进步和科技创新提供支撑。

三、轻工业标准化工作重点任务

（一）指导思想

今后一段时期，轻工业标准化工作的指导思想是：以科学发展为主题，以加快转变方式为主线，促进科技进步和技术创新，改造提升传统产业，培育发展战略性新兴产业，以提升轻工标准化发展整体质量效益为核心目标，按照“系统管理、重点突破、整体提升”的工作要求，加强标准的顶层设计，加快制定轻工业急需、具有创新成果和国际水平的重要技术标准，加快建立适应轻工业发展需要的技术标准体系，带动标准技术水平的整体提升，促进轻工业平稳较快发展。

（二）2012年重点工作

2012年，轻工业标准化工作要深入贯彻2012年全国标准化工作会议及全国工业行业标准化工作会议精神，把握标准化工作的科学性、民主性、系统性、权威性、服务性，创新工作机制，推进系统管理，加强标准制修订全过程管理，促进标准与科技紧密结合，努力实现战略性新兴产业、参与国际标准化活动等领域的新突破，促进整体提升。

1. 努力创新工作机制，推进轻工标准化系统管理。

今年国家将完善标准分类管理机制，将强化对公益性标准的主导与支持。轻工国家标准以强制性和基础通用、管理、方法以及关键共性技术、重要产品为重点，主要涉及人身健康、公共安全、消费者利益、环境保护、资源节约等领域标准，以及基础通用方法和产业发展的关键技术标准。国家将在标准制修订、标准化科研、经费投入等方面加大支持力度。同时，国家将加强强制性标准管理，特别是立项和审查环节。强制性标准是技术法规在我国的主要表现形式，并已得到国内外认可，在我国经济社会发展中，发挥了重要作用。国家将对现有强制性标准进行梳理，做好顶层设计，提炼整合一类标准中的健康、安全、环保等强制性要求，制定通用共性强制性国家标准，并结合标准复审适时修订有关标准，对超范围制定的标准将及时废止或转变为推荐性标准。

轻工行业标准要围绕传统产业改造提升，切实做好行业标准复审和修订工作，重点制定代表产业先进水平，有利淘汰落后产能的新技术、新工艺、新产品和先进管理标准，提高轻工产品在质量、安全、卫生、可靠性和检测等方面的标准水平。

2. 突出重点，加快轻工重要技术标准制定，推进新兴产业、新材料、新技术标准化进程。

一是配合国家积极推进消费品安全标准体系研究，参与基础通用安全标准研制。继续加大玩具、家具、文具、化妆品等重要消费品安全标准和检测方法标准的制修订力度。积极参与卫生部牵头制定的食品及相关产品安全标准的制修订工作，不断完善与食品安全标准衔接的涵盖食品基础、管理、产品分等分级及非食品安全的质量要求等标准体系。二是加强新兴产业、新材料、新技术标准制定工作。推动LED照明电器、特种玻璃、功能陶瓷、塑木材料的标准体系研究，加快相关标准的立项、制定工作。开展工具酶等基础性领域标准体系建设，研制生物制造等领域重点产品标准。为加快轻工产业结构调整和升级、建设资源节约型和环境友好型社会发挥标准的支撑、引领和保障作用。

3. 进一步增强参与国际标准化活动的能力。

要配合国家标准委等部门，为企业、标准化技术组织参与国际标准化活动创造有利环境，支持有条件的企业或标准化技术组织主导国际标准研制，承担国际标准化组织秘书处或领导职务，推动具有创新成果的技术标准走向国际，占领行业竞争制高点。提升实质性参与国际标准化活动的能力和水平。建立一支相对稳定的专家队伍，形成长期参与国际标准化活动的经费保障机制，力争有更广泛的领域、更多数量的国际标准由我们的技术委员会参与或主持起草，有效推动我国轻工优势技术与标准成为国际标准。继续推进国际标准转化，在现有基础上，努力提高与国际标准的一致性程度。

为做好以上工作，必须加强和改进技术委员会的管理。为此，根据国家标准化管理委员会相关规定，中轻联制定了《全国轻工行业专业标准化技术委员会管理暂行办法》及《全国轻工行业专业标准化技术委员会换届工作暂行办法》。关于“管理暂行办法”，主要是更好的贯彻落实国家标准化管理委员会关于《全国专业标准化技术委员会管理规定》，并针对轻工各技术委员会运行中的问题提出的，管理办法进一步明确了各协会与标委会的关系，即协会要把行业急需制修订的标准要求带到技术委员会并形成共识，同时纳入年度计划，标委会要以行业需求为导向，更好的为行业发展服务，“管理暂行办法”还就工作程序，财务公开透明提出要求，同时明确了不允许以企业出资多少，作为起草单位排序依据等纪律。关于“换届工作暂行办法”，主要是考虑各标委会换届中遇到的问题，如不协调、不按期换届等，作好换届前期筹备和思想工作，协调各方意见，筹组换届领导小组，根据协商意见提出建议名单，最终由国标委确定。根据实际情况，两个“暂行办法”还需在听取各方面意见的基础上，进一步研究完善。

4. 努力推进轻工标准化与科技相结合。

标准化需要科技创新驱动，科技创新需要标准化支撑。一是，针对应急性、培育性、基础通用技术标准研究，各专业标准化技术委员会要积极争取承担质检公益性科研专项标准化项目，特别是标准预研、有一定科研基础的重要标准研制。二是，行业承担的科研项目，可把标准研制实施作为科技研发和成果转化的重要措施，充分发挥标准在科技成果转化中的桥梁纽带作用，使创新成果通过标准快速转化为现实生产力，依靠科技创新提升标准质量水平和竞争力。三是，以新材料、新产品、新技术研发和产业化应用为重点，促进科技成果转化为技术标准。

5. 继续深化标准化军民融合，做好国家军用标准化工作。

继续组织轻工有关行业开展向国家总装备部申报2012年国家军用标准制修订项目计划，督促项目归口单位和项目承担单位按期、保质完成2011年下达的军用标准制修订项目工作。

6. 加快“十二五”标准化工作规划编制工作。

“十二五”是轻工业发展的重要时期，应对调整、转型、升级、全面提升轻工业整体素质、构建现代产业体系的战略目标，标准发挥的作用越来越关键，对标准的水平要求越来越高，标准涉及的领域越来越广泛。因此，发挥标准的综合性、成套性、整体协调性要求更加迫切，推进标准化工作势在必行，完善标准化体系的任务更加繁重。同时，标准工作必须同轻工业“十二五”发展规划相衔接，也是标准工作必须认真解决的重要问题。为此，各行业协会和相应的标委会，要根据各行业“十二五”规划，共同研究，认真开展标准化“十二五”规划工作。规划要按“系统管理、重点突破、整体提升”的要求，全面总结标准化工作的成绩和存在的问题，全面分析标准与国外同行的差距，全面把握标准的先进性、适用性和有效性，明确“十二五”标准工作的整体思路、目标，坚持以服务科学发展为主题，以支撑加快转变发展为主线，坚持以提升标准化发展整体质量、效益为核心目标，全面提升标准水平，缩小同国外差距。《工业转型升级规划(2011—2015)》提出：“十二五”重点领域和新兴产业的技术标准要取得突破，主要工业品质量标准接近和达到国际先进水平，规划要紧紧围绕这一目标，要围绕标准的系统化要求，进行编制。为做好这一工作，各协会要与标委会特别是要与标委会秘书处组成专门班子，进行这项工作。首先，要认真进行对标分析，找出差距，明确方向，提高国际标准采标率，全面提升标准水平。希望各单位要抓紧时间开展此项工作，质量标准部要对各行业标准规划编制给予指导，提出要求，并在各行业规划基础上编制轻工业联合会的标准规划。

四、工作要求

做好2012年轻工标准化各项工作，需要各行业协会大力支持，需要广大企业的积极参与，需要各轻工行业标准化技术委员会技术支撑。在此，我强调以下几点：

1. 转变思想观念，深刻认识标准化工作对轻工行业发展的促进作用。

目前，轻工标准化工作所处的形势、环境正在发生着深刻的变化，需要我们创新工作思路和方法，及时转变观念，努力适应新形势的要求。轻工各行业协会、各标准化技术组织要充分认识、高度重视“系统管理、重点突破、整体提升”的内涵要求，将标准化工作与行业的总体工作统一起来，合力做好轻工标准化工作。轻工各行业协会要加强本行业情况研究工作，充分发挥行业协会贴近行业、熟悉企业的优势，深入开展行业基本情况、标准体系研究工作，提升标准化对行业发展的促进和支撑水平。轻工各标准化技术组织，要建立健全标准化工作规章制度，重视标准化工作人员的配备和能力的培养，提高技术和服务能力。

2. 轻工国家标准、行业标准要努力提高“先进性、适用性、有效性”。

首先，强调先进性，是要求标准讲科学、用科学，提高标准的科技含量和标准的质量技术水平，要积极推动更多的轻工标准达到或高于相关联的国际标准水平。当然，提升先进性并不是技术指标越高越好，还必须与中国国情相适应；第二，强调适用性，需要标准在制修订过程中要广泛听取行业、企业、科研、监督机构、消费者等各方意见，满足实际需要，标准必须紧贴需求，服务大局；最后，强调有效性，需要标准得到应用。协会、技术委员会要重视标准的宣贯，只有让所有标准使用方能够得到标准、理解标准、执行标准，标准才是有效的。

3. 加强轻工国家标准、行业标准制修订全过程的管理。

首先是把好立项关。技术委员会在提出标准立项时要切实以需求为导向，对项目的必要性、可行性进行充分的论证，充分听取全体委员的意见并达成共识。要注意国家标准与行业标准的配套，突出各级标准的制定重点，避免标准之间交叉、重复、矛盾。其次是加强制修订过程的监督。要落实技术委员会工作责任，严格标准制修订程序，确保标准编写质量。

4. 按期完成标准制修订计划，确保计划的严肃性。

标准制修订项目一旦列入计划，标准化技术委员会要抓紧时间组织落实。要处理好数量、速度、结构、质量、效益等要素的关系，控制好计划实施进度安排，否则，无法保持计划的严肃性，也不利于解决标准缺失、老化、滞后的问题。今后，中轻联将加强对这方面的考核，并采取必要的处理措施。

5. 加强标准制修订经费管理。

中轻联下发的《全国轻工行业专业标准化技术委员会管理暂行办法》中对技术委员会经费的筹集、使用和管理提出了明确的要求，并强调“标委会、分标委会在标准起草过程中，不得采取摊派、有偿署名、及以企业出资多少作为标准起草单位顺序的依据等方式收取不合理费用。”随着标准制修订数量的增加和社会各界对标准的重视，一些技术委员会标准经费年收支额度较大，经费管理需要高度重视，严加管理。

同志们！今年轻工业面临着调结构、转方式、促发展的关键时期，对轻工标准化工作提出了更高的要求，任务十分艰巨。我们要在国家有关部门、各级地方政府的大力支持下，继往开来，开拓创新，努力扎实，共同做好轻工标准化各项工作，为轻工业平稳较快发展作出新的贡献，以优异的成绩迎接党的十八大的胜利召开。

2012年发布塑料相关国家标准、行业标准

标准代号	标准名称
GB/T 15343—2012	滑石化学分析方法(2012年国家标准42号)
GB/T 15344—2012	滑石物理检验方法(2012年国家标准42号)
GB/T 17497.2—2012	柔性版装潢印刷品 第2部分:塑料与金属箔类(2012年国家标准42号)
GB/T 29365—2012	塑木复合材料人工气候老化试验方法(2012年国家标准42号)
GB/T 29418—2012	塑木复合材料产品物理力学性能测试(2012年国家标准42号)
GB/T 29419—2012	塑木复合材料铺板性能等级和护栏体系性能(2012年国家标准42号)
GB/T 29460—2012	含缺陷聚乙烯管道电熔接头安全评定(2012年国家标准42号)
GB/T 29461—2012	聚乙烯管道电熔接头超声检测(2012年国家标准42号)
GB 8624—2012	建筑材料及制品燃烧性能分级(2012年国家标准41号)
GB/T 29284—2012	聚乳酸(2012年国家标准41号)
GB/T 29288—2012	热塑性硬质聚氨酯泡沫塑料通用技术条件(2012年国家标准41号)
GB/T 29336—2012	化妆品用共挤出多层复合软管(2012年国家标准41号)
GB/T 29333—2012	模内装饰(IMD)用硬化薄膜耐湿热老化性能测定方法(2012年国家标准41号)
GB/T 29330—2012	模内装饰(IMD)用薄膜油墨粘接性能测定方法(2012年国家标准41号)
GB/T 15342—2012	滑石粉(代替GB 15342—1994)(2012年国家标准41号)
GB 11655.1—2012	合成材料制造业卫生防护距离第1部分:聚氯乙烯制造业(2012年国家标准31号)
GB/T 16716.7—2012	包装与包装废弃物第7部分:生物降解和堆肥(2012年国家标准28号公告)
GB/T 28765—2012	包装材料塑料薄膜、片材和容器的有机气体透过率试验方法(2012年国家标准28号公告)
GB/T 28797—2012	室内塑料垃圾桶(2012年国家标准28号公告)
GB/T 28798—2012	塑料收纳箱(2012年国家标准28号公告)
GB/T 28799.1—2012	冷热水用耐热聚乙烯(PE—RT)管道系统第1部分:总则(2012年国家标准28号公告)
GB/T 28799.2—2012	冷热水用耐热聚乙烯(PE—RT)管道系统第2部分:管材(2012年国家标准28号公告)
GB/T 28799.3—2012	冷热水用耐热聚乙烯(PE—RT)管道系统第3部分:管件(2012年国家标准28号公告)
GB/Z 28820.1—2012	聚合物长期辐射老化 第1部分:监测扩散限制氧化的技术(2012年国家标准28号公告)
GB/Z 28820.2—2012	聚合物长期辐射老化 第2部分:预测低剂量率下老化的程序(2012年国家标准28号公告)
GB/Z 28820.3—2012	聚合物长期辐射老化 第3部分:低压电缆材料在役监测程序(2012年国家标准28号公告)
GB/T 28886—2012	建筑用塑料门(2012年国家标准28号公告)
GB/T 28887—2012	建筑用塑料窗(2012年国家标准28号公告)
GB/T 28889—2012	复合材料面内剪切性能试验方法(2012年国家标准28号公告)
GB/T 28891—2012	纤维增强塑料复合材料单向增强材料Ⅰ型层间断裂韧性GIC的测定
GB/T 28897—2012	钢塑复合管(2012年国家标准28号公告)
GB 18173.1—2012	高分子防水材料 第1部分:片材(2012年国家标准24号公告)
GB/T 19089—2012	橡胶或塑料涂覆织物耐磨性的测定马丁代尔法(2012年国家标准13号公告)
GB/T 28461—2012	碳纤维预浸料(2012年国家标准13号公告)
GB 28481—2012	塑料家具中有害物质限量(2012年国家标准13号公告)
GB/T 28494—2012	热塑性塑料截止阀(2012年国家标准13号公告)
GB/T 28596—2012	内壁碳涂层聚对苯二甲酸乙二醇酯瓶(2012年国家标准13号公告)

续表

标准代号	标 准 名 称
GB/T 28605—2012	生活饮用水用橡胶或塑料软管和非增强软管及软管组合件(2012年国家标准13号公告)
GB/T 28609—2012	光学功能薄膜聚对苯二甲酸乙二醇酯(PET)薄膜双折射测定方法(2012年国家标准13号公告)
GB 25936.1—2012	橡胶塑料粉碎机械第1部分：刀片式破碎机安全要求(2012年行业标准1号公告)
GB 25936.2—2012	橡胶塑料粉碎机械第2部分：拉条式切粒机安全要求(2012年行业标准1号公告)
GB 25936.3—2012	橡胶塑料粉碎机械第3部分：切碎机安全要求(2012年行业标准1号公告)
HG/T 4386—2012	增塑剂环氧大豆油(2012行业标准70号)
HG/T 4453—2012	塑料　增塑剂使用控制技术规范(2012行业标准70号)
HG/T 4454—2012	塑料　增塑剂迁移的测定(2012行业标准70号)
HG/T 4455—2012	塑料　增塑剂损失的测定热空气法(2012行业标准70号)
HG/T 4456—2012	塑料　增塑剂在压缩应力下渗出的测定(2012行业标准70号)
HG/T 4457—2012	塑料　增塑剂在潮湿条件下渗出的测定(2012行业标准70号)
HG/T 4458—2012	塑料　增塑剂损失的测定活性炭法(2012行业标准70号)
HG/T 4459—2012	塑料　增塑剂在液体介质条件下抽出的测定(2012行业标准70号)
HG/T 4395—2012	太阳能热水器用聚氨酯硬泡组合聚醚(2012行业标准70号)
HG/T 4304—2012	耐蚀聚烯烃(PO)塑料衬里技术条件(2012行业标准70号)
JC/T 2112—2012	塑料防护排水板(2012行业标准70号)
JC/T 2129—2012	电致液晶夹层调光玻璃(2012行业标准70号)
JC/T 587—2012	玻璃纤维缠绕增强热固性树脂耐腐蚀立式贮罐(2012行业标准70号)
JC/T 718—2012	玻璃纤维缠绕增强热固性树脂耐腐蚀卧式贮罐(2012行业标准70号)
FZ/T 51006—2012	膜级聚己内酰胺切片(2012行业标准70号)
FZ/T 51007—2012	阻燃聚酯切片(PET)(2012行业标准70号)
FZ/T 54057—2012	聚对苯二甲酸丁二醇酯(PBT)预取向丝(2012行业标准70号)
FZ/T 54065—2012	聚丙烯腈基碳纤维原丝(2012行业标准70号)
QB/T 1046—2012	凹版塑料薄膜表印油墨(2012行业标准70号)
QB/T 2024—2012	凹版塑料薄膜复合油墨(2012行业标准70号)
QB/T 4395—2012	硬质聚氯乙烯(PVC—U)低发泡中空格子板(2012行业标准70号)
QB/T 4396—2012	软体沼气池用聚氯乙烯涂覆织物膜材(2012行业标准70号)
QB/T 4397—2012	自洁型聚氯乙烯涂覆织物建筑膜材(2012行业标准70号)
QB/T 4398—2012	聚全氟乙丙烯(FEP)薄膜(2012行业标准70号)
QB/T 4415—2012	软体聚氯乙烯涂覆织物沼气池(2012行业标准70号)
BB/T 0060—2012	包装容器聚对苯二甲酸乙二醇酯(PET)(2012行业标准70号)
YD/T 2433.1—2012	650nm塑料光纤传输设备用光模块技术条件第1部分：155Mb/s光收发合一模块(2012行业标准70号)
HG/T 3690—2012	工业用钢骨架聚乙烯塑料复合管(代替HG/T 3690—2001)(2012行业标准55号)
HG/T 3691—2012	工业用钢骨架聚乙烯塑料复合管件(代替HG/T 3691—2001)(2012行业标准55号)
HG/T 3707—2012	工业用孔网钢骨架聚乙烯复合管件(代替HG/T 3707—2003)(2012行业标准55号)
HG/T 4371—2012	化工用聚氯乙烯复合衬里塔器(2012行业标准55号)
HG/T 4372—2012	化工用复合材料管及管件(2012行业标准55号)
HG/T 4373—2012	化工用塑料衬里复合管和管件(2012行业标准55号)
HG/T 4375—2012	改性超高分子量聚乙烯管材衬里专用料

续表

标准代号	标 准 名 称
HG/T 3183—2012	氟塑料衬里单级单吸化工离心泵技术条件(代替 HG/T 3183—1989)(2012 行业标准 55 号)
HG/T 4182—2012	尼龙 66 切片(2012 行业标准 55 号)
YS/T 451—2012	塑覆铜管(2012 行业标准 55 号)
SH/T 1774—2012	塑料聚丙烯等规指数的测定低分辨率脉冲核磁共振法(2012 行业标准 55 号)
SH/T 1775—2012	塑料线型低密度聚乙烯(PE—LLD)组成的定量分析碳—13 核磁共振波谱法(2012 行业标准 55 号)
QB/T 4370—2012	家具用软质阻燃聚氨酯泡沫塑料(2012 行业标准 55 号)
BB/T 0037—2012	双面涂覆聚氯乙烯阻燃防水布和篷布(2012 行业标准 55 号)
JB/T 8734. 1—2012	额定电压 450/750V 及以下聚氯乙烯绝缘电缆电线和软线第 1 部分：一般规定(代替 JB/T 8734. 1—1998)(2012 年行业标准 20 号公告)
JB/T 8734. 2—2012	额定电压 450/750V 及以下聚氯乙烯绝缘电缆电线和软线第 2 部分：固定布线用电缆电线(代替 JB/T 8734. 2—1998)(2012 年行业标准 20 号公告)
JB/T 8734. 3—2012	额定电压 450/750V 及以下聚氯乙烯绝缘电缆电线和软线第 3 部分：连接用软电线和软电缆(代替 JB/T8734. 3—1998)(2012 年行业标准 20 号公告)
JB/T 8734. 4—2012	额定电压 450/750V 及以下聚氯乙烯绝缘电缆电线和软线第 4 部分：安装用电线(代替 JB/T 8734. 4—1998)(2012 年行业标准 20 号公告)
JB/T 8734. 5—2012	额定电压 450/750V 及以下聚氯乙烯绝缘电缆电线和软线第 5 部分：屏蔽电线(代替 JB/T 8734. 5—1998)(2012 年行业标准 20 号公告)
JB/T 8734. 6—2012	额定电压 450/750V 及以下聚氯乙烯绝缘电缆电线和软线第 6 部分：电梯电缆(2012 年行业标准 20 号公告)
JB/T 11340. 2—2012	阀控式铅酸蓄电池安全阀　第 2 部分：塑料壳体(2012 年行业标准 20 号公告)
QB/T 2901—2012	口腔清洁护理用品牙膏用铝塑复合软管(2012 年行业标准 20 号公告)
QB/T 4317—2012	浸塑衣架(2012 年行业标准 20 号公告)
QB/T 4330—2012	带衬里 PVC 庭院鞋(2012 年行业标准 20 号公告)
QB/T 4331—2012	儿童旅游鞋(2012 年行业标准 20 号公告)
QB/T 4332—2012	工艺鞋(2012 年行业标准 20 号公告)
QB/T 4336—2012	注塑塑料鞋跟(2012 年行业标准 20 号公告)
QB/T 4341—2012	抗菌聚氨酯合成革抗菌性能试验方法和抗菌效果(2012 年行业标准 20 号公告)
QB/T 4342—2012	服装用聚氨酯合成革安全要求(2012 年行业标准 20 号公告)
QB/T 4343—2012	合成革用水性色浆(2012 年行业标准 20 号公告)
QB/T 4344—2012	裙腰带用聚氯乙烯人造革(2012 年行业标准 20 号公告)
QB/T 4345—2012	防护鞋底用聚氨酯树脂(2012 年行业标准 20 号公告)
QB/T 4346—2012	织物复合用干法聚氨酯薄膜(2012 年行业标准 20 号公告)
QB/T 4347—2012	汽车用聚氯乙烯薄膜和片材(2012 年行业标准 20 号公告)
HG/T 4288—2012	偏光眼镜用三醋酸纤维素酯(TAC)薄膜(2012 年行业标准 20 号公告)
HG/T 4302—2012	耐候阻隔绝缘性功能薄膜(2012 年行业标准 20 号公告)
HG/T 4303—2012	表面硬化聚酯薄膜耐磨性测定方法(2012 年行业标准 20 号公告)
BB/T 0059—2012	医疗器械吸塑包装用共挤膜(2012 年行业标准 20 号公告)

(中国塑料加工工业协会　田岩　倪国庆　钟雁)

2012 年国家标准计划项目汇总表

序号	计划编号	项目名称	标准性质	制/修订	代替标准号	采用国际标准	完成时间	主管部门	技术归口单位	起草单位
第一批										
1	20120293 – T – 469	无缝铝塑共挤出复合软管	推荐	制定			2013	国家标准化管理委员会	全国包装标准化技术委员会	深圳市通产丽星股份有限公司
2	20120315 – T – 469	超滤膜测试方法	推荐	制定			2014	国家标准化管理委员会	全国分离膜标准化技术委员会	天津膜天膜科技股份有限公司
3	20120316 – T – 469	反渗透膜测试方法	推荐	制定			2014	国家标准化管理委员会	全国分离膜标准化技术委员会	贵阳时代沃顿科技有限公司、太仓华辰净化设备有限公司、深圳嘉泉水处理科技有限公司
4	20120507 – T – 469	塑料吹塑平托盘	推荐	制定			2013	国家标准化管理委员会	全国物流标准化技术委员会	张家港市同大机械有限公司、中国物流与采购联合会托盘专业委员会
5	20120756 – T – 604	注塑机用伺服变频控制设备	推荐	制定			2014	中国电器工业协会	全国变频调速设备标准化技术委员会	天津电气传动设计研究所、广州市珠峰电气有限公司等
6	20120913 – T – 609	玻璃纤维增强热固性树脂管 湿态环境下长期极限弯曲应变和长期环变形的测定	推荐	制定			2014	中国建筑材料联合会	全国纤维增强塑料标准化技术委员会	北京玻璃钢研究设计院、武汉理工大学、同济大学
7	20120914 – T – 609	玻璃纤维增强热固性树脂管和管件长期静水压试验方法	推荐	制定			2014	中国建筑材料联合会	全国纤维增强塑料标准化技术委员会	北京玻璃钢研究设计院、武汉理工大学、同济大学

续表

序号	计划编号	项目名称	标准性质	制/修订	代替标准号	采用国际标准	完成时间	主管部门	技术归口单位	起草单位
8	20120915－T－609	建筑用玻璃纤维增强酚醛树脂板	推荐	制定			2014	中国建筑材料联合会	全国纤维增强塑料标准化技术委员会	中国建筑材料科学研究总院、济南同镒节能材料有限公司
9	20120916－T－609	纤维增强塑料 试验板制备 第4部分：预浸料模塑	推荐	制定			2012	中国建筑材料联合会	全国纤维增强塑料标准化技术委员会	北京玻璃钢研究设计院
10	20120999－T－606	光学功能薄膜 表面硬化薄膜 硬化层厚度测试方法	推荐	制定			2014	中国石油和化学工业联合会	全国光学功能薄膜材料标准化技术委员会	中国乐凯胶片集团公司
11	20121000－T－606	光学功能薄膜术语及其定义	推荐	制定			2014	中国石油和化学工业联合会	全国光学功能薄膜材料标准化技术委员会	中国乐凯胶片集团公司
12	20121056－T－606	LED 灯罩用聚碳酸酯	推荐	制定			2014	中国石油和化学工业联合会	全国塑料标准化技术委员会	上海日之升新技术发展有限公司
13	20121059－T－606	塑料 聚苯硫醚(PPS)的模塑和挤塑材料 第1部分：命名系统和基础规范	推荐	制定		ISO 28078－1：2009	2014	中国石油和化学工业联合会	全国塑料标准化技术委员会	中蓝晨光化工研究设计院有限公司、四川得阳特种新材料有限公司
14	20121060－T－606	塑料 聚苯硫醚(PPS)的模塑和挤塑材料 第2部分：试样制备和性能测定	推荐	制定		ISO 28078－2：2009	2014	中国石油和化学工业联合会	全国塑料标准化技术委员会	中蓝晨光化工研究设计院有限公司、四川得阳特种新材料有限公司
15	20121061－T－606	塑料 聚碳酸酯(PC)模塑和挤出材料 第1部分：命名系统和基础规范	推荐	制定		ISO 7391－1	2014	中国石油和化学工业联合会	全国塑料标准化技术委员会	中国蓝星(集团)股份有限公司

续表

序号	计划编号	项目名称	标准性质	制/修订	代替标准号	采用国际标准	完成时间	主管部门	技术归口单位	起草单位
16	20121062 - T - 606	塑料　聚碳酸酯(PC)模塑和挤出材料　第2部分：试样制备和性能测试	推荐	制定		ISO 7391 - 2	2014	中国石油和化学工业联合会	全国塑料标准化技术委员会	中国蓝星(集团)股份有限公司
17	20121063 - T - 606	塑料　聚酰胺模塑和挤出材料　第1部分：命名系统和规范基础	推荐	制定		ISO 1874 - 1：2010	2015	中国石油和化学工业联合会	全国塑料标准化技术委员会	金发科技股份有限公司
18	20121064 - T - 606	塑料　聚酰胺模塑和挤出材料　第2部分：试样制备和性能测定	推荐	制定		ISO 1874 - 2：2006	2015	中国石油和化学工业联合会	全国塑料标准化技术委员会	上海金发科技发展有限公司
19	20121065 - T - 606	塑料　热塑性聚酯(TP)模塑和挤出材料 第2部分：试样制备和性能测定	推荐	制定		ISO 7792 - 2：1997	2013	中国石油和化学工业联合会	全国塑料标准化技术委员会	中国石化仪征化纤股份有限公司
20	20121066 - T - 606	塑料　热塑性塑料熔体质量流动速率(MFR)和熔体体积流动速率(MVR)的测定　第1部分：标准方法	推荐	修订	GB/T 3682—2000	ISO 1133 - 1：2011	2014	中国石油和化学工业联合会	全国塑料标准化技术委员会	中国石化北京燕山分公司树脂应用研究所、中蓝晨光化工研究设计院、中国石化北京化工研究院燕山分院
21	20121067 - T - 606	塑料　热塑性塑料熔体质量流动速率(MFR)和熔体体积流动速率(MVR)的测定　第2部分：对时间 - 温度历史和/或湿度影响敏感的材料用试验方法	推荐	制定		ISO 1133 - 2：2011	2014	中国石油和化学工业联合会	全国塑料标准化技术委员会	中蓝晨光化工研究设计院、国家合成树脂质量监督检验中心

续表

序号	计划编号	项目名称	标准性质	制/修订	代替标准号	采用国际标准	完成时间	主管部门	技术归口单位	起草单位
22	20121068 - T - 606	塑料 乙烯/乙酸乙烯酯(E/VAC)模塑和挤出材料 第1部分：命名系统和分类基础	推荐	制定		ISO 4613 - 1：1993	2013	中国石油和化学工业联合会	全国塑料标准化技术委员会	中国石油化工股份有限公司北京燕山分公司树脂应用研究所、中国石油化工股份有限公司北京燕山分公司质量监督检验中心
23	20121069 - T - 606	橡塑材料中增塑剂含量的测定 - 气相色谱质谱联用法	推荐	制定			2013	中国石油和化学工业联合会	全国塑料标准化技术委员会	福建省产品质量检验研究院、国家塑料制品质量监督检验中心(福州)
24	20121113 - T - 606	橡胶或塑料涂覆织物 抗刺穿性测试方法	推荐	制定			2013	中国石油和化学工业联合会	全国橡胶与橡胶制品标准化技术委员会	中国人民解放军总后勤部油料研究所、凯迪西北橡胶有限公司
25	20121126 - T - 606	输送带 具有橡胶或塑料覆盖层的煤矿井下用织物芯输送带规范	推荐	制定		ISO 22721：2007	2013	中国石油和化学工业联合会	中国石油和化学工业联合会	青岛科技大学等
26	20121128 - T - 606	输送带——具有橡胶或塑料覆盖层的普通用途织物芯输送带规范	推荐	制定		ISO 14890：2003	2014	中国石油和化学工业联合会	中国石油和化学工业联合会	青岛橡六输送带有限公司、青岛科技大学等
第二批										
1	20121821 - T - 609	聚氯乙烯卷材地板 第2部分：同质聚氯乙烯卷材地	推荐	修订	GB/T 11982.2—1996	ISO10581：2011	2015	中国建筑材料联合会	全国轻质与装饰装修建筑材料标准化技术委员会	上海市建筑科学研究院(集团)有限公司、上海建科检验有限公司
2	20121824 - T - 609	玻璃纤维增强塑料波纹板	推荐	修订	GB/T 14206—2005	JISA 5701：1999	2014	中国建筑材料联合会	全国纤维增强塑料标准化技术委员会	秦皇岛耀华玻璃钢股份公司

续表

序号	计划编号	项目名称	标准性质	制/修订	代替标准号	采用国际标准	完成时间	主管部门	技术归口单位	起草单位
3	20121867-T-607	密胺塑料餐饮具	推荐	制定			2013	中国轻工业联合会	全国食品直接接触材料及制品标准化技术委员会	轻工业塑料加工应用研究所、台州市希尔家庭用品有限公司
4	20121868-T-607	食品塑料包装容器中顶空气体含量的测定 传感器法	推荐	制定			2014	中国轻工业联合会	全国食品直接接触材料及制品标准化技术委员会	北京市海淀区产品质量监督检验所、济南兰光机电技术有限公司
5	20121869-T-607	节水灌溉器材 第1部分：单翼迷宫式滴灌带	推荐	修订	GB/T 19812.1—2005		2013	中国轻工业联合会	全国塑料制品标准化技术委员会	新疆天业股份有限公司、中国水利水电科学研究院
6	20121870-T-607	节水灌溉器材 第2部分：压力补偿式滴头及滴灌管	推荐	修订	GB/T 19812.2—2005		2013	中国轻工业联合会	全国塑料制品标准化技术委员会	中国水利水电科学研究院、新疆天业股份有限公司
7	20121871-T-607	节水灌溉器材 第3部分：内镶式滴灌管、带	推荐	修订	GB/T 19812.3—2008		2013	中国轻工业联合会	全国塑料制品标准化技术委员会	新疆天业股份有限公司、中国水利水电科学研究院
8	20121872-T-607	聚乙烯滚塑导引和隔离墩通用技术条件	推荐	制定			2013	中国轻工业联合会	全国塑料制品标准化技术委员会	佛山市顺德区爱得乐绅谊滚塑制品有限公司、中国标准化协会等
9	20121873-T-607	埋地排水用聚丙烯（PP）双壁波纹管材	推荐	制定		ISO 21138：2006	2013	中国轻工业联合会	全国塑料制品标准化技术委员会	永高股份有限公司
10	20121874-T-607	热塑性塑料及其复合材料热封面热粘性能测定	推荐	制定			2014	中国轻工业联合会	全国塑料制品标准化技术委员会	北京市海淀区产品质量监督检验所、济南兰光机电技术有限公司
11	20121875-T-607	软质泡沫聚合材料 滞后损失试验方法	推荐	制定		ASTM D3574-2008X6	2014	中国轻工业联合会	全国塑料制品标准化技术委员会	全国塑料制品标准化中心、江苏省化工研究所有限公司、浙江圣诺盟顾家海绵有限公司

续表

序号	计划编号	项目名称	标准性质	制/修订	代替标准号	采用国际标准	完成时间	主管部门	技术归口单位	起草单位
12	20121876 - T - 607	软质泡沫聚合材料 低温柔性试验方法	推荐	制定		BS 4023：1975 Appendix C	2014	中国轻工业联合会	全国塑料制品标准化技术委员会	全国塑料制品标准化中心、江苏省化工研究所有限公司、浙江圣诺盟顾家海绵有限公司
13	20121877 - T - 607	硬聚氯乙烯管材 差示扫描量热法（DSC）第 1 部分：加工温度的测量	推荐	制定		ISO 18373 - 1：2007	2014	中国轻工业联合会	全国塑料制品标准化技术委员会、全国质量监管重点产品检验方法标准化技术委员会	广州市质量监督检测研究院
14	20121878 - T - 607	粘合软质聚氨酯泡沫塑料	推荐	制定		ISO 5999：2007(E)	2013	中国轻工业联合会	全国塑料制品标准化技术委员会	全国塑料制品标准化中心、浙江圣诺盟顾家海绵有限公司
15	20121939 - T - 606	塑料 使用体积排阻色谱测定聚合物的平均分子量和分子量分布 第 1 部分：通则	推荐	制定		ISO 16014 - 1：2003	2014	中国石油和化学工业联合会	全国塑料标准化技术委员会	广州市质量监督检测研究院
16	20121940 - T - 606	塑料 抗冲击聚苯乙烯防静电材料	推荐	制定			2013	中国石油和化学工业联合会	全国塑料标准化技术委员会	金发科技股份有限公司
17	20121941 - T - 606	塑料 热机械分析法（TMA） 第 1 部分：通则	推荐	制定		ISO 11359 - 1	2013	中国石油和化学工业联合会	全国塑料标准化技术委员会	金发科技股份有限公司
18	20121942 - T - 606	塑料 热机械分析法（TMA） 第 2 部分：线性膨胀系数和玻璃化转变温度的测定	推荐	制定		ISO 11359 - 2	2013	中国石油和化学工业联合会	全国塑料标准化技术委员会	金发科技股份有限公司

（中国塑料加工工业协会　田岩　倪国庆　钟雁）

2012年塑料相关行业标准制修订计划

序号	计划号	项目名称	性质	制/修订	代替标准	采标情况	完成年限	部内主管司局	技术委员会或技术归口单位	主要起草单位
第一批										
1	2012－0019T－HG	等离子电视(PDP)滤光膜	推荐	制定			2012	原材料工业司	全国光学功能薄膜材料标准化技术委员会	山东天诺光电材料有限公司、四川长虹电子集团有限公司
2	2012－0020T－HG	光学级聚酯薄膜	推荐	制定			2012	原材料工业司	全国光学功能薄膜材料标准化技术委员会	合肥乐凯科技产业有限公司、中国乐凯胶片集团公司
3	2012－0021T－HG	透明电磁波屏蔽膜	推荐	制定			2012	原材料工业司	全国光学功能薄膜材料标准化技术委员会	乐凯胶片股份有限公司、中国乐凯胶片集团公司
4	2012－0002T－HG	化工用塑料管道粘接　剥离检测方法	推荐	制定			2012	原材料工业司	全国非金属化工设备标准化技术委员会	温州赵氟隆有限公司，国家塑料制品质量监督检验中心，广州市特种承压设备检测研究院
5	2012－0003T－HG	化工用塑料管道粘接　剪切检测方法	推荐	制定			2012	原材料工业司	全国非金属化工设备标准化技术委员会	温州赵氟隆有限公司，国家塑料制品质量监督检验中心，广州市特种承压设备检测研究院
6	2012－0004T－HG	化工用塑料管道粘接　拉伸检测方法	推荐	制定			2012	原材料工业司	全国非金属化工设备标准化技术委员会	温州赵氟隆有限公司，国家塑料制品质量监督检验中心，广州市特种承压设备检测研究院
7	2012－0005T－HG	塑料焊接机具　挤出焊枪	推荐	制定			2013	原材料工业司	全国非金属化工设备标准化技术委员会	温州赵氟隆有限公司、莱丹塑料焊接技术（上海）有限公司

续表

序号	计划号	项目名称	性质	制/修订	代替标准	采标情况	完成年限	部内主管司局	技术委员会或技术归口单位	主要起草单位
8	2012－0006T－HG	塑料焊接机具　热风焊枪	推荐	制定			2013	原材料工业司	全国非金属化工设备标准化技术委员会	温州赵氟隆有限公司、莱丹塑料焊接技术（上海）有限公司
9	2012－0040T－HG	聚氨酯原料发泡反应特性的测定方法	推荐	制定			2012	原材料工业司	全国塑料标准化技术委员会聚氨酯分会	江苏省化工研究所有限公司、江苏省聚氨酯产品质量监督检测站、常熟一统聚氨酯有限公司、黎明化工研究院
10	2012－0041T－HG	塑料　二羟基聚醚多元醇	推荐	制定			2012	原材料工业司	全国塑料标准化技术委员会聚氨酯分会	中国石化集团资产经营管理有限公司上海高桥分公司、江苏钟山化工有限公司、山东蓝星东大化工有限责任公司、天津石化聚醚部、黎明化工研究院
11	2012－0042T－HG	塑料　六羟基聚醚多元醇	推荐	制定			2012	原材料工业司	全国塑料标准化技术委员会聚氨酯分会	山东蓝星东大化工有限责任公司、天津石化聚醚部、江苏钟山化工有限公司、中国石化集团资产经营管理有限公司上海高桥分公司、黎明化工研究院
12	2012－0038T－HG	高抗冲聚苯乙烯（HIPS）色母料	推荐	制定			2012	原材料工业司	全国塑料标准化技术委员会、全国塑料制品标准化技术委员会	宁波色母粒有限公司、北京化工大学
13	2012－0039T－HG	聚丙烯（PP）色母料	推荐	制定			2012	原材料工业司	全国塑料标准化技术委员会、全国塑料制品标准化技术委员会	宁波色母粒有限公司、北京化工大学

续表

序号	计划号	项目名称	性质	制/修订	代替标准	采标情况	完成年限	部内主管司局	技术委员会或技术归口单位	主要起草单位
14	2012－0026T－HG	消光用二氧化硅	推荐	制定			2012	原材料工业司	全国化学标准化技术委员会无机化工分会	中海油天津化工研究设计院、冷水江三A化工有限责任公司
15	2012－0028T－HG	紫外阻隔材料用合成水滑石	推荐	制定			2012	原材料工业司	全国化学标准化技术委员会无机化工分会	中海油天津化工研究设计院、北京化工大学
16	2012－0261T－QB	防护手套用聚氨酯超细纤维合成革	推荐	制定			2012	消费品工业司	全国塑料制品技术标准化技术委员会	上海华峰超纤材料股份有限公司
17	2012－0262T－QB	聚氯乙烯发泡垫技术条件	推荐	制定			2012	消费品工业司	全国塑料制品技术标准化技术委员会	佛山远华塑料实业有限公司
18	2012－0263T－QB	内墙装饰用水性聚氨酯壁革	推荐	制定			2012	消费品工业司	全国塑料制品技术标准化技术委员会	浙江优耐克科技发展有限公司
19	2012－0264T－QB	人造革合成革试验方法　成雾性的测定	推荐	制定			2012	消费品工业司	全国塑料制品技术标准化技术委员会	昆山阿基里斯人造皮有限公司
20	2012－0265T－QB	人造革合成革试验方法　透气性的测定	推荐	制定			2012	消费品工业司	全国塑料制品技术标准化技术委员会	安徽安利合成革股份有限公司
21	2012－0266T－QB	人造革合成革用颜色色卡	推荐	制定			2012	消费品工业司	全国塑料制品技术标准化技术委员会	浙江深蓝轻纺科技有限公司
22	2012－0267T－QB	休闲鞋用聚氨酯合成革	推荐	制定			2012	消费品工业司	全国塑料制品技术标准化技术委员会	安徽安利合成革股份有限公司
23	2012－0268T－QB	游艇用聚氯乙烯人造革	推荐	制定			2012	消费品工业司	全国塑料制品技术标准化技术委员会	佛山市高明威仕达塑料有限公司

续表

序号	计划号	项目名称	性质	制/修订	代替标准	采标情况	完成年限	部内主管司局	技术委员会或技术归口单位	主要起草单位
第二批										
1	2012-0780T-SH	塑料 乙烯-丙烯共聚聚丙烯单体含量及序列结构分析 碳-13核磁共振波谱法	推荐	制定			2013	原材料工业司	全国塑料标准化技术委员会石化塑料树脂产品分技术委员会(TC15/SC1)	中国石油化工股份有限公司北京燕山分公司树脂应用研究所
2	2012-0781T-SH	土工膜用高密度聚乙烯树脂	推荐	制定			2014	原材料工业司	全国塑料标准化技术委员会石化塑料树脂产品分技术委员会(TC15/SC1)	中国石油化工股份有限公司北京化工研究院
3	2012-0811T-JC	壁纸胶粘剂	推荐	修订	JC/T 548—1994	JIS A 6922—2003，MOD	2013	原材料工业司	全国装饰装修标准化技术委员会	上海建科检验有限公司
4	2012-0812T-JC	木塑复合材料耐氯水色牢度试验方法	推荐	制定			2014	原材料工业司	全国装饰装修标准化技术委员会	广州赫尔普复合材料科技有限公司
5	2012-0813T-JC	注塑专用木塑复合粒料	推荐	制定			2014	原材料工业司	全国装饰装修标准化技术委员会	惠东美新木塑型材制品有限公司
6	2012-0815T-HG	工业用孔网钢骨架聚乙烯复合管	推荐	修订	HG/T 3706—2003		2013	原材料工业司	全国非金属化工设备标准化技术委员会	江苏法尔胜新型管业公司，四川东泰新材料科技有限公司，东泰(成都)工业有限公司
7	2012-0816T-HG	整体浇铸乙烯基树脂混凝土电解槽	推荐	制定			2013	原材料工业司	全国非金属化工设备标准化技术委员会	天华化工机械及自动化研究设计院、金川集团有限公司、中国恩菲工程技术有限公司、中国瑞林工程技术有限公司、北京矿冶研究总院、长沙有色冶金设计研究院有限公司

续表

序号	计划号	项目名称	性质	制/修订	代替标准	采标情况	完成年限	部内主管司局	技术委员会或技术归口单位	主要起草单位
8	2012-0817T-HG	光学功能薄膜颜色的测量方法	推荐	制定			2013	原材料工业司	全国光学功能薄膜材料标准化技术委员会	中国兵器工业集团第五三研究所
9	2012-0893T-HG	橡胶或塑料提升带	推荐	修订	HG/T 2577—2006		2013	原材料工业司	全国带轮与带标准化技术委员会输送带分会	无锡宝通带业股份有限公司、青岛新干线技术咨询有限公司、青岛科技大学等
10	2012-0916T-HG	电线电缆用热塑性弹性体材料	推荐	制定		ASTM D4245—2002, MOD	2014	原材料工业司	全国橡胶与橡胶制品标准化技术委员会	浙江三博聚合物有限公司、沈阳橡胶研究设计院
11	2012-0931T-HG	橡塑铺地材料 第3部分：阻燃聚氯乙烯地板	推荐	修订	HG/T 3747.3—2006		2014	原材料工业司	全国橡胶与橡胶制品标准化技术委员会橡胶杂品分技术委员会	来安县亨通橡塑制品有限公司、安徽省亨威塑胶制品有限公司
12	2012-1073T-BB	包装容器 钢塑复合桶	推荐	制定			2012	消费品工业司	全国包装标准化技术委员会	国家包装产品质量监督检验中心(广州)、无锡四方友信股份有限公司
13	2012-1075T-BB	包装用镀铝薄膜	推荐	修订	BB/T 0030—2004		2012	消费品工业司	全国包装标准化技术委员会	中国包装联合会
14	2012-1076T-BB	包装用单向拉伸热收缩型聚酯薄膜	推荐	制定			2012	消费品工业司	全国包装标准化技术委员会	富维薄膜(山东)有限公司
15	2012-1077T-BB	聚偏二氯乙烯涂布薄膜	推荐	修订	BB/T 0012—2008		2012	消费品工业司	全国包装标准化技术委员会	海南赛诺实业有限公司
16	2012-1078T-BB	聚乙烯卧式吹塑罐	推荐	制定			2012	消费品工业司	全国包装标准化技术委员会	陕西科龙塑业有限公司
17	2012-1079T-BB	运输包装用拉伸缠绕膜	推荐	修订	BB/T 0024—2004		2012	消费品工业司	全国包装标准化技术委员会	中国包装联合会

续表

序号	计划号	项目名称	性质	制/修订	代替标准	采标情况	完成年限	部内主管司局	技术委员会或技术归口单位	主要起草单位
18	2012-1144T-QB	箱包配件 塑料插扣耐用性能试验方法	推荐	制定			2013	消费品工业司	全国皮革标委会	东莞市恒宇仪器有限公司、中国皮革和制鞋工业研究院
19	2012-1202T-QB	服装用聚氨酯定岛型超细纤维合成革	推荐	制定			2013	消费品工业司	全国塑料制品标准化技术委员会	绍兴东泰聚合材料有限公司、烟台万华超纤股份有限公司、上海华锋超纤材料股份有限公司、浙江梅盛实业股份有限公司
20	2012-1203T-QB	钢板和钢带包装用聚乙烯低发泡片材	推荐	制定			2013	消费品工业司	全国塑料制品标准化技术委员会	武汉太行冶金材料有限公司
21	2012-1204T-QB	工业用均聚聚丙烯(β-PPH)管道系统 第1部分：管材	推荐	制定		DIN 8077，NEQ；DIN 8078，NEQ	2013	消费品工业司	全国塑料制品标准化技术委员会	江苏兴隆防腐设备有限公司
22	2012-1205T-QB	工业用均聚聚丙烯(β-PPH)管道系统 第2部分：管件	推荐	制定		DIN 16962，NEQ；DIN 8078，NEQ	2013	消费品工业司	全国塑料制品标准化技术委员会	江苏兴隆防腐设备有限公司
23	2012-1206T-QB	海洋油围栏用聚氯乙烯涂层膜材	推荐	制定			2013	消费品工业司	全国塑料制品标准化技术委员会	广东亿龙新材料科技有限公司
24	2012-1207T-QB	聚苯乙烯(PS)片材混配专用色母粒	推荐	制定			2013	消费品工业司	全国塑料制品标准化技术委员会	浙江七色鹿色母粒有限公司、北京化工大学
25	2012-1208T-QB	聚全氟乙丙烯管材	推荐	制定		ASTM D3296-03，NEQ	2013	消费品工业司	全国塑料制品标准化技术委员会	上海市塑料研究所
26	2012-1209T-QB	聚四氟乙烯薄膜	推荐	修订	QB/T 3627—1999	ASTM D3308—2006，NEQ	2013	消费品工业司	全国塑料制品标准化技术委员会	北京市塑料研究所

续表

序号	计划号	项目名称	性质	制/修订	代替标准	采标情况	完成年限	部内主管司局	技术委员会或技术归口单位	主要起草单位
27	2012－1210T－QB	聚四氟乙烯管材	推荐	修订	QB/T 3624—1999	ASTM D3295—2006(2011)，NEQ	2013	消费品工业司	全国塑料制品标准化技术委员会	上海市塑料研究所
28	2012－1211T－QB	聚四氟乙烯双向拉伸薄膜	推荐	制定			2013	消费品工业司	全国塑料制品标准化技术委员会	上海市凌桥环保设备厂有限公司
29	2012－1212T－QB	冷热水用聚丙烯（PP－R）管材专用色母粒	推荐	制定			2013	消费品工业司	全国塑料制品标准化技术委员会	浙江七色鹿色母粒有限公司、北京化工大学
30	2012－1213T－QB	摩托车鞍座用聚氨酯合成革	推荐	制定			2013	消费品工业司	全国塑料制品标准化技术委员会	昆山协孚人造皮有限公司
31	2012－1214T－QB	人造革合成革用水性聚氨酯表面处理剂	推荐	制定			2013	消费品工业司	全国塑料制品标准化技术委员会	合肥市科天化工有限公司
32	2012－1215T－QB	湿法水性聚氨酯合成革	推荐	制定			2013	消费品工业司	全国塑料制品标准化技术委员会	潮州市金山塑胶有限公司
33	2012－1216T－QB	水性聚氨酯超细纤维合成革	推荐	制定			2013	消费品工业司	全国塑料制品标准化技术委员会	浙江繁盛超纤制品有限公司、上海华锋超纤材料股份有限公司
34	2012－1217T－QB	塑料经编遮阳网	推荐	修订	QB/T 2000—1994		2013	消费品工业司	全国塑料制品标准化技术委员会	嵊州市德利经编网业有限公司
35	2012－1218T－QB	硬质聚氯乙烯（PVC－U）挤出中空板材	推荐	制定			2013	消费品工业司	全国塑料制品标准化技术委员会	安徽国风塑料建材有限公司
36	2012－1219T－QB	再生聚苯乙烯挤出发泡线材	推荐	制定			2013	消费品工业司	全国塑料制品标准化技术委员会	上海英科实业有限公司等

续表

序号	计划号	项目名称	性质	制/修订	代替标准	采标情况	完成年限	部内主管司局	技术委员会或技术归口单位	主要起草单位
37	2012－1220T－QB	再生塑料拼装沼气发生器	推荐	制定			2013	消费品工业司	全国塑料制品标准化技术委员会	保定广顺再生资源开发利用有限公司
38	2012－1441T－QB	电子包装用聚丙烯泡沫塑料	推荐	制定			2012	消费品工业司安徽省经信委员会	全国塑料制品标准化技术委员会	合肥会通中科材料有限公司
第三批										
1	2012－1515T－HG	颜料和体质颜料 塑料加工过程中颜色热稳定性的试验 第1部分：总则	推荐	制定			2013	原材料工业司	全国涂料和颜料标准化技术委员会	百合花集团有限公司、北京化工大学、美利达颜料工业有限公司
2	2012－1516T－HG	颜料和体质颜料 塑料加工过程中颜色热稳定性的试验 第2部分：注塑成型法	推荐	制定			2013	原材料工业司	全国涂料和颜料标准化技术委员会	百合花集团有限公司、江苏双乐化工颜料有限公司、美利达颜料工业有限公司
3	2012－1517T－HG	颜料和体质颜料 塑料加工过程中颜色热稳定性的试验 第3部分：烘箱法	推荐	制定			2013	原材料工业司	全国涂料和颜料标准化技术委员会	百合花集团有限公司、上海捷虹颜料化工集团股份有限公司、江苏双乐化工颜料有限公司
4	2012－1518T－HG	颜料和体质颜料 塑料加工过程中颜色热稳定性的试验 第4部分：两辊机法	推荐	制定			2013	原材料工业司	全国涂料和颜料标准化技术委员会	百合花集团有限公司、上海捷虹颜料化工集团股份有限公司、江苏双乐化工颜料有限公司
5	2012－1519T－HG	颜料和体质颜料 塑料中分散性的评定 第1部分：总则	推荐	制定			2013	原材料工业司	全国涂料和颜料标准化技术委员会	百合花集团有限公司、北京化工大学、江苏双乐化工颜料有限公司

续表

序号	计划号	项目名称	性质	制/修订	代替标准	采标情况	完成年限	部内主管司局	技术委员会或技术归口单位	主要起草单位
6	2012－1520T－HG	颜料和体质颜料塑料中分散性的评定　第2部分：两辊机法测定增塑聚氯乙烯中颜料分散性	推荐	制定			2013	原材料工业司	全国涂料和颜料标准化技术委员会	百合花集团有限公司、江苏双乐化工颜料有限公司、美利达颜料工业有限公司
7	2012－1521T－HG	颜料和体质颜料塑料中分散性的评定　第3部分：两辊机法测定聚乙烯中着色颜料分散性	推荐	制定			2013	原材料工业司	全国涂料和颜料标准化技术委员会	百合花集团有限公司、江苏双乐化工颜料有限公司、美利达颜料工业有限公司
8	2012－1522T－HG	颜料和体质颜料塑料中分散性的评定　第4部分：两辊机法测定聚乙烯中白色颜料分散性	推荐	制定			2013	原材料工业司	全国涂料和颜料标准化技术委员会	百合花集团有限公司、龙口联合化学有限公司、江苏双乐化工颜料有限公司
9	2012－1523T－HG	颜料和体质颜料塑料中分散性的评定　第5部分：加热熔融挤出机法测定着色剂分散性	推荐	制定			2013	原材料工业司	全国涂料和颜料标准化技术委员会	百合花集团有限公司、龙口联合化学有限公司、江苏双乐化工颜料有限公司
10	2012－1524T－HG	颜料和体质颜料增塑聚氯乙烯中着色剂的试验　第1部分：基础混合料的组成和制备	推荐	制定			2013	原材料工业司	全国涂料和颜料标准化技术委员会	上海捷虹颜料化工集团股份有限公司、北京化工大学、百合花集团有限公司
11	2012－1525T－HG	颜料和体质颜料增塑聚氯乙烯中着色剂的试验　第2部分：试验样品的制备	推荐	制定			2013	原材料工业司	全国涂料和颜料标准化技术委员会	上海捷虹颜料化工集团股份有限公司、百合花集团有限公司、江苏双乐化工颜料有限公司

续表

序号	计划号	项目名称	性质	制/修订	代替标准	采标情况	完成年限	部内主管司局	技术委员会或技术归口单位	主要起草单位
12	2012－1526T－HG	颜料和体质颜料 增塑聚氯乙烯中着色剂的试验 第3部分：白色颜料相对消色力的测定	推荐	制定			2013	原材料工业司	全国涂料和颜料标准化技术委员会	上海捷虹颜料化工集团股份有限公司、百合花集团有限公司、江苏双乐化工颜料有限公司
13	2012－1527T－HG	颜料和体质颜料 增塑聚氯乙烯中着色剂的试验 第4部分：迁移性的测定	推荐	制定			2013	原材料工业司	全国涂料和颜料标准化技术委员会	上海捷虹颜料化工集团股份有限公司、龙口联合化学有限公司、百合花集团有限公司
14	2012－1613T－JB	塑料电缆桥架	推荐	制定			2014	装备工业司	全国电器附件标准化技术委员会	中国电器科学研究院有限公司
15	2012－1656T－JB	塑料焊缝无损检测方法 通用要求	推荐	制定			2014	装备工业司	全国焊接标准化技术委员会	温州赵氟隆有限公司
16	2012－1657T－JB	塑料焊缝无损检测方法 目视检测	推荐	制定			2014	装备工业司	全国焊接标准化技术委员会	温州赵氟隆有限公司
17	2012－1658T－JB	塑料焊缝无损检测方法 射线检测	推荐	制定			2014	装备工业司	全国焊接标准化技术委员会	温州赵氟隆有限公司
18	2012－1659T－JB	塑料焊缝无损检测方法 超声检测	推荐	制定			2014	装备工业司	全国焊接标准化技术委员会	温州赵氟隆有限公司
19	2012－2139T－QC	汽车用真空吸塑仪表板表皮技术条件	推荐	修订	QC/T 29089—1992		2013	装备工业司	全国汽车标准化技术委员会非金属制品分委会	长春富维－江森自控汽车饰件系统有限公司
20	2012－2154T－QB	木塑衣架	推荐	制定			2013	消费品工业司	全国日用杂品标准化中心	北京市轻工产品质量监督检验一站、桂林毛嘉工艺品有限公司

（中国塑料加工工业协会　田岩　倪国庆　钟雁）

重点企业介绍

广东正茂精机有限公司

广东正茂精机有限公司(原东莞市步明精机有限公司)是生产全液压精密注塑机的专业厂家，公司创办人黄步明先生是享受国务院特殊津贴专家，中国塑机行业协会资深专家，教授级高工。是我国第一项注塑机发明专利的发明者，也是我国第一个获得美、欧、日等国家注塑机发明专利的发明者。

其专利产品——BM系列内循环二板直压式注塑机属自主创新、世界首创。BM系列内循环二板直压式注塑机是在总结20余年设计制造全液压注塑机的经验和吸收国外先进技术的基础上研制而成。它既有全液压式注塑机和肘杆式(机铰式)注塑机的优点，又没有两者明显缺点，在结构设计及产品质量上迅速缩短了我国注塑机设计制造技术与世界先进水平之间的差距，整机性能达到或超过国际先进水平。它的面世，填补了我国研发生产内循环二板直压式注塑机的空白，开创了中国研发生产高档、精密二板直压式注塑机的新时代。

BM系列二板直压式注塑机在锁模结构及其整机技术上有重大突破，为市场提供一种能替代进口高端精密注塑机，可用于医用塑料产品、PET瓶胚、粉末冶金、微型、精密电子产品及光学产品等的生产。它节能、减耗；高速、高效、精密；洁净、环保、安全、便捷、寿命长。主要体现在(见图1)开合模最大速度≥800mm/s，比传统直压式注塑机提高30%，比国内肘杆式注塑机提高20%；制品重量重复精度≤0.15%，比国内肘杆式注塑提高4~5倍；能耗比传统全液压注塑机配置普通电机配定量泵减少75%；与国内肘杆式注塑机相比，整机长度短20%，整机的使用寿命提高2倍以上。综上所述，还可以为塑料制品加工企业节省塑料原料消耗，减少废气和废油的排放，保护环境，提高塑料制品的品质，延长模具寿命二倍以上，节省使用空间，使塑料制品企业升级换代。

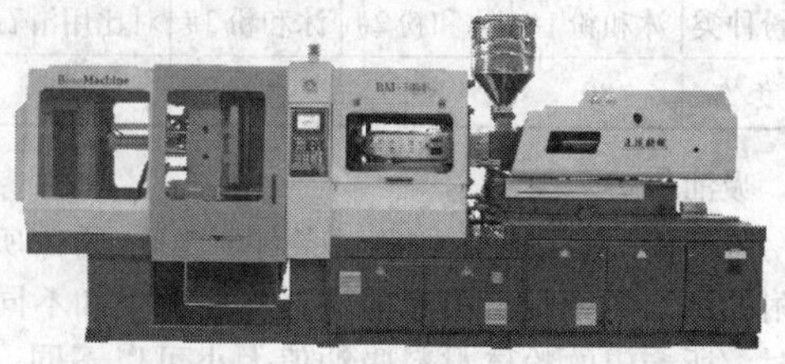

产品主要特点：

省电　节约用电40%~80%。

省料　运行稳定、产品重量重复误差小于0.15%，节省料耗1%~4%。

省时　升压时间短，移模速度高达800mm/s，开、合模时间短，比普通机省时10%~35%。

省油　锁模内润滑设计，节省润滑油100%，洁净环保，符合GMP认证标准。

省工　节省润滑工序与人工。

省调模　不需要调模。

省机器　机器损耗极小，机器寿命提高1倍以上。

省模具　模具受力均匀、低压护模灵敏可靠，模具寿命提高1~2倍。

省空间　机身短20%，占地面积少20%。

广东正茂精机有限公司

地址：广东省东莞市横沥镇山厦工业区

电话：(0086)769-38921039，89182111

传真：(0086)769-38921061，38921060

网址：www.bloomachine.com

邮箱：bmsales@bloomachine.com

沐和矿业有限公司

位于安徽省宿松县的沐和矿业有限公司于2012年建立。公司以安徽省宿松县特有的多种化合物共生矿石为原料，采用国际先进水平的气流磨将其粉碎至1250目以上，年加工能力可达100kt。

经有关专家和用户酝酿探讨，认为该种粉体的矿物组成成分复杂，很难用传统的“滑石”、“方解石”、“白云石”、“石英”等概念界定，但这种粉体又具有单纯的滑石粉或方解石粉所不具备的使用效果，故将此种新型矿物粉体材料命名为硅钙复合粉体，商品名为沐和粉。

沐和粉(硅钙复合粉体)的技术特性：

1. 矿物组成

沐和粉(硅钙复合粉体)由硅、钙等化学元素组成的复合共生矿物加工而成，按照传统的矿物组成观念。国家建筑材料工业地质工程勘查研究院测试中心的检测结果如表1如示。

表1　宿松矿山矿物组成　%

滑石	方解石	白云石	石英	石棉
38.3	39.9	13.7	8.1	0

化学元素分析：

沐和粉(硅钙复合粉体)所含化学元素为硅(Si)、钙(Ca)、镁(Mg)、氧(O)，取自不同矿点的矿石加工而成的粉体其几种元素的含量也不尽相同。采用扫描电子显微镜—能谱仪对宿松三个矿点的化学元素种类及含量进行了定量分析，结果表明三个矿点样本中的氧(O)元素含量基本相同，约为64% ~ 65%，其他 Si、Ca、Mg 三种元素总和为35% ~ 36%，只是三种元素的比例略有变化，而典型的滑石粉样本中只有 Si、、Mg 和 O 三种元素，不含有 Ca 元素。宿松三个矿点样本的 Si、Ca、Mg 三种元素的含量比例如表2所示。(详见宁波益可达新材料有限公司的试验评价报告附件Ⅰ)。

表2　三个矿点样本的化学元素含量比值

矿点	Si: Ca: Mg: O
1#	11: 14: 10: 65
2#	13: 12: 11: 64
3#	11: 6: 19: 64

2. 粉体颗粒几何形态

宁波益可达新材料有限公司对沐和粉(硅钙复合粉体)三种样本用扫描电镜进行了观察拍照，并和传统滑石粉的电镜照片进行了对照。他们认为沐和粉三个样本的颗粒形态基本一致，呈不规颗粒状，其中含有一定比例的片状颗粒，而做为对比样的滑石粉颗粒为具有一定长径比的棒状结构体，片状颗粒数量很少。

北京石油化工学院提供的沐和粉颗粒及辽宁海城滑石粉颗粒的扫描电镜照片也表明，取自不同矿点矿石加工而成的、颗粒粒径1250目或2500目的沐和粉(硅钙复合粉体)都呈现出一定比例的片状结构体，而辽宁海城二氧化硅(SiO_2)含量高达50% ~ 60%的滑石粉(通常以 SiO_2 含量高低做为评判滑石粉档次的依据)反而呈现出“球状或片状”微细颗粒组成的松散聚集体，其片状结构特征远不如沐和粉(硅钙复合粉体)。(详见北京石油化工学院材料科学与工程系的电镜照片及分析评价一文)。

粒度及粒径分布：

沐和矿业有限公司采用具有国际先进水平的气流粉碎研磨设备将天然复合共生的硅、钙、镁、氧等元素组成的矿石加工成粒径微细的粉体，极大限度地保留了对粉体材料增强起至关重要作用的片状结构，而且由于粉碎研磨设备先进，工艺技术得当，所得到粉体粒径最大值得以精确控制，粒径分布窄，对粉体在塑料材料中发挥填充改性作用十分有利。

宁波益可达新材料有限公司对三种沐和粉颗粒粒径大小及分布测试结果如表3所示。

表3　沐和粉(硅钙复合粉体)颗粒的粒径及分布

沐和粉	平均粒径 Dn/μm	表面积平均粒径 Dw/μm	体积平均粒径 Dn/μm	粒径分布指数/μ
1#	7.94	20.05	5.37	3.73
2#	7.33	26.78	5.65	4.37
3#	9.03	10.61	6.42	1.65
对比用滑石粉	6.24	15.01	4.72	3.99

宁波益可达新材料有限公司的试验评价报告指出，沐和粉(硅钙复合粉体)三个样本的粒度约为7 ~ 9μm，粒度分布几种样本中除沐和粉3#较窄外，其它两种和对比用滑石粉相似。(具体情况可见宁波益可达新材料有限公司的试验评价报告附件Ⅱ)

密度：

宁波益可达新材料有限公司对沐和粉(硅钙复合粉体)及对比用滑石粉的真实密度和堆积密度进行了测试，其结果见表4。

表4　沐和粉(硅钙复合粉体)和对比用滑石粉的密度

矿粉种类	沐和粉1#	沐和粉2#	沐和粉3#	对比用滑石粉
堆积密度/(g/cm^3)	0.6060	0.6396	0.6526	0.5883
真实密度/(g/cm^3)	2.7798	2.5728	2.2205	2.6353

从表4数据看出沐和粉(硅钙复合粉体)与该公司在线使用的滑石粉相比，堆积密度稍大一些，而真实密度除3#粉稍低外，另外两种(1#和2#)粉基本上与对比用滑石粉相同。

白度：

宁波益可达新材料有限公司对沐和粉(硅钙复合粉体)的白度进行了测试，结果表明所有沐和粉(硅钙复合粉体)的白度都高于对比用滑石粉的白度(见表5)。

表5　沐和粉(硅钙复合粉体)和对比用滑石粉的白度

矿粉种类	沐和粉1#	沐和粉2#	沐和粉3#	对比用滑石粉
白度/%	89	89	87	81

吸油值：

吸油值是指在规定的测试条件下100g粉体所能吸附的试剂的数量。填充的塑料不同种类和不同用途时，所希望的粉体材料吸油值大小可以不同。对制作聚烯烃塑料改性填充母料或改性专用料而言，粉体的吸油值宜低不宜高。宁波益可达新材料有限公司对沐和粉(硅钙复合粉体)及对比用滑石粉的吸油值进行了测定，结果如表6所示。

表6　沐和粉(硅钙复合粉体)和对比用滑石粉的吸油值

矿粉种类	沐和粉 1#	沐和粉 2#	沐和粉 3#	对比用滑石粉
吸油值/(mL/100g)	19	20	20	19

从表6数据可知，沐和粉(硅钙复合粉体)与在线使用的滑石粉具有同档次吸油值。

沐和粉(硅钙复合粉体)的重要意义：

改革开放以来，我国塑料加工业获得持续快速发展，已成为全世界范围内的生产大国和消费大国，正在朝着世界强国大步迈进。

我国非金属矿资源丰富。在塑料中科学地、适量添加非金属矿物粉体材料具有极其重要的意义，既可以降低原材料成本，又可少用以石油为原料制造的高分子树脂，还能改善塑料材料及制品某些方面的性能或增加高分子材料本不具有的功能，在当今倡导科学发展观、实现可持续发展的时代，建设资源、能源节约型和环境友好型社会，非金属矿物粉体材料在塑料中应用具有广阔的市场前景和显著的经济社会效益。

滑石粉是塑料改性用的重要非金属矿粉体材料，目前塑料加工行业每年使用12000kt非金属矿粉体材料，滑石粉约占总量25%即达到3000kt左右。

我国是滑石及滑石粉的重要生产大国，消费大国，同时也是世界上重要的出口大国。由于我国滑石开采历史悠久，加之多年来的过渡开采，多地传统滑石产地面临资源枯竭的局面，尤其是高档滑石日渐稀少。目前市场上流通的滑石粉已和几十年前的同类产品在成分上大不相同，而且价格一路飚升，高档滑石粉售价已从近千元/吨涨到数千元/吨。

滑石的化学名称为水合偏硅酸镁，分子式为$Mg_3Si_4O_{10}(OH)_2$。纯滑石中SiO_2占63.47%，MgO占31.68%，H_2O占4.75%。商品流通过程中往往将SiO_2含量当成水合偏硅酸镁即滑石含量的标志，“SiO_2含量越高，则滑石的档次越高”成为业内共识。

众所周知，滑石粉在塑料中起到增加材料刚性的作用取决于它的层状基本结构单元，即两层由硅(Si)原子和氧原子构成的四面体夹着一层由镁(Mg)原子、氧原子(O)和羟基构成的八面体。实际上颗粒的这种片状形态越明显，所占的比例越高，其粉体在塑料基体中分散又好的话，对填充体系的刚性(弯曲强度和弯曲模量)贡献越大。

多样性和复杂性是滑石的显著特点，也就是说世界上找不到两块完全相同的滑石。实际上滑石只是一种很宽阔范围的矿石的总称，不同的矿石在纯度、形态及应用后所表现的作用都不尽相同。自然界中存在滑石都是多种矿物的共生体，只不过按照化学元素的种类和含量区分滑石的纯度而已。

另一种经常使用判断指标是烧失量，认为烧失量低于8%才是高档的滑石，增刚作用显著的其烧失量应当在6.5%以下。由于与滑石共生的矿物种类很多，此种判断方法不能适用于所有情况。

位于安徽省宿松县的矿山出的矿石与传统意义上的滑石矿石有所不同，虽然按照化学元素的种类和含量推断为滑石、方解石、白云石和石英的天然复合共生矿物，因有钙(Ca)元素的存在且占一定比例，这与传统的标准滑石矿有所不同，但能否在塑料中做为增刚性填料应用主要取决于其粉末颗粒是否呈现片状形态。

通过扫描电镜观察和能谱分析，表明沐和粉颗粒中有片状结构形态的粒子存在，沐和矿业有限公司的先进设备和加工技术使得这种片状结构得以完好地保留，为在塑料中应用起到增强增刚作用奠定了坚实基础。我们认为将具有多种元素组成的多种化合物天然复合共生而成的矿物加工制成的粉体称之为硅钙复合粉体，有别于传统意义上的滑石粉和方解石粉，是完全正确的，也是十分必要的。

通过对该新型矿物粉体的加工及应用试验，可以得出如下结论：

采用先进的气流粉碎、研磨、分级设备，可将硅钙、镁等多种元素组成的化合物天然复合共生的矿物制成粒度为1250目或更细小的粉体，同时最大限度地保持住粉体颗粒的片状形态。

硅钙复合粉体在塑料加工行业中可以用于传统滑石粉改性的材料及制品的领域，使用的方法和工艺与滑石粉相同。

硅钙复合粉体在塑料材料制品中的改性效果基本与传统滑石粉的改性效果相当，但较之滑石粉改性塑料材料，硅钙复合粉体改性塑料的断裂伸长率更高。

经SGS(通标标准技术服务公司)检测中心检测，硅钙复合粉体不含石棉，铅、镉、汞、砷等有害元素的含量极低，可在塑料加工过程及使用过程中确保安全无害。

为便于宣传，宿松沐和矿业有限公司制作的硅钙复合粉体商业名称称之为“沐和粉”。

综上所述，“沐和粉”(硅钙复合粉体)是一种全新的非金属矿物粉体材料，在塑料加工行业中具有广泛的用武之地和光明的市场前景，“沐和粉”(硅钙复合粉体)的问世和推广应用将产生显著的经济和社会效益!

地址:安徽省宿松县工业园区宏业路10号
电话:400－181－3399
传真:0556－5665555
网址:www. mhky. com. cn

南京聚隆科技股份有限公司

南京聚隆科技股份有限公司前身南京聚隆化学实业有限责任公司1999年4月创立于南京高新技术产业开发区。2009年9月改制为南京聚隆科技股份有限公司。13年来,聚隆公司以改性塑料的研发、生产和销售作为经营方向,在艰难中崛起,在创新中发展,从名不见经传的小厂发展为拥有2个全资子公司、550名员工、年产值6亿元的科技型企业。近年来,公司先后被评为国家重点高新技术企业、江苏省高新技术企业、江苏省创新型企业、中国改性塑料行业十佳企业,中国化工500强企业,走出一条依靠科技创新推动企业发展之路。

在艰难中起步准确把握战略定位

聚隆公司成立初期,国内改性塑料面临复杂的市场形势和激烈的竞争,其高端市场有杜邦、巴斯夫这样的国际公司,而在中低端市场,则有江浙一带大大小小的塑料厂,产品主要应用领域为家用电器、办公设备、电子电气等,用于对性能要求不太高的外观装饰件等产品上。大企业依靠资金、技术和人才的绝对优势垄断市场,开发和生产优质批量产品;小企业只能接单定做,生产小批量、多品种的产品,但由于研发投入不足,产品上不了档次,质量问题较多。

聚隆公司是小企业中的小企业,没有第一桶金,没有国企改制的优惠政策,由13位自然人集资118万元,租赁了一间厂房和一条双螺杆生产线。但面临的挑战与机遇是同样的。挑战在于:每一个行业、每一个企业都有自己的资质和壁垒。产品要想进入汽车领域,必须接受汽车总厂和汽车零部件厂的联合论证;要想进入铁路系统,必须经过铁科院检验测试和上道审查;要想进入电子电器、电动工具等行业,都须经过反复数十次的检测和试料才能最后确认。机遇在于:聚隆公司的产品一旦为客户所接受,结成较为牢固的产业链利益共同体,双方都会尽力去维护培育,形成长效机制。

聚隆公司确定了以"通用塑料工程化,工程塑料高性能化"为目标的中高端产品路线,将公司定位于以国有改性工程塑料替代进口产品的中高端汽车、交通运输以及电子电器等领域塑料制品的原料供应商,努力推动企业向高端化、规模化、品牌化方向发展。

由此形成聚隆使命:创新塑料世界,成就聚隆伟业,坚持为国家支柱产业、重点工程和广大客户提供个性化的基础材料和全方位的技术服务,推动中国改性塑料行业的发展。

构建以知识产权为核心的企业创新体系

技术创新是知识的运用与创新,要使企业创造持久的竞争优势,必须拥有以知识产权为核心的创新体系。聚隆公司以建立现代企业制度为目标,将企业的信息、情报、技术、研究集中起来,构建有利于企业自主创新的体制和机制,推动企业持续创新。

知识产权管理机制。聚隆公司承担了国家高科技计划(863计划)、国家科技支撑计划、国家火炬计划、国家重大科技成果转化等国家级项目,两次实施江苏省科技成果转化项目,形成一批研发和产业化成果。"几种无机纳米材料的制备及应用研究"和"有机化无机颗粒改性聚合物复合材料制备关键技术"荣获2005年和2009年国家科技进步二等奖。通过知识产权贯标和推进计划,初步建立知识产权运行体系,确立了"战略引领,合理规划,持续创新,开拓未来"的知识产权方针,建立了专利数据库和各项管理制度。专利申请81项,授权59项,其中发明专利17项;拥有省市著名商标3项,省市名牌产品4项。

研发平台创新机制。聚隆公司建立了研究院,归口管理经省有关部门批准依托公司建立的江苏省企业技术中心、江苏省改性塑料工程技术研究中心、江苏省塑木复合材料工程技术研究中心,江苏省企业院士工作站、江苏省博士后科研工作站和江苏省企业研究生工作站,配备专用于新品试验的TS－53型双螺杆挤出试验机和常规测试的全套检测设备40余台,特别是引进了美国辛辛那提－米拉克龙制造的国际上最先进的TC86锥型双螺杆挤出机,研发经费投入销售额的3%～5%,有效地推动了科研成果的问世。

产学研合作机制。聚隆公司长期与南京大学、华东理工大学、南京理工大学、南京林业大学、南汽研究所、扬子石化研究院、中科院化学所等20等高校和科研院所紧密合作。与有关单位合作成立了"中国聚酰胺产业技术创新战略联盟"、"江苏省纤维增强热塑性塑料产业联盟",把从原材料到制品各环节相关单位组织起来,实现高端产业链集聚,加快产业化过程。

信息化管理平台。聚隆公司建立并运营的“中国工程塑料网”和“中国塑木网”，成为行业协会的指定网站；与中国塑料加工协会合作经营《国外塑料》和《中国塑木》杂志，紧密联系行业动态，做好外部信息搜集和整合；以现代信息技术为载体建立了内部局域网和OA系统，拓宽和优化了信息资源空间和管理平台，使技术创新管理工作更加科学化、规范化、精细化。

以质量为核心的科学管理机制。聚隆公司在创建初期困难情况下，就建立了QAQC现场质量管理和标准化工作流程，对原料采购、产品生产和售后服务实行全程质量监控。2002年通过了ISO9001认证，2004年在国内率先通过ISO/TS16949汽车管理体系国际认证，还通过了UL94、ROHS、FDA、EN71、VALEO1000等认证。聚隆公司主导和参与编制5项国家标准，已公布实施2项；企业标准经江苏省标准化研究院评估，已达到国际先进水平。公司质量信用评价体系通过了江苏省企业质量信用评价审定委员会的A级评审。

整合市场资源铸造民族自主品牌

技术创新的根本是产品创新，要求企业不断拿出能占领市场、有竞争力的产品。聚隆公司新品开发的重点是研究专有的技术配方、独特的工艺路线、准确高效的配色及个性化的技术服务。不仅使产品以最佳性能价格比立足市场，而且成为企业做强做大的核心竞争要素。13年来，公司不断探索，勇于实践，整合市场资源铸造民族自主品牌，从最初的尼龙产品扩展到PP、PBT、PC、PPO等多种产品，形成了高性能改性尼龙、高性能工程化聚丙烯和塑木环境工程材料三大产品系列群，广泛应用于汽车、铁路、电子电器、仪器仪表、机械、体育休闲等领域，创造了“以塑代钢”、“以塑代木”、“塑木结合”的奇迹。

一批民族自主品牌应运而生，脱颖而出。“增强增韧高性能尼龙”和“环保型塑木复合材料”被认定为国家重点新产品，“增强增韧高性能聚丙烯”被认定为江苏省高新技术产品和江苏省重点新产品，“汽车用改性聚丙烯复合材料”和“环保型塑木建材”被认定为江苏省自主创新产品。聚隆公司自主开发的高性能尼龙和汽车用改性聚丙烯已应用于神龙富康、马自达、标致、福特、通用、日产等中高档车型的保险杠、仪表板、车门内板、后护板、空调器壳体、风扇等部件上。全球最大的汽车空调器零配件供应商法国VALEO集团将公司评定为A级供应商，产品通过VALEO使用在全球各大车型上。广大客户反映，聚隆公司部分产品的品质已经完全达到甚至超过国际著名企业产品的品质。

在我国自主设计的第一条准高速铁路秦沈铁路建设之际，聚隆公司接到了国家铁路交通体系全线提速工程塑料配件的攻关任务，要求产品能够长时间承受各种恶劣环境的考验，在反复震动下不脆裂、重压下不变形。经过无数次实验和理论分析研究，聚隆公司终于掌握了产品的核心技术和关键技术。产品应用于秦沈铁路路轨专用尼龙套筒上，填补了国内空白，经受了提速到200km/h的考验。在国家拉动内需投资计划中，铁路建设被列为重中之重。聚隆公司通过技术创新和技术集成，提升了铁路专用尼龙材料的综合力学性能，产品不仅具备长期热稳定、优良的机械性能和电性能以及良好的流动性和表观，还具有抗冲击、高刚性等特性，通过全国范围内300万次火车抗疲劳试验，达到国家高速铁路的技术要求和建设标准。产品应用于武广、京沪、福厦、哈大、成绵乐高速铁路的轨距块、挡板座、套管等绝缘扣件上，并经受了486.1km/h的考验。

从2002年开始，聚隆公司就组织研发塑木复合材料。塑木复合材料利用地膜、电线皮、包装袋等废旧塑料和稻壳、秸秆、锯木等农林废弃物为主要原料制成，耐水性和耐老化等性能优于优质木材，使用报废后仍可回收利用，为废旧塑料和农林废弃物的再生利用开辟了一条新路。近年来，相继承担了国家科技支撑计划、资源节约和环境保护、江苏省科技成果转化专项资金等项目，在江苏率先建成了年产20kt环保型塑木复合材料及制品的科研生产基地，研制出高强度、阻燃型、耐磨型、低密度及高流动性等5种具有特定性能的专用塑木建材。产品60%出口到欧洲、美国、加拿大和中国台湾等国家和地区。受金融危机影响，外贸业务一度停止。公司积极转变发展方式，把扩大内需放在更加突出的位置。受塑木专委会委托，举办了以“绿色低碳，迎接腾飞”为主题的中国第四届国际塑木高峰论坛，不仅推动了对发展我国的塑木产业产生深远的影响，也提高了公司在国内外塑木行业的知名度。公司产品已广泛应用于北京故宫修复重建工程、上海世博会、广州亚运会、西安大明宫遗址公园、黄山风景区、海口美兰区改造项目等。

在转型升级中建设现代化的科研生产基地

经过13年的艰苦奋斗和持续快速发展，聚隆公司顺利地度过了创业期，进入成长期。在总结历史经验，研究发展战略过程中，公司高层领导审时度势，从长远角度和战略高度形成共识，公司面临的是一个机遇与挑战并存、积极变化和不利影响同时显现的复杂环境，但总体形势回升向好，要趁势而上，积极作为，依靠科技支撑和引领，将传统的生产经营方式转到科学发展的轨道上来。

在转型升级中，聚隆公司开始实现了四个转变：一是从传统的作坊式经营模式向以技术创新为中心的经营模式转变，二是从跟风式产品开发向创建自主知识产权和自主品牌方向转变，三是由服务传统产业向服务高端领域转变，四是由产业经营向产业经营与资本经营相结合的方向转变。经过较长时间的酝酿和谋划，编制了3年发展规划，明确了奋斗目标、主要任务和具体措施。

2011年，聚隆公司在南京高新区征地114亩，建设高起点、高标准的新材料产业园，努力打造环境一流、装备一流、管理一流的科研生产基地。经过一年努力，现已建成年产24kt高性能改性尼龙、年产28kt高性能工程化聚丙烯、年产15kt塑木环境工程材料的生产线和科技综合楼。

聚隆公司站在新的起点上开始腾飞。

地址：南京高新开发区创业路6号

邮编：210061

瑞士乔治费歇尔管路系统

乔治费歇尔（Georg Fischer，简称GF）创立于1802年，总部设在瑞士，并在瑞士证券交易所（SWX SwissExchange）上市。GF作为一家全球运营的工业集团，在全球拥有135个分支机构、25个研发中心。GF集团专注于三大核心业务：GF汽车产品、GF管路系统和GF阿奇夏米尔精密机床。

GF旗下的管路系统集团是世界领先的高品质塑料管路系统制造商，拥有145年的管路系统产品生产经验和50多年的塑料管路系统产品研发技术，可提供6万种以上的产品因而实现采购一站式服务。GF在业内拥有众多第一：生产第一个铸铁管接头、生产出第一个塑料管件、第一个把PB用于塑料管路工业化生产。

目前GF管路系统在中国拥有2个全资工厂、9个合资工厂。GF管路系统的产品在中国同样被广泛应用，在民用建筑领域，GF与朗诗、当代、万科等地产企业有着良好的合作，许多国家级大型项目、中高端住宅项目和民用节能建筑也都使用了GF的产品，如奥运“鸟巢”、世博轴、国家大剧院、MOMA等。在工业领域，GF的产品被用于制药、化工、水处理、造船、半导体等行业，是Intel、AMD、英利等许多知名企业的首选供应商。

佛山巴顿菲尔辛辛那提塑料设备有限公司

佛山巴顿菲尔辛辛那提塑料设备有限公司（BCC），是巴顿菲尔辛辛那提集团成员之一，联合巴顿菲尔辛辛那提挤出技术奥地利有限公司（BCA），巴顿菲尔辛辛那提挤出技术德国有限公司（BCG），美国玛普兰挤出技术有限公司（BCU），这四家公司共同组成全球最大的管材、型材、薄膜和片材挤出生产设备供应商：巴顿菲尔辛辛那提挤出技术集团。

“巴顿菲尔-辛辛那提”品牌荟萃了其来自欧洲的最先进技术、最专业知识，和来自挤出行业超过50年的经验积累。“巴顿菲尔-辛辛那提”品牌在全球得到用户广泛认同，并因此成为业界公认杰出的挤出机械供应商之一。

佛山巴顿菲尔辛辛那提塑料设备有限公司生产基地位于广东顺德，占地面积17800m^2，雇员约180人。我们传承欧洲的先进技术和生产理念，在中国制造和组装高性价比的挤出设备并提供优质的服务，为国内外客户提供领先的挤出解决方案并带给他们决定性的竞争优势和技术优势。

佛山巴顿菲尔辛辛那提的主营业务包括：塑料管材挤出生产线，如用于生产燃气管道、饮用水管、排污管、电讯、卫浴以及灌溉用管道；塑料型材挤出生产线，用于生产窗型材、建筑型材、技术型材如密封条、装饰条、线槽等；PVC造粒生产线；模具和下游设备。

地址：广东省佛山市顺德大良凤翔工业区金翔路2号

邮编：528300

电话：+86(757)22380110

传真：+86(757)29975631

电邮：China@battenfeld-cincinnati.com

网址：www.battenfeld-cincinnati.com/China

川路塑胶集团

成都川路塑胶集团创建于1986年，是一家专业生产新型化学建材的中外合资企业，总部位于中国·成都国家经济技术开发区，是目前国内同行业中成立早、规模大、品种齐、质量优、开发能力强，品牌价值和企业固定资产近十亿元的名牌企业。

川路塑胶集团是四川省高新技术企业和政府培

育型大企业，是中国塑料加工工业协会理事及管道分会副理事长单位和全国塑料制品标准化技术委员会委员兼SC3副主任委员单位。拥有国家授权的博士后科研工作站及数项国家产品专利，是四川大学高分子材料实验基地。荣获了中国驰名商标、中国环境标志产品荣誉称号，通过了ISO9001质量管理体系认证、ISO14001环境管理体系认证、GB/T 28001—2001职业健康管理体系等认证，被评为中国市场用户满意第一品牌及中国管材管件业最具影响力品牌称号。

川路塑胶集团在全国拥有分公司、总经销、特约经销800余家，组成了较完善的营销与服务网络，并与万科、保利、招商、恒大等著名地产公司形成战略合作。“川路管材”、“川路型材”等系列产品广泛应用于国内(外)城市化建设的建筑给(排)水、建筑门窗、电器穿线、电网改造、市政建设、农网改造、石油化工、新农村建设等众多领域。主要工程包括：毛主席纪念堂改造、小平故里、钓鱼台国宾馆、多国驻我国大使馆、布达拉宫改造、四位机库、二滩水电站、北京2008奥运主体育馆、上海世博园、三亚博鳌论坛会址、重庆朝天门广场、成都地铁、5·12灾后重建工程、喀麦隆议会大厦、赛班国际五星级酒店、巴哈马国家体育馆、非洲农场喷灌给水工程等。

川路人以责任为己任，20多年来始终坚持一个产品品牌(“川路”唯一品牌)，一个产品质量等级(国家标准等级)服务于市场，高品质的产品与服务获得了众多使用者的认可，川路品牌赢得了广泛的美誉度与忠诚度。

张家港市贝尔机械有限公司

张家港市贝尔机械有限公司是一家具自主进出口经营权的省级高新技术企业、省著名商标、省级塑机产品出口基地企业，成立于1998年，集研发、生产与销售塑料机械的科技型企业，坐落于交通便利的江苏省张家港市省级经济技术开发区，是第一家落户市民营科技园的企业。公司目前占地面积108亩，现代化科研楼及标准化车间60000m^2，现有员工300余人，大中专以上人员占职工总人数的50%以上。近年来，公司以创新为主导，紧随世界塑机创新的时代潮流，不断自主创新。公司产品以挤出类为主，尤其是高效高速类挤出生产线赶超国际先进技术水平，在国内外很多知名企业的生产过程中被广泛认可及高度评价，产品大部分出口远销亚、非、欧等地区。公司在市内同行业自2006年起，据海关部门及商务局统计，连续七年产品出口销售第一名。2012年公司实现销售1.9亿元，利税2802万元，出口销售1600万美金。

公司建有江苏省级废塑料工程技术研究中心，通过近几年的努力，已申请国家专利50项，其中发明专利20项，实用新型专利30项，授权专利26项，2003年至今先后获省高新技术产品7只，2006、2009、2012三次被被省科技厅认定为江苏省高新技术企业，今年公司还与南京航空航天大学与江苏科技大学共建企业博士后工作站，项目进展迅速，使企业走上了快速、高效、发展道路。

公司在企业内部推行6S现代化、科学化管理，尤其注重人才的引进和培养。公司现有大专以上科技人员100余名，涵盖了塑料加工与成型、机械制造、电气自动化等相关专业，每年投入销售净利润的5%作为培训基金对技术、生产、营销等岗位的工作人员进行科学化培训。公司始终坚持创新为主导，贯切实行“质为本、诚为信、创双赢”的发展方针，注重科技创新，与国内高校(北京化工大学、南京航空航天大学等)、国内外权威机构研究所等保持长期的科研合作关系，每年投入不低于销售额的6%作为科研经费，用于新产品的开发和老产品的技术升级，至今已形成公司成熟的产品系列，具备提供一体化成套设备和承接“交钥匙”工程的能力。

网址：www. beierpm. com
电话：0512－58682198
传真：0512－58682126

富强鑫集团

富强鑫集团成立于1974年，为目前中国台湾地区规模最大的塑料射出成型机专业制造厂商之一，并且是中国台湾注塑机专业厂商中唯一股票上柜之公司。富强鑫拥有30年以上的研发与生产经验，主要从事各类油压机器及注塑机之研发、生产及销售，包括：双色双料注塑机、夹层混色注塑机、高速闭回路精密注塑机、油电复合式注塑机、全电式注塑机、PET瓶胚注塑机、电木注塑机、二板式注塑机、超大型注塑机等。

富强鑫(宁波)机器制造有限公司系由中国台湾富强鑫精密工业股份有限公司于2001年12月与中策动力机电集团公司合资成立，主要从事精密注塑机之生产。目前投资总额为690万美元。宁波富强鑫新厂位于宁波市江北投资创业中心B区，占地约$34000m^2$(50亩)，于2004年8月兴建完工并陆续启用。目前员工约200人，规划年生产量可达1000台。

四川广汉锐星塑胶有限公司

四川广汉锐星塑胶有限公司是由原四川省广汉塑料厂改制成立的民营企业，是中国塑料加工协会注塑专委会理事单位，与四川大学、西南科技大学、西南石油大学建立了《产学研实习基地》。

公司位于古蜀文化三星堆遗址发源地——广汉市，距成都市30km，交通运输条件十分便捷。从德国、日本引进的中空容器吹塑生产线，大型注塑机等先进设备，为提供质量优良稳定的产品奠定了装备技术基础，与相关大学建立的合作关系和具有丰富专业实践经验的职工队伍铸就了高水准的人才技术基础，在行业中具有较强综合竞争能力。

公司按照ISO9001：2000《质量管理体系要求》建立的质量保证体系，取得了《食品质量安全生产许可证》、《危险化学品包装物容器生产许可证》、《出口商品包装质量许可证》，保证了公司产品质量和服务质量的高标准，“鱼跃牌”商标连续多年为德阳市知名商标，2012年获得四川省著名商标。

公司产品主要系列有：中空吹塑容器(容积2～200L)、周转箱及日用制品及家电塑料配件等，广泛应用和服务于国民经济各领域。

地址：四川省广汉市玉溪路一段69号
电话：0838－5103587　5103597
传真：0838－5102222
网址：http：//www. ghrxsj. com
邮箱：rx5102222@163. com
邮编：618300

青州市金诺尔塑胶有限公司

青州市金诺尔塑胶有限公司位于山东半岛中部，东邻风筝都潍坊，西接工业重镇淄博，南依水果之乡临沂，北傍石化基地东营。青州古九州之一，交通便利，人杰地灵。青州市有着五千年的悠久历史和灿烂文化，是古代“东夷文化”的发祥地。自西汉以来为历史名域重镇，公司坐落于青州市经济开发区下万工业园。

青州市金诺尔塑胶有限公司成立于2003年8月，法人代表赵庆太，注册资金228万元，占地面积$15600m^2$，办公楼面积$1200m^2$，车间$5600m^2$，现有职工50人，其中技术人员10名，占职工总人数的20%。

公司现有三层共挤CPP流延线3条，设备采用全程微机控制，自动化程度高，居国内领先水平，年设计能力10000吨，生产厚度为20－100um，宽250－3600mm的流延膜，年产值过亿元。产品广泛应用于食品、医药包装、制袋及镀铝行业，产品畅销全国各地。

公司自2003年投产以来，以优越的环境、先进的设备、过硬的技术生产一流的产品，得到了客户的认可和赞同。公司本着质量第一，信誉至上的原则，与新老客户携手共进，共创辉煌。

地址：青州经济开发区下万工业园内
电话：0536－3292993
传真：0536－3298192
网址：www. jnesj. com
邮编：262500

南京金陵化工厂有限责任公司

南京金陵化工厂有限责任公司创建于1958年，是国内最大的塑料稳定剂生产厂家之一，2008年响应南京市市政府绿色环保的号召，公司开始环保搬迁，经过为期二年的建设，一座崭新的集科研、生产、检测、销售及服务于一体的现代化工厂在南京化学工业园落成并正式投入生产运行。

新工厂中，自动化设备的应用及先进的生产工艺能为客户提供稳定的产品质量：生产现场数据化传输和网络管理系统将大大提升生产效率；现代化的产品研发中心和实验室将为技术创新提供坚实的基础；高效的技术团队，我们能为客户提供迅捷、有力的技术服务和技术支持；完善的ERP管理系统，实现了对整个公司内部流程和供应链的精确管理。

公司已有铅盐类、硬脂酸盐类、无尘复合盐等系列化工产品，其中无尘复合盐为主打产品。目前公司已具有6条无尘复合盐生产线，生产能力达30kt/a，产品主要分型材及板材、管材及管件、电线电缆三大系列50多个品种型号，包括高铅、中铅、低铅到无铅的钙锌复合稳定剂，金陵化工复合稳定剂具有优异的热稳定性、良好的加工性能、析出低、卓越的物理性能及耐候性，质量居国内同行业领先水平，在同行业中享有较高的声誉，广泛应用于

PVC产品的加工，如门窗型材、发泡材料、板材、光壁管、波纹管以及电线电缆等，另外，根据客户的不同需求，可提供片状、粉状等不同形态的产品，产品行销全国各地，并远销东南亚、俄罗斯等国际市场。

山东万达化工有限公司

山东万达化工有限公司成立于2001年11月3日，注册资金9000万，是中国万达控股集团的全资子公司，属国家大型一档企业。公司是国家火炬计划重点高新技术企业，以研发和生产石油化工和精细化工为主导方向，是亚洲最大、世界第三MBS生产企业和国内最大的ODA生产企业。

公司位于万达百亿工业园内，拥有资产25亿多元，占地6万多平方米，员工900名，95%以上的员工具有中专（高中）以上学历，其中高、中级技术人员40余名。拥有国家级技术研发中心和国务院批准设立的博士后科研工作站，具备雄厚的科研基础和完全自主研发能力，被中国塑料加工工业协会授予副会长单位。

顺丁橡胶项目自建设以来，以优质的产品质量赢得市场的认可和广大客户的好评，现二期产能扩产至50kt/a，产品网络覆盖国内各省市地区。

丁二烯项目投资9亿元，总建设规模150kt/a，该项目充分利用周边C4资源，大大改变区域内化工产品原材料供应紧张的局面，有效降低公司主打产品MBS、ABS、顺丁橡胶的成本，扩大成本优势，有效抵御市场风险。

对于打造公司的核心竞争力，进一步完善集团公司上下游一体化发展的产业格局有着重要的战略意义。也使企业逐步成长为我国较大规模的顺丁橡胶生产商与丁二烯供应商。

公司ABS项目拥有300kt/aABS颗粒、60kt/a高胶粉生产能力，该项目采用自主研发新技术，攻克了世界上高分子颗粒增大技术，生产过程采用DCS自动控制系统，产品性能更加优越和稳定。

MBS塑料抗冲剂产品，综合性能国际领先，产销量稳居国内首位，并占国内市场份额的70%以上，并远销中国台湾、东南亚等国家和地区。其抗冲性、透明度等关键指标均优于或等同于进口产品，已列入“国家重点火炬计划”。

公司主要生产顺丁橡胶、丁二烯、ABS颗粒、高胶粉、MBS塑料抗冲剂、聚丙烯酰胺、ACR塑料加工助剂、ODA(4，4′－二氨基二苯醚)、破乳剂等几十种系列产品，并提供油田开采过程中的技术服务。

联系电话：0546－2065369
传真：0546－2079999
网址：http：//www.wandahg.com
E－mail：wdhgbgs@163.com
公司地址：山东省东营市永莘路68号
邮编：257506

上海天力实业集团

上海天力实业集团是以始创于1993年的上海天力实业（集团）有限公司以及浙江天兴管业有限公司为核心的企业群，旗下拥有上海天力实业集团卫浴有限公司、上海天力瑞家销售有限公司等企业。

天力集团总部位于上海，在上海、浙江拥有两大生产基地，集团所属企业总注册资本逾一亿元人民币，总占地面积约125亩，已建厂房建筑面积约60000m^2，形成年产15000t的生产能力。上海天力实业（集团）有限公司系上海市建筑材料行业协会副会长单位，天力PP－R产品系上海名牌，天力商标系上海市著名商标。

天力集团领军中国新型建筑给排水管道的研发与制造，旗下产品包括新型塑料管道、铜管道、不锈钢管道等三大国际先进的主流管道系统，涉及PP－R管材管件、PE－RT管材管件、铜管材管件、不锈钢管材管件、PVC－U排水管、线管和管件等产品，共200个产品系列、1800多个产品品种，产品广泛应用于建筑给排水、空调制冷、地板采暖、热交换系统等领域以及建筑、食品、医药、化工、石油等行业，销售往中国、美国、加拿大、澳洲、东南亚、非洲、中东等国家与地区。

天力以科技创新为己任，拥有专业的研发团队及试验室，目前拥有22项专利，2000年天力PP－R产品列入建设部科技成果推广转换项目，2008年获技术改造项目政府补贴。

天力创新提出“管道产品本身只是半成品”的理念，在中国创立研发、制造、销售、管道系统设计、施工、系统测试、售后一条龙服务模式，将完整可靠的系统交付予千家万户。

全国热线：400－920－1898
上海热线：800－620－1666
地址：上海市奉贤区金汇工业园金斗路288号
传真：021－37561122
网址：www.teilei.com

厦门市台亚塑胶有限公司

厦门市台亚塑胶有限公司位于厦门市翔安区巷北工业区，公司成立于2001年，是一家专业研发生产PVC-U给排水管、PP-R热水管、PE给水管、PVC-M抗冲改性给水管、PVC-U中空(单壁)螺旋消音管、PVC-U电工套管、CPVC埋地式高压电力电缆护套管、PE通信电缆用非开挖顶管、MPP电力电缆用非开挖顶管、各式球阀/蝶阀/底阀等系列产品及农业节水灌溉管材管件的生产骨干企业。厂区占地75亩，标准厂房6.5万平方米，员工总人数800多名，管材生产直径可达ϕ1200mm，管件产品备有2000多种规格，年生产能力达5万多吨。企业通过ISO质量管理体系及出口产品质量双认证，拥有30多种实用新型专利产品和40多份外观设计专利，产品销往国内各个省份及出口20多个国家，是国内管材管件行业中较大规模生产制造企业。公司及产品先后荣获厦门市重点民营企业、中国驰名商标、国家高新技术企业、福建省名牌产品、福建省著名商标、福建省企业知名字号等荣誉，被阿里巴巴和中国制造网评为“金牌全球供应商”及福建省甲控设备材料供应商。

公司始终秉承“科学提升效益，创新提高价值，智本赢得市场”的经营宗旨，在借鉴国内外先进的生产技术的基础上，不断科研创新、不断研发和生产优质产品，为客户提供更良好服务。我们将自强自立、与时俱进、开拓创新，为国家的现代农业、水利、电力、交通、通信的开发建设做出自己的贡献。

公司网址： www. taiyacn. com

邮箱： sale@ taiyacn. com

地址： 厦门市翔安区马巷镇巷北工业区

华大化学集团有限公司

华大化学集团有限公司(简称“华大化学)，前身为烟台华大化学工业有限公司，成立于1993年2月8日，曾为中日合资企业、烟台万华合成革集团的子公司，2004年9月30日改制为股份制企业。2013年7月18日，取得企业集团登记证，华大化学集团成立；2013年7月22日，烟台华大化学工业有限公司更名为华大化学集团有限公司。

华大化学主要从事人造革用聚氨酯树脂、鞋底用聚氨酯树脂、水性聚氨酯树脂和聚酯多元醇系列产品的研发、生产和销售，是国内第一家专业从事聚氨酯树脂的企业，开创了中国聚氨酯树脂之先河，所生产产品广泛应用于鞋、箱包、沙发、镜面、服装革制品及涂料、黏合剂、弹性体、黏合层、树脂产品的制作。2008年，华大化学开始着力投入水性聚氨酯树脂和水性聚氨酯在合成革上应用技术的开发，在这短短几年时间，即实现了水性聚氨酯树脂产品的从无到有的重大突破，解决了水性聚氨酯树脂在合成革上应用的诸多难点，开始了将水性聚氨酯树脂及水性合成革产业化、规模化的步伐，开创了水性环保合成革的新纪元。

华大化学根据战略发展需要，稳步实施战略布局，自2004年改制以来，先后在浙江、江苏、山东、福建、辽宁、河南等地建立多家子公司及分支机构，形成自珠三角、长三角、环渤海经济圈向外全面幅射态势，年生产能力达到300kt，并与南美、中东、东南亚、欧洲多地建立贸易往来关系，不断加强“华大化学”品牌在国内国际的影响力，使华大化学这个聚氨酯树脂行业的知名品牌更加深入人心。

华大化学团结一心，励精图治，公司取得了一系列荣誉：改制之初的2005年，华大化学就被烟台市委、市政府授予“烟台市中小信用企业”，成为烟台市直企业唯一一家入选企业；2006年，获山东省“全省轻纺系统烟草工会系统企业文化建设先进单位”；2007年11月被山东省科技厅认定为“山东省高新技术企业”；2008年10月被评为“山东省第七届全省消费者满意单位”；2009年6月被评为“山东省轻工系统第七批企业文化建设示范单位”、“合成革用水性聚氨酯树脂的研究与产业化”列为烟台市科技局重点研究项目；2011年，“水性合成革技术改造项目”列为国家经信委重点技术改造项目、“华大化学”牌被评为“山东省著名商标”、10月被评为“烟台市第八届消费者满意单位”；2012年，获“全国十佳皮化企业称号”。

浙江耐和实业有限公司

耐和实业创建于1994年，至今已有18年的历史。2003年，公司进驻丽水，坐落于省级经济开发区，占地7万平方米，东接远期干道，西临330国道，北距金丽温高速，自然环境优雅，交通十分便捷。公司部门健全，设置合理，技术力量雄厚，管理队伍素质过硬。现有员工350人，技术人员52人，其中高级技术职称5人，中级技术职称20人。

公司拥有两条水性合成革生产线，新生产线采用水性树脂作为制革原材料，原材料本身就是无害化的环保产品，因此在生产过程中没有任何有害气体、液体排放，从源头上实现清洁生产并减少回收“三废”需要的大量成本。同时，用水性树脂加工的合成革，由于皮膜中含有大量亲水基团和微孔结构，具备并拥有透气、透湿性能以及和真皮一样的触感，安全性能更好，是真正意义上的绿色、环保产品，并因此荣获2012年中国人造革合成革行业绿色企业。

公司拥有PU/PVC生产线和两条高档水刺无纺布生产线，专业生产各种PU/半PU革，如服装革、鞋面革、玩具革、箱包革等革产品。产品以其优良的透气性、耐磨性、真皮感等高性能赢得了市场，也为公司赢得了声誉。

公司秉承“脚踏实地，吃苦耐劳”的企业精神，为企业稳定发展，规模不断扩大，提供强有力的精神支柱。公司的发展得到了开发区相关部门、领导的充分肯定，获得“成长型企业”荣誉称号，2006年开始连续被评为开发区“纳税大户”，开发区“明星企业”，合成革商会副会长单位。

地址：丽水市水阁工业园区平谷三路12号
邮编：323000
电话：0578－2690111　2690112
传真：0578－2690102
网址：http：//www. naihe. com
http：//naihe. cn. alibaba. com

广东德塑科技有限公司

广东德塑科技有限公司始创于1989年，是一家专业生产塑料管道及塑料生产设备的大型民营科技企业。公司位于广东省鹤山市，占地面积300多亩，现有员工700多人(其中大、中专以上185人，技术人员95人)，公司拥有80多条先进的挤出生产线和60多台注塑生产设备，并建有配套齐全的综合实验室和模具加工中心，是国内最先采用端面注塑工艺进行配件生产的企业，年生产能力100kt以上。

公司主要生产“德塑”牌PE给水管、PE燃气管、PE通信子管、PE－RT地暖管、HDPE双壁波纹管、HDPE中空壁缠绕管、PP－R冷热水管、PVC－U给/排水管、PVC难燃线槽/线管、PVC－U通信管、PVC－C高压电力电缆管、PVC－U双壁波纹管以及各类开关、插座和配电箱等系列产品。产品广泛应用于市政排污、乡镇供水、农业排灌、民用建筑、燃气输送和电力通信等领域。

公司已通过ISO9001：2008质量管理体系、ISO14001：2004环境管理体系和OHSAS18001：2001职业健康安全管理体系认证；“德塑”商标被认定为“广东省著名商标”；德塑产品通过并获得“新华节水产品认证”、“中国环境标志产品认证”、“中国国家强制性产品认证”、“标准化良好行为证书”、工程建设新技术新产品证书”、“采用国际标准产品标志证书”、“采用国际标准产品认可证书”和“科学技术成果鉴定证书”，并入选《全国农村饮水安全工程材料设备产品信息年报》；公司荣获“重合同守信用”、“全国质量信用企业”、“民营科技企业”和“计量保证体系合格企业”等称号，并拥有多项产品专利；“德塑”产品质量和品牌知名度得到了广大用户的肯定和赞誉。

德塑公司将始终坚持以优质的产品和完善的服务，满足客户需求，善尽社会责任；并通过不断创新实现对产品、服务和管理的持续改善。

广东三凌科技集团有限公司

广东三凌科技集团有限公司总部位于汕头市濠江区南山湾工业园，旗下拥有广东金嘉泰投资有限公司、广东三凌塑料管材有限公司、汕头市三凌市政建设有限公司等三家全资子公司和研发机构——广东省工程技术研究开发中心。广东省金嘉泰投资有限公司是集团公司发展的重要板块，涉足城市建设、工程项目、房地产业、实业、商业贸易、教育、高新科技的项目投资和创业投资等领域。广东三凌塑料管材有限公司是集团公司的产业支柱，是国家高新技术企业、广东省新型塑料管道创新产业化示范基地，被评为“广东省模范劳动关系和谐企业”、“连续十一年广东省守合同重信用企业”、“汕头市十大诚信企业”。公司研发生产的“和塑”品牌PVC、PE、PPR等系列塑料管道产品，广泛应用于国内供水管网、排水管网、通信管网、电力管网和燃气管网等领域，荣获“中国塑管行业十大品牌”、“中国消费者信赖质量放心品牌”、“广东省著名商标”、“广东省名牌产品”、“广东省高新技术产品”等称号。公司拥有数十项发明专利，多项创新研发成果荣获国家级、省级和市级的科技奖，多项自主创新技术列入“国家级星火计划项目”，部分管道产品填补国内空白。

汕头市三凌市政建设有限公司是具有二级市政工程总承包资质的施工企业，成立十余年来致力于市政管网工程的配套安装，承担了粤东地区大部分农村水改工程项目的施工和水厂的建设，参与了汕头南澳岛引韩供水工程项目的建设，合作建设了一定规模的房屋住宅和市政项目工程，是集团公司组成的重要部分。

广东省工程技术研究开发中心是通过专家论证鉴定，经广东省科技厅、发改委和经信委联合批准，以三凌塑料管材公司为依托的省级技术研发机构。它对于提升塑料管道行业的整体技术水平，增强行业竞争力和发展后劲，具有重要的战略意义。研发中心主要是通过对新型塑料管道工程技术的深入研究，创新改性复合材料在塑料管道领域的技术，研究开发各类新产品、新材料，形成具有自主知识产权的核心技术，为同行业提供技术示范、技术咨询和技术服务，促进研发成果产业化。

集团公司现拥有厂房和办公配套楼房 10 万多平方米，生产设备和研发设备几百台套；共有员工 800 多人，拥有各类专业技术和管理人才 200 多人。其中具备中高级技术职称的人才 80 多人，大专以上学历的人员占员工总数 32%。

三斯达(福建)塑胶有限公司

三斯达(福建)塑胶有限公司系中国台湾证券交易所上市公司，前身为三斯达(福建)鞋业有限公司。公司座落在福建著名侨乡有中国鞋都之称的晋江市，于 1982 创建，从成立至今致力于废旧塑料袋、鞋类边角废料等橡塑废料的回收循环再利用，从回收到改性设备的设计、制造总成独创发明了一系列先进的废品回收技术和生产工艺，拥有发明和实用新型专利 20 多项，专业生产应用于鞋材、箱包衬垫、体育用品、拼图、地垫、汽车及家装建材等广泛领域之各式 EVA 发泡材料，年产超 30 万立方，是福建省乃至全国最具规模的 EVA 发泡专业生产厂商之一。

得益于鞋都和福建、广东两地市场的产业集聚优势和产业链供应优势，公司回收利用的鞋用边角废料和 PE 废旧塑料源源不断，公司 2010 ~ 2012 三年的年废塑处理分别达 42000t、45000t 和 50000t，不仅有效得降低了原料成本，提升公司经济效益，同时，也极大得减少了废塑对环境的污染和资源的浪费，提升了社会效益，践行节能减碳的社会责任。公司生产的各式发泡材料，可就近销往福建及广东、江浙地区的鞋厂、箱包公司及体育用品、玩具加工公司，下游市场成熟、稳定。

公司在立足本业的同时，也积极推进资本市场运营步伐。通过合理评估和精心的规划布局，于 2011 年 8 月成功登入中国台湾证交所主板挂牌交易，募集新台币 13 亿多(折人民币约 2.9 亿)，资金全部用于返程投资。经过公司的全面规划和布局，福建公司增购土地 137 亩，投建“三斯达废塑循环回收利用产业化基地”(2012 ~ 2013 年度泉州市重点项目)，现总占地面积达 250 亩，建有标准厂房超 80000m^2，拥有专业的研发团队和先进发泡生产设备 32 组，并随着扩厂不断提升产能，预计到 2013 年底，发泡生产设备可扩充到 42 组，预计年产各式 EVA 发泡材料可达 35 万立方，规模在国内同行中首屈一指。

同时，公司于 2011 年上半年在江苏省句容市经济开发区新成立三斯达(江苏)公司，占地 150 亩，预计总投资达 9000 万美金，拟配备发泡生产设备比齐晋江公司，预计至 2013 年全面投产后，公司产能将在现有基础上再翻一番。江苏公司已经完成土地平整及桩基等基础工作，工程施工陆续开展。

经过三十多年的不懈努力，公司已发展成为全国最具规模的 EVA 发泡研发中心和制造基地，产品畅销国内市场并远销欧美等地。

“创新，源于涅槃重生”，三斯达人清楚，创新是一个企业不断进步、发展的灵魂。公司逐年加大研发投入的同时，积极寻求同相关科研机构、行业协会的进一步合作。2009 年公司当选为中国塑料加工工业协会副会长单位，并被协会命名为“中国 EVA 循环再利用产业化研发基地”，显示了公司对国内塑胶发泡行业建设的高度重视和责任感，也进一步提高了公司在行业内的地位和影响力。同时公司还计划跟国内高校共同成立研发基地，就阻燃、隔热、抗静电等新型 EVA 发泡材料的研发进行紧密合作。

公司建立了优秀卓越的企业文化体系和科学、完善的管理制度，通过了 ISO9001、ISO14000 质量认证体系，多次被评为“AAA 级信用企业”、“甲类纳税企业”。公司的“EVA 回收循环利用项目”先后被评为“2006 年度晋江市第一批科技项目”和“2009 年第一批省级循环经济资金项目”，“2009 年泉州市 6.18 项目成功转化资金补助项目”。2012 年通过福建省高新技术企业认定，同时积极起草行业国家标准的制定。

慈溪市德顺容器有限公司

慈溪市德顺容器有限公司成立于 1999 年，一直注重滚塑行业，专业生产塑料储罐及滚塑制品加工、模具设计制造及设备制造。公司拥有多项发明专利，是滚塑行业里综合实力最强的企业之一，并是中国塑协滚塑专委会主任单位。

公司主导滚塑产品是塑料水箱、保温箱、冷藏箱、包装箱，近几年德顺设备模具远销往美国、俄罗斯、澳大利亚、法国、东南亚、西班牙以及中东大部分国家，内销通及全国各地。

德顺无论在硬件设施、技术水平，还是市场销售、团队精神上均在行业前列。德顺将秉承着“技术一流、品质至上、行业领先、顾客满意”经营理念和“用品德做每一件事”的企业精神与国内外朋友们共同发展，努力争做中国的滚塑事业的领头羊！

福建宝利特集团有限公司

福建宝利特集团有限公司系外商独资企业，地处福州市江阴工业集中区。前身为福建宝利特制革工业有限公司，创办于1994年。宝利特集团注册资本2000万美元，总投资额5000万美元，下属拥有福建宝利特纺织涂层有限公司、福建宝利特新材料科技有限公司、福建宝利特合成材料有限公司、福建利达化工(福建)有限公司。宝利特集团总占地面积442亩，现拥有五条国际先进水平的PU/PVC人造革生产线、一条压延生产线和一条纺织涂层生产线以及整厂配套设备，并拥有十余套生产各种高分子材料的专用设备，专业生产各种中高档PU/PVC人造革系列产品、高档织物涂层面料、油性/水性PU树脂、各种特殊高分子材料、处理剂及环保增塑剂等产品，年产值达15亿元。产品主要物性指标符合GB/T 8948—2008、GB/T 8949—2008国家标准，并达到欧盟EN－71、ROHS、REACH及美国ASTM等各项标准，质量达到国内外同类产品的先进水平。

福建宝利特集团通过ISO9001质量管理体系认证、ISO14001环境管理体系、ISO28001职业健康安全管理体系，连续多年获得各级政府及有关部门授予：“全国外商投资双优企业”、“福建省百家明星侨资企业”、“全国明星侨资企业”、“省级花园式单位”、“纳税信用A级企业”、“福州市产品质量奖”、“福州市级企业技术中心”、“福州市知识产权示范企业”、“福建省技术创新工程创新型试点企业”、“福建名牌产品”、“福建省著名商标”、“福建省高新技术企业”、“福建省装饰革企业工程技术研究中心”等荣誉称号。截至2013年5月，集团总共申请发明专利12项，其中4项获得国家发明专利证书；申请实用新型专利9项，其中7项获得国家实用新型专利证书。

地址：福建省福清市江阴工业集中区圣发路
邮编：350309
电话：0591－85698818
传真：0591－85698828
网站：http：//www. cnpolytech. com
邮箱：info@ cnpolytech. com
baolite@ cnpolytech. com

浙江众成包装材料股份有限公司

浙江众成包装材料股份有限公司成立于2001年，是一家集科研、设计、生产、销售及售后服务于一体的全过程制造企业，是全球知名的高品质POF热收缩膜制造商和国内优秀的POF热收缩膜整体包装解决方案提供商。公司产能规模达22.7kt，在职员工380余人。2012年，公司实现销售收入44852万元，利税15056万元。

公司自成立以来，始终坚持“赢在领先”的企业精神、“诚信拥抱客户，真情温暖员工”的经营理念和“差异化、个性化”市场战略，重视新产品、新工艺、新设备的自主研发，先后承担“国家火炬计划项目”3项，多项产品被认定为省级新产品，获得“浙江省著名商标”、“浙江名牌产品”、“浙江省知名商号”、“浙江出口名牌”、“浙江省转型升级引领示范企业”、“浙江省绿色企业”、“中国轻工业塑料行业十强企业”、“国家高新技术企业”、“国家火炬计划重点高新技术企业”等多项荣誉。

公司产品不断推陈出新，品种齐全，现已远销全球60多个国家和地区，成为国内市场占有率排名第一、全球市场占有率排名第二的POF热收缩膜行业领军企业。

公司总投资5.4亿的募投项目即将陆续竣工，届时产能、效益将大大提高。

无锡市佳盛高新改性材料有限公司

无锡市佳盛高新改性材料有限公司建于2002年初，是江苏省高新技术企业和国家火炬计划锡山新材料产业基地的成员企业。公司位于风景秀丽、富饶发达的无锡市锡山区荡口镇鹅湖工业园，紧靠沪宁高速公路，交通十分便利。

公司专业生产“佳盛”牌新型高分子材料改性剂和Pams树脂系列产品，可作挤压和模塑成型加工助剂、改性剂、黏合剂、黏结剂、增黏剂、增强剂、增塑剂、抗氧剂、分散剂、润滑剂、高效燃料及热载体等用途，具体应用于高浓度、高阻燃、高填充塑料色母粒、塑料改性、橡塑鞋材、电线电缆料、热塑性弹性体、橡胶材料、热熔胶、油漆油墨、涂料、颜料、精密铸造等领域(详细应用说明向公司技术开发部索取资料)。

公司坚持务实、创新、求精的企业精神，奉行“市场是天、安全是地、质量是命、管理是根”的宗旨。公司严把生产环节，加强技术改进，实行制度化、规范化内部质量管理，形成较强的科研开发能力、规模生产能力和经营管理能力，已获ISO9001：2000国际质量体系认证和ISO14001：2004环境管理体系认证。产品参照美国阿莫科AmocoResin18－210、18－240、18－290系列树脂标准进行生产检测，质量性能相同，同时产品符合欧盟SGS的(ROHS、PHAS)检测标准，是用户的最佳选择。产品销往全球，佳盛公司董事长—潘林根愿意同中外各界新老朋友携手合作、共同发展、再创辉煌。

地址：中国江苏省无锡市锡山区荡口镇鹅湖工业园
邮编：214116
电话：0086－510－88520858，88748136
传真：0086－510－88748340，512－65390573
网址：//www. wx－jiasheng. com
电子邮件：webmaster@ wx－jiasheng. com
联系人：潘林根 0086－13906202341，13306202341
李晓勇 0086－13338762870，18962121918

普立万 polyone

普立万是全球领先的特种聚合材料、服务和解决方案供应商。总部位于美国俄亥俄州，是一家在北美、南美、欧洲、非洲和亚洲都有业务运营的跨国公司。普立万在全球拥有近七千名员工，分布于80多个工厂和仓库，十余个创新中心和实验室，及位于五大洲的销售和服务网点。普立万在全球范围内的客户数以万计，服务的应用行业包括包装、建材、医疗、运输、电子电气、家电、线缆、消费品、纺织和其他工业应用，为客户提供35000种以上的聚合物解决方案，包括颜色和添加剂、嘉洛斯，寇兰和GSDI、特种工程塑料、吉力士热塑性弹性体、Glasforms高级复合材料、设计结构与解决方案、特种油墨和聚合物系统、Geon高性能材料、特种涂层、生产商服务并向客户提供聚合物分销服务。通过紧密合作，帮助各行各业的客户开发创新产品和服务，改善产品性能并提升其竞争优势。

地址：上海市浦东新区郭守敬路88号
电话：021－50805768
网站：www. polyone. com
微博：www. weibo. com/polyone
电邮：jennifer. huang@ polyone. com

山东日科化学股份有限公司

山东日科化学股份有限公司股票代码：300214。公司位于山东省昌乐县经济开发区，占地面积32万平方米。是由泰山学者、归国留日博士赵东日先生于2003年创办的集科研、生产、销售和技术服务于一体的现代化高新技术企业，注册资本2.025亿元。下设山东日科新材料有限公司、山东日科橡塑科技有限公司、山东日科塑胶有限公司、山东日科进出口贸易有限公司四个子公司。公司2005年被认定为山东省高新技术企业，2008年重审认定为省第一批高新技术企业；2009年被评为国家火炬计划重点高新技术企业；山东省专利明星企业；山东省创新型试点企业。是第三大国际丙烯酸酯类PVC改性剂制造供应商，全国最大的丙烯酸酯类PVC改性剂生产商，是国内首家将丙烯酸酯类PVC抗冲加工改性剂(ACR)产业化的厂家，是塑料助剂行业首家采用自行开发计算机控制系统进行生产工艺控制的企业；是塑料助剂行业首家上市企业。

公司自成立以来，坚持自主创新和知识产权保护。报国资委批准在民政部注册成立了中国塑料加工工业协会新材料研究开发工作委员会；建立了山东省塑料改性工程技术研究中心和潍坊市工程中心、企业技术中心，并拥有96人的研发队伍。先后承担了国家、省、市科技计划15项，公司承担的国家“十二五”科技支撑计划《节能门窗用，耐候高性能塑料型材的研究开发与应用示范》进展顺利；公司申请了国家发明专利17项、已获授权13项，申请美国发明专利1项、已获得授权；获得省级科技成果4项，获得山东省技术发明奖三等奖2项，行业技术发明奖三等奖1项，市级科学技术进步二等奖1项；是山东省“泰山学者”设岗单位。经过几年的努力工作，创立了塑料加工行业知名的“”合力品牌和“”日科品牌。“”商标被评为山东省著名商标；“”商标和“”商标已经在美国和欧盟进行了注册。到现在，公司的每一个产品都有自己的知识产权；新型高分子材料ACM树脂被评为山东省名牌产品。

华伦皮塑(苏州)有限公司

华伦皮塑(苏州)有限公司成立于2000年9月，公司位于美丽的长江之滨。是一家中外合资企业，总投资1600多万元，主要从事各种PU人造革的研发、生产和销售，目前公司主要产品有：服装革、沙发革、箱包革、球革、鞋革、手套革、汽车革以及其他特种革等。

公司引进国际先进的氨基酸柔软皮生产线，拥有干式生产线四条，湿式生产线五条，高档压纹机十余台、双色印刷机五台及多台意大利ROLLMAC辊涂机、喷光生产线等。公司有强大的后段研发团队，提高商品附加值，可为市场提供花样繁多的人造革产品。2007年以来公司被认定为“江苏省高新技术企业”，2010年再次通过“江苏省高新技术企业”认定。“WARREN”商标被认定为“江苏省著名商标”。2008年以来被评为苏州市“循环经济试点企业”，苏州市节能“先进单位”，太仓市“环保诚信企业”。产品通过了欧盟REACH法标准和ROHS标准和美国、英国的阻燃标准，公司于2006年通过了ISO9001：2008质量管理体系认证，2010年通过了ISO14001：2004环境管理体系认证。公司被太仓市促进就业工作领导小组办公室认定为大学生见习基地。公司具有自主知识产权的“合成革用环保型干法PU浆料”被列入《2008－2009国家重点新产品计划项目》，并获得江苏省“高新技术产品认定证书”，“苏州名牌产品”，“苏州市知名字号”，2009年获“国家发明专利”2项。2009年NBA扣篮大赛冠军使用的篮球是由华伦皮塑公司提供的PU人造革制成。箱包革，鞋革也分别被“耐克”“阿迪达斯”等全球知名品牌制造商广泛使用。“WARREN”被江苏省工商行政管理局认定为知名商标。

华伦皮塑(苏州)有限公司管理严谨，技术力量雄厚，专业技术人员占公司总人数的30%以上，采用先进的工艺配方，年产量2300万米人造皮革，年销售额达五亿元人民币，产品远销欧美、非洲、中东、香港等地区，产品质量受到客户一致评。

公司紧邻苏州、无锡、常熟、南京、上海，所处位置交通便利，地理位置优越，目前常熟至上海高速公路已修通并即将通车，最近处上下高速路口离公司不足一公里。公司秉承“待客诚信”的企业宗旨，保证一流的质量和优质的服务。

公司新开发的优力神系列TPU复合材料与其他合成革制品比较具有强度高、韧性好、耐磨、耐寒、耐老化、防霉、抗紫外线等优异功能。特别是该系列产品可以重复利用，埋入地下可以完全降解，是一种理想的环保产品。在生产过程中，与传统的合成革制品相比，该制品具有明显的节约劳动力、降低能耗、零排放等特点，在制造过程中不产生废气，废水，残渣。优力神系列TPU复合材料是一种全环保节能型新材料，这一系列产品的问世，开拓了环保合成革制品的应用市场，是未来合成革制品的发展方向，我们相信，将来这一系列产品会在应用领域里为全球的环保领域占领一定市场，可以说，绿色环保合成革的梦，华伦实现了！

电话：0512－81612558

邮箱：hl_syj@163.com，gaojingang.warren@gmail.com

手机：13823506393，13606245625

网址：http：//www.warren.cn

山东陆宇塑胶工业有限公司

山东陆宇塑胶工业有限公司坐落于黄河三角洲高效生态经济区——东营市经济技术开发区，是一家集科研、生产、营销和服务为一体的综合性企业。公司致力于各类塑胶管道的研发与生产，注册资本壹亿零捌拾万元人民币，总投资8.6亿元人民币，占地面积300余亩。

公司管理科学、技术领先，产品品质优良、服务信誉卓著，已发展成为国内产销量最大的塑胶管生产企业之一，综合实力位居同行业前列。公司先后通过ISO9001质量管理体系、ISO14001环境管理体系和OHSAS18001职业健康安全管理体系认证，顺利获得新华节水产品认证和中国环境标志产品认证，连续多年被评定为省级守合同重信用企业，是中国塑料加工工业协会、中国水利企业协会、中国工程建设标准化协会会员单位、水利部农村饮水安全重点推广单位。2008年荣获山东名牌，2009年荣膺中国建材500强。

2010年，公司被认定为“国家级高新技术企业”，并经山东省科技厅批准组建“山东省塑料管道系统工程技术研究中心”。“陆宇检测中心”通过中国合格评定国家认可委员会(CNAS)认可，标志着公司的检测资质和检测服务能力列居行业榜首。2011年公司在“市级企业技术中心”的基础上经山东省经信委专家评审，正式升格为“省级企业技术中心”。科研技术创新方面，公司先后获得塑料加工技术专利35项，发明2项。

公司成套引进奥地利辛辛那提等国内外先进生

产线和检测设备，凭借多年来积累的生产和管理经验结合不断的技术创新，所生产的“陆宇”牌系列塑胶产品，屡次通过国家塑料制品质量监督检验中心、中国疾病预防控制中心等权威机构的检测，产品各项性能指标完全符合国家标准，部分指标超越标准要求。目前，公司年产能达150kt以上，主导产品四大类九个系列，分别为：硬质聚氯乙烯类(PVC－U给水、排水、电工、PVC－M给水管材及管件)；聚乙烯类(HDPE给水、燃气、双壁波纹排污管材及管件)；无规共聚聚丙烯类(PP－R冷热水管材及管件)；耐热聚乙烯类(PE－RT地板采暖管材及管件)。公司产品种类繁多，用途广泛，可充分满足各工程领域用户对产品的需求。

陆宇产品销售区域广泛，内销涉及全国26个省市，同时远销海外10多个国家。为使顾客方便快捷的采购陆宇系列产品，公司在各地设置经销商并通力合作，以期共同拓展市场，保证交货和服务时效。产品推广过程中，还建立健全了售前、售中、售后服务体系，解除了顾客的后顾之忧，深获顾客信赖。为及时了解客户的更高需求，公司通过多种渠道和方式进行顾客满意度调查，通过对反馈讯息的分析和评估及时加强产品和服务的适宜性，努力做到准时无缺，让顾客满意。

地址：东营市经济技术开发区北一路103号(第Ⅰ工业园区)/126号(第Ⅱ工业园区)

电话：0546－776777(0～9)

传真：0546－7767700

邮编：257091

网址：www. sdluyu. com. cn

E－mail：168@ sdluyu. com. cn

山东天鹤塑胶股份有限公司

山东天鹤塑胶股份有限公司是国内大型塑料加工企业，占地面积145亩，员工238人，注册资本5587万元。公司集20年生产吹塑膜经验，拥有强大的生产技术力量和产品开发能力，企业技术中心为省级企业技术中心，年加工能力70000t。产品除供应中国市场外，还远销26个国家和地区。

公司已通过国际质量和环境管理体系认证多年、产品先后获得山东名牌和国家质量免检证书；开发的PO膜荣获山东省科学进步二等奖；公司先后被评为中国塑料行业3A级信用企业、中国塑料行业先进单位、中国土工合成材料聚乙烯土工膜生产出口基地、国家高新技术企业、2011年度轻工系统卓越绩效企业、山东省塑料行业50强、2012年被省政府授予山东省行业龙头骨干企业、山东省守合同重信用企业等荣誉；公司现为中国塑料加工工业协会副会长、中国塑料加工工业协会农膜专委会副理事长、山东省农塑工程学会副会长单位。

公司共取得了17项国家专利，其中发明专利3项。

涂覆型流滴消雾膜的设备制造、生产工艺、涂覆剂的配方，为公司的农膜产品核心技术。该产品在2009年获得国家专利，该项科技成果于2012年11月获山东省科技进步二等奖。公司主持制订的《涂覆型持久性聚乙烯流滴棚膜QB/T 4475—2013》标准，将于2013年12月发布执行。

集装箱液袋膜：该技术于2006年根据国外需求开发，主要应用于集装箱的液体类食品和非危险化学品的运输，拓展了集装箱的适用范围，该产品已占国际50%的市场份额；公司主持制订的《集装箱运输液体用聚乙烯袋内衬膜QB/T 4474—2013》标准，将于2013年12月发布执行。该产品2012年已申请国家发明专利。

糙面土工膜的产品和生产方法：该技术获得2项国家发明专利。公司现为中国唯一能生产符合国际标准的糙面土工膜的生产厂家。该产品已经销售澳大利亚、香港、菲律宾、哈萨克斯坦等国家和地区。公司作为第二起草人，2005年参加了《GB/T 17643—2010土工合成材料聚乙烯土工膜》标准制定，并于2010年正式发布。

公司主营三大系列产品，阳光系列高端农膜市场容量大，盈利能力强，是公司的主打产品；土工膜随着国家水利、环保设施的持续投入，市场前景广阔；液体包装膜的开发，将极大的促进集装箱的高效能的运输。

联系方式：山东省博博市临淄区南一路2号

电话：0533－7126666　土工专线：7119206

传真：0533－7118318　7118328

网址：www. tianhesd. com

www. chinatianhe. com. cn

E－mail：tianhe@ tianhesd. com

神塑科技有限公司

神塑科技有限公司，成立于2007年4月16日，公司位于交通便利、风景优美的长沙市金洲新区金洲大道西208号，是一家集塑胶管道系列产品的生产、研发、销售、技术咨询与技术服务于一体的高新技术企业，员工360余人，注册资金1.5亿元。公司先后通过了ISO9001质量管理体系、ISO14001环境管理体系和OHSAS18001职业健康安全管理体系认证，先后获得了“高新技术企业”“湖南省建设科技成果推广项目证书”，“2007～2008、2008～2009年度湖南省‘守合同重信用’单位”，“湖南省质量信用等级A级企业”(由质监部门颁发)，“湖南名牌产品”，“湖南省著名商标”，“质量、信用、品牌信誉AAA级企业(工商部门颁发)”等各类认证和荣誉证书。公司产品包括PE、PVC、PPR管道系列，现有管材生产线76条，管件生产设备80台，年生产能力300kt，年产值20亿元以上。

地址：湖南长沙市金洲新区金洲大道西208号神塑科技园

电话：400－6666－198

传真：0731－88721399

网址：www.shensukeji.com

四川国丰管业有限公司

四川国丰管业有限公司成立于2009年8月，注册资金5500万，座落于成都市大邑县工业发展区，占地面积60000余平方米，毗邻成温邛高速，交通便捷，并在同行业中首家入驻成都市青羊工业总部基地设立市场运营中心。是一家专注于塑料管道研发、制造、销售、安装于一体的高新技术企业。公司目前有员工300人，其中工程技术人员42人，行政管理人员36人，具有规模庞大的生产车间及完善的生产设备。每年向市场提供80kt规格聚乙烯(PE)管道及检查井制品，是西南地区规模最大，规格最全的聚乙烯(PE)管道及检查井的专业生产企业。现拥有国内多条一流的生产设备和检测设备，技术力量居国内领先水平。同时还有一支创新务实的管理团队和完善有效的质保体系。专业生产HDPE双壁波纹管、PVC－U双壁波纹管、PE给水管、PE燃气管及PE煤矿用管等与之配套的管件。产品广泛应用于供水、燃气、通讯光缆套管．高速公路排水，各种市政、工业、矿山、养殖、农业排水、排污、通风等领域。

公司现已通过ISO9001质量管理体系认证。产品通过国家级、省级检测和鉴定，因各项技术指标稳定，价格合理，服务周到，受到了广大客户的一致好评，被市场广泛认可。公司通过战略联盟，分别在上海、广州、天津等地建设生产分厂并组建销售公司，以强化“国丰”品牌的市场渗透率和提高产品市场占有率。

西安高科建材科技有限公司

高科建材是西安大型国由西安大型国有企业西安高科(集团)公司投资组建的现代化新型建材企业，是国家火炬计划重点高新技术企业，中国有机锡环保型材创新示范基地。总资产超10亿元，员工2000多人。

经过十余年发展壮大，高科建材已成长为中国塑料型材行业领先企业、西部管道龙头企业。高科建材品牌影响力位列行业三甲。旗下拥有三个生产基地，两个控股公司。产业横跨型材、管道、门窗、楼宇智能及电子元器件五大门类，形成了产业化、规模化、集约化、现代化、高端化、国际化的新型建材产业集群。

高科建材拥有各类专利技术二十多项，是西安市技术中心和陕西省技术中心。先后通过了ISO9001、ISO14001、ISO18001国际质量、环境和安全体系认证，先后获得西安市名牌、陕西省名牌、陕西省著名商标和中国驰名商标，在全国建有100多个销售部、500多家经销商，产品同时出口美国、德国、加拿大、俄罗斯、澳大利亚、巴西、韩国、印度等19个国家和地区。

2013年开始，高科建材着眼于长远和更大的发展，按照“总体规划，分步实施”的原则，规划建设高科集团新型建材产业园，到“十二五”末将形成高科集团新型建材产业集群。

安徽国通高新管业股份有限公司

安徽国通高新管业股份有限公司始建于1993年，是中国塑料加工工业协会塑料管道专业委员会副理事长单位、国家高新技术企业、PE双壁波纹管材国家标准(GB/T 19472.1—2004)第一起草单位、国内首家专业生产新型塑料管材的上市公司(股票代码：600444)，年生产能力100kt以上。公司控股股东合肥通用机械研究院是央企中国机械工业集团有限公司旗下以技术研发为主的科研型企业，在技术研发、内外部资源等方面优势明显，为公司的技术研发及品牌建设等提供了有力的支撑。公司以安徽合肥为大本营，并在广东南沙投资设立生产基地(广东国通)，已经成为全国知名的新型塑料管材专业生产企业。未来，公司将利用自身在产品市场和资本市场的综合优势，努力提高公司综合经济实力和市场竞争力，铸造更为坚实、响亮的国通品牌。

汕头市华鹰软包装设备总厂有限公司

汕头市华鹰软包装设备总厂有限公司成立于1986年，集科研、设计、制造、销售、服务为一体，是我国中、高档印刷软包装设备与涂层加工设备的主要供应商。“华鹰设备，中国精品”是华鹰人孜孜不倦的追求，“敬业、诚信、创新、永攀”是华鹰人的经营理念，公司坚持“品质第一”的宗旨，使产品始终保持在高档次、高品质的水平。

2011年公司与瑞士保利泰(Polytype)加工设备有限公司正式达成资金、技术、品牌等引进合作协议，成功转型为外商投资企业，并设立涂布设备制造分厂专注于高端特种涂层加工设备的研发、生产和销售。

公司注重产品科研开发投入，成立印刷涂布设备工程技术研究开发中心，下设机械设计与制造、工业自动化控制技术、高分子化学技术等专业技术室；连年承担多项国家级火炬计划、国家级重点新产品计划，公司先后被评定为国家级高新技术企业、国家火炬计划重点高新技术企业、广东省第一批创新帮扶高成长型中小企业，是“全国复合膜行业委员会理事单位”、“广东省食品包装机械协会理事单位”，并通过ISO9001质量管理体系认证，产品获欧盟CE安全认证。

公司已建立广东省省级工程技术研究开发中心，先后完成国家级重点新产品项目5项，国家火炬计划项目4项，广东省重点新产品、创新产品、高新技术产品7项，省级以上科研项目近20项；获专利授权证书25项、软件著作权证书2项；主导起草行业标准1项；获市级以上科学技术进步奖10多项。

公司拥有一支素质高、业务精的员工队伍：现有职工近200人，其中研发人员32人，占员工总人数的16%；具有国家工人等级证书的一线技工93人，占工人总人数的47%，高水平的员工队伍，保证了各项管理业务的有效开展。

主要产品有：印刷软包装设备：凹版印刷机系列、干式复合机系列、全自动制袋机系列、检品复卷机系列、环保节能减排成套设备；特种涂层加工设备：食品/医药包装材料系列、烟酒包装系列、标签材料系列、家电家装系列、新兴材料系列、特殊订货。

公司一贯以优质的设备、超值的服务，受到客户广泛的赞扬，在行业中享有良好的信誉。市场已由中国市场扩展到世界各地，企业生产的产品畅销国内20多个省市和地区，并出口加拿大、俄罗斯、南非、土耳其、印度、菲律宾、泰国、印度尼西亚、日本、韩国、中国台湾等国家和地区。

企业名称： 汕头市华鹰软包装设备总厂有限公司
联系地址： 广东省汕头市潮汕路金园工业区9片区B2-B4
邮政编码： 515064
销售联系电话： 0754-88213139/88226231/88227042
网址： www. hyspe. com
E-Mail： sales@ hyspe. com

长沙天卓塑胶有限公司

长沙天卓塑胶有限公司座落在湖南省望城经济开发区，占地14余万平方米，是一家拥有资产数亿元的新型化学建筑材料生产基地，集研发、生产、销售于一体的高科技企业，并拥有一批专业的化学建筑材料研发人才和生产技术队伍，并与高校建立产学研合作平台。

目前公司的主要项目为HDPE给水管、双壁波纹管、钢带增强螺旋波纹管、燃气管、垃圾填埋透水管、煤矿井下用管、非开挖用管的生产销售，年生产能力100kt。生产项目采用国际先进技术和行业最先进的全自动电脑控制生产设备，产品品种、规格齐全，全系列产品都经过国家权威机构检测，各项力学性能和理化卫生指标均达到相关标准要求。于2009年以来产品两度被评为湖南省名牌，2011年获得湖南省著名商标，2012年通过环境标志产品认证。工厂获得ISO9001质量体系认证、ISO14001环境管理体系认证和OHSAS18001职业健康体系认证，依靠数据科学管理，建立了从原辅材料进厂筛选，工艺配方，在线品质监控到成品出厂全过程的质量保证体系，具有可追溯性，是目前国内最专业的HDPE管道生产厂商之一。产品广泛应用于市政给排水、农村安全饮水工程、建筑给排水、水利、农林排灌、工矿、燃气等几大建设领域当中，产品品质深得用户信赖，服务同样受到用户的好评。

福建亚通新材料科技股份有限公司

福建亚通新材料科技股份有限公司创建于1994

年，是一家专业从事塑料管道产品研究和制造的国家级重点高新技术企业。亚通产品主要用于市政建设(道路、通讯、电力、燃气、供水、排水、排污等基础设施建设)、水务投资运营(城市供水、排污、输水管网建设改造)、建筑工程、农业节水排灌系统、现代园艺等各种领域，产品种类及配套之全，位居全国同行业领先地位。

亚通经国家人事部批准设立国家博士后科研工作站，现系建设部全国塑料管道科技产业化基地，全国化学建材骨干企业，中国塑料加工工业协会副理事长单位。亚通拥有福建、北京、内蒙古、黑龙江、河南、重庆、湖北、甘肃、新疆等10多个生产基地和覆盖全国的生产、销售和服务网络。从2004年起，亚通产品陆续销往俄罗斯、马耳他、新加坡、沙特阿拉伯、圭亚那、伊朗、蒙古等国家和地区。

亚通是中国塑料管材及管件市场的知名品牌，是国家工商总局认定的“中国驰名商标”。企业的系列产品荣获了“中国名牌产品”、“国家重点新产品”、“福建名牌产品”等多项荣誉。

台塑集团

台塑集团创建于1954年，截至2011年止，资产总额达6994亿元人民币，集团营业总额高达3703多亿元人民币，集团首创于中国台湾，初期以石化工业为主，后续投资遍及美国、东南亚，20世纪90年代起更积极投入中国市场。

南亚塑胶公司对PVC管材、管件给予国家社会带来的经济效益，有深入体会，为将此经济效益扩展至中国大陆，从1995年起南亚公司陆续投入中国管材市场，现已分别创建南亚厦门公司、重庆公司、广州公司、山东东营公司、安徽芜湖公司、河南郑州公司、辽宁鞍山公司等。目前，PVC－U管材年产能达300kt，PVC－U管件达15kt，2007年再陆续开发PE、PPR管材、管件。后续并将加快速度在国内各地增建管材厂，未来，将在国内每省份至少投建一个管材厂，年产量目标将达1000kt以上，对国内PVC管材、管件推广与应用，十足体现领头羊的角色。

总结中国台湾、美国50余年丰富经验，南亚塑料公司在国内投建的管材厂，充分展现九大特色：

1. 采用奥地利辛西那提挤出机、日本东芝注塑机等最先进生产设备；

2. 原料混合采用美国西门子计算机监控系统；封闭式螺旋供料系统，配方稳定、质量可靠；

3. 从供料、挤出、成型、喷字、切断以至于捆包，全程采用自动工艺流程，人为影响可以完全排除；

4. 产品质量标准，除完全符合GB国家标准外，部分产品更采取ISO国际标准，质量水平媲美国际先进国家。

5. 率先采用有机锡稳定剂(非铅盐稳定剂)，卫生性能完全符合国家饮用水卫生指标及蒸馏水卫生指标，充分体现环保建材的优势；

6. 彻底落实质量检测，确保用户权益，并加上售前、售后服务体系，建立拥护信得过首选品牌；

7. 产品规格齐全，管材口径从 ϕ16mm～ϕ630mm，一应俱全；并配套427种给水管件，193种排水管件及21种电工管件，可完全满足各类工程设计需要；

8. 各地管材厂年产能达高30kt以上，成品存货量允足，供应灵活快速，可充分搭配各类工程进度；

9. 采用台塑经营管理模式，不断推动生产销售5S活动，更坚持突破、创新、彻底、圆满的经营理念，对国内员工水平有效促进，火速推动本土经营目标。产品质量、品牌形象经由国家建设部、各省建委建设系统、建设工程行业协会、各层级质量评选单位，先后认定与推荐，同时获得国家免检证书，并已通过ISO9001认证，目前已奠立行业前导地位。

颐通集团

颐通集团是一家大型专业生产市政工程用高密度聚乙烯(HDPE)管道的现代化企业，注册资金2.36亿元，公司集研发、生产、销售、服务于一身，以“德益社会、共担责任、开放进取、永不放弃”为核心的价值观整体服务于客户。集团目前拥有湖南、辽宁、甘肃、河北四大生产基地，销售机构遍布全国，拥有高水准持续供货和敏捷的全方位服务能力。产能规模居同行业领先水平，品牌享誉海内外。

公司主要产品有PE给水管、PE燃气管、PE双壁波纹管、PE钢带增强螺旋波纹管、PE矿用管以及与管材配套的各种管件。产品广泛应用于城市供水、排水、排污工程，农业喷灌、滴灌、节水灌溉工程，引流、治沙工程，输油管道，燃气管网，低压弱电和通信光缆护套等，是市政工程、厂矿建设、小城镇建设和文明生态村建设的首选产品。该类产品具有重量轻、耐腐蚀、耐低温、不渗漏、环保节能、成本低、寿命长等优良特性，项目产品环保节能无污染，并可回收再利用，符合建设节约型社会和发展循环经济的要求，是水泥管和铸铁管的最佳替代产品。

安全、质量、环保、速度、信誉是颐通集团生存和发展的立身之本。公司在业内率先通过了ISO9001：2008质量管理体系认证、ISO14001环境管理体系认证和OHSAS18001职业健康安全管理体系三合一认证。产品经国家、省、市三级质量技术监督部门抽检和监督检验，其化学成分、力学性能等各项指标全部达到甚至超过国家标准。公司产品先后被评为“高新技术产品”“消费者信得过产品”“环境标志产品”“节水标志产品”“湖南省名牌产品”。企业先后被评为“高新技术企业”“重合同守信用单位”“质量信用AAA级企业”“中国工程建设重点推广单位”“中国PE管材生产十强企业”等，同时，颐通商标被评为“湖南省著名商标”。颐通集团目前是中国塑料加工工业协会理事单位、中国塑料管道专业委员会会员单位、中国防腐协会会员单位，为国家首批一级资质获证企业。

总部地址：湖南省岳阳县生态工业园

全国免费服务热线：400－612－3188

传真：0730－7603308

邮编：414100

青岛顺德塑料机械有限公司

青岛顺德塑料机械有限公司公司始建于1991年，是中国最早生产塑料机械和塑料制品的专业化公司之一，经过二十年的发展，现已在国内外塑料挤出行业中处于领先地位。是国家十一个五年计划支撑计划木塑料课题组组长单位，青岛市高新技术企业，青岛市AAA级信誉企业，中国专利山东明星企业……其产品已通过ISO9001国际标准质量管理体系认证和欧州CE认证。生产的塑料挤出机被评为山东省名牌产品，公司所用“同飞”牌商标被评为山东省著名商标。

公司重视技术创新，拥有完善的创新机制，有专门研发机构和试制车间，不断推出新产品，为中国塑料机械和塑料制品的发展做出了重大贡献，受到国家科技部、质检总局等部委的大力扶持。

公司加大了对国外市场的开拓，塑料挤出自动化生产线是国内最早占领欧美市场的企业之一，而且份额不断扩大，彻底打破了欧美企业在塑机挤出业的垄断地位。我们在产品质量上精益求精，在技术上不断完善，不断为用户提供优质、可靠、价格合理的新产品，帮助用户创造最大的利润和商机是我们最终的目标。

电话：0532－87285708；0532－82299626

传真：0532－82299621

邮箱：info@shunde－qd.com

南亚塑胶工业股份有限公司南通厂

南亚塑胶工业股份有限公司南通厂区成立于1996年，总投资3.8亿美元，主要生产线34条，生产PVC软、硬质胶布、PVC、PU人造革、PVC、PET粘合装饰材、PVC、PE保鲜膜、BOPP薄膜、珠光纸、40.5KV/20KV/10KV高低压开关柜等产品，用于车辆内饰、鞋类、家具、皮包箱、球、吹气制品、胶带、文具、吸塑包装、真空成型、折叠成型、装潢建材、包装用膜及配电设备控制系统等。

南通厂区全面导入母公司各项管理制度，大力推动产品别、机台别经营负责制度，依照产品、机台特性成立产品别、机台别经营小组，发挥专业团队优势，提升整体经营绩效。较早推动计算机ERP管理，整个经营活动全面纳入电脑管理，提高管理绩效。已通过ISO9001、ISO14001、OHSAS18001、TS16949及3C认证，

公司秉持“勤劳朴实、止于至善、永续经营、奉献社会”，推行全面质量管理活动，追求永续改善，提供客户完全满意的产品与服务，贡献社会。

地址：中国江苏省南通市通京大道101号

电话：0513－85291811(总机)

网址：http：www.nypc.com.cn

佑利控股集团有限公司

佑利控股集团有限公司成立于1998年。是目前我国塑胶行业产品种类最齐全的大型企业集团，国家塑料制品标准化委员会(TC48/SC3)核心成员单位；国家CPVC产品标准主任起草单位；国家UPVC、ABS标准第一起草单位。设有北京化工大学“佑利”博士创新基金；全国氯碱行业“佑利杯”论文赛奖金。中国农业银行AAA级信誉单位；中国人民保险公司产品质量受保护单位；中国氯碱工业协会会员单位；国家标准环保排放达标单位；浙江省优秀科技型企

业。“佑利”商标为浙江省著名商标。

佑利控股集团有限公司，是我国首家生产 CPVC 系列产品的大型合资企业，美国 NOVEON 诺誉化学公司创建于 1870 年，是世界 CPVC 产品标准的制定者和指导者。高标准的规模投资，高技术的科学引用，高层次的企业管理，高诚信的经营理念，使公司始终具有先进的生产设备，完整的测试工艺，雄厚的技术人才，一流的产品质量。公司通过 ISO9001；ISO14001，GB/T 28001，ABS，CCS，DNV，特种压力生产许可证等。是太钢、大连造船厂、新疆华泰股份公司、秦山核电等国家重大工程建设合格供应商。产品销往全国各地及出口海外，深受国内外新老客户的信赖与爱戴。

公司生产的管道、管件、阀门、板材、填料、焊条等系列产品，具有高强度、耐高温、耐酸、阻燃、无毒等特性。是国家主导推行的非金属绿色管道。产品完全符合 GB/T 18998、GB/T 18993、ISO 15493、美国 ASTM 标准 F438、F439、F441 和德国 DIN 标准 8079、8080、以及日本 JIS6776 标准的规定，广泛应用于矿山、石油、冶金、化工、油田、电力、造船、造纸、核电、制革、医药、印染、电镀、食品、饮料、家电、航天航空、军事工业、电子半导体、污水处理、消防系统等工业部门和宾馆、饭店等行业。该产品非但具有其他管道系统无法替代的优越性，而且价格便宜、安装方便。同时，公司生产的 ABS、UPVC 等管道、管件、阀门、填料等系列产品，仍占国内市场领先地位。

地址：浙江省乐清市柳市镇兴业北路 8 - 88 号
电话：0577 - 62767777
传真：0577 - 62771236
手机：13806868951
网址：www. chinayouli. com
E - mail：sale@ chinayouli. com

美吉特塑料中心

东莞(常平)美吉特塑料中心位于广深黄金走廊中段，是拥有“京九物流第一镇”和“华南商贸重镇”等称号的的东莞市常平镇物流园区。挟有毗邻虎门、蛇口、香港三大码头的地理位置优势，且坐拥京九、广深、广梅汕三大铁路交汇枢纽，瞬间可达广、深、港三大机场。交通发达，物流便捷，区位优势得天独厚。

塑料中心一、二期用地达 140 亩，总建筑面积 14 万平方米，是一个专为国内外塑料行业全产业链提供精品展示、商品交易、质量检测、信息发布、技术转让、电子商务、仓储物流的多功能现代化的大型商务平台。以全方面的规划思考层面，打造美吉特塑料中心成为便捷舒适塑料之都，将东莞(常平)在塑料行业的影响力扩及全国。

此外，为了更便捷美吉特塑料中心业主的生活需求，以及提升常平东区的商业价值，三期用地将规划成为建筑面积 9 万平方米的美吉特(商业)广场。提供常平地区一个以高端硬件设施和完美配套服务的现代商务平台。并以品位高雅、品牌汇集为鲜明特点，成为珠三角具有重大影响力的购物美食天堂、娱乐休闲胜地。地段增值前力，无限可期!

美吉特塑料中心着眼于大品牌定位，挟带着集团 20 於年全国化经营的资源优势，大空间招商，大范围辐射，大产业链经营，强势打造一个以塑料全产业链为主体的品牌汇集中心。经营触角立足东莞、依托珠三角，辐射国内外；并以专业化塑料市场为核心，进行科学化、现代化、国际化的产业升级，打造出崭新型态华南塑料总部基地，成为国内运营能力最强大的塑料专业市场!

辽宁华塑实业集团有限公司

华塑集团座落于经济发达、风景秀丽素有“湿地之都”、“鹤乡”美誉的海滨城市——辽宁盘锦。

公司创建于 2002 年 4 月，2010 年 8 月成立辽宁华塑实业集团有限公司，占地 310 亩，总投资 10 亿元，建筑面积达 12 万平方米。是一家专业从事石油化工产品销售、塑料原料贸易、塑料制品生产、仓储物流、电子商务、融投资为一体的大型民营企业。

2012 年 6 月由华塑集团全资投资建设的辽宁海塑(营口)高分子新材料产业园成立，注册资金 2 亿元，占地面积 2050 亩，总投资 60 亿元。

集团目前拥有员工 1500 余人，年销售收入近百亿元。集团下设华塑塑料产业园、营口高分子新材料产业园，旗下拥有近 20 家企业。

经过 10 多年的发展，与盘锦石化、燕山石化、大庆石化、抚顺石化、天联石化、齐鲁石化、上海赛科、吉林石化等大型石化企业建立了密切的合作关系，同时与日本伊藤忠商社、美国埃克森、日本住友、美国陶氏、韩国三星等国外知名石化企业有着良好的合作。公司经销的产品覆盖东北三省，逐步向华北、华东、华南地区延伸，形成了具有华塑特色的营销网络。

高速发展中的华塑集团按照“产业生态组织者”战略规划，各部门正全面布局、构建和组织实施东北亚塑料产业圈项目，现已建成交易平台、制品营销网络和两个工业产业园区，中国东北沈阳塑胶城选址工作正在进行之中。华塑集团将成为全球最大原料交易商和制品生产商。项目建成后，预计三到五年集团公司贸易和工业总产值将超过三百亿，中国东北亚塑胶城将成为东北亚地区最大的塑料产品交易中心。同时将实现“创新发展、产业报国”的经营宗旨，实现“做一个负责任的企业公民”的社会责任和企业价值。

科倍隆集团

科倍隆集团隶属于美国上市公司(Hillenbrand Inc.)，Hillenbrand是一家设立在美国，进行全球多元化战略的实业公司，其在纽约证券交易市场上市，于2012年底正式收购科倍隆集团。

科倍隆为Hillenbrand工艺设备集团(PEG)中的一员。PEG是设计，制造，销售和维修广泛应用于各工业市场的加工设备和系统的领导者。

科倍隆集团是配混系统，物料输送系统和服务全世界范围内的市场和技术的引领者，并为塑料，化学，制药，食品和矿产行业设计，开发，制造和维修系统，设备和零部件。其总部设在德国，旗下的四家主要生产基地累积拥有300多年的历史。科倍隆集团的技术也深远影响了中国塑料挤出机行业的质量标准。全球所有新型塑料材料中超过75%是在科倍隆的测试实验室中进行开发和研究的。科倍隆南京严格遵守科倍隆集团的质量标准，充分确保了每道生产工序的高质量完成。

科倍隆(南京)机械有限公司负责生产、销售双螺杆挤出机并提供技术服务，而作为科倍隆集团全球三大研发中心之一，科倍隆南京有助科倍隆集团公司更快更好地为中国及亚洲的客户提供系统解决方案。

由科倍隆南京设计制造的STS advanced系列配混挤出机，比扭矩达10Nm/cm^3，扭矩实现了15%的提升。由于扭矩的提升，双螺杆(STS)配混机的产品质量也得到大幅度的提升，而产量更有高达20%的提高。STSadvanced设备综合了科倍隆工艺方面的专业技术和全球网络的优势，它完全贯彻了“德国技术”的精髓，全球统一的质量标准和中国制造的价格优势，这样的高性价比使配混机能在更短的时间内为您实现投资回报。

苏州奥美材料科技有限公司

苏州奥美材料科技有限公司(www.pc-film.com)位于美丽的苏州国家高新产业开发区，总投资2亿元人民币，拥有多条当今世界最先进的挤出压延生产线，年设计生产能力20，000吨，是中国最大的集研发、制造、销售、服务于一体的聚碳酸酯(Polycarbonate，简称PC)薄膜及片材生产基地。

苏州奥美材料科技有限公司(以下简称“苏州奥美”)前身为成立于2003年的苏州奥美光学材料有限公司。经过十年的发展，苏州奥美现拥有六十余项国家专利(授权二十四篇)，并主导了PC薄膜产业国家标准制定，是江苏省著名商标及名牌产品、江苏省高新技术企业、江苏省民营科技型企业。

苏州奥美专注于研究、开发、制造国内外高端市场所需的特殊聚碳酸酯薄膜产品。目前应用于光平板显示、高铁航空、LED照明等领域的十大系列，二百多个品种的产品，业务遍及60多个国家和地区，连续多年产销量及市场占有率中国第一。

2003年4月，苏州奥美成立使得中国成为即美国、日本、德国后世界上第四个可以生产该产品的国家；2005年9月，在国内率先成功研制出环保阻燃级PC薄膜；2008年8月，成功研制出非卤素高阻燃级PC薄膜；2011年5月，承担“江苏省科技支撑计划(工业部分)”—“新型平板显示用光学面板”项目开发；2011年10月，与日本帝人集团的战略协作计划启动；2012年7月高铁航空桌椅系统用板开发成功；2013年3月LED照明及背光模组用光扩散板开发成功；2013年4月，建筑面积达7000m^{2}的奥美新厂区即将破土动工建设。预订到2017年，苏州奥美年产能达到25，000t，年产值超过10亿元，并力争在创业板上市。

丽水市南城区控制性详细规划

公共设施用地规划总则：

为了推动丽水经济开发区持续、健康建设发展，科学合理指导丽水经济开发区东扩区块的开发建设，进而加快特色制造业基地的形成，实现与中心城区(北城)互动，强化丽水中心城市接受辐射的能力，推动丽水中心城市跨越式发展，特制定本规划。

规划范围位于丽水市区南部，南至大梁山脚规划中的丽龙高速公路，西邻水阁工业区快速干道，北至南明山脚。用地范围面积约 $35km^2$，金丽温高速公路将它分成东北和西南两大片区。其中东北片区(富岭组团)约 $10km^2$，西南片区(七百秧工业组团)面积约 $25km^2$。

发展规划：

充分利用目前中国经济发展所处的重要战略机遇期，抓住发展的有利时机和山区用地优势，以担当丽水经济增长中心为目标，从扩大产业规模和提升产业高度两个方面同时入手，进一步加快南城的发展步伐。

利用大型区域性基础设施，抓住国际产业和区域产业转移的时机，引导企业落户开发区，促进南城健康发展。

转变政府管理方式、管制体制，优化南城软环境，同时改善基础设施等硬环境，提高对周边城市的产业吸引力和辐射力。

提高生态环境保护意识，促进南城的可持续发展。

结合山地地形条件，最大可能减少工程投资。

适应丽水市城市总体发展的需要，引导第二产业的有序发展，集聚丽水市内外企业，吸引区域产业转移，形成高标准、高起点、具有一定高新技术含量的工业园区，促进丽水第二产业上一个新的台阶，打造丽水特色制造业基地。

功能定位为浙西南地区工业发展的重要集聚中心，工贸业综合发展与人居环境优越的丽水城市新区。

总体布局：

规划形成"一心、二带、二片"的结构与总体布局形式。其中"一心"：指城市南部地区中心，位于水阁东侧南北向干路和金丽温高速公路之间，七百秧组团(工业区东扩区块)北部，配置有行政、办公、文化、娱乐、商务等服务与管理设施；"二带"为丽龙高速公路与金丽温高速公路沿线形成的防护景观林带；"二片"指以中一路七百秧组团(工业区东扩区块)及金丽温高速公路为界形成的南、北各一个功能片，其中北侧功能片以富岭组团为主，为居住片；南侧为以七百秧组团(工业区东扩区块)为主，形成工业片。其中七百秧水库公园以现状七百秧水库为基础，保留主要水体，并加以改造。仓储区位于交通枢纽东北角，功能独立，结合高速公路接口可作为物流区。

规划区居住人口 17.0 万人，就业人口 12.3 万人。

规划用地总面积 3528.05 万平方米，其中居住用地 619.07 万平方米，公共设施用地 141.34 万平方米，道路广场用地 411.04 万平方米，工业用地 1220.57 万平方米，物流用地 54.30 万平方米，市政设施用地 58.25 万平方米，绿化用地 794.04 万平方米(含保留山体及边坡绿化用地)，水域和其他用地 92.59 万平方米。

本规划包括：公共设施用地规划、居住用地规划、工业仓储用地规划、道路交通及相关设施规划、绿地系统规划、景观规划、市政基础设施规划、道路平面定位与竖向规划、水系及七百秧水库保护、改造规划、环境保护规划、土地使用和建筑规划等。

北京禧天龙塑料制品有限公司

北京禧天龙塑料制品有限公司始创于 1990 年，前身为浙江华兴塑业，公司一直致力于科技创新与品牌发展战略，历经 20 余年的开拓进取，公司目前已跃居国内集研发、制造、销售网络等综合实力最强的塑料家居用品生产、销售企业行列。

公司总部座落于首都北京，占地面积 90 亩，建筑面积达到 6 万平米，员工 500 余人，并拥有北京、天津、哈尔滨、成都四大生产基地，在北京、上海、天津、哈尔滨、沈阳、山东、石家庄、成都、西安、郑州、福建、武汉等地设有办事处。公司拥有成熟庞大的销售与服务网络，辐射全国，成为家乐福、沃尔玛、乐购、百安居、物美、华润万家等国内外知名大型连锁超市的优质供应商与首选品牌，同时与遍及全国的 300 余家经销商建立了良好的合作关系。公司拥有自营进出口权，产品远销韩国、日本、澳大利亚、新加坡及欧美等市场并在新加坡设有分公司。

公司具备成熟专业的研发团队和精密塑模的制作能力，拥有精加工中心及 120T ~ 1400T 国内先进的节能型全电脑注塑设备 100 余台，配置了伺服机械手及意大利全自动大型中央供料系统，确保了产品质量的稳定性，并大幅度减轻了员工的劳动强度，提高了生产效率。公司于 2008 年顺利通过了 ISO9000 质量管理体系认证，并取得了"QS"生产安全许可证。目前已经开发出数百款产品，并获得了十多项实用新型及产品外观设计专利，可以满足不同顾客需求。凭借时尚的产品、卓越的品质、优良的服务，"禧天龙 Citylong"、"禧仕多"、"华兴"以及"乖乖兔 Cute Bunny"深受广大消费者的喜爱，已经成为广大消费者耳熟能详的品牌。

地址：北京市通州区台湖镇东下营村

网址：www. citylong. com

邮箱: vip@ citylong. com
电话: 010 - 61537313

东莞艾尔发自动化机械有限公司

艾尔发是天行自动化机械股份有限公司的子公司，专业制造、销售射出成型专用机械手臂及周边自动化设备，可搭配20~6000t各型注塑机，机型有斜臂式、横走式、纵走式、侧取式及全伺服马达型等机台供客户针对不同需求来做搭配，年产销超过1万台，总销售已超过10万台，经过多年的努力成为世界知名的自动化机械领导品牌之一。

艾尔发建立了一套完整个营销服务体系，在中国大陆有东莞厂及苏州厂，中国直营销售服务点有超过95个。在国外市场上，除了欧洲、美洲、非洲、澳洲及亚洲原有的专业代理商外，天行自去年起也陆续在河内、胡志明、曼谷直接设直营服务点(技术支持中心)，未来预计还会在菲律宾、马来西亚等国家设直营站以服务东南亚地区越来越多的跨国客户。

联络人: 黄俊钦　总经理
电话: 0769 - 8318 - 0326
传真: 0769 - 8318 - 0329
E - mall: info@ alfarobot. com
Web: www. alfarobot. com

南亚塑胶工业(郑州)有限公司

台湾台塑集团创建于1954年(前身为台湾塑胶公司)，初期以石化工业为主。随着规模不断扩大，截至2012年底，台塑集团共有百余家分子企业及关系企业，员工达10.2万多人，资产总额6400亿人民币，资产净值与营业收入均超过4900亿人民币，占台湾国民生产总值13%，是台湾最大的民营企业。董事长王永庆被称为台湾的“经营之神”，世界“塑胶大王”。

台塑集团经营范围十分广泛，包括炼油、石化原料、塑胶加工、纤维、纺织、电子材料、半导体、汽车、发电、机械、运输、生物科技、教育与医疗事业等。尤其是在石化工业领域，建立起从原油进口、运输、冶炼、裂解、加工制造到成品油零售等一体化的完整产业链，这在台湾是独一无二的企业集团。

台塑集团于2004年再在河南省投资兴建南亚塑胶工业(郑州)有限公司。南亚塑胶工业(郑州)有限公司位于郑州经济技术开发区航海东路与新107国道交叉口处，厂区占地面积120亩，一期投资总额2000万美金，将投入16条生产线，2007年3月正式投产销售。目前已投入12条生产线，可年产南亚牌PVC - U管材35kt，是目前中原地区最大的塑胶管材生产基地之一。

公司产品包括：PVC - U给水管($\phi20-\phi630$)，PVC - M给水管($\phi20-\phi630$)，PVC - U排水管($\phi50-\phi500$)，PVC - U电工管($\phi16-\phi40$)，PE100给水管材($\phi20-\phi630$)，PE100燃气管材($\phi20-\phi630$)，PP - R给水管材($\phi20-\phi110$)，PE - RT给水管材($\phi20-\phi32$)。

常州嘉仁禾化学有限公司

常州嘉仁禾化学有限公司是中国塑料加工工业协会理事单位、中国塑协助剂专委会理事单位、台塑关系企业合格分供方、江苏省清洁化生产示范单位、省级高新企业、常州市生态园林单位。公司位于美丽富饶的江南水乡天目湖畔，被誉为现代化园林式工厂。

公司秉承德国技术，凭借公司投资创办的有中科院院士、教授、博士等数十位国内外化工专家组建的鸿博(溧阳)新材料技术研究院的技术平台，研发并生产新型材料，包括环保建材、石化产品专业用的相关助剂，适用于PVC等各种新型塑材，公司研发的具有国际先进水平的环保钙锌、钡锌和高端无酚产品，在近百家台资、大陆工厂的宽幅压延线和大型挤出、浸塑、注塑和吹塑等设备上得到成功使用，被南亚塑胶等高知名度塑胶企业确定为长期供应商。产品广泛适用于环保汽车革、发泡板、地板胶(医院、机场、学校、科研院所、舰艇等用)、人造革、透明膜、玩具膜、车身贴、PVC手套、PVC医用塑料、百叶窗、电线电缆料、油墨和涂料等。北京化工大学、东南大学、中国林化研究所和常州大学为公司产学研合作单位，是常州大学的实习基地。公司现有“常州市塑料助剂工程技术研究中心”，承担高科技新产品的开发工作，公司开发的符合欧盟市场标准的无酚产品填补了国内空白，由公司和中国林化所合作研发的无金属生态型稳定剂已被国家科技部列入“十二五”规划，研发工作已全面启动。

2012年常州嘉仁禾化学有限公司承担的国家十二五科技攻关项目：“生物基PVC热稳定剂制备技术”是目前全球新兴的前沿战略性研究课题，我公司通过与中国林化所产学研合作研发生物基 PVC 热稳定剂产品已达国际国内先进水平。

公司董事长沈卫锋先生现为中国青年企业家协会会员，首届长三角年度青商人物“杰出青商”和常州市“831 高层次创新创业人才”，“东南大学聘为校外辅导导师”，“常州市十大大学生创业导师”，公司现为“常州市大学生创业实践基地”。

长虹塑料集团英派瑞塑料有限公司

长虹塑料集团英派瑞塑料有限公司(下简称“公司”)成立于2010年8月，注册资金7000万元，主要生产和销售：尼龙扎带、钢钉线卡、定位片、压线帽、接线端子、号码管、缠绕管、冷压端头”等“CHS”品牌的塑料制品，是长虹塑料集团的六个子公司之一。公司坚持“诚信、高效、创新、共赢”的经营理念，管理上坚持以市场为导向，采用现代企业管理制度，集售前、售中、售后服务于一身的营销服务模式，为广大用户提供最优质的产品。凭藉过硬的产品质量和优质的服务，赢得了国内外广泛客户的厚爱，产品已销往：欧洲、北美洲、南美洲、大洋洲、非洲、亚洲等100多个国家和地区。

成立到现在短短几年时间的市场竞争洗礼，已迅速发展成为全国较具规模的配线器材产品生产企业：拥有大型节能注塑机130多台；自主研发热流道模具达150多台套；新引进6条挤出式塑料机流水线入驻；开发80多套高端配线槽新产品模具；2013年内完成二期工程，续建10万平方米的标准厂房及配套建筑，届时公司占地面积将达到20万平方米，建筑面积将达到30万平方米。业务范围涉及电器、电子、建筑、汽车、农业、服装、食品等多个应用领域，已整合形成研、产、销一条龙的庞大的产业群体，产品获得国家专利10多项。为了进一步落实国家科教兴国战略，促进科技创新，加快企业经济发展和社会进步，2013年7月9日，公司与北京工商大学正式签订了校企合作协议，促进企业进行传统产业改造和高新技术产业发展，研究高新技术项目和攻克企业技术难题，支持企业技术创新。这标志着公司在规范化发展的道路上迈出了重要的一步，为做大企业规模、提高经济效益，实现企业战略化经营格局，进一步奠定了良好的基础。

电话：0577－62799888

传真：0577－62793006

网址：www. chs. com. cn

山东通佳机械有限公司

山东通佳机械有限公司地处孔孟之乡的山东省济宁市国家高新技术产业开发区，创始于1953年，员工628人，占地面积18万平方米。年产塑料机械2000台套，塑料制品10000t。山东通佳机械有限公司是中国塑料机械工业协会副会长单位，中国轻工机械协会理事单位，山东省塑料加工协会常任理事单位，全国轻工系统技术创新先进单位，中国专利山东明星企业。产品遍及全国各地和世界六十多个国家和地区。

公司设有国家级塑料机械技术研发中心，山东省企业技术中心，先后研制开发出九大类180多种规格的具有国际先进水平的塑料机械装备，其中有多项产品填补了国内空白，获得多项省部级科技进步奖和国家专利，并分别被列为国家级重点新产品、山东名牌产品、国家级火炬计划项目、国家技术创新基金项目、山东省技术创新重点项目。

贵州康塑实业股份有限公司

贵州康塑实业股份有限公司(原贵阳文峰塑料管业有限公司)自1992年开始从事塑料管材、管件的研究、设计、工艺的配方、模具开发和生产工作，是一个快速发展中的民营企业，也是目前贵州规模较大、实力较强的塑料管材生产厂家。公司总部位于金华镇金龙村(321国道14公里处)，瓮安分厂位于县城南区，交通十分便利。

公司系国家管道协会理事长单位、贵州省塑料协会会员单位，贵州省消协保名优推荐单位、贵州省质量技术监督局诚信企业AAA级单位，已率先通过ISO9001：2000国际体系认证。

康塑管业占地总面积70000多平方米，固定资产1亿元，技术实力雄厚。高级职称12人，中级职称24人，员工400人，拥有先进设备。PE管材生产线15条，PVC管生产线8条，RR－R生产线5条，PE管件生产线3条。其中PE管材年产量7000多吨，产品规格为DN16－DN630，PVC管材年产量4000多吨，RR－R管材年产量3000多吨。

公司主要产品有：HDPE给水、燃气、通信、喷灌等平壁管材、管件，PE多孔梅花管、子管和双壁波纹管；PVC给水管及双壁波纹管、绝缘电工套管。广泛用于建筑工程、市政工程、通信工程、宽带网络工程、有限电视网络工程、高速公路工程、电力工程、煤气工程、自来水工程、高尔夫球场、农业排灌、水产养殖、化工排污、矿山通风等领域。

公司把"以人为本，以质取胜，以诚服务"作为企业经营理念，凭着以质量求生存，以成本求竞争，以信誉求发展，秉诚"以人、以诚、以效"的管理理念，靠优异的产品质量赢得用户，凭完善的销售服务拓展市场。特别是公司二期工程增加了 HDPE 缠绕双壁波纹管，多孔梅花管，各种套管生产线，适应于城镇地下排污、通信电务、高、低压用套管，挖掘了我司潜力，适应市场需求；为公司持续发展增加了后劲。成为贵州省政府的重点发展对象。

公司供销部专门设有客户服务部(附设施工队)，其职能是更好地为客户服务，让客户满意，做好我公司产品的售前、售中、售后服务，做到用户的期望和要求是我们努力的方向，用户的满意和信任是我们生存的保证。

地址：贵阳市金阳新区金华镇金龙村 12 组(321 国道 14KM 处)

邮编：550023

电话：0851－4759980　0851－4720363

传真：0851－4766900

上海优珀斯材料科技有限公司

上海优珀斯材料科技有限公司(以下简称"公司")成立于 2008 年，是一家集研发、生产、销售、服务于一体的环保科技型企业。公司凭借自身研发专利技术，生产产品用于防水、防渗、防腐、保温市场的先进高分子膜材料——强力膜、亲水膜、降解膜膜、土工膜及配套产品，所生产的产品属于国家战略性新兴产业中的新材料产业领域。公司产品种类多样，质量服务优越，深受广大客户认可，不仅广销中国各个地区，每年还大宗销往非洲、中东、南亚、东南亚等地区。

公司自成立以来，凭借自身技术实力和自主创新的潜力，致力于打造一个以上海总部为管理中枢覆盖华北、华南、华东和华西四大区域生产基地的集团化企业。截至现今，已在华北地区－河北任丘设立了生产分公司，还在华东地区－江苏太仓设立了生产分公司。另外，华南地区－广东顺德和华西地区－四川成都设立生产分公司的计划也已提到公司议程。

2011 年，公司根据国际国内同行业领域的发展情况，发起"SDM 膜开发"高新技术产品成果转化项目一，目前已通过轻工部专家组鉴定，认定该产品属国际先进水平。SDM 膜项目同类产品目前需要国外进口来供应，在国内相关领域还处于空白期，因此，这项项目能填补国内空白，市场前景十分广阔，对国内相关领域也有着里程碑式的影响。

地址：上海市青浦区华新镇嘉松中路 799 弄 26 号

网址：www. upasschina. com

电话：021－51210658(总机)

传真：021－59797857

销售热线：4003－7003

四川省海维塑胶有限公司

四川省海维塑胶有限公司创建于 1998 年，现有自贡大安高硐二分厂、自贡伍家坡三分厂、自贡盐马路四分厂及公司总部 4 个生产经营场所。主要产品为"海维"牌 PVC 给排水管材、管件、PVC 电工套管、PP－R 给水管、PE 给水管、PE 埋地燃气管、波纹管、梅花管及高压电力电缆管等系列工程管道。公司拥有现代化的大型注塑设备和挤塑设备，设备数量达 100 余套(台)，中、高级工程技术人员 40 人，年生产能力达 36kt，占地 4.8 万平方米，为西南地区知名度颇高的大型塑胶企业。

公司为中国塑料加工工业协会常务理事单位、中国塑料加工工业协会管道专业委员会会员单位、中国工业防腐蚀技术协会会员单位，中国农业节水和农村供水技术协会会员单位，全国行业质量示范企业、中国塑料行业 AAA 级信用企业、中国优秀民营企业家企业、中国著名品牌企业、中国绿色环保产品企业、中国环境标志产品认证企业、全国质量检验稳定合格产品企业、全国质量诚信优秀示范企业，"四川名牌产品"企业、"四川省著名商标"企业、四川省创业之星企业、四川省质量信誉 AAA 级企业、四川省质量管理先进企业、四川放心产品示范单位，四川用户满意企业、四川实施卓越绩效先进单位、四川省重合同守信用企业、"3.15"质量无投诉先进单位、银行系统 AA＋级企业。

公司严格按照国家标准设计、生产、管理，通过 ISO9001：2008 国际质量体系认证和中国环境标志产品认证。其注册的"海维"牌、"名苑"牌 PVC－U、PP－R、PE 管材、管件系列产品因其质量稳定、性能优良、抗冲击强度高、耐腐蚀、抗压耐热、绝缘、液体阻力小、施工方便、使用寿命长、用途广泛、社会信誉好而闻名于国内同行业。公司在西南、西北地区有成熟良好的销售市场和广大的用户群。销售网络遍及川、渝、滇、黔、湘、鄂、桂、陕、新、宁、甘、内蒙等省市、自治区及哈萨克斯坦、乌兹别克等中亚地区，成为众多重大建筑工程项目的首选产品，受到广大用户的信赖。

地址：四川自贡市贡井盐马路98号
电话：0813－3301537
传真：0813－3308098
网址：www. schwsj. com

常州晶雪冷冻设备有限公司

常州晶雪冷冻设备有限公司是国内领先的冷藏库和节能厂房整体解决方案供应商，也是国内最大的节能保温板材生产厂家。经过20多年的发展，晶雪目前已经建成两个生产基地和遍布全国的销售网络，形成了200万平方米各类节能板材、20000扇冷库门和工业门及5000个升降平台的年生产能力，能够为客户提供节能保温系统设计、生产、施工及维护的的全方位服务。公司生产“晶雪”“晶诺”品牌的各类PU、PIR等新型节能板材、“晶道”品牌的各类冷冻冷藏库门、工业滑升门、升降平台，产品均具有较高的市场占有率。

公司生产的“晶雪”“晶诺”品牌的各类PU、PIR等新型节能板材、“晶道”品牌的各类冷冻冷藏库门、工业门和升降平台，广泛的应用于冷链物流、超市、食品加工、生物医药、餐饮酒店、机场、科研院校、工业厂房和建筑外墙等行业，具有较高的市场占有率，并积累了大量的中高端客户，拥有良好的口碑。

公司是中国制冷学会会员、上海冷藏库协会副会长单位、中国塑料加工协会聚氨酯制品专业委员会副理事长单位、中国食品工业协会物流委员会副理事长单位，中国仓储协会会员，中国绝热节能材料协会会员，常州市重合同守信用企业、常州市知名品牌、常州市免检企业，江苏省著名商标，上海海洋大学食品学院校外实习基地。

2006年，公司被国家环保总局批准列为首批国家ODS淘汰技改单位，淘汰氟利昂发泡工艺，采用更为环保的发泡技术，并获国际多边基金奖励。2008年公司产品又率先通过国内新消防标准测试。2009年公司主要产品：金属面聚氨酯硬质夹芯板和轻型平移门被江苏省科学技术厅评定为“高新技术产品”。2010年被评为国家级高新技术企业。2011年被中国塑料加工工业协会综合评审为2010年度行业排名第一位。

公司参与起草、修订了13项国家、行业标准，其中参与GB/T 21558—2008标准修订工作获而得了“中国轻工业联合会科学技术进步三等奖”。

公司近几年加大对新产品、新技术研究投入力度，目前公司职工近500人，安装施工员工200多人，技术人员50多人，拥有各类专利12项。为不断满足公司日益扩展的销售市场，将公司做大做强，保持在行业内的领先地位，公司在武进经济开发区一期征地100亩，自筹资金2.6亿元投资建设现代化的新工厂46000m^2，并分别从德国、意大利引进两条当今世界最先进的全自动连续生产线。

公司的发展得到了当地政府的大力支持及肯定，并获得了常州市武进区2011年度工业先进企业，2011年度成长型工业企业，2011年度创新投入先进企业等荣誉称号。

吉林中粮生化包装有限公司

吉林中粮生化包装有限公司创建于1995年末，厂址位于吉林省东丰县工业集中区，占地面积13万平方米，建筑面积3万平方米，现有员工550人。

公司主要产品有塑料编织袋、塑料桶、集装袋等塑料包装制品及阀口纸袋等纸包装制品。年产纸塑包装物10kt。企业于2004年通过ISO－9001质量管理体系认证；2007年8月，阀口纸袋产品获得两项国家专利权；2008年通过国家QS认证。公司成为东北地区规模较大的食品级包装物生产企业。

公司拥有雄厚的技术力量，生产设备先进，检测手段完备，是食品包装的骨干企业。

公司始终如一地贯彻“以人为本”的经营理念，秉承“诚信、团队、专业、创新”的中粮企业精神，坚持“奉献营养健康的食品，高品质的生活空间及生活服务，使客户、股东、员工价值最大化”的中粮使命，以实现双赢为目的，不断推陈出新，以上乘的品质、良好的信誉，为客户提供优质的服务。

上海永利带业股份有限公司

上海永利带业股份有限公司是一家集研发、生产、销售各种规格型号新型材料输送带于一体的专业公司。公司自1989年成立以来取得了许多荣誉和成绩：上海市高新技术企业、上海市科技小巨人(培育)企业、上海市著名商标、上海名牌产品。多项技术被上海市科委认定为上海市高新技术成果转化项目，其中高强度精密石材带被认定为国家重点新产品。2008 年与同济大学共同设立国内第一家“轻型输送带研发中心”。2009 年于东华大学共同设立“轻型输送带增强基材研发中心”。

目前，公司共申请国家专利近 70 项，其中授权的发明专利 11 项，产品技术经上海科学技术情报研究所查新检索，达到国际先进水平。

2009 年，永利在荷兰注册了永利欧洲公司，2010 年，在韩国设立了永利韩国，在土耳其和印度分别设定了代理商，专业销售永利产品，产品已出口世界各地。永利公司商标产品在全国市场的占有率分别为 15%。公司始终以完善的服务、创新的思维、卓越的管理，打造世界新材料轻型输送带的生产基地。

地址：上海市青浦区徐泾镇徐旺路 58 号
电话：0086 - 21 - 59884057
传真：0086 - 21 - 59884157
网址：www. yonglibelt. com
邮箱：info@ yonglibelt. com

中国联塑集团控股有限公司

中国联塑集团控股有限公司(简称：中国联塑，香港上市代号：2128)是中国领先的大型建材家居产业集团，产品及服务涵盖管道产品、卫浴产品、整体厨房、型材门窗、装饰板材、消防器材及卫生材料等领域。销售额突破 100 亿元人民币。

随着联塑全球化、国际化进程步伐的推进，中国联塑已拥有逾 30 家控股子公司，拥有超过 25 个生产基地，分布于全国 15 个省份及加拿大和美国(加利福利亚科罗纳)，形成了覆盖全国，辐射全球的生产基地和销售网络，能够及时、高效地为顾客提供产品和服务。

中国联塑建有国际领先，国内一流的研究院，拥有各类科研人员 1000 多名，设有博士后科研工作站、CNAS 国家认可实验室。目前，中国联塑拥有和正在申请的专利有近 1000 项。科研成果先后入选国家火炬计划项目、国家重点新产品、全国建设行业科技成果推广项目和政府绿色采购清单；先后被国家有关部门授予国家高新技术企业、国家认定企业技术中心、中国建设科技自主创新优势企业、知识产权优势企业、建设部产业化示范基地、广东省政府质量奖等荣誉称号和奖项。

现阶段，中国联塑拥有 10000 多种产品，是国内建材家居领域产品体系最为齐全的生产商之一。中国联塑的产品被广泛应用于家居装修、民用建筑、市政给水、排水、电力通信、燃气、消防及农业等领域。在 2008 年北京奥运会、2010 年广州亚运会及上海世博会的部分场馆建设中，联塑均被指定为产品供货商。

随着全球化、国际化战略发展目标的推进，中国联塑将秉着“为居者构筑轻松生活”的品牌信仰，以全新的姿态，致力于将中国联塑打造成泛家居领域，世界领先的大型建材家居产业集团，为客户提供更多高性价比的产品的服务，缔造舒适、高品质居家生活。

浙江明日控股集团股份有限公司

浙江明日控股集团股份有限公司为浙江省塑料行业协会会长、中国塑料加工工业协会副理事长单位，隶属于浙江省供销社，是浙江农资集团核心成员企业，前身浙江农资石化有限公司成立于 1998 年，公司注册地杭州滨江区，总股本 11600 万股，总资产逾 15 亿元，员工 500 余人，公司主营塑料原料、化工产品贸易和农用薄膜、包装材料、软包装制品生产业务，汇总经营收入超 100 亿元，进出口总额 1.5 亿美元，多年来年均增速达到 30% 水平，公司已发展成为中国最大的塑化分销服务商之一。

公司坚持以发展为主线，通过国内贸易与国际贸易相结合、现货业务与期货业务相结合、通用料与专用料相结合、商品经营与资本运作相结合，不断拓展业务领域和品种，成为了全国知名的塑化专业化公司。目前，公司塑化业务年销售量逾 1200kt，其中，聚烯烃业务 700kt，聚氯乙烯业务超 400kt，ABS、PS、EVA、茂金属、弹性体等业务量 50kt，甲醇、乙二醇、天胶等化工产品业务量近 100kt。目前，公司已成为中石化系统紧密合作伙伴，成为新疆天业浙江省、安徽省核心经销商，成为上海赛科、扬子 - 巴斯夫 LDPE、绍兴三圆 PP 最大分销商和核心客户，与福建联合、宁波禾元、海天石化、中海壳牌、山西榆社、中盐吉兰泰、陕西金泰、陕西北元等单位建立起了紧密合作关系；公司坚持国际化战略，连续多年与美国埃克森美孚化工建立起“浙江省战略合作伙伴”关系，与沙特阿美建立起福建省战略合作关系，并与博禄化工、美国道化学、住友化学、SABIC、美科联合、英利士、三井化学、三菱商事、卡塔尔石油、巴塞尔等单位建立起紧密合作关系，进口塑料原料 10 万余吨。

公司紧抓塑化分销网络建设，立足华东、面向全国，商品直销率在80%以上，已在浙江省各地市、上海、江苏、福建、安徽、江西、山东、广东、四川和宁波港、上海港、广州港、天津港等设立分销机构，在华东地区形成了畅通、高效的分销网络体系。公司还在新加坡、中国香港成立境外离岸公司，开展转口贸易、美金业务。

公司塑化工业，主营农用薄膜、包装材料、软包装制品的生产，拥有加工产能70kt、产值6亿元，是浙江包装工业50强企业，“星光”农(地)膜被授予国家免检产品，“新光”塑料薄膜被授予“浙江名牌产品”称号，被中塑协授予“促进农膜行业发展突出贡献奖”。

公司始终坚持“开拓、创新、诚信、共赢”的企业精神，树立起了良好的商业信誉和企业形象，公司被国家工商行政管理总局授予了全国“守合同重信用”单位，2008－2012年连续被全国工商业联合会授予“中国民营企业500强企业”，2005年以来连续被浙江省工商局授予“重合同守信用AAA级单位”称号，被浙江省人行、农行评为“信用等级AAA级企业”称号。

地址(Add)：中国杭州市滨江区泰安路199号浙江农资大厦

NO. 199 Taian Road Binjiang DistrictHangzhou China

电话(Tel)：0571－87661222

邮编(P. C)：310052

传真(Fax)：0571－87661333

网址：www. zjmr. cn

贵州森瑞管业有限公司

贵州森瑞管业有限公司成立于2003年9月，位于贵阳市国家高新技术产业开发区，占地面积123000余平方米，公司注册资金10000万元，总资产数亿元，是贵州省规模最大的专业从事新型塑料管材、管件研发、制造、销售的新型环保企业，并在武汉市东西湖区设有控股公司——武汉森瑞管业有限公司。

公司目前装备了50余条国际、国内先进的生产线，建立了完善的检测设备手段，贵州总部年生产量达50kt以上，武汉公司年产量30kt以上。主要产品有埋地用聚乙烯(PE)给水管、燃气用埋地聚乙烯(PE)管、煤矿用聚乙烯(PE)管材；埋地排水用HDPE双壁波纹管、PVC－U双壁波纹管、钢带增强聚乙烯(PE)螺旋波纹管；地下通信管道用管、埋地用PVC－C电力电缆护套管；建筑用PP－R上水管和PVC－U下水管、难燃型PVC电线槽、工业线槽、电工套管等，以及与管材相应管、配件系统，产品覆盖了国家标准或行业标准所列全部规格。

公司以“向社会提供环保、节能、安全、经济的塑料管道系统”为质量方针，坚持内抓质量管理，外抓市场开拓，以顾客为中心，不断提高产品质量和服务质量，满足顾客要求。公司先后通过ISO9001－2000质量管理体系认证，ISO10012计量检测体系认定，ISO14001环境管理体系认证，OHSAS18001职业健康安全管理体系认证和压力管道元件认证等。公司先后被评定为“国家高新技术企业”，“省级企业技术中心”，省级“守合同、重信用”单位，“贵州质量诚信5A级品牌企业”。并获得“贵州省‘五一’劳动奖状”单位，国家质量监督检验检疫总局授权的“聚乙烯(PE)管道焊工考试委员会”单位，中国质量诚信企业协会“副会长单位”，住房和城乡建设部科技发展促进中心《建设科技》“理事单位”等，公司所有产品均被建设部列为“全国建设行业科技成果推广项目”、“贵阳市名牌产品”和“贵州省名牌产品”。

河南佰利联化学股份有限公司

诚信永远，追求卓越。河南佰利联化学股份有限公司是一家极具革新精神的大型精细无机化工企业。中国化工企业500强，国家级高新技术企业，中国钛白行业最具发展潜力的上市公司(002601)。

佰利联化学，被越来越多的业界人士关注。金红石型钛白粉现产能200kt/a，近期目标300kt/a(氯化法100kt)，远期规划500kt/a。力争国内领先，世界一流。

创新和循环经济是公司的核心竞争力！实施“项目和项目带动”战略，依托人本、资金、科技优势，致力于做全球优秀的化学品生产商。始于客户需求，立于持续改进，终于客户满意，佰利联与您共发展。

地址：河南省焦作市中站区焦克路

邮编：454191

电话：0391－3126699

传真：0391－3126818

邮箱：sales@ billionschem. com　hnbllxsgs@ 126. com

网站：http：//www. billionschem. com

四川中装科技有限公司

四川中装科技有限公司是具有较强技术实力专

业同向双螺杆挤出成套设备制造商，公司的中心业务致力于同向平行双螺杆挤出设备的开发、设计、制造与技术服务，是中国塑料机械工业学会理事会会员单位。

四川中装科技有限公司是由一批国内最早制造和应用双螺杆挤出机的技术人员组建的技术型企业，在近三十年制造和应用平行同向双螺杆挤出机的过程中积累了大量宝贵经验，并通过自己的摸索和参考国外的先进技术，突破了挤出机传动技术的关键问题，形成了具有自主知识产权的核心传动技术，使中装科技的挤出机产品具有高扭矩、高效率、低能耗、高性价比、综合生产成本低等优点，其主要技术指标远远高于国内同业厂家的技术指标，自商业化生产以来一直保持着国内技术领先的地位，同时与国外一流的挤出装备制造厂保持着同步的技术水平。

中装科技公司在传动技术方面的优势，源于其对高效混炼设备有较多的经验总结和较深的系统性解读，并且能针对有故障的国外一线品牌挤出机给出系统性的解决方案，已经为沙伯基础塑料、彩艳集团、富士康集团、中蓝蓝星公司、出光等多家客户交出满意答卷，对德国 ZSK 系列、ZSE 系列、日本 TEM 系列、TX 系列等多个一线品牌的挤出机齿轮箱实施过恢复性能的手术，同时也可提供同机型高性能的螺杆元件耗材。

山东英科环保再生资源股份有限公司

山东英科环保再生资源股份有限公司是一家中外合资公司，位于淄博市临淄区齐鲁化学工业园清田路，共占地 158 亩，年产值约 5000 万美元。

英科环保专业生产高分子材料仿木线材及其相关的框类产品，如各种尺寸和花色的成品像框、画框、镜框等，主要用于家居装饰行业和终端家居用品消费者，产品 100% 出口海外。由于产品的主要特色在于利用国内废弃的 PS 白色泡沫包装材料，重新回收利用，运用公司特殊塑料动态成型加工技术加工将废旧的塑料加工成各种精美的墙面装饰产品，有“变废为宝”的作用，年可利用 50kt 废旧塑料，所以公司在创始之初，即获得了国家环保鼓励类项目。

塑料框材相对传统木框材料，更具有美观性、耐磨性、抗腐蚀性等特色，在表面处理工艺上更简洁，效果更精美，所以产品一经推出，即受到国内外客户的广泛欢迎；这种以塑代木，变废为宝的工艺，打破了木制框的生产传统，改变了原先繁复的生产工序，极大地提高了生产效率，降低了生产成本；同时，废旧塑料的处理是环保业关注的焦点，英科环保始终致力于开发废旧塑料产品市场，回收国际市场上各类废旧塑料，重新利用资源，将塑料产品加工成各类精美生活用品，为国家节省了大量的木材。2011 年，共生产约 120 万箱的塑料线材，避免了约 200 万颗树木被砍伐，为保护生态环境，实现循环经济，资源再利用做出了不小的贡献。我公司成立以来获得山东省资源综合利用企业；山东省循环经济十大示范工程；高新技术企业等荣誉。

英科环保经过多年的培训和累积，拥有一支敬业钻研的专业制造队伍，不断地开发出新产品以满足客户的需要，同时还拥有一支年轻高学历，务实求新的销售团队，不断地与客户保持良好地、积极地沟通。正是由于公司始终秉持精益求精的品质要求、务实创新的企业文化，才使得英科环保近几年在激烈的国际市场竞争中脱颖而出，成为目前国内规模大，质量佳，产品种类全，交货及时的高分子材料框类产品专业制造商。

上海邦中高分子材料有限公司

上海邦中高分子材料有限公司成立于 2004 年，主营高科技新材料的研发、生产和销售，并且致力于循环经济的探索，拥有 400 亩生产基地，包括上海邦中新材料有限公司、江苏邦中高分子材料有限公司、上海邦中投资有限公司等子公司。在上海市申报成立三个省级研发中心——上海市高分子粘接树脂研发中心、上海市导电复合材料研发中心、上海市循环经济研发中心，为公司的持续发展提供了有力的技术支持。以“掌握核心技术，每天进步 1%”为宗旨的邦中公司将成为中国最具成长价值的新材料高新技术企业之一。

公司拥有粘接功能树脂、阻燃树脂、导电树脂、碳纤维及其复合材料等四大系列自主知识产权产品，年生产能力超过 100kt。广泛应用于汽车、家电、建材、电子、电工电器、航空航天、军工、包装等多种行业。

上海邦中建立了以企业技术研发中心为主体，以国家认可实验室、ULCTDP 认可实验室和上海市高分子粘接树脂研发中心、上海市导电复合材料研发中心、上海市循环经济研发中心为依托，以上海交通大学、华东理工大学、复旦大学等高校为支撑的先进的研发平台。

公司视质量为企业的生命，先后通过了 ISO9001 质量管理体系认证、ISO14000 环境管理体系认证、TS16949 汽车产品质量管理体系认证。

服务热线：021－67891573 57893826；67891089 67891657

公司网址：http：//www.banzan.com

公司地址：上海市松江区新浜工业园新工路 215 号

山东金达双鹏集团有限公司

山东金达双鹏集团有限公司，位于山东半岛中部，东邻美丽的海滨城市—青岛，西于世界风筝之都—潍坊毗邻，南距济青高速高密出口 2km，交通条件便利。

山东金达双鹏集团有限公司是中国建筑工程金属结构协会、中国塑料加工工业协会、山东建设机械协会会员单位。公司拥有先进的混料系统（均化恒温系统，真空上料系统）、高速双螺杆挤出机 60 条。主要产品有：60 平开系列、65 三密封平开系列、80、88 推拉系列、高耐候双色共挤、浮雕纹彩、白色高耐候、塑胶共挤、PVC 护栏、百叶窗等系列产品。现已形成年产塑料异型材 30000t 的规模。公司依靠国际化先进的生产设备、先进的科学生产技术和 ISO9001 国际质量管理体系，产品经国家化学建筑材料检测中心测试，个项性能指标均达到和超过国家规定的标准，是中国塑料加工工业协会定点生产企业。公司先后获得省级先进单位、农业银行 AAA 级信用企业、山东省建材行业十强企业、塑料异型材八强企业、山东省建设机械行业名牌产品。2006 年金达双鹏塑料异型材被评为“山东名牌”，“双鹏”商标被评为山东著名商标，2011 年被认定为“中国驰名商标”。

德科摩橡塑科技（东莞）有限公司

德科摩橡塑科技（东莞）有限公司隶属于香港上市公司大同机械企业有限公司下属企业，2003 年由德科摩国际和德国 DEKUMA GmbH 在东莞合作组建亚洲研发制造中心，专注于挤出生产线的设计、生产、销售与售后服务，为顾客提供整套挤出技术及橡胶技术交钥匙方案。

产品源于德国先进的设计理念，根植于大同集团强大的机械加工能力，秉承欧洲机器的特性：高精度、功能完善、稳定可靠、耐用。拥有德国优秀的设计师队伍，汇同国内顶级设计工程师形成强大的技术实力。

德科摩公司是行业首家国际级高新技术企业，国家塑料管道协会会员，与中国化工大学、华南理工大学、东莞理工学院等国内外众多知名企业长期合作。

公司采用先进的加工和检测设备，如柔性制造系统、加工中心、数控车床（70 台）、数控钣金设备（6 台）、光学对刀仪、三坐标测量机、超声波探伤仪等。全面推行欧洲质量管理和质量保证体系，对每一道生产工序实行定人、定岗、定职三级检验法，每道工序和每个产品都进行严格的科学测试；完善的质量保证体系，技术精良的制造队伍以确保产品的加工和装配精度，从而保证产品的性能和可靠性。

德科摩优势项目：

ϕ16mm～ϕ2000mm PE/PPR/PERT 单/多层共挤高速挤出生产线

25∶1/33∶1/36∶1 高挤出量·低能耗·高性能单螺杆挤出机

PPR/PERT 尼龙 3 层/5 层管材高速挤出生产线

全系列平行异向双螺杆挤出机（PVC 专用）

ϕ16mm～ϕ2000mm 管材高速无屑切割机

100 米/分钟 PE/PP 超高速管材挤出生产线

PE/PPR/PERT 双管高速挤出生产线

地址：广东省东莞市东城区周屋工业区银珠路

PC：523118

Tel：+86－769－22667200

Fax：+86－769－22667227

Website：http：//www.dekuma.com

E－mail：info@dekuma.com

中塑集团

中塑集团（全称“成都中塑投资集团有限公司”）主要经营业务涉及投资、地产、市场运营等，是集涉塑全产业链、居家采购、休闲娱乐等业务于一体的多功能、集约化、网络化、专业化的产城商贸综合体开发商、运营商和管理商。

公司开发建设的“中塑·成都国际贸易中心”，着力打造“中国西部塑料化工产业商贸总部基地”。总规划占地 1100 亩，总建筑面积 300 万平方米，总投资约 60 亿元人民币。项目分两期开发建设，一期规划用地 560 亩，配套建设 500 亩专属仓储物流基地。

中塑·成都国际贸易中心升级专业市场理念、领跑第五代专业市场。以成都北部发达交通网络为依托，以仓储物流为基础，以信息化为手段，以批量采购、集中供应、电子商务、拍卖交易等为主要经营方式，构建国际产业综合服务平台，做大“塑料化工”，整合涉塑家居、灯饰产业，打造塑料产业商贸集群，搭建行业B2B电子商务平台，发布塑料价格指数，整合全球塑料相关产业商家，举办国际塑料、化工，橡胶产业商品博览会、交流，促进线下与线上交易的互动，建设塑料交易所和塑料产业研究院，提供金融担保和小额信贷服务，扶持或者自主承担重大重点科技项目和企业委托开发项目，提供检验测试、咨询等服务，开展行业政策法规，行业信息、行业技术、产品报价等全方位的配套交流服务。

中塑集团以“精诚至心，精准致胜”之道，坚持诚信、创新、务实的工作作风，实现并继续创造着公司规模和品牌的跨越式发展。中塑集团在“产城一体”和“双化互动”的背景下，首创了“产业商贸综合体”概念，为成都多产业商贸和“产城一体”的发展树立了参考榜样。“中塑·成都国际贸易中心”，不仅是中塑集团旗下一个投资60亿的超大型、省级重点项目，也是中塑集团整合产城资源，驱动产业财富的绝佳样板。

中塑·成都国际贸易中心项目前开发建设的是一组团中国塑料城和二组团中塑博美居家MALL。

一组团中国塑料城总建筑面积约11万平方米，是新都区政府为实现国家产业转移，引进东部产业和龙头企业而实施的重大产业服务型项目。由中塑集团建设、运营和管理，已于2011年11月18日正式投入运营，着力于促进涉塑及化工全产业链发展，打造“西部涉塑第一镇”，并于2012年10月18日授牌为“西部塑料化工产业商贸总部基地”。

中塑集团首创“中塑博美模式”，以“居家与世界同步”的理念打造中塑·成都国际贸易中心二组团中塑博美居家MALL。中塑博美居家MALL建筑面积约33万平方米，定位为以居家为中心，集购物与生活为一体的时尚居家生活聚集地，整合国内一线居家品牌，同时规划有诸多中高端餐饮、娱乐业态，打造一个与世界同步的，集休闲娱乐、购物、生活于一体的时尚居家生活中心。中塑博美居家MALL自2012年6月28日开盘以来，取得了良好的销售业绩，名列成都商业地产销售排行榜榜首。

在未来的发展中，中塑集团仍将全力以赴，构建具有行业影响力的多元企业集团：商业地产开发将以成都为起点，布局西南，落子全国，甚至走出国门，建立真正意义上的国际贸易平台；塑料全产业链的打造仍是集团重要工作，将陆续完善涉塑仓储、电子商务、产业园区、研究机构等的开发、建设和组建；中塑博美居家MALL将作为集团新兴板块进行重点发展，力争成为西南地区最具影响力的中高端家居连锁品牌。

深圳市通产丽星股份有限公司

深圳市通产丽星股份有限公司是国有控股专业从事文化创意、新材料科技、循环经济的A股上市公司，国家级高新技术企业。公司可提供产品及服务包括创意设计、工艺装备及精密模具设计制造、碳纳米材料、高分子材料改性及环保材料、高端化妆品及食品包装解决方案和产品、汽车轻量化解决方案和产品、新能源包装材料、RFID信息化智能包装、包装废弃物循环利用等。

公司成立于1984年，注册资本25806.8956万元，总部位于深圳市龙岗区，在深圳、广州、上海、苏州等地设立了大型生产基地；在欧洲、美国设立了海外仓储基地；在深圳、广州设立了主要研发基地。公司拥有国家“863”表面技术研究中心、国家认定企业技术中心。是中国包装联合会副会长单位、中国塑料加工协会副理事长单位、全国印刷电子产业技术创新联盟副理事长单位、中国标准化协会常务理事单位、深圳市新材料行业协会会长单位、国际ISO/TC122/SC4工作组(WG1包装和包装废弃物ISO标准使用要求)成员单位。

地址：深圳市龙岗区坂田五和南路49号

电话：0755－28482022

网址：www. beautystar. cn

苯领高分子

苯领是全球领先的苯乙烯系列产品供应商，在不同的行业和区域拥有超过80年的经验。苯领为各种行业提供苯乙烯系列产品，这些行业包括汽车、电气与电子、建筑与建材、家用电器、玩具与休闲、包装和医疗保健与诊断。

苯领只专注于苯乙烯系列产品领域，提供了业内最完善的普通和特种苯乙烯产品组合。这包括：

- 苯乙烯单体(SM)

- 聚苯乙烯(PS)
- 丙烯腈-丁二烯-苯乙烯共聚物(ABS)
- 苯乙烯-丁二烯嵌段共聚物(SBC)
- 其他苯乙烯共聚物(SAN、AMSAN、ASA、MABS)
- 共聚共混物(ABS/PA、ASA/PA、ASA/PC)

苯领致力于为客户提供最佳解决方案。我们了解并始终关注客户需求。

凭借士气高昂的团队、业内领先的生产基地以及无人能及的研发实力，苯领将准确、高效地满足客户的独特需求。

从汽车、建筑建材到电子、医疗保健、包装和休闲，苯领的客户几乎遍及所有行业。在每一个领域，苯领都致力于帮助客户充分利用全球市场趋势带来的机遇。

网址： www. styrolution. com

广东伊之密精密机械股份有限公司

广东伊之密精密机械股份有限公司是专注于“模压成型”专用机械设备的设计、研发、生产，销售及服务的高新技术企业。始创于2002年，位于中国著名的工业之都——顺德(国家级高新技术产业区)，占地面积达80000m^2。以高精度注射成型机、高性能铝镁合金压铸机、高品质橡胶机为主导产品。

成立至今，伊之密凭借雄厚的资金与规模实力支持，结合业界优秀的研发、设计、制造、服务、营销团队，秉持“让中国装备技术与世界同步，并为全球客户创造更佳的投资回报及客户体验”的企业宗旨，致力成为一家经营好、管理好、文化好，让员工引以为傲，为社会仰慕及尊敬的企业。

伊之密拥有省级企业技术中心、工程中心并设立了博士后科研工作站，目前已成为中国最具竞争力和发展潜力的大型装备综合服务商、中国最具规模的装备制造企业之一、国家级高新技术企业及国家级火炬计划项目实施企业单位。2009年以来，公司持续快速增长，2009~2011年营业收入年复合增长率超过60%。

在国内，伊之密除顺德容桂生产基地外，还建有顺德五沙、苏州吴江两大生产基地，全面投产以后，伊之密每年产能将翻倍，成为业内最大厂商之一。

在全球，伊之密建有多个海外办事处和服务点，业务覆盖数十个国家和地区。2011年3月，伊之密成功收购了美国百年企业HPM公司的全部知识产权，迈出了伊之密全球化的重要一步。

另外，伊之密计划三年内在印度、巴西、俄罗斯三个国家之一建立海外生产基地，计划2014年底投入使用，通过更多的海外生产基地为全球客户提供更好的产品和服务。

广东伊之密精密机械股份有限公司是以“模压成型”为主题的机械装备制造商，致力于让中国装备技术与世界同步，并为全球客户创造更佳的投资回报及客户体验。公司以高精度注射成型机、高性能铝镁合金压铸机、高品质橡胶机为主导产品。

伊之密始创于2002年，总部位于顺德国家级高新技术产业区，占地面积达80000m^2，还建有顺德五沙、苏州吴江两大生产基地。在全球，目前伊之密建有30多个海外办事处和服务点，业务覆盖达近50个国家和地区。2011年3月，伊之密成功收购了美国百年企业HPM公司的全部知识产权，这将是伊之密迈向全球化的重要里程碑。

地址： 中国广东省佛山市顺德高新区(容桂)科苑三路22号
电话(TEL)： +86-757-2926 2000
传真(FAX)： +86-757-2926 5164
E-mail： yzm@ yizumi-group. com
网址： www. yizumi-group. com

广州海狮软件科技有限公司

广州海狮软件科技有限公司是一家专业致力于工业控制系统研发、生产、销售为一体的高新技术企业。公司以高科技项目为主体，以高素质人才为支柱。专业领域涉及硬件EDA开发、底层DSP开发；VC软件开发、电气控制系统设计等。几年来，海狮公司全体员工不断努力、更新、完善，使产品(米重控制系统，超声波在线测厚测偏系统……)达到国际先进水平。为广大客户降低制造成本、提高生产质量、增加公司收益。深受广大客户的认可及赞誉。

电话： 020-66692618/23374475
传真： 020-32028792

上海白蝶管业科技股份有限公司

上海白蝶管业科技股份有限公司是一家从事高

科技、高性能、环保型的新型管材、管件的生产和销售的股份制企业。1997年底在国内率先开发生产了“给水用三型聚丙烯(PP-R)管道”产品，广泛应用于工业及民用冷热水给水系统、纯净饮用水系统、采暖及中央空调等系统，是传统金属管道的理想替代产品。

公司建立了三大生产基地，拥有德国进口克劳斯玛菲、奥地利辛辛那提、巴顿菲尔等全自动在线检测管材挤出生产线和众多的注塑设备，并配备有多台进口管件焊制设备及检测试验设备，可生产口径自16~450mm多种压力等级的PP-R管、PE管、PE-RT管、PP-R稳态复合管、3S聚丙烯静音排水管、PVC-U排水管、PVC-U电工套管、β.PP-R管材和相配套的管配件，产品广泛应用于市政供水、饮用水、建筑给排水、化工、医疗、采暖等领域，进一步扩大了白蝶产品的应用领域和市场占有率。

公司从1993年国家对塑料管道产品进行监督抽查开始，连续多年通过了国家和上海市地方的产品质量监督抽查，产品质量稳定、可靠，在用户中有很高的信任度。白蝶管已成为市场首选品牌之一。

公司作为中国塑协塑料管道专业委员会副理事长单位，全国塑料制品标准化技术委员会(TC48/SC3)委员单位，在把产品推向市场的同时，注重了配套的应用技术和相关产品的研究开发，先后完成了“PP-R国家标准”的制订，编制了“PP-R管道设计、施工、验收规范”、“PP-R空调管施工规程”、“PP-R施工图集”等。

公司从投产塑料管道开始就把产品质量放在生产经营工作的首位，从1993年开始，已连续多年通过了国家和上海地方的产品质量监督抽查，产品质量稳定、可靠，并以全国的营销网络为基础建立了售后服务体系，开设了800-820-0166的全国服务热线，以保证跟广大用户的直接联系，在用户中有很高的信任度。先后获得上海市著名商标、上海名牌产品称号。

汕头市东田转印有限公司

汕头市东田转印有限公司是广东省高新技术企业，是国内最早从事热转移印刷技术和产品的研究、开发、生产和销售并提供相关技术服务的大型专业公司，已通过ISO9001质量管理体系认证和ISO14001环保管理体系认证。公司一直秉承“诚信经营、质量第一、真诚服务”的宗旨，连续八年评为“守合同重信用”单位。

公司目前的主要产品有各式热转印膜，适用于塑料、玻璃、金属、木材等制品表面的烫印装饰，提高制品的档次和价值。产品注册商标为“東田DONGTIAN”。

公司技术力量雄厚，生产设备先进，工艺成熟配套，检测手段完善，产品质量稳定，服务及时优质，拥有良好信誉，产品曾获广东省和汕头市科技进步奖，热转印膜被中国包装联合会评为“中国包装名牌产品”。“東田DONGTIAN”商标评为“广东省著名商标”。目前采用本公司转印膜装饰的产品已遍及国内外各地。

江门市辉隆塑料机械有限公司

江门市辉隆塑料机械有限公司成立于1996年，是一家专业研制高档挤出复合生产设备的国家级高新技术企业，是中国塑料机械研究权威华南理工大学博士后科研流动站博士后科研基地，是中国包装联合会理事单位和广东省包装技术协会常务理事单位。

十多年来，辉隆公司通过与华南理工大学等高校的技术交流与合作，组建了一支博士、博士后、教授、高级工程师领衔的专业技术研发队伍，投入了大量的研发资金，研制高效、精密、节能、环保的挤出复合生产线，承担国家省市区科技研发项目6项，拥有国际首创的“混沌混炼型低能耗挤出机”等20项发明和创新专利技术。公司产品广泛应用于生产纸塑铝砖包、枕包(牛奶、凉茶、饮料)等快速食品饮料无菌包装材料。2007年8月，由辉隆公司和华南理工大学共同合作的“基于混沌混炼的高性能高分子包装材料成型关键装备及技术研发”项目通过了广东省科技成果鉴定，并获得国家教育部“2007年度科学技术进步奖二等奖”，该项目“混沌混炼型低能耗挤出机”名义比功率仅为国标的一半，节能显著，属国际首创，整体技术及产品达到国际先进水平。

至2012年12月止，辉隆公司挤出复合机全球销量超过450台/套，年生产能力可达50台/套。著名企业如黄山永新、奇妙包装、青岛人印、永大集团、皇冠胶粘、印度U-FLEX及全球包装领袖加铝包装都在使用多条辉隆的挤出复合生产线。辉隆公司所研制的国际最高端共挤挤出复合机，畅销十多个国家和地区，是世界高端挤出复合机的主要制造商之一。

地址：广东省江门市高新技术开发区德发路12号

电话：0750－3866989　3866988
传真：0750－3866987
E－mail：hl@ huilongpm. com

成都市岷江自来水厂双流聚乙烯管材生产车间

成都市岷江自来水厂是一家多产业结合的大型集中式供水企业，供水区域覆盖全县24个乡镇，日最大供水量达20余万吨。其下属企业成都市岷江自来水厂双流聚乙烯管材生产车间是专业从事聚乙烯(PE)给水、燃气管材、管件的生产、销售和管材焊接技术指导服务的国有企业，其生产的产品统一注册商标为“清润”。

车间荣获了国家质量监督检验检疫总局颁发的《特种设备制造许可证》—A级证书、国家水利部灌排中心、四川省建设厅、四川省农田水利局、中国建筑金属结构协会给水排水设备分会颁发的产品推荐证书、成都市工商行政管理局颁发的《成都市著名商标》证书。目前已通过ISO9001：2000质量管理体系和ISO14001：2004环境管理体系认证。75%以上的车间员工拥有大专以上学历，并聘请四川大学高分子材料系教授吴智华为技术顾问，以四川大学高分子材料系毕业生为技术骨干力量组建了技术部以来，依靠完善的管理，先进的科技，短短几年间取得了飞速的发展。2008年7月30日被成都市委、成都市人民政府评为“抗震救灾过渡安置房建设先进单位”。

清润管材历来坚持以质量为中心，以管理求效益，依靠科技进步求发展的经营方针，建立不断发展具有“清润”特色的技术创新体系、生产管理体系、市场供需体系和服务体系，以“提高质量，保护环境，持续改善，永续经营”为基本理念。

“清润”牌给水管和燃气管是车间两大环保节能型产品，符合产业发展政策具有不生锈、质量轻、强度高、韧性好、耐腐蚀、施工维护方便、使用寿命长等优点。清润管材对产品的高要求，对销售人员严格的技术培训，对售后服务的不断完善，成就了清润，其产品得到了广大客户的认可，目前，清润管材已在四川、云南、甘肃、贵州、湖南、西藏、宁夏等省、市、自治区建立了营销服务网络。

巴斯夫

巴斯夫是全球领先的化工公司：The Chemical Company。公司的产品涵盖化学品、塑料、特性产品、作物保护产品以及石油与天然气。

公司将经济上的成功、社会责任和环境保护相结合。通过科学与创新，我们帮助各行各业的客户满足当前及未来社会的需求。

产品和系统解决方案为保护资源、保障营养以及提高生活质量做出贡献。

企业宗旨概括了这样的贡献：“创造化学新作用——追求可持续发展的未来”。

若想获得更多关于巴斯夫的信息，请访问：www. basf. com。

（王浩　郭齐　刘英俊）

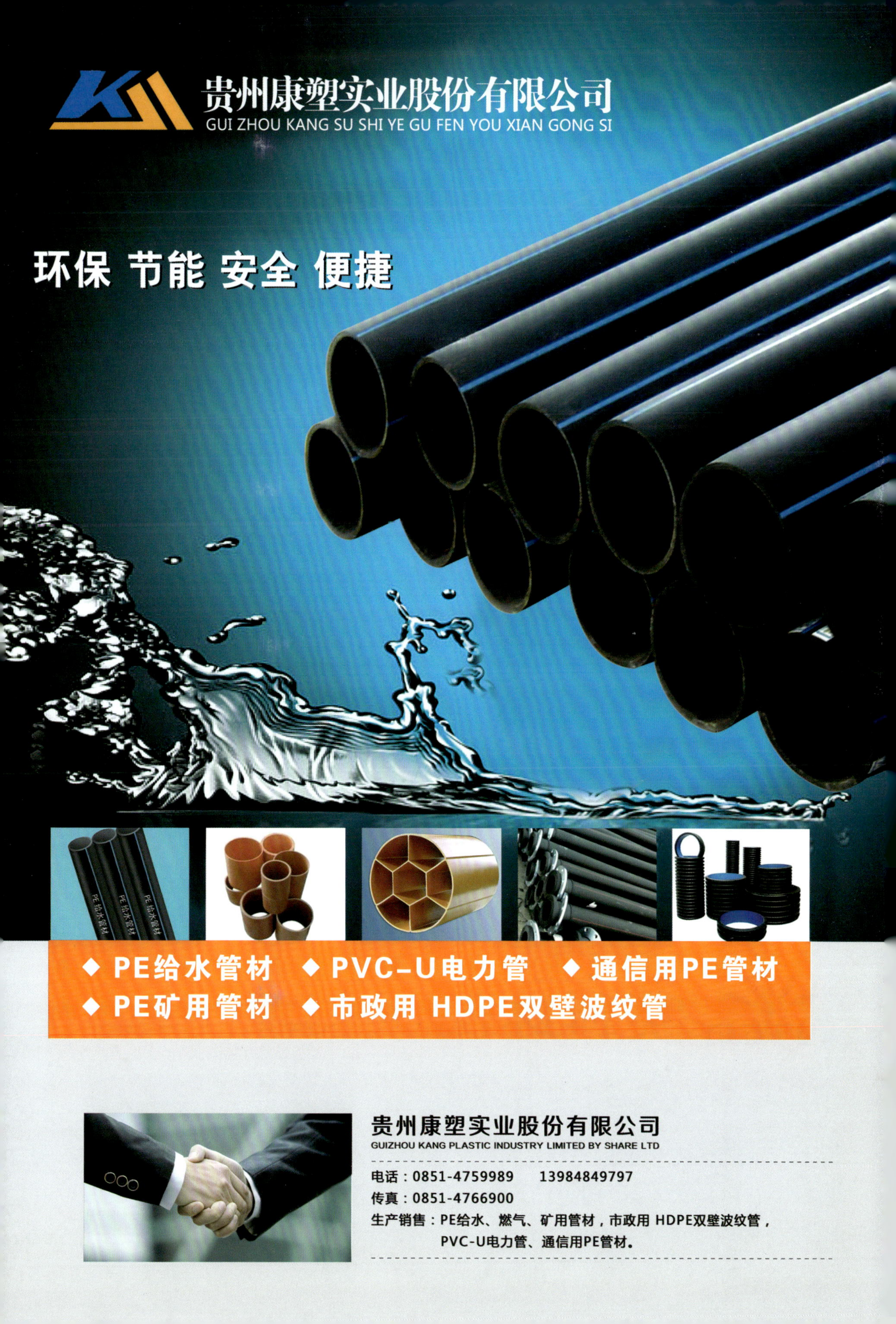

丽水市南城区控制性详细规划

公共设施用地规划总则

丽水经济开发区为省开发区，规划面积近50平方公里，金丽温高速公路贯穿而过，距离温州 108 公里。其中东北片区（富岭组团）约 10 平方千米，西南片区（七百秧工业组团）面积约 25 平方千米；14.4 平方公里的水阁工业区已基本建成，主要产业有通专用设备制造业、金属制品制造业、汽车配件制造业、生物医药制造业等。

发展规划

充分利用目前中国经济发展所处的重要战略机遇期，抓住发展的有利时机和山区用地优势，以担当丽水经济增长中心为目标，从扩大产业规模和提升产业高度两个方面同时入手，进一步加快南城的发展步伐。

利用大型区域性基础设施，抓住国际产业和区域产业转移的时机，引导企业落户开发区，促进南城健康发展。

转变政府管理方式、管制体制，优化南城软环境，同时改善基础设施等硬环境，提高对周边城市的产业吸引力和辐射力。

提高生态环境保护意识，促进南城的可持续发展。

结合山地地形条件，最大可能减少工程投资。

适应丽水市城市总体发展的需要，引导第二产业的有序发展，集聚丽水市内外企业，吸引区域产业转移，形成高标准、高起点、具有一定高新技术含量的工业园区，促进丽水第二产业上一个新的台阶，打造丽水特色制造业基地。

功能定位为浙西南地区工业发展的重要集聚中心，工贸业综合发展与人居环境优越的丽水城市新区。

总体布局

规划形成“一心、二带、二片”的结构与总体布局形式。其中“一心”：指城市南部地区中心，位于水阁东侧南北向干路和金丽温高速公路之间，七百秧组团（工业区东扩区块）北部，配置有行政、办公、文化、娱乐、商务等服务与管理设施；“二带”为丽龙高速公路与金丽温高速公路沿线形成的防护景观林带；“二片”指以中一路七百秧组团（工业区东扩区块）及金丽温高速公路为界形成的南、北各一个功能片，其中北侧功能片以富岭组团为主，为居住片；南侧为以七百秧组团（工业区东扩区块）为主，形成工业片。其中七百秧水库公园以现状七百秧水库为基础，保留主要水体，并加以改造。仓储区位于交通枢纽东北角，功能独立，结合高速公路接口可作为物流区。

规划区居住人口 17.0 万人，就业人口 12.3 万人。

规划用地总面积 3528.05 万平方米，其中居住用地 619.07 万平方米，公共设施用地 141.34 万平方米，道路广场用地 411.04 万平方米，工业用地 1220.57 万平方米，物流用地 54.30 万平方米，市政设施用地 58.25 万平方米，绿化用地 794.04 万平方米（含保留山体及边坡绿化用地），水域和其他用地 92.59 万平方米。

本规划包括：公共设施用地规划、居住用地规划、工业仓储用地规划、道路交通及相关设施规划、绿地系统规划、景观规划、市政基础设施规划、道路平面定位与竖向规划、水系及七百秧水库保护、改造规划、环境保护规划、土地使用和建筑规划等。

丽水生态产业集聚区（经济开发区）

地　　址：丽水市水阁工业区绿谷大道238号　邮政编码：323000

招商电话：0578-2990299　0578-2990099

网　　址：http://kfq.lishui.gov.cn/

公司简介

浙江华泰塑胶股份有限公司

Zhejiang Huatai plastic Limited by Share Ltd

浙江华泰塑胶股份有限公司创建于1998年，注册资本3270万元。是一家集科研、生产、销售为一体的塑料压延薄膜生产基地龙头企业。公司具有先进的生产装备，拥有3条台湾引进的压延生产线、一条日本引进的压延生产线及干式复合生产线两条，涂布机两条，分切机5台。公司拥有一流的生产工艺和完善的检测手段，通过ISO9001、ISO14001质量/环境管理体系认证。公司年产3万吨以上PVC薄膜，几百个品种的中高档系列产品满足不同客户的需求，产品辐射国内各省市，远销东南亚、中东欧、非洲等地区。公司连续多年名列中国塑胶百强，国家重合同守信用企业，中国质量信用AAA企业，浙江高新技术企业，浙江省优秀民营企业。2013年，“浙塑”牌商标被浙江省工商行政管理局认定为省著名商标。

公司拥有雄厚的技术实力，建有省塑料行业研发中心一个、拥有各种专利10多余个，省科技新产品5项，1项填补了国内空白，曾参与高光亮度广告膜PVC----PET复合膜，三维彩虹膜等多种产品标准的制定，并与中科技院长春应化所，浙江大学、武汉工程大学等大院名校合作，不断研发新产品，满足日新月异的市场需求。

公司坚持“以人为本、科技创新、科学管理、精益求精、诚实守信、客户至上”的理念，秉持“求实、求变、求高、求强”的企业文化理念，致力于塑料工业的科学创新、协调、稳定，可持续发展的目标前进。

产品堆放区

车间环境

地板膜

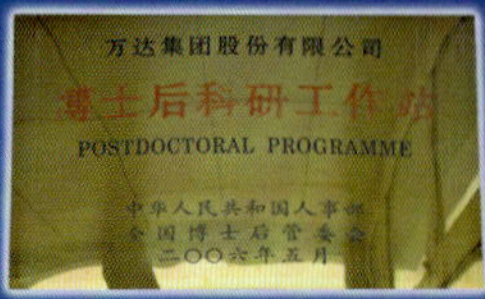

台亚
TAIYA
中国驰名商标

上海永利带业股份有限公司

上海永利带业股份有限公司创建于2002年，坐落于上海市，办公地位于上海市虹桥枢纽附近的青浦区徐泾镇徐旺路58号，占地30亩。公司是一家以研发、生产制造、销售各种规格型号轻型输送带产品的专业公司，也是目前国内专业性、配套性最强的新材料类轻型输送带研发生产高科技企业。系国内具备替代进口轻型输送带的民营企业，当前综合实力在行业内排名前列2009年初完成公司股份制改造。

公司自成立以来取得了许多荣誉和成绩：上海市文明单位、上海市高新技术企业、上海市科技小巨人（培育）企业、上海市著名商标、上海名牌产品、上海市模范职工之家。多项技术被上海市科委认定为上海市高新技术成果转化项目，其中高粘结强度多功能PVC-TPE输送带材被上海市科委认定为上海市火炬计划项目，高摩擦PVC-TPE花色输送带被认定为上海市重点新产品，高强度精密石材带被认定为国家重点新产品。2008年与同济大学共同设立“轻型输送带研发中心”。2009年于东华大学共同设立“轻型输送带增强基材研发中心”。目前，公司共申请国家专利近70项，其中授权的发明专利11项，产品技术经上海科学技术情报研究所查新检索，达到国际先进水平。

图案（永利皮带）

被推荐为 二○一二年度

上海名牌

公司产品被广泛地应用在各种行业，国内市场占有率达到30%。公司在天津、沈阳等地设有8个办事处，拥有接头设备及输送带仓库。 2009年，永利在荷兰注册了永利欧洲公司，2010年，在韩国设立了永利韩国，在土耳其和印度分别设定了代理商，专业销售永利产品，产品已出口世界各地。公司始终以完善的服务、创新的思维、卓越的管理，打造世界新材料轻型输送带的生产基地。

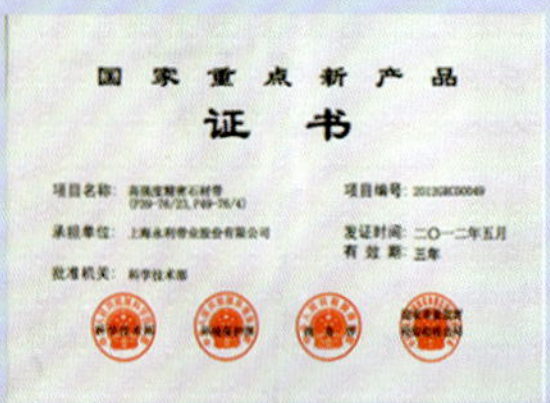
国家重点新产品
证书

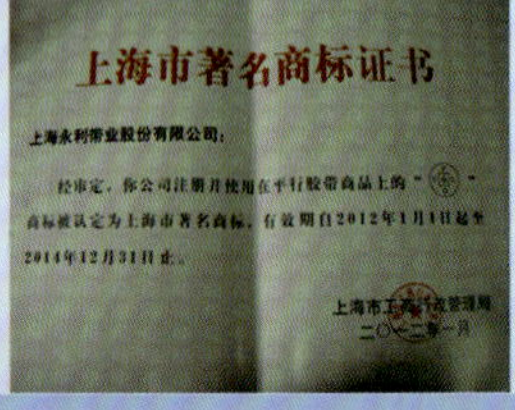
上海市著名商标证书

上海永利带业股份有限公司：

高新技术企业
证书

金诺尔塑胶

青州市金诺尔塑胶有限公司位于山东半岛中部，东邻风筝都潍坊，西接工业重镇淄博，南依水果之乡临沂，北傍石化基地东营。青州古九州之一，交通便利，人杰地灵。青州市有着五千年的悠久历史和灿烂文化，是古代“东夷文化”的发祥地。自西汉以来为历史名域重镇，公司坐落于青州市经济开发区卞万工业园。

青州市金诺尔塑胶有限公司成立于2003年8月，法人代表赵庆太，注册资金228万元，占地面积15600平方米，办公楼面积1200平方米，车间5600平方米，现有职工80人，其中技术人员10名，占职工总人数的20%。

公司现有三层共挤CPP流延线3条，设备采用全程微机控制，自动化程度高，居国内领先水平，年设计能力10000吨，生产厚度为20-100um,宽250-3600mm的流延膜，年产值过亿元。产品广泛应用于食品、医药包装、制袋及镀铝行业，产品畅销全国各地。

公司自2003年投产以来，以优越的环境、先进的设备、过硬的技术生产一流的产品，得到了客户的认可和赞同。公司本着质量第一，信誉至上的原则，与新老客户携手共进，共创辉煌。

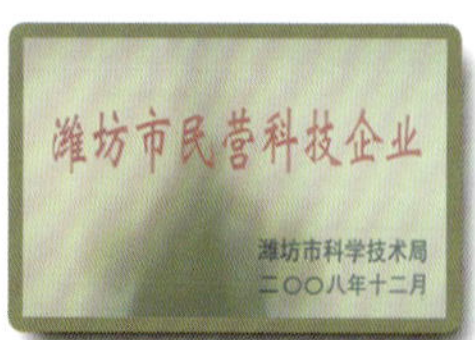

青州市金诺尔塑胶有限公司

地址：青州经济开发区卞万工业园内
电话：0536-3292993
传真：0536-3298192
网址：www.jnesj.com
邮编：262500

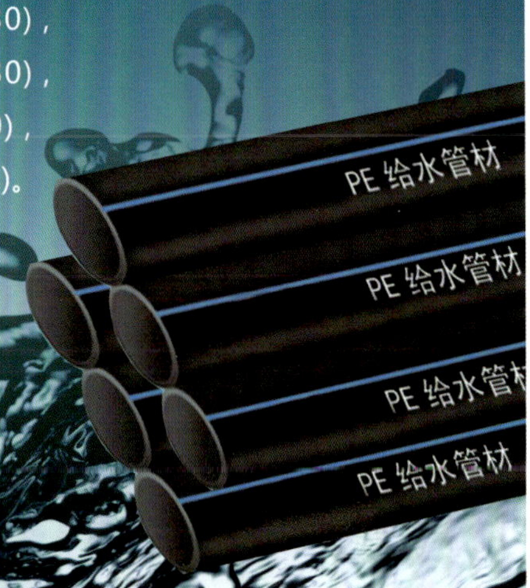

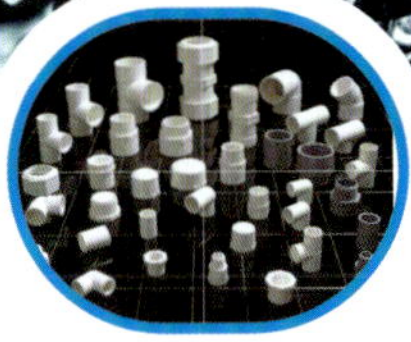

清润®
QINGRUN
成都岷江水厂
Chengdu Minjiang Waterworks
双流聚乙烯管材生产车间

四川省著名商标

清润管材50年不变

通过 ISO9001：2008 ISO14001：2004 国际质量环境管理体系认证

成都岷江水厂是一家多产业结合的大型集中式供水企业，供水区域覆盖全县24个乡镇，日最大供水量达20余万吨。其下属企业成都市岷江自来水厂双流聚乙烯管材生产车间是专业从事聚乙烯（PE）给水、燃气管材、管件的生产、销售和管材焊接技术指导服务的国有企业，其生产的产品统一注册商标为“清润”。

清润管业拥有PE管材生产线8条，具备dn20～630mm型号管材生产能力，管件生产设备10台，焊接设备200余台，差热分析仪、熔体流动速率仪、碳黑含量测试仪、电子拉力试验机、爆破耐压试验机等各性能检测设备20余台，具备从原材料进厂到dn20～630mm型号管材出厂检测能力，年最大产量17000吨，现固定资产达3000余万元。

清润管业聘请四川大学高分子材料系教授吴智华为技术顾问，以四川大学高分子材料系优秀人才为技术骨干力量。通过ISO9001：2008和ISO14001：2004国际质量环境管理体系认证，取得《涉及饮用水卫生安全产品卫生许可批件》、《特种设备制造许可证》A级、四川建设领域科技成果或应用技术备案等证书，荣获“四川省著名商标”、“成都市著名商标”、成都市AA级守合同重信用企业称号，入选《全国农村饮水安全工程材料设备产品信息年报》、《成都市地方产品配套目录》，信用等级达到AA级。因抗震救灾表现突出，2008年7月30日上级单位成都市岷江自来水厂被成都市委、成都市人民政府评为抗震救灾过渡安置房建设先进单位。2009年至2010年，连续二年荣获双流县“纳税攀登奖”。2010年与四川大学合作成立高分子科学与工程学院科研、人才培养、实习基地。清润管业还是中国塑料加工工业协会塑料管道专业委员会理事和中国工业防腐蚀技术协会、四川燃气协会、四川省村镇供水协会、重庆市燃气行业协会会员。

清润管业在四川、云南、甘肃、贵州、湖南、西藏、宁夏、重庆等省、市、自治区建立了营销服务网络。质量与信誉是清润管业永恒的主题。

地址：四川省成都市双流县东升镇西安路三段25号
厂址：四川省成都市双流县金桥镇金马村 邮编：610200
电话：028-67085966(销售部) 028-67085981(技术部) 传真：028-67085985

南通华盛新材料股份有限公司

NANTONG HUASHENG PLASTIC PRODUCTS CO.,LTD

大厅

车间

中转区

仓库

南通华盛新材料股份有限公司，地处长江三角洲沿海地区中部，江苏省南通市通州区，厂区占地面积10万平方米，主要从事聚乙烯薄膜製品和生物降解膜的技术研发、生产和销售。主要产品有各类购物袋、食品袋、垃圾袋、服装袋、多层共挤膜、工业包装膜、抗菌抗静电膜、生物降解膜及制品等。年产量超过4万吨，是国内同行业大型的企业之一。华盛拥有雄厚的技术实力与国内多所高校及研究所建立合作关系，聚集了一批业内精英，使公司稳步发展。在生产上，通过对工艺和品质的严格控制，使产品品质可靠，赢得了国内外客户的信赖。在研发上，凭藉大量的投入和人才引进，致力于全降解材料PBS,PPC改性薄膜专用料技术的研究与应用，使华盛不断推出新的功能性薄膜产品，引领塑胶制品行业的锐新变革，以卓越的产品与服务超越顾客需求，提升人类社会生活品质。

华盛之道，贵在视野广阔而学有专精。视野广阔，使我们能在复杂分坛的市场竞争中准确把握前进的方向。学有专精，让我们有能力在所耕耘的领域中向客户提供更专业、更优质的服务。我们的目标是通过对国际上先进技术的跟踪，通过对新材料、新工艺的探索，向客户提供更优质的产品，帮助客户提高竞争力，与客户共同发展。

地址：江苏省通州经济开发区杏园路289号

网址：www.huasheng-nt.com

电话：（+86-513）86199900

传真：（+86-513）86199911

中国塑料加工工业协会简介

理事长 钱桂敬

中国塑料加工工业协会（简称中国塑协），英文名称CHINA PLASTICS PROCESSING INDUSTRY ASSOCIATION（缩写为CPPIA），成立于1989年，是中国塑料加工业的行业组织，由从事塑料加工及其相关产业生产、经营的企业、事业单位、社会团体、科研院所等单位及个人自愿组成的全国性、非营利性、具法人地位的社会团体组织。中国塑协是在民政部注册登记的一级社团法人，在业务上接受国务院国有资产监督管理委员会和中国轻工业联合会指导和监督管理。

协会宗旨： 遵守宪法、法律、法规，贯彻国家有关方针、政策，遵守社会道德风尚，反映行业诉求，维护会员合法权益，引导并促进本行业健康和持续发展，为会员、行业和政府服务。

基本职能： 反映行业愿望，研究行业发展方向，编制行业发展规划，协调行业内外关系；代表会员权益，向政府反映行业的意见和要求；组织技术交流和培训，参与质量管理监督，承担技术咨询；实行行业指导，促进产业发展，维护产业安全。

会　员： 中国塑协现设有33个专业委员会，2000余家会员单位。

分支机构： 农用薄膜、塑料节水器材、塑料管道、异型材及门窗制品、泡沫塑料EPS、人造革合成革、双向拉伸聚酯薄膜、双向拉伸聚丙烯薄膜、复合薄膜制品、中空制品、塑料编织制品、工程塑料、医用塑料、塑木制品、聚氨酯制品、氟塑料加工、聚氯乙烯板制品、硬质PVC低发泡制品、注塑制品、滚塑、改性塑料、降解塑料、多功能母料、塑料再生利用、塑料助剂、流延薄膜、塑料配线器材、镀铝膜、密胺塑料制品、塑料技术协作委员会、专家委员会、新材料研究开发工作委员会、教育与培训委员会等。

出版物 主办期刊：《中国塑料》、《国外塑料》；

编辑出版：《中国塑协通讯》、《中国塑料工业年鉴》以及多种专题会议文集等。

中国塑料加工工业协会农用薄膜专业委员会

中国塑料加工工业协会改性塑料专业委员会

中国塑料加工工业协会中空制品专业委员会

中国塑料加工工业协会人造革合成革专业委员会

中国塑料加工工业协会异型材及门窗制品专业委员会

中国塑料加工工业协会注塑制品专业委员会

中国塑料加工工业协会复合膜制品专业委员会

中国塑料加工工业协会聚氨酯制品专业委员会

中国塑料加工工业协会聚氯乙烯板制品专业委员会

中国塑料加工工业协会塑料编织制品专业委员会

中国塑料加工工业协会塑料管道专业委员会

中国塑料加工工业协会双向拉伸聚丙烯薄膜专业委员会

中国塑料加工工业协会双向拉伸聚酯薄膜专业委员会

中国塑料加工工业协会泡沫塑料EPS专业委员会

中国塑料加工工业协会硬质PVC发泡制品专业委员会

中国塑料加工工业协会滚塑专业委员会

中国塑料加工工业协会塑料技术协作委员会

中国塑料加工工业协会塑料节水器材专业委员会

中国塑料加工工业协会塑料再生利用专业委员会

中国塑料加工工业协会医用塑料专业委员会

中国塑料加工工业协会降解塑料专业委员会

中国塑料加工工业协会氟塑料加工专业委员会

中国塑料加工工业协会多功能母料专业委员会

中国塑料加工工业协会工程塑料专业委员会

中国塑料加工工业协会塑木制品专业委员会

中国塑料加工工业协会专家委员会

中国塑料加工工业协会塑料助剂专业委员会

中国塑料加工工业协会日科新材料研究开发工作委员会

中国塑料加工工业协会流延薄膜专业委员会

中国塑料加工工业协会塑料配线器材专业委员会

中国塑料加工工业协会镀铝膜专业委员会

中国塑料加工工业协会教育与培训委员会

中国塑料加工工业协会密胺塑料制品专业委员会

地址：北京东长安街6号

邮编：100740

电话：（8610）65592885，65267869，65268096，65122056，65281529

传真：（8610）65278590，65225254　　网址：http://www.cppia.com.cn

Email: cppia@cppia.com.cn

WARREN
华伦皮塑（苏州）有限公司
环境友好，绿色环保合成革梦，华伦实现。
无溶剂合成革、tpu合成革
电话：0512-81612558
邮箱：hl_syj@163.com gaojingang.warren@gmail.com
手机：13823506393 13606245625
网址：http://www.warren.cn